The Mississippi Almanac

The Ultimate Reference on the State
2001 - 2002

Compiled and Written by James L. Cox

COMPUTER SEARCH & RESEARCH

The manuscript for this book was prepared in electronic form.
All graphics layouts and book design by James L. Cox

The Mississippi Almanac
The Ultimate Reference on the State
2001 - 2002

Copyright © 2001 by James L. Cox — All rights reserved
Printed in the United States of America

Lithography by Rose Printing Company, Inc.
Tallahassee, Florida

ISBN 0-9643545-2-7

The names, addresses and telephone numbers in this book were obtained from
phone directories, computer databases and other sources the publisher regards as reliable.
Although compiled under strict guidelines with numerous cross-checks, the publisher cannot and
does not guarantee the correctness or completeness of all information presented — because of
the possibility of human error and the fact that addresses and phone numbers sometimes change
— hence no responsiblity for same can be or is assumed.
We request that inaccuracies and/or omissions be brought to our attention
so that corrections can be made in a succeeding edition.

No part of this book may be reproduced in any manner whatsoever, stored in a retrieval system,
or transmitted in any form, electronic, mechanical, or other means, now known or hereafter
invented, without permission of the publisher, except in the case of brief quotations
embodied in critical articles and reviews, and the usual allowable nonprofit use by
educational organizations, including school libraries and public libraries.
For information, to make comments or suggestions for people or topics
to be included in future editions, or to order additional copies
please contact
Computer Search & Research
340 North Street
Yazoo City, MS 39194-4245
(662) 746-1919

Contents

INTRODUCTION & ACKNOWLEDGMENTS	vii
A Chronology of Mississippi History	1
Geography of Mississippi	50
Map Coordinates and Elevation of Mississippi Cities	53
Mississippi Weather: Statewide	54
Temperatures and Precipitation Data for Selected Major Cities	54
Seasonal/Annual Temperatures and Precipitation; Freeze Data: 30-Year Means	58
General; Weather Records & Extremes; Weather Phone Numbers	59
Violent Weather: Hurricanes; Tornadoes	60
Mississippi Weather: Jackson	62
Temperatures (Hot)	62
Temperatures (Cold)	63
Precipitation (Rain)	64
Precipitation (Snow)	65
Jackson Records/Data: Daily Record Hi/Lo & Normal Temps, Record & Normal Precip.	67
People of Mississippi	73
General; Population Statistics	73
Estimated Population as of July 1, 1998 — Breakdown by Age Group (Table)	74
Housing	75
Education; Labor; Some Selected Vital Statistics; Veterans	76
Profiles of Famous & Notable Mississippians	77
Famous & Notable Mississippians Listed by Name	224
Famous & Notable Mississippians Listed by Birth Date	236
Famous & Notable Mississippians Listed by Death Date	249
Famous & Notable Mississippians Listed by Profession	254
Number of Famous & Notable Mississippians in Each Profession	257
Birth Places of Native-Born Famous & Notable Mississippians	258
Number of Famous & Notable Mississippians Born in Each County	262
Other Mississippi Blues Artists	263
"Miss Mississippi" Titleholders	268
Mississippi's "Miss Hospitality" Titleholders	269
Mississippians in The Super Bowl	270
Mississippi's College Football Bowl Games (through 1999)	272
Mississippi First-Round Picks in NFL and NBA Drafts	273
Members of the Mississippi Sports Hall of Fame (Through 2000)	274
Mississippians Who Received The Congressional Medal of Honor	275
Movies Filmed in Mississippi	276
Almost 500 Movies Mississippians Helped Make	281
Mississippi Superlatives & Trivia	294
The Mississippi Gulf Coast	294
Business & Commercial Ventures	295
Agriculture; Plants and Trees	298
Churches & Religion; Mississippi Colleges & Universities	299
Mississippi College Women	300
Other Notable Mississippi Women	301
Mississippi's Beautiful Women; The First State To...	302
The Civil War	303

Contents

Mississippi Superlatives & Trivia (continued)
- World War II; Other Military Facts --- 304
- Mississippi's Medal of Honor Recipients --- 305
- Black Mississippi Achievers --- 306
- More Mississippi Achievers --- 307
- Sports --- 309
- Gaming/Gambling --- 312
- Mississippi Birthplaces; It Originated In Mississippi; Inventive Mississippians --- 313
- Aviation Firsts & Feats --- 314
- Medical Breakthroughs & Milestones --- 315
- Hi-Tech Stuff --- 317
- Politically Correct --- 318
- "Capitals" of the World; Standing Tall --- 320
- Mississippi Media; Gotta Travel On --- 321
- Mississippi Placenames --- 322
- Mississippi County Names --- 324
- Over the County Line; Old Buildings & Things --- 325
- Mississippi Movie Makers --- 327
- Mississippi Music Makers - Blues --- 330
- Mississippi Music Makers - Soul/R&B --- 332
- Mississippi Music Makers - Rock/Pop --- 334
- Mississippi Music Makers - Country --- 337
- Mississippi Music Makers - Jazz --- 341
- Mississippi Music Makers - Gospel --- 342
- Literary Legacy; Burial Places of the Famous --- 343
- The Great Mississippi Outdoors; Miss-cellaneous --- 345

Government of Mississippi --- 348
- Number of Mississippi State Government Employees (Table) --- 349

Governors of Mississippi (list of) --- 352

Alphabetical List of Mississippi Governors --- 354

Short Profiles of Mississippi Governors (In the Order They Served) --- 355

Mississippi Legislative Sessions 1875-2000 --- 364

Members of the U.S. Senate From Mississippi (1817 - 2001) --- 365

Members of the U.S. House of Representatives From Mississippi (1817-2001) --- 366

State & Federal Government Phone Numbers --- 369
- Mississippi Congressional Delegation; Top Mississippi Elected Officials --- 369
- Branches & Departments of State Government --- 370
- State Government Toll-Free Numbers --- 372
- Federal Government Toll-Free Numbers; Other Federal Government Phone Numbers --- 373

Assorted Mississippi Associations/Organizations --- 374
- Business & Trade Associations; Education Associations; Political Parties --- 374
- Professional Associations; Miscellaneous Associations & Organizations --- 375

Economy of Mississippi --- 376
- Income; General Business --- 376
- Taxes; Construction; Labor --- 377
- Employment Averages, 1998 & 1999 (table); Selected Miss. Leading Economic Indicators --- 378
- Energy & Environment --- 379
- Ports; Miscellaneous; Fortune 500 Companies with Operations in Mississippi, 1999 --- 380

Contents

Largest Publicly Traded Miss.-Based Companies (Capitalization/Stock Performance)	381
Market Shares for Top-10 Banks in Mississippi; Manufactures Summary, 1996	381
For Each Mississippi County: Per Capita Income, 1998 & Cost of Living Index, 1999	382
Members of the Mississippi Business Hall of Fame (Through 2000)	**383**
Health in Mississippi	**384**
Number of Live Births and Deaths in Cities of 10,000 or More, 1998 (Table)	386
Hospitals in Mississippi	**387**
Ambulatory Surgical Facilities	389
County Health Departments in Mississippi	**390**
Law Enforcement Units in Mississippi	**391**
Sheriff's Departments by County	391
Local Police Departments	392
Dept. of Public Safety (Highway Patrol); Driver's License Examining Stations	394
Crime in Mississippi	**396**
Number of Major Offenses in Selected Cities With Pop. 10,000 or More, 1999	396
No. of Major Offenses, 1999: By Area; For the Jackson MSA	397
Fire Departments in Mississippi	**398**
Statistics from the Office of the Mississippi State Fire Marshall	401
Education in Mississippi	**402**
General; Public Schools, Elementary & Secondary	402
Higher Education: The 8 State-Supported University; The 15 Public Community Colleges	403
Colleges & Universities in Mississippi	**404**
Libraries in Mississippi	**405**
Public Libraries	405
University & College Libraries; Community College Libraries; Other Libraries	410
Mississippi Agriculture	**411**
Crops	411
Livestock; Aquaculture (Catfish); General	412
Mississippi Farm Income and Expenses, 1996 - 1998 (Table)	413
Value Added to the U.S. Economy by the Agriculture Sector in Miss., 1996 - 1998 (Table)	413
Mississippi Agriculture (Charts)	**414**
Top-10 Producing Counties for Cotton, Soybeans and Wheat, 1999	414
Top-10 Producing Counties for Corn & Rice and Top-7 Counties for Sorghum, 1999	415
Tree Species of Mississippi	**416**
Champion Trees of Mississippi	**417**
Wildflowers of Mississippi	**424**
Road Mileage Between Mississippi Cities (Shortest Route)	**428**
Travel and Recreation in Mississippi	**430**
Welcome Centers in Mississippi	431
Mississippi Welcome Centers - Where Visitors Came From; Number of Visitors (Tables)	432
Tourist Attractions in Mississippi	**433**
Conventions & Visitors Bureaus of Mississippi	**450**
Chambers of Commerce in Mississippi	**452**
Mississippi Outdoor Sportsmen's Records	**455**
Boone & Crockett Deer Heads Taken in Mississippi	455
Miss. Best Bucks Taken with Bow & Arrow; Animals Harvested in the 1998-99 Season	456
Official State Record Fish; Some Freshwater Fish Found in Mississippi	457

Contents

State Parks in Mississippi	458
Public & Private Golf Courses in Mississippi	462
Casinos in Mississippi	464
Mississippi Casinos Gross Gaming Revenues	466
State Tax Revenue From Casinos	467
Places in Mississippi with Indian Names	468
Broadcasting Stations in Mississippi	470
Public/Educational TV Stations; Commercial TV Stations; Public Radio Stations	470
Commercial Radio Stations	471
Commercial Radio Networks; College/University Radio Stations	475
Newspapers in Mississippi	476
Daily Newspapers; Weekly Newspapers	476
College/University Newspapers	478
Wire Services; Media Associations; Religious; Business & Professional Journals	479
Jackson MSA (Metropolitan Statistical Area)	480
Geography; People, General; Population Statistics; Housing	480
Income; Economy; Labor	481
Major Employment Sectors of the Jackson MSA (Table); Crime; Health; Education	482
Transportation; Arts; Sports; Veterans	483
How Mississippi Ranks Among All the Southern States in Selected Categories	484
Mississippi Phone Exchanges	486
Mississippi Phone Exchanges — Numerical Cross Reference	491
Mississippi ZIP Codes	496
Mississippi ZIP Codes — Numerical Cross Reference	503
Population of Mississippi Cities & Towns (Numerically — 1998 Census Estimates)	508
Population of Mississippi Cities & Towns (Alpha. Cross Reference)	510
Counties of Mississippi by Population (Ranking by Census Estimates of 7/1/1999)	512
The County 1999 Population Pie	512
Miss. Counties Population Charts (1998 Est.), Top-10 Counties: White, Non-White & Total	513
Analysis of Mississippi Population Figures (1998 Census Estimates)	514
Analysis of Population of MSAs (Metropolitan Statistical Areas)	514
Analysis of Counties Population	514
Analysis of Municipalities Population	514
Population Growth in Mississippi 1830 - 1999	515
The Changing Population of Mississippi	515
The Counties of Mississippi by Area	516
The Counties of Mississippi (Map)	517
The Counties of Mississippi (Data)	518
Former Names of Some Mississippi Communities	559
The Counties of Mississippi with Placenames	565
Master List of Mississippi Placenames	580
Selected Bibliography	597
Index of People	599
General Index	614

Introduction & Acknowledgments

The first two editions of *The Mississippi Almanac* were well received and brought us much positive feedback. We're also very appreciative of the praise we received from the media.

We've re-formatted much of the book and hope you like the new look. We continue to use larger print than most information almanacs, although we had to reduce the size of print in some chapters to accommodate the much larger volume of information we provide in this edition. We've tried to keep the book as accurate as possible by checking the data many times, but please let us know about mistakes. Two years of research went into each of the previous two editions plus over three years into this edition. The culmination of seven years of labor-intensive research, this book is a continuous work in progress. It continues to be a labor of love and your satisfaction is our greatest reward. We sincerely hope that you'll find the book informative, interesting and useful.

It would be impossible to compile a book of this magnitude without a great deal of help. We've been fortunate in receiving assistance and information from a multitude of people. Thanks to several agencies of the Federal Government, especially the U.S. Census Bureau. Many state government agencies were very helpful. Thanks to: Dr. Marianne Hill and Dr. Darrin M. Webb with the Center for Policy Research and Planning at Mississippi Institutions of Higher Learning; the State Board for Community and Junior Colleges; Bill Lunceford and Dennis Riecke at the Mississippi Department of Wildlife, Fisheries and Parks; Tom Van Hyning with the Tourism Division of the Mississippi Development Authority; Wayne Gasson, Director of the Labor Market Information Department at the Mississippi Employment Security Commission; Rick Olson, Community Assistance Forester with the Mississippi Forestry Commission; Serial Kenerson, Deputy State Statistician with the Mississippi Agricultural Statistics Service; the Mississippi Forestry Commission; the Mississippi Department of Corrections; the Mississippi Library Commission; the Mississippi State Tax Commission; the Department of Public Safety; the State Gaming Commission; the State Department of Education; the State Department of Health; Arlene Davis with the Mississippi State Board of Medical Licensure; the State Department of Mental Health; the Department of Human Services; and Farrah Cox, Administrative Assistant of Publications with the Mississippi Secretary of State's Office.

Thanks also to Michael Rubenstein and his friendly staff at the Mississippi Sports Hall of Fame and Museum; Glen Waddle on the selection committee with the Jackson Touchdown Club and Mississippi Sports Hall of Fame, Inc.; the ACT (American College Test) headquarters in Iowa; Larry Greer, Regional Director - Corporate and External Affairs with BellSouth in Jackson; Tim Pepper, Extension agent with the Yazoo County Extension Service; Cory Neill of Carrollton, Mississippi, record keeper with the Mississippi Bowhunters Association; LaRee Callahan, Mississippi Miss Hospitality Coordinator with the Hattiesburg Convention & Visitors Bureau; and the Miss Mississippi Corporation of Vicksburg. Thanks to Henry E. Thompson, Sergeant First Class, Army (retired) of Laurel, Mississippi, for his help in gathering information on some of the Congressional Medal of Honor recipients. Special thanks also to Nancy Jacobs, an English teacher at Starkville High School. She and her students are the authors of the Mississippi Writers and Musicians Web Project. I highly recommend this excellent Website, which features brief biographical profiles and some interviews. The Website now includes Mississippi Artists plus Stage, Screen and TV Stars (http://shs.starkville.k12.mswm/MSWritersAndMusicians/music.html).

It is almost impossible to thank everyone who made a contribution, so to those we might have missed, please forgive us.

And, once again, a very special thank you to Lou. Without her help, encouragement and sacrifice, this book would not have been published. Lou, I love you!

James L. Cox • Yazoo City, Mississippi • November 2000

Dedication
Dedicated to the people of Mississippi, the most persevering people on earth!

A Chronology of Mississippi History

1519
Alonso de Pineda leads a group of Spanish explorers along the Gulf of Mexico and discovers the mouth of a great river they name "Rio del Espiritu Santo" or "River of the Holy Ghost," thought by some to be the Mississippi.

1540
Spanish explorers led by Hernando De Soto first enter Mississippi in December near Columbus after wandering for a year and a half through the wilderness of Florida, Georgia, North and South Carolina, Tennessee and Alabama.

1541
De Soto discovers the Mississippi River on May 8 at a place called Quizquiz, the location of which is a matter of debate. Memphis, Tunica, and Sunflower Landing are mentioned in different theories. Most evidence seems to favor Council Bend or Walnut Bend in Tunica County. After a month of barge and canoe building, De Soto and his men cross the Mississippi.

1542
De Soto returns to the eastern side of the Mississippi River, then dies from fever on Mississippi soil in May. Some historians say it is near Natchez, while others say it is in Bolivar County. To conceal his death and protect his body from desecration by the Indians, his men place it in a trough made of live-oak and at midnight, sink it to the bottom of the mighty river that De Soto had discovered just a year earlier.

1673
Father Jacques Marquette and trader Louis Jolliet explore the Mississippi River as far south as the mouth of the Arkansas.

1682
La Salle (full name and title: Robert Rene Cavalier, Sieur de La Salle) and his party explores the Mississippi River, passing by Vicksburg, Grand Gulf and other places. On March 23, they spend the night near Natchez. The first Christian religious service held in what will later become the State of Mississippi takes place when Father Zenobius Membre celebrates Mass on Easter Sunday, March 29 at the area later known as Fort Adams in Wilkinson County. The expedition party reaches the mouth of the Mississippi River on April 7. On April 9, La Salle claims all of the lower Mississippi River area for France and calls it Louisiana in honor of King Louis XIV.

1684
On July 24, La Salle sails from France with 4 ships and 400 men on his 2nd voyage to the New World. It's a failed expedition as La Salle fails to find the mouth of the Mississippi and lands too far to the west on the coast of Texas.

1687
La Salle is killed by one of his own men during a mutiny on March 19. With him goes the dream of France establishing a colony at the mouth of the Mississippi...at least for now.

1693
On the Discovery of the Mississippi, the memoirs of Henry de Tonty, is published. In it, he describes his travels with Robert Cavelier, Sieur de La Salle, and his claim of the Louisiana territory for France. It will be translated into English by Thomas Falconer in 1844.

1698
Father Davion of the Catholic Church builds a chapel near Fort Adams. He and his followers (including Indians) are a great influence in the French gaining control of the valley.

1699
On Feb. 13, Iberville and his men first step ashore in present-day Biloxi to affirm the claims of King Louis XIV of France. French colonists, led by Pierre le Moyne, Sieur d'Iberville, start to build Fort Maurepas on April 8, the first permanent colony in Mississippi (now Ocean Springs), also the first European settlement in the Mississippi Valley.

1713
Antoine de la Mothe Cadillac, a French explorer, becomes governor general of Louisiana.

1716
The French, under orders of Cadillac, build Fort Rosalie at the site of present-day Natchez.

1717
Financier John Law, on orders from King Louis, launches the Mississippi Scheme to bring 6,000 settlers, 3,000 slaves & commercial development to the French-held Mississippi River Valley. Although the plan is fairly successful, it falls apart in 1720 and almost brings France to financial collapse.

1720
Le Moyne de Bienville abandons Old Biloxi (Ocean Springs) and establishes New Biloxi (at present day Biloxi) as the new capital of the French Colony of Louisiana.

1721
Two French ships arrive at Ship Island on January 3 with 300 settlers for Pascagoula and Bay Saint Louis.

1729
The massacre at Fort Rosalie on Nov. 28 is the worst Indian massacre to ever take place on Mississippi soil with Indians killing 138 Frenchmen, 35 French women, and 56 children. Fort Rosalie is destroyed. The revolt spreads throughout the area with a massacre at Fort St. Pierre overlooking the Yazoo River near present-day Redwood.

1736
In retaliation for the attack on Fort Rosalie, French forces under Bienville, along with some Choctaw Indians, attack the Chickasaws at Ackia near of the site of present-day Tupelo on May 25. The Chickasaws are helped by some English traders. The French are defeated and retreat, hastening the French decline in the Mississippi Valley.

1750
A line of Plantations extend from New Orleans on both sides of the river to Natchez and beyond.

1763
In the Treaty of Paris at the end of the French and Indian War, all lands east of the Mississippi, except New Orleans, are ceded to the English, ending 64 years of French rule. Mississippi is placed in the colony of British West Florida.

1779
Fort Panmure (formerly Fort Rosalie and rebuilt by the English) at Natchez is occupied by the Spanish on September 21 leading to Spanish rule of the territory that will later become the State of Mississippi.

1781
On April 22, the English re-occupy Fort Panmure. On July 23, the Spanish reclaim the fort.

1783
U.S. gets northern Mississippi in the Revolutionary War. Spain gets southern Mississippi as part of West Florida.

1784
A census of the Natchez District indicates there are 1,619 people, including 498 black slaves.

1785
Georgia organizes southern Mississippi as Bourbon County which they will sell in the "Yazoo Fraud" in 1795.

1791
Father William Savage dedicates the Church of Our Savior of the World at Natchez.

A Chronology of Mississippi History

1792
The census compiled by Governor Gayoso now shows 4,346 people in the Natchez District.

1793
Eli Whitney invents the cotton gin, reviving southern slavery. A black male sells for $400, while a black female brings $300.

1795
In the Treaty of San Lorenzo signed Oct. 27, the Spaniards surrender Natchez to the U.S. and let Americans ship goods to New Orleans; The cotton gin is first introduced in Natchez.

1797
An epidemic of fever decimates the Natchez District, forcing hundreds to flee. Dysentery, smallpox, measles, scarlet fever, cancer, cholera, and venereal disease plague the settlers.

1798
On Mar. 23, the Spanish evacuate Fort Nogales in what is now Vicksburg; After 19 years under Spanish rule, Natchez passes into the control of Americans. On March 30, the Spanish flag is lowered for the last time. The U.S. takes possession of Natchez area on March 3; The Mississippi Territory and Adams County are established on April 7; On May 7, Winthrop Sargent becomes first territorial governor; The Woodville Baptist Church is established..

1799
The territorial seal, patterned after the Great Seal of the U.S., arrives by boat at Natchez in Jan. and presented to the first territorial governor Winthrop Sargent; In April, Tobias Gibson, a 27-year-old circuit rider from South Carolina and the first preacher appointed to become a Methodist missionary to Mississippi, preaches his first sermon in Natchez — the Washington United Methodist Church is established; On April 2, the second county in Mississippi, Pickering (the name is later changed to Jefferson) is organized.

1800
Benjamin M. Stokes begins publication of the state's first newspaper, the *Mississippi Gazette* in Natchez, during the early part of the year; Territory east of the Pearl River is organized as Washington County.

1801
Claiborne and Wilkinson Counties are organized, giving the territory 5 counties; The government gets permission from the Choctaw and Chickasaw Indians to build a wagonway through their territory from Nashville to Natchez. The road, 450 miles long, is to follow the old Natchez Trace, a trail long used by the Indians. The road is known as "Road From Nashville In The State of Tennessee To The Grindstone Ford of The Bayou Pierre In The Mississippi Territory" (map makers refuse to use that name), "Natchez Road", Nashville Road", "Mail Road" and "Cumberland Road"; The new territorial governor, W.C.C. Claiborne, arrives in Natchez on Nov. 23.

1802
On Feb. 1, the territorial capital is moved only 6 miles from Natchez to Washington, Mississippi. That's where Jefferson College is chartered this year; On Apr. 24, the U.S. Government agrees to pay the State of Georgia $1,250,000 to relinquish claims to disputed territory in the Mississippi Territory; On July 26, the *Mississippi Herald*, the first newspaper of any stability, is printed by Andrew Marschalk.

1803
The Natchez Trace opens. The state's third oldest settlement, Port Gibson (1729), is chartered as a town on Mar. 12; On April 9, Natchez is incorporated as a city of the U.S.; The U.S. buys the Louisiana Territory for $11,250,000 in bonds plus $3,750,000 indemnities to American citizens with claims against France. The U.S. takes title on Dec. 20. The purchase doubles the area of the United States.

1804
Congress adds all the northern part of what is now Mississippi and Alabama to the Mississippi Territory. Almost all this land is held by the Indians and is not yet open to white settlement; Rev. Joseph Bullen of Vermont comes to Mississippi and organizes the first Presbyterian Church in the state, the Bethel at Uniontown in Jefferson County. The first church camp meeting held in Mississippi takes place at a site on Clear Creek in Adams County in November.

1805
On March 1, Robert Williams becomes territorial governor; On June 11, the U.S. Army orders that Fort Rosalie be dismantled. Only the flag pole is left standing; The Natchez (Charity) Hospital is founded.

1806
Congress appropriates money for the improvement of the Natchez Trace. The wagonway is to be "...twenty feet wide with a causeway over all marshes and bridges over all streams less than forty feet wide." If the streams were more than forty feet wide, they were to "have trees fallen across them so as to admit the passage of a mail carrier with his mail." The Natchez Trace is the first improved road in the state; With a combined membership of 706, the six Baptist churches in the state group themselves together to form the Mississippi Baptist Association. The charter members of the association are: Salem in Jefferson County, Bayou Pierre in Clairborne County, New Hope in Adams County, Bethel in Wilkinson County, and New Providence and Ebenezer in Amite County.

1807
The Franklin Academy is established in Jefferson County by the Franklin Society on Jan. 8; the Three-Chopped Way road is opened from Natchez eastward to Georgia.

1808
The Bethany Presbyterian Church is established near Liberty in Amite County, Mississippi.

1809
David Holmes becomes the last territorial governor on Mar. 3; Land offices are doing a booming business selling Mississippi land to eager buyers; The "Bank of Mississippi" is chartered; Amite, Franklin, Warren and Wayne counties are organized; Madison Academy is established in Clairborne County.

1810
Madison County is established.

1811
Farmers suffer the ravages of "rot" which lays waste to the cotton fields. They also endure devastating floods; the first steamboat, the *New Orleans*, cruises the Mississippi River.

1812
The U.S. declares war against England in June. During the War of 1812, Miss. Choctaw Indian Chief Pushamataha holds the rank of Colonel in the U.S. Army. Under his command, Choctaw Chief Greenwood Leflore is a Major.

1813
Andrew Marschalk launches his most successful of many editorial ventures, the *Washington Republican*.

1815
After the end of the War of 1812 early this year, the price of cotton in the New Orleans market immediately rises to a seven-year high of 18 cents a pound, a price more than double the average of the past five years; On May 13, the post office is established at Monticello with Hiram Runnels (later to be governor) as the first postmaster.

A Chronology of Mississippi History

1816
Madison Co. has a population of 14,200 and Adams Co. 10,131; On Sept. 20, Generals Andrew Jackson and David Meriwether and "the whole Chickasaw Nation...," sign the Treaty of Chickasaw Council House in Lee County.

1817
On Oct. 17, David Holmes officially becomes the State of Mississippi's first governor. He has been governor of the Mississippi Territory since Mar. 3, 1809; The State constitution is framed and Mississippi admitted as a state, with 14 counties, on December 10. The four periods in Mississippi history until now are: Spanish Dominion, 1540-1699; French Dominion, 1699-1763; English Dominion, 1763-1779; and the Mississippi Territory, 1798-1817; The only Catholic church in the state is at Natchez, and it dates back to the Spanish period.
Deaths: Former Mississippi Territorial Governor William C.C. Claiborne dies in New Orleans on Nov. 23.

1818
The Great Seal of Mississippi is adopted by the legislature on Jan. 19; The 6 Mississippi Methodist circuits report ministering to 1,846 whites and 389 blacks.

1819
On Feb. 17, the state grants a charter to Elizabeth Female Academy in Washington, Mississippi. It is the first school in the U.S. authorized to grant degrees to young women.

1820
George Poindexter becomes governor Jan. 5; On Oct. 18, the Treaty of Doak's Stand (with Chief Pushmataha) provides for large land cession from the Choctaws; The Land Act of 1820 lowers the minimum price of land from $2 to $1.25 per acre; Since 1817, academies incorporated include one at Pass Christian, four in the Natchez region, and one in Lawrence Co.; Rev. Adam Cloud organizes the first Episcopal church in the state, Christ Church at Church Hill in Jefferson County; The Jackson Military Road across the state is completed.
Deaths: The first Governor of the Mississippi Territory, Winthrop Sargent, dies in New Orleans on June 3 at age 65.

1821
On Feb. 21, the legislature declares that land ceded to the U.S. by the Choctaw Indians 4 months earlier would become Hinds County, named for Maj. Gen. Thomas Hinds, a hero of the Battle of New Orleans. Four more counties, Copiah, Madison, Rankin and Yazoo, are soon created from this large area; The first State Bar Association in the U.S. is organized in Natchez on May 26; Franklin Academy, founded by Gideon Lincecum, opens in Columbus, the first free public high school in the state. Wayne County reports 6 schools. Franklin, Lawrence, and Pike Counties report "hardly any schools," and Greene and Perry Counties report they have no schools; Columbia is chosen as capital of the state; Walter Leake is elected governor by a vote of 4,730 to 1,269 over Charles B. Green.

1822
On Jan. 7, Walter Leake is inaugurated as governor; LeFleur's Bluff becomes the state capital (later renamed Jackson after Andrew Jackson). The legislature moves from Columbia to Jackson a few weeks later; The name of the post office in Franklin County, established May 10, 1815, is changed from Franklin to Meadville Dec. 18. On Dec. 23, the legislative session begins in the first state capitol building.

1823
Bainbridge County is created on Jan. 17, but has a brief life of only a year before the name is changed to Covington County; Walter Leake is re-elected governor winning against David Dickson and William Lattimore.

1824
Mississippi becomes the first state to abolish imprisonment for debtors on Jan. 23; The *Woodville Republican* newspaper is established (the oldest business in the state today); The Woodville United Methodist Church is established; Miss. Baptists organize the first State Convention (disbanded 1829);
Deaths: On December 24, Choctaw Chief Pushmataha dies in Washington, D.C. Highly respected by whites and Indians, he is given a military funeral with internment in the nation's capital with other American heroes. He was a Colonel in the Mississippi militia serving in the War of 1812. Senator Andrew Jackson eulogized him as "the greatest and bravest Indian" he had ever known.

1825
The rapidly growing community around Walnut Hills is incorporated into the town of Vicksburg, named after settler Newet Vick; In the gubernatorial election in August, David Holmes wins over Cowles Mead by the overwhelming margin of 7,746 to 1,499; On November 17, Lt. Governor Gerard C. Brandon becomes governor upon the death of Walter Leake. He is the first native Mississippian to become governor; The Gallman Baptist Church is established.

1826
On Jan. 7, David Holmes becomes governor for the 2nd time. On July 25, Governor Holmes resigns and Lt. Governor Gerald C. Brandon becomes governor for the 2nd time, replacing a governor who was also holding the office for a 2nd time; Hampstead Academy is established at Clinton, later to become Mississippi College, first a Presbyterian Church school then later a Baptist School; In Natchez, a home that cares for 15 homeless children says it spent $1,109.07 for their support; In Dec., a group of citizens buys the *Mississippi Statesman* newspaper and hire Andrew Marschalk as publisher, who merges his *Natchez Gazette* with the new journal and starts the *Mississippi Statesman and Natchez Gazette*; With parishes at Church Hill, Natchez, Port Gibson & Woodville, the Episcopal Diocese of Mississippi is established with 5 clergymen and 100 communicants.

1827
In February, the legislature changes the name of Hampstead Academy in Clinton to Mississippi Academy; In the gubernatorial election in August, Gerald Brandon receives 5,842 votes to 5,380 for all 4 of his opponents combined.

1828
The only black-owned financial institution in the state, Penny Savings Bank of Indianola, closes its doors.

1829
The first Disciples of Christ churches are converted from Baptist churches at Wells Creek in Franklin County and Mt. Moriah and Ebenezer in Wilkinson Co; On Sept. 28, the post office in Hinds County known as Mount Salus is changed to Clinton; On Dec. 9, the name of the post office at Flagg Spring in Yazoo County is changed to Benton.

1830
The first predominately black land-grant college in the nation begins as Oakland College (later Alcorn State University), a school for white males at first; The Treaty of Dancing Rabbit Creek (principal Indian Chief Greenwood Leflore) is signed on Sept. 27 by 172 Choctaw leaders and several U.S. leaders. It provides for cession of the last of the Choctaw lands; The Bank of Mississippi, chartered in 1809, closes; Cotton production in the state is 100,000 bales (500 pounds each); Dr. Rush Nutt becomes the first Mississippi planter to use steam power to drive his ginstand.

A Chronology of Mississippi History

1831

On Dec. 19, the Vicksburg & Clinton Railroad becomes the first chartered in Mississippi. The Woodville (Mississippi) & Saint Francisville (Louisiana) railway, also chartered this year, is the first actually constructed in the state and among the first in the nation; In Aug., Abram Scott is elected governor with 3,958 votes to 3,711 for Hiram Runnels, 2,902 for Charles Lynch, 1,440 for W. P. Harris, and 492 for Adam Gordon.

1832

Abram M. Scott becomes governor on Jan. 9; A constitutional convention convenes in Jackson on Sept. 10 and soon frames the second state constitution; In the Treaty of Pontotoc (principal Indian Chief is Levi Colbert) signed on Oct. 20, the Chickasaws cede more than six million acres of their lands in the northern part of the state, their last substantial property. Soon forced to leave the state, they will travel over the "Trail of Tears" west toward Oklahoma; There are 3 land offices in the state at Augusta, Washington, and Mount Salus (now Clinton). Vicksburg City Hospital is founded; In June, Mississippi College grants its first degrees; Two more Baptist congregations embrace the Disciples of Christ, one at Grand Gulf and another eight miles west of Jackson at Battle Springs.
Deaths: The man who was the last Gov. of the Mississippi Territory and the first Gov. of the State of Mississippi, David Holmes, dies at his home near Winchester, Va. on Aug. 20.

1833

On February 26, Gov. Abram Scott approves an act providing $95,000 "for the erection of a State House and suitable offices for the Secretary of State, State Treasurer, Auditor of Public Accounts and Attorney General," and $10,000 "for the erection of a suitable house for the Governor, in the town of Jackson."; Seventeen counties are organized, the so-called Choctaw Cession counties: Attala, Carroll, Choctaw, Clarke, Holmes, Jasper, Kemper, Lauderdale, Leake, Neshoba, Noxubee, Oktibbeha, Scott, Smith, Tallahatchie, Winston and Yalobusha; Dr. Rush Nutt and other farmers in the Rodney area develop a new variety of cotton known as Petit Gulf Cotton. Soon sold to other cotton-growing states, it becomes the ancestor of all later American breeds; Gov. Abram Scott dies June 12 and Charles Lynchbecomes governor. On Nov. 21, Hiram Runnels replaces Charles Lynch as governor.

1834

The Rose Hill Baptist Church is established in Natchez.

1835

On Aug. 10, the name of the post office in Taladega (est. 2/9/1833) in Noxubee County is changed to Macon; On Dec. 3, John Quitman becomes governor; Land sales in the state this year total 2,931,181 acres; The First Baptist Church and the First Christian Church are established in Jackson; Baptists report 107 churches with membership of 4,865, white and colored; The Synod of Mississippi Presbytery now consists of 24 churches with a combined membership between 800 and 900; On Dec. 7, the post office is established at Holly Springs, 2 months before Marshall County is formed; Irate citizens of Vicksburg hang 5 professional gamblers for murder; Henry Voss, editor of the *Grand Gulf Advertiser*, estimates that circulation of out-of-state newspapers in Mississippi is almost as large as those published in the state.

1836

On Jan. 7, Charles Lynch becomes governor of the state for the second time; Thirteen counties are organized on Feb. 14, the so-called Chickasaw Cession counties: Bolivar, Chickasaw, Coahoma, DeSoto, Itawamba, Lafayette, Marshall, Newton, Panola, Pontotoc, Tippah, Tishomingo, and Tunica; On Mar. 29, the name of the post office at Pittsburg, established on Feb. 28, 1834, is changed to Grenada; Eleven railroad companies are chartered: Jackson & Brandon Railroad & Bridge, Mississippi & Alabama Railroad, Mississippi Springs Railroad, Benton & Manchester (Yazoo City) Railroad, Lake Washington & Deer Creek Railroad & Banking, Mississippi Railroad, Aberdeen & Pontotoc Railroad & Banking, Tallahatchie Railroad, Tombigbee Railroad, Yazoo Railroad and Gainesville & Narkeetah Railroad. These companies do more banking than constructing railroads; More than a million acres of cotton are planted in the state and the price reaches twenty cents a pound in the New Orleans market; The senatorial election has a tragic ending with a duel at Clinton witnessed by 400 people. Isaac Caldwell is killed instantly and Samuel Gwin, severely wounded, dies two and a half years later; The Citizens Theatre is erected in Vicksburg.
Deaths: Former Governor of the Mississippi Territory, Robert Williams dies in Monroe, Louisiana on Jan. 25 at age 62.

1837

On Feb. 18, the *Eastern Clarion* newspaper, which will later become *The Clarion-Ledger*, is founded in Paulding in Jasper County; The first court decision in the U.S. to grant property rights to women takes place when Betsy Allen, a young Chickasaw women from Toccopola in Pontotoc Country takes her legal fight for property rights to the State Supreme Court and wins; Five more railroad companies are chartered; Seven million acres of land in the state have been sold since 1833, much of it on credit; State bank closings follow a nationwide financial panic. A great depression starts and will last until 1845; Pope Gregory XVI establishes the Diocese of Natchez.

1838

Alexander G. McNutt becomes governor on Jan. 8; Biloxi is first incorporated as a town on Feb. 8; The legislature establishes the Union Bank; Four railroad companies are chartered in the state — Raymond Railroad, Paulding & Pontotoc Railroad, Newton & Lauderdale Railroad & Turnpike Company, and Eagle Railroad & Lumber Company; In Oct., the infamous "Trail of Tears," which will later involve the Indians of Mississippi, starts in Georgia where the Cherokees are forced to move westward toward Oklahoma.

1839

The new state capitol is occupied. Construction starts this year on the governor's mansion, more than 6 years after the original appropriation was made in 1833. It will cost 5 times the $10,000 appropriated; The state legislature passes an "anti-tippling" bill that forbids sale of intoxicating liquors in places where it is to be consumed; The Natchez (Charity) Hospital is officially designated as a state hospital; The Kosciusko Railroad Company is chartered; Cotton production is 386,803 bales (500 pounds each) of seed cotton and the state also harvests 196,626 bushels of wheat; This past decade of the 30s has produced 61 incorporated secondary schools (academies).

1840

The old General and ex-President Andrew Jackson accepts an invitation to visit Jackson. He arrives in Vicksburg on the steamboat "Clarksdale" on Jan. 16. He arrives in Jackson Jan. 19 to a huge welcome. After much celebration and festivity, he leaves on Jan. 21. This was Jackson's first and only visit to the state capital named in his honor; On Feb. 20, the legislature establishes the University of Mississippi and determines its location out of 7 possible sites: Brandon, Kosciusko, Louisville, Middleton, Mississippi City, Monroe Missionary Station, and Oxford; The state's first prison is built in Jackson; Mississippi has 60 counties; Blacks now outnumber whites in

A Chronology of Mississippi History

the state. It will be 100 years later, in 1940, before whites are again the majority race; On May 7, a deadly tornado at Natchez kills 317 people & destroys property valued at $5 million (in 1840 dollars); It is estimated there are 382 public schools with about 8,000 students and there are 2,553 pupils attending 71 academies in the state; The first Baptist congregation in Vicksburg is established with 30 members.

1841
On the seventh ballot and by a vote of 58 to 57, Oxford is selected over Mississippi City on the Gulf Coast for the location of the University of Mississippi; Harrison county is organized; The first Jewish congregation is organized in Vicksburg where there are 25-30 Jewish families. It is first known as the Hebrew Benevolent Congregation of the Men of Mercy, but will change the name to Congregation Anshe Chesed when they formally incorporate in 1862.

1842
On Jan. 10, Tilghman M. Tucker becomes Governor of the State of Mississippi; On Feb. 20, famous orator Henry Clay arrives in Vicksburg aboard the steamship "Ambassador" on his way to speak at Jackson.

1843
The *Vicksburg Sentinel* editor's columns during a crusade against banks so infuriated an opponent that editor James Hagan was challenged and killed on the street in Vicksburg during the spring of the year; On June 7, the name of the post office in Leesville is changed to Kilmichael; The Jews of Natchez organize the Congregation B'nai Israel.

1844
On Jan. 10, Albert G. Brown becomes Governor; Issaquena and Sunflower counties are organized; The University of Mississippi is incorporated and a board of trustees is selected; The first public school is started in Vicksburg.

1845
On Mar. 6, Robert J. Walker, a prominent Natchez lawyer, is appointed Secretary of the Treasury by President Polk, the first Mississippian to become a member of a U.S. President's cabinet; Jefferson Davis is elected to Congress; Mississippi Baptists report 25 associations representing 400 churches with a total membership of 21,485; German and Alsatian Jews organize the Congregation B'nai Israel in Columbus.

1846
A formal declaration of war against Mexico comes on May 13, and Mississippians rally to the cause; The first public school is started in Jackson; Membership in the Methodist Conference has increased to 10,095 whites and 854 blacks; The first Lutheran church in the state, New Hope Lutheran, is built near Sallis in Attala County. The Mississippi Baptist Convention sends its first delegates to the Southern Baptist Convention.

1847
John Quitman's distinguished service during the Mexican War earned him a promotion to major general on April 14, the first Mississippian to gain that rank. Mississippi volunteers under Colonel Jefferson Davis also render distinguished service at Buena Vista in the battle against Mexico. Davis is wounded and returns to Mississippi where he is appointed to the U.S. Senate; The State Baptist Convention appropriates $800 to subsidize the building of churches. Natchez, Port Gibson, Vicksburg, Yazoo City, and Grand Gulf each receive $100.

1848
On Jan. 10, Joseph W. Matthews becomes governor; The legislature establishes the School for the Blind on March 2; The University of Mississippi opens its first session on November 6 with eighty students enrolled, of which 47 complete the first year; Oxford outlaws the sale of liquor. **Deaths**: Former Governor Alexander G. McNutt dies in DeSoto County, Mississippi on Oct. 22 at age 46.

1849
Total production of cotton in the state this year is 484,292 bales (400 pounds each) ginned, the crop diminished by at least one-third by unfavorable weather; During this past decade of the 40s, about 43 academies were chartered in the state; The Order of the Eastern Star, the Masonic women's auxiliary, is organized near Lexington, Mississippi.

1850
On Jan. 10, John Quitman becomes governor for the 2nd time; There are 6,628 pupils attending 171 academies and private schools and 18,746 pupils in 782 "public" schools. Expenditures for schools is estimated at $254,159. Only 8 counties report no schools; The production of upland rice reaches a peak of 3 million pounds, most of it grown in such coastal counties as Harrison and Perry, where it is used to feed cattle; Figures show 216 planters in the state own a hundred or more slaves each; The largest planter residing in the state and perhaps "the greatest planter and slaveowner in the U.S. in the fifties" is Dr. Stephen Duncan of Natchez. This year, he liquidates most of his holdings in Adams County and shifts most of his operation to Issaquena County. He owns more than 1,000 slaves, of which more than 700 are on five absentee cotton plantations in Issaquena County. By 1860, Duncan's Issaquena County property alone will be valued at $1,340,700; The Green Creek Baptist Church is established in Petal. **Deaths**: Former two-term Governor Gerard C. Brandon dies near Fort Adams, Mississippi on March 28 at age 61.

1851
On Jan. 31, Gail Borden of Liberty in Amite County announces invention of evaporated milk; John Guion becomes the state's 17th governor on Feb. 3 following John Quitman's resignation; Jefferson Davis resigns from the U.S. Senate to run for governor. He's defeated by Harry Foote by a margin of only 959 — official returns gave Foote 29,318 to 28,359 for Davis. Foote carried 31 counties to Davis' 28; One of the first colleges for women in the state, the Yalobusha Baptist Female Institute is started (reopened as a private school named Emma Mercer Institute after the war, and later renamed Grenada Female Academy); James Whitfield replaces John Guion as governor on Nov. 24; A Mrs. Mahala Roach in Vicksburg trims the first Christmas tree ever decorated in the state.

1852
When Harry Foote becomes the Governor on Jan. 10, he becomes the fourth governor the state has had in the past year; Calhoun county is organized; There are about 6,000 Catholics in the state served by 11 priests at 11 churches.

1853
Jefferson Davis is appointed U.S. Secretary of War by President Pierce; Hillman College is founded in Clinton as Central Female Academy. **Deaths**: Former two-term Governor Charles Lynch dies near Jackson on Feb. 9; Former Gov. George Poindexter dies in Jackson on Sept. 5.

1854
John J. Pettus becomes governor on Jan. 6. On Jan 10, John J. McRae replaces John Pettis, who has been governor for only 4 days; The legislature establishes the University of Mississippi Law School and a School for the Deaf; Beth Eden Lutheran Church is built at Louisville; Two new political parties make their appearance in Mississippi to compete with the Democrats and the fast-disappearing Whigs — the Republicans (called "Black Republicans" in the South because of their antislavery

A Chronology of Mississippi History

stance, and later because most of their members were black) and the Know-Nothings (the American party); Henry Hughes of Port Gibson publishes his book, *Treatise on Sociology*. Sociologists later call him "the first American sociologist," and credit him with coining the word "sociology."

1855
On Mar. 13, the "Heroine," a 94-ton steamboat explodes on the Tombigbee River killing 8 people; The first state mental hospital is built in Jackson and a second one built later at Meridian; Warren County planter, John Hebron, finds fruit more profitable than cotton and averages $600 per acre from the sale of peaches and pears; The Episcopal Church now has 33 parishes, 30 clergymen, and 941 communicants; Large numbers of Catholic churches are now found in Natchez, Biloxi, Pass Christian, Bay St. Louis, Vicksburg, Port Gibson, Jackson and Yazoo City. **Deaths**: Former Governor John I. Guion dies in Jackson on June 26 at the age of 52.

1856
By constitutional amendment, future general elections in Mississippi will be held in Oct. with the governor's term commencing in Nov.; Two more Lutheran churches are built in the state — Providence at Burns and Bethlehem at Forest; Dairyman Gail Borden of Liberty produces the first can of evaporated condensed milk in the world.

1857
The Dred Scott decision by the U.S. Supreme Court on Mar. 6 holds that slaves did not become free in a free state, Congress could not bar slavery from a territory, and blacks could not be citizens; Jefferson Davis, after retiring from Pierce's cabinet, enters the Senate where he'll have much influence for the rest of the decade; Jacob Thompson becomes the 3rd Mississippian to serve on the cabinet when appointed Secretary of the Interior by President Buchanan; In the gubernatorial election, William McWillie, a states-rights Democrat, receives 27,376 votes to 14,095 for Edward Yerger, the American Party candidate. McWillie becomes governor in November; Luther Chapel Lutheran Church is started in Pulaski, Mississippi. **Deaths**: Former Governor Hiram Runnels dies on Dec. 17.

1858
The Mississippi Historical Society is founded; A board of levee commissioners is established with jurisdiction over the entire Mississippi Delta. **Deaths**: Former Gov. John A. Quitman dies near Natchez on July 17 at age 58.

1859
On July 28, *The Meridian*, that city's first newspaper is published, edited by W.L. Spinks; John J. Pettus becomes governor for the second time Nov. 21; Mississippi leads the nation in cotton production with this year's 1,202,507 bales (400 pounds each) ginned, over 22% of total U.S. production. Yazoo County led the state with 64,075 bales, a figure exceeded by only 2 other counties in the U.S. — Carroll and Tensas parishes in Louisiana. The state also harvests 29 million bushels of corn (38 bushels per capita), and 587,925 bushels of wheat; Whitworth College (for women) is founded by Reverend M. J. Whitworth; Preparations are being made for war. In Dec., Gov. Pettus is told the village of Shuqualak has organized the Quitman Light Infantry and needs aid in securing a cannon, and the young men of Sharon wish to organize a corps of mounted riflemen to defend the South. **Deaths**: Former Governor Tilghman Tucker dies at his father's home in Bexar, Alamaba on April 3 at the age of 57.

1860
The Census shows 3,552 people in the state who own more than 30 slaves each. However, the average slaveowner holds fewer than 30 slaves. Out of 30,943 slaveowners, 27,391 hold 30 slaves or less each. The average price of an adult field hand slave on the New Orleans market has risen to $1,800, and the total value of Mississippi's slave property is estimated at $350 million. The number of free blacks in the state is only 773, one of smallest numbers of any southern state. Of Mississippi's 791,305 people, 436,631, or over 55%, are black; Of all the farms containing three or more acres, only 2,349 are 500 acres or larger, the majority of the remaining 34,658 farms being between 20 and 100 acres in size. Total real and personal property in the state is valued at $754,900,768. The value of livestock is $41,891,692. Improved land sells for $18 per acre; School enrollment has increased to 30,970 students in 1,116 schools funded by $385,677. Mississippi is spending more for public schools than the states of California, Connecticut, Delaware, Maryland, Minnesota, New Hampshire, or Rhode Island; Methodists have the largest church membership in the state with 606 churches reporting membership of 50,000 whites and 11,008 blacks; Baptists claim a membership of 41,482, being served by 305 ordained ministers in 596 churches. There are 148 Presbyterian churches. The number of Catholics in the state is about 10,000 with 1 Bishop and 18 priests maintaining 13 parishes and 28 mission stations. The Catholic Church of the Holy Cross is built in Neshoba County. Estimates give about 2,450 Disciples of Christ members. There are only 9 Lutheran churches in the state; There are 41 newspapers in the state; The railroads are so popular, there are two north-and-south lines and one east-and-west line across the state, with a total 872 miles of rails; Since 1850, the number of factories producing textiles in the state has increased from 2 to 6, while the number of textile workers rose from 58 to 717; The *Jackson Mississippian* discusses the Lincoln presidential victory in an editorial entitled, "The Deed is Done — Disunion the Remedy."

1861
At the start of the year, Mississippi is ranked fifth wealthiest in the nation of 34 states; Six railroads have been started (none finished) in the state: the New Orleans, the Jackson, the Great Northern, the Canton & Jackson, the Mississippi Central & Tennessee, and the Mobile & Ohio; The State Convention in Jackson votes 84-15 to withdraw from the Union and Mississippi secedes on January 9, the second (after South Carolina) of eleven states. The official document is signed by 98 of the 100 delegates. On Jan. 20, Mississippi state troops seize Fort Adams on Ship Island in the Mississippi Sound off the shore of Biloxi, a key refueling point for Union vessels and key to the defense of New Orleans; On Feb.4, Confederate constitutional convention meets for the first time in Montgomery, Alabama, Alabama, Georgia, Florida, Louisiana, Mississippi & South Carolina elect Jefferson Davis president of the Confederacy. Davis takes his oath of office in Montgomery on February 18; Confederates fire on Ft. Sumter in Charleston, S.C. on Apr. 12. War begins! In April, President Davis calls on Mississippi for 8,000 men to serve for 12 months. Many a farmer is willing to risk foreclosure by pledging his crops to the government in hopes that it would help fight off the creditors. By May, 11 states have seceded. On Sept. 16, the Confederacy, in the face of growing Federal naval power in the Gulf, withdraws from Ship Island. A Union force from the *USS Massachusetts* occupies the island. On Sept. 28, the governor orders the assembling of 10,000 men at Grenada and Vicksburg. On Nov. 27, a Federal expedition sails from Hampton, Virginia, to Ship Island. By Dec. 3, Ship Island is occupied by Federal forces under Major General

A Chronology of Mississippi History

Benjamin Butler with assistance of the *USS Constitution*. Federal troops raid Biloxi at the end of the year. War has come to Mississippi; In the fall, only four students appear at the University of Mississippi, so it closes; In the election Oct. 7, Gov. Pettus receives 30,467 votes, Jacob Thompson 3,556 votes; Jews organize Congregation Beth Israel in Jackson.

1862

On Feb. 6, Ulysses S Grant begins his military campaign in Mississippi; On Feb. 15, a Federal expedition from Cairo, Illinois, moves down the Tennessee River to Eastport in Tishomingo County and continues through Feb. 22; Shortly after daybreak on April 6, the Battle of Shiloh, Tenn. begins. The Confederate forces are led by Gen. Albert Sidney Johnston out of Corinth, Miss. against the Union forces under Gen. Ulysses S. Grant. There is savage fighting at Shiloh Church, the Sunken Road, the Hornet's Nest, and Peach Orchard. Grant gets reinforcements when Gen. Buell arrives. Gen. Johnston is killed in the fighting and General Beauregard assumes command. The next day, Beauregard realizes he is far outnumbered and wisely retreats back to Corinth. Union casualties at Shiloh are 12,163, while Confederate losses are listed at 10,699 killed and wounded. On April 28, Beauregard is reinforced by Van Dorn's Army, but they're still outnumbered two to one. They turned their troops to fortifying Corinth. The Battle of Farmington on May 9 pits Union Maj. Gen. John Pope's men against Confederate Maj. Gen. Earl Van Dorn's forces 11½ miles southeast of Corinth. By late May, it is apparent to Beauregard that his army will soon be encircled, so orders are given to withdraw to Tupelo. The evacuation of Corinth begins the night of May 29; In Yazoo City, even though an invading army might be expected at any moment, people "engaged an old man to play the fiddle for the children to dance" on May Day, and the schoolgirls have their May Queen; On May 13, Natchez is occupied by Federal naval forces under Flag Officer Daniel Farragut. The first attack on Vicksburg comes by way of the river from the south by Admiral Farragut's gunboats on May 18. Natchez had surrendered without a shot, but at Vicksburg, it was a different story. The ironclad ram, the *CSS Arkansas* commanded by Lt. Charles W. Read, casts off from Yazoo City and starts down the Yazoo River on July 14. The next day, the ship enters the Mississippi and fights her way past ocean-going warships, river ironclads, and rams. She takes a severe pounding, but makes it and ties up in front of Vicksburg. Farragut is enraged and for the next week, tries every way he can to destroy the *Arkansas*, but she escapes destruction. The first Union attack on Vicksburg has failed. Farragut leaves the Vicksburg area on July 27 and returns his big boats to New Orleans. Ironically, the Confederates themselves destroy the *Arkansas* on Aug. 6 when her machinery fails for the second time in as many days; On June 15, Brig. Gen. William Sherman leads an expedition to Holly Springs in Marshall County and skirmishes at the Tallahatchie River Bridge. Fighting there continues through June 18; In mid Sept., there is heavy fighting at Iuka where Union Maj. Gen. William Rosecrans defeats Maj. Gen. Sterling Price on Sept. 19 with casualties numbering about 2,350; In early Oct., the Battle of Corinth is one of the war's bitterest fights with Union losses totaling 2,359 and Confederate, 4,838; On Nov. 5, a disastrous explosion at a Jackson arsenal just a few blocks north of the Capitol kills 47 employees; On Dec. 12, the Union gunboat, the *USS Cairo*, strikes a Confederate torpedo and sinks in the Yazoo River just north of Vicksburg. All 160 men aboard escape without injury; On Dec. 20, Confederate forces under Gen. Earl Van Dorn raid General Grant's supply depot at Holly Springs and destroy or confiscate over $1,000,000 of Federal supplies; On Dec. 27 & 28, Confederates turn back Gen. Sherman's forces ending the second campaign against Vicksburg. The Confederates suffer 206 casualties, the Federals 1,929. Throughout 1862 Federal naval and military expeditions against Vicksburg have failed; Confederate soldiers in Jackson use an old covered bridge across the Pearl River as a make-shift prison to hold 401 Union troops; Pushed to their capacity by the demands of wartime, textile mills of the state are using 2,000 pounds of wool and 20 bales of cotton a day.

Deaths: Former Governor Joseph W. Matthews dies in Palmetto, Georgia on Aug. 27.

1863

On Jan. 1, President Lincoln issues the Emancipation Proclamation freeing "all slaves in areas still in rebellion."; At the beginning of the year, an army under Gen. Grant descends the river to the Louisiana shore near Vicksburg, and assisted by a strong fleet under Admiral Porter, strives for 3 months to cross the river and attack the city from the rear. On the high bluffs commanding a bend in the river, Confederate batteries prevent the passage of Federal vessels and make impossible cooperation between Federal troops above and below the city; By March, private factories in the state are producing 10,000 garments a week; Anti-war feelings are not widespread, although there remain some counties that are against the war. The northeastern county of Tishomingo, with very few slaves, remains mainly Unionist and to a lesser degree, its neighboring counties of Pontotoc and Itawamba. Jones County even went so far as to secede from the Confederacy late last year and later will be called the "Republic of Jones" in the newspapers around the country. A large number of Confederate deserters are hiding in Choctaw, Attala, Leake, and Winston Counties; As the war progresses, life for Mississippians becomes extremely difficult, to say the least. They learn to make "coffee" out of parched corn and okra or dried sweet potatoes, tea from dried raspberry leaves, soda from sour milk or vinegar mixed with lye burnt out of corn cobs, wax candles by adding quicklime to mutton suet, ink and dyes from berries and tree bark, and horse collars out of plaited cornshucks; Even in the dark days of Vicksburg, many farmers offer supplies free to Confederate commissaries; In March, Gen. Grant prepares to launch his final Vicksburg offensive. Vicksburg has defied large-scale land and river expeditions for more than a year; Starting Apr. 17, Gen. Grierson and his forces destroy $4 million worth of property in their two-week raid across the state; On Apr. 30, in the largest amphibious operation in U.S. history (until North Africa in WWII), Grant puts 24,000 men and 60 cannon ashore at Bruinsburg near Grand Gulf. After a battle with Confederate forces on May 1, Grant's columns occupy Port Gibson. After Grant declares "This town is too beautiful to burn," his forces drive northward; The bloodiest action of the Vicksburg campaign occurs on May 16 at Champion Hill about 12 miles east of Vicksburg. Federals number 32,000, Confederates total 23,000. Vicksburg defender Gen. John C. Pemberton loses nearly 4,000 men, not counting Loring's division. Grant sustains casualties of 2,500, with Hovey losing one-third of his division killed or wounded. Historians later call the battle the most decisive of the Civil War. On May 17, the Union army continues its march toward Vicksburg with another battle near Bovina — the Big Black River Bridge Battle claims 276 Union troops killed and wounded with 1,751 Confederates captured or killed. On May 18, Union guns open

A Chronology of Mississippi History

on the city — the 47-day Siege of Vicksburg has begun; Thousands of shells are hurled into the city. Citizens dig caves into the sides of the hills. Vicksburg's defenders run out of food. The ration for a soldier near the end of the siege is one biscuit and a small piece of bacon per day. Vicksburg surrenders! At 10 a.m., on July 4 the Confederate army, 29,500 strong, marches out and stack arms. Grant's army marches in, takes possession of Vicksburg and raises the "Stars and Stripes" over the Warren County Courthouse. Gen. Grant would later say in his memoirs, when Vicksburg fell "the fate of the Confederacy was sealed." Grant then sends a force under Sherman to capture Jackson, which is soon occupied by Union troops. Points as far south as Natchez and as far north as Yazoo City are occupied by Federal troops; Vicksburg and Natchez become refuges for Negro runaways; On Aug. 6, the state capitol is moved from Meridian to Macon where it remains until the end of the war; Charles Clark is Governor starting November 16.

1864

There is a skirmish at the Big Black River Bridge on Feb. 4; Union Gen. Sherman moves out of Vicksburg in early Feb. with his army of 25,000 men. They destroy property between Jackson and Meridian — some estimates place property loss as high as $50,000,000. The Federals reach Meridian on Feb. 14 and destroy the city; the State legislature tries to provide relief from war-caused inflation by fixing prices. The schedule for April was "...bacon, $1.40 to $1.50 per pound; coffee, $5 per pound; corn, $1.75 to $3.10 per bushel; corn meal, $2.25 to $3.00 per bushel; flour, extra, $50 per barrel; horses, first class, $700; good jeans, $8 per yard; molasses, $7 per gallon; salt, $15 per bushel; army shoes, $10 per pair; soap, 75 cents per pound; woolen socks, $2 per pair; sugar, $2 per pound; green tea, $10 per pound; vinegar, $3 per gallon; and wool, $5 per pound."; Groups of women at Natchez form "Needle Regiments" to sew for the soldiers. One of the boxes contains "60 pairs of socks, 25 blankets, 13 pairs of gloves, 14 flannel shirts, 16 towels, 2 handkerchiefs, 5 pairs of trousers, and one bushel of dried apples."; Parents and friends send gift boxes to loved ones fighting. A typical one contains blackberry cordial, honey, dried apples, pecans, letter paper, stamps, shirts and socks; People had to be self-sufficient. Attala County, for example, this year produces corn, wheat, flour, rice, indigo, wine, bacon, lard, leather, shoes, boots, jugs, jars, cups, saucers, hats, buttons, buckets, brooms, furniture, and wagons; There is a Confederate victory at Brice's Cross Roads on June 10; On July 12 there is heavy fighting near Pontotoc. On July 13-15, the Battle of Harrisburg, near Tupelo, is a fierce and deadly one. A local Confederate Regiment of 279 strong, lose 235 men killed and wounded including every field and line officer of the 38th Mississippi Company A (mounted infantry), except one. All losses, nearly 85%, were Mississippians; the town of Oxford is almost completely burned by the Union Army under the command of Gen. A. J. Smith on Aug. 22; On Oct. 7, Jackson is called "Chimneyville" for the first time when the *Illustrated Newspaper* shows an illustration of the ruins of the city; When Union commanders hear that some trains were again running, cavalry columns are given the mission of destroying those railroads. Col. Embury Osband strikes first. Leaving Vicksburg on Nov. 23 with his reinforced brigade, they ride up the Benton Road and strike the Mississippi Central near Vaughan. They burn the railroad bridge across the Big Black at Way's Bluff, then follow the railroad to Goodman, burning bridges and trestles as they advance. When the Federals reach Yazoo City, they are harassed by a brigade from Wirt Adams's command. At Concord Church on Dec. 1, there is a bitter battle between Odband's patrols and the Confederates. The Yanks are bested, and the next day, Osband pulls out of Yazoo City and returns to Vicksburg. On Dec. 21, Gen. Grierson leaves Memphis with 3,500 horsemen. Before reaching Vicksburg on Jan. 4, 1865, they burn railroad bridges and trestles, twist rails, and destroy other property as they march through towns such as Lamar, Ripley, Booneville, Egypt, Houston, Bankston, Grenada and Durant.

1865

On Feb. 6, Robert E. Lee is named Confederate General in Chief; On Mar. 18, the Congress of the Conferderate States of America adjourns for the last time; On Apr. 16, a large crowd gathers in front of the Warren County Courthouse in Vicksburg as news of Lincoln's assassination is received; Some battles still rage across the state during the first part of this year. Gen. Richard Taylor, commanding troops in Alabama, Mississippi and East Louisiana, surrenders to Gen. Edward Canby on May 4 at Citronelle, Alabama. On May 10, President Davis is captured by Union Cavalry near Irwinville, Georgia. Gov. Clark surrenders the government to Gen. E.D. Osband on May 22. The Civil War is over — for Mississippi, the Confederacy, and for the Nation. The South had been crushed. Much of Mississippi had been devastated and the economy ruined. The *New Orleans Times* reports soon after the end of the war that "extreme poverty rules in almost every household" in Mississippi. The crop of 1865 was small, and as a result most people in the state experience a bleak winter. Confederate deaths from the war total 133,821, to which should be added 26,000 to 31,000 who died in Union prisons. An estimated total of 78,000 Mississippians, about 50% of the white men between 16 and 50 years of age, had served in the Confederate armies, of which 59,000 were killed or wounded. Mississippi suffers the largest percentage of casualties of any state in the Confederacy. Five Mississippians held the rank of Major General and 29 the rank of Brigadier General. During the war, it became necessary to move the seat of government several times. The capitol is moved to Enterprise in Clarke County, then to Meridian, then back to Jackson, then briefly to Columbus in Lowndes County, then back to Meridian, then to Macon, and finally back to Jackson; President Andrew Johnson appoints Judge W. L. Sharkey provisional governor June 13; The post- war legislature estimates the state's wartime indebtedness as $8,842,837.73; On Aug. 31, the body of Choctaw Chief Greenwood Leflore is wrapped in the U.S. Flag and buried near his home in Malmaison; William Sharkey is governor from June 13 to Oct. 16, then Benjamin Humphreys is governor, effective Oct. 16; The Constitution of 1865 is framed that abolishes slavery in Mississippi. Over 400,000 Negroes in the state gain their freedom; The legislature brings in a bill entitled "An Act to confer Civil Rights or Freedmen, and for other purposes." The bill extends few rights of substance to blacks, and becomes the basis of the controversial Black Code, the first enacted by a Southern state after the Civil War; By the fall, virtually all 13,000 men of the military occupation force in the state are former slaves. Not until racial tensions subside does the War Dept. order disbandment of Negro regiments; The Pearl Street African Methodist Episcopal Church is established in Jackson.

1866

The state legislature refuses to ratify the 13th amendment (abolishing slavery) and 14th amendment (citizenship rights not to be abridged) to the United States Constitution.

A Chronology of Mississippi History

1867
On the eve of the imposition of Reconstruction, the legislature repeals most of the features of the Black Code; Reconstruction Act passes and Mississippi is placed under Federal military rule; Tupelo is chosen as the county seat of Lee County on April 15; Jefferson Davis is released from prison in May.
Deaths: Former Governor John J. Pettus dies in Pulaski County, Arkansas on Jan. 28.

1868
On Jan. 7, the Mississippi constitutional convention meets in Jackson; Money virtually disappears from circulation. When courts intervene to force the debtors to pay up, they usually sell their land at prices of 25 to 30 cents an acre. Thousands of acres of land are forfeited to authorities for nonpayment of taxes; A state constitution is made, but rejected by the voters in June. By a margin of only 7,629 votes out of 120,091 cast, Mississippi Democrats do what no other conservative party in the South is able to do — reject a Black and Tan constitution; Gov. Humphreys is removed from office by Federals and replaced by Adelbert Ames June 15; Throughout the summer, registrars under the direction of Maj. Gen. Edward Ord and his 2,100 bluecoats, move from precinct to precinct enrolling voters. Of a voting population of about 160,000, some 137,000 men register to vote — 79,176 blacks and 58,385 whites; R.H. Henry, who later founds *The Clarion-Ledger* newspaper, starts his career at the *Forest Register* in Scott Co.
Deaths: Former Governor John J. McRae dies in British Honduras (now Belize) in Central America on May 31 while there visiting his brother. Buried in that country, he is the only Mississippi governor buried outside the U.S.

1869
The Constitution of 1868 is approved; The *Oxford Falcon* reports the sale of land at $20 an acre which during the years just following the war could have been purchased for $2 an acre; The State Fair is held in Jackson for the first time; The Brotherhood of Locomotive Engineers is organized in Water Valley, the first local union established in Mississippi. Later, a member of two of the early lodges in Water Valley will be the legendary railroad engineer, Casey Jones, one of the great heroes of American folklore; With blacks flocking to the polls to cast Republican ballots and with thousands of angry whites staying home in protest, the Alcorn-Lynch-Ames ticket wins a landslide victory in the fall with 76,000 votes to the opposition's 38,000. Republicans also win an overwhelming majority in the legislature and elect all of the congressmen.
Deaths: Former Gov. William McWillie dies on March 3.

1870
Mississippi is readmitted to the Union on Feb. 23, the 10th of 11 states. Three days later military rule ends in the state; Gov. James Alcorn is inaugurated; Adelbert Ames & Hiram Revels (1st black U.S. senator) are seated in the Senate on Feb. 25; In July, Gov. Alcorn secures legislation prohibiting the use of masks and disguises by night riders, an early effort to break up the Ku Klux Klan; The Methodist Episcopal Church establishes a college for blacks, Shaw University (later Rust College) at Holly Springs, Mississippi; About 990 miles of virtually inoperable railroads exist in the state; The state now holds more than 2 million acres of tax-delinquent lands.
Deaths: Writer, jurist, and educator Augustus Longstreet, who headed 4 universities and was the second chancellor of the University of Mississippi, dies in Oxford on July 9 at age 79.

1871
Alcorn A&M College is established from Oakland College (1830), which makes 3 Negro colleges in the state with Rust College (1870) and Tougaloo College (1869); During its first year in operation, the public school system has 66,257 students in 3,000 school units with 3,600 teachers of whom 399 are black; Liberty in Amite County erects the first Confederate Monument in the U.S.; On Sept. 7, Jackson's first ice plant begins operation with a 3,000 pounds per day output; On Nov. 30, Ridgley Powers becomes governor after James Alcorn, the state's 1st Republican governor, resigns to take a U.S. Senate seat; Clinton and Starkville ban liquor sales.

1872
The town of Tougaloo bans liquor sales; Congress gives amnesty to most Confederates; With only 32 Negroes in the House, John R. Lynch, born into slavery, is chosen speaker of the house; The legislature passes a popular measure allowing tax refunds for manufacturing firms showing a profit of less than 4%; By special act of the legislature, the city of McComb if granted its charter on April 5; Rail terminals at Winona and Canton are so busy that cotton shipments are often delayed for several days; In June, a 180-foot riverboat, the *Iron Mountain*, leaves Vicksburg carrying 55 passengers and crew with a cargo of molasses and towing barges of cotton. Cotton barges are found, but no trace of the boat or survivors is ever found!

1873
Adelbert Ames is elected gov. the second time; Even though many Negroes are elected as Republicans, a majority of the state's counties are under Democratic-conservative control.
Deaths: Former Gov. William L. Sharkey dies in Washington, D.C. on April 29 at the age of 74.

1874
On Feb. 3, Blanche K. Bruce becomes the first black elected to a full six-year term in the U.S. Senate. Negro membership in the legislature has increased to 60. Most conservatives fear Gov. Ames will resign for a Senate post and thus elevate the black Lt. Governor, Alexander Davis, into the governorship; There's race trouble in Warren County in late summer as blacks and whites riot over political offices held by blacks. Two whites and 29 blacks are killed; Property tax reaches an all-time high of 14 mills; The last documented duel in the state takes place on April 18 at Bay St. Louis; The Mount Hermon Female Seminary for Negro women is opened at Clinton.

1875
The bustling Monroe County town of Camargo has its incorporation repealed on Apr. 5. The town dies as its residents move to nearby Nettleton; The Mississippi Dental Association is formed in Vicksburg on Apr. 21; On July 4, White Democrats kill several blacks in terrorist attacks in Vicksburg; On Sept. 1, white Democrats attacked Republicans at Yazoo City. One white and 3 blacks are killed; There's intense political strife as race riots at Clinton, Mississippi on Sept. 4 result in the deaths of 3 white men. Democrats warn that a race war is imminent; Democrats win the election around the state on Nov. 4 giving control back to whites; Charles Caldwell is the first black in Mississippi accused of the murder of a white man and found "not guilty" by an all-white jury. Later elected to the state senate, he is assassinated on Dec. 25 in Clinton.
Deaths: Former Gov. James Whitfield dies on June 25.

1876
Aldelbert Ames resigns as governor after the threat of impeachment; John Stone becomes governor on March 29; Elections result in sweeping Democratic victories. Of the nearly 165,000 votes cast, only 52,605 were Republican.
Deaths: Elizabeth Taylor Greenfield, a Natchez native (b. 1818), who became the first African-American concert singer who was known as "the Black Swan" dies this year.

A Chronology of Mississippi History

1877
The State Board of Health is established Feb. 1; The Chicago, St. Louis & New Orleans Railroad system becomes part of the Illinois Central Railroad Company; The Seminary For Freedmen is established at Natchez by the Negro Baptist Associations; Perry Co. Courthouse in New Augusta burns.
Deaths: Former Governor Charles Clark dies in Bolivar County on Dec. 18 at the age of 67.

1878
Yellow-fever epidemic strikes all over the state affecting 46 towns and killing over 3,000; The legislature establishes the Agricultural and Mechanical College at Starkville, later known as Mississippi State College and then as Mississippi State University, chartered on Feb. 23; In the fall, there are 155,679 white and 190,211 black children of school age, yet average daily attendance is only 64,318 whites and 71,658 blacks.

1879
On June 28, Congress creates the Mississippi River Commission to prevent flooding and improve navigation; 75% of blacks over 10 years old in the state cannot read or write.
Deaths: Poet Irwin Russell from Port Gibson dies in New Orleans 2 days before Christmas, one year after publishing his famous poem, *Christmas Night in the Quarters.*

1880
Railroads are taking business away from steamboats with 1,119 miles of railroad tracks and 2,000 Mississippians employed by railroad companies; A&M College opens its first session on Oct. 6 with 354 students; Mississippians number 1,131,597, about 650,000 blacks and 480,000 whites — 123,000 classified as farmers and planters with over 215,000 agricultural laborers. The value of livestock in the state is $24,285,717, down substantially since 1860. Lawrence County is the first county in the state to ban liquor sales.
Deaths: Former Governor Henry S. Foote dies at his home in Nashville, Tennessee on May 20 at age 76; Overcome by apoplexy, former Gov. Albert G. Brown falls face down in a shallow pond and dies near Terry, Miss. on June 12 at age 67.

1881
On Oct. 28, the Union Co. Courthouse is destroyed by a fire set by an arsonist to destroy his criminal record; New Orleans, Mobile & Chattanooga Railroad merges with the Louisville & Nashville system; Telephone lines are installed in Natchez.

1882
Robert Lowry becomes governor on Jan. 29; The legislature passes a bill exempting new industries from taxation for ten years. On Mar. 9, the legislature passes a law prohibiting the sale of intoxicating liquors within five miles of the University of Mississippi; Ole Miss becomes the first college in the state to go co-educational; The Yazoo & Mississippi Valley Railroad is organized; On April 22, a fierce tornado destroys Monticello, the Lawrence County seat, leaving only three homes standing; There is a devastating Mississippi River flood this year. For a time, the river is so wide that a person could take a boat from Vicksburg to Monroe, Louisiana!; The Bay Street Presbyterian Church is Hattiesburg is established.
Deaths: Former Governor Benjamin G. Humphreys dies in Leflore County on Dec. 20 at the age of 74.

1883
On April 22, a single tornado hits Beauregard, Mississippi killing 40 people; The Seminary For Freedmen is moved from Natchez to Jackson and renamed Jackson College; The Main Street Baptist Church in Hattiesburg is founded.

1884
The city of Hattiesburg is incorporated on Mar. 11. First known as Twin Forks, it is named for Hattie Lott Hardy, wife of city founder Capt. William H. Hardy; A college for women is established in Columbus on Mar. 12, first as Industrial Institute and College, then Mississippi State College for Women (1920) and later as Mississippi Univ. for Women.
Deaths: Historian J.F.H. Claiborne dies on May 17 at age 76.

1885
A second institution for the care and treatment of the insane, On Jan. 12, the East Mississippi State Insane Asylum is opened in Meridian; L.Q.C. Lamar becomes the fourth Mississippian to serve on the cabinet when he is appointed as Secretary of the Interior by President Cleveland. He is the second Mississippian to head the department; The Mississippi Education Association is organized as the State Teachers' Association; Industrial Institute and College in Columbus, authorized last year, begins its first session with 341 students.

1886
On Jan. 4, the Mississippi State Bar Association is formed in Jackson; On March 17, twenty blacks are killed in the Carrollton Massacre; On March 25, the Bolivar County village of Sims is chartered as a town and renamed Cleveland after U.S. President Grover Cleveland; Out of a total of 471,622 educable children in the state, only 270,774 are enrolled, and average daily attendance is 163,864. There are 6,112 teachers of which 2,752 are black. Teacher salaries in county schools average $33 a month for whites, $23.50 a month for blacks. In city schools, the figures are $52 and $32; An electric light plant is started in Natchez to provide lights for a casino.

1887
L.Q.C. Lamar, a U.S. senator during the 1870s and 1880s, is appointed to the U.S. Supreme Court; The all-black town of Mound Bayou is founded by Isaiah T. Montgomery, a Warren County native; The African Methodist Episcopal Church establishes Campbell College in Vicksburg and Friars Point.

1888
John Logan Power, a native of Ireland, who owns and publishes *The Clarion* in Jackson consolidates his paper with the *Brookhaven Ledger*, owned and published by R.H. Henry. *The Clarion-Ledger* is born; The legislature passes laws providing separate accommodations for blacks on railroads. Other "Jim Crow" laws are soon enacted. The legislature establishes the first Agricultural Experiment Station.

1889
On June 5, a fire in downtown Biloxi destroys 25 buildings while firefighters stand by helplessly due to a lack of water; The last professional bare-knuckle fight in America takes place near Richburg in Lamar County between the great John L. Sullivan and challenger Jake Kilrain; The Neshoba County Fair is first held; Receipts of state government this year total $1,151,055; The Mississippi Bankers Association is formed; The New York Life Insurance Company has 1,434 policies in force worth $4,073,810, more than any insurer in the state.
Deaths: Former President of the Confederacy Jefferson Davis dies Dec. 6 at Beauvoir on the Gulf Coast where he had spent his last years. His body is first buried in the Metarie Cemetary in New Orleans and is reburied in 1893 in Jefferson Davis Circle, Hollywood Cemetary, in Richmond, Virginia.

1890
On Jan. 13, John M. Stone becomes governor for the second time; On Feb. 17, the largest antebellum home ever built in the state, Windsor near Port Gibson in Clairborne County, burns to the ground. The fire is caused by a careless smoker; Expenses of the legislature run to $75,485, the greatest single expenditure of state government; In April, up to 1,200 people

A Chronology of Mississippi History

a day arrive in Aberdeen by train to hear famous evangelist Sam Jones; Statewide, there are 4,334 white teachers paid an average of $32 a month, and 3,212 Negro teachers paid $20 per month, and they all receive pay for only the 4 months of school a year. About 80% of schools in the state are one room-one teacher. There are 272,682 school-age blacks in the state with 183,290 enrolled in public schools, but the average attendance is only 101,710. The average daily attendance for whites is 90,716 out of a possible 191,792. Only 12,900 whites and 2,244 blacks attend private schools, a mere 7% of total school attendance; The University of Mississippi has 232 students with 9 professors and 24 students graduate. The name of Shaw University, the black college at Holly Springs, is changed to Rust College; the new state constitution of 1890 is made. The final vote on its adoption, 104 to 8, comes on Nov. 1. The only black delegate at the Constitutional Convention is Isaiah T. Montgomery, who founded the all-black town of Mound Bayou in 1887; Most cities in the state now have a duel cemetery policy and newspapers have their own policies for handling black advertisements and announcements; A guide book to Vicksburg published this year states that houses have recently been numbered, several streets are being paved at a cost of 50¢ per square yard, the city pays the water company $65 per year for each of the 95 fire hydrants in use and an electric company is paid $108 per year for each of 50 arc street lights. In addition, 3½ miles of electric street railroad is also in operation; Prevailing statewide prices: beef, 4¢ a pound; bacon, 6¢ a pound; eggs, 14¢ per dozen; Forty-six banks in the state have resources of $10 million, including $635,631 cash; Confederate soldiers, sailors, and their servants who lost a limb in the service, or who suffered incapacitating wounds, receive a pension of $17.85 a year, if they own less than $500 property; There are 2,333 miles of railroad track and over 4,000 railroad employees in the state; Black churches in the state include 1,385 Negro Baptist churches with 136,647 members, 293 Colored Methodist Episcopal churches with 20,107 members, 195 Northern Methodist Episcopal churches with 14,869 members, 42 African Methodist Episcopal churches with 10,270 members, and 64 African Methodist Episcopal Zion churches with 8,519 members.

1891
Census figures for 1890 are released, showing Mississippi with 1,289,600 people — 744,749 black and 544,851 white. Vicksburg has a population of 13,373, Meridian 10,624, Natchez 10,101 and Jackson only 5,920. Hinds County has 28,368 blacks, 10,892 whites. The total urban population of the state is 69,966 with only 12 places in the state with 2,500 or more inhabitants. Census figures also show the state has 305,000 horses and mules, 915,000 cattle and calves including 96,000 draft oxen, 452,000 sheep and lambs, over one million hogs, and about 6 million chickens and turkeys. The value of all livestock in the state is $33,936,435. Rosa Wiss, born in Meridian c. 1868, graduates from Industrial Institute and College (Miss. University for Women). She will become the first woman in Mississippi to receive a medical degree.

1892
The state auditor reports 46 property and liability insurance companies and 3 life insurance companies doing business in the state with 2 fire insurance companies, Mississippi Home Insurance Co. of Vicksburg and Columbus Banking and Insurance Co. of Columbus, being chartered in the state; Millsaps College opens in Jackson.

1893
There is a financial panic, like the one in 1837, with 15,000 businesses bankrupt nationwide and hundreds in Mississippi; On Oct. 1, a fierce hurricane (before they were named) hits the Mississippi Gulf Coast killing more people and causing more damage than any previous storm. It wrecks the seafood industry and knocks out Biloxi's week-old electric light system
Deaths: L.Q.C. Lamar, who was a member of the U.S. House of Representatives, a U.S. Senator, a U.S. Presidential Cabinet member, and the only Mississippian to ever serve on the U.S. Supreme Court, dies on Jan. 23 in Georgia at the age of 67.
Sports: Ole Miss has its first football win Nov. 11 by crushing Southwestern Baptist University at Jackson, Tenn. 56-0.

1894
The present state flag, along with Coat of Arms, is adopted by the legislature. The statute will later be repealed in 1906.
Deaths: former Governor James Alcorn dies on Dec. 20.
Sports: On Oct. 27, Ole Miss plays football in Jackson for the first time, losing to Alabama 6-0.

1896
Anselm J. McLaurin becomes governor Jan. 20; A law school is opened at Millsaps College on Sept. 23 (it will operate for 22 years until 1918 when nearly all the students join the service during World War I).

1897
Jimmie Rodgers, "The Singing Brakeman," is born on Sept. 8 at Pine Springs near Meridian; William Faulkner, Mississippi's most famous writers, is born on Sept. 25 in New Albany.
Deaths: U.S. Sen. James Z. George of Carroll Co., known as the "father of the U.S. Dept. of Agriculture" and the architect of the state constitution of 1890, dies on Aug. 14 at age 71 in Mississippi City where he had gone in search of health.
Sports: Ole Miss plays no football this year when a yellow fever epidemic causes a cancellation of the season.

1898
The first free public library in the state is established at Biloxi with a total of about 100 books; Yellow fever returns with 1,385 reported cases in 28 locations in Mississippi. Eighty-four people die from the disease. There have also been 2,876 cases of smallpox reported in the state in the past two years.
Deaths: Blanche K. Bruce, the first African-American ever to serve a full term in the U.S. Senate, dies in Washington on March 17; and Annie C. Peyton, founder of Mississippi University for Women in Columbus, dies this year.

1899
A capital investment of $10,800,000 in 608 sawmills produces more than one billion board feet of lumber. Mississippi has become one of the leading timber-producing states.

1900
On Jan. 16, Andrew Longino becomes Mississippi's first governor of the new century. Plans are drawn for construction of a new state capitol; On Apr. 30, John Luther (Casey) Jones, dies in the Cannonball Express train wreck at Vaughan in Yazoo County; About 92% of Mississippians live on farms, although manufacturing establishments now number 4,772, up from 1,479 in 1880; Value of lumber is $15,650,110 while cotton is $10,368,904; Railroads in the state have 2,934 miles of track; Mississippi has 12 national banks and 101 state banks; Enrollment at Alcorn College is 425. Enrollment in all colleges in the state is 2,727; The name of the Miss. State Lunatic Asylum is changed to Miss. State Insane Hospital; On Nov. 9, a fire of unknown origin burns 90 buildings in the business district and a posh residential area of Biloxi; The Scared Heart Catholic Church is Hattiesburg is established.
Deaths: Former two-time Gov. John M. Stone dies in Holly Springs, Mississippi on March 26 at the age of 69.

A Chronology of Mississippi History

1901
On Mar. 20, "Concord" in Natchez burns. It was the residence of Manuel Gayoso de Lemos, the first Spanish Governor of the Mississippi territory; Work begins on the new capitol building in March when funds become available after courts order the Illinois Central Railroad to pay almost $1 million in back taxes; In Apr., another epidemic of smallpox in the state causes 595 deaths out of 2,720 cases in the past five months.
Deaths: On Jan. 16, Hiram Revels, the first black U.S. senator from the state, dies in Aberdeen, Mississippi at the age of 73.
Sports: Mississippi A&M College (later to become Mississippi State University) has its first football victory with a 17-0 win over the University of Mississippi.

1902
A Department of Insurance is created, and the first Insurance Commissioner is W.Q. Cole of Yalobusha County; A State Department of Archives and History, the second such department in the nation, is established. The first Director, Dr. Dunbar Rowland, assumes his duties March 27; Mississippi experiences a record-setting heat wave (through the summer of 2000, the year of 1902 still holds the record as being the hottest summer in state history); the Teddy Bear gets its start from an incident in Mississippi this year. President Theodore "Teddy" Roosevelt was on a hunt in Sharkey County near Onward. By Nov. 14, the second day of the hunt, Roosevelt was disappointed that he had had no real opportunity to shoot a bear. So his friends and his guide, Holt Collier, a Mississippi native, cornered a young, 235-pound bear cub and tie it to a tree for Roosevelt to shoot. But Roosevelt declines to shoot this little bear, believing such an act to be beneath his dignity as a hunter and as a man: "If I shot that little fellow I couldn't be able to look my boys in the face again." News of the day's events quickly reached the press, notably including Washington Post political cartoonist Clifford Berryman. It wasn't long before the appearance of "Teddy's Bear," later the "Teddy Bear." The great success of that toy bear led to the formation of the Ideal Toy Corp. in 1903.

1903
On Jan. 2, President Roosevelt shuts down the post office in Indianola, Mississippi for refusing to accept its appointed postmistress because she is black; Headline in the *Weekly Clarion-Ledger* of June 4: "The Largest Crowd Ever Assembled in the City of Jackson" — it's the dedication of the new capitol, which draws about 25,000 people. Cost of the building, including the grading of the grounds, the pavements, and additional granite steps is $1,093,641. There is $101,000 worth of genuine marble, $36,000 worth of Scagliola, and $212,000 worth of Bedford Limestone. The electric and gas fixtures cost $15,000. There are 4,750 incandescent electric lights, of which 750 are placed in the central dome and rotunda. The eagle atop the dome, made of copper with a heavy coating of gold leaf, measures 15 feet in wing-spread, is 8 feet tall, and costs $1,500; The Matty Hersee Hospital is founded in Meridian; In December, 21 life insurance companies have $68,233,889 of insurance in force in the state.

1904
On Jan. 19, James K. Vardaman becomes governor with the support of small farmers and others, ending the control of the plantation "planter class."; In Jan., the legislature meets for the first time in the new Capitol Building; On Feb. 9, Jackson city officials pass an ordinance requiring all houses and buildings to have a uniform numbering system; In Feb., there are 167 banks in the state reporting $46,427,948 in resources, as compared to 149 banks with resources of $34,037,321 the previous year. There are 11 banks owned and operated by Negroes; On May 25, a devastating fire in Yazoo City nearly destroys the town. Along with some 200 or more residences, nearly every business and industry is gone. A total of 324 buildings are destroyed with only one livery stable, one drug store and two black churches left standing. The city will be rebuilt within a year; On Sept. 30, Picayune in Pearl River County is incorporated; This year, the Memphis-to-Vicksburg segment of the Mississippi River carries 87,581,000 tons of cotton, 76,357,000 tons of lumber and 463,629,000 tons of logs. South from Vicksburg to New Orleans, the amounts are 46,997,000 tons of cotton, 25,358,000 tons of lumber and 133,683,000 tons of logs; A new Perry County Courthouse is finished in New Augusta to replace the one that burned in 1877; The Rhodes Scholarship is first established and Ebenezer James Ford of Columbia, is the first in the state to have the prestigious honor of being a "Rhodes Scholar."
Deaths: Adams County, Mississippi native Prentiss Ingraham, the third most prolific author in the U.S. with more than 600 books to his credit, dies at Beauvoir in Biloxi on Aug. 16.
Sports: The Ole Miss Rebels win over Southwestern Baptist University (now Union Univ.) in Jackson, Tenn. 114-0. That remains the most one-sided football win in Ole Miss history.

1905
As of March 1, there are 184 insurance companies licensed in the state; On May 24, the village of Moorhead in Sunflower Co., pop. 437, is officially made a town by Gov. Vardaman. On Oct. 14, a town charter is granted to Richton in Perry Co.

1906
Streetcars start operation in Yazoo City on Jan. 2. It's the second municipal streetcar system in the nation; On Feb. 25, Lamar Mutual Life Insurance Co. is organized in Jackson; Jackson passes an ordinance to deal with that controversial machine, the automobile. Speed limits are set at 12 mph for straight-away driving and 7 mph for turning; The hurricane of Sept. 21 (before they were named) kills 350 people in Mississippi and Louisiana; On Nov. 19, twenty-three buildings including the post office and *The Chronicle* newspaper burn to the ground in Fayette; Out of a total population of 1,708,272, members of churches in the state number 657,381. Baptists have 371,518, Methodists 212,105, and Roman Catholics 28,576 members. There are 17 congregations of Jews with 746 families.

1907
There are 3 towns in the state with population of 10,000 or more: Meridian 16,444, Vicksburg 15,856 and Natchez 13,680; On Sept. 20 the boll weevil is first detected in Mississippi in a cotton field about 6 miles south of Natchez.

1908
Edmond F. Noel is inaugurated governor on Jan. 21; The legislature passes a statewide liquor prohibition law; On Mar. 4, the state's first full-fledged Mardi-Gras parade is held in Bay St. Louis with 17 floats and several bands; On April 24, a series of tornadoes kills 155 and injures 970 statewide — 102 dead in Lamar and Wayne counties alone; A School of Pharmacy is started at the University of Miss.; Mississipppi ranks third in the nation in lumber production; On Dec. 27, the first cotton ever exported from Gulfport, 9,520 bales, leaves on the British steamer *Conway* bound for Liverpool, England.
Deaths: Stephen Dill Lee, the youngest Lt. General in the Confederacy and the officer who ordered the first shot in the Civil War, later became a state senator, and was the first president of Mississippi A&M College (later Mississippi State University), dies in Vicksburg on May 28 at the age of 74.

A Chronology of Mississippi History

1909
The Mississippi Library Association is founded. The first free library of significant size (see 1898) is established at Houston, Mississippi with the help of the Andrew Carnegie program; The *USS Mississippi* becomes the first and only first-class battleship to visit an inland city anywhere in the U.S. when it navigates up the Mississippi River to Natchez on May 20; On November 1, President William Howard Taft is honored at a special luncheon in the Governor's Mansion in Jackson; The 1,761 saw mills in the state produce 2,572,669,000 board feet of lumber; Mississippi has 10 miles of stone-surfaced road, 125 miles of gravel road, and 50 miles of sand and clay roads, for a total of 185 miles of "improved" roads — out of 38,698 miles of mostly mud-bound so-called public highways in the state; This year, there are 36 life insurance companies operating in the state with $113,462,910 of insurance in force.
Deaths: Former Gov. Anselm McLaurin dies on Dec. 22.

1910
Mississippi Normal College is established by an act of the state legislature. The school, later to become the University of Southern Mississippi, won't open until 1912; The Consolidated School Law is passed. Woolmarket Consolidated School is the first such school in the state, organized on July 16; Farmers in the state report having 1,292,119 hogs, 1,012,632 cattle and 195,245 sheep worth a total of $75 million, plus over $50 million worth of horses and mules; There are now 4,506 miles of railroad tracks in Mississippi.
Deaths: Former Gov. Robert Lowry dies in Jackson Jan. 19.

1911
Tennessee Williams, famous dramatist, is born in Columbus on February 26; On March 11, former President Theodore Roosevelt speaks to a crowd of around 6,000 in McComb in an effort to gain support for the building of the Panama Canal; Violence erupts in McComb, an important railroad terminal, when most of the 1,500 railroad workers there go on strike. Strikebreakers are brought in, martial law is declared, machine guns are placed on top of buildings, and barbed wire surrounds the shops. A number of men are killed and Illinois Central wins. This is a costly lesson for labor unions in Mississippi, for it will be 1922 before shop crafts along the Illinois Central main line attempt another strike; Belhaven College is founded in Jackson as a school for young women.

1912
Earl L. Brewer becomes governor on Jan. 16; Constuction begins on the first concrete highway in the state between Tupelo and Verona in Lee County. Highway 45 is the first hard surface road in the South; A Bureau of Vital Statistics is created and the first state income tax law is passed on Mar. 16; Mississippi State Charity Hospital in Jackson opens June 1; Hattiesburg has six lumber mills, a cotton oil mill, a compress, two railroad shops, the state's largest machine shop, and two phone companies; Mississippi Normal College opens in Hattiesburg on Sept. 18 with a faculty of 18 and 220 students. It'll later be known as the University of Southern Mississipppi.
Deaths: Democrat Hernando De Soto Money, a U.S. congressman and senator who was minority leader from 1909-1911, dies near Biloxi on Sept. 18 at age 73; Former Gov. Ridgely C. Powers dies in Los Angeles, Calif. on Nov. 11 at age 75.

1913
The Piney Woods Country Life School, founded by Dr. Laurence C. Jones, is chartered in Rankin County.

1914
Since 1907, at least 100 banks in the state have failed. On March 9, Senate Bill Number 48 becomes effective, the first comprehensive banking law ever passed in Mississippi; There are 625 deaths from typhoid fever in the state; The state has 5,694 motor vehicles. The first state-aid highway law is passed. Up until now, Mississippi had been one of 6 states in the South which had taken no legal step to build state roads.

1915
On Feb. 4, experiments to find the cause of pellagra begin at the Mississippi State Penitentiary at Parchman; Lee County Road 681 opens — the first concrete road in the South; In Dec., 281 state banks reporting total resources of $72,732,627.
Sports: Edwin "Goat" Hale leads the Mississippi College Collegians (now Choctaws) to a 74-0 victory over Ole Miss.

1916
Theodore Gilmore Bilbo becomes governor on Jan. 18; The legislature establishes a State Tax Commission, a Highway Commission, a State Board of Law Examiners, a Board of Pardons, a Department of Game and Fish, an Education Commission, the Mississippi Illiteracy Commission, and a state-run sanitarium to treat tuberculosis (TB) patients. The legislature also passes a law prohibiting public hangings.
Deaths: the founder of Millsaps College in Jackson, Reuben Millsaps, dies on June 28 and is buried on the college campus.

1917
The state's Centennial year; U.S. enters World War One and 66,000 Mississippian men and women serve including 56,740 young men who are inducted or enlisted. Camp Shelby is a principal training center; Possibly the first major airplane activity in the state is at West Point where "Jenny" planes fly out of Payne Flying Field; The State Tax Commission's total assessed value of all lands in the state is $417,124,293, up from $253,708,655 in 1915; Bank deposits in the state now total $98 million; The state spends about $1,000 on roads this year; The South Mississippi Charity Hospital opens in Laurel.
Deaths: Noted politician "Private" John Allen, who served 8 terms in the U.S. House of Representatives from 1885 to 1901, dies on Oct. 30 at the age of 71.

1918
On Jan. 8, Mississippi becomes the first state to ratify the 18th amendment (prohibition); On Mar. 28, Humphreys County is the last county in the state to be organized; There are 5 prison farms in the state: Belmont, Lambert, Oakley, Parchman, and Rankin; A severe epidemic of "Spanish Flu" sweeps through the U.S. with the first cases in the state reported in Jackson on Sept. 28. There are 6,219 deaths from the disease recorded in Mississippi this year; Nov. 11 marks the end of World War I, in which 704 Mississippians gave their lives. The state had six Brigadier Generals and one Major General in that war.
Deaths: Infamous artist, George Ohr, "The Mad Potter of Biloxi," dies in his hometown of Biloxi on April 7 at age 61.

1919
On March 3, General John J. Pershing personally awards the Distinguished Service Cross to Bay St. Louis native Sgt. Henry J. Tudury, Mississippi's most decorated soldier of World War I; The "Spanish Flu" epidemic continues with the number of deaths in Mississippi in 1918 and 1919 at 9,234, most of which occurred in the last three months of 1918 and the first three months of this year. A total of 213,104 cases are reported for these two years; The first Jitney Jungle store opens in Jackson, later to become one of the first "Super Market" chains in the U.S.; On Nov. 13, the Mississippi Confederate Monument is dedicated at the Vicksburg National Battlefield; The state now has 59,000 motor vehicles.

A Chronology of Mississippi History

1920
On Jan. 20, Gov. Lee M. Russell is inaugurated; There is a legislative effort to move the University of Mississippi from Oxford to Jackson; A State Board of Accountancy, Board of Optometry and Board of Pharmacy are created; The name of the Mississippi Industrial Institute and College is changed, effective Feb. 12, to Mississippi State College for Women; On Mar. 27, a law is passed authorizing the creation of county health departments; On Apr. 4, the Mississippi State School for the Mentally Handicapped is established at Ellisville; On Apr. 5, a tornado in east central Mississippi kills 130 and injures 659; Jackson sets an auto speed limit of 15 miles per hour for straight-away driving and 7½ miles per hour for turning, not much change since 1906 when the last speed limits were set; On Dec. 23, the first steamboat to carry bananas from Central America arrives in Gulfport with 30,000 stalks of the fruit. Gulfport will go on to become the number-one banana port in the nation; There are 667 tractors on Mississippi farms, or one for every 405 farms. The number of horses and mules in the state has peaked at 523,000; There are 43 life insurance companies, including 5 state-chartered, doing business with $263,703,040 worth of insurance in force in the state; For the first time in the nation's history, urban population (51.2%) outnumbers rural population (48.8%). In Mississippi, figures show 13.4% urban and 86.6% rural; Enrollment in colleges in the state this fall is 4,238.

1921
The Mississippi Poetry Society is first organized; An ad in the *Jackson Daily News* on May 29 shows Batte Furniture Company of Jackson offering new refrigerators from $20 to $45. Another ad has Capitol Auto Sales of Jackson offering a Studebaker 2-passenger Roadster for $1300; A McCarty-Holman Stores ad in the *Jackson Daily News* in June advertises Masons quart fruit jars at 90¢ a dozen, pure lard 15¢ a pound and Irish potatoes 1¢ per pound. An ad for The Emporium, "Jackson's Greatest Store," offers ladies silk or wool sport skirts from $6.95 to $19.95; Millsaps College gives 24 graduates their diplomas on June 7; On Sunday, June 19, a wind-assisted fire sweeps through Pascagoula destroying 50 buildings. Damage is held to $500,000; Enrollment in A & M College (later Mississippi State University) in the fall is 1,421 students; The *Jackson Daily News* reports a total of 52 lynchings in the U.S. in the first 10 months of this year — 4 whites and 48 blacks including 1 woman — with Mississippi pushing Georgia for first place with the most lynchings. **Sports**: The Ole Miss football team plays the University of Havana in Cuba and loses to the Cubans 14-0 on Dec. 30.

1922
The legislature authorizes a system of junior colleges, the first in the nation. The first established are Pearl River Junior College and then Hinds County Junior College; Mississippi is a pioneer in the use of airplanes in farming with some of the first experiments tried in the Delta cotton fields; The Federal estimated value of all tangible property in the state as of Dec. 31 is $2,177,795,000 with assessed value of $708,395,755.

1923
On May 18, aviator Charles Lindbergh lands his "Jenny" plane northeast of Maben, Mississippi, and damages the propeller. While waiting in Maben for a new one, he spends several days selling rides on his airplane for $5 each to defray his expenses; U.S. Sen. John Sharp Williams announces his retirement by stating, "I would rather be a hound dog and bay at the moon from my Mississippi plantation than remain in the U.S. Senate." He then went home to Cedar Grove in Yazoo Co; The electric systems of Greenville, Jackson & Vicksburg are organized into Mississippi Power and Light Co. with 10,200 customers, 157 miles of lines and a value of $6,500,000; In the first state gubernatorial election after women are granted voting rights, Henry Whitfield is elected governor in a landslide victory over Theodore Bilbo.

1924
Henry L. Whitfield becomes governor Jan. 22; The legislature establishes Delta State Teachers College at Cleveland, changes the name of the Mississippi Normal College at Hattiesburg to Mississippi State Teachers College, establishes the State Insurance Commission, abolishes the Board of Pardons, and passes a new graduated income tax law; Dr. Felix J. Underwood is appointed full-time executive officer of the State Board of Health; Belle Kearney of Madison Co. wins a state senate seat, the first woman in the South to hold that position; Masonite Corp., the inventor of particle board, is founded in Laurel; On Dec. 28, an entire city block of Corinth catches fire and burns in 5° below zero weather.

1925
The Tung oil tree, native to China, is introduced to Mississippi; The first electrically powered cotton gin in the state is installed at Iuka; Riley King, later known as B.B. King, is born Sept. 16 at Itta Bena; A train wreck in Victoria (Marshall Co.) kills 21 people on Oct. 27; The first milk condensing plant in the South, Borden's, begins operation in Starkville. Gail Borden had created his first can of condensed milk at Liberty in 1856; Mississippi Power and Light Co. replaces Jackson Public Service and eventually operates electric, gas, and street-railroad service in the city; The 1,279 sawmills in the state produce an all-time high of three billion board feet of lumber; The state is maintaining 2,632 miles of roads and has financed work on an additional 1,294 miles from federal funds; On Dec 8, a tornado strikes Yazoo City, killing 2, injuring 99, and causing $500,000 damage.

1926
The State Library Commission is established; The first natural gas field is discovered near Amory.

1927
On Apr. 21, the levee breaks near Greenville bringing the Mississippi River flood with the loss of over $40,000,000 worth of property. In Greenville, where the flood stage was 42 feet, the river rises to 54.6 feet! The river's depth was 57.2 feet at Vicksburg (flood stage 45 feet) and 56.1 feet at Natchez (flood stage 46 feet). In some places, the river is 100 miles wide! The flood covers 2,722,005 acres of land, of which 976,905 acres were devoted to agriculture. The population of the flooded area is 185,495, with 41,673 homes flooded, 21,362 buildings destroyed, 62,089 buildings damaged, and 2,836 work animals, 6,873 cattle, 31,740 hogs & over 266,000 poultry drowned. The flood drives 100,000 Mississippians from their homes with some places under water for 12 weeks. The American Red Cross assists over 157,000 Mississippians; On Oct. 7, Charles Lindbergh lands his airplane — the Spirit of St. Louis — at Davis Field (later Hawkins Field) in Jackson as one stop on his 22,000 mile barnstorming tour of 82 American cities; The Mississippi Folklore Society is formed at Ole Miss; A natural gas field near Amory is developed and pipelines laid to carry gas to Amory, Tupelo and Aberdeen. **Deaths**: Gov. Henry L. Whitfield dies in Jackson on Mar. 18 at the age of 58; Former Gov. Edmond Favor Noel dies in Lexington, Mississippi on July 30 at the age of 71.

A Chronology of Mississippi History

1928
On Jan. 17, Theodore G. Bilbo becomes governor for a second time; The legislature establishes the Mississippi Agriculture Service Department, a State Board of Architecture, a State Commission for the Blind, a Junior College Commission, the Misssssippi Athletic Commisssion, and legalizes boxing and wrestling; When the Crystal Springs School opens Sept. 3, it is the largest consolidated school in the United States! The brick structure is 3 stories tall, 325 feet long and had 88 rooms with a 1,500 student capacity; Mississippi receives $1,307,879 in road-aid money from the federal government this year.
Deaths: Larry Semon, born in West Point, Mississippi, who became one of the earliest movie directors, dies after a nervous breakdown in California on Oct. 8 at only 39 years old.

1929
Delta Air Lines begins regular passenger service from Dallas to Atlanta including a stop in Jackson; William Faulkner's *The Sound and the Fury* is published; By Aug., there are 18 airplanes licensed in the state; On Aug. 29, airplane stunt-pilot and barnstormer Capt. Roscoe Turner of Corinth lands his plane in New York after a 19½ hour flight from Los Angeles, the first coast-to-coast, non-stop passenger flight ever made.
Sports: The Ole Miss football team plays its first night game.

1930
The Municipal Airport in Hattiesburg is dedicated on Sept. 23; Kudzu, a fast-growing vine, is brought to the state from Japan to help check soil erosion; Money and jobs erode as Mississippians suffer the beginning of the Great Depression years; Fifty-nine banks in the state fail; A natural gas field is opened in Hinds & Rankin Counties. Natural gas is turned into Jackson's mains for the first time on Oct. 29; There are now 11 junior colleges in the state with 1,619 students enrolled; Mississippi spends $1,774,612 this year to maintain roads.
Deaths: Former Governor James K. Vardaman dies in Birmingham, Alabama on June 25 at the age of 68.

1931
Census figures of 1930 show Mississippi with a population of 2,009,821 (the first time the state has passed the 2-million mark), an increase of 219,203 since 1920. Whites number 998,077—blacks 1,009,622. Rural population has increased by 120,424 to 1,670,971; On June 2, the statues of Mississippians Jefferson Davis and U.S. Senator James Z. George are unveiled in Statuary Hall at the U.S. Capitol in Washington; The average price of a pound of cotton is 5.66 cents, way down from 22.88 cents in 1922; Another 56 banks in the state fail; Because of the many "little red schoolhouses," there are over 5,000 school administrative units in the state.
Deaths: Ida Bell Wells-Barnett of Holly Springs, journalist and Civil Rights pioneer, dies on March 25 at age 69.

1932
On Jan. 19, Martin S. Conner becomes governor; Mississippi's economy is devastated by the Great Depression and other factors. The Bilbo administration had left only $1,326 in the state treasury. The state debt totals $50 million. The state has no credit. Per capita income in the state is only $126 a year. Thousands lose their homes because they don't have money to pay taxes. Average teacher salary is now $414 per year, down from the 1929-30 average of $637; The Great Depression bank failures, for the most part, seem to be over. "Only" 12 banks in the state fail this year; The first state sales tax, 2 percent, goes into effect on May 1. Collections in the first 6 months total $1,173,721; The lumber industry is in a decline. The state has only 257 lumber mills with an output of just 500 million board feet, less than any year since 1880; Enrollment in all colleges in Mississippi this fall is only 8,069, with 3,350 in five state institutions, 1,400 in private senior colleges, 2,631 in eleven public junior colleges, and 688 in eight private junior colleges.
Deaths: Noted politician John Sharp Williams of Yazoo Co., a former U.S. Senator, dies on Sept. 7 at the age of 77.

1933
Dr. Felix Underwood, executive officer of the State Board of Health states "In the days of Imperial Rome the span of life stood at 20 years. In 1700 when the first statistical tables were compiled it stood at 25 years. Today (in Mississippi) it stands at 59."; Tupelo becomes the first city in the country to receive electricity from the Tennessee Valley Authority (TVA); The first Civilian Conservation Corps (CCC) camp is started in the state — 33 camps will be established between now and 1941;
Deaths: Martha Mattox, Natchez native and silent screen actress, dies on May 2 at age 53; Singing legend Jimmie Rodgers dies from TB on May 26 at age 35; Former Governor Adelbert Ames dies in Florida on April 12 at the age of 97, the last survivor of all the Generals of the Civil War.

1934
Tupelo becomes the first city in the U.S. to receive electric power from TVA (Tennessee Valley Authority) on Feb. 7. The Alcorn Electric Power Association becomes the first rural electric cooperative in the U.S.; The Mississippi Game and Fish Commission establishes the Mississippi Museum of Natural Science in Jackson; School plant (buildings, etc.) investment in the state is $41,166,373; Mississippi Congressman Jeff Busby introduces a resolution asking the Interior Department to make "a survey of the old Indian trail known as the Natchez Trace, with a view to constructing a national road on the route to be known as the Natchez Trace Parkway."
Deaths: Blues legend Charley Patton, a native of Edwards, Miss., dies in Indianola, Miss. on April 28 at the age of 47; Dorothy Dell (Goff), a native of Hattiesburg who was Miss Universe of 1930 and starred in 3 movies, dies in an auto accident June 8 at 19 years old; and Wilbur Higby, a Meridian native and silent screen actor, dies on Dec. 1 at age 67.

1935
Elvis Presley is born in Tupelo on Jan. 8; The new State Hospital at Whitfield is first occupied, the 9-day move from the institution on North State Street in Jackson begins on Mar. 4; Out of 278,510 men and 19,035 women registered to work, 57,728 have been placed on Civil Works Administration (CWA) projects; Al and Fred Key, brothers from Meridian, set a world's record for sustained endurance in the air — 653 hours and 34 minutes (over 27 days) in a flight over Meridian in their plane the "Ole Miss". They started their historic flight on June 4, and traveled a total distance of 52,320 miles and consumed 6,000 gallons of gasoline (refueled in the air) and 300 gallons of oil. Key Field will later be named for them; The state has 35 public libraries with a total of 338,000 volumes; "The Rebel," the South's first diesel-powered streamliner locomotive, makes its debut in Jackson. When the Rural Electrification Administration (REA) is started, less than one percent of Mississippi's 311,683 farm houses have electricity.

1936
On Jan. 21, Hugh L. White is inaugurated as governor; There are only 922 miles of hard-surfaced highways in the state's 6,215-mile system. A Good Roads Program is adopted; Farm income is $185 million while the total industrial payroll is only $14 million. A Balance Agriculture with Industry program is adopted; The State Dept. of Public Welfare and a Board of State Park Supervisors are established; On Mar. 17, the Monroe County Electric Power Association becomes the

A Chronology of Mississippi History

first REA-financed co-op in the nation to electrify its system. On April 5, a twister hits Tupelo cutting a path of destruction a half-mile wide and 4 miles long killing 216 people, injuring 659 and causing $4-8 million damage; Harvest season brings an all-time high average yield of 306 pounds of cotton per acre, compared to 140 pounds 4 years earlier. The state makes a world record on 17 acres of oats, averaging 135 bushels per acre; There are 138 cases of polio in the state; Dr. Leslie Rush of Meridian performs the first bone-pinning operation ever; The state's first dial telephone system is installed at Lake.
Sports: Out of 200 suggested new nicknames for the University of Mississippi "Flood" football team, five are selected and sent to a panel of sports writers, who pick "Rebels." Since then the team has been known as the Ole Miss Rebels. Catholic University slips by the Ole Miss Rebels 20-19 in the Orange Bowl.

1937
On Apr. 8, about 450 workers at the Tupelo Cotton Mill are fired after 100 of them go on strike for higher pay; On Aug. 1, the state's first Krystal Hamburger Restaurant opens at 436 Capitol Street in Jackson; On Sept. 26, the "World's Greatest Blues Singer," Bessie Smith (a native of Chattanooga), is killed in an automobile accident near Clarksdale; Roads financed in Mississippi by New Deal projects have amounted to $40,343,039.14; The epidemic of poliomyelitis continues with another 385 cases reported in Mississippi this year.
Deaths: Dunbar Rowland, one of Mississippi's best-known historians and writers and the first director of the Miss. Dept. of Archives and History, dies on Nov. 1 at the age of 73.
Sports: On Sept. 30, the Ole Miss Rebels football team is the first college squad in the U.S. to fly on an airplane when they fly from Memphis to Philadelphia, Pa. on American Airlines; Duquesne slips by Miss. State 13-12 in the Orange Bowl.

1938
The Legislature makes the magnolia the state tree. The homestead exemption program begins; Construction begins on the 435-mile Natchez Trace Parkway from Natchez to Nashville; Ingalls Shipyard begins operation in Pascagoula.
Deaths: The state's best known bluesman, the legendary Robert Johnson, a Hazlehurst native, dies in Greenwood on Aug. 16, a few days after he was reportedly poisoned by a jealous husband who had slipped something into his whiskey.

1939
There are about 4,000 miles of paved highways in the state, thanks to Gov. White's Good Roads Program; The first oil field starts production at Tinsley in Yazoo Co. on Aug. 29.
Deaths: Belle Kearney, a Madison County native who served as the first female state senator in the South and a was a feminist writer, dies at the home of a friend in Jackson on Feb. 27 at the age of 75; John Roy Lynch, who was born a slave in Louisiana, but became Mississippi's first black member of the U.S. House of Representatives and the only black for over 100 years, and at the age of 25, the youngest ever elected to the House, dies in Chicago on Nov. 2 at the age of 92.

1940
In Jan. 16, Paul B. Johnson, Sr. of Hattiesburg is inaugurated as governor; The free school textbook program is enacted; A state college for blacks, Mississippi Negro Training School (later Jackson State University), is founded; Black Mississippi writer Richard Wright publishes *Native Son*; The Rhythm Club dance hall in Natchez catches fire on Apr. 23 — 209 die in the state's worst fire disaster; The B.G. Humphreys Bridge over the Mississippi River between Greenville, Miss. and Lake Village, Ark., opens on Sept. 17; Beginning Oct. 16, 260,000 Mississippians register for the draft with their selective service boards. Camp Shelby near Hattiesburg is reactivated and will train hundreds of thousands of troops during WWII; Per capita income in the state is $218; Enrollment in all colleges in the state this fall is 14,019; The year's cotton crop of 1.25 million bales is valued at only $61 million; There are 63 life insurance companies (10 state firms) doing business in the state with $496,694,895 worth of insurance in force; For the first time in 100 years, whites are again the majority race in Mississippi.

1941
On June 29, the world's first all-welded passenger ship, the *African Comet*, is launched at Ingalls Shipyard at Pascagoula; Eleven Mississippians, ten Navy men and one Marine, die on board the *USS Arizona* on Dec. 7 when Japan attacks Pearl Harbor. They are among hundreds of Americans who go down to a watery grave on that ship. On Dec. 10, the U.S. declares war on Japan — the U.S. has entered World War II; Keesler Air Force Base is established in Biloxi. A peak military population of 69,000 will make it the largest airbase in the world. During the war 141,000 mechanics and 336,000 trainees will be schooled there; Another large army training center is Camp McCain, built eight miles south of Grenada. At its peak, Camp McCain serves as many as 50,000 troops.
Deaths: Noted politician Pat Harrison, a Crystal Springs native who became a U.S. Congressman and Senator who served as President pro temp of the Senate, dies in Washington on June 22 at age 59. His funeral service is held in the chamber of the U.S. Senate; Frank L. Cooley, a Natchez native and silent screen actor, dies in Hollywood on July 6; Hamilton Smith, a Scott County native, who was one of the early film directors, dies in Los Angeles on Oct. 29 at the age of 54.
Sports: The Mississippi State Bulldogs football team defeats Georgetown 14-7 in the Orange Bowl in Miami, Florida.

1942
On Mar. 16, tornadoes kill 65 and injure 500 from central to northeast Mississippi; Foster General Hospital in Jackson is activated for military use on Dec. 14. State school plant 9buildings, land, etc.) investment is estimated at $61,658,821.
Deaths: William Alexander Percy, a Greenville native and noted poet, dies on Jan. 21 at the age of 56; Former Governor Andrew H. Longino dies in Jackson on Feb. 24. Former Gov. Earl LeRoy Brewer dies in Jackson on March 10 at age 72.

1943
Work starts Feb. 7 on permanent buildings at Jackson's Army General Hospital; Gov. Paul B. Johnson, Sr. becomes the only Governor of the state to ever entertain a member of a royal family at the Governor's Mansion. The Netherland's Princess Juliana was reviewing her Royal Dutch Air Force training in Jackson; Camp Shelby is home to as many as 75,000 soldiers at a time; The Miss. Baptist Seminary is founded to train ministers; A Jitney-Jungle supermarket ad in *The Clarion-Ledger* advertises Blue Plate peanut butter, 16-ounce jar 32¢; Silver Cow milk, small can 5¢; and tomatoes, 15¢ a pound;
Deaths: Former Gov. Lee M. Russell dies in Jackson on May 16; Charles Graham, a Carthage native and silent screen actor, dies in Los Angeles on Oct. 9 at age 48; After a severe heart attack on Dec. 20, Gov. Paul Johnson, Sr. dies Dec. 26, only 3 weeks before the completion of his term. For the second time, Lt. Gov. Dennis Murphree becomes governor.

1944
On Jan. 18, Thomas L. Bailey is inaugurated governor; The legislature chooses the mockingbird as the official state bird; On Jan. 29, famous entertainer and stripper, Gypsy Rose Lee, performs at Camp Shelby near Hattiesburg; Dr. Felix

A Chronology of Mississippi History

Underwood, who heads the state Board of Health, says "During December (1943), Mississippi had 687 reported cases of whooping cough, 450 of mumps, 128 of diphtheria and 52 cases of scarlet fever."; In March, Jackson Postmaster A.C. Griffin has to tell his patrons that in-city postal rates have increased from 2 to 3 cents for a letter; Also in March, Gov. Bailey signs into law a state teachers retirement system; In April, State Highway Dept. Director E.D. Kenna estimates flood waters have done $400,000 damage to state roads; On July 28, a 100-mile-per-hour windstorm topples four buildings at the Greenwood Air Base, killing one soldier, injuring a dozen and damaging 23 buildings, 11 vehicles and 64 planes; In Sept., International Harvester gives the first public demonstration of their mechanical cotton pickers, with 8 models crawling through a field near Clarksdale. More than 2,000 people gather around the field on the Hopson Plantation to watch machines pick cotton 60 times faster than a man. The 8 machines "together were doing the work of 480 pairs of hands." It was the first cotton crop commercially produced entirely by machinery in the nation; In November, Mississippi votes for President Roosevelt's re-election and Gov. Bailey wires him the state is the "Number one Democratic state."
Deaths: William Hollingsworth, a celebrated artist, who painted about his hometown of Jackson, despondent over the death of his father a year earlier, takes his own life on Aug. 1.

1945
The State Treasury starts the year with over $22 million — $14,971,907 in the general fund and $7,251,104 in the special fund; On Jan. 5 & 6, two tornadoes batter the Delta counties of Washington, Sunflower & Carroll, plus Wilkinson and Amite counties, leaving 8 dead and causing much property loss; On Jan. 10, Ingalls Shipbuilding launches the 18,000-ton transport, the *USS Sea Tarpon* — its 61st ship in 55 months; On Feb 12, at least 43 are killed and hundreds injured by a tornado that sweeps across parts of Mississippi & Alabama. Property damage is extensive; *Jackson Daily News* headline on Monday, May 7: **"Tuesday is Designated V-E Day as Germany Surrenders."** Germany surrenders unconditionally to the Western Allies and Russia at 7:41 p.m. Jackson time, Sunday, May 6. The war in Europe is over! The *Jackson Daily News* headline on Monday, August 6: **"U.S.- Developed Atomic Bomb Equals 20,000 Tons of TNT; First One Dropped on Japan"**. The new bomb was used for the first time Sunday, Aug. 5 on Hiroshima — a second bomb dropped on Nagasaki on Aug. 9. Japan surrenders on Aug. 14, ending World War II! During the war, 4,185 Mississippi servicemen and women died; Of the $4 billion spent on war plants in the South, Mississippi received only $64 million, less than any other southern state; Mississippi's death rate has declined from 12.3 per 100,000 in 1920 to 8.5 per 100,000 this year. The number of farms with tractors has doubled since 1940, yet there are still 328,687 mules. This year's 9,779,000-bale cotton crop is the smallest since 1934. **Deaths**: One of the greatest military leaders ever from the state, full Admiral John Sidney McCain, a native of Teoc in Carroll County, and one of several from that military family, dies on Sept. 6, just 4 days after he witnessed the Japanese surrender aboard the *USS Missouri* in Toyko Bay on Sept. 2.

1946
The legislature establishes the Mississippi Commission on Hospital Care; Per capita income in the state is $605, almost triple the amount in 1940; In April, seven Dominican Sisters of Springfield, Ill. purchase the 75-bed Jackson Infirmary for $100,000, and it becomes St. Dominic's Hospital; The Foster General Army Hospital in Jackson is redesignated a Veterans Administration Hospital. Columbus airfield is declared permanent. Most of the other military bases around the state are deactivated and closed; In June, Hodding Carter of the *Greenville Delta Democrat-Times* receives the Pulitzer for his editorial, *Go For Broke*, which was published Aug. 27, 1945, on the subject of racial, religious and economic intolerance;
Deaths: On Nov. 2, Governor Thomas L. Bailey dies from cancer, slightly less than 3 years after taking office. He is succeeded by Fielding L. Wright of Rolling Fork.

1947
The Mississippi Association for Teachers in Colored Schools is renamed the Mississippi Teachers' Association; On Sept. 19 a strong hurricane (before they were named) hits the coast killing 27 Mississippians and causing considerable damage.
Deaths: Well-known big band orchestra leader Jimmie Lunceford, a Fulton native, dies in Oregon on July 12 at the age of 44. It's thought he was poisoned by a racist restaurant owner who resented serving him and his band; former two-term Governor Theodore Bilbo dies in New Orleans, Louisiana on Aug. 21 at the age of 69.

1948
The legislature starts its session in Jan. and is the youngest in 50 years with a total of 57 members under age 40. In the house, 78 of the 140 members are new to the body and practically all first-termers are veterans of WWII. They enact a Workmen's Compensation Law and place emphasis on educational needs; On May 28, the Beverly Drive-In Theatre, the state's largest, opens in Hattiesburg; Gov. Fielding L. Wright is the first Mississippian to be a candidate for vice-president of the U.S.; Mississippi-born playwright Tennessee Williams receives a Pulitzer Prize for Drama for his play *A Streetcar Named Desire*; Morris Futurion, a Russian immigrant, establishes the first furniture factory in the state and the furniture industry's first assembly line in New Albany. He is called the "the Henry Ford of furniture"; The Museum of Classical Archaeology opens at Ole Miss; On Oct. 21, Jesse Leroy Brown of Hattiesburg becomes America's first black naval aviator; In Oct. the Allison's Wells Art Colony is founded by artists Karl and Mildred Wolfe of Jackson.
Deaths: John A. Lomax, a Goodman, Miss. native and blues archivist, who, with the help of his son, made over 10,000 recordings of early blues artists for the Library of Congress, dies on Jan. 26 at age 80; Blues singer Lucille Bogan, an Amory, Miss. native, dies in Los Angeles on Aug. 10 at age 51; Helen Carloss, a Yazoo City native, the first woman in the nation to argue cases before the U.S. Circuit Court of Appeals and the U.S. Supreme Court, dies Dec. 23 at the age of 55.
Sports: The Ole Miss Rebels beat Texas Christian University 13-9 in the Delta Bowl in Memphis, Tennessee.

1949
The Natchez Times daily newspaper begins publication Feb. 6; On Mar. 24, six people are killed and 23 injured in a tornado that hits the Washington County communities of Tralake, Lake Jackson, Glen Allen and Foote; On Apr. 22, Yazoo County residents vote an overwhelming 99.9% in favor of a $750,000 bond issue to finance the startup of farmer-owned Mississippi Chemical Corporation; On April 27, the Mississippi Highway Department awards contracts in the amount of $821,669 to build roads. State-maintained primary road mileage in Mississippi now stands at 4,461.5 miles.
Deaths: Former Gov. Dennis Murphree dies Feb. 9; Major League baseball player Eric McNair of Meridian dies Mar. 11.

A Chronology of Mississippi History

1950
The legislature provides for a system of secondary roads and the hard-surfacing of 11,658 miles of roads and establish University Medical Center, a medical school and teaching hospital in Jackson as part of the University of Mississippi; On June 25, the Korean War begins; Per capita income in the state is $755; Union membership in the state stands at 50,000; There are 91 insurance companies (13 Mississippi companies) conducting business in the state with $1,126,419,705 worth of insurance in force; Enrollment in colleges this fall is 21,716 with 7,984 enrolled in the 15 junior colleges; The 1950 census shows urban population of the state at 607,162, or 27.9% of total population, living in 54 urban places. Nearly half of the urban population is living in seven cities of 25,000 or more. For the first time Mississippi has a Standard Metropolitan Area: the Jackson SMA has a total population of 142,164.
Deaths: B.J. Barrier, Jr., Yazoo City native and aviation pioneer, is killed in a plane crash on Feb. 9 near Dallas, Texas; Former Governor Mike Conner dies in Jackson on Sept. 16 at age 59; In Korea on Dec. 4, Ensign Jesse Leroy Brown, a native of Hattiesburg, becomes America's first black naval aviator to lose his life in combat.

1951
The state's first female mayor, Dorothy Painter Crawford, is sworn in as Mayor of Madison on Jan. 2; From Jan. 28 through Feb. 1, one of the worst ice storms ever hits northern Mississippi, Alabama, Georgia and Tennessee causing $100 million damage from downed trees, broken power lines and collapsed roofs. Human toll: 22 dead (6 in Miss.) and over 500 seriously injured; Mississippi Valley State University is founded on June 4; "Hacksaw" Mary Cain of Summit becomes the first female candidate for governor of Mississippi.

1952
Hugh White is sworn in as governor for the 2nd time on Jan. 22; The average salary of classroom teachers in the state is $1,534 per year, while the average for the South is $2,559; A recognition strike of the Amalgamated Clothing Workers of America (ACWA) in Water Valley, Mississippi turns into a bitter labor dispute; In December, a ground breaking ceremony is held for Mississippi Medical Center in Jackson.
Deaths: Henry Herschel Brickell, a native of Senatobia, Miss., considered one of the best professional literary critics of the 20th century who wrote short stories on the Civil War set in Yazoo City, Miss. (where he lived for a time), dies on May 29 at age 63; Actor Olin Frances, a native of Mooreville in Lee County native, dies in Hollywood on June 30 at age 61.
Sports: Glenn Cain quarterbacks Millsaps to a 27-7 victory over Howard College on Oct. 31. It is the first college game to be played at the new Hinds County Stadium, later called the Mississippi Veterans Memorial Stadium.

1953
On Jan. 20, 1953, WJTV-TV (CBS), channel 25 (later channel 12), in Jackson begins broadcasting; On June 27, there is a Truce ending the Korean War. The number of Mississippi lives lost in the war totaled 409; On Sept. 27, WTOK-TV (ABC/CBS), channel 11, in Meridian begins broadcasting; On Dec. 5, a tornado hits Vicksburg killing 38, injuring 270 and causing tremendous damage; On Dec. 20, WLBT-TV (NBC), channel 3, in Jackson begins broadcasting for the first time.
Deaths: Ben Ames Williams, Macon native (grandnephew of Confederate Gen. James Longstreet) who wrote 32 books including many best-sellers in the 1930s, dies Feb. 4 at age 63.
Sports: St. Louis Cardinal Dizzy Dean, of Bond, Mississippi (Stone County) is inducted into the Baseball Hall of Fame in Cooperstown, N.Y.; The Ole Miss Rebels beat Chattanooga 39-6 at Mississippi Veterans Memorial Stadium. It is the first appearance by the Rebels in Jackson in 18 years and is the first *major* college game played at the new stadium (see 1952); and in football Georgia Tech beats Ole Miss 24-7 in the Sugar Bowl in New Orleans and Pacific of California whips Southern Mississippi 26-7 in the Sun Bowl in El Paso, Texas.

1954
Oprah Winfrey is born in Kosciusko on Jan. 29. She will become a famous TV talk show host and the highest paid female entertainer in the U.S.; On Feb. 24, the legislature passes a right-to-work law, though not without considerable opposition from organized labor; On May 17, the U.S. Supreme Court renders a decision in the *Brown vs. Board of Education* case which voids the doctrine of "separate but equal" educational facilities, and decrees that states must integrate public schools. The legislature sets up plans for the complete reorganization of the public school system on a segregated basis; On May 26, the St. Dominic-Jackson Memorial Hospital is dedicated; On July 11, the first Citizens Council is formed in Indianola; On July 30, Tupelo, Mississippi native Elvis Presley makes his public debut at Overton Park Shell in Memphis; The *Vicksburg Sunday Post-Herald* receives a Pulitzer Prize for local reporting.
Deaths: Blue singer Lillian "Lil" Green, a Clarksdale native dies April 14; R.W. Blackwood, an Ackerman native and member of the Blackwood Brothers, is killed in a plane crash on June 24; James Howell Street, a Lumberton, Miss. native who became the youngest ordained Baptist minister in the U.S. in 1924, then left the ministry to write several best-selling novels, dies in Chapel Hill, N.C. on Sept. 28.

1955
The sales tax increases from 2% to 3%; A member of a state 4-H Club raises 304 bushels of corn on one acre, a world record for corn production; State-born dramatist Tennessee Williams receives a Pulitzer Prize for Drama for his play *Cat On A Hot Tin Roof*; Mississippi writer William Faulkner gets the Pulitzer Prize for Fiction for *A Fable*; A 14-year-old black youth, Emmett Till, visiting the Delta from Chicago, was pulled from his bed on Aug. 28 by two white men who then brutally beat him and shoot shot him through the head before throwing his body into the Tallahatchie River. The men are tried in Sumner for murder, but the all-white jury acquits them. Historians will say this incident sparked the birth of the Civil Rights movement in the state; Construction of the first phase of the Medical Center in Jackson is completed and dedication ceremonies are held Oct. 24; Late this year, after 146 years assets of all banks in the state finally top $1 billion.
Deaths: Novelist Frances Jones Gaither, born in Tennessee, but reared in Corinth, Mississippi, dies on Oct. 28 at age 66.
Sports: In football, Mississippi State defeats Alabama 26-7, making it 2 years in a row the Bulldogs beat the Tide; Southern Mississippi makes it two years in a row they've lost in the Sun Bowl — this year to Texas Western 37-14; and Navy shuts out the Ole Miss Rebels 21-0 in the Sugar Bowl.

1956
On Jan. 17, J.P. Coleman becomes governor; Six paper mills in the state produce 1,296,000 tons of paper valued at $50 million from 2,135,000 cords of wood for which $32 million was paid, and pay 8,000 employees $33,500,000 in wages; The value of crops, livestock and forestry production in the state totals $652 million; The infamous state spy agency, the Sovereignty Commission, is created; Elvis Presley's first nationwide hit, *Heartbreak Hotel*, tops the charts on March 10

A Chronology of Mississippi History

and stays at No. 1 for 8 weeks. He has 10 more hits this year including 4 more No. 1s. Two, *Don't Be Cruel* and *Hound Dog* (back-to-back on the same single), both stay No. 1 for 11 weeks making them the biggest R&R singles of all time. His first movie, *Love Me Tender*, is also released; WCBI-TV, channel 4, in Columbus begins broadcasting on July 13.
Deaths: Former Gov. Fielding Wright dies in Jackson on May 4; B. Reeves Eason, a Friars Point, Miss. native and one of the early movie directors (he did the burning of Atlanta scene in *Gone With the Wind*), dies of a heart attack in Calif. on June 9; Bluesman Tommy Johnson, a Terry, Miss. native dies Nov. 1.
Sports: Ole Miss slips by Texas Christian University 14-13 in the Cotton Bowl in Dallas.

1957
WTWV-TV (now (WTVA), channel 9, in Tupelo-Columbus begins broadcasting Mar. 18; On Apr. 29, Congress approves the first Civil Rights bill since Reconstruction; The first class of 24 students graduate in June from the four-year medical school at Mississippi Medical Center (later University of Mississippi Medical Center) in Jackson; June 25-30, Hurricane Audrey kills 390 in Mississippi, Alabama, Louisiana and Texas; Out of 500,000 pupils in the state, only about 15,500 are attending private or parochial schools; On Nov. 8, a tornado kills 13 and injures 200 in Mississippi and Louisiana; Mississippians write checks this year totaling $4,281,203,000.
Deaths: Kate Freeman Clark of Holly Springs. One of her paintings hangs in the U.S. Ambassador's residence in Paris. She owned the largest single private art collection in the world, 1,200 paintings, which she willed to Holly Springs.
Sports: West Texas State defeats the Southern Mississippi football team 20-13 in the Tangerine Bowl.

1958
Figures released Jan. 8 estimate the cost of Mississippi's share of the new Federal interstate highway system has climbed to $353 million; On Jan. 29, the state senate votes 35-11 to allow women to serve on juries; Mississippi State College is renamed Mississippi State University; On Feb 26, tornadoes kill 13 persons, injure 70, and cause extensive damage in south central Mississippi; Mary Ann Mobley of Brandon wins the Miss America crown, receiving more votes from the judges in Atlantic City than anyone up until now; One in four Mississippians qualifies for Federal surplus food commodities; Mississippi tax collections for the year total $113,174,535.
Deaths: W.C. Handy, an Alabama native who lived in Clarksdale for a time and "discovered" the blues in nearby Tutwiler, dies in New York City on March 28 at the age of 84; Big Bill Broonzy, a Scott County native and one of the early blues legends, dies in Chicago on Aug. 14 at age 65; Rod Brasfield, a native of Smithville in Monroe Co. and member of the Grand Ole Opry in Nashville and the show's top comedian for 14 years, dies on Sept. 12 of a heart attack at age 48.
Sports: the Ole Miss football team beats Florida 7-3 in the Gator Bowl in Jacksonville; the Ole Miss Rebels defeat Texas 39-7 in the Sugar Bowl in New Orleans; and the Southern Miss. Golden Eagles lose the Tangerine Bowl in Orlando for the second year in a row, this year to East Texas State, 10-9.

1959
On the night of Jan. 23, Old Main at Mississippi State, the largest college dormitory under one roof in the country, burns to the ground. All but one of the 900 residents escape. Allen Williamson, 19, of Columbus dies in the blaze; Lynda Lee Mead of Natchez wins the Miss America 1960 crown, making it two years in a row for Mississippi. The only other time this has happened was in 1935 and 1936 when Pennsylvania took the crown 2 years running; On Oct. 20, WABG-TV (ABC), channel 6, in Greenwood-Greenville begins broadcasting; An ad in *The Clarion-Ledger* newspaper on Dec. 4 has A & P® offering these prices: salt meat, 5 lbs. for $1.00—Eight O'Clock® coffee, 1 lb. 51¢—pork sausages, 27¢ per lb.—bacon, 29¢ per lb.—lettuce, 2 heads for 29¢—potatoes, 10 lb. bag 49¢—large Dash® laundry detergent, 39¢—Swanson® meat pies, 3 for 59¢—sugar, 5 lb. bag, 39¢—and apples, 12 for 49¢. A service station ad shows gasoline prices at 25.9¢ and 28.9¢ per gallon; Some end-of-the-year figures: the amount of life insurance sold in the state is $2.75 billion, up 28% from 1958 — value of residential construction is almost $69 million, value of all construction in the state, $250 million — nearly 50 million barrels of oil were produced this year, a record high. There are 2,578 producing oil wells in 156 fields — retail sales for the year are up at least 18%, gasoline sales up 6% — non-farm employment is above 400,000. About 2,500 manufacturing companies employ more than 100,000 workers receiving over $300 million in wages. For the year, income taxes totaled $18,669,567, sales tax collections $64,477,906, total state tax collections a record $126,177,278.
Deaths: Felix J. Underwood, a Nettleton native and physician who was Mississippi's Health Officer for 34 years, dies on Jan. 9; Blues singer/guitarist Eddie "Guitar Slim" Jones, a Greenwood native, dies of pneumonia in New York City on Feb. 7 at age 32; Lester Young, a native of Woodville, who played tenor sax and was a bop pioneer with Count Basie and others, and in 1956 was voted "Greatest Tenor Saxophonist Ever," dies in New York City on Mar. 15 at the age of 49.
Sports: The Mississippi State Bulldog basketball team wins the school's first Southeastern Conference championship.

1960
Ross R. Barnett is inaugurated governor Jan. 19; Enrollment in all colleges in the state this fall is 35,473; There are now 329 banks, including branches and offices, in the state; There are 272 insurance companies (27 Miss. firms) doing business in the state with $3,492,399,555 worth of insurance in force.
Deaths: Archie Brownlee, who led the Five Blind Boys of Mississippi, dies in New Orleans on Feb. 8 at age 35; David L. Cohn, Greenville native who was an historian, author of several books and political speech writer for many national figures including Averell Harriman, Adlai Stevenson, and Sam Rayburn, dies on Sept. 12;.Richard Wright, a Natchez native and black novelist whose works include *Uncle Tom's Children* ('38), *Native Son* ('40), *12 Million Black Voices* ('41) & *Black Boy* ('45) among others, dies in Paris, France on Nov. 28.
Sports: The Ole Miss Rebels win the national football championship; The Rebels blank LSU 21-0 in the Sugar Bowl in New Orleans; Ralph Boston of Laurel breaks the record set by Jesse Owens as he wins the Gold Medal in the running broad jump at the Summer Olympics in Rome.

1961
On May 23, two buses of "Freedom Riders" arrive in Jackson. Although accompanied by federal marshals, all 27 Riders are arrested for entering a "white" washroom and failure to obey police. The Riders continue coming and by the end of June, 163 had been arrested and convicted in Jackson; In June, the Justice Department files the first of many voter discrimination suits in the state; Restoration of the Old Capitol is completed for use as an historical museum; Intense rain during a 2-week period causes flooding from nearly every stream in the state. On Dec. 21, the Pearl River at Jackson reaches 37.24 feet, 9.24 feet above flood stage. Nearly 600 homes are flooded and 3,000 people affected; There is the first use of electrical

A Chronology of Mississippi History

anesthesia at the University Medical Center in Jackson; A large oil refinery is located at Pascagoula; NASA selects Mississippi for testing Saturn rocket motors for the space program; Litton Industries purchases Ingalls Shipyard; The Natchez Trace Parkway Museum is opened in Tupelo; Brice's Crossroads Civil War Museum opens in Prentiss County. **Sports**: The Ole Miss Rebels football team beats Rice 14-6 making it two years in a row they've won the Sugar Bowl.

1962

The U.S. Supreme Court on March 26 backs the "one-man, one-vote" apportionment of seats in states legislatures; A plan for redistricting representation in the Mississippi legislature is approved; The first McDonald's restaurant in the state opens May 23 on Pass Road in Biloxi; The Grand Gulf State Historical Park Museum opens near Port Gibson; The world's first human kidney transplant takes place at the University Medical Center in Jackson; The first black, James Meredith, is admitted to the University of Mississippi Oct. 1 after great opposition from Governor Ross Barnett causes the Federal government to deploy 3,000 troops to put down riots that leaves 2 dead, 175 injured, and 212 arrested; On Oct. 15, WLOX-TV, channel 13, in Biloxi-Gulfport begins broadcasting; Farmers and ranchers report more than 2,100,000 cattle in the state. There are 85 meat-packing plants in Mississippi; Manufacturing employment in the state has increased significantly since 1950, yet union membership stands at 52,000, an increase of only 2,000 in 12 years. **Deaths**: Actor Willie Best, a Sunflower native dies from cancer in Hollywood on Feb. 27 at age 48; Actor Roscoe Ates, Lawrence Co. native, dies from lung cancer in Hollywood on March 1 at age 70; Film director and playwright Will A. Price, a McComb native, dies on July 4. During the filming of the movie, *Gone With the Wind*, Price coached Clark Gable and Vivian Leigh on how to speak "Southern."; and famed novelist William Faulkner dies from a thrombosis on July 6 in Byhalia. **Sports**: Texas defeats the Mississippi State University Buldogs 12-7 in the Cotton Bowl in Dallas, Texas.

1963

Civil rights campaigns throughout the South start with a voter registration drive in April in Greenville. They continue in May in Jackson and several other cities; The first lung transplant in the U.S. takes place on June 11 at University Medical Center in Jackson. Dr. James D. Hardy and his team replace the patient's left lung in the 3-hour operation. The patient, John Richard Russell, survives 18 days; The first adrenal glands transplanted in humans also takes place there this year; NAACP leader Medger Evers is murdered, shot in the back on the night of June 12, at his Jackson home. Byron De La Beckwith, a Greenwood Citizens Council activist, is charged in the slaying and is tried twice in 1964, both times ending in mistrials; The Jackson Municipal Airport at Thompson Field is dedicated on July 8 in Rankin County — passenger boardings at the airport total 105,623 by the end of the year; In Sept., schools peacefully integrate throughout most of the South; A Chevron refinery is built in Pascagoula; On Sept. 26, the Edgewater Mall opens at Biloxi/Gulfport. It's the first regional shopping center on the Mississippi Gulf Coast; The state has 154 textile and clothing plants — 81 of the state's 82 counties now have at least one industry; Ira B. Harkey, Jr. of the *Pascagoula Chronicle* receives a Pulitzer for his editorials; William Faulkner receives another Pulitzer for *The Reivers*; The Kate Freeman Clark Art Gallery, with the largest collection by one artist in the world, opens in Holly Springs. **Deaths**: In addition to Medgar Evers (see above), Stark Young, a native of Como and leading New York drama critic who also wrote plays, novels and nonfiction, dies Jan. 6 at age 81; Ruth Campbell, Yazoo City native and first women attorney admitted to the Mississippi bar, dies on March 3 at age 76; John Faulkner, brother of William, Ripley native who wrote several novels himself, dies on March 28; Legendary bluesman Elmore James, a Holmes Co. native, dies of a heart attack on May 24; Writer Mildred Spurrier Topp, reared in Greenwood, dies Aug. 15 at age 66; Walter Davis, early blues pianist born in Grenada dies in St. Louis on Oct. 22 at age 51; **Sports**: The Mississippi State Bulldog basketball team wins its first trip to the NCAA Tournament; Willye B. White from Money in Leflore County wins the Gold Medal in the long jump in the Olympics; The Mississippi State Bulldog football team wins over North Carolina State 16-12 in the Liberty Bowl in Memphis; and the Ole Miss Rebels football team wins over Arkansas 17-13 in the Sugar Bowl in New Orleans.

1964

On Jan. 21, Paul B. Johnson, Jr. becomes governor. His father served as governor from Jan. 16, 1940 until his death on Dec. 26, 1943; The first heart transplant operation in the world, which is also the first animal-to-human transplant, is carried out at the University Medical Center in Jackson on Jan. 23. Dr. James D. Hardy heads the team of 12 that transplants the heart of a chimpanzee into a 64-year-old patient. The heart continues beating for 90 minutes; On Feb. 17, the U.S. Supreme Court orders that congressional districts have equal populations; On Feb. 28 Clifford Walker, 36, is killed returning home from International Paper Co. in Natchez, a center of White Knights activity. His bullet-riddled body and car is found off U.S. 61. It is reportedly the first slaying authorized in Mississippi by the White Knights. No one is ever prosecuted; On May 2, Charles Eddie Moore and Henry Hezekiah Dee, both 19, are beaten to death and thrown in the Mississippi River. Charles Marcus Edwards and James Ford Seale are arrested. Edwards confesses, but neither are ever prosecuted; On June 21, three civil rights workers, Michael Schwerner, 24, James Chaney, 21, and Andrew Goodman, 20, were shot to death by Klansman. Their bodies are found buried in an earthen dam on Aug. 4 and 21 white men are arrested. Testimony reveals that Imperial Wizard Sam Bowers ordered the killings. A jury convicts Bowers and six other Klansman of federal conspiracy charges. No murder charges are ever filed; In special session, the state legislature states "the 1964 Federal Civil Rights Act is unconstitutional and that the citizens of this state should resist the enforcement of this Act by all legal means." By the end of this racially-tense summer, casualties include 6 murders, 80 beatings, 35 shootings, 68 bombings or burnings of churches, businesses and homes, and 1,000 arrests. The are reportedly responsible for most of the violence; On Oct. 4-7, Hurricane Hilda kills 38 in Mississippi, Georgia and Louisiana; On Oct. 22, a 5-kiloton nuclear device is exploded inside the Tatum salt dome in Lamar County. It is the first nuclear detonation east of the Mississippi River; Hazel Brannon Smith of the *Lexington Advertiser* receives a Pulitzer Prize for her editorial writing, making it 2 years in a row that Mississippians have received the award; Mississippi is the nation's leading producer of tung nuts (64% of the U.S. crop), ranks 2nd in cotton production, 5th in broilers, 5th in pecans, 7th in soybeans, 6th in sweet potato production, 17th in number of cattle, 12th in eggs and 18th in farm income. **Deaths**: Frances "Fannye" Cook, a Crystal Springs native, research biologist, writer of the classic reference book *The Freshwater Fishes of Mississippi* (1959),

A Chronology of Mississippi History

who established and was director of what would later be the Mississippi Museum of Natural History, dies on April 30 at age 70; Bo Carter, a Bolton native and influential early bluesman, dies in Memphis on Sept. 21; Sam Cooke, born in Clarksdale, one of the first soul singers with many No. 1 hits, is shot to death in Los Angeles by a female motel manager on Dec. 11 at age 29. **Sports**: The Ole Miss Rebels football team gets beaten twice this year in bowl games — by Tulsa 14-7 in the Bluebonnet Bowl and by Alabama 12-7 in the Sugar Bowl.

1965
On Aug. 15, Earl Hodges, 47, is beaten to death after he reportedly tried to leave the Klan. No one is ever prosecuted. Sept. 7-12, Hurricane Betsy kills 74 in Mississippi, Florida and Louisiana; On Oct. 7, Hinds General Hospital is opened; All banks in the state become FDIC insured banks. Already the state's largest bank, Deposit Guaranty National, merges with 3 existing banks to become the first $300 million banking establishment in the state. Total assets of all banks in the state pass the $2 billion level (the $1 billion mark was reached just a little over 10 years ago); Enrollment in colleges this fall is 55,790. There are 8 state-supported institutions of higher learning and 17 junior colleges; Mississippi is the No. 1 tree farming state in the nation, and has been for the past 5 years. This year, there are 3,474 tree farms covering 3,267,433 acres; The value of major manufactured forest products in the state exceeds $700 million; Manufacturing employment in the state stands at over 150,000, surpassing agricultural employment for the first time; Mississippi now supplies nearly one-half of the nation's canned oysters and one-fourth of the shrimp. **Deaths**: Major league baseball player Jim Edwards, dies in his native Calhoun County on Jan. 19; Silent screen actor William David, a Vicksburg native, dies in New York State on April 10 at age 82; One of the Delta's most famous bluemen, harmonica player Sonny Boy Williamson II (b. Aleck Ford "Rice" Miller) dies of TB in Helena, Arkansas on June 23 at age 57; Former two-time Governor Hugh L. White dies in Jackson on Sept. 20; Walter Anderson, a painter, sculptor and potter, who grew up on the Mississippi Gulf Coast, dies on Nov. 30 at age 62. **Sports**: The Ole Miss Rebels football team beats Auburn 13-7 in the Liberty Bowl in Memphis, Tenn.

1966
On Jan. 10, Klansmen fire-bomb the store and house of NAACP leader Vernon Dahmer, 58, who fires back as his family escapes. Four Klansmen are arrested, including Imperial Wizard Sam Bowers. Three Klansmen are sentenced to life, but Bowers is freed after mistrials result from hung juries (Bowers will be retried and found guilty in 1999); On March 3, a tornado sweeps through central Mississippi killing 57, including 12 in Jackson's Candlestick Park area, and injuring 504. Damages in Hinds county alone total $12 million. This twister stays on the ground for 200 miles; On Apr. 23, the engines of the second stage of the Apollo Saturn V rocket are tested at the Mississippi Test Facility near Bay St. Louis; James Meredith, who had integrated Ole Miss, begins a march around the state to encourage 450,000 blacks to register. He is shotgunned from ambush and wounded near Hernando on June 6. The march is completed June 26 with a 15,000-person rally in Jackson at which Meredith, Stokely Carmichael, and Dr. Martin Luther King share the podium; Doctors Hospital in Jackson opens on July 10; The U.S. Supreme Court rules that a change in the Mississippi River channel had shifted an oil well site from Louisiana into Mississippi; In Sept., 200 whites in Grenada armed with pipes, chains and ax handles, beat 30 black students and parents integrating the high school; The Census Bureau reports some 454,200 people have out-migrated from the state since 1950. **Deaths**: Major league baseball player Andy Reese, a Tupelo native, dies on Jan. 10; William Lockhart Clayton, Tupelo native who drafted the Marshall Plan following World War II when he was Under Secretary of State for economic affairs in 1947, dies on Feb. 8 at age 67; Blues harmonica player William "Jazz" Gillum, an Indianola native, dies on March 29; Mississippi John Hurt, well-known bluesman and native of Teoc, dies in Grenada, Miss. on Nov. 2 at the age of 73; and Hubert Creekmore, Water Valley native, a novelist and poet. **Sports**: Texas blanks Ole Miss 19-0 in the Bluebonnet Bowl.

1967
On Feb. 27, Armstrong Rubber Co. of Natchez employee Wharlest Jackson, 37, is killed by a car bomb after he was offered a promotion previously held by whites only; The space age comes to the state as NASA's Space Technology Laboratories opens in Hancock County; On Aug. 11, Marine Lance Corporal Roy M. Wheat, a native of Moselle in Jones County, throws himself on a land mine to save his fellow marines. He is the only Mississippian to receive the Medal of Honor during the Vietnam War; On Oct. 20, an all-white federal jury convicts 7 men of conspiracy in the slayings of 3 civil rights workers in 1964; Robert Clark of Ebenezer is the first black elected to state legislature since the Reconstruction period; Per capita income in Mississippi is now $1,896. **Deaths**: Bluesman J.B. Lenoir, a Monticello native, dies in Urbana, Illinois on Apr. 29 at age 37 after an auto accident. **Sports**: Univ. of Texas beats Ole Miss 14-7 in the Sun Bowl.

1968
John Bell Williams is sworn in as governor on Jan. 16; On June 10, WHTV-TV (now WTZH), channel 24, in Meridian begins broadcasting; In July, President Johnson signs a bill establishing a federal marijuana farm at the University of Mississippi to be used as a research center for "...the botany, chemistry, and cultivation of the drug," and will become the main supplier of marijuana used for official medical research in America; Catfish Farmers of America is chartered in Mississippi; The college enrollment increase, measured at an average of about 10% per year over the past 15 years, drops to only 1.25% in Mississippi's eight public institutions of higher learning; Per capita income this year is $2,081, but is still $1,340 under the national figure; In Oct., United Parcel Service announces it will deliver small packages throughout Mississippi; 1968's oil production of over 59 million barrels surpasses the 1963 record of 58.6 million; The state has 299 sawmills, 10 pulpwood/paper mills, 27 plywood/ veneer mills, 29 wood-processing plants and 37 miscellaneous timber-industry plants; Mississippi has 9,762 miles of state roads and 49,356 miles of rural roads, of which 2,611 miles are unsurfaced. In addition, 530 miles of the federal interstate highway system, out of 678 miles planned in the state, have been completed; The state has 3,635 miles of railroad track. **Deaths**: Two Canton natives die this year: painter John McCrady and bluesman Johnnie 'Geechie' Temple, Nov. 22. **Sports**: The Ole Miss Rebels football team beats Virginia Tech 34-17 in the Liberty Bowl in Memphis, Tennessee.

1969
On Jan. 23, a tornado kills 32 people in Copiah, Simpson and Smith counties; Rankin General Hospital in Jackson opens in March; On Apr. 2, Jackson Mayor Allen C. Thompson announces that "beginning today, anyone in the Jackson area needing emergency help can get it by telephoning 911."; On June 29, Jackson's high reaches 102 degrees for the seventh

A Chronology of Mississippi History

consecutive day of 100 degrees or above. It is the hottest June in 67 years; On July 8, U.S. forces begin withdrawal from Vietnam. Mississippi losses in that conflict include 637 dead; The strongest hurricane to ever hit the U.S. mainland, category 5 Great Hurricane Camille hits Mississippi's Gulf Coast with deadly force the night of August 17 and 18 causing 144 deaths and $1.3 billion (1969 dollars) property damage in the state. Packing winds of over 200 mph with a record storm surge of 22-25 feet, it leaves 3,880 Mississippi homes completely destroyed with another 41,785 homes sustaining major damage. It hits the timber industry hard with 1.2 billion board feet of saw timber blown down or twisted beyond use, and 900,000 cords of pulpwood destroyed or severely damaged. The volume of timber destroyed equals two-years growth in the second forest in the 15 counties affected. It initiates the greatest forest salvage operation in history. Mississippi will lose $5.1 million in tax revenues because of Hurricane Camille; Charles Evers is elected mayor in Fayette, the first black mayor in the state since Reconstruction; On Sept. 11, the first of a fleet of ocean-going ships docks at the Mississippi River port in Greenville as officials proclaim the port "the nation's fifth seacoast"; In early Oct., a special session of the legislature approves most of Gov. John Bell Williams' programs; Also in early Oct., the University of Mississippi School of Pharmacy opens for public view the nation's only legally grown crop of marijuana; After 15 years of resistance to court-ordered integration, the beginning of the end comes late this year with several new court decisions mandating unitary school systems. In Jackson, an estimated 8,000 white students flee the public schools for segregated academies during the first year; There are 88,000 farm tractors in the state; The work force in textiles and allied industry is 44,000 (the 1890 Census 79 years ago showed 1,184 working in cotton mills); There are 1,120,224 autos and 290,134 trucks and buses registered in the state; State-maintained roads now total 9,861 miles, 9,350 paved, and the state is spending $12,104,166 ($1,227 per mile) this year for maintenance; The state has 67 public and 86 private airports on which the state and federal governments have spent $24 million; Banks in the state reach the $3 billion aggregate asset plateau; There are now 424 insurance companies (28 Mississippi firms) doing business in Mississippi with $8,479,926,980 worth of insurance in force. Death payments to Mississippi residents is over $48 million this year; and Librarians at the University of Mississippi compile a *Preliminary Identification List of Mississippi Authors* that contains just over 1,400 names!
Deaths: Commodore S. Cochran, a Richton native who won the Gold Medal as part of the U.S. 1,600-meter relay team in the 1924 Olympics at Paris, dies on Jan. 3 at age 66; Skip James, Bentonia native and one of the earliest and most influential bluesmen, dies in Philadelphia, Penn. on Oct. 3 at age 67; Bluesman Magic Sam (Samuel Maghett), a Grenada native, dies in Chicago on Dec. 1 at age 32; Broadcast pioneer Hoyt Wooten, who started the first radio station in Mississippi in Coldwater in 1922, dies at his home in Memphis on Dec. 6.

1970

In Jan., Mississippi Baptist Hospital officials announce they'll build a new 600-bed hospital at a cost of $25 million; On Feb. 1, the PBS station WMAA, TV channel 29, in Jackson begins broadcasting; Construction begins on the Walter Sillers State Office Building in Jackson on April 9. It will be the state's tallest building at 20 stories high; In the early morning hours of May 15, two black students at Jackson State College, Phillip L. Gibbs, 21, and James Earl Green, 17, are killed by police firing on a dormitory. This followed two days of protests of the Vietnam War and human rights violations; On May 25, officials announce plans for a $450,000 catfish processing plant to be located on a 20-acre site near Belzoni; The Waterways Experiment Station, run by the Army Corps of Engineers, opens in Vicksburg; There is a work force of 22,800 in lumber and wood-products manufacturing. Growing and processing trees bring $800 million yearly to the state's economy with about 30% of that economy based on forestry. Trees cover 57% of the land; Union membership in the state is estimated to be around 80,000, an increase of 28,000 in the 8 years since 1962; On Aug. 17, the first anniversary of hurricane Camille, ceremonies are held at Camp Shelby where Major General Walter Johnson decorates 21 National Guard members for acts of heroism during Camille rescue operations. Fourteen receive the Army Commendation Medal and 7 are awarded the Soldier's Medal, the nation's highest peacetime decoration. Most of the men had continued rescuing people after being ordered to take shelter; On Oct 3, WAPT-TV, channel 16, in Jackson begins broadcasting; The number of passengers boarding at Thompson Field this year is 259,995 with scheduled airlines operating 43 flights a day; The state has 3,495 producing oil wells with an annual output of 65,119,072 barrels and natural gas production this year is 154,144,017 million cubic feet; There are 182 banking institutions in the state with an additional 348 branches and offices; The state has 20 daily and 113 weekly newspapers plus the nation's first color educational TV station; School plant (buildings, improvements, etc.) investment in the state is approximately $500 million; Out of a total of 600,000 enrollment, about 62,000 are now attending private schools (See 1957); Enrollment in all colleges in the state this fall is 71,089; Census figures show 276 incorporated places in Miss., of which 76 are urban. The state's population is 44.5% urban 55.5% rural. Urban population is approaching a million at 986,642. The state has two Standard Metropolitan Areas, Jackson with 258,906 and Biloxi-Gulfport with 134,582.
Deaths: Ishmon Bracey, a Bryam native and one of the early giants of Delta blues, dies in Jackson on Feb. 12; Bluesman Earl Zebedee Hooker (John Lee's cousin), a Clarksdale native, dies in Chicago on April 21; Otis Spann, Jackson native who played piano in the Muddy Waters band and claimed he was Waters half-brother, considered the greatest blues piano player of all time, dies in Chicago on April 24; Roscoe Turner, a Corinth, Miss. native who was an aviation pioneer who set many records and won many trophies and is the only Mississippian in the National Aviation Hall of Fame, dies on June 23. Some of his planes and awards are on display at the Smithsonian Museum; Cid Ricketts Sumner, a Brookhaven native who gained worldwide fame for her "Tammy" novels, several made into movies, dies on Oct. 15 at the age of 80.
Sports: The Ole Miss Rebels football team defeats Arkansas 27-22 in the Sugar Bowl.

1971

On Feb. 4, a tornado hits a house trailer in Grenada killing 7; On Feb. 21, a series of twisters hit the state. A tornado, considered one of the most deadly single twisters ever, kills 58 in Pugh City. Another twister hits Yazoo County destroying Little Yazoo then going on to Benton and Midway leaving 9 dead and damage of $1.5 to $2 million with 50 homes and businesses destroyed and 70 others damaged. As many as 50 other tornadoes hit the Delta the same day with damage and/or deaths at Cary, Inverness, Delta City, Belzoni, Moorhead, Greenwood & Oxford. The twisters kill 111, injure 1,511 &

A Chronology of Mississippi History

cause $17 million in damage; On Aug. 27, the Jackson School Board releases their 1971-72 budget for Jackson public schools — $22,923,518, down slightly from last year; On Aug. 30, the Jackson City Council announces their new city budget, a little over $27 million, up only about 3% from the current year's budget; On Oct. 13, WTZH-TV, channel 24 in Meridian begins broadcasting; Fayette Mayor Charles Evers becomes the first black statewide candidate when he unsuccessfully challenges Bill Waller in the governor's race; Seven blacks are sworn into office in Port Gibson on Dec. 31.
Deaths: Roy Blackwood, original member of the Blackwood Brothers, dies March 21 at the age of 70; Thomas Wayne (Perkins), Batesville native who had the hit *Tragedy* (1959), dies in an auto accident on Aug. 15 at age 31; Mississippian Sylvester Mack Magee, the last survivor of the Civil War dies Nov. 15, supposedly at the advanced age of 130!; Bluesman Junior Parker, Clarksdale native, dies Nov. 18 at the age of 39.
Sports: In Jan., Auburn beats Ole Miss 35-28 in the Gator Bowl; and in Dec., the Ole Miss Rebels football team whips Georgia Tech 41-18 in the Peach Bowl in Atlanta, Georgia.

1972

Mississippi's tallest building, the 263-foot high Walter Sillers State Office Building in Jackson is officially dedicated on Jan. 14; Also on Jan. 14 the PBS stations WMAH TV, channel 19 in Biloxi, WMAU-TV, channel 17, in Bude and WMAW-TV, channel 14, in Meridian begin broadcasting; William L. Waller becomes the state's 55th governor on Jan. 18; On Feb. 3, Governor Waller names educator Amos Wright to be on the board of the Mississippi Authority for Educational Television, the first black to be appointed to an administrative position on a state board; On Feb. 8, Waller proposes tax increases to pay for a $600 million highway program; Lt. Governor William Winter warns the senate on Feb. 11 that it must get to work soon on 346 bills if the session's work is to be completed within the scheduled 125 days; On May 19, PBS station WMAV-TV, channel 18, in Oxford begins broadcasting; On Sept. 15, PBS station WMAO-TV, channel 23, in Greenwood begins broadcasting; By the end of October, Mississippi has added $852 million worth of new or expanded industry.
Deaths: Hodding Carter, Pulitzer Prize-winning journalist who started the *Delta Democrat-Times* in Greenville and wrote 20 books, dies on April 4; Mississippi Fred McDowell, blues legend who influenced artists such as Bonnie Raitt and the Rolling Stones, dies in Memphis on July 3 at age 68;
Sports: Coach Paul Gregory takes his Mississippi State Bulldog baseball team to its first College World Series.

1973

On Jan. 2, the legislature opens a 90-day session to tackle 500 pre-filed bills and to decide what to do with the over $100 million all-time record high surplus in the state treasury; On Jan. 30 Senator John Stennis, 73, is shot twice in an apparent robbery attempt after he got out of his car in front of his residence in Washington, D.C.; On Mar. 1, Nettleton becomes the first town in the state to have delivery of mail to corner "cluster boxes."; Mississippian Eudora Welty receives the Pulitzer Prize for Fiction for *The Optimist's Daughter*; Charles Hickson and his friend Calvin Parker, Jr., both of Pascagoula, make national headlines when they claim to be UFO abductees. They say that on the night of October 11, three creatures from a flying object landed near where they had been fishing, took them inside their craft and gave them some type of physical examination before releasing them; In Dec., Jackson stores show shortages of blue jeans, antifreeze, towels, drapes, electric heaters, paper bags, toys, and many other items; On Dec. 30, First Baptist Church of Jackson, with the largest congregation in the state, names Rev. Frank Pollard of Dallas as its new pastor; Investment in new and expanded industry in the state passes the billion dollar mark in 1973.
Deaths: Willie Mitchell, Mississippi's first baseball legend, who was the first Mississippian to play in the major leagues (Cleveland Indians) and was the first pitcher to face Babe Ruth in an American League game (he struck out Babe!), dies from a stroke on Nov. 23, about a week before his 84th birthday.

1974

A power shift begins in the legislature when Valley Park farmer C.B. "Buddie" Newman, filling in for ailing Speaker John R. Junkin, is elected speaker pro tem; On Mar. 15, Delta State Teachers College (est. 1924) is renamed Delta State University and Alcorn A&M is changed to Alcorn State University. Mississippi State College for Women also gets a name change to Mississippi University for Women this year; On April 3 & 4, an outbreak of 148 twisters kills 350, injures 5,484 in Miss. & 11 other states; On June 17, the U.S. Supreme Court refuses to stay an order by the 5th Circuit Court of Appeals requiring the Mississippi Highway Patrol to revise its racially discriminatory hiring procedures; The largest sternwheeler ever built, the *Sprague*, burns at Vicksburg.
Deaths: Bluesman Arthur "Big Boy" Crudup, a native of Forest, who wrote *That's All Right Mama* — the first song Elvis released — dies on Mar. 28 at age 68; Blues singer/ songwriter Johnny Young, a Vicksburg native, dies April 18; Dizzy Dean, who grew up in Bond and was a baseball pitcher who helped the Cardinals win the World Series in 1934, a member of the Baseball Hall of Fame, dies on July 11 at age 63; Major league baseball player Buddy Myer, an Ellisville native, dies Oct. 31; and member of the Blackwood Brothers gospel group, Doyle Blackwood, dies in Oct. at the age of 63.
Sports: The Mississippi State Bulldogs football team gets by North Carolina 26-24 in the Sun Bowl in El Paso, Texas.

1975

On Jan 10, a tornado levels a shopping center and several homes in McComb killing 12 people, injuring about 200, and causing property damage estimated in the millions. Several other places are hit by the twister, but McComb took the brunt of the only severe wind storm of the year; In March, the state's two largest teacher organizations, the MEA and the MTA, vote to merge as the Mississippi Association of Educators; The Mississippi Band of Choctaw Indians elect Phillip Martin, their first chief in 145 years; On June 24, the first Wendy's hamburger restaurant in the state opens at 241 W. Northside Drive in Jackson; At the beginning of summer, public swimming pools in Jackson, closed since 1963, open as integrated facilities; A federal three-judge panel orders into effect a new legislative apportionment plan for 3 counties, Hinds, Harrison and Jackson, in the face of lawsuits asking complete redistricting of the entire state; Civil rights attorneys file a series of federal lawsuits against the Mississippi State Hospital at Whitfield citing the living conditions, care of patients, and the condition of the facilities; The U.S. Supreme Court rules that the City of Jackson and Mississippi are not liable in the Jackson State shootings of 1970; Construction begins on the new federal building in downtown Jackson; The Deposit Guaranty Plaza opens; A strike by construction workers delays over twenty major projects in Jackson for 2 months; Contruction finally begins on the long- awaited Tennessee-Tombigbee Waterway as work gets underway on a dam at Columbus; The Tennessee Valley Authority announce plans to build a nuclear power plant at Iuka in Tishomingo

A Chronology of Mississippi History

County; The Blue Laws of the state are rescinded and stores start opening Sundays; Helen Ford of Hattiesburg, an alumna of Jackson State University, is chosen as "Miss Black America"; Evangelist Billy Graham brings his crusade to Jackson; Elvis Presley returns to his home state with a soldout concert in Jackson and comes back for a second concert to accommodate the demand; An encephalitis epidemic causes numerous deaths; Batesville attorney Cliff Finch stuns political observers by sweeping two of three state elections in winning the gubernatorial election. He loses to Lt. Gov. William Winter in the first primary, but beats him in the second. He beats his Republican opponent Gil Carmichael in Nov.; The year closes with gasoline up to 68¢ a gallon.
Deaths: Frank Hains, amusements editor of the *Jackson Daily News*, is murdered; Bluesman Walter Vinson (Mississippi Sheiks), Bolton native, dies on April 22; Dr. Laurence Jones, founder of Piney Woods School, dies on July 15; Blues singer K.C. Douglas, dies Oct. 18; John R. Junkin, long-time speaker of the House, resigns a few weeks before his death; Two separate plane crashes kill Jacksonian businessman Roger Stribling and five others and Doxey Fisher and his companions on the eve of the election in which he was a candidate for state treasurer; and Blues singer 'Hound Dog" Taylor, a Natchez native, dies on Dec. 17.

1976
Cliff Finch becomes governor on Jan. 20. It's reported he spent $1 million on his election; Feb. 18, an early morning tornado hits a Clinton trailer park and parts of North Jackson, injuring 50 people. A tornado-related death and 9 injuries occur March 20 during a storm that sweeps through parts of Clay, Monroe, and Webster counties. On March 29 a tornado slashes through the center of Canton, killing 3 people and injuring 177 others. At the same time Canton is being hit, another twister cuts a continuous path through 6 counties hitting the towns of Gallman and Newton and passing just north of Meridian. This tornado causes 8 injuries, but no deaths. All-toll this year, Mississippi is hit by 34 tornadoes which kill 5 people, injure 292, and cause almost $40 million in damages; On May 7, a disgruntled former employee files a lawsuit against Bankers Trust saying it could no longer be trusted. This causes a full-scale run on deposits on May 10 which causes the collapse of the savings and loan and eventually costs its 60,000 depositors a lose of 13.5 cents on the dollar. By mid-June, the crisis had spread to several other privately-insured savings and loans and threatened the rest. Gov. Finch calls a special session of the legislature and during the weekend of June 19-20, lawmakers pass a bill forcing all state-chartered savings and loans to obtain federal insurance; On July 4, Mississippi observes the nation's bicentennial with the official ceremony held at historic Jefferson College in Adams County; America's celebrated Freedom Train derails at Hog Chain, a small community four miles north of Bogue Chitto in Lincoln County; Hinds County Chancellor George Haynes, making a final judgment on a suit originally filed in 1969, rules on Aug. 9 that the NAACP's 1960s boycott of Port Gibson white merchants was illegal and the NAACP would have to pay 12 of the merchants $1.25 million to cover economic damages and attorney's fees. The NAACP says the decision would practically bankrupt them; The first State Park to open in 25 years opens on the coast; In the Nov. general election, Mississippi's vote is credited for putting Jimmy Carter over the top in his win as president; A severe summer drought that continues through the fall causes farmers much distress and force many out of business as crops, especially cotton, wither as market prices remain low. This caps a 4-year period of losses for farmers and causes the Secretary of Agriculture to declare 56 Mississippi counties agricultural disaster areas; Racially divided factions of the Democratic party merge and pick state NAACP President Arron Henry as one of two co-chairman. In the legislature, three Hinds County blacks are elected to the House, joining Holmes County Rep. Robert Clark, who had been the lone black member since 1967.
Deaths: Blues legend "Howlin' Wolf" (Chester Arthur Burnett), a West Point native, dies during surgery for an aneurysm on Jan. 10 at age 63 in Chicago; Jimmy Reed, a native of Dunleith, Miss. who recorded the blues and R&B hits *Hush Hush*, *Big Boss Man* and *Bright Lights, Big City*, dies in Oakland, California on Aug. 29, a week before his 51st birthday; and Ray Lum, a Rocky Springs native and renowned mule trader and storyteller, dies on Dec. 17 at age 85.

1977
Mississippians suffer through high winds, freezing temps and a crippling ice storm in Jan. in one of the worst winters ever. Some rural residents are without electricity for five days; On Apr 4, tornadoes kill 22 in Mississippi, On June 6, Joseph Lawson Howze is installed as bishop of the diocese of Biloxi. He is the first black bishop of the Catholic Church in the U.S; President Jimmy Carter flies into Jackson aboard Air Force One on July 12. He addresses a crowd of 8,000 at Thompson Field, attends a reception, then helicopters to Yazoo City where he answers questions before an audience of 2,000 at a nationally-televised Town Hall Meeting. He spends the night at the Yazoo City home of retired industrialist Owen Cooper. The visit is mostly a show of gratitude for the Mississippi vote that put Carter over the top in the 1976 election; The infamous state spy agency, the Sovereignty Commission, is disbanded; Bay St. Louis becomes the first city in the state to change to the mayor-council form of government; On Oct. 20, a plane crash at Gillsburg near McComb kills 3 members of the Southern-rock band Lynyrd Skynyrd including lead singer Ronnie Van Zant. Three others are also killed, the band's road manager, the pilot and co-pilot. Nineteen survive the crash.
Deaths: Bukka White, Texas-born blues legend, who spent a lot of time in Mississippi, dies in Memphis on Feb. 26 at age 70; Painter Theora Hamblett, a Lafayette County native, dies March 6; Civil Rights leader Fannie Lou Hamer, Montgomery County native, dies March 14; and Tupelo native and superstar Elvis Presley dies on Aug. 16 in Memphis of a heart attack.
Sports: In July, Ron Polk replaces Paul Gregory as baseball coach at Mississippi State University.

1978
When Metrocenter opens in Jackson on Mar. 1, it's the largest mall in the Southeast; An early morning dormitory fire at Ellisville State School that kills 15 mentally retarded women is blamed on an arsonist; State Senator Bill Burgin, chairman of the Senate Appropriations Committee, and former state Senator Flavous Lambert are convicted in federal court for conspiracy to defraud the government. Burgin resigns from the Senate; Yazoo City Police Chief David Overton heads for a trial in Vicksburg, but does not return. A Yazoo City grand jury indicts him on charges of embezzlement; U.S. Sen. James Eastland does not seek re-election to the seat he's held for 36 years. U.S. Rep. Thad Cochran is elected, giving Mississippi its first Republican senator since Reconstruction and the state's first ever popularly elected Republican senator. Fayette Mayor Charles Evers, a black, unsuccessfully ran for the seat.
Deaths: Willie Foster, a Texas native who grew up in Lorman and played baseball at Alcorn University, where he later

A Chronology of Mississippi History

coached, one of the greatest pitchers in the old Negro Leagues and a member of the Baseball Hall of Fame (1996), dies in Lorman on Sept. 16 at age 74; Wyatt Cooper, Clarke County native who wrote the TV screenplay for *The Chapman Report* and collaborated with Truman Capote on *The Glass House*, married New York socialite Gloria Vandervilt and lived in New York, dies there this year after a series of heart attacks; William Grant Still, a Woodville native known as the Dean of Afro-American Composers, dies on Dec. 3 at 83.

1979

Canton businessman Arthur Tate breaks the racial barrier in the state Senate; The legislature passes an ethics bill and an $83.3 million tax cut that includes $69.5 million in increased income tax exemptions; From April 11-13, almost 20 inches of rain falls in the upper Pearl River Basin. The Pearl crests in Jackson on April 17 at 43.28 feet, 15.28 feet above flood stage. Some 1,935 homes and 775 businesses are flooded and more than 6,000 people affected. The Great Easter Flood is the second worst recorded flood in the state's history, after the Great Mississippi Flood of 1927. The final cost is almost $100 million; Jackson hosts the International Ballet Competition in July, offering world-class ballet to state residents; The narrowest recorded percentage win in an election anywhere occurs in Mississippi on Aug. 7. In the Southern District Highway Commissioner race, Robert E. Joiner is declared the winner over W. H. Pyron, with 133,587 votes to 133,582. This world record means that the loser got more than 49.999% of the vote!; In late summer, Hurricane David is headed for Mississippi, but it changes course just in time and heads away from the state. Hurricane Frederic strikes the Gulf Coast between Mobile, Ala. and Pascagoula on Sept. 12 causing hundreds of millions of dollars damage in Mississippi with more than 400,000 people evacuated from coastal areas of Mississippi, Alabama, Florida and Louisiana; Aides to former Governor Finch, Jimmy Means and Edgar Lloyd, are indicted and Chester Blalock is convicted. Charges against aid Bob Perry are dropped in exchange for cooperation with the Justice Department in its investigation of the former governor; Cheryl Prewitt of Ackerman wins Miss America, 1980; Elections produce a democratic sweep as William Winter wins over Republican Gil Carmichael for governor. Seventeen blacks win seats in the 1980 legislature. The black success is due to the settlement this year of the state's 14-year reapportionment case; Fidelity Bank of Jackson fails without warning; Nap Cassibry, an 11-year state senator, is indicted by a Harrison County grand jury Dec. 18 on a conflict of interest charge. He resigns during an investigation by the state Attorney General; and work begins on restoration of the Capitol Building in Jackson using $19 million in federal revenue sharing money.
Deaths: Former Lt. Gov. Charles Sullivan dies in a plane crash just 14 miles from his Clarksdale home; pioneering black librarian Charlemae Rollins, a Yazoo City native, dies in Chicago on Feb. 3; Frederick H. Coe, a native of Alligator, Miss. and one of leading TV producers of the 1940s & 50s and producer of several movies including the award winner, *The Mircle Worker* ('62), dies April 29; Gus "Banjo Joe" Cannon, native of Marshall County, best known of all the jug band musicians, who wrote the hit *Walk Right In*, sung by the Rooftop Singers (No. 1 pop 1963), dies in Memphis on Oct. 15 at age 94; Jackie Brenston, native of Clarksdale whose No. 1 hit record *Rocket 88* ('51) was considered to be the first true Rock and Roll record, dies in Memphis on Dec. 15 at age 49.

1980

William Winter becomes governor on Jan. 22; Before leaving office, Gov. Finch suspends and commutes prison sentences for 26 Parchman inmates — including 11 serving life terms for murder and rape; About 64 percent of the farms in all but three of the state's 82 counties are parched by drought as the South swelters in a killer heat wave. Sixty-five die of heat-related injuries, making the heat wave the state's deadliest disaster since tornadoes swept through the Delta killing 113 people in 1971. It is the state's second-hottest summer on record (the hottest was 1902); The Public Service Commission approves a record rate increase, including a $48.3 million hike for MP&L, the biggest in the state's history; Mississippi goes Republican for president as the majority vote for Ronald Reagan. Representative Jon Hinson is re-elected despite revelations linking him with Washington, D.C.'s homosexual community;
Deaths: major league baseball player Hughie Critz, a Starkville native, dies on Jan. 10 at age 80; Rockabilly singer Warren Smith, a Louise native, dies on Jan. 30; Don Scott, Olympic Champ in 1924, dies on Oct. 10. Scott Field at Mississippi State University is named in his honor; painter Marie Atkinson Hull, a Summit native, dies on Nov. 21 at 89.
Sports: The MSU Bulldogs football team pulls off the greatest upset ever with a 6-3 win over No. 1-rated Alabama; Mississippi State goes 9-3, losing to Nebraska 31-17 in the Sun Bowl; Ole Miss qualifies for the National Invitation Tournament, but loses in the first round; Southern Mississippi, behind the running of Reggie Collier, goes 9-3 and defeats McNeese State 16-14 in the Independence Bowl.

1981

On Apr. 22, the Joint Center for Political Studies report 2,991 Blacks holding elective offices in 45 states and the District of Columbia, compared with 2,621 in April 1973 and 1,185 in 1969. The Center reports 108 Black mayors. Michigan had the largest number of Black elected officials (194), followed by Mississippi (191); Fourth District U.S. Rep. Jon Hinson resigns his seat after his arrest on an oral sodomy charge in Washington, D.C.; Jackson native Beth Henley, a playwright, receives a Pulitzer for Drama for *Crimes of the Heart* (later made into a successful movie); In July, the Adolph Coors Co. of Boulder, Colorado begins distribution of Coors Beer in the state; At one minute past midnight on Aug. 1, MTV, Music Television Video, goes on air for the first time. It's a brainchild of Mississippian Bob Pittman from Brookhaven; On Sept. 17, Peggy Lowe is abducted from her Unifirst Savings & Loan office in Jackson. Self-described "mad-dog killer" Marion Albert Pruitt leads police to her body in Livingston, Alabama on Oct. 28; Business and personal bankruptcies in the state increase with a Nov. total of 4,858, well ahead of the 4,608 for all of 1980. Unemployment in the state rose faster in Mississippi this year than the national average. It hits a seasonally adjusted rate of 9.5% in Nov. — the highest since the deep downturn in 1974-75. The number of Mississippians employed making durable goods, which make up more than half of the state's manufacturing sector, drops to 116,700 in Nov., down from 135,300 a year ago. December sees more layoffs as manufacturers slow production to keep inventories in line. Despite the sluggish economy, 60 new firms announced plans during the year to invest more than $556 million in plants in Mississippi that would provide more than 5,000 new jobs. In the first 11 months of the year, 59 existing industries in Mississippi announced expansion plans that would provide an additional 3,200 jobs in the state;
Deaths: Major league baseball player Gerald "Gee" Walker, a Gulfport native, dies March 20; Actor Kelly Brown, a Jackson native, dies in March; Bluesman Walter 'Furry' Lewis, a

A Chronology of Mississippi History

Greenwood native, dies on Sept. 14; Roy Cochran, a Richton native who won two Gold Medals in track events in the 1948 Olympics at London, dies on Sept. 26 at age 62; Herbie Holmes, Yazoo City native and big band leader who taught Lawrence Welk his emcee style, dies on Dec. 1 at age 68; Blues harpist Walter Horton, a Horn Lake native, dies Dec. 8. **Sports**: Veterans Memorial Stadium in Jackson is host to the largest crowd (64,112) to ever witness a sporting event in the state: The USM Golden Eagles defeat the MSU Bulldogs 7 to 6; Marcus Dupree, with 87 TDs, breaks Herschel Walker's prep TD record while playing for Philadephia High; Mississippi State, 46-17 in baseball, earns a trip to the College World Series; Ole Miss wins the SEC Tournament in Birmingham and earns the first NCAA tournament bid in the school's history; Mississippi State makes its second consecutive bowl appearance, defeating Kansas 10-0 in the Hall of Fame Bowl in Birmingham; and Southern Mississippi loses to Missouri 19-17 in the Tangerine Bowl.

1982

In Washington, Mississippi-born Lennie Skutnik becomes an instant hero in Jan. when he jumps into the Potomac River to rescue Air Florida crash victim Priscilla Tirado. The Biloxi native is publicly complimented for his actions by President Ronald Reagan; The major utilities ask for big rate hikes: South Central Bell for $92 million, Mississippi Power Co. for $21.9 million, Mississippi Power and Light Co. for $93.9 million, and Mississippi Valley Gas for $14.2 million. The requests provoke consumer protests; A January snow and ice storm blankets much of the central and northern part of the state. Also in January, a tornado touches down south of Newton, killing one person, injuring 27 others and causing widespread property damage. Another tornado in early April hits Neshoba County, killing 3 people and leaving 40 injured; The 90-day legislative session is marked by money shortages and political wars. At the end of the session, lawmakers had killed bills for a state-supported kindergarten program and left the rest of Governor William Winter's educational reform program in a shambles. However, when Winter summons lawmakers into special session in early Dec. to consider a comprehensive education package, both chambers approve sweeping educational reforms, including mandated kindergartens beginning in 1986, and tax increases to support them. No money was allocated for salary increases for schoolteachers, state employees, or colleges; County singer George Jones is arrested by the Highway Patrol in Jackson in March on charges of speeding and possession of cocaine. The next day, Jones is involved in a one-car accident in Monroe County and charged with driving while intoxicated; Two men are killed in blasts at a cottonseed plant in Jackson in March. In Pascagoula, two chemical company workers are killed in May when overcome by fumes while inspecting the inside of a new railroad tank car. Two more men die in an explosion and fire at a plastics factory at Gulfport in June; Marion Albert Pruett is convicted in April of killing Peggy Lowe of Brandon after taking her captive during the Sept. 1981 robbery of a Jackson savings and loan. Pruett is later convicted of slayings in Arkansas and Colorado; Franklin County Sheriff James Posey, 38, is shot to death by a gunman in rural Lincoln County shortly after he exchanged himself for hostages. Officers then kill the gunman; Unemployment reaches a record 12.6% in August, but improves slightly by the end of the year; After the state gives $750,000 in matching funds, the Mississippi Firefighters Memorial Burn Center opens in Greenville; Four men are convicted during 1982 of the New Year's eve, 1981, death of State Trooper Billy Morris Langham, killed after stopping a car on U.S. 49 near Collins. The last conviction comes in Sept., when Samuel Johnson of Springfield, Louisiana is sentenced to die in the gas chamber; In Nov., Haley Barbour, 34, a Yazoo City lawyer runs as a republican candidate for senator against democrat John Stennis, but loses; Former Tchula Mayor Eddie Carthan, 33, accused of hiring two men to kill Alderman Roosevelt Granderson, a longtime political foe, is acquitted by a jury in Lexington on Nov. 4; Choking smoke from smoldering polyurethane foam pours from a padded cell of a former mental patient at the Harrison County Jail in Biloxi on Nov. 8, killing 27 prisoners and injuring 61 inmates and rescue personnel. Two of the injured later die. Authorities charge Robert Eugene Pates, a 31-year-old drifter from Illinois, with 27 of the deaths, saying he deliberately set the blaze; On Dec. 2, James Billiot is convicted in Gulfport for killing his stepfather. He later stands trials in the deaths of his stepsister and mother. The 3 were beaten to death with a sledgehammer at their rural Hancock County home on Thanksgiving Day, 1981; On Dec. 21, Governor Winter signs the 1982 Education Reform Act; Lenore Loving Prather becomes the first woman to serve on the state Supreme Court; Dr. Robert Harrison, a dentist of Yazoo City, is elected as the first black to serve as chairman of the state College Board; The Tennessee Valley Authority cancels plans to build a nuclear power plant in Iuka in Tishomingo County after spending about $1 billion; The Hederman family sells *The Clarion-Ledger* and *Jackson Daily News* to Gannett, a nationwide news and information company headquartered in Virginia that publishes several dozen daily newspapers, including *USA Today*, the national newspaper. **Deaths**: John T. Kelly, who had served as special agent in charge of the FBI in Mississippi since 1978, dies in Jackson in March following a heart attack; Lehman Engel, Jackson native, composer/conductor who worked with some of the biggest names on major record labels, won 3 Tony Awards, conducted over 150 musicals, and even wrote books on music, dies on Aug. 29; Aviation pioneer and record-holder H.T. 'Dick' Merrill, a native of Iuka, dies on Oct. 31 at the age of 88; Big Joe Williams, a native of Crawford and notable bluesman dies in Macon, Miss. on Dec. 17 at the age of 79. **Sports**: Calvin Smith of Bolton records the fastest time in the world for 100 meters, a wind-assisted 9.91 seconds; Jackson Mets player Darryl Strawberry is voted the Texas League MVP; Archie Manning is traded from New Orleans to Houston; Steve Sloan leaves Ole Miss for Duke; USM's football program is placed on probation by the NCAA; and Bobby Collins is replaced as coach at USM by Jim Carmody.

1983

Construction is under way on a $25 million state prison to house 505 inmates near the State Hospital at Whifield in Rankin County; Mississippi Power and Light Co. asks for a $94 million rate hike in Jan., but the PSC allows only $47.5 million. Later in the year, South Central Bell asks for a $98.2 million increase and the PSC says no; The legislature, in its regular session, approves a utility reform act that prohibits utilities from the old practice of putting rate hikes into effect under bond before the PSC decides on the matter; the LDDS company, which will later evolve into MCI WorldCom, is formed; In Feb., Jackson voters reject a $42 million school bond issue; An Unusually mild winter ends with a record-breaking cold spell, then floods in north Mississippi, tornado damage in April and a major flood in Jackson in late May. The Pearl River reaches 39.58 feet in Jackson, or 11.5

A Chronology of Mississippi History

feet above flood stage. At its peak on May 25, more than 700 homes and 280 businesses are flooded and about 5,000 people are affected; Also in May, Edward L. Cates, a 55-year-old Jackson attorney and former City Commissioner, is thought to have died in his burning car in rural Madison County. Cates turns up, very much alive, in June in Lawrenceville, Georgia. He is indicted in Hinds County for embezzling $223,336 from a corporate client and for capital murder and arson for the death of the still-unidentified person whose charred body was found in his car; The restored Capitol Building is dedicated on June 3; Governor Winter proclaims June 12 Medgar Evers Day. Riding in the parade in Jackson that day was former World-Champion boxer Muhammed Ali, bluesman B.B. King, the Rev. Jesse Jackson, and former Governor Ross Barnett, who fought to keep segregation alive in the 1960s!; In Aug., the College Board asks for the resignation of Jackson State University President John A. Peoples, Jr., who does step down; Mississippi returns to capital punishment with the Sept. 3 execution of Jimmy Lee Gray in the gas chamber at the State Penitentiary at Parchman. Gray was the first execution in 19 years and one of the first in the nation after the U.S. Supreme Court allowed restoration of the death penalty; Ole Miss Chancelor Porter Fortune announces his retirement. In early Dec., the state College Board asks outgoing Governor William Winter to take the job. Winter first says yes, then changes his mind; The Jackson *Clarion-Ledger* receives a Pulitzer Prize gold medal for distinguished and meritorious public service; A Warren Central High School teacher says she was horrified, but not surprised, when a student pulled a gun on her; Several episodes of the TV show, *The Mississippi*, starring Ralph Waite of *The Waltons* fame, are filmed around Natchez and in Vicksburg; In Oct., state finances stand at $52.5 million in the red. In a special session in Nov., the legislature agrees to a $90 million tax increase bill to help bail out the state; Bill Allain is elected governor Nov. 8 despite allegations from Republicans that he had been involved with male prostitutes; On Dec. 1, the sales tax rate goes from 5% to 6%; Lenore Prather becomes Mississippi's first woman Supreme Court Justice.
Deaths: Bolton native and bluesman Sam Chatmon dies Feb. 2 at age 86; Columbus native and world-renowned dramatist Tennessee Williams dies Feb. 25, one day before his 72nd birthday; College football great Edwin "Goat" Hale, a Jackson native, dies on Mar. 25; Former Gov. John Bell Williams dies in Brandon on Mar. 25; Actor Gavin Gordon, a Waybe Co. native, dies April 7; Jackson native actress Ernestine Wade, who played Sapphire Stevens on the TV comedy series *The Amos 'n' Andy Show* in the early 1950s, dies April 15; Turner Catledge, a native of Ackerman, worked for the *New York Times* for more than 40 years, including top management jobs, dies April 27 at age 82; Rolling Fork native and blues legend "Muddy Waters" (McKinley Morganfield) dies April 30 at 68.
Sports: Mississippian Calvin Smith wins a gold medal at the World University Games; Ole Miss basketball coach Lee Hunt is voted SEC Coach of the Year. His team finishes the year tied for 2nd place in the SEC and receives an NIT bid, the school's 4th straight; Under new coach Billy Brewer, Ole Miss goes 6-5 and loses to Air Force 9-3 in the Independence Bowl; Jerry Rice is named SWAC Player of the Year; Ole Miss' Ralph Spry wins the NCAA long jump; Mississippi State's Jeff Malone is a first-round NBA pick; and Archie Manning is traded from Houston to Minnesota.

1984
In Jan., the legislature meets for the first time in the restored Capitol Building; Bill Allain is sworn in as governor on Jan. 10; On Mar. 14, the guided missile cruiser, the *Vincennes*, is christened at Ingalls Shipbuilding in Pascagoula; On April 21, the evening before Easter Sunday, tornadoes race across 10 counties in northern Mississippi, leveling the heart of Water Valley in Yalobusha County, killing 15 people and causing $21 million in damage; In July, 49-year-old West Cole becomes the first person in the state to be sentenced to die by lethal injection; On Sept. 12, Northpark Mall opens 800,000 square feet of shopping space after completion of the first phase of the $101 million mall in Ridgeland; On Sept. 4, Jacksonians overwhelmingly approve a change from the city's 72-year-old commission form of government to the mayor-council form, a victory for Mayor Dale Danks; United Airlines becomes the 4th major airline to serve Jackson in Oct. when it begins 2 daily round-trip flights to Chicago via Memphis; The state's first garbage-powered energy plant begins operation at Moss Point on Oct. 31; Records show about 5% of Mississippi's school bus drivers are teenagers; In the Nov. general election, Ronald Reagan carries Mississippi by the widest margin since the Nixon landslide of 1972;
Deaths: Karl Wolfe, one of the premier artists of Mississippi, born in Brookhaven in 1903, dies in Jackson on Nov. 16.
Sports: Mississippian Calvin Smith wins a Gold Medal in the Summer Olympics; On Sept. 10, the Jackson Mets win their second Texas League championship, defeating the Beaumont Golden Gators 6-4 and taking 4 games in the best of 7 series; Walter Payton becomes the NFL's all-time leading rusher; Marcus Dupree signs a multi-million dollar contract with the USFL's New Orleans Breakers; Mississippi Valley and Alcorn State play before 64,000 fans at Memorial Stadium.

1985
Laurel native Leontyne Price gives her last Metropolitan Opera performance on Jan. 3; On Jan. 11, Judge Reuben Anderson becomes the first black state Supreme Court Justice in Mississippi; On Jan. 12, the first commercial tow prepares to start its trip up the 234-mile Tenn-Tom Waterway as it opens to provide direct shipping on the Tennessee River to the Gulf of Mexico. A total of 350 million cubic yards of earth were removed from the entire Tenn-Tom Waterway, or nearly twice that removed for the construction of the Panama Canal, making the Tenn-Tom Waterway the largest single earth excavation project in history!; On Jan. 17, around 10,000 teachers brave cold weather to rally at the state capitol for higher salaries and to scoff at Gov. Bill Allain's proposed $1,500 pay hike. After the governor vetoes a $77.6 million pay raise, an estimated 9,100 teachers begin a 3-week strike on Feb. 24; On Jan. 23, the Personnel Board approves an extensive reorganization of the Department of Education, the first in 20 years; On Feb. 14, State Rep. Fred Banks, Jr. of Jackson becomes Misissippi's only black circuit judge when he replaces his former law partner, Rueben Anderson, on the bench for Hinds and Yazoo counties; In Feb., there is a record 86 straight hours of subfreezing temperatures in Jackson; On July 1, Grand Gulf Unit 1 near Port Gibson in Clairborne County begins operation as the nation's largest operating nuclear power plant; The state reports spending $5,710,230 on the 1985 regular legislative session and the short special session of June 1984; On Sept. 2, hurricane Elena hits the coast, causing one death and $10 million damage; Tommy Brooks, president pro tem of the state Senate, receives a 9-year sentence for conspiring to extort money to push a horse-racing bill; Marcus Dilworth, a 17-year-old black of Yazoo City, is picked from 500,000 boys across the nation to become the first Mississippian to be chosen president of the American Legion

A Chronology of Mississippi History

Boys Nation; Susan Akin of Meridian wins the Miss America 1986 crown. This makes 4 times Mississippians have won (also in '58, '59 & '79); Mrs. Donna Hild Russell, from Brandon, is chosen Mrs. America 1985. A graduate of Ole Miss, she is selected as third runner-up in the 1986 Mrs. World Pageant held in Honolulu, Hawaii on Sept. 21; On Dec. 9, the Jackson Municipal Airport is closed after a Delta Air Lines jetliner rolls off a runway and becomes mired in mud.

Deaths: Borden Deal, whose book, *Dunbar's Cove* (1957), was made into the movie *Wild River* (1960), dies on Jan. 22; Sports referee A.C. "Butch' Lambert, a Holcut native, dies on Jan. 26; Musician and songwriter, Hoyt Lester Ming, an Ackerman native, dies on April 28; Evelyn Allen Hammett, a Jefferson County native who was head of the Department of Languages and Literature at Delta State University from 1947-54 and wrote the well-known children's book, *I, Priscilla,* dies on June 16, four days after her 91st birthday; Guy Bush, a native of Aberdeen, Miss. who played for the Chicago Cubs for 17 seasons, dies at Shannon, Miss. on July 2 at age 83. Babe Ruth hit his last two home runs off balls pitched by Bush during the World Series May 25, 1935. He's in the Mississippi Sports Hall of Fame; Frank "Bruiser" Kinard, a Pelahatchie native and tackle for the New York Dodgers for 9 playing seasons from 1938-47, inducted into the College Football Hall of Fame in 1951, the first Mississippian selected for the Pro Football Hall of Fame, and was inducted into the Mississippi Sports Hall of Fame in 1961, dies on Sept. 7; Blind John Davis, a Hattiesburg native and bluesman, dies in Chicago on Oct. 12; Former Governor Paul B. Johnson, Jr. dies on Oct. 14 at age 69; Elsie McWilliams, Harpersville native who wrote many of the songs recorded by her famous brother-in-law Jimmie Rodgers, dies on Dec. 31 at age 89.

Sports: MSU finishes in third place in the 1985 College World Series. Will Clark and Rafael Palmeiro are first-round draft choices; Walter Payton helps the Chicago Bears to the Super Bowl; and Emory Bellard is fired as coach at Mississippi State after his fourth consecutive losing season.

1986

On Jan. 23, the House of Representatives overwhelmingly approves a measure abolishing Mississippi's blue laws that restrict Sunday sales; On Jan. 24, Mississippi inventor Joseph W. Newman delivers a prototype of his energy machine to federal engineers in Washington, D.C. for testing. Newman claims his machine produces more energy than it uses; On Feb. 4, Shondra May, 17, of the Pea Ridge community disappears. Her body is found Feb. 26 by a fisherman in a Bolton area creek. Two autopsies fail to establish what killed her; On Feb. 4, a natural gas explosion devastates the Watkins Furniture and Appliance store in downtown Crystal Springs, and kills 8 people including 4 members of the Watkins family. On June 15, explosions at a First Chemical Corp. plant in Pascagoula caused by a chemical reaction result in a fire that lasts more than 11 hours. Damage estimates are several millions of dollars. On July 22, 14 people were injured during a gas explosion at Enterprise Products loading facility at Petal. On Dec. 16, an explosion at another Enterprise Products' site, two miles from the first blast, forces the evacuation of nearly 200 people. Officials say the two blasts are not related; In Feb., the Eudora Welty Library opens at 300 North State Street in Jackson as the state's largest public library; On Feb. 9, Walter L. Nixon, Jr., 57, of Biloxi, chief judge of the Southern District of Mississippi, becomes only the second sitting federal judge to be convicted of crimes committed while in office. Nixon is sentenced in March to two 5-year prison terms after being convicted on two counts of perjury involving his July 18, 1984, appearance before a special federal grand jury in Hattiesburg; On Sept. 7, about 700 people are evacuated from Collins after 25 Illinois Central Gulf railroad cars derail. Five derailed tankers contain toxic chlorine gas, and a hole in one spews deadly fumes, prompting the 6-day evacuation and closure of a nine-mile portion of U.S. Highway 49. On Sept. 18, nearly 1,500 Madison County residents are forced to leave their homes after a motor home strikes a 68-car ICG train derailing 20 cars. Several cars contain toxic substances, but only one propane gas car bursts into flames; In the Nov. 4 election, Mike Espy of Yazoo City is elected in the 2nd district, the first black congressman from Mississippi since 1883 during Reconstruction. Major news organizations, from the *New York Times* to *ABC News* profile Espy after his election. On Nov. 4, voters reverse a 96-year-old ban prohibiting state governors from succeeding themselves in office; A 9-year-old tradition ends on Dec. 12 as U.S. District Judge William Barbour issues a temporary injunction prohibiting the lighted display of a Christian cross on the eastern face of the Sillers Building — that in answer to a suit filed by the American Civil Liberty Union alleging violation of separation of church and state; Arkabutla native James Earl Jones receives the Tony Award for his role in the Broadway play *Fences*; Native Mississippian Richard H. Truly, an astronaut, becomes head of the NASA Space Shuttle program.

Deaths: On Jan. 18, Claude Ramsey, the Moss Point labor union chief who led Mississippi organized labor for more than a quarter century, dies at his Jackson home at age 69; On Feb. 19, former U.S. Sen. James Eastland, the "godfather of Mississippi politics," the Doddsville country lawyer and plantation owner who rose to fame as the iron-fisted chairman of the Senate Judiciary Committee, the state's senior senator known for his adamant opposition to Civil Rights legislation; Actor Alvin Childress, a Meridian native who played Amos Jones in the TV comedy series *The Amos 'n' Andy Show* in the early 1950s, dies April 19 at age 78; On April 22, former Governor Cliff Finch, of a massive heart attack at age 59; Novelist William Attaway, a Greenville native, dies on June 17; Major league baseball player 'Skeeter' Webb, a Meridian native, dies July 8; Major league baseball player S.B. 'Sam' Vick, a Batesville native, dies Aug. 17; Joseph Paul Treen, A Purvis native who invented the bicycle and motorcycle kickstand (among other inventions) and father of Louisiana Governor David Treen, dies Aug. 24; On Sept. 16, Thomas S. "Dick" Hitt of Jackson, the Marion Co. native who made his mark in athletics as a player, coach and administrator, became the first manager of Mississippi Memorial Stadium and member of the Mississippi Sports Hall of Fame; On Nov. 2, Herman B. DeCell, former state senator, intellectual and humanitarian, dies at his Yazoo City home from a heart attack; On Nov. 8, Owen Cooper, Yazoo City resident, founder of Mississippi Chemical Corporation and one of the most influential Mississippians of the last four decades as a leader in religion, Civil Rights and politics, dies of cancer at age 78; On Nov. 29, Madison Co. Sheriff for 22 years, Billy Noble, dies of a heart attack; On Dec. 21, State Sen. Howard Dyer of Greenville, champion of a new state constitution and a state lottery, dies of an apparent heart attack; and Coldwater native and historian Dumas Malone dies on Dec. 27 at the age of 94.

Sports: Violation of NCAA recruiting regulations earn the Ole Miss Rebels a two-year probation and a ban on TV and bowl appearances during '87. The Ole Miss athletic committee still recommends extension of head coach Billy Brewer's contract;

A Chronology of Mississippi History

Archie Cooley leaves Mississippi Valley State for Arkansas-Pine Bluff; Rockey Felker leads State to a 6-5 record in his first season as coach; Ed Murphy replaces Lee Hunt as basketball coach at Ole Miss; and the Ole Miss Rebels football team goes 8-3-1 and beats Texas Tech 20-17 in the Independence Bowl in Shreveport.

1987

On Feb. 12, the U.S. Attorney's office began arresting county supervisors in the FBI undercover probe Operation Pretense. They are accused of bribery, extortion, accepting kickbacks, mail fraud, rigging bids and false billing. By year's end, the sting results in the arrests of 49 supervisors in 23 counties; On Feb. 28, a tornado strikes the Glade community in Jones County, killing 7 people and ripping a path of destruction 20 miles long; On Mar. 26, five members of the Chi Omega sorority at the University of Mississippi are killed when a one-ton truck plows into them on state highway 6. The women were walking between Batesville and Oxford to raise funds for the Kidney Foundation; State representative Buddie Newman, 66, of Valley Park, a legislator for 40 years and Speaker of the House since 1976, announces on Mar. 31 that he will not seek re-election; Mound Bayou, the nation's oldest and largest all-black city, observes its centennial on July 12; On July 18, Toni Seawright, 23-year-old Moss Point resident and Mississippi University for Women graduate, becomes the first black to win the Miss Mississippi Pageant in Vicksburg. Seawright is picked as 4th alternate in the Miss America Pageant in Atlantic City, N.J., on Sept. 19; U.S. Senator John Stennis, 86, of DeKalb announces Oct. 19 that he will not seek re-election to the post he has held since 1948; Also on Oct. 19, it is Black Monday on Wall Street as the stock market plummets 508 points — the biggest one-day loss in history. Mississippi-based stocks don't suffer much from the crash; On Nov. 3, voters elect 39-year-old Harvard graduate Ray Mabus from Ackerman as governor. Mabus, the current State Auditor, defeats Republican Jack Reed, 63, a Tupelo businessman, for the post 385,689 to 336,006. Other youthful candidates winning include Mike Moore, 35, elected attorney general, and Pete Johnson, 39, chosen state auditor; The year produced a homicide a week in Jackson, matching the record of 52 in 1982; In late Dec., Mississippi is ruled out as a possible site for the $4.4 billion Superconducting Super Collider atom smasher, for which the legislature had authorized spending $2.5 million for filing the proposal and promoting the project; **Deaths**: Physician and medical pioneer Leslie Vaughn Rush, a Meridian native, dies on Feb. 8; Bluesman Robert Wilkins, Hernando native, dies on May 26 at age 91; Harrison County Circuit Court Judge Vincent Sherry and his wife, former Biloxi City Councilwoman Margaret Sherry are found dead in their Biloxi home on Sept. 14. Autopsies reveal they were shot at close range; Actress Ruth Attaway, a Greenville native, dies on Sept. 21 at the age of 77; O.B. McClinton, a black singer born in Senatobia, Miss. who had the country hit *Don't Let the Green Grass Fool You* in 1973, dies of cancer on Sept. 23 at the age of 45; On Nov. 6, former Governor Ross Barnett dies at age 89. He tried to preserve segregation in the 1960s and will be remembered for his 1962 confrontation with federal officials when he tried to block registration of James Meredith as the first black student at the University of Mississippi. **Sports**: Ole Miss struggles through to a 3-8 year while battling under NCAA probation; Curley Hallman replaces Jim Carmody as football coach at the University of Southern Mississippi; and USM wins the NIT championship.

1988

Ray Mabus becomes governor Jan. 12; On Apr. 6, Sunburst takes over a failing Baton Rouge bank, becoming the first Mississippi bank to have an operation outside the state; A disaster is declared in the state in the worst drought and heat wave since the 1930s; On Aug. 4, an arson fire destroys Phi Beta Sigma, the first black fraternity house on Ole Miss' Frat Row; Socialite Annie Laurie Hearin, wife of Mississippi Valley Gas CEO Robert Hearin, is abducted from her Jackson home; The famous Norman Rockwell art exhibit touring America, is displayed at the University of Southern Mississippi, the only university in the nation to have the exhibit; A British Airways Concorde supersonic jet lands in Mississippi for the first time at the Jackson Municipal Airport. **Deaths**: Singer Harold Dorman, a Sledge native who had the first hit of *Mountain of Love* (another Sledge native, Charley Pride, would later also make a hit of it), dies on Oct. 8; Eddie James "Son" House, a native of Lyon, Miss. and legendary early bluesman, dies on Oct. 19 in Detroit; Columbus native Henry Armstrong, the only boxer to hold three world titles simultaneously (in the 1930s) dies Oct. 24 in Los Angeles of heart failure at age 75; Writer and cartoonist Edwin Phillips Granberry, a Meridian native famous for his *Buz Sawyer* comic strip that ran for over 30 years, dies on Dec. 5 at age 91. **Sports**: Lewis Tillman replaces Walter Payton as Jackson State's all-time leading rusher; JSU wins their 4th straight SWAC title of the decade; Chris Jackson (will later be named Mahmoud Abdul-Rauf) leads Gulfport to the state basketball title, then signs with LSU; At the Olympics, Jennifer Gillom wins a Gold Medal and Larry Myricks wins bronze; USM goes 10-2 for the season and wins 38-18 over the UT, El Paso in the Independence Bowl in Shreveport; and Ole Miss tight end Wesley Walls is named Associated Press All-America.

1989

In Jan., John Stennis steps down from the U.S. Senate seat he first won in 1948; In March, Newton Alfred Winn, a native of Florida, is arrested in connection with last year's abduction of Jackson socialite Annie Laurie Hearin; On Apr. 27, the Jackson Municipal Airport is officially renamed the Jackson International Airport; The controversial movie *Mississippi Burning*, is released nationwide. The movie, the story of three Civil Rights workers killed in the state in 1964 and the FBI's involvement in the investigation, stars Gene Hackman and Willem Dafoe and was filmed in Mississippi; Leo Edwards is executed in the state gas chamber on June 21. It will be Mississippi's last execution in the 20th Century; The state's two charity hospitals officially close during the summer as Governor Ray Mabus had proposed, and the state and its residents begin a struggle to provide health care for the indigent and the working poor; On July 27, James Finneran of California becomes the first deaf principal of the Mississippi School for the Deaf; Mississippian Richard H. Truly is promoted to head the National Aeronautics and Space Administration (NASA), the first astronaut to become that agency's administrator; Clyda S. Rent becomes the first permanent female president of Mississippi University for Women; The U.S. Senate strips convicted perjurer Walter Nixon of his federal judgeship and his $89,500 annual salary. **Deaths**: Two-time Olympic Champion (1956 & '60) Lee Calhoun, Laurel native, dies June 21; Military leader, Admiral Means Johnston, Jr., a Greenwood native, dies July 14; Major league baseball player Hal Lee, a Ludlow native, dies Sept. 4; Jazz drummer Freddie Waits, a Jackson native, dies Nov. 18; and Freshman U.S. Rep. Larkin Smith dies in a plane crash.

A Chronology of Mississippi History

Sports: Archie Manning is inducted into the College Football Hall of Fame; Jerry Rice wins MVP of Super Bowl XXIII; Will Clark leads the San Francisco Giants to the World Series; Chucky Mullins and Allen Moore sustain paralyzing injuries playing for Ole Miss; the Ole Miss Rebels football team goes 7-4 and then defeats Air Force 42-29 in the Liberty Bowl in Memphis; and former MSU head football coach Jim Carmody becomes defensive coordinator at Mississippi State University.

1990

On Jan 4, federal regulators take control of First Guaranty Bank for Savings, a Hattiesburg-based savings and loan with branches in 8 Mississippi cities; On Jan. 10, the state Public Service Commission orders South Central Bell to refund to customers $1.06 million in overearnings; Deposit Guaranty National Bank completes its $23.1 million purchase of Commerce National Bank of Shreveport on Feb. 8. On Feb. 12, Hancock Bank of Gulfport buys Metropolitan Bank of Biloxi for $6.75 million; Despite the efforts of over 100 firefighters, the Perry County Courthouse in New Augusta burns to the ground on Feb. 27. The courthouse had been completed in 1904 to replace the one that burned in 1877; Mississippi's first life-care retirement community, St. Catherine's Village, is dedicated on March 12; On June 28, a Nashville medical group agrees to buy Mercy Regional Medical Center in Vicksburg; On Aug. 3, the Mississippi Employment Security Commission says it will close 16 of 35 job offices around the state and fire 100 workers because of a $4.6 million loss in federal funds; Delta Pride Catfish workers begin a strike over wages and working conditions at the nation's largest catfish processor. The strike which begins Sept. 13 lasts for 3 months before it is finally settled on Dec. 14; The Weyerhaeuser Company dedicates a $500 million pulp mill in Lowndes County near Columbus on Oct. 8;
Deaths: Fashion designer Patrick Kelly, Vicksburg native, dies in Paris, France on Jan.1; Greenville writer Walker Percy dies of cancer in Covington, La. on May 10 at age 73; Jim Henson, Greenville native and creator of the Muppets, dies of a rare form of strepp pneumonia on June 16; Jazz tenor saxophonist Frank Wright, a Grenada native, dies on May 17; Murry Kellum, who went to high school in Florence, Miss. and recorded novelty songs, dies on Sept. 15; Robert Hearin, Sr., 73, dies of a heart attack in Nov. He was the multi-millionaire Mississippi Valley Gas CEO whose wife, Annie Laurie, was kidnapped from their Jackson home in 1988.
Sports: North Carolina State defeats Southern Mississippi 31-27 in the All-American Bowl; Clifton Davis III of North Panola sets a new state high school record for touchdown passes in one game as he throws 10 in a game against Coldwater. It also ties the national high school record!

1991

Families along the Gulf Coast and in Vicksburg evacuate their flooded homes in early Jan; Census figures released early this year show the state with: a population of 2,573,216 — 47% urban & 53% rural; 1,230,512 males (47.82%) and 1,342,704 females (52.18%); 1,633,461 whites (63.48%) and 915,057 blacks (35.56%); 3 MSAs wholly within the state — Jackson with 395,396 in the 3 counties of Hinds, Madison, and Rankin — Gulfport-Biloxi with 197,125 — Pascagoula with 115,243; households number 911,374; and 29 cities with population over 10,000; On Feb. 18, a Jackson school bus carrying 34 Siwell Junior High students overturns, sending 26 to the hospital with minor injuries; On Apr. 4, Jackson fire chief LaMar Chamblee quits after 33 years to become a Methodist minister; Three Cuban dancers are refused entrance visas to perform in Jackson May 18-19 at the International Ballet Competition because of Cuba's stance on the Persian Gulf war; On June 4, Jackson voters approve a $35.2 million school bond issue; On July 30, officials announce that Annie Laurie Hearin, kidnapped wife of Jackson millionaire Robert Hearin, has been declared legally dead; On Aug. 1, Donald Leroy Evans captures national attention after confessing to the abduction, rape and murder of Beatrice Louise Routh, 10, in Gulfport and claiming responsibility for as many as 60 murders across the country since 1977; A lawsuit against Tom Hamby, publisher of the defunct *Pearl Press*, is dismissed in Rankin County Circuit Court on Aug. 14. The suit sought $1 million in the Aug. 20, 1988, slaying of John Hester, Jr., 17; An Aegis guided missile cruiser, the *USS Vicksburg*, is christened at Ingalls Shipbuilding in Pascagoula on Sept. 12; On Nov. 13, the U.S. Supreme Court hears arguments over whether Mississippi has done enough to desegregate its 8 universities; Hinds County voters kill a $17.7 million school bond on Nov. 19; On Dec. 19, fire destroys the Vicksburg Laundry, site of the nation's first Coca-Cola bottling plant;
Deaths: James Thomas "Papa" Bell, a native of Starkville and longtime pro baseball player in the Negro Leagues, probably the fastest player ever, the only native Mississippian in the Baseball Hall of Fame and also a member of the Mississippi Sports Hall of Fame, dies in St. Louis on Mar. 7 at age 87; David Ruffin, born in the community of Whynot near Meridian, the co-lead singer of the Temptations from 1963-68, had his own Top-10 hit records *My Whole World Ended (The Moment You Left Me)* in '69 and *Walk Away From Love* in '76, dies on June 1 at age 49, his life cut short by drugs; On June 16, *Hattieburg American* editor Buddy Baker, 55, dies of cancer; On June 19, Matt Devenney, 33, director of the Community Stewpot in Jackson, is shot to death outside the food kitchen. John D. Smith, 37, an unemployed drifter, is charged with murder; George Moody, retired in 1990 after 20 years as executive director of the state Board for Community and Junior Colleges, dies of a heart attack on July 1 while vacationing with his wife in Yellowstone National Park; Samuel L. Reed, one of Mississippi's first professional catfish farmers, founder of the Humphreys County World Catfish Festival, and former mayor of Belzoni, dies of heart failure; and former Gov. James Plemon "J.P." Coleman, dies Sept. 28.
Sports: In Jan., Michigan whips Ole Miss 35-3 in the Gator Bowl in Jacksonville; Under coach Richard Williams, the Mississippi State basketball team wins another SEC title; The Jackson Generals baseball team becomes a Houston Astros affiliate after being with the New York Mets from 1975-90; and Air Force beats the Mississippi State Bulldogs 38-15 in the Liberty Bowl in Memphis, Tennessee.

1992

On Jan. 6, First District Congressman Jamie Whitten enters the record books for the longest service in the U.S. House of Representatives — over 50 years; Jan. 14, Kirk Fordice is sworn in as governor — the first Republican governor since 1876; Richard Truly, a Mississippi native and first astronaut to head NASA, resigns as director of that agency on Feb. 12 over differences with the administration; On Apr. 11, the Gulfport Police Dept. becomes the first in the state to establish a bicycle patrol; The state sales tax goes from 6% to 7% on July 1; On Aug. 1, the Isle of Capri Casino, the first dockside gaming operation in the state, opens in Biloxi; On Nov. 21 & 22, several tornadoes hit the state. Brandon & Flowood take the brunt. Ten of the 15 who die statewide were from Rankin County, where more than 400 dwellings are damaged or

A Chronology of Mississippi History

destroyed. On Dec. 24, President Clinton appoints Mike Espy of Yazoo City to the cabinet as Secretary of Agriculture. When elected from the second district in 1986, he was the first black congressman from Mississippi since Reconstruction. **Deaths**: Willie Dixon, Vicksburg native and one of the most famous blues singers and songwriters, dies in Burbank, Calif. on Jan. 29 at age 76; Ethel Wright Mohamed, who was born at Fame, but spent most of her life in Belzoni, called the Grandma Moses of stitchery, has a permanent collection at the Smithsonian Institute in Washington, and received the 1991 Governor's Lifetime Achievement Award for "Excellence in the Arts," dies on Feb. 15 at the age of 84; Rockabilly entertainer Luke McDaniel, an Ellisville native, dies on June 27; Journalist Richard "Dick" Armstrong, a Jackson native, who worked for *Time* and *Saturday Evening Post* magazines and became executive editor of *Fortune* magazine, dies on Aug. 16; Actor Frederick O'Neal, a Brooksville native, dies on Aug. 15; Businessman-industralist Dumas Milner, Attala County native, dies on Oct. 6; Walter "Red" Barber, a native of Columbus and famous radio sportscaster for more than 30 years and a member of the Baseball Hall of Fame dies on Oct. 22; Dana Andrews, a native of Collins, Mississippi, an actor who starred in 69 films, dies on Dec. 17 at age 83; and Bluesman Albert King, an Indianola native, dies on Dec. 21. **Sports**: The Ole Miss Rebels football team blanks Air Force 13-0 in the Liberty Bowl in Memphis, Tennessee.

1993

In Jan., Mike Espy starts work as Secretary of the Department of Agriculture, the fourth largest department of the federal government with 115,000 employees and a budget of over $60 billion.. He is the first ever Secretary of Agriculture from the state and the 5th person from Mississippi to serve in the cabinet. He is the first black, the first Southerner and the youngest person to ever serve as secretary of agriculture; On Apr. 17, a Rabbi at Jackson's Temple Beth Israel reads from their recently acquired Torah No. 599 to a crowd of over 600 people. It was the first reading from the sacred document in over 50 years since it was stolen from a synagogue in Prague, Czechoslovakia by the Nazi's during World War II; At about 3 a.m. on Sept. 22, the Amtrak Sunset Limited passenger train has just left Mississippi headed east when all 3 engines and 4 of the 8 cars plunge off a bridge into foggy Bayou Canot about 11 miles north of Mobile, Ala. The bridge had been struck by a wayward barge in fog not long before. It's the worst Amtrak accident ever with the final death toll 47 including 2 Mississippians (fortunately, 163 people survive). The dead range in age from 2 months to 86 years. Up until now, the total deaths in Amtrak's 23-year history had been 48; About 1,400 workers at NASA's Yellow Creek plant near Iuka receive notices on Oct. 20 that the plant is closing after Congress voted to kill the billion dollar advanced Solid Rocket Motor program; Final '93 figures show Mississippi's timber has become the first agricultural commodity to break the billion dollar mark — more than $1.01 billion worth of forest products compared to $904 million for poultry & eggs, and $623 million for cotton; First American Bank opens in Jackson. It is the first black-owned financial institution in the state since Penny Savings Bank in Indianola closed in 1928. **Deaths**: Frank Williams, a Smithdale native and gospel singer with the Jackson Southeraires who founded the Mississippi mass Choir, dies on March 22 in Savannah, Ga.; Sculptor Leon Z. Koury, a Greenville native, dies on April 11; Blues harpist Isaiah 'Doctor" Ross, a Tunica native, dies on May 28; Conway Twitty, born Harold Lloyd Jenkins at Friars Point, Miss., a rock/country superstar who had more No. 1 hits (55) than any other artist in any genre, the only artist in the history of popular music to have 21 consecutive top-5 hits, won 40+ awards including a Grammy, dies on June 5 at age 59 from a ruptured blood vessel in his stomach; and James "Son" Thomas, a blues musician & sculptor born in Eden (Yazoo County), dies on June 26. **Sports**: In football, North Carolina gets by Mississippi State 21-17 in the Peach Bowl.

1994

On Jan. 27, the third trial of Byron De La Beckwith begins in Jackson. Charged with killing Medgar Evers on June 12, 1963, he was tried twice in 1964 with all-white juries, both trials ending in mistrials. This time the jury of eight blacks and four whites deliberate about six hours before returning the verdict — guilty. Evers widow, Myrlie, and two of his children cheer and embrace as the murder verdict is announced at 10:35 a.m. on Feb. 5. White supremacist Beckwith, age 73, shows no emotion when the verdict is read. Hinds County Circuit Judge L. Breland Hilburn announces the sentence — life in prison; On Feb. 10, a fierce ice storm hits north Mississippi. In a 26-county area, the storm leaves over 200,000 households (over 500,000 residents) without electricity and affects 491 water systems serving over 740,000 people. A 3 to 6-inch sheet of ice coats the area and leaves towns resembling war zones with snapped trees and downed power lines and phone lines. Even some 95-foot steel transmission poles with 42-inch concrete bases just fold. Lost communications effectively isolates entire cities and counties from the outside world. Even with thousands of workers on the job, it will still take weeks to restore power to some places. South Central Bell will later report they recorded 53,000 trouble calls from its 313,000 customers in the storm area. The company replaces more than 1,600 telephone poles, repairs more than 5,000 cables and fixes more than 46,000 dropped lines — all at a cost of over $20 million. Although no lose of lives is blamed on the weather, it is the worst ice storm to hit the state since January 1951. The final damage figure will top $1.6 billion with timber losses over about 3.7 million acres set at $1.28 billion; On April 5, first district congressman Jamie Whitten announces he will not seek another term. He was first elected to Congress on Nov. 4, 1941. He had served 52 years as of Jan. 1994, more than any congressman ever; The legislative session, which was supposed to end April 3, comes to an end on April 12. They set the next fiscal year's budget at $2.45 billion, 19% more than this year's. They gave raises to teachers, higher education professors, state employees and highway patrol troopers — passed bonds to take care of road and bridge repairs, repairs to state-owned buildings and improvements to state parks — provided for more prison cells and more space for juvenile training schools — made it illegal for minors to possess guns, lowered the age for being tried as an adult from 18 to 17, increased the minimum driver's license age from 15 to 16, added a $25 dollar fine to the seat-belt law and passed hate-crime legislation and some lobbyist reform. They did not approve Governor Fordice's proposal for an income-tax cut and they gave themselves a 50% raise, which the governor vetoes; On Apr. 12, a tornado hits Woolmarket in Harrison County killing two people; On May 2, Jackson Mayor Kane Ditto fires police chief Jimmy Wilson for incompetence; On May 11, President Clinton nominates former Mississippi Governor Ray Mabus as ambassador to Saudi Arabia. He is the second Mississippian appointed to an ambassadorship. The first was Gulfport native Tom Anderson who served as U.S. envoy to Barbados from 1984 until 1986;

A Chronology of Mississippi History

In May, Attorney General Mike Moore files a lawsuit against the tobacco industry, making Mississippi the first state to sue to recover Medicaid costs spent on people with tobacco-related illnesses; By midyear the state's economy is experiencing unprecedented growth. Housing starts are up 21%, gross sales increased 9%, and gross production is up 7.2%. There have been 530 manufacturing locations or expansions in the state during the past year. Calls to the state's tourism dept. jumped from 80 to 1,000 per day. The state is fast becoming a telecommunications hub of the South and a major player in goods distribution by rail. The gaming industry gets much of the credit for the economic turnaround, with 31 casinos open as of August 1; At mid-year the state College Board plans to close Mississippi University for Women in Columbus and Mississippi Valley State University in Itta Bena as a solution to the Ayers desegregation case; In July, the *Clarion-Ledger* and the Mississippi Municipal Association choose Bay St. Louis, Clinton, and Tupelo as the state's "Most Livable Communities" for 1994; On July 30, the largest drug bust ever made in the state — a whole tractor-trailer 3,000-pound-load, valued at almost $100 million, is confiscated. For fear of possible violent attacks to steal the dope, the entire shipment of 1,420 pounds of cocaine and 1,600 pounds of marijuana is burned; On Aug. 15 the state legislature convenes in a special session mainly to address the problem of overcrowded jails and prisons. On the first day of the session, the Senate approves bills to speed appeals involving the death penalty and eliminate parole in capital murder cases. The session lasts through Aug. 23 and the legislators produce 2 prison bills, one authorizing construction of 4,116 new prison beds, 2,000 of them private, the other budgets $65 million for prison construction. They also reauthorize the 5-member state Parole Board and make more prisoners ineligible for parole. One provision would take TVs, radios and weight-lifting equipment away from most inmates. The 9-day special session cost taxpayers $267,844 for legislators' salaries and expenses, or an average of $29,760 a day; On Aug. 17, groundbreaking ceremonies are held in Yazoo City for a federal prison. The first phase project includes a $50 million low security correctional unit. Eventually, there will be a 4-unit complex located on the 1,000-acre site purchased by Yazoo City and county and donated to the Federal Bureau of Prisons. It will be the first federal prison in the state; On Sept. 21, a federal indictment charges former Mississippi College President Lewis Nobles of diverting $1.7 million in donations to the private school and wasting the money on prostitutes, lavish gifts and personal investments. His trial is to begin in Feb. 1995; On Sept. 29, police in Spartanburg, S.C. arrest a man for car theft and find out that he is Phillip Dean Fleming, wanted in Mississippi on kidnap charges. Fleming is accused in the Sept. 12 abduction of 8-year-old Santana Renee Boyd from Bramlett Elementary School in Oxford. She was released 18 hours later in a Jackson, Tenn. McDonald's restaurant. Although Fleming is wanted in other states on sex-related charges, he will first be tried in Mississippi on kidnapping, which carries a life sentence; On Oct. 3, Secretary of Agriculture Mike Espy announces he is resigning, effective at the end of 1994, amid a scandal that included a federal investigation of him for allegedly taking illegal gifts from companies his department regulates. President Clinton appointed him Secretary of Agriculture on Dec. 24, 1992; On Nov. 2, a national crime study report shows Mississippi has had the greatest overall increase in crime in the nation from 1960-92 — 508 percent!; Also on Nov. 2, Jackson Mayor Kane Ditto announces he has chosen Robert Johnson, chief of the Jackson, Michigan, Police Dept., as Jackson's new police chief. Johnson will be the city's 4th permanent police chief in 5 years. His appointment marks the third time Ditto, elected in 1989, has chosen a candidate from outside the Jackson Police Department; Also on Nov. 2, a jury deliberates only 20 minutes before convicting Paul Hill, 40, a former minister who graduated from Belhaven College in Jackson, of murder in the slayings of an abortion doctor and his bodyguard in Pensacola, Florida. The jury recommends death in the electric chair for Hill; In the general election on Nov. 8 Roger Wicker, 43, a Republican state senator from Tupelo scores a solid victory by securing retiring U.S. Representative Jamie Whitten's First District seat. Republican Senator Trent Lott is also re-elected to a second 6-year term. This followed a wave of Republican victories across the nation that gives the GOP control of both houses of Congress in January. It's the first time in 40 years the Repulican Party has had control of both houses of Congress. Bucking the Republican trend, Democrats Bennie Thompson (Dist. 2), Sonny Montgomery (Dist. 3), Mike Parker (Dist. 4), and Gene Taylor (Dist. 5) are all re-elected to the U.S. House; The Jackson *Clarion-Ledger*, which just joined the list of the 100 largest newspapers in the nation, breaks ground on Nov. 22 for a $30 million new building and expansion project. The 60,000-square-foot building on Congress Street should be ready in Dec. 1995; On Nov. 27, Jackson reports its 87th homicide of the year, tying the record number of murders for all of last year; On Sunday night, Nov. 27, tornadoes and high winds leave more than 100 homes damaged plus 12 homes completely destroyed. A tree falls on a mobile home in Magee killing a woman and her 2-year-old son. Gov. Fordice declares a state of emergency in the six counties involved — Hinds, Issaquena, Kemper, Neshoba, Simpson and Smith; On Dec 2, Senator Trent Lott claims a one-vote victory to become the Republicans' No. 2 Senate leader, the majority whip. He leapfrogged over Mississippi's senior senator, Thad Cockran, who was unopposed for another term as Republican Conference chairman, the No. 3 post; This year's figures show poultry and eggs products beat out the timber industry by a mere $8 million with $1.078 billion to timber's $1.070 billion; **Deaths**: Gospel blues singer Willie Mae Ford Smith, a Rolling Fork native, dies on Feb. 2; Bilbo "Mule" Monaghan, a native of Amory, Mississippi who became the first deaf player in the country to play a full year of pro football and later taught and coached at the Mississippi School for the Deaf and served as president of the Mississippi Association for the Deaf, dies on Feb. 10 at age 83 from pneumonia; Hazel Brannon Smith, who was a Pulitzer Prize-winning journalist at the *Lexington Advertiser*, dies on May 17; Bluesman Eddie Boyd, a Stovall native, dies on July 13; Soul singer Major Lance, a Winstonville native, dies on Sept. 3; Blues harpist Louis Myers, a Byhalia native, dies on Sept. 5; Choreographer Hollis Pippin, a Jackson native, dies on Sept. 26; Johnny R. "Jack" Spinks, Toomsuba native and first black Mississippian to be drafted by the NFL when he was picked by the Pittsburgh Steelers in the 11th round in 1952 and coached at his alma mater Alcorn from 1959-85, dies in Jackson on Sept. 29 of complications from diabetes. Alcorn named its 22,000-seat, $9 million stadium after him in 1992. He was inducted into the Mississippi Sports Hall of Fame in 1985 and Southwestern Athletic Conference Hall of Fame in 1992; James E. "Buster" Poole, a Gloster native and the first of 14 Poole family members to play football at Ole Miss, was a 3-time All-Pro

A Chronology of Mississippi History

defensive end during his seven seasons in the NFL, and is in the Mississippi Sports Hall of Fame, dies in Oxford on Nov. 16; Harvey "Pop" Watkins, Sr., gospel singer and songwriter and original member of the Canton Spirituals, dies Nov. 16. **Sports**: On July 12, Ole Miss Chancellor Gerald Turner announces he had fired head football coach Billy Brewer for "engagement in deliberate and serious violations of NCAA and Southeastern Conference legislation." Brewer was 67-56-3 in 11 seasons at Ole Miss, 33-42 in Southeastern Conference games. He coached the Rebels to five bowl games and was three times named SEC Coach of the Year. He was the longest-serving active football coach in the SEC and the second winningest coach in Ole Miss history. On Dec 2, Tommy Tuberville, an assistant on three of Miami's national championship teams, is named new head football coach; the Jackson Generals baseball team tied the record for the best month in Jackson franchise history, going 22-8 in the month of July. The 1984 league-champion Mets were 22-8 in June under Sam Perlozzo; Groundbreaking ceremonies are held on Aug. 20 for the Mississippi Sports Hall of Fame in Jackson. The first induction ceremonies for 6 former Mississippi sports greats is planned for March 17, 1995. The 6 to be inducted are James "Cool Papa" Bell, Willie Brown, Roland Dale, Doug Hutton, Freddie Little, and Crawford Mims; On Sept. 5, Mississippi Valley alumnus and native Mississippian Jerry Rice, wide receiver of the San Francisco 49ers, gets 3 TDs to set an all-time record, making Rice the NFL's career leader with 127 touchdowns!; Marcus Dupree's 87 touchdown state record is broken Oct. 14 by Gary "Turk" McGill of Taylorsville who scores 3 times to take his high-school total to 88; On Oct. 1, quarterback Steve "Air" McNair surpasses former Portland State Neil Lomax (1977-80, 13,345 yards) as the Division 1-AA all-time total offense leader with 13,531 yards. On Oct. 22, McNair surpasses Ty Detmer's total offense record of 14,665 yards for all divisions. Following his college career, McNair's name goes in the record books of Alcorn State, the SAC and the NCAA — no player in any division has gained more yards in a college career than McNair's 16,823! On Dec. 10, McNair finishes third place for the Heisman behind Colorado's Rashaan Salaam and Penn State's Ki-Jana Carter. McNair joins Gordie Lockbaum of Holy Cross, who finished third for the Heisman in 1987, as the highest Heisman finisher below the NCAA Division I-A level.

1995

Eight people die in 3 separate fires on New Year's Day. A 77-year-old man dies, in Mendenhall, 3 children and their grandmother die in a blaze in Lauderdale County and the fire that kills an elderly couple and their young child in Forest was arson, according to Scott County officials; On Jan. 25, a Jones County Circuit Court jury hits Trustmark National Bank with $38 million in damages. The jury finds Trustmark, based in Jackson, guilty of charging an auto loan customer with more than $9,000 in questionable insurance fees by signing him up for the policy without his consent. The amount, the largest jury award in the state's history up until now, is later reduced to $5.5 million by a judge; Former Mississippi College President Lewis Nobles flees the state early in the year. He was charged in 1994 with mail fraud, money laundering, tax evasion and violating the Mann Act by having women cross state lines to commit sex acts. On Jan. 26, he swallows poison when FBI agents attempt to arrest his at a San Francisco hotel. He later undergoes emergency surgery for an ulcer. After his recuperation, U.S. District Judge William H. Barbour, Jr. orders him taken to the federal facility in Springfield, Mo. for an extensive mental evaluation. He remains there most of the year before being brought back to Mississippi; In Jan., the State Public Service Commission orders Mississippi Power & Light to cut rates and give customers refunds of $57 million. That brings the total amount to $88 million that MP&L has had to cut rates since March 1994; After a Feb. 23 traffic accident in which he drives off the road and hits some trees in Flowood, State Supreme Court Justice Chuck McRae fails several field sobriety tests. McRae, 55, arrested on a charge of first offense DUI and refusal of breath test, pleads no contest after a fierce battle to keep his driver's license. His driving privileges are automatically revoked for 90 days, but Hinds County Judge William Barnett grants the justice's request for a hardship exception, permitting McRae to get behind the wheel again after 30 days. Much controversy follows the case throughout the year with many officials calling for his ouster from the high court. Northern District Highway Commissioner Zach Stewart and state Representative Keith Montgomery will also be charged with drunken driving later this year; On March 7 severe thunderstorms that spawned as many as 26 tornadoes are blamed for the deaths of 2 Savannah, Georgia guardsman when high winds and heavy rains caused their truck to hydroplane off the highway near Wiggins, Mississippi. These are the only two people killed by twisters in the state this year, although a total of 54 tornadoes also result in 21 injuries by year's end; On March 7, U.S. District Judge Neal Biggers finally issues a ruling in the long-awaited 20-year-old Ayers case. It states that the state College Board can not close Mississippi Valley State University and Mississippi University for Women as part of its federally ordered plan to desegregate the state's higher education system. He further orders the state to spend about $30 million to improve programs at predominantly black Jackson State and Alcorn State. Plaintiffs in the case, brought by the late Jake Ayers, appealed the ruling to the 5th U.S. Circuit Court of Appeals, saying it falls short of needed improvements at historically black schools; An unremarkable legislative session ends with legislators finally getting around to ratifying the 13th Amendment on Mar. 16 that bans slavery that was rejected on Dec. 4, 1865; In the spring, Albertson's Inc. of Boise, Idaho, the nation's largest grocery store chain, announces plans to build at least 6 new stores in the Jackson metro area by 1997, spurring heated opposition from Mississippi-based Jitney Jungle Stores of America, Inc; On May 3, the *Mississippi Almanac: The Ultimate Reference on the State* by James Cox is published for the first time. Cox, a Yazoo City resident, spent over two years compiling the volume, the state's first information almanac; On May 9-10 flash floods from torrential rains damaged over 1,000 homes on the Mississippi coast. Harrison County bore the brunt with 611 homes damaged; On June 11, thousands greeted the world's largest sternwheeler, the *American Queen*, as she makes her first port of call in Natchez; On July 1, Robert Khayat succeeds Gerald Turner as chancellor at the Unversity of Mississippi. Turner resigned to become president of Southern Methodist University in Dallas; In July the Atlanta-based ValuJet Airlines begins operations at Jackson International Airport. With low fares and no-frills, they carry 10,137 passengers in and out of Jackson during their first month, boosting overall traffic at the airport 6.7%. However, ValuJet's low fares cause dominant Delta Airlines' numbers to fall to 43,850 customers, a 14% drop for the month. A month after ValuJet starts, TWA Airlines begins flying from Jackson to St. Louis; McCarty Farms, Mississippi's second largest

A Chronology of Mississippi History

poultry company, is bought out by Tyson Foods, the nation's largest poultry producer. The sale of McCarty, a family owned company founded in 1943, completed on Sept. 1 is said to be worth $130 million; On Sept. 10, the Amtrak "City of New Orleans" passenger train makes its first stops in Greenwood and Yazoo City. Those will now be the only two stops between Memphis and Jackson. Amtrak gave up its old route which had stops in Batesville, Grenada, Winona, Durant, and Canton because it was too costly; On Sept. 19, Mobile Telecommunications Technologies Corp. launches its revolutionary SkyTel 2-Way paging network with initial service available in 150 major U.S. markets. Industry analysts speculate Jackson-based Mtel's $300 million gamble puts the company 6 months to a year ahead of competition; Also in Sept. BellSouth announces that it would sell MobileComm, the nation's second largest paging company, for $945 million to MobileMedia of New Jersey and that the headquarters would be moved from Jackson; On Oct. 4, Lloyd Jones, sometimes controversial sheriff of Simpson County, is shot to death at his home in the Shady Grove Community. A county jail trusty, R. V. Lewis, is also killed. Carl Ray Johnson of Magee is charged with capital murder in the deaths; In Oct., U.S. Representative G.V. "Sonny" Montgomery, 75, of Meridian announces his retirement after 30 years in Congress; On Oct. 12, popular Warren County Sheriff Paul Barrett is convicted in a federal court of two counts of lying under oath about the value of a motorcycle he was given. Despite his conviction, voters re-elect Barrett in November; On Nov. 2, a Hinds County Court jury slaps British Columbia-based Loewen Group Inc. with $500 million in damages, the largest award ever in Mississippi. The award is to Jerry O'Keefe, a Biloxi funeral home owner who claimed Loewen damaged his business with unfair trade practices; In the November election Governor Kirk Fordice easily turns back a challenge from Democratic Secretary of State Dick Molpus to become the state's first chief executive to win back-to-back terms since Reconstruction. Democrat Ronnie Musgrove is chosen by voters as Lt. Governor over incumbent Republican Eddie Briggs. Democrats win every statewide office other than governor and retain control of both the state House and Senate. Voters reject term limits for public officials from the statehouse to city halls. Three convicted felons are elected as sheriffs — Gary W. Mauney in Tippah County, John Allen Jones in Humphreys County and Jacob Cartlidge in Sharkey County. A quirk in state laws allowed their election, but law forbids them to carry guns; In Nov., Fourth District Representative Mike Parker, 46, changes over to the Republican Party after being elected four times as a Democrat; On Nov. 14, a federal government shutdown due to lack of funding causes the furloughing of 2.1 million federal civilian workers including some in Mississippi. It forces the temporary closing of the Vicksburg Military Park and the National Wildlife Refuges in the state to hunting; On Nov. 16, Jitney Jungle Stores of America Inc. announces plans by its stockholders to sell a majority of shares in the family-owned business to the New York group Bruckmann, Rosser & Sherrill. The offering, valued at $400 million, was said to be a prelude to a public offering of stock. Jitney Jungle, the state's largest retailer and the 128th largest private company in the nation with $1.2 billion in revenues, operates 104 stores in six states, including the warehouse-style Sack and Save chain; On Nov. 20, furniture heiress Jacqueline Levitz is reported missing from her Vicksburg home; On Nov. 28, Mirage Resorts Inc. announces a $300 million budget for a planned 18-acre luxury resort on Biloxi's strip. The project includes a 1,200-room hotel and casino and will employ 2,000 people directly, and another 3,000 people indirectly; On Dec. 9, the nuclear-powered super-aircraft-carrier, *USS John C. Stennis*, is commissioned before a crowd of 20,000 in Norfolk, Virginia; On Dec. 20, Warren County Sheriff Paul Barrett resigns and leaves office after 27 years when the state Supreme Court dissolves a stay that kept him at his post. Barrett's attorneys had unsuccessfully argued that he should keep his job until he was sentenced on Jan. 26, 1996. After Barrett resigns, Warren County supervisors appoint Chief Deputy Otha Jones as interim sheriff; The state's unemployment rate drops to 4.9% for December with more people working than at any time in the history of Mississippi. New capital investment is flowing into the state at a record level with gambling still providing much, but not all, of the state's economic good news. The number of state companies that are publicly traded increased to 25 in 1995 with initial offerings by Bellmont Homes and MS Financial. Major gains in stocks were posted by 17 of those firms this year including D&PL (Delta and Pine Land cotton producer), up 177%; FirstMiss Gold (mining operation of First Mississippi Corp.), up 158%; WorldCom Inc., up 81.9%; Gulf South Medical Supply, up 62.4%; Microtek Medical, up 47.8%; Deposit Guaranty Corp., up 47.7%; and Parkway Co., up 47.1%. The six Mississippi companies that lost ground in the stock market during the year were River Oaks, down 45.7%; Casino Magic Corp., down 41.9%; Sanderson Farms, down 29.4%; KLLM, down 28.2%; and Callon Petroleum Co., down 8%; On average, stock prices of Mississippi-based companies rose a respectable 28.6%; Mississippi had two close misses from hurricanes during the year — Erin on Aug. 3 and Opal on Oct. 4, both of which hit the Florida panhandle causing considerable damage; Columbus and Meridian end the year breathing easier after their military bases were spared closure; Former Mississippi College President Lewis Nobles is brought back to Mississippi after a lengthy mental evaluation in Missouri. He spends the last few months of the year in the Madison County Jail.

Deaths: Norris Weese, an Ole Miss football standout who played pro ball for Denver and remains third on the Broncos' all-time proficiency list among quarterbacks, dies in Denver on Jan. 20 at age 43 after a long fight against bone cancer; Margaret Wade, born in McCool, Mississipi in 1912, the "First Lady of Basketball" coached girls basketball at Cleveland High School and her alma mater Delta State in the 1970s where she won three national championships in six years, the first women inducted into the Mississippi Sports Hall of Fame in 1974, and in 1986 was the first women inducted into the National Basketball Hall of Fame, dies on Feb. 16, 1995 in Cleveland, Miss; Blues pianist Sunnyland Slim (Albert Luandrew), a Vance native, dies on March 17; Former Senator John C. Stennis, native of DeKalb, dies on April 23 at the age of 93. The Democrat served 41 years in the U.S. Senate before retiring in 1989; Five prominent Mississippi journalists die this year: newspaper chain owner John O. Emmerich, Jr., 65, on Feb. 25 from a heart attack after collapsing outside his Greenwood home following a morning jog — James S. Saggus, 69, of Brandon, who spent 30 years with the Associated Press, on Apr. 3 from leukemia — James K. Cazalas, 56, editor of the *Delta Democrat Times* in Greenville since 1984, on June 1 of cancer — Robert H. "Ace" Cleveland, Sr., a Hattiesburg native who started as a teen-aged sports writer at the *Hattiesburg American*, went on to become sports editor there, and later worked at the *Jackson Daily News*

A Chronology of Mississippi History

and then served as sports information director at the University of Southern Mississippi, dies at age 69 on April 17 from a stroke — and Eugene Butler, a Starkville native who was editor-in-chief of the *Progressive Farmer* magazine for many years and founded *Southern Living* magazine, dies in Dallas, Texas on June 5 only 6 days before his 101st birthday; Major league baseball player Harry "Popeye" Craft, a native of Ellisville, who played in both the 1939 and 1940 World Series and managed the Kansas City Athletics from 1957-59 where he signed Mickey Mantle to his first contract, a member of the Mississippi Sports Hall of Fame, dies in Houston on Aug. 3 at age 80; Former U.S. Representative Jamie Whitten, 85, dies on Sept. 9. The Democrat retired in 1994 after serving 53 years in Congress, longer than any other person; College head John Tyler Caldwell, a Yazoo City native, who was president of the University of Arkansas (1952-59) and chancellor of North Carolina State University (1959-75), dies on Oct. 13; and high school football coach Charles S. Thomas, Sr., a Winona native reared in Moorhead and member of the Miss. Sports Hall of Fame (1975), dies on Nov. 23 at the age of 82.

Sports: In Jan., North Carolina State defeats the Mississippi State Bulldogs football team 28-24 in the Peach Bowl; The Mississippi State basketball team makes the Sweet 16 of the NCAA Tournament for the first time in 32 years on March 19, losing to eventual champion UCLA 86-67 on March 23. The Bulldogs begin the 1995-96 season ranked No. 8 in the country; Former USM standout and Kiln native Brett Farve wins the National Football League MVP Award by throwing 38 TDs to lead the Green Bay Packers to the NFC Central Division title and 11 victories; Mount Olive native and former Alcorn great Steve McNair signs a rookie-record $28.7 million contract with the Houston Oilers, then sits for 3 months before leading the Oilers to victories in the final 2 games; Former Mississippi Valley State great Jerry Rice breaks several more NFL records, but finishes only third in NFL Offensive Player of the Year voting; Tommy Tuberville achieves a winning record and an Egg Bowl victory 13-10 over Mississippi State at Starkville in his first season as Ole Miss Coach. He finishes 3rd behind Steve Spurrier and Danny Ford in SEC Coach of the Year voting; Jackson State finishes strong to win its first Southwestern Athletic Conference football championship since 1990 and the first since James Carson became the Tigers' head coach; Mississippi College's new president, Howell Todd, announces in March that the school will drop down from NCAA Division II to Division III status for all sports; Ed Dougherty, 47, makes the Deposit Guaranty Golf Classic his first PGA Tour victory. Mississippi's only PGA Tour stop breaks all attendance records; After State's Bulldogs finish the season 3-8, defensive and offensive coordinators Bill Clay and Bruce Arians resign; Jackson Academy loses coach Sherard Shaw to cancer, but then, under new coach David Blount they have 3 playoff victories to win the Academy AAA state championship, beating Jackson Prep for the first time in the process; The Jets-Eagles pre-season game draws an estimated 52,000 in Jackson's first NFL exhibition since 1970; Ole Miss makes the NCAA Baseball Tournament field and finishes 2nd to host Florida State in the Atlanta I regional; Jake Gibbs, the Ole Miss legend, finally makes the College Football Hall of Fame; and Jackson almost got a Canadian Football League franchise. The deal falls through completely on April 4.

1996

Kirk Fordice made history four years ago when he became the state's first Republican governor since reconstruction. On Jan. 9, he makes history for the second time when he becomes the only Mississippi governor this century sworn in for back-to-back terms; Mississippi's oldest and largest daily newspaper, *The Clarion-Ledger*, opens its new $32 million building at 201 South Congress Street in Jackson, just in time for the paper's 108th birthday; The Commission on Judicial Performance says in a Jan. 12 recommendation to the Mississippi Supreme Court that Supreme Court Justice Chuck McRae should be publicly censured for his conviction last year for DUI; On Jan. 23, a federal judge sentences former Warren County Sheriff Paul Barrett to 15 months in prison, a $2,000 fine and two years probation for convictions of making false statements under oath in a federal trial and before a grand jury. Barrett, one of the longest serving sheriffs in the state, remains free pending his appeal; On Jan. 24, best-selling author John Grisham wins an actual court case in Brookhaven. The jury awards $683,500 in damages to Grisham's client, the widow of John Wayne King, a railroad brakeman killed in 1991 after being pinned between two cars. That was slightly more than the $665,000 Grisham had asked for in the case and was one of the biggest settlements in Lincoln County in years. It was the first time Grisham had lawyered since 1991; On Jan. 29, unusually heavy fog, along with some electronic landing equipment failure, forces the Jackson International Airport to close — the first such instance in more than a decade. Twenty-seven planes are affected during a 15-hour period; On Feb. 2, an ice storm moves through central and northern Mississippi. While not quite as intense as the ice storm of 1994, it covers a larger area and causes widespread power outages with about 115,000 customers losing power during the peak of the storm. Record cold temperatures followed the storm paralyzing the upper two-thirds of the state. There are new record lows for the dates in Jackson of 8 degrees on Feb. 4 and 10 degrees on Feb. 5. The temperature in Jackson finally reaches 32 degrees at 11:57 a.m. Feb. 5, ending a stretch of 76 hours and 32 minutes of subfreezing weather. The record period was 86 hours set in Feb. 1985. At least 14 deaths are blamed on the cold with one drowning after a car slid into a stream, four freezing to death, and seven others in a fire that kills members of three generations of a Newton family on Feb. 3.; On Feb. 16, Governor Kirk Fordice sues Attorney General Mike Moore, saying that Moore did not have the authority to sue tobacco companies. Mississippi was the first state in the nation to sue tobacco companies when Moore filed the lawsuit in May 1994; On Feb. 27, Betty Frezzell of Crystal Springs drives her van into a state car at an intersection about 15 miles southwest of Magee. In the brand-new state car are Highway Patrol officer Cpl. Mike Wilke and Lt. Governor Ronnie Musgrove. Wilke was driving Musgrove to a Prentiss Chamber of Commerce banquet to make a speech. All three are hospitalized with serious injuries. A neurosurgeon at University Medical Center says that an airbag probably saved the Lt. Governor's life. All three recuperate with Musgrove released from the hospital in ten days; One of the greatest cultural events in the state's history starts on March 1 — *The Palaces of St. Petersburg: Russian Imperial Style* exhibition opens at the Mississippi Arts Pavilion in downtown Jackson. The exclusive American appearance in Jackson offers recreations of five opulent rooms and six galleries from the four "string of pearls" palaces encircling St. Petersburg, Russia. The exhibition showcases the most extensive collection of imperial Russian treasures (over 600 rare objects) ever exhibited on this continent. The exhibition will run for 6 months; Despite problems earlier in the year with fog, electronic equipment problems and the ice storm, the Jackson

A Chronology of Mississippi History

International Airport reports 69,913 passengers in Feb., 25 percent more than Feb. 1995; In Dec. 1994, Lisa Herdahl of Ecru, a town of 696 people, joined with civil liberties groups to sue North Pontotoc school officials, seeking to stop Bible classes and prayers over the intercom. Five of her 6 children attend school at Ecru. That trial starts the first week of March 1996 in U.S. District Court in Oxford, keeping Mississippi in the national spotlight. U.S. District Judge Neal Biggers, who hears arguments for 3 days, will rule for Herdahl and against the Pontotoc County School District on June 3. Biggers does say, however, that students may continue to meet before school to participate in prayers and devotionals; The State Board of Education formally takes over North Panola schools on Mar. 8 after the systems goes broke; On Mar. 12, Super Tuesday, GOP candidate Bob Dole carries Mississippi, collecting all of the state's 33 delegates. The primaries went on without 3rd District U.S. Rep. Sonny Montgomery, who had announced he would not seek re-election and would retire next Jan. after 30 years. Congress will soon pass a resolution to name the Veterans Affairs Medical Center in Jackson in honor of Montgomery; On March 13, the nation's fifth-largest tobacco company, the Liggett Group, announces it will settle part of lawsuits by Mississippi and four other states. The suits seek reimbursement of costs in treating tobacco-related illnesses. Mississippi receives its first yearly installment — $200,000 — on April 8. Yearly payments over the next 25 years will be $400,000; On Mar. 15, speed limits climb to 70 mph on the state's rural interstate highways and will be raised from 55 to 65 mph a few weeks later on many of the state's major 4-lane highways such as U.S. Highways 45, 49, 61, 82, and 98; On Mar. 26, new State Agriculture Commissioner Lester Spell said that the Jim Buck Ross administration had left his department with a deficit and he might have to furlough 165 workers, about half of the agency's work force, if the legislature doesn't approve $1.2 million in additional funding; On March 29, the Old Country Store and Museum at Lorman closes its doors after more than 105 years; On Apr. 12, white supremacist Larry Wayne Shoemake hides inside the abandoned PoFolks Restaurant on Ellis Avenue with a vast arsenal of assault weapons and ammunition.. The 53-year-old Jackson man, who believes in a coming "race war" and has strong neo-Nazi views, begins a barrage of gunfire that lasts 40 minutes and leaves one man dead and seven wounded. The gunfire is so intense, it keeps hundreds of police officers and rescue personnel pinned down outside and unable to reach the shooter. All the victims are black including the dead man, D.Q. Holyfield, 49, of Forest. Among the wounded is Jackson *Clarion-Ledger* police reporter Pamela Berry, 26, who is shot in the neck, but is expected to fully recover, and a 10-year-old boy. Shoemake finally sets fire to the building and kills himself with a Ruger .357 Magnum. Coincidentally or not, the date of one of the most horrifying events to ever hit Jackson came on the anniversary of the start of the Civil War at Fort Sumter, S.C. in 1861; Another uneventful legislative session ends on April 13. From May 1, 1995 until April 30, 1996, it cost $4.05 million to run the Senate, $6.67 million to run the House, plus $714,759 in shared expenses for a total of $11.4 million to run the state legislature; On April 21, St. Dominic's Hospital in Jackson celebrates its 50th anniversary. Since April 1946, when seven Dominican Sisters of Springfield, Ill. purchased the Jackson Infirmary for $100,000, it has grown from a 75-bed hospital to a 500-bed facility; On Apr. 24, less than two weeks after the Shoemake rampage, another horrible event, a massacre, hits Jackson. Black firefighter Kenny Tornes goes into a rage and commits a daylong act of mass violence as he first kills his wife at their home, then goes to Jackson's Central Fire Station. There he walks into a meeting of top officials and shoots and kills four top-level fire officers — District Chief Dwight Craft, District 1 Chief Rick Robbins, Capt. Stanley Adams and Capt. Don Moree. He also wounds two others. Tornes then flees to Northpark Mall where he wounds one Ridgeland police officer. Another Ridgeland officer, Randy Gooch, draws his 9 mm pistol and drops Tornes with a shot to the head. Tornes will recover to face not only five murder charges, but three additional murders that occurred on Oct. 4, 1994. Ballistic test results show that Tornes is the one who murdered Victoria Minor, her 2-week-old baby and a man friend one-and-a-half years ago. The International Association of Fire Fighters will later state that the Tornes killing spree was the deadliest nonfire-related event in U.S. firefighter history!; On May 2, the trial of Lewis Nobles, which started on Jan. 17 this year, ends with his conviction. Nobles had pleaded guilty to two counts of mail fraud, two counts of income tax evasion and one count of money laundering, but did not say why he kept $2.8 million in donations he solicited for Mississippi College that he headed for 25 years. U.S. District Judge William Barbour, Jr. sentences the 70-year-old ailing Nobles to a 7-year Federal prison term; On May 3, Fire Chief Joe Donovan announces that he is resigning from the Jackson Fire Department and retiring, effective Aug. 31. He gives no reasons, but calls the recent Tornes killings "very, very traumatic."; On May 25, several dozen notable Mississippians act as torchbearers carrying the Olympic torch through the towns and cities of Sandy Hook, Columbia, Prentiss, Mendenhall, Puckett, Brandon, Pearl, and then to the greater Jackson area for a 22-minute ceremony at Jubilee Jam. From there, it makes it way to Vicksburg before going on through other states on its way to Atlanta; On June 3, the state's first privately run prison, the Marshall County Correctional Facility opens. The 205,398-square-foot, 1,000-inmate medium-security prison is located about three miles north of downtown Holly Springs; On June 12, a day after Bob Dole resigns from the U.S. Senate to run for president of the U.S., Senator Trent Lott of Mississippi is elected to replace him as Senate Majority Leader, the most powerful member of the Senate. Republican senators voted 44-8 to elevate Lott, who was second in leadership as majority whip, to the top job over fellow Mississippian Thad Cochran, who remains third in leadership as Republican Conference Chairman. It's the first time two senators from the same state were candidates for the majority leader's post and Lott is the first Mississippian elected to the spot since it was created in 1920; On June 13, a three-judge panel for the 5th U.S. Circuit Court of Appeals in New Orleans upholds the decision by U.S. District Judge William H, Barbour Jr. to make public the files of the Mississippi Sovereignty Commission; On June 26, the Mississippi Municipal Association and the *Clarion-Ledger* announce Mississippi's Most Livable Communities: Belzoni, Monticello and Natchez. This makes two years in a row for Natchez, the only two-time winner of the award since it began in 1993; For the fiscal year that ended June 30, private gifts to the University of Mississippi totaled $25.3 million, the largest amount ever in one year; On July 10, Insurance Commissioner George Dale announces that Prudential Life Insurance Co. has agreed to pay a $250,000 fine to the Mississippi Insurance Department over improper sales practices by agents; The Senate meets in a special session on July 11 called by

A Chronology of Mississippi History

Governor Fordice to reconsider his nomination of four white men to the State College Board. The Senate Universities and Colleges Committee votes by a razor-thin margin to kill the nominations. The center of controversy since March, several suits have been filed by the Governor and others in the case; On July 18, the College Board selects Georgia educator Horace W. Fleming Jr. as the new head of the University of Southern Mississippi. He succeeds President Aubrey Lucas who retires in Dec; On Aug. 12, the 36th Republican National Convention starts in San Diego with Mississippians wielding much power with the presence of Republican National Committee Chairman Haley Barbour of Yazoo City, Co-Chairwoman Evelyn McPhail of Bay St. Louis, Senate Majority Leader Trent Lott, and Senator Thad Cochran, who holds the No. 3 spot in the Senate GOP leadership as chairman of the Republican Conference. The GOP formally nominates the team of Robert Dole for president and Jack Kemp for vice-president; The Democrats open their 42nd Democratic National Convention in Chicago on Aug. 26 with 44 Mississippi delegates present. All the Mississippi votes go to the party's nominees, Bill Clinton for president and Al Gore for vice-president; When the fall semester of school starts in Mississippi in August, there are about 40,000 students in private schools; The great cultural exhibit, *The Palaces of St. Petersburg: Russian Imperial Style*, comes to an end. There was a sell-out crowd of 7,650 on the last day of the exhibit, Saturday, Aug. 31, with Royce and Barbara Moore of Gulfport buying the last two tickets. Final total ticket sales for the six-month run reached 553,894 — the most successful event of its kind in the state's history and the second highest attended exhibit in the U.S. this year! Officials say the exhibit had an economic impact of more than $61 million in Jackson and the state. Plans begin for a *Splendors of Versailles* exhibit in 1998; On Sept. 9, Bernie Ebbers, CEO of WorldCom, the nation's 4th-largest telecommunications company, announces they will move their headquarters from Jackson to Clinton in 1997; On Sept. 26, U.S. District Judge Walter Gex in Biloxi fines Florida-based Arizona Chemical $2.5 million for trying to hide hazardous waste in Mississippi by falsifying water reports. The penalty is the largest federal criminal fine in state history. The company is also ordered to pay an additional $1.5 million in restitution to a state environmental cleanup fund and $150,000 to the state to resolve civil charges; In the early morning hours of Sept. 28, four Mississippi College students are killed instantly when their car apparently hydroplanes off rain-soaked I-20 in Jackson and crashes onto a street below; During the last week of Sept., it's announced that Jackson beat out Savannah, Ga. as the site of the 1999 Southern Economic Development Council convention; The Jackson International Airport ends Sept. with passenger traffic of 71,210 compared to 71,989 in Sept. a year ago. This slight drop ended a 14-month streak of increases; State Auditor Steve Patterson announces Oct. 10 that he is resigning effective Nov. 1. He is facing a misdemeanor charge of failing to pay taxes on a motor vehicle he owned. Patterson has been state auditor since 1991. He is the first statewide elected official in modern Mississippi history to resign from office. On Oct. 16, Gov. Fordice appoints Phil Bryant, 41, a five-year Republican state representative from Brandon to serve the remaining three years and two months of Patterson's term; On election day, Nov. 5, Gov. Kirk Fordice, driving alone, apparently loses control of his vehicle heading south on I-55 at the 220-mile marker near Tillatoba in Yalobusha County. The 1996 Jeep Grand Cherokee hits several trees, hits a bump and flies through the air before flipping end over end and then catching on fire. Sardis truck driver Bill Lowe, 53, and other passing motorists pull the governor from the burning wreckage. The governor is taken first to the Grenada Hospital and then to University Medical Center in Jackson where he was hospitalized in serious condition with bruised heart, lungs and liver, a collapsed left lung, four broken left ribs, broken vertebrae, broken left shoulder blade and collarbone, bruises and abrasions and a partially-severed left ear. The trauma team at UMC is the same group that attended Lt. Gov. Ronnie Musgrove after a Feb. 27 automobile accident just eight months ago; President Clinton wins reelection in a coast-to-coast landslide, although Bob Dole barely carries Mississippi 49% to Clinton's 45%. There aren't many surprises in the other races — Senator Thad Cochran easily wins reelection over his two opponents with 71% of the vote. The incumbents in the 1st, 2nd, 4th and 5th Congressional Districts all win reelection including Mike Parker (4th Dist.), who had switched from the Democratic to the Republican Party. For the first time in 30 years, the 3rd Congressional District got a new representative with Charles "Chip" Pickering (R) of Laurel winning the seat of retiring Democrat Sonny Montgomery. Parker's switch and Pickering's election make three Republicans in the House counting Roger Wicker in the 1st District, the first time in the state's history that the GOP has had a majority in the House of Representatives. Even though their candidate for president lost, the Republican Party sets a milestone — not since 1930 has the GOP won both chambers of Congress in consecutive elections. For one thing, this assures that Senator Trent Lott of Mississippi will remain in his top position as Senate Majority Leader. For the third time in six years, DeSoto County voters reject legalized gambling; In ceremonies on Veterans Day, Nov. 11, the VA Medical Center in Jackson officially becomes the G.V. "Sonny" Montgomery VA Medical Center as the hospital also celebrates its 50th anniversary; In mid-November, authorities arrest two Moss Point men, Paul Walls, Sr. and Dock Eatman on charges they illegally used the highly toxic cotton insecticide methyl parathion in homes and businesses. Hundreds of buildings had been sprayed and many have to be evacuated. Officials start calling it the worst case of pesticide misuse in U.S. history; After 24 days in the hospital, Gov. Fordice is released on Nov. 30 with his physician, Dr. Keith Thomae, saying that his recovery progress will be monitored closely over the next few weeks. He has been in the hospital since his near-fatal auto crash on Nov. 5; On Dec. 6, Trustees of the Department of Archives and History announce the selection of five people elected to the State of Mississippi Hall of Fame: Choctaw Chief Greenwood Leflore (elected chief in 1830), former U.S. Senator Hiram R. Revels (the first black in the U.S. Congress in 1870), Dr. Felix J. Underwood (a past director of the Mississippi Board of Health), and former newspaper publishers William Hodding Carter, Jr. of the *Delta-Democrat Times* in Greenville and George McLean, founder of *The Northeast Mississippi Daily Journal* in Tupelo, the largest Mississippi-owned newspaper. Elections for the Hall of Fame are only held every five years; On Dec. 14, Lt. Gov. Ronnie Musgrove, his wife and 7 law school buddies and their wives are in the Riverwalk in New Orleans when a 69,000 freight ship losses power and slams into the dockside mall causing considerable damage and over 100 injuries, but no deaths. Musgrove and his party are not hurt. This has been a year of close calls for Lt. Gov. Musgrove; On Dec. 16, the Mississippi Gaming Commission, by a vote of 2-1, denies a

A Chronology of Mississippi History

permit for a casino on the Big Black River between Jackson and Vicksburg. Horseshoe Gaming had wanted to build a $125 million casino/hotel/auto racing facility in Warren County, but the commission said it would have an overwhelming adverse economic impact on the City of Vicksburg and Warren County and stifle Vicksburg tourism. Multi-Gaming Management had originally filed the license application for the site, but withdrew on Oct. 1 after the issue became controversial; A Chancery Court in Benton County had terminated Melissa Brooks' visitation rights to her children. She was blocked from appealing the case because she couldn't afford the $2,352 worth of court reporter's transcripts. The Mississippi Supreme Court in Aug. 1995 refused to waive the fees and dismissed her appeal. The U.S. Supreme Court rules on Dec. 16 that the poor have the right to appeal and that the Mississippi Supreme Court *will* hear her case. The American Civil Liberties Union had pursued Brooks' case and said the impact of the ruling would be felt nationally; On Dec. 20, WorldCom stockholders approve a $12.6 billion merger with MFS Commmunications of Omaha, the fifth-largest in U.S. history. WorldCom's stock rose 48% for the year. Other Mississippi gainers on Wall Street for the year: Parkway Properties up 104%, Callon Petroleum up 90%, Sanderson Farms up 60%, and Deposit Guaranty up 39%. The year's losers include MS Financial down 86%, MTel down 60%, River Oaks Furniture down 50% and Casino America down 48%; Mississippi's unemployment rate for the year was 5.9%, the lowest in 17 years; At year's end, Gov. Fordice is back at work after recovering from his near-fatal auto accident on Nov. 5; Hattiesburg philanthropist Oseola McCarty pushes the button to lower the ball in Times Square in New York to bring in the New Year of 1997.

Deaths: Mamie Davis Willoughby, born in Liberty in 1916, wrote a weekly column, *Along the RFD*, for the Jackson *Clarion-Ledger* for nearly 50 years and wrote 3 books under the pen name Rose Budd Stevens, dies Jan. 9 at her home in Liberty; Charlie Conerly, a Clarksdale native and one of Mississippi's earliest and most renowned football heroes, who played pro 14 years for the New York Giants and one of the sport's first great passers, a member of the Mississippi Sports Hall of Fame, dies Feb. 13 in Memphis at age 74; Roosevelt "Booba" Barnes, blues singer and musician, dies of lung cancer on Apr. 3 at age 58; William Wade Guice, Harrison County's civil defense director since 1961, best known for his work with Hurricane Camille in 1969, dies at age 69 of cancer on Aug. 18, a day after the 27th anniversary of Camille; Louis Westerfield, Dean of the University of Mississippi School of Law who made history when he became the first black in that position in 1994, dies on Aug. 24 at age 47 of a heart attack in New Orleans; and Charlotte Capers dies on Dec. 23 at age 83. The Archives and History Building, where she worked for 45 years including director from 1955-69, is named after her.

Sports: On Mar. 10, the Mississippi State Bulldog basketball team wins its first Southeastern Conference Tournament title. The Dogs win the NCAA Tournament's Southeast Regional to earn a return trip to the NCAA Sweet 16 for the second consecutive season. On Mar. 24, it happens! — the 19th ranked Dogs upset No. 7 Cincinnati 73-63 for the Southeast Regional championship and become Mississippi's first Final Four team! But, State's hot steak ends as Syracuse beats them 77-69 on Mar. 30. Coach Richard Williams and other Mississippians are still extremely proud of the team as they end the best season in school history with a 26-8 record, winning 15 of their last 17 games while defeating Kentucky, Connecticutt and Cincinnati, the 1st, 3rd and 7th ranked teams in the nation; On Mar. 12, M.K. Turk announces his resignation, ending his 20-year reign as head basketball coach at USM where he compiled a 300-267 record. James Green, an Iowa State assistant coach and New Albany, Miss. native, is named to replace Turk; One year after coaching Ole Miss' baseball team to its first NCAA Tournament appearance in 18 seasons, Don Kessinger resigns on May 25 to accept an administrative job in the Rebel athletic department. This follows a very disappointing '96 season in which the team set a school record for losses in a season and tied a Southeastern Conference record for most losses in league play; Mississippi sees its four-game win streak broken as Alabama claims a 17-14 victory in the 9th annual Alabama/Mississippi All-Star Classic Football game on June 15; After years of planning, the $4.5 million Mississippi Sports Hall of Fame and Museum in Jackson opens July 4. It is the most technologically advanced museum in the state and one of the most advanced in the nation; Willy Wood wins the Deposit Guaranty Golf Classic at the Annadale course in Madison on July 21. Wood, a veteran golfer, earned $180,000 for his first Tour victory by shooting a tournament-record 20-under-par 268 to finish one shot ahead of Kirk Tripplet. The 145-player field was considered the strongest in the tournament's 29-year history, due partly to the $1 million purse, up $300,000 from last year; The Centennial Olympic Games in Atlanta end on Aug. 4 with three Mississippians making strong showings. Hattiesburg resident (Georgia native) Angel Martino was the first American to win a medal at the games, winning a bronze in the 100-meter freestyle. At 29 years old, she was also the oldest American swimmer to ever win an Olympic medal. Martino added three more medals, two Gold Medals and another bronze. Falilatu Ogunkoya, a native of Nigeria and former track star at Mississippi State, won a bronze medal in the 400-meter run, the first individual medal ever claimed by a Nigerian women. Ogunkoya later added a silver medal in the 4x400 relay. And, Ruthie Bolton, a McLain, Mississippi native, helped the U.S. women's basketball team win the last Gold Medal awarded at the games; On Aug. 17, native Mississippians Walter Payton and Wilbert Montgomery, two of football's greatest running backs, are inducted into the College Football Hall of Fame; On Aug. 28, Jerry Rice becomes a San Franciso 49er for life when he signs a 7-year pact worth $32 million that runs through 2002. The deal replaces a contract due to expire following the 1997 season and includes a $4 million signing bonus; On Sept. 9, Ole Miss athletic director Pete Boone outlines plans for a $13 million expansion of Vaught-Hemingway Stadium to 50,157 seat-capacity by the 1998 football season; On Sept. 10, the Jackson Generals beat Wichita, Kansas, to win their second Texas League championship title in three years and the fifth in the franchise's 22-season history; On Nov. 2, the USM Golden Eagles, ranked No. 23, wins its 7th consecutive football game of the season and clinches a tie for the first-ever Conference USA championship with a 21-17 victory over Cincinnati; In the 49ers 24-17 win over the Saints on Nov. 3, Jerry Rice becomes the first NFL player with 1,000 career receptions; Playing on a soggy field before 23,678 fans at Vaught- Hemingway Stadium, the Mississippi State Bulldogs beat the Ole Miss Rebels 17-0 in the Egg Bowl on Nov. 30. It was the first time State has shut out Ole Miss since 1941 and the first time since 1963 the Bulldogs have had an SEC shutout on the road; On Dec. 3, Delta State University freshman Treg Thomas is the first person to be awarded the Conerly Trophy, which goes to the state's top college player. The trophy was established this year after Charlie Conerly

A Chronology of Mississippi History

died on Feb. 13. Thomas set the Gulf South Conference record for rushing yards in a season — 1,604 — one of the five best single-seasons ever by a four-year college in Mississippi; The Intercollegiate Tennis Association releases rankings on Dec. 10 showing that the nation's top four college tennis players are in Mississippi — Mississippi State with the top-2, Thomas Duprè and Matthieu Ballay with Sebastien DeChaunac and Johan Landsberg of Ole Miss right behind. In the team rankings, State is third and Ole Miss fifth. That means Mississippi has the top four tennis players and two of the top five tennis teams in the nation! The Mississippi State tennis team had advanced to the NCAA Team Championships in the spring; In other sports news of the year: the Mississippi Sea Wolves, the state's first pro hockey team draw about 5,500 fans a game to the Mississippi Coast Coliseum while winning 13 of their first 16 home games; Jackson State won its second straight SWAC football title and made the NCAA 1-AA playoffs for the 11th time, again losing in the first round; Mississippi State had another losing football season but managed one of the year's biggest upsets, 17-16 over 8th-ranked Alabama for only its second win over the Crimson Tide in 39 years; The Delta State women's basketball team advanced to the NCAAs for the 10th time in 11 years; Ole Miss and USM both played in the women's NCAA basketball tournament for the 3rd straight year. The Lady Eagles even won a game before being eliminated; The New Hope Trojans baseball team went 43-0, winning the State Class 4A championship and setting state records for single-season victories and consecutive wins. They also set a national high school record for victories by an undefeated team!; What a year it was for Brett Favre! He threw 39 TDs to break his own NFC-record 38 he threw in '95, had 3,899 passing yards, made All-Star for the 2nd straight year, and on Dec. 30, Favre became only the second player in NFL history to win consecutive MVP awards. Favre's agent, James "Bus" Cook of Hattiesburg, is negotiating a record 7-year, $50 million contract!; AND, Richard Williams ends 1996 as the winningest men's basketball coach in Mississippi State history. State's 62-60 victory over Fresno State on Dec. 31 gives Williams 170 career victories in his 10+ seasons!!

1997
On Jan. 14, Curtis Giovanni Flowers, 26, of Winona, Mississippi is jailed in Plano, Texas and charged with four counts of capital murder in the July 16, 1996, shootings of Bertha Tardy, owner of Tardy Furniture Co. of Winona, and three of her employees. Flowers had worked briefly at the furniture store; Appearing in public for the first time since his near-fatal vehicle crash two months ago, a noticeably thinner Gov. Fordice delivers his State of the State address on Jan. 14. His speech is short on legislative proposals, but long on thanks and humility. The next day, the governor holds a news conference and tells the media that he has no recollection of the accident; On Feb. 18, state Rep. Barney Schoby (D-Natchez), an African-American, is confirmed for a seat on the Workers' Compensation Commission; Victor L. Bowles, 48, a decorated Vietnam veteran from Ethel in Attala County reportedly depressed over his poor health, walks into the G.V. "Sonny" Montgomery Veterans Medical Center in Jackson on Feb. 19, kills Dr. Ralph R. Carter, 46, a pulmonologist, with a shotgun blast to his chest and neck delivered at point-blank range, then kills himself with a shot to the head with the same weapon; On Feb. 21, Eric Snow, 21, a Bassfield resident with a lengthy criminal record, shoots to death Jefferson Davis County Sheriff's deputies Tommy Bourne and J.P. Rutland, who were transporting him to jail in Pearl; On Mar. 1, at least 4 twisters hit northern Mississippi, mainly Union and Pontotoc Counties. In Randolph, Mississippi, a 50-year-old man, Huey Totor, is killed and over 20 people injured with many homes destroyed; On March 13, a federal jury convicts Dock Eatman, 62, a Moss Point lay minister, of 21 misdemeanor counts of violating the federal pesticide law by spraying 11 south Mississippi homes and a day-care center with highly toxic farm chemicals, including methyl parathion; Also on March 13, the Mississippi Supreme Court rejects Gov. Fordice's petition to block Attorney General Mike Moore's lawsuit against the nation's cigarette manufacturers; On March 24, Mississippi State University President Donald Zacharias announces his retirement after tests showed he's suffering from multiple sclerosis; On April 5, legislators wrap up their regular session having passed the Mississippi Adequate Education Program, an equity-funding bill to overhaul the way Mississippi pays for public schools, a welfare-reform plan that meets federal mandates, a tax cut for married couples, pay raises for teachers, state employees and a host of state and local elected officials, a pilot program for charter schools, funding for the Bureau of Narcotics so they can hire 105 officers over the next three years, and bans on same-sex marriages and partial-birth abortions; On May 2, a federal jury in Hattiesburg convicts Paul Wall, Sr., 61, or Moss Point on 48 counts of misusing farm insecticides to kill roaches in private homes, delivering the most significant blow yet to the "cotton poison" black market; On May 19, Evelyn McPhail, former co-chairperson of the Republican National Committee, is critically injured after her car hydroplanes on a wet road and crashes into a tree; On June 3, Harvey Johnson, a Democrat, makes history by soundly defeating Republican Charlotte Reeves, 30,310 (70%) to 13,282 (30%), to become Jackson's first black mayor — the nation's 418th black mayor; In one of the decades biggest stories, it's announced on June 20 that there is a $368.5 billion settlement with the tobacco industry in a nationwide suit led by Mississippi Attorney General Mike Moore. The state could reap $75 to $100 million a year with most of the money going to health care in Mississippi; On July 3, Mississippi becomes the first state to settle the tobacco lawsuit with the state's share being 1.7 percent of the national figure — an estimated $3.366 billion over the next 25 years!; Eleven Illinois Central railroad cars derail near Flora on July 18 spilling Chlorophene, a highly flammable liquid. The next day, more than 4,000 residents are evacuated from Flora and surrounding areas so emergency environmental teams can explode 35,000 gallons of the toxic chemical; In July, former Biloxi mayor Pete Halat is convicted and sentenced to 18 years in prison. He was accused of participating in a conspiracy whose members arranged the 1987 slayings of his friends and prominent Biloxi residents Judge Vincent Sherry and his wife Margaret; In late July the Mississippi Municipal Association announces this year's most livable communities — Clinton, Petal and West Point; Jitney Jungle Stores of America Inc. finalizes its purchase of Delchamps Inc. for $260 million on Sept. 12, making Jitney the 39th largest grocery chain in the nation; The headline in *The Clarion-Ledger* on Thursday, Oct. 2: **"2 dead, 7 hurt in shooting at Pearl High; student held."** Pearl sophomore Luke Woodham, 16, drives to the school shortly before 8 a.m. on Oct. 1 armed with a 30-30 rifle. He opens fire on his classmates in the building's commons area killing senior Lydia Kaye Dew, 17, and Christina Menefee, 16, Woodham's ex-girlfriend. Those injured are senior Alan Westbrook, 18, sophomore Denise

A Chronology of Mississippi History

Magee, 15, junior Deepika Dhawan, 17, freshman Joni Palmer, 14, freshman Robert Harris, Jr., 14, sophomore Jerry Safley, 17, and sophomore Stephanie Wiggins, 15. At 9:30 a.m., police discover the body of Woodham's mother, 50-year-old Mary Anne Woodham, at their 323 Barrow St. home. Woodham had allegedly stabbed her to death at 5 a.m. that morning. Woodham is charged with three counts of murder and seven counts of aggravated assault. Grieving students descriptions of cult-like activities and an alleged plot lead to the arrests of six more students on Oct. 6 and 7. Arrested on conspiracy to commit murder are Pearl High students Donald P. Brooks II, 17, Wesley Brownell, 17, Delbert "Alan" Shaw, 16, Justin Sledge, 16, and Daniel "Lucas" Thompson, 16. Marshall "Grant" Boyette, Jr., 18, a Hinds Community College student, is also arrested on charges of conspiracy to commit murder, and will later be called the "mastermind" of a group called the "Kroth." The national spotlight will be focused on this tragic story for some time as it is the first of several school shootings by students that will occur in other states around the country in the next year or so; On Oct. 23, WLBT's nearly 2,000-foot TV tower collapses killing three workers, all from Quebec, Canada; Mississippi Superintendent of Education Tom Burnham resigns from the job he has held since July 1, 1992. State Board of Education members accept his resignation on Oct. 24; Jackson Police Chief Robert Johnson resigns on Nov. 3 under pressure from City Hall. Johnson, who came from Jackson, Mich. in 1994, is replaced in the interim by Assistant Chief Bracy Coleman; It is announced on Nov. 10 that Clinton-based WorldCom will join MCI Communication Corp. in a $37 billion agreement — the largest corporate merger in U.S. history!; On Dec. 8, Deposit Guaranty Corp. announces a $2.7 billion merger with Nashville, Tennessee-based First American Corp.; A surprise snowstorm on Dec. 14 dumps up to 8 inches of the white stuff in central Mississippi, including 4.8 inches at the Jackson International Airport. It is Jackson's worst one-day snowfall in Dec. in almost 70 years since 7.5 inches fell Dec. 22, 1929. The storm leaves 17,000 households without electricity; On Dec. 22, the Mississippi Supreme Court denies his appeal and upholds white supremacist Byron De La Beckwith's conviction in the slaying of NAACP Field Secretary Medgar Evers over 34 years ago; There were more than 19,000 business and personal bankruptcies filed in Mississippi this year, compared to 15,761 cases in 1996 and 11,832 in calendar year 1995; When final figures are in, Missisppi's only Fortune 500 company, WorldCom, reports revenues of $7.35 billion for the year, up 64 percent over 1996's $4.49 billion. However, net income of $357.2 million will be down from 1996's $414.9 million, due to WorldCom's acquisition of MFS Communications in late '96; And, Jackson International Airport passes the million-passenger mark for the first time.

Deaths: College and pro football great Thomas "Shorty" McWilliams, a Meridian native, dies on Jan. 9; Bluesman Jack Owens, a Bentonia native, dies on Feb. 9; Former state Senator Ellis Bodron of Vicksburg, dies of brain cancer on Feb. 18 at age 73. He had been around the Capitol for 48 years, 36 of them as a lawmaker and the last 12 as a lobbyist; Frank D. Barber, a Hattiesburg native and state Appeals Court judge, former state senator, who early in his career worked on the Washington staff of then-U.S. Senator James Eastland, dies on March 4, two weeks after he slipped and fell at his Jackson home. He was 67 years old; Rockabilly singer Ernie Chaffin, a Water Valley native, dies in a tractor accident on his farm in Hattiesburg on April 16; Civil Rights leader Aaron Henry, a Clarksdale native who was head of the state NAACP, dies on May 19; Writer and politician Frank E. Smith, a former state senator and member of the U.S. House, dies Aug. 2; Mississippi State Bulldog senior tailback Keffer McGee, drowns in a Starkville apartment complex swimming pool on Aug. 5. An autopsy reveals previously unknown heart disease; Major General William "Bud" Miley, "Father of American Paratroopers," dies in his adopted hometown of Starkville on Sept. 25 at the age of 99; and bluesman Jimmy Rogers (James A. Lane, and not to be confused with country singer Jimmie Rodgers), a Ruleville native, dies on Dec. 19 at the age of 73.

Sports: Along the way to its first-ever SEC regular season title, the Ole Miss basketball team upsets defending national champion Kentucky and attains its first-ever Top 25 ranking. The Rebels make it to the NCAA Tournament, but suffer a first-round 62-40 loss to Temple; Ron Polk announces his resignation after 22 seasons as Mississippi State's baseball coach on June 5, just two days after the Bulldogs are eliminated from their fifth College World Series under Polk, the only coach in the SEC with 1,000 career victories. He hasn't had a losing season in 26 seasons (the first 4 at Georgia Southern) and has a career record of 1,043-486; The Ole Miss Rebels football team wins their first game against a top 10 team, 36-21 at LSU, and earn a Top 25 ranking. The team wins 7 games and earns a bowl berth in its first season after NCAA probation. After a last-minute TD and 2-point conversion to beat Mississippi State 15-14 in their regular season finale, the Rebels earn their first bowl berth since 1992 — they win 34-31 against Marshall in the Motor City Bowl; The University of Mississippi bans flag sticks at its stadium; The University of Southern Mississippi Golden Eagles football team goes 8-3 again this year, but unlike last year they win the Conference USA title outright. USM clinches its first bowl berth since 1990 with a 33-0 victory over Houston, the same team that last year ended the Eagles seven-game winning streak and forced a tie for the C-USA title. USM wins the Liberty Bowl 41-7 against Pttsburgh; Mississippi State's football team get off to a great 7-2 start to put them in a position to win their first Southeastern Conference Western Division title and a bowl berth, but they lose their last two games to Arkansas and Ole Miss; The Jackson State Tigers football team makes its third straight NCAA Division I-AA appearance. With a fourth- quarter lead in a first-round game at Western Illinois, they lose 31-24 to fall to 0-12 in the playoffs; Van Chancellor, the only person to coach the Ole Miss women's basketball team in the SEC, leaves Oxford after 19 seasons to coach the new Women's NBA Houston Comets; South Panola ends the regular season as Mississippi's No. 1 high school football team for the second consecutive year, but again lose to Moss Point in the Class 5A championship game. Moss Point becomes the first 5A team to win back-to-back championships and three overall. Weir wins its third Class 1A title in four years, making coach Joe Gant the first Mississippi coach to win five high school football state championships; In Dec., Ole Miss quarterback Stewart Patridge becomes the second person to win the (Charlie) Conerly Trophy given annually to the state's top college football player; In the pro ranks of the NFL, former Mississippi Valley star Jerry Rice makes a return for San Francisco just four months after a supposedly season-ending knee injury. He catches a touchdown in the 15th game of the season and becomes the first non-kicker to score 1,000 career points in the NFL. Former University of Southern Mississippi star Brett Farve, the NFL's MVP the last two seasons, leads Green Bay to a

A Chronology of Mississippi History

30-13 Super Bowl win over the New England Patriots and follows that feat with another great season. Steve McNair, the NCAA career total offense leader from Alcorn State, is successful in his first season as a full-time starting quarterback for the Tennessee Oilers And, former Ole Miss standout Wesley Walls of the Carolina Panthers is named to the Pro Bowl for the second straight year.

1998

The year starts with many cultural activities planned for Jackson, all billed as the Great Jackson Renaissance — *The Splendors of Versailles Exhibition* April 1-Aug. 31 at the Mississippi Arts Pavillon, *Our Nation's Colors: A Celebration of American Painting* March 7-July 27 at the Mississippi Museum of Art, USA International Ballot Competition June 13-28 at Thalia Mara Hall, *Alsace to America: Discovering a Southern Jewish Heritage* May 29-Aug. 31 at Mtel Centre, and *The King's Astronomers: Science and Strategic Interest in the Court of Versailles* April 3-Sept. 3 at the Russell C. Davis Planetarium; On Jan. 5, William "Bill" L. Waller Jr. is sworn in as the newest justice on the Mississippi Supreme Court. Waller, 45, calls the death penalty in Mississippi "the poster child of justice gone wrong."; Also on Jan. 5, Dr. Mack Portera spends his first day on the job as president of Mississippi State University, succeeding retiring president Dr. Donald Zacharias. Portera oversees a $300 million budget and more than 4,000 employees; Heavy rains Jan. 5 through Jan. 7 cause widespread flooding around the state, with major rainfall reported in the eastern and southeastern areas. Gov. Fordice declares a state of emergency for 9 counties; A year after being charged with scheming to bilk Madison County taxpayers of $3.65 million, theme park promoter and Kountry Tyme Sports Foundation President Larry Foley enters a guilty plea on Jan. 22; On Feb. 10, the first installment of Mississippi's tobacco lawsuit settlement goes to the state treasury — $175,276,772.90; Four generations of family ownership spanning a century ends on Feb. 26 for Hederman Brothers Printing with the company's sale to Memphis-based Master Graphics Inc. Hederman Brothers once owned *The Clarion-Ledger* and *Jackson Daily News*. The firm will still operate with the same management and personnel at its headquarters in Ridgeland, where it moved to from downtown Jackson in 1993; On the morning of Feb. 26, a six-block area of historic Natchez is hit by raging winds many believe to be a tornado. But, National Weather Service radar data strongly suggests that the $30 million damage to schools, churches, homes and businesses is caused by a bow echo and associated straight line winds in excess of 70 mph, although 2 separate F1 (minimum) tornadoes are produced nearby. Amazingly, no lives are lost with only four minor injuries reported; On March 17, records of the Sovereignty Commission, Mississippi's segregation watchdog agency, are finally opened to the public at the Department of Archives and History. The documents, locked away in a state vault for two decades since the agency's demise, are brought to light after pressure from Civil Rights organizations and a federal court order; The legislative session ends on April 3. This year, lawmakers passed funding for the Adequate Education Program, handed out pay raises to teachers and state employees, provided $5 million for a local law enforcement grant program, including increased funding for the Highway Patrol and Narcotics Bureau, passed a campaign finance reform bill that will give voters more information on who contributes to candidates, approved a start-up plan to take advantage of a federal Children's Health Insurance Program, and approved a $43 million Capitol Complex bond bill; On April 3, a Hinds County Circuit Court jury takes less than 3 hours to decide the fate of former Jackson firefighter Kenneth Tornes, whose shooting rampage left four fire officials dead in 1996. The 8 women and 4 men say Tornes should die by lethal injection for the slayings of two of his victims, District Chiefs Willie Dwight Craft, 48, and John Richard Robbins, 47. Another jury later will decide his penalty for killing Captains Stan Adams, 45, and Don Moree, 49, the same day at Central Fire Station on April 24, 1996; On April 6, Yazoo City elects its first black mayor, Wardell Leach; On April 7, Gov. Fordice calls a special session of the Senate for May 3 over Seante Economic Development, Tourism and Parks Committee Chairman John Horhn's refusal to act on Fordice's nomination of Brandon businessman Mike Marsh as chairman of the state Workers Compensation board. In the special session, the Senate adjourns without voting on the nomination; On April 8, several tornadoes hit Mississippi, Alabama and Georgia killing 39 people, including a 16-year-old boy in a mobile home in Pontotoc County, the only death in Misssissippi from tornadoes for the entire year, although there are other deaths from storms; North Carolina educator Lester C. Newman is named the new president of Mississippi Valley State University on April 30; On June 5, a 10-woman, 2-man jury in Philadelphia, Mississippi finds Luke Woodham, the 17-year-old accused Pearl High School gunman, guilty of killing his mother, Mary Woodham, on Oct. 1, 1997. They had deliberated about 3 hours. Woodham makes no statement before he is sentenced to life in prison. However, the heavily guarded teen repeatedly calls the verdict "God's will," as he is taken from the courthouse. A week later on June 12, another jury in Hattiesburg finds Woodham guilty on all counts in the Pearl High School shooting rampage that left two dead and seven wounded. He receives two life terms plus 20 years each on seven assault counts; Fast-moving thunderstorms rake Forrest, Lamar and Perry counties about 10:40 p.m. on June 5. Hardest hit was southeast Hattiesburg, where falling trees strike vehicles killing two motorists in separate accidents within a 30-minute period. Although it appears to be the work of a tornado, the National Weather Service says it was a line of severe thunderstorms with strong straight-line winds; Inmates Mario Centobia and Jeremy Granberry escape on June 25 while being taken from the Parchman prison to a court hearing in Laurel. They overpower Jones County Sheriff Maurice Hooks and another man, leaving them tied up in an old barn in Rankin County. Hooks, and his friend, Ray Butler are found the next day suffering from only minor injuries. After driving Hook's patrol car to Alabama, Centobia and Granberry shoot and wound a Tuscaloosa policeman after he pulls them over. Two days later, officer Keith Turner is fatally shot in Moody, Ala., where Granberry surrenders. Centobie eluded officials for eight days before slipping past them and hijacking a car to south Mississippi, where he is finally captured. Centobie escapes again in Oct., this time from a maximum-security cell in Gadsden, Ala., where he was awaiting trial in the shooting death of Turner. He was captured twelve days later in an Atlanta suburb; Richard Thompson returns for a second time as state superintendent of education on July 1. Thompson was previously held that position from 1990-92; After spending 8 months evaluating acting Police Chief Bracy Coleman, Jackson Mayor Harvey Johnson names him to the permanent post on July 9; Rankin County District Attorney John Kitchens on July 21 asks the court to dismiss conspiracy charges against Danny Brooks, 18, Wesley Brownell, 18, and

The Ultimate Reference on the State

A Chronology of Mississippi History

Delbert Allen Shaw, 19, in connection to the shooting rampage of convicted killer Luke Woodham. Accessory to murder charges remain against Grant Boyette, 19, and Justin Sledge, 17, in that case; On Aug. 21, former Ku Klux Klan Imperial Wizard Sam Bowers is convicted in Hattiesburg for the killing of Vernon Dahmer Sr. in 1966. The racially mixed jury reaches the verdict in less than 4 hours. Afterwards, Ellie Dahmer, Vernon's 73-year-old widow, cries. Bowers is given a life sentence. Four previous trials in the turbulent 1960s, at least two of them in front of all-white juries, ended in deadlock. Dahmer fought off two carloads of Klansmen at his Hattiesburg home and grocery store during the predawn hours of Jan. 10, 1966, while his family fled. His lungs seared by the intense heat from the fire the Klansmen set, Dahmer died 12 hours later; *The Splendors of Versailles* exhibition ends Aug. 31. Although attendance was only about 271,000 for its 5-month run, well under the break-even goal of 417,000, it was still the second-most attended art and cultural event in the Southeast U.S. during 1998 and had a $40 million economic impact on the state; One of the biggest corporate mergers of all time between Jackson-based WorldCom and MCI is finalized after Federal Communications Commission approval on Sept. 14; After leaving hundreds dead in the Caribbean, Hurricane Georges skirts the Louisiana coast, then suddenly turns into the eastern part of the Mississippi coast during the early morning hours of Sept. 28. With winds as high as 174 mph and torrential rains up to 20 inches, it drives hundreds from their homes, especially in the Pascagoula area, leaving a trail of damage and thousands without electricity. Seventeen counties are declared federal disaster areas, although there are no deaths or serious injuries from the storm. Mississippi took a $310 million hit from Georges, which caused at least $2.5 billion in insured damages in the U.S., making it the third costliest hurricane on record; On Oct. 21, Jackson City Council President Louis and his son Artie are indicted on bribery and extortion charges for accepting money to influence the rezoning of a topless dance club. They both enter pleas of innocent; In Oct., a three-judge federal panel ends Mississippi's status as the only holdout in implementing the National Voter Registration Act, known as the Motor Voter law. Previously, Mississippi had operated separate registrations for state and federal elections. Motor Voter allows voters to register when getting driver's licenses or applying for welfare benefits; U.S. Rep. Mike Parker's decision not to seek re-election attracts a big field in the Fourth Congressional District, where Southern District Transporatation Commissioner Ronnie Shows, a Democrat, defeats Republican tax lawyer Delbert Hosemann. The state's other four congressmen easily win re-election; On Dec. 2, former Agriculture Secretary Mike Espy is acquitted on all 30 counts of his corruption case involving sports tickets and travel he accepted from companies that did business with the Dept. of Agriculture. Federal prosecutor Donald Smaltz had spent almost $20 million during the 4-year investigation that left Espy owing $1.5 million in legal fees; On Dec. 19, President Bill Clinton is impeached! Two of the 4 articles pass the House roll-call vote. Four of the five in Mississippi's delegation to the House of Representatives — all except Bennie Thompson — vote for impeachment; A Christmas Eve and Christmas Day ice storm hits several southeastern states including a large part of Mississippi, especially the central and northern sections of the state. While not near as severe as the ice storm of Feb. 1994, it still darkens the homes and Christmas spirits of more than 200,000 families across the state as power is lost and millions of tons of fallen trees, branches and debris is left behind; It wasn't a good year for Mississippi stocks...most were down for the year with Halter Marine down a whopping 82.11%, the greatest percentage loss, and Friede Goldman the next biggest loser at 60.09% down. The few exceptions were: MCI WorldCom, up an astounding 140.17%; Isle of Capri Casinos, up 47.54%; Delta & Pine Land, up 23.33%; SkyTel Communications, up 4.73%; Sanderson Farms, up 3.36%; and Trustmark, a 1.69% gain.

Deaths: Business executive Joe Frank Sanderson (Sanderson Farms), a Jackson native, dies on Jan. 4; Bluesman Junior Kimbrough, Marshall County native, dies on Jan. 16; On March 7, Melia M. Peavey, Peavey Electonics president and CEO Hartley Peavey's wife, dies from heart failure caused by a diabetic coma at age 43; On April 6, country music legend Tammy Wynette, "The First Lady of Country Music," dies at her home in Nashville from a blood clot to the lungs at the age of 55; On April 16, Jane Reid-Petty, a Meridian native who was an actor, writer, director, and founder of New Stage Theatre in Jackson, Mississippi's first and only professional theater, dies in Jackson after a long battle with cancer; Junie Hovious, a Vicksburg native, who was assistant football coach for 29 years and head golf coach for 25 years at Ole Miss, a member of the Mississippi Sports Hall of Fame (1967), dies on May 7; Ole Miss student-athlete Joey Embry, 21, drowns on May 19 while retrieving golf balls at the Mississippi State University Golf Course; Mississippi State football great E.B. "Buddy" Elrod, dies on June 13; Journalist Frank Trippett, a Columbus native who worked for *Newsweek* and *Time* magazines and won many awards, dies on June 18; Jazz Trumpter Bobby Bryant, a Hattiesburg native, dies in June; Gulfport journalist Robert P. McHugh, who won many awards, dies on July 23; On Aug. 4, Jerry Clower dies of cardiorespiratory failure at Baptist Medical Center in Jackson on Aug. 24 at the age of 71, just five days after undergoing sextuple bypass heart surgery. The renowned member of the Grand Ole Opry was the first country humorist to earn a Gold record. He received 9 consecutive awards for "Country Comic of the Year." His *Greatest Hits* album sold more than 500,000 copies; Rockabilly singer and songwriter Charlie Feathers, a Myrtle native, dies on Aug. 29; Golf great Cary Middlecoff, dies on Sept. 1; A Hattiesburg native and distinguished graduate of the University of Southern Mississippi, Julie Ann Cook Sperber, and her husband, Tom, of California, were two of 229 people killed when Swissair Flight 111 plunges into the Atlantic Ocean off the coast of Nova Scotia during the evening of Sept. 2; Grand Ole Opry announcer T. Tommy Cutrer, a Pike County native, dies on Oct. 11; Bluesman Lonnie Pitchford, a Lexington native, dies on Nov. 8; Evelyn McPhail, a Bay St. Louis native who became co-chairperson of the National Republican Committee (with Haley Barbour), dies on Nov. 26, about a year and a half after a serious car accident; Noted writer Margaret Walker Alexander, professor at Jackson State University, dies on Nov. 30; and pro world boxing champ Archie Moore, a Benoit native, dies on Dec. 9.

Sports: On Jan. 3, both Southern Mississippi and Ole Miss football teams finish in the Top 25 in the final Associated Press and *USA Today*/ESPN polls, USM at No. 19 in both and Ole Miss at No. 22. The Rebels are 8-4 and winners of the Motor City Bowl and the Eagles only losses for the season were to No. 4 Florida, No. 7 Tennessee and unranked Alabama, all on the road; On Jan. 25, the Denver Broncos upset the Green Bay Packers 31-24, despite and outstanding performance by Mississippian Brett Farve, the Green Bay

A Chronology of Mississippi History

quarterback who completed 25 of 42 passes for 256 yards and three touchdowns. Mississippi still had a player on the winning side, Willie Green with the Broncos; On March 11, Ole Miss forward Ansu Sesay is named Associated Press Southeastern Conference player of the year. Sesay, who had just been named a second-team AP All-American the day before, was a unanimous choice by 10 AP voters and in voting among SEC coaches. The 6-foot-9 Sesay led the league in scoring with a 19.2 average and was fifth in rebounding with a 7.5 average. He was also one of the top defenders and passers for Ole Miss as the Rebels won their second consecutive Western Division championship; on March 11, Southern Mississippi ends their basketball season with a 77-62 loss to Auburn in the National Invitation Tournament. USM finishes 22-11, ten more wins than last year's team and only the second Eagles team since 1961 to win at least 22 games; USM missed out on an NCAA berth. But, Ole Miss' best basketball season ends on March 13 when unranked Valparaiso stuns No. 13 Ole Miss 70-69 on a buzzer-beating 3-pointer in the opening round of the NCAA Tournament. After that, Ole Miss is ranked 20th in the *USA Today*/ESPN poll. The Rebels, 22-7, are the first team in school history to be ranked in the final polls; The winningest coach in Mississippi State University basketball history, Richard Williams, retires March 12, two years after taking the Bulldogs to the NCAA Final Four and one week after completing his second consecutive sub-par season; On April 9, Rod Barnes, a native of Satartia, Miss., is promoted from assistant to head coach of the Ole Miss basketball team; The Mississippi State baseball team beats Texas A&M 11-5 to win the NCAA Regional on May 24. They are knocked out of the College World Series by Southern Cal 7-1 on June 2. The Bulldogs finish a great season 42-23; On June 3, Georgia senior associate athletic director John Shafter is named the new athletic director at Ole Miss; On June 20, Mississippi beats Alabama 9-0 in the 11th All-Star Classic. The first shutout in Alabama/Mississippi history snaps Alabama's two-game winning streak and trims Mississippi's deficit in the series 6-5; Houston Comets assistant coach, Peggie Gillom, former player and assistant women's basketball coach at Ole Miss for 16 seasons, is hired as head coach of Texas A&M women's basketball on June 26; On July 19, the Deposit Guaranty Golf Classic at Annandale Golf Club is won by PGA Tour pro Fred Funk. His 72-hole total of 18-under 270 was worth $216,000 from the $1.2 million purse; Hattiesburg native Tim Floyd is introduced as the Chicago Bulls new basketball coach on July 23; Jackson State beats Alcorn State 56-26 on Nov. 21, its fourth straight win over its biggest rival in the Capital City Classic; On Nov. 26, Mississippi State beats Ole Miss 28-6 in the Egg Bowl to earn the Southeastern Conference Western Division championship, the school's first championship since an SEC title in 1941; Five days after Tommy Tuberville abruptly leaves to coach Auburn, David Cutcliffe signs on as the 34th head football coach of the Ole Miss Rebels on Dec. 2; On Dec. 9, it's announced Mississippi will get a professional football team in the new Regional Football League. The Mississippi Pride will have their first kickoff in April 1999 in Miss. Veterans Memorial Stadium; In tennis, Ole Miss' women and men make the national quarterfinals. State's men make the national semifinals!; The Murrah High School Lady Mustangs basketball team went 36-0, becoming the first unbeaten Class 5A girls team in 10 years; Mississippi State senior tailback J.J. Johnson, who set school records for rushing yards in a season and in a game and led the SEC in rushing this season, is the third to win the Conerly Trophy, given annually to the state's top college football player; All three Mississippi Division I-A universities go to bowl games in the same season for the first time: the University of Southern Mississippi loses to Idaho 42-35 in the Humanitarian Bowl on Dec. 30; the Ole Miss Rebels, under new football coach David Cutcliffe, close out the year with a win over Texas Tech University 35-18 in the Independence Bowl on Dec. 31; and Mississippi State comes off their 24-14 loss to the University of Tennessee in the Southeastern Conference Championship game to play New Year's Day against the University of Texas in the Cotton Bowl.

1999

Self-professed serial killer Donald Leroy Evans, 41, is stabbed to death by another death-row inmate at the State Penitentiary at Parchman on Jan. 4. He was sentenced to death in 1993 on a capital murder charge for the killing of 10-year-old Beatrice Louise Routh, a homeless girl whom he kidnapped from a park in Gulfport, then sexually assaulted before killing her. He claimed to have killed more than 60 people in 22 states; On Jan. 6, Attorney General Mike Moore drops out of the governor's race. Instead, the 46-year-old Democrat says he'll seek a fourth term as attorney general; On Feb. 11, Attorney General Mike Moore arrives at Jefferson Todd Educational Center to assist in negotiations with Michael Martin, 47, who took four women hostage at the school in Purvis. The gunman had requested to talk to Moore. The 12-hour-long standoff ends at 10:30 p.m. when the four hostages were released and Martin was taken into custody and charged with kidnapping. No students had been taken hostage. Martin, a disabled veteran who has a history of mental problems and drug abuse said he was protesting failure by the school system to hire black teachers and educate students about black history; Although Senate Majority Leader Trent Lott and fellow Mississippi Republican Sen. Thad Cochran vote on Feb. 12 to convict Bill Clinton on two articles of impeachment, the president is found not guilty; Jackson City Council President Louis Armstrong, a fixture in city government for 14 years, pleads guilty on Feb. 16 to conspiring to commit extortion and accepting a $25,000 bribe to influence a council vote on rezoning a topless bar. On Feb. 23, his son Artie Armstrong, 30, also pleads guilty, admitting that he accepted $28,500 from topless bar owner Jon Adams; On March 16, Amtrak's City of New Orleans passenger train collides with a flatbed tractor-trailer truck loaded with steel at Bourbonnais, Illinois just south of Chicago. Among the 11 confirmed dead are four Mississippians — Tougaloo College senior Sheena Johnson Dowe, 22, and three DeSoto County residents, June Bonnin, 47, of Nesbit, and Raney Lipscomb, 10, and her sister Lacey Lipscomb, 8, both of Lake Cormorant and Bonnin's granddaughter, Jessica Whitaker, 12, of Memphis. Among the more than 100 injured in the disaster was Bonnin's 9-year-old daughter, Ashley, who had her foot amputated, and Suzanne Cole of Clinton (Miss.) High School, who suffers a broken back. Clinton High students Michael Freeman and Caleb McNair and others from a group of 17 youths from Clinton High and Covenant Christian School of Clinton, who were all passengers on the train, are heroes as they pull others to safety; On Mar. 25, the merger of Canadian National and Illinois Central railroad companies is approved; The legislature ends its 1999 regular session on April 1, one of the most productive sessions in many years with lawmakers approving an 8 percent teacher pay increase and pay increase for state workers, approving funds to create more nursing home beds in Mississippi, expanding the state/federal Children's Health

A Chronology of Mississippi History

Insurance Program, providing funding for a statewide hospital trauma care system, expanding pay and job slots for the state Crime Lab, and approving a "whistleblower law" to protect state workers from being punished for reporting waste, abuse, and dangerous practices within government; On April 1, Willie B. Southern Jr., 34, ends a 5-day standoff with Jackson police at his hotel room at Best Suites of America off I-55 South. Southern threw out a .45-caliber pistol and emerged with his 9-year-old son, then surrendered to police in front of TV cameras — live on the 6 o'clock news. Police Chief Bracy Coleman says charges could be pending, but first Southern would be mentally evaluated; A gunman who says he is seeking "social change" takes 10 hostages at a downtown Jackson bank on April 8, creating a 7-hour standoff. It ends peacefully when Terrance D. Stamps, 22, of Jackson surrenders to police after holding 7 bank employees and 3 customers at the Trustmark National Bank branch at 504 S. State Street; On April 12, Marion Albert Pruitt, 49, is executed by lethal injection in Arkansas for the Oct. 12, 1981, kidnapping and slaying of convenience store clerk Bobbie Jean Robertson, 30, of Fort Smith. Peggy Lowe, an employee of the Metrocenter branch of Unifirst Saings & Loan in Jackson, and Robertson were killed in a week-long spree of terror that led Pruitt to dub himself a "mad-dog killer." Pruitt later kills two convenience store clerks in Colorado. Earlier in 1981, Pruitt had killed his common-law wife in New Mexico. He received life sentences for the four killings outside Arkansas, but got the death penalty for his conviction in the state; On Apr. 14, a deadly F3 (158-206 mph winds), half-mile wide tornado hits Covington, Jasper & Jones counties damaging over 50 homes in Hot Coffee, SoSo, Moss, and Hebron, where it kills one person; On April 20, two young men in black trench coats sweep through Columbine High School in Littleton, Colorado, a Denver suburb, attacking with guns and explosives. Eric Harris, 18, and Dylan Klebold, 17, both juniors at the school, massacre 12 of their fellow students and a teacher and wound more than 30 others before taking their own lives. With 15 dead, it is by far the bloodiest in a series of shootings that have rocked U.S. communities since Luke Woodham killed 2 and injured 7 at Pearl High School on Oct. 1, 1997. It brings back horrible memories to everyone in Pearl and all of Mississippi; Mississippi Supreme Court Justice Chuck McRae is riding his motorcycle northbound on I-55 on May 18 when he is stopped and charged with DUI and refusing to take a breath test. It is his second DUI charge — the first was in 1995. On July 6, Hinds County Justice Court Judge Clyde Chapman finds McRae innocent citing lack of evidence; On May 29, the Vicksburg National Military Park commemorates its 100th anniversary; There are announcements of three mergers of Jackson-based companies in less than a week. Birmingham-based AmSouth Bancorp announces June 1 plans to buy First American Corp. of Tennessee, parent of Deposit Guaranty National Bank, the state's largest bank. The next day Friede Goldman International makes known their plans to merge with Gulfport-based Halter Marine in a $218 million deal, and both those deals are only a few days after telecommunications giant MCI WorldCom announced a $1.3 billion buyout of SkyTel, the paging and messaging company; WLBT-Channel 3 breaks this news story in early June: Gov. Kirk Fordice walks through the Memphis airport on June 6 with Ann Creson, a Memphis widow whom the station identifies as Fordice's high school sweetheart. They say the governor vacationed in France the previous week with her, while his wife, Pat, remained in Mississippi. After a tumultuous week of revelations about marital problems, Gov. Fordice states on June 10 that he wants to divorce his wife of nearly 44 years and marry Ann Creson; On June 24, Governor Fordice sets a July 22 special session of the legislature to consider a tax cut. On July 22, legislators meet for 3 and a half hours before adjourning without voting on a 10 percent income tax cut or any of Fordice's other four proposals; On June 30, a Humphreys County jury finds that Dennis Howell Newton, 50, was a bystander in the killing of a 54-year-old one-armed sharecropper. The jury — made up of 10 women and 2 men, 7 whites and 5 blacks — deliberated 3 hours before acquitting the Yazoo City construction worker of murder in the April 12, 1970, death of Rainey Pool. A white mob beat Pool lifeless before throwing him into the Sunflower River. Newton's three co-defendants will be tried in Nov.; The Publishers Clearing House Prize Patrol finally comes calling in Mississippi on June 30. They deliver a $10,000 check to Earlean Madison of Jackson, who works at *The Clarion-Ledger* newspaper; For the first time ever, a woman takes the helm of one of Mississippi's largest corporate entities. On July 1, Carolyn Shanks, 37, becomes president and CEO of Entergy Mississippi, succeeding retiring Don Meiners; On July 6, President Clinton visits Clarksdale, Mississippi on a four-day cross-country tour to promote economic expansion in impoverished areas; On July 20, a federal grand jury accuses Jackson City Councilman Robert Williams of attempting to extort money to influence his vote on a cable television franchise and the zoning of a topless bar. U.S. Attorney Brad Pigott states the indictment is expected to mark the end of a federal investigation of Jackson city government; After the election on Aug. 3, it's Musgrove vs. Parker for the Governor's Mansion. Lt. Gov. Ronnie Musgrove coasts to an easy win in the Democratic primary, while Mike Parker edges out a majority victory over Eddie Briggs for the Republican nomination; Former Jackson City Council President Louis Armstrong and his son Artie get off with light sentences Aug. 20. U.S. District Judge Henry T. Wingate sentences Louis Armstrong, 48, to serve 15 months and his son Artie, 30, to 9 months. Both must also pay a $4,000 fine. Both are expected to testify against Councilman Robert Williams when he goes to trial in Oct; On Oct. 12, Jitney Jungle Stores of America, one of the largest supermarket operators in the Southeast, files for Chapter 11 bankruptcy protection. The company owns 192 retail grocery stores, 54 gas stations and 10 liquor stores in six states, but says as many as 55 stores could be closed in the coming year; Former University of Mississippi football coach Billy Brewer declares himself vindicated by the $221,355 the Lafayette County Circuit Court jury awards him Oct. 12. The university fired Brewer amid a 1994 NCAA investigation that led to sanctions against the Ole Miss football program. The amount awarded Brewer was the unpaid compensation from the final 3 years of his contract, minus $79,000 he earned from other jobs since his firing. Brewer had sought $2 million in other damages; Sheriff Marvin M. Farrior of Wayne County retires after serving 31 years (elected 8 times), longer than any other sheriff in state history; On Oct. 31, an EgyptAir 767 jetliner bound for Cairo plunges 33,000 feet in two minutes, crashing into the ocean off Nantucket Island. Most of the 217 on board were American tourists including Edmund Miller Sr. and his wife, Hannah, a West Point, Mississippi couple in their 70s, who had boarded the flight in New York on their way to a vacation in Egypt and Israel; It is the closest gubernatorial election of the 20th Century in Mississippi on Nov. 2. Final

A Chronology of Mississippi History

results show democrat Ronnie Musgrove leads his republican opponent Mike Parker in the popular vote by only 8,343 votes. Musgrove had 379,034 votes, or 49.62 percent to Parker's 370,691, or 48.52 percent. They tied with electoral votes — each had 61 of the state's 122. The state constitution mandates that a candidate must receive a majority of the popular votes (50% + 1) and a majority of the electoral votes, and since Parker refuses to concede, the race will have to be decided in the Mississippi House of Representatives at the beginning of the 2000 regular session. Incumbent legislators take a beating as many lose their seats in the election; On Nov. 13, a Humphreys County jury convicts former Klansman James "Doc" Caston, 66, of Satartia, his brother Charles E. Caston, 64, of Holly Bluff, and their half brother, Hal Crimm, 51, of Vicksburg each of manslaughter for the 1970 beating death of one-armed sharecropper Rainey Pool near Louise. They are each sentenced to 20 years in prison. A fourth man, Dennis Howell Newton, 50, of Yazoo City, was acquitted earlier this year on June 30; Jackson International Airport handles 1,347,104 passengers this year, up 24.7% from the figure of 1,080,771 passengers just two years ago in 1997; A 1987 transportation program's first three phases called for 1,088 miles in the state to be increased to four-lane highways. By the end of this year, 585.2 miles have been completed, 349.7 miles are under construction, and 153.1 miles remain untouched; The state's largest newspaper, *The Clarion-Ledger* of Jackson, conducted a series of special millennium polls asking readers to pick their all-time favorite Mississippian in each of several categories. The results were printed at various intervals, most of them released during late summer and fall. Here are the top choices of some of those polls: All-Time Favorite Entertainer, Elvis Presley; Favorite Pop/Rock Singer, Elvis Presley; Mississippi's Man of the Century, Elvis; Mississippi's Woman of the Century, Eudora Welty; Favorite Country Music Singer/Musician, Faith Hill; Favorite Blues/Jazz/R&B Singer/ Musician, B. B. King; Performer in "Other" Music, Leontyne Price (opera singer); Favorite Actor, Morgan Freeman; Favorite TV Personality, Woodie Assaf; Favorite Fiction Writer, William Faulkner; Favorite Non-Fiction Writer, Willie Morris; Favorite Miss Mississippi, Mary Ann Mobley; Top Humanitarian, Oseola McCarty; and Favorite Politician, John C. Stennis. Readers also choose the world's first heart transplant as the state's top scientific contribution. Dr. James D. Hardy and a team of surgeons at University Medical Center in Jackson transplanted the heart of a chimpanzee into the chest of a 64-year-old dying man on Jan. 23, 1964. Also the first animal-to-human transplant in the world, the heart continued beating for 90 minutes. Readers picked their favorite Recurring Events as the Neshoba County Fair (No. 1) and the Mississippi State Fair (No. 2); The 64-bed Central Mississippi Medical Center North Campus on Ridgewood Road in Jackson is forced by court order to close its doors on the last day of the year because it didn't have a valid Certificate of Need; As the Second Millennium ends, Mississippians wonder what the New Millennium will bring.
Deaths: Lillian McMurry, blues record producer who founded Trumpet Records in Jackson, dies on March 18; Howard Miller, a Vicksburg businessman who fought as state Wildlife Commissioner to expand opportunities for Mississippi outdoorsmen, dies on April 1 at age 57 after a two-month battle with cancer; Thomas J. Biggs, an architect who designed many buildings and churches in Jackson, dies at his Jackson home on April 5; World-famous writer Willie Morris, a Jackson native who grew up in Yazoo City, who became the youngest editor ever (32) of the nation's oldest magazine (*Harper's*), and wrote 19 books starting with *North Toward Home* (1967), dies suddenly of a heart attack on Aug. 2; Major league baseball player, Harry "The Hat" Walker, a Pascagoula native, dies on Aug. 8; On Sept. 11, Alton Wayne Roberts, 61, dies of heart failure in Meridian. He was the former nightclub bouncer who was one of 7 Klansmen convicted of federal conspiracy charges in connection with the June 21, 1967, killings of Civil Rights workers Michael Schwerner, Andrew Goodman and James Chaney. Testimony pointed to Roberts as the triggerman; Pro baseball coach Paul Gregory, a native of Tomnolan, dies on Sept. 16; Mystery novelist and book reviewer for *The Clarion-Ledger*, Neil McGaughey, a Natchez native reared in Prentiss, where he dies of heart failure on Sept. 21 at age 47; Philanthropist- humanitarian Oseola McCarty, a Hattiesburg native who donated $150,000 (about 60 percent of her earnings in a lifetime of washing and ironing) to the University of Southern Mississippi to establish scholarships, dies of cancer on Sept. 26 at the age of 91; James "Big Daddy" Carson, dies on Oct. 7 at age 59. He had coached Jackson State's football team to a 54-25-1 record in his seven seasons; One of the greatest pro football players of all time, Walter Payton, a Columbia native, dies on Nov. 1 from bile duct cancer that developed from a rare liver disease. Thousands attend several memorial services in Mississippi and Chicago where he played; legendary deejay Early Wright of Clarksdale, dies on Dec. 10; And former Ag Commissioner of Mississippi, Jim Buck Ross, dies on Dec. 14 at the age of 82.
Sports: In Jan., Texas beats Mississippi State 38-11 in the Cotton Bowl in Dallas; On Jan. 15, Southern Mississippi Athletic Director Bill McLellan, 66, announces his retirement after 13 years on the job. He got USM into the C-USA football conference after years as an independent; The Alcorn State Braves basketball team assures itself a spot in the NCAA Tournament with an 89-83 win over Southern University in the SWAC Tournament championship game on March 6; Mississippi State basketball team's 84-79 overtime loss to No. 2 Arkansas on March 6 also loses them a NCAA Tournament at-large berth. Instead, they play in the National Invitation Tournament, where they falter to Colorado State 69-56 in the first round; On March 12, Ole Miss gets the first NCAA men's basketball tournament victory in school history. Ninth-seeded Ole Miss wins over eight-seeded Villanova 72-70 in a first-round game of the Midwest Regional. The Rebels snap a six-game postseason losing streak dating back 16 years as they become 0-3 in the NCAA Tournament. Ole Miss, 20-12, then advances to play top-seeded Michigan State on March 14. It's a heartbreaker as the Spartans end the Rebs' crusade with a 74-66 win; On May 24, all three Mississippi Big 3 baseball teams are picked as No. 3 seeds to play in the NCAA Baseball Tournament. The University of Southern Mississippi, the University of Mississippi and Mississippi State University are picked — in that order — the first time three Mississippi schools have been chosen for the tournament in the same season; Legendary Mississippi State baseball coach Ron Polk is introduced on June 3 as the new coach of the Georgia Bulldogs baseball team. He retired from coaching at Miss. State after the 1997 College World Series but stayed in Starkville as an assistant athletic director for special projects while still working with the U.S. national team; On June 6, the best-attended sports event in the state's history comes to a close. The U.S. Women's Open golf championship in West Point, Mississippi drew 102,735 spectators to the Old Waverly Golf Club event. Juli Inkster from Los Altos, California wins

A Chronology of Mississippi History

the $315,000 first prize in record fashion by shooting a 16-under-par 272. The previous low for an Open was 10-under. The event drew 14 hours of live TV coverage and hundreds of reporters from around the world. George Bryan built Old Waverly and was the person who coaxed the USGA into bringing the Open to Mississippi; It's announced on Aug. 24 that the Texas-Louisiana League will field a pro baseball team in Jackson after the Jackson Gererals, the Class AA Texas League affiliate of the Houston Astros, leave Smith-Wills after this season; When the AP football poll is released on Sun., Oct. 10, all three Division I-A teams are ranked: MSU 12, Ole Miss 22, and USM 25; It took Mississippi State University 105 years, 100 football seasons, more than 900 games, and 30 head coaches but, finally the Bulldogs go 7-0 as they rally to defeat Louisiana State University 17-16 on Oct. 23 — the first time in school history that the Bulldogs have started a season with 7 consecutive victories! The team moves into a tie at No. 8 with Nebraska in the AP Top 25 poll. Then the Bulldogs make it an unbelievable 8-0 season start as they beat the University of Kentucky 23-22 on Nov. 4!; On Nov. 1, Brian Henninger wins the Southern Farm Bureau Classic. In his seven years on the PGA Tour, the 37-year-old Oregon native has won twice, both times at Annandale Golf Club in Madison. Henninger's other win was in 1994 — when it was called the Deposit Guaranty Golf Classic — in a tournament shortened to 36 holes by rain. This year's tournament was shortened by 18 holes for memorial services following the death of pro golfer Payne Stewart. Henninger's 54-hole total of 14-under 202 was worth $360,000 from the $2 million purse; On Nov. 20, the University of Southern Mississippi Golden Eagles football team wins 30-27 over the University of Louisville to give USM the Conference USA championship. It was the Eagles 3rd championship in 4 years. They also won in 1996 and '97. Jackson State University finishes a perfect SWAC Division season with a 58-6 blowout of Alcorn State in the Capital City Classic at Mississippi Veterans Memorial Stadium; On Thanksgiving night, Nov. 25, the 18th-ranked Mississippi State Bulldogs get a 23-20 victory over No. 23 Ole Miss in the Egg Bowl. Scott Westerfield's 44-yard field goal with 4 seconds to play caps yet another improbable comeback, the Bulldog's 4th of the season. The win moves the Dawgs to 9-2, 6-2, and a second place finish in the Southeastern Conference Western Division. The Ole Miss Rebels are 7-4 and 4-4; In the SWAC's first-ever championship football game, a crowd of almost 48,000 at Legion Field in Birmingham watches Southern University claim a 31-30 victory over the Jackson State Univsersity Tigers; Running back Deuce McAllister, after finishing No. 2 in the Southeastern Conference in all-purpose yardage and No. 8 nationally, is the fourth person to win the (Charlie) Conerly Trophy given annually to the state's top college football player. He is the second Ole Miss player to receive the trophy — the first was quarterback Stewart Patridge, who received the second Conerly in 1997; The Mississippi State football team beats Clemson 17-7 in the Peach Bowl in Atlanta, making the Bulldogs 10-2 overall for the season. State rates No. 12 in the final Associated Press Top 25; The University of Mississippi gets by Oklahoma 27-25 in the Independence Bowl in Shreveport; and the University of Southern Mississippi Golden Eagles football team beats Colorado State 23-17 in the Liberty Bowl in Memphis — the state's first ever 3-game bowl sweep!; A few sports tidbits we might have missed: Mississippi College makes the Division III Sweet 16 — Mississippi State's women's basketball team makes its first trip to the NCAA Tournament — Ole Miss plays in the Women's NIT — Delta State again wins the Gulf South Conference to reach the NCAA Tournament Elite Eight — Southern Miss' Courtney Blades sets the NCAA season strikeout record (497) while leading USM to the softball College World Series — and Savante Stringfellow of Ole Miss places 3rd in the NCAA long jump with 26-7 & 3/4; In *The Clarion-Ledger* millennium polls, readers pick their all-time favorites: Favorite Male Athlete, Archie Manning (football); Favorite Female Athlete, Jennifer Gillom (basketball); No. 1 to Head the First Team of the Miss. Division I Men's Basketball Team of the Century, Bailey Howell (some players picked for the team were Erick Dampier, Lindsey Hunter, Jeff Malone & Clarence Weatherspoon).

2000 (through June)

The new Twenty-First Century and Third Millennium dawns in the state with Mississippians celebrating after realizing that Y2K is AOK! Many had feared that the much-hyped, so-called Y2K (Year 2000) computer bug would create havoc when the midnight hour struck. It didn't happen...in Mississippi or elsewhere. Only a few minor computer glitches were reported anywhere on the planet; The state legislative session begins on Jan. 4 and the first order of business is to settle the undecided governor's race of last Nov. 2 — the closest gubernatorial election of the 20th Century in Mississippi. It takes the House just 12 minutes to resolve the governor's race — Ronnie Musgrove receives 86 votes (70.5%) to Mike Parker's 36 votes (29.5%). It was the first gubernatorial election ever decided in the House; On Jan. 6, Democrat Amy Tuck takes the oath of office administered by Mississippi Supreme Court Justice Lenore Prather, becoming only the second woman ever elected lieutenant governor in the state; On Jan 10, Gov.-elect Musgrove appoints Batesville banker J.C. Burns, 55, as director of the Mississippi Department of Economic and Community Development. He names interim Jackson State University President Bettye Ward Fletcher, 51, as director of the Department of Human Services; After 24 years as head of the Mississippi Bureau of Narcotics, Tom Blain resigns on Jan. 11; At noon on Jan. 11, David Ronald Musgrove, a former two-term state senator and one-term lieutenant governor, takes the oath and becomes Mississipppi's 62nd governor. A host of dignitaries, including U.S. Senate Majority Leader Trent Lott, attends the ceremony; On Jan. 11, analysts predict that Mississippi native Bob Pittman could be the crown prince of America Online, Time Warner once those companies complete their merger, waiting only for incoming CEO Jerry Levin to retire. Pittman, 46, the creator of MTV, in the president and chief operating officer of AOL, the world's largest Internet service provider; On Jan. 27, Charter's Georgia-based corporate offices announce that within days, they are closing their 110-bed psychiatric hospital in Flowood along with 32 other Charter locations nationwide. Charter had already closed 18 hospitals in the last six months. The Charter 66-bed hospital in DeSoto County at Olive Branch will remain open; On Jan. 28, a winter storm hits northern parts of the state dumping the most snow in decades. Snowfall was recorded in 17 counties with a foot or more falling in the cities of Cleveland and Grenada; On Feb. 3, Gov. Musgrove promotes David Huggins, 52, of Brandon from associate commissioner to commissioner of the Department of Public Safety. Huggins then appoints African-American Col. L.M. Claiborne Jr., 43, as associate commissioner and chief of the Highway Patrol; On Feb. 4, Millsaps College trustees name Frances Lucas-Tauchar, 43, as president, the first woman to

A Chronology of Mississippi History

lead the 110-year-old liberal arts college. The Jackson native and Mississippi State University graduate will succeed retiring 22-year President George Harmon on July 1; On Feb. 8, Grant Boyette, the alleged mastermind behind the Pearl High shootings in 1997, pleads guilty to conspiring to impede a public official. In exchange, prosecutors drop the more serious murder-accessory charges that directly tied Boyette, 20, to three slayings on Oct. 1, 1997. Boyette is sentenced to a 6-month boot camp-style program and 5 years supervised probation. He is the last defendant to be prosecuted in the shooting rampage by Luke Woodham; The Mississippi Band of Choctaw Indians unveils a plan for their second gaming casino on Feb. 8. In addition to their Silver Star Resort and Casino near Philadelphia, plans call for a $250 million casino complex with the tentative name of Golden Moon that will feature 90,000 feet of gaming space, a 600-room hotel and an 80-foot diameter golden globe restaurant perched atop the building. Tribal Chief Phillip Martin says the casino and other developments, such as a retail center and villas at the Dancing Rabbit Golf Course, will take place over the next four years and create nearly 10,000 jobs; On Feb. 9, Gov. Musgrove delivers his first State of the State address to the Legislature, pitching unity and vowing to work with lawmakers. Reaction to the governor's speech is mostly positive; On Feb. 12, Jitney Jungle Stores of America close 10 grocery stores as part of the their bankruptcy restructuring. The only Mississippi store closed is in Tupelo. However, a week later on Feb. 19, they close the Jitney stores at 3366 Terry Road and 311 W. Northside Drive in Jackson, plus the 189 Peace Street store in Canton; Jessie Stringer, 65, a former concert promoter and liquor store and lounge owner, known as "The Godfather" of Jackson cocaine dealers, is sentenced Feb. 15 to 10 years in prison; Elizabeth Slater, 39, wanted for allegedly causing a fatal accident while fleeing Jackson police, is captured in St. Louis on Feb. 15. Slater had been wanted on a manslaughter charge since Jan. 13 when Jackson police said she crashed into a car driven by Jamie Boyll, 50, of Brandon, while trying to avoid capture on a check forgery charge. Mrs. Boyll died on Jan. 14; On Feb. 17, it is announced that 200 workers in McRae's Jackson headquarters will lose their jobs as the result of consolidation of operations with sister company Proffitt's in Knoxville, both of which are a part of Saks Inc.; Madison, Mississippi's Raytheon Aerospace will continue to maintain Air Force One and C-9 aircraft for the Navy, Air Force and Marines, thanks to a $475 million contract announced on Feb. 17; State College Board members on Feb. 17 decide to give a four-year contract extension to embattled Mississippi University for Woman President Clyda Rent. Ending months of uncertainty, the board votes 9-3 to keep the MUW leader on the $134,000-per-year job after weighing criticism from faculty members against alumnae support; On Feb. 21, Gov. Musgrove appoints retired U.S. Drug Enforcement agent Don Strange to lead the state Bureau of Narcotics and former Jackson Police Chief Robert Johnson as the new Department of Corrections commissioner; Gov. Musgrove ends a two-decade debate on Feb. 23 when he signs into law mandatory auto liability insurance. The new law takes effect Jan. 1, 2001; The casino industry in Mississippi sets records for the first quarter of 2000 with total revenues over $695.2 million, up 14 percent from the $611.2 million first quarter record of 1999! The two regions each set records for each of the three months and for the quarter — the Gulf Coast casinos rose 21 percent to about $290.4 million, compared to $240.1 million in 1999, and the Mississippi River casinos had $404.9 million for the quarter, a 9 percent increase over the $371 in 1999. In the 7 years and 8 months (exactly 400 weeks or 2,800 days) since the first casino in the state started operation in Biloxi on Aug. 1, 1992, the gaming industry in Mississippi has grossed over $13.3 billion and paid almost $1.6 billion in gaming taxes to the state; On April 11, Public Safety Commissioner David Huggins names Ken Winter as director of the state Crime Lab. Winter was director of the Mississippi Delta Law Enforcement Training Academy and former Wisconsin Crime Lab forensic specialist and Indianola police chief; Former Jackson City Council President Louis Armstrong is released from a federal prison in Florida on April 11 after serving 13 months of a 15-month sentence. He was released early for good behavior; On April 17, BancorpSouth of Tupelo and First United Bancshares of El Dorado, Akansas, announce a $455 million merger that would make BancorpSouth the largest state-based bank corporation in terms of assets. The combined operation would cover 6 states — Mississippi, Louisiana, Arkansas, Tennessee, Alabama, and Texas — with assets of $8.6 billion and deposits of $7.25 billion; Two of the oldest community banks in the state announce merger plans on April 20. Greenwood-based Valley Bank, with $290 million in assets, will merge with State Bank and Trust Co. of Brookhaven, with $135 million in assets. After the union, all the banks of the new company would be known as State Bank and Trust; On April 24, Mississippi-based Jitney Jungle Stores of America announce the closing of 7 stores in Alabama, bringing to 44 the number of stores closed of sold since the company's Chapter 11 bankruptcy reorganization filing in Oct. 1999. They have closed all their stores in Birmingham, Memphis and Little Rock; On April 26, a bank is robbed in Pearl, the sixth bank robbery during April in the Jackson Metro area; On April 27, MCI WorldCom announces earnings of nearly $1.3 billion on about $10 billion in sales for the first quarter of 2000, up from $712 million in earnings on $8.7 billion in sales for the first quarter of 1999; On April 28, a 2:30 a.m. wind-assisted fire at Ross Barnett Reservoir at the Main Harbor Marina completely destroys two piers (E & F) and 62 boats. Damage is expected to top $3 million. The cause of the blaze was not immediately known; On April 29, the legislature tweaks the final touches on a record $3.6 billion state budget; As the legislature starts its final week of the regular session April 30, a group of angry black senators has an injunction served on Lt. Gov. Amy Tuck at the Senate podium to keep her from enforcing a ruling that grew out a flap about some members wanting the state flag changed. The injunction was issued by Hinds County Chancery Judge Denise Sweet; The Casey Jones Museum State Park in eastern Yazoo County commemorates the 100th anniversary of the train wreck near the Vaughan station on April 30, 1900, that took the life of legendary railroad engineer Casey Jones; On May 1, Gov. Musgrove signs into law a bill to raise teachers' pay. The largest teacher pay plan in state history, a five-year $337.9 million package, easily passed the House 102-19 on April 18. the state's 30,000 public school teachers would start seeing larger paychecks in 2001. Since the raise is contingent upon the state's economy growing at 5 percent annually, reaction to the bill is mixed; On May 2, the full Senate approves Gov. Musgrove's choice of Ben Barrett Smith as chairman of the Workers Compensation Commission; The regular session of the legislature is officially over on May 7, but most of the work is done on May 4 and most members depart for home; Officials of the Mississippi Symphony Orchestra announce May 5 that Crafton Beck will be its new conductor and artistic director. Beck, a 43-year-old

A Chronology of Mississippi History

Arkansas native and two-time Grammy nominee, had been the conductor of the Lima Symphony Orchestra in Lima, Ohio and the Boca Pops Orchestra in Boca Raton, Florida. He will be the fourth conductor to take the podium in the Mississippi Symphony's 55-year history; Many wonder whether the teacher pay hike will be in jeopardy when it is announced on May 15 the state's revenue collections for April were $4.6 million below estimates showing an economic growth of only 3.7 percent, the second lowest in the last 12 years. However, it is quickly pointed out that if the economy doesn't grow at 5 percent, lawmakers can still grant the teacher raises by voting to ignore the triggering provision; The bidding competition for KLLM Transport Services apparently ends on May 26. The Richland, Mississippi-based firm's board of directors entered an agreement with its chief executive officer, Jack Liles, and billionaire CEO of WorldCom Bernie Ebbers, to sell the 4.1 million outstanding shares of stock at $8.05 apiece; A special session of the state legislature on June 29 kills a controversial legislative retirement plan slipped into a bill in the closing days of the regular session in early May. Lawmakers overwhelming vote to repeal the legislation that would have given them double the retirement of the average state worker. The House voted 102-15 with two members voting present and three absent. In the Senate, 48 voted to repeal with two voting present and two absent. The governor had called the special session to try to get the measure repealed before it became law on July 1; During the last week in June, regulators in Europe and the U.S. Dept. of Justice announce they will block the planned merger of Sprint and WorldCom; On June 30, Gov. Musgrove names former Gov. William Winter to head the 17-person Advisory Commission on the State Flag and Coat of Arms. Musgrove created the commission in May following a Mississippi Supreme Court ruling that the flag used since 1894 was not the official flag because the statute making the flag the official emblem was repealed in 1906. The court ruled that the flag and coat of arms were in use by custom only. The state flag has been a source of division with many Mississippians believing the Confederate battle flag part of the emblem symbolizes racism while others defend it as part of their heritage; Brig. General George Walker resigns June 30 as senior assistant adjutant general, a position Gov. Ronnie Musgrove created for him after a Senate committee rejected his appointment to head the Mississippi National Guard; and the fiscal year ends showing "only" a 2.8 percent growth in the state's revenues over the past 12 months. Misssiiippi still collected $92.3 million more than it did in fiscal year 1999.

Deaths: Craig Claiborne, a Sunflower native, who was a food critic for the *New York Times* and author of many cookbooks, dies on Jan. 22 at the age of 79; Record producer John Vincent Imbragulio (aka Johnny Vincent), who founded the Ace record label and produced early rock hits such as Huey "Piano" Smith's *Rockin' Pneumonia & Boogie Woogie Flu* and *Don't You Just Know It*, plus Frankie Ford's R&R classic *Sea Cruise*, dies at his Jackson home of heart failure on Feb. 4 at age 74; Sculptor and outdoorsman Bruce H. Brady, a Brookhaven native, dies on Feb. 8; On Feb. 27, Mississippi Supreme Court Justice Michael Sullivan dies at his Jackson home from lung cancer at the age of 61; Tellis "T.B." Ellis, a Vicksburg native who grew up in Jackson and was athletic director at JSU for 31 years and became known as "the father of Jackson State athletics," dies on March 15 at age 87; Dick Livingston, a Democrat from Pulaski in Scott County, who served 28 years in the Mississippi House, dies on March 28 of cancer at the age of 60; Kenneth Tornes, 36, dies from a blood clot to his lung on April 9 in Parchman prison hospital. The former Jackson firefighter, on death row for taking the lives of his wife and four firefighters in a 1996 shooting spree, pleaded guilty March 19, 1998, to four counts of capital murder. A jury sentenced him to die by lethal injection for two of the five slayings. His execution had been scheduled for June 2, 2000; and college/pro football great and Mississippi Sports Hall of Famer J.T. "Blondy" Black, a native of Philadelphia, Miss., dies of respiratory failure in Jackson on May 4 at age 79.

Sports: Although Mississippian Steve McNair gives a very impressive performance in Super Bowl XXXIV on Jan. 30 that brings the Tennessee Titans back even from a 16-point deficit, the St. Louis Rams still win the game 23-16 in what many call the best Super Bowl ever. McNair's 64 yards rushing was a Super Bowl record for a quarterback; On Feb. 13, Jackson State defeats Arkansas-Pine Bluff 9-2 handing JSU baseball coach Bob Braddy his 800th career victory!; On Feb. 16, J.L. Holloway, co-owner of the Jackson Bandits minor league hockey team, announces plans for construction of a 7,500-seat entertainment and sports arena to be built within the year. Plans are for the $25 million arena to be built on the state Fairgrounds, not far from the team's current home in the Mississippi Coliseum; Coach Dave Whitney's Alcorn State Braves basketball team races past Texas Southern 82-65 on Feb. 28 to capture its second straight regular season SWAC championship. Alcorn, 18-9 overall and 15-3 in the SWAC, has an 8-game winning streak and a home court winning streak of 26 games; Coach Sharon Fanning's Mississippi State Lady Bulldogs (No. 17) beat No. 2 Georgia 62-61 on March 4 to reach the SEC championship game for the first time. The next day, the Lady Bulldogs, 23-6, play their hearts out against Tennessee (also No. 2), but the Lady Vols win it 70-67. The 12th-ranked Lady Bulldogs crush St. Peter's Peahens 94-60 on March 17, earning their first NCAA Tournament victory; Even with a 14-point halftime deficit, the Jackson State Tigers mens basketball team roars back to beat Southern 76-61 on March 11 for the SWAC title. On March 16, the Arizona Wildcats run over Jackson State 71-47 in the opening round of the West Regional NCAA Men's Basketball Tournament; On March 11, Coach Shirley Walker's Alcorn State Lady Braves blast Grambling 83-58 in the SWAC final for an NCAA berth. Top-seeded Louisiana Tech, 29-2, overwhelm the Lady Braves 95-53 on March 18 in the first round of the NCAA Tournament Midwest Regional; Delta State's Lady Statesmen roll over Rollins 74-44 on March 11 in the championship game of the NCAA Division II South Regional to earn a spot in the Elite Eight; Coach Patrick Nutter's Yazoo County Lady Panthers start their season with a 63-48 victory over No. 7 Tupelo. They finish with a 39-0 record when they win their 62nd straight game with a 43-30 victory over No. 5 Forest on March 9 to claim their second straight Class 3A championship. The Panthers three Dandy Dozen, center Jackie Gainwell, forward Seneca Anderson, and guard Latrisha Graves, all signed with Mississippi State. Yazoo County is picked the No. 1 girls basketball team in *The Clarion-Ledger* poll; Ebony Felder of Murrah High in Jackson averages 18.6 points, 12.2 rebounds, 4.4 steals, 3.3 assists and 2 blocked shots to lead the Lady Mustangs to a 32-1 record and their 3rd straight Class 5A state title. She signs with Georgia; The East Coach Hockey League team, the Jackson Bandits, wrap up their inaugural season on April 4, barely missing the Kelly Cup playoffs by one point. They finish the season 32-32-6; At Claremont, California on April 14, Ole Miss junior Savante Stringfellow leaps to a new

A Chronology of Mississippi History

personal best in the long jump. With a jump of 26-9 & 1/4, the Jackson native set both a meet record (almost 3 feet over the old record) and track record (more than a foot over the old record). Lady Rebels junior Teneeshia Jones set meet records in the 100 meters and 200 meters. Her 200-meter time of 23.47 provisionally qualifies her for the NCAA Championships and ranks her fourth in the nation and second in the Southeasternn Conference this season. Lady Rebel Brandy Mack also provisionally qualifies for the NCAA Championships by winning the 400-meter hurdles with her season-best time of 58.61; On April 14, Jackson State University captures its 13th SWAC title in golf, the Tigers gaining an automatic bid to the NCAA Regionals. This will be the second trip to the NCAA Regionals for JSU — the first was in 1995. JSU is the only historically black school to participate in the 105-year history of the event; On April 15, ten players with Mississippi ties are taken in rounds 1 through 3 of the NFL football draft, including wide receiver Sylvester Morris and cornerback Rashard Anderson, both from Jackson State and both first round picks (21st & 23rd). The selection of Anderson and Morris gives JSU seven first-rounders since 1972, the most of any school in the state; During the same middle-of-April weekend, Mississippi State senior Alex Rocha from Sao Paulo, Brazil, shoots a school-record 10-under-par 62 in the first round of the Hitchcock Invitational, a golf event he goes on to win. That makes 4 victories this spring. Rocha was featured in the April 3 issue of *Sports Illustrated* for the 8-under 208 he shot to win the Seminole Intercollegiate in Florida. Rocha, the SEC's top-rated golfer, holds 14 school records, including best single round (63), best three-round score (18 under 198), best career scoring average (72.68), and the school's lowest season scoring average (69.97) by almost three strokes. Rocha led the after the second round of the SEC Golf Championship until slipping to 1-over-par 73 in the final round to finish second on April 23; The Mississippi State baseball team wins over the University of Tennessee 4-2 on April 29. The win push the 12th-ranked Bulldogs, 32-12 and 13-7 in the SEC, into first place in the West after LSU's 6-4 loss at Ole Miss on April 29; It is announced on May 1 that Alcorn State will not be allowed to play in the Southwestern Athletic Conference baseball tournament because they did not play enough games; Terry McMillan resigns on May 1 as athletic director and football coach at Mississippi College citing the need for "a new challenge." McMillan, 53, had worked at Mississippi College for 28 years, the last nine in the dual capacity; It shocks the experts when Darius Rice, a 6-foot-9, 200-pound McDonald's All-America forward from Jackson's Lanier High School signs with Miami, the Big East Conference school on May 2. Rice was widely considered the nation's top unsigned prospect with most observers predicting he would sign with Mississippi State, Memphis or Kentucky; The new Jackson Diamond Kats baseball team make their debut in Greenville on May 5. They play their first home game in Jackson on May 9. The D-Kats treated a crowd of 2,389 to a 5-4 Texas-Louisiana League victory over the Alexandria Aces, which now makes the D-Kats 2-3 on the season; On May 7, the Jackson State Tigers rally from an 8-3 deficit to defeat Grambling State 12-11 in a dramatic winner-take-all title game that will take them to their fourth NCAA Regional appearance and JSU's first since 1989; Needing a win to reach the SEC Tournament, Ole Miss blows it when the Rebels lose to the Arkansas Wildcats 9-5 on May 14; Following a series of meetings with athletic director John Shafer, Pat Harrison resigns as Ole Miss baseball coach on May 17. He had lost his last five Sotuheastern Conference series; On May 19, USM loses to Alabama-Birmingham 10-6 in the Conference USA Baseball Tournament. The Golden Eagles, once 24-11 and closing in on a second straight trip to an NCAA regional, kept going downhill after an extra-inning loss to Alabama on April 11; On May 20, the U.S. Olympic Team Trials for cyclists is held in Jackson, the first Olympic qualifying event ever held in the state. The winners — Nicole Freedman in the women's and Antonio Cruz in the men's, both California natives — qualified for the U.S. cycling team that will participate in the 2000 Summer Olympics in Sydney, Australia; In 1999, Courtney Blades set the NCAA season strikeout record (497) while leading USM to the softball College World Series. On April 29, 2000, Blades struck out 16 batters in an 8-0 victory at North Carolina Charlotte, breaking her year-old NCAA single-season mark. Blades was 39-5 for the 2000 season after compiling a 43-6 record and earning first-team All-America honors as a junior. She was leading the nation with 12.2 strikeouts per 7 innings! At this year's Women's College World Series, the University of Southern Mississippi Lady Eagles softball team was one victory short of the WCWS title game when they are defeated by UCLA on May 28, 2000. It was USM's second consecutive trip to the World Series. Just three days before on May 25, Courtney Blades pitched the second perfect game in Women's World College Series history. Blades, 52-8, finished the season with NCAA records for victories and strikeouts (663). She had 166 more strikeouts than her own single-season record of 497 strikeouts she set in 1999. She also holds the career mark for victories (151) and strikeouts (1,773); On May 31, Ole Miss junior Savante Stringfellow soars 26 feet, 9¾ inches and had four of the five best jumps at the NCAA Track and Field Championships. Stringfellow is fourth in the world as he heads into the U.S. Olympic trials in July; The Mississippi State Bulldogs baseball team loses to Clemson 9-4 in the Super Regional on June 3. One day earlier, they lost the series opener 11-4. That, after their earlier two and out at the Southeastern Conference Tournament, means that trip to Omaha will have to wait until another year; Rett Chrowder wins the State Am title on June 4, becoming one of only four players in the history of the State Am to win it three consecutive times. He did it at the Country Club of Jackson, where he won the first of his four State Ams in 1992. Crowder's 72-hole total of 275 (67-68-69-71) was four shots better than that of runner-up Robert Dreyfus. He is 50-under par for the four times he's won the State Am; Mike Bianco, 33, is hired as the Ole Miss baseball coach to succeed Pat Harrison, who resigned on May 17. Bianco has been head coach at McNeese State for the past three years and before that was assistant coach at LSU; On June 22, Meridian native Pam Posey clinches the Mississippi Women's Amateur golf title at the Beau Pré Country Club in Natchez with a 5 and 3 victory over three-time defending champion Cissye Gallagher. A Greenwood resident, eight-time champion Gallagher has finished second five times.; and Mississippians are pushing the the candidacy of "Deuce" McAllister for the Heisman Trophy. That's the way it was in Mississippi for just the first half of the first year of the new Third Millennium.

Last minute BULLETIN as this book goes to press: Nissan Motor Company announces on Nov. 9, 2000, that it is going to build a billion dollar truck manufacturing plant in Madison County just south of Canton that will initially employ about 3,000 people and eventually as many as 4,000 workers!

Geography of Mississippi

Rank In Size: 32nd in the nation
Surface Area: **Total** — 48,433.59 square miles (32,997,498 acres), rank 32
(approx. 1/78th of U.S. area or 1/4,066th of earth's surface area)
Land Area — 46,913.64 square miles (30,024,730 acres), rank 31
(approximately 1/1,234th of the total land surface area of earth)
Water Area — 1,519.95 sq. miles: 781 sq. miles of inland water surface; 739 sq. mi. coastal.
Coastline: The Gulf of Mexico; 44 miles general (rank 18), and 359 miles tidal [shoreline] (rank 22)
Noncontiguous Areas (Islands): Cat Island, Horn Island, Petit Bois Island, and Ship Island.
Total Distance Around State Boundary: Approx. 1,024 miles (along all river, gulf & inland curves), 464 miles natural and 560 miles geometric perimeter. Mississippi River shoreline is 410 miles.
Geographic Center: 9 miles W/NW of Carthage in Leake County at approx. **32°47' north latitude and 89°40' west longitude**, about a half mile from the community of Saint Ann.
Physiographic Region: Gulf Coast Plains (Division defined by Census Bureau)
Political-Geographic Division: East South-Central (Census Bureau). Mississippi lies within one day's drive of 55% of the U.S. population. Fourteen large urban centers are located within a 500 mile radius from the center of the state.
Ports: The two main Mississippi ports, Gulfport and Pascagoula, are closer to the Panama Canal than either New Orleans, Louisiana or Mobile, Alabama.
Extreme Length: North to South - 340 miles
Extreme Breadth: East to West - 180 miles (170 miles, approximate mean)
Highest Point: Woodall Mountain, 806 ft., rank 47 (located in Tishomingo Co. in extreme NE of state)
Lowest Point: Gulf of Mexico, sea level (rank 3)
Approximate Mean Elevation: 300 feet (rank 45)   *Gulf of Mexico: 582,100 sq. miles with an avg. depth of 5,297 feet*
State Boundary: Alabama to the east, the Mississippi River and Arkansas to the west, Louisiana to the upper south and west, the Gulf of Mexico to the extreme south, and Tennessee to the north.
Northernmost Point: The border with the State of Tennessee at **34°56'55" north latitude**.
Southernmost Point: Lighthouse Point is **30°10'25" north latitude** at 89°27'47" west longitude.
Easternmost Point: 7 miles E/NE of Iuka in Tishomingo County at a point bordering Pickwick Lake at Eastport approximately **88°06'01" west longitude** at 34°53'18" north latitude.
Westernmost Point: About 20 miles W/SW of Woodville in Wilkinson County at a point bordering the Miss. River at approx. **91°37'37" west longitude** at 30°59'59" north latitude.
Major Watersheds: Ten with 100 million gallons daily minimum flow — Amite River, Bayou Pierre-Coles Creek, Big Black River, Biloxi-Jourdan-Wolf River, Hatchie-Tuscumbia-Wolf River, Homochitto River, Noxubee-Tombigbee River, Pascagoula River, Pearl River, and Yazoo River.
Minor Watersheds: 306 ranging is size from 20,000 to 250,000 acres.
Major Rivers: The Big Black (330 miles long from its source in Webster Co.), the Homochitto and the Yazoo (169 miles long) are tributaries that flow into the Mississippi. Main tributaries that feed the Yazoo are the Sunflower, the Yalobusha and the Tallahatchie (301 miles long from its source in Tippah Co.). The Pearl (411 miles long from its source in Neshoba Co.) flows through the center of the state directly into the Gulf of Mexico. The southeastern part is drained by the Pascagoula, Chickasawhay & Leaf Rivers. The northeastern section is drained by the Tombigbee River (525 miles long from its source in Prentiss Co.), which flows into Mobile River.
Other Rivers: Amite, Biloxi, Bogue Chitto, Bogue Phalia, Buffalo, Buttahatchie, Chuquatonchee, Coldwater, Escatawpa, Fair, Hatchie, Homochitto, Hushpuckena, Loosa-Scoona, Noxubee, Old, Quiver, Skuna, Strong, Tangipoahoa, Tchoutacabouffa, Wolf, Yockanookany, Yocona
Creeks: Abiaca, Archusa, Arkabutla, Ascalmore, Atkinson, Bahala, Bakers, Bear, Beaver, Beaverdam, Besa Chitto, Big, Big Brown, Big Cedar, Big Cypress, Big Sand, Big Spring, Black, Blackwater, Bluff, Boguefala, Boone, Bowie, Bridge, Broken Pumpkin, Brushy, Bucatunna, Bynum, Calabrella, Cameron, Campbell, Cane, Caney, Caston, Catahoula, Catalpa, Chambers, Chiwapa, Chunky, Chuqutonchee, Clark, Clear, Cobbs, Coles, Conehatta, Copiah, Cuffawa, Cypress, Dabbs, Darling, Deer, Doaks, Dry, Eucutta, Fairchilds, Fannegusha, Flint, Fourteenmile, Gaines, Gum, Harland, Hashuqua, Hickahala, Hinkle, Hobolochitto, Hobuck, Holiday, Hominy, Horn, Hotopha, Houlka, Hurricane, Hushpuckena, Indian, Jackson, James, Johnson, Jordan, Labutcha,

Geography of Mississippi

Lenoir's, Line, Little, Little Bear, Little Black, Little Brown, Little Sand, Little Teoc, Little Yellow, Long, Luxapallila, Mackeys, Magby, Magees, Mattubby, Maynor, Mays, McCall, McGee's, Middle Fork, Mud, Mudd Island, Muddy, Mulberry, Mussacuna, Nanih Waiya, Oakey Woods, Oakohay, Okatibbee, Okatoma, Okafoma, Okatibbee, Old, Otoucalofa, Pammegusha, Pawticfaw, Pelahatchie, Percy, Perry, Persimmon, Petticocowa, Pigeon Roost, Piney, Piney Woods, Pinishook, Plum, Ponta, Poplar, Porters, Pumpkin, Pushepatapa, Red, Red Banks, Richland, Richmond, Rocky, Sand, Sand Hill, Sandy, Second, Seneasha, Shackaloo, Shongelo, Shubuta, Shuqualak, Silver, Sipsey, Snake, Souinlovey, South Tippah, Spring, Straight, Sucarnoochee, Sykes, Tallahaga, Tallahalla, Tallahatta, Tallahoma, Tenmile, Teoc, Thompson, Tiger, Tillatobia, Tilton, Topisaw, Town, Trim Cane, Turkey, Tuscalameta, Tuscumbia, Tuxachanie, Twenty Mile, Wahalak, Walls, Warrior, Weaver, Wet Water, Whiskey, White Oak, White Sand, Wolf, Yellow, Young, Zilpha.

Major Lakes/Reservoirs: Six (6) — Arkabutla, Enid, Grenada, Okatibbee, Ross Barnett, Sardis ((Ross Barnett is the largest with 33,000 acres [5.16 square miles] and 105 miles of shoreline)

Other Lakes: Aaron, Adair, Adam, Airey, Airplane, Albemarle, Aldrich, Alec, Alexander, Algar, Allen, Alligator, American Legion, Anchor, Annie Carter, Artonish, Ashley, Askew, Backbone, Bailey, Baker, Bangs, Barnes, Barrett, Bear, Beardslee, Beasley, Beaver, Beaverdam, Bee, Bell, Belmont, Beulah, Big, Big Black, Big Blue, Big Eddy, Bill Waller, Bird, Black, Blue, Bluff, Board, Bobo, Bobs, Boles, Bolivar, Boneyard, Breland, Broad, Buck, Buckatunna, Buckskin, Burnside, Bush, Butler, Cane, Car, Carlisle, Carruth, Carter, Castle, Cat, Catfish, Catherine, Causey, Cedar Hill, Centennial, Choctaw, Chute, Claiborne, Clark, Clear, Coaker, Cook, Cooks, Cooley, Coon Creek, Coon Island, Corn, Corner, County, Cow Oak, Crawford, Creswell, Cunningham, Cypress, Dace, Dads, Darr, Davis, Dead, Deep, Dear, Delta, Democrat, Denman, Dent, Dickerson, Dixie Springs, Dixon, Dollar, Dry, Duck, Dumas, Dump, Durden, Eagle, Elbow, Elks, Ferguson, Fish, Fishhook, Five Mile, Flag, Flat, Flea Harbor, Fletcher, Flower, Gator, George, Gibbs, Gill, Gin, Glory, Goggle Eye, Gooden, Goose, Gorman, Graham, Grass, Graves, Greasy, Green, Gum, Hadley, Hamilton, Hamp, Hampton, Hard Cash, Hico, Hide-A-Way, Holmes, Horn, Horseshoe, Hurricane, Jeff Davis, Johnson, Kaiser-Carlton, Kemper County, Lake Comorant, Lamar Bruce, Lee, Liddon, Lincoln, Little Whiting, Loakfoma, Long, Lorman, Malone, Marathon, Marsh, Mary Crawford, Mohawk, Monroe, Moon, Okhissa, Oktibbeha County, Old River, Paul H. Barrett, Perry, Pickwick, Pipes, Puskus, Risher, Russell, Sandridge, Sansing, Saw Grass, Serene, Shelby, Simpson, Stribling, Swan, Tackett, Tangipahoa, Tiak O'Khata, Tillatoba, Tippah County, Tithelo, Tom Bailey, Ton, Tully Seale, Tunica, Vista, Walthall, Washington, Waukomis, Whiting, Whittington, Williams, Wolf.

Topography/Terrain: The state falls into two natural regions, the Mississippi Floodplain and the Gulf Coastal Plain. Except for alluvial deposits and a strip in the northeast, soils are red and yellow clays in the north and center and sandy in the south. The Mississippi Floodplain along the western edge of the state was built up by successive floods. From the southwestern corner upstream to Vicksburg this region extends inland only a few miles. North of Vicksburg the area becomes a leaf-shaped plain with an average width of 65 miles. This region between the Mississippi and Yazoo Rivers is the Yazoo Basin, or Delta, one of the most fertile areas in the world. The Gulf Coastal Plain covering all the rest of the state may be divided into 9 distinct areas. The Tombigbee and Tennessee River Hills occupy a 120-mile strip along the Alabama border in the northeast. West of these hills lies the Black Prairie, a crescent-shaped belt of fertile lowland with few trees. Elevation varies from 250 to 500 feet. The Pontotoc Ridge rises along the western border of the Black Prairie from the Tennessee state line to near Ackerman. This low range varies in width from 2 to 21 miles. The fourth distinct area of northeastern Mississippi is the Flatwoods, a narrow crescent of sticky clay soil extending to the Tennessee and Alabama borders. The North Central Hills occupy all of the north-central area and extend as far southeast as Clarke County. To the west, along the edge of the Mississippi Floodplain, is another series of uplands, called the Loess Hills (or Bluff Hills), 5 to 15 miles wide, bordering the eastern edge of the Delta in the north and curving westward to follow the Mississippi River below Vicksburg. South of the North Central Hills, the Jackson Prairies run northwest to southeast from Yazoo County into Wayne County. This is a belt of fertile farmland with an extreme width of 40 miles. South of the Jackson Prairies, all of southern Mississippi is known as the Piney Woods, except for a strip along the gulf known as the Coastal Meadows.

Geography of Mississippi

Natural Resources: Petroleum, natural gas, sand, gravel, timber, 53 salt domes.
Land Use: Cotton, rice, soybeans, corn — cattle & other livestock, catfish, poultry, timber
Cropland: 7,191,480 acres, or 11,237 square miles (23.2%)
Pasture Land: 3,998,711 acres, or 6,248 square miles (12.9%)
Forested Area, 1998: 18,587,300 acres, or 29,043 square miles (almost 62% of the state)
Wildfires, FY 1999: 43,082 acres in 4,360 fires (5-yr. avg., FY '95-'99 — 47,235 acres in 3,924 fires)
FY 1998: 35,451 acres in 3,238 fires (worst FY '95-'99: 1996 — 95,014 acres in 6,344 fires)
Federally-Owned Land, 1997: 1,276,358.8 acres, or 1,994.31 square miles (4.223%)
Non-Federal Lands, 1997: 29,626,681 acres, or 46,291.7 square miles (95.78%)
Nat'l. Forests (6): Bienville, Delta, DeSoto, Holly Springs, Homochitto, Tombigbee (1,158,000 acres)
National Parks (4): Brice's Crossroads (battlefield site), Gulf Islands Nat'l Seashore (105,900 acres), Tupelo Battlefield Monument, Vicksburg National Military Park (1,620 acres)
Land In National Parks: 107,500 acres (168.1 square miles)
Land In State Parks: 23,000 acres (35.94 square miles)
State Parks (29): Buccaneer, Casey Jones Railroad Museum, Clarko, Florewood River Plantation, George P. Cossar, Golden Memorial, Great River Road, Gulf Marine, Holmes County, Hugh White, J.P. Coleman, John Kyle, Lake Lincoln, Lake Lowndes, LeFleur's Bluff, Legion, Leroy Percy, Nanih Waiya, Natchez, Paul Johnson, Percy Quin, Roosevelt, Sam Dale Historic Site, Shepard, Tishomingo, Tombigbee, Trace, Wall Doxey, and Winterville Mounds Historic Site.
State Historical Sites (5): (considered State Parks) Casey Jones Museum, Florewood River Plantation, Nanih Waiya, Sam Dale, and Winterville Mounds.
National Wildlife Refuges (10): Bogue Chitto, Dahomey, Hillside, Horn Island, Mathews Brake, Morgan Brake, Noxubee, Panther Swamp, Sandhill Crane and Yazoo
Wilderness Areas (3): Black Creek, Gulf Islands National Seashore and Leaf River
Wildlife Management Areas: 36 (Dept. of Wildlife Fisheries & Parks has 21 fishing lakes-5,111 acres)
Federal Indian Reservations & Trust Lands: Over 8,500 members of the Mississippi Band of Choctaws live on the 20,486 acres of tribally-owned land near Philadelphia in Neshoba County.
Climate: semi-tropical, abundant rainfall, long growing season, extreme temperatures unusual.
Annual Rain: 52.8 inches. This is equivalent to 136.4 million acre-feet of water, or 185.4 billion short tons, or 44.5 trillion gallons, or an average of 122 billion gallons a day.
Fresh Water Withdrawn, 1995: 3.204 billion gallons per day (1,191 gallons per capita)
Annual Soil Erosion: 55,300,000 tons
Largest County (in area): Yazoo — 933 square miles (920 square miles land area).
Of the 3,142 counties in the U.S., there are 788 counties larger than Yazoo (in land area). Of Alaska's 27 counties (called divisions or boroughs), all except one are larger than Yazoo, with the largest (Yukon) being a huge 145,287 square miles, over 3 times bigger than the state of Mississippi! The largest county in the U.S., excluding Alaska, is San Bernardino, California — 20,106 sq. miles — 21.5 times larger than Yazoo! San Bernardino County is over 16 times larger than Rhode Island, the nation's smallest state. At 1,231 square miles, Rhode Island is just 298 square miles (32%) bigger than Yazoo County! A total of 45 of California's 58 counties are larger than Yazoo. All 15 counties in Arizona and all 23 counties in Wyoming are larger than Yazoo, with the average size of counties in those two states being 7,576 and 4,222 square miles, respectively! All of New Mexico's 33 counties, except one, are larger than Yazoo. Texas has 109 counties (out of 254) that are larger than Yazoo, 53 of Montana's 56 counties are bigger, 23 of Utah's 29 are larger, 30 of Washington's 39 are bigger, and 14 of Nevada's 16 counties are larger.
Smallest County (in area): Alcorn — 401 sq. miles (400 sq. miles land area. By state code, Mississippi counties cannot legally be less than 400 square miles). There are 564 counties in the U.S. that are smaller than Alcorn County. All of Rhode Island's 5 counties, except one, are smaller than Alcorn. Neighboring Tennessee has 37 counties (out of 95) that are smaller than Alcorn. A total of 103 counties in Georgia (out of 159) are smaller, 87 of Kentucky's 120 counties are smaller, 50 of Virginia's 95 counties are smaller, and even Texas has 12 counties with less area than Alcorn! The smallest county in the U.S. is Kalawao, Hiwaii — 13 square miles. Mississippi's smallest county, Alcorn, is over 30 times larger than the smallest county in the United States!

Map Coordinates and Elevation of Mississippi Cities

City	Coordinates (Center)	Elevation (ft.)	City	Coordinates (Center)	Elevation (ft.)
Aberdeen	N33° 49.518' W88° 32.609'	243	Macon	N33° 06.332' W88° 33.652'	200
Amory	N33° 59.068' W88° 29.285'	252	Madison	N32° 27.716' W90° 06.917'	341
Baldwyn	N34° 30.580' W88° 38.114'	388	Magee	N31° 52.433' W89° 44.020'	433
Batesville	N34° 18.697' W89° 56.664'	244	Magnolia	N31° 08.605' W90° 27.530'	311
Bay Saint Louis	N30° 18.532' W89° 19.802'	28	McComb	N31° 14.626' W90° 27.188'	424
Belzoni	N33° 11.061' W90° 29.365'	118	Mendenhall	N31° 57.717' W89° 52.213'	340
Biloxi	N30° 23.675' W88° 53.602'	17	Meridian	N32° 21.858' W88° 42.218'	353
Booneville	N34° 39.497' W88° 34.002'	538	Moorhead	N33° 27.018' W90° 30.339'	121
Brandon	N32° 16.399' W89° 59.154'	455	Morton	N32° 21.225' W89° 39.280'	475
Brookhaven	N31° 34.746' W90° 26.443'	495	Moss Point	N30° 24.292' W88° 32.055'	23
Canton	N32° 36.762' W90° 02.200'	241	Mound Bayou	N33° 52.693' W90° 43.640'	151
Carthage	N32° 43.965' W89° 32.170'	357	Natchez	N31° 33.650' W91° 23.191'	197
Charleston	N34° 00.418' W90° 03.396'	220	Nettleton	N34° 05.347' W88° 37.340'	268
Clarksdale	N34° 12.014' W90° 34.261'	180	New Albany	N34° 29.652' W89° 00.470'	363
Cleveland	N33° 44.640' W90° 43.490'	144	Newton	N32° 19.279' W89° 09.803'	434
Clinton	N32° 20.495' W90° 19.310'	368	Ocean Springs	N30° 24.686' W88° 49.672'	30
Collins	N31° 38.753' W89° 33.301'	298	Okolona	N34° 00.110' W88° 45.328'	343
Columbia	N31° 15.106' W89° 50.253'	154	Olive Branch	N34° 57.701' W89° 49.776'	388
Columbus	N33° 29.740' W88° 25.635'	217	Oxford	N34° 21.989' W89° 31.164'	509
Corinth	N34° 56.063' W88° 31.340'	446	Pascagoula	N30° 21.949' W88° 33.372'	13
Crystal Springs	N31° 59.242' W90° 21.422'	471	Pass Christian	N30° 18.945' W89° 14.856'	18
D'Iberville	N30° 25.582' W88° 53.451'	20	Pearl	N32° 16.483' W90° 07.921'	282
Drew	N33° 48.577' W90° 31.585'	134	Petal	N31° 20.789' W89° 15.602'	162
Durant	N33° 04.519' W89° 51.271'	265	Philadelphia	N32° 46.302' W89° 07.017'	425
Ellisville	N31° 36.243' W89° 11.736'	273	Picayune	N30° 31.528' W89° 40.769'	79
Eupora	N33° 32.448' W89° 16.029'	390	Pontotoc	N34° 14.873' W88° 59.929'	499
Flowood	N32° 18.579' W90° 08.333'	276	Poplarville	N30° 50.411' W89° 32.057'	315
Forest	N32° 21.879' W89° 28.458'	482	Purvis	N31° 08.605' W89° 24.581'	391
Fulton	N34° 16.439' W88° 24.552'	346	Quitman	N32° 02.405' W88° 43.685'	230
Gautier	N30° 23.149' W88° 36.696'	13	Raymond	N32° 15.566' W90° 25.369'	327
Greenville	N33° 24.614' W91° 03.707'	135	Richland	N32° 14.432' W90° 09.951'	266
Greenwood	N33° 30.969' W90° 10.767'	135	Ridgeland	N32° 25.708' W90° 07.943'	363
Grenada	N33° 46.151' W89° 48.504'	219	Ripley	N34° 43.789' W88° 57.046'	502
Gulfport	N30° 22.049' W89° 05.564'	24	Rolling Fork	N32° 54.398' W90° 52.694'	107
Hattiesburg	N31° 19.634' W89° 17.424'	176	Rosedale	N33° 51.218' W91° 01.678'	154
Hazlehurst	N31° 51.622' W90° 23.764'	484	Ruleville	N33° 43.545' W90° 33.094'	141
Hernando	N34° 49.438' W89° 59.627'	403	Senatobia	N34° 37.063' W89° 58.136'	295
Hollandale	N33° 10.136' W90° 51.240'	118	Shaw	N33° 36.102' W90° 46.423'	135
Holly Springs	N34° 46.059' W89° 26.931'	627	Shelby	N33° 57.056' W90° 46.064'	157
Horn Lake	N34° 57.206' W90° 02.919'	322	Southaven	N34° 59.505' W90° 00.505'	346
Houston	N33° 53.910' W88° 59.958'	361	Starkville	N33° 27.027' W88° 49.102'	340
Indianola	N33° 27.060' W90° 39.311'	125	Tchula	N33° 10.974' W90° 13.376'	118
Itta Bena	N33° 29.710' W90° 19.184'	135	Tupelo	N34° 15.460' W88° 42.203'	291
Iuka	N34° 48.709' W88° 11.397'	589	Verona	N34° 11.660' W88° 43.186'	324
Jackson	N32° 17.900' W90° 11.000'	292	Vicksburg	N32° 21.154' W90° 52.663'	252
Kosciusko	N33° 03.461' W89° 35.258'	492	Water Valley	N34° 09.085' W89° 37.888'	295
Laurel	N31° 41.643' W89° 07.840'	273	Waveland	N30° 17.211' W89° 22.573'	23
Leland	N33° 24.334' W90° 53.868'	130	Waynesboro	N31° 40.485' W88° 38.773'	197
Lexington	N33° 06.798' W90° 03.197'	238	West Point	N33° 36.461' W88° 39.028'	232
Long Beach	N30° 21.036' W89° 09.168'	33	Wiggins	N30° 51.490' W89° 08.128'	265
Louisville	N33° 07.432' W89° 03.293'	577	Winona	N33° 28.919' W89° 43.688'	382
Lucedale	N30° 55.456' W88° 35.537'	282	Yazoo City	N32° 51.319' W90° 24.348'	115

The Ultimate Reference on the State

Mississippi Weather: Statewide

TEMPERATURE AND PRECIPITATION DATA FOR SELECTED MAJOR CITIES

BILOXI

Month	Average Daily Max Temp.	Average Daily Min Temp.	Record High Temp. (Latest Year)	Record Low Temp. (Latest Year)	Normal Monthly Rainfall	Record Monthly Rainfall (Year)	Record Daily Rainfall (Year)
Jan.	59.6	42.3	77 (1952)	10 (1963)	5.38	12.48 (1978)	8.96 (1965)
Feb.	63.2	45.3	78 (1969)	14 (1951)	5.90	11.52 (1979)	4.37 (1979)
Mar.	69.2	52.1	85 (1975)	22 (1980)	5.30	12.66 (1980)	6.45 (1953)
Apr.	76.4	59.6	90 (1955)	30 (1975)	4.35	17.15 (1980)	7.73 (1980)
May	82.8	66.5	98 (1953)	45 (1960)	4.80	12.02 (1972)	6.33 (1978)
June	88.2	72.6	101 (1953)	55 (1956)	4.96	13.03 (1970)	5.33 (1961)
July	90.0	74.5	103 (1980)	60 (1967)	6.49	16.52 (1979)	7.82 (1970)
Aug.	89.7	73.9	104 (2000)	61 (1967)	6.57	14.90 (1970)	4.02 (1971)
Sept.	86.9	70.1	101 (1954)	45 (1967)	5.25	17.25 (1957)	8.55 (1957)
Oct.	79.6	59.6	92 (1969)	32 (1957)	3.29	11.86 (1967)	9.80 (1967)
Nov.	70.6	52.0	84 (1971)	25 (1970)	4.07	7.93 (1975)	3.54 (1961)
Dec.	63.3	45.8	79 (1964)	9 (1962)	5.40	9.37 (1953)	3.42 (1972)

Annual: Mean Temp — 68.1; Mean Max Temp — 76.6; Mean Min Temp — 59.5; Avg. Precipitation — 61.76 inches
Record Monthly Snowfall (Inches): Dec. — 5.0 in 1963; Jan. — 8.0 in 1964; Feb. — 2.0 in 1973; Mar. — 2.0 in 1954

BROOKHAVEN

Month	Average Daily Max Temp.	Average Daily Min Temp.	Record High Temp. (Latest Year)	Record Low Temp. (Latest Year)	Normal Monthly Rainfall	Record Monthly Rainfall (Year)	Record Daily Rainfall (Year)
Jan.	56.3	34.3	82 (1952)	5 (1962)	5.55	10.18 (1972)	2.98 (1963)
Feb.	60.6	36.9	83 (1980)	5 (1951)	5.61	10.46 (1966)	3.93 (1975)
Mar.	69.0	45.1	89 (1974)	14 (1980)	6.42	15.85 (1961)	4.02 (1962)
Apr.	76.5	52.8	92 (1952)	31 (1971)	5.70	15.05 (1974)	6.88 (1955)
May	82.5	60.1	102 (1951)	40 (1960)	5.43	13.69 (1953)	5.98 (1978)
June	88.5	67.0	104 (1952)	49 (1966)	3.99	10.00 (1957)	5.16 (1957)
July	90.5	69.9	102 (1980)	54 (1967)	4.73	10.84 (1979)	3.21 (1964)
Aug.	90.2	69.0	104 (1951)	56 (1967)	4.67	10.76 (1970)	3.59 (1960)
Sept.	85.9	64.1	102 (1980)	37 (1967)	3.50	10.10 (1957)	2.92 (1971)
Oct.	77.5	52.2	95 (1963)	29 (1980)	3.43	9.61 (1964)	6.84 (1964)
Nov.	68.1	44.7	86 (1961)	19 (1979)	4.58	9.71 (1957)	3.59 (1961)
Dec.	59.8	37.4	84 (1951)	8 (1962)	6.48	14.81 (1971)	6.75 (1971)

Annual: Mean Temp — 64.1; Mean Max Temp — 75.5; Mean Min Temp — 52.8; Avg. Precipitation — 60.09 inches
Record Monthly Snowfall (Inches): Dec. — 4.7 in 1963; Jan. — 4.8 in 1977; Feb. — 5.0 in 1960; Mar. — 4.0 in 1968

Mississippi Weather: Statewide

TEMPERATURE AND PRECIPITATION DATA FOR SELECTED MAJOR CITIES

CLARKSDALE

Month	Average Daily Max Temp.	Average Daily Min Temp.	Record High Temp. (Latest Year)	Record Low Temp. (Latest Year)	Normal Monthly Rainfall	Record Monthly Rainfall (Year)	Record Daily Rainfall (Year)
Jan.	47.8	29.8	80 (1975)	0 (1962)	4.22	10768 (1974)	3.70 (1951)
Feb.	52.8	33.5	81 (1962)	0 (1951)	4.77	10.74 (1956)	5.77 (1966)
Mar.	62.9	41.6	87 (1963)	18 (1980)	5.34	12.43 (1973)	4.40 (1955)
Apr.	73.4	51.4	93 (1952)	32 (1975)	4.73	11.01 (1973)	3.67 (1955)
May	81.9	60.4	101 (1953)	40 (1954)	5.21	14.27 (1953)	4.20 (1974)
June	89.5	68.1	107 (1953)	53 (1956)	4.31	10.77 (1974)	5.95 (1980)
July	92.2	71.4	107 (1952)	58 (1972)	3.93	10.21 (1958)	4.10 (1980)
Aug.	90.5	69.5	107 (1951)	55 (1974)	2.88	5.86 (1975)	3.34 (1970)
Sept.	84.9	63.3	105 (1951)	41 (1967)	3.17	8.74 (1958)	3.90 (1959)
Oct.	75.2	51.1	96 (1954)	31 (1952)	2.97	7.05 (1970)	3.40 (1957)
Nov.	63.2	42.2	87 (1971)	16 (1970)	5.30	11.68 (1957)	4.95 (1972)
Dec.	52.2	34.0	80 (1951)	5 (1962)	5.59	9.64 (1951)	3.71 (1957)

Annual: Mean Temp — 61.8; Mean Max Temp — 72.2; Mean Min Temp — 51.4; Avg. Precipitation — 52.39 inches

Record Monthly Snowfall (Inches): Dec. — 9.0 in 1963; Jan. — 5.0 in 1962; Feb. — 4.0 in 1951; Mar. — 13.0 in 1968

COLUMBUS

Month	Average Daily Max Temp.	Average Daily Min Temp.	Record High Temp. (Latest Year)	Record Low Temp. (Latest Year)	Normal Monthly Rainfall	Record Monthly Rainfall (Year)	Record Daily Rainfall (Year)
Jan.	52.0	30.2	81 (1952)	-1 (1962)	5.69	13.50 (1979)	4.24 (1979)
Feb.	57.1	33.2	84 (1962)	1 (1951)	5.38	10.31 (1956)	4.24 (1965)
Mar.	66.4	41.9	88 (1967)	13 (1980)	6.41	15.49 (1980)	5.15 (1951)
Apr.	75.6	50.1	90 (1978)	29 (1958)	6.18	16.51 (1979)	8.58 (1979)
May	82.5	58.4	96 (1962)	35 (1976)	4.98	12.05 (1978)	3.13 (1980)
June	89.0	65.8	105 (1954)	42 (1956)	3.70	7.32 (1957)	2.50 (1956)
July	91.9	69.2	108 (1952)	53 (1967)	4.95	18.93 (1968)	15.68 (1968)
Aug.	91.5	68.4	108 (2000)	50 (1956)	3.84	7.13 (1970)	4.04 (1962)
Sept.	86.2	62.2	105 (1954)	36 (1967)	3.80	12.07 (1979)	3.28 (1979)
Oct.	76.6	48.8	98 (1954)	25 (1957)	3.29	7.37 (1975)	4.52 (1975)
Nov.	66.4	40.7	87 (1961)	15 (1955)	4.79	10.00 (1957)	2.97 (1979)
Dec.	56.2	33.4	83 (1978)	4 (1962)	6.05	13.52 (1951)	4.00 (1973)

Annual: Mean Temp — 62.3; Mean Max Temp — 74.3; Mean Min Temp — 50.2; Avg. Precipitation — 59.06 inches

Record Monthly Snowfall (Inches): Dec. — 8.0 in 1958; Jan. — 14.0 in 1964; Feb. — 10.3 in 1960; Mar. — 7.0 in 1968

Mississippi Weather: Statewide

TEMPERATURE AND PRECIPITATION DATA FOR SELECTED MAJOR CITIES

GREENWOOD

Month	Average Daily Max Temp.	Average Daily Min Temp.	Record High Temp. (Latest Year)	Record Low Temp. (Latest Year)	Normal Monthly Rainfall	Record Monthly Rainfall (Year)	Record Daily Rainfall (Year)
Jan.	51.5	33.5	82 (1972)	-2 (1977)	4.86	12.12 (1951)	3.76 (1973)
Feb.	56.6	36.9	81 (1962)	-4 (1951)	4.52	10.42 (1956)	3.82 (1959)
Mar.	65.7	45.1	88 (1963)	15 (1980)	5.80	16.84 (1973)	6.83 (1955)
Apr.	74.8	53.1	92 (1972)	31 (1975)	5.09	10.91 (1964)	4.64 (1953)
May	82.3	61.6	100 (1951)	31 (1943)	5.25	14.18 (1953)	4.48 (1962)
June	89.4	68.7	104 (1954)	49 (1956)	4.28	8.98 (1976)	4.69 (1980)
July	91.5	71.7	105 (1980)	56 (1953)	4.25	11.12 (1963)	4.24 (1959)
Aug.	90.7	70.4	106 (2000)	55 (1976)	2.63	7.69 (1964)	3.56 (1964)
Sept.	85.7	64.6	102 (1964)	35 (1967)	3.32	19.65 (1958)	8.07 (1958)
Oct.	76.3	52.2	97 (1954)	27 (1952)	3.64	10.22 (1970)	4.10 (1970)
Nov.	65.3	44.1	89 (1972)	17 (1976)	4.99	13.20 (1957)	3.67 (1957)
Dec.	55.5	36.8	81 (1951)	8 (1962)	5.86	11.13 (1961)	6.15 (1954)

Annual: Mean Temp — 63.5; Mean Max Temp — 73.8; Mean Min Temp — 53.2; Avg. Precipitation — 54.49 inches

Record Monthly Snowfall (Inches): Dec. — 4.0 in 1963; Jan. — 5.9 in 1966; Feb. — 8.0 in 1960; Mar. — 6.0 in 1968

HATTIESBURG

Month	Average Daily Max Temp.	Average Daily Min Temp.	Record High Temp. (Latest Year)	Record Low Temp. (Latest Year)	Normal Monthly Rainfall	Record Monthly Rainfall (Year)	Record Daily Rainfall (Year)
Jan.	57.8	34.3	83 (1957)	7 (1963)	5.78	10.36 (1979)	4.95 (1975)
Feb.	62.3	37.2	84 (1962)	7 (1951)	5.71	17.59 (1961)	7.02 (1961)
Mar.	70.4	45.2	89 (1974)	17 (1980)	6.27	13.94 (1961)	4.43 (1974)
Apr.	78.2	53.9	94 (1955)	31 (1973)	4.79	13.24 (1979)	5.60 (1979)
May	84.1	60.8	104 (1951)	40 (1971)	5.19	10.45 (1980)	4.91 (1978)
June	90.0	67.6	106 (1963)	49 (1972)	4.22	10.45 (1975)	2.58 (1951)
July	91.8	70.7	102 (1980)	57 (1953)	5.46	14.52 (1979)	2.70 (1978)
Aug.	91.5	70.3	106 (2000)	55 (1952)	5.23	9.43 (1969)	3.54 (1953)
Sept.	87.5	65.2	100 (1954)	44 (1975)	3.64	14.82 (1957)	4.94 (1958)
Oct.	79.6	52.0	97 (1954)	23 (1952)	3.17	11.37 (1959)	3.73 (1960)
Nov.	69.8	44.1	87 (1972)	20 (1976)	4.83	7.95 (1961)	3.60 (1957)
Dec.	61.5	37.6	84 (1951)	7 (1962)	6.29	14.79 (1953)	4.47 (1967)

Annual: Mean Temp — 65.2; Mean Max Temp — 77.0; Mean Min Temp — 53.0; Avg. Precipitation — 60.58 inches

Record Monthly Snowfall (Inches): Jan. — 7.0 in 1964; Feb. — 3.0 in 1960

Mississippi Weather: Statewide

TEMPERATURE AND PRECIPITATION DATA FOR SELECTED MAJOR CITIES

MERIDIAN

Month	Average Daily Max Temp.	Average Daily Min Temp.	Record High Temp. (Latest Year)	Record Low Temp. (Latest Year)	Normal Monthly Rainfall	Record Monthly Rainfall (Year)	Record Daily Rainfall (Year)
Jan.	58.4	35.4	83 (1950)	0 (1962)	4.33	12.14 (1947)	4.54 (1972)
Feb.	61.8	37.7	85 (1982)	8 (1951)	4.86	12.89 (1961)	5.61 (1961)
Mar.	68.7	43.4	90 (1974)	15 (1980)	6.21	16.47 (1976)	7.00 (1979)
Apr.	78.4	52.3	91 (1970)	29 (1950)	5.10	16.82 (1964)	6.36 (1964)
May	85.2	59.5	99 (1951)	38 (1971)	3.84	9.70 (1980)	5.84 (1952)
June	91.3	67.0	103 (1969)	45 (1956)	3.68	7.81 (1961)	2.65 (1974)
July	92.5	69.9	107 (1980)	55 (1967)	5.12	15.29 (1959)	6.95 (1959)
Aug.	92.2	69.1	106 (2000)	53 (1952)	3.89	8.55 (1960)	3.37 (1963)
Sept.	86.9	63.6	105 (1990)	34 (1967)	3.29	10.24 (1957)	4.67 (1979)
Oct.	78.8	50.8	97 (1954)	24 (1952)	2.18	10.65 (1970)	6.04 (1970)
Nov.	67.7	40.7	87 (1946)	16 (1976)	3.51	13.93 (1948)	4.50 (1957)
Dec.	59.8	36.0	82 (1982)	4 (1962)	5.57	14.79 (1973)	8.13 (1973)

Annual: Mean Temp — 64.1; Mean Max Temp — 76.3; Mean Min Temp — 51.8; Avg. Precipitation — 56.71 inches

Record Monthly Snowfall (Inches): Dec. — 17.6 in 1963; Jan. — 5.8 in 1948; Feb. — 3.1 in 1960; Mar. — 1.5 in 1968

TUPELO

Month	Average Daily Max Temp.	Average Daily Min Temp.	Record High Temp. (Latest Year)	Record Low Temp. (Latest Year)	Normal Monthly Rainfall	Record Monthly Rainfall (Year)	Record Daily Rainfall (Year)
Jan.	48.8	30.9	80 (1972)	-12 (1966)	4.89	14.81 (1974)	4.20 (1951)
Feb.	54.4	34.0	83 (1977)	-1 (1951)	4.72	9.32 (1953)	3.70 (1966)
Mar.	64.3	43.2	88 (1963)	7 (1980)	6.07	17.20 (1980)	9.40 (1955)
Apr.	73.9	51.0	90 (1961)	23 (1973)	5.25	11.28 (1956)	7.26 (1962)
May	80.9	59.5	98 (1977)	30 (1976)	5.72	17.96 (1978)	5.26 (1970)
June	87.8	66.5	104 (1954)	41 (1966)	3.84	9.52 (1957)	3.22 (1978)
July	90.7	70.6	106 (1952)	50 (1967)	4.30	11.52 (1964)	5.01 (1963)
Aug.	89.9	69.3	107 (1937)	50 (1967)	3.05	10.32 (1961)	7.10 (1961)
Sept.	84.7	63.3	104 (1980)	40 (1916)	3.60	10.03 (1958)	3.61 (1979)
Oct.	74.9	49.8	95 (1963)	24 (1980)	3.42	9.03 (1970)	4.40 (1970)
Nov.	63.5	41.7	84 (1971)	11 (1976)	4.85	14.89 (1957)	3.70 (1961)
Dec.	52.8	34.1	81 (1951)	-1 (1963)	6.16	11.30 (1961)	4.10 (1951)

Annual: Mean Temp — 61.7; Mean Max Temp — 72.2; Mean Min Temp — 51.2; Avg. Precipitation — 55.87 inches

Record Monthly Snowfall (Inches): Nov. — 1.0 in 1969; Dec. — 6.0 in 1958; Jan. — 13.0 in 1966; Feb. — 4.2 in 1960; Mar. — 11.0 in 1968 (Average Annual Snowfall is 2.4 inches)

Mississippi Weather: Statewide

Seasonal/Annual Temperatures and Precipitation

	TEMPERATURE (°F)					PRECIPITATION (INCHES)				
DIVISION	WIN.	SPRING	SUM.	FALL	ANNUAL	WIN.	SPRING	SUM.	FALL	ANNUAL
Upper Delta	44	64	80	62	63	23.1	30.7	8.8	10.9	74.5
North Central	45	63	79	61	62	24.8	32.0	9.6	10.0	76.4
Northeast	44	63	79	61	62	27.5	37.8	9.9	9.2	84.4
Lower Delta	47	66	81	64	64	22.1	31.4	9.4	9.8	72.7
Central	48	65	79	63	64	18.8	32.9	9.8	9.2	70.7
East Central	47	65	79	62	63	18.2	33.6	10.9	8.5	71.2
Southwest	51	67	80	65	66	20.8	29.6	12.3	11.9	74.6
South Central	51	68	80	65	66	21.7	28.3	12.1	12.9	75.0
Southeast	51	67	79	64	65	18.9	28.6	14.2	9.8	71.5
Coastal	54	68	80	66	67	26.3	32.0	17.8	11.9	88.0

Winter: December, January, and February. Spring: March, April, and May. Summer: June, July & August. Fall: September, October, and November. Source: National Weather Service Forecast Office for 1991.

NOAA Weather Radio broadcasts nationwide on these frequencies:
162.400, 162.425, 162.450, 162.475, 162.500, 162.525 and 162.550 MHz
In Mississippi, tune to one of the following stations closest to your location:

Ackerman (KIH-51)	162.475	Gulfport (KIH-21)	162.400	Melba (KIH-47)	162.475
Booneville (KIH-53)	162.550	Inverness (KIH-50)	162.550	Meridian (KIH-49)	162.550
Bude (KIH-48)	162.550	Jackson (KIH-38)	162.400	Oxford (KIH-52)	162.400
Columbia (Repeater)	162.400	Kosciusko (WWG-38)	162.425	Parchman (WWG-39)	162.500

Freeze Data, 30-Year Means

	LAST SPRING DATE		FIRST FALL DATE		NO. DAYS BETWEEN DATES	
City	24° or below	32° or below	32° or below	24° or below	24° or below	32° or below
Biloxi	None	Feb 16	Nov 4	None	---	261
Clarksdale	Feb 17	Mar 31	Nov 2	Nov 4	260	216
Columbus	Feb 17	Feb 27	Nov 3	Nov 4	260	249
Corinth	Mar 10	Mar 31	Oct 7	Nov 4	239	190
Greenville	Feb 17	Feb 26	Nov 4	Nov 5	261	251
Hernando	Feb 16	Mar 31	Nov 2	Nov 4	261	216
Jackson	Feb 16	Mar 15	Nov 2	Nov 5	262	232
Kosciusko	Feb 17	Mar 31	Nov 2	Nov 4	260	216
Laurel	Feb 17	Mar 11	Nov 4	Nov 5	261	238
Meridian	Feb 16	Mar 11	Nov 3	Nov 5	262	237
Natchez	None	Feb 16	Nov 4	Nov 9	---	261
Tupelo	Feb 16	Mar 31	Nov 3	Nov 4	261	217
Tylertown	Feb 16	Mar 11	Nov 4	None	---	238

Source: National Weather Service Forecast Office for 1991. Data based on 30 years of records.

Mississippi Weather: Statewide

Average Temperatures Statewide: 80° summer/42° winter.
Monthly Average Temperatures: highest 92.5°; lowest 34.9°; spread 57.6° (rank 47).
Average Annual Precipitation Statewide: 52.86 inches of rain (very little snow) — equivalent to 136.4 million acre-feet, or 185.4 billion short tons, or 44.5 trillion gallons, or an average of 122 billion gallons a day. The average for the continental U.S. is about 4.14 trillion gallons a day. Therefor, Mississippi receives on average approximately 1/34th (almost 3%) of the nation's total rainfall.
Average Precipitation by Season (inches): Winter 15.26; Spring 14.86; Summer 13.44; Fall 9.30
Average Annual Surface Runoff: about 25 inches, almost half the amount of annual precipitation.

WEATHER RECORDS & EXTREMES

Highest Temperature: 115° on July 29, 1930, at Holly Springs. That same day, the temperature reached 114° at Aberdeen, 111° at Oxford and Starkville, and 110° in Yazoo City.
Lowest Temperature: -19° on Jan. 30, 1966, near Corinth. A low of -13° was recorded at the University of Mississippi on Jan. 21,1985. A reading of -12° was recorded at Holly Springs on Dec. 24, 1963. Unofficially, the temperature in Macon in Noxubee County dipped to -23° on Jan. 23, 1940.
Driest Year: For one location, Yazoo City holds the record — only 25.97 inches for the entire year of 1936.
Most Rainfall (Inches): In 24 hours — 15.68 on July 9, 1968 at Columbus. Jackson had 6.97 on 10/4/64.
Greatest monthly rainfall — 30.75 inches in July 1916 at Merrill in George County.
Greatest annual rainfall — 114.86 in 1973 in Jackson County. Beaumont had 102.89 in 1961.
Greatest one-hour rainfall — 4.06 on Apr. 11, 1979, in Jackson (Meridian had the previous record one-hour rainfall of 3.73 on Aug. 13, 1906). Exactly one year later, on Apr. 11, 1980, there was a record 4.80 inches for the date for Jackson, but that was for an entire day.
Most Snowfall: In 24 hours — 18.0 inches at Mt. Pleasant and Tunica on Dec. 23, 1963.
Unofficially, Macon in Noxubee County recorded 24 inches in about 10 hours on Jan. 17, 1940.
Greatest snowfall in a month — 23.0 inches at Cleveland in January 1966.
Greatest snowfall in a single season — 25.2 inches at Senatobia during the winter of 1967-68.
Most Destructive Ice Storms: Thirty-eight deaths were attributed to an ice storm that hit Miss., Ark. and S.C. on **Jan 24-31, 1948**; On **Jan 28-Feb 1, 1951**, one of the worst ice storms ever hit Ala., Ga., Tenn. and northern Mississippi causing an estimated $100 million damage from downed trees, broken power lines and collapsed roofs. It left 22 dead (6 in Miss.) and over 500 seriously injured. On **Feb 10, 1994**, a fierce ice storm hit northern Miss. In a 24-county area, the storm left over 200,000 households (over 500,000 residents) without electricity and affected 491 water systems serving over 740,000 people. A 3 to 6-inch sheet of ice coated the area and left snapped trees and downed power lines. Some of the hardest hit major communities were Greenville, Drew, Oxford and Cleveland. Although no deaths were reported, it was the worst ice storm to hit the state since Jan. 1951. Damage estimates exceeded $1.6 billion with damage to 3.7 million acres of timber. A **1998 Christmas Eve** ice storm hit a large part of Mississippi, especially central and northern sections. While not near as severe as the ice storm of Feb. 1994, power was lost in more than 200,000 homes and millions of tons of fallen trees, branches and debris were left behind.
Most Unusual Weather Occurrence: On May 11, 1894, at Bovina, 8 miles east of Vicksburg, a gopher turtle measuring 6 by 8 inches and entirely encased in ice fell with the hail.
Highest Wind: Not counting tornadoes, the greatest wind was produced by Great Hurricane Camille (the only category 5 hurricane to ever hit the U.S. mainland), which hit the Mississippi coast the night of Aug 17-18, 1969. A wind gust of 229 mph was recorded at Biloxi on Aug. 17! The winds were high enough to break many of the wind gauges before accurate readings could be taken.
National Weather Service radar data strongly suggests that the $30 million damage in Natchez on Feb. 26, 1998, was caused by a bow echo and associated straight-line winds in excess of 70 mph, although 2 separate F1 (minimum) tornadoes were produced nearby.
The greatest sustained wind speed ever recorded in Jackson was 68 mph on March 10, 1952. There were probably higher gusts.

WEATHER PHONE NUMBERS
Federal Aviation Administration, Pilot Weather Briefing Flight Planning   1-800-962-2318
Weather Service/Administration, Special Weather Info & To Report Bad Weather; Jackson   (601) 936-2189
National Weather Service; Thompson Field; Jackson, Miss. on the Internet — http://www.jannws.state.ms.us

Mississippi Weather: Statewide

VIOLENT WEATHER

Hurricanes (from 1906-11/1/2000, MS felt the effects of 10 hurricanes—one category 1, two category 2s, six category 3s and one category 5)

Hurricane of Sept. 19-24, 1906, killed 350 in Mississippi and Louisiana.

Hurricane of Sept. 29, 1915, left 500 dead in Mississippi and Louisiana.

Hurricane of Sept. 19, 1947, killed 27 people in Miss. & caused much damage.

Hurricane Audrey, June 25-30, 1957, killed 390 in Miss., Ala., Lou. & Tex.

Hurricane Hilda of Oct. 4-7, 1964, killed 38 in Mississippi, Georgia & Louisiana.

Hurricane Betsy of Sept. 7-12, 1965, killed 74 in Mississippi, Florida and Louisiana.

Hurricane Camille of Aug. 17 & 18, 1969, caused 144 deaths in Mississippi and floods in Virginia that drowned 112 more people. It had a record storm surge in excess of 25 feet, and had winds in excess of 200 mph. Camille did $1.3 billion (in 1969 dollars) property damage in Mississippi.

Hurricane Frederic on Sept. 12, 1979, struck the coast between Pascagoula and Mobile, Alabama causing hundreds of millions of dollars damage in Mississippi alone with 400,000 people evacuated from coastal areas of Mississippi, Alabama, Florida and Louisiana.

Hurricane Elena made landfall on the Mississippi coast on Sept. 2, 1985, after looping near the west coast of Florida and causing storm-surge flooding from Florida to Mississippi. The death toll was 4 and damage estimates of $1 to 1.5 billion.

Hurricane Georges made landfall at Ocean Springs about 4 a.m. Sept. 28, 1998, with 105 mph winds. About 1.5 million people had evacuated the coastal areas of Florida, Alabama, Mississippi, and Louisiana. There were no deaths of serious injuries in the state, but it caused widespread flooding after stalling over Mississippi for a day and dumping 2 feet of rain. Total U.S. damage: $5 billion.

> Through Oct. 2000, there have been no deaths from hurricanes in Mississippi for over 31 years — since Camille in Aug. 1969.

> The number of recorded tornadoes in the U.S. has risen sharply — 1950s: 4,796; 1960s: 6,813; 1970s: 8,580; 1980s: 8,196; and 1990s (through July 1999): 10,804. That's 39,189 tornadoes in 5 decades! The number of *reported* tornadoes has more than doubled from the 1950s to the 1990s. And, evidence suggests that many tornadoes go undetected! Of the more than 1,400 reported tornadoes and 130 tornado-related deaths nationwide in 1998, four twisters were responsible for 82 of the fatalities. Mississippi ranks 5th nationally in the number of tornadoes (1,303 from 1/1/1950-12/31/1999), but second (after Texas) in the number ranked "strong and violent" and first in tornado-related deaths with 1,183 killed since 1916 (389 killed from 1/1/1950-12/31/99). Figures for 8 decades show an average of 15 people in Mississippi die from twisters each year, with annual deaths ranging from 0 to 118 in 1971. Since 1950 (thru 1999), 48 Mississippi counties have reported deaths from tornadoes with 34 counties reporting no deaths. On a national average, 37 percent of all tornadoes are considered unusually powerful. In Miss. the average is 60 percent. Winds in that category (F-5) range as high as 300 mph!

Worst Tornadoes (Through Oct. 2000)

1840 — May 7: one of the worst tornadoes in history killed 317 people in Natchez (48 on land and 269 on the river) and did $1,260,000 property damage, a huge sum in the dollar value of 1840. This 2-mile wide twister is still considered to be "the most destructive single-location tornado" ever in the U.S.!

1882 — April 22: one of the worst tornadoes in history completely destroyed Monticello, Mississippi.

1883 — April 22: a single tornado hit Beauregard, Mississippi killing 40 people.

1884 — February 19: an outbreak of storms that produced a swarm of 60+ tornadoes killed an estimated 800 in Mississippi and five other Southern states plus Indiana.

1908 — April 24: a series of tornadoes killed 155 and injured 970 statewide — 102 dead in Wayne and Lamar Counties alone, including 47 dead and over 300 injured in the town of Purvis.

1920 — April 5: a tornado in east central Mississippi killed 130 and injured 659; On April 20, a lone twister killed 37 people in West Point and Aberdeen, Mississippi, and injured hundreds more.

1921 — April 26: a tornado demolished the town of Braxton (Simpson Co.) causing 10 deaths & 40 injuries.

1925 — December 8: a twister struck Yazoo City killing 2, injuring 99 and causing $500,000 damage.

1932 — March 21: a swarm of 27 tornadoes killed 268 & injured 1,874 in Miss., Ala., Ga. & Tenn.

1936 — April 5: a twister hit Tupelo cutting a path of destruction a half-mile wide and 4 miles long killing 216 people, injuring 659 and causing over $3 million damage.

1942 — March 16: a series of tornadoes killed 75 and injured 500 from central to northeast Mississippi.

1945 — January 5 & 6: two tornadoes battered the Delta counties of Washington, Sunflower and Carroll plus Wilkinson and Amite counties causing 8 deaths and extensive property damage.

1945 — February 12: a tornado killed 43 and injured hundreds in Miss. & Ala. Property damage extensive.

1949 — March 24: six were killed by a tornado in Washington County, Mississippi.

1952 — March 21 & 22: 31 twisters killed 208 and injured 1,154 in Miss., Ala., Ark., Tenn. & Mo.

Mississippi Weather: Statewide

1953 — Dec. 5: a tornado hit Vicksburg killing 38, injuring 270 and causing $25 million property damage.

1955 — February 1: tornadoes in Tunica, Mississippi killed 31 persons and injured at least 100 others.

1957 — November 8: 13 persons were killed and 200 injured in a tornado in Mississippi and Louisiana.

1958 — February 26: 13 persons killed & 70 injured with extensive property damage in south central Miss.

1966 — March 3: an F-5 tornado (the strongest) swept through central Mississippi killing 57 people, including 12 in Jackson's Candlestick Park area, and injuring 504. Damages in Hinds county alone totaled $12 million. This twister stayed on the ground for 200 miles!

1969 — January 23: a tornado killed 32 people in Copiah, Simpson and Smith counties.

1970 — April 19: a twister hit Corinth and Ripley killing 5, injuring 70 and causing much property damage.

1971 — February 4: a tornado ripped apart a mobile home in Grenada killing 7; On Feb. 21, one of the most deadly single tornadoes of all time killed 58 in Pugh City. Another hit Yazoo County, destroying Little Yazoo, then raking Benton and Midway — 9 dead and damage of $2 million with 50 businesses and homes destroyed and 70 severely damaged. Up to 50 other tornadoes hit the Delta the same day with damage and/or deaths & injuries at Cary, Belzoni, Inverness, Delta City, Oxford, Moorhead and Greenwood. All toll on Feb. 21: 110 dead, 1,511 injured and $17 million in damage. This was one of Mississippi's worst years for tornadoes with 118 killed.

1974 — April 3 & 4: a Palm Sunday outbreak of 148 twisters killed 350 and injured 5,484 in Mississippi and eleven other states. Total damage estimates were close to $1 billion.

1975 — January 10: a tornado leveled a shopping center in McComb killing 12 people, injuring about 200, with property damage estimated in the millions of dollars.

1976 — Mississippi was hit by 34 tornadoes that killed 5 people, injured 292 & caused $40 million damage: February 18, a twister hit a Clinton mobile home park, injuring 50 and causing $2.2 million in damage. Twisters in Leake & Neshoba counties killed 1, injured 27 and caused $11 million damage; March 20, a tornado hit parts of Clay, Webster & Monroe counties killing 1, injuring 9 and causing $1.5 million damage; March 29, a twister hit Canton killing 3 people and injuring 177. Another half-mile wide twister cut a 107-mile long path through 6 counties hitting the towns of Gallman and Newton and just missing Meridian. It injured 8 people & caused $9.3 million damage

1977 — April 4: tornadoes killed 22 in Mississippi, Alabama and Georgia.

1982 — In January, a tornado touched down south of Newton, killing one person and injuring 27 others; In early April, a twister hit Neshoba County, killing 3 and injuring 40.

1984 — April 21: tornadoes raced across 10 counties in northern Mississippi, leveling the heart of Water Valley in Yalobusha County, killing 15 people and causing $21 million in damage.

1987 — February 28: a devastating tornado, the strongest in the U.S. in 2 years, hit Jones County killing 7 people in its 20-mile long path. Hardest hit was the town of Glade with 900 residents.

1992 — March 10: a twister hit the Zero community in Lauderdale County killing 3 people, injured 58 and damaged or destroyed 200 homes; November 21 & 22: several tornadoes hit the state. Brandon and Flowood took the brunt. Ten of the 15 who died statewide were from Rankin County, where more than 400 dwellings were damaged or destroyed. For the entire year of 1992, there were 54 tornadoes, resulting in 18 deaths and 353 injuries. While only 4 percent of the nation's tornadoes were in Mississippi, the state accounted for 46% of total U.S. deaths and 27% of injuries in 1992.

1994 — April 12: a tornado hit Woolmarket in Harrison County killing 2 people; November 27: tornadoes and high winds left more than 100 homes damaged and 12 homes destroyed in 6 counties. A tree fell on a mobile home in Magee in Simpson County killing a woman and her 2-year-old son.

1995 — Two people were killed and 21 injured during the year as 54 tornadoes were reported.

1997 — March 1: at least 4 twisters hit northern Mississippi, mainly Union and Pontotoc Counties. In Randolph, Mississippi, a 50-year-old man was killed, over 20 injured and many homes destroyed.

1998 — April 8: several tornadoes hit Miss., Ala. & Ga. killing 39 people and injuring over 200. Most of the 33 killed in Ala. were in Jefferson County just outside Birmingham where an F-5 tornado hit. Five people were killed in Ga. For the most part, Mississippi was spared, but one 16-year-old boy was killed in a mobile home in Pontotoc County; The NWS says that severe thunderstorms with strong straight-line winds caused the falling trees that killed 2 people in vehicles at Hattiesburg on June 5.

1999 — April 14: a deadly F3 (158-206 mph winds), half-mile wide tornado hit Covington, Jasper & Jones counties damaging 50+ homes in Hot Coffee, SoSo, Moss, and Hebron, where it killed one person.

Weather in Mississippi: Jackson

TEMPERATURES (HOT) — THROUGH OCT. 2000

Highest Temperature: 107° (four times) — September 6 & 7, 1925; July 29, 1930; and Aug. 30, 2000.

No. of Days with 100° or Above: 1902 — 46 days; 1980 — 29 days; 1954 — 27 days; 1952 — 26 days; 1924 & 1930 — 23 days each; 1925, 1951 & 2000 — 21 days each; 1943, 1947 & 1969 — 15 days each; 1921 — 13 days; 1896, 1897, 1944 & 1990 — 12 days each; and 1914 — 10 days.

The temperature was 100° or higher for 12 straight days twice in Jackson — Aug. 13-24, 1902 and June 22-July 2, 1969. The years with the least number of 100° or above days were 1906, 1919, 1934, 1942 and 1995 with only one day each year. There were just two 100° or higher readings in 1999 — 100° on Aug. 7 and 104° on Aug. 19 (broke the record set in 1902). The temp didn't reach 100° in 2000 until July 15 when it hit 101°, then 102° July 16, 102° July 17, 101° July 19 (tied record), and 102° July 20 (record). August was the 6th hottest Aug. on record with 12 days above 100°: 102° Aug. 10 (tied record); 101° Aug. 16; 103° Aug. 17; 103° Aug. 18; 101° Aug. 20; 103° Aug. 21 (record); 101° Aug. 25 (tied record); 102° Aug. 26; 102° Aug. 28; 104° Aug. 29 (tied record); 107° Aug. 30 (highest in 70 years, highest ever for August, and ties the highest ever recorded in Jackson); and 106° Aug. 31 (record). That was 17 days in July and August above 100° — 101° to 107° (avg. of 102.5°) — setting 4 daily records and tying 4 more to make the summer of 2000 the hottest in 20 years! Then, Sept. started with 4 days in a row above 100°. The temp has hit 100° or above in 55 of 105 years (1896-2000). All 100° or above readings occurred on 481 days, or 2.4% of the 19,997 days of the 55 years (54 years + Jan. 1-Sept. 30, 2000). Over the 104.75-year period (1/1/1896-9/30/2000), the 481 days represent about 1.26% of the 38,259 days of the period. Almost 10% of the 100° days occurred in 1902 and almost half (49.27%) in 9 years: 1902, 1924, 1925, 1930, 1951, 1952, 1954, 1980 and 2000. The longest period of years that had 100° or above was 1933 through 1944, a 12-year stretch. Through Sept. 2000, the earliest date the temp reached 100° of higher in Jackson is May 28 (100° in 1911) and the latest in the year is Sept. 24 (101° in 1921). Temperatures in Jackson have always been below 100° in Jan., Feb., March, April, Oct., Nov. and Dec. with all 100° or above readings occurring in May, June, July, Aug. & Sept.

> READ ABOUT HEATWAVE 2000 ☞

Years That Had No 100° Readings (with the highest temperature for the year):
1898 (99); 1903 (98); 1904 (98); 1905 (97); 1907 (99); 1908 (99); 1910 (99); 1912 (98); 1916 (98); 1920 (98); 1922 (98); 1923 (97); 1926 (98); 1929 (97); 1932 (98); 1945 (97); 1946 (97); 1949 (98); 1950 (99); 1955 (97); 1956 (99); 1957 (96); 1958 (95); 1959 (94); 1961 (94); 1962 (99); 1964 (99); 1965 (99); 1967 (96); 1968 (97); 1971 (98); 1972 (99); 1973 (98); 1974 (96); 1975 (95); 1976 (97); 1977 (98); 1978 (99); 1979 (98); 1982 (98); 1983 (99); 1984 (98); 1985 (99); 1989 (98); 1991 (99); 1992 (97); 1993 (99); 1994 (95); 1996 (99); 1997 (99) [lowest max temp was 94 in 1959 & 1961] Max temp of 99° recorded 17 of the years; 98° in 16; 97° in 9; 96° in 3; 95° in 3; & 94° in 2 years. That's 50 years (of 105 years between 1896-2000) in which Jackson has had all below 100° readings. The longest period of consecutive years with below 100° readings was 1971-1979, a 9-year stretch.

> From Jan. 1 thru Oct. 2000, 12 daily temp. records (10 highs & 2 lows) were set or tied in Jackson.

Hottest Year: 1921, when the annual maximum temperature averaged 82.0° **(normal annual high is 76)**

Hottest Seasons (Winter — Dec., Jan. & Feb.; Spring — Mar., Apr. & May; Summer — June, July & Aug.; Autumn — Sept., Oct. & Nov.)
- **Warmest Winter**: 1927, when temperatures for the 3-month period averaged 57.4° (normal is 46.6)
- **Hottest Spring**: 1908, when temperatures for the 3-month period averaged 69.9° (normal is 64.4)
- **Hottest Summer**: 1952, when temperatures for the 3-month period averaged 84.5° (normal is 80.4)
- **Hottest Autumn**: 1927, when temperatures for the 3-month period averaged 71.2° (normal is 65.5)

Record Highs for Each Month: 85° on Jan. 10, 1949; 89° on Feb. 25, 1918; 95° on Mar. 24, 1929; 94° on Apr. 29, 1899 & Apr. 21, 1987; 100° on May 28, 1911; 105° on June 20, 1936; 107° on July 29, 1930; 107° on Aug. 30, 2000; 107° on Sept. 6 & 7, 1925; 98° on Oct. 4, 1911; 89° on Nov. 4, 1922 & Nov. 1, 1927; 84° on Dec. 3, 1922, Dec. 16, 1924, Dec. 6, 1951 & Dec. 7, 1978.

Normal (Average) Highs for Each Month: Jan. — 56; Feb. — 60; Mar. — 69; Apr. — 77; May — 84; June — 91; July — 92; Aug. — 92; Sept. — 88; Oct. — 79; Nov. — 69; Dec. — 59

Hottest/Warmest Months (based on average high temperatures for the entire month):

Month	Avg High	High Mean
Jan:	68.4° in 1950	High Mean was 59.8° in 1950
Feb:	72.0° in 1927	High Mean was 61.8° in 1927
Mar:	78.5° in 1907	High Mean was 67.8° in 1921
Apr:	84.2° in 1925	High Mean was 71.6° in 1925
May:	91.0° in 1899	High Mean was 78.2° in 1896
June:	98.5° in 1902	High Mean was 84.6° in 1952
July:	98.2° in 1902	High Mean was 85.8° in 1980
Aug:	99.3° in 1954	High Mean was 86.0° in 1954
Sept:	98.3° in 1925	High Mean was 85.2° in 1925
Oct:	85.5° in 1919	High Mean was 75.4° in 1919
Nov:	78.2° in 1909	High Mean was 63.8° in 1927
Dec:	69.2° in 1933	High Mean was 58.3° in 1984

> Since 1896, the daily *low* temperature in Jackson, Miss. has been 80 degrees or above only 3 times: September 1, 1905, July 26, 1980 and July 9, 1998.

> The winter of 1998-99 was the 4th warmest & winter of 1999-00 the 3rd warmest on record in Jackson.

> During Heatwave 2000, there were 8 days in a row above 100° in Jackson — the last 4 days of August and the first 4 days of September. It was the longest stretch of 100° or above temperatures since 1988 when there were 8 straight days of 100° or above.

Weather in Mississippi: Jackson

TEMPERATURES (COLD) — THROUGH OCT. 2000

Lowest Temperature: -5° on Jan. 27, 1940. The temperature has only been below zero one other time in Jackson and that was a reading of -1° on Jan. 12, 1962. Single-digit temperatures have been recorded only 37 times in Jackson, including these two readings.

Earliest First Freeze Date on Record: October 9, 1917 (Average First Freeze Date is November 2).

Latest Last Freeze Date on Record: April 25, 1910 (Average Last Freeze Date is March 15).

Coldest Weather; Number of Days per Year w/Maximum Temp. 32° or Less: 8 in 1940; 7 in 1978; 6 in 1905 & 1963; 5 in 1983, 1985 & 1989; and 4 days each of the years 1900, 1961, 1958 & 1981.

Coldest Weather; Number of Days per Year with Minimum Temp. 32° or Less: 74 in 1968; 72 in 1978; 68 in 1977; 63 in 1979; 61 in 1976; 60 in 1900 & 1963; 58 in 1967; 57 in 1958 & 1980; 55 in 1983. The year with the least number of freezing days is 1921 with 8.

Coldest Continuous Period: The record for *continuous* below 32 degree readings was 86 hours set in February 1985. A stretch of 76 hours and 32 minutes of subfreezing weather ended at 11:57 a.m. on February 5, 1996. From January 14-February 3, 1940, the low each day was 32° or below for 21 consecutive days. During that period, the low was 10° or less for 6 consecutive days, January 23-28!

Greatest Temperature Falls: 24 hrs—57° (82° to 25°); 12 hrs—50° (82° to 32°); 6 hrs—40° (83° to 43°)

Coldest Year: 1900, when the annual minimum temperature averaged 49.4° (**normal annual low is 52°**)

Coldest Seasons (Winter—Dec., Jan. & Feb.; Spring—Mar., Apr. & May; Summer—June, July & Aug.; Autumn—Sept., Oct. & Nov.)
  Coldest Winter: 1921, when temperatures for the 3-month period averaged 41.2° (normal is 46.6)
  Coolest Spring: 1971, when temperatures for the 3-month period averaged 60.8° (normal is 64.4)
  Coolest Summer: 1900, when temperatures for the 3-month period averaged 77.2° (normal is 80.4)
  Coolest Autumn: 1976, when temperatures for the 3-month period averaged 60.6° (normal is 65.5)

Record Lows for Each Calender Month: -5° on January 27, 1940; 1° on February 2, 1951; 15° on March 3, 1980; 27° on April 4, 1987; 38° on May 4, 1971; 47° on June 1, 1984; 51° on July 15, 1967; 54° on August 23, 1956; 35° on September 29, 1967; 26° on October 31, 1993; 15° on November 27, 1903; 4° on December 23, 1989.

Normal (Average) Lows for Each Month: Jan. — 33; Feb. — 36; Mar. — 44; Apr. — 52; May — 60; June — 67; July — 71; Aug. — 70; Sept. — 64; Oct. — 50; Nov. — 42; Dec. — 36

Coldest/Coolest Months (based on average low temperatures for the entire month):

Month	Coldest	Low Mean
Jan:	21.9° in 1940	Low Mean was 31.9° in 1940
Feb:	28.2° in 1978	Low Mean was 38.4° in 1905
Mar:	37.6° in 1960	Low Mean was 47.5° in 1960
Apr:	49.7° in 1901	Low Mean was 59.6° in 1898
May:	54.1° in 1900	Low Mean was 67.8° in 1954
June:	61.9° in 1903	Low Mean was 73.5° in 1903
July:	64.8° in 1900	Low Mean was 77.3° in 1967
Aug:	66.7° in 1992	Low Mean was 77.0° in 1967
Sept:	58.2° in 1967	Low Mean was 69.8° in 1967
Oct:	42.6° in 1952	Low Mean was 58.9° in 1952
Nov:	35.6° in 1976	Low Mean was 47.2° in 1976
Dec:	28.8° in 1989	Low Mean was 38.6° in 1963

April 1997 was the first time since 1938 that April was cooler than March in Jackson

There was no freeze at all in Jackson during the entire month of Dec. 1931. During Dec. 1940, the temperature was as low as the freezing mark on only one day. During the month of Jan. there have been as few as 2 days in which the low was at or below 32° — in Jan. in 1921, 1950 and 1953. From Jan. 7 through Feb. 21, 1911, the low never reached as low as the freezing mark — a period of 45 consecutive days when the temperature was always above 32°! Several of the daily lows during the period were in the 60s. In 1898, it remained above 32° for 27 consecutive days from Jan. 5th through Jan. 31st in Jackson.

Monthly Mean Season Average Temperature:
  Winter: Highest — 57.4° in 1927   Lowest — 41.2° in 1978
  Spring: Highest — 69.9° in 1908   Lowest — 60.8° in 1971
  Summer: Highest — 84.5° in 1952   Lowest — 77.2° in 1900
  Autumn: Highest — 71.2° in 1927   Lowest — 60.6° in 1976

Annual Mean Temperature for a Year: Highest — 69.1° in 1927; **Lowest** — 62.4° in 1979.

No. of Winter Heating Degree Days: Normal 1,586; Highest 2,106 in 1978; Lowest 810 in 1927

No. of Seasonal Heating Degree Days: Normal 2,389; Highest 2,971 in 1978; Lowest 1,472 in 1927

Percentage of Possible Sunshine, Monthly Average: Jan 47%; Feb 56%; Mar 59%; Apr 63%; May 63%; June 70%; July 65%; Aug 64%; Sept 61%; Oct 66%; Nov 55%; and Dec 49%.

Lo/Hi Temps in Jackson on the Last Day of the 20th Century / 2nd Millennium, 12/31/1999: 51°/71°

Lo/Hi Temps in Jackson on the First Day of the 21st Century / 3rd Millennium, 01/01/2000: 49°/68°

Weather in Mississippi: Jackson

PRECIPITATION (RAIN) — THROUGH OCT. 2000

Normal Yearly Precipitation: 55.37 inches. This is equivalent to 321,884 acre-feet of water, or 14.02 billion cubic feet, or 874.93 billion pounds, or 437,463,532 short tons, or 105.07 billion gallons — about 287.86 million gallons a day average for Jackson.

No. of Days per Year with Measurable Rain: Most — 148 in 1912; Least — 46 in 1899; Avg. — 110

15 Wettest Years (Inches): 1979 — 92.75; 1982 — 75.63; 1983 — 73.27; 1923 — 72.75; 1964 — 71.45; 1975 — 70.23; 1912 — 65.63; 1961 — 65.07; 1919 — 63.39; 1932 — 63.32; 1980 & 1991 — 63.06; 1971 — 62.06; 1898 — 61.94; 1905 — 61.61.

1912 had the most days with measurable rain — 148, but it was only the 7th wettest year.

15 Driest Years (Inches): 1952 — 31.66; 1963 — 35.03; 1924 — 35.10; 1943 — 37.20; 1964 — 37.70; 1969 — 38.90; 1917 — 39.48; 1930 — 40.29; 1904 — 40.36; 1962 — 40.49; 1910 — 41.89; 1903 — 42.11; 1951 — 42.25; 1933 — 42.36; 1941 — 43.09 **(1999 was 17th driest yr. — 43.24)**

1899 had the least number of days with measurable rain — 46 (yet it was *not* a driest year)

Wettest Seasons (Winter—Dec., Jan. & Feb.; Spring—Mar., Apr. & May; Summer—June, July & Aug.; Fall—Sept., Oct. & Nov.)
- **Winter**: 1982-83, with monthly average of 10.81 inches.
- **Spring**: 1980, with monthly average of 11.50 inches.
- **Summer**: 1979, with monthly average of 8.36 inches.
- **Autumn**: 1906, with monthly average of 7.44 inches.

Driest Seasons (Inches)
- **Winter**: 1999-00, w/monthly average of 1.98 (normal 5.34)
- **Spring**: 1992, with a monthly average of 1.60 (normal 5.48)
- **Summer**: 1930, with a monthly average of 1.49 (normal 3.82)
- **Autumn**: 1903, with a monthly average of 0.46 (normal 3.87)

> On Mar. 27, 1997, the Mississippi River at Vicksburg was at 49.0 ft., higher than any Mar. 27 in the 20th century, including years with record floods. In 1983, it crested at 49.3 ft., but the level on Mar. 27 was 24.5 ft. The year the river reached 51.6 ft., 1973, saw a Mar. 27 level of 44 ft. In 1927, the year of the century's worst Mississippi River flood, the Mar. 27 measurement was 46.3 ft. The level of 1997 was one of the earliest high-water marks ever. At flood stage, the Mississippi at Vicksburg passes 1.4 million cubic feet of water p/second (equal to 60 million garden hoses). Souce: U.S. Army Corps of Engineers

Normal Monthly Precip. (Inches): Jan.—5.24; Feb.—4.70; Mar.—5.82; Apr.—5.57; May—5.05; June—3.18; July—4.51; Aug.—3.77; Sept.—3.55; Oct.—3.26; Nov.—4.81; Dec.—5.91

Wettest Months, by Month (Inches): Jan. 1979—14.10; Feb. 1896—12.94; Mar. 1976—15.13; Apr. 1991—15.95; May 1909—12.23; June 1909—9.69; July 1979—13.25; Aug. 1942—11.39; Sept. 1906—14.77; Oct. 1918—10.58; Nov. 1948—15.76; Dec. 1982—17.70

15 Wettest Months (Inches): Dec. 1982 — 17.70; Apr. 1991 — 15.95; Nov. 1948 — 15.76; Apr. 1983 — 15.53; Mar. 1976 — 15.13; Sept. 1906 — 14.77; Dec. 1932 — 14.50; Apr. 1979 — 14.38; Apr. 1980 — 14.33; Jan. 1979 — 14.10; Apr. 1921 — 14.06; Apr. 1900 — 13.86; Mar. 1980 — 13.57; July 1979 — 13.25; July 1955 — 13.13

Of the 15 wettest months, 6 of them have been in April, 2 each for March, July & Dec., and one each in the months of January, September and November.

> August 2000 was the 2nd driest Aug. on record (0.26), missing the all time driest Aug. (1946 - 0.23) by only 0.03 inch.

Driest Months, by Month (Inches): Jan. 1979 — 0.75; Feb. 1947 — 1.15; Mar. 1911 — 1.29; Apr. 1903 — 0.55; May 1951 — 0.16; June 1930 — Trace; July 1924 — 0.21; Aug. 1946 — 0.23; Sept. 1956 — 0.04; Oct. 1904, 1924 & 1963 — 0.00; Nov. 1924 — Trace; Dec. 1980 — 0.91

15 Driest Months (Inches): Oct. 1904 — 0; Oct. 1924 — 0; Oct. 1963 — 0; June 1930 — Trace; Nov. 1924 — Trace; Oct. 1952 — Trace; Nov. 1949 — 0.01; Sept. 1956 — 0.04; Oct. 1908 — 0.08; Oct. 1909 — 0.09; Oct. 1971 — 0.09; June 1988 — 0.10; May 1951 — 0.16; July 1924 — 0.21; Sept. 1955 — 0.22 (Seven of the 15 driest months were in October.)

Wettest Days (The Wettest Day for Each Calender Month, in Inches): Jan. 27, 1994 — 4.72; Feb. 2, 1896 — 5.69; Mar.19, 1906 — 5.00; Apr. 16, 1921 — 6.30; May 10, 1925 — 4.40; June 10, 1997 — 6.49; July 17, 1933 — 4.98; Aug. 26, 1992 — 4.04; Sept. 27, 1906 — 6.52; Oct. 4, 1964 — 6.97; Nov. 13, 1957 — 3.97; Dec. 27, 1942 — 5.73

Wettest Single Day: Oct. 4, 1964 — 6.97 inches.

> The Ross Barnett Reservoir was at a record low of 292.84 ft. on Oct. 31, 2000. Normal level is 297 ft. above sea level.

Barometric Pressure (Sea Level, In Inches)
- **Highest**: 30.83 on Feb. 9, 1981, Dec. 23, 1989 and sometime during Dec. 1972 (exact date n/a)
- **Lowest**: 28.94 on Aug. 17-18, 1969 (during Great Hurricane Camille)

Average Wind Direction and Speed in Jackson: 9.8 mph from the Southwest

Greatest Wind: Greatest sustained speed ever recorded in Jackson was 68 mph on March 10, 1952. There were probably higher gusts.

Weather in Mississippi: Jackson

❄ PRECIPITATION (SNOW) — THROUGH APRIL 2000 ❄

November: Since 1896, only 14 snow (or sleet) events have been recorded in Jackson on a total of 17 days in November, of which only one instance was a measurable amount of snow, 0.2 inch on Nov. 24, 1938. November has accounted for only 0.15% of all snow recorded in Jackson.

December: Snow has been recorded in Jackson a total of 69 days in December, but measurable amounts (0.1 inch or more) were recorded on only 13 days. Cumulative total snowfall for Dec. is 24 inches for a 104-year period, or 0.23 inch per year average. Historically, it snows on 2.2% of Dec. days, yet only 0.4% of the December days account for measurable amounts. Jackson has **not** had a White Christmas since record keeping began in 1896. A trace was recorded on each Christmas Eve of 1943, 1975 and 1990, but it melted as it fell. Trace amounts were recorded on Christmas Day in 1953 and 1983, but it melted as it fell. On Dec. 22, 1935, a total of 2.5 inches fell, but it melted the next day. On Dec. 22, 1929, a total of 7.5 inches of snow fell, the largest amount ever recorded for Dec., but it melted before Christmas Day. The 2nd biggest snowfall for Dec. in Jackson was 4.8 inches on Dec. 14, 1997. This surprise snow storm was the biggest December snow in 68 years (since 1929) and the biggest snow since January 13, 1982. December snowfall has accounted for 17.5% of all snow recorded in Jackson since Jan. 1, 1896.

January: Snow has been recorded in Jackson a total of 119 days in January, but measurable amounts were recorded on only 32 days. Cumulative total snowfall for Jan. during the 104-year period is 77.3 inches, or about 0.74 inch per year average. Historically, it snows on 3.69 percent of Jan. days, yet less than 1% of Jan. days receive measurable amounts. On Jan. 28, 1904, a total of 11.7 inches of snow was recorded. It was the only day that year that it snowed, yet that day's snowfall is the overall record one-day, one-week, one-month, and one-year all-time record total amount. Snowfall in January has accounted for 56.26% of all snow recorded in Jackson.

February: Snow has been recorded in Jackson a total of 69 days in February, but measurable amounts were recorded on only 11 days. The largest snowfall recorded in Feb. was 6 inches on Feb. 13, 1960. Cumulative total snowfall for Feb. during the 104-year period is 27.8 inches, or about 0.27 inch per year average. Historically, it snows on 2.35% of Feb. days, yet only 0.37% of the days receive measurable amounts. February has accounted for 20.2% of all snow in Jackson.

March: Snow has been recorded in Jackson a total of 45 days in March, but measurable amounts were recorded on only 4 days. The largest snowfall recorded in March was 5 inches on March 22, 1968. The next day there was an additional 0.3 inch. The only other instances were 0.1 inch on March 4, 1978 and 1.6 inches on March 12, 1993. The other 41 instances were officially "traces." Cumulative total snowfall for March for the 104-year period is 7.0 inches, or an average of less than 0.07 inch per year. Historically, it snows on 1.4% of the March days, yet less than 0.12% of March days receive measurable amounts. March has accounted for only 5.09% of all snow recorded in Jackson.

April: It has snowed only 5 times (days) in April. Snow started falling at 7:53 pm on April 2, 1987 and it fell non-stop until 3:05 am on April 3. Yet, the amount was only 0.5 inch on the 2nd and 0.6 inch on the 3rd. That's a total of 1.1 inches of snow ever in April and it was from one snow event over a two-day period. The other instances were trace amounts on April 6, 1971, April 19, 1983 (the latest spring snow in Jackson) and on April 10, 1989. April has accounted for less than one percent (0.8%) of all snow recorded in Jackson since 1896.

Summary: Jackson has recorded snow during some of the six months of November through April since 1896. There have been many years with no snow, not even flurries. There've been a total of 18,971 snow-season days from Jan. 1, 1896 through Apr. 30, 2000. It has snowed in Jackson on 326 (about 1.7%) of those days, or about 3.13 snow days per year average. Measurable snow fell on only 64 days, 19.6% of the total snow days. The 64 days of measurable snow represent only 0.34% (about one-third of 1%) of the total of all the snow-season days, or about .61 of a measurable snow day per year average. There were only trace amounts on 262 of the 326 days. There has been 137.4 total inches of snow for the 64 days with measurable snow. That's about 1.32 inches of snow per year average.

Weather in Mississippi: Jackson

Largest Snowfalls in Jackson (Inches): 11.7 on Jan. 28, 1904 — 10.0 on Jan. 2, 1919 — 7.5 on Dec. 22, 1929 — 7.0 on Jan. 22, 1940 — 6.0 on Feb. 13, 1960 — 5.5 on Jan. 13, 1982 — 5.0 on Mar. 22, 1968 — 4.8 on Dec. 14, 1997 — 4.5 on Jan. 23, 1948 — 4.0 on Feb. 23, 1901, Jan. 30, 1949 and Jan. 9, 1962 — 3.6 on Feb. 23, 1968 — 3.5 on Jan. 23, 1940 — 3.1 on Feb. 12, 1960 — 2.7 on Jan. 30, 1977 — 2.6 on Jan. 22, 1918 and Jan. 23, 1935 — 2.5 on Dec. 31, 1899, Dec. 22, 1935 and Feb. 10, 1958 — 2.2 on Jan. 4, 1905 — and 2.0 on Feb. 14, 1914.

That's 23 snowfalls of 2 inches or more — 15 snowfalls of 3 inches or greater — 12 snowfalls of 4 inches or greater — 7 snowfalls 5 inches or greater — 5 snowfalls 6 inches or greater — 4 snowfalls 7 inches or greater — just 2 snowfalls 10 inches or greater — and only 1 snowfall 11 inches or greater. These 23 snowfalls, with a cumulative total of 103.8 inches (average 4.51 inches per snowfall), account for 75.55% of the 137.4 total inches Jackson has received in the 64 days with measurable snowfall. There's been measurable snow on only 19.63% of the 326 snow days. Since 1896, it's snowed in Jackson on 1.72% of the total season days between Nov. 1 & Apr. 30, yet only 0.33% (one-third of 1%) of the total 18,971 snow-season days have been measurable amounts.

At the NWS at Thompson Field in Jackson as of April 30, 2000, the last time it snowed as much as...

- 0.10 inch was on Jan. 27, 2000
- 0.50 inch was on Dec. 14, 1997
- 1.00 inch was on Dec. 14, 1997
- 2.00 inches was on Dec. 14, 1997
- 2.50 inches was on Dec. 14, 1997
- 3.00 inches was on Dec. 14, 1997
- 3.50 inches was on Dec. 14, 1997
- 4.50 inches was on Dec. 14, 1997
- 5.00 inches was on Jan. 13, 1982
- 5.50 inches was on Jan. 13, 1982
- 6.00 inches was on Feb. 13, 1960
- 6.50 inches was on Jan. 22, 1940
- 7.00 inches was on Jan. 22, 1940
- 7.50 inches was on Dec. 22, 1929
- 8.00 inches was on Jan. 2, 1919
- 8.50 inches was on Jan. 2, 1919
- 9.00 inches was on Jan. 2, 1919
- 9.50 inches was on Jan. 2, 1919
- 10.00 inches was on Jan. 2, 1919
- 10.50 inches was on Jan. 28, 1904
- 11.00 inches was on Jan. 28, 1904
- 11.50 inches was on Jan. 28, 1904
- 12.00 inches was...NEVER...

....at least, not since Jan. 1, 1896)

GREATEST TOTAL SNOW/SLEET ACCUMULATION IN A SEASON
1903-04: 11.7 inches (fell in one day, Jan 28th)
1939-40: 11.6 inches (fell on 4 separate days)
1918-19: 10.0 inches (fell on one day, Jan 2nd)

GREATEST 24 HOUR SNOWFALL
DECEMBER: 7.5 inches on Dec. 22, 1929
JANUARY: 11.7 inches on Jan. 28, 1904
FEBRUARY: 6.0 inches on Feb. 13, 1960
MARCH: 5.3 inches on Mar. 22-23, 1968
APRIL: 1.1 inches on Apr. 2-3, 1987

MAXIMUM MONTHLY SNOWFALL
NOVEMBER: 0.2 inches in 1938
DECEMBER: 8.0 inches in 1929
JANUARY: 11.7 inches in 1904
FEBRUARY: 6.0 inches in 1960
MARCH: 5.3 inches in 1968
APRIL: 1.1 inches in 1987

GREATEST DEPTH ON THE GROUND (WHOLE INCHES)
DECEMBER: 8 inches on Dec. 22, 1929
JANUARY: 12 inches on Jan. 28, 1904
FEBRUARY: 6 inches on Feb. 14, 1960
MARCH: 5 inches on Mar. 22, 1958
APRIL: 1 inch on Apr. 3, 1987

THE LONGEST PERIOD OF TIME WITHOUT ANY SNOW ON THE GROUND IN JACKSON, MISSISSIPPI, WAS NEARLY 7 YEARS, FROM MARCH 1905 TO DECEMBER 1911.

The Surprise Snowstorm: Light to moderate snow began falling shortly after midnight Sunday, December 14, 1997, as a deep upper level storm system moved slowly along the northern Gulf coast. By the time the snow ended about 7 hours later, 8 inches accumulation was common from the Jackson and Vicksburg metro areas of Mississippi east to just north of Meridian into west central Alabama. A total of 4.8 inches of snow fell officially at the Jackson International Airport, which was the 8th largest on record, and the largest so early in the winter (actually late fall). It was the second largest one day snowfall in the month of December (the largest December snow was 7.5 inches on December 29, 1929). The only mention of snow that the National Weather Service at Jackson had in the forecast for Saturday night and Sunday was "flurries."

❄❄❄❄❄❄❄❄❄❄❄❄❄❄

Mississippi Weather: Jackson Records/Data

Date	Record High (latest date)	Record Low (latest date)	Normal Temp. High / Low	Record Precip. (date)	Normal Precip. Month-to-Date	Normal Precip. Year-to-Date
Jan. 1	81 (1952)	17 (1984)	56 / 34	3.99 (1911)	0.18	0.18
2	80 (1952)	15 (1979)	56 / 33	2.02 (1919)	0.36	0.36
3	78 (1950)	08 (1919)	56 / 33	2.35 (1926)	0.54	0.54
4	78 (1997)	04 (1919)	56 / 33	1.87 (1949)	0.72	0.72
5	78 (1921)	11 (1969)	56 / 33	3.24 (1950)	0.90	0.90
6	79 (1989)	10 (1924)	56 / 33	2.44 (1932)	1.08	1.08
7	78 (1989)	16 (1924)	56 / 33	1.84 (1947)	1.26	1.26
8	78 (1937)	10 (1942)	55 / 33	1.80 (1953)	1.43	1.43
9	80 (1957)	09 (1970)	55 / 33	2.38 (1977)	1.60	1.60
10	85 (1949)*	04 (1962)	55 / 33	2.50 (1925)	1.77	1.77
11	80 (1916)	01 (1962)	55 / 33	2.83 (1980)	1.94	1.94
12	80 (1916)	-01 (1962)	55 / 33	2.68 (1932)	2.11	2.11
13	82 (1972)	04 (1918)	55 / 32	1.97 (1947)	2.28	2.28
14	80 (1937)	15 (1982)	55 / 32	1.38 (1971)	2.45	2.45
15	82 (1947)	13 (1982)	55 / 32	1.70 (1954)	2.62	2.62
16	80 (1932)	15 (1977)	55 / 32	1.82 (1947)	2.79	2.79
17	81 (1943)	10 (1977)	55 / 32	3.16 (1926)	2.96	2.96
18	78 (1974)	10 (1948)	55 / 32	1.88 (1936)	3.13	3.13
19	81 (1982)	06 (1977)	55 / 32	3.42 (1979)	3.30	3.30
20	81 (1935)	02 (1985)	55 / 32	2.86 (1979)	3.47	3.47
21	80 (1938)	02 (1985)	55 / 32	2.59 (1998)	3.64	3.64
22	81 (1937)	12 (1984)	56 / 32	2.09 (1980)	3.80	3.80
23	82 (1943)	09 (1940)	56 / 33	2.04 (1923)	3.96	3.96
24	82 (1972)	01 (1948)	56 / 33	2.30 (1990)	4.12	4.12
25	79 (1909)	02 (1940)	56 / 33	1.25 (1976)	4.28	4.28
26	81 (1952)	01 (1940)	56 / 33	3.56 (1996)	4.44	4.44
27	80 (1975)	-05 (1940)*❋	56 / 33	4.72 (1994)*	4.60	4.60
28	83 (1911)	05 (1940)	56 / 33	1.17 (1904)	4.76	4.76
29	81 (1917)	09 (1966)	56 / 33	2.23 (1999)	4.92	4.92
30	81 (1917)	03 (1904)	57 / 33	2.27 (1999)	5.08	5.08
31	82 (1911)	16 (1940)	57 / 33	3.69 (1951)	5.24	5.24
Feb. 1	82 (1911)	08 (1951)	57 / 33	2.28 (1973)	0.16	5.40
2	81 (1990)	01 (1951)*	57 / 33	5.69 (1896)*	0.32	5.56
3	86 (1896)	04 (1951)	57 / 33	2.88 (1936)	0.48	5.72
4	82 (1957)	10 (1996)	57 / 34	1.75 (1956)	0.64	5.88
5	81 (1927)	10 (1996)	58 / 34	2.42 (1914)	0.80	6.04
6	78 (1927)	18 (1988)	58 / 34	1.58 (1972)	0.96	6.20
7	81 (1999)	12 (1988)	58 / 34	1.95 (1903)	1.12	6.36
8	83 (1937)	15 (1933)	58 / 34	2.54 (1933)	1.28	6.52
9	82 (1957)	12 (1933)	59 / 34	4.01 (1946)	1.44	6.68
10	81 (1937)	13 (1971)	59 / 34	2.43 (1965)	1.60	6.84
11	84 (1922)	18 (1973)	59 / 35	2.45 (1965)	1.77	7.01
12	84 (1922)	14 (1968)	59 / 35	2.56 (1945)	1.94	7.18
13	82 (1962)	11 (1905)	60 / 35	3.57 (1950)	2.11	7.35
14	82 (1990)	10 (1960)	60 / 35	3.78 (1917)	2.28	7.52
15	86 (1911)	13 (1905)	60 / 36	2.78 (1974)	2.45	7.69
16	84 (1927)	18 (1991)	60 / 36	2.00 (1903)	2.62	7.86
17	81 (1927)	15 (1900)	61 / 36	1.48 (1921)	2.79	8.03
18	82 (1911)	15 (1900)	61 / 36	3.12 (1927)	2.96	8.20
19	82 (1986)	18 (1978)	61 / 37	2.33 (1991)	3.13	8.37
20	83 (1986)	20 (1978)	61 / 37	1.89 (1953)	3.30	8.54
21	83 (1909)	18 (1978)	62 / 37	1.62 (1955)	3.47	8.71
22	82 (1980)	16 (1978)	62 / 37	2.04 (1950)	3.64	8.88
23	83 (1996)	17 (1964)	62 / 38	3.26 (1979)	3.81	9.05
24	83 (1927)	18 (1968)	63 / 38	1.52 (1985)	3.98	9.22
25	89 (1918)*	20 (1967)	63 / 38	1.19 (1919)	4.16	9.40
26	83 (1917)	19 (1974)	63 / 39	2.52 (1987)	4.34	9.58
27	86 (1918)	21 (1934)	64 / 39	2.21 (1913)	4.52	9.76
28	87 (1918)	20 (1935)	64 / 39	1.41 (1916)	4.70	9.94
29	83 (1932)	24 (1968)	64 / 39	0.52 (1920)	N/A	N/A

* Monthly record. ❋ All-time record — lowest temperature ever recorded in Jackson.
Precipitation record for the month of: January — 14.10" in 1979   February — 12.94" in 1896

The Ultimate Reference on the State

Mississippi Weather: Jackson Records/Data

Date	Record High (latest date)	Record Low (latest date)	Normal Temp. High / Low	Record Precip. (date)	Normal Precip. Month-to-Date	Normal Precip. Year-to-Date
Mar. 1	83 (1972)	18 (1968)	64 / 40	2.19 (1994)	0.18	10.12
2	86 (1918)	19 (1980)	65 / 40	2.18 (1964)	0.36	10.30
3	84 (1953)	15 (1980) *	65 / 40	2.93 (1934)	0.54	10.48
4	88 (1910)	19 (1968)	65 / 41	2.75 (1983)	0.72	10.66
5	85 (1918)	19 (1978)	66 / 41	2.72 (1935)	0.90	10.84
6	86 (1918)	23 (1960)	66 / 41	2.55 (1941)	1.08	11.02
7	86 (1911)	21 (1966)	67 / 42	2.22 (1998)	1.26	11.20
8	84 (1910)	23 (1996)	67 / 42	2.66 (1976)	1.45	11.39
9	90 (1911)	16 (1996)	67 / 42	2.35 (1913)	1.64	11.58
10	88 (1911)	19 (1932)	68 / 42	2.34 (1922)	1.83	11.77
11	93 (1911)	24 (1998)	68 / 43	1.44 (1912)	2.02	11.96
12	87 (1975)	23 (1998)	68 / 43	3.11 (1921)	2.21	12.15
13	87 (1918)	21 (1932)	68 / 43	2.27 (1956)	2.40	12.34
14	86 (1989)	19 (1993)	69 / 44	3.68 (1964)	2.59	12.53
15	88 (1982)	22 (1988)	69 / 44	2.14 (1946)	2.78	12.72
16	87 (1982)	25 (1988)	69 / 44	2.62 (1980)	2.97	12.91
17	88 (1907)	29 (1931)	70 / 44	2.54 (1945)	3.16	13.10
18	90 (1908)	28 (1960)	70 / 45	1.82 (1951)	3.35	13.29
19	88 (1982)	25 (1923)	70 / 45	5.00 (1906)*	3.54	13.48
20	89 (1907)	23 (1923)	71 / 45	2.28 (1941)	3.73	13.67
21	88 (1907)	19 (1965)	71 / 46	2.44 (1982)	3.92	13.86
22	88 (1995)	23 (1986)	71 / 46	3.37 (1929)	4.11	14.05
23	89 (1929)	26 (1914)	72 / 46	2.25 (1923)	4.30	14.24
24	95 (1929) *	22 (1968)	72 / 46	2.70 (1973)	4.49	14.43
25	89 (1907)	25 (1966)	72 / 47	3.40 (1949)	4.68	14.62
26	89 (1907)	25 (1955)	72 / 47	2.75 (1946)	4.87	14.81
27	88 (1935)	23 (1955)	73 / 47	2.07 (1949)	5.06	15.00
28	90 (1910)	31 (1978)	73 / 47	3.07 (1944)	5.25	15.19
29	88 (1974)	30 (1930)	73 / 48	3.83 (1991)	5.44	15.38
30	88 (1946)	30 (1964)	73 / 48	2.26 (1976)	5.63	15.57
31	87 (1981)	29 (1987)	74 / 48	3.10 (1922)	5.82	15.76
Apr. 1	87 (1927)	31 (1994)	74 / 48	1.84 (1938)	0.19	15.95
2	90 (1918)	30 (1992)	74 / 49	1.99 (1988)	0.38	16.14
3	90 (1918)	32 (1971)	74 / 49	2.43 (2000)	0.57	16.33
4	87 (1988)	27 (1987)*	75 / 49	2.49 (1977)	0.76	16.52
5	89 (1955)	28 (1987)	75 / 49	3.06 (1964)	0.95	16.71
6	90 (1911)	32 (1971)	75 / 50	4.50 (1983)	1.14	16.90
7	88 (1986)	31 (1990)	75 / 50	1.35 (1983)	1.33	17.09
8	89 (1967)	30 (1971)	76 / 50	2.16 (1938)	1.52	17.28
9	89 (1908)	33 (2000)	76 / 50	2.83 (1943)	1.71	17.47
10	89 (1922)	34 (1914)	76 / 50	1.65 (1919)	1.90	17.66
11	88 (1927)	30 (1989)	76 / 51	4.80 (1980)	2.09	17.85
12	89 (1948)	32 (1989)	77 / 51	4.40 (1974)	2.28	18.04
13	88 (1972)	30 (1940)	77 / 51	4.93 (1983)	2.47	18.23
14	89 (1972)	34 (1959)	77 / 51	2.64 (1896)	2.66	18.42
15	91 (1925)	36 (1957)	77 / 52	2.51 (1912)	2.85	18.61
16	92 (1925)	33 (1983)	78 / 52	6.30 (1921) *	3.04	18.80
17	91 (1925)	37 (1951)	78 / 52	4.00 (1900)	3.23	18.99
18	89 (1948)	33 (1997)	78 / 52	2.43 (1944)	3.41	19.17
19	92 (1987)	35 (1983)	78 / 53	1.72 (1982)	3.59	19.35
20	91 (1987)	38 (1956)	79 / 53	2.65 (1995)	3.77	19.53
21	94 (1987) *	37 (1934)	79 / 53	3.47 (1951)	3.95	19.71
22	92 (1925)	36 (1993)	79 / 54	4.55 (1928)	4.13	19.89
23	93 (1925)	36 (1986)	79 / 54	2.03 (1988)	4.31	20.07
24	93 (1925)	39 (1910)	79 / 54	2.59 (1913)	4.49	20.25
25	90 (1925)	31 (1910)	80 / 54	3.48 (1929)	4.67	20.43
26	90 (1989)	36 (1910)	80 / 55	2.22 (1920)	4.85	20.61
27	93 (1987)	40 (1903)	80 / 55	2.74 (1921)	5.03	20.79
28	92 (1899)	41 (1920)	80 / 55	2.68 (1918)	5.21	20.97
29	94 (1899) *	40 (1965)	80 / 55	4.85 (1953)	5.39	21.15
30	93 (1943)	38 (1965)	81 / 56	2.19 (1940)	5.57	21.33

* Monthly record.   Precipitation record for the month of: March — 15.13" in 1976   April — 15.95" in 1991

Mississippi Weather: Jackson Records/Data

Date	Record High (latest date)	Record Low (latest date)	Normal Temp. High / Low	Record Precip. (date)	Normal Precip. Month-to-Date	Normal Precip. Year-to-Date
May 1	92 (1952)	40 (1908)	81 / 56	4.17 (1954)	0.18	21.51
2	94 (1902)	40 (1909)	81 / 56	1.66 (1950)	0.36	21.69
3	92 (1943)	44 (1970)	81 / 57	2.40 (1916)	0.54	21.87
4	93 (1949)	38 (1971)*	81 / 57	3.20 (1989)	0.72	22.05
5	96 (1952)	44 (1978)	81 / 57	4.24 (1908)	0.90	22.23
6	96 (1952)	43 (1957)	82 / 57	2.44 (1935)	1.08	22.41
7	94 (1952)	44 (1944)	82 / 57	3.42 (1915)	1.26	22.59
8	93 (1927)	41 (1992)	82 / 58	2.02 (1961)	1.44	22.77
9	93 (1927)	39 (1917)	82 / 58	0.92 (1971)	1.62	22.95
10	95 (1899)	41 (1906)	83 / 58	4.40 (1925)*	1.80	23.13
11	96 (1902)	42 (1900)	83 / 59	2.10 (1926)	1.98	23.31
12	96 (1902)	42 (1989)	83 / 59	2.69 (1990)	2.15	23.48
13	93 (1916)	42 (1960)	83 / 59	1.10 (1903)	2.32	23.65
14	92 (1991)	42 (1971)	83 / 60	2.32 (1976)	2.49	23.82
15	92 (1915)	41 (1917)	84 / 60	3.12 (1983)	2.66	23.99
16	94 (1899)	44 (1917)	84 / 60	1.95 (1980)	2.83	24.16
17	95 (1899)	47 (1967)	84 / 60	1.85 (1953)	3.00	24.33
18	94 (1951)	45 (1973)	84 / 61	2.64 (1989)	3.16	24.49
19	94 (1951)	46 (1976)	85 / 61	3.65 (1930)	3.32	24.65
20	97 (1964)	48 (1958)	85 / 61	3.10 (1931)	3.48	24.81
21	97 (1902)	45 (1981)	85 / 61	3.07 (1967)	3.64	24.97
22	98 (1902)	46 (1993)	85 / 62	2.58 (1959)	3.79	25.12
23	95 (1948)	50 (1931)	86 / 62	1.78 (1905)	3.94	25.27
24	95 (1996)	46 (1931)	86 / 62	1.19 (1932)	4.09	25.42
25	97 (1902)	46 (1979)	86 / 62	2.70 (1948)	4.24	25.57
26	99 (1964)	44 (1979)	86 / 63	3.80 (1909)	4.38	25.71
27	98 (1953)	46 (1961)	87 / 63	2.70 (1976)	4.52	25.85
28	100 (1911)*	43 (1961)	87 / 63	1.34 (1915)	4.66	25.99
29	99 (1911)	51 (1961)	87 / 63	2.02 (1912)	4.79	26.12
30	99 (1911)	45 (1984)	87 / 64	2.93 (1986)	4.92	26.25
31	99 (1951)	43 (1984)	88 / 64	2.54 (1946)	5.05	26.38
June 1	102 (1951)	47 (1984)*	88 / 64	3.90 (1909)	0.12	26.50
2	99 (1911)	49 (1966)	88 / 64	1.51 (1896)	0.24	26.62
3	102 (1911)	48 (1956)	88 / 65	1.43 (1957)	0.36	26.74
4	99 (1985)	55 (1955)	89 / 65	2.04 (1897)	0.47	26.85
5	98 (1985)	53 (1946)	89 / 65	3.24 (1979)	0.58	26.96
6	101 (1902)	55 (1897)	89 / 65	1.57 (1901)	0.69	27.07
7	100 (1953)	55 (2000)	89 / 66	3.22 (1901)	0.80	27.18
8	99 (1963)	51 (1977)	90 / 66	2.13 (1989)	0.90	27.28
9	99 (1953)	51 (1930)	90 / 66	0.90 (1903)	1.00	27.38
10	101 (1911)	51 (1930)	90 / 66	6.49 (1997)*	1.10	27.48
11	104 (1902)	50 (1988)	90 / 66	1.56 (1992)	1.20	27.58
12	103 (1902)	52 (1988)	90 / 67	1.10 (1959)	1.30	27.68
13	102 (1953)	51 (1985)	91 / 67	2.97 (1956)	1.40	27.78
14	103 (1902)	54 (1985)	91 / 67	3.89 (1945)	1.50	27.88
15	101 (1963)	52 (1933)	91 / 67	2.49 (1935)	1.60	27.98
16	101 (1911)	51 (1933)	91 / 67	3.21 (1982)	1.70	28.08
17	103 (1902)	50 (1917)	91 / 68	5.19 (1934)	1.80	28.18
18	103 (1902)	56 (1899)	91 / 68	2.38 (1956)	1.90	28.28
19	104 (1902)	57 (1899)	91 / 68	1.65 (1975)	2.00	28.38
20	105 (1936)*	56 (1985)	91 / 68	2.94 (1920)	2.10	28.48
21	102 (1953)	57 (1976)	92 / 68	2.62 (1909)	2.20	28.58
22	101 (1969)	57 (1976)	92 / 68	2.50 (1957)	2.30	28.68
23	101 (1897)	56 (1992)	92 / 69	2.31 (1943)	2.40	28.78
24	101 (1897)	57 (1902)	92 / 69	2.67 (1994)	2.50	28.88
25	101 (1969)	56 (1974)	92 / 69	1.94 (1999)	2.61	28.99
26	102 (1930)	55 (1974)	92 / 69	1.19 (1939)	2.72	29.10
27	104 (1988)	55 (1974)	92 / 69	2.09 (1929)	2.83	29.21
28	103 (1988)	56 (1974)	92 / 69	2.04 (1898)	2.94	29.32
29	105 (1988)	58 (1974)	92 / 69	1.53 (1943)	3.06	29.44
30	103 (1902)	54 (1974)	92 / 69	1.75 (1904)	3.18	29.56

* Monthly record. Precipitation record for the month of: May — 12.23" in 1909   June — 9.69" in 1909

The Ultimate Reference on the State

Mississippi Weather: Jackson Records/Data

Date	Record High (latest date)	Record Low (latest date)	Normal Temp. High / Low	Record Precip. (date)	Normal Precip. Month-to-Date	Normal Precip. Year-to-Date
July 1	104 (1954)	58 (1923)	92 / 69	4.95 (1981)	0.12	29.68
2	104 (1902)	58 (1924)	92 / 70	3.15 (1959)	0.25	29.81
3	103 (1902)	57 (1924)	92 / 70	1.94 (1942)	0.38	29.94
4	105 (1902)	58 (1924)	92 / 70	2.12 (1922)	0.51	30.07
5	102 (1948)	59 (1922)	92 / 70	1.63 (1959)	0.65	30.21
6	104 (1902)	59 (1972)	92 / 70	3.28 (1940)	0.79	30.35
7	105 (1902)	55 (1972)	92 / 70	2.07 (1946)	0.93	30.49
8	103 (1907)	60 (1972)	92 / 70	4.14 (1963)	1.07	30.63
9	102 (1969)	61 (1947)	92 / 70	3.45 (1925)	1.22	30.78
10	100 (1966)	60 (1947)	92 / 70	1.51 (1898)	1.37	30.93
11	104 (1930)	61 (1947)	92 / 70	2.26 (1979)	1.52	31.08
12	106 (1930)	61 (1900)	92 / 70	2.13 (1943)	1.67	31.23
13	105 (1930)	60 (1900)	92 / 70	3.64 (1979)	1.82	31.38
14	105 (1980)	58 (1967)	92 / 70	0.80 (1955)	1.97	31.53
15	105 (1980)	51 (1967)*	92 / 70	2.40 (1982)	2.12	31.68
16	106 (1980)	54 (1967)	92 / 71	1.68 (1938)	2.27	31.83
17	104 (1902)	61 (1926)	92 / 71	4.98 (1933)*	2.42	31.98
18	104 (1944)	61 (1967)	92 / 71	2.71 (1912)	2.57	32.13
19	101 (2000)	64 (1984)	92 / 71	2.25 (1923)	2.73	32.29
20	102 (2000)	61 (1984)	93 / 71	2.92 (1938)	2.88	32.44
21	101 (1951)	62 (1900)	93 / 71	3.04 (1955)	3.03	32.59
22	103 (1924)	59 (1947)	93 / 71	1.92 (1953)	3.18	32.74
23	103 (1934)	57 (1947)	93 / 71	1.31 (1949)	3.33	32.89
24	105 (1924)	59 (1915)	93 / 71	1.91 (1931)	3.48	33.04
25	103 (1952)	61 (1904)	93 / 71	4.65 (1975)	3.63	33.19
26	101 (1952)	58 (1911)	93 / 71	1.34 (1928)	3.78	33.34
27	103 (1952)	58 (1911)	93 / 71	2.28 (1950)	3.93	33.49
28	102 (1930)	60 (1911)	93 / 71	2.00 (1898)	4.08	33.64
29	107 (1930)*❋	61 (1994)	93 / 71	1.07 (1972)	4.23	33.79
30	104 (1930)	61 (1897)	93 / 71	1.53 (1996)	4.37	33.93
31	103 (1930)	62 (1897)	93 / 71	1.69 (1975)	4.51	34.07
Aug. 1	104 (1896)	60 (1965)	93 / 71	3.25 (1982)	0.14	34.21
2	102 (1947)	59 (1965)	93 / 71	2.60 (1908)	0.28	34.35
3	103 (1952)	60 (1965)	93 / 71	2.52 (1914)	0.41	34.48
4	102 (1897)	62 (1973)	93 / 71	1.76 (1995)	0.54	34.61
5	102 (1902)	58 (1974)	93 / 71	2.45 (1995)	0.67	34.74
6	102 (1947)	60 (1974)	93 / 71	1.30 (1996)	0.80	34.87
7	102 (1947)	62 (1900)	93 / 70	1.96 (1983)	0.93	35.00
8	104 (1935)	58 (1989)	92 / 70	2.74 (1948)	1.06	35.13
9	105 (1935)	55 (1990)	92 / 70	3.99 (1942)	1.18	35.25
10	102 (2000)	59 (1990)	92 / 70	2.62 (1966)	1.30	35.37
11	103 (1954)	59 (1990)	92 / 70	1.51 (1984)	1.42	35.49
12	104 (1954)	58 (1931)	92 / 70	1.49 (1923)	1.54	35.61
13	104 (1954)	55 (1931)	92 / 70	3.07 (1997)	1.66	35.73
14	105 (1954)	57 (1931)	92 / 70	1.07 (1937)	1.78	35.85
15	105 (1902)	59 (1963)	92 / 70	0.80 (1975)	1.90	35.97
16	105 (1943)	58 (1992)	92 / 70	3.95 (1985)	2.02	36.09
17	104 (1952)	58 (1992)	92 / 70	1.82 (1958)	2.14	36.21
18	105 (1909)	60 (1992)	92 / 70	2.91 (1969)	2.26	36.33
19	104 (1999)	61 (1943)	92 / 70	1.74 (1960)	2.38	36.45
20	104 (1925)	60 (1976)	92 / 69	2.54 (1942)	2.50	36.57
21	103 (2000)	55 (1991)	92 / 69	1.73 (1901)	2.61	36.68
22	101 (1990)	55 (1956)	92 / 69	3.11 (1960)	2.72	36.79
23	103 (1924)	54 (1956)*	92 / 69	1.12 (1934)	2.83	36.90
24	103 (1924)	57 (1931)	92 / 69	0.85 (1939)	2.94	37.01
25	101 (2000)	58 (1917)	91 / 69	1.47 (1967)	3.05	37.12
26	104 (1902)	55 (1966)	91 / 69	4.04 (1992)*	3.17	37.24
27	105 (1943)	57 (1958)	91 / 69	1.57 (1996)	3.29	37.36
28	106 (1943)	57 (1958)	91 / 69	1.62 (1931)	3.41	37.48
29	104 (2000)	55 (1992)	91 / 68	3.00 (1902)	3.53	37.60
30	107 (2000)*❋	56 (1992)	91 / 68	1.67 (1976)	3.65	37.72
31	106 (2000)	57 (1946)	91 / 68	0.89 (1938)	3.77	37.84

*Monthly record. ❋All-time record high temperature (also on 9/6 & 9/7/1925). Precip. record: July — 13.25" in 1979 Aug. — 11.39" in 1942

Mississippi Weather: Jackson Records/Data

Date	Record High (latest date)	Record Low (latest date)	Normal Temp. High / Low	Record Precip. (date)	Normal Precip. Month-to-Date	Normal Precip. Year-to-Date
Sept. 1	104 (2000)	52 (1903)	91 / 68	1.85 (1930)	0.12	37.96
2	103 (1951)	52 (1903)	91 / 68	1.41 (1992)	0.24	38.08
3	102 (2000)	54 (1952)	90 / 68	1.34 (1981)	0.36	38.20
4	105 (1899)	51 (1952)	90 / 67	2.37 (1949)	0.48	38.32
5	105 (1925)	51 (1934)	90 / 67	1.48 (1906)	0.60	38.44
6	107 (1925)*❋	52 (1934)	90 / 67	3.35 (1906)	0.72	38.56
7	107 (1925)*❋	52 (1896)	90 / 67	1.06 (1976)	0.84	38.68
8	104 (1925)	49 (1934)	90 / 67	1.15 (1906)	0.96	38.80
9	103 (1925)	52 (1918)	90 / 66	1.51 (1990)	1.08	38.92
10	103 (1980)	51 (1955)	89 / 66	4.10 (1965)	1.20	39.04
11	99 (1951)	51 (1976)	89 / 66	3.96 (1965)	1.32	39.16
12	102 (1980)	44 (1940)	89 / 65	1.90 (1998)	1.44	39.28
13	101 (1921)	45 (1940)	89 / 65	1.53 (1979)	1.56	39.40
14	102 (1921)	42 (1902)	89 / 65	1.62 (1962)	1.68	39.52
15	104 (1980)	42 (1902)	88 / 64	1.44 (1949)	1.80	39.64
16	103 (1927)	42 (1902)	88 / 64	4.59 (1971)	1.92	39.76
17	102 (1925)	50 (1961)	88 / 64	1.05 (1913)	2.04	39.88
18	103 (1925)	46 (1981)	88 / 63	1.53 (1964)	2.16	40.00
19	105 (1925)	43 (1981)	87 / 63	1.94 (1899)	2.28	40.12
20	104 (1925)	44 (1938)	87 / 62	4.20 (1979)	2.40	40.24
21	103 (1925)	43 (1918)	87 / 62	2.66 (1909)	2.52	40.36
22	101 (1925)	41 (1983)	87 / 62	0.84 (1912)	2.64	40.48
23	102 (1925)	41 (1982)	86 / 61	3.69 (1914)	2.76	40.60
24	101 (1921)	46 (1982)	86 / 61	2.24 (1991)	2.88	40.72
25	98 (1921)	46 (1975)	86 / 60	1.72 (1974)	3.00	40.84
26	96 (1936)	44 (1975)	86 / 59	3.30 (1970)	3.11	40.95
27	99 (1915)	43 (1899)	85 / 59	6.52 (1906)*	3.22	41.06
28	99 (1953)	41 (1967)	85 / 59	2.00 (1902)	3.33	41.17
29	99 (1953)	35 (1967)*	85 / 58	2.12 (1989)	3.44	41.28
30	97 (1927)	37 (1967)	84 / 57	3.70 (1915)	3.55	41.39
Oct. 1	97 (1911)	36 (1984)	84 / 57	4.04 (1905)	0.11	41.50
2	96 (1911)	34 (1984)	84 / 56	1.28 (1925)	0.21	41.60
3	97 (1911)	39 (1984)	83 / 56	3.00 (1995)	0.31	41.70
4	98 (1911)*	38 (1987)	83 / 55	6.97 (1964)**	0.41	41.80
5	96 (1954)	38 (1987)	83 / 55	2.17 (1976)	0.51	41.90
6	97 (1911)	36 (1932)	82 / 54	2.25 (1982)	0.61	42.00
7	96 (1911)	35 (1932)	82 / 54	2.86 (1982)	0.71	42.10
8	96 (1928)	35 (1987)	82 / 53	1.43 (1930)	0.81	42.20
9	95 (1948)	32 (1917)	81 / 53	1.31 (1982)	0.91	42.30
10	94 (1928)	36 (1917)	81 / 52	1.66 (1934)	1.01	42.40
11	93 (1928)	35 (1964)	81 / 52	1.35 (1897)	1.11	42.50
12	93 (1928)	35 (1932)	80 / 51	3.45 (1970)	1.21	42.60
13	93 (1963)	33 (1977)	80 / 51	1.90 (1959)	1.31	42.70
14	95 (1899)	35 (1977)	80 / 51	1.88 (1995)	1.41	42.80
15	94 (1899)	35 (1987)	79 / 50	1.90 (1905)	1.51	42.90
16	91 (1899)	35 (1987)	79 / 50	6.35 (1975)	1.61	43.00
17	93 (1915)	31 (1943)	79 / 49	1.56 (1932)	1.71	43.10
18	93 (1926)	30 (1948)	78 / 49	1.38 (1941)	1.81	43.20
19	93 (1921)	31 (1948)	78 / 49	2.36 (1970)	1.91	43.30
20	90 (1939)	29 (1989)	78 / 48	1.30 (1957)	2.01	43.40
21	92 (1899)	30 (1917)	77 / 48	4.15 (1984)	2.11	43.50
22	92 (1941)	31 (1987)	77 / 48	1.50 (1972)	2.22	43.61
23	92 (1927)	32 (1916)	77 / 47	1.95 (1918)	2.33	43.72
24	91 (1921)	28 (1917)	77 / 47	1.81 (1918)	2.44	43.83
25	92 (1921)	31 (1982)	76 / 47	2.75 (1981)	2.55	43.94
26	92 (1927)	30 (1955)	76 / 47	2.54 (1932)	2.66	44.05
27	90 (1919)	29 (1898)	76 / 46	1.74 (1985)	2.78	44.17
28	90 (1919)	27 (1914)	75 / 46	1.29 (1935)	2.90	44.29
29	90 (1927)	27 (1910)	75 / 46	3.34 (1918)	3.02	44.41
30	89 (1927)	27 (1910)	75 / 46	1.65 (1949)	3.14	44.53
31	90 (1912)	26 (1993)*	74 / 46	1.21 (1942)	3.26	44.65

*Monthly record. ❋All-time record high temperature (also recorded on 7/29/30 and 8/30/2000). **All-time record wettest day.
Precipitation record: September — 14.77" in 1906   October — 10.58" in 1918

The Ultimate Reference on the State

Mississippi Weather: Jackson Records/Data

Date	Record High (latest date)	Record Low (latest date)	Normal Temp. High / Low	Record Precip. (date)	Normal Precip. Month-to-Date	Normal Precip. Year-to-Date
Nov. 1	89 (1927)*	24 (1993)	74 / 45	1.90 (1929)	0.13	44.78
2	88 (1971)	21 (1966)	74 / 45	1.79 (1934)	0.26	44.91
3	87 (1922)	17 (1966)	73 / 45	1.49 (1950)	0.39	45.04
4	89 (1922)*	25 (1966)	73 / 45	1.95 (1925)	0.53	45.18
5	85 (1909)	23 (1991)	73 / 44	0.80 (1905)	0.67	45.32
6	87 (1911)	26 (1991)	72 / 44	0.98 (1975)	0.81	45.46
7	86 (1909)	23 (1959)	72 / 44	2.45 (1989)	0.95	45.60
8	86 (1986)	24 (1951)	72 / 44	2.01 (1911)	1.10	45.75
9	86 (1920)	24 (1896)	71 / 44	1.83 (1979)	1.25	45.90
10	85 (1927)	23 (1991)	71 / 44	3.64 (1946)	1.40	46.05
11	85 (1911)	25 (1900)	71 / 43	1.47 (1935)	1.55	46.20
12	85 (1985)	24 (1900)	71 / 43	1.98 (1929)	1.70	46.35
13	86 (1955)	23 (1907)	70 / 43	3.97 (1957)*	1.86	46.51
14	88 (1921)	21 (1907)	70 / 43	2.27 (1993)	2.02	46.67
15	87 (1902)	20 (1969)	69 / 42	1.61 (1944)	2.18	46.83
16	86 (1931)	21 (1940)	69 / 42	2.21 (1987)	2.34	46.99
17	85 (1906)	21 (1920)	69 / 42	1.17 (1974)	2.51	47.16
18	87 (1930)	20 (1959)	68 / 42	2.56 (1948)	2.68	47.33
19	86 (1930)	17 (1903)	68 / 42	2.05 (1983)	2.85	47.50
20	81 (1933)	21 (1914)	68 / 41	2.06 (1973)	3.02	47.67
21	82 (1913)	21 (1937)	67 / 41	2.57 (1977)	3.19	47.84
22	84 (1921)	22 (1937)	67 / 41	3.26 (1979)	3.36	48.01
23	85 (1913)	22 (1903)	67 / 41	1.95 (1983)	3.54	48.19
24	86 (1921)	19 (1970)	66 / 41	1.89 (1986)	3.72	48.37
25	84 (1908)	18 (1950)	66 / 40	2.46 (1979)	3.90	48.55
26	84 (1985)	21 (1900)	66 / 40	3.64 (1948)	4.08	48.73
27	83 (1989)	15 (1903)*	65 / 40	3.49 (1982)	4.26	48.91
28	81 (1908)	16 (1938)	65 / 40	2.54 (1963)	4.44	49.09
29	81 (1970)	20 (1955)	65 / 39	3.45 (1977)	4.62	49.27
30	82 (1981)	17 (1976)	64 / 39	1.53 (1936)	4.81	49.46
Dec. 1	81 (1991)	20 (1965)	64 / 39	2.00 (1936)	0.19	49.65
2	83 (1922)	20 (1960)	63 / 39	2.68 (1991)	0.38	49.84
3	84 (1922)*	18 (1935)	63 / 39	4.92 (1982)	0.57	50.03
4	82 (1922)	20 (1989)	63 / 38	4.01 (1897)	0.76	50.22
5	81 (1916)	21 (1935)	62 / 38	2.26 (1971)	0.95	50.41
6	84 (1951)*	20 (1937)	62 / 38	2.51 (1971)	1.14	50.60
7	84 (1978)*	14 (1937)	62 / 38	1.85 (1989)	1.33	50.79
8	82 (1922)	19 (1965)	62 / 37	3.00 (1978)	1.52	50.98
9	80 (1972)	14 (1917)	62 / 37	2.45 (1931)	1.71	51.17
10	80 (1943)	16 (1937)	61 / 37	1.93 (1932)	1.90	51.36
11	82 (1931)	15 (1937)	61 / 37	2.29 (1964)	2.09	51.55
12	81 (1971)	12 (1962)	60 / 37	2.76 (1932)	2.28	51.74
13	79 (1929)	08 (1962)	60 / 37	2.25 (1919)	2.47	51.93
14	81 (1987)	18 (1958)	60 / 36	4.00 (1901)	2.67	52.13
15	80 (1948)	15 (1958)	59 / 36	1.98 (1940)	2.87	52.33
16	84 (1924)*	12 (1901)	59 / 36	2.00 (1948)	3.07	52.53
17	82 (1924)	16 (1932)	59 / 36	2.85 (1922)	3.26	52.72
18	82 (1908)	13 (1901)	59 / 36	2.19 (1995)	3.45	52.91
19	76 (1984)	14 (1901)	58 / 35	1.48 (1987)	3.64	53.10
20	81 (1978)	13 (1901)	58 / 35	2.16 (1972)	3.83	53.29
21	79 (1970)	12 (1901)	58 / 35	1.49 (1908)	4.02	53.48
22	77 (1991)	07 (1989)	58 / 35	3.21 (1941)	4.21	53.67
23	80 (1931)	04 (1989)*	58 / 35	3.00 (1974)	4.40	53.86
24	80 (1955)	06 (1989)	57 / 35	2.82 (1973)	4.59	54.05
25	80 (1942)	07 (1983)	57 / 34	4.15 (1926)	4.78	54.24
26	78 (1971)	09 (1983)	57 / 34	3.33 (1934)	4.97	54.43
27	77 (1982)	16 (1935)	57 / 34	5.73 (1942)*	5.16	54.62
28	76 (1990)	13 (1925)	57 / 34	2.19 (1915)	5.35	54.81
29	79 (1990)	18 (1995)	57 / 34	3.10 (1927)	5.54	55.00
30	80 (1984)	10 (1917)	56 / 34	1.87 (1972)	5.73	55.19
31	80 (1951)	10 (1983)	56 / 34	1.57 (1981)	5.91	55.37

* Monthly record.   Precipitation record for the month of: Nov. — 15.76" in 1948   Dec. — 17.70" in 1982

The Mississippi Almanac

People of Mississippi

GENERAL (1990 Figures)

Ethnic Origins: 63% European, 36% African, 1% Other

Ancestry (no. per 100,000 people): Arab 130.7; Austrian 27.6; Belgian 16.8; Canadian 32.8; Czech 44.7; Danish 59.6; Dutch 770.6; English 7,732.6; Finnish 35.8; French (except Basque) 2,293.2; French Canadian 602.6; German 6,860.0; Greek 68.1; Hungarian 38.2; Irish 10,669.7; Italian 990.8; Lithuanian 13.1; Norwegian 101.8; Polish 275.1; Portuguese 3.6; Romanian 10.7; Russian 48.0; Scotch Irish 3,014.0; Scottish 986.9; Slovak 61.5; Subsaharan African 137.4; Swedish 206.4; Swiss 57.5; Ukrainian 13.5; United States or American 12,757.4; Welch 200.7: West Indian 29.7; and Yugoslavian 28.6 (to derive actual no., multiply no. given by 25.7322)

Born in Mississippi: 77.3% of total population, rank 5 [State Native(s): noun - Mississippian(s)]

Foreign-Born Population: 20,383 (0.8%), rank 51 (entered U.S. 1980-1990: 8,206)

People Speaking Foreign Language at Home (1990 Census figures of Americans age 5 and over): 86 non-English languages are spoken by 66,516 individuals (2.6%, rank 48), including 25,061 (1.0%) who speak Spanish; 12,728 (0.50%) who speak French; 6,563 (0.26%) who speak German; and 4,410 (0.17%) who speak Choctaw & other Indian dialects.

Religions:
- Christian: 1,720,521 (94.20%, rank 3)[1] — 32% Baptist, 10% Methodist, 3.8% Catholic
- Jewish: 10,959 (00.60%, rank 25)
- Agnostic: 9,132 (00.50%, rank 27)
- Other: 23,744 (01.30%, rank 24)
- None: 51,141 (02.80%, rank 47)

IMMIGRANTS TO:		
	The U.S.	Mississippi
1994	798,394	810
1995	720,461	757
1996	915,900	1,073
1997	798,378	1,118

POPULATION STATISTICS

Population, 1990: 2,575,475 (rank 31) Urban: 47.1% Rural: 52.9%

Change in Population: 1980-1990: +2.1%   1990-1998: +6.86%   1990-1999: +7.5%

Population (Census Estimate) 7/1/1999: 2,768,619
  7/1/1998: 2,751,335 (1,394,843, or 50.7%, live in incorporated places)

Population Density (persons per square mile): **1999** — 57.3 **1998** — 57 **1990** — 54.9 **1960** — 46

Voting Age Pop.: **1998** — 1,995,217   **1997** — 1,977,503

Population, White: **1990** — 1,625,131 (63.10%)   **1998** — 1,719,483 (62.48%) +5.81% from '90
Black: **1990** — 913,270 (35.46%)   **1998** — 1,003,173 (36.45%) +9.84% from '90
Hispanic: **1990** — 16,076 (0.62%)   **1998** — 22,755 (0.9%) +41.6% from 1990

(In 1998, U.S. Immigration & Naturalization Service estimated there were 4,000 illegal residents in Miss.)

Native American Pop.: **1990** — 8,311 (0.33%) [most on one Choctaw Reservation of 20,486 acres]
  1998 — 10,129 (0.37%) 21.87% increase from 1990

Asian/Pacific Islanders Pop.: **1990** — 12,687 (0.49%)   **1998** — 19,307 (0.70%) +52.18% from '90

Total Nonwhite Population: **1990** — 950,344 (36.9%)   **1980-1990**: 3.50% increase
  1998 — 1,032,609 (37.52%)   **1990-1998**: 8.66% increase.

Total Male and Female Never Married, 1990: 26.7%, rank 20

Single Adult Females, 1990: 484,444 (46.6% of females age 15 & over)
  Married: 555,135 (53.4% of females age 15 & over)
  Never Married: 245,341 (23.6% of females age 15 & over)
  Separated: 34,306 (3.3% of females age 15 & over)
  Divorced: 89,404 (8.6% of females age 15 & over)
  Widowed: 149,699 (14.4% of females age 15 & over)

Single Adult Males, 1990: 368,137 (40.3% of males age 15 & over)
  Married: 546,268 (59.8% of males age 15 & over)
  Never Married: 274,961 (30.1% of males age 15 & over)
  Separated: 22,655 (2.48% of males age 15 & over)
  Divorced: 64,858 (7.10% of males age 15 & over)
  Widowed: 27,770 (3.04% of males age 15 & over)

> A 1995 survey showed that of the 1.1 million baby-boomers born in Mississippi, 471,441 (43%) had left the state. The trend seems to be reversing as there was a net gain each year from July 1991 to July 1995 with 29,998 more people moving to the state than leaving it. Census Bureau figures show that from 4/1/1990 to 7/1/1999, the state had a net international migration of 6,887 and a net domestic migration of 44,639.

Couples Married in 1998: 20,911 Bride — White 14,222 Non-White 6,689 (12,260 first marriages)
  Groom — White 14,158 Non-White 6,753 (12,310 first. marriages)

Number of Divorces Granted in Miss., 1998: 13,748 (White 10,310; Non-White 3,004; Unknown 434)

---

[1] Rank for religions is national rank of percentage and not of the absolute numbers. Many of the 1990 population figures have been revised.

People of Mississippi

ESTIMATED POPULATION JULY 1, 1998 — BREAKDOWN BY AGE GROUP

Age Group	Number	Percentage	White	Percentage	NonWhite	Percentage
Under 5 Years	202,072	7.34	108,481	53.68	93,591	46.32
Male	102,916	50.93	55,823	54.24	47,093	45.76
Female	99,156	49.07	52,658	53.11	46,498	46.89
5 to 17 Years	554,803	20.16	296,818	53.50	257,985	46.50
Male	283,540	51.11	152,730	53.87	130,810	46.13
Female	271,263	48.89	144,088	53.12	127,175	46.88
18 to 24 Years	299,779	10.89	164,682	54.93	135,097	45.07
Male	148,779	49.63	84,382	56.72	64,397	43.28
Female	151,000	50.37	80,300	53.18	70,700	46.82
25 to 44 Years	795,300	28.90	498,750	62.71	296,550	37.29
Male	384,769	48.38	249,729	64.90	135,040	35.10
Female	410,531	51.62	249,021	60.66	161,510	39.34
45 to 64 Years	563,827	20.49	402,236	71.34	161,591	28.66
Male	265,923	47.16	195,114	73.37	70,809	26.63
Female	297,904	52.84	207,122	69.53	90,782	30.47
16 Years & Over	2,088,488	75.89	1,364,204	65.32	724,284	34.68
Male	980,141	46.93	654,877	66.81	325,264	33.19
Female	1,108,347	53.07	709,327	64.00	399,020	36.00
Under 16 Years	663,604	24.11	355,020	53.50	308,584	46.50
Male	338,799	51.05	182,416	53.84	156,383	46.16
Female	324,805	48.95	172,604	53.14	152,201	46.86
18 Years & Over	1,995,217	72.50	1,314,184	65.87	681,033	34.13
Male	932,484	46.74	628,999	67.45	303,485	32.55
Female	1,062,733	53.26	685,185	64.47	377,548	35.53
Under 18 Years	756,875	27.50	405,299	53.55	351,576	46.45
Male	386,456	51.06	208,553	53.97	177,903	46.03
Female	370,419	48.94	196,746	53.11	173,673	46.89
21 Years & Over	1,856,160	67.45	1,240,176	66.81	615,984	33.19
Male	862,713	46.48	590,927	68.50	271,786	31.50
Female	993,447	53.52	649,249	65.35	344,198	34.65
Under 21 Years	895,932	32.55	479,307	53.50	416,625	46.50
Male	456,227	50.92	246,625	54.06	209,602	45.94
Female	439,705	49.08	232,682	52.92	207,023	47.08
65 Years & Over	336,311	12.22	248,516	73.89	87,795	26.11
Male	133,013	39.55	99,774	75.01	33,239	24.99
Female	203,298	60.45	148,742	73.16	54,556	26.84
Under 65 Years	2,415,781	87.78	1,470,967	60.89	944,814	39.11
Male	1,185,927	49.09	737,778	62.21	448,149	37.79
Female	1,229,854	50.91	733,189	59.62	496,665	40.38
85 Years & Over	40,052	1.46	27,487	68.63	12,565	31.37
Male	11,389	28.44	7,402	65.00	3,987	35.00
Female	28,663	71.56	20,085	70.07	8,578	29.93
TOTAL POP.	2,752,092	100.00	1,719,483	62.48	1,032,609	37.52
Male	1,318,940	47.92	837,552	63.50	481,388	36.50
Female	1,433,152	52.08	881,931	61.54	551,221	38.46

Source: The U.S. Census Bureau

People of Mississippi

Estimated Pop. (July 1st each year): 1998 — 2,751,335 1997 — 2,731,826 1996 — 2,709,925
1999 — 2,768,619 1995 — 2,690,788 1994 — 2,663,450 1993 — 2,635,574
1992 — 2,610,193 1991 — 2,591,230 1990 — 2,577,426

Median Age of Population: 1998 — 33.4 years (male 31.8 yrs; female 34.9 yrs)
1995 — 31.7 years (male 29.8 yrs; female 33.4 yrs)) 1990 — 31.1 years

No. of Households: 1998: 972,868 ('90-'98: +6.8%) **Persons P/Household:** 1998: 2.8 1990: 2.75

Household Information, 1990:
- **Tot. Number of Households:** 910,574 (1980-90: +10.1%)
- **Family Households:** 679,191 (74.6%, rank 2)
- **Nonfamily Households:** 231,383 (25.4%, rank 50)
- **Married Couple Households:** 498,522 (54.7% of households)
- **Households with Children:** 257,007 (28.2% of households)
- **Two Person Households:** 269,767 (29.6% of households)
- **Over 7-Person Households:** 20,962 (2.3% of households)

> In late summer 2000, some preliminary results of the 2000 Census trickling in showed Mississippi's population was
> 1,728,520 white (61.9%, up 5.6%)
> 1,010,216 black (36.2%, up 10.1%)
> 23,975 Hispanics (0.86%, up 49.9%)
> 19,601 Asian/Pacific Islanders (+49.7%)
> 10,282 Native American (+20%)
> = 2,792,594 TOTAL (+8.3% from 1990).

Pop. Below The Poverty Level: 1998 — 17.1% 1997 — 18.6%
Total Medicaid Eligibles, April 2000: 408,594
Projected Population: 2005 — 2,969,905 2010 — 3,104,296

> Projections by Mississippi Institutions of Higher Learning, Center for Policy Research and Planning; Jackson, Miss.

HOUSING

Housing Units, 1990: 1,010,423 (urban — 249,574 or 24.7%; suburban — 239,470 or 23.7%; rural units — 521,378 or 51.6% of total) 2.55 persons per housing unit, rank 4

Median Year Structures Built: 1971 **Homes Built Before 1940:** 8.6%
Occupied Housing Units: 911,402 (90.2% of total units) **Persons per Housing Unit:** 2.72
Occupied Housing Units with More Than 1 Person per Room: 5.8%, rank 11
Homes with: 1-3 rooms — 12.2% 4-8 rooms — 83.8% 9 or more — 4.0% Avg. — 5.3 rooms
Home Ownership: 1998 — 75.1% '90 — 71.5%

> In 1998, Miss. tied with Kentucky for 3rd highest home-ownership rate in the U.S., at 75.1%, up from 73.7% (6th) in 1997, and from 71.1% (11th) in 1995. In metro Jackson, 4,730 homes were sold in 1998 and 4,693 in 1999. The median price for homes in Jackson was $95,100 in 1999 and $93,200 in 1998. The median price on the Mississippi Gulf Coast was $89,000 in 1999 and $86,000 in 1998.

Owner-Occupied Units: 651,587
- **Percent of Total Units:** 64.49%
- **Percent of Occupied Units:** 71.5%
- **Persons per Unit:** 2.78
- **Valued:** less than $49,999: 56.4%; $50,000-$99,999: 35.3%; $100,000-$249,999: 7.6%
  $250,000-$499,999: 0.5%; over $500,000: 0.1%; **Median Value:** $45,600
- **Median Monthly Homeowner Costs:** $511
- **Owners with Monthly Cost...**below $500—48.5%; $500-$999—43.6%; $1,000-$1,999—7.3%
- **Average Owner's Income Spent for Housing:** 20.8%
- **Value of Residential Remodeling:** $44,954,083 ($17.47 p/capita)

New Single Family Housing Permits: 1999 — 11,000 1998 — 12,880
Existing Single Family Home Sales: 1999 — 51,100 1998 — 48,200
1997 — 43,500 1990 — 28,200

> Mississippi had the fastest growth in the Southeast in the number of single-family building permits issued in the first quarter of 1999 — 10,384 — up 32% from 7,870 in the first quarter of 1998.

Vacant Homes: For Sale: 12.8% of all vacant homes **For Rent:** 27.5% of all vacant homes
Renter-Occupied Units: 259,787
- **Percent of Total Units:** 25.71%, rank 46
- **Percent of Occupied Units:** 28.5%, rank 49
- **Persons per Unit:** 2.65, rank 4
- **Median Contract Rent:** $215 monthly
- **Renters with Monthly Rent:** under $200, 45.9%; $200-$499, 50.8%; $500-$749, 2.9%
- **Renters Income Spent for Rent:** 27.1% **Rental Vacancy Rate:** 9.5%, rank 18

> Manufactured housing in Mississippi had a record $1.1 billion impact on the state's economy during 1998. The seven manufacturing plants, plus 227 retail sales centers, provided Mississippi with more than 4,500 jobs and a $52 million payroll!

Manufactured Housing (Mobile Homes), Trailers & Other: 16.38% of total housing units, rank 9
Total Energy Use by Residences, 1995: 192 trillion Btu (71.2 million Btu per capita)
Electric Energy Use by Residences, 1997: 49.48 trillion Btu (18.1 million Btu per capita)
Homes Heating with: gas 40.8%; electricity 30.6%; wood 7.8%; solar energy 0.02%
Homes With: water wells 12.1%; septic systems 38.3%
Households with Telephone, 1999: approx. 90% (households with no phone 10%, rank 51)
Percent of Households with Internet Access, Dec. 1998: 13.6%, the lowest in the nation.

The Ultimate Reference on the State

People of Mississippi

EDUCATION

Percentage with Bachelor's Degree or Higher (25 Years of Age or Older), Mar. 1999: 19.2% of pop.
Percentage with Bachelor's Degree or Higher (25 Years of Age or Older), 1990: 14.7%, rank 48
   Associate Degree: Black adults 4.0%; White adults 5.7%; Hispanic adults 6.4%; Native American adults 5.6%; Asian American adults 5.3%; all adults 5.2%
   Bachlor's Degree: Black adults 5.8%; White adults 11.4%; Hispanic adults 11.1%; Native American adults 6.0%; Asian Amer. adults 16.7%; all adults 9.7%
   Graduate Degree: Black adults 3.0%; White adults 5.9%; Hispanic adults 4.7%; Native American adults 2.5%; Asian American adults 18.7%; all adults 5.1%
High School Graduates 25 Years of Age & Older, March 1999: 78.0% of population
   1990: 64.3% of population, rank 51
High School Diploma Only: Black adults 22.1%; White adults 30.1%; Hispanic adults 23.2%; Native American adults 29.6%; Asian American adults 17.9%
Less Than 9th. Grade Education: Black adults 26.6%; White adults 26.4%; Hispanic adults 12.8%; Native American adults 28.0%; Asian American adults 18.0%; all minorities 26.4%; all adults 15.7%
(For more complete statistics on education, see the later chapter "Education in Mississippi.")

LABOR

Manufacturing Avg. Weekly Earnings: 1999 — $461.73   1998 — $444.22   1997 — $432.02
   Avg. Hourly Earnings: 1999 — $11.18   1998 — $10.73   1997 — $10.41
Average Pay Statewide: 1998 — $23,822 ($33,381 in U.S.)   1997 — $22,767 ($31,734 in U.S.)
Employees in Nonfarm Establishments, April 2000 (in thousands): Construction 53.5; Manufacturing 244.1; Transportation & Public Utilities 57; Wholesale & Retail Trade 248.6; FIRE (Finance, Insurance & Real Estate) 42; Services 273.2; Government 233.9; TOTAL 1,158 (1,158,000).
Employment Distribution, May 1999: 23.2% services; 21.8% trade; 21.1 mfg.; 19.9% government
Total Civilian Labor Force, 1999: Yr. — 1,270,000   Nov. — 1,289,700   Dec. — 1,305,400
   2000: Feb. — 1,307,400   Mar. — 1,312,800   Apr. — 1,306,700   July — 1,339,000
   1997 — 1,262,300 (men 662,200; women 600,100 — white 818,000; black 429,000)
Employment, 2000: Feb. — 1,235,600   Mar. — 1,238,000   Apr. — 1,243,400   July — 1,260,400
Employment, Annual Average: 1999 — 1,205,300   1998 — 1,199,200   1997 — 1,189,800
Average Unemployment & Rate for the Year, 1999: 64,700 (5.1%, rank 40)
Unemployment Rate: July 2000 — 5.9%   July 1999 — 5.3%
Number Unemployed: July 2000 — 78,600   July 1999 — 67,400
(see the later chapter "Economy of Mississippi" for more statistics on labor)

> **Median household income in Miss. in 1999 was $32,540.**
> SOURCE: U.S. Census Bureau

SOME SELECTED VITAL STATISTICS

Total Live Births:	1998 — 42,917	1997 — 41,527	1996 — 40,978	1995 — 41,332
Number of Deaths:	1998 — 27,737	1997 — 27,380	1996 — 26,566	1995 — 26,910
No. of Infant Deaths:	1998 — 436	1997 — 440	1996 — 451	1995 — 435
Abortions Performed:	1998 — 3,955	1997 — 4,325	1996 — 4,206	1995 — 3,563
Number of Marriages:	1998 — 20,911	1997 — 21,338	1996 — 21,550	1995 — 22,150
Number of Divorces:	1998 — 13,748	1997 — 13,860	1996 — 14,263	1995 — 13,182

Life Expectancy in Years (National Averages for Those Born in 1998):
   Female — 79.4   **Male** — 73.9   **Both Sexes** — 76.7
(See many additional vital statistics in the later chapter "Health in Mississippi.")

VETERANS

World War II: 58,000
Korean War: 40,000

> Of 16 million Americans who served in World War II, only 6.6 million were alive in mid-1998.

Vietnam War: 67,000 (60,000 with no prior wartime service)
Persian Gulf War: 28,000 (24,000 with no prior wartime service)
Total: War Veterans — 176,000   Peacetime Veterans — 48,000

> Mississippi has a higher percentage of veterans receiving disability compensation than any other state. Over 40,000 veterans in Mississippi received $322,669,000 in total veterans benefit payments in 1998.

Total No. of Veterans, July 1, 1998: 223,774 (24.8 million nationwide as of 7/1/1999). In spring 2000, about 1,567 veterans were dying nationwide every day. About 5,200 veterans in Mississippi, including 3,000 who served in World War II, are expected to die during the year 2000.

Profiles of Famous & Notable Mississippians

Mahmoud Abdul-Rauf

Born in Gulfport on Mar. 9, 1969, his name was Chris Jackson before he converted to Islam in the early 1990s. This basketball guard once made 283 consecutive free throws in high school practice and once scored 55 points in a college game. The 6-ft.-1 two-time LSU All-American averaged 30.2 points as an LSU freshman in 1988-89. He was the third pick overall in the 1990 NBA draft and averaged 15.2 ppg in 8 NBA seasons. He was named the NBA's Most Improved Player in 1992-93. During the 1993-94 season, Abdul-Rauf led the Denver Nuggets to their first playoff since 1990. He led Denver in scoring with 18 points per game and 3.62 assists. He was also the NBA's best free-throw shooter with 95.6% (season record second only to the .958 of Calvin Murphy in 1980-81 and this still held through the end of 1998) and had his best shooting percentage from the field in his career, 46.0, the second-best in NBA history. In 1994-95, he led the Nuggets to the playoffs for the second year in a row. During the 1995-96 season, he gained notoriety by refusing to stand during the national anthem claiming it was against his Islamic faith. The NBA suspended him, but after it cost Abdul-Rauf $31,707 for a game missed, he agreed to stand and say a silent prayer during the anthem. He led Denver in scoring (19.2 points per game) and assists (6.8 per game), and was the NBA season free-throw percentage leader with 93.0 during the 1995-96 season. Nevertheless, the Nuggets traded him to the Sacramento Kings at season's end. The 1997-98 season was the worst of his seven in the NBA as he averaged 7.3 points and 1.2 rebounds in only 31 games of 82, averaging just 17 minutes per outing. He spent much of the season on the injured list.. His five-year $13.5 million package netted him $3.3 million for the season. After his contract with the Kings expired in the summer of 1998, Abdul-Raul left the NBA and signed a two-year $3.4 million contract to play basketball in Turkey. After sitting out the 1999 season, he signed with the Vancouver Grizzlies on Aug. 19, 2000.

Susan Diane Akin

Born on Aug. 12, 1964, in Meridian. She was "Little Miss America" at age 6. After being crowned Miss America 1986, she traveled with Bob Hope, performing at conventions in Las Vegas and Atlantic City. Now Susan Akin-Lynch, she has been spokesperson for the National Down's Syndrome Association and seatbelt safety, among other causes.

Margaret Walker Alexander

Born July 27, 1915, in Birmingham, she grew up in Alabama, Louisiana & Mississippi. She received her B.A. from Northwestern University in 1935, and M.A. and Ph.D. from the University of Iowa. She taught at Livingstone College, West Virginia State College, the University of Iowa, Northwestern University and Jackson State University, where she taught English. At Jackson State, she founded the Institute for the Study of the History, Life and Culture of Black People in 1968. For 11 years, she was director of the center that was renamed The Margaret Walker Alexander National Research Center in her honor. She received a Rosenwald Fellowship in 1944. In 1954, she was a Ford Fellow at Yale University. She received a literary fellowship in 1968, a Fulbright Hayes Fellowship in 1971 and a Senior Fellowship from the National Endowment for the Humanities. Her writing first appeared in *Crisis* magazine in 1934. Alexander began writing poetry at age 15. In 1942, she received the Yale Award for Younger Poets for her book, *For My People*. She authored nine books including five volumes of poetry. Her first novel *Jubilee* (1966), about slave life, won a Houghton Mifflin Literary Fellowship Award and became an international best seller. It even inspired an opera. She sued author Alex Haley in 1988, claiming that his book *Roots* infringed on *Jubilee*'s copyright. The case was dismissed. Her other books include *Prophets for a New Day* (1970), *How I Wrote Jubilee* (1972) and *October Journey* (1973). Alexander lectured at seminars and literary festivals around the country. A Jackson Public Library and a Jackson street are named for her. She received the Living Legacy Award from President Jimmy Carter. At her last public appearance in Chicago, Alexander was inducted into the African American Literary Hall of Fame and received the Lifetime Achievement Award from Chicago State University. She received the Lifetime Achievement Award, the highest honor of the Mississippi Governor's Awards for Excellence in the Arts. She was the recipient of many honorary degrees from around the country including the first ever presented by Jackson State University in the spring of 1998. Alexander, along with Eudora Welty and Thalia Mara, were the first recipients of the (Jackson) Mayor's Arts Achievement Honors on July 30, 1998. Novelist, poet, biographer, scholar, teacher, humanitarian and Civil Rights leader Margaret Walker Alexander died after a bout with cancer at her daughter's home in Chicago on Nov. 30, 1998, at the age of 83. She is buried in the Garden Memorial Park in Jackson.

Mary Alice

Born Dec. 3, 1941, in Indianola, Mississippi. She's a black supporting actress who's been onscreen since the 1970s. She earned Emmy nominations on NBC-TV's *I'll Fly Away* in 1993 and starred with James Earl Jones in both Broadway's *Fences* and TV's *The Vernon Johns Story*. She received a nomination in 1995 for a Tony Award as Best Actress in a Play for her role in *Having Our Say*. She played "Annie Lamb" in *Bonfire of the Vanities* (1990), a movie with fellow Mississippian Morgan Freeman, she was "Nurse Margaret" in the Robin Williams hit movie *Awakenings* (1990), "Lottie" in *A Perfect World* (1993), plays "Alice" in *Bed of Roses* (1996), played "Rosa Lynn Sinclair" in *Down in the Delta* (1998) and appeared in *Catfish in Black Bean Sauce* (2000).

John Allen

Born John Mills Allen on July 8, 1846, in Tishomingo County, Mississippi. "Private" John Allen served 8 terms in the U.S. Congress from 1885 to 1901. While everybody in politics seemed to have been nothing less than a brigadier general in the Civil War, Allen boasted that he "had been one of the few privates, if not the only one." He often entertained House members with humorous speeches. He died on Oct. 30, 1917, and is buried in Glenwood Cemetery in Tupelo.

Mose Allison

Born Mose John Allison, Jr. on Nov. 11, 1927 in Tippo, Tallahatchie County, Mississippi. He attended Ole Miss and has a B.A. degree in English and philosophy from Louisiana State. This jazz pianist and vocalist worked with jazz masters Stan Getz, Gerry Mulligan, Al Cohn and Zoot Sims, and has toured much. He has recorded almost 40 albums including *Lessons in Living* (1983) and *Ever Since The World Ended* (1989), both nominated for Grammy Awards, *Gimcracks and Gewgaws* (1997). Also quite a prolific songwriter, the Yardbirds, the Who, Van Morrison, Leon Russell and Bonnie Raitt have all drawn upon his 100-plus original songs such as *Hello There, Universe*, *I Don't Worry About A Thing*, and *Parchman Farm*. Allison lives on Long Island, New York.

Alyce Alston

Born Alice Alston on June 12, 1964, in Jackson, Mississippi, her parents are Alex Alston, Jr., a Jackson attorney and Sarah

Profiles of Famous & Notable Mississippians

Jane Alston, a former Jackson City School Board member. Alyce graduated from Murrah High School. After graduating from Southern Methodist University in Dallas, she landed her first job in advertising sales for the *American Journal of Nursing* in New York. While studying for her masters of business administration degree from Pepperdine University between 1990 and 1995, she was West Coast manager of *TV Guide*. In Dec. 1995, Alston was named associate publisher of *Allure*, a women's magazine, and then publisher of *YM*, a teen magazine, from 1996-99. After spending most of 2000 as publisher of *O, The Oprah Magazine*, Alston announced in August that she was leaving to become publisher of the fashion magazine *W*. Alston is known in the magazine trade as "the turn-around queen" because of her success in making winners out of publications in need of an overhaul. Alston lives in Manhattan with her husband, Tom Biggs, an Internet consultant, and their two children.

Lance Alworth

Born Lance Dwight Alworth on Aug. 3, 1940, in Houston, Texas, he grew up in Brookhaven, Mississippi. Nicknamed "Bambi" for his smooth, graceful, spectacular moves. He was an Arkansas All-America in 1961. In pro football he was a flanker/wide receiver for the San Diego Chargers (1962-70 and the Dallas Cowboys (1971-72). He was the yearly leader in receptions in 1966 with 73 carries producing 1,383 yards and 13 TDs, and also in 1968 going 1,312 yards with 68 receptions and scoring 10 TDs. He had more than 1,000 receiving every year from 1963 to '69. His pro career record: 542 receptions, 10,266 yards and 85 receiving TDs. His total of 87 career TDs ranks 20th (as of 1998) on the list of Leading Lifetime Touchdown Scorers. He caught passes in 96 straight games. He was the AFL receiving leader three years, played in seven AFL All-Star games and scored the first Dallas TD in Super Bowl VI. He's listed on Pro Football Digest's All-Time All-Pro Football Team. He's in the College Football Hall of Fame and was the first AFL star to be enshrined in the Pro Football Hall of Fame (1978). He was inducted into the Mississippi Sports Hall of Fame in 1988. He was among 48 players picked to be on the NFL's 75th Anniversary All-Time Team in 1994. He was one of only 4 Mississippians picked (Alworth, Ray Guy, Walter Payton & Jerry Rice) and one of only 2 Mississippians (Rice) out of the four wide receivers.

Andy Anderson

Born May 15, 1935, in Memphis, he grew up in Clarksdale, Miss. Andy became a Rock 'n' Roll singer, songwriter and musician who formed a group called "The Rolling Stones" while attending Mississippi State University in Starkville in the mid-1950s, long before the famous British group took that name. By 1955 the group was playing all around campus, in neighboring towns, and on the road. While still in school, Andy and the group cut an album at Sun Records in Memphis, but it was never released because Sun was using its funds to pay its long roster of artists. At Sun and on the road, Andy and the Rolling Stones played with Elvis Presley, Jerry Lee Lewis, Johnny Cash and Roy Orbison. At one time Andy and Elvis shared the same voice teacher in Memphis, Zelma Lee Whitfield. Andy and the other group members graduated from Mississippi State in 1957. After Murray Nash and Associates in Nashville signed the Rolling Stones in 1957, a deal was struck with a subsidiary of London Records (same label that later signed the famous Rolling Stones) for the recording of *Johnny Valentine*. The song was written by Andy as an answer to *The Naughty Lady of Shady Lane*, a popular song at the time by the Mills Brothers. Studio musicians were used in Nashville because the Rolling Stones members didn't belong to the union. The recording of *Johnny Valentine* featured Andy on lead vocals, Hank Garland on lead guitar, Buddy Harmon on drums, Bobby Moore on bass, and the Jordanaires on background vocals. It holds a unique place in musical history — it was the first Rock and Roll record to be distributed on a worldwide basis! It sold over 600,000 copies. Later in 1957 at Fidelity Studio in Nashville Andy and his group cut *You Shake a Me Up* for a 45 single record, which was picked up by Apollo, a New York label. It became one of the few songs in history to be the Pick Hit of the Week in *Cashbox*, *Billboard*, and *Music Reporter* all in the same week. Andy also started another Rock 'n' Roll group, The Dawnbreakers, in 1960. In 1974, he teamed up with J.J. Hettinger, a talented songwriter, and together they wrote many songs, cut some tracks at Malaco Studios in Jackson, and toured under the name of The Eagle and the Hawk. In addition to music, Andy even pursued an acting career while living in California. From 1966-68, under the guidance of Aaron Spelling and the William Morris Agency, Andy was successful playing small parts in films and recording new songs with the group, The Association. Andy and his manager also formed their own management company and began managing other hot groups such as The Seeds, Canned Heat and Jefferson Airplane. In the late 1970s Bison Bop Records, a major distributor of old Rock and Roll in Europe, released Andy's entire catalog in Germany. The success of Andy's album in Germany led to the release of his old Sun recordings in England, Sweden and Japan. In Europe, Andy is considered one of the original founders of Rock 'n' Roll. Anderson has also been an entrepreneur and has founded and operated several businesses, including a wholesale electric supply company he started in Jackson in 1960, Big Valley Land & Construction Co. in Taos, New Mexico, and others. Since 1987, he's been selling medical supplies for a company in Jackson, where he still lives with his wife, the former Kay Norcom. Andy still finds time to make music. This is a very condensed version of Andy's interesting and varied life. For a longer version, check the www.rockabillyhall.com Website. Andy is a member of the Rockabilly Hall of Fame.

Reuben Anderson

Born in Jackson on Sept. 16, 1942. In 1967, he became the first black graduate of the University of Mississippi School of Law. Anderson started out handling Civil Rights cases and representing such figures as activist Fannie Lou Hamer and Aaron Henry of Clarksdale, former head of the Mississippi state NAACP. He later served as a city and county judge and was the state's first black Circuit Court judge since Reconstruction, appointed by former Gov. William Winter to preside in the Hinds/Yazoo district. Gov. Bill Allain appointed him to the state high court in 1985 and Anderson became Mississippi's first black Supreme Court Justice. He was elected to the job in 1986 and unopposed in 1989. He resigned in 1990 to return to private practice. Anderson became the first black to head the Mississippi Bar Association when the 5,200 attorneys in the state elected him to that position in Feb. 1996.

Walter Anderson

Born Walter Inglis Anderson on Sept. 29, 1903, in New Orleans, he grew up on the Mississippi Gulf Coast. He was educated at a private boarding school, then attended the Parsons Institute of Design in New York and the Pennsylvania Academy of Fine Arts, where his drawings earned him a scholarship for study abroad. He traveled extensively throughout Europe. An oil painter, watercolorist, sculptor, naturalist, wood carver, decorator, and potter, Anderson

Profiles of Famous & Notable Mississippians

produced award-winning pottery for Shearwater Pottery in Ocean Springs, founded by his older brother Peter in 1928. He painted many naturalist murals and his block prints and children's book illustrations were featured in the Brooklyn Museum. In the late 1930s, Anderson was diagnosed with schizophrenia and spent three years in and out of hospitals. He died on Nov. 30, 1965. The largest Anderson book ever published, *Symphony of Animals*, with 175 full-color plates and 70 ink and pencil sketches of animals and amphibians of Mississippi, was released in 1996.

Dana Andrews

Born Carver Dana Andrews on Jan. 1, 1909, in the Dont Community near Collins, Miss. He was already a qualified accountant and a trained singer before starting his work in movies. He became an actor and made his screen debut in *Lucky Cisco Kid* in 1938, but had his first worthwhile part in *The Westerner* in 1939. He made a total of sixty-nine films, including his last one, *Prince Jack*, in 1984. Some of his other movies are *Swamp Water* (1941), *Tobacco Road* (1941), *Ball of Fire* (1942), *The North Star* (1943), *The Ox-Bow Incident* (1943, added to the National Film Registry in the Library of Congress in 1998), *The Purple Heart* (1943), *Up in Arms* (1944), *Laura* (1944), *Boomerang* (1947), *Night Song* (1947), *My Foolish Heart* (1949), *Edge of Doom* (1950), *Beyond a Reasonable Doubt* (1956), *In Harm's Way* (1961), *Brainstorm* (1965), *Airport 1975* (1974) and *The Last Tycoon* (1976). His movie, *The Best Years of Our Lives* (1946), was rated No. 37 on The American Film Institute's list of the Top 100 Greatest American Movies of All Time announced in 1998. He was in the TV daytime soap opera *Bright Promise* in the late 1960s. Andrews died on December 17, 1992. Actor Steve Forrest, born in Huntsville, Texas on Sept. 29, 1924, is his brother.

John Armistead

Born June 14, 1941, in Mobile, Ala. He earned a B.A. from Mississippi College in 1963, a masters from Golden Gate Baptist Theological Seminary in 1966 and a doctorate from New Orleans Theological Seminary in 1975. He moved to Mississippi in 1979 and became pastor of Calvary Baptist Church in Tupelo. He resigned as pastor after his first mystery novel, *A Legacy of Vengeance* (1994), was published and became a religion journalist for the Tupelo *Daily Journal* newspaper. He followed up on his first novel with two more, *Cruel As The Grave* (1996) and *A Homecoming for Murder* (1998). All his novels feature Grover Bramlett, the Sheriff of fictional Chakchiuma County, Mississippi.

Henry Armstrong

Born Henry Jackson on Dec. 12, 1912, in Columbus, Mississippi, the 11th of 15 children. His father, also named Henry, was a mix of Indian, Irish and black. His mother, America, was half-Cherokee Indian. When Armstrong was 4, the family moved to St. Louis. His mother died a year later, and he was raised by his grandmother. As an amateur boxer Armstrong fought under the name Melody Jackson. On his debut as an 18-year-old pro, he was knocked out in the third round by Al Iovino on July 27, 1931, in Pennsylvania. It was one of only two knockouts Armstrong would suffer in his career. Armstrong moved to Los Angeles, where he resumed his amateur status. He teamed up with — and took the surname of — a trainer and former boxer named Henry Armstrong. He officially turned pro a year later after failing to make the 1932 Olympic team, but lost his first two fights in Los Angeles. Boxing as a featherweight, he gained a lot of experience from 1933 to 1935, fighting 46 times, mostly in California and Mexico. In 1936 legendary singer Al Jolson purchased Armstrong's contract. The next year Armstrong fought 27 times and won all of them — 26 by a knockout. Armstrong knocked out featherweight champion Petey Sarron in the 6th round on Oct. 29, 1937. He won 14 fights before bypassing the lightweight title and challenging welterweight champion Barney Ross for his crown on May 31, 1938. Armstrong overwhelmed Ross to gain the 15-round decision. Armstrong took away Lou Ambers' lightweight crown on Aug. 17, 1938 in Madison Square Garden, but not without much difficulty. Despite almost blacking out in the 15th round from a badly cut lip and other injuries, Armstrong won a split decision to make history. The 5-foot-5 "Homicide Hank" was the World Champion Featherweight Champion in 1937-38, the World Welterweight Champion 1938-40 and the World Lightweight Champion in 1938 — the only boxer to ever hold three world titles simultaneously! And he managed this unique feat back when there were only eight weight classes! On March 1, 1940, in Los Angeles, Armstrong tried to become a four-division champion when he attempted to take the middleweight crown from Ceferino Garcia, but it ended in a draw enabling Garcia to keep the title. Seven months later, Armstrong finally lost his welterweight title after 19 successful defenses, including six in 1940. In 1943, he lost a 10-round decision to an up-and-coming Sugar Ray Robinson. Armstrong had a 151-21-9 record in his 15-year pro career, including 101 knockouts! He played himself in 3 movies: *Keep Punching* (1939), *The Pittsburgh Kid* (1941) and *Joe Palooka, Champ* (1946). Armstrong's purses had totaled almost $1 million, but most of the money was gone when he retired at age 32. He overcame alcoholism and became an ordained Baptist minister in 1951 before returning to St. Louis. Armstrong died of heart failure in Los Angeles on Oct. 24, 1988, at age 75 and is buried in Rosedale Memorial Park. He was inducted into the International Boxing Hall of Fame on June 10, 1990.

Richard "Dick" Armstrong

Born on Aug. 29, 1929, in Jackson, Mississippi. He attended the University of Missouri School of Journalism and Columbia University. Armstrong worked for *Time* magazine, the *Saturday Evening Post*, and was executive editor of *Fortune* magazine. He retired in 1989. He died of cancer on Aug. 16, 1992, in New York City at the age of 62.

Woodie Assaf

This living-legend in Mississippi broadcasting was born in McComb on March 15, 1917. He graduated from McComb High School, then attended Southwest Junior College and Louisiana State University. Woodie worked at McComb's first radio station, WSKB (now WHNY) from 1937 to 1940, then left to attend Columbia Radio College in Chicago. He entered the army as a private in 1941, advanced to the rank of 1st Lieutenant and was a training officer during World War II. After discharge, he again entered broadcasting and worked for 5 months at WQBC in Vicksburg and then WJDX in Jackson in 1945. He stayed there for 9 years, then switched over to WLBT-TV the day it went on the air, Dec. 20, 1953. He worked between WJDX radio and WLBT-TV for about 2 years before going full-time on TV recording commercials, reporting news, sports, and weather, and selling advertising. It wasn't long before he settled on just reporting the weather and selling. As of Dec. 20, 1999, he had been the weatherman on WLBT for 46 years — with the same TV station longer than any other TV weatherman in the nation. He is Jackson's (and Mississippi's) most-watched, most-popular and most-trusted weatherman. He's a very active member of his community — Past President of the Mississippi Sportscasters Association,

Profiles of Famous & Notable Mississippians

Past President of his Kiwanis Club, and on numerous boards and committees. In 1982, he was chosen Alumnus of the Year at Southwest Community College. He's been honored with many awards such as the Sales and Marketing Award in 1972 and 1986, the American Advertising Federation Silver Medal in 1978, the MBA Outstanding Public Service Award in 1970, the Germain-Monteil Volunteer Activist Award presented by McRae's in 1979, the Lindsey Nelson Lifetime Achievement Award in Sportscasting from the All-American Football Foundation in March 1996 and the Hope Award for philanthropic generosity and community service from the Mississippi Chapter of the National Multiple Sclerosis Society in Sept. 1998 — to name just a few. And, Woodie says one of the greatest honors he's ever received was carrying the Olympic Torch on May 25, 1996. After Hurricane Camille hit Mississippi in 1969, Woodie hosted a benefit that starred Bob Hope and raised more than $2.5 million including a donation of $5,000 from Elvis Presley obtained by Woodie through Col. Tom Parker. After the 1979 Easter Flood, he hosted another benefit show that raised $88,000. He has been the host and producer of the annual Easter Seal Telethon since 1975 that's raised almost $4 million helping over 345,000 Mississippians with thousands of services. In addition, since 1985, Woodie has hosted the Santa's Toy Chest at WLBT, collecting thousands of toys for needy children. His benefits and public service work has raised over $10 million! In May 1999, Woodie underwent angioplasty to remove obstructions in a heart value. Doctors at Baptist Medical Center in Jackson performed double bypass surgery and heart value replacement on July 7, 1999. On Aug. 23, Woodie underwent surgery for the third time in as many months when surgeons operated on him to repair a ruptured abdominal aortic aneurysm. After a couple of months, Woodie was back on the air again on Nov. 4 doing what he loves best. In a special poll conducted by *The Clarion-Ledger* newspaper of Jackson in 1999, readers picked Woodie (172 votes out of 305) as their favorite Mississippi TV personality of the millennium! Woodie's closest competitor was his own colleague and stand-in, feature reporter Walt Grayson (see profile), who received 65 votes.

Roscoe Ates

Born Jan. 20, 1892, in Grange, Lawrence County, Mississippi. He spent a great deal of his childhood overcoming a severe stammer, but revived it for comic effect when he became a vaudeville, stage, screen and TV actor and became known for his stutter. He was in over 95 movies from *South Sea Rose* (1929 - ship's cook) to *The Errand Boy* (1961). In between, he appeared in some sizable roles in such films as *The Champ* (1931), *Freaks* (1932, on the National Film Registry, Library of Congress) and *Alice in Wonderland* (1933). He also had some minor roles in some big films, such as a "Press Photographer" (uncredited) in *King Kong* (1933) and a convalescent soldier (uncredited) in *Gone with the Wind* (1939). He played the recurring character "Soapy Jones," a comic sidekick to singing cowboy Eddie Dean, in a series of 15 low-budget westerns in the 1940s including *Tumbleweed Trail* (1946), *Colorado Serenade* (1946), *Stars Over Texas* (1946), *Wild West* (1946), *Range Beyond the Blue* (1947), *Shadow Valley* (1947), *West to Glory* (1947), *Tornado Range* (1948), and *The Westward Trail* (1948). Ates appeared in several Columbia and Universal shorts (1937) and in the *Wild Bill Hickock* serial (1938). He played Deputy Roscoe in the 1950 TV series, *The Marshal of Gunsight Pass*. Notable TV guest appearances include: *Whispering Smith* in the episode "Three for One" on 7/3/1961; *Alfred Hitchcock Presents* in the episode "Road Hog" on 12/6/1959 and playing "Ben White" in the episode "And The Desert Shall Blossom" on 12/21/1958; and on *Wagon Train* in the episode: "The Sacramento Story" on 6/25/1958. Ates died from lung cancer on March 1, 1962, in Hollywood, California at the age of 70.

Ruth Attaway

Born in Greenville, Mississippi on June 28, 1910, she is best known for her work in theater. She debuted on Broadway in 1936 and went on to work on various stages, on and off Broadway, for over 40 years. Attaway was the first director in the New York Players Guild. She had supporting roles in several movies. Her film debut was as "Moll" in *The President's Lady* (1953). Her other movie credits: played "Philomena" in *The Young Don't Cry* (1957), an uncredited bit part in *Raintree County* (1957), portions of which were filmed in Mississippi; "Serena" in *Porgy and Bess* (1959); "Mayor's nurse" in *The Taking of Pelham One Two Three* (1974); "Edna" in *Conrack* (1974); and "Louise" in *Being There* (1979). She also work some in radio and TV. Attaway played "Delia" in the TV movie *The Bermuda Depths* (1978). When not acting, she worked for the American Red Cross and for the state of New York. She died in New York City on Sept. 21, 1987, from injuries she received in a fire. She was 77.

William Attaway

Born Nov. 19, 1911, in Greenville, Miss., his family moved to Chicago when he was very young. He dropped out of the University of Illinois and spent his time as a hobo, laborer and seaman before returning to finish his schooling. He moved to New York where he published his first novel, *Let Me Breathe Thunder*, in 1939. His second novel was *Blood on the Forge* (1941). In the 1950s he turned to writing for radio, films and TV. He was the first black writer to write scripts for TV and films. He wrote *A Hundred Years of Laughter*, an hour long special on black humor that aired in 1964 and featured comedians Redd Fox, Moms Mabley, and Flip Wilson in their very first appearance on TV. He also wrote for such TV programs as *Wide, Wide World* and *The Colgate Hour*. Attaway was a composer as well as a writer and arranged songs for Harry Belafonte. He composed over 500 songs, some 150 of which are calypsos He also wrote the *Calypso Song Book* (1957). Attaway died of heart failure on June 17, 1986, at age 74 in Los Angeles, California.

James A. Autry

Born Mar. 8, 1933, in Memphis, he grew up in Benton County, Mississippi. He received a B.A. degree in journalism from the University of Mississippi in 1955 and was later elected to the Ole Miss Alumni Hall of Fame. He was president of the Meredith Corporation's Magazine Group, publisher of *Ladies' Home Journal*, *Better Homes and Gardens* and *Successful Farming*. He retired from Meredith in 1991 to pursue a career as lecturer and management consultant. His books include *Love and Profit: The Art of Caring Leadership* (1991), *Life & Work: A Manager's Search for Meaning* (1994) and *Confessions of an Accidental Businessman: It Takes a Lifetime to Learn Wisdom* (1996). He's had two volumes of poetry published, *Nights Under a Tin Roof* (1983) and *Life After Mississippi* (1989).

Blaine Baggett

Born Austin Blaine Baggett on July 20, 1951, at Horn Lake, Miss., he attended Northwest Mississippi Community College in Senatobia and received his degree in English literature from Millsaps College in Jackson in 1973. After a one-year stint in the Peace Corps, a friend at ETV in Jackson hired him in 1974 to write station breaks. He then worked for PBS-TV in

Profiles of Famous & Notable Mississippians

Washington and from there to KCET, the public station in Los Angles, where he is now director of public affairs and feature documentaries. Baggett was executive producer and co-writer of the monumental 8-hour PBS series on World War I called *The Great War and the Shaping of the 20th Century*. He also directed one of the 8 one-hour episodes which aired 4 consecutive nights in Nov. 1996. He co-authored *The Great War*, a companion book to the series. He co-authored another book, *Secret Intelligence*, a history of the CIA, a companion book to the TV series of the same name, which Baggett produced. His international and award-winning body of work also includes *Spy Machines*, *The Astronomers* and *Spaceflight*, one of the highest-rated PBS miniseries ever. Baggett has also produced many programs in the award-winning PBS *Nova* series. He was one of the U.S. finalists for the First Journalist in Space competition, a program placed on indefinite hold following the Challenger space shuttle disaster.

Howard Bahr

Born Howard Leslie Hereford on Aug. 3, 1946 in Meridian, Mississippi, his mother remarried and he adopted the surname of his stepfather, Bahr. In the U.S. Navy from 1964 to 1968, he served in Vietnam. He has held several jobs, including one with Illinois Central Railroad for 5 years. Bahr worked at William Faulkner's Rowan Oak home in Oxford from 1976 to 1993, serving as curator from 1984 to 1993. For several years now, he's been an assistant professor of English at Motlow Community College in Fayetteville, Tennessee. It took him three years to finish his first novel, *The Black Flower: A Civil War Story* (1997), a gripping story about the brutal battle of Franklin, Tennessee (a real battle) as told through the eyes of one common soldier. It's a riveting blend of history and fiction that Bahr, a long-time Civil War re-enactor, wrote after 20 years of research. Many reviewers compared it to another novel, *Cold Mountain*, which also came out in 1997 and climbed to No. 1 on the *New York Times* bestseller list, although many reviewers said *The Black Flower* was even better. Bahr's novel won the prestigious Harold D. Vursell Memorial Award from the American Academy of Arts and Letters. Bahr's second Civil War novel, *The Year of Jubilo*, was published in May 2000. It's the story of a 33-year-old teacher from Mississippi who was shamed into joining the war, then returns home only to find things curiously different. Bahr also authored the book, *Home for Christmas* (1997), a family story for children and adults.

Coolidge Ball

Born Nov. 6, 1951, in Inverness, he grew up in Indianola (both places are in Sunflower County, Miss.). The 6-foot-4 basketball player's nickname is "Cool-Aid." Ball was the first black athlete at the University of Mississippi when he signed a basketball scholarship at Ole Miss in 1970. He was selected as the best freshman basketball player in the SEC in 1970, was All-SEC in 1972 and 1973, and was elected Captain of the Ole Miss team in 1974. He averaged 22.7 ppg and 16.4 rebounds in his freshman year. His sophomore-through-senior stats include 1,072 points (14.1 ppg), 754 rebounds, and 131 assists in 76 games played. He shot 43.3% from the field and 72% from the free throw line. Ball graduated from Ole Miss in 1975 with a B.S. degree in recreation leadership. He coached basketball at Northwest Community College in Senatobia, Mississippi from 1975-79. In the fall of 1979, he started his own business, Ball Sign Company in Oxford. Ball was inducted into the Ole Miss Sports Hall of Fame in 1991.

Glen Ballard

This musician (bass guitar, keyboards and synthesizer), songwriter and record producer was born in Natchez on May 1, 1953. He studied journalism and political science at Ole Miss with the intention of going to law school. The day after graduation, he drove to Los Angeles where he landed a job as a gofer with Elton John's band and eventually wound up playing piano for singer Kiki Dee. Ballard later wrote songs for artists Quincy Jones was producing. Ballard's studio career began with actor-singer Jack Wagner's 1984 album *All I Need*, which launched the hit title track. He worked with other artists including Teddy Pendergrass and Ava Cherry, also playing synthesizer on Michael Jackson's 1987 effort *Bad*. After working on Barbra Streisand's *Till I Loved You* and Paula Abdul's *Forever Your Girl*, Ballard's production breakthrough came with the 1990 release of Wilson Phillips' smash self-titled debut. Ballard co-wrote Michael Jackson's smash hit, *Man in the Mirror*. He won a Grammy in 1990 for Best Instrumental Arrangement Accompanying Vocals for his song *The Places You Find Love*, recorded by Chaka Khan. In 1996, he won a Grammy for Best Rock Song, *You Oughta Know*, and the singer Ballard produced, Canadian artist Alanis Morissette, also won a Grammy for the song and another one for the album it was taken from, *Jagged Little Pill*, which Ballard also produced. Morissette was nominated in 6 categories and Ballard received 5 nominations. Ballard wrote the music for her No. 1 album which went multi-platinum, the 3rd best-seller of 1995 (over 4 million) and the top best-selling album of 1996 — 10 million copies — making it the best-selling album ever by a woman. By the end of 1998, *Jagged Little Pill* had sold over 28 million copies! In the spring of 1998, Ballard teamed with Capitol Records to form a new label, Java. Their first action was to sign Lisa Presley to an exclusive contract. In Nov. 1998, Morissette released a new album, *Supposed Former Infatuation Junkie*, co-produced and co-written by Glen Ballard. The album set a record for first-week sales when it sold 469,000 copies and entered the *Billboard* chart at No. 1! It went on to go multi-platinum in 1998, selling over 3 million copies!

Louis Baloni

Born Aug. 28, 1934, in Shaw, Mississippi. He received his B.S. degree in accounting from Delta State University of Cleveland in 1956. Baloni is the executive vice president and chief financial officer of Dunavant Enterprises of Memphis, Tennessee, the world's largest cotton merchant. He was named DSU's Outstanding Alumnus of 1996.

Moe Bandy

Born Feb. 12, 1944, in Meridian. This Country singer and songwriter gave up the rodeo for music. He had the hit singles *Bandy The Rodeo Clown*, *Hank Williams, You Wrote My Life*, *It's A Cheatin' Situation*, and *I Cheated Me Right out of You* (#1 in 1979) and a No. 1 hit single with Joe Stampley, *Just Good Ol' Boys* (1979). He and Joe received the Country Music Association Vocal Duo of the Year Award in 1980.

Walter Lanier "Red" Barber

Born in Columbus, Miss. on Feb. 17, 1908. He was a famous radio sportscaster with his own unique style for more than 30 years. He had a flair for developing such catch phrases as "rhubarb" and "sittin' in the catbird seat!" His radio career started in 1933 when he was hired as team announcer for the Cincinnati Reds. In 1939 he became the announcer for what would later be called the Brooklyn Dodgers Radio Network. By 1953 Barber's broadcasts were picked up by 117 stations nationwide. He left Brooklyn and began the 1954 season as

Profiles of Famous & Notable Mississippians

sportscaster for the New York Yankees where he stayed for 12 years. In 1978 he was elected to the Baseball Hall of Fame. In 1981, he began a weekly sports commentary show on National Public Radio, and he won the Peabody Award for his radio commentary in 1991. His books include the autobiographical *Rhubarb in the Catbird Seat* (1968) and *1947, When All Hell Broke Loose in Baseball* (1982). He died on Oct. 22, 1992.

Haley Barbour

Born Oct. 22, 1947, in Yazoo City. Barbour started in Republican politics while still a student at Ole Miss. In 1968 at age 21, he organized 20 Mississippi counties for Richard Nixon's presidential campaign. Later, as a student at Ole Miss Law School, he worked as executive director of the state Republican Party. He soon moved into a job with the Southern Association of Republican Chairmen. Barbour has made only one bid for public office. He lost a Senate race to John Stennis in 1982, but still managed to garner 36 percent of the vote, quite a feat against Stennis. He became Mississippi's Republican National Committeeman in 1984. He was the White House Political Director in the Reagan administration in 1988 and a senior advisor to George Bush's successful presidential campaign. Barbour became Chairman of the Republican National Committee in Jan. 1993. He can take much credit for the GOP sweep across the country in the election in Nov. 1994, in which Republicans gained control of both the Senate and House for the first time in 40 years! The polished 36th GOP convention in San Diego in Aug. 1996 went so smoothly it was called "Haley's Show." Republicans retained control over both houses of Congress in the Nov. 1996 election. Not since 1930 had the GOP won both chambers of Congress in consecutive elections. He gave up chairmanship of the RNC after his 2nd term expired in Jan. 1997 and resigned his national committee-man post in Aug. 1998. He now travels extensively as a Washington lobbyist and political consultant. In the March 20, 2000 issue of *Forbes* magazine's list of the top 100 highest paid celebrities, Barbour, one of 3 Mississippians on the list, ranked No. 70 with his 1999 income of $7.5 million. The Highway 3 bypass at Yazoo City is named Haley Barbour Parkway.

Van T. Barfoot

Born Van Thomas Barfoot on June 15, 1919, near Edinburg, Leake County, Mississippi. He was living in Carthage when he entered the U.S. Army. Barfoot is one of only 4 *native* Mississippians (of 7 Mississippians) to be awarded the Congressional Medal of Honor (CMOH) during World War II. Barfoot was presented the Medal on Oct. 4, 1944, for the bravery he showed on May 23, 1944. Here are the actual words of his citation: "For conspicuous gallantry and intrepidity at the risk of life above and beyond the call of duty on 23 May 1944, near Carano, Italy. With his platoon heavily engaged during an assault against forces well entrenched on commanding ground, 2d Lt. Barfoot (then Tech. Sgt.) moved off alone upon the enemy left flank. He crawled to the proximity of 1 machinegun nest and made a direct hit on it with a hand grenade, killing 2 and wounding 3 Germans. He continued along the German defense line to another machinegun emplacement, and with his tommygun killed 2 and captured 3 soldiers. Members of another enemy machinegun crew then abandoned their position and gave themselves up to Sgt. Barfoot. Leaving the prisoners for his support squad to pick up, he proceeded to mop up positions in the immediate area, capturing more prisoners and bringing his total count to 17. Later that day, after he had reorganized his men and consolidated the newly captured ground, the enemy launched a fierce armored counterattack directly at his platoon positions. Securing a bazooka, Sgt. Barfoot took up an exposed position directly in front of 3 advancing Mark VI tanks. From a distance of 75 yards his first shot destroyed the track of the leading tank, effectively disabling it, while the other 2 changed direction toward the flank. As the crew of the disabled tank dismounted, Sgt. Barfoot killed 3 of them with his tommygun. He continued onward into enemy terrain and destroyed a recently abandoned German fieldpiece with a demolition charge placed in the breech. While returning to his platoon position, Sgt. Barfoot, though greatly fatigued by his Herculean efforts, assisted 2 of his seriously wounded men 1,700 yards to a position of safety. Sgt. Barfoot's extraordinary heroism, demonstration of magnificent valor, and aggressive determination in the face of pointblank fire are a perpetual inspiration to his fellow soldiers." Barfoot later rose through the ranks to become a Colonel. Barfoot's Medal was one of 17 Medals of Honor that have been officially accredited to Mississippi in all wars, although we can claim 5 more that were accredited to other states because the recipients with Mississippi ties were in other states when they went into service. Barfoot is one of only 13 native Mississippians (of 22 Mississippians — 15 Army, 4 Marines and 3 in the Navy) in all wars to have received the CMOH. Of 3,433 total recipients of the Medal, only 151 were still living as of Nov. 1, 2000 (living recipients by conflict: WWII - 63; Korean War - 21; Vietnam - 68). Col. Barfoot was one of those 151 and one of only 2 *native* Mississippians (of 3 Mississippians) who received the CMOH still alive. The other native Mississippian still alive is General Louis H. Wilson Jr., and the "adopted" Mississippian is Jack H. Lucas. Barfoot now lives in Virginia.

James Barksdale

Born Jan. 24, 1943, in Jackson. He graduated from Murrah High School and earned a bachelor's degree in business from Ole Miss. He was CEO of Federal Express during most of the 1970s into the early 1990s. President and CEO of McCaw Cellular Communications until it merged with AT&T Wireless Services, he became chief executive of their wireless division. Then he became CEO of the new California-based Netscape that makes computer software called "browsers" to navigate the Internet. Barksdale led Netscape from 1995 until its sale to America Online, completed in early 1999. That sale, originally valued at $4 billion, had a final price tag of $15 billion due to AOL's skyrocketing stock price. Barksdale now serves on the board of directors for AOL, but holds no management positions at AOL. He is now co-chairman of the Internet Policy Institute. In 1996, Barksdale and his wife, Sally, made a record $5.4 million gift to create an Honors College at the University of Mississippi — the largest private gift to Ole Miss since it opened in 1848. In Jan. 2000, the Barksdales donated $100 million to create the Barksdale Reading Institute at the University of Mississippi Foundation, which will seek to ensure every child leaves third grade reading at grade level. It's believed to be the largest single donation to advance literacy in the nation's history! Barksdale was inducted into the Ole Miss Hall of Fame in 1996. The Barksdales now live in Jackson.

Prentiss Barnes

He was an original member of the Moonglows, one of the early doo wop groups of the 1950s, and one the best groups of that period. He was born on April 12, 1925, in Magnolia in Pike County, Mississippi. Barnes was in Cleveland, Ohio in the early Fifties when he joined Harvey Fuqua and Bobby Lester, who had previously sung together in their hometown of Louisville, Kentucky. They first called their group the Crazy

Profiles of Famous & Notable Mississippians

Sounds, but were renamed the Moonglows by deejay Alan Freed, the man who gave Rock and Roll music its name. Barnes was the bass singer for the group that also made some recordings as the Moonlighters. In 1952 the first Moonglows record, *I Just Can't Tell No Lie*, was released on Champagne Records, owned by Freed. In 1953, the group had five singles on the Chance label. In 1954, things really started clicking when they debuted on the Chicago-based Chess label with *Sincerely*, the biggest hit of their career (#1 R&B, #20 pop). In 1956, the Moonglows second-biggest hit, *See Saw*, reached No. 6 R&B chart and No. 25 pop. The last of their singles to chart was the Platters-influenced *Ten Commandments of Love* in 1958 (#9 R&B, #22 pop). Other songs by the group included *The Beating of My Heart, Please Send Me Someone to Love, Let's Go, Shoo Doo Be Doo (My Loving Baby), When I'm With You, We Go Together*, and *Most of All*. In 1959 after Barnes had left the Moonglows, a young Marvin Gaye became a member of the group. The Moonglows disbanded in 1960, although singles were released under their name by Chess into 1961. Barnes pursuit of a solo career ended in 1969 on a San Antonio railroad track when his car was hit by a train he never saw coming. Hospitalized for two years, his left arm was amputated and he underwent 10 operations. Barnes was in New York when he and the other original members of the Moonglows were inducted into the Rock and Roll Hall of Fame on March 6, 2000. They were inducted alongside Eric Clapton, Earth, Wind & Fire, The Lovin' Spoonful, Bonnie Raitt and James Taylor. Prentiss Barnes now lives in Jackson.

Roosevelt "Booba" Barnes
Born Sept. 25, 1936, in Longwood, Washington County, Mississippi. Barnes was a vocalist and harmonica and guitar player who started playing in juke joints in the Delta when he was 13. Barnes began playing music professionally in 1960, playing guitar in a Mississippi band named the Swinging Gold Coasters. After living for a time in Chicago, he moved back to Greenville in 1971, where he formed a band called The Playboys and opened a nightclub, The Playboy Club, in 1985. He continued rocking the Delta juke joints during the 80s, but after the release of his debut album, *The Heartbroken Man* (1990) on Rooster Blues Records, he headed back to Chicago to follow the trail of his idols Howlin' Wolf and Little Milton. Barnes and the Playboys also toured the U.S. and Europe. His last performance was at the Rock 'n' Roll Hall of Fame in Cleveland, Ohio. Barnes died of lung cancer on April 3, 1996.

Fred Barnett
Born June 17, 1966, in Shelby, Mississippi. He attended Rosedale High School, where he was All-district and team MVP in only year of high school football. He was a law enforcement major at Arkansas State, where he set school records with 95 receptions and 1,571 receiving yards, caught 38 passes for 643 yards and four touchdowns as a senior. The 6-foot, 200 pound Barnett was selected by the Philadelphia Eagles in the third round (77th pick overall) of the 1990 NFL Draft. He was signed by the Dolphins in 1996 and came back after major knee surgery to play the last half of the season. Barnett retired from pro football during the 1997 season.

Lem Barney
Born Lemuel J. Barney Jr. on Sept. 8, 1945, in Gulfport, Miss. His nickname is "Stroll." The 6-foot-2, 190-pound Barney was an all-star cornerback with Jackson State, where he intercepted 27 passes in three seasons and also did the team's punting. He was a second-round draft pick by the Detroit Lions in 1967 and played for them until he retired in 1977. In his first season, he ran back 3 of his league-leading 10 interceptions for TDs and was selected the NFL's defensive rookie of the year. Barney was named to the all-pro team in 1968, '69 and '72 and played in 10 Pro Bowls. During his career, Barney intercepted 56 passes and returned them for 1,077 yards, an average of 19.2, and scored 8 touchdowns; he returned 143 punts for 1,312 yards, a 9.2 average, and 2 touchdowns; and he had 50 kickoff returns for 1,274 yards, a 25.5 average, and 1 touchdown. Barney also punted 113 times for a 35.5-yard average. He was inducted into the Mississippi Sports Hall of Fame in 1986. He was inducted into the Pro Football Hall of Fame in 1992, only the fifth cornerback to enter the Hall. He played himself in the movie *Paper Lion* (1968) and played "Frenchy LaBoise" in the film *The Black Six* (1974).

Nevada Barr
Born in Nevada in Mar. 1, 1952, she grew up in California, where she attended California Polytechnic Institute and graduate school at the University of California. She was living in New York City when she started writing in 1978. She moved to Clinton, Mississippi in 1993. A former park ranger who once worked along the Natchez Trace in Mississippi, her books are about a female park ranger whose specialty is the investigative side of law enforcement. Her first book was *Bittersweet* (1984) followed by *Track of the Cat* (1993), which won the Agatha and Anthony Mystery Writers' Awards. Her other books are *A Superior Death* (1994), *Ill Wind* (1995), *Firestorm* (1996) *Endangered Species* (1997), *Blind Descent* (1998), *Liberty Falling* (1999), which is set on Statue of Liberty Island in New York City, and *Deep South* (2000), which is set on the Natchez Trace Parkway in Mississippi. She and her husband still live in Clinton, Mississippi.

Johnny Barranco
Born June 26, 1951, in Bossier City, Louisiana, his family moved to Jackson when he was only three. After playing in bands around Mississippi, he moved to New York in 1972 at age 21 and got into the jingle business. Barranco's voice was on several national commercials including Juicy Fruit® ("The taste is gonna move ya"), the U.S. Army Reserves ("Be all that you can be") and beer commercials for Coors Light®, Old Milwaukee® and Stroh's®. He co-wrote the theme songs for the soap operas *Search for Tomorrow* and *The Edge of Night*. Barranco gave up his 20-year jingle career and moved back to Jackson in 1995 to establish a children's ministry which included Judah Records. He produced the children's Christmas album, *Happy Birthday Lord Jesus* and *He Created Me*. Barranco is now living in Nashville. His latest Christian children's album is titled *Let's Go Fishing!*

Bucky Barrett
Born Raymond Samuel Barrett on Sept. 19, 1944, in Pensacola, Fl., he grew up in Jackson and Canton, Mississippi. He played guitar with the Versatiles, the Nightriders, Tim Whitsett and the Imperial Show Band, and other regional bands in the Jackson area in the early and mid-1960s. Barrett went on to a music career in Nashville. The first star that he worked with was Dottie West. He has since played with hundreds of artists. He toured all around the world as lead guitarist for Roy Orbison from 1981-88. He was a nominee for the Guitar Player Awards, Best Studio Guitarist for six years running, 1980-85. He was a Country Music Association nominee for Instrumentalist of the Year in 1984. Barrett played on the Neil Young gold album, *Comes a Time*, and on the 1989 Grammy winner for best Country Collaboration, *Cryin'* by Roy Orbison and k.d. lang. Barrett has played on over 1,500 albums. He has three CDs of his own — *Killin' the Wind: The Nashville Superpickers* (1981); *Long Time Coming:*

Profiles of Famous & Notable Mississippians

A Tribute to Roy Orbison by His Guitarist, Bucky Barrett; and one for Christmas, *Bucky Barrett: 12 Songs of Christmas* (1998). Barrett is one of 6 guitarists on a 1999 CD called *The Great Mississippi Jazz Guitarists Reunion*, released by the Mississippi Musicians Hall of Fame (available on their website & area record stores). The other artists are Steve Blailock, Mundell Lowe, Skeets McWilliams, Bob Saxton & Lloyd Wells (all are profiled in this chapter). Barrett has appeared on TV on *The Tonight Show, Late Show, Saturday Night Live, Today Show, Farm Aid* and *Austin City Limits*.

B. J. Barrier, Jr.
Aviation pioneer born in Yazoo City on June 26, 1906. He served in WWII as a U.S. Navy pilot instructor. He was killed in a plane crash on Feb. 9, 1950, close to Dallas, Texas. Barrier Airfield in Yazoo City is named in his honor.

Marion S. Barry, Jr.
Born in Itta Bena, Miss. on Mar. 6, 1936. He was forced to resign as mayor of Washington, D.C. after a drug conviction for smoking crack cocaine in 1990. He served a 6-months prison term in 1991 and Washington voters returned him to the mayor's office in 1994. Barry did not seek a fifth term.

Dee Barton
Born Sept. 18, 1937, in Houston, Mississippi. When he was about 4, he moved with his family to Starkville, where his dad was the high school band director until 1955. After graduating from Starkville High in 1955, he attended North Texas State where he received a B.A. in education, with an emphasis on musical composition, in 1960. In 1961, he joined the Stan Kenton Orchestra and played trombone & drums through most of the 1960s. He then formed the Dee Barton Orchestra, a 22-piece band which made a big impact in Los Angeles. He composed, arranged, conducted, and was musical consultant for Tony Bennett, Frank Sinatra, Peggy Lee, John Lennon and the Rolling Stones. John Williams, composer for *Star Wars*, has also been Barton's close friend and mentor in the music business. Clint Eastwood gave him his first big break in the movies when he got Barton to score the music for the 1971 movie, *Play Misty For Me*. He's written scores to more than 50 other movies including 3 more Clint Eastwood hits — *High Plains Drifter* (1973), *Every Which Way But Loose* (1978) and *Thunderbolt and Lightfoot* (1974). He wrote supplemental compositions for all of Eastwood's five Dirty Harry movies: *Dirty Harry* (1971); *Magnum Force* (1973); *The Enforcer* (1976); *Sudden Impact* (1983) and *The Dead Pool* (1988). He has written scores for TV shows including *The Odd Couple*, *Red Skelton*, *The Rockford Files*, *Soul Train* and *Batman*. He's also written music for hundreds of radio and TV commercials. In 1994, Barton moved back to Jackson, where he is now composer in residence at Jackson State University. Barton was one of the first 27 inducted into the inaugural Mississippi Musicians Hall of Fame on April 1, 2000.

Harry Basch
Born March 17, 1915, in Greenville, Miss. He's a supporting actor who's had roles in a few theatrical movies, such as a doctor in *Coma* (1978), but most of his appearances have been on TV. He played "Vince Caproni" in the TV series *Falcon Crest* from 1982-84, appeared on the soap *General Hospital* in 1983, and made guest appearances on TV series such as *Star Trek* (1966), *Gunsmoke* (1967) and *Bonanza* (1972).

Jack Bass
Born June 24, 1934, in a town named North located in South Carolina (famed singer Eartha Kitt was also born there). A journalism professor at the Ole Miss since 1987, he won the 1993 Robert F. Kennedy Award for his nonfiction book, *Taming the Storm: The Life and Times of Judge Frank M. Johnson, Jr.* That book was edited by the late Jacqueline Kennedy Onassis, who was a close friend of the Judge. Bass co-authored the book (with Marilyn W. Thompson), *Ol' Strom — An Unauthorized Biography of a Political Master* (1998).

Lance Bass
James Lansten "Lance" Bass was born on May 4, 1979, in Laurel, Mississippi. In 1989, his family moved to Clinton. In the eighth grade Lance auditioned for the Mississippi Show Stoppers, a statewide group sponsored by the Mississippi Agricultural and Forestry Museum. He later became a member of a competition choir called Attache. Garth Brooks was one of his major influences. The best day of his life, he says, was when he was called to audition for the R&B and pop, dance quintet, 'N Sync. 'N Sync is made up of four other guys — J.C. Chasez, 21, from Baltimore; Justin Timberlake, 17, from Memphis, Chris Kirkpatrick, 27, from Pennsylvania, and Joey Fontane, 21, from New York. Lance is the fifth member of the group as bass singer. The name 'N Sync is an acronym formed by the last letter of all the guy's first names. The group has been compared to others such as Backstreet Boys and New Kids On The Block. A solid group since 1995, 'N Sync first hit it big in Europe. 'N Sync's self-titled debut album was released on March 24, 1998 and went multi-platinum in the U.S. in 1998 selling over 4 million copies! Their first single, *I Want You Back*, was the fastest-rising single and had the longest stay on the charts for a new act. The single went platinum within four months of its release. By the end of Feb. 1999, their single, *(God Must Have Spent) A Little More Time on You*, was on the Top-10 singles chart followed by another hit *I Drive Myself Crazy*. In mid-March 2000, their new album, *No Strings Attached*, was released with the songs "Bye, Bye, Bye", "This I Promise You," "Just Got Pair," and "It's Gonna Be Me" (the No. 1 single by the first week in Aug. 2000). It was the fastest selling album in history!! By the end of its first day in stores, the CD had sold more than a million copies, doing in a single day what the previous record-holder — the Backstreet Boys' album *Millennium* — took a week to do. By its second week, *No Strings Attached* had racked up a phenomenal 2.4 million units, more than double the 1.13 million sales of the Backstreet Boys album! Tickets for the group's 2000 summer tour went on sale on March 25, 2000, and by the end of the day, more than 600,000 tickets had been sold nationwide! The group had 6 nominations in 2000 for the MTV Video Awards and won Best Pop Video for *Bye, Bye, Bye*. Lance appeared on the 1999 TV series, *Jack of All Trades*, and played himself on guest appearances on the TV shows *Total Request with Carson Daly* (1998), *Sabrina, the Teenage Witch* (1999), *Loveline* (1999), and *Clueless* (1999). Lance currently resides in Orlando, headquarters of the group, but his family still lives in Clinton, Mississippi, and his mother, Diane, is a sixth grade teacher in Brandon, Miss.

Luster Bayless
Born Oct. 26, 1937, in Ruleville, Mississippi. He worked in Hollywood from age 20 designing costumes for John Wayne and other stars. Wayne's personal costume designer for many years, Bayless is credited in 13 John Wayne movies. Some of his major film credits include the John Wayne westerns *Rio Lobo* (1970), *The Train Robbers* (1973), *Rooster Cogburn* (1975), and *The Shootist* (1976, Wayne's last movie), plus other films such as *Telefon* (1977, men's costumes), *Comes a Horseman* (1978) and *Tom Horn* (1979). Bayless also worked 5 years for Walt Disney. He founded and is CEO of United American Costume Corporation in North Hollywood.

Profiles of Famous & Notable Mississippians

T. Bubba Bechtol

Born James Terryl Bechtol on May 1, 1945, in Biloxi, Mississippi, he grew up in rural Gautier and Fountainblue. He attended public schools in Ocean Springs and graduated from Long Beach High, where he says, "I grabbed a football and ran out of poverty with it." He attended Perkinston Junior College in Wiggins, Mississippi on a scholarship. Bubba attended the University of Southern Mississippi for one year until, Bubba says, "I tore my knees up and left to make money!" Even though he would later become a comedian, he was an entrepreneur most of his working life. He was president of the United States Jaycees in 1980 and president of the Freedom's Foundation at Valley Forge in 1983. He served as executive director of Commitment 1980, the Reagan for President Campaign and served on the transition team as a speech writer for two years. Bechtol ran for the U.S. House as a Republican in Florida in 1982 and won in the primary, but lost the general election. He joined the National Speakers Association (NSA) in 1978 and began his career as a speaker/humorist on the convention circuit. He became the No. 1 most-requested humorist in the country in the NSA. He traveled to 56 foreign countries and even wrote a book, *Bubba's Book*. He also wrote an essay about his native state called *Mississippi, My Mississippi*, which commentator Paul Harvey read twice on his radio show. Bubba founded The Bubba's of America, an organization he claims has over 100,000 members and also serves as his fan club. Now (2000) 19 years old, it was chartered to preserve the "Bubba Lifestyle" and is 42% female (Bubba calls them Bubbettes!). When Southern writer Lewis Grizzard became too ill to perform his shows, he called on Bubba to fill in for him. Bubba did so until Grizzard's untimely death — thus began Bubba's career in show business. He appeared on *Crook and Chase* on The Nashville Network (TNN) many times and is now with Opryland Productions as their headliner comedian. Bubba has appeared on the Grand Ole Opry many times and is now a full time comedian in the country music market. His first album entitled, *Bill Ain't No Bubba* (1994), a comedic jab at President Clinton, received national attention. He also released another album, *Bubba: Unclogged*, in 1996. In Bubba's terms, "when you are raised to be laid back, and like to fish, hunt, and drive four-wheel drive vehicles, you may be a Bubba!" Currently living in Pensacola, Florida, he is "the epitome of Bubbaism."

William Beckwith

Born March 13, 1952, in Greenville, Mississippi. He graduated with bachelor's and masters degrees in sculpture from the University of Mississippi. He began studying with Greenville sculptor Leon Koury at the age of 15. Beckwith uses the same technique used by his mentor, the late Koury, and classical sculptor Auguste Rodin — he builds an armature and adds clay to it, rather than taking away from a block of material. He has produced realistic sculptures in bronze and hydrostone. Beckwith's work includes the full-size sculpture of William Faulkner on the town square in Oxford, which was unveiled on Sept. 25, 1997, the 100th anniversary of Faulkner's birth. He created the 8-foot tall bronze sculpture at the Jefferson Davis Presidential Library at Beauvoir Mansion in Biloxi. Beckwith did the sculpture of three children in a fountain in the atrium of Mississippi Methodist Rehabilitation Center in Jackson. Beckwith sculpted a statue of a flag bearer of the 11th Mississippi Infantry that was unveiled at Gettysburg National Battlefield on May 27, 2000. He also sculpted a bust of Faulkner for the Hattiesburg Public Library, the first of a numbered series of 32 busts, which coincides with the number of books written by Faulkner. Beckwith says he has an affinity with Faulkner because he now lives in Lafayette County, the county that became Yoknawpatawpha County in Faulkner's novels. In fact, Beckwith lives in Taylor, the very town where Faulkner's *Sanctuary* took place, and part of the story actually took place in Beckwith's yard on the property where the old railroad depot used to be!

Carey Bell

Born Carey Bell Harrington on Nov. 14, 1936, in Macon, Mississippi, he was already playing the harp when he was eight and working professionally with his godfather, pianist Lovie Lee, at 13. Lee took him to Chicago in 1956 where Bell took up electric bass, playing behind Robert Nighthawk, Johnny Young, and his mentor Big Walter Horton. After learning his harmonica riffs from Chicago's very best, Big Walter, Little Walter and Sonny Boy Williamson II, he became one of the great blues harp players. He was a sideman with Muddy Waters and Willie Dixon in the early 1970s, touring and recording with both legends. He cut his first album as a singer/harmonica player for Delmark in 1969. Four cuts by Bell were included on the first batch of Alligator's *Living Chicago Blues* anthologies in 1978. In 1990 he participated in the 1990 harmonica summit meeting *Harp Attack!*, which brought him into the studio with fellow greats James Cotton, Junior Wells, and Billy Branch. His recent solo set for Alligator was called *Deep Down*.

Charles G. Bell

Born Charles Greenleaf Bell on Oct. 31, 1916, in Greenville. This protégé of William Alexander Percy received a B.S. in physics from the University of Virginia in 1936. Graduating as a Rhodes Scholar from Oxford, he received a B.A. in 1938, an M.A. in 1938, and a Litt.D. in 1939. Bell became an instructor in English at Blackburn College (1939-40) before leaving for Iowa State University, where he taught English (1940-43) and then physics (1943-45). Later, Bell joined the University of Chicago as an assistant professor of humanities. Leaving Chicago in 1956, he became a Fulbright professor in Munich, Germany. Bell then went to St. John's College in Maryland as a tutor until 1967. Next, he went to St. John's College in New Mexico as a tutor (1968) and director of graduate preceptorial (1972-73). Bell worked as a lecturer at several colleges such as Black Mountain College and the University of Rochester. He also served as a guest professor at the University of Frankfurt in Germany, the State University of New York, and the University of Puerto Rico. His books of poetry include *Songs for a New America* (1953) and *Delta Return* (1956). He's had over 50 poems published in *The Atlantic Monthly, Harper's Bazaar, & The Ladies' Home Journal*. His other works include *The Married Land* (1st novel in a trilogy), *The Half Gods* (2nd novel in a trilogy), and *Five Chambered Hearth*. Bell's works in progress are: *The Third Kingdom* (completing the trilogy); *Loves Five-Fold*, a collection of verse; *See It Whole*, a volume of articles; *Symbolic History*, a series of slide-tape dramas; and a study of western arts and soul. Among his awards and honors are the Rockefeller post-war fellow in 1948, the Ford Foundation fellow in 1952-53, and the Fulbright fellow. Bell is also a member of Phi Beta Kappa and the Raven Society.

James "Cool Papa" Bell

Born James Thomas Bell May 17, 1903, in Starkville, Miss., he was nicknamed "Cool Papa" because of his coolness before crowds. The switch-hitting center fielder played for the Negro Leagues, playing for the St. Louis Stars, the Pittsburgh Crawfords, the Homestead Grays and the Kansas City Stars between 1922 and 1950 — and 21 of those years he also

Profiles of Famous & Notable Mississippians

competed in winter ball. He was probably the fastest man ever to play baseball — in 1933 he stole 175 bases and is said to have once rounded the bases in 12 seconds (the *official* record is 13.3 seconds, set by Evar Swanson of the Reds in 1931)! In 1933, he also hit 63 doubles, 17 triples, 11 home runs and batted .379. His .437 batting average in 89 games in 1940 was the highest in the history of the Mexican League. He never hit below .300 in any season and his lifetime batting average was estimated at .419, second in the Negro Leagues to legendary Josh Gibson. He never got a chance to play in the American and National leagues, retiring in 1950 at the age of 47. On July 3, 1994, the road into Smith-Wills Stadium and the Mississippi Sports Hall of Fame in Jackson was dedicated "Cool Papa Bell Drive" in his honor. Bell is the only native Mississippian in the Baseball Hall of Fame, inducted in Aug. 1974. He was inducted into the Mississippi Sports Hall of Fame in 1995. Bell died in St. Louis on March 7, 1991, at age 87 and is buried in St. Peter's Cemetery in Hillsdale, Mo.

Charles C. Bennett

Born Mar. 31, 1940, in Independence, Louisiana, he spent his childhood summers in Mississippi and stills spends a lot of time in the state, especially in Wesson, which he says "looks like a movie set." Bennett has designed the sets for over 50 film and TV projects and has been nominated for 7 Emmy Awards including 3 that he won for the TV mini- series *Roots*, *Evergreen* (1985) and *Oldest Living Confederate Widow Tells All* (1994). He also did set work on these other TV mini-series: *Kane & Abel* (1985); *I'll Take Manhattan* (1987); *A Season in Purgatory* (1996); *Bella Mafia* (1997) and *Chiefs*. Bennett counts among his TV movies and specials: *Rappaccini's Daughter* (1980); *We're Fighting Back* (1981); *Noon Wine* (1985); *Doubletake* (1985); *Women of Valor* (1986); *Her Secret Life* (1987); *Mayflower Madam* (1987); the Hallmark Hall of Fame's *Home Fires Burning* (1989); *Roxanne: The Prize Pulitzer* (1989); *Murder in Mississippi* (1990); *Grass Roots* (1992); *Sunstroke* (1992); *Labor of Love: The Arlette Schweitzer Story* (1993); *Past the Bleachers* (1995); *A Horse for Danny* (1995); *Bye Bye Birdie* (1995); *Miss Evers' Boys* (1997); *1 Get to the Heart: The Barbara Mandrell Story* (1997); *Mama Flora's Family*; *A Lesson Before Dying*. He's also worked on the TV series *Savannah*, *Fame* and *I'll Fly Away*. His theater movie credits include *McBain* (1991), *New Jack City* (1991), *Shakedown* (1988) and *Hoodlum* (1997).

Lerone Bennett, Jr.

Born in Clarksdale, Mississippi on Oct. 17, 1928. He worked for the *Atlanta Daily World* (1949-53), *Jet* magazine (1953), and for *Ebony* magazine as associate editor 1954-57 and as senior editor (1958-present). Bennett is an historian, critic, poet, essayist, and writer of short stories. His book *Before the Mayflower: A History of the Negro in America, 1619-1966* is considered by many to be the "Bible of black history."

Willie Best

Born May 27, 1913, in Sunflower, Mississippi. He was 17 years old when he made his film debut in 1930. A veteran of a traveling show, Best fell victim to the stereotyping of the era when he first came to Hollywood. The studio he worked for claimed that not only did Best enjoy humiliating himself in "darkie" roles such as the shuffling, watermelon-consuming "Yassuh boss' character billed as "Sleep 'N' Eat," but that the only compensation he wanted for his screen work was three squares a day and a warm place to sleep. However, his consummate skill as a performer and his perfect comic timing resulted in Bob Hope, who worked with him in *The Ghost Breakers* (1940) and *Nothing But the Truth* (1940), referring to Best as "the finest actor I knew." Best appeared in 95 films from *Feet First* (1930) to *South of Caliente* (1951). He was in *Little Miss Marker* (1934, added to the National Film Registry in the Library of Congress in 1998) along with another Mississippian, Dorothy Dell from Hattiesburg (see her profile). Best also made some TV appearances: as "Willie" in the series *The Stu Erwin Show*, a/k/a *The Trouble with Father* (1950-55), as "Charlie" in the series *My Little Margie* (1952) and as "Willie Slocum" in the series *Waterfront* (1954). He died from cancer on Feb. 27, 1962, in Hollywood at age 48.

Thomas J. Biggs

Born Thomas Jones Biggs in Arkansas on Jan 28, 1912. This architect was in charge of architecture and engineering during the construction of the Pentagon. He was an area engineer for construction of Woodrow Wilson General Hospital in Virginia, the Reading, Pennsylvania Army Air Base and the Aberdeen Proving Grounds. Biggs was a lieutenant in the U.S. Army Corps of Engineers in 1945 when he helped establish Biggs and Weir Architects in Jackson. He designed many notable buildings in Jackson, including the Russell Davis Planetarium, the Mississippi Arts Center, Millsaps College Academic Complex, Northminster Baptist Church, St. Philips Episcopal Church, Covenant Presbyterian Church, and St. Richard's Catholic Church, for which he received the National Liturgical Design Award. Biggs earned the Design of Public Space Award in the Governor's Awards for Excellence in the Arts in 1995. Biggs died of cardio-pulmonary arrest on April 5, 1999, at his home in Jackson, Mississippi, at the age of 87.

J.T. "Blondy" Black

Born Aug. 20, 1920, in Philadelphia, Mississippi. He was a graduate of Philadelphia High School, where he excelled in field and track. Black held the Mississippi high school 100-yard dash record for 27 years. He also won the Southeastern Conference 100-yard dash championship. Black was an outstanding football player at Mississippi State University, starring on their undefeated 1941 Orange Bowl championship team that finished ninth in the nation in the Associated Press poll. In 1941, the *San Francisco Examiner* called Black the fastest man in the world over 200 pounds! After graduating from Mississippi State, he served as a lieutenant in the U.S. Marine Corps during World War II. Black later trained for the 1944 Olympics, which was canceled due to the war. He played football two seasons in the pros — in 1946 for the Buffalo Bisons and in 1947 for the Baltimore Colts. In the 1950s, Black operated a car dealership in Yazoo City. He later moved to Jackson, where he became a land developer and business owner. He was inducted into the Mississippi Sports Hall of Fame in 1976. Black died of respiratory failure at G.V. "Sonny" Montgomery Veterans Affairs Medical Center in Jackson on May 4, 2000, at age 79.

John C. Black

John Charles Black was born Jan. 27, 1839, in Lexington, Holmes County, Mississippi. His family moved to Danville, Illinois in 1847 when Black was 8 years old. He attended the common schools and Wabash College in Crawfordsville, Ind., but did not graduate until after the close of the Civil War. Black served in the Union Army from Apr. 14, 1861, to Aug. 15, 1865. He entered service in Danville, Ill. as a private, and was successively sergeant major, major, lieutenant colonel, and colonel. He was a brevetted brigadier general for service in the storming of Fort Blakeley on Apr. 9, 1865. Lieutenant Colonel Black was with the 37th Illinois Infantry at Prairie Grove, Arkansas during the Civil War when he performed an act of bravery on Dec. 7, 1862, that earned him the Medal of

Profiles of Famous & Notable Mississippians

Honor (MOH). The Medal was presented to him on Oct. 31, 1893. Here are the actual words of his citation: "Gallantly charged the position of the enemy at the head of his regiment, after 2 other regiments had been repulsed and driven down the hill, and captured a battery; was severely wounded." There were 53 Medals of Honor awarded for action "on the ground" in Mississippi during the Civil War, of which only one (awarded to August Dorley-see his profile) was officially accredited to Mississippi, with the other 52 accredited to other states. Black's Medal of Honor is officially accredited to Illinois, his adopted state. Black was one of only 2 native Mississippians (of 5 Mississippians-3 Union Army & 2 Union Navy) to receive the Medal of Honor during the Civil War. The Medal was awarded to only those that fought for the North — the Medal was not given to Confederates. In all wars, 17 Medals of Honor have been officially accredited to Mississippi, although we claim 5 more that were accredited to other states because the recipients had Mississippi ties. Black is one of 13 native Mississippians (of 22 Mississippians) in all wars to have received the Congressional Medal of Honor, out of 3,433 recipients of the Medal through Nov. 1, 2000. Of all Mississippi MOH recipients, 15 were in the Army, 4 in the Marines and 3 in the Navy. After the war, Black studied law in Chicago, was admitted to the bar in 1867 and started practice in Danville, Ill. He was appointed U.S. Commissioner of Pensions by President Cleveland and served from Mar. 17, 1885, to Mar. 27, 1889. He was elected as a Democrat to the 53rd Congress and served from Mar. 4, 1893, to Jan. 12, 1895, when he resigned. Black was a U.S. attorney for the northern district of Illinois 1895-99 and commander in chief of the Grand Army of the Republic in 1903-04. A member of the U.S. Civil Service Commission 1904-13, he served as its president. Black died in Chicago on Aug. 17, 1915, at age 76 and is buried in the Spring Hill Cemetery in Danville. There is no Medal of Honor marker on his grave.

Blackwood Brothers Quartet

One of the most influential singing groups in the country, the quartet was formed in Ackerman, Mississippi by sons of sharecroppers. Evangelist Roy Blackwood (b. 12-24-1900 at Fentress, Miss.; d. 3-21-1971), oldest brother in the Blackwood family, formed the quartet in 1934, and at that time, the members all lived in Choctaw County. Brothers Roy Blackwood, Doyle Blackwood (b. 8-22-1911 in Ackerman; d. 10-??-1974), their youngest brother, James (b. 8-4-1919 in Ackerman), along with Roy's oldest son R.W. Blackwood, age 13 (b. 10-23-1921 in Ackerman; d. 6-24-1954), comprised the original quartet. Roy was the lead singer, Doyle sang bass and played guitar, James sang baritone and Roy's son, R.W., sang tenor. The Blackwoods sang at area churches during the mid-1930s. By 1937, they began working a radio show in Kosciusko, Miss. The quartet moved to WJDX radio in Jackson later that year, singing pop and country in addition to gospel. After two years in Jackson, they were popular enough to move to KWKH in Shreveport, a regional superstation that broadcast over much of the South. World War II took them to San Diego, Calif., where they temporarily quit singing so that they could work in defense plants. When they re-formed in 1946, Doyle Blackwood had been replaced by Don Smith. The Blackwoods began their own record company, and became so popular that Doyle soon returned to start another group, the Blackwood Gospel Quartet. By 1950, Roy had retired and was replaced by Bill Lyles. The Blackwoods moved to Memphis, signed a contract with RCA Victor and began recording in 1952. In 1954, the quartet gained national recognition when they won the talent contest on the *Arthur Godfrey* TV program, broadcast over CBS. They joined the McGuire Sisters to sing *Lead Me To That Rock*. R.W. Blackwood and Bill Lyles were killed in a plane crash on June 24, 1954, in Clanton, Alabama. The Blackwood Brothers immediately disbanded and vowed to never perform again. Fortunately they returned several years later, gradually adding J.D. Sumner (b. 1925; d. 11-16-1998) as a replacement for Lyles, plus Roy's son Cecil Blackwood (b. 10-28-1934 in Ackerman) and James' son James Blackwood, Jr. (b. 7-31-1943 in San Diego). In the early 1950's, Cecil Blackwood organized a teenage gospel group called the Songfellows. A young Elvis Presley, one of the Blackwood Brothers greatest fans, auditioned for the group in 1953, and was turned down because he couldn't sing harmony. The Blackwood Brothers organized the National Quartet Convention in 1956. They also organized the Gospel Music Association, were founders of the Skylite Record Company and owned the Stamps Music Company and other music companies. From the 1950s to the 1970s, the Blackwoods were one of the most popular gospel groups in the U.S. The were the first gospel group to record a long play album (*Hymn Sing*) in gospel music history. They have recorded over 200 albums and toured in 47 countries. They won the first of their 9 Grammy Awards for Best Gospel Performance in 1966 and they have won a total of 27 Dove Awards. James Blackwood alone won 7 Dove Awards for Male Vocalist of the Year during the 1970s. He was inducted into the Gospel Music Hall of Fame in 1974 and is still known as "Mr. Gospel Singer of America." The Blackwood Brothers Quartet were inducted into the Gospel Music Association Hall of Fame on April 2, 1998. James Blackwood/the Blackwood Brothers was one of the first 27 inducted into the Miss. Musicians Hall of Fame April 1, 2000.

Steve Blailock

Born July 9, 1944, in McComb, Miss. Blailock is a great jazz guitarist who has played with such artists as Betty Carter, Annette Cobb, Eddie Vinson, Willie Mae "Big Mama" Thorton, Jimmy Weatherspoon, Pete Fountain, Al Hirt, Wynton Marsalis and Harry Connick, Jr. Blailock was influenced by jazz early on. He started out on the piano, then picked up the guitar and trumpet in the third grade! One of his mentors in his youth was Mississippian Lloyd Wells. Blailock started playing professionally at age twelve and went on the road at age sixteen with a group from Florida. That band managed to get a million-seller on the charts. Blailock soon moved to Nashville, where he studied with famous guitarist Hank Garland and found lots of work as a studio guitarist, working with such artists as Hank Crawford, Don Bowman, Willie Nelson, Ray Price and many others. After four years in Nashville, he moved to Los Angeles, where he was hired by soul singer Lou Rawls. In L.A., Blailock became a big part of the jazz and blues scene while he continued to record in New York, Nashville and Los Angeles over the next 20 years. In 1981 he played guitar for fellow Mississippian Bucky Barrett on the album *Killin' the Wind*. Blailock wanted to get back to his musical roots of jazz and blues, so in 1984 he moved to New Orleans. There, he's worked with such artists as Herb Tassin, Leroy Jones and clarinetist Dr. Michael White, and he even branched out into Cajun and zydeco genres. In the 1990s, Blailock and his band, "Swing Thing," made a total of 26 tours in Italy, France, Germany, Finland, Norway, Holland, Belgium, Japan, Switzerland and the Beijing International Jazz Festival in China. He performed at the 1996 Summer Olympic Games in Atlanta. Since 1992, he has been an instructor of

Profiles of Famous & Notable Mississippians

Jazz Studies at Dillard University in New Orleans. Blailock now plays banjo for Greg Staffod's Young Tuxedo Brass Band. He has a self-produced disc entitled *Mixed Bag*, and is working on another CD. Blailock was voted All Star Guitar/Banjo Player for 1997 by *New Orleans Magazine*. He has picked guitar on more than 900 CDs! He is one of 6 guitarists on a 1999 CD called *The Great Mississippi Jazz Guitarists Reunion*, released by the Miss. Musicians Hall of Fame (available on the MMHOF Website or at area record stores). The other artists on the album are Bucky Barrett, Mundell Lowe, Skeets McWilliams, Bob Saxton and Lloyd Wells.

Felix "Doc" Blanchard

Born Felix Blanchard on Dec. 11, 1924, in Bishopville, S.C. He played 4 years of high school football at St. Stanislaus High in Bay St. Louis, Miss. as a standout running back from 1938-42. As a senior, he scored 165 points and led his team to an undefeated season. He donated his Heisman Trophy, Maxwell Cup and Sullivan Trophy to St. Stanislaus. Blanchard was the first football player to win the Sullivan, awarded to the nation's best amateur athlete! He starred on the University of North Carolina freshman team, was drafted into the Army in the spring of 1943 and received an appointment to West Point in 1944. He became Army's greatest fullback. At Army, Blanchard and Glenn Davis formed one of the greatest backfields in college football history. They were known as "Mr. Inside" and "Mr. Outside," and "The Touchdown Twins." During their playing days, Army won 3 straight national titles. Blanchard and Davis won the Heisman Trophy in 1945 and 1946, respectively. It was only the second time in history that a school has produced different back-to-back Heisman winners. From 1944-46, he was a 3-year letterman and 3-time All-American at Army. He scored 19 TDs during his Heisman Trophy season. Blanchard ranks third on the Army career scoring list with 231 points. He produced 1,935 all-purpose yards during his 3-year career. Blanchard's in the College Football Hall of Fame and the Miss. Sports Hall of Fame ('94). He now lives in Bulverde, Texas.

David Blankenhorn

Born May 25, 1955, in Jackson, he lived there until age 17, attending Callaway High before his family moved to Virginia. He graduated magna cum laude from Harvard and received his master's from the University of Warwick in England on a John Knox Fellowship. His book, *Fatherless America: Confronting Our Most Urgent Social Problem*, was published in 1995. His ideas have received attention in *The New York Times*, *The Washington Post*, *Time*, *Newsweek* and *U.S. News & World Report*. Blankenhorn is founder and president of the Institute of American Values in New York City, where he now lives.

Don Blasingame

Born Don Lee Blasingame on Mar. 16, 1932, in Corinth, Miss. Making his major league baseball debut on Sept. 20, 1955, with St. Louis, he stayed with the Cardinals until 1959. He played for the San Francisco Giants (1960-61), the Cincinnati Reds (1961-63), the Washington Senators (1963-66) and the Kansas City Athletics in 1966. Blasingame played in the 1958 All-Star game and in the 1961 World Series. His career stats show 1,366 hits in 5,296 at bats (.258 batting avg.), 731 runs, 21 homers and 308 RBIs in 1,444 games played. He was inducted into the Mississippi Sports Hall of Fame in 1980.

Blind Melon

This hard-rock group of five has three Mississippians — Glen Graham, drummer, born in Columbus on Dec. 5, 1967; Brad Smith, bass guitarist, born in Columbus on Sept. 29, 1968; and Thomas Roger Stevens, guitarist, born in West Point on Oct. 31, 1969. The group rated a cover photo nude (but "tastefully" done with their hands placed strategically), on the Nov. 11, 1993 issue of *Rolling Stone* magazine. Their first album, *Blind Melon* (1993), went double-platinum with a hit single and video called *No Rain*. Their follow-up single was *Tones of Home*. Right after the release of their second album, *Soup* ('95), the group's lead singer, Shannon Hoon, was found dead on the band's tour bus in New Orleans of a reported drug overdose. He was 28 years old. The group's 3rd album, *Nico*, (named after Hoon's one-year old daughter) a collection of outtakes and rarities, was released in late 1996. After releasing that album, Blind Melon announced that the remaining members would carry on performing under a different name. Blind Melon received a 1998 Grammy nomination for the music video for their 1997 hit, *Letters From A Porcupine*.

Lucille Bogan

Born Lucille Armstrong on April 1, 1897, in Amory, Miss., she grew up in Birmingham, Alabama. As early as 1923, Bogan started recording but never worked in a true jazz band atmosphere. After a shaky first recording session, her voice deepened, and by 1927 she was singing the blues. Bogan made some important recordings in the late 1920s and early 1930s. After scoring a "race" hit in 1927 with *Sweet Petunia*, she changed her name to Bessie Jackson. Her best known tune, *Shave 'Em Dry*, has shown up on numerous compilations of bawdy blues material. Bogan sang about prostitution (*Tricks Ain't Walking' No More*), abusive men (*Women Don't Need Men*), alcoholism (*Sloppy Drunk Blues*) and her lyrics often had sexual themes. She seldom strayed into pop-style music, remaining a straight-ahead blues stylist with songs that had feminist overtones. Big-voiced, big-hearted Bogan died of coronary sclerosis in Los Angeles on Aug. 10, 1948 at age 51.

Ruthie Bolton-Holifield

Born on May 25, 1967, in McLain, Miss. She played basketball at Auburn from 1986-89, helping them to a 119-13 record and was named to 1988 and 89 NCAA Mideast Region All-Tournament teams, the 1988 NCAA Final Four All-Tournament Team and the 1989 All SEC second team. She helped the U.S. women's basketball team win an Olympic gold medal, the last one contested, at the games in Atlanta on Aug. 4, 1996. Ruthie was the only player on the US Olympic team that was not All-American in college. She started all 8 games in the Olympics and scored 15 points, made 5 steals, 5 assists and 5 rebounds. Her excellent defense helped the U.S. defeat Brazil 111-87. Ruthie was selected as the 1996 *Clarion-Ledger* Sports Person of the Year! The 5-foot-9 shooting guard was the leading scorer for the Sacramento Monarchs during her rookie 1997 season. Ruthie has the distinct honor of being named as the first WNBA Player of the Week on July 1, 1997. She posted a 21.5 average in the preceding 4 games and was third in the league in rebounding. On June 7, 1998, Ruthie hit two 3-pointers in the final 2 minutes as the U.S. team rallied to beat Russia 71-65 and win the 13th Women's World Championship at Berlin. It was the first world title for the U.S. since 1990, and their sixth overall! As of July 27, 2000, she had made 339 points for the season, averaging 14.1 points per game in 24 games played for the Sacramento Monarchs.

Brendon Boone

Born Norman Brendon Boone, Jr. on Feb. 26, 1938, in Meridian. His father was a Methodist minister and the family moved a lot — about once every five years. He graduated high school in Columbia, Mississippi in 1956. After that he attended Georgia Tech studying architectural design. Later he entered Emory University studying theology, then went on to

Profiles of Famous & Notable Mississippians

complete a B.A. Degree in English and journalism in less than three years at Mississippi Southern University. Thereafter followed a year of formal dramatic training toward his Masters in the Theatre Arts Department of Rollins College in Florida. Most of his work has been on TV, but he has had supporting roles in a few movies, namely as "Barney" in *The Creeping Terror* ('64), a military policeman (uncredited) in the sci-fi film *Fantastic Voyage* ('66) and as "Jim Handley" in *The Big Game* ('72). In made-for-TV movies, he was "Private Huffman" in *The Hanged Man* ('74), "Dr. Michaels" in *The Hostage Heart* ('77), a hitman on *Hanging by a Thread* ('79), and "Marty" on *The Night the Bridge Fell Down* ('83). He was the "Chief" on the TV series *Garrison's Gorillas* ('67). Notable TV guest appearances have been on *The Red Skelton Show*, *Cade's County*, *B.J. and the Bear*, *Falcon Crest* ('81) playing "Architect" in several episodes of *Airwolf* ('84) playing "security guard," *Dragnet*, several episodes of *Adam 12*, *Rawhide* ('65), several episodes of *Gomer Pyle, U.S.M.C.* ('66), *Bonanza* (5/8/66), *The Virginian*, *Gunsmoke* (10/20/69), *Emergency!* (2/16/74 & 3/9/74), *Switch* (3/21/75), *Fantasy Island* (12/9/78), *Quincy* (3/13/80, 2/24/81 & 9/29/82), *Code Red* (11/1/81), *General Hospital*, *Lottery!* (3/8/84), *Knight Rider* (3/10/85), *Jake and the Fatman*, ('91), & *The Young and the Restless*, playing "Attorney" in recurring episodes ('95).

Jerry H. Booth

Born Mar. 24, 1941, in Mathiston, Miss., Booth was an award-winning physicist. He graduated from Mississippi State University in 1964. Booth did doctoral work in physics at the University of Alabama. He worked with NASA's Saturn V and Apollo space programs from 1965 to 1970 and was involved in pioneering research involving lasers in holography. He then became an aerospace engineer with the Naval Weapons Engineering Support Activity at the Washington Navy Yard, where he worked on the Sikorsky H53 helicopter. From 1979 to 1985, he was a warheads engineer with the Office of Naval Intelligence. In 1985, Booth joined the Defense Intelligence Agency. His research there disclosed the strategic and mechanical capabilities of the Chinese Silkworm missile. While at the DIA, he received a Joint Meritorious Unit Award for work in aiding U.S. forces in the Persian Gulf War. He was recognized as an expert on conventional explosives, nuclear warheads, missiles, and exotic explosives. Booth was a member of the nuclear weapons working group of the Joint Atomic Energy Intelligence Committee. He was fluent in 5 languages and was a member of the Washington Judo Club, where he attained a brown belt. He was a founding member, with NASA Director Werner Von Braun, of the Astronomy Association in Huntsville and helped Von Braun in efforts to build an observatory there. He had worked for the government for 30 years and was living in Arlington, Va., where he died on Aug. 31, 1995, at the age of 54.

Ralph Boston

Born May 9, 1939, in Laurel, Mississippi. He graduated from Oak Park High School in 1957, then became a track star at Tennessee State University, where he received a graduate degree in biochemistry. The first track and field athlete to win a medal three straight times in the long jump (1960-68), Ralph Boston broke Jesse Owens' coveted 24-year-old Olympic mark in Rome in Aug. 1960 (that record stood until Bob Beamon's jump in Mexico City in 1968). Boston's jump reached 26-feet, 7 3/4 inches, shattering Owens' world record (26-4 1/4) by over three inches, and this just two weeks before the Olympic Games, in which Boston won gold. Facing a brisk head wind in the 1964 Olympics in Tokyo, Boston finished second for the silver, but only after he advised Great Britain's Lynn Davies on how to deal with the wind. The advice allowed Davies to take the gold medal. Four years later, in Mexico City, Boston again gave advice to a competitor — this time to teammate Bob Beamon. Beamon moved his approach back a few inches so he could get a clean jump, as suggested by Boston, and then set a new world record. The unselfish Boston collected the bronze. Boston is on the U.S. Olympic Committee's Top 100 Golden Olympians of all the modern games! He's in the National Track & Field Hall of Fame (1974), the Olympic Hall of Fame (1985) and the National Black College Hall of Fame in Atlanta (1995). He was the first African-American inducted into the Mississippi Sports Hall of Fame in 1977. Boston now has a cleaning business in Atlanta.

Marshall Bouldin III

Born Sept. 6, 1923, in Dundee (Tunica County), Mississippi. This painter came home to Mississippi from New York in 1950 and now lives in Clarksdale. He has painted the famous — from the daughters of presidents to military leaders — and the not so famous. The *New York Times* dubbed him "the South's foremost portrait painter." He received the Artists Achievement Award of the Governor's Awards in 1997.

Tim Bowens

Born Feb. 7, 1973, in Okolona, Miss. The 6-4, 310-pound Bowens played football for the Ole Miss Rebels, then went pro with the Miami Dolphins as a defensive tackle in 1994. Through the 1998 season, he had a pro career total of 13 sacks and 174 tackles in 80 games. He was picked for his first Pro Bowl on Dec. 16, 1998. Seven players from Mississippi were picked, including the great Jerry Rice, but only Jimmy Smith (Jacksonville wide receiver) and Bowens were voted onto the team as starters for the game in Honolulu on Feb. 7, 1999.

Jeff Bower

Born on May 28, 1953, in Roswell, Georgia. First as a record-setting quarterback, then as an assistant coach, and finishing his 10th season as head football coach in 1999, Jeff Bower has been a mainstay in the University of Southern Mississippi football program. A prep All-American at Roswell High, Bower guided his team to a pair of state championships in football. Following his senior season, Bower was named the Class AAA Georgia back of the year and played in the Georgia High School All-Star Game. After first signing with the University of Georgia, Bower instead headed to the University of Southern Mississippi. After sitting out a redshirt season in 1972, Bower took over as the Eagles' starting quarterback in 1973 and guided the team to a successful 6-4-1 mark. In his first season, he threw for 1,495 yards while completing 116 of 199 passes, nine of which were touchdowns. His .583 passing percentage during the 1973 season stood as a single-season record at USM for 23 years — falling by the side in 1996 at the hands of Lee Roberts. As a senior in 1975, Bower was named team captain and team MVP as he led the Eagles to an 8-3 record. Bower's career totals as a player included completing 278 of 506 passes for 3,589 yards and 20 touchdowns. He still holds the USM career mark for completion percentage among players with a minimum 200 pass attempts with a .549 mark. Only Brett Favre (1987-90), Reggie Collier (1979-82) and Lee Roberts (1995-98) rank ahead of Bower's 4,062 yards of career total offense (Bower coached all three during their playing days at USM). Bower still stands seventh in career passing yardage (3,589), completions (278) and attempts (506), and he is still fourth in career touchdown passes with 20. After Bower completed his bachelor's degree in 1975 he decided to stay at USM in order

Profiles of Famous & Notable Mississippians

to pursue a master's degree. Coach Bobby Collins asked Bower to remain with the Golden Eagle program as a graduate assistant. During his first season, the Golden Eagles struggled to a 3-8 record, but during his second year, the team defeated national power Auburn as well as state foes Ole Miss and Mississippi State. Bower received his MBA in management from Southern Miss in 1978. At Coach Collins request Bower remained from 1978 through 1981 working as receivers coach. In 1980 the Eagles finished with a victory in the Independence Bowl, and in 1981 USM went to the Tangerine Bowl. When Collins left USM in 1982 to become head coach at Southern Methodist University, Jeff Bower went with him to become the Mustangs' quarterback coach. During the period between 1982 and 1986, USM won the Cotton Bowl (1982) and the Aloha Bowl (1984) and played in the Sun Bowl (1983). In 1987 Bower moved on to coach the quarterbacks at Wake Forest University. The Demon Deacons finished that season with a 7-4 record, their best in 44 years. The next season Bower returned to his alma mater as assistant head coach, offensive coordinator and quarterbacks coach, a job he held for two seasons. During his first season back in 1988, the Eagles set numerous passing records and finished the season with a 10-2 record and an Independence Bowl victory. During that season the Eagles put up the highest per game passing average in school history at 235.3 yards per game. In 1988, Bower was voted into the Southern Miss Sports Hall of Fame. Bower moved on to Oklahoma State in 1989 to serve in the same capacity, assistant head coach/offensive coordinator and quarterbacks coach. Although the team managed only a 4-7 record, Bower's offensive attack produced the nation's leading rusher in Gerald Hudson. His recognition as an outstanding offensive coach continued to grow after he took as head coach of the Golden Eagles for the final game of the 1990 season, becoming the 17th head football coach in USM history. Quarterback Brett Favre, under Bower's guidance, completed 28 of 39 passes for 341 yards and two touchdowns during the 1990 All-American Bowl against North Carolina State. In 1992, Bower took a team with only four starters returning, but finished the season with a 7-4 record. After suffering through a rare losing season in 1993, the Golden Eagles bounced back with consecutive 6-5 winning seasons in 1994 and 95. In 1996, Bower guided the Eagles to an 8-3 record and a share of the inaugural Conference USA Championship. The Eagles enjoyed 7 consecutive victories during the year, which helped put Southern Miss into the nation's top 25 polls for the first time since the 1989 season. During the 1997 season Bower guided the Eagles to a 9-3 record and sole possession of the Conference USA crown. The Eagles spent two weeks in the national polls during the year. After scoring the most lopsided victory of any bowl victor, a 41-7 rout of Pittsburgh in the Liberty Bowl, Southern Miss scored a final national ranking of 19th in both the AP and ESPN/*USA Today* coaches polls, marking the first time in school history a Golden Eagles squad finished the year in the top 25. The 1998 Eagles rebounded from a 1-3 start to the season by winning 6 of their final 7 games, earning a second consecutive bowl trip. For the second time in as many seasons Southern Miss was one of just a hand full of schools to produce a 2,000-yard passer, a 1,000-yard rusher and a 1,000-yard receiver, and was one of just two schools to repeat the accomplishment from the previous season. Bower has coached numerous All-America and All-Conference selections. Besides Favre and Collier, Bower has had a hand in the careers of former USM offensive players Glen Howe, Mike Landrum, Marvin Harvey, Louis Lipps, Sammy Winder, Fred Brock and Tony Smith, all of whom went on to play professional football. The 1997 Golden Eagles sent seven players into various camps around the NFL. The 1999 Eagles had two All-Americans in defensive lineman Adalius Thomas and receiver Sherrod Gideon. Thomas, an AFCA first team All-American in 1998, was named by College Football News as the best defensive lineman in the nation for the 1999 season. Gideon, who already owns virtually every school receiving record, was the second leading returning receiver in the nation. In addition, while at Southern Methodist, Bower's quarterbacks received first team all-conference honors for three consecutive seasons. At Wake Forest, Bower coached Mike Elkins, the second quarterback taken in the 1989 NFL draft. In 1997, Lee Roberts, the latest in a long line of successful quarterbacks to play under Bower, solidified his position as one of the great passers in school history by becoming just the second player in school history to pass for more than 2,000 yards in a season, a feat he repeated in 1998, breaking the school record with 2,680 yards passing. Bower guided the program at his alma mater into a new era as a founding member of Conference USA. The Eagles' first season in C-USA was an unqualified success as the team put together a seven-game win streak and earned a share of the inaugural Conference USA title. In USM's fourth year with the new conference in 1999, Bower led the Golden Eagles to their third Conference USA crown. He also took the Eagles to their third consecutive bowl game in 1999, earning a berth in the Liberty Bowl, which the Eagles won 23-17 over Colorado State. After that, Southern Miss achieved the highest rankings in school history, 14th in the AP poll and 13th in the USPN/*USA Today* coaches' poll. After a 9-3 record in 1999, Bower's career record as a head coach stood at 59-43-1, which tied him with Reed Green for second place, behind only Pie Vann on the career victories list at Southern Mississippi.

Dennis "Oil Can" Boyd

Born Dennis Ray Boyd on Oct. 6, 1959, in Meridian, Miss. A graduate of Jackson State, he became a star pitcher for the Boston Red Sox, making his major league debut on Sept. 13, 1982. He stayed with the Red Sox until 1989. He pitched in the 1986 World Series for the ill-fated BoSox club that lost to the New York Mets in seven games. Boyd pitched for the Montreal Expos in 1990 and 1991. His 10-year career in the major leagues ended in 1991 with the Texas Rangers. For his major league career Boyd was 78-77 with a 4.04 ERA after pitching in 214 games. In 1994 and '95, he played in the independent, Class A Northern League with the Sioux City Explorers, and was 4-1 with a 1.89 ERA before his season was cut short by a blood clot in his right shoulder. In Jan. 1995, Boyd declared his intentions to sign a contract with the Chicago White Sox, dispite the ongoing baseball strike. He, instead, opted to play for the Bangor Blue Ox in the Northeast League in 1996 and went 10-0 for the season. Boyd also pitched in Mexico and various independent leagues such as the Greenville (Miss.) Bluesmen, a Big South minor league team, until 1998. Now, Boyd is back in his hometown of Meridian, where he is trying to bring a Texas-Louisiana League franchise and also wants to start a baseball academy for kids.

Eddie Boyd

Born on Nov. 25, 1914, in Stovall, Coahoma Co., Miss., he was a half-brother to Memphis Slim and a first cousin to Muddy Waters. In the 1930s he moved to Memphis where he started playing piano. In 1941 Boyd settled in Chicago and did session work for the Bluebird record label. He backed harp legend Sonny Boy Williamson on his 1945 classic *Elevator*

Profiles of Famous & Notable Mississippians

Woman, and also accompanied stars Jazz Gillum and Tampa Red. Boyd made his own recording debut on RCA in 1947 and stayed with Victor through 1949. He reportedly paid for the date that produced *Five Long Years* himself, peddling the track to JOB Records. The record topped the R&B charts in 1952 and is a certified blues classic since covered by B.B. King, Muddy Waters, Jimmy Reed, Buddy Guy, and many others. Deejay Al Benson (a Mississippian) signed Boyd to a contract with his Parrot label, then promptly sold the pact to Chess, inaugurating a stormy few years with Chicago's top blues outlet. There he recorded *24 Hours* and *Third Degree*, both big R&B hits in 1953, and a host of other Chicago blues gems. A serious auto wreck in 1957 stalled his career for a while. Boyd became enamored of Europe during his tour with the 1965 American Folk Blues Festival, so he moved to Belgium. The recording opportunities long denied him in his native land were plentiful overseas. Boyd cut prolifically during the late 1960s. In the early 1970s, he settled in Helsinki, Finland, where he played often and lived comfortably until his death there on July 13, 1994, at the age of 79.

Jimmy Boyd

Born Jan. 9, 1939, in McComb, Miss. a singer and actor, he's best-known as Howard on the 1960s TV weekly sitcom *Bachelor Father*. He's also had supporting roles in several movies, including: *Racing Blood* (1954-as David); *The Second Greatest Sex* (1955-as Newt McClure); *Platinum High School* (1960-as Bud Starkweather); *Inherit the Wind* (1960-as Howard); *High Time* (1960-as Higgson); *The Two Little Bears* (1961-as Tina's boy friend); *Norwood* (1970-as Jeeter); and *That's the Way of the World* (1975-as Gary Page).

Ishmon Bracey

Ishmon (or Ishman) Bracey was born in Byram, Miss. on Jan. 9, 1900. One of the early giants of the Delta blues, he often worked with local Jackson legends like Tommy Johnson and Charlie McCoy. He cut a small handful of sides for the Paramount label in 1930, some of the most coveted discs in blues history. He did *Suitcase Full of Blues* and *Bust Up Blues*. Bracey died in Jackson on Feb. 12, 1970, at age 70.

Bruce H. Brady

Nationally acclaimed sculptor Bruce Holmes Brady was born on Aug. 28, 1934, in Brookhaven, Miss. He was a graduate of the University of Mississippi (1957) and the UM School of Law (1961). He practiced law in Brookhaven for ten years before becoming an editor for *Outdoor Life Magazine* in 1972. A self-taught sculptor, he didn't start his career in that art until 1983. His sculpture of an American bison, *Tatanka*, was given to former president Ronald Reagan before he left office and is now housed in the Reagan Library in California. Brady's portrait bust of president Theodore Roosevelt was presented to Bob Dole on his final day as a U.S. Senator. Brady is also well-known for his sculptor of novelist William Faulkner. His commissioned works include the Mississippi Sports Hall of Fame's *Charlie Conerly Memorial Trophy*. Brady was the featured sculptor of the Southeastern Wildlife Art Exposition and served on the advisory board of the Lauren Rogers Museum of Art. He worked in the medium of bronze sculpture and combined his love of the outdoors with his art. He served as commissioner with the Mississippi Dept. of Wildlife Conservation and as a board member of the Mississippi Wildlife Federation. His many awards include being named Sportsman of the Year and Outdoor Communicator of the Year. He received the president's Award for Lifetime Achievement from the Mississippi Wildlife Federation. An anthology of his hunting articles, *Bruce Brady's Game Trails*, was published in 1990, and his poem *Autumn* has been published several times. Attorney, artist, writer, and outdoorsman Brady died in Brookhaven on Feb. 8, 2000, at age 65 of heart failure following a three-year battle with esophageal cancer. He is buried in the Brady Family Cemetery.

Bonnie Lynn Bramlett

Born Bonnie Lynn O'Farrell in Pontotoc County on November 8, 1944. She was with the group Delaney & Bonnie and married to Delaney. A little bit of trivia — she even sang for a short time in Ike Turner's soul group, the Ikettes!

Delaney Bramlett

Born July 1, 1939, in Pontotoc County, Mississippi. While still a teenager, Delaney made some demos for another Mississippian, Elvis Presley, and played a cardboard box as a drum on a George Jones record. Once grown, Delaney joined the Navy for three years. After service he moved his family to Los Angeles to be with him, where he has remained ever since. After moving to L.A., he became a regular on the TV show *Shindig* as a Shindog, the house band. He was already busy writing with the likes of Mac Davis and Jackie DeShannon. Over the years, some of his songs have reached standard status such as *Superstar*, *Never Ending Song of Love* and *Let It Rain*, among others. A few of the artists who have recorded Delaney compositions are Luther Vandross, Ray Charles, Phoebe Snow, the Staple Singers, the Osmonds, The Carpenters, The Everly Brothers, Crystal Gale and even Lawrence Welk used *Never Ending Song of Love* as an opener for one of his shows. Over the years songwriting partners have included longtime friends like Leon Russell, Steve Cropper, John Lennon, Eric Clapton, Billy Burnette, Dorsey Burnette, George Harrison, Mac Davis and Tony Joe White. Then, there are his (their) hit recordings: *Only You Know & I Know* (#20 in 1971) as "Delaney & Bonnie" and *Never Ending Song of Love* (#13 in 1971) as "Delaney & Bonnie & Friends." "Friends" were backing artists making up a virtual Who's Who of rock music, who included, at various times, Eric Clapton, Duane Allman, Joe Cocker, Rita Coolidge, Dave Mason, Billy Preston, Leon Russell and Jim Gordon. Jimi Hendrix joined the "Friends" for a couple weeks of touring. John Lennon and Delaney collaborated together and Delaney played the friend role as a member of Lennon's Plastic Ono Band. Jerry Lee Lewis requested Delaney's presence during the recording of his famous *London Sessions* album in England. But the late Duane Allman and Delaney became very best friends sharing ideas, musical licks and a never-ending friendship. Clapton, Gordon and other "friends" formed Derek & the Dominoes after performing together on Delaney & Bonnie's 1969-70 tour. After Eric Clapton joined him on tour, Delaney produced and co-wrote songs for Clapton's first solo LP. Due to contractual obligations he relinquished the writer credit to his wife, Bonnie Bramlett, enabling him to keep the rights in the family. Clapton still credits Delaney for pushing him to sing and teaching him. Known as a songwriter, singer and musician, Delaney has also been a mentor to some of the very best. George Harrison had his first slide bottle placed in his hand by Delaney who quickly taught George how to play slide and write a Gospel song, which resulted in Harrison's hit *My Sweet Lord*. Delaney produced the late King Curtis' last LP and taught Curtis to sing. He has produced artists such as Etta James and Dorothy Morrison (on *Happy Day*), and wrote for and produced Elvin Bishop, John Hammond, Bobby Whitlock and the Staple Singers. Delaney recorded a total of 16 albums, solo and with Bonnie and "friends." Delaney & Bonnie dissolved their marriage and the group in 1972.

Profiles of Famous & Notable Mississippians

Brandy
Born Brandy Norwood on Feb. 11, 1979, in McComb, Miss., her family moved to Los Angeles in 1983. She signed a record contract with Atlantic Records in 1994 and soon had a No. 1 R&B hit, *I Wanna Be Down*. By the time she turned 16, she had a Platinum album and two Grammy nominations. She had the number 10 R & B hit of all of 1995, called *Baby*, which was taken from her self-titled debut album that had gone quadruple platinum by 1998. She started 1996 with a Top 10 R&B single, *Sittin' Up In My Room* from the *Waiting to Exhale* movie soundtrack, that also entered the Top Singles pop chart a few weeks later. It was 8th on the list of Top R&B Singles of all of 1996. Other hits include *Best Friend*, *Brokenhearted* and the No. 1 hit in 1998, a duet with Monica, *The Boy Is Mine*, which went platinum. That song was taken from her second album, *Never Say Never*, and a second single, *Top of the World*, made the Top-10 on several charts. She started out 1999 with her *Have You Ever?* on top of the singles and R&B charts. The American Music Awards show in 1996 named Brandy the favorite new soul-R&B artist. She has won five *Soul Train* awards including the Soul Train Lady of Soul Entertainer of the Year Award in 1996. On TV, she portrayed shy student Danesha on the now-defunct weekly series *Thea* and the title character in the comedy *Moesha*. She starred in ABC-TV's *Wonderful World of Disney* feature *Cinderella* in Nov. 1997. Diana Ross and Brandy played singing mother-and-daughter on the ABC-TV movie, *Double Platinum*, which aired May 16, 1999. Brandy received two 1998 Grammy nominations — for Female R&B Performance for *Sittin' Up in My Room* and Pop Collaboration with Vocals for *Missing You* with Tamia, Gladys Knight and Chaka Khan. In 1999, Brandy was nominated with Monica for Record of the Year and Best R&B Performance By a Duo or Group With Vocal for the record *The Boy Is Mine*. Brandy was in the 1998 movie *I Still Know What You Did Last Summer*. She even has her own DC Comics book! And, Brandy was selected as a spokeswoman for Cover Girls Cosmetics.

William T. Brannon
Born March 6, 1906, in Pachuta (Clarke County), Mississippi. He wrote more than 2,500 crime articles and mystery stories under a variety of pseudonyms including Lawrence Gardner, Jack Hamilton, Peter Hermanns, William Tibbetts, and others. He received the Edgar Allen Poe Award in 1950 and 1951.

Jeff Branson
Born Jeffery Glenn Branson on Jan. 26, 1967, in Waynesboro, Mississippi. He made his major league baseball debut with Cincinnati on April 12, 1992, and this infielder stayed with the Reds until 1997. He played second base for the Cleveland Indians in 1997 and 1998. Branson went to the minor league Indianapolis Indians for the 1999 season. The 2000 season found him with the Los Angeles Dodgers. His career stats through the 2000 season show 377 hits in 1,534 at bats (.246 batting average), 170 runs, 34 home runs and 156 RBIs in 681 games played. He now resides in Millry, Alabama.

Jeff Brantley
Born on Sept. 5, 1963, in Florence, Alabama. He became the best pitcher in school history at Mississippi State. He made his major league baseball debut on Aug. 5, 1988, with the San Francisco Giants, where he stayed until 1993. He pitched in the 1989 World Series and in the 1990 All-Star game. He switched to the Cincinnati Reds for the 1994 season. During the first month of the season, he had a team-high 15 saves and a 2.48 earned-run average with 63 strikeouts, compared to just 28 walks, in 65 innings pitched. He appeared in 50 games, third-most on the team, and made $1 million in bonuses to go with his $500,000 base salary. On Oct. 27, 1994, he signed a two-year, $2.5 million contract to stay with the Cincinnati Reds. During the strike-abbreviated 1995 season, he had 28 saves, three wins and a 2.82 ERA in 56 games for the National League Central champs. On Sept. 20, 1996, Brantley made his 40th save, a team-record and second in the National League. Before the game, he signed a three-year contract extension with the Reds worth $8.4 million. Brantley ended his 1996 season with club-record 44 saves and a 2.41 ERA in 66 appearances. With the St. Louis Cardinals for the 1998 season, he was 0-5 with a 4.44 ERA and 14 saves. The Cardinals sent Brantley to the Philadelphia Phillies on Nov. 19, 1998. Brantley, who had shoulder surgery in 1997, just got started in the 1999 season when he had to have another operation on his shoulder that would take him out for the rest of the season. Then, after becoming a free agent, he re-signed with the Phillies on Dec. 7, 1999, agreeing to a one-year contract. In March 2000, Brantley found out that a slightly strained triceps would probably keep him from making the opening day roster, but wouldn't end his career. Brantley's career stats through the 2000 season: 43 wins, 45 losses, 172 saves and a 3.35 ERA in 597 games. Brantley has a home in Clinton, Mississippi.

Rod Brasfield
Born Aug. 22, 1910, in Smithville in Monroe County, Mississippi. He made his first appearance on the Grand Ole Opry in Nashville on July 15, 1944, and was that show's top comedian for the next 14 years until Sept. 12, 1958, when he died of a heart attack at age 48. Brasfield received critical praise for his dramatic role opposite Andy Griffith in his only film, *A Face in the Crowd* (1957). He was elected to the Country Music Hall of Fame in 1987.

Jackie Brenston
Born August 15, 1930, in Clarksdale, Mississippi. He had a No. 1 hit record *Rocket 88* in 1951. The Rock and Roll Hall of Fame says that "among many music scholars, *Rocket 88*, by Jackie Brenston - the singer and sax player in Ike Turner's Band - is regarded as the first rock and roll record. It was produced by Phillips at Sun in March 1951 and released on the Chess label." *Rockett 88* climbed to the top of the R&B charts and was the second most successful R&B record of 1951, behind only *Sixty Minute Man* by the Dominoes. The success of Brenston's record helped keep Sam Phillips' fledging Sun Records label in business. *Rockett 88* was written by Mississippians Ike Turner (who played with Jackie on the record) and Delta bluesman James Cotton. Brenston died in Memphis, Tennessee on Dec. 15, 1979.

Jim Brewer
Born on Sept. 7, 1933, in Hattiesburg. He received all his higher education, including his doctorate, at the University of Southern Mississippi. A lifelong educator, Dr. Brewer is the founder and former president of Associated Consultants in Education. With offices in Clinton, Mississippi and Suffern, New York, his company developed training materials and programs for education and business. His BEST Instrument personality inventory series is sold in seven countries (translated into 4 languages) and is used by many Fortune 500 companies, including Readers Digest, IBM, Liberty Insurance, Century 21, Harley Davidson, and the U.S. Postal Service, just to name a few. He developed more than 50 customized video programs used for training employees of TVA and other power companies in several states, including Mississippi, Illinois and Louisiana, plus Central America. Dr. Brewer has been rated top trainer and consultant in Mississippi, Louisiana and

Profiles of Famous & Notable Mississippians

Michigan. He and his company have also produced video programs for parents that won four national awards and are used by over 2,000 schools around the nation. Dr. Brewer was recently recognized by the Americanism Foundation for his work in education of character and values. Dr. Brewer is also founder and Chairman of the Board of the Mississippi Musicians Hall of Fame and its Mississippi Music Heritage Museum in Clinton. The first 27 artists were inducted into the Mississippi Musicians Hall of Fame on Apr. 1, 2000.

Henry Herschel Brickell

Born in Senatobia on Sept. 13, 1889, he also lived in several other Mississippi towns, including Yazoo City. Considered to be one of the best professional literary critics of the 20th century, he was well-traveled, cultured, and an expert on the short story. He served as the third editor of the *O. Henry Memorial Award Prize Stories* (1940-46), and *Prize Stories: The O. Henry Awards* (1947-51). He was literary editor for the *New York Evening Post* (1923-28), editor with Henry Holt & Co. 1928-33, and wrote some editorials for the *New York Sun*. In addition to book reviews for magazines like *The Saturday Review of Literature*, *Virginia Quarterly*, *The Atlantic Monthly*, and *The Nation*, he wrote short stories on the Civil War set in Yazoo City. He died in Jackson on May 29, 1952.

James F. Brieger

Born April 9, 1930, in Newton County, Mississippi. He wrote and published *Hometown Mississippi* in 1980. This detailed reference work, reissued in trade paperback in 1997, is an exhaustive compilation of Mississippi placenames, both present and past (many towns & places are now extinct) and gives in-depth information on how these places came to be, how they got their names, and some of their early history. Research for this large book took 15 years!

Big Bill Broonzy

Born William Lee Conley Broonzy in Scott, Bolivar County, Mississippi on June 26, 1893. His recording career spanned 5 decades, taking him from Mississippi to Chicago and even to Europe. A songwriter, vocalist, and guitarist, he recorded over 250 songs prior to WWII & hundreds more after. Among his hundreds of titles are standards like *All by Myself* and *Key to the Highway*. He also wrote many songs and was a Chicago studio sideman on countless sessions for bluesmen Sonny Boy Williamson, Bumble Bee Slim and others. He played several styles — down-home finger-picking, ragtime, and single-string electric. He was instrumental in the growth of the Chicago Blues sound, and his travels abroad rank him as one of the leading blues ambassadors. He was one of a family of 17 who learned to fiddle on a homemade instrument and was performing by age ten at social functions and in church. After brief stints on the pulpit and in the Army, he moved to Chicago where he switched from violin to guitar. Broonzy began his recording career with Paramount in 1927. He label-hopped from Paramount to Bluebird to Columbia to Chess to Okeh!. In the early 1930s he cut some great blues and hokum. In 1938, Broonzy was at Carnegie Hall, purportedly filling in for Robert Johnson, who had just passed away. The following year he appeared with Benny Goodman and Louis Armstrong in the film production *Swingin' the Dream*. Broonzy spent a good part of the early 1940s barnstorming the South with Lil Green's road show or in Chicago with Memphis Slim until 1951. Then, he spent a considerable amount of time doing live performances and recording overseas in Europe and worldwide. Broonsy worked with a long list of artists from Blind John Davis to Pete Seeger. In 1955, the book *Big Bill Blues*, his life as told to a Danish writer, was published. In 1957, after one more British tour, the pace began to catch up with Broonzy. He spent the last year of his life in and out of hospitals and finally succumbed to throat cancer. Broonzy died on Aug. 15, 1958, in Chicago and is buried there. He's in the Blues Foundation's Hall of Fame.

Jesse Leroy Brown

Born in Hattiesburg on Oct. 13, 1926. He was salutatorian at Eureka High in Hattiesburg. He then attended Ohio State University's college of engineering where he maintained a straight "A" average for three years. Brown enlisted in the Naval Air Reserve in 1946, went to Pensacola for flight training in 1947 and became the first black pilot in the Navy when he received his wings on Oct. 21, 1948, at the age of 22. He became the nation's first black aviator to be killed in combat when he was shot down behind enemy lines over North Korea on Dec. 4, 1950. Brown flew 20 missions in Korea between October 1950 and his death. He was posthumously awarded the Air Medal, the Distinguished Flying Cross and a purple heart for heroism and extraordinary achievement in action. The Navy knox class ocean escort vessel, the *USS Jesse L. Brown*, launched from New Orleans in 1972 and commissioned in 1973, was named in his honor. Brown was the first black naval officer to have a ship named in his honor. The ship was decommissioned at Pensacola in 1994. In 1994, a monument to Brown was unveiled in Hattiesburg on Jesse Brown Street.

Kelly Brown

Born Sept. 24, 1928, in Jackson, Miss. He is a movie character actor who played "Carl" in *Seven Brides for Seven Brothers* (1954), "Jimmy McBride" in *Daddy Long Legs* (1955), "Sam" in *The Girl Most Likely* (1957), and appeared in the TV movie *Meet Me in St. Louis* (1959). He owned and operated a Ballet Studio in Phoenix, Arizona in the late 1960s. Brown died in Scottsdale, Arizona in March 1981 at age 52.

Larry Brown

Born the son of sharecroppers on July 9, 1951, in Yocona, Mississippi and raised in Potlockney near Oxford. He graduated from Lafayette High School in 1969. He adapted his highly popular and successful novel *Joe* (1992) for the stage and also wrote the novels, *Facing the Music* (1988), *Dirty Work*, and *Big Bad Love* — all raw, realistic tales of the rural South. He wrote the non-fiction book, *On Fire, A Personal Account of Life and Death and Choices* (1994), a story of his life as a captain with the Oxford Fire Department. Brown's sixth book, the novel *Father and Son* (1996) received the Southern Book Critics Circle award in 1997. Brown was the first two-time winner of the award, his novel *Joe* having won the 1992 award. His latest work is *Fay* (1999). His short stories have appeared in several magazines and anthologies. Brown received the Artist's Achievement Award of the 2000 Governor's Awards for Excellence in the Arts.

Paul T. Brown

Born May 14, 1949, in Greenwood, he grew up in Yazoo City from age one and now lives in Brandon. He graduated from Mississippi State. This outdoorsman and award-winning photographer released 102 of his favorite nature and wildlife photos from 20 years of work in his first book, *Wildlife of the South*, in 1994. Included is Brown's photo of a great blue heron with a bluegill empaled on its beak — the Southeastern Outdoor Press Association's 1994 Photo of the Year. Another book of amazing photographs of animals, *Wild Visions*, was released in 1998. His photos have appeared in many wildlife magazines, including *Field & Stream* and *Southern Outdoors*.

Profiles of Famous & Notable Mississippians

Richard Jess Brown, Jr.
Born Sept. 13, 1956, in Jackson, Miss. He received a degree in music education from Memphis State University and his master's in music performance from DePaul University. He has performed with many great classical and jazz artists such as Ella Fitzgerald, Pearl Bailey, Andre Watts, Lester Bowie, Ed Wilderson and others. He has played on Top-10 albums and received international recognition performing extensively in Europe including Paris, Zurich, London, Vienna and Venice. Articles about him have appeared in *Newsweek*, *Downbeat*, *Coda* and *Atlantic Monthly*.

Willie Brown
Born in Yazoo City on Dec. 2, 1940. Played as a linebacker at Grambling State. He played defensive back for the Denver Broncos from 1967-78 and the Oakland Raiders from 1963-78. He was All-AFL in his second season. He was MVP of the 1965 AFL All-Star game, as well as the Raiders' MVP in 1969. Brown, who played in 205 pro games, was an All-Pro 12 consecutive years during his 16-year career. He played in five AFL All-Star games, four AFC-NFC Pro Bowls and nine AFL/AFC title games — was All-AFL/AFC seven times. He shares the Raider career pass interception record with 39 and holds the NFL record for most consecutive seasons with at least one interception in 16 consecutive seasons. He played in Super Bowl II in 1968 and in Super Bowl XI in 1977, he intercepted a Fran Tarkinson pass and returned it 75 yards for a TD in Oakland's 32-14 win over Minnesota. He was a defensive backfield coach in Super Bowls XV and XVIII, both Raiders' wins. On Jan. 15, 1992, he was hired as head coach at Long Beach State in California. Selected to the AFL's all-time team and enshrined in the Pro Football Hall of Fame in 1984 in his first year of eligibility, Brown is also a member of the Grambling State University Hall of Fame, Louisiana Sports Hall of Fame and the SWAC Hall of Fame. He was inducted into the Mississippi Sports Hall of Fame on March 17, 1995.

Wilson Brown
Born in 1841 in Natchez, Adams County, Miss. Brown was a Landsman with the U.S. Navy when he performed an act of bravery on Aug. 5, 1864, which earned him the Medal of Honor (MOH). The Medal was awarded to him on Dec. 31, 1864. Here are the actual words of his citation: "On board the flagship *U.S.S. Hartford* during successful attacks against Fort Morgan, rebel gunboats and the ram Tennessee in Mobile Bay on 5 August 1864. Knocked unconscious into the hold of the ship when an enemy shellburst fatally wounded a man on the ladder above him, Brown, upon regaining consciousness, promptly returned to the shell whip on the berth deck and zealously continued to perform his duties although 4 of the 6 men at this station had been either killed or wounded by the enemy's terrific fire." Brown was one of only 2 native Mississippians (of 5 Mississippians) to receive the Medal of Honor during the Civil War. The Medal was awarded to only those that fought for the North — the Medal was not given to Confederates. Brown's MOH was officially accredited to "Mississippi River, Mississippi." Brown's Medal was one of 17 Medals of Honor that have been officially accredited to Mississippi in all wars, although we claim 5 more that were accredited to other states because the recipients had Mississippi ties. Brown is one of 13 native Mississippians (of 22 Mississippians — 15 Army, 4 Marines and 3 Navy) in all wars to have received the MOH, out of 3,433 recipients of the Medal through Nov. 1, 2000. Of Mississippi MOH recipients, Brown was the only *native* Mississippian (of 2 Mississippians) to serve in the Navy during the Civil War (the other was "adopted" Mississippian Martin Freeman-see his profile) and the only *native* Mississippian (of 3 Mississippians) to receive the MOH for service in the Navy in all wars. Brown was buried in the Natchez National Cemetery in Natchez on Jan. 24, 1900. A Medal of Honor marker is on his grave.

Archie Brownlee
Born in 1925, Brownlee started attending the Piney Woods School in Mississippi when only 6 years old. There he formed and led the Five Blind Boys of Mississippi, a traditional Black gospel group, in the 1930s. Archie Brownlee's amazing vocal flights and theatrics helped make the group one of the greatest quartets of all time. They were originally recorded by the Library of Congress in 1937 doing comic and game tunes. Brownlee became a star in the 1940s and early '50s. His importance to the development of gospel/R&B can be compared to Mississippian Lester Young's contribution to jazz sax. Some have said that without Brownlee, there might not be a Ray Charles or James Brown. Brownlee died of pneumonia in the New Orleans Charity Hospital Feb. 8, 1960, at age 35.

Blanche K. Bruce
Born Blanche Kelso Bruce on Mar. 1, 1841, in Prince Edward County, Virginia. In the 1870s, he was the most recognized black political leader in Mississippi. When the Mississippi legislature elected him to the U.S. Senate in 1874, Bruce became the first African-American ever to serve a full term in the U.S. Senate. Although shunned by his Mississippi colleague, James L. Alcorn, Bruce enjoyed a friendlier relationship with Alcorn's successor, L.Q.C. Lamar. On Feb. 14, 1879, Bruce became the first black senator to preside over a Senate session. Whites recaptured political control, and in 1880 James Z. George was chosen to succeed Bruce. President Garfield appointed Bruce registrar of the treasury, where he served until 1885. President Harrison appointed Bruce recorder of deeds for the District of Columbia in 1889. After leaving this office in 1893, Bruce was a trustee of the public schools in Washington, and again registrar of the treasury from 1897 until his death on March 17, 1898.

Paul Brummett
Born Aug. 10, 1939, in Jackson. He graduated from Murrah High School in 1957 and received a B.S. degree in industrial technology from Mississippi State University in 1963. Brummett has since worked for Supreme Electronics, U.S. Industries, and television manufacturers RCA and Sylvania. In 1970, while working for the Jerold Corporation, Brummett patented a way of storing clothing on hangers in one-20th of the space. After he started his own first company, Applied Microcomputer, he developed a way to manage industrial plants' peak energy demand to save costs and also a way to read and apply bar codes. In 1987, he started another company, Brummett Computers, which he soon sold. In 1996, he started a third company, Television Corporation of America (TCA). Envisioning a day soon when all communications services will be on cable — TV, telephone, Internet — Brummett developed and patented a process for making electronic circuitry combining artificial intelligence with digital TV that will enable transmissions at narrower bandwidths. This will mean many benefits, including more TV channels with higher picture quality, clearer phone reception, and much faster computer connections to the Internet.

John H. Bryan, Jr.
Born in West Point Oct. 5, 1936. He was a student at Mississippi State University in 1959-60 and is an economics and business graduate of Rhodes College of Memphis. Consolidated Foods (later Sara Lee Corporation), a Fortune

Profiles of Famous & Notable Mississippians

500 company, acquired his family business, Bryan Brothers Packing of West Point (est. 1936) in 1967. Bryan became president and a director of Sara Lee in 1974, was named CEO a year later and was elected Chairman of the Board in 1976. He's in the Mississippi Business Hall of Fame. An active supporter of the arts, Bryan is a member of the President's Committee on the Arts and Humanties and a member of the Trustees Council of the National Gallery of Art. He has received Holland's Order of Orange Nassau, France's Chevalier de la Legion of Honneur, and the National Humanitarian Award of the National Conference of Christians and Jews. Mississippi State awarded its first honorary degrees during commencement ceremonies on May 13, 1999, and one of the three initial recipients was John Bryan. According to *Forbes* magazine, Bryan's pay in 1999 was almost a million dollars with close to $1.5 million in bonuses. When his "other compensation" of $12 million and stock gains of over $10 million are counted, it makes his total 1999 compensation almost $25 million, placing him in the top 10 highest paid CEOs in America! John retired from Sara Lee on July 1, 2000. John's brother George is senior vice president of Sara Lee Corp., the second largest food company in America (after Conagra) with 1999 revenues of over $20 billion!

Bobby Bryant

Born on May 19, 1934, in Hattiesburg, Miss. A jazz trumpet player, he also played the flugelhorn. Early on Bryant played trumpet and tenor before settling on the trumpet. He moved to Chicago in 1952, graduating from the Cosmopolitan School of Music in 1957. He freelanced for 3 years, working with Red Saunders, singer Billy Williams, and appearing with smaller groups. He spent 1960 in New York and then relocated to Los Angeles the following year where he permanently settled. Bryant toured with Vic Damone, then headed his own groups, playing with big bands such as Charles Mingus (1964), Gerald Wilson and Oliver Nelson. In addition to big band work, Bryant was active in the studios and as a jazz educator. As a leader, Bryant led big band dates for VeeJay (1961), two for Pacific Jazz in 1969 and one for Cadet (1971) in addition to a sextet set for Cadet in 1967. His last album was *Swahili Strut* in 1971. Bryant died in June 1998.

Bill Buchanan

Born Jan. 23, 1953, in Mobile, Ala., he grew up in Mississippi and graduated from Meridian High in 1971. He received a masters in electrical engineering from Mississippi State after working as a graduate assistant at NASA. As a former captain in the U.S. Air Force Electronic Systems Division, he helped develop and test a prototype radar designed to penetrate foliage. He is now a successful engineer with Bell Laboratories in New Hampshire, where he develops control systems and communication protocols for computer networks. On the side, he's been writing novels. His first work was released in Feb. 1997. Nearly 300,000 copies of the paperback *Virus* have been distributed nationwide. It was a long road — he first got the idea for *Virus* back in 1983. After his manuscripts were rejected over 50 times, Buchanan finally found an agent in New York in 1995. In all, it took Buchanan 14 years to get his book published. *Virus*, which made *USA Today*'s list of top selling books in the country, is the tense story about an unstoppable computer super virus that worms its way into the U.S. strategic defense system causing the country's own antimissile lasers to target commercial jetliners, holding the nation and the world hostage. *Virus* is based on the concept of the Strategic Defense Initiative, or Star Wars, a technology first made public in 1983 during the Reagan Administration.

Buchanan is finishing his second novel, *Clear Water*, a techno-thriller involving submarines. Buchanan says "Someday, I hope to get good enough at this to make a living. My dream is to move back home to Wren, Mississippi, and write on my grandparents' farm."

Jimmy Buffett

This R&R and pop singer/songwriter was born on Christmas Day, Dec. 25, 1946, in Pascagoula, Mississippi, but grew up in Mobile, Alabama. His nickname is Bubba. He has a B.S. degree in history and journalism from the University of Southern Mississippi. After working in New Orleans, he moved to Nashville in 1969, where he landed a job writing for *Billboard* magazine. In 1971, he settled in Key West, Florida. A big hit single record that helped jump-start his career was *Margaritaville* (#8 in 1977 on the Pop Chart & it also hit the Country Chart). Other single hits include *Come Monday* and *Fins*. He has recorded lots of albums including *Songs You Know By Heart* (Platinum in 1985), *Feeding Frenzy* (Gold in 1990), and *Boats, Beaches, Bars & Ballads* (Platinum in 1992), *Fruitcakes* (1994), *Barmeter Soup* (1995), *Banana Wind* (1996), and *Beach House on the Moon* (1999), his 31st album. He's co-authored two children's books with his daughter Savannah Jane, *The Jolly Mon* (1993) and *Trouble Dolls* (1997), and three books of his own, *Tales from Margaritaville* (1990), *Where is Joe Merchant?* (1992) and *A Pirate Looks At Fifty* (1998). Buffett wrote music and lyrics for the movie *Arachnophobia* (1990). He's been in a few movies: playing himself in *Rancho Deluxe* (1975) and *FM* (1978); as "additional blond agent" in *Repo Man* (1984); *Doctor Duck's Super Secret All-Purpose Sauce* (1985); as "the armless guy" in *Cobb* (1994); and as a 727 pilot in *Congo* (1995). He owns a restaurant/bar chain named Margaritaville in Key West, Orlando, New Orleans and Charleston, S.C. He also markets a line of clothing. He has a huge beach/party-crowd following of fans who call themselves "Parrotheads." There are a total of 80 Parrothead fan clubs worldwide. Buffett was one of the first 27 inducted into the inaugural Miss. Musicians Hall of Fame on April 1, 2000.

Ellis Rena Burks

Born Sept. 11, 1964, in Vicksburg. He made his major league baseball debut on Apr. 30, 1987, with the Boston Red Sox where he stayed until 1992. In his rookie year he became the third Red Sox player in history to achieve 20 home runs and 20 stolen bases in a season. He played for the Chicago White Sox in 1993. In 1994 he went with the Colorado Rockies. At the end of the 1996 season as a Colorado Rockies outfielder, he had an injury-free year and joined Hank Aaron as the only players with 40 homers, 200 hits and 30 steals in a season! He played in 2 All-Star games, 1990 and 1996. He was acquired by the San Francisco Giants in July 1998. On Nov. 12, 1998, Burks agreed to a $10 million, two-year contract. He got $4.5 million in 1999 and $5.5 million in 2000. The two-time All-Star hit .292 with 21 homers and 76 RBIs in the 1998 season. During the 1999 season, he batted .282 with 31 home runs and 96 RBIs. His careers stats through the 2000 season include 1,770 hits in 6,044 at bats (.293 batting avg.), 1,045 runs, 285 home runs, and 1,012 RBIs in 1,672 games played.

Charles Burnett

Born Apr. 13, 1944, in Vicksburg, he's an African-American independent filmmaker. His *Killer of Sheep*, produced in 1973 but not shown until 1977, won multiple awards. Though it never received commercial release, the film was added to the National Film Registry by the Library of Congress in 1990. Burnett's first theatrical release, *To Sleep With Anger* (1990),

Profiles of Famous & Notable Mississippians

starred Danny Glover and cost less than $1.5 million. It was nominated for the New York Film Critics Award for Best Screenplay. The National Society of Film Critics cited Burnett's *Nightjohn* at its 32nd annual meeting in New York in 1998. They cited the work, about slaves teaching one another to read, as "a film whose special qualities and origins challenged the strictures of the marketplace." Burnett directed *The Annihilation of Fish*, starring James Earl Jones, which made its world premiere at the Toronto Film Festival in 1999.

Chester Arthur Burnett (see Howlin' Wolf)

Eddie "Guitar" Burns

Born Feb. 8, 1928, in Belzoni, Miss. He's one of Detroit's finest bluesmen, best known for working with John Lee Hooker. Burns picked up his early blues training from the 78 rpm records of Sonny Boy Williamson, Tommy McClennan and Big Bill Broonzy. He is a harp player in Detroit. He cut *Notoriety Woman*, his first single, in 1948. Burns added guitar the next year, cutting sessions with Hooker. Burns's own discography includes the singles: *Hello Miss Jessie Lee* ('52), *Biscuit Baking Mama* ('54) *Treat Me Like I Treat You* ('57). In 1961, Burns cut *Orange Driver* and several more R&B-slanted sides. Blues talent runs in the Burns family — brother Jimmy is a blues-soul performer based in Chicago.

R.L. Burnside

Born Nov. 23, 1926, in Oxford, Mississippi. The guitarist, singer and songwriter now makes his home in Holly Springs, in the hill country where he's lived most of his life. In fact, he lives right next door to the juke joint owned by his friend and fellow bluesman, the late Junior Kimbrough (1930-1998). Burnside first learned his music from his neighbor, "Mississippi" Fred McDowell. His other influences include Muddy Waters, John Lee Hooker and Lightnin' Hopkins. Up until the mid-1980s, Burnside was primarily a farmer and fisherman. In the late 1980s he was invited to perform at several European blues festivals. In 1992, he was featured alongside Junior Kimbrough in a documentary film, *Deep Blues*. His albums, *Bad Luck City* (1993), *Too Bad Jim* (1994), *A Ass Pocket of Whiskey* (1996), *Mr. Wizard* (1997) and *Come on In* (1998), were released on the Oxford-based Fat Possum label. Burnside is accompanied by his small family band known as the Sound Machine, which includes his son Dwayne on bass and son-in-law Calvin Jackson on drums, plus Kenny Brown on guitar. Burnside's recordings showcase the raw, downhome-style, unadulterated blues that Burnside has played for over 30 years at Kimbrough's juke joint.

Ode Burrell

Born Sept. 15, 1939, in Goodman, Mississippi, he grew up in nearby Durant. He attended Holmes Junior College at Goodman before playing for two seasons at Mississippi State. He not only played as a starting tailback, but also as a left cornerback, punter, kickoff specialist and kick returner. At Mississippi State, Burrell was the Bulldogs' leading rusher, punter, punt returner, and kickoff returner for the 1962 season. He was named to the Coaches All-American Team, the All-Southeastern Conference Team, and was MVP in the 1963 Liberty Bowl victory over North Carolina State. He also was named best offensive back in the Senior Bowl and Blue-Gray game in 1963. After graduating from State in 1964, Burrell was drafted by both the NFL-champion Green Bay Packers and the AFL's Houston Oilers. He played six seasons for the Oilers (1964-68), who traded LSU Heisman Trophy winner Billy Cannon to make room for Burrell on the roster. The first time Burrell touched the football for Houston, he ran a kickoff back for a touchdown. He was the Oilers' MVP and leading rusher in 1967 and among the top five in the American Football League in rushing and receiving, and in 1968 he played in the Pro Bowl. He's in the Sports Halls of Fame at Holmes Community College and MSU (1995) and in the Mississippi Sports Hall of Fame (1997). Burrell is retired after being on the coaching staff of Gulf Coast Community College for six years and currently lives in Gautier, Mississippi.

Guy T. Bush

Guy Terrell Bush was born on Aug. 23, 1901, in Aberdeen, Mississippi. Nicknamed "The Mississippi Mudcat," he made his major league baseball debut on Sept. 17, 1923, with Chicago and stayed with the Cubs through 1934. He played for the Pittsburgh Pirates (1935-36), the Boston Bees (1936-37), the St. Louis Cardinals in 1938 and the Cincinnati Reds in 1945. Bush won 176 games (lost 136 games) with a 3.86 ERA in over 17 major league seasons. He pitched in 542 games, including pitching 151 complete games. Babe Ruth hit his last two home runs off balls pitched by Bush during the World Series on May 25, 1935. He was inducted into the Mississippi Sports Hall of Fame in 1973. Bush died at Shannon, Mississippi on July 2, 1985 at age 83.

Eugene Butler

Born June 11, 1894, in Starkville, Miss. He graduated from Mississippi A&M (Mississippi State) in 1913. He was editor-in-chief of the *Progressive Farmer* magazine for many years and founded *Southern Living* magazine. Butler died in Dallas, Texas on June 5, 1995, only 6 days before his 101st birthday.

Jack Butler

Born in Alligator, Mississippi on May 8, 1944. He received his B.A. and B.S. degrees from Central Missouri State and an M.F.A. in creative writing from the University of Arkansas. His books include *West of Hollywood* (1980), *Hawk Gumbo and Other Stories* (1982), and *The Kid Who Wanted to Be a Spaceman* (1984). He has also published frequently in literary journals including the *New Yorker* and *New Orleans Review*.

Jerry Butler

Born on Dec. 8, 1939, in Sunflower Co., Miss., he moved to Chicago at an early age. Butler helped shape the history of soul music in 1958, when he and Curtis Mayfield formed the group, The Impressions. That same year, he wrote *For Your Precious Love*, a landmark, gold-selling record (#11 in '58). Butler went on to become one of the biggest R&R and soul singers of all time. Philadelphia DJ Georgie Woods dubbed him "The Iceman" in 1959 for his cool delivery and effortless on-stage style. It stuck. The Iceman's other big hit records were *He Will Break Your Heart* (# 7 in '60), *Moon River* (#11 in '61), *Hey, Western Union Man* (#16 in '68) and *Only The Strong Survive* (# 4 million- seller in '69). He had a hit record with Betty Everett (from Greenwood, Miss.) *Let It Be Me* (# 5 in '64). He has had a total of 16 Top 40 hits and a prodigious 62 albums! Butler is currently serving his fourth 4-year term as commissioner of Cook County, Illinois, the 2nd most-populous county in the United States (5.5 million) while continuing to entertain on stage during weekends.

John Tyler Caldwell

Born Dec. 9, 1911, in Yazoo City, Mississippi. After receiving his bachelor's degree from Mississippi State College in 1932, he earned master's degrees from Duke University (1936) and Columbia University (1937) and a doctoral degree from Princeton University in 1939 as a Julius Rosenwald Fellow. A political science instructor, he taught at Holmes Junior College in Goodman, Mississippi from 1932-36 and at Vanderbilt University in Nashville from 1939-47. He entered the U.S. Navy as an Ensign in 1942. In 1946, he left the Navy with the

Profiles of Famous & Notable Mississippians

rank of Lt. Commander. He was president of Alabama College from 1947-52 and president of the University of Arkansas from 1952-59. Dr. Caldwell served as chancellor of North Carolina State University from 1959 to 1975. At NCSU, Caldwell distinguished himself as a champion of education and Civil Rights. He was credited with calming fears about integration and social change and with encouraging campus diversity. During his tenure, the school's enrollment grew from 6,000 to more than 15,000, and was transformed from a regional technical school to a major research university with broad emphasis on science and humanities. North Carolina Governor Jim Hunt, a senior at NCSU when Caldwell arrived as chancellor, said that under Caldwell's leadership, the school "rose to a new level as a great comprehensive university." After stepping down as NCSU chancellor in 1975, Caldwell taught political science there, served as president of the Triangle Universities Center for Advanced Studies, and served as a trustee of Harvard University and the National Humanities Center. In 1987, he won the North Carolina Award, the state's highest honor. In 1988, the National Association of State Universities and Land-Grant Colleges named Caldwell one of Mississippi State's 10 distinguished alumni. Caldwell died in Raleigh, N.C. on Oct. 13, 1995, at the age of 83.

Lee Calhoun
Born Feb. 23, 1933, in Laurel. Calhoun was the first man to win the gold medal in the Olympic 110-meter hurdles *twice*, in 1956 and '60, and remained the only man to do it until Roger Kingdom won his second gold in the event in 1988. In both races, Calhoun led U.S. medal sweeps, including an Olympic-record performance in 1956. Calhoun served as head coach for the 1968 U.S. Olympic Team, and as an assistant coach in '76. A seven-time national champion, he broke five world records during his great career. He was inducted into the National Track & Field Hall of Fame in 1974 and into the Olympic Hall of Fame in 1991. Calhoun died on June 21, 1989.

Milton Campbell (see "Little Milton")

V. Ruth Campbell
Born Virginia Ruth Campbell on Jan. 20, 1887, in Yazoo City. She was the first women attorney admitted to the Mississippi state bar. She died in Yazoo City on Mar. 3, 1963, at age 76.

Will D. Campbell
Born Will Davis Campbell on July 18, 1924, in East Fork in Amite County, Miss. He now lives and writes in Mount Juliet, Tenn. A graduate of Yale University Divinity School, Campbell is the only minister to ever become a comic strip character! His friend, Pulitzer-Prize-winning cartoonist Doug Marlette, had lived in Mississippi for a few years when he first drew the comic strip, *Kudzu*. Campbell performed the ceremony when Doug got married and, to thank him, the cartoonist invented a new character, the round-hatted preacher Will B. Dunn for the nationally-syndicated comic strip. From 1954-56, Campbell was campus chaplain at Ole Miss before becoming a consultant on race relations for the National Council of Churches 1956-63. A longtime Civil Rights activist, he was one of the founders, along with Dr. Martin Luther King, Jr., of the Southern Christian Leadership Conference. Campbell is the author of *Race and Renewal of the Church* (1962), the award-winning *Brother to a Dragonfly* (1977, about his upbringing in Miss.), *The Glad River* (1982, about the Southern Baptist Convention), *The Stem of Jesse: The Costs of Community at a 1960s Southern School* (1995), the children's book, *The Pear Tree that Bloomed in the Fall* (1996), a collection of commentaries titled *Soul Among Lions: Musings of a Bootleg Preacher* (1999), plus numerous essays.

He received the 1998 Mississippi Institute of Arts and Letters award in the non-fiction category for *And Also With You: Duncan Gray and the American Dilemma*, a 1997 work about the struggles of Ole Miss as the enrollment of the first black student there, James Meredith, sparked riots. He has received many other awards and was honored by The American Civil Liberties Union in Nashville with its Lifetime Achievement Award. In Dec. 1999, Campbell was presented with an honorary doctorate from the University of Southern Mississippi. It was only the second honorary doctorate ever awarded by USM. The first one went to the late humanitarian Oceola McCarty. Another famous native of East Fork, the late Jerry Clower, was Campbell's cousin.

Ace Cannon
Born John Henry Cannon, Jr. on May 5, 1934, in Grenada, Mississippi. Ace Cannon, saxophone virtuoso, is a musician whose records have consistently appeared on *Billboard*'s and *Cashbox*'s charts. The "Godfather of Sax" started his career in Memphis, Tennessee, recording on many of the 1950's hits on Sun Records. Sam Phillips says that "Ace Cannon is the greatest saxophone player who ever lived." In 1959 he started playing with the Bill Black Combo, one of the most popular instrumental groups of their era. Cannon played lead sax on all the combo's original recordings. They appeared on the most prominent TV shows of that era, including *The Ed Sullivan Show*, *The Merv Griffin Show* and Dick Clark's *American Bandstand*. In 1962 Ace recorded the instrumental smash *Tuff*. Since that time he has recorded 37 singles and 52 albums, including *Ace in the Hole*, *Ace of Sax*, *Aces High*, etc.

Gus "Banjo Joe" Cannon
Born in Red Banks on Henderson Newell's plantation in Marshall County, Mississippi on Sept. 12, 1884, the son of sharecroppers. His father had been a slave. When Gus was 12 he went to Clarksdale to work in the cotton fields. Around this time Gus took an interest in music and made a banjo from a guitar neck and a bread pan. Gus got his first real banjo when he was 15. There were several banjo/fiddle groups in Clarksdale at the time, including W.C. Handy (see his profile) and his band. By 1901 Gus had gotten a job working for the rail road at Belzoni, Mississippi. It was at this time that he formed his first jug band. By 1914 Gus was playing the medicine show circuit around Mississippi and Tennessee under the name "Banjo Joe". Gus also made visits to Beale Street in Memphis. Gus lived off and on in Memphis during the 1920s and became the best known of all the jug band musicians. Cannon led his "Jug Stompers" on banjo and jug with the ensemble usually including a second banjoist and sometimes a kazoo. The group made historic recordings on the Victor label in 1928-30, which later became a favorite source of material for the Grateful Dead. The first recordings were made on Jan 30, 1928 when they recorded 4 sides in an old auditorium. The 4 cuts were *Minglewood Blues*, *Big Railroad Blues*, *Madison Street Rag* and *Springdale Blues*. These recordings did well and in Sept. 1928 an additional 10 sides were cut. Cannon's Jug Stompers recorded a total of 26 sides between Jan. 30, 1928 and Nov. 28, 1930. Cannon's *Walk Right In*, sung by the Rooftop Singers, made No. 1 on the pop chart in 1963. Gus Cannon died in Memphis on Oct. 15, 1979.

Robert Canzoneri
Born Nov. 21, 1925, in San Marcos, Texas, he grew up in Clinton. He received his B.A. from Mississippi College in 1948, his M.A. from Ole Miss in 1951 and his Ph.D. from Stanford. He has been at Ohio State since 1965 where he directs the creative writing program. His books include *I Do*

Profiles of Famous & Notable Mississippians

So Politely: A Voice from the South (1965), *Watch Us Pass* (1968), *Men with Little Hammers* (1969), and *Barbed Wire & Other Stories* (1970). *A Highly Ramified Tree* (1976) won the Ohioana Award as best autobiographical book of the year.

Charlotte Capers
Born June 28, 1913, in Columbia, Tenn., she grew up in Jackson, attended Millsaps College and received her B.A. from Ole Miss in 1934. She worked at the Mississippi Dept. of Archives and History for 45 years, serving as its first woman director from 1955-69. In 1972, she was appointed head of the $2.5 million restoration of the Governor's Mansion. Capers also oversaw the restoration of the Old Capitol to a museum. The Archives and History Building was named after her when she retired in 1983. She wrote historical articles for the *Encyclopedia Britannica* and *Americana*, 99 book reviews for *The New York Times*, edited several books on the history of Mississippi and the South, and was editor-in chief of the *Journal of Mississippi History* from 1956-1969. Her book, *The Capers Papers*, is a collection of essays from her *Jackson Daily News* and *Star-Times* columns. She died Dec. 23, 1996.

Helen Carlisle
Born Mary Helen Carlisle on Nov. 25, 1917, in Vossburg, Jasper Co., Mississippi. She graduated from Mississippi State College for Women (now Mississippi University for Women) in 1939. Carlisle was Director of Home Economics at McCormick and Company in Baltimore, Maryland, the largest spice company in the world, when she wrote the book, *Spices of the World Cookbook* (1964), under the name "Mary Collins" (like "Betty Crocker"). She also contributed articles in the U.S. Dept. of Agriculture's yearbook *Food For Us All* and in the *Handbook of Food Preparation* for the American Home Economics Association. Carlisle represented the U.S. Dept. of Agriculture and the Grocery Manufacturers of America in international food exhibits in Japan, Sweden and England. She's been listed in several publications, including *The Two Thousand Women of Achievement* (1969, London, England), *Foremost Women in Communications* (1970) and the 1st and 2nd editions of *Who's Who in American Women*. Carlisle has lived in Jacksonville, Fl. since the early 1980s.

Jennifer Carlisle
Born Nov. 7, 1982, in Flowood. She lived with her family in Brandon until they moved to Flowood in 1997. Carlisle made a perfect 36 score on the ACT (American College Test) when she took the test in Feb. 1999. Carlisle is one of the youngest (16 years and 3 months) Mississippi students to ever make a perfect ACT score. The youngest was Shayon Ghosh, a senior at Jackson Prep when he took the test in Dec. 1999 at age 13 years, 2 months. Carlisle was a sophomore at Jackson Preparatory School, which she has attended since the 7th grade. She scored a 26 on the ACT in the 7th grade, 33 on the ACT in the 9th grade, and reached her goal of a perfect 36 in the 10th grade. In the 7th grade Carlisle achieved national recognition in the TIPS program as well as winning the First in State Award in Life Sciences in the Academic Betterment Competition. In the 8th grade she: was a Mississippi Council of Teachers of English writing award finalist; was a Promising Young Writers Program winner in the National Council of Teachers of English competition; ranked 3rd in the state in the Academic Betterment Competition in Physical Sciences and received a silver medal for the National Latin Exam for Latin I. In the 9th grade Carlisle: won the First in State in English in the Academic Betterment Competition; was 2nd in the state in the Mississippi School for Math and Sciences geometry competition; received a silver medal for the National Latin Exam for Latin II; was co-editor of the junior high newspaper; editor-in-chief of the junior high literary magazine; was elected to the National Junior Honor Society and to Chi Alpha Mu; won the Jackson Prep Honors English Award and the National Junior Honor Society Volunteer Service Award. In the 10th grade she was First in State in the Mississippi School for Math and Sciences Algebra II competition. Carlisle is a member of the debate team, Mu Alpha Theta, Science Club, Astronomy Club, Key Club, and others. She has had poems published in several anthologies and magazines, including *Southern Voices*. Jackson Prep is proud of the fact that 3 of their students have scored a perfect 36 on the ACT. In addition to Jennifer and Shayon Ghosh, Steven Shackleford, Jr., aced the test in 1994. Jackson Prep ties Hattiesburg High School, which has also had 3 students to ace the ACT, for first place in the state for the greatest number of students making the top score on the ACT. Carlisle is one of 7 students in Mississippi to score 36 during 1999. Although seven is not a record for a single state as far as the absolute number, ACT headquarters says it might very well be a record for Mississippi as far as per capita state population and compared with the total number of students in a state taking the test during a single calendar year. Carlisle is one of only 12 students from the state to ever make a 36 score (either a "perfect" 36 or a composite 36) on the test through June 2000, according to ACT.

Helen Carloss
Born April 18, 1893, in Yazoo City, Mississippi. A 1913 graduate of Industrial Institute and College (now Mississippi University for Women), she became a successful attorney and tax expert who was the first woman in the nation to argue cases before the U.S. Circuit Court of Appeals and the Supreme Court. She argued before the Supreme Court several times. She died on December 23, 1948, at age 55, and is buried in Glenwood Cemetery in Yazoo City.

Joe Frank Carollo
This R&R singer/musician was born in Leland, Mississippi on September 3, 1939. He was with group Hamilton, Joe Frank & Reynolds who had 2 big hit records *Don't Pull Your Love* (Top-5 million-seller 1971) and *Fallin' In Love* (No. 1 million-seller 1975). Carollo studied music at Delta State in Cleveland, Mississippi, but didn't graduate.

Sam Carr
Born at Friar's Point, Mississippi on April 17, 1926. Carr's father, legendary Bluesman Robert Nighthawk would take Sam along on his gigs when he was only 8 or 9 years old. Sam Carr has worked with Frank Frost for so many years that their names have become inseparable to a lot of blues fans. While doing gigs up and down the "Blues Highway" they joined up with Sonny Boy Williamson and became his last band. Carr has consistently been chosen as the best blues drummer in *Living Blues* magazine. He now lives in Dundee, Mississippi.

Anne Carsley
Born in Jackson on Apr. 11, 1935. She received a B.A. from Millsaps College in 1957 and an M.A. from Ole Miss in 1959. She wrote these romantic novels with historical settings: *This Ravished Rose* (1980), *The Winged Lion* (1981), *This Triumphant Fire* (1982), *Defiant Desire* (1983), *The Golden Savage* (1984) and *Tempest* (1985).

Bo Carter
Born Armenter Chatmon in Bolton, Miss. on March 21, 1893. He made over 100 recordings of mostly "hokum" blues, which was Delta blues with bawdy lyrics. Some of his songs are *Bo Carter's Advice, Who's Been Here, Pussy Cat Blues, Banana In Your Fruit Basket, Pin in Your Cushion,* and *Your Biscuits Are*

Profiles of Famous & Notable Mississippians

Big Enough for Me. He was influenced by John Hurt and Big Bill Broonzy. One of the most popular bluesmen of the 1930s, he recorded enough material for several reissue albums. He was also the first to record the standard *Corrine Corrina* (1928). Carter's influence can be heard on early Bob Dylan records. Bo and his brothers Lonnie and Sam Chatmon (see profile) also recorded as members of the Mississippi Sheiks with Walter Vinson (see profile). Bo died Sept. 21, 1964, of a brain hemorrhage in Memphis.

Hodding Carter, Jr.
Born Feb. 3, 1907, in Hammond, Louisiana. One of Mississippi's best known newspaper men, he came to Greenville in 1936 and started the *Delta Democrat-Times* through which he was an early champion of Civil Rights in the 1950s and 60s. He wrote over 20 books and articles for nationally published magazines and newspapers. His literary work includes fiction, poetry, biography, autobiography, books of the river, and history. Books he wrote include *The Lower Mississippi* (1942), *Winds of Fear* (1945), *Flood Crest* (1947), *Southern Legacy* (1950), *Angry Scar* (1959), *First Person Rural* (1950) and *Man and the River, the Mississippi* (1970). He won a Neiman Fellowship to Harvard (1940), a Guggenheim Writing Fellowship (1945) and a Pulitzer Prize for his editorials (1946). He died on April 4, 1972. Trustees of the Mississippi Dept. of Archives and History elected him to the Mississippi Hall of Fame on Dec. 6, 1996.

Hodding Carter III
Born Apr. 7, 1935, in New Orleans, he grew up in Greenville. The son of newspaperman Hodding Carter, this award-winning journalist became widely known in the late 1970s as the U.S. State Department spokesman for the administration of President Carter. Also the former assistant Secretary of State, he is now president and CEO of the John S. and James L. Knight Foundation in Miami, Florida.

Johnny Carver
Born in Jackson on Nov. 24, 1940, he recorded the country albums, *Afternoon Delight* and *The Best of Johnny Carver* and had a country Top 10 hit single, *Tie A Yellow Ribbon*, in 1973.

Turner Catledge
Born William Turner Catledge on Mar. 17, 1901, in New Prospect, 6 miles from Ackerman. He started his newspaper career at *The Neshoba Democrat* in Philadelphia in 1921. He went on to work for the *New York Times* for more than 40 years, became managing editor in 1951, executive editor in 1964, and company vice-president in 1968. Retiring in 1970, he published his autobiography, *My Life and The Times* (1971). Catledge died in New Orleans on April 27, 1983. His papers are preserved in the Mitchell Memorial Library on the campus at Mississippi State University in Starkville.

Lacey Chabert
Born Sept. 30, 1982, in Purvis, Mississippi, her family later moved to California. She started taking voice lessons at age five. At nine years old she was discovered by an agent when her parents took the family to New York for a two-week summer vacation. Chabert was a junior vocalist finalist on *Star Search 1991*. She originated the role of Bianca, Erica Kane's (Susan Lucci's) daughter in the TV soap series *All My Children*. She has appeared in TV movies such as *A Little Piece of Heaven* and *Gypsy*. She gained her break in a cough syrup commercial before auditioning for the Broadway production of *Les Miserables*, where she played young Cosette for two years. She played Claudia on the Fox Network show *Party of Five*, which won the Golden Globe for Best Dramatic Series in 1995 and was nominated for the same award in 1996. Chabert won *The Hollywood Reporter*'s young star award for her portrayal of Claudia. Boasting an active voice-over career, Chabert has given life to characters in many animated features including *Babes in Toyland*, *Anastasia* (singing voice of young Anastasia, 1997), *Journey Beneath the Sea* (voice of Merla, 1997), Disney's *Little Redux Riding Hood* (voice of Little Red, 1997) and *Lion King II: Simba's Pride* (voice of young Kiara, 1998), Steven Speilberg's *An American Tale III*, Mikail Barishnikov's *Stories From My Childhood*, and as "Eliza Thornberry" in the Saturday morning TV series, *The Wild Thornberries*. She made her big-screen debut as "Penny" in *Lost In Space* (1998), based on the 1960s sci-fi TV series.

Ernie Chaffin
Born Jan. 1, 1928, in Water Valley, Yalobusha County, Mississippi. He was a rockabilly artist who recorded *Laughin' and Jokin'* (1957) and some other tracks for Sun Records in Memphis. Chaffin died on April 16, 1997, following a tractor accident on his farm in Hattiesburg, Mississippi. He was 69. He is a member of the Rockabilly Hall of Fame.

The Chambers Brothers
Originally a black Mississippi gospel group formed in Lee County. Members of the group are George, bassist/singer, born 9/26/31; Willie, guitarist and singer, born 3/3/38; Lester, Harmonicist/singer, born 4/13/40; and Joe, guitarist/singer, born 8/24/42. All were born in Flora in Madison County, except Joe, who was born in Scott County. The four brothers moved to Calif. and became Rock/R&B singers with the psychedelic hit record *Time Has Come Today* (#11 in 1968) and also charted with *I Can't Turn You Loose* (#37 in 1968).

Clifford E. Charlesworth
Born Nov. 29, 1931, in Jackson, Mississippi. A Hinds Junior College honor graduate who was named 1969 "Alumnus of the Year," he went on to work for NASA and was flight director for two of the Apollo space flights.

Armenter Chatmon (see Bo Carter)

Sam Chatmon
Brother of Bo Carter (see his profile), he was born in Bolton, Miss. on Jan. 10, 1899. Aso the brother of Lonnie Chatmon, who led the famous Mississippi Sheiks. Sam was a member of the Sheiks at times, but launched his own solo career in the early 1930s. He continued Bo's tradition of double-entendre-lyrics blues, but also showed a serious side in the early anthology *I Have To Paint My Face*. While he performed and recorded as a solo act, he would still record with the Sheiks and with his brother Lonnie. Throughout the 1930s, Sam traveled throughout the south, playing with a variety of minstrel and medicine shows. He stopped traveling in the early 1940s, making himself a home in Hollandale, where he worked on plantations. For the next two decades, Sam Chatmon was essentially retired from music. When the blues revival arrived in the late 1950s, he managed to capitalize on the genre's resurgent popularity. In 1960, he signed a contract with Arhoolie and recorded a number of songs for the label. Throughout the 1960s and '70s, he played clubs and blues and folk festivals across America. Chatmon was an active performer and recording artist right up until his death. He died in Hollandale on Feb. 2, 1983, at the age of 84 and is buried in the Sanders Memorial Garden Cemetery in Hollandale.

Alvin Childress
Born on Sept. 10, 1907, in Meridian, Miss. A graduate of Rust College in Holly Springs, actor Childress made his first New York stage appearance in 1931. This black character actor, onscreen from the 1930s in films made for black audiences, began appearing in Hollywood films in the 1950s. He is best

Profiles of Famous & Notable Mississippians

known as Amos Jones in the TV series, *The Amos 'n' Andy Show*, which debuted June 28, 1951 and ran through June 11, 1953. Two other Mississippians were in the cast: Ernestine Wade (b. in Jackson) played Sapphire Stevens and Spencer Williams (attended high school in Natchez) played Andy. The Amos 'n' Andy Show was the 13th highest rated show during its first year on the air. Childress played a janitor in the Clint Eastwood movie *Thunderbolt and Lightfoot* (1974) and had some other minor film roles in the 1970s. Childress also appeared on a few TV series, such as *Sanford and Son* and *The Jeffersons*. He died on Apr. 19, 1986, in Inglewood, Calif.

Craig Claiborne
Born Sept. 4, 1920, in Sunflower, Mississippi. He attended Mississippi State and received a degree from the University of Missouri in 1942. He studied cooking art in Switzerland. Editor of *Gourmet* magazine for a time, he was food editor for the *New York Times* in 1957-72 and again starting in 1974. He authored 20 books including: *The New York Times Cook Book* (1961), *An Herb and Spice Cook Book* (1963), his autobiography, *A Feast Made For Laughter* (1982), *The New York Times Food Encyclopedia* (1985), *Craig Claiborne's Memorable Meals* (1985), and *The Best of Craig Claiborne* (1999). Claiborne died on Jan. 22, 2000, at the age of 79.

J.F.H. Claiborne
Born John Francis Hamtranck Claiborne on Apr. 24, 1807, in Natchez when Mississippi was still a territory, he was a nephew of William Charles Cole Claiborne. A planter, politician, and popular journalist, he also had a great interest in the state's history. He received his education in Mississippi and Virginia. He studied law and was admitted to the bar, but he didn't stay long in the legal profession. In 1828, he became active in politics, first as an editor of the *Natchez Statesman and Gazette*, then as a Mississippi legislator and then was elected to the U.S. Congress and served from 1835 to 1837. In 1835 he established a plantation using borrowed money, but lost everything in the Panic of 1837. The following year, he lost his congressional seat in a disputed election. For the next few years, he struggled to overcome his political defeat and financial ruin, as well as consumption, which would plague his health throughout his life. In 1841 he became editor of the *Natchez Mississippi Free Trader*, and from 1842 to 1844, he was appointed by President John Tyler to serve as Chairman of the Board of Choctaw Commissioners to investigate claims under the Treaty of Dancing Rabbit Creek (1830). He returned to journalism in 1844, editing the *Jeffersonian* 1844-46, the *Statesman* 1849-51, and the *Louisiana Courier* 1850-53, all of them near New Orleans. During this time he made money speculating in cotton, earning enough to purchase in 1849 a seashore plantation in Shieldsboro in Hancock County, where he lived until it burned in 1870. A Jacksonian Democrat, Claiborne was popular as a newspaper editor, partly because he wrote clearly and forcefully and partly because of political views he espoused. A white supremacist, he defended slavery as morally right and upheld the right of states to secede from the union, though he opposed secession. His most important journalistic contributions were two series of essays about his travels through the piney woods of Mississippi and Louisiana. The essays represent a detailed description of the people he met, their homes, dress and habits. The essays would serve as an important resource for future historians on rural folk. His accumulation of numerous historical documents and artifacts after the Civil War would become the principal source for his major work: *Mississippi as a Province, Territory, and State, with Biographical Notices of Eminent Citizens* (1880). His collection of papers and documents is now located in three repositories: the Department of Archives and History in Jackson, Mississippi; the Library of Congress in Washington; and the Library of the University of North Carolina. The collection is an indispensable source for historians. In 1964, historian John K. Bettersworth praised Claiborne as the author of the best history of the state ever written. The history he published was volume one of a two-volume set. Volume two was never published. The manuscript was completed in 1884, but was lost in a fire that destroyed Claiborne's home in March 1884. The "father of Mississippi history," died at his estate, "Dumbarton," near Natchez on May 17, 1884, at age 76 and is buried in the Trinity Churchyard in Natchez.

Dave Clark
Born David Earl Clark on Sept. 3, 1962, in Tupelo. He set the high school record for home runs in a single season with 23 while at Shannon High School in 1980. A standout at Jackson State, he was named outfielder on *The Sporting News* college All-America team in 1983. He was selected by the Cleveland Indians in the first round (11th pick overall) of the 1986 free-agent draft and made his major league debut on Sept. 3, 1986. With the Indians through 1989, he went to the Chicago Cubs in 1990 and the Kansas City Royals in 1991. Clark was signed by the Pittsburgh Pirates as a free agent to a minor-league contract on Jan 24, 1992. Signing on with the Los Angeles Dodgers in 1996, he came off the bench to bat .308 while amassing a team-record 22 RBIs in the pinch. Clark signed with the Houston Astros as a free agent in the off-season and was used primarily as a left-handed pinch hitter during the 1998 season. Consequently, Clark hit just .204 with no home runs and four RBIs in 131 at bats that season. His career stats through 1998: 518 hits in 1,964 at bats (.264 batting avg.), 248 runs, 62 home runs & 284 RBIs in 905 games played. He wasn't listed on any major league rosters for 1999 or 2000.

Kate Freeman Clark
Born in 1875 in Holly Springs, she spent her first 10 years in Vicksburg where her father, Edward Clark, practiced law. In 1891, Clark traveled with her mother to New York City to enter a finishing school. She joined the Art Students League in 1894 and studied art at some of the finest schools. Beginning at the turn of the century, Clark's landscapes and still lifes were exhibited at the Carnegie Institute in Pittsburgh and the Corcoran Gallery of Art in Washington. Clark exhibited under the masculine name of Freeman Clark. Her career as a painter ended with the death of her mother and her return to Holly Springs in 1923. Her painting, *Work Out In Mississippi Grove*, one of only two of her paintings known to have been painted in the South, hangs in the U.S. Ambassador's residence in Paris. She died in 1957, willing the largest single privately-owned art collection in the world, over 1,200 paintings, to Holly Springs. The museum that houses her paintings next to her family house opened in 1963.

Tena Clark
Born on Dec. 19, 1953, in Waynesboro, Miss., she graduated from Waynesboro Central High School in 1971. Clark now lives and works in Los Angeles, where she's a successful film producer as well as a songwriter. She produces and writes for hit movies such as *Twins* (1988), *French Kiss* ('95), *My Best Friend's Wedding* ('97), and *Hope Floats* ('98). She was lyricist and composer of the *Love Lessions* ('92) album by Rita Coolidge and has been writer, arranger and/or producer for several other recording artists, including Pattie LaBelle, CeCe Winans, Gladys Knight, Dionne Warwick, Shanice Williams and Olivia Newton-John. She also wrote McDonald's® "Have

Profiles of Famous & Notable Mississippians

You Had Your Break Today," and other national commercials for Oldsmobile®, and Pillsbury® and 7-Up®. In 1997, Clark created a new company, Disc Marketing, in Pasadena, California that creates CDs and CD-ROMs for corporations and retailers worldwide. The company also produces all the music for United Airlines and the president's and vice-president's planes, Air Force I and II.

Will Clark

Born on March 13, 1964, in New Orleans. In his high school senior year in New Orleans in 1982, this left-handed first baseman had 10 home runs and 32 RBIs to earn him honors as a High School All-American. In 1984, his second year at Mississippi State, he was an All-American for the Bulldogs and hit 28 home runs, 93 RBIs and had a .368 batting average. That spring, Clark made the U.S. Olympic team which took the 2nd place silver medal. He was on Ron Polk's celebrated 1985 Diamond Bulldogs team, which also featured future major league stars Rafael Palmeiro, Jeff Brantley (see their profiles), and Bobby Thigpen. They became the first State team to hit the 50 win mark, finishing with a 50-15 record and a 3rd place tie in the NCAA College World Series at Omaha. Clark was the only former Mississippi collegian selected as one of the all-time top 50 players in the College World Series in the Spring of 1999, the 50th anniversary of the tournament's move to Omaha. During his time at State, Clark hit .391 with 61 home runs and 199 RBIs and helped the Bulldogs to 3 NCAA Tournament appearances and a berth in that 1985 College World Series. Clark was drafted by San Francisco Giants who placed him on their Class A team in Fresno where he played his first pro game on June 21, 1985. After only 65 minor league games, the Giants moved Clark up to the major leagues in San Francisco where he started as first baseman. He made his major league debut on April 8, 1986. Clark's performance helped the Giants win the National League West in 1987. A six-time All-Star, Clark was the MVP of the 1989 NLCS, leading the Giants to the World Series marred by an earthquake that struck just before Game 3. The Oakland A's swept the Giants in 4 games. After that, the Giants signed Will to a $15 million, 4-year contract, making him the highest paid player in baseball history at the time. The Texas Rangers signed him for the 1994 season and he was with the Rangers through 1998. In late 1998, Clark signed a two-year $11 million contract with the Baltimore Orioles. Clark had to undergo surgery on his left elbow in late Aug. 1999, which put him out for the rest of the season. In the 2000 season, Clark was hitting .301 with 9 homers and 28 RBIs in 79 games when Baltimore traded him to the St. Louis Cardinals on July 31. Subbing for an injured Mark McGwire, Clark batted .345 with 12 homers and 42 RBIs for the Cardinals in the final two months of the 2000 season. He went on to bat .345 in the postseason, and his three-run, first inning homer in Game 2 of the NL division series helped send St. Louis into its first NL championship series since 1996. But, the Cards were losers in the NLCS to the New York Mets. On Nov. 2, 2000, to the surprise of most fans, Clark announced that he was retiring from baseball. And, even though he never got the World Series ring he always wanted, he left with some great careers stats: 2,176 hits in 7,173 at bats (.303 batting avg.), 1,186 runs, 284 home runs, and 1,205 RBIs in 1,976 games played.

William Lockhart Clayton

Born in Tupelo, Miss. on Feb. 7, 1880, he was the originator of the historic Marshall Plan following World War II when he was Assistant Secretary of State for Economic Affairs (1944-46) and Undersecretary of State of Economic Affairs (1946-47). Clayton held many other positions with the federal government, including: member of the War Industries Board (1918); vice-president of the Export-Import Bank (1940-42); Assistant Secretary of Commerce (1942-45); Alternate Governor of the World Bank (1946-49); Member of the National Security Training Commission (1951-54); Chairman of the National Committee on Campaign Contributions and Expenditures (1960). He authored *We Must Trade Sovereignty for Freedom* ('50), *The Road to Peace* ('55), *What Price Oil?* (1958, and quite ahead of its time), and *We Are Losing the Cold War* ('58). A collection of his official papers from 1897-1966 would stack 34 feet high! Clayton died in Houston, Texas on Feb. 8, 1966, the day after his 86th birthday.

Eddy Clearwater

Born Eddy Harrington on Jan 10, 1935, in Macon, Miss. Once dismissed as a Chuck Berry imitator, this blues and rock singer/musician has a wide-ranging repertoire from country to Motown to rockabilly to disco to R&R to gospel. His albums feature his westside brand of blues, heavily influenced by Otis Rush and Magic Sam, both Mississippians. He lived in Birmingham, Ala. before moving to Chicago in 1950. Initially billing himself as Guitar Eddy, he soon cut two singles including the Berry-derived *Hillbilly Blues*. Drummer Jump Jackson invented Eddy's stage name as a takeoff on the name of Muddy Waters. As Clear Waters, he cut another Berry knockoff, *Cool Water*. By the time he journeyed to Cincinnati in 1961 to cut the rockers *I Was Gone*, *A Real Good Time* and *Twist Like This*, he was officially Eddy Clearwater. He also uses the nickname "The Chief" because of his penchant for donning native American headdresses on stage. Rooster Blues Records of Clarksdale, Mississippi released an album called *The Chief* in 1980. Two encores albums for Rooster were *Help Yourself* (1992) and *Mean Case of the Blues* (1996). His *Cool Blues Walk* album followed in 1998.

Robert H. "Ace" Cleveland, Sr.

Born Aug. 6, 1926, in Hattiesburg. He started as a teen-aged sports writer at the *Hattiesburg American*, went on to become sports editor there, and later worked at the *Jackson Daily News*. Cleveland began his career as sports information director at the University of Southern Mississippi in 1955, when it was called Mississippi Southern. He was very active as the school's publicist, promoting the school and especially sports. All of his colleagues agree that he did as much for USM as anybody ever involved with the school. Former USM football coach P.W. Underwood credited Cleveland for helping punter Ray Guy become an All-American. Behind the scenes, Cleveland also worked promoting the Deposit Guaranty Golf Classic for its first 26 years in Hattiesburg, as it grew from a $20,000 novelty in 1968 to a $300,000 event in 1993, right before it was moved to Jackson. USM named the M.M. Roberts Stadium press box after Cleveland. He was selected as a member of USM's Sports Hall of Fame in 1985, a year before he retired. Cleveland died on April 17, 1995, in Hattiesburg from complications from a stroke. He is one of five charter members of the Mississippi Sportswriters Association Hall of Fame. He was inducted into the Mississippi Sports Hall of Fame in 1998. His sons followed him into sports writing — Rick is sports columnist and Bobby is outdoors editor for *The Clarion-Ledger* in Jackson.

Jerry Clower

Born Howard Gerald Clower in East Fork, near Liberty, in Amite County, Mississippi on Sept. 28, 1926. He joined the Navy at the age of 16 and served three years as a radioman during WWII. He later attended Mississippi State University.

Profiles of Famous & Notable Mississippians

Clower, who once said "I don't tell funny stories, I tell stories funny," sold more country-comedy albums than any other artist and was the first country humorist to earn a gold record. He never recorded for any other label than MCA Records and was with that prestigious record company longer than any other artist. Tandy Rice of Nashville, Clower's manager and publicist, was his only agent during that time. Clower's 26th album was released in the fall of 1998. For 10 consecutive years, he earned the top comedian awards from *Billboard*, *Cashbox* and *Record World* magazines and received 9 consecutive awards for "Country Comic of the Year." His *Greatest Hits* album sold more than 500,000 copies. Most of Clower's stories were about the fictitious Ledbetter clan of Amite County — Marcel, Ardel, Burnell, Raynell, W.L., Lanell, Udell, Odell, Claud, Newgene and Clovis — 11 siblings raised by Aunt Pet and Uncle Versie. His most popular story was *Knock 'Em Out, John*, a tale about coon hunting that was included in his first album. A devout Southern Baptist, Clower stated that he never recorded an album that couldn't be played in church. He wrote 3 books, *Ain't God Good, Let The Hammer Down* and *Life Everafter*. Clower started his comedy career while working as a fertilizer salesman for Mississippi Chemical Corp. in Yazoo City where he lived for over 34 years from Mar. 1954 until Oct. 1988 when he returned to Amite County. On Sept. 19, 1995, Jerry donated 2 of his 3 gold record albums, *Yazoo Talkin'* and *Mouth of Mississippi*, to Yazoo City's Jerry Clower Exhibition Center. A stretch of State Highway 49E through Yazoo City is named Jerry Clower Boulevard in his honor. Clower became the first Grand Ole Opry entertainer to be honored by the National Football Foundation and Hall of Fame. The former Mississippi State defensive left tackle received the organization's Distinguished American Award presented on Feb. 17, 1997 in ceremonies in Natchez. Another famous native of East Fork, preacher, writer and Civil Rights activist Will B. Campbell, was a cousin (see his profile). On Aug. 4, 1998, Clower missed his first show in 32 years after becoming ill while preparing to perform at the Mountain State Fair in Hiawassee, Georgia. Clower died of cardiorespiratory failure at Baptist Medical Center in Jackson on Aug. 24, 1998, at the age of 71, just five days after undergoing sextuple bypass heart surgery. About 250 mourners, including Bob Whittaker, president and general manager of the Grand Ole Opry, crowded into East Fork Baptist Church for the funeral services. Superstar singer Garth Brooks sent 12 dozen roses. Wreaths and flower arrangements from Dolly Parton, Ricky Skaggs, Mel Tillis and others lined the plot where Clower was buried next to his mother in the East Fork Cemetery.

Willie Cobbs
Born in Smale, Arkansas on July 15, 1932. This Delta Blues artist's recording career has spanned five decades and he's performed with many Blues artists, including Muddy Waters and Little Milton. After years of harp work and recording 45's, Willie gave up the studio and became a club owner; running the Blue Flame in Stuttgart, Ark. and later opening Turning Point in Itta Bena, Miss. In 1978 he relocated to Greenwood, Mississippi and opened Mr. C's Bar-B-Que. Willie's fame spread when the Allman Brothers recorded his song *You Don't Love Me (You Don't Care)*, which became an international hit. In 1986 he teamed up with Jim O'Neal of Rooster Blues in Clarksdale and put together a cassette of his 45 releases. He recorded his first CD, *Down To Earth*, on Rooster Blues in 1994. Willie can be seen in several movies, most notably as a down and out bluesman in *Mississippi Masala*.

Commodore Cochran
Commodore Shelton Cochran was born in Richton, Miss. on Jan. 20, 1902. He graduated from Richton High school at age 15. Cochran was a standout track athlete at Mississippi A&M (Mississippi State) in 1920-23 where he became one of the school's greatest track stars, running the 100-, 220-, 440-, and 880-yard dashes, among other events. He was captain of the 1923 team. He was inducted into the MSU Sports Hall of Fame in 1997. Commodore won the Gold Medal as part of the U.S. 1,600-meter relay team in the 1924 Olympics at Paris. His younger brother Roy won two Gold Medals in the 1948 Olympics in London. They are the only brothers ever to win Olympic gold. Both were second cousins to Mississippi Senator Thad Cochran. Commodore died on Jan. 3, 1969.

Hank Cochran
Born Garland Perry Cochran on Aug. 2, 1935, in Isola, Humphreys County, Mississippi. He became one of the greatest songwriters in Nashville and on the entire planet! He first went to California and appeared on the "California Hayride" and "Town Hall Party" and worked at Pamper Music's California office. In 1960, he moved to Nashville where he was hired by Pamper Music there to write and plug songs. He became a co-owner and stayed with Pamper until 1967. In 1961, he recorded his first record as a solo artist for Liberty Records. A singer with several hits, his real talent is songwriting. In 1961, he also had his first hit as a songwriter when he teamed up with Harlan Howard to write *I Fall to Pieces*, recorded by Patsy Cline. He went on to write or co-write many, many more hits including: *A Little Bitty Tear* (Burl Ives, 1961); *Funny Way of Laughin'* (Burl Ives, 1962); *Tears Break Out On Me* (Eddy Arnold, 1962); *I'd Fight the World Before I'd Ever Let You Go* (Jim Reeves, 1974); *He's Got You* (Patsy Cline, 1962 & Loretta Lynn, 1977); *You Comb Her Hair* (George Jones, 1963); *Make the World Go Away* (Ray Price, 1963 & Eddy Arnold, 1965, and Elvis Presley); *I Want to Go With You* (Eddy Arnold, 1966); *Don't Touch Me* (Jeannie Seely, 1966); *It's Not Love (But It's Not Bad)* (Merle Haggard, 1973); *Montego Bay* (Merle Haggard); *Can I Sleep in Your Arms* (Jeannie Seely, 1973); *Lucky Ladies* (Jeannie Seely, 1973); *Why Can't He Be You* (Loretta Lynn, 1978); *What Would Your Memories Do* (Vern Gosdin, 1984); *The Chair* (George Strait, 1985); *Ocean Front Property* (George Strait, 1988); *Don't You Ever Get Tired of Hurting Me* (Ronnie Milsap, 1989); *Set 'Em Up Joe* (Vern Gosdin, 1989); *Who You Gonna Blame It On This Time* (Vern Gosdin, 1989); *Right In the Wrong Direction* (Vern Gosdin, 1990); *This Ain't My First Rodeo* (Vern Gosdin, 1990); and *Is It Raining At Your House* (Vern Gosdin, 1991). Songs written (or co-written) by Cochran that have been...*Billboard* No. 1 Singles — *Don't You Ever Get Tired of Hurting Me, He's Got You, I Fall to Pieces, I Want to Go With You, It's Not Love (But It's Not Bad), Make the World Go Away, Ocean Front Property, Set 'Em Up Joe, That's All That Matters to Me* and *The Chair*; ...*Billboard* Top 5 Singles — *A Little Bitty Tear, Don't Touch Me, Make the World Go Away, Who You Gonna Blame It On This Time* and *You Comb Her Hair*; ...and *Billboard* Top 10 Singles — *Can I Sleep In Your Arms, Funny Way of Laughing, Is It Raining At Your House, Right In the Wrong Direction, Tears Break Out On Me, What Would Your Memories Do* and *Why Can't He Be You*. Cochran and the songs he's written have won many awards including 33 BMI (Broadcast Music Inc,) Awards. Among those were five BMI Awards for One Million Airplays for *I Fall to Pieces, Don't Touch Me, He's Got You, The Chair* and *Don't You Ever Get Tired of Hurting Me*, plus

Profiles of Famous & Notable Mississippians

one BMI Award for Two Million Airplays for *Make the World Go Away*. He also received a Country Music Association Award for *Walkway of Stars* (1967). Cochran performed his song, *Make the World Go Away*, in the feature film *Honeysuckle Rose* (1980) starring Willie Nelson. When he was elected to the Nashville Songwriters Hall of Fame in 1974, he got all the votes! It was the only year that only one writer got elected. Cochran got Willie Nelson his first break after Willie moved to Nashville. Hank convinced Pamper Music to hire Willie, forgoing his own $50.00 raise to help pay Nelson's salary. Also, when Joe Allison, head of Liberty Record's country division at the time, offered Cochran a recording deal, Cochran told Allison to hire Willie Nelson first. Liberty soon signed Cochran anyway. From 1989, Cochran has been co-owner, writer and professional consultant of Co-Heart Music Group in Nashville.

Roy Cochran
Leroy Braxton Cochran was born in Richton, Mississippi on Jan. 26, 1919. After being a star quarterback at Richton High School, he turned down a football scholarship at Tulane to run track at Indiana, where he was a three-time All-American. He earned a graduate degree at Southern California after World War II. At age 29, he won two gold medals in the 1948 Olympics at London. He won the 400-meter hurdles in the then-Olympics record time of 51.1 seconds and garnered the second gold medal as part of the 1,600-meter relay team. His older brother, Commodore Cochran (see his profile), won an Olympic Gold Medal in the 1924 Olympics at Paris. They are believed to be the only brothers ever to win Olympic Gold. Both were second cousins to Mississippi Senator Thad Cochran. Roy died on Sept. 26, 1981. He was inducted into the Mississippi Sports Hall of Fame on Feb. 28, 1997.

Thad Cochran
Born Dec. 7, 1937, in Pontotoc, Mississippi. He graduated from Byram High School in 1955, from the University of Mississippi in 1959, and the University of Mississippi Law School 1965. He studied international law for a year from 1963-64 at the University of Dublin, Ireland. Cochran served in the U.S. Navy from 1959-1961. Admitted to the Mississippi bar in 1965, he started his practice in Jackson. He received the Outstanding Young Man of the Year Award from the Junior Chamber of Commerce in Mississippi in 1971. Cochran was elected as a Republican to the 93rd Congress in 1972, reelected to the 94th and 95th Congresses and served from Jan. 3, 1973 until his resignation on Dec. 26, 1978. He was chairman of the Senate Republican Conference in the 102nd through 104th Congresses. First elected to the U.S. Senate on Nov. 7, 1978, and subsequently appointed by the governor on Dec. 27, 1978 to fill the vacancy caused by the resignation of Senator James O. Eastland, Cochran became the first Republican Senator from Mississippi since reconstruction. He served as chair on the subcommittees on Agriculture, Rural Development and Related Agencies, and Production and Price Competitiveness, and was on these committees: Appropriations, Governmental Affairs, Agriculture, Nutrition and Forestry and Rules Administration, Joint Committee on the Library, and Joint Committee on Printing. He was reelected without opposition in 1990 to his third term in the Senate and easily won reelection for a fourth term against two opponents in Nov. 1996, garnering 71% of the vote for the term ending Jan. 3, 2003. Cochran is third in leadership in the U.S. Senate as Republican Conference Chairman. Two research facilities in Mississippi bear Cochran's name. Mississippi State University's National Warmwater Aquatics Center in Stoneville was named for Cochran in 1998, and in 1999, a building at the University of Mississippi on the Oxford campus became the Cochran National Center for Natural Products Research. A longtime champion of the arts, Cochran received the Arts Leadership Award of the 2000 Governor's Awards for Excellence in the Arts.

Frederick H. Coe
Born Dec. 23, 1914, in Alligator, Miss. He was a leading TV producer during television's golden age of the late 40s and early 50s, producing *Televison Playhouse* (1948-52), *Mr. Peepers* (1952-53) & *Philco-Goodyear Playhouse* (1954-55). He also produced several Broadway plays including *The Trip to Bountiful* and the play and movie versions of *The Mircle Worker* (1962), which won a Tony. He was co-screenwriter (with Francis Ford Coppola) for the movie *This Property Is Condemned* (1966, filmed in Miss.). He died in Los Angeles on April 29, 1979 at age 64. A state historical marker was dedicated at his place of birth in Alligator on March 24, 1997.

David L. Cohn
Born David Lewis Cohn in Greenville, Miss. on Sept. 30, 1897, the son of Jewish immigrants from Poland. He studied law at the University of Virginia and Yale, where he took classes under former U.S. President William H. Taft. For two years, he lived in the household of William Alexander Percy where he wrote *God Shakes Creation*, published in 1935 and reissued in 1948 under the title *Where I Was Born and Raised*. Cohn wrote political speeches for many nationally-known political figures, including William J. Fulbright, Averell Harriman, Adlai Stevenson and Sam Rayburn. He also published more than 60 articles in the *Atlantic Monthly*. His books include *Picking America's Pockets: The Story of the Costs and Consequences of Our Tariff Policy* (1936), *The Good Old Days: A History of American Morals and Manners as Seen Through the Sears Roebuck Catalogs 1905 to the Present* (1940), *New Orleans and Its Living Past* (1941) and *This Is the Story* (1947). He died on Sept. 12, 1960.

Harry A. Cole, Sr.
Born Jan. 9, 1888, in Jackson. He invented the popular household cleaner "Pine-Sol," selling his first case in 1929 to Walgreen Drugs. Initially sold as a janitorial cleaner, it was later bottled for household use. By 1949, Pine-Sol was a regional product manufactured by Dumas Milner (see profile) in Jackson. The American Cyanamid Company acquired Pine-Sol in 1963 and maintained the product as a regional brand until the early 1970s. The product and name were acquired by the Clorox Co. in 1990. Cole died in July 1969.

Reggie Collier
Born on May 14, 1961, in D'Iberville, Mississippi. He became an All-America quarterback at Southern Mississippi and led USM to consecutive bowl games. A Black quarterback when black quarterbacks weren't fashionable, he destroyed Alabama 38-29 in 1982 and ended the Tide's 57-game home winning streak. Collier was the first quarterback in NCAA history to pass and rush for 1,000 yards in a season. Collier didn't start as a freshman at USM, but he piled up 2,304 yards rushing and 3,662 passing for a total of 5,966 yards in three seasons as USM's starting quarterback. He placed 9th in the Heisman Trophy voting as a junior. The Dallas Cowboys drafted Collier in the sixth round, but he signed for more money with the United States Football League. He was the first player chosen by the Birmingham Stallions. Collier played in 7 games, going 47-108 passing for 604 yards, 1 TD and 7 INTs. Traded to the Federals after Birmingham signed Cliff Stoudt, he saw action in 9 games, completing 82 of 160 passes for 969 yards, 6

Profiles of Famous & Notable Mississippians

scores, 12 INTs. He continued improvement with the Renegades in 1985 — 229-427 for 2,578 yards, 13 TDs, 16 INTs and ran 92 times for 606 yards and 12 TDs including a 71 yarder, and ran for 171 yards in one game, the pro record for a QB. He joined Dallas in 1987. Collier, who never did find big success in pro football, was released by the Cowboys after one season and then played for the Pittsburgh Steelers one season in 1988. He now works at a recreation center in New York City. On Oct. 7, 2000, Collier and ex-teammate Sammy Winder were inducted into the new Legends Society, which honors former Southern Miss athletic greats. The pair join Brett Favre, Janice Felder, Ray Guy, Nick Revlon and Clarence Weatherspoon in the exclusive club.

Bobby Collins

Born Thurmon L. Collins, Jr. on Oct. 25, 1933, in Laurel, Mississippi He was an outstanding quarterback at Laurel High School, then played football at Mississippi State from 1951 through 1954. A four year letterman, Bobby led MSU in punting every year he played. In his senior year, Collins was elected a co-captain and started at quarterback. MSU complied a record of 20-15-3 while Collins was on the team. After graduation in 1955, Bobby remained in Starkville as a graduate assistant coach. In 1956 he was selected as offensive backfield coach at Colorado State, but returned to Mississippi State to coach the freshman squad in 1957. Collins became offensive backfield coach for the Bulldogs in 1959 and coached at State through the 1960 season. In 1961 he was hired as backfield coach. at George Washington University. Bobby went to Virginia Tech in 1964 as defensive coordinator, but went to lead the North Carolina offense in 1967. In 1971 he was named assistant head coach and defensive coordinator of the Tar Heels. The North Carolina offense led the ACC in total offense and scoring in 3 of the 5 years Collins coached at Chapel Hill. In 1975, Southern Mississippi picked Collins as head coach of the Golden Eagles football program. In his 7 years as head coach of the Eagles (1975-1981), his teams racked up 48 wins, 30 losses, and only 2 ties with consecutive 9 win seasons. In his tenure, the Golden Eagles won three of their last four games against in-state rival Ole Miss and their final six (one by forfeit) against their other in-state rival and Collins' alma mater, Mississippi State. They also had key victories over Florida State and Auburn. Under Collins, the Golden Eagles made USM's first two bowl appearances as a division I-A team their first ever national TV appearance. His best two teams were the 1980 and 1981 squads as the 1980 team finished 9-3 with a win in the Independence Bowl and the 1981 team completing a 9-2-1 season and played in the Tangerine Bowl. Despite the 19-17 loss to Missouri in the Tangerine Bowl, Collins' team ended the year ranked 18th nationally and Bobby was named District Four National Coach of the Year by the American Football Coaches Association. His players at USM included such names as Sammy Winder, Reggie Collier, Hanford Dixon, Richard Byrd, Ricky Floyd, and Stoney Parker. He was so popular on campus and in the Hattiesburg community that alumni and fans produced a song about Bobby and the Eagles, and cranked out slogans such as "Eagle Fever," "I Believe" and "Seas of Gold." After several years of turning down offers to coach elsewhere, Collins was approached by Southern Methodist University, and Collins reluctantly left the Golden Eagles and headed to Dallas. He led the Mustangs from 1982 through 1986 to Top Twenty national rankings and bowl wins. His first team in 1982 was unbeaten at 11-0-1, beat Pittsburgh 7-3 in the 1983 Cotton Bowl, and finished No. 2 in the national rankings. The 1982 Mustangs captured the SWC Championship and was the only unbeaten team in the nation, gaining SWC Coach of the Year Honors for Collins. He kept the Mustangs on the winning track in 1983 and 1984 finishing 10-2 with a loss to Alabama in the 1983 Sun Bowl and a win over Notre Dame in the 1984 Aloha Bowl. The 3 straight bowl games was a school record. His early 37-9-1 record was the best 4 year mark for any coach in SMU history. Before Collins' Mustangs won 10 or more games from 1982 to 1984, no SMU coach has ever led the team to back-to-back 10-win seasons. The 3 consecutive 10-win campaigns were a first for any SWC school, and Collins didn't have a losing record against any SWC school in the time He produced 26 All Southwest Conference players while leading SMU, including the most productive backfield pair in NCAA history — Craig James and Eric Dickerson who rewrote the SWC record books. Another Collins player, Lance McIlhenny, was the all-time winningest starting quarterback in conference history. His 1983 SMU squad had the unique distinction of playing in three bowl games in one season — the Cotton Bowl in Jan., the Mirage Bowl in Tokyo, Japan, in Nov., and the Sun Bowl in Dec. 1983. Overall, Bobby's SMU teams racked up 43 wins, 14 losses, and one tie. In 12 years as a head college football coach, Bobby's teams at USM and SMU amassed 91 wins, 44 losses, and 3 ties. Collins returned to Mississippi following the 1986 season after SMU's program was shut down for two years due to recruiting violations caused by overly zealous Mustang boosters. Collins had racked up more than 30 years coaching experience. He returned home to Hattiesburg and entered the insurance business. From 1992, Collins spent seven years helping USM's fund-raising efforts. Under his guidance, the USM Eagle Club set new fundraising records with $1.1 million dollars in 1998 and an all-time membership high of 2,924 before his retirement in Jan. 1999. Collins was inducted into the USM Athletic Hall of Fame in 1999 and enshrined in the Mississippi Sports Hall of Fame in 2000.

Henry A. Commiskey, Sr.

Born on Jan. 10, 1927, in Hattiesburg, Miss. He was the first U.S. Marine to win the Congressional Medal of Honor in the Korean conflict for his brave actions on Sept. 20, 1950. Commiskey was one of only 4 native Mississippians (of 5 Mississippians) to receive the Medal during the Korean conflict and the only Marine from Miss. to receive it for service in Korea. He was personally presented the Medal by Pres. Harry S. Truman on Aug. 1, 1951. Here are the actual words of his citation: "For conspicuous gallantry and intrepidity at the risk of his life above and beyond the call of duty while serving as a platoon leader in Company C, in action against enemy aggressor forces. Directed to attack hostile forces well dug in on Hill 85, 1st Lt. Commiskey, spearheaded the assault, charging up the steep slopes on the way. Coolly disregarding the heavy enemy machinegun and small arms fire, he plunged on well forward of the rest of his platoon and was the first man to reach the crest of the objective. Armed only with a pistol, he jumped into a hostile machinegun emplacement occupied by 5 enemy troops and quickly disposed of 4 of the soldiers with his automatic pistol. Grappling with the fifth, 1st Lt. Commiskey knocked him to the ground and held him until he could obtain a weapon from another member of his platoon and killed the last of the enemy guncrew. Continuing his bold assault, he moved to the next emplacement, killed 2 more of the enemy and then led his platoon toward the rear nose of the hill to rout the remainder of the hostile troops and destroy them as they fled from their

Profiles of Famous & Notable Mississippians

positions. His valiant leadership and courageous fighting spirit served to inspire the men of his company to heroic endeavor in seizing the objective and reflect the highest credit upon 1st Lt. Commiskey and the U.S. Naval Service." Commiskey died on Aug. 16, 1971, at the age of 44. His body was cremated and his ashes scattered at sea. Commiskey's Medal was one of 17 Medals of Honor that have been officially accredited to Mississippi in all wars, although we claim 5 more accredited to other states because the recipients had Mississippi ties. Commiskey is one of only 13 native Mississippians (of 22 Mississippians — 15 Army, 4 Marines and 3 Navy) in all wars to receive the Medal of Honor out of 3,433 total recipients of the Medal through Nov. 1, 2000.

Charlie Conerly

Born Charles Albert Conerly, Jr. on Sept. 19, 1921, in Clarksdale, Mississippi. His football nickname was "Chunkin' Charlie," but his closest friends called him "Roach." He was one of Mississippi's earliest and most renowned football heroes and one of the sport's first great passers. He played for Ole Miss in one of the all-time great Mississippi college games in 1947. Charley outdueled LSU's Y. A. Tittle as he scored all three Rebel Touchdowns to win 20-18 over LSU. That year Conerly led Ole Miss to its first Southeastern Conference championship and was the SEC player of the year in 1947. He still holds the Ole Miss record of 18 touchdown passes in a season. He also had a baseball batting average of .451, still a Rebels' season record. Conerly finished in 4th place for the Heisman Trophy in 1947, the first Mississippi collegian to make a serious run the Heisman. He earned All-Pro honors three times and threw for 19,488 yards and 173 TDs in a 14-year career as quarterback with the New York Giants. He became the 1948 NFL rookie of the year when he set a rookie record of 22 TD passes in a season, a record Conerly held for 50 years until Peyton Manning made 3 touchdown passes on Dec. 13, 1998 to give him 23 for a season. Conerly led the Giants to the NFL title in 1956. He played in the first sudden-death game in NFL championship history: on Dec. 28, 1958 at Yankee Stadium in New York, it was 8 minutes and 15 seconds into sudden-death overtime when Baltimore fullback Alan Ameche crashed into the end zone from the 1-yard line to defeat the Giants 23-17. That game is credited with popularizing pro football on a national scale. Conerly received the prestigious Jim Thorpe Trophy, the oldest and highest pro football award, as most valuable NFL player in 1959. He retired after the 1961 season at age 40, replaced by 35-year-old Y.A. Tittle. The Giants retired his No. 42 in 1962. Although Conerly didn't make it to the Pro Football Hall of Fame, he was inducted into the College Football Hall of Fame in 1965 and the Mississippi Sports Hall of Fame in 1966. He was the original Marlboro Man appearing in many magazine advertisements and TV commercials as the early "Marlboro Cowboy" for Phillip Morris. Conerly died in a Memphis hospital on Feb. 13, 1996, after a long illness. Burial was in his hometown of Clarksdale. A special award, the Conerly Trophy, is now given annually to the state's top college football player. Delta State freshman running back Treg Thomas was the first winner of the Conerly Trophy presented in 1996. Other winners include Ole Miss quarterback Stewart Patridge in 1997, Mississippi State senior tailback J.J. Johnson in 1998, and junior running back Deuce McAllister in 1999, the 2nd Ole Miss player to receive the trophy.

Francis "Fannye" A. Cook

Born on July 19, 1889, in Crystal Springs, Mississippi. She graduated in 1911 from Industrial Institute and College (now Mississippi University for Women) and is considered to be the finest writer ever produced at that school. After teaching in Mississippi, Wyoming and Panama, she pursued graduate studies in Washington, D.C. and Colorado, bypassing a master's degree to work directly on a doctorate. She returned to Mississippi to champion the cause of conservation, organizing the Mississippi Association for Conservation of Wildlife in 1927. Her work lead to the establishment of the first state Game and Fish Commission and she worked as a research biologist with them for 27 years. Her original research and field work resulted in her book *The Freshwater Fishes of Mississippi*, published in 1959. That volume remains a valuable scientific reference today. She also established and was director of the state wildlife museum for the State Game and Fish Commission, now the Mississippi Museum of Natural History, from its inception in 1933 until her retirement on Dec. 31, 1958. Cook died on April 30, 1964, at age 74.

Sam Cooke

Born Samuel Cook (without the "e"). Most biographers list his birthplace as Chicago, but he was born Jan. 22, 1935, in Clarksdale, Mississippi, and his family moved to Chicago when he was just a toddler. Son of a Baptist minister, he sang in the choir from age 6. He joined the gospel group, the highway Q.C.'s and later became lead singer of the Soul Stirrers from 1950-56. Cooke started singing secular songs in 1956. From 1957-65, he had 29 single records as Top-40 hits, including 13 in the Top-15 and 4 in the Top-10. His big No. 1 hit was also his first hit, *You Send Me* (1957, #1 both pop and R&B), written by his brother, Charles "L.C." Cooke. Some of his other hits: *Only Sixteen* (#28 pop in 1959), *Chain Gang* (1960, #2 pop and R&B), *Cupid* (1961, #17 pop and #20 R&B), *Twistin' The Night Away* (1962, #9 pop and #1 R&B), *Bring It On Home To Me* (#13 pop in 1962, with backing vocal by Lou Rawls), *Another Saturday Night* (#10 pop in 1963), *Good News* (#11 pop in 1964), and *Shake* (#7 pop in 1965). His hit *Wonderful World* (1960, #12 pop and #2 R&B) was revived in 1965 by the British Invasion group Herman's Hermits and was prominently featured in the 1985 hit movie *Witness*, which starred Harrison Ford. In June of 1964, Cooke created a minor sensation in New York City by spending $10,000 of his own money to erect a 20-by-100-foot billboard in Times Square emblazoned with the question, "Who's the biggest Cook in Town?" Several days later the a 45-foot, 1,500-pound photograph of Cooke was added with the message: "Sam's the biggest Cooke in town." Cooke was shot to death at age 29 in Los Angeles by a female motel manager on Dec. 11, 1964, under mysterious circumstances. He is buried in Forest Lawn Cemetery in Glendale, California. Cooke is revered as the definitive soul singer. He was inducted into the R&R Hall of Fame in 1986. Three of his songs, *A Change Is Gonna Come*, *Bring It On Home to Me* and *You Send Me* are included on the Rock & Roll Hall of Fame & Museum's list of 500 Songs That Shaped Rock & Roll. Cooke was one of the first 27 inducted into the Mississippi Musicians Hall of Fame on April 1, 2000.

Frank L. Cooley

Born in 1870 in Natchez, Mississippi. A silent screen actor, he first entered films with the Keystone Company in 1912. His films included *The First Year* (1926), *More Pay - Less Work* (1926), *Wanted: A Coward* (1927), and *Honor Bound* (1928). Cooley died on July 6, 1941, in Hollywood, California.

Dorree Cooper

Born Mar. 5, 1952, in New Orleans, her family moved to Pass Christian, Miss. when she was 10 years old. She majored in art

Profiles of Famous & Notable Mississippians

at South Carolina's Converse College and the University of Kentucky, where she received her B.A. degree in art. She first planned to teach but became an artist specializing in large sculptures. She had her own show at the Mississippi Museum of Art in Jackson in 1980. She started working in motion pictures as a set decorator in 1983. The list of hit movies to her credit include *A Nightmare on Elm Street* ('84), *Runaway Train* ('85 - assistant set decorator), *Honey, I Shrunk the Kids* ('89), *Honey, I Blew Up the Kid* ('92), *Fat Man and Little Boy* ('89), *The Distinguished Gentleman* ('92), *A Time to Kill* ('96), *Batman & Robin* ('97), and *Message in a Bottle* ('99). She received an Oscar® nomination for her set decorations on *Legends of the Fall* ('95) starring Brad Pitt.

Forrest Lamar Cooper
Born Oct. 12, 1944, in Jackson, Mississippi, he now lives in Florence, Mississippi. He wrote the popular series of books *Mississippi Trivia, Volumes 1, 2, 3* (1985) and *Volume 4* (1990). He has been interested in state history since he started keeping a scrapbook in 1956. He has also been a frequent contributor to *Mississippi*, having written over 50 articles for the popular magazine and has released his *Matters-of-Fact Mississippi Calendar* for several years running.

Owen Cooper
Lawrence Owen Cooper was born on Apr. 19, 1908, in Vicksburg. He was one of the most influential Mississippians during the last 4 decades of his life. When President Jimmy Carter came to Yazoo City for a nationally televised Town Hall Meeting on July 12, 1977, he spent the night at Cooper's home. He was the founder and CEO of Mississippi Chemical Corp. of Yazoo City, the largest farmer-owned fertilizer cooperative in the world at the time. A leader in Civil Rights, politics, economics, and especially religion, he served as head of the Southern Baptist Convention. Former Gov. William Winter called Cooper "an authentic Mississippi hero." He died on Nov. 8, 1986, of cancer. The Mississippi Department of Transportation set up the Owen Cooper Award to honor individuals who have been instrumental in supporting and promoting transportation in the state. The first Owen Cooper Memorial Award was presented in 1998 to John Pennbaker, a former mayor of New Albany, who served from 1975-92 in the state legislature, where he was instrumental in getting the 1987 Four-Lane Highway Program passed. Cooper is a member of the Mississippi Business Hall of Fame.

Wyatt Cooper
Born Wyatt Emory Cooper on Sept. 1, 1927, in Quitman, Mississippi. Cooper attended the University of California. He wrote the TV screenplay for *The Chapman Report* and collaborated with Truman Capote on the screenplay for *The Glass House*. As a stage and screen actor in Hollywood and New York City, he appeared in *Kraft Television Theatre*, *Robert Montgomery Presents* and *Philco Playhouse* in the early 1950s. Cooper played "Tommy" in the movie *Sanctuary* (1961). He married socialite Gloria Vandervilt on Dec. 24, 1963, and lived in New York City until his death. Cooper died on Jan. 5, 1978, after a series of heart attacks.

The Cotton Blossom Singers
The group was first formed by Grace Jones, wife of Piney Woods School founder Laurence Jones, in 1927. Some of the first members later formed the group, The Five Blind Boys of Mississippi. Today, the 40-member Cotton Blossom Singers performs nationally and inter- nationally with a repertoire that includes standard choral arrangements by African-American composers with an emphasis on preserving spirituals. The group was the recipient of the Heritage Award of the 1998 Mississippi Governor's Awards for Excellence in the Arts.

James Cotton
This blues harmonica player was born on July 1, 1935, in Dundee, Tunica Co., Miss. Cotton was only a child when he first heard Sonny Boy Williamson's fabled radio broadcasts for King Biscuit Time over KFFA out of Helena, Ark. Cotton moved into Williamson's home at age 9, learning to play the harp from one of the masters. Six years later, Cotton was ready to unleash his own sound. He started gigging around West Memphis, and soon had his own radio show over KWEM in 1952. It was about this time that Cotton co-wrote, with fellow Mississippian Ike Turner, what was probably the first Rock 'n' Roll hit, *Rocket 88* (See Jackie Brenston). Sam Phillips invited Cotton to record for him on his new Sun label, and two singles emerged: *Straighten Up Baby* in 1953 and *Cotton Crop Blues* the next year. When Muddy Waters rolled through Memphis minus his harpist Junior Wells, Cotton hired on and went to Chicago. But, Chess Records insisted on using Little Walter on the majority of Waters's records until 1958, when Cotton blew behind Waters on *She's Nineteen Years Old* and *Close to You*. At Cotton's urging, Waters added the Ann Cole tune *Got My Mojo Working* to his repertoire. Walter played on Muddy Waters's first studio take of it, but that's Cotton on the 1960 album cut live at the Newport Jazz Festival. By 1966, Cotton started to make it on his own. He recorded for several labels before his official full-length album debut on Verve Records in 1967. Throwing a touch of soul into his debut set, Cotton ventured into the growing blues-rock field. He stayed with Verve through the end of the decade. In 1974, Cotton signed with Buddah and released *100% Cotton* with Matt "Guitar" Murphy (see profile) backing him. Alligator issued 2 other Cotton LPs, *High Compression* and *Harp Attack!* in 1990. Antone's Records was responsible for the 1991 album, *Mighty Long Time*. Due to throat problems, Cotton has some trouble with vocals, but remains a great instrumentalist.

Tommy Couch
Born Nov. 12, 1942, in Tuscumbia, Alabama. Couch first became hooked on soul and blues as a pharmacy student at Ole Miss while booking bands for his fraternity, Pi Kappa Alpha. The student who would become president and founder of Malaco Records teamed up with fraternity brother Gerald "Wolf" Stephenson to attract white musicians from Muscle Shoals recording studio in the Alabama town of the same name. After graduating in 1965, Couch moved to Jackson, but the temptation of the music industry lured Couch away from pharmacy. Couch started laying the foundation for one of the nation's oldest independent labels when he formed a partnership with his brother-in-law Mitchell Malouf of Jackson. Combining their last names, the two started Malaco Attractions, a company specializing in booking groups for appearances in Mississippi. Three years later, Malaco Records was formed in 1968 and started producing music to release to major recording companies. It was a blues singer from Como who put Malaco in the national spotlight in the late 1960s. Fred McDowell cut an album called *I Do Not Play No Rock-'n'-Roll*. The album was nominated for a Grammy. After the success of McDowell on Capitol Records, Malaco Records formed Chimneyville, their independent record label, and produced its first album in 1970. King Floyd's *Groove Me* sold more than 2 million singles and put the Jackson-based record company on the map. In 1997, Couch and Stephenson, who is now one of Malaco's vice presidents, enjoyed the successes of a string of hit records. Malouf left the company for other pursuits in 1975. Malaco, along with its affiliated Savoy label,

Profiles of Famous & Notable Mississippians

dominated the 1997 coveted Stellar nominations for gospel music with a total of 15, ten of which they won, including the Song of the Year, Group of the Year, Choir of the Year and Traditional Album of the Year awards. Four Malaco recording artists drew multiple nominations. Malaco's current roster of recording artists include R&B stars Bobby "Blue" Bland, Shirley Brown, The Controllers, Tyrone Davis*, King Floyd, Denise LaSalle*, Latimore, Little Milton*, Bobby Rush, Johnnie Taylor and Artie White*, plus many gospel greats such as James Cleveland, The Dallas-Fort Worth Mass Choir, The Georgia Mass Choir, The Jackson Southernaires, The Men of Standard, The Miami Mass Choir, The Mississippi Children's Choir, The Mississippi Mass Choir*, Dorothy Norwood and numerous others (artists with asterisks are profiled in this chapter). The company has 125 employees and five labels that produce about 50 contemporary Christian, gospel, blues, and urban music albums a year. Couch's Malaco Records has grown from a student-run operation on the Ole Miss campus at Oxford to the largest independent R&B and gospel label in the U.S. Malaco was one of the first 27 nominees, and the only record label, inducted into the Miss. Musicians Hall of Fame April 1, 2000.

Joe Courtney
Born Oct. 17, 1969, in Jackson, he graduated from Callaway High School. This 6-9 forward played basketball 2 years at Mississippi State before transferring to Southern Mississippi. He started his pro career by playing 12 games with the Chicago Bulls and Golden State Warriors in 1992-93. He started the 1993-94 season with the Phoenix Suns and finished with the Milwaukee Bucks, averaging 5.2 points and 1.1 rebounds. In 1994, he signed a free-agent contract with the Charlotte Hornets, his 5th NBA team in 3 years.

Calvin Cox
Born Dec. 19, 1918, this Mississippian was a paper boy for *The Greenwood Commonwealth*. When he was 16, he was working for the paper as a Linotype operator and photographer. He worked for *The Atlanta Constitution* Newspaper in Atlanta, Georgia for 37 years as news editor, copy editor, assistant managing editor and associate editor. He helped start the Atlanta Press Club. Cox retired in 1982 and currently lives in Austell, Georgia, right outside of Atlanta.

Harry "Popeye" Craft
Born Harry Frances Craft on April 19, 1915, in Ellisville, Miss. His nicknames were "Popeye" and "Wildfire." He was one of the most outstanding *football* players in Mississippi College's history. He signed a pro baseball contract in 1935, joined the Cincinnati Redlegs as an outfielder in 1937 and stayed with them 6 years until 1942, playing in the 1939 and 1940 World Series. His career totals: 533 hits in 2,104 at-bats (.253 batting avg.), 237 runs, 44 home runs, and 267 RBIs in 566 games. He managed the Kansas City Athletics from 1957-59 where he signed Mickey Mantle to his first contract. From 1962-64, he was the manager of the Houston Colt .45s, the forerunner of the Houston Astros. Craft's teams were 360-485-4. He was inducted into the Mississippi Sports Hall of Fame in 1975. He was a scout for the Astros prior to his death in Houston, Texas on Aug. 3, 1995.

Hubert Creekmore
Born on Jan. 16, 1907, in Water Valley, Miss., he also lived in Jackson, Miss. and New York City. Creekmore wrote 4 novels and 5 volumes of poetry: *Personal Sun* (1940), *The Stone Ants* (1943), *The Long Reprieve* (1946), *Formula* (1947), and *No Harm to Lovers* (1950). He edited *A Little Treasury of World Poetry* (1952). Creekmore died in 1966.

Jack Cristil
Born in Memphis on Dec. 10, 1925, he has lived in Tupelo since 1955. He has been the voice of the Mississippi State Bulldogs football team since 1953 — and has never missed a game! Cristill broadcast his 500th game on Nov. 20, 1999! He has also been the radio voice of State basketball since 1957 and has broadcast more than 1,100 of their games. In 1988 his SEC peers named him the league's best play-by-play man. In 1997 Cristil received the Chris Schenkel Award for broadcasting excellence, given by the National Football Foundation. He has received the Outstanding Broadcaster in Mississippi award 23 times and became the first non-athlete ever inducted into the Mississippi Sports Hall of Fame when he was enshrined in the Media category in 1991.

Hughie Critz
Born Hugh Melville Critz on Sept. 17, 1900, in Starkville, Miss. He made his major league baseball debut on May 31, 1924, with the Cincinnati Reds. Critz played for the New York Giants from 1930-1935 including the 1933 World Series. His career stats: 1,591 hits in 5,930 at bats (.268 batting avg.), 832 runs, 38 homers, and 531 RBIs in 1,478 games played. Critz was inducted into the Mississippi Sports Hall of Fame in 1963 and into the Mississippi State University Sports Hall of Fame in 1970. He died on Jan 10, 1980, in Greenwood, Mississippi.

Harold Cross
Born in Ripley on Sept. 28, 1946, he grew up in Falkner (both towns in Tippah County). Cross now lives in Brandon. He received his bachelors degree from Mississippi State and his masters from Mississippi College. His book, *They Sleep Beneath the Mockingbird* (1994), is about Confederate generals buried in Mississippi. Brigadier General Cross is also Commander of the Mississippi Air National Guard.

Rett Crowder
Born June 16, 1970, in New Orleans, Louisiana. When he was 6 years old, his family moved to Jackson, Mississippi. He attended Louisiana State University on a golf scholarship, were he graduated in 1992 with a degree in economics. On May 14, 1999, Crowder was playing in the Country Club of Jackson Four-Ball when he shot a 58 — a lower 18-hole golf score than anybody has ever shot on the PGA Tour! The lowest score in Tour history is 59, set by five players — David Duval, Chip Beck and Al Geiberger on the PGA Tour and Doug Dunakey and Notah Begay on the Nike Tour. Shigeki Maruyama of Japan shot a 58 (and just missed shooting 57) on June 5, 2000, at Harrison, N.Y. during qualifying for the U.S. Open, but his 58 is not recognized as a PGA Tour record because it wasn't scored during a Tour event. Crowder's 58 may equal the best score ever shot on a par-72 course. Homero Blancas shot a 55 on a par-69 course in Longview, Texas, in 1961. *The Guinness Book of World Records* states that three pro players have scored 57 on a long course (over 6,000 yards), but one was 6,389 yards, par 71, another at 6,098 yards, par 70, with the length of the third not listed. *The Guinness Book* no longer lists lowest 18-hole rounds, but its 1992 edition says at least four players shot a 58 on a course longer than 6,000 meters (6,561 yards). Country Club of Jackson played to about 6,400 yards for Crowder's round. No club rule changes were made for his round and he didn't get to improve his ball's lie in the fairway or pick up any gimme putts. Crowder's 14-under-par round included 12 birdies, one eagle and five pars. He grew up playing Country Club of Jackson, where the previous course record was 62. There's where Crowder won his first State Am in 1992 with a score of 10-under. He then had a short career as a touring pro and once

Profiles of Famous & Notable Mississippians

shot a course-record 61 in South Africa. He regained his amateur status in 1996 after a two-year stint as a pro and has dominated the Mississippi scene since. At the State Am at the Dancing Rabbit Golf Club in Philadelphia, Mississippi in 1998, Crowder ran away from the field with a 72-hole total of 16-under 272 — the lowest winning score in the 83-year history of the tournament! In 1999, Crowder captured the State Am by a 7-stoke margin, shooting an 11-under-par 277 at Timberton Golf Club in Hattiesburg. On June 4, 2000, he won his third straight State Am title with a 72-hole total of 13-under 275 while playing at Country Club of Jackson. Crowder is one of only four players in the 84-year history of the State Am to win it three consecutive times. He is 50-under par for the four times he's won the State Am tournament. Crowder won the Farm Bureau Invitational on July 18, 1999, at Clarksdale Country Club. He won the Mid-Am at The Refuge in Flowood on Aug. 1, 1999. He shot a course record opening round 63 and finished with a 3-day total of 10-under 203. Crowder is the first person to win the Mississippi Am, the MPGA Invitational and the Mid-Am in the same year. His combined score in the 3 events was 25-under par with a margin of 14 strokes. In 1999, he was selected MGA player of the year for the third consecutive year. Crowder works as a broker at J.C. Bradford & Company of Jackson.

Mart Crowley
Born Aug. 21, 1936, in Vicksburg, Mississippi. He graduated from St. Aloysius High School in Vicksburg in 1953, then attended UCLA in California to work on an art degree. He was production assistant and writer for *Baby Doll*, *The Last Mile* with Mickey Rooney, *The Fugitive Kind* with Marlon Brando, *Butterfield 8* with Elizabeth Taylor, *Splendor in the Grass* starring Natalie Wood and Warren Beatty, and other movies. He later became executive story editor and eventually producer of ABC-TV's *Hart to Hart*. He wrote the screenplay for the made-for-TV movie *There Must Be A Pony*, which starred Robert Wagner and Elizabeth Taylor and first aired on ABC-TV on Oct. 5, 1986. His plays include *The Boys in the Band* (1968), *Remote Asylum* (1970), *Breeze From the Gulf* (1973) and *For Reasons That Remain Unclear*. First appearing off-Broadway, *The Boys in the Band* was getting a New York revival in 1996 and *USA Today*'s David Patrick Stearns called it "The *Uncle Tom's Cabin* of homosexual literature."

Arthur "Big Boy" Crudup
Born in Forest on Aug. 24, 1905, he was also known as Elmore Jones and Percy Crudup. This bluesman was a big influence on Elvis Presley. He wrote *That's All Right Mama* — the first song Elvis released. Elvis also recorded two other Crudup compositions, *So Glad You're Mine* and *My Baby Left Me*. He also wrote *Rock Me Mama* and other rockabilly standards and is a member of the Rockabilly Hall of fame. He sang in church as a child and in the late 1930s joined a gospel group called the Harmonizing Four. In 1940, Crudup migrated to Chicago from Mississippi. He was playing for spare change on the streets and living in a packing crate underneath an elevated train track when RCA/Bluebird producer Lester Melrose dropped a few coins in Crudup's hat. Melrose hired Crudup to play a party at Tampa Red's house attended by the cream of Melrose's stable — Big Bill Broonzy, Lonnie Johnson and Lil Green. By September of 1941, Crudup himself was an RCA artist. He reached the top of the R&B lists during the mid-1940s with *Who's Been Foolin' You*, *Keep Your Arms Around Me*, *So Glad You're Mine* and *Ethel Mae*. He cut the original *That's All Right* in 1946, but it wasn't a hit at the time. Crudup recorded only sporadically, and often on other labels under the name Elmore Jones or Percy Crudup (his son's name). Crudup quit Victor in 1954. Retired from music, he was digging and selling sweet potatoes, when, during the 1960s, Philadelphia blues promoter Dick Waterman took an interest in him and his business problems. Dick began working with the American Guild of Artists and Composers in an attempt to collect some of the royalties withheld from Crudup. He eventually received $60,000 from BMI and reached a settlement with the music publishers. In 1961, he surfaced after a long layoff with an album dominated by remakes of his Bluebird hits. Crudup resumed his music career in 1968 and toured the U.S. and Europe until his death from a heart attack. He died in Nassawadox, Va. on March 28, 1974.

T. Tommy Cutrer
Born Thomas Clinton Cutrer on June 29, 1924, in Osyka, Pike County, Mississippi, he made his life's work in broadcasting. For many years he was the featured announcer on WSM's Grand Ole Opry in Nashville, Tennessee. He was inducted into the Country Music DJ Hall of Fame in 1980. Cutrer died in Nashville on Oct. 11, 1998, at the age of 74.

Roland Dale
Born Oct. 30, 1927, in Magee, Mississippi, he attended Magee High and was a standout student athlete. Widely recruited, he signed at Ole Miss where he played one season for NFL Hall of Famer Edwin "Goat" Hale (see his profile) as a 205-lb. two-way tackle for the Rebels in 1945. After a 14-month hitch in the Marine Corps, Dale returned to Ole Miss to play for John Vaught's first 3 teams. He was left tackle on two of the Rebel's finest teams, the 1947 SEC champions and the team of 1948, which posted a combined 7-3 record. Dale served as captain of the 1949 Rebel squad. He was selected to play in the Blue-Gray postseason college All-Star game. He also received his masters degree in physical education at Ole Miss. Dale was drafted by the Brooklyn Dodgers, but played pro in the NFL as a defensive end with the Washington Redskins in 1950. A shoulder injury forced an early retirement from the pro ranks and he entered coaching, first at Jones Junior College in Ellisville, Mississippi, then at Greenwood High School and as athletic director and coach at Gulfport High School, where he was named Big Eight Coach of the Year. Dale coached in the Mississippi High School All-Star Football Game. He was selected as line coach at Mississippi Southern College (now Univ. of Southern Mississippi) by Mississippi Sports Hall of Fame members Reed Green and Pie Vann in 1955. During his coaching stint, Southern racked up a 26-3-1 record and was invited to the Tangerine Bowl twice. Dale was called back to Ole Miss by Mississippi Sports Hall of Famers Tad Smith and John Vaught where he became one of the most successful football coaches in Ole Miss history for 12 seasons. He served as head football coach at Southeast Louisiana for two seasons (1972-74), where he hired Billy Brewer as a defensive backfield coach. Dale become Athletic Director at University of Southern Mississippi in 1974. While at USM, Dale developed and advanced the USM Athletic Department to new heights unparalleled in school history. Dale bought in a remarkable lineup of coaches to Hattiesbrg including football coach Bobby Collins, men's basketball coach M.K. Turk, women's basketball coach Kay James, and baseball coach Hill Denson. Dale was instrumental in obtaining USM's present day affiliation with the Metro Conference plus the upgrading of the athletic facilities, including the expansion and renovation of M.M. Roberts Stadium. When he retired in 1986, USM immediately gave Dale the permanent appointment of Director of Athletics Emeritus. He was

Profiles of Famous & Notable Mississippians

inducted into the University of Mississippi Athletic Hall of Fame in 1987, the Miss. Sports Hall of Fame in 1995, and the University of Southern Miss. Sports Hall of Fame in 1996.

Erick Dampier

Born July 14, 1974, in New Hebron, Miss. In 3 seasons at Mississippi State, the 6-foot-11 basketball center became only the 5th player in the school's history to earn first team All-SEC honors for 2 consecutive seasons, 1994-95 and 1995-96. During his collegiate career, he averaged 13.2 points, 9.2 rebounds, and shot 58.7 percent from the floor. He established a school record with 249 blocked shots, including a Mississippi State season record of 106 in 1995-96. Dampier is 4th on MSU's career rebounding list (859) and 7th all-time in career rebounding average. His efforts helped the Bulldogs to a 66-27 record and make it into postseason play for 3 years running — the NIT in 1994, the NCAA tournament in 1995 and all the way to the Final Four in 1996. He gave up his final year of college eligibility to enter the draft and was chosen by the Indiana Pacers as the 10th overall pick on June 26, 1996. He was with the Golden State Warriors for the 1997-98 and 1998-99 seasons. During the 1998-99 season, Dampier averaged 8.8 points and 7.6 rebounds. The Warriors re-signed him to a multi-year $48 million contract on Aug. 24, 1999. He was expected to be on the injured list at the start of the 1999-2000 season after knee surgery on Sept. 16. Dampier's pro career stats through the 1998-99 season: started all 154 games (24.1 mins.); 1,341 points (8.7 ppg. avg.); 1,009 rebounds (6.6 avg.); 58 steals (0.38 avg.); 212 blocks (1.38 avg.); and 137 assists (0.89 avg.). His career percentages are .429 field goal and .660 free throw. In 1999, Dampier was chosen a member of the first team in *The Clarion-Ledger* Division I Men's Basketball Team of the Century!

William David

Born Oct. 5, 1882, in Vicksburg. A stage actor and silent screen actor, he appeared in the early films: *Arms and the Girl* (1917), *Here Comes the Bride* (1919), *The Girl Problem* (1919), *Outcast* (1922), *Received Payment* (1922), and *Fog Bound* (1923). He died April 10, 1965 in East Islip, N.Y.

Blind John Davis

Born in Hattiesburg on Dec. 7, 1913, his blues piano work was featured on dozens of blues records during the 1930s and '40s, accompanying artists such as Sonny Boy Williamson, Tampa Red, and Big Bill Broonzy. He was the first blues pianist to do a European tour (with Broonzy in 1952). He died in Chicago on Oct. 12, 1985, at the age of 71.

Jefferson Davis

He was the first and only President of the Confederate States of America. He was born in a log cabin in Christian County, Kentucky (now Fairview, Todd County), on June 3, 1808. While young, he moved with his parents to Louisiana and from there to a plantation near Woodville, Wilkinson County, Mississippi. Davis attended the Wilkinson County Academy, Jefferson College near Natchez, St. Thomas College in Washington County, Kentucky, and Transylvania University in Lexington, Kentucky. He graduated from the U.S. Military Academy in West Point, N.Y., in 1828. Davis served in the Black Hawk War in 1832 and was promoted to the rank of first lieutenant in the First Dragoons in 1833, and served until 1835, when he resigned. He then moved to his plantation, 'Brierfield,' in Warren County, Mississippi, and farmed cotton. Davis was elected as a Democrat to the 29th Congress and served from March 4, 1845, until June 1846, when he resigned to command the First Regiment of Mississippi Riflemen in the war with Mexico. He was appointed to the U.S. Senate to fill the vacancy caused by the death of Jesse Speight. He was subsequently elected and served from Aug. 10, 1847, until Sept. 23, 1851, when he resigned. Davis was chairman of the Committee on Military Affairs in the 30th through 32nd Congresses. He was an unsuccessful candidate for Governor of Mississippi in 1851. Davis was appointed Secretary of War by President Franklin Pierce and served in that position from 1853-1857. Again elected as a Democrat to the U.S. Senate and served from March 4, 1857, until Jan. 21, 1861, when he withdrew with other secessionist Senators. He was chairman of the Committee on Military Affairs and the Militia in the 35th and 36th Congresses. Davis was commissioned major general of the Mississippi State militia in Jan. 1861. He was chosen President of the Confederacy by the Provisional Congress and inaugurated in Montgomery, Al. on Feb. 18, 1861. Davis was then elected President of the Confederacy for a term of six years and inaugurated in Richmond, Va., on Feb. 22, 1862. Captured by Union troops in Irwinsville, Ga., on May 10, 1865, he was imprisoned in Fortress Monroe, indicted for treason, and was paroled in the custody of the court in 1867. He lived most of his last days in poverty at Beauvoir on the Mississippi Gulf Coast, a home willed to him by Sarah A. Dorsey, a friend of Mrs. Davis. There, he spent three years writing *The Rise and Fall of the Confederate Government*. Davis died in New Orleans on Dec. 6, 1889, at the age of 81. Interment was in the Metairie Cemetery in New Orleans with reinterment on May 31, 1893, in Hollywood Cemetery in Richmond, Va. Inscribed upon his gravestone are the words, "At Rest, An American Soldier And Defender of the Constitution." Davis was posthumously restored to the full rights of citizenship, retroactively effective Dec. 25, 1868, pursuant to a Joint Resolution of Congress, approved on Oct. 17, 1978.

Paul Davis

Born in Meridian on April 21, 1948. His biggest hit records to hit *Billboard*'s Top-40 were *I Go Crazy* (#7 in 1978) and *'65 Love Affair* (# 6 in 1982). He had 6 other records that hit the Top-40 charts from 1974-1982. His country hits include a No. 1 with Marie Osmond *You're Still New to Me* (1986), and a No. 1 with Tanya Tucker & Paul Overstreet *I Won't Take Less than Your Love* (1987). He wrote the No. 1 country hit, *Meet Me In Montana*, recorded by Marie Osmond with Dan Seals in 1985. He has also produced many hits by other artists.

Tyrone Davis

Born May 4, 1938, in Greenville, Mississippi. Davis debuted on record in 1965 as "Tyrone the Wonder Boy." This soul singer had two million-selling hit single records, *Can I Change My Mind* (#5 in 1969) and *Turn Back The Hands of Time* (#3 in 1970), plus 3 others that made the Top-40. He left Greenville for Michigan when he was 14, settled into the Chicago soul scene by age 19, then returned to his Mississippi musical roots in 1996 with a series of albums for Malaco Records in Jackson. He has recorded over 30 albums including *Pleasin' You* (1997). In 1998, Davis was awarded the R&B Foundation's Pioneer Award for lifetime career achievements.

Walter Davis

An early blues pianist born March 1, 1912, in Grenada, Mississippi, he relocated to St. Louis during the mid-1920s. Also known as 'Hooker Joe," he was a two-fisted piano player who was one of the brightest stars of the 1930s Bluebird period of blues' development. Davis was among the most prolific blues performers to emerge from the pre-war St. Louis scene, cutting over 150 sides between 1930 and 1952, such as *Ashes In My Whiskey* and *Blue Blues*. A stroke prompted him

Profiles of Famous & Notable Mississippians

to move from music to the ministry during the early 1950s. Davis was still preaching at the time of his death in St. Louis, Missouri on October 22, 1963, at the age of 51.

John De Chiaro
Born John Paul De Chiaro on Jan. 19, 1953, in the Bronx, New York. De Chiaro received his B.S. in musical education at Kean College and his M.A. at New York University. He is now Professor of Music at the University of Southern Mississippi. He played classical guitar at New York's Carnegie Hall when he was 23 years old, and performed several solo concerts there in the 1970s. He was named Young Artist of the Year by *Musical America Magazine* in 1982. In 1989, NASA commissioned him to compose a theme for the space program. On Sept. 14, 1994, John Paul played guitar for Pope John Paul II in Rome! On Dec. 26, 1997, De Chiaro performed at a candlelight concert at the White House, which was attended briefly by President Clinton, and he was invited to perform at the White House again during Christmas 1998. De Chiaro recorded a 4-CD set of the *complete* piano works of Scott Joplin performed on guitar, a feat never before accomplished!

Borden Deal
Born Oct. 12, 1922, in Pontotoc, Miss. He received his B.A. from the University of Alabama in 1949, then did graduate study at Mexico City College in 1950. Deal held many jobs including employment at the U.S. Labor Department. He was also a correspondent for Associated Films (1950-55), a tracer for an auto finance company in Birmingham, Alabama, a telephone solicitor in New Orleans, and a radio copywriter in Mobile, Ala. Deal was awarded a Guggenheim Fellowship in 1967 and a Literary Award by the Alabama Library Association in 1963. His book, *Dunbar's Cove* ('57), was made into the movie *Wild River* ('60), which starred Montgomery Cliff and Lee Remick. His other novels, many about "the New South," include *Walk Through the Valley* ('56), *It's Always Three O'clock* ('61), *Devil's Whispers* ('61), *The Spangled Road* ('62), *A Long Way To Go* ('65), *The Tobacco Men* ('65), *The Least One* ('67), *The Advocate* ('68), *Interstate* ('70), and *The Other Room* ('74). Deal also wrote under the pseudonyms of Lee Borden and Leigh Borden. His books have been translated into over twenty languages and adapted for the stage, movies, radio and TV. *The Insolent Breed* ('59) was the basis for the Broadway musical *A Joyful Noise*. Deal died in Sarasota, Florida on Jan. 22, 1985.

Dizzy Dean
Born Jay Hanna Dean (he also used Jerome Herman Dean) on Jan. 16, 1910, in Lucas, Arkansas, he grew up in Bond, Miss. A colorful pitcher for the St. Louis Cardinals "Gashouse Gang" (major league debut Sept. 28, 1930) in the 1930s, he averaged 24 wins a season for 1932-36, leading the National League in strikeouts for 4 of the 5 years (1932-35). In 1934, he won 30 regular-season games, and the MVP award. His 2 World Series victories that season, combined with his brother Paul's 2 wins, gave the Cardinals the World Series championship. Dean became the first National League pitcher to win an All-Star game in 1936. He remained with the Cardinals until 1938, when he was traded to the Chicago Cubs. He last pitched for the Cubs during the 1940 season, bringing his lifetime record to 150 victories and 83 defeats. After retiring from baseball in 1941, he became a TV sports commentator. Dean was elected to the Baseball Hall of Fame in 1953. In 1967 he announced and then withdrew his candidacy for the governorship of Mississippi. The Dizzy Dean Museum is located in the Mississippi Sports Hall of Fame in Jackson, where Dean was inducted in 1990. Dean died on July 17, 1974, in Reno, Nevada and is buried in the Bond Cemetery in Stone County, Mississippi. The Wiggins Post Office building was named in honor of Dean on Aug. 15, 2000 and Dean was among 20 legends of baseball to appear on commemorative postage stamps issued by the Postal Service.

Dorothy Dell
Born Dorothy Goff on Jan. 30, 1915, in Hattiesburg, Mississippi. This "Miss America" of 1930 and "Miss Universe" of 1930 became a stage actress who starred in the Zigfield Follies and also starred in three 1934 films for Paramount Pictures before dying at age 19 that same year. The movies were *Wharf Angel*, *Little Miss Marker* (added to the National Film Registry by the Library of Congress in 1998), and *Shoot The Works*, which was never released due to her death in an auto wreck in Pasadena, Calif. on June 8, 1934.

S. Gale Denley
Born in Coffeeville in Yalobusha County on Feb. 23, 1936. This third-generation newspaper publisher began working as a child at *The Coffeeville Courier*, founded in 1907 by his grandfather. In 1953, he and his father, the late Sellers Vanhoozer Denley, established *The Calhoun County Journal* in Bruce. Denley has worked at that paper since, serving as publisher since 1970. Since 1984, he has written a syndicated political and general interest column that appears in about a dozen Mississippi newspapers including *The Clarion-Ledger* of Jackson. He is also a stockholder and director of *The Scott County Times* in Forest and *The South Reporter* in Holly Springs. He served for a year on the journalism faculty at the University of Southern Mississippi. In 1963, he began his career at Ole Miss where he served as associate professor of journalism and director of the Student Media Center supervising *The Daily Mississippian* campus newspaper, the college FM radio station and the Ole Miss yearbook until his retirement in Dec. 1996. Denley was inducted into the Mississippi Press Association's Hall of Fame June 22, 1996.

James H. Diamond
Born on April 22, 1925, in New Orleans, he was living in Gulfport when he entered the U.S. Army. PFC Diamond was in Co. D, 21st Infantry, 24th Infantry Division in Mintal, Mindanao, Philippine Islands when he performed an act of bravery, which took his life on May 14, 1945. He was awarded the Congressional Medal of Honor posthumously on March 6, 1946. Here are the actual words of his citation: "As a member of the machinegun section, he displayed extreme gallantry and intrepidity above and beyond the call of duty. When a Japanese sniper rose from his foxhole to throw a grenade into their midst, this valiant soldier charged and killed the enemy with a burst from his submachine gun; then, by delivering sustained fire from his personal arm and simultaneously directing the fire of 105mm. and .50 caliber weapons upon the enemy pillboxes immobilizing this and another machinegun section, he enabled them to put their guns into action. When 2 infantry companies established a bridgehead, he voluntarily assisted in evacuating the wounded under heavy fire; and then, securing an abandoned vehicle, transported casualties to the rear through mortar and artillery fire so intense as to render the vehicle inoperative and despite the fact he was suffering from a painful wound. The following day he again volunteered, this time for the hazardous job of repairing a bridge under heavy enemy fire. On 14 May 1945, when leading a patrol to evacuate casualties from his battalion, which was cut off, he ran through a virtual hail of Japanese fire to secure an abandoned machine gun. Though mortally wounded as he reached the gun, he succeeded in drawing sufficient fire upon

Profiles of Famous & Notable Mississippians

himself so that the remaining members of the patrol could reach safety. Pfc. Diamond's indomitable spirit, constant disregard of danger, and eagerness to assist his comrades, will ever remain a symbol of selflessness and heroic sacrifice to those for whom he gave his life." Although born in another state, Diamonds's Medal of Honor is accredited to his adopted state of Mississippi. Diamond's Medal was one of 17 Medals of Honor that have been officially accredited to Mississippi in all wars, although we claim 5 more that were accredited to other states because the recipients had Mississippi ties. Diamond is one of 7 Mississippians (4 native Mississippians) to be awarded the Congressional Medal of Honor (CMOH) during WWII. Diamond was one of only 2 non-native Mississippians (of 6 Mississippians) to be awarded the CMOH posthumously. The other was Milton L. Olive III. Diamond was one of 22 Mississippians (13 native)[15 Army, 4 Marines & 3 Navy] in all wars to be awarded the CMOH out of 3,433 recipients through Nov. 1, 2000. Diamond is buried in the Evergreen Cemetery (Block 29, Lot 12, Space 6) in Gulfport. A Medal of Honor marker is on his grave.

Bo Diddley

Born Otha Ellas Bates McDaniel on Dec. 30, 1928, in McComb, Mississippi, his family moved to Chicago when he was 5. Before taking up blues and R&B, Diddley actually studied classical violin, but shifted gears after hearing John Lee Hooker. When he started recording, he adopted the name "Bo Diddley," black slang for a mischievous child and also the name of a one-stringed African guitar. His music is punctuated by pulsating beats and his style is flamboyant as he plays square fur-covered guitars and swivels his hips. One of the key figures in the development of R&B, Rock 'n Roll and modern popular music, his R&B hits include *Bo Diddley*, *I'm A Man* (covered by The Yardbirds), *Mona* (covered by The Rolling Stones), *Who Do You Love*, *You Don't Love Me*, *Diddley Daddy*, *Pretty Thing*, Diddy Wah Diddy, *You Can't Judge a Book by Its Cover* and *Road Runner*, plus a Top-20 pop hit *Say Man* (1959). In Great Britain, he is revered as a giant on the order of Chuck Berry and Muddy Waters. Buddy Holly covered *Bo Diddley* and used a modified Bo Diddley beat on his own hit *Not Fade Away*. He has recorded nearly 50 albums. He received a 1997 Grammy nomination and in 1998, he received the Grammy's prestigious Lifetime Achievement Award. He's also received the Lifetime Achievement Award from the Rhythm & Blues Foundation. Diddley was one of the first members inducted into the Rock & Roll Hall of Fame in 1986. His song, *Bo Diddley*, is included on the Rock and Roll Hall of Fame and Museum's list of 500 Songs That Shaped Rock And Roll. He played a pawnbroker in the Eddie Murphy movie *Trading Places* (1983) and has been in other movies with Roll & Roll themes. He appeared as a pool player in the video of George Thorogood's *Bad to the Bone*. Diddley was one of first 27 inducted into the inaugural Mississippi Musicians Hall of Fame on April 1, 2000.

Louisa Dixon

Born in Stanford, Connecticut on March 31, 1950, she grew up in New Canaan, Connecticut, a suburb of New York City. She attended Antioch College in Yellow Springs, Ohio, where she studied for two quarters. She graduated Summa Cum Laude from Ohio State University with a B.S. in Clinical Psychology. Later, she attended Creighton University School of Law in Omaha, Nebraska, where she got her J.D. in 1977. Dixon has worked many different and interesting jobs: a clerk for Judge Albert Schatz in the U.S. Federal District Court in Omaha, Nebraska; a job in the Special Counsel's office at the Department of Energy in Washington, D.C.; a campaign worker in the John Glenn Presidential Campaign; and in 1984 she became Director of Investigations in the State Auditor's office of Mississippi. In 1988, she became the Commissioner of Public Safety for the State of Mississippi (which includes the Highway Patrol). In 1992, Dixon resigned that position to raise her young son Ben Johnson, who was two at the time. She is now president of Greenfield Plantation, her family owned timber farm in Natchez, Mississippi. With all this, she has still found the time to become a novelist. Her books include *Next to Last Chance: A Mississippi Mystery* (1998), *Outside Chance* (1999), *No Chance*, slated for September 2000, and *Never Had A Chance* (a work in progress).

Willie Dixon

Born Willie James Dixon in Vicksburg on July 1, 1915. He was one of the most important figures of the Chicago blues scene. A gifted bassist, arranger, promoter & record producer, but is best known for the hundreds of blues songs he wrote over the course of 5 decades: *Little Red Rooster*, *Wang Dang Doodle*, *I Ain't Superstitious*, *Pretty Thing*, *My Babe*, *Back Door Man*, and *Seventh Son*—songs recorded by artists around the world such as the Doors, Bo Diddley, Johnny Rivers, Eric Clapton, Led Zeppelin, & the Rolling Stones. He was inducted into the R&R Hall of Fame in 1994 in the "Early Influences" category. Dixon died in Burbank, Calif. on Jan. 29, 1992. He is buried in the Burr Oak Cemetery in Alsip, Illinois (Aracia Lawn, Lot 18, Grave 1 right by the road).

Jim Dollarhide

Born June 8, 1952, in Greenwood, he grew up in Jackson, where he attended Hinds Junior College. Dollarhide started in photography in high school and continued in college. He has worked more than 20 years as a commercial cinematographer and film producer. He's won many advertising awards including Addys, Clios, Tellys, and, in Oct. 1994, he received the Chicago Film Festival's highest award, the Golden Hugo, for his 25-minute film *Harmonies: A Mississippi Overture*, produced for the Mississippi Department of Economic Development. The film also garnered top honors by winning 2 Addys from the Jackson Avertising Federation, Best of Show at the Mercury Awards, Best of Show at the Cindy Awards, plus an International Monitor Award for Best Director for Dollarhide Imageworks, his Jackson-based film and video production company. Dollarhide dismantled Imageworks in 1997 and started a new company, Dollarhide Film. He was cinematographer for the movie, *The Rising Place*, filmed in Jackson, Canton and Yazoo City in the spring of 1999.

David Herbert Donald

Born Oct. 1, 1920 in Goodman, Holmes County, Mississippi. He attended the public schools, then Holmes Junior College and graduated with the highest honors from Millsaps College in Jackson in 1941. Donald did his graduate work in history at the University of North Carolina and graduated from the University of Illinois, where he was research assistant for the great Lincoln scholar J.G. Randall. Donald has taught at some of America's greatest universities including Columbia and Princeton. He was the first Harry C. Black Professor of American History at Johns Hopkins University, where he was the founder and director of the Institute of Southern History. Donald has held visiting appointments at the University College of North Wales, at Amherst College, and at Oxford University. In 1973, he came to Harvard University as Charles Warren Professor of American History, and for six years he was chairman of the graduate program of the History of American Civilization. Donald has received honorary degrees

Profiles of Famous & Notable Mississippians

from Millsaps College, the College of Charleston, Oxford University, the University of Illinois, Harvard University, and Lincoln University. He has been the recipient of two Guggenheim Fellowships. Donald has authored many books, most of them about Lincoln and the Civil War. He is a two-time Pulitzer Prize-winner in the Biography category, one for *Charles Sumner and the Coming of the Civil War* in 1961 and another for *Look Homeward: A Life of Thomas Wolfe* in 1988. His crowning achievement was *Lincoln* (1996), for which he received both the Christopher Award and the Lincoln Award, which included $35,000 cash. Many consider it the best biography of Abraham Lincoln ever written. Professor Donald is acknowledged to be the top Lincoln scholar in the nation! Now retired, he holds the title of Charles Warren Professor Emeritus of American History at Harvard. He and his wife, Aida DiPace Donald, the editor-in-chief of the Harvard University Press, live in Lincoln, Mass.

August Dorley
Born in Baden, Germany in Dec. 1842. He entered the Union Army in Mississippi. Private Dorley was in Company B, 1st Louisiana Cavalry when he performed an act of bravery at Mount Pleasant, Alabama, on April 11, 1865, that earned him the Medal of Honor (MOH). His citation reads simply "Capture of flag." Of 53 Medals of Honor awarded for action "on the ground" in Mississippi during the Civil War, Dorley's was the only one officially accredited to Mississippi. The other 52 were accredited to other states. Mississippi had two other Medals of Honor accredited during the Civil War, but the two men served in the Union Navy and not "on the ground." Dorley's MOH was officially accredited to Natchez, one of three Medals of Honor to be accredited to Mississippi for action during the Civil War. Dorley was one of only 5 Mississippians (2 *native* Mississippians) to be awarded the MOH during the Civil War (3 Union Army & 2 Union Navy). The Medal was awarded to only those that fought for the North. Dorley's Medal was one of 17 Medals of Honor that have been officially accredited to Mississippi in all wars, although we claim 5 more that were accredited to other states because the recipients had Mississippi ties. Dorley was one of 22 Mississippians (13 native Mississippians)[15 Army, 4 Marines and 3 Navy] in all wars to have received the Medal of Honor out of 3,433 recipients through Nov. 1, 2000. Dorley died on Oct. 17, 1867, at age 24 and is buried in the Natchez City Cemetery. A Medel of Honor marker is on his grave.

Harold Dorman
Born on Dec. 23, 1931, in Sledge, Mississippi. He moved to Memphis in 1955 and recorded for Sun Records starting in 1957. His biggest hit and only song to hit the Top-40 was *Mountain of Love* (#21 in 1960) which Charley Pride (also from Sledge) recorded and turned into a No. 1 country hit in 1982. Dorman suffered two strokes in 1984. He died in Memphis, Tennessee on Oct. 8, 1988, at age 56.

Ben H. Douglas
Born Feb. 20, 1935, in Sontag, Mississippi. He received a B.S. in chemistry and zoology from Mississippi College in 1956 and his doctorate in physiology and biophysics from the University of Mississippi Medical Center in 1964. Now retired, Dr. Douglas is Professor Emeritus of Anatomy and Obstetrics and Gynecology, and former assistant vice chancellor for graduate studies at UMC. Dr. Douglas was the first to demonstrate that there is a transient increase in blood volume and interstitial pressure prior to the onset of hypertension. He received the Mississippi Academy of Sciences Award for Outstanding Contribution to Science in 1983. He was president of the Mississippi Academy of Sciences 1985-86 and president of the International Society for the Study of Pathophysiology of Pregnancy 1990-91. Douglas was also president of the Mississippi Writer's Association in 1994. He wrote *Reset Your Appestat* and *Ageless: Living Younger Longer* (1994) and the children's books, *What is There to Do in the Country?* (1996) and *Willie Roy Dewberry's Panther* (1998). Dr. Douglas has also lectured to medical groups all over the world.

Ellen Douglas
Born in Natchez on July 12, 1921, she's also lived in Greenville, Miss. Ellen Douglas is the pen name of Josephine Haxton, who now lives in Jackson. She graduated from Ole Miss in 1942. Her prose has earned critical acclaim and praise from fellow Mississippi authors Shelby Foote, Richard Ford, Walker Percy and Eudora Welty. She was the first recipient of the Mississippi Institute of Arts and Letters Literature Award in 1979 for *The Rock Cried Out* (also a Book-of-the-Month Alternate). Her other works: *A Family's Affair* (1962), winner of the Houghton Mifflin-Esquire Fellowship Award and named by a *New York Times* critic as one of the 5 best novels of the year; *Black Cloud, White Cloud* (1963); *Where the Dreams Cross* (1968); *Apostles of Light* (1973), nominated for the National Book Award; *A Lifetime Burning* (1982), won the Mississippi Institute of Arts & Letters (MIAL) Literature Award; *Can't Quit You, Baby* (1988); and won the MIAL award in the fiction category presented May 8, 1999, for her short story collection, *Truth: Four Stories I Am Finally Old Enough to Tell* (1998). *Truth* was also a finalist for the Robert F. Kennedy Book Award given annually for books dealing with Civil Rights issues. Douglas was also the recipient of the Hillsdale Award for Fiction from the Fellowship of Southern Writers. On March 19, 1999, she received the Artist's Achievement Award of the Governor's Awards in 1999.

K.C. Douglas
Born Nov. 21, 1913, in Sharon, Miss., he transplanted himself to California in 1945. His first album was titled *K. C. Douglas, A Dead Beat Guitar and the Mississippi Blues*. A song he wrote, *Mercury Boogie*, was redone by the Steve Miller Band. He died of a heart attack on Oct. 18, 1975, in Berkeley, Calif.

Steve Douglas
Born in Greenville Feb. 17, 1951, his family moved to Silsbee, Texas in 1964 when he was 13 years old. A sax player from a young age, Douglas has appeared on many rock albums by big-name artists starting back in the early 1960's. He has played the sax (and sometimes flute) on albums by artists such as Jan and Dean, Dion, The Letterman, Leon Russell, Bette Midler, Elvis Presley, and several by Bob Dylan. His own debut country album, *This Is True* (1980), was a hit. He's also recorded the albums *Hot Sax*, *Beyond Broadway*, *My Kind of Music*, *Music of Cheops*, and *Twist*. Douglas has also worked as arranger and producer on many albums.

Mary Angie Douglass
Born on Mar. 26, 1908, in X-Prairie, Noxubee Co., Miss. She graduated from Mississippi State College for Women (now Miss. Univ. for Women) in 1931. She was on the secretarial staff of FBI Director J. Edgar Hoover in Washington, D.C. Douglass died in Macon, Miss. on June 9, 1981, at age 73.

Peggy Dow
Born Peggy Josephine Varnadow on March 18, 1928, in Columbia, Miss. Her family moved to Covington, Louisiana right before Peggy became a teenager. The blonde actress was signed by Universal Pictures in 1949, and the studio condensed her name down to Peggy Dow. Her first movie was

Profiles of Famous & Notable Mississippians

Woman in Hiding (1949). Dow was good in the female-lead role with James (Jimmy) Stewart in *Harvey* (1950), and even better as the steadfast girlfriend of blind veteran Arthur Kennedy in *I Want You* (1951). After her ninth movie, *Bright Victory* (1951), Dow ended her burgeoning film career when she married wealthy Oklahoma oil man Walter Helmerich III. She and her family now live in Tulsa.

Bill Dunlap
Born Jan. 21, 1944, in Mathiston, Webster County, Mississippi, he gained national attention in 1985 when his huge 112-foot narrative painting on 14 canvases titled *Corcoran Panorama* hung in the rotunda of the Corcoran Gallery in Washington. His second solo exhibit, *In the Spirit of the Land*, was on display at the Corcoran Gallery and New Orleans Center for Contemporary Art. This mixed-media selection consisted of 16 constructions and paintings combining elements of painting, sculpture & assemblage with a national historical theme. He received the 1998 Mississippi Institute of Arts and Letters award in the visual arts category for *In the Spirit of the Land*. Dunlap now lives in McLean, Va., but still maintains a studio in his hometown of Mathiston, where he works frequently.

Marcus Dupree
Born May 22, 1964. From 1978-81, this 220-pound running back scored a high school state-record 87 touchdowns at his hometown of Philadelphia, Mississippi, where he also had 5,283 rushing yards. His senior year, he was the nation's top recruit and went on to star at Oklahoma. At 19, he turned pro when he signed with the USFL Breakers in 1984, where he played in 15 games, running 145 times for 684 yards and 9 TDs. A major knee injury limited him to just 17 carries for 69 yards and a TD in 1985. After knee surgery, he played briefly with the NFL's L.A. Rams in 1990-91. Dupree's 87 TD high school state record was broken on Oct. 14, 1994 by Gary "Turk" McGill of Taylorsville who scored 3 times to take his high school total to 88 touchdowns.

Buddy Durr
Born on Sept. 15, 1956, in Isola, Mississippi, he is a former All-State punter at Delta State. After trying to make it in pro football in the NFL at Dallas and Washington with no success, he later turned to archery. In competition at Valdosta, Ga., Durr won the titles of 1994 Archery Shooters Association World Champion and Shooter of the Year in the Men's Limited Division. It was his first year of national competition.

John Dye
Born John Carroll Dye on Jan. 31, 1963, in Amory, Miss. When he was in junior high, he wanted to be an architect. When he graduated from Tupelo High School and started to college, he wanted to be a Civil Rights attorney. John received "Best Actor" awards from Mississippi State before transferring his sophomore year to the University of Memphis (then Memphis State University). He landed his first film role in *Makin' The Grade* in 1984 while still attending Memphis State. John really got his first big break with Taco Bell commercials — he was the one with toy chickens stuck all over his jacket. He also did the music video *Sleeping Bag* with ZZ Top. His TV roles have been in CBS' *Tour of Duty* (as "Doc Hock"), ABC's *Jack's Place*, and he is currently "Andrew, the Angel of Death" on the CBS drama *Touched By An Angel* and he also appears on the spin-off *Promised Land*.

Charles W. Eagles
Born Sept. 22, 1946, in Spartanburg, S.C. He received his B.A. from Presbyterian College, and his M.A. and Ph.D. from the University of North Carolina. He has taught at North Carolina State University (1977-80), Southeast Missouri State University (1980-82), and Vanderbilt University (1982-83). A history professor at the University of Mississippi since 1983, Dr. Eagles won the 1993 Lilian Smith Award in non-fiction for *Outside Agitator: Jon Daniels and the Civil Rights Movement in Alabama*. His other books include *Jonathan Daniels and Race Relations: The Evolution of a Southern Liberal* (1982), *The Civil Rights Movement in America* (1986), *Democracy Delayed: Congressional Reapportionment and the Urban-Rural Conflict in the 1920s* (1990), *"The Mind of the South" After Fifty Years* (1992), and *Is There a Southern Political Tradition?* (1996). Some of his many articles, essays and reviews have appeared in publications such as *The Historian, Journal of American History* and *The New York Times*. Eagles has been a contributor to several encyclopedias, including the *Encyclopedia of Southern Culture* (1989), which was co-edited by Mississippian William Ferris (see profile).

B. Reeves Eason
Born Oct. 2, 1886, in Friars Point, Mississippi. He left the produce business and broke into films as a journeyman actor in stock and vaudeville. Eason became one of the earliest movie directors. He got his first chance to yell "Action!" through a megaphone in 1913 while working for the Amercian Film Company. He earned the nickname "Breezy" because he liked to shoot his films fast and rush them out for release. Quite prolific, he's listed as Director on 101 movies starting with *The Spirit of Adventure* in 1915 to *Rimfire* in 1949. Eason is also writer on 9 films, actor in 2 films, producer in one, composer in one, and as second unit director in 12 films, including *Charge of the Light Brigade* (1936). That picture landed Eason in trouble with the ASPCA after his climatic scene resulted in the deaths of several horses. Although most of his movies were westerns and serials, he was involved with the original classic *Ben-Hur* (1926). Although the director of the film was officially credited to Fred Niblo, it was Eason, listed as associate director and second unit director, who handled the film's chariot-race centerpiece! Eason was also the second-unit director (uncredited) responsible for the burning of Atlanta sequence in the smash movie *Gone With the Wind* (1939). He continued to helm second-echelon actioners and serials until his retirement in 1950. Eason died of a heart attack on June 9, 1956, in Sherman Oaks, California at age 69.

James O. Eastland
James Oliver Eastland was born on Nov. 28, 1904, in Doddsville, Sunflower County, Mississippi, he moved with his parents to Forest, Scott County, Mississippi, in 1905. He attended the public schools, the University of Mississippi at Oxford, Vanderbilt University in Nashville, Tennessee, and the University of Alabama at Tuscaloosa. Eastland studied law, was admitted to the bar in 1927 and started his practice in Forest. He was a member of the Mississippi House of Representatives from 1928-32. He moved to Ruleville, Mississippi, in 1934. Eastland was appointed as a Democrat to the U.S. Senate to fill the vacancy caused by the death of Pat Harrison in 1941. He was not a candidate in the special election, which was won by Wall Doxey, a member of the House since 1929. In 1942, Eastland defeated Doxey in the race for a full term in the U.S. Senate. A leader in agriculture and national security, he was also known as an untiring opponent of Civil Rights legislation. He was chairman of the powerful Senate Judiciary Committee in the 84th through the 95th Congresses (1956-78). He served as President pro tempore of the Senate during the 92nd through the 95th Congresses until his retirement in 1978. As president pro temp

of the Senate in the early 1970s, he became acting vice president twice, after the resignations of vice presidents Spiro Agnew and Gerald Ford. Thus, Eastland held the highest national office ever held by a Mississippian. Eastland served six terms in the Senate from 1943-78, or 36 years, before choosing not to seek reelection in 1978. Eastland's colleague in the Senate for most of his tenure was John Stennis. In fact, Eastland and Stennis represented Mississippi concurrently in the Senate for 31 years, the longest period of simultaneous service of any state in the Union. Eastland died in Doddsville, Mississippi, on Feb. 19, 1986. He is buried in Forest Cemetery in Forest, Miss. Thad Cochran won his senate seat.

Bernie Ebbers

Born Bernard J. Ebbers on Aug. 27, 1941, in Canada, he first came to Mississippi to play basketball at Mississippi College, where he received his B.A. in 1967. In 1985, he was recruited to help then-financially failing LDDS recover. The company went public four years later and Ebbers became president and CEO. The firm changed its name to WorldCom in 1995. It bought Omaha-based MFS Communications Co. in 1996 for over $12 billion, the 5fth-largest business merger in history at the time. After the merger, WorldCom became the nation's 4th largest long-distance company and Mississippi's only state-based Fortune 500 company, first entering the rankings in 1995 at No. 498. It moved up to number 309 in 1996, then soared up 99 points to No. 210 for 1997 after announcing plans to merge with MCI. The $37 billion merger, the largest in history at the time, was completed on Sept. 14, 1998. The company moved up to position No. 25 on the Fortune 500 list for 1999, up from No. 80 in 1998. MCI WorldCom announced on May 28, 1999, a $1.3 billion stock-trade deal to acquire SkyTel. The Jackson-based paging company operates as a separate subsidiary. After having made more than sixty acquisitions in a decade, MCI WorldCom announced on Oct. 5, 1999, that it was seeking to acquire Sprint, the nation's third largest U.S. long-distance phone company. The deal was valued at $115 billion, the largest merger in U.S. history at the time. On July 13, 2000, WorldCom and Sprint jointly announced that the deal was off after European regulators and the FCC said they would block the merger. WorldCom showed 1998 revenues of $17.678 billion and earnings of $1.2 billion. Earnings grew an estimated 194%, to $3.8 billion, in 1999. Earnings were nearly $1.3 billion on about $10 billion in sales for the first quarter of 2000, up from $712 million in earnings on $8.7 billion in sales for the first quarter of 1999. During the 2nd quarter of 2000, WorldCom's revenues were $10.2 billion, up 12.4 percent from the 2nd quarter of 1999. Third quarter earnings were almost $1.4 billion on sales of $10.4 billion. *Forbes* reported Ebbers' total compensation (salary, bonuses and stock) was $8.5 million in 1999, a 5 percent increase over the $8.1 million he received in 1998. Ebbers ranked No. 1 among 37 executives in the telecommunications industry and among the 800 other executives in *Forbes' Most Powerful People Annual Directory* of 1999. According to *Forbes* magazine's 1999 list of "400 Richest Americans," Ebbers ranked as the 251st richest person in the country with his net worth of $1.4 billion, more than double his reported wealth of $690 million in 1998. Ebbers was the state's first and only billionaire! Because of declining stock prices, Ebber's net worth dropped to $780 million in 2000, which put him in the 368th position of *Forbes* list released in Sept. 2000. MCI WorldCom has been recognized by *Forbes, Fortune, Business Week* and *Financial World* magazines for its rapid growth and stock performance. *Business Week* named MCI WorldCom the 14th largest company in the world in its July 6, 1999, issue. The ranking, based on the company's market cap of $152 billion, was up 57 slots from the 1998 position of 71. Previously, *Financial World* listed Ebbers among 16 outstanding CEOs, and he was selected as one of *Business Week*'s 25 Top Managers. In 1992, Ebbers received the Alumnus of the Year award from Mississippi College and the school granted him an honorary Doctor of Law degree. He's also in the Mississippi Business Hall of Fame. In 1998, the Metro-Jackson Chamber of Commerce presented the Business of the Year Award to MCI WorldCom. The company relocated its headquarters from Jackson to nearby Clinton, in 1998.

Brad Edwards

Born June 10, 1971, in Jackson, Miss., he was a 4-sport athlete at Jackson Academy. A 1994 University of Alabama graduate, his resume includes a stint in sports information at Alabama as well as jobs with the NFL's Indianapolis Colts, U.S. Olympic Committee and the now-defunct Birmingham Barracudas of the CFL. Since 1996, he's been the top statistical researcher for ESPN, the TV cable sports network operating out of Bristol, Conn. During the week, Edwards compiles information packages for use on as many as seven games to be televised by ESPN. He's also in charge of producing graphics for the network's football halftime and scoreboard shows.

David "Honeyboy" Edwards

Born David Edwards on June 28, 1915, in Shaw, Miss., this blues guitarist was a staple on the Delta Blues circuit. His childhood pals included Tommy McClennan and Robert Petway and he later worked with Rice Miller, Elmore James and many other early blues legends. He impressed Big Joe Williams enough to take him under his wing. Rambling around the South, Honeyboy experienced Charley Patton and played often with Robert Johnson. Musicologist Alan Lomax went to Clarksdale in 1942 and captured Edwards on tape for the Library of Congress. In 1951 he cut a 78 for Artist Record Co., *Build a Cave* (as Mr. Honey), and four 1953 sides for Chess that laid unissued until *Drop Down Mama* turned up 17 years later on an anthology. Edwards was in Chicago from the mid-1950s on. The guitarist met young harpist and blues aficionado Michael Frank in 1972. Four years later, they formed the Honeyboy Edwards Blues Band. When Frank inaugurated his Earwig label, he enlisted Honeyboy and long-time pals Sunnyland Slim, Big Walter Horton, Floyd Jones, and Kansas City Red to cut an album, *Old Friends* (1979). His album, *Delta Bluesman* ('92), is mixed with some of Edwards' Library of Congress masters and recent performances.

Jim Edwards

Born James Corbette Edwards on Dec. 14, 1894, in Banner, Calhoun Co., Miss. His nickname was "Little Joe." The 6-2, 185-pound Edwards made his major league baseball debut on May 14, 1922, with Cleveland. He pitched for the Indians until 1925, then pitched for the Chicago White Sox (1925-26) and the Cincinnati Reds in 1928. He pitched in 145 games (including 23 complete games) with 26 wins and 37 losses for a 4.37 ERA and he pitched 6 shutouts. Edwards died on Jan. 19, 1965, in Sarepta, Calhoun Co., Miss. He was inducted into the Mississippi Sports Hall of Fame the next year, 1966.

Theodore "Teddy" Edwards

Born Theodore Marcus Edwards in Jackson, Miss. on Apr. 26, 1924. He played his first professional job at age 12. He moved to Detroit, then to Los Angeles in 1944 where he became known as an outstanding innovator of bebop and a brilliant improviser and arranger. He switched from alto to tenor sax when he worked with Howard McGhee in the 1940s. He

Profiles of Famous & Notable Mississippians

performed in Europe and Japan and appeared with such greats as Hank Jones, Ernie Fields, Roy Milton, Charley Parker, Benny Carter and Gerald Wilson. His records include *Around the Clock* with Wyonnie Harris and *Up in Dodo's Room* with Howard McGee. He's been a band leader since 1958.

Marietta Eichelberger

Born on Aug. 20, 1891 in Macon, Noxubee County, Miss. She graduated from Industrial Institute and College in 1912. She also taught some at that school in Columbus. Head of nutrition research for the Evaporated Milk Institute of America in Chicago for many years, it was largely through Dr. Eichelberger's research that the canning of milk and safe baby formulae was perfected. She died during February 1982.

Tellis "T.B." Ellis

Tellis B. Ellis was born on May 26, 1912, in Vicksburg, his family moved to Jackson at an early age. He graduated from the high school department of Jackson State College, then received his bachelor's degree from Moorhead College and was a letterman in basketball and football at both schools. He received his master's in education from Boston University, where he also held a doctoral teaching fellowship. He also studied at the University of Southern Mississippi. Ellis served in the U.S. Army Air Force during WWII. He served as head coach for basketball and football at Jackson State University, where he was chairman of the department of health and physical education and was also associate professor. In 1946, he was appointed athletic director and served in that position until his retirement in 1977. His many honors include Coach of the Year for the South Central Athletic Conference, the NCAA Centennial Football Award, and the American Football Foundation General Robert R. Nyland Lifetime Achievement Award. Ellis received special commendations from the Mississippi legislature and the Mississippi Association of Health, Physical Education and Recreation. He was inducted into the Association of Collegiate Directors Hall of Fame, the Southwestern Athletic Conference Hall of Fame and the Jackson State University Hall of Fame. Ellis had a great ability to hire successful coaches, including football's Bob Hill and W.C. Gordon and men's basketball coach Paul Covington. He developed a practice schedule and a game-day schedule that many coaches follow today. Ellis, called "the father of Jackson State athletics," died at his home on March 15, 2000, at age 87 and is buried in the Garden Memorial Cemetery in Jackson.

Tim Ellis

Born on May 10, 1956, in Louisville, Miss. On Sept. 17, 1977, Ole Miss was playing 3rd-ranked Notre Dame. Backup quarterback Ellis, who had been sidelined all season, thrilled a Memorial Stadium crowd of 48,200 by leading a game-winning drive in the final minutes of the game. Tapped to play with less than 5 minutes left and Ole Miss down 13-10, Ellis first threw a 50-yard pass to tight end L.Q. Smith. Then, a 13-yard run by James Storey set up Ellis' 10-yard TD pass to Storey to win the game for the Rebels 20-13. In a 1994 poll of readers by *The Clarion-Ledger*, this game was rated as Mississippi's No. 1 greatest college football game ever!

E. B. "Buddy" Elrod

Born Erwin Brice Elrod on Oct. 28, 1918, in Sherman, Texas. He played football at Mississippi State University and was the first player there to be named to the All-American team. He didn't graduate, instead leaving Mississippi State in 1941 to join the U.S. Air Force. Elrod was the base commander at Los Alamos AFB in New Mexico and Tinker AFB in Oklahoma. He was a prisoner of war for 11 months during World War II. He also served in the Korean War and the Vietnam War. Elrod retired from service with the rank of colonel. He was inducted into the Mississippi State University Sports Hall of Fame in 1971 and into the Mississippi Sports Hall of Fame in 1975. Elrod died in Olathe, Kansas on June 13, 1998, at age 79.

Ward Emling

Born Jan. 21, 1954, in New Orleans, his family moved to Jackson in 1964 when he was 10 years old. He graduated from Murrah High School in 1972 and from Millsaps College cum laude with a degree in English in 1976. Appearing in more than a dozen stage productions at Millsaps, he won several awards for his acting. His first experience with Hollywood filmmaking came in 1973 with the feature film *Huckleberry Finn*, which was shot in Natchez, Mississippi. Emling was an extra and a wardrobe assistant. It was his summer job after his first year at Millsaps. After graduating from Millsaps, Emling studied at the select British drama school, Guildhall School of Music and Drama in London, from 1977 to 1979. Several years later, the head of the Mississippi Film Office (MFO) remembered Emling's film work and called him to fill a three-month position. Soon promoted to director, he ended up staying from 1980 to 1983. The MFO, established in 1973, is in the Division of Tourism, itself within the Department of Economic and Community Development. When CBS-TV renewed the series *The Mississippi*, Emling left to become its location manager. From 1983 to 1990, he pursued acting in Los Angeles, appearing in the TV series *St. Elsewhere*, *Knot's Landing*, *Matlock*, *Our House*, and the miniseries *Beulah Land* among others. He also did production, location work and some acting on feature films such as *D.A.R.Y.L.*, *Problem Child*, *K-9*, and *The Premonition* (filmed in Miss.). He returned to the MFO as director in 1990. During his tenure, several big movies have been filmed in Mississippi, contributing greatly to the state's economy. In 1995 and 1996 alone, three movies — *A Time to Kill*, *The Chamber* and *The Ghosts of Mississippi* — brought in about $12 million to the state. On *A Time to Kill*, filmed in Canton, almost $2 million was paid out in salaries to many Mississippians who worked as security guards, crew and extras. Emling was recently elected president of the Association of Film Commissioners International, a 23-country, 268-member organization of film commissions.

John O. Emmerich, Jr.

Born in McComb, Miss. Apr. 16, 1929, the son of the late John Oliver Emmerich, Sr., who published the *Enterprise Journal* for 55 years, and was nationally known for his moderate editorial stands during the Civil Rights struggles of the 1960s. John, Jr. worked for the *Minneapolis Tribune*, the *Baltimore Sun* and the *Houston Cronicle*. Emmerich served 9 years on The Associated Press board, including one as vice chairman. He was a past president of the Mississippi Press Association, Louisiana-Mississippi AP Editors and chaired the Southern Newspaper Publishers Association Foundation. As president of Emmerich Enterprises, he published 12 daily and weekly newspapers in Mississippi and one in Louisiana. His Mississippi papers included the dailies *The Greenwood Commonwealth*, the McComb *Enterprise Journal*, and the *Clarksdale Press Register*, plus the bi-weekly *The Yazoo Herald* and weeklies in Carrollton, Charleston, Columbia, Indianola, Jackson, Magee, Mendenhall and Winona. He was Mississippi's first and only publisher of a chain of newspapers located in the state. He died from a heart attack on Feb. 25, 1995, collapsing outside his Greenwood home after a morning jog. Emmerich was inducted into the Mississippi Press Association's Hall of Fame on June 22, 1996.

Profiles of Famous & Notable Mississippians

Lehman Engel
Born Sept. 14, 1910, in Jackson. In a music career that spanned more than 5 decades, he worked with Aaron Copland, Leonard Bernstein, John Gielgud, Lillian Gish, Rosalind Russell, Mary Martin, Bing Crosby, Nelson Eddy, Liza Minelli, Barbara Streisand, Tennesee Williams, Pearl Bailey and many others. He won 3 Tonys and conducted over 150 musicals including *Li'l Abner*, *Call Me Mister*, and *Wonderful Town*, as well as operas, symphonies and ballets. Engel conducted over 50 recordings of shows for top labels such as RCA, Decca, and Columbia and was guest conductor of the Boston Symphony and St. Louis Opera. He also wrote books on music: *Words with Music* ('71), *Getting Started in the Theatre* ('73), and *The Making of the Musical* ('77). He died on Aug. 29, 1982. Engel was one of the first 27 inducted into the inaugural Miss. Musicians Hall of Fame on April 1, 2000.

Mike Espy
Born Albert Michael Espy on Nov. 30, 1953, in Yazoo City, Miss. He received his B.A. from Howard University in Washington, D.C., in 1975 and his J.D. from the University of Santa Clara Law School, California, in 1978. He worked as assistant secretary of state, chief, Mississippi Legal Services, 1978-1980, assistant secretary of Public Lands Division, 1980-1984 and assistant State attorney general, 1984-1985. Elected to Congress from the 2nd district in Nov. 1986, he was the first black congressman from Mississippi since reconstruction. Espy won re-election in 1988, 1990 and 1992. He served on the House Budget Committee, House Agriculture Committee, and was vice chairman of the Democratic Leadership Council. President Clinton appointed him Secretary of Agriculture on Dec. 24, 1992. He was the only cabinet member from Mississippi in the 20th Century and only the 5th cabinet member ever from the state. Espy was the first black, the first Southerner and the youngest person to ever serve as secretary of agriculture, overseeing a department with 115,000 employees with a budget of over $60 billion. In a move to streamline the department, he closed 1,300 offices, eliminated 7,000 jobs and merged 14 departments of agriculture. On Oct. 3, 1994, Espy announced he was resigning amid a scandal and federal investigation of him for allegedly taking gifts from companies his department regulated. Espy joined a Jackson law firm at the start of 1996. After federal prosecutor Donald Smaltz spent about $20 million during a 4-year investigation, on Dec. 2, 1998, a jury in Washington acquitted Espy of all 30 counts brought against him. On Feb. 16, 1999, Espy was listed "of counsel" in the Jackson office of Butler, Snow, O'Mara, Stevens & Cannada, Mississippi's largest law firm. It was announced in March 1999 that Espy had accepted a nonpaying position as a senior advisor for the U.S. Department of Energy.

Kevin Etheridge
Born Sept 21, 1975, in Flowood, Miss. He attended Natchez High through the 10th grade, then transferred to the Mississippi School for Mathematics and Science where he graduated in 1994. In April 1994, he scored a perfect 36 on the ACT (American College Test). When Etheridge enrolled as a freshman, he was the first student ever at Mississippi State to have a perfect ACT score. He was the first of only twelve Mississippi students to ever make 36 ACT scores (through June 2000), according to ACT headquarters in Iowa. Graduating with a B.S. in mechanical engineering from Mississippi State in 1998, he's now employed with Howard Industries in Laurel, Mississippi.

Betty Everett
Born on Nov. 23, 1939, in Greenwood, Miss. She sang gospel growing up in Greenwood before relocating to Chicago in 1957 and moving into secular music. She began recording for Cobra in 1958, then joined Vee-Jay in the early 1960s. Her original version of *You're No Good* didn't make much impact until it was turned into a No. 1 pop hit by Linda Ronstadt in 1975. Everett's next single was her one big Top-10 hit *The Shoop Shoop Song (It's In His Kiss)* (#6 in '64). She then had a big Top-5 hit record with Jerry Butler (also from Miss.) *Let It Be Me* (#5 in '64), the former Everly Brothers hit of the 1950s. Everett's song, *There Comes a Time* ('69), reached No. 2 on the R&B charts and also cracked the pop Top 30 at No. 26. Everett also hit the R&B charts in 1969 with *I Can't Say No To You* and *It's Been A Long Time*. She charted R&B in 1971 with *I Got To Tell Somebody* and *Ain't Nothing Gonna Change Me*. Everett quit the music business in 1980.

John Daniel "J.D." Evermore
He was born Johnny Moore on No. 5, 1968, in Leland, Mississippi and grew up in Greenville, Jackson and on the coast around Gulfport. He adopted the screen name "J.D. Evermore" because his real name is so common. Starting in 1990, he studied theater at the University of Southern Mississippi, but left before getting his degree to take the male lead in a theater production in Los Angeles. After some time and only a few bit parts, he left L.A. to live in Austin, Texas. There, he landed a few parts, including three episodes of the TV series *Walker, Texas Ranger* playing bad guys in each. Evermore plays a police officer in the *Kraft Premier Movie: Picnic*, which stars Josh Brolin and Mary Steenburgen and aired on CBS on April 16, 2000. The made-for-TV movie is a remake of the 1955 movie that starred William Holden and Kim Novak. In another TV movie, *Hell Swarm* (2000), a thriller about a swarm of killer bees, he played an undercover cop whose body was taken over by an alien. In theatrical films, Evermore plays a hospital orderly in *Where the Heart Is* (2000), a movie that stars Ashley Judd, Stockard Channing and Sally Field. Evermore has also written a screenplay, *If Only Eden*, scheduled for shooting sometime in 2001. Evermore moved back to Los Angeles in the spring of 2000.

Charles Evers
Born Sept. 11, 1922, in Decatur, Miss. He replaced his slain brother, Medgar, as field secretary of the NAACP in 1963. He helped avert a student riot at Jackson State College in 1964 and co-leader of the biracial Loyal Democrat coalition that unseated the all-white Mississippi delegation to 1968 at the Democratic National Convention. Elected mayor of Fayette, Miss. in 1969, he was the first black mayor of a biracial town in the South since Reconstruction. He was the first black candidate for governor in 1971. His autobiography is *Have No Fear: A Black Man's Fight for Respect in America* (1997).

Medgar Evers
This Civil Rights leader was born Medgar Wiley Evers on July 2, 1925, in Decatur, Miss. He was inducted into the army in 1943, serving in Normandy. After the war, he attended Alcorn College (now Alcorn State University), majoring in business administration. While at Alcorn, he was a member of the debate team, the college choir, and the football and track teams, editor of the campus newspaper for two years and the annual for one year. He was listed in *Who's Who in American Colleges*. At Alcorn he met Myrlie Beasley, of Vicksburg, and they were married on Dec. 24, 1951. He received his B.A. degree the next semester and they moved to Mound Bayou, during which time Evers began to establish local chapters of

Profiles of Famous & Notable Mississippians

the NAACP throughout the Delta. Evers was the first known black applicant to the Ole Miss law school in 1952. Denied admission, Evers and his wife moved to Jackson, where they set up an NAACP office, and he began investigating violent crimes committed against blacks. His boycott of Jackson merchants in the early 1960s attracted national attention, and his efforts to have James Meredith admitted to the University of Mississippi in 1962 brought federal help. Meredith was admitted to Ole Miss, a major step in securing Civil Rights in the state, but a riot on campus left two people dead, and Evers' involvement increased the hatred many people felt toward him. He was field secretary for the NAACP when he was shot from ambush — murdered at his home in Jackson on June 12, 1963. He is buried in Section 36 of Arlington National Cemetery. After three trials, Byron De La Beckwith was convicted for his murder on Feb. 5, 1994. Evers was awarded the Springarn Medal, the highest honor given by the NAACP. When Evers died in 1963, only 28,000 blacks were registered voters. By 1971, there were 250,000 and by 1982 over 500,000. In May 1999, the Jackson City Council voted unanimously to create a legal holiday in his honor. Medgar Wiley Evers Day will coincide with the 4th of July holiday.

Myrlie Evers-Williams

The widow of slain Civil Rights leader Medgar Evers was born Myrlie Beasley on March 17, 1933, in Vicksburg. She met Evers when they were both attending Alcorn College (now Alcorn State University). After Medgar was murdered, she moved to California, ran for a seat in Congress in 1970, but lost, and was then appointed as a public works commissioner for Los Angeles. In 1987, she finished third in a 12-way race for a seat on the Los Angeles City Council. She was overjoyed when Byron De La Beckwith, the avowed white supremacist accused for the murder of Medgar, was finally convicted in his third trial on Feb. 5, 1994. A little over a year later on Feb. 18, 1995, in a close vote of 30-29, Myrlie became the first Mississippian and the first women elected to chair the national NAACP board. Her husband of 18 years, Walter Williams, died of cancer just four days later. Evers did not seek a fourth one-year term as head of the NAACP and stepped down in Jan. 1999. Whoopi Goldberg plays Myrlie in *The Ghosts of Mississippi* (1996), a movie about the 1993-94 trial of Byron De La Beckwith that was filmed in Jackson. Her book, *For Us, The Living* (1967), was re-released in paperback in late 1996. On July 16, 1998, Evers-Williams was awarded the Springarn Medal by the NAACP. It was the first time the medal had gone to two members of the same family (it was awarded years earlier to Medgar). Her autobiography, *Watch Me Fly: What I Learned on the Way to Becoming the Woman I Was Meant to Be*, was published in 1999.

Terry Ewert

He was born on May 9, 1951. His dad was in the military and he was born in Las Vegas, but grew up in Jackson from age six. He graduated from Murrah High School in 1969 and from Ole Miss in 1973. Ewert is now executive producer of CBS-TV Sports where he coordinates and manages such events as NCAA Tournaments, NASCAR car races and the Masters Golf Classic. He was head of production for Atlanta Olympic Broadcasting, NBC's coordinating producer for Olympics Cable in Barcelona and the 1988 Seoul Olympics.

Robert Fairley

Born July 18, 1976, in Lucedale, Miss. At George County High School in Lucedale, Fairley earned All-County and All-State as his team's top scorer and rebounder. Fairley averaged 12 points, 7 rebounds, and 4 blocks as a junior and 19 points, 12 rebounds, and 7 blocks as a senior. The 6-10 forward helped Jackson State capture the SWAC title and advance to the NCAA Tournament for the first time in the school's history. Fairley earned first team All-SWAC honors and Most Improved Player while at JSU. He started 54 of 57 games for the Tigers and averaged 9.8 points and 5.0 rebounds per game as a senior. Fairley is a former member of the Harlem Globetrotters, signing with them in 1999.

Julie Kaye Fanton

Born May 14, 1958, in Oxford, Miss. She earned her degree in theater arts in 1979 at Ole Miss. Fanton has lived in Los Angeles since 1979 where she was set decorator for the ABC-TV sitcom, *Sabrina, The Teenage Witch*. She received a 1998 Emmy nomination as set decorator for the TV special, *Rodgers and Hammerstein's Cinderella*, which aired on ABC's *Wonderful World of Disney* in Nov. 1997. She has also worked on other TV series, several made-for-TV movies, as well as major feature films including *Darkman* (1990) and *The Mightly Duck*s (1992). Fanton serves as lay minister at the Prince of Peace Episcopal Church in Los Angeles.

Jamaa Fanaka

Born Walter Gordon on Sept. 6, 1942, in Jackson, Miss., he is a movie director, producer and writer. He directed *Street Wars* (1972), *Soul Vengeance* (1975), *Emma Mae* (1976), and *Penitentiary I, II, & III* (1979, 1982 & 1987).

John Faulkner

Younger brother of William, he was born John Wesley Thompson Falkner, III (after his grandfather) on Sept. 24, 1901, in Ripley and spent most of his life in Oxford, Mississippi. He received a B.A. from Ole Miss. He worked with the State Highway Dept., was a pilot for Mid-South Airways, and was a farmer, painter, lecturer and writer. His novels include *Men Working* (1941), *Dollar Cotton* (1942), *Chooky* (1950), *Cabin Road* (1951), *Ain't Gonna Rain No More* (1959), and *Uncle Good's Weekend Party* (1960). He died on March 28, 1963, just 9 months after William died.

William Faulkner

Born William Cuthbert Falkner (he added the 'u') on Sept. 25, 1897, in New Albany and raised in nearby Oxford as the oldest of four sons of an old-line southern family. He dropped out of high school to work in his grandfather's bank in 1915. Claiming to be an Englishman, he lied in order to join the Royal Canadian Air Force when he was 20 years old. However, he didn't see combat action, as he had wanted, because World War I ended before he finished his training as a fighter pilot. Back in Oxford, he was admitted to Ole Miss as a veteran, but soon quit to write, supporting himself with odd jobs. His first book, *The Marble Faun*, a collection of poems, was privately printed in 1924. The next year he moved to New Orleans and worked as a journalist. Although his books received favorable reviews, only one, *Sanctuary*, sold well. In 1946 the critic Malcolm Cowley put together *The Portable Faulkner*, arranging extracts from Faulkner's novels into chronological sequence. Many of Faulkner's works, long out of print, began to be reissued, and his national popularity soared. He was awarded the Nobel Prize for Literature in 1949 and received Pulitzer Prizes for Fiction in 1955 for *A Fable* and in 1963 for *The Reivers* (made into a movie starring Steve McQueen and filmed in Mississippi). Faulkner's other works include: *Soldier's Pay* (1926), *Mosquitoes* (1927), *Sartoris* [originally *Flags in the Dust*](1929), *The Sound and the Fury* (1929) [originally *Twilight*], *As I Lay Dying* (1930), *Sanctuary* (1931), *Light in August* (1932), *Pylon* (1935), *Absalom, Absalom!* (1936), *The Unvanquished* (1938), *Wild Palms*

Profiles of Famous & Notable Mississippians

(1939), *The Hamlet* (1940), *Go Down Moses* (1942), *Intruder in the Dust* (1948, made into a movie filmed in Mississippi and released in 1949), *Knight's Gambit* (1949), *Requiem for a Nun* (1951), *The Town* (1957), and *The Mansion* (1959). His short fiction appears in *Collected Stories* (1950) and *Uncollected Stories* (1979). He worked on the screenplays of over two dozen movies including screen adaptations of several of his own novels and several Howard Hawks films. In addition to some of his own novels, he was screenwriter for the films *Today We Live* (1933), *Road to Glory* (1936), *Slave Ship* (1937), *Four Men and a Prayer* (1938, uncredited), *Drums Along the Mohawk* (1939, uncredited), *To Have and Have Not* (1944), *The Southerner* (1945, uncredited), *God Is My Co-Pilot* (1945, uncredited), *Mildred Pierce* (1945, uncredited — listed on the National Film Registry in the Library of Congress), *The Big Sleep* (1946), *Deep Valley* (1947, uncredited), *Adventures of Don Juan* (1948, uncredited), and *Land of the Pharaohs* (1955). In his novels, Faulkner created his own mythical county and called it Yoknapatawpha and named the capital of it Jefferson. You'll easily recognize the county as Lafayette County and the capital of Jefferson as Oxford. Faulkner was one of three Mississippi writers, along with Eudora Welty and Richard Wright, featured at Atlanta's Olympic Games in July 1996 in a special literary exhibition of nine Southern writers called *The American South: Past, Present and Future*. They are the only three Mississippians to have won the coveted Pulitzer Prize for fiction, Faulkner being the first. Three of Faulkner's novels are on the "100 Best Novels of the Century" compiled in 1998 by the editorial board of Modern Library, a division of Random House — *The Sound and the Fury* (No. 6), *As I Lay Dying* (No. 35), and *Light in August* (No. 54). At the end of 1999, World on the Web published a list of "The Century's Top 100 Books" with the books given no particular ranking. Faulkner's *The Collected Stories* (1950) was on the list. In a 1999 special millennium poll by *The Clarion-Ledger* of Jackson, readers picked Faulkner as their No. 1 all-time favorite fiction writer from Mississippi. In her 4-volume anthology, *Mississippi Writers: Reflections of Childhood and Youth*, editor Dorothy Abbott said of Faulkner, "He is considered by many critics to be the finest writer America has produced and one of the finest writers in the English language." Faulkner died from a thrombosis on July 6, 1962, in Byhalia, Miss. He is buried in Saint Peter's Cemetery in Oxford. A life-size statue of Faulkner, sculpted by Mississippi artist William Beckwith (see his profile), was unveiled in Oxford on Sept. 25, 1997, the 100th anniversary of Faulkner's birth.

Brett Favre

Born Brett Lorenzo Favre on Oct. 10, 1969, at Pass Christian, Mississippi, he grew up in another coastal community, the town of Kiln (pronounced "Kill"). A University of Southern Mississippi star, he played in the one of the all-time great Mississippi college games in 1989 when he led the Golden Eagles to a 30-26 upset of the sixth-ranked Florida State Seminoles at Jacksonville. Favre passed for 282 yards and 2 TDs. He started his Pro-football career with the Green Bay Packers in 1992. Favre went from 18 interceptions in '192 to 24 in 1993. He led the league with 522 pass attempts in 1993, 51 more than he had in 1992. Favre's mistakes were offset with huge plays like 1993's 28-24 triumph over the Lions, in which he threw a perfect 48-yard crossfield touchdown pass to Sterling Sharpe with 55 seconds left that won their first-round playoff game at Detroit. He led the Packers to 9-7 records during his first two seasons as starter and went to two Pro Bowls. Favre took the Packers to the playoffs in 1993 for the first time in a non-strike year since 1972. In Green Bay's last seven games of the 1994 season, he completed 64.9 percent of his passes with 20 TDs and 6 interceptions. Favre was 363-for-582 for 3,882 yards with 33 TDs, only 14 interceptions and was ranked No. 2 in the NFC and in the league with a 90.7 rating for the 1994 season. He had an incredible 1995 season, throwing for and NFL-best 4,413 yards and 38 TDs while leading Green Bay to an 11-5 season, its first 11-victory season since 1966, and its first NFC Central title in 23 years. Favre is only the third quarterback in the 75-year history of Packer football to throw for more than 4,000 yards in a season. This followed three straight 3,000 yard-passing seasons! He holds the Packers' record for highest completion percentage (62.4%). Only Hall of Famer Bart Starr enjoyed more success. Favre was chosen 1995 NFL Offensive Player of the Year and also named the National Football League's MVP, receiving 69 of a possible 88 first-place votes from a panel of sports writers and broadcasters. He became only the third Mississippian to receive the NFL MVP honor after running back Walter Payton with the Chicago Bears in 1977 and quarterback Charley Conerly with the New York Giants in 1959. Favre led all selections with 86 votes for the 1995 Associated Press All-Pro Team. On Jan. 24, 1996, Favre was named the NFL's Player of the Year. In the Pro Bowl game at Honolulu on Feb. 4, 1996, he threw a pass to fellow Mississippian Jerry Rice that resulted in a 1-yard TD that helped the NFC to a 20-13 victory over the AFC. Favre was selected on Dec. 12, 1996 for the NFC team to play in the 1997 Pro Bowl on Feb. 2 in Honolulu. On Dec. 22, 1996, the Packers won over the Vikings 38-10 to take them to the playoffs. Favre's three touchdown passes in that game gave him 39, the most ever by an NFC quarterback, to break his own NFC record 38 he threw in 1995. During the 1996 season, he completed 325 of 543 passes for 3,899 passing yards while throwing just 13 interceptions and had a 95.8 rating, second in the league to San Francisco's Steve Young. Favre is one of only three athletes who appeared on the cover of *Sports Illustrated* three times in 1996. On Jan. 12, 1997, Favre led his team to a 30-13 win over the Carolina Panthers in the NFC championship game to take the Packers to the Super Bowl for the first time in 29 years! In Super Bowl XXXI on Jan. 26, 1997, Favre threw for 246 yards, including two long touchdown passes in Green Bay's 35-21 victory over New England! One of the TD passes was for 81 yards — a Super Bowl record! He ran, then dove into the corner of the end zone for another score. He also threw for a 2-point conversion. He threw no interceptions and the Packers had no turnovers. It was Green Bay's first Super Bowl victory in almost 30 years! Favre had told his teachers when he was a little boy, "I'm going to quarterback in the Super Bowl, and I'm gonna win." He made that promise good on Super Bowl Sunday 1997! Favre threw 2 touchdowns on Dec. 7, 1997, to become the first quarterback in NFL history to throw 30 TD passes or more in 4 consecutive seasons! In 1997, Favre led the league in TD passes with 35 (59.3%), was second in passing yards with 3,867, and had 16 interceptions. He was named the top pro male Athlete of the Year by *The Clarion-Ledger*, was selected to the AP All-Pro team for the 3rd consecutive year, and on Dec. 27, 1997, Favre earned the NFL MVP award for an unprecedented 3rd straight year. Favre helped take his team to the Super Bowl for the second consecutive year, but even though he completed 25 of 42 passes for 256 yards and 3 TDs, it was not enough as the Denver Broncos upset the Packers 31-24 in Super Bowl XXXII on Jan. 25, 1998. He finished the

Profiles of Famous & Notable Mississippians

1998 season with a league-high 4,212 yards passing and 31 TDs to become the first player ever with five 30-touchdown seasons! Farve started the 1999 season on Sept. 12 throwing 28-of-47 for 333 yards and four touchdowns in leading the Packers to a victory over Oakland 28-24. He engineered a fourth-quarter 11-play, 82-yard comeback drive that culminated with a 1-yard TD pass to Jeff Thomason. His 14 four-TD games put him 3rd on the NFL's career list behind only Dan Marino (21) & Johnny Unitas (17). Farve led the Packers to another comeback win on Sept. 26, 1999. His 23-yard TD pass with 12 seconds left gave Green Bay a 23-20 victory over the Minnesota Vikings. Former Jackson State star Corey Bradford's catch capped a 77-yard, 104-second drive led by Favre. On his 30th birthday, Oct. 10, Favre led Green Bay on his third last-minute, game-winning drive of the season. Favre hit Antonio Freeman with a 21-yard TD pass with 1:05 left as the Packers beat the Tampa Bay Buccaneers 26-23. The winning pass capped a six-play, 73-yard drive directed by Farve. It was the 16th game-winning drive and the 13th fourth-quarter comeback of his career. Other than those three comeback wins, Favre had a poor 1999 season. He threw more interceptions (23) than TD passes (22) for the first time since 1993. His quarterback rating was 74.7, ranking him 25th among the league's quarterbacks after never being lower than 10th in his career. Through the '99 seaon, Favre had 235 touchdowns more than any other QB in the 1990s and his streak of 125 consecutive regular season starts was the longest in NFL history by a QB. On July 25, 2000, the league picked Favre as second-team NFL All-Decade (1990s) Quaterback. His pro career stats through the the first 8 games of the 2000 season show 2,832 completions on 4,637 attempts with 32,867 passing yards, 245 touchdowns 150 interceptions in 137 games. He also recorded 1,481 yards and 11 TDs rushing. Favre owns 460 acres near Hattiesburg, Mississippi, where he's building a large house. In 2000 Favre was inducted into the just-established Legends Society, which honors former Southern Miss athletic greats.

Charlie Feathers
Born Charles Arthur Feathers on June 12, 1932, at Myrtle near Holly Springs, Miss. Feathers was a rockabilly singer who was an early member of the rock 'n' roll scene in Memphis in the early 1950s. He sometimes used pseudonyms such as Charlie Morgan and Jess Hooper. Feathers consistently claimed until his death that he taught Elvis Presley how to sing and helped pick songs for Elvis to record at Sun Records in Memphis. Indeed, he is the co-writer of Elvis' hit *I Forgot To Remember To Forget* (also an early Sun record for Johnny Cash). Feathers had two records of his own on the Sun label, both country honky tonkers, *I've Been Deceived* backed with *Peepin' Eyes* and *Wedding Gown of White* backed with *Defrost Your Heart*. He also recorded four records on the King label in Cincinnati, Ohio, including *One Hand Loose*. In 1973 he began to play regularly with his family band at Harpers Lounge in Memphis where he was filmed by the BBC as part of a documentary on the creators of popular music. Feathers was among the first rockabilly singers to travel to England to perform in the mid-1970s at the beginning of the rockabilly revival. In 1977, a gig at London's Rainbow Theatre drew raves from rockabilly fans. Feathers died of a stroke on Aug. 29, 1998, in Memphis at age 66. There is a excellent display of Feather's memorabilia at the Memphis Music Museum. He's a member of the Rockabilly Hall of Fame.

Robert B. Ferguson
Born on Dec. 30, 1927, in the Missouri Ozarks town of Willow Springs, where he was raised. He received his B.A. degree in Radio and TV production and the Speech Department at Washington State University in 1954. His graduate studies were at Vanderbilt University pursuing a doctorate in Anthropology. He came to the Choctaw Indian Reservation near Philadelphia, Mississippi in early 1978 to become Tribal Historian in charge of the Tribal Archives, Museum, historical publications, and head of the media production facilities. He retired from those positions in 1999. Before coming to Mississippi, he had an illustrious and varied career in the entertainment business. From 1954 to 1956, he was personal manager of country music artist Ferlin Husky. From 1956-61, he was a movie producer for the Tennessee Game & Fish Commission, writing, filming and producing outdoor films. The first series, *The World Outdoors*, received the award as Best North American Conservation TV Production for 1958. He was also a pioneer in the production of ecology education films. He remained an independent movie producer while running his Robert B. Ferguson Music and Backwoods Music publishing companies from 1961-63. From 1963-77, he was Senior Record Producer and A&R man at RCA Records in Nashville, reporting directly to the man who hired him, Vice-President Chet Adkins. Ferguson produced the records of country giants Chet Adkins, Charley Pride, Dolly Parton, Porter Wagoner, Danny Davis, Connie Smith, Dottie West, and 50+ other recording artists. RCA was the leading producer of country records in the world during Ferguson's tenure. Ferguson wrote *Wings of A Dove*, a huge hit by Ferlin Husky, which was BMI's (Broadcast Music Inc.) Outstanding Best-Selling Song in both pop and country fields in 1960 and went on to receive the "Million-Aires" Award for over one-million air plays from BMI in 1988. He also wrote *Carrol County Accident*, a hit by Porter Wagoner, which won the CMA Best Country Song of the Year in 1969, a writers award. His published writings include *So You Want To Be In Music* (1972), *Indians of the Southeast: Then and Now*, with Dr. Jesse Burt (1973), as well as articles in many books about the Choctaw and other Indian cultures. In 1979, he taught a course in Choctaw Culture History at Mississippi State as well as other courses and lectures to various community/education groups about the Choctaws, conservation and archaeological subjects. He has received many honors and awards including the Iron Eyes Cody Peace Medal in 1986.

William R. Ferris
Born Feb. 5, 1942, near Vicksburg. He received a B.A. in English from Davidson College in North Carolina, an M.A. in English from Northwestern University (Chicago), an M.A. and Ph.D. in folklore from the University of Pennsylvania, and a Doctor of Fine Arts degree from Rhodes College in 1997. Dr. Ferris taught at Jackson State 1970-72, at Yale 1972-79 and was a professor of anthropology at Ole Miss from 1979 until President Clinton nominated him to head the National Endowment for the Humanities in Washington in late 1997. he was a visiting fellow at the Stanford Humanities Center at Stanford University in Palo Alto, California in 1989 and 1990. Ferris helped found the Center for Southern Folklore, a nonprofit media center in Memphis. In 1979, he became the first director of the Center for the Study of Southern Culture at the Ole Miss. Ferris has produced many recordings and films about southern life. He called himself "The Blues Doctor" as deejay on a weekly Mississippi public radio program. Ferris is the author of over 100 publications in the fields of folklore, American literature, fiction and photography. He is author of these books: *Blues from the Delta* ('70), *Mississippi Black*

Profiles of Famous & Notable Mississippians

Folklore ('71), *Images of the South: Visits with Eudora Welty and Walker Evans* ('78), *Afro-American Folk Art and Crafts* ('78), *Local Color* ('82), and *"You Live and Learn. Then You Die and Forget It All": Ray Lum's Tales of Horses, Mules and Men* ('92). Ferris was co-editor of *The Encyclopedia of Southern Culture* ('89), a large reference work which has sold over 100,000 copies. He was a consultant for the movies *The Color Purple* ('85), *Crossroads* ('86) and *Heart of Dixie* ('89). Ferris was the only Mississippian of 5 recipients to receive the Charles Frankel Award presented by President Clinton in 1995. He was named a "Chevalier in the Order of Arts and Letters" in 1985 and an "Officer in the Order of Arts and Letters" in 1994 by the French government.

Dave "Boo" Ferriss

Born David Meadow Ferriss on Dec. 5, 1921, in Shaw, Miss. He became one of baseball's brightest young pitching stars, making his major league debut on Apr 29, 1945, with Boston. He opened his major league career with twenty-two scoreless innings — a record that still endures to this day. Ferriss won 21 games (21-10 with a 2.96 ERA) as a rookie for the Red Sox in 1945. In 1946, Ferriss had a 25-6 record, the best winning percentage of any pitcher in the league. He won 13 straight at Fenway Park in 1946, still a major league record. He contributed two solid outings to the team's World Series effort, but the Sox fell to the St. Louis Cardinals in 7 games. After suffering a shoulder injury, he won only 12 games in 1947, seven in 1948 and then pitched only briefly in 1949 and 1950. He returned to the Sox as a coach in 1955 and later served as coach at Delta State in Mississippi. Ferriss was inducted into the Mississippi Sports Hall of Fame in 1964 and the Mississippi State University Sports Hall of Fame in 1970.

Arty Finkelberg

Born Jan. 6, 1954, in Brooklyn, he grew up in the Bronx, New York City. He came to Jackson, Mississippi in 1975 as a comptroller for Continental Can, then went with Merrill Lynch in 1982. Since 1988, he's been with A.G. Edwards, where he's now senior vice president of investments, a Charter Financial Analysis and a Certified Financial Planner. The Sept. 1994 cover story of the magazine *Financial Planning on Wall Street* listed Finkelberg as one of the 100 best "new style" financial brokers in America. In 2000, he had over $130 million in assets under his management.

The Five Blind Boys

Formed in 1930s in Jackson, Mississippi. The group's origins date back to the 1930s, when Archie Brownlee (Brownley in some accounts), Joseph Ford, Lawrence Abrams, and Lloyd Woodard formed a quartet. They were students at the Piney Woods School in Rankin County. They began in the group The Cotton Blossom Singers, and did both spiritual and secular material. The quartet sang on the school grounds in 1936, then were recorded in 1937 by Alan Lomax for the Library of Congress. After graduation, they decided to become professional singers and for a time performed under dual identities — they were The Cotton Blossom Singers for popular songs and The Jackson Harmoneers for gospel. They became a quintet when Melvin Henderson joined. When Percell Perkins replaced Henderson in the mid-'40s, they became The Five Blind Boys. Perkins, who doubled as their manager, was not blind. They made their recording debut for Excelsior in 1946 and when they joined the Peacock label in 1950, The Five Blind Boys became superstars. The single *Our Father* was a Top 10 R&B hit, one of the few gospel records ever to make the *Billboard* rhythm and blues charts. The group became a prolific ensemble, recording 27 singles and five albums for Peacock through the 1960s. Brownlee died in New Orleans in 1960. Perkins left the group soon after becoming a minister. The list of replacements included Rev. Sammy Lewis, Rev. George Warren, and Tiny Powell. Roscoe Robinson took over for Brownlee, and was assisted by second lead Willmer Broadnax, who was also a masterful singer. The Five Blind Boys continued through the 1970s and '80s and even into the '90s, though Woodard died in the mid-1970s, and Lawrence Abrams passed away in 1982.

John M. Floyd

Born on Nov. 25, 1947, in Kosciusko, Mississippi, he grew up in nearby Sallis (Attala County) and now lives in Brandon. He attended Kosciusko High School and Mississippi State. He is a former Air Force captain, and spent 26 years with IBM, where he installed and taught finance applications throughout the U.S. and abroad. Since 1994 he has published more than 250 short stories and fillers in magazines like *Writer's Digest*, *Woman's World*, *The Strand*, and *Alfred Hitchcock's Mystery Magazine*. His stories have been nominated for both the Pushcart Prize and the Derringer Award, and one has been distributed worldwide in Braille and on audio tape.

Tim Floyd

Born Timothy F. Floyd on Feb. 25, 1954, in Hattiesburg. His father, the late Lee Floyd, was the head men's basketball coach at Southern Mississippi for 14 years (1949-54 & 1962-71), recording a 246-147 overall record. Tim would follow in his father's footsteps. He attended Southern Mississippi where he was a walk-on from 1972-74 before transferring to Louisiana Tech where he played on a scholarship in 1976 & '77. In 1976 and '77, Floyd was a student assistant coach at Louisiana Tech where he graduated with a degree in health and physical education in 1977. He was assistant coach at Texas-El Paso for nine years, then he set out on his own. First, two seasons as head coach at Idaho and six years at New Orleans before taking the head coaching position at Iowa State in 1994. On July 22, 1998, Floyd resigned at Iowa State to go pro — as the head-coach-in-waiting of the World Champion Chicago Bulls! Floyd officially became head coach on Jan. 15, 1999, just 2 days after Michael Jordan announced his retirement. Before going to Chicago, Floyd had an 81-47 record at Iowa State. He recorded 20 or more wins in seven of 11 seasons as head coach at three schools with an overall record of 243-130.

Shelby Foote

Born Nov. 17, 1916, in Greenville, Mississippi. He wrote several novels including *Tournament* (1949), *Follow Me Down* (1950), *Love in a Dry Season* (1951), *Shiloh* (1952), *Jordan County* (1954), and *September, September* (1977), but his massive 1.2 million word, 3-volume historical reference *The Civil War: A Narrative* (Vol.1-1958, Vol. 2-1963, & Vol. 3-1974) made him the nation's top Civil War historian and earned him a nomination for a Pulitzer Prize. Near the end of the 20th Century, *The Civil War* appeared on several lists: It was No. 15 on the Modern Library's "100 Best Nonfiction Books of the Century"; No. 93 on National Review's "The Top 100 Nonfiction Books of the Century"; listed as one of "The Century's Top 100 Books" compiled by World on the Web; and listed as one of "The Fifty Best Books of the Century" compiled by the Intercollegiate Studies Institute. Foote was co-narrator for the acclaimed PBS-TV series *The Civil War* in 1990 and provided commentary for the 1994 PBS 18-hour series, *Baseball*. He was presented the Lifetime Achievement Award in the 1995 Governor's Awards for Excellence in the Arts. Foote makes his home in Memphis.

Profiles of Famous & Notable Mississippians

Steve Forbert
Born Dec. 13, 1954, in Meridian, he started playing guitar at age 10. At 21, this folk artist was in New York City, playing on the streets for spare change. His debut album *Alive on Arrival* (1978) stayed in the Top 100 for months and his next album, *Jackrabbit Slim*, with the hit *Romeo's Tune*, got into the Top 20. The albums *Little Stevie Orbit* and *Steve Forbert* came in the early 80s followed by *Streets of This Town* ('88), *The American In Me* ('92), *Mission of the Crossroad Palms* ('95), *Rocking Horse Head* ('96), *Here's Your Pizza* ('97) and *Evergreen Boy* (2000). In the early 1990s, he opened for Elton John in Europe. He's written hits for several country artists.

Richard Ford
Born Feb. 16, 1944, in Jackson, Mississippi. He received a B.A. from Michigan State University and an M.F.A. from the University of California. Ford has been a Guggenheim fellow (1977-78) and a two-time National Endowment of the Arts fellow (1979-80 & 1985-86). He has published widely in periodicals such as *Esquire* and *Harpers*. In 1995, he won the annual $25,000 Rea Award for the Short Story, one of his collections being *Rock Springs*. A previous winner of that prize was fellow Jacksonian Eudora Welty. Ford wrote the best-selling novels *The Ultimate Good Luck* (1981), *The Sportswriter* (1986-won the PEN/Faulkner citation for fiction award), *A Piece of My Heart* (1987), *Wildlife* (1990) and *Independence Day* (1995). *Independence Day* became a fiction nominee for the National Book Circle Award and the PEN/Faulkner Award in 1996 and Ford won the 1996 Pulitzer Prize for fiction for that work. He's only the 3rd Mississippian to win the Pulitzer for fiction award. He follows literary giants William Faulkner of Oxford and Eudora Welty of Jackson. Ford received France's coveted Officer of the Order of Arts and Letters medal in 1996. A trio of his short stories appeared as the book *Women with Men: Three Stories* (1997).

Ruth Ford
Born Ruth Elizabeth Ford on July 7, 1915, in Hazlehurst, Mississippi. Onscreen since 1941, she appeared in mostly supporting roles in over 2 dozen films from *Secrets of the Lone Wolf* (1941) to *Too Scared to Scream* (1985). Her most memorable role was in the film *The Keys of the Kingdom* (1944). She was in the play *Dinner at Eight* (1966) and has acted mainly on the stage in recent years. She was married to actor Zachary Scott from 1952 until his death in 1965.

Willie Foster
Born William Hendrick Foster on June 12, 1904, in Calvert, Texas, but was reared by his grandmother in Lorman, Miss. He played baseball at Alcorn University briefly, but started playing professionally in 1923. A big man at 6-feet-1, 195 pounds, he was perhaps the greatest left-handed pitcher ever in the Negro Leagues with whom he played from 1923-1937. Foster, a half-brother of Negro National League founder Rube Foster, won 137 games in the league, more than Satchel Paige (129) and outpitched the Hall of Famer in head-to-head competition. He pitched for the Chicago American Giants, the Homestead Grays, and the Pittsburgh Crawfords. In 1926, Foster won 26 straight games and went 11-4 to take a doubleheader as the Giants clinched the pennant. In 1927, he was 21-3 in the regular season and won three more times in the Negro League World Series, in 1927, '28 and '33. In the East-West All-Star Classic in 1933, Foster got a complete game victory against an East squad loaded with players like Cool Papa Bell, Josh Gibson, Oscar Charleston, and many other Negro League greats. His playing career ended in 1938, nine years before the game was integrated. Foster became baseball coach and dean of men at his alma mater, Alcorn State, in 1960 until right before his death in Lorman on Sept. 16, 1978. Eighteen years after he died, Foster was elected to the Baseball Hall of Fame — inducted on Aug. 4, 1996.

Pete Fountain
Born Peter Dewey Fountain in Bay St. Louis on July 3, 1930. A clarinetist who worked with Monk Hazel, Phil Zito's International Dixieland Express, the Junior Dixieland Band, The Dukes of Dixieland, Al Hirt and others in the 1940s. Fountain and the late Al Hirt (b: 1922, d: 4-27-99) started out together with day jobs as exterminators, killing rats and roaches by day and playing music at night. Fountain spent 4 years with the Basin Street Six, then hit it big when he signed on for 2 years with Lawrence Welk, host of the nation's most popular TV show, in 1957. Fountain and Welk were largely attributed with preserving Dixieland jazz. He has recorded over 40 albums including *Basin Street Blues*, *Bourbon Street*, *Dixieland*, *Lawrence Welk Presents Pete Fountain*, and *Mr. New Orleans*. From the 60s on, many people identified New Orleans music with either Fountain or Al Hirt.

Jo Foxworth
Born June 30, 1918, in Tylertown, Miss. She graduated from Tylertown High School, then attended Mississippi College for Women (now Mississippi University for Women), where in 1937 she was named editor of *The Spectator*, the college newspaper. She went on to the Missouri School of Journalism. Her first job was advertising manager for Kennington's, a now-defunct department store in Jackson. From there, she went to work for McCann-Erickson, the giant ad firm in New York City. Foxworth began as a copywriter, was promoted to group supervisor and then vice president and creative director on accounts such as Coca Cola, Westinghouse, Nestle, Chesterfield, Owens-Corning Fiberglass and Hilton Hotels. In 1968, she founded her own advertising agency, Jo Foxworth, Inc., attracting such accounts as JCPenny and Chiquita Bananas. She has been named an Advertising Woman of the Year numerous times and holds many honors bestowed on her by the ad industry: President of Advertising Women of New York; Governor of the American Advertising Federation, which also presented her with their Silver Medal Award; a columnist for 11 years for Advertising Age; winner of the National Headliner Award of Women in Communications; and election to the American Advertising Federation's Hall of Fame (1996), the highest honor of the advertising industry. At the time, she was only the sixth woman to be elected to the 130 member Hall of Fame in the 48 years of its existence. Foxworth is the author of 3 books, all about woman making it to the top in a male-dominated society: *Boss Lady: An Executive Woman Tells About Making It* (1978); *Wising Up* (1980); and *The Bordello Cookbook* (1996). The latter is about "America's first female entrepreneurs — the millionaire madams who made their mark in the only business open to them at the time." Reflecting Foxworth's well-known wit, it's described as "a rollicking review of the most colorful madams in the nation's history, with 138 contemporary recipes inspired by their showmanship woven into the text."

Jim Fraiser
A lawyer, actor, teacher, editor, and best-selling author, he was born John James Fraiser III on Oct. 27, 1954, in New Orleans, the son of Chief Judge John Fraiser, Jr. of Greenwood, Miss. He grew up in Greenwood, graduating from Greenwood High in 1972. He received his B.A. in English and history in 1976 and his law degree three years later, both from the University of Mississippi. He served as an assistant district attorney in

Profiles of Famous & Notable Mississippians

Hinds County from 1980-82, then was in private practice until 1995, when he became a special assistant attorney general in the Civil Litigation Division, a position he still holds today. From 1981-91 he performed professionally with Jackson's New Stage Theater. Several unpublished plays which he wrote have been performed, including adaptations of Walker Percy's novel *Love in the Ruins* ('89) and Ernest Hemingway's *The Sun Also Arises* ('90), and the original plays *Cosmos by Copernicus* ('91) and *The Judas Principle* ('92). A member of the Screen Actors Guild since 1988, he had roles in the feature films *Good Ole Boy* (1988), *Mississippi Burning* ('89), *Blind Vengeance* ('92) and as a veterinarian in *My Dog Skip* (2000), the movie based on the book by the late Willie Morris. From 1988-90, he was the philosophy columnist for *Down South Magazine*, which published his short story *The Plutonian Chronicles* ('89). Between 1990 and 1993, he served as a paralegal instructor at the University of Mississippi and the Mississippi University for Women. He's written free-lance articles for *Greenwood Commonwealth*, the *Daily Mississippian*, *The Clarion Ledger*, *North Mississippi Business Journal*, *National Women Lawyers Journal*, *Mississippi Lawyer Magazine* and *The American Bar Journal*. He is a contributing editor for the *Jackson Business Journal* and a contributing writer for the *Northside Sun*. His first book was the humorous *M is for Mississippi: An Irreverent Guide to the Magnolia State* ('91). *Shadow Seed* ('97), set in present-day Jackson, was his first novel. It sold out in hardcover after only two months and was released in paperback in 1998. His latest book is *Mississippi River Country Tales* (1999).

Olin Francis

Born Sept. 13, 1891, in Mooreville, Lee Co., Miss. He became a character actor who was in 39 films from *A Knight of the West* in 1921 to *Rollin' Home to Texas* in 1940, including many westerns in the 1930s. He played "Fulad" in *Gunga Din* (1939). Francis died on June 30, 1952, in Hollywood, Calif.

Rev. C.L. Franklin

Born Clarence LeVaughn Franklin on Jan. 22, 1915, in Clarksdale, Miss. A widely-known Baptist preacher with over 70 albums of his sermons issued on the famous Chess record label, he is probably better known for being the father of famous soul singer Aretha Franklin, who was born Mar. 25, 1942, in Memphis and grew up in Detroit. Rev. Franklin moved to Detroit in 1946. By the middle 1950s, he had earned the nickname "The Man With The Million-Dollar Voice" and garnered up to $4,000 a personal appearance. He founded the Bethel Baptist Church and was pastor there until his death. He was also a close confidant of Martin Luther King, Jr. In 1979, seven robbers trying to steal antique windows shot Rev. Franklin in his home in Detroit. His wounds left the Baptist minister semi-comatose for 5 years until his death July 27, 1984. Shortly before the shooting Franklin had celebrated his 33rd anniversary as a pastor. Over 3,000 people attended the funeral service inside the church with another 6,000 outside to hear Rev. Jesse Jackson eulogize his friend and colleague. Franklin was buried in the Woodlawn Cemetery in Detroit.

Cliff Freeman

Born Feb. 14, 1941, in Vicksburg, his family moved to Florida when he was 5 years old. He's now living in New York. Freeman is an advertising executive and ad creator who, in the early 1980s, penned the memorable line "Where's the beef?" for Wendy's hamburger chain. That campaign earned him industrywide fame and helped his firm land the Little Caesars account in 1987. Freeman's wacky, funny "Pizza, Pizza!" commercials started airing in 1988 and helped build the Detroit-based pizza chain from a $900 million regional chain to a $2 billion national company. During 1993 and 1994, Little Caesars won 10 Clio awards, 11 Addys and 8 Andys and his company, Cliff Freeman and Partners, was named ad agency of the year by the industry's trade association. Little Caesars ads were rated the 2nd-most recognized by consumers (after Coca-Cola ads) in 1994. Cliff Freeman and Partners won 9 Addys in 1998 including 2 for ads for office retailer Staples, 2 for ads for Fox sports and one for Little Caesars. The voice of the cartoon character who chants "Pizza, Pizza!" in Little Caesars commercial is Freeman's. Freeman also wrote "Sometimes you feel like a nut, sometimes you don't" for Almond Joy/Mounds® candy bars.

Martin Freeman

Born May 14, 1814, in Stettin, Germany he entered service in Louisiana. Freeman was a pilot in the Union Navy when he performed an act of bravery on Aug. 5, 1864, that earned him the Medal of Honor (MOH). He was awarded the Medal on Dec. 31, 1864. Here are the actual words of his citation: "As pilot of the flagship, *U.S.S. Hartford*, during action against Fort Morgan, rebel gunboats and the ram Tennessee, in Mobile Bay, 5 August 1864. With his ship under terrific enemy shellfire, Freeman calmly remained at his station in the maintop and skillfully piloted the ships into the bay. He rendered gallant service throughout the prolonged battle in which the rebel gunboats were captured or driven off, the prize ram Tennessee forced to surrender, and the fort successfully attacked." Freeman's MOH was officially accredited to Ship Island, Mississippi, one of three Medals of Honor to be accredited to Mississippi for action during the Civil War. Freeman was one of only 5 Mississippians (2 *native* Mississippians) to be awarded the MOH during the Civil War (3 Union Army & 2 Union Navy). The medal was awarded to only those that fought for the North — the medal was not given to Confederates. Of MOH recipients, Freeman was one of only 2 Mississippians to serve in the Navy during the Civil War (the other was native Mississippian Wilson Brown-see his profile) and one of only 3 Mississippians to receive the MOH for service in the Navy in all wars. Freeman's Medal was one of 17 Medals of Honor that have been officially accredited to Mississippi in all wars, although we claim 5 more that were accredited to other states, but the recipients had Mississippi ties. Freeman was one of 22 Mississippians (13 native)[15 Army, 4 Marines & 3 Navy] in all wars to have received the MOH out of 3,433 recipients through Nov. 1, 2000. He died on Sept. 11, 1894, in Pascagoula and was buried in an unmarked grave in the Greenwood Cemetery in Pascagoula. There is now a Medal of Honor marker on his gravesite.

Morgan Freeman

Born in Memphis on June 1, 1937. He split his childhood years between the Mississippi Delta cities of Greenwood, Charleston, and Bruce, and the streets of Chicago. In 1955 he graduated from high school in Greenwood, then joined the Air Force and served 4 years. In 1959 he moved to Los Angeles to become an actor and attended Los Angeles City College. He settled in New York in 1963 and in 1967 he made his stage debut off Broadway in *Niggerlover*. He played many stage roles, both on and off Broadway, from Rudolph in the Pearl Bailey version of *Hello, Dolly!* to the title role of *Purlie!* to Shakespearean performer, winning the off-Broadway's Obie Award for *Coriolanus* in 1979. He continued his stage work after starting in films, winning another Obie for his work in *The Gospel of Collonus*, both off-Broadway and later on Broadway (1984-88). He was "Easy Reader" on the PBS-TV

Profiles of Famous & Notable Mississippians

children's show *The Electric Company* from 1971-76. He made his film debut in *Who Says I Can't Ride a Rainbow?* (1971). He received critical acclaim playing volatile pimp "Fast Black" in the film *Street Smart* (1987) and with a reprisal of his off-Broadway Obie-winning role as a chauffeur in the South in *Driving Miss Daisy* (1989). Other films include *Brubaker* (1980), *Eyewitness* (1981), *Harry and Son* (1984), *Teachers* (1984), *Clean and Sober* (1988), *Glory* (1989), *Lean On Me* (1989), *Bonfire of the Vanities* (1990), *Robin Hood: Prince of Theives* (1991), *The Shawshank Redemption* (1994), for which he received the 1995 nomination for the leading film actor award by the Screen Actors Guild, *Outbreak* (1995), *Seven* (1995), *Chain Reaction* (1996), *The Flood* (1997), *Kiss the Girls* (1997), *Amistad* (1997), *Deep Impact* (1998), *Hard Rain* (1998), *Water Damage* (1999), *Third Degree* (2000), *Nurse Betty* (2000), *Long Way to Freedom* (2000, playing Nelson Mandela), and *Rendezvous with Rama* (2000). Another movie in which Freeman starred, the Clint Eastwood western *Unforgiven*, was the Oscar-winning Best Picture of 1992 and was rated No. 98 on The American Film Institute's list of the Top 100 Greatest American Movies of All Time, announced in 1998 in celebration of the 100th anniversary of film making. He was on TV in 1993 in *Amos, the Story of an Old Dog and His Couch*. In 1995, he narrated the TV documentary miniseries, *The Promised Land* and narrated the 1997 documentary about the plight of post-Holocaust Jews, *The Long Way Home*. He is a three-time Academy Award® nominee (*Street Smart*, *Driving Miss Daisy* and *The Shawshank Redemption*) and a two-time Golden Globe winner. For stage work, he has won 3 Obies, Drama Desk and Clarence Derwent Awards and a Tony nomination. Freeman made his directorial debut in the story of a black South African policeman and his son divided by apartheid in *Botha!* in 1993. By 1999, he had turned producer — his first effort was the TV movie, *The Mutiny*, which aired on NBC on March 28, 1999. In 1996, Gov. Fordice presented Freeman with the Lifetime Achievement Award. He was only the fifth person to receive this highest honor of the Governor's Awards for Excellence in the Arts, joining notables Eudora Welty, Leontyne Price, Margaret Walker Alexander and Shelby Foote. In a special millennium poll by *The Clarion-Ledger* of Jackson, readers overwhelming (over half of the 800 votes) chose Freeman as their favorite actor from Mississippi. The results were announced on Oct. 4, 1999. Freeman has a 44-acre ranch in Charleston, Mississippi. He is co-owner of Madidi, a new fine-dining restaurant in Clarksdale, Mississippi.

Edward O. Fritts

Born Feb. 21, 1941 in Cape Girardeau, Missouri. He first came to Mississippi in 1959 to attend the University of Mississippi. After graduating from Ole Miss, he bought his first radio station in Indianola, Mississippi in 1963. Operating out of Indianola, he soon built a broadcast group consisting of one AM and one FM station in each of the cities of Indianola, Tupelo, Mississippi, Helena, Arkansas, and Winnsboro, Louisiana. But, Fritts was destined to face a much greater challenge. In Oct. 1982 Fritts became president and CEO of the National Association of Broacasters (NAB) in Washington, D.C. He sold his eight radio stations soon after taking the helm of the NAB to become the broadcast industry's chief spokesman and lobbyist. NAB's members include the ABC, NBC, CBS and Fox networks, their affiliated stations and independent TV and radio stations in large, medium and small markets. Under Fritts's leadership, the NAB has gotten each of the 1,600 broadcast companies: a second TV channel for digital broadcasts for free; persuaded Congress to make it easier for TV and radio companies to own more stations and keep their licenses longer; and forced rival cable companies to carry local TV stations on their systems. Fritts is considered one of the most effective lobbyists in Washington. Known for promoting the public service commitments of broadcasters, he has served on the boards of The Ad Council, the National Commission Against Drunk Driving, the Centers for Disease Control's Business Responds to AIDS program, and the U.S. Chamber of Commerce. Fritts has also served on the Individual Investors Advisory Committee of the New York Stock Exchange. Stressing the NAB's growing international involvement, Fritts has served as vice chairman of the State Department's International Media Fund, assisting Eastern European nations in establishing their own private broadcast systems. He was vice chairman of President Reagan's White House Private Sector Initiatives Board. Fritts is the recipient of numerous national and international awards, including the French Medal of Arts and Letters, the Golden Ambrosiana of Milano and the Lion of Venice. The Media Institute awarded Fritts its prestigious American Horizon Award for leadership in promoting the vitality and independence of American media and communications. While still living in Mississippi, Fritts received the first Ole Miss Silver Mike Award for significant contributions to broadcast journalism. Still involved in Mississippi, he serves on the board of the University of Mississippi Foundation. Eddie and his wife Martha Dale are involved in civic, educational and charitable organizations, including the Wolf Trap Foundation, Arlington Hospital Foundation and the National Museum for Women in the Arts.

Frances Jones Gaither

Born in Tennessee on May 21, 1889, she grew up in Corinth, Mississippi. She married Rice Gaither, an editorial writer for the *New York Times*. She wrote the novels *The Scarlet Coat* (1940), *Follow the Drinking Gourd* (1940), *The Red Cock Crows* (1944), and *Double Muscadine*, the Book-of-the-Month selection in March 1949. She also wrote children's books including *The Painted Arrow* (1931) and *Little Miss Cappo* (1937). She died on Oct. 28, 1955, at the age of 66.

Jim Gallagher, Jr.

Born Mar. 24, 1961, in Pennsylvania, he grew up in Indiana. Gallagher moved to Mississippi in 1988 when he married Cissye, a Greenwood native and eight-time Mississippi Women's Amateur champion (she won her 3rd straight title in 1999). He's been one of the top players on the PGA Tour since 1985 when he won the Deposit Guaranty Golf Classic at Hattiesburg. Gallagher won $1,078,870 in 1993, capped the season by winning the Tour Championship, then played a key role on the U. S. Ryder Cup team. He won two PGA Tour events in 1995 to finish 6th on the money list with $1.06 million. From 1989 through 1995, he won five tournaments. He finished 76th, 145th and 161st on the money list in 1996, 1997 and 1998, respectively. Going into the Southern Farm Bureau Classic at Annadale in Madison, Mississippi, in Oct. 1999, Gallagher was 179th on the money list with $127,458. He went into the 2000 Southern Farm Bureau Classic at No. 152 on the money list with $226,827.

Evelyn Gandy

Born Sept. 4, 1920, in Hattiesburg. She was the only woman in the University of Mississippi School of Law class of 1943 and was president of the student body. Gandy was the first woman in Mississippi to be appointed assistant attorney general and the first women appointed commissioner of public welfare. Gandy also served in the state legislature, the first woman from

Profiles of Famous & Notable Mississippians

Forrest County to be elected state representative. As state treasurer from 1960-64, she was the first woman in Mississippi elected to a constitutional statewide office. She served a second term as treasurer from 1968-72. Gandy was the first woman in Mississippi to be elected commissioner of insurance. On Jan. 14, 1976, she became the first woman lieutenant governor in the state, serving until Jan. 16, 1980. She attempted twice to be the first woman elected governor of Mississippi, but lost in the Democratic Primary to William Winter in 1979 and to Bill Allain in 1983. Gandy was awarded the 1997 Margaret Brent Women Lawyers of Achievement Award. In 1998, she was given the Lifetime Achievement Award by the Mississippi Women Lawyers Association and was also given the Lindy Boggs Award for public service by the Southern Women in Public Service.

Cynthia Lynn Geary

Born March 21, 1965, in Jackson. She graduated from Jackson Prep, earned a degree from Ole Miss, then moved to Los Angeles in 1987. She was an Outstanding Supporting Actress Emmy nominee for her role as Shelly Tambo on the TV series *Northern Exposure*. Winner of the 1992 Emmy Award for Outstanding Drama Series, it was canceled after the 1994-95 season. Geary also appeared on other TV series: *Us* ('91); *Hostile Force* ('96); and *You're the One* ('98). She's been in several TV movies: *To Grandmother's House We Go* ('92, as "Rhonda Thompson"); *The Awakening* ('93, as "Sara"); and *When Time Expires* ('97, as "June Kelly"). She's been in these feature films: *Eight Seconds* ('94, as "Kellie Frost"); *The Killing Grounds* ('97, as "Janice Harper"); *Smoke Signals* ('98, as "Cathy the gymnast"); *The Break Up* ('98); and *John John in the Sky* ('99, as "Annette").

Bobbie Gentry

Born Roberta Lee Streeter on July 27, 1944, in Chickasaw County, Miss. Brought up in Greenwood, Mississippi by her grandparents from the time she was 6 years old, she got her stage name from the 1952 movie *Ruby Gentry*, starring Charlton Heston and Jennifer Jones. Gentry had a huge multi-million-selling, No. 1 record *Ode To Billie Joe* (1967) which she also wrote. She won 3 Grammys for her hit (all in 1967) and the Academy of Country Music voted her Most Promising Female Vocalist for 1967. Her hit song was made into a movie of the same title filmed in Mississippi and released in 1976. Her album *Ode to Billy Joe* (1967) went Gold as did the album *Bobbie Gentry and Glen Campbell*. Gentry and Campbell's cover version of the Everly Brothers' *Let It Be Me* reached No. 14 on the country charts in 1969 and their cover of another Everly's hit, *All I Have To Do Is Dream*, hit No. 6 on the country chart in 1970. She recorded 8 albums and at least three compilation albums of her hits have been released including *The Golden Classics of Bobbie Gentry*, released in January 1998. Gentry now lives in California.

James Z. George

James Zachariah George was born Oct. 20, 1826, in Monroe Co., Georgia. His family moved to Noxubee Co., Miss. when he was eight and settled in Carroll Co., Miss. two years later. George joined the Mississippi Rifles in 1846 and served in Mexico until discharged for ill health. Having grown up getting only a rudimentary education from the "field schools" of the day, George was self-taught. He studied law, was admitted to the bar in 1847 and started practice in Carrollton. George was a reporter of the Mississippi Supreme Court in 1854. As a member of the Mississippi secession convention, he signed the ordinance of secession. George served in the Confederate Army during the Civil War, attaining the rank of brigadier general of State troops. He lived in Jackson from 1872-87, when he returned to Carrollton. He was appointed judge of the State Supreme Court in 1879 and was elected chief justice. He was elected as a Democrat to the U.S. Senate in 1880, reelected in 1886, and again in 1892, and served from March 4, 1881, until his death in 1897. He was chairman of the Committee on Agriculture and Forestry in the 53rd Congress, and his crowning contribution in that body was in the creation of the U.S. Department of Agriculture. Known in Congress as "the Great Commoner," he helped in framing the Sherman Antitrust Act and worked for aid to education and civil service reform. A member of the constitutional convention of 1890, he is considered the architect of the state's present constitution. George is one of only two Mississippians (with Jefferson Davis) honored with a statue in the U.S. Capitol. George died on Aug. 14, 1897, in Mississippi City, Mississippi, and is buried in the Evergreen Cemetery in Carrollton. George County, Mississippi is named for him.

Shayon Ghosh

He is the youngest person in Mississippi (and one of the youngest in the nation) to ever make a perfect 36 score on the ACT (American College Test)! Born on Oct. 3, 1986, in Ames, Iowa, his family moved to the Jackson area when he was just one and a half years old. Shayon was only 13 years and two months old when he made the perfect 36 score on the ACT in Dec. 1999. He previously took the test twice when he was only 12 years old, making 34 the first time and 35 on the second try. Even at age 13, this Clinton resident was a high school senior at Jackson Prep. Shayon also scored 1,590 out of 1,600 on his Scholastic Aptitude Test (SAT). His mother says he was reading at age 3. She said that although Shayon is a certified genius, she doesn't know his IQ, because the last time he took an IQ test, it was off the scale — too high to read! On April 14, 2000, Shayon was named Mississippi's top STAR (Student-Teacher Achievement Program) student, the youngest ever to received the prestigious award that comes with a $24,000 college scholarship. When he graduated from high school in 2000, he already had two semesters of college work behind him from advanced placement classes at Jackson Prep. Ghosh, who wants to major in computer science and computer engineering, was courted by colleges across the nation but chose to stay at home and spend the 2000-01 school year at Jackson State University. He's attending JSU as a Presidential Scholar with all expenses paid. Ghosh is the youngest person ever admitted in the 20-year history of JSU's honors program and the only student ever at the school to have a perfect score on the ACT. After one year at Jackson State, Ghost will transfer to prestigious Carnegie-Mellon Uniiversity in Pittsburgh, Pa., where he's been promised more than $15,000 a year in scholarship aid. His father, Dr. Kunal Ghosh, a native of India, chairs the physics department at Jackson State University and his mother, Dr. Susmita Ghosh, a native of Bangladesh, is a post doctoral research fellow at JSU in environmental science. Jackson Prep is proud of the fact that three of their students have scored a 36 on the ACT. In addition to Shayon, Jennifer Carlisle did it in Feb. 1999 and Steven Shackleford, Jr., aced the test while at Jackson Prep in 1994. Jackson Prep ties with Hattiesburg High School, which has also had 3 students to ace the ACT, for first place in the state for the greatest number of students making the top score on the ACT. Shayon is one of 7 students in Mississippi to score 36 during 1999 (either a so-called "perfect" 36 with no mistakes or a composite 36). Shayon is one of only 12 students from the state to ever score a 36 on the test through June 2000.

Profiles of Famous & Notable Mississippians

Jake Gibbs

Born Jake Dean Gibbs on Nov. 7, 1938, in Grenada, Miss. He played quarterback and defensive back for Ole Miss from 1958-60. He made All-SEC as a junior in 1959 when he led the league in passing with 755 yards. During his senior year, he ran for 246 yards, passed for 970, accounted for 17 TDs and was named SEC Player of the Year. Gibbs was a consensus All- America after leading Ole Miss to a 9-0-1 record and a national championship in 1960. He finished 3rd place for the Heisman Trophy in 1960. In his three years at Ole Miss, he played on football teams that lost only 3 games and went 3-0 in bowl games. During the 1960 Sugar Bowl, with just 30 seconds left in the half, Gibbs threw a pass to unguarded receiver, halfback Cowboy Woodruff, who took the ball 43 yards for the TD and a 7-0 Ole Miss lead over LSU at halftime. The Rebels won 21-0 and were chosen by the Associated Press as the SEC Team of the Decade. He was selected the Most Outstanding Player of the 1961 Sugar Bowl when he scored both Rebel TDs in a 14-6 victory over Rice. *Sports Illustrated* magazine picked Gibbs as the eighth best college quarterback in the modern era. He also made All-American as an Ole Miss baseball player. He turned down several pro football offers to play 10 seasons as catcher for the New York Yankees. In 1971, he quit pro baseball to become the Rebel baseball coach. In 19 seasons as coach, Gibbs compiled a record of 486-389-9, a SEC record of 188-230-4 (.450) and led the Rebels to two SEC titles. Inducted into the Mississippi Sports Hall of Fame in 1976, he became the 8th Rebel player in the College Football Hall of Fame in 1995.

Ellen Gilchrist

Born Feb. 20, 1935, in Vicksburg, Mississippi. She received a B.A. from Millsaps College in Jackson, then did graduate work in creative writing at the University of Arkansas. Her first collection of short stories, *In the Land of Dreamy Dreams* (1981), won the Miss. Institute of Arts and Letters Literature Award. Her collection of stories, *Victory Over Japan*, also won the MIAL Award and the American Book Award, both in 1984. Her *The Courts of Love* (1996), was a National Book Award winner. She has written 3 novels and 10 story collections, including *Drunk With Love* (1986), *Light Can Be Both Wave and Particle* (1989), *Anabasis: A Journey to the Interior* ('94), *Starcarbon* ('94), *Sarah Conley* (1997), *Flights of Angels* (1998), and *The Cabal and Other Stories* (2000).

Mickey Gilley

A country singer/pianist born Mar. 9, 1936, in Natchez, he grew up in nearby Ferriday, Louisiana. He received the Academy of Country Music Award for Single Record of the Year, *Bring It On Home* ('76). His first hit was *Room Full of Roses* ('74) followed by 17 No. 1 hits like *I Overlooked An Orchid* and *Stand By Me* that also went Pop (#22 in '80). He was once part-owner of Gilley's nightclub in Pasadena (a suburb of Houston, Tex.), at one time considered the largest honky-tonk in the world seating 5,000 people. Gilley and the club were prominently featured in the 1980 John Travolta hit movie *Urban Cowboy*. Mickey is first cousin of singer Jerry Lee Lewis and former TV evangelist Jimmy Swaggart.

Jennifer Gillom

Born June 13, 1964 in Abbeville, Lafayette County, Miss. Her nickname is "Jent," from childhood. Jennifer graduated from the University of Mississippi in 1986 with a degree in education. With 2,186 career points, Jennifer is the third leading scorer in Mississippi basketball history, behind only her sister Peggy, in first place with 2,486 points, and John Stroud, in second place with 2,328 career points. Jennifer is in second place among women players, behind only her sister. Jennifer won a silver medal at the 1985 World University Games. She was selected 1985 Basketball Sportswoman of the Year by the U.S. Ollympic Committee and also by *Olympian* magazine. In 1986, she was Mississippi Sportswoman of the year, Kodak All-American, and SEC Female Athlete of the Year. Jennifer was a member of the 1986 Goodwill Games and World Championship teams, won gold at the 1987 pan Am Games, and was a member of the 1988 U.S. Olympic basketball team which claimed the gold medal. She later played professionally in Italy for eight seasons (1987-96) and then played for Athens, Greece in 1996-97. Jennifer started playing for the WNBA's Phoenix Mercury in 1997. She reached the WNBA Semifinals in 1997 and was named to the All-WNBA Second Team after leading the Mercury in scoring (15.7 points per game). She ranked 5th in the WNBA in scoring and 10th in free-throw percentage (.777). In 1998, Jennifer was named to the All-WNBA First Team. In the WNBA for 1998, she was ranked: 2nd in points per game (20.8); 4th in rebounds per game (7.3); 14th in field goal percentage (.463); 6th in three-point field goal percentage (.378); 11th in steals per game (1.67); 8th in three-point field goals made (31); and 16th in minutes per game (32.1). Jennifer played in 32 games in 1999 and her stats show: 485 points (15.2 avg.); 163 field goals (5.1 avg.); 428 field-goal assists 13.4 avg.); .381 field goal percentage; 141 free throws (4.4 avg.); 177 free-throw assists (5.5 avg.); and .797 free throw percentage. Her sister, Peggy, is the head basketball coach at Texas A&M and Jennifer would like to follow in her footsteps as a pro coach. Jennifer and Peggy Gillom were both honored by the University of Mississippi on March 30, 1999, as recipients of the 10th annual Awards of Distinction, the first time two members of the same family were so honored. Jennifer was inducted into the Ole Miss Hall of Fame on Sept. 11, 1999. In 1999 Jennifer was voted by readers of *The Clarion-Ledger* as Mississippi's favorite female athlete of the millennium! *The Clarion-Ledger* picked Jennifer as the No. 1 Pro Athlete of The Year of 1999 in women's basketball. In the summer of 2000, Jennifer was one of only four WNBA players picked to be national spokespersons for the Be Active health and fitness campaign sponsored by Nike.

Peggy Gillom

Born April 14, 1958, in Abbeville, Mississippi. Peggie earned a bachelor's degree in social work from the Univerity of Mississippi. She is the all-time leading scorer and rebounder in Ole Miss Lady Rebel basketball. A 4-year starter for the Lady Rebel basketball team from 1976 through 1980, she scored 2,486 points and grabbed 1,271 rebounds, setting records that still stand in both categories at Ole Miss and state records by male or female. Peggie is still the only Lady Rebel to ever score over 2,000 points and pull down over 1,000 rebounds in a career. Her numbers even surpass the Ole Miss men's basketball team all-time career leaders John Stroud, with 2,328 points and Joe Harvell, with 2,078 points. During her career at Ole Miss, the Lady Rebel basketball team compiled a 99-46 record. She helped lead the team to the Mississippi AIAW Region III playoffs in her freshman year and to the AIAWQ Nationals as a sophomore. She played her last two seasons under Van Chancellor in 1978-79 and 1979-1980. The 1978-79 Lady Rebels finished with a 31-9 record and played in the AIAW Region III. In her senior year, Ole Miss again played in the Mississippi AIAW tourney, the predecessor for the NCAA playoffs. Peggie was named to the Southeastern Conference All Tournament team and she was a finalist for the

Profiles of Famous & Notable Mississippians

Wade Trophy, the award named after Margaret Wade of Delta State to honor the top college women's basketball player. She holds 8 other Lady Rebel game, season and career records. She was drafted by the Dallas Diamonds of the Women's Professional Basketball League where she played one year. Peggie was named as an assistant to Van Chancellor in 1981. In her 16-year coaching career, she led the Lady Rebels to 12 NCAA Tournaments including nine Sweet 16 and four Elite Eight appearances. The 1991-92 Lady Rebels won the regular season SEC title, a first for the program. The Lady Rebs had 355 wins and only 108 losses for a 76% winning average during Peggy's coaching tenure. As a player and assistant coach, she was involved in 454 wins and only 154 losses since 1977 for a 74% winning percentage. She followed Coach Chancellor to the WNBA's Houston Comets in the league's inaugural season in 1997. Peggie coached her sister Jennifer from 1982-86. Jennifer scored 2,186 points, 300 short of Peggie's record, but good enough to place Jennifer second behind her sister on the all-time Lady Rebel scoring list. Peggie and Jennifer are the only two Lady Rebels to score over 2,000 career points. Jennifer now plays for the WNBA's Phoenix Mercury. Peggy is now head basketball coach at Texas A&M. On Oct. 26, 1996, Peggie became only the third woman in Ole Miss history to be inducted into the Ole Miss Athletic Hall of Fame, joining Sheila Sullivan and the late Eugenia Conner. She was inducted into the Miss. Sports Hall of Fame in 1998. Peggy and Jennifer were both recipients of the Ole Miss 10th annual Awards of Distinction in 1999, the first time two members of the same family received the award.

William M. "Jazz" Gillum

Born William McKinley Gillum on Sept. 11, 1904, in Indianola, Mississippi he was teaching himself how to play harmonica by the tender age of six. After running away from home in 1911 to live with relatives in Charleston, Mississippi, Jazz spent the next dozen years working a day job and spending his weekends playing for tips on local street corners. When he visited Chicago in 1923, he liked it so much he put down roots there. There he met guitarist Big Bill Broonzy and the two of them started working club dates around the city as a duo. By 1934, Gillum started showing up on recording dates for Bluebird, RCA Victor's budget label. Chicago producer Lester Melrose frequently called on Gillum as a sideman — as well as cutting sides on his own — as part of the "Bluebird beat" house band. A couple of his own sides were *Got To Reap What You Sow* and *Your're Laughing Now*. His career came to a halt when the label folded in the late 1940s and aside from a Memphis Slim session in 1961, he seems to have been largely inactive throughout the 1950s until his death from a gunshot wound as a result of an argument. Gillum died in Chicago on Mar. 29, 1966. Next to John Lee "Sonny Boy" Williamson, no harmonica player was as much in demand on Chicago recording sessions during the 1930s as Jazz Gillum.

Michael Goggin

Born on June 5, 1982, in Hattiesburg, Mississippi. In 1999, he made perfect scores on both the ACT and SAT, the two major college entrance exams, the first time in Mississippi history that a student has aced both tests! There have only been a few in the nation to ever make a perfect score on both tests (exact figures are not available). Goggin attended Hattiesburg High, and was a junior there when he scored 36 on the ACT in June 1999. He was a senior when he scored a 1600 on the SAT in Nov. 1999. Goggin, ranked first in his class with a perfect 4.00 GPA, is also a National Merit Semi-Finalist. On April 14, 2000, he received 2nd place honors and a $20,000 scholarship as a STAR (Student-Teacher Achievement Program) student. He plays the violin and was selected to All-State Orchestra and was concertmaster of the regional orchestra of South Mississippi. In debate, he was a member of the Hattiesburg High Debate Team. He was also treasurer of the school's chapter of the National Forensics League and was a two-time competitor at Catholic Forensic League's national competition. Goggin was a member of the Mock Trial Team, which won second place in the state. He was elected Democratic Party Leader at the Mississippi Youth Congress two years in a row. In soccer, he played on the junior varsity team. In addition, he was treasurer of the school chapter of the National Honor Society, captain of the Quiz Bowl Team, and served on the Mayor's Youth Advisory Council. Goggin plans to attend Harvard. His parents, William and Cheryl Goggin, are both professors at the University of Southern Mississippi, he in psychology and she in art history. Michael Goggin is one of 7 students in Mississippi to make 36 on the ACT during 1999 (either a "perfect" 36 with no mistakes or a composite 36). Although seven for one calendar year is not a record for a single state as far as the absolute number, ACT headquarters in Iowa says it might very well be a record for Mississippi as far as per capita state population and also compared with the total number of students in a state taking the test during a single calendar year. Goggin is one of only 12 students from the state to ever make a 36 score on the test through June 2000. Hattiesburg High is proud of the fact that three of their students have scored a 36 on the ACT. In addition to Goggin, Christine Varnado did it in 1997 and Kimberly R. Smith aced the test in 1994. Hattiesburg High School ties Jackson Prep, which has also had 3 students to ace the ACT, for the greatest number of students in the state making the top ACT score.

W.C. Gorden

Born June 30, 1930 in Nashville, he came to Mississippi in 1956. He was football coach at Jackson State University from the 1967-91. Gorden also served as head baseball coach in 1972 & '73, winning the SWAC championship in 1972. He coached Jackson State football to a 119-48-5 record and won eight SAC championships in 15 seasons. Gorden's teams won a SWAC-record 28 straight games from 1985-89 and advanced to the NCAA Division I-AA playoffs nine times. Gorden was named SWAC coach of the year six times. After stepping down as coach, he served as athletic director at Jackson State in 1992 and 1994. Gorden was inducted into the Mississippi Sports Hall of Fame on Feb. 28, 1997.

Chuck and Larry Gordon

They're probably the most commercially-successful brother team of movie producers in film history! Lawrence A. "Larry" Gordon was born on Mar. 25, 1936, in Yazoo City and grew up in Belzoni, Mississippi. He began his career as an assistant to TV-Producer Aaron Spelling after attending Tulane University studying business. Larry was President of 20th Century-Fox from 1984-86. Charles Gordon was born in Belzoni on May 13, 1947. Producers of both independent and studio-based films, some hit movies they have produced (together or separately) include *Dillinger* ('73), *Hard Times* ('75), *Hooper* ('78), *48 Hours* ('82), *Brewster's Millions* ('85), *Jumpin' Jack Flash* ('86), *Predator* ('87), *Die Hard* ('88), *Lock Up* ('89), *Field of Dreams* (Academy Award® nominated for Best Picture of the Year in 1989), *Die Hard 2* ('90), *Another 48 HRS* ('90), *Predator 2* ('90), *The Rocketeer* ('91), *Boogie Nights* ('97), *The Devil's Own* ('97), *Event Horizon* ('97), *October Sky* ('99), *Thieves* ('99), *Mystery Men* ('99), *Tomb Raider* (2001) and *Hellboy* (2001). The Gordon brothers also

Profiles of Famous & Notable Mississippians

produced *Waterworld* (1995) starring Kevin Costner and Dennis Hopper, the second-most expensive film ever made, which cost from $175 to $200 million, an amount exceeded only by the 1997 movie *Titanic*.

Gavin Gordon
Born Fred Gavin Gordon on April 8, 1901, in Waynesboro, Mississippi, he grew up in the small community of Chicora, also in Wayne County. After finishing 10th grade, he went to work in a railroad office in Mobile, where he had a few parts in Little Theatre. He soon went to Baltimore and took a course in dramatic art. He then went to the legitimate stage and then to Hollywood. Hawknosed Gordon was one of many stage actors drafted for the movies in the first years of sound. Some of his bigger roles were opposite Greta Garbo in her second talkie, *Romance* (1930), as the missionary fiancée of Barbara Stanwyck in Frank Capra's *The Bitter Tea of General Yen* (1933) and as Lord Byron in *Bride of Frankenstein* (1935). He appeared in *The Scarlett Express* (1934), which starred Marlene Dietrich, and in another Garbo film, *Camille* (1936). The first movie he appeared in was *His First Command* in 1929. His last film was *Patsy* in 1964. He was in 59 pictures during that 35-year period, playing mostly small character roles in films such as Otto Preminger's musical *Centennial Summer* (1946), *White Christmas* (1954), *Knock on Wood* (1954), *The Ten Commandments* (1956), and the Vincent Price gothic thriller, *The Bat* (1959). He made appearances on the TV shows *Alfred Hitchcock Presents*, *The Red Skelton Show* and *The Jack Benny Show*. He was close friends with all three celebrities. Gordon, who specialized in "English gentleman" roles, cultivated a British accent so perfect that many actually thought he was an Englishman. Gordon died at Canoga Park, California on April 7, 1983, just one day before his 82nd birthday. His ashes were flown to Mobile and buried with his sisters and mother in Magnolia Cemetery. Gordon, who had never married and had no close relatives, left his quite sizable personal library to the Waynesboro Memorial Public Library.

Phil Gordon
Born May 5, 1922, in Meridian Miss. The actor who played "Jasper DePew" on *The Beverly Hillbillies* TV series in 1962 and 1963, he also made several guest appearances on the 1960s TV shows *Green Acres* and *Petticoat Junction*.

Samuel Marshall Gore
Born of Mississippi parents on Nov. 24, 1927, in Coolidge, Texas, his family moved back to Mississippi when he was 5. Gore received his B.F.A. degree at Atlanta College of Art, his B.A. at Mississippi College, his masters at the University of Alabama and his doctorate at Illinois State University. This Clinton sculptor is the former chairman of the Mississippi College Art Department. Among his most familiar works are *Christ the Healer* (dedicated Nov. 8, 2000) and *Student Nurse* (1989), bronze sculptures in the main lobby of Mississippi Baptist Medical Center in Jackson and *The Working Man* (1992), located in front of the Jim Buck Ross Agriculture Museum. Gore also travels around the country sculpting clay into the *Head of Christ*, *Madonna and Child* and other religious figures before live audiences. The performance art sessions last about 30 minutes each. Dr. Gore received the Career in the Arts Award of the Governor's Awards in 1997.

Charles Graham
Born Feb. 16, 1895, in Carthage, Miss. A silent screen actor, he was in 24 movies from *Checkers* in 1913 to *The Untamed Lady* in 1926. Graham died Oct. 9, 1943, in Los Angeles.

Edwin Phillips Granberry
Born April 18, 1897, in Meridian, Miss. He created and wrote the comic strip *Buz Sawyer* for more than 30 years. He also wrote four novels and was awarded the O' Henry Prize for one of his short story collections in 1932. Granberry was living in Winter Park, Florida when he died on Dec. 5, 1988, at age 91.

Mark Gray
Singer/songwriter Gray was born on Oct. 24, 1952, in Vicksburg, the youngest of seven children. His mother died when he was two, and he was raised on Lookout Mountain, Georgia by his aunt and uncle. It was there that he began singing gospel music and learned to play piano. He returned to his father's 250-acre Mississippi farm when he was 15 and later became a finalist on the *Ted Mack Amateur Hour*. In 1972, Gray was performing in Meridian with the Revelations, a gospel group he founded, when the Oak Ridge Boys asked him to join their publishing company and appear on their tours. Gray moved to Nashville, but had several lean years. He eventually left the Oaks to join another gospel group, the Downings. He became so popular that the group fired him, and he returned to Vicksburg, where he performed in Jackson nightclubs. In 1979, he was invited to join Exile. Gray honed his songwriting skills when not performing with the group, and two songs co-written with J.P. Pennington, *Take Me Down* (1982) and *The Closer You Get* (1983), became major hits for the group Alabama. Gray recorded two albums with Exile and remained with them until 1981, when he left to pursue a solo career and write songs. He later signed with Columbia Records as a writer and performer. His first solo single, *If It Ain't Real (It Ain't You)*, made it to the Top 30 in 1983 and *Wounded Hearts* made it to the Top 20. Performers such as Engelbert Humperdinck and Melissa Manchester continued to record his songs. In 1984, Gray scored 4 Top 10 hits, including *Diamond in the Dust*, from his second album, *This Ol' Piano*. In 1985, he had 2 more Top 10 hits, but in about a year his career came to a halt. Released from his Columbia contract, he has continued to record for independent labels.

Paul Gray
This former Jacksonian is a senior writer and book reviewer on staff at *Time* magazine. He wrote the *Man of the Year* cover story on Pope John Paul II in a Dec. 1994 issue. More recently he wrote the obituary of Joe DiMaggio in 1999.

Walt Grayson
Born Mar. 17, 1949, in Greenville and grew up there. He got his start in broadcasting at WJPR radio while still in high school. In 1969 Walt moved to Jackson to continue his broadcast career at WRBC radio. Over the next few years, he managed to squeeze in a degree from Mississippi College in Clinton while still working at several other Jackson radio stations. After graduation and while working for WSLI radio in Jackson, Walt got a taste of television, taking over the weekend weather duties at WJTV-TV right next door. In 1984 Walt left radio for good when he moved full time to Jackson's WLBT-TV, doing 10 pm weather duties as well as producing feature programs such as *Spirit of Mississippi* in the 1980s and *Look Around Mississippi* and *Mississippi Seen* in the 1990s. People have come to better appreciate what Mississippi is all about and the rich heritage of the state through Walt's features. Many schools in the state use tapes of his shows in their Mississippi History and Social Studies classes. Walt's features are on video tapes for sale at bookstores and other outlets and are very popular. Walt writes all the features himself as well as doing his own photography, editing and narration. His stories have won several awards including two "Best of Show" awards in 1994 and 1998 at the Mississippi Broadcasters Association annual competition. Walt and his colleague at WLBT, Woodie

Profiles of Famous & Notable Mississippians

Assaf (see profile), continue to be the state's two most popular TV weathercasters. Walt is married to his high school sweetheart, Susan. And their only daughter, Keri, married her high school sweetheart, Bryan Horn.

Hugh Green

Born Hugh Donell Green on July 27, 1959, in Natchez, Mississippi, he attended North High School in Natchez, where he was Mississippi's top lineman. Green finished 2nd for the Heisman Trophy in 1980 as a defensive end at Pittsburgh — the closest to winning the award of any native Mississippian. He won the Lombardi and Maxwell awards at Pitt in 1980. Green later played for the Tampa Bay Buccaneers and Miami Dolphins and played in two Pro Bowls. He was inducted into the College Football Hall of Fame in 1996.

Lillian "Lil" Green

Born Dec. 22, 1919, in Clarksdale, Miss. She learned the blues in church and juke joints. In Chicago in the 30s she teamed up with one of Mississippi's finest bluesmen, Big Bill Broonzy, and they worked the chitlin' circuit together. Her composition, *Romance In the Dark*, was a 1940 Bluebird hit and in 1941 she followed with *Why Don't You Do Right?*, later covered by Peggy Lee. It's said that Green served time in prison for her involvement in a juke-joint killing, although it not confirmed. She died in Chicago on April 14, 1954, of pneumonia.

L. C. Greenwood

Born Sept 7, 1947 in Canton, Mississippi. His nickname is "Hollywood Bags." He didn't play football until he was a junior at Rogers High School. By his senior year, he was good enough to be recruited by Jackson State, Tennessee State and Arkansas AM&N. The 6-6½, 250-pound Greenwood went with the small Arkansas school. After college, he was picked in the 10th round by the Pittsburgh Steelers. He was voted the league's best defensive end in 1976. Greenwood appeared in 6 Pro Bowls and has 4 Super Bowl rings: IX (1975); X (1976); XIII (1979); and XIV (1980) in which Greenwood had 3 sacks. The Steelers won in all four Super Bowls. Over his 14 NFL seasons, Greenwood piled up 73½ sacks, leading the Steelers in that category. He retired from pro football in 1981. He had played in over 160 pro games. Greenwood was inducted into the Mississippi Sports Hall of Fame in 1996.

Jack Gregory

Born Earl Jackson Gregory, Jr. on Oct. 3, 1944, in Tupelo, he grew up in Okolona, Mississippi. A 4 year football letterman at Okolona High, Jack also played on the basketball team and was a member of the track squad in his senior year, when he was active in the shot put, relay, and high jump events. He finished first in the shot put in the conference finals, 2nd in the District, and 4th place in the state championship meet. He was a member of the first Okolona High School track team to win the Tombigbee Conference meet and a District title in 1962. He was an All Tombigbee Conference player on the gridiron and the basketball court in 1962, his senior year. He received the Sportsmanship Award in 1961 football. After graduating from high school in 1962, Jack went to the University of Chattanooga (same school where his father played), where he played tight end and defensive end for the Moccasins from 1962 through 1965. Jack was drafted by two pro football teams — in the 9th round of a special NFL draft by the Cleveland Browns and by the AFL's Buffalo Bills. Instead of going pro, he came home to Mississippi at mid-semester his junior year, transferring to Delta State, where he again played tight end, defensive end and linebacker. Gregory set a Statesmen school record in 1966 by gaining 557 yards on pass receptions at the tight end position. As a member of the Delta State track team, he broke another record by taking first place in the shot put in the 1966 Southwestern Invitational Track Meet in Memphis. Jack's father, John, was a guard for the 1941 Cleveland Rams. Jack began his pro football NFL career as a defensive end with the Cleveland Browns. Nicknamed "Big Jack," Gregory was a dominating defensive end in the NFL. After he two years apprenticeship, Jack emerged as an All Pro player. At 6-5, 250 pounds, he was perfect for the linebacker position. He spent the first two seasons at defensive end or tackle and was excellent in pass rushing. Succeeding Browns standout Bill Glass in 1968, Jack became one of the best quarterback sackers in the league. After a great year in 1969, he was selected for the Pro Bowl along with 7 other teammates including former Ole Miss guard Gene Hickerson (member Miss. Sports Hall of Fame). Following his pro bowl year in 1970, he was named the Stan Cofall Award winner as the Outstanding Defensive Player of the Year by the Cleveland Touchdown Club. During the opening of the 1970 season against the New York Jets, Gregory sacked QB Joe Namath in the first ABC Monday Night football game ever aired. During the off season of his pro career, Jack operated a farm in Okolona. His first stint with the Browns lasted from 1967 through 1972 when he played out his contract and made history by becoming the first Cleveland player to become a free agent. After negotiating with the Miami Dolphins, the Washington Redskins, and several other teams, Gregory signed with New York. He played for the Giants for the next 7 seasons. In 1972, Jack had his finest season by leading the NFL in quarterback sacks with 21 and he was runner-up to NFL Defensive Player of the Year honors. He finished second in the balloting for the MVP award in the league. He was also presented the Phil King Memorial Award by the Giants. Jack was named first team All NFL by UPI and the Pro Football Writers and appeared in his second Pro Bowl. He played in his third Pro Bowl after a great 1974 season. During the 1975 season, Jack again had the most quarterback sacks on the team and was named the Giants' MVP and Defensive Player of the Year. He was captain of the Giants defense for 5 seasons in New York. Through 6 seasons, Gregory had 73 quarterback sacks, one of the leading totals in the league. During his playing days in the NFL, Jack only missed 4 games: the last 3 games of the year in 1976 when he sat out due to a knee injury and one exhibition game He scored his only touchdown in a pro game in 1977, when he scooped up a fumble and ran it 38 yards into the end zone in a pre-season game against his old team, the Browns. It was another banner year in 1977 as he racked up a Giants team record 91 tackles with 32 solos, 59 assists, and 9 QB sacks. Following the 1977 season, Jack once again became a free agent, but eventually came to terms with the Giants through the 1979 season. He played his 13th and final season of pro football in 1979 at his old stomping grounds in Cleveland His numbers for QB sacks in a career rank among the best in the NFL record book. In the all-time records of the Giants, Jack ranks 6th with 65 sacks in his 6 seasons. He is second on the Browns QB sack leaders for a season, trailing the man he replaced, Bill Glass, by only half a sack with 14 in 1970. After his pro football career, Gregory returned home, where in 1978 the State of Mississippi in House Concurrent Resolution No. 67 commended Gregory for his pro football playing career. He was enshrined into the Delta State Sports Hall of Fame in 1985 and named to the All-time Kappa Alpha Fraternity Alumni Pro Football Hall of Fame. He was inducted into the Mississippi Sports Hall of Fame in March 2000. Jack is noted in Mississippi for his

Profiles of Famous & Notable Mississippians

tremendous devotion of time and talent to Easter Seals. He participated in the Easter Seal Telethon from 1975-91. From 1978 through 1984, he organized and hosted the Jack Gregory Easter Seal Rodeo which gathered over $40,000 in contributions. Since 1980, Jack has co-hosted the Easter Seal telethon along with WLBT-TV's weatherman Woodie Assaf. Together they have raised millions of dollars. Gregory served as President of the Easter Seal Board of Directors in 1988. He was honored in 1990 for 15 years of service to the Easter Seal Society and the Telethon. In 1991, he was honored at the Easter Seal National Convention with an award for the longest service by a professional athlete in America as a telethon host. Following his football career, Jack has been a diversified businessman. He served as a scout for the Denver Broncos for 3 years. A well known auctioneer, Jack worked for the Yokiey & Lundy Auction Company of Belzoni, Mississippi and was the Founder, Vice President, Ring Master, and Auctioneer for the Rebel Auction Company. He currently is President of Jack Gregory, Jr. Enterprises, a furniture company, and remains active as a cattleman. He has been Executive Director of the Mississippi Association of Supervisors in Jackson since 1993.

Paul Gregory
Paul Edwin Gregory was born on June 9, 1908, in Tomnolen, Webster County, Miss. He spent his high school days as a standout athlete at Leland High School in Washington County. Gregory was a three-sport letterman at Mississippi State, where he graduated. He earned his master's degree from the University of Washington. He started his pro baseball career with the Southern League's Atlanta Crackers before being traded to the Chicago White Sox, making his pitching debut with the Sox on Apr. 20, 1932. During his short major league career from 1932 to 1933, he pitched against the likes of Babe Ruth, Lou Gehrig and Joe Demaggio in 56 (8 complete) games, winning 9 and losing 14 for a 4.72 ERA. He also played for the Seattle Rainers and was a player/coach for the Hollywood Stars. After serving in the Navy during WWII, he began a 27-year coaching career at Mississippi State when he was hired in 1947 by Athletic Director Dudy Noble, Gregory's former MSU baseball coach. After coaching basketball from 1948 to 1955, Gregory made his mark as the Bulldogs' baseball coach. He led MSU to a 328-200-1 record and 15 winning seasons from 1957-74, including 4 SEC titles and a College World Series appearance in 1971. He was named SEC and NCAA District III Coach of the Year several times. Gregory was given the Distinguished American Award by the National Football Foundation and the College Hall of Fame. He was inducted into the 1977 American Baseball Coaches Association Hall of Fame, was MSU Alumnus of the Year, and was inducted into the MSU Hall of Fame. Gregory was the oldest living member of the Mississippi Sports Hall of Fame (1982) when he died of heart failure in Tunica on Sept. 16, 1999, at age 91. He is buried in Tunica.

Dick Griffin
This jazz artist and composer was born James Richard Griffin on Jan. 28, 1940, in Fannin (Rankin County), Mississippi. He attended public schools in Jackson, where he studied trombone and piano at an early age. He graduated from Jackson State and received his Master's degree from Indiana University. Griffin taught school in Columbus, Mississippi before going to New York to make his recording debut. He's recorded with Ella Fitzgerald, Duke Ellington, Marvin Gaye, Lou Rawls, and played for many Broadway productions, including *The Wiz*, *Black and Blue* and *Lena*. Griffin's composition *World Vibration Suite* was premiered by the Brooklyn Philharmonic.

John Grisham
Born Feb. 8, 1955, in Jonesboro, Arkansas, his family moved to Southaven, Miss. when he was 12 years old. He received a degree in accounting from Mississippi State University in 1977 and received his law degree from the University of Mississippi School of Law in 1981. He was elected in the State Legislature in 1983. Before his second novel, *The Firm*, was published Paramount Pictures purchased the film rights in 1990 for $600,000. *The Firm* spent 47 weeks on *The New York Times* best-seller list in hardback and became the longest-selling paperback on the *Publishers Weekly* best-seller list. After the success of his second novel, he left his law practice in Southaven, resigned from the House of Representatives and moved to Oxford to become a full-time novelist. He also bought a home in a secluded area near Charlottesville, Virginia in 1994. Grisham's novels *Pelican Brief* and *The Client* also became successful movies in 1993 and 1994, respectively. He sold the movie rights for his first novel, *A Time to Kill* (originally titled *Deathknell*), for $6 million and with the stipulation that he have approval over the script, screenwriters, and much of the cast. The film was shot in Canton, Mississippi in the fall of 1995, made its world premiere in Jackson on July 13, 1996 and was released nationwide July 24. The movie grossed over $100 million after 8 weeks, qualifying it as a blockbuster. The film finished 9th of all movies at the box office for 1996, grossing $108.8 million (153rd on the list of movies with the highest all-time grosses as of 12-5-1999). Movie rights for his fifth novel, *The Chamber* (1994), were sold before the book was finished. That movie, too, was filmed in Mississippi and released nationwide Oct. 11, 1996. A movie based on his 6th novel, *The Rainmaker*, was filmed in Memphis during the fall of 1996 and released in 1997. Grisham's other novels, all best-sellers, are *The Runaway Jury* (1996), *The Partner* (1997), *The Street Lawyer* (1998), *The Testament* (1999), and *The Brethren* (2000). Many of his novels have been the No. 1 best-seller for the entire year, such as *The Firm* in 1991, *The Chamber* in 1994, *The Rainmaker* in 1995, *The Runaway Jury* in 1996, *The Partner* in 1997, and *The Street Lawyer* in 1998. Many of these also became the nation's No. 1 for the year in paperback in the year following the hardback editions. Grisham was listed in the *Guinness Book of World Records*™ after his 6th, 7th & 8th books each had a record 2.8 million first-run release! Over 70 million copies of his books are in print. One of the world's best-selling authors, his books have been translated into 31 languages. Grisham's first screenplay, *The Gingerbread Man*, was filmed in Savannah, Ga. in 1997 with Robert Downey, Jr. and Daryl Hannah starring. In the March 20, 2000, issue of *Forbes* magazine's list of the top 100 highest paid celebrities, Grisham ranked No. 27 with his 1999 income of over $36 million. Grisham is also publisher of *The Oxford American* magazine. His novel, *The Painted House*, ran in serial form in six consecutive bi-monthly issues of that magazine starting in Jan. 2000. Grisham's papers are preserved in the Mitchell Memorial Library on campus at Mississippi State in Starkville.

Gary Grubbs
Born Nov. 14, 1949, in Amory, Miss., he grew up in Prentiss, Miss. from age one. He is a 1972 graduate of the University of Southern Mississippi, where he was a three year letterman for the Golden Eagles football team. He was inducted into the USM Hall of Fame in Nov. 1999. Grubbs has lived in Los Angeles since 1977. He is a writer and a prolific character actor who has been in several feature films: *The Border* ('82, as "Honk"), *Honkytonk Man* ('82, as "Jim Bob"); *Silkwood* ('83,

Profiles of Famous & Notable Mississippians

as "Randy Fox"); *And God Created Woman* ('87, as "Rupert Willis"); *Nadine* ('87, as Cecil); *JFK* ('91, as "Al Oser"); *Gone Fishin'* ('97, as "Phil Beasly"); *X-Files: The Movie* ('98, as "Fire Capt. Miles Cooles") and *The Astronaut's Wife* ('99, as head of NASA). Grubbs has appeared in at least 25 made-for-TV movies: *Willa* ('79, as "Junior"); *The Return of Frank Cannon* ('80, as "Mechanic"); *Gideon's Trumpet* ('80, as "Deputy Hamilton"); *Fatal Vision* ('84, as "James Blackburn"); *Ernie Kovacs: Between the Laughter* ('84, as "Nigel Edmunds"); *The Burning Bed* ('84, as "District Attorney"); *Convicted* ('86, as "Tom Cowan"); *Guilty of Innocence: The Lenell Geter Story* ('87, as "Martin Nash"); *Poker Alice* ('87, as "Marshall"); *Carly's Web* ('87); *Foxfire* ('87, as "Prince"); *Davy Crockett: Rainbow in the Thunder* ('88); *The Court-Martial of Jackie Robinson* ('90); *Without Warning: The James Brady Story* ('91, as "Larry Speakes"); *Honor Thy Mother* ('92); *A Child Lost Forever* ('92); *Telling Secrets* ('93, as "Detective Ron Taylor"); *The Ernest Green Story* ('93, as "Mr. Loomis"); *Miracle Child* ('93); *The Positively True Adventures of the Alleged Texas Cheerleader- Murdering Mom* ('93, as Detective Helton); *River of Rage: The Taking of Maggie Keene* ('93, as "C.W. Hardgrave"); *Midnight Runaround* ('94, as "Lester"); *The Stranger Beside Me* ('95); *Love's Deadly Triangle: The Texas Cadet Murder* ('97); and *Journey of the Heart* ('97). Grubbs was in the TV mini-series movies, *North and South II* ('86, as "Lieutenant Pickles") and *Heaven & Hell: North & South, Book III* ('94). Grubbs also appeared in these TV series: *For Love and Honor* ('83, as "Capt. Steven Wiecek"); *Half Nelson* ('85, as "Detective Hamill"); *Hull High* ('90, as "Mr. Brawley"); and *Will & Grace* ('98, as "Harlan Polk"). Notable TV guest appearances include: *Charlie's Angels* (9/19/79); *Young Maverick* (1/16/80); *Hill Street Blues* (1/15/81); *The Greatest American Hero* (12/16/81); *The Dukes of Hazzard* (3/16/79 & in '82); *The A-Team* (2/25/86); *T.J. Hooker* (5/28/86); *Married...with Children* (9/27/87); *Hunter* (1/6/90); *Time Trax* (11/8/93); *The X Files* (5/12/95); *Second Noah* (3/2/96); *Boston Common* (3/25/96); *Caroline in the City* (4/15/97); *ER* (5/7/98); *Dr. Quinn, Medicine Woman* (5/9/98); *Touched by an Angel* ('98); and *JAG* ('98). Grubbs had a role in the first play he wrote, *As the Crow Flies*, during its world premiere at New Stage Theatre in Jackson on March 12, 1999. He is married to Miss Mississippi of 1972, Glenda Meadows of Richton.

Ray Guy

Born in Thomson, Georgia on Dec. 22, 1949. Probably the best punter Mississippi ever had, he played football at the University of Southern Mississippi before turning pro. However, he didn't graduate from USM until 1978, after his pro career. Guy kicked the second-longest punt in college football history — a 93-yarder against Ole Miss in 1972 (the record, 99 yards, is held by Pat Brady of Nevada-Reno against Loyola-Marymount in 1950). Guy's punting average for 1971-72 was 44.67. He was voted an all-American player by *Time* magazine, *Sporting News* and Football Writer's Association of America. He was picked in the first round of the NFL draft by the Oakland Raiders in 1973. A seven-time Pro Bowl punter for the Raiders, Guy led the league in punting in 1974, '75 and '77. He punted 619 times without a kick being blocked, the second-longest streak in history. Guy was inducted into the Mississippi Sports Hall of Fame in 1994. He was among 48 players picked by a 15-person panel of NFL and Pro Football Hall of Fame officials, former players and media members, to be on the NFL's 75th Anniversary All-Time Team announced in Sept. 1994. Guy was one of only four Mississippians picked (Guy, Lance Alworth, Walter Payton and Jerry Rice) and the only punter picked. Guy was the only punter nominated in 1999 for the Football Hall of Fame! Guy was picked as punter for the 27-player NFL All-Time team selected by the 36 Pro Football Hall of Fame voters. Two other Mississippians, Jerry Rice (as one of the wide receivers) and the late Walter Payton (as one of the running backs) were selected for the team announced on Aug. 1, 2000. In 2000 Guy was inducted into the just-established Legends Society, which honors former Southern Miss athletic greats. Guy now lives in his hometown of Thomson, Georgia.

Arthur C. Guyton

Born Arthur Clifton Guyton on Sept. 8, 1919, in Oxford, Mississippi. He completed his undergraduate work at Ole Miss in 3 years, graduating at the top of his class in 1939, then attended Harvard Medical School. He served his surgical internship and residency at Massachusetts General and with the U.S. Navy at the National Naval Medical Center in Bethesda, Maryland. Doctor Guyton wrote the world's most widely used medical textbook, *Textbook of Medical Physiology* (1956), which is now in its 10th edition. He holds patent designs for a motorized wheelchair, a special medical hoist and a walking brace. His inventions earned him a Presidential Citation. The $14.5 million Arthur C. Guyton Laboratory Research Center at University Medical Center in Jackson was dedicated in his honor on June 18, 1993. In Nov. 1996, he received the Abraham Flexner Award for Distinguished Service to Medical Education presented by the Association of American Medical Colleges at their meeting in San Francisco. The association said Guyton "has made an unparalleled impact on medical education and cardiovascular physiology as a teacher, administrator and writer, earning him a variety of honors from all corners of the globe." In June 1997, Dr. Timothy Johnson, medical reporter for ABC-TV's *Good Morning America*, featured Dr. Guyton and his family — 10 children, all physicians — on the program! Dr. Guyton is professor emeritus of physiology and biophysics at University Medical Center. Dr. Guyton, whose research has saved countless lives, came in second in a poll of Mississippi's Top Humanitarians of the 20th Century. Results of the reader poll by *The Clarion-Ledger* were released on Aug. 9, 1999. In first place was philanthropist Oseola McCarty of Hattiesburg.

Toxey Haas

Haas (pronounced Hays) was born Jan. 21, 1960, in West Point, Mississippi. At age 6, he began following his dad on hunting trips. He developed definite ideas on camouflage and later said, "I always dreamed of being invisible to game while in the woods." At age 25, he walked into a fabric mill with a fist full of dirt, bark, leaves and limbs and told them to duplicate it on fabric. A few months later, his first pattern "Bottomland" was in production. Thus, the company, Haas Outdoors, was born in West Point in 1986. Haas went on to invent "Greenleaf," "Treestand," "Break-Up" (the company's No. 1 all-time best seller) and other patterns — a total of about a dozen Mossy Oak® designs — that have won the hearts of hunters across the country as "America's Most Effective Concealment System." His latest pattern is 'Forest Floor" introduced in Jan. 2000. Haas, the sole owner of all the copyrights and trademarks related to his Mossy Oak® patterns, has redefined camouflage and made Haas Outdoors the clear national leader in the industry. The company has over 50 employees and manufactures over 1,500 items for men, women and children. In addition, Haas has almost 500 sporting goods manufacturer licensees nationwide including

Profiles of Famous & Notable Mississippians

Browning®, Columbia® and Remington®. Haas has added a fully computerized state-of-the-art video production facility at their headquarters, where they produce two TV programs for TNN. The company also operates an outdoor-oriented Website (outdoors.com or mossyoak.com), buys and sells hunting real estate, and develops feed and seeds for conservationists and wildlife managers. Haas is a dedicated bowhunter of whitetail deer and turkey. In March 2000, it was announced that Haas Outdoors, Inc., was being sold to Russell Corp. of Atlanta, which will continue to operate the business in West Point.

Travis Haddix
Born in Walnut, Miss. on Nov. 26, 1938, his nickname is "Moonchild." He was inspired in his early years by B.B. King's broadcasts on WDIA out of Memphis. He's lived in Cleveland, Ohio since 1959, where he's become a fine bluesman, recording albums such as *Wrong Side Out* (1988), *Winners Never Quit* (1991), *What I Know Right Now* (1992), *I Got a Sure Thing* (1993) and *Big Ole Goodun'* (1994).

Alice Haining
Born in Jackson on Oct. 8, 1959, she was valedictorian of both her high school, Woodland Hills Academy, and her 1981 class at Mississippi College, where she had a double major in English and modern languages. On TV soap operas, she has played: "Jodie Fields" on TV's *Search For Tomorrow*; "Liza Colby Chandler" on *All My Children* (1984); "Cecilia Thompson" in *Loving* (1985-86); and "Angel Lange Snyder" on *As the World Turns* (1989, 1990-93). A notable TV guest appearance was on *Spenser: For Hire* in the episode "Autumn Thieves" in 1985. She acted in Broadway's *On Borrowed Time* in 1991 and in off-Broadway's *The Cover of Life* in 1994.

Fred W. Haise, Jr.
Born Fred Wallace Haise, Jr. on Nov. 14, 1933, in Biloxi. He graduated from Biloxi High School when he was 16. Haise worked for the *Biloxi Daily Herald* as a delivery boy, then as a sports reporter. He studied aeronautical engineering at the University of Oklahoma, completed training as a test pilot at Edwards Air Force Base and then joined NASA as a test pilot in 1959. He was selected as an astronaut in 1966, the first astronaut chosen from Mississippi. He served on the backup crew for Apollo 8, along with Neil Armstrong and Buzz Aldrin. He backed up Aldrin on Apollo 11, then John Young on Apollo 16. Haise's first flight in space was on Apollo 13 launched April 11, 1970. This third lunar landing attempt was aborted when a liquid-oxygen tank in the service module exploded, forcing the crew to return home after 142 hours. There was serious doubt whether the three-man crew would make it back to Earth alive. A movie version of their narrow escape, *Apollo 13* ('95) with Bill Paxton playing Haise was a big box-office hit. During 1977, Haise was the chief pilot for approach and landing tests with the Space Shuttle Enterprise. He retired from NASA in 1979 to become a vice-president of Grumman Aerospace Corp. He was presented the Presidential Medal of Freedom in 1970, only the second Mississippian to receive the nation's highest civilian award (the first was Laurel native Leontyne Price). Haise is one of only 3 astronauts born in Mississippi. The other two are Donald H. Peterson, born in Winona and Richard H. Truly, born in Fayette (see profiles).

Edwin "Goat" Hale
Born on Jan. 29, 1896, in Jackson. He earned his nickname "Goat" at Jackson Central High when he ran through the end zone and butted his head into a wooden building, loosening some planks. He played football at Mississippi College twice. In 1915, his first season there, he led the Collegians (before they were "Choctaws") to a 74-0 victory over Ole Miss. Hale left Mississippi College after the 1916 season to enter World War I. He returned after the war to finish his college career in 1920. In 1921, his last year at MC, he scored 23 TDs and all 23 extra points. After whipping Alabama, one fan remarked that Hale was "the best team I've ever seen." He coached at Ole Miss in the 1940s. He was inducted into the Mississippi Sports Hall of Fame in 1961 and the College Football Hall of Fame in 1963. Hale died in Clinton, Miss. on March 25, 1983.

John E. Hall
Born Aug. 8, 1946, in Milo, West Virginia. Hall received his doctorate in physiology at Michigan State University in 1974. He came to Mississippi that same year and did postdoctoral training at the University of Mississippi Medical Center before joining the faculty. There he stayed to become one of the state's leading research scientists. Today, Dr. Hall is the Guyton Professor, Chairman of the Physiology and Biophysics Department, and Director of the Center of Excellence in Cardiovascular-Renel Research at UMC. His major research interests include cardiovascular and renal physiology, mechanisms of hypertension, obesity and insulin resistance, and computer modeling and simulation of the cardiovascular-renal systems. Hall's early research proved instrumental in the development of a drug known as Captopril, the first clinically proven drug to lower blood pressure and prevent kidney damage resulting from sustained hypertension that can cause kidney failure or a heart attack. Dr. Hall's most recent work examined insulin in relation to hypertension in obese diabetics and may have uncovered the mechanism in obesity that leads to hypertension and kidney disease. For his work in this field, Hall received the world medical community's coveted Merck, Sharp and Dohme International Award from the International Society of Hypertension, presented to him in July 1998 in Amsterdam, the Netherlands. His many other awards and honors include the Harry Goldblatt Award of the American Heart Association, the Lewis Dahl Lectureship of the American Heart Association, the Marion Young Scholar Award of the American Society of Hypertension, the Ernest Starling Lectureship of the American Physiological Society, the Distinguished Research Achievment Award of the American Heart Association, and the A.P. Barnard Distinguished Professorship of the University of Mississippi. He has authored or co-authored over 360 articles that have appeared in the nation's most prestigious medical journals as well as in journals abroad. He has also written or edited 7 books. Hall is editor of *The American Journal of Physiology: Regulatory, Integrative and Comparative Physiology*.

Theora Hamblett
Born Jan. 15, 1895, in Paris, Lafayette County, Miss. She taught school near her home from 1915-36. In 1939, Theora moved to Oxford where she became a seamstress and turned her home into a boardinghouse. She didn't start painting until the early 1950s. She painted scenes of southern country life, children's games, and her most unusual works are the 300+ religious paintings of biblical subjects and of Hamblett's own dreams and visions. Her first such painting she did in 1954, *The Golden Gate* and later renamed *The Vision*, is owned by the Museum of Modern Art in New York. Her work has been exhibited in Canada, Mexico, Europe, and throughout the U.S. She left many of her paintings to University Museum at Ole Miss in Oxford, Mississippi when she died on March 6, 1977. She is buried in the Hamblett family cemetery about halfway between Water Valley and Paris, Mississippi.

Profiles of Famous & Notable Mississippians

Fannie Lou Hamer
Born Fannie Lou Townsend on Oct. 6, 1917, in Montgomery County, her family moved to Sunflower County, Miss. when she was 2 years old. The youngest of 20 children born to sharecropper parents, Fannie had only 6 years of schooling (a year of schooling was only 4 months for black students then) and was a polio victim, yet she became one of the most recognized women of the Civil Rights movement in the early 1960's. She helped get Head Start & better low-income housing into Mississippi. She spoke nationwide and became one of America's most admired Civil Rights leaders. She died on Mar. 14, 1977, and is buried in Ruleville, Miss. Incribed on her tombstone are the words, "I'm sick and tired of being sick and tired." Her autobiography, *This Little Light of Mine*, was published in 1994. In 1995 the post office in Ruleville was dedicated to her. She's in the National Women's Hall of Fame.

Evelyn Allen Hammett
Born in Jefferson County on June 12, 1894. Head of the Department of Languages and Literature at Delta State University from 1947-54, she wrote the well-known children's book, *I, Priscilla*. Hammett died on June 16, 1985.

Earle W. Hammons
Born on Dec. 2, 1882, in Winona, Mississippi. An early movie producer, he started in the silent screen era with *Ride on a Runaway Train* (1920) and produced two more silent films. Most of the movies he produced were in the 1930s after sound came along. He produced *Those We Love* and two other films in 1932 including *Come On, Tarzan*. His last movie was *Happy Heels* in 1936. All toll, he was producer on a dozen films, executive producer on most of them. Hammons died in New Rochelle, New York on July 31, 1962, at the age of 79.

W.C. Handy
William Christopher Handy was born on Nov. 16, 1873, in Florence, Ala., the son of former slaves. As a 15-year-old he left home to work in a traveling minstrel show. He attended Teachers A&M College in Huntsville, then worked as a school teacher and bandmaster. In 1893, he formed a quartet to perform at the World's Columbian Exposition in Chicago. For several years he drifted around the country working at different jobs. From 1903 to 1905, he lived on Issaquena Avenue in Clarksdale, Mississippi. It was near there that he "discovered" the blues in 1903. Handy wrote that "One night in Tutwiler, as I nodded in the railroad station waiting for a train...a Negro had commenced plunking a guitar beside me while I slept. As he played, he pressed a knife on the string of the guitar in the manner popularized by Hawaiian guitarists who used steel bars. The effect was unforgettable. His song, too, struck me instantly. 'Goin' Where the Southern Cross the Dog'." Eventually he settled in Memphis, where he wrote *Memphis Blues* and published it on Sept. 27, 1912. It was considered to be the first song composed and published with the word "blues" in it Handy also composed the immortal *St. Louis Blues* (1914), and other classics such as *Beale Street Blues*, *Memphis Blues*, *Careless Love*, and *Yellow Dog Blues*. He wrote during the period of transition from ragtime to jazz using the influences of spirituals, work songs, and folk ballads in addition to ragtime and the 12-bar blues notes that he inserted. His own chosen instrument was the coronet. In all, he wrote some 60 compositions plus his autobiography, *Father of the Blues*. Handy was inducted into the Songwriters Hall of Fame in 1983. The man who forever changed the course of American music spent his last years in New York City, where he died March 28, 1958, and is buried in the Woodlawn Cemetery (Cosmos Section, Block 203/198) in the Bronx.

Barry Hannah
Born Apr. 23, 1942, in Meridian, Mississippi, he grew up in Forest, Pascagoula, and Clinton. He received a B.A. from Mississippi College and an F.M.A. from the University of Arkansas. He has been writer-in-residence at Clemson University, Memphis State University, the University of Alabama, the University of Iowa, the University of Montana and at Ole Miss since 1985. His novels include *Geronimo, Rex* (1972), which won a Faulkner Prize, and *Nightwatchmen* (1973). Hannah's *Airships* (1978), a collection of short stories, received critical acclaim and won the Arnold Gingrich Short Fiction Award. *Ray* (1980) and *The Tennis Handsome* (1983) both received international acclaim. *Captain Maximus* was published in 1985. His short story, *Nicodemus Bluff*, appeared in *New Stories from the South: The Year's Best 1994*. *High Lomesome* (1996), a collection of his short stories that previously appeared in *Esquire*, *Sports Afield*, *The Oxford American* and other magazines, was published in Oct. 1996. His collection of short stories, *Bats Out of Hell*, also won the prestigious Faulkner Award for Literature in 1997.

Jack G. Hanson
Born Sept. 18, 1930, in Escatawpa, Jackson Co., Mississippi, he was living in Galveston, Texas, when he entered the U.S. Army. Hanson was in Company F, 31st Infantry Regiment near Pachi-dong, Korea when he performed an act of bravery that took his life on June 7, 1951. He was awarded the Congressional Medal of Honor posthumously on Feb. 1, 1952. Here are the actual words of his citation: "Pfc. Hanson, a machine gunner with the 1st Platoon, Company F, distinguished himself by conspicuous gallantry and intrepidity at the risk of his life above and beyond the call of duty in action against an armed enemy of the United Nations. The company, in defensive positions on two strategic hills separated by a wide saddle, was ruthlessly attacked at approximately 0300 hours, the brunt of which centered on the approach to the divide within range of Pfc. Hanson's machinegun. In the initial phase of the action, 4 riflemen were wounded and evacuated and the numerically superior enemy, advancing under cover of darkness, infiltrated and posed an imminent threat to the security of the command post and weapons platoon. Upon orders to move to key terrain above and to the right of Pfc. Hanson's position, he voluntarily remained to provide protective fire for the withdrawal. Subsequent to the retiring elements fighting a rearguard action to the new location, it was learned that Pfc. Hanson's assistant gunner and 3 riflemen had been wounded and had crawled to safety, and that he was maintaining a lone-man defense. After the 1st Platoon reorganized, counterattacked, and resecured its original positions at approximately 0530 hours, Pfc. Hanson's body was found lying in front of his emplacement, his machinegun ammunition expended, his empty pistol in his right hand, and a machete with blood on the blade in his left hand, and approximately 22 enemy dead lay in the wake of his action. Pfc. Hanson's consummate valor, inspirational conduct, and willing self-sacrifice enabled the company to contain the enemy and regain the commanding ground, and reflect lasting glory on himself and the noble traditions of the military service." Although born in Mississippi, his Medal of Honor is accredited to Texas, his adopted state. In all wars, 17 Medals of Honor have been officially accredited to Mississippi, although we claim 5 more that were accredited to other states because the recipients had Mississippi ties. Hanson was one of 4 native Mississippians (out of a total of 5 Mississippians) to earn the Congressional Medal of Honor (CMOH) during the

Profiles of Famous & Notable Mississippians

Korean conflict, and one of only two Mississippians (both native - see Mack A. Jordan profile) in the Korean conflict to be awarded the Medal posthumously. He was one of only 4 native Mississippians (of 6 Mississippians) to be awarded the CMOH posthumously. Hanson is one of only 13 native Mississippians (of 22 Mississippians — 15 Army, 4 Marines and 3 Navy) in all wars to be awarded the CMOH out of 3,433 recipients through Nov. 1, 2000. Hanson is buried in the Robinson Cemetery in Escatawpa, Mississippi. There is no Medal of Honor marker on his grave.

Mel Hardin (see ":Mel & Tim")

Phil Hardwick

Born on June 20, 1948, in Mendenhall, Miss. He received his B.S. in Real Estate and Finance Business Administration from Belhaven College and his MBA from Millsaps College. One of Mississippi's foremost experts on real estate, he's written many professional papers and articles and was an adjunct professor at Millsaps College and an instructor at the Mississippi Realtors Institute. Hardwick is the real estate columnist for the *Mississippi Business Journal*. He was president of the Mississippi Economic Development Council, 1997-98. He has held the positions of Deputy Administrator and Chief Investigator and Administrator of the Miss. Real Estate Commission, Director of Economic and Community Development for the City of Jackson, and is currently VP of Community and Economic Development at Mississippi Valley Gas. His book, *Two Hours of Real Estate: One Minute at a Time*, was published in 1993. He ventured into fiction with a self-published 3-cassette audiobook mystery/thriller called *The Real Estate Agent*. He's also written *Mississippi Mysteries*, a series of printed novellas, which include *Found in Flora* ('96), *Justice in Jackson* ('97), *Captured in Canton* ('97), *Newcomer in New Albany* ('97), *Vengeance in Vicksburg* ('98), *Collision in Columbia* ('98), and *Conspiracy in Corinth* ('99).

James D. Hardy

Born May 14, 1918, in Birmingham, Alabama. He attended the University of Alabama, then received his MD in 1942 from the University of Pennsylvania, where he also served his internship and residency. He started his active duty in the U.S. Army in 1944. He moved to Jackson, Mississippi in 1955. Dr. Hardy was Chairman of the Department of Surgery at UMC from its establishment in 1955 until his retirement in 1987. Dr. Hardy and his team at the University Medical Center in Jackson performed the world's first human kidney autotransplant in 1962, the first lung transplant in the world on June 11, 1963 (they replaced the left lung of patient John Richard Russell in the 3-hour operation—he survived 18 days), the first adrenal glands autotransplant in humans in 1963, and the first animal-to-human transplant operation in the world on Jan. 23, 1964. The heart of a chimpanzee was transplanted into a 64-year-old Boyd Rush, who was dying. The heart continued beating for 90 minutes. It was actually the first heart transplant of any kind in the world! Thirty-five years later in mid-1999, readers of *The Clarion-Ledger* in Jackson overwhelmingly selected that operation as the state's greatest scientific accomplishment of the millennium! Dr. Hardy's autobiography, *The World of Surgery, 1945-1985; Memoirs of One Participant* was published in 1986. He has received numerous awards and honors for his pioneering work. The $7.8 million James D. Hardy Clinical Sciences Building at the University Medical Center in Jackson was dedicated in his honor on February 25, 1994. Dr. Hardy was featured in the final segment of the 4-part PBS documentary *Knife to the Heart* which aired in 1997.

Ira B. Harkey, Jr.

Born Jan. 15, 1918, in New Orleans. Harkey graduated from Tulane with a degree in commerce in 1938. He first came to Mississippi in 1949. Harkey received a Pulitzer Prize in 1963 for his editorials on Civil Rights in the *Pascagoula Chronicle*. In the 1960s, he was a professor of journalism at Ohio State University. He also wrote his autobiography titled *The Smell of Burning Crosses* (1967), about his experiences as a journalist in Mississippi at the time he won the Pulitzer. His second book was the biographical *Pioneer Bush Pilot, the Story of Noel Wien* (1974), reflecting Harkey's experiences in the late 1960s when he taught at the University of Alaska at Fairbanks. Harkey co-authored the biography *Alton Ochsner, Surgeon of the South* (1990). Harkey has written articles that have appeared in the *Wall Street Journal* and other national publications. Harkey now lives in Keerville, Texas.

Greg Harkins

Born Mar. 21, 1953, in Jackson, Mississippi. "Chairmaker to the Presidents," this master craftsman had built rocking chairs for four U.S. Presidents — Jimmy Carter, Ronald Reagan, George Bush, and Bill Clinton. His numerous celebrity clients include Nancy Reagan, Dan Quayle, Bob Hope, Paul Harvey, the late George Burns, Oprah Winfrey, and even Pope John Paul II! He's also sold his chairs to hundreds of just plain folks across the nation and in about 20 foreign countries. A huge rocking chair built by Harkins is on display at the Jim Buck Ross Agricultural and Forestry Museum in Jackson. He was nominated for the 1995 Governor's Award for Excellence and also received a grant from the Mississippi Arts Commission. He has been featured in *Esquire* magazine and appeared on the cover of the October 1995 issue of *American Woodworker* magazine. Crews from Australia and Japan have visited Vaughn to film his work. His shop is located in Yazoo County on Possum Bend Road in Vaughn not far off I-55.

Robert Harper

Born in Jackson, Mississippi in 1931. This character actor has appeared in over 2 dozen movies since playing a night watchman in his first film, *The Premonition* (1975), which was filmed entirely in Mississippi. Some of the other recognizable movies in which he has a part include *Mommie Dearest* ('81, as David), *Creepshow* ('82, as Charlie Gereson in "The Crate"), *Once Upon a Time in America* ('84, as Sharkey), *Twins* ('88, as Gilbert Larsen), *War of the Roses* ('89, as Heath), *Final Analysis* ('92, as Alan Lowenthal), *Gunman* ('94, as Rance), *Deconstructing Harry* ('97, as Harry's doctor), *Molly* ('99, as Dr. Simmons), and *The Insider* ('99, as Mark Stern). He helped produce the film, *Rookie of the Year* ('93). He's had minor roles in over a dozen TV movies. His notable TV guest appearances include: *Wiseguy* as "Dewitt Clipton" ('89); *Roseanne* playing "Edgar" on 2/28/89; *Star Trek: The Next Generation* playing "Lathal" in the episode "The Host" on 5/11/91; and on *Michael Hayes* on 3/4/98.

Eddy Harrington (see Eddy Clearwater)

Othella Harrington

Born on Jan. 31, 1974, in Jackson. He attended college at Georgetown. This 6-9 power forward began his pro basketball career in the NBA with the Houston Rockets in the 1996-97 season. He played the 1999-2000 season with the Vancouver Grizzlies. His career stats: played in 115 games (15.3 minutes avg.); 623 points (5.4 avg.); 405 rebounds (3.5 avg.); 22 steals (0.19 avg.); 49 blocks (0.43 avg.); and 42 assists (0.37 avg.). His career percentages, field goal .513 & free throw .695.

Lusia Harris (see Lusia Harris Stewart)

Profiles of Famous & Notable Mississippians

Thomas Harris
Born William Thomas Harris III on Sept. 22, 1940, in Jackson, Tennessee, he moved to Rich, Coahoma County, Mississippi at a young age. He attended Clarksdale High School, where his mother taught biology. Spenting most of his time reading and writing, Hemmingway was his favorite writer. After high school, he went to Baylor University in Waco, Texas, to earn a major in English. While at Baylor, Harris wrote numerous stories for magazines like *True* and *Argosy*. He also worked for the Waco *News-Tribune* as a police reporter. After college Harris moved to New York and held a job as a reporter for the Associated Press from 1968-74. His experiences as a crime reporter gave him information he used in his later writings. His first book, *Black Sunday* ('75), is about Arab terrorist and a Vietnam veteran who commandeer the Goodyear Blimp and try to bomb the Super Bowl. It became a best seller and a successful 1977 movie starring Bruce Dern and Robert Shaw. Harris does a lot of research for his fiction, so his second book *Red Dragon* was not published until 1981. This novel is the story of an FBI agent's search for a serial killer and introduces us to Harris' psychotic character, psychiatrist-turned-madman Hannibal "The Cannibal" Lecter. *Red Dragon* also became a popular movie called *Manhunter* (1986). His third novel once again brings us Hannibal "The Cannibal," and is considered a masterpiece of suspense, *The Silence of the Lambs* (1988). The film version was the biggest grossing movie of 1991, taking in almost $131 million in the U.S. alone! It became only the third movie ever to win the top five Academy Awards® — Best Actor (Anthony Hopkins), Best Actress (Jodie Foster), Best Screenplay (Ted Dally), Best Director (Jonathan Demme), and Best Picture! Harris' fourth novel, *Hannibal*, quickly became a No. 1 Bestseller after it was released in June 1999. And, a movie sequel titled *Hannibal* with Sir Anthony Hopkins again playing Hannibal Lecter has a release date of Feb. 2001. Harris has homes in Rich, Miss., Long Island, N.Y., and Miami.

David E. Harrison
Born in Oct 17, 1937, in Mann, W.Va., he moved to Columbus, Mississippi in 1969. As senior product designer for Sanderson Plumbing for 20 years, he was responsible for several patents that company holds, including "the soft toilet seat" he designed in 1986, of which over a million are sold each year. Harrison died of a heart attack on July 7, 1996.

Pat Harrison
Born Byron Patton Harrison on Aug. 29, 1881, at Crystal Springs, Copiah Co., Miss. He briefly attended the University of Mississippi and the University of Louisiana at Baton Rouge. He taught school at Leakesville, Miss. and also studied law. He was admitted to the bar in 1902 and started his practice in Leakesville. Harrison was district attorney for the second district of Mississippi 1906-1910, when he resigned. He moved to Gulfport in 1908. He was elected as a Democrat to the 62nd and to the three succeeding Congresses and served from March 4, 1911 until March 3, 1919. Harrison was elected as a Democrat to the U.S. Senate in 1918 and was reelected in 1924, 1930, and 1936 and served from March 4, 1919 until his death. He served as President pro tempore of the Senate during the 77th Congress and was chairman of the Committee on Finance in the 73rd through 77th Congresses. Harrison died in Washington, D.C. on June 22, 1941, and services were held in the chamber of the United States Senate. He is buried in the Evergreen Cemetery in Gulfport, Miss. The Pat Harrison Waterway District of Mississippi was named in his honor.

Antonio Harvey
Born July 6, 1970, in Pascagoula, Miss. This basketball player was the Missouri Valley Freshman of the Year at Southern Illinois before transferring to Georgia. He left Georgia after one season and went on to become the Carolina Conference Player of the Year at NAIA Pfeiffer College. He led the NAIA in blocked shots as a junior (4.8) and senior (5.3). In the 1993-94 season this 6-10, 245-pound forward-center averaged 2.6 points and 2.2 rebounds in 27 games as a reserve center in his rookie season with the NBA Los Angeles Lakers. He played for the Lakers through the 1994-95 season, then a season for the Vancouver Grizzlies, then to the L.A. Clippers for the 1995-96 season, and for the Seattle Supersonics during the 1996-97 season. He played for the Portland Trail Blazers during the 1999-2000 season. His 6-season career stats: He played in 147 games (11.3 minutes avg. p/game); 468 points (3.2 avg.); 371 rebounds (2.5 avg.); 50 steals (0.34 avg.); 111 blocks (0.76 avg.); and 44 assists (0.30 avg.). His career field goal percentage is .396 and free throw percentage is .494.

Sam Haskell
Born June 24, 1955, in Mobile, Alabama, where his mother worked as a nurse, he grew up in Amory, Mississippi from about age 4. Haskell graduated from Ole Miss in 1977. He is the senior vice president and former west coast head of TV for the William Morris Agency, the huge talent agency in Los Angeles. He is still a senior vice president, but in Sept. 1999 he was promoted to the position of Worldwide head of Television. Haskell started in the mailroom at William Morris in 1978 and in 12 years worked his way to become the agency's youngest senior vice president ever. Haskell now runs the entire TV arm of William Morris, overseeing about 100 agents and their staffs in Los Angeles, Nashville, Rome, London, Munich and Sydney. Haskell has been responsible for the development and/or production of such hit shows as *Cosby*, *Murphy Brown*, *Suddenly Susan*, *Mad About You*, *Second Noah*, *Roseanne* and others. Haskell's top Hollywood clients have included Kathie Lee Gifford, Jo Beth Williams, Martin Short, Lucie Arnaz, Marilyn McCoo, Jaleel White, Joan Van Ark, Malcolm Jamal Warner, Debbie Allen, Stephanie Zimbalist, and Donna Mills. His work with children earned him 1997 Man of the Year honors from the Alliance for Children's Rights presented to him in Beverly Hills. For several years running, he has used his position as leverage in staging Stars Over Mississippi, a fundraiser that has brought big-name celebrities to Amory. Created in memory of his mother, Mary Kirkpatrick Haskell, the event has raised over $1 million in scholarship money. Haskell is married to Mary Donnelly, Miss Mississippi of 1977.

Ted Hawkins
A blues singer-guitarist born on Oct. 28, 1936, in Lakeshore, Mississippi, he grew up in Biloxi in poverty. An abused and illiterate child, Hawkins was sent to reform school when he was 12 years old. At age 15, he stole a leather jacket and spent 3 years at Parchman Farm. Roaming from Chicago to Philadelphia to Buffalo after his release, Hawkins finally purchased a one-way ticket to L.A. in 1966. After several recording deals went sour, Hawkins became a street musician playing for change. Then, in 1971, producer Bruce Bromberg recorded Hawkins and his original material. Bromberg lost touch with Hawkins for a while after recording him — Hawkins had fallen afoul of the law once again. In 1982, those tapes finally emerged on Rounder Records as *Watch Your Step*, and Hawkins began to receive some acclaim. *Rolling Stone* magazine gave his album a five-star review. Bromberg corralled him again for the 1986 encore album *Happy Hour*, which contained the touching *Cold & Bitter Tears*. At the

Profiles of Famous & Notable Mississippians

suggestion of a British deejay, Hawkins moved to England in 1986 and was treated like a star for four years, performing in Great Britain, Ireland, France, even Japan. But when he came home, he was faced with the same old situation. Once again, he set up his tip jar on the beach and played for passersby, until 1994. That's when DGC/Geffen Records issued *The Next Hundred Years*, his breakthrough album, released to critical acclaim. Just when he was finally getting a break, he died of a stroke on Jan.. 1, 1995, in Los Angeles. For a year or so, he was even a star in his own country. His album, *Love You Most of All: More Songs from Venice Beach*, was issued in 1998.

Brooks Haxton
Born in Greenville on Dec. 1, 1950. A National Endowment of the Arts fellow, he has gained critical acclaim for his books of poetry *Dominion, Dead Reckoning,* and *The Lay of Eleanor and Irene*. Another book of poetry, *The Sun at Night*, was published in May 1995. He has also written some screen plays including *Tennessee Williams: Orpheus of the American Stage*, which aired on PBS on Dec. 18. 1994. Brooks, who now lives in Syracuse, N.Y., is the son of acclaimed Jackson novelist Josephine Haxton, whose pen name is Ellen Douglas.

Josephine Haxton (see Ellen Douglas)

Charlie Hayes
Born on May 29, 1965, in Hattiesburg. He made his major league baseball debut on Sept. 11, 1988, with San Francisco. He stayed with the Giants until 1989, then to the Philadelphia Phillies (1989-1995), the New York Yankees (1992-96), the Colorado Rockies (1993-94) and the Pittsburgh Pirates and the New York A's in 1996. In 1996, Hayes was a key contributor to the Yankees in the World Series as he helped them win their first world title in 18 years. Hayes recorded the final out by catching a foul pop in Game 6 against Atlanta. He played in 1998 and 1999 with the San Francisco Giants. He played for the Milwaukee Brewers in 2000. His career stats through the 2000 season include 1,369 hits in 5,212 at bats (.263 batting avg.), 576 runs, 144 homers, 736 RBIs in 1,516 games played.

Saul Haymond, Sr.
Born Jan. 4, 1947, in Ebenezer, Holmes County, Miss. This black artist, who now lives in Tchula, specializes in paintings of plantation life in the 1800, but even paints futuristic scenes. He has received grants from institutions such as the Adolph and Esther Gottlieb Foundation of New York, the Mississippi Arts Commission, and the Southern Art Federation in Atlanta which has also sponsored exhibitions of his works. He sold his first painting in 1967 to the governor of California for $500. His painting, *Morganfield Plantation*, brought $24,600. He received a John Simon Guggenheim Memorial Foundation Latin American Fellowship in 1995. He also received a Pollock-Krasner Foundation Fellowship in 1995. He is a man of many talents. Even though he has only a formal fourth-grade education, he has taught himself to write in four different languages and has rendered some 10,000 blueprints for various projects including two on which he holds patents. Many of his visionary inventions deal with farm machinery.

Spencer Haywood
Born Apr. 22, 1949, in Silver City, Humphreys County, Miss. The 6-foot-8 Haywood starred on the U.S. basketball team in the 1968 Olympics, where he was a Gold Medal winner who set a USA individual competition record for the most points (145) and had the 2nd highest field goal percentage with .719 (64-89). He became the first college player to Test the ABA Hardship Draft Rule in 1969 when he left the University of Detroit after his sophomore season to go pro, signing for $50,000 a year with the Denver Rockets. There, he was voted Rookie of the Year in 1970 and was voted the ABA's MVP in 1970 when he led the league in scoring (30.0 ppg) and rebounding (19.5 p/game). He was also MVP of the 1969-70 ABA All-Star Game. He is: the second rookie (behind Wilt Chamberlain) to score 2,500 points in a first pro season; the ABA Record Holder for most field goals (986) and rebounds (1,637) in a season; the ABA Record Holder for Highest Rebound per Game Average (19.5 in 1969-70); and a member of 1969-70 ABA All-Pro Team. He later played for the NBA's Seattle Supersonics and 4 other teams during a 14-year period.

John W. Heard
Born John William Heard on March 27, 1860, in Woodstock (now Money), Leflore Co., Miss. He graduated from West Point Military Academy in 1883. He was a 1st Lt. in the 3d U.S. Cavalry at the Mouth of the Manimani River, west of Bahia Honda, Cuba, fighting in the Spanish-American War when he performed an act of bravery on July 23, 1898, that earned him the Medal of Honor, which was awarded on June 21, 1899. Here are the actual words of his citation: "After 2 men had been shot down by Spaniards while transmitting orders to the engine-room on the Wanderer, the ship having become disabled, this officer took the position held by them and personally transmitted the orders, remaining at his post until the ship was out of danger." Heard was one of two native Mississippians (see Ira C. Welborn) to receive the Medal of Honor for the Spanish-American War. Heard's was one of 17 Medals of Honor officially accredited to Mississippi in all wars, although we claim 5 more that were accredited to other states because the recipients had Mississippi ties. Hanson is one of 13 native Mississippians (of 22 Mississippians — 15 Army, 4 Marines and 3 Navy) in all wars to have received the Medal of Honor out of 3,433 total recipients of the Medal through Nov. 1, 2000. Heard retired with the rank of Brigadier General. He died on Feb. 4, 1922, and is buried in the West Point Post Cemetery in New York (Sec. VIII, Row B, Grave 112). There is no Medal of Honor marker on his grave.

Jimmy Heidel
Born in Benton, Yazoo County, Mississippi on Dec. 1, 1943. He was in economic development for many years in Vicksburg. In 1992, he became Director of the Mississippi Department of Economic and Community Development and was considered to be one of the best directors of economic development in the nation. He resigned that position in Jan. 2000. Heidel can take much credit for the economic boom in Mississippi during the 1990s. During his eight-year tenure, Heidel oversaw the creation of 194,000 jobs with economic investments by companies totaling more than $20 billion. From 1992 through 1999, the state reported several economic gains, including a 17.6 percent increase in disposable personal income, the highest increase in the U.S., and the highest number of new business start-ups nationwide during 1998. Heidel is once again working in Vicksburg as the executive in charge of the Warren County Port Commission, the Chamber of Commerce and the Economic Development Foundation. A football standout at Ole Miss, Heidel also played pro football as a defensive back with the New Orleans Saints.

Jimmy Henderson
Born May 20, 1954, in Jackson, Miss. This jazz musician plays trombone and sometimes guitar in the big band/swing style. He has played on many albums with such artists as Bobby Bryant, Glen Miller, the Dorsey Brothers, B.B. King, Dean Parks, the Platters, and Ernie Watts. Also a songwriter, Henderson's songs have been recorded by Little Anthony, Paul Anka, Fats Domino, Peggy Lee, & Charlie Rich.

Profiles of Famous & Notable Mississippians

Mike Henderson
Born on July 7, 1951, in Yazoo City, Mississippi. Guitarist, singer and songwriter Henderson carved a niche for himself as a session man over the years in the Nashville studio scene before he began recording under his own name with his own blues band, the Bluebloods. Henderson's albums include *Edge of Night* (1994), *First Blood* (1996) and *Oakland Blues* (1998). He and his band have recorded and performed with Emmy Lou Harris, Kevin Welch, Stevie Ray Vaughan, Lonnie Mack, Aaron Neville, Johnny Cash, Al Kooper and Delbert McClinton. The band got some radio attention on its second release for their song, *Pay Bo Diddley*, a song that addressed the inequities in U.S. record royalty laws. *First Blood* was recorded in the studio in Nashville over two days, with almost all the songs recorded on the first take with no overdubs. The band lends their own spin to classic blues material like Sonny Boy Williamson's *So Sad to Be Lonesome*, J.B. Hutto's *Hip Shakin'* and Hound Dog Taylor's *Give Me Back My Wig*.

Beth Henley
Born Elizabeth Becker Henley on May 8, 1952, in Jackson, Mississippi. While still a sophomore in college, she wrote the play, *Crimes of the Heart*, for which she received the Pulitzer Prize in 1981 — the first female to win the Pulitzer for Drama in 21 years — and won the New York Critics' Circle Award for 1980-81. In 1986, her screen adaptation of the play earned her an Oscar® nomination for Best Adapted Screenplay. She wrote the off-Broadway play *The Miss Firecracker Contest* which became the movie *Miss Firecracker* (1989) starring Holly Hunter and filmed in Yazoo City, Mississippi. It won critical acclaim, but didn't fare so well at the box office. Her other screenwriter credits include *True Stories* (1986), *No Mercy* (1986) and *Nobody's Fool* (1986), a romantic comedy starring fellow Mississippian Eric Roberts. Henley also had a bit part in that movie as a bridesmaid and also appears as a "Bible pusher" in the film *Swing Shift* (1984). Her other plays include *Abundance*, *The Wake of Jamey Foster*, *Am I Blue* and *Revelers*. Her play, *Impossible Marriage*, starring Holly Hunter, opened on Broadway on Oct. 15, 1998.

Aaron Henry
This Civil Rights leader and activist was born on July 2, 1922, in Clarksdale, Miss., the son of sharecroppers. By profession he was a pharmacist and owned Fourth Street Drug Store in Clarksdale. He was easy-going and his quiet diplomacy accomplished much. Henry was a key figure in bringing better housing, health services, more employment, and the Head Start program to the state. He headed up the formation of the Mississippi Freedom Democratic Party and the Council of Federated Organizations. He became state president of the NAACP in 1959. Henry was one of the nation's foremost grassroots fighters of equality on the local, state and national levels, according to the biography titled, *Aaron Henry: The Fire Ever Burning*, by Henry Aaron with Constance Curry (University Press of Mississippi), published in early 2000. He never fully recovered from a stoke he suffered on Christmas Day 1996. Aaron Henry died on May 19, 1997, in Clarksdale.

Robert T. Henry
Born Nov. 27, 1923, in Greenville, Miss. He was a Private in the U.S. Army, 16th Infantry, 1st Infantry Division in Germany when he performed an act of bravery, which took his life on Dec. 3, 1944. The Congressional Medal of Honor (CMOH) was awarded posthumously on June 12, 1945. Here are the actual words of his citation: "Near Luchem, Germany, he volunteered to attempt the destruction of a nest of 5 enemy machineguns located in a bunker 150 yards to the flank which had stopped the advance of his platoon. Stripping off his pack, overshoes, helmet, and overcoat, he sprinted alone with his rifle and hand grenades across the open terrain toward the enemy emplacement. Before he had gone half the distance he was hit by a burst of machinegun fire. Dropping his rifle, he continued to stagger forward until he fell mortally wounded only 10 yards from the enemy emplacement. His single-handed attack forced the enemy to leave the machineguns. During this break in hostile fire the platoon moved forward and overran the position. Pvt. Henry, by his gallantry and intrepidity and utter disregard for his own life, enabled his company to reach its objective, capturing this key defense and 70 German prisoners." Henry is one of 4 native Mississippians (of 7 Mississippians) to be awarded the CMOH during WWII. He was one of 4 *native* Mississippians (of 6 Mississippians) to be awarded the CMOH posthumously. Henry's Medal was one of 17 Medals of Honor that have been officially accredited to Mississippi in all wars, although we claim 5 more accredited to other states because the recipients had Mississippi ties. Henry is one of 13 *native* Mississippians (of 22 Mississippians — 15 Army, 4 Marines & 3 Navy) in all wars to be awarded the CMOH out of 3,433 total recipients through Nov. 1, 2000. Henry is buried in the Greenville Cemetery in Greenville, Mississippi. A Medal of Honor marker is on his grave.

Jim Henson
This world-famous puppeteer was born James Maury Henson on Sept. 24, 1936, in Greenville, Mississippi. His "Muppets" were first seen in 1954 on a Washington, D.C. TV station. By 1969 Kermit, the Frog , Miss Piggy, Big Bird and his other characters formed the core of the children's program "Sesame Street." Kermit ("the former tadpole from Mississippi"), the first of Henson's 3,000 muppet creations, was named after one of Henson's Leland friends, Kermit Scott, now a professor at Purdue University in Indiana. Kermit has starred in 5 feature films, hosted the TV shows *Nightline*, *The Tonight Show* and *Larry King Live*, and served as the Grand Marshall of the 1996 Tournament of Roses Parade. The feature films of Kermit and Henson's other muppet creations include *The Muppet Movie* ('79), *The Great Muppet Caper* ('81), *The Dark Crystal* ('82), *The Muppets Take Manhattan* ('84), and *Teenage Mutant Ninja Turtles* (1989). Henson directed the children's fantasy movie *Labyrinth* (1986) which stars David Bowie and is based on one of Henson's stories. He also designed the creatures for the film. Henson created the popular show *Fraggle Rock* for HBO and the reptilian comedy *Dinosaurs*, which debuted on ABC-TV on Apr. 26, 1991. Henson even had a couple of Top-40 hit records — he was the voices of Ernie on *Rubber Duckie* (#16 in '70) and Kermit on *Rainbow Connection* (#25 in '79). His characters have been featured in many books and toys. Henson received many awards including an Emmy in 1978 for their weekly TV series *The Muppet Show* (1976-81), seen in over 100 countries. Right before Henson's death, the Walt Disney Company was considering a purchase of the Muppets, reportedly for $100 million! He died on May 16, 1990, from *Streptococcus pneumoniae*, a rare form of Strep-A pneumonia. His body was cremated. The Jim Henson Muppet Museum opened in Leland, Mississippi on Aug. 28, 1991.

Ty Herndon
Born on May 2, 1962 in Meridian, Mississippi, he grew up in Butler, Alabama, where he sang gospel music and learned how to play piano. After graduating from high school, he moved to Nashville. He spent 10 years without making much progress getting into the music business, so he left Music City for Texas, where he played in local honky tonks and developed a

Profiles of Famous & Notable Mississippians

dedicated following. In 1993, he won the Texas Entertainer of the Year. Later that year, he signed to Epic Records. Ty Herndon's first single *What Mattered Most* hit No. 1 in the spring of 1995. An album of the same name was released in April and it became a Top 10 country hit. Herndon's second single, *I Want My Goodbye Back*, became a No. 7 hit. The third single, *Heart Half Empty*, was a hit and Herndon's second album, *Living in A Moment*, debuted at No. 6 in the summer of 1996. Herndon followed with the albums *Big Hopes* (1998) and *Steam* (1999), both big sellers.

Anthony Herrera

Born Jan. 19, 1944, in Wiggins, Mississippi. He played "Jack Curtis" on the soap *The Young and the Restless* in 1976-77. He also played the soap operas villains "Dane Hammond" in 1984-86 on *Loving*, and "James Stenbeck" on *As The World Turns* (1980-1983; 1986-1987; 1989; 1996; 1997-). He also appeared in these made-for-TV movies: *Helter Skelter* (1976), *The Night Rider* (1979), *Mandrake* (1979), *Money, Power, Murder* (1989), *Writer's Block* ('91), and *Taking Back My Life: The Nancy Ziegenmeyer Story* ('92). He was director of the TV movie *The Wide Net* ('97) and was also a writer on that film. A TV guest appearance was on *Silk Stalkings* playing "Ted Meyerson" in the episode "The Queen is Dead" on 12/3/92.

Wilbur Higby

Born Wilbur Higby Jones on Aug. 21, 1867, in Meridian, Mississippi. He was a silent screen actor who played in 36 movies from *Strathmore* in 1915 to *God's Great Wilderness* in 1927. He was in one "talkie," *Hat, Coat and Glove* (1934). Higby died of pneumonia Dec. 1, 1934, in Hollywood, Calif.

Faith Hill

Born Sept. 21, 1967, in Star, Rankin County, Mississippi. Adopted when she was only three days old, her new parents named her Audrey Faith Perry. She was voted most beautiful, most popular and class favorite at McLaurin High School. She went to Nashville in 1987 at the age of 19. It wasn't long before she signed a record contract, and after her debut album she went on tour with Reba McEntire. In the 5-year period ending in mid-1999, Faith has become a superstar garnering 7 No. 1 singles, 9 No. 1 videos, 3 multiplatinum albums and numerous awards! The single *Wild One*, taken from her debut million-selling album in 1993, *Take Me As I Am*, spent 4 consecutive weeks at *Billboard*'s top spot, the longest stint ever for a female country music singer's debut song! That album produced two more No. 1 hits including *Piece of My Heart*, the former Janis Joplin hit, and *Take Me As I Am*. The hit single, *Let's Go To Vegas*, was included in her 2nd album, *It Matters To Me*, released in late summer 1995. By Jan. 1996, the title song from that album was the No. 1 country single in the U.S. and stayed on top for 3 consecutive weeks. Another hit single, *Someone Else's Dream*, was released as her 2nd album also went platinum in the spring of 1996. By the fall of 1996, her single *You Can't Lose Me* was in the Country Top 10. Her single *I Can't Do That Anymore* was in the Country Top 10 by the end of Jan. 1997. Her third album, *Faith*, was released in the spring of 1998 with the song *This Kiss* rapidly climbing to No. 1 on the country chart and crossing over to garner airplay on rock stations. *This Kiss* was her 7th No. 1 hit. Her 8th No. 1 single came in the fall of 1999 with *The Secret of Life*. At the end of 1999, her album *Breathe* was No. 3 and the single of the same title was No. 1 (her 9th) on the country charts. By mid-Feb. 2000, the album had already gone double platinum (2 million copies). Hill is the first female country artist ever to achieve double platinum status on both her debut and follow up albums. Hill was named one of *People* magazine's "50 Most Beautiful People" of 1995. She sang at the closing ceremony of the Centennial Olympics in Atlanta on Aug. 4, 1996. Hill was named Academy of Country Music's Top New Female Performer in 1994, *Billboard*'s Top Female Country Artist of 1994 and won the 1995 TNN/*Music City News* Star of Tomorrow Award. She was nominated for the 1995 American Music Awards Best New Country Artist, nominated for the 1996 American Music Awards as Best Female Country Artist, nominated as CMA Female Vocalist of the Year for 1996 and received 3 Academy of Country Music nominations for 1996. She was nominated for Female Artist of the Year for the TNN/*Music City News* Country Awards in 1997. On Oct. 6, 1996, Hill married country singer Tim McGraw, the son of former Philadelphia Phillies major league baseball pitcher Tug McGraw. By mid-1997, Tim and Faith had a Top-10 country hit, *It's Your Love*, which went on to become the No.2 country hit for all of 1997! That record received two 1998 Grammy nominations for Country Song and for Country Collaboration with Vocals. Faith & Tim's record, *Just to Hear You Say You Love Me*, received the 1998 CMA nomination for Vocal Event of the Year. Faith was nominated for three 1999 Grammys and Faith and Tim's performance won the Top Vocal Event of the Year Award at the 34th annual Academy of Country Music Awards in 1999. Faith, with a leading six nominations of her own, won the Top Video Award for *This Kiss*, plus Top Female Vocalist of the Year and Single Record of the Year. She had more nominations than anyone for the 1999 TNN/*Music City News* Country Awards — a total of 7 nominations. Hill and her hit, *Breathe*, also dominated the nominations for the TNN Awards in 2000 with eight — for best entertainer and female vocalist, with *Breathe* up for best single, video, song and album. Not far behind Hill was husband Tim, who had 5 nominations. At the 35th annual Academy of Coutry Music Awards on May 3, 2000, Faith and Tim each won their second consecutive Vocalist of the Year awards and Faith won top video prize for *Breathe*. Hill led all performers with 8 nominations and McGraw had 5 nods for the 2000 TNN Awards to be handed out June 15 in Nashville. In Dec. 1996, Faith performed on the annual nationally televised special, *Christmas In Washington*, attended by President and Mrs. Clinton. Faith made her acting debut on the 1998 season premieres of two highly rated CBS-TV hit shows. She played a night club singer who is the estranged wife of a character played by Richard Thomas (*The Waltons*). This was a two part story that started on *Touched by an Angel* and concluded on *Promised Land*. In the spring of 1999, Faith was selected as a spokeswoman for Cover Girls Cosmetics. In a millennium poll conducted by *The Clarion-Ledger* of Jackson in 1999, readers picked Hill as their all-time favorite country music singer. Faith had the honor of singing the national anthem at Super Bowl XXXIV in Atlanta, Georgia on Jan. 30, 2000.

Rebecca Hill

Born Jan. 18, 1944, in Memphis. In 1946 her family moved to Soso, Miss., and in 1953 she moved to Palos Park, Ill. She graduated Phi Beta Kappa from Grinnell College and studied at Manchester University in England before receiving an M.A. from Harvard in 1967. She was a screenwriter for King Screen Productions in Seattle for one year in 1970. She then became a free-lance writer for four years. From 1976-1978 she was a television writer and producer for the Veterans Administration Hospital in St. Cloud, Minnesota. Remaining in St. Cloud, she decided to be a full-time writer. Her first novel, *Blue Rise* (1983), was set in Mississippi and won the Mississippi

Profiles of Famous & Notable Mississippians

Institute of Arts and Literature Award. Her other books include *Aspera Among Birches* and *A Killing Time in St. Cloud* (co-author) and *Cotton House*.

Arthur "Art" Hillery
This jazz pianist, organist, composer and arranger was born on Oct. 31, 1925, in New Orleans, but grew up in Jackson. He graduated from Jackson State University in 1949. He began playing with local groups at an early age. He has accompanied and recorded with a variety of big-name artists such as Ruth Brown, Joe Williams, Al Hibbler, and Ella Fitzgerald. He has performed in Brazil, Japan, Norway, Italy and other countries.

Milt Hinton
Born Milton John Hinton on June 23, 1910, in Vicksburg, Mississippi. Hinton's family moved to Chicago when he was 11 years old. As a young adult, Hinton moved to Queens, New York, where he still resides. "The Judge" is a key big band, jazz, swing-bop artist who plays bass and has played in several jazz bands including those of Count Basie, Louis Armstrong Dizzy Gillespie and Cab Calloway. He recorded eight albums of his own, mostly in the 1950s, but also in 1977, 1986 and 1990. But as an a studio musician, Hinton has probably appeared on more records than anyone else in the world! This jazz legend and composer was awarded the American Jazz Master Fellowship from the National Endowment for the Arts. He received a New York State Governor's Arts Award in 1996 and was the recipient of the Artist's Achievement Award of the 1998 Mississippi Governor's Awards for Excellence in the Arts. Hinton was one of the first 27 inducted into the inaugural Mississippi Musicians Hall of Fame on April 1, 2000.

Eddie Hodges
Born March 5, 1947, in Hattiesburg, Mississippi. He was the child actor who starred as Frank Sinatra's son in the movie *A Hole In The Head* (1956). Little Eddie and the late Sinatra sang the Academy Award®-winning song *High Hopes*. Hodges played "Huck Finn" in the movie *The Adventures of Huckleberry Finn* (1960). He had a small part in the Elvis movie *Live a Little, Love a Little* (1968) and a few other bit parts before retiring from his movie career in his late teens due to problems with drugs. He recorded two songs that made the *Billboard* Top 20: *I'm Gonna Knock On Your Door* (#12 in 1961) and *(Girls, Girls, Girls) Made To Love* (#14 in 1962).

W.G. "Mickey" Holliman, Jr.
Born Sept 24, 1937, in Shuqualak, Noxubee Co., Miss. He is president and CEO of St. Louis, Missouri-based Furniture Brands International, the nation's largest residential furniture manufacturer and parent company of Action Industries in Tupelo, Miss. In 1970, with Alvin "Bo" Bland, he cofounded Action Industries, specializing in upholstered reclining chairs. Under his leadership, Action expanded its product line to include motion furniture, sleeper sofas, and a complete line of reclining chairs. Holliman assumed his current position in 1996 with the conglomerate that also manages the Broyhill, Lane, and Thomasville furniture manufacturers. A graduate of Mississippi State, class of 1960, he's on the board of directors of the Mississippi State University Foundation, and in 1993 was named the college's Alumni Fellow. He was Mississippi State College of Business and Industry's 1998 Alumnus of the Year and Mississippi State's National Alumnus of the Year for 1998! All five of Holliman's children attended Mississippi State, and four received undergraduate degrees.

Gerald M. Hollingsworth
Born in Centreville, Miss. c. 1929. He earned a bachelor's in engineering at Ole Miss in 1953, finished his medical degree at Harvard in 1955 and completed his surgical residency in Jacksonville, Fl. From 1957-59, he was a Navy flight surgeon and then started his private medical practice in 1959 in Ft. Walton Beach, Fl. In 1995, he made a $2 million donation to Ole Miss, the single largest gift ever made to the school's athletic department. It helped fund the Manning-Hollingsworth Memorabilia Room in the Starnes Athletic Training Center. Later, at a crucial phase in plans to attract private funds for the $13 million football stadium expansion at Ole Miss, Hollingsworth stepped forward with $3 million, which brought his contributions to more than $5 million. His support led university officials to name the football field at Vaught-Hemingway Stadium in his honor. He was inducted into the Ole Miss Alumni Hall of Fame on Oct. 23, 1998.

William Hollingsworth
Born Feb. 17, 1910, in Jackson. His prodigious output of paintings, drawings, lithographs and watercolors were widely displayed. The main theme of his artwork was his hometown of Jackson. Nearly 300 of his works belong to the Mississippi Museum of Art which held a special display of them in 1998. Hollingsworth, despondent over the death of his father in 1943, took his own life on Aug. 1, 1944.

Herbie Holmes
Herbert Payne Holmes was born on Sept. 27, 1912, in Yazoo City. He played in a small band at Yazoo City High before graduating in 1929. When he enrolled at Ole Miss, he joined the college orchestra, The Mississippians, which he soon began to lead. During Holmes' junior year, the NBC radio affiliate in Memphis, WMC, and Loew's State Theater sponsored a vocal competition. The first prize was trip to New York, an audition at the NBC studios, and a guest appearance on the Eddie Cantor radio program. Holmes won. In 1935, the band went on the road and before long it was the Herbie Holmes Orchestra. In late 1935, the band signed with a large booking agency which handled talent such as Count Basie, Benny Goodman, Tommy Dorsey, and Guy Lombardo. Gaining more popularity as their tour schedule grew, they evolved into a swing-style band playing jazz and Dixieland. Later signing with a new agency and with a new vocalist, Nancy Hutson, the orchestra was booked solid playing in more fashionable venues, including the roof gardens of some of the finest hotels in the country. Holmes adopted the slogan, "Music Served Southern-Style." The press referred to him as "The Young Maestro from the Mississippi Delta." Bassist Fay Anderson from Yazoo City joined the band in 1938. Holmes, Nancy, and the orchestra ushered in the New Year 1939 with a national radio broadcast from the Edgewater Beach Hotel in Chicago. It was about this time when Lawrence Welk was just starting. Their mutual agency urged Welk to study Holmes' emcee style and asked Holmes to emulate Welk's musical style. As a result, the Herbie Holmes Orchestra moved toward a more mellow style of music for dining and dancing. The band continued to succeed, now in bigger and better hotels. In June 1941, Herbie and Nancy married. Through 1940 and 1941 the band was constantly touring. They recorded four sides for the Okeh label. One was Herbie's rendition of *Ida* and Nancy was featured on *A Little Love is a Dangerous Thing*. Then, the war years came and disrupted everything. Holmes became associated with the USO and entertained troops around the country. In 1943, he dissolved the band and joined the Navy. After the war, he and Nancy and their two children moved back to Yazoo City. Holmes died on Dec. 1, 1981. In 1989, he was inducted into the Ole Miss Jazz Alumni Hall of Fame. His beloved wife, Nancy, died of a heart attack in Yazoo City on Aug. 8, 1998, at the age of 83.

Profiles of Famous & Notable Mississippians

Richard E. Holmes

Born Richard Earl Holmes on Feb. 17, 1944 in Starkville, Miss. The first black student at Mississippi State, he enrolled there in 1965, completed a bachelor's in 1969, a master's in 1972, then attended medical school at Michigan State University. The Holmes Cultural Diversity Center at MSU was named for him in 1991. And, the endowment at MSU initially known as the Black Student Scholarship Fund is now known as the Dr. Richard E. Holmes Endowed Scholarship Fund. Holmes spent 55 days in Saudi Arabia in 1991 as part of Desert Storm. Holmes, who has practiced emergency medicine since 1984 in four states and in 30 emergency rooms, is now an emergency room physician in Birmingham, Alabama.

Morris Holt (see "Magic Slim")

Glenn Honeycutt

Born May 2, 1933, in Belzoni, Miss. Elvis Presley's cousin, Honeycutt moved to Memphis in 1940 and later attended Humes High School with Elvis. After holding several jobs and playing guitar part time, he entered the Army in 1952. After the Army, he formed Glenn Honeycutt and the Rhythmaires in 1955. A member of the group, Jack Clement, introduced Honeycutt to Sam Phillips at Sun Records. A couple of sides he cut at Sun were *Rock All Night* ('57) and *Campus Love* ('58). He's worked for the U.S. Postal Service since 1958. Honeycutt is a member of the Rockabilly Hall of Fame.

Earl Zebedee Hooker

Born Jan. 2, 1930, in Clarksdale, Mississippi. Generally acknowledged by his peers as the finest all-around guitarist in Chicago blues circles, his slide guitar work was the most technically advanced of all bluesmen. He recorded 18 albums and was sideman on numerous sessions. Cousin of John Lee Hooker. Died of TB Apr. 21, 1970, in Chicago.

John Lee Hooker

This legendary bluesman and father of the boogie was born August 22, 1917, near Clarksdale, Miss., the son of sharecroppers. His stepfather, Will Moore, taught him how to play guitar, and as a young man Hooker encountered such blues legends as Charley Patton and Blind Lemon Jefferson. In his early teens, Hooker ran off to Memphis. He also lived in Cincinnati and Knoxville before settling down in Detroit in 1943. He made his debut recording *Boogie Chillun'* in 1948, which became a No. 1 jukebox hit and his first million-seller. This was followed by an even bigger hit with I'm *In The Mood* and other classics such as *Crawling Kingsnake* and *Hobo Blues*. More than 100 of Hooker's songs were recorded on Vee Jay Records during the 1950's and 1960's. His foot-stomping boogie was adapted and amplified in the 1960s and 70s by a great number of Rock and Roll artists, including the Rolling Stones, the Yardbirds, John Mayall, Ten Years After, Foghat, ZZ Top and George Thorogood. Johnny Rivers cut some of his songs in the early 60s and Hooker's hit *Boom Boom* was covered by The Animals. By 1970 Hooker had moved to California and began working with rockers Van Morrison and Canned Heat, who modeled their sound after Hooker's boogie and collaborated on several albums and tours. During the 1970's and much of the 80's Hooker toured the U.S. and Europe. He appeared in *The Blues Brothers* movie (1980). He sang the title role on Pete Townshend's concept album *The Iron Man*. His album, *The Healer* ('89), received critical acclaim, had sales of over a million copies and won a Grammy. In 1990, musical greats Bonnie Raitt, Joe Cocker, Huey Lewis, Carlos Santana, Robert Cray, Al Kooper, Johnny Winter and several others paid tribute to Hooker with a performance at Madison Square Garden. He shared a 1989 Grammy with Bonnie Raitt for Best Traditional Blues Recording for their album *I'm in the Mood*. Hooker's album *Chill Out* (1995) won the 1996 Grammy for Traditional Blues Album and the Traditional Blues Album of the Year in the 1996 W.C. Handy Blues Awards. Hooker was presented with the Blues Foundation's second annual Lifetime Achievement Award in 1996. He won a 1997 Grammy for Traditional Blues Album for *Don't Look Back* and was nominated for another Grammy in for Pop Callaboration with Vocals for the *Don't Look Back* single he did with Van Morrison. Hooker was inducted into the Rock & Roll Hall of Fame in 1991. Two of his songs, *Boogie Chillun'* and *Boom Boom*, are included on the Rock and Roll Hall of Fame and Museum's list of 500 Songs That Shaped Rock And Roll. John Lee Hooker Lane was dedicated in his hometown of Clarksdale on Nov. 14, 1998. Hooker has utilized his star status to help those less fortunate with his active support for projects such as Blues Against Blindness and the Blues Heaven Foundation, which was founded by fellow Mississippian and blues great, the late Willie Dixon. After receiving the Lifetime Achievement Award from the Rhythm & Blues Foundation in 1999, Hooker gave back the $20,000 that came with the award, telling the sponsors to use the money for the less fortunate.

Houston Hoover

Born Feb. 6, 1965, in Yazoo City, Miss. He played football at Yazoo City High School (class of 1983). Hoover played football at Jackson State for 5 years, but he turned pro and didn't graduate. This offensive tackle was drafted by the Atlanta Falcons in 1988 and played for them for 5 years. Hoover played for the Cleveland Browns for one year (1993) and the Miami Dolphins for one year (1994) before retiring from pro football. He now makes his home in Atlanta, Ga.

Gerald Hopkins

Born Dec. 26, 1965, in Biloxi, Mississippi. This actor played A.J. (Alan Jr.) Quartermaine on the TV soap *General Hospital* in 1991-92 and was in the feature films *Midnight Man* (1994) and *Pentathlon* (1994). His notable TV guest appearances include an episode of *Matlock* playing "Young Hubert" on 12/12/1989 and on *Shannon's Deal* (1990).

Clay Hopper

Born Robert Clay Hopper on Oct. 3, 1900, in Greenwood, Miss. He played at Mississippi State, where he graduated in 1926. He managed the Montreal Royals minor league baseball team, the Brooklyn Dodgers top farm club, (from 1928-56). This was the team Jackie Robinson, an African-American, first played on when he broke the so-called "color barrier." Robinson spent his first season with Montreal and electrified baseball, pushing the Royals to their second straight pennant. Batting a league-leading .349, Robinson led the team to their best record ever, 18 games ahead of Syracuse. Clay Hopper was inducted into the Mississippi State University Sports Hall of Fame in two categories, baseball and football, in 1970. He died in Greenwood in April 1976 at the age of 75.

"Big" Walter Horton

Born Apr. 6, 1917, at Horn Lake, Mississippi, his nickname was "Shakey." He recorded with a Memphis Jug Band in 1927, but made his mark when he recorded a couple of records for Sam Phillips. One of them was called *Easy*. The other one, a slow, simple instrumental version of *I Almost Lost My Mind*, featuring only harmonica and guitar, is one of the classic harmonica records of all time. Horton went on to a brief stint in Muddy Waters' band, and played the classic harp part on *Forty Days and Forty Nights*. He played backup harp for bluesman Jimmy Rogers. He recorded his first solo album in

Profiles of Famous & Notable Mississippians

the mid-sixties, and cut a series of albums in the late sixties and early seventies. One of the all-time great blues harp players, he helped define modern amplified harp. He died in Chicago on Dec. 8, 1981, and is buried in the Westvale Cemetery (Section J-1, Lot 39) in Worth, Illinois.

Eddie James "Son" House

This legendary early bluesman was born Edward James House, Jr. on March 21, 1902, in Riverton in Coahoma County. By the age of 15, Son was preaching the gospel in various Baptist churches as the family wandered from one plantation to the next. He didn't even bother picking up a guitar until he turned 25. In fact, House said that he didn't like to hear a guitar. He hated plantation labor even more and had developed a taste for corn whiskey. He drunkenly started singing the blues at a house party in Lyon, Mississippi, one night and made a little money doing it. After that, Son House leaned more and more toward the blues. Later, at another house frolic in Lyon, he shot a man dead and was sentenced to Parchman Farm. Claiming self defense, he ended up serving only two years. After he was released, a Clarksdale judge told him never to set foot in town again, so, he started a new life in the Delta as a bluesman. After hitchhiking and hoboing the rails, he made it to Lula, Mississippi, where he ran into Charley Patton, the most legendary character the blues had to offer at that point. The two of them argued and bickered constantly and the only thing these two seemed to have in common was imbibing. Though House would later refer in interviews to Patton as a "jerk" (among other things), it was Patton's success as a bluesman that got Son's foot in the door as a recording artist. He followed Patton to Wisconsin and recorded a handful of sides for Paramount. These records today are rare and some of the most highly prized collector's items of Delta blues recordings. House laid down some superb performances on these 78s: *My Black Mama*, *Preachin' the Blues*, and *Dry Spell Blues*, with an unreleased test acetate of *Walkin' Blues* showing up decades later. It was those recordings that led Alan Lomax to Son's door in 1941 to record him for the Library of Congress. Son was still playing, but had backed off of it a bit since Charley Patton died in 1934. House did some tunes solo, but also cut a session backed by a little string band. Just as House had gone a full decade without recording, after the Lomax recordings, he just as quickly disappeared, moving to Rochester, N.Y. When folk blues researchers finally found him in 1964, he told them that he hadn't touched a guitar in years. One of the researchers, a young guitarist named Alan Wilson (later of the blues-rock group Canned Heat) sat down and literally retaught Son House how to play like Son House. After that, it was off on the festival and coffeehouse circuit and he also recorded again. In 1965, he played Carnegie Hall and was the subject of a film documentary four years later. Hailed as the greatest living Delta singer still performing, nobody dared call themselves the king of the blues as long as Son House was around. In the early 1970s, he came down with both Alzheimer's and Parkinson's diseases that first affected his memory and his ability to recall songs onstage and later, his hands, which shook so badly he had to later give up the guitar and live performing altogether by 1976. He lived quietly in Detroit for another 12 years, passing away on Oct. 19, 1988. House was inducted into the Blues Foundation's Hall of Fame in 1980. The last great voice of the first-generation bluemen, he was a tremendous influence on Robert Johnson, Muddy Waters, and many others. A teenage Robert Johnson heard Son House and abandoned the harmonica for the guitar. Several students of the blues have stated that Son House was the blues.

Thelma Houston

Born on May 7, 1943, in Leland, Mississippi, this soul singer had a No. 1 hit record *Don't Leave Me This Way* (1977) for which she received a 1977 Grammy for Best Female R&B Vocal. Houston was a protégé of composer Jimmy Webb in the late 1960s. She appeared in the films *Death Scream* (1975) and Oprah Winfrey's *Beloved* (1998).

Junie Hovious

Born John Alexander Hovious, Jr. on Oct. 4, 1919, in Vicksburg, Mississippi. He lettered in football, basketball and baseball at the University of Mississippi. Hovious played halfback for the Ole Miss Rebels football team from 1938-42. He was All-SEC and still holds the Ole Miss record of 1,142 punt return yards. His 96-yard punt return against Georgia in 1940 ranks third in school history. He was a member of Omicron Delta Kappa and Delta Tau Delta fraternities while at Ole Miss. After playing pro football for the NFL's New York Giants in 1945, he returned to Ole Miss, where he worked as a Rebel assistant football coach for 29 years. He was head golf coach there for 25 years. He is a member of the Ole Miss Alumni Hall of Fame and was inducted into the Mississippi Sports Hall of Fame in 1967. Hovious died of heart failure in Oxford on May 7, 1998, at the age of 78.

Guy Hovis

Born on Sept. 24, 1941, in Tupelo. He graduated from Ole Miss where he studied accounting. To Los Angeles in 1967, he was on Art Linkletter's TV show *House Party* for one year, then on ABC Records as one-half of the duo Guy & David. He and his wife Ralna joined *The Lawrence Welk Show* as singers in 1970 and stayed through 1982. They recorded 15 albums together. Hovis has also appeared on the Johnny Carson, Mike Douglas, Merv Griffin, Jim Nabors, Bob Hope and Dinah Shore shows. He's also been a frequent guest on game shows and telethons. He was nominated by members of the recording industry as both producer and artist of the year. Hovis came back to Mississippi in 1989 and is state director for Senator Trent Lott. Fans can still see Hovis on stage twice a year at the Lawrence Welk Theater in Branson, Missouri, and at Mississippi festivals and churches.

Bailey Howell

Born on Jan. 20, 1937. He was a basketball prodigy in his hometown, the small community of Middleton, Tenn. (pop. 300), just five miles above the Mississippi-Tennessee line. When he played at Mississippi State, he became not only the best basketball player in that school's history, but also the best in Mississippi's history! Howell, a consensus All-American in 1958-59, holds State's records for career scoring average and rebound average. This 6-foot-7 center averaged 27.1 points and 17 rebounds over three seasons at State and nobody before or after has even come close. He averaged 25.9 points per game his first year, leading the nation in field-goal percentage with 56.8 percent, while pulling down 19.7 rebounds per game! As a sophomore in 1957, he scored 37 points and grabbed 22 rebounds as State beat Kentucky for the first time in school history. Howell led State to a 61-14 record over three years, once scoring 47 points in a game, another time getting 34 rebounds in one game. Howell's biggest thrill as a collegian was when State won the SEC championship in 1959. State was then chosen to play in the NCAA Tournament, but the Mississippi governor barred the Bulldogs from participating because State would have faced integrated teams. That was Howell's biggest disappointment. Scoring 2,030 points in his college career, he left with 27 school records, and remains one of only four SEC players to score more than 2,000 points and

Profiles of Famous & Notable Mississippians

collect 1,000 or more rebounds! Another Mississippi State great, Jeff Malone, has since eclipsed Howell's career scoring mark, but most of Howell's other records still hold, like his career rebounding numbers of 1,277 total, 17.0 career average, 19.7 season average and game-high 34. He was the second pick in the first round of the 1959 NBA draft. A six-time NBA All-Star, he scored 17,770 points, grabbed more than 2,000 rebounds and passed out over 2,000 assists in a 12-year pro career with Detroit, Baltimore, Boston and Philadelphia. Howell averaged 20 points per game when the Boston Celtics won the world championship in 1968. He was inducted into the Mississippi State University Sports Hall of Fame in 1971 and into the Mississippi Sports Hall of Fame in 1977. Howell, who now lives in Starkville, became the first male basketball player from Mississippi to be inducted into the Naismith Memorial Basketball Hall of Fame in 1997, and as of July 2000, he's still the only Mississippian enshrined there. In early 1999, Howell was chosen No. 1 to head the first team by readers in voting for *The Clarion-Ledger* Division I Men's Basketball Team of the Century!

Grady Howell, Jr.

Born Hamilton Grady Howell, Jr. on April 7, 1947, in Biloxi, he is a ninth generation Mississippian whose ancestors landed with D'Iberville at the close of the 17th century. He received his bachelors and master's degrees in history from Southeastern Louisiana University. He also studied at the National Archives Institute and the Georgia Dept. of Archives and History Institute at Emory Unversity in 1974. This historian's works, endorsed by Shelby Foote and Ed Bearss, include: *Going to Meet the Yankees, A History of the "Bloody Sixth" Mississippi Infantry, C.S.A.* (1981); *To Live and Die in Dixie, A History of the Third Regiment Mississippi Infantry, C.S.A.* (1991); *Hill of Death, The Battle of Champion Hill* [monograph] (1993); and *A Southern Lacrimosa, The Mexican War Journal of Dr. Thomas Neely Love, Surgeon, Second Regiment Mississippi Volunteer Infantry, U.S.A.* (1995). The first volume of his monumental multi-volume set, *For Dixie Land, I'll Take My Stand! A Muster Listing of All Known Mississippi Confederate Soldiers and Sailors, 1861-1865,* was published in 1998. There will be least 4 volumes, each over a thousand pages! This set should prove an invaluable reference source for genealogists and other researchers. Another work in progress is *Mississippi Rifles: A History of Mississippi Volunteers in the Mexican War, 1846-1848.* Howell also indexed *Military History of Mississippi, 1803-1898* by Dunbar Rowland (1978) and *The UnCivil War* by Thomas B. Keyes ('91). Howell now lives in Madison, Mississippi.

"Howlin' Wolf"

Born Chester Arthur Burnett on June 10, 1911, at West Point, Mississippi. The Wolf was six-foot-six and weighed close to 300 pounds in his prime and had a raspy, sandpaper growl of a voice. Wolf's childhood idol was country singer Jimmie Rodgers, who was noted for his "blues-yodel." Wolf tried to emulate the yodel but found that his efforts sounded more like a howl. He didn't start recording until the 50s, first at Sun Records in Memphis and then at Chess in Chicago. He quickly racked up such blues classics as *How Many More Years, Riding In The Moonlight, Spoonful, I Ain't Superstitious* and *Back Door Man.* Known as the founder of Chicago electric blues, he recorded a prodigious 67 albums. Wolf was very popular in England where such greats as the Beatles, Eric Clapton, and the Rolling Stones were devoted fans. He was inducted into Rock & Roll Hall of Fame in 1991. Three of his songs, *Smokestack Lightnin', Spoonful* and *The Red Rooster* are included on the Rock and Roll Hall of Fame's list of 500 Songs That Shaped Rock And Roll. In 1994 the U. S. Postal Service issued postage stamps commemorating eight "Legends of Blues and Jazz." Howlin' Wolf was one of three Mississippians (other 2 were Robert Johnson and Muddy Waters) honored. Howlin' Wolf gave his last performance in Chicago in Nov. 1975 with fellow blues titan B.B. King. He died during surgery for an aneurysm on January 10, 1976, in Chicago's Veterans Hospital and is buried in the Oakridge Cemetery (Section 18, Lot 325 right by the road) in Hillside, Illinois. A Life-size granite statue of him was unveiled in his hometown of West Point in 1997.

Robert Hubbard

Born Apr. 15, 1945, in Dayton, Ohio. He earned a B.A. and master's in music from the University of Southern Mississippi. He taught music 8 years at Pearl River Junior College, where he developed an interest in photography and started his own photography business. He has many photos in permanent collections at the Mississippi Museum of Art and the New Orleans Museum of Art. He has won awards in regional art shows and has been widely published in national publications. In 1990 the Rembrandt Society of the Mississippi Museum of Art named him "Artist of the Year," only the 5th person to be so honored. He provided the photos for the book, *Ghosts! Personal Accounts of Modern Mississippi Hauntings* (1992), written by his wife Sylvia. He's also written articles published in national and regional magazines, including *The National Rifleman* and *South Mississippi Magazine.*

Kent Hull

Born Jan. 13, 1961, in Greenwood. A four-year letterman at Mississippi State (1979-82), he signed a free-agent contract with the Buffalo Bills in 1986. Hull is one of only 8 players that played in all 4 of the Bills' Super Bowls (they lost all 4) and he was a three-time Pro Bowl selection. On Dec. 30, 1996, he announced his retirement after 11 seasons with Buffalo. He moved back to his farm in Greenwood, Mississippi.

Marie Atkinson Hull

Born Sept. 28, 1890, in Summit, Miss. She studied at the Pennsylvania Academy of Fine Arts and the Art Students League in New York and painted in France, Spain, Morocco, Canada, and Mexico. Her work was exhibited at the New York World's Fair and the San Francisco Golden Gate Exhibition in 1939, the Chicago Art Institute, and the All-American National Shows in New York. One of Mississippi's all-time, best-known artists, her art covered a period of more than 60 years and varied in style from traditional to very abstract. Hull died on Nov. 21, 1980 in Jackson.

Michael Humphreys

Born Michael Conner Humphreys in 1985 in Independence, Miss. Michael played young Forrest in the Academy Award-winning *Forrest Gump* (1994), the 6th biggest box office film of all time after *Titanic, Star Wars, Star Wars Episode I: The Phantom Menace, E.T.* and *Jurassic Park*. Released on July 6, 1994, it grossed $329,452,287 in the U.S. The movie was No. 1 in rental and No. 2 in sales of video tapes in 1995. This film was No. 71 on the American Film Institute's list of Top 100 Greatest American Movies of All Time announced in 1998.

Lindsey Hunter

Born Dec. 3, 1970, in Utica, Mississippi. The 6-2, 195-pound guard graduated from Murrah High in Jackson, then went to Alcorn State for one year before transferring to Jackson State. After sitting out a year, Hunter turned in three great seasons at JSU, averaging better than 20 points per game each year. As a senior, he was fifth in the nation in scoring (26.7 ppg) and was

Profiles of Famous & Notable Mississippians

the Black College Player of the year. He scored a school-record 907 points that season, including a JSU-best 48 points against Kansas in which he hit eleven 3-pointers. He made 39 points against Connecticut during an NIT game. He was SWAC MVP and honorable mention All-America. Hunter finished his college career as JSU's second all-time leading scorer with 2,226 points. He holds numerous collegiate records including most points in a season and most points in a game. He was the 10th overall pick by the Detroit Pistons for the 1992-93 season. Hunter averaged 10.3 points, 4.8 assists and 26.5 minutes playing during his rookie season. On Dec. 27, 1992, he fired up 26 field goal attempts (11 made), the NCAA record for the most 3-point-attempts. Hunter led the team in steals and was named to the NBA's All-Rookie second team. During the 1996-97 season, Hunter averaged 14.2 points and 1.9 assists. During the 1997-98 season, he shot 971 points (11.8 per game), ranked 16th in the NBA in Blocks Per Game (1.70) with a total of 139, and ranked 16th in the NBA in Rebounds Per Game (8.7). Following his 7th season with the Pistons, his career stats through the 1999-2000 season: played in 357 games (30.2 minutes avg. p/game); 3,864 points (10.8 avg. p/game); 938 rebounds (2.6 avg. p/game); 508 steals (1.42 avg. p/game); 69 blocks (0.19 avg. p/game); and 1,115 assists (3.12 avg.). His career field goal percentage is .386 and free throw percentage is .742. In early 1999, Hunter was chosen as a member of the first team on *The Clarion-Ledger* Division I Men's Basketball Team of the Century!

Mississippi John Hurt

Born John Smith Hurt on March 8, 1892. That's the date on his tombstone. The Social Security Death Index gives his birth date as July 3, 1893. Born in Teoc, Carroll County, his family moved to Avalon, Mississippi, where he grew up. Although he learned to read and write, he didn't attend school past the fourth grade. He was a sharecropper for many years. For fun and extra cash, Hurt joined other local guitarists and fiddlers for church suppers and dances. Hurt soon became a popular favorite. In the late 1920s, Okeh Records decided to record Hurt and he recorded two songs in Feb. 1928 in Memphis, *Frankie* and *Nobody's Dirty Business*. In Dec. 1928, Hurt traveled to New York City to record five more sides, including *Candy Man* and *Spike Driver Blues*. After his records made few sales, Hurt returned to Avalon and went back to sharecropping and performing in towns surrounding his home. That could have been the end of Hurt's national career had not two young blues musicians from Washington. Tom Hoskins and Mike Stewart, came across the original Okeh recording of *Avalon Blues* in 1963. The two blues archivists headed south armed with a tape recorder. They found Hurt, 71 years old, but still able to sing and play. They recorded him and returned to Washington with the tapes that resulted in the rediscovery of Mississippi John Hurt. He was a complete and instant success in the folk/blues scene. From the Spring of 1963, when he was brought to Washington to perform, until his death in 1966, Hurt played all over the Northeast at clubs and many folk festivals, including twice at the Newport Folk Festival. He was much admired by his new-found audience and was befriended by fellow performers like Doc Watson and Fred McDowell. In the end, he retired to a small home in Granada. His song, *Stagger Lee Blues*, is included on the Rock and Roll Hall of Fame's list of 500 Songs That Shaped Rock And Roll. Hurt died of a heart attack in Grenada on Nov. 2, 1966, and is buried in the Saint James Cemetery in Avalon, Mississippi.

Doug Hutton

Born Mar. 17, 1942, in Bolton, Mississippi. He broke the state tournament basketball scoring record as a Clinton High senior with 47 points in the semi-finals against Florence and topped that with 54 in the final against Philadelphia, a record which would stand for 14 years. A *Parade* All-America, Hutton later set the Mississippi High School All-Star record of 32 points, which still stands. He had a 3-sport career at Mississippi State (class of 1965), earning seven letters in basketball, baseball, and track during his four years as a Bulldog in the early 1960s. With Hutton's help, Babe McCarty's basketball team won SEC championships in 1962 with a 24-1 record and in 1963 with a 22-6 record. Hutton spent a year as a graduate assistant at Mississippi State before launching his 33-year coaching career. He coached at Hazlehurst for 2 years, Florence for 14 and at Clinton for 17 years, his teams garnering several state championships. Hutton was inducted into both the Mississippi State University Sports Hall of Fame and the Mississippi Sports Hall of Fame in 1995. 1999

Greg Iles

He was born April 8, 1960, in Stuttgart, Germany, where his father headed the U.S. Embassy medical clinic. He grew up in Natchez and majored in English at Ole Miss, graduating in 1983. His first two novels, focusing on WWII, became instant hits — *Spandau Phoenix* (1993), sold 32,000 copies in hardcover and 600,000 in paperback and *Black Cross* (1995), 100,000 copies hardcover and one million in paperback. His third novel, *Mortal Fear* (1997), a high-tech thriller about murder on the Internet, is set in the Mississippi Delta. Two of his first three novels were *New York Times* bestsellers, and *Black Cross* was awarded the Mississippi Author's Award for Fiction. Iles's fourth novel, *The Quiet Game* (1999), is set in Mississippi and deals with a 30-year-old murder that explodes into the present with devastating consequences. His fifth novel, *24 Hours* (2000), is a thriller set in the Jackson area that features the kidnapping of the five-year-old daughter of a wealthy anesthesiologist and his wife from their Madison county mansion. Iles' latest contract was a two-book deal with Putnam of New York for more than $1 million.

John Vincent Imbragulio

Dick Clark called Imbragulio, the founder of Ace Records, Ace Music Publisher and Avanti Records, one of the true pioneers of American music. Born on Oct. 3, 1925, in Hattiesburg, he grew up in Laurel, Mississippi. His first involvement with the music business was in 1945 when he purchased ten jukeboxes from Canadian-born David C. Rockola, the so called Rock-Ola Jukeboxes. By 1947, Johnny was a salesman for Music Sales of New Orleans, which took him all over Alabama, Florida, Louisiana and Mississippi. He learned the music business from the ground up. He soon opened a record shop in Jackson, Mississippi, selling mostly black music to customers and jukebox operators. He even began his own label, Champion Records, recording artists such as Junior Blackman, Arthur "Big Boy" Crudup, Tommy Lee Thompson, and Bonnie Williams. In 1950, he joined Specialty Records of New Orleans as an A&R man, recording one of the great blues classics of all time, *The Things I Used to Do*, by Guitar Slim with the quest pianist and arranger being a young Ray Charles. It went to No. 1 on the R&B charts in 1954. Now using the name Johnny Vincent, he also recorded many other artists, including Earl King and John Lee Hooker. In Aug. 1955, he started Ace Records, taking the name from a popular pocket comb, with offices in Jackson, Miss. and distribution in New Orleans — New Orleans' only independent record company at the time. Johnny quickly began recording and releasing an eclectic mix of blues and country music on the

Profiles of Famous & Notable Mississippians

new label. He was involved with dozens of artists, many of whom would later make a big name for themselves: Doctor John, Frank Fields, Allen Toussaint, Joe Tex, Sammy Myers, Buddy Guy, Lightnin' Slim, and Elmore James, just to name a few. Johnny's very first release on Ace was the swamp pop classic *Those Lonely, Lonely Nights* by Earl King. Between 1957 and 1960, Ace Records had 8 records on the R&B charts and 15 recordings hit the *Billboard* Top 100, including Huey "Piano" Smith's *Rockin' Pneumonia & Boogie Woogie Flu* and *Don't You Just Know It* (#9 pop 1958), Frankie Ford's classic *Sea Cruise* (#14 pop 1959), which has remained one of the most requested oldies of all times, plus hits by teen idol Jimmy Clanton. From 1958 to 1962, Clanton alone had 7 hits on the Top 40, including 3 that made the Top 10: *Just A Dream* (#4, 1958); *Go, Jimmy, Go* (#5, 1959 & '60); and *Venus in Blue Jeans* (#7, 1962). Ace Records and the master recordings are now owned by a British firm, which is fast re-releasing those hits. Johnny produced five albums by R&B and blues singer Willie Clayton since 1993 and he formed another label, Avanti Records, just a few years before his untimely death. Johnny was back living in Jackson, Mississippi, when he died of heart failure on Feb. 4, 2000, at age 74. Many people in the music industry attended the funeral service and Willie Clayton sang a soulful *Amazing Grace*. He is buried in Parkway Memorial Cemetery in Ridgeland, Mississippi. In the music business for almost half a century, Johnny was a living legend who made a big impact on blues and early Rock 'n' Roll music.

Birney Imes

Born Aug, 21, 1951, in Columbus, Miss., where he still lives. In the mid-1970s, this professional photographer started traveling the backroads of the state with his camera. His work is contained in 3 books — *Juke Joint* (1990), about Delta honky tonks, *Partial To Home* (1994), and *Whispering Pines* (1994), about a former night spot 15 miles north of Macon. Imes is a two-time winner of the Mississippi Institute of Arts and Letters Photography Award.

Michael Jabaley

Dr. Jabaley was born July 12, 1934, in Copperhill, Tenn. He was the first member of his Lebanese family to attend college. He received his B.A. from Vanderbilt in Nashville where he played football and earned membership in Phi Beta Kappa and Omicron Delta Kappa. He received his medical degree from Johns Hopkins University in Baltimore. He served as a major in the U.S. Army Medical Corps, including a tour of duty in Vietnam, before coming to Jackson in 1972 as head of the plastic surgery residency at the University of Mississippi Medical Center. He left for private practice in 1979. Every hand surgeon in the world knows his name — he is president of the Sunderland Society, a prestigious international organization of hand surgeons who specialize in microsurgery on nerves. There are no more than 70 members worldwide! Among the many positions he has held: past president of The American Society for Surgery of the Hand, past president of the Mississippi Chapter of The American College of Surgeons, past vice-president of The American Board of Plastic Surgeons and past president of the American Association of Plastic Surgeons. Jabaley has lectured in the U.S. and around the world and has also written in many medical publications.

Becca Jackson

Born in 1968 in Kosciusko, Miss., she grew up in Smithdale in Amite County. She moved to Nashville at age 19 to make her mark in country music. Folk rock artists such as Jackson Browne and Rita Coolidge influenced her music. For three years, she sang at Opryland and worked for music publishing companies, made demo tapes and sang ad jingles. In 1995, she signed with the Word gospel label. In 1996, Jackson recorded a CD with 10 songs, 2 of which she wrote and another two she co-wrote. The CD, titled *It'll Sneak Up On You*, was released in 1997 and a cut, *Hands Tied*, quickly hit the Contemporary Christian Music charts nationwide.

Carl Jackson

Born on Sept. 18, 1953, in Louisville, Miss. Jackson started in the music business at age 14 when he spent his summers playing banjo for Jim & Jesse and the Virginia Boys, a bluegrass Grand Ole Opry act. After high school, he joined the group full time on the road. At 19, Jackson spent about six months on tour with The Sullivan Family, a gospel group, before forming a bluegrass band with Keith Whitley called The Country Store. That lasted only about a week. Then Jackson met Glen Campbell at the Ohio State Fair. Glen listened to Jackson play and hired him on the spot. Jackson stayed with Glen for 12 years. Jackson recorded a couple of songs, *She's Gone, Gone, Gone* and *Dixie Train*, that made the top-40 country charts in 1984. And in 1991, he and John Starling released a bluegrass album that won a Grammy. But, it's been his songwriting talents that have really shined. Jackson and fellow Mississippian Jim Weatherly won a 1991 Dove Award for the gospel song *Where Shadows Never Fall*, recorded by Glen Campbell. In 1984, Glen Campbell recorded a song written by Jackson's called *Letter to Home*. It was a song he'd written basically as a letter to his folks when he moved out to Los Angeles to work with Glen. It became Jackson's first top-10 record. Since then, Jackson has penned songs recorded by Diamond Rio, Patty Loveless, Pam Tillis, Steve Wariner and Trisha Yearwood. Garth Brooks recorded Jackson's *Against the Grain* and his *Fit for a King* was on Brooks's album, *Sevens*. Vince Gill recorded 2 Carl Jackson tunes, including the chart-topper *No Future in the Past*.

George Jackson

Born March 12, 1945, in Indianola, he grew up in Greenville. Jackson has written many pop and R&B hits. He was living in Memphis when he wrote *I Belive I'll Go Back Home* for the Ovations, which a Top 20 R&B hit in 1965. He also wrote *Too Weak To Fight* for Clarence Carter, *A Man And A Half* for Wilson Pickett, *One Bad Apple* for the Osmond Brothers, and *Old Time Rock & Roll* for Bob Seger. He's also written songs for James Brown, Tina Turner, Tyrone Davis, and others. Since the early 80s, he's been a staff writer for Malaco in Jackson, where he's written songs for Latimore, Bobby "Blue" Bland, Denise LaSalle, and Johnnie Taylor, among others. Jackson's song *Down Home Blues*, a big hit by Z.Z. Hill, was inducted into the Blues Hall of Fame in Feb. 2000. Jackson and that song previously won the W.C. Handy Award from the Blues Foundation. Jackson has written over 1,000 songs!

D. Clayton James

Born on Feb. 13, 1931, in Winchester, Kentucky, he grew up Natchez, Miss. He received a B.A. degree at Southwestern College in Memphis (1953), a B.D. from Louisville (KY) Theological Seminary (1956), his M.A. from the University of Texas (1959) and his Ph.D.. from the University of Texas in 1964. This Mississippi State University Professor Emeritus of History is most noted for his three-volume biography of the late General Douglas MacArthur titled *The Years of MacArthur*. He also wrote *Refighting the Last War: Command and Crisis in Korea 1950-53* (1992), *Antebellum Natchez* (1993), *From Pearl Harbor to V-J Day: The American Armed Forces in World War II* (1995), and *America and the Great War, 1914-1920*, cowritten with Anne Sharp Wells.

Profiles of Famous & Notable Mississippians

Elmore James

Born Jan. 27, 1918, at Richland, Holmes County, Mississippi, he grew into his teens in nearby Poplar Springs. Both places are near Ebenezer, Mississippi. As a teenager and young man he also spent some time in Belzoni, Mississippi. Elmore was born the illegitimate son of Leola Brooks and later given the surname of his stepfather. At an early age he learned to play bottleneck on a homemade instrument fashioned out of a broom handle and a lard can. By the age of 14, he was already a weekend musician, working juke joints in the Belzoni area under the names "Cleanhead" or "Joe Willie James" (his stepfather's name). Although he confined himself to a home base area around Belzoni, he would join up and work with traveling players like Robert Johnson, Howlin' Wolf and Sonny Boy Williamson. Heavily influenced by Robert Johnson, Elmore later became well known after recording his own version of Johnson's *I Believe I'll Dust My Broom*. In fact, Elmore named his band the Broom Dusters. After spending three years in the Navy stationed in Guam during World War II, he moved to Memphis, working in clubs for a while. Elmore was also one of the first "guest stars" on the popular King Biscuit Time radio show on KFFA in Helena, Arkansas, and also doing stints on the *Talaho Syrup Show* on Yazoo City's WAZF and the *Hadacol* Show on KWEM in West Memphis. At Trumpet Records in Chicago, Elmore was recorded at the tail end of a Sonny Boy session doing his now signature tune, *Dust My Broom*. The record became the surprise R&B hit of 1951, making the Top Ten and making a recording star out of Elmore. Over the next 12 years he would record more than 100 songs for Modern, Chess, Chief, Fire, Fury, and Enjoy Records, and help define the modern electric Chicago blues sound of today. The most influential slide guitarist of the postwar period, the "King of the Slide Guitar" helped shape the rural sounds of the Mississippi Delta Blues into a wrenching raw music that eventually bled to Rock 'n' Roll. He played throughout the Delta rending emotional blues that drove audiences wild. He influenced many blues guitarists including Hound Dog Taylor, James "Son" Thomas, Joe Carter, J.B. Hutto, Johnny Littlejohn, Duane Allman, Jimi Hendrix, Johnny Winter, Eric Clapton, ZZ Top, Stevie Ray Vaughan, and others. His single-string work also had an effect on B.B. King and Chuck Berry. No one attempting to play slide guitar today can do it without being compared to Elmore. His many albums contained songs such as *Standing at the Crossroads*, *The Sky Is Crying*, *Look Over Yonder Wall*, and *Something Inside of Me*. A radio repairman by trade, Elmore reworked his guitar amplifiers in his spare time, getting them to produce distorted sounds that wouldn't be heard again until the advent of heavy rock amplification in the late 1960s. In later years, a recurring heart condition would send him back home to Jackson, Mississippi, where he temporarily set aside his playing for work as a disc jockey or radio repairman. In early 1963, Elmore returned to Chicago, ready to resume his playing career when he suffered his final heart attack. Elmore died in Chicago on May 24, 1963, and his wake was attended by over 400 blues luminaries before his body was shipped back to Mississippi. He is buried in the Newport Missionary Baptist Church Cemetery about 3 miles from Ebenezer, Holmes County, Miss. He was elected to the Blues Foundation's Hall of Fame in 1980. He was inducted into the Rock & Roll Hall of Fame in 1992. Elmore's songs, *Dust My Broom* and *Shake Your Moneymaker*, are included on the R&R Hall of Fame's list of 500 Songs That Shaped Rock and Roll.

Skip James

Born Nehemiah Curtis James on June 9, 1902, in Bentonia, Yazoo County, Mississippi, he was one of the most influential early Delta bluesmen. His *Hard Time Killing Floor Blues* has been rated as one of the three or four Great Depression songs. He recorded 26 songs at his first session in 1931. He waited a little while to record again — 33 years in fact! After being "discovered" in a hospital in Tunica, Mississippi, Skip James appeared at the 1964 Newport Folk Festival and subsequently recorded two superb albums for Vanguard, the better of which is *Skip James Today!* The album features his best known compositions. The legendary Robert Johnson recorded James' *Devil Got My Woman*, which he retitled as *Hellhound On My Trail*. Eric Clapton recorded James' *I'm So Glad* on the first Cream album. Skip James died of cancer in Philadelphia, Pa. on Oct. 3, 1969, at the age of 67.

Valerie Jaudon

Born Aug. 6, 1945, in Greenville. She studied at the Memphis Academy of Art in 1965, graduated from Mississippi University for Women in 1967 and did post-graduate work at University of the Americas in Mexico City from 1967-68 and St. Martin's School of Art in London from 1968-69. In late 1969 she settled in New York and has since become an internationally recognized contemporary artist. She once titled a series of her works after Mississippi cities including *Jackson*, *Natchez*, and *Yazoo City*. Her works are part of big-name national collections, including those at the Hirshhorn Museum and Sculpture Garden and the National Museum of Women in the Arts in Washington, D.C., the Museum of Modern Art in New York and the Fogg Art Museum at Harvard University. Jaudon is also known for large-scale public projects such as steel fences, ceramic wall murals, floor mosaics, stained-glass windows and gardens. In 1988, she was among the first artists commissioned to create architectural projects for New York's mass transit system. In 1989, she designed a tile mural for an indoor pool at the Equitable Center in New York. In 1993, she received an award from the American Society of Landscape Architects for her design of a garden at the Birmingham Museum of Art. She designed a floor mosaic installed at the Washington National Airport. In the summer of 1996, thirty-three of her abstract paintings were shown at the Mississippi Museum of Art. She received a Mississippi Institute of Arts and Letters award in 1997 for her collection of paintings, *Run Silent, Run Deep*.

Don Jeffcoat

Born Feb. 16, 1975, in Gulfport. This young actor already has quite a long filmography, most of it on TV: *After the Promise* as Richard 2 ('87), *The Wonder Years* as Eric Antonio (1988-'89), *Broken Angel* as Brad ('88), *General Hospital* as Craig ('90) and *One Life to Live* as Joe Riley, Jr.('97). His notable TV guest appearances include: *Dr. Quinn, Medicine Woman* ('93), *7th Heaven* ('96), *Step by Step* on 1/3/92, *Murder, She Wrote* on 10/3/93, *Malibu Shores* in the pilot episode on 3/9/96 and on 3/16/96, *The John Larroquette Show* in the episode "Hello, Baby Hello" on 4/30/96, *Pacific Blue* in the episode "Wheels of Fire" on 11/17/96, *Party of Five* in the episode "I Do" on 11/27/96, *Sliders* on 3/28/97, and *Touched by an Angel* playing "Gordon" in the episode "Jones vs. God" on 10/19/97. He's been in 3 feature films: *Ghoulies II* ('87 - as "Eddie"), *Night of the Demons* ('87 - as "Billy") and *Wish Upon a Star* ('96 as "Kyle Harding").

Bert Jenkins

Born Nov. 29, 1924 in Richton, Perry Co., Miss. Considered to be the greatest high school basketball coach ever from

Profiles of Famous & Notable Mississippians

Mississippi, he graduated from Starkville High and attended Mississippi State for one year before serving in World War II. He fought under Generals Omar Bradley and George Patton, was wounded in the Battle of the Bulge and lost a leg in a German prisoner of war camp. After the war, Jenkins received his bachelor's degree in English at Mississippi Southern in 1947 and his master's at Alabama in 1949. He began his teaching and coaching career at Gulfport in 1950. Jenkins' legendary Gulfport Admiral teams won 7 state championships, 13 Big Eight championships, numerous district crowns, and had twenty-five 20-win seasons, eighteen 30-win seasons, and three 40-win seasons. His teams won over 82 percent of the time! Jenkins received numerous coaching awards, including national coach of the year in 1989. He retired in 1989 with a state-record 866 wins and only 180 losses in over 28 seasons! One of his players, Chris Jackson, became NBA star Mahmoud Abdul-Rauf (see his profile). Jenkins is a member of the Miss. Association of Coaches Hall of Fame and he was inducted into the Mississippi Sports Hall of Fame in 1999. Jenkins and his wife, Lil, live on the Mississippi Gulf Coast.

Daron Jenkins

Born on Feb. 22, 1968, in Mendenhall, Mississippi. He played basketball at Mendenhall High, Copiah-Lincoln Community College and the University of Southern Mississippi. He later played in the Milwaukee, Los Angeles and Dallas summer leagues and for the Global Basketball Association and Professional European Basketball Association. He is a former player with the Harlem Globetrotters, signing with them in '96.

Jaimoe Jai Johanny

Born Johnny Lee Johnson on July 8, 1944, in Gulfport, Miss., he also uses the name Jaimoe Jai Johanny Johansen. A rock drummer who was one of the original members of the Allman Brothers Band, he's also worked with Paul Hornsby, Charlie Daniels, the Marshall Tucker Band and other artists on a couple dozen albums since 1969.

"Big" Jack Johnson

Born July 30, 1940, in Lambert, Miss. "The Oilman" is one of the best Blues guitarists ever to come out of the Clarksdale area. Unlike many Bluesmen, Big Jack stayed in the Delta where he continues to make his home. In 1962 Big Jack teamed up with Frank Frost and Sam Carr (see his profile) and formed what most blues fans think of as the perfect Blues trio. They were Frank Frost and the Nighthawks then Little Sam Carr and The Blues Kings. In 1978, after a lengthy breakup, they became the Jelly Roll Kings. After recording *Rockin' The Juke Joint Down*, the Jelly Roll Kings did sporadic performances while continuing to perform separately as well. They reunited for the Chicago Blues Festival in 1987 and '91. They also regrouped for another Jelly Roll Kings CD, *Off Yonder Wall*, on Fat Possum Records released in 1996. Big Jack Johnson has also enjoyed a successful career fronting his own band. Big Jack sings about the troubles of today's world — hate, violence, disease — but, he also sings about hope, living together in peace, and making the world a better place. Big Jack has been named "Best Live Performer" in The *Living Blues* Magazine Critic's Poll and his song *We Gotta Stop This Killin'* was voted best song of the year. Tours have taken him to Japan, Germany, and other European countries. He's also in regular demand at festivals all over the U.S. Big Jack spends a lot of time on the road with his band, but occasionally you can catch him at home in one of the jukes around Clarksdale.

George Ellis Johnson

Born June 16, 1927, in Richton, Miss. In 1954, Johnson, living in Chicago, turned a $500 loan into a multi-million dollar cosmetics business, founding the Johnson Products Company. In 1971, Johnson Products became the first African American-owned company to be listed on the American Stock Exchange. Johnson became the first African American to be elected a director of the board of Commonwealth Edison in Chicago in 1971. *Ebony* magazine honored Johnson in 1978 with its American Black Achievement Award.

Jimmy Johnson

Born in Lanett, Alabama on Feb. 19, 1952. His editorial cartooning for the now-defunct *Jackson Daily News* (from Aug. 1979 through 1985) was honored by the Robert F. Kennedy Journalism Awards. While still working in Jackson, Johnson created the comic strip *Arlo and Janis*, which premiered on July 29, 1985. The popular strip has appeared since in *The Clarion-Ledger* and over 600 other newspapers nationwide distributed by United Media of New York. Johnson now lives in Alabama and in Pass Christian, Mississippi, which he says he considers home, too.

Jimmy Johnson

Born Jimmy Thompson on Nov. 25, 1928, in Holly Springs, Mississippi. Johnson moved to Chicago in 1950. His guitar playing remained a hobby for years, but in 1959, Johnson began gigging with harpist Slim Willis around the West side. Since there was more money to be realized playing R&B during the 1960s, Johnson concentrated on that for a while. He led house bands behind Otis Clay, Denise LaSalle, and Garland Green, cutting an occasional instrumental 45 on the side. Johnson found his way back to the blues in 1974 as Jimmy Dawkins's rhythm guitarist. He toured Japan behind Otis Rush in 1975. Johnson didn't release his first album until he was 50 years old. He's made up for lost time since, establishing himself as one of the Windy City's premier blues artists. With the 1978 release of four sides on Alligator's first batch of Living Chicago Blues anthologies, the album *Whacks on Delmark* (1979), the Delmark follow-up *North/South* (1982) and the 1983 release of *Bar Room Preacher* by Alligator, Johnson continued his climb into the top ranks of Chicago blues. Then tragedy struck. On Dec. 2, 1988, Johnson had a car wreck in Indiana, which injured him and killed his bassist and keyboardist. After Johnson recovered, he cut a solid album for Verve in 1994 called *I'm a Jockey*.

Johnny Lee Johnson (see Jaimoe Jai Johanny)

Luther "Guitar Jr." Johnson

Born April 11, 1939, in Itta Bena, Mississippi. While he performed gospel and blues while growing up, blues was his main passion after he moved to Chicago in the mid-1950s. Magic Sam became a major inspiration to Johnson during the mid-1960s when Johnson spent a couple of years in Sam's band. Of the three blues guitarists answering to the name of Luther Johnson, this blues veteran is probably the best-known. Like Luther "Georgia Boy/Snake Boy" Johnson, "Guitar Junior" spent a stint in the top-seeded band of Muddy Waters from 1972 to 79). His 1976 debut album, *Luther's Blues*, was cut during a European tour with Muddy. By 1980, Johnson was on his own, recording with the Nighthawks as well as four tracks on Alligator's second series of Living Chicago Blues anthologies. He moved to Boston during the early 1980s. With his own band, the Magic Rockers, Johnson released *Doin' the Sugar Too* on Rooster Blues in 1984. Since 1990, Johnson has had three albums on the Bullseye Blues label.

Robert Johnson

Legendary bluesman born May 8, 1911, at Hazlehurst, Miss., he grew up in and around Robinsonville, Miss. He recorded only 2 albums (29 songs) in five sessions in Texas during Nov.

Profiles of Famous & Notable Mississippians

1936 and June 1937. Songs include *Rambling On My Mind*, *Walking Blues* and *Honeymoon Blues*. One the most influential 20th century blues artists, Johnson was inducted into the Rock & Roll Hall of Fame in 1986 in the "Early Influences" category. Four of Johnson's songs, *Cross Road Blues*, *Hellhound On My Trail*, *Love in Vain* and *Sweet Home Chicago*, are included on the Rock and Roll Hall of Fame and Museum's list of 500 Songs That Shaped Rock And Roll. The 1986 movie *Crossroads*, loosely based on Johnson's life, was filmed on location in the Delta towns of Beulah, Bolivar, Chatham, Greenville, Vicksburg and Winterville. Legend has it that Johnson sold his soul to the devil in exchange for his ability to play and sing the blues better than any other man. The real story is that Johnson had large hands with long fingers, and this was probably how he was able to play such strange and innovative chords and notes. Johnson's life came to a premature end after his whiskey was poisoned by the jealous husband of a woman he began seeing during a stint at the Three Forks juke joint just outside Greenwood, Miss. The poisoning occurred on the night of Aug. 13, 1938. Johnson died 3 nights later on Aug. 16, 1938. There are four locations that are listed in various reference sources as his possible burial place — 1) In the Zion Church Cemetery in Morgan City, Miss., about 30 miles southeast of Cleveland, where there's a four-sided gray granite marker placed there April 20, 1991. On one side is a list of his 29 songs. On another side is a line from one of his songs: "You may bury my body down by the highway side..." (the words to the rest of that verse: "...so my evil old spirit can get a Greyhound bus and ride." is not on the stone); 2) In the Payne Chapel Memorial Baptist Church Cemetery in Quito, Miss.; 3) Near Hazlehurst; and 4) an unmarked grave at Little Zion Missionary Baptist Church just north of Greenwood is the most likely burial site. In 1994 the U.S. Postal Service issued postage stamps commemorating 8 "Legends of Blues and Jazz." Robert Johnson was one of three Mississippians honored. The other two were Howlin' Wolf and Muddy Waters. Johnson was one of the first 27 inducted into the inaugural Miss. Musicians Hall of Fame on April 1, 2000.

Tommy Johnson
Born in 1896 in Terry, Miss., his family moved to Crystal Springs in 1910. By age 16, Johnson had run away from home to become a "professional" musician, largely supporting himself by playing on the street for tips. By his late teens, Johnson was frequently enjoying the company of rising local stars Charley Patton, Dick Bankston and Willie Brown, all sowing the seeds of what would become the Mississippi Delta blues. Johnson spent most of the 1920s drinking, womanizing, gambling, and playing with Charley McCoy, Walter Vincent, and Ishmon Bracey. He cut his first records for Victor in Memphis in 1928. Johnson's first releases inspired up and coming disciples like Howlin' Wolf, Robert Nighthawk, Floyd Jones, "Boogie" Bill Webb, K.C. Douglas, Johnny "Geechie" Temple, and Otis Spann. He cut some great records for the Paramount label in 1930, largely through the maneuvering of fellow drinking buddy Charley Patton. One of his early admirers, Howlin' Wolf, took Johnson's *Cool Water Blues* in the 1950s and the song became *I Asked for Water (She Brought Me Gasoline)*. Another signature piece, his *Maggie Campbell*, came with a chord progression that was used for many variations by blues players dating all the way back to Charley Patton through Robert Nighthawk. Two of his best-known songs have survived into modern times; *Big Road Blues* is probably best known to contemporary blues fans from adaptations by Floyd Jones and others, while his *Canned Heat Blues*, an account of his addiction to alcohol, was the tune that gave the California blues-rock band their name. Johnson only recorded from 1928 to 1930, but the legend of Tommy Johnson is hard to ignore — like his uncontrolled womanizing and alcoholism. Years before the deal with the Devil at a deserted Delta crossroads was being used as an explanation of the other-worldly abilities of young Robert Johnson, the story was being told repeatedly about Tommy, often by the man himself to reinforce his abilities to doubting audiences. At his live performances he would play the guitar behind his neck in emulation of Charley Patton's showboating while hollering the blues at full throated level for hours without a break. He worked on a medicine show with Ishmon Bracey in the 1930s, but mostly stayed on the juke and small party circuit the rest of his days. He was playing a local house party when he suffered a fatal heart attack. He died in Crystal Springs on Nov. 1, 1956, at the age of 60 and is buried there at the Warm Springs Methodist Church Cemetery. He's in the Blues Foundation's Hall of Fame. Next to Son House and Charley Patton, no one was more important to the development of pre-Robert Johnson Delta blues than Tommy Johnson.

John Johnston
Born Feb. 10, 1965, in Jackson. He was a 1983 graduate of Jackson Prep and got a degree at Millsaps College in 1989. Soon after, he went to work in Hollywood, California as a production assistant. At first, he worked mainly on commercials, casting spots for Post Raisin Bran and NFL products and helping coordinate ads for American Express and Levi's 501 jeans. He moved into feature films and worked with such stars as John Travolta, Tony Curtis, Charlie Sheen and Arnold Schwarzenegger. He now works as a locations manager, finding and securing places for movies to be filmed and he worked in that capacity on *The Chamber* when it was being filmed in Jackson in spring 1996. Johnston also worked on *Pulp Fiction*, *Volcano*, *X-Files: The Movie*, and the NBC-TV series, *The Pretender*. His latest movie brought him back to his hometown, again. He was locations manager for *The Rising Place*, written and directed by another native Jacksonian, Tom Rice (see his profile), and filmed in Jackson, Canton and Yazoo City in the spring of 1999. John's brother, Bob Johnston is producer of *The Rising Place*.

Means Johnston, Jr.
Born Dec. 5, 1916, in Greenwood. This four-star Admiral had ten major commands at sea and was commander of the Allied Forces of Southern Europe, part of NATO. He died of cancer on July 14, 1989, at age 72 at Walter Reed Army Hospital in Washington and is buried in Arlington National Cemetery.

Deacon Jones
Born David Deacon Jones on Dec. 9, 1938 in Eatonville, Florida. The 6-5, 272-pound Jones played college football at Mississippi Industrial before turning pro. He was drafted in 1961 in the 14th round by the Los Angeles Rams and stayed with them until 1971. He was a 5-time All-Pro (1965-69) with the LA Rams. He played for the San Diego Chargers in 1972 and '73 and for the Washington Redskins in 1974. Jones is the unofficial all-time NFL sack leader with 173½ in 14 years. Jones is in Pro Football Hall of Fame (1980) and was among 48 players picked for The All-Time NFL Team in 1994.

Eddie "Guitar Slim" Jones
Born Dec. 10, 1926, in Greenwood, he grew up in Hollandale, Miss. Best known for the R&B classic hit record, *The Things That Used To Be*, which topped the R&B charts for 6 weeks in 1953 and has become a blues standard (Ray Charles backed him on piano). Eddie sometimes used 500 feet of microphone

Profiles of Famous & Notable Mississippians

cord because he liked to be carried out onto the street on his valet's shoulders while still performing! He died of pneumonia on Feb. 7, 1959, in New York City at the age of 32.

Hayes Jones
Born Aug. 4, 1938, in Starkville, Miss. He won the Gold Medal in the high hurdles in the 1964 Olympics. He was inducted into the National Track & Field Hall of Fame in '76.

Henry "Hank" Jones
Born in Vicksburg, Mississippi on July 31, 1918. This jazz pianist played in local bands while a teenager and in 1944 moved to New York to play with Hot Lips Page. He had stints with John Kirby, Howard McGhee, Coleman Hawkins, Andy Kirk and Billy Eckstine and was influenced by Teddy Wilson and Art Tatum. He was on several Jazz at the Philharmonic tours (starting in 1947), worked as accompanist for Ella Fitzgerald (1948-53) and recorded with Charlie Parker. In the 1950s Jones performed with Artie Shaw, Benny Goodman, Lester Young, Cannonball Adderley and many others. He was on the staff of CBS during 1959-1976 but always remained active in jazz. In the late 1970s Jones was the pianist in the Broadway musical *Ain't Misbehavin'* and he recorded with a pickup unit dubbed the Great Jazz Trio which at various times includes Ron Carter, Buster Williams or Eddie Gomez on bass and Tony Williams, Al Foster or Jimmy Cobb on drums. Among the many labels that Hank Jones has recorded for as a leader are Verve, Savoy, Epic, Golden Crest, Capitol, Argo, ABC-Paramount, Impulse, Concord, East Wind, Muse, Galaxy, Black & Blue, MPS, and Inner City.

James Earl Jones
Born Todd Jones on Jan. 17, 1931, at Arkabutla, Mississippi, the son of Mississippian and actor Robert Earle Jones. Raised in Michigan from the early age of about 5 by his maternal grandparents, he overcame a stutter while in high school and won a scholarship to the University of Michigan where he studied drama. He moved to New York City in 1955 to pursue a stage career and was reunited with his father who had left the family before James Earl's birth. After years of playing bit parts, Jones won recognition for his performance in *The Blacks* ('61), *Mr. Johnson, Moon on a Rainbow Shawl* and many other plays. Jones worked in 18 plays in thirty months during the early sixties. In 1962 he won an Obie Award as best off-Broadway actor. In 1964 he appeared in Othello for the first time, a role he repeated several times. He gained prominence on the New York stage, particularly in *The Great White Hope* (Tony Award for Best Actor, '69), a role that earned him an Oscar® nomination when he reprised it for the screen in 1970. He received the 1987 Tony Award for Best Actor & the Outer Critics Circle Award for his role in the Broadway play *Fences*. Some of his movies include *Dr. Strangelove* ('64), *The Comedians* ('67), *End of the Road* ('70), *The Last Remake of Beau Geste* ('77), *A Piece of the Action* ('77), *Conan, The Barbarian* ('82), *My Little Girl* ('86), *Gardens of Stone* ('87), *Matewan* ('87), *Coming To America* ('88), *Field of Dreams* ('89), *The Hunt for Red October* ('90), *Patriot Games* ('92), *Sneakers* ('92), *Clear and Present Danger* ('94), *Cry, The Beloved Country* ('95), *A Famiy Thing* ('96), *Gang Related* ('97), and as one of the hosts in Walt Disney's *Fantasia 2000* ('99). He was the voice of "Darth Vader" in the *Star Wars* trilogy ('77, '80, '83 & re-released '97), the voice of Mufasa in Disney's animated feature *The Lion King* ('94) and *The Lion King II: Simba's Pride* ('98), the voice during the opening segment of *Judge Dredd* ('95), the voice of Kibosh in *Casper: A Spirited Beginning* ('97), the voice of the Mountain King in the NBC-TV miniseries *Merlin* in 1998, and the voice on CNN station-break IDs. Two of his films, *Star Wars* and *Dr. Strangelove*, were rated No. 15 and No. 26, respectively, on The American Film Institute's list of the Top 100 Greatest American Movies of All Time announced in 1998. By the way, for being the voice of Darth Vader in *Star Wars* (1977), he was paid only $2,500 and his name wasn't listed in the credits! On TV, he starred in the mini-series *Roots II: The Next Generation*, the detective series *Paris* (1979-80), co-starred in the crime series *Pros and Cons*, and won an Emmy as best actor in a dramatic series for *Gabriel's Fire*. In 1997, he appeared in *Alone, The Second Civil War*, and co-starred in *What the Deaf Man Heard* on CBS. He was in the PBS movie *Hallelujah* (1993). He received a 1994 Emmy nomination for Best Guest in a Drama Series for an episode of *Picket Fences*. He's in the Theater Hall of Fame, was awarded the National Medal of the Arts, and holds honorary doctorates from the University of Michigan, Princeton, Columbia and Yale.

Laurence Clifton Jones
Born Nov. 21, 1884, in St. Joseph, Mo. While in high school, he moved to Iowa and became the first black graduate of Marshalltown, Iowa, High School. He graduated from the University of Iowa in 1907. Considered one of the pioneers of black education in Mississippi, Jones taught at Utica in Hinds County, and made it his goal to help poor, uneducated blacks. He traveled 20 miles a day on foot throughout Rankin County, promoting Booker T. Washington's idea for a practical black school. One day as Jones sat reading a book, a black child came up and told Jones about his desire to read. Jones agreed to teach the child, who returned the next day with two friends. As the days passed, the number of students increased and the weather grew colder. Jones acquired a sheep shelter, fifty dollars, and forty acres of land from an educated former slave. A white owner of a sawmill donated lumber, and local blacks helped build the school in 1909. It's now known as the Piney Woods Country Life School, one of only four black boarding schools in the nation. Dr. Jones wrote several books about the school and education — *The Pine Torch* (1911), *Piney Woods and Its Story* ('22), *The Spirit of Piney Woods* ('31), and *The Bottom Rail* (1935). Jones died on July 15, 1975, at age 91.

Robert Earl Jones
Born Feb. 3, 1910, in Coldwater, Miss. A former prizefighter, he's an accomplished actor who's appeared in minor roles in the movies *Hang 'Em High* (1967), *The Sting* (1973), *Trading Places* (1983), *The Cotton Club* (1984) and *Witness* (1985). He's also starred in several Broadway productions including Shakespeare's *Othello*, and made numerous appearances on TV shows. He is the father of actor James Earl Jones.

Daniel P. Jordan
Born July 22, 1938, in Philadelphia, Miss., he received his B.A. (English and history) and his M.A. in history from the University of Mississippi, where he was a scholarship athlete in baseball and basketball and served as student body president. He received his Ph.D. in history from the University of Virginia in 1970. Since 1985, Dr. Jordan has headed the nonprofit Thomas Jefferson Memorial Foundation, which owns and operates Monticello, the home of Thomas Jefferson, in Charlottesville, Virginia, which has a $19 million operating budget and 353 employees. It's the only house in America on the United Nations' prestigious World Heritage List of sites that must be preserved at all costs. The Pyramids of Egypt and the Great Wall of China also are on the list. Dr. Jordan is also a Scholar in Residence at the University of Virginia. He has written three books: *Political Leadership in Jefferson's Virginia*; *A Richmond Reader*; and *Tobacco Merchant: The*

Profiles of Famous & Notable Mississippians

Story of Universal Leaf Tobacco Company. He has been a book reviewer for the *Richmond Times-Dispatch*, a contributor to *Commonwealth Magazine*, and has written over 60 articles, essays and reviews in scholarly journals and reference works. His national media appearances include ABC-TV (twice), CBS-TV, NBC-TV (7 times), CNN, C-SPAN (numerous times), the A&E, Discovery and Learning Channels, and Voice of America. Dr. Jordan played a central role in the commemoration of the 250th anniversary of the birth of Thomas Jefferson in 1993, including a private tour of Monticello conducted by he and his wife for President and Mrs. Clinton and Vice President and Mrs. Gore. He has chaired and served as a member of boards of numerous national and Virginia organizations. He has received many awards and honors, including the University of Virginia's Raven Alumni Award, presented by Katy Couric on NBC-TV's *Today Show* in 1993. A famous Mississippian, as well as a famous Virginian, Dr. Jordan was inducted into the Ole Miss Alumni Hall of Fame in 1990.

Mack A. Jordan
Born Dec. 8, 1928, in Collins, Mississippi. He was a Private First Class in the U.S. Army, Company K, 21st Infantry Regiment, 24th Infantry Division near Kumsong, Korea when he performed an act of bravery on Nov. 15, 1951 that took his life. He was awarded the Congressional Medal of Honor posthumously on Jan. 8, 1953. Here are the actual words of his citation: "Pfc. Jordan, a member of Company K, distinguished himself by conspicuous gallantry and indomitable courage above and beyond the call of duty in action against the enemy. As a squad leader of the 3d Platoon, he was participating in a night attack on key terrain against a fanatical hostile force when the advance was halted by intense small-arms and automatic-weapons fire and a vicious barrage of hand grenades. Upon orders for the platoon to withdraw and reorganize, Pfc. Jordan voluntarily remained behind to provide covering fire. Crawling toward an enemy machinegun emplacement, he threw 3 grenades and neutralized the gun. He then rushed the position delivering a devastating hail of fire, killing several of the enemy and forcing the remainder to fall back to new positions. He courageously attempted to move forward to silence another machinegun but, before he could leave his position, the ruthless foe hurled explosives down the hill and in the ensuing blast both legs were severed. Despite mortal wounds, he continued to deliver deadly fire and held off the assailants until the platoon returned. Pfc. Jordan's unflinching courage and gallant self-sacrifice reflect lasting glory upon himself and uphold the noble traditions of the infantry and the military service." Jordan was one of only 4 native Mississippians (out of 5 Mississippians) to earn the Medal of Honor for their service in the Korean conflict and one of only 4 *native* Mississippians (out of 6) to be awarded the Medal posthumously. Jordan's Medal was one of 17 Medals of Honor officially accredited to Mississippi in all wars, although we claim 5 more accredited to other states because the recipients had Mississippi ties. Jordan is one of 13 *native* Mississippians (of 22 Mississippians — 15 Army, 4 Marines & 3 Navy) in all wars to be awarded the Medal of Honor out of 3,433 recipients through Nov. 1, 2000. Jordan is buried in the Station Creek Cemetery in Collins, Mississippi. There is no Medal of Honor marker on his gravesite.

Winthrop D. Jordan
Born Nov. 11, 1931, in Worcester, Mass. He has been at the University of Mississippi since 1982. Dr. Jordan is the first holder of the endowed William F. Winter Professorship of History, which he has held since 1993, and a professor of Afro-American studies. He won the 1993 Bancroft Prize (his 2nd) and the Kayden National University Press Award for his book *Tumult and Silence at Second Creek: An Inquiry into a Civil War and Slave Conspiracy*. Jordan was a recipient of a Barnard Distinguished Professorship, 1998-2003.

Margie Joseph
Born in Pascagoula in 1950. She has lived for some time in New Orleans, where she attended Dillard University. Jazz and gospel music play a big part in the vocal style of Margie, who cites Sarah Vaughan and Aretha Franklin as influences. She debuted on Okeh records in 1967. Margie specializes in lushly orchestrated revivals of R&B classics, like Al Green's *Let's Stay Together*, and the Supremes *Stop! In the Name of Love*. Her biggest hit was *My Love* in 1974. She sang with the group Blue Magic on *What's Come Over Me* (1975), which made the R&B Top 20. Her dance-flavored *Ready for the Night* was a small R&B hit in 1984. She has recorded 6 albums.

Belle Kearney
Born Mar. 6, 1863, near Flora, Miss. With a considerable gift of oratory, at age 26 she joined the Temperance Movement and traveled throughout the U.S. lecturing on that subject. In 1902, she became the first women to address a joint session of the Mississippi legislature. On a world tour in 1904-05, she spoke in a number of European countries. In addition to her involvement in the Temperance Movement, Kearney was a strong advocate of women's suffrage and she served as president of the Mississippi Woman Suffrage Association from 1906-08. After spending several years away from the state in Washington and New York, she ran for the U.S. Senate in 1921, losing to James K. Vardaman for the seat held by retiring John Sharp Williams (see his profile). She was the first woman in the South to become a state senator when she defeated three male opponents in Madison County in 1923. She served two terms. She wrote three books including her autobiography, *A Slaveholder's Daughter* (1900). Kearney spent her last years on the plantation where she was born. She died of cancer at the home of a friend in Jackson on Feb. 27, 1939, at age 75 and is buried in in Madison County.

Don Lee Keith
Born on Oct. 25, 1940, in Wheeler, Prentiss Co., Miss. He attended Ole Miss in 1960-61 before moving to New Orleans to join the staff of the *Times-Picayune*. In 1976 he became associate editor of the *Courier* in New Orleans and later editor-in-chief of the *New Orleans Magazine*. Keith was twice nominated for the Pulitizer and has been the recipient of many journalism awards from the Press Club of New Orleans. He's now journalist-in-residence at the University of New Orleans.

Murry Kellum
Born Dec. 31, 1942, in Jackson, Tennessee, he graduated from Florence (Miss.) High School in 1960. He was fairly successful in recording novelty-type songs of country humor such as *Long Tall Texan* (1964), *Tell Her Lies and Feed Her Candy* and *Joy To The World*. Kellum died on Sept. 15, 1990.

Patrick Kelly
Born Sept. 24, 1954, in Vicksburg. He was the first American designer ever inducted into the Chamble Syndicale, the elite French fashion-industry union. He made his home in Paris where he marketed his clothing, sunglasses and fragrance under the name Patrick Kelly Paris. He was pictured on the cover of the May 1989 issue of *Essence* magazine and was also featured in *Vogue, Mademoiselle, Time* and others. Kelly died in Paris on Jan. 1, 1990, at the age of 35.

Profiles of Famous & Notable Mississippians

Randolph Keys
Born on Apr. 19, 1966, in Collins, Miss. Keys was the MVP in the NIT and led the Southern Mississippi basketball team to the tournament title as a senior. Keys was a first-round draft pick by Cleveland in 1988. He played for the Cavaliers for 1½ seasons before being traded to Charlotte. He played for the Hornets for one and a half seasons before playing in Italy for one season and Spain for two years. He returned to the NBA by signing with the Lakers in 1994 and then he played for the Milwaukee Bucks in 1995. After that, a series of knee operations sidelined him for a while.

Robert C. Khayat
Born Robert Conrad Khayat on Apr. 18, 1938, in Moss Point, Mississippi. He was a two-sport college athlete at Ole Miss and went on to become a lineman/place-kicker for the Washington Redskins from 1960-64 and made it to a Pro Bowl. As a Rebel football player, he led the nation's place-kickers in scoring in 1958 and 1959. In Rebel baseball, he caught for two Southeastern Conference title teams. A former law professor, Dr. Khayat became the chancellor of the University of Mississippi on July 1, 1995, when Gerald Turner resigned to become president of Southern Methodist University in Dallas. The ceremonies were held on April 11, 1996, installing him as Ole Miss' 25th chief executive since the Oxford school opened in 1848. One of the speakers at the event was Khayat's friend, author John Grisham. On Mar. 30, 1998, the NFL Alumni board of directors presented Khayat with its Careeer Achievement Award for his achievements on and off the playing field. As a student at Ole Miss in the 1960s, he was featured as a member of the Student Hall of Fame, the only Chancellor to have received this honor. He was inducted into the Mississippi Sports Hall of Fame in March 2000 in the football category. Dr. Kyayat was elected chairman of the Commission on Colleges of the Southern Association of Colleges and Schools for 2000, which accredits about 12,000 public and private schools. On Oct. 21, 2000, delegates at the Phi Beta Kappa national convention in Philadelphia, Pennsylvannia, voted overwhelmingly in favor of establishing a chapter at Ole Miss. Dr. Khayat had worked for some time to make Ole Miss the first public institution of higher learning in Mississippi chosen for a chapter of Phi Beta Kappa, considered the nation's most prestigious honor society.

"Junior" Kimbrough
Born David Kimbrough on July 28, 1930, in Hudsonville, Marshall Co., Miss. This bluesman was named as a prime early influence by rockabilly pioneer Charlie Feathers (see his profile). Kimbrough ran his own juke joints for more than 30 years and sang the blues for most of his life. But, his brand of blues remained a regional sensation for most of his career. That changed somewhat in the early '90s, when he appeared in the 1991 movie *Deep Blues* and on its Anxious/Atlantic soundtrack, leading to his own debut for Fat Possum Records, where he cut three albums: *All Night Long, Sad Days, Lonely Nights* and *Most Things Haven't Worked Out*. Some things didn't — Kimbrough died of a heart attack in Holly Springs, Misssssippi on Jan. 17, 1998, at the age of 67.

Frank "Bruiser" Kinard
Born Frank Manning Kinard on Oct. 23, 1914, in Pelahatchie, Mississippi. He played football for Ole Miss, but also started for the basketball team and ran the 440 in track. He went into pro football as a tackle for the Dodgers as a second-round draft pick in 1938 and played for 9 years from 1938-47. He was out with injuries only once. He was the First man to earn both All-NFL, All-AAFC honors — All-NFL, 1940, 1941, 1943 & 1944 and All-AAFC in 1946. He was All-service in 1945. Inducted into the College Football Hall of Fame in 1951, he was the first Rebel player inducted. He was the first Mississippian to be selected for the Pro Football Hall of Fame, enshrined in 1971! Kinard was inducted into the Mississippi Sports Hall of Fame in 1961. He died Sept. 7, 1985, at age 70.

Albert King
Born Albert Nelson on April 25, 1923, in Indianola, Miss., he grew up in Forrest City, Ark. King taught himself how to play guitar as a child, building his own instrument out of a cigar box. He played drums for bluesman, then went on his own with blues and R&B hits such as *Laudromat Blues* and *Don't Throw Your Love On Me So Strong*. Along with B.B. King and Freddie King, Albert King was one of the major influences on blues and rock guitar players. Albert King played guitar left-handed, without re-stringing the guitar after the right-handed setup. This "upside-down" playing accounts for his difference in tone. King was a major influence on blues and rock guitar players like Stevie Ray Vaughan, Robert Cray and Otis Rush. Eric Clapton copied King's *Personal Manager* guitar solo note-for-note on Cream's song *Strange Brew*. King's song, *Born Under A Bad Sign*, is included on the Rock and Roll Hall of Fame and Museum's list of 500 Songs That Shaped Rock And Roll. King died from a heart attack in Memphis on Dec. 21, 1992, at age 69. He is buried in Paradise Gardens Cemetery in Edmonson, Arkansas.

B.B. King
Legendary bluesman born Riley B. King on a plantation at Itta Bena on Sept. 16, 1925. B.B. is not related to singer Albert King, although B.B.'s father was named Albert. His stage name started in the 1940s when he was a Memphis DJ known as "the Beale Street Blues Boy," which was shortened to "Blues Boy," then to "B.B." A superb showman and one of the world's greatest guitar soloists, the "King of the Blues" is the best-known and most influential bluesman. Back in the 1950s, he rescued his guitar from a fire started in a dance hall in Twist, Arkansas by two men who knocked over a heater in a fight over a woman named Lucille. Since then he has called his guitar "Lucille." His first record was *Miss Martha King* ('49), followed by *Three O'Clock Blues*, a major national R&B hit of 1950. His *Billboard* Top 40 hits are: *Rock Me Baby* ('64), *Paying the Cost to be the Boss* ('68), *The Thrill is Gone* ('70), *Ask Me No Questions* ('71), *To Know You is to Love You* ('73), and *I Like to Live the Love* ('74). He has recorded about 40 albums from the first titled *The Unexpected... Instrumental; B.B. King...Just Sweet Guitar* in the 1960s to *Riding With the King* (with Eric Clapton) in July 2000. In 1971, the *Live at the Regal* album was his first to cross over from the blues charts to the pop charts. Other albums include *Indianola Mississippi Roots* ('70), *Six Silver Strings* ('85), and *There Is Always One More Time* ('91). He has won 8 regular Grammys — for the song *The Thrill is Gone* ('71) and the albums *There Must Be a Better World Somewhere* ('81), *Blues 'n' Jazz* ('84), *My Guitar Sings the Blues* ('86), *Live at San Quentin* ('90), *Live at the Apollo* ('91), *Blues Summit* ('92) and one in 1997 for his performance with seven other artists in *SRV Shuffle*, which won for best rock instrumental. Plus King won the special Grammy, the Lifetime Achievement Award, in 1988. King received a 1999 Grammy nomination for Best Contemporary Blues Album for *Deuces Wild*. A few of his many other awards: inducted into the Blues Foundation Hall of Fame in 1984; inducted into the Rock & Roll Hall of Fame in 1986 (Two of B.B.'s songs, *Sweet Little Angel* and *The Thrill Is Gone*, are included on the Rock and Roll Hall of Fame and

Profiles of Famous & Notable Mississippians

Museum's list of 500 Songs That Shaped Rock & Roll); Lifetime Achievement Award from the Songwriters Hall of Fame in 1990; the Presidential Medal of Honor in 1990, the same year he got his Star on the Hollywood Walk of Fame; National Heritage Fellowship from the National Endowment of the Arts in 1991; and the Kennedy Center Honor in 1995. He has an honorary Doctorate from Yale. On Jan. 21, 1987, King donated his personal record collection, including more than 3750 LP's, 2400 old 78's and 500 single 45's of jazz, blues, soul, R&B, rock, pop and country, to the Blues Archives at Ole Miss. The computer CD-ROM, *On the Road With B.B. King*, was released in 1996 as the world's first interactive musical biography. On Aug. 4, 1996, King sang in the closing ceremony of the 1996 Summer Olympic Games in Atlanta. In 1996, he cut back to about 250 dates a year. In 1956, he performed 342 one-night stands. In a millennium poll conducted by *The Clarion-Ledger* of Jackson released on Aug. 30, 1999, readers picked King as their all-time favorite in the Blues/Jazz/R&B category. He was one of the first 27 inducted into the Miss. Musicians Hall of Fame on April 1, 2000.

Pat Kirby
Born Oct. 8, 1956, in Tylertown, he grew up in Newton, Miss. He attended East Central Community College, Millsaps College, and earned a business degree from the University of Southern Mississippi in 1978. After college, he moved to Atlanta where he works as a furniture manufacturers' sales rep. Being an almost dead ringer for country superstar Garth Brooks, he performs all over the country. He was a regular at the Opryland Showpark and drew critics' applause with *Legends in Concert* in Vegas. He has appeared on *Geraldo* and TNN's *Dancing at the Hot Spots* and *Country News*.

Fred Knobloch
Born April 28, 1953, in Jackson, Mississippi. A country singer and songwriter, his own hit records include the self-penned *Why Not Me* (No. 1 on the *Billboard* adult contemporary chart and No. 18 on the Hot 100), *Killin' Time* (#28 in 1981 - a duet with actress Susan Anton), plus a No. 1 country single with the group Schuyler, Knobloch & Overstreet (Mississippian Paul), *Baby's Got a New Baby*, in 1986. He co-wrote the B.J. Thomas hit *The Whole World's In Love When You're Lonely* and he has written several hits for country stars like Lorrie Morgan (*Back in Your Arms Again*), Sawyer Brown (*Used to Blue*), and Faith Hill (*If My Heart Had Wings*). He's also written songs for Kenny Rogers, Trisha Yearwood, and George Strait, including his No. 1 hit of 1999, *Meanwhile*. He has even composed for TV (*Melrose Place* and *Beverly Hills 90210*) and feature films. Knobloch is a featured vocalist on the album, *Jelly Roll Johnson and a Few Close Friends* ('98).

Leon Z. Koury
Born Nov. 3, 1909, in Greenville, Mississippi. While Koury was still young, poet William Alexander Percy encouraged him to pursue art. Koury exhibited in the New York World's Fair in 1939. He headed up the W.P.A. Art Programs in Greenville during World War II. He also taught for the Greenville Art Association for many years. Sculptor William Beckwith, a native of Greenville now living in Taylor, Mississippi, was one of Koury's students (see his profile). Koury was best known for his lifelike portrait busts of notables such as William Faulkner and Hodding Carter. One of his pieces, *The Compress Worker*, is in the permanent collection of the Brook's Museum in Memphis. Koury died in Greenville April 11, 1993, at age 83.

Sylvia Howell Krebs
Born Sept. 9, 1937, in Jackson. Basketball star Sylvia Howell scored 4,205 points in 4 seasons at Forest High School and won 150 of 164 games from 1952-55. Forest won 81 straight games during her junior and senior seasons as Sylvia led the school to 3 consecutive state championships. She wasn't slack in academia either as she was salutatorian of her 1955 class after finishing with straight A's. Her studies dominated while attending Belhaven College, although she did play on the college team. She received her bachelor of arts in 1959. He earned her masters of arts in 1963 and Ph.D. in 1968, both at the University of Alabama. Dr. Krebs taught for many years at 11 different colleges and universities in Alabama, Georgia, and the People's Republic of China. She was inducted into the Mississippi Sports Hall of Fame in 1996.

Diane Ladd
Born Rose Diane Ladner on Nov. 29, 1932, in Merdian, Miss. She moved to New York City as a teenager, finding work as a model and as a dancer at the Copacabana nightclub. Ladd made her New York stage debut in Tennessee Williams' *Orpheus Descending*. Debuting onscreen in *Something Wild* (1961), she went on to star in three movies that brought her Academy Award® nominations: Martin Scorsese's *Alice Doesn't Live Here Anymore* (1975) [she played Flo], *Wild at Heart* (1990), which co-starred her daughter Laura Dern and was filmed in Mississippi, and *Rambling Rose* (1991). Ladd and daughter Laura Dern both received Academy Award® nominations for their roles in *Rambling Rose*, the first real-life mother and daughter to be nominated for one film in the same year. She has been in about 2 dozen films including *The Reivers* (1969), *WUSA* (1970), *White Lightning* (1973), *Chinatown* (1974), *All Night Long* (1981), *Black Widow* (1986), *National Lampoon's Christmas Vacation* (1989), *A Kiss Before Dying* (1991), *Mother* (1996), *Citizen Ruth* (1996, again with daughter Laura), *Ghosts of Mississippi* (1996), *James Dean: Race with Destiny* (1997), *Late Last Night* (1998), *Primary Colors* (1998), *Daddy and Them* (1999), *28 Days* (2000), and *Redemption of the Ghost* (2000). *Chinatown* (1974) was rated No. 19 on The American Film Institute's list of the Top 100 Greatest American Movies of All Time announced in 1998. Ladd received a 1994 Emmy nomination as Best Guest Actress in a Comedy Series for her role as the eccentric yet sympathetic mother of Grace on an episode of ABC-TV's *Grace Under Fire*. She directed her former husband, actor Bruce Dern (they divorced in 1967), and stars with him in *Mrs. Munck*, a made-for-TV movie that aired on Showtime several times in 1996. Some of the other recent TV movies that she has done include *Ruby Ridge: An American Tragedy* (1996), *Cold Lazarus* (mini-series in '96), *The Westing Game* (1997) and *The Staircase* (1998).

L.Q.C. Lamar
Lucius Quintus Cincinnatus Lamar was born Sept. 17, 1825, near Eatonton in Putnam County, Georgia. He attended schools in Baldwin and Newton Counties in Georgia and graduated from Emory College in Oxford, Georgia in 1845. He studied law in Macon and was admitted to the bar in 1847. Lamar moved to Oxford in 1849, where he practiced law and served one year as professor of mathematics in the University of Mississippi at Oxford. He moved to Covington, Georgia in 1852 and practiced law. Lamar was a member of the Georgia State house of representatives in 1853. He returned to Mississippi in 1855. Elected as a Democrat to the 35th and 36th Congresses, he served from March 4, 1857, until his retirement in December 1860 to become a member of the secession convention of Mississippi. Lamar drafted the Mississippi ordinance of secession. During the Civil War, he

Profiles of Famous & Notable Mississippians

served in the Confederate Army as lieutenant colonel until 1862. He entered the diplomatic service of the Confederacy in 1862 and was sent on a special mission to Russia, France, and England. After the Civil War, he again practiced law and was a professor of metaphysics, social science, and law at the University of Mississippi. Lamar was a member of the State constitutional conventions in 1865, 1868, 1875, 1877, and 1881. He was elected to the 43rd and 44th Congresses and served from March 4, 1873 until March 3, 1877. He was chairman of the Committee on Pacific Railroads in the 44rth Congress. He was elected to the U.S. Senate from 1877-85 and served from March 4, 1877, until March 6, 1885, when he resigned to accept a Cabinet post. He was chairman of the Committee on Interior and Insular Affairs and the Committee on Railroads in the 46th Congress. Lamar served as Secretary of the Interior in the Cabinet of President Grover Cleveland from 1885-1888. He was appointed by President Cleveland to be Associate Justice of the U.S. Supreme Court and served from Jan. 16, 1888 until his death. Lamar is the only Mississippian to ever serve on the nation's highest court. In fact, he is the only Mississippian to have served in all the following: U.S. House, U.S. Senate, as a member of the president's cabinet, and as a Supreme Court Justice. Lamar was the son-in-law of Augustus B. Longstreet (1790-1870), an author and second chancellor of Ole Miss (see his profile). Lamar died in Vineville, Georgia Jan. 23, 1893. First buried in the Riverside Cemetery in Macon, Georgia, his body was reburied in St. Peter's Cemetery in Oxford, Miss. in 1894. Lamar County in south Mississippi is named after him.

A.C. "Butch" Lambert

Born Aaron Colus Lambert on Feb. 27, 1923, in Holcut, Tishomingo County, Mississippi. His family moved to Red Bay, Alabama, where they lived 4 years before settling in Fulton in Itawamba Co., Mississippi in 1938. Lambert played every sport at Itawamba Agricultural High School, where he graduated in 1941. He volunteered and served in the U.S. Navy from 1943 through 1946. He played football at Ole Miss after World War II, but a leg injury pushed him into the role of team manager and trainer for football, basketball and baseball. Lambert coached the first three seasons in Itawamba Community College history before leaving to become a field representative with the Mississippi Tax Commission in 1952. He became Rockwell International's director of employee relations from 1956-80, then went back to the state tax commission from 1980-85. He also served in the Mississippi legislature as a representative from Lee and Itawamba counties from 1960-64 and as a Lee county representative from 1968-80. In his spare time, he was a sports referee, officiating at hundreds of South- eastern Conference football games from 1953-82, primarily as a line judge. He officiated in 10 bowl games, including two for the national championship: the 1975 Orange Bowl between Notre Dame and Alabama and the 1982 Orange Bowl between Clemson and Nebraska. He also officiated basketball in the SEC for 20 years and worked 4 NCAA regionals. He was the SEC's supervisor of officials from his retirement until his death on Jan. 26, 1985. He became only the second referee in the Mississippi Sports Hall of Fame when he was inducted in Mar. 2000 (the other is "Ju" Burghard). Itawamba Community College's stadium and the playing field at Mississippi Veterans Memorial Stadium in Jackson are both named after Lambert.

Major Lance

Born Apr. 4, 1941, in Winstonville, Bolivar County, Mississippi, Major Lance moved to Chicago as a child. While studying at Wells High School — where Curtis Mayfield and Jerry Butler also attended — Lance began boxing, but his attention soon turned to music. In 1962, Lance was signed to the revived OKeh Records. Later that year, Lance recorded his first single, *Delilah*, for the label. Like most of the Major's material, the song was written by Mayfield. Though *Delilah* wasn't a hit, Lance's second single, *The Monkey Time*, was a monster. Released in the summer of 1963, it reached No. 2 on the R&B charts and No. 8 pop. *Hey Little Girl* was a Top 15 pop and R&B hit later that year, followed by the Top 5 pop hit *Um, Um, Um, Um, Um, Um* early in 1964. Over the next year and a half, he continued to turn out a series of Mayfield-written songs, nearly all of which reached the R&B Top 40, but only a few were pop hits — *The Matador* (#20 in 1964), *Rhythm* (#24 in 1964), and *Come See* (#40 in 1965). After he had a few Top 20 R&B hits in 1965, *Ain't It A Shame*, *Too Hot to Hold*, and *Everybody Loves a Good Time*, Lance was sent to work with Billy Sherrill in Nashville. Out of these sessions, *It's the Beat* became Lance's only Top 40 hit. Since the teaming with Sherrill wasn't working out, Lance worked with a number of producers during 1966 and 1967, with only *Without a Doubt* barely touching the R&B charts in 1968. Over the next few years, Lance had a handful of Top 40 R&B hits on various labels including *Follow the Leader*, *Stay Away From Me (I Love You too Much)* [#13], and *Must Be Love Coming Down*. In 1972, Lance relocated to England and appeared on the "Soul Circuit," but returned to Atlanta in 1974. He signed with Playboy and released a disco version of *Um, Um, Um, Um, Um, Um* that became a minor hit, which was followed by a pair of minor hits in 1975. Shortly afterward, his career entered a downward spiral, and in 1978 he was convicted of selling cocaine. Lance spent the next four years in prison. Upon his release, he began playing the Beach Music circuit on the Carolina coast until he had a heart attack in 1987. In 1994, he gave a final, triumphant performance at the Chicago Blues Festival, which turned out to be his last. Lance died of heart failure on Sept. 3, 1994, in Decatur, Georgia at the age of 53.

Denise LaSalle

Born Denise Allen on July 16, 1939, in Leflore County, she grew up in Belzoni, Mississippi. LaSalle's early influences from jukeboxes and radio included Ruth Brown, Lavern Baker, and Dinah Washington. LaSalle moved to Chicago in her early 20s. This soul singer/songwriter had a million-selling gold record *Trapped By A Thing Called Love* in 1971, No. 1 on the R&B/Soul charts for 16 weeks and No. 13 on the pop charts. Other hit singles include *Now Run and Tell That*, *A Man Size Job* and *Married, But Not to Each Other*, which was also recorded by country star Barbara Mandrell. In 1976 she signed with ABC Records and recorded, *Second Breath* (1976), *The Bitch Is Bad* (1977), and *Under The Influence* (1978). Her first album for MCA, *Unwrapped* had many notable hits. The most popular, a 15-minute remake of *Trapped By A Thing Called Love*, which scored again in a medley with *Make Me Yours* and *Precious Precious*. In 1982, a Malaco Records executive in Jackson called to ask her to write a song for Z.Z. Hill. She's been with Malaco ever since. LaSalle's first album on Malaco was *Lady In The Street*. *Right Place, Right Time*, her 2nd Malaco release featured the late Z.Z. Hill's *Down Home Blues*. Other albums include *Love Talkin'*, *Rain & Fire*, *It's Lying Time Again*, *Hittin' Where It Hurts*, *Still Trapped* and *Love Me Right*. She has recorded over 20 albums including *Smokin' in Bed* ('98). LaSalle is now based in Jackson, Tennessee.

Profiles of Famous & Notable Mississippians

Jerome F. Leavell

Born on Feb. 14, 1928, in Blue Mountain in Tippah County, he grew up in Oxford, Mississippi. Jerome Fontaine Leavell is not only one of the finest legal minds ever born in Mississippi, he has to be near the top on any short list of the state's greatest intellectuals of all time. After serving in the U.S. Army as part of the occupation forces in Japan following World War II, Leavell graduated from the University of Mississippi receiving two degrees, his B.A. and LL.B.-J.D., on the same day in 1951! He then started his law career as an attorney for the War Claims Commission and later the Federal Trade Commission's Anti-Monopoly Division in Washington, D.C. In 1952, he was selected from among several young legal scholars to serve as law clerk to Judge Edwin R. Holmes, the then Senior Judge of the U.S. Court of Appeals for the Fifth Circuit in New Orleans. Leavell lived in Yazoo City, Mississippi at the time. Later in the 1950s, he was associated with the Wall Street law firm of Cadwalader, Wickersham and Taft, the oldest law firm in the nation. From 1958 to 1964 he was an assistant to the General Counsel in the law department of the second largest bank in the country, the Chase Manhattan Bank. During that period, he was also an assistant of the General Counsel of the world's largest brokerage firm, Merrill Lynch, Pierce, Fenner & Smith in New York City and was one of the ten attorneys who established the law department at firm. He also became the first lawyer from that firm to be admitted to practice before the U.S. Supreme Court. From 1962 to 1963, Leavell was a Trial Attorney for the Legal Enforcement Division of the New York State Tax Commission and at the same time maintained his general practice in Manhattan. In 1964 he was granted a Master's Degree in Law (LL.M.) at Yale Law School after having been invited to spend a year there as a Sterling Fellow. He also holds the highest earned research degree from Yale University, the Juridical Science Doctoris (J.S.D.), one of only four Mississippians to hold such a degree. In 1969 Dr. Leavell attended Oxford University in England as a Ford Foundation Fellow and visiting scholar. He was invited to the University of Edinburgh in Scotland as a Post-Doctorate Fellow in 1974 and invited as a Visiting Scholar to Harvard Law School in 1975. For three years, he was a professor of law at historic William and Mary Law School in Virginia, the oldest in the nation. He received tenure his first year there and was the recipient of a certificate of merit for outstanding teaching and distinguished writing. Dr. Leavell also taught at Louisiana State University. He taught at and was co-founder of the law schools of the University of Arkansas at Little Rock, and Mississippi College. After teaching in Clinton from 1975 to 1977, Dr. Leavell retired from the education field and returned to law practice in Oxford. He is a member of the bar in five states — Arkansas, Georgia, New York, Virginia, and Mississippi. The only honorary member of Delta Theta Phi, the international legal fraternity, Dr. Leavell is widely known and recognized as an authority in several fields of law — Torts, Conflict of Laws, and Legal Medicine. He has also studied Copyright Law extensively. He served on the Commission for the Protection of Human Subjects of Biomedical and Behavioral Research and has held many other important positions. Dr. Leavell's many written works include *A Treatise on the Law and Ethics of Organ Transplants* and *The Return of Caveat Venditor As the Law of Products Liability*. He's received enough awards and honors to fill a book and has been listed in *Who's Who Among Lawyers*, *Who's Who in America*, *Who's Who in the World*, *Directory of American Scholars*, *A Biographical Record of Contemporary Achievement*, *The Dictionary of International Biography*, and *Who's Who Among Authors and Journalists*. He is much in demand as a speaker and lecturer. In the 1970s, the White House nominated him for a federal judgeship. Now retired, Dr. Leavell and his wife, the former Martha Naomi Roll of Natchez, live in Oxford, Mississippi.

Chris LeDoux

Born Oct. 2, 1948, in Biloxi, he spent a good portion of his teen years in Texas. He started his career as a rodeo rider, winning a world championship title in bareback bronc riding in 1976 when he was 24 years old. He started writing, singing, and recording songs while still on the rodeo circuit, beginning in 1972. His big break came when Garth Brooks sang that he listened to "a worn-out tape of Chris LeDoux" in his 1989 hit *Much Too Young (To Feel This Damn Old)*. When everybody started asking who Chris Ledoux was, Brooks label signed him to a contract. Before signing with Capitol Nashville in 1991, LeDoux had recorded 22 albums on his own label. He has recorded eight albums with Capitol. His duet with Garth Brooks, *Whatcha Gonna Do With a Cowboy?* reached the Top 10 and received a Grammy nomination. The album of the same title was certified gold in 1993. Another album, *The Best of Chris LeDoux* was certified gold in 1997. He has an attention-getting stage show in Garth's style. In Sept. 2000, LeDoux was diagnosed with primary sclerosing cholangitis, the same disease that contributed to the death of Walter Payton in 1999. In early Oct., LeDoux received a liver transplant.

Hal Lee

Born Feb. 15, 1905, in Ludlow, Scott Co., Miss. His nickname was "Sheriff." He made his major league baseball debut on Apr. 19, 1930, with the Brooklyn Robins. Lee also played for the Philadelphia Phillies (1931-33), the Boston Braves (1933-35) and the Boston Bees in 1936. His career stats include 755 hits in 2,750 at bats (.275 batting average), 316 runs, 33 home runs and 323 RBIs in 752 games played. He was inducted into the Mississippi Sports Hall of Fame in 1974. Lee died on Sept. 4, 1989, in Pascagoula, Miss. at age 84.

Hubert L. Lee

Hubert Louis Lee was born on Feb. 2, 1915, in Arburg, Mo., but he was living in Leland, Miss. when he entered the U.S. Army. Master Sergeant Lee was in Company I, 23d Infantry Regiment, 2d Infantry Division near Ip-ori, Korea when he performed an act of bravery on Feb. 1, 1951, that earned him the Congressional Medal of Honor (CMOH). He was awarded the Medal on Feb. 5, 1952. Here are the actual words of his citation: "M/Sgt. Lee, a member of Company I, distinguished himself by conspicuous gallantry and intrepidity above and beyond the call of duty in action against the enemy. When his platoon was forced from its position by a numerically superior enemy force, and his platoon leader wounded, M/Sgt. Lee assumed command, regrouped the remnants of his unit, and led them in repeated assaults to regain the position. Within 25 yards of his objective he received a leg wound from grenade fragments, but refused assistance and continued the attack. Although forced to withdraw 5 times, each time he regrouped his remaining men and renewed the assault. Moving forward at the head of his small group in the fifth attempt, he was struck by an exploding grenade, knocked to the ground, and seriously wounded in both legs. Still refusing assistance, he advanced by crawling, rising to his knees to fire, and urging his men to follow. While thus directing the final assault he was wounded a third time, by small-arms fire. Persistently continuing to crawl forward, he directed his men in a final and successful attack which regained the vital objective. His intrepid

Profiles of Famous & Notable Mississippians

leadership and determination led to the destruction of 83 of the enemy and withdrawal of the remainder, and was a vital factor in stopping the enemy attack. M/Sgt. Lee's indomitable courage, consummate valor, and outstanding leadership reflect the highest credit upon himself and are in keeping with the finest traditions of the infantry and the U.S. Army." Although born in another state, Lee's CMOH is accredited to Mississippi. He was one of only 5 Mississippians (4 native) to receive the CMOH for service in Korea. Lee's Medal was one of 17 Medals of Honor that have been officially accredited to Mississippi in all wars, although we claim 5 more accredited to other states because the recipients had Mississippi ties. Lee is one of only 22 Mississippians (13 native Mississippians)[15 Army, 4 Marines & 3 Navy] in all wars to have received the CMOH out of 3,433 total recipients of the Medal through Nov. 1, 2000. Lee died on Nov. 5, 1982, and is buried in the Leland-Stoneville Cemetery in Stoneville, Mississippi. A Medal of Honor marker is on his grave.

Stephen Dill Lee

Born Sept. 22, 1833, in Charleston, S.C. He entered West Point at age 17 and graduated in 1854. He served frontier duty in Kansas, Texas, the Dakotas, and as assistant adjutant general of Florida during the Seminole War. He resigned his commission of first lieutenant in the U.S. Army after South Carolina seceded from the Union and joined with the Southern cause in 1861. In his book, *Sons of the South* (1961), Clayton Rand states that "By ordering the first shot fired at Fort Sumter on April 12, 1861, at half past four in the morning, Stephen Dill Lee started the Civil War." Lee was the youngest Lt. General in the Confederacy and Jefferson Davis called him one of the Confederacy's best soldiers. Lee made Mississippi his home after the war. He was a farmer, then became a state senator, then the first president of Mississippi Agricultural and Mechanical College (now Mississippi State Univ.). He was also a leading figure in the United Confederate Veterans, serving as Commander-in-Chief from 1904 until his death in Vicksburg on May 28, 1908. He's buried in Columbus, Miss.

Chet Lemon

Born Chester Earl Lemon in Jackson on Feb. 12, 1955. He made his major league baseball debut on Sept. 9, 1975, with Chicago. He stayed with the White Sox until 1981, then played for the Detroit Tigers (1982-90). He played in 3 All-Star games, 1978, '79 & '84 and in the 1984 World Series. His career stats: 1,875 hits in 6,868 at bats (.273 batting avg.), 973 runs, 215 homeruns, and 884 RBIs in 1,988 games.

J.B. Lenoir

He was born J.B. Lenoir on May 5, 1929, at Monticello, Miss. J.B. doesn't stand for anything, the initials were his legal name. His early influences were Blind Lemon Jefferson, Lightnin' Hopkins and Arthur "Big Boy" Crudup. Lenoir spent time in New Orleans before arriving in Chicago in the late 1940s. His first single for Chess in 1951 was *Korea Blues*, a bit of topical commentary. Parrot Records quickly recalled his politically charged *Eisenhower Blues* (1954) when it became controversial, and replaced it with the slightly less dissentious *Tax Paying Blues*. Lenoir recorded his most durable piece, the often-covered *Mama Talk to Your Daughter* (1954) for the Parrot label. Lenoir's 1954-57 Parrot and Checker Records output included *Don't Touch My Head* and *Natural Man*. In 1965-66, he recorded *Alabama Blues* and *Down in Mississippi*, done in Chicago under blues great Willie Dixon's supervision. Later came *Alabama March, Vietnam Blues* and *Shot on James Meredith*. New listeners sometimes question Lenoir's gender upon first hearing his records because of his exceptionally high-pitched vocal range. A wild and popular stage performer, he was starting to inject African percussion & rhythms into his music at the time of his death in Urbana, Ill. on April 29, 1967. He had been in an auto accident just three weeks earlier.

Sam Leslie

Born Samuel Andrew Leslie on July 26, 1905, in Moss Point, Miss. He made his major league baseball debut on Oct. 6, 1929, for New York. He played for the Giants until 1938, except the three seasons he played for the Brooklyn Dodgers (1933-35). He played in the 1936 and '37 World Series. His career stats include 749 hits in 2,460 at bats (.304 batting avg.), 311 runs, 36 homers and 389 RBIs in 822 games. He was inducted into the Mississippi Sports Hall of Fame in 1968. Leslie died on Jan. 21, 1979, in Pascagoula, Miss. at age 73.

Tom Lester

Born Sept. 23, 1938, in Jackson, his family moved to Laurel when he was two. He graduated from Ole Miss. He is best known for playing gawky farmhand Eb Dawson on the TV comedy series *Green Acres* in the 1960s and later in syndicated reruns. He appeared in a few movies including *Benji* (1974) and *Return to Green Acres* (1990).

Walter "Furry" Lewis

This Blues singer/guitarist was born Mar. 6, 1895, in Greenwood, Miss. and went to Memphis at an early age. He recorded a couple songs for Vocalion in 1927 — *A Chicken Ain't Nothin' But A Bird* and *East St. Louis*. One of the very best blues storytellers, he was equally adept at blues and ragtime, and made the most out of an understated, rather than an overtly flamboyant style. Lewis achieved much popularity in Memphis in the years prior to his death in Memphis on Sept. 14, 1981. He appeared in a film with Burt Reynolds, was a guest on Johnny Carson's *Tonight Show* and opened for the Rolling Stones when they played Memphis.

Jerry Lee Lewis

Born Sept. 29, 1935, in Ferriday, Louisiana. He moved to Nesbit, Mississippi in 1973 and still lives there. He enrolled in Texas Bible Institute after graduating from high school, but was kicked out after playing a boogie-woogie version of *God Is Real*. Lewis has played the piano since age 9, professionally since age 15. He first recorded for Sun Records in Memphis. Songwriter Jack Clement discovered and recorded Jerry Lee while Sam Phillips was away in Florida. The first track Lewis recorded was *End of the Road*, cut in Nov. 1956. Jerry Lee's unique piano-pounding, boogie style gave him 3 top-10 gold records: *Whole Lot Of Shakin' Goin' On* (#3 in 1957), *Great Balls of Fire* (#2 in 1958), which became the best-selling record in Sun Records' history, and *Breathless* (#7 in 1958). His first record, *Whole Lotta Shakin' Goin' On* was recorded in one take. Right after its release Lewis performed to a national TV audience on *The Steve Allen Show* on July 28, 1957. He had 3 more records in the Top-40: *High School Confidential* (#21 in '58), *What'd I Say* (#30 in '61) and *Me And Bobby McGee* (#40 in '72). For a five month period, he was concurrently married to both wife #2 and wife #3. He married his 13-year-old 2nd cousin, Myra Gale Brown (his 3rd wife), in Hernando on Dec. 12, 1957 (divorced in '70) and it almost ruined his career. Lewis was in the movies *Disc Jockey Jamboree* and *High School Confidential* ('58). In 1958, his 12-day engagement at the Paramount Theatre in New York broke all previous attendance records, including those set by Frank Sinatra. He was among the first inductees into the Rock & Roll Hall of Fame on Jan. 23, 1986, along with Elvis. Two of Jerry Lee's songs, *Great Balls of Fire* and *Whole Lotta Shakin' Goin' On*, are included on the Rock and Roll Hall of

Profiles of Famous & Notable Mississippians

Fame and Museum's list of 500 Songs That Shaped Rock And Roll. On June 13, 1989, Lewis got his star on the Hollywood Walk of Fame. Dennis Quaid played Jerry (Jerry singing) and Winona Ryder played Myra in the 1989 biographical movie *Great Balls of Fire*. "The Killer" made a comeback in country music and between 1968 and 1972 he chalked up 15 country charters, including the No. 1 hits *To Make Love Sweeter for You* (1968), *There Must Be More to Love than This* (1970), *Would You Take Another Chance on Me* (1971) and *Chantilly Lace* (1972). He's had his share of family tragedy: wife #4 Jaren Gunn was found dead in a swimming pool; wife #5 Shawn Stevens died of a methadone overdose two and a half months after the wedding; his 19-year-old Jerry Lee Lewis, Jr. was killed in a car accident; son #2 drowned as an infant; and Lewis himself has survived some serious illnesses in the past few years. Lewis is first cousin to singer Mickey Gilley (born in Natchez) and TV evangelist Jimmy Swaggart.

Ken Lindsay

Born July 3, 1943, in Gadsden, Alabama. He has lived in the Jackson area and worked at the Colonial Country Club in Madison since coming to Mississippi in Jan. 1970. Lindsay's apprenticeship in golf began at the age of 10 when he became a caddy at the country club in Gadsden. An excellent golfer, Lindsay played collegiately at Memhis State (now University of Memphis) where he won 40 of 44 matches over 4 years. After graduation, he served in the U.S. Air Force advancing to the rank of captain and winning 10 military golf tournaments, including the 1968 Air Force Worldwide Championship. Lindsay had several high finishes in the Magnolia Classic at Hattiesburg, which later moved to Jackson to became the Deposit Guaranty Golf Classic and then the Southern Farm Bureau Classic. Although he would have probably done great on the Tour, he chose to be a club pro and stay at Colonial, where in 1992 — shortly after Colonial acquired Deerfield Country Club — Lindsay became director of golf and general manager. He was chairman of the PGA Rules Committee from 1984 to 1989 and served as a rules official at some of the most prestigious tournaments in the world, including the U.S. Open. He has officiated at all four of golf's major tournaments and on the PGA Tour. The PGA vice-president in 1995-96, Lindsay was the No. 1 club pro in the U.S. as president of the PGA of America from 1997 to 1998. He was only the second Mississippian elected as head of the 24,000-member, world's largest working sports organization. James Ray Carpenter of Hattiesburg was president of the PGA in 1987-88. Ken Lindsay will be enshrined in the Mississippi Sports Hall of Fame on March 23, 2001.

Jake W. Lindsey

Jake William Lindsey was born May 1, 1921, in Isnay, Alabama. He grew up in Lucedale, Mississippi, where he was living when he entered the U.S. Army. Technical Sergeant Lindsey was in the 16th Infantry, 1st Infantry Division near Hamich, Germany when he performed an act of bravery on Nov. 16 1944, that earned him the Congressional Medal of Honor (CMOH). He was the 100th infantry soldier of World War II to receive the CMOH. President Harry S. Truman personally presented Lindsey the Medal on May 30, 1945, during a joint session of Congress, the only time the Medal has been so awarded. Presidents usually personally award the CMOH, but not before a joint session of Congress. Here are the actual words of his citation: "For gallantry and intrepidity at the risk of his life above and beyond the call of duty on 16 November 1944, in Germany. T/Sgt. Lindsey assumed a position about 10 yards to the front of his platoon during an intense enemy infantry-tank counterattack, and by his unerringly accurate fire destroyed 2 enemy machinegun nests, forced the withdrawal of 2 tanks, and effectively halted enemy flanking patrols. Later, although painfully wounded, he engaged 8 Germans, who were reestablishing machinegun positions, in hand-to-hand combat, killing 3, capturing 3, and causing the other 2 to flee. By his gallantry, T/Sgt. Lindsey secured his unit's position, and reflected great credit upon himself and the U.S. Army." Lindsey's Medal of Honor is accredited to his adopted state of Mississippi. Lindsey was one of only 7 Mississippians (4 native) to receive the CMOH for service during WWII (out of 441 awarded). Lindsey's Medal is one of 17 Medals of Honor that have been officially accredited to Mississippi, although we claim 5 more accredited to other states, because the recipients had Mississippi ties. Lindsey is one of only 22 Mississippians (13 native)[15 Army, 4 Marines & 3 Navy] in all wars to have received the CMOH out of 3,433 recipients through Nov. 1, 2000. He died July 18, 1988, at age 67 and is buried in the White House Cemetery in Waynesboro, Miss. A Medal of Honor marker is on his grave.

Freddie Little

Born April 25, 1936, in Picayune, Mississippi. He attended George Washington Carver High School, where he was a four sport letterman. Little was a 9.7 sprinter, averaged 12 points per game in basketball, was captain and co-captain as a running back on his football team and once struck out 14 as a baseball pitcher. He fought his first professional fight in his hometown of Picayune in April, 1957. Little was offered scholarships by 24 colleges and attended Dillard University in New Orleans on an academic scholarship. He boxed from 1957 to 1972, winning the 24 of his first 25 fights, and held the WBC World Junior Middleweight Championship from Oct. 1968 until Oct. 1969. He went 50-6-1 during his pro career with 32 KOs. He continued to fight until his retirement in 1972 going out in style with a seventh round knock out of Billy Walker in Stateline, Nevada. He was the first boxer inducted into the Mississippi Sports Hall of Fame (1995) and through the 2001 inductees he remained the only one in the boxing category. Freddie later had a successful career as a teacher and in state government. He was a member of the Nevada State Boxing Commission for many years and presently is Deputy Director of the Dept. of Transportation of the State of Nevada.

"Little Howlin' Wolf"

Born Jessie Sanders on July 26, 1930, in Florence, Mississippi, where he grew up along Highway 49. He's lived in Chicago most of his adult life, during which time he spent many hours in blues clubs and on the road with Howlin' Wolf. Jessie first took to the stage with Howlin' Wolf (Chester Arthur Burnett) in 1950. Wolf took Jessie under his wing and often referred to Jessie as his "son". Out of respect and admiration for his long time friend and mentor Jessie began performing as "Lil Howlin' Wolf". Jesse later married Howlin' Wolf's niece, whom he met at Wolf's funeral. In 1945 he went to work for the City of Chicago Police Department and worked for them for 47 years. He performed on weekends with blues greats such as Howlin Wolf, Jimmy Reed, Hound Dog Taylor, Albert King, Magic Sam, Freddie King, and Little Junior Parker. During a visit home in 1947 while at WDIA in Memphis he met B.B. King and Bobby Blue Bland. A decade later he would share the bill with not only B.B. King and Bobby Blue Bland but also the likes of Little Milton, Chuck Berry, Bobby Taylor, and Jimmy Reed. He's also shared the stage with legendary greats James Brown, Aretha Franklin, and Millie Jackson. Little Wolf's career has taken him across the U.S. and

Profiles of Famous & Notable Mississippians

overseas to Germany and France. Little Wolf performed for two of our country's presidents, Carter and Reagan. After performing for President Reagan in 1985 he recorded *White House Blues* in Washington, DC. Sometime before Little Howlin Wolf retired in 1992 he purchased two Greyhound buses. He ran a bus service for touring groups and musicians until 1996 when he sold one of his buses to his good friend Bobby Rush who keeps it hot on the Blues Highway. Since his retirement and move to Memphis, Little Howlin' Wolf has made several appearances at festivals such as the Memphis In May Music Festival. He also does occasional shows at the casinos in Tunica, Mississippi.

"Little Milton"

Born Milton Campbell on Sept. 7, 1934, in Inverness, Mississippi, he grew up in the Greenville-Leland area and was influenced by T-Bone Walker, B.B. King, Roy Brown and Big Joe Turner. He began recording for Sun Records in Memphis in 1953, backed by Ike Turner's band. In 1958, he moved to St. Louis and, with Oliver Sain, started the Bobbin label, famous for signing Albert King. He signed to the Chess label's subsidiary Checker in 1961. There, over a nine year span, he cut over a hundred sides, several of which made it to the top ten on the national R&B charts. His first recording success came in 1962 with *So Mean To Me*. He had the No. 1 R&B hit *We're Gonna Make It* in 1965 followed by *Who Cheatin' Who* that same year. He also recorded on the Checker and Stax labels before signing with Malaco Records in Jackson in 1984. Some other hits include *Grits Ain't Grocery, Little Bluebird, The Blues Is Alright, Nobody's Sleeping in My Bed, Annie Mae's Cafe, Feel So Bad, If Walls Could Talk, Baby I Love You* and *I'll Catch You On Your Way Down*. Some important album releases include 2 from MCA in 1986, *Sings Big Blues* and *We're Gonna Make It*, and *Back To Back* on Malaco in 1988. Little Milton is a member of the Blues Hall of Fame and a multiple winner of the W.C. Handy Awards including Male Artist of the Soul/Blues category in 1996. He was the recipient of a 1997 Rhythm & Blues Foundation Pioneer Award on Feb. 27, 1997. He has recorded about 30 albums.

John A. Lomax

Born John Avery Lomax Sept. 23, 1867, in Goodman, Miss. John, along with his son, Alan (born in Texas), created the Archive of American Folk Song at the Library of Congress and published many anthologies of black music, including *Negro Folk Songs as Sung by Lead Belly* (1936), *Our Singing Country* (1941) plus *American Ballads and Folk Songs* and *Folk Songs of North America*. All toll, they collected about 10,000 early folk and blues recordings for the Library of Congress. In 1941, John and Alan went to Stovall's plantation, where Muddy Waters was employed, and recorded his earthy unamplified country blues several years before Muddy became famous. John Lomax died in Greenville, Miss. Jan. 26, 1948.

Augustus B. Longstreet

Born Augustus Baldwin Longstreet on Sept. 22, 1790, in Augusta, Georgia. After law school, Longstreet rode as a circuit lawyer in rural Georgia. During these trips he heard folk stories and experienced the back-country lifestyles that he would later record in his writings. He served as a superior court judge and representative in the Georgia Assembly. Moved by the death of his eldest son, Longstreet pursued a career in the Methodist ministry. He went on to serve as president of four universities, including a newly founded Emory College from 1839 to 1848 and was the second chancellor of the University of Mississippi from 1849 to 1856. Longstreet was the first of four Yale graduates to serve as president of Ole Miss, and he was the first of three presidents to be an ordained minister. During his tenure at the University of Mississippi, several social fraternities were organized and the School of Law was started. After resigning from Ole Miss because of political pressure, he lived briefly in Abbeville, Mississippi, before becoming president of the University of South Carolina in 1858. When the Civil War began in 1861, he returned to Mississippi, where he supported the southern cause with his writings. Longstreet's book of humorous sketches entitled *Georgia Scenes, Characters, Incidents, etc.., in the First Half Century of the Republic* (1835), marks the beginning of the literary genre known as Southwestern Humor, which flourished from 1835 to 1861. Set in what were then the southwestern states of Georgia, Alabama, Mississippi, Louisiana, Arkansas, Tennessee, and Missouri, Southwestern humor originated in the political and oral traditions of this growing region. Southwestern humor became hallmarks of late-nineteenth century realism and local color, particularly in the writings of Mark Twain. Longstreet's nephew, Gen. James Longstreet, served as one of the South's principal military commanders, and his son-in-law, L.Q.C. Lamar (see his profile), saw action against Union Gen. George McClellan in Virginia in 1862 and later became the only Mississippian to serve on the U.S. Supreme Court. Longstreet lived the latter part of his life in Oxford, Miss., where he died on July 9, 1870. He is buried in St. Peter's Cemetery in Oxford.

Trent Lott

Born Chester Trent Lott on Oct. 9, 1941, in Grenada, Mississippi, the family moved to Pascagoula when he was still a toddler. He graduated from Pascagoula public schools, then received a B.P.A. degree (1963) and his law degree (1967) from the University of Mississippi. Lott served as a field representative for Ole Miss from 1963-1965. Admitted to the Mississippi bar in 1967, he started practice in Pascagoula. In 1968 he started his Washington career working 4 years as administrative assistant for 5th District U.S. Rep. Bill Colmer. Lott was elected as a Republican to the U. S. House in 1972 and was re-elected 7 times, serving a total of 16 years for the 5th District, serving in the 93rd through the 100th Congresses from Jan. 3, 1973 until Jan. 3, 1989. He was minority whip in the 97th through the 100th Congresses. First elected to the Senate in 1988, then re-elected in 1994, he was Republican whip in 1995 and 1996. A day after Bob Dole resigned from the Senate on June 11, 1996, to run for president, Lott was elected to replace him as Majority Leader. Republican senators voted 44-8 to elevate Lott, who was second in leadership as majority whip, to the top job over fellow Mississippian Thad Cochran. Lott won a new two-year term as Majority Leader on Dec. 1, 1998, despite the rank and file members' discontent about the party's poor showing in the election the previous month. The University of Mississippi recognized Lott, one of its most famous alumni, by establishing the Trent Lott Leadership Institute in 1999. Lott easily won re-election for his third six-year Senate term on Nov. 7, 2000.

Mundell Lowe

Born James Mundell Lowe on April 21, 1922, in Laurel, Mississippi. This composer, arranger, and jazz guitarist has worked with Billie Holliday, Charlie Parker, Hank Jones, Georgie Auld, Ruby Braff, Ben Webster, Harold Ashby, Helen Humes, Sarah Vaughan, Carmen McRae, and fellow Mississippian Lester Young. He began playing guitar at age six under instruction of his father who was a Baptist minister. Soon after he graduated from high school in 1940, he was drafted. After military service, Lowe played for a year and a

Profiles of Famous & Notable Mississippians

half with Ray McKinley, who had been with the Glenn Miller Band. He later moved to New York and in 1950 became musical arranger at the NBC network, working on the *Today Show* and other shows. In 1965, Lowe moved to California where Jackie Cooper hired him as a composer for films and television. He composed the music for the movies *A Time for Killing* (1967), *Billy Jack* (1971), *Everything You Always Wanted to Know About Sex* (1972) and the TV movie *Tarantulas: The Deadly Cargo* (1977). In the late 1970s, Lowe made a special appearance with Peggy Lee at the White House and toured Japan with Benny Carter. He played at the Monterey Jazz Festival and from 1981-86 served as director of that festival. Lowe has recorded over two dozen albums from *Guitar Moods* (1950) to the movie soundtrack *Satan in High Heels* (1997), for which he composed and directed the music, and *Second Time Around* (1998). He received an honorary doctorate of music from Millspas College of Jackon, Mississippi in 1999. Lowe is one of six guitarists on a 1999 CD called *The Great Mississippi Jazz Guitarists Reunion*, released by the Mississippi Musicians Hall of Fame (available from the MMHOF Website or at area record stores). The other artists on the album are Bucky Barrett, Steve Blailock, Skeets McWilliams, Bob Saxton and Lloyd Wells (all these artists are profiled). Lowe, as well as McWilliams and Wells were among the first 27 inducted into the inaugural Mississippi Musicians Hall of Fame on April 1, 2000.

Beverly Lowry

Born Beverly Fey on August 10, 1938, in Memphis, Tenn., she grew up in Greenville, Miss. She spent 2 years at Ole Miss and graduated from Memphis State in 1960. Lowry now lives in San Marcos, Texas, where she has been associate professor of fiction writing at Southwest Texas State University since 1976. And she's also been busy writing novels. Her first two were *Come Back, Lolly Ray* (1977 and *Emma Blue* (1978). Her third novel, *Daddy's Girl*, won the Jesse Jones Award for the best work of fiction written in 1981. Her first two novels are set in Mississippi, but the locale changes to Texas for the third novel. Her fourth and fifth novels are *The Perfect Sonya* (1987) and *Breaking Gentle* (1988). Her sixth novel, *The Track of Real Desires* (1994), returns to Mississippi as the setting in a fictional town named Eunola (Greenville). For that book, Lowry received the 1995 Mississippi Institute of Arts and Letters most-coveted Fiction Award. Lowry has held many positions and received many honors. She was a member of the Cultural Arts Council of Houston, Texas. She was also a member of the International P.E.N., the Author's Guild, and the Poets and Writers Texas Institute. Lowry taught creative writing at the University of Houston, and her short stories and articles have appeared in the *Black Warrior Review*, *Vanity Fair*, *Viva*, *Houston Review*, *Texas Monthly*, *Mississsippi Review*, and the *New York Times Book Review*. She was a winner of the National Endowment for the Arts Fellowship in 1979 and received a Guggenheim Fellowship in 1983.

Albert Luandrew (see "Sunnyland Slim")

Jack H. Lucas

Jacklyn 'Jack" Harold Lucas was born on Feb. 14, 1928, in Plymouth, North Carolina. His Congressional Medal of Honor (CMOH) is officially accredited to Virginia, where he entered the service. He was the youngest Marine ever and the youngest man in the 20th century to be given the CMOH. When Lucas was 14, he forged his mother's name on a consent form and entered the Marines. On Iwo Jima during World War II, Lucas threw himself on a Japanese grenade and pulled another one under him to protect his buddies. Mercifully only one of the grenades exploded. That extreme act of bravery occurred less than a week after Lucas' 17th birthday! Here are the actual words of his citation: "For conspicuous gallantry and intrepidity at the risk of his life above and beyond the call of duty while serving with the 1st Battalion, 26th Marines, 5th Marine Division, during action against enemy Japanese forces on Iwo Jima, Volcano Islands, 20 February 1945. While creeping through a treacherous, twisting ravine which ran in close proximity to a fluid and uncertain frontline on D-plus-1 day, Pfc. Lucas and 3 other men were suddenly ambushed by a hostile patrol which savagely attacked with rifle fire and grenades. Quick to act when the lives of the small group were endangered by 2 grenades which landed directly in front of them, Pfc. Lucas unhesitatingly hurled himself over his comrades upon 1 grenade and pulled the other under him, absorbing the whole blasting forces of the explosions in his own body in order to shield his companions from the concussion and murderous flying fragments. By his inspiring action and valiant spirit of self-sacrifice, he not only protected his comrades from certain injury or possible death but also enabled them to rout the Japanese patrol and continue the advance. His exceptionally courageous initiative and loyalty reflect the highest credit upon Pfc. Lucas and the U.S. Naval Service." Although severely injured by the blast, Lucas was not knocked out. Lucas stated that had he been unconscious, he would have drowned in his own blood. He received 16 pints of blood before being evacuated from the island. Back in the states, he underwent 22 surgeries in seven months to remove schrapnel. Twenty-two Marines in the Pacific received the Medal of Honor for jumping on grenades to protect their comrades. Lucas was one of only three who lived to tell about it! Lucas was discharged from the Marines on Sept. 18, 1945 for reasons of disability. President Harry Truman presented the Medal of Honor to Lucas at the White House on Oct. 5, 1945. He has met ever president since Truman, except Jimmy Carter. Lucas is one of only 7 Mississippians (4 native) to receive the Congressional Medal of Honor for service during World War II, and Lucas and Louis H. Wilson were the only two Marines among those seven. Of Mississippi Medal of Honor recipients, Lucas is one of only 4 Marines to ever earn the Medal. In all wars, 17 Medals of Honor have been accredited to Mississippi, although we can claim 5 more that were accredited to other states because the recipients with Mississippi ties were in other states when they went into service. Lucas is one of only 22 Mississippians (13 native Mississippians)[15 Army, 4 Marines and 3 Navy] in all wars to have received the Medal of Honor out of the 3,433 total recipients through Nov. 1, 2000. Of the 3,411 recipients, only 151 were still living as of Nov. 1, 2000 (living recipients by conflict: WWII - 62; Korean War - 21; Vietnam - 68). Lucas was one of those 151 and one of only 3 Mississippians who received the Medal of Honor who are still alive. The two native Mississippians still alive are Van T. Barfoot and former Commandant of the U.S. Marine Corps, retired General Louis H. Wilson, Jr. While working for the Veterans Administration in Winston-Salem, N.C., Lucas finished high school. After two years at Duke University, he enrolled at High Point College and graduated in 1956 with a degree in business. In 1961, Lucas enlisted in the U.S. Army Paratroopers and asked to go to Vietnam, but he was assigned to Fort Bragg to train troops. He was honorably discharged in 1965 with the rank of captain. Lucas later entered the retail meat business in the Washington, D.C. area, eventually opening five stores and making a lot of money. He and his wife, Erlene, were living in a mansion in Clinton, Maryland.

Profiles of Famous & Notable Mississippians

They had two children and had been married for 20 years in 1977, when Erline, then 38, was charged with conspiring to murder Jack, presumably for his money. The man Erlene hired to kill him was an undercover state trooper. Lucas asked the judge to be lenient. The judge gave her ten years, but suspended the sentence. Following their divorce, Lucas revisited Iwo Jima in 1985. Shortly thereafter, Nick Kolinsky of Petal, Mississippi, whom he had never met, saw a CBS-TV documentary on Lucas and invited him down for a visit. Lucas decided to move to Hattiesburg, Mississippi, where he's been since 1986. Lucas was a special guest during President Clinton's State of the Union address on Jan. 24, 1995. He received a five-minute standing ovation from Congress.

Ray Lum

This mule trader and storyteller extraordinaire was born on June 25, 1891, in Rocky Springs in Claiborne County. Mississippi writer William Ferris (see his profile) wrote a book about Ray and his tall tales called *"You Live and Learn. Then You Die and Forget It All": Ray Lum's Tales of Horses, Mules and Men* (1992). Famed Mississippi author Eudora Welty wrote the foreword. Lum died in Vicksburg, Mississippi on December 17, 1976, at the age of 84.

Jimmie Lunceford

Born James Melvin Lunceford on June 6, 1902, in Fulton, Mississippi. While teaching music at Manassa High School in Memphis, Tenn. in 1927, Lunceford organized a student band called the Chichasaw Syncopators, recording two songs that year and two more in 1930. After leaving Memphis, the Jimmie Lunceford Orchestra played in Cleveland and Buffalo. It was the first orchestra to feature high-note trumpeters starting with Tommy Stevenson in 1934 and had a strong influence on the early Stan Kenton Orchestra, and later Benny Goodman. In 1934 the orchestra was a big hit at New York's Cotton Club. They recorded a few songs for Victor and then switched to Decca. Among their many hits were *Ain't She Sweet, Rhythm Is Our Business, My Blue Heaven, Swanee River, Organ Grinder's Swing, For Dancers Only,* and *'Tain't What You Do, It's the Way That Cha Do It*. In 1939, Tommy Dorsey lured arranger and vocalist Sy Oliver away from Lunceford, but trumpeters Gerald Wilson and Snooky Young were added to the band. In 1942 several key players left for jobs elsewhere and the orchestra gradually declined. In 1947, Lunceford suddenly collapsed and rumors have persisted that he was poisoned by a racist restaurant owner reluctant about serving his band. He died July 12, 1947, in Seaside, Oregon.

John Roy Lynch

Born a slave on Sept. 10, 1847, in Vidalia, Louisiana, then taken to Natchez with his mother after his father's death in 1863. He was freed when Union forces occupied Natchez. After emancipation, he engaged in photography and attended evening school. When Governor Ames appointed his Justice of the Peace in 1869 at age 21, he was the first black to hold public office in Mississippi. A member of the State house of representatives 1869-1873, he served the last term as speaker. Lynch was elected as a Republican to the 43rd and 44th U.S. Congresses and served from Mar. 4, 1873 to Mar. 3, 1877. He became Mississippi's first black member of the U.S. House and, at the age of 25, the youngest ever elected to the House and the only black for over 100 years. Lynch was an unsuccessful candidate for reelection in 1876. He successfully contested the election of James R. Chalmers to the 47th Congress and served from April 29, 1882, to March 3, 1883. After being an unsuccessful candidate for reelection in 1882, he returned to his plantation in Adams County, Mississippi to farm. He was chairman of the Republican State executive committee 1881-1889, a member of the Republican National Committee for the State of Mississippi 1884-1889, and a delegate to the Republican National Conventions in 1872, '84, '88, '92, and 1900. As temporary chairman of the Republican National Convention in Chicago in 1884, Lynch became the first black American to deliver the keynote address at a national political convention. He was the 4th Auditor of the Treasury for the Navy Dept. under President Harrison 1889-93. Lynch studied law and admitted to the Mississippi bar in 1896. He returned to Washington in 1897, where he practiced law until 1898, when he was appointed a major and additional paymaster of Volunteers during the Spanish-American War by President McKinley, who also appointed him as a paymaster in the Army with the rank of captain in 1901. Lynch was promoted to major in 1906 and retired from the army in 1911. He served as president of Capital Savings Bank in Washington, the first black bank in the nation. After moving to Chicago in 1912, Lynch authored *The Facts of Reconstruction* (1913), his personal account of the politics of post-Civil War Mississippi. He died in Chicago on Nov. 2, 1939, at age 92 and is buried in Arlington National Cemetery.

James J. Madison

Born James Jonas Madison on May 20, 1884, in Jersey City, N.J., he was appointed his commission to the service from Mississippi. He was a Lt. Commander in the U.S. Naval Reserve Force when he performed an act of bravery on Oct. 4, 1918, that earned him the Medal of Honor (MOH). Here are the actual words of his citation: "For exceptionally heroic service in a position of great responsibility as commanding officer of the *U.S.S. Ticonderoga*, when, on 4 October 1918, that vessel was attacked by an enemy submarine and was sunk after a prolonged and gallant resistance. The submarine opened fire at a range of 500 yards, the first shots taking effect on the bridge and forecastle, 1 of the 2 forward guns of the Ticonderoga being disabled by the second shot. The fire was returned and the fight continued for nearly 2 hours. Lt. Comdr. Madison was severely wounded early in the fight, but caused himself to be placed in a chair on the bridge and continued to direct the fire and to maneuver the ship. When the order was finally given to abandon the sinking ship, he became unconscious from loss of blood, but was lowered into a lifeboat and was saved, with 31 others, out of a total number of 236 on board." Madison was the only Mississippian to receive the MOH for World War I. He is one of only three Mississippi MOH recipients to serve in the Navy. The other two, August Dorley and Martin Freeman, received their Medals of Honor during the Civil War. Madison's Medal was one of 17 Medals of Honor that have been officially accredited to Mississippi in all wars, although we can claim 5 more that were accredited to other states because the recipients had Mississippi ties. Madison is one of only 22 Mississippians (13 *native* Mississippians)[15 Army, 4 Marines & 3 Navy] in all wars to have received the CMOH out of 3,433 recipients of the Medal through Nov. 1, 2000. Madison died on Dec. 27, 1922, at age 38 and is buried in Fairview Cemetery in Fairview, New Jersey. There is no Medal of Honor marker on his grave.

"Magic Sam"

Born Samuel Maghett in Grenada, Miss. on Feb. 14, 1937. He drew on the church-based soul styling favored by B.B. King and Otis Rush to record some of the best blues to come out of Chicago in the late 1960s. His early sides included hits like *All Your Love, Easy Baby* and *She Belongs To Me*. Delmark Records recorded Magic Sam's two seminal albums, *West Side*

Profiles of Famous & Notable Mississippians

Soul (1967) and *Black Magic* (1968). Sam died of a heart attack in Chicago on Dec. 1, 1969. He was only 32. He is buried in the Restvale Cemetery in Alsip, Ill. (Section D, Lot 106, Grave 3, look for the "Graham" marker nearby).

Jim Majure
Born Aug. 29, 1938, in Durant, Mississippi, he lived in Madison for many years. He graduated from Ole Miss in 1963 with a degree in advertising. His first novel, *The Delta Triangle* (1995), sold out its first two printings totaling 12,500 copies. His second novel, *Reluctant Reunion*, was released Sept. 25, 1996. Majure, also a songwriter, won a trip to Nashville in 1992 in the Governor's Songwriting Contest for a tune called *Cowboys, Cap Guns and Cracker Jacks*, which he wrote for his 5-year-old son. Majure died in Jackson on Oct. 20, 1996, from a heart attack at age 58.

Dumas Malone
Born Jan. 10, 1892, in Coldwater, Miss. He received his B.A. from Emory and his M.A. and Ph.D. from Yale. He taught history at the University of Virginia, Yale and Columbia Universities. He won the Pulitzer Prize for History in 1975 for his monumental six-volume biography of Thomas Jefferson titled *Jefferson and His Time*. That book was on the list of "The 50 Best Books of the Century" released in 1999 by the Intercollegiate Institute. Malone died on Dec. 27, 1986, in Charlottesville, Va., just two weeks before his 95th birthday.

Jeff Malone
Born on June 28, 1961, in Macon, Georgia. This 6-foot-4 guard *was* Mississippi State University basketball from 1979-83 — the school's all-time scoring leader with 2,142 points! Some of his other Mississippi State records include Most Points Scored in a Season: 777 (1982-83); Most Field Goals Made in a Season: 323 (1982-83); Most Field Goals in a Career: 906 ; Most Field Goals Attempted in a Career: 1,768; Highest Minutes Played-Per-Game Average in a Four-Year Career: 35.0; and Most Minutes Played in a Career: 3,851. Malone, a four-year starter at Mississippi State, was chosen as UPI's SEC Player of the Year for the 1982-83 season and earned All-America honors from the *Sporting News*. A three-time All-SEC pick, he was the nation's No. 2 scorer (26.8 ppg) as a senior. He was drafted as the 10th overall pick by the Washington Bullets in 1983 and was an NBA All-Star in 1986 and '87 with the Bullets. He then played for the Utah Jazz, the Philadelphia 76ers and other NBA teams before ending his 13-year NBA career in 1996 to play ball in Greece. He was a first-year assistant coach with the Yakima Sun Kings for one year, then in 1999 he signed as assistant coach with the San Diego Stingrays. In 1999, Malone was chosen as a member of the first team on *The Clarion-Ledger* Division I Men's Basketball Team of the Century!

Tom "Bones" Malone
Born Thomas Hugh Malone on June 16, 1947, in Hattiesburg, he grew up in Sumrall, Mississippi. A jazz trombonist, he has also worked in classical, rock and blues playing sax, tuba, flute, piccolo, and electric bass. He has arranged for and played with Jimmy Dorsey, Woody Herman, Doc Severinson, James Brown, B.B. King, Pink Floyd, Paul Simon, Diana Ross, and many others. He was an original member of the *Saturday Night Live* band and became the band's musical director. Malone did arrangements for Lionel Ritchie and Stevie Wonder and contributed about 25 arrangements to the *Late Show with David Letterman* in the late 1980s and early 90s. Malone was a member of the Blues Brothers band and was in the movies *The Blues Brothers* (1980) and *Blues Brothers 2000* (1998). He played network themes on the 1992 Olympics on CBS as well as themes for *CBS This Morning* and *Murder She Wrote*. He joined the CBS-TV Orchestra on Nov. 1, 1993. Malone, who has also recorded dozens of jazz albums, currently lives in Manhattan.

Kris Mangum
Born Aug. 15, 1973, in Magee, Miss., a town that was once named Mangum. During his first 3 years at Ole Miss, the 6-4, 245-pound Mangum caught 74 passes for 729 yards and four TDs, averaging 9.9 yards per catch. His 74 catches rank 2nd among UM tight ends, trailing only Jim Poole's 94 (1969-71). Mangum was the 36th Ole Miss player to earn first-team All-America honors. He was selected to the *Football Digest* All-America first team, the *Football News* All-America second team and All-Southeastern Conference first team in 1997. He was selected by the Carolina Panthers in the 7th round (228th pick overall) of the 1997 NFL draft. Mangum was released by the Panthers on Sept. 2, then re-signed by the Panthers to their practice squad on Sept 4. He was still playing for the Panthers in 2000. Kris is the son of John Mangum, who was defensive tackle with Boston Patriots in 1966 and 1967, and the brother of John Mangum, cornerback with the Chicago Bears.

Archie Manning
Born Elisha Archibald Manning III on Mar. 19, 1949, in Drew, Miss. He graduated from Drew High School in 1967. The 6'3" Manning started as an Ole Miss Rebel quarterback in his sophomore year in 1968. The next year, he became a folk hero when Ole Miss played Alabama in the 3rd game of the season. Even though Ole Miss lost to Alabama 33-32, Manning's effort set a Southeastern Conference record for total defense of 540 yards which still stands. He completed 33 of 53 passes, which is a school record that still stands. Also in 1969, an injured Manning rallied the Rebels late in the 3rd quarter, down 17-13, to win 25-17 over Georgia. He ran for 30 yards and passed for 159 to help the Rebels defeat unbeaten and 2nd-ranked Tennessee 38-0. During 1969, Archie scored 86 points, the single-season scoring record for Ole Miss football that still stands. Sportscasters called him "Super" Manning. A postal clerk in Magnolia, Miss. wrote a song called *The Ballad of Archie Who*, which quickly sold 35,000 copies. Then, he broke his arm ruining his chances for the Heisman trophy, although he finished in the top four in Heisman voting in 1969. In 1970, he was pictured on the covers of *College Football* and *Sports Illustrated* magazines. Manning's college career statistics showed he completed 402 of 761 passes (52.8%) for 4,753 yards for 31 TDs and he rushed 316 times for 823 yards. Manning shared the career TD pass record of 31 with Kent Austin, Mark Young and later Romaro Miller until Miller set the new record of 32 on Oct. 7, 2000. Manning singly held the career record of 25 rushing TDs until it was tied by "Deuce" McAllister on Sept. 2, 2000 (the same day Archie's son Eli made his Rebel debut). Manning was picked by the New Orleans Saints in the 1971 NFL draft. He passed for 23,911 yards in the NFL and his 14-year pro career included 2 Pro Bowls and selection as the league's MVP. He retired in 1985 after brief stays with the Houston Oilers and Minnesota Vikings. He was inducted into both the College Football Hall of Fame and the Miss. Sports Hall of Fame in 1989. A color analyst for the Saints since 1985, Archie quit his radio broadcasts at the end of 1997 to follow the career of son Peyton with the Indianapolis Colts. In a poll in 1999, readers of *The Clarion-Ledger* voted Archie Manning as Mississippi's favorite male athlete of the millennium! In Sept. 2000, the book, *Manning: A Father, His Sons, and a Football Legacy*, was released. Archie co-wrote the book with son Peyton.

Profiles of Famous & Notable Mississippians

Danny Manning

Born May 17, 1966, in Hattiesburg. He played basketball at Kansas. This 6-10 forward-center made his NBA basketball debut with the Los Angeles Clippers in 1988 and played for them until 1994. He also played for the Atlanta Hawks in 1993-94. With the Phoenix Suns since 1994, Manning was acquired during the 1998-99 offseason by the Orlando Magic who then traded him to the Milwaukee Bucks on Aug. 19, 1999. His career stats through the 1999-2000 season: played in 625 games (31.8 minutes avg.); 10,779 points (17.2 avg.); 3,848 rebounds (6.2 avg.); 825 steals (1.32 avg.); 632 blocks (1.01 avg.); and 1,748 assists (2.80 avg.). His career field goal percentage is .517 and free throw percentage is .732.

Thalia Mara

Born June 28, 1911, in Chicago. She was living in New York City in 1975 and was considering a job as artistic director of the Metropolitan Opera, but instead, decided to move to Jackson. This professional dancer was founder of the former Jackson Ballet troupe, which later became Ballet Mississippi. She is the founder and artistic director of the quadrennial USA International Ballet Competition, which she brought to Jackson for the first time in 1979. The sixth USA IBC in 1998 brought artists from about 3 dozen countries to the Jackson Municipal Auditorium. In 1994, the name of that auditorium was changed to Thalia Mara Hall. Mara, along with Eudora Welty and Margaret Walker Alexander, were the first recipients of the (Jackson) Mayor's Arts Achivement Honors on July 30, 1998. Mara has also authored ten books.

Florence Mars

Born Jan 1, 1923, in Philadelphia, she grew up in this Neshoba County city. She attended Millsaps College and received a B.S. from Ole Miss in 1944. Her photographs have appeared in the *New York Times* and *Time* magazine and are used as illustrations in her book, *Witness in Philadelphia* (1977), about the 1964 murders of three Civil Rights workers. A sequel to that book was *The Bell Returns to Mount Zion* (1996), a reference book she wrote for libraries.

Phillip Martin

Born Mar. 13, 1926, in Philadelphia, Mississippi. He is the elected Chief of the Mississippi Band of Choctaw Indians, a tribe of over 10,000 members, most of them living on 21,000 acres of reservation land in east central Mississippi near Philadelphia. Martin was elected to his seventh 4-year term as Chief in June 1999. He spent three years as the tribe's first business manager, five years as director of the Choctaw Community Action Agency and 29 years as the tribe's principal elected official — a total of over 40 years of service to the tribal government. He has been responsible for the establishment of numerous tribal business enterprises: an industrial park; a construction company; the Choctaw Transit Authority; the Choctaw Utility Commission; the Chahta Enterprise which assembles automotive wiring harnesses in three plants for the Ford Motor Company and small motors for United Technologies; a company that manufactures audio speakers and electronic components for Ford, Chrysler, and Westinghouse; Navistar, that hand-finishes greetings cards for the American Greetings Corporation of Cleveland, Ohio; and another company that makes plastic cutlery for McDonald's franchises. These, along with several other enterprises, have produced tribal sales of over $100 million yearly and provided 3,300 non-casino jobs on the reservation. On July 1, 1994, Martin and the tribe opened its first gaming operation, the Silver Star Hotel and Casino which provide 2,700 jobs. During his tenure as tribal Chief, reservation unemployment had declined 70 percent to its current level of less than 10 percent. Since 1979, the Mississippi Band of Choctaw Indians has made a $174 million capital investment in the state. Nationally, Martin has served in many positions including President of the National Tribal Chairmen's Association, founder and past President of the United South and Eastern Tribes, an association of all 22 federally-recognized tribes in the eastern U.S., and in 1992, he founded the United South and Eastern Tribes Gaming Association of which he serves as its current president. Chief Martin and his various business enterprises have received numerous awards including the Jay Silverheels Award and many awards from federal government agencies. In 1996, he was inducted into Junior Achievement's Mississippi Business Hall of Fame and Vice-President Al Gore presented him with the Hammer Award from the National Performance Review Board. A 1998 book, *The Choctaw Revolution: Lessons for Federal Indian Policy*, praised the Mississippi Band of Choctaws and Chief Martin for overcoming poverty and finding economic prosperity. The book was authored by Peter Ferrara of Americans for Tax Reform, a group that also presented Martin with a Taxpayer Hero Award on Sept. 16, 1998. On Feb. 8, 2000, Chief Martin unveiled plans for the Mississippi Band of Choctaw's second casino. The plans call for a $250 million casino complex with the name Golden Moon that will feature 90,000 feet of gaming space, a 600-room hotel and an 80-foot diameter golden globe restaurant perched atop the building. Groundbreaking ceremonies for the Golden Moon were held Nov. 16, 2000. Martin said the casino and other developments, such as a retail center and villas at the Dancing Rabbit Golf Course, will take place over the next four years and create nearly 10,000 jobs.

Roy M. Martin

Born Jan. 31, 1895, in Rosebud, Arkansas. A pioneer in establishment of school bands in the U.S., he organized the first school band in Arkansas in 1916, In 1930, he organized the Arkansas School Band Association. In 1932, Martin moved to Greenwood as director for Greenwood High School Band, one of only 8 in the state at the time. He held that position until his retirement in 1952. In 1934, he organized the Dixie School Band Association and held the Dixie Band Contest in 1935. In 1936, he started the Delta Band Festival, which has continued over the years. In 1940, Martin organized First Chair of America to honor First Chair players in bands and orchestras. He served as manager of the Mississippi Lions Club All State Band for 19 years from 1950 to 1969. In 1960, Martin established the Mac Award to honor band directors. In 1962, he started the United States of America High School Band composed of members from all around the country. This band played concerts in the U.S., Canada, Mexico and Europe, and was the official Bi-Centennial representative of the U.S. in Nice, France in 1976. He established the National High School Band Achievement Award in 1980. A few of the many honors and awards Martin received include the E.F. Goldman Award of the American School Band Directors Association, the Cross of Malta of the Veterans of Foreign Wars, the American Legion Gold Medal, the Gold Record from the University of Southern Mississippi, the Gold Medal from the University of Rome, the Lions International Banner of Excellence, and the Greenwood Lions Club Outstanding Citizen Award. The state legislature passed a resolution in 1984 recognizing his accomplishments. He was the first person inducted into the Miss. Band Directors Hall of Fame. Martin died in Greenwood on Jan. 23, 1985, just a week short of his 90 birthday.

Profiles of Famous & Notable Mississippians

Eleni Matos
Born Feb. 11, 1966, in Jackson, she is a 1988 graduate of Millsaps College. One of the world's rising opera stars, this mezzo-soprano trained at Chicago's Lyric Opera Center, sang at Boston Lyric Opera and debuted at the New York City Opera. Matos has performed under the direction of Daniel Barenboim and Leonard Slatkin, and now sings with the renowned Lyric Opera of Chicago where maestro Zubin Mehta calls her 'the Greek mezzo." One of her roles there was singing Siegrune in Richard Wagner's *Die Walkure* in the full Ring Cycle. She has won 31 vocal competitions including the Maria Callas International Opera Competition in Athens, the International Luciano Pavarotti Competition, the Licia Albanese/Puccini Foundation Competition, and the Queen Elizabeth International Competition in Belgium. She recently performed at the foot of the Acropolis in Athens.

Aubrey D. Matthews
Born Sept. 15, 1962, in Pascagoula, Miss. He graduated from high school in Moss Point and is an alumnus of Gulf Coast Community College and Delta State. He played pro football for the Jacksonville Bulls, the Atlanta Falcons, the Green Bay Packers, and nine seasons for the Detroits Lions through 1994. He played in the NFC championship game in 1991.

Martha Mattox
Born in June 19, 1879, in Natchez, Miss. This screen actress was prolific with an output of 81 films from *The Hungry Actors* in 1914 to Frank Capra's *The Bitter Tea of General Yen* in 1933 (she played "Miss Avery"). Most of her films were in the silent screen era, but she did almost 2 dozen talkies. Mattox died on May 2, 1933, in Sidney, New York.

John Maxwell
Born on July 12, 1944, in Jackson, he grew up in Pickens, Mississippi and Seattle, Washington. Maxwell is best known for his one-man play *Oh, Mr. Faulkner, Do You Write?*, based on the life of Mississippi's Nobel Prize-winning author William Faulkner. Maxwell has performed his play in 12 foreign countries and most of the U.S. since its premiere at New Stage in 1981. He performs another one of his plays, *The Last Epistle*, in churches. He moved from Seattle, Washington to Jackson in June 1995 after the New Stage Theater named him as artistic director. His play, *Buck Nekkid*, had its world premiere at New Stage on Oct. 18, 1996.

Richard E. Mayo
Born Richard Earl Mayo on July 20, 1935, in Meridian, Mississippi. He received his B.S. degree in chemical engineering at the University of Mississippi in 1959. He also studied education for public management on a fellowship at Stanford University in 1971-72. Mayo went on to have a very impressive career with the National Aeronautics and Space Administration (NASA), and his work helped put the first man on the moon, later put several more astronauts on the lunar surface, and turned the Space Shuttle into a viable space vehicle. He first joined NASA in 1959 as a subsystem project engineer for the Echo project at Langley Research Center in Hampton, Virginia. Mayo transferred to the Manned Spacecraft Center in Houston in 1962, where he served as test engineer for Project Mercury and was also subsystem manager for the lunar module environmental control system. By 1968, he was directing a staff of 70 engineers and technicians at Kennedy Space Center in Florida. Mayo and his crew helped prepare astronaut Neil Armstrong for his history-making launch to the moon and man's first landing and walk on the moon. Part of their work was on the Extravehicular Mobility Unit (EMU) and Mayo also acted as liaison between the work being done at Kennedy Space Center and the work at Houston. In 1970, Mayo returned to Houston as Special Assistant to the Chief, Crew Systems Division, and directed efforts to extend the capability of the Apollo EMU for increased lunar exploration time. He also served in mission control center as technical advisor on the EMU during the last several Apollo missions. Mayo became Chief of Laboratory Operations Office at Johnson Space Center in 1972. For his next several years at Houston, Mayo's work concerned the Space Shuttle with testing of equipment and training of Shuttle crews. Between 1975 and 1979, he was Chief of the Engineering Division at JSC. From 1979 to 1981, Mayo served as Executive Assistant to the Director of Engineering. As Deputy Chief of the Crew and Thermal Systems Division from 1981 to 1987, he was responsible for all division testing and flight preparations including space suits, life support, the Shuttle Manned Maneuvering Unit and the Shuttle EMU. In 1987, Mayo became Director of the European Program Division of NASA's Space Station Freedom Program Office in Reston, Va. He was still involved with the Space Station Freedom Project when he moved back to Houston as Assistant Director of Engineering at JSC. Mayo retired in 1990 after a 31-year career with NASA, but still does consulting work for them, including support for the International Space Station's Russian Integration Office. He is married to the former Betty Addy of Decatur, Mississippi, where they now live.

Mac McAnally
Born Lyman McAnally, Jr., on July 1, 1959, in Belmont, Miss., he grew up there. He cut his teeth on gospel, playing piano in church. By age 13, he was already gigging with a band in the "stateline" clubs along the Mississippi-Tennessee line. He took up the guitar and became a session musician at a recording studio at Muscle Shoals, Ala. His debut single from his first album, *It's A Crazy World*, went to No. 2 on the adult contemporary charts and broke into the pop Top 40 in 1977. His Top-10 country hit, *Back Where I Come From* ('90), mentions his hometown of Belmont. His latest album is *Word of Mouth* ('99). Jimmy Buffett, a fellow Mississippian, has recorded 5 of his songs including *It's My Job*. He's wrote *Old Flame* for Alabama, *Two Dozen Roses* for Shenandoah, *Precious Thing* for Steve Wariner, *Thank God For You* for Sawyer Brown, and *Crime of Passion* for Ricky Van Shelton. McAnally has produced artists such as Jimmy Buffet, Sawyer Brown and Ricky Skaggs. As a session guitarist, he's appeared on albums by Reba McEntire, Dolly Parton, Lyle Lovett, Trisha Yearwood, George Jones, and many others. McAnally, who lives in Nashville, has been compared to literary figure William Faulkner and singer/musician James Taylor.

Jim McCafferty
Born Mar. 12, 1954, in Tupelo, he currently practices law in Jackson. He has written 2 children's books, *Holt and the Cowboys* and *Holt and the Teddy Bear*. Holt in the books is real-life Holt Collier, son of a slave, bear hunter, and guide for Teddy Roosevelt when he went on the famous bear hunt near Onward, Mississippi, then refused to shoot a bear captured by Holt. The Teddy Bear was born out of that incident. McCafferty plans more books in the series.

John Sidney McCain
He was a member of the famous military family called the "Fighting McCains" that started in Mississippi. John Sidney McCain was born at Teoc, Carroll County, Mississippi on Aug. 9, 1884. He was a student at the University of Mississippi in 1901 and 1902. After graduating from the U.S. Naval Academy in 1906, McCain was commissioned an

Profiles of Famous & Notable Mississippians

Ensign and was promoted through the ranks, attaining the rank of Rear Admiral in 1941, then to Vice Admiral in 1943. McCain served as Chief of the Naval Bureau of Aeronautics from Sept. 1942 until July 1943 when he became Deputy Chief of Naval Operations for Air. When he was Commander of Carrier Task Force 38 during World War II, planes under his command took part in action over Peleliu, Leyte Gulf, Philippine Sea, Mindoro, Luzon, Formosa, Ruyukyus, and Japan. Between July 10 and Aug. 14, 1945, McCain's aviators located and destroyed 3,000 grounded enemy planes. He witnessed the Japanese surrender aboard the *USS Missouri* in Toyko Bay on Sept. 2, 1945. He died just four days later on Sept. 6, 1945, at age 61, having attained the rank of full Four-Star Admiral. He is buried in Section 2 of Arlington National Cemetery among other family members, including his brother William Alexander McCain, who was born in Carroll County on Aug. 25, 1878. William McCain attained the rank of Brigadier General in the U.S. Army. John Sidney McCain's son, John Sidney McCain, Jr., born in Council Bluff, Iowa on Jan. 17, 1911, also reached the rank of Admiral in the U.S. Navy. He died in Washington, D.C. on March 22, 1981, and is buried in the family plot in Arlington. John S. McCain, Junior's son, John S. McCain III was serving in the U.S. Navy when he became a prisoner of war after being shot down while on an air mission over North Vietnam. He was a U.S. Senator from Arizona and a candidate for the Republican nomination for President of the U.S., until dropping out of the race on March 9, 2000. Sen. Cain says he remembers spending many happy summers at his grandfather's home in Teoc.

Oseola McCarty

Born Mar. 7, 1908, in the Hattiesburg area. She became a worldwide celebrity in 1995 when she donated $150,000 to the University of Southern Mississippi in Hattiesburg to establish a scholarship that especially targets black students. The money represented about 60 percent of McCarty's earnings in a lifetime of washing and ironing! Companies and individuals have contributed thousands more to the scholarship fund. McCarty was interviewed in numerous magazines, newspapers, and on TV programs including NBC's *Today Show*, on CNN, the Barbara Walters' hosted ABC special *The 10 Most Fascinating People of 1995*, Robin Leach's program, *Heroes America*, *The David Letterman Show*, *The Oprah Winfrey Show*, and many others. The 88 year old, who never made it past the sixth grade, received an honorary Doctor of Humane Letters degree during Harvard University's 345th commencement in June of 1996. She authored an advise book, *Oseola McCarty's Simple Wisdom for Rich Living* (1996). On Feb. 20, 1996, she was a torch bearer for the Centennial Summer Olympics. McCarty was on hand to help New York City Mayor Rudolph Giuliani lower the illuminated ball in Times Square to usher in the New Year of 1997. It was the first time *anyone* had ever been invited to help the mayor with this annual event. McCarty said at the time that it was the first time she'd ever stayed up until midnight. Her generosity lead to numerous awards including the Presidential Citizens Medal, the nation's second highest civilian award. McCarty was awarded USM's first honorary degree, the doctor of humane letters, in the spring of 1998. McCarty took first place in a *Clarion-Ledger* poll of Mississippi's Top Humanitarians of the 20th Century, released in 1999. Dr. Arthur C. Guyton, whose medical research has saved countless lives, came in second in that poll. McCarty died on Sept. 26, 1999, in her small frame house in Hattiesburg from complications of liver cancer. She was 91 years old. Accolades poured in from admirers worldwide, including the White House. President Clinton described her as a "true American hero." The statement added, "While we mourn her passing, Oseola McCarty's commitment to the dignity of work, her belief in the power of education and her extraordinary generosity ensure that her memory will live on for generations to come. Our country needs more people like her who don't just talk about responsibility and community, but who live those values everyday." She is buried in the Highland Park Cemetery in Hattiesburg.

Eric McClellan

Born Nov. 14, 1959 in Tampa, Florida, his family moved to Brandon, Miss. in Jan. 1973 when he was 13 years old. He attended University of Southern Mississippi for one year. From his first job cutting silk screens in a stop sign shop in Pearl, Miss. to being named Executive Creative Director of TBWA Chiat Day in New York at age 36, McClellan's career has taken him to Atlanta, New York, California, Kenya, the Czech Republic, and many places in between. His career as an art director in the advertising business began in 1983 with a newspaper ad for student loans for the Bank of Tupelo. After a series of agency jobs in Jackson, McClellan moved to Atlanta, where he worked two years for the Babbitt & Reiman agency. In 1989, he moved to New York City to work for the Deutsch agency. There, he created the memorable campaigns of "Your Mother Wears Nike" for British Knights and "It's a Big Country, Someone's Got to Furnish It" for IKEA. For those efforts, McClellan garnered two Gold Lions from Cannes. He was then named creative director for the Pepsi International account at the giant ad agency, BBD&O in New York. For two years, McClellan traveled around the world producing spots for Pepsi with Michael Jackson and Diet Pepsi with Ray Charles. In 1992 he was named Outstanding TV Art Director on *Adweek*'s Creative All-Star Team. The next year, 4 of his commercials were placed in the permanent collections of both the Museum of Modern Art and the Museum of Television and Radio. In 1994, McClellan joined Chiat/Day as Group Creative Director for the New York Life and America Online accounts. He spent 1995 in the agency's Venice, California office as Creative Director on the Infiniti account. Returning to New York in 1996, he was named Managing Partner and Executive Creative Director of TBWA/Chiat/Day. During the next two years, the agency gained over $250 million in new billings from ABC, barnesandnoble.com, Outback Steakhouse, Champion, Promus Hotels, Prodigy Internet, Comcast and Seagram's. McClellan now lives in New York City.

O.B. McClinton

This black country singer was born Obie Burnett McClinton on April 25, 1940, in Senatobia. The son of a preacher, he attended Rust College in Holly Springs, where he sang in their acapella choir. His biggest hit was *Don't Let the Green Grass Fool You* in 1973. After becoming terminally ill, he recorded *When I Die, Take Me Back To Senatobia*. He died of cancer on Sept. 23, 1987, and was buried in Senatobia, Mississippi.

Herschel McCoy

Born in Meridian, Miss. He became a Hollywood costume designer for such movies as *Joan of Arc* (1948), starring Ingrid Bergman, *Tulsa* (1949), with Susan Hayward, and *Quo Vadis?* (1951), starring Robert Taylor and Deborah Kerr. *Joan of Arc* received the Academy Award® nomination for Best Costume Design and McCoy himself was named in the Academy Award nomination for Best Costume Design for *Quo Vadis?*

John McCrady

Born Sept. 5, 1911 in Canton, Miss., he spent much of his life in New Orleans. McCrady studied at Ole Miss, where his

Profiles of Famous & Notable Mississippians

father, an Episcopal Minister, served on the faculty. There he painted the acclaimed *Portrait of a Negro*, which earned him a fellowship at the Art Students League in New York City. He also studied at the New Orleans Art School and the University of Pennsylvania. Known as a painter of life in the South in the period between the two world wars, in 1937 he received acclaim and a 5-page spread in *Life* magazine when his famous *Swing Low, Sweet Chariot* and other paintings were shown in New York. *Life* later commissioned him to do a series of paintings. He received a Guggenheim Foundation Fellowship in 1939. McCrady founded the McCrady Art School in 1942 on Bourbon Street in the French Quarter, where he taught and influenced a generation of aspiring Louisiana artists. Some of his paintings are on display at the City Art Museum in St. Louis, Mo. and at the U.S. Post Office in Amory, Miss. On March 22, 1997, one of McCrady's paintings at New Orleans Auction Galleries brought $308,000, the highest price ever paid for a painting in that city. McCrady died in 1968.

Luke McDaniel

Born February 3, 1927, in Ellisville, Miss. McDaniel began his career as a mandolin player and, after gathering a backup band, began playing professionally in 1945. They opened for Hank Williams in New Orleans in the late 1940's. In 1952 they recorded *Whoa Boy* for Trumpet Records in Jackson, Miss. The record was indicative of the rockabilly music that was soon to come. In 1953, McDaniel recorded for King Records in Cincinnati, but got no results. By 1954 McDaniel was back in New Orleans recording for the Mel-A-Dee label and playing the Louisiana Hayride regularly, where he met Elvis Presley. Around this time, McDaniel wrote *Midnight Shift* under the pseudonym of "Earl Lee," which Buddy Holly would later record. In 1956 Elvis and Carl Perkins urged McDaniels to submit a demo to Sam Phillips. He did so, and was quickly signed to a contract with Sun Records. After recording two sessions, McDaniel was told that he would only be paid for cuts that were released, not the entire sessions. He left in anger and never returned. He later managed to pitch songs to George Jones and Jim Reeves, but had no further success with his own recordings. He recorded five singles on the Big Howdy label under the name "Jeff Daniels". One of these, *Foxy Dan*, was written for him by Carl Perkins. Even though none of his Sun material was issued at the time, subsequent release by Charly Records has made McDaniel a popular artist to current generations of rockabilly fans, with songs like *My Baby Don't Rock* and *Huh Babe*. He is a member of the Rockabilly Hall of Fame. McDaniel was living in Wilmer, Alabama when he died on June 27, 1992, at the age of 65.

Jimmie McDowell

Born Mar. 24, 1926, in Brookhaven, he's one of the most famous sportswriters in Mississippi history. He started writing at age 11 for the *Brookhaven Leader* newspaper publishing a column called "Pop Flies and Errors." McDowell, a 1949 Ole Miss graduate, was a sportswriter or editor for the *Jackson Daily News*, the *Meridian Star*, the *State Times* in Jackson, the *Commercial Appeal* in Memphis and the *Trenton Times* in New Jersey. He is the founder of the Mississippi Sports Hall of Fame. It was McDowell who, in 1960, came up with the idea of starting an organization to honor Mississippi's greatest athletes. Radio personality Farmer Jim Neal helped McDowell get the MSHOF off the ground. Almost 40 years later, in 1999, McDowell himself was inducted into the Mississippi Sports Hall of Fame. He worked for the National Football Foundation and College Football Hall of Fame from 1964-91 and served as executive director for 21 years, traveling extensively across the nation. In 1994 he helped form the All American Football Foundation and serves as that organization's president. McDowell lives in Jackson and still writes freelance columns for newspapers across Mississippi.

"Mississippi" Fred McDowell

This blues legend was born Jan. 12, 1906, in Rossville, Tenn. and was playing the guitar by the age of 14 with a slide hollowed out of a steer bone. His parents died when Fred was a youngster and he soon adopted the life of a traveling musician. The 1920s saw him playing for tips on the street around Memphis, the hoboing life eventually setting him down in Como, Mississippi, where he lived the rest of his life. There he split his time between farming and playing his music on weekends for various local fish fries and house parties. This pattern stayed largely unchanged for the next 30 years until he was discovered in 1959 by folklorist Alan Lomax, who taped him and released the recordings on the Atlantic label. Two albums, *Fred McDowell, Volume 1* and *Volume 2*, were released on Arhoolie Records in the mid-1960s. The success of these recordings suddenly found McDowell much in demand on the folk and festival circuit, working everything from the Newport Folk Festival to coffeehouse dates to becoming a member of the American Folk Blues Festival in Europe. He was also well documented on film, with appearances in *The Blues Maker* (1968), his own documentary *Fred McDowell* (1969) and *Roots of American Music: Country and Urban Music* (1970). At the end of the decade, he signed to do an album for Capitol Records while his tunes were being mainstreamed by artists like Bonnie Raitt (who recorded several of his tunes, including versions of *Write Me a Few Lines* and *Kokomo*) and the Rolling Stones, who included a version of his classic *You Got to Move* on their Sticky Fingers album. One of his last albums in the late 1960s, *I Do Not Play No Rock 'n' Roll*, was recorded for Capitol Records at the then-new Malaco Recording Studio in Jackson and helped bring them national attention. The album was nominated for a Grammy. McDowell knew he was the real deal and while others were changing their sound to keep pace with the changing times, Mississippi Fred stood out from the rest of the pack simply by not changing his style. Although generally lumped in with other blues "rediscoveries" from the 1960s, the amazing thing about him was that he never recorded in the 1920s or '30s, didn't get "discovered" until 1959, and didn't become a full-time professional musician until the mid-1960s. McDowell was diagnosed with cancer while performing dates in 1971. He died in Memphis on July 3, 1972.

Antonio McDyess

Born Sept. 7, 1974, in Quitman, Mississippi. He averaged 25.8 points and 14.7 rebounds at Quitman High in 1991-92 & 1992-93. He then played for Alabama. The Clippers took the 6-foot-9 McDyess as the No. 2 overall pick of the 1995 NBA, but immediately traded him to Denver. He averaged 13.4 points and 7.5 rebounds a game during the 1996 season with the Denver Nuggets and was fourth in balloting for the NBA's all-rookie team chosen by the league's coaches. He had some of the Nugget's best rookie numbers during the 1997 season — 1,020 points (18.3 avg., the 2nd highest on the team), 572 rebounds (9.3 avg.) & 126 blocks. Denver offered McDyess $70 million over 6 years, but he wanted $30 million more, which would have made him the NBA's first $100 million man, So, the Nuggets swapped him to the Phoenix Suns on Oct. 1, 1997. McDyess was the main reason the Suns rebounded from a dismal 1996-97 season to finish third in the Pacific Division. During the 1997-98 season, he averaged 15.1

Profiles of Famous & Notable Mississippians

points (1,225) and 7.6 rebounds in 81 games and ranked 7th in the NBA in Field-Goal Percentage (.536). In the final days of a three-year $7.4 million deal that paid him $2.876 million in the 1997-98 season, McDyess became a free agent in the summer of 1998. On Jan. 22, 1999, he signed a six-year, $67.5 million contract with the Denver Nuggets, the team that traded him to Phoenix just 15 months earlier. With the Nuggets, he was one of only six players in the NBA with 20 ppg and 10 rpg in 1998-99. His career stats through the 1999-2000 season: played in 231 games (31.5 minutes. avg.); 3,597 points (15.6 avg.); 1,722 rebounds (7.5 avg.); 216 steals; 375 blocks; 287 assists, a goal percentage of .492 and free throw percentage of .700. McDyess won a Gold Medal as a member of the U.S. Olympic men's basketball team in the 2000 Olympics in Sydney. He was the only Mississippian on the team.

Neil McGaughey

Born on Oct. 3, 1951, in Natchez. A mystery book reviewer for *The Clarion-Ledger* in Jackson for the decade of the 80s, he turned out 300-400 reviews. He didn't critique books he didn't like, so most of his reviews were positive. He was also a writer of four successful mystery novels: *Otherwise Known As Murder* (1993), *And Then There Were Ten* (1995), *The Best Money Murder Can Buy* (1996) and *A Corpse By Any Other Name* (1998). Noel and Lula McGaughey adopted Neil from a Natchez hospital when he was 6 weeks old, and he grew up in Prentiss, Miss. That's where he died of heart failure on Sept. 21, 1999, at the age of 47. Several months before his death, he had been diagnosed with Peyronie's disease, a rare condition of unknown cause, characterized by the collapse of the body's tiny capillaries that carry blood to the extremities.

Gary "Turk" McGill

Born Apr. 12, 1976, in Taylorsville, Miss. On Oct. 14, 1994, this 5-9, 175-pound senior tailback scored 3 TDs to surpass, by one, Marcus Dupree's high school state record 87 touchdowns set in 1978-81 at Philadelphia, Miss. In 1994, McGill also tied the state record of 40 TDs in one season set by Tim Moffett, also of Taylorsville, in 1980. Kevin Jones with South Panola set a new state record of 41 season rushing TDs on Dec. 6, 1996, but the record stood for less than a day until broken by Dicenzo Miller (Weir TB, see his profile) when he finished with 42 on Dec. 7. Miller scored 4 touchdowns on Oct. 31, 1997, giving him 106 in 4 years, the most ever by a high school player in Mississippi, breaking the previous career record of 105 set by McGill.

Mike McGregor

Born April 14, 1939, in Tibbs (near Sledge), Miss. He was jeweler, leather craftsman and horse wrangler for Elvis Presley from 1967 to 1976. Mike operated a shop on Highway 7 near Oxford until his untimely death from lung cancer on Jan. 6, 1999. His shop is still open where you can buy replicas of Elvis' show belts plus Elvis-inspired jewelry and leatherwork.

Robert P. McHugh

Born Robert Paul McHugh on Feb. 14, 1917, in Cedar Rapids, Iowa. He graduated from Loras College and the University of Iowa. This veteran journalist had lived in Gulfport, Mississippi for almost 30 years at the time of his death. McHugh was a photographer during World War II. He later worked for the *Waterloo Courier* and then as editor in the Balitmore Bureau of the Associated Press for 12 years starting in 1950. He covered the funeral of President John F. Kennedy in 1963, the year he became an editor at *The State* newspaper in Columbia, South Carolina. McHugh moved to the Mississippi Gulf Coast in 1969 as associate editor of *The Daily Herald*. One of his first big stories was Hurricane Camille. McHugh reported on the Category 5 storm, dictating stories until the line went dead. In 1973, he was named executive editor of a new morning newspaper, *South Mississippi Sun*, which was later combined with the *Daily Herald* to form *The Sun Herald*. He served as executive editor until 1982, then moved to full-time editorial writing in 1982 until retiring in 1986. McHugh won several awards for his editorial writing and columns, as well as his news coverage. During his Baltimore years in the 1950s, he was as associate of H.L. Mencken, writing an introduction for a compilation of Mencken's essays in 1958. McHugh served as president of the Mississippi Institute of Arts and Letters and the Gulf Coast Opera. In 1992, the Mississippi Press Asociation inducted McHugh into its Hall of Fame. McHugh died of kidney failure in Gulfport on July 23, 1998, at age 81.

Derrick McKey

Born Oct. 10, 1966, in Meridian, this 6-9 Alabama standout left school one year early when he was the 9th pick overall in the NBA draft in 1987. He spent 6 years with the Supersonics and ranks in the top 10 on Seattle's all-time list in 12 categories, including 9th in scoring and 10th in rebounding. Traded to the Pacers for the 1993-94 season, he averaged 12.0 points, 5.3 rebounds and 4.3 assists to help Indiana come within one game of the NBA finals in his first year there. McKey was named to the NBA All-Defensive 2nd team in 1995 and helped the Pacers to the conference finals and a franchise-high 52 victories. He averaged 13.3 points with a team-high 125 steals. McKey's career stats through the 1999-2000 season: played in 785 games (31.3 minutes avg.); 9,803 points (12.5 avg.); 3,908 rebounds (5.0 avg.); 942 steals; 577 blocks; and 2,087 assists. His career field goal percentage is .489 and free throw percentage is .779.

Lillian McMurry

Born Lillian Shedd on Dec. 30, 1921, in Purvis, Mississippi. She founded Trumpet Records in Jackson, a record label that made historic contributions to blues and the genesis of rock 'n' roll. McMurry was the record producer who first recorded Elmore James (in 1951) and Sonny Boy Williamson II. McMurry wrote Sonny Boy's hit *Red Hot Kisses*. A member of the Blues Hall Of Fame, McMurry died March 18, 1999, of a heart attack at the age of 77.

Eric McNair

Born Donald Eric McNair on Apr. 12, 1909, in Meridian. His nickname was "Boob." He made his major league baseball debut on Sept. 20, 1929, with the Philadelphia Athletics, where he stayed until 1935. He also played for the Boston Red Sox (1936-38), the Chicago White Sox (1939-40), and the Detroit Tigers (1941-42) and then back to the Philadelphia Athletics in 1942. He played in the 1930 and '31 World Series. His career stats: 1,240 hits in 4,519 at bats (.274 batting avg.), 592 runs, 82 home runs & 633 RBIs in 1,251 games played. McNair died on Mar. 11, 1949, in Meridian at age 39. He was inducted into the Mississippi Sports Hall of Fame in 1963.

Steve McNair

Born Feb. 14, 1973, in Mount Olive, Mississippi, he played at Mount Olive High and was a two-time All State selection at defensive back. His high school career total of 30 interceptions tied a state record. On Oct. 1, 1994, the Alcorn State quarterback, playing with an injured shoulder, surpassed former Portland State star Neil Lomax as the Division 1-AA all-time total offense leader in a game against Mississippi Valley State. Lomax played from 1977-80 and finished with 13,345 yards. McNair had 13,531 yards. During the Oct. 22 home game against MSU, McNair surpassed Ty Detmer's total offense record of 14,665 yards for all divisions. McNair had

Profiles of Famous & Notable Mississippians

the new record of 15,049 yards and became the most prolific offensive player in NCAA's 125-year history. He gained 649 yards in that game, a Division I-AA record. McNair's last regular season game of his college career was on Nov. 19 when Alcorn beat Jackson State 52-34. McNair's college highlights: the only player in NCAA history to gain over 16,000 yards (16,823) in total offense during his college career; set a collegiate record by averaging 400.55 yards in total offense per game; became only the third player in Division I-AA to throw for 100 TDs in a career (119); owns every Alcorn State game, season and career passing and total offense record — he set seven I-AA records, including Division I-AA season records for Total Offense (5,799 yards in 1994) and Passing Yards (4,863 in 1994). He set 40 NCAA records. He won player of the Year honors for 4 consecutive years. McNair finished with 928 completions in 1,673 attempts (55.5%) for 14,496 yards passing (a Division I-AA career record) with 119 TDs and 58 INTs, added 2,327 yards and 33 TDs on 375 rushing attempts (6.2 avg.), and was Unanimous All-America choice. On Dec 9, 1994, he received the first Eddie Robinson Award. The Sept. 26, 1994 issue of the prestigious New York-based magazine *Sports Illustrated*, featured a picture of 6-3, 218-pound McNair on the cover along with the caption in large print "Hand Him the Heisman" and a 4-page article inside. He was the first Mississippi collegian to be featured on that magazine's cover since former University of Mississippi quarterback Archie Manning in 1970. McNair finished in third place for the Heisman behind Colorado running star Rashaan Salaam and Penn State running back Ki-Jana Carter. McNair was the top quarterback in the voting, but he received only 111 of the 792 first-place votes while Salaam got 400. McNair joins Gordie Lockbaum of Holy Cross, who finished 3rd in 1987, as the highest Heisman finisher below the NCAA Division I-A level. McNair is the 3rd Mississippi collegian to finish third, following Ole Miss' Jake Gibbs in 1960 and Archie Manning in 1970. On Dec. 19, 1994, McNair won the Walter Payton Award as the top player in NCAA Division I-AA football. Only one other SWAC player had won the Payton Award since its inception in 1987 — running back Walter Dean of Grambling in 1990. McNair was also chosen as the 1994 College Offensive Player of the Year by the Mississippi Sports Writers Association and named *The Clarion-Ledger* Sportsperson of the Year 1994. On April 22, 1995, McNair was the first quarterback selected when the Houston Oilers chose him as the third pick overall in the NFL draft. He signed a $28.7 million contract, a record amount for a rookie at the time. Houston kept him on the sidelines until the 14th week of the 1995 season. In his 2nd NFL season in 1996, McNair started 4 games and threw 6 touchdown passes (a 90.6 rating) and 4 interceptions. After moving to Tennessee, the Oilers (later changed to the Titans) sank to 29th in passing in 1997. In McNair's first season as a starter in 1997 — he completed 52% of his passes for 2,665 yards with 14 touchdowns and 13 interceptions. He led the team in rushing TDs with 8 and his 674 yards ranked 2nd. In 1998, McNair became the fourth quarterback in franchise history to pass for more than 3,000 yards — he finished with 3,228 yards and 15 touchdowns, all career-highs, with 10 interceptions. In the 1999 season opening game on Sept. 12, McNair thrilled the fans when he finished 21-of-32 for 341 yards and three TDs to lead the Titans to a come-from-behind 36-35 victory over the Cincinnati Bengals. After having started 34 straight games, McNair missed six weeks of play after undergoing surgery on his spine on Sept. 19, 1999. He was back in the game on Oct. 31. In his 10th game of the 1999 season, McNair completed 23 of 33 passes and had a pro career-high 5 TD passes in the Titans 41-14 win over Jacksonville, keeping alive the Titans hopes for their first AFC Central Division title since 1993. McNair's efforts through the playoffs took the Titans to Jacksonville on Jan. 23, 2000, where they defeated the Jaguar's 33 - 14 to win the AFC title. Even with a sore turf toe, McNair scored two rushing touchdown and gained 91 yards. He also tossed a touchdown pass and gained 112 yards in the air. Although McNair gave an impressive performance in Super Bowl XXXIV on Jan. 30, including 64 yards rushing, a Super Bowl record for a quarterback, which brought the Titans back even from a 16-point deficit, the St. Louis Rams still won the game 23-16 in what many called the best Super Bowl ever. McNair's stats for the 1999 season: in 11 games played, he made 331 pass attempts with 187 completions for 2,179 yards and 12 TDs. He had an additional 74 yards and 8 TDs rushing. His pro career stats through Oct. 30, 2000: in 67 games played, he made 1,639 pass attempts with 933 completions for 11,092 yards & 59 TDs. He had 1,933 yards, 22 TDs rushing.

Evelyn McPhail

Born June 9, 1930, in Bay St. Louis. She was head of the state GOP and served as director of political education and training at the Republican National Committee from 1987-93. In Jan. 1995, she was elected co-chairperson to serve alongside fellow Mississippian, Haley Barbour. She retired from the RNC when her term ended in Jan. 1997. She was honored in 1998 as the National Republican Women's Leadership Forum's Woman of the Year. On May 19, 1997, McPhail was seriously injured when her car hydroplaned off I-59 in Jasper County and slid backwards into a tree. She spent the rest of 1997 in the Mississippi Methodist Rehablitation Center. Mrs. McPhail died on Nov. 26, 1998, in the Diamondhead community on the Gulf Coast. She was 68 years old.

Tim McPherson (see "Mel & Tim")

Richard D. McRae, Sr.

Born Feb. 14, 1921, in Jackson. After graduating from the University of Mississippi's School of Business in 1942, he joined McRae's Department Store chain that his father, Sam P. McRae, had started as McRae's Dry Goods in 1902 in Jackson. He became chairman of the board of McRae's chain of 28 stores in Mississippi, Alabama, Louisiana and Florida that employed 5,000 people and had yearly sales close to a half billion dollars. In 1994, McRae's merged with another department store chain, Proffitt's. The parent company became Saks, Inc. (the famous Saks Fifth Avenue) in 1998 when Saks acquired both Proffit's and McRae's. Richard McRae, Sr. is a member on numerous boards and in 1964 established the McRae Foundation, a philanthropic organization. McRae is in the Mississippi Business Hall of Fame.

Gerald McRaney

Born Aug. 19, 1948, in Collins, Miss., he attended Ole Miss. He held several jobs before becoming an actor. He worked as a mud-logger in the oil fields of New Orleans. He was a surveyor (on-shore and off-shore), a taxi driver, a carpenter, and a rough-neck. He co-starred with Jamison Parker in TV's private eye series *Simon & Simon* in the 80s for 8 seasons, starred in the TV sitcom series *Major Dad* and in the weekly TV drama *Promised Land* which started in the fall of 1996 on CBS. He's been in several made-for-TV movies such as *Someone She Knows* (NBC Oct. 3, 1994), *Jake Lassiter: Justice on the Bayou* (NBC Jan. 9, 1995), *Not Our Son* (CBS Jan. 31, 1995), *Dream of Murder, Nothing Lasts Forever, A Stranger Beside Me, Deadly Vows, A Nightmare Come True*

Profiles of Famous & Notable Mississippians

(1997), and *A Thousand Men and a Baby* (1997). He has also made guest appearances on several TV series, including *The Rockford Files* and *Gunsmoke*. He's been in a few feature films, most notably *The NeverEnding Story* (1984), a fantasy filmed in Germany. He was pictured on the June 12, 1989 cover of *People* magazine with his then new bride (his third wife), actress Delta Burke (b. 7-30-1956 in Florida). They live in New Orleans and have a farm in Mississippi.

Elsie McWilliams

Born June 1, 1896, in Harperville, Scott Co., Miss., she later moved to Meridian and attended high school there. She wrote or cowrote 38 of the 110 songs recorded by her brother-in-law, the legendary Jimmie Rodgers, including *The Sailor's Plea, My Old Pal, You and My Old Guitar, Daddy and Home, I'm Lonely and Blue, Lullaby Yodel, Never No Mo' Blues, Waiting For a Train, Home Call* and *Mississippi Moon*. Her songs appeared on eight of Rodgers' albums. She worked with Roy Huskey, Jr., Shot Jackson, Grady Martin, Buddy Spicher, Doc Watson, and many others. Her songs have been recorded by Gene Autry, the Carter Family, Lefty Frizzell, Merle Haggard, Robert John, Grandpa Jones, Hank Snow, Ernest Tubb, Tanya Tucker, and others. She was elected to the Songwriters Hall of Fame in Nashville in 1979. McWilliams died in Meridian on Dec. 31, 1985, at the age of 89. She was one of the first 27 inducted into the inaugural Mississippi Musicians Hall of Fame on April 1, 2000.

Henry "Skeets" McWilliams

Born Aug. 6, 1924, in Jackson, he spent much of his childhood in Chicago. He came back to Jackson and ran a guitar shop. In the navy during WWII, he appeared regularly on the radio network show *Meet Your Navy* and later toured the South Pacific entertaining troops with Ray Anthony's Band. In Chicago after the war, he played the big jazz clubs in the "Loop." Jazz critic Pat Harris in *Downbeat Magazine* called him "The Fair-Haired Boy of Chicago Guitarists." He was on Jackson's first regular live music TV program on WLBT in the early 1950s. He did a concert in England in '94 and another in France in '95. McWilliams is one of six artists on a 1999 CD called *The Great Mississippi Jazz Guitarists Reunion*, released by the Mississippi Musicians Hall of Fame (available on the MMHOF Website or at area record stores). The other artists are Bucky Barrett, Steve Blailock, Mundell Lowe, Bob Saxton and Lloyd Wells (see their profiles). McWilliams is considered to be one of the all-time great jazz guitarists. McWilliams, as well as Lowe and Wells were among the first 27 inducted into the inaugural Miss. Musicians Hall of Fame on April 1, 2000.

Thomas E. "Shorty" McWilliams

Born May 12, 1926, in Meridian, Mississippi. A standout tailback at Mississippi State University, he finished 10th in the Heisman voting as a freshman in 1944. He was second-team All-Amerca and first-team All-Southeastern Conference. After the outbreak of World War II McWilliams played for the 1945 undefeated Army team in the backfield with Heisman winners Doc Blanchard and Glenn Davis. He placed 8th in the Heisman voting that year, won by his backfield teammate Doc Blanchard. McWilliams returned to Mississippi State after the one season with Army. He was first-team All-SEC three more times, from 1946-48. He played with the Los Angeles Dons in 1949 and with the Pittsburgh Steelers in 1950, his brief pro career hobbled by a knee injury. McWilliams came home to Meridian in 1955, purchasing the Weidmann's Restaurant, which his family still owns. He was inducted into the Mississippi Sports Hall of Fame in 1962 and into the Mississippi State University Sports Hall of Fame in 1970. He died from a stroke in Meridian on Jan. 9, 1997, at age 70.

Lynda Lee Mead

Born on April 17, 1939, in New Orleans, she was 5 years old when her family moved to Natchez. She was Miss America, 1960. Now Lynda Shea, she is a founding member and former director of Memphis Development Foundation, and founder and first president of Subsidium, a support organization for The Memphis Oral School for the Deaf. A successful businesswoman in Memphis since 1984, she owns/operates Shea Designs, an interior design firm, and French Country Imports, an antique company that imports from France.

"Mel & Tim"

Cousins Mel Hardin and Tim McPherson were born in Holly Springs, Miss. They eventually went to Chicago, and in 1969, hooked up with Gene "Duke of Earl" Chandler, a producer for the Bamboo label. Chandler produced Mel & Tim's first million-selling single *Backfield In Motion* (1969), a Top 10 pop hit and No. 3 R&B. The follow-up a few months later, *Good Guys Only Win in the Movies*, reached No. 45 pop and No. 17 R&B, after which the duo parted company with Chandler. By 1972, Mel & Tim were on Stax Records, and hit No. 19 pop and No. 4 R&B that summer with the ballad *Starting All Over Again*, which Daryl Hall & John Oates remade in 1991. After one additional top forty R&B hit, Mel & Tim disappeared from the charts. They were in the film *Wattstax* (1973) doing *I May Not Be What You Want*.

Frederic Frances Mellen

A geologist and writer born on Aug. 21, 1911, in Starkville, Miss. He discovered the Tinsley oil dome in Yazoo County, which led to the first commercial oil production in the state. Mellen was living in Clinton when he died on Nov. 6, 1989.

James Meredith

Civil rights activist born June 25, 1933, in Kosciusko, Miss. It caused rioting that took two lives at the University of Mississippi in 1962, but by Federal court order and the presence of about 3,000 Army troops, Meredith was finally admitted and became the first black enrolled in Ole Miss. He graduated on Aug. 18, 1963 with a major in government and politics. In 1966, while on a Civil Rights march, he was wounded by a shotgun blast shot from ambush near Hernando. He has published 2 books: *Three Years in Mississippi* (1966) and *Mississippi: A Volume of Eleven Books* (1995).

H. T. "Dick" Merrill

Born Henry Tyndall Merrill on Feb. 1, 1894, in Iuka, Tishomingo County, Mississippi. Merrill was an early aviation pioneer who became a legend in his own time. Merrill got his nickname in his first year at Ole Miss, where he pitched baseball both right-handed and left-handed. His fellow students compared him with a Yale University fictional character named Dick Merrywell, who was an ambidextrous pitcher, so he was tagged "Dick" and the moniker stuck. He quit college after his first year and signed on as a pitcher for a Class-D ballclub in Jonesboro Arkansas, where he became the youngest professional player in the league. In the fall of 1914, Merrill attended the Mississippi State Fair and saw something that would change the course of his life. He witnessed the plane flying talents of another native Mississippian, Katherine Stinson, one of the first American women to fly. She was the first woman to fly at night, do a loop-de-loop and the first woman to fly in Japan. Merrill was impressed. After a couple more years of baseball, he joined a U.S. Naval Unit in 1917 to learn to fly. He was sent to France where he flew some, but the war ended before he saw any combat action. After the war, he joined a flying outfit as a barnstormer. In 1920, he bought a

Profiles of Famous & Notable Mississippians

used military JN-4 "Jenny" for $600 from a war surplus dealer and took a job as an airmail pilot flying from Richmond, Virginia to Atlanta, Georgia. He became quite popular with journalists because of his mascots. Like fellow barnstormer Roscoe Turner from Corinth, Mississippi (not far from Merrill's hometown of Iuka), Merrill flew with a lion cub, "Princess Doreen." But, unlike Turner, Merrill flew with several mascots — his pet Doberman, raccoons, foxes, a groundhog, and once, even a big, black King snake! In 1936, he and his co-pilot, entertainer Harry Richman, made the first round-trip Atlantic flight in a plane loaded with 40,000 ping pong balls to make the craft buoyant just in case they had to ditch her in the ocean. They landed in South Wales having established a new speed record for crossing the Atlantic of 18 hours and 36 minutes. After they flew back to the U.S., a New York journalist referred to them as "the only two American aviators who ever 'double-crossed' the ocean." By 1937, Merrill was a pilot for Eastern Airlines. On May 6, 1937, the German airship Hindenburg crashed and burned in Lakehurst, New Jersey. Merrill was flying for the William Randolph Hearst newspaper chain when he carried pictures of that crash to London, landing there on May 10, the same day King George VI was crowned King of England. He flew back to the states with 51 enlarged photographs of the coronation, landing in Massachusetts on May 14. The flight lasted just over 22 hours, a new world record for a westerly crossing of the Atlantic. Merrill flew a C-46 military transport plane into China during WWII. After the war, he was Gen. Eisenhower's personal pilot during Ike's presidential campaign. Merrill retired from Eastern Airlines in 1961. In 1966, he and TV personality Arthur Godfrey teamed up for a record-setting, around-the-world flight. Flying a jet, they flew 23,523 miles with stops in eleven countries. On April 15, 1966, the National Aernautics Association presented the two with certificates confirming 21 new speed records they established during their flight. In 1972, at the age of 78, Merrill set a new speed record on the delivery flight of the new wide-bodied Lockheed L-1011 Tri-Star jet from Palmdale, Calif. to Miami. — 3 hours and 33 minutes, a record that still stands. Merrill died on Oct. 31, 1982, at his home in Lake Elsinore, Calif. He was 88.

Eddie Merrins

Born Aug. 4, 1932, in Meridian, Mississippi. Perhaps the most accomplished golf instructor in the world, he is now director of golf for the famed Bel-Air Country Club in Los Angeles, California. Known as "The Little Pro," Merrins starting playing golf in 1944 at age 11 in his hometown of Meridian. At 17, he won the first of his three State Amateur titles. In 1950, he won the National Jaycee Junior Tournament and a scholarship to Louisiana State University. He led LSU and later UCLA to collegiate championships. Merrins also won the Gulf Coast Open and the New Orleans Invitational in 1954 and the 1955 Colonial Invitational in Memphis. After turning pro in 1957, he went on to play in 8 U.S. Opens and 6 PGA Championships. He won the Long Island Open and the Metropolitan PGA Championship in 1961 and the Southern California PGA medal play titles in 1974 and 1975. However, Merrins greatest success has come as a teacher and coach. At UCLA, he has coached hundreds, including current PGA Tour greats Steve Pate, Corey Pavin and Duffy Waldorf, for whom he still works. He was 1985 NCAA Coach of the Year and won the 1988 NCAA championship. In addition to the pros, he has tutored such celebrities as Tom Cruise, Jack Nicholson, Bing Crosby, Clark Gable and many others. Merrins founded the Friends of Golf program, which has raised over $2.5 million to support UCLA golf and junior golf programs in Southern California. He has been Southern California's Player of the Year, Professional of the Year and Teacher of the Year. *Golf* magazine has him on their list of Top 100 Golf Pros and he's a member of the magazine's Teaching Panel. Merrins has been the recipient of many honors, including his induction into the Mississippi Sports Hall of Fame in March 2000.

Cary Middlecoff

Born on Jan. 6, 1921, in Halls, Tennessee, he moved at an early age to Memphis, where he attended high school. He graduated from Ole Miss, where he became the Rebels' first golf All-American in 1939. He joined the professional golf tour in 1947 and won more than 40 PGA victories including the U.S. Open titles in 1949 (score 286) and 1956 (score 281). Middlecoff won the Masters by a margin of 7 shots (score 279) in 1955, his best season with 6 wins. He received the Byron Nelson Award in 1955 for the most victories on tour and the Vardon Trophy in 1956, awarded each year to the PGA player who posts the season's best scoring average. His average was 70.35 in 66 rounds played in 1956. Middlecoff is tied in 7th place with Walter Hagen on the list of All-Time Tournament winners, both with 40 points. He was a member of 3 victorious Ryder Cup teams. Middlecoff is listed in the PGA Tour record book for being in the longest sudden-death playoff. Middlecoff and Lloyd Mangrum played 11 extra holes after they had tied for the 72-hole lead in the 1949 Motor City Open in Detroit without deciding the title. When darkness intervened, they were declared co-champions. There have been longer playoffs, but all started with an 18-hole stroke round, which was tied, then went on to more holes. Retiring from the tour in 1961 after back surgery, Middlecoff served 15 years as a network TV golf commentator. He was elected into the PGA Hall of Fame in 1974 and inducted into the Mississippi Sports Hall of Fame in 1996. Middlecoff died of heart failure in Memphis on Sept. 1, 1998, at age 77.

William "Bud" Miley

Born in Fort Mason, Calif. in Dec 26, 1897, he retired to Starkville, Miss. in 1955 after becoming known as the "father of American paratrooping". A 1918 graduate of West Point, he was a champion college gymnast. For 14 years in the 1920s and 1930s, Miley was a lieutenant in the U.S. Army. When he was selected to be the first commander of the 501st Parachute Battalion at Fort Benning.in 1940, he had never made a jump! Miley figured out the type of equipment paratroopers should have (such as jumpsuits with multiply pockets), how they should be trained and even how they should carry their rifles (in a side bag). Miley led troops who defended the Panama Canal. He also organized the 503rd Paratroop Regiment and the 17th Airborne Division that provided ground support to the 101st Airborne during the Battle of the Bulge in 1944. The 17th Airborne also made the famous jump across the Rhine River in March 1945. He retired with the rank of Major General. Miley died in Starkville, Miss. on Sept. 25, 1997, at the age of 99. A segment of Mississippi State Highway 389 in Starkville was named in his honor on Sept. 24, 1998.

Dicenzo Miller

Born July 9, 1980, in Eupora, Miss., Miller was a running and defensive back that played football four years at Weir High in Choctaw County and never missed a game in 51 varsity appearances. During the 1997 season, the 5-10, 185-pound Miller became Mississippi's all-time high school TD leader (118), broke his own record for touchdowns in a season (47) and led Weir to a 15-0 record, a second straight Class 1A state championship and third in four years (only one other

Profiles of Famous & Notable Mississippians

Mississippian has made more than 100 TDs in their high school career — Gary McGill of Taylorsville scored 105 TDs from 1991-94). During the 1997 season, Miller had 3,185 all-purpose years — 2,291 on 200 carries, 324 on 12 catches and 570 on 19 kick returns. On defense, he had 36 tackles and 10 interceptions. In the final three rounds of the playoffs, Miller helped Weir stretch its winning streak to 29 games. He also played baseball and basketball some in high school. He was Player of the Year on *The Clarion-Ledger* All-State team of 1997. Miller signed with the Mississippi State Bulldogs in 1998. Just halfway through the 2000 Southeastern Conference season, Miller ranked fourth in the league with 83.2 rushing yards per game, more than Ole Miss' Duece McAllister, the Heisman candidate. Miller is also State's No. 2 receiver.

John Ramsey Miller

Born Oct. 3, 1949, in Greenville, he graduated from Cleveland High School and Delta State. He started out as a commercial photographer, shooting album covers for Amy Grant and David Allen Coe, among others, then went into advertising, working in New Orleans and Miami. He tried for six years to become a novelist, writing four novels which received many rejections. Even when a couple of them were published, they went nowhere. His fifth book, the mystery-thriller *The Last Family*, was rejected 40 times. But, he finally hit paydirt with it when Bantam Books gave Miller a $150,000 advance and a two-book $1 million contract. *The Last Family*, released in June 1996, quickly became a Literary Guild main selection and was *People* magazine's Beach Book of the Week in early July. Larry King gave it Five Stars in his weekly *USA Today* column. Miller reworked an earlier novel, *Comfort* (1998), and was also working on a mystery-thriller titled *Lost and Found*. He currently lives in Concord, North Carolina.

Mary Carol Miller

Born on Mar. 27, 1954, in Greenwood, Mississippi. A Graduate of the University of Mississippi School of Medicine, this physician turned writer started out with a simple idea for a magazine article in 1992. It turned into a three year research project that resulted in the book, *Lost Mansions of Mississippi*, a photographic and historical review of 57 notable, but long-vanished antebellum mansions, including Windsor, Annandale, Malmaison, and Morro Castle. One surprise, she says, was the small amount of damage done to Mississippi homes during the Civil War. Of the 100 homes she researched, only six were intentionally destroyed during the war. Miller's latest book is *Written in the Bricks: A Visual and Historical Tour of Fifteen Mississippi Hometowns* (1999). The photographs in that book were taken by Mary Rose Carter, another native of Greenwood. Miller and Carter have also worked together on articles for *Mississippi* magazine.

Mulgrew Miller

Born in Greenwood on Aug. 13, 1955, he began playing piano at an early age. At age 21, he was chosen by Mercer Ellington to fill the chair of Duke Ellington and he spent 3 years in that position. He also trained with jazz notables Johnny Griffin, Woody Shaw, Betty Carter, and Tony Williams and has worked with Branford Marsalis, Freddie Hubbard and others. Among his albums are *Keys to the City* and *Work*.

Romaro Miller

Born Sept. 12, 1978, in Shannon, Miss., 6-foot-2, 190-pound Miller is the second-most productive quarterback in high school history. In 4 seasons at Shannon High School, he accounted for 12,315 total yards, second only to the all-time 14,448 yards by Ken Hall of Sugarland, Texas (1950-53)! In that time, Miller passed or ran for 127 TDs, a state record. He compiled amazing numbers in the 1996 season as he led the Red Raiders, 12-2, to their first Class 3A championship 43-30 over Prentiss. He passed for a state-record 3,579 yards and 38 TDs and ran for 1,064 yards and 13 TDs — a state-record 4,643 total yards and 51 touchdowns. He finished as No. 2 career passer with 9,070 yards and 89 TDs, behind Clifton Davis III of North Panola, who threw for 9,309 yards and 104 TDs from 1988-91. He was featured in the Nov. 1996 issue of *Sports Illustrated* and selected 1996 Player of the Year on *The Clarion-Ledger* All-State football team and as a *Parade* magazine All-American. He was named Mississippi's high school football Player of the Year for 1996 by the state's Associated Press sports writers. Miller signed with Ole Miss and after mainly sitting on the sidelines for his first season, the sophomore had a dazzling debut as the Rebel's starting quarterback on Sept. 5, 1998. Before a record crowd of 46,191 at Vaught-Hemingway Stadium, Miller completed 26-of-40 passes for 332 yards and two TDs in the Rebel's 30-10 victory over Memphis. The 332 passing yards were the most ever by a first-time Ole Miss starter. The 355 total yards he compiled was the fourth-best total in Ole Miss history! During 1998, Miller threw for 2,273 yards as he guided his team to an Independence Bowl win. Miller earned offensive MVP honors with an Independence Bowl record three TD passes to lead the Rebels to a 35-18 victory over Texas Tech on Dec. 31. Ole Miss had it second consecutive Independence Bowl victory in 1999. At the start of the 2000 season, Miller had 4,299 college-career passing yards, 25 touchdown passes and had amassed more 200-yard passing games (13) than any other Rebel player. In the game against Arkansas State on Oct. 7, 2000, Miller broke the Ole Miss record for touchdown passes. Miller's 32nd career TD pass broke the mark he which he has shared with Archie Manning Kent Austin and Mark Young.

Reuben W. Millsaps

Reuben Webster Millsaps was born on May 30, 1833, on a farm about 14 miles from Hazlehurst, Mississippi. He picked cotton, worked hard at other jobs and squeezed his pennies. With his savings, he caught a river boat at Natchez and made his way to Hanover College in Indiana. In his third year, he transferred to Indiana Asbury University (now De Pauw), where he graduated in 1854. After teaching school for two years, he entered Harvard Law School in 1856 and finished the 4-year course in 3 years. He started his law practice at Pine Bluff, Arkansas. At the outbreak of the Civil War, he enlisted in the Confederacy, fought in the battles of Shiloh, Franklin and Nashville, was wounded twice, and advanced from a private to the rank of major. After the war, Millsaps quit law practice and got a job hauling cotton to Natchez. In 1969 he became a country merchant at Brookhaven. In 1881 he moved to St. Louis, where he operated a wholesale and commission business. In 1885 he sold out, retired and traveled abroad. After a few years, he moved to Jackson and soon became the financial wizard of Mississippi. Millsaps had interest in banks in Jackson, Clarksdale, Forest, Hazlehurst and New Orleans. He was also director of the Illinois Central Railway. A shrewd investor, Millsaps soon became wealthy. Then came payback time. Bishop Charles B. Galloway, a close friend of Millsaps, raised $50,000 to establish a Methodist college. Millsaps matched the $50,000 and the Bishop dedicated the college in Jackson in 1893. Out of modesty, the Major at first objected to the college bearing his name, but he endowed Millsaps College with $500,000 and the institution stands today. He not only gave of his money, but his time and attention to the school and other philanthropies over the years. Millsaps had been only 17

Profiles of Famous & Notable Mississippians

years old when he made his convenant "If God prospers me I will make it possible for every young man desiring a Christian education to get it within the borders of our State." He kept his promise. Major Millsaps died on June 28, 1916, at the age of 83 and is buried with his wife on the campus at Millsaps College in Jackson, Mississippi.

Dumas Milner

Born Robert Ernest Milner on Jan. 28, 1917, on a farm in Attala County, Mississippi. In his youth, he often trailed after a hired hand named Dumas, so his older sisters started calling him Dumas and it stuck. He attended high school in the nearby town of Ethel, where he graduated in 1935. He hated farming, so while still a poor country boy he vowed to become the richest man in Mississippi. Dumas Milner was probably the closest Mississippi ever came to having a Howard Hughes. In fact, in some early pictures, he somewhat resembles a young Hughes. After high school, Milner attended Chillicothe Business College in Missouri on a three-month scholarship. Following that, he worked briefly at a number of jobs, getting himself fired from several of them by being too free with advice to his employers. He worked for a federal farm-loan office, a Shell Oil branch in Memphis, an oil distributor in Arkansas, and the Chevrolet dealer in Ethel. While he was selling cars Milner decided to go in business for himself. He soon turned a $3,500 loan into Milner Oil Company. By the time the company had expanded to eleven filling stations in 1940, Milner felt it was time to branch out. He bought the Chrysler-Plymouth and International Harvester dealerships in Kosciusko, Mississippi. He was also in the hauling business with a large fleet of trucks. When he was drafted into the Army Air Force in 1942, he liquidated his little empire, selling everything except the Chrysler-Plymouth dealership. For his first four years as an entrepreneur he had only $21,000 to show. But even in service he made money. He made $68 a month as a sergeant, but $5,000 a month selling used cars to his fellow servicemen. After the war, he reassumed management of his car dealership in Kosciusko, joined by his new bride, Myrtle Ruth, who kept the books. Milner started branching out. He became a wholesale army surplus dealer and made millions. He had loaned some money to a small janitors' supply company in Jackson and in 1949 found himself its reluctant owner. Its main product was the pine-oil cleaner Pine-Sol, invented in the 1920s by Jacksonian Harry A. Cole, Sr. Milner felt Pine-Sol could be sold to housewives as well as janitors and by the early 1950s, he was making a profit distributing Pine-Sol and other cleaning aid products nationwide. By the time Milner sold Pine-Sol to American Cyanamid in 1963, he and the other stockholders reportedly received stock in that company valued at $17 million. Also in the early 1950s, Milner started collecting car dealerships. He first started a Chevrolet dealership in Jackson. Next, he talked General Motors officials into selling him a Chevrolet dealership in New Orleans. By 1957, Milner Chevrolet was the biggest dealership in New Orleans, making almost $500,000 that year! In the early 1960s, it was billed as "The South's Largest Chrovelet Dealership" with 7 locations in the New Orleans area. By the 1960s, Milner controlled as many as 30 GM dealerships in Kansas City, Fort Lauderdale, Los Angeles, San Diego, Philadelphia, Tampa, Tulsa and San Antonio, and other locations across the country. In addition to Jackson, his Mississippi dealerships included Brookhaven, Laurel and Vicksburg. At the time, Milner was considered the world's largest General Motors dealer! Next, Milner started constructing office-buildings. The 10-story Milner Building in downtown Jackson was finished in July 1954. Although the building cost $2 million, Milner financed it for $250,000 by arranging to lease half the space to long-term tenants. Milner moved his office to the top floor, collected $500,000 in rent in the first two years, then sold his $250,000 equity for $750,000! Milner built several other office buildings including the 25-story Kroger Building in Cincinnati, Ohio, the 12-story Petroleum Bulding in Jackson, a 12-story building in Mobile, a 15-story building in Midland, Texas, and the Edgewater Plaza Center in Biloxi, the first air-conditioned shopping mall on the entire Gulf Coast. He was also in the motel business, at one time controlling Sun-N-Sands motels in Jackson and Biloxi, the King Edward Hotels in Jackson, Mississippi and Beaumont, Texas, the Edgewater Gulf Hotel in Biloxi, the Markham in Gulfport, and the El Tropican Motel in San Antonio, Texas. One venture that didn't fare so well was the *State Times*, a Jackson daily newspaper which Milner and other investors started in 1955. The paper, which never showed a profit, was eventually sold to Jackson's longtime newspaper family, the Hedermans. Milner did better with another media venture, WJQS, a radio station he owned in Jackson. He also owned several insurance companies and car rental agencies. He received numerous honors and awards including his selection as Most Outstanding Young Man for 1951 by the Junior Chamber of Commerce of Mississippi, the first Special Horatio Alger Award in 1956, the Obie Award presented by the Orange Bowl Committee in 1966, and many others. Feature articles about Milner appeared in national magazines such as *Life* and *Fortune*, and he was among financial giants profiled in newspapers and on radio and TV. Milner said he never made the kind of money he was rumored to have made, although businesses he owned did clear about $100 million a year during the peak years. He had as many as 2,500 employees across the country and many of them often received a share of the profits. In Oct. 1969, at age 52, Milner suffered a cerebral hemorrhage that totally incapacitated him. He spent much of the remaining part of his life fighting back, while his attorneys were busy selling off most of his empire. Dumas Milner died on Oct. 6, 1992, at the age of 75.

Crawford Mims

Born Mar. 21, 1933, in Carroll County, Mississippi. He played football at J.Z. George High School, then freshman football at Ole Miss in 1950 and went on the become an All-American lineman. Mims was All-Conference in 1951, All-American in 1953, Most Valuable Player in the North-South Shrine game in 1953, and in 1954 he played in the Senior Bowl and the 1954 College All-Star game. After graduating from Ole Miss in 1954, Mims was picked in the draft by the New York Giants, but couldn't go to camp because of a bad kidney bruise he had suffered in the All-Star game. He came home to Mississippi and coached on John Vaught's staff during 1955. Then Mims moved to Vicksburg and in 1960 started a chain of convenience stores called Shop-A-Minit. He was inducted into the Mississippi Sports Hall of Fame in 1995.

Hoyt Lester Ming

Born Oct 6, 1902, in Choctaw County near Ackerman, Miss. He played the fiddle and could perfectly imitate the fiddle with his voice. One of his fiddle and mouth-music tunes, *Indian War Whoop*, is in the Smithsonian Institute in Washington, D.C.. Ming's tune, *Rattle Snake Daddy*, was used as music in the soundtrack for the movie *Ode to Billy Joe* (filmed in Mississippi). Still making his home in Choctaw County at the time of his death, Ming died of a heart attack while making a public appearance in Attlala County on Apr. 28, 1985. Ming,

Profiles of Famous & Notable Mississippians

although the name sounds Chinese, was of German ancestry and the surname was originally spelled M-e-n-g.

The Mississippi Mass Choir

This group of 150 Mississippians is headquartered in Jackson and is led by Jerry Mannery. The group was formed in early 1988 by Frank Williams (1947-93, see profile), a member of the Jackson Southeraires. Their first album on Malaco Records, *Mississippi Mass Choir Live*, was certified the No. 1 Gospel Album in the nation by *Billboard* in the spring of 1989, just 5 weeks after its release. The album remained No. 1 on *Billboard's* chart for 45 consecutive weeks, setting a new record for a recording in any music genre. *Billboard* presented the choir with a special achievement award in 1991. Their 2nd album, *God Gets the Glory*, was the No. 1 gospel album by *Billboard* on Dec. 26, 1992, which also named it the 1992 Gospel Record of the Year. The group's third album, *It Remains to Be Seen*, was *Billboard's* No. 1 gospel album for 53 weeks, although not consecutive weeks. They recorded their 4th album, *I'll See You in The Rapture*, in Jan. 1996. At the time the group performed for Pope John Paul II at his summer home near Rome on Mar. 31, 1997, that album was in its 43rd week on *Billboard's* Top Gospel Albums chart. The album also received a 1997 Grammy nomination for Gospel Album by a Choir or Chorus. The group has toured Italy, France and Greece, where they were the first gospel group to sing at the ancient Acropolis! They've been nominated for the Soul-Train Music Awards and Dove Awards, plus the group and their albums have won many awards including both the Choir of the Year Award and Traditional Choir of the Year Award at the Stellar Awards in 1996. The group's latest album, *Emmanuel*, made its history-making worldwide premiere on the Internet on Aug. 5, 1999. Frank Williams/the Mississippi Mass Choir was one of the first 27 inducted into the inaugural Miss. Musicians Hall of Fame on April 1, 2000.

The Mississippi Sheiks

One of the classic string bands of the late 1920s and early '30s, this group featured the talents of Mississippians Walter Vinson, brothers Bo Carter and Sam Chatmon (see their profiles) plus Lonnie Chatmon. Both Carter and Sam also had successful solo careers, which occasionally prevented them from performing with the group. Formed in Jackson in 1926, the group took their name from the Rudolph Valentino movie *The Sheik*. Several years after they began performing, the group recorded their first session in 1930. Over the next five years, they cut nearly 70 songs. The Sheiks retained their popularity until the end of the 1930s when they disbanded.

Judith Paige Mitchell

Born Judith Segel (she later legally changed her name) on Nov. 24, 19??, in New Orleans, she spent her early years in Jackson, where she began her writing career as acclaimed novelist Paige Mitchell (her husband was well-known Jackson attorney, the late Al Binder). Her novels include *A Wilderness of Monkeys* (1965), *Love Is Not a Safe Country* (1967), *The Covenant* (1973), *Act of Love: The Killing of George Zygmanik* (1976) and *Wild Seed* (1982). Since 1985, she has lived in California, working as a screenwriter and producer for Lorimar and Warner Brothers. She has written scripts for several TV movies, including *The Client*, based on the novel by John Grisham, *Young at Heart*, which starred Frank Sinatra and aired on CBS in 1995, and an ABC movie, *Dalva*.

Willie Mitchell

Born William Mitchell on Dec. 1, 1889, in Pleasant Grove, Panola County, he was Mississippi's first baseball legend. Pitching for Mississippi A&M College in 1909, Mitchell pitched an almost perfect game against LSU in Baton Rouge striking out 26 of 27 batters. That same year, he struck out a Texas League record 20 batters pitching for San Antonio in a game against Galveston. He then joined the Cleveland Indians to become the first Mississippian to play in the major leagues. His major league debut was on Sept. 22, 1909. He made four American League All-Star teams and was the first pitcher to face Babe Ruth in an American League game. He struck out the Babe! He was inducted into the Mississippi Sports Hall of Fame in 1966 and inducted into the Mississippi State University Sports Hall of Fame in 1970. Mitchell died from a stroke in Sardis, Mississippi on Nov. 23, 1973, at age 83.

Willie Mitchell

Born Mar. 1, 1928, in Ashland, Miss. Influenced by Roy Eldridge and Harry James, Mitchell took up the trumpet at age eight and later became a very versatile: trumpeter, keyboardist, composer, arranger, producer and businessman. He went to Memphis at an early age. He formed his own band in 1954, which became the house band of Hi Records. He later became president of that record label. He signed Al Green to Hi in 1969 and produced Green's records. Willie Mitchell had a successful recording career of his own during the mid-1960s. From the 1950s to the mid-1960s, he had a string of hits — mostly blues/R&B/soul dance numbers — during the middle and late 1960s, when he became extremely popular on college campuses. He had two Top-40 hit single records *20-75* (#31 in 1964) [title refers to the record's label number] and *Soul Serenade* (#23 in 1968), and has cut over 20 albums.

Mary Ann Mobley

Born Feb. 17, 1939, in Biloxi, she grew up in Brandon, Miss. and graduated from Brandon High. She was then selected as the first Carrier Scholar to Ole Miss. Mobley won the 1959 Miss America crown by singing an aria from *Madame Butterfly* and the pop hit *There'll Be Some Changes Made*. The first and best known of the four Miss Americas from Mississippi, her score from the judges was the highest ever voted a Miss America, up until that time. One of the most popular and most successful Miss Americas, she is the only Miss America ever to achieve success in some many fields — personal appearances, Broadway, film, TV, and as a documentary filmmaker. Within a year, Mobley was a featured vocalist on the CBS-TV variety series, *Be Our Guest*. Shortly after finishing her year as Miss America, she made her Broadway debut in the play *Nowhere to Go But Up*. She also appeared in off-Broadway productions of *The King and I*, *Oklahoma*, *Cabaret*, and *Hello, Dolly*. She went to Hollywood in the early 1960s where she danced & sang with Elvis Presley in back-to-back MGM movie musicals, *Girl Happy* (1965) and *Harum Scarum* (1965). In TV, Mobley was a guest on virtually every prime-time dramatic series of the 1960s. She later played a recurring role on the ABC daytimer *General Hospital*, and in 1985 replaced Dixie Carter in the part of Conrad Bain's wife on the weekly sitcom *Diff'rent Strokes*. She was also the first *Girl From U.N.C.L.E.* when she appeared in the pilot episode titled *The Moon Glow Affair*. In a 1999 reader poll conducted by *The Clarion-Ledger*, Mary Ann was selected as the favorite and all-time best Miss Mississippi. She received 217 votes out of more than 470 cast. Mary Ann is active for many charitable causes. She and longtime husband, Emmy-winning actor Gary Collins, were married in Brandon.

Ethel Wright Mohamed

Born Oct. 13, 1907, at Fame in Webster Co., Miss. Often called the Grandma Moses of stitchery, she sewed her pictures with intricate, colorful stitches. Her work appears in a

permanent collection at the Smithsonian in Washington, D.C. She received numerous awards and including the 1991 Governor's Lifetime Achievement Award for "Excellence in the Arts." Many of her works can be seen at a museum, in a display called "Mama's Dream World," at her homeplace in Belzoni. She died of cancer on Feb. 15, 1992, at the age of 84.

Bilbo "Mule" Monaghan

Born on June 23, 1910, in Amory, Miss. Monaghan lost his hearing when he was 5 because of measles. He went to the Mississippi School for the Deaf and Dumb (later the Mississippi School for the Deaf) when he was 12 years old. He read every book he could get his hands on and finished high school when he was only 15. He also worked hard at sports. He played all sports at MSDD, was a four-sport letterman at Gallaudet University in Washington, D.C. and is a Hall of Fame member at both schools. Monaghan was only the second MSDD graduate to receive a college degree, graduating from Gallaudet in 1932. Then, he became the first deaf player to play a full year of pro football. At Memphis, he played end and returned interceptions 75 and 85 yards for TDs to highlight his one and only professional season. After the year of pro ball, Monaghan returned to MSDD to teach and coach. His coaching career spanned from 1933-46, all at MSD, where the best and most popular sport was basketball. Bilbo's 1938 team made the state semifinals for just the second time in school history. Against deaf schools in the South, his teams lost only once in 13 years. Even against hearing schools, MSD held its own. A man of many talents, Monagahn was a woodworker, wrote poetry, operated a Linotype at the Memphis *Commercial Appeal* (they say he was the best), and was a master printer who worked for the Government Printing Office in Washington, D.C. for 6 years. He served as president of the Mississippi Association for the Deaf and he and his wife, Kathryn, are generally recognized as the first deaf parents in America to legally adopt hearing children. They adopted daughters Sharon and Patricia in 1951. Monaghan died on Feb. 10, 1994, at age 83 from pneumonia. He was inducted into the Mississippi Sports Hall of Fame in 1996.

Hernando De Soto Money

Born Aug. 26, 1839, in Zeiglerville, which at the time was in Holmes County, Mississippi (Zeiglerville would later be in Yazoo County). In his early childhood, his family moved to Carrollton, Carroll County, Mississippi. Money received his early education in the public schools and from a private tutor, then graduated from the law department of the University of Mississippi at Oxford. Admitted to the bar, he began his practice in Carrollton about 1860. He served in the Confederate Army throughout the Civil War. He returned to Carrollton and edited the *Conservative* newspaper, then moved to Winona, Montgomery County, Mississippi, and edited the *Winona Advance* from 1873-1875. Money was the mayor of Winona in 1873 and 1874. He was elected as a Democrat to the 44th Congress and to the four succeeding Congresses and served from March 4, 1875 to March 3, 1885. He declined to be a candidate for renomination in 1884. He was chairman of the Committee on Post Office and Post Roads in the 46th and 48th Congresses. He engaged in the practice of law in Washington, D.C., until 1891, when he returned to Carrollton, Mississippi. Money was elected to the 53rd and 54th Congresses and served from March 4, 1893 to March 3, 1897. In January 1896, he was elected as a Democrat to the United States Senate for the term starting March 4, 1899. During that term, he was appointed and subsequently elected to the U.S. Senate to fill the vacancy caused by the death of James Z. George (see profile). He was reelected in 1906 and served from Oct. 8, 1897, to March 3, 1911. Money was minority leader in the Senate from 1909 to 1911. He declined to be a candidate for reelection and returned to his home near Biloxi, Mississippi, where he died on Sept. 18, 1912. He is buried in the family vault at Carrollton, Mississippi.

G.V. "Sonny" Montgomery

Born Gillespie Montgomery in Meridian on Aug. 5, 1920. During military service in World War II, he adopted the middle initial V. (which stands for nothing in particular, although it's been said he picked it for "Victory") because he was tired of putting N.M.I. — No Middle Initial — on forms he had to fill out. He attended the public schools in Meridian and the McCallie Military School in Chattanooga, Tennessee. He graduated from Mississippi State College (later Mississippi State University) in Jan. 1943. On Feb.3, 1943, he became an Army private and in less than three months was commissioned a 2nd lieutenant. His unit served in France and Germany during the end of WW II. Montgomery received the Bronze Star, the European Theater Ribbon, and a Commendation Ribbon. During the Korean War, Montgomery was called to duty as commander of a tank company in the Mississippi National Guard's 31st Dixie Division, but didn't have to go overseas. He was elected to the Mississippi Senate in Nov. 1955, where he served for ten years with a perfect attendance record. One of his major accomplishments was the introduction of legislation creating the Mississippi Authority for Educational Television. In Nov. 1966, he was elected as a Democrat to the U.S. House of Representatives from what then the state's 4th District for the first of his 15 two-year terms in Congress, serving in the 90th through the 104th Congresses from Jan. 3, 1967 until Jan. 3, 1997. He was chairman of the Select Committee on Military Involvement in Southeast Asia in the 91st Congress, the Select Committee on Missing in Action in Southeast Asia in the 94th Congress, and the Committee on Veterans' Affairs in the 97th through the 103rd Congresses. In 1970, he became president of the Congressional Prayer Breakfast Group. In Dec. 1970, he was assigned a seat on the House Armed Services Committee. In Dec. 1980, Montgomery became chairman of the House Veterans Committee and held that position until Republicans won a majority in the House in the 1994 elections. With Republicans as the congressional majority in Jan. 1995, Montgomery became the ranking Democrat on the Veterans Affairs Committee. In Jan. 1981, he retired from the Mississippi National Guard after 35 years of service. In Aug. 1981, the G.V. Montgomery National Guard Complex in Meridian was dedicated and the congressman was promoted to the rank of major general in the Guard during those ceremonies. Of his many achievements in Congress, he is proudest of the Montgomery GI Bill which President Reagan signed into law in Oct. 1984. Montgomery was the first member of Congress to lead the House of Representatives in the Pledge of Allegiance when it became a part of daily operations on Sept. 13, 1988. In June 1995, the Federal Base Closure Committee spared Columbus Air Force Base and Meridian NAS — another victory for Montgomery and other congressional delegation members who fought hard to keep the bases open. In 1995, he was presented the Defense Department Medal for Distinguished Service, the agency's highest civilian award. Montgomery did not seek re-election in 1996 and Republican Chip Pickering was elected to fill his congressional seat. On Veterans Day, Nov. 11, 1996, about 1,000 officials, veterans and friends gathered in Jackson to rename the Veterans Affairs

Profiles of Famous & Notable Mississippians

Medical Center the G.V. "Sonny" Montgomery VA Medical Center. Some of the many places and things named after him: a gymnasium at Naval Air Station Meridian; a housing complex at Columbus Air Force Base; a meeting room at the headquarters of the National Guard Association of the U.S. in Washington; a lock on the Tennessee-Tombigbee Waterway, about 12 miles north of Fulton; and an industrial park east of Meridian. On Dec. 12, 1996, He received the Army's Distinguished Civilian Service Award, the highest honor the Army bestows on a civilian. Montgomery, "Mr. Veteran," retired after Jan. 3, 1997, his last official day as Third District congressman. He received many special awards and honors in 1997: on Feb. 20, the Mississippi State Society of Daughters of the American Revolution, which has about 5,000 members in 80 chapters around the state, awarded Montgomery its highest honor, the Medal of Honor; on Dec. 17, he was presented with the Air Force 50th anniversary Pioneer Award, one of only 4 presented nationwide; and on Dec. 20, he received the 1997 Liberty Bowl Distinguished Citizen Award. Past recipients include Danny Thomas, Bear Bryant and Elvis Presley. He is owner of Montgomery Insurance Agency and vice president of the Greater Mississippi Life Insurance Company, both in Meridian. Montgomery's papers are preserved in the Mitchell Memorial Library on the campus at Mississippi State University in Starkville. In a *Clarion-Ledger* Millennium poll released Oct. 25, 1999, readers voted Montgomery the state's second all-time favorite politician, behind only the late John C. Stennis. Montgomery received 106 votes, only 19 less than Stennis. Even though he is retired from public office, he still champions rights for veterans.

Wilbert N. Montgomery

Born Sept. 16, 1954, in Greenville. He went to Jackson State where he was a teammate of Walter Payton for a short while. Also a running back, being in Payton's shadow was just too much for Montgomery, so he signed with Abilene Christian College. The first time he was handed the ball at Abilene, he ran it in for a touchdown. He went on to score 37 TDs as a freshman at that school. Montgomery scored an NAIA record 76 TDs while at Abilene Christian. He went pro with the Philadelphia Eagles and played in two Super Bowls. He rushed for more than 1,200 yards three times with the Eagles. Montgomery became one of the 608 members of the College Football Hall of Fame on Aug. 17, 1996, the same day Payton was inducted. He now divides his time between his sales job and his radio/TV duties with the Philadelphia Eagles.

Anne Moody

A writer and Civil Rights activist born Sept. 15, 1940, in Centreville, Wilkinson Co., Miss. She attended Natchez Junior College and received a B.S. from Tougaloo College. While at Tougaloo College, she worked with the NAACP, CORE (Congress of Racial Equality) and SNCC (Student Non-Violent Coordinating Committee), culminating in her personal involvement in the integration of Woolworth's lunch counter in Jackson. Her first book, *Coming of Age in Mississippi* (1968), received the American Library Association Best Book of the Year Award, the Gold Medal Award from the National Council of Catholics and Jews, and a rave review from Senator Edward Kennedy writing for the *New York Times*. She also received the silver medal from *Mademoiselle* magazine for her short story *New Hopes for the Seventies*. Her other works include *Dial, 1969*, and *Mr. Death: Four Stories*. Moody also has sound recordings of her novel *Mr. Death* and her short story *Bobo*. *Coming of Age In Mississippi*, with over 30 printings, has become a classic used as a high school and college textbook throughout the world, and has been translated into seven languages. Moody now lives in New York City.

Archie Moore

Born Archibald Lee Wright on Dec. 13, 1913, in Benoit, Bolivar Co., Mississippi. Moore became a world-champion boxer whose nickname was "The Mongoose." He won his first professional fight when he was 23 years old with a decision over Murray Allen in Quincy, Illinois. He first won the light heavyweight title at age 39 with a victory over Joey Maxim. He successfully defended his title nine times, but along the way lost to heavyweight champs Rocky Marciano, Floyd Patterson and Muhammad Ali. Moore was the only boxer to ever fight both Marciano and Ali. He was the last man to fight Marciano, and that was on Sept. 21, 1955. Moore floored Marciano in the second round, but Maricano wore him down and won on a ninth-round knockout. He held the light heavyweight title for 11 years with a career record of 195-25-8, knocking out 141 opponents (the record for KOs) in 228 bouts, according to the *Boxing Record Book*. Other sources list his knockout total at 145, while others say it was 129. Moore retired in 1963 at age 49 after a 27-year boxing career. Fighting in an era when fixed fights were not uncommon, Moore told *Sports Illustrated* in a 1969 interview that he never took a dive. He was inducted into the International Boxing Hall of Fame on June 10, 1990. Moore had some minor roles in a few movies, most notably as "Jim" in *The Adventures of Huckleberry Finn* (1960), "Jedediah" in *The Carpetbaggers* (1964), as "Mr. Jackson" in *Fortune Cookie* (1966), as "Parkard" in *The Outfit* (1973) and as "Carlos" in the Charles Bronson western *Breakheart Pass* (1976). Moore died in San Diego on Dec. 9, 1998, just 4 days before his 85th birthday. His body was cremated and his urn is on display at Cypress View Mausoleum in San Diego, Calif.

Dorothy Moore

Pop-Soul singer born Oct. 13, 1947, in Jackson, Mississippi. While attending Jackson State University, Dorothy and two high school friends formed The Poppies. Their single, *Lullaby of Love* on Epic Records made the top 40 charts in 1966. After a short time with other labels, Dorothy united with Malaco Records in 1975 and recorded *Misty Blue*, one of 1976's biggest international hits. This gold record topped the charts in the U.S., Canada and the United Kingdom. There was renewed interest and sales of the song when it was prominently featured in the 1996 movie *Phenomenon* starring John Travolta. So much so, in fact, that it prompted Malaco to release a new compilation album, *Misty Blue and Other Greatest Hits*. Moore's other memorable tunes include *With Pen In Hand*, *I Believe You* and *Funny How Time Slips Away*. She's has 10 albums including *Stay Close to Home* (1993) and *More Moore* (1996). She received Grammy nominations for both *Misty Blue* and *I Believe You*. Actually, this "Sweetheart of Rhythm and Blues" has won two Grammys out of five nominations. She won *Billboard* magazine's 1976 No. 1 Female R&B Vocalist Award, the NATRA Female R&B Vocalist of the Year award, the NAACP Image Award and many other awards. Moore received the Artist's Achievement Award of the 1996 Governor's Awards for Excellence in the Arts.

Johnny Moore (see John Daniel "J.D." Evermore)

McKinley Morganfield (see "Muddy Waters")

Willie Morris

William Weaks Morris was born Nov. 29, 1934, in Jackson, he grew up in Yazoo City, Misssissippi from age six. In high school, he was editor of the school newspaper and played football, basketball, and baseball. He was voted most versatile,

Profiles of Famous & Notable Mississippians

wittiest, and most likely to succeed. Morris graduated class valedictorian at Yazoo City High School in 1952. He was editor of the school paper, *The Daily Texan*, at the University of Texas and was elected *Phi Beta Kappa*. He graduated there with a degree in English in 1956. Morris received a Rhodes Scholarship and studied modern history at New College in England until 1960. He was editor of the *Texas Observer* in Austin, Texas from 1960-63. He started work for *Harper's Magazine* in New York in 1963 and became editor-in-chief in 1967 at age 32, the youngest editor ever of the nation's oldest magazine. Morris resigned from *Harper's* in 1971 in an editorial dispute. Morris lived in Oxford for a time starting in 1980 as writer-in-residence at the University of Mississippi. Morris wrote 19 books: Nonfiction — *North Toward Home* (1967), *Yazoo, Integration in a Deep Southern Town* (1971), *A Southern Album: Recollections of Some People and Places and Times Gone By* (1975), *James Jones: A Friendship* (1978), *The Courting of Marcus Dupree* (1983), *Faulkner's Mississippi* (1990), *New York Days* (1993), *My Dog Skip* (1995), *The Ghosts of Medgar Evers: A Tale of Race, Murder, Mississippi, and the Movies* (1998) and *My Cat Spit McGee* (1999, released after his death); Fiction — *The Last of the Southern Girls* (1973); Essay Collections — *The South Today: 100 Years After Appomattox* (1965), *Terrains of the Heart and other Essays on Home* (1981), *Always Stand in Against the Curve and Other Sports Stories* (1983), *Homecomings* (1989), *My Two Oxfords* (1992), and *After All, It's Just a Game* (1992); Books for Children — *Good Ole Boy: A Delta Boyhood* (1971), and *Good Ole Boy and the Witch of Yazoo* (1989). *Good Old Boy: A Delta Boyhood* was made into a movie released in 1988, then re-released in 1994 as *The River Pirates*. The movie, *My Dog Skip*, based on Morris' book about his childhood in Yazoo City, was filmed in the spring of 1998 in Canton, Jackson and Yazoo City. Released nationwide in Mar. 2000, it did vary well at the box office. Morris received the Governor's Award for Excellence in the Arts in 1994. At the Natchez Literary Festival in 1996 he received the third annual Richard Wright Medal for Literary Excellence. Morris wrote the introductory essay, *A Prayer Before the Feast*, for the official souvenir program of Atlanta's Centennial Olympic Games of 1996. In a 1999 poll by *The Clarion-Ledger*, readers picked Morris as their No. 1 favorite nonfiction writer. He had lived in Jackson since 1990. Literary genius Willie Morris died of a heart attack on Aug. 2, 1999, at the age of 64. Reaction to the writer's death came from many quarters, including the White House. President Clinton issued the statement, "Hillary and I were greatly saddened by the death of our good friend. Willie Morris was not only my friend, he was a national treasure." Public visitation was on Aug. 5 in the Rotunda of the Old Capitol Museum. Morris was the first to lie in state there since Senator John C. Stennis in 1995. The memorial service that followed that day at First United Methodist Church in Yazoo City was attended by over 400 people. The service was led by the Rev. Will D. Campbell, minister, author and activist. Others there eulogizing Morris were former U.S. Agriculture Secretary Mike Espy, former Governor William Winter, and former Ole Miss football coach Billy Brewer. The "power crowd" also included film producers Fred Zollo (*Mississippi Burning, Ghosts of Misssissippi*) and Mark Johnson (*Rain Man, My Dog Skip*), plus a host of authors — Richard Ford (*Independence Day*), Marshall Frady (*Jesse Jackson: A Biography, Wallace*), Kaye Gibbons (*A Virtuous Woman*), John Grisham (*A Time To Kill*), Winston Groom (*Forrest Gump*), David Halberstam (*The Powers That Be*), Josephine Haxton (pen name Ellen Douglas), and William Styron (*Sophie's Choice*). Willie was buried in Glenwood Cemetery in Yazoo City, just 13 paces south of the grave of the witch he immortalized in his book, *Good Old Boy and The Witch of Yazoo*. The gravesite is close to the front entrance in the center (Plot I-Odd Fellows) of the old part of the cemetery. The University of Mississippi dedicated its seventh annual Oxford Conference for the Book held in April 2000 to Morris. The book, *Conversations with Willie Morris*, compiled and edited by Jack Bales, was released by University Press in May.

Davis K. Mortensen

Born Apr. 25, 1932, in Charles City, Iowa, his parents moved to Jackson County, Mississippi when he was one year old. They lived in the small community of Harleston until 1941, then moved to Moss Point, Mississippi. Mortensen enrolled at Mississippi State in 1954 with the aid of the GI Bill after two years at Mississippi Gulf Coast Community College. After receiving his degree in 1956, he began his career with Alcoa Aluminum in East Tennessee as an industrial engineer. He became associated with the giant Fortune 500 company, Georgia-Pacific, in 1962 while working in Arkansas. Georgia-Pacific, the world's largest forest products company, is a significant player in Mississippi's economy. It employs 4,000 people, operates 21 production facilities, 2 distribution centers and has offices or facilities in Bay Springs, Centreville, Columbia, Eupora, Gloster, Grenada, Hattiesburg, Jackson, Louisville, Monticello, New Augusta, Oxford, Roxie, and Taylorsville. G-P's investment in Mississippi totals over $1.2 billion. Georgia-Pacific owns 800,000 acres of timberland in Mississippi. Mortensen rose through corporate ranks until he became executive vice president of building products for G-P in Atlanta, Georgia in 1989. In this position, Mortensen was responsibility for almost half of G-P's 52,000 employees, the company's six million acres of timber holdings, manufacturing facilities, and the sales/distribution of products the company manufactures. In 1989, Mortensen received Georgia-Pacific's coveted Distinguished Service Award. He is proud of his safety record. During Mortensen's tenure, Georgia-Pacific led the forest products industry with the lowest Occupational Safety and Health Administration incident rate in the U.S. from 1993 through 1997, the year Mortensen retired from the company. He currently lives in Georgia.

Alice Moseley

Born Dec, 21, 1909, in Birmingham, Alabama. After marriage, she moved to the Batesville, Mississippi area, where she taught school for many years. She has lived at Bay St. Louis since late 1988. This painter's work, described as "idyllic" folk art, has received much acclaim in Mississippi and elsewhere. Her best-known painting is probably *The House is Blue But the Old Lady Ain't*. She has appeared on WLOX-TV in Biloxi and the Mississippi Educational TV network, talking about her art. Recent articles about her have appeared in national publications, such as *Southwest Airlines Magazine* and *Traveling Leisure Magazine*. The children's playroom at Hancock Memorial Hospital, where about 30 of her prints are hanging, was dedicated in her name in late 1998.

Eric Moulds

Born July 17, 1973, in Lucedale, Miss. Moulds ranks third on Mississippi State's career receiving list with 118 catches for 2,022 yards. His 17.1 yards average per catch ranks sixth on the school's all-time list. With the NFL Buffalo Bills, he had a good rookie year in 1996, highlighted by 2 TD receptions as he caught 20 passes for 279 yards (14.0 avg.). In 1997, he played in all 16 games and made 8. Moulds received a game

Profiles of Famous & Notable Mississippians

ball for his special teams play at Detroit on Oct. 5 when he set up the Bills first TD with a 53-yard KOR. He set the Bills receiving record in 1998 with 1,368 yards! He was among 7 Mississippi players picked for the 1999 Pro Bowl in Honolulu. This wide receiver's pro career stats through Oct. 29, 2000, shows 3,767 receiving yards on 240 receptions and 22 TDs and 2,126 yards on 95 kickoff returns in 70 games played.

"Muddy Waters"

This legendary bluesman was born McKinley Morganfield on April 4, 1915, at Rolling Fork, Mississippi, where he was discovered in 1940 by folk music archivists Alan Lomax and John Work. Raised in the Delta in Clarksdale, where he began to sing, compose and play the blues. Moving to Chicago, he made his first recordings in 1941, including *I Can't Be Satisfied*. Beginning in the late 50s, his band appeared at the folk and jazz festivals of Newport, Rhode Island, and Monterey, California. In the 1950s & 60s, he had over a dozen hits including *She Moves Me* (1952), *Caledonia, Baby Please Don't Go, Mannish Boy, Hoochie-Coochie Man, Just make Love To You, Rolling Stone* and *Got My Mojo Workin'*. He became known as the "Father of electric blues." A songwriter as well as guitarist and singer, he led his band on numerous recordings including *They Call Me Muddy Waters* (1971) and *London Sessions* (1972), both of which won Grammys. He won 6 Grammy awards. Bluesmen Little Walter, Jimmy Rogers, Junior Wells, James Cotton and Buddy Guy all played in Waters' band. His songs have been sung by the Rolling Stones and other rockers. In a serious car accident in 1973, but went on a short, but well-received U.S. tour in 1977 and cut a comeback album produced by albino blues guitarist Johnny Winter (born in Leland, Miss.). He was inducted into the Rock and Roll Hall of Fame in 1986. Four of Muddy's songs, *Got My Mojo Working, Hoochie Coochie Man, Mannish Boy* and *Rollin' Stone*, are included on the Rock and Roll Hall of Fame's list of 500 Songs That Shaped Rock And Roll. In 1994, the Postal Service issued stamps commemorating eight "Legends of Blues and Jazz," including Waters and Mississippians Howlin' Wolf and Robert Johnson. He died in Westmont, Ill. on Apr. 30, 1983, and is buried in the Restvale Cemetery (Section H, right by the office) in Worth, Illinois.

Dot Murphy

Dorothy Easterwood was born on Sept. 20, 1952, in Jackson. She was a standout basketball player at Starkville High School and at Mississippi University for Women. She averaged 33 points per game during high school, a performance that helped Starkville to two state basketball championships. At MUW, she was All-America and made the World University Games in 1973, the highest level of competition for women's basketball at the time. Dot has been an assistant coach of *football*, that's right, football, at Hinds Community College at Raymond, Mississippi since 1984, and an assistant football coach to her husband, Gene Murphy (b. Oct. 1, 1954 in Columbus, Miss.), at Hinds since 1987. Dot is the first full-time female assistant football coach on the collegiate level in the U.S. The teams the Murphys have coached have captured five state and regional championships since 1987 and 22 of their players have been drafted by the NFL. The Murphys have been featured in *Sports Illustrated* and other national magazines. They were on NBC's *Today Show* and the *NFL/TNT Football America* TV program on which they were featured won an Emmy! Dot was honored by Outstanding Women of America once in 1974 for playing basketball and again in 1986 for coaching football. Dot was inducted into the Mississippi Sports Hall of Fame in 1999.

Matt "Guitar" Murphy

Born Dec. 29, 1927, in Sunflower, Miss. Blues legend Willie Dixon called Matt the best blues guitar player! Murphy was a sideman with Memphis Slim and Bobby Bland. A band member with the Blues Brothers, he had a memorable scene with Aretha Franklin in *The Blues Brothers* movie (1980).

Charlie Musselwhite

This blues harmonica player was born Jan. 31, 1944, in Kosciusko, Miss., grew up in Memphis from age 3, then went to Chicago in the early 1960s. His debut album was *Stand Back, Here Comes Charlie Musselwhite's South Side Blues Band* on Vanguard. He also made recordings in the late 1980s & early 90s for Alligator Records. He is a Grammy nominee and a six-time W.C. Handy Blues Award winner from the Blues Foundation of Memphis, the latest in 1999. Musselwhite received the Artist's Achievement Award of the 2000 Governor's Awards for Excellence in the Arts. The late Big Joe Williams once said, "Charlie Musselwhite is one of the greatest living harp players of country blues. He is right up there with Sonny Boy Williamson (I), and he's been my harp player ever since Sonny Boy got killed."

Buddy Myer

Born Charles Solomon Myer on Mar. 16, 1904, in Ellisville, Mississippi. He made his major league baseball debut on Sept. 26, 1925, with the Washington Nationals and stayed with them until 1941, except for 2 seasons with the Boston Red Sox (1927-28). He played in the 1925 and 1933 World Series and in 2 All-Star games in 1935 and 1937. His career stats include 2,131 hits in 7,038 at bats (.303 batting avg.), 1,174 runs, 38 home runs and 850 RBIs in 1,923 games played. He was inducted into the Mississippi Sports Hall of Fame in 1971 and the Mississippi State University Sports Hall of Fame in 1972. Myer died Oct. 31, 1974, in Baton Rouge, Louisiana at age 70.

Louis Myers

Born Sept. 18, 1929, at Byhalia, Miss. A member of Little Walter's band, the Aces, Myers was one of the blues' finest guitar and harp players. Louis moved to Chicago with his family in 1941. As fate would have it, the family moved next door to blues great Lonnie Johnson, whose complex riffs caught young Louis's ear. Myers also played with guitarist Arthur "Big Boy" Spires before teaming with his brother David on guitar and young harpist Junior Wells to form the Aces (who were initially known as the Three Deuces). Little Walter, just breaking nationally with his classic *Juke*, moved into the front man role with the Aces. Myers and the Aces backed Walter on his seminal *Mean Old World, Sad Hours, Off the Wall*, and *Tell Me Mama* and at New York's famous Apollo Theater before Louis left in 1954. Myers also played with Otis Rush, Earl Hooker, and many more. But his own recording career was practically non-existent, except for a few singles, including *Just Whaling/Bluesy* (1956). The Aces reformed during the 1970s and visited Europe often as a trusty rhythm section for touring acts. Myers cut a fine set for Advent in 1978, *I'm a Southern Man*. Myers suffered a stroke while recording his last album for Earwig, 1991's *Tell My Story Movin'*. He completed the disc but was limited to playing only harp. He died on Sept. 5, 1994, in Chicago at age 64.

Pamela Nail

Born Aug. 6, 1962, in Crawfordsville, Indiana, she grew up in Baton Rouge, Louisiana. She was Miss Louisiana in 1983. Nail has lived in Jackson, Mississippi since 1985. She was Mrs. Mississippi 1987 and was also Mrs. America 1987. She won the title of Mrs. World 1988 in Australia, and is the only American to have ever won Mrs. World!

Profiles of Famous & Notable Mississippians

Ellis Nassour

Born Oct. 25, 1941, in Vicksburg. From the time he was in fifth grade, when anyone asked "What will you do when you grow up?", Ellis replied "Work for the *New York Times*." He prepared himself for the task by earning a bachelor's degree in journalism from the University of Mississippi in 1964 and a master's in journalism from Columbia University in 1966. Later, Ellis was touring the *New York Times* when, by chance, he met Turner Catledge, a native of Philadelphia, Mississippi, who was managing editor. Catledge offered him a job. He started off at the bottom as a copy boy and worked his way to reporter, covering metropolitan, family, style, foreign, UN, photo and finally culture news, where he wrote extensively about the arts. In 1970, Ellis met the young composer Andrew Lloyd Webber and lyricist Tim Rice from England, who told him they were writing an opera about Jesus. Ellis felt it would be epic, and so pitched their idea to music industry executives. This resulted in Webber and Rice coming to the states where Ellis joined them in the development of the landmark musical production *Jesus Christ Superstar*. Ellis' experiences from this resulted in his first book, *Rock Opera: The Creation of Jesus Christ Superstar* (1973). While working for Universal Studios/MCA from 1970-73, Ellis introduced then unknown Elton John in his American debut and first U.S. tour. Ellis also did press and public relations work for Rick Nelson, Millie Jackson, Gloria Gaynor, The Who, Neil Diamond, Bill Cosby, Brenda Lee, Conway Twitty and Loretta Lynn. His friendship with Lynn resulted in numerous stories about her friend, the late Patsy Cline, whom Ellis wrote about in a series of 1979-80 magazine articles. These pieces were the basis for his first Patsy Cline bio, *Patsy Cline: An Intimate Biography* (1981). Interviews Ellis conducted with Jackson, Mississippi native Louise Seger contained in that book would be the basis for the later hit musical revue, *Always, Patsy Cline*. Besides working as a ghost writer on celebrity books and an international entertainment freelance journalist for such publications as the *New York Times*, the *Daily News* and the *London Times*, Ellis did media consultant work with such stars as Mae West, Bette Davis and Joan Crawford. His third book was *Honky Tonk Angel: the Intimate Story of Patsy Cline* (1993). That book has been adapted by Ellis into the stage musical *Honky Tonk Angel*, with the Patsy Cline classics and an original score by George Leonard and Ellis. He was associate editor (music, film and theater) and contributing editor for *American National Biography* (1999), a multi-volume set published by Oxford University Press. Ellis is now at work on his first novel, *The Scent of Magnolia*, which is set against a Vicksburg, Mississippi backdrop.

Frances E. Neal

Born June 27, 1921, in Carrollton, Miss. This actress was in only four films: *Lady Scarface*, playing "Ann Rogers" ('41); *Citizen Kane*, uncredited for the role of "Ethel" ('41); *Powder Town*, playing "Carol" ('42); and *Come on Danger*, playing "Ann Jordan" ('42). But, she had a part (although not listed in the picture credits) in the top movie of all time — *Citizen Kane* — rated No. 1 on The American Film Institute's 1998 list of the Top 100 Greatest American Movies of All Time.

Ben Nelson

Born Aug. 1, 1944, in Canton, Miss. He received a liberal arts degree from Mississippi State in 1966. Today, he is one of the two PGA Tournament Directors. Nelson has been involved with the game of golf most of his life. His association with the PGA Tour came after a stint on the Mississippi State golf team, one year as an assistant pro at Vicksburg Country Club, and 19 years as the head professional and co-owner of Live Oaks Golf Club in Jackson. His reputation for knowing the rules of the game soon spread and in 1986 the PGA Tour called. After working part time for two years, Nelson became a full-time rules official for the PGA Tour in 1988 and was named Tournament Director of competitions in Sept. 1995. For 30 weeks out of the year, Nelson works PGA Tour events. During some 40-plus PGA Tour events each year, Nelson and the other rules officials are responsible for making sure that the game is played by the rules, and that play moves at an acceptable speed. The Tournament Director has additional responsibilities such as having the final word on all rules disputes and coordinating TV coverage. Nelson has worked every PGA Tour event at least once. He's also worked the Masters, the U.S. Open, the PGA Championship, the British Open, and the Ryder Cup, events recognized, but not directly sponsored by the PGA. Nelson was inducted into the Mississippi State University Sports Hall of Fame in 1997.

Jack Nelson

Born Oct. 11, 1929 in Talladega, Alabama, his family moved to Biloxi, Miss. when he was in eighth grade. He has served as Washington Bureau chief for *The Los Angeles Times* since the mid-1970s. One of Washington's foremost investigative and political reporters, his journalism career began at *The Atlanta Constitution* where he won a Pulitzer for Reporting in 1960 for a series exposing irregularities at a Georgia mental institution. He joined *The Los Angeles Times* in 1965 as chief of its Atlanta bureau, before being transferred to Washington. He has won a number of other distinguished prizes, including a Drew Pearson award in 1975 for investigative reporting. He's well-known to TV audiences, having been a regular on PBS's "Washington Week in Review" and other network appearances. He wrote the book *Terror In The Night* (1993), the story of how Jews in Jackson and Meridian, Mississippi worked with FBI agents to set a trap for a Klan terrorist bomber in 1968. In May 1999, Nelson received the Robert F. Kennedy Lifetime Achievement Award in Journalism.

Joseph W. Newman

Born Joseph Westly Rogers on July 2, 1936, in Mobile, Ala., he grew up in Lucedale, Miss. He claims about 40 inventions, of which 10 have received patents, such as plastic-covered barbells, an orange picker, an automatic rake, a vibrating electromagnetic fishing lure, and several other unusual devices. Newman is probably best known for his attempts to patent an "energy machine" that he says produces more power than it consumes. Since 1979, the U.S. Patent Office has continued to turn down his patent application, calling his machine a bogus perpetual motion device. Most physicists say his machine is impossible because it violates the second law of thermodynamics. Newman now lives in Scottsdale, Arizona.

Leedell W. Neyland

Born Leedell Wallace Neyland on Aug. 4, 1921, at Gloster, Amite County, Mississippi. This longtime resident of the state of Florida wrote *The History of Florida A&M University*.

Lewis Nordan

Born Aug. 23, 1939, in Itta Bena, Mississippi. Once a firecracker salesman, he now teaches at the University of Pittsburgh. He has also worked as a high school teacher, orderly, nightwatchman and clerk. After spending two years in the U.S. Navy, he received his B.A. from Millsaps College in Jackson, his M.A. from Mississippi State University, and his Ph.D. from Auburn University in Alabama. Dr. Jordan has received many awards since his first one in 1977 — the University of Arkansas's John Gould Fletcher Award for

Profiles of Famous & Notable Mississippians

fiction for his short story, *Rat Song*. A year later, he received a National Endowment for the Arts grant. All four of his novels, *Music of the Swamp* (1991), 1993's award-winning *Wolf Whistle*, *The Sharpshooter Blues* (1995) and *Lightning Song* (1997), are set in the Mississippi Delta with a cast of eccentric Southern characters. He has also written three collections of short stories, including *Welcome to the Arrow-Catcher Fair* (1983), *The All-Girl Football Team* (1986) and *Sugar Among the Freaks* (1996). Nordan took a turn at nonfiction to unload about his personal life with the release of his memoir, *Boy with Loaded Gun*, in the early part of 2000.

Willie "Ray-J" Norwood, Jr.
Born Jan. 17, 1981, in McComb, Mississippi, his family moved to Los Angeles in 1983. He made his TV debut in 1993 playing Little John on Fox Network's weekly sitcom *Sinbad*. Brother of R&B singer and actress Brandy.

Ralph Null
Born Apr. 2, 1946, in Lauderdale, Miss. An internationally recognized leader in the floral arts, he was with Mississippi State for 25 years, where he advanced to full professor and retired as Professor Emeritus. Listed in *Who's Who in America Colleges and Universities*, he's received many professional awards. His floral creations have graced state dinners and receptions for the past 4 U.S. Presidents, and the windows at Macy's Department Store. Photographs of his work have appeared in several national publications and in Neiman Marcus catalogues. He has judged national and international exhibitions and competitions and given more than 500 lectures and demonstrations throughout the U.S. including the Smithsonian Institute in Washington and in London, Cape Town, Tokyo, Sidney and other places around the globe. A frequent contributor to trade publications, he wrote *A Floral Guide to Successful Weddings. A Christmas Collection* (1995).

Carrie Nye
Born Caroline Nye McGeoy in 1937 in Greenwood, Miss. An actress, her first screen role was "Norine" in the movie *Group* in 1966. She also had supporting roles as: "Aldena Kittner" in *The Seduction of Joe Tynan* ('79); "Sylvia" in *Creepshow* ('82); "Grazietta" in *Too Scared to Scream* ('85); "Regina Holt" in *Hello Again* ('87) and a few other movies. She's been married to TV host/commentator Dick Cavett since 1964.

Frederick O'Neal
Born Aug. 27, 1905, in Brooksville, Noxubee Co., Miss., this black actor played Officer Wallace in the TV series *Car 54, Where Are You?* ('62) and was "Jacques Serac" in the TV movie *Strategy of Terror* ('69). His theatrical releases include *Pinky* ('49) as "Jake Walters," *Tarzan's Peril* ('51) as "King Bulam," *Something of Value* ('57) as "Adam Marenga," *Anna Lucasta* ('58) as "Frank"; *Take a Giant Step* ('59); *The Sins of Rachel Cade* ('60 as "Buderga"; and *Free, White and 21* ('63) playing "Ernie Jones." O'Neal died in New York City on Aug. 25, 1992, just two days before his 87th birthday.

Jack H. Oakman
Born on May 27, 1923, at Panther Burn, Sharkey County, Mississippi. He spent his childhood at Panther Burn and graduated from Hollandale High School in 1942. Oakman enrolled at Mississippi State University in Sept. 1942, but a few months later in Feb. 1943, he was called to active duty by the Army Air Corps for air cadet training. He was serving as a navigator of a B-17 Flying Fortress out of England when his plane was shot down in Nov. 1944. Oakman spent 6 months as a prisoner of war in several German P.O.W. camps during the last part of World War II. After the war, Oakman returned to Mississippi State and received his B.S. degree in agriculture in May 1949. After holding several positions in the field of agriculture, he started a career as an independent agricultural consultant in 1962. Oakman is considered an expert on southern agriculture and was elected to the Agricultural Consultants Hall of Fame in 1987. On the side, he's had a really interesting hobby. He has one of the largest collections of movie memorabilia in the South, which he's been collecting for over 30 years. Along with his hobby of collecting, he has become a film historian and has authored or co-authored articles on movies and also lectured about the subject at colleges. He has been active at film festivals since the early 1990s. His direct involvement in films include assisting with the production of two movies shot in Mississippi, *Heart of Dixie* (1989) and *The Gun in Betty Lou's Handbag* (1992). Oakman also appeared in those films as an extra and had roles as an extra in several other films, including *Miss Firecracker* (1989), *Great Balls of Fire* (1989), *The Firm* (1993), and *Separated by Murder* (1994). He was a Deacon in a church scene in the TV series *Young Elvis* (1990).

Falilatu Ogunkoya
Born in Ode-Lime, Nigeria, Africa on Dec. 5, 1968. She is a former track star at Mississippi State (class of 1992), where she holds the school records for the Indoor 55-Meter Dash (6.89 in '88), the Indoor 200-Meter Dash (23.89 in '88), the Indoor 400-Meter Dash (53.03 in '90), the Outdoor 100-Meter Dash (11.40 in '88), the Outdoor 200-Meter Dash (22.82 in '89) and the Outdoor 400-Meter Dash (51.26 in '89). She won the bronze medal in the 400-meter run at the 1996 Centennial Olympic Games in Atlanta. It was the first individual medal ever claimed by a Nigerian women. Ogunkoya went on to add a silver medal in the 4x400 relay. She was inducted into the MSU Sports Hall of Fame on Oct. 10, 1998.

George Ohr
Born George Edgar Ohr on July 12, 1857, in Biloxi. "The Mad Potter of Biloxi" was a tall man with white hair and 18-inch handlebar mustache who rode a motorcycle. This eccentric self-promoter proclaimed himself the "Greatest art potter on Earth." He was considered the town lunatic, but modern artists say his abstract work was decades ahead of its time. He could hardly give away his creations, but now one pot sells at upscale auction houses for more than Ohr earned in his lifetime. Ohr pots have sold for as much as $100,000 each. New Jersey antiques dealer, James Carpenter, purchased 7,000 pieces of Ohr's pottery in 1968 and offered it for sale in the New York area. Ohr's work astounded the art world. Not really mad, but egocentric, he knew acting "crazy" attracted tourists to his shop, the Pot-Ohr-E. He died in Biloxi on Apr. 7, 1918. The George E. Ohr Arts and Cultural Center, opened Oct. 22, 1994, in Biloxi and features more than 250 of his creations.

Milton L. Olive III
Born Milton Lee Olive III on Nov. 7, 1946, in Chicago, he grew up from about age 4 with his grandfather near Ebenezer, Holmes County, Mississippi. He had returned to Chicago when he entered the Army and his Congressional Medal of Honor is officially accredited to Illinois. Private First Class Olive was in the U.S. Army, Company B, 2d Battalion (Airborne), 503d Infantry, 173d Airborne Brigade in Phu Cuong, Republic of Vietnam when he performed an act of bravery on Oct. 22, 1965 that cost him his life. He was posthumously awarded the Congressional Medal of Honor by President Johnson at the White House on April 21, 1966. Here are the actual words of his citation: "For conspicuous gallantry and intrepidity at the risk of his life above and beyond the call of duty. Pfc. Olive was a member of the 3d Platoon of

Profiles of Famous & Notable Mississippians

Company B, as it moved through the jungle to find the Viet Cong operating in the area. Although the platoon was subjected to a heavy volume of enemy gunfire and pinned down temporarily, it retaliated by assaulting the Viet Cong positions, causing the enemy to flee. As the platoon pursued the insurgents, Pfc. Olive and 4 other soldiers were moving through the jungle together when a grenade was thrown into their midst. Pfc. Olive saw the grenade, and then saved the lives of his fellow soldiers at the sacrifice of his own by grabbing the grenade in his hand and falling on it to absorb the blast with his body. Through his bravery, unhesitating actions, and complete disregard for his safety, he prevented additional loss of life or injury to the members of his platoon. Pfc. Olive's extraordinary heroism, at the risk of his life above and beyond the call of duty are in the highest traditions of the U.S. Army and reflect great credit upon himself and the Armed Forces of his country." Olive was one of only two Mississippians to be awarded the Congressional Medal of Honor for service in the Vietnam War. The other, and only *native* Mississippian, was Roy M. Wheat of Hattiesburg. Olive was one of only two non-native Mississippians (of 6 Mississippians) to be awarded the CMOH posthumously. The other was James H. Diamond. In all wars, 17 Medals of Honor have been officially accredited to Mississippi, although we claim 5 more because the recipients had Mississippi ties (as is the case with Olive). Olive was one of 22 Mississippians (13 native Mississippians)[15 Army, 4 Marines & 3 Navy] in all wars to be awarded the CMOH out of 3,433 total recipients of the Medal through Nov. 1, 2000. Olive is buried in the West Grove Missionary Baptist Church Cemetery halfway between Ebenezer and Lexington in Holmes County, Mississippi. A Congressional Medal of Honor marker is on his grave.

Paul Ott

This entertainer and conservationist was born Paul Ott Holland on Sept. 25, 1934, in McComb and raised in Dixie Springs, Mississippi. His father died shortly after he was born and his mother remarried, so he then became Paul Ott Holland Carruth. Also a songwriter, his best known song is *Plant A Tree*. Another song, *Seeds of Life*, that Ott wrote for Yazoo City-based Mississippi Chemical Corp., is popular with grade-school children. He also wrote *Cotton Man* for the National Cotton Council of America. *I'm The South*, a 14 minute music-video, has been broadcast all over the world by Voice of America and Ott uses his *The American Farmer: Heart of Our Land* in a motivational program at conventions and other gatherings. Ott was previously a spokesman for the Mississippi Game and Fish Commission and the National Wildlife Federation and he is currently the host of a weekly TV and radio program produced by his own Listen to the Eagle Network. In March 1999, Ott announced that he had formed the Listen to the Eagle Outdoorsman's Association, an organization that will provide sportsmen a united front to protect the traditions and rights of hunters and fisherman. Paul Ott now lives in Dixie Springs, Mississippi.

Charles L. Overby

Born Sept 18, 1946 in Jackson, Mississippi. His journalism career began in high school as a part-time sports reporter in Jackson. He went on to work in various positions at newspapers in Nashville, Cocoa Beach, Florida, and Jackson. As a reporter, he covered the White House, presidential campaigns, Congress and the Supreme Court. He traveled over 100,000 miles with Jimmy Carter and Gerald Ford while covering the 1976 presidential campaign for Gannett News Service. When Gannett bought his hometown newspaper, he returned to Jackson as executive editor of *The Clarion-Ledger*. Overby was at the helm when the paper was awarded the 1983 Pulitzer Prize for Distinguished Public Service for its coverage of Mississippi's education reform act, which led to public kindergartens and a major upgrading of education standards. Overby worked for 16 years as reporter, editor and corporate executive for the Gannett Company, the nation's largest newspaper company with over 39,000 employees and $5.1 billion in operating revenue in 1998. He was vice president for news and communications for Gannett and served on the management committees of Gannett and *USA TODAY*. He was named president and CEO of the Gannett Foundation in 1989. The foundation was renamed The Freedom Forum in 1991. He became chairman and CEO in 1997. The Freedom Forum is an independent, nonpartisan foundation dedicated to First Amendment and media issues. The foundation, with more than $1 billion in assets, is one of the nation's largest. Overby oversees The Freedom Forum's offices and programs on five continents. He is also chairman and chief executive officer of two affiliate organizations, the $50 million Newseum, a state-of-the-art museum of news that is Washington, D.C.'s newest major tourist attraction, and the Freedom Forum First Amendment Center at Vanderbilt University in Nashville, Tennessee. Overby has served two stints in government. He was press assistant to Sen. John Stennis, D-Mississippi, and special assistant for administration to Gov. Lamar Alexander, R-Tennessee. Overby serves on the Board of Regents of Baylor University and is a member of the foundation board of the University of Mississippi, his alma mater. Overby and his wife, Andrea, received honorary doctorates from Mississippi University for Women in the spring of 2000.

Paul Overstreet

Born Mar. 17, 1955, in Newton, he grew up in Vancleave, Miss. His own hits include *Heroes* and *Ball and Chain*. He had a No. 1 country hit with the group Schuyler, Knobloch & Overstreet, *Baby's Got a New Baby* (1986). He had another No. 1 country hit with Tanya Tucker and Paul Davis, *I Won't Take Less Than Your Love* (1987). One of the most successful writers in country music, Overstreet wrote *Same Ole Me*, a No. 5 hit by George Jones in 1982. Overstreet co-wrote *Diggin' Up Bones* ('85), *On The Other Hand* ('86) and *Forever and Ever, Amen* ('87), all No. 1 hits for Randy Travis, the latter winning him and co-writers, Randy Travis and Don Schlitz, a Grammy Songwriter Award in 1987 for Best Country Song. He shared the Grammy Best Country Song Award in 1991 with Naomi Judd and John Jarvis for co-writing the Judds hit *Love Can Build A Bridge*. Overstreet also co-wrote *I Fell in Love Again Last Night*, a No. 1 hit for the Forrester Sisters in 1985. He received a nomination for the 1995 *Music City News* Country Awards as Christian Country Artist and received the same nomination in 1997. His latest CD is titled *A Songwriter's Project, Volume I* with Paul singing many of his timeless hits that have been recorded by other artists.

Garry Owen

Born on Feb. 18, 1902, in Brookhaven, Miss. He became an actor who was in a prodigious 90 films from *Men with Wings* in 1931 to *Scandal Sheet*, released in 1952. Most of his roles were small parts such as bartenders, cab drivers, and especially reporters, and most of the films were B movies. Owen, who was sometimes credited as Gary Owen II, died of a heart attack on June 1, 1951, in Hollywood, California.

Jack Owens

Like Skip James, Owens hails from Bentonia, Yazoo County, Mississippi, where he was born L.F. Nelson on Nov. 17, 1904.

Profiles of Famous & Notable Mississippians

In fact, Skip James was his ex-brother-in-law. Owens parents were Celica Owens and George Nelson and he was raised by Sam Owens. Not "discovered" until late in life when noted folklorist and blues scholar David Evans made several recordings with Owens in the late 1960s and early 1970s, he pioneered the style known as Bentonia Country Blues. You can hear his dark, haunting Bentonia blues in the album cut by Owens and Bud Spires (on harp), *It Must Have Been the Devil* — it's Bentonia country blues at its best! Owens received the 1995 National Hertiage Award presented by the National Endowment for the Arts. With the award he received a $10,000 fellowship, induction into the nation's Folk Arts Hall of Fame and an opportunity to play for President Clinton. He was also presented with the W.C. Handy Award in Memphis. In 1995, he was featured in a TV commercial outside the Blue Front Cafe in Bentonia for a national jeans maker. Owens, who had a following in several foreign counties as well as in the U.S., died on Feb. 9, 1997, in Yazoo City at the age of 92.

Jim Pace

Born Feb. 1, 1961, in Monticello, Miss. He was a pre-med student at Mississippi State and medical student at University Medical Center in Jackson. Thirteen years after graduating from Mississippi State, and nine years after exiting a promising career in medicine, the Jackson resident became part of the top team of big-league road racing, driving an Oldsmobile-powered Riley & Scott Mk3 for Doyle Racing. He piloted a 550-horsepower, carbon-fiber, gasoline-filled bathtub, a 'World Sports Car,' to overall wins in the 24 Hours at Daytona, the 12 Hours of Sebring, and the Texas 500, earning a place among the sport's ranking endurance racers. The 6'1" Pace first entered professional racing in 1987. That year Pace won Rookie of the Year honors in the Skip Barber Racing Series. In 1988-89, he ran the Skip Barber Pro Series, which led to his first race at Daytona in 1990. His major wins have included the 24 Hours of Daytona GTU in 1990, the 12 hours of Sebring GTP Lights in 1991, and the 1994 Exxon Supreme GTU championship after victories at Road Atlanta and Indianapolis Raceway. He gained worldwide attention during the weekend of Feb. 3-4, 1996 by winning the Rolex 24 Hours of Daytona sports-car endurance race. Pace teamed with fellow American Scott Sharp and South African Wayne Taylor to win the most grueling race on the annual International Motor Sports Association World Sports Car Series circuit. They drove an Oldsmobile Mark III powered by an Aurora V-8 Oldsmobile engine and covered 697 laps for 2,481.32 miles on Daytona's 3.56-mile road circuit. Their average speed was 103.324 mph. They competed with some of the world's top drivers in Ferraris, Porsches, Mazdas, Dodges, Fords and Chevrolets. Seventy-eight cars from 27 different countries started the race. By co-piloting a winning car during the 12 Hours of Sebring Race in 1996, Pace claimed two legs of the world endurance racing triple crown. Now Pace's name, along with his teammates, is in the record book after the wins at Daytona and Sebring — the first all-American chassis and engine combination ever to sweep the Florida events.

Rafael Palmeiro

Born Sept. 24, 1964, in Havana, Cuba. He was a baseball star at Mississippi State University on their most celebrated team, Ron Polk's 1985 Diamond Bulldogs, which also featured future major league stars Jeff Brantley, Will Clark, and Bobby Thigpen. They became the first State team to hit the 50 win mark, finishing with a 50-15 record and a 3rd place tie in the NCAA College World Series at Omaha. Palmeiro made his major league debut on Sept. 8, 1986, for Chicago, and played for the Cubs through the 1988 season. He played for the Texas Rangers from 1989 through 1993. From 1994 through 1998, he played first base for the Baltimore Orioles. During the off-season, the Texas Rangers re-signed Palmeiro to a five-year $45 million contract. Palmeiro had knee surgery in Feb. 1999. Soon after the start of the 1999 season on May 2, he made his 2,000 career hit! He was the AL Player of the Month for June. He was named to the American League team for the All-Star game on July 13, 1999. *The Clarion-Ledger* newspaper of Jackson picked Palmeiro as the No. 1 Male Athlete of the Year for 1999. Palmeiro, mostly a designated hitter, ended the 1999 season batting .324 47 home runs and 148 RBIs. In Oct., he was picked as *The Sporting News* Player of the Year, beating 1998's winner, Chicago Cub's outfielder Sammy Sosa, 74 votes to 57½ in balloting by nearly 400 major leaguers for the award given annually since 1936. Despite playing just 28 games at first base in 1999, he still won his 3rd straight American League Gold Glove announced Nov. 9. On Sept. 23, 2000, Palmeiro became the 32nd man in baseball history to his 400 home runs. His career stats through the 2000 season: 2,321 hits in 7,846 at bats (.296 batting avg.), 1,259 runs, 400 home runs, and 1,347 RBIs in 2,098 games.

John N. Palmer, Sr.

Born July 14, 1934, in Corinth, Miss. He sold his Jackson-based company, Mobil Communications Corp. to BellSouth, then founded Mobile Telecommunications Technologies, or Mtel, in Nov. 1988. Under Chairman of the Board Palmer's leadership, Mtel grew from a company that started with 30 employees and a few thousand customers to one of the nation's largest paging companies with 2,200 employees, more than one million customers and a positive cash flow of $100 million in 1996. Mtel introduced SkyTel 2-Way, the nation's first two-way paging network, in Sept. 1995. Mtel changed its corporate name to SkyTel in 1998. Mississippi-based MCI WorldCom acquired SkyTel in a $1.3 billion stock-trade deal in 1999, but operates it as a separate subsidiary. Palmer is in the Mississippi Business Hall of Fame. A longtime patron of the arts, Palmer received the Arts Patron Award of the 2000 Governor's Awards for Excellence in the Arts.

Dave Parker

Born David Gene Parker on June 9, 1951, in Calhoun City, Mississippi. He made his major league baseball debut on July 12, 1973, for the Pittsburgh Pirates and stayed with that team until 1983. In 1977 and 1978 he won Batting Champion both years with .338 & .334 averages. he was chosen the Baseball Writers Association NL MVP in 1978. When Parker played for the Cincinnati Reds (1984-1987), when he was the RBI leader with 125 in 1985. He also played for Oakland Athletics (1988-1989), the Milwaukee Brewers in 1990, the California Angels in 1991, and the Toronto Blue Jays in 1991. He was an All-Star and played in 3 World Series games — in 1979, 1988 and 1989. In his first World Series game in 1979, Parker got the game-winning hit in Game 6 and batted .345 overall as Pittsburgh beat Batimore in Game 7. On the list of All-Time Home Run Leaders with 339, some of his other career stats include 2,712 hits in 9,358 at bats (.290 batting average), 1,272 runs and 1,493 RBIs in 2,466 games played.

Little Junior Parker

Born Herman Parker in Clarksdale, Mississippi on March 27, 1932. Worked with Howlin' Wolf & B.B. King around Memphis. He recorded *Mystery Train* on the Sun label, later a hit by Elvis Presley. Parker had a top-10 R&B hit *Driving Wheel*. He toured a lot with Bobby "Blue" Bland. Parker recorded 23 albums. He died on Nov. 18, 1971.

Profiles of Famous & Notable Mississippians

Laurie E. Parker
Born July 24, 1963, in Bruce, Miss. When she completed her degree in education at Mississippi State in 1985, she was planning a career as a teacher. Now, she's living in her hometown of Starkville, designing jewelry, and has authored and illustrated a book titled *Everywhere in Mississippi*, written in rhyming narrative about the adventures of a man's state-wide search for his beloved dog, Skippy, and includes the names of 305 Mississippi towns. Parker also wrote the children's books, *Mississippi Alphabet* (1998) and *All Over Alabama*. Parker received the children's book award from the Mississippi Library Association in Oct. 2000.

Claude Passeau
Born on Apr. 9, 1909, in Waynesboro, Mississippi, he was an outstanding athlete at Millsaps College from 1928-32. Passeau made his major league baseball debut on Sept. 29, 1935. He pitched 13 seasons for the Pittsburgh Pirates, Philadelphia Phillies (1936-39) and Chicago Cubs (1939-47). He played in 5 straight All-Star games (1941-46), the starting pitcher in 3 of those, and pitched a 1-hit shutout for the Cubs in game 3 of the 1945 World Series. His career stats: 444 games played (188 complete), 162 wins and 150 losses with a 3.32 ERA. He was inducted into the Miss. Sports Hall of Fame in 1964.

Carolyn Bennett Patterson
Born in April 12, 1922, in Kosciusko, Mississippi. Her family moved to Jackson when she was just a toddler. They then moved to Yazoo City, Mississippi, in 1933 when she was 11 years old, and she attended high school there. She attended Mississippi State University for one year and graduated from Louisiana State University. Patterson began her journalism career as the first female police reporter for the *New Orleans States*. She worked as a Capitol Hill reporter for several newspapers in Ohio. Patterson was working as public relations consultant for several musical acts when she applied for a job at the *National Geographic* magazine in 1949. First hired as a library research assistant, she soon became a writer for the publication. Patterson covered Winston Churchhill's funeral in London. She walked 180 miles through the mountains of southern France, with her pack donkey in tow, for the story retracing the route of Robert Louis Stevenson's *Travels with a Donkey in Cevennes*. She appeared on the cover of *National Geographic* for that story. She also wrote about the New York World's Fair, about skiing in the Swiss Alps, and other stories. In 1960, she became the first female editor at *National Geographic* and retired in 1986 as senior assistant editor. She details her adventures around the world in her book, *Lands, Legends & Laughter* ('98). In 1999, Patterson donated her personal and professional papers to Mississippi State, where they will be preserved in the Mitchell Memorial Library.

Charley Patton
This legendary blues singer was born in Edwards, Miss. in April 1887. The Delta's first great blues star, the original "King of the Delta Blues" was a major influence on artists like Robert Johnson, Howlin' Wolf, John Lee Hooker and many others. When he played at plantation dances and juke joints, he'd draw big crowds. Even though Patton was only five-feet-five and weighed only 135 pounds, he sounded much bigger. Sleepy John Estes claimed Patton was the loudest blues singer he ever heard and it was rumored that his voice was loud enough to carry outdoors at a dance up to 500 yards away without amplification. And, he had the "image." He was easy to provoke, capable of downing much food and liquor, and often had a woman on each arm. His slide work — played in his lap like a Hawaiian guitar and fretted with a pocket knife or played with a brass pipe for a bottleneck — influenced contemporaries like Son House and up and coming youngsters like Robert Johnson. He popped his bass strings (a technique he developed some 40 years before funk bass players started doing the same thing), beat his guitar like a drum and stomped his feet to reinforce certain beats. Most of the now-common guitar gymnastics modern audiences have come to associate with the likes of a Jimi Hendrix, originated with Patton. He would "entertain the peoples" and rock the house with everything from blues, ballads, ragtime to gospel. His records, especially his first and biggest hit, *Pony Blues*, could be heard on phonographs throughout the South. Although he was certainly not the first Delta bluesman to record, he quickly became one of the most popular. He first recorded in 1929 for Paramount and within a year's time, he was not only the largest-selling blues artist but also the most prolific. He recorded some 60 odd tracks. His final session was done only months before his death. Patton was responsible for getting Willie Brown and Son House their first chances to record. Patton died from a heart ailment in Indianola, Miss., on April 28, 1934, and is buried in a cemetery in nearby Holly Ridge.

Walter Payton
Born Walter Jerry Payton July 25, 1954, in Columbia, Mississippi. In 1974, while at Jackson State University, he became the leading scorer in NCAA history with 464 points. He scored 46 points in one game when he scored 7 touchdowns for Jackson State against Lane College in 1972! That was also the game in which Payton rushed for 279 yards, his career best rushing performance. His college career rushing total at Jackson State was 3,563 yards. He received a B.A. in special education in 3½ years. He was picked 4th in the first-round of the 1974 NFL draft. Payton played his entire pro career (1975-87) with the Chicago Bears and became one of the NFL's greatest performers. His career stats: 16,726 yards, 100 TDs rushing; 492 receptions for 4,538 yards; 21,803 combined net yards; 125 touchdowns. Records he holds: the All-Time Leading NFL Rusher, combined net yards, 1976-80 with 16,726 yards in 3,838 attempts (also a league record); All-Purpose Yards (21,803); number of games in which he gained at least 100 yards rushing (77); and he is tied for the NFL record for the most times of running 1,000 yards or more in a season — 10 times in 1976-81 and 1983-86. He held the NFL record for most rushing yards in a single game, 275 against Minnesota on Nov. 20, 1977, until Corey Dillon ran for 278 on Oct. 22, 2000; Payton's in fifth place for the Most Yards Gained in a Season, 1,852, in 339 attempts in 1977. He's in fifth place among the All-Time Leading Touchdown Scorers (through the 1998 season) with a career total of 125 TDs (110 rushing), behind only fellow Mississippian Jerry Rice, plus Marcus Allen, Emmit Smith and Jim Brown. Payton was named to the Associated Press All-Pro team 5 times and was selected to play in the Pro Bowl 9 times. He received the Jim Thorpe Trophy as NFL's MVP in 1977. Payton played in Super Bowl XX in 1986. He was the first football player (the 5th major athlete) to be pictured on the Wheaties® cereal box. His image appeared on Wheaties ® eight times (including a special edition package after he died), more than any other athlete, except Michael Jordan. In 1999, he was voted one of the 10 all-time Favorite Wheaties Champions! Payton missed only one game out of 191 during his entire NFL career. He played his last pro game on Jan. 10, 1988. His uniform number at Jackson State and with the Chicago Bears was 34. He was inducted into the Mississippi Sports Hall of Fame and the Pro Football Hall of Fame in 1993. Payton was among 48 players

Profiles of Famous & Notable Mississippians

picked to be on the NFL's 75th Anniversary All-Time Team, announced in 1994. He was one of only 4 Mississippians picked (Payton, Lance Alworth, Ray Guy & Jerry Rice) and the only Mississippian of the 6 running backs picked. Payton was enshrined in the College Football Hall of Fame in 1996. His college and pro performances, and his disposition, earned him the nickname "Sweetness." On Feb. 2, 1999, Payton disclosed that he was suffering from primary sclerosing cholangitis, a rare liver disease, and he would die within two years if he didn't get a liver transplant. Soon after that news conference, doctors also discovered bile duct cancer and Payton's fight lasted only nine more months. He died on Nov. 1, 1999, at age 45. Several memorial services were held for Payton including one at Jackson State. About 20,000 fans, including his former teammates and the entire Chicago Bears 1999 team, turned out to honor him at Soldier Field in Chicago for the service led by Rev. Jesse Jackson. Michael Jordan paid proper homage to Payton by acknowledging him as "an icon long before I arrived." On Dec. 10, 1999, Payton was among a group of 3 (the other 2 were former Texas A&M RB Johnny Bailey & former North Dakota QB Jeff Bentrim) who made up the first induction class of the NCAA Division II Football Hall of Fame in Florence, Ala. A press released on Jan. 25, 2000, stated: "Payton has been voted NFL Player of the Century by fans in a poll conducted on nfl.com." He received 124,170 votes. The closest was Joe Montana with 114,210 votes. Payton was picked as one of the running backs for the 27-player NFL All-Time team selected by the 36 Pro Football Hall of Fame voters. Two other Mississippians, Ray Guy (as punter) and Jerry Rice (as one of the wide receivers) were selected for the team announced Aug. 1, 2000. In the fall of 2000, Jackson State University broke ground on a large athletic complex that will be named after Payton with one of the streets running through it also named in honor of Payton.

Hartley Peavey

Born Dec. 30, 1941, in Meridian. After getting a B.A. degree in business from Mississippi State University in 1965, this self-proclaimed "frustrated rocker" set out, with only $8,000, to manufacture electric guitar amplifiers. The result — Peavey Electronics Corporation, the third largest private company in Mississippi, with sales of $370 million in 1997. Peavey's 31 plants in Mississippi employ over 2,000 people and there is one plant in Corby, England. The only U.S. company that makes every "link in the audio chain," their products include over 3,000 items ranging from audio cables to guitars to amplifiers to sophisticated digital sound systems and recording studio equipment. The company exports products to 103 countries. Those products can be seen in hit movies, on the sets of some of the most-popular TV shows, on the floor of the U.S. Senate, and in countless rock and roll, country and blues bands around the world. The company builds guitars for the likes of Eddie Van Halen and Merle Haggard, and supplies PA systems for Opryland and many other organizations. Peavey produced a first-of-its-kind sound system used at the 2000 Summer Olympics. Peavey's all-digital system (from mikes to speakers) was installed at Stadium Australia. Hartley Peavey is a member of Hollywood's Rock and Roll Walk of Fame. On June 27, 1985, Peavey became the first firm in the state to receive the U.S. Dept. of Commerce's rare Presidential E-Star Award. The company and its products have received numerous industry awards. In 1995, the book, *Making It In America — Proven Paths to Success from 50 Top Companies*, cited Peavey Electronics in a league with Xerox, Microsoft, Motorola, Harley Davidson and other top firms! On Feb. 24, 1996, CNN featured Peavey, the CEO of the Meridian-based company, on its documentary program, *Pinnacle*, which was seen in 210 countries. A one-hour documentary, *Hartley and Melia Peavey: To Build a Dream*, was produced and broadcast by Mississippi ETV in 1997. Melia M. Peavey, Hartley's wife, was president of the company until her untimely death from heart failure caused by a diabetic coma on March 7, 1998. She was 43. Hartley and Melia were both charter members of the Mississippi Business Hall of Fame in 1991.

John Clifford Pemberton

He was a native Northerner, but he fought whole-heartedly for the South. Pemberton was born on Aug. 10, 1814, in Philadelphia, Pennsylvania. He was educated in Philadelphia then graduated from West Point Military Academy in 1837. He fought in the Mexican War and was cited for bravery in many of the crucial battles of 1846 and 1847. After the Civil War started, he went to Richmond in 1861 to offer his services to the Confederacy. After being made a lieutenant colonel on April 28, 1861, Pemberton began organizing the cavalry and artillery in Virginia. On May 8 he was promoted to colonel, on June 17 to brigadier general, and on Feb. 13, 1862, he became a major general in command of South Carolina, Georgia, and Florida. In October 1862 Pemberton was made lieutenant general and given command over Mississippi, Tennessee, and eastern Louisiana. Ordered by President Jefferson Davis to hold Vicksburg at all costs, Pemberton directed a stubborn defense despite his lack of adequate food, ammunition, and fighting men. Gen. U.S. Grant laid siege on both land and water, and by early July 1863 the Confederate defenders were suffering from starvation and exhaustion. After Union forces had held the city in a 47-day siege, he was forced to surrender Vicksburg to Gen. Ulysses S. Grant on July 4, 1863. The capturing of Vicksburg secured all of the Mississippi River for the Union and ensured the defeat of the Confederacy. Shortly after the surrender of Vicksburg, Pemberton resigned his commission as lieutenant general and served out the rest of the war as an ordnance inspector with the rank of colonel. He then retired to a farm near Warrenton, Va. In 1876, he moved to Philadelphia. Permberton died on July 13, 1881, and is buried in the Laurel Hill Cemetery in Philadelphia, Pa. (Section 9, Lot 53). In July 2000, a man from Ohio donated a handwritten account of the Siege of Vicksburg penned by Gen. Pemberton to the Mississippi Department of Archives and History.

Walker Percy

Born in Birmingham, Alabama on May 28, 1916, and raised in Greenville, Mississippi. He became a physician, but retired from medicine after contracting TB during internship in 1942. He started writing, and his first novel, *The Moviegoer* (1961), won the National Book Award. Since then his fiction and nonfiction works include *The Last Gentleman* (1966), *Love in the Ruins* (1971), *The Message in the Bottle* (1975), *Lancelot* (1977), and *The Second Coming* (1980), which received the Mississippi Institute of Arts and Letters Literature Award. His *Lost in the Cosmos* (1983) was on the list of "The Century's Top 100 Books" compiled by the World on the Web in late 1999 and also made the list of "The Fifty Best Books of the Century" compiled by the Intercollegiate Institute. Percy's first novel, *The Moviegoer*, was No. 60 on the "100 Best Novels of the Century" drawn up in 1998 by the editorial board of Modern Library, a division of Random House. The poet William Alexander Percy (see his profile), who was Walker's cousin, served as his guardian after the death of Walker's parents. Walter Percy died of cancer in Covington, Louisiana on May 10, 1990, just 18 days before his 74th birthday.

Profiles of Famous & Notable Mississippians

William Alexander Percy
Born May 14, 1885, in Greenville, Miss. He started his career as a lawyer and was appointed Chairman of the Flood Relief Committee of the Red Cross during the 1927 Mississippi flood. Among his books of poetry are: *Sappho in Levkas, and Other Poems* (1915), *In April Once, and Other Poems* (1920), *Enzio's Kingdom, and Other Poems* (1924), *Selected Poems* (1930), *The Collected Poems of William Alexander Percy* (1943), *Of Silence and Stars* (1953). His best-known work was the autobiographical *Lanterns on the Levee* (1941), published just a year before his death on Jan. 21, 1942.

Pinetop Perkins
Born Joe Willie Perkins on July 7, 1913, in Belzoni, Mississippi. He began his blues career primarily as a guitarist, but a mid-1940s encounter with an outraged chorus girl toting a knife at a Helena, Arkansas nightspot left him with severed tendons in his left arm. That dashed his guitar aspirations, but Perkins came back strong from the injury, concentrating solely on piano from that point on. In the early years, he appeared with the King Biscuit Boys, Robert Nighthawk, and Earl Hooker. He recorded *Pinetop's Boogie Woogie* for Sam Phillips in 1953. He replaced Otis Spann in the Muddy Waters Band in 1969. He is one of the world's top blues pianists.

Ray Perkins
Born Walter Ray Perkins Nov. 6, 1941, in Mount Olive, Mississippi, he grew up Petal near Hattiesburg. Perkins was a 4 sport letterman in football, basketball, baseball and track at Petal High. He led the Petal High School gridiron team to a 1961 undefeated season and he made the All Conference teams once in basketball and twice in football. Perkins was chosen as a 1961 high school All American fullback at Petal. He signed with Alabama in 1961, where he ended up playing wide receiver. In a 1962 freshman year practice with the Crimson Tide, Perkins collided with a teammate and suffered a serious head injury that required brain surgery in Birmingham. When he returned to the playing field, Perkins established himself as one of the finest wide receivers to ever play college football. The fastest man on the team, Perkins led Alabama to national championships in 1964 and 1965 and he was elected a permanent captain of the undefeated 1966 Tide team that finished 11-0. During his playing days from 1964-66, the Crimson Tide record was 20-2-1. Alabama captured the SEC Championship all three years and Perkins was chosen as the Atlanta Touchdown Club's SEC Player of the Year for 1966 and was named a consensus All American and All SEC player in his senior year. He was a receiver for Joe Namath, Steve Sloan and Ken Stabler. His nine catches against Ole Miss in his senior year set a single game. Alabama record and he tied a Crimson Tide record of 63 career receptions. He played in three bowl games — 1965 Orange Bowl (Texas 21-Ala. 17); 1966 Orange Bowl (Ala. 39-Nebraska 28) and 1967 Sugar Bowl (Ala. 34 - Nebraska 7). He set an Orange Bowl record in the 1966 contest with nine catches, all in the first half. He also set records for most yards receiving in the Orange and Sugar Bowls and the most TD receptions in the Orange Bowl. The Orange Bowl picked Perkins for the All-Time Orange Bowl Team in the 1950-1966 era. Bear Bryant called Perkins "a truly great athlete, and our best football player. If we played him on defense, he would be our best defensive player." He played in the Senior Bowl following the 1967 Sugar Bowl. Perkins was also a track star. One year he competed in the 100 yard dash, the broad jump, triple jump and relay teams. In one meet, he won the 100 yard dash, placed in the broad jump, ran on relay teams, and was the leading individual scorer. He graduated from Alabama on May 28, 1867 with a B.S. in Education. Perkins was drafted by the Baltimore Colts in the 7th round of the NFL draft and played for Baltimore for 5 years from 1967-1971. He helped the Colts win two NFL crowns (1968 and 1971) and he was a passing target of Hall of Fame quarterback Johnny Unitas. He played in Super Bowls III and V and during his NFL playing days, he caught 93 passes for 1,538 yards and 11 TDs. After a knee injury shortened his pro career, he entered the college coaching ranks as a receiver coach at Mississippi State in 1973. After one season at State, Perkins joined the New England Patriots again as a receivers coach. After serving 4 years (1974-1977) with the Patriots, he was named offensive coordinator for the San Diego Chargers and helped direct an offensive that scored 355 points and tied the NFL in passing. In 1979 Perkins was selected as head coach of the New York Giants where he faced a complete rebuilding job. He brought the Giants back from losing seasons to the first playoff squad in 18 years. He coached the South in the 1979 Senior Bowl. Following the 1982 strike year with the Giants, the Alabama Alumni Association named him "Man of the Year." Perkins shocked the college world by taking over for his mentor, legend Paul "Bear" Bryant. His teams rolled up a 32-15-1 record during the four years he coached the Crimson Tide. Under Perkins, Alabama captured 3 bowl games — the 1983 Sun Bowl (Ala. 28 - SMU 7); the 1985 Aloha Bowl (Ala. 23 - Southern Cal 3); and the 1986 Sun Fowl (Ala. 28- Wash. 6). Following Bama's 9-2-1 record in 1985, Perkins was named as the SEC Coach of the Year by the *Birmingham News*. In 1987, he became head coach of the Tampa Bay Buccaneers. He departed Tampa in 1990 and, in 1992, was named head coach at Arkansas State. He rejoined the Patriots as offensive coordinator in 1993 and revamped the New England offense. The Patriots led the AFC in scoring in 1996 and played in Super Bowl XXI. Perkins next job was offensive coordinator for the Oakland Raiders. Perkins is a member of the Alabama Sports Hall of Fame and has his own coaching corner in the Paul "Bear" Bryant Museum on the Tuscaloosa campus. The Ray Perkins Most Improved Receiver Award is given annually after spring football practice. Perkins was inducted into the Mississippi Sports Hall of Fame in 1998.

Vernon Perry
Born Sept. 22, 1954, in Jackson, Miss. He was a standout at Jackson State. He was playing with the Houston Oilers in the 1979 playoff game against the San Diego Chargers when he intercepted four passes, more than anyone in history.

Ben Peters
Born Ben James Peters on June 20, 1933, in Greenville, Miss., he grew up in nearby Hollandale, where he started playing and singing in local bands when he was 14. Ben attended High school in Hollandale from 1945 to 1952 and the University of Southern Mississippi from 1952 to 1956. After graduating from college, he completed flight training and spent the next four years in the Navy. It was during this period that he turned to songwriting, and would later become one of the greatest and most prolific songwriters to ever hit Nashville, Tennessee. On July 10, 1966, Peters moved to Nashville to write and become Professional Manager of Fingerlake Publishing Co. Shortly thereafter he wrote his first No. 1 song in 1967, *Turn the World Around*, recorded by Eddy Arnold. In 1970, he started his own publishing company, Ben Peters Music. Among over 1,000 recordings of his songs in the U.S. and abroad are *Love Put a Song in My Heart* (hit by Johnny Rodriguez in 1975), *Daytime Friends* (hit by Kenny Rogers in 1977), *Tell Me What It's Like* (hit by Brenda Lee), *Before My Time* (hit by John

Profiles of Famous & Notable Mississippians

Conlee in 1979), *Heart, Soul, Body and Mind* (hit by Johnny Mathis), plus many, many more. His songs have really helped the career of fellow Mississippian Charley Pride. Peters won a Grammy in 1972 for *Kiss An Angel Good Morning*, a No. 1 record by Pride. A gospel song Peters wrote, *Let Me Live*, won a Grammy for Pride for Best Gospel Vocal Performance. Other songs that Peters wrote that were hits for Charley Pride include *It's Gonna Take a Little Bit Longer* (1972), *A Whole Lotta Things to Sing About* (1976), *More to Me* (1977) and *Burgers and Fries* (1978). Other artists who have recorded songs written by Peters include Tom Jones, Dionne Warwick, Perry Como, Bobby Darin, Dean Martin, Waylon Jennings, Lou Rawls, Ronnie Milsap, Bobby Vinton, Dolly Parton, Connie Francis, Ray Charles, Loretta Lynn, George Jones, Barbara Mandrell, Ray Price, T.G. Shepperd and fellow Mississippians Conway Twitty, Tammy Wynette and Jerry Lee Lewis, plus dozens and dozens of other artists. Peters co-wrote, with Vivian Keith, *Before the Next Teardrop Falls*, a big hit by Freddy Fender in 1975. It was the Music Operators of America Record of the Year on juke boxes and Record World magazine's Top Country Single of the Year. Peters was *Billboard* magazine's Best Male Country Writer (973), Nashville Songwriters Association's Songwriter of the Year (1975), and was inducted into the Nashville Songwriters Hall of Fame in 1980. He has won 27 BMI writer awards and 17 publisher awards! Peters was one of the first 27 inducted into the inaugural Mississippi Musicians Hall of Fame on April 1, 2000. He has had many No. 1 hits in Australia, England and other countries in Europe. His songs have sold well over 100 million copies and been played on radio and TV over 15 million times! He has had 3 songs that have played over a million times each in the U.S. alone, and many of his songs have been featured in movies.

Donald H. Peterson
Born Oct. 22, 1933, in Winona, Miss. He received a B.S. degree from the U.S. Military Academy and a master's in nuclear engineering from the U.S. Air Force Institute of Technology. Peterson is also a graduate of the Air Force Test Pilot School and the War College. He became an astronaut in 1969. Peterson flew on only one mission, but what an important one! He flew aboard the STS-6 mission, the very first Shuttle Mission in 1983. The first spacewalk of the Shuttle program was performed by Peterson and fellow astronaut F. Story Musgrave during that mission. It lasted 4-hours and 17 minutes. Peterson logged more than 120 hours on that one space flight, which lasted from April 4 until April 9, 1983, completing 80 orbits of the earth. Colonel Peterson is retired from the Air Force and is now President of Aerospace Operations Consultants, Inc. Peterson is one of only three astronauts born in Mississippi. The other two are Fred W. Haise, Jr. (b. Biloxi) and Richard H. Truly (b. Fayette).

Annie C. Peyton
Annie Coleman was born in Madison County on Sept. 12, 1852. She received a degree from Whitworth College. After her marriage to Ephraim G. Peyton in 1872, they first lived in Gallatin, then the seat of Copiah County, and later moved to Hazlehurst. Mrs. Peyton had a dream that Mississippi should have a college to educate its young women. And it was a cause she ardently pursued. She wrote articles in many Mississippi newspapers in 1880 urging the establishment of a state-supported school for young women. She signed the articles simply as "A Mississippi Woman." It was mainly through Mrs. Peyton's efforts that Mississippi became the first state to establish a state-endowed college for the higher education of women. Industrial Institute and College opened in Columbus in 1884. It later became Mississippi State College for Women and is know today as Mississippi University for Women. After the death of her husband, she moved to Columbus to be superintendent of the new college. She died there in 1898.

Thomas Hal Phillips
Born Oct. 11, 1922, in Corinth, Miss. He is a 1943 graduate of Mississippi State. His novels include *The Bitterweed Path* (1950), *The Golden Lie* (1951), *Search for a Hero* (1952), *The Kangaroo Hollow* (1954), and *The Loved and the Unloved* (1955). He has received several literary awards including the Rosenwald, Fulbright, and Guggenheim Fellowships. Screen credits include the made-for-TV Emmy award winning movie *The Autobiography of Miss Jane Pittman* (1974, filmed in Natchez) plus the movies *Huckleberry Finn* (1974, filmed in Miss.), *Ode To Billy Joe* (1976, filmed in Miss.), *Walking Tall II* (1975), *Barn Burning* (1978 TV movie filmed in Miss.), *Roll of Thunder; Hear My Cry* (1978), and several Tarzan movies. He has been involved in several Robert Altman films, including *Thieves Like Us* (1974, filmed in Miss.), *California Split* (1974), *Nashville* (1975), and *Buffalo Bill* (1976).

Cory Philpot
Born May 15, 1970 in Savannah, Georgia. This former Ole Miss running back (1991-93) set a Canadian Football League record in 1995 with 22 touchdowns for the British Columbia Lions. He carried 229 times for 1,308 yards and 17 touchdowns, caught 41 passes for 542 yards and four TDs, and returned 24 kickoffs for 572 yards and one TD.

Hollis Pippin
Born May 3, 1950, in Jackson. A speech and dramatic arts graduate of Jackson State Univerity, he studied drama and dance at North Carolina A & T University. He was the first black man to join the Greensboro Civic Ballet Company. He also studied at the University of Southern Mississippi, the Broadway Dance Center in New York, Jacob's Pillow School of Dance in Lee, MA, and R'Wanda Lewis Afro-American Dance Studio in Los Angeles. He performed with Ballet Mississippi, Mississippi Opera Association and Opera South. As a member of the Soul Train Gang, a R&B/pop recording group, he performed on TV's *American Bandstand* and *Soul Train*, for which he co-wrote the show's theme song, *Soul Train '76*. He appeared in many stage plays, TV commercials, and 2 movies, *The Ministrel Man* and *Mississippi Masala* ('91). He was a jazz dance instructor for Jackson Public Schools. He died in Jackson on Sept. 26, 1994.

Lonnie Pitchford
Born Oct. 8, 1955, and raised five miles out of Lexington, Miss. Pitchford was a most versatile musician. He played one room jook joints and Carnegie Hall. A carpenter by trade, he built his own house and built his own guitars. Lonnie could be seen around Clarksdale wearing his carpentry belt and carrying on his trade. He began making one string guitars as a child and taught himself to play them. He often constructed one on stage and then proceeded to amaze audiences with his ability to get incredible sounds from it. He also built a one-string guitar known as the Diddley Bow. In 1974 Lonnie became an overnight wonder when the Smithsonian Institute discovered his ability to bring the material of the legendary Robert Johnson to life. He was 18 years old when he went off to Washington D.C. to play at the National Folk Festival. He banged together his one string guitar on stage at the festival and proceeded to teach the audience about the Blues. Not limited to his Diddley Bow, he was equally at home with the Strat. On his latest CD, *All Around Man*, he played acoustic

Profiles of Famous & Notable Mississippians

guitar, diddley bow, electric slide, lead, rhythm, bass, piano, and mouth harp. Pitchford died of pneumonia (from HIV) on Nov. 8, 1998, in Clarksdale at age 43 and is buried in the Newport M.B. Church Cemetery near Ebenezer, Mississippi.

Bob Pittman

Born Robert W. Pittman on Dec. 28, 1953, in Jackson, he grew up in Brookhaven, Mississippi. In the late 1960s, Pittman went to work at top-40 radio station WRBC in Jackson. He soon graduated from Millsaps College. By the time he turned 23, he was program manager of WNBC radio in New York City. By the time he was 25, he had helped make WBNC the top-rated radio station in the country. Next, Pittman created MTV, Music Television Video, on the air for the first time Aug. 1, 1981 — the first 24-hour music video channel. He served as the CEO of MTV Networks. He was later head the Six Flags theme parks as president and CEO of Time Warner Enterprises. In a little over 3 years, he guided that company to significant growth and when he left the firm in 1995, he was paid $20 million for a buyout of his contract with Time Warner as well as a fee for arranging the sale of 51 percent in the park operation. He then became managing partner and CEO of Century 21 Real Estate. Next he became president and CEO of AOL Networks of America Online, the world's biggest Internet company. Pittman was president and chief operating officer of the company when it bought Netscape, the computer browser firm in early 1999 (the head of that firm was Mississippian James Barksdale). The deal was valued at almost $10 billion. AOL announced on Jan. 10, 2000, its intention to acquire entertainment/communications giant Time Warner in a stock deal worth $162 billion (when first announced), the largest merger in U.S. history! Pittman will be co-CEO for the new company and heir apparent Chief Executive Officer. AOL made history when it became the first purely Internet company to make the Fortune 500 at No. 337 (based on 1999 revenue) on the list released in early April 2000. A special issue of *Life* magazine in 1996 listed Pittman as one of the Top-50 most influential baby boomers. Pittman maintains close ties to Mississippi as part owner of the *DeSoto Times Today* and as a member of the Millsaps College board of directors.

John A. Pittman

John Albert Pittman was born Oct. 15, 1928, in Carrollton, Miss., and grew up near Tchula, Miss. He was still living in Mississippi when he service in the U.S. Army. Pittman was in Company C, 23rd Infantry Regiment, 2nd Infantry Division near Kujangdong, Korea, when he performed an act of bravery on Nov. 26, 1950, that earned him the Congressional Medal of Honor (CMOH). The Medal was presented to him on June 4, 1951. Here are the actual words of his citation: "Sgt. Pittman, distinguished himself by conspicuous gallantry and intrepidity above and beyond the call of duty in action against the enemy. He volunteered to lead his squad in a counterattack to regain commanding terrain lost in an earlier engagement. Moving aggressively forward in the face of intense artillery, mortar, and small-arms fire he was wounded by mortar fragments. Disregarding his wounds he continued to lead and direct his men in a bold advance against the hostile standpoint. During this daring action, an enemy grenade was thrown in the midst of his squad endangering the lives of his comrades. Without hesitation, Sgt. Pittman threw himself on the grenade and absorbed its burst with his body. When a medical aid man reached him, his first request was to be informed as to how many of his men were hurt. This intrepid and selfless act saved several of his men from death or serious injury and was an inspiration to the entire command. Sgt. Pittman's extraordinary heroism reflects the highest credit upon himself and is in keeping with the esteemed traditions of the military service." Pittman was the third person to earn the CMOH in Korea for that particular act — throwing himself on a grenade — and the only one of the three to survive. He was one of only 4 native Mississippians (out of 5 Mississippians) that received the CMOH for service in the Korean conflict. Pittman's Medal was one of 17 Medals of Honor that have been officially accredited to Mississippi in all wars, although we claim 5 more that were accredited to other states because the recipients had Mississippi ties. He is one of 13 native Mississippians (of 22 Mississippians — 15 Army, 4 Marines & 3 Navy) in all wars to have received the CMOH out of 3,433 recipients of the Medal through Nov. 1, 2000. Pittman was photographed with President Harry S. Truman for the May 28, 1951, issue of *Time* magazine. He had been living in Greenwood, Miss., for many years at the time of his death on April 8, 1995, at age 66. Pittman in buried in the New Hope Church Cemetery in Greenwood. There is no Medal of Honor marker on his grave.

William Pittman II

Born on April 4, 1972, in Birmingham, Alabama, he grew up in Florence, Mississippi, where he graduated from McLaurin High School. In high school, he wasn't voted most likely to become a professional cowboy, but he did. Pittman says "One of my football teammates bet me I couldn't ride a bucking horse. And I did." Pittman became a high school rodeo champion. Then he went pro in 1992. Every year since, he has returned home to compete in the Dixie Nationals, where he finished second in 1999, his highest placing in Jackson. Pittman has become the world's seventh-ranked bareback horse rider! He now participates in specialized rodeos, which features three roughstock events — bareback riding, bull riding and saddle bronc riding instead of the traditional six rodeo events. Just coming off a PRCA event in Houston, Texas, where he won $14,000, he was in Jackson again for the Ultimate Cowboys Roughstock National Tour in May 2000. Jackson was among 12 stops on the Ultimate Cowboys tour. Pittman, who has been traveling to about 125 rodeos per year, hopes to cut back to about 30 a year in the specialized field.

Sterling Plumpp

Born Jan. 30, 1940, in Clinton, Miss., and reared by his maternal grandparents, who were sharecroppers. As a young boy, Plumpp never attended school a full year. At the age of 15 he moved to Jackson, where he completed grammar and high school, graduating as class valedictorian in 1960. Later, he spent two years at St. Benedict's College, before quitting and joining the Army. He went to Chicago in the fall of 1962. Today Plumpp is a professor of English and African-American Studies at the University of Illinois, where he has won two Amoco-Silver Circle Awards for excellence in teaching. He also won the Carl Sandburg Literary Prize for poetry for *The Mojo Hands Call, I Must Go* ('83). His other books include: *Hornam, Harriet Tubman* (autobiographical); *Ornate With Smoke*; *Blues: The Story Always Untold*; *Half Black, Half Blacker*; *Black Rituals* ('87); *Superbad and the Hip Jesus*; and is *Steps To Break the Circle* about his life in Clinton in the 1940s and early 50s. Plumpp conducts poetry workshops and was advisor for the TV series *The Promised Land*.

Frank and Sandra Polanski

Sandra Paschal was born in Grenada, Miss. on May 17, 1939. She received her bachelor's degree from Miss. University for Women. Frank was born on Sept. 29, 1939 in Kenosha, Wisconsin. They met at the University of Michigan, where they both earned master of music degrees in piano. They wed

Profiles of Famous & Notable Mississippians

in 1963 and debuted as a piano duo soon after they moved to Jackson in 1965. They've played with the Mississippi Symphony Chamber Orchestra, for Millsaps College theatrical productions, and in the Mississippi Symphony Orchestra's opening Ovation concert in 1994, and also in many solo and duo recitals. Frank is a former associate professor who taught piano theory and pedagogy at Millsaps College through the spring of 1995. Sandra is music chairman at Jackson Public Schools' Academic & Performing Arts Complex (APAC).

Ron Polk

Born Jan. 12, 1944, in Boston, Mass., he grew up in Phoenix, Arizona. For the last three decades of the 20th Century, few men have had such an impact on amateur baseball as Ron Polk. Since graduating from Grand Canyon (Arizona) College in 1968, Polk has known one profession — coaching. He began his career as a graduate assistant on the staff of at the University of Arizona. He assisted the Wildcats in their drive to the 1966 NCAA College World Series. He accepted a graduate assistant position at the University of New Mexico in 1968. In 1969, Polk accepted his first full-time coaching post as assistant at Miami Dade-South Community College, where he served until being named head coach at Georgia Southern College in 1971. In his 4 years with Georgia Southern, he led the Eagles to a 155-64 record. His 1973 and '74 Eagle teams played in the NCAA District III playoffs held at MSU's Dudy Noble Field. The 1973 team won the district title and earned a 5th place tie with Oklahoma in the NCAA College World Series, an achievement that brought Polk his first National Coach of the Year Award. He left Georgia Southern briefly to serve as an assistant coach at the University of Miami during 1975. Polk was invited to come to Mississippi State in Nov. 1975 and was named the Bulldogs 13th head baseball coach. At Mississippi State and Georgia Southern, Polk's teams complied a phenomenal record of 1,043 wins and 486 losses making him the 16th All-Time winningest division one baseball coach. He guided six teams to the NCAA College World Series and 17 squads to the NCAA regional tournament appearances. Polk and his Bulldog teams racked up 888 wins and only 422 loses (.678 percentage), making him the winningest coach in Mississippi State and SEC history. While Polk was at State, MSU teams advanced to the NCAA College World Series five times (1979, 1981, 1985, 1990 and 1997), competed in 15 NCAA regional tournaments, and captured 4 SEC titles in 1979, 1985, 1987 and 1989. Polk's 1979 team established new SEC marks for wins (48) and winning percentage in the SEC (17-2, .895) and captured the first SEC title for the school in any sport since the 1971 SEC baseball crown. His most celebrated team was the 1985 Diamond Bulldogs, which featured future major league stars Jeff Brantley, Will Clark, Rafael Palmeiro and Bobby Thigpen. They became the first State team to hit the 50 win mark, finishing with a 50-15 record and a 3rd place tie in the NCAA College World Series. For his coaching efforts of this super Bulldog team, Polk was awarded his second National Coach of the Year honor and he was singled out by the major league scouting directors top collegiate coach. Polk's 1989 team posted the second of the school's three 50 win campaigns with a 51-14 record and won MSU's 10th SEC title in baseball. Polk was named SEC Coach of the Year in 1979, 1985, 1987 and 1989. In 1995, Baseball America rated Polk ninth on its list of top 10 power brokers in all of amateur/collegiate baseball. He served from 1985-86 as President of the 5,000 member American Baseball Coaches Association and was honored by his peers as the recipient of the association's top honor, The Lefty Gomez Award. Polk was inducted into the ABCA's Hall of Fame in 1995. On March 20, 1994, he notched his 900th career coaching victory against instate rival Ole Miss. Polk became only the 16th coach in college baseball history to reach the 1,000 win pinnacle on Feb. 2, 1997, as his Bulldogs defeated Delta State 11-4 at Dudy Noble Field. At State, Polk coached 18 All Americans and 101 players who signed to play professional baseball. The list of Polk's coaching pupils include: one major league manager plus four others on major league staffs; 16 college head coaches; 10 college assistants; and 15 high school coaches around the nation who have either played for or coached under Polk at Mississippi State or Georgia Southern. A total of 47 of his former players and assistant coaches have continued in the coaching field, six of whom are high school coaches in Mississippi. He served six times (1977, 1987, 1988, 1995, 1996 & 1998) on the USA Baseball teams that have played in the Summer Olympics. In 1991, Polk managed Team USA to a bronze medal in the Pan American Games in Havana. In 1998, Polk was inducted into both the Mississippi Sports Hall of Fame and the Mississippi State University Sports Hall of Fame. Polk, at odds with the NCAA over some of their regulations, resigned from college baseball in 1997, a day after Mississippi State was eliminated from the College World Series. On June 3, 1999, it was announced that Polk would be the new head baseball coach of the Georgia Bulldogs. Many Mississippi State fans were highly disappointed because Polk would now be competing against Mississippi.

James E. "Buster" Poole

Born Sept. 9, 1915, in Gloster, Mississippi. He played football at the University of Mississippi from 1934-36, the first of 14 Poole family members to play at Ole Miss. Poole graduated in 1937. He has a three-time All-Pro defensive end during his seven seasons in the NFL with the New York Giants and Chicago Cardinals. He played for the Giants when the team won one world's pro football title in 1938, and lost championship titles in 1939, 1941 and 1946. Poole and his former Ole Miss teammate Bruiser Kinard played against each other on the day the Japanese bombed Pearl Harbor. Kinard was All-Pro with the Brooklyn Dodgers at the time. In 1947, Poole was the first coach hired by Rebel coach . He retired from his Ole Miss coaching job in 1970. He was inducted into the Mississippi Sports Hall of Fame in 1964. Poole died on Nov. 16, 1994 in Oxford, Miss. at the age of 79.

Malcolm Portera

Born Jan. 31, 1946, in West Point, Miss. Mississippi State alumnus Dr. Portera returned to his alma mater at the beginning of 1998 to succeed retiring Dr. Donald Zacharias. Portera became MSU's 16th president after more than 22 years in progressive administrative roles in the University of Alabama system. Portera was the first student in the West Point school system's history to have perfect attendance for 12 years. He considered medicine and architecture, but after enrolling at Mississippi State, Portera decided to major in general science. His subsequent degrees are in political science. Portera received bachelor's and master's degrees from Mississippi State in 1969 and 1971. In 1974 he went to work for the Board of Trustees, State Institutions of Higher Learning, in the Mississippi Research and Development Center. The following year, he was named director of extended instructional programs and assistant to the vice president for academic affairs at the University of Alabama in Tuscaloosa, while pursuing a doctorate in political science, which he earned in 1977. Portera became Alabama's assistant vice

Profiles of Famous & Notable Mississippians

president for research and public service in 1979. He also taught part-time in the Department of Political Science. Eight months later, he was asked to serve as executive assistant to the president. In that role, he assisted in day-to-day operations of the university, acted as liaison officer with the Board of Trustees and the University of Alabama system office, and directed the work of five campus units. In 1983, he was named vice president for external affairs, a position he held for seven years until becoming vice chancellor for external affairs for the University of Alabama system, comprising the Tuscaloosa, Birmingham, and Huntsville campuses. In 1991, he chaired the Japan/U.S. Information Technology Conference. He's been a member of the Institute for the Study of International Affairs, the Alabama delegation to Japan-U.S. Southeast Meetings, the (Alabama) Governor's Welcoming Delegation for the People's Republic of China Trade Delegation, and an adjunct senior associate of the Population Institute of the East-West Center. Portera is an international associate of the Foundation for Advanced Information and Research and of the Institute of Fiscal and Monetary Policy for the Japan Ministry of Finance, and has been a consultant for Hyundai Precision Industries in Korea. He has been a member of the Southern Growth Policies Board, the American Economic Development Council, the Society of College and University Planners, and the U.S. Senate Committee on Productivity Awards. He was deeply involved in economic development initiatives in Alabama as a member of the Governor's Task Force on Economic Development. Dr. Portera serves as a member of the board of directors of several corporations including Sanderson Plumbing, Mid-South Industries, and Furniture Brands International. He also serves on the board of the Mississippi Economic Council and the Institute for Technology Development, both based in Jackson, and Regional Technology Strategies, Inc. of Chapel Hill, N.C. In March 1996, he retired from the University of Alabama and formed a strategic planning company, Portera and Associates. A year and a half later, the opportunity to lead his alma mater into the 21st century presented itself. He was officially inaugurated as Mississippi State University President on Feb. 6, 1999. He is married to the former Olivia Catledge, also a 1969 Mississippi State graduate and West Point native.

Parker Posey

Born Parker Christian Posey on Nov. 8, 1968, in Baltimore, Md. (her dad was in Army Intelligence at the time), she came to Laurel, Miss. at age 12. He twin brother, Christopher Posey, is an attorney in Atlanta, and her father and mother are Chris and Lynda Posey — her dad is owner of Posey Chevrolet-Nissan in Laurel and her mother a professional chef. She graduated from R.H. Watkins High School in Laurel and attended college at the prestigious State University of New York, where she roomed with Sherry Stringfield of TV's *ER*. When Parker was growing up, she wanted to be a ballerina, but decided on acting. Her first role was playing "Tess Shelby" on the TV soap *As the World Turns* (1991-1992). She played "Connie Bradshaw" in two TV mini-series, *Tales of the City* (1993) and *More Tales of the City* (1998). She was uncredited as a "beachgoer" in her first theatrical release, *The Wake*, in 1993. That same year, she appeared, with listings in the credits, in 3 other films: *Joey Breaker*, *Dazed & Confused*, and as "Stephanie" in *Coneheads*. She's been real busy since appearing in supporting roles in about two dozen additional films. She plays "Patricia Eden," Tom Hanks' girlfriend, in the Hanks/Meg Ryan movie, *You've Got Mail*. She also appears in *Scream 3*, the first blockbuster of the New Millennium — the biggest-grossing movie of 2000 through March.

Lenore L. Prather

Born Lenore L. Loving on Sept. 17, 1931, in West Point, Clay County, Mississippi. She graduated in 1949 from West Point High School. She graduated from Mississippi University for Women in 1953. Listed in *Who's Who in American Colleges & Universities* at the time, Prather went on to set many firsts, including being the first female Chief Justice of the State Supreme Court. She graduated from the University of Mississippi School of Law in 1955 with a J.D. degree. She was in private practice with her father and subsequently with her husband from 1955 until 1971. In 1965, she was appointed Municipal Judge in West Point. In 1971, Governor John Bell Williams appointed Prather as Chancery Judge for the 14th Chancery District — the first woman to hold a Chancellorship in Mississippi. Governor William F. Winter appointed her to the Mississippi Supreme Court in 1982 — the first female Supreme Court Justice for the state. Prather became a Presiding Justice in Jan. 1993. She was inducted into the University of Mississippi Alumni Hall of Fame in 1986, and in 1995 she was selected as the Ole Miss Law Alumna of the Year. Mississippi University for Women presented her with the Medal of Excellence in 1990, and the Alumni Achievement Award in 1993. The Mississippi Women Lawyers Association presented Prather with the Outstanding Mississippi Woman Lawyer Award in 1998. Prather is a member of The Mississippi Bar, The Mississippi Bar Foundation, the Conference of Mississippi Judges and the American Bar Association. A member of Rotary International and Daughters of the American Revolution, Prather has been listed in *Who's Who in America* from 1984 through 1998. She lost her bid for re-election on Nov. 7, 2000, the first sitting Supreme Court Chief Justice in Mississippi to ever be defeated in an election. The widow of Robert B. Prather, she has three daughters and two grandchildren and resides in Columbus, Mississippi.

Elvis Presley

Born Elvis Aron Presley in Tupelo, Mississippi on January 8, 1935. The National Audubon Society claims that Elvis was named after Elvis Stahr, former head of the Society, although Presley's father was named Vernon *Elvis* Presley. His twin brother, Jesse Garon Presley, was stillborn. Elvis was truly a Superstar, even a Megastar — the most famous and successful singer/performer of all-time! The "King of Rock & Roll" sold over a billion records worldwide. His biggest year was 1956 when he topped the charts (on 3/10) with his first national hit *Heartbreak Hotel* which stayed at number one for 8 weeks. He had 10 more hits in 1956 including 4 more No. 1s. *Don't Be Cruel* and *Hound Dog* were released back-to-back on one single and both went to No. 1 and stayed 11 weeks making them the biggest Rock & Roll hits of all time. Following that release, his *Love Me Tender* not only stayed No. 1 for 5 weeks, but was the first single in history to sell more than a million *advance* copies! Three of his songs *Jailhouse Rock*, *Don't Be Cruel* and *Teddy Bear* were all No. 1 on 3 charts (R&R, R&B and Country) at the same time! On Jan. 24, 1958, *Jailhouse Rock* became the first record ever to debut on the British singles chart in the No. 1 position! Some of the records Elvis and his recordings set: Most charted singles on the Hot-100 of *Billboard* magazine (149 from 1956 to May 1990); Most Top-40 records (107) Most Top-10 records (38); Most weeks holding No. 1 position (80) with his 18 number-one hits; the Most Hit Albums (94 from 1956 to April 1989); and the solo artist to receive the most RIAA awards (56 including 16 Gold singles, 33 Gold albums and 8 Platinum albums). In 1992, the 15th anniversary of his death, Elvis was honored with an

Profiles of Famous & Notable Mississippians

astounding 110 record certification awards — the largest number ever bestowed on a single artist or group in pop history! Up until his death, Elvis had 21 albums that each sold a million copies or more, more than any other artist. It is estimated that Presley's total of million-selling singles worldwide is now more than 80. He received 3 Grammy awards, all for his gospel albums *How Great Thou Art* in 1967 and again in 1974, and *He Touched Me* in 1972. He sang Red Foley's song *Old Shep* to win his first talent show on Oct. 3, 1945 at age 10 — second prize at the Mississippi-Alabama Fair and Dairy Show. When he was 13, the family moved to Memphis, where Elvis graduated from L.C. Humes High School on June 14, 1953. On July 18, 1953, the 17-year-old Presley went into the recording studio at Sun Records and paid $5 to record a two-sided single as a birthday present for his mother. One of the sides was *My Happiness*. Sam Phillips (b. 1/5/1923), owner of the label, finally signed Elvis and he made his first professional recordings in 1954. The first song Sun released was *That's All Right, Mama*, written by black Mississippi songwriter Arthur "Big Boy" Crudup. That record received its first radio play ever at 9:30 pm on July 10, 1954, on WHBQ in Memphis. Presley joined the Memphis Federation of Musicians, Local 71, on July 30, 1954, the same day he made his public debut at Overton Park Shell in Memphis. Phillips sold Presley's contract, along with the rights to his 5 Sun singles to RCA for $35,000 on Nov. 22, 1955. The only manager Elvis had during his career was "Colonel" Tom Parker (born Andreas Cornelis van Kuijk on 6/26/1909 in the Netherlands, died from a stroke on 1/21/1997), who reportedly received 50% of Presley's earnings. Elvis performed on both the "Louisiana Hayride" and "The Grand Ole Opry" at age 19. His first TV appearance was on Jackie Gleason's *The Stage Show* starring Jimmy and Tommy Dorsey on Jan. 28, 1956, on which he sang *Blue Suede Shoes*. Elvis made his first appearance on the national TV *Ed Sullivan Show* on Sept. 9, 1956. He made his 7th & final appearance on the Sullivan Show on Jan. 6, 1957. His first film was *Love Me Tender*, which premiered in New York City at the Paramount Theater on Nov. 16, 1956. He starred in 30 additional films. Most critics agree that the best were *Jailhouse Rock* (1957), the western, *Flaming Star* (1960), and *Viva Las Vegas* (1964) which co-stars Ann-Margret (see the chapter "Almost 500 Movies Mississippians Helped Make" for a complete listing of all 31 Elvis movies). Elvis signed a 5-year film contract with Hal Wallis on Jan. 21, 1961. He was in the Army from Mar. 24, 1958 to Mar. 5, 1960. His mother, Gladys Love Smith Presley (b. 4/25/1912), died on Aug. 14, 1958, during Elvis' Army tour. His father, Vernon Elvis Presley (b. 4/10/1916), died on June 26, 1979. Elvis was promoted to the rank of Sergeant on Jan. 14, 1960. His serial number (dog tag) was 53310761 and Selective Service number was 40-86-35-16. Elvis' Social Security number was 409-52-2002. His checking account number at the National Bank of Commerce in Memphis was 011-143875. He married Priscilla Beaulieu (b. 5/24/45) on May 1, 1967, they divorced Oct. 11, 1973. Their only child, Lisa Marie, was born Feb. 1, 1968 (Lisa Marie married entertainer Michael Jackson on 5/26/94 and filed for divorce on 1/18/96). Elvis was made an agent of the Bureau of Narcotics and Dangerous Drugs by President Nixon in 1970 (Elvis has a connection to another U.S. president. According to two noted genealogists who published two separate books in 1991, Elvis and former president Jimmy Carter share a 17th-century German ancestor. According to the two experts, the immigrant ancestor of Presley's paternal line, and also Jimmy Carter, was Valentine Preslar, born in Germany around 1669, who immigrated to New York with his wife, Anna Christina Framse, in 1709). On Jan. 14, 1973, Elvis broadcast his "Aloha From Hawaii" live telecast, which was reportedly viewed by more than a billion people worldwide. His last live performance was at Indianapolis June 26, 1977. Elvis liked to give expensive gifts, including cars, to friends and even strangers. He presented his close friend, country singer T.G. Sheppard (Bill Browder), with the gift of a completely outfitted customized touring bus! Elvis was among the first group of inductees into the Rock and Roll Hall of Fame on Jan. 23, 1986. Six Presley's songs, the most of any single artist, are included on the R&R Hall of Fame's list of 500 Songs That Shaped Rock And Roll. Those songs are *Heartbreak Hotel*, *Jailhouse Rock*, *Love Me Tender*, *Mystery Train*, *Suspicious Minds* and *That's All Right*. On Jan. 17, 1972, a section of Memphis' Highway 51 South was renamed Elvis Presley Blvd. Elvis died Aug. 16, 1977 at his Graceland mansion of an accidental drug overdose while sitting on the toilet. He was 42 years old. In the last 7 months of his life, Elvis had 5,300 uppers, downers, and painkillers prescribed for him. His last snack was 4 scoops of ice cream and 6 chocolate chip cookies. He weighed 230 pounds at his death. The autopsy listed the cause of death as a heart attack. Since his death, he's been practically worshipped by fans worldwide. On the 58th anniversary of his birth, Jan. 8, 1993, the Elvis Commemorative Postage Stamp went on sale. He was inducted into the Country Music Hall of Fame in 1998. In a Millennium poll conducted by *The Clarion-Ledger* in 1999, readers overwhelmingly picked him No. 1 in two categories — as their All-Time Favorite Entertainer and All-Time Favorite Pop/Rock Singer. In another Millennium poll, *The Clarion-Ledger* readers picked Elvis as Mississippi's Man of the Century! The national publication *Entertainment Weekly* magazine picked Elvis No. 2 on their list of "The Top 100 Entertainers of the Last 50 Years (of the 20th Century)" in the issue released in Nov. 1999. Would you believe the Beatles took the top spot?! However, in its last issue of the 20th Century, *TV Guide* picked Elvis as "The Entertainer of the Century"! Elvis was one of the first 27 inducted into the Mississippi Musicians Hall of Fame on April 1, 2000.

Cheryl Prewitt
Born on Feb. 15, 1957, in Ackerman, Mississippi. Prewitt was Miss America, 1980. She is married to Harry Salem, former vice-president of the Oral Roberts Evangelistic Organization. Cheryl is an accomplished author, speaker, musician, songwriter, and teacher who ministers the gospel with her husband throughout the world. She has written a dozen books and completed nine music recording projects.

George Baker Price
Born on Aug. 28, 1929, in Laurel, Miss. Brig. Gen. Price was the first black Mississippian to advance to the rank of General in the U.S. Army. Retired from the military, he is now the manager of his sister, opera star Leontyne Price.

Leontyne Price
Born Leontyne Mary Violet Price on Feb. 10, 1927, in Laurel, Mississippi. She achieved international renown with her brilliant voice. She received her B.A. degree in art in 1948 from the College of Education and Industrial Arts in Wilberforce, Ohio, then attended the Juilliard School of Music in New York on a scholarship (1948-52). In 1952, she sang the role of Mistress Ford in Verdi's *Falstaff*, the lead in Thomson's *Four Saints in Three Acts*, and toured as Bess in Gershwin's *Porgy and Bess*. Her important debuts include: *Town Hall*

Profiles of Famous & Notable Mississippians

(1954), in the New York premiere of Samuel Barber's *Hermit Songs*; TV (1955), with NBC Opera Company in Puccini's *Tosca*; the Vienna Opera (1958), in Verdi's *Aida*; La Scala (1960), and the Metropolitan Opera as Leonora in Verdi's *Trovatore* (Jan. 27, 1961). She has sung with the San Francisco Opera Company, the Vienna State Opera, La Scala in Milan, Italy, Covent Garden in London. She was with "The Met" from 1961 until her final performance on Jan. 3, 1985 in which she sang the title role in Verdi's *Aida*. *Time* magazine once hailed her as the "diva di tutte le dive" (diva of all divas). In 1977, she was awarded the San Francisco Opera Medal in honor of the 20th anniversary of her debut with the company. She has won 3 Emmy Awards and 19 Grammy Awards, including a lifetime Grammy in 1989. Awarded the Presidential Medal of Freedom in 1965 by President Johnson, she was the first Mississippian and the first opera singer to receive the nation's highest civilian award. In 1986, the government of France named her a Commandeur of the French Order of Arts and Letters. She also received the Kennedy Center Honor and the Lifetime Achievement Award, the highest honor of the Mississippi Governor's Awards for Excellence in the Arts. She's a member of the Metropolitan Opera Association, the Board of Directors of the Dance Theater of Harlem, and on the Board of Trustees of New York University. She wrote a children's book, *Aida*, in 1990. Her brother, retired Brig. Gen. George Price is her manager. In a special millennium poll conducted by *The Clarion-Ledger* of Jackson in 1999, readers picked Price as their favorite all-time Mississippi music performer in the category of "Other Music." Price was one of the first 27 inducted into the inaugural Mississippi Musicians Hall of Fame on April 1, 2000. Price received a Lifetime Achievement Award from the Mississippi Institute of Arts and Letters on April 28.

Will A. Price
This screenwriter was born in McComb. As technical advisor and dialogue director for *Gone With The Wind* (1938), he coached Clark Gable and Vivien Leigh on how to speak Southern. Quoting from the production notes released in 1939: "To insure Vivien Leigh's mastery of the Southern accent, Will A. Price of McComb, Mississippi, an expert on Southern dialects, and Susan Myrick, of Macon, Georgia, were engaged to assist her." The film was rated No. 4 on The American Film Institute's list of the Top 100 Greatest American Movies of All Time announced in 1998 on the 100th anniversary of film making. Price was also the director of three movies: *Strange Bargain* (1949); *Tripoli* (1950, also story writer); and *Rock, Rock, Rock* (1956). He was also story writer for the film *Northwest Frontier* (1959). Price was married to actress Maureen O'Hara from 1941 to 1953. He died on July 4, 1962.

Charley Pride
Country singer and entertainer born Charles Frank Pride in Sledge, Miss. on Mar. 18, 1938. He began his career in sports and played 2 seasons for the Memphis Red Sox of the old Negro League before a stint in the service. After service, tryouts as a pitcher & outfielder for the Los Angeles Angels and New York Mets in the early 60s failed to get him signed. He changed to music after almost 3 years in baseball. His first hit record was *The Snakes Crawl at Night* (1964). He followed that with 35 No. 1s including 5 in a row. He has sold more than 30 million records including 6 gold singles hits and 40 albums including 12 gold albums in the U.S., 31 gold and 4 platinum records worldwide, making him one of the Top-15 best-selling artists of all time! Single record hits like these number-ones: *Is Anybody Goin' to San Antone* (1970), *Kiss An Angel Good Morning* (1971), *Someone Loves You Honey* (1978), *Where Do I Put Her Memory* (1979), and *Mountain of Love* (1982). Pride was RCA's best-selling artist since Elvis. He made his Grand Ole Opry debut in Jan. 1967. Some of his awards: Country Music Association Male Vocalist of the Year two years in a row, 1971 & 72; Entertainer of the Year in 1971; and *Music City News* Male Artist of the Year for 5 straight years (1969-73). He received country male vocalist awards by the Country Music Association, *Billboard*, *Cashbox* & Music Operators of America. He garnered three Grammys in 1971 as both a country and gospel singer. Charley received his star on the Hollywood Walk of Fame on July 20, 1999. On Oct. 4, 2000, Charley will become the 73rd member inducted into the Country Music Hall of Fame.

Will Primos
Born Wilbur Rivers Primos on March 2, 1952, in Jackson. His early influences were his grandfathers, Wilbur Rogers Rivers, from Little Rock, Mississippi, and Angelo Pop Primos, his father, Kenneth Primos, and three uncles, Aleck, Gus and Billy. Exposing Will to the woods, streams, rivers and lakes of Mississippi when he was young, they instilled in him a tremendous love and appreciation for wild things and the great outdoors. In 1974, Will graduated from Belhaven College with a major in business and a minor in biology. In 1976, he combined his education with his love of hunting, fishing and the outdoors to begin a small manufacturing business making turkey calls. The company, first known as Primos Yelpers, evolved into Primos Hunting Calls, which now has 49 employees and manufactures, markets and distributes its 200 products all over the United States, Canada, and Europe. Primos Hunting Calls has acquired intellectual property rights in the form of some 10 patents and 20 trademarks which the company uses to protect its position within the industry. As part of its marketing plan, Primos began producing "The Truth®" video series in 1987. There are currently 22 titles in the series with more planned. It has become the most watched hunting video series in the U.S. Because of the marketing strength, media exposure, and recognition of Primos Hunting Calls, "The Truth®" video series is sponsored by many hunting industry companies including Remington® Arms, Whitewater® Outdoor Clothing, PSE® archery equipment, Advantage® Camouflage, and Scent Shield®.

James "Snooky" Pryor
Born James Edward Pryor in Lambert, Miss. on Sept. 15, 1921. He was playing harmonica at the age of eight. The two Sonny Boys were influential to Pryor's emerging style, as he played around the Delta. Pryor contributed solid harp work to numerous early Chicago blues classics as both a leader and sideman, and has worked with just about every bluesman. His instrumental *Boogie* (1948) became the basis for Little Walter's hit *Juke*, while his *Someone To Love* (1956) was adapted by the Yardbirds. He hit Chicago for the first time in 1940. Armed with a primitive amp, he dazzled folks with his massively amplified harp. Pryor made some groundbreaking 78s during the immediate postwar Chicago blues era through the 1950s, but commercial success never materialized. He wound down his blues-playing in the early 1960s, finally in 1967 he moving to downstate Illinois and got lost. The 1987 Blind Pig album, *Snooky*, announced to the world that the veteran harpist was alive and well. A pair of CDs for Antone's, *Too Cool to Move* and *In This Mess Up to My Chest*, followed.

Trent Pulliam
Born Aug. 13, 1975, in Houston, Miss. He earned All-County and All-District honors and was named All-Area Player of the

Profiles of Famous & Notable Mississippians

Year after averaging 25 points and 15 rebounds as a senior at Houston High School. He finished his three-year career at Jackson State ranked 15th on the school's all-time scoring list with 1,179 points. As a senior in 1997-98, Pulliam led the Tigers in scoring, rebounding, steals, three-point field goals made and minutes played. He earned the team's Most Valuable Player honors as a junior after averaging a career-high 14.1 points and 7.9 boards per game. He started all but one of 84 games at Jackson State. Pulliam was considered the best all-around player in the Southwestern Athletic Conference in 1997-98. He is a former member of the Harlem Globetrotters, signing with them in 1999.

Janos Radvanyi

Born Aug. 24, 1922, in Hungary. At age 21, he was rescuing Jews being marched to machine-gun executions during WWII. At age 25, he was a diplomat for the Hungarian government. While he was Hungary's highest-level official in the U.S. during the Vietnam War era, he defected in 1967 and applied for political asylum in the U.S. This earned him a death sentence in Hungary that was removed only when communism collapsed. After earning a doctorate at Stanford, he took a job with Mississippi State, where, in 1983, he formed and became director of the school's Center for International Security and Strategic Studies. In 1990, Dr. Radvanyi helped develop the Japan-U.S. Committee for Promoting Economic Development of East Central Europe, an international group of academic, business and government officials that received $1 billion in pledges from Japan and resources from the U.S. to clean major environmental problems in Europe. He also persuaded leaders from Japan, Russia and the U.S. to talk about nuclear waste dumping at sea in 1995. After stepping down as the center's director in 1996, he was selected to chair the department at MSU and his name was bestowed permanently on that endowed chair in 1998. He is now Professor Emeritus. Dr. Radvanyi's work has earned high praise from the U.S. Environmental Protection Agency and his native Hungary.

William Raspberry

Born Oct. 12, 1935, in Okolona, Miss. He received his B.S. from Indiana Central College. He taught journalism at Howard University and the University of Maryland. The Capital Press Club presented Raspberry with the Journalist of the Year award in 1965 for his coverage of the Watts riot in California, which also won him a nomination for a Pulitzer. He authored the book *Looking Backward at Us*, filled with his opinions about education, family and racial matters. He has honorary degrees from the universities of Georgetown, Maryland and Indianapolis. Raspberry, now a nationally syndicated columnist for the *Washington Post*, was inducted into the Mississippi Press Association Hall of Fame on June 16, 2000.

William Silas "Si" Redd

Born Nov. 16, 1911, in Philadelphia, Neshoba Co., Miss. He attended East Central Community College and is an Ole Miss dropout. The son of a sharecropper/preacher, he founded Mississippi Vending Machine Company in the 1930s, which specialized in penny pinball machines. He built it into a 1,000 machine enterprise, then sold it and moved to Sterling, Ill. in the mid-1940s where he got into the jukebox business. From there, he moved to Boston where he operated a six-state distributorship for jukeboxes. He moved to Nevada in 1967 and became associated with Bally Distributing, eventually becoming a majority stockholder in the company that placed slot machines in casinos. He later formed International Game Technology, which now manufactures 75 percent of the slot machines in the U.S. Redd sold his controlling interest in that company in the late 1980s and started another company, International Technical Systems. In the town of Mesquite, Nevada (5,500 pop.), about 80 miles northeast of Reno, he owns the Si Redd Oasis Resort Casino with a 1,019-room hotel, 3 golf courses and 2,200 acres of land. He estimates his wealth at about $100 million. He was an innovator in the slot business, coming up with the ideas of the video poker machine, the elimination of lemons on slot reels, higher payoffs for higher denomination machines, and multi-coin machines. He is known as the "slot machine king" in Nevada. Also called "the father of gaming in Mississippi," Redd first brought legal gaming to the state when he docked a cruise ship at Gulfport in 1989. He is credited with pushing the gaming issue until it was adopted by the Mississippi legislature.

Jimmy Reed

Born Mathis James Reed in Dunleith, Mississippi on September 6, 1925. He moved to Gary, Indiana, in 1948, and two years later, at age 25, quit his job in a steel foundry to become a full-time musician. He signed with a new label, Vee-Jay Records, in 1953, and cracked the R&B charts in 1955 with *You Don't Have to Go*. He went on to have the blues and R&B record hits *Hush Hush*, *Big Boss Man* and *Bright Lights, Big City* and recorded 56 albums during his career. He was revered by musicians such as the Rolling Stones, who covered *Honest I Do*, and Van Morrison, who recorded *Bright Lights, Big City* while with the group Them. Reed's influence extended to such groups as the Grateful Dead, who performed his songs in their jugband days and recorded *Big Boss Man* on a 1971 live album. Reed was inducted into the Rock and Roll Hall of Fame in 1991. Two of his songs, *Big Boss Man* and *Bright Lights, Big City*, are included on the Rock and Roll Hall of Fame's list of 500 Songs That Shaped Rock And Roll. The Rock and Roll Hall of Fame says "no one, save for B.B. King, so effectively reached both black and white audiences in the Fifties and Sixties." Reed died of an epileptic seizure in Oakland, California on Aug. 29, 1976, only about a week before reaching age 51. He is buried in the Lincoln Cemetery in Blue Island, Illinois.

Walter Reed

Born Sept. 20, 1933, in Meridian. Reed lettered four years in track and played fullback in football at Jackson State University. He also served as an assistant football coach and head baseball coach in 1965-66. Reed led the Tigers to their first winning season in baseball in 1966. He received his master's degree at Indiana University and his doctor's degree at the University of Miami. Dr. Reed was athletic director at Jackson State from 1977-1988 and held the same position at Florida A&M from 1988 until he retired in 1994. His athletic programs had great success at both schools. Jackson State won SWAC championships every year and won the all-sports trophy every year for the men and some years for the women. While Reed was at Jackson State, the Lady Tigers were the first historically black women's basketball team to play in the NCAA Tournament. He scheduled the first football game in Mississippi history between a Division 1-AA school (Jackson State) and a Division 1-A school (Southern Mississippi). During his tenure at Florida A&M, the school won the all-sports trophy in the Mid-Eastern Athletic Conference four straight years for the men and two consecutive years for the women. Reed was named SWAC Athletic Director of the Year in 1983 and 1984. He's won many more awards and honors, but he is most proud that in all his years as athletic director, his programs never operated at a deficit. He's also proud of the coaching staff that he had at both schools. Reed has been busy

The Ultimate Reference on the State

Profiles of Famous & Notable Mississippians

since he retired in 1994. He has been a member of 27 professional and charitable organizations, including the National Association of College Directors of Athletics, the Fellowship of Christian Athletes and the Boy Scouts of America. He chaired the NCAA Division 1-AA football committee and served as a faculty representative for Jackson State to the NCAA, the NAIA and the SWAC. He even served as a volunteer at the Mississippi Sports Hall of Fame. Dr. Reed is a member of the Jackson State Hall of Fame and was only the 9th athletic administrator to be inducted into the Miss. Sports Hall of Fame when he was enshrined on Mar. 12, 1999.

Andy Reese
Born Andrew Jackson Reese on Feb. 7, 1904, in Tupelo. He played baseball with the New York Giants from 1927 to 1930, making his major league debut on Apr. 15, 1927. His career stats include 321 hits in 1,142 at bats (.281 batting avg.), 166 runs, 14 home runs and 111 RBIs in 331 games played. Reese died on Jan. 10, 1966, in Tupelo at the age of 61. He was inducted into the Mississippi Sports Hall of Fame in 1969.

Anna Reeves
Born Mar. 8, 1959, in Winona, she grew up in Carrollton and now lives in Brookhaven, Miss. She was named Bowhunter of the Year by the Mississippi Bowhunter's Association for two years in a row, 1994 and 1995. She was the first women to win the title in competition against men. In Sept. 1994, she won the Women's Open title at the World Archery Championships in Valdosta, Georgia. She has won other titles since then.

Jane Reid-Petty
Born on June 12, 1927, in Meridian. She received her B.A. degree in English at the University of Alabama. She studied acting with Uta Hagen and acting technique with Bill Hickey at HB Studio in New York. After moving to Jackson, she later returned to New York for a short time in 1969 to produce the play, *A Home Away From*. She was arts editor, theater critic and daily columnist for the *State Times* in Jackson from 1956-60. Reid-Petty founded New Stage Theatre in Jackson in 1965, Mississippi's first and only professional theater, and was its managing director from its beginning until 1970. The first play produced at New Stage in 1966 was *Who's Afraid of Virginia Woolf?* The last play she directed there was *Molly Sweeney* in Oct. 1997. In between, Reid-Petty authored the award-winning play *Seasons of Dreams* based on works by Eudora Welty. The play was performed at New Stage and later broadcast by Mississippi Educational TV. The production won the prestigious Peabody Award. She was development director/media consultant for the New Stage world premiere of Welty's *The Ponder Heart* in 1982 and adapted that story in 1987 into a one-woman show, *Edna Earle*, which she toured nationally. She launched the Eudora Welty New Plays Series in 1985 and, under her leadership, the theater started its Arts in Education program and its touring program, Shakespeare in the Schools. Reid-Petty was New Stage Theatre's producing artistic director from 1983-92. She was narrator for the PBS special *Southern Writers*, and script writer and narrator for *One Time One Place*, an exploration of Welty's photographs. She received the Governor's Award for Excellence in the Arts and the Institute for Arts and Letters Performing Arts Award in 1992. New Stage in Jackson was renamed the Jane Reid-Petty Theatre Center in 1997. Reid-Petty died on April 16, 1998, at age 70 following a lengthy battle with cancer.

Hiram Rhodes Revels
Born Sept. 27, 1827, in Fayetteville, North Carolina. He attended various schools and seminaries and Knox College in Bloomington, Illinois. He became a barber and an ordained a minister in the African Methodist Episcopal Church at Baltimore, Maryland in 1845. He carried on his religious work in Illinois, Indiana, Kansas, Kentucky, Missouri, and Tennessee, and finally accepted a pastorate in Baltimore, Maryland in 1860. At the outbreak of the Civil War, he assisted in recruiting two regiments of African American troops in Maryland and served in Vicksburg as chaplain of a Negro regiment and organized African American churches in Mississippi. Revels established a school for freedmen in St. Louis, Missouri in 1863. He then settled in Natchez, Mississippi in 1866. He was elected alderman in 1868 and a member of the State senate in 1870. Upon the readmission of Mississippi, he was elected as a Republican to the U.S. Senate and served from Feb. 23, 1870 to March 3, 1871 and was the first African American Senator. He was secretary of State ad interim of Mississippi in 1873. Revels was president of the Alcorn Agricultural College in Rodney, Miss. from 1876-82. He later moved to Holly Springs and continued his religious work. Revels died in Aberdeen, Miss. on Jan. 16, 1901. Burial was in the Hill Crest Cemetery in Holly Springs, Mississippi.

Jerry Rice
Born Jerome Lee Rice on Oct. 13, 1962, in Starkville, Oktibbeha Co., he grew up in Crawford, Lowndes Co., Miss., where he attended B.L Moor High School. In high school and college, he wore number 88. Willie Totten was his college quarterback when Jerry attended Mississippi Valley State from 1981 to 1984. Rice and Totten, "the Satellite Connection," combined to set over 75 NCAA records. Totten passed to Rice for 47 touchdowns, 27 during the 1984 season when Valley won games 86-0 and 83-11. On March 25, 2000, Rice and Totten were both on hand as Valley renamed its football facility Rice-Totten Stadium. Rice once caught 24 passes in a single game. He never missed a game. Rice holds the NCAA records, Division 1-AA, for Most Reception Yards (4,693) and set a total of 18 NCAA Division II records: consensus All-America, totaling more than 100 receptions in both his junior and senior seasons; recorded 1,845 yards and scored 28 touchdowns as a senior in 1984; exceeded 1,000 yards receiving during 3 consecutive years; MVP in the Blue-Gray Game, and played in the Freedom Bowl All-Star game; and was named to the SBN Sports Network's Black College Football All-Time team (Rice held the NCAA, Division 1-AA record for Most Career Receptions [301] until it was tied and then broken by Scott Pingel [302] of Westminster when he caught two in a game on Sept. 4, 1999). Rice became a wide receiver for the San Francisco 49ers and it turned into a 15-year career with them through 1999. Rice's first pro touchdown came on a 25 yard pass from Joe Montana. On Labor Day, Sept. 5, 1994, Rice, starting his 10th year with the 49ers, made 3 touchdowns in the season-opening game against the L.A. Raiders. The first TD tied him with fellow Mississippian Walter Payton, the 2nd tied Jim Brown's record 126 career TDs, and the 3rd TD made him the "Touchdown King" — the NFL's career leader with 127! Rice then had 120 touchdowns on pass receptions (most in NFL history) and tied Brown with 7 on the ground. Today, Rice owns just about every major NFL record, at last count 14 NFL records, plus 12 Pro Bowl invitations, 2 NFL Player of the Year Awards, 12 Super Bowl Records and 3 Super Bowl rings. Her is a list of just some of his First Place Records through the the first 9 games of the 2000 season (thru 10/29): Career TDs (184); Career Receiving TDs (174); Career Receptions (1,248); Career Receiving Yards (18,917); Career TD Connections [Rice & Steve Young](87); Season Receiving Yards (1,848, in

Profiles of Famous & Notable Mississippians

1995); Season Receiving Touchdowns (22, in 1987); Seasons with 50+ Receptions (13); Seasons with 100+ Receptions (4); Consecutive Seasons with 100+ Receptions (3); Game Receiving Touchdowns (5); Games with 100+ Receiving Yards (64); Consecutive 1,000-Yard Receiving Seasons (11, from 1986 through 1996); Consecutive 1,000-Yard Seasons (11); Most 1,000+ Yards Receiving Seasons (12); Consecutive Games with a Reception (195); Consecutive Games with a Reception TD (14); Consecutive Post Season Games with a Reception (23); 49ers Most Career Points (1,074); MNF Most Touchdowns (30); Pro Bowl Consecutive Visits (10); Pro Bowl Total Visits (12); Pro Bowl 1995-1996 MVP; Career Pro Bowl Yards (439, after Rice's 60 yards in 1998, which broke the 408 Pro Bowl career yards held by Tim Brown of the Oakland Raiders); Super Bowl Points in a Game (18 in Super Bowl XXIX, ties record also held by Roger Craig and Ricky Watters who also got his 18 points in Super Bowl XXIX); Super Bowl TDs in a Game (3, ties record also shared by Roger Craig and Ricky Watters); Super Bowl Reception TDs in a Game (3); Super Bowl Receptions in a Game (11, ties with Dan Ross); Super Bowl Receiving Yards in a Game (215); Super Bowl Fastest Touchdown (84 seconds in Super Bowl XXIX on Jan. 29, 1995); Super Bowl Career TDs (7); Super Bowl Career Reception TDs (7); Super Bowl Career Receptions (28); Super Bowl Career Points (42); Super Bowl Career Receiving Yardage (512); and Super Bowl Career Combined Net Yardage (527). That's an incredible 33 records, including 12 Super Bowl records!! Rice was MVP of Super Bowl XXIII in 1989. He was the first NFL player with 1,000 career receptions, the first receiver with 1,000 catches, and the first player with 16,000 receiving yards. In 1985, Rice was All-Rookie, NFC Rookie of the Year, and NFC Offensive Rookie of the Year. He the 1993 NFL Offensive Player of the Year. He was the *Sports Illustrated* Player of the Year in 1986, '87, '90 and '93. He was *Sports Illustrated* All-Pro in 1992, '93 and '94. He was the *Sporting News* NFL Player of the Year in 1987 and '90. He was All-NFC 8 times — in 1986, '87, '88, '89, '90, '92, '93 and '94. Rice was the NFL Player of the Year in 1987 and '90. He won the Len Eshmont Award in 1987 and again in '93. Rice is 7-Time All-Pro — in 1987, '88, '89, '90, '92, '93 and '94. On Dec. 16, 1998, Rice was selected to the Pro Bowl for the 12th time. Rice has been an All-Pro every year except 1985, his rookie season, and 1991. Rice was among 48 players picked to be on the NFL's 75th Anniversary All-Time Team announced in Sept. 1994. Rice was one of only four Mississippians picked (Rice, Lance Alworth, Ray Guy and Walter Payton) and one of only two Mississippians (Alworth) out of the 4 wide receivers picked. Rice, who had never missed a game because of injuries — a streak of 188 games, including 21 postseason games — was put out of action when he hurt his left knee on the opening game of the 1997 season. After surgery and 3½ months of grueling rehab, Rice returned to play on Dec. 14, 1997 and scored his 166th career TD and became the first non-kicker in NFL history to score 1,000 points! But, he cracked his left kneecap and had to undergo surgery again along with more months of rehab. Before the start of the 1998 season, Rice signed a $36 million contract with the 49ers that included a $4 million signing bonus. The new pact that runs through 2003 replaced a seven-year $31.6 million deal he had signed just 2 years earlier. It made Rice the league's highest-paid receiver with the annual average of $6 million topping the league's previous high of $5.875 million for Minnesota's Cris Carter. Considered to be the greatest wide receiver ever, Rice was named the greatest player in NFL history by TodaySports.com (on the Internet) in Aug. 1999! On July 25, 2000, the league picked Rice and 4 others as unanimous selections to the NFL All-Decade team for the 1990s. During the decade, Rice led receivers with 12,078 receiving & 103 TDs for San Francisco. Rice was picked as one of the wide receivers for the 27-player NFL All-Time team selected by the 36 Pro Football Hall of Fame voters. Two other Mississippians, Ray Guy (as punter) and the late Walter Payton (as one of the running backs) were selected for the team announced on Aug. 1, 2000.

"Sir" Mack Rice

Born Bonny Rice on Nov. 10, 1933, in Clarksdale, Miss., he moved at an early age to Detroit where he has been a major figure in the music business since the 1950s. He was a member of the Falcons along with Eddie Floyd, Willie Schofield and Joe Stubbs. The group recorded *You're So Fine*, which reached No. 17 on the *Billboard* pop chart in 1959. In his book, *The Heart of Rock and Roll* (1989), Dave Marsh called that song "arguably the first soul hit." Although he is a vocalist, Rice's real talent seems to be his songwriting. In 1965, he wrote *Mustang Sally*. Rice's own version of the song reached No. 15 on the R&B chart in 1965. But, the record of that song by Wilson Pickett in 1966 topped the R&B charts and reached No. 23 on the Top 40 chart. Mercury Records was so proud of the success of that tune that they "knighted" Rice and he's been "Sir" Mack Rice since. The song, *Mustang Sally*, has since been recorded by several other artists including the Young Rascals. Rice became involved with Stax Records of Memphis as a songwriter, producer and arranger in 1969. Some of the songs he wrote for Stax and the artists who recorded them include *Respect Yourself* by the Staple Singers (#12 pop in 1971), *Cheaper to Keep Her* by Johnny Taylor (#15 pop in 1973), and *Cadillac Assembly Line* (Albert King). Rice's songs have also been recorded by Eddie Floyd, Ike & Tina Turner, Bruce Willis, Buddy Guy and the Blues Brothers.

Tom Rice

Born Nov. 12, 1973, in Jackson, Mississippi, he attended Jackson Preparatory School. In 1991, Rice began publishing a movie review magazine, *The Marquee*, which he distributed in the Jackson area. After receiving the Presidential Scholarship at the School of Visual Arts in New York, he moved to Manhattan. He directed a staged reading of his script, *Chasing Rainbows*, at the Lambs Theatre on Broadway. Soon after he wrote and directed *Just In Time* (1996), a short film shot in Nashville. After working in various capacities on Broadcast shows, TV sitcoms and made-for-TV movies, Rice wrote and directed *The Rising Place*, his first feature film, shot in Canton and other Mississippi locations in May 1999. Rice currently resides in Los Angeles, California.

Beah Richards

Born Beulah Richardson on July 12, 1920, in Vicksburg. An understated black actress, she began her career in the theater. After college at Dillard University, she served a three-year acting apprenticeship in San Diego, then moved to New York in 1951. In 1954, she made her professional debut in the off-Broadway play *Take a Giant Step*. She starred in her first film, *The Mugger*, in 1958. After touring with the national company of *A Raisin in the Sun* in the early 1960s, she garnered much attention in the lead role of the play *The Amen Corner*, a role which earned her a Tony nomination. Impressed by her work, director Otto Preminger cast her in a central supporting role in *Hurry Sundown* (1967), her first movie of any importance. Richards played two roles in the hit movie *In the Heat of the Night* (1967), which was nominated for 6

Profiles of Famous & Notable Mississippians

Academy Awards®, winning 5 Oscars®, including Best Picture. Next, she played Sidney Poitier's mother in *Guess Who's Coming to Dinner* (1967), the top-grossing movie of 1967, a role for which she received an Academy Award® nomination for Best Supporting Actress and a Golden Globe nomination. The movie, which received 11 Academy Award® nominations and won two Oscars®, was rated No. 99 on The American Film Institute's list of the Top 100 Greatest American Movies of All Time, announced in 1998. Richards also appeared with fellow Mississippian James Earl Jones in *The Great White Hope* (1970) and she played "Baby Suggs" in *Beloved* (1998), which stars fellow Mississippian Oprah Winfrey. Some of her other films include *The Miracle Worker* (1962), *Mahogany* (1975) and *Drugstore Cowboy* (1989). She was in many TV series including *Roots: The Next Generation*, *Hill Street Blues*, *ER* and she won an Emmy in 1998 for a guest appearance on *Frank's Place*. Just days before her death, Richards received a 2000 Emmy for a guest appearance on the ABC-TV law drama *The Practice*. Richards, who has just returned home to Vicksburg in May 2000, died in her hometown on Sept. 14, 2000, from emphysema. She was 80 years old. She was elected to the Black Filmakers Hall of Fame in 1974. She wrote the books *A Black Woman Speaks* (1950) and *One in a Crowd* (1951).

LeAnn Rimes

Born Aug. 28, 1982, in Pearl, Mississippi, she now lives in Garland, Texas near Dallas. She was a two-week winner on *Star Search* in 1990. Her first single record, *Blue*, was released June 3, 1996. In a month it hit the nation's Top-10 country charts. LeAnn's album, *Blue*, made its debut on *Billboard*'s pop chart at No. 4 the week of July 20, 1996, having sold more than 129,000 copies in its first week in stores! By the end of 1996, the album had sold more than 2 million copies. By mid-1999, *Blue*, her 1996 debut album, had surpassed the 7 million sales mark. Her album, *You Light Up My Life: Inspirational Songs*, also a multi-platinum LP, debuted at No. 1 on three *Billboard* charts: Pop, Country and Contemporary Christian, the first time that has ever been achieved by a country artist. *Early years: Unchained Melody*, a compilation album of LeAnn's early work, was released in early 1997 and sold multi-platinum. To top off 1997, she had a No. 1 one pop single with *How Do I Live*. Her other hits include the No. 1 country single *One Way Ticket (Because I Can)* (1996), *Unchained Melody* (Top 10 country single 1997), *On the Side of Angels*, hit the Top-10 Country Singles Chart in 1998 and *Sittin' on Top of the World* (Top-10 Album in 1998) with the Top-10 single, *Commitment*. By the middle of Nov. 1999, her album *LeAnn Rimes* was No. 1 on the country album chart and as the 20th Century ended and the 21st Century (& Third Millennium) began, her single *Big Deal* was on the Top 10 country chart. LeAnn scored the No. 1 county record for the year in 1997 with *How Do I Live*, the No. 7 country hit with *You Light Up My Life* and the No. 8 country hit for the year with *The Light In Your Eyes*. *How Do I Live* also placed 9th Top Single of the Year and *Blue* was the 6th Top Album of the Year in 1997. She received two Country Music Association nominations in 1996 — the youngest person ever nominated for a CMA award. In 1997, she captured an American Music Award, followed by two Grammys (including Best New Artist, the first time a country artist ever captured that honor), three Academy of Country Music Awards, a TNN Music City Award and a CMA Horizon Award. LeAnn closed 1997 with 4 *Billboard* Music Awards, including Artist of the Year. Overseas, she was awarded the BBC's prestigious Rising Star Award. LeAnn's acting debut was in Dec. 1997 when she starred in the ABC-TV movie, *Holiday in Your Heart*, based on the book of the same title, which LeAnn co-wrote. She made guest appearances on 3 episodes on the TV soap *Days of Our Lives* in 1998. Her singing was featured in the 1998 Disney animated movie, *Camelot*.

Jim Ritchie

This self-described "storyteller" was born on April 12, 1937, in Brookhaven, Mississippi and now lives in Shocco in Madison County. Ritchie worked for IBM for 15 years, then started his own computer sales and consulting business in 1978. He retired from that in late 1999 to start the Website southernstories.com that promotes books written by Southern authors plus artwork and music produced by Southern artists. Ritchie is the author of *Shocco Tales: Southern Fried Sagas* (1991), a collection of his down-home stories. In 1996, a series of four audio cassettes was released with some of the tales from the book narrated by Ritchie. The recording deal was with the same company that recorded the first tapes of comedian Jeff Foxworthy. Ritchie also writes newspaper columns and his articles have appeared in several magazines, plus he had a speaking part in the hit movie *A Time To Kill*.

Eric Roberts

Born Eric Anthony Roberts on April 18, 1956, in Biloxi. His parents founded and ran an actors workshop in Georgia, and Roberts first appeared on stage at age five. He moved to London at age 17 and studied theater at the Royal Academy of Dramatic Arts and then the American Academy of Dramatic Arts. His professional stage debut was in *Rebel Women*. He did considerable stage work after that, at one point even taking over the lead from John Malkovich in the Broadway play *Burn This*. Before he became a movie star, he appeared in at least two soap operas, *Another World* and *How To Survive a Marriage*. His film debut was in *King of the Gypsies* in 1978. Since then, he's been in over 50 movies, his most notable: *Raggedy Man* (1981), *The Pope of Greenwich Village* (1984), *The Coca-Cola Kid* (1985), *The Runaway Train* (1985, Academy Award® nomination for Best Supporting Actor), *Nobody's Fool* (1986, from the play written by Mississippian Beth Henley), *The Ambulance* (1990), *The Specialist* (1994). *It's My Party* (1995), *The Immortals* (1995), *Heaven's Prisoner* (1996), *Past Perfect* (1996), *The Grave* (1996), *American Strays* (1996), *The Shadow Men* (1997), *Making Sandwiches* (1997), *Two Shades of Blue* (1998), The *Prophecy II* (1998), *Bittersweet* (1998), *TripFall* (1999), *Hitman's Run* (1999) and *A Better Way to Die* (1999). His more recent TV movies include: *Saved by the Light* (1995), *Doctor Who* (1996), *Dark Angel* (1996), *In Cold Blood* (1996), *Purgatory West of the Pecos* (1999), and he plays Bugsy Siegel in *Lansky* (1999). He appeared in the TV mini-series *The Odyssey*, which aired May 1997. In 1981, Roberts was seriously injured in a car accident and spent three days in a coma. He's the brother of actress Julia Roberts (b. 10/28/67 in Georgia).

James Robinson

Born Aug. 31, 1970, in Jackson. He was a basketball standout at Murrah High School, where he averaged 40.7 ppg in 1988-89, his senior year — a Class 5A record. Robinson then played for Alabama. The 6-foot-2, 180 pound guard was the 21st overall pick in the 1993 draft and averaged 4.8 points in 11.6 minutes per game as a guard in his rookie 1993-94 season with the Portland Trail Blazers. With the Los Angeles Clippers during the 1997-1998 season, his stats include 541 points (7.7 per game), 10 blocks and 37 steals. He was with the Minnesota Timberwolves in 1998-99. His career stats through the

Profiles of Famous & Notable Mississippians

1998-99 season: started 344 games (18.5 minutes avg. p/game); 2,689 points (7.8 avg. p/game); 590 rebounds (1.7 avg. p/game); 179 steals (0.52 avg. p/game); 62 blocks (0.18 avg. p/game); and 659 assists (1.92 avg. p/game). His career field goal percentage is .397 and free throw percentage is .664.

Jimmie Rodgers

Born James Charles Rodgers on Sept. 8, 1897, at Pine Springs near Meridian. Before Rodgers became famous, he worked as a brakeman on the New Orleans and North East Railroad. He also worked as a truck driver, cab driver, farmhand, mechanic, janitor, dishwasher, day laborer and a city detective in Asheville, N.C. A legendary figure known as "The Singing Brakeman," "The Blue Yodeler," "The Yodeling Cowboy," and "The Father of Country Music." The first nationally known country star — he was "the man that started it all, " to quote his plaque at the Country Music Hall of Fame in Nashville. His first radio performance was on WWNC in Asheville, N.C. on April 18, 1927 with his band, the Jimmie Rodgers Entertainers. Jimmie (along with the Carter Family) cut his first recordings for Victor Records in Bristol, Tennessee on August 1-4, 1927. Ralph Peer was the RCA man that recorded him. His first record was released on Oct. 7, 1927 with the two songs *The Soldier's Sweetheart* and *Sleep, Baby, Sleep*. Another record, *Blue Yodel*, went on to sell a million copies. It was the first of 12 blue yodels he recorded. At a stage appearance at the Earle Theater in Washington, D.C., Rodgers performed *Frankie and Johnnie* as an encore and came back for 16 curtain calls! He was one of the first three members elected into the Country Music Hall of Fame in 1961, and one of the first elected to the Songwriters Hall of Fame in 1970 for writing songs like *T for Texas (Blue Yodel Number 1), Any Old Time, The Soldier's Sweetheart, TB Blues, Waiting For A Train, Travelin' Blues, Train Whistle Blues, In the Jailhouse Now, My Little Old Home in New Orleans* and *Mule Skinner Blues (Blue Yodel Number 8)*. In Hollywood, he recorded with Louie Armstrong and in 1931 he toured with humorist Will Rogers to raise money for Dustbowl victims. During Rodgers' recording career (1927-1933), he recorded 110 sides for the Victor label and sold around 12 million records. Rodgers once stated "The underest dog is just as good as I am; and I'm just as good as the toppest dog." Sixty-seven albums of Rodgers songs have, so far, been released. Rodgers recorded his final song, *Fifteen Years Ago Today*, just two days before his death. His 6-year career cut short by Tuberculosis. He died in New York City on May 26, 1933, at the age of 35 and is buried in the Oak Grove Cemetery in Meridian. The Jimmie Rodgers Society was formed on Sept. 26, 1947. He's a member of the Bluegrass Hall of Fame and was inducted into the Rock & Roll Hall of Fame in 1986 in the "Early Influences" category. Rodgers is the only musician in four major halls of fame! His song, *Blue Yodel No. 9*, is included on the Rock & Roll Hall of Fame's list of 500 Songs That Shaped Rock And Roll. The R&R Hall of Fame quotes Bob Dylan's liner notes to the Jimmie Rodgers tribute album that became the first release on Dylan's Egyptian Records in 1997: "Jimmie Rodgers, of course, is one of the guiding lights of the Twentieth Century, whose way with song has always been an inspiration to those of us who have followed the path....He was a performer of force without precedent with a sound as lonesome and mystical as it was dynamic. He gives hope to the vanquished and humility to the mighty." Rodgers was the first country star to have a stamp dedicated to him — the Jimmie Rodgers Commemorative Postage Stamp issued in 1978 honoring the "Father of Country Music." In 1984, Rodgers became the first white person to win the W.C. Handy Blues Award for his contribution to the blues. Rodgers was one of the first 27 inducted into the inaugural Mississippi Musicians Hall of Fame on April 1, 2000.

Jimmy Rogers

Born James A. Lane on June 3, 1924, in Ruleville, Miss. He played the guitar, harmonica and piano. A major figure in the development of post-war Chicago blues in the 40s and 50s, he's best known for his Chess recordings: *That's All Right* (1950), a blues standard, and *Walking by Myself* (1956). He retained his own style and is one of the few who never adapted the B.B. King styles of string-bending. One of the last great Chicago blues artists, he died of cancer on Dec. 19, 1997.

Charlemae Rollins

Born June 20, 1897, in Yazoo City, Mississippi. She studied library science at Columbia University. Rollins was one of the first librarians to stress pride in black heritage. When the George C. Hall Branch of the Chicago Public Library opened in Jan. 1932, Rollins was put in charge of the children's department. She led a lifelong crusade to change the image of African Americans in children's literature and promote the publication of books about the African American experience. She gained national attention in 1941 by editing *We Build Together: A Reader's Guide to Negro Life and Literature for Elementary and High School Use*, an annotated bibliography of children's books about African Americans published by the National Council of Teachers of English. Rollins died on Feb. 3, 1979, in Chicago, Illinois.

Eric H. "Rick" Rommerdale

Born Nov. 27, 1941, in Erie, Penn., he has been a Mississippi resident since retiring from the Navy in 1974, where he was a dental lab technician. He invented the Easy Hold by Trim toenail clippers while working as chief of dental laboratory technology at the University of Mississippi School of Dentistry (he retired in April 1998). These clippers have unique finger grips designed to be slip proof and also catch the clippings. His invention really took off after national attention garnered when Chicago-based syndicated columnist Mike Royko praised the clippers in two different columns within two weeks in late Oct. and early Nov. 1994. The columns appeared in over 600 newspapers around the nation.

Stuart A. Roosa

Born Stuart Allen Roosa on Aug. 16, 1933, in Durango, Colorado, he grew up in Claremore, Oklahoma. He left the University of Colorado after two years to earn his Air Force wings, then returned to school to get a bachelor's degree in aeronautical engineering. He was a graduate of the aerospace test pilot school and was an experimental test pilot at Edwards Air Force Base before becoming one of 19 people picked for the astronaut class of 1966. He served with NASA for 10 years. A member of the support crew for the Apollo 9 space flight before he flew his sole mission on Apollo 14 from Jan. 31-Feb. 9, 1971. Roosa piloted the command module Kitty Hawk that orbited the moon while astronauts Alan Shepard and Edgar Mitchell descended to the surface in the lunar module Antares. After carrying out their assignments on the moon, the two other astronauts rejoined Colonel Roosa and he brought them back to Earth. Roosa was one of only six men to fly the command module on the Apollo moon-landing missions. He later served as backup command pilot for the Apollo 16 and 17 missions and was assigned to the Space Shuttle Program until his retirement in 1976. "Stuart Roosa was one of the 'can-do' space-farers that helped take America and all humankind to the moon," said Daniel S. Goldin, chief

Profiles of Famous & Notable Mississippians

of the National Aeronautics and Space Administration. "He exemplified the talents that all of NASA strives for: service to our nation, technical know-how and an unbridled creative spirit." He had more than 216 cumulative hours of space flight. Roosa became president and owner of Gulf Coast Coors, a beer distributor in Gulfport in 1981. He and his family lived in Sessums, Mississippi. Roosa died Virginia of complications from pancreatitis on Dec. 12, 1994, at the age of 60. Colonel Roosa and his wife were visiting a son, who lives in Arlington, at the time of his death. He is buried in Section 7-A of Arlington National Cemetery, not far from the Tomb of the Unknowns and the Memorial Amphitheater.

Craig Ross

Born Stanley Craig Ross on Oct. 27, 1981, in Vicksburg, Mississippi. Ross was a junior at Vicksburg High School when he scored a 36 on the ACT (American College Test) in June 1999. A member of the class of 2000, Ross has kept a perfect 4.0 Honor Roll grade point average through high school. He has been a member of the Beta Club, the Junior Classical League, and the Technology Student Association for four years. He's been on the Quiz Bowl for all 4 years of high school and won first place at the MSMS competition for four years. He's also been on the junior varsity tennis team since 8th grade. Ross has been a member of Mu Alpha Theta since the 10th grade and is treasurer of the organization in his senior year. He's still found time to be of service in his community by tutoring math and science all through high school, teaching Latin to 4-6th grade students during his 10th grade, as well as helping with the Special Olympics and Run Through History. He has won many awards including the U.S. Achievement Academy History Award. Ross is a National Merit Semifinalist and is listed in *Who's Who among High School Students*. He hasn't yet decided where he will attend college, but he plans on majoring in math and computer or electrical engineering. After his education, he wants to work in the computer field, either programming or designing. A self-admitted "video game junkie," Ross says he would love to design the programs for those popular computer games. Ross is one of 7 students in Mississippi to score 36 on the ACT during 1999. Although 7 for one calendar year is not a record for a single state as far as the absolute number, ACT headquarters says it might very well be a record for Mississippi as far as per capita state population and compared with the number of students in a state taking the test during a calendar year. Ross is one of only 12 Mississippi students to ever make a 36 score through June 2000.

Isaiah "Doctor" Ross

This blues guitarist, harpist, and vocalist was born Charles Isaiah Ross in Tunica, Miss. on Oct. 21, 1925. He had a unique and unusual style — he essentially played backwards! He played his guitar left-handed and upside-down and played harmonica turned around with the low notes to his right. He recorded two classics on the Sun Records label in Memphis, *Chicago Breakdown* and *Boogie Disease*. Ross is a member of the Blues Hall of Fame. He died May 28, 1993, at age 67.

Jim Buck Ross

Born in Pelahatchie, Mississippi on Aug. 14, 1917. He was a graduate of Mississippi State University (class of 1939) and the Jackson School of Law (later the Mississippi College law school). After law school, Ross served in the U.S. Army during World War II. After the war, he served one term as mayor of Pelahatchie and one term in the Mississippi Senate. He was elected Commissioner of Agriculture and Commerce in 1968 and served in that capacity until his retirement in 1995, one of the nation's longest serving agriculture commissioners. Ross was well-known for promoting Mississippi farm-raised catfish and the state poultry industry. He was instrumental in the creation of the College of Veterinary Medicine at Mississippi State University in 1974. He founded the Jim Buck Ross Mississippi Agriculture and Forestry/National Agricultural Aviation Museum in Jackson, considered to be one of the finest of its kind in the nation. Under his direction as chairman of the Mississippi State Fair Commission, the Dixie National Livestock Show held in February every year grew to be the largest livestock show east of the Mississippi River. Ross was instrumental in obtaining legislation and financing for the Mississippi Sports Hall of Fame. He was also known for giving hilarious speeches at the Neshoba County Fair. After suffering numerous health problems over the past few years, Ross died of a stroke on Dec. 14, 1999, at the age of 82.

James C. "Butch" Rosser, Jr.

Born on Sept. 14, 1954, in Rome, Mississippi, he grew up in Moorhead (both in Sunflower County). As a black child growing up in the Delta, young Rosser was inspired by the TV program, *Ben Casey, M.D.* He also had a love for remote-controlled airplanes. Now, as a physician, he has combined those two things to become a leading international authority on minimally invasive cybersurgery. He graduated from Gentry High School in Indianola, then accepted a football scholarship at the University of Florida because his first choice, the University of Mississippi, did not accept black football players when he applied in 1971. Because his participation in sports was lowering his grades, he later changed to Ole Miss to pursue a medical degree and became the third black to receive a degree in medicine from the University of Mississippi. Upon completing his residency at Akron General Medical Center in Ohio, he taught at Northeastern Ohio College of Medicine. It was there that he heard about doctors in Germany trying to remove a gall bladder using a laparoscope. After traveling to Europe to learn more about the procedure, Rosser removed his first gall bladder by laparoscopy in early 1990. Since then, laparoscopy, where only small incisions are made in the patient, has become his specialty. He started doing research and more complex procedures and became internationally known. Now, Dr. Rosser is on the cutting-edge. From his office in Connecticut, Rosser uses his computer and telecommunications technology to videoconference with doctors in other countries and direct their surgery techniques via satellite as they operate. He lectures around the world and was selected as one of the chairmen for the Fourth World Endoscopic Congress. He has been a contributing editor of several medical journals, has contributed chapters to major laparoscopic textbooks and has written two books on the subject. In 1991, Rosser was honored on the Children's Mircle Telethon and with the Kent State Minority Achievement Award. He received the Smithsonian Award for Technical Achievement in Medicine in 1997 and 1998. This Mississippi University Medical Center graduate has been featured on CNN, the *CBS Morning Show*, the Learning Channel and the Discovery Channel.

Dunbar Rowland

Born Aug. 25, 1864, in Oakland, Yalobusha Co., Miss. He was the first director of the Mississippi Dept. of Archives and History from Mar. 14, 1902 until his death on Nov. 1, 1937. A pioneer in the archival field in the U.S., he received his B.A. from Mississippi A & M College (Miss. State) and L.L.B. from the Ole Miss and practiced law for a few years before becoming director of the Archives. He published his 3-volume

Profiles of Famous & Notable Mississippians

Encyclopedia of Mississippi History in 1907, his series of *Official and Statistical Registers of the State of Mississippi* from 1904 through 1928, the 10-volume *Jefferson Davis, Constitutionalist* in 1923, plus several other history books.

David Ruffin

Born Jan. 18, 1941, in the community of Whynot near Meridian, Mississippi. He was the co-lead singer of The Temptations from 1963-68. He also had some Top-10 hit records on his own: *My Whole World Ended (The Moment You Left Me)* (#9 in 1969), and *Walk Away From Love* (#9 in 1976) plus 12 albums. The Temptations were inducted into the Rock and Roll Hall of Fame in 1989. Three of The Temptations' songs, *Ain't Too Proud To Beg*, *My Girl* and *Papa Was A Rollin' Stone*, are included on the Rock and Roll Hall of Fame's list of 500 Songs That Shaped Rock And Roll. Ruffin's life was cut short by drug abuse when he died on June 1, 1991, at age 50. He is buried in the Woodlawn Cemetery in Detroit, Michigan. Much of his life and career was portrayed on the NBC-TV mini-series, *The Temptations*, which aired on Nov. 1 & 2, 1998. He was the brother of singer Jimmy Ruffin.

Jimmy Ruffin

Soul singer born on May 7, 1939 in Collinsville, Miss. He had Top-10 record hits *What Becomes of The Broken-hearted* (#7 in 1966) and *Hold On To My Love* (#10 in 1980). He also had *I've Passed This Way Before* (#17 in 1967) and *Gonna Give Her All The Love I've Got* (#29 in 1967). He has 13 albums. Brother of Mississippian David Ruffin.

Bobby Rush

Born Emmit Ellis Jr. on Nov. 10, 1940, in Homer, Louisiana, he and his family relocated to Chicago in 1953, where he fronted various blues bands on the West Side blues circuit in the 1960s. His first hit was the single *Chicken Heads* (1971) followed by *Bow-Legged Woman*. He recorded for several labels until 1979 when his hit album *Rush Hour* was released on Philadelphia International. During the 1980s, Rush cut the funky albums *Gotta have Money* (1984) and *What's Good for the Goose Is Good for the Gander* (1985). During the mid-1990s, Rush signed with Waldoxy, a label belonging to Malaco of Jackson. This marked a return to a soul-blues sound including the albums *One Monkey Don't Stop No Show* (1995), *Lovin's a Big Fat Woman* (1997), and *Hoochie Man* (2000). Rush has lived in Jackson since the early 1990s. He received the 1997 Living Blues Award for Best Live Performance, the 1997 *Real Blues Magazine* Award for Best Soul/R&B Live Performer for the second consecutive year, plus he's been nominated for two W.C. Handy Awards. Rush writes over 99 percent of his material and has written over 500 songs.

Leslie Vaughn Rush

Born Feb. 16, 1905, in Meridian. A medical pioneer and physician, Dr. Rush pioneered the use of bone-pinning, performing the first successful intramedullary bone-pinning operation in 1936 at Rush Memorial Hospital (now Rush Foundation Hospital) in Meridian. The Rush pin used today was perfected in 1948. Dr. Rush died on Feb. 8, 1987.

Otis Rush

This blues guitarist and singer was born Apr. 29, 1934, in Philadelphia, Mississippi. With his unique style he has influenced many young guitarists including Jimmy Page, Eric Clapton and Stevie Ray Vaughan. He has recorded 20 albums, including *Ain't Enough Comin' In* (1994). Also a songwriter, he wrote *She's A Good 'Un*, an early hit, and *Homework*, a big single in 1962. Rush's song, *I Can't Quit You Baby*, is included on the Rock and Roll Hall of Fame & Museum's list of 500 Songs That Shaped Rock And Roll.

Felder Rushing

Born June 19, 1952, in Indianola, Miss. An honor graduate of Louisiana State Landscape School of the South, he also holds two degrees from Mississippi State. He's been a horticulture agent for the Cooperative Extension Service for Hinnds County since 1980. Rushing also writes a garden column for *The Clarion-Ledger* and has written for several national gardening magazines such as *Fine Gardening*, *Garden Design* and *Country Living Gardens*. He's also appeared on many radio and TV programs. In 1992, he was featured in the *New York Times* for his interest in "yard art." He was honored as Mississippi Author of the Year in 1988 for his first book, *Gardening Southern Style*, and the Garden Writers Association of America named his *Passalong Plants* the best garden book of 1994, giving it their Quill and Trowel Award. He co-authored *Taylor's Guide to Southern Landscaping* ('90) and *Great Garden Shortcuts* ('96), along with other garden experts. His book, *Scarecrows: Making Harvest Figures and Other Yard Folks*, was published in 1998.

Donna Hild Russell

Born June 27, 1954, in Brandon, Mississippi. She was Miss University 1974. Russell graduated from Ole Miss in 1976. She won the title of Mrs. America 1985, and was third runner up for Mrs. World 1986. Her daughter, Heather, 20, competed for the Miss Mississippi 2000 title as Miss Madison.

Johnny Russell

This country singer, songwriter and comedian was born on Jan. 23, 1940, in Moorhead, Mississippi. Russell's family moved to California when he was 11 and he grew up there acting and appearing in clubs and on local TV. A songwriter from an early age, Jim Reeves put the Russell-penned *In A Mansion Stands My Love* on the B side of his No. 1 country hit of 1959, *He'll Have to Go*. Russell wrote *Act Naturally*, a big country hit for Buck Owens and also a pop/rock hit by former Beatle Ringo Starr. Other big country and pop stars that have recorded songs written by Russell include George Jones, Dolly Parton, Patti Page, Del Reeves, George Strait and Bobby Vinton. He wrote Gene Watson's hit *Got No Reason Now For Going Home*. He's also recorded several hits of his own. Starting in the early 1970s he had *Mr. And Mrs. Untrue*, *Rain Falling on Me*, *Rednecks*, *White Socks and Blue Ribbon Beer*, *Catfish John*, *The Baptism of Jesse Taylor*, *Hello I Love You* and *Song of the South*. Russell was on the long running syndicated TV show *Hee Haw*. He's been a member of the Grand Ole Opry in Nashville since 1985. In 1990, Russell's performance at the International Music Festival at Wembley Arena in London was the first country performance to be aired live on the new cable and satellite TV network, British Satellite Broadcasting.

James Saggus

Born Aug 15, 1925, in Alexandria, Louisiana, he become one of Mississippi's most renowned journalists. His career began at the *Daily Town Talk* in Alexandria. He began working for The Associated Press in New Orleans in 1949 and joined the AP bureau in Jackson as correspondent in 1958. Colleagues and state officials have praised Saggus for his coverage of a wide range of government activities and political campaigns beginning with the administration of Governor J.P. Coleman in the mid-1950s. He covered James Meredith's admission to the University of Mississippi in 1962, the murder of Medgar Evers in 1963, and many other top stories in the state through the years. He also covered high school and college football and was inducted into the Mississippi Sportwriters Hall of Fame in 1990. The 1988 Mississippi legislature voted unanimously to

Profiles of Famous & Notable Mississippians

commend Saggus for his career. He retired from the AP after that session ended. Saggus died of leukemia at his Brandon, Mississippi home on Apr. 4, 1995.

Sidney L. "Sid" Salter
Born on Jan. 16, 1959, at Philadelphia, Mississippi. He was a John C. Stennis Scholar in Political Science at Mississippi State from 1977-80 and received his B.A. degree in political science there in 1988. He also studied on a Eastern European Economics Fellowship in 1993 at the European Academy of Berlin, Germany. Salter began his journalism career as assistant sports editor of *The Starkville Daily News* in Aug. 1981. He has been associate editor of *The Neshoba Democrat* in Philadelphia, managing editor of *The Bolivar Commercial* in Cleveland and president and CEO of Monroe Publishing, Inc., publisher of *The Aberdeen Examiner* and *The Amory Advertiser*. Since 1983, he has been publisher and editor of *The Scott County Times/The Times Plus* in Forest where he now lives. He is also a syndicated newspaper columnist appearing in 58 Mississippi daily and weekly newspapers, including *The Clarion-Ledger* Sunday "Perspective" section, currently the most widely-published op/ed column in the state. Since 1992, he has been political analyst/commentator on newscasts on WTOK-TV in Meridian and is also chief commentator on that station for all election coverage. He takes pride in the many community activities in which he has been involved and has received much recognition and many awards for the leadership positions he has held. Also, he and his paper have received numerous journalism awards. In Aug. 1996, Salter became the first journalist chosen for the $1 million endowed Kelly Gene Cook, Sr. Chair in Journalism and Associate Professor of Journalism in the Department of Journalism at the University of Mississippi in Oxford.

Jessie Sanders (see "Little Howlin' Wolf")

Joe Frank Sanderson
Born Aug. 3, 1925, in Jackson, Mississippi. Sanderson was an Air Force veteran and graduated from Mississippi State in 1947 with degrees in business and accounting. He was co-founder and chairman of the board of Sanderson Farms Inc. based in Laurel, Mississippi. He was director and chairman of the National Broiler Council and of the Mississippi Poultry Association. Sanderson was director of the Southeastern Poultry and Egg Association and president of the Business and Industry Political Education Committee. He was a past president of the Mississippi State University Foundation and a trustee of Millsaps College. He also served as a member of the board of trustees of the Laurel Separate Municipal School District, president of the Laurel Chamber of Commerce, and president of the Jones County United Way. Sanderson was named to the Mississippi Business Hall of Fame in 1991 and received the Mississippi Business All-Star award from the Mississippi Economic Council that same year. He was the Mississippi Philanthropist of the Year in 1994, and in 1995, the Laurel Junior Auxiliary named him Humanitarian of the Year. He was the Mississippi State University Alumni Association's Alumnus of the Year in 1990. He provided a substantial portion of the funding for the $19.2 million Joe Frank Sanderson Center, an indoor recreation facility at Mississippi State. He died in Laurel on Jan 4, 1998, at age 72.

Bob Saxton
Born Aug. 16, 1932, on a farm in Newton County, Miss. He graduated from Shady Grove High School near Laurel. Saxton finished a four-year hitch in the U.S. Air Force in 1955. This country music and jazz guitarist has appeared with and played with many artists. He lived in Anchorage, Alaska for several years, where he played at churches and prisons in the 1970s. In 1984, he worked for 9 months with country music star Charlies Louvin. Saxton has performed with the Dorsey Brothers, Patsy Cline and fellow Mississippian Bobbie Gentry. He played on the Grand Ole Opry with Billy Walker and even appeared once with Chet Atkins. Saxton won the Merle Travis National Thumb Pickers Contest twice, in 1989 and 1995. He's also had his share of appearances overseas. He performed in June 1998 at the Intrernational Guitar Festival at Reinheim on the French-German border. He also recorded a CD in Germany in 1998 entitled *The Guitar Styles of Bob Saxton*. He still stays pretty busy with personal appearances. Saxton made an appearance in New York with fellow Mississippian Johnny Russell (see his profile) in May 1999. From there, he went on to Reno and California. He lives in Goodlettsville near Nashville and when he's not busy touring, he tunes pianos. One of his clients in country superstar Trisha Yearwood. Saxton is one of six artists on a 1999 CD called *The Great Mississippi Jazz Guitarists Reunion*, released by the Mississippi Musicians Hall of Fame (available from the MMHOF website or at area record stores). The other artists are Bucky Barrett, Steve Blailock, Mundell Lowe, Skeets McWilliams and Lloyd Wells (all are profiled in this chapter).

Chuck Scarborough
Born Nov. 4, 1943, in Pittsburgh, Pa., he entered television news in 1966 at Biloxi's WLOX-TV after he was discharged from his four-year stint in the U.S. Air Force at Keesler Air Force Base. Scarborough worked as an anchor and was in charge of all on-air operations for the station. From 1968 through 1969, he worked for WDAM-TV in Hattiesburg as a reporter and anchor, while working on a degree at University of Southern Mississippi. He received his B.S. degree, Phi Kappa Phi, from the department of radio, television and film at USM in 1969. In 1969, he moved to WAGA-TV in Atlanta, where he remained until 1972. While there, he served as managing news editor, in addition to his duties as reporter and anchor of the 6 and 11 p.m. newscasts. After two years as the anchorman at WNEV-TV in Boston, Scarborough went to work at WNBC-TV in New York in 1974, where he remains today drawing a $2 million a year salary. Among his awards are 22 Emmys and several awards from the Associated Press. He won the *Washington Review of Journalism*'s Best in the Business Award in 1984, the Working Press Association Terry Anderson Award in 1992, and an Honorary Doctor of Letters from Mercy College. He was recently asked by the National Urban League to present a humanitarian award to Oseola McCarty (see her profile) from Hattiesburg, Mississippi, who donated her $150,000 life savings to set up scholarship funds at the University of Southern Mississippi — Scarborough's alma mater. An accomplished writer, Scarborough has authored 3 novels, *Stryker* ('78), *The Myrmidon Project* ('80), and *Aftershock* ('91); as well as articles published in *New York*, *Boston*, and *American Home* magazines.

Don Scott
Born Don Magruder Scott on Nov. 5, 1894 in Woodville, Mississippi. He was Mississippi A&M's (class of 1917) first national track champion, winning the AAU half mile in 1916. An Olympian in 1916, 1920 and 1924, he won the Gold Medal in the 1924 modern pentathlon. He was inducted into the Mississippi Sports Hall of Fame in 1963, the oldest enshrined there. Mississippi State University in Starkville inducted Scott into their Sports Hall of Fame in 1970, and the school also named its stadium, Scott Field, in his honor. Scott died in San Antonio, Texas on Oct. 10, 1980.

Profiles of Famous & Notable Mississippians

George "Boomer" Scott
Born George Charles Scott on Mar. 23, 1944, in Greenville. He made his major league baseball debut on Apr. 12, 1966, with Boston and stayed with the Red Sox until 1971. He also played for the Milwaukee Brewers (1972-76) and for 3 other major league teams in 1979, his last season — the Kansas City Royals, the New York Yankees, and then back with the Bosten Red Sox, where he finished up his pro career. He won two-thirds of a triple crown as an American Leaguer in 1975 while playing first base for the Milwaukee Brewers. That year, he hit a league-high 36 homers with a league-high 109 RBIs. His home-run title was shared with the Oakland Athletics' Reggie Jackson. He played in 3 All-Star games, 1966, 1975 and 1977, and he played in the 1967 World Series. His career stats include 1,992 hits in 7,433 at bats (.268 batting avg.), 957 runs, 271 home runs and 1,051 RBIs in 2,034 games.

Johnny Sea
Born on July 15, 1940, in Gulfport, Mississippi, he grew up in Atlanta, Ga. Singer/songwriter Sea had a few country hits in 1959 and the mid-'60s. He got his start at age 17, when he won a state talent show, signed with a record label and began appearing on the Louisiana Hayride. He remained there two years before debuting on the Grand Ole Opry. Sea first appeared on the country charts in 1959 with the Top 15 single *Frankie's Man Johnny*. His follow-up, *Nobody's Darling But Mine* (1960), did equally well. When his music career slowed down, he headed west to become a cowboy, living in different areas ranging from Los Angeles to Oklahoma. Sea returned to recording in 1964, when *My Baby Walks All Over Me* reached the Top 30. Then came another hit with *My Old Faded Love* (1965), which landed him a contract with Warner Brothers and his biggest hit, *Day for Decision* (1966). The song, a reply to Barry McGuire's protest song *Eve of Destruction*, not only reached the Top 15 on country charts, but also crossed over to Top 40 pop. He moved to Columbia Records and had a minor hit in 1968 with *Goin' to Tulsa*, recorded under his birthname Johnny Seay. That year he also had his final chart song with *Three Six Packs, Two Arms and a Juke Box*. Sea soon left again to become a cowboy in Justiceburg, Texas.

James L. Seawright, Jr.
Born in Jackson on May 22, 1935, he grew up in Greenwood, Mississippi. Well known as an electronic sculptor, he now lives in New York and is head of the visual arts department at Princeton University. Some of his pieces are on permanent display at the Museum of Modern Art and the Guggenheim in New York and in other places around the country. He also has a piece on permanent display at the Seattle Airport and another in Honolulu. He is the brother of Joseph Seawright (see his profile below) and both are cousins of Mississippian Richard Truly, the only astronaut to ever head NASA.

Joseph P. Seawright
Born in Greenwood on Aug. 19, 1945. A designer for Baldwin Piano and Organ Company in Greenwood since 1974, he is believed to be the only single person in Mississippi to have designed and built his own hot air balloon. After a year-and-a-half of research, he spent almost 6 months sewing the balloon together on an industrial sewing machine and finished it in 1995. The balloon, called the "Baby Grand," holds almost 74,000 cubic feet of air when fully inflated and has a piano keyboard design on it. He is the brother of James Seawright (see profile above) and both are cousins of Mississippian Richard Truly, the only astronaut to ever head NASA.

Larry Semon
Born Lawrence Semon in West Point, Miss. on July 6, 1889. His father, professional magician Zera the Great, and mother were touring the South at the time. He became a slapstick comedian known for his charming, white-painted face and clownish smile. He started out as a cartoonist for the New York *Sun*. In 1916, he was hired by Vitagraph to write and direct comedy short films. Soon, he became one of the most popular and highest paid comedians of the early 20s. After starring himself in his company's films, his popularity approached that of Charlie Chaplin, Buster Keaton and Harold Lloyd. He also became popular in Europe. He directed most of his own films and was often supported by a villainous Oliver Hardy (before Laurel). He directed the original silent screen version of *Wizard of Oz* (1925), in which he also played the part of the scarecrow. His career was marred by personal problems and he squandered his fortune. Semon declared bankruptcy in March 1928. He was penniless when he died at the Garcelon Ranch, near Victorville, Calif. on Oct. 8, 1928, from pneumonia after a nervous breakdown He was 39.

Floyd D. Shaman
Born Dec. 20, 1935 in Wheatland, Wyoming. After studying art at the University of Wyoming and receiving a degree in painting, he apprenticed with a stone carver for three years and completed his master's degree in sculpture. Shaman moved to Cleveland, Miss. in 1970 to teach at Delta State. When he couldn't find stone, he started carving and sculpting wood. He now works primarily with laminated wood to create furniture items such as chairs and benches, and humorous life-size wood figures. He is currently working on women figures such as Cleopatra, the Statue of Liberty, Madame Butterfly, and other pieces for galleries. The late Malcolm Forbes had a piece of his work, and Mississippian Thomas Harris, author of *Silence of the Lambs*, owns a piece of Shaman's work.

Billy Shaw
Born in Dec. 15, 1938, in Natchez and raised in Vicksburg, Mississippi, he played football his junior year at long-defunct Jett High School. Shaw ranks among the greatest Georgia Tech linemen, playing both ways at tackle and from 1957-61 and earning All-American and All Southeastern Conference honors. He make the All- SEC third team in 1959 and first team in 1960. In 1961, Shaw went pro playing offensive guard for the Buffalo Bills of the American Football League. In 119 games over 9 seasons, he was 7 times captain and most valuable lineman. After the Bills won league championships in 1964 and 1965, the team came up one game shy of making their first Super Bowl in 1966. He was named to the All-AFL first team from 1962-1966. Shaw earned All-Pro honors 7 times and made 8 trips to the AFL Pro Bowl. He retired after the 1969 season. Shaw was inducted into the Mississippi Sports Hall of Fame in 1996. When inducted into the Pro Football Hall of Fame on Aug. 7, 1999, Shaw became the first member to have spent his entire career in the AFL, which merged with the NFL in 1970.

Jackie Sherrill
The year 2000 was his 10th season as head football coach at Mississippi State University. Born Nov. 28, 1943, in Duncan, Oklahoma, he spent part of his youth in Biloxi, where he played football at Biloxi High. In his senior year, he earned high school all-America and was the team's MVP before graduating in 1962. Sherrill played for the legendary Paul "Bear" Bryant at the University of Alabama from 1962-65. He lettered 3 years and played on the 1964 and '65 national championship teams. After earning a degree in business administration in 1966, Sherrill served on Bryant's staff as a graduate assistant coach in 1966, and held a similar position at

Profiles of Famous & Notable Mississippians

Arkansas in 1967. His first full-time coaching job came in 1968 at Iowa State where he served as an assistant. Sherrill served as assistant head coach for the Pittsburgh Panthers from 1973-75. He landed his first head coaching post in 1976 at Washington State University. A year later, he returned as the Panthers' head coach. During the 1970s and '80s, Sherrill posted a 105-45-2 record, guiding teams at Pittsburgh and Texas A&M to 8 bowl appearances and 6 top-10 finishes. His final three Pittsburgh teams (1979-81) posted a 33-3 record and played in the Fiesta, Gator and Sugar Bowls. His 5-year tenure at Pittsburgh resulted in a 50-9-1 record, 5 straight bowl games and 4 top-10 national rankings. His 1980 team finished the year ranked second in the nation and his 1981 Panthers beat SEC champ Georgia in the Sugar Bowl. Sherrill was honored as the Eastern Coach of the Year in 1979 and 1980. His 1985-87 Texas A&M teams had a 29-7-1 record, advancing to 3 straight Cotton Bowls as champions of the SWC. During Sherrill's 7-years, the Aggies posted a 52-28-1 overall record, 36-17-1 within the SWC. A&M posted 10-win campaigns in 1985 and '87, and Sherrill was named SWC Coach of the Year both years. Those teams beat Auburn (36-16) and Notre Dame (35-10) in respective Cotton Bowls. He was named national coach of the year by *Playboy* magazine in 1988. He arrived as Mississippi State University's 30th head football coach in late 1990. In 1991, Sherrill molded the State football team into a competitive force in the SEC with a remarkable first season at MSU, including a nationally televised wins over Texas and Auburn, a triumph in the Egg Bowl against Mississippi, and a berth in the 1991 Liberty Bowl. State fans responded in 1992 by purchasing every available season ticket, a first at MSU. In succeeding years, State helped set attendance records at both the Liberty and Peach Bowls and set records in season ticket sales and attendance. Sherrill led MSU to its most TV appearances in one year ever in 1991, 1992, 1996, 1997, 1998 and 1999. He led the Bulldogs to a national ranking of 23rd by the Associated Press in 1992, the school's highest postseason showing since 1981. In 1992, MSU beat both Texas and Auburn for a second-straight year and defeated Top-10 ranked Florida. The Dawgs went on to play in the Jan. 1993 Peach Bowl. In 1993, for the second time in three years, State defeated arch-rival Mississippi in the Egg Bowl. State won 8 games in 1994, defeating Tennessee, South Carolina, Mississippi, Kentucky & Arkansas. The five league wins were accomplished only two other times in school history. For the third time in four years, he led the Bulldogs to victory over in-state rival Mississippi, the first time that had occurred since 1939-42. That 1994 win over the Rebels was a third-straight SEC road victory, a feat unmatched in 37 years. For the second time in three seasons, he led the Dawgs to the Peach Bowl, MSU's third postseason showing in four years. Mississippi State had six 1994 seniors selected in the NFL draft, the most from the school in 47 years, and supplied the NFL with 2 first-round draft choices from its 1995 team, two-thirds of the entire SEC's first-round selections that year. In 1996, Mississippi State defeated Alabama for the first time in 16 years and also defeated Mississippi for the fourth time in Sherrill's first six years. The 1997 Bulldogs beat Alabama for a second-straight season and defeated South Carolina, Kentucky and Auburn. State's eight victories in 1998 marked the second time a Sherrill-coached State team had reached that win total. Prior to Sherrill's arrival, it had been 10 years since the school had an eight-win season. The 1998 team was undefeated at home, a first at State since 1989, when the Bulldogs only played one SEC contest at Scott Field. MSU won six SEC games in 1998 for the first time ever. State beat Alabama for a third-straight season, a first at the school since 1912-14. Sherrill had his 150th career win when his 1998 team defeated Auburn. The Western Division champion Bulldogs played for a league title for the first time in 57 years at the 1998 SEC championship game on Dec. 5 in Atlanta. After they came from behind to defeat LSU on Oct. 23 (for the first time since 1991), the Bulldogs were 7-0 for the 1999 season, the best start in the school's 105-year history and 100 football seasons that saw more than 900 games under 30 head coaches! The Bulldogs moved up from No. 12 to No. 8 in both The Associated Press Top 25 poll (tied with Nebaska) and the ESPN/*USA Today* Top 25 coaches poll! With 4 games to play, the '99 Bulldogs had already won more games than 81 of the previous 99 Mississippi State football teams! State went to 8-0 in the next game. After that they lost two straight, then finished the regular season 9-2 by winning the Egg Bowl against Ole Miss 23-20 on Nov. 25, 1999 (making State's record in the Egg Bowl under Sherrill 6-3), another come-from-behind victory that was won in the last few seconds of play, something the Bulldogs were noted for in the 1999 season. With a 17-7 Peach Bowl win over Clemson Dec. 30 (Sherrill's first bowl victory), the Bulldogs finished the 1999 season 10-2 overall, second in the Western Division to Southeastern Conference champion Alabama. State was No. 12 in the final Associated Press Top 25. Sherrill has directed the Dawgs to five bowl berths — the only head coach ever to take MSU to more than two bowl games. He has posted 18 winning seasons in his 22 years as a college head coach and gone to 13 bowl games. He is one of only 3 active head coaches to lead 3 different schools to bowl games. Sherrill, 63-46-2 at State through Oct. 28, 2000, is one win shy of tying Allyn McKeen's school record. Sherrill owns the school record of 38 SEC victories, nine more than runner-up McKeen. Sherrill is 169-91-4 in his 22 seasons as head coach (through 10/28/2000). He has won 11 games during a season on three different occasions, and 10 twice. Twenty of the top 25 crowds including 9 of the best 10 ever at MSU's Scott Field have come during Sherrill's tenure. This includes the record crowd of 43,917 on Oct. 7, 2000. He coached Heisman candidate and All-Pro quarterback Dan Marino, Lombardi Trophy & Maxwell Trophy winner Hugh Green, and Outland Trophy winner Mark May. Over 100 of his pupils have advanced to careers in pro football. Sherrill, a popular speaker, was honored by Success Motivational Institute as recipient of its 1991 International Achiever Award. Sherrill's ranks fifth in overall pay among SEC coaches. His base pay is $175,000 and his total annual compensation package is $750,000.

Purvis Short

Born Aug. 24, 1956, in Hattiesburg. Purvis received more than 150 scholarship offers, but decided to attend Jackson State University where his older brother, Eugene, was a basketball star. Purvis, himself, was a basketball standout at JSU from 1974-78. Eugene set JSU's career scoring record with 2,017 points from 1972-75. Purvis eclipsed his brother's record with a new mark of 2,434 points (23.7 ppg avg.), which remains the record. Purvis led the Tigers to a 83-23 record and a SWAC title in 1975. Even in his freshman year, he led the team in field goal percentage. As a sophomore, he established several school records including the highest scoring average (29.5 ppg), most field goal attempts (635) and most field goals made (324). Purvis was the fifth player selected in the NBA draft in 1978, one of the highest selections ever for a Mississippian at

Profiles of Famous & Notable Mississippians

the time. He made the All-Rookie team and paced the Golden State Warriors in scoring seven of his nine seasons with them. He scored 59 points for the Warriors in a game against the Nets in 1984. The 1984-85 season was his best, when he finished fourth in the league in scoring. In 1987, the Warriors traded him to Houston where he played two seasons. After playing a year for New Jersey, he played a year overseas. When he retired from pro basketball in 1992 after 11 seasons with 3 NBA teams, scoring 14,607 points for a 17.3 per game average. He was among the league's top 20 career scorers. He was inducted into the SWAC Hall of Fame in 1998. Purvis Short now makes his home in Houston. Still involved with pro basketball as a counselor for the NBA Players Association, he travels around the country talking to players about substance abuse and other topics. Short was inducted into the Mississippi Sports Hall of Fame in March 2000.

Jean F. Simmons
Born Jean Elstner Frazer on May 10, 1936, in Monroe, Louisiana, her nickname since childhood has been "Sister." She is married to Dr. Heber Simmons, Jr., a children's dentist. She received her B.S. degree at Memphis State University in 1957, her master's at Mississippi College in 1966 and her doctorate in Early Childhood Development at Jackson State University in 1990. She also studied at other Mississippi schools including Delta State University, Millsaps College and the University of Southern Mississippi. Dr. Simmons has been with the Jackson School System since 1962. Involved in the arts in a big way, she's been associated with the Arts Alliance of Jackson/Hinds County, the Mississippi Arts Association, the Mississippi Arts Festival, the New Stage Theatre, the Jackson Music Association, the Mississippi Symphony Orchestra, the Mississippi Ballet and the International Ballet Competition. In 1979, she co-authored the book, *A Child's Guide to Mississippi*. She has received many honors including a listing in *Outstanding Young Women of America* in 1966, in *Who's Who of American Women with World Notables* in 1970-71, in the *Who's Who of American Women* in 1972-73 and again in 1974-75. Dr. Jean Simmons put together the Academic and Performing Arts Complex/ Performing Arts Division for the Jackson Public School System in 1981 and was director of that program from its inception until she resigned her position as performing arts coordinator on June 18, 1999. The program received the 1988 Mississippi Arts Commission's Governor's Awards in the Arts. Simmons received the Arts Education Award of the Governor's Awards in 1997.

"Jumpin'" Gene Simmons
Born July 10, 1933, in Tupelo. He started in music at age 15 playing dances in Tupelo and Memphis. He recorded for Sun Records after moving to Memphis in the late 1950s. He has also recorded for Hi, Epic, and his own studio in Tupelo. Simmons played shows throughout the South until 1959 when he went on tour in Canada. He came back to the U.S. in 1960 and worked at the Cotton Club in Memphis in 1961. Then he joined the Bill Black Combo and worked for Hi Records. He also wrote several songs at the time. Simmons had one big hit record, *Haunted House*, that almost made it to the Top-10 (#11) in 1964. He's a member of the Rockabilly Hall of Fame.

Prescilla D. Slade
Born on Sept. 16, 1951, in Shaw, Bolivar Co., Miss., she grew up from age six in Yazoo City, Miss. After graduating from Yazoo City High, she received her bachelor's in business administration from Mississippi State, an MPA degree in accounting from Jackson State and her doctorate in accounting from the University of Texas in Austin. Dr. Slade taught at Tougaloo College and the University of Texas. She joined the faculty at Texas Southern University in 1991 as chairman of the accounting department. She was named dean of the School of Business in 1992. Dr. Slade took the school through the legislative process and was responsible for the construction of the Jesse H. Jones School of Business. She was appointed as acting president of TSU in Feb. 1999. After serving in the interim position for almost a year, at the start of 2000 Dr. Slade was appointed president of Texas Southern University. Thirty-five individuals had applied for the position. She is a member of the National Association of Black Accountants, the American Association of Women Accountants, and many other organizations and serves on the boards of numerous organizations. Slade is the daughter of Mrs. Percy Dean of Yazoo City and the late Rev. Dean.

Jackie Slater
Born May 27, 1954, in Jackson, this former Jackson State offensive lineman became the first player in the NFL to stay with the same team for two decades, setting an NFL record by playing in 259 games with the Los Angeles/St. Louis Rams from 1976 to 1995. He retired after the 1995 season.

James D. Slaton
Born James Daniel Slaton on Apr. 2, 1912, in Laurel, Mississippi, he was living in Gulfport when he entered the U.S. Army. Corporal Slaton was in the 157th Infantry, 45th Infantry Division near Oliveto, Italy when he performed an act of bravery on Sept. 23, 1943, that earned him the Congressional Medal of Honor. He was presented the Medal on May 30, 1944. Here are the actual words of his citation: "For conspicuous gallantry and intrepidity at the risk of life above and beyond the call of duty in action with the enemy in the vicinity of Oliveto, Italy, on 23 September 1943. Cpl. Slaton was lead scout of an infantry squad which had been committed to a flank to knock out enemy resistance which had succeeded in pinning 2 attacking platoons to the ground. Working ahead of his squad, Cpl. Slaton crept upon an enemy machinegun nest and, assaulting it with his bayonet, succeeded in killing the gunner. When his bayonet stuck, he detached it from the rifle and killed another gunner with rifle fire. At that time he was fired upon by a machinegun to his immediate left. Cpl. Slaton then moved over open ground under constant fire to within throwing distance, and on his second try scored a direct hit on the second enemy machinegun nest, killing 2 enemy gunners. At that time a third machinegun fired on him 100 yards to his front, and Cpl. Slaton killed both of these enemy gunners with rifle fire. As a result of Cpl. Slaton's heroic action in immobilizing 3 enemy machinegun nests with bayonet, grenade, and rifle fire, the 2 rifle platoons which were receiving heavy casualties from enemy fire were enabled to withdraw to covered positions and again take the initiative. Cpl. Slaton withdrew under mortar fire on order of his platoon leader at dusk that evening. The heroic actions of Cpl. Slaton were far above and beyond the call of duty and are worthy of emulation." Slaton is one of only 4 *native* Mississippians (of 7 Mississippians) awarded the Congressional Medal of Honor during WWII. Slaton's Medal was one of 17 Medals of Honor officially accredited to Mississippi in all wars, although we claim 5 more accredited to other states because the recipients had Mississippi ties. Slaton is one of only 13 *native* Mississippians (of 22 Mississippians — 15 Army, 4 Marines & 3 Navy) in all wars to receive the Medal of Honor out of 3,433 total recipients of the Medal through Nov. 1, 2000. Slaton died on Feb. 2, 1961. He is buried in the Harmony Cemetery in Laurel. There is no Medal of Honor marker on his gravesite.

Profiles of Famous & Notable Mississippians

Torrance Small
Born Sept. 6, 1970, in Tampa, Fl. He was an education major at Alcorn, he finished his football career as the leading receiver in Alcorn State history with 140 catches for 2,527 yards and 16 TDs, was first-team All-Southwest Athletic Conference selection as a senior and a sophomore; and he set a then school-record by catching 55 passes for 1,068 yards and 7 TDs as a senior. In his 7-year NFL pro career as a wide receiver for Indianapolis, Torrance played in 85 games and has 208 catches for 2,668 yards and 17 TDs (thru 1999).

Calvin Smith
This world-class sprinter was born on Jan. 8, 1961, in Bolton, Miss. He attended the University of Alabama and was one of the best ever in their track program — 8 times All-America, 4 times Southeastern Conference champion, holder still of school records for the 100 meters (9.93 seconds) and 200 meters (19.99 seconds). He set the 100-meter world record of 9.93 seconds on July 3, 1983 at the National Sports Festival in Colorado Springs and held that record until Sept. 24, 1988, when Carl Lewis beat it by one second. He gained Olympic Gold at the 1984 Los Angeles Games running the third leg of the 4x100 relay which turned a world-record time of 37.83 seconds. In the 1988 Games at Seoul, Korea, Smith gained bronze in the 100 meter after Canada's Ben Johnson was stripped of his win for steroid use. He was assistant track coach at the University of Alabama from 1995-97. He now lives in Tampa, Fl., where he teaches underprivileged children.

Frank E. Smith
Born Frank Ellis Smith in Sidon, Miss. on Feb 21, 1918. He attended the public schools of Sidon and Greenwood, Sunflower Junior College in Moorhead, Miss., and received a B.A. from Ole Miss in 1941. Smith entered the U.S. Army as a private on Feb. 9, 1942, graduated from Field Artillery officers candidate school and served in Europe as a captain with the 243rd Field Artillery Battalion of the Third Army. He was discharged to the reserves as a major of Field Artillery on Feb. 13, 1946. He was a student at American University in Washington, D.C. in 1946. He was Managing editor of the Greenwood *Morning Star* in 1946-47. He was a legislative assistant to U.S. Senator John Stennis 1947-1949. He was a member of State Senate 1948-1950. Smith was elected as a Democrat to the 82nd and to the five succeeding Congresses and served from January 3, 1951 until his resignation Nov. 14, 1962. He was unsuccessful for renomination in 1962 to the 88th Congress. He then became director of the Tennessee Valley Authority for ten years from Nov. 14, 1962 to May 18, 1972. Before returning to Mississippi, he was associate director of the Illinois State board of higher education from 1973-1974, and was a professor at Virginia Tech from 1977-1979. Smith was a special assistant to Governor William Winter of Mississippi from 1980-1983. He was elected a life fellow to the Southern Regional Council in 1984. Smith was among the first of Mississippi politicians to denounce segregation and expounds on his thinking in his autobiographical book, *Congressman from Mississippi* (1964). His other books include *The Yazoo* (1954), *Dixie* (1965), *The Politics of Conservation* (1966) and *Mississippians All* (1968). Smith died on Aug. 2, 1997, in Jackson, Mississippi.

Frederick W. Smith
Born Frederick Wallace Smith on Aug. 11, 1944, in Marks, Quitman County, Miss. He attended Yale University, where he earned a B.S. in economics in 1966. Smith served as an officer in the U.S. Marine Corps, including tours of duty in Vietnam from 1966-70. He founded Federal Express in 1971 in an abandoned military hangar at Memphis International Airport. The company began operations on Apr. 17, 1973. Within 10 years, Federal Express had racked up $1 billion in revenue, becoming the first American company to reach the billion-dollar mark in one decade without mergers or acquisitions. In 1990, it was the first company to win the Malcolm Baldrige National Quality Award. The company has won many other awards. Smith has been a leader in regulatory reform and can take much credit for government deregulation of the airline industry, for both cargo and passengers. FedEx has become the largest express delivery company in the world with 1998 revenues of $12 billion. Fred Smith is Chairman, President and CEO of FDX Corporation, a $16 billion global transportation and logistics holding company, established on Jan. 27, 1998. The companies under the FDX umbrella — Federal Express, RPS, Viking Freight, Roberts Express, Caliber Logistics and Caliber Technology — operate in 211 countries with more than 190,000 employees worldwide who handle an average daily shipping volume of 5 million items! Vance Trimble wrote a book called *Overnight Success: Federal Express and Frederick Smith, Its Renegade Creator*.

Hamilton Smith
Born Oct. 22, 1887, in Muskegon, Scott County, Mississippi. He was a movie director and writer in the early days of the silent screen. He was director of *The Ventures of Marguerite* (1915), *Isle of Doubt* (1922) and *The Inner Man* (1922). He wrote the stories for *The Barricade* (1917) and *The Man Unconquerable* (1922). He wrote the scenarios for *Her Second Husband* (1917) and *American Maid* (1917). He died on Oct. 29, 1941, in Los Angeles, California at the age of 54.

Hazel Brannon Smith
Born Feb. 5, 1914, in Gadsden, Ala. She received a Pulitzer in 1964 for her editorial writing at the now-defunct *Lexington Advertiser* in Lexington, Miss. She died in Lexington on May 17, 1994. Smith was one of 25 "outstanding communicators" inducted into the Communications Hall of Fame at the University of Alabama in 1998.

Janet Marie Smith
Born on Dec. 13, 1957, in Jackson. Her father, Thomas Henry Smith, has his own architectural firm in Jackson. She is a 1981 graduate of the Mississippi State University School of Architecture. She received a masters degree in urban planning form City College in New York. Smith worked in New York City as coordinator of architecture and design for Battery Park City, a project in downtown Manhattan with an estimated cost of $3 billion. From there she moved to the West Coast and became president and chief operating officer for downtown Los Angeles' oldest city park, Pershing Square. It was back to the East Coast in 1989, where she joined the Baltimore Orioles organization. As vice president for planning and development, Smith was responsible for the overall look of Oriole Park at Camden Yards. The $105 million ballpark, an important part of Baltimore's urban renaissance, received the prestigious American Institute of Architects' Honor Award in 1992, and was the site of the 1993 All-Star Game. Smith's next job took her to Atlanta. As the vice president for sports facilities for TBS Properties, she was responsible for the development of facilities that support entrepreneur Ted Turner's professional sports teams — Major League Baseball's Atlanta Braves and the National Basketball Association's Atlanta Hawks. Smith also was director of planning and development for the Braves. Part of her responsibilities at TBS Properties, a division of Turner Broadcasting Network, included overseeing design of the $150 million stadium that was used for the 1996 Olympic

Profiles of Famous & Notable Mississippians

games. After the Olympics, it became the permanent home for the Atlanta Braves, seating 48,000 baseball fans. Smith also used her design talents to improve the CNN Center, and is working on new spring training facilities for the Braves in Jupiter, Florida. She still has all those responsibilities, and more, after her recent promotion. Smith is now president of Turner Sports and Entertainment Development. Smith was the 1994 Alumnus of the Year for the School of Architecture at Mississippi State. She and her husband, Bart, live in Baltimore and she commutes to her job in Atlanta.

Jimmy Smith

Born Feb. 9, 1969, in Detroit, Michigan. He was a Callaway High School graduate and Jackson State University football standout who graduated in 1992 with a degree in business management. The 6-ft-1, 205-pound Smith's college highlights: completed his career with 107 receptions for 2,047 yards (19.1-yard average) and 16 TDs, adding 19 rushing attempts for 138 yards and one TD. In his junior year, he teamed with Tim Barnett (former Kansas City Chief) as the top wide receiver tandem in the nation. In his NFL pro career as a wide receiver for Jacksonville: 1996 — led the conference in receiving yards (1,244) although he started only nine games; 1997 — voted to the Pro Bowl for the first time in his career...caught 82 passes to rank second on the Jaguars (behind Keenan McCardell's 85), third in the AFC and seventh in the NFL...had a career-high and team-record 1,324 receiving yards, first on the team, third in the AFC and fourth in the NFL...and his 16.1-yard average per catch the sixth best in the league for players with 50 or more receptions. He led the AFC in combined receiving yardage with 165 receptions for the 1997 and '98 seasons. He had 16 touchdowns in three seasons (1996, '97 & '98), ranking second to James Stewart on the Jaguars career list of all-time leaders for receivers. He was voted to the Pro Bowl for the 2nd time on Dec. 16, 1998. Of 7 players with Missispi connections picked (including Jerry Rice), only Tim Bowens (Miami Dolphins) and Smith were voted onto the team as starters. At the 37th annual award ceremonies of the Mississippi Sports Hall of Fame on Mar. 12, 1999, Smith was named the Mississippi Professional Athlete of the Year. He started all 16 games of the 1999 season and had an NFL-leading 116 receptions for 1,636 yards (14.1 yards avg.) and 6 TDs. The receptions and yardage were the sixth most in NFL history. Smith's career stats through Oct. 22, 2000, show 430 receptions for 6,331 yards (14.7 yards avg.) and 34 touchdowns in 88 games played.

Kimberly R. Smith

Born Kimberly Rose Smith to Mississippi-born parents on Sept. 21, 1977, in Forth Worth, Texas. Her family moved to Jackson, Tenn. in 1978 and then to Hattiesburg, Miss. in 1984 when Kimberly was 6. She made a perfect 36 on the ACT (American College Test) when she took it in the fall of 1994 (she also scored 1,430 out of 1,600 on the SAT). Officials with the Iowa-based ACT say only 36 of the 900,000 students who took the test nationwide in the fall of 1994 made a 36 score. At Hattiesburg High, Smith was secretary and president of the National Forensic League, the head attorney on the Mock Trial team that became state champions, a STAR student, and had the female lead in the stage production of the musical *Oklahoma*. She graduated valedictorian of the class of 1995 with a perfect 4.0 GPA and maintained that average through undergraduate and graduate school at Ole Miss. Her achievements and honors at Ole Miss are numerous. She was a member of the Chancellor's Leadership Class, administration section editor of the Ole Miss annual staff, and class Marshall for the College of Liberal Arts during the May 1998 commencement. Smith was a member of the Delta Gamma Sorority and was vice president of programming and director of scholarship for that organization. She worked on several faculty committees that rendered decisions that had a great impact on the university, such as the Honors Advisory Council to create the University of Mississippi's McDonnell-Barksdale Honors College and the Faculty Search Committee for Director of that organization. Smith was director of campus activities for the Ole Miss Ambassadors and was musical director and member of the Baptist Student Union's "Gift of Song" ensemble. In the Oxford community, she did volunteer work for the Chamber of Commerce Mathematics Homework Hotline. Smith won the Newman Scholarship of $26,000, the largest single scholar- ship offered by Ole Miss at the time. She has since been the recipient of a Delta Gamma Foundation Scholarship, a National Merit Scholarship, a Robert Byrd Scholarship, and a graduate fellowship to study mathematics. Smith was a Taylor Medalist, the highest academic honor at Ole Miss. She received the Governor's Award in Political Science and the Alfred Hume Memorial Award for Outstanding Mathematics Undergraduate and was selected for *Who's Who in American Colleges*. She received her B.A. degree in Mathematics in 1998 and her M.A. in Mathematics in 1999. Smith was one of eight alumni inducted into the Ole Miss Hall of Fame in 1999. She started law school in the fall of 1999. Smith is one of only twelve students from the state to ever make a 36 score (either a 36 with no mistakes, or a composite 36) on the ACT through June 2000, according to the people at ACT headquarters in Iowa. Hattiesburg High is proud of the fact that three of their students have scored a 36 on the ACT. In addition to Smith, Michael Goggin did it in 1999 and Christine Varnado aced the test in 1997. Hattiesburg High School ties Jackson Prep, which has also had three students to ace the ACT, for first place in the state for the greatest number of students making the top score on the ACT.

L. T. Smith

Born Leroy Taylor Smith on Sept. 10, 1918, in Jackson. He attended the school he would put on the athletic map, Lanier High School, from 1932-1938. He played end in football and a forward in basketball for the Bulldogs and he was selected to the football All Big 8 Second team. L.T. attended college on and off from 1938-1945 beginning at Jackson State, where he played basketball and football for the Blue Bengals. In 1939, he enrolled at Tougaloo College where he played hoops and football. He was named to the First Team of the All South Central Athletic Conference in football. From 1942-45, he taught social sciences and coached football, basketball and track at Alexander High School in Brookhaven. From 1944-46, Smith became athletic director and social science teacher at Bell Street High in Grenada. He entered military service in 1945 and upon discharge from the from the Navy, L.T. returned to Tougaloo College and received his B.S. degree in 1946. He launched his 23-year high school coaching career by returning to his prep alma mater at Lanier High in Jackson. As Athletic director and social science teacher, Coach Smith had great success in football and basketball. His Lanier football teams compiled a record of 104 wins, 16 losses and 6 ties. Smith's basketball players set the modern day standard for all future Lanier teams. Under his guidance, Lanier won 341 games, losing only 34 contests, and they captured 7 Big 8 conference and 5 state championship titles. Under Smith, Lanier won the state title in hoops for 5 years — in 1951, '52 and '56 through '58. The Bulldogs captured conference honors

Profiles of Famous & Notable Mississippians

for 7 years — in 1951, 1952 and 1954 through 1958. L.T.'s Lanier track team won the state title in 1959. Smith officiated SWAC football and basketball games from 1950 through 1980 and received a plaque from the conference for outstanding service. Coach Smith has received a number of awards and honors including two Certificates of Excellency in Basketball from the National High School Athletic Association in 1958 and 1959. He is a member of the elite Sports Trail Century Club of Chicago, recognizing his 100 coaching victories. He was the 1967 Lanier Alumnus of the Year and received a 1964 annual dedication in addition to the 1957 and 1965 team awards. Tougaloo College presented him with a Molder of Champs Award. Tougaloo College inducted L.T. into their Hall of Fame in 1993 and the Mississippi Association of Coaches (MAC) put him in their Hall of Fame in 1979 after 25 years of coaching. He was inducted into the Mississippi Sports Hall of Fame in 1998. One of his former players, Robert Hathron of Ruleville, is also in the MAC Hall of Fame making L.T. and Robert the only coach and player combination in the coaching shrine. Smith currently lives in Jackson.

Patrick D. Smith
Born Oct. 8, 1927, in Mendenhall, Miss. He graduated from Hinds Junior College and holds a B.A. and M.A. in English from Ole Miss. He has written several books, including *The River Is Home* (1953) and 3 that were nominated for Pulitzers — *Forever Island* (1973), *Angel City* (1978) and *A Land Remembered* (1984). *Angel City* was made into a 1980 TV movie. Smith has also been nominated six times for the Nobel Prize for Literature. Smith, who has lived in Florida for a long time, was selected for induction into the 1999 Florida Artists Hall of Fame. Writers previously inducted include Marjorie Rawlings, Ernest Hemingway and Tennessee Williams. Smith is only the second writer inducted during his lifetime.

Symba Smith
Born July 6, 19??, in Gulfport, Miss. She was Miss Teen All American in 1989 and runner-up in the 1990 Venus Swimsuit Competition. Smith was on the cover of the first *Girls of the Gulf Coast* calendar, the *Star Search* Model of the Year in 1991, and did commercials for McDonald's® & Keebler®. She was "Annihilator Girl" in the movie *Beverly Hills Cop III* ('94) and played "Jack's Dancing Partner" in *L..A. Confidential* ('97). Notable TV guest appearances include *Veronica's Closet* ("Veronica's Man in a Suitcase," 4/9/98) and *Star Trek: Deep Space Nine* (as "Aluura" in "Profit and Lace" on 5/11/98).

Warren Smith
Born Feb. 7, 1933, in Louise, Humphreys Co., Miss., he lived mostly in Texas, apart from periods in Memphis from 1955-59 and Hollywood from 1959-62. Smith recorded for Sun, Liberty, Mercury, Skill and Jubal record labels. He recorded some excellent Sun rockabilly recordings including *Rock & Roll Ruby* (1956), *Miss Froggie* (1957), *Red Cadillac And A Black Mustache* (1957), *So Long I'm Gone* (1957), *Ubangi Stomp* (1957), *Sweet Sweet Girl* (1958) and *Uranium Rock* (1958). Cub Koda, writing for the *All-Music Guide*, said, "For sheer, heartfelt vocalizing abilities, of all the folks who stood in front of the microphone at Sun studio, Warren Smith may have been the most talented." Though typecast as a rocker, Smith left Sun and achieved minor success in the 1960s singing country music, his first love. Although he became a personnel manager in Longview, Texas, he toured England in a rockabilly revival show. He once had "Warren Smith-The Rock 'n' Roll Ruby Man" painted on the back of his new Cadillac. Smith died Jan. 30, 1980, of a heart attack, a week before his 47th birthday. He's in the Rockabilly Hall of Fame.

Willie Mae Ford Smith
Born June 23, 1904, in Rolling Fork, Mississippi. Sometimes known as "Mother Smith," she had a 1937 gospel hit *If You Just Keep Still*. She was also known for *Take Your Burdens to the Lord*. She was one of the most important gospel singers in the blues/pentecostal traditions to emerge in the 1930s. She died on Feb. 2, 1994 at the age of 89.

John "Big Bad" Smitty
Born John Smith on Feb. 11, 1940, in Vicksburg, he was raised in the tiny Delta town of Schlater. When he was ten his father bought a guitar for Smitty's older brother Nelson, and Smitty would play it when no one was around. By his mid teens he was gigging in the Greenville area with his schoolmate, Roosevelt "Booba" Barnes. By his twenties he had moved to Jackson. In the fertile Jackson blues scene of the fifties Smitty played regularly with artists including John Littlejohn, Sam Myers, King Edward and King Mose. He was recorded at this time by Johnny Vincent of Ace Records whose most famous artists were Frankie "Sea Cruise" Ford and Huey "Piano" Smith of *Rockin' Pneumonia and Boogie Woogie Blues* fame. Two of these cuts, *Smokestack Lightnin'* and *How Many More Years* appeared on the Ace 1970 anthology *Genuine Mississippi Blues* alongside cuts by greats Fred McDowell, Littlejohn, Myers, Frankie Lee Sims and Elmore James, on whose cuts Smitty played lead guitar. On the James cuts on this album you can hear James say "take it Smitty" before the solos. By his thirties Smitty had moved to St. Louis. After a return to Mississippi, he led his own band, Big Bad Smitty and the Upsetters. Smitty has performed abroad in Holland, Switzerland, Italy, Germany, Belgium and England. *Block Magazine* in Holland and *Il Blues* in Italy put Smitty on their covers. The June 1993 *Living Blues* featured Smitty on the cover with an interview inside. With bandmates Bennie Smith, one of the finest guitarists around, and Arthur Williams (see profile), one of the few remaining authentic Mississippi harmonica players, Big Bad Smitty is a bluesman of great power who plays the blues in the tradition of Muddy Waters and Howlin' Wolf. In 1993, Smitty suffered a stroke. After recuperating, he made his first public appearance at the Dusk 'til Dawn Festival in Oklahoma, then made a guest appearance at the St. Louis Blues and Heritage Festival.

Otis Spann
This Blues pianist was born March 21, 1930, in Jackson, Miss. He began playing piano by age eight and by age 14, he was playing in bands around Jackson. He went to Chicago in 1946 or 1947. Spann gigged on his own before hooking up with Muddy Waters in 1952. Spann claimed that Waters was his half-brother. He was a member of the Muddy Waters band of the 1950s and 1960s and played on most of Waters' classic Chess recordings between 1953 and 1969. Waters classics sporting Spann's ivories include *Hoochie Coochie Man, I'm Ready, Just Make Love to Me* and Waters' seminal 1960 live version of *Got My Mojo Working* (cut at the Newport Jazz Festival, where Spann dazzled the crowd with some sensational boogies). Spann's own Chess output was limited to a 1954 single, *It Must Have Been the Devil*, that featured B.B. King on guitar, and sessions in 1956 and 1963 that remained in the can for decades. So Spann looked elsewhere, waxing a stunning album for Candid with guitarist Robert Lockwood, Jr. in 1960, a largely solo outing for Storyville in 1963 that was cut in Copenhagen, a set for British Decca the following year that found him in the company of Waters and Eric Clapton, and a 1964 LP for Prestige where Spann shared vocal duties with bandmate James Cotton. Testament and Vanguard both

Profiles of Famous & Notable Mississippians

recorded Spann as a leader in 1965. *The Blues Is Where It's At*, Spann's 1966 album for ABC-Bluesway, sounded like a live recording but was actually a studio date enlivened by people in the studio, including Waters, guitarist Sammy Lawhorn, and George "Harmonica" Smith. A Bluesway encore, *The Bottom of the Blues* followed in 1967 and featured Otis's wife, Lucille, helping out on vocals. Spann's last few years with Muddy Waters were memorable for their collaboration on the Chess set *Fathers and Sons*, but the pianist was clearly ready to launch a solo career. He recorded a set for Blue Horizon with British blues-rockers Fleetwood Mac that produced Spann's *Hungry Country Girl*. He finally turned the piano in the Waters band over to Pinetop Perkins (see his profile) in 1969. He was stricken with cancer and died in Chicago on April 24, 1970, at the young age of 40. He is buried in the Burr Oak Cemetery in Alsip, Illinois. Only a piece of plywood marked his grave until June 6, 1999, when a gravestone was finally installed thanks to funds raised by readers of *Blues Revue* magazine. Many Blues aficionados and critics alike consider him (then and now) as Chicago's leading postwar blues pianist.

Larry Speakes

Born Sept. 13, 1939 in Cleveland, Mississippi. He began his career as a reporter for small newspapers in Mississippi. He went to Washington in 1968 as press secretary to Mississippi Senator James O. Eastland. He was also staff assistant in the Nixon administration (1974), assistant press secretary to President Gerald Ford (1974-77), with the Washington public relations firm of Hill and Knowlton as a vice-president (1977-81), and deputy press secretary for President Ronald Reagan (1981-88). He became the chief White House spokesman for the Reagan administration after Press Secretary Jim Brady was severely wounded in an assassination attempt against the president.

Britney Spears

This teenage singing and dancing sensation was born Britney Jean Spears on Dec. 2, 1981, in Kentwood, Louisiana, close to the Mississippi state line. Britney, whose nicknames are "Brit" and "Boo Boo," has several connections to Mississippi. She and her older brother Bryan attended Parklane Academy in McComb, Mississippi, and her 9-year-old sister, Jamie Lynne, is still in school (as of early 2000) at Parklane. Britney's father, Jamie Spears, is a contractor for a Jackson construction company. On those rare occasions when she can make it home, she still likes to hang out with friends in McComb. After several years of singing in church choirs and showcases around her home base, she was a winner on *Star Search* at the age of 10. Brit was really discovered in the fifth grade when she auditioned for the *Mickey Mouse Club* show televised on the Disney Channel. She was named most beautiful eight-grader and a beauty her freshman year at Parklane — her final year at the private school. After a series of TV commercials and stage appearances, at age 11 Brit finally joined the *Mickey Mouse Club* in Orlando, Florida, where she remained from 1992 to 1994. In 1998, she took the world by storm with her first single recording, *Baby One More Time*, on Jive records. After releasing her first album of the same title in Jan. 1999, she released two more singles. That album remained in the Top 10 all through 1999 and by the end of the year, had sold 10 million copies, more than any other artist. Britney is the youngest artist ever to sell so many copies of an album. She is the first solo artist to have a No. 1 album and No. 1 single on the *Billboard* charts at the same time with a debut! Her other hit singles have been *Crazy*, *Somtimes* and *From the Bottom of My Heart*. Spears' CD, *Oops...I Did It Again*, released in spring 2000, set a one-week record for a female artist by selling 1.3 million copies in its first week! Like her first album, it debuted at No. 1 on the charts. Her 1999 earnings totaled $15 million, and in 2000 she's expected to make at least $15 million on just Britney dolls alone. Her concert promoter has guaranteed Britney at least $200,000 per show for a 100-show tour. She has advertising deals worth $6 million with Clairol, Polaroid and the Got Milk? campaign. She was nominated for 2 Grammys in 2000. Britney has made guest appearances on TV shows, mainly playing herself: *TRI* ('98); *The Howie Mandel Show* ('99); *The View* (6/9/99); *Sabrina, the Teenage Witch* (9/24/99); *TRI* (9/28/99); and *The Simpsons* (voice in the episode "The Mansion Family" on 1/23/2000). In 1999, Britney was named one of *Teen People* magazine's "21 Hottest Stars Under 21" and was on *People* magazine's "50 Most Beautiful People" list. On June 30, 2000, she performed on NBC's *Today* program at Rockefeller Plaza in New York. An estimated 6,000-plus fans on hand made Spears appearance the biggest *Today* concert ever, surpassing Ricky Martin and Bon Jovi, who each drew about 5,000.

Lake Speed

Born in Jackson, Mississippi on Jan. 17, 1948. In the right sport for his name, he has been a professional race car driver on the NASCAR circuit until 1998. His lone Winston Cup victory was in the TranSouth 500 at Darlington, S.C. on March 26, 1988. Speed finished 2nd in the 1985 Daytona 500 and 14th in the 1994 Daytona. He made his 15th appearance at Daytona in 1998 and finished 17th. He finished the 1994 season in 11th place in point standings with winnings for the year of more than $750,000 and started the 1995 season ranked No. 29 on the all-time NASCAR money list with $2,861,337. He finished the 1996 season in 23rd place for the second year in row and also had a disappointing 1997 season. At only 34th in the point standings in July 1998, and after suffering serious injuries in a pair of accidents, Speed said he would take the rest of the year off. He had had 402 starts in Winston Cup races and won nearly $5 million! In March, 1999, Midwest Transit Racing hired Speed as the team's general manager. Speed lives at Kannapolis, N.C.

Elizabeth Spencer

Born July 19, 1921, in Carrollton, Mississippi. She received a B.A. in English from Belhaven College of Jackson in 1942. She received her master's degree in English from Vanderbilt. She taught at Northwest Mississippi Junior College, at Belmont College, Nashville, and at the University of Mississippi. She was also a reporter for the *Nashville Tennessean* before publishing her first novel, *Fire in the Morning*. *The New York Times* Book Review called it one of the three best books of 1948. Her other novels include *This Crooked Way* (1952), *The Voice at the Back Door* (1956), *The Light in the Piazza* (1960), *Knights and Dragons* (1965), *No Place for an Angel* (1967), *The Snare* (1972), *The Salt Line* (1984), and others. A full-time writer since 1953, she has written 16 books and published articles and short stories in national publications such as *The New Yorker*, *The Atlanta Monthly* and *The Texas Quarterly*, among others. Spencer has received many awards including a Guggenheim Fellowship (1953), the Rosenthal Foundation Award of the American Academy of Arts and Letters (1957), the McGraw-Hill Fiction Award (1960), and others. Belhaven College honored Spencer with an honorary doctorate on May 8, 1999. After living and teaching in Montreal, Canada for a decade, Spencer has lived in Chapel Hill, North Carolina since 1986.

Profiles of Famous & Notable Mississippians

Johnny R. "Jack" Spinks
Born Feb. 4, 1930, in Toomsuba, Miss. Nicknamed "Jack-the-Ripper," he was a six-foot-two, 230-pound standout running back at Alcorn State who led the Braves to a 29-11 record and 3 South Central Athletic Conference championships. Spinks was named a three-time All-American by the *Pittsburgh Courier*. He was the first black Mississippian to be drafted by the NFL when picked by the Pittsburgh Steelers in the 11th round in 1952. He also played with the then-Chicago Cardinals (1954), Green Bay Packers (1955-56) and New York Giants (1956-57). He returned to Alcorn in 1959 and worked on the coaching staff until 1985. Alcorn named its new 22,000-seat, $9 million stadium after him in 1992. He was inducted into the Mississippi Sports Hall of Fame in 1985 and the Southwestern Athletic Conference Hall of Fame in 1992. He died in Jackson on Sept. 29, 1994, from diabetes.

Billy Stacey
Born Billy McGovern Stacey July 30, 1936, in Winona, Miss. He was Mississippi State All-American quarterback in 1957 and the No. 1 draft choice of the St. Louis Cardinals in 1959. One of pro-football's top defensive backs, he was inducted into the Miss. State University Sports Hall of Fame in 1970.

Roebuck "Pop" Staples
Born Dec. 28, 1915, in Winona, Miss., he grew up in Drew, Miss. He moved to Chicago when he was 21. Patriarch of the family gospel and soul group "The Staple Singers," which included his daughter Cleotha and son Pervis, both born in Drew, Mississippi in the mid 1930s. Some of the Staple Singers many hits include the No. 1, million-selling *I'll Take You There* (1972) and *Let's Do It Again* (1975), among other hits like *Respect Yourself* (#12 in 1971), *If You're Ready (Come Go With Me)* (#9 in 1973), a million-seller Top-10, and *Touch A Hand, Make A Friend* (#23 in 1974). On his own, Pop Staples recorded *Peace to the Neighborhood* featuring Bonnie Raitt, Jackson Brown and Ty Cooder. His CD, *Father, Father*, won the 1995 Grammy Award for Best Contemporary Blues Album. The Staples have had over 40 albums. The Staple Singers were inducted into The Rock and Roll Hall of Fame in 1999. Also in 1999, Pop received the Lifetime Achievement Award of the Governor's Awards. The Staples' song, *Respect Yourself*, is on the Rock and Roll Hall of Fame and Museum's list of 500 Songs That Shaped Rock And Roll.

Mike Starnes
Born Feb. 22, 1945, in Baton Rouge, Louisiana, his family moved to Oxford, Mississippi when he was about 3 years old. He is a University of Mississippi graduate. He and his wife Nancye started M.S. Carriers, a Memphis-based trucking company, in 1978 with $10,000 in savings. Starnes is chief executive officer of the company which now has annual revenues of about $350 million and is the seventh-largest truckload company in the U.S. Starnes was chairman of the U.S. Chamber of Commerce in Washington for a one-year term from Feb. 24, 1997 through Feb. 1998.

John C. Stennis
Born John Cornelius Stennis on Aug. 3, 1901, in Kemper County. Stennis graduated from Mississippi State in 1923 and from the University of Virginia Law School in 1928. A Democrat, Stennis served in the state legislature (1928-32), as a prosecuting attorney (1931-37), and as a circuit judge (1937-47). He was elected to the U.S. Senate on Nov. 4, 1947 to fill the vacancy caused by the death of Theodore G. Bilbo and served from Nov. 5, 1947 until Jan. 3, 1989. He had served 41 years and 2 months, the longest tenure ever in the senate at that time. He served on the Armed Services (chairman 1969-80) and Appropriations committees. In Jan. 1987, his colleagues elected him president pro tem during the 100th Congress, making him third in line to the presidency of the U.S. He was also chairman of the Select Committee on Standards and Conduct in the 89th through the 93rd Congresses, the Committee on Armed Services in the 91st through the 96th Congresses, and the Committee on Appropriations in the 100th Congress. He became one of the leaders of the Southern conservative wing of the Democratic party and one of the Senate's experts on defense. Stennis' colleague in the Senate for most of his tenure was James Eastland. In fact, Stennis and Eastland represented Mississippi concurrently in the Senate for 31 years (1947-78), the longest period of simultaneous service of any state in the Union. Stennis was a resident of Starkville, and later, Madison, Mississippi, until his death from pneumonia in a Jackson hospital April 23, 1995. On April 26, Stennis became only the second Mississippian to lie in state at the Old Capitol this century. The first was J.P. Coleman, governor from 1956-60, who died in Sept. 1991. Stennis was laid to rest in the Pinecrest Cemetery in his native DeKalb. In 1997, Columbus Lock & Dam was renamed for Stennis, a longtime Tenn-Tom supporter. The John C. Stennis Institute of Government at Mississippi State — established in 1976 and funded by federal and corporate grants/contracts plus private donations — promotes citizen involvement in government and provides assistance to state agencies and local governments. In a *Clarion-Ledger* millennium poll released on Oct. 25, 1999, readers voted Stennis the state's all-time favorite politician.

Rose Budd Stevens (see Mamie Davis Willoughby)

Stella Stevens
Born Estelle Eggleston on Oct. 1, 1936, in Yazoo City, Miss. and *not* Hot Coffee, Miss. as is often printed. Stevens was a wife, mother and divorcee before she was 17. While studying medicine at Memphis State, she became interested in modeling and acting and even had a nude spread in *Playboy* magazine. She posed again for *Playboy* in 1968, this time, she said, to get people to attend her films. While quite prolific with over 70 movies to her credit since her debut film *Say One for Me* (1959), most are of the B-movie variety with a few 1960s cult favorites. Stevens forte has been in the comedy genre, although she has been delighted with a few "bad girl" roles. Stella's better movies include *Li'l Abner* (1959), the Elvis Presley movie *Girls! Girls! Girls!* (1962), *Too Late Blues* (1962), *The Courtship of Eddie's Father* (1963), *The Nutty Professor* (1963), *Advance to the Rear* (1964), *The Silencers* (1966), *The Ballad of Cable Hogue* (1970), *The Poseidon Adventure* (1972) and *Nickelodeon* (1976). She directed a documentary, *The American Heroine*, in 1979 and the movie *Ranch*, which casts her son, Andrew Stevens, in 1988.

Lisa Stewart
Born on Aug. 6, 1968, in Louisville, Mississippi. She attended Mississippi University for Women, then transferred to Belmont University in Nashville where she graduated in 1999 with a degree in music. She started out as a country music singer with her self-titled solo album, *Lisa Stewart* (1992). In 1993, she co-hosted a syndicated TV show called *#1 Country*. Stewart opened for Kenny Rogers in 1994 and 1995, and also opened for the Statler Brothers in 1996. She was a featured performer on TNN's *Music City Tonight* and in 1995, and also co-hosted *Yesteryear* on TNN. She did a USO tour overseas in Bosnia. Since Jan. 1997, Stewart has been co-hosting *This Week in Country Music*, a one-hour program that airs each Saturday night on TNN. Stewart now lives in Nashville.

Profiles of Famous & Notable Mississippians

Lusia Harris Stewart

Lucy was born Feb. 10, 1955, in Minter City and graduated from Amanda Elzy High in Greenwood, Miss. The 6-foot-3, 185-pound center starred for Coach Margaret Wade's three AIAW national-champion teams at Delta State in the mid 1970s and averaged 25.9 points per game during her career with the Lady Statesmen. As a sophomore, she scored a game-high 32 points in the 90-81 championship game victory against Immaculata that capped the Lady Statesmen's 29-0 season and their 93-4 record during the championship run. In the 1976 Montreal Games, Stewart scored the first-ever basket in Olympic women's basketball competition! Her pro career began in 1980 when she played for the WBL's Houston Angels. Harris later returned to Delta State as an admissions counselor and assistant basketball coach. Stewart is a member of the National Basketball Hall of Fame. She and her coach at Delta State, Margaret Wade, were both charter inductees in the Women's Basketball Hall of Fame when it opened in Knoxville, Tennessee on June 4, 1999, and were the only two of the initial 25 inductees with Mississippi ties.

Tonea Stewart

Born in Greenwood, her nickname is "Tommie." A Jackson State University graduate in 1970, she was also a professor there for 20 years. She also attended Florida State University and the University of California. She is a veteran of New Stage Theatre of Jackson. She played the role of Virgil Tibb's Aunt Etta for five years on the CBS-TV weekly series *In The Heat of the Night* and the role of "Mama Paige" in the made-for-TV movie *Don't Look Back: the Story of Leroy 'Satchel' Paige* (1981). She has been in several feature films including *Mississippi Burning* (1988) and she had the major role of Gwen in the movie *A Time To Kill* (1996), the John Grisham movie filmed in Canton. She also appeared in *Livin' Large* (1991) and *Body Snatchers* (1994). A notable TV guest appearance was on *Walker, Texas Ranger* playing "Judge Lonetta Paxton" in the episode "Trial of LaRue" on 3/8/1997. On Sept. 29, 1995, she was inducted into the National Black College Hall of Fame in Atlanta. Dr. Stewart is now professor and chairman of theater arts at Alabama State University.

William Grant Still

Born at Woodville, Mississippi on May 11, 1895. He attended Wilberforce University and Oberlin Universty and received honorary degrees from both universities. He earned the title Dean of Afro-American Composers because of the successful fusion in his orchestral works of black and European musical traditions. He began composing seriously in the late 20s, and won acclaim with such works as *Afro-American Symphony* (1931) and the operas *Troubled Island* and *A Bayou Legend* (1940). According to the *Negro Almanac*, "In 1936, Still became the first Negro to conduct a major American orchestra when he gave a program of his own compositions at the Hollywood Bowl." Still received the Harmon Award in 1927. He died in Los Angeles, Calif. on Dec. 3, 1978, at age 83. Still was one of the first 27 inducted into the inaugural Mississippi Musicians Hall of Fame on April 1, 2000.

James Howell Street

Born Oct. 15, 1903, in Lumberton, he also lived in Laurel and Hattiesburg. In 1924 he became the youngest ordained Baptist minister in the U.S. at age 21. He left the ministry and worked as a reporter for several newspapers. His novels include *Oh, Promised Land* (1940), *In My Father's House* (1941), and *The Gauntlet* (1945). Three of his books were make into movies: *The Biscuit Eater* (1941), *Tap Roots* (1942), and *Good-bye, My Lady* (1954). Nearly all his novels were best sellers with some selling over a million copies. His total output was 17 books, 35 short stories and 20 magazine articles. He died of a heart attack in Chapel Hill, N.C. on Sept. 28, 1954.

Roberta Streeter (see Bobbie Gentry)

Barrett Strong

A R&B singer and songwriter born Feb. 5, 1941, in West Point, Miss. A hit record of his own was *Money (That's What I Want)* (#23 Pop & #2 R&B in 1960), later recorded by the Beatles. That song is included on the Rock and Roll Hall of Fame and Museum's list of 500 Songs That Shaped Rock And Roll. Barrett Strong was a key associate and friend of Berry Gordy. It was his hit, *Money*, that provided the money for Gordy to expand his operation in the early days of Motown. Strong co-wrote many hits for Motown: Marvin Gaye's *I Heard It Through the Grapevine* and *Too Busy Thinking About My Baby*; Edwin Starr's *War*; *Take Me in Your Arms and Love Me* for Gladys Knight and The Pips; plus many of the Temptations' top-10 hits including *Just My Imagination, Ball of Confusion, Cloud Nine* and *Papa Was A Rolling Stone*. That last song is also included on the Rock and Roll Hall of Fame's list of 500 Songs That Shaped Rock And Roll. Strong left Motown when they moved to Los Angeles in 1972.

Marty Stuart

This country singer/songwriter was born Sept. 30, 1958, in Philadelphia, Mississippi. A whiz on the mandolin at 12 years old, he played in Lester Flatt's band from 1972 until Flatt's death in 1979. He played in Vassar Clements' jazz/bluegrass fusion group, Doc Watson's road band and, in the early 1980s, in the Johnny Cash band (was briefly Cash's son-in-law). His first solo album was *Busy Bee Cafe* (1982). Marty signed a recording contract with CBS Records and, in 1986, they released the album *Marty Stuart*. The first single off the album, *Arlene*, broke the *Billboard* Top 20 and he was nominated for Best New Male Vocalist by the Academy of Country Music. However, the album garnered little chart success. He signed with MCA Records in 1989 breaking the top 10 for the first time in 1990 with the album *Hillbilly Rock*, which went gold. His second album *Tempted*, went gold with four hits: *Tempted, Little Things, Till I Found You* and *Burn Me Down*. He wrote two songs that became award-winning duets with his friend Travis Tritt. Collaboration on *The Whiskey Ain't Workin'* and *This One's Gonna Hurt You* brought the team a Country Music Association Award for Vocal Event of the Year (1992) and "Whiskey" won a Grammy (1993). His album, *This One's Gonna Hurt You*, went Gold. He became a member of the Grand Ole Opry in 1992, twenty years after his first appearance on the Opry stage at age 13 with Lester Flatt's band. His "Marty Party" series of specials hit TNN TV network in 1994 and he played TV host for two years. The series also inspired a Marvel Comics special edition comic book, *The Marty Party in Space*. Marty was nominated for the 1995 Music City News Country Awards as Male Artist of the Year. Stuart also received a 1997 Grammy nomination. The CD, *Honky Tonkin's What I Do Best*, was released in 1996 with another rocking duet with Travis Tritt as the title track for which the two received the 1996 Country Music Association nomination for Vocal Event of the Year and the Vocal Collaboration Award for the 31st TNN/*Music City News* Country Awards presented in 1997. On July 9, 1997, he married the "Sweetheart of the Grand Ole Opry," Connie Smith, whom he met when she was appearing in Marty's hometown of Philadelphia. In 1999, he received his third Grammy for a song he wrote and produced, *Same Old Train*, from the *Tribute to Tradition* album with Merle Haggard, Joe

Profiles of Famous & Notable Mississippians

Diffie, Pam Tillis and others. On his album, *The Pilgrim* (1999), Marty is joined by Emmy Lou Harris, Johnny Cash, Ralph Stanley and George Jones. In 1999, Marty scored and produced the music for the Billy Bob Thornton movie, *Daddy and Them* and the soundtrack album with Dwight Yoakam, Sheryl Crow and Marty. On March 19, 1999, Stuart received the Artist's Achievement Award of the (Mississippi) Governor's Awards. Also a photographer, Marty has had photos published in *Country Music* magazine, *People, Southern Living* and other publications. His book *Pilgrims: Sinners, Saints & Prophets*, essays and photos of country stars, hit the bookstores in 1999.

Hubert Sumlin
Born Nov. 16, 1931, in Greenwood, Miss. A longtime Wolf sideman, he did the great guitar work on all the Howlin' Wolf Chess classic singles of the late 1950s and early 60s, such as *Spoonful, I Ain't Superstitious, Back Door Man, Smokestack Lightin' & Red Rooster*. Guitarist Jimi Hendrix once wrote "My favorite guitar player is Hubert Sumlin."

Cid Ricketts Sumner
Born Bertha Ricketts in Brookhaven, Miss. on Sept. 27, 1890. She gained worldwide fame for her "Tammy" novels: *Tammy Tell Me True, Tammy in Rome*, and *Tammy Out of Time*. The movies made from her books (*Tammy and the Bachelor*, 1957; *Tammy and the Doctor*, 1963; and *Tammy Tell Me True*, 1961) made actresses Debbie Reynolds and Sandra Dee famous. Sumner didn't publish her first novel until she was 48. She died in Massachusetts on October 15, 1970, at age 80.

Nan Sumrall
Born Nov. 23, 1965, in Hattiesburg. She was Miss Mississippi in 1985. Sumrall graduated from the University of Southern Mississippi in 1988 with a degree in communications. After successfully auditioning for a job at the Opryland theme park, she moved to Nashville in 1989. For two years, she sang and danced at Opryland and performed background vocals for country artist Brenda Lee. For a while, Sumrall worked for the producer of country star George Strait and also for singer Tracy Byrd's manager. She was the TV talk show sidekick for host Gary Chapman on TNN's *Prime Time County* from July 27, 1998, until it went off the air in late 1999.

"Sunnyland Slim"
Born Albert Luandrew on Sept. 5, 1907, in Vance, Miss. on the Quitman County/Tallahatchie County line. He adopted his stage name from the title of one of his best-known songs, the mournful *Sunnyland Train*, the song that immortalized the St. Louis-to-Memphis locomotive. A barrelhouse-style piano man, he's probably been on more recordings, both as sideman and leader, than any other blues pianist. After entertaining at juke joints and movie houses in the Delta, Luandrew made Memphis his homebase during the late 1920s, playing along Beale Street and hanging out with the likes of Little Brother Montgomery and Ma Rainey. He moved to Chicago in 1939 and played for a while with John Lee "Sonny Boy" Williamson before cutting eight sides for RCA Victor in 1947 under the name of "Doctor Clayton's Buddy." If it hadn't been for the helpful Sunnyland, Muddy Waters may not have found his way onto the Chess label. It was at the pianist's 1947 session for Aristocrat that the Chess brothers made Waters's acquaintance. Aristocrat was but one of many labels that Sunnyland recorded for between 1948-56. In 1960, he traveled to Englewood Cliffs, N.J., to cut his debut LP for Prestige's Bluesville subsidiary with King Curtis supplying tenor sax breaks on many cuts. The album, *Slim's Shout*, ranks as one of his finest, with renditions of *The Devil Is a Busy Man, Shake It, Brownskin Woman*, and *It's You Baby*. As late as 1985, Sunnyland Slim recorded *Chicago Jump* for the Red Beans label. For a time, he even headed his own label, Airway Records. Coming home from a gig one night, he slipped and fell on ice, which led to numerous complications. Sunnyland Slim died of kidney failure in Chicago on March 17, 1995, at age 87. For more than 50 years, Sunnyland had rumbled the ivories around the Windy City, playing with virtually every bluesman imaginable and backing the great majority of them in the studio at one time or another.

Dave C. Swalm
Born Nov. 8, 1932, in Los Angeles. A chemical engineering graduate of Mississippi State University (1955), he is the retired chairman and chief executive officer of Texas Olefins Co. in Houston, the nation's largest privately-owned producer of petrochemical raw materials. In Sept. 1994, Swalm made the single largest donation in Mississippi State's 116-year history when he gave $7 million to fund a 4-story chemical engineering building on the Starkville campus.

Eugenia Ann Talbott
Born July 31, 1947, in Pascagoula, she was influenced by Mississippi painter Walter Anderson. Reflecting her travels in Europe, Africa, Central American, and North America, particularly in the Canadian Arctic, Talbott's paintings center mainly on human and animal subjects, but she also paints portraits. She has worked in many mediums— pencil, ink, oils, and watercolors. Her "Painted Pets" animal subjects, done with oils on wooden pieces and large room divider screens and fireplace screens, are very popular. She also paints furniture in fancy designs and faux finishes. Talbott's paintings have been exhibited extensively around Mississippi as well as in Canada and Paris. She has taught art, even to the Inuit natives of the Arctic, and has lectured widely on her work, animal rights and conservation. Many articles about her work have appeared in regional and national publications. She studied art at Mississippi University for Women and settled in the small town of Mayhew near Columbus. She currently owns and operates the Eugenia Talbott Studio and Gallery in Columbus, which features stone carvings of people and animals made by the Inuits, called "Soapstone," plus many of her own works.

Donna Tartt
Born Dec. 23, 1963 in Greenwood, she grew up in Grenada, Mississippi. She wrote her first poem at age five and published her first sonnet in a Mississippi literary review at age 13. She entered the University of Mississippi at Oxford in 1981. After her freshman year at Ole Miss, she transferred to Bennington College in Vermont. She received critical acclaim for her 1992 novel, *The Secret History*, her only novel to date. Kropf Publishing paid a massive $450,000 for the book and ordered a 75,000-copy first printing. Demand for the book was heavy enough for additional printings. It remained on the *Publishers Weekly* bestseller list for 13 weeks, reaching as high as No. 2! Tartt is now writing short stories.

Clifton Taulbert
Born Feb. 19, 1945 in Glen Allan, Miss., he was valedictorian at O'Bannon High School in Greenville. At age 17, he moved to Tulsa, where he graduated from Oral Roberts University. Taulbert received a Pulitzer nomination for his book *The Last Train North*. His book, *Once upon a Time...When We Were Colored*, was made into a movie with the same title ('96). The movie, with Taulbert as co-producer, was filmed in Wilmington, N.C. Set in 1946, in recounts his memories of growing up in a poor, all-black community. More of his memoirs are in his books, *Watching Our Crops Come In* ('97)

Profiles of Famous & Notable Mississippians

and *Eight Habits of the Heart* (1997). In 1998, Taulbert began writing a series of children's books with illustrator E.B. White with the first titled *Little Cliff and the Porch People*.

"Hound Dog" Taylor
Born Theodore Roosevelt Taylor in Natchez on Apr. 12, 1917. An influential slide guitarist, he was the first blues artist to record on Alligator Records in 1971. His debut album, *Hound Dog Taylor & The Houserockers*, was inducted into the Blues Hall of Fame in 1996. Taylor died in Chicago Dec. 17, 1975, and is buried in the Restvale Cemetery in Alsip, Illinois.

Mike Taylor
Born July 28, 1946, in New Orleans, he grew up in Meridian. He played golf for Brigham Young University from 1965-68 and was All-America in 1966. He won 10 amateur state championships in the 1960s and '70s. No other player has won more than six. Taylor's record has earned him the distinction of being the best player ever to play in the State Amateur. He was inducted into the Mississippi Sports Hall of Fame in 1997.

Mildred D. Taylor
Born Sept. 13, 1943, in Jackson, Mississippi, she grew up in Toledo, Ohio, with yearly trips back to Mississippi. In the newly-integrated town of Toledo, she was the only black child in her school class. She graduated from the University of Toledo, then served 2 years with the Peace Corps in Ethiopia. When she returned, she attended the University of Colorado School of Journalism, where she earned a Master of Arts degree. While attending school, she worked with university officials and fellow students in structuring a Black Studies program at the university. She now lives in Colorado and writes. Her first book, *Song of the Trees* (1975), won the Council on Interracial Books Award in the African-American category and was also a *New York Times* Outstanding Book of the Year in 1975. Her second book, *Roll of Thunder, Hear My Cry* (1976), won the Newbery Medal in 1977 and was made into a movie (1978) that stars Morgan Freeman. A sequel to the book, *Let the Circle be Unbroken*, was published in 1981.

W. C. Taylor, Jr.
Born Nov. 10, 1945, in Grenada, Miss. In 1996, he was a Christian Country Music Association Top-5 male vocalist and his video was voted a Top-5 video of the year in 1995. In 1995, the *Nashville Tracker* magazine named Taylor Christian Artist of the Year and the International Country Gospel Music Association voted him Country Gospel Male Vocalist. In late 1995, the readers of Nashville's *Music City News* nominated Taylor as the top Christian country artist in the nation. Taylor received the Great Plains Christian Country Male Entertainer in 1996 and Airplay International Christian Country Male Vocalist and Christian Album of the Year in 1997. In Jan. 1998, Taylor became the first singer inducted into the North American Country Music Association International Hall of Fame in Gatlinburg, Tenn. His No. 1 songs on *Cashbox*, *The Nashville Tracker*, *Music City News* and other charts include *Smile If You Love Jesus*, *He Is There*, *Moving Through Me*, *The House That Jack Built*, *The Carpenter Man* and *Never Give Up the Faith*. In addition to singing, Taylor owns 2 record labels, Circuit Rider Records for country gospel music and Rider Records for country and bluegrass music. Taylor is also president of the National Fellowship of Baptist Performing Artists. He and his wife Annelle are the founders of the Country Gospel Music Guild, which compiles playlists from 60 reporting radio stations across the U.S. and publishes a Top 80 music chart that appears monthly in the *U.S. Gospel News*. With a circulation in excess of 100,000, it is the biggest country gospel chart in the world!

Johnnie "Geechie" Temple
Born in Canton, Mississippi on Oct. 18, 1906. He is one of the great unsung heroes of the blues. A contemporary of Son House, Skip James, and other Delta legends, he was the first to develop the now-standard bottom-string boogie bass figure, generally credited to . Two of the songs he recorded were *Big Leg Woman* and *Gimme Some of That Yum Yum Yum*. Temple died of cancer on Nov. 22, 1968, at age 62 .

Byron Thames
Born on April 23, 1969, in Jackson Miss. He played Matt in the TV series *Father Murphy* and appeared in the TV shows *Chips*, *Silver Spoons*, and *Just Pals*. His movie debut was in *Heart Like a Wheel* (1983). He played the young Johnny in the 1985 movie *Johnny Dangerously*, which stars Michael Keaton as the grown Johnny. In his sixth film, *84 Charlie Mopic* (1989), Thames plays a Vietnam combat cameraman.

Herbert Theriot
Born Sept. 27, 1966, in Franklin, La., his family moved to Wiggins, Miss. when he was 14. He now lives in Poplarville, Mississippi. He learned calf roping from his father, Ernest, a horse trainer and rodeo competitor. Herbert went pro in 1986. In 1994, he became Mississippi's first world rodeo champion when he won the calf-roping competition of the Professional Rodeo Cowboys Association. His all-time record to lasso a running calf, dismount his horse, get the calf to the ground and tie up three of its legs is 6.5 seconds! In 1996, he finished 3rd in the National Finals Rodeo in Las Vegas to bring his season winnings to $151,644. He was the only man to qualify in two categories, steer wrestling and calf roping. He also won the Southeastern Circuit All-Around Cowboy title in 1996. Theriot donated the saddle he won in that competition to the Mississippi Sports Hall of Fame. He spends 300 nights on the road all over the country competing in over 100 rodeos a year.

Kathy Thibodeaux
Born on Nov. 9, 1956, in Memphis, she has made Mississippi her home for many years. She was a Silver Medalist in the 1982 International Ballet Competition. She started her own ballet company, Ballet Magnificat, in 1986, the only Christian ballet school and touring company in the U.S. She is the wife of actor-singer Keith Thibodeaux.

Keith R. Thibodeaux
Born Dec. 1, 1950, in Lafayette, Louisiana. He lived in Laurel, Mississippi from 1969-76 and in Jackson since 1976. Thibodeaux was the child actor who played "Little Ricky" Ricardo on the top-rated and award-winning TV series *I Love Lucy* from 1956-60 (his character was officially "born" on 1/19/1953). In the early 1960s, Thibodeaux played Opie's best friend Johnny Paul Jason on *The Andy Griffith Show*. From 1969-89, he was with David & the Giants, at first a rock, then gospel-rock group, that recorded for CBS & Word record labels. Keith tells his life story in his book *Life After Lucy* (1994). He is now executive director of Ballet Magnificat, the Christian dance troupe founded by his wife, Kathy.

Charles S. Thomas, Sr.
Charles S. "Chuck" Thomas was born Oct. 22, 1913, in Winona, Miss. When he was still a baby, his family moved to Moorhead, Mississippi, where he grew up. He attended the public schools, Sunflower Junior College (now Mississippi Delta Community College), and Delta State University. He was Delta State's first football All-American and was only the second All-American from Mississippi after Bruiser Kinard. Thomas led the nation in scoring with 119 points in 1936 and was named to the Little All-American team in 1937. After graduating from Delta State in 1938 with a B.S. double major

Profiles of Famous & Notable Mississippians

in social studies, Thomas served as high school football coach in Itta Bena, Yazoo City and Winona and was a football official for 25 years. He was inducted into the Mississippi Sports Hall of Fame in 1975. Thomas died of heart failure in Greenville, Mississippi on Nov. 23, 1995, at the age of 82. He was one of the 15 charter members inducted into the new Delta Community College Hall of Fame in early 1999.

James "Son" Thomas

A blues musician and sculptor born on Oct. 14, 1926, in Eden, Yazoo Co., Miss. He played in juke joints before he began recording in the late 1960s. He appeared in the films *Delta Blues Singer: James "Sonny Ford" Thomas* ('70) and *Give My Poor Heart Ease: Mississippi Delta Bluesmen* ('75), plus the short *Mississippi Delta Blues* ('74). Thomas also made festival appearances in the 1970s and '80s. He died from emphysema and a stoke in Greenville, Mississippi on June 26, 1993.

Rufus Thomas

R&B singer and songwriter born on March 26, 1917, at Cayce, Miss. The self-proclaimed "World's Oldest Teenager" has been a staple on the Memphis music scene since the 20s. He was a deejay in Memphis 1953-74. He had the first hit ever recorded on Sun Records, *Bear Cat* in 1953. His biggest pop record was the Top-10 hit *Walking The Dog* (#10 in 1963). In the early 1970s Thomas recorded three records for Stax that all made it into the R&B top 5 — *Do the Funky Chicken, The Breakdown,* and *(Do the) Push and Pull*, the latter giving Thomas his first No. 1 hit. He is the father of singers Carla and Vaneese Thomas. He appeared in the film *Wattstax* (1973).

Treg Thomas

Born Tregnel Kynta Thomas on Mar. 14, 1977, in Pascagoula, Mississippi, he graduated from Pascagoula High. While still a freshman at Delta State University, Thomas received the first annual Conerly Trophy, established in honor of Mississippi football great, the late Charlie Conerly. A panel of 55 sports reporters and broadcasters from across the state selected Thomas, who set a DSU-record 1,604 yards on 275 carries with 11 touchdowns and the Gulf South Conference record for rushing yards in a season. The Gulf South's Freshman of the Year averaged 160.4 yards per game and 5.8 yards per carry. The 5 feet 7 inch, 175 pound Thomas was awarded the trophy on Dec. 3, 1996. The trophy was presented by ABC-TV sportscaster Frank Gifford and former vice presidential candidate Jack Kemp, both of whom had been teammates with Conerly on the New York Giants team. His chance for a pro career was dimmed when he blew out his knee four games into his junior year and had to undergo three surgeries.

Larry A. Thompson

Born on Aug. 1, 1944, in Clarksdale, Miss. Thompson has been the producer or executive producer on these TV shows, movies and specials: *The Eagle and the Bear* ('85); *Convicted* ('86); *Original Sin* ('89); *Little White Lies* ('89); *Lucy & Desi: Before the Laughter* ('91 special); *Broken Promises: Taking Emily Back* ('93); *Face of Evil* ('96); *Replacing Dad* ('98); *And the Beat Goes On: The Sonny and Cher Story* ('99 special); and *Murder in the Mirror* (2000). He also produced these feature theater movies: *Crimes of Passion* ('84); *My Demon Lover* ('87); and *Breaking the Rules* ('92). Thompson owns the Los Angeles management/production firm that manages actors William Shatner (*Star Trek*), Donna Mills and several others.

Paul Thorn

Born in Kenosha, Wisconsin on July 13, 1964, his family moved to Mooreville in Lee County, Miss. when he was five years old. He started out as a professional boxer. When he fought Roberto Duran in April 1987, Thorn was a 160- pound middleweight ranked 28th in the world by the WBC. Thorn lost to Duran and after a few more fights, he quit the ring with a pro record of 17-3. He next tried songwriting and singing. He wrote or co-wrote songs for Tanya Tucker, Joe Diffee, the group Shenandoah, Ronnie Milsap and others. In 1996, he co-wrote a song with singer/songwriter Carole King. After his 12-song CD, *Hammer and Nail* (1997), was released by A&M records, he went on tour with the popular artist Sting. After A&M folded, Thorn recorded his next album, *Ain't Love Strange* (1999), on his own label, Perpetual Obscurity Records. In 1999, he was opening for Willie Nelson, Richard Thompson and other artists. When he's not on the road touring, Thorn calls Nettleton, Mississippi home.

Mildred Spurrier Topp

Born Mildred Spurrier on Jan. 5, 1897, in Forest City, Ill., she grew up from age 10 in Greenwood, Miss. She graduated from Greenwood High School, then received her degree in 1917 from Industrial Institute and College (Miss. University for Women). Married to Robert G. Topp in 1917, she taught English at Greenwood High from 1918-22. She served in the Mississippi legislature 1932-36 as a representative of Leflore County. She raised 2 children, then at age 50, turned to writing, authoring two autobiographical works. *Smile Please* (1948) became an immediate best seller. Critics said it was funny and "...and a masterpiece of pure wit." Her other best seller was *In the Pink* (1950). In 1954, she received her M.A. degree from Ole Miss, where she also taught composition and creative writing. The Erma Bombeck of her generation, Mrs. Topp died on Aug. 15, 1963, at the age of 66.

Joseph Paul Treen

Born May 1, 1900, in Purvis, Lamar County, Miss. Credited with over 60 inventions, his most famous was the kickstand for bicycles and motorcycles. He was also first with the idea of putting thermostats in the radiators of motor vehicles. The father of former Louisiana Governor David Treen, Joseph Treen died in New Orleans on Aug. 24, 1986.

Frank Trippett

Born July 1, 1926, in Columbus, he grew up in Aberdeen, Miss. He attended Mississippi College, Ole Miss, Duke University, Vandercook College of Music, and New York State University. His first job as a journalist was in Mississippi with the *Meridian Star*. He worked with the Fredericksburg, Virginia *Free Lance-Star* and the St. Petersburg *Florida Times* before joining the staff of *Newsweek* in 1961. He became senior writer and essayist on the staff of *Time* magazine in 1977. He received many journalism awards including the 1981 American Bar Association Silver Gavel for distinguished writing on law and the 1982 National Space Club citation for distinguished writing on space. Trippett's articles have appeared in the *New York Times Sunday Magazine*, *Saturday Review*, *People*, *Life*, and *Reader's Digest*. Trippett died in New York state on June 18, 1998.

Richard H. Truly

Born Richard Harrison Truly on Nov. 12, 1937, in Fayette, he attended schools in Fayette and Meridian, Miss. He graduated from the Georgia Institute of Technology in 1959 with a bachelor's degree in aeronautical engineering, then joined the Navy. Following flight school, he was designated a naval aviator in 1960. His initial tour of duty was aboard the *USS Intrepid* and the *USS Enterprise*, and he made more than 300 carrier landings. From 1963-65, he was a student and then instructor at the U.S. Air Force Aerospace Research Pilot School at Edwards Air Force Base, Calif. He advanced to the rank of rear admiral, then was transferred to the astronaut

Profiles of Famous & Notable Mississippians

corps. In 1965, Truly became one of the first military astronauts selected to the Air Force's Manned Orbiting Laboratory program in Los Angeles and transferred to NASA in Aug. 1969. He served as capsule communicator for all three Skylab missions in 1973 and the Apollo-Soyuz mission in 1975. As a naval aviator, test pilot, and astronaut, Truly logged over 7,500 hours in numerous military and civilian jet aircraft. He was pilot for one of the two-astronaut crews that flew the 747/Space Shuttle Enterprise approach and landing test flights during 1977. He then was backup pilot for STS-1, the first orbital test of the Shuttle. His first space flight was Nov. 12-14, 1981, as pilot of Space Shuttle Columbia (STS-2), significant as the first piloted spacecraft to be reflown in space. His second flight (STS-8, Aug. 30-Sept. 5, 1983) was as commander of Space Shuttle Challenger, the first night launch and landing in the Shuttle program. He left NASA in 1983 to head the new Naval Space Command, but returned in 1986 after the Challenger disaster. Truly became NASA's Associate Administrator for Space Flight on Feb. 20, 1986 and led the painstaking rebuilding of the Space Shuttle program. This was highlighted by NASA's celebrated "return to flight" on Sept. 29, 1988, when Discovery lifted off from Kennedy Space Center, Florida, on the first Shuttle mission in almost 3 years. On Jan. 18, 1989, Truly was awarded the Presidential Citizen's Medal by President Reagan. His NASA awards include two Distinguished Service Medals, the Outstanding Leadership Medal, two Exceptional Service Medals and two NASA Space Flight Medals. His military decorations include the Defense Distinguished Service Medal, the Defense Superior Service Medal, two Legions of Merit, the Navy Distinguished Flying Cross, and the Meritorious Service Medal. He also received the American Astronautical Society's Flight Achievement Award ('77), the Air Force Association's David C. Shilling Award ('78), the Society of Experimental Test Pilot's Ivan C. Kincheloe Award ('78), the American Institute of Aeronautics and Astronautics Haley Space Flight Award ('80), the Harmon International Trophy ('82), the Thomas D. White Space Trophy ('82), the Robert J. Collier Trophy twice (1982 & '89), the Robert H. Goddard Memorial Trophy twice (1982 & '89), the Federation Aeronautique Internationale Gold Space Medal ('84), the James H. Doolittle Award ('88), the John F. Kennedy Astronautics Award ('90), the Veterans of Foreign Wars Aviation and Space Gold Medal ('91), and many other awards. Truly served as the eighth NASA administrator (the first astronaut administrator) from May 14, 1989-March 31, 1992, when he resigned in a policy dispute. After leaving NASA, Admiral Truly became Vice President and Director of the Georgia Tech Research Institute at the Georgia Institute of Technology in Atlanta. Truly is one of only three astronauts born in Mississippi. The other two are Fred W. Haise, Jr. (b. Biloxi) and Donald H. Peterson (b. Winona)[see profiles].

Ike Turner

Born Izear Turner on Nov. 5, 1931, in Clarksdale, Mississippi. At age 11, Ike was backing pianist for bluesman Sonny Boy Williamson. He later formed the group Ike & Tina Turner. Ike and Tina (b. Anna Mae Bullock 11/26/1939 in Nutbush, Tenn.) were married from 1958 to 1976. Their stormy marriage was depicted in the biopic *What's Love Got to Do with It?* (1993) with Ike played by Laurence Fishburne and Tina played by Angela Bassett. In 1960, Ike developed a dynamic stage show around Tina. Their biggest hit record was the Top-5 million-seller *Proud Mary* (#4 Top-40 in 1971). Ike has had 14 solo albums and 87 Ike & Tina albums have been released. They were inducted into the Rock and Roll Hall of Fame in 1991. Ike & Tina's song, *River Deep, Mountain High*, is included on the Rock and Roll Hall of Fame and Museum's list of 500 Songs That Shaped Rock And Roll. Ike has played himself in several films including *Taking Off* (1971). Ike co-wrote, with bluesman James Cotton, what was probably the first Rock 'n' Roll hit, *Rocket 88*, and Turner played on Jackie Brenston's recording of it in the early 1950s.

Roscoe Turner

This aviation pioneer was born on Sept. 29, 1895, near Corinth, Mississippi. At the age of sixteen, Roscoe made his way to Memphis where he eventually became an ice truck driver, then a taxi driver and finally an expert auto mechanic for local Packard and Cadillac dealers. Just before World War I, he tried to enlist in the aviation section of the Signal Corps, but was turned down because he lacked the required two years of college education. During World War I, Turner enlisted in the Ambulance Corps and was sent to France. He transferred to the Aviation Section, but the Armistice was signed before he could see combat action. After the war, Turner and a partner form the Roscoe Turner Flying Circus in 1919 and for five years they put on death-defying performances. In addition to having his own flying circus and being a barnstorming stuntman, wingwalker and parachutist, Turner even became a movie stuntman and actor in Howard Hughes' World War I movie *Hell's Angels* (1930). On Aug. 25, 1929, he landed his plane in New York after a 19½ hour flight from Los Angeles, the first coast-to-coast, non-stop passenger flight. He received the coveted Harmon Trophy for "Outstanding Achievement in Aviation" on Nov. 11, 1932, for setting an east-to-west transcontinental flight record of 12 hours and 33 minutes. Among his many accomplishments were numerous transcontinental records, from west to east and east to west. In 1933 he won the Shell Speed Dashes and the famous Bendix Trophy. In 1934 he won the Thompson Trophy Race, was second in the Shell Speed Dashes and finished second in the Speed Division of the MacRobertson International Air Race. He and his two-man crew were the only Americans to finish the grueling London-to-Melbourne race. Turner appeared on the cover of *Time* magazine on Oct. 29, 1934. In 1938 Roscoe placed second in the Golden Gate Trophy Race and won the Thompson Trophy Race for the second time. He also receives the Allegheny-Ludlum Trophy for setting a world's lap record of 293 miles per hour. At the close of the 1939 Cleveland National Air Races where he won the Thompson Trophy for an unprecedented third time, Turner announced his retirement from active competition. Turner then founded a regional airline and directed a school for pilots and mechanics. He formed the Turner Aviation Institute in 1940 to train flight instructors, pilots and mechanics needed during World War II. After the war Turner says: "Aviation is going to control the world economically and militarily whether we like it or not. Airpower is not merely military aviation, it is also civilian aviation and airpower is peace power." Throughout the 1950s and 60s he continued to contribute to the development of aviation through his flight school and aircraft sales facility at Indianapolis. As America's premier speed flyer, Turner was a multiple winner of the Harmon and Henderson Trophies, and received a special Distinguished Flying Cross by Act of Congress in 1952. Turner and Jimmy Doolittle are the only people in history to have won both the Bendix cross-country race and the Thompson Race. Turner was the only pilot to have won the Thompson air race three times. During his stunt show days, he flew in pink jodhpurs, gleaming cavalry boots, a brass-button tunic, sported a needle-pointed waxed mustache

Profiles of Famous & Notable Mississippians

and flew with his animal mascot "Gilmore," an African Lion cub until it grew too big for the cockpit. He stuffed the animal when it died. Turner's planes, trophies and Gilmore are in the Smithsonian Museum in Washington. Turner is the only Mississippian in the National Aviation Hall of Fame, inducted in 1975. He is also enshrined in the Motor Sports Hall of Fame (Aviation Division). Roscoe Turner died on June 23, 1970, but is still remembered in the Roscoe Turner Hot Air Balloon Race held annually in Corinth. His biography, *Roscoe Turner: Aviation's Master Showman*, written by Carroll V. Glines, was published in 1995 by the Smithsonian Institution Press.

Conway Twitty

This rock and country superstar was born Harold Lloyd Jenkins on Sept. 1, 1933, at Friars Point, Miss. His father was a riverboat pilot who taught the boy his first guitar chords at age 4. He also learned music from a black neighbor Conway called "Uncle Fred" and spent many hours on a ditch bank listening to gospel music from a nearby church. He formed his first singing group when he was 10 years old. By the age of 12, his family had moved up the river to Helena, Arkansas. Conway attended Central High School in Helena 1952-53. After high school, he was offered a contract to play professional baseball with the Philadelphia Phillies, but before he could sign, he was drafted by the U.S. Army. In the early 1950s, he joined a service band, the Cimmarons, in Japan when he was in the Army. In 1956, Conway entered the music scene playing a rock 'n' roll song, *Born to Sing the Blues*, the first of 8 unreleased songs recorded on the Sun label. In 1957, he chose his stage name from the towns of Conway, Arkansas and Twitty, Texas. His first No. 1 record was the million-selling ballad, *It's Only Make Believe* ('58). In 1965, he became the first major rock star to change to country. "The Twitty Bird" had more No. 1 hits (55) than any other artist in *any* genre (that includes Elvis, the Beatles, Frank Sinatra and Michael Jackson) — the only artist in the history of popular music to have had 21 consecutive top-5 hits! In 1990, Conway recorded and released his 55th #1 single, *Crazy In Love*, which stayed on the charts for 5 months. During the first 15 years of R&R's (Radio and Records) country chart histories, Conway reigned unchallenged as Top Artist based upon points tallied for the most No. 1's, most Top 5 and most Top 10 hits during that time, and that doesn't even count a later five-year period of Conway's hits! His hits include *Hello Darling* ('70), *Baby's Gone* ('73), *You've Never Been This Far Before* ('73), *I'm Not Through Loving You Yet* ('74), *(Lying Here With) Linda On My Mind* ('75), *I Can't Believe She Gives It All To Me* ('76), *I've Already Loved You In My Mind* ('77), *Don't Take It Away* ('78), *I May Never Get To Heaven* ('79), *I'd Love To Lay You Down* ('79) and *Tight Fittin' Jeans* ('80). He wrote or co-wrote 25% of his hits, writing over 200 songs. Conway was inducted into the Nashville Songwriters Hall of Fame in 1993. *Hello Darling* became the first song broadcast in space when played during the Apollo-Soyuz mission. The "High Priest of Country Music" had numerous awards including a Grammy, 4 CMA awards, 6 Academy of Country Music awards, 14 *Music City News* awards, 13 *Billboard* awards and 2 Truckers' awards. In performance awards, he received 23 from BMI, 8 from ASCAP, and 20 from SESAC. He also received a Special Citation of Achievement Award from BMI for over 2 million performances of *It's Only Make Believe*. He was made an honorary chief of the Choctaws and given the Indian name "Hatako-Chtokchito-A-akni-Toloa" meaning "Great Man of Country Music." A teamup with Loretta Lynn in 1970 was followed by several years with many awards together, and hits such as *As Soon As I Hang Up the Phone* ('74), *The Letter* ('76), *Lead Me On*, and *Louisiana Woman, Mississippi Man*. He appeared in the film *College Confidential* ('61) and two other teen movies, *Platinum High School* and *Sex Kittens Go To College*. In 1989, Conway celebrated the 7th anniversary of "Twitty City," his 9-acre tourist complex just outside Nashville. He died June 4, 1993, at age 59 from a stomach aneurysm following a concert at Springfield, Mo. He is buried in Sumner Memorial Park in Gallatin, Tenn. His album, *Final Touches* (1993), was released after his death. Conway was inducted into the Country Music Hall of Fame in 1999.

Dan Tyler

Born on Nov. 22, 1950, in McComb, Mississippi. He got his B.A. at Ole Miss in 1972 and his law degree there in 1975, then moved to Nashville to pursue his dream of being a songwriter. Since then, dozens of major country music artists have recorded songs he's written. Among his hits are *Modern Day Romance* by the Nitty Gritty Dirt Band, *Baby's Got a New Baby* by SKO and *Twenty Years Ago* by Kenny Rogers. His songs have been released by B.J. Thomas, Glen Campbell, Juice Newton, Marie Osmond, Keith Whitley, and in 1981, the Oak Ridge Boys topped the charts with *Bobbie Sue*, which was written by Tyler and his wife of 26 years, Adele Brown Tyler. He has had five No. 1 hits! His most recent was *The Light in Your Eyes* from LeAnn Rimes' *Blue* album. As of July 2000, more than 70 of his songs have been recorded by major artists of varying genres. Tyler also wrote a novel, *Music City Confidential* (1996), based on his experiences in Nashville.

Felix J. Underwood

Born on Nov. 21, 1882, in Nettleton, Miss. He graduated from the University of Tennessee Medical School in 1908. He first practiced medicine in Nettleton, then became a part-time health officer for Monroe County from 1909-15, then full-time 1916-21. In 1921, he was appointed director of the Bureau of Child Hygiene with the Mississippi State Board of Health. In July 1924, Dr. Underwood was appointed State Health Officer of Mississippi and remained in that position until the Retirement Law forced his retirement on June 23, 1958. The State Board of Health made great progress during Dr. Underwood's 34-year tenure. He died on Jan. 9, 1959. Trustees of the Department of Archives and History elected him to the State of Mississippi Hall of Fame on Dec. 6, 1996.

Del Unser

Born Delbert Bernard Unser in Decatur, Illinois on Dec. 9, 1944. He was a three-year baseball outfield starter at Mississippi State from 1964-66, making All-SEC in 1965 and 1966 and was chosen All-American by *The Sporting News* in 1966. Unser was drafted in the first round by the Washington Senators in 1966 and made his major league debut on Apr. 10, 1968. He played 17 years in pro baseball, 15 in the major leagues with the Washington Senators (1968-71), the Cleveland Indians (1972), the Philadelphia Phillies (1973-74 & 1979-82), the New York Mets (1975-76), and the Montreal Expos (1976-78). He played for the Phillies in the 1980 World Series. Unser's career stats include 1,344 hits in 5,215 at bats (.258 batting avg.), 617 runs, 87 home runs and 481 RBIs in 1,799 games played. After sitting out 1983 in retirement, he returned to the Phillies working in various jobs until he became director of player personnel in 1989. The last we heard, he was still on the job there. Unser was inducted into the Mississippi State University Sports Hall of Fame in 1981 and into the Mississippi Sports Hall of Fame on Feb. 28, 1997.

Peggy Varnadow (see Peggy Dow)

Profiles of Famous & Notable Mississippians

Christine M. Varnado

Born Jan. 29, 1980, in Metairie, La., the daughter of Carey and Peggy Varnado, her family moved to Hattiesburg when she was just 4-months old. In the fall of 1997, Varnado scored a perfect 36 on the ACT (American College Test). She was the only Mississippi student and one of only 27 nationwide that scored a perfect 36 in 1997. The test was taken by 645,000 students in the fall of 1997, including 22,000 in Mississippi. At Hattiesburg High, Varnado was involved in community theater productions, academic quiz bowl teams, and winning 53 awards in speech and debate tournaments. Varnado, with a 100.55 grade-point average, won a $24,000 academic scholarship as the Mississippi Economic Council's No.1 STAR student. She won $2,000 in the Laws of Life contest for her winning essay on race relations, which included an interview with Ellie Dahmer, whose husband, voting rights activist Vernon Dahmer, Sr., was killed in the firebombing of his home for helping black citizens register to vote. An aspiring writer with published essays and poems, Varnado penned an award-winning tribute letter to author Harper Lee, who wrote *To Kill A Mockingbird*. Lee sent her a handwritten reply. *USA Today* newspaper mentioned this when they named her as one of only two Mississippi students to their All-USA High School Academic Team. Each year, two Presidential Scholars, one male and one female, are named from each state. Varnado was the female Presidential Scholar for 1998 in Mississippi and the only recipient ever from Hattiesburg. Varnado graduated as valedictorian of her 1998 class at Hattiesburg High and is now studying English and public policy at Duke University. She is one of only 12 students in Mississippi to score a 36 score on the ACT through June 2000

Johnny Vaught

Born John Howard Vaught on May 6, 1909, in Olney, Texas. Since 1947 he's lived in Mississippi, where he's become one of the state's greatest football coaching legends. During the last year of the 20th Century, *The Clarion-Ledger* newspaper of Jackson ranked Ole Miss' glory days of football as the No. 2 sports story of the century. Those Glory Days of Rebel football were from 1947 until 1970 under head coach Vaught. In his first year as coach at the University of Mississippi, he led the team to the school's first SEC championship and a berth at the Delta Bowl in Memphis. With Charlie Conerly and Barney Poole just two of the many talented players on the '47 squad, the team went 9-2, losing only to Arkansas and Vanderbilt. Vaught brought the Rebels their first National Championship in 1960 and another one in 1962. With Vaught at the helm, the Ole Miss Rebels football team won a total of six SEC titles and played in 27 bowl games (15 consecutive), 16 of which they won. The Rebels were the SEC Team of the Decade for 1950-59. From 1957-59, ten Rebel players and coaches were inducted into the College Football Hall of Fame! Vaught also coached the last 8 games of the '73 season. He compiled a 190-61-12 record as head football coach at Ole Miss. Vaught was inducted into the Mississippi Sports Hall of Fame in 1976. His name was added to the Ole Miss football stadium on Oct. 16, 1982. Long known as Hemingway Stadium after Judge William Hemingway (1869-1937), the stadium is now known as Vaught-Hemingway Stadium. Johnny Vaught now lives in Oxford.

S.B. "Sam" Vick

Born Samuel Bruce Vick on Apr. 12, 1895, in Batesville, Miss. He made his major league baseball debut on Sept. 20, 1917, for the New York Yankees and stayed with them through the 1920 season. He played for the Boston Red Sox in 1921. He is the only man to ever pinch hit for Babe Ruth! His career stats show 159 hits in 641 at bats (.248 batting average), 90 runs, 2 home runs, and 50 RBIs in 213 games played. He was inducted into the Mississippi Sports Hall of Fame in 1967. He died on Aug. 17, 1986, in Memphis, Tennessee.

Johnny Vincent (see John Vincent Imbragulio)

Walter Vinson

Born Walter Jacobs Vinson (sometimes spelled Vincson or Vincent) on Feb. 2, 1901, in Bolton, Miss. Singer and guitarist Vinson was among the most noteworthy blues accompanists of his era. He began performing as a child, and during his teen years was a fixture at area parties and picnics. He rarely if ever appeared as a solo act, seemingly much more at home in duos and trios. During the 1920s he worked with Charlie McCoy, Rubin Lacy and Son Spand before forging his long-lasting union with Lonnie Chatmon in 1928. In addition to teaming with Chatmon in the legendary Mississippi Sheiks, Vinson also recorded with him in the Mississippi Hot Footers and worked with Chatmon's brothers Bo Carter (see his profile) and Harry. When the Sheiks' broke up in 1933 Vinson recorded with various players in areas ranging from Jackson to New Orleans to Chicago. An active club performer during the early 1940s, by the middle of the decade he had begun a lengthy hiatus from music which continued through 1960, at which point he returned to recording and festival appearances. Bad health forced Vinson into retirement during the early 1970s. He died in Chicago on April 22, 1975, at the age of 74.

Ernestine Wade

Born on Aug. 7, 1906, in Jackson, Miss. She played Sapphire Stevens on the TV series, *The Amos 'n' Andy Show*, which debuted June 28, 1951 and ran through June 11, 1953. The Amos 'n' Andy Show was the 13th highest rated show during its first year on the air. Two other Mississippians were in the cast: Alvin Childress (b. in Meridian) played Amos Jones and Spencer Williams (b. Vidalia, Louisiana, but attended high school in Natchez) played Andy. After the TV series ended, Wade played the organ in funeral parlors, worked as a legal secretary and bookkeeper, and occasionally appeared on radio and TV. Wade died in Los Angeles April 15, 1983, at age 77.

Margaret Wade

Born Dec. 30, 1912, in McCool, Miss. She starred in basketball at Delta State University for 3 years until the school dropped the sport before her senior season, 1932-33. She graduated from Delta State in 1933. After playing two years of semiprofessional ball, Wade spent 19 years as the high-school coach in Cleveland, Miss., where her teams tallied a 453-89-6 record. In 1959, she returned to Delta State to become the school's women's physical education director. When the school resurrected its women's basketball program in 1973, Wade was named coach. After a 16-2 campaign in Wade's first season as coach, Delta State won three consecutive national championship AIAW titles. The Lady Statesmen compiled a 93-4 record during the championship run. Wade retired in 1979 with a 157-23 collegiate coaching record in 23 seasons. In 1974, she was the first women inducted into the Mississippi Sports Hall of Fame. In 1986, Wade was the first women inducted into the National Basketball Hall of Fame. The NCAA women's player of the year trophy bears her name. The "First Lady of Basketball" died on Feb. 16, 1995, in Cleveland, Mississippi. Wade and one of her players at Delta State, Lusia Harris Stewart, were both charter inductees in the Women's Basketball Hall of Fame when it opened in Knoxville, Tennessee on June 4, 1999, and they were the only two of the initial 25 inductees with Mississippi ties.

Profiles of Famous & Notable Mississippians

Freddie Waits

Born Apr. 27, 1943, in Jackson, he graduated from Jackson State, where he majored in flute. He soon switched to drums. Some of his early gigs were for blues artists, including Memphis Slim and John Lee Hooker, and he also picked up experience performing soul music. He played with the Jimmy Wilkins orchestra in Detroit in 1962, was in Paul Winter's band from 1963-65, and worked in Los Angeles with Gerald Wilson's Orchestra. Waits worked as a drummer for Motown Records, where he played with hitmakers Marvin Gaye, Stevie Wonder, and Martha & The Vandellas. He later settled in New York and recorded with Ella Fitzgerald and Lena Horn. Unfortunately, he never led any record dates of his own. Waits died on Nov. 18, 1989, in New York City at age 46.

Charles C. Walker

Born Dec 11, 1934, in Hattiesburg. He loves the game of checkers, so he built the International Checker Hall of Fame in Petal, Miss. It contains Ripley's Believe It-or-Not largest and 2nd largest checkerboards in the world. This self-made, rags-to-riches millionaire built the checkered palace in 1979 as part of his 30-acre estate. He has garnered several championship titles and played 201 simultaneous games in New Orleans in 1988. Walker set a Guinness World Record in Oct. 1994 by playing checkers with 306 people simultaneously and winning 300 of those games! It was Walker's 4th Guinness World Record and the event was sponsored by Dollywood.

Dontae Walker

Born on January 31, 1980, in Jackson, Mississippi, this Clinton High School football standout recorded 1,880 yards for 33 touchdowns — the best in Class 5A in the state in both categories — in 1998, his senior year! During his three-year career with the Arrows, Walker rushed for 5,153 yards, scored 79 touchdowns and averaged 8.8 yards per carry. The 5' 10", 200-pound Walker has a top-end speed of 4.41.40! He was the 1998 *Clarion-Ledger* Player of the Year and a *USA Today* first-team All-America selection. In 1998, *SuperPrep* magazine ranked Walker as the nation's No. 1 running back. Walker committed to Mississippi State University.

Gerald Walker

Born on Mar. 19, 1908, in Gulfport, Mississippi. An Ole Miss letterman, "Gee" made his major league baseball debut on April 14, 1931, with Detroit. On the opening day of his last season with the Tigers in 1937, Walker homered, tripled, doubled and singled in consecutive at-bats! That remains the only opening day cycle in major league history! Walker went on to play for the Chicago White Sox (1938-39), the Washington Nationals (1940), the Cleveland Indians (1941), and the Cincinnati Reds (1942-45). Walker played in two World Series, 1934 and 1935, and in the 1937 All-Star game. His career stats: 1,991 hits in 6,771 at bats (.294 batting avg.), 954 runs, 124 home runs, and 997 RBIs in 1,784 games played. He was inducted into the Mississippi Sports Hall of Fame in 1969. Walker died in Whitfield, Mississippi on Mar. 20, 1981, the day after his 73rd birthday.

Harry "The Hat" Walker

Born Harry William Walker on Oct. 22, 1916, in Pascagoula, Mississippi, the son of the first Alabamian to go to baseball's major leagues - Ewart "Dixie" Walker, who pitched for Washington in 1909. Harry made his major league baseball debut on Sept. 25, 1940, with the St. Louis Cardinals, was traded to the Phils in 1947, then went to the Chicago Cubs at the end of 1948. This left-handed hitter was nicknamed for his habit of adjusting his cap between pitches. He led the National League in hitting and triples in 1947 when he batted .363 while playing 130 games for Philadelphia and 10 games with St. Louis. In 1949 he played for the Chicago Cubs and Cincinnati Reds and was the first player in the NL to lead in hitting while playing with more than one club during the same season. He played in 2 All-Star games, 1943 & '47. He played in 3 World Series games, 1942, '43 & '46. Walker made the hit that scored Enos Slaughter from first base with the winning run for St. Louis in Game 7 of the 1946 World Series. After a 22-year pro career, including 11 seasons in the majors, his stats show 786 hits in 2,651 at bats (.296 batting avg.), 385 runs, 10 home runs, and 214 RBIs in 807 games played. Walker spent 20 years as a manager, including major-league stints with the Cardinals ('55), the Pittsburg Pirates (1965-67) and the Houston Astros (1968-72). After that, he worked in various capacities for the Cardinals' organization for six years, including hitting coach, minor league farm director and scout. Walker then went to Alabama-Birmingham, where he became the first head coach for the baseball program from 1979-1986. He led the Blazers to Sun Belt Conference North Division titles in 1981-82 and had an eight-year record of 211-171. Walker finished his UAB career with four consecutive 20-plus victory seasons. Walker died on Aug. 8, 1999, in Birmingham, Alabama, from complications of a stroke. He was 82.

Rebecca Walker

Born in Jackson, Mississippi in 1969. She is the daughter of writer Alice Walker (from Alabama), who wrote the book, *The Color Purple*, which was made into the movie of the same title. Rebecca is a 1992 graduate of Yale University. She is cofounder and president of Third Wave Direct Action Corp., "an organization devoted to young feminist activism." Rebecca is the author of the book *To Be Real: Telling the Truth and Changing the Face of Feminism*, a collection of essays. Her godmother is Gloria Steinem, the feminist icon. She was on *Time* magazine's list of 50 future leaders in America. She's also a contributing writer to *Harper's*, *Essence*, *Sassy*, and *Ms* magazines. As an actress, she played "March Cunningham" in the movie *Primary Colors* (1998).

Bobby Wallace

Born Robert Hue Wallace on Sept. 17, 1954, in Magnolia, Arkansas, his family later moved to Jackson, Mississippi. He lettered in football, basketball and track three years at Callaway High School in Jackson, where he graduated in 1972. He also lettered in football three years at Mississippi State University, where he received his B.S. degree in physical education in 1976. His coaching experience includes: graduate assistant at Mississippi State (1976-77); defensive secondary at East Carolina (1977-80); defensive backs at Wyoming (1980-81); defensive secondary at Auburn (1981-85); defensive coordinator at Mississippi State (1986-87); defensive backs at Illinois (1987) and head coach at the University of North Alabama (1988-97). In 1993 Wallace and his UNA Lions produced the first perfect season, 14-0, in school and Gulf South Conference history. The Lions then won their first national championship in the 45-year history of UNA football and broke more than 70 school and conference records in the process. In 1994 Wallace guided the team to a 13-1 mark and another national championship title. In 1995, he coached North Alabama to its third NCAA Division II football championship. No other NCAA football team, at any level, has won 3 consecutive national titles! Among the many records broken, UNA became the first college team in history to win as many as 40 games in a three-year period! Wallace was named GSC Coach of the Year for a third consecutive season, the first coach in the 24-year history of the league to be so honored. He

Profiles of Famous & Notable Mississippians

also received many other awards. Wallace signed a five-year deal as head football coach for the Temple University Owls in Philadelphia, Pa. on Dec. 5, 1997.

Wesley Walls

Born Charles Wesley Walls on Mar. 26, 1966, in Batesville, Mississippi. He graduated Valedictorian of his class at Pontotoc High. Walls attended all 4 years at Ole Miss on a football scholarship and had the highest grade-point average in the SEC for 3 years. He graduated with a 3.31 GPA and an engineering degree. He was named an Associated Press All-American in 1988 and received the NCAA Hall of Fame scholarship that same year. The 6-foot-5, 250 pound Walls was a second-draft choice with the San Francisco 49ers as a tight end in 1989. He played with the 49ers in Super Bowl XXIV in his rookie year (1990), catching a pass in San Francisco's 55-10 win over Denver. After 5 seasons with the 49ers, he went to the New Orleans Saints as a free agent at the start of the 1994 season. During his second year with the Saints, he had the all-time team record for highest number of catches for a tight end. The Carolina Panthers lured Walls away from the Saints on Feb. 21, 1996, with a 3-year $4 million contract and made him a full-time starter for the first time in his 8-year career. In 1999, Walls' contract was re-negotiated for about $8 million. At the end of 1996, Walls' season stats totaled 61 catches and his 10 TDs tied for second-most in the NFC and he was the Terry Bradshaw pick as Free Agent of the Year. His 1997 season included these Single-Game Highs: Receptions — 8 (Nov. 30, 1997, vs. New Orleans); Yards — 147 (Sept. 7, 1997, vs. Atlanta); and TD Receptions — 2 (Sept. 14, 1997, vs. San Diego). The Panthers leading receiver in 1997, he also had two 100-yard receiving games. Walls had another great year in 1998, followed by his best season in 1999. Walls started all 16 games of the season and caught a career-high 63 passes for 822 yards and tied the NFL record for single-season touchdown catches by a tight end with 12. He played in the last 4 Pro Bowls and was Carolina's second-leading receiver in 2000 with 31 catches for 422 yards and 2 TDs. Walls suffered season-ending tears in the ligaments of his left knee in a game on Oct. 29, 2000. His pro career stats through Oct. 29, 2000, showed 4,376 receiving yards on 368 receptions and 44 TDs. Walls holds the Carolina Panthers all-time records for most touchdown receptions (35) and most TDs (35).

Ray Walston

Born on Dec. 2, 1914, in Laurel, Mississippi, he grew up in New Orleans. He has numerous stage, screen & TV credits. Made his film debut in *Kiss Them For Me* (1957). Had key roles in *Damn Yankees* (1958), for which he received a 1956 Tony award for Best Actor, and *South Pacific* (1958), both on Broadway and in the movies. Other movies include *The Apartment* (1960), *Tall Story* (1960), *Kiss Me Stupid* (1964), *Paint Your Wagon* (1969), *The Sting* (1973), *Popeye* (1980) and *Of Mice and Men* (1981). *The Apartment*, a 1960 release in which Walston played, was rated No. 93 on The American Film Institute's list of the Top 100 Greatest American Movies of All Time, announced in 1998. He co-starred with the late Bill Bixby on the 1963-66 CBS-TV weekly comedy series *My Favorite Martian*, also made into a 1999 movie in which Walston also stars. He played the colorful judge Henry Bone on the CBS-TV series *Picket Fences*, a role for which he won an Emmy two years in a row, 1995 & '96, as Best Supporting Actor in a Drama Series (also nominated in 1994). The last *Picket Fences* aired April 24, 1996. He played Professor Glen Bateman on ABC-TV's 8-hour miniseries, *The Stand*, based on Stephen King's 1978 epic novel, which aired in May 1994. He has been a guest star on numerous TV shows, including *Star Trek: The Next Generation*, on which he played Captain Picard's Starfleet Academy mentor, Boothby.

Sela Ward

Born in Meridian on July 11, 1956, she graduated from the University of Alabama where she was a cheerleader for the Crimson Tide football team. Heading to New York after college, she began work at an advertising agency, but soon started modeling. She signed with the Wilhemina agency and did about 20 national TV commercials. Ward moved to L.A. in 1983 and within weeks landed her first movie role in the Burt Reynolds vehicle, *The Man Who Loved Women*. She's been in over a dozen films since, including *Rustler's Rhapsody* ('85), *Nothing in Common* ('86), *Hello Again* ('87) and a small part as the "woman in bar" in *Runaway Bride* ('99). Starring as the wife of Dr. Richard Kimble (Harrison Ford) in the 1993 hit, *The Fugitive*, her character is murdered in the first part of the movie. Ward was on *People* magazine's list of 50 Most Beautiful People in 1992. She won an Emmy Award for Best Actress in a Drama Series in 1994 for her role as the free-spirited artist Teddy on NBC-TV's weekly series *Sisters*. She received Golden Globe nominations for best lead actress in a drama series for *Sisters* three times, in 1992, '94 and in 1996, when she actually won the award. The last episode of that series aired May 4, 1996, after 6 seasons. She played the late newswoman Jessica Savitch on the Lifetime Cable Network movie *Almost Golden* (1995), a role that earned her an Emmy nomination, a Screen Actors Guild nod & a Cable Ace Award. In the fall of 1999, she starred in ABC-TV's *Once and Again*, a new romantic comedy, a role that earned Ward an Emmy for Best Actress in a Drama Series on Sept. 10, 2000.

Wyatt Waters

Born March 16, 1955, in Brookhaven, Mississippi. He graduated from Clinton High School in 1973 and received his Masters of Arts degree from Mississippi College. This watercolor artist had the first book of his paintings, *Another Coat of Paint: An Artist's View of Jackson, Mississippi*, published in 1995. Jackson's Lemuria Bookstore owner John Evans said it was "one of the biggest books we've ever had." Waters' second book, *Painting Home*, was released in the fall of 1998 to much fanfare and excitement. Unlike his first volume, which consisted primarily of existing paintings, *Painting Home* was created from the canvas up with Waters traveling around the state for three years and painting on-location. He painted *Shadow on the Sun* at Sun Record Studio in Memphis on the day rock 'n' roll legend Carl Perkins died. *Harp and Angels* depicts the Tutwiler grave of blues great Sonny Boy Williamson II. And, a quiet scene of a church in Sherard, Mississippi is called *Double Crossed*.

Harvey "Pop" Watkins, Sr.

Born in Canton, Miss. on Dec. 5, 1929. This singer-songwriter was a founding member of the internationally known gospel group, the Canton Spirituals, and began singing in the group at age 14. The group's album, *Live in Memphis*, received a Grammy nomination in 1994. *Live in Memphis* was the longest running album on Billboard's Gospel Music Chart as of Nov. 1994. In July 1994, Watkins received a Legend Award at the Miss. Gospel Music Awards, the same month that Second Street in Canton was renamed Harvey Watkins, Sr. Drive in his honor. He also received the Vision Award and numerous other awards. Watkins, who died of cancer in Jackson on Nov. 16, 1994, was the only original member still with the Canton Spirituals. The group he helped form was inducted into the Gospel Music Hall of Fame in Detroit in 1998.

Profiles of Famous & Notable Mississippians

Brad Watson

Born July 24, 1955, in Meridian, he has been a teacher, carpenter, truck tire changer, fire alarm system salesman, and Hollywood garbageman. When he left Mississippi fresh out of high school, he headed for Hollywood with the intention of making a name for himself. After working as a garbageman to pay his rent in Hollywood, he came home to Meridian and got a job as a carpenter. He finally enrolled at Meridian Junior College and got into an Honors English class, where he studied Southern literature. Watson enrolled at Mississippi State University in Starkville in the summer of 1976 and graduated in 1978 with a bachelor's degree in English. Next, he earned a Master of Fine Arts degree in creative writing and American literature at the University of Alabama. Watson's first published short story appeared in *Intro*, an anthology of stories by people in writing programs around the country. Nothing ever came of it. Watson was 23 years old. He worked on the Alabama Gulf Coast with a weekly newspaper, then became a correspondent for the *Montgomery Advertiser*, where he eventually was promoted to state editor. When he left the paper, he worked for an ad agency in Montgomery writing ad copy. He returned to the University of Alabama in 1988 to teach part-time and to get back into writing. Watson finally found success as the author of *Last Days of the Dog-Men*, a highly acclaimed collection of short stories with dogs as real characters who illuminate human inter- personal relations in events such as divorce and other failures. Sales of the book, published by Norton in April 1996, have far exceeded expectations. Norton sold the rights to German and British publishers, and Dell published the paperback version in 1997. Positive reviews appeared in such publications as *The New York Times*, *Publishers Weekly*, *Newsday*, and *Globe*. *Last Days of the Dog-Men* won the 1997 Sue Kaufman Prize for first fiction from the American Academy of Arts and Letters and the Great Lakes Colleges Association New Writers Award for 1997. Regardless of the success he achieves as a writer, Watson plans to continue teaching. He is now teaching at Harvard. Watson and his family live in Alabama and Boston.

Libby Rae Watson

Born Jan. 5, 1954, in Pascagoula. She sings and plays in a style rooted in the 1920s. Blues legend Sam Chatmon of Hollandale befriended her and taught her many songs including *Sitting on Top of the World*, which she sang at his funeral in 1983. Some of her performances include the Mississippi Crossroads Blues Festival in Greenwood, Miss., the King Biscuit Festival in Helena, Ark., the Gulf Coast Blues Festival in Biloxi, Miss., and the Columbus, Ohio Traditional Blues Festival. She also helped coordinate the first Mississippi Delta Blues Festival in Greenville, Mississippi. Libby Rae is currently performing with her band, The Liberators. They have one CD called *Saltwater Blues*, which consist of original songs. A new CD, also of original material, was released in 1999.

Thomas Wayne

Born Thomas Wayne Perkins on July 22, 1940, in Batesville, Mississippi. He first recorded for Mercury Records in 1956. He had a top-10 record, *Tragedy*, in 1959. He was the brother of Luther Perkins, guitarist for Johnny Cash's band from 1955-67. Thomas worked as a session guitarist in Nashville until his death in an auto accident on Aug. 15, 1971 at the age of 31. Wayne is in the Rockabilly Hall of Fame.

Jim Weatherly

This Pop/county singer/songwriter was born March 17, 1943, in Pontotoc, Miss. Weatherly played football at Ole Miss in the Rebels' only undefeated season. In the off-season and in the summers, he was lead singer for his band, Jim Weatherly & The Vegas. Weatherly's career began moving at a steady pace when he and a group of buddies moved to Los Angeles shortly after graduating from Ole Miss. In L.A., their band became The Gordian Knot, cut an album and played clubs and a USO tour with Nancy Sinatra before splitting up four years later. A friend of Weatherly's, actor Lee Majors, who was on the TV series *Big Valley* at the time, introduced Weatherly to Jim Nabors. Nabors liked Weatherly's music and told him if he ever wanted a job writing songs to call him. After the group split up, Weatherly wrote for Nabors' publishing company for two and a half years while Nabors had his variety show on TV. Though Nabors recorded a number of his songs, Weatherly really wanted to try his hand in a different genre, such as country or rock, music that would get more air time. So, when Nabors' show was canceled, Weatherly hooked up with L.A. publisher Larry Gordon. The record deal that Gordon arranged allowed Weatherly to cut seven albums that included country and pop music. Weatherly's *The Need to Be* hit No. 11 in pop, and his single *I'll Still Love You* went to No. 5 on the country charts. A song Weatherly originally titled *Midnight Plane to Houston* brought added fame and fortune to Gladys Knight when she cut it as *Midnight Train to Georgia*. The song won her a Grammy for Best Rhythm and Blues Vocal Recording. Weatherly's first No. 1 hit *Neither One of Us*, also recorded by Knight, won her a Grammy for Best Pop Vocal. For 25 years, Weatherly divided his time between Los Angeles and Nashville, writing songs and performing, before moving back to the South in 1988. Though Weatherly can still be seen on stage at local writers' nights, he says his large-scale performance days are behind him. He prefers song writing to singing. Country artist Bryan White topped the charts in 1996 with *Someone Else's Star*, a song that Weatherly co-wrote. Weatherly continues to actively pen new tunes with such artists as Steve Wariner, Jeff Carson and Vince Gill. His song *Love Never Broke Anyone's Heart* was included on Gill's award-winning album, *I Still Believe in You*.

Clarence Weatherspoon

Born Sept. 8, 1970, in Crawford, Miss., hometown of football great Jerry Rice. This 6-foot-7 basketball small forward was a three-time Metro Conference Player of the Year at the University of Southern Mississippi where he averaged 18.2 points and 11.3 rebounds in 117 games over four seasons from 1988-92. He finished as USM's second all-time leading scorer (2,130 points) behind Nick Revon. He finished as the Golden Eagles' all-time leading rebounder (1,230) and the Metro Conference all-time leader with 11.3 per game. During Weatherspoon's years at USM, the Golden Eagles posted back-to-back 20-win seasons (1989-90 & 1990-91) and played in the NCAA Tournament twice. He was the 9th choice in the first round by the Philadelphia 76ers in the 1992 draft and made the NBA All-Rookie 2nd team. During the 1993-94 season with the 76ers, he was one of only five NBA players to have 100 points, 100 rebounds, 100 steals, 100 blocked shots and 100 assists. Only 5 players had more rebounds in a game than Weatherspoon. He had 23 against Orlando. He led the 76ers in points and rebounds and was second in field goal percentage and blocked shots. After he went with the Golden State Warriors, he averaged 18.1 points and was 2nd on the 76ers in rebounds, assists and steals during the 1994-95 season. He averaged 16.7 points and 9.7 rebounds in 1995-96. He started all 82 games and averaged 12.2 points and 8.3 rebounds in 1996-97. After averaging 15 points per game in 6 NBA seasons (mostly with Philadelphia), his average dropped

Profiles of Famous & Notable Mississippians

steadily. During the 1997-98 season with the Warriors, he started only 31 games and averaged 10.7 points and 8.3 rebounds with 22 blocks and 42 steals. He was free to negotiate after his 4-year $14.6 million contract ran out on in 1998. On Jan. 24, 1999, Weatherspoon signed a 3-year deal with the Miami Heat totaling almost $5.8 million. His pro career stats through the 1999-2000 season: played in 479 games (35.8 minutes avg.); 7,198 points (15.0 ppg avg.); 3,973 rebounds (8.3 avg.); 571 steals; 518 blocks; and 941 assists. His career field goal percentage is .468 and free throw percentage is .726. In 1999, Weatherspoon was chosen as a member of the first team for *The Clarion-Ledger* Division I Men's Basketball Team of the Century! On Aug. 30, 2000, Weatherspoon was traded to the Cleveland Cavaliers. In 2000 Weatherspoon was inducted into the just-established Legends Society, which honors former Southern Miss athletic greats.

Peggy Webb
Born Peggy Elaine Hussey on Feb. 8, 1942, in Mooreville in Lee Co., close to Tupelo, where she now lives. A former English teacher and magazine writer, Webb started writing romance novels at age 43. Her first novel, *Taming Maggie* (1985), reached No. 1 on Waldenbooks' Romance Novels Bestsellers list. Webb was the first romance novelist ever to have their first book reach the top of that list! She's been quite prolific since then, turning out romance novels at the average rate of three per year. Her latest two are *Summer Hawk* (1999) and *Warrior's Embrace* (May 2000), her 48th novel.

"Skeeter" Webb
Born James Laverne Webb on Nov. 4, 1909, in Meridian, Mississippi. He made his major league baseball debut on July 20, 1932, with the St. Louis Cardinals. He played only one season for St. Louis and was out of the major leagues from 1934-37. Back in the majors in 1938, he played for the Cleveland Indians (1938-39), the Chicago White Sox (1940-44), the Detroit Tigers (1945-47) and the Philadelphia Athletics in 1948. His career stats include 498 hits in 2,274 at bats (.219 batting average), 216 runs, 3 home runs and 166 RBIs in 699 games played. He was inducted into the Mississippi Sports Hall of Fame in 1978. Webb died on July 8, 1986, in Meridian at the age of 76.

Ted J. Webb, Jr.
Born Ted Johnson Webb, Jr. on Nov. 1, 1956, in Yazoo City, Mississippi. A commercial banker in Hattiesburg, he invented a popular children's toy, Air Pogo, in 1992. First invented for the Webb's two children, Caroline and Julia, it proved so popular with them and the neighborhood kids, it just took off. Air Pogo, the original bouncing swing that is made to hang from a tree limb or swing set, is made for children ages 5 to 10 and retails for about $100. Air Pogo has received quite a few honors and awards, including the Parent's Choice Gold Award (the "Oscar" of children's products) in 1993, listed as one of Dr. Toy's Top 100 Children's Products in 1994, and listed as one of *Parents Magazine*'s Best Summer Toys in 1995. The toy has been featured in *The Wall Street Journal*, *USA Today* and was even seen on the *Live with Regis and Kathie Lee* TV show in May 1995. Ted's wife, Sarah, is president of the company that markets the toy. Air Pogo is made in Laurel, Mississippi and shipped throughout the United States.

Norris Weese
Born in Aug. 12, 1951, in Baton Rouge, Louisiana. He was a 1973 graduate of Ole Miss, where he was a three-year starting quarterback. As co-captain of the Rebels' 1973 team, he threw just one interception in 55 pass attempts. He was named MVP in the Hula Bowl and in the 1971 Peach Bowl as he guided the Rebels to a 41-18 win over Georgia Tech. Weese ranks 6th in career total offense at Ole Miss with 3,179 yards and was inducted into the Ole Miss Athletic Hall of Fame in 1994. He was the Jackson Touchdown Club's Sportsman of the Year in 1974. Drafted in 1974 by the Los Angeles Rams, Weese played for the World Football League before being signed by the Denver Broncos in 1976. He played for Denver until 1979 as a backup quarterback to Craig Morton. In the 1978 Super Bowl, Weese replaced Morton in the 3rd quarter and guided Denver to its only TD. He completed 4 of 10 passes and ran three times for 26 yards in the championship against Dallas. He also took over for Morton in 1978 in the playoff game with Pittsburgh. He passed for 118 yards and finished as the Broncos' top rusher with 43 yards. He was a starter in 6 games in 1979 before injuring his knee. He retired the following season and became a certified public accountant in Denver. Weese remains third on the Broncos' all-time proficiency list among quarterbacks. His pro career totals are 143 completions of 251 pass attempts for 1,887 yards and 7 TDs and he ran 69 times for 362 yards. Weese, age 43, died in Denver on Jan. 13, 1995, after a long fight against bone cancer.

Ira C. Welborn
Born Ira Clinton Welborn on Feb. 13, 1874, in Mico (now Shady Grove), Jones Co., Miss. He graduated from West Point Military Academy in 1898 and went directly to Santiago, Cuba. Welborn was a Second Lieutenant with the 9th U.S. Infantry at Santiago when he performed an act of bravery on July 2, 1898, that earned him the Medal of Honor (MOH). He was presented the Medal on June 21, 1899. Here are the actual words of his citation: "Voluntarily left shelter and went, under fire, to the aid of a private of his company who was wounded." Welborn was one of only two Mississippians to receive the MOH in the Spanish-American War. The other serviceman was John W. Heard (see his profile). Welborn also held the distinguished service medal. His foreign duty included service in the Philippines and China. He was later commandant at Mississippi A&M, and an honor graduate of the Army School of the Line in 1916. From 1918-20 he was with the tank corps in Washington, during which time Dwight D. Eisenhower was on his staff as a major. Welborn's was one of 17 Medals of Honor that have been officially accredited to Mississippi in all wars, although we claim 5 more accredited to other states because the recipients with Mississippi ties were in other states when they entered service. Welborn is one of only 13 native Mississippians (of 22 Mississippians — 15 Army, 4 Marines & 3 Navy) in all wars to have received the MOH out of 3,433 recipients of the Medal through Nov. 1, 2000. Welborn died at the Biloxi Veterans Hospital on July 13, 1956, at age 82. He was laid to rest with full military honors in the Biloxi National Cemetery. There is a Medal of Honor marker on his grave.

Lloyd Wells
Born April 22, 1938 in Gulfport, he grew up in Laurel. He graduated from Mississippi Southern in 1960. Wells went on to a career as a jazz musician, arranger, producer and director. He was on many recordings with big bands including an album with Glenn Miller. He was a guitarist on several TV shows including *Sesame Street*, *The Electric Company*, *The Merv Griffin Show*, *The Toast of the Town/The Ed Sullivan Show*, and *The Tonight Show with Johnny Carson*. He was involved in 18 Broadway plays including *Caberet*. Wells arranged and conducted the only Gershwin estate-sanctioned *Gershwin Review* which played in 90 U.S. cities. He was music director of Opryland USA in Nashville for 23 years from 1975-98. Wells, who was the music conductor and arranger for

Profiles of Famous & Notable Mississippians

Tennessee Ernie Ford's orchestra, is proud of the fact that he talked the late singer into donating the arrangements of his many audio recordings and video recordings to the University of Southern Mississippi. Wells was inducted into USM's Alumni Hall of Fame in 1992. He is one of six artists on a 1999 CD called *The Great Mississippi Jazz Guitarists Reunion*, released by the Mississippi Musicians Hall of Fame. The other artists are Bucky Barrett, Steve Blaylock, Mundell Lowe, Skeets McWilliams and Bob Saxton (all are profiled). Wells now lives in Nashville. Wells, as well as Lowe and McWilliams were among the first 27 inducted into the Miss. Musicians Hall of Fame April 1, 2000.

Mary Ann Wells
Born July 2, 1944, at Agricola, Miss. Her work as a professional photographer, photo journalist, and journalist has received national, state, and regional awards. Her writing and photography has appeared in over 100 publications. Her books include *A Guide to Mississippi's Festivals, Fairs & Flea Markets*, *A History Lovers Guide to Mississippi*, *A History Lovers Guide to Louisiana*, and *Native Land*.

Ida Bell Wells-Barnett
Born the daughter of slaves in Holly Springs, Miss. on July 16, 1862. Educated at Rust College, a high school and industrial school for freed slaves in Holly Springs, she later attended Fisk University. When she was 14, both her parents died within 24 hours of each other. Lying about her age, she became a teacher in the Memphis area and was the sole support of her five brothers and sisters. Her pay was $25 a month. In 1908, she co-founded the National Association for the Advancement of Colored People (NAACP). She brought a lawsuit in Tennessee against a railroad that tried to force her to leave a "whites-only" car. Although she eventually lost the case, Wells-Barnett continued to be a militant defender of black rights. She bought an interest in the *Memphis Free Speech* and used the newspaper to denounce lynchings. She later moved to New York and then Chicago after she married Ferdinand Barnett, who owned a newspaper there. They used the newspaper to fight for equal rights. Wells in her time was perhaps the most famous journalist in the country. She also became active in organizing local black women in causes ranging from anti-lynching campaigns to the suffrage movement. She died on Mar. 25, 1931. On Feb. 1, 1990, she was honored by the U.S. Postal Service with a commemorative stamp issued at the Museum of Science and Technology in Chicago. She's in the National Women's Hall of Fame.

Eudora Welty
Born Eudora Alice Welty on April 13, 1909, in Jackson. She attended Industrial Institute and College (now Mississippi University for Women) for two years, then received a B.A. from the University of Wisconsin in 1929. Her first job was at Jackson radio station WJDX, which Welty's father founded. Many of the stories that brought her fame first appeared in *The New Yorker* magazine. She received the Pulitzer Prize in 1973 for *The Optimist's Daughter* ('69). She also wrote *A Curtain of Green* ('41), *The Robber Bridegroom* ('42), *The Wide Net and Other Stories* ('43), *Delta Wedding* ('46), *The Golden Apples* ('49), *The Ponder Heart* ('54), *The Bride of the Innisfallen and Other Stories* ('55), *The Shoe Bird* ('64, her only book written for children), *Losing Battles* ('70), *One Time, One Place* ('74), *The Eye of the Story* ('77), *The Collected Stories of Eudora Welty* ('80) and *One Writer's Beginnings* ('84). In a compilation, *Eudora Welty: A Writer's Eye* ('94), she sizes up the works of other authors, writing 69 reviews of books published from 1942-84, most of them from the *New York Times* best seller lists. In 1998, filmmaker/actress Jodie Markell released a film adaptation of Welty's classic short story *Why I Live at the P.O.* Welty's *The Ponder Heart*, shot for PBS' *Masterpiece Theater* in Canton, Edwards and Raymond in the spring of 2000, will air in 2001. Welty is also an accomplished professional photographer and has had several books of her pictures released including *Country Churchyards* (2000). The state's largest public library in Jackson is named in her honor. Welty twice received the Presidential Medal of Freedom, from presidents Carter and Reagan. In 1992, she became only the 4th person to receive the National Book Foundation's Medal for Distinguished Contribution to American Letters. Welty lived in Paris in 1949 and 50 and France has long translated her novels and short stories. In 1987, she was knighted by the French government and in 1996, they presented her with The Legion of Honor, France's highest civilian award in ceremonies at Jackson's Old Capitol Museum. She has also received the Lifetime Achievement Award, the highest honor of the Governor's Awards for Excellence in the Arts. Welty was one of 3 Mississippi writers (with William Faulkner and Richard Wright) featured at Atlanta's Centennial Olympic Games in 1996 in a special literary exhibition of 9 Southern writers called *The American South: Past, Present & Future*. Welty has honorary degrees from Millsaps College, Smith College, Harvard University, and received the first honorary degree awarded by the Mississippi University for Women in 1998. Welty, along with Margaret Walker Alexander and Thalia Mara, were the first recipients of the (Jackson) Mayor's Arts Achivement Honors in 1998. In a special millennium poll released the last week of 1999, readers of *The Clarion-Ledger* overwhelming picked Eudora Welty as Mississippi's Woman of the Century! Welty was inducted into the National Women's Hall of Fame on October 7, 2000, along with 19 others.

Louis Westerfield
Born July 31, 1949, in Kemper Co., Miss., he grew up in New Orleans. He received a master's degree from Columbia University Law School in New York and a Juris Doctor degree from Loyola University's School of Law. Westerfield began his legal career in 1974 as an assistant district attorney in New Orleans, became assistant professor of law at Southern University's School of Law in 1975, then joined Loyola's law faculty in 1978. He became the first tenured African-American law professor at Ole Miss in 1983. In 1986, he became the first black law dean at North Carolina Central University. He became law dean at Loyola in 1990. He made history in 1994 when he was named dean of the University of Mississippi School of Law, the first black to hold that position. His promising future was cut short by his premature death from a heart attack in New Orleans on Aug. 24, 1996, at age 47.

Roy M. Wheat
Roy Mitchell Wheat was born July 24, 1947, in Moselle, Jones County, Mississippi. He entered the U.S. Marine Corps in Jackson, Miss. Wheat was a Lance Corporal with Company K, 3d Battalion, 7th Marine, 1st Marine Division in the Republic of Vietnam when he performed the ultimate sacrifice — an act of bravery that took his life on Aug. 11, 1967. He was awarded the Congressional Medal of Honor posthumously in 1969. Here are the actual words of his citation: "For conspicuous gallantry and intrepidity at the risk of his life above and beyond the call of duty. L/Cpl. Wheat and 2 other marines were assigned the mission of providing security for a Navy construction battalion crane and crew operating along Liberty Road in the vicinity of the Dien Ban District, Quang Nam

Profiles of Famous & Notable Mississippians

Province. After the marines had set up security positions in a tree line adjacent to the work site, L/Cpl. Wheat reconnoitered the area to the rear of their location for the possible presence of guerrillas. He then returned to within 10 feet of the friendly position, and here unintentionally triggered a well concealed, bounding type, antipersonnel mine. Immediately, a hissing sound was heard which was identified by the 3 marines as that of a burning time fuse. Shouting a warning to his comrades, L/Cpl. Wheat in a valiant act of heroism hurled himself upon the mine, absorbing the tremendous impact of the explosion with his body. The inspirational personal heroism and extraordinary valor of his unselfish action saved his fellow marines from certain injury and possible death, reflected great credit upon himself, and upheld the highest traditions of the Marine Corps and the U.S. Naval Service. He gallantly gave his life for his country." Wheat was the only *native* Mississippian (of 2 Mississippians) to earn the Congressional Medal of Honor (CMOH) during the Vietnam War. The other serviceman awarded the CMOH for service in Vietnam was adopted Mississippian Milton L. Olive III (Army). Both Wheat and Olive were awarded their Medals posthumously. Wheat was one of only 4 native Mississippians (of 6 Mississippians) ever awarded the Medal posthumously. Wheat's Medal was one of 17 Medals of Honor that have been officially accredited to Mississippi in all wars, although we claim 5 more that were accredited to other states because the recipients had Mississippi ties. Wheat is one of 13 native Mississippians (of 22 Mississippians — 15 Army, 4 Marines & 3 Navy) in all wars to be awarded the CMOH out of 3,433 total recipients of the Medal through Nov. 1, 2000. Wheat is buried in the Eastabutchie Cemetery in Eastabutchie, Mississippi. A Medal of Honor marker is on his grave.

Artie White

Born April 16, 1937, in Vicksburg. He sang gospel with the Harps of David at the age of 11 prior to going to Chicago in 1956, where he sang with the Full Gospel Wonders. White claims that he was lured into singing the devil's music by a well-heeled dude who drove up in a Cadillac and promised him $10,000 to record some blues songs! Very few Chicago blues artists were able to pierce the R&B charts during the 1970s, but smooth-voiced "Blues Boy" White managed it with his 1977 single *Leanin' Tree*. For a while, he tried his hand at running a blues club, Bootsy's Lounge. He cut an album in 1985 for Shreveport-based Ronn Records called *Blues Boy*. He signed with Ichiban in 1987 and recorded six sets (enough for a Best Of CD in 1991). On 1989's *Thangs Got to Change*, White enjoyed the presence of fellow Mississippian Little Milton Campbell, one of his prime influences, on lead guitar. His latest CD is *Shades of Blue* on Waldoxy, one of the labels of Malaco Music Group of Jackson, Mississippi.

Bukka White

This Blues legend was born Booker T. Washington White on Nov. 12, 1909 (the Social Security Death Index says Nov. 12, 1900), on a farm near Houston, Mississippi, a cousin of Blues great B.B. King. Bukka got a guitar for his 9th birthday. His grandfather was a preacher, but Bukka showed an early preference for the blues after a meeting with the legendary Charley Patton. Bukka hoboed everywhere from the Delta to Buffalo, NY. He boxed in Chicago and K.O.'d many opponents. In Chicago, Bukka met Tampa Red, Memphis Minnie and Big Bill Broonzy. In the 1960s he performed with Son House, Skip James, John Hurt and Sleepy John Estes. Many of his songs detail his experiences as a prisoner for two years at Parchman Farm for shooting a man in the thigh after the man ambushed Bukka on a road in 1937. Singing in the tradition of Son House, he'd work his guitar like a drum on train songs about his hobo life, and on classics like *Bukka's Jitterbug Swing* and *Fixing To Die*. He died of cancer in Memphis on Feb. 26, 1977, at the age of 67 (or 76).

Frank White

Born in Greenwood, Mississippi on September 4, 1950. He made his major league baseball debut on June 12, 1973. He played second base for the Kansas City Royals for 12 years form 1973-1990. He played in 5 All-Star games, 1978, 1979, 1981, 1982 and 1986. He played in two World Series, in 1980 and 1985. In Game 3 of the 1985 World Series, White hit a home run that helped Kansas City to win the title. In a total of 2,324 games played, his career stats show 2.006 hits in 7,859 at-bats (.255 batting avg.), 912 runs, 160 homers & 886 RBIs.

Willye B. White

Born Jan. 1, 1936, in Money, Mississippi. A 5-time Olympian, she won the Silver Medal in the long jump in 1956 and another in the 4x100-meter relay in 1964. Inducted into both the National Track & Field Hall of Fame and the Miss. Sports Hall of Fame in 1981, she was inducted into the International Women's Sports Hall of Fame in Track & Field in 1988.

Jamie L. Whitten

Born Jamie Lloyd Whitten in Cascilla, Miss. on April 18, 1910. First elected to Congress on Nov. 4, 1941, he entered the record books on Jan. 6, 1992 by breaking the record for the longest service in the House. He officially retired in January 1995 after 53 years, longer than any other member in congressional history. He went to congress a month before the Japanese attack on Pearl Harbor. On Dec. 8, 1941, Whitten voted to send the U.S. into World War II. He was the last person still in congress who voted on that historic resolution. He served under 11 presidents, from Franklin D. Roosevelt to Bill Clinton and witnessed almost a quarter of the nation's history. Whitten accomplished much for his district and Mississippi including highway construction, farmers' aid, public works, and flood control projects such as the construction of Arkabutla, Sardis, Enid and Grenada reservoirs. He led the 20-year fight to create the Tennessee-Tombigbee Waterway. It was through his efforts that north Mississippi was included in the Appalachian Regional Commission making the region eligible for federal assistance. Considered a major force in American agriculture, he came to be known on Capitol Hill as "the permanent secretary of agriculture." He was chairman of the Appropriations Agriculture Subcommittee from 1949 and chairman of the full committee from 1979 up until the 1993-94 congressional session. Whitten was also known for work on the powerful House Appropriations Committee, which controls the purse strings. He lost those jobs after illness made it difficult for him to handle the schedule. Roger Wicker, Republican, of Tupelo, won Whitten's seat in the election in Nov. 1994. Whitten died on Sept. 9, 1995, of heart and kidney failure in Oxford, Mississippi. A lock on the Tennessee-Tombigbee Waterway was named after Whitten in 1997.

Tom Wilburn

Thomas L. "Tom" Wilburn was born Nov. 30, 1918, in Columbus, Miss. He grew up on a farm in Artesia, just south of Columbus. There, he learned to love horses. He trained Air Force fighter pilots during World War II, but went back to training horses and racing after he got out of the service. After racing for a few years, he decided that he wanted to be a professional harness racing driver, so, in the summer of 1947, he left to follow his dream. He wound up in Chicago, where he

Profiles of Famous & Notable Mississippians

earned $1,500 that summer and fall. For the next 26 years, Wilburn spent May until December racing all around the country. He served as a horse trainer for up to 12 owners at a time, earning a training fee plus 10 percent of the earnings as a driver. Over his career that lasted until 1973, he raced thousands of times, producing 1,667 wins and $2.9 million in earnings! He's proud of the fact that for his first 20 years as a professional, from 1947 until 1967, he was the only national harness racing driver from Mississippi. Wilburn ranks among the 100 all-time leading racers in the U.S. Because so many of his victories occurred at a track just outside Chicago, he was voted into the Illinois Harness Racing Hall of Fame in 1989. After returning to oversee the same 1,700 acre farm on which he grew up, he won the 1991 Cattleman of the Year Award from the Mississippi Cattleman's Association.

Robert Wilkins

This blues singer-guitarist was born Robert Timothy Wilkins on Jan. 16, 1896, in Hernando, DeSoto County, Mississippi. He was working as a Pullman porter in Memphis when he first recorded for Victor in 1928. His 1929 song *That's No Way to Get Along* was later recorded by the Rolling Stones as *Prodigal Son*. Wilkins recorded a one-chord song called *Rollin' Stone*. Because of a violent altercation at a house party at which he was playing, he quit the blues in 1936 and became a minister of the Church of God in Christ and remained so until his death in Memphis on May 26, 1987, at age 91.

Ben Williams

Born Robert Jerry Williams in Yazoo City, Mississippi on Sept. 1, 1954, he played football at Yazoo City High. On Dec. 11, 1971, "Gentle" Ben and James Reed of Meridian became the first black football players to sign with Ole Miss. Williams became a four-year starter, a three-time All-SEC player (1973-75) and made the first team All-American in 1975. During his college career, Williams had 377 tackles, including 116 his senior year. He had 18 quarterback sacks in 1973, an Ole Miss record that still stands. He was named to the Ole Miss Team of the Century in 1992. Williams was taken in the 3rd round of the 1976 NFL draft and played 11 seasons and 150 games for the Buffalo Bills, starting in 143 games. He led the Bills in tackles 5 of his last 6 seasons and led in sacks in 1980, 1981 and 1983. He had a total of 51 career sacks. He was inducted into the Mississippi Sports Hall of Fame in 1997.

Ben Ames Williams

Born March 3, 1889, in Macon, Mississippi. Williams was the grandnephew of James Longstreet, the Confederate general. He lived as a boy in Jackson, Ohio, then attended school in West Newton, Mass. in 1904. The next year, he went to Cardiff, Wales, where his father was Consul, and entered Dartmouth College in the fall of 1906 and received his B.A. degree there in 1910. he worked at the Boston *American* from 1901-1916, where he started writing novels. His first book was *All the Brothers Were Valiant* (1919). His best-sellers include *Honeyflow* (1932), *Come Spring* (1932), *Mischief* (1933), *Pascal's Mill* (1933), *Crucible* (1937), *The Strange Woman* (1941), *Leave Her to Heaven* (1944), and *The Unconquered* (1953). Williams wrote a total of 32 books. He was also associated with almost 2 dozen movies — he wrote the screenplays for some and others were based on his books. Williams died on Feb. 4, 1953, at the age of 63.

"Big" Joe Williams

Born Joe Lee Williams on Oct. 16, 1903, in Crawford, Miss. Cantankerous Big Joe could practically do it all as far as blues — sing and play guitar, harmonica, accordion & kazoo. In his early Delta days, he played work camps, jukes, store porches, streets and alleys from New Orleans to Chicago. He recorded for 5 decades for Vocalion, Okeh, Paramount, Bluebird and other labels. His song, *Baby Please Don't Go*, is included on the Rock and Roll Hall of Fame's list of 500 Songs That Shaped Rock And Roll. He's in the Blues Foundation's Hall of Fame. Williams died in Macon, Mississippi on Dec. 17, 1982.

Frank Williams

Born on June 27, 1947, in Smithdale, Amite County, Mississippi, he was probably the most influential of the many Williams Brothers, all born in Smithdale. He was a member of the Jackson Southernaires and was the man who founded the Mississippi Mass Choir (see that profile). Williams died on March 22, 1993, in Savannah, Georgia. Frank Williams/the Mississippi Mass Choir was one of the first 27 inducted into the Mississippi Musicians Hall of Fame on April 1, 2000.

John Sharp Williams

Born July 30, 1854, in Memphis. After the death of his parents, he moved to Yazoo County, Miss. Williams, whose grandfather had been a U.S. Rep. from Tennessee, served eight terms in the U.S. House (1893-1909), the last three as minority leader. Williams attended private schools, the Kentucky Military Institute near Frankfort, the University of the South in Sewanee, Tenn., the University of Virginia at Charlottesville, and the University of Heidelberg at Baden, Germany. After that, he studied law at the University of Virginia and in Memphis, Tenn. Admitted to the bar in 1877, he moved to Yazoo City, Mississippi in 1878, where he practiced law and planted cotton. He was elected as a Democrat to the 53rd U.S. Congress and to the seven succeeding Congresses and served from March 4, 1893 to March 3, 1909. He was minority leader in the 58th, 59th, and 60th Congresses and was chairman of the Committee on Party Leaders in the 58th through 60th Congresses. Williams was elected as a Democrat to the U.S. Senate in 1910, reelected in 1916 and served from March 4, 1911, to March 3, 1923. Williams has the distinction of being the first U.S. Senator in the nation to be elected by popular ballot! In the Senate, he was chairman of the Committee to Audit and Control the Contingent Expense (63rd Congress), Committee on the Library (64th and 65th Congresses) and the Committee on the University of the United States (66th Congress). He declined to be a candidate for renomination in 1922 and retired from public life after making the statement, "I would rather be a hound dog and bay at the moon from my Mississippi plantation than remain in the U.S. Senate." He lived on his plantation, 'Cedar Grove,' near Yazoo City, Mississippi, until his death there on Sept. 27, 1932. He is buried in the family cemetery on the plantation.

Milan B. Williams

Born in Okolona on March 28, 1948. He played keyboards with the group, the Commodores, although he can also play trombone, drums and guitar. They toured and performed with The Jackson Five for 5 years before signing up with Motown as The Commodores in 1972. From 1974-85, the group had 41 albums and 17 Top-40 hit singles which included 10 in the Top-10 (actually 8 of those were in the top-5) with 2 of those as No. 1s, and they garnered 10 gold records and 5 platinum records. Their biggest was the smash hit *Three Times A Lady*. He was in the film *Thank God It's Friday*. Milan was valedictorian at his high school in Okolona and was a senior at Tuskegee Institute in Alabama studying electrical engineering when he joined up with Lionel Richie and the rest of the guys.

Spencer Williams, Jr.

Born July 14, 1893, in Vidalia, Louisiana, he received his high school education at Wards Academy in Natchez. He enjoyed a

Profiles of Famous & Notable Mississippians

long stage career before entering films in the early 1930s. He appeared in dozens of movies, mostly those designed for black audiences of the 1930s and 40s, but is best known for playing Andy Hogg Brown on the popular, early TV comedy series, *The Amos 'n' Andy Show*, which debuted June 28, 1951. Two other Mississippians were in the cast: Alvin Childress of Meridian played Amos Jones and Ernestine Wade of Jackson played Sapphire Stevens. Williams died on Dec. 13, 1969.

Tennessee Williams

Thomas Lanier Williams was born on Mar. 26, 1911, in Columbus, Miss. in the rectory of St. Paul's Episcopal Church, where his maternal grandfather was the rector. Williams lived in Columbus until age 3, then spent most of his youth in Clarksdale, Miss. and Saint Louis, Mo. He later moved to New Orleans, then to Los Angeles and finally to New York. He attended the University of Missouri and Washington University and received a B.A. in 1938 from the University of Iowa, where his fraternity brothers teased him about him about his Southern accent and dubbed him "Tennessee." Williams liked his new nickname and he had many ancestors from that state, so eventually he adopted it as his professional name. The first work to bear his new name was *The Field of Blue Children* (1939). He wrote these plays, all made into successful movies: *The Glass Menagerie* (the play, a revision of an earlier script called *The Gentleman Caller*, won the New York Critics' Circle Award for 1944-45, and 2 movies were made, one in 1950 and another in 1987); *The Rose Tattoo* (movie in 1950); *Cat On A Hot Tin Roof* (play won the 1955 Pulitzer Prize for Drama, plus the movie received an Oscar® nomination for Best Picture of 1958); *Suddenly, Last Summer* (movie of 1959); and *The Night of the Iguana* movie of 1964 won the New York Critics' Circle Award for 1961-62. The play, *A Streetcar Named Desire*, received the 1948 Pulitzer Prize for Drama & New York Critics' Circle award for 1947-48 and the movie received the Academy Awards® nomination for Best Picture of 1951 and rated No. 45 on The American Film Institute's list of the Top 100 Greatest American Movies of All Time. Williams also wrote the plays *Camino Real* ('53), *Sweet Bird of Youth* ('59), and *Summer and Smoke* ('48), rewritten and produced in 1964 as *Eccentricities of a Nightingale*. He wrote the script for the movie *Baby Doll* ('56) based on his *27 Wagons Full of Cotton*, and even wrote an opera *Lord Byron's Love Letter* ('54). Two collections of Williams's one-act plays were published: *27 Wagons Full of Cotton* ('46) and *American Blues* ('48). There were 4 volumes of short stories — *One Arm and Other Stories* ('48), *Hard Candy* ('54), *The Knightly Quest* ('69) and *Eight Mortal Women Possessed* ('74). One of his last plays was *Clothes for a Summer Hotel* ('80) based on the writer F. Scott Fitzgerald. His total output was 20 full-length plays, 25 short plays, 2 novels (*The Roman Spring of Mrs. Stone* in 1950 and *Moise and the World of Reason* in 1975), 60 short stories, 2 books of poetry and his autobiography! He received the Kennedy Center Honors Award in 1979 and the Presidential Medal of Freedom in 1980, the nation's highest civilian award. He died in New York City Feb. 25, 1983, at age 71 and is buried in the Calvary Cemetery in Saint Louis. The Columbus/Lowndes County Chamber of Commerce purchased the rectory in which Williams was born, moved it to Main Street and restored it. In 1995 the Greater Golden Triangle Welcome Center opened offices in the Victorian-style twin-gabled house, built in 1875.

Sonny Boy Williamson II

Born Aleck Ford "Rice" Miller on March 11, 1908, in Glendora, Miss., although nobody is sure about his birth date because he was known to lie about it. He was one of the finest blues harp players who ever lived. Having written classics like *One Way Out*, *Help Me*, *Fattening Frogs for Snakes* and more, he was also one of the blues' greatest songwriters. He started recording late in life, after achieving fame as the host of the King Biscuit radio show in Helena, Ark. In the early 1950s, he recorded a series of sides for Lillian McMurry's (see profile) Trumpet Records label that included classics like *Pontiac Blues* and *Mighty Long Time*. A great influence on the English R&B scene, he recorded with the Yardbirds, the Animals and Jimmy Page. Ike Turner (from Clarksdale) played piano for Sonny Boy when he was only 11 years old. Sonny Boy died from TB in Helena on June 23, 1965. He is buried in the Whitfield Baptist Church Cemetery in Tutwiler, Mississippi.

Mamie Davis Willoughby

Born Nov. 3, 1915, near Liberty, Mississippi. She wrote a weekly column, *Along the RFD*, for the Jackson *Clarion-Ledger* newspaper for nearly 50 years and her work appeared in *Progressive Farmer*, *Collier's* and *Atlantic Monthly* magazines. She wrote 3 books under the name Rose Budd Stevens. *Along the RFD with Rose Budd Stevens* and *Sweetly Be!* were collections of her columns and *From Rose Budd's Kitchen* was a book of favorite recipes. She died on Jan. 9, 1996, at the age of 80 at her home in Liberty, Miss.

Al Wilson

This soul singer/drummer was born on June 19, 1939, in Meridian, Miss. Wilson moved to San Bernadino, Calif. in the late 1950s and sang with the Rollers from 1960-62. After going solo, his first hit was *The Snake* (#27 in 1968). He followed with the No. 1, million-seller *Show And Tell* (1973/74). Wilson made the Top 40 with 2 other singles, *La La Peace Song* (#30 in 1974) and *I've Got A Feeling (We'll Be Seeing Each Other Again)* (1976, #29 pop & #3 R&B).

Cassandra Wilson

Born Cassandra Fowlkes on Dec. 4, 1955, in Jackson, the daughter of the late Herman B. Fowlkes, jazz bassist, and Mary Fowlkes, who still lives in Jackson. She attended Milsaps College and was an AKA sorority member at Jackson State University. After graduating from Jackson State in 1981, Wilson took a job as public relations director at a New Orleans TV station. Now living in New York, she has taken that city by storm since the mid-1980s with her unique blending of jazz, free-form, R&B, and soul styles with her critically acclaimed albums and many concerts, in the U.S. and abroad. She had a very successful concert at New York's Lincoln Center in 1994. Her debut album was *Point of View* in 1985. Other albums: *Days Aweigh* (1987), *Blue Skies* (1988), *Jumpworld* (1989), *Live* (1990), *She Who Weeps* (1990), the critically acclaimed *Cassandra Wilson Live* (1992), *Dance To The Drums Again* (1993) and the Grammy-nominated *Blue Light 'Til Dawn* in 1993, which really thrust her into the limelight. Her CD, *New Moon Daughter* (1995), crossed Wilson over to national celebrity status. The album received the 1996 Soul Train award nomination for Best Jazz Album, won Wilson a 1997 Grammy for Best Jazz Vocal and was No. 1 on *Time* magazine's Best Music of 1996. A *New York Times* critic called it one of the best pop albums of the decade! In 1996 she was featured on CBS-TV's *This Morning* and in *People*, *Time*, *Vibe*, *Jazz Times*, and *USA Today*. *Ebony* magazine selected her one of America's "15 most beautiful black women." A *Down Beat* magazine critics poll picked her Female Vocalist of the Year in 1996 and their readers chose her in 1995 and 1996. The Aug. 1996 issue of *Esquire* magazine named Wilson as one of "The People We Love,"

Profiles of Famous & Notable Mississippians

along with women like Sharon Stone and Princess Di. The July 1996 issue of *Essence* magazine had Wilson on the cover and called her "this generation's first lady of jazz." She was selected to receive the 1997 Governor's Award for Excellence in the Arts. Unfortunately, she was unable to accept the award (which is not given unless accepted in-person) due to her tour with Wynton Marsalis. Her tour, entitled *Blood on the Fields*, was Grammy nominated for best vocal performance. In early 1999, Wilson's tribute album to Miles Davis was released. She had worked on the album, *Traveling Miles*, since late 1997.

Charles Wilson

Born Aug 2, 1939, in Kennett, Mo. His father, grandfather and uncle were all physicians, so Wilson studied pre-med at Westminster College in Missouri. When he was 22, he moved to north Mississippi near Aberdeen. After becoming a successful farmer, he went on to become a builder, land developer, oil and gas syndicator and then a mystery writer. He currently lives in Brandon, Miss. Each of his novels has outsold its predecessor. His first 4 books were police-thrillers: *Nightwatcher* ('90), *Silent Witness* ('92), *The Cassandra Prophecy* ('93) and *When First We Deceive* ('94). In 1995, he changed to scientific suspense with *Direct Descendant*. After an initial paperback printing of 70,000, the book quickly went into a 2nd printing. His sixth book was *Fertile Ground* ('96). *Extinct*, released in early 1997 had a first printing of 200,000 copies and by the first week in May it made the *USA Today* best-seller list. His 8th novel, *Embryo* ('99), had an initial printing of 500,000! His ninth novel, *Donor*, was released as a paperback original in Nov. 1999. *Donor* ends with a 14-page teaser for the followup and Wilson's tenth novel, *Game Plan*, which was released in hardback in Jan. 2000. Many of his novels are set in Mississippi: *Nightwatcher* and *Silent Witness* are set in central Mississippi; *When First We Deceive* and *The Cassandra Prophecy* are set on the Mississippi Gulf Coast; and *Fertile Ground* takes place in Jackson. His book *Extinct*, about a prehistoric animal attacking humans on the Pascagoula River, is being made into an NBC-TV movie. *Donor*, described by reviewer J. C. Patterson as *Coma* meets *The Firm*, is set in Biloxi's Coastal Regional Hospital. The action in *Game Plan* takes place at University Medical Center and the Belhaven area in Jackson.

Elder Roma Wilson

Born December 22, 1910, in Hickory Flat, Benton Co., Miss., he grew up in Blue Springs in Union County. Wilson began playing harmonica at the age of 13. Upon becoming an ordained minister in the Pentecostal Church in 1929, he began traveling the northern Mississippi area. Wilson relocated to Michigan during the early 1940s, settling in Detroit in 1942. There he performed on street corners with his children for spare change. While playing harmonica in a local record shop in 1948, he was secretly recorded by the store's owner who, without Wilson's knowledge or consent, licensed the tracks for release. For years after, folklorists attempted to find him, but couldn't. After the death of his wife, he moved back to Mississippi during the early 1970s. In the years that followed, Wilson began to realize that he was renowned among roots music scholars, finally hearing his decades-old recordings for the first time. He started appearing on the festival circuit with performances at the Chicago Blues Festival and the New Orleans Jazz & Heritage Festival, among others. In 1994, he was named a National Hertiage Fellow receiving a $10,000 fellowship and induction into the nation's Folk Arts Hall of Fame. A year later, he issued the LP *This Train*, which included his first new recordings in decades. He is considered among the premier gospel harmonica masters of his era.

Gerald Stanley Wilson

Born Sept. 4, 1918, in Shelby, Miss. He learned trumpet while attending college in Detroit. He played with Jimmie Lunceford (see profile) and his band from 1939-42, then moved to Los Angeles. After playing for Count Basie and Dizzy Gillespie in 1947-48, Wilson quit the music business for a while. After a tentative return as a bandleader in 1952, it took awhile for Wilson to gradually ease his way back into jazz full-time. One tune that he wrote, *Viva Tirado*, became a surprise hit single for the Latin rock group El Chicano in 1970. He scored films and TV programs, worked as an arranger for singers such as Al Hibbler, Bobby Darin and Johnny Hartman, contributed arrangements to the Duke Ellington band, and wrote music for the Los Angeles Philharmonic. He also started a series of hugely entertaining and informative classes in jazz history at California State University, Northridge (then San Fernando Valley State College) in 1970, moving them to UCLA in 1992, and had his own radio program on L.A.'s KBCA-FM from 1969 to 1976. Wilson continued to lead big bands off and on through the 1980s and '90s, as well as running the orchestra for Redd Foxx's NBC shows. In 1995, he celebrated more than half a century as a leader by releasing *State Street Sweet*, and scoring a solid hit at the Playboy Jazz Festival. Wilson has been a popular leader, arranger, and musical director.

Louis Hugh Wilson, Jr.

Born Feb. 11, 1920, in Brandon, he became the highest-ranking military officer ever from Mississippi! On Oct. 25, 1945, he was awarded the Congressional Medal of Honor for his heroic action in a 2-day battle on Guam on July 25 and 26, 1944. Here are the actual words of his citation: "For conspicuous gallantry and intrepidity at the risk of his life above and beyond the call of duty as commanding officer of a rifle company attached to the 2d Battalion, 9th Marines, 3d Marine Division, in action against enemy Japanese forces at Fonte Hill, Guam, 25-26 July 1944. Ordered to take that portion of the hill within his zone of action, Capt. Wilson initiated his attack in mid-afternoon, pushed up the rugged, open terrain against terrific machinegun and rifle fire for 300 yards and successfully captured the objective. Promptly assuming command of other disorganized units and motorized equipment in addition to his own company and 1 reinforcing platoon, he organized his night defenses in the face of continuous hostile fire and, although wounded 3 times during this 5-hour period, completed his disposition of men and guns before retiring to the company command post for medical attention. Shortly thereafter, when the enemy launched the first of a series of savage counterattacks lasting all night, he voluntarily rejoined his besieged units and repeatedly exposed himself to the merciless hail of shrapnel and bullets, dashing 50 yards into the open on 1 occasion to rescue a wounded marine lying helpless beyond the frontlines. Fighting fiercely in hand-to-hand encounters, he led his men in furiously waged battle for approximately 10 hours, tenaciously holding his line and repelling the fanatically renewed counterthrusts until he succeeded in crushing the last efforts of the hard-pressed Japanese early the following morning. Then organizing a 17-man patrol, he immediately advanced upon a strategic slope essential to the security of his position and, boldly defying intense mortar, machinegun, and rifle fire which struck down 13 of his men, drove relentlessly forward with the remnants of his patrol to seize the vital ground. By his indomitable leadership, daring combat tactics, and valor in the face of overwhelming odds, Capt. Wilson succeeded in capturing and

Profiles of Famous & Notable Mississippians

holding the strategic high ground in his regimental sector, thereby contributing essentially to the success of his regimental mission and to the annihilation of 350 Japanese troops. His inspiring conduct throughout the critical periods of this decisive action sustains and enhances the highest traditions of the U.S. Naval Service." Wilson was one of only 4 native Mississippians (of 7 Mississippians) to receive the Congressional Medal of Honor (CMOH) during WWII, and Wilson and Jack H. Lucas were the only 2 Marines with Mississippi ties. Wilson's Medal is one of 17 Medals of Honor that have been officially accredited to Mississippi in all wars, although we claim 5 more accredited to other states because the recipients with Mississippi ties were in other states when they went into service. Wilson is one of 13 native Mississippians (of 22 Mississippians — 15 Army, 4 Marines and 3 Navy) in all wars to have received the CMOH out of 3,433 total recipients through Nov. 1, 2000. Of the 3,433 recipients, only 151 were still living as of Nov. 1, 2000 (by conflict: WWII - 62 Korean War - 21; Vietnam - 68). Wilson is one of those 151 and one of only 2 native Mississippians (of 3 Mississippians) who received the CMOH still alive. Native Mississippian Van T. Barfoot and adopted Mississippian Jack H. Lucas were the other two still alive. Wilson went on to become a four-star general and Commandant of the U.S. Marine Corps (1975-79), which made him a member of the Joint Chiefs of Staff and, as such, the highest ranking, most senior military officer from Mississippi in the history of the state. General Wilson now lives in California. Although no Medal of Honor recipients from Mississippi are now buried in Arlington National Cemetery, General Wilson told the author of this book that he will be laid to rest there.

Mary Wilson

Born in Greenville, Mississippi on March 6, 1944. Even though her family moved to Detroit when she was only 3, her grandparents and other relatives still live in Greenville and Wilson visits the Delta every other summer. At age 13, she was a founding member of the Primettes which later evolved into the Supremes, one of the most famous and successful vocal groups in music history. During 13 years with the Motown Records' group, she lent her voice to a dozen number one hits: *Where Did Our Love Go* (1964), *Baby Love* (1964), *Come See About Me* (1964), *Stop! In the Name of Love* (1965), *Back In My Arms Again* (1965), *I Hear A Symphony* (1965), *You Can't Hurry Love* (1966), *You Keep Me Hangin' On* (1966), *Love Is Here and Now You're Gone* (1967), *The Happening* (1967), *Love Child* (1968), and *Someday We'll Be Together* (with the Temptations in 1969). When Diana Ross left the group to go solo in 1970, Wilson led the Supremes and sustained them through 1977 with 4 million-selling albums: *Stoned Love*, *Up the Ladder to the Roof*, *Floy Joy*, and *Everybody's Got the Right to Love*. In 1992, she released her own acclaimed solo disc, *Walk the Line*. She has written two best-selling autobiographies, *Dreamgirl...My Life as a Supreme* and *Supreme Faith*. After more than 30 years in show business, she still travels all over the world during concerts as "The Supreme's Mary Wilson," including shows at some of the casinos in her home state of Mississippi.

Richard Wiman

Born on July 31, 1950, in Brandon, Miss. In the ministry since 1976, he's been the pastor of the First Presbyterian Church in Belzoni, Miss. since 1981. He's also written and self-published two books, *Tired Tubes and Ten-Speed Turkeys* (1991) and *Long Shots From the Flat Lands* (1995). Wiman also writes a weekly column for *The Belzoni Banner* newspaper.

Sammy Winder

Born July 15, 1959, in Madison, Miss. He attended Madison-Ridgeland High School from 1974-77 where he was an All Conference running back and Honorable Mention All State and was voted Outstanding Athlete. He lettered 4 years in track and was the 100 yard dash conference champion. Not highly recruited out of high school, he walked on at Southern Mississippi in 1977. A broken foot kept him on the sidelines and he received red shirt status from USM head coach, Bobby Collins. After seeing spot duty early in the 1978 season, he burst onto the scene in the fourth game at home against the Mississippi State Bulldogs. Trailing 17-0, Winder helped rally the team to a 22-17 come-from-behind win that propelled USM to a 7-4 winning record. In 1979, Sammy led USM in rushing with 173 carries for 748 yards and 3 TDs as the Golden Eagles has a 6-4-1 record. Winder led the nation in scoring in 1980 as he scored 20 TDs and fell just short of 1,000 yards rushing with 237 carries for 996 yards. The Golden Eagles finished 8-3 and defeated McNeese State in the Independence Bowl — the first bowl win in school history. Winder's most spectacular play in college occurred on Oct. 4, 1980, in Mississippi Veterans Memorial Stadium when he scored the winning TD against Ole Miss in the 28-22 Eagle victory. He leaped from the five yard line and soared over a Rebel defensive back. In his senior year, USM had one of its finest seasons as the team went 9-1-1, were ranked as high as no. 8 in the country and the team advanced to the Tangerine Bowl where USM lost to Missouri. Team captain for his last year at USM, Winder had 228 rushes for 1,029 yards and 12 TDs. He completed his career at Southern Mississippi as the second all-time leading rusher with 3,114 yards on a school record 736 attempts and his 39 rushing TDs are the most in school history. He ran for over 100 yards in a game 9 times including a career high 175 yards in a 10-0 win over Memphis on Oct. 17, 1981. Winder was named to the All South Independent Team in 1980 and '81 and also earned Honorable Mention All America honors for those seasons. During his years at USM, the Eagles had a record of 31-13 including 4 straight wins over archrival Mississippi State and a pair of wins against Ole Miss. Following his final season at USM, Winder played in the East-West Shrine Bowl and the Senior Bowl. He was a 5th round selection of the Denver Broncos in the 1982 draft, launching an 8 year NFL career. From 1983-88, he started 77 of 88 regular season games, playing fullback and tailback. He became a starter in 1983 despite missing two games and most of the third with a sprained ankle. Winder played in 128 games for Denver and he had 97 regular season starts. His career rushing stats put him second on the all-time Broncos list with 1,493 rushes for 5,428 yards and 39 TDs. He topped the 100 yard mark in games 7 times, including a career high 165 yards against the Houston Oilers in 1983. Winder led the Broncos in rushing for 5 straight years from 1983-87. His best season was 1984, when he ran 296 times for 1,153 yards plus 44 catches for 1,302 yards. Winder was chosen Co-Offensive MVP of the Broncos following the '88 season, sharing the honor with John Elway. He is 2nd on the all-time Denver TD list with 14 in 1986, a single season franchise record. He was the leading scorer in the AFC in 1987. Winder had a knee injury against San Diego in a 1985 game, underwent surgery the next day, and started against Pittsburgh just 13 days later. He was once an opening day starter for the Broncos despite missing most of training camp with an appendectomy. He played in 3 Super Bowls ('86, '87 & '89) and saw action in 11 post-season games. Winder had 144

Profiles of Famous & Notable Mississippians

carries for 461 yards and one rushing TD in the playoffs along with 20 receptions for 193 yards and 2 TDs. He played in 2 Pro Bowls ('84 & '86) and he was 2nd team UPI All-NFL in 1984. Before the end of his pro career, he formed his own construction company in Jackson. He was inducted into the Miss. Sports Hall of Fame in 1998. On Oct. 7, 2000, Winder and ex-teammate Reggie Collier were inducted into the new Legends Society, which honors former Southern Miss athletic greats. The pair join Brett Favre, Janice Felder, Ray Guy, Nick Revlon and Clarence Weatherspoon in the exclusive club.

Oprah Winfrey

Born Jan. 29, 1954, in Kosciusko, Mississippi, where she lived until age 6, then moved to Milwaukee with her mother. At age 13 she went to live with her father in Nashville. At age 17 Winfrey was a part-time radio news announcer. She won a full scholarship to Tennessee State and while attending college she was crowned Miss Black Tennessee. She also became the first black woman to anchor a newscast for Nashville's CBS-TV affiliate. After graduation, she worked as a newscaster and hosted the local TV talk-show *People Are Talking* in Baltimore from 1977-83. She then became host of the TV talk show *A.M. Chicago*. In 1985 the show was renamed *The Oprah Winfrey Show* and achieved national syndication in 1986. Winfrey became the nation's richest entertainer in 1993 by owning the show she hosts and produces (her production company is named Harpo), the Chicago studio where it's taped, plus a chunk of the company that distributes it. She was the first woman to ever rank No. 1 on *Forbes*' list of 40 highest paid entertainers. Winfrey appeared twice in the No. 1 spot on *Forbes* Top 40 Richest Entertainers list 1987-1997. The *Forbes* list of "The 400 Richest Americans," released Sept. 23, 1999, listed Winfrey's net worth as $725 million, the 348th wealthiest American. The Mar. 20, 2000, issue of *Forbes* listed her 1999 income as $150 million, in second place on the list of the 100 top-earning celebrities. The Oprah Winfrey show started its 14th season in the fall of 1999. Winfrey and her show have won a total of 32 daytime Emmys, plus a Lifetime Achievement Emmy in 1998. She received the Academy Award® nomination for Best Supporting Actress for her role as "Sofia" in *The Color Purple*, the top grossing film of 1985 ($94 million). She played "Mrs. Thomas" in *Native Son* (1986). She produced and costarred in the TV miniseries *The Women of Brewster Place* and was as actress in, as well as producer of, the ABC network's made-for-TV movie *There Are No Children Here* (1993). Her 1993 TV special, an exclusive interview with reclusive superstar Michael Jackson, was highly rated as was her exclusive interview with Madonna in late 1996. Winfrey produced the TV miniseries *The Wedding* (1998) on the ABC network. She was among 25 women inducted into the National Women's Hall of Fame on Sept. 24, 1994. On Sept. 29, 1995, she was inducted into the National Black College Hall of Fame in Atlanta. In 1996, *Life* magazine listed Winfrey as one of the Top-50 most influential "baby boomers" in the nation. In 1996, *Time* listed her as one of the 25 most influential people in America and *TV Guide* picked her as Performer of the Year. *People* magazine listed Winfrey in their annual list of "The 50 Most Beautiful People in the World" in 1997. In early 1998, Winfrey defended herself against a suit brought by a group of Texas cattlemen who blamed a collapse in cattle prices on a 1996 *Oprah Winfrey Show* they said falsely warned American beef could spread mad-cow disease. The five-week case ended in Amarillo when the jury found in Winfrey's favor by rejecting the $11 million suit. Winfrey produced and stars in the movie *Beloved* (1998) with fellow Mississippians Beah Richards and Thelma Houston. The film proved to be a big disappointment at the box office. Costing $53 million to make, it grossed less than $23 million. Winfrey's new women's magazine, *O, the Oprah Magazine*, debuted Apr. 19, 2000, with another Mississippian, Alyce Alston, a Jackson native, as publisher.

Hattie Winston

Born Mar. 3, 1945, in Greenville, she's an actress who started out in TV as "Sylvia" on *The Electric Company* in 1971. She was in several other TV series and TV movies including *The Dain Curse* ('78 mini-series), *Nurse* ('81), *Homefront* ('91), *One Woman's Courage* ('94), *The Cherokee Kid* ('96) and *Becker* ('98, as "Margaret Wyborn"). She had minor roles in 7 theatrical films: *Without a Trace* ('83); *Good to Go* ('86); *Clara's Heart* ('88); *A Show of Force* ('90); *Beverly Hills Cop III* ('94); *Sunset Park* ('96) and *Jackie Brown* ('97).

Johnny Winter

Born John Dawson Winter III on Feb. 23, 1944, in Leland, Miss., he grew up in Beaumont, Tex. This albino blues guitarist formed his first band at 14 with his brother Edgar in Beaumont and spent his youth in recording studios cutting regional singles and albums and in bars playing the blues. His discovery on a national level came via an article in *Rolling Stone* magazine which led to a record deal with Columbia. Winter became a major star in the late 1960s and early '70s. His debut pro album, *Johnny Winter*, reached the charts in 1969. Starting out with a trio, Winter later formed a band with former members of The McCoys, including second guitarist Rick Derringer. It was called Johnny Winter And. He achieved a sales peak in 1971 with the gold-selling *Live/Johnny Winter And*. He returned in 1973 with *Still Alive and Well*, his highest-charting album. His albums became more blues-oriented in the late '70s and he also produced several albums for Muddy Waters and toured with him. In the 1980s he switched to the blues label Alligator for three albums, and has since recorded for the MCA and Pointblank/Virgin labels.

Elizabeth Wolfe

Born in Jackson on May 20, 1949, she is the daughter of famed Mississippi artists Karl & Mildred Wolfe. She attended Jackson City public schools, Millsaps College, the University of Southern Mississippi, and received her B.F.A. from the Portland School of Art in Portland (now the Maine College of Art). She has worked in many mediums, including clay sculpture and stained glass. Her recent work, a group of *17 Oil on Paper Paintings*, exhibited at the Andy Young Gallery in Jackson in Oct. 1994. Wolfe has taught art at APAC and Millsaps College. "Bebe" also works at the Wolfe Studio in Jackson with her mother Mildred (see her profile).

Karl Wolfe

One of the premier artists of Mississippi, he was born in Brookhaven on Jan. 25, 1903. He graduated from high school in Columbia, Miss., then attended Soule' Business College in New Orleans and the Chicago Art Institute. He won a William French scholarship for study in Europe in 1928-29. Wolfe exhibited widely in the 1930s and 40s. His WPA mural, now in the Louisville Post Office, represented Mississippi at the Chicago World's Fair and the New York World's Fair. He married fellow artist Mildred Nungester in 1944. After serving in the Air Force 1942-44, he returned to Jackson and painted many portraits, including those of governors, educators, and other notable people. His work is represented in permanent collections of the Mississippi Museum of Art, Montgomery Museum of Art, Millsaps College, Belhaven College, and at other institutions, as well as in many private collections. He

Profiles of Famous & Notable Mississippians

died in Jackson Nov. 16, 1984. His wife Mildred and daughter Elizabeth, both artists, continue their work in Jackson.

Mildred Wolfe
Born Mildred Nungester in Celina, Ohio, on Aug. 23, 1912. After graduating from high school in Decatur, Ala. in 1928, she received her A.B. from Alabama College for Women (Univ. of Montevallo) in 1932 and her M.A. from Colorado College in 1944. From 1932 to 1942, she taught in Decatur Junior High School and studied art in the summer months at Dixie Art Colony of Alabama with J. Kelly Fitzpatrick, the Chicago Art Institute, New York Art Students League, and the Colorado Springs Fine Arts Center. She married fellow artist, Mississippian Karl Wolfe, in 1944. She exhibited widely in the 1930s and 40s. She has worked in oils, watercolors, lithographs, woodcuts, stained glass design and has painted mostly landscapes, but also some portraits. Her work is well represented in collections at Millsaps College, Belhaven College, and the National Portrait Gallery in Washington, DC. Listed in *Who's Who in American Art*, the *International Biographical Dictionary of Art*, and *Mothers of Achievement in American Art*. She and her daughter, Elizabeth ("Bebe"), continue their art work at the Wolfe Studio in Jackson.

Hoyt B. Wooten
Born Sept. 29, 1893, in Coldwater, Tate County, Miss. This broadcasting pioneer owned and operated Mississippi's first commercial radio station, KFNG, broadcasting from his home in Coldwater, operating on 1370 kc with 10 watts. The station went on the air on Sept. 22, 1922. The station was moved to the Whitehaven section of Memphis in 1926 and the call letters changed to WREC (**W**ooten's **R**adio-**E**lectric **C**ompany). The station then operated on the frequency of 600 kilocycles (kilohertz) with 200 watts power. After moving to the basement of Hotel Peabody in 1929, power was increased to 500 watts, then shortly after that to 1,000 watts. In 1936, power was increased to 5,000 watts (the man who would later discover Elvis Presley, , worked at WREC as a DJ and engineer starting in 1945 until he started in 1950). WREC-FM went on the air in stereo on March 1, 1969. Less than a year later, on Dec. 6, 1969, Hoyt Wooten died at his home at the age of 76. WREC-AM & FM still operate in Memphis. Wooten was also a pioneer in TV. On July 19, 1928, Wooten was granted one of the first six permits in the U.S. to build and operate a closed-circuit experimental Composite V.T. television transmitter. On Jan. 1, 1956, WREC-TV began regular broadcasting on channel 8. The TV station was sold to *The New York Times* in 1971.

Charlie Worsham
Born in Jackson, his family moved to Grenada, Miss., when he was two years old. Charlie is a banjo-picking prodigy who started playing when he was about eight years old. Only 14 years old on Sept. 1, 1999, he had already performed on the Grand Ole Opry, appeared on The Nashville Network, and opened for country/bluegrass singer Ricky Skaggs. Charlie performed during a month-long tour of Ireland in June 1999.

Charles Wright
Born April 6, 1942, in Clarksdale. At age 12 he moved with his family to Los Angeles. This singer, pianist and guitarist was founder and leader of an 8-member band, a soul-funk group recruited from the Watts section of L.A. Originally known as the Soul Runners, they changed their name to "The Watts 103rd Street Rhythm Band." Bill Cosby helped get the band off the ground by giving them appearances at his gigs. The group had the hit records *Do Your Thing* (#11 pop 1969), *Love Land* (#16 pop 1970) and *Express Yourself* (#12 pop 1970). *Your Love (Means Everything to Me)* was their final R&B hit in 1971, hitting No. 9 R&B & 12 pop.

Early Wright
Born on Feb. 10, 1915, in Jefferson, Carroll Co., Miss. After farming and tending cattle for awhile, in 1937 Wright moved to Clarksdale, where he spent the rest of his life. He learned to drive a train, then became a mechanic and opened his own business, Simmons and Wright Garage. On the side, he was the manager of the Four Star Quartet gospel group at the time he was hired by Clarksdale's WROX radio in 1947. Wright was Mississippi's first black disc jockey. His nightly "Soul Man" broadcast spanned more than half a century and made Wright a living legend, not only in his hometown, but around the state and the nation. His show lasted 51 years until his retirement in 1998, one of the longest continuous-running radio shows in the nation. Some of the musical greats who appeared live on his program were Elvis Presley, B.B. king, Muddy Waters, Ike and Tina Turner, Bobby Rush, Sonny Boy Williamson II, Little Milton, Robert Nighthawk, Pinetop Perkins, Charley Pride, and Rufus Thomas, just to name a few. He was profiled often by the national media including ABC-TV, CBS-TV, CNN, *The Washington Post*, *Los Angeles Times* and *Atlanta Journal Constitution*. Wright suffered a heart attack on Nov. 8, 1999. He died on Dec. 10, 1999, and is buried in Heavenly Rest Cemetery in Clarksdale.

Frank Wright
Born July 9, 1935, in Grenada, Mississippi, he was an ordained minister who played jazz tenor sax. Throughout his career Wright always played free, or avant-garde, jazz. Early on he was an electric bassist who played R&B. However, upon meeting Albert Ayler he was inspired to switch to tenor. He moved to New York in the early 1960s and played with many musicians including Larry Young, Sunny Murray and briefly with Cecil Taylor and John Coltrane. After 1969, Wright spent much of the rest of his career living and playing in Europe. He died in Germany on May 17, 1990, at the age of 54.

Richard Wright
Born Richard Nathaniel Wright Sept. 4, 1908, near Natchez, he moved to Memphis with his family when he was 6, then to Jackson when he was 12. Wright was the first black novelist to achieve fame and fortune in the U.S. His books of fiction include *Uncle Tom's Children: Four Novellas* ('38), *Uncle Tom's Children: Five Long Stories* ('38), *Bright and Morning Star* ('38), *Native Son* ('40), *The Outsider* ('53), *Savage Holiday* ('54), *The Long Dream* ('58), *Eight Men* ('61) and *Lawd Today* ('63). His books of nonfiction include *How "Bigger" Was Born; the Story of Native Son* ('40), *12 Million Black Voices: A Folk History of the Negro in the United States* ('41), *Black Boy: A Record of Childhood and Youth* ('45), *Black Power: A Record of Reactions in a Land of Pathos* ('54), *The Color Curtain: Report on the Bandung Conference* ('56), *Pagan Spain* ('57), *White Man, Listen!* ('57), *Letters to Joe C. Brown* ('68) and *American Hunger* ('77). Wright was a member of the Communist Party from 1927-44. He died in Paris on Nov. 28, 1960. A film titled *Richard Wright: Black Boy*, produced by ETV and the BBC, made its world premiere screening on Mississippi ETV in 1994, with the national TV premiere in 1995. Wright was one of 3 Mississippi writers (the other two were William Faulkner and Eudora Welty) featured at Atlanta's Centennial Olympic Games in 1996 in a literary exhibition of 9 Southern writers called *The American South: Past, Present & Future*. Wright's novel, *Native Son*, was No. 20 on the "100 Best Novels of the Century" compiled by the editorial board of Modern Library, a division of Random

Profiles of Famous & Notable Mississippians

House, and *Black Boy* was No. 13 on their list of "100 Best Nonfiction Books of the Century."

Tammy Wynette

Born Virginia Wynette Pugh on May 5, 1942, in the Bounds community near Tremont in Itawamba County, Mississippi. She picked cotton as a child and later worked as a waitress, a factory hand and as a hairdresser for a time in Tupelo. She was given her stage name by her producer, Billy Sherrill, who said she look like a "Tammy." With over 35 No. 1 hits (21 in a row) and 11 No. 1 albums (out of 50+), she was called "The First Lady of Country Music," but was also known as the "Heroine of Heartbreak." Her biggest hit was the No. 1 smash *Stand By Your Man* ('68), which sold 6 million copies! She received a Grammy for the album of the same title for Best Country Performance, Female ('69); voted Female Vocalist of the Year ('69) by the Academy of Country Music, Country Music Association's Female Vocalist of the Year for 3 years straight, 1968-70, plus many more awards including the American Music Awards' most-coveted Award of Tribute presented on Jan. 29, 1996. She also had another Number-One hit in 1968 that has become a country standard, *D-I-V-O-R-C-E*. Her *Greatest Hits* album was certified Platinum in 1989. And, would you believe, Tammy was turned down by 5 record companies before she was signed by Epic Records? The made-for-TV autobiographical movie, *Stand By Your Man* ('81), starred Annette O'Toole as Tammy. In 1992, Wynette recorded with the British dance group KLF, including *Justified and Ancient*, an electronic dance tune which went No. 1 in 18 countries. Her album, *Without Walls*, is a collection of duets with country and pop stars such as Sting, Elton John, and Joe Diffy. There was a stormy marriage to George Jones from 2/16/69 to 3/13/75, during which time they had many duet hits such as *We're Gonna Hold On* (#1 in '71) and *Golden Ring* (#1 in '76). Tammy and George reunited professionally in 1995 and their album *One* received the 1996 Country Music Association nomination for Vocal Event of the Year. She was married 5 times (Jones was her middle husband), in addition to relationships that included Burt Reynolds. Tammy Wynette, with a long history of health problems, died in her sleep at her Nashville home from a blood clot to the lungs on April 6, 1998, at age 55. She is buried in Woodlawn Memorial Park in Nashville. A tribute album, *Tammy Wynette Remembered*, released Sept. 8, 1998, had fellow Mississippian and fan Faith Hill singing Wynette's 1976 hit *'Til I Can Make It on My Own*, Rosanne Cash with *D.I.V.O.R.C.E.*, and Elton John doing Wynette's signature song, *Stand By Your Man*! Trisha Yearwood, Lorrie Morgan, and others are also on the album. Wynette was inducted into the Country Music Hall of Fame on Sept. 23, 1998, and was one of the first 27 inducted into the inaugural Miss. Musicians Hall of Fame April 1, 2000. Wynette was presented the Pioneer Award at the 35th annual Academy of Country Music Awards on May 3, 2000, the first time the academy had given the award posthumously.

Steve Yarbrough

He was born Aug. 29, 1956, in Indianola, Miss. He graduated from Indianola Academy in 1975, from Ole Miss in 1979, then studied at the University of Arkansas. Yarbrough taught at Virginia Tech for 4 years, then in 1988 moved to Fresno, where he is professor of creative writing at Cal State. His first book of short stories was *Family Men*. His second, *Mississippi History* ('94), is a collection of short stories set in Mississippi. Another of his short story collections is *Veneer*. Yarbrough won a National Endowment for the Arts Fellowship in fiction writing, and recently won a Pushcart Prize for nonfiction for a piece titled *Preacher*. His first novel, *The Oxygen Man*, released in spring of 1999, won the Mississippi Institute of Arts and Letters Awards for fiction in 2000, as well as the Mississippi Library Association Award. Yarbrough was named the John and Renee Grisham Visiting Southern Writer-In-Residence at Ole Miss for 1999-2000.

Al Young

Born on May 31, 1939, in Ocean Springs, Mississippi. He lived there for half of his childhood life, until his father was discharged from the Navy. Following his father's discharge, the entire family moved to Detroit. After graduating from high school, Young attended the University of Michigan where he majored in Spanish. Young moved to San Francisco in 1961. There, he pursued a music career and worked at many jobs — as a musician, disk jockey, medical photographer, janitor, railroad man, editor, and screenwriter. Young graduated with honors and obtained his B.A. degree from the University of California at Berkley in 1969. That same year, *Dancing*, his first volume of poetry was published. Young has written an additional three books of poetry, five novels, and four books of prose. Other books of poetry include *The Song Turning Back Into Itself* (1971), *Geography of the Near Past* (1976), and *The Blues Don't Change* (1982). His novels include *How Is Angelina?* (1975), *Sitting Pretty* (1976), and *Ask Me Now* (1980). Books of essays on music include *Snakes* and *Bodies & Soul* (1981). Young has written for *Rolling Stone*, the *Chicago Sun-Times*, the *New York Times*, *Harpers* and others. He's cofounder and editor of the *Yardbird Reader* and the editor of the anthology *African American Literature*. His prose/poetry have been translated into more than a dozen languages. Film assignments have included scripts for Dick Gregory, Sidney Poitier, Richard Pryor, and Bill Cosby. Young's many awards/honors include the Joseph Henry Jackson Award, the Pushcart Prize, the American Book Award, and the Wallace Stegner Fellowship Award. He also received the National Endowment for the Arts, and Guggenheim and Fulbright fellowships. He has taught writing and literature at the University of Washington, Stanford, Colorado College, the University of California and was visiting writer-in-residence at the University of Arkansas in 1997. Young now resides in Polo Alto, California.

Billie Jean Young

Born on July 21, 1947, in Pennington, Alabama, she moved to Jackson, Mississippi in 1981. She is an actress, playwright, poet and former Jackson State University professor. She is best known for her one-woman show *Fannie Lou Hamer...This Little Light*. A tape of her poetry, *My Name Is Black*, was released in Dec. 1994. The Mississippi Arts Commission awarded Young the coveted Artist's Achievement Award in the 1995 Governor's Awards for Excellence in the Arts. She appeared as "Mrs. Williams" in the Oscar®-winning *Mississippi Burning* (1988), a movie filmed in Mississippi. She played the part of "Coral" in the made-for-TV movie *Blue Bayou*, which aired on NBC in 1990. Young is currently working on another volume of poetry with the working title of *Five Decades of Living*. Young is now living back home in Pennington, Alabama, but visits Mississippi often.

Johnny Young

Born on Jan. 1, 1918, in Vicksburg. He used an unusual instrument to play the blues, the mandolin. His first hit was the Chicago blues classic *Money Taking Women*. A couple more of his songs were *All My Money Gone* and *Bad Blood*. He worked with the major figures of blues history, including Sonny Boy Williamson, Muddy Waters, Walter Horton, and

Profiles of Famous & Notable Mississippians

Otis Spann. He was, he insisted, born to be a musician. He died of a heart attack in Chicago on Apr. 18, 1974, at age 56.

Lester Willis Young

Born Aug. 27, 1909, in Woodville, Mississippi. The nickname "Pres" was given to him by Billie Holliday. He played tenor sax and was a bop pioneer with Count Basie & others. He became popular with, and influenced, many jazz greats including John Coltrane, Sonny Rollins, and Stan Getz. Young and his music were featured in the 1944 movie, *Jammin' the Blues*, a film included on the National Film Registry at the Library of Congress. In 1956, he was voted "Greatest Tenor Saxophonist Ever." In the annual poll of both readers and critics conducted by *Downbeat* magazine, Young took top jazz honors in 1959. His impact on jazz was profound. He died in New York on March 15, 1959, at age 49 and is buried in the Evergeen Cemetery (Redemption Section, Grave 11418) in Brooklyn, N.Y. Young was one of the first 27 inducted into the inaugural Miss. Musicians Hall of Fame on April 1, 2000.

Stark Young

Born Oct. 11, 1881, at Como, Mississippi. He received his B.A. from Ole Miss and his M.A. from Columbia. While teaching at the University of Mississippi, the University of Texas and Amherst College, he also published poetry, plays, and criticism. After moving to New York in 1921, he became a theater drama critic for the *New Republic* and was soon recognized as the leading New York Critic. He continued working for the *New Republic*, writing more than a thousand essays in 40 years, until he resigned in 1947. He wrote the plays *The Colonnade* (1924) and *The Saint* (1925). He also wrote non-fiction books concerning the theater, *The Flower in Drama* (1923), *Glamour* (1925), *Theatre Practice* (1926), and *The Theatre* (1927). His novels include *The Three Fountains* (1924), *Heaven Trees* (1926), *The Torches Flare* (1928), *River House* (1929), and *So Red the Rose* (1934). Young died in New York City on Jan. 6, 1963, at age 81. He is buried in Friendship Cemetery in Como, Mississippi.

Luigi Zaninelli

Born March 30, 1932, in Raritan, N.J. A graduate of the Curtis Institute of Music in Philadelphia, Penn., where he studied with Gian-Carlo Menotti and Bohuslav Martinu. He also studied in Italy with Rosario Scalero. Since 1973, he has been composer-in-residence and professor of music at University of Southern Mississippi in Hattiesburg. During his tenure there, he has produced over 200 published works including the operas *Snow White* and *Mr. Sebastian*. The Kennedy Center for the Performing Arts in Washington has had productions of his works, *The Tale of Peter Rabbit* and *A Musical Banquet for Children*, both receiving critical acclaim. Zaninelli has fulfilled commissions from the Seattle Symphony, the New Orleans Symphony, the Memphis Ballet, and the New York Metropolitan Opera Ballet. His original PBS-TV scores for *The Islander* with James Best and *Passover* with Edward Asner both received international acclaim. In 1992, he became the first three-time winner of the Mississippi Institute of Arts and Letters Award (MIAL) for Music. He was a MIAL winner again in 1998 for his compositions, *Three American Hymns* for soprano and *Wind Ensemble*. Zaninlli won the MIAL in music an unprecedented 5th time in 2000 for his composition *A Crown, A Mansion and A Throne*.

Jim Ziglar

Born James W. Ziglar on Dec. 8, 1945, in Pascagoula, Miss. He and his friend, Trent Lott, U.S. Senator and majority leader, briefly attended Pascagoula High School together and they both sang in the church choir at the First Baptist Church. Ziglar worked for a short time as copy boy in the newsroom of *Mississippi Press* of Pascagoula. After graduating from high school, Ziglar moved to Washington, where he worked as an aide to U.S. Sen. James Eastland of Mississippi during the daytime and attended George Washington University in the evenings. He also worked as a law clerk for U.S. Supreme Court Judge Harry Blackmon and as an assistant secretary of the interior. He finally went to Wall Street in New York as a lawyer and investment banker as managing director at Paine Webber. At the urging of Senator Lott, Ziglar left Wall Street in Dec. 1998 to became the U.S. Senate Sergeant at Arms and doorkeeper, whose responsibilities include overseeing a staff of 775 and a budget of $120 million.

Zig Ziglar

Born Hillary Ziglar on Nov. 6, 1926, in a rural area of Coffee County in southern Alabama. When he was 4 years old, his family moved to Yazoo City, where he grew up and attended high school. He began his career as a cookware salesman in Mississippi. Ziglar's book *See You at The Top* (1984) was a best-seller that put Ziglar "on top" and made him famous throughout the world. His other books include *Confessions of a Happy Christian* (1982), *Dear Family* (1984), *Raising Positive Kids in a Negative World* (1985), *Steps to the Top* (1985), *Zig Ziglar's Secrets of Closing the Sale* (1985), *Zig Ziglar's Favorite Quotations* (1990), *Ziglar on Selling: The Ultimate Handbook for the Complete Sales Professional* (1991), *Courtship after Marriage* (1992), *Over the Top* (1994) and *Top Performance, by Zig Ziglar and Jim Savage* (1995). Ziglar has also produced scores of albums, tapes and films, such as *How To Be A Winner*, *Secrets of Closing the Sale*, *Sell Your Way to the Top*, and *Goals—Setting & Achieving Them*. His successful motivation/public relations company is headquartered in Dallas, Texas. Much in demand as a speaker, he's shared the podium with many famous people, including Presidents Jimmy Carter, Gerald Ford, Ronald Reagan and George Bush, plus General Norman Schwarzkopf, General Colin Powell, Norman Vincent Peale and Paul Harvey.

Famous & Notable Mississippians Listed by Name

NAME	PROFESSION(S)	PLACE OF BIRTH	BIRTH DATE	DIED
Abdul-Rauf, Mahmoud	Sports: pro basketball player	Gulfport	03-09-1969	
Akin, Susan Diane	Miss America (1986)	Meridian	08-12-1964	
Alexander, Margaret Walker	Writer-professor	Birmingham, AL	07-27-1915	11-30-1998
Alice, Mary	Actress	Indianola	12-03-1941	
Allen, John	Politician (historical figure)	Tishomingo Co.	07-08-1846	10-30-1917
Allison, Mose	Jazz musician/songwriter	Tippo	11-11-1927	
Alston, Alyce	Magazine publisher	Jackson	06-12-1964	
Alworth, Lance	Sports: pro football player	Houston, TX	08-03-1940	
Anderson, Andy	R&R singer/musician	Memphis, TN	05-15-1935	
Anderson, Rueben	Jurist-attorney	Jackson	09-16-1942	
Anderson, Walter	Artist: potter	New Orleans, LA	09-29-1903	11-30-1965
Andrews, Dana	Actor	Collins	01-01-1909	12-17-1992
Armistead, John	Mystery writer	Mobile, AL	06-14-1941	
Armstrong, Henry	Sports: pro boxing champ	Columbus	12-12-1912	10-24-1988
Armstrong, Richard "Dick"	Journalist-editor	Jackson	08-29-1929	08-16-1992
Assaf, Woodie	Broadcaster (TV weatherman)	McComb	03-15-1917	
Ates, Roscoe	Actor	Grange	01-20-1892	03-01-1962
Attaway, Ruth	Actress	Greenville	06-28-1910	09-21-1987
Attaway, William	Novelist-script writer	Greenville	11-19-1911	06-17-1986
Autry, James A.	Writer-business consultant	Benton County	03-08-1933	
Baggett, Blaine	TV producer/writer	Horn Lake	07-20-1951	
Bahr, Howard	Writer-historian-professor	Meridian	08-03-1946	
Ball, Coolidge	Sports: college basketball	Inverness	11-06-1951	
Ballard, Glen	Songwriter-record producer	Natchez	05-01-1953	
Baloni, Louis	Business executive	Shaw	08-28-1934	
Bandy, Moe	Country music singer/songwriter	Meridian	02-12-1944	
Barber, Walter Lanier "Red"	Sportscaster	Columbus	02-17-1908	10-22-1992
Barbour, Haley	Political Party leader-attorney	Yazoo City	10-22-1947	
Barfoot, Van T.	Medal of Honor recipient	near Edinburg	06-15-1919	
Barksdale, James	Corporate CEO	Jackson	01-24-1943	
Barnes, Prentiss	Singer-Rock and Roll pioneer	Magnolia	04-12-1925	
Barnes, Roosevelt "Booba"	Blues guitarist-singer	Longwood	09-25-1936	04-03-1996
Barnett, Fred	Sports: pro football player	Shelby	06-17-1966	
Barney, Lem	Sports: pro football player	Gulfport	09-08-1945	
Barr, Nevada	Mystery writer	California	03-01-1952	
Barranco, Johnny	Commercial jingle singer	Bossier City, LA	06-26-1951	
Barrett, Bucky	Musician: jazz guitarist	Pensacola, FL	09-19-1944	
Barrier, B.J. (Jr.)	Aviation pioneer	Yazoo City	06-26-1906	02-09-1950
Barry, Marion S. (Jr.)	Former mayor Washington, D.C.	Itta Bena	03-06-1936	
Barton, Dee	Composer-conductor-musician	Houston, MS	09-18-1937	
Basch, Harry	Actor	Greenville	03-17-1915	
Bass, Jack	Professor-writer	North, SC	06-24-1934	
Bass, Lance	Singer w/rock group 'N Sync	Laurel	05-04-1979	
Bayless, Luster	Movie costume designer	Ruleville	10-26-1937	
Bechtol, T. Bubba	Country comedian/comic	Biloxi	05-01-1945	
Beckwith, William	Artist: sculptor	Greenville	03-13-1952	
Bell, Carey	Blues harmonica player	Macon	11-14-1936	
Bell, Charles G.	Poet	Greenville	10-31-1916	
Bell, James "Cool Papa"	Sports: pro baseball player	Starkville	05-17-1903	03-07-1991
Bennett, Charles C.	Movie set designer	Independence, LA	03-31-1940	
Bennett, Lerone (Jr.)	Journalist-writer	Clarksdale	10-17-1928	
Best, Willie	Actor	Sunflower	05-27-1913	02-27-1962
Biggs, Thomas J.	Architect	Arkansas	01-28-1912	04-05-1999
Black, J.T. "Blondy"	Sports: college/pro football	Philadelphia, MS	08-20-1920	05-04-2000
Black, John C.	Medal of Honor recipient	Lexington	01-27-1839	08-17-1915
Blackwood, Cecil	w/Blackwood Bros. Quartet	Ackerman	10-28-1934	
Blackwood, Doyle	w/Blackwood Bros. Quartet	Ackerman	08-22-1911	10-??-1974
Blackwood, James	w/Blackwood Bros. Quartet	Ackerman	08-04-1919	
Blackwood, R.W.	w/Blackwood Bros. Quartet	Ackerman	10-23-1921	06-24-1954
Blackwood, Roy	w/Blackwood Bros. Quartet	Fentress	12-24-1900	03-21-1971
Blailock, Steve	Musician: jazz guitarist	McComb	07-09-1944	
Blanchard, "Doc" Felix	Sports: college football player	South Carolina	12-11-1924	
Blankenhorn, David	Writer	Jackson	05-25-1955	
Blasingame, Don	Sports: major league baseball	Corinth	03-16-1932	

Famous & Notable Mississippians Listed by Name

NAME	PROFESSION(S)	PLACE OF BIRTH	BIRTH DATE	DIED
Bogan, Lucille	Blues singer	Amory	04-01-1897	08-10-1948
Bolton-Holifield, Ruthie	Olympic Champion (1996)	McLain	05-25-1967	
Boone, Brendon	Actor (TV)	Meridian	02-26-1938	
Booth, Jerry H.	Scientist: physicist	Mathiston	03-24-1941	08-31-1995
Boston, Ralph	Olympic Champion (1960)	Laurel	05-09-1939	
Bouldin, Marshall (III)	Artist: portrait painter	Dundee	09-06-1923	
Bowens, Tim	Sports: pro football player	Okolona	02-07-1973	
Bower, Jeff	Sports: college coach/player	Roswell, GA	05-28-1953	
Boyd, Dennis "Oil Can"	Sports: major league baseball	Meridian	10-06-1959	
Boyd, Eddie	Blues singer/pianist	Stovall	11-25-1914	07-13-1994
Boyd, Jimmy	Actor	McComb	01-09-1939	
Bracey, Ishmon	Blues singer/guitarist	Byram	01-09-1900	02-12-1970
Brady, Bruce H.	Artist: sculptor-outdoorsman	Brookhaven	08-28-1934	02-08-2000
Bramlett, Bonnie Lynn	Rock singer	Pontotoc County	11-08-1944	
Bramlett, Delaney	Rock singer	Pontotoc County	07-01-1939	
Brandy (Norwood)	R&B Singer-actress	McComb	02-11-1979	
Brannon, William T.	Mystery writer	Pachuta	03-06-1906	
Branson, Jeff	Sports: major league baseball	Waynesboro	01-26-1967	
Brantley, Jeff	Sports: major league baseball	Florence, AL	09-05-1963	
Brasfield, Rod	Country comedian	Smithville	08-22-1910	09-12-1958
Brenston, Jackie	History-making singer	Clarksdale	08-15-1930	12-15-1979
Brewer, Jim	Educator	Hattiesburg	09-07-1933	
Brickell, Henry Herschel	Literary critic	Senatobia	09-13-1889	05-29-1952
Brieger, James F.	Author-researcher	Newton County	04-09-1930	
Broonzy, Big Bill	Legendary bluesman	Scott	06-26-1893	08-15-1958
Brown, Jesse Leroy	Military aviator-hero	Hattiesburg	10-13-1926	12-04-1950
Brown, Kelly	Actor	Jackson	09-24-1928	03-??-1981
Brown, Larry	Author-playwright	Yocona	07-09-1951	
Brown, Paul T.	Photographer-outdoorsman	Greenwood	05-14-1949	
Brown, Richard Jess (Jr.)	Jazz musician	Jackson	09-13-1956	
Brown, Willie	Sports: pro football	Yazoo City	12-02-1940	
Brown, Wilson	Medal of Honor recipient	Natchez	1841	01-24-1900
Brownlee, Archie	Gospel blues singer	?, Mississippi	1925	02-08-1960
Bruce, Blanche K.	Politician (historical figure)	Virginia	03-01-1841	03-17-1898
Brummett, Paul	Inventor-scientist	Jackson	08-10-1939	
Bryan, John H. (Jr.)	Corporate CEO	West Point	10-05-1936	
Bryant, Bobby	Musician: jazz trumpetist	Hattiesburg	05-19-1934	06-??-1998
Buchanan, Bill	Novelist-engineer	Mobile, AL	01-23-1953	
Buffett, Jimmy	R&R-Pop singer-writer	Pascagoula	12-25-1946	
Burks, Ellis Rena	Sports: major league baseball	Vicksburg	09-11-1964	
Burnett, Charles	Film director	Vicksburg	04-13-1944	
Burns, Eddie "Guitar"	Blues singer/guitarist	Belzoni	02-08-1928	
Burnside, R.L.	Blues singer/guitarist	Oxford	11-23-1926	
Burrell, Ode	Sports: college/pro football	Goodman	09-15-1939	
Bush, Guy T.	Sports: major league baseball	Aberdeen	08-23-1901	07-02-1985
Butler, Eugene	Journalist-editor	Starkville	06-11-1894	06-05-1995
Butler, Jack	Writer	Alligator	05-08-1944	
Butler, Jerry	R&R-Soul singer	Sunflower County	12-08-1939	
Caldwell, John Tyler	Educator: college chancellor	Yazoo City	12-09-1911	10-13-1995
Calhoun, Lee	Olympic champion (1956/'60)	Laurel	02-23-1933	06-21-1989
Campbell, V. Ruth	History-making attorney	Yazoo City	01-20-1887	03-03-1963
Campbell, Will D.	Minister-writer-activist	East Fork	07-18-1924	
Cannon, Ace	Saxophonist	Grenada	05-05-1934	
Cannon, Gus "Banjo Joe"	Early bluesman	Red Banks	09-12-1884	10-15-1979
Canzoneri, Robert	Writer-educator	San Marcos, TX	11-21-1925	
Capers, Charlotte	Writer-administrator	Columbia, TN	06-13-1913	12-23-1996
Carlisle, Helen	Writer-home economist	Vossburg	11-25-1917	
Carlisle, Jennifer	Top student: perfect ACT score	Flowood	11-07-1982	
Carloss, Helen	History-making attorney	Yazoo City	04-18-1893	12-23-1948
Carollo, Joe Frank	R&R singer/musician	Leland	09-03-1939	
Carr, Sam	Musician: blues drummer	Friar's Point	04-17-1926	
Carsley, Anne	Novelist	Jackson	04-11-1935	
Carter, Bo	Early bluesman	Bolton	03-21-1893	09-21-1964
Carter, Hodding (Jr.)	Journalist-writer	Hammond, LA	02-03-1907	04-04-1972

Famous & Notable Mississippians Listed by Name

NAME	PROFESSION(S)	PLACE OF BIRTH	BIRTH DATE	DIED
Carter, Hodding (III)	Journalist-government service	New Orleans, LA	04-07-1935	
Carver, Johnny	Country music singer	Jackson	11-24-1940	
Catledge, Turner	Journalist	near Ackerman	03-17-1901	04-27-1983
Chabert, Lacey	Actress	Purvis	09-30-1982	
Chaffin, Ernie	Rockabilly singer	Water Valley	01-01-1928	04-16-1997
Chambers, George	w/Chambers Bros. rock group	Flora	09-26-1931	
Chambers, Joe	w/Chambers Bros. rock group	Scott County	08-24-1942	
Chambers, Lester	w/Chambers Bros. rock group	Flora	04-13-1940	
Chambers, Willie	w/Chambers Bros. rock group	Flora	03-03-1938	
Charlesworth, Clifford E.	NASA official	Jackson	11-29-1931	
Chatmon, Sam	Blues singer	Bolton	01-10-1899	02-02-1983
Childress, Alvin	Actor-comic	Meridian	09-10-1907	04-19-1986
Claiborne, Craig	Columnist (food critic)	Sunflower	09-04-1920	01-22-2000
Claiborne, J.F.H.	Historian	Natchez	04-24-1807	05-17-1884
Clark, Dave	Sports: major league baseball	Tupelo	09-03-1962	
Clark, Kate Freeman	Artist: painter	Holly Springs	1875	1957
Clark, Tena	Movie score writer	Waynesboro	12-19-1953	
Clark, Will	Sports: college/pro baseball	New Orleans, LA	03-13-1964	
Clayton, William Lockhart	Government service	Tupelo	02-07-1880	02-08-1966
Clearwater, Eddy	Blues-rock singer/musician	Macon	01-10-1935	
Cleveland, Rob't. "Ace" (Sr.)	Journalist-publicist	Hattiesburg	08-06-1926	04-17-1995
Clower, Jerry	Country humorist	East Fork	09-28-1926	08-24-1998
Cobbs, Willie	Bluesman	Smale, AR	07-15-1932	
Cochran, Commodore	Olympic Champion (1924)	Richton	01-20-1902	01-03-1969
Cochran, Hank	Country songwriter/singer	Isola	08-02-1935	
Cochran, Roy	Olympic Champion (1948)	Richton	01-26-1919	09-26-1981
Cochran, Thad	U.S. Senator	Pontotoc	12-07-1937	
Coe, Frederick H.	TV Producer	Alligator	12-23-1914	04-29-1979
Cohn, David L.	Writer-essayist	Greenville	09-30-1897	09-12-1960
Cole Harry A. (Sr.)	Inventor	Jackson	01-09-1888	07-??-1969
Collier, Reggie	Sports: college football player	D'Iberville	05-14-1961	
Collins, Bobby	Sports: college football coach	Laurel	10-25-1933	
Commiskey, Henry A. (Sr.)	Medal of Honor recipient	Hattiesburg	01-10-1927	08-16-1971
Conerly, Charlie	Sports: pro football player	Clarksdale	09-19-1921	02-13-1996
Cook, Frances "Fannye" A.	Research biologist-writer	Crystal Springs	07-19-1889	04-30-1964
Cooke, Sam	Soul-Pop singer	Clarksdale	01-22-1935	12-11-1964
Cooley, Frank L.	Actor (silent screen)	Natchez	1870	07-06-1941
Cooper, Dorree	Artist-movie set decorator	New Orleans, LA	03-05-1952	
Cooper, Forrest Lamar	Writer	Jackson	10-12-1944	
Cooper, Owen	Industrialist-religious leader	Vicksburg	04-19-1908	11-08-1986
Cooper, Wyatt	Screenwriter-actor	Quitman	09-01-1927	01-05-1978
Cotton Blossom Singers, The	Spiritual Singing Group	Rankin County	1928 (formed)	
Cotton, James	Blues harmonica player	Dundee	07-01-1935	
Couch, Tommy	Music industry CEO	Tuscumbia, AL	11-12-1942	
Courtney, Joe	Sports: pro basketball player	Jackson	10-17-1969	
Cox, Calvin	Journalist-photographer	Greenwood	12-19-1918	
Craft, Harry "Popeye"	Sports: major league baseball	Ellisville	04-19-1915	08-03-1995
Creekmore, Hubert	Poet-novelist	Water Valley	01-16-1907	1966
Cristil, Jack	Sports broadcaster	Memphis, TN	12-10-1925	
Critz, Hughie	Sports: major league baseball	Starkville	09-17-1900	11-10-1980
Cross, Harold	Historical writer	Ripley	09-28-1946	
Crowder, Rett	Sports: amateur golfer	New Orleans, LA	06-16-1970	
Crowley, Mart	Playwright	Vicksburg	08-21-1936	
Crudup, Arthur "Big Boy"	Bluesman	Forest	08-24-1905	03-28-1974
Cutrer, T. Tommy	Grand Ole Opry announcer	Osyka	06-29-1924	10-11-1998
Dale, Roland	Sports: football player/coach	Magee	10-30-1927	
Dampier, Erick	Sports: college/pro basketball	Newhebron	07-14-1974	
David, William	Actor (silent screen)	Vicksburg	10-05-1882	04-10-1965
Davis, Blind John	Blues singer/pianist	Hattiesburg	02-07-1913	10-12-1985
Davis, Jefferson	President of the Confederacy	Todd County, KY	06-03-1808	12-06-1889
Davis, Paul	Singer-songwriter-producer	Meridian	04-21-1948	
Davis, Tyrone	Soul singer	Greenville	05-04-1938	
Davis, Walter	Early blues pianist	Grenada	03-01-1912	10-22-1963
De Chiaro, John	Classical guitarist-professor	Bronx, New York, NY	01-19-1953	

Famous & Notable Mississippians Listed by Name

NAME	PROFESSION(S)	PLACE OF BIRTH	BIRTH DATE	DIED
Deal, Borden	Writer	Pontotoc	10-12-1922	01-22-1985
Dean, Dizzy	Sports: major league baseball	Lucas, AR	01-16-1910	07-17-1974
Dell, Dorothy	Miss Universe (1930)-actor	Hattiesburg	01-30-1915	06-08-1934
Denley, S. Gale	Journalist-publisher-professor	Coffeeville	02-23-1936	
Diamond, James H.	Medal of Honor recipient	New Orleans, LA	04-22-1925	05-14-1945
Diddley, Bo	R&B-pop singer/guitarist	McComb	12-30-1928	
Dixon, Louisa	Novelist	Stanford, CT	03-31-1950	
Dixon, Willie	Bluesman	Vicksburg	07-01-1915	01-29-1992
Dollarhide, Jim	Film producer	Greenwood	06-08-1952	
Donald, David Herbert	Biographer-historian-professor	Goodman	10-01-1920	
Dorley, August	Medal of Honor recipient	Baden, Germany	12-??-1842	10-17-1867
Dorman, Harold	Pop-country singer	Sledge	12-23-1931	10-08-1988
Douglas, Ben H.	Scientist-professor-writer	Sontag	02-20-1935	
Douglas, Ellen	Novelist-short story writer	Natchez	07-12-1921	
Douglas, K.C.	Blues singer/guitarist	Sharon	11-21-1913	10-18-1975
Douglas, Steve	Musician (country & rock)	Greenville	02-17-1951	
Douglass, Mary Angie	Administrator-secretary	X-Prarie	03-26-1908	06-09-1981
Dow, Peggy	Actress	Columbia	03-18-1928	
Dunlap, Bill	Artist: painter	Mathiston	01-21-1944	
Dupree, Marcus	Sports: pro football player	Philadelphia, MS	05-22-1964	
Durr, Buddy	Sports: pro archery	Isola	09-15-1956	
Dye, John	Actor	Amory	01-31-1963	
Eagles, Charles W.	Historian-professor	Spartanburg, SC	09-22-1946	
Eason, B. Reeves	Movie director-screenwriter	Friars Point	10-02-1886	06-09-1956
Eastland, James O.	Politician: U.S. senator	Doddsville	11-28-1904	02-19-1986
Ebbers, Bernie	Corporate CEO	Canada	08-27-1941	
Edwards, Brad	Sports statistician	Jackson	06-10-1971	
Edwards, David "Honeyboy"	Blues singer/guitarist	Shaw	06-28-1915	
Edwards, Jim	Sports: major league baseball	Banner	12-14-1894	01-19-1965
Edwards, Theodore "Teddy"	Jazz saxophonist/arranger	Jackson	04-26-1924	
Eichelberger, Marietta	Scientist-medical researcher	Macon	08-20-1891	02-??-1982
Ellis, Tellis "T.B."	Sports: college athletic director	Vicksburg	05-26-1912	03-15-2000
Ellis, Tim	Sports: college football player	Louisville, MS	05-10-1956	
Elrod, E.B. "Buddy"	Sports: college football player	Sherman, TX	10-28-1918	06-13-1998
Emling, Ward	Gov'mt. administrator-actor	New Orleans, LA	01-21-1954	
Emmerich, John O. (Jr.)	Newspaperman	McComb	04-16-1929	02-25-1995
Engel, Lehman	Conductor-composer	Jackson	09-14-1910	08-29-1982
Espy, Mike	former U.S. Ag Secretary	Yazoo City	11-30-1953	
Etheridge, Kevin	Top student: perfect ACT score	Flowood	09-21-1975	
Everett, Betty	R&B singer	Greenwood	11-23-1939	
Evermore, John Daniel "J.D."	Actor	Leland	11-05-1968	
Evers, Charles	Civil Rights leader/activist	Decatur	09-11-1922	
Evers, Medgar	Civil Rights leader/activist	Decatur	07-02-1925	06-12-1963
Evers-Williams, Myrlie	Chairwoman of the NAACP	Vicksburg	03-17-1933	
Ewert, Terry	TV producer	Las Vegas, NV	05-09-1951	
Fairley, Robert	Sports: Harlem Globetrotter	Lucedale	07-18-1976	
Fanton, Julie Kaye	Set decorator for TV/movies	Oxford	05-14-1958	
Fanaka, Jamaa	Movie director	Jackson	09-06-1942	
Faulkner, John	Novelist-painter	Ripley	09-24-1901	03-28-1963
Faulkner, William	Novelist-screenwriter	New Albany	09-25-1897	07-06-1962
Favre, Brett	Sports: pro football player	Pass Christian	10-10-1969	
Feathers, Charlie	Rockabilly singer/songwriter	Myrtle	06-12-1932	08-29-1998
Ferguson, Robert B.	Songwriter-historian-scholar	Willow Springs, MO	12-30-1927	
Ferris, William R.	Writer-folklorist-scholar	near Vicksburg	02-05-1942	
Ferriss, Dave "Boo"	Sports: major league baseball	Shaw	12-05-1921	
Finkelberg, Arty	Financial broker	Brooklyn, NY	01-06-1954	
Five Blind Boys, The	Gospel-pop group	Rankin Co. (formed)	1930s (formed)	
Floyd, John M.	Writer-computer engineer	Kosciusko	11-25-1947	
Floyd, Tim	Sports: college & pro coach	Hattiesburg	02-25-1954	
Foote, Shelby	Historian-novelist	Greenville	11-17-1916	
Forbert, Steve	Folk singer/songwriter	Meridian	12-13-1954	
Ford, Richard	Writer-novelist	Jackson	02-16-1944	
Ford, Ruth	Actress	Hazlehurst	07-07-1915	
Foster, Willie	Sports: pro baseball player/coach	Calvert, TX	06-12-1904	09-16-1978

Famous & Notable Mississippians Listed by Name

NAME	PROFESSION(S)	PLACE OF BIRTH	BIRTH DATE	DIED
Fountain, Pete	Musician: clarinetist	Bay Saint Louis	07-03-1930	
Foxworth, Jo	Advertising CEO-writer	Tylertown	06-30-1918	
Fraiser, Jim	Writer-attorney	New Orleans, LA	10-27-1954	
Francis, Olin	Actor	Mooreville	09-13-1891	06-30-1952
Franklin, Rev. C.L.	Minister	Clarksdale	01-22-1915	07-27-1984
Freeman, Cliff	Advertising executive-creator	Vicksburg	02-14-1941	
Freeman, Martin	Medal of Honor recipient	Stettin, Germany	05-14-1814	09-11-1894
Freeman, Morgan	Actor	Memphis, TN	06-01-1937	
Fritts, Edward O.	President/CEO of the NAB	Cape Girardeau, MO	02-21-1941	
Gaither, Frances Jones	Novelist-writer	Tennessee	05-21-1889	10-28-1955
Gallagher, Jim (Jr.)	Sports: pro golfer	Pennsylvania	03-24-1961	
Gandy, Evelyn	History-making politician	Hattiesburg	09-04-1920	
Geary, Cynthia Lynn	Actress	Jackson	03-21-1965	
Gentry, Bobbie	Pop & county singer-writer	Chickasaw County	07-27-1944	
George, James Z.	Politician (historical figure)	Monroe Co., GA	10-20-1826	08-14-1897
Ghosh, Shayon	Top student: perfect ACT score	Ames, Iowa	10-03-1986	
Gibbs, Jake	Sports: college football player	Grenada	11-07-1938	
Gilchrist, Ellen	Writer	Vicksburg	02-20-1935	
Gilley, Mickey	Country singer/pianist	Natchez	03-09-1936	
Gillom, Jennifer	Sports: college-pro basketball	Abbeville	06-13-1964	
Gillom, Peggy	Sports: college basketball	Abbeville	04-14-1958	
Gillum, William M. "Jazz"	Blues harmonica player	Indianola	09-11-1904	03-29-1966
Goggin, Michael	Top student: perfect ACT & SAT	Hattiesburg	06-05-1982	
Gorden, W.C.	Sports: college coach	Nashville, TN	06-30-1930	
Gordon, Charles "Chuck"	Movie producer/director	Belzoni	05-13-1947	
Gordon, Gavin	Actor	Chicora	04-08-1901	04-07-1983
Gordon, Larry	Movie producer-CEO	Yazoo City	03-25-1936	
Gordon, Phil	Actor	Meridian	05-05-1922	
Gore, Samuel Marshall	Artist: sculptor-professor	Coolidge, TX	11-24-1927	
Graham, Charles	Actor: silent screen	Carthage	02-16-1895	10-09-1943
Graham, Glen	with rock group Blind Melon	Columbus	12-05-1967	
Granberry, Edwin Phillips	Cartoonist-writer	Meridian	04-18-1897	12-05-1988
Gray, Mark	Country music songwriter/singer	Vicksburg	10-24-1952	
Gray, Paul	Journalist-book reviewer	Jackson	19??	
Grayson, Walt	Broadcaster (TV weatherman)	Greenville	03-17-1949	
Green, Hugh	Sports: college football	Natchez	07-27-1959	
Green, Lillian "Lil"	Blues singer	Clarksdale	12-22-1919	04-14-1954
Greenwood, L.C.	Sports: pro football player	Canton	09-07-1947	
Gregory, Jack	Sports: pro football player	Tupelo	10-03-1944	
Gregory, Paul	Sports (baseball): coach / pro	Tomnolen	06-09-1908	09-16-1999
Griffin, Dick	Jazz musician/composer	Fannin	01-28-1940	
Grisham, John	Novelist-attorney	Jonesboro, AR	02-08-1955	
Grubbs, Gary	Actor: movies & TV	Amory	11-14-1949	
Guy, Ray	Sports: pro football punter	Thomson, GA	12-22-1949	
Guyton, Arthur C.	Physician-writer-inventor	Oxford	09-08-1919	
Haas, Toxey	Inventor-entrepreneur	West Point	01-21-1960	
Haddix, Travis	Blues singer/guitarist	Walnut	11-26-1938	
Haining, Alice	Actress	Jackson	10-08-1959	
Haise, Fred W. (Jr.)	Astronaut	Biloxi	11-14-1933	
Hale, Edwin "Goat"	Sports: college football player	Jackson	01-29-1896	03-25-1983
Hall, John E.	Medical research scientist	Milo, WV	08-08-1946	
Hamblett, Theora	Artist: primitive painter	Paris, MS	01-15-1895	03-06-1977
Hamer, Fannie Lou	Civil Rights leader/activist	Montgomery Co.	10-06-1917	03-14-1977
Hammett, Evelyn Allen	Educator-writer	Jefferson Co.	06-12-1894	06-16-1985
Hammons, Earle W.	Early film producer	Winona	12-02-1882	07-31-1962
Handy, W.C.	Ledendary jazz/bluesman	Florence, AL	11-16-1873	03-28-1958
Hannah, Barry	Novelist	Meridian	04-23-1942	
Hanson, Jack G.	Medal of Honor recipient	Escatawpa	09-18-1930	06-07-1951
Hardin, Mel	With R&B duo Mel & Tim	Holly Springs	19??	
Hardwick, Phil	Writer-administrator	Mendenhall	06-20-1948	
Hardy, James D.	Pioneering surgeon	Birmingham, AL	05-14-1918	
Harkey, Ira B. (Jr.)	Journalist	New Orleans, LA	01-15-1918	
Harkins, Greg	Craftsman: chairmaker	Jackson	03-21-1953	
Harper, Robert	Actor	Jackson	1931	

Famous & Notable Mississippians Listed by Name

NAME	PROFESSION(S)	PLACE OF BIRTH	BIRTH DATE	DIED
Harrington, Othella	Sports: pro basketball player	Jackson	01-31-1974	
Harris, Thomas	Novelist	Jackson, TN	09-22-1940	
Harrison, David E.	Inventor	Mann, WV	10-17-1937	07-07-1996
Harrison, Pat	Politician (historical figure)	Crystal Springs	08-29-1881	06-22-1941
Harvey, Antonio	Sports: pro basketball player	Pascagoula	07-06-1970	
Haskell, Sam	Entertainment executive	Mobile, AL	06-24-1955	
Hawkins, Ted	Blues singer-guitarist	Lakeshore	10-28-1936	01-01-1995
Haxton, Brooks	Poet-screenwriter	Greenville	12-01-1950	
Hayes, Charlie	Sports: major league baseball	Hattiesburg	05-29-1965	
Haymond, Saul (Sr.)	Black artist: painter	Ebenezer (Holmes Co.)	01-04-1947	
Haywood, Spencer	Sports: pro basketball player	Silver City	04-22-1949	
Heard, John W.	Medal of Honor recipient	Woodstock (Money)	03-27-1860	02-04-1922
Heidel, Jimmy	Government administrator	Benton	12-01-1943	
Henderson, Jimmy	Jazz musician	Jackson	05-20-1954	
Henderson, Mike	Rock bass player	Yazoo City	07-07-1951	
Henley, Beth	Playwright-actress	Jackson	05-08-1952	
Henry, Aaron	Civil Rights leader/activist	Clarksdale	07-02-1922	05-19-1997
Henry, Robert T.	Medal of Honor recipient	Greenville	11-27-1923	12-03-1944
Henson, Jim	Puppeteer	Greenville	09-24-1936	05-16-1990
Herndon, Ty	Country music singer	Meridian	05-02-1962	
Herrera, Anthony	Actor	Wiggins	01-19-1944	
Higby, Wilbur	Actor (silent screen)	Meridian	08-21-1867	12-01-1934
Hill, Faith	Country music singer	Star	09-21-1967	
Hill, Rebecca	Novelist	Memphis, TN	01-18-1944	
Hillery, Arthur "Art"	Jazz musician/composer	New Orleans, LA	10-31-1925	
Hinton, Milt	Jazz & big band bassist	Vicksburg	06-23-1910	
Hodges, Eddie	Actor	Hattiesburg	03-05-1947	
Holliman, W.G. "Mickey" (Jr.)	Corporate CEO	Shuqualak	09-24-1937	
Hollingsworth, Gerald M.	Philanthropist-physician	Centreville	c. 1929	
Hollingsworth, William	Artist: painter	Jackson	02-17-1910	08-01-1944
Holmes, Herbie	Orchestra/Band leader leader	Yazoo City	09-27-1912	12-01-1981
Holmes, Richard E.	History-making physician	Starkville	02-17-1944	
Honeycutt, Glenn	Rockabilly singer	Belzoni	05-02-1933	
Hooker, Earl Zebedee	Blues guitarist/singer	Clarksdale	01-02-1930	04-21-1970
Hooker, John Lee	Legendary bluesman	Clarksdale	08-22-1917	
Hoover, Houston	Sports: pro football player	Yazoo City	02-06-1965	
Hopkins, Gerald	Actor (TV)	Biloxi	12-26-1965	
Hopper, Clay	Sports: manager	Greenwood	10-03-1900	04-??-1976
Horton, "Big" Walter	Blues harmonica player	Horn Lake	04-06-1917	12-08-1981
House, Eddie "Son"	Legendary early bluesman	Riverton	03-21-1902	10-19-1988
Houston, Thelma	Soul singer-actress	Leland	05-07-1943	
Hovious, Junie	Sports: college football coach	Vicksburg	10-04-1919	05-07-1998
Hovis, Guy	Singer	Tupelo	09-24-1941	
Howell, Bailey	Sports: college/pro basketball	Middleton, TN	01-20-1937	
Howell, Grady (Jr.)	Historian-writer	Biloxi	04-07-1947	
"Howlin' Wolf"	Blues singer	West Point	06-10-1911	01-10-1976
Hubbard, Robert	Photographer-writer	Dayton, Ohio	04-15-1945	
Hull, Kent	Sports: pro football player	Greenwood	01-13-1961	
Hull, Marie Atkinson	Artist: painter	Summit	09-28-1890	11-21-1980
Humphreys, Michael	Actor	Independence	1985	
Hunter, Lindsey	Sports: pro basketball player	Utica	12-03-1970	
Hurt, Mississippi John	Blues singer/guitarist	Teoc	03-08-1892	11-02-1966
Hutton, Doug	Sports: basketball player/coach	Bolton	03-17-1942	
Iles, Greg	Novelist	Stuttgart, Germany	04-08-1960	
Imbragulio, John Vincent	Record producer-label founder	Hattiesburg	10-03-1925	02-04-2000
Imes, Birney	Photographer	Columbus	08-21-1951	
Jabaley, Michael	Hand surgeon (plastic surgeon)	Copperhill, TN	07-12-1934	
Jackson, Becca	Gospel singer/songwriter	Kosciusko	1968	
Jackson, Carl	Country music songwriter	Louisville, MS	09-18-1953	
Jackson, George	R&B/soul/pop songwriter	Indianola	03-12-1945	
James, D. Clayton	Author-biographer	Winchester, KY	02-13-1931	
James, Elmore	Legendary blues guitarist	Richland (Holmes Co)	01-27-1918	05-24-1963
James, Skip	Blues guitarist/singer	Bentonia	06-09-1902	10-03-1969
Jaudon, Valerie	Artist: contemporary painter	Greenville	08-06-1945	

The Ultimate Reference on the State

Famous & Notable Mississippians Listed by Name

NAME	PROFESSION(S)	PLACE OF BIRTH	BIRTH DATE	DIED
Jeffcoat, Don	Actor: TV	Gulfport	02-16-1975	
Jenkins, Bert	Sports: basketball coach	Richton	11-29-1924	
Jenkins, Daron	Sports: former H. Globetrotter	Mendenhall	02-22-1968	
Johanny, Jaimoe Jai	Musician: rock percussionist	Gulfport	07-08-1944	
Johnson, "Big" Jack	Musician: blues guitarist	Lambert	07-30-1940	
Johnson, George Ellis	Business executive	Richton	06-16-1927	
Johnson, Jimmy	Cartoonist	Lanett, AL	02-19-1952	
Johnson, Jimmy	Blues singer/guitarist	Holly Springs	11-25-1928	
Johnson, Luther "Guitar Jr."	Blues singer/guitarist	Itta Bena	04-11-1939	
Johnson, Robert	Legendary bluesman	Hazlehurst	05-08-1911	08-16-1938
Johnson, Tommy	Early bluesman	Terry	1896	11-01-1956
Johnston, John	Film locations manager	Jackson	02-10-1965	
Johnston, Means (Jr.)	Military leader: Admiral	Greenwood	12-05-1916	07-14-1989
Jones, Deacon	Sports: pro football player	Eatonville, FL	12-09-1938	
Jones, Eddie "Guitar Slim"	Blues singer/guitarist	Greenwood	12-10-1926	02-07-1959
Jones, Hayes	Olympics Champion (1964)	Starkville	08-04-1938	
Jones, Henry "Hank"	Musician: jazz pianist	Vicksburg	07-31-1918	
Jones, James Earl	Actor-announcer	Arkabutla	01-17-1931	
Jones, Laurence Clifton	Educator-writer	St. Joseph, MO	11-21-1884	07-15-1975
Jones, Robert Earl	Actor-Sports: boxer	Coldwater	02-03-1910	
Jordan, Daniel P.	Historian-scholar	Philadelphia, MS	07-22-1938	
Jordan, Mack A.	Medal of Honor recipient	Collins	12-08-1928	11-15-1951
Jordan, Winthrop	Professor-historian-writer	Worcester, MA	11-11-1931	
Joseph, Margie	R&B-soul singer	Pascagoula	1950	
Kearney, Belle	Feminist-writer-state senator	near Flora	03-06-1863	02-27-1939
Keith, Don Lee	Journalist	Wheeler	10-25-1940	
Kellum, Murry	Pop singer	Jackson, TN	12-31-1942	09-15-1990
Kelly, Patrick	Fashion designer	Vicksburg	09-24-1954	01-01-1990
Keys, Randolph	Sports: pro basketball player	Collins	04-19-1966	
Khayat, Robert C.	Educator-administrator	Moss Point	04-18-1938	
Kimbrough, "Junior"	Bluesman	Hudsonville	07-28-1930	01-16-1998
Kinard, Frank "Bruiser"	Sports: pro football player	Pelahatchie	10-23-1914	09-07-1985
King, Albert	Blues-R&B-soul guitarist	Indianola	04-25-1923	12-21-1992
King, B.B.	Legendary bluesman	Itta Bena	09-16-1925	
Kirby, Pat	Country singer & look-a-like	Tylertown	10-08-1956	
Knobloch, Fred	Country music singer/songwriter	Jackson	04-28-1953	
Koury, Leon Z.	Artist: sculptor	Greenville	11-03-1909	04-11-1993
Krebs, Sylvia Howell	Sports: high school basketball	Jackson	09-09-1937	
Ladd, Diane	Actress	Meridian	11-29-1932	
Lamar, L.Q.C.	Statesman-jurist	Georgia	09-17-1825	01-23-1893
Lambert, A.C. "Butch"	Sports: referee official	Holcut	02-27-1923	01-26-1985
Lance, Major	Soul singer	Winstonville	04-04-1941	09-03-1994
LaSalle, Denise	Soul singer	Leflore County	07-16-1939	
Leavell, Jerome F.	Educator-attorney-writer	Blue Mountain	02-14-1928	
LeDoux, Chris	Country music singer/songwriter	Biloxi	10-02-1948	
Lee, Hal	Sports: major league baseball	Ludlow	02-15-1905	09-04-1989
Lee, Hubert L.	Medal of Honor recipient	Arburg, MO	02-02-1915	11-05-1982
Lee, Stephen Dill	Educator-state senator	Charleston, SC	09-22-1833	05-28-1908
Lemon, Chet	Sports: major league baseball	Jackson	02-12-1955	
Lenoir, J.B.	Blues singer/musician	Monticello	05-05-1929	04-29-1967
Leslie, Sam	Sports: major league baseball	Moss Point	07-26-1905	01-21-1979
Lester, Tom	Actor	Jackson	09-23-1938	
Lewis, Walter "Furry"	Blues singer/guitarist	Greenwood	03-06-1895	09-14-1981
Lewis, Jerry Lee	R&R/country music singer	Ferriday, La.	09-29-1935	
Lindsay, Ken	Sports: club golf pro	Gadsden, AL	07-03-1943	
Lindsey, Jake W.	Medal of Honor recipient	Isnay, AL	05-01-1921	07-18-1988
Little, Freddie	Sports: pro-boxing champ	Picayune	04-25-1936	
"Little Howlin' Wolf"	Bluesman	Florence	07-26-1930	
"Little Milton"	Blues singer/guitarist	Inverness	09-07-1934	
Lomax, John A.	Blues collector/archivist	Goodman	09-23-1867	01-26-1948
Longstreet, Augustus B.	Educator-jurist-writer	Augusta, GA	09-22-1790	07-09-1870
Lott, Trent	Politician: U.S. Senator	Grenada	10-09-1941	
Lowe, Mundell	Composer-guitarist	Laurel	04-21-1922	
Lowry, Beverly	Writer	Memphis, TN	08-10-1938	

Famous & Notable Mississippians Listed by Name

NAME	PROFESSION(S)	PLACE OF BIRTH	BIRTH DATE	DIED
Lucas, Jack H.	Medal of Honor recipient	Plymouth, NC	02-14-1928	
Lum, Ray	Mule trader-storyteller	Rocky Springs	06-25-1891	12-17-1976
Lunceford, Jimmie	Big band/orchestra leader	Fulton	06-06-1902	07-12-1947
Lynch, John Roy	Politician-writer	Vidalia, LA	09-10-1847	11-02-1939
Madison, James J.	Medal of Honor recipient	Jersey City, NJ	05-20-1884	12-27-1922
Magic Sam	Blues singer/guitarist	Grenada	02-14-1937	12-01-1969
Majure, Jim	Novelist	Durant	08-29-1938	10-20-1996
Malone, Dumas	Historian	Coldwater	01-10-1892	12-27-1986
Malone, Jeff	Sports: pro basketball	Macon, GA	06-28-1961	
Malone, Tom "Bones"	Musician (trombonist)/arranger	Hattiesburg	06-16-1947	
Mangum, Kris	Sports: college/pro football	Magee	08-15-1973	
Manning, Archie	Sports: college/pro football	Drew	03-19-1949	
Manning, Danny	Sports: pro basketball player	Hattiesburg	05-17-1966	
Mara, Thalia	Professional dancer	Chicago	06-28-1911	
Mars, Florence	Writer-photographer	Philadelphia, MS	01-01-1923	
Martin, Phillip	Indian Chief-entrepreneur	Philadelphia, MS	03-13-1926	
Martin, Roy M.	Band director	Rosebud, AR	01-31-1895	01-23-1985
Matos, Eleni	Opera singer	Jackson	02-11-1966	
Matthews, Aubrey D.	Sports: pro football player	Pascagoula	09-15-1962	
Mattox, Martha	Actress	Natchez	06-19-1879	05-02-1933
Maxwell, John	Playwright	Jackson	07-12-1944	
Mayo, Richard E.	NASA administrator	Meridian	07-20-1935	
McAnally, Mac	Country music songwriter/singer	Belmont	07-01-1959	
McCafferty, Jim	Writer-attorney	Tupelo	03-12-1954	
McCain, John Sidney	Military leader: Admiral	Teoc	08-09-1884	09-06-1945
McCarty, Oseola	Philanthropist-humanitarian	Hattiesburg	03-07-1908	09-26-1999
McClellan, Eric	Advertising executive	Tampa, FL	11-14-1959	
McClinton, O.B.	Country music singer	Senatobia	04-25-1940	09-23-1987
McCoy, Herschel	Movie costume designer	Meridian	?	
McCrady, John	Artist: painter	Canton	09-05-1911	1968
McDaniel, Luke	Rockabilly singer/musician	Ellisville	02-03-1927	06-27-1992
McDowell, Jimmie	Sports journalist	Brookhaven	03-24-1926	
McDowell, "Mississippi" Fred	Blues legend	Rossville, TN	01-12-1906	07-03-1972
McDyess, Antonio	Sports: pro basketball player	Quitman	09-07-1974	
McGaughey, Neil	Mystery novelist-journalist	Natchez	10-03-1951	09-21-1999
McGill, Gary "Turk"	Sports: high school football	Taylorsville	04-12-1976	
McGregor, Mike	Craftsman: jeweler	Tibbs	04-14-1939	01-06-1999
McHugh, Robert P.	Journalist	Cedar Rapids, IA	02-14-1917	07-23-1998
McKey, Derrick	Sports: pro basketball player	Meridian	10-10-1966	
McMurry, Lillian	Blues record producer	Purvis	12-30-1921	03-18-1999
McNair, Eric	Sports: major league baseball	Meridian	04-12-1909	03-11-1949
McNair, Steve	Sports: college football player	Mount Olive	02-14-1973	
McPhail, Evelyn	Political party official	Bay St. Louis	06-09-1930	11-26-1998
McPherson, Tim	With R&B duo Mel & Tim	Holly Springs	19??	
McRae, Richard D. (Sr.)	Corporate CEO-philanthropist	Jackson	02-14-1921	
McRaney, Gerald	Actor	Collins	08-19-1948	
McWilliams, Elsie	Songwriter	Harperville	06-01-1896	12-31-1985
McWilliams, Henry "Skeets"	Jazz /swing-style guitarist	Jackson	08-06-1924	
McWilliams, T.E. "Shorty"	Sports: college-pro football	Meridian	05-12-1926	01-09-1997
Mead, Lynda Lee	Miss America (1960)	New Orleans, LA	04-17-1939	
Mellen, Frederic Frances	Geologist-writer	Starkville	08-21-1911	11-06-1989
Meredith, James	Civil Rights activist	Kosciusko	06-25-1933	
Merrill, H. T. "Dick"	Aviation pioneer	Iuka	02-01-1894	10-31-1982
Merrins, Eddie	Sports: golf pro & pro golfer	Meridian	08-04-1932	
Middlecoff, Cary	Sports: pro golfer	Halls, TN	01-06-1921	09-01-1998
Miley, William "Bud"	Military leader: General	Fort Mason, CA	12-26-1897	09-25-1997
Miller, Dicenzo	Sports: high school football	Eupora	07-09-1980	
Miller, John Ramsey	Novelist	Greenville	10-03-1949	
Miller, Mary Carol	Writer-physician	Greenwood	03-27-1954	
Miller, Mulgrew	Jazz pianist	Greenwood	08-13-1955	
Miller, Romaro	Sports: hi sch'l/college football	Shannon	09-12-1978	
Millsaps, Reuben W.	College founder	near Hazlehurst	05-30-1833	06-28-1916
Milner, Dumas	Businessman-industrialist	Attala County	01-28-1917	10-06-1992
Mims, Crawford	Sports: college football player	Carroll County	03-21-1933	

Famous & Notable Mississippians Listed by Name

NAME	PROFESSION(S)	PLACE OF BIRTH	BIRTH DATE	DIED
Ming, Hoyt Lester	Musician-songwriter	near Ackerman	10-06-1902	04-28-1985
Mississippi Mass Choir, The	Gospel group	Jackson	1988 (formed)	
Mississippi Sheiks, The	Blues-folk group	Jackson (formed at)	1926 (formed)	
Mitchell, Judith Paige	Novelist-screenwriter-producer	New Orleans, LA	11-24-19??	
Mitchell, Willie	Sports: major league baseball	Pleasant Grove	12-01-1889	11-23-1973
Mitchell, Willie	Musician-composer	Ashland	03-01-1928	
Mobley, Mary Ann	Miss America (1959)-actress	Biloxi	02-17-1939	
Mohamed, Ethel Wright	Artist: embroiderer	Fame	10-13-1907	02-15-1992
Monaghan, Bilbo "Mule"	Sports: pro football-coach	Amory	06-23-1910	02-10-1994
Money, Hernando De Soto	Politician (historical figure)	Holmes County	08-26-1839	09-18-1912
Montgomery, G.V. "Sonny"	U.S. congressman	Meridian	08-05-1920	
Montgomery, Wilbert N.	Sports: college/pro football	Greenville	09-16-1954	
Moody, Anne	Writer-Civil Rights activist	Centreville	09-15-1940	
Moore, Archie	Sports: pro boxing champ	Benoit	12-13-1913	12-09-1998
Moore, Dorothy	Pop-Soul singer	Jackson	10-13-1947	
Morris, Willie	Writer-novelist	Jackson	11-29-1934	08-02-1999
Mortensen, Davis K.	Business executive	Charles City, IA	04-25-1932	
Moseley, Alice	Artist: painter	Birmingham, AL	12-21-1909	
Moulds, Eric	Sports: college/pro football	Lucedale	07-17-1973	
"Muddy Waters"	Legendary bluesman	Rolling Fork	04-04-1915	04-30-1983
Murphy, Dot	Sports: basketball-coach	Jackson	09-20-1952	
Murphy, Gene	Sports: football coach	Columbus	10-01-1954	
Murphy, Matt "Guitar"	Blues guitarist	Sunflower	12-29-1927	
Musselwhite, Charlie	Blues harmonica player	Kosciusko	01-31-1944	
Myer, Buddy	Sports: major league baseball	Ellisville	03-16-1904	10-31-1974
Myers, Louis	Blues guitarist/harp player	Byhalia	09-18-1929	09-04-1994
Nail, Pamela	Mrs. World (1988)	Crawfordsville, IN	08-06-1962	
Nassour, Ellis	Writer	Vicksburg	10-25-1941	
Neal, Frances E.	Actress	Carrollton	06-27-1921	
Nelson, Ben	PGA Tour golf official	Canton	08-01-1944	
Nelson, Jack	Journalist-author	Biloxi	10-11-1929	
Newman, Joseph W.	Inventor	Mobile, AL	07-02-1936	
Neyland, Leedell W.	Writer	Gloster	08-04-1921	
Nordan, Lewis	Novelist	Itta Bena	08-23-1939	
Norwood, Willie "Ray-J" (Jr.)	Actor	McComb	01-17-1981	
Null, Ralph	Floral designer	Lauderdale	04-02-1946	
Nye, Carrie	Actress	Greenwood	1937	
O'Neal, Frederick	Actor	Brooksville	08-27-1905	08-25-1992
Oakman, Jack H.	Movie expert/collector	Panther Burn	05-27-1923	
Ogunkoya, Falilatu	Olympic Champion (1996)	Nigeria, Africa	12-05-1968	
Ohr, George	Artist: potter	Biloxi	07-12-1857	04-07-1918
Olive, Milton L. III	Medal of Honor recipient	Chicago, IL	11-07-1946	10-22-1965
Ott, Paul	Entertainer-conservationist	McComb	09-25-1934	
Overby, Charles L.	Journalist-CEO	Jackson	09-18-1946	
Overstreet, Paul	Country music singer-songwriter	Newton	03-17-1955	
Owen, Garry	Actor	Brookhaven	02-18-1902	06-01-1951
Owens, Jack	Blues singer/musician	Bentonia	11-17-1904	02-09-1997
Pace, Jim	Sports: sports car racing	Monticello	02-01-1961	
Palmeiro, Rafael	Sports: college/pro baseball	Havana, Cuba	09-24-1964	
Palmer, John N. (Sr.)	Corporate CEO	Corinth	07-14-1934	
Parker, Dave	Sports: major league baseball	Calhoun City	06-09-1951	
Parker, Junior	Blues singer/musician	Clarksdale	03-27-1932	11-18-1971
Parker, Laurie E.	Writer-crafts artist	Bruce	07-24-1963	
Passeau, Claude	Sports: major league baseball	Waynesboro	04-09-1909	
Patterson, Carolyn Bennett	Journalist-writer	Kosciusko	04-12-1922	
Patton, Charley	Legendary blues singer	Edwards	04-??-1887	04-28-1934
Payton, Walter	Sports: pro football player	Columbia	07-25-1954	11-01-1999
Peavey, Hartley	Corporate CEO	Merdian	12-30-1941	
Pemberton, John Clifford	Military leader/historical figure	Philadelphia, PA	08-10-1814	07-13-1881
Percy, Walker	Writer-physician	Birmingham, AL	05-28-1916	05-10-1990
Percy, William Alexander	Poet-lawyer	Greenville	05-14-1885	01-21-1942
Perkins, "Pinetop"	Blues pianist	Belzoni	07-07-1913	
Perkins, Ray	Sports: college football coach	Mount Olive	11-06-1941	
Perry, Vernon	Sports: pro football player	Jackson	09-22-1954	

Famous & Notable Mississippians Listed by Name

NAME	PROFESSION(S)	PLACE OF BIRTH	BIRTH DATE	DIED
Peters, Ben	Country-Pop songwriter	Greenville	06-20-1933	
Peterson, Donald H.	Astronaut	Winona	10-22-1933	
Peyton, Annie C.	College founder	Madison County	09-12-1852	??/??/ 1898
Phillips, Thomas Hal	Novelist-screen writer	Corinth	10-11-1922	
Philpot, Cory	Sports: pro football player	Savannah, GA	05-15-1970	
Pippin, Hollis	Choreographer-director	Jackson	05-03-1950	09-26-1994
Pitchford, Lonnie	Blues musician	Lexington	10-08-1955	11-08-1998
Pittman, Bob	Entertainment business	Jackson	12-28-1953	
Pittman, John A.	Medal of Honor recipient	Carrollton	10-15-1928	04-08-1995
Pittman, William (II)	Sports: pro rodeo champion	Birmingham, AL	04-04-1072	
Plumpp, Sterling D.	Poet	Clinton	01-30-1940	
Polanski, Frank	Musician: pianist	Kenosha, WI	09-29-1939	
Polanski, Sandra	Musician: pianist	Grenada	05-17-1939	
Polk, Ron	Sports: college baseball coach	Boston, MA	01-12-1944	
Poole, James E. "Buster"	Sports: pro football-coach	Gloster	09-09-1915	11-16-1994
Portera, Malcolm	Educator: college president	West Point	01-31-1946	
Posey, Parker	Actress	Baltimore, MD	11-08-1968	
Prather, Lenore L.	History-making jurist	West Point	09-17-1931	
Presley, Elvis	Singer-performer-actor	Tupelo	01-08-1935	08-16-1977
Prewitt, Cheryl	Miss America (1980)	Ackerman	02-15-1957	
Price, George Baker	Military leader	Laurel	08-28-1929	
Price, Leontyne	Soprano opera singer	Laurel	02-10-1927	
Price, Will A.	Playwright	McComb	?	07-04-1962
Pride, Charley	Country singer	Sledge	03-18-1938	
Primos, Will	Entrepreneur-inventor	Jackson	03-02-1952	
Pryor, James "Snooky"	Blues harmonica player	Lambert	09-15-1921	
Pulliam, Trent	Sports: former H. Globetrotter	Houston, MS	08-13-1975	
Radvanyi, Janos	Professor-environmentalist	Hungary	08-24-1922	
Raspberry, William	Journalist	Okolona	10-12-1935	
Redd, William Silas "Si"	Businessman-innovator	Philadelphia, MS	11-16-1911	
Reed, Jimmy	Blues singer	Dunleith	09-06-1925	08-29-1976
Reed, Walter	Sports: administrator/coach	Meridian	09-20-1933	
Reese, Andy	Sports: major league baseball	Tupelo	02-07-1904	01-10-1966
Reeves, Anna	Sports: pro archery	Winona	03-08-1959	
Reid-Petty, Jane	Actor-writer-director	Meridian	06-12-1927	04-16-1998
Revels, Hiram Rhodes	Politician (historical figure)	Fayetteville, NC	09-27-1827	01-16-1901
Rice, Jerry	Sports: pro football player	Crawford	10-13-1962	
Rice, "Sir" Mack	R&B songwriter/singer	Clarksdale	11-10-1933	
Rice, Tom	Movie director/screenwriter	Jackson	11-12-1973	
Richards, Beah	Actress	Vicksburg	07-12-1920	09-14-2000
Rimes, LeAnn	Country music singer	Pearl	08-28-1982	
Ritchie, Jim	Writer-storyteller	Brookhaven	04-12-1937	
Roberts, Eric	Actor	Biloxi	04-18-1956	
Robinson, James	Sports: pro basketball player	Jackson	08-31-1971	
Rodgers, Jimmie	Country music singer/songwriter	Meridian	09-08-1897	05-26-1933
Rogers, Jimmy	Blues singer/guitarist	Ruleville	06-03-1924	12-19-1997
Rollins, Charlemae	Librarian-writer	Yazoo City	06-20-1897	02-03-1979
Rommerdale, Rick	Inventor	Erie, PA	11-27-1941	
Roosa, Stuart A.	Astronaut-businessman	Durango, CO	08-16-1933	12-12-1994
Ross, Craig	Top student: perfect ACT score	Vicksburg	10-27-1981	
Ross, Isaiah "Doctor"	Blues guitarist/harpist	Tunica	10-21-1925	05-28-1993
Ross, Jim Buck	Miss ag commissioner	Pelahatchie	08-14-1917	12-14-1999
Rosser, James C. "Butch"	Physician: pionering surgeon	Rome	09-14-1954	
Rowland, Dunbar	Historian-writer-official	Oakland	08-25-1864	11-01-1937
Ruffin, David	Soul singer	Whynot	01-18-1941	06-01-1991
Ruffin, Jimmy	Soul singer	Collinsville	05-07-1939	
Rush, Bobby	Soul/R&B singer	Homer, LA	11-10-1940	
Rush, Leslie Vaughn	Medical pioneer-physician-	Meridian	02-16-1905	02-08-1987
Rush, Otis	Blues guitarist/singer	Philadelphia, MS	04-29-1934	
Rushing, Felder	Horticultural agent-writer	Indianola	06-19-1952	
Russell, Donna Hild	Mrs. America (1985)	Brandon	06-27-1954	
Russell, Johnny	Country music singer-comedian	Moorhead	01-23-1940	
Saggus, James	Journalist	Alexandria, LA	08-15-1925	04-04-1995
Salter, Sidney L. "Sid"	Journalist-publisher-professor	Philadelphia, MS	01-16-1959	

Famous & Notable Mississippians Listed by Name

NAME	PROFESSION(S)	PLACE OF BIRTH	BIRTH DATE	DIED
Sanderson, Joe Frank	Business executive	Jackson	08-03-1925	01-04-1998
Saxton, Bob	Musician: country/jazz guitarist	Newton County	08-16-1932	
Scarborough, Chuck	TV journalist	Pittsburgh, PA	11-04-1943	
Scott, Don	Olympic Champion (1924)	Woodville	11-05-1894	10-10-1980
Scott, George "Boomer"	Sports: major league baseball	Greenville	03-23-1944	
Sea, Johnny	Country music singer/songwriter	Gulfport	07-15-1940	
Seawright, James L. (Jr.)	Art: sculptor-educator	Jackson	05-22-1935	
Seawright, Joseph P.	History-making designer	Greenwood	08-19-1945	
Semon, Larry	Actor & director	West Point	07-06-1889	10-08-1928
Shaman, Floyd D.	Artist: sculptor	Wheatland, WY	12-20-1935	
Shaw, Billy	Sports: college & pro football	Natchez	12-15-1938	
Sherrill, Jackie	Sports: college football coach	Duncan, OK	11-28-1943	
Short, Purvis	Sports: college/pro basketball	Hattiesburg	08-24-1956	
Simmons, Jean F.	Educator	Monroe, LA	05-10-1936	
Simmons, "Jumpin' " Gene	R&B singer	Tupelo	07-10-1933	
Slade, Prescilla D.	Educator-college president	Shaw	09-16-1951	
Slater, Jackie	Sports: pro football player	Jackson	05-27-1954	
Slaton, James D.	Medal of Honor recipient	Laurel	04-02-1912	02-02-1961
Small, Torrance	Sports: college/pro football	Tampa, FL	07-06-1970	
Smith, Brad	with rock group Blind Melon	Columbus	09-29-1968	
Smith, Calvin	Sports: sprinter	Bolton	01-08-1961	
Smith, Frank E.	Politician-writer	Sidon	02-21-1918	08-02-1997
Smith, Frederick W.	Businessman-entrepreneur	Marks	08-11-1944	
Smith, Hamilton	Movie director/screenwriter	Muskegon, MS	10-22-1887	10-29-1941
Smith, Hazel Brannon	Journalist	Gadsden, AL	02-05-1914	05-17-1994
Smith, Janet Marie	Architect-business executive	Jackson	12-13-1957	
Smith, Jimmy	Sports: college/pro football	Detroit, MI	02-09-1969	
Smith, Kimberly R.	Top student: perfect ACT score	Fort Worth, TX	09-21-1977	
Smith, L.T.	Sports: high school coach	Jackson	09-10-1918	
Smith, Patrick D.	Novelist	Mendenhall	10-08-1927	
Smith, Symba	Actress	Gulfport	07-06-19??	
Smith, Warren	Rockabilly singer/musician	Louise	02-07-1933	01-30-1980
Smith, Willie Mae Ford	Gospel blues singer	Rolling Fork	06-23-1904	02-02-1994
Smitty, John "Big Bad"	Bluesman	Vicksburg	02-11-1940	
Spann, Otis	Blues pianist/singer	Jackson	03-21-1930	04-25-1970
Speakes, Larry	Journalist	Cleveland	09-13-1939	
Spears, Britney	Pop singer/dancer	Kentwood, LA	12-02-1981	
Speed, Lake	Sports: pro racecar driver	Jackson	01-17-1948	
Spencer, Elizabeth	Novelist	Carrollton	07-19-1921	
Spinks, Johnny R. "Jack"	Sports: pro football player	Toomsuba	02-04-1930	09-29-1994
Stacey, Billy	Sports: pro football player	Winona	07-30-1936	
Staples, Roebuck "Pop"	Gospel-Soul singer	Winona	12-28-1915	
Starnes, Mike	Corporate CEO	Baton Rouge, LA	02-22-1945	
Stennis, John C.	U.S. senator	Kemper Co.	08-03-1901	04-23-1995
Stevens, Stella	Actress	Yazoo City	10-01-1936	
Stevens, Thomas Roger	with rock group Blind Melon	West Point	10-31-1969	
Stewart, Lisa	TV host-country music singer	Louisville, MS	08-06-1968	
Stewart, Lusia Harris	Sports: college/pro basketball	Minter City	02-10-1955	
Stewart, Tonea	Actress	Greenwood	19??	
Still, William Grant	Musician-composer	Woodville	05-11-1895	12-03-1978
Street, James Howell	Novelist-journalist	Lumberton	10-15-1903	09-28-1954
Strong, Barrett	R&B singer/songwriter	West Point	02-05-1941	
Stuart, Marty	Country music singer/songwriter	Philadelphia, MS	09-30-1958	
Sumlin, Hubert	Blues guitarist	Greenwood	11-16-1931	
Sumner, Cid Ricketts	Novelist	Brookhaven	09-27-1890	10-15-1970
Sumrall, Nan	Miss Mississippi-TV personality	Hattiesburg	11-23-1965	
Sunnyland Slim	Blues pianist	Vance	09-05-1907	03-17-1995
Swalm, Dave C.	Engineer-CEO-philanthropist	Los Angeles, CA	11-08-1932	
Talbott, Eugenia Ann	Artist: painter	Pascagoula	07-31-1947	
Tartt, Donna	Novelist	Greenwood	12-23-1963	
Taulbert, Clifton L.	Writer	Glen Allan	02-19-1945	
Taylor, "Hound Dog"	Blues singer/guitarist	Natchez	04-12-1917	12-17-1975
Taylor, Mike	Sports: amateur golfer	New Orleans	07-28-1946	
Taylor, Mildred D.	Writer	Jackson	09-13-1943	

Famous & Notable Mississippians Listed by Name

NAME	PROFESSION(S)	PLACE OF BIRTH	BIRTH DATE	DIED
Taylor, W.C. (Jr.)	Christian country music singer	Grenada	11-10-1945	
Temple, Johnnie "Geechie"	Bluesman	Canton	10-18-1906	11-22-1968
Thames, Byron	Actor	Jackson	04-23-1969	
Theriot, Herbert	Rodeo world champion	Franklin, LA	09-27-1966	
Thibodeaux, Kathy	Ballet dancer/instructor	Memphis, TN	11-09-1956	
Thibodeaux, Keith R.	Actor-singer	Lafayette, LA	12-01-1950	
Thomas, Charles S. (Sr.)	Sports: hi school football coach	Winona	10-22-1913	11-23-1995
Thomas, James "Son"	Blues musician-sculptor	Eden	10-14-1926	06-26-1993
Thomas, Rufus	R&B singer/songwriter	Cayce	03-26-1917	
Thomas, Treg	Sports: college football player	Pascagoula	03-14-1977	
Thompson, Larry A.	Movie producer-impresario	Clarksdale	08-01-1944	
Thorn, Paul	Pro boxer-songwriter/singer	Kenosha, WI	07-13-1964	
Topp, Mildred Spurrier	Writer-teacher	Forest City, IL	01-05-1897	08-15-1963
Treen, Joseph Paul	Inventor	Purvis	05-01-1900	08-24-1986
Trippett, Frank	Journalist	Columbus	07-01-1926	06-18-1998
Truly, Richard H.	Astronaut-head of NASA	Fayette	11-12-1937	
Turner, Ike	R&B singer/musician	Clarksdale	11-05-1931	
Turner, Roscoe	Aviation pioneer	Corinth	09-29-1895	06-23-1970
Twitty, Conway	Rock-Country music superstar	Friars Point	09-01-1933	06-05-1993
Tyler, Dan	Songwriter-author	McComb	11-22-1950	
Underwood, Felix J.	State health officer-physician-	Nettleton	11-21-1882	01-09-1959
Unser, Del	Sports: college/pro baseball	Decatur, IL	12-09-1944	
Varnado, Christine M.	Top student: perfect ACT score	Metairie, LA	01-29-1980	
Vaught, Johnny	Sports: college football coach	Olney, TX	05-06-1909	
Vick, S.B. "Sam"	Sports: major league baseball	Batesville	04-12-1895	08-17-1986
Vinson, Walter	Bluesman	Bolton	02-02-1901	04-22-1975
Wade, Ernestine	Actress-comic	Jackson	08-07-1906	04-15-1983
Wade, Margaret	Sports: basketball coach	McCool	12-30-1912	02-16-1995
Waits, Freddie	Musician: jazz drummer	Jackson	04-27-1943	11-18-1989
Walker, Charles C.	Checkers champion	Hattiesburg	12-11-1934	
Walker, Dontae	Sports: high school football	Jackson	01-31-1980	
Walker, Gerald	Sports: major league baseball	Gulfport	03-19-1908	03-20-1981
Walker, Harry "The Hat"	Sports: major league baseball	Pascagoula	10-22-1916	08-08-1999
Walker, Rebecca	Writer-feminist-actress	Jackson	1969	
Wallace, Bobby	Sports: college football coach	Magnolia, AR	09-17-1954	
Walls, Wesley	Sports: pro football player	Batesville	03-26-1966	
Walston, Ray	Actor	Laurel	12-02-1914	
Ward, Sela	Actress	Meridian	07-11-1956	
Waters, Wyatt	Artist: watercolorist	Brookhaven	03-16-1955	
Watkins, Harvey "Pop" (Sr.)	Gospel singer/songwriter	Canton	12-05-1929	11-16-1994
Watson, Brad	Writer-professor	Meridian	07-24-1955	
Watson, Libby Rae	Blues singer/musician	Pascagoula	01-05-1954	
Wayne, Thomas	R&R/Pop singer	Batesville	07-22-1940	08-15-1971
Weatherly, Jim	Pop-county singer/songwriter	Pontotoc	03-17-1943	
Weatherspoon, Clarence	Sports: pro basketball player	Crawford	09-08-1970	
Webb, Peggy	Writer: romance novelist	Mooreville	02-08-1942	
Webb, "Skeeter"	Sports: major league baseball	Meridian	11-04-1909	07-08-1986
Webb, Ted J. (Jr.)	Inventor-banker	Yazoo City	11-01-1956	
Weese, Norris	Sports: college-pro football	Baton Rouge, LA	08-12-1951	01-13-1995
Welborn, Ira C.	Medal of Honor recipient	Mico (Shady Grove)	02-13-1874	07-13-1956
Wells, Lloyd	Musician: jazz guitarist	Gulfport	04-22-1938	
Wells, Mary Ann	Writer-journalist	Agricola	07-02-1944	
Wells-Barnett, Ida Bell	Civil Rights pioneer	Holly Springs	07-16-1862	03-25-1931
Welty, Eudora	Writer-novelist	Jackson	04-13-1909	
Westerfield, Louis	Educator-attorney	Kemper County	07-31-1949	08-24-1996
Wheat, Roy M.	Medal of Honor recipient	Moselle	07-24-1947	08-11-1967
White, Artie	Blues singer	Vicksburg	04-16-1937	
White, Bukka	Blues legend	Houston, MS	11-12-1906	02-26-1977
White, Frank	Sports: major league baseball	Greenwood	09-04-1950	
White, Willye B.	Olympic Champion (1964)	Money	01-01-1936	
Whitten, Jamie L.	U.S. Congressman	Cascilla	04-18-1910	09-09-1995
Wilburn, Tom	Sports: horse harness racing	Columbus	11-30-1918	
Wilkins, Robert	Blues singer/guitarist	Hernando	01-16-1896	05-26-1987
Williams, Ben	Sports: college/pro football	Yazoo City	09-01-1954	

Famous & Notable Mississippians Listed by Name

NAME	PROFESSION(S)	PLACE OF BIRTH	BIRTH DATE	DIED
Williams, Ben Ames	Novelist-writer	Macon	03-07-1889	02-04-1953
Williams, "Big" Joe	Blues singer/musician	Crawford	10-16-1903	12-17-1982
Williams, Frank	Gospel singer/group founder	Smithdale	06-27-1947	03-22-1993
Williams, John Sharp	Politician (historical figure)	Memphis, TN	07-30-1854	09-07-1932
Williams, Milan B.	Musician: keyboardist	Okolona	03-28-1948	
Williams, Spencer (Jr.)	Actor-comic	Vidalia, LA	07-14-1893	12-13-1969
Williams, Tennessee	Dramatist	Columbus	03-26-1911	02-25-1983
Williamson, Sonny Boy (II)	Early bluesman	Glendora	03-11-1908	06-23-1965
Willoughby, Mamie Davis	Writer	near Liberty	11-03-1915	01-09-1996
Wilson, Al	Soul singer/drummer	Meridian	06-19-1939	
Wilson, Cassandra	Jazz vocalist	Jackson	12-04-1955	
Wilson, Charles	Mystery writer	Kennett, MO	08-02-1939	
Wilson, Elder Roma	Gospel blues musician	Hickory Flat	12-22-1910	
Wilson, Gerald Stanley	Jazz trumpeter/arranger	Shelby	09-04-1918	
Wilson, Louis Hugh (Jr.)	Military leader/MOH recipient	Brandon	02-11-1920	
Wilson, Mary	Motown soul singer	Greenville	03-06-1944	
Wiman, Richard	Writer-minister	Brandon	07-31-1950	
Winder, Sammy	Sports: pro football player	Madison	07-15-1959	
Winfrey, Oprah	Talk show host-actress	Kosciusko	01-29-1954	
Winston, Hattie	Actress	Greenville	03-03-1945	
Winter, Johnny	Musician: blues guitarist	Leland	02-23-1944	
Wolfe, Elizabeth	Artist: painter-sculptor	Jackson	05-20-1949	
Wolfe, Karl	Artist: painter	Brookhaven	01-25-1903	11-16-1984
Wolfe, Mildred	Artist: painter	Celina, OH	08-23-1912	
Wooten, Hoyt B.	Broadcast pioneer	Coldwater	09-29-1893	12-06-1969
Worsham, Charlie	Musician: banjo prodigy	Jackson	09-01-1985	
Wright, Charles	Soul/funk singer	Clarksdale	04-06-1942	
Wright, Early	Legendary disc jockey	Jefferson (Carroll Co.)	02-10-1915	12-10-1999
Wright, Frank	Jazz tenor saxophonist	Grenada	07-09-1935	05-17-1990
Wright, Richard	Novelist	Natchez	09-04-1908	11-28-1960
Wynette, Tammy	Country music singer	Tremont	05-05-1942	04-06-1998
Yarbrough, Steve	Writer-professor	Indianola	08-29-1956	
Young, Al	Writer-musician	Ocean Springs	05-31-1939	
Young, Billie Jean	Actress-playwright-poet	Pennington, AL	07-21-1947	
Young, Johnny	Blues singer	Vicksburg	01-01-1918	04-18-1974
Young, Lester Willis	Jazz musician & composer	Woodville	08-27-1909	03-15-1959
Young, Stark	Drama critic-writer	Como	10-11-1881	01-06-1963
Zaninelli, Luigi	Music composer-professor	Raritan, NJ	03-30-1932	
Ziglar, Jim	Government service-attorney	Pascagoula	12-08-1945	
Ziglar, Zig	Motivational writer-speaker	Alabama	11-06-1926	

Famous & Notable Mississippians Listed by Birth Date

BIRTH DATE	NAME	PROFESSION(S)	PLACE OF BIRTH
Jan. 01, 1909	Dana Andrews (d.)	Actor	Collins
Jan. 01, 1918	Johnny Young (d.)	Blues singer	Vicksburg
Jan. 01, 1923	Florence Mars	Writer-photographer	Philadelphia, MS
Jan. 01, 1928	Ernie Chaffin (d.)	Rockabilly singer	Water Valley
Jan. 01, 1936	Willye B. White	Olympic Champion (1964)	Money
Jan. 02, 1930	Earl Zebedee Hooker (d.)	Blues guitarist-singer	Clarksdale
Jan. 04, 1947	Saul Haymond, Sr.	Black artist: painter	Ebenezer (Holmes County)
Jan. 05, 1897	Mildred Spurrier Topp (d.)	Writer-teacher	Forest City, IL
Jan. 05, 1954	Libby Rae Watson	Blues singer/musician	Pascagoula
Jan. 06, 1921	Cary Middlecoff (d.)	Sports: pro golfer	Halls, TN
Jan. 06, 1954	Arty Finkelberg	Financial broker	Brooklyn, New York, NY
Jan. 08, 1935	Elvis Presley (d.)	Singer-performer-actor-superstar	Tupelo
Jan. 08, 1961	Calvin Smith	Sports: sprinter	Bolton
Jan. 09, 1888	Harry A. Cole, Sr. (d.)	Inventor	Jackson
Jan. 09, 1900	Ishmon Bracey (d.)	Blues singer/guitarist	Byram
Jan. 09, 1939	Jimmy Boyd	Actor	McComb
Jan. 10, 1892	Dumas Malone (d.)	Historian	Coldwater
Jan. 10, 1899	Sam Chatmon (d.)	Blues singer	Bolton
Jan. 10, 1927	Henry A. Commiskey, Sr. (d.)	Medal of Honor recipient	Hattiesburg
Jan. 10, 1935	Eddy Clearwater	Blues/rock singer/musician	Macon

Famous & Notable Mississippians Listed by Birth Date

BIRTH DATE	NAME	PROFESSION(S)	PLACE OF BIRTH
Jan. 12, 1906	"Mississippi" Fred McDowell (d.)[1]	Blues legend	Rossville, TN
Jan. 12, 1944	Ron Polk	Sports: college football coach	Boston, MA
Jan. 13, 1961	Kent Hull	Sports: pro football player	Greenwood
Jan. 15, 1895	Theora Hamblett (d.)	Artist: primitive painter	Paris, MS
Jan. 15, 1918	Ira B. Harkey, Jr.	Journalist	New Orleans, LA
Jan. 16, 1896	Robert Wilkins (d.)	Blues singer/guitarist	Hernando
Jan. 16, 1907	Hubert Creekmore (d.)	Poet-novelist	Water Valley
Jan. 16, 1910	Dizzy Dean (d.)	Sports: major league baseball	Lucas, AR
Jan. 16, 1959	Sidney L. "Sid" Salter	Journalist-publisher-professor	Philadelphia, MS
Jan. 17, 1931	James Earl Jones	Actor-announcer	Arkabutla
Jan. 17, 1948	Lake Speed	Pro racecar driver-manager	Jackson
Jan. 17, 1981	Willie 'Ray-J' Norwood, Jr.	Actor	McComb
Jan. 18, 1941	David Ruffin (d.)	Soul singer	Whynot
Jan. 18, 1944	Rebecca Hill	Novelist	Memphis, TN
Jan. 19, 1944	Anthony Herrera	Actor	Wiggins
Jan. 19, 1953	John De Chiaro	Classical guitarist-professor	Bronx, New York, NY
Jan. 20, 1887	V. Ruth Campbell (d.)	History-making attorney	Yazoo City
Jan. 20, 1892	Roscoe Ates (d.)	Actor	Grange
Jan. 20, 1902	Commodore Cochran (d.)	Olympic Champion (1924)	Richton
Jan. 20, 1937	Bailey Howell	Sports: college pro basketball	Middleton, TN
Jan. 21, 1944	Bill Dunlap	Artist: painter	Mathiston
Jan. 21, 1954	Ward Emling	Government administrator-actor	New Orleans, LA
Jan. 21, 1960	Toxey Haas	Inventor-entrepreneur	West Point
Jan. 22, 1915	Rev. C. L. Franklin (d.)	Minister-recording artist	Clarksdale
Jan. 22, 1935	Sam Cooke (d.)	Soul/pop singer	Clarksdale
Jan. 23, 1940	Johnny Russell	Country music singer	Moorhead
Jan. 23, 1953	Bill Buchanan	Novelist-engineer	Mobile, AL
Jan. 24, 1943	James Barksdale	Corporate CEO-philanthropist	Jackson
Jan. 25, 1903	Karl Wolfe (d.)	Artist: painter	Brookhaven
Jan. 26, 1919	Roy Cochran (d.)	Olympic Champion (1948)	Richton
Jan. 26, 1967	Jeff Branson	Sports: major league baseball	Waynesboro
Jan. 27, 1839	John C. Black (d.)	Medal of Honor recipient	Lexington
Jan. 27, 1918	Elmore James (d.)	Legendary blues guitarist/singer	Richland (Holmes County)
Jan. 28 1912	Thomas J. Biggs (d.)	Architect	Arkansas
Jan. 28, 1917	Dumas Milner (d.)	Businessman-industrialist	Attala County
Jan. 28, 1940	Dick Griffin	Jazz musician-composer	Fannin
Jan. 29, 1896	Edwin "Goat" Hale (d.)	Sports: college football	Jackson
Jan. 29, 1954	Oprah Winfrey	Talk show host-actress	Kosciusko
Jan. 29, 1980	Christine M. Varnado	Top student: perfect ACT score	Metairie, LA
Jan. 30, 1915	Dorothy Dell (d.)	Miss Universe (1930)-actress	Hattiesburg
Jan. 30, 1940	Sterling D. Plumpp	Poet	Clinton
Jan. 31, 1895	Roy M. Martin (d.)	High School band director	Rosebud, AR
Jan. 31, 1944	Charlie Musselwhite	Blues harmonica player	Kosciusko
Jan. 31, 1946	Malcolm Portera	Educator: president of MSU	West Point
Jan. 31, 1963	John Dye	Actor	Amory
Jan. 31, 1974	Othella Harrington	Sports: pro basketball player	Jackson
Jan. 31, 1980	Dontae Walker	Sports: high school/pro fooball player	Jackson
Feb. 01, 1894	H.T. "Dick" Merrill (d.)	Aviation pioneer	Iuka
Feb. 01, 1961	Jim Pace	Sports: sports car racing	Monticello
Feb. 02, 1901	Walter Vinson (d.)	Bluesman	Bolton
Feb. 02, 1915	Hubert L. Lee (d.)	Medal of Honor recipient	Arburg, MO
Feb. 03, 1907	Hodding Carter, Jr. (d.)	Journalist-writer	Hammond, LA
Feb. 03, 1910	Robert Earl Jones	Actor-Sports: boxer	Coldwater
Feb. 03, 1927	Luke McDaniel (d.)	Rockabilly singer/musician	Ellisville
Feb. 04, 1930	Johnny R. "Jack" Spinks (d.)	Sports: pro football player	Toomsuba
Feb. 05, 1914	Hazel Brannon Smith (d.)	Journalist	Gadsden, AL
Feb. 05, 1941	Barrett Strong	R&B singer/songwriter	West Point
Feb. 05, 1942	William R. Ferris	Writer-folklorist-scholar	near Vicksburg
Feb. 06, 1965	Houston Hoover	Sports: pro football player	Yazoo City
Feb. 07, 1880	William Lockhart Clayton (d.)	Government service	Tupelo
Feb. 07, 1904	Andy Reese (d.)	Sports: major league baseball	Tupelo
Feb. 07, 1913	Blind John Davis (d.)	Blues singer/pianist	Hattiesburg
Feb. 07, 1933	Warren Smith (d.)	Rockabilly singer/musician	Louise

[1] (d.) INDICATES THAT PERSON IS DECEASED. ALL PLACES LISTED UNDER "PLACE OF BIRTH" ARE IN MISSISSIPPI UNLESS OTHERWISE INDICATED.

The Ultimate Reference on the State

Famous & Notable Mississippians Listed by Birth Date

BIRTH DATE	NAME	PROFESSION(S)	PLACE OF BIRTH
Feb. 07, 1973	Tim Bowens	Sports: pro football player	Okolona
Feb. 08, 1928	Eddie "Guitar" Burns	Blues singer/guitarist	Belzoni
Feb. 08, 1942	Peggy Webb	Writer: romance novelist	Mooreville
Feb. 08, 1955	John Grisham	Novelist-attorney	Jonesboro, AR
Feb. 09, 1969	Jimmy Smith	Sports: college/pro football player	Detroit, MI
Feb. 10, 1915	Early Wright (d.)	Legendary disc jockey	Jefferson (Carroll County)
Feb. 10, 1927	Leontyne Price	Opera singer	Laurel
Feb. 10, 1955	Lusia Harris Stewart	Sports: college/pro basketball	Minter City
Feb. 10, 1965	John Johnston	Film locations manager	Jackson
Feb. 11, 1920	Louis Hugh Wilson, Jr.	Military leader-MOH recipient	Brandon
Feb. 11, 1940	John "Big Bad" Smitty	Bluesman	Vicksburg
Feb. 11, 1966	Eleni Matos	Opera singer	Jackson
Feb. 11, 1979	Brandy (Norwood)	R&B singer-actress	McComb
Feb. 12, 1944	Moe Bandy	Country music singer/songwriter	Meridian
Feb. 12, 1955	Chet Lemon	Sports: major league baseball	Jackson
Feb. 13, 1874	Ira C. Welborn (d.)	Medal of Honor recipient	Mico (Shady Grove)
Feb. 13, 1931	D. Clayton James	Author-biographer	Winchester, KY
Feb. 14, 1917	Robert P. McHugh (d.)	Journalist	Cedar Rapids, IA
Feb. 14, 1921	Richard D. McRae, Sr.	CEO-philanthropist	Jackson
Feb. 14, 1928	Jerome F. Leavell	Educator-attorney-writer	Blue Mountain
Feb. 14, 1928	Jack Lucas	Medal of Honor recipient	Plymouth, NC
Feb. 14, 1937	Magic Sam (d.)	Blues singer/guitarist	Grenada
Feb. 14, 1941	Cliff Freeman	Advertising executive/creator	Vicksburg
Feb. 14, 1973	Steve McNair	Sports: college-pro football player	Mount Olive
Feb. 15, 1905	Hal Lee (d.)	Sports: major league baseball	Ludlow
Feb. 15, 1957	Cheryl Prewitt	Miss America (1980)	Ackerman
Feb. 16, 1895	Charles Graham (d.)	Actor (silent screen)	Carthage
Feb. 16, 1905	Leslie Vaughn Rush (d.)	Medical pioneering physician	Meridian
Feb. 16, 1944	Richard Ford	Writer-novelist	Jackson
Feb. 16, 1975	Don Jeffcoat	Actor (TV)	Gulfport
Feb. 17, 1908	Walter Lanier "Red" Barber (d.)	Sportscaster	Columbus
Feb. 17, 1910	William Hollingsworth (d.)	Artist: painter	Jackson
Feb. 17, 1939	Mary Ann Mobley	Miss America (1959)-actress	Biloxi
Feb. 17, 1944	Richard E. Holmes	History-making physician	Starkville
Feb. 17, 1951	Steve Douglas	Musician (country & rock)	Greenville
Feb. 18, 1902	Garry Owen (d.)	Actor	Brookhaven
Feb. 19, 1945	Clifton Taulbert	Writer	Glen Allan
Feb. 19, 1952	Jimmy Johnson	Cartoonist	Lanett, AL
Feb. 20, 1935	Ben H. Douglas	Scientist-professor-writer	Sontag
Feb. 20, 1935	Ellen Gilchrist	Writer	Vicksburg
Feb. 21, 1918	Frank E. Smith (d.)	Politician-writer	Sidon
Feb. 21, 1941	Edward O. Fritts	President/CEO of the NAB	Cape Giradeau, MO
Feb. 22, 1945	Mike Starnes	Corporate CEO	Baton Rouge, LA
Feb. 22, 1968	Daron Jenkins	Sports: former Harlem Globetrotter	Mendenhall
Feb. 23, 1933	Lee Calhoun (d.)	Olympic Champion (1956 & 1960)	Laurel
Feb. 23, 1936	S. Gale Denley	Journalist-publisher-professor	Coffeeville
Feb. 23, 1944	Johnny Winter	Musician; blues guitarist	Leland
Feb. 25, 1954	Tim Floyd	Sports: college/pro coach	Hattiesburg
Feb. 26, 1938	Brendon Boone	Actor (TV)	Meridian
Feb. 27, 1923	A.C. "Butch" Lambert (d.)	Sports: referee official	Holcut
Mar. 01, 1841	Blanche K. Bruce (d.)	Politician (historical figure)	Virginia
Mar. 01, 1912	Walter Davis (d.)	Musician: early blues pianist	Grenada
Mar. 01, 1928	Willie Mitchell	Musician-composer	Ashland
Mar. 01, 1952	Nevada Barr	Novelist: mystery writer	California
Mar. 02, 1952	Will Primos	Entrepreneur-inventor	Jackson
Mar. 03, 1938	Willie Chambers	with Chamber Bros. rock group	Flora
Mar. 03, 1945	Hattie Winston	Actress	Greenville
Mar. 05, 1947	Eddie Hodges	Actor	Hattiesburg
Mar. 05, 1952	Dorree Cooper	Movie set designer-artist	New Orleans, LA
Mar. 06, 1863	Belle Kearney (d.)	Feminist-writer-state senator	near Flora
Mar. 06, 1895	Walter "Furry" Lewis (d.)	Blues singer/guitarist	Greenwood
Mar. 06, 1906	William T. Brannon	Novelist: mystery writer	Pachuta
Mar. 06, 1936	Marion S. Berry, Jr.	former Mayor of Washington, DC	Itta Bena
Mar. 06, 1944	Mary Wilson	Soul singer (with the Supremes)	Greenville

Famous & Notable Mississippians Listed by Birth Date

BIRTH DATE	NAME	PROFESSION(S)	PLACE OF BIRTH
Mar. 07, 1889	Ben Ames Williams (d.)	Novelist-writer	Macon
Mar. 07, 1908	Oseola McCarty (d.)	Phllanthropist-humanitarian	Hattiesburg
Mar. 08, 1892	"Mississippi" John Hurt (d.)	Blues singer/guitarist	Teoc
Mar. 08, 1933	James A. Autry	Writer-business consultant	Benton County
Mar. 08, 1959	Anna Reeves	Spoof heart failure ro archery	Winona
Mar. 09, 1936	Mickey Gilley	Country music singer/pianist	Natchez
Mar. 09, 1969	Mahmoud Abdul-Rauf	Sports: pro basketball player	Gulfport
Mar. 11, 1908	Sonny Boy Williamson II (d.)	Early bluesman	Glendora
Mar. 12, 1945	George Jackson	R&B/soul/pop songwriter	Indianola
Mar. 12, 1954	Jim McCafferty	Writer-attorney	Tupelo
Mar. 13, 1926	Phillip Martin	Indian Chief-entrepreneur	Philadelphia, MS
Mar. 13, 1952	William Beckwith	Artist: sculptor	Greenville
Mar. 13, 1964	Will Clark	Sports: college/pro baseball player	New Orleans, LA
Mar. 14, 1977	Treg Thomas	Sports: college football player	Pascagoula
Mar. 15, 1917	Woodie Assaf	Broadcaster: TV weatherman	McComb
Mar. 16, 1904	Buddy Myer (d.)	Sports: major league baseball	Ellisville
Mar. 16, 1932	Don Blasingame	Sports: major league baseball	Corinth
Mar. 16, 1955	Wyatt Waters	Artist: watercolorist	Brookhaven
Mar. 17, 1901	Turner Catledge (d.)	Journalist	near Ackerman
Mar. 17, 1915	Harry Basch	Actor (Films & TV)	Greenville
Mar. 17, 1933	Myrlie Evers-Williams	former Chariwoman of the NAACP	Vicksburg
Mar. 17, 1942	Doug Hutton	Sports: basketball player/coach	Bolton
Mar. 17, 1943	Jim Weatherly	Pop-country songwriter/singer	Pontotoc
Mar. 17, 1949	Walt Grayson	Broadcaster: TV weatherman-writer	Greenville
Mar. 17, 1955	Paul Overstreet	Country music songwriter/singer	Newton
Mar. 18, 1928	Peggy Dow	Actress	Columbia
Mar. 18, 1938	Charley Pride	Country music singer	Sledge
Mar. 19, 1908	Gerald Walker (d.)	Sports: major league baseball	Gulfport
Mar. 19, 1949	Archie Manning	Sports: college/pro football player	Drew
Mar. 21, 1893	Bo Carter (d.)	Early bluesman	Bolton
Mar. 21, 1902	Eddie "Son" House (d.)	Legendary early bluesman	Riverton
Mar. 21, 1930	Otis Spann (d.)	Blues pianist/singer	Jackson
Mar. 21, 1933	Crawford Mims	Sports: college football player	Carroll County
Mar. 21, 1953	Greg Harkins	Craftsman: chairmaker	Jackson
Mar. 21, 1965	Cynthia Lynn Geary	Actress	Jackson
Mar. 23, 1944	George "Boomer" Scott	Sports: major league baseball	Greenville
Mar. 24, 1926	Jimmie McDowell	Sports journalist	Brookhaven
Mar. 24, 1941	Jerry H. Booth (d.)	Scientist (physicist)-gov'ment service	Mathiston
Mar. 24, 1961	Jim Gallagher Jr.	Sports: pro golfer	Pennsylvania
Mar. 25, 1936	Larry Gordon	Movie producer-CEO	Yazoo City
Mar. 26, 1908	Mary Angie Douglass (d.)	Administrator-secretary	X-Prairie
Mar. 26, 1911	Tennessee Williams (d.)	Dramatist	Columbus
Mar. 26, 1917	Rufus Thomas	R&B singer/songwriter	Cayce
Mar. 26, 1966	Wesley Walls	Sports: pro football player	Batesville
Mar. 27, 1860	John W. Heard (d.)	Medal of Honor recipient	Woodstock (now Money)
Mar. 27, 1932	Little Junior Parker (d.)	Blues singer/musician	Clarksdale
Mar. 27, 1954	Mary Carol Miller	Writer-physician	Greenwood
Mar. 28, 1948	Milan B. Williams	Musician: keyboardist	Okolona
Mar. 30, 1932	Luigi Zaninelli	Music composer-professor	Raritan, NJ
Mar. 31, 1940	Charles C. Bennett	Movie set designer	Independence, LA
Mar. 31, 1950	Louisa Dixon	Novelist	Stanford, CT
Apr. 01, 1897	Lucille Bogan (d.)	Blues singer	Amory
Apr. 02, 1912	James D. Slaton (d.)	Medal of Honor recipient	Laurel
Apr. 02, 1946	Ralph Null	Floral designer	Lauderdale
Apr. 04, 1915	"Muddy Waters" (d.)	Legendary bluesman	Rolling Fork
Apr. 04, 1941	Major Lance (d.)	Soul singer	Winstonville
Apr. 04, 1972	William Pittman II	Sports: pro rodeo champion	Birmingham, AL
Apr. 06, 1917	"Big" Walter Horton (d.)	Blues harmonica player	Horn Lake
Apr. 06, 1942	Charles Wright	Soul/funk singer	Clarksdale
Apr. 07, 1935	Hodding Carter III	Journalist-government service	New Orleans, LA
Apr. 07, 1947	Grady Howell, Jr.	Historian-writer	Biloxi
Apr. 08, 1901	Gavin Gordon (d.)	Actor	Chicora
Apr. 08, 1960	Greg Iles	Novelist	Stuttgart, Germany
Apr. 09, 1909	Claude Passeau	Sports: major league baseball	Waynesboro

Famous & Notable Mississippians Listed by Birth Date

BIRTH DATE	NAME	PROFESSION(S)	PLACE OF BIRTH
Apr. 09, 1930	James F. Brieger	Author-researcher	Newton County
Apr. 11, 1935	Anne Carsley	Novelist	Jackson
Apr. 11, 1939	Luther "Guitar Jr." Johnson	Blues singer/guitarist	Itta Bena
Apr. 12, 1895	S.B. "Sam" Vick (d.)	Sports: major league baseball	Batesville
Apr. 12, 1909	Eric McNair (d.)	Sports: major league baseball	Meridian
Apr. 12, 1917	"Hound Dog" Taylor (d.)	Blues singer/guitarist	Natchez
Apr. 12, 1922	Carolyn Bennett Patterson	Journalist-writer	Kosciusko
Apr. 12, 1925	Prentiss Barnes	Singer-Rock and Roll pioneer	Magnolia
Apr. 12, 1937	Jim Ritchie	Writer-storyteller	Brookhaven
Apr. 12, 1976	Gary "Turk" McGill	Sports: high school football player	Taylorsville
Apr. 13, 1909	Eudora Welty	Writer-novelist	Jackson
Apr. 13, 1940	Lester Chambers	with the Chambers Bros. rock group	Flora
Apr. 13, 1944	Charles Burnett	Film director	Vicksburg
Apr. 14, 1939	Mike McGregor (d.)	Craftsman: jeweler	Tibbs
Apr. 14, 1958	Peggy Gillom	Sports: college basketball player	Abbeville
Apr. 15, 1945	Robert Hubbard	Photographer-writer	Dayton, OH
Apr. 16, 1929	John O. Emmerich, Jr. (d.)	Journalist-newspaper owner	McComb
Apr. 16, 1937	Artie White	Blues singer	Vicksburg
Apr. 17, 1926	Sam Carr	Musician: blues drummer	Friar's Point
Apr. 17, 1939	Lynda Lee Mead	Miss America (1960)	New Orleans, LA
Apr. 18, 1893	Helen Carloss (d.)	History-making attorney	Yazoo City
Apr. 18, 1897	Edwin Phillips Granberry (d.)	Cartoonist-writer	Meridian
Apr. 18, 1910	Jamie L. Whitten (d.)	Politician: U.S. Congressman	Cascilla
Apr. 18, 1938	Robert C. Khayat	Educator-Chancellor of UM	Moss Point
Apr. 18, 1956	Eric Roberts	Actor	Biloxi
Apr. 19, 1908	Owen Cooper (d.)	Industrialist-religious leader	Vicksburg
Apr. 19, 1915	Harry "Popeye" Craft (d.)	Sports: major league baseball	Ellisville
Apr. 19, 1966	Randolph Keys	Sports: pro basketball player	Collins
Apr. 21, 1922	Mundell Lowe	Musician: jazz guitarist/composer	Laurel
Apr. 21, 1948	Paul Davis	Singer-songwriter-producer	Meridian
Apr. 22, 1925	James H. Diamond (d.)	Medal of Honor recipient	New Orleans, LA
Apr. 22, 1938	Lloyd Wells	Musician: jazz guitarist	Gulfport
Apr. 22, 1949	Spencer Haywood	Sports: pro basketball player	Silver City
Apr. 23, 1942	Barry Hannah	Novelist	Meridian
Apr. 23, 1969	Bryon Thames	Actor	Jackson
Apr. 24, 1807	J.F.H. Claiborne (d.)	Historian	Natchez
Apr. 25, 1923	Albert King (d.)	Blues-R&B-soul guitarist	Indianola
Apr. 25, 1932	Davis K. Mortensen	Business executive	Charles City, IA
Apr. 25, 1936	Freddie Little	Sports: pro boxing champ	Picayune
Apr. 25, 1940	O.B. McClinton (d.)	Country music singer	Senatobia
Apr. 26, 1924	Theodore "Teddy" Edwards	Jazz saxophonist/arranger	Jackson
Apr. 27, 1943	Freddie Waits (d.)	Musician: jazz drummer	Jackson
Apr. 28, 1953	Fred Knobloch	Country music singer/songwriter	Jackson
Apr. 29, 1934	Otis Rush	Blues singer/guitarist	Philadelphia, MS
Apr. ??, 1887	Charley Patton (d.)	Legendary blues singer	Edwards
May 01, 1900	Joseph Paul Treen (d.)	Inventor	Purvis
May 01, 1921	Jake W. Lindsey, Sr. (d.)	Medal of Honor recipient	Isnay, AL
May 01, 1945	T. Bubba Bechtol	Country comedian/comic	Biloxi
May 01, 1953	Glen Ballard	Songwriter-record producer	Natchez
May 02, 1933	Glenn Honeycutt	Rockabilly singer	Belzoni
May 02, 1962	Ty Herndon	Country music singer	Meridian
May 03, 1950	Hollis Pippin (d.)	Choreographer-director	Jackson
May 04, 1938	Tyrone Davis	Soul singer	Greenville
May 04, 1979	Lance Bass	Singer w/the group 'N Sync	Laurel
May 05, 1922	Phil Gordon	Actor	Meridian
May 05, 1929	J.B. Lenoir (d.)	Blues singer/musician	Monticello
May 05, 1934	Ace Cannon	Musician: saxophonist	Grenada
May 05, 1942	Tammy Wynette (d.)	Country music singer	Tremont
May 06, 1909	Johnny Vaught	Sports: college football coach	Olney, TX
May 07, 1939	Jimmy Ruffin	Soul singer	Collinsville
May 07, 1943	Thelma Houston	Soul singer	Leland
May 08, 1911	Robert Johnson (d.)	Legendary bluesman	Hazlehurst
May 08, 1944	Jack Butler	Writer	Alligator
May 08, 1952	Beth Henley	Playwright-actress	Jackson

Famous & Notable Mississippians Listed by Birth Date

BIRTH DATE	NAME	PROFESSION(S)	PLACE OF BIRTH
May 09, 1939	Ralph Boston	Olympic Champion (1960)	Laurel
May 09, 1951	Terry Ewert	TV producer	Las Vegas, NV
May 10, 1936	Jean F. Simmons	Educator	Monroe, LA
May 10, 1956	Tim Ellis	Sports: college football player	Louisville, MS
May 11, 1895	William Grant Still (d.)	Musician-composer	Woodville
May 12, 1926	Thomas "Shorty" McWilliams (d.)	Sports: college/pro football player	Meridian
May 13, 1947	Charles "Chuck" Gordon	Movie producer/director	Belzoni
May 14, 1814	Martin Freeman (d.)	Medal of Honor recipient	Stettinn, Germany
May 14, 1885	William Alexander Percy (d.)	Poet-attorney	Greenville
May 14, 1918	James D. Hardy	Pioneering surgeon	Birmingham, AL
May 14, 1949	Paul T. Brown	Photographer-outdoorsman	Greenwood
May 14, 1958	Julie Kaye Fanton	TV-movie set decorator	Oxford
May 14, 1961	Reggie Collier	Sports: college football player	D'Iberville
May 15, 1935	Andy Anderson	R&R singer-musician	Memphis, TN
May 15, 1970	Cory Philpot	Sports: pro football player	Savannah, GA
May 17, 1903	James "Cool Papa" Bell (d.)	Sports: pro baseball player	Starkville
May 17, 1939	Sandra Polanski	Musician: pianist	Grenada
May 17, 1966	Danny Manning	Sports: pro basketball player	Hattiesburg
May 19, 1934	Bobby Bryant (d.)	Musician: jazz trumpetist	Hattiesburg
May 20, 1884	James J. Madison (d.)	Medal of Honor recipient	Jersey City, NJ
May 20, 1949	Elizabeth Wolfe	Artist: painter/sculptor	Jackson
May 20, 1954	Jimmy Henderson	Jazz musician	Jackson
May 21, 1889	Frances Jones Gaither (d.)	Novelist-writer	Tennessee
May 22, 1935	James L. Seawright, Jr.	Artist: sculptor-educator	Jackson
May 22, 1964	Marcus Dupree	Sports: pro football player	Philadelphia, MS
May 25, 1955	David Blankenhorn	Writer	Jackson
May 25, 1967	Ruthie Bolton-Holifield	Olympic Champion (1996)	McLain
May 26, 1912	Tellis "T.B." Ellis (d.)	Sports: college athletic director	Vicksburg
May 27, 1913	Willie Best (d.)	Actor	Sunflower
May 27, 1921	Jack H. Oakman	Movie expert/collector	Panther Burn
May 27, 1954	Jackie Slater	Sports: pro football player	Jackson
May 28, 1916	Walker Percy (d.)	Writer-physician	Birmingham, AL
May 28, 1953	Jeff Bower	Sports: college football coach/player	Roswell, GA
May 29, 1965	Charlie Hayes	Sports: major league baseball	Hattiesburg
May 30, 1833	Reuben W. Millsaps (d.)	College founder	near Hazlehurst
May 31, 1939	Al Young	Writer-musician	Ocean Springs
June 01, 1896	Elsie McWilliams (d.)	Songwriter	Harperville
June 01, 1937	Morgan Freeman	Actor	Memphis, TN
June 03, 1808	Jefferson Davis (d.)	President of the Confederacy	Todd County, KY
June 03, 1924	Jimmy Rogers (d.)	Blues singer/guitarist	Ruleville
June 05, 1982	Michael Goggin	Top student: perfect ACT & SAT	Hattiesburg
June 06, 1902	Jimmie Linceford (d.)	Big band/orchestra leader	Fulton
June 08, 1952	Jim Dollarhide	Film Producer	Greenwood
June 09, 1902	Skip James (d.)	Blues guitarist/singer	Bentonia
June 09, 1908	Paul Gregory (d.)	Sports (baseball): coach/pro player	Tomnolen
June 09, 1930	Evelyn McPhail (d.)	Political party official	Bay St. Louis
June 09, 1951	Dave Parker	Sports: major league baseball	Calhoun City
June 10, 1911	"Howlin' Wolf" (d.)	Blues singer	West Point
June 10, 1971	Brad Edwards	Sports statistician	Jackson
June 11, 1894	Eugene Butler (d.)	Journalist-editor	Starkville
June 12, 1894	Evelyn Allen Hammett (d.)	Educator-writer	Jefferson County
June 12, 1904	Willie Foster (d.)	Sports: pro basketball player/coach	Calvert, TX
June 12, 1927	Jane Reid-Petty (d.)	Actress-director-writer	Meridian
June 12, 1932	Charlie Feathers (d.)	Rockabilly singer/songwriter	Myrtle
June 12, 1964	Alyce Alston	Magazine publisher	Jackson
June 13, 1913	Charlotte Capers (d.)	Writer-administrator	Columbia, TN
June 13, 1964	Jennifer Gillom	Sports: college/pro basketball	Abbeville
June 14, 1941	John Armistead	Novelist: mystery writer	Mobile, AL
June 15, 1919	Van T. Barfoot	Medal of Honor recipient	near Edinburg
June 16, 1927	George Ellis Johnson	Business executive	Richton
June 16, 1947	Tom "Bones" Malone	Musician (trombonist)/arranger	Hattiesburg
June 16, 1970	Rett Crowder	Sports: amateur golfer	New Orleans, LA
June 17, 1966	Fred Barnett	Sports: pro football player	Shelby
June 19, 1879	Martha Mattox (d.)	Actress	Natchez

Famous & Notable Mississippians Listed by Birth Date

BIRTH DATE	NAME	PROFESSION(S)	PLACE OF BIRTH
June 19, 1939	Al Wilson	Soul singer/drummer	Meridian
June 19, 1952	Felder Rushing	Writer-horticulture agent	Indianola
June 20, 1897	Charlemae Rollins (d.)	Librarian-writer	Yazoo City
June 20, 1933	Ben Peters	Country-pop songwriter	Greenville
June 20, 1948	Phil Hardwick	Writer-administrator	Mendenhall
June 23, 1904	Willie Mae Ford Smith (d.)	Gospel blues singer	Rolling Fork
June 23, 1910	Milt Hinton	Big band bassist	Vicksburg
June 23, 1910	Bilbo "Mule" Monaghan (d.)	Sports: pro football player/coach	Amory
June 24, 1934	Jack Bass	Writer-professor	North, SC
June 24, 1955	Sam Haskell	Entertainment executive	Mobile, AL
June 25, 1891	Ray Lum (d.)	Storyteller-mule trader	Rocky Springs
June 25, 1933	James Meredith	Civil Rights activist	Kosciusko
June 26, 1893	Big Bill Broonzy (d.)	Legendary bluesman	Scott
June 26, 1906	B.J. Barrier, Jr. (d.)	Aviation pioneer	Yazoo City
June 26, 1951	Johnny Barranco	Commercial jingle singer	Bossier City, LA
June 27, 1921	Frances E. Neal	Actress	Carrollton
June 27, 1947	Frank Williams (d.)	Gospel singer-group founder	Smithdale
June 27, 1954	Donna Hild Russell	Mrs. America (1985)	Brandon
June 28, 1910	Ruth Attaway (d.)	Actress	Greenville
June 28, 1911	Thalia Mara	Professional dancer	Chicago, IL
June 28, 1915	David "Honeyboy" Edwards	Blues singer/guitarist	Shaw
June 28, 1961	Jeff Malone	Sports: pro basketball player	Macon, GA
June 29, 1924	T. Tommy Cutrer (d.)	Grand Ole Opry announcer	Osyka
June 30, 1918	Jo Foxworth	Advertising CEO-writer	Tylertown
June 30, 1930	W.C. Gordon	Sports: college coach	Nashville, TN
July 01, 1915	Willie Dixon (d.)	Blues singer/songwriter	Vicksburg
July 01, 1926	Frank Trippett (d.)	Journalist	Columbus
July 01, 1935	James Cotton	Blues harmonica player	Dundee
July 01, 1939	Delaney Bramlett	Rock singer	Pontotoc County
July 01, 1959	Mac McAnally	Country music songwriter/singer	Belmont
July 02, 1922	Aaron Henry (d.)	Civil Rights leader/activist	Clarksdale
July 02, 1925	Medger Evers (d.)	Civil Rights leader/activist	Decatur
July 02, 1936	Joseph W. Newman	Inventor	Mobile, AL
July 02, 1944	Mary Ann Wells	Journalist-writer	Agricola
July 03, 1910	Pete Fountain	Musician: clarinetist	Bay St. Louis
July 03, 1943	Ken Lindsay	Sports: club golf pro	Gadsden, AL
July 06, 1889	Larry Semon (d.)	Actor & film director	West Point
July 06, 1970	Antonio Harvey	Sports: pro basketball player	Pascagoula
July 06, 1970	Torrance Small	Sports: college/pro football player	Tampa, FL
July 06, 19??	Symba Smith	Actress	Gulfport
July 07, 1913	"Pinetop" Perkins	Musician: blues pianist	Belzoni
July 07, 1915	Ruth Ford	Actress	Hazlehurst
July 07, 1951	Mike Henderson	Rock bass player	Yazoo City
July 08, 1846	John Allen (d.)	Politician (historical figure)	Tishomingo County
July 08, 1944	Jaimoe Jai Johanny	Musician: rock percussionist	Gulfport
July 09, 1935	Frank Wright (d.)	Musician: jazz tenor saxophonist	Grenada
July 09, 1944	Steve Blailock	Musician: jazz guitarist	McComb
July 09, 1951	Larry Brown	Author-playwright	Yocona
July 09, 1980	Dicenzo Miller	Sports: high school/college football	Eupora
July 10, 1933	"Jumpin' " Gene Simmons	R&B singer/songwriter	Tupelo
July 11, 1956	Sela Ward	Actress	Meridian
July 12, 1857	George Ohr (d.)	Artist: potter	Biloxi
July 12, 1920	Beah Richards (d.)	Actress	Vicksburg
July 12, 1921	Ellen Douglas	Novelist-short story writer	Natchez
July 12, 1934	Michael Jabaley	Hand surgeon (plastic surgeon)	Copperhill, TN
July 12, 1944	John Maxwell	Playwright	Jackson
July 13, 1964	Paul Thorn	Songwriter/singer- pro boxer	Kenosha, WI
July 14, 1893	Spencer Williams, Jr. (d.)	Actor-comic	Vidalia, LA
July 14, 1934	John N. Palmer, Sr.	Corporate CEO	Corinth
July 14, 1974	Eric Dampier	Sports: college/pro basketball	Newhebron
July 15, 1932	Willie Cobbs	Bluesman	Smale, AR
July 15, 1940	Johnny Sea	Country music singer/songwriter	Gulfport
July 15, 1959	Sammy Winder	Sports: pro football player	Madison
July 16, 1862	Ida Bell Wells-Barnett (d.)	Civil Right pioneer	Holly Springs

Famous & Notable Mississippians Listed by Birth Date

BIRTH DATE	NAME	PROFESSION(S)	PLACE OF BIRTH
July 16, 1939	Denise LaSalle	Soul singer	Leflore County
July 17, 1973	Eric Moulds	Sports: college/pro football player	Lucedale
July 18, 1924	Will D. Campbell	Minister-writer-activist	East Fork
July 18, 1976	Robert Fairley	Sports: former Harlem Globetrotter	Lucedale
July 19, 1889	Frances "Fannye" A. Cook (d.)	Research biologist-writer	Crystal Springs
July 19, 1921	Elizabeth Spencer	Novelist	Carrollton
July 20, 1935	Richard E. Mayo	Administrator for NASA	Meridian
July 20, 1951	Blaine Baggett	TV producer/writer	Horn Lake
July 21, 1947	Billie Jean Young	Actress-playwright-poet	Pennington, AL
July 22, 1938	Daniel P. Jordan	Historian-scholar	Philadelphia, MS
July 22, 1940	Thomas Wayne (d.)	R&R-Pop singer	Batesville
July 24, 1947	Roy M. Wheat (d.)	Medal of Honor recipient	Moselle
July 24, 1955	Brad Watson	Writer-professor	Meridian
July 24, 1961	Laurie E. Parker	Writer-crafts artist	Bruce
July 25, 1954	Walter Payton (d.)	Sports: pro/college football player	Columbia
July 26, 1905	Sam Leslie (d.)	Sports: major league baseball	Moss Point
July 26, 1930	Little Howlin' Wolf	Bluesman	Florence
July 27, 1915	Margaret Walker Alexander (d.)	Writer-professor	Birmingham, AL
July 27, 1944	Bobbie Gentry	Pop/Country singer/songwriter	Chickasaw County
July 27, 1959	Hugh Green	Sports: college football player	Natchez
July 28, 1930	"Junior" Kimbrough (d.)	Bluesman	Hudsonville
July 28, 1946	Mike Taylor	Sports: amateur golfer	New Orleans, LA
July 30, 1854	John Sharp Williams (d.)	Politician (historical figure)	Memphis, TN
July 30, 1936	Billy Stacey	Sports: pro football player	Winona
July 30, 1940	"Big" Jack Johnson	Musician: blues guitarist	Lambert
July 31, 1918	Henry "Hank" Jones	Musician: jazz pianist	Vicksburg
July 31, 1947	Eugenia Ann Talbott	Artist: painter	Pascagoula
July 31, 1949	Louis Westerfield (d.)	Educator-attorney	Kemper County
July 31, 1950	Richard Wiman	Writer-minister	Brandon
Aug. 01, 1944	Ben Nelson	PGA Tour golf official	Canton
Aug. 01, 1944	Larry A. Thompson	Movie producer-impresario	Clarksdale
Aug. 02, 1935	Hank Cochran	Country music songwriter/singer	Isola
Aug. 02, 1939	Charles Wilson	Novelist: mystery writer	Kennett, MO
Aug. 03, 1901	John C. Stennis (d.)	U.S. Senator	Kemper County
Aug. 03, 1925	Joe Frank Sanderson (d.)	Business executive	Jackson
Aug. 03, 1940	Lance Alworth	Sports: pro football player	Houston, TX
Aug. 03, 1946	Howard Bahr	Writer-historian-professor	Meridian
Aug. 04, 1919	James Blackwood	with the Blackwood Bros. Quartet	Ackerman
Aug. 04, 1924	Leedell W. Neyland	Writer	Gloster
Aug. 04, 1932	Eddie Merrins	Sports: golf pro & pro golfer	Meridian
Aug. 04, 1938	Hayes Jones	Olympic Champion (1964)	Starkville
Aug. 05, 1920	G.V. "Sonny" Montgomery	U.S. Congressman	Meridian
Aug. 06, 1924	Henry "Skeets" McWilliams	Musician: jazz guitarist	Jackson
Aug. 06, 1926	Rob't. H. "Ace" Cleveland, Sr. (d.)	Journalist-publicist	Hattiesburg
Aug. 06, 1945	Valerie Jaudon	Artist: contemporary painter	Greenville
Aug. 06, 1962	Pamela Nail	Mrs. World (1988)	Crawfordsville, IN
Aug. 06, 1968	Lisa Stewart	TV host-country music singer	Louisville, MS
Aug. 07, 1906	Ernestine Wade (d.)	Actress-comic	Jackson
Aug. 08, 1946	John E. Hall	Medical research scientist	Milo, WV
Aug. 09, 1884	John Sidney McCain (d.)	Military leader: Admiral	Teoc
Aug. 10, 1814	John Clifford Pemberton (d.)	Military leader/historical figure	Philadelphia, PA
Aug. 10, 1938	Beverly Lowry	Writer	Memphis, TN
Aug. 10, 1939	Paul Brummett	Inventor-scientist	Jackson
Aug. 11, 1944	Frederick W. Smith	Businessman-entrepreneur	Marks
Aug. 12, 1951	Norris Weese (d.)	Sports: college-pro football player	Baton Rouge, LA
Aug. 12, 1964	Susan Diane Akin	Miss America (1986)	Meridian
Aug. 13, 1955	Mulgrew Miller	Musician: jazz pianist	Greenwood
Aug. 13, 1975	Trent Pulliam	Sports; former Harlem Globetrotter	Houston, MS
Aug. 14, 1917	Jim Buck Ross (d.)	Miss. agriculture commissioner	Pelahatchie
Aug. 15, 1925	James Saggus (d.)	Journalist	Alexandria, LA
Aug. 15, 1930	Jackie Brenston (d.)	History-making singer	Clarksdale
Aug. 15, 1973	Kris Mangum	Sports: college/pro football player	Magee
Aug. 16, 1932	Bob Saxton	Musician: country & jazz guitarist	Newton County
Aug. 16, 1933	Stuart A. Roosa (d.)	Astronaut-businessman	Durango, CO

The Ultimate Reference on the State

Famous & Notable Mississippians Listed by Birth Date

BIRTH DATE	NAME	PROFESSION(S)	PLACE OF BIRTH
Aug. 19, 1945	Joseph P. Seawright	History-making designer	Greenwood
Aug. 19, 1948	Gerald McRaney	Actor	Collins
Aug. 20, 1891	Marietta Eichelberger (d.)	Scientist-medical researcher	Macon
Aug. 20, 1920	J.T. "Blondy" Black (d.)	Sports: college/pro football	Philadelphia, MS
Aug. 21, 1867	Wilbur Higby (d.)	Actor (silent screen)	Meridian
Aug. 21, 1911	Frederic Frances Mellen (d.)	Geologist-writer	Starkville
Aug. 21, 1936	Mart Crowley	Playwright	Vicksburg
Aug. 21, 1951	Birney Imes	Photographer	Columbus
Aug. 22, 1910	Rod Brasfield (d.)	Country comedian	Smithville
Aug. 22, 1911	Doyle Blackwood (d.)	with the Blackwood Bros. Quartet	Ackerman
Aug. 22, 1917	John Lee Hooker	Legendary bluesman	Clarksdale
Aug. 23, 1901	Guy T. Bush (d.)	Sports: major league baseball	Aberdeen
Aug. 23, 1912	Mildred Wolfe	Artist: painter	Celina, OH
Aug. 23, 1939	Lewis Nordan	Novelist	Itta Bena
Aug. 24, 1905	Arthur "Big Boy" Crudup (d.)	blues singer/songwriter	Forest
Aug. 24, 1921	Janos Radvanyi	Professor-environmentalist	Hungary
Aug. 24, 1942	Joe Chambers	with the Chambers Bros. rock group	Scott County
Aug. 24, 1956	Purvis Short	Sports: college/pro basketball	Hattiesburg
Aug. 25, 1864	Dunbar Rowland (d.)	Historian-writer-gov'ment official	Oakland, MS
Aug. 26, 1839	Hernando De Soto Money (d.)	Politician (historical figure)	Holmes County
Aug. 27, 1905	Frederick O'Neal (d.)	Actor	Brooksville
Aug. 27, 1909	Lester Willis Young (d.)	Jazz musician/composer	Woodville
Aug. 27, 1941	Bernie Ebbers	Corporate CEO	Canada
Aug. 28, 1929	George Baker Price	Military leader	Laurel
Aug. 28, 1934	Louis Baloni	Business executive	Shaw
Aug. 28, 1934	Bruce H. Brady (d.)	Artist: sculptor-outdoorsman	Brookhaven
Aug. 28, 1982	LeAnn Rimes	Country music singer	Pearl
Aug. 29, 1929	Richard "Dick" Armstrong (d.)	Journalist-editor	Jackson
Aug. 29, 1881	Pat Harrison (d.)	Politician (historical figure)	Crystal Springs
Aug. 29, 1938	Jim Majure (d.)	Novelist	Durant
Aug. 29, 1956	Steve Yarbrough	Writer-professor	Indianola
Aug. 31, 1970	James Robinson	Sports: pro basketball player	Jackson
Sept. 01, 1927	Wyatt Cooper (d.)	Screenwriter-actor	Quitman
Sept. 01, 1933	Conway Twitty (d.)	Rock-Country superstar	Friar's Point
Sept. 01, 1954	Ben Williams	Sports: college/pro football player	Yazoo City
Sept. 01, 1985	Charlie Worsham	Musician: banjo podigy	Jackson
Sept. 03, 1939	Joe Frank Carollo	R&R singe/musician	Leland
Sept. 03, 1962	Dave Clark	Sports: major league baseball	Tupelo
Sept. 04, 1908	Richard Wright (d.)	History-making black novelist	Natchez
Sept. 04, 1918	Gerald Stanley Wilson	Musician: jazz trumpeter/arranger	Shelby
Sept. 04, 1920	Craig Claiborne (d.)	Food critic columnist	Sunflower
Sept. 04, 1920	Evelyn Gandy	History-making politician	Hattiesburg
Sept. 04, 1950	Frank White	Sports: major league baseball	Greenwood
Sept. 05, 1907	Sunnyland Slim (d.)	Musician: blues pianist	Vance
Sept. 05, 1911	John McCrady (d.)	Artist: painter	Canton
Sept. 05, 1963	Jeff Brantley	Sports: major league baseball	Birmingham, AL
Sept. 06, 1923	Marshall Bouldin III	Artist: portrait painter	Dundee
Sept. 06, 1925	Jimmy Reed (d.)	Blues singer	Dunleith
Sept. 06, 1942	Jamaa Fanaka	Movie director	Jackson
Sept. 07, 1933	Jim Brewer	Educator-founder MS Musician's HOF	Hattiesburg
Sept. 07, 1934	Little Milton	Blues singer/guitarist	Inverness
Sept. 07, 1947	L.C. Greenwood	Sports: pro football player	Canton
Sept. 07, 1974	Antonio McDyess	Sprots: pro basketball player	Quitman
Sept. 08, 1897	Jimmie Rodgers (d.)	Country music singer/songwriter	Meridian (Pine Springs)
Sept. 08, 1919	Arthur C. Guyton	Physician-writer-inventor	Oxford
Sept. 08, 1945	Lem Barney	Sports: pro football player	Gulfport
Sept. 08, 1970	Clarence Weatherspoon	Sports: pro basketball player	Crawford
Sept. 09, 1915	James E. "Buster" Poole (d.)	Sports: pro football player/coach	Gloster
Sept. 09, 1937	Sylvia Howell Krebs	Sports: high school basketball	Jackson
Sept. 10, 1847	John Roy Lynch (d.)	Politician-writer	Louisiana
Sept. 10, 1907	Alvin Childress (d.)	Actor-comic	Meridian
Sept. 10, 1918	L.T. Smith	Hi school football/basketball coach	Jackson
Sept. 11, 1904	William M. "Jazz" Gillum (d.)	Blues harmonica player	Indianola
Sept. 11, 1922	Charles Evers	Civil Rights leader/activist	Decatur

Famous & Notable Mississippians Listed by Birth Date

BIRTH DATE	NAME	PROFESSION(S)	PLACE OF BIRTH
Sept. 11, 1964	Ellis Rena Burks	Sports: major league baseball	Vicksburg
Sept. 12, 1852	Annie C. Peyton (d.)	College founder	Madison County
Sept. 12, 1884	Gus "Banjo Joe" Cannon (d.)	Early bluesman	Red Banks
Sept. 12, 1978	Romaro Miller	Sports: hi school/college football	Shannnon
Sept. 13, 1891	Olin Frances (d.)	Actor	Mooreville
Sept. 13, 1899	Henry Herschel Brickell (d.)	Literary critic	Senatobia
Sept. 13, 1939	Larry Speakes	Journalist-government service	Cleveland, MS
Sept. 13, 1943	Mildred D. Taylor	Writer	Jackson
Sept. 13, 1956	Richard Jess Brown, Jr.	Jazz musician	Jackson
Sept. 14, 1910	Lehman Engel (d.)	Conductor-composer	Jackson
Sept. 14, 1954	James C. "Butch" Rosser	Physician: pioneering surgeon	Rome
Sept. 15, 1921	James "Snooky" Pryor	Blues harmonica player	Lambert
Sept. 15, 1939	Ode Burrell	Sports: college/pro football player	Goodman
Sept. 15, 1940	Anne Moody	Writer-Civil Rights activist	Centreville
Sept. 15, 1956	Buddy Durr	Sports: pro archery	Isola
Sept. 15, 1962	Aubrey D. Matthews	Sports: pro football player	Moss Point
Sept. 16, 1925	B.B. King	Legendary bluesman	Itta Bena
Sept. 16, 1942	Rueben Anderson	History-making attorney/jurist	Jackson
Sept. 16, 1951	Prescilla D. Slade	Educator: college president	Shaw
Sept. 16, 1954	Wilbert N. Montgomery	Sports: college/pro football player	Greenville
Sept. 17, 1825	L.Q.C. Lamar (d.)	Statesman-jurist (historical figure)	Georgia
Sept. 17, 1900	Hughie Critz (d.)	Sports: major league baseball	Starkville
Sept. 17, 1931	Lenore L. Prather	History-making jurist	West Point
Sept. 17, 1954	Bobby Wallace	Sports: college football coach	Magnolia, AR
Sept. 18, 1929	Louis Myers (d.)	Blues guitarist/harp player	Byhalia
Sept. 18, 1930	Jack G. Hanson (d.)	Medal of Honor recipient	Escatawpa
Sept. 18, 1937	Dee Barton	Composer-conductor-musician	Houston, MS
Sept. 18, 1946	Charles L. Overby	Journalist-CEO	Jackson
Sept. 18, 1953	Carl Jackson	Country music songwriter	Louisville, MS
Sept. 19, 1921	Charlie Conerly (d.)	Sports: pro football player	Clarksdale
Sept. 19, 1944	Bucky Barrett	Musician: jazz guitarist	Pensacola, FL
Sept. 20, 1933	Walter Reed	Sports: coach & administrator	Meridian
Sept. 20, 1952	Dot Murphy	Sports: basketball/football coach	Jackson
Sept. 21, 1975	Kevin Etheridge	Top Student: perfect ACT score	Flowood
Sept. 21, 1967	Faith Hill	Country music singer	Star
Sept. 21, 1977	Kimberly R. Smith	Top student: perfect ACT score	Fort Worth, TX
Sept. 22, 1790	Augustus B. Longstreet (d.)	Educator-jurist-writer	Augusta, GA
Sept. 22, 1833	Stephen Dill Lee (d.)	Educator-state senator-CSA Gen.	Charleston, SC
Sept. 22, 1940	Thomas Harris	Novelist	Jackson, TN
Sept. 22, 1946	Charles W. Eagles	Historian-professor	Spartanburg, SC
Sept. 22, 1954	Vernon Perry	Sports: pro football player	Jackson
Sept. 23, 1867	John A. Lomax (d.)	Blues collector-archivist	Goodman
Sept. 23, 1938	Tom Lester	Actor	Jackson
Sept. 24, 1901	John Faulkner (d.)	Novelist-artist: painter	Ripley
Sept. 24, 1928	Kelly Brown (d.)	Actor	Jackson
Sept. 24, 1936	Jim Henson (d.)	Puppeteer	Greenville
Sept. 24, 1937	W.G. "Mickey" Holliman Jr.	Corporate CEO	Shuqualak
Sept. 24, 1941	Guy Hovis	Singer-entertainer	Tupelo
Sept. 24, 1954	Patrick Kelly (d.)	Fashion designer	Vicksburg
Sept. 24, 1964	Rafael Palmeiro	Sports: college-pro baseball player	Havana, Cuba
Sept. 25, 1897	William Faulkner (d.)	Novelist-screenwriter	New Albany
Sept. 25, 1934	Paul Ott	Entertainer-conservationist	McComb
Sept. 25, 1936	Roosevelt "Booba" Barnes (d.)	Blues guitarist/singer	Longwood
Sept. 26, 1931	George Chambers	with the Chamber Bros. rock group	Flora
Sept. 27, 1827	Hiram Rhodes Revels (d.)	Politician (historical figure)	Fayetteville, NC
Sept. 27, 1890	Cid Ricketts Sumner (d.)	Novelist	Brookhaven
Sept. 27, 1912	Herbie Holmes (d.)	Orchestra/big band leader	Yazoo City
Sept. 27, 1966	Herbert Theriot	Rodeo World Champion	Franklin, LA
Sept. 28, 1890	Marie Atkinson Hull (d.)	Artist: painter	Summit
Sept. 28, 1926	Jerry Clower (d.)	Country humorist	East Fork
Sept. 28, 1946	Harold Cross	Historian	Ripley
Sept. 29, 1893	Hoyt B. Wooten (d.)	Broadcast pioneer	Coldwater
Sept. 29, 1895	Roscoe Turner (d.)	Aviation pioneer	Corinth
Sept. 29, 1903	Walter Anderson (d.)	Artist: potter	New Orleans, LA

Famous & Notable Mississippians Listed by Birth Date

BIRTH DATE	NAME	PROFESSION(S)	PLACE OF BIRTH
Sept. 29, 1935	Jerry Lee Lewis	R&R/country music singer	Ferriday, LA
Sept. 29, 1939	Frank Polanski	Musician: pianist	Kenosha, WI
Sept. 29, 1968	Brad Smith	member of Blind Melon rock group	Columbus
Sept. 30, 1897	David L. Cohn (d.)	Writer-essayist	Greenville
Sept. 30, 1958	Marty Stuart	Country music sing/songwriter	Philadelphia, MS
Sept. 30, 1982	Lacey Chabert	Actress	Purvis
Oct. 01, 1920	David Herbert Donald	Biographer-historian-professor	Goodman
Oct. 01, 1936	George Butler	Blues singer/musician	Hernando
Oct. 01, 1936	Stella Stevens	Actress	Yazoo City
Oct. 01, 1954	Gene Murphy	Sports: college football coach	Columbus
Oct. 02, 1886	B. Reeves Eason (d.)	Movie director/screenwriter	Friar's Point
Oct. 02, 1948	Chris LeDoux	Country music singer/songwriter	Biloxi
Oct. 03, 1900	Clay Hopper (d.)	Sports: pro baseball manager	Greenwood
Oct. 03, 1925	John Vincent Imbragulio (d.)	Record producer/label founder	Hattiesburg
Oct. 03, 1944	Jack Gregory	Sports: pro football player	Tupelo
Oct. 03, 1949	John Ramsey Miller	Novelist	Greenville
Oct. 03, 1951	Neil McGaughey (d.)	Mystery novelist-journalist	Natchez
Oct. 03, 1986	Shayon Ghosh	Top student: perfect ACT score	Ames, IA
Oct. 04, 1919	Junie Hovious (d.)	Sports: college football coach	Vicksburg
Oct. 05, 1882	William David (d.)	Actor (silent screen)	Vicksburg
Oct. 05, 1936	John H. Bryan Jr.	Corporate CEO	West Point
Oct. 06, 1902	Hoyt Lester Ming (d.)	Musician- songwriter	near Ackerman
Oct. 06, 1917	Fannie Lou Hamer (d.)	Civil Rights leader/activist	Montgomery County
Oct. 06, 1959	Dennis "Oil Can" Boyd	Sports: major league baseball	Meridian
Oct. 08, 1927	Patrick D. Smith	Novelist	Mendenhall
Oct. 08, 1955	Lonnie Pitchford (d.)	Blues musician	Lexington
Oct. 08, 1956	Pat Kirby	Country music singer/look-a-like	Tylertown
Oct. 08, 1959	Alice Haining	Actress	Jackson
Oct. 09, 1941	Trent Lott	Politician: U.S. Senator	Grenada
Oct. 10, 1966	Derrick McKey	Sports: pro basketball player	Meridian
Oct. 10, 1969	Brett Favre	Sports: pro football player	Pass Christian
Oct. 11, 1881	Stark Young (d.)	Drama critic-writer	Como
Oct. 11, 1922	Thomas Hal Phillips	Novelist-screenwriter	Corinth
Oct. 11, 1929	Jack Nelson	Journalist-writer	Biloxi
Oct. 12, 1922	Borden Deal (d.)	Writer	Pontotoc
Oct. 12, 1935	William Raspberry	Journalist	Okolona
Oct. 12, 1944	Forrest Lamar Cooper	Writer	Jackson
Oct. 13, 1907	Ethel Wright Mohamed (d.)	Artist: embroiderer	Fame
Oct. 13, 1926	Jesse Leroy Brown (d.)	History-making military aviator-hero	Hattiesburg
Oct. 13, 1947	Dorothy Moore	Pop/soul singer	Jackson
Oct. 13, 1962	Jerry Rice	Sports: college/pro football player	Crawford
Oct. 14, 1926	James "Son" Thomas (d.)	Blues musician-sculptor	Eden
Oct. 15, 1903	James Howell Street (d.)	Novelist-journalist	Lumberton
Oct. 15, 1928	John A. Pittman (d.)	Medal of Honor recipient	Carrollton
Oct. 16, 1903	"Big" Joe Williams (d.)	Blues singer/musician	Crawford
Oct. 17, 1928	Lerone Bennett, Jr.	Writer-journalist	Clarksdale
Oct. 17, 1937	David E. Harrison (d.)	Inventor	Mann, WV
Oct. 17, 1969	Joe Courtney	Sports: pro basketball player	Jackson
Oct. 18, 1906	Johnnie "Geechie" Temple (d.)	Bluesman	Canton
Oct. 20, 1826	James Z. George (d.)	Politician (historical figure)	Monroe County, GA
Oct. 21, 1925	Isaiah "Doctor" Ross (d.)	Blues guitarist/harpist	Tunica
Oct. 22, 1887	Hamilton Smith (d.)	Move director/screnwriter	Muskegon, MS
Oct. 22, 1913	Charles S. Thomas, Sr. (d.)	Sports: high school football coach	Winona
Oct. 22, 1916	Harry "The Hat" Walker (d.)	Sports: major league baseball	Pascagoula
Oct. 22, 1933	Donald H. Peterson	Astronaut	Winona
Oct. 22, 1947	Haley Barbour	Political party leader-attorney	Yazoo City
Oct. 23, 1914	Frank "Bruiser" Kinard (d.)	Sports: pro football player	Pelahatchie
Oct. 23, 1921	R.W. Blackwood (d.)	with the Blackwood Bros. Quartet	Ackerman
Oct. 24, 1952	Mark Gray	Country music songwriter/singer	Vicksburg
Oct. 25, 1933	Bobby Collins	Sports: college football coach	Laurel
Oct. 25, 1940	Don Lee Keith	Journalist	Wheeler
Oct. 25, 1941	Ellis Nassour	Writer	Vicksburg
Oct. 26, 1937	Luster Bayless	Movie costume designer	Ruleville
Oct. 27, 1954	Jim Fraiser	Writer-attorney	New Orleans, LA

Famous & Notable Mississippians Listed by Birth Date

BIRTH DATE	NAME	PROFESSION(S)	PLACE OF BIRTH
Oct. 27, 1981	Craig Ross	Top student: perfect ACT score	Vicksburg
Oct. 28, 1918	E.B. "Buddy" Elrod (d.)	Sports: college football player	Sherman, TX
Oct. 28, 1934	Cecil Blackwood	with the Blackwood Bros. Quartet	Ackerman
Oct. 28, 1936	Ted Hawkins (d.)	Blues singer/guitarist	Lakeshore
Oct. 30, 1927	Roland Dale	Sports: football player/coach	Magee
Oct. 31, 1916	Charles G. Bell	Poet	Greenville
Oct. 31, 1925	Arthur "Art" Hillery	Jazz musician/composer	New Orleans, LA
Oct. 31, 1969	Thomas Roger Stevens	member of Blind Melon rock group	West Point
Nov. 01, 1956	Ted J. Webb Jr.	Inventor-banker	Yazoo City
Nov. 03, 1909	Leon Z. Koury (d.)	Artist: sculptor	Greenville
Nov. 03, 1915	Mamie Davis Willoughby (d.)	Writer	near Liberty
Nov. 04, 1909	"Skeeter" Webb (d.)	Sports: major league baseball	Meridian
Nov. 04, 1943	Chuck Scarborough	TV journalist	Pittsburgh, PA
Nov. 05, 1894	Don Scott (d.)	Olympic Champion (1924)	Woodville
Nov. 05, 1931	Ike Turner	R&B singer/musician	Clarksdale
Nov. 05, 1968	John Daniel "J.D." Evermore	Actor (TV & movies)	Leland
Nov. 06, 1926	Zig Ziglar	Motivational writer/speaker	Alabama
Nov. 06, 1941	Ray Perkins	Sports: college football player	Mount Olive
Nov. 06, 19511	Coolidge Ball	Sports: college basketball player	Inverness
Nov. 07, 1938	Jake Gibbs	Sports: college football player	Grenada
Nov. 07, 1946	Milton L. Olive III (d.)	Medal of Honor recipient	Chicago, IL
Nov. 07, 1982	Jennifer Carlisle	Top student: perfect ACT score	Flowood
Nov. 08, 1932	Dave C. Swalm	Philanthropist-CEO-engineer	Los Angeles, CA
Nov. 08, 1944	Bonnie Lynn Bramlett	Rock singer w/Delaney & Bonnie	Pontotoc County
Nov. 08, 1968	Parker Posey	Actress	Baltimore, MD
Nov. 09, 1956	Kathy Thibodeaux	Ballet dancer/instructor	Memphis, TN
Nov. 10, 1933	"Sir" Mack Rice	R&B songwriter/singer	Clarksdale
Nov. 10, 1940	Bobby Rush	Soul/R&B singer	Homer, LA
Nov. 10, 1945	W.C. Taylor, Jr.	Christian country singer	Grenada
Nov. 11, 1927	Mose Allison	Jazz musician/songwriter	Tippo
Nov. 11, 1931	Winthrop Jordan	Historian-writer-professor	Worcester, MA
Nov. 12, 1906	Bukka White (d.)	Legendary bluesman	Houston, MS
Nov. 12, 1937	Richard Harrison Truly	Astronaut-head of NASA	Fayette
Nov. 12, 1942	Tommy Couch	Music industry CEO	Tuscumbia, LA
Nov. 12, 1973	Tom Rice	Movie director/screenwriter	Jackson
Nov. 14, 1933	Fred W. Haise, Jr.	Astronaut	Biloxi
Nov. 14, 1936	Carey Bell	Musician: blues harmonica player	Macon
Nov. 14, 1949	Gary Grubbs	Actor (movies & TV)	Amory
Nov. 14, 1959	Eric McClellan	Advertising executive	Tampa, FL
Nov. 16, 1873	W.C. Handy (d.)	Legendary jazz/bluesman	Florence, AL
Nov. 16, 1911	William Silas "Si" Redd	Businessman-innovator	Philadelphia, MS
Nov. 16, 1931	Hubert Sumlin	Musician: blues guitarist	Greenwood
Nov. 17, 1904	Jack Owens (d.)	Blues singer/musician	Bentonia
Nov. 17, 1916	Shelby Foote	Historian-novelist	Greenville
Nov. 19, 1911	William Attaway (d.)	Novelist-script writer	Greenville
Nov. 21, 1882	Felix J. Underwood (d.)	State health officer-physician	Nettleton
Nov. 21, 1884	Laurence Clifton Jones (d.)	Educator-writer	St. Joseph, MO
Nov. 21, 1913	K.C. Douglas (d.)	Blues singer/guitarist	Sharon
Nov. 21, 1925	Robert Canzoneri	Writer-educator	San Marcos, TX
Nov. 22, 1950	Dan Tyler	Songwriter-author	McComb
Nov. 23, 1926	R.L. Burnside	Blues singer/guitarist	Oxford
Nov. 23, 1939	Betty Everett	R&B singer	Greenwood
Nov. 23, 1965	Nan Sumrall	Miss Mississippi-TV personality	Hattiesburg
Nov. 24, 1927	Samuel Marshall Gore	Artist: sculptor-professor	Coolidge, TX
Nov. 24, 1940	Johnny Carver	Country music singer	Jackson
Nov. 24, 19??	Judith Paige Mitchell	Novelist-screenwriter-producer	New Orleans, LA
Nov. 25, 1914	Eddie Boyd (d.)	Blues singer/pianist	Stovall
Nov. 25, 1917	Helen Carlisle	Writer-home economist	Vossburg
Nov. 25, 1928	Jimmy Johnson	Blues singer/guitarist	Holly Springs
Nov. 25, 1947	John M. Floyd	Writer-computer engineer	Kosciusko
Nov. 26, 1938	Travis Haddix	Blues singer/guitarist	Walnut
Nov. 27, 1923	Robert T. Henry (d.)	Medal of Honor recipient	Greenville
Nov. 27, 1941	Rick Rommerdale	Inventor	Eric, PA
Nov. 28, 1904	James O. Eastland (d.)	U.S. Senator	Doddsville

Famous & Notable Mississippians Listed by Birth Date

BIRTH DATE	NAME	PROFESSION(S)	PLACE OF BIRTH
Nov. 28, 1943	Jackie Sherrill	Sports: college football coach	Duncan, OK
Nov. 29, 1924	Bert Jenkins	Sports: high school basketball coach	Richton
Nov. 29, 1931	Clifford E. Charlesworth	NASA official	Jackson
Nov. 29, 1932	Diane Ladd	Actress	Meridian
Nov. 29, 1934	Willie Morris (d.)	Novelist-writer	Jackson
Nov. 30, 1918	Tom Wilburn	Sports: horse harness racing	Columbus
Nov. 30, 1953	Mike Espy	Politician-U.S. Ag Secretary	Yazoo City
Dec. 01, 1889	Willie Mitchell (d.)	Sports: major league baseball	Pleasant Grove
Dec. 01, 1943	Jimmy Heidel	State government administrator	Benton
Dec. 01, 1950	Brooks Haxton	Poet-screenwriter	Greenville
Dec. 01, 1950	Keith R. Thibodeaux	Actor-singer	Lafayette, LA
Dec. 02, 1882	Earle W. Hammons (d.)	Early film producer	Winona
Dec. 02, 1914	Ray Walston	Actor	Laurel
Dec. 02, 1940	Willie Brown	Sports: pro football player	Yazoo City
Dec. 02, 1981	Britney Spears	Pop singer/dancer	Kentwood, LA
Dec. 03, 1941	Mary Alice	Actress	Indianola
Dec. 03, 1970	Lindsey Hunter	Sports: pro basketball player	Utica
Dec. 04, 1955	Cassandra Wilson	Jazz vocalist	Jackson
Dec. 05, 1916	Means Johnston, Jr. (d.)	Military leader: Admiral	Greenwood
Dec. 05, 1921	Dave "Boo" Ferriss	Sports: major league baseball	Shaw
Dec. 05, 1929	Harvey "Pop" Watkins, Sr. (d.)	Gospel singer/songwriter	Canton
Dec. 05, 1967	Glen Graham	member of Blind Melon rock group	Columbus
Dec. 05, 1968	Falilatu Ogunkoya	Olympic Champion (1996)	Nigeria, Africa
Dec. 07, 1937	Thad Cochran	U.S. Senator	Pontotoc
Dec. 08, 1928	Mack A. Jordan (d.)	Medal of Honor recipient	Collins
Dec. 08, 1939	Jerry Butler	R&B/pop singer	Sunflower County
Dec. 08, 1945	Jim Ziglar	Government service-attorney	Pascagoula
Dec. 09, 1911	John Tyler Caldwell (d.)	Educator: college chancellor	Yazoo City
Dec. 09, 1938	Deacon Jones	Sports: pro football player	Eatonville, FL
Dec. 09, 1944	Del Unser	Sports: college/pro football player	Decatur, IL
Dec. 10, 1925	Jack Cristil	Sports announcer	Memphis, TN
Dec. 10, 1926	Eddie "Guitar Slim" Jones (d.)	Blues singer/guitarist	Greenwood
Dec. 11, 1924	Felix "Doc" Blanchard	Sports: college football player	South Carolina
Dec. 11, 1934	Charles C. Walker	Checkers champion	Hattiesburg
Dec. 12, 1912	Henry Armstrong (d.)	Sports: pro boxing champ	Columbus
Dec. 13, 1913	Archie Moore (d.)	Sports; pro boxing champ	Benoit
Dec. 13, 1954	Steve Forbert	Folk singer/songwriter	Meridian
Dec. 13, 1957	Janet Marie Smith	Architect-business executive	Jackson
Dec. 14, 1894	Jim Edwards (d.)	Sports: major league baseball	Banner
Dec. 15, 1938	Billy Shaw	Sports: college/pro football player	Natchez
Dec. 19, 1918	Calvin Cox	Journalist-photographer	Greenwood
Dec. 19, 1953	Tena Clark	Movie score writer	Waynesboro
Dec. 20, 1935	Floyd D. Shaman	Artist: sculptor	Wheatland, WY
Dec. 21, 1909	Alice Moseley	Artist: painter	Birmingham, AL
Dec. 22, 1910	Elder Roma Wilson	Gospel blues musician	Hickory Flat
Dec. 22, 1919	Lillian "Lil" Green (d.)	Blues singer	Clarksdale
Dec. 22, 1949	Ray Guy	Sports: pro football punter	Thomson, GA
Dec. 23, 1914	Frederick H. Coe (d.)	TV producer	Alligator
Dec. 23, 1931	Harold Dorman (d.)	Pop/country music singer	Sledge
Dec. 23, 1963	Donna Tartt	Novelist-short story writer	Greenwood
Dec. 24, 1900	Roy Blackwood (d.)	with the Blackwood Bros. Quartet	Fentress
Dec. 25, 1946	Jimmy Buffett	Pop singer	Pascagoula
Dec. 26, 1897	William "Bud" Miley (d.)	Military leader: General	Fort Mason, CA
Dec. 26, 1965	Gerald Hopkins	Actor (TV)	Biloxi
Dec. 28, 1915	Roebuck "Pop" Staples	Gospel/pop singer	Winona
Dec. 28, 1953	Bob Pittman	Entertainment CEO	Jackson
Dec. 29, 1927	Matt "Guitar" Murphy	Musician: blues guitarist	Sunflower
Dec. 30, 1912	Margaret Wade (d.)	Sports: basketball coach	McCool
Dec. 30, 1921	Lillian McMurry (d.)	Blues record producer/label founder	Purvis
Dec. 30, 1927	Robert B. Ferguson	Songwriter-historian-scholar	Willow Springs, MO
Dec. 30, 1928	Bo Diddley	R&B/pop singer/guitarist	McComb
Dec. 30, 1941	Hartley Peavey	Corporate founder/CEO	Meridian
Dec. 31, 1942	Murry Kellum (d.)	Pop singer	Jackson, TN
Dec. ??, 1842	August Dorley (d.)	Medal of Honor recipient	Baden, Germany

Famous & Notable Mississippians Listed by Death Date

DEATH DATE	NAME	PROFESSION(S)	PLACE OF BIRTH	D.O.B.
1867 (Oct. 17)	August Dorley	Medal of Honor recipient	Baden, Germany	12-??-1842
1870 (July 9)	Augustus B. Longstreet	Educator-jurist-writer	Augusta, GA	09-22-1790
1881 (July 13)	John Clifford Pemberton	Military leader/historical figure	Philadelphia, PA	07-10-1814
1884 (May 17)	J.F.H. Claiborne	Historian	Natchez	04-24-1907
1889 (Dec. 6)	Jefferson Davis	President of the Confederacy	Todd County, KY	06-03-1808
1893 (Jan. 23)	L.Q.C. Lamar	Statesman-jurist (historical figure)	Georgia	09-17-1825
1894 (Sept. 11)	Martin Freeman	Medal of Honor recipient	Stettin, Germany	05-14-1814
1897 (Aug. 14)	James Z. George	Politician (historical figure)	Monroe County, GA	10-20-1826
1898 (Mar. 17)	Blanche K. Bruce	Politician (historical figure)	Virginia	03-01-1841
1898	Anne C. Peyton	College founder	Madison County	09-12-1852
1900 (Jan. 24)	Wilson Brown	Medal of Honor recipient	Natchez	??-??-1841
1901 (Jan. 16)	Hiram Rhodes Revels	Politician (historical figure)	Fayetteville, NC	09-27-1827
1908 (May 28)	Stephen Dill Lee	Educator-state senator	South Carolina	09-22-1833
1912 (Sept. 18)	Hernando De Soto Money	Politician (historical figure)	Holmes County	08-26-1839
1915 (Aug. 17)	John C. Black	Medal of Honor recipient	Lexington	01-27-1839
1916 (June 28)	Reuben W. Millsaps	College founder	near Hazlehurst	05-30-1833
1917 (Oct. 30)	John Allen	Politician (historical figure)	Tishomingo County	07-08-1846
1918 (Apr. 7)	George Ohr	Artist: potter	Biloxi	07-12-1857
1922 (Feb. 4)	John W. Heard	Medal of Honor recipient	Woodstock (Money)	03-27-1860
1922 (Dec. 27)	James J. Madison	Medal of Honor recipient	Jersey City, NJ	05-20-1884
1928 (Oct. 8)	Larry Semon	Actor & film director	West Point	07-06-1889
1931 (Mar. 25)	Ida Bell Wells-Barnett	Civil Right pioneer	Holly Springs	07-16-1862
1932 (Sept. 7)	John Sharp Williams	Politician (historical figure)	Memphis, TN	07-30-1854
1933 (May 21)	Martha Mattox	Actress	Natchez	06-19-1879
1933 (May 26)	Jimmie Rodgers	Country music singer/songwriter	Meridian (Pine Springs)	09-08-1897
1934 (Apr. 28)	Charley Patton	Legendary blues singer	Edwards	04-??-1887
1934 (June 8)	Dorothy Dell	Miss Universe (1930)-actress	Hattiesburg	01-30-1915
1934 (Dec. 1)	Wilbur Higby	Actor (silent screen)	Meridian	08-21-1867
1937 (Nov. 1)	Dunbar Rowland	Historian-writer-gov'ment official	Oakland, MS	08-25-1864
1938 (Aug. 16)	Robert Johnson	Legendary bluesman	Hazlehurst	05-08-1911
1939 (Feb. 27)	Belle Kearney	Feminist-writer-state senator	near Flora	03-06-1863
1939 (Nov. 2)	John Roy Lynch	Politician-writer	Louisiana	09-10-1847
1941 (June 22)	Pat Harrison	Politician (historical figure)	Crystal Springs	08-29-1881
1941 (July 6)	Frank L. Cooley	Actor (silent screen)	Natchez	??-??-1870
1941 (Oct. 29)	Hamilton Smith	Move director/screenwriter	Muskegon, MS	10-22-1887
1942 (Jan. 21)	William Alexander Percy	Poet-attorney	Greenville	05-14-1885
1943 (Oct. 9)	Charles Graham	Actor (silent screen)	Carthage	02-16-1895
1944 (Aug. 1)	William Hollingsworth	Artist: painter	Jackson	02-17-1910
1944 (Dec. 31)	Robert T. Henry	Medal of Honor recipient	Greenville	11-27-1923
1945 (May 14)	James H. Diamond	Medal of Honor recipient	New Orleans, LA	04-22-1925
1945 (Sept. 6)	John Sidney McCain	Military leader: Admiral	Teoc	08-09-1884
1947 (July 12)	Jimmie Linceford	Big band/orchestra leader	Fulton	06-06-1902
1948 (Jan. 26)	John A. Lomax	Blues collector-archivist	Goodman	09-23-1867
1948 (Aug. 10)	Lucille Bogan	Blues singer	Amory	04-01-1897
1948 (Dec. 23)	Helen Carloss	History-making attorney	Yazoo City	04-18-1893
1949 (Mar. 11)	Eric McNair	Sports: major league baseball	Meridian	04-12-1909
1950 (Feb. 9)	B.J. Barrier, Jr.	Aviation pioneer	Yazoo City	06-26-1906
1950 (Dec. 4)	Jesse Leroy Brown	Military aviator-hero	Hattiesburg	10-13-1926
1951 (June 1)	Garry Owen	Actor	Brookhaven	02-18-1902
1951 (June 7)	Jack G. Hanson	Medal of Honor recipient	Escatawpa	09-18-1930
1951 (Nov. 15)	Mack A. Jordan	Medal of Honor recipient	Collins	12-08-1928
1952 (May 29)	Henry Herschel Brickell	Literary critic	Senatobia	09-13-1889
1952 (June 30)	Olin Frances	Actor	Mooreville	09-13-1891
1953 (Feb. 4)	Ben Ames Williams	Novelist-writer	Macon	03-07-1889
1954 (Apr. 14)	Lillian "Lil" Green	Blues singer	Clarksdale	12-22-1919
1954 (June 24)	R.W. Blackwood	with the Blackwood Bros. Quartet	Ackerman	10-23-1921
1954 (Sept. 28)	James Howell Street	Novelist-journalist	Lumberton	10-15-1903
1955 (Oct. 28)	Frances Jones Gaither	Novelist-writer	Tennessee	05-21-1889
1956 (June 9)	B. Reeves Eason	Movie director/screenwriter	Friar's Point	10-02-1886
1956 (July 13)	Ira C. Welborn	Medal of Honor recipient	Mico (Shady Grove)	02-13-1874
1956 (Nov. 1)	Tommy Johnson	Early bluesman	Terry	??-??-1896
1957	Kate Freeman Clark	Artist: painter	Holly Springs	??-??-1875
1958 (Mar. 28)	W.C. Handy	Legendary jazz/bluesman	Florence, AL	11-16-1873
1958 (Aug. 15)	Big Bill Broonzy	Legendary bluesman	Scott	06-26-1893

Famous & Notable Mississippians Listed by Death Date

DEATH DATE	NAME	PROFESSION(S)	PLACE OF BIRTH	D.O.B.
1958 (Sept. 12)	Rod Brasfield	Country comedian	Smithville	08-22-1910
1959 (Jan. 9)	Felix J. Underwood	State health officer-physician	Nettleton	11-21-1882
1959 (Feb. 7)	Eddie "Guitar Slim" Jones	Blues singer/guitarist	Greenwood	12-10-1926
1959 (Mar. 15)	Lester Willis Young	Jazz musician/composer	Woodville	08-27-1909
1960 (Feb. 8)	Archie Brownlee	Gospel singer	?, Mississippi	??-??- 1925
1960 (Sept. 12)	David L. Cohn	Writer-essayist	Greenville	09-30-1897
1960 (Nov. 28)	Richard Wright	History-making black novelist	Natchez	09-04-1908
1961 (Feb. 2)	James D. Slaton	Medal of Honor recipient	Laurel	04-02-1912
1962 (Feb. 27)	Willie Best	Actor	Sunflower	05-27-1913
1962 (Mar. 1)	Roscoe Ates	Actor	Grange	01-20-1892
1962 (July 4)	Will A. Price	Movie director/playwright	McComb	?
1962 (July 6)	William Faulkner	Novelist-screenwriter	New Albany	09-25-1897
1962 (July 31)	Earle W. Hammons	Early film producer	Winona	12-02-1882
1963 (Jan. 6)	Stark Young	Drama critic-writer	Como	10-11-1881
1963 (Mar. 3)	V. Ruth Campbell	History-making attorney	Yazoo City	01-20-1887
1963 (Mar. 28)	John Faulkner	Novelist-artist: painter	Ripley	09-24-1901
1963 (May 24)	Elmore James	Legendary blues guitarist/singer	Richland (Holmes Co.)	01-27-1918
1963 (June 12)	Medger Evers	Civil Rights leader/activist	Decatur	07-02-1925
1963 (Aug. 15)	Mildred Spurrier Topp	Writer-teacher	Forest City, IL	01-05-1897
1963 (Oct. 22)	Walter Davis	Musician: early blues pianist	Grenada	03-01-1912
1964 (Apr. 30)	Frances "Fannye" A. Cook	Research biologist-writer	Crystal Springs	07-19-1889
1964 (Sept. 21)	Bo Carter	Early bluesman	Bolton	03-21-1893
1964 (Dec. 11)	Sam Cooke	Soul/pop singer	Clarksdale	01-22-1935
1965 (Jan. 19)	Jim Edwards	Sports: major league baseball	Banner	12-14-1894
1965 (Apr. 10)	William David	Actor (silent screen)	Vicksburg	10-05-1882
1965 (June 23)	Sonny Boy Williamson II	Early bluesman	Glendora	03-11-1908
1965 (Oct. 22)	Milton L. Olive III	Medal of Honor recipient	Chicago, IL	11-07-1946
1965 (Nov. 30)	Walter Anderson	Artist: potter	New Orleans, LA	09-29-1901
1966 (Jan. 10)	Andy Reese	Sports: major league baseball	Tupelo	02-07-1904
1966 (Feb. 8)	William Lockhart Clayton	Government service	Tupelo	02-07-1880
1966 (Mar. 29)	William M. "Jazz" Gillum	Blues harmonica player	Indianola	09-11-1904
1966 (Nov. 2)	"Mississippi" John Hurt	Blues singer/guitarist	Teoc	03-08-1892
1966	Hubert Creekmore	Poet-novelist	Water Valley	01-16-1907
1967 (Apr. 29)	J.B. Lenoir	Blues singer/musician	Monticello	05-05-1929
1967 (Aug. 11)	Roy M. Wheat	Medal of Honor recipient	Moselle	07-24-1947
1968 (Nov. 22)	Johnnie "Geechie" Temple	Bluesman	Canton	10-18-1906
1968	John McCrady	Artist: painter	Canton	09-05-1911
1969 (Jan. 3)	Commodore Cochran	Olympic Champion (1924)	Richton	01-20-1902
1969 (July ??)	Harry A. Cole, Sr.	Inventor	Jackson	01-09-1888
1969 (Oct. 3)	Skip James	Blues guitarist/singer	Bentonia	06-09-1902
1969 (Dec. 1)	Magic Sam	Blues singer/guitarist	Grenada	02-14-1937
1969 (Dec. 6)	Hoyt B. Wooten	Broadcast pioneer	Coldwater	09-29-1893
1969 (Dec. 13)	Spencer Williams, Jr.	Actor-comic	Vidalia, LA	07-14-1893
1970 (Feb. 12)	Ishmon Bracey	Blues singer/guitarist	Byram	01-09-1900
1970 (Apr. 21)	Earl Zebedee Hooker	Blues guitarist/singer	Clarksdale	01-02-1930
1970 (Apr. 25)	Otis Spann	Blues pianist/singer	Jackson	03-21-1930
1970 (June 23)	Roscoe Turner	Aviation pioneer	Corinth	09-29-1895
1970 (Oct. 15)	Cid Ricketts Sumner	Novelist	Brookhaven	09-27-1890
1971 (Mar. 21)	Roy Blackwood	with the Blackwood Bros. Quartet	Fentress	12-24-1900
1971 (Aug. 15)	Thomas Wayne	R&R-Pop singer	Batesville	07-22-1940
1971 (Aug. 16)	Henry A. Commiskey, Sr.	Medal of Honor recipient	Hattiesburg	01-10-1927
1971 (Nov. 18)	Junior Parker	Blues singer/musician	Clarksdale	03-27-1932
1972 (Apr. 4)	Hodding Carter, Jr.	Journalist-writer	Hammond, LA	02-03-1907
1972 (July 3)	"Mississippi" Fred McDowell	Blues legend	Rossville, TN	01-12-1906
1973 (Nov. 23)	Willie Mitchell	Sports: major league baseball	Pleasant Grove	12-01-1889
1974 (Mar. 28)	Arthur "Big Boy" Crudup	blues singer/songwriter	Forest	08-24-1905
1974 (Apr. 18)	Johnny Young	Blues singer	Vicksburg	01-01-1918
1974 (July 17)	Dizzy Dean	Sports: major league baseball	Lucas, AR	01-16-1910
1974 (Oct. 31)	Buddy Myer	Sports: major league baseball	Ellisville	03-16-1904
1974 (Oct. ??)	Doyle Blackwood	with the Blackwood Bros. Quartet	Ackerman	08-22-1911
1975 (Apr. 22)	Walter Vinson	Bluesman	Bolton	02-02-1901
1975 (July 15)	Laurence Clifton Jones	Educator-writer	St. Joseph, MO	11-21-1884
1975 (Oct. 18)	K.C. Douglas	Blues singer/guitarist	Sharon	11-21-1913
1975 (Dec. 17)	"Hound Dog" Taylor	Blues singer/guitarist	Natchez	04-12-1917

Famous & Notable Mississippians Listed by Death Date

DEATH DATE	NAME	PROFESSION(S)	PLACE OF BIRTH	D.O.B.
1976 (Jan. 10)	"Howlin' Wolf"	Blues singer	West Point	06-10-1911
1976 (Apr. ??)	Clay Hopper	Sports: pro baseball manager	Greenwood	10-03-1900
1976 (Aug. 29)	Jimmy Reed	Blues singer	Dunleith	09-06-1925
1976 (Dec. 17)	Ray Lum	Storyteller-mule trader	Rocky Springs	06-25-1891
1977 (Feb. 26)	Bukka White	Legendary bluesman	Houston, MS	11-12-1906
1977 (Mar. 14)	Theora Hamblett	Artist: primitive painter	Paris, MS	01-15-1895
1977 (Mar. 14)	Fannie Lou Hamer	Civil Rights leader/activist	Montgomery County	10-06-1917
1977 (Aug. 16)	Elvis Presley	Singer-entertainer-actor	Tupelo	01-08-1935
1978 (Jan. 5)	Wyatt Cooper	Screenwriter-actor	Quitman	09-01-1927
1978 (Sept. 16)	Willie Foster	Sports: pro basketball play./coach	Calvert, TX	06-12-1904
1978 (Dec. 3)	William Grant Still	Musician-composer	Woodville	05-11-1895
1979 (Jan. 21)	Sam Leslie	Sports: major league baseball	Moss Point	07-26-1905
1979 (Feb. 3)	Charlemae Rollins	Librarian-writer	Yazoo City	06-20-1897
1979 (Apr. 29)	Frederick H. Coe	TV producer	Alligator	12-23-1914
1979 (Oct. 15)	Gus "Banjo Joe" Cannon	Early bluesman	Red Banks	09-12-1884
1979 (Dec. 15)	Jackie Brenston	History-making singer	Clarksdale	08-15-1930
1980 (Jan. 10)	Hughie Critz	Sports: major league baseball	Starkville	09-17-1900
1980 (Jan. 30)	Warren Smith	Rockabilly singer/musician	Louise	02-07-1933
1980 (Oct. 10)	Don Scott	Olympic Champion (1924)	Woodville	11-05-1894
1980 (Nov. 21)	Marie Atkinson Hull	Artist: painter	Summit	09-28-1890
1981 (Mar. 20)	Gerald Walker	Sports: major league baseball	Gulfport	03-19-1908
1981 (Mar. ??)	Kelly Brown	Actor	Jackson	09-24-1928
1981 (June 9)	Mary Angie Douglass	Administrator-secretary	X-Prairie	03-26-1908
1981 (Sept. 14)	Walter "Furry" Lewis	Blues singer/guitarist	Greenwood	03-06-1895
1981 (Sept. 26)	Roy Cochran	Olympic Champion (1948)	Richton	01-26-1919
1981 (Dec. 1)	Herbie Holmes	Orchestra/big band leader	Yazoo City	09-27-1912
1981 (Dec. 8)	"Big" Walter Horton	Blues harmonica player	Horn Lake	04-06-1917
1982 (Feb. ??)	Marietta Eichelberger	Scientist-medical researcher	Macon	08-20-1891
1982 (Aug. 29)	Lehman Engel	Conductor-composer	Jackson	09-14-1910
1982 (Oct. 31)	H.T. "Dick" Merrill	Aviation pioneer	Iuka	02-01-1894
1982 (Nov. 5)	Hubert L. Lee	Medal of Honor recipient	Arburg, MO	02-02-1915
1982 (Dec. 17)	"Big" Joe Williams	Blues singer/musician	Crawford	10-16-1903
1983 (Feb. 2)	Sam Chatmon	Blues singer	Bolton	01-10-1899
1983 (Feb. 25)	Tennessee Williams	Dramatist	Columbus	03-26-1911
1983 (Mar. 25)	Edwin "Goat" Hale	Sports: college football	Jackson	01-29-1896
1983 (Apr. 7)	Gavin Gordon	Actor	Chicora	04-08-1901
1983 (Apr. 15)	Ernestine Wade	Actress-comic	Jackson	08-07-1906
1983 (Apr. 27)	Turner Catledge	Journalist	near Ackerman	03-17-1901
1983 (Apr. 30)	"Muddy Waters"	Legendary bluesman	Rolling Fork	04-04-1915
1984 (July 27)	Rev. C. L. Franklin	Minister-recording artist	Clarksdale	01-22-1915
1984 (Nov. 16)	Karl Wolfe	Artist: painter	Brookhaven	01-25-1903
1985 (Jan. 22)	Borden Deal	Writer	Pontotoc	10-12-1922
1985 (Jan. 23)	Roy M. Martin	High School band director	Rosebud, AR	01-31-1895
1985 (Jan. 26)	A.C. "Butch' Lambert	Sports: referee official	Holcut	02-27-1923
1985 (Apr. 28)	Hoyt Lester Ming	Musician- songwriter	near Ackerman	10-06-1902
1985 (June 16)	Evelyn Allen Hammett	Educator-writer	Jefferson County	06-12-1894
1985 (July 2)	Guy T. Bush	Sports: major league baseball	Aberdeen	08-23-1901
1985 (Sept. 7)	Frank "Bruiser" Kinard	Sports: pro football player	Pelahatchie	10-23-1914
1985 (Oct. 12)	Blind John Davis	Blues singer/pianist	Hattiesburg	02-07-1913
1985 (Dec. 31)	Elsie McWilliams	Songwriter	Harperville	06-01-1896
1986 (Feb. 19)	James O. Eastland	U.S. Senator	Doddsville	11-28-1904
1986 (Apr. 19)	Alvin Childress	Actor-comic	Meridian	09-10-1907
1986 (June 17)	William Attaway	Novelist-script writer	Greenville	11-19-1911
1986 (July 8)	"Skeeter" Webb	Sports: major league baseball	Meridian	11-04-1909
1986 (Aug. 17)	S.B. "Sam" Vick	Sports: major league baseball	Batesville	04-12-1895
1986 (Aug. 24)	Joseph Paul Treen	Inventor	Purvis	05-01-1900
1986 (Nov. 8)	Owen Cooper	Industrialist-religious leader	Vicksburg	04-19-1908
1986 (Dec. 27)	Dumas Malone	Historian	Coldwater	01-10-1892
1987 (Feb. 8)	Leslie Vaughn Rush	Medical pioneering physician	Meridian	02-16-1905
1987 (May 26)	Robert Wilkins	Blues singer/guitarist	Hernando	01-16-1896
1987 (Sept. 21)	Ruth Attaway	Actress	Greenville	06-28-1910
1987 (Sept. 23)	O.B. McClinton	Country music singer	Senatobia	04-25-1940
1988 (July 18)	Jake W. Lindsey, Sr.	Medal of Honor recipient	Isnay, AL	05-01-1921
1988 (Oct. 8)	Harold Dorman	Pop/country music singer	Sledge	12-23-1931

Famous & Notable Mississippians Listed by Death Date

DEATH DATE	NAME	PROFESSION(S)	PLACE OF BIRTH	D.O.B.
1988 (Oct. 19)	Eddie "Son" House	Legendary early bluesman	Riverton	03-21-1902
1988 (Oct. 24)	Henry Armstrong	Sports: pro boxing champ	Columbus	12-12-1912
1988 (Dec. 5)	Edwin Phillips Granberry	Cartoonist-writer	Meridian	04-18-1897
1989 (June 21)	Lee Calhoun	Olympic Champion (1956/1960)	Laurel	02-23-1933
1989 (July 14)	Means Johnston, Jr.	Military leader: Admiral	Greenwood	12-05-1916
1989 (Sept. 4)	Hal Lee	Sports: major league baseball	Ludlow	02-15-1905
1989 (Nov. 6)	Frederic Frances Mellen	Geologist-writer	Starkville	08-21-1911
1989 (Nov. 18)	Freddie Waits	Musician: jazz drummer	Jackson	04-27-1943
1990 (Jan. 1)	Patrick Kelly	Fashion designer	Vicksburg	09-24-1954
1990 (May 10)	Walker Percy	Writer-physician	Birmingham, AL	05-28-1916
1990 (May 16)	Jim Henson	Puppeteer	Greenville	09-24-1936
1990 (May 17)	Frank Wright	Musician: jazz tenor saxophonist	Grenada	07-09-1935
1990 (Sept. 15)	Murry Kellum	Pop singer	Jackson, TN	12-31-1942
1991 (Mar. 7)	James "Cool Papa" Bell	Sports: pro baseball player	Starkville	05-17-1903
1991 (June 1)	David Ruffin	Soul singer	Whynot	01-18-1941
1992 (Jan. 29)	Willie Dixon	Blues singer/songwriter	Vicksburg	07-01-1915
1992 (Feb. 15)	Ethel Wright Mohamed	Artist: embroiderer	Fame	10-13-1907
1992 (June 27)	Luke McDaniel	Rockabilly singer/musician	Ellisville	02-03-1927
1992 (Aug. 16)	Richard "Dick" Armstrong	Journalist-editor	Jackson	08-29-1929
1992 (Aug. 25)	Frederick O'Neal	Actor	Brooksville	08-27-1905
1992 (Oct. 6)	Dumas Milner	Businessman-industrialist	Attala County	01-28-1917
1992 (Oct. 22)	Walter Lanier "Red" Barber	Sportscaster	Columbus	02-17-1908
1992 (Dec. 17)	Dana Andrews	Actor	Collins	01-01-1909
1992 (Dec. 21)	Albert King	Blues-R&B-soul guitarist	Indianola	04-25-1923
1993 (Mar. 22)	Frank Williams	Gospel singer-group founder	Smithdale	06-27-1947
1993 (Apr. 11)	Leon Z. Koury	Artist: sculptor	Greenville	11-03-1909
1993 (May 28)	Isaiah "Doctor' Ross	Blues guitarist/harpist	Tunica	10-21-1925
1993 (June 5)	Conway Twitty	Rock-Country superstar	Friar's Point	09-01-1933
1993 (June 26)	James "Son" Thomas	Blues musician-sculptor	Eden	10-14-1926
1994 (Feb. 2)	Willie Mae Ford Smith	Gospel blues singer	Rolling Fork	06-23-1904
1994 (Feb. 10)	Bilbo "Mule" Monaghan	Sports: pro football player/coach	Amory	06-23-1910
1994 (May 17)	Hazel Brannon Smith	Journalist	Gadsden, AL	02-05-1914
1994 (July 13)	Eddie Boyd	Blues singer/pianist	Stovall	11-25-1914
1994 (Sept. 3)	Major Lance	Soul singer	Winstonville	04-04-1941
1994 (Sept. 5)	Louis Myers	Blues guitarist/harp player	Byhalia	09-18-1929
1994 (Sept. 26)	Hollis Pippin	Choreographer-director	Jackson	05-03-1950
1994 (Sept. 29)	Johnny R. "Jack" Spinks	Sports: pro football player	Toomsuba	02-04-1930
1994 (Nov. 16)	James E. "Buster" Poole	Sports: pro football player/coach	Gloster	09-09-1915
1994 (Nov. 16)	Harvey "Pop" Watkins, Sr.	Gospel singer/songwriter	Canton	12-05-1929
1994 (Dec. 12)	Stuart A. Roosa	Astronaut-businessman	Durango, CO	08-16-1933
1995 (Jan. 1)	Ted Hawkins	Blues singer/guitarist	Lakeshore	10-28-1936
1995 (Jan. 13)	Norris Weese	Sports: college-pro football player	Baton Rouge, LA	08-12-1951
1995 (Feb. 16)	Margaret Wade	Sports: basketball coach	McCool	12-30-1912
1995 (Feb. 25)	John O. Emmerich, Jr.	Journalist-newspaper owner	McComb	04-16-1929
1995 (Mar. 17)	Sunnyland Slim	Musician: blues pianist	Vance	09-05-1907
1995 (Apr. 4)	James Saggus	Journalist	Alexandria, LA	08-15-1925
1995 (Apr. 8)	John A. Pittman	Medal of Honor recipient	Carrollton	10-15-1928
1995 (Apr. 17)	Rob't. H. "Ace" Cleveland, Sr.	Journalist-publicist	Hattiesburg	08-06-1926
1995 (Apr. 23)	John C. Stennis	U.S. Senator	Kemper County	08-03-1901
1995 (June 5)	Eugene Butler	Journalist-editor	Starkville	06-11-1894
1995 (Aug. 3)	Harry "Popeye" Craft	Sports: major league baseball	Ellisville	04-19-1915
1995 (Aug. 31)	Jerry H. Booth	Scientist (physicist)-gov'ment	Mathiston	03-24-1941
1995 (Sept. 9)	Jamie L. Whitten	Politician: U.S. Congressman	Cascilla	04-18-1910
1995 (Oct. 13)	John Tyler Caldwell	Educator: college chancellor	Yazoo City	12-09-1911
1995 (Nov. 23)	Charles S. Thomas, Sr.	Sports: high school football coach	Winona	10-22-1913
1996 (Jan. 9)	Mamie Davis Willoughby	Writer	near Liberty	11-03-1915
1996 (Feb. 14)	Charlie Conerly	Sports: pro football player	Clarksdale	09-19-1921
1996 (Apr. 3)	Roosevelt "Booba" Barnes	Blues guitarist/singer	Longwood	09-25-1936
1996 (July 7)	David E. Harrison	Inventor	Mann, WV	10-17-1937
1996 (Aug. 24)	Louis Westerfield	Educator-attorney	Kemper County	07-31-1949
1996 (Oct. 20)	Jim Majure	Novelist	Durant	08-29-1938
1996 (Dec. 23)	Charlotte Capers	Writer-administrator	Columbia, TN	06-13-1913
1997 (Jan. 9)	Thomas "Shorty" McWilliams	Sports: college/pro football player	Meridian	05-12-1926
1997 (Feb. 9)	Jack Owens	Blues singer/musician	Bentonia	11-17-1904

Famous & Notable Mississippians Listed by Death Date

DEATH DATE	NAME	PROFESSION(S)	PLACE OF BIRTH	D.O.B.
1997 (Apr. 16)	Ernie Chaffin	Rockabilly singer	Water Valley	01-01-1928
1997 (May 19)	Aaron Henry	Civil Rights leader/activist	Clarksdale	07-02-1922
1997 (Aug. 2)	Frank E. Smith	Politician-writer	Sidon	02-21-1918
1997 (Sept. 25)	William "Bud" Miley	Military leader: General	Fort Mason, CA	12-26-1897
1997 (Dec. 19)	Jimmy Rogers	Blues singer/guitarist	Ruleville	06-03-1924
1998 (Jan. 4)	Joe Frank Sanderson	Business executive	Jackson	08-03-1925
1998 (Jan. 16)	"Junior" Kimbrough	Bluesman	Hudsonville	07-28-1930
1998 (Apr. 6)	Tammy Wynette	Country music singer	Tremont	05-05-1942
1998 (Apr. 16)	Jane Reid-Petty	Actress-director-writer	Meridian	06-12-1927
1998 (May 7)	Junie Hovious	Sports: college football coach	Vicksburg	10-04-1919
1998 (June 13)	E.B. "Buddy" Elrod	Sports: college football player	Sherman, TX	10-28-1918
1998 (June 18)	Frank Trippett	Journalist	Columbus	07-01-1926
1998 (June ??)	Bobby Bryant	Musician: jazz trumpetist	Hattiesburg	05-19-1934
1998 (July 23)	Robert P. McHugh	Journalist	Cedar Rapids, IA	02-14-1917
1998 (Aug. 24)	Jerry Clower	Country humorist	East Fork	09-28-1926
1998 (Aug. 29)	Charlie Feathers	Rockabilly singer/songwriter	Myrtle	06-12-1932
1998 (Sept. 1)	Cary Middlecoff	Sports: pro golfer	Halls, TN	01-06-1921
1998 (Oct. 11)	T. Tommy Cutrer	Grand Ole Opry announcer	Osyka	06-29-1924
1998 (Nov. 8)	Lonnie Pitchford	Blues musician	Lexington	10-08-1955
1998 (Nov. 26)	Evelyn McPhail	Political party official	Bay St. Louis	06-09-1930
1998 (Nov. 30)	Margaret Walker Alexander	Writer-professor	Birmingham, AL	07-27-1915
1998 (Dec. 9)	Archie Moore	Sports; pro boxing champ	Benoit	12-12-1913
1999 (Jan. 6)	Mike McGregor	Craftsman: jeweler	Tibbs	04-14-1939
1999 (Mar. 18)	Lillian McMurry	Blues record producer/founder	Purvis	12-30-1921
1999 (Apr. 5)	Thomas J. Biggs	Architect	Arkansas	01-28-1912
1999 (Aug. 2)	Willie Morris	Novelist-writer	Jackson	11-29-1934
1999 (Aug. 8)	Harry "The Hat" Walker	Sports: major league baseball	Pascagoula	10-22-1916
1999 (Sept. 16)	Paul Gregory	Sports (baseball): coach/pro player	Tomnolen	06-09-1908
1999 (Sept. 21)	Neil McGaughey	Mystery novelist-journalist	Natchez	10-03-1951
1999 (Sept. 26)	Oseola McCarty	Phllanthropist-humanitarian	Hattiesburg	03-07-1908
1999 (Nov. 1)	Walter Payton	Sports: pro/college football player	Columbia	07-25-1954
1999 (Dec. 10)	Early Wright	Legendary disc jockey	Jefferson (Carroll Co.)	02-10-1915
1999 (Dec. 14)	Jim Buck Ross	Miss. agriculture commissioner	Pelahatchie	08-14-1917
2000 (Jan. 22)	Craig Claiborne	Food critic columnist	Sunflower	09-04-1920
2000 (Feb. 4)	John Vincent Imbragulio	Record producer/label founder	Hattiesburg	10-03-1925
2000 (Feb. 8)	Bruce H. Brady	Artist: sculptor-outdoorsman	Brookhaven	08-28-1934
2000 (Mar. 15)	Tellis "T.B." Ellis *	Sports: college athletic director	Vicksburg	05-26-1912
2000 (May 4)	J.T. "Blondy" Black	Sports: college/pro football	Philadelphia, MS	08-20-1920
2000 (Sept. 14)	Beah Richards	Actress	Vicksburg	07-12-1920

Famous & Notable Mississippians Listed by Profession

Actors & Actresses
Mary Alice
Dana Andrews
Roscoe Ates
Ruth Attaway
Harry Basch
Willie Best
Brendon Boone
Jimmy Boyd
Kelly Brown
Lacey Chabert
Frank L. Cooley
William David
Peggy Dow
John Dye
John Daniel "J.D." Evermore
Ruth Ford
Olin Francis
Morgan Freeman
Cynthia Lynn Geary
Gavin Gordon
Phil Gordon
Charles Graham
Gary Grubbs
Alice Haining
Robert Harper
Anthony Herrera
Wilbur Higby
Eddie Hodges
Gerald Hopkins
Michael Humphreys
Don Jeffcoat
James Earl Jones
Robert Earl Jones
Diane Ladd
Tom Lester
Martha Mattox
Gerald McRaney
Frances E. Neal
Willie "Ray-J" Norwood, Jr.
Carrie Nye
Frederick O'Neal
Garry Owen
Parker Posey
Beah Richards
Eric Roberts
Larry Semon
Symba Smith
Stella Stevens
Tonea Stewart
Byron Thames
Keith R. Thibodeaux
Ray Walston
Sela Ward
Hattie Winston
Billie Jean Young
Advertising
Johnny Barranco
Jim Dollarhide
Jo Foxworth
Cliff Freeman
Eric McClellan
Architects
Thomas J. Biggs
Janet Marie Smith

Artists (Painters, Sculptors, Potters, Etc.)
Walter Anderson
William Beckwith
Marshall Bouldin III
Bruce H. Brady
Kate Freeman Clark
Bill Dunlap
Samuel Marshall Gore
Theora Hamblett
Saul Haymond, Sr.
William Hollingsworth
Marie Atkinson Hull
Valerie Jaudon
Leon Z. Koury
John McCrady
Ethel Wright Mohamed
Alice Moseley
George Ohr
James L. Seawright, Jr.
Floyd D. Shaman
Eugenia Ann Talbott
Wyatt Waters
Elizabeth Wolfe
Karl Wolfe
Mildred Wolfe
Astronauts / NASA Officials
Clifford E. Charlesworth
Fred W. Haise, Jr.
Richard E. Mayo
Donald H. Peterson
Stuart A. Roosa
Richard H. Truly
Attorneys / Jurists
Rueben Anderson
Haley Barbour
Helen Carloss
V. Ruth Campbell
L.Q.C. Lamar
Lenore L. Prather
Aviation Pioneers
B.J. Barrier, Jr.
Alton Parker
H. T. "Dick" Merrill
Roscoe Turner
Beauty Contest Winners
Susan Diane Akin
Dorothy Dell
Lynda Lee Mead
Mary Ann Mobley
Pamela Nail
Cheryl Prewitt
Donna Hild Russell
Bluesmen (& Women)
Roosevelt "Booba" Barnes
Carey Bell
Lucille Bogan
Eddie Boyd
Ishmon Bracey
Big Bill Broonzy
Archie Brownlee
Eddie "Guitar" Burns
R.L. Burnside
Gus "Banjo Joe" Cannon
Sam Carr

Bo Carter
Sam Chatmon
Eddy Clearwater
Willie Cobbs
James Cotton
Arthur "Big Boy" Crudup
Blind John Davis
Walter Davis
Willie Dixon
K.C. Douglas
Dave "Honeyboy" Edwards
William M. "Jazz" Gillum
Lillian "Lil" Green
Travis Haddix
W.C. Handy
Ted Hawkins
Earl Zebedee Hooker
John Lee Hooker
"Big" Walter Horton
Eddie "Son" House
"Howlin' Wolf"
Mississippi John Hurt
Elmore James
Skip James
"Big" Jack Johnson
Jimmy Johnson
Luther "Guitar Jr." Johnson
Robert Johnson
Tommy Johnson
Eddie "Guitar Slim" Jones
"Junior" Kimbrough
Albert King
B.B. King
J.B. Lenoir
Walter "Furry" Lewis
"Little Howlin' Wolf"
"Little Milton"
Magic Sam
Mississippi Fred McDowell
"Muddy Waters"
Matt "Guitar" Murphy
Charlie Musselwhite
Louis Myers
Jack Owens
Little Junior Parker
Charley Patton
Pinetop Perkins
Lonnie Pitchford
James "Snooky" Pryor
Jimmy Reed
Jimmy Rogers
Isaiah "Doctor" Ross
Otis Rush
Willie Mae Ford Smith
John "Big Bad" Smitty
Otis Spann
Hubert Sumlin
Sunnyland Slim
"Hound Dog" Taylor
Johnnie "Geechie" Temple
James "Son" Thomas
Walter Vinson
Libby Rae Watson
Artie White
Bukka White

Robert Wilkins
"Big" Joe Williams
Sonny Boy Williamson II
Elder Roma Wilson
Johnny Winter
Johnny Young
Broadcasters / Sportscasters
Woodie Assaf
Walter Lanier "Red" Barber
Jack Cristil
T. Tommy Cutrer
Walt Grayson
Chuck Scarborough
Hoyt B. Wooten
Early Wright
Business Executives / CEOs
Louis Baloni
James Barksdale
John H. Bryan, Jr.
Owen Cooper
Tommy Couch
Bernie Ebbers
Sam Haskell
W.G. "Mickey" Holliman, Jr.
George Ellis Johnson
Richard D. McRae, Sr.
Dumas Milner
Davis K. Mortensen
Charles L. Overby
John N. Palmer, Sr.
Hartley Peavey
Bob Pittman
Will Primos
William Silas "Si" Redd
Joe Frank Sanderson
Frederick W. Smith
Mike Starnes
Cartoonists
Edwin Phillips Granberry
Jimmy Johnson
Choreographers / Dancers
Thalia Mara
Hollis Pippin
Kathy Thibodeaux
Civil Rights Leaders / Activists
Charles Evers
Medgar Evers
Myrlie Evers-Williams
Fannie Lou Hamer
Aaron Henry
James Meredith
Anne Moody
Ida Bell Wells-Barnett
Comedians / Humorists
T. Bubba Bechtol
Rod Brasfield
Alvin Childress
Jerry Clower
Ernestine Wade
Spencer Williams, Jr.
Composers / Conductors
Lehman Engel
William Grant Still
Luigi Zaninelli

Famous & Notable Mississippians Listed by Profession

Critics
Henry Herschel Brickell
Craig Claiborne
Stark Young
Educators / College Founders
John Tyler Caldwell
Evelyn Allen Hammett
Laurence Clifton Jones
Robert C. Khayat
Jerome F. Leavell
Stephen Dill Lee
Augustus B. Longstreet
Reuben W. Millsaps
Annie C. Peyton
Malcolm Portera
Jean F. Simmons
Prescilla D. Slade
Louis Westerfield
Government Service
Marion S. Barry, Jr.
William Lockhart Clayton
Ward Emling
Mike Espy
Jimmy Heidel
Jim Buck Ross
Jim Ziglar
Historians / Biographers
J.F.H. Claiborne
David Herbert Donald
Charles W. Eagles
Robert B. Ferguson
Shelby Foote
Grady Howell, Jr.
D. Clayton James
Daniel P. Jordan
Winthrop Jordan
Dumas Malone
Dunbar Rowland
Inventors
Paul Brummett
Harry A. Cole, Sr.
Toxey Haas
David E. Harrison
Joseph W. Newman
Rick Rommerdale
Joseph Paul Treen
Ted. J. Webb, Jr.
Journalists / Editors / Publishers
Alyce Alston
Richard "Dick" Armstrong
Lerone Bennett, Jr.
Eugene Butler
Hodding Carter, Jr.
Hodding Carter III
Turner Catledge
Rob't H. "Ace" Cleveland, Jr.
Calvin Cox
S. Gale Denley
John O. Emmerich, Jr.
Paul Gray
Ira B. Harkey, Jr.
Don Lee Keith
Jimmie McDowell
Robert P. McHugh

Jack Nelson
Carolyn Bennett Patterson
William Raspberry
James Saggus
Sidney L. "Sid" Salter
Hazel Brannon Smith
Larry Speakes
Frank Trippett
Military Heroes and Medal of Honor Recipients
Van T. Barfoot
John C. Black
Jesse Leroy Brown
Wilson Brown
Henry A. Commiskey, Sr.
James H. Diamond
August Dorley
Martin Freeman
Jack G. Hanson
John W. Heard
Robert T. Henry
Mack A. Jordan
Hubert L. Lee
Jake W. Lindsey, Sr.
Jack Lucas
James J. Madison
Milton L. Olive III
John A. Pittman
James D. Slaton
Ira C. Welborn
Roy M. Wheat
Military Leaders
Means Johnston, Jr.
John Sidney McCain
William "Bud" Miley
John Clifford Pemberton
George Baker Price
Louis Hugh Wilson, Jr. (also Medal of Honor recipient)
Movie / TV Costume & Set Designers
Luster Bayless
Charles C. Bennett
Dorree Cooper
Julie Kaye Fanton
Herschel McCoy
Movie Directors / Producers
Charles Burnett
B. Reeves Eason
Jamaa Fanaka
Charles "Chuck" Gordon
Larry Gordon
Earle W. Hammons
Will A. Price
Tom Rice
Hamilton Smith
Larry A. Thompson
Movie Score Writers
Dee Barton
Tena Clark
Movie Screenwriters
Wyatt Cooper
Judith Paige Mitchell
Thomas Hal Phillips

Musicians
Ace Cannon
John De Chiaro
Steve Douglas
Pete Fountain
Glen Graham
Mike Henderson
Jaimoe Jai Johanny
Hoyt Lester Ming
Willie Mitchell
Frank Polanski
Sandra Polanski
Bob Saxton
Brad Smith
Thomas Roger Stevens
Milan B. Williams
Charlie Worsham
Musicians (Jazz)
Mose Allison
Bucky Barrett
Steve Blailock
Richard Jess Brown, Jr.
Bobby Bryant
Theodore "Teddy" Edwards
Dick Griffin
Jimmy Henderson
Arthur "Art" Hillery
Milt Hinton
Henry "Hank" Jones
Mundell Lowe
Tom "Bones" Malone
Henry "Skeets" McWilliams
Mulgrew Miller
Freddie Waits
Lloyd Wells
Gerald Stanley Wilson
Frank Wright
Lester Willis Young
Philanthropists
Gerald M. Hollingsworth
Oseola McCarty
Dave C. Swalm
Playwrights
Mart Crowley
Beth Henley
John Maxwell
Jane Reid-Petty
Tennessee Williams
Photographers
Paul T. Brown
Robert Hubbard
Birney Imes
Florence Mars
Physicians
Arthur C.. Guyton
James D. Hardy
Michael Jabaley
James C. "Butch" Rosser
Leslie Vaughn Rush
Felix J. Underwood
Politicians
John Allen
Blanche K. Bruce
Thad Cochran
James O. Eastland

Evelyn Gandy
James Z. George
Trent Lott
John Roy Lynch
Pat Harrison
Hernando De Soto Money
G.V. "Sonny" Montgomery
Hiram Rhodes Revels
Frank E. Smith
John C. Stennis
Jamie L. Whitten
John Sharp Williams
Record Producers
Glen Ballard
John Vincent Imbragulio
Lillian McMurry
Researchers
James F. Brieger
Frances "Fannye" A. Cook
Scientists
Jerry H. Booth
Marietta Eichelberger
Ben H. Douglas
John E. Hall
Singers
Andy Anderson
Moe Bandy
Prentiss Barnes
Lance Bass
Cecil Blackwood
Doyle Blackwood
James Blackwood
R.W. Blackwood
Roy Blackwood
Delaney Bramlett
Bonnie Lynn Bramlett
Brandy (Norwood)
Jackie Brenston
Jimmy Buffett
Jerry Butler
Joe Frank Carollo
Johnny Carver
Ernie Chaffin
George Chambers
Joe Chambers
Lester Chambers
Willie Chambers
Sam Cooke
Paul Davis
Tyrone Davis
Bo Diddley
Harold Dorman
Betty Everett
Charlie Feathers
Steve Forbert
Bobbie Gentry
Mickey Gilley
Mel Hardin
Ty Herndon
Faith Hill
Glenn Honeycutt
Thelma Houston
Guy Hovis
Pat Kirby
Becca Jackson

The Ultimate Reference on the State

Famous & Notable Mississippians Listed by Profession

Margie Joseph
Murry Kellum
Fred Knobloch
Major Lance
Denise LaSalle
Chris LeDoux
Jerry Lee Lewis
Mac McAnally
Luke McDaniel
O.B. McClinton
Tim McPherson
Dorothy Moore
Paul Overstreet
Elvis Presley
Charley Pride
LeAnn Rimes
Jimmie Rodgers
David Ruffin
Jimmy Ruffin
Bobby Rush
Johnny Russell
Johnny Sea
"Jumpin'" Gene Simmons
Warren Smith
Britney Spears
Roebuck "Pop" Staples
Barrett Strong
Marty Stuart
W.C. Taylor, Jr.
Rufus Thomas
Ike Turner
Conway Twitty
Harvey "Pop" Watkins, Sr.
Thomas Wayne
Frank Williams
Al Wilson
Cassandra Wilson
Mary Wilson
Charles Wright
Tammy Wynette
Singers: Opera
Eleni Matos
Leontyne Price
Songwriters
Hank Cochran
Mark Gray
Carl Jackson
George Jackson
Elsie McWilliams
Ben Peters
"Sir" Mack Rice
Paul Thorn
Dan Tyler
Jim Weatherly
Sports: Coaches / Administrators
Jeff Bower
Bobby Collins
Roland Dale
Tellis "T.B." Ellis
Tim Floyd
W.C. Gorden
Paul Gregory
Junie Hovious
Doug Hutton

Bert Jenkins
A.C. "Butch" Lambert
Gene Murphy
Ron Polk
Walter Reed
Jackie Sherrill
L.T. Smith
Charles S. Thomas, Sr.
Johnny Vaught
Margaret Wade
Bobby Wallace
Sports: College Basketball
Coolidge Ball
Erick Dampier
Jennifer Gillom
Peggy Gillom
Sports: College Football
Felix "Doc" Blanchard
Reggie Collier
Tim Ellis
E.B. "Buddy" Elrod
Jake Gibbs
Hugh Green
Edwin "Goat" Hale
Kris Mangum
Archie Manning
Steve McNair
T.E. "Shorty" McWilliams
Crawford Mims
Ray Perkins
Treg Thomas
Sports: Hi School Football
Gary "Turk" McGill
Dicenzo Miller
Romaro Miller
Dontae Walker
Sports: Olympic Champions
Ruthie Bolton-Holifield ('96)
Ralph Boston (1960)
Lee Calhoun (1956 & 1960)
Commodore Cochran (1924)
Roy Cochran (1948)
Hayes Jones (1964)
Falilatu Ogunkoya (1996)
Don Scott (1924)
Willye B. White (1964)
Sports: Pro / Major League Baseball
James "Cool Papa" Bell
Don Blasingame
Dennis "Oil Can" Boyd
Jeff Branson
Jeff Brantley
Ellis Rena Burks
Guy T. Bush
Dave Clark
Will Clark
Harry "Popeye" Craft
Hughie Critz
Dizzy Dean
Jim Edwards
Dave "Boo" Ferriss
Willie Foster
Charlie Hayes
Hal Lee

Chet Lemon
Sam Leslie
Eric McNair
Willie Mitchell
Buddy Myer
Rafael Palmeiro
Dave Parker
Claude Passeau
Andy Reese
George "Boomer" Scott
Del Unser
S.B. "Sam" Vick
Gerald Walker
Harry "The Hat" Walker
"Skeeter" Webb
Frank White
Sports: Pro Basketball
Mahmoud Abdul-Rauf
Joe Courtney
Othello Harrington
Antonio Harvey
Spencer Haywood
Bailey Howell
Lindsey Hunter
Randolph Keys
Jeff Malone
Danny Manning
Antonio McDyess
Derrick McKey
James Robinson
Purvis Short
Lusia Harris Stewart
Clarence Weatherspoon
Sports: Pro Boxers
Henry Armstrong
Freddie Little
Archie Moore
Sports: Pro Football
Lance Alworth
Fred Barnett
Lem Barney
J.T. "Blondy" Black
Tim Bowens
Willie Brown
Ode Burrell
Charlie Conerly
Marcus Dupree
Brett Favre
L.C. Greenwood
Jack Gregory
Ray Guy
Houston Hoover
Kent Hull
Deacon Jones
Frank "Bruiser" Kinard
Aubrey D. Matthews
Bilbo "Mule" Monaghan
Wilbert N. Montgomery
Eric Moulds
Walter Payton
Vernon Perry
Cory Philpot
James E. "Buster" Poole
Jerry Rice
Billy Shaw

Jackie Slater
Torrance Small
Jimmy Smith
Johnny R. "Jack" Spinks
Billy Stacey
Wesley Walls
Norris Weese
Ben Williams
Sammy Winder
Sports: Pro Golfers
Jim Gallagher, Jr.
Eddie Merrins
Cary Middlecoff
Sports: Racecar Drivers
Jim Pace
Lake Speed
Sports: Others
Brad Edwards (statistician)
Rett Crowder (amateur golfer)
Buddy Durr: Pro archer
Robert Fairley (former
   Harlem Globetrotter)
Clay Hopper (manager)
Daron Jenkins (former
   Harlem Globetrotter)
Sylvia Howell Krebs
   high school basketball
Ken Lindsay (club golf pro)
Dot Murphy (high school &
   college basketball coach +
   college football coach)
Ben Nelson
   (PGA Tour golf official)
William Pittman II
   Rodeo champ
Trent Pulliam (former
   Harlem Globetrotter)
Anna Reeves: Pro archer
Calvin Smith (sprinter)
Mike Taylor (amateur golfer)
Herbert Theriot (rodeo champ)
Charles C. Walker
   (checkers champion)
Tom Wilburn
   (horse harness racing)
Top Students - 36 ACT Score
Jennifer Carlisle
Kevin Etheridge
Shayon Ghosh
Michael Goggin
Craig Ross
Kimberly R. Smith
Christine M. Varnado
TV Hosts / Talk-Show Hosts
Lisa Stewart
Nan Sumrall
Oprah Winfrey
TV Producers / Writers
Blaine Baggett
Frederick H. Coe
Terry Ewert
Writers / Novelists
Margaret Walker Alexander
John Armistead
William Attaway

Famous & Notable Mississippians Listed by Profession

James A. Autry	Greg Iles	Richard Wright	John Johnston
Howard Bahr	Beverly Lowry	Steve Yarbrough	(Film locations manager)
Nevada Barr	Jim Majure	Al Young	Belle Kearney
Jack Bass	Jim McCafferty	Zig Ziglar	(Feminist/state senator)
David Blankenhorn	Neil McGaughey	**Writers (Poets)**	Patrick Kelly (Fashion designer)
William T. Brannon	John Ramsey Miller	Charles G. Bell	John A. Lomax (Archivist)
Larry Brown	Mary Carol Miller	Hubert Creekmore	Ray Lum
Bill Buchanan	Willie Morris	Brooks Haxton	(Mule trader/storyteller)
Jack Butler	Ellis Nassour	William Alexander Percy	Jimmie Lunceford (Big band
Will D. Campbell	Leedell W. Neyland	Sterling D. Plumpp	musician/leader)
Robert Canzoneri	Lewis Nordan	**Others: Miscellaneous**	Phillip Martin (Indian Chief
Charlotte Capers	Laurie E. Parker	Jim Brewer (educator &	& entrepreneur)
Anne Carsley	Walker Percy	founder of the Miss.	Roy M. Martin
Forrest Lamar Cooper	Jim Ritchie	Musicians Hall of Fame)	(Hi School band director)
David L. Cohn	Felder Rushing	Helen Carlisle (writer)	Mike McGregor
Harold Cross	Patrick D. Smith	Jefferson Davis	(Craftsman: jeweler)
Borden Deal	Elizabeth Spencer	(President of the C.S.A.)	Evelyn McPhail
Louisa Dixon	James Howell Street	Mary Angie Douglass	(Political party official)
Ellen Douglas	Cid Ricketts Sumner	(Administrator/secretary)	Frederic Frances Mellen
John Faulkner	Donna Tartt	Arty Finkelberg	(Geologist/writer)
William Faulkner	Clifton L. Taulbert	(Financial analysis)	Ralph Null (Floral designer)
William R. Ferris	Mildred D. Taylor	Rev. C.L. Franklin (Minister)	Jack H. Oakman
John M. Floyd	Mildred Spurrier Topp	Edward O. Fritts	(Film expert & collector)
Richard Ford	Rebecca Walker	(President/CEO of NAB)	Paul Ott (Entertainer/
Jim Fraiser	Brad Watson	Greg Harkins	conservationist)
Frances Jones Gaither	Peggy Webb	(Craftsman: chairmaker)	Janos Radvanyi (Professor/
Ellen Gilchrist	Mary Ann Wells	Jim Henson (Puppeteer)	environmentalist)
John Grisham	Eudora Welty	Herbie Holmes (Big band	Charlemae Rollins (Librarian)
Barry Hannah	Ben Ames Williams	musician/leader)	Joseph P. Seawright
Phil Hardwick	Mamie Davis Willoughby	Richard E. Holmes	(Designer/history-maker)
Thomas Harris	Charles Wilson	(history-maker/physician)	
Rebecca Hill	Richard Wiman		

NOTE: Persons are listed by their main profession, or that profession in which they have made the greatest impact. Many have also made significant contributions in other fields (i.e., many listed as singers are also songwriters, although we list only 10 as songwriters, and many professors, instead of being listed as educators, are listed as writers or artists).

The Number of Famous & Notable Mississippians Listed in Each Profession

Actors & Actresses	55	Inventors	8	Songwriters	10
Advertising	5	Journalists / Editors / Publishers	24	Sports: Coaches / administrators	20
Architects	2	Military Heroes-MOH Recipients	21	Sports: College Basketball	4
Artists (painters, potters, etc.)	24	Military Leaders	6	Sports: College Football	14
Astronauts / NASA Officials	6	Movie Costume / Set Designers	5	Sports: Hi School Football	4
Attorneys / Jurists	6	Movie Directors / Producers	10	Sports: Olympic Champions	9
Aviation Pioneers	4	Movie Score Writers	2	Sports: Major League Baseball	33
Beauty Contest Winners	7	Movie Screenwriters	3	Sports: Pro Basketball	16
Bluesmen (& Women)	82	Musicians	16	Sports: Pro Boxers	3
Broadcasters / Sportscasters	8	Musicians (Jazz)	20	Sports: Pro Football	36
Business Executives / CEOs	21	Philanthropists	3	Sports: Pro Golfers	3
Cartoonists	2	Playwrights	5	Sports: Racecar Drivers	2
Choreographers / Dancers	3	Photographers	4	Sports: Others	18
Civil Rights Leaders / Activists	8	Physicians	6	Top students-ACT score of 36	7
Comedians / Humorists	6	Politicians	16	TV Hosts / Talk-Show Hosts	3
Composers/Conductors	3	Record Producers	3	TV Producers / Writers	3
Critics	3	Researchers	2	Writers / Novelists	71
Educators / College Founders	13	Scientists	4	Writers (Poets)	5
Government Service	7	Singers	80	Others: Miscellaneous	28
Historians / Biographers	11	Singers: Opera	2	**Total No. People Listed**	**805**

Birth Places of Native-Born Famous & Notable Mississippians

Abbeville (Lafayette County)
Jennifer Gillom
Peggy Gillom
Aberdeen (Monroe County)
Guy Bush
Ackerman (Choctaw County)
Cecil Blackwood
Doyle Blackwood
James Blackwood
R.W. Blackwood
Turner Catledge
Cheryl Prewitt
Agricola (George County)
Mary Ann Wells
Alligator (Bolivar County)
Jack Butler
Frederick H. Coe
Amory (Monroe County)
Lucille Bogan
John Dye
Gary Grubbs
Bilbo "Mule" Monaghan
Arkabutla (Tate County)
James Earl Jones
Ashland (Benton County)
Willie Mitchell (the musician)
Attala County
Dumas Milner
Banner (Calhoun County)
Jim Edwards
Batesville (Panola County)
S.B. "Sam" Vick
Wesley Walls
Thomas Wayne
Bay Saint Louis (Hancock County)
Pete Fountain
Evelyn McPhail
Belmont (Tishomingo County)
Mac McAnally
Belzoni (Humphreys County)
Eddie "Guitar" Burns
Charles "Chuck" Gordon
Glenn Honeycutt
Pinetop Perkins
Benoit (Bolivar County)
Archie Moore
Benton (Yazoo County)
Jimmy Heidel
Benton County
James A. Autry
Bentonia (Yazoo County)
Skip James
Jack Owens
Biloxi (Harrison County)
T. Bubba Bechtol
Fred W. Haise, Jr.
Gerald Hopkins
Grady Howell, Jr.
Chris LeDoux
Mary Ann Mobley
George Ohr
Eric Roberts
Blue Mountain (Tippah County)
Jerome F. Leavell

Bolton (Hinds County)
Bo Carter
Sam Chatmon
Doug Hutton
Calvin Smith
Walter Vinson
Brandon (Rankin County)
Donna Hild Russell
Louis Hugh Wilson, Jr.
Richard Wiman
Brookhaven (Lincoln County)
Bruce H. Brady
Jimmie McDowell
Garry Owen
Jim Ritchie
Cid Ricketts Sumner
Wyatt Waters
Karl Wolfe
Brooksville (Noxubee County)
Frederick O'Neal
Bruce (Calhoun County)
Laurie E. Parker
Byhalia (Marshall County)
Louis Myers
Byram (Hinds County)
Ishmon Bracey
Calhoun City (Calhoun County)
Dave Parker
Canton (Madison County)
L.C. Greenwood
John McCrady
Ben Nelson
Johnnie "Geechie" Temple
Harvey "Pop" Watkins, Sr.
Carroll County
Crawford Mims
Carrollton (Carroll County)
Frances E. Neal
John A. Pittman
Elizabeth Spencer
Carthage (Leake County)
Charles Graham
Cascilla (Tallahatchie County)
Jamie L. Whitten
Cayce (Marshall County)
Rufus Thomas
Centreville (Wilkinson County)
Gerald M. Hollingsworth
Anne Moody
Chicora (Wayne County)
Gavin Gordon
Choctaw County
Hoyt Lester Ming
Clarksdale (Coahoma County)
Lerone Bennett, Jr.
Jackie Brenston
Charlie Conerly
Sam Cooke
Rev. C.L. Franklin
Lillian "Lil" Green
Aaron Henry
Earl Zebedee Hooker
John Lee Hooker
Little Junior Parker
"Sir" Mack Rice

Larry A. Thompson
Ike Turner
Charles Wright
Cleveland (Bolivar County)
Larry Speakes
Clinton (Hinds County)
Sterling D. Plumpp
Coffeeville (Yalobusha County)
S. Gale Denley
Coldwater (Tate County)
Robert Earl Jones
Dumas Malone
Hoyt B. Wooten
Collins (Covington County)
Dana Andrews (in Dont community)
Mack A. Jordan
Randolph Keys
Gerald McRaney
Collinsville (Lauderdale County)
Jimmy Ruffin
Columbia (Marion County)
Peggy Dow
Walter Payton
Columbus (Lowndes County)
Henry Armstrong
Walter Lanier "Red" Barber
Glen Graham
Birney Imes
Gene Murphy
Ralph Null
Brad Smith
Frank Trippett
Tom Wilburn
Tennessee Williams
Como (Panola County)
Stark Young
Corinth (Alcorn County)
Don Blasingame
John N. Palmer, Sr.
Thomas Hal Phillips
Roscoe Turner
Crawford (Lowndes County)
Jerry Rice
Clarence Weatherspoon
"Big" Joe Williams
Crystal Springs (Copiah County)
Frances "Fannye" Cook
Pat Harrison
D'Iberville (Harrison County)
Reggie Collier
Decatur (Newton County)
Charles Evers
Medgar Evers
Doddsville (Sunflower County)
James O. Eastland
Drew (Sunflower County)
Archie Manning
Dundee (Tunica County)
Marshall Bouldin III
James Cotton
Dunleith (Washington County)
Jimmy Reed
Durant (Holmes)
Jim Majure

Birth Places of Native-Born Famous & Notable Mississippians

East Fork (Amite County)
Will D. Campbell
Jerry Clower
Ebenezer (Holmes County)
Saul Haymond, Sr.
Eden (Yazoo County)
James "Son" Thomas
Edinburg (Leake County)
Van T. Barfoot
Edwards (Hinds County)
Charley Patton
Ellisville (Jones County)
Harry "Popeye" Craft
Luke McDaniel
Buddy Myer
Escatawpa (Jackson County)
Jack G. Hanson
Eupora (Webster County)
Dicenzo Miller
Fame (Webster County)
Ethel Wright Mohamed
Fannin (Rankin County)
Dick Griffin
Fayette (Jefferson County)
Richard H. Truly
Fentress (Choctaw County)
Roy Blackwood
Flora (Madison County)
George Chambers
Lester Chambers
Willie Chambers
Belle Kearney
Florence (Rankin County)
Little Howlin' Wolf
Flowood (Rankin County)
Jennifer Carlisle
Kevin Etheridge
Forest (Scott County)
Arthur "Big Boy" Crudup
Friars Point (Coahoma County)
Sam Carr
B. Reeves Eason
Conway Twitty
Fulton (Itawamba County)
Jimmie Lunceford
Glen Allan (Washington County)
Clifton L. Taulbert
Glendora (Tallahatchie County)
Sonny Boy Williamson II
Gloster (Amite County)
Leedell W. Neyland
James E. "Buster" Poole
Goodman (Holmes County)
Ode Burrell
David Donald
John A. Lomax
Grange (Lawrence County)
Roscoe Ates
Greenville (Washington County)
Ruth Attaway
William Attaway
Harry Basch
William Beckwith
Charles G. Bell
David L. Cohn

Tyrone Davis
Steve Douglas
Shelby Foote
Walt Grayson
Brooks Haxton
Robert T. Henry
Jim Henson
Valerie Jaudon
Leon Z. Koury
John Ramsey Miller
Wilbert N. Montgomery
William Alexander Percy
Ben Peters
George "Boomer" Scott
Mary Wilson
Hattie Winston
Greenwood (Leflore County)
Paul T. Brown
Calvin Cox
Jim Dollarhide
Betty Everett
Clay Hopper
Kent Hull
Means Johnston, Jr.
Eddie "Guitar Slim" Jones
Walter "Furry" Lewis
Mary Carol Miller
Mulgrew Miller
Carrie Nye
Joseph P. Seawright
Tonea Stewart
Hubert Sumlin
Donna Tartt
Frank White
Grenada (Grenada County)
Ace Cannon
Walter Davis
Jake Gibbs
Trent Lott
Magic Sam
Sandra Polanski
W.C. Taylor, Jr.
Frank Wright
Gulfport (Harrison County)
Mahmoud Abdul-Rauf
Lem Barney
Don Jeffcoat
Jaimoe Jai Johanny
Johnny Sea
Symba Smith
Gerald Walker
Lloyd Wells
Harperville (Scott County)
Elsie McWilliams
Hattiesburg (Forrest County)
Jim Brewer
Jesse Leroy Brown
Bobby Bryant
Robert H. "Ace" Cleveland, Jr.
Henry A. Commiskey, Sr.
Blind John Davis
Dorothy Dell
Tim Floyd
Evelyn Gandy
Michael Goggin

Charlie Hayes
Eddie Hodges
John Vincent Imbragulio
Tom "Bones" Malone
Danny Manning
Oseola McCarty
Purvis Short
Nan Sumrall
Charles C. Walker
Hazlehurst (Copiah County)
Ruth Ford
Robert Johnson
Reuben W. Millsaps
Hernando (DeSoto County)
Robert Wilkins
Hickory Flat (Benton County)
Elder Roma Wilson
Holcut (Tishimingo County)
A.C. "Butch" Lambert
Holly Springs (Marshall County)
Kate Freeman Clark
Mel Hardin
Jimmy Johnson
Tim McPherson
Ida Bell Wells-Barnett
Holmes County
Hernando De Soto Money
Horn Lake (DeSoto County)
Blaine Baggett
"Big" Walter Horton
Houston (Chickasaw County)
Dee Barton
Bobbie Gentry
Trent Pulliam
Bukka White
Hudsonville (Marshall County)
"Junior" Kimbrough
Independence (Tate County)
Michael Humphreys
Indianola (Sunflower County)
Mary Alice
William M. "Jazz" Gillum
George Jackson
Albert King
Felder Rushing
Steve Yarbrough
Inverness (Sunflower County)
Coolidge Ball
Little Milton
Isola (Humphreys County)
Hank Cochran
Buddy Durr
Itta Bena (Leflore County)
B.B. King
Marion S. Barry, Jr.
Luther "Guitar Jr." Johnson
Lewis Nordan
Iuka (Tishomingo County)
H.T. "Dick" Merrill
Jackson (Hinds County)
Alyce Alston
Rueben Anderson
Richard "Dick" Armstrong
James Barksdale
David Blankenhorn

The Ultimate Reference on the State

Birth Places of Native-Born Famous & Notable Mississippians

Jackson (continued)
Kelly Brown
Richard Jess Brown, Jr.
Paul Brummett
Anne Carsley
Johnny Carver
Clifford E. Charlesworth
Harry A. Cole, Sr.
Forrest Lamar Cooper
Joe Courtney
Brad Edwards
Theodore "Teddy" Edwards
Lehman Engel
Jamaa Fanaka
Richard Ford
Cynthia Lynn Geary
Paul Gray
Alice Haining
Edwin "Goat" Hale
Greg Harkins
Robert Harper
Othello Harrington
Jimmy Henderson
Beth Henley
William Hollingsworth
John Johnston
Fred Knobloch
Sylvia Howell Krebs
Chet Lemon
Tom Lester
Eleni Matos
John Maxwell
Richard D. McRae, Sr.
Henry "Skeets" McWilliams
Dorothy Moore
Willie Morris
Dot Murphy
Charles L. Overby
Vernon Perry
Hollis Pippin
Bob Pittman
Will Primos
Tom Rice
James Robinson
Joe Frank Sanderson
James L. Seawright, Jr.
Jackie Slater
Janet Marie Smith
L.T. Smith
Otis Spann
Lake Speed
Mildred D. Taylor
Byron Thames
Ernestine Wade
Freddie Waits
Dontae Walker
Rebecca Walker
Eudora Welty
Cassandra Wilson
Elizabeth Wolfe
Jefferson (Carroll County)
Early Wright
Jefferson County
Evelyn Allen Hammett

Kemper County
John C. Stennis
Louis Westerfield
Kosciusko (Attala County)
John M. Floyd
Becca Jackson
James Meredith
Charlie Musselwhite
Carolyn Bennett Patterson
Oprah Winfrey
Lakeshore (Hancock County)
Ted Hawkins
Lambert (Quitman County)
"Big" Jack Johnson
James "Snooky" Pryor
Laurel (Jones County)
Lance Bass
Ralph Boston
Lee Calhoun
Bobby Collins
Mundell Lowe
George Baker Price
Leontyne Price
James D. Slaton
Ray Walston
Leflore County
Denise LaSalle
Leland (Washington County)
Joe Frank Carollo
John Daniel "J.D." Evermore
Thelma Houston
Johnny Winter
Lexington (Holmes County)
John C. Black
Lonnie Pitchford
Liberty (Amite County)
Mamie Davis Willoughby
Longwood (Washington County)
Roosevelt "Booba" Barnes
Louise (Humphreys County)
Warren Smith
Louisville (Winston County)
Tim Ellis
Carl Jackson
Lisa Stewart
Lucedale (George County)
Robert Fairley
Eric Moulds
Ludlow (Scott County)
Hal Lee
Lumberton (Lamar County)
James Howell Street
Macon (Noxubee County)
Carey Bell
Eddy Clearwater
Marietta Eichelberger
Ben Ames Williams
Madison County
Annie C. Peyton
Sammy Winder
Magee (Simpson County)
Roland Dale
Kris Mangum
Magnolia (Pike County)
Prentiss Barnes

Marks (Quitman County)
Frederick W. Smith
Mathiston (Choctaw County)
Jerry H. Booth
Bill Dunlap
McComb (Pike County)
Woodie Assaf
Steve Blailock
Jimmy Boyd
Brandy (Norwood)
Bo Diddley
John O. Emmerich, Jr.
Willie "Ray-J" Norwood, Jr.
Paul Ott
Will A. Price
Dan Tyler
McCool (Attala County)
Margaret Wade
McLain (Greene County)
Ruthie Bolton-Holifield
Mendenhall (Simpson County)
Phil Hardwick
Daron Jenkins
Patrick D. Smith
Meridian (Lauderdale County)
Susan Diane Akin
Howard Bahr
Moe Bandy
Brendon Boone
Dennis "Oil Can" Boyd
Alvin Childress
Paul Davis
Steve Forbert
Edwin Phillips Granberry
Phil Gordon
Barry Hannah
Wilbur Higby
Ty Herndon
Diane Ladd
Richard Mayo
Herschel McCoy
Derrick McKey
Eric McNair
Thomas E. "Shorty" McWilliams
Eddie Merrins
G.V. "Sonny" Montgomery
Hartley Peavey
Walter Reed
Jane Reid-Petty
Leslie Vaughn Rush
Sela Ward
Brad Watson
"Skeeter" Webb
Al Wilson
Mico [now Shady Grove] (Jones Co.)
Ira C. Welborn
Minter City (Leflore County)
Lusia Harris Stewart
Money (Leflore County)
Willye B. White
Montgomery County
Fannie Lou Hamer
Monticello (Lawrence County)
J.B. Lenoir
Jim Pace

Birth Places of Native-Born Famous & Notable Mississippians

Mooreville (Lee County)
Olin Francis
Peggy Webb
Moorhead (Sunflower County)
Johnny Russell
Moselle (Jones County)
Roy M. Wheat
Moss Point (Jackson County)
Robert C. Khayat
Sam Leslie
Mount Olive (Covington County)
Steve McNair
Ray Perkins
Muskegon (Scott County)
Hamilton Smith
Myrtle (Union County)
Charlie Feathers
Natchez (Adams County)
Glen Ballard
Wilson Brown
J.F.H. Claiborne
Frank L. Cooley
Ellen Douglas
Mickey Gilley
Hugh Green
Martha Mattox
Neil McGaughey
Billy Shaw
"Hound Dog" Taylor
Richard Wright
Nettleton (Lee County)
Felix J. Underwood
New Albany (Union County)
William Faulkner
Newhebron (Lawrence County)
Erick Dampier
Newton (Newton County)
Paul Overstreet
Newton County
James F. Brieger
Bob Saxton
Oakland (Yalobusha County)
Dunbar Rowland
Ocean Springs (Jackson County)
Al Young
Okolona (Chickasaw County)
Tim Bowens
Milan B. Williams
William Raspberry
Osyka (Pike County)
T. Tommy Cutrer
Oxford (Lafayette County)
R.L. Burnside
Julie Kaye Fanton
Arthur C. Guyton
Pachuta (Clarke County)
William T. Brannon
Panther Burn (Sharkey County)
Jack H. Oakman
Paris (Lafayette County)
Theora Hamblett
Pascagoula (Jackson County)
Jimmy Buffett
Antonio Harvey
Margie Joseph

Aubrey D. Matthews
Eugenia Ann Talbott
Treg Thomas
Harry "The Hat" Walker
Libby Rae Watson
Jim Ziglar
Pass Christian (Harrison County)
Brett Favre
Pearl (Rankin County)
LeAnn Rimes
Pelahatchie (Rankin County)
Frank "Bruiser" Kinard
Jim Buck Ross
Philadelphia (Neshoba County)
J.T. "Blondy" Black
Marcus Dupree
Daniel P. Jordan
Florence Mars
Phillip Martin
William Silas "Si" Redd
Otis Rush
Sidney L. "Sid" Salter
Marty Stuart
Picayune (Pearl River County)
Freddie Little
Pine Springs (Lauderdale County)
Jimmie Rodgers
Pleasant Grove (Panola County)
Willie Mitchell (the baseball player)
Pontotoc (Pontotoc County)
Thad Cochran
Borden Deal
Jim Weatherly
Pontotoc County
Delaney Bramlett
Bonnie Lynn Bramlett
Purvis (Lamar County)
Lacey Chabert
Lillian McMurry
Joseph Paul Treen
Quitman (Clarke County)
Wyatt Cooper
Antonio McDyess
Red Banks (Marshall County)
Gus "Banjo Joe" Cannon
Richland (Holmes County)
Elmore James
Richton (Perry County)
Commodore Cochran
Roy Cochran
Bert Jenkins
George Ellis Johnson
Ripley (Tippah County)
Harold Cross
John Faulkner
Riverton (Coahoma County)
Eddie "Son" House
Rocky Springs (Claiborne County)
Ray Lum
Rolling Fork (Sharkey County)
"Muddy Waters"
Willie Mae Ford Smith
Rome (Sunflower County)
James C. "Butch" Rosser

Ruleville (Sunflower County)
Luster Bayless
Jimmy Rogers
Scott (Bolivar County)
Big Bill Broonzy
Scott County
Joe Chambers
Senatobia (Tate County)
Henry Herschel Brickell
O.B. McClinton
Shannon (Lee County)
Romaro Miller
Sharon (Madison County)
K.C. Douglas
Shaw (Bolivar County)
Louis Baloni
David "Honeyboy" Edwards
Dave "Boo" Ferriss
Prescilla D. Slade
Shelby (Bolivar County)
Fred Barnett
Gerald Stanley Wilson
Shuqualak (Noxubee County)
W.G. "Mickey" Holliman, Jr.
Sidon (Leflore County)
Frank E. Smith
Silver City (Humphreys County)
Spencer Haywood
Sledge (Quitman County)
Harold Dorman
Charley Pride
Smithdale (Amite County)
Frank Williams
Smithville (Monroe County)
Rod Brasfield
Sontag (Lawrence County)
Ben H. Douglas
Star (Rankin County)
Faith Hill
Starkville (Oktibbeha County)
James "Cool Papa" Bell
Eugene Butler
Hughie Critz
Richard E. Holmes
Hayes Jones
Frederic Frances Mellen
Stovall (Coahoma County)
Eddie Boyd
Summit (Pike County)
Marie Atkinson Hull
Sunflower (Sunflower County)
Willie Best
Craig Claiborne
Matt "Guitar" Murphy
Sunflower County
Jerry Butler
Taylorsville (Smith County)
Gary "Turk" McGill
Teoc (Carroll County)
Mississippi John Hurt
John Sidney McCain
Terry (Hinds County)
Tommy Johnson
Tibbs (Tunica County)
Mike McGregor

The Ultimate Reference on the State

Birth Places of Native-Born Famous & Notable Mississippians

Tippo (Tallahatchie County)
Mose John Allison
Tishomingo County
John Allen
Tomnolen (Webster County)
Paul Gregory
Toomsuba (Lauderdale County)
Johnny R. "Jack" Spinks
Tremont (Itawamba County)
Tammy Wynette
Tunica (Tunica County)
Isaiah "Doctor" Ross
Tupelo (Lee County)
Dave Clark
William Lockhart Clayton
Jack Gregory
Guy Hovis
Jim McCafferty
Elvis Presley
Andy Reese
"Jumpin'" Gene Simmons
Tylertown (Walthall County)
Jo Foxworth
Pat Kirby
Utica (Hinds County)
Lindsey Hunter
Vance (Quitman County)
Sunnyland Slim
Vicksburg (Warren County)
Ellis Rena Burks
Charles Burnett
Owen Cooper
Mart Crowley
William David
Willie Dixon
Tellis "T.B." Ellis
Myrlie Evers-Williams
William R. Ferris

Cliff Freeman
Ellen Gilchrist
Mark Gray
Milt Hinton
Junie Hovious
Henry "Hank" Jones
Patrick Kelly
Ellis Nassour
Beah Richards
Craig Ross
John "Big Bad" Smitty
Artie White
Johnny Young
Vossburg (Jasper County)
Helen Carlisle
Walnut (Tippah County)
Travis Haddix
Water Valley (Yalobusha County)
Ernie Chaffin
Hubert Creekmore
Waynesboro (Wayne County)
Jeff Branson
Tena Clark
Claude Passeau
West Point (Clay County)
John H. Bryan, Jr.
Toxey Haas
"Howlin' Wolf"
Malcolm Portera
Lenore L. Prather
Larry Semon
Thomas Roger Stevens
Barrett Strong
Wheeler (Prentiss County)
Don Lee Keith
Whynot (Lauderdale County)
David Ruffin

Wiggins (Stone County)
Anthony Herrera
Winona (Montgomery County)
Earle W. Hammons
Donald H. Peterson
Anna Reeves
Billy Stacey
Roebuck "Pop" Staples
Charles S. Thomas, Sr.
Winstonville (Bolivar County)
Major Lance
Woodstock [now Money] **(Leflore Co.)**
John W. Heard
Woodville (Wilkinson County)
Don Scott
William Grant Still
Lester Willis Young
Yazoo City (Yazoo County)
Haley Barbour
B.J. Barrier, Jr.
Willie Brown
John Tyler Caldwell
V. Ruth Campbell
Helen Carloss
Mike Espy
Larry Gordon
Mike Henderson
Herbie Holmes
Houston Hoover
Charlemae Rollins
Stella Stevens
Ted. J. Webb, Jr.
Ben Williams
Yocona (Lafayette County)
Larry Brown
X-Prairie (Noxubee County)
Mary Angie Douglass
?, Mississippi Archie Brownlee

The Number of Famous & Notable Mississippians Born in Each County

County	#	County	#	County	#	County	#
Adams	12	Grenada	8	Lincoln	6	Simpson	5
Alcorn	5	Hancock	3	Lowndes	14	Smith	1
Amite	6	Harrison	18	Madison	12	Stone	1
Attala	8	Hinds	74	Marion	2	Sunflower	18
Benton	3	Holmes	9	Marshall	9	Tallahatchie	3
Bolivar	12	Humphreys	8	Monroe	6	Tate	7
Calhoun	3	Issaquena	0	Montgomery	6	Tippah	4
Carroll	7	Itawamba	2	Neshoba	9	Tishomingo	3
Chickasaw	7	Jackson	13	Newton	5	Tunica	4
Choctaw	10	Jasper	1	Noxubee	7	Union	2
Claiborne	1	Jefferson	2	Oktibbeha	6	Walthall	2
Clarke	3	Jefferson Davis	0	Panola	5	Warren	22
Clay	8	Jones	14	Pearl River	1	Washington	28
Coahoma	19	Kemper	2	Perry	4	Wayne	5
Copiah	5	Lafayette	7	Pike	13	Webster	3
Covington	6	Lamar	4	Pontotoc	5	Wilkinson	5
DeSoto	3	Lauderdale	33	Prentiss	1	Winston	3
Forrest	19	Lawrence	5	Quitman	6	Yalobusha	4
Franklin	0	Leake	2	Rankin	11	Yazoo	19
George	3	Lee	12	Scott	5	Unknown county	1
Greene	1	Leflore	26	Sharkey	3	**Total**	**659**

Other Mississippi Blues Artists

Name and Nickname[1]	Associated Songs/Albums & Notes	Place of Birth	D.O.B.	Died
Adams, Woodrow Wilson	(guitarist with Sun Records)	Tchula	04-09-1917	
Akers, Garfield	"Cottonfield Blues"/"Dough Roller Blues"	Batesville	c. 1902	c. 1962
Alexander, James "J.W."	(worked with The Rolling Stones & others)	Hamilton	01-21-1916	07-08-1996
Allen, Pete	(worked with Artie White & Carey Bell)	McComb	08-11-1949	
Anderson, Brint	"Homage to Elmore" (1995)	Natchez	04-12-1954	
Anderson, Jimmy	"House Rockin' & Hip Swingin'"	Natchez	11-21-1934	
Andrews, Ruby	"Casanova (Your Playing Days Are Over)"	Hollandale	03-12-1947	
Armstead, Joshie "Jo"	(with the Ikettes & worked with B.B. King)	Yazoo City	10-18-1944	
Armstrong, Walter Zuber	(tenor sax jazz artist)	Tupelo	09-09-1936	03-01-1998
Austin, Jesse "Wild Bill"	"Steel Trap (1992)/"Baby's Back" (1995)	Longwood	09-25-1930	03-22-1996
Baker, "King Ernest"	"I Feel Alright"/"That's When I Woke Up"	Natchez	05-30-1939	03-04-2000
Baker, Sam	"No Love Lost" ('96)/"Bringing U Some Soul"	Jackson	06-14-1941	
Bankhead, Tommy	"Message to St. Louis" (2000)	Lake Comorant	10-24-1931	
Banks, Willie	(leader of gospel group, the Southeraires)	Raymond	05-11-1929	02-01-1993
Bankston, Dick	?	Crystal Springs	??-??-1899	?
Barnes, Walter	(a bandleader who played clarinet & sax)	Vicksburg	07-08-1905	04-23-1940
Bates, Leroy "Lefty"	(with Jimmy Reed/Eddie Taylor/Willie Dixon)	Pelahatchie	05-07-1924	03-02-1991
Batts, Will	"Sounds of Memphis (1933-39)"	Michigan City	01-24-1902	02-18-1956
Beard, Joe	"No More Cherry Rose" & "It's Up To You"	Ashland	02-04-1938	
Beauregard, Nathan	"Nobody's Business But My Own"	Ashland	??-??-1863	??-??-1970
Beckett, Frederic Lee	(jazz trombonist with Lionel Hampton)	Nettleton	01-23-1917	01-30-1946
Bell, Earl	(guitarist)	Hernando	02-19-1914	07-??-1977
Benson, Al	(produced Albert King-owned Parrot Records)	Jackson	06-30-1908	09-06-1978
Bertrand, Jimmy	(worked w/Johnny Dodds/Louis Armstrong)	Biloxi	02-24-1900	?
Bevel, Charles	(wrote songs for & worked with Jerry Butler)	Swiftown	12-07-1938	
Billington, "Mr." Johnnie	(blues guitarist who now lives in Lambert)	Crowder	04-11-1935	
Binder, Dennis "Long Man"	"Long Man Blues"	Rosedale	08-13-1907	07-??-1998
Blackman, Junior	(drummer with Howlin' Wolf & others)	Leland	08-30-1935	
Blakeney, Andrew "Andy Blake"	(worked some with Lionel Hampton)	Quitman	06-10-1898	02-12-1992
Blakes, Clennon Lee	(harp player known as "Sonny Blake")	Dundee	01-04-1923	
Boines, Huston	"Blow It 'Til You Like It: Memphis" (1990)	Hazlehurst	12-30-1918	11-08-1970
Booker, Charlie	"Memphis Blues Caravan, Vol. 2" (1994)	Moorhead.	09-03-1919	09-20-1989
Boyd, Little (real given name)	(harmonica player)	Carthage	08-24-1924	02-??-1978
Boyson, Cornelius "Boysaw"	(played bass with Koko Taylor)	Tunica	09-05-1936	07-09-1994
Braddy, Pauline	(drummer w/the Sweethearts of Rhythm)	Mendenhall	02-14-1922	01-??-1996
Bradford, Bobby Lee	(trumpet player/composer w/Quincy Jones)	Cleveland	07-19-1934	
Bradley, Addie "Jan"	"We Girls" (worked with Curtis Mayfield)	Byhalia	07-06-1943	
Brewer, James "Blind Jim"	"I Don't Want No Woman If She Got Hair Like Drops of Rain"	Brookhaven	10-03-1921	06-03-1988
Brooks, "Big" Leon	"Let's Go to Town"	Sunflower	11-19-1933	01-22-1982
Brooks, Columbus	(guitarist for Sam Myers)	Jackson.	11-16-1927	02-04-1976
Brown, Andrew	"Can't Let You Go"	Jackson	02-25-1937	12-11-1985
Brown, Arelean	(vocalist)	Tchula	06-10-1924	04-27-1981
Brown, Cleo	"Living in the Afterglow" (1996)	Meridian	12-08-1903	04-15-1995
Brown, Dusty	"Chicago Blues Harmonica" (1998)	Tralake	03-11-1929	
Brown, John Henry "Bubba"	(vocalist and piano player)	Brandon	12-05-1902	12-??-1985
Brown, James Thomas "J.T."	"Windy City Boogie" (1951)	?, Miss.	04-02-1918	11-24-1969
Brown, Mel	"I'd Rather Be Sucking My Thumb" (1969)	Jackson	10-07-1939	
Brown, "Smoky Babe" Robert	(played around Baton Rouge in early 1960s)	Itta Bena	12-24-1927	01-??-1976
Brown, Willie Lee	"Future Blues" and "M&O Blues"	Clarksdale	08-06-1900	12-30-1952
Buford, George "Mojo"	(harp player for Muddy Waters)	Hernando	11-10-1929	
Burks, Eddie	"Vampire Woman" and "This Old Road"	Rising Sun	09-15-1931	11-20-1997
Burns, Jimmy	"Leaving Here Walking" (1996)	Dublin	02-27-1943	
Burton, Aron	"Garbage Man"	Thyatira	06-15-1938	
Burton, Larry	(guitarist on many albums-Aron's brother)	Coldwater	03-16-1951	
Butler, George "Wild Child"	(played harmonica/guitar w/Muddy Waters)	Hernando	10-01-1936	
Cage, James "Butch"	"Raise a Ruckus Tonight"	Hamburg	03-16-1894	12-??-1973
Calhoun, Eddie	(played bass for Erroll Garner, et al.)	Clarksdale	11-13-1921	01-27-1994
Calicott, "Mississippi Joe"	"Great Long Ways From Home"	Nesbit	11-10-1900	10-??-1969
Campbell, Eddie C.	"King of the Jungle" (1977, reissued 1996)	Duncan	05-06-1939	
Campbell, Lucie E.	(gospel songwriter)	Duck Hill	04-30-1885	01-03-1963

[1] This is a list of 305 blues men and women (some rather minor and/or obscure) not profiled or listed in previous chapters. A few gospel, jazz, R&B and Soul/Rock artists are also included. All cities and towns listed under "Place of Birth" are Mississippi locations.

The Ultimate Reference on the State

Other Mississippi Blues Artists

Name and Nickname[1]	Associated Songs/Albums & Notes	Place of Birth	D.O.B.	Died
Campbell, Walter "Choker"	(played tenor sax for Big Joe Turner, et al.)	Shelby	03-21-1916	07-20-1993
Carr, James	"You've Got My Mind Messed Up" (1966)	Coahoma County	06-13-1942	
Carroll, Jeanne — — —	(aka Alberta Jean Simmons)	Ruleville	01-15-1931	
Carter, Calvin	(producer of many blues/R&B hits)	Tunica	05-27-1925	07-15-1986
Caston, Leonard "Baby Doo"	"Blues At Midnight" (pianist w/Willie Dixon)	Sumrall	06-02-1917	08-22-1987
Christian, "Little" Johnny	(vocalist)	Cleveland	08-19-1936	01-27-1993
Clark, "Big" Sam	"I Fell in Love With This Woman"	Glover	07-01-1916	08-06-1981
Clay, Otis	"Trying to Live My Life Without You"	Waxhaw	02-11-1942	
Clayton, Willie	"Tell Me" and "What a Way to Put It"	Indianola	03-29-1955	
Coday, Bill	"Get Your Lie Straight" (#14 R&B 1971)	Coldwater	05-10-1942	
Colbert, John (aka "J. Blackfoot")	"Taxi" (Top-10 R&B in 1984)	Greenville	11-20-1946	
Collins, Louis Bo "Mr. Bo"	"If Trouble Was Money" (1996)	Indianola	04-07-1933	09-15-1995
Comfort, Joe	(bassman w/Nat King Cole/Lionel Hampton)	Alcorn	07-18-1917	10-29-1988
Cooper, "Uncle" Joe	(guitarist)	Yazoo City	06-30-1914	
Covington, "Blind" Ben	(worked with Jaybird Coleman)	Columbus	??-??- 1900	??-??- 1935
Covington, Robert	(drummer for Sunnyland Slim)	Yazoo City	12-13-1941	01-17-1996
Craig, "Left Hand" Frank	'Living Chicago Blues" (anthology 1978)	Greenville	10-05-1935	01-14-1992
Crockett, George "G.L."	"It's a Man Down There" (Top-10 R&B)	Carrollton	09-18-1928	02-15-1967
Crook, General	(songwriter/arranger/vocalist w/L.V. Johnson)	Mound Bayou	02-28-1945	
Cummings, George	(steel guitarist w/Dr. Hook & Medicine Show)	Meridian	07-28-1938	
Curry, Pinell	(drummer)	Greenville	08-09-1934	05-20-1982
Curtis, James "Peck"	"Mississippi Delta Blues in the 1960s"	Benoit.	03-07-1912	11-01-1970
Darby, "Big" Ike	"Cryin' The Blues"	Philadelphia	12-07-1933	09-06-1988
Davenport, Lester "Mad Dog"	"When the Blues Hits You"	Tchula	01-16-1932	
Davis, Charles	(sax player)	Goodman	05-20-1933	
Davis, "Little" Sammy (or Sam)	"I Ain't Lyin' " (1995)	Winona	11-28-1928	
Davis, Mamie "Galore"	(vocalist)	Erwin	09-24-1940	
Dawkins, James Henry "Jimmy"	"Fast Fingers" & "All for Business"	Tchula	10-24-1936	
DeShay, James	(guitarist)	Benoit	05-16-1919	11-11-1998
Diamond, William "Do Boy"	(worked with Fats Domino)	Canton	03-12-1913	01-??-1982
Dixon, Wylie	(songwriter & vocalist)	Columbus	03-19-1939	09-13-1996
Dobbs, C. D.	(guitarist)	Okolona	05-19-1917	05-30-1993
Donley, Jimmy	"Born to Be a Loser" (worked w/Fats Domino)	Gulfport	08-17-1929	03-??-1963
Drain, Charles	"The Dependable" [jazz album](w/the Tabs)	Eupora	05-31-1939	03-18-1995
Dunbar, Scott	(worked w/Shawn Pittman on "Burnin' Up")	Wilkinson Co.	07-01-1909	10-15-1994
Dyer, Johnnie	"Shake It!"	Rolling Fork	12-07-1938	
Eatem, Robert "Big Mojo"	"Sweet Home Chicago" (1988)	Inverness	01-22-1928	
Eatmon, Narvel "Cadillac Baby"	?	Cayuga	10-08-1912	03-18-1991
El, Eddie	"Chess Rhythm & Roll" (1994)	Mound Bayou	06-27-1914	06-01-1982
Evans, Leo "Lucky Lopez"	"Southside Saturday Night" (1994)	Eastabutchie	05-01-1937	
Evans, "Miss" Jo	(vocalist with Bullet Records)	Hazlehurst	02-10-1921	
Ezell, Ralph	(bass guitarist w/Dobie Gray & Shenandoah)	Union	06-26-1953	
Floyd, "Harmonica" Frank	"Married Man's Blues"	Toccopola	10-11-1908	08-07-1984
Ford, James "T-Model"	"Pee-Wee Get My Gun"	Forest	09-04-1914	09-09-1998
Fortune, Jesse	"Too Many Cooks" & "Fortune Tellin' Man"	Macon	02-28-1930	
Foster, Bobby	(vocalist)	Tchula	02-28-1942	
Foster, Leroy "Baby Face"	"The Devil Is Going To Get You"	Algoma	02-01-1920	05-26-1958
Foster, "Little" Willie	(says he was "born on a cotton sack")	near Leland	04-05-1922	
Frye, Theodore	(gospel singer/songwriter)	Fayette	09-07-1895	11-??-1976
Fuller, Johnny	"All Night Long" & original "Haunted House"	Edwards	04-20-1929	05-20-1985
Funchess, John Wesley — —	(slide guitarist aka "Johnny Littlejohn")	Lake	04-16-1931	02-01-1994
Gaines, Otho Lee	(played bass w/The Delta Rhythm Boys)	Houston	04-26-1914	06-15-1987
Gilbert, Lafayette "Shorty"	(with Eddie Shaw on "Too Many Highways")	Lena	11-30-1951	
Gilmore, Boyd	"Blues Masters, Vol. 18: More Slide" (1998)	Belzoni	06-01-1910	12-23-1976
Goodman, Al	(blues/soul record producer)	Jackson	03-31-1947	
Graves, Roosevelt "Blind"	"Blind Roosevelt Graves (1929-36)"	Summerland	12-09-1909	12-30-1962
Green, Garland	"Jealous Kind of Fella" (1995)	Dunleith	06-14-1942	
Green, Henry	(singer & producer)	Smithville	03-23-1943	
Green, L. C.	(guitarist)	Minter City	10-23-1921	08-24-1985
Griffith, Shirley	"Walkin' Blues" and "Bad Luck Blues"	Brandon	04-26-1908	06-18-1974
Hall, Rick	(studio owner/producer in Muscle Shoals, AL)	Franklin City	01-31-1932	

[1] This is a list of 305 blues men and women (some rather minor and/or obscure) not profiled or listed in previous chapters. A few gospel, jazz, R&B and Soul/Rock artists are also included. All cities and towns listed under "Place of Birth" are Mississippi locations.

Other Mississippi Blues Artists

Name and Nickname	Associated Songs/Albums & Notes	Place of Birth	D.O.B.	Died
Handy, "Captain" John	(tenor sax) "John Handy's Quintet" (1966)	Pass Christian	06-24-1900	01-12-1971
Harney, Richard "Hacksaw"	(childhood nickname was "Candy")	Money	07-16-1902	12-25-1973
Harper, Joe	(worked with Sleepy John Estes)	Raymond	05-05-1930	02-24-1973
Harris, Homer	(worked with Muddy Waters)	Drew	05-06-1916	
Hatch, "Little" Provine (Jr.)	Harp & vocals on "Well, All Right" (1993)	Sledge	10-25-1921	
Hayes, P. T.	(harmonica player)	Byhalia	04-03-1923	05-02-1983
Hayes, Roland "Blue Boy"	(harmonica player)	Laurel	10-18-1922	12-31-1976
Hemphill, Jessie Mae	"Feelin' Good" and "She-Wolf"	Senatobia	10-18-1933	
Hemphill, Sidney "Sid"	"Southern Journey, Vols. 1 & 3" (1997)	Como	10-17-1926	08-28-1996
Henderson, Joe	"Snap Your Fingers" (pop/R&B hit in 1962)	Como	??-??- 1938	10-24-1964
Henley, John Lee	(worked with "Honeyboy" Edwards)	Canton	02-13-1919	03-12-1995
Hill, Lillie Mae	(vocalist)	Clarksdale	02-24-1935	12-23-1985
Hill, Raymond	(played tenor sax on Brenston's "Rocket 88")	Clarksdale	04-29-1933	04-16-1996
Hill, Rosa Lee	(country and Delta blues style)	Como	09-25-1910	10-22-1968
Holiday, Jimmy	(R&B, Soul singer and songwriter)	Sallis	07-24-1934	02-15-1987
Hollins, Tony	"Crawlin' King Snake"	Starkville	??-??- 1900	??-??- 1959
Holmes, Joe "King Solomon Hill"	"Gone Dead Train"/"Down on Bended Knees"	McComb	??-??- 1897	??-??- 1949
Holt, Isaac "Redd"	"Look Out!" (w/Young-Holt Unlimited)	Rosedale	05-16-1932	
Holt, Morris "Magic Slim"	"Grand Slam" ('82) & "Black Tornado" ('98)	Grenada	08-07-1937	
Holts, Roosevelt	"Presenting the Country Blues" (1968)	Tylertown	01-15-1905	02-27-1994
Huff, Luther Henry	"Delta Blues: 1951" (1990)	Fannin	12-05-1910	11-18-1973
Huff, Percy	"Delta Blues: 1951" (1990) [Percy's bro.]	Fannin	11-07-1911	02-??-1979
Hunter, Lurleen	"Lonesome Gal" and "Night Life" (1956)	Clarksdale	12-01-1928	
Jackson, Fruteland	"I Claim Nothing But the Blues"	Doddsville	06-09-1953	
Jackson, George "G.P."	"American Blues Legends" (1974)	Alligator	05-16-1920	02-28-1990
Jackson, Jim	"Kansas City Blues" (a blues hit & classic)	Hernando	??-??- 1890	??-??- 1937
Jackson, Lee (aka Warren Lee)	"All Around Man"	Jackson	08-18-1921	07-01-1979
Jackson, Louvette	(vocalist with Spivey Records)	Meridian	11-17-1945	02-18-1988
Jackson, Vasti "Vas-Tie"	"Vas-Tie Jackson" (1996)	McComb	10-20-1959	
James, Michael "Dr. Mike"	(guitarist)	Cleveland	06-10-1965	
Jefferson, Wesley — —	(vocalist aka "Mississippi Junebug")	Roundaway	03-23-1944	
Johnson, James "Super Chikan"	"Blues Come Home to Roost" (1997)	Darling	02-16-1951	
Johnson, Johnny "Johnny Cool"	(worked with Dwight Twilley & Tom Petty)	Clarksdale	??-??- 1967	
Johnson, Major	(guitarist)	Crystal Springs	12-07-1905	06-??-1986
Johnson, Oliver "Dink"	"Dink's (Final) Blues"	Biloxi	10-28-1892	11-29-1954
Johnson, "Signifyin' " Mary	(born a Williams, married Lonnie Johnson)	Eden (or Jackson)	1905	?
Johnson, Sylvester "Syl"	"Take Me to the River" (#7 R&B 1975)	Holly Springs	07-01-1939	
Johnson, Willie Lee "Guitar"	(guitarist in Howlin' Wolf's band)	Lake Cormorant	03-04-1923	02-26-1995
Jones, Albennie	(vocalist with Savoy & National Records)	Gulfport	11-29-1914	06-15-1989
Jones, Arthneice "Gas Man"	(with Lonnie Shields on "Portrait" 1992)	Glendora	07-16-1946	
Jones, Calvin "Fuzz"	(bass player) "Through High Places"	Greenwood	06-09-1926	
Jones, Casey	"(I-94) On My Way to Chicago"	Nitta Yuma	07-26-1939	
Jones, "Little" Johnny	"Big Town Playboy" (Elmore James' pianist)	Jackson	11-01-1924	11-19-1964
Kent, Willie	"Ain't It Nice" and "Too Hurt to Cry"	Inverness	02-24-1936	
Kidd, "Prez" Kenneth	(guitarist)	Newton	12-29-1934	06-27-1995
Kimball, Jeanette S.	(plays piano: jazz and blues)	Pass Christian	12-18-1908	
Kinsey, Lester "Big Daddy"	"Bad Situation" (1984) w/The Kinsey Report	Pleasant Grove	03-18-1927	
Kirkland, Bo	(lead singer with the group Censations)	Yazoo City	10-11-1946	
Kizart, Lee	(played with Ike Turner)	Glendora	03-01-1905	01-??-1971
Kizart, Willie	(guitarist on Jackie Brenston's "Rocket 88")	Dundee	07-16-1896	01-??-1971
Lacy, Reubin "Rube"	"Mississippi Jail House Groan"	Pelahatchie	06-18-1911	01-??-1983
Lane, Ernest	(worked with Canned Heat)	Clarksdale	03-16-1933	
Leake, Lafayette	(pianist on scores of albums w/many bluesmen)	Winona	06-01-1919	08-14-1990
Lee, George W. (Sr.)	(played some with B.B. King)	Lake (Scott Co.)	10-07-1907	08-06-2000
Lightfoot, Alexander — —	(aka "Papa George") "Night Time"	Natchez	03-02-1924	11-28-1971
Logan, Andrew — —	(harp player aka "Flying Black Eagle")	Crawfordsville	04-08-1921	04-11-1995
London, Mel	(producer w/Junior Wells-wrote "Poison Ivy")	?, Miss.	04-09-1932	05-16-1975
Love, Clayton	"She Made My Blood Run Cold"	Mattson	11-15-1927	
Love, Willie	"Take It Easy, Baby"	Duncan	11-04-1906	08-19-1953
Macon, John Wesley — —	(guitarist aka "Mr. Shortstuff")	Crawford	??-??- 1923	12-28-1973
Magee, Sterling	"Mother Mojo" (Satan of Satan and Adam)	Mount Olive	05-20-1936	
Martin, "Fiddlin' " Joe	(worked with legend Son House)	Edwards	01-08-1900	11-21-1975
May, "Brother" Joe	"Search Me Lord" 1949 (gospel)	Macon	11-09-1912	07-14-1972

The Ultimate Reference on the State

Other Mississippi Blues Artists

Name and Nickname[1]	Associated Songs/Albums & Notes	Place of Birth	D.O.B.	Died
McClennan, Tommy	"Bottle It Up and Go" and Catfish Blues"	Yazoo City	04-08-1908	c. 1958
McCoy, "Papa" Charlie	"Sweet Home Chicago" (Joe McCoy's bro.)	Jackson	05-26-1909	01-28-1950
McCoy, "Kansas" Joe	"Oh Red" and "Yes, I Got Your Woman"	Raymond	05-11-1905	01-28-1950
McElroy, Sollie (Jr.)	(original lead singer with the Flamingos)	Gulfport	07-16-1933	01-15-1995
Minter, Iverson "Louisiana Red"	"Dead Stray Dog"/"Sittin' Here Wonderin' "	Vicksburg	03-23-1936	
Mitchell, James	(saxophonist with Hi/Stax Records)	Ashland	05-15-1931	
Mitchell, McKinley	"The Town I Live In"	Jackson	12-25-1934	01-18-1986
Montgomery, Marion	(modern jazz singer)	Natchez	11-17-1934	
Montgomery, Robbie	(member of the Ikettes & worked w/Dr. John)	Columbus	06-16-1941	
Moore, Johnny	(worked with Nat King Cole)	West Point	09-01-1940	01-06-1969
Moore, Johnny B. (Belle)	"Hard Times" (guitarist)	Clarksdale	01-24-1950	
Moore, Milton A. "Brew" (Jr.)	(tenor sax player with Claude Thornhill)	Indianola	03-26-1924	08-19-1973
Morris, Willie	(guitarist with Adelphi Records)	Bolton	06-08-1906	
Myers, David "The Thumper"	(with the Aces - Bob Myers' brother)	Byhalia	10-30-1926	
Myers, Robert L. "Bob"	(David Myers' brother)	Byhalia	05-02-1925	05-01-1983
Myers, Sam	"Sleeping in the Ground"	Laurel	03-19-1936	
Needham, Theresa	(owned Theresa's Lounge in Chicago)	Meridian	05-30-1912	10-16-1992
Nichols, Alvin "Youngblood"	(worked with Johnny Littlejohn)	Camden	02-10-1947	
Norris, William James	(aka "Dead Eye" or "Sonny Mack")	Jackson	10-12-1951	
Norwood, Sam "One Leg"	(aka "Peg Leg")	Crystal Springs	??-??-1900	??-??-1967
Perkins, Al	(worked w/Stephen Stills/Dolly Parton)	Brookhaven	08-01-1933	02-13-1983
Phillips, Brewer	(worked with Hound Dog Taylor)	Coila	11-21-1933	08-15-1999
Plunkett, Robert	(drummer with Eddie Shaw and Otis Rush)	Benton	10-19-1931	
Porter, David "Pecan"	(bass guitarist)	Sumner	03-24-1943	
Porter, Gene	(played tenor sax with Fats Waller)	Pocahantas	06-07-1910	02-24-1993
Powell, Eugene	(aka "Sonny Boy Nelson")	Utica	12-23-1908	11-04-1998
Primer, John	"The Real Deal" (1995)	Camden	03-03-1946	
Ramsey, James	(aka "The Lone Black Ranger")	Jackson	02-01-1932	
Rasberry, Eddie	"Mississippi Burnin' Blues, Vol. 2" (1995)	Jackson	06-20-1955	12-09-1995
Richard, Willie "Hip Linkchain"	"Airbusters"	Jackson	11-10-1936	02-13-1989
Riggins, Richard	(aka "Harmonica Slim")	Tupelo	07-01-1921	
Rivers, Boyd	(guitarist with L&R Records)	Pickens	12-25-1934	11-22-1993
Robinson, Rev. Cleophus	"Wrapped Up, Tied Up, Tangled Up" (Gospel)	Canton	03-18-1932	07-??-1998
Robinson, Fenton	"Somebody Loan Me A Dime"	Minter City	09-23-1935	11-25-1997
Robinson, George	(worked with Fats Waller)	Aberdeen	06-12-1934	03-11-1997
Rosby, Rasberry "Raz"/"Butch"	(worked with Elmore James & Sonny Boy II)	Lexington	06-28-1904	12-??-1970
Rushen, Tom	(worked with legend Charley Patton)	Tylertown	02-22-1898	09-22-1990
Sain, Oliver	"Party Hearty" (Top 20 R&B in 1976)	Dundee	03-01-1932	
Sandifer, John	(aka "Mississippi Johnny Waters")	Jackson	05-24-1935	01-29-1987
Sane, Dan	(guitarist with Frank Stokes & Will Batts)	Michigan City	09-22-1896	02-18-1956
Satterfield, Louis	(with B.B. King/Muddy Waters/Howlin' Wolf)	Shaw	04-03-1937	
Savage, David	"The Jewell" (1991)	Greenville	09-10-1927	06-23-1992
Scott, Esther Mae "Mother"	(gospel singer) "Mam Ain't Nobody's Fool"	Bovina	03-25-1893	10-16-1979
Scott, James (Jr.)	(guitarist with Sun Records in Memphis)	Lexington	01-21-1913	07-18-1983
Scott, Kenneth "Buddy"	"Bad Avenue" (1993)	Jackson	01-09-1935	02-05-1994
Scruggs, Irene (aka Dixie Nolan)	(worked with Blind Blake & King Oliver)	?, Miss.	12-07-1901	
Sellers, "Brother" John	(worked with legend Big Bill Broonzy)	Clarksdale	05-27-1924	03-27-1999
Shaw, Charles "Bobo"	Drummer w/Muse on "Bugle Boy Bop" ('77)	Pope	09-05-1947	
Shaw, Eddie	"In the Land of the Crossroads"	Stringtown	03-20-1937	
Shaw, Eddie "Vann" (Jr.)	"Morning Rain" (on Lonnie Shields' "Portrait")	Greenville	11-08-1980	
Shelby, Beau	(guitarist for Clayton Love)	Indianola	01-01-1962	
Short, J. D. "Jellyjaw"	"You're Tempting Me"/"It's Hard Time"	Port Gibson	02-26-1902	10-21-1962
Shower, "Little" Hudson	(guitarist)	Anguilla	09-06-1919	
Sims, Henry "Son"	(worked with Charley Patton/Muddy Waters)	Anguilla	08-22-1890	12-23-1958
Smith, "Barkin' " Bill	"Gotcha!" (1994)	Cleveland	08-18-1928	
Smith, Byther Claude Earl John	(sideman/songwriter-cousin to J.B. Lenoir)	Monticello	04-17-1933	
Smith, "Wadada" Leo	(trumpeter-has taught at Cal Arts since 1993)	Leland	12-18-1941	
Smith, Lucius	(banjo player)	Panola County	11-09-1884	05-18-1980
Smith, "Whispering" Moses	"A Thousand Miles From Nowhere"	Union Church	01-25-1932	04-28-1984
Smothers, Albert "Little Smokey"	"Bossman: Chicago Blues of Little Smokey..."	Tchula	01-02-1939	
Smothers, Otis 'Big Smokey'	"I Got My Eyes on You" (Albert's brother)	Lexington	03-14-1929	07-23-1993

[1] This is a list of 305 blues men and women (some rather minor and/or obscure) not profiled or listed in previous chapters. A few gospel, jazz, R&B and Soul/Rock artists are also included. All cities and towns listed under "Place of Birth" are Mississippi locations.

Other Mississippi Blues Artists

Name and Nickname	Associated Songs/Albums & Notes	Place of Birth	D.O.B.	Died
Solomon, King S.	(vocalist with Combo Records)	Jackson		
Spann, Lucille	(worked with her husband, Otis Spann)	Bolton	06-23-1938	08-02-1994
Sparks, Milton 'Lindberg'	(vocalist w/his twin brother Aaron "Pinetop")	Tupelo	05-22-1910	05-??-1963
Spires, Arthur "Big Boy"	"Chicago Blues: The Change Era" (1998)	Yazoo City	02-25-1912	10-22-1990
Spires, Benjamin "Bud"	(Big Boy's son-played harp for Jack Owens)	Anding	05-20-1931	
Stackhouse, Houston	(mentor/teacher of Robert Nighthawk)	Wesson	09-28-1910	09-23-1980
Staples, Cleotha	(member of Staple Singers-Pops' daughter)	Drew	04-11-1934	
Staples, Pervis	(member of Staple Singers-Pops' son)	Drew	??-??- 1935	
Stepney, Billy	(drummer for Sonny Boy Williamson II)	Grenada	01-16-1930	
Stevenson, Arthur Lee	(aka "Kansas City Red"/w.w/"Honeyboy")	Drew	05-07-1926	05-07-1991
Stovall, Jewell "Babe"	"South Mississippi Blues"	Tylertown	10-04-1907	09-21-1974
Streeter, "Big Time" Sarah	"Lay It on 'em Girls" (1993)	Coldwater	01-31-1953	
Strother, Percy L.	"A Good Woman Is Hard to Find"	Vicksburg	07-23-1946	
Stuckey, Henry	(mentor to Skip James)	Bentonia	12-12-1896	03-09-1966
Suggs, James Douglas "J.D."	(guitarist)	Kosciusko	03-09-1886	06-19-1955
Summers, Jimmy	(guitarist)	Schlater	05-03-1923	01-12-1983
Swan, Frank	(with Earl Hooker and "Big" Walter Horton)	Amory	12-12-1940	
Taylor, Eddie	(played guitar on all the Jimmy Reed hits)	Benoit	01-29-1923	12-25-1985
Taylor, Melvin	"Blues on the Run"	Jackson	03-13-1959	
Terry, Doc	"St. Louis Blues Today" (1998)	Sunflower	??-??- 1921	
Thomas, Willie B.	(on album "Country Negro Jam Sessions")	Lobdell	05-25-1912	11-??-1977
Thompson, A. Sonny	"Long Gone"/"Late Freight" (R&B hits, 1948)	Centreville	08-22-1916	08-11-1989
Thompson, Charles W. "Maxwell Street Jimmy Davis"	"Takoma Blues" (1987, reissued 1998)	Tippo or Vance	03-02-1925	12-28-1995
Thompson, Dave	"Little Dave and Big Love" (1995)	Jackson	05-22-1969	
Thompson, Mac "Mac Johnson"	(bassman for Magic Sam)	Lamar	01-28-1934	10-10-1991
Townsend, Henry J. — —	(aka "Too Tight Henry") "Mule"	Shelby	10-27-1909	
Turner, Othar	"Everybody Hollerin' Goat"	Rankin County	06-02-1907	
Valery, Joseph (Jr.) "Little Joe Blue"	"Dirty Work is Going On" (a blues standard)	Vicksburg	09-23-1934	04-22-1990
Veal, C. V.	(drummer with Ike Turner)	Bobo	10-04-1926	
Venson, "Playboy"	(on the Sun Records roster)	Belzoni	01-04-1913	02-24-1985
Vincent, Monroe — — —	aka "Polka Dot Slim" (with Lightnin' Slim)	Woodville	12-09-1919	
Vinson, Mose	(did session work for Sam Phillips)	Holly Springs	08-07-1917	
Walker, James	(co-lead w/gospel group Dixie Humingbirds)	Mileston	05-24-1926	10-30-1992
Walker, Johnny "Big Moose"	"I'm Gonna Tell My Mama"	Stoneville	06-27-1927	12-02-1999
Walker, Robert "Bilbo"	"Promised Land" (plays blues, R&B, rock)	Clarksdale	02-19-1937	
Walton, Wade	"Shake 'em on Down" (1958)	Lombardy	10-10-1923	01-10-2000
Ware, Hayes	"Ghetto Woman" (1979) [Bass player]	Ruleville	11-04-1927	12-18-1987
Washington, Leon	(tenor sax player)	Jackson	06-27-1909	02-??-1973
Watts, Louis "Kid" Thomas	(played with Elmore James and Bo Diddley)	Sturgis	06-20-1934	04-13-1970
Weathersby, Carl	"Don't Lay Your Blues on Me" (1996)	Jackson	02-24-1953	
Weaver, "Little" Robert	(guitarist for Big Bad Smitty)	Starkville	06-15-1933	10-19-1993
Webb, "Boogie" Bill	"Drinkin' & Stinkin' " (1989)	Jackson	03-24-1924	08-22-1990
Wells, Ben	(drummer with Tommy Bankhead)	Lucedale	10-30-1938	
Wells, John "Boogie Daddy"	"Stormy" (1995)	Starkville	05-04-1947	
Whitsett, Carson	(keyboardist with the MGs [after Booker T.])	Jackson	05-01-1945	
Wilborn, Nelson "Dirty Red"	"Piano Blues Rarities 1933-37" (1991)	Sumner	08-31-1907	03-??-1970
Wilkins, Joe Willie	(worked with Sonny Boy Williamson II)	Davenport	01-07-1923	03-28-1979
Williams, Arthur "Mississippi"	(harp on Big Bad Smitty's "Cold Blood" CD)	Tunica	07-08-1937	
Williams, Bunny	(tenor sax player at Trumpet Records)	Magnolia	03-10-1924	
Williams, Douglas	(lead singer of the Williams Brothers)	Smithdale	09-03-1956	
Williams, Lee "Shot"	"Love Will Go All the Way" (1998) [gospel]	Tchula	05-21-1938	
Williams, Pearlis	(drummer with The Harlem Hamfats)	Gloster	05-14-1909	03-11-1999
Willing, "Brother" John	(harmonica player)	DeKalb	c. 1949	08-06-1983
Wilson, Robert Lee "Smokey"	"Smoke N' Fire"	Glen Allen	07-11-1936	
Witherspoon, Matilda — — —	(vocalist aka "Mississippi Matilda")	Hattiesburg	01-27-1914	11-15-1978
Woods, Johnny "Mississippi"	(on Shawn Pittman's album "Burnin' Up")	Looxahoma	11-19-1917	02-01-1990
Wrencher, John Thomas "One-Armed John"	"Rockin' Chair Blues" and "Conductor Took My Baby To Tennessee"	Sunflower	02-12-1923	07-15-1977
Young, Ed	(worked with W.C. Handy & Robert Steele)	?, Miss.	02-22-1908	07-17-1974
Young, G. D.	(fife & drums)	Tyro	03-31-1895	03-08-1979
Young, Zora	"Travelin' Light"	West Point	01-21-1948	

"Miss Mississippi" Titleholders

YEAR	MISS MISSISSIPPI	REPRESENTING	YEAR	MISS MISSISSIPPI	REPRESENTING
1935	LaFrance Boyette	Sumner	1968	Mary Linda Mills	MSU/McComb
1936	Rachel Ann Smith[1]	Booneville	1969	Jane Carol Foshee	Hattiesburg
1937	Virginia Helen Riley	West Point	1970	Christine Joyce McClamroch[8]	Columbus
1938	Frances Carlisle Sykes	Aberdeen	1971	Jennifer Jo Blair	Miss. State/Tupelo
1939	Doris Coggins[2]	Baldwyn	1972	Glenda Cheryl Meadows	Richton
1940	Carolyn Simon	Greenville	1973	Kathleen (Kathy) Ann Coole	MSCW/Gulfport
1941	Madeline Theresa Smith	Winona	1974	Carol Diane Bounds	Miss. State/Gulfport
1942	Dorothy Elizabeth Fox[3]	Columbus	1975	Mollie Magee	MSU/Mendenhall
1943	Arminta Scott	Corinth	1976	Bobbye Wood	Wm. Carey College/Hattiesburg
1944	Sarah Ann Topp	Tupelo	1977	Mary Donnelly	University/Oxford
1945	Harriet Jane Carr	Marks	1978	Cheri Lynn Brown[9]	Meridian
1946	Lennie Josephine Nobles	Greenwood	1979	Cheryl Prewitt ✽	Ackerman
1947	Kitty Bevens Bailey	Oxford	1979	Sherye Simmons	Jackson
1948	Virginia Joyce Hollingsworth	Kosciusko	1980	Donna Marie Pope[10]	Pearl River County/McNeil
1949	Katherine Wright	Pascagoula	1981	Karen Hopson[11]	Vicksburg
1950	Annie Laurie Roberts	Hattiesburg	1982	Dianne Evans[12]	Wm. Carey/Taylorsville
1951	Jessie Wynn Morgan	Newton	1983	Wanda Gayle Geddie[13]	Wm. Carey/Hattiesburg
1952	Dora Lee Livingston	Yazoo City	1984	Kathy Manning[14]	Drew
1953	Suzanne Dugger	Picayune	1985	Susan Akin ✽	Meridian
1954	Celeste Hill Luckett	Clarksdale	1985	Nan Sumrall	Hattiesburg
1955	Carolyn Cockran	Lucedale	1986	Kimberly McGuffee[15]	Mendenhall
1956	Martha Annette Teasdale	Hattiesburg	1987	Toni Seawright[16]	Moss Point
1957	Mary Imogene Allen	Yazoo City	1988	Carla Haag[17]	Hattiesburg
1958	Mary Ann Mobley[4] ✽	Brandon	1989	Cherry Busby	Tupelo
1958	Margie Lou Wilson	Itta Bena	1990	Beth Howell[18]	Clinton
1959	Lynda Lee Mead ✽	University/Natchez	1991	Missy Hurdle[19]	Holly Springs
1959	Betty Jane Porter	Brookhaven	1992	Kandace Williams	Tupelo
1960	Patricia Ann McRaney	McComb	1993	Lenena Holder[20]	Booneville
1961	Annice Ray Jernigan	University/New Albany	1994	Becky Blouin[21]	Miss Dixieland/Batesville
1962	Charlotte Ann Carroll[5]	Eupora	1995	Monica Louwerens	Miss Magnolia/Greenville
1963	Barbara Jan Nave	MSCW/McComb	1996	Kari Litton	Miss New South/Pontotoc
1964	Judith Marion Simino	Vicksburg	1997	Myra Barginear[22]	Belhaven College/Grenada
1965	Patricia (Patsy) Alice Puckett[6]	Columbus	1998	Melinda King	Miss Hattiesburg
1966	Robbie Lee Robertson	MSU/Hattiesburg	1999	Heather Soriano	Miss East Central/Philadelphia
1967	Joan Stephanie Myers[7]	Miss. College/Forest	2000	Christy May[23]	Miss Pontotoc

[1] Sixteen-year-old Rachel Smith made it to the finals at the Miss America Pageant, then moved to Colorado and won that state's crown, and so returned to Atlantic City, New Jersey to compete a second time.

[2] The first in the nation to win the title of "Miss Congeniality" when it was first instituted at the pageant in Atlantic City in 1939.

[3] The second Miss Mississippi to win the title of "Miss Congeniality" at the Miss America Pageant at Atlantic City.

[4] The first and best known of the four Miss Americas from Mississippi, her score from the judges was the highest ever voted a Miss America, up until that time. After finishing her year as Miss America, she made her Broadway debut in the play *Nowhere to Go But Up*. She appeared in the off-Broadway productions of *The King and I*, *Oklahoma*, *Cabaret*, and *Hello, Dolly*. To Hollywood in the early 1960s where she danced & sang with Elvis in back-to-back movie musicals, *Girl Happy* and *Harum Scarum*. She and her longtime husband, actor Gary Collins, were married in Brandon.

[5] Top 10 finalist and Talent Preliminary winner at the Miss America Pageant.

[6] First Alternate to Miss America and Preliminary Swimsuit Winner.

[7] First Alternate to Miss America.

[8] Third Alternate to Miss America.

[9] Preliminary Swimsuit Winner.

[10] Second Alternate to Miss America and Preliminary Swimsuit Winner.

[11] Top 10 finalist in Miss America and Preliminary Swimsuit Winner.

[12] Second Alternate to Miss America and Preliminary Talent Winner.

[13] Second Alternate to Miss America and Preliminary Swimsuit Winner.

[14] Second Alternate to Miss America and Preliminary Swimsuit Winner. She also won the Miss Mississippi USA Pageant in 1986.

[15] Top 10 finalist in Miss America.

[16] The first black Miss Mississippi

[17] Top 10 finalist in Miss America and Preliminary Swimsuit Winner.

[18] Preliminary Swimsuit Winner.

[19] Fourth Alternate to Miss America.

[20] Preliminary Talent Winner at the Miss America Pageant.

[21] Miss Mississippi winners for 1994 (Blouin), 1995 (Louwerens) and 1996 (Litton) were all Top 10 finalists in the Miss America Pageant.

[22] Second Alternate to Miss America.

[23] Third Alternate to Miss America.

> While Mississippi has not claimed the most Miss America titles (California and Ohio tie for 1st with 6 wins each and Pennsylvania has 5 wins), the state leads the nation in total points for all wins including swimsuit, talent, alternates, etc. Mississippi has had 4 Miss Americas, 2 runners-up, 9 Top-5 finishers and 7 Top-10 finishers (through 2000)!

> ✽ **Won The Miss America Crown**. Cheryl Prewitt and Susan Akin were also Preliminary Swimsuit Winners.

Mississippi's "Miss Hospitality" Titleholders

YEAR	MISS HOSPITALITY	HOMETOWN (COUNTY)	YEAR	MISS HOSPITALITY	HOMETOWN (COUNTY)
1949	Katherine Wright	Pascagoula (Jackson)	1975	Karen Alexander	Union (Newton)
1950	Betty Denton	Tupelo (Lee)	1976	Jennie Jones	McComb (Pike)
1951	Jo Ann Turner	Yazoo City (Yazoo)	1977	Laura Parish	Carson (Jefferson Davis)
1952	Suzanne Paul	Meridian (Lauderdale)	1978	Tami Oliver	Clinton (Hinds)
1953	Edna Khayat	Moss Point (Jackson)	1979	Shane Pittman	Tylertown (Walthall)
1954	Anne Bush	Laurel (Jones)	1980	Tena Rayborn	Oak Grove
1955	Emily Hall	Leland (Washington)	1981	Patra Massey	Mendenhall (Simpson)
1956	No Pageant Held	N/A	1982	Renee Henderson	Columbus (Lowndes)
1957	Jane Fatherbee	West Point (Clay)	1983	Lucy Jenkins	McComb (Pike)
1958	Elaine Lipsey	Prentiss (Jefferson Davis)	1984	Jill Sanders	Amory (Monroe)
1959	Sandra Scarborough	Meadville (Franklin)	1985	Suzanne Wilkerson	Woodville (Wilkinson)
1960	June Wood	Hattiesburg (Forrest)	1986	Mary Beth Fisher	Okolona (Chickasaw)
1961	Joann Watts	Poplarville (Pearl River)	1987	Elizabeth Pharr Wyatt	Cleveland (Bolivar)
1962	Loren Ormond	Forest (Scott)	1988	Amy Jo Skelton	Olive Branch (DeSoto)
1963	Diane Cox	Clarksdale (Coahoma)	1989	Tammy Johnson	Jackson (Hinds)
1964	Roseanne Burleson	Fulton (Itawamba)	1990	Amy Harrison	Grenada (Grenada)
1965	Ann Kitchens	Batesville (Panola)	1991	Toni Price	Mendenhall (Simpson)
1966	Carolyn Anderson	Gulfport (Harrison)	1992	Leigh Lucas	(Newton County)
1967	Mary Kathrine Morphis	Greenville (Washington)	1993	Mary Elizabeth Gill	(Noxubee County)
1968	Brenda Wiygul	Starkville (Otibbeha)	1994	Kimber Lynn Pitts	(Covington County)
1969	Sharon Applegate	Starkville (Oktibbeha)	1995	Fisher Fleming	Batesville (Panola)
1970	Maianne Mullens	West Point (Clay)	1996	Kristen Earles	Magee (Simpson)
1971	Susan Broom	Columbia (Marion)	1997	Mary Lacy Montgomery	Hattiesburg (Forrest)
1972	Deborah Karls	Greenville (Washington)	1998	Jeanna Runnels	Hattiesburg (Forrest)
1973	Becky Black	Brookhaven (Lincoln)	1999	Olivia Irons	Philadelphia (Neshoba)
1974	Robin Matulich	Columbia (Marion)			

A Short History of the Mississippi Miss Hospitality Pageant

The Agriculture and Industry Board first came up with the idea of a Miss Hospitality pageant in 1949. The pageant, which started that year under Governor Fielding Wright and the Mississippi Legislature, turned 50 years old in 1999. The purpose of the Mississippi Miss Hospitality continues to be the identification and presentation of a knowledgeable young lady to help promote the state in tourism and economic development.

In 1985 the legislature voted to discontinue the pageant. The Starkville Area Chamber of Commerce asked and received the sponsorship. The pageant was incorporated in 1987, and remained in Starkville until 1997, at which time the Starkville Board of Directors began searching for another city to serve as the pageant's new location. Hattiesburg petitioned and received the honor of hosting the pageant in December of 1997.

The pageant is now presented by the Hattiesburg Convention and Visitors Bureau, the City of Hattiesburg and the University of Southern Mississippi. During pageant week every year, contestants are provided with opportunities to polish their public speaking and interview skills, as well as their poise and interpersonal relations among fellow contestants, judges and pageant officials.

Mississippi Miss Hospitality represents the state through the Mississippi Department of Economic and Community Development and makes countless appearances throughout Mississippi during her reign.

Mississippi remains the only state in the nation to have a Miss Hospitality Pageant.

Mission Statement

The mission of the Mississippi Miss Hospitality Pageant shall be to identify, honor, and utilize a young lady between the ages of 18 and 22 for the purpose of promoting Mississippi's tourism, industry, and economic development internally and externally by serving as the state's goodwill ambassador.

Thanks to LaRee Callahan, Mississippi Miss Hospitality Coordinator, Hattiesburg Convention & Visitors Bureau, for the information on this page.

Mississippians in The Super Bowl

	Position	NFL Team	Miss. Connection
Super Bowl I (1967)			
Jim Taylor	RB	Greenbay Packers*	Hinds CC
Jerrell Wilson	P	Kansas City Chiefs	Southern Miss
Super Bowl II (1968)			
Willie Brown	DB	Oakland Raiders	Yazoo City
Jim Harvey	G	Oakland Raiders	Ole Miss
Super Bowl III (1969)			
Roy Hilton	DE	Baltimore Colts	Jackson State
Ray Perkins	WR	Baltimore Colts	Petal
Willie Richardson	WR	Baltimore Colts	Jackson State
John Williams	OL	Baltimore Colts	Jackson
Verlon Biggs	DE	New York Jets*	Jackson State
Larry Grantham	LB	New York Jets	Ole Miss
Super Bowl IV (1970)			
Jim Marsallis	DB	Kansas City Chiefs*	Pascagoula
Jerrell Wilson	P	Kansas City Chiefs	Southern Miss
Super Bowl V (1971)			
Tom Goode	C	Baltimore Colts*	Mississippi State
Roy Hilton	DE	Baltimore Colts	Jackson State
Ray Perkins	WR	Baltimore Colts	Petal
John Williams	OL	Baltimore Colts	Jackson
D.D. Lewis	LB	Dallas Cowboys	Mississippi State
Gloster Richardson	WR	Dallas Cowboys	Jackson State
Super Bowl VI (1972)			
Lance Alworth	WR	Dallas Cowboys*	Brookhaven
D.D. Lewis	LB	Dallas Cowboys	Mississippi State
Gloster Richardson	WR	Dallas Cowboys	Jackson State
Super Bowl VII (1973)			
Willie Young	DE	Miami Dolphins*	Alcorn State
Verlon Biggs	DE	Washington Redskins	Jackson State
Super Bowl VIII (1974) — NONE			
Super Bowl IX (1975)			
L.C. Greenwood	DL	Pittsburgh Steelers*	Canton
Super Bowl X (1976)			
D.D. Lewis	LB	Dallas Cowboys	Mississippi State
L.C. Greenwood	DL	Pittsburgh Steelers*	Canton
Super Bowl XI (1977)			
Willie Brown	DB	Oakland Raiders*	Yazoo City
Ray Guy	P	Oakland Raiders	Southern Miss
Floyd Rice	DB	Oakland Raiders	Alcorn State
Super Bowl XII (1978)			
D.D. Lewis	LB	Dallas Cowboys*	Mississippi State
Larry Evans	LB	Denver Broncos	Mississippi College
Norris Weese	QB	Denver Broncos	Ole Miss
Super Bowl XIII (1979)			
D.D. Lewis	LB	Dallas Cowboys	Mississippi State
L.C. Greenwood	DL	Pittsburgh Steelers*	Canton
Super Bowl XIV (1980)			
Jackie Slater	OL	Los Angeles Rams	Jackson State
L.C. Greenwood	DL	Pittsburgh Steelers*	Canton
Super Bowl XV (1981)			
Ray Guy	P	Oakland Raiders*	Southern Miss
Richard Blackmore	DB	Philadelphia Eagles	Mississippi State
Perry Harrington	RB	Philadelphia Eagles	Jackson State
Super Bowl XVI (1982)			
Jim Miller	P	San Francisco 49ers*	Ole Miss
Ricky Patton	RB	San Francisco 49ers	Jackson State
Lawrence Pillers	DE	San Francisco 49ers	Alcorn State
Super Bowl XVII (1983)			
Cleveland Green	OL	Miami Dolphins	Utica
Richard Caster	TE	Washington Redskins*	Jackson State
Clarence Harmon	RB	Washington Redskins	Miss. State
Virgil Seay	WR	Washington Redskins	East Miss. CC
Greg Williams	DB	Washington Redskins	Miss. State
Otis Wonsley	RB	Washington Redskins	Miss. State
Super Bowl XVIII (1984)			
Ray Guy	P	Los Angeles Raiders*	Southern Miss
Cle Montgomery	KR	Los Angeles Raiders	Greenville
Virgil Seay	WR	Washington Redskins	East Miss. CC
Otis Wonsley	RB	Washington Redskins	Miss. State
Super Bowl XIX (1985)			
Bud Brown	DB	Miami Dolphins	Southern Miss
Joe Carter	RB	Miami Dolphins	Starkville
Cleveland Green	OL	Miami Dolphins	Utica
Lawrence Pillers	DE	San Francisco 49ers*	Alcorn State
Super Bowl XX (1986)			
Leslie Frazier	DB	Chicago Bears*	Alcorn State
Tyrone Keyes	DE	Chicago Bears	Mississippi State
Walter Payton	RB	Chicago Bears	Jackson State
Super Bowl XXI (1987)			
Gene Lang	RB	Denver Broncos	Pass Christian
Andre Townsend	DL	Denver Broncos	Ole Miss
Sammy Winder	RB	Denver Broncos	Southern Miss
Super Bowl XXII (1988)			
Gene Lang	RB	Denver Broncos	Pass Christian
Bruce Plummer	CB	Denver Broncos	Mississippi State
Andre Townsend	DL	Denver Broncos	Ole Miss
Sammy Winder	RB	Denver Broncos	Southern Miss
Barry Wilburn	CB	Washington Redskins*	Ole Miss
Super Bowl XXIII (1989)			
Jerry Rice	WR	San Francisco*	Miss. Valley State
Super Bowl XXIV (1990)			
Andre Townsend	DL	Denver Broncos	Ole Miss
Sammy Winder	RB	Denver Broncos	Southern Miss
Jerry Rice	WR	San Francisco*	Miss. Valley State
Wesley Walls	TE	San Francisco	Ole Miss
Super Bowl XXV (1991)			
Kent Hull	C	Buffalo Bills	Mississippi State
Leon Seals	DL	Buffalo Bills	Jackson State
Kirby Jackson	DB	Buffalo Bills	Mississippi State
Don Smith	RB	Buffalo Bills	Mississippi State
Johnie Cooks	LB	New York Giants*	Mississippi State
Lewis Tillman	RB	New York Giants	Jackson State
Super Bowl XXVI (1992)			
Kent Hull	C	Buffalo Bills	Mississippi State
Leon Seals	DL	Buffalo Bills	Jackson State
Kirby Jackson	DB	Buffalo Bills	Mississippi State
Super Bowl XXVII (1993)			
Kent Hull	C	Buffalo Bills	Mississippi State
Kirby Jackson	DB	Buffalo Bills	Mississippi State
Leon Lett	DL	Dallas Cowboys*	Hinds CC
Issiac Holt	DB	Dallas Cowboys	Alcorn State
Jimmy Smith	WR	Dallas Cowboys	Jackson State
Super Bowl XXVIII (1994)			
Kent Hull	C	Buffalo Bills	Mississippi State
Richard Harvey	LB	Buffalo Bills	Mississippi State
Leon Lett	DL	Dallas Cowboys*	Hinds CC
Super Bowl XXIX (1995)			
Jerry Rice	WR	San Francisco*	Miss. Valley State
Super Bowl XXX (1996)			
Alundis Brice	LB	Dallas Cowboys*	Ole Miss
Leon Lett	DL	Dallas Cowboys	Hinds CC
Fred McAfee	RB	Pittsburgh Steelers	Miss. College
Super Bowl XXXI (1997)			
Brett Favre	QB	Green Bay Packers*	Southern Miss
Super Bowl XXXII (1998)			
Willie Green	WR	Denver Broncos*	Ole Miss
Brett Favre	QB	Green Bay Packers	Southern Miss
Super Bowl XXXIII (1999)			
Willie Green	WR	Denver Broncos*	Ole Miss
Super Bowl XXXIV (2000)			
Dexter McCleon	DB	St. Louis Rams*	Meridian
Greg Favors	LB	Tennessee Titans	Mississippi State
Steve McNair	QB	Tennessee Titans	Alcorn State
Perry Phenix	DB	Tennessee Titans	Southern Miss

Players from Mississippi colleges are listed by their college, even if their hometown is also in Mississippi. * Winning team.

Compiled by Bill Hetrick and used with his permission.

Mississippians in The Super Bowl

FACTOIDS ABOUT MISSISSIPPIANS IN THE SUPER BOWL

Mississippians have played in every Super Bowl game (Super Bowl I in 1967 through XXXIV in 2000), except one — Super Bowl VIII in 1974. Mississippians have been on the winning side 52.5% of the time. By Mississippians, we mean those from the state or those who played at colleges in Mississippi.

Sixty-seven (67) Mississippians played in 33 of the 34 Super Bowls. Of the 66 teams fielded in the 33 games, Mississippians played on 53 of them. Twenty-one Mississippians have played in more than one Super Bowl.

Mississippians occupied 101 playing positions in the 33 games. Fifty-three of those playing positions were on the winning teams (52.5%) with 48 playing positions on the losing teams (47.5%). The 21 players in multiple games represented 55 of the playing positions — 26 winning positions and 29 losing positions.

In 30 of the 33 games, there was at least one Mississippi player on the winning team. Mississippians were only on the teams that lost in Super Bowls II (1968), XXI (1987) and XXVI (1992).

In 20 of the 33 Super Bowls, at least one Mississippian played on each of the two teams in each game. Conversely, in 13 of the 33 Super Bowls, Mississippi players were on only one of the two teams.

The greatest number of Mississippians in a single Super Bowl was six players in each of four games: Super Bowl III (1969); Super Bowl V (1971); Super Bowl XVII (1983); and Super Bowl XXV (1991). In none of those 4 games were all 6 Mississippians on the same team. The greatest number of Mississippians on a single team was in Super Bowl XVII in 1983 when five were with the winning Washington Redskins.

There were five Mississippians in each of two Super Bowls: XXII (1988) and XXVII (1993).

There were four Mississippians in each of four Super Bowls: XVIII (1984); XIX (1985); XXIV (1990); and XXXIV (2000).

> Mississippian Jerry Rice holds these Super Bowl Records: Most Points, Career (42); Most Touchdowns, Career (7); Most Receptions, Career (28); PASS RECEIVING: Most Yards Gained, Career (512) and Combined Net Yards Gained (527); Most Yards Gained, Game (215 in 1989); plus he has tied several other Super Bowl Records.

There were three Mississippians in each of ten Super Bowls with all three players on the same side in six of those games.

There were two Mississippians in each of eight Super Bowls with both players on the same side only twice.

There was only one Mississippi player in each of the following five Super Bowls: IX (1975, L.C. Greenwood); XXIII (1989, Jerry Rice); XXIX (1995, Jerry Rice); XXXI (1997, Brett Favre); & XXXIII (1999, Willie Green).

D.D. Lewis was one of only 10 players to ever play in 5 Super Bowls. Lewis played for the Dallas Cowboys in all of the following 5 games: V (1971); VI (1972); X (1976); XII (1978); and XIII (1979). Lewis was on the winning side in 2 Super Bowls, VI & XII. Only one player (Mike Lodish) has ever played in 6 Super Bowls.

There have been only 2 Mississippians to play in 4 Super Bowls (8 playing positions). L.C. Greenwood played for the Pittsburgh Steelers 4 times & all were winning games. Kent Hull played for the Buffalo Bills 4 times and all 4 were losing games.

> In Super Bowl XXXIV on Jan. 30, 2000, Mississippian Steve McNair rushed for 64 yards, a Super Bowl Record for Most Rushing Yards for a quarterback.

There have been only 6 Mississippians to play in 3 Super Bowls (18 playing positions). Ray Guy, Leon Lett and Jerry Rice were each on the winning team in all 3 of their Super Bowls. Kirby Jackson, Andre Townsend and Sammy Winder were each on the losing team in all 3 of their Super Bowls.

There have been 12 Mississippians to play in two Super Bowls each (24 playing positions):
Verlon Biggs (1 win); Willie Brown (1 win); Brett Favre (1 win); Cleveland Green (no wins); Willie Green (both wins); Roy Hilton (1 win); Gene Lang (no wins); Ray Perkins (1 win); Lawrence Pillers (both wins); Gloster Richardson (1 win); Leon Seals (no wins); and Virgil Seay (1 win).

A total of 46 Mississippians have played in only one Super Bowl — 27 on winning teams / 19 on losing teams.

Mississippian Brett Favre holds the Super Bowl Record for Longest Pass Completion — 81 yards to Antonio Freeman (TD) in XXXI in 1997.

The analysis on this page by James L. Cox

Mississippi's College Football Bowl Games (through 1999)

BOWL GAME	YEAR	TEAMS & SCORE
All-American Bowl (1 loss)	1990	N. Carolina State 31, Southern Mississippi 27
Bluebonnet Bowl; Houston, TX	1964	Tulsa 14, Mississippi 7
(2 games: 2 losses)	1966	Texas 19, Mississippi 0
Cotton Bowl; Dallas, TX	1956	Mississippi 14, TCU 13
(3 games: 1 win, 2 losses)	1962	Texas 12, Mississippi State 7
	1998	Texas 38, Mississippi State 11 (Jan. 1999 game)
Delta Bowl; Memphis, TN (1 win)	1948	Mississippi 13, Texas Christian 9
Gator Bowl; Jacksonville, FL	1958	Mississippi 7, Florida 3
(3 games: 1 win, 2 losses)	1971	Auburn 35, Mississippi 28 (Jan. game)
	1991	Michigan 35, Mississippi 3 (Jan. game)
Hall of Fame Bowl; Birmingham, AL (1 win)	1981	Mississippi State 10, Kansas 0 (Dec. game)
Humanitarian Bowl; Boise, ID (1 loss)	1998	Idaho 42, Southern Mississippi 35 (Dec. game)
Independence Bowl; Shreveport, LA	1980	Southern Miss. 16, McNeese State 14
(6 games: 5 wins, 1 loss)	1983	Air Force 9, Mississippi 3
	1986	Mississippi 20, Texas Tech 17
	1988	Southern Mississippi 38, UT El Paso 18
	1998	Mississippi 35, Texas Tech 18
	1999	Mississippi 27, Oklahoma 25
Liberty Bowl; Memphis, TN	1963	Mississippi State 16, N. Carolina State 12
(8 games: 7 wins, 1 loss)	1965	Mississippi 13, Auburn 7
	1968	Mississippi 34, Virginia Tech 17
	1989	Mississippi 42, Air Force 29
	1991	Air Force 38, Mississippi State 15
	1992	Mississippi 13, Air Force 0
	1997	Southern Mississippi 41, Pittsburgh 7
	1999	Southern Mississippi 23, Colorado State 17
Motor City Bowl; Pontiac, MI (1 win)	1997	Mississippi 34, Marshall 31 (Dec. game)
Orange Bowl; Miami, FL	1936	Catholic University 20, Mississippi 19
(3 games: 1 win, 2 losses)	1937	Duquesne 13, Mississippi State 12
	1941	Mississippi State 14, Georgetown 7
Peach Bowl; Atlanta, GA	1971	Mississippi 41, Georgia Tech 18
(4 games: 2 wins, 2 losses)	1993	North Carolina 21, Mississippi State 17
	1995	N. Carolina State 28, Miss. State 24 (Jan. game)
	1999	Mississippi State 17, Clemson 7
Sugar Bowl; New Orleans, LA	1953	Georgia Tech 24, Mississippi 7
(8 games: 5 wins, 3 losses)	1955	Navy 21, Mississippi 0
	1958	Mississippi 39, Texas 7
	1960	Mississippi 21, LSU 0
	1961	Mississippi 14, Rice 6
	1963	Mississippi 17, Arkansas 13
	1964	Alabama 12, Mississippi 7
	1970	Mississippi 27, Arkansas 22
Sun Bowl; El Paso, TX	1953	Pacific (CA) 26, Southern Mississippi 7
(5 games: 1 win, 4 losses)	1954	Texas Western 37, Southern Miss. 14
	1967	Univ. Texas El Paso 14, Mississippi 7
	1974	Mississippi State 26, North Carolina 24
	1980	Nebraska 31, Mississippi State 17
Tangerine Bowl; Orlando, FL	1957	West Texas State 20, Southern Mississippi 13
[Florida Citrus Bowl since 1983]	1958	East Texas State 10, Southern Mississippi 9
(3 games: 0 wins, 3 losses)	1981	Missouri 19, Southern Mississippi 17

Total of 50 bowl games played from 1936 through Dec. 1999 (64 years) with 26 wins & 24 losses.
Ole Miss: 28 — 17 wins, 11 losses   MSU: 11 — 5 wins, 6 losses   USM: 11 — 4 wins, 7 losses
All 3 Mississippi NCAA Division 1-A schools went to bowls in 1998, the first time ever in the same year.
All three teams went to bowl games again in 1999 and all three won for the first time ever!!

Mississippi First-Round Picks In NFL and NBA Drafts

FOOTBALL

Year	Player	Pick No.	Position	College[1]	NFL Team
2000	Sylvester Morris	21	WR	Jackson State	Kansas City Chiefs
	Rashard Anderson	23	CB	Jackson State	Carolina Panthers
1998	Duane Starks	10	DE	Holmes Comm. College	Baltimore Ravens
	John Avery	29	RB	Ole Miss	Miami Dolphins
1997	Dwayne Rudd	20	LB	Alabama	Minnesota
1996	Walt Harris	13	DB	Mississippi State	Chicago
	Eric Moulds	24	WR	Mississippi State	Buffalo
1995	Steve McNair	3	QB	Alcorn State	Houston/Tennessee
1994	John Thierry	11	DE	Alcorn State	Chicago
	Tim Bowens	20	DT	Ole Miss	Miami
1993	Lester Holmes	19	OL	Jackson State	Philadelphia
1992	Terrell Buckley	5	CB	Florida State	Green Bay
	Tony Smith	19	RB	Southern Mississippi	Atlanta
1990	Tony Bennett	18	LB	Ole Miss	Green Bay
	Kelvin Pritchett	20	DT	Ole Miss	Dallas
1985	Jerry Rice	16	WR	Miss. Valley State	San Francisco
	Freddie Joe Nunn	18	LB	Ole Miss	Arizona
1984	Louis Lipps	23	WR	Southern Mississippi	Pittsburgh
1983	Michael Haddix	8	RB	Mississippi State	Philadelphia
1982	Johnie Cooks	2	LB	Mississippi State	Indianapolis
	Glen Collins	26	DE	Mississippi State	Cincinnati
1981	Hugh Green	7	LB	Pittsburg	Tampa Bay
	Hanford Dixon	22	DB	Southern Mississippi	Cleveland
1980	Roynell Young	23	DB	Alcorn State	Philadelphia
1975	Walter Payton	4	RB	Jackson State	Chicago
	Robert Brazile	6	LB	Jackson State	Tennessee
	Jimmy Webb	10	DT	Mississippi State	San Francisco
1974	Donald Reese	26	DE	Jackson State	Miami
1973	Ray Guy	23	P	Southern Mississippi	Oakland
1972	Jerome Barkum	9	WR	Jackson State	New York Jets
1971	Archie Manning	2	QB	Ole Miss	New Orleans
1966	Lance Alworth	--	WR	Arkansas	San Francisco
	Mike Dennis	--	RB	Ole Miss	Buffalo
	Stan Hindman	--	DE	Ole Miss	San Francisco
1963	Jim Dunaway	--	OL	Ole Miss	Minnesota
1961	Bobby Crespino	--	TE	Ole Miss	Cleveland
1959	Bill Stacy	--	B	Mississippi State	St. Louis
1956	Art Davis	--	B	Mississippi State	Pittsburgh
1942	Merle Hapes	--	B	Ole Miss	New York Giants
1954	Ed Beatty	--	C	Ole Miss	Los Angeles Rams
1939	Parker Hall	--	B	Ole Miss	St. Louis

* The selection of Anderson and Morris gave JSU seven first-rounders since 1972, the most of any school in Mississippi. Through the 1999 season, Ole Miss had sent 153 players to the NFL or AFL, MSU 98, JSU 77 and Southern Miss 73.

BASKETBALL

Year	Player	Pick No.	College or City	NBA Team
1999	Jonathan Bender	5	Picayune High School**	Toronto (then to Indiana)
1996	Erick Dampier	10	Mississippi State	Indiana
	Dontaé Jones	21	Mississippi State	New York
1995	Antonio McDyess	2	Quitman	L.A. Clippers
1993	Lindsey Hunter	10	Jackson State	Detroit
1992	Clarence Weatherspoon	9	Southern Mississippi	Philadelphia
1990	Chris Jackson	3	Gulfport	Denver
	Gerald Glass	20	Ole Miss	Minnesota
1988	Randolph Keys	22	Southern Mississippi	Cleveland
1983	Jeff Malone	10	Mississippi State	Washington
1980	Rickey Brown	13	Mississippi State	Golden State
1979	Wiley Peck	19	Mississippi State	San Antonio
1978	Purvis Short	5	Jackson State	Golden State
1975	Eugene Short	9	Jackson State	New York
1959	Bailey Howell	2	Mississippi State	Detroit

[1] Players from Miss. & those who played at 4-year schools in the state. **First player ever in Miss. to be drafted directly from high school.

The Ultimate Reference on the State

Members of the Mississippi Sports Hall of Fame (Through 2001)

Sports Administration
W.C. "Pop' Allen, 1994[1]
Bernard Blackwell, 2001
Roland Dale, 1995*
Doss Golden Fulton, 1986
Reed Green, 1966
T.S. "Dick" Hitt, 1965
Carl Maddox, 1989
C.R. "Dudy" Noble, 1961
Walter Reed, 1999*
Tad Smith, 1969

Baseball
"Cool Papa" Bell, 1995*
Don Blasingame, 1980*
Guy Bush, 1973*
Harry "Popeye" Craft, 1975*
"Hughie" Critz, 1963*
Jim Davenport, 1983
Jay "Dizzy" Dean, 1990*
Jim Edwards, 1966*
Dave "Boo" Ferriss, 1964*
Paul Gregory, 1982*
Donnie Kessinger, 1984
Hal "Sheriff" Lee, 1974*
Sam Leslie, 1968*
Eric McNair, 1963*
Willie Mitchell, 1966*
C.S. "Buddy" Myer, 1971*
Claude Passeau, 1964*
Ron Polk, 1998*
Andy Reese, 1969*
T.K. "Tom" Swayze, 1978
Del Unser, 1997*
S.B. "Sam" Vick, 1967*
Gerald Walker, 1969*
J.L. "Skeeter" Webb, 1978*

Basketball
Bonner Arnold, 1978
James Ashmore, 1983
Therman Blacklidge, 1971
Denver Brackeen, 1982
Lee Floyd, 1991
J.C. "Joe" Gibbon, 1979
Peggy Gillom, 1998*
Bonnie Graham, 1963
Bailey Howell, 1977*
Doug Hutton, 1995*
Sylvia Howell Krebs, 1996*
Wendell Ladner, 1988
Carla 'Shorty" Lowry, 1985
"Babe" McCarthy, 1974
Dot Murphy, 1999*
Purvis Short, 2000*
Lusia Harris Stewart, 1990*
W.D. "Red" Stroud, 1990

Lily Margaret Wade, 1974*
Charlie Ward, 1979
Davey Whitney, Jr., 1991

Boxing
Freddie Little, 1995*

Football
Billy Ray Adams, 1987
Lance Alworth, 1988*
Johnny Baker, 1986
Lem Barney, 1986*
Doby Bartling, 1977
James Baxter, 1969
J.T. "Blondy" Black, 1976*
"Doc" Blanchard, 1994*
Leon Bramlett, 1988
Willie Brown, 1995*
Jackson Brumfield, 2001
Ode Burrell, 1997*
Marino Casem, 1994
Gene Chadwick, 1973
Bobby Collins, 2000*
Charlie Conerly, 1966*
Hamp Cook, 1996
Hunter Corhern, 1989
Bobby Crespino, 1994
Harper Davis, 1980
Arthur "Art" Davis, 1981
Eagle Day, 1981
John "Kayo" Dottley, 1971
Jim Dunaway, 1990
Doug Elmore, 1993
"Buddy" Elrod, 1975*
Nollie "Papa" Felts, 1967
Charlie Flowers, 1985
Joe Fortunato, 1978
Smylie Gebhart, 1987
Kline Gilbert, 1977
T.G. "Tom" Goode, 1990
W.C. Gorden, 1997*
Larry Grantham, 1980
L.C. Greenwood, 1996*
Jack Gregory, 2000*
Ray Guy, 1994*
L.P. "Parker" Hall, 1970
Marion Henley, 1993
Gene Hickerson, 1979
Stan Hindman, 1988
Joel Hitt, 1972
T.D. "Dobie" Holden, 1970
"Junie" Hovious, 1967*
Harold Jackson, 1989
Doug Kenna, Jr., 1970
Robert Khayat, 2000*
"Bruiser" Kinard, 1961*
Ike Knox, 1964
Jimmy "King" Lear, 1991

D.D. Lewis, 1987
James Harol Lofton, 1999
Archie Manning, 1989*
Bucky McElroy, 1981
David McIntosh, 1973
Allyn McKeen, 1977
Shorty McWilliams, 1963*
Abe Mickal, 1985
Crawford Mims, 1995*
Bilbo Monaghan, 1996*
"Bucky" Moore, 1965
George Morris, 1983
Thomas Neville, Jr., 1984
Jack C. Nix, 1988
J.D. "Jackie" Parker, 1972
Jimmy Patton, 1972
Walter Payton, 1993*
Hugh Pepper, 1977
Ray Perkins, 1998*
J.M. "Bubba" Phillips, 1972
George D. Pillow, 1983
Barney Poole, 1965
J.E. "Buster" Poole, 1964*
Ray Smith Poole, 1968
Joe Renfroe, 1982
Nick Revon, 1985
Willie Richardson, 1979
Stanley L. Robinson, 1961
W.C. "Billy" Sam, 1965
W.L. "Billy" Shaw, 1996*
Riley H. Smith, 1984
Jack Spinks, 1984*
Billy M. Stacy, 1979*
H.L. "Hook" Stone, 1972
Billie Scott Suber, 1993
W.R. "Polie" Sullivan, 1973
R.B. "Bull" Sullivan, 1984
Marvin Terrell, 2001
"Chuck" Thomas, 1975*
"Bear" Underwood, 1986
Thad "Pie" Vann, 1971
Johnny Vaught, 1976
Ben Williams, 1997*
Pat Wilson, 1969
Sammy Winder, 1998*

Golf
Mickey Bellande, 1974
Agnes M. Fitzhugh, 1975
Ken Lindsay, 2001*
Eddie Merrins, 2000*
Cary Middlecoff, 1996*
Mary Bentley Mills, 1987
Johnny Pott, 1993
M.D. "Mike" Taylor, 1997*
H.G. Weddington, 1983
B.F. "Spec" Wilson, 1967

Sports Media
Robert H. "Ace" Cleveland, Sr., 1998*
Jack Cristil, 1991*
Bob Hartley, 1994
Jimmie McDowell, 1999*
Carl Walters Sr., 1993

Multi-Sports
Charles Armstrong, 1976
Calvin Barbour, 1983
"Buck" Cameron, 1987
A.G. Crawford, 1972
Jess Fatheree, 1964
Tranny Lee Gaddy, 1965
Jerry "Jake" Gibbs, 1976*
Edwin "Goat" Hale, 1961*
Johnny Montgomery, 1974
Clyde "Heifer" Stuart, 1968
B.O. Van Hook, 1981
J.E. "Fred" Walters, 1971

Tennis
Bobby Brien, 1985
Mark Cameron, 1999
W.E. "Slew" Hester, 1968
Lester M. Sack, 1991
R. Tom Sawyer, 1992
Dorothy Vest, 1980

Track and Field
Ralph Boston, 1976*
Roy Cochran, 1997*
K.P. Gatchell, 1966
Glen "Slats" Hardin, 1991
Larry Myricks, 2001
Don M. Scott, 1963*
William O. Spencer, 1968
Paul L. Wells, 1970
Willye B. White, 1981*

Swimming & Diving
M.C. Johnson, 1978

Coaching & Officials
Julius "Ju" Burghard, 1970
J.W. "Wobble" Davidson, 1986
Bert Jenkins, 1999*
Orsmond Jordan, Jr., 2001
Butch Lambert, Sr., 2000*
L.T. Smith, 1998*
Pete Taylor, 1990

[1] Each member's name is followed by the year they were inducted. The first female inductee was Margaret Wade, inducted in 1974. The first black inductee was Ralph Boston in 1976. The Hall of Fame now has 23 black members (11.4%) and 10 women members (5.0%) out of 201 members.
*An asterisk indicates that the member is profiled in the previous chapter, "Profiles of Famous & Notable Mississippians."
Source: The Jackson Touchdown Club and Mississippi Sports Hall of Fame, Inc.

Mississippians Who Received The Congressional Medal of Honor

Name	Place of Birth	Date of Birth	Branch of Service	War/ Conflict	Date of Heroic Act	Date Medal Awarded	Date of Death
Ames, Adelbert[1]	Rockland, Maine	31 October 1835	Union Army	Civil War	21 July 1861	22 June 1894	12 April 1933
Barfoot, Van T. ** +	Edinburg, Mississippi	15 June 1919	Army	World War II	23 May 1944	4 October 1944	Still Living
Black, John C.	Lexington, Mississippi	27 January 1839	Union Army	Civil War	7 December 1862	31 October 1893	17 August 1915
Brown, Wilson * +	Natchez, Mississippi	1841	Federal Navy	Civil War	5 August 1864	31 December 1864	24 January 1900 (buried)
Commiskey, Henry A. Sr.+	Hattiesburg, Mississippi	10 January 1927	Marine Corps	Korean Conflict	20 September 1950	1 August 1951	16 August 1971
Diamond, James H. * +	New Orleans, Louisiana[2]	22 April 1925	Army	World War II	14 May 1945	6 March 1946 (P)	14 May 1945
Dorley, August * +	Baden, Germany	?? December 1842	Union Army	Civil War	11 April 1865	Unknown	17 October 1867
Freeman, Martin * +	Stettin, Germany	14 May 1814	Federal Navy	Civil War	5 August 1864	31 December 1864	11 September 1894
Hanson, Jack G. *	Escatawpa, Mississippi	18 September 1930	Army	Korean Conflict	7 June 1951	1 February 1952 (P)	7 June 1951
Heard, John W. +	Woodstock (Money) MS	27 March 1860	Army	Spanish-American	23 July 1898	21 June 1899	4 February 1922
Henry, Robert T. * +	Greenville, Mississippi	27 November 1923	Army	World War II	3 December 1944	12 June 1945 (P)	3 December 1944
Jordan, Mack A. * +	Collins, Mississippi	8 December 1928	Army	Korean Conflict	15 November 1951	8 January 1953 (P)	15 November 1951
Lee, Hubert L. * +	Arburg, Missouri[1]	2 February 1915	Army	Korean Conflict	1 February 1951	5 February 1952	5 November 1982
Lindsey, Jake W. * +	Isnay, Alabama[4]	1 May 1921	Army	World War II	16 November 1944	30 May 1945	18 July 1988
Lucas, Jack H. **	Plymouth, N.C.[5]	14 February 1928	Marine Corps	World War II	20 February 1945	5 October 1945	Still Living
Madison, James J. +	Jersey City, New Jersey	20 May 1884	Navy	World War I	4 October 1918	Unknown	27 December 1922
Olive, Milton L. III*	Chicago, Illinois	7 November 1946	Army	Vietnam	22 October 1965	21 April 1966 (P)	22 October 1965
Pittman, John A. * +	Carrollton, Mississippi	15 October 1928	Army	Korean Conflict	26 November 1950	4 June 1951	8 April 1995
Slaton, James D. * +	Laurel, Mississippi	2 April 1912	Army	World War II	23 September 1943	30 May 1944	2 February 1961
Welborn, Ira C. * +	Mico (Shady Grove), Miss.	13 February 1874	Army	Spanish-American	2 July 1898	21 June 1899	13 July 1956
Wheat, Roy M. [6]* +	Moselle, Mississippi	24 July 1947	Marine Corps	Vietnam	11 August 1967	1969 (P)	11 August 1967
Wilson, Louis H. Jr.[7] ** +	Brandon, Mississippi	11 February 1920	Marine Corps	World War II	25 & 26 July 1944	25 October 1945	Still Living

(P) after "Date Medal Awarded" means awarded posthumously. *There are 18 MOH recipients buried in Miss. — the 14 here marked with a single asterisk, plus 4 non-Mississippians not listed: Charles C. Bessey (buried in Biloxi); James Snedden (buried in Lexington); Hilliard A. Wilbanks (buried in Fayette); and George Wilhelm (buried in Greenville).   + These 17 Medals of Honor are officially accredited to Miss.
** Still living as of 11/1/2000 (of 151 living out of 3,433 MOH recipients. Living recipients by conflict: WWII-62; Korea-21; Vietnam-68).

[1] The only Gov. of Miss. who was a Medal of Honor recipient (Civil War). His MOH is officially accredited to Maine, where he was born.
[2] He was living in Gulfport, Mississippi, when he entered service, so his CMOH is officially accredited to Mississippi.
[3] He was living in Leland, Mississippi, when he entered service, so his CMOH is officially accredited to Mississippi.
[4] He was living in Lucedale, Mississippi, when he entered service, so his CMOH is officially accredited to Mississippi.
[5] He has lived in Hattiesburg, Mississippi, since 1986. He is the youngest Marine ever and the youngest man in the 20th century to be given the Congressional Medal of Honor. He was just 17 years, 6 days old at the time of his heroic action. His CMOH is accredited to Virginia.
[6] The only *native* Mississippian to be given the Congressional Medal of Honor for the Vietnam War.
[7] A Capt. when he received the CMOH, he reached the rank of 4-star general and became Commandant of the U.S. Marine Corps (1975-79), which made him a member of the Joint Chiefs of Staff and thus the highest ranking, most senior military officer ever from Mississippi.

The Ultimate Reference on the State

 ## Movies Filmed in Mississippi

1916[1] ***The Crisis*** — Civil War Drama. Directed by Colin Campbell IV. Cast includes Marshall Neilan, Eugenie Besserer, Sam D. Drane, George Fawcett, and Cecil Holland as Gen. Sherman. Filmed on location in St. Louis, Mo., with some scenes at Vicksburg Memorial Park (later Vicksburg National Military Park), Miss.

1949 ***Intruder in the Dust*** — Drama. Directed by Clarence Brown. Cast includes David Brian, Juano Hernandez, Claude Jarman, Jr., Elizabeth Patterson, Porter Hall, Charles Kemper, Will Geer, David Clarke, Elzie Emanuel and Lela Bliss. A black man (Hernandez) is accused of murder in a Southern town, and a gathering mob wants to lynch him. An adaptation of the William Faulkner novel, filmed in Oxford.

1956 ***Baby Doll*** — Drama. Directed by Elia Kazan. Cast includes Carroll Baker, Karl Malden, Mildred Dunnock, Lonny Chapman, Eades Hogue and Noah Williamson. The story revolves around a 19-year-old virgin bride, her witless and blustery husband, and a smarmy business rival bent on using both of them. Condemned by the Catholic Legion of Decency when it was released, this Tennessee Williams script, although tame by today's standards, still sizzles. Film debuts of Eli Wallach and Rip Torn (in an uncredited bit part). Baker received an Academy Award® nomination as Best Actress and the picture received an additional 3 nominations. Filmed in Benoit, Bolivar County, Mississippi.

1957 ***Raintree County*** — Historical Drama. Directed by Edward Dmytryk. Cast includes Elizabeth Taylor, Montgomery Clift, Lee Marvin, Agnes Moorehead, Eva Marie Saint, and Rod Taylor. Mississippian Ruth Attaway had an uncredited bit part. Elizabeth Taylor stars as a spoiled Civil War-era belle who discovers marriage isn't all it's cracked up to be. Solid acting and a memorable Johnny Green score. Montgomery Clift was disfigured in a near-fatal car accident during production. Taylor received an Academy Award® nomination as Best Actress and the picture three Oscar® nominations. The Ruins of Windsor, historical landmark near Port Gibson, serves as a prominent backdrop in some scenes. Some filming in Natchez.

1959 ***The Horse Soldiers*** — Civil War Drama. Directed by John Ford. Cast includes John Wayne, William Holden, Ken Curtis, Hoot Gibson, Strother Martin, Denver Pyle, Constance Towers, Judson Pratt, Willis Bouchey, Bing Russell, O.Z. Whitehead, Hank Worden and Chuck Hayward. Ford's only feature set during the Civil War is factually based. Union Colonel Wayne leads a sabotage party deep into Rebel territory, accompanied by a somewhat pacifistic doctor, Major Hank Kendall (Holden). A large-scale action picture filmed near Natchez, Mississippi and in Louisiana and Texas.

1960 ***Home from the Hill*** — Drama. Directed by Vincente Minnelli. Cast includes Robert Mitchum, Eleanor Parker, Constance Ford, George Hamilton, George Peppard, Everett Sloane, Luana Patten, Anne Seymour, Sarah Halstead, Ken Renard and Ray Teal. A film with gritty subject matter, this drama is about a Southern landowner's conflicts with his wife and two sons, one of them illegitimate. This movie gave George Hamilton and George Peppard their first big break. Portions were filmed in Oxford.

1966 ***This Property Is Condemned*** — Drama/Romance. Directed by Sydney Pollack. Cast includes Natalie Wood, Robert Redford, Charles Bronson, Robert Blake, Dabney Coleman, Kate Reid, Mary Badham, Alan Baxter, John Harding, Ray Hemphill, and Brett Pearson. This version of Tennessee Williams' one-act play has Wood falling for Redford, the out-of-towner staying in her mama's boarding house. Screenwriter credits list Mississippian Fred Coe and Francis Coppola. Filmed in Bay St. Louis, Miss. and Louisiana.

1969 ***The Reivers*** — Comedy/Drama. Directed by Mark Rydell. Cast includes Steve McQueen, Sharon Farrell, Lonny Chapman, Rupert Crosse, Will Geer, Juano Hernandez, and Meridian native Dianne Ladd. Narrated by Burgess Meredith. From Faulkner's novel, it's about a young boy (Vogel) in 1905 Mississippi who takes off for an adventurous automobile trip with devil-may-care Steve McQueen and his buddy Rupert Crosse, who received an Academy Award® nomination for Best Supporting Actor. John Williams received an Oscar® nomination for Best Original Score. Filmed in Carrollton and Carroll County, Mississippi.

1972 ***Tomorrow*** — Drama. Directed by Joseph Anthony. Cast includes Robert Duvall, Olga Bellin, Sudie Bond, Richard McConnell, Peter Masterson, William Hawley, James Franks, Johnny Mask, Effie Green, Ken Lindley, R.M. Weaver, Dick Dougherty, Jeff Williams VII, Jack Simley and Billy Summerford. This is an overlooked William Faulkner story about a handyman who cares for and eventually falls in love with an abandoned pregnant woman. Bellin & Duvall are both excellent in this best-ever screen adaptation of the author's work. Filmed in Oakland (Yalobusha County), Mississippi and Tupelo, Mississippi.

---

[1] Year of movie's release. Some movies listed were filmed entirely in Mississippi, while only segments of others were filmed in the state. Probably the first movie ever filmed in the state was *Love and Duty*, made in Biloxi in 1915, which starred several Gulf Coast residents and was first shown at the Airdome Theatre in Biloxi.   Main Source: Mississippi Film Commission.

 # Movies Filmed in Mississippi

1974 *Thieves Like Us* — Crime Drama. Directed by Robert Altman. Cast includes Keith Carradine, Shelley Duvall, Louise Fletcher, Ann Latham, Bert Remsen, John Schuck, and Tom Skerritt. Three misfits escape from a prison camp in 1930s South and go on a crime spree. The youngest (Carradine) falls in love with a simple, uneducated girl (Duvall). Altman digs deep into period atmosphere. A remake of *They Live by Night*, the fictional story takes place in Yazoo County, although it was filmed in Pickens in neighboring Holmes County and in Canton. Corinth native Thomas Hal Phillips worked some on the script.

1974 *Huckleberry Finn* — Musical. Directed by J. Lee Thompson. Cast includes Jeff East (as Huckleberry Finn), Paul Winfield (as Jim), Harvey Korman, David Wayne, Arthur O'Connell, Gary Merrill, Natalie Trundy, Lucille Benson, Kim O'Brien, Jean Fay, Ruby Leftwich, Odessa Cleveland, Joe Boris, Danny Lantrip and Van Bennett. A musical version of the Mark Twain classic, filmed in Natchez, Mississippi.

1975 *The Premonition* — Horror. Directed by Robert A. Schnitzer. Cast includes Ellen Barber, Edward Bell, Jeff Corey, Richard Lynch and Jackson native Robert Harper. A supernatural tale with an eerie atmosphere and the use of parapsychology to find clues to a young girl's disappearance. Filmed entirely in Mississippi.

1976 *Ode to Billy Joe* — Drama. Directed by Max Baer, Jr. (Jethro on TV's *The Beverly Hillbillies*) Cast includes Robby Benson (as Billy Joe McAllister), James Best, Terence Goodman, Joan Hotchkis, Sandy McPeak, Glynnis O'Connor and Becky Bowen. Mississippian Bobbie Gentry's 1967 song hit provided the basis for this film. Mississippian Hal Thomas Phillips was screen writer. Filmed entirely in Mississippi.

1978 *Pretty Baby* — Drama. Directed by Louis Malle. Cast includes Brooke Shields, Keith Carradine, Susan Sarandon, Antonio Fargas, Frances Faye, Gerrit Graham, Mae Mercer, Diana Scarwid, Barbara Steele, Matthew Anton, Seret Scott and Cheryl Markowitz. Malle's first American film is a beautiful, low-keyed story of marriage between a 12-year-old New Orleans prostitute and an older photographer, set at the time of World War I. Shields is striking in the title role. Jerry Wexler received an Academy Award® nomination for Music Scoring (1978). Filmed in Hattiesburg, Mississippi and New Orleans, Louisiana.

1981 *This Is Elvis* — Biography. Directed by Malcolm Leo and Andrew Solt. Cast includes David Scott, Paul Boensh, III, Johnny Harra, Rhonda Lyn, Furry Lewis and Larry Raspberry. An examination of Elvis's life that combines documentary footage with sequences of actors playing Presley at various stages of his life.

1982 *The Beast Within* — Horror. Directed by Philippe Mora. Cast includes Ronny Cox, Bibi Besch, Paul Clemens, R.G. Armstrong, Don Gordon & L.Q. Jones. Besch was raped and impregnated by a hairy-legged "thing" while on her honeymoon. Several years later, her son (Clemens), now a teenager, changes into a monster and starts the raping and killing cycle all over again. Filmed in Raymond, Mississippi.

1986 *Crossroads* — Drama. Directed by Walter Hill. Cast includes Ralph Macchio, Joe Seneca, Harry Carey, Jr., Jami Gertz, Robert Judd, Joe Morton, Robert Judd, Steve Vai, Dennis Lipscomb, John Hancock, Allan Arbus and Tim Russ (as Robert Johnson). A cocky young white musician (Macchio) tracks down a legendary bluesman (Seneca) in a Harlem hospital and agrees to bring him back to his Mississippi home in return for some long-lost songs. There is a subplot about the old-timer having sold his soul to the devil. Based loosely on the life of Mississippi bluesman Robert Johnson. Filmed in the Mississippi Delta.

1986 *Down by Law* — Comedy/Drama. Directed by Jim Jarmusch. Cast includes Tom Waits, John Lurie, Ellen Barkin, Roberto Benigni, Billie Neal, Rockets Redglare, Vernel Bagneris, L.C. Drane, Carrie Lindsoe, and Dave Petitjean. About three mismatched miscreants on the run from the law in the Louisiana bayous.

1988 *Mississippi Burning* — Historical Drama. Directed by Alan Parker. Cast includes Gene Hackman, Willem Dafoe, Frances McDormand, Brad Dourif, R. Lee Ermey, Gailard Sartain, Stephen Tobolowsky, Michael Rooker, Pruitt Taylor Vince, Kevin Dunn, Frankie Faison, Tom Mason, Geoffrey Nauffts and Jim Fraiser (Jackson, Mississippi attorney). Two FBI agents — one a by-the-book type (Dafoe), the other an experienced Southern lawman who knows how to handle people (Hackman) — head the government investigation into the disappearance of three civil rights workers in Mississippi during the summer of 1964. A vivid recreation of the period and setting which was inspired by real-life events. Hackman gives a dynamic performance as the former small-town sheriff who figures out how to crack the case. Peter Biziou's cinematography won an Oscar®. The film received six other nominations: Best Picture, Best Director (Parker), Best Actor (Hackman), Best Supporting Actress (McDormand), Best Film Editing & Best Sound. Filmed in Mississippi in Jackson, Vicksburg, Bovina, the Ross Barnett Reservoir and Vaiden, with the town square scenes shot in Lafayette, Louisiana. This film grossed $34.6 million in U.S. theaters.

 **Movies Filmed in Mississippi**

1988 *Good Ole Boy: A Delta Boyhood* — Adventure/Comedy. Directed by Tom G. Robertson. Cast includes Curtis Caine Jr., Richard Council (as Willie Morris' father), Douglas Emerson, Richard Farnsworth, Jim Fraiser (of Jackson, Miss.), Ryan Francis (as Willie Morris), Dule Hill, Gennie James, Kevin Joseph, Christopher Luckey, Richard Luckey, Jordan Marder, Ritchie Montgomery, Maureen O'Sullivan, Anne Ramsey (as "The Hag," or witch, the last role before she died), Caron West (as Willie Morris' Mother) and Ralph Waite as narrator. A coming-of-age adventure that has Willie and his boyhood friends clashing with a gang of notorious river pirates in a swamp near Yazoo City. They also imagine encounters with the Yazoo Witch and outwit rivals. Based on the book by the late Willie Morris, *Good Ole Boy: A Delta Boyhood*, it was re-released in 1994 as *The River Pirates*. This movie was filmed in and around Natchez.

1989 *Heart of Dixie* — Drama. Directed by Martin Davidson. Cast includes Ally Sheedy, Virginia Madsen, Phoebe Cates, Treat Williams, Don Michael Paul, Kyle Secor, Francesca Roberts, Peter Berg I, Jenny Robertson and Lisa Zane. The story of an Alabama college sorority in the late 1950s and one girl's awakening to life's realities — including the mistreatment of blacks. Filmed in Oxford and Holly Springs.

1989 *Miss Firecracker* — Comedy/Romance. Directed by Thomas Schlamme. Cast includes Holly Hunter, Mary Steenburgen, Tim Robbins, Alfre Woodard, Scott Glenn, Ann Wedgeworth and Trey Wilson (his last role before he died). Mississippian Beth Henley's off-Broadway play, *The Miss Firecracker Contest*, becomes a movie, with Hunter recreating her stage role. In the Mississippi town of Yazoo City, a lonely, pitiful (and hilarious) Hunter yearns for love and self-esteem. This sweet-natured comedy, scripted by Henley, is reminiscent of 1930s screwball films. Director Schlamme's feature debut—that's his real-life wife, Christine Lahti, as a neighbor (holding their own newborn baby) in the movie. Filmed in Yazoo City with the exception of one short scene in each of the cities of Belzoni, Jackson and Lexington, Mississippi.

1990 *Wild at Heart* — Comedy/Drama/Romance. Directed by David Lynch. Cast includes Nicolas Cage, Laura Dern, Diane Ladd, Willem Dafoe, Isabella Rossellini and Crispin Glover. He's Elvis, she's Marilyn, they're madly in love and on the lam. They hop in her convertible and make an odyssey through Hell. A violent Southern Gothic melodrama with formidable performances all around, including real-life mother and daughter, Diane Ladd (from Meridian, Mississippi) and Laura Dern. It grossed $14.6 million in the U.S.

1991 *Mississippi Masala* — Drama/Romance. Directed by Mira Nair. Cast includes Denzel Washington, Sarita Choudhury, Roshan Seth, Charles Dutton, Joe Seneca and the late Mississippi choreographer Hollis Pippin. Family racism threatens to destroy the romance between an Afro-American (Washington) and an East Indian immigrant (Choudhury). Shot in Biloxi, Ocean Springs & Greenwood, Miss. Grossed $7.3 million.

1992 *The Gun In Betty Lou's Handbag* — Comedy. Directed by Allan Moyle. Cast includes Penelope Ann Miller, Eric Thal, William Forsythe, Cathy Moriarty, Alfre Woodard, Julianne Moore, Andy Romano, Ray McKinnon, Christopher John Fields, Billie Neal, Gale Mayron and Faye Grant. Shy librarian Betty Lou Perkins (Penelope Ann Miller) was a nobody until somebody found a gun in her handbag. Then, when Betty Lou confesses to a crime she didn't commit, her world turns upside down! The bogus confession launches a series of uproariously funny events as a new, sexy Betty Lou captures headlines, rocks out in nightclubs, outwits the mob and wins cheers from the townspeople. Filmed in Oxford, Miss. and Louisiana.

1993 *The Adventures of Huckleberry Finn* — Adventure. Directed by Stephen Sommers. Cast includes Elijah Wood (as Huck Finn), Courtney B. Vance (as Jim), Robbie Coltrane, Jason Robards, Ron Perlman, Dana Ivey, Anne Heche, James Gammon, Paxton Whitehead, Tom Aldredge and Mary Louise Wilson. An excellent retelling of the Mark Twain classic. Filmed mainly on the Natchez Trace Parkway in Mississippi.

1996 *The Chamber* — Drama/Thriller. Directed by James Foley. Cast includes Gene Hackman, Chris O'Donnell, Faye Dunaway, Lela Rochon, Bo Jackson, Raymond Barry, Robert Prosky, Josef Summer, David Marshall Grant, Nicholas Pryor, Harve Presnell, Richard Bradford and Millie Perkins. Young lawyer Adam Hall (O'Donnell) takes on the pro bono case of Sam Cayhall (Hackman), his grandfather. Cayhall was sentenced to the gas chamber in a KKK bombing that killed a Mississippi Jewish lawyer and his two young sons. Based on the best-selling novel by Mississippian John Grisham. Filmed mostly in Mississippi at Jackson, Indianola and Parchman prison. This movie grossed $14.4 million at the U.S. box office.

1996 *The People vs. Larry Flynt* — Drama. Directed by Milos Forman. Cast includes Woody Harrelson (as Larry Flynt), Courtney Love, Edward Norton II, Brett Harrelson, Donna Hanover, Ruth Carter Stapleton, James Cromwell, Crispin Glover and James Carville. A story of the controversial pornography publisher and how he became a defender of free speech. Filmed in Oxford & Memphis. It grossed $20.2 million.

 **Movies Filmed in Mississippi**

1996 *A Time to Kill* — Thriller. Directed by Joel Schumacher. Cast includes Matthew McConaughey, Samuel L. Jackson, Sandra Bullock, Kevin Spacey, Donald Sutherland, Kiefer Sutherland, Tonea Stewart, Brenda Fricker, Ashley Judd, Oliver Platt, Charles Dutton, Patrick McGoohan, and Joe Seneca (his last role before he died). McConaughey defends a black man (Jackson) on trial for the murder of two white men who raped his young daughter. Based on Mississippian John Grisham's first novel. Dorree Cooper, of Pass Christian, Mississippi, worked as set decorator. This blockbuster grossed $108.7 million (over $100 million its first 8 weeks) at the U.S. box office and $145.6 million worldwide. Filmed entirely in Mississippi, mostly in and around the City of Canton with a scene at Jackson International Airport in Jackson, Mississippi. In a special millennium poll conducted by *The Clarion-Ledger* newspaper of Jackson and the results released on Oct. 4, 1999, readers picked this movie as their all-time favorite movie filmed in and/or about Mississippi!

1997 *Ghosts of Mississippi* — Thriller. Directed by Rob Reiner. Cast includes Whoopi Goldberg, Alec Baldwin, James Woods, Craig T. Nelson (as Ed Peters), Susanna Thompson, Lucas Black II, Joseph Tello, Alexa Vega, William H. Macy, Ben Bennett II, Darrell Evers, Yolanda King, James Van Evers, Jerry Levine, Sky Rumph, and Meridian, Miss. native Diane Ladd. Hinds Co. Assistant District Attorney Bobby DeLaughter (Baldwin) finally brings Byron De La Beckwith (Woods) to trial 30 years after the death of civil rights worker Medgar Evers. Goldberg plays Evers widow, Myrlie. Woods received an Academy Award® nomination for Supporting Actor. Filmed in Jackson, Natchez, Woodville and 3 locations in Yazoo County — Yazoo City, Bentonia and Satartia. This picture grossed $13.05 million in U.S. box office receipts.

1997 *The Sore Losers* — Sci-Fi Action. Directed by John Michael McCarthy. Cast includes Jack Oblivian, Kerine Elkins, Mike Maker, D'Lana Tunnell, Hugh Brooks, Ghetty Chasun, Jim Townsend, David F. Friedman, Mary Wills II, Lydia Martini, Gray Burnhart, Dave Dunlap, Dave Shipp, and Jennifer Stevens. Filmed in Tupelo and Guntown, Mississippi, plus Memphis, Tennessee and Anniston, Alabama.

1997 *Blossom Time* — Drama. Directed by David Orr (III). Cast includes Laurel Holloman, David Orr (III), Greg Farnese, Daniel Gavin, Anthony Gavin, Michelle Bronson, Shannon Hile, and John Philbin. A young woman struggles to leave her suffocating farm life. Director Orr says the film is a "homage to the great American playwright Tennessee Williams and was shot in the small Mississippi town where Tennessee was born." That town is Columbus.

1998 *Finding Graceland* (aka *The Road to Graceland*) — Drama. Directed by David Winkler. Cast includes Harvey Keitel (as Elvis), Johnathon Schaech, Gretchen Mol, David Stewart, Susan Traylor, Tammy Isbell, and Trae Thomas. After losing his wife, a man (Schaech) decides to go on a journey from New Mexico to Memphis to see Graceland in his beat-up car. En route, he picks up a hitchhiker (Harvey Keitel) in a pink sports jacket who proclaims himself to be Elvis, who is trying to return home to Graceland. Bridget Fonda appears as a Mississippi casino Marilyn Monroe impersonator who helps Schaech out of his situation. This movie was first shown at the Toronto film festival in Canada on Sept 12, 1998. The script had to be approved by Priscilla Presley, who enjoyed it so much that she decided to be Executive Producer. Filmed in Hollywood and Tunica (both places are in Tunica County, Mississippi) and in Memphis, Tennessee.

1999 *Cookie's Fortune* — Mystery. Directed by Robert Altman. Cast includes Glenn Close, Chris O'Donnell, Ned Beatty, Courtney Vance, Donald Moffat, Liv Tyler, Julianne Moore, Patricia Neal, Charles S. Dutton and Lyle Lovett. A murder-mystery tale in a small town in Mississippi involving two sisters with O'Donnell playing a Mississippi sheriff. Filmed in Holly Springs, Miss. It grossed $11 million in the U.S.

1999 *Double Jeopardy* — Revenge Drama. Directed by Bruce Beresford (*Driving Miss Daisy, Crimes of the Heart, Tender Mercies*). Cast includes Tommy Lee Jones, Ashley Judd, Annabeth Gish, Bruce Greenwood, Roma Maffia, Davenia McFadden, Jay Brazeau, Gillian Barber, Benjamin Weir and Spencer Treat Clark. The movie is about a woman (Judd) who has served 6 years in prison for killing her husband, who actually faked his own death and framed her for the murder in an insurance scam. Jones plays a parole officer who has to track her down. The film opened on Sept. 24, 1999, and was No. 1 at the box office grossing $23.2 million its first weekend. Although most of the movie was filmed in Vancouver, Canada and New Orleans, Louisiana, a crucial underwater scene was shot in a huge 250,000-gallon water tank at the John C. Stennis Space Center near Bay St. Louis, Mississippi. The scene, which took about 2 weeks to set up and shoot but is less than a minute on screen, pumped about $100,000 into Hancock County because Paramount Pictures used local labor, materials and security. This movie grossed $116.5 million at the U.S. box office.

1999 *Red Dirt* — Drama. Directed and written by Tag Purvis. Cast includes Karen Black, Walt Goggins, Aleksa Pallindino, and Glenn Shadix. Independent movie filmed in and around Meridian, Mississippi.

 **Movies Filmed in Mississippi**

1999 — *The Insider* — Drama. Directed by Michael Mann. Cast includes Al Pacino (as Lowell Bergman), Russell Crowe (as Jeffrey Wigand), Christopher Plummer (as Mike Wallace), Jackson native Robert Harper, Lindsay Crouse, Gina Gershon, Bruce McGill, Rip Torn, and Diane Venora. The true story of tobacco executive-turned-whistleblower Jeffrey Wigand and his relationship with "60 Minutes" producer Lowell Bergman. Shot in Pascagoula, Miss., Mobile, Ala. and other locations. Released on Nov. 7, 1999, it grossed $28 million in theaters. It received 5 Golden Globe nods and 7 Academy Award nominations (won none).

2000 — *My Dog Skip* — Comedy-Drama. Directed by Jay Russell. Cast includes Kevin Bacon and Diane Lane as Willie's Dad & Mom, Frankie Muniz (as Willie), Bradley Coryell, Peter Crombie, Daylan Honeycutt, Clint Howard, Cody Linley, Caitlin Wachs, Jordan Williams, plus Nathaniel Lee and Jim Fraiser (both Mississippians). The movie takes place during World War II and is based on book by the late Willie Morris (1934-1999) about his childhood in Yazoo City, Miss. It was filmed in the late spring and early summer of 1998 in Canton, Jackson and Yazoo City. Before its nationwide release on March 3, 2000, text showings in New York, Los Angeles and Austin, Texas resulted in these rave reviews: "It's a family movie with a heart and a brain. And if you aren't moved to tears, you might need an organ transplant." (*USA Today*); & "It will have you sitting up begging for more. I loved every minute of it." (Joel Siegel, *Good Morning America*). Costing only $15 million to make, the movie grossed $34,099,640 in U.S. theaters.

2000 — *O Brother, Where Art Thou?* — Comedy. Directed, produced and written by Joel and Ethan Coen, whose credits include *Raising Arizona* and *Fargo* (1997 Academy Award® for Best Original Screenplay). Cast includes George Clooney, John Turturro, Charles Durning, Tim Blake Nelson and Holly Hunter. The film, a rural road comedy set in the 1930s, is about three chain gang members who break free and have a variety of adventures, including a bank robbery. It was filmed in the summer of 1999 at locations in Mississippi, including downtown Jackson, Edwards, Madison County, Yazoo City and other locales in Yazoo County.

2001 — *The Rising Place* — Drama. Directed by Tom Rice (born in Jackson). Rice wrote the screenplay based on the novel by David Armstrong of Natchez. Los Angeles-based assistant director Thomas Keith was a member of the first graduating class at Jackson Preparatory School. The cinematographer is Mississippian Jim Dollarhide, based in Jackson. Cast includes Laurel Holloman (*Boogie Nights*), Tess Harper (Oscar® nominee for *Crimes of the Heart*), Elise Neal (*Scream 2*), Gary Cole (*The Brady Bunch Movie*) and Frances Fisher (*Titanic*). The story revolves around an idealistic northern lawyer who moves to a small Mississippi town and two young ladies, Emily Hodge (Holloman) and her best friend, Wilma Watson (Neal), as they come of age during WWII. Filming began in Canton and other Mississippi locales in May 1999.

200? — *John John in the Sky* — Drama. An independent film directed, produced and written by Jefferson Davis, a native of Midway, Yazoo Co., Miss. Cast includes Christian Craft, age 9, of Richland, Miss., as young John John; native Jacksonian Cynthia Geary ("Shelly Tambo" on TV series *Northern Exposure*), who plays "Annette"; Matt Letscher (*The Mask of Zorro*), who plays the grown up John John, husband to Geary's Annette; country singer Randy Travis plays Billy Joe Claiborne, John John's father; Romy Rosemont plays Sandra Claiborne, John John's mother; and Rusty Schwimmer as Zeola. It's the story of a boy's adventures and his dreams of building a plane and flying away from a world where he finds too many demands placed upon him. Filmed in Yazoo County in Midway and Yazoo City, and in Jackson, during the summer of 1999. It was shown at the Crossroads Film Festival in April 2000. Any comercial release date is uncertain.

In addition to the 41 theatrical films listed, many TV series have been filmed in the state, including 3 episodes of *Promised Land* shoot in Natchez in 1999. TV movies filmed in Miss. include *The Minstrel Man* (1975), *Nighmare in Bedham County* (1976, in Moorhead), *Roll of Thunder, Hear My Cry* (1977), *Barn Burning* (1978), *Freedom Road* (1978), *Love's Savage Fury* (1979), *The Bear* (1979), *Don't Look Back: the Story of Leroy 'Satchel' Paige* (1981), *The Dark Secret of Black Bayou* (1981), *The Further Adventures of Tom Sawyer and Huckleberry Finn* (1981), *Mistress of Paradise* (1981), *Courtship* (1986), *The Wide Net* (1986), *Uncle Tom's Cabin* (1987), *Blind Vengeance* (1990), *Taking Back My Life: The Story of Nancy Ziegenmeyer* (1991), and Eudora Welty's *The Ponder Heart*, shot for PBS' *Masterpiece Theater* in Canton, Edwards and Raymond in the spring of 2000.

TV mini-series filmed in the state include *The Autobiography of Miss Jane Pittman* (1974, filmed in Woodville), *I Know Why the Caged Bird Sings* (1979), *Beulah Land* (1980), *North and South: Book I* (1985) and *Book II* (1986).

Documentaries and shorts filmed in Mississippi include *Life on the Mississippi* (1978), *Mississippi Blues* (1983), *Portrait of America* (1985), *Eyes on the Prize* (1987), *Return to the River* (1989), *Deep Blues* (1990), *The Search for Robert Johnson* (1991), *Southern Justice: American Undercover* (1991), *Freedom on My Mind* (1993), *The Promised Land* (1993), *Southern Writers* (1993), *America's War on Poverty* (1994), *A Public Voice* (1994) *Mississippi* (1994), *Highway 61* (1995), *Transplants* (1995), *Lost in Mississippi* (1996), *The Fifties* (1997), *Standing on My Sister's Shoulders* (1997), Eudora Welty's *Why I Live at the P.O.* (1998, filmed in Como & Tunica, Miss. in late summer 1997), and *No Time to Cry: The Vernon Dahmer Story* (1999).

 **Almost 500 Movies Mississippians Helped Make**

28 Days (2000) — Meridian, Mississippi native Diane Ladd costars with Sandra Bullock in this drama.
48 HRS. (1982) — The producer of this top box office hit, which stars Eddie Murphy and Nick Nolte, is Lawrence Gordon, who was born in Yazoo City, Mississippi and reared in Belzoni, Mississippi.
84 Charlie Mopic (1989) — Jackson, Mississippi native Byron Thames plays a Vietnam combat cameraman.
Advance to the Rear (1964) — Yazoo City native Stella Stevens costars with Glenn Ford in this slapstick comedy.
Adventures of Huckleberry Finn, The (1960) — Two Mississippians are in this film. Hattiesburg native Eddie Hodges plays Huck and Benoit native and former world boxing champ Archie Moore plays Jim.
Air Force (1943) — Mississippian William Faulkner (1897-1962) wrote dialogue for this Howard Hawk's film.
Airport 1975 (1974) — This film stars Collins, Mississippi native, the late Dana Andrews (1909-1992), along with an all-star cast including Charlton Heston, George Kennedy and Karen Black.
Alice Doesn't Live Here Anymore (1975) — Meridian, Mississippi native Diane Ladd received an Academy Award® nomination for Supporting Actress for her role as "Flo." Ellen Burstyn and Jodie Foster also co-star.
Alice in Wonderland (1933) — Grange, Mississippi native Roscoe Ates appears with some of the top Paramount stars of the time, Cary Grant, Gary Cooper, W.C. Fields and Edward Everett, in this Lewis Carroll story.
All Night Long (1981) — Meridian native Diane Ladd costars with Gene Hackman and Barbra Streisand.
Ambulance, The (1990) — Biloxi native Eric Roberts costars with fellow Mississippian James Earl Jones.
American Strays (1996) — Biloxi native Eric Roberts plays "Martin," one of many travelers (Scott Plank, Melora Walters, John Savage, James Russo and Luke Perry) who stop to eat at Red's Desert Oasis and find they are involved in the showdown of their life in this action comedy.
Amistad (1997) — Mississippian Morgan Freeman costars with Anthony Hopkins in this Steven Spielberg film.
Another 48 HRS. (1990) — This hit sequel was also produced by Lawrence Gordon from Belzoni, Mississippi.
Apartment, The (1960) — Laurel native Ray Walston costars with Jack Lemmon and Shirley MacLaine in this film rated No. 93 on the American Film Institute's list of the Top 100 Greatest American Movies of All Time.
Armageddon (1998) — Michael Duncan, who attended Alcorn State University in Miss., costars with Bruce Willis.
Assignment Paris (1952) — The late Dana Andrews, a native of Collins, Mississippi, costars with George Sanders.
Astronaut's Wife, The (1999) — Mississippian Gary Grubbs played the director of NASA in this sci-fi thriller.
Awakenings (1990) — Black Indianola, Mississippi native Mary Alive is "Nurse Margaret" in this Robin Williams hit.
Ball of Fire (1942) — The late Dana Andrews (1909-1992), a native of Collins, Mississippi stars.
Ballad of Cable Hogue, The (1970) — Yazoo City native Stella Stevens costars with Jason Robards, Jr.
Batman & Robin (1997) — Pass Christian, Mississippi native Dorree Cooper was set decorator for this film that stars George Clooney, Arnold Schwarzenegger and Chris O'Donnell.
Battle of the Bulge (1965) — The Dana Andrews (1912-1992), a native of Collins, Miss., costars in this war movie with Henry Fonda, Robert Ryan. Charles Bronson, George Montgomery and a host of other big-name stars.
Being There (1979) — Mississippian Ruth Attaway plays "Louise" in this rags-to-riches satiric comedy/drama that stars Richard Basehart, Melvyn Douglas, Shirley MacLaine and Peter Sellers. Sellers' performance as "Chance," the gardener who becomes so influential, won a long-overdue Academy Award® as Best Actor.
Belle Starr (1941) — The late Dana Andrews, a native of Collins, Mississippi, costars with Randolph Scott..
Beloved (1998) — Kosciusko, Mississippi native and talk-show queen Oprah Winfrey produced and stars in this film that also stars Danny Glover. The late Beah Richards, a Vicksburg native, also had a part in this film.
Ben-Hur (1926) — B. Reeves Eason of Friars Point, Miss., directed the film's chariot-race centerpiece in this classic.
Benji (1974) — Jackson, Mississippi native Tom Lester (TV's *Green Acres*) costars with the "top dog".
Berlin Correspondent (1942) — Stars Dana Andrews (1912-1992), a native of Dont near Collins, Mississippi.
Best of the Best (1989) — Native Mississippians James Earl Jones and Eric Roberts star in this kickboxing flick.
Best Years of Our Lives, The (1946) — Collins native Dana Andrews (1909-1992) costars with Myrna Loy, Fredric March, and Teresa Wright in this film that won 7 Oscars® including Best Picture. This movie was rated No. 37 on the American Film Institute's 1998 list of the Top 100 Greatest American Movies of All Time.
Better Way to Die, A (1999) — Biloxi, Mississippi native Eric Roberts plays a Chicago cop threatened by the Mafia.
Beverly Hills Cop III (1994) — Two Mississippians have supporting roles in this movie. Gulfport native Symba Smith is "Annihilator Girl" and Greenville, Mississippi-born Hattie Winston also had a part in it.
Beyond a Reasonable Doubt (1956) — Stars Collins, Mississippi native Dana Andrews with Rhonda Fleming.
Big Sleep, The (1946) — The co-screenwriter for this Howard Hawks film starring Humphrey Bogart, Lauren Bacall and Karl Malden was Mississippian William Faulkner (1897-1962).
Billy Jack (1971) — Mississippian Mundell Lowe was music director and composer for this film starring husband and wife team Tom Laughlin and Delores Taylor. This top grossing film of 1971 has become a cult classic.
Bitter Tea of General Yen, The (1933) — Mississippian Gavin Gordon plays the fiancée of Barbara Stanwyck. Another Mississippian, Martha Mattox, a native of Natchez, plays "Miss Avery" in this movie.
Bittersweet (1998) — Biloxi native Eric Roberts costars with Angie Everhart and James Russo.
Black Sunday (1977) — Bruce Dern and Robert Shaw star in this film about an Arab terrorist and a Vietnam veteran who commandeer the Goodyear Blimp and try to bomb the Super Bowl. Based on the bestselling book written by Mississippian Thomas Harris, who also gave us *The Silence of the Lambs*.

Almost 500 Movies Mississippians Helped Make

Black Widow (1986) — Meridian native Diane Ladd costars with Debra Winger and Dennis Hopper.
Blood Red (1988) — Film debut of Julia Roberts & the only film in which she appears with her brother Eric Roberts.
Blue Hawaii (1961) — Elvis sings the pretty song *Can't Help Falling In Love* and Angela Lansbury plays his mother.
Blues Brother, The (1980) — Mississippi Bluesman John Lee Hooker appears in this popular box-office hit which stars Dan Aykroyd and the late John Belushi.
Bonfire of the Vanities, The (1990) — Mississippians Morgan Freeman (from Charleston) and Mary Alice (from Indianola) appear in this comedy with Tom Hanks and Bruce Willis.
Boogie Nights (1997) — Yazoo City-born/Belzoni-reared Larry Gordon was executive producer of this movie which stars Burt Reynolds and Mark Wahlberg in a drama about the underworld of pornography.
Boom! (1968) — Based on the play, *The Milktrain Doesn't Stop Here Anymore*, written by Columbus, Mississippi native Tennessee Williams, the film stars Elizabeth Taylor and Richard Burton.
Boomerang (1947) — This film stars the late Dana Andrews (1909-1992), a native or Dont near Collins, Mississippi.
Bopha! (1993) — Charleston, Mississippi resident Morgan Freeman and award-winning actor made his directorial debut with this picture that stars Danny Glover, Malcolm McDowell and Alfre Woodard.
Brainstorm (1965) — Collins, Miss. native, the late Dana Andrews, costars with Jeffrey Hunter and Anne Frances.
Breakheart Pass (1976) — Benoit, Mississippi native and former world boxing champ Archie Moore plays "Carlos" in this western that stars Charles Bronson.
Brewster's Millions (1985) — The producer of this film, which stars Richard Pryor and the late John Candy, is Lawrence Gordon, who was born in Yazoo City, Mississippi and reared in Belzoni, Mississippi.
Bride of Frankenstein (1935) — Mississippian Gavin Gordon plays Lord Byron in this sci-fi/horror classic.
Brubaker (1980) — Morgan Freeman's 2nd movie was this prison flick starring Robert Redford & Jane Alexander.
Butterfield 8 (1960) — Vicksburg native Mart Crowley worked as production assistant and writer on this film that stars Elizabeth Taylor, who won on Oscar® for her role.
California Split (1974) — Corinth native Thomas Hal Phillips wrote for this and other Robert Altman films.
Canyon Passage (1946) — The late Dana Andrews, a native of Collins, Mississippi, costars with Susan Hayward.
Carpetbaggers, The (1964) — Benoit, Mississippi native and former world boxing champ Archie Moore plays "Jedediah" in this film, which some describe as a biopic of Howard Hughes. It stars George Peppard, Elizabeth Ashley, Carroll Baker, Alan Ladd and a host of other big names.
Casper: A Spirited Beginning (1997) — Arkabutla, Mississippi native James Earl Jones is the voice of Kibosh.
Catfish in Black Bean Sauce (2000) — Indianola, Mississippi black supporting actress Mary Alice has a part.
Cat On A Hot Tin Roof (1958) — This movie starring Paul Newman and Elizabeth Taylor received the Academy Award nomination for Best Picture of 1958 and was based on the play written by Columbus native Tennessee Williams (1911-1983), who received the 1955 Pulitzer Prize for his work.
Chain Reaction (1996) — Charleston, Mississippi resident Morgan Freeman costars with Keanu Reeves.
Champ, The (1931) — Grange, Lawrence Co., Miss. native Roscoe Ates plays the stuttering manager of a washed-up boxer, played by Wallace Beery, who won an Academy Award® for his *tour de force* performance.
Change of Habit (1969) — Elvis Presley plays a doctor in his last movie and co-star Mary Tyler Moore plays a nun!?
Charro! (1969) — Victor French is one of the costars in this Elvis western. *Flaming Star* was a better western.
Chinatown (1974) — Meridian native Diane Ladd stars with Jack Nicholson, Faye Dunaway, and John Huston. The movie received 11 Academy Award® nominations, winning one Oscar® for writing. This film was rated No. 19 on the American Film Institute's list of the Top 100 Greatest American Movies of All Time.
Citizen Kane (1941) — Frances Neal, a native of Carrollton, Mississippi, played the part of "Ethel" (uncredited) in this Orson Wells vehicle, which was No. 1 on the American Film Institute's list of the Top 100 Greatest American Movies of All Time, announced in 1998 in celebration of the 100th anniversary of film making.
Citizen Ruth (1996) — Meridian, Mississippi native Diane Ladd plays Ruth's Mother and Ladd's real-life daughter Laura Dern plays "Ruth Stoops" in this comedy that also stars Burt Reynolds.
Clambake (1967) — Tupelo, Mississippi native Elvis stars. His costars are Gary Merrill and Shelly Fabares.
Clean and Sober (1988) — Charleston, Mississippi resident Morgan Freeman costars in this Michael Keaton drama.
Clear and Present Danger (1994) — Arkabutla, Mississippi native James Earl Jones costars. Harrison Ford plays CIA agent Jack Ryan with Willem Dafoe and Anne Archer in this smash hit, the third Tom Clancy movie.
Coca-Cola Kid, The (1985) — Biloxi native Eric Roberts (bro. of actress Julia Roberts) costars with Greta Scacchi.
College Confidential (1960) — Friar's Point, Mississippi native Conway Twitty stars in this B-movie.
Color Purple, The (1985) — Kosciusko native and talk-show host Oprah Winfrey received an Academy Award® nomination as Best Supporting Actress for her film debut in this Steven Spielberg movie, the top grossing film of 1985 ($94 million). The movie also stars Danny Glover and Whoopi Goldberg.
Comedians (1967) — Contrary to its title, this was a drama that stars Elizabeth Taylor and Richard Burton and was Arkabutla, Mississippi native James Earl Jones' second movie.
Coming To America (1988) — Arkabutla, Mississippi native James Earl Jones appears with Eddie Murphy.
Comes A Horseman (1978) — Ruleville, Mississippi native Luster Bayless was the costume designer for this modern western which stars James Caan, Jane Fonda, Mark Harmon and Jason Robards, Jr.

 **Almost 500 Movies Mississippians Helped Make**

Conan, The Barbarian (1982) — Miss. native James Earl Jones plays the antagonist of Arnold Schwartzenegger.
Coneheads (1993) — Parker Posey, who grew up in Laurel, Mississippi, plays the best friend of the teenage offspring of parental units "Beldar" (Dan Aykroyd) and "Prymaat" (Jane Curtin) in this sci-fi comedy.
Conrack (1974) — Mississippian Ruth Attaway plays "Edna" in biographical movie about author Pat Conroy's job as a young teacher that stars Hume Cronyn, Paul Winfield and Jon Voight as Pat Conroy.
Convicts (1991) — Arkabutla, Mississippi native James Earl Jones costars with Robert Duvall and Lukas Haas.
Cotton Club, The (1984) — Robert Earl Jones, a native of Coldwater, Mississippi and father of actor James Earl Jones, appears in this film with Richard Gere, Nicolas Cage, Fred Gwynne and many others.
Courtship of Eddie's Father, The (1963) — Yazoo City native Stella Stevens plays "Dollye Daly" in this romantic comedy that also features Glenn Ford, Ron Howard and Shirley Jones.
Couch Trip, The (1988) — Mississippian Lawrence Gordon is producer of this comedy starring Dan Aykroyd.
Crack in the World (1965) — The late Dana Andrews, a native of Collins, Mississippi, stars in this sci-fi thriller.
Crash Dive (1943) — The late Dana Andrews, a native of Collins, Mississippi, costars with Tyrone Power.
Creepshow (1982) — Jackson, Mississippi native Robert Harper plays the part of "Charlie" in one of the stories and Geenwood, Mississippi native Carrie Nye plays "Sylvia" in another segment.
Crimes of the Heart (1986) — Jackson native Beth Henley wrote the screenplay based on her Pulitzer Prize-winning play. The movie stars Diane Keaton, Sissy Spacek, Tess Harper, Jessica Lange, and Sam Shepard.
Crowded Sky, The (1960) — The late Dana Andrews, a native of Collins, costars with Rhonda Fleming.
Curse of the Demon (1958) — Dana Andrews (1912-1992), a native of Collins, Mississippi, stars in this one.
Daddy and Them (1999) — Meridian, Miss. native Diane Ladd is once again in a movie with her real-life daughter Laura Dern. Ben Affleck, Billy Bob Thornton and Andy Griffith are some of the other actors in this dark comedy where a married couple (Thornton & Dern) come to the aid of a jailed uncle (the late Jim Varney).
Daddy Long Legs (1955) — Jackson native Kelly Brown plays "Jimmy McBride" in this Fred Astaire musical.
Daisy Kenyon (1947) — Dana Andrews, a native of Collins, Miss., costars with Joan Crawford & Henry Fonda.
Damn Yankees (1958) — Laurel native Ray Walston reprised his Tony Award-winning Broadway role.
Dark Crystal, The (1982) — This film has creature characters created by Jim Henson (1936-90), born in Greenville.
Dark Man (1990) — Oxford, Miss. native Julie Kaye Fanton worked as assistant set decorator for this sci-fi thriller that stars Liam Neeson, Larry Drake and Frances McDormand.
Dead Pool, The (1988) — The string cues (supplemental musical compositions) for Clint Eastwood's fifth Dirty Harry movie were written by Dee Barton from Starkville, Mississippi. Liam Neeson costars.
Deep Impact (1998) — Charleston, Mississippi resident Morgan Freeman costars with Robert Duvall in this disaster/thriller about an enormous comet hitting earth. "Oceans rise. Cities fall. Hope survives."
Deep Waters (1948) — Dana Andrews (1912-1992), a native of Collins, Mississippi, costars with Jean Peters.
Devil's Brigade (1968) — The late Dana Andrews, a native of Collins, Mississippi, costars with William Holden.
Devil's Own, The (1997) — Mississippian Larry Gordon produced this thriller, which stars Harrison Ford & Brad Pitt.
Diary of an American Family (1999) — Mississippian James Earl Jones stars with Sean Patrick Flanery.
Die Hard (1988) — The producer of this hit, starring Bruce Willis & Alan Rickman, is Mississippian Larry Gordon.
Die Hard 2 (1990) — This hit sequel was also produced by Lawrence Gordon of Yazoo City/Belzoni, Mississippi.
Dillinger (1973) — The executive producer of this film, which stars Warren Oates and Richard Dreyfuss, is Lawrence Gordon, born in Yazoo City, Mississippi and reared in Belzoni, Mississippi.
Dirty Harry (1971) — The string cues for this Clint Eastwood movie were written by Mississippian Dee Barton.
Distinguished Gentleman, The (1992) — Dorree Cooper of Pass Christian, Mississippi was the set decorator for this comedy, which stars Eddie Murphy.
Dr. Strangelove - or- How I Learned to Stop Worrying and Love the Bomb (1964) — This was the debut movie for Mississippi native James Earl Jones. This black comedy spoof stars Peter Sellers and George C. Scott and received 4 Academy Award® nominations. This film was rated No. 26 on the American Film Institute's list of the Top 100 Greatest American Movies of All Time, announced in 1998.
Double Trouble (1967) — Tupelo, Mississippi native Elvis Presley stars and Annette Day costars.
Down in the Delta (1998) — Indianola, Mississippi native Mary Alice plays "Rosa Lynn" in this movie that stars Alfre Woodard, Wesley Snipes, Al Freeman Jr., and the late Esther Rolle.
Driver, The (1978) — The producer of this film, which stars Ryan O'Neal & Bruce Dern, is Larry Gordon, who was born in Yazoo City and grew up in Belzoni, Mississippi.
Driving Miss Daisy (1989) — Charleston resident Morgan Freeman received an Academy Award® nomination for Best Performance by an Actor in a Supporting Role. The movie, which also stars Jessica Tandy and Dan Aykroyd, received an additional 8 nominations and won 4 Oscars® including Best Picture of the Year.
Drugstore Cowboy (1989) — The late Beah Richards, a Vicksburg native, plays a drug counselor to Matt Dillon.
Duel in the Jungle (1954) — The late Dana Andrews, a native of Collins, Mississippi, costars with Jeanne Crain.
Easy Come, Easy Go (1967) - Another Elvis Presley musical. One of his costars is Dodie Marshal.
Edge of Doom (1950) — Collins native, the late Dana Andrews (1909-1992), costars with Farley Granger.
Eight Seconds (1994) — Jackson native Cynthia Lynn Geary costars with Luke Perry in this true-story rodeo movie.

The Ultimate Reference on the State

Almost 500 Movies Mississippians Helped Make

Elephant Walk (1954) — The late Dana Andrews, a native of Collins, Mississippi, costars with Elizabeth Taylor.
End, The (1978) — The producer of this Burt Reynolds/Sally Fields film is Larry Gordon, Belzoni, Miss. native.
End of the Road (1970) — Arkabutla, Mississippi native James Earl Jones costars with Stacy Keach.
Enforcer, The (1976) — Mississippian Dee Barton wrote the string cues for Clint Eastwood's third Dirty Harry movie.
Event Horizon (1997) — Mississippian Larry Gordon is producer of this sci-fi thriller starring Laurence Fishburne.
Every Which Way But Loose (1978) — Mississippian Dee Barton wrote the string cues for this Clint Eastwood movie.
Everything You Always Wanted to Know About Sex, But Were Afraid to Ask (1972) — Laurel, Mississippi native Mundell Lowe composed the music for this Woody Allen film that stars a host of actors, mainly in cameos.
Eyewitness (1981) — Charleston, Miss. resident Morgan Freeman appears with William Hurt & Sigourney Weaver.
Face in the Crowd, A (1957) — Rod Brasfield (1910-1958), Monroe County native and Grand Ole Opry's top country comedian for 14 years (1944-1958) and member of the Country Music Hall of Fame, received critical praise for his dramatic role opposite Andy Griffith in this, his only film.
Fallen Angel (1945) — Dana Andrews (1912-1992), a native of Collins, Mississippi, costars with Alice Faye.
Family Business (1989) — The producer of this film, which stars Sean Connery and Dustin Hoffman, is Larry Gordon, who was born in Yazoo City, Mississippi and raised in Belzoni, Mississippi.
Family Thing, A (1996) — Arkabutla, Mississippi native James Earl Jones costars with Robert Duvall.
Fantasia 2000 (1999) — James Earl Jones plays one of the hosts in this Walt Disney live/animated feature.
Fast Times at Ridgemont High (1982) — Laurel's Ray Walston costars with Sean Penn and Jennifer Jason Leigh and he also starred in the TV spin off, *Fast Times*, in 1985-86.
Fat Man and Little Boy (1989) — Dorree Cooper of Pass Christian, Mississippi was the set decorator for this movie which stars Paul Newman and Bonnie Bodelia.
Fearmakers, The (1958) — Stars the late Dana Andrews (1912-1992), a native of Dont near Collins, Mississippi.
Final Analysis (1992) — Biloxi, Mississippi native Eric Roberts plays "Jimmy Evans" and Jackson native Robert Harper plays "Alan Lowenthal" in this mystery that also stars Richard Gere and Kim Basinger.
Firm, The (1993) — Stars Tom Cruise and is from the best-selling book by Oxford, Miss. novelist John Grisham.
Field of Dreams (1989) — This movie has three Mississippi connections. Arkabutla native James Earl Jones stars with Kevin Costner and the late Burt Lancaster in this sports fantasy produced by Lawrence Gordon from Belzoni, Mississippi. In a short scene in Fenway Park, you can see Meridian's Oil Can Boyd pitching for the Red Sox. The movie received the Academy Award® nomination for Best Picture of the Year.
Flaming Star (1960) — This western was one of the better pictures Tupelo native Elvis Presley made. He plays a half-breed Indian and his costars are Barbara Eden and Steve Forrest.
Follow That Dream (1962) — Tupelo native Elvis Presley stars with Anne Helm and Arthur O'Connell.
Forbidden Street (1949) — Dana Andrews (1912-1992), a native of Collins, Miss., costars with Maureen O'Hara.
Forrest Gump (1994) — Michael Humphreys of Independence, Miss., plays the young Forrest in one of the biggest movies of 1994. The film received 13 Academy Award® nominations, winning 6 Oscars® and was rated No. 71 on the American Film Institute's list of the Top 100 Greatest American Movies of All Time.
Fortune Cookie (1966) — Benoit, Mississippi native and former world boxing champ Archie Moore plays "Mr. Jackson" in this comedy that stars Jack Lemon and Walter Matthau.
Frankie and Johnny (1966) — Donna Douglas (TV's *Beverly Hillbillies*) and Harry Morgan costar with Elvis.
Freaks (1932) — Grange, Lawrence Co., Miss. native Roscoe Ates plays a member of a traveling-circus freak show.
Frogmen, The (1951) — The late Dana Andrews, a native of Collins, Mississippi, costars with Richard Widmark.
Fugitive, The (1993) — Meridian native Sela Ward costars with Harrison Ford, playing his wife who is murdered, in one of the biggest movies of 1993. Co-star Tommy Lee Jones won an Oscar® for Best Supporting Actor and the film received 6 more Academy Award® nominations including Best Picture of the Year.
Fugitive Kind, The (1959) — Stars Marlon Brando and Joanne Woodward and is based on Tennessee Williams' play *Orpheus Descending*. Vicksburg, Mississippi native Mart Crowley was production assistant and writer.
Fun In Acapulco (1963) — Tupelo, Mississippi native Elvis Presley stars, and his "main squeeze" is Ursala Andress.
G.I. Blues (1960) — Costar Juliet Prowse dances with Tupelo, Mississippi native Elvis Presley in this one.
Gang Related (1997) — James Earl Jones costars with James Belushi and Dennis Quaid in this crime drama.
Gardens of Stone (1987) — A war drama with Mississippian James Earl Jones, James Caan and Anjelica Huston.
Gingerbread Man, The (1998) — Mississippian John Grisham's first screenplay. It stars Robert Downey, Jr.
Girl Happy (1965) — Brandon native Mary Ann Mobley, Miss America 1959, danced and sang with fellow Mississippian Elvis Presley in this movie musical. Shelley Fabares also costars.
Girl Most Likely, The (1957) — Jackson, Mississippi native Kelly Brown plays "Sam" in this musical comedy.
Girls! Girls! Girls! (1962) — One of his biggest moneymakers, Tupelo native Elvis Presly costars with fellow Mississippian Stella Stevens. Wouldn't you know Elvis would make a movie with this title?!
Glass Menagerie, The (1950) — Based on the play by Columbus, Miss. native Tennessee Williams (1911-1983). Williams was also co-screenwriter for the first movie in 1950 starring Jane Wyman and Kirt Douglas. Another movie in 1987 stars Joanne Woodward and was directed by her husband, Paul Newman. A 1973 version marked the TV debut of Katharine Hepburn.

 **Almost 500 Movies Mississippians Helped Make**

Glory (1989) — Charleston, Mississippi resident Morgan Freeman costars with Denzel Washington.

Gone with the Wind (1938) — McComb, Mississippi native Will Price (who married actress Maureen O'Hara), as dialogue director, coached Clark Gable and Vivien Leigh on how to speak Southern. B. Reeves Eason, a native of Friars Point, Miss., was 2nd-unit director and handled the burning of Atlanta scene. Roscoe Ates, a Lawrence Co., Miss. native, played a convalescent soldier (uncredited). This film was rated No. 4 on the American Film Institute's list of the Top 100 Greatest American Movies of All Time, announced in 1998.

Good Guys Wear Black (1979) — The late Dana Andrews (1912-1992), a native of Collins, Mississippi, costars with Chuck Norris. Collins would make only one other movie after this, *Prince Jack*, in 1984.

Grave, The (1996) — Biloxi native Eric Roberts plays "Cass" in this horror movie about two prisoners who escape with the help of their jailer to search for a treasure that is supposedly buried with a dead millionaire.

Great Balls of Fire (1989) — Dennis Quaid plays Jerry and Winona Ryder also stars, but "The Killer" himself, Jerry Lee Lewis, a longtime resident of Nesbit, Mississippi, is the one singing and playing his hit songs.

Great White Hope, The (1970) — Arkabutla, Mississippi native James Earl Jones won the Tony Award for Best Actor in 1969 for his stage performance and an Oscar® nomination when he reprised the role for this film. Making an appearance as "Mama Tiny" is the late Beah Richards, a Vicksburg native.

Green Mile, The (1999) — Michael Duncan, who attended Alcorn State University in Miss., costars with Tom Hanks. Duncan was nominated for an Oscar® for Best Supporting Actor and the movie for Best Picture.

Guess Who's Coming to Dinner (1967) — Vicksburg, Mississippi native Beah Richards got an Academy Award® nomination as Best Supporting Actress for her role as Sidney Poitier's mother in this movie, which also stars Spencer Tracy and Katharine Hepburn. The movie received 11 Academy Award® nominations and won 2 Oscars® and was the top-grossing movie of 1967. This film was rated No. 99 on the American Film Institute's list of the Top 100 Greatest American Movies of All Time, announced in 1998.

Gunga Din (1939) — Mississippian William Faulkner was co-screenwriter for this film starring Cary Grant. Mooreville, Lee County, Mississippi native Olin Francis plays "Fulad" in this movie.

Hang 'Em High (1967) — Mississippian Robert Earl Jones had a small part in this Clint Eastwood western.

Hannibal (Silence of the Lambs 2) (2001) — Sir Anthony Hopkins once again plays the evil Hannibal Lecter in this film based on the novel written by Rich, Mississippi native Thomas Harris (filming began in May 2000).

Hard Rain (1998) — Charleston, Mississippi resident Morgan Freeman costars with Christian Slater.

Hard Times (1975) — Charles Bronson stars in this film produced by native Mississippian Lawrence Gordon.

Harry and Son (1984) — Charleston, Miss. resident Morgan Freeman stars with Paul Newman and Robby Benson.

Harum Scarum (1965) — Brandon native Mary Ann Mobley, Miss America 1959, danced and sang with fellow Mississippian Elvis Presley in this MGM movie musical. Michael Ansara also costars.

Harvey (1950) — Columbia, Mississippi native Peggy Dow plays the romantic-lead role with James Stewart.

Heart Like a Wheel (1983) — Jackson, Mississippi native Byron Thames made his debut in this movie that stars Bonnie Bedelia as a real-life auto racing champion.

Heaven's Prisoner (1995) — Biloxi native Eric Roberts plays a mean Cajun crime boss.

Hello Again (1987) — Two Mississippians have a part in this musical comedy: Meridian native Sela Ward plays "Kim Lacey" and Greenwood native Carrie Nye plays "Regina Holt." Corbin Bernsen stars.

High School Confidential (1958) — Longtime Nesbit, Miss. resident Jerry Lee Lewis sings & pounds the piano.

High Plains Drifter (1973) — The score for this Clint Eastwood western was written by Dee Barton of Starkville.

High Time (1960) — McComb, Miss. native Jimmy Boyd appears with stars Bing Crosby, Fabian and Tuesday Weld.

Hitman's Run (1999) — Biloxi, Mississippi native Eric Roberts stars in this independent film about the mob.

Hole In the Head, A (1956) — Hattiesburg native Eddie Hodges plays Frank Sinatra's son. Hodges and the late Sinata sing the Academy Award®-winning song, *High Hopes*, in the film.

Honey, I Blew Up the Kid (1992) — Dorree Cooper of Pass Christian, Miss. was set decorator for this sequel.

Honey, I Shrunk the Kids (1989) — Dorree Cooper of Pass Christian, Mississippi was the set decorator for this comedy/sci-fi film which stars Rick Moranis.

Honeysuckle Rose (1980) — Isola, Mississippi native, country songwriter/singer Hank Cochran performed his song, *Make the World Go Away*, in the feature film which stars Willie Nelson and Dyan Cannon.

Hoodlum (1997), Wesson, Mississippi resident Charles C. Bennett was the set designer for this 1930s urban drama starring Laurence Fishburne, Andy Garcia and Venessa Williams.

Hooper (1978) — The executive producer of this film, which stars Burt Reynolds and Sally Fields, is Lawrence Gordon, born in Yazoo City, Mississippi and reared in Belzoni, Mississippi.

Hot Rods to Hell (1967) — Stars the late Dana Andrews (1912-1992), a native of Dont near Collins, Mississippi.

Hunt for Red October, The (1990) — Arkabutla native James Earl Jones stars with Sean Connery, Alec Baldwin, and Scott Glenn in this big hit thriller that received 3 Academy Award® nominations and won one Oscar®.

Hurry Sundown (1967) — This was the first important picture for Vicksburg, Mississippi native Beah Richards, who played "Rose Scott." It also stars Michael Caine, Diahann Carroll, Faye Dunaway and other big names.

I Want You (1951) — Dana Andrews (1912-1992), a native of Collins, Mississippi costars with Dorothy McGuire. Columbia, Mississippi native Peggy Dow plays the steadfast girlfriend of blind veteran Arthur Kennedy.

Almost 500 Movies Mississippians Helped Make

I Still Know What You Did Last Summer (1998) — McComb, Mississippi native Brandy (Norwood) costars with Jennifer Love Hewitt and Freddie Prinze, Jr. in this horror/slasher sequel.

Immortals, The (1995) — Biloxi native Eric Roberts plays "Jack," a crafty nightclub owner who brings together a group of small time hoods (Joe Pantoliano, Clarence Williams III, William Forsythe, Chris Rock) and teams them up for a series of heists and a battle with Jack's nemesis Dominic (Tony Curtis).

In Harm's Way (1961) — This Otto Preminger war film stars Collins native, the late Dana Andrews (1909-1992) along with John Wayne, Kirk Douglas, Henry Fonda and a host of other stars.

Innocent Bystanders (1973) — Dana Andrews (1912-1992), a native of Collins, Miss., costars with Stanley Baker.

In The Heat of the Night (1967) — Vicksburg, Mississippi native Beah Richards plays 2 roles, "Mama Caleba" and "Mrs. Bellamy". It stars Rod Steiger and Sidney Poitier and was nominated for 7 Academy Awards®, winning 5 Oscars® including Best Picture and Rod Syeiger winning Best Actor. The film, set in Sparta, Mississippi (filmed in Tennessee), later spawned a TV series (filmed in Georgia).

Inherit The Wind (1960) — McComb, Miss. native Jimmy Boyd plays "Howard" in this acclaimed film about the famous "Scopes Monkey Trail" that stars Fredric March, Spencer Tracy, Gene Kelly and Donna Anderson.

Iron Curtain (1948) — The late Dana Andrews costars with Gene Tierney.

It Happened at the World's Fair (1963) — Elvis is at the Seattle World's Fair. Joan O'Brian and Gary Lockwood co-star. Young Kurt Russell, who would later play Elvis in a TV movie, makes his film debut in a small role.

It's My Party (1996) — Biloxi native Eric Roberts stars as architect who decides to throw himself a farewell party, then end his own life, after learning that he has AIDS.

JFK (1991) — Gary Grubbs, who grew up in Prentiss, has a part in this Oliver Stone film that stars Kevin Kostner.

Jailhouse Rock (1957) — One of the better Elvis Presley movies. Dean Jones costars.

James Dean: Race with Destiny (1997) — Meridian, Mississippi native Diane Ladd stars with Robert Mitchum and Carrie Mitchum (Robert's real-life granddaughter) who, at the time, was married to Casper Van Dien who plays James Dean in this flick. Got all that?

Jefferson In Paris (1995) — Arkabutla, Miss. native James Earl Jones costars with Nick Nolte and Greta Scacchi.

Joan of Arc (1948) — Meridian native Herschel McCoy was the costume designer of this film which starred Ingrid Bergman in the title role. The picture received an Academy Award nomination for Best Costume Design.

Johnny Dangerously (1984) — Jackson, Mississippi native Byron Thames plays the young Johnny, while the grown Johnny in played by Michael Keaton. Laurel, Mississippi native Ray Walston has a supporting role.

Johnny Handsome (1989) — Charleston, Mississippi resident Morgan Freeman costars with Mickey Rourke.

Judge Dredd (1995) — It's the voice of James Earl Jones in the opening segment of this Sylvester Stallone vehicle.

Jumpin' Jack Flash (1986) — The producer of this big box office hit, which stars Whoopi Goldberg and Jim Belushi, is Lawrence Gordon, who was born in Yazoo City and raised in Belzoni, Mississippi.

Jury Duty (1995) — Jackson native John Fortenberry directed this exploitation comedy/satire designed to take some cheap shots at the overblown O.J. Simpson trial. It stars Tia Carrere, Charles Napier and Abe Vigoda.

K-9 (1989) — The producer of this cop and dog film, which stars James Belushi with the mutt, is Lawrence Gordon, who was born in Yazoo City, Mississippi and raised in Belzoni, Mississippi.

Keys of the Kingdom, The (1944) — Hazlehurst, Mississippi native Ruth Elizabeth Ford has a small part in this film which stars Gregory Peck, Vincent Price, and Roddy McDowall.

Kid Galahad (1962) — Tupelo native Elvis Presley plays a boxer and Gig Young and Charles Bronson co-star.

King Creole (1958) — Set in New Orleans, it's one of the better Elvis Presley movies and costars Carolyn Jones.

King Kong (1933) — Roscoe Ates, who was born in Grange, Lawrence County, Miss., plays an uncredited role.

King of the Gypsies (1978) — Biloxi-born Eric Roberts costars with Judd Hirsch, Susan Sarandon, Annette O'Toole.

Kiss Before Dying, A (1991) — Meridian, Mississippi native Diane Ladd is a co-star in this film.

Kiss Me, Stupid (1964) — Laurel native Ray Walston costars with Dean Martin and Kim Kovak.

Kiss the Girls (1997) — Charleston, Mississippi resident Morgan Freeman stars along with Ashley Judd.

Kiss Them for Me (1957) — Laurel native Ray Walston's debut movie with costars Cary Grant & Jayne Mansfield.

Kissin' Cousins (1964) — This Elvis movie costars Glenda Ferrell, Arthur O'Connell and Jack Albertson.

Kit Carson (1940) — This film stars Collins, Mississippi native, the late Dana Andrews (1909-1992).

L.A. Confidential (1997) — Gulfport, Mississippi native Symba Smith plays "Jack's Dancing Partner" in this film, which stars Kevin Spacey and Kim Basinger.

Labyrinth (1986) — Greenville, Miss. native Jim Henson directed this children's fantasy movie which stars David Bowie and is based on one of Henson's stories. Henson also designed the creature puppets for the film.

Land of the Pharaohs (1955) — Co-screenwriter of this film starring Joan Collins was William Faulkner.

Last Remake of Beau Geste, The (1977) — James Earl Jones costars with Marty Feldman and Ann-Margret.

Last Mile, The (1959) — Vicksburg native Mart Crowley was production assistant/writer. It stars Mickey Rooney.

Last of the Mobile Hot-Shots (1970) — Based on the play, *Seven Descents of Myrtle*, written by Columbus, Mississippi native Tennessee Williams (1914-1983), the film stars James Coburn and Lynn Redgrave.

Last Tycoon, The (1976) — Collins, Miss. native Dana Andrews costars with Robert De Niro and many other stars.

Late Last Night (1998) — Meridian, Miss. native Diane Ladd plays a psychiatrist and Emilio Estevez plays "Dan."

 **Almost 500 Movies Mississippians Helped Make**

Laura (1944) — Collins native Dana Andrews costars with Gene Tierney and Vincent Price in this 4-star Otto Preminger film that received 5 Academy Award® nominations including an Oscar® for Cinematography.
Lean On Me (1989) — Charleston, Mississippi resident Morgan Freeman has the central role in this popular film.
Legends of the Fall (1995) — Dorree Cooper of Pass Christian, Miss. received an Academy Award® nomination for her set decorations for this movie which stars Brad Pitt and Sir Anthony Hopkins.
Leviathan (1989) — The producer of this underwater horror film, which stars Peter Weller and Richard Crenna, is Lawrence Gordon, who was born in Yazoo City, Mississippi and raised in Belzoni, Mississippi.
Lion King, The (1994) — Arkabutla native James Earl Jones is the voice of Mufasa in this top box-office smash Disney animated feature that received 4 Academy Award® nominations and won 2 Oscars® for its music.
Lion King II: Simba's Pride, The (1998) — Once again, Mississippian James Earl Jones is the voice of Mufasa.
Li'l Abner (1959) — Yazoo City, Mississippi native Stella Stevens plays "Appassionata Von Climax" in this musical comedy that also stars Stubby Kaye and Julie Newmar.
Live a Little, Love a Lot (1968) — Elvis with Michele Carey. Hattiesburg native Eddie Hodges has a small part.
Lock Up (1989) — The producer of this box office favorite, which stars Sylvester Stallone and Donald Sutherland, is Lawrence Gordon, who was born in Yazoo City, Mississippi and raised in Belzoni, Mississippi.
Long Hot Summer, The (1958) — Stars Paul Newman & Joanne Woodward and based on William Faulkner's novel.
Long Way to Freedom (2000) — Charleston, Mississippi resident Morgan Freeman plays Nelson Mandela.
Lost In Space (1998) — Action-packed sci-fi thriller based on the 1960s TV series and loaded with special effects. Purvis, Mississippi native and TV star Lacey Chabert plays "Penny Robinson" in her big-screen debut.
Love Me Tender (1956) — Elvis Presley's film debut. A Civil War-period movie with Debra Paget & Richard Egan.
Loved One, The (1965) — The late Dana Andrews (1912-1992), a native of Collins, Mississippi, costars with James Coburn, Rod Steiger and a host of other stars.
Loving You (1957) — Elvis' second movie costars Lizabeth Scott and Wendall Corey and "El" sings *Teddy Bear*.
Lucas (1986) — The producer of this film, which stars Charlie Sheen and Winona Ryder, is Lawrence Gordon, who was born in Yazoo City, Mississippi and raised in Belzoni, Mississippi.
Lucky Cisco Kid (1938) — Collins, Mississippi native Dana Andrews made his film debut in this movie.
Macho Callahan (1970) — Meridian, Mississippi native Diane Ladd costars with David Janssen and Jean Seberg.
Madison Avenue (1962) — The late Dana Andrews, a native of Collins, Mississippi, costars with Eleanor Parker.
Magnum Force (1973) — The string cues (supplemental musical compositions) for Clint Eastwood's second Dirty Harry movie, and the other Dirty Harry films, were written by Dee Barton from Starkville, Mississippi.
Mahogany (1975) — Vicksburg native Beah Richards plays "Florence" in this movie that stars singer Diana Ross.
Making Sandwiches (1997) — Biloxi native Eric Roberts costars with Matthew McConaughey and Sandra Bullock. Bullock also wrote and directed this feature.
Manhunter (1986) — Based on Mississippian Thomas Harris' book *Red Dragon*, it introduces the psychotic character, psychiatrist Hannibal "The Cannibal" Lecter, who turns up later in *Silence of the Lambs*.
Man-Trap (1961) — Yazoo City, Mississippi native Stella Stevens costars with Jeffrey Hunter and David Janssen.
Man Who Loved Women, The (1983) — Meridian, Mississippi native Sela Ward made her film debut opposite Burt Reynolds in this romantic comedy which also stars Julie Andrews and Kim Basinger.
Marie (1985) — Charleston, Mississippi resident Morgan Freeman costars with Sissy Spacek and Jeff Daniels.
Matewan (1987) — This first-class drama stars Mississippian James Earl Jones, Mary McDonnell, and Cris Cooper.
Mighty Ducks, The (1992) — Oxford, Mississippi native Julie Kaye Fanton worked as assistant set decorator on this movie that has Emilio Estevez coaching a peewee hockey team.
Miracle Worker, The (1962) — Alligator, Mississippi native, the late Frederick H. Coe (1914-1979), produced this film as he did the Tony-winning Broadway play on which it is based. The film, a biography about blind, deaf Helen Keller, stars Patty Duke as Keller. Vicksburg native Beah Richards plays the role of "Viney."
Mommie Dearest (1981) — Mississippian Robert Harper is in this biopic starring Faye Dunaway as Joan Crawford.
Monster in the Closet (1986) — Yazoo City native Stella Stevens costars with Claude Akins and Howard Duff.
Mother (1996) — Meridian, Mississippi native Diane Ladd stars in this horror thriller with Olympia Dukakis.
Muppet Movie, The (1979) — This movie, and the other muppet films, star Miss Piggy, Kermit the Frog, and the other muppet creations of Greenville native, the late Jim Henson (1936-1990).
Muppets Take Manhattan, The (1984) — Another hit movie with muppets created by Jim Henson of Greenville.
My Best Friend's Wedding (1997) — Waynesboro, Miss. native Tena Clark wrote music for this Julia Roberts film.
My Favorite Martian (1999) — Jeff Daniels and Christopher Lloyd play Earthling and Martian and Laurel native Ray Walston, the original Martian of the TV series, has the cameo role of "Armitan" in this sci-fi comedy.
My Foolish Heart (1949) — Collins native, the late Dana Andrews (1909-1992) costars with Susan Hayward.
My Little Girl (1986) — Mississippian James Earl Jones appears with Mary Stuart Masterson and Geraldine Page.
Mystery Men (1999) — Mississippian Larry Gordon is the producer of this comic-book spoof of super heroes.
Nashville (1975) — Corinth native Thomas Hal Phillips was involved with this and other Robert Altman films.
National Lampoon's Christmas Vacation (1989) — Meridian, Mississippi native Diane Ladd costars with Chevy Chase and Beverly D'Angelo in this comedy.

The Ultimate Reference on the State

 **Almost 500 Movies Mississippians Helped Make**

Native Son (1986) — Talk show host and Kosciusko, Mississippi native Oprah Winfrey plays "Mrs. Thomas" in this remake of the 1951 film, based on the book and play written by Natchez, Miss. native Richard Wright.
NeverEnding Story, The (1984) — Collins native Gerald McRaney had a role in this fantasy filmed in Germany.
New Jack City (1991) — Louisiana native, but longtime visitor and resident of Wesson, Miss., Charles C. Bennett was production designer (set decorator) for this film that stars Judd Nelson, Ice-T and Wesley Snipes.
Nickelodeon (1976) — Yazoo City, Mississippi native Stella Stevens costars with Ryan O'Neal and Burt Reynolds.
Night of the Iguana, The (1964) — The movie starring Ava Gardner, Deborah Kerr and Richard Burton was based on the play written by Columbus native Tennessee Williams (1911-1983).
Night Song (1947) — Merle Oberon costars with Collins, Miss. native Dana Andrews, who plays a blind pianist.
Nightmare on Elm Street, A (1984) — Pass Christian, Miss. native Dorree Cooper was set decorator for this film.
No Mercy (1986) — Beth Henley was one of 3 screenwriters for this film starring Richard Gere and Kim Basinger.
No Minor Vices (1948) — The late Dana Andrews (1912-1992), a native of Collins, Miss., costars with Lili Palmer.
Nobody's Fool (1986) — Biloxi native Eric Roberts costars with Rosanna Arquette in this romantic comedy based on the play written by fellow Mississippian Beth Henley of Jackson, who has a bit part as a bridesmaid.
North Star, The (1943) — The late Dana Andrews (1909-1992), a native of Collins, Mississippi, costars in another war movie with Anne Baxter and Walter Huston. This film received 6 Academy Award® nominations.
Norwood (1970) — McComb, Mississippi native Jimmy Boyd plays "Jeeter" in this comedy-adventure that also stars Glen Campbell, Kim Darby, Dom DeLuise, Pat Hingle, and Carol Lynley.
Nothing in Common (1986) — Meridian, Mississippi native Sela Ward plays "Cheryl Ann Wayne" in this comedy/drama with Tom Hanks at the helm. This was the last film in which Jackie Gleason appears.
Nurse Betty (2000) — Charleston resident Morgan Freeman costars with Greg Kinnear & Chris Rock in this comedy.
Nutty Professor, The (1963) — Mississippian Stella Stevens costars in a Jerry Lewis parody of Dr. Jekyll/Mr. Hyde.
October Sky (1999) — Produced by Charles "Chuck' Gordon, born and reared in Belzoni, Humphreys County, Miss.
Of Mice and Men (1981) — Laurel, Mississippi native Ray Walston costars with John Malkovich and Gary Sinise.
O'Hara's Wife (1982) — Laurel, Mississippi native Ray Walston costars with Edward Asner and Jodie Foster.
Once Upon a Time in America (1984) — Jackson, Mississippi native Robert Harper plays "Sharkey" in this film that stars Robert de Niro and several other big name actors.
Once Upon a Time...When We Were Colored (1996) — Based on the book by Mississippian Clifton Taulbert.
Outbreak (1995) — Mississippian Morgan Freeman costars with Dustin Hoffman and Rene Russo in this thriller.
Outfit, The (1973) — Benoit, Mississippi native and former world boxing champ Archie Moore plays "Parkard" in this melodrama that stars Robert Duvall, Joe Don Baker and Karen Black.
Ox-Bow Incident (1943) — Collins native Dana Andrews stars with Henry Fonda & Anthony Quinn.
Paint Your Wagon (1969) — Laurel native Ray Walston costars with Clint Eastwood, Lee Marvin and others.
Paradise, Hawaiin Style (1966) — Elvis in Hawaii again, this time with costars Suzanna Leigh and James Shigeta.
Past Perfect (1996) — Biloxi native Eric Roberts plays "Dylan Cooper," a cop who tries to protect a juvenile he arrested from a murderous band of time-traveling truant officers. Laurie Holden and Nick Mancuso costar.
Paternity (1981) — The producer of this film, which stars Burt Reynolds, is Belzoni native Larry Gordon.
Patriot Games (1992) — Mississippian James Earl Jones, Harrison Ford, and Anne Archer in a top action/thriller.
Pelican Brief (1992) — From the best-selling book written by Oxford, Mississippi novelist John Grisham.
Penitentiary (1979) — Jamaa Fanaka (Jackson, Mississippi-born Walter Gordon) was producer, director and screenwriter for this film (and the 2 sequels) about a young black man who is falsely convicted of murder and sent to prison, where his only means of survival is his skill as a boxer in matches against other convicts.
Period of Adjustment (1962) — Based on the play written by Mississippian Tennessee Williams, it stars Jane Fonda.
Piece of the Action, A (1977) — Arkabutla native James Earl Jones costars with Sidney Poitier and Bill Cosby.
Pinky (1949) — Brooksville, Miss. native Frederick O'Neal plays "Jake Walters" in this 4-star movie about racial intolerance in the South. It stars Ethel Barrymore and Ethel Waters with Jeanne Crain in the title role.
Platinum College (1960) — Friar's Point, Mississippi native Conway Twitty appears in this B-movie.
Platinum High School (1960) — McComb, Mississippi native Jimmy Boyd plays "Bud Starkweather" in this crime drama that stars Andy Rooney, Dan Duryea and Yvette Mimieux.
Player, The (1992) — Stars Tim Robbins, Whoopi Goldberg, Laurel native Ray Walston and scores of star cameos.
Play Misty For Me (1971) — Musical score for this Clint Eastwood movie was written by Dee Barton of Starkville.
Pope of Greenwich Village, The (1984) — Biloxi native Eric Roberts plays "Paulie" as he costars with Daryl Hannah and Geraldine Page, who received the Academy Award® nomination for Best Supporting Actress.
Popeye (1980) — Laurel-born Ray Walston plays Popeye's (Robin Williams') Pappy. Shelley Duvall plays Olive Oyl.
Porgy and Bess (1959) — Mississippian Ruth Attaway plays "Serena" in this Otto Preminger musical that stars a plethora of big names such as Pearl Bailey, Diahann Carroll, Sammy Davis, Sr. and Sidney Poitier.
Portrait in Black (1960) — Laurel's Ray Walston costars with Lana Turner, Sandra Dee, and Anthony Quinn.
Poseidon Adventure, The (1972) — Yazoo City's Stella Stevens costars with Gene Hackman, Shelley Winters, and a host of other stars in one of the most popular "disaster" movies — it was the top grossing film of 1972. This movie received 10 Academy Award® nominations, winning 3 Oscars®.

 **Almost 500 Movies Mississippians Helped Make**

Power 98 (1996) — Biloxi native Eric Roberts plays a Los Angeles radio talk show host talking to a killer.
Power of One (1992) — Charleston, Mississippi resident Morgan Freeman costars with Stephen Dorff.
Predator (1987) — The producer of this hit sci-fi action film, which stars Arnold Schwarzenegger and Carl Weathers, is Lawrence Gordon, who was born in Yazoo City, Mississippi and raised in Belzoni, Miss.
Predator 2 (1990) — This hit sequel, which stars Danny Glover and Gary Busey, was produced by Lawrence Gordon, who was born in Yazoo City and raised in Belzoni, Mississippi.
President's Lady, The (1953) — Mississippian Ruth Attaway plays "Moll" in this historical drama that stars Charlton Heston as Andrew Jackson and Susan Hayward as his wife Rachel.
Primary Colors (1998) — Meridian native Diane Ladd plays Mamma Stanton in this comedy/drama with an all-star cast, including John Travolta (Gov. Stanton). Jackson native Rebecca Walker also has a part. Arkabutla, Mississippi native James Earl Jones does a CNN voiceover.
Prince Jack (1984) — This was the last movie Collins, Mississippi native Dana Andrews made.
Prophecy II, The (1998) — Biloxi native Eric Roberts costars with Christopher Walken in this horror fantasy.
Purple Heart, The (1943) — The late Dana Andrews (1909-1992), a native of Collins, Mississippi, stars.
Quest for Atlantis (1999) — Arkabutla, Miss. native James Earl Jones costars with Regina King and Jennifer Rubin.
Quo Vadis? (1951) — Meridian native Herschel McCoy was the costume designer of this film starring Robert Taylor and Deborah Kerr, and was named in the Academy Award® nomination for Best Costume Design.
Raggedy Man (1981) — Biloxi native Eric Roberts costars with Sissy Spacek and Sam Shepard.
Rainmaker, The (1997) — Francis Ford Coppola directed this film adapted from Mississippian John Grisham's novel and stars Matt Damon, Jon Voight, Mickey Rourke, and Danny DeVito. It was filmed in Memphis.
Rambling Rose (1991) — Meridian native Diane Ladd and daughter Laura Dern both received Academy Award® nominations for their roles, the first real-life mother and daughter to be nominated in the same year.
Rebel Rousers (1970) — Meridian native Diane Ladd costars with Cameron Mitchell, Jack Nicholson, and Bruce Dern, her real-life ex-husband. Ladd and Dern divorced in 1967.
Redemption of the Ghost (2000) — Meridian, Mississippi native Diane Ladd stars.
Rendezvous with Rama (2000) — Charleston, Mississippi resident Morgan Freeman plays Commander William T. Norton in this adventure/sci-fi feature based on the science fiction novel by Arther C. Clark.
Rio Lobo (1970) — Ruleville, Miss. native Luster Bayless was costume designer for this John Wayne western.
Road to Glory, The (1936) — Mississippian William Faulkner (1897-1962) co-wrote the screenplay.
Robin Hood: Prince of Thieves (1991) — Charleston, Miss. resident Morgan Freeman costars with Kevin Costner.
Rocketeer, The (1991) — The producer of this film is Lawrence Gordon, originally of Belzoni, Mississippi.
Rollin' Home to Texas (1940) — This western was the last movie (of 39) made by Mooreville native Olin Francis.
Rolling Thunder (1977) — The executive producer of this film, which stars Tommy Lee Jones and Dabney Coleman, is Lawrence Gordon, born in Yazoo City, Mississippi and raised in Belzoni, Mississippi.
Roll of Thunder; Hear My Cry (1978) — Based on a book written by Jackson native Mildred D. Taylor and stars Mississippian Morgan Freeman. Corinth native Hal Thomas Phillips also did some screenwriting for it.
Roman Spring of Mrs. Stone, The (1961) — This movie is based on the novel written by playwright Tennessee Williams (1914-1983), a native of Columbus, Mississippi. It stars Vivien Leigh and Warren Beatty.
Romance (1930) — Mississippian Gavin Gordon plays opposite Greta Garbo in her second "talkie."
Rookie of the Year (1993) — Jackson, Miss. native Robert Harper is one of the 3 producers of this sports comedy.
Rooster Cogburn (1975) — Mississippian Luster Bayless was costume designer for this sequel to the 1969 western *True Grit* in which John Wayne reprises his role as the grizzled lawman. Katharine Hepburn costars.
Rose Tattoo, The (1955) — Stars Burt Lancaster. The co-screenwriter was Columbus native Tennessee Williams.
Roustabout (1964) — This one finds Elvis working in Barbara Stanwyck's carnival. Leif Erickson also costars.
Runaway Bride (1999) — Meridian native Sela Ward has a small part as "woman in bar" in this Julia Roberts vehicle.
Runaway Train, The (1985) — Biloxi native Eric Roberts received an Academy Award® nomination for Supporting Actor for his role opposite Jon Voight, who received a nomination for Best Actor. Dorree Cooper, a native of Pass Christian, Mississippi, was assistant set decorator for this film.
Rustler's Rhapsody (1985) — Meridian, Mississippi native Sela Ward plays Col. Ticonderoga's (Andy Griffith's) daughter in this spoof of Saturday-matinee westerns that also stars Tom Berenger.
Sailor's Lady (1940) — The late Dana Andrews (1912-1992), a native of Collins, Mississippi, stars.
Sanctuary (1961) — Based on Mississippian William Faulkner's novel, it stars Lee Remick and Bradford Dillman.
Satan Bug, The (1965) — Dana Andrews, a native of Collins, Miss., costars with Ed Asner & Richard Basehart.
Saving Private Ryan (1998) — Historian Stephen Ambrose, a resident of Bay St. Louis, who was a consultant for this Steven Spielberg top-grossing film of 1998 ($216 million), called it "The best war movie ever make."
Say One for Me (1959) — This musical comedy was Yazoo City native Stella Stevens' debut film and also stars Laurel, Mississippi native Ray Walston along with Debbie Reynolds, Bing Crosby and Robert Wagner.
Scream 3 (2000) — Parker Posey, who grew up in Laurel, Miss., is in the first blockbuster of the new millennium.
Sealed Cargo (1951) — The late Dana Andrews (1912-1992), a native of Collins, Miss., costars with Claude Rains.
Second Greatest Sex, The (1955) — McComb, Mississippi native Jimmy Boyd plays "Newt McClure" in this musical.

 **Almost 500 Movies Mississippians Helped Make**

Secrets of the Lone Wolf (1941) — Hazlehurst, Mississippi native Ruth Ford plays "Helene de Leon" in this mystery.
Seduction of Joe Tynan, The (1979) — Greenwood, Mississippi native Carrie Nye plays "Aldena Kittner" in this political suspense/drama that stars Rip Torn as Senator Kittner and Alan Alda as "Joe Tynan."
Seven (1995) — Brad Pitt is a young cop teamed with Mississippi's Morgan Freeman as a veteran detective in this hit.
Seven Brides for Seven Brothers (1954) — Jackson, Mississippi native Kelly Brown plays "Carl" in this musical.
Sex Kittens Go to College (1960) — Friar's Point, Mississippi native Conway Twitty stars in this B-movie.
Shadow Men, The (1997) — Biloxi native Eric Roberts stars. After a family Ryan Barrett) has an alien encounter, they call the Air Force which leads to a visit by "Men In Black," who turn out to be alien-human mutants.
Shakedown (1988) — Louisiana native, but longtime visitor and resident of Wesson, Mississippi, Charles C. Bennett was production designer (set decorator) for this film that stars Richard Brooks, Sam Elloit & Peter Weller.
Shawshank Redemption (1994) — Charleston resident Morgan Freeman received an Academy Award® nomination for Best Actor. He costars with Tim Robbins in this prison pic that got 6 more Oscar® nods.
Shootist, The (1976) — Ruleville, Mississippi native Luster Bayless was one of the three costume designers for this, John Wayne's last movie. This western featured a host of other big name stars including James Stewart, Lauren Becall, Richard Boone, Hugh O'Brian, Harry Morgan and John Carradine.
Silence of the Lambs, The (1991) — This blockbuster was based on the best selling novel written by Mississippian Thomas Harris and again brings us his psychotic character Dr. Hannibal "The Cannibal" Lecter. The biggest grossing movie of 1991 ($131 million in the U.S.), it became only the third movie ever to win the top five Academy Awards® — Best Actor (Anthony Hopkins), Best Actress (Jodie Foster), Best Screenplay (Ted Dally), Best Director (Jonathan Demme), and Best Picture! It was rated No. 65 on the American Film Institute's list of the Top 100 Greatest American Movies of All Time, announced in 1998.
Silencers, The (1966) — This was the late Dean Martin's first role as secret agent Matt Helm and one of his costars is Yazoo City, Mississippi native Stella Stevens, who plays "Gail, Big O's Girl".
Silver Streak (1976) — Laurel's Ray Walston puts up with the wild comic antics of Gene Wilder and Richard Pryor.
Sins of Rachel Cade, The (1960) — Brooksville, Mississippi native Frederick O'Neal plays "Buderga" in this movie about an American nurse (Angie Dickinson as "Rachel Cade") working in Africa who falls in love with Roger Moore's character, but Peter Finch's character is the one who really loves her. Got all that?
Slave Ship (1937) — Mississippian William Faulkner (1897-1962) co-wrote the film adaptation & additional dialogue
Smoke Signal (1955) — The late Dana Andrews (1912-1992), a native of Collins, Miss., costars with Piper Laurie.
Sneakers (1992) — Mississippian James Earl Jones stars with Robert Redford, Dan Aykroyd, and Sidney Poitier.
Something of Value (1957) — Brooksville, Mississippi native Frederick O'Neal plays "Adam Marenga" in this flick about tribal war in Africa. It stars Rock Hudson, Juano Hernandez, Sidney Poitier and Dana Wynter.
Something Wicked This Way Comes (1983) — Meridian, Miss. native Diane Ladd costars with Jason Robards.
Something Wild (1961) — Meridian, Mississippi native Diane Ladd is a co-star with Carol Baker.
Sommersby (1993) — Arkabutla, Mississippi native James Earl Jones costars with Richard Gere and Jodie Foster.
Sound and the Fury, The (1959) — Based on William Faulkner's novel, it stars Yul Brynner and Joanne Woodward.
South Pacific (1958) — Laurel native Ray Walston reprised his Broadway role in this movie musical.
Specialist, The (1994) — Biloxi native Eric Roberts costars with Sylvester Stallone, Sharon Stone & James Woods.
Speedway (1968) — Elvis' second car-racing movie has costars Nancy Sinatra and the late Bill Bixby.
Spinout (1966) — Once again, Shelley Fabares costars with Tupelo native Elvis Presley. His first car-racing flick.
Spitfire Grill, The (1996) — Winner of the Audience Award at the 1996 Sundance Film Festival, it was financed by Gregory Productions formed by the Sacred Heart League, a Catholic organization based in Walls, Miss.
Splendor in the Grass (1961) — Vicksburg native Mart Crowley worked as production assistant and writer on this film that stars Natalie Wood and Warren Beatty, who made his film debut in this movie.
Spring Reunion (1957) — The late Dana Andrews, a native of Collins, Mississippi, costars with Betty Hutton.
Star 80 (1983) — Biloxi native Eric Roberts plays a real baddie in this one. This biopic stars Meriel Hemingway as Dorothy Stratten, the Playboy model who is murdered by her husband, Paul Snider, played by Roberts.
Star Wars Trilogy (*Star Wars*, '77, 7 Oscars®; *The Empire Strikes Back*, '80, 2 Oscars®; and *Return of the Jedi*, '83, 1 Oscar®) — Arkabutla native James Earl Jones is the voice of villain "Darth Vader" in this series, 3 of the biggest hits of all time. All three were digitally-enhanced and re-released in 1997 with great success at the box office. *Star Wars* was rated No. 37 on the American Film Institute's list of the Top 100 Greatest American Movies of All Time, announced in 1998 in celebration of the 100th anniversary of film making.
State Fair (1945) — The late Dana Andrews (1912-1992), a native of Collins, Mississippi, costars in this musical that contains the Oscar®-winning Rodgers and Hammerstein song *It Might As Well be Spring*.
Stay Away Joe (1968) — Some critics say it was Elvis' worst movie. It costars Joan Blondell and Burgess Meredith.
Sting, The (1973) — Laurel native Ray Walston has a part. Robert Earl Jones, a native of Coldwater, Miss. and father of actor James Earl Jones, also appears in this film which stars Paul Newman and Robert Redford.
Strange Lady in Town (1955) — The late Dana Andrews, a native of Collins, Miss., costars with Greer Garson.
Street Smart (1987) — Charleston resident Morgan Freeman received critical acclaim and an Academy Award® nomination for Best Supporting Actor playing volatile pimp "Fast Black." It also stars Christopher Reeve.

 **Almost 500 Movies Mississippians Helped Make**

Streetcar Named Desire, A (1951) — Stars Marlon Brando and was nominated for the Academy Award® Best Picture of 1951. Based on the play written by Columbus, Miss. native Tennessee Williams (1911-1983), which received the 1948 Pulitzer Prize. Williams was also co-screenwriter for the movie. Costars Kim Hunter, Vivien Leigh, and Karl Malden all received Oscars® for their roles. The movie rated No. 45 on the American Film Institute's list of the Top 100 Greatest American Movies of All Time, announced in 1998.

Sudden Impact (1983) — The string cues (supplemental musical compositions) for Clint Eastwood's fourth Dirty Harry movie, as well as the other four Dirty Harry films, were written by Dee Barton from Starkville.

Suddenly, Last Summer (1959) — Stars Elizabeth Taylor, Montgomery Clift, and Katharine Hepburn. Based on the play written by Columbus, Miss. native Tennessee Williams (1911-1983), who was also co-screenwriter.

Summer and Smoke (1961) — Based on the play written by Columbus, Mississippi native Tennessee Williams.

Swamp Water (1941) — Dana Andrews, a native of Collins, Miss., costars with Walter Brennan and Anne Baxter.

Sweet Bird of Youth (1962) — Based on the play written by Tennessee Williams, it stars Paul Newman.

Swing Shift (1984) — Jackson native Beth Henley had a minor role as the "Bible pusher" in the romantic-comedy drama set during WWII. the movie has several big stars including Ed Harris, Kurt Russell, Goldie Hawn, Holly Hunter and Christine Lahti received an Academy Award® nomination for her role of Hazel.

Sword in the Desert (1949) — The late Dana Andrews, a native of Collins, Mississippi, costars with Jeff Chandler.

Tall Story (1960) — Laurel native Ray Walston costars with Anthony Perkins and Jane Fonda.

Take a Hard Ride (1975) — Dana Andrews, a native of Collins, Miss., costars with Lee Van Cleef in this western.

Taking of Pelham One Two Three, The (1974) — Mississippian Ruth Attaway plays the mayor's (Lee Wallace) nurse in this subway terrorists/hostages movie that stars Martin Balsam, Walter Matthau and Robert Shaw.

Tall Story (1960) — Jane Fonda's film debut in a comedy with Anthony Perkins and Mississippian Ray Walston.

Tammy and the Bachelor (1957) — This first Tammy movie (of 3) stars Debbie Reynolds as Tammy and was based on the novels written by Brookhaven, Mississippi native Cid Ricketts Sumner (1890-1970).

Tammy and the Doctor (1963) — This third, and last, Tammy movie stars Sandra Dee and Peter Fonda.

Tammy Tell Me True (1961) — This second Tammy movie (of 3) stars Sandra Dee as Tammy and was based on the novel of that title written by Brookhaven, Mississippi native Cid Ricketts Sumner.

Tarnished Angels, The (1958) — Based on the novella *Pylon*, written by Mississippian William Faulkner, this film stars Rock Hudson and Dorothy Malone.

Tarzan's Peril (1951) — Brooksville, Mississippi native Frederick O'Neal plays Bulam, the Evil Chieftain. Lex Barker plays Tarzan and Virginia Huston is Jane.

Teachers (1984) — Charleston, Miss. resident Morgan Freeman costars with Nick Nolte and JoBeth Williams.

Teenage Mutant Ninja Turtles (1990) — This movie has characters created by Mississippian Jim Henson (1936-1990)

Telefon (1977) — Mississippian Luster Bayless was men's costume designer for this film starring Charles Bronson.

Ten Commandments, The (1956) — Mississippian Gavin Gordon has a small role in this Charleton Heston movie.

That Was Then, This Is Now (1985) — Charleston, MIssissippi resident Morgan Freeman stars with Emilio Estevez.

That's the Way of the World (1975) — McComb, Mississippi native Jimmy Boyd plays "Gary Page" in this movie, a behind-the-scenes look at the music industry. It stars Harvey Keitel and Ed Nelson.

Thieves (1999) — Belzoni native Larry Gordon is the producer of this crime drama, which stars Jennifer Lopez.

Third Degree (2000) — Charleston, Miss. resident Morgan Freeman costars with Gene Hackman in this crime drama.

Three Fugitives (1989) — This comedy features Arkabutla native James Earl Jones, Nick Noltle, and Martin Short.

Three Hours to Kill (1954) — The late Dana Andrews, a native of Collins, Mississippi, costars with Donna Reed.

Throw Mama From the Train (1987) — Stars Billy Crystal, Danny DeVito and Oprah Winfrey has a small part.

Thunderbolt and Lightfoot (1974) — The musical score for this movie, which stars Clint Eastwood, Jeff Bridges and George Kennedy, was written by Dee Barton from Starkville, Mississippi. Black character actor Alvin Childress (Amos of *Amos 'N' Andy*), a Meridian, Mississippi native, plays a janitor in this film.

Tickle Me (1965) — Typical Elvis fare with Julie Adams and Jocelyn Lane costarring with "the King."

Time for Killing, A (1967) — Laurel, Mississippi native Mundell Lowe was music director and composer for this western that stars Glenn Ford, George Hamilton and Inger Stevens.

To Have and Have Not (1944) — The screenplay was cowritten by Oxford, Mississippi's own William Faulkner. The picture stars Humphrey Bogart and Lauren Bacall.

Tobacco Road (1941) — Dana Andrews of Collins, Mississippi costars with Charley Grapewin and Gene Tierney.

Today We Live (1933) — Oxford, Mississippi's William Faulkner (1897-1962) cowrote the screenplay for this Howard Hawk's film that stars Joan Crawford, Robert Young, and Gary Cooper.

Tom Horn (1980) — Mississippian Luster Bayless was the costume designer for this Steve McQueen western.

Tomorrow (1972) — Oxford's William Faulkner (1897-1962) wrote the story for this film starring Robert Duvall.

Too Late Blues (1962) — Yazoo City native Stella Stevens costars with Bobby Darin and John Cassavetes.

Too Scared to Scream (1985) — Two Mississippians have a part in this mystery/horror/suspense thriller about a serial killer. Hazlehurst native Ruth Ford plays "Irma" and Greenwood native Carrie Nye plays "Grazietta."

Tomb Raider (2001) — Mississippian Larry Gordon is producer of this action/adventure/mystery movie.

Town Tamer (1965) — The late Dana Andrews, a native of Collins, Miss., and Pat O'Brian costar in this western.

 **Almost 500 Movies Mississippians Helped Make**

Trading Places (1983) — Robert Earl Jones, native of Coldwater, Mississippi and father of actor James Earl Jones, appears in this Eddie Murphy film. Magnolia, Mississippi native Bo Diddley also has a small part.

Train Robbers, The (1973) — Mississippian Luster Bayless was costume designer for this John Wayne western.

TripFall (1999) — Biloxi native Eric Roberts plays "Mr. Eddie" in this film that costars Katy Boyer, Rachel Hunter, Tyler Cole Malinger, Christina Ann Moore, Ken Palmer, Michael Raynor and John Ritter.

Trouble With Girls, The (1969) — Elvis' last movie has Marlyn Mason and Vincent Price as costars.

True Stories (1986) — The screenplay was written by Jackson native Beth Henley. Drew, Mississippi native Roebuck "Pop" Staples (The Staple Singers) plays 'Mr. Tucker' in this satire that stars John Goodman.

Tulsa (1949) — Meridian native Herschel McCoy was the costume designer of this film starring Susan Hayward.

Twins (1988) — Jackson native Robert Harper plays "Gilbert Larsen" with Arnold Schwarzenegger & Danny DeVito. Waynesboro, Miss. native Tena Clark also wrote some of the music for this movie.

Two Little Bears, The (1961) — McComb, Mississippi native Jimmy Boyd plays "Tina's (Brenda Lee) boy friend" in this children's fantasy that also stars Nancy Kulp, Eddie Albert, Jane Wyatt and Soupy Sales.

Two Shades of Blue (1998) — Biloxi native Eric Roberts costars with Gary Busey, Rachel Hunter & Marlee Matlin.

Unforgiven (1992) — Mississippian Morgan Freeman costars with Clint Eastwood and Gene Hackman in this western that received 9 Academy Award® nominations, winning 4 Oscars® including Best Picture of 1992. This film was rated No. 98 on the American Film Institute's list of the Top 100 Greatest American Movies of All Time, announced in 1998 in celebration of the 100th anniversary of film making.

Up In Arms (1944) — The late Dana Andrews (1909-1992), a native of Collins, Mississippi stars.

Urban Cowboy (1980) — Stars John Travolta, Debra Winger, plus Natchez native Mickey Gilley and features the nightclub Mickey owned in Houston, Texas — Gilley's — at the time the largest beer-joint in the world.

Viva Las Vegas (1964) — Ann-Margret costars with Elvis Presley in one of his best movies.

Walk in the Sun, A (1945) — Dana Andrews (1912-1992), a native of Collins, Miss., costars with Lloyd Bridges.

Walking Tall II (1975) — Corinth native Thomas Hal Phillips did some screenwriting for this movie.

War of the Roses (1989) — Jackson, Mississippi native Robert Harper plays "Heath" in this black comedy that stars Michael Douglas and Kathleen Turner as a married couple that fight it out to the bittersweet end.

Water Damage (1999) — Charleston, Mississippi resident Morgan Freeman stars in this crime thriller.

Waterworld (1995) — The second most expensive movie ever made (almost $200 million & 2 years in the making) stars Kevin Costner and Dennis Hopper and was produced by Lawrence "Larry" Gordon, who credits his brother Chuck as producer. Both Larry and Chuck Gordon are from Belzoni, Mississippi.

Westerner, The (1939) — Collins, Mississippi native Dana Andrews had his first significant role in this film.

Where the Heart Is (2000) — Mississippian Johnny Moore (aka J.D. Evermore) plays a hospital orderly.

Where the Sidewalk Ends (1950) — Dana Andrews, a native of Collins, Mississippi, costars with Gary Merrill.

White Christmas (1954) — Mississippian Gavin Gordon plays the role of General Carlton in this musical classic.

White Lightning (1973) — Meridian native Diane Ladd appears in this film which stars Burt Reynolds.

Whole Nine Yards, The (2000) — Michael Duncan, who attended Alcorn State University, costars with Bruce Willis.

Who's Minding the Store (1963) — Laurel native Ray Walston costars with Jerry Lewis and Jill St. John.

Who Says I Can't Ride a Rainbow (1971) — Morgan Freeman made his film debut with co-star Jack Klugman.

Wing and a Prayer (1944) — The late Dana Andrews, a native of Collins, Mississippi, costars with Don Ameche.

Wild In the Country (1961) — Elvis Presley stars along with Hope Lange, Tuesday Weld, & John Ireland.

Wild River (1960) — Stars Montgomery Cliff and Lee Remick and was adapted from the book, *Dunbar's Cove* ('57), written by Pontotoc, Mississippi native Borden Deal. Bruce Dern, former husband of actress Dianne Ladd from Meridian, Mississippi, and father of actress Laura Dern, made his film debut in this movie.

Witness (1985) — Mississippian Robert Earl Jones has a small part in this drama that stars Harrison Ford.

Wives and Lovers (1963) — Laurel, Miss. native Ray Walston is a performer with Janet Leigh and Shelly Winters.

Wizard of Oz (1925) — This original silent-screen version was directed by Larry Semon, born in West Point, Miss.

WUSA (1970) — Meridian, Mississippi native Diane Ladd costars with Paul Newman and Joanne Woodward.

X-Files: The Movie (1998) — Prentiss, Mississippi native Gary Grubbs plays the fire chief in this sci-fi blockbuster.

You've Got Mail (1998) — Former Laurel resident Parker Posey is in this romantic comedy about two co-workers (Tom Hanks and Meg Ryan) who hate each other at the office but fall in love over the Internet.

Zero Hour (1957) — The late Dana Andrews (1912-1992), a native of Collins, Mississippi, stars. This was the movie that was spoofed by *Airplane*, the 1980 comic blockbuster film.

 This list contains 12 movies included in the American Film Institute's list of the Top 100 Greatest American Movies of All Time, announced in 1998 in celebration of the 100th anniversary of film making. It also contains 33 of the biggest box office hits of all time, each film grossing over $100 million (see the next page). This list includes all 31 Elvis Presley films. The list does not include movies filmed in Mississippi. See the preceding chapter for a list of those 41 films.

 **Almost 500 Movies Mississippians Helped Make**

Through May 28, 2000, a total of 206 films had grossed over $100 million each in the U.S. Only 8 of the movies were released prior to 1970. Of the 206 films, 18 were released in 1998 and 21 in 1999 and two in 2000 (No. 111, *The Gladiator* and No. 126, *Erin Brockovich*). The movies range from *Titanic* (No. 1), which grossed $600,743,440 to *Die Hard With a Vengeance* (No. 206), which grossed $100,012,000. The grosses include all revenue at theaters in the U.S. since the films original release date and includes revenue from any re-releases. At least 33 (16%) of the 206 films had Mississippians involved in some way — acting, directing, producing, costume designing, set decorating, writing, or writing music. Mississippians had a part in making four of the Top 10 films! The 33 top-grossing movies Mississippians helped make grossed $5,497,723,192, an average of $166,597,672 per film! Below is a list of those 33 films.

ALL-TIME TOP GROSSING MOVIES MISSISSIPPIANS HELPED MAKE

Title of Film	Year	Mississippian(s)	Role In Film	Total Gross	Rank
Star Wars	1977	James Earl Jones	Voice of "Darth Vader"	$460,935,665	2
Forrest Gump	1994	Michael Humphreys	Actor (young Gump)	$329,452,287	6
The Lion King	1994	James Earl Jones	Voice of "Musafa"	$312,775,367	7
Return of the Jedi	1983	James Earl Jones	Voice of "Darth Vader"	$309,125,409	8
The Empire Strikes Back	1980	James Earl Jones	Voice of "Darth Vader"	$290,158,751	11
Saving Private Ryan	1998	Stephen Ambrose	Consultant	$216,119,491	25
Armageddon	1998	Michael Duncan	Actor	$201,551,346	29
Gone with the Wind	1939	Roscoe Ates	Actor (bit part)	$198,514,494	30
		B. Reeves Eason	Second Unit Director		
		Will A. Price	Technical advisor		
The Fugitive	1993	Sela Ward	Actress	$183,752,965	36
Robin Hood: Prince of Thieves	1991	Morgan Freeman	Actor	$165,493,908	53
The Firm	1993	John Grisham	Based on his novel	$158,348,367	60
The Sting	1973	Robert Earl Jones	Actor	$156,000,000	62
		Ray Walston	Actor		
Runaway Bride	1999	Sela Ward	Actress	$152,149,590	68
Deep Impact	1998	Morgan Freeman	Actor	$140,387,792	85
The Green Mile	1999	Michael Duncan	Actor	$136,801,374	91
Teenage Mutant Ninja Turtes	1990	Jim Henson	Designer of creatures	$135,265,915	95
The Silence of the Lambs	1991	Thomas Harris	Based on his novel	$130,726,716	101
Honey I Shrunk the Kids	1989	Dorree Cooper	Set designer	$130,724,172	102
Coming to America	1988	James Earl Jones	Actor	$128,152,301	109
My Best Friend's Wedding	1997	Tena Clark	Scored some music	$126,805,112	113
Clear and Present Danger	1994	James Earl Jones	Actor	$121,985,472	123
The Hunt for Red October	1990	James Earl Jones	Actor	$120,709,866	128
Die Hard 2	1990	Larry Gordon	Producer	$117,323,878	137
Double Jeopardy	1999	Various Mississippians	Filmed partially in Miss.	$116,735,231	139
You've Got Mail	1998	Parker Posey	Actress	$115,731,542	142
Twins	1988	Tena Clark	Scored some music	$111,936,388	151
A Time to Kill	1996	John Grisham	Based on his novel	$108,285,000	159
		Various Mississippians	Filmed entirely in Miss.		
Batman and Robin	1997	Dorree Cooper	Set designer	$107,285,004	163
Driving Miss Daisy	1989	Morgan Freeman	Actor	$106,578,049	167
Every Which Way But Loose	1978	Dee Barton	Scored music	$105,918,400	170
Unforgiven	1992	Morgan Freeman	Actor	$101,100,000	192
The Pelican Brief	1993	John Grisham	Based on his novel	$100,768,000	196
Seven	1995	Morgan Freeman	Actor	$100,125,340	203

The Ultimate Reference on the State

Mississippi Superlatives and Trivia

The Mississippi Gulf Coast

The Singing River at Pascagoula makes a sound like the humming of bees. This has never been explained, but there's the legend about Anola, an Indian princess of the Biloxi tribe who loved Altama, a young chieftain of the Pascagoulas. She was betrothed to a chieftain of her own tribe, but fled with Altama to his people. Faced with enslavement by the Biloxi tribe, the Pascagoula braves, with women and children leading the way, joined hands and began chanting a song of death as they walked into the river until the last voice was hushed by the dark, engulfing waters...or was it!?!

•••

The first settlement in the Mississippi Valley was at Fort Maurepas, now Ocean Springs, in 1699.

•••

A record eight flags have flown over Biloxi including French, Spanish, British, Confederacy, and U.S.

•••

The world's longest & largest man-made beach is along the Mississippi Coast from Biloxi to Henderson Point, averaging 200 feet wide and 26 miles long. The Gulf Coast is the lowest and flattest in the U.S.

•••

The nation's second oldest yacht club, the Pass Christian Yacht Club, organized in 1849, is only 5 years younger than the New York City Yacht Club — the nation's oldest.

•••

The world's largest shrimp (size of a medium lobster) is at the Old Spanish Fort Museum in Pascagoula.

•••

Located on 13,500 acres in Hancock County, NASA's John C. Stennis Space Center employs over 4,300 people (35% are scientists or engineers & 29% are technicians) and adds almost a half billion dollars to the local economy annually. Stennis Space Center has tested all of NASA's rocket engines, including the Saturn booster rockets, which propelled the Apollo astronauts into space on their journeys to the moon. The Stennis Space Center had more than 112,00 visitors go through its visitors center in 1998.

•••

Some of the U.S. Navy's most advanced ships are constructed by the Ingalls Division of Litton Industries in Pascagoula. The world's first all-welded iron ship, the *SS Exchequer*, was built at Ingalls in 1939, only one year after the shipyard opened. The world's first all-welded passenger ship, the *African Comet*, was launched at Ingalls in 1941. The first nuclear submarine built in the South, the *U.S.S. Sculpin*, was built at Ingalls in 1960. Ingalls was awarded a contract in 1998 to build 2 guided-missile destroyers for the U.S. Navy, bringing to 21 the number of Aegis destroyers under contract. In 1999 Ingalls signed a contract to construct the two largest cruise ships ever built in America, the two $600 million ships to be delivered by January 2003 and 2004. The two ships will be the first ocean-going cruise ships to be built in the U.S. since 1958, when Ingalls built two of the largest and most luxurious passenger ships ever built, the *SS Brasil* and the *SS Argentina*, the last two cruise ships built in the U.S.
The state's largest single private employer, Ingalls Shipyard has over 11,000 workers.

•••

The oldest edifice in the U.S. west of the Atlantic coast is the Old Spanish Fort in Pascagoula. Built between 1715-1726, this historic structure was once the carpentry shop of Joseph Simon de La Pointe.

•••

The largest sculpture in the U.S., also the largest sculpture of a shark head in the world, is located on the Mississippi Gulf Coast in front of T-Shirt City on highway 90 in Biloxi. The 32,000 pound (16 tons) sculpture consists of a steel frame covered with polystyrene Each of its eyes is over a yard wide and its teeth range from 22 to 24 inches long. The sculpture, designed by Kern Studios of New Orleans and built by Florida Foam Company of Jacksonville, was hauled to the Biloxi business in May 1999 on 4 flatbed 18-wheelers. The load was so wide they couldn't take the Mobile Tunnel and had to circle Mobile Bay.

•••

The two main Mississippi ports, Gulfport and Pascagoula, are closer to the Panama Canal than either New Orleans, Louisiana or Mobile, Alabama. Gulfport is the No. 1 banana port in the U.S.

•••

The first national bank branch legally operated in the U.S. was chartered in Moss Point on Mar. 14, 1907.

Mississippi Superlatives and Trivia

Harrison County, Mississippi was the 2nd county in the U.S. to establish a Board of Health. In the early 1900's, Gulfport had several cases of yellow fever and the city was under quarantine often. An inspection station was established when the quarantine station was withdrawn. It evolved into a Board of Health.

●●●

The largest tree in the world ever transplanted, a live oak weighing almost 300 tons, was picked up and moved 100 yards during the weekend of April 13-14, 1996 in Biloxi, Miss. This giant tree — 593,049 pounds, 50 feet tall, a trunk 52 inches in diameter and branch circumference 95 feet wide — was actually the largest of 3 giant live oaks that Grand Casino contracted to be moved in order to preserve them. This world-record transplant was performed by Environmental Design, a Houston, Texas firm. The cost was $35,000 for the actual uprooting and moving, with the total contract for the project around $60,000.

●●●

The last documented duel in Mississippi took place on April 18, 1874, in Bay Saint Louis.

●●●

Barq's Root Beer, now the nation best-selling root beer, was first developed and bottled in 1898 in Biloxi, Mississippi, by chemist Edward C. Barq. The first franchise was issued in 1934 in Mobile, Alabama. Coca-Cola (which now owns Barq's) and the City of Biloxi placed a state historical marker in the original plant at 140 Kellar Avenue in Biloxi in 1998 to mark the soft drink's 100th anniversary.

Business & Commercial Ventures

The popular Oreck vacuum cleaners are made in only one place in the world— Long Beach, Mississippi! The New Orleans-based company say the vacuums were originally produced in Michigan by Bissell, but are now manufactured only on the Mississippi Gulf Coast at the rate of about 150,000 units per month.

●●●

The oldest family-owned telephone company in the nation, The Hughes Telephone Company, is now located at Bailey in Lauderdale County. It originally began at Obadiah, Mississippi in January 1911.

●●●

The only Fortune 500 company based in Mississippi is WorldCom, headquartered in Clinton. The firm became the nation's 2nd largest long-distance company after it acquired MCI, a $37 billion deal and the largest merger in U.S. history when announced in 1997. A later plan to merge with communications giant, Sprint, a $115 billion deal when first announced, fell through in 2000. *Business Week* magazine named MCI WorldCom the 14th largest company in the world in its issue dated July 6, 1999.

●●●

Mtel in Jackson, introduced SkyTel 2-Way, the nation's first two-way paging network, in 1995. The company changed its corporate name to SkyTel in 1998. Skytel was first in the U.S. with programmable Internet services via pagers. On Aug. 11, 1999, the company introduced the SkyTel Message Center, through which people can manage their E-mail, faxes and voice mail — the first unified messaging product to offer both wireless and Internet platforms. MCI WorldCom acquired Skytel in mid-1999.

●●●

Auto World Weekly magazine, launched in June 2000, is a national publication with its editorial offices on the Mississippi Gulf Coast in Pass Christian. The editor-in-chief is William Jeanes, a Corinth, Miss. native and 25-year veteran of auto magazines, including a stint as editor-in-chief of *Car and Driver*.

●●●

The largest "frozenated" beverage company in the United States, ICEE® "The Coldest Drink in Town," is owned and managed by Fred Montalvo, who lives at Edwards in Hinds County, Mississippi.

●●●

The first brand of personal computers to be mass-produced by a Mississippi-based company, Howard Computers, made its debut Nov. 9, 1998. The company is a division of Howard Industries of Laurel, which has manufactured electric power transformers for 30 years. The firm competes against the major PC brands, such as Compaq, Dell and Gateway and sells computers on a built-to-order basis.

●●●

The first standard-gauge railroad in the U.S. and among the first regular-running railroads in the nation was the Woodville (Mississippi) and Saint Francisville (Louisiana) railway, chartered in 1831 — transporting and in full operation by the summer of 1836.

Mississippi Superlatives and Trivia

The furniture industry's first assembly line was started in 1948 in New Albany at the Mohasco-Futurion Corp., a company started by Russian immigrant, Morris Futurion, called the Henry Ford of furniture.

•••

With 54,000 pieces of furniture produced daily in Mississippi, the state is now the upholstery capital of the world, a designation formerly held by North Carolina. More than 70 percent of the upholstered furniture produced in the U.S. in made in Mississippi, much of it in and near Tupelo!

•••

The South's largest retail furniture store is Miskelly Furniture on Airport Road in Pearl, Mississippi.

•••

The largest syndicator of outdoors media programming (hunting and fishing programs) in the U.S. is Baer Media located in Southaven, Mississippi. Max Baer, Sr., a native of Memphis, Tennessee, co-owns and operates the business he founded in 1986 with his two sons, Max, Jr. and Chris.

•••

The most watched hunting video series in the U.S. is produced by a Mississippi company founded by a native Mississippian. Will Primos, born in Jackson, and his company Primos, Inc., began producing "The Truth®" video series in 1987. As of this writing, there are 22 titles in the series with more planned.

•••

In Oct. 1998, two Mississippi firms were on *Inc.* magazine's list of the 500 fastest-growing privately-held companies in the nation! Triton Systems of Long Beach, the nation's second largest manufacturer of off-premises ATMs (Automated Teller Machines) with over 35,000 machines in 15 countries, was listed No. 123. Number 30 in 1997, they made the list for the third consecutive year in 1999. Triton made 11,553 machines in 1999, up from 2,928 in 1995! Triton was also named the Mississippi Exporter of the Year for 1998. In its first year of eligibility, SIMOD Telecommunications of Pearl was on *Inc.* magazine's list at No. 247. In 1997, *Entrepreneur* magazine named SIMOD (Success Is Made Of Dreams) one of the 100 hottest new businesses in America. They sell, install and maintain telephone equipment & networks.

•••

A Mississippi company was listed as one of the fastest growing small businesses in the country in 1999. Pinnacle Construction of Ridgeland was rated No. 38 on *Entrepreneur* magazine's Hot 100 list and was the only Mississippi-based firm on the 1999 list! The company, founded and headed by Mississippian Donnie Young, started business on Sept. 1, 1997, and had $170,000 in income in the last 4 months of that year. In its first full year of operation in 1998, the company had a gross of almost $9 million and was making a profit. Pinnacle Construction specializes in general commercial construction.

•••

W.G. Yates & Sons Construction Co., with offices in Jackson and Philadelphia, Mississippi, became the state's largest construction company after announcing on Nov. 18, 1999, the purchase of Memphis-based Eagles Ventures, the owner of several construction companies. The privately-held Yates Companies will have annual revenues of $600 million with over 2,000 workers in Mississippi, Alabama, Georgia and Tennessee. Yates built the Beau Rivage Hotel & Casino in Biloxi, Sam's Town and Hollywood casinos in Tunica, and a hotel at the famous and historic Biltmore Estate in Charlotte, North Carolina.

•••

A Mississippi company was named the best small corporation in the nation for 1999. *Business Week*, which ranks small companies (under $500 million in annual sales) based on sales, return on capital and earnings growth, named Friede Goldman International to the top spot. Headquartered in Jackson, Friede Goldman is a marine company that specializes in building and refurbishing oil drilling platforms and most of its 5,000 employees work on the Mississippi Gulf Coast. In winning the honor, the Mississippi company headed by J.L. Holloway, beat out more than 10,000 publicly traded firms tracked by *Business Week*. Holloway had been named to the Mississippi Business Hall of Fame less than a month before. In 1999 Friede Goldman acquired Halter Marine Group in Gulfport, adding 8,000 workers!

•••

The world's largest and heaviest mobile off-shore self-elevating oil rigs were built at Vicksburg by the Marathon LeTourneau Company. The first one, the "Gorilla," stands over 600 feet tall, weighs approximately 38 million pounds (19,000 tons), and can move under its own power across land at the speed of 100 feet per day. Proportionately, this is far slower than a snail. Now, there are Gorilla VI & VII models.

Mississippi Superlatives and Trivia

The longest board in the world was cut in Madison, Mississippi on May 7, 1998. The *Guinness Book of World Records*™ witnessed and documented the 113-foot, 4-inch board cut from a 13-story tall pine tree brought from southern Mississippi. Logosol Chainsaw, a Swedish company with an office in Madison, made the cut with 8 of its "one-man sawmills" lined up. The board was given to the city of Madison who dubbed it the "State Board of Education" and moved it to the Jim Buck Ross Agriculture and Forestry Museum where visiting students are encouraged to sign the plank pledging to remain in school.

●●●

The Flexible Flyer, probably the best snow sled made, is made in only one place — at West Point, Miss. by Blazon-Flexible Flyer, Inc. One of the original Flyers is on display in the Smithsonian Institute.

●●●

A Mississippi company's product has been on the moon! When astronauts landed on the moon, the lunar vehicle they drove had wire in its tires made by Delta Wire Corporation of Clarksdale, Mississippi.

●●●

Another Mississippi company's products are out of this world! Pioneer Aerospace of Columbia (Marion County) manufactures parachutes used by NASA Space Shuttle missions, the Mars Pathfinder spacecraft and the Galileo probe, which orbited the planet Jupiter. A Pioneer parachute helped the Galileo probe descend through Jupiter's thick atmosphere and a cluster of Pioneer chutes eased the fall of the space shuttle's solid rocket boosters. The company, in Columbia since 1933, made parachutes for the military during WWII and today still makes personnel and cargo chutes for the U.S. and 14 foreign countries, including Canada. The big cargo rigs support up to 5,000 pounds, but can be clustered together to drop up to 40,000 pounds — even a vehicle. Each month Pioneer Aerospace uses more than 400,000 yards of fabric, 500,000 yards of tape and webbing, 2,300 yards of cord and 3,000 pounds of thread!

●●●

The world's largest industrial forklift, the Y-120BW Lift Truck, is designed and built in Mississippi by Taylor Machine Works at Louisville in Winston County. Only 4 of these 95-ton monster machines exist.

●●●

Mississippian Billy Mounger II founded Tritel in 1999 with an initial investment of $180 million. On Feb. 29, 2000, Jackson-based Tritel Inc. agreed to sell its shares to another young wireless telephone company, Virginia-based TeleCorp PCS Inc. for $5.3 billion! Mounger will serve as chairman of the board of the new company called Telecorp, based in Virginia. The firm will continue to operate its stores in the Southeast and continue to expand selling the AT&T wireless service under the SunCom brand.

●●●

The Aug. 1999 issue of *Consumer Reports* magazine gave a Mississippi-made product its top rating! The respected national publication, known for its impartiality as an independent tester, named Viking Range Corporation's oven/stove combination the best consumer product of its type available — the best range they has ever tested! The Greenwood-based company's 36-inch dual electric and gas oven/stove beat out 4 competitors in the range category and earned the only "excellent" rating from the magazine's editors. The Viking range is a high-end, pro-style range that sells for $5,000.

●●●

Peavey Electronics Corporation in Meridian, founded in 1965 by Hartley Peavey, has 2,000 employees at 33 facilities totaling 2.5 million square feet of manufacturing space, making Peavey the largest manufacturer of musical instruments and portable sound equipment in the U.S. It is the only U.S. company that makes every "link in the audio chain" and the only major U.S. manufacturer of musical instrumentation and amplification where the founder still owns and actively manages the company. ♫♪

●●●

The first can of evaporated condensed milk was produced in Liberty, Mississippi, in 1856 by Gail Borden (d.1/11/1874). The first bottle of Dr. Tichener's antiseptic was also produced in Liberty.

●●●

The world's largest hardboard manufacturing plant is located at Laurel in Jones County. Operated by the Masonite Corporation, it was also the first plant in the United States to manufacture hardboard products.

●●●

Every commercial airplane in the free world has at least one hydraulic component that was designed and manufactured in Miss. — at Vickers in Jackson, the world's largest maker of aerospace hydraulic pumps.

Mississippi Superlatives and Trivia

A native Mississippian was once considered the world's largest General Motors dealer! In the 1960s, Dumas Milner in Jackson controlled as many as 30 GM dealerships in Kansas City, Fort Lauderdale, Los Angeles, San Diego, Philadelphia, Tampa, Tulsa and San Antonio, and other locations across the country. His Mississippi dealerships included Brookhaven, Jackson, Laurel and Vicksburg.

●●●

The nation's largest producer and distributor of fresh shell chicken eggs is headquartered in Jackson, Mississippi! Cal-Maine Foods, Inc., sells most of its eggs in 26 states across the southeastern, southwestern, midwestern and mid-Atlantic sections of the U.S.

Agriculture

Mississippi is the 4th largest poultry-producing state in the nation — a $1.4 billion industry in 1998! Timber became the state's first $1 billion ag commodity in 1993. In 1994, timber came in 2nd to poultry and eggs which surged to $1.078 billion in value — the first time poultry passed the $1 billion mark.

●●●

Before going public in 1994, Mississippi Chemical Corp., headquartered in Yazoo City, was the world's first farmer-owned nitrogen plant and the world's largest farmer-owned fertilizer plant.

●●●

The first cotton crop commercially produced entirely by machinery in the U.S. was near Clarksdale, Mississippi in Sept. 1944. Eight International Harvester machines "did the work of 480 pairs of hands."

●●●

The largest gin laboratory in the world is the USDA Cotton Ginning Research Laboratory at Stoneville.

●●●

The nation's leading center for catfish research is the Stoneville Research Center in Washington County. The construction of a $5 million-plus national warm water aquaculture center was begun in Aug. 1996.

●●●

The first and only federal marijuana farm in the nation was established in July 1968 when President Johnson signed the bill establishing the farm at the University of Mississippi to be used as a research center for "...the botany, chemistry, and cultivation of the drug." That farm became the main supplier of marijuana used for official medical research in America. That farm is still in operation.

Plants and Trees

The world's only cactus plantation, located near Edwards in Hinds County, grows over 3,000 varieties.

●●●

Mississippi is one of only two states in the nation where the state flower is the blossom of the state tree. The official state tree/flower is the Magnolia for Mississippi and Virginia has its Dogwood tree/flower.

●●●

Mississippi has more tree farms than any other state, according to the American Forest Institute, and has been the "number one tree farm state in the nation" for over 34 years. The world's largest cottonwood tree plantation is the Fitler Plantation in Issaquena County.

●●●

Mississippi's largest tree is a Baldcypress located 8 miles north of Belzoni in Humphreys County on property owned by Mark Simmons. It's 46 feet, 4 inches in circumference, about 15 feet in diameter, 70 feet in height and is believed to be over 2,000 years old! This state champion tree is located within 300 feet of the former champion bald cypress which is only slightly smaller. The smaller tree remains the 2nd largest tree in the state and would produce enough lumber to build six ordinary houses. The state's tallest champion tree, a Mockernut Hickory (156 feet), is also located in Humphreys County.

●●●

Delta & Pine Land Company in Scott (pop. 130), Bolivar County, Mississippi is the world's largest commercial breeder, producer and seller of cotton planting seed. The company was founded in Scott in 1911 by a group of British textile workers.

●●●

Nine of the ten most successful varieties of "paper-shell" pecans in the world were developed in Jackson County, Mississippi — Alley, Delmas, Hall, Lewis, Papst, Russell, Schley, Stuart and Success.

Mississippi Superlatives and Trivia

Churches & Religion

Mississippi's largest church, First Baptist of Jackson, received the fourth largest church organ in the United States in 1990, a $2-million-dollar gift from Canadian Baptist Edgar Morgan.

• • •

Dr. Charles Bryant, an amateur archaeologist and former president of Chamberlain Academy in Port Gibson, discovered the lost Biblical town of Trogylium in the late 1960s. The remains of the town are located on the eastern shore of Samos Island in the Aegean Sea near the southern coastline of Turkey.

• • •

The first successful Biblical novel ever published was *Prince of the House of David*, written by Joseph Holt Ingraham of Natchez. Between 1824 and 1847, he wrote and published eighty novels, about 10% of all novels published in the United States during the period!

• • •

Mississippi has more churches *per capita* than any other state in the country.

• • •

The nation's oldest Episcopal church building west of the Allegheny mountains is Saint Paul's Episcopal Church located in Woodville in Wilkinson County. It was erected in 1824.

• • •

The first Catholic seminary for black priests in the U.S. was opened in Bay Saint Louis on 9/16/1923. The first black Catholic bishop consecrated in the U.S. was J.O. Bowers at Bay St. Louis on 4/22/1953.

• • •

The largest Bible rebinding company in the nation is Norris Bookbinding in Greenwood, Mississippi.

• • •

The world's first Eskimo Catholic priest was ordained in Pass Christian, Mississippi in 1963.

• • •

The first Jewish congregation in the U.S. to call a woman to exercise a rabbi's function was in Meridian, Miss. on Jan. 26, 1951.

Mississippi Colleges & Universities

The oldest book in the nation is an ancient Biblical manuscript at the University of Mississippi. The oldest bathtub in the western hemisphere is in the archaeology museum at Ole Miss. The world's largest collection of Blues music is in the Blues Archive at Ole Miss in Oxford.

• • •

The world's largest collection of original manuscripts and illustrations of children's books is at the University of Southern Mississippi Library in Hattiesburg. The only university in the U.S. privileged to display the important Norman Rockwell exhibit, which toured the nation in 1988, was Southern Miss.

• • •

The first preparatory school established in the Mississippi Territory was Historic Jefferson College, located in Washington in Adams County, and established in 1802.

• • •

The first state in the nation to have a planned system of junior colleges was Mississippi.

• • •

The first Rhodes Scholar from Mississippi was Ebenezer James Ford (1886-1947) from Columbia. He achieved this honor in 1904, the year the prestigious scholarship was established.

• • •

The nation's oldest land grant college for African-Americans is Alcorn State Univ. (est. 1871). Many famous people have attended Alcorn including *Roots* author Alex Haley when his father taught there.

• • •

When the Industrial Institute and College (now Mississippi University for Women) opened in Columbus in 1884, it was the first state-operated university exclusively for women in the U.S.

• • •

The first school in the U.S. to grant degrees to women was Elizabeth Female Academy at Washington in Adams County, Mississippi, established on Feb. 17, 1819. The first *co-educational* college in the nation to grant degrees to women was Mississippi College.

The Ultimate Reference on the State

Mississippi Superlatives and Trivia

It is believed to be the largest single donation to advance literacy in U.S. history. We're referring to the $100 million donated in January 2000 by Jackson, Mississippi native Jim Barksdale and his wife, Sally, to create the Barksdale Reading Institute to be administered by the University of Mississippi Foundation. The Barksdale Reading Institute will seek to ensure every child leaves third grade reading at his/her grade level. Jim Barksdale, an Ole Miss alumnus, made his fortune as the CEO of Netscape, the computer browser company that was bought by America Online (AOL) in early 1999.

•••

When a spokesman for the University of Southern Mississippi said that "It's the most unusual gift that we have ever seen," he has talking about the donation to the school of a Wendy's restaurant! Gene Carlisle of Memphis, a 1964 graduate of USM, owns 46 Wendy's outlets in Mississippi. In 1999, he decided to donate the one on Westover Drive in Hattiesburg to his alma mater. The Wendy's will continue to be managed by the Carlisle Corporation under a lease arrangement and USM will collect about $90,000 annually in rent which will go into scholarship funds. The university has the option of eventually selling the $700,000 property back to the Carlisle Corporation. The gift of a fast-food restaurant, or any restaurant, to an institution of higher learning is quite unique and probably a first anywhere!

Mississippi College Women

Mary Angie Douglass, a 1931 graduate of Mississippi State College for Women (now Miss. University for Women) was on the secretarial staff of J. Edgar Hoover, FBI Director in Washington, D.C.

•••

Mississippi State College (now Mississippi University for Women) graduate Nell Neill James (1895-1997), a native of Grenada, is credited with introducing the silk industry to Ajijic, Mexaco. She also authored several travel books including the *Petticoat Vagabond* series.

•••

Industrial Institute for Women (Mississippi University for Women) graduate Dr. Marietta Eichelberger (class of 1912) was head of nutrition research for the Evaporated Milk Institute of Chicago for many years. Largely through her research and efforts, the canning of milk and safe baby formula was perfected.

•••

A big corporate entity in Mississippi started the 21st Century/Third Millennium with a Mississippi woman at the helm. Carolyn C. Shanks has been Entergy Mississippi president and CEO since July 1, 1999. She joined Entergy in 1983 as a accountant with Mississippi Power & Light and later transferred to System Energy Resources, the subsidiary responsible for the operation of Grand Gulf Nuclear Station. Shanks was instrumental in the consolidation of Entergy's five nuclear units and the decision to expand their nuclear arm into a national company. She graduated from Senatobia High School, got an associate degree from Northwest Mississippi Junior College and received her bachelor of professional accountancy degree from Mississippi State University. She has been a Certified Public Accountant since 1988.

•••

Cynthia Ivy Pharr, from Richton, Perry Co., Mississippi, is president of Marketing Communications in Dallas, Texas, the Southwest's largest public relations firm. She is on the boards of directors for ShowBiz Pizza Time Inc. and Spaghetti Warehouse, and is chair of the board of GuestCare Inc. In 1985, she was named one of *Glamour* magazine's Ten Outstanding Working Women, and in 1990 was named Outstanding Alumna of the Year in the College of Arts and Sciences at Mississippi State University.

•••

Tougaloo College graduate Anne Moody, a Civil Rights activist born in Centreville, Mississippi, authored the book, *Coming of Age In Mississippi*, published in 1968. It received the American Library Association "Best Book of the Year Award," plus many other awards, and a rave review from Senator Edward Kennedy writing for the *New York Times*. The book, with over thirty printings, is a classic used as a high school and college text throughout the world and has been translated into seven languages.

•••

A successful University of Southern Mississippi graduate is Margaret Loesch (class of 1968), manager of production and the creative services at the ABC-TV network, then director of children's programming at NBC in the 1970s, executive vice-president at Hanna-Barbera Productions in the 1980s, then president of FOX children's programming, and is now president of the Jim Henson TV Group.

Mississippi Superlatives and Trivia

Pretty actress Kate Jackson, who played one of "Charlie's Angels" alongside costars Farrah Fawcett and Jaclyn Smith in the 1970s, attended the University of Mississippi in Oxford.

●●●

The idea for *Grandparents Magazine* was conceived by a University of Mississippi student Rhonda Gooden from Clarksdale. She dreamed up the idea as part a school journalism project. The Meredith Corp., which publishes over a dozen magazines including *Better Homes and Gardens* and *Ladies Home Journal*, paid Gooden $5,000 for the rights and issued the debut issue of the magazine in January 1987.

●●●

Vivian Brown Swain (Vivian Brown on the air), a graduate of the Jackson State University department of physics and atmospheric sciences, is a meteorologist with the Weather Channel in Atlanta, Georgia.

●●●

Industrial Institute for Women (now Mississippi University for Women) 1913 graduate Helen Carloss (1890-1948) from Yazoo City, Mississippi, was a successful attorney and tax expert and the first women in the nation to argue cases before the U.S. Circuit Court of Appeals and the U.S. Supreme Court.

●●●

Blanche C. Williams (1879-1944), a native of Kosciusko, Miss. and 1898 graduate of Industrial Institute for Women (now Miss. Univ. for Women) was a novelist and founder of the O. Henry Short Story Awards in 1918 when she was Chair of the English department at Hunter College in New York State.

Other Notable Mississippi Women

Yazoo City native V. Ruth Campbell (1887-1963) was the first woman admitted to the Miss. state bar.

●●●

The first women federal judge in the U.S. was Burnita Shelton Matthews (1895-1988) of Hazlehurst, Mississippi. She served the Washington, D.C. Federal District.

●●●

The first court decision in the United States to grant property rights to women took place in Mississippi. In 1837, Betsy Allen, a young Chickasaw women from Toccopola in Pontotoc County, carried her legal fight for property rights to the Mississippi Supreme Court, and won.

●●●

Carol Fowler, who grew up in Jackson, became news director of Chicago TV station WGN in late 1999.

●●●

In mid-year of 2000, Hattiesburg anesthesiologist Dr. Candace Keller became the first female president of the Mississippi State Medical Association.

●●●

Inverness, Mississippi native Anne Hudson was selected as best professor at a master's degree-granting university or college in the U.S. in 1996 by both the Carnegie Foundation for the Advancement of Teaching and the Council for Advancement and Support of Education. The first women to receive a doctorate in mathematics from Tulane, Dr. Hudson left a tenured position at Syracuse University in New York to move back to her native South to teach at Armstrong Atlantic State University in Savannah.

●●●

Oprah Winfrey, born in Kosciusko, was the first woman to ever rank No. 1 on *Forbes* magazine's list of 40 highest paid entertainers in 1993 with estimated total gross earnings at $98 million for 1992-93. In 1996 she was again on top with 1995-96 earnings of $171 million! The *Forbes* list of "The 400 Richest Americans" in 1999 listed Winfrey's net worth as $725 million, the 348th wealthiest American.

●●●

The first Mississippian and first woman to chair the board of the NAACP was Myrlie Evers-Williams, widow of slain civil rights leader Medgar Evers. Elected Feb. 18, 1995, she served through Jan. 1999.

●●●

The first female rural route mail carrier in the U.S. was Mrs. Mamie Thomas, who delivered mail by horse-drawn buggy in 1914 to the area southwest of Vicksburg, Mississippi.

●●●

The first woman in the South to become a state senator was Belle Kearney (1863-1939) from Madison County. She served two terms starting in 1924.

Mississippi Superlatives and Trivia

The first writer to have a romance novel reach No. 1 on Waldenbooks' Romance Novels Bestsellers list was Peggy Webb, a native of Mooreville, Mississippi, who now resides in Tupelo. Her first romance novel, *Taming Maggie*, reached No. 1 on that list in 1985. She has written a total of 48 romance novels counting *Warrior's Embrace*, released in May 2000 by Silhouette Books.

Mississippi's Beautiful Women

Miss Mississippi / Miss America

With four Miss America wins, Mississippi has not claimed the most Miss America titles (California is first with 6 wins and Ohio and Pennsylvania tie with 5 wins each), but does lead the nation in total points for all wins including swimsuit, talent, number of alternates, etc. Mississippi has had four Miss Americas, two runners-up, eight Top 5 finishers and seven Top 10 finishers (through 1999)!

●●●

Sixteen-year-old Rachel Ann Smith of Booneville, Miss Mississippi 1936, made it to the Miss America finals, then moved to Colorado and won that state's crown to compete at Atlantic City a second time.

●●●

Helen Ford of Hattiesburg, an alumna of Jackson State, was chosen "Miss Black America, 1975."

●●●

The first "Miss Congeniality" in America was Miss Mississippi Doris Coggins of Baldwyn, who was the first to win that title when the category was first instituted in 1939 in Atlantic City!

●●●

The first and best known of the four Miss Americas from Mississippi, Mary Ann Mobley of Brandon, had the highest score from the judges ever voted a Miss America, up until that time. She was crowned Miss America 1958. Mary Ann co-starred in two movies with Elvis Presley. In a 1999 poll, readers of *The Clarion-Ledger* newspaper of Jackson voted Mary Ann as their favorite all-time Miss Mississippi!

●●●

Brandon, Mississippi native Donna Hild Russell was Mrs. America 1985 and third runner up in the 1986 Mrs. World Pageant. Pamela Nail, a resident of Jackson, Mississippi won the title of Mrs. World, 1988, in Australia, and is the only American to have ever won Mrs. World! Before that, she was Miss Louisiana in 1983, Mrs. Mississippi, 1987, and was also , 1987.

●●●

Mississippi is the only state to ever have a Miss Hospitality Pageant (now held in Hattiesburg) to select a young lady to promote state tourism and economic development. There have been 51 Miss Hospitalities from Katherine Wright from Pascagoula in 1949 to Olivia Irons from Philadelphia, Mississippi, in 1999.

The First State to...

The first state in the nation to abolish imprisonment for debtors was Mississippi in 1824.
The first state to abolish leasing convicts to private enterprise was Mississippi in 1894.
The first state to adopt a homestead exemption law for homeowners was Mississippi.

●●●

The first city in the United States to use electricity from the Tennessee Valley Authority, the country's largest power producer, was Tupelo, Mississippi on February 7, 1934.
the first rural electric cooperative in the nation was Alcorn Electric Power Association in Corinth, Miss. The Monroe County Electric Power Association in Amory, Mississippi, was the first co-op in the U.S. financed by the Rural Electrification Administration (REA) to electrify its system on March 17, 1936.

●●●

Jackson was the first city in the world in which Digital Satellite Systems mini-dishes (18-36 inches in diameter) for receiving TV programs were sold. Cowboy Maloney's first sold them on June 17, 1994.

●●●

The first anti-pollution law in America was passed under the Spaniards in Natchez in 1783 when livestock owners complained about the noxious wastes from the indigo industry pouring into streams from which their cattle drank. The Governor issued an ordinance against the practice and fined those guilty.

●●●

The first state to organize a State Bar Association was Mississippi — in Natchez on May 26, 1821.

Mississippi Superlatives and Trivia

The Civil War

Mississippi suffered the largest percentage of casualties of any state in the Confederacy. An estimated 78,000 Mississippians served in the Confederate armies, of which 59,000 were either killed or wounded. Confederate deaths totaled 133,821 plus 26,000 to 31,000 more who died in Union prisons.

●●●

Of over 200,000 African-American men that served for the Union during the Civil War, 38,000 of them were killed and 14 of them won the Medal of Honor, the nation's highest award! About 38,000 blacks fought for the South. One of the South's best snipers was a black Confederate.

●●●

Historians say the foremost cavalry officer the U.S. ever produced was Lt. Gen. Nathan Bedford Forrest. Reared in Tippah and Hernando Counties, Miss., he joined the Confederate Army at age 40 as a private.

●●●

According to most historians, the most decisive battle of the Civil War was fought in Mississippi — the Battle of Champion Hill, fought May 16, 1863, near Edwards. It enabled the later capture of Vicksburg.

●●●

In pre-Civil War 1861, Mississippi ranked as the fifth wealthiest state in the nation of thirty-four states.

●●●

The first war vessel ever sunk by a water-floated mine, or electrically detonated "torpedo," was the *U.S.S. Cairo*, which sank in the Yazoo River on Dec. 12, 1862. All 160 men aboard escaped injury. The Cairo was raised Dec. 12, 1964. Now restored, it is a museum at the Vicksburg National Military Park.

●●●

The Old Courthouse Museum in Vicksburg has the South's largest collection of Civil War memorabilia.

●●●

The first state to erect a Confederate monument was Mississippi at Liberty in Amite County in 1871. Forty-four of Mississippi's 82 counties, over half of them, have Confederate monuments. Ironically, Jefferson Davis County, organized in 1906, is one of the counties where there are no such monuments. The National Military Park in Vicksburg has over 1,200 monuments, both Confederate & Union.

●●●

The last survivor of all the Generals of the Civil War was Mississippi Gov. Adelbert Ames, a native of Rockland, Maine, had been a Brigidier General in the Federal Army. Appointed provisional Governor in 1868, he was elected in 1874, but resigned under threat of impeachment in 1876. He died in Florida in 1933 at the age of 97. The last survivor of the Civil War, according to *Blue and Gray* magazine, was Sylvester Magee, a former slave bought at a slave market in Enterprise, Mississippi in 1858 and taken to a plantation in Covington County. He ran away, joined the Union Army and served at Vicksburg. When he died in Marion County, Mississippi on Oct. 15, 1971, he was supposedly at the advanced age of 130!

●●●

Mississippi native Major Lamar Fontaine, a scout under Generals Thomas "Stonewall" Jackson & Joseph E. Johnston, wrote *All Quiet Along the Pontomac*, one of the most popular songs of the Civil War.

●●●

The national holiday, Memorial Day, actually started in Mississippi. A group of women decided to do their part to help heal the wounds of war. They placed home-grown flowers on the graves of Confederate *and* Union soldiers for the first time on Apr. 25, 1866, at Friendship Cemetery in Columbus. This gesture was immortalized in the poem, *The Blue and the Gray*, by Francis Miles Finch in the *Atlantic Monthly*, September 1887 issue. This first "Decoration Day" soon developed into our National Memorial Day.

●●●

The only Confederate soldier given the honor of lying in state in the Old Capitol in Jackson, Mississippi was General William Barksdale, a Tennessee native, killed in the Battle of Gettysburg on July 2, 1863. He commanded Mississippi troops at the first battle of Manassas, Virginia and Antietam.

●●●

The first and only President of the Confederate States of America was Jefferson Davis, a Mississippian.

Mississippi Superlatives and Trivia

The world's only documented case of "Pregnancy by Bullet" happened in Mississippi!! The Nov. 7, 1874, issue of *American Medical Weekly* relates the bizarre episode which began during the Battle of Raymond during the Civil War on May 12, 1863: "According to Dr. T. G. Capers of Vicksburg, a soldier friend of his was hit in the scrotum by a bullet, which carried away his left testicle. The same bullet apparently penetrated the left side of the abdomen of a 17-year-old girl in a nearby house. Two hundred and seventy-eight days later, the young lady gave birth to a healthy 8-pound boy 'to the surprise of herself and the mortification of her parents and friends'. Three weeks later, Dr. Caper operated on the infant and removed a smashed miniball. He concluded that this was the same ball that had carried away the testicle of his young friend. It had penetrated the ovary of the young lady and, with some spermatozoa upon it, impregnated her! With this conviction, the doctor talked to his young friend and told him about the situation. Skeptical at first, he consented to visit the young mother. A friendship ensued which soon blossomed into a happy marriage. The couple had three more children, none of whom resembled their father as closely as the first!"

World War II

D'Lo, a small town in Simpson County, sent more men to war in World War II than any town its size in the U.S. — out of a population of 400, nearly 150, or 38% of them served (46 volunteers).

●●●

Eleven Mississippians died on the ship, the *U.S.S. Arizona*, at Pearl Harbor on Dec. 7, 1941, the incident that brought the U.S. into WWII. About 235,000 Mississippians served during that war.

Other Military Facts

Mississippi's most decorated soldier of WWI, Sgt. Henry Jetton Tudury, a native of Bay St. Louis, was personally awarded the Distinguished Service Cross by General John J. Pershing on Mar. 3, 1919.

●●●

Mississippians killed: World War I—704 (of 56,740 that served); World War II — 4,185 (of 235,000 that served); Korea—409; Vietnam War—637; Total—5,935 Mississippians lost their lives in all 4 wars.

●●●

The first national guard unit in the U.S. to receive the giant C-141B Starlifter transport jet was the Mississippi Air National Guard in Jackson on Aug. 10, 1986. This huge plane is 168 feet long, 39 feet high and can carry up to 90,000 pounds of cargo, 200 troops, 155 paratroopers or 103 litter patients.

●●●

Camp Shelby near Hattiesburg is the largest National Guard and reserve training camp in the nation.

●●●

The last battle between the United States Navy and a foreign foe in American waters was near Bay St. Louis when American ships battled the British Fleet in the Gulf of Mexico in the War of 1812.

●●●

Frank M. Adams (b. 9/25/1925 - d. 5/20/1990), a native of Tunica, Miss., was Lieutenant Commander (the second in command) of the *USS Nautilus*, the world's first nuclear-powered submarine when it became the first vessel to go under the Arctic ice cap. It was located at 90 degrees north, the geographic North Pole, at 11:15 pm EST on Aug. 3, 1958. He retired as a captain in 1969 after having commanded two nuclear subs and having held high administrative posts in the nuclear propulsion program initiated by Vice Admiral Hyman Rickover. The Triton submarines were designed at that time. Adams went on to a successful business career as a top executive with several large companies including the Bendix Corp.

●●●

Means Johnston, Jr., a Greenwood, Mississippi native, was a four-star Admiral who had the command of the Allied Forces of Southern Europe, part of NATO. Another four-star Admiral from Mississippi was John Sidney McCain, born in Teoc, Carroll County, one of several from his famous military family.

●●●

The highest ranking, most senior military officer in the entire history of the state is Lewis H. Wilson, Jr. born in Brandon in Rankin County. He was a Four-Star General who was also Commandant of the U.S. Marine Corps from 1975-79, which made him a member of the Joint Chiefs of Staff. He was a Captain when he received the Congressional Medal of Honor during World War II (see next page).

Mississippi Superlatives and Trivia

Mississippi's Medal of Honor Recipients

Mississippi has had a total of 22 men who have earned the Congressional Medal of Honor (CMOH), the highest award the U.S. gives people in the military: **The Civil War** (5, out of 1,520 awarded) — Adelbert Ames (Union Army-accredited to ME-buried in MA), John C. Black (Union Army-accredited to IL-buried in IL), Wilson Brown+ (Union Navy), August Dorley+ (Union Army) and Martin Freeman+ (Union Navy); The **Spanish-American War** (2, out of 109 awarded) — John W. Heard (Army-buried in NY) and Ira C. Welborn+ (Army); **World War I** (1, out of 124 awarded) — James J. Madison (Navy-buried in NJ); **World War II** (7, out of 441 awarded) — Van T. Barfoot (Army), James H. Diamond*+ (Army); Robert T. Henry*+ (Army), Jake W. Lindsey+ (Army), Jack H. Lucas (Marines-accredited to VA), James D. Slaton+ (Army) and Louis H. Wilson Jr. (Marines); **Korean Conflict** (5, out of 131 awarded) — Henry A. Commiskey (Marines-ashes scattered at sea), Jack G. Hanson*+ (Army-accredited to TX), Mack A. Jordan*+ (Army), Hubert H. Lee+ (Army) and John A. Pittman+ (Army); and the **Vietnam War** (2, out of 241 awarded) — Roy M. Wheat*+ (Marines) and Milton L. Olive III*+ (Army-accredited to IL). Thirteen of the 22 are native Mississippians born in the state. The 9 "adopted" Mississippians are Adelbert Ames (born in ME), James H. Diamond (born in LA), August Dorley & Martin Freeman (both born in Germany), Hubert L. Lee (born in MO), Jake W. Lindsey (born in AL), Jack H. Lucas (born in NC), James J. Madison (born in NJ) and Milton L. Olive III (born in IL). Most of those born in other states lived in Mississippi when they went into the service. Jack Lucas came to live in Mississippi after the service. Milton Olive was born in Chicago, grew up in Mississippi, then entered the service in Chicago. Adelbert Ames was the only Mississippi governor to be a MOH recipient. The 6 listed with asterisks were awarded the Medal posthumously (4 were native Mississippians). There were 53 Medals of Honor awarded for action "on the ground" in Mississippi during the Civil War, of which only one (awarded to August Dorley) was officially accredited to Mississippi, with the other 52 accredited to other states. In all wars, 17 Medals of Honor have been officially accredited to Mississippi, although we claim 5 more accredited to other states because the recipients had Mississippi ties. Of the 22 Mississippi recipients, 15 were Army, 4 Marines and 3 Navy. As of Nov. 1, 2000 — 2,386 Medals have been awarded to the Army, 745 to the Navy, 295 to Marines, 16 to the Air Force, 1 to the Coast Guard and 9 Unknowns. There have been 3,433 recipients (last 22 Medals awarded 6-21-2000) and 3,452 Medals awarded — 19 received the Medal twice. Of the 3,433 recipients, only 151 were living as of Nov. 1, 2000 (living recipients by conflict: WWII - 62; Korean War - 21; Vietnam - 68). Of those 151, three are Mississippi recipients: Van T. Barfoot, Jack H. Lucas and Louis H. Wilson, Jr. No Mississippi CMOH recipient is buried in Arlington National Cemetery. Eighteen CMOH recipients are buried in the state, including 14 Mississippians (8 native) listed here with a plus sign (+) and 4 non-Mississippians. (see "Famous & Notable Mississippians" for profiles of all Miss. recipients)

•••

Jack Lucas of Hattiesburg, Mississippi, was the youngest Marine ever and the youngest man in the 20th Century to be given the Congressional Medal of Honor on Feb. 20, 1945. He received the award at the age of 17 for throwing himself on a grenade to protect his buddies on Iwo Jima during World War II. Mr. Lucas was a special guest during President Clinton's State of the Union address on Jan. 24, 1995.

•••

Tech. Sgt. Jake W. Lindsey, a resident of Lucedale, Mississippi, was the 100th infantry soldier of WWII to receive the Medal of Honor. President Harry S. Truman personally presented Lindsey the medal on May 30, 1945, during a joint session of Congress, the only time the medal has been so awarded.

•••

Only one *native* Mississippian received the Congressional Medal of Honor during the Vietnam War. Lance Corporal Roy Mitchell Wheat, from Moselle in Jones County, sacrificed his life by throwing himself on a mine to save two fellow marines on Aug. 11, 1967 (two other MOH recipients were from Jones County — James D. Slaten from Laurel and Ira C. Welborn from Mico, now called Shady Grove). Army Private First Class Milton L. Olive, III, an African-American born in Chicago and reared near Ebenezer, Mississippi, sacrificed his life to save his companions by throwing himself on a grenade on Oct. 22, 1965, in Vietnam. Medal of Honor recipient Olive is buried in Holmes County, Mississippi.

Mississippi Superlatives and Trivia

Black Mississippi Achievers

The first black pilot in the U.S. Navy and the nation's first black aviator to be killed in combat was Ensign Jesse L. Brown (b. 10/13/26 in Hattiesburg), shot down in Korea on Dec. 4, 1950. The *USS Jesse L. Brown*, a knox-class escort vessel commissioned on Mar. 18, 1973, was named in honor of Brown.

•••

The first African-American from Mississippi to advance to the rank of General in the U.S. Army was Brig. General George Baker Price of Laurel, brother to former Metropolitan Opera star Leontyne Price.

•••

The first black to achieve international stardom in opera was Leontyne Price, a native of Laurel, Miss.

•••

The first African-American symphonic work to be performed in the U.S. was composed by William Grant Still of Woodville, Mississippi. It was called the *Afro-American Symphony*.

•••

The first black in the U.S. Senate was Hiram Revels (1822-1901), elected in 1870 during Reconstruction. He helped found Alcorn A&M College, now Alcorn State University. Trustees of the Department of Archives & History elected him to the State of Mississippi Hall of Fame on Dec. 6, 1996.

•••

John Roy Lynch was a Natchez house slave. In 1873, he became Mississippi's first black representative and, at age 25, the youngest man ever elected to the House of Representatives at the time. In 1884, he was the first black American to deliver the keynote address before a national political convention.

•••

The first African-American owned and operated bank in the United States was The Lincoln Bank in Vicksburg, established during Reconstruction in the 1870s.

•••

Reuben Anderson was the first black graduate of the University of Mississippi School of Law in 1967. He was the state's first black Circuit Court judge since Reconstruction, appointed by former Gov. William Winter to preside in the Hinds/Yazoo district. He became Mississippi's first black state Supreme Court justice when appointed by Governor Bill Allain in 1985. He was elected to the job in 1986 and again in 1989. In Feb. 1996, Anderson became the first black to head the Mississippi Bar Association when the 5,200 attorneys in the state elected him to start serving in that position in the summer of 1997.

•••

When Mike Espy of Yazoo City was elected from the second district in 1986, he was the first black congressman from Mississippi since Reconstruction. He became Secretary of Agriculture in 1993 — the first for that post from Mississippi, the only cabinet member from Mississippi in the 20th Century, and only 5th cabinet member ever from the state. He was the first black, the first Southerner and the youngest person ever to head the 4th-largest federal agency with 115,000 employees and a $60 billion budget.

•••

The first federal building in the United States to be named for an African-American is the McCoy Federal Building in Jackson, named for Dr. A. H. McCoy, a prominent dentist & business leader.

•••

Louis Westerfield (1949-1996) became the first tenured African-American law professor at Ole Miss in 1983. In 1994, he was named the first black dean of the University of Mississippi School of Law.

•••

The first black writer to write scripts for TV and films was William Attaway (1911-1986), a native of Greenville, Mississippi. He wrote *A Hundred Years of Laughter*, an hour long special on black humor that aired in 1964 and featured comedians Redd Fox, Moms Mabley and Flip Wilson in their very first appearance on TV. He was also a published novelist and songwriter who composed over 500 songs.

•••

Richton, Mississippi native George Ellis Johnson parlayed a small loan of $500 into a multi-million dollar cosmetics business, founding the Johnson Products Company in Chicago in 1954. In 1971, Johnson Products became the first African American-owned company to be listed on the American Stock Exchange. *Ebony* magazine honored Johnson in 1978 with its American Black Achievement Award.

Mississippi Superlatives and Trivia

Lerone Bennett, Jr., a native of Clarksdale, who worked for the *Atlanta Daily World* (1949-53), *Jet* ('53), & *Ebony* magazine as associate editor 1954-57 and as senior editor (1958-present), wrote *Before the Mayflower: A History of the Negro in America, 1619-1966*, considered be the "bible of black history."

●●●

Mississippian W.A. Scott founded the 1st black-owned newspaper in the U.S., *The Atlanta Daily World*.

●●●

The first Mississippian to be chosen president of the American Legion Boys Nation was Marcus R. Dilworth, age 17, of Yazoo City, chosen from almost 500,000 boys from across America in 1985.

●●●

A Mississippi native and African-American, Patrick Kelly (1954-1990) of Vicksburg, was the first American designer to be inducted into the Chamble Syndicale, the elite French fashion-industry union.

More Mississippi Achievers

Dr. Daniel Jordan of Philadelphia, Miss., an Ole Miss graduate, is the head of the Thomas Jefferson Memorial Foundation, which owns and operates Monticello, the home of Thomas Jefferson.

●●●

Joe Price of Meridian became chief of the Science and Technology Division of the Library of Congress.

●●●

A Hinds Junior College honor student, Clifford E. Charlesworth, who was named 1969 "Alumnus of the Year," worked for NASA and was flight director of two Apollo space missions.

●●●

A native of Clinton, Miss., James D. Byrd, is a polymer scientist who holds seven patents and developed the plastic used as heat shields for NASA space vehicles. He has written over 40 technical publications.

●●●

A Mississippi native coined the word "sociology." Colonel Henry Hughes, C.S.A., of Port Gibson in Clairborne County, coined the word when he published his *Treatise on Sociology* in 1854.

●●●

Bob Pittman, who grew up in Brookhaven, Mississippi, founded MTV (Music Television Video) in 1981

●●●

Mississippi native, Frances Witherspoon, born in Meridian on July 8, 1886, was the co-founder of the Legal Advice Bureau in 1915, the forerunner of the American Civil Liberties Union.

●●●

The first Mississippian elected to the Smithsonian Institution's Board of Directors was Charlie Kemp of Hazlehurst in Copiah County. He was elected in April 1985.

●●●

Native Mississippian Turner Catledge (1901-1983), born near Ackerman, worked for the *New York Times* for over 40 years as managing editor, then executive editor, then company vice-president.

●●●

Jerry Clower (1926-1998) was born at East Fork, Miss., but lived in Yazoo City for 34 years (1954-88). He was working there as a fertilizer salesman for Mississippi Chemical when he first started recording. Jerry sold more country-comedy albums than any other artist and received 9 consecutive awards for "Country Comic of the Year." He recorded his 30th album in 1996 at Dollywood in Tennessee.

●●●

Will D. Campbell, a native of East Fork near Liberty in Amite County, is the only minister in the world to ever become a comic strip character! The round-hatted preacher Will B. Dunn, in the nationally-syndicated comic strip *Kudzu*, was modeled after Campbell by his good friend, Pulitzer-Prize-winning cartoonist Doug Marlette, who lived in Mississippi when he first created the comic strip.

●●●

James D. "Jimmy" Dean, a lawyer and municipal judge in Corinth in Alcorn County, was the first Mississippian ever elected National Commander of the 2.7 million-member American Legion (1986-87).

●●●

A Mississippi native, William Lockhart Clayton (1880-1966) of Tupelo, was the originator of the Marshall Plan in 1947 following WWII when he was Undersecretary of State for Economic Affairs.

Mississippi Superlatives and Trivia

The top Abraham Lincoln scholar in the nation is acknowledged to be David Donald, born in Goodman, Mississippi in 1920. A two-time Pulitzer Prize winner, his latest work, *Lincoln*, was published in 1995. He is the Charles Warren Professor Emeritus of American History at Harvard University.

●●●

Through June 2000, there have been only 12 Mississippi students to ever make the top score (either a so-called "perfect 36," or a composite 36) on the ACT (American College Test). The first was Kevin Etheridge, who lived in Flowood and was attending Mississippi School for Math and Science when he aced the test in spring 1994. Later that year, Stephen Shackleford, Jr. of Jackson Prep and Kimberly R. Smith of Hattiesburg High both made the top score. The only student from Mississippi to ace the ACT in 1997 was Christine Varnado of Hattiesburg High. In 1999, an amazing 7 Mississippians made the 36 score: Jennifer Carlisle, a sophomore at Jackson Prep (16 years, 3 months old at the time); Shayon Ghosh, a senior at Jackson Prep, who was just past 13 years old and the youngest person ever in the state to make a 36; Michael Goggin of Hattiesburg High (also made a top 1,600 on the SAT); David Griswold of Tupelo High; William Phillips of Jackson Academy; Ronnie Robertson of Pillow Academy in Greenville; and Stanley Craig Ross of Vicksburg High School. Ruopeng Zhu, a 16-year-old sophomore at Jackson Academy, was the only Mississippian to get the top score of 36 on the ACT in June 2000.

●●●

As of the Fall of 1998, U.S. Marshall David Crews, 44, was assigned to the U.S. District Court in his hometown of Oxford, Mississippi. Of the country's 95 U.S. Marshalls at the time, Crews was the only one who held membership in Phi Beta Kappa, the nation's most elite academic honor society. In fact, a Department of Justice spokesperson stated that Crews is "one of only a few people in the history of the Marshall service to have the honor." He was inducted into the prestigious academic organization when he was a junior at the University of the South, where he graduated with a degree in history in 1976.

●●●

If you picked up a copy of *Good Housekeeping* magazine in late summer 1999, you probably noticed the name of Gail Pittman. This artistic Mississippian designed the ceramic dinnerware for NBC-TV's *Today* co-host Katie Couric for her newly decorated apartment in Manhattan, which is featured in the cover story of the magazine. Pittman and her partner, Helaine Maley, operate Gail Pittman Studio in Ridgeland, Mississippi, which has over 100 employees. The company manufactures hand-painted dinnerware and accessories. Artist/businesswoman Pittman had previously enjoyed success in supplying dinnerware for the Italian-theme restaurant, La Cucina, at Biloxi's Beau Rivage Resort and Casino.

●●●

Yes, there is a *real* "Karate Kid," and he's from Mississippi! Jordan Morrison of Florence, Mississippi, was only 14 years old when he won a gold medal as a world karate champion in Japan on Aug. 14, 1999! Morrison beat out 84 competitors to win in his 13-15 age group in Seibukan Shorin-Ryu and then bested the top winners in other karate styles for the championship in the Okinawan Traditional Karate-do and Kobudo World Tournament in Naha, Okinawa. Jordan was the only competitor under 21 from the U.S. The junior black belt had previously finished fifth in 1997 in the Junior World Karate Cup in Budapest, Hungary, won the Seibukan World Cup in Atlanta in Oct. 1998, and won 19 national AAU, USANKF and Junior Olympic gold medals! Morrison hopes to represent the U.S. in the Pan Am Games when he becomes 16 years old and to compete in the Olympics if karate becomes part of the games.

●●●

Cliff Freeman, a Vicksburg native, is the man responsible for some of the most successful/memorable TV ad campaigns in recent years. An advertising executive and ad creator, in the early 80s he penned the memorable line "Where's the beef?" for the Wendy's hamburger chain. Freeman's funny "Pizza, Pizza!" commercials started airing in 1988. During 1993 and 1994 alone, Little Caesars ads won 10 Clio awards, 11 Addys and 8 Andys. Little Caesars ads were rated the second-most recognized by consumers (after Coca-Cola) in 1994. The voice of the cartoon gnome character who chants "Pizza, Pizza!" is Freeman's. Freeman also wrote the Almond Joy® candy bar ad "Sometimes I feel like a nut, sometimes I don't."

●●●

A Mississippi native, Wallace Saunders, composed the original ballad *Casey Jones*. Saunders, an engine wiper at the railroad shop in Water Valley, was a personal friend of Jones. He didn't get credit for writing the song. Some railroad people reportedly talked him out of his rights to the song for just a bottle of gin.

Mississippi Superlatives and Trivia

Native Mississippian Charles C. Walker built the International Checker Hall of Fame in Petal, Miss. in 1979 as part of his 30-acre estate. It contains Ripley's Believe It-or-Not largest and 2nd largest checkerboards in the world. This self-made millionaire has garnered several championship titles and in Oct. 1994, Walker set a Guinness World Record by playing checkers with 306 people simultaneously and winning 300 of those games! It was Walker's 4th Guinness World Record. He began with 201 simultaneous games in New Orleans in 1988.

Sports

The first Mississippian to play in baseball's major leagues was Willie Mitchell (1889-1972), who joined the Cleveland Indians in 1909. Mississippi's first baseball legend, he made four American League All-Star teams and was the first pitcher to face Babe Ruth in an American League game. He struck out the Babe! He's a member of the Mississippi Sports Hall of Fame, inducted in 1966.

●●●

The only man to ever pinch hit for Babe Ruth was S.B. "Sam" Vick of Oakland in Yalobusha County, who played for the New York Yankees from 1917 to 1920. Babe Ruth's last two homers (Nos. 713 & 714) were off balls pitched by Guy Bush of Tupelo on May 25, 1935. Bush was with the Chicago Cubs.

●●●

Gerald "Gee" Walker, a Gulfport native and Ole Miss letterman, was playing for the Detroit Tigers on opening day of the 1937 season when he homered, tripled, doubled and singled in consecutive at-bats! That remains the only opening day cycle in major league baseball history!

●●●

The only *native* Mississippian in the Baseball Hall of Fame is James Thomas "Cool Papa" Bell (1903-1991), inducted in 1974. He played in the Negro Leagues from 1922-50. Probably the fastest man ever to play baseball — in 1933 alone he stole 175 bases! His .437 batting average in 89 games in 1940 was the highest in the history of the Mexican League. He never hit below .300 in any season and his lifetime batting average was estimated at .419, second in the Negro Leagues to Josh Gibson. "Cool Papa Bell Drive" into Smith-Wills Stadium in Jackson was dedicated in 1994. He was inducted into the Mississippi Sports Hall of Fame in 1995. Fellow Negro League player Willie Foster, reared in Lorman, Mississippi, was inducted into the Baseball Hall of Fame in 1996, but he was a Texas native.

●●●

The nucleus, or "pill," of every baseball used in the major leagues is made in only one place — at Muscle Shoals Rubber Co. in Batesville, Miss. The cores, made of rubber with a little cork and smaller than a golf ball, have been made in Batesville since 1965 when the company moved there from Alabama.

●●●

At the Women's College World Series, the University of Southern Mississippi Lady Eagles softball team was one victory short of the title game when they were defeated by UCLA on May 28, 2000. It was USM's second consecutive trip to the World Series, both times behind the fantastic pitching of Courtney Blades. Three days before (May 25) Blades pitched the second perfect game in WCWS history. Blades, 52-8, finished the season with NCAA records for victories and strikeouts (663). She had 166 more strikeouts than her own single-season record of 497 strikeouts she set in 1999. She also holds the career mark for victories (151) and strikeouts (1,773)! Blades didn't quite make the cut for the 2000 Olympics.

●●●

During his incredible 1996 season Mississippian Brett Favre threw a NFC-record 39 TDs in leading the Green Bay Packers to Super Bowl XXXI, which they won 35-21 against New England on Jan. 26, 1997, the game in which Favre threw a Super-Bowl-record 81 yard TD pass! He threw 2 TDs on Dec. 7, 1997, to become the first quarterback in NFL history to throw 30 TD passes or more in 4 consecutive seasons! On Dec. 27, 1997, Favre earned the NFL MVP award for an unprecedented 3rd straight year. In 1998, Favre became the first player ever with five 30-touchdown seasons!

●●●

Alcorn State quarterback and Heisman candidate, Steve "Air" McNair ended his college career on Nov. 19, 1994 with 16,823 yards, more than anyone in history!! On Apr. 22, 1995, the Houston Oilers chose him as the 3rd pick in the NFL draft. He signed a $28 million contract, then a record for a rookie. And in 1999, McNair's plays took the Tennessee Titans though the playoffs and on to Super Bowl XXXIV!

Mississippi Superlatives and Trivia

After Mississippi State came from behind to defeat LSU Oct. 23 (first time since '91), Jackie Sherrill's Bulldogs were 7-0 for the 1999 season, the best start in the school's 105-year history and 100 seasons that saw more than 900 games played under 30 head coaches! After that, the Bulldogs moved up No. 8 in both national polls! With 4 games to play, the '99 Bulldogs had already won more games than 81 of the previous 99 Miss. State football teams! They won their next game to make it an 8-0 season start.

●●●

The first Mississippian selected for the Pro Football Hall of Fame was Frank "Bruiser" Kinard (1914-1985), a native of Pelahatchie. Kinard was enshrined in the Pro Football Hall of Fame in 1971. He played tackle for the Dodgers from 1938-47. He was the first Ole Miss Rebel player inducted into the College Football Hall of Fame in 1951. In addition to Kinard, Mississippi claims six other players in the Pro Football Hall of Fame! They are Mississippians Lance Alworth, Lem Barney, Willie Brown, and Walter Payton and we also claim Ray Guy and David "Deacon" Jones, both from other states (Georgia and Florida respectively), but they played college football for Mississippi schools.

●●●

Walter Payton (1954-1999) of Columbia, Miss. was the first football player pictured on the Wheaties cereal box. In 1999, he was voted one of the 10 all-time Favorite Wheaties® Champions! He was one of the NFL's greatest performers with these records: the All-Time Leading NFL Rusher, 1976-80 with 16,726 yards; Most All-Purpose Yards (21,803); number of games in which he gained at least 100 yards rushing (77); the NFL record for the most rushing yards in a single game, 275; and the NFL record for the most times of running 1,000 yards or more in a season — 10 times in 1976-81 and 1983-86. He's 5th in All-Time Leading TD Scorers with a career total of 125. Payton's in the Mississippi Sports Hall of Fame (1993), the Pro Football Hall of Fame (1993) and the College Football Hall of Fame (1996).

●●●

There are three Mississippians on the list of pro football's top 20 "Leading Lifetime Touchdown Scorers" through the 1998 season: Jerry Rice in 1st place with 175 TDs; Walter Payton in 5th place with 125 TDs; and Lance Alworth in 20th place with 87 TDs. The 20 players scored 2,177 TDs through the 1998 season with our 3 Mississippians (15% of the group) having a combined total of 387 TDs (18% of the total)! The top 5 players scored a combined total of 705 TDs, so the two Mississippians in the top 5, Rice and Payton, make up 40% of the group and their 300 combined TDs account for 42% of the top 5 TDs!

●●●

Mississippian Jerry Rice, wide receiver for the San Francisco 49ers, is an incredible football player! Here are just a few of his First Place Career Records through the 1999 season: Total TDs (180); Receiving TDs (169); Receptions (1,206); Receiving Yards Gained (18,442); Season Receiving Yards (1,848); Seasons with 50+ Receptions (13); Seasons with 100+ Receptions (4); Game Receiving Touchdowns (5); Games with 100+ Receiving Yards (64); Consecutive 1,000-Yard Receiving Seasons (11); Consecutive 1,000-Yard Seasons (11); Consecutive Games with a Reception (195) & Consecutive Games with a Reception TD (14). That's not even counting all his post season, Pro Bowl and Super Bowl records!

●●●

Duece McAllister set 2 Ole Miss records in the game against Arkansas State on Oct. 7, 2000 — 2,730 career rushing yards (broke Kayo Dottley's 2,654) and 210 career points (broke Brian Lee's record).

●●●

The first deaf player in U.S. history to play a full year of pro football was Mississippian Bilbo "Mule" Monaghan (1910-1994). He was only the second Mississippi School for the Deaf graduate to receive a college degree. He also had a distinguished coaching career at the MSD from 1933-46. He and his wife, Kathryn, are generally recognized as the first deaf parents in America to legally adopt hearing children, adopting two daughters in 1951. He was inducted into the Mississippi Sports Hall of Fame in 1996.

●●●

On May 14, 1999, Jacksonian Rett Crowder was playing at the Country Club of Jackson when he shot a 58 — a lower 18-hole golf score than anybody has ever shot on the PGA Tour! He won his first State Am in 1992 at Country Club with a score of 10-under. At the Dancing Rabbit Golf Club in Philadelphia, Miss. in 1998, Crowder scored a 72-hole total of 16-under 272 — the lowest winning score in the 83-year history of the State Am! He also captured the State Am in 1999 and 2000, becoming one of only four players in the history of the State Am to win it three consecutive times.

Mississippi Superlatives and Trivia

In 1996-97, Ken Lindsay of Madison, was president of the Professional Golfers Association of America (PGA), the 24,000-member, world's largest working sports organization. Lindsay was only the second Mississippian to hold this position. James Ray Carpenter of Hattiesburg was PGA president in 1987-88. Lindsay will be enshrined in the Mississippi Sports Hall of Fame on March 23, 2001.

•••

Archie Moore (1913-1998), a native of Benoit, Miss. was World Light-Heavyweight Champion from 1952-60. Moore was the only boxer to fight both Muhammad Ali and Rocky Marciano and was the last to fight Marciano (Sept. 21, 1955). Moore's overall career record was 195-25-8 with a record 141 KOs!

•••

Columbus native Henry Armstrong (1912-1988) is the only boxer to ever hold 3 world champion titles simultaneously — World Featherweight (1937-38), World Welterweight (1938-40) and World Light-weight in 1938. And the man who owned his contract during that time period was none other than the legendary singer Al Jolson, who had purchased Armstrong's contract in 1936. Armstrong was inducted into the International Boxing Hall of Fame in 1990.

•••

Major boxing matches in the U.S. started at Mississippi City on the Gulf coast where the first championship fight in history was fought in Feb. 7, 1882, when John L. Sullivan KO'd Paddy Ryan. The last bare knuckles sanctioned fight in the U.S. was at Richburg in Perry County on July 8, 1889, when John L. Sullivan defeated Jake Kilrain. The timekeeper was Bat Masterson, former legendary old-west Sheriff of Dodge City, Kansas, a sportswriter for the New York *Morning Telegraph* at the time.

•••

The $4.5 million Mississippi Sports Hall of Fame and Museum opened July 4, 1996, as "Mississippi's First Museum for the 21st Century" and the most advanced of its kind in the world. The 21,542 sq.-ft building is three stories tall. Counting year 2001 inductees, there are 201 members in the Hall of Fame.

•••

Mississippi has had many athletes participate in the Olympic Games with many of them winning medals:
- Don Scott, born in Woodville, was Mississippi A&M's first national track champion, winning the AAU half mile in 1916. He was an Olympian in 1916, 1920 and 1924, winning the Gold Medal in the 1924 modern pentathlon. He was the first person inducted into the Mississippi Sports Hall of Fame (1963). Mississippi State University's Scott Field in Starkville is named after him.
- Long jumper Edward Lansing Gordon, Jr., a Jackson native, won a Gold Medal in the 1932 Olympics.
- Money (Leflore County) native Willye B. White was a 5-time Olympian. She won the Silver Medal in the long jump in 1964. She's in the National Track & Field Hall of Fame and the Mississippi Sports Hall of Fame.
- High hurdler Hayes Jones, a Starkville native, won the Gold Medal in the 1964 Olympics.
- Boxer Quicy Daniels, a native of Biloxi, won bronze in the 1960 Olympics and middleweight boxer Alfred Jones, born in Grace in Issaquena County, won bronze in the 1968 Olympic Games.
- Laurel native Lee Calhoun was the first man to win the Gold Medal in the Olympic 110-meter hurdles *twice*, in 1956 and 1960, and remained the only man to win twice until 1988.
- The Cochran brothers from Richton are only brothers to win Olympic Gold. Commodore (1902-1969) won his in the 1924 Olympics in Paris as part of the U.S. 1600-meter relay team. Roy (1919-1981) won 2 Gold Medals at the 1948 Olympics in London, one in the 400-meter hurdles in the then-Olympic record time of 51.1 seconds, and another one as part of the 1600-meter relay team.
- Mississippian Calvin Smith was the fastest man on earth, holding the 100-meter world record of 9.93 seconds from July 3, 1983, until Carl Lewis broke it by 1 second on Sept. 24, 1988. Smith gained Gold in 1984 running the 3rd leg of the 4x100 relay which turned a world-record time of 37.83 seconds
- Alice Regina Brown, a Jackson native, won the Gold Medal as a 4x100 relay runner in the 1988 Olympics.
- Ruthie Bolton-Holifield, a native of McLain, helped the U.S. women's basketball team win the last Gold Medal awarded at the 1996 Olympics. She received her second Gold as a member of the same team in the 2000 Summer Olympics in Sydney, Australia. Mississippians Neil Fortner and Peggie Gillom also won Gold Medals as coach and assistant coach, respectively, of that team.
- Other Mississippi medalists in the 2000 Olympics were Roy Oswalt on the U.S. baseball team who won Gold, Antonio McDyess on the U.S. men's basketball team who won Gold, and U.S. Army Sgt. First Class Todd Graves, a native of Laurel, who won the bronze in international skeet shooting.

The U.S. Olympic Team Trials for cyclists held in Jackson on May 20, 2000, was the first Olympic qualifying event ever held in Mississippi. Nicole Freedman and Antonio Cruz, both California natives, qualified for the U.S. cycling team that participated in the 2000 Summer Olympics in Sydney, Australia.

Mississippi Superlatives and Trivia

Basketball great Purvis Short had a standout high school career in Hattiesburg, then at Jackson State he set the JSU scoring record with 2,434 points (avg. of 23.8 p/game), a record he still held through 1999! Short was the 5th player selected in the 1978 National Basketball Association (NBA) draft by the Golden State Warriors. He played 12 pro seasons, averaging 17.3 points, 4.3 rebounds and 2.5 assists per game. Short was inducted into the SWAC Hall of Fame in '98 and the Mississippi Sports Hall of Fame in 2000.

•••

The first Mississippian to go directly to the NBA (National Basketball Association) from high school was 18-year-old Jonathan Bender of Picayune. The only Mississippian picked in the first round of the NBA draft in 1999, Toronto selected Bender fifth overall on June 30. He was the highest drafted prep player since Minnesota took Kevin Garnett fifth overall in 1995. After the Raptors picked Bender, they traded him to the Indiana Pacers, who signed him to 3-season contract worth almost $7 million. In the McDonald's All-American Game, Bender scored 31 points to break Michael Jordan's record of 30!

•••

Here are a few state high school records. The New Hope baseball team set a national high school record for victories by an undefeated team in 1996. They went 43-0, which also set new state records for single-season wins and consecutive wins. Robert Woodard is Mississippi's high school basketball career scoring leader with 4,274 points (Houlka High, 1981-86). In football, Clifton Davis III of North Panola holds the state high school record for TD passes in one game, 10 in a game against Coldwater in 1990, also tying the national high school record! He also holds the state record of 9,309 career passing yards and 89 high school career TD passes (1988-91). In 1996, Kevin Jones (S. Panola RB) set 2 state records of 46 points in a game and 322 points in a season. His record 41 TDs stood for less than a day until Dicenzo Miller (Weir TB) finished with 42 on Dec. 7. Miller scored 47 TDs in 1997 and 118 during his high school career, both state records. Only one other Mississippian has scored more than 100 TDs during a high school career — Gary McGill of Taylorsville scored 105 from 1991-94. In 1997, Romaro Miller (Shannon QB) set new state records with 3,579 passing yards for a season, 4,643 total yards (3,579 passing & 1,064 rushing) and 51 total TDs (38 passing & 13 rushing). On Oct. 15, 1999, senior running back Marvin Vaughan of Velma Jackson set the state high school record for most rushing yards in a career with 6,594 yards, surpassing James Cooper's 6,557 yards (Raymond, 1977-80). Vaughan finished his high school career with 7,416 yards to become Mississippi's first ever 7,000-yard rusher. Vaughan had 2,936 yards in 1998, a state-record for a season until that was broken by Noah Ingram (Ruleville RB) on Nov. 12, 1999, when he finished with 3,168 yards, 232 yards over Vaughan's previous record. Ingram set the state single-game rushing record with 480 yards on Nov. 5, 1999, then broke his own record with 506 yards on Sept. 9, 2000! That stood only until Oct. 13 when Troy Staten (D'Iberville RB) set the state single-game rushing record with 517 yards! On Oct. 13, 2000, Noah Ingram became the state's career leading rusher with 7,562 career yards! On Sept. 9, 2000, Michael Spurlock (Indianola Gentry QB) set a new state-record 544 passing yards, surpassing the 497 yards set by Hillcrest Christian's Seth Smith in 1998. And, George County High junior Christy Fairley broke the state meet record in the 400 meters on May 5, 2000, with a blazing time of 53.57 seconds to become the fastest female quarter-miler in state history!. Fairley erased the mark of 54.94 set by Janet Davis of Gentry in 1983.

Gaming/Gambling

Mississippi is the third biggest gaming state in the nation after Nevada and New Jersey in terms of revenue and second in gaming space, behind only Nevada! The first casino, the Isle of Capri, opened in Biloxi on Aug. 1, 1992. Cumulative revenues of all casinos passed the billion dollar mark during Jan. 1994, reached the 2 billion mark just 8 months later during Sept. 1994, and reached the 5 billion mark in June 1996. Gaming revenues passed the $2 billion mark for one year for the first time in 1998. Through March 2000, seven years and eight months (exactly 2,800 days or exactly 400 weeks) after gaming began in the state, cumulative gross gaming revenue of all casinos totaled $13,330,893,168 — an average of $1,733,016,133 per year, $144,901,013 per month, $33,327,232.92 per week, or $4,761,033.27 per day!

•••

The largest floating casino in the world is the 140,000-square-foot Grand Casino in Tunica County. The largest casino between Las Vegas and Atlantic City, the world's 3rd largest casino has the 3rd largest surveillance system with 1,100 cameras to keep watch on its 3,100 slot machines and 160 table games.

Mississippi Superlatives and Trivia

Mississippi "Birthplaces"

The birthplace of the Order of the Eastern Star was in Richland in Holmes County in 1847.

●●●

The birthplace of the PTA (Parents-Teachers Association), was in Crystal Springs, Miss., in 1909.

●●●

The birthplace of corn clubs, later to evolve into 4-H Clubs, was in Holmes County in 1907. In 1955, a member of a Mississippi 4-H Club grew 304 bushels of corn on one acre, a world record at the time.

●●●

The birthplace of the National Association of Junior Auxiliaries was in Greenville, Mississippi, in 1941.

●●●

The birthplace of the Blues, the only truly original America music, was in the Mississippi Delta. The blues was "discovered" in Mississippi in 1903 by W.C. Handy, who adapted the music and popularized it in classics like *St. Louis Blues*. Handy wrote, "One night in Tutwiler, as I nodded in the railroad station waiting for a train, a Negro had commenced plunking a guitar beside me while I slept. As he played, he pressed a knife on the string of the guitar in the manner popularized by Hawaiian guitarists who used steel bars. The effect was unforgettable. His song, too, struck me instantly, 'Goin' Where the Southern Cross the Dog'."

It Originated In Mississippi

The Teddy Bear originated in Mississippi. President Theodore "Teddy" Roosevelt, while on a hunt in Sharkey County on Nov. 14, 1902, refused to shoot a bear captured by his guide, Holt Collier. That incident gave birth to "Teddy's Bear," later the "Teddy Bear." The great success of that toy bear led to the formation of the Ideal Toy Corp. in 1903. The Onward Store, on Highway 61 about 25 miles north of Vicksburg, built in 1913 and located near the site, displays photographs of the hunt.

●●●

Coca-Cola in bottles originated in Mississippi. In the summer of 1894, a young candy merchant named Joseph A. Biedenharn of Vicksburg took the popular fountain beverage Coca-Cola, put it into bottles and shipped it into rural areas — the first time Coke had been sold in bottles. This created a new concept of marketing and established the cornerstone of franchised bottlers who now distribute the drink all over the world. Coca-Cola, the world's largest soft-drink company, is based in Atlanta, Georgia. The Biedenharn family eventually acquired bottling franchises is four states and helped start Delta Airlines.

Inventive Mississippians

Toxey Haas started his company, Haas Outdoors, in his hometown of West Point, Miss. in 1986 to create his inventions of "Bottomland," "Greenleaf" and other patterns that have redefined camouflage. His Mossy Oak® patterns been called "America's Most Effective Concealment System." Haas Outdoors was sold in the spring of 2000 to Russell, Inc. of Atlanta, which will keep the company in West Point.

●●●

Inventor David E. Harrison (1937-1996) of Columbus, Mississippi, was responsible for several patents, the most successful seller being the soft toilet seat, of which over a million are sold each year.

●●●

A Mississippi native born in Clinton, James D. Byrd, is a polymer scientist who holds seven patents and developed the plastic used as heat shields by NASA. Mississippians were granted 182 patents in 1997.

●●●

You might have been to a sporting event and seen the small (about 10-15 feet long) blimps flying around. Well, the mechanical parts of these miniature blimps which allow them to fly are created by three men of the Jackson, Mississippi area. Bob Cheesman, a music professor at Hinds Community College, engineer Hank Cooper and bank branch manager Thomas Harvey, got together and started working on blimps that could fly by remote control in 1988. Their first sale was in 1991 to the Minnesota Timberwolves. The 3 model airplane enthusiasts have since turned their hobby into a part-time international business. Their blimps are used by the Chicago Bulls, Houston Rockets, Charlotte Hornets and other basketball teams. Also flown by other sports teams, including the Jackson Bandits hockey team, the blimps are designed by the threesome in the shapes of mascots, UFOs, dragons,...whatever...and sell for $8,000 to $50,000.

Mississippi Superlatives and Trivia

The inventor of the popular household cleaner "Pine-Sol®" was Harry A. Cole, Jr., born in Jackson.

•••

Joseph Paul Treen (1900-1986), a native of Purvis, Miss. is credited with over 60 inventions, the most popular being the kickstand for bicycles and motorcycles. His son, David, was governor of Louisiana.

Aviation Firsts & Feats

Some of the first aerial crop dusting in the nation was conducted on cotton near Leland, Miss. in 1927. As of August 1929, there were 18 licensed airplanes in the state.

•••

The world's first round trip transoceanic flight was performed in 1928 by H.T. "Dick" Merrell, a native of Iuka, Mississippi. The flight to England was made in a plane loaded with ping pong balls.

•••

The first coast-to-coast, non-stop passenger flight in the U.S. was made by Captain Roscoe Turner, a native of Corinth in Alcorn County. He landed his plane in New York after a 19½ hour flight from Los Angeles. He also set an east-to-west transcontinental flight record of 12 hours and 33 minutes, a feat for which this aviation pioneer received the coveted Harmon Trophy for "Outstanding Achievement in Aviation" on Nov. 11, 1932. He is the only three-time winner of the Thompson Trophy Race and the only Mississippian in the National Aviation Hall of Fame at Dayton, Ohio. During his stunt shows, he flew with his animal mascot "Gilmore," an African Lion cub, until it grew too big. A stuffed Gilmore and Turner's plane are featured in the National Air and Space Museum at the Smithsonian Institute.

•••

Rosser "Ross" A. Collins (1880-1968), a native of Collinsville in Lauderdale County, Mississippi served as a representative in the U.S. Congress from 1921 to 1942 and was credited with being the "Father of the Flying Fortress" by Major General H. "Hap" Arnold, Chief of the U.S. Army Air Corps.

•••

Maj. Gen. William "Bud" Miley (1898-1997), known as the "Father of American Paratrooping," was born in California, but in 1955 retired to Starkville, Miss., where he lived the rest of his life. A 1918 graduate of West Point, Miley was selected as the first commander of the 501st Parachute Battalion at Fort Benning, Ga. in 1940. Though he'd never made a jump, Miley figured out the equipment needed by paratroopers (jumpsuits with multiply pockets), how they were trained and how they could carry their rifles (in a side bag). Miley led troops who defended the Panama Canal. He organized the 503rd paratroop regiment and the 17th Airborne Division that provided support to the 101st Airborne during the Battle of the Bulge in 1944. The 17th Airborne made the famous jump across the Rhine River in 1945

•••

Navy pilot Lt. George Anderson, Rear Admiral Richard E. Byrd's personal pilot during Byrd's fourth expedition to Antartica in 1946-47, is buried in Hill Crest Cemetery in his hometown of Holly Springs, Mississippi. Anderson, who served with distinction in the South Pacific during World War II, died Aug. 7, 1948, in a plane crash near his base in Jacksonville, Florida.

•••

The first American to set foot on the continent of Antartica and the first American to fly a plane over Antartica was Alton N. Parker, a native of Crystal Springs, Mississippi.

•••

The world's record for sustained endurance in the air — 653 hours and 34 minutes (over 27 days) — was set by Al and Fred Key, brothers from Meridian, in a flight over Meridian in their plane the "Ole Miss" starting on June 4, 1935. Key Field in Meridian is named after them.

•••

General Frank Gregory, of Shelby, Mississippi, is one of the principal developers of the helicopter.

•••

The first college football squad in America to fly on an airplane was the Ole Miss team when it flew from Memphis, Tennessee to Philadelphia, Pennsylvania on American Airlines on September 30, 1937.

•••

So far, there have been three astronauts who were born in Mississippi. They are Fred W. Haise, Jr., born in Biloxi, Donald H. Peterson born in Winona and Richard H. Truly, born in Fayette, Mississippi.

Mississippi Superlatives and Trivia

The first astronaut chosen from Mississippi was Fred W. Haise, Jr. from Biloxi. He served on the backup crew for Apollo 8, along with Neil Armstrong and Buzz Aldrin. He backed up Aldrin on Apollo 11, the flight that first landed man on the moon. His first flight in space was on the ill-fated Apollo 13 flight, the third lunar landing attempt, which had to abort because of the explosion of an oxygen tank.

●●●

The first astronaut to ever head the National Aeronautics and Space Administration was from Mississippi. In 1989, Richard H. Truly from Fayette was promoted to the top position of NASA, the first astronaut to head that federal agency.

●●●

The first hot-air balloon allowed in New York Central Park was the Mississippi Balloon when it highlighted Mississippi Day in 1988. Owned by the Mississippi Printing Company of Greenwood, it is 80 feet high, 56 feet in diameter and holds 90,000 cubic feet of air when fully inflated.

●●●

The nation's first naval aviator to be killed in a plane crash was a Mississippian. Ensign William Devotie Billingsley, a native of Winona, lost his life when his plane was struck by a wind shear and crashed into the Chesapeake Bay near Annapolis, Maryland on June 20, 1913.

●●●

First Lt. Karen Fuller Tribbett, 25, a native of Athens, Georgia, became the first female combat jet pilot in the U.S. Marine Corps when she earned her wings at the Naval Air Station in Meridian, Mississippi, in mid-October 1997. Her next assignment was learning to fly the F-18 Hornet, one of the military's most effective combat aircraft. Only those most elite with top grades are assigned F-18s!

●●●

Columbus Air Force Base in Mississippi boasts the first female wing commander in the U.S. Air Force! Col. Teresa M. Peterson took command of The 14th Flying Training Wing on July 10, 1998. Peterson had served as the wing's vice commander since October 1997.

Medical Breakthroughs & Milestones

Physician/researcher/inventor/writer, Dr. Arthur C. Guyton, a native of Oxford, Miss., wrote the world's most widely used medical textbook, *Textbook of Medical Physiology* (1956). He holds patent designs for a motorized wheelchair, a special medical hoist and a walking brace, inventions that earned him a Presidential Citation. He also did pioneering research on heart/blood vessel function and hypertension. Dr. Guyton is Professor Emeritus of physiology and biophysics at University Medical Center in Jackson.

●●●

Dr. James D. Hardy was head of the surgical team at University Medical Center in Jackson that performed the world's first kidney transplant in 1962. They performed the first lung transplant in the world on June 11, 1963, by replacing the patient's left lung. The patient, John Richard Russell, survived 18 days. They performed the first adrenal glands transplant in humans in 1963. On Jan. 23, 1964, Dr. Hardy and his team performed the first heart transplant in the world (also the first animal-to-human transplant), putting the heart of a chimpanzee into a 64-year-old dying man. The heart beat for 90 minutes.

●●●

In late spring 1997, University Medical Center began a five-year test of a new Magnetic Resonance Imager, the Interventional MRI. As of mid-1999, UMC is one of only 3 test sites in the U.S. for the twin-magnet interventional MRI. The others are at Harvard and Stanford Universities' teaching hospitals. The interventional MRI takes images in an open area without the "tunnel" of the conventional MRI and produces sharper enhanced images that provide improved diagnostic procedures.

●●●

University Medical Center in Jackson, Mississippi was the first in the U.S. to use Cryoablation, a new cancer therapy that destroys kidney cancer cells by using sub-zero temperatures! Tumors are blasted with argon gas at a temperature of minus 186 degrees Celsius with a probe guided by an Interventional MRI. The probe was approved by the Food and Drug Administration on July 20, 1998, and it was first used in this country the next day at University Medical Center. During May 1999, UMC physician Patrick Sewell, assistant professor of radiology, performed renal cryosurgery on 23 patients. One year later in May 2000, no cancer had returned in the 23 patients he treated.

Mississippi Superlatives and Trivia

University of Mississippi Medical Center radiologist Dr. Patrick Sewell has developed a new procedure to treat lung cancer called radiofrequency lung tumor ablation. Dr. Sewell, considered the world's authority on the procedure, inserts a radiofrequency (hot) probe into the tumor through a small quarter-inch incision in the patient's chest. The probe, guided by viewing a interventional CAT scan, literally cooks the tumor as if it were in a microwave. The incision is closed with a single suture or a Band-Aid and the patient usually goes home is a day or two. Costing about $2,000, it is much cheaper than conventional lung surgery. The procedure was performed for the first time in the world at UMC in the spring of 1999. Dr. Sewell also performed the procedure in China in Oct. 1999 with another test on ten patients during Feb. 2000. Although not yet a widely-accepted or proven treatment, post-surgery PET scans for detecting live cancer cells showed the procedure was killing 100 percent of targeted tumors!

●●●

The University of Mississippi Medical Center in Jackson, the state's health sciences campus, is one huge operation. There are 2.5 million square feet under roof on the 164-acre campus. The Center has $211 million in construction and renovation projects authorized that are estimated to create over 5,700 jobs with a $449 million in economic impact over several years. Over half of Mississippi's practicing physicians are graduates of UMC and more than two-thirds of the School of Medicine's graduates are still in the state. University Medical Center's $440,975,350 budget for FY 1998 had almost a $1 billion economic impact on Jackson and the state! The more than 1,800 students add an additional $30 million to the state's income flow. With about 6,500 employees and an annual payroll of $185 million, UMC is the greater Jackson area's largest employer and close to the top on the list of largest employers in the state. The teaching hospital admits more than 25,000 patients yearly and treats about 300,000 in its emergency room. Counting staff, students, patients and visitors, the daily peak "population" of UMC ranges from 10,000 to 12,000, which exceeds the population of 87 to 89 percent of Mississippi's incorporated municipalities and 10 Mississippi counties! The annual utility bill alone is $4.5 million. In a year, 4 million pounds (2,000 tons) of linens are laundered and 45 tons of eggs are cooked for breakfast!

●●●

The first endowed chair of nursing in the state was also the first worldwide when the University Medical Center in Jackson announced the creation of the Harriet G. Williamson Chair of Nephrology Nursing on June 30, 1999. The chair was funded by a $1 million gift from the Kidney Care Foundation of Jackson.

●●●

The first successful intramedullary bone-pinning operation in the world took place in Mississippi, performed by Dr. Leslie Vaughn Rush, a native of Meridian. Dr. Rush performed the operation in 1936 at Rush Memorial Hospital (now Rush Foundation Hospital) in Meridian. The Rush pin used today was perfected in 1948 and is used worldwide in the treatment of bone fractures.

●●●

Compared to all other cities the same size in the U.S., Hattiesburg is rated No. 1 in medical services!

●●●

On Jan. 8, 1997, Ladora Brown of Kokomo, Miss., gave birth to healthy Tashaila Brown who weighed 15 lbs., 5 oz. and was 25 inches in length. Her head circumference was 16 inches compared to a 12-inch norm. This was the largest baby ever born at Forrest General Hospital in Hattiesburg and is the second largest ever born in the state. The biggest baby, 16 lbs. 4 oz., was born at Bolivar Co. Hospital in 1982. A 15 lbs. 3oz. baby was born at Gulfport Memorial in 1981 and a 15-pounder was born at Golden Triangle Hospital in Columbus (year not available). Bryant Crosby, weighing 14 lbs. 13 oz. and 22 inches in length, was born Sept. 19, 1995 at Methodist Medical Center in Jackson. On his first birthday Bryant weighed an amazing 44 pounds! According to the *Guinness Book of World Records*™, the heaviest single birth ever born to a healthy mother was a boy weighing 22 lbs. 8 oz. born to Signora Carmelina Fedele in Italy in Sept. 1955. The Brown baby weighed 68% as much as the world's largest baby and Mississippi's largest baby ever checked in at 73% the weight of the world's largest infant.

●●●

Two University of Southern Mississippi scientists helped develop a new material for repairing torn retinas, a major cause of blindness. Robert Lockhead and Lon Mathias, polymer science professors at USM, were part of a five-man team awarded a patent in early 1999 for their new polymeric material that mimics the special property of the retina, the thin layer of tissue lining the inside of the eyeball.

Mississippi Superlatives and Trivia

Hi-Tech Stuff

Four state universities — Mississippi State, the University of Mississippi, the University of Southern Mississippi, and Jackson State University — have developed curriculum designed especially for the growing telecommunications industry in the state. Ole Miss already offers specialized degrees in telecommunications at its Center of Wireless Communication. Mississippi State and Hinds Community College are the only institutions in the nation to allow U.S. Marines to earn degrees via interactive computer courses, no matter where they are on the planet!

•••

Mississippi has 84,800 miles of fiber optics in place (as of mid-1999), with more being installed daily.

•••

BellSouth, the primary provider of telecommunications in Mississippi, offers the latest in technology. The company was approaching the 100% digital mark (about 99%) at start of 2000. BellSouth also pioneered the Mississippi FiberNet 2000 project, the nation's first fiber optic-based, fully digital, interactive two-way distance learning network.

•••

Telecommunications services in Mississippi rival those of any state in the U.S.! In addition to being the home of telecommunications giants MCI WorldCom, the nation's second largest long distance company, and SkyTel (a subsidiary of MCI WorldCom), an international wireless communications firm, the state is also the home of NATCOM, the largest pager refurbisher in the United States.

•••

A company in Starkville, NewIDEAS — New Institute for Design and Electronic Applications and Service — is on the cutting edge of computer animation. Owned by Patty O'Conner-Seger, a computer animator and designer and former professor at Mississippi State, NewIDEAS has done animation work on TV commercials and is a national training center for Silicon Studios, a top-of-the-line computer hardware company that enabled Hollywood to create the prehistoric creatures in the hit movie *Jurassic Park*. NewIDEAS also created graphics for an interactive TV display for a large store chain, the first such system in the nation. CNN broadcast a report on NewIDEAS in 1996.

•••

Mississippi is the supercomputer center of the South with the most Cray processors of any state in the region. Mississippi ranked third in the nation behind New Mexico and California for supercomputing, according to Mannheim University's Top-500 list of high-performance computers in the world released in 1998. Mississippi provides 41 percent of supercomputing power for the Defense Department with two of its four Shared Resource Centers in the state — at the Naval Oceanographic Office at the John C. Stennis Space Center in Hancock County and at the U.S. Army Corps of Engineers Waterways Experiment Station in Vicksburg. An upgrade made in 1998 enabled the system in Vicksburg to do 600 billion calculations per second ! That's 1,000 times faster than 1999's fastest desktop PCs (600 megahertz)! The third center in the state at Mississippi State University ranked 20th in the nation and fourth in the southeast for supercomputing power. Mississippi State's computer has approximately 1,000 times more memory than the average PC! Computer codes for the simulation of fluid flow around ships developed at MSU were selected by the Navy for use in construction of its ships.

•••

The largest research, testing and development facility of the United States Army Corps of Engineers is at the Waterways Experiment Station in Vicksburg, which also has the world's largest hydrology laboratory and the world's most powerful research centrifuge, a $6-million machine dedicated on Nov. 20, 1997.

•••

The first nuclear detonation east of the Mississippi River was in Mississippi. On October 22, 1964, a 5-kiloton nuclear device was exploded inside the Tatum salt dome in Lamar County.

•••

A study released March 3, 2000, showed that the John C. Stennis Space Center added $405 million the economy of southwest Mississippi and northeast Louisiana in 1999, about 10 percent more than the $336 million in 1998. Most of the money goes for payrolls. The center is Hancock County's largest employer. Of the 4,357 employees, 35 percent are scientists or engineers and 29 percent are technicians.

Mississippi Superlatives and Trivia

The most accurate mine-hunting devise the U.S. Army has was developed by a University of Mississippi scientist. The land mine detector was devised by James Sabatier, a research scientist at the National Center for Physical Acoustics at Ole Miss. In a series of blind tests at Fort A.P. Hill in Virginia in 1999, Sabatier's system, which uses sound waves and a laser Doppler vibrometer, detected 95 percent of hidden antitank mines with only one false alarm and 100 percent of antipersonnel mines with four false alarms.

Politically Correct

Sen. James Eastland (1904-1986) became president pro temp of the U.S. Senate in the early 1970s. He was only the second Mississippian to hold that post. The first was Pat Harrison of Harrison County who served in that position from Jan. 6 to July 9, 1941. As president pro temp of the Senate, James Eastland became Acting Vice President twice, after the resignations of vice presidents Spiro Agnew and Gerald Ford. In that capacity, Eastland held the highest national office ever by a Mississippian.

●●●

James Eastland (1904-1986) and John Stennis (1901-1995) represented Mississippi concurrently in the Senate for 31 years (1947-1978), the longest period of simultaneous service of any state in the nation.

●●●

In a *Clarion-Ledger* special millennium poll released on Oct. 25, 1999, readers voted John C. Stennis the state's all-time favorite politician. He received 125 votes out of 467 cast. The readers second place choice was retired U.S. Congressman G. V. "Sonny" Montgomery, receiving only 19 votes less than Stennis.

●●●

The record for longest service in the U.S. House of Representatives is held by Mississippi First District congressman Jamie Whitten (1910-1995). He entered the record books Jan. 6, 1992, when he had served 50 years, first being elected on Nov. 4, 1941. He retired in January 1995 after having served 53 years!

●●●

Roger Wicker made history in the Nov. 6, 1994, election when he was elected to replace retiring Jamie Whitten in the 1st Congressional District. Wicker, an attorney and former Republican state senator from Tupelo, was the first Republican to win the seat in the First District in the 20th Century. The last Republicans to hold the seat were Joesph Morphis of Pontotoc and George Harris of Hernando in 1869, when each represented only part of the current district. Wicker was the only Republican representative from Mississippi until the election on Nov. 5, 1996, when two other Republicans were elected.

●●●

John Sharp Williams (1854-1932), a plantation owner from Yazoo City, was the first U.S. Senator in the nation to be elected by popular ballot! He was elected to the Senate in 1910 and remained there until 1923. He had previously served 8 terms in the U.S. House (1893-1909), the last three as minority leader.

●●●

When first elected to the U.S. Senate in 1978, Thad Cochran was Mississippi's first Republican senator since Reconstruction and the state's first ever popularly elected Republican senator.

●●●

On June 12, 1996, U.S. Senator Trent Lott became the most powerful member of the Senate when he was elected to replace Bob Dole (who resigned to run for president) as Senate Majority Leader. Lott was the first Mississippian elected to the post since it was created in 1920. Mississippi's senior senator, Thad Cochran, ran against him, the first time 2 senators from the same state had run for the position.

●●●

The 36th Republican National Convention held in San Diego, California in mid-August 1996 probably had more Mississippians wielding more power than at any convention in the GOP's history. Present were Senate Majority Leader Trent Lott, and Senator Thad Cochran, who held the No. 3 spot in the Senate GOP leadership as chairman of the Republican Conference, Republican National Committee Chairman Haley Barbour, and Co-Chairwoman Evelyn McPhail. Haley Barbour of Yazoo City was chairman of the Republican National Committee from Jan. 1993 - Jan. 1997 and Bay St. Louis native Evelyn McPhail held the RNC's No. 2 post from Jan. 1995 to Jan. 1997.

●●●

Already the longest-serving elected insurance commissioner in the U.S., George Dale was re-elected on Nov. 2, 1999, to serve a seventh term. Dale is one of 12 elected insurance commissioners in the country.

Mississippi Superlatives and Trivia

Mississippi Attorney General Mike Moore was named "Lawyer of the Year" for 1997 by The National Law Journal, a publication for lawyers. He was cited for his leadership and success as chief negotiator in the $368.5 billion settlement with the tobacco industry and as the first state AG to sue. On July 14, 1998, Moore was sworn in as president of the National Association of Attorneys General. Moore was re-elected on Nov. 2, 1999, to serve his fourth term as Attorney General of the State of Mississippi.

●●●

The closest gubernatorial election of the 20th Century in Mississippi was on Nov. 2, 1999. After the final results were finally tabulated about 3 weeks after the election, Democrat Ronnie Musgrove led his Republican opponent Mike Parker in the popular vote by only 8,343 votes. Musgrove had 379,034 votes, or 49.62 percent, to Parker's 370,691, or 48.52 percent. They tied with electoral votes — each had 61 of the state's 122. Because the state constitution mandates that a candidate must receive a majority of the popular votes (50% + 1) and a majority of the electoral votes, and since Parker refused to concede, the race had to be decided in the Mississippi House of Representatives. On Jan. 4, 2000, the first day of the regular session, it took the House just 12 minutes to resolve the governor's race — Musgrove received 86 votes (70.5%) to Parker's 36 votes (29.5%). It was the first governor's race ever decided in the House.

●●●

The narrowest recorded percentage win in an election anywhere occurred in Mississippi on August 7, 1979. In the Southern District Highway Commissioner race, Robert E. Joiner was declared the winner over W.H. Pyron, with 133,587 votes to 133,582, a difference of only 5 votes. According to the *Guinness Book of World Records*™, this means that the loser got more than 49.999 percent of the vote!

●●●

Marshall Bennett, Mississippi's state treasurer, was named the nation's best fiscal leader when he was awarded the 1998 Jesse M. Unruh Award. Bennett was the first Mississippian to receive the honor given by the National Association of State Treasurers who cited Bennett's creation of the National Public Finance Institute and his work in crafting state college savings and prepaid tuitions plans.

●●●

Each state is allowed a statue or bust of only two people in the Statuary Hall of the U.S. Capitol in Washington. The Mississippians honored are Jefferson Davis, president of the Confederacy and James Z. George, architect of the Mississippi Constitution of 1890. Their statutes were unveiled on June 2, 1931.

●●●

L.Q.C. Lamar, a U.S. senator during the 1870s and 1880s, was appointed to the U.S. Supreme Court in 1887, the only Mississippian to ever serve on the nation's highest court and the only Mississippian to serve in all the following: U.S. House, U.S. Senate, presidential cabinet member, and Supreme Court.

●●●

The first Presidential Cabinet member from Mississippi was Robert J. Walker, a prominent Natchez lawyer who was appointed Secretary of the Treasury by President James K. Polk on Mar. 6, 1845. The other four cabinet members from Mississippi were: Jefferson Davis, Secretary of War, appointed by President Pierce in 1853; Jacob Thompson, Secretary of the Interior, appointed by President Buchanan in 1857; L.Q.C. Lamar, Secretary of the Interior, appointed by President Cleveland in 1885; and Mike Espy, Secretary of Agriculture, appointed by President Clinton in 1993, who was the only presidential cabinet appointee from Mississippi in the Twentieth Century.

●●●

Mississippi only *officially* agreed to allow women to vote on Mar. 16, 1984 (64 years late) by being the last state to ratify the 19th Amendment, which became part of the Constitution in Aug. 1920. The state has still *not* ratified: the 17th Amendment (U.S. senators shall be elected) which became a part of the constitution in May 1913; the 21st Amendment (repealed the 18th Amendment of prohibition); the 23rd Amendment (gives the District of Columbia representation in the Electoral College) which became part of the Constitution in April 1961; the 24th Amendment (citizens cannot be denied the right to vote if they fail to pay poll taxes) which became part of the Constitution in Feb. 1964; the 26th Amendment (gives citizens 18 and older the right to vote), which became part of the Constitution in July 1971; nor the 27th Amendment (puts limits on the timing of congressional pay raises) which became part of the Constitution in May 1992. The legislature also rejected the 13th Amendment, which abolished slavery, on Dec. 4, 1865, but lawmakers finally did ratify it on Mar. 16, 1995 — over 129 years after the fact!

Mississippi Superlatives and Trivia

Prohibition ended in the U.S. on December 5, 1933 — but not in Mississippi. It was almost 33 years later, in 1966, that the state finally allowed its individual counties the option to vote to go wet or remain dry. Mississippi, the first state to ratify the Prohibition Amendment on Jan. 8, 1918, was the last state to allow legally sold alcoholic beverages, although Mississippi has still not ratified the 21st Amendment to the Constitution which repealed the 18th Amendment — Prohibition.

•••

Since Mississippi officially became a state on Dec. 10, 1817, the following cities have served as the seat of government, some of them the capital more than one time: Columbia (Marion County); Columbus (Lowndes County); Enterprise (Clarke County); Jackson (Hinds County); Macon (Noxubee County); Meridian (Lauderdale County); Monticello (Lawrence County); and Natchez and Washington (Adams County). The capital was moved several times during the Civil War between May 1863 and May 1865 — first to Enterprise, then to Meridian, back to Jackson, then to Columbus, then back to Meridian, then to Macon, then back to Jackson. Jackson has been the capital since the end of the Civil War.

"Capitals" of the World

The "Catfish Capital of the World" is Belzoni in Humphreys County. Mississippi produces about 60% of the world's supply of catfish and Humphreys County has 27.6% of the state's catfish water surface acres.

•••

The "Cotton Capital of the World" is Greenwood. The second largest cotton exchange in the U.S. is on Cotton Row in Greenwood, Mississippi, located in Leflore County.

•••

The "Upholstered Furniture Capital of the World" is Tupelo, Mississippi, a designation formerly held by North Carolina! About 54,000 pieces of upholstery are produced daily in Mississippi, more than 70 percent of the upholstered furniture produced in the United States, much of it in and near Tupelo.

•••

The "Sweet Potato Capital of the World" is Vardaman, Mississippi, located in Calhoun County.

•••

The "Towboat Capital of the World" is Greenville, Mississippi, located in Washington County.

•••

Crystal Springs, Mississippi was once known as the "Tomato Capital of the World."

Standing Tall

The Tower Building in Jackson, built in less than 6 months in 1929, is the second largest reinforced concrete building in the world. It was the state's tallest (260 feet) until the 263-foot high Sillers State Office Building in Jackson was finished in 1971. Now, the tallest building in the state is the 1,200-room hotel at Goldstrike Casino in Tunica, which opened in 1997. That 31-story structure stands 317 feet tall!

•••

The tallest free-standing structure in Mississippi is the 520-foot cooling tower at the Grand Gulf Nuclear Power Plant near Port Gibson. The second tallest free-standing structure in the state is the 400-foot test stand at the National Space Technology Laboratory (NASA) in Hancock County. The highest natural point in the state is Woodall Mountain, 806 feet, located two miles south of Iuka in Tishomingo County.

•••

Mississippi claims two TV towers that are among the tallest in the nation! WLBT-TV in Jackson started using their new tower in late July 1999. That tower is 1,999 feet above ground. That's 549 feet taller than the Sears Tower in Chicago, the tallest building in the U.S.! It cost $3.5 million, weighs 1.2 million pounds (600 tons), and includes more than 7 miles of guy wire. When WLBT's first 1,999-foot tower was erected in 1967, it was the tallest structure east of the Mississippi. That tower replaced a 1,500-foot tower that was toppled by the Candlestick Park tornado on Mar. 3, 1966. WLBT's first 1,999-foot tower collapsed on Oct. 23, 1997, killing three workers employed by a Canadian firm working on the tower. WABG-TV in Greenville has a tower that is one foot taller at 2,000 feet above the ground. However, the WLBT tower reaches 304 feet higher in the sky because it rises 2,419 feet above sea level, while the WABG tower is only 2,115 feet above sea level. Both of Mississippi's tall towers are only a few dozen feet shorter than the tallest structure in the U.S. — a 2,063-foot TV tower in Blanchard, North Dakota.

Mississippi Superlatives and Trivia

Mississippi Media

The first commercial radio station in the Mississippi was KFNG at Coldwater in Tate County. It went on the air September 22, 1922, and was owned & operated by broadcasting pioneer Hoyt Wooten. The station was later moved to Memphis, Tennessee and became WREC. The first *network* radio station in Mississippi was WJDX in Jackson. It went on the air in the Lamar Life Building on November 30, 1929.

•••

Woodie Assaf started broadcasting the weather on WLBT-TV the day it went on the air, Dec. 20, 1953. As of Dec. 20, 1999, he had been the weatherman on WLBT for 46 years — with the same TV station longer than any other TV weatherman in the nation, a record he has held for several years running!

•••

The first TV station in Mississippi was WJTV in Jackson. It first went on the air Jan. 20, 1953, as a UHF station, channel 25. The station obtained additional power and became channel 12, VHF, on July 1, 1954.

•••

Mississippi Educational Television earned a national Emmy Award, announced in late Aug. 1999. The National Academy of Television Arts and Sciences presented the statewide public TV network with the Public Service Announcement Award for *Ticktock Minutes*, a series of educational music videos for children ages 4-12. The one-minute segments feature Dr. Ticktock, a puppet with a doctorate in E.U.S. (Everything Under the Sun). *Ticktock Minutes* previously won 7 regional Emmys and two first-place Chris Awards from the annual Columbus International Film and Video Festival in Columbus, Ohio. *Ticktock Minutes* not only airs on ETV in Mississippi, it is distributed to other public stations around the country by satellite. Mississippi ETV and two of Jackson's commercial TV stations have won regional Emmys in the past, but this was the first national Emmy for any broadcaster in the area!

•••

Mississippi's first and only publisher of a chain of newspapers located in the state was John O. Emmerich, Jr. (1929-1995), born in McComb. He published 12 daily and weekly newspapers in the state, including *The Greenwood Commonwealth*, the McComb *Enterprise Journal* and *The Yazoo Herald*.

•••

Four Mississippi journalists have won Pulitzers: three for **Editorials** — Hodding Carter (1907-1972) with the *Delta Democrat Times* in 1946, Ira B. Harkey, Jr. (1918 -) with the *Pascagoula Chronicle* in 1963, and Hazel Brannon Smith (1914-1994) with the *Lexington Advertiser* in 1964; and for **Reporting** — Jack Nelson (1929-) in 1960.

Gotta Travel On

The total miles driven on all Mississippi roads in 1998 was 34,208,624,000 miles, (over 34 billion miles) which is equivalent to 184 trips from the earth to the Sun and back!

•••

Statistics show that in 1996, Mississippians had $3,352,000,000 in domestic travel expenditures — the amount of money they spent on overnight trips and day trips of 100 miles or more within the U.S.

•••

If all the registered motor vehicles in the state were placed bumper-to-bumper, they would stretch from Jackson, Mississippi to Mexico City, Mexico and back...twice — a distance of over 5,600 miles!

•••

The first hard surface road in the South was Highway 45 between Tupelo and Verona in Lee County, Mississippi. Concrete paving of the road was done in 1912.

•••

According to the Mississippi Department of Transportation, the longest stretch of highway in the U.S. with no horizontal or vertical curves (completely flat) is a 29.8 mile section of U.S. Highway 61, beginning just north of Clarksdale to just south of Tunica.

•••

According to a recent nationwide highway study conducted by the University of North Carolina in Charlotte, North Carolina, Mississippi has the best highway system in the South and the fourth best in the nation! Mississippi has also been commended by the Federal Highway Administration for the best record in planning and execution of highway improvements.

Mississippi Superlatives and Trivia

Mississippi Placenames

Mississippi placenames — names of cities, towns, villages and communities — are varied and colorful. In the Index of Mississippi Placenames, the last chapter in this book, there are nearly 4,000 listings. Some of the more interesting ones are listed below with the name of their county in parentheses:

Names of Foreign Countries — Africa (Coahoma), Brazil (Tallahatchie), Cuba (Alcorn), Denmark (Lafayette), Ireland (Wilkinson), Scotland (Yazoo) and Egypt (Chickasaw and Holmes).

Names of Foreign Cities — Athens (Monroe), Aberdeen (Monroe), Cairo (Prentiss), Canton (Madison), Dublin (Coahoma), Moscow (Kemper), Paris (Lafayette) and Rome (Sunflower & Winston).

Names of Major U.S. Cities — Akron (Kemper), Anchorage (Humphreys), Atlanta (Chickasaw), Austin (Tunica), Birmingham (Lee), Brooklyn (Forrest & Humphreys), Buffalo (Wilkinson), Charleston (Tallahatchie), Cleveland (Bolivar & Kemper), Hollywood (Tunica), Houston (Chickasaw & Lauderdale), Knoxville (Franklin), Manhattan (Washington), Nashville (Lowndes), New York (Chickasaw), Philadelphia (Neshoba), Phoenix (Jefferson & Yazoo), Raleigh (Smith), Richmond (Lee & Rankin), Tampa (Winston), Topeka (Lawrence) & Waco (Sunflower).

Names of Other States — Michigan (Benton), Nevada (Hinds), Oklahoma (Carroll), Oregon (Holmes) and Texas (Kemper & Stone).

Animal Names — Alligator (Bolivar), Bear Town (Pike), Birdie (Quitman), Buzzard Bay (Perry), Coon Box (Jefferson), Coon Tail (Monroe), Crow (Alcorn & Noxubee), Dogtown (Lafayette), Duck Hill (Montgomery), Falcon (Quitman), Fox (Montgomery), Frogtown (Scott), Goose Pond (Monroe), Panther Burn (Sharkey), Wolf (Scott), Wolf Lake (Humphreys) and Wren (Monroe).

Biblical People/Places — Bethany (Lee), Bethel (Newton), Bethlehem (Marshall), Calvary (Winston), Canaan (Benton), Corinth (Alcorn), Damascus (Kemper & Scott), Eden (Yazoo), Galilee (Rankin), Hebron (Amite, Jefferson Davis, Jones & Pontotoc), Moses (Kemper), Palestine (Clay, Hinds, Pearl River & Yalobusha), Sampson (Lauderdale), Sidon (Leflore) and Thyatira (Tate).

Body Parts — Arm (Lawrence), Foote and Heads (both in Washington County) and Gums (Yalobusha).

Car Names — Cadillac (Jefferson), Ford (Jackson and Winston) and Fordsville (Marion).

Colorful Names — Black (Holmes), Gray (Leake), Orange (Franklin & Jasper), Magenta (Washington) and Pink (Tunica). [also see Lilac and violet in flower names below]

Flower Names — Flowers (Walthall and Warren), Lilac (Montgomery) and Violet (Jefferson).

Food and Beverage Names — Bacon (Chickasaw), Coke (Tishomingo), Goodfood (Pontotoc), Hot Coffee (Covington) and Lunch (Itawamba).

Friendly Names — Bewelcome (Amite), Darling (Quitman), Goodluck (Forrest), Love (DeSoto), Fellowship (Jasper), Friendship (Attala, Covington, Lincoln & Pontotoc), and Tryus (Lawrence).

Growth — Improve (Marion), Increase (Lauderdale), Needmore (Tallahatchie) & Success (Harrison).

Heavenly Names — Moon (Coahoma), Lone Star (Covington), Morning Star (Hinds), Orion (Marshall), Pluto (Holmes), Rising Sun (Leflore), Star (Rankin), Sun (Scott), Sunrise (Forrest & Leake) and Sunset (Covington & Oktibbeha).

Holiday Names — Get a "Gift" (Alcorn) for "Christmas" (Bolivar).

Industry Names — Electric Mills (Kemper), Energy (Clarke), Industrial (Pearl River), Oil City (Yazoo), Tie Plant (Grenada) and Veneer (Marion).

Monetary Names — Cash (Scott), Deposit (Winston), Hard Cash (Humphreys), Money (Leflore), Rich (Coahoma), Value (Rankin).

Hard-to-Say Names — Gautier (Jackson), Kosciusko (Attala), Satartia (Yazoo) and Saucier (Harrison)

Royal Names — King (Rankin), Kings (Warren), Kings Corner (Panola), Kings Ferry (Warren), Kings Point (Jefferson), Monarch (Jones) and Queensburg (Jones).

Weather Names — Cyclone (Simpson), Hurricane (Attala, Pontotoc and Warren) and Rain (Lincoln).

Worship Places — Double Churches (Jefferson Davis), Synagogue (Alcorn) and Tabernacle (Attala).

●●●

Some slogans, past and present, of selected Mississippi cities and towns: "Welcome to Columbia, city of charm on the Pearl River"; "Welcome to Crystal Springs, refreshing as it sounds"; "Gulfport — where your ship comes in"; "Jackson — the bold new city"; "Welcome to Newton, home of Ford Ice Cream"; and our personal favorite, "Welcome to Puckett, 300 friendly folks...and a few old soreheads."

Mississippi Superlatives and Trivia

Some other interesting and unusual placenames in Mississippi: Busy Corner (Amite), Coatraw (Newton), Complete (Lauderdale), Congress (Chickasaw), Dont (Covington), Expose (Marion), Finis Hook (Winston), Forty (Rankin), Hardscrabble (Lawrence), Heartease (Harrison), Hells Halfacre (Leflore), Hero (Jasper), Hog Chain (Lincoln), Hercules Station (Perry), Hooker (Lawrence), It (Copiah), Jayess (Lawrence), King And Anderson (Coahoma), King Bee (Neshoba), Lar-eli-do (Lee), Limerick (Yazoo), Lost Gap (Lauderdale), Merry Hell (Simpson), Oliverfried (Quitman), Partee (Calhoun), Possumneck (Attala), Red Lick (Jefferson), Rough Edge (Pontotoc), Roundaway (Coahoma), Sandy Hook (Marion), Six Towns (Newton), Snowdown (Tishomingo), Soso (Jones), Speedtown (Covington), Triplets Corners (Winston), Veto (Franklin), plus Whynot and Zero (both in Lauderdale County).

●●●

Out-of-place placenames: the place named Adams is in Hinds County, *not* Adams County. Other county namesakes with their counties in parentheses: Benton (Yazoo); Claiborne (Jasper); Clay (Itawamba); DeSoto (Clarke); Forrest (Attala); Franklin (Holmes); Humphreys (Claiborne); Issaquena (Sharkey); Lawrence (Monroe & Newton); Leflore (Grenada); Marion (Lauderdale); Monroe (Franklin), Montgomery (Holmes & Lincoln), Oktibbeha (Kemper); Prentiss (Jefferson Davis); Quitman (Clarke); Simpson (Smith); Smith (Covington & Lauderdale); Union (Covington, Jones, Lee, Simpson & Smith); Washington (Adams); Webster (Winston). Alcorn *is* in Alcorn Co., but there's also one in Claiborne Co.

●●●

The shortest placenames in the state are "By" in Alcorn County and "It" in Copiah County, the only two 2-letter placenames in Mississippi. There are 22 three-letter placenames in the state: Arm in Lawrence County, Asa in Panola County, Cam in Lincoln County, Coy in Kemper County, Eli in Noxubee County, Fox in Montgomery County, Hoy in Jones County, Hub in Marion County, Joe in Rankin County, Lux in Covington County, Nod in Yazoo County, Oma in Lawrence County, Ora in Covington County, Pat in Rankin County, Ras in Jasper County, Rio in Kemper County, Roy in Clarke County, Rye in Monroe County, Sun in Scott County, Ted in Smith County, Una in Clay County, and Way in Madison County.

●●●

Here's how some selected Mississippi places got their names: **Alligator**, because there were so many alligators in the nearby lake — **Appeal**, because a sawmill owner "appealed" so often to the Yazoo and Mississippi Valley to build a railroad spur line to move his logs that they finally did build it — **Ecru** means "beige," the color of nearby clay deposits or the color of the railroad depot — **Isola** is short for "isolated," after a school superintendent referred to "that isolated schoolhouse" located on the other side of the county — **King Bee** was named for a race horse belonging to local sawmill operator Jim Mack Johnson — **Panther Burn** was named for the many panthers early settlers saw in the surrounding area and "Burn" was one of their other words for creek — **Red Lick**, because the local soil was red, contained salt deposits, and early settlers brought their cattle there to lick the soil — **Red Star** was named for a large red star painted on the side of a store building by the Star Tobacco Company — **Reform**, because a mailman named Hanna on that route made the statement that he was going to "reform" the people there — **Rough Edge** probably took its name from the first schoolhouse built there which was constructed of "rough" lumber — **Roundaway**, because it was hard to reach — **Sandy Hook**, because extra oxen had to be hooked to wagons to pull them across the sandy river bottom — **Soso**, from a man who, when asked about his health, would always reply, "Oh, just so-so." — **Electric Mills**, for an electrically operated sawmill — **Veneer**, for a veneer mill located in nearby Foxworth — **Tie Plant**, for a manufacturing plant there that produced creosote used to preserve railroad ties — **Bobo, Darling, Money, Expose** and **Touchstone** were all named after men with those surnames — **Pink** for a man with that first name — **Jayess** took its name from the initials of J.S. Butterfield, a local lumberman — **Dont,** when they were trying to name it, every suggestion was met with "Don't name it that." So many "Don'ts" were received, the people finally settled on Dont — **Veto** was the name they agreed upon after the authorities at the new post office there had vetoed all names submitted — **Rising Sun** had poker players that played all night until sunup and established a club called the Rising Sun Club. Later, a town built there took the name — and **Midnight** was named by a man who won the land in a poker game at the stroke of midnight.

●●●

Hattiesburg is known as the "Hub City," Vicksburg is known as "Hill City," Meridian is known as "The Queen City" and Greenville is known as the "Queen City of the Delta."

Mississippi Superlatives and Trivia

The City of Belzoni in Humphreys County was named for Giovanni Battista Belzoni (1778-1823), an Italian inventor, explorer, showman, and Egyptologist. He was the world's strongest archaeologist who, in the year 1800, "walked around a stage supporting on his shoulders an iron frame on which stood 11 men (over 1,700 lbs.)." There is only one other place named Belzoni in the U.S. — in Oklahoma in the County of Pushmataha. That county is named for one of Mississippi's famous Choctaw Indian Chiefs.

Mississippi County Names

Of the 3,141 counties in the U.S., the only one named for the city of Grenada, Spain, is in Mississippi. The only county in the nation named for Simon Bolivar (1783-1830), whom historians call "the George Washington of South America," is in Mississippi. The other Mississippi counties (31 in all) with names not used by other counties are Alcorn, Amite, Attala, Coahoma, Copiah, Forrest, George, Hinds, Issaquena, Itawamba, Kemper, Leake, Leflore, Neshoba, Noxubee, Oktibbeha, Pearl River, Prentiss, Rankin, Sharkey, Sunflower, Tallahatchie, Tate, Tippah, Tishomingo, Tunica, Walthall, Yalobusha and Yazoo.

●●●

Eight Mississippi counties were named for officers/heroes of the American Revolutionary War: General Nathaniel **Greene**, Sargent **Jasper**, John Paul **Jones**, General Marquis de **LaFayette**, General Francis **Marion**, General Richard **Montgomery**, Joseph **Warren**, and General Anthony **Wayne**.

●●●

Five Mississippi counties were named for signers of the Declaration of Independence: John **Adams** (also President), Charles **Carroll**, Benjamin **Franklin**, John **Hancock**, and Thomas **Jefferson** (also President).

●●●

Mississippi counties named for Presidents (7): John **Adams** (the 2nd), William Henry **Harrison** (9th), Thomas **Jefferson** (3rd), Abraham **Lincoln** (16th), James **Madison** (4th), James **Monroe** (5th) and George **Washington** (the first). Only one county is named for a Vice President — John C. **Calhoun**.

●●●

Seven Mississippi counties were named for officers/heroes of the War of 1812: General Leonard **Covington**, General Andrew **Jackson** (also U.S. President), Colonel James **Lauderdale** (killed at the Battle of New Orleans in 1815), Captain James **Lawrence**, Major Greenwood **Leflore** (Choctaw Indian Chief), Commodore Oliver **Perry**, and General James **Wilkinson**.

●●●

Five Mississippi counties were named for officers of the Confederate States of America: Colonel Samuel **Benton**, Lt. General Nathan Bedford **Forrest**, Lt. Colonel L.Q.C. **Lamar**, General Robert E. **Lee**, and Major General Edward C. **Walthall**.

●●●

Nine Mississippi counties were named for former Mississippi Governors: James L. **Alcorn**, William C.C. **Claiborne**, David **Holmes**, Benjamin G. **Humphreys**, Walter **Leake**, John A. **Quitman**, Abram M. **Scott**, W.L. **Sharkey**, and John Marshall **Stone**.

●●●

There are only three counties in Mississippi in which the county and the county seat share the same name — Grenada, Pontotoc, and Tunica.

●●●

Three Mississippi counties are named for Indian Chiefs — Itawamba, Leflore and Tishomingo. Two counties are named for Indian tribes — Chickasaw and Choctaw. Fifteen additional counties in the state have Indian words, mostly Choctaw, as their names: Amite, Attala, Coahoma, Copiah, Issaquena, Neshoba, Noxubee, Oktibbeha, Panola, Pontotoc, Tallahatchie, Tippah, Tunica, Yalaobusha and Yazoo.

●●●

Three counties started with different names — **Clay** began as Colfax in 1871 (changed 1876); **Jefferson** began as Pickering in 1799 (changed 1802); and **Webster** began as Sumner in 1874 (changed 1882).

●●●

Mississippi has 92 county seats because 10 counties have duel seats: Bolivar (Cleveland & Rosedale), Carroll (Carrollton & Vaiden), Chickasaw (Houston & Okolona), Harrison (Gulfport & Biloxi), Hinds (Jackson & Raymond), Jasper (Bay Springs & Paulding), Jones (Ellisville & Laurel), Panola (Batesville & Sardis), Tallahatchie (Charleston & Sumner), and Yalobusha (Coffeeville & Water Valley).

Mississippi Superlatives and Trivia

Over the County Line

According to the U.S. Census Bureau, there are now 16 incorporated municipalities in Mississippi that straddle county lines. They are (with July 1, 1998 population estimates): **Baldwyn** (3,416 — 1,834 in Prentiss County & 1,582 in Lee County); **Centreville** (1,543 — 1,255 in Wilkinson County & 288 in Amite County); **Crenshaw** (1,007 — 784 in Panola County & 223 in Quitman County); **Crosby** (443 — 281 in Wilkinson County & 162 in Amite County); **Crowder** (794 — 459 in Quitman County & 335 in Panola County); **Hattiesburg** (48,806 — 45,996 in Forrest County & 2,810 in Lamar County); **Jackson** (188,419 — 187,433 in Hinds County, 853 in Madison County, & 133 in Rankin County); **Lake** (364 — 343 in Scott County & 21 in Newton County); **Lumberton** (2,563 — 2,553 in Lamar County & 10 in Pearl River County); **Maben** (742 — 491 in Oktibbeha County & 251 in Webster County); **Mathiston** (832 — 734 in Webster County & 98 in Choctaw County); **Nettleton** (2,612 — 1,404 in Monroe County & 1,208 in Lee County); **Shaw** (2,290 — 2,283 in Bolivar County & 7 in Sunflower County); **Sherman** (620 — 449 in Pontotoc County & 171 in Union County); **State Line** (425 — 269 in Greene County & 156 in Wayne County); **Union** (1,873 — 1,407 in Newton County & 466 in Neshoba County).

Old Buildings & Things

The largest number of antebellum, or pre-Civil War, structures in the U.S. is in Natchez, Miss., which has over 600 buildings (100 houses) on the Nat'l. Register of Historic Places. Natchez once had over 500 millionaires, more than any city in the U.S., except New York.

•••

As of mid-1999, there were 571 Mississippi Landmarks (historically significant public buildings and sites) in the state, according to Elbert R. Hilliard, State Historic Preservation Officer and director of the Mississippi Department of Archives and History. The total number of state entries on the National Register of Historic Places stood at 1,175!

•••

Longwood, circa 1858-61, in Natchez, Mississippi, is the largest remaining octagonal house in the U.S. A superb example of the mid-19th century Oriental style, it was originally designed by it's owner, Dr. Haller Rush Nutt, with solar panels (strategically place mirrors) to reflect the sun's rays for the purpose of heating water. However, when the Civil War began, the workmen who were from the north, returned home. Dr. Nutt, also a northerner, lost his wealth and plantations across the river in Louisiana and died a broken man. Longwood remains unfinished today. Visitors to this most unusual house can still see the workmen's tools left where they were dropped, abandoned in their haste to exit the South.

•••

Two popular dinner silverware patterns produced by the Gorham Silver Company, "Melrose" and "Stanton Hall," were named for the famous antebellum homes in Natchez. The designs on the Melrose settings are reproductions of the intricate carvings found on the rosewood furniture at the Melrose home.

•••

Natchez-Under-The-Hill was called Natchez Landing at the turn of the nineteenth century, when it began to acquire an infamous reputation as "the most notorious spot on the Mississippi River." Above the hill the wealthy of Natchez looked down upon the rougher elements of river life — the gaming halls, saloons and dens of vice where the lawless gathered, as well as bustling wharves, cluttered warehouses and shops. Much of the area has been washed away by the river and all that remains today is busy Silver Street where scenes were filmed for the TV movie *North and South*. Gaming has also returned to this historic district in the form of the Lady Luck Casino.

•••

The second largest Indian mound in the U.S. is the Emerald Mound, 10 miles northeast of Natchez on the Natchez Trace Parkway. Built between 1250-1600 A.D. by ancestors of the Natchez Indians, the ceremonial mound covers 8 acres, measures 770 by 435 feet at its base and is 35 feet high.

•••

The second oldest executive residence in the U.S. that has been continuously occupied as a gubernatorial residence is the Governor's Mansion in Jackson, circa 1842. The Mansion was designated a National Historic Landmark by the U.S. Department of Interior in 1975.

Mississippi Superlatives and Trivia

The largest sternwheeler towboat ever built, the Sprague, was for a number of years docked at Vicksburg. This popular old sternwheeler burned in Vicksburg in 1974.

●●●

Windsor, near Port Gibson, was the largest antebellum mansion ever built in Mississippi. Built in 1860, it survived the Civil War, but was destroyed in 1890 by a fire reportedly set by a careless smoker. All that remain today are 23 huge columns. The Ruins of Windsor were featured in the major motion pictures *Raintree County* (1957) starring Elizabeth Taylor and *Ghosts of Mississippi* (1997) with Alec Baldwin.

●●●

Springfield Plantation (circa 1786-91) off the Natchez Trace Parkway, near Fayette, was where Andrew Jackson and Rachel Robards were married in 1791. Springfield was one of the first houses in America built with a full colonnade across the entire facade and was the first such mansion built in the Mississippi Valley. Springfield remains almost entirely original and is on the National Register of Historic Places.

●●●

The cost of the state capitol building, when completed in July 1903, was $1,093,641 — $101,000 worth of genuine marble, $36,000 worth of Scagliola, and $212,000 worth of Bedford Limestone. Only 4 kinds of wood are used in the building — Maple, Oak, Walnut and Mahogany. Electric and gas fixtures cost $15,000. There are 4,750 incandescent electric lights — 750 in the central dome and rotunda.

●●●

The world's only two-row stationary Dentzel menagerie in existence is in Meridian. The Dentzel Carousel, c. 1895-99, has original paintings adorning the top of the carousel and all animals were intricately handcarved of basswood and poplar. It was used in the 1904 St. Louis World's Fair before it was sold to Meridian in 1909 for $2,000. Experts estimate that it would bring between $1 million and $5 million on today's open market!! The menagerie is listed on the National Register of Historic Places.

●●●

The only lighthouse in the U.S. that stands in the middle of a four-lane highway is the Biloxi Lighthouse, a 62-foot-tall cast-iron structure that was erected in 1848.

●●●

The oldest existing industrial building in the state is a three-story structure in Corinth, Mississippi. The building was constructed in 1869 and although it stood largely deserted for the first 20 years, it has seen several owners who used it for various purposes. First used as a cotton and woolen mill, it later became Corinth Machinery Co., which produced sawmills they sold and erected worldwide. The company made portable sawmills for the government during WWII. Today, the building is owned by a Canadian firm.

●●●

The oldest university building and the second oldest school building in Mississippi is the Chalmers Institute building in Holly Springs, erected in 1837.

●●●

When the Crystal Springs School opened Sept. 3, 1928, it was the largest consolidated school in the U.S.! The brick structure was 3 stories tall, 325 feet long & had 88 rooms with a 1,500 student capacity.

●●●

The Petrified Forest, located near Flora, Mississippi, is estimated to be about 36 million years old. This National Registered Landmark is the only petrified forest in the eastern United States.

●●●

The City of Jackson, Mississippi rests directly on an ancient island and the mouth of the volcano that created that island is directly beneath the Mississippi Coliseum. Jackson's extinct volcano, a profound geologic feature in the state, is 144 million years old and has been quiet for about 75 million years.

●●●

The oldest campground fair in the U.S. is the Neshoba County Fair®, known as "Mississippi's Giant Houseparty®." It started in 1889 and is still held yearly the first week of Aug. near Philadelphia, Miss.

●●●

The oldest field game in America is Stickball, played by the Choctaw Indians of Mississippi. Stickball is played on a large field with goalposts (precursors of the modern-day football goals) erected at each end of the field. Demonstrations of this sport can be seen at the Annual Choctaw Indian Fair, a weeklong event held every July on the Choctaw Indian Reservation near Philadelphia, Mississippi.

Mississippi Superlatives and Trivia

Mississippi Movie Makers

Eric Roberts, a native of Biloxi, has starred in the movies *King of the Gypsies* ('78), *Raggedy Man* ('81), *The Pope of Greenwich Village* ('84), *The Coca-Cola Kid* ('85), *The Runaway Train* ('85), for which he received the Academy Award® nomination for Supporting Actor and *Nobody's Fool* ('86) from the play written by fellow Mississippian Beth Henley. He is the brother of actress Julia Roberts (born in Georgia).

•••

Dana Andrews, a native of Collins, Miss. (1909-1992) made 69 films from *Lucky Cisco Kid* in 1938 to *Prince Jack* in 1984. Some of his other movies were *Tobacco Road* (1941), *The Ox-Bow Incident* (1943), *Laura* (1944), *The Best Years of Our Lives* (1946), *Night Song* (1947), *Brainstorm* ('65) & *Airport 1975*.

•••

James Earl Jones, a native of Arkabutla, Miss., received an Academy Award® nomination for *The Great White Hope*, a role for which he had already received a Tony Award for Best Actor in 1969 for the play. Some of his other movies include *Dr. Stranglove* (1964), *Conan, The Barbarian* (1982), *Gardens of Stone* (1987), *Matewan* (1987), *Coming To America* (1988), *Field of Dreams* (1989), *The Hunt for Red October* (1990), *Patriot Games* (1992), *Clear and Present Danger* (1994), *Cry, The Beloved Country* (1995) and *A Family Thing* (1996). In addition, he was the voice of villain "Darth Vader" in the *Star Wars* trilogy (1977, '80 & '83), and the voice of Mufasa in Disney's animated feature *The Lion King* ('94). In addition to his many roles on TV, Laurel native Ray Walston has been in several feature films including *South Pacific* ('58, and in the Broadway production) *The Apartment* ('60), *Tall Story* ('60), *Kiss Me Stupid* ('64), *Paint Your Wagon* ('69), *The Sting* ('73), *Popeye* ('80) and *Of Mice and Men* (1981).

•••

Morgan Freeman, although born in Memphis, spent his childhood between the Mississippi Delta and Chicago and currently has a ranch in Charleston, Miss. He has been in some big movies including *Brubaker* ('80), *Eyewitness* ('81), *Harry and Son* ('84), *Teachers* ('84), *Clean and Sober* ('88), *Street Smart* ('87), *Driving Miss Daisy* ('89), *Glory* ('89), *Lean On Me* ('89), *Robin Hood: Prince of Theives* ('91), *Unforgiven* (the Oscar-winning Best Picture of 1992), *The Shawshank Redemption* ('94), *Outbreak* ('95), *Seven* ('95), *Chain Reaction* ('96), *Kiss the Girls* ('96), *The Flood* ('97) and *Deep Impact* ('98). He is a three-time Academy Award® nominee (*Street Smart*, *Driving Miss Daisy*, and *The Shawshank Redemption*) and a two-time Golden Globe winner, in addition to many awards for his stage work. In 1996, Gov. Fordice presented Freeman with the Lifetime Achievement Award. Freeman was only the fifth person to receive this highest honor of the Governor's Awards for Excellence in the Arts.

•••

In a previous chapter, "Almost 500 Movies Mississippians Helped Make," Collins native Dana Andrews has 63 movies, Charleston resident Morgan Freeman has 32 films, Arkabutla native James Earl Jones has 37, Biloxi native Eric Roberts 26, and Laurel native Ray Walston has 20 movies on the list. Combined with all 31 Elvis movies, these 6 Mississippians have a total of 209 films, about 44% of all movies listed!

•••

These six silent screen actors were native-born Mississippians: Frank L. Cooley (1870-1941) and Martha Mattox (1979-1933), both born in Natchez; William David (1882-1965), born in Vicksburg; Charles Graham (1895-1943), born in Carthage; William Higby (1867-1934), born in Meridian; and Larry Semon (1889-1928), born in West Point (best known as a director, he also acted in several films).

•••

One of the earliest movie directors was B. Reeves Eason (1886-1956), born in Friars Point, Mississippi. He is listed as director on 101 movies, including the second unit director who handled the famous chariot race in the original *Ben-Hur* (1926) and the burning of Atlanta sequence for the smash movie *Gone With the Wind* (1939). Another film director from Mississippi was Larry Semon (1889- 1928), born in West Point. He directed the original silent screen version of *Wizard of Oz* (1925), and was also one of the highest paid silent screen comic actors whose popularity approached that of Charlie Chaplin, Buster Keaton and Harold Lloyd. Other early movie directors from Mississippi were Hamilton Smith (1887-1941), born in Muskegon in Scott County, and Lawrence B. McGill, born in Courtland in Panola County about 1869. An early movie producer was Earle W. Hammons (1882-1962), born in Winona.

The Ultimate Reference on the State

Mississippi Superlatives and Trivia

Larry and Charles Gordon, natives of Belzoni, Mississippi, are probably the most commercially-successful brother team of movie producers in film history! Top box-office hit movies they have produced (together or separately), include *Hard Times* (1975), *Hooper* (1978), *48 Hours* (1982), *Brewster's Millions* (1985), *Jumpin' Jack Flash* (1986), *Predator* (1987), *Die Hard* (1988), *Lock Up* (1989), *Field of Dreams* (Academy Award® nomination for Best Picture of the Year in 1989), *Die Hard 2* (1990), *Another 48 HRS* (1990), *Predator 2* (1990), *Waterworld* (1995), *Boogie Nights* (1997), and *October Sky* (1999). Larry Gordon was President of 20th Century-Fox from 1984-86.

•••

Mississippians helped make 12% of the greatest movies of all time, including the movie rated Number One! The chapter in this book titled "Almost 500 Movies Mississippians Helped Make" shows Mississippians involved in twelve movies on The American Film Institute's list of the Top 100 Greatest American Movies of All Time announced in 1998 in celebration of the 100th anniversary of film making. Those movies with ranking in the Top 100 and Mississippian(s) involved are: 1—*Citizen Kane* (Frances Neal); 4—*Gone with the Wind* (Will Price and B. Reeves Eason); 15—*Star Wars* (James Earl Jones); 19—*Chinatown* (Dianne Ladd); 26—*Dr. Strangelove* (James Earl Jones); 37—*The Best Years of Our Lives* (Dana Andrews); 45—*A Streetcar Named Desire* (Tennessee Williams); 65—*The Silence of the Lambs* (Thomas Harris); 71—*Forrest Gump* (Michael Humphreys); 93—*The Apartment* (Ray Walston); 98—*Unforgiven* (Morgan Freeman); and 99—*Guess Who's Coming To Dinner* (Beah Richards).

•••

Frances E. Neal, a native of Carrollton, Mississippi, had a part in the No. 1 movie of all time! She played "Ethel" in *Citizen Kane* (1941), No. 1 on The American Film Institute's list of the Top 100 Greatest American Movies of All Time, announced in 1998 on the 100th anniversary of film making.

•••

Mississippians helped make 16 of the 250 films listed in the National Film Registry in the Library of Congress through 1998 (most are movies, but some are shorts, cartoons, newsreels, etc.). Films that are "Culturally, historically, or esthetically significant" are selected. Films with Mississippians involved are: *The Apartment* (1960 - Ray Walston, actor); *Ben-Hur* (1926 - B. Reeves Eason, 2nd unit director); *The Best Years of Our Lives* (1946 - Dana Andrews, actor); *The Big Sleep* (1946 - William Faulkner, screenwriter); *Chinatown* (1974 - Dianne Ladd, actress); *Citizen Kane* (1941, Frances Neal, actress); *Dr. Strangelove* (1964 - James Earl Jones, actor); *Freaks* (1932 - Roscoe Ates, actor); *Gone with the Wind* (1939 - Will Price, technical advisor; B. Reeves Eason, 2nd unit director; & Roscoe Ates, actor); *Jammin' the Blues* (1944 - Lester Young, music performer); *Killer of Sheep* (1977 - Charles Burnett, Producer); *Little Miss Marker* (1934 - Dorothy Dell [Goff], actress & Willie Best, actor); *Mildred Pierce* (1945 - William Faulkner, writer); *Nashville* (1975 - Thomas Hal Phillips, writer); *The Ox-Bow Incident* (1943, Dana Andrews, actor); and *Star Wars* (1977 - James Earl Jones, voice of "Darth Vader").

•••

Mississippians had a part in the filming of 33 of the biggest box office hits in movie history! Through May 28, 2000, a total of 206 films had grossed over $100 million each in the U.S. and people in the movie industry with Mississippi roots or connections were involved in the making of 16 percent of them. Mississippians help make four of the Top 10 grossing films: No. 2, *Star Wars* (1977, James Earl Jones); No. 6, *Forrest Gump* (1994, Michael Humphreys); No. 7, *The Lion King* (1994, James Earl Jones); and No. 8, *Return of the Jedi* (1983, James Earl Jones)! Those 33 films Mississippians helped make grossed $5,497,723,192 in the U.S. alone, an average of $166,597,672 per film! One of the 33 movies, *A Time to Kill* (No. 159), was filmed entirely in Mississippi, and the underwater scene of *Double Jeopardy* (No. 139), was shot in a huge water tank at the John C. Stennis Space Center near the Mississippi Coast. (see the complete list of the 33 biggest box office movies Mississippians helped make on the last page of the preceding chapter titled "Almost 500 Movies Mississippians Helped Make").

•••

The first real-life mother and daughter to receive an Academy Award® nomination for one film in the same year was Mississippian Diane Ladd, a native of Meridian, and her daughter, actress Laura Dern, for their roles in *Rambling Rose*, a big movie of 1991. Two other films brought Ladd Academy Award® nominations, *Alice Doesn't Live Here Anymore* (1974), in which she played Flo, and *Wild at Heart* (1990) which also co-starred her daughter Laura and was filmed in Mississippi.

Mississippi Superlatives and Trivia

Oprah Winfrey, a native of Kosciusko, Mississippi, is not only the highest paid female entertainer in the country and the most successful talk show host ever, but she also starred in the movie *The Color Purple* in 1985, a role for which she received the Academy Award® nomination for Best Supporting Actress. Winfrey produced the movie, *Beloved* (1998). She also starred in the film with fellow Mississippians Beah Richards and Thelma Houston. Although it received critical acclaim, the movie proved to be a box-office disappointment. Costing $53 million to make, it grossed less than $23 million in the U.S.

●●●

Stella Stevens, a Yazoo City, Mississippi native, is an actress who has been in several Hollywood feature films including *Li'l Abner* (1959), *Girls! Girls! Girls!* (Elvis movie of '62), *Too Late Blues* ('62), *The Courtship of Eddie's Father* ('63), *The Nutty Professor* ('63), *Advance to the Rear* ('64), *The Silencers* ('66), *The Ballad of Cable Hogue* ('70) *The Poseidon Adventure* ('72), and *Nickelodeon* (1976).

●●●

Dee Barton, a native of Houston, Mississippi who grew up in Starkville, wrote the supplemental music compositions for all 5 of Clint Eastwood's Dirty Harry movies plus he wrote the complete music scores for four other Eastwood films: *Play Misty For Me* (1971), *High Plains Drifter* (1973), *Every Which Way But Loose* (1978) and *Thunderbolt and Lightfoot* (1974). He has also scored over 50 other films.

●●●

McComb native Will Price, as technical director and dialogue director for *Gone With The Wind* (1938), coached Clark Gable & Vivien Leigh on how to speak Southern. Price married actress Maureen O'Hara.

●●●

The "Tammy" novels written by Brookhaven native Cid Sumner (1890-1970) made her famous and were made into the movies *Tammy and the Bachelor* (1957), *Tammy and the Doctor* (1963) and *Tammy Tell Me True* (1961) that made actresses Debbie Reynolds and Sandra Dee famous for their title roles.

●●●

Luster Bayless, a native of Ruleville, Mississippi, worked in Hollywood from age 20 designing costumes for actors and actresses. He was superstar John Wayne's personal costume designer for many years.

●●●

Herschel McCoy, a Meridian native, was a costume designer for the movies *Joan of Arc* (1948), which received the Academy Award® nomination for Best Costume Design and McCoy himself was named in the Academy Award nomination for Best Costume Design for *Quo Vadis?* (1951).

●●●

Dorree Cooper, a native of Pass Christian, is a movie set decorator with an impressive list of hit movies: *Honey, I Shrunk the Kids* (1989); *Honey, I Blew Up the Kid* (1992); *Fat Man and Little Boy* (1989); *The Distinguished Gentleman* (1992); and *A Time to Kill* (1996). She got an Academy Award® nomination for her set decorations on *Legends of the Fall* (1995), which stars Brad Pitt and Sir Anthony Hopkins.

●●●

Charles Bennett was born in Louisiana, but spent his childhood summers in Mississippi and now lives in Wesson, Mississippi. A movie set designer, he's been nominated for 7 Emmy Awards and has won three.

●●●

African-American Michael Clarke Duncan, the big, muscular actor who played "Bear" in the blockbuster Bruce Willis movie *Armageddon* (1998) was a student at Alcorn State University in Mississippi in the early 1980s. Duncan, who also stars with Tom Hanks in the hit movie *The Green Mile* (1999), was nominated for a Golden Globe Award as Best Supporting Actor for his role in that film. Duncan also received an Oscar® nomination for Best Supporting Actor and the movie received the Academy Award® nomination for Best Picture. Duncan appears again with Bruce Willis in *The Whole Nine Yards* (2000).

●●●

Parker Posey, who grew up in Laurel, Mississippi, is an actress who had a role in the first blockbuster movie of the 21st Century/Third Millennium. *Scream 3*, released on 3,467 screens on Feb. 4, 2000, was No. 1 as it grossed an amazing $34,713,000 its opening weekend, a record amount for a movie for that time of the year. Through April 2, this movie grossed $86,520,105, making it the biggest box office hit of 2000 up until that time. Parker appeared with Tom Hanks and Meg Ryan in *You've Got Mail* in 1998.

●●●

Actress Ruth Ford of Hazlehurst was married to actor Zachary Scott from 1952 until his death in 1965.

The Ultimate Reference on the State

Mississippi Superlatives and Trivia

Mississippi Music Makers — Blues

Willie Dixon (1915-1992), a Vicksburg native, was one of the most important figures to emerge from the Chicago blues scene. A gifted bassist, arranger, promoter and record producer, but is best known for the hundreds of blues songs he wrote over the course of 5 decades: *Little Red Rooster*, *Wang Dang Doodle*, *I Ain't Superstitious*, *Pretty Thing*, *My Babe*, *Back Door Man*, and *Seventh Son* — songs recorded by artists around the world, such as the Doors, Bo Diddley, Johnny Rivers, Eric Clapton, Led Zeppelin and the Rolling Stones. Dixon was inducted into the Rock & Roll Hall of Fame in 1994.

●●●

John Lee Hooker, the legendary bluesman born in Clarksdale, Mississippi, had a major influence on R&B and R&R. He made his debut recording *Boogie Chillen'* in 1948. His hit *Boom Boom* was covered by the Animals. He shared a 1989 Grammy with Bonnie Raitt for Best Traditional Blues Recording for their album *I'm in the Mood*. Hooker's album *Chill Out*, released in Feb. 1995, won the 1996 Grammy for Traditional Blues Album. That album also won the Traditional Blues Album of the Year in the 1996 W.C. Handy Blues Awards given by the Blues Foundation of Memphis. On Nov. 7, 1996, Hooker was presented with the Blues Foundation's second annual Lifetime Achievement Award. Hooker was inducted into the Rock & Roll Hall of Fame in 1991. Two of his songs, *Boogie Chillun* and *Boom Boom*, are on the Rock and Roll Hall of Fame and Museum's list of 500 Songs That Shaped Rock And Roll.

●●●

Sonny Boy Williamson II (1899-1965), born Aleck Ford "Rice" Miller in Glendora, Mississippi, was one of the finest blues harmonica men who ever lived. He was a great influence on the English R&B scene and recorded with the Yardbirds, the Animals and Jimmy Page.

●●●

Jimmy Reed (1925-1976), a native of Dunleith, Miss., had great blues and R&B hits. Reed was inducted into the Rock & Roll Hall of Fame in 1991. Two of his songs, *Big Boss Man* and *Bright Lights, Big City*, are included on the Rock and Roll Hall of Fame's list of 500 Songs That Shaped Rock and Roll.

●●●

Ishmon Bracey (1900-1970) of Byram, Hinds County, Miss. was one of the early giants of the blues who worked with legends Tommy Johnson and Charlie McCoy. One Bracey song was *Suitcase Full of Blues*.

●●●

Harmonica player Charlie Musselwhite, born in Kosciusko, Mississippi, is a Grammy nominee and a six-time W.C. Handy Blues Award winner from the Blues Foundation of Memphis, the latest in 1999.

●●●

"Howlin' Wolf" (1910-1978), born Chester Arthur Burnett at West Point, Mississippi, recorded such blues classics as *How Many More Years*, *Riding In The Moonlight*, *I Ain't Superstitious* and *Back Door Man*. He recorded a prodigious total of 67 albums. He was inducted into Rock & Roll Hall of Fame in 1991. Three of his songs, *Smokestack Lightnin'*, *Spoonful* and *The Red Rooster*, are on the Rock and Roll Hall of Fame and Museum's list of 500 Songs That Shaped Rock And Roll.

●●●

Elmore James (1918-1963), born at Richland in Holmes County, Mississippi, helped define the modern electric Chicago blues sound of today. "The King of the Slide Guitarists" influenced many modern blues artists including Duane Allman, Jimi Hendrix, Johnny Winter, Eric Clapton and others. He recorded albums containing songs such as *Standing at the Crossroads*, *The Sky Is Crying*, *Look Over Yonder Wall*, and *Something Inside of Me*. He was inducted into the Rock & Roll Hall of Fame in 1992. Two of Elmore's songs, *Dust My Broom* and *Shake Your Moneymaker*, are included on the Rock and Roll Hall of Fame's list of 500 Songs That Shaped Rock and Roll. He is buried in Holmes County near Ebenezer.

●●●

Otis Rush of Philadelphia, Mississippi, is a blues artist who influenced many young guitarists with his unique style including Jimmy Page, Eric Clapton and Stevie Ray Vaughan. His song, *I Can't Quit You Baby*, is included on the Rock and Roll Hall of Fame's list of 500 Songs That Shaped Rock and Roll.

●●●

Big Joe Williams (1903-1982), born in Crawford, Mississippi, wrote a song, *Baby Please Don't Go*, that is included on the Rock and Roll Hall of Fame's list of 500 Songs That Shaped Rock And Roll.

Mississippi Superlatives and Trivia

Skip James (1902-1069), a native of Bentonia in Yazoo County, Mississippi, was one of the most influential early Delta bluesmen. The legendary Robert Johnson recorded his *Devil Got My Woman* retitled as *Hellhound On My Trail*. Eric Clapton recorded James' *I'm So Glad* on the first Cream album.

●●●

Robert Johnson (1911-1938) was probably the most famous of the legendary early bluesmen. Born at Hazlehurst, he grew up in and around Robinsonville, Mississippi. He recorded only 2 albums (29 songs), but was one the most influential 20th century blues artists. He was inducted into the Rock & Roll Hall of Fame in 1986 in the "Early Influences" category. Four of Johnson's songs, *Cross Road Blues, Hellhound On My Trail, Love in Vain* and *Sweet Home Chicago*, are included on the Rock and Roll Hall of Fame's list of 500 Songs That Shaped Rock and Roll. The 1986 movie *Crossroads* was based loosely on Johnson's life and was filmed on location in the Mississippi Delta. It's been said that Johnson sold his soul to the devil in exchange for his ability to play and sing the blues better than any other man.

●●●

Albert King (1923-1992), a native of Indianola, Mississippi, was a major influence on blues and rock guitar players like Stevie Ray Vaughan, Robert Cray, Otis Rush, Eric Clapton and others. In fact, Eric Clapton copied King's *Personal Manager* guitar solo note-for-note on Cream's song *Strange Brew*. One of his songs, *Born Under A bad Sign*, is included on the Rock and Roll Hall of Fame's list of 500 Songs That Shaped Rock and Roll. He is no relation to B.B. King, although B.B.'s daddy was named Albert.

●●●

Legendary bluesman B.B. King was born on a plantation at Itta Bena, Mississippi. The "King of the Blues" is the best-known and most influential modern bluesman. His first record was *Miss Martha King* ('49), followed by *Three O'Clock Blues*, a major R&B hit of 1950. His *Billboard* Top 40 hits are: *Rock Me Baby* (1964), *Paying the Cost to be the Boss* (1968), *The Thrill is Gone* (1970), *Ask Me No Questions* (1971), *To Know You is to Love You* (1973), and *I Like to Live the Love* (1974). He has recorded over 40 albums from *The Unexpected...Instrumental; B.B. King...Just Sweet Guitar* in the 60s to *Heart and Soul* in 1995. In 1971, the *Live at the Regal* album was his first to cross over from blues to pop charts. He has won 8 regular Grammys — for the song *The Thrill is Gone* (1971) and the albums *There Must Be a Better World Somewhere* (1981), *Blues 'n' Jazz* (1984), *My Guitar Sings the Blues* (1986), *Live at San Quentin* (1990), *Live at the Apollo* (1991), *Blues Summit* (1992) and in 1997 with 7 other artists on *SRV Shuffle*, best rock instrumental, plus the special Grammy Lifetime Achievement Award in 1988. He received the Lifetime Achievement Award from the Songwriters Hall of Fame (1990), the Presidential Medal of Honor (1990), a National Heritage Fellowship (1991) and the Kennedy Center Honor in 1995. He's in the Blues Foundation Hall of Fame (1984), Rock & Roll Hall of Fame (1986) and has a star on the Hollywood Walk of Fame. Two of King's songs, *Sweet Little Angel* and *The Thrill Is Gone*, are included on the Rock and Roll Hall of Fame's list of 500 Songs That Shaped Rock and Roll.

●●●

Charley Patton (1891-1934) was the Delta's first great blues star. The original "King of the Delta Blues" was a major influence on artists like Robert Johnson, Howlin' Wolf, John Lee Hooker and many others.

●●●

Legendary bluesman "Muddy Waters" was born McKinley Morganfield (1915-1983) at Rolling Fork, and raised in the Delta in Clarksdale. He moved to Chicago where he made his first recordings in 1941. In the 50s & 60s, he had over a dozen hits including *She Moves Me* ('52), *Caledonia, Baby Please Don't Go, Mannish Boy, Hoochie-Coochie Man, Just make Love To You, Rolling Stone* and *Got My Mojo Workin'*. He became known as the "Father of electric blues." He won 6 Grammy awards and his songs have been recorded by the Rolling Stones and other rockers. In a serious car accident in 1973, he went on a short, well-received U.S. tour in 1977 and cut a comeback album produced by albino blues guitarist Johnny Winter (b. Leland, Miss.). He was inducted into the Rock & Roll Hall of Fame in 1986. Four of Muddy Waters' songs, *Got My Mojo Working, Hoochie Coochie Man, Mannish Boy* and *Rollin' Stone*, are included on the Rock and Roll Hall of Fame's list of 500 Songs That Shaped Rock and Roll.

●●●

Little Milton (Campbell), a native of Inverness, Miss., was one of the best-selling blues artists of the 1960s with hit singles like *Feel So Bad, Baby I Love You* and the No. 1 R&B hit *We're Gonna Make It*. He won the Male Artist of the Year in the Soul/Blues category in the 1996 W.C. Handy Blues Awards.

Mississippi Superlatives and Trivia

Blues pianist Pinetop Perkins, a native of Belzoni, Mississippi, had a song, *Pinetop's Boogie Woogie*, included on the Rock and Roll Hall of Fame's list of 500 Songs That Shaped Rock And Roll.

●●●

Blues artist, Mississippi John Hurt, born in Teoc, Carroll County, Mississippi, has a song, *Stagger Lee Blues*, included on the Rock and Roll Hall of Fame's list of 500 Songs That Shaped Rock And Roll.

●●●

Matt "Guitar" Murphy, a native of Sunflower, Mississippi was a band member with the Blues Brothers in the 80s and had a memorable scene with Aretha Franklin in *The Blues Brothers* movie. Blues great Willie Dixon once called Matt the best guitar player in the blues!

Mississippi Music Makers — Soul/R&B

David Ruffin (1941-1991) was born in the community of Whynot near Meridian. He was the co-lead singer of The Temptations from 1963-68. He also had some Top-10 hit records on his own: *My Whole World Ended (The Moment You Left Me)* (#9 in '69), and *Walk Away From Love* (#9 in '76). Three of the Temptation's songs, *Ain't Too Proud To Beg*, *My Girl* and *Papa Was A Rollin' Stone*, are included on the Rock and Roll Hall of Fame's list of 500 Songs That Shaped Rock and Roll.

●●●

Jimmy Ruffin (David's bro.), a soul singer born in Collinsville, Miss., had the Top-10 record hits *What Becomes of The Brokenhearted* (#7 in '66) and *Hold On To My Love* (#10 in '80). His other Top 40 hits were *I've Passed This Way Before* (#17 in '67) and *Gonna Give Her All The Love I've Got* (#29 in 67).

●●●

Jerry Butler, a native of Sunflower County, Miss., helped shape the history of soul in 1958 when he wrote and recorded *For Your Precious Love*, a gold record (#11 in '58). He had a total of 16 Top 40 hits including *He Will Break Your Heart* (# 7 in '60), *Moon River* (#11 in '61), *Hey, Western Union Man* (#16 in 1968) and *Only The Strong Survive* (# 4 million-seller in 1969). He had a hit record with Betty Everett (from Greenwood, Miss.) *Let It Be Me* (# 5 in 1964) and he has produced a prodigious 62 albums!

●●●

Betty Everett, a native of Greenwood, is an R&B singer whose one solo hit record was *The Shoop Shoop Song (It's In His Kiss)* (#6 in '64). She also had a Top-5 hit with Jerry Butler, *Let It Be Me* (#5 in 1964).

●●●

♫Shoo Doo Be Doo♪...Mississippi had at least two members of two doo wop groups in the early and mid 1950s. Prentiss Barnes (1925-), born in Magnolia, Mississippi, was the bass singer of the Moonglows, the group that gave us such gems as *Sincerely* (#1 R&B, #20 pop in 1955), *See Saw* (#6 R&B, # 25 pop in 1956) and *Ten Commandments of Love* in 1958 (#9 R&B, #22 pop in 1958). Barnes now lives in Jackson. The other was Sollie McElroy, Jr. (1933-1995), born in Gulfport, Mississippi, the original lead singer of the Flamingos. After McElroy left the group in 1954, the Flamingos had two hits, *I Only Have Eyes For You* (#3 R&B, #11 pop in 1959) and *Nobody Loves Me Like You* (#30 pop in 1960 and written by another native Mississippian, Sam Cooke). But, while McElroy was still with the group, the two groups both recorded for Chance Records in Chicago and they even came out with an album together in 1953 called *The Flamingos Meet the Moonglows*, which was reissued 40 years later in 1993.

●●●

Bo Diddley was born Otha Ellas Bates McDaniel in McComb, Mississippi. His music is punctuated by a pulsating beat that has become known as the "Bo Diddley beat" and his style is flamboyant. One of the key figures in the development of rock/R&B music, his records have been covered by the Yardbirds, the Rolling Stones and others. Inducted into the Rock & Roll Hall of Fame in 1986, his song, *Bo Diddley*, is on the Rock and Roll Hall of Fame and Museum's list of 500 Songs That Shaped Rock And Roll.

●●●

Barrett Strong, a native Mississippian, had a hit record of his own called *Money (That's What I Want)* (#23 in '60), which he wrote. It was later a hit by the Beatles. Strong co-wrote many of the Temptations' Top-10 hits including *Just My Imagination*, *Papa Was A Rolling Stone*, *Ball of Confusion* and *Cloud Nine*. *Money (That's What I Want)* and *Papa Was A Rolling Stone* are both listed on the Rock and Roll Hall of Fame's list of the Top 500 Songs That Shaped Rock and Roll. Barrett co-wrote another song on that list, Marvin Gaye's *I Heard It Through the Grapevine*.

Mississippi Superlatives and Trivia

Jim Weatherly (born in Pontotoc, Miss.), a pop/county singer and songwriter, wrote the Gladys Knight's soul hits *Neither One of Us*, *Midnight Train To Georgia* and *Best Thing That Ever Happened To Me*.

●●●

Roebuck "Pop" Staples, who was born in Winona, Mississippi, and grew up in Drew, Mississippi, is the patriarch of the family gospel and soul group The Staple Singers, which includes daughter Cleotha and son Pervis, both born in Drew, Mississippi in the mid 1930s. The group had the No. 1 million-selling records *I'll Take You There* (1972) and *Let's Do It Again* (1975) among other hits like *Respect Yourself* (#12 in 1971), *If You're Ready (Come Go With Me)* (#9 in 1973), a million-seller Top-10, and *Touch A Hand, Make A Friend* (#23 in 1974). Pop Staples received the 1995 Grammy Award for Best Traditional Blues Album for his *Father, Father*. One of the Staples' songs, *Respect Yourself*, is included on the Rock and Roll Hall of Fame's list of 500 Songs That Shaped Rock and Roll and was written by another Mississippian, Sir Mack Rice, born in Clarksdale.

●●●

Sir Mack Rice, the man who wrote Wilson Pickett's smash soul hit *Mustang Sally*, was born in Clarksdale, Mississippi, and grew up in Detroit. Rice's own version of the song reached No. 15 on the R&B chart in 1965. But, the record of that song by Wilson Pickett in 1966 topped the R&B charts and reached No. 23 on the Top 40 chart. Rice is a producer and arranger as well as a songwriter. Some of the songs he wrote and the artists who recorded them include *Respect Yourself* (#12 pop in 1971 by the Staple Singers), *Cheaper to Keep Her* (#15 pop in 1973 by Johnny Taylor), and *Cadillac Assembly Line* (Albert King). Rice's songs have also been recorded by Eddie Floyd, Ike & Tina Turner, Bruce Willis, Buddy Guy, the Blues Brothers and the Commitments. He started off as a member of the Falcons along with Eddie Floyd, Willie Schofield and Joe Stubbs. The group recorded *You're So Fine*, which reached No. 17 on the *Billboard* pop chart in 1959 and has been called "arguably the first soul hit."

●●●

Mary Wilson was born in Greenville, Mississippi. At the young age of 13, she was a founding member of the Primettes which later evolved into the Supremes, one of the most famous and successful vocal groups in music history. During 13 years with the Motown Records' group, she lent her voice to a dozen number one hits: *Where Did Our Love Go* ('64), *Baby Love* ('64), *Come See About Me* ('64), *Stop! In the Name of Love* ('65), *Back In My Arms Again* ('65), *I Hear A Symphony* ('65), *You Can't Hurry Love* ('66), *You Keep Me Hangin' On* ('66), *Love Is Here and Now You're Gone* ('67), *The Happening* ('67), *Love Child* ('68), and *Someday We'll Be Together* (with the Temptations in '69). When Diana Ross left the group to go solo in 1970, Wilson led the Supremes and sustained them through 1977 with 4 million-selling albums: *Stoned Love*, *Up the Ladder to the Roof*, *Floy Joy*, and *Everybody's Got the Right to Love*. Two of the Supreme's songs, *Stop! In The Name Of Love* and *You Can't Hurry Love*, are included on the Rock and Roll Hall of Fame's list of 500 Songs That Shaped Rock and Roll.

●●●

Milan B. Williams, a native of Okolona, Mississippi, played keyboards with a group that toured and performed with The Jackson Five for 5 years before signing up with Motown as The Commodores in 1972. From 1974 through 1985, the group had 41 albums and 17 Top-40 hit singles which included 10 in the Top-10 (actually 8 were in the top-5) with 2 of those No. 1s, and they garnered 10 gold records and 5 platinum records. Their biggest was the smash hit *Three Times A Lady*.

●●●

Dorothy Moore is a Pop-Soul singer born in Jackson. The "Sweetheart of R&B" has been nominated for 5 Grammys and won 2 of them for *Misty Blue*, a #3 gold record of 1976, and *I Believe You*. Her other memorable tunes include *With Pen In Hand*, *I Believe You* and *Funny How Time Slips Away*. She won *Billboard* magazine's 1976 No. 1 Female R&B Vocalist Award and the NAACP Image Award. Moore received the Artist's Achievement Award of the 1996 Governor's Awards for Excellence in the Arts.

●●●

Ike Turner, a Clarksdale, Mississippi, native married Anne Mae Bullock (Tina) from Tennessee in 1958 and then developed a dynamic stage show around her. Their biggest hit record was the Top-5 million-seller *Proud Mary* (#4 in 1971). Ike & Tina Turner were inducted into the Rock & Roll Hall of Fame in 1991. Ike and Tina's song, *River Deep, Mountain High*, is included on the Rock and Roll Hall of Fame's list of 500 Songs That Shaped Rock And Roll.

Mississippi Superlatives and Trivia

Al Wilson (1939-1970), a native of Meridian, had a No. 1 gold record with *Show and Tell* in 1973-74.

•••

Thelma Houston, a native of Leland, Mississippi, is the soul singer that had a No. 1 hit record with *Don't Leave Me This Way* (1977), for which she received a 1977 Grammy for Best Female R&B Vocal.

•••

Tyrone Davis, born in Greenville, is the soul singer who had the million-selling hit single records *Can I Change My Mind* (#5 in '69) and *Turn Back The Hands of Time* (#3 in '70). He has recorded 27 albums.

•••

Revered as the definitive soul singer, Sam Cooke (1935-1964) was a Mississippian. Although most biographers list his birthplace as Chicago, he was born in Clarksdale and his family moved to Chicago when he was a baby. From 1957-65, twenty-nine of his singles were Top-40 hits, including 13 in the Top-15 and 4 in the Top-10. His big No. 1 hit was also his first hit, *You Send Me* (1957). Some other hits: *Only Sixteen* (#28 in '59), *Chain Gang* (#2 in '60), *Cupid* (#17 in '61), *Twistin' The Night Away* (#9 in '62), *Bring It On Home To Me* (#13 in '62, with backing vocal by Lou Rawls), *Another Saturday Night* (#10 in '63), *Good News* (#11 in '64), and *Shake* (#7 in 1965). He was inducted into the R&R Hall of Fame in 1986. Cooke has 3 songs on the Rock and Roll Hall of Fame and Museum's list of 500 Songs That Shaped Rock And Roll — *A Change Is Gonna Come*, *Bring It On Home to Me* and *You Send Me*.

•••

Soul singer Brandy was born Brandy Norwood in McComb in 1979. In 1994, she captured national attention with her No. 1 R&B hit, *I Wanna Be Down*. She had the number 10 R&B hit of all of 1995 called *Baby*. Her No. 1 R&B single, *Sittin' Up In My Room* from the *Waiting to Exhale* movie soundtrack was the No. 8 R&B song of all of 1996 and also made the Top Singles pop chart. Other hits include *Best Friend* and *Brokenhearted*. Brandy was named favorite new soul-R&B artist on the American Music Awards show in 1996. She has won 5 *Soul Train* awards including the Soul Train Lady of Soul Entertainer of the Year Award in 1996. By the time she turned 16, she had a Platinum album and two Grammy nominations. She received two Grammy nominations in 1997 and 2 nominations in 1998. Brandy has sold over 4 million albums. She portrayed shy student Danesha on ABC-TV's now-defunct weekly series *Thea* and now plays the title character in *Moesha*, a weekly comedy series.

•••

Soul recording artist Major Lance, although he grew up in Chicago, was born in Winstonville, Bolivar County, Mississippi. His second single *The Monkey Time*, was a monster. Released in the summer of 1963, it reached No. 2 on the R&B charts and No. 8 pop. *Hey Little Girl* was a Top 15 pop and R&B hit later that year, followed by the Top 5 pop hit *Um, Um, Um, Um, Um, Um* early in 1964. Over the next year and a half, he continued to turn out a series of Curtis Mayfield-written songs, nearly all of which reached the R&B Top 40 (and a few pop hits), such as *The Matador* (#20 in 1964), *Rhythm* (#24 in 1964), and *Come See* (#40 in 1965), and he had a few Top 20 R&B hits in 1965.

Mississippi Music Makers — Rock/Pop

Most music industry experts consider *Rocket 88*, released in 1951, the first true Rock 'n' Roll record. It was recorded by Jackie Brenston (1930-1979), a native of Clarksdale. The song was written by two other Mississippians, Ike Turner (who played with Brenston on the record) and Delta bluesman James Cotton.

•••

Joe Frank Carollo, a native of Leland, Miss., was the "Joe Frank" in the group Hamilton, Joe Frank & Reynolds that had 2 big hit songs records: *Don't Pull Your Love* (Top-5 million-seller in '71) and *Fallin' In Love* (No. 1 million-seller in 1975). He studied music at Delta State in Cleveland, but didn't graduate.

•••

The rock band Blind Melon has 3 Mississippians — Glen Graham, drummer and Brad Smith, bass guitarist, both born in Columbus, plus Thomas Roger Stevens, guitarist, born in West Point. The group rated a nude cover photo on the Nov. 11, 1993 issue of *Rolling Stone* magazine.

•••

Johnny Rivers, rock star of the 1960s and 70s, songwriter, record producer and owner of Soul City Records, cut his very first recording in Mississippi. New York-born Rivers, who grew up in Louisiana, was only 14 when he recorded *Hey, Little Girl* at Suede Label Records in Natchez. It didn't make a hit.

Mississippi Superlatives and Trivia

The Grammy-winning Pointer Sisters with multi-platinum record sales had their first recording session in Mississippi! They were still teens when they recorded at Malaco Records in Jackson in the early 1970s.

●●●

Pop singer Jimmy Buffett is a native of Pascagoula, Mississippi. A big hit single record that helped jumpstart his career was *Margaritaville* (#8 in 1977). He settled in Key West, Florida in 1971 and began churning out hit albums. He has recorded 31 albums including *Songs You Know By Heart* (Platinum in 1985), *Feeding Frenzy* (Gold in '90), and *Boats, Beaches, Bars & Ballads* (Platinum in '92), *Fruitcakes* ('94), *Barometer Soup* ('95), and *Banana Wind* ('96), and *Beach House on the Moon* (1999). His huge beach/party-crowd following of fans call themselves "Parrotheads" and have 80 fan clubs worldwide.

●●●

Lance Bass, a native of Laurel, who grew up from age 10 in Clinton, Mississippi, is the bass singer in the nationally and internationally famous pop/dance group 'N Sync. Their self-titled debut album released in 1998 went double platinum in the U.S. and Canada. Their first single, *I Want You Back*, was the fastest-rising single with the longest stay on the charts for a new act, and quickly went platinum within four months. Their *No Strings Attached* album, released in March 2000, was the fastest selling album in history, selling more than one million copies in its first day and 2.4 million in its first week!!

●●●

Four members of the modern rock band 3 Doors Down are longtime friends from Escatawpa in Jackson County, Mississippi: singer Brad Arnold, who also writes their songs; guitarists Matt Roberts and Chris Henderson; and bassist Todd Harrell. The drummer is Richard Liles, a Hattiesburg native. The band's debut album, *The Better Life*, went gold by mid-April, 2000 and by Oct., it had gone triple platinum and in the *Billboard* Top 10. Cuts from the album include *Life of My Own*, *Duck and Run*, *Be Like That*, and their hit single, *Kryptonite*, which they performed on Jay Leno's *The Tonight Show* in mid-May, 2000.

●●●

Glen Ballard, a Natchez native, started out in the music business working with Elton John, then played piano for singer Kiki Dee, wrote songs for artists Quincy Jones was producing and also co-wrote Michael Jackson's smash hit, *Man in the Mirror*. Ballard won a Grammy in 1990 for Best Instrumental Arrangement Accompanying Vocals for his song, *The Places You Find Love*, recorded by Chaka Khan. In 1996, he won a Grammy for Best Rock Song, *You Oughta Know*, and the singer Ballard produced, Canadian artist Alanis Morissette, also won a Grammy for the song and another one for the album it was taken from, *Jagged Little Pill*, which Ballard also produced. Ballard also wrote the music for that No. 1 multi-platinum album, the best-selling album of 1996 (10 million), making it the best-selling album ever by a woman. Through 1998, it sold 28 million copies! Ballard received 5 Grammy nominations in 1996.

●●●

Megastar Elvis Presley (1935-1977), the "King of Rock & Roll," has sold over a billion records worldwide. *Don't Be Cruel* and *Hound Dog* were released back-to-back on one single in 1956 and both went to No. 1 and stayed 11 weeks making them the biggest R&R hits of all time. *Love Me Tender* (1956) became the first single in history to sell a million *advance* copies! Three songs *Jailhouse Rock*, *Don't Be Cruel* and *Teddy Bear* were each No. 1 on 3 charts (R&R, R&B and Country) at the same time! Some records Elvis set: Most charted singles on the Hot-100 of *Billboard* (149 from 1956 to May 1990); Most Top-40 records (107); Most Top-10 records (38); Most weeks holding No.-1 position (80) with his 18 No. 1 hits; the Most Hit Albums (94 from 1956-Apr. '89); and the solo artist to receive the most RIAA awards (57 — 16 Gold singles, 33 Gold albums and 8 Platinum albums). In 1992, the 15th anniversary of his death, Elvis was honored with an astounding 110 record certification awards — the largest number ever bestowed on a single artist or group in pop history! Up until his death, Elvis had 21 albums that each sold a million copies or more, more than any other artist. It is estimated that Presley's total of million-selling singles worldwide is now over 80. He received 3 Grammy awards for his gospel albums *How Great Thou Art* in 1967 and again in 1974, and *He Touched Me* in 1972.

●●●

Six Elvis Presley songs, more than any other single artist, are included on the Rock and Roll Hall of Fame's list of 500 Songs That Shaped Rock And Roll! Those songs are *Heartbreak Hotel*, *Jailhouse Rock*, *Love Me Tender*, *Mystery Train*, *Suspicious Minds* and *That's All Right*. Another Elvis song, *Hound Dog* (the version by Willie Mae "Big Mama" Thornton, who wrote it), is included on that list.

Mississippi Superlatives and Trivia

Mississippians can take credit for 48 (almost 10%) of the songs on the Rock and Roll Hall of Fame and Museum's list of 500 Songs That Shaped Rock and Roll. The list by artists: Sam Cooke (3 songs - *A Change Is Gonna Come, Bring It On Home to Me & You Send Me*); Bo Diddley (*Bo Diddley*), Marvin Gaye (*I Heard It Through The Grapevine* — co-written by Mississippian Barrett Strong); John Lee Hooker (2 songs - *Boogie Chillun & Boom Boom*); Howlin' Wolf (3 songs - *Smokestack Lightnin', Spoonful & The Red Rooster*); Mississippi John Hurt (*Stack O' Lee Blues*); Elmore James (2 songs - *Dust My Broom & Shake Your Moneymaker*); Robert Johnson (4 songs - *Cross Road Blues, Hellhound On My Trail, Love in Vain & Sweet Home Chicago*); Albert King (*Born Under A Bad Sign*); B.B. King (2 songs - *Sweet Little Angel & The Thrill Is Gone*); Jerry Lee Lewis (2 songs - *Great Balls of Fire & Whole Lotta Shakin' Goin' On*) Pinetop Perkins (*Pinetop's Boogie Woogie*); Elvis Presley (6 songs, more than any other single artist - *Heartbreak Hotel, Jailhouse Rock, Love Me Tender, Mystery Train, Suspicious Minds & That's All Right*); Jimmy Reed (2 songs - *Big Boss Man & Bright Lights, Big City*); Jimmie Rodgers (*Blue Yodel No. 9*); Otis Rush (*I Can't Quit You Baby*); The Staple Singers [leader is Mississippian "Pop" Staples] (*Respect Yourself* — written by Mississippian Sir Mack Rice); Edwin Starr (*War* — cowritten by Mississippian Barrett Strong); Barrett Strong (*Money [That's What I Want]*); The Supremes [Mississippian Mary Wilson was a member] (2 songs - *Stop! In The Name Of Love & You Can't Hurry Love*); The Temptations [David Ruffin was a member and *Papa...* was co-written by Mississippian Barrett Strong] (3 songs - *Ain't Too Proud To Beg, My Girl & Papa Was A Rollin' Stone*); Willie Mae 'Big Mama' Thornton [one of Elvis Presley's hits](*Hound Dog*); Ike & Tina Turner [Ike Turner is from Clarksdale, MS] (*River Deep, Mountain High*); Muddy Waters (4 songs - *Got My Mojo Working, Hoochie Coochie Man, Mannish Boy & Rollin' Stone*); and Big Joe Williams (*Baby Please Don't Go*).

•••

Here's are the 48 songs by Mississippians on the list of 500 Songs That Shaped Rock And Roll, listed alphabetically by song: *Ain't Too Proud To Beg; Baby Please Don't Go; Big Boss Man; Blue Yodel No. 9; Bo Diddley; Boogie Chillun; Boom Boom; Born Under A Bad Sign; Bright Lights, Big City; Bring It On Home to Me; Change Is Gonna Come, A; Cross Road Blues; Dust My Broom; Got My Mojo Working; Great Balls of Fire; Heartbreak Hotel; Hellhound On My Trail; Hoochie Coochie Man; Hound Dog; I Can't Quit You Baby; I Heard It Through The Grapevine; Jailhouse Rock; Love in Vain; Love Me Tender; Mannish Boy; Money (That's What I Want); My Girl; Mystery Train; Papa Was A Rollin' Stone; Pinetop's Boogie Woogie; Respect Yourself; River Deep, Mountain High; Rollin' Stone; Shake Your Moneymaker; Smokestack Lightnin'; Spoonful; Stack O' Lee Blues; Stop! In The Name Of Love; Suspicious Minds; Sweet Home Chicago; Sweet Little Angel; That's All Right; The Red Rooster; Thrill Is Gone, The; War; Whole Lotta A Shakin' Goin' On; You Can't Hurry Love;* and *You Send Me*.

•••

There are 16 Mississippians, all native-born except one (Jerry lee Lewis), in the Rock and Roll Hall of Fame in Cleveland, Ohio. They are (year they were inducted follows their name): Sam Cooke (1986), Bo Diddley (1986), Willie Dixon (1994), John Lee Hooker (1991), Howlin' Wolf (1991), Elmore James (1992), Robert Johnson (1986), B.B. King (1986), Jerry Lee Lewis (1986), Muddy Waters (1986), Elvis Presley (1986), Jimmy Reed (1991), Jimmie Rodgers (1986), The Temptations [David Ruffin] (1989), The Staple Singers ["Pop" Staples] (1999) and Ike and Tina Turner [Ike Turner] (1991).

•••

Rock 'n' Roll legend Jerry Lee Lewis was born in Ferriday, Louisiana, but has lived much of his life in Nesbit, Mississippi (since 1973). He first recorded for Sun Records in Memphis in 1956. His unique piano-pounding, boogie style gave him 3 top-10 gold records: *Whole Lot Of Shakin' Going On* (#3 in 1957), *Great Balls of Fire* (#2 in 1958) and *Breathless* (#7 in 1958) with 3 more records in the Top-40: *High School Confidential* (#21 in 1958), *What'd I Say* (#30 in 1961) and *Me And Bobby McGee* (#40 in 1972). In 1958, his 12-day engagement at the New York Paramount Theatre broke all previous attendance records, including those set by Frank Sinatra. "The Killer" made a comeback in country music in 1968 and followed with several No. 1 country hits, including *To Make Love Sweeter for You* (1968), *There Must Be More to Love than This* (1970), *Would You Take Another Chance on Me* (1971) and *Chantilly Lace* (1972). He was inducted into the Rock and Roll Hall of Fame in 1986. Two of his songs, *Great Balls of Fire* and *Whole Lotta Shakin' Goin' On*, are included on the Rock and Roll Hall of Fame's list of 500 Songs That Shaped Rock And Roll.

Mississippi Superlatives and Trivia

About the biggest singing sensation in the nation during the final year of the 20th-Century was Mississippian Britney Spears. Well, we'll claim her as a Mississippian. Although born in Kentwood, Louisiana, just over the state line, she traveled to McComb, Mississippi to attend the private school, Parklane Academy. Her brother also attended Parklane and her younger sister was still attending in early 2000. Britany's father is a contractor for a construction company in Jackson, Miss. Even after Britney became famous, she still likes to hang out in McComb. Britney was a member of Walt Disney's *Mickey Mouse Club* TV show from 1992 to 1994. In 1998, she took the world by storm with her first single recording, *Baby One More Time*, on the Jive record label. After releasing her first album of the same title in Jan. 1999, she released two more singles. That album remained in the Top 10 all through 1999 and by the end of the year, had sold over 9 million copies (multi-platinum). Britney is the youngest artist ever to sell so many copies of an album. She is the first solo artist to have a No. 1 album and No. 1 single on the *Billboard* charts at the same time with a debut! In 1999, Britney was named one of *Teen People* magazine's "21 Hottest Stars Under 21" and was one of *People* magazine's "50 Most Beautiful People."

Mississippi Music Makers — Country

Mac McAnally's debut single from his first album, *It's A Crazy World*, went to number 2 on the adult contemporary charts and broke into the pop Top 40. His 1990 Top-10 country hit, *Back Where I Come From*, mentions his hometown of Belmont, Mississippi. Jimmy Buffett, a fellow Mississippian, has recorded 5 of his songs including *It's My Job*. He has also written such hits as *Old Flame* for Alabama, *Two Dozen Roses* for Shenandoah, *Precious Thing* for Steve Wariner and *Crime of Passion* for Ricky Van Shelton. McAnally has been compared to pop musicians like James Taylor and Jimmy Buffett.

●●●

Marty Stuart was born in Philadelphia, Mississippi. He played in Lester Flatt's band, in Vassar Clements' jazz/bluegrass fusion group, Doc Watson's road band and in the Johnny Cash band. His first solo album was *Busy Bee Cafe* (1982), followed by the albums *Hillbilly Rock* (1989) which yielded the hit singles *Western Girls*, *Hillbilly Rock*, *Tempted* (1991) and *Burn One Down*. His 1991 duet with Travis Tritt, *The Whiskey Ain't Workin' Anymore*, won a Grammy Award for Vocal Performance By A Duo or Group. Another big hit with Tritt was *This One's Gonna Hurt You (For A Long, Long Time)* in 1993 — the album went Gold. He was nominated for the 1995 *Music City News* Awards as Male Artist of the Year. The CD, *Honky Tonkin's What I Do Best*, was released in 1996 with another duet with Travis Tritt as the title track for which the two received the 1996 CMA nomination for Vocal Event of the Year plus the Vocal Collaboration Award for the 1997 TNN/*Music City News* Country Awards. Stuart received a 1997 Grammy nomination. He shared three 1999 Grammy nominations with several other artists in each category: Best Bluegrass Album (*Home Sweet Home*); Best Country Instrumental Performance (*Reuben's Train*); & Best Country Collaboration With Vocals (*Same Old Train*, which Stuart wrote). In 1997, he married country music legend and "Sweetheart of the Grand Ole Opry," Connie Smith. On March 19, 1999, Stuart received the Artist's Achievement Award of the 1999 Governor's Awards.

●●●

Bobbie Gentry, born Roberta Lee Streeter in Chickasaw Co., Miss., had a huge multi-million-selling, No. 1 hit record *Ode To Billie Joe* ('67) which she also wrote. She won 3 Grammys for her hit (all in 1967), and the song was made into a movie of the same title filmed in Mississippi and released in 1976. Her album *Ode to Billy Joe* ('67) went Gold as did the album *Bobbie Gentry and Glen Campbell*.

●●●

Mickey Gilley, a Natchez native, received the Academy of Country Music Award for Single Record of the Year, *Bring It On Home* (1976). His first hit was *Room Full of Roses* (1974) followed by 17 number-one hits like *I Overlooked An Orchid* and *Stand By Me* that also went Pop (#22 in 1980). He was once part-owner of Gilley's nightclub in Pasadena, TX (suburb of Houston), at one time considered the largest honky-tonk in the world seating 5,000 people. Gilley and the club were prominately featured in the film *Urban Cowboy* (1980). Mickey is first cousin to Rock & Roll legend Jerry Lee Lewis.

●●●

The last public performance of country music great Hank Williams was at the USO Community House in Biloxi on December 7, 1952. He died just three weeks later, on Jan. 1, 1953, in the back of his car on his way to scheduled performances in Oak Hill, West Virginia and Canton, Ohio.

Mississippi Superlatives and Trivia

The youngest person ever nominated for a Country Music Association award was LeAnn Rimes (at age 14), a native of Pearl, Mississippi. Actually, she was nominated for *two* 1996 CMA awards — the Horizon Award for best newcomer in country music and for Single of the Year for her hit song *Blue*. In 1997, she received 5 CMA nominations and won two Grammys out of 4 nominations (including Best New Artist, the first time a country artist ever captured that honor). Also in 1997, Rimes won 3 Academy of Country Music Awards, a TNN/ Music City Award, a CMA Horizon Award, 4 *Billboard* Music Awards (including Artist of the Year), and overseas, the BBC's Rising Star Award. By mid-1999, *Blue*, her 1996 debut album, had surpassed the 7 million sales mark. Her album, *You Light Up My Life: Inspirational Songs*, also a multi-platinum LP, debuted at No. 1 on three *Billboard* charts: Pop, Country and Contemporary Christian, the first time that has ever been achieved by a country artist. *Early years: Unchained Melody*, an album of her early work, was released in 1997 and quickly sold multi-platinum.

●●●

Paul Davis, a Meridian native, has had some big pop/country records including *I Go Crazy* (#7 in '77), *'65 Love Affair* (# 6 in '82), a No. 1 with Marie Osmond *You're Still New to Me* ('86), and a No. 1 with Tanya Tucker and Mississippian Paul Overstreet *I Won't Take Less than Your Love* ('87). He wrote the No. 1 country hit *Meet Me In Montana* ('85) and others. He has also produced many hits by other artists.

●●●

Country singer/songwriter Fred Knobloch was born in Jackson. His hit records include *Why Not Me* (#18 in '80), which he wrote, *Killin' Time* (#28 in '81), a duet with TV/film actress Susan Anton, and a No. 1 country single with the group Schuyler, Knobloch & Overstreet (fellow Mississippian Paul), *Baby's Got a New Baby*, in 1986. He co-wrote the B.J. Thomas hit *The Whole World's In Love When You're Lonely*.

●●●

In the 5-year period ending in mid-1999, Star, Mississippi native Faith Hill became a superstar garnering 7 No. 1 singles, 9 No. 1 videos, 3 multi-platinum albums and numerous awards! Hill's first single *Wild One*, taken from her debut million-selling album, *Take Me As I Am*, spent 4 consecutive weeks at *Billboard*'s top spot at the close of 1993, the longest stint ever for a female country music singer's debut song! The album produced two more No. 1s including *Piece of My Heart* and *Take Me As I Am*. By Jan. 1996, the title song from her 2nd album, *Let's Go To Vegas*, was the No. 1 country single and stayed on top for 3 weeks running. Her 2nd album also went platinum in the spring of 1996. She was named Academy of Country Music's Top New Female Performer in '94, *Billboard*'s Top Female Country Artist of 1994 and won the 1995 TNN/*Music City News* Star of Tomorrow Award. She was nominated for the 1995 American Music Awards Best New Country Artist, nominated as CMA Female Vocalist of the Year for 1996 and received 3 Academy of Country Music nominations for 1996. On Oct. 6, 1996, Hill married county singer Tim McGraw. By mid-1997, Tim and Faith had a Top-10 country hit called, *It's Your Love*, which became the No. 2 County hit for 1997! That record received two 1998 Grammy nominations for Country Song and Country Collaboration with Vocals. Faith & Tim's record, *Just to Hear You Say You Love Me*, received the 1998 CMA nomination for Vocal Event of the Year. Faith was nominated for three 1999 Grammys. Faith and Tim's song, *Just to Hear You Say You Love Me*, won the Top Vocal Event of the Year Award at the 1999 Academy of Country Music Awards. Faith, with a leading 6 nominations of her own, won the Top Video Award for *This Kiss*, plus Top Female Vocalist of the Year and Single Record of the Year. She had more nominations than anyone for the 1999 TNN/*Music City News* Country Awards — a total of 7 nominations including Best Female Artist. Her song, *This Kiss*, was nominated for Best Single, Best Video and Best Song. Her duet with Husband Tim McGraw, *Just to Hear You Say You Love Me*, received nominations for Best Vocal Collaboration and Best Song. Hill was named one of *People* magazine's "50 Most Beautiful People" of 1995.

●●●

Born in Vancleave, Miss., Paul Overstreet's own solo hits include *Heroes* and *Ball and Chain*. He had a Nno. 1 country hit with the group Schuyler, Knobloch (Jackson's Fred) & Overstreet, *Baby's Got a New Baby* ('86) and another number-one country hit with Tanya Tucker & Paul Davis, *I Won't Take Less Than Your Love* ('87). He co-wrote *On The Other Hand* (#1 in '86) and *Forever and Ever, Amen* (#1 in '87) hits for Randy Travis, the latter winning him and co-writers, Randy Travis and Don Schlitz, a Grammy Songwriter Award in 1987 for Best Country Song. He shared the Grammy Best Country Song Award in 1991 with Naomi Judd and John Jarvis for co-writing the Judds hit *Love Can Build A Bridge*.

Mississippi Superlatives and Trivia

Mississippian Ben Peters, born in Greenville and reared in Hollandale, is a super country music songwriter who has written hundreds of hits. Just a few are: *Turn the World Around* (Eddy Arnold, 1967); *Tell Me What It's Like* (hit by Brenda Lee); *Kiss An Angel Good Morning* (Charley Pride, a No. 1 Grammy winner in 1972, plus Peters has written many more recorded by Charley); *Love Put a Song in My Heart* (hit by Johnny Rodriguez in 1975); *Before the Next Teardrop Falls* (Freddy Fender, 1975); *Daytime Friends* (Kenny Rogers, 1977); and *Before My Time* (hit by John Conlee in 1979), *Heart, Soul, Body and Mind* (hit by Johnny Mathis), plus many, many more. There have been over 1,000 recordings of his songs in the U.S. and abroad! Other artists who have recorded songs written by Peters include Tom Jones, Dionne Warwick, Perry Como, Bobby Darin, Dean Martin, Waylon Jennings, Lou Rawls, Ronnie Milsap, Bobby Vinton, Dolly Parton, Connie Francis, Ray Charles, Loretta Lynn, George Jones, Barbara Mandrell, Ray Price, T.G. Shepperd and fellow Mississippians Conway Twitty, Tammy Wynette and Jerry Lee Lewis. He's won many awards and is a member of the Songwriters Hall of Fame.

●●●

When Hank Cochran, a native of Isola, Humphreys County, Mississippi, was elected to the Nashville Songwriters Hall of Fame in 1974, he got all the votes! It was the only year that only one writer got elected. Cochran also got Willie Nelson his first break after Willie moved to Nashville. Hank convinced Pamper Music to hire Willie, forgoing his own $50.00 raise which went to pay Nelson's salary. Just a few of the many, many hit songs written or co-written by Cochran include: *I Fall to Pieces* (Patsy Cline, 1961); *A Little Bitty Tear* (Burl Ives, 1961); *I'd Fight the World Before I'd Ever Let You Go* (Jim Reeves, 1974); *He's Got You* (Patsy Cline, 1962 & Loretta Lynn, 1977); *You Comb Her Hair* (George Jones, 1963); *Make the World Go Away* (Ray Price, 1963 & Eddy Arnold, 1965), *I Want to Go With You* (Eddy Arnold, 1966); *Don't Touch Me* (Jeannie Seely, 1966); *It's Not Love (But It's Not Bad)* (Merle Haggard, 1973); *Montego Bay* (Merle Haggard); *Why Can't He Be You* (Loretta Lynn, 1978); *The Chair* (George Strait, 1985); *Ocean Front Property* (George Strait, 1988); *Don't You Ever Get Tired of Hurting Me* (Ronnie Milsap, 1989) and many, many more. Cochran and the songs he's written have won many awards including 33 BMI (Broadcast Music, Inc.) Awards.

●●●

Conway Twitty (1933-1993), the first rock *and* country superstar, was born Harold Lloyd Jenkins at Friars Point, Miss. He started out in R&R with a No. 1, million-selling ballad, *It's Only Make Believe* (1958). In 1965, he became the first major rock star to change over to the country field. "The Twitty Bird" had more No. 1 records (55) than any other artist in *any* genre including Elvis, the Beatles and Michael Jackson — the only artist in the history of popular music to have 21 consecutive Top-5 hits! His many hits include *Hello Darling* ('70), *You've Never Been This Far Before* ('73), *Don't Take It Away* ('78), *I May Never Get To Heaven* ('79), *I'd Love To Lay You Down* ('79) and *Tight Fittin' Jeans* (1980). He wrote or co-wrote 25% of his hits, writing over 200 songs during his career. *Hello Darling* became the first song broadcast in space when played during the Apollo-Soyuz mission. He had more than 40 awards including a Grammy, 4 CMA awards, 6 Academy of Country Music awards, 14 *Music City News* awards and 13 *Billboard* awards. A successful teamup with Loretta Lynn in 1970 was followed with many awards together and duo hits such as *Lead Me On* and *Louisiana Woman, Mississippi Man*.

●●●

Jimmie Rodgers (1897-1933) was born at Pine Springs near Meridian. This legendary figure is known as "The Singing Brakeman," "The Blue Yodeler," "The Yodeling Cowboy," and "The Father of Country Music" The first nationally known country star — he was "the man that started it all." Jimmie cut his first recordings for Victor Records in Bristol, Tennessee on August 1-4, 1927. He was the first person elected into the Country Music Hall of Fame in 1961, and one of the first elected to the Songwriters Hall of Fame ('70) for writing songs like *T for Texas (Blue Yodel Number 1), Any Old Time, TB Blues, Waiting For A Train, Travelin' Blues, Train Whistle Blues* and *Mule Skinner Blues (Blue Yodel Number 8)*. Rodgers sold more than 20 million records in the last 6 years of his life. He was inducted into the Rock & Roll Hall of Fame in 1986 in the "Early Influences" category. One of his songs, *Blue Yodel Number 9*, is included on the Rock and Roll Hall of Fame's list of 500 Songs That Shaped Rock and Roll.

●●●

Elsie McWilliams (1897-1985), a Meridian native, wrote or cowrote 38 of the 110 songs recorded by her famous brother-in-law Jimmie Rodgers. She was elected to the Songwriter's Hall of Fame in 1979.

Mississippi Superlatives and Trivia

Tammy Wynette (1942-1998) was born Virginia Wynette Pugh in Tremont, Miss. With over 35 No. 1 hits (21 in a row) and 11 No. 1 albums (out of 50+), she was called "The First Lady of Country Music," but was also known as the "Heroine of Heartbreak." Her biggest hit was *Stand By Your Man* (1968), which sold 6 million copies! She received a Grammy for the album of the same title for Best Country Performance, Female (1969); voted Female Vocalist of the Year (1969) by the Academy of Country Music, Country Music Association's Female Vocalist of the Year for 3 years straight, 1968-70, plus many other awards including the American Music Awards' most-coveted Award of Tribute presented in 1996. She also had another No. 1 hit in 1968 that has become a country standard, *D-I-V-O-R-C-E*. Her *Greatest Hits* album was certified Platinum in 1989. There was the stormy marriage to George Jones 1969-1975, during which time they had many duet hits such as *We're Gonna Hold On* (#1 in 1971), and *Golden Ring* (#1 in 1976). Tammy and George reunited professionally in 1995 and their album *One* received the 1996 Country Music Association nomination for Vocal Event of the Year.

●●●

McComb, Mississippi native Dan Tyler got his B.A. (1972) and his law degree (1975) from Ole Miss, then moved to Nashville to become a songwriter. He's been quite successful as dozens of major country music artists have recorded songs he's written, including *Modern Day Romance* by the Nitty Gritty Dirt Band, *Baby's Got a New Baby* by SKO and *Twenty Years Ago* by Kenny Rogers. Many more of his songs have been released by such artists as B.J. Thomas, Glen Campbell, Juice Newton, Marie Osmond and Keith Whitley. In 1981, the Oak Ridge Boys topped the charts with *Bobbie Sue*, written by Tyler and his wife, Adele Brown Tyler. He has had five No. 1 hits, including *The Light in Your Eyes* from LeAnn Rimes' *Blue* album. As of July 1999, more than 60 of his songs have been recorded by major artists. Tyler wrote a novel, *Music City Confidential* (1996), based on his experiences in Nashville.

●●●

Louisville, Mississippi native Carl Jackson played with Glen Campbell for 12 years. In 1991, he and John Starling released a bluegrass album that won a Grammy. And, he's a great songwriter! Jackson and fellow Mississippian Jim Weatherly won a 1991 Dove Award for the gospel song *Where Shadows Never Fall*, recorded by Glen Campbell. Campbell also had a recording of his song, *Letter to Home* (1984), which was Jackson's first top-10 record. Since then, Jackson has had songs recorded by Diamond Rio, Patty Loveless, Pam Tillis, Steve Wariner and Trisha Yearwood. Garth Brooks recorded Jackson's *Against the Grain* and Jackson's *Fit for a King* has been released on Brooks's album, *Sevens*. Vince Gill has recorded 2 Carl Jackson tunes, including the chart-topper *No Future in the Past*.

●●●

Paul Thorn, who grew up in Lee County, Miss., started out as a professional boxer and even fought Roberto Duran. Thorn was a middleweight ranked 28th in the world by the WBC when he lost to Duran and soon after quit the ring with a pro record of 17-3. He then tried songwriting — writing or co-writing songs for Tanya Tucker, Joe Diffee, Shenandoah and Ronnie Milsap. In 1996, he co-wrote a song with singer/songwriter Carole King. His own CD, *Hammer and Nail*, was released on A&M records in 1997. Thorn's next album, *Ain't Love Strange* (1999), was released on his own Perpetual Obscurity Records. Thorn, who has toured with pop star Sting, makes his home in Nettleton, Mississippi.

●●●

Charley Pride was born in Sledge, Mississippi. He wanted to be a pro baseball player and actually tried out for the Los Angeles Angels and New York Mets in the early 1960s, but failed to get signed. He changed to music and his first hit record was *The Snakes Crawl at Night* (1964). He followed that with 35 Number Ones including 5 in a row. He has sold more than 30 million records including 6 gold singles hits and 40 albums including 12 gold albums in the U.S., 31 gold and 4 platinum records worldwide, making him one of the Top-15 best-selling recording artists of all time! His single records include these No. 1 hits: *Is Anybody Goin' to San Antone* (1970), *Kiss An Angel Good Morning* (1971), *Someone Loves You Honey* (1978), *Where Do I Put Her Memory* (1979), and *Mountain of Love* (1982). Pride was RCA's best-selling artist since Elvis. Some of his awards: CMA Male Vocalist of the Year two years in a row, 1971 & 72; CMA Entertainer of the Year in 1971; and *Music City News* Male Artist of the Year for 5 straight years (1969-73). He received country male vocalist awards by the Country Music Association, *Billboard*, *Cashbox* & Music Operators of America. He won three Grammys in 1971 as both a country and gospel singer. Charley got his star on the Hollywood Walk of Fame in July 1999. He lives in Dallas.

Mississippi Superlatives and Trivia

Harold Dorman (1931-1988), a native of Sledge, Miss., had only one Top-40 hit, *Mountain of Love* (#21 in 1960), which Charley Pride (also from Sledge) later recorded and made a No. 1 country hit in 1982.

Mississippi Music Makers — Jazz

Cassandra Wilson, born Cassandra Fowlkes in Jackson, now lives in New York. Her unique style of music fuses jazz, free-form, R&B and soul. Her debut album was *Point of View* in 1985 and others followed, many to critical acclaim. Her album *Blue Light 'Til Dawn* (1993) received a Grammy nomination. Her *New Moon Daughter* CD in 1995 crossed Wilson over to national celebrity status. The album received the 1996 Soul Train award nomination for Best Jazz Album, won Wilson a 1997 Grammy for Best Jazz Vocal and was No. 1 on *Time* magazine's Best Music of 1996. The Aug. 1996 issue of *Esquire* magazine named Wilson as one of "The People We Love." The July 1996 issue of *Essence* magazine, with Wilson on its cover, called her "this generation's first lady of jazz."

●●●

Jazz guitarist Lloyd Wells was born in Gulfport and grew up in Laurel, Mississippi. In his long career as a jazz musician and music arranger, producer and director, he has played on many recordings with big bands, including an album with Glenn Miller. Wells was the music conductor and arranger for Tennessee Ernie Ford's orchestra for a number of years. He was a guitarist on several TV shows including *Sesame Street*, *The Electric Company*, *The Merv Griffin Show*, *The Toast of the Town/The Ed Sullivan Show*, and *The Tonight Show with Johnny Carson*. He also was involved in 18 Broadway plays including *Caberet*. Wells was music director of Opryland USA in Nashville for 23 years from 1975-98.

●●●

Jazz and country music guitarist Bob Saxton was born in Newton County, Mississippi. He worked for 9 months with country music star Charlies Louvin. Saxton has performed with the Dorsey Brothers, Patsy Cline and fellow Mississippi Bobbie Gentry. He played on the Grand Ole Opry with Billy Walker and even appeared once with Chet Atkins. Saxton won the Merle Travis National Thumb Pickers Contest twice, in 1989 and 1995. He's also had his share of appearances overseas. He performed in June 1998 at the International Guitar Festival at Reinheim on the French-German border. He also recorded a CD in Germany in 1998 entitled *The Guitar Styles of Bob Saxton*.

●●●

Jazz guitarist Steve Blailock, born in McComb, Mississippi, has played with such artists as Eddie Vinson, Willie Mae "Big Mama" Thorton, Jimmy Weatherspoon, Pete Fountain, Al Hirt, Wynton Marsalis and Harry Connick, Jr. A studio musician in Nashville for 4 years, he worked with such artists as Don Bowman, Willie Nelson, Ray Price and many others. In Los Angeles, Blailock was hired by soul singer Lou Rawls and became a big part of the jazz and blues scene. In 1984 he moved to New Orleans, where he worked with such artists as Herb Tassin, Leroy Jones and clarinetist Dr. Michael White, and he even branched out into the Cajun and zydeco genres. In the 1990s, Blailock made a total of 26 tours in Italy, France, Germany, Finland, Norway, Holland, Belgium, Japan, and other countries, including the Beijing International Jazz Festival in China. He also performed at the 1996 Summer Olympic Games in Atlanta. Blailock has picked guitar on more than 900 CDs, including a couple of his own!

●●●

Henry "Skeets" McWilliams, a native Jacksonian, is considered to be one of the all-time great jazz guitarists in the country. In the navy during WWII, he toured the South Pacific entertaining troops with Ray Anthony's Band. In Chicago after the war, he played the big jazz clubs in the "Loop." He did a concert in England in 1994 and another in France in 1995.

●●●

Jazz guitarist Bucky Barrett was born in Florida, but grew up in Jackson and Canton, Mississippi. Best known as guitarist for superstar Roy Orbison for 8 years (1981-1988), he's also worked with hundreds of other artists. Barrett played on the Neil Young gold album, *Comes a Time*, and on the 1989 Grammy winner for best Country Collaboration, *Cryin'* by Roy Orbison and k.d. lang. Barrett has played on over 1,500 albums. He has three CDs of his own — *Killin' the Wind: The Nashville Superpickers* (1981); *Long Time Coming: A Tribute to Roy Orbison by His Guitarist, Bucky Barrett*; and a Christmas CD. He was a nominee for the Guitar Player Awards, Best Studio Guitarist for six years running, 1980-1985. He was a Country Music Association nominee for Instrumentalist of the Year in 1984.

Mississippi Superlatives and Trivia

Jazz guitarist Mundell Lowe was born in Laurel, Mississippi. Also a composer and arranger, he has worked with Billie Holliday, Charlie Parker, Hank Jones, Sarah Vaughan, Carmen McRae, fellow Mississippian Lester Young, and many other artists. He moved to New York and in 1950 became musical arranger at the NBC network, working on the *Today Show* and other shows. In 1965, Lowe moved to California where Jackie Cooper hired him as a composer for films and television. He composed the music for the movies *A Time for Killing* (1967), *Billy Jack* (1971), *Everything You Always Wanted to Know About Sex* (1972) and the TV movie *Tarantulas: The Deadly Cargo* (1977). In the late 1970s, Lowe made a special appearance with Peggy Lee at the White House and toured Japan with Benny Carter. He played at the Monterey Jazz Festival and from 1981-86 served as director of that festival. Lowe has recorded over two dozen albums from *Guitar Moods* (1950) to the movie soundtrack *Satan in High Heels* (1997), for which he composed and directed the music, and *Second Time Around* (1998).

•••

The six guitarists listed above — Bucky Barrett, Steve Blailock, Mundell Lowe, Skeets McWilliams, Bob Saxton and Lloyd Wells — all play on a special 1999 CD called *The Great Mississippi Jazz Guitarists Reunion*, released by the Mississippi Musicians Hall of Fame. It's great!

•••

Lester Young (1909-1959), born in Woodville, Mississippi, played tenor sax and was a bop pioneer with Count Basie and influenced many jazz greats including John Coltrane, Sonny Rollins, and Stan Getz. In 1956, he was voted "Greatest Tenor Saxophonist Ever" In the annual poll of readers & critics conducted by *Downbeat* magazine, Young took top jazz honors in 1959. His impact on jazz was profound.

Mississippi Music Makers — Gospel

W.C. Taylor, Jr. a native of Grenada, Mississippi was: *Nashville Tracker* magazine's Christian Artist of the Year (1995); International Country Gospel Music Association's Country Gospel Male Vocalist (1995); Christian Country Music Association Top-5 male vocalist (1996); Great Plains Christian Country Male Entertainer (1996) and Airplay International Christian Country Male Vocalist (1997). In Jan. 1998, Taylor became the first singer inducted into the North American Country Music Association International Hall of Fame. He and wife, Annelle, publish a Top 80 music chart monthly in the *U.S. Gospel News*. With a circulation over 100,000, it is the biggest country gospel chart in the world!

•••

Jackson, Mississippi native Ginny Owens was just 24 years old when her first single record, *Free* (from her debut album *Without Condition*) hit No. 1 on the Adult Contemporary Christian charts in late Aug. 1999. Owens, who was born with little sight and lost that as a toddler, graduated as valedictorian of her high school class at Mississippi School for the Blind (while also taking classes at Murrah High School!). She then attended Belmont University in Nashville on a full scholarship, where she studied music and graduated cum laude. She then began writing songs for BMG Publishing in Nashville and soon signed a record deal with Rocketown Records. As you can see, Ginny Owens is on her way!

•••

One of the most influential singing groups in the country, the Blackwood Brothers Quartet was formed in Ackerman, Mississippi in 1934 by 3 brothers, Roy, Doyle, and James Blackwood.

•••

The Mississippi Mass Choir, a group of 125 Mississippians, was formed in 1988. Their first album, *Mississippi Mass Choir Live*, was certified the No. 1 Gospel Album in the nation by *Billboard* just 5 weeks after release. The album remained No. 1 on *Billboard's* chart for a record 45 consecutive weeks. Their 2nd album, *God Gets the Glory*, was the No. 1 gospel album and named 1992 Gospel Record of the Year by *Billboard*. Their 3rd album, *It Remains to Be Seen*, was *Billboard* magazine's No. 1 gospel album for 53 weeks (not consecutive). Their 4th album was *I'll See You in The Rapture* (1996).

•••

Malaco Records of Jackson, Mississippi is the nation's largest independent R&B and Gospel label!

•••

Harvey "Pop" Watkins, Sr., born in Canton, Miss., was a founding member of the internationally-known gospel group, the Canton Spirituals. Their album, *Live in Memphis*, received a Grammy nomination and was the longest running album on *Billboard's* Gospel Chart at the time of Watkins death in Nov. 1994.

Mississippi Superlatives and Trivia

Literary Legacy

In Millennium polls conducted by *The Clarion-Ledger* of Jackson in 1999, readers chose William Faulkner as their favorite all-time fiction writer from Mississippi and the late Willie Morris (1934-1999) as their all-time favorite non-fiction writer from Mississippi. Morris became the youngest editor of the nation's oldest magazine when he became editor-in-chief of *Harper's Magazine* in 1967 at age 32.

●●●

Mississippians wrote 5 of the books listed as the "100 Best Novels of the Century," compiled by the editorial board of Modern Library, a division of Random House. Included on the list are three novels by William Faulkner (their position on the list noted in parentheses): (6) *The Sound and the Fury*; (35) *As I Lay Dying*; and (54) *Light in August*. The other 2 were (20) *Native Son* by Richard Wright and (60) *The Moviegoer* by Walker Percy. On the Modern Library's list of "100 Best Nonfiction Books of the Century," *Black Boy* by Richard Wright was No. 13 and *The Civil War* (3 vols., 1958, '63, '74) by Shelby Foote was No. 15. On the National Review's list of "The Top 100 Nonfiction Books of the Century," *The Civil War* by Shelby Foote was No. 93. The Intercollegiate Studies Institute's list of "The Fifty Best Books of the Century" (books not ranked) contained works by 3 Mississippians: Shelby Foote (*The Civil War*); Dumas Malone (*Jefferson and His Time*, 1948-81); and Walker Percy (*Lost in the Cosmos*, 1983).

●●●

Only 3 Mississippians have won the prestigious and coveted Pulitzer Prize for fiction — William Faulkner of Oxford in 1955 and 1963, Eudora Welty of Jackson in 1973, and Richard Ford in 1996.

●●●

Eleven Mississippians have won a total of 14 Pulitzer Prizes, with three of them winning twice — **For Editorial Writing**: Hodding Carter (1946), Ira B. Harkey, Jr. (1963) and Hazel Brannon Smith (1964); **For Reporting**: Jack Nelson (1960); **For Fiction**: William Faulkner (1955 & 1963), Eudora Welty (1973) and Richard Ford (1996); **For History**: Dumas Malone (1975); **For Biography**: David Herbert Donald (1961 & 1988); and **For Drama**: Tennessee Williams (1948 & 1955) and Beth Henley (1981). Plus, The *Vicksburg Sunday Post-Herald* newspaper received a Pulitzer in 1954 for **Local Reporting** and *The Clarion-Ledger* newspaper in Jackson received a Pulitzer Gold Medal for distinguished and meritorious **Public Service** in 1983. Several other Mississippians have been *nominated* for the Pulitzer.

●●●

In a special literary exhibition of nine Southern writers called *The American South: Past, Present and Future*, featured at Atlanta's Centennial Olympic Games of 1996, Mississippi was one-third of the show, claiming three of the nine writers — William Faulkner, Eudora Welty, and Richard Wright.

●●●

Adams County, Mississippi native Prentiss Ingraham (1843-1904) is the third most prolific writer in literary history with over 600 novels and 400 novelettes to his credit!

Burial Places of the Famous

The oldest known death date cut on a tombstone in Mississippi is that of William Gilbert, who died Nov. 16, 1796. That tombstone is located in Foster Mound Cemetery in Natchez. In Howard Hill Cemetery near Lexington in Holmes County, there is a stone with the name "Allen Green" and a birth date of 1770 and a death date of 1932, which would have make him 162 years old!! Old papers that might have verified the dates were burned in a Holmes County courthouse fire in 1995.

●●●

Buried in Natchez City Cemetery are Jose Vidal, governor of the Natchez Spanish District in 1798, Issac Guion, commander of U.S. Forces that took control of the Natchez Territory, General John A. Quitman, Mexico War hero and Governor of Mississippi, T.P. Leathers, Captain of the steamboat Natchez in the famous race with the steamboat Robert E. Lee, General W.T. Martin, Mississippi's highest ranking Confederate officer, and August Dorley, a Medal of Honor recipient during the Civil War.

●●●

The famous inventor of the "Bowie Knife", Resin Bowie, is buried in the Catholic Cemetery in Port Gibson. The knife was made famous by his younger brother, Jim Bowie, in a duel in Natchez.

The Ultimate Reference on the State

Mississippi Superlatives and Trivia

There are 18 Medal of Honor recipients buried in Mississippi. The 8 native Mississippians are: Wilson Brown (Natchez National Cemetery); Jack G. Hanson (Robinson Cemetery, Escatawpa); Robert T. Henry (Greenville Cemetery, Greenville); Mark A. Jordan (Station Creek Cemetery, Collins); John A. Pittman (New Hope Church Cemetery, Greenwood); James D. Slaton (Harmony Cemetery, Laurel); Ira C. Welborn (Biloxi National Cemetery); and Roy M. Wheat (Eastabutchie Cemetery). The 6 "adopted' Mississippians are: James H. Diamond (Evergreen Cemetery in Gulfport); August Dorley (Natchez City Cemetery); Martin Freeman (Greenwood Cemetery in Pascagoula); Hubert L. Lee (Leland-Stoneville Cemetery in Stoneville); Jake W. Lindsey (White House Cemetery in Waynesboro); and Milton L. Olive III (West Grove MB Church Cemetery halfway between Ebenezer and Lexington). Four non-Mississippians who were Medal of Honor recipients are buried in the state. They are Charles C. Bessey (Old Biloxi Cemetery), James Snedden (Odd Fellow Cemetery, Lexington), Hilliard A. Wilbanks (Methodist Cemetery, Fayette), and George Wilhelm (Greenville Cemetery, Greenville).

●●●

Greenville Cemetery in Greenville is the only cemetery in Mississippi where more than one Medal of Honor recipient is buried. Two Medal of Honor recipients are buried there — Greenville native Robert T. Henry and George Wilhelm, whose hometown was Lancaster, Ohio.

●●●

The Friendship Cemetery in Columbus, Mississippi, is famous for being the place where our National Memorial Day started as Decoration Day way back in 1866. It is also the final resting place of two Mississippi governors (Henry Lewis Whitfield and James Whitfield), four Confederate generals, several politicians and soldiers from every U.S. war from the American Revolution to the Vietnam War. The 60-acre cemetery that now has about 18,000 graves was founded and operated by the Independent Order of Odd Fellows until 1957 and has since been owned by the City of Columbus.

●●●

In Greenwood Cemetery in Jackson are the graves of 6 Mississippi Governors (Albert G. Brown, John I. Guion, Charles Lynch, Alexander G. McNutt, Abram M. Scott and William L. Sharkey), 4 State Supreme Court justices, 4 Episcopal bishops and one Methodist bishop.

●●●

Three Mississippi Governors, Martin "Mike" Conner, Lee M. Russell and James K. Vardaman, are buried in Lakewood Memorial Park Cemetery in Jackson, Mississippi.

●●●

Kelly and Emil Mitchell, the queen and king of all gypsies in North America, were buried in Rose Hill Cemetery in Meridian — the queen in 1915, the king in 1942. Nine other gypsies are also buried there.

●●●

Buried in Rose Hill Cemetery in Meridian is Charles W. "Savez" Read, born in Yazoo County and reared in Jackson. Lt. Read was the sterngun commander of the *CSS Arkansas*, the iron-clad ship that made it past 50 Yankee vessels on the Mississippi River at Vicksburg on July 15, 1862. This, and Read's other exploits in the Confederate Navy, earned him the nickname "the John Paul Jones of the Confederacy."

●●●

In Glenwood Cemetery in Yazoo City, you'll find the graves of Helen Carloss (1893-1948), an attorney and tax expert who was the first women ever to argue cases before the U.S. Supreme Court and V. Ruth Campbell (1887-1963), the first women attorney admitted to the state bar. There is also the grave of another women — the famous Yazoo Witch — complete with chains around it to hold her in! The city placed a grave marker there, upon which these words are inscribed: "According to local legend...on May 25, 1904, the Witch of Yazoo City broke out of these curious chain links surrounding her grave and burned down Yazoo City. Writer Willie Morris's classic, *Good Old Boy*, brought national renown to this vengeful women and her shameful deed." The man who immortalized her, Willie Morris, one of Mississippi's most renowned writers, was buried 13 paces south of her grave on Aug. 5, 1999.

●●●

The nation's second largest national cemetery is Vicksburg National Cemetery (est. 1866), where nearly 17,000 Union soldiers are buried (about 13,000 are unknown). In addition, the cemetery is the final resting place for veterans of the Spanish-American War, World Wars I and II, and the Korean Conflict. It was closed to further burials in 1961. The largest national cemetery is Arlington National Cemetery.

Mississippi Superlatives and Trivia

In an old cemetery near Jacinto in Alcorn County are the graves of 17 children who belonged to one mother. Each child died at the age of sixteen months!

●●●

The man who invented the dollar sign ($), Oliver Pollock, is buried in Pinckneyville, Wilkinson County, Mississippi, where he died in 1832. Pollock, refusing to use the sign for the British pound, instead wrote an "S" over a "U" (U.S.). The U.S. Treasury slightly modified it and adopted Pollock's sign. Quite wealthy, he was also the largest individual financial contributor to the American War of Independence.

●●●

Here are three interesting epitaphs. Was the late William L. Hamel (April 23, 1921 - Aug. 18, 1999) a prophetic, but unheeded hypochondriac? The headstone on his grave in Vicksburg's Cedar Hill Cemetery, which was placed there quite some time before his death, reads, "See, I told you I was sick." Not far away in the same cemetery is the grave of Thomas M. Morrissey (1929 - 1985). Inscribed upon his tombstone are the words, "Adverse to the plow, prone to the fiddle and jug." State Representative Steve Holland of Tupelo, a funeral home director by profession, is referred to by his legislative colleagues as, 'the gentleman from Lee (County)." Holland, still alive as of Oct. 1, 2000, already has his epitaph etched and the stone is place. It reads, "Beloved gentleman from Lee. He lived 'til he died."

The Great Mississippi Outdoors

A World Record!! — the No. 1 deer ever killed by a hunter with a firearm was killed by Tony Fulton of Louisville, Mississippi on Jan. 5, 1995, in Winston County! Originally scored at 255 & 6/8, Fulton's buck was re-scored in April 1998 by Boone & Crockett judges in Reno, Nevada at 295 & 7/8! The Boone & Crockett Club, keepers of North American Big Game records, made it official at their 23rd annual Awards Banquet in Reno on June 13, 1998. The Boone & Crockett record is the second for Fulton's buck, which was previously ranked the No. 1 record buck under the Buckmaster scoring system at 321 & 7/8!

●●●

Ronnie Young of Hernando, DeSoto County, Mississippi performed a feat accomplished by only 75 hunters in the world in one year! During the spring of 1999 over a three-month period, Young made a Royal Slam. He harvested all four species of North American turkey — Osceola (in Florida), Eastern (in Mississippi), Rio Grande (in Texas) and Merriam's (on the Nebraska/South Dakota line), plus he took a Gould's turkey in Mexico. In all five cases, Young killed at least two of each species, so he actually got a double Royal Slam. Only a few of the 75 hunters have ever made a double Royal Slam. Veterinarian Dr. Eddie Lipscomb of Port Gibson, Mississippi made a Royal Slam in the spring of 2000.

Miss-cellaneous

Famed hatmaker John Stetson practiced his trade at Dunn's Falls near Meridian right after the Civil War.

●●●

The Corinth-Alcorn County Convention and Agri-Exposition Center has the largest arena floor in the state, 150 by 300 feet. The $6 million facility, opened in 1999, has 3,100 fixed seats expandable to 7,500.

●●●

During its six-month run in Jackson from Mar. 1 through Aug. 31, 1996, the great cultural exhibit, *The Palaces of St. Petersburg: Russian Imperial Style*, had 553,894 visitors — the most successful event of its kind in the state's history and the second highest attended exhibit in the U.S. in 1996!

●●●

"The Divide Cut," on the Tenn-Tom Waterway, is the topographic divide line (line of hills) between the Tennessee and Tombigbee River basins separating Bay Springs Lake on the Tenn-Tom and Pickwick Lake on the Tennessee River. Over 150 million cubic yards of earth were removed to form the 39-mile long Divide Cut — more than that excavated for the Suez Canal! A total of 350 million cubic yards of earth were removed from the entire Tennessee-Tombigbee Waterway, or nearly twice that removed for the construction of the Panama Canal, making it the largest single earth excavation project in history!

●●●

The "Devil's Punch Bowl," located near Natchez, Mississippi, is one of nature's anomalous formations. It is a gigantic, semi-circular pit, somewhat cone-shaped. Connected with this spot are countless tales of runaway slaves, river pirates, buried treasure, and other stories of adventure and romance.

Mississippi Superlatives and Trivia

The State Historical Museum in the Old Capitol in Jackson has over 30,000 catalogued artifacts. In the Civil War section, there's an authentic and rare Sherman necktie — a railroad rail heated over a fire and then bent around a tree. Gen. William T. Sherman used this method to destroy the South's rail system. The "necktie" in Jackson was found buried in a muddy bank of the Pearl River, just a few hundred yards from the museum — the same museum that borders some of the very tracks Sherman destroyed.

●●●

Under construction for 18 months, the brand new $18 million Mississippi Museum of Natural Science opened at LeFleur's Bluff State Park in Jackson on March 3, 2000. The 73,000-square-foot museum has triple the exhibit space of the old museum, including 100,000 gallons of aquarium space and a multi-media center/auditorium that holds 200 people, classrooms and space for special traveling exhibits.

●●●

The only federal prison in Mississippi is in Yazoo City — a $50 million low-security correctional unit housing 1,536 male prisoners. The facility officially opened on March 5, 1997, on a 1,000-acre site. Construction of a second federal prison in Yazoo City, a $101 million medium-security facility, is scheduled to begin sometime in the year 2000 and will be built adjacent to the current prison.

●●●

Grand Boulevard in Greenwood, Mississippi, 80 feet wide and lined with pin oaks planted early in the 20th Century, was once described in the *New York Times* as the "most beautiful street in America."

●●●

Phil Gilbert's Shoe Parlor on Washington Street in Vicksburg, Mississippi, was the first place in the nation to sell shoes in boxes in pairs (one right foot and one left foot). That was in 1884.

●●●

Under the category of "I bet you didn't know that.": Harry Moses Horwitz (1897-1975) of Brooklyn, New York, better known as Moe Howard of the Three Stooges, got his start in show business in 1914 on a Mississippi riverboat that docked at Jackson, Mississippi, and cruised the Pearl River.

●●●

In 1821, Captain Isaac Ross, whose plantation was in Lorman, Mississippi, freed his slaves and arranged for them to be sent to Africa where they helped found Liberia, now the oldest black republic in Africa.

●●●

The first Southerner to use Negro dialect in poetry was Irwin Russell (6/3/1853-12/23/1879), born in Port Gibson. His long poem, *Christmas Night In the Quarters*, earned him the stamp of genius.

●●●

In 1940, Brooksville, Noxubee Co., Miss. resident Simeon Orr held the record of breeding and marketing the largest hog and ox in the world! The hog weighed 1,604 pounds, the ox tipped the scales at 3,000 lbs!

●●●

Although the well-known *Guinness Book of World Records*® no longer list world records on homegrown fruits and vegetables, their 1981 edition listed an okra stalk 17 feet tall grown in 1979 by P.C. Cain of Kosciusko, Mississippi! The book also listed a sweet pepper plant owned by Ralph Savarese of Pascagoula, Mississippi, which grew to be 56 inches tall and yielded 53 peppers in 1978!

●●●

The Clarion-Ledger of Jackson conducted a series of special Millennium polls asking readers to pick their all-time favorite Mississippian in each of several categories. The results were printed in the newspaper at various intervals during 1999. Here are the top choices of some of those polls: All-Time Favorite Entertainer — Elvis Presley; Favorite Pop/Rock Singer — Elvis Presley; Mississippi's Man of the Century — Elvis Presley; Mississippi's Woman of the Century — Eudora Welty; Favorite Country Music Singer/Musician — Faith Hill; Favorite Blues/Jazz/R&B Singer/Musician — B. B. King; Favorite Performer in "Other" Music — Leontyne Price (opera singer); Favorite Actor — Morgan Freeman; Favorite TV Personality — Woodie Assaf; Favorite Fiction Writer — William Faulkner; Favorite Non-Fiction Writer — Willie Morris; Favorite Miss Mississippi — Mary Ann Mobley; Favorite Male Athlete — Archie Manning (football); Favorite Female Athlete — Jennifer Gillom (basketball); No. 1 to Head the First Team of the Miss. Division I Men's Basketball Team of the Century — Bailey Howell (some players picked to be on the team were Erick Dampier, Lindsey Hunter, Jeff Malone and Clarence Weatherspoon); Top Humanitarian — Oseola McCarty; and Favorite Politician — John C. Stennis.

Mississippi Superlatives and Trivia

In 1872, the 180-foot paddle wheeler Iron Mountain left Vicksburg for New Orleans with 55 passengers and crew, a cargo of molasses and towing barges of cotton. Two hours after it left Vicksburg, another steamer, The Iroquois Chief, almost collided with a string of runaway cotton barges. The Iron Mountain had simply vanished, leaving no debris or survivors. No trace of the Iron Mountain was ever found.

•••

Willie Fulgear, owner of a Los Angeles salvage business, was in the news in March 2000. He discovered 52 stolen Oscar® statuettes in a trash heap and turned them in. His reward was $50,000 and two tickets to the 2000 Academy Awards® ceremony. Willie Fulgear was born in Hazlehurst, Mississippi.

•••

Two nationally-famous cartoon strips are drawn by artists who, while not native Mississippians, lived in the state at the time their strips were created. Pulitzer-Prize-winning cartoonist Doug Marlette lived in Mississippi when he first created the comic strip *Kudzu*. He modeled one of the characters, the round-hatted preacher Will B. Dunn, after his close friend, Will Campbell, a minister, activist and writer from East Fork, Mississippi. While working for the now-defunct *Jackson Daily News* newspaper, Jimmy Johnson created the comic strip *Arlo and Janis*, which premiered on July 29, 1985. The popular strip has appeared since in *The Clarion-Ledger* and over 600 other newspapers nationwide. Johnson now lives in his home state of Alabama and in Pass Christian, Mississippi, which he says he considers home, too.

•••

What's in a name? The U.S. Census Bureau has a database with 88,799 surnames in the nation. The 10 most common surnames in the U.S. are Smith, Johnson, Williams, Jones, Brown, Davis, Miller, Wilson, Moore and Taylor. More than 46,000 different last names exist in Mississippi, where the 10 most common surnames are Smith, Williams, Jones, Johnson, Brown, Davis, Moore, Taylor, Jackson and White. These top ten surnames in Mississippi account for over 70,000 phone listings, or about 9% of all listed residential phones in the state! The top 100 most common surnames in the state account for about a quarter of a million phone listings, or about 28% of all residential listings! The most common given (Christian) names in Mississippi, as well as in the United States, are James and Mary.

•••

The largest rural mail carrier in the U.S. was William Edward Rankin (1890-1943) who lived and worked in Sandy Hook near Columbia in Marion County, Mississippi. He weighed over 460 pounds.

•••

The true value of all real and personal property in Mississippi in 1998 was $85,365,262,427! That much money in brand new one-hundred dollar bills would stack over 58 miles high! Tilt the stack over to lay on the ground and it would extend from the center of Jackson to the center of Brookhaven, Mississippi!

•••

♫Money...money...money...mon-ney♪. There were 3 Mississippians on the list of the Top 100 Highest Paid Celebrities in *Forbes* March 20, 2000 issue: TV talk-show queen Oprah Winfrey, rated No. 2 with 1999 earnings of $150 million (2nd only to *Star Wars* movie producer George Lucas with $400 million); best-selling novelist John Grisham, rated No. 27 with 1999 earnings of $36 million; and lobbyist/political consultant Haley Barbour, rated No. 70 with his 1999 earnings of $7.5 million. Telecommunications executive Bernie Ebbers, CEO of Mississippi-based MCI-WorldCom, was No. 174 on the 1999 *Forbes* list of 400 Richest Americans with a net worth of $1.4 billion, the 367th richest person in the world!

•••

Mississippi was the second state in the nation to establish an official State Archives Department (1902).

•••

Murrah High School in Jackson, Mississippi placed among the nation's top-ranked schools in a report in *Newsweek* magazine in a March 2000 issue. The only high school in Mississippi making the list, Murrah ranked No. 226 among 472 public high schools in America for its high rate of graduates and the number of students taking advanced-level college placement courses.

•••

The rarest of North American cranes, the Sandhill Crane, lives in the grassy savannas of Jackson County.

•••

The home of Mr. & Mrs. Charles Ramsey in Pass Christian is reputed to be the largest home in the state. Within its 20,000 square feet are 19 bathrooms and 15 bedrooms! (Know of one larger? Let us know.)

Government of Mississippi

Official Name: State of Mississippi
State Nicknames: The Magnolia State and The Hospitality State
Origin of Name Mississippi: The state got its name from the river named by the Indians. First written records indicate it was spelled Malabouchia or Muchee Supee. Later spellings were Mechasipi, Mitchisipi, Misisipi, Micissippi, and Mississippi (this would be a more accurate spelling). The Choctaw "mish sha sippukrie" translates either as "Father of Waters," or "Beyond Age," according to the translator. The name was likely derived from the Chippewa Indian words mici (great) & zibi (river) or "gathering-in of all the waters." Also, Algonquin Indian word "Messipi". It was first written by La Salle's Lt. Henri de Tonti as "Michi Sepe".
First European Permanent Settlement: At Biloxi Bay by the French in 1699
Admitted to the Union: Dec. 10, 1817 (20th State admitted)
Seceded: January 9, 1861 (2nd of 11 states)   **Readmission**: February 23, 1870 (9th of 11 states)
Present Constitution Adopted: 1890
Capital: Jackson
Executive Term: 4 years
Governor: Ronnie Musgrove (D), to Jan 2004 (salary $101,800)
Lt. Governor: Amy Tuck (D) to Jan 2004 (salary $48,835)
Attorney General: Mike Moore (D), to Jan 2004 (salary $90,800)
Secretary of State: Eric Clark (D), to Jan 2004 (salary $75,000)
Auditor: Phil Bryant (R), to Jan 2004 (salary $75,000)
Treasurer: Marshall Bennett (D), to Jan 2004 (salary $75,000)
Ag. Commissioner: Lester Spell (D), to Jan 2004 (salary $75,000)
Insurance Commissioner: George Dale (D), to Jan 2000 (salary $75,000)
Legislators, 1999: House 122 — 83 Democrats, 36 Republicans, 3 Ind. — 35 blacks, 18 women
    Senate 52 — 34 Democrats, 18 Republicans — 10 blacks, 3 women
Legislators, 2000: House 122 — 86 Democrats, 33 Republicans, 3 Ind. — 35 blacks, 16 women
    Senate 52 — 34 Democrats, 18 Republicans — 10 blacks, 6 women
Minority Members, 2000: Blacks — 45 (26.2%)   Women — 22 (12.6%)   Total — 67 (38.5%)
Judiciary: Supreme Court — 9 justices; term, 8 years. Chancery Court — 39 judges; term, 4 years.
    Circuit Court — 40 judges; term, 4 years.
Electoral Votes: 7
U.S. Senators: Thad Cochran (R) 'til Jan. 2003, Trent Lott (R) 'til Jan. 2007
Number of U.S. Representatives: 5 (all were re-elected on Nov. 7, 2000)
    First District: Roger Wicker (R)   Fourth District: Ronnie Shows (D)
    Second Dist.:   Bennie Thompson (D)   Fifth District: Gene Taylor (D)
    Third District: Charles "Chip" Pickering (R)
Black Elected Officials, Jan. '97: State Legislature 46; City & County Offices 519; Law Enforcement 98;
    Education 140 = Total 803 (more than any other state).
Number of Registered Votors, 1996: 1,732,529 (voting age population of 1,966,000)
Voters, 1996 Presidential Election: 886,082 cast votes for the 3 top presidential candidates
    2000 Presidential Election: 985,402 cast votes for the 3 top presidential candidates (a state record)
(From the Reconstruction period through 1960, Mississippi cast its electoral votes for the Democratic candidate for president in all elections except that of 1948, when the States' Rights Democratic candidate received the votes. The state's popular vote supported the Republican candidate in 1964, 1972, 1980, 1984, 1988, 1992, 1996 and 2000.)
Flag: 3 horizontal stripes of blue, white & red with Confederate battle flag in upper left corner.
Motto: **Virtute et Armis** (by valor and arms), suggested by James R. Preston, a native of Virginia, who was, at the time (1894), Superintendent of Education in the State of Mississippi.
Coat of Arms: On Feb. 7, 1894, a legislative-appointed committee recommended a "Shield in color blue, with an eagle upon it with extended pinions, holding in the right talon a palm branch and a bundle of arrows in the left talon, with the word 'Mississippi' above the eagle; the lettering on the shield and the eagle to be in gold; below the shield two branches of the cotton stalk, saltierwise, as in submitted design, and a scroll below extending upward and on each side three-fourths of the length of the shield; upon the scroll, which is to be red, the motto be printed in gold letters upon white spaces, as in design accompanying, the motto to be — **Virtute et Armis**."

U.S. CABINET MEMBERS FROM MISSISSIPPI
1) Robert J. Walker, Treasury, appointed by President Polk 1845
2) Jefferson Davis, War, appointed by President Pierce 1853
3) Jacob Thompson, Interior, appointed by President Buchanan 1857
4) L.Q.C. Lamar, Interior, appointed by President Cleveland 1885
5) Mike Espy, Agriculture, appointed by President Clinton 1993

U.S. Senators receive an annual salary of $141,300 ($157,000 for Majority and Minority leaders).

As of May 2000, Miss. had 55 black mayors, more than any other state.

Government of Mississippi

State Symbol: The Great Seal of the State of Mississippi — eagle with olive branch and arrows.
Other State Symbols (Scientific name in parenthesis and year adopted in brackets):
    Beverage — Milk [1984]
    Bird — Mockingbird (Mimus polyglottos) [1944]
    Butterfly — Spicebush swallowtail (Pterourus troilus) [1991]
    Fish — Largemouth Bass (Micropterus salmoides) [1974]
    Flower — Evergreen magnolia (Magnolia grandiflora) [1952]
    Folk Dance — The Square Dance [1995]
    Fossil — Prehistoric whale [1981] (fossil found in Yazoo County in 1971 & nicknamed "Ziggy")
    Insect — Honeybee (Apis mellifera) [1980]
    Land Mammals — White-tailed deer (Odocoileus virginianus) [1974]
                      — Red Fox (Vulpes fulva) [1997]
    Shell — Oyster shell (Crassostrea virginica) [1974]
    Song — "Go, Mississippi" - words & music by Houston Davis [1962]
    Stone — Petrified wood [1976]
    Tree — Evergreen magnolia (Magnolia grandiflora) [1938]
    Water Mammal — Bottle-nosed Dolphin or Porpoise (Tursiops truncatus) [1974]
    Waterfowl — Wood Duck (Aix sponsa) [1974]

> Arkansas, Florida, Tenessee & Texas also claim the mockingbird as the state bird.

> No more than one state symbol has been adopted in any given year, except in 1974 when five symbols were adopted.

State Paid Holidays (Any holiday that falls on Sunday is observed the following Monday):
    New Years Day (1st day of Jan.); Martin Luther King's & Robert E. Lee's Birthday (3rd Mon. in Jan.); Washington's Birthday (3rd Mon. in Feb.); Confederate Memorial Day (Last Mon. in Apr.); Jefferson Davis's Birthday & National Memorial Day (Last Mon. in May); Independence Day (July 4th); Labor Day (1st Mon. in Sept.); Armistice or Veteran's Day (Nov. 11th); Thanksgiving Day (4th Thurs. in Nov.); and Christmas Day (Dec. 25th).

NUMBER OF MISSISSIPPI STATE GOVERNMENT EMPLOYEES

Job Group*	1997	1998	% Change
Higher Education (staff)	13,309	14,710	+10.5
Higher Education (instructional)	7,741	7,823	+1
Other Educational (i.e., handicapped training)	1,817	1,576	-13
Hospitals	9,493	9,761	+2.8
Corrections	4,120	4,142	+0.5
Natural Resources	4,064	3,781	-7
Streets & Highways	3,336	3,282	-1.6
Health	3,314	3,070	-7.3
Public Welfare	3,201	3,110	-2.8
Finance Administration	1,211	1,180	-2.5
Social Security Administration	1,087	1,085	-0.2
Police	979	927	-5.3
Parks and Recreation	525	503	-4.2
Central Administration	472	489	+3.6
Judicial and Legal	418	473	+13.1
Alcohol Beverage Control	123	128	+4
Water Transportation	52	56	+7.7
Other (non-category positions)	2,733	2,673	-2.2
TOTAL ALL STATE EMPLOYEES*	**57,995**	**58,769**	**+1.3**

* does not include employees in primary & secondary education. Source: U.S. Census Bureau

State Employees: approximately 55% female, 45% male; 60% white and 40% black.
State Employee Averages: education 14 years; age 40; service 8 years, 5 months; salary $23,137.

The Ultimate Reference on the State

Government of Mississippi

Fed'l. Funds Miss. Received, 1993: $13,080,000,000 ($4,970 per capita) 0.01% of $1.27 trillion spent.
         1998: $15,314,467,000 ($5,566 per capita)
         Defense: $ 2,429,000,000
         Non-Defense: $12,885,000,000

> Mississippi defense facilities will receive over $2.7 billion in federal funds in 2001 for equipment and research.

Grants to State & Local Governments, 1998: $3,025,000,000
Federal Defense Programs Spending in Miss., FY 2000: $3,170,000,000
Military Contracts in Mississippi, 1997: $1,431,000,000 ($1,277,000,000 payroll)
Military Installations, 1997: 12,362 military personnel & 9,677 civilian employees
Number of Veterans, Including All Wars, 7/1/1998: 223,774
Veterans Medical Services and Administrative Costs, FY 1998: $261,462,480
Veterans Benefit Payments by the Federal Government, 1998:

Pension and Disability Payments	$ 297,249,000
Readjustment Benefits & Vocational Rehab	11,298,000
Life Insurance Benefit Payments	13,830,000
Other Assistance to Veterans	292,000
Total (In Addition to Medical Benefits)	**$ 322,669,000**

> Litton Industries, parent company of Ingalls Shipyard in Pascagoula, received $1,602,659,000 in defense contracts in Fiscal Year 1997.

> The State of Mississippi has a higher percentage of veterans receiving disability benefits than any other state in the country.

Temporary Assistance To Needy Families (TANF) FY 1998: 23,722 average monthly number of families. There were 60,097 average monthly recipients (47,242 children) for payments totaling $93,436,000 (average monthly payment was $129.56 per person or $328.23 per family).
Food Stamps: 1998 — $246,450,000   1997 — $296,408,000   1996 — 365,904,000
    1995 — $379,769,000   1994 — $393,013,000
School Lunch Program, FY 1998: $92 milion (403,000 enrolled).   1999 — 284,975 children ate free.
Licensed Child Care Centers, Feb. 1998 — 1,543   **Licensed Child Care Providers, Feb. 1998** — 908
Number of Foster Care Homes, 1995: 978 (with 2,945 children).
Social Security (Old Age, Survivors, & Disability Insurance Payments), 1998: $3,723,946,000
Supplemental Security Income (SSI), 1998: 136,000 recipients received payments of $527,872,000.
Medicare, 1998: $2,201,037,000 was paid on behalf of over 400,000 enrollees.
Medicaid & Other Public Assistance Med'l. Care, 1998: $1,741,379,000 paid 500,000+ people.
Federal Aid for Medicaid, Year Ending 9/30/1998: $1,393,000,000
Total Medicaid Eligibles, April 2000: 408,594
Total Federal Transfer Payments to Mississippi, 1998: $10,306,970,000
Unemployment Insurance Benefit Payments, 1998: $116,661,000
Workers' Compensation, 1998: 16,235 claims filed. Total of $234,700,133 paid to claimants.
State Government Revenues, FY 1997: $9,400,000,000
State Government Expenditures, FY 1997: $9,006,000,000 ($3,298 per cap.)
State Government Indebtedness, FY 1997: $2,455,000,000 ($899 per capita)
State General Fund, FY 2001: $3.6 billion, up from $3.5 billion for FY 2000
Mississippi's Bond Ratings, 4th. Quarter, 1998: Standard & Poor's—AA; Moody's—Aa3; Fitch—AA

> Median household income in Miss. in 1999 was $32,540.
> SOURCE: U.S. Census Bureau

Mississippi Wet Counties (Liquor/Wine) 7/1/2000: (44)
    Adams, Amite, Bolivar, Carroll, Claiborne, Clay, Coahoma, Copiah, DeSoto, Forrest, Grenada, Hancock, Harrison, Holmes, Humphreys, Issaquena, Jackson, Jefferson, Jefferson Davis, Kemper, Lafayette, Lauderdale, Lee, Leflore, Lowndes, Madison, Marion, Marshall, Montgomery, Noxubee, Oktibbeha, Panola, Perry, Pike, Quitman, Sharkey, Sunflower, Tallahatchie, Tunica, Warren, Washington, Wilkinson, Yalobusha, and Yazoo.
    Partial (2 co. seats): Chickasaw (2nd dist.), Hinds (1st dist.), Jones (2nd dist.) & Jasper (1st dist.).

Mississippi Dry Counties (as of 7/1/2000): (26)
    Alcorn, Attala, Benton, Calhoun, Choctaw, Clarke, Franklin, George, Greene, Lamar (except the city of Hattiesburg), Leake, Lincoln, Monroe (except the City of Aberdeen), Neshoba (except the Silver Star Casino & Silver Star Golf Course owned by the Choctow Indians), Newton, Pearl River, Pontotoc, Prentiss, Rankin, Scott, Simpson, Smith, Tate, Tishomingo, Wayne, and Webster.
    Partial (2 co. seats): Chickasaw (1st dist.), Hinds (2nd dist.), Jones (1st dist.) & Jasper (2nd dist.)

Mississippi Counties That Have Not Voted (thus remain dry as of 7/1/2000): (8)
    Covington, Itawamba, Lawrence, Stone, Tippah, Union, Walthall, and Winston.

Beer: legal in 46 counties; illegal in 35 counties (19 legal beer *cities* are within those 35 counties).

Government of Mississippi

No. ABC Permit Holders (10/29/99): 1,241 (package stores—446; on premises—761; misc.—34)
Total Wine & Liquor Sales (Incl. Taxes), FY 1999: $180,733,899 by 1,349 permittees (2,003,085 cases)
Alcohol Taxes, FY 1999: ABC Div. collected $28,130,103 taxes/fees + $30,766,800 profit = $58,896,903.
Age of Buying Alcohol: 21
Age of Marriage: With Consent — Male 17, Females 15   **Without Consent:** 21 (male & female)
Age of Leaving School: after age 17   **Age of Majority-full civil rights:** 18
Governmental Units, 1997: 936 (82 county, 295 municipal, 164 school districts & 395 special districts)
Most Populated County, 7/1/1998: Hinds — 247,144 (282.45 persons per square mile).

    Mississippi's most populated county has over 151 times the population of Issaquena, the state's least populated county. There are 206 counties in the U.S. that have greater populations than Hinds. That means that Hinds is the 207th most-populated county in the U.S. Every state, except six, has at least one county with a population that exceeds Hinds County. All counties in Montana, North Dakota, South Dakota, Vermont, West Virginia, and Wyoming have less population than Hinds. The most populated county in the nation is Los Angeles County, California with a 1998 population of 9,213,533 — over 37 times the population of Hinds County! California alone has 21 counties with greater populations than Hinds, including 8 counties that exceed a million each! The top 25 most populated counties in the U.S. each have a population exceeding 1.3 million!

Least Populated County, 7/1/1998: Issaquena — 1,629 (4.01 persons per square mile).

    There are 50 counties in the U.S. with less population than Issaquena County. So, Issaqena is the nation's 51st least populated county. Those 50 counties are located in the following 14 states: Alaska (2 counties); California (1 county); Colorado (3 counties); Hawaii (1 county); Idaho (2 counties); Montana (7 counties); Nebraska (13 counties); Nevada (1 county); New Mexico (1 county); North Dakota (2 counties); Oregon (1 county); South Dakota (3 counties); Texas (11 counties); and Utah (2 counties). The populations of those 50 counties range from 1,603 (Wheeler County, OR) on down to 74 in Kalawao County, Hawaii, which is the least populated county in the U.S. (also the smallest in area at 13 sq. mi. - see below). The total aggregate population of those 50 counties is 47,371, or an average of only 947 per county. The 10 least populated counties in the U.S. had 1997 population figures ranging from 578 down to 74. The least populated county in Mississippi, Issaquena, has over 22 times the population of the least populated county in the U.S.!

Largest County (in area): Yazoo — 933 square miles (920 square miles land area).

    Of the 3,142 counties in the U.S., there are 788 counties larger than Yazoo based on land area (conversely, 2.353 countries smaller than Yazoo). Of Alaska's 27 counties (called divisions or boroughs), all except one are larger than Yazoo, with the largest (Yukon) being a huge 145,287 square miles, over 3 times bigger than the whole state of Mississippi! The largest county in the U.S., excluding Alaska, is San Bernardino, California — 20,106 sq. miles — 21.5 times larger than Yazoo! San Bernardino County is over 16 times larger than Rhode Island, the nation's smallest state (at 1,231 square miles, Rhode Island is just 298 square miles [32%] bigger than Yazoo County!). A total of 45 of California's 58 counties are larger than Yazoo. All 15 counties in Arizona and all 23 counties in Wyoming are larger than Yazoo, with the average size of counties in those two states being 7,576 and 4,222 square miles, respectively! All of New Mexico's 33 counties, except one, are larger than Yazoo. Texas has 109 counties (out of 254) that are larger than Yazoo, 53 of Montana's 56 counties are bigger, 23 of Utah's 29 are larger, 30 of Washington's 39 are bigger, and 14 of Nevada's 16 counties are larger.

Smallest County (in area): Alcorn — 401 square miles (400 square miles land area. By state code, Mississippi counties cannot legally be less than 400 square miles). There are 564 counties in the U.S. that are smaller than Alcorn County (conversely, there are 2,577 counties larger than Alcorn). All of Rhode Island's 5 counties, except one, are smaller than Alcorn. Neighboring Tennessee has 37 counties (out of 95) that are smaller than Alcorn. A total of 103 counties in Georgia (of 159 counties) are smaller, 87 of Kentucky's 120 counties are smaller, 50 of Virginia's 95 counties are smaller, and even Texas has 12 counties with less area than Alcorn! The smallest county in the United States is Kalawao, Hiwaii — 13 square miles. Mississippi's smallest county, Alcorn, is over 30 times larger than the smallest county in the U.S.!

Oldest County: Adams — Established 1798   **Youngest County:** Humphreys — Established 1918

Governors of Mississippi

Mississippi Territory 1798-1817

Winthrop Sargent	May 7, 1798 to May 25, 1801
William Charles Cole Claiborne	May 25, 1801 to Mar. 1, 1805
Robert Williams	Mar. 1, 1805 to Mar. 3, 1809
David Holmes	Mar. 3, 1809 to Oct. 17, 1816

State of Mississippi since 1817

David Holmes	Oct. 17, 1817 to Jan. 5, 1820
George Poindexter	Jan. 5, 1820 to Jan. 7, 1822
Walter Leake	Jan. 7, 1822 to Nov. 17, 1825
Gerard Chittocque Brandon[1]	Nov. 17, 1825 to Jan. 7, 1826
David Holmes[2]	Jan. 7, 1826 to July 25, 1826
Gerard Chittocque Brandon[3]	July 25, 1826 to Jan. 9, 1832
Abram Marshall Scott[4]	Jan. 9, 1832 to June 12, 1833
Charles Lynch	June 12, 1833 to Nov. 21, 1833
Hiram George Runnels	Nov. 21, 1833 to Nov. 20, 1835
John Anthony Quitman	Dec. 3, 1835 to Jan. 7, 1836
Charles Lynch	Jan. 7, 1836 to Jan. 8, 1838
Alexander Gallatin McNutt	Jan. 8, 1838 to Jan. 10, 1842
Tilghman Mayfield Tucker[5]	Jan. 10, 1842 to Jan. 10, 1844
Albert Gallatin Brown[6]	Jan. 10, 1844 to Jan. 10, 1848
Joseph W. Matthews	Jan. 10, 1848 to Jan. 10, 1850
John Anthony Quitman	Jan. 10, 1850 to Feb. 3, 1851
John Isaac Guion	Feb. 3, 1851 to Nov. 4, 1851
James Whitfield	Nov. 24, 1851 to Jan. 10, 1852
Henry Stuart Foote	Jan. 10, 1852 to Jan. 6, 1854
John Jones Pettus[7]	Jan. 6, 1854 to Jan. 10, 1854
John Jones McRae[8]	Jan. 10, 1854 to Nov. 16, 1857
William McWillie	Nov. 16, 1857 to Nov. 21, 1859
John Jones Pettus	Nov. 21, 1859 to Nov. 16, 1863
Charles Clark	Nov. 16, 1863 to May 22, 1865
William Lewis Sharkey	June 13, 1865 to Oct. 16, 1865
Benjamin Grubb Humphreys	Oct. 16, 1865 to June 15, 1868
Adelbert Ames[9]	June 15, 1868 to Feb. 23, 1870

[1] Was lieutenant governor and became governor upon the death of Walter Leake. He was the first *native* Mississippian to become governor.
[2] The state's only governor to resign from office, except Aldelbert Ames (see his footnote).
[3] Was lieutenant governor and became governor upon the resignation of Governor David Holmes.
[4] Died in office of Asiatic Cholera.
[5] Was the first governor to live in the Governor's Mansion.
[6] The youngest governor to ever serve. He was 30 years old when he went into office.
[7] Pettus' first term lasted 4 days, the shortest gubernatorial term in state history. John Quitman's first term was 35 days and Gerald Brandon's first term just 46 days. James Whitfield served just 47 days for his one & only term.
[8] He died while on a trip to join his brother in British Honduras in Central America and was buried in the country of Belize on May 31, 1868 — the only Mississippi governor to be buried outside the continental United States.
[9] A native of Maine. Appointed provisional governor in 1868 and elected in 1874. He resigned under threat of impeachment in 1876. He died in Florida in 1933 at the age of 97 — the last survivor of all the generals of the Civil War (he was a Brigadier General for the Federals and a Medal of Honor recipient).

Governors of Mississippi

James Lusk Alcorn[10]	Mar. 10, 1870 to Nov. 30, 1871
Ridgley Ceylon Powers	Nov. 30, 1871 to Jan. 4, 1874
Adelbert Ames	Jan. 4, 1874 to Mar. 29, 1876
John Marshall Stone[11]	Mar. 29, 1876 to Jan. 29, 1882
Robert Lowry	Jan. 29, 1882 to Jan. 13, 1890
John Marshall Stone	Jan. 13, 1890 to Jan. 20, 1896
Anselm Joseph McLaurin	Jan. 20, 1896 to Jan. 16, 1900
Andrew Houston Longino	Jan. 16, 1900 to Jan. 19, 1904
James Kimble Vardaman	Jan. 19, 1904 to Jan. 21, 1908
Edmond Favor Noel	Jan. 21, 1908 to Jan. 16, 1912
Earl LeRoy Brewer	Jan. 16, 1912 to Jan. 18, 1916
Theodore Gilmore Bilbo	Jan. 18, 1916 to Jan. 20, 1920
Lee Maurice Russell	Jan. 20, 1920 to Jan. 22, 1924
Henry Lewis Whitfield[12]	Jan. 22, 1924 to Mar. 18, 1927
Dennis Herron Murphree[13]	Mar. 18, 1927 to Jan. 17, 1928
Theodore Gilmore Bilbo	Jan. 17, 1928 to Jan. 19, 1932
Martin Sennett "Mike" Conner	Jan. 19, 1932 to Jan. 21, 1936
Hugh Lawson White	Jan. 21, 1936 to Jan. 16, 1940
Paul Burney Johnson, Sr.	Jan. 16, 1940 to Dec. 26, 1943
Dennis Herron Murphree[14]	Dec. 26, 1943 to Jan. 18, 1944
Thomas Lowry Bailey	Jan. 18, 1944 to Nov. 2, 1946
Fielding Lewis Wright[15]	Nov. 2, 1946 to Jan. 22, 1952
Hugh Lawson White	Jan. 22, 1952 to Jan. 17, 1956
James Plemon "J. P." Coleman	Jan. 17, 1956 to Jan. 19, 1960
Ross Robert Barnett	Jan. 19, 1960 to Jan. 21, 1964
Paul Burney Johnson, Jr.	Jan. 21, 1964 to Jan. 16, 1968
John Bell Williams	Jan. 16, 1968 to Jan. 18, 1972
William Lowe "Bill" Waller	Jan. 18, 1972 to Jan. 20, 1976
Charles Clifton "Cliff" Finch	Jan. 20, 1976 to Jan. 22, 1980
William Forrest Winter	Jan. 22, 1980 to Jan. 10, 1984
William Aloysius "Bill" Allain	Jan. 10, 1984 to Jan. 12, 1988
Raymond Edwin "Ray" Mabus, Jr.	Jan. 12, 1988 to Jan. 14, 1992
Daniel Kirkwood "Kirk" Fordice[16]	Jan. 14, 1992 to Jan. 11, 2000
David Ronald "Ronnie" Musgrove[17]	Jan. 11, 2000 to Present

[10] Mississippi's first Republican governor. He resigned from office on Nov. 30, 1871, to take a U.S. Senate seat.
[11] Counting both his terms, he was governor for twelve years — longer than any other governor of Mississippi.
[12] The oldest governor to ever serve, he was 65 years old when he went into office.
[13] Was lieutenant governor and became governor upon the death of Governor Henry L. Whitfield. Murphree was the only governor to ever be lieutenant governor 3 times. Only one other person, Brad Dye, Jr., has ever been lt. governor 3 times. Murphree was lieutenant governor for 3 separate terms, Brad Dye for 3 straight terms.
[14] Was lieutenant governor and became governor upon the death of Gov. Paul B. Johnson, Sr.
[15] Was lieutenant governor and became governor upon the death of Gov. Thomas L. Bailey.
[16] Mississippi's first Republican governor since 1876, he also became the first governor in the 20th century to win back-to-back terms when he was re-elected on Nov. 7, 1995.
[17] He was in the closest gubernatorial race of the 20th Century with Mike Parker and the outcome had to be decided in the Mississippi House of Representatives. On Jan. 4, 2000, it took the House just 12 minutes to decide — Musgrove received 86 votes (70.5%) to Parker's 36 votes (29.5%). It was the first gubernatorial election ever decided in the House.

Alphabetical List of Mississippi Governors

Name of Governor	Birthdate	Place of Birth	Died	Place of Death	Dates Served
Alcorn, James Lusk	11/04/1816	Golconda, IL	12/20/1894	Coahoma Co., MS	03/10/1870 - 11/30/1871
Allain, William Aloysius "Bill"	02/14/1928	Washington, MS	Living	N/A	01/10/1984 - 01/12/1988
Ames, Aldelbert	10/31/1835	near Rockland, ME	04/12/1933	Ormond, FL	06/15/1868 - 02/23/1870
					01/04/1874 - 03/29/1876
Bailey, Thomas Lowry	01/06/1888	near Maben, MS	11/02/1946	Jackson, MS	01/18/1944 - 11/02/1946
Barnett, Ross Robert	01/22/1898	Leake Co., MS	11/06/1987	Jackson, MS	01/19/1960 - 01/21/1964
Bilbo, Theodore Gilmore	10/13/1877	near Poplarville, MS	08/21/1947	New Orleans, LA	01/18/1916 - 01/20/1920
					01/17/1928 - 01/19/1932
Brandon, Gerard Chittocque	09/15/1788	near Natchez, MS	03/28/1850	nr. Fort Adams, MS	11/17/1825 - 01/07/1826
					07/25/1826 - 01/09/1832
Brewer, Earl LeRoy	08/11/1869	Carroll Co., MS	03/10/1942	Jackson, MS	01/16/1912 - 01/18/1916
Brown, Albert Gallatin	05/31/1813	Chester District, SC	06/12/1880	near Terry, MS	01/10/1844 - 01/10/1848
Clark, Charles	02/19/1810	Cincinnati, OH	12/18/1877	Bolivar Co., MS	11/16/1863 - 05/22/1865
Claiborne, William Charles Cole Gov. of Miss. Territory	??/??/1775	Sussex Co., VA	11/23/1817	New Orleans, LA	05/25/1801 - 03/01/1805
Coleman, James Plemon "J.P."	01/09/1914	Ackerman, MS	09/28/1991	Ackerman, MS	01/17/1956 - 01/19/1960
Conner, Martin Sennett "Mike"	08/31/1891	Hattiesburg, MS	09/16/1950	Jackson, MS	01/19/1932 - 01/21/1936
Finch, Charles Clifton "Cliff"	04/04/1927	near Pope, MS	04/22/1986	Batesville, MS	01/20/1976 - 01/22/1980
Foote, Henry Stuart	02/28/1804	Fauquier Co., VA	05/20/1880	Nashville, TN	01/10/1852 - 01/06/1854
Fordice, Daniel K. "Kirk"	02/10/1934	Memphis, TB	Living	N/A	01/14/1992 - 01/11/2000
Guion, John Isaac	11/18/1802	near Natchez, MS	06/26/1855	Jackson, MS	02/03/1851 - 11/04/1851
Holmes, David (Territory Gov.) First State Governor	03/10/1770	near Hanover, PA	08/20/1832	nr. Winchester, VA	03/03/1809 - 10/17/1817
					10/17/1817 - 01/05/1820
Humphreys, Benjamin Grubb	08/26/1808	Claiborne Co., MS-T	12/20/1882	Leflore Co., MS	10/16/1865 - 06/15/1868
Johnson, Paul Burney (Sr.)	03/23/1880	Hillsboro, MS	12/26/1943	Hattiesburg, MS	01/16/1940 - 12/26/1943
Johnson, Paul Burney (Jr.)	01/23/1916	Hattiesburg, MS	10/14/1985	Hattiesburg, MS	01/21/1964 - 01/16/1968
Leake, Walter	05/25/1762	Albemarle Co., VA	11/17/1825	Mount Salis, MS	01/07/1822 - 11/17/1825
Longino, Andrew Houston	05/16/1855	Lawrence Co., MS	02/24/1942	Jackson, MS	01/16/1900 - 01/19/1904
Lowry, Robert	03/10/1831	Chesterfield Dist., SC	01/19/1910	Jackson, MS	01/29/1882 - 01/13/1890
Lynch, Charles	??/??/1783	South Carolina	02/09/1853	near Jackson, MS	06/12/1833 - 11/21/1833
					01/07/1836 - 01/08/1838
Mabus, Raymond Edwin "Ray" (Jr.)	10/11/1948	Choctaw Co., MS	Living	N/A	01/12/1988 - 01/14/1992
Matthews, Joseph W.	??/??/1812	near Huntsville, AL	08/27/1862	Palmetto, GA	01/10/1848 - 01/10/1850
McLarrin, Anselm Joseph	03/26/1848	Brandon, MS	12/22/1909	Brandon, MS	01/20/1896 - 01/16/1900
McNutt, Alexander Gallatin	01/03/1802	Rockbridge Co., VA	10/22/1848	DeSoto Co., MS	01/08/1838 - 01/10/1842
McRae, John Jones	01/10/1815	Sneedsboro, NC	05/31/1868	British Honduras	01/10/1854 - 11/16/1857
McWillie, William	11/17/1795	Kershaw District, SC	03/03/1869	Madison Co., MS	11/16/1857 - 11/21/1859
Murphree, Dennis Herron	01/06/1886	Pittsboro, MS	02/09/1949	Jackson. MS	03/18/1927 - 01/17/1928
					12/26/1943 - 01/18/1944
Musgrove, David Ronald "Ronnie"	07/29/1956	Batesville, MS	Living	N/A	01/11/2000 -
Noel, Edmond Favor	03/04/1856	near Lexington, MS	07/30/1927	Lexington, MS	01/21/1908 - 01/16/1912
Pettus, John Jones	10/09/1813	Wilson Co., TN	01/28/1867	Pulaski Co., AR	01/06/1854 - 01/10/1854
					11/21/1859 - 11/16/1863
Poindexter, George	??/??/1779	Louisa Co., VA	09/05/1853	Jackson, MS	01/05/1820 - 01/07/1822
Powers, Ridgely Ceylon	12/24/1836	Mecca, OH	11/11/1912	Los Angeles, CA	11/30/1871 - 01/04/1874
Quitman, John Anthony	09/01/1799	Rhinebeck, NY	07/17/1858	near Natchez, MS	12/03/1835 - 01/07/1836
					01/10/1850 - 02/03/1851
Runnels, Hiram George	12/17/1796	Hancock Co., GA	12/17/1857	Houston, TX	11/21/1833 - 11/20/1835
Russell, Lee Maurice	11/16/1875	Dallas, MS	05/16/1943	Jackson, MS	01/20/1920 - 01/22/1924
Sargent, Winthrop (Territory Gov.)	05/01/1755	Gloucester, MA	06/03/1820	New Orleans, LA	05/07/1798 - 05/25/1801
Scott, Abram Marshall	??/??/1785	South Carolina	06/12/1833	Jackson, MS	01/09/1832 - 06/12/1833
Sharkey, William Lewis	07/12/1798	eastern Tennessee	04/29/1873	Washington, DC	06/13/1865 - 10/16/1865
Stone, John Marshall	04/30/1830	Milan, TN	03/26/1900	Holly Springs, MS	03/29/1876 - 01/29/1882
					01/13/1890 - 01/20/1896
Tucker, Tilghman Mayfield	02/05/1802	North Carolina	04/03/1859	Bexar, AL	01/10/1842 - 01/10/1844
Vardaman, James Kimble	07/26/1861	near Edna, TX	06/25/1930	Birmingham, AL	01/19/1904 - 01/21/1908
Waller, William Lowe "Bill"	10/21/1926	Lafayette Co., MS	Living	N/A	01/18/1972 - 01/20/1976
White, Hugh Lawson	08/19/1881	Whitestown, MS	09/20/1965	Jackson, MS	01/21/1936 - 01/16/1940
					01/22/1952 - 01/17/1956
Whitfield, Henry Lewis	06/20/1868	near Brandon, MS	03/18/1927	Jackson, MS	01/22/1924 - 03/18/1927
Whitfield, James	12/15/1791	Elbert Co., GA	06/25/1875	Columbus, MS	11/24/1851 - 01/10/1852
Williams, John Bell	12/04/1918	Raymond, MS	03/25/1983	Brandon, MS	01/16/1968 - 01/18/1972
Williams, Robert (Territory Gov.)	07/12/1773	Prince Edward Co., VA	01/25/1836	Monroe, LA	03/01/1805 - 03/03/1809
Winter, William Forrest	02/21/1923	Grenada, MS	Living	N/A	01/22/1980 - 01/10/1984
Wright, Fielding Lewis	05/16/1895	Rolling Fork, MS	05/04/1956	Jackson, MS	11/02/1946 - 01/22/1952

Short Profiles of Mississippi Governors (In the Order They Served)

Winthrop Sargent
Born May 1, 1755, in Gloucester, Massachusetts; graduated from Harvard University; enlisted as a lieutenant in Gridley's Regiment of Massachusetts Artillery on July 7, 1775, and after serving 8 years during the American Revolution, he left the service as a Brevet-Major; was elected Secretary of the Mississippi Territory in 1787. He served in that capacity until the second U.S. President, John Adams, appointed him Governor of the Mississippi Territory, a position he held from May 7, 1798 to May 25, 1801; after his term as governor, he became a planter at his home "Glochester" near Natchez; died in New Orleans on June 3, 1820; interment at Glochester in Natchez.

William Charles Cole Claiborne
Born in 1775 in Sussex County, Virginia; moved in his early youth to New York City; later studied law in Richmond, Virginia, was admitted to the bar and started his practice in Sullivan County, Tennessee; a delegate to the Tennessee State Constitutional Convention in 1796; appointed Tennessee state court judge, 1796; elected as a Republican from Tenn. to the 5th and 6th Congresses, and served from Nov. 23, 1797, to March 3, 1801, in spite of the fact that he was still initially under the constitutional age requirement of 25 years; appointed Governor of Mississippi Territory, May 25, 1801 to Mar. 1, 1805; appointed in Oct. 1803 one of the commissioners to take possession of Louisiana when purchased from France and served as Governor of the Territory of Orleans 1804-1812; Governor of Louisiana 1812-1816 (the only man to have ever been governor of both Mississippi and Louisiana); elected as a Democrat from Louisiana to the U.S. Senate and served from March 4, 1817, until his death of a liver ailment in New Orleans on Nov. 23, 1817; original interment at Basin St. Louis Cemetery, New Orleans, Louisiana, re-interment at Metairie Cemetery, New Orleans. Claiborne counties in three states — Louisiana, Mississippi and Tennessee — are named for him.

Robert Williams
Born on July 12, 1773, in Prince Edward County, Virginia, he soon moved with his parents to Surry County, North Carolina; studied law and was admitted to the bar and started his practice in what is now Rockingham County, N.C; was elected a member of North Carolina state senate and served from 1792 to 1795; elected as a Republican to the 5th, 6th, and 7th Congresses (March 4, 1797-March 3, 1803); appointed by President Thomas Jefferson in 1803 as a member of a commission to ascertain the rights of persons claiming lands west of the Pearl River in Mississippi Territory and served in this capacity until 1807; Governor of Mississippi Territory from March 1, 1805, to March 3, 1809, when he resigned; subsequently resided in Mississippi and North Carolina, where he practiced law and engaged in planting; adjutant general of North Carolina; moved to Louisiana, where he died on Jan. 25, 1836; interment on his plantation near Monroe, Louisiana.

David Holmes
Born at Mary Ann Furnace, near Hanover, York County, Pennsylvannia on March 10, 1770; moved to Virginia as a child and attended Winchester Academy in Winchester; studied law, was admitted to the bar in 1791 and started practice in Harrisonburg, Va; held several local offices; was elected to the 5th Congress and to the five succeeding Congresses (March 4, 1797-March 3, 1809); was not a candidate for renomination in 1808; chairman, Committee on Claims (9th and 10th Congresses); moved to the Mississippi Territory and was Governor of Mississippi Territory, Mar. 3, 1809 to Oct. 17, 1817; the first Governor of the State of Mississippi, Oct. 17, 1817 to Jan. 5, 1820; appointed to the U.S. Senate from Mississippi as a Republican to fill the vacancy caused by the resignation of Walter Leake; was subsequently elected and served from Aug. 30, 1820, to Sept. 25, 1825, when he resigned; chairman, Committee on Indian Affairs (16th Congress); was again Governor of Mississippi from Jan. 7, 1826 to July 25, 1826, when he stepped down due to ill health, the state's only Governor to resign from office, except Aldelbert Ames; died at Jordan's Sulphur Springs near Winchester, Va. Aug. 20, 1832; interment at Mount Hebron Cemetery in Winchester; Holmes County, Mississippi is named for him.

George Poindexter
Born in Louisa County, Va. in 1779; had a sporadic education; studied law; was admitted to the bar in 1800 and started practice in Milton, Va.; moved to the Territory of Mississippi in 1802 and practiced law in Natchez; attorney general of the Territory; member Territorial general assembly 1805; elected as a Delegate from Mississippi Territory to the 10th, 11th, and 12th Congresses (March 4, 1807-March 3, 1813); U.S. district judge for the Territory 1813-1817; served in the War of 1812; upon the admission of Mississippi as a State was elected to the 15th Congress and served from Dec. 10, 1817, to March 3, 1819; chairman, Committee on Public Lands (15th Congress); Governor of Mississippi, Jan. 5, 1820 to Jan. 7, 1822; unsuccessful candidate for election in 1820 to the 17th Congress and in 1822 to the 18th Congress; appointed in 1830 to the U.S. Senate to

Short Profiles of Mississippi Governors (In the Order They Served)

fill the vacancy caused by the death of Robert H. Adams; subsequently elected and served Oct. 15, 1830, to March 3, 1835; unsuccessful candidate for reelection; served as President pro tempore of the Senate during the 23rd Congress; chairman, Committee on Private Land Claims (22nd Congress), Committee on Public Lands (23rd Congress); moved to Lexington, Kentucky and practiced law; returned to Jackson and continued the practice of law until his death on Sept. 5, 1853; interment in Greenwood Cemetery in Jackson.

Walter Leake

Born in Albemarle County, Va., on May 25, 1762; served in the Revolutionary War; studied law; admitted to the bar and practiced; appointed by President Thomas Jefferson as one of the U.S. judges for the Mississippi Territory in 1807; moved to Hinds County, Mississippi, and engaged in the practice of law; upon the admission of Mississippi as a State into the Union, was elected as a Republican to the U.S. Senate and served from Dec. 10, 1817-May 15, 1820, when he resigned; chairman, Committee on Indian Affairs (16th Congress); appointed U.S. Marshal for Mississippi in 1820; Governor of Mississippi, Jan. 7, 1822 to Nov. 17, 1825; died in Mount Salus, Mississippi (later Clinton), Nov. 17, 1825; interment in a private or family cemetery in Hinds Co., Miss; Leake County, Mississippi, is named for him.

Gerard Chittocque Brandon

Born Sept. 15, 1788, near Natchez, Mississippi; Lieutenant Governor of Mississippi, 1824-25 and again in 1826; Governor of Mississippi, Nov. 17, 1825 to Jan. 7, 1826 (just 46 days-was Lieutenant Governor and became Governor upon the death of Walter Leake) and July 25, 1826 to Jan. 9, 1832 (was Lieutenant Governor and became Governor upon the resignation of Gov. David Holmes); was the first *native* Mississippian to become Governor; died near Fort Adams, Mississippi, on Mar. 28, 1850; burial location is unknown.

Abram Marshall Scott

Born in 1785 in South Carolina; Member of Miss. state senate, 1822 and 1826-27; Lt. Gov., 1828-32; Governor of Mississippi, Jan. 9, 1832 to June 12, 1833; died in office of Asiatic cholera on June 12, 1833; interment in Greenwood Cemetery, Jackson.

Charles Lynch

Born in 1783 in South Carolina; settled in Lawrence County, Mississippi about 1821; held public office for the first time when the legislature elected him probate judge of Lawrence County; member of Mississippi state senate, 1827, 1832-33; candidate for the U.S. Senate in Jan. 1829, but was defeated; became Governor of Mississippi upon the death of Governor Abram Scott on June 12, 1833 and served until Nov. 21, 1833; again Governor of Mississippi, Jan. 7, 1836-Jan. 8, 1838; died near Jackson on Feb. 9, 1853; interment in Greenwood Cemetery, Jackson.

Hiram George Runnels

Born Dec. 17, 1796, in Hancock County, Ga; settled in Lawrence County, Mississippi in 1810; Mississippi state auditor, 1822-30; member of Mississippi legislature, 1830-41; candidate for governor in 1931, but was defeated; Governor of Mississippi, Nov. 21, 1833 to Nov. 20, 1835; delegate to Texas state constitutional convention, 1845; died in Houston, Texas on his 61th birthday, Dec. 17, 1857; interment at Glenwood Cemetery, Houston; Runnels County, Texas named for him.

John Anthony Quitman

Born in Rhinebeck, New York on Sept. 1, 1799; graduated from Hartwick Seminary in 1816; instructor in Mount Airy College, Pennsylvania, in 1818; studied law; was admitted to the bar; moved to Chillicothe, Ohio, in 1820, and then to Natchez in 1821, where he practiced law; member of the State house of representatives in 1826 and 1827; chancellor of the State from 1828 until 1835, when he resigned; member of the State constitutional convention in 1832; served in the State senate in 1835 and 1836 and was made its president; Governor of Mississippi, Dec. 3, 1835 to Jan. 7, 1836 (just 35 days); judge of the high court of errors and appeals in 1838; appointed brigadier general of volunteers July 1, 1846, during the Mexican War; commissioned a major general. in the Regular Army April 14, 1847, and thus the highest ranking Mississippian during the Mexican War, and honorably discharged July 20, 1848; again Governor of Mississippi, Jan. 10, 1850 to Feb. 3, 1851; elected as a Democrat to the 34th and 35th Congresses and served from March 4, 1855, until his death; chairman, Committee on Military Affairs (34th and 35th Congresses); He died on July 17, 1858, on his plantation, "Monmouth," near Natchez, presumably from the effects of National Hotel disease contracted in Washington during the inauguration of President Buchanan. At the time of his death, Governor Quitman was said to be the most popular man in all America; interment in the Natchez National Cemetery.

Alexander Gallatin McNutt

Born Jan. 3, 1802, in Rockbridge County, Va.; practiced law in Jackson, Mississippi for a short time, then moved to Vicksburg, where he continued practicing law; member of Mississippi state senate, 1835-37; Gov. of Mississippi, Jan. 8, 1838 to Jan. 10, 1842; died in DeSoto County, Miss. on Oct. 22, 1848; interment at Greenwood Cemetery in Jackson, Mississippi.

Short Profiles of Mississippi Governors (In the Order They Served)

Tilghman Mayfield Tucker
Born near Lime Stone Springs, North Carolina on Feb. 5, 1802; completed preparatory studies, then farmed; moved to Hamilton, Miss.; studied law, was admitted to the bar and began practice in Columbus, Miss.; member of the State House of Representatives 1831-1835; served in the State Senate 1838-1841; Gov. of Miss., Jan. 10, 1842 to Jan. 10, 1844 (was the first Governor to live in the Governor's Mansion); elected as a Democrat to the 28th Congress (March 4, 1843-March 3, 1845); retired to his plantation, "Cottonwood," in Louisiana; died at the home of his father near Bexar, Marion County, Alabama, April 3, 1859; interment in a private or family cemetery.

Albert Gallatin Brown
Born May 31, 1813 in Chester District, South Carolina, he moved with his parents to Copiah County, Mississippi in 1823; at age 16 he entered Mississippi College at Clinton; at the end of his third year, he transferred to Jefferson College in Washington, Mississippi; studied law, was admitted to the bar in 1833; started practice in Gallatin, Miss., the seat of Copiah County; elected as a Democrat to the 26th Congress and served from March 4, 1839 to March 3, 1841; declined to be a candidate for renomination in 1840; judge of the circuit superior court in 1842 and 1843; Governor of Mississippi from Jan. 10, 1844 to Jan. 10, 1848, he is known as the father of the University of Mississippi and the public school system, both of which were established during his term as governor; youngest man to ever serve as governor of Miss. — 30 years old when he went into office; elected to the 30th, 31st, and 32nd Congresses and served from March 4, 1847 to March 3, 1853; chairman of the Committee on the District of Columbia in the 31st Congress; elected to the U.S. Senate in 1854 to fill the vacancy in the term beginning March 4, 1853, reelected in 1859 and served from Jan. 7, 1854 until Jan.12, 1861, when he withdrew; chairman of the Committee on the District of Columbia 34th through 36th Congresses; entered the Confederate Army as a captain during the Civil War; elected a member of the Confederate Senate in 1862 and served in the 1st and 2nd Confederate Congresses; overcome by apoplexy, he fell face down in a shallow pond and died near Terry, Mississippi on June 12, 1880; interment at Greenwood Cemetery in Jackson, Miss; Brown County, Kansas is named for him.

Joseph W. Matthews
Born near Huntsville, Ala. in 1812; member of Mississippi state house of representatives, 1840-44; member of Mississippi state senate, 1844-48; Gov. of Mississippi, Jan. 10, 1848 to Jan. 10, 1850; died in Palmetto, Ga. on Aug. 27, 1862; interment in a private or family cemetery in Benton County, Mississippi.

John Isaac Guion
Born on Nov. 18, 1802, near Natchez in Adams County in the Mississippi Territory; member of the state senate, 1842-46 and 1846-50; Governor of Mississippi, Feb. 3, 1851 to Nov. 4, 1851; died in Jackson on June 26, 1855; interment in Greenwood Cemetery in Jackson, Mississippi.

James Whitfield
Born on Dec. 15, 1791, in Elbert County, Ga.; moved to Columbus and established a business; member of Mississippi House of Representatives, 1842-50 & 1858-62; member of Mississippi Senate, 1851; Governor of Mississippi, Nov. 24, 1851 to Jan. 10, 1852, his term in office was only 47 days long, the shortest of any single-term governor of Mississippi; died in Columbus on June 25, 1875; interment in the Friendship Cemetery in Columbus, Mississippi.

Henry Stuart Foote
Born Feb. 28, 1804, in Fauquier County, Va.; graduated from Washington College (now Washington and Lee University), Lexington, Va. in 1819; studied law, admitted to the bar in 1823, and started practice in Ala. in 1825; moved to Mississippi in 1826 and practiced law in Jackson, Natchez, Vicksburg, and Raymond; elected as a Democrat to the U.S. Senate and served from March 4, 1847, until Jan. 8, 1852, when he resigned to become Governor; chairman, Committee on Foreign Relations (31st and 32nd Congresses); Governor of Mississippi, Jan. 10, 1852 to Jan. 6, 1854; moved to Calif. in 1854; returned to Vicksburg, Miss., in 1858; later settled near Nashville; elected to the 1st & 2nd Confederate Congresses; moved to Washington, D.C. and practiced law; appointed by Pres. Rutherford Hayes as superintendent of the mint at New Orleans 1878-80; became an author; died in Nashville May 20, 1880; Interment at Mount Olivet Cemetery in Nashville.

John Jones Pettus
Born on Oct. 9, 1813, in Wilson County, Tenn.; served as a representative in the Mississippi legislature from Kemper County from 1846-57; Governor of Mississippi, Jan. 6, 1854 to Jan. 10, 1854 (the shortest gubernatorial term at only 4 days) and again Nov. 21, 1859 to Nov. 16, 1863; after the war, amnesty was refused him, and he became a fugitive; the manhunt continued until his death in Pulaski County, Arkansas on Jan. 28, 1867; interment at Flat Bayou Burial Ground in Wabbaseka, Arkansas.

Short Profiles of Mississippi Governors (In the Order They Served)

John Jones McRae
Born on Jan. 10, 1815, in Sneedsboro (now McFarlan), N.C.; moved with his parents to Winchester, Wayne Co., Miss., in 1817; graduated from Miami University, Oxford, Ohio, in 1834; studied law in Pearlington, Miss.; was admitted to the bar and practiced law; founded the *Eastern Clarion* newspaper at Paulding, Mississippi; member state house of representatives 1848-1850, serving as speaker in 1850; appointed as a Democrat to the U.S. Senate to fill the vacancy caused by the resignation of Jefferson Davis and served from Dec. 1, 1851, to March 17, 1852, when a successor was elected and qualified; Governor of Mississippi, Jan. 10, 1854 to Nov. 16, 1857; elected as a Democrat to the 35th Congress to fill the vacancy caused by the death of John A. Quitman; reelected to the 36th Congress and served from Dec. 7, 1858, until he withdrew Jan. 12, 1861; representative from Miss. in the Confederate Congress, 1862-1864; died May 31, 1868, while on a trip to join his brother in British Honduras in Central America and was buried in Belize, the only Miss. governor buried outside the continental United States.

William McWillie
Born in Kershaw District, S.C. on Nov. 17, 1795; served in the War of 1812 as adjutant in his father's regiment; graduated from South Carolina College in 1817; studied law; admitted to the bar in 1818 and started practice in Camden, S.C.; president of the Camden Bank in 1836; member of the State senate 1836-1840; moved to Madison County, Mississippi, in Sept. 1845 and engaged in planting; elected as a Democrat to the 31st Congress (March 4, 1849-March 3, 1851); chairman, Committee on Expenditures in the Post Office Department (31st Congress); unsuccessful candidate for reelection in 1850 to the 32nd Congress; Governor of Mississippi, Nov. 16, 1857 to Nov. 21, 1859; active in the support of the Confederacy; died on his estate "Kirkwood" in Madison County on Mar. 3, 1869; interment in St. Philip's Churchyard in Madison County, Mississippi.

Charles Clark
Born Feb. 19, 1810, in Cincinnati, Ohio; moved to Mississippi at age 21 and settled in Jefferson County, where he taught school while studying law; elected to the lower house of the legislature from Jefferson County in 1838 and was reelected and served until 1844; fought in the Mexican War, then moved to Bolivar County, Mississippi; General in the Confederacy; Governor of Mississippi, Nov. 16, 1863 to May 22, 1865; removed from office by U.S. troops and imprisoned in Savannah, Ga.; died in Bolivar County on Dec. 18, 1877; interment in a private or family cemetery in Bolivar County.

William Lewis Sharkey
Born July 12, 1798, in eastern Tenn.; his father brought him and settled in Warren County, Miss. when he was about 6 year old; enlisted in the military in a Mississippi Company and fought in the Battle of New Orleans; after the Army, he studied law first in Tenn., then in Natchez and was admitted to the bar in 1822; was a member of the lower house of the legislature from Warren County, 1828-29; circuit judge in 1832 before being elected to the high Court of Errors and Appeals, where he was chosen Chief Justice; resigned from the court 1850 and practiced law in Jackson; Governor of Mississippi, June 13, 1865 to Oct. 16, 1865; died in Washington, D.C. on April 29, 1873; interment at Greenwood Cemetery in Jackson; Sharkey Co., Miss. is named for him.

Benjamin Grubb Humphreys
Born Aug. 26, 1808, in Claiborne County in the Mississippi Territory; member of Mississippi state legislature, 1837; member of Mississippi senate, 1839; general in the Confederate Army during the Civil War; Governor of Mississippi Oct. 16, 1865 to June 15, 1868; physically ejected from the governor's office by an armed force under the orders of the U.S. military commander of Mississippi; died in Leflore County, Mississippi on Dec. 20, 1882; interment at Greenwood Cemetery in Port Gibson, Mississippi; Humphreys County, Mississippi is named for him.

Adelbert Ames
Born at East Thomaston near Rockland, Knox County, Maine, on Oct. 31, 1835; attended the common schools and graduated from the U.S. Military Academy at West Point in 1861; entered military service at Rockland, Maine; during the Civil War served with the Union Army from 1861 to 1865 as lieutenant, colonel, and brigadier general; was a First Lieutenant in the 5th U.S. Artillery at Bull Run, Virginia when he performed an act of bravery on July 21, 1861, that earned him the Medal of Honor; was presented the medal on June 22, 1894. Here are the actual words of his citation: "remained upon the field in command of a section of Griffin's Battery, directing its fire after being severely wounded and refusing to leave the field until too weak to sit upon the caisson where he had been placed by men of his command." Ames Medal of Honor (MOH) is officially accredited to Maine, his home state. Ames was one of only five men with Mississippi ties to receive the MOH during the Civil War. He is one of only 22 Mississippians (13 native Mississippians)[15 Army, 4 Marines and 3 Navy] in all wars to have

Short Profiles of Mississippi Governors (In the Order They Served)

received the MOH out of the 3,433 total recipients of the medal through July 1, 2000. Ames was the only Governor of Mississippi to have received the Medal of Honor; was a captain in the Fifth Artillery of the Regular Army 1864-1866; Lt. Colonel of the Twenty-fourth U.S. Infantry from 1866 until 1870, when he resigned; was appointed provisional Governor of Mississippi, June 15, 1868 to Feb. 23, 1870;.was appointed to the command of the fourth military district (Department of Mississippi) March 17, 1869; upon the readmission of the State of Mississippi to representation was elected as a Republican to the U.S. Senate, and served from Feb. 23, 1870, until Jan. 10, 1874, when he resigned, having been elected Governor in 1873; chairman, Committee on Enrolled Bills (53rd Congress); served as Governor again from Jan. 4, 1874 to Mar. 29, 1876; resigned under threat of impeachment in 1876; moved to New York City and later to Lowell, Mass.; engaged in the flour business, with mills in Minnesota, also in various manufacturing industries in Lowell; appointed Brigadier General of Volunteers in the Spanish-American War 1898-1899; Lived in retirement in Lowell; when he died at his winter home in Ormond, Florida on Apr. 12, 1933, at the age of 97, he was the last survivor of all the generals of the Civil War; interment in the Hildreth Family Cemetery in Lowell, Massachusetts.

James Lusk Alcorn

Born near Golconda, Illinois on Nov. 4, 1816; attended the public schools of Livingston County, Ky., and graduated from Cumberland College, Ky.; deputy sheriff of Livingston County 1839-1844; member of the Kentucky house of representatives in 1843; studied law; was admitted to the bar in 1844 and started practice in Delta, Panola County, Miss.; member of the Miss. House 1846, 1856, and 1857; served in the State Senate 1848-54; unsuccessful candidate for election to the 35th Congress in 1856; declined the nomination for Governor in 1857; founder of the Miss. levee system and was made president of the levee board of the Mississippi-Yazoo Delta in 1858; served in the Confederate Army as a brigadier general; presented credentials as a U.S. Senator-elect in 1865 but was not permitted to take his seat; elected first Republican Governor of Miss. in 1869 and served from March 10, 1870, until his resignation on Nov. 30, 1871, having previously been elected Senator; elected as a Republican to the U.S. Senate on Jan. 18, 1870, for the term beginning March 4, 1871, but did not assume duties until Dec. 1, 1871, preferring to continue as Governor; served as Senator from Dec. 1, 1871, to March 3, 1877; unsuccessful candidate for Governor in 1873; resumed the practice of law in Friars Point; died at his plantation home, "Eagles Nest," in Coahoma County, Miss. on Dec. 20, 1894; interment in the family cemetery on his estate; Alcorn County, Mississippi is named for him.

Ridgely Ceylon Powers

Born in Mecca, Ohio on Dec. 24, 1836; graduated from the University of Michigan and got his advanced degree from Union College in Schenectady, New York in 1862; Colonel in the Union Army during the Civil War; appointed sheriff of Noxubee County, Miss. in 1868; Lt. Gov. of Mississippi, 1870-71; Governor of Miss., Nov. 30, 1871 to Jan. 4, 1874; in 1879, moved to Prescott, Arizona, then to California; died in Los Angeles Nov. 11, 1912; burial location unknown.

John Marshall Stone

Born on April 30, 1830, in Milan, Gibson County, Tenn.; served in the Confederate Army during the Civil War; elected to the Miss. Senate in 1969 from Alcorn, Itawamba, Prentiss, and Tishomingo Counties and served throughout Reconstruction; elected Pro Tem of the Senate in 1826; Governor of Mississippi, Mar. 29, 1876 to Jan. 29, 1882 and Jan. 13, 1890 to Jan. 20, 1896. Altogether he was governor for twelve years — longer than any other governor of Mississippi; elected the second President of Agricultural and Mechanical College (later Mississippi State University) to replace retiring Stephen Dill Lee; died in Holly Springs, Mississippi on March 26, 1900; interment at Oak Grove Cemetery in Iuka, Mississippi. Stone County, Mississippi is named for him.

Robert Lowry

Born Mar. 10, 1831, in Chesterfield District, S. C.; General in the Confederate Army during the Civil War; after the war, practiced law in Brandon, Miss.; elected to the state Senate from Rankin and Smith Counties in 1865; Governor of Mississippi, Jan. 29, 1882 to Jan. 13, 1890; died in Jackson, Mississippi on Jan. 19, 1910; interment at City Cemetery, Brandon, Mississippi.

Anselm Joseph McLaurin

Born in Brandon, Mississippi on March 26, 1848. Served in the Confederate Army during the Civil War; after the war, he studied law and was admitted to the bar in 1868; Governor of Mississippi, Jan. 20, 1896 to Jan. 16, 1900; U.S. Senator from Mississippi, 1894-95 and 1901-09; died in Brandon, Miss. on Dec. 22, 1909; interment at Brandon Cemetery in Brandon.

Andrew Houston Longino

Born May 16, 1855, in Lawrence County, Mississippi; graduated from Mississippi College in Clinton in 1875; studied law at the University of Virginia Law School starting in 1880; started his

Short Profiles of Mississippi Governors (In the Order They Served)

practice of law at Monticello; Member of Mississippi state senate, 1880-84; in 1888, was appointed U.S. District Attorney for the Southern District of Mississippi; he next moved to Greenwood to practice law, then after an appointment as Chancellor of the 7th District by Gov. Stone, he moved to Greenville; Governor of Mississippi Jan. 16, 1900 to Jan. 19, 1904; after his term as governor, he practiced law in Jackson; died in Baptist Hospital in Jackson on Feb. 24, 1942; interment at Cedarlawn Cemetery in Jackson.

James Kimble Vardaman

Born near Edna, Texas on July 26, 1861; his family settled in Yalobusha Co., Miss. in 1868; attended public schools; studied law in Carrollton, Miss.; admitted to the bar in 1881 and started practice in Winona, Miss.; became editor of the *Winona Advance* newspaper; moved to Greenwood, Miss., where he practiced law and also engaged in the newspaper business; member, state house of representatives, 1890-1896, and served as speaker 1894; unsuccessful candidate for governor of Mississippi in 1895 and again in 1899; served as a major in the U.S. Army in Cuba during the Spanish-American War; presidential elector on the Democratic ticket in 1892 and 1896; publisher of the *Greenwood Commonwealth* 1896-1903 and the *Issue* 1908-1912; Governor of Mississippi, Jan. 19, 1904 to Jan. 21, 1908; unsuccessful candidate for election to the U.S. Senate in 1907 and 1910; elected as a Democrat to the U.S. Senate in 1912 and served from March 4, 1913, to March 3, 1919; unsuccessful candidate for reelection in 1918 and for election in 1922; chairman, Committee on the Conservation of Natural Resources (63rd through 65th Congresses), Committee on Expenditures in the Post Office Department (63rd Congress), Committee on Manufacturers (65th Congress); in 1922, moved to Birmingham, Ala., where he died on June 25, 1930; interment in Lakewood Memorial Park, Jackson, Mississippi.

Edmond Favor Noel

Born March 4, 1856, near Lexington, Mississippi; member of Mississippi state house of representatives, 1881; member of Mississippi state senate, 1895 and 1899; served in the U.S. Army during the Spanish-American War; Gov. of Mississippi, Jan. 21, 1908 to Jan. 16, 1912; died in Lexington, Mississippi on July 30, 1927; interment at Odd Fellows Cemetery in Lexington.

Earl LeRoy Brewer

Born Aug. 11, 1869, in Carroll County, Miss.; member of Miss. state senate, 1896-1900; Brewer had opposed Noel for governor in 1907, but was defeated. In 1911 no one ran against Brewer and he was nominated and elected without a contest; Governor of Mississippi, Jan. 16, 1912 to Jan. 18, 1916; died in Jackson Mar. 10, 1942; burial location is unknown.

Theodore Gilmore Bilbo

Born Oct. 13, 1877, on a farm near Poplarville, Pearl River County, Mississippi; attended the public schools, then Peabody College in Nashville, studied law at Vanderbilt University, and the University of Michigan; teacher in district and high schools of Mississippi for 5 years; was admitted to the bar in 1908 and started practice in Poplarville; member, State senate 1908-1912; elected Lt. Gov. 1912-1916; twice elected Governor of Mississippi, Jan. 18, 1916 to Jan. 20, 1920 and Jan. 17, 1928 to Jan. 19, 1932; elected as a Democrat to the U.S. Senate in 1934, 1940 and again in 1946 and served from Jan. 3, 1935, until his death in New Orleans on Aug. 21, 1947; did not take the oath of office in 1947 at the beginning of the 80th Congress; chairman, Committee on District of Columbia (78th and 79th Congresses), Committee on Pensions (78th Congress); interment in Juniper Grove Cemetery, near Poplarville, Miss.

Lee Maurice Russell

Born Nov. 16, 1875, at Dallas in Lafayette County, Mississippi.; attended the public schools in Lafayette County, graduating from Tocopola Normal School in 1879; in 1901, received a B.P. degree from the University of Mississippi, where he also studied law; was elected to the state house of representatives and served from 1908-10; elected to the State Senate on Nov. 7, 1911; Lt. Governor of Mississippi, 1916-20; Governor of Mississippi Jan. 20, 1920 to Jan. 22, 1924; charged by a former stenographer with breach of promise and seduction, he was tried in federal court and a jury found in his favor; died at his home in Jackson on May 16, 1943; interment at Lakewood Memorial Park in Jackson, Mississippi.

Henry Lewis Whitfield

Born near Brandon, Mississippi on June 20, 1868; a teacher by profession; Governor of Mississippi, Jan. 22, 1924 to Mar. 18, 1927; the oldest Governor — was 65 years old when he went into office; during his administration, the state hospital for the mentally ill was moved from Jackson to Rankin County, where a new well-equipped hospital was named Whitfield in his honor; died at the Governor's Mansion in Jackson on March 18, 1927; interment in the Friendship Cemetery in Columbus, Mississippi.

Dennis Herron Murphree

Born Jan. 6, 1886, in Pittsboro, Calhoun Co., Miss.; Lt. Gov. of Mississippi 3 times (only one other person, Brad Dye, has been lt. gov. that many times and Dye was never gov.) — 1924-27,

Short Profiles of Mississippi Governors (In the Order They Served)

1932-36, and 1940-43; Governor of Mississippi, Mar. 18, 1927 to Jan. 17, 1928 (was lt. gov. and became governor upon the death of Gov. Henry L. Whitfield) and also governor, Dec. 26, 1943 to Jan. 18, 1944 (was lt. gov. and became governor upon the death of Gov. Paul B. Johnson, Sr.); died of a stroke in Jackson on Feb. 9, 1949; burial in the Pittsboro Cemetery in Calhoun County, Misissippi.

Martin Sennett 'Mike' Conner
Born on Aug. 31, 1891, in Hattiesburg, he grew up in Seminary, Miss.; attended the University of Mississippi and Yale University; political career began in 1916, when he was elected to the state House of Representatives, where he later became speaker of the House; Governor of Mississippi, Jan. 19, 1932 to Jan. 21, 1936; served as Southeastern Conference Baseball Commissioner; died in Jackson on Sept. 16, 1950; Interment at Lakewood Memorial Park in Jackson, Mississippi.

Hugh Lawson White
Born Aug. 19, 1881, in Whitestown, Wilkinson County, Mississippi; was mayor of Columbia, Mississippi; Governor of Mississippi, Jan. 21, 1936 to Jan. 16, 1940 and again from Jan. 22, 1952 to Jan. 17, 1956; under his leadership, the "Balance Agriculture with Industry (BAWI)" program was implemented, which was quite successful, and the state highway patrol was established; died on Sept. 20, 1965, in Jackson; interment at Hollywood Cemetery in McComb, Mississippi.

Paul Burney Johnson, Sr.
Born Mar. 23, 1880, in Hillsboro, Scott Co., Miss; attended the public schools, Harpersville College, and Millsaps College; studied law; was admitted to the bar in 1903 and started practice in Hattiesburg, Miss.; judge of the city court, 1907-08; circuit judge of the 12th judicial district, 1910-19; elected as a Democrat to the 66th and 67th Congresses (March 4, 1919-March 3, 1923); declined to be a candidate for renomination in 1922; resumed the practice of his profession and also farmed; served as Governor of Mississippi, Jan. 16, 1940 until his death in Hattiesburg on Dec. 26, 1943; interment in Oaklawn (City) Cemetery in Hattiesburg, where his son Paul Burney Johnson, Jr. (Governor of Mississippi from 1964-68), is also buried.

Thomas Lowry Bailey
Born near Maben, Webster County, Mississippi on Jan. 6, 1888; graduated from Millsaps College; after teaching school for awhile, he began to practice law in Meridian; served in the state legislature for 24 years and was speaker of the House; Governor of Mississippi, Jan. 18, 1944 to Nov. 2, 1946; died in the Governor's Mansion in Jackson on Nov. 2, 1946; burial in the Magnolia Cemetery in Meridian (Section 76, Lot 75).

Fielding Lewis Wright
Born May 16, 1895, in Rolling Fork, Sharkey Co., Mississippi; served in the U.S. Army during World War I; member of the state legislature and was speaker of the House; Governor of Mississippi, Nov. 2, 1946 to Jan. 22, 1952 (Lt. Gov. since 1944 and became Governor upon the death of Gov. Thomas L. Bailey). During his tenure as governor, a workmen's compensation law was passed; candidate for Vice President of the U.S. in the States' Rights party in 1948; died in Jackson on May 4, 1956; interment in the Wright family cemetery in Rolling Fork, Mississippi.

James Plemon "J.P." Coleman
Born Jan. 9, 1914, in Ackerman, Mississippi; graduated from high school in 1931; attended the University of Mississippi; while studying law at George Washington University in Washington, D.C., he worked as secretary to U.S. Rep. Aaron Lane Ford of Mississippi; admitted to the bar of Mississippi in 1937; circuit judge, 1947-50; Justice of the State Supreme Court, 1950; state attorney general, 1950-56; unopposed in the general election in Nov. 1955, Coleman pledged to maintain segregated education in Miss.; Governor of Mississippi, Jan. 17, 1956 to Jan. 19, 1960; was the first head of the State Sovereignty Commission (segregationist "spy" organization) when it was established in 1956; member of Mississippi state house of representatives, 1960-64; Judge of U.S. Court of Appeals, 1965; died in Ackerman on Sept. 28, 1991; burial in Enon Cemetery in Ackerman.

Ross Robert Barnett
Born Jan. 22, 1898, in the Standing Pine community of Leake Co., Miss.; paid his way through public high school and college working as a barber; served in the U.S. Army during World War I; attended Mississippi College in Clinton, where he graduated in 1922; taught high school in Pontotoc, Miss. for two years before studying law at the University of Mississippi, where he received his law degree in 1926; practiced law in Jackson; entered politics in 1951 in an unsuccessful bid for the Democratic nomination for governor; Governor of Mississippi, Jan. 19, 1960 to Jan. 21, 1964; an ardent segregationist and white supremacist, he tried to block the enrollment of James Meredith, the first black admitted to the University of Mississippi in Sept. 1962, which caused the Federal government to deploy 3,000 troops to put down riots that left 2 dead and 375 injured; he ran unsuccessfully for governor in 1967; practiced law in Jackson until his death there on Nov. 6, 1987; burial in the Barnett Cemetery in Leake Co.; the largest reservoir in the state, the Ross Barnett Reservoir near Jackson, is named after him.

Short Profiles of Mississippi Governors (In the Order They Served)

Paul Burney Johnson, Jr.
Born Jan. 23, 1916, in Hattiesburg, Miss.; attended the public schools in Forrest County and Columbia Military Academy in Columbia, Tenn; graduated from the University of Mississippi, where he was a member of the Rebels football team and had the distinction of being the first sophomore ever elected president of the student body; studied law and was admitted to the bar in 1940; practiced law in Hattiesburg and Jackson; served in the U.S. Marine Corps during World War II where he rose from the rank of private to captain; served as assistant U.S. Attorney for the Southern District of Mississippi, 1948-51; Lt. Gov. of Mississippi, 1960-64; Governor of Mississippi, Jan. 21, 1964 to Jan. 16, 1968; died in Hattiesburg on Oct. 14, 1985; burial in Oaklawn (City) Cemetery in Hattiesburg; where his father Paul B. Johnson (Gov. of Miss. 1940-43) is also buried.

John Bell Williams
Born Dec. 4, 1918, in Raymond, Mississippi; attended the public schools; graduated from Hinds Junior College, Raymond, Miss., in 1936, from the University of Mississippi at Oxford in 1938, and from Jackson (Miss.) School of Law in 1940; was admitted to the bar in 1940 and started practice in Raymond; enlisted as an aviation cadet in the U.S. Army, Nov. 5, 1941; was commissioned as a pilot July 3, 1942; As an Army Air Forces pilot in WWII, he lost an arm in an airplane crash; retired from active service because of his injuries on April 29, 1944; prosecuting attorney of Hinds County, Miss., from May 20, 1944, to October 1, 1946; elected as a Democrat to the 80th and to the ten succeeding Congresses, and served from Jan. 3, 1947, to Jan. 16, 1968, when he resigned, having been elected Gov. of Mississippi for the four-year term commencing on that date and served as governor Jan. 16, 1968 to Jan. 18, 1972; practiced law in Jackson, Miss., until retiring January 1, 1981; resident of Brandon, Miss., until his death there on March 25, 1983; interment in Raymond Cemetery, Raymond, Mississippi.

William Lowe "Bill" Waller
Born Oct. 21, 1926, in rural Lafayette Co., Miss. near Oxford; attended public schools and graduated from Oxford High School; received his B.A. degree from Memphis State University in business administration and law degree from the University of Mississippi; also holds an honorary Doctor of Laws degree from Whitworth College; served in the U.S. Army during the Korean Conflict; after service, he practiced law in Jackson, Mississippi; elected district attorney of Hinds County in 1959 and reelected in 1963; Governor of Mississippi from Jan. 18, 1972 to Jan. 20, 1976.

Charles Clifton "Cliff" Finch
Born near Pope, Panola County, Miss. on Apr. 4, 1927; attended the public schools; at age 18, he enlisted in the service and served in the Army in Italy during World War II; in 1958, he earned a B.A. degree and a law degree from the University of Mississippi; began to practice law in Batesville; was elected to the state house of representatives from Panola County; served as District Attorney for the 17th District, 1964-72; In 1971, ran for Lt. Gov. losing to William Winter, but getting more votes than any other first-time candidate for a statewide office in Mississippi history; Governor of Mississippi, Jan. 20, 1976 to Jan. 22, 1980; was instrumental in bringing the USA International Ballet Competition to Jackson; after serving as governor, he unsuccessfully ran for president of the United States; died of a heart attack in his office in Batesville on Apr. 22, 1986; burial in the Magnolia Cemetery in Batesville.

William Forrest Winter
Born Feb. 21, 1923, in Grenada, Miss.; graduated from Grenada High School as valedictorian in 1940; received his B.A. and law degrees from the University of Mississippi, where he was named Outstanding Law Graduate in 1949; elected to the Mississippi House of Representatives while still a law student in 1947 and reelected to a second term in 1951 without opposition; served in the U.S. Army during World War II and the Korean Conflict, advancing from the rank of private to major; legislative assistant to U.S. Senator John Stennis, 1950-51; state tax collector, 1956-64; state treasurer, 1964-68; Lt. Governor from 1972-76; Governor of Mississippi from Jan. 22, 1980 to Jan. 10, 1984; fought successfully as governor for education reform; past president of the Mississippi Historical Society and president of the board of trustees of State Archives and History; the. new William F. Winter Archives and History Building named after him is being built at the corner of North and Amite streets in Jackson.

William Aloysius "Bill" Allain
Born Feb. 14, 1928, in Washington just outside Natchez in Adams County, Mississippi, the son of a riverboat pilot; educated in the public schools and graduated from Natchez High School; studied pre-law at Notre Dame and received his law degree from the University of Mississippi School of Law; served in the U.S. Army during the Korean conflict with much of his service taking place in combat zones; after service, he practiced law in Natchez until 1962 when he became assistant attorney general of Mississippi (1962-75); attorney general of Mississippi from 1979 to 1983; Governor of Mississippi from Jan. 10, 1984 to Jan. 12, 1988.

Short Profiles of Mississippi Governors (In the Order They Served)

Raymond Edwin "Ray" Mabus, Jr.

Born Oct. 11, 1948, in Choctaw County, Miss., he attended public schools in Ackerman; received his B.A. from the University of Mississippi, an M.A. from Johns Hopkins University, and a law degree from Harvard; served in the U.S. Navy; was counsel to a subcommittee of the U.S. House of Representatives; was legal counsel to Mississippi Governor William Winter, 1980-83; in his first try for elective office, he was elected state auditor in 1983; he was just 39 years old when elected Governor of Mississippi and he served from Jan. 12, 1988 to Jan. 14, 1992; In the 1991 election, the Democrat had a chance to become the first Mississippi governor to succeed himself in the 20th Century, but lost to Republican Kirk Fordice; after his term as governor, he was appointed U.S. ambassador to Saudi Arabia by President Bill Clinton and served in that position from 1994-96.

Daniel Kirkwood 'Kirk' Fordice

Born Feb. 10, 1934, in Memphis, Tenn; received his B.S. in civil engineering and an M.S. in industrial management from Perdue University; member of the U.S. Army Reserves for 20 years, retiring with the rank of colonel; was president of Fordice Construction Company in Vicksburg, Mississippi, 1962-91, which specialized in heavy construction and highway bridge construction and handled mostly U.S. Corps of Engineers river embankment projects; Governor of Mississippi, Jan. 14, 1992 to Jan. 9, 1996, and was reelected to a second term Jan. 9, 1996 to Jan. 11, 2000; Mississippi's first Republican Governor since John M. Stone in 1876, and the first Governor in the 20th Century to win back-to-back terms when re-elected on Nov. 7, 1995; was the first Vicksburg resident elected governor since Alexander McNutt in 1838; it was the first and only public office Fordice ever held; although the state's growing economy was excellent during his tenure, Fordice had only a fair working relationship with the legislature and a very poor relationship with the news media; Fordice could not seek a third term.

David Ronald "Ronnie" Musgrove

Born July 29, 1956, in Batesville, Panola County, Mississippi; graduated from Northwest Mississippi Community College, then the University of Mississippi with a bachelor's degree in business administration, and the University of Mississippi Law School in 1981; was elected state president of the Mississippi Chapter of Phi Beta Lambda and national president in 1977; was elected president of the Student Body Association of the University of Mississippi School of Law in 1980; is a partner in the law firm Smith, Musgrove and McCord in Batesville, Mississippi; in 1987, was elected to the Mississippi State Senate representing Tate and Panola Counties and reelected in 1991 and '92; chaired the Senate Education Committee and served on the Education, Aappropriations, Fees, Salaries and Administration, Judiciary, and Local, Private, and Public Utilities Committees; was selected for membership in the American Inns of Court in 1986; inducted as a fellow into the Mississippi Bar Foundation in 1995; chaired the National Conference of Lieutenant Governors 1998-1999; served as Lt. Governor of Mississippi from January 1996 until January 11, 2000, when he became Governor; was in the closest gubernatorial election of the 20th Century in Mississippi on Nov. 2, 1999. Final results showed Democrat Musgrove led his Republican opponent Mike Parker in the popular vote by only 8,343 votes. Musgrove had 379,034 votes, or 49.62 percent to Parker's 370,691, or 48.52 percent. Each had 61 of the state's 122 electoral votes. The state constitution mandates that a candidate must receive a majority of the popular votes (50% + 1) and a majority of the electoral votes, and because Parker refused to concede, the race had to be decided in the Mississippi House of Representatives. On Jan. 4, 2000, the first day of the session, it took the House just 12 minutes to resolve the governor's race — Musgrove received 86 votes (70.5%) to Parker's 36 votes (29.5%). It was the first gubernatorial election ever decided in the House.

Mississippi Legislative Sessions 1817 - 2000

Oct. 1817 - Feb. 1818	Oct. 1865 - Dec. 1865	Dec. 1932 - Dec. 1932	June 18, 1976 - June 20, 1976
Jan. 1819 - Feb. 1819	Oct. 1866 - Oct. 1866	Jan. 1934 - Apr. 1934	Jan. 4, 1977 - Apr. 3, 1977
Jan. 1820 - Feb. 1820	Jan. 1867 - Feb. 1867	Oct. 1935 - Dec. 1935	Aug. 12, 1977 - Aug. 13, 1977
Jan. 1821 - Feb. 1821	Jan. 1870 - July 1870	Jan. 1936 - Mar. 1936	Jan. 3, 1978 - Apr. 7, 1978
Nov. 1821 - Nov. 1821	Jan. 1871 - May 1871	Sept. 1936 - Sept. 1936	Jan. 2, 1979 - Apr. 1, 1979
June 1822 - June 1822	Jan. 1872 - Apr. 1872	Nov. 1936 - Dec. 1936	May 1, 1979 - May 3, 1979
Dec. 1822 - Jan. 1823	Jan. 1873 - Apr. 1873	Jan. 1938 - Apr. 1938	Jan. 8, 1980 - May 11, 1980
Dec. 1823 - Jan. 1824	Oct. 1873 - Oct. 1873	July 1938 - Aug. 1938	Jan. 6, 1981 - Apr. 8, 1981
Jan. 1825 - Feb. 1825	Jan. 1874 - Apr. 1874	Jan. 1940 - May 1940	Aug. 25, 1981 - Aug. 27, 1981
Jan. 1826 - Jan. 1826	Dec. 1874 - Dec. 1874	Jan. 6, 1942 - Mar. 23, 1942	Jan. 5, 1982 - Apr. 10, 1982
Jan. 1827 - Feb. 1827	Jan. 1875 - Mar. 1875	Jan. 4, 1944 - Mar. 31, 1944	Dec. 6, 1982 - Dec. 21, 1982
Jan. 1828 - Feb. 1828	July 1875 - July 1875	Nov. 2, 1944 - Nov. 3, 1944	Jan. 4, 1983 - Apr. 21, 1983
Jan. 1829 - Feb. 1829	Jan. 1876 - Apr. 1876	Jan. 8, 1946 - Apr. 10, 1946	June 24, 1983 - June 24, 1983
Jan. 1830 - Feb. 1830	Jan. 1877 - Feb. 1877	Mar. 4, 1947 - Mar. 15, 1947	Nov. 16, 1983 - Nov. 19, 1983
Nov. 1830 - Dec. 1830	Jan. 1878 - Mar. 1878	Nov. 12, 1947 - Nov. 15, 1947	Jan. 3, 1984 - May 15, 1984
Nov. 1831 - Dec. 1831	Jan. 1880 - Mar. 1880	Jan. 6, 1948 - Apr. 14, 1948	June 25, 1984 - June 27, 1984
Jan. 1833 - Mar. 1833	Jan. 1882 - Mar. 1882	Nov. 14, 1949 - Dec. 17, 1949	Jan. 8, 1985 - Apr. 11, 1985
Nov. 1833 - Dec. 1833	Jan. 1884 - Mar. 1884	Jan. 3, 1950 - Apr. 20, 1950	Jan. 7, 1986 - Apr. 15, 1986
Jan. 1835 - Jan. 1835	Jan. 1886 - Mar. 1886	Jan. 8, 1952 - Apr. 17, 1952	May 28, 1986 - June 1, 1986
Jan. 1836 - Feb. 1836	Jan. 1888 - Mar. 1888	Nov. 3, 1953 - Dec. 28, 1953	Jan. 6, 1987 - Apr. 5, 1987
Apr. 1837 - May 1837	Jan. 1890 - Feb. 1890	Jan. 5, 1954 - May 6, 1954	Aug. 27, 1987 - Aug. 29, 1987
Jan. 1838 - Feb. 1838	Jan. 1892 - Apr. 1892	Sept. 7, 1954 - Sept. 30, 1954	Jan. 5, 1988 - May 8, 1988
Jan. 1839 - Feb. 1839	Jan. 1894 - Feb. 1894	Jan. 11, 1955 - Apr. 7, 1955	Aug. 10, 1988 - Aug. 16, 1988
Jan. 1840 - Feb. 1840	Jan. 1896 - Mar. 1896	Jan. 3, 1956 - Apr. 6, 1956	Jan. 3, 1989 - Apr. 10, 1989
Jan. 1841 - Feb. 1841	Apr. 1897 - May 1897	Nov. 5, 1957 - Dec. 14, 1957	Apr. 17, 1989 - Apr. 19, 1989
Jan. 1842 - Feb. 1842	Jan. 1898 - Feb. 1898	Jan. 7, 1958 - May 10, 1958	Jan. 2, 1990 - Apr. 14, 1990
July 1843 - July 1843	Jan. 1900 - Mar. 1900	Dec. 2, 1959 - Dec. 24, 1959	June 18, 1990 - June 30, 1990
Jan. 1844 - Feb. 1844	Jan. 1902 - Mar. 1902	Jan. 5, 1960 - May 11, 1960	Jan. 8, 1991 - May 6, 1991
Jan. 1846 - Mar. 1846	Jan. 1904 - Mar. 1904	Aug. 23, 1961 - Aug. 25, 1961	Dec. 18, 1991 - Dec. 20, 1991
Jan. 1848 - Mar. 1848	Jan. 1906 - Apr. 1906	Oct. 17, 1961 - Oct. 21, 1961	Jan. 7, 1992 - May 12, 1992
Jan. 1850 - Mar. 1850	Jan. 1908 - Mar. 1908	Jan. 2, 1962 - June 2, 1962	Sept. 16, 1992 - Sept. 16, 1992
Nov. 1850 - Nov. 1850	Jan. 1910 - Apr. 1910	Sept. 18, 1962 - Oct. 6, 1962	Jan. 5, 1993 - Apr. 4, 1993
Jan. 1852 - Mar. 1852	Nov. 1911 - Nov. 1911	Nov. 13, 1962 - Dec. 21, 1962	Jan. 4, 1994 - Apr. 3, 1994
Oct. 1852 - Oct. 1852	Jan. 1912 - Mar. 1912	Feb. 25, 1963 - Mar. 2, 1963	Aug. 15, 1994 - Aug. 23, 1994
Jan. 1854 - Mar. 1854	June 1913 - June 1913	Jan. 7, 1964 - June 12, 1964	Jan. 3, 1995 - Apr. 11, 1995
Jan. 1856 - Mar. 1856	Jan. 1914 - Mar. 1914	June 23, 1964 - July 15, 1964	Jan. 2, 1996 - Apr. 19, 1996
Dec. 1856 - Feb. 1857	Jan. 1916 - Apr. 1916	June 14, 1965 - July 10, 1965	July 11, 1996 - July 11, 1996
Nov. 1857 - Nov. 1857	Sept. 1917 - Oct. 1917	Jan. 4, 1966 - June 17, 1966	Oct. 11, 1996 - Oct. 11, 1996
Nov. 1858 - Dec. 1858	Jan. 1918 - Mar. 1918	Nov. 9, 1966 - Jan. 6, 1967	Jan. 7, 1997 - Apr. 10, 1997
Nov. 1859 - Feb. 1860	Jan. 1920 - Apr. 1920	June 20, 1967 - June 30, 1967	Apr. 23, 1997 - Apr. 23, 1997
Nov. 1860 - Nov. 1860	Jan. 1922 - Apr. 1922	Jan. 2, 1968 - Aug. 9, 1968	Jan. 6, 1998 - Apr. 5, 1998
Jan. 1861 - Jan. 1861	Jan. 1924 - Apr. 1924	July 22, 1969 - Oct. 11, 1969	Jan. 5, 1999 - Apr. 1, 1999
July 1861 - Aug. 1861	Jan. 1926 - Mar. 1926	Jan. 6, 1970 - Apr. 6, 1970	May 3, 1999 - May 4, 1999
Nov. 1861 - Jan. 1862	Jan. 1928 - Apr. 1928	Jan. 5, 1971 - Apr. 5, 1971	July 22, 1999 - July 22, 1999
Dec. 1862 - Jan. 1863	Oct. 1928 - Dec. 1928	Jan. 4, 1972 - May 9, 1972	Jan. 4, 2000 - May 7, 2000
Nov. 1863 - Dec. 1863	June 1929 - Sept. 1929	Jan. 2, 1973 - Apr. 2, 1973	June 29, 2000 - June 29, 2000
Mar. 1864 - Apr. 1864	Jan. 1930 - May 1930	Jan. 8, 1974 - Apr. 7, 1974	Aug. 28, 2000 - Aug. 30, 2000
Aug. 1864 - Aug. 1864	Sept. 1931 - Oct. 1931	Jan. 7, 1975 - Apr. 6, 1975	Nov. 6, 2000 - Nov. 6, 2000
Feb. 1865 - Mar. 1865	Jan. 1932 - May 1932	Jan. 6, 1976 - May 9, 1976	

Each Regular Session of the Legislature convenes on the first Tuesday after the first Monday in January. Each Regular Session is 90 days long, except for the first year of a new term, like 2000, when it lasts 125 days. The Governor may call extraordinary sessions when he deems it necessary. During the 1999 regular session, the Senate had 1,257 bills introduced and the House had 1,754 bills introduced with 654 bills passing both houses. Of those, 11 bills were vetoed by Governor Fordice (9 House bills + 2 Senate bills). For the fiscal year ending June 30, 2000, the budget appropriated for: the House — $3,727,380 salaries/expenses, plus $3,880,874 contingent fund = $7,608,254 total; the Senate — $1,674,887 salaries/expenses, plus $3,383,703 contingent fund = $5,058,590 total.

Members of the U.S. Senate From Mississippi (1817 - 2001)

Member's Name	Birthdate	Place of Birth	Died	Place of Death	Dates Served
Adams, Robert Huntington (Jacksonian)[1]	??/??/1792	Rockbridge Co., VA	07/02/1830	Natchez, MS	01/06/1830 - 07/02/1830
Adams, Stephen (D) *	10/17/1807	Pendleton Dist., SC	05/01/1857	Memphis, TN	03/17/1852 - 03/03/1857
Alcorn, James Lusk (R) +	11/04/1816	Golconda, IL	12/19/1894	Coahoma Co. MS	12/01/1841 - 03/03/1877
Ames, Adelbert (R) +	10/31/1835	Rockland, ME	04/12/1933	Ormond, FL	02/23/1870 - 01/10/1874
Bilbo, Theodore Gilmore (D) +	10/13/1877	Poplarville, MS	08/21/1947	New Orleans, LA	01/03/1935 - 08/21/1947
Black, John (Whig)	unknown	Massachusetts	08/29/1854	Winchester, VA	11/12/1832 - 03/03/1833
					11/22/1833 - 01/22/1838
Brooke, Walker (Whig)	12/25/1813	Page Brooke, VA	02/18/1869	Vicksburg, MS	02/18/1852 - 03/03/1853
Brown, Albert Gallatin (D) * +	05/31/1813	Chester District, SC	06/12/1880	near Terry, MS	01/07/1854 - 01/12/1861
Bruce, Blanche Kelso (R)	03/01/1841	near Farmville, VA	03/17/1898	Washington, DC	03/04/1875 - 03/03/1881
Chalmers, Joseph Williams (D)	??/??/1807	Halifax Co., VA	06/16/1853	Holly Springs, MS	11/03/1845 - 03/03/1847
Cochran, William Thad (R) *	12/07/1937	Pontotoc, MS	Living	N/A	01/03/1979 -
Davis, Jefferson (D)*	06/03/1808	Fairview, KY	12/06/1889	New Orleans, LA	08/10/1847 - 09/23/1851
					04/04/1857 - 01/21/1861
Doxey, Wall (D) *	08/08/1892	Holly Springs, MS	03/02/1962	Memphis, TN	09/29/1941 - 03/03/1943
Eastland, James Oliver (D)	11/28/1904	Doddsville, MS	02/19/1986	Doddsville, MS	06/30/1941 - 09/28/1941
					01/03/1943 - 12/27/1978
Ellis, Powhatan	01/17/1790	Red Hill, VA	03/18/1863	Richmond, VA	09/28/1825 - 01/28/1826
					03/04/1827 - 07/16/1832
Foote, Henry Stuart (D) +	01/28/1804	Fauquier Co., VA	05/20/1880	Nashville, TN	03/04/1847 - 01/08/1852
George, James Zachariah (D)	10/20/1826	Monroe Co., GA	08/14/1897	Miss. City, MS	03/04/1881 - 08/14/1997
Gordon, James	12/06/1833	Cotton Gin Port, MS	11/28/1912	Okolona, MS	12/27/1909 - 02/22/1910
Harrison, Byron Patton (Pat) (D) *	08/29/1881	Crystal Springs, MS	06/22/1941	Washington, DC	03/04/1919 - 06/22/1941
Henderson, John (Whig)	02/28/1797	Cumberland Co., NJ	09/15/1857	Pass Christian, MS	03/04/1839 - 03/03/1845
Holmes, David (R) +	03/10/1769	near Hanover, PA	08/20/1832	nr. Winchester, VA	08/30/1820 - 09/25/1825
Lamar, Lucius Quintus Cincinnatus (D) *	09/17/1825	Eatonton, GA	01/23/1893	Vineville, GA	03/04/1877 - 03/06/1885
Leake, Walter (R) +	05/25/1762	Albermarle Co., VA	11/17/1825	Mount Salus (now Clinton), MS	12/10/1817 - 05/15/1820
Lott, Chester Trent (R) *	10/09/1941	Grenada, MS	Living	N/A	03/03/1989 -
McLaurin, Anselm Joseph (D) +	03/26/1848	Brandon, MS	12/22/1909	Brandon, MS	02/07/1894 - 03/03/1895
					03/04/1901 - 12/22/1909
McRae, John Jones (D) * +	01/10/1815	Sneedsboro (now McFarlan), NC	05/31/1868	British Honduras (now Belize)	12/01/1851 - 03/17/1852
Money, Hernando De Soto (D) *	08/26/1839	Holmes County, MS	09/18/1912	near Biloxi, MS	10/08/1897 - 03/03/1911
Pease, Henry Roberts (R)	02/19/1835	Winsted, Conn.	01/02/1907	Watertown, SD	02/03/1874 - 03/03/1875
Percy, Le Roy (D)	11/09/1860	near Greenville, MS	12/24/1929	Memphis, TN	02/23/1910 - 03/03/1913
Poindexter, George * +	??/??/1779	Louisa Co., VA	09/05/1853	Jackson, MS	10/15/1830 - 03/03/1835
Reed, Thomas Buck	05/07/1787	near Lexington, KY	11/26/1829	Lexington, KY	01/28/1826 - 03/03/1827
					03/04/1829 - 11/26/1929
Revels, Hiram Rhodes (R)	09/27/1827	Fayetteville, NC	01/16/1901	Aberdeen, MS	02/23/1870 - 03/03/1871
Speight, Jesse (D)	09/22/1795	Greene County, NC	05/01/1847	Columbus, MS	03/04/1845 - 05/01/1847
Stennis, John Cornelius (D)	08/03/1901	near DeKalb, MS	04/23/1995	Jackson, MS	11/05/1947 - 03/03/1989
Stephens, Hubert Durrett (D) *	07/02/1875	New Albany, MS	03/14/1946	New Albany, MS	03/04/1923 - 01/03/1935
Sullivan, William Van Amberg (D) *	12/18/1857	near Winona, MS	03/21/1918	Oxford, MS	05/31/1898 - 03/03/1901
Trotter, James Fisher (D)	11/05/1802	Brunswick Co., VA	03/09/1866	Holly Springs, MS	01/22/1838 - 07/10/1838
Vardaman, James Kimble (D) +	07/26/1861	near Edna, TX	06/25/1930	Birmingham, AL	03/04/1913 - 03/03/1919
Walker, Robert John (D)	07/19/1801	Northumberland, PA	11/11/1869	Washington, DC	03/04/1835 - 03/05/1845
Walthall, Edward Cary (D)	04/04/1831	Richmond, VA	04/21/1898	Washington, DC	03/09/1885 - 01/24/1894
					04/04/1895 - 04/21/1898
Williams, John Sharp (D) *	07/30/1854	Memphis, TN	09/27/1932	Yazoo County, MS	03/04/1911 - 03/03/1923
Williams, Thomas Hickman (D)	01/20/1801	Williamson Co., TN	05/03/1851	near Pontotoc, MS	11/12/1838 - 03/03/1839
Williams, Thomas Hill (R)	??/??/1780	North Carolina	??/??/1840	Robertson Co., TN	12/10/1817 - 03/03/1829

[1] Party affiliation in parentheses — (D) for Democrat, (R) for Republican, other parties are spelled out. * Also served as a Representative in the Congress of the United States. + Also served as Governor of the State of Mississippi. SOURCE: The United States Congress Website

The Ultimate Reference on the State

Members of the U.S. House of Representatives From Mississippi (1817-2001)

Member's Name	Birthdate	Place of Birth	Died	Place of Death	Dates Served
Abernethy, Thomas Gerstle (D)[1]	05/16/1903	Eupora, MS	06/11/1998	Jackson, MS	01/03/1943 - 01/03/1973
Adams, Stephen (D) *	10/17/1807	Pendleton Dist., SC	05/01/1857	Memphis, TN	03/04/1845 - 03/03/1847
Allen, John Mills (D)	07/08/1846	Tishomingo Co., MS	10/30/1917	Tupelo, MS	03/04/1885 - 03/03/1901
Anderson, Chapman Levy (D)	03/15/1845	near Macon, MS	04/27/1924	Kosciusko, MS	03/04/1887 - 03/03/1891
Barksdale, Ethelbert (D)	01/04/1824	Smyrna, TN	02/17/1893	Yazoo City, MS	03/04/1883 - 03/03/1887
Barksdale, William (D)	08/21/1821	Rutherford Co., TN	07/02/1863	Gettysburg, PA	03/04/1853 - 01/12/1861
Barry, Frederick George (D)	01/12/1845	Woodbury, TN	05/07/1909	West Point, MS	03/04/1885 - 03/03/1889
Barry, Henry W. (R)	04/??/1840	Schoharie Co., NY	06/07/1875	Washington, DC	02/23/1870 - 03/03/1875
Barry, William Taylor Sullivan (D)	12/10/1821	Columbus, MS	01/29/1868	Columbus, MS	03/04/1853 - 03/03/1855
Beeman, Joseph Henry (D)	11/17/1833	near Gatesville, NC	07/31/1909	near Lena, MS	03/04/1891 - 03/03/1893
Bennett, Hendley Stone (D)	04/07/1807	near Franklin, TN	12/15/1891	Franklin, TN	03/04/1855 - 03/03/1857
Bowen, David Reece (D)	10/21/1932	Houston, MS	Living	N/A	03/03/1973 - 03/03/1983
Bowers, Eaton Jackson (D)	05/17/1865	Canton, MS	10/26/1939	New Orleans, LA	03/04/1903 - 03/03/1911
Brown, Albert Gallatin (D) * +	05/31/1813	Chester Dist., SC	06/12/1880	near Terry, MS	03/04/1839 - 03/03/1841
					03/04/1847 - 03/03/1853
Busby, Thomas Jefferson (D)	07/26/1884	Short, MS	10/18/1964	Houston, MS	03/04/1923 - 01/03/1935
Byrd, Adam Monroe (D)	07/06/1859	Sumter Co., AL	06/21/1912	Hot Springs, AR	03/04/1903 - 03/03/1911
Cage, Harry (Jacksonian)	unknown	Sumner Co., TN	??/??/1859	New Orleans, LA	03/04/1833 - 03/03/1835
Candler, Ezekiel Samuel, Jr. (D)	01/18/1862	Belleville, FL	12/18/1944	Corinth, MS	03/04/1901 - 03/03/1921
Catchings, Thomas Clendinen (D)	01/11/1847	Brownsville, MS	12/24/1927	Vicksburg, MS	03/04/1885 - 03/03/1901
Chalmers, James Ronald (D)	01/12/1831	near Lynchburg, VA	04/09/1898	Memphis, TN	03/04/1877 - 04/291882
					06/25/1884 - 03/03/1885
Claiborne, John Francis Hamtramck (Jacksonian)	04/24/1807	Natchez, MS	03/17/1884	near Natchez, MS	03/04/1835 - 03/03/1837
					07/18/1837 - 02/05/1838
Cochran, William Thad (R) *	12/07/1937	Pontotoc, MS	Living	N/A	01/03/1973 - 12/26/1978
Collier, James William (D)	09/28/1872	near Vicksburg, MS	09/28/1933	Washington, DC	03/04/1909 - 03/03/1933
Collins, Ross Alexander (D)	04/25/1880	Collinsville, MS	07/14/1968	Meridian, MS	03/04/1921 - 01/03/1935
					01/03/1937 - 01/03/1943
Colmer, William Meyers (D)	02/11/1890	Moss Point, MS	09/09/1980	Pascagoula, MS	03/04/1933 - 01/03/1973
Davis, Jefferson (D) *	06/03/1808	Fairview, KY	12/06/1889	New Orleans, LA	03/04/1845 - 06/??/1846
Davis, Reuben (D)	01/18/1813	Winchester, TN	10/14/1890	Huntsville, AL	03/04/1857 - 01/12/1861
Denny, Walter McKennon (D)	10/28/1853	Moss Point, MS	11/05/1926	Pascagoula, MS	03/04/1895 - 03/03/1897
Dickson, David (Whig)	unknown	Georgia	07/31/1836	Hot Springs, AR	03/04/1835 - 07/31/1836
Dickson, William Alexander (D)	07/20/1861	Centreville, MS	02/25/1940	Centreville, MS	03/04/1909 - 03/03/1913
Dowdy, Charles Wayne (D)	07/27/1943	Fitzgerald, GA	Living	N/A	07/07/1981 - 01/03/1989
Doxey, Wall (D) *	07/08/1892	Holly Springs, MS	03/02/1962	Memphis, TN	03/04/1929 - 09/28/1941
Dunn, Aubert Culberson (D)	11/20/1896	Meridian, MS	01/04/1987	Mobile, AL	01/03/1935 - 01/03/1937
Ellett, Henry Thomas (D)	03/08/1812	Salem, NJ	10/15/1887	Memphis, TN	01/26/1947 - 03/03/1947
Ellzey, Lawrence Russell (D)	03/20/1891	near Wesson, MS	12/07/1977	Jackson, MS	03/15/1932 - 01/03/1935
Espy, Albert Michael (D)	11/30/1953	Yazoo City, MS	Living	N/A	01/03/1987 - 01/22/1993
Featherston, Winfield Scott (D)	07/08/1820	nr. Murfreesboro, TN	05/28/1891	Holly Springs, MS	03/04/1847 - 03/03/1851
Ford, Aaron Lane (D)	12/21/1902	Potts Camp, MS	07/08/1983	Jackson, MS	01/03/1935 - 01/03/1943
Fox, Andrew Fuller (D)	04/26/1849	Reform, AL	08/29/1926	West Point, MS	03/04/1897 - 03/03/1903
Franklin, William Webster (R)	12/13/1941	Greenwood, MS	Living	N/A	01/03/1983 - 01/03/1987
Freeman, John D. (Unionist)	unknown	Cooperstown, NY	01/17/1886	Canon City, CO	03/04/1851 - 03/03/1853
Gholson, Samuel Jameson (D) (Jacksonian, then a Demo.)	05/19/1808	near Richmond, KY	10/16/1883	Aberdeen, MS	12/01/1836 - 03/03/1837
					07/18/1837 - 02/05/1838
Griffin, Charles Hudson (D)	05/09/1926	near Utica, MS	09/10/1989	Utica, MS	03/12/1968 - 01/03/1973
Gwin, William McKendree, MD (D)	10/09/1805	near Gallatin, TN	09/03/1885	New York, NY	03/04/1841 - 03/03/1843
Haile, William	??/??/1797	unknown	03/07/1837	near Woodville, MS	07/10/1826 - 09/12/1828
Hall, Robert Samuel (D)	03/10/1879	Williamsburg, MS	06/10/1941	Arlington, VA	03/04/1929 - 03/03/1933

[1] Party affiliation in parentheses — (D) for Democrat, (R) for Republican, other parties are spelled out.
* Also served in the United States Senate.   + Also served as Governor of the State of Mississippi.
SOURCE: The United States Congress Website

Members of the U.S. House of Representatives From Mississippi (1817-2001)

Member's Name	Birthdate	Place of Birth	Died	Place of Death	Dates Served
Hammett, William Henry (D)[1]	03/25/1799	Don Manway, County Cork, Ireland	07/09/1861	Washington Co., MS	03/04/1843 - 03/03/1845
Harris, George Emrick (R)	01/06/1827	Orange Co., NJ	03/19/1911	Washington, DC	02/23/1870 - 03/03/1873
Harris, Wiley Pope (D)	11/09/1818	Holmesville, MS	12/03/1891	Jackson, MS	03/04/1853 - 03/03/1855
Harrison, Byron Patton "Pat" (D) *	08/29/1881	Crystal Springs, MS	06/22/1941	Washington, DC	03/04/1911 - 03/03/1919
Henry, Patrick (D)	02/12/1843	Cynthia, MS	05/18/1930	Brandon, MS	03/04/1897 - 03/03/1901
Henry, Patrick (D)	02/15/1861	near Helena, AR	12/28/1933	Vicksburg, MS	03/04/1901 - 03/03/1903
Hill, Wilson Shedric (D)	01/19/1863	near Lodi, Choctaw Co., MS	02/14/1921	Greenwood, MS	03/04/1903 - 03/03/1909
Hinds, Thomas (D)	01/09/1780	Berkeley Co., VA	08/23/1840	Greenville, MS	10/21/1828 - 03/03/1831
Hinson, Jon Clifton (R)	03/16/1942	Tylertown, MS	07/21/1995		01/03/1979 - 04/13/1981
Hooker, Charles Edward (D)	??/??/1825	Union, SC	01/08/1914	Jackson, MS	03/04/1875 - 03/03/1883
					03/04/1887 - 03/03/1895
					03/04/1901 - 03/03/1903
Howe, Albert Richards (R)	01/01/1840	Brookfield, MA	06/01/1884	Chicago, IL	03/04/1873 - 03/03/1875
Humphreys, Benjamin Grubb (D)	08/17/1865	Claiborne Co., MS	10/16/1923	Greenville, MS	03/04/1903 - 10/16/1923
Humphreys, William Yerger (D)	09/09/1890	Greenville, MS	02/26/1933	Greenville, MS	11/27/1923 - 03/03/1925
Jeffords, Elza (R)	05/23/1826	Ironton OH	03/19/1885	Vicksburg, MS	03/04/1883 - 03/03/1885
Johnson, Paul Burney, Sr. (D) +	03/23/1880	Hillsboro, MS	12/26/1943	Hattiesburg, MS	03/04/1919 - 03/03/1923
Kyle, John Curtis (D)	07/17/1851	near Sardis, MS	07/06/1913	Sardis, MS	03/04/1891 - 03/03/1897
Lake, William Augustus (American Party)	01/06/1808	near Cambridge, MD	10/15/1861	Hopefield, AR	03/04/1855 - 03/03/1857
Lamar, Lucius Quintus Cincinnatus (D)*	09/17/1825	Eatonton, GA	01/23/1893	Vineville, GA	03/04/1857 - 12/??/1860
					03/04/1873 - 03/03/1877
Lewis, Clarke (D)	11/08/1840	Huntsville, AL	03/13/1896	near Macon, MS	03/04/1889 - 03/03/1893
Lott, Chester Trent (R) *	10/09/1941	Grenada, MS	Living	N/A	01/03/1973 - 01/03/1989
Love, William Franklin (D)	03/29/1850	near Liberty, MS	10/16/1898	Gloster, MS	03/04/1897 - 10/16/1898
Lowrey, Bill Green (D)	05/25/1862	Kossuth, MS	09/02/1947	Olive Branch, MS	03/04/1921 - 03/03/1929
Lynch, John Roy (R)	09/10/1847	near Vidalia, LA	11/02/1939	Chicago, IL	03/04/1873 - 03/03/1877
					04/29/1882 - 03/03/1883
Manning, Vannoy Hartrog (D)	07/26/1839	near Raleigh, NC	11/03/1892	Branchville, MD	03/04/1877 - 03/03/1883
McGehee, Daniel Rayford (D)	09/10/1883	Little Springs, MS	02/09/1962	Meadville, MS	01/03/1935 - 01/03/1947
McKee, George Colin (R)	10/02/1837	Joliet, IL	11/17/1890	Jackson, MS	03/04/1869 - 03/03/1875
McLain, Frank Alexander (D)	01/29/1852	near Gloster, MS	10/10/1920	Gloster, MS	12/12/1898 - 03/03/1909
McRae, John Jones (D) * +	01/10/1815	Sneedsboro, NC	05/31/1868	British Honduras	12/07/1858 - 01/12/1861
McWillie, William (D) +	11/17/1795	Kershaw Dist., SC	03/03/1869	Madison Co., MS	03/04/1849 - 03/03/1851
Money, Hernando De Soto (D) *	08/26/1839	Zeigerville (Holmes County), MS	09/18/1912	near Biloxi, MS	03/04/1875 - 03/03/1885
					03/04/1893 - 03/03/1897
Montgomery, Gillespie V. "Sonny" (D)	08/05/1920	Meridian, MS	Living	N/A	01/03/1967 - 01/03/1997
Morgan, James Bright (D)	03/14/1833	near Fayetteville, TN	06/18/1892	near Horn Lake, MS	03/04/1885 - 03/03/1891
Morphis, Joseph Lewis (R)	04/17/1831	near Pocahantas, TN	07/29/1913	Cleveland, OK	02/23/1870 - 03/03/1873
Muldrow, Henry Lowndes (D)	02/08/1837	nr. Tibbes Stat., MS	03/01/1905	Starkville, MS	03/04/1877 - 03/03/1885
Nabers, Benjamin Duke (Unionist)	11/07/1812	Franklin, TN	09/06/1878	Holly Springs, MS	03/04/1851 - 03/03/1853
Niles, Jason (R)	12/19/1814	Burlington, VT	07/07/1894	Kosciusko, MS	03/04/1873 - 03/03/1875
Parker, Michael (Mike) (D)	10/31/1949	Laurel, MS	Living	N/A	01/03/1989 - 11/10/1995
as a Republican.....					11/10/1995 - 01/03/1999
Perce, Legrand Winfield (R)	06/19/1836	Buffalo, NY	03/16/1911	Chicago, IL	02/23/1870 - 03/03/1873
Pickering, Charles W. (Chip), Jr. (R)	08/10/1963	Laurel, MS	Living	N/A	01/03/1997 -

[1] Party affiliation in parentheses — (D) for Democrat, (R) for Republican, other parties are spelled out.
 * Also served in the United States Senate.   + Also served as Governor of the State of Mississippi.
SOURCE: The United States Congress Website

Members of the U.S. House of Representatives From Mississippi (1817-2001)

Member's Name	Birthdate	Place of Birth	Died	Place of Death	Dates Served
Plummer, Franklin E. (Jacksonian)	unknown	Massachusetts	09/24/1847	Jackson, MS	03/04/1831 - 03/03/1835
Poindexter, George * [1]	??/??/1779	Louisa Co., VA	09/05/1853	Jackson, MS	12/10/1817 - 03/03/1819
Prentiss, Seargent Smith	07/30/1808	Portland, ME	07/01/1850	near Natchez, MS	05/30/1838 - 03/03/1839
Quin, Percy Edwards (D)	10/30/1872	near Liberty, MS	02/04/1932	Washington, DC	03/04/1913 - 02/04/1932
Quitman, John Anthony (D) +	09/01/1799	Rhinebeck, NY	07/17/1858	near Natchez, MS	03/04/1855 - 07/17/1858
Rankin, Christopher	??/??/1788	Washington Co., PA	03/14/1826	Washington, DC	03/04/1819 - 03/14/1826
Rankin, John Elliott (D)	03/29/1882	Bolanda, MS	11/26/1960	Tupelo, MS	03/04/1921 - 01/03/1953
Roberts, Robert Whyte (D)	11/28/1784	Kent Co., DE	01/04/1865	near Hillsboro, MS	03/04/1843 - 03/03/1847
Shows, Ronnie (D)	01/26/1947	Jones County, MS	Living	N/A	01/03/1999 -
Singleton, Otho Robards (D)	10/14/1814	Nicholasville, KY	01/11/1889	Washington, DC	03/04/1853 - 03/03/1855 03/04/1857 - 01/12/1861
Sisson, Thomas Upton (D)	09/22/1869	near McCool, MS	09/26/1923	Washington, DC	03/04/1909 - 03/03/1923
Smith, Frank Ellis (D)	02/21/1918	Sidon, MS	08/02/1997	Jackson, MS	01/03/1951 - 11/14/1962
Smith, Larkin I. (R)	06/26/1944	Poplarville, MS	08/13/1989	plane crash in MS (DeSoto Nat'l. Forest)	01/03/1989 - 08/13/1989
Spencer, James Grafton (D)	09/13/1844	nr. Port Gibson, MS	02/22/1926	Port Gibson, MS	03/04/1895 - 03/03/1897
Spight, Thomas (D)	10/25/1841	near Ripley, MS	01/05/1924	Ripley, MS	07/05/1898 - 03/03/1911
Stephens, Hubert Durrett (D) *	07/02/1875	New Albany, MS	03/14/1946	nr. New Albany, MS	03/04/1911 - 03/03/1921
Stockdale, Thomas Ringland (D)	03/28/1828	W. Union Church, PA	01/08/1899	Summit, MS	03/04/1887 - 03/03/1895
Sullivan, William Van Amberg (D) *	12/18/1857	near Winona, MS	03/21/1918	Oxford, MS	03/04/1897 - 05/31/1898
Taylor, Gary Eugene "Gene" (D)	09/17/1953	New Orleans, LA	Living	N/A	10/17/1989 -
Thompson, Bennie (D)	01/28/1948	Bolton, MS	Living	N/A	04/13/1993 -
Thompson, Jacob (D)	05/15/1810	Leasburg, NC	03/24/1885	Memphis, TN	03/04/1839 - 03/03/1851
Tompkins, Patrick Watson (Whig)	??/??/1804	Kentucky	05/08/1853	San Francisco, CA	03/04/1847 - 03/03/1849
Tucker, Tilghman Mayfield (D) +	02/05/1802	near Lime Stone Springs, NC	04/03/1859	Bexar, AL	03/04/1843 - 03/03/1845
Van Eaton, Henry Smith (D)	09/14/1826	Anderson Township, OH	05/30/1898	Woodville, MS	03/04/1883 - 03/03/1887
Venable, William Webb (D)	09/25/1880	Clinton, MS	08/02/1948	New Orleans, LA	01/04/1916 - 03/03/1921
Walker, Prentiss Lafayette (R)	08/23/1917	nr. Taylorsville, MS	06/05/1998	Jackson, MS	01/03/1965 - 01/03/1967
Wells, Guilford Wiley (Independent Republican)	02/14/1840	Conesus Center, NY	03/21/1909	Santa Monica, CA	03/04/1875 - 03/03/1877
Whitten, Jamie Lloyd (D)	04/18/1910	Cascilla, MS	09/09/1995	Oxford, MS	11/04/1941 - 01/03/1995
Whittington, William Madison (D)	05/04/1878	Little Springs, MS	08/20/1962	Greenwood, MS	03/04/1925 - 01/03/1951
Wicker, Roger F. (R)	07/05/1951	Pontotoc, MS	Living	N/A	01/03/1995 -
Wilcox, John A. (Unionist)	04/18/1819	Greene County, NC	02/07/1864	Richmond, VA	03/04/1851 - 03/03/1853
Williams, John Bell (D) +	12/04/1918	Raymond, MS	03/25/1983	Brandon, MS	01/03/1947 - 01/16/1968
Williams, John Sharp (D) *	07/30/1854	Memphis, TN	09/27/1932	nr. Yazoo City, MS	03/04/1893 - 03/03/1909
Wilson, Thomas Webber (D)	01/24/1893	Coldwater, MS	01/31/1948	Coldwater, MS	03/04/1923 - 03/03/1929
Winstead, William Arthur (D)	01/06/1904	nr. Philadelphia, MS	03/14/1995	Philadelphia, MS	01/03/1943 - 01/03/1965
Witherspoon, Samuel Andrew (D)	05/04/1855	near Columbus, MS	11/24/1915	Meridian, MS	03/04/1911 - 11/24/1915
Word, Thomas Jefferson (Whig)	unknown	Surry County, NC	unknown	unknown	05/30/1838 - 03/03/1839
Wright, Daniel Boone (D)	02/17/1812	near Mount Pleasant, TN	12/27/1887	Ashland, MS	03/04/1853 - 03/03/1857

[1] Party affiliation in parentheses — (D) for Democrat, (R) for Republican, other parties are spelled out.
 * Also served in the United States Senate.   + Also served as Governor of the State of Mississippi.
SOURCE: The United States Congress Website

State & Federal Government Phone Numbers

Mississippi Congressional Delegation

Senate

THAD COCHRAN (R); 326 Senate Russell Bldg; 1st & C Streets, NE; Washington, DC 20510 .... (202) 224-5054
    District Office: 188 E Capitol, Suite 614; Jackson, MS 39201 (Neal Flowers, Mgr.) .... (601) 965-4459
    Federal Courthouse, 2nd Floor; Oxford, MS .... (662) 236-1018
    E-Mail — senator@cochran.senate.gov   Web Page — www.senate.gov/~cochran

TRENT LOTT (R); 487 Senate Russell Bldg; 1st & C Streets, NE; Washington, DC 20510 .... (202) 224-6253
    District Offices: Federal Bldg; 200 E Washington St, Rm 145; Greenwood, MS 38930 ...... (662) 453-5681
    1 Government Plaza, Suite 428; Gulfport, MS 39501 .... (228) 863-1988
    245 E Capitol St, Suite 226; Jackson, MS 39201 (Guy Hovis, Mgr.) .... (601) 965-4644
    911 Jackson Ave, Suite 127 (PO Box 1474); Oxford, MS 38655 .... (662) 234-3774
    3100 S Pascagoula St; Pascagoula, MS 39567 .... (228) 762-5400
    E-Mail — senatorlott@lott.senate.gov   Web Page — www.senate.gov/~lott

U. S. House of Representatives

DISTRICT 1: ROGER WICKER (R); 206 Cannon Office Bldg; Washington, DC 20515 .... (202) 225-4306
    District Offices: 8700 Northwest Dr, Suite 102 (PO Box 70); Southaven, MS 38671 .... (662) 342-3942
    500 W Main St; Room 210 (PO Box 1482); Tupelo, MS 38801 .... (662) 844-5437
    E-Mail — roger.wicker@mail.house.gov   Home Page — www.house.gov/wicker

DISTRICT 2: BENNIE THOMPSON (D); 1408 Longworth; Washington, DC 20515 .... (202) 225-5876
    District Offices: 107 W Madison; Bolton, MS 39041 .... 1-800-355-9003 or (601) 866-9003
    910 Courthouse Lane; Greenville, MS 38701 .... (662) 335-9003
    509 US Hwy 82 West; Greenwood, MS 38930 .... (662) 455-9003
    Quitman County Courthouse; 230 Chestnut St; Marks, MS 38646 .... (662) 326-9003
    City Hall, Suite 134; 106 N Green St; Mound Bayou, MS 38762 .... (662) 741-9003
    E-Mail — thompsonms2nd@mail.house.gov Web Page — www.house.gov/thompson

DISTRICT 3: CHARLES "CHIP" PICKERING (R); 427 Cannon Bldg; Washington, DC 20515 .... (202) 225-5031
    District Offices: P. O. Box 5618; Meridian, MS 39302 .... (601) 693-6681
    110-D Airport Rd; Pearl, MS 39208 .... (601) 932-2410

DISTRICT 4: RONNIE SHOWS (D); Longworth Bldg; Washington, DC 20515 .... (202) 225-5865
    District Offices: 245 E Capitol St, Suite 222; Jackson, MS 39201 .... (601) 352-1355
    122 S Broadway; McComb, MS 39648 .... (601) 684-9449
    242 John R. Junkin Dr, Suite C; Natchez, MS 39120 .... (601) 446-8825
    728 1/2 Sawmill Rd; Laurel, MS 39440 .... (601) 425-5257
    250 Broad St, Suite 9; Columbia, MS 39429 .... (601) 731-1622
    E-Mail — ronnie.shows@mail.house.gov

DISTRICT 5: GENE TAYLOR (D); 2311 Rayburn Bldg; Washington, DC 20515 .... (202) 225-5772
    District Offices: 2424 14th St; Gulfport, MS 39501 .... 1-800-273-4363 or (228) 864-7670
    701 Main St, Suite 215; Hattiesburg, MS 39401 .... (601) 582-3246
    Hancock County; Bay St. Louis, MS .... (228) 466-3972
    1215-B Government St; Ocean Springs, MS 39564 .... (228) 872-7950

Top Mississippi Elected Officials

MISSISSIPPI STATE GOVERNMENT INFORMATION .... (601) 359-1000
GOVERNOR'S OFFICE; Jackson (www.govoff.state.ms.us   E-mail: governor@govoff.state.ms.us) .... (601) 359-3100
GOVERNOR'S MANSION; 300 E Capitol St; Jackson 39205 .... (601) 359-3175
LIEUTENANT GOVERNOR; Jackson (www.ls.state.ms.us   E-mail: atuck@mail.senate.state.ms.us) .... (601) 359-3200
ATTORNEY GENERAL; Jackson (www.ago.state.ms.us   E-mail: msago@ago.state.ms.us) .... (601) 359-3680
SECRETARY OF STATE, Jackson; (www.sos.state.ms.us   E-mail: administrator@sos.state.ms.us) .... (601) 359-1350
STATE TREASURER; Jackson (www.treasury.state.ms.us   E-mail: mbennett@treasury.state.ms.us) .... (601) 359-3600
STATE AUDITOR; Jackson (www.osa.state.ms.us   E-mail: auditor@osa.state.ms.us) .... (601) 364-2888
AGRICULTURE COMMISSIONER; Jackson (www.mdac.state.ms.us E-mail: Webmaster@mdac.state.ms.us) (601) 359-1111
INSURANCE COMMISSIONER; Jackson (www.doi.state.ms.us   E-mail: georgedale@mid.state.ms.us) ..... (601) 359-3569
MISSISSIPPI SENATE, MEMBERS DURING SESSIONS .... (601) 359-3770
MISSISSIPPI SENATE, PRESIDENT PRO TEMPORE .... (601) 359-3209
SECRETARY OF THE SENATE .... (601) 359-3202
HOUSE OF REPRESENTATIVES; Members during sessions .... (601) 359-3770
HOUSE OF REPRESENTATIVES, CLERK OF THE HOUSE .... (601) 359-3360
SPEAKER OF THE HOUSE .... (601) 359-3300
HOUSE OF REPRESENTATIVES, SPEAKER PRO TEMPORE .... (601) 359-3304

Mississippi Legislature Internet Address — www.ls.state.ms.us

The Ultimate Reference on the State

State & Federal Government Phone Numbers

Branches & Departments of State Government

AGRICULTURE & COMMERCE DEPT, FARMERS MARKET OFFICE	(601) 354-6573
AGRICULTURE & FORESTRY MUSEUM; Lakeland Dr; Jackson	(601) 354-6113
BARNETT RESERVOIR OFFICE; 115 Madison Landing Circle; Madison 39110	(601) 354-3448
BIRTH & DEATH CERTIFICATES; Jackson	(601) 960-7981
DEPT. OF ARCHIVES AND HISTORY; Charlotte Capers Bldg; 100 S State St; Jackson 39205	(601) 359-6876
DEPT. OF BANKING & CONSUMER FINANCE; 304 Sillers Bldg; Jackson	(601) 359-1031
INDUSTRIES FOR THE BLIND; 2501 N West; Jackson	(601) 355-0212
INSTITUTIONS OF HIGHER LEARNING; 3825 Ridgewood Rd; Jackson 39211-6453	(601) 432-6611
MISSISSIPPI AIR NATIONAL GUARD; Thompson Field; Jackson	(601) 939-3633
MISSISSIPPI ARCHIVES AND HISTORY DEPT; 100 S State; Jackson	(601) 359-6850
MISSISSIPPI AUTHORITY FOR EDUCATIONAL TELEVISION; 3825 Ridgewood; Jackson	(601) 432-6565
MISSISSIPPI BOARD OF NURSING; 1935 Lakeland Dr; Jackson 39216	(601) 987-4188
MISSISSIPPI BUREAU OF NARCOTICS, Headquarters; Jackson	(601) 359-1570
MISSISSIPPI COLISEUM; 1207 Mississippi; Jackson	(601) 961-4000
MISSISSIPPI DEPT OF CORRECTIONS, Central Office; 723 N President: Jackson 39202-3097	(601) 359-5600
Mississippi Dept. of Corrections; STATE PENITENTIARY; PO Box 1057; Parchman 38738	(662) 745-6611
Mississippi Dept. of Corrections; Central MS Correctional Facility; PO Box 88550; Pearl 39288	(601) 932-2880
Mississippi Dept. of Corrections; South MS Correctional Institution; Box 1419; Leakesville 39451	(662) 394-5600
Mississippi Dept. of Corrections; Flowood Restitution Center/CWC; 1632 Hwy 80E; Flowood	(601) 936-7213
Mississippi Dept. of Corrections; Greenwood Restitution Ctr; Hwy 7N; Box 1346; Greenwood	(662) 453-5134
Mississippi Dept. of Corrections; Hinds County Restitution Ctr; 429 S Gallatin St; Jackson 39203	(601) 354-0062
Mississippi Dept. of Corrections; Pascagoula Restitution Ctr; 1721 E Kenneth Ave; Pascagoula	(228) 762-1331
Mississippi Dept. of Corrections; Alcorn County Community Work Center (CWC); Corinth	(662) 287-8105
Mississippi Dept. of Corrections; Bolivar County CWC; Hwy 8; Rosedale 38769	(662) 759-3535
Mississippi Dept. of Corrections; Forest County CWC; 112 Alcorn Ave; Hattiesburg 39401	(601) 544-5030
Mississippi Dept. of Corrections; George County CWC; 106 Industrial Park; Lucedale 39452	(601) 947-7581
Mississippi Dept. of Corrections; Harrison County CWC; 3920 8th Ave; Gulfport 39501	(228) 865-0020
Mississippi Dept. of Corrections; Jackson County CWC; 1717 Kenneth Ave; Pascagoula 39567	(228) 762-0255
Mississippi Dept. of Corrections; Jefferson County CWC; Rt 2 Box 35-F; Fayette 39069	(601) 786-3556
Mississippi Dept. of Corrections; Leflore County CWC; Rt 3 Box 127-M; Greenwood 38930	(662) 453-9720
Mississippi Dept. of Corrections; Madison County CWC; 140 Corrections Dr; Canton 39046	(601) 859-7711
Mississippi Dept. of Corrections; Noxubee County CWC; 110 Industrial Park Dr; Macon 39341	(662) 726-2375
Mississippi Dept. of Corrections; Pike County CWC; Industrial Park Rd; Magnolia 39652	(601) 783-5514
Mississippi Dept. of Corrections; Quitman County CWC; Rt 1 Box 246; Lambert 38643	(662) 326-2133
Mississippi Dept. of Corrections; Simpson County CWC; Rt 1 Box 138-A; Magee 39111	(601) 849-3281
Mississippi Dept. of Corrections; Washington Co. CWC; 1398 N Beauchamp Ext; Greenville 38703	(662) 332-6358
Mississippi Dept. of Corrections; Wilkinson County CWC; 84 Prison Lane; Woodville 39669	(601) 888-4378
Mississippi Dept. of Corrections; Yazoo Co. CWC; Box 1047; 625 W Jefferson; Yazoo City 39194	(662) 746-2085
Mississippi Dept. of Corrections; Carroll/Montgomery Cor'l. Facility (private); Po Box 291; Carrollton	(662) 464-5221
Mississippi Dept. of Corrections; Delta Correctional Facility (private); 3800 Baldwin Rd; Greenwood	(662) 455-4546
Mississippi Dept. of Corrections; East Miss. Correctional Facility (private); PO Box 4217; Meridian	(601) 553-8550
Mississippi Dept. of Corrections; Issaquena Co. Cor'l. Facility (private); Po Box 220; Mayersville	(662) 873-2150
Mississippi Dept. of Corrections; Jefferson/Franklin Cor'l. Facility (private); Rt. 2, Box 29; Fayette	(601) 786-2284
Mississippi Dept. of Corrections; Leake Co. Correctional Facility (private); 399 C.O. Brooks St; Carthage	(601) 298-9003
Mississippi Dept. of Corrections; Marion/Walthall Cor'l. Facility (private); 503 S Main St; Columbia	(601) 736-3621
Mississippi Dept. of Corrections; Marshall Co. Cor'l Facility (private); 833 West St; Holly Springs	(662) 252-7111
Mississippi Dept. of Corrections: Wilkinson Co. Correctional Facility (private); PO Box 11079; Woodville	(601) 888-3199
Mississippi Dept. of Corrections; Winston/Choctaw Co. Cor'l. Facility (private); 2460 Hwy 25N; Louisville	(662) 773-5881
MISSISSIPPI DEPARTMENT OF MARINE RESOURCES; 1141 Bayview; Biloxi 39530	(228) 385-5860
MISSISSIPPI DEPARTMENT OF PUBLIC SAFETY/HIGHWAY PATROL; Jackson	(601) 987-1212
MISSISSIPPI DEPARTMENT OF TRANSPORTATION; Administration Bldg; 401 North West St; Jackson	(601) 359-7685
MISSISSIPPI DEPARTMENT OF TRANSPORTATION; Woolfork State Office Bldg; Jackson 39201	(601) 359-1209
Mississippi Department of Transportation; District 1 Headquarters; 1909 N Gloster; Tupelo 38801	(662) 842-1122
Mississippi Department of Transportation; District 2 Headquarters; 150 Hwy 51N; Batesville 38606	(662) 563-4541
Mississippi Department of Transportation; District 3 Headquarters; 1240 Hwy 49W; Yazoo City 39194	(662) 746-2513
Mississippi Department of Transportation; District 5 Headquarters; 7759 Hwy 80W; Newton 39345	(601) 683-3341
Mississippi Department of Transportation; District 6 Headquarters; 6356 Hwy 49N; Hattiesburg 39401	(601) 544-6511
Mississippi Department of Transportation; District 7 Headquarters; Hwy 51N; McComb 39648	(601) 684-2111
Mississippi Department of Transportation; State Highway Commission; Commissioner-Central District	(601) 359-7041

State & Federal Government Phone Numbers

Mississippi Department of Transportation; State Highway Commission; Commissioner-Northern District	(601) 359-7040
Mississippi Department of Transportation; State Highway Commission; Commissioner-Southern District	(601) 359-7039
MISSISSIPPI DEPARTMENT OF WILDLIFE, FISHERIES & PARKS; 1505 Eastover Dr; Jackson 39211	(601) 432-2400
MISSISSIPPI EDUCATION & RESEARCH CENTER; 3825 Ridgewood Rd; Jackson	(601) 432-6476
MISSISSIPPI EMPLOYMENT SERVICE; 5959 I-55 N. Frontage Rd; Jackson	(601) 961-7931
Mississippi Employment Service; 400B Wise Wilkins Rd; Columbus 39701	(662) 328-6876
Mississippi Employment Service; 800 Hiway 1 S; Delta Plaza Greenville 38703	(662) 332-8101
Mississippi Employment Service; 315 Lamar St; Greenwood 38930	(662) 453-7141
Mississippi Employment Service; 2229 22nd St; Gulfport 39501	(228) 864-1771
Mississippi Employment Service; 4100 Mamie St; Hattiesburg 39402	(601) 264-0502
Mississippi Employment Service; 2350 Hiway 80 W; Jackson	(601) 961-7802
Mississippi Employment Service; 1100 17th Ave; Meridian 39301	(601) 483-1406
Mississippi Employment Service; 538 Magazine St; Tupelo 38801	(662) 842-4371
Mississippi Employment Service; 1625 Monroe St; Vicksburg 39180	(601) 638-1452
MISSISSIPPI FAIR COMMISSION; 1207 Mississippi; Jackson	(601) 961-4000
MISSISSIPPI FILM COMMISSION; Walter Sillers Bldg; Jackson	(601) 359-3449
MISSISSIPPI FORESTRY COMMISSION; 301 North Lamar; Jackson 39201	(601) 359-1386
MISSISSIPPI GAMING COMMISSION; 202 E Pearl St; Jackson 39201	(601) 351-2800
MISSISSIPPI LEVEE BOARD; 211 S Walnut St; Greenville 38701	(662) 332-6732
MISSISSIPPI LIBRARY COMMISSION; 1221 Ellis Ave; Jackson 39209	(601) 359-1036
MISSISSIPPI NATIONAL GUARD; Recruiting; Hwy 468; Brandon	(601) 825-0274
MISSISSIPPI NATIONAL GUARD; Recruiting; 1500 E Northside Dr; Clinton	(601) 924-9283
MISSISSIPPI NATIONAL GUARD; Recruiting; 505 E Main; Raymond	(601) 857-8596
MISSISSIPPI PAROLE BOARD; 201 W Capital Street, Suite 800; Jackson 39201	(601) 354-7716
MISSISSIPPI SCHOOL FOR THE BLIND; 1252 Eastover Dr; Jackson	(601) 987-3911
MISSISSIPPI SCHOOL FOR THE DEAF; Jackson	(601) 987-3911
MISS. STATE BOARD OF MEDICAL LICENSURE; 3000 Old Canton Rd., Suite 111; Jackson 39216	(601) 987-3079
MISSISSIPPI STATE CRIME LAB; 1900 E Woodrow Wilson; Jackson 39216	(601) 987-1600
Mississippi State Crime Lab; Batesville	(662) 563-5681
Mississippi State Crime Lab; Gulfport	(228) 832-9641
Mississippi State Crime Lab; Meridian	(601) 483-5273
MISSISSIPPI STATE HOSPITAL; Whitfield 39193	(601) 939-1221
MISSISSIPPI STATE TAX COMMISSION; Central Office; 1577 Springridge Rd; Raymond 39154	(601) 923-7000
Mississippi State Tax Commission; District Office; 212 S First St; Brookhaven 39601	(601) 833-4761
Mississippi State Tax Commission; District Office; 3580 Hwy 45N; Columbus 39701	(662) 328-3271
Mississippi State Tax Commission; District Office; 111 E Market St; Greenwood 38930	(662) 453-1742
Mississippi State Tax Commission; District Office; 318 Courthouse Rd; Gulfport 39501	(228) 896-1393
Mississippi State Tax Commission; District Office; 1318 Hardy St; Hattiesburg 39401	(601) 545-1261
Mississippi State Tax Commission; District Office; 2418 9th. St; Meridian 39301	(601) 483-2273
Mississippi State Tax Commission; District Office; 115 S Ward St; Senatobia 38668	(601) 562-4489
Mississippi State Tax Commission; District Office; 4008 W Main St; Tupelo 38801	(662) 842-4316
MISSISSIPPI STATE VETERANS' HOME; 4607 Lindburgh Dr; Jackson	(601) 353-6142
MISSISSIPPI TRADEMART; 1200 E Mississippi; Jackson	(601) 354-7051
MISSISSIPPI VETERANS MEMORIAL STADIUM; 2531 N. State St; Jackson	(601) 981-4664
MISSISSIPPI VOCATIONAL REHAB FOR THE BLIND; 5455 Executive Place; Jackson	(601) 364-2650
MISS. WATER RESOURCES ASSN; PO Box 4200; Jackson 39296 (E-mail: insightltd@email.msn.com)	(601) 355-8538
MISSISSIPPI WILDLIFE & CONSERVATION; Lake Monroe Rd; Amory 38821	(662) 256-9637
MISSISSIPPI WILDLIFE FEDERATION; 520 N President St; Jackson 39201	(601) 353-6922
MISSISSIPPI WILDLIFE MANAGEMENT; Hwy 364; Iuka 38852	(662) 423-1455
MISSISSIPPI WORKER'S COMPENSATION COMMISSION; 1428 Lakeland Dr; Jackson 39216	(601) 987-4200
MUSEUM OF NATURAL SCIENCE; in Lefluer's Bluff State Park off Lakeland Drive; Jackson	(601) 354-7303
STATE ALCOHOL BEVERAGE CONTROL BOARD; Jackson	(601) 856-1301
STATE ARTS COMMISSION; 239 N Lamar; Jackson 39201	(601) 359-6030
STATE BOARD OF ARCHITECTURE; 502 Robert E. Lee Bldg; Jackson	(601) 359-6020
STATE BOARD OF COMMUNITY & JUNIOR COLLEGES; 3825 Ridgewood Rd; Jackson 39211	(601) 432-6518
STATE BOARD OF COSMETOLOGY; 1804 N State; Jackson 39202	(601) 354-6623
STATE BOARD OF DENTAL EXAMINERS; 600 E Amite St., Suite 100; Jackson 39201	(601) 924-9622
STATE BOARD OF ENGINEERS & LAND SURVEYORS; Robert E. Lee Bldg; Jackson	(601) 359-6160
STATE BOARD OF FUNERAL SERVICES; 802 N State St, Suite 401; Jackson 39202	(601) 354-6903
STATE BOARD OF PROFESSIONAL COUNSELING EXAMINERS; Mississippi State Univ.	(662) 325-8182

The Ultimate Reference on the State

State & Federal Government Phone Numbers

STATE BOARD OF PUBLIC ACCOUNTANCY; 653 N State St.; Jackson 39202	(601) 354-7320
STATE CONTRACTOR'S BOARD; 2001 Airport Rd; Jackson 39208	(601) 354-6161
STATE DEPARTMENT OF EDUCATION; 501 Sillers Bldg; Jackson 39201	(601) 359-3513
STATE DEPARTMENT OF ENVIRONMENTAL QUALITY; 2380 Hwy 80W; Jackson 39204	(601) 961-5650
STATE DEPARTMENT OF FINANCE & ADMINISTRATION; Jackson	(601) 359-3402
STATE DEPARTMENT OF HEALTH; Jackson	(601) 960-7400
STATE DEPARTMENT OF HUMAN SERVICES; Jackson	(601) 960-4245
STATE ETHICS COMMISSION; 146 E Amite: Jackson 39201	(601) 359-1285
STATE FIRE ACADEMY; 1400 Old Whitfield Rd; Jackson 39208	(601) 932-2444
STATE HISTORICAL MUSEUM; Old Capitol; Jackson	(601) 359-6920
STATE MENTAL HEALTH DEPT; Robert E. Lee Bldg; Jackson	(601) 359-1288
STATE MILITARY DEPT; Jackson	(601) 973-6000
STATE MOTOR VEHICLE COMMISSION; Jackson	(601) 987-3995
STATE OIL AND GAS BOARD; 500 Greymont Ave; Jackson 39202	(601) 354-7142
STATE P E E R COMMITTEE; 222 N President; Jackson 39201	(601) 359-1226
STATE PARKS & RECREATION; Jackson	(601) 364-2010
STATE PERSONNEL BOARD; 301 N Lamar; Jackson 39201	(601) 359-1406
STATE PHARMACY BOARD; 625 N State St; Jackson 39204	(601) 354-6750
STATE PSYCHOLOGICAL EXAMINERS BOARD; 812 N President; Jackson 39202	(601) 353-8871
STATE PUBLIC SERVICE COMMISSION; Jackson	(601) 961-5431
STATE REAL ESTATE COMMISSION; Jackson	(601) 987-3969
STATE SOIL & WATER CONSERVATION COMMISSION; Jackson	(601) 359-1281
STATE TESTING LABORATORY; 1912 Military Rd; Columbus 39701	(662) 327-4490
STATE VETERANS AFFAIRS BOARD; 206 W Pearl St; Jackson 39201	(601) 354-7377
SUPREME COURT OF MISSISSIPPI, General Information; 450 Gartin Bldg; Jackson 39201	(601) 359-3697

State Government Toll-Free Phone Numbers

AGRICULTURE DEPT, POULTRY HOTLINE	800-535-4555
CONSUMER PROTECTION DIVISION OF THE ATTORNEY GENERAL'S OFFICE	800-281-4418
DEPARTMENT OF BANKING & CONSUMER FINANCE; 550 High St; W. Sillers Bldg; Jackson 39201	800-844-2499
DEPARTMENT OF WILDLIFE, FISHERIES & PARKS; to report hunting accidents	800-237-6278
GOVERNOR'S SERVICE LINE	800-832-6123
MEDICAID FRAUD UNIT OF THE ATTORNEY GENERAL'S OFFICE	800-852-8341
MISSISSIPPI BUREAU OF NARCOTICS; Headquarters Hot Line	800-844-6272
MISSISSIPPI DEPARTMENT OF HUMAN SERVICES; Main Information	800-345-6347
MISSISSIPPI DEPARTMENT OF HUMAN SERVICES; Aging & Adult Services	800-948-3090
MISSISSIPPI DEPARTMENT OF HUMAN SERVICES; Child Abuse Hotline	800-222-8000
MISSISSIPPI DEPARTMENT OF HUMAN SERVICES; Child Support Enforcement	800-948-4010
MISSISSIPPI DEPARTMENT OF HUMAN SERVICES; Children & Youth	800-877-7882
MISSISSIPPI DEPARTMENT OF HUMAN SERVICES; Community Services	800-421-0762
MISSISSIPPI DEPARTMENT OF HUMAN SERVICES; Economic Assistance Inquiry	800-948-3050
MISSISSIPPI DEPARTMENT OF HUMAN SERVICES; Family & Children Services; Adoption	800-821-9157
MISSISSIPPI DEPARTMENT OF HUMAN SERVICES; Statewide Hotline	800-345-6347
MISSISSIPPI DEPARTMENT OF PARKS & RECREATION	800-467-2757
MISSISSIPPI DEVELOPMENT AUTHORITY	800-222-7622
MISSISSIPPI GOVERNMENT MEDICAID; 4785 I-55N; Jackson	800-421-2408
MISSISSIPPI HIGHWAY PATROL; Statewide Crimestoppers Tipline & Connections School Safety	888-827-4637
MISSISSIPPI INSURANCE COMMISSION; Jackson	800-562-2957
MISSISSIPPI LIBRARY COMMISSION; 1221 Ellis Ave; Jackson 39209	800-359-1036
MISSISSIPPI PUBLIC EMPLOYEES RETIREMENT SYSTEM; 429 Mississippi St; Jackson 39201	800-647-7542
MISSISSIPPI PUBLIC SERVICE COMMISSION; Northern District	800-356-6428
MISSISSIPPI PUBLIC SERVICE COMMISSION; Southern District	800-356-6429
MISSISSIPPI PUBLIC SERVICE COMMISSION; Central District	800-356-6430
MISSISSIPPI REGIONAL POISON CONTROL CENTER	800-738-9898
MISSISSIPPI SECRETARY OF STATE'S OFFICE	800-256-3494
MISSISSIPPI WILDLIFE FEDERATION; To report wildlife violations	800-237-6278
STATE CRIME VICTIM COMPENSATION PROGRAM	800-829-6766
STATE DEPT OF EDUCATION, Community & Outreach Services	800-264-3516
STATE DEPARTMENT OF HEALTH	800-227-7308
STATE GAMING COMMISSION; 202 E Pearl St; Jackson 39201	800-504-7529
TENNESSEE TOMBIGBEE WATERWAY; 518 2nd Ave. N; Columbus	800-457-9739

State & Federal Government Phone Numbers

Federal Government Toll-Free Phone Numbers

ADMINISTRATION ON AGING; Free legal advice for elderly age 60 or over, regardless of income	888-660-0008
CENTER FOR FOOD SAFETY AND NUTRITION	800-332-4010
CONSUMER PRODUCT SAFETY COMMISSION	800-638-2772
DEPT. OF HOUSING & URBAN DEVELOPMENT (HUD); Housing Discrimination & Information	800-669-9777
EQUAL EMPLOYMENT OPPORTUNITY COMMISSION	800-669-3362
FEDERAL TRADE COMMISSION; to report a consumer fraud complaint: (877) FTC-HELP	877-382-4357
FEDERAL TRADE COMMISSION — ID Theft Hotline	877-438-4338
GENERAL SERVICES ADMINISTRATION; Ofc Inspector Gen; Fraud, Waste & Abuse	800-424-5210
INTERNAL REVENUE SERVICE, Tape Recorded Tax Information	800-829-4477
INTERNAL REVENUE SERVICE, Federal Tax Forms Only	800-829-3676
INTERNAL REVENUE SERVICE, Federal Tax Info, Assistance & Problem Resolution	800-829-1040
INTERNAL REVENUE SERVICE, Tax Assistance For The Deaf (TDD)	800-829-4059
MEDICARE FRAUD HOTLINE, U.S. Dept. of Health & Human Services (business hrs, Mon-Fri)	800-447-8477
NATIONAL FRAUD INFORMATION.CTR, NAT'L. CONSUMERS LEAGUE; Washington, DC	800-876-7060
World Wide Web — www.fraud.org	
SOCIAL SECURITY ADMINISTRATION; McCoy Federal Bldg; Jackson	800-772-1213
SOCIAL SECURITY ADMINISTRATION — Fraud Hotline	800-269-0271
SOCIAL SECURITY EARNINGS/BENEFITS ESTIMATE REQUEST APPLICATION	800-772-1213
TRANSPORTATION DEPT, FAA, Pilot Weather Briefing/Flight Planning	800-962-2318
US NAVY FAMILY SERVICE CENTER; Bldg 29; Gulfport	800-342-3525
U.S.D.A. MEAT AND POULTRY HOTLINE	800-535-4555
U.S. POSTAL SERVICE; Express Mail Info & Pickup Service	800-222-1811
UNITED STATES GOVERNMENT; Federal Information Center	800-688-9889
VETERANS ADMINISTRATION MEDICAL CENTER (G.V. "SONNY' MONTGOMERY); 1500 E Woodrow Wilson Dr; Jackson (automated phone service)	800-949-1009
VETERANS AFFAIRS DEPARTMENT; Inspector General Complaint Center	800-368-5899
VETERANS AFFAIRS DEPARTMENT/VA MEDICAL CENTERS; Nationwide Hotline	800-827-1000

Other Federal Government Phone Numbers (Toll Calls)

DEPARTMENT OF AGRICULTURE; A S C S State Office; 6310 I-55N; Jackson	(601) 965-4300
DEPARTMENT OF AGRICULTURE; Agricultural Marketing Service; Poultry Division	(601) 965-4664
DEPARTMENT OF AGRICULTURE; Federal Crop Insurance Corporation	(601) 965-4328
DEPARTMENT OF AGRICULTURE; Forest Service; Soil Conservation Service	(601) 965-4559
DEPARTMENT OF AGRICULTURE; Nat'l Agricultural Statistics Service-State Statistician: Jackson	(601) 965-4575
DEPARTMENT OF AGRICULTURE; National Forests in Mississippi; Supervisor's Office	(601) 965-4391
DEPARTMENT OF AGRICULTURE; Soil Conservation Service	(601) 965-5205
DEPARTMENT OF AGRICULTURE; Veterinary Services, Jackson Area Ofc; 345 Keyway St; Flowood	(601) 965-4307
DEPARTMENT OF DEFENSE; Contract Audit Agency; Federal Bldg; Jackson	(601) 965-5710
DEPARTMENT OF HOUSING & URBAN DEVELOPMENT (HUD); Jackson	(601) 965-4752
DEPARTMENT OF TRANSPORTATION, FAA; Hawkins Field Airport Control Tower; Jackson	(601) 965-5790
DEPARTMENT OF VETERANS AFFAIRS; VA Medical Center; 1500 E Woodrow Wilson Dr; Jackson	(601) 362-4471
FARMERS HOME ADMINISTRATION; 100 W Capitol St; Fed'l Bldg, Suite 831; Jackson	(601) 965-4318
FEDERAL BUREAU OF INVESTIGATION; 100 W Capitol; Fed'l Bldg, Suite 1553; Jackson	(601) 948-5000
FEDERAL DEPOSIT INSURANCE CORPORATION; 118 Patton Dr; Pearl	(601) 932-6744
FOOD AND DRUG ADMINISTRATION; Federal Bldg; Jackson	(601) 965-4581
GENERAL SERVICES ADMINISTRATION; Federal Protective Service; Federal Bldg; Jackson	(601) 965-4452
INTERIOR DEPARTMENT; Bureau of Land Management; 411 Briarwood Dr; Jackson	(601) 977-5400
INTERIOR DEPARTMENT; Fish & Wildlife Service; 6578 Dogwood View Parkway; Jackson	(601) 965-4900
INTERIOR DEPARTMENT; National Park Service; Natchez Trace Parkway; Ridgeland	(601) 856-7321
NATIONAL WEATHER SERVICE; Administration, weather info, to report severe weather; Jackson	(601) 936-2189
PROBATION & PAROLE; 234 E Capitol St; Jackson	(601) 965-4447
RAILROAD RETIREMENT BOARD; Federal Bldg; Jackson	(601) 965-4229
SMALL BUSINESS ADMINISTRATION; 101 W Capitol, Suite 400; Jackson 39201	(601) 965-4378
SOCIAL SECURITY ADMINISTRATION	(601) 965-5001
World Wide Web — www.ssa.gov/atlanta/ms/offices/0641.htm	
TREASURY DEPARTMENT, ALCOHOL, TOBACCO & FIREARMS DIVISION; Enforcement; Jackson	(601) 965-4205
TREASURY DEPARTMENT, SECRET SERVICE; 100 W Capitol; Jackson	(601) 965-4436
U.S. BANKRUPTCY COURT CLERK; 100 E Capitol; Jackson	(601) 965-5301
U.S. DISTRICT COURT-SOUTHERN DISTRICT OF MISSISSIPPI; 245 E Capitol; Jackson	(601) 965-4439
U.S. POSTAL SERVICE, PASSPORT INFORMATION; Jackson	(601) 968-1614

The Ultimate Reference on the State

Assorted Mississippi Associations/Organizations

BUSINESS & TRADE ASSOCIATIONS

American Pulpwood Association; 606 Hwy 80W; Clinton 39056	(601) 924-1830
American Subcontractors Association Of Mississippi; 741 Harris; Jackson	(601) 352-9273
Catfish Farmers of America; 1100 Hwy 82E; Indianola 38751	(662) 887-2699
Home Builders Association of Mississippi; 6531 Dogwood View Parkway; Jackson	(601) 969-3446
Mississippi Asphalt Pavement Association; 711 N President; Jackson	(601) 948-5495
Mississippi Associated Builders & Contractors; 805 E River Place; Jackson	(601) 944-0421
Mississippi Association of Convenience Stores; 808 N President St; Jackson	(601) 353-5559
Mississippi Association of Cooperatives; 233 E. Hamilton; Jackson 39202	(601) 354-2750
Mississippi Association of Life Underwriters; 5475 Executive Place; Jackson	(601) 981-1522
Mississippi Association of Realtors Inc; 555 Park Dr; Flowood 39208	(601) 932-5241
Mississippi Automobile Dealers Association; 800 Woodlands Pkwy; Jackson	(601) 948-6868
Mississippi Automotive Wholesalers Association; 4500 I-55N; Jackson 39211	(601) 981-8150
Mississippi Bankers Association; 640 N State St; Jackson 39202	(601) 948-6366
Mississippi Cattlemen Association; 680 Monroe St; Jackson 39202	(601) 354-8957
Mississippi Concrete Industries Association; 6700 Old Canton Rd; Jackson	(601) 957-5274
Mississippi Consumer Finance Association; 15 Northtown Dr; Jackson 39211	(601) 956-0117
Mississippi Credit Union System; 1400 Lakeover Rd; Jackson 39213	(601) 981-4552
Mississippi Hospitality/Beverage Association; 1009 N West St; Jackson	(601) 352-4528
Mississippi Hotel & Motel Association; 5135 Galaxie Dr; Jackson 39206	(601) 981-1160
Mississippi Independent Auto Dealers; 6649 Richmond Grove Rd; Jackson	(601) 957-1010
Mississippi Insurance Underwriting Association; 2685 Insurance Center Dr; Jackson	(601) 981-2915
Mississippi League of Savings Institutions; 720 N President St, Jackson	(601) 354-4431
Mississippi Loggers Association; 104 Artsian Place; Quitman 39355	(601) 776-5754
Mississippi Lumber Manufacturers Association; 490 E Woodrow Wilson; Jackson	(601) 982-1731
Mississippi Malt Beverage Association; 4785 I-55N; Jackson 39206	(601) 987-9098
Mississippi Manufactured Housing Association; 320-A Edgewood Terrace Dr; Jackson	(601) 981-3916
Mississippi Manufacturers Association; 720 N President St; Jackson 39202	(601) 948-1222
Mississippi Natural Gas Association; 452Luckney Rd; Flowood 39208	(601) 992-6006
Mississippi Pawnbrokers Association; 1500-B Terry Rd; Jackson 39204	(601) 352-9192
Mississippi Pest Control Association; 220 Office Park Plaza; Jackson 39206	(601) 982-3385
Mississippi Petroleum Marketers Association; 808 N President St; Jackson	(601) 353-1624
Mississippi Poultry Association; 720 N President; Jackson 39202	(601) 355-0248
Mississippi Quarter Horse Association; 206 Main; Tupelo 38801	(662) 844-4988
Mississippi Railroad Association; 814 N President St; Jackson 39202	(601) 948-3514
Mississippi Restaurant Association; 4506 Office Park Dr; Jackson 39206	(601) 982-4281
Mississippi Road Builders Association; 601 George St; Jackson 39202	(601) 948-8825
Mississippi Soft Drink Association; 3000 N State; Jackson 39216	(601) 982-3332
Mississippi Trucking Association; 767 N President St; Jackson 39202	(601) 354-0616
Miss. Water Resources Assn; PO Box 4200; Jackson 39296 (E-mail: insightltd@email.msn.com)	(601) 355-8538
National Cosmetology of Mississippi Inc; 806 E Fortification; Jackson 39202	(601) 948-5434
National Cutting Horse Association; 1207 Mississippi; Jackson 39202	(601) 948-2000
National Federation of Independent Business; 620 N State; Jackson 39202	(601) 355-6696
Retail Association of Mississippi; 4785 I-55N; Jackson 39206	(601) 362-8900

EDUCATION ASSOCIATIONS

Mississippi American Federation of Teachers; 1140 Pass Rd; Gulfport	(228) 868-1397
Mississippi American Federation of Teachers; 218 S State; Jackson 39201	(601) 352-7613
Mississippi Association of Educators; 775 N State St; Jackson 39202	(601) 354-4463
Mississippi Association of Independent Colleges; Clinton 39056	(601) 925-3400
Mississippi Community College Association; 704 N President; Jackson	(601) 969-7694
Mississippi Community College Foundation; 5935 Hwy 18W; Jackson	(601) 982-0308
Mississippi Congress of Parents & Teachers; 400 E South St; Jackson	(601) 352-7383
Mississippi High School Activities Association; 1201 Clinton-Raymond Rd; Clinton	(601) 924-6400
Mississippi Private School Association; 5727 Country Cork Rd; Jackson 39206	(601) 956-6872
Mississippi Professional Educators; 629 N Jefferson St; Jackson 39202	(601) 355-5517
Mississippi School Boards Association; 489A Springridge Rd; Clinton 39056	(601) 924-2001

POLITICAL PARTIES

Mississippi Democratic Party Headquarters; 832 N Congress St; Jackson 39202	(601) 969-2913
Mississippi Republican Party Headquarters; 555 Tombigbee St; Jackson 39201	(601) 948-5191

Assorted Mississippi Associations/Organizations

PROFESSIONAL ASSOCIATIONS

American Civil Liberties Union Of Mississippi; 921 N Congress; Jackson	(601) 355-6464
American Institute of Architects, Mississippi. Chapter; 812 N President; Jackson	(601) 948-6735
American Society of Plastic And Reconstructive Surgeons; Jackson	(601) 969-9050
Clinical Psychology & Psychiatry Association; Highland Village, Ste 234; Jackson	(601) 982-8531
Independent Nursing Home Association; 620 N State St; Jackson 39202	(601) 355-5445
Jackson Police Officers Association; 116 Claiborne Ave; Jackson 39209	(601) 353-1946
Mississippi Academy of Family Physicians; 4800 McWillie Cr; Jackson	(601) 981-0774
Mississippi Academy of Sciences; 405 Briarwood Dr; Jackson 39206	(601) 977-0627
Mississippi Association for Home Care; 840 East River Pl; Jackson 39202	(601) 355-8900
Mississippi Association of Alcohol & Drug Abuse Counselors; Jackson	(601) 982-4009
Mississippi Association of Broadcasters; 15 Northtown Dr; Jackson	(601) 957-9121
Mississippi Association of Chiefs Of Police; 937 Madison Ave; Madison	(601) 853-1289
Mississippi Association of Coaches; 505 E Main St; Raymond 39154	(601) 857-9926
Mississippi Association of Supervisors; 793 N President; Jackson 39202	(601) 353-2741
Mississippi Dental Association; 2630 Ridgewood Rd; Jackson 39216	(601) 982-0442
Mississippi Engineering Society; 5425 Executive Place; Jackson 39206	(601) 366-1312
Mississippi Forestry Association; 620 N State; Jackson 39202	(601) 354-4936
Mississippi Funeral Directors Association; Jackson	(601) 969-6789
Mississippi Hospital Association; 6425 Lakeover Rd; Jackson 39213	(601) 982-3251
Mississippi Medical Association; 735 Riverside Dr; Jackson 39202	(601) 354-5433
Mississippi Municipal Association; 200 N State St; Jackson 39201	(601) 353-5854
Mississippi Nurses' Association; 135 Bounds St; Jackson 39206	(601) 982-9182
Mississippi Optometric Association; 5420 I-55N; Jackson 39211	(601) 956-7412
Mississippi Pharmacists Association; 341 Edgewood Terrace Dr; Jackson	(601) 981-0416
Mississippi Press Association; 351 Edgewood Terrace Dr; Jackson 39206	(601) 981-3060
Mississippi Society of Certified Public Accountants; 4500 I-55N; Jackson	(601) 366-3473
Mississippi State Bar; 643 N State St; Jackson 39202	(601) 948-4471
Mississippi Trial Lawyers Association; 727 N Congress St; Jackson 39202	(601) 948-8631
National Association of Accountants; Jackson	(601) 960-4832
National Association of Social Workers, Mississippi Chapter; 2906 N State; Jackson	(601) 981-8359
State Employee Association of Mississippi; 455 N Lamar St; Jackson 39202	(601) 353-3844

MISCELLANEOUS ASSOCIATIONS & ORGANIZATIONS

Arts Alliance of Jackson & Hinds County Hotline	1-800-667-4977 or (601) 948-8643
Better Business Bureau of Mississippi; Jackson (www.bbbmississippi.org)	(601) 987-8282
Homework Hot Line; Jackson	(800) 888-5331
City of Jackson Mayor's Action Line	(601) 960-1111
Junior Chamber of Commerce; 201 S President St; Jackson 39201	(601) 969-7689
Junior League of Jackson; 805 Riverside Dr; Jackson 39202	(601) 948-2357
Mississippi Animal Rescue League; 4395 South Dr; Jackson 39209	(601) 969-1631
Mississippi Federation of Women's Clubs; 2407 N State St; Jackson	(601) 366-2652
Mississippi Jaycees; 4833 Jaycee Dr; Meridian 39301	(601) 483-2221
Mississippi Nature Conservancy; 809 N President St; Jackson 39202	(601) 355-5357
National Association of Junior Auxiliaries; 845 S Main St; Greenville	(662) 332-3000
Volunteer Resource Center; 843 N President St; Jackson 39202	(601) 354-1765

THE THREE MAJOR NATIONAL CREDIT BUREAUS:

Equifax	(800) 525-6285
Experian	(800) 301-7195
Trans Union	(800) 680-7289

Economy of Mississippi

INCOME

Total Personal Income: 1999 — $56,773,382,000 (**$20,506 Income Per Capita** - U.S. $28,518)
1998 — $54,410,139,000 (**$19,776 Income Per Capita** - U.S. $27,203)
$22,980 metropolitan; $17,985 nonmetropolitan
$35,688,337,000 Net Earnings ($12,971 per capita)
$10,306,970,000 Transfer Payments ($3,746 per capita)
$ 8,414,832,000 Dividends, Interest, & Rent ($3,058 per capita)

> The Bureau of Economic Analysis found Mississippi's per capita income growth rate of 79% from 1986 to 1996 to be among the highest in the nation.

Earnings in Mississippi, 1998: $36,726,408,000 Total
$28,590,982,000 Wages & Salaries
$ 4,011,895,000 Other Labor Income
$ 4,123,531,000 Proprietors Income

> 84 companies from 18 foreign countries had 144 businesses in the state during 1997 and contributed about $800 million to the state's economy. Of the 82 Mississippi counties, 45 of them had at least one foreign-owned business.

Wages & Salaries: 1997 — $26,657,297,000   1996 — $25,139,336,000
Transfer Payments: 1997 — $10,146,989,000   1996 — $ 9,696,280,000
Farm Income: 1998 — $ 839,778,000   1997 — $ 828,297,000

Selected Components of Government Transfer Payments, 1998:
$3,831,003,000 Retirement & Disability Insurance Payments
$3,966,619,000 Med'l. Payments ($2,201,037,000 Medicare; $1,741,379,000 pub. assist. med'l.)
$1,404,265,000 Income Maintenance Benefit Payments ($527,872,000 SSI; $59,185,000 family assistance; $246,450,000 food stamps; $570,758,000 other)

Total Disposable Personal Income: 1999 — $50,503,749,000 (**$18,241 Per Capita** - U.S. $24,297)
1998 — $48,524,989,000 (**$17,637 Per Capita** - U.S. $23,238)
1997 — $46,205,009,000 (**$16,914 Per Capita** - U.S. $22,312)

Median Household Income: 1999 — $32,540 (U.S. $40,800)   **Avg. Household Income, 1998:** $55,928
Below Poverty Level: 1999—16.9%; '98—17.1%; '97—18.6% (poverty threshold family of 4: $16,400)

GENERAL BUSINESS

Banks, 6/30/1999: 109 banks with assets of $29,410,751,000 and deposits of $26,554,679,000.
Insurance Companies, 1998: More than 1,700 companies licensed in Mississippi with $4,877,250,257 direct premiums written and $3,526,241,675 direct losses paid (664 life, health and accident companies — $2,351,293,707 premiums written and $1,618,059,228 direct losses paid; 787 fire and casuality companies — $2,361,111,676 premiums written and $1,752,180,849 losses paid).

Gross State Product, 1999:

$64,007,000,000 **Total** (Projected 2000: $66.488 billion)
14,456,000,000 Manufacturing
2,628,000,000 Contract Construction
460,000,000 Mining
6,775,000,000 Transportation, Communications, Utilities
9,982,000,000 Wholesale & Retail Trade
7,555,000,000 Finance, Insurance & Real Estate
10,805,000,000 Services
1,524,000,000 Farm
359,000,000 Ag Services, Forestry & Fisheries
$ 9,464,000,000 Government

> All GSP figures are preliminary estimates in current dollars.

TOP MANUFACTURING EMPLOYERS IN MISSISSIPPI
JANUARY 2000
1. Ingalls Shipbuilding, Pascagoula   11,000
2. Friede Goldman Halter,   "   8,000
3. Howard Industries, Laurel   4,000
4. Heatcraft Inc., Grenada   2,700
5. Bryan Foods, West Point   2,500
SOURCE: Mississippi Manufacturers Directory

Total Retail Sales: Year Ending 6/30/1999 — $34,030,579,307
Year Ending 6/30/1998 — $31,272,146,307
Total Businesses, 1998: 51,500 with employees + 95,000 self-employed persons = 146,500
1996: 48,300 firms employed 883,300 and had receipts of $116 billion.
New Businesses: 1999 — 1,205   1998 — 1,347 (+15%, the greatest rate increase in the U.S.)
Jobs Created by New Businesses: 1999 — 6,391   1998 — 8,197 (+23.1%, greatest rate increase in U.S.)
Shopping Centers/Malls, 1999: $787 million in sales taxes, $11.2 billion in sales, 117,900 employees.
1998: 433 with 42 million sq. ft., $10.5 billion in sales, 112,700 employees.
Three Mississippi malls exceeded the national average of $308 per square foot in sales in 1998. Northpark Mall in Ridgeland (958,183 sq. ft.) and the Mall at Barnes Crossing in Tupelo (909,655 sq. ft.) each had $345 in sales per sq. ft., and Edgewater Mall in Biloxi (900,000 sq. ft) reported $310 in sales per sq. foot.

Tourism: Tourism is the state's 2nd largest industry after health care in the service sector of Mississippi, producing $5.1 billion in FY 1998, up from $4.8 billion in FY 1997. Tourism accounted for 86,000 jobs in FY 1998 compared to 79,000 jobs in FY 1997.

Economy of Mississippi

TAXES

Total Mississippi Tax Commission Receipts, FY Ending 6/30/99: $4,900,005,896
Assessed Value of All Property, 1999: Real — $7,651,259,695   Personal — $5,635,442,552
Assessed Value of All Real Property, 1998: $7,304,229,113 (true value of $59,367,865,756)
Assessed Value of All Personal Property, 1998: $5,241,720,774 (true value of $25,997,396,671)
Sales Tax Collected by Mississippi, FY 1999: $1,988,088,523
State Income Tax Rate for Individuals: 1st $5,000 — 3%; Next $5,000 — 4%; Over $10,000 — 5%
Individual State Income Tax Collected By Mississippi, FY 1999: $128,248,661
Personal Gross Income Taxes, FY 1999: $774,310,864 ($279.67 per capita)
    996,767 Mississippi residents with **net taxable income of $16,121,079,879**
Corporate Taxes Collected By Mississippi, FY 1999: $330,158,582
Corporate State Income/Franchise Taxes Paid, FY 1999: $281,189,126
    Paid by 57,294 corporate taxpayers — 19,532 from out-of-state

> The true value of all real and personal property in Mississippi in 1998 was **$85,365,262,427!**

Total State: Revenue, FY '97 — $9.4 billion   Expenditures, FY '97 — $9.006 billion ($3,298 p/cap.)
Total State Debt, FY 1997: $2,455,000,000 ($899 per capita)
Fed'l. Spending, '97: $5.871 billion   **Fed'l. Taxes, '97**: $3.637 billion

> The state budget for FY 2001 is $3.6 billion, up from $3.5 billion for FY 2000.

Individual Income Taxes & Social Security Taxes Paid to the IRS, 1998: $6,452,000,000
Mississippi's Proportionate Share of the National Debt:
   00:00:01 EST on 1/1/2000: $58,541,224,770 (1.014% of total National debt $5,776,091,314,225.33)
   00:00:01 EST on 9/1/2000: $57,421,317,830 ($20,562 p/Capita) Nat'l. debt $5,677,822,307,077.83

CONSTRUCTION

New Housing Starts, 1999: 14,500 (11,000 single-family units)
                    1998: 12,880 single & multi-family units ($890 million)
                    1997: 10,282 single & multi-family units ($716 million)
Construction, Nonresidential: 1998 $1,245,000,000   1997 $1,038,000,000
            Residential: 1999 $ 922,600,000   1998 $1,101,000,000

> Mississippi had the fastest growth in the Southeast in the number of single-family building permits issued in the first quarter of 1999 — 10,384 — up 32% from 7,870 in the first quarter of 1998.

Total Value of Construction (including non-building), 1998: $3.291 billion
Income from Construction, 1995: $1,853,231,000 (direct $1,031,866,000 indirect $821,365,000)

LABOR

Principal Manufactured Goods: chemicals & plastics, food & kindred products, furniture, lumber & wood products, electrical machinery, transportation equipment.
Manufacturing Avg. Weekly Earnings: 1999 — $461.73   1998 — $444.22   1997 — $432.02
        Avg. Hourly Earnings: 1999 — $11.18   1998 — $10.73   1997 — $10.41
Hourly Wages, 1997: $5.15 or less (13.8%); $5.16-7.79 (26.6%); $7.80-9.99 (15.6%); $10.00+ (43.9%).
Avg. Earnings per Job: 1998 — $25,108 (wages/salaries $23,203; nonfarm proprietors' inc. $18,558)
                1997 — $24,114 (wages/salaries $22,141; nonfarm proprietors' inc. $17,987)
Largest Non-Government Employer, 1/1/2000: Pascagoula-based shipbuilder Ingalls w/11,500.
   Litton Industries, parent company of Ingalls Shipyard, received $1,602,659,000 in defense contracts in FY 1997.
Employment Distribution, May 1999: 23.2% services; 21.8% trade; 21.1 mfg.; 19.9% government
Manufacturing, 1999: 3,930 firms with 266,561 employees   **No. of Union Members, 1998**: 61,200
Employees in Nonfarm Establishments, April 2000 (in thousands): Construction 53.5; Manufacturing 244.1; Transportation & Public Utilities 57; Wholesale & Retail Trade 248.6; Finance, Insurance & Real Estate 42; Services 273.2; Government 233.9; TOTAL 1,158 (1,158,000).
Total Civilian Labor Force, 1999: Year — 1,270,000   Nov. — 1,289,700   Dec. — 1,305,400
    2000: Feb. — 1,307,400   Mar. — 1,312,800   Apr. — 1,306,700   July — 1,339,000
    1997 — 1,262,300 (men 662,200; women 600,100 — white 818,000; black 429,000)
Employment, 2000: Feb. — 1,235,600   Mar. — 1,238,000   Apr. — 1,243,400   July — 1,260,400
Employment, Annual Average: 1999 — 1,205,300   1998 — 1,199,200   1997 — 1,189,800
Average Unemployment & Rate, 1999: 64,700 (5.1%, rank 40)
Unemployment Rate: July 2000 — 5.9%   July 1999 — 5.3%
Number Unemployed: July 2000 — 78,600   July 1999 — 67,400

> Mississippi had the fastest-growing median wage in the nation from 1989 to 1998! The median hourly wage was $10 in 1998, up 17.92% from $8.48 in 1989.

Unemployment Insurance Benefit Payments, 1998: $116,661,000
Workers' Compensation, 1998: 16,235 claims filed. Total of $234,700,133 paid to claimants.

Economy of Mississippi

No. Workers in State Government: April 2000 — 62,100 **1999** — 59,900 **1998** — 58,800
No. Federal Government Employees: April 2000 — 25,700 **1999** — 26,100 **1998** — 26,200
Main Federal Facilities: Columbus Air Force Base; John C. Stennis Space Center, Hancock County; Keesler Air Force Base, Biloxi; Meridian Naval Air Station; Pascagoula Naval Home Port; U.S. Army Corps of Engineers Waterway Experiment Station, Vicksburg; and the Federal Correctional Facility in Yazoo City. (Keesler AF Base, with 12,055 military & 3,600 civilians, boosted the Miss. Gulf Coast economy by a record $1.4 billion in FY ending 9/30/1999.)
Military Bases, 1997: 45,536 (19,394 active duty, 18,301 family members & 7,841 civilian workers.)
Military Contracts: FY 2000 — $3,170,000,000   1996 — $1,912,000,000 (payroll $1.3 billion)

ANNUAL EMPLOYMENT AVERAGES BY SECTOR IN MISSISSIPPI (IN THOUSANDS)

Sector	1999	1998	Sector	1999	1998
Mining (incl. Oil & Gas Extraction)	5.2	6.3	Service Producing Industries	849.0	827.5
Construction	55.7	54.4	Transportation & Utilities	55.5	53.8
Total Manufacturing	244.9	245.5	Transportation	33.9	32.9
Durable Goods Mfg.	153.3	151.6	Communications	11.6	11.3
Lumber & Wood Products	26.2	27.8	Total Trade	252.4	245.2
Furniture & Fixtures	30.6	28.0	Wholesale Trade	46.9	47.5
Stone, Clay & Glass	6.2	5.9	Retail Trade	205.5	197.7
Metal Products	17.8	18.4	Finance, Insurance, Real Estate	42.4	42.5
Industrial Machinery	19.1	18.7	Banks & Credit Institutions	21.4	21.7
Electronic Equipment	22.0	22.0	Insurance	12.5	12.6
Transportation Equipment	26.4	26.1	Services	269.9	262.6
Nondurable Goods Mfg.	91.6	93.9	Hotels & Lodging	33.4	27.9
Food & Kindred Products	29.7	29.0	Amusements (incl. movies)	26.1	26.2
Textile Mill Products	4.6	4.7	Health Services	75.9	76.7
Apparel	17.6	21.1	Total Government	228.9	223.4
Paper & Allied Products	8.7	9.0	Federal Government	26.1	26.2
Printing & Publishing	8.0	7.9	State & local government	202.8	197.3
Chemicals & Allied Products	7.5	7.4	State government	59.9	58.1
Petroleum & Coal	2.5	2.3	Local government	142.9	139.2
Rubber & Plastics	12.9	12.2	**Total Nonfarm Employment**	1,154.8	1,133.7

SOURCE: Mississippi Employment Security Commission. 1998 figures are benchmarked to 1999.

SELECTED MISSISSIPPI ECONOMIC INDICATORS

	JUNE 2000	JUNE 1999	% CHANGE
Coincident Indicator Index	106.1	106.1	0.0
Nonagricultural Employment (thousands)	1,150.7	1,156.3	-0.5
Merchandise Retail Sales (millions of 1982-84 dollars)	246.3	259.6	-5.1
Leading Indicator Index	102.4	102.4	0.0
Manufacturing Employment (thousands)	241.7	244.9	-1.3
Service Sector Employment (thousands)	270.2	269.9	0.1
Value of Building Permits (thousands of 1982-84 $)	43,340.5	50,089.3	-13.5
Initial Unemployment Claims (thousands)	12.0	13.5	-11.1
Length of Average Workweek (hours)	40.9	41.3	-1.0
Miscellaneous—Consumer Price Index, U.S. (1982-84 = 100)	172.3	166.2	3.7
Unemployment Rate (percentage, non-seasonably adjusted)	6.9	6.1	13.1
Unemployment Rate (percentage)	6.1	5.1	19.6
Continued Unemployment Claims	75,874	85,636	-11.4
Average Manufacturing Wage (dollars per hour)	11.61	11.10	4.6
Total Retail Sales (millions of current $)	2,839.6	2,895.6	-1.9
Morgage Rates (30 year conventional)	8.29	7.55	9.8

Note: The data are seasonally adjusted unless otherwise noted. The information for the Economic Indicators and some other data in this chapter, courtesy of the Mississippi Institutions of Higher Learning, Center for Policy Research and Planning, Jackson, Mississippi.

Economy of Mississippi

ENERGY & ENVIRONMENT

Nonfuel Minerals: 1998 — $190 million (sand & gravel, portland cement, clays and crushed stone)
  1997 — $175 million   1996 — $144 million   1995 — $131 million
Crude Petroleum Production (millions of barrels):   1997 — 21 (value $356 million)
  1995 — 20 (value $294 million)   1990 — 30 (value $630 million)
Natural Gas Marketed Production, 1997: 107 billion cubic feet (value $186 million)
Gas Utility Industry, 1997:   Customers — 396,000 residential; 442,000 total
  Sales (trillions of Btu) — 27 residential, 78 total
  Revenues — $166 million residential; $370 million total
Electric Energy Production, 1998: 31,900,000,000 kWh **total all sources**
  11,700,000,000 kWh from coal (36.7%)   9,200,000,000 kWh from nuclear energy (28.8%)
  5,600,000,000 kWh from natural gas (17.6%)   5,400,000,000 kWh from petroleum (16.9%)
Electric Energy Sales, 1998: 40.1 bil. kWh (14.8 residential, 36.9%; 10.0 commercial, 24.9%; 14.6 industrial, 36.4%)
Average Cost of Electricity, 1998: 5.98 cents per kWh (all residential, commercial & industrial users)
Nuclear Power Plants: One — Grand Gulf in Claiborne Co. near Port Gibson (capacity 7.2 mil. kW).
Total Energy Consumption (trillions of Btu): 1997 — 1,123.7 (rank 30)   1996 — 1,098.4
Energy Consumption Per Capita: 1997 — 411.3 million Btu (rank 14)   1996 — 405.3 million Btu
Total Energy Consumption, 1995: 1,058.8 trillion Btu (rank 29), 393.5 million Btu per capita.
Energy Expenditures (End-Use Sector), 1995 (millions of dollars): $5,325 ($1,979 per capita)
  $1,223 residential (23%); $692 commercial (13%); $1,182 industrial (22.2%); $2,228 transportation (41.8%)
Electric Power Associations of Mississippi:
  1. Alcorn County Electric Power Association - Corinth
  2. Central Electric Power Association - Carthage
  3. Coahoma Electric Power Association - Lyon
  4. Coast Electric Power Association - Bay St. Louis
  5. Delta Electric Power Association - Greenwood
  6. Dixie Electric Power Association - Laurel
  7. East Mississippi Electric Power Association - Meridian
  8. Four-County Electric Power Association - Columbus
  9. Magnolia Electric Power Association - McComb
  10. Monroe County Electric Power Association - Amory
  11. Natchez Trace Electric Power Association - Houston
  12. Northeast Mississippi Electric Power Association - Oxford
  13. North Central Mississippi Electric Power Association - Byhalia
  14. Pearl River Valley Electric Power Association - Columbia
  15. Pontotoc Electric Power Association - Pontotoc
  16. Prentiss County Electric Power Association - Booneville
  17. Singing River Electric Power Association - Lucedale
  18. Southern Pine Electric Power Association - Taylorsville
  19. Southwest Mississippi Electric Power Association - Lorman
  20. Tallahatchie Valley Electric Power Association - Batesville
  21. Pippah Electric Power Association - Ripley
  22. Tishomingo County Electric Power Association - Iuka
  23. Tombigbee Electric Power Association - Tupelo
  24. Twin County Electric Power Association - Hollandale
  25. Yazoo Valley Electric Power Association - Yazoo City

> As of Jan. 1, 2000, there were 10 new wholesale, gas-fired electric power plants in operation, under construction, or proposed for Mississippi.

> A report by the U.S. Census Bureau released June 29, 2000, showed that Mississippi led the nation in service industry job growth between 1992 and 1997 with a 66.9% increase in employment from 108,222 to 180,615 jobs and a 94.3% hike in receipts in the service sector, up from $5.5 billion to $10.7 billion. Mississippi's hotel/motel receipts grew from $235 million in 1992 to $1.34 billion in 1997, when the state's hotel industry was dominated by casino hotels.

> According to *Forbes* magazine, the Mississippi Gulf Coast and Jackson rank among the top 100 places in the nation to do business. The coast ranked No. 82 and Jackson ranked No. 85 in the article, which appeared in the May 29, 2000, edition. *Forbes* surveyed a total of 294 metropolitan areas, including 200 large and 94 small locales.

Daily Water Use (gallons), 1995: 3,204,000,000 (1,191 p/cap.) Ground Water 2,590m; Surface Water 614m
Selected Water Uses (millions of gallons p/day): Irrigation 1,740; Public Supply 377; Industrial 294; Thermoelectric 375; Consumptive Use 1,570
Number of Landfills, 1/1/1997: 18 (there were 120 operating in 1988)
Hazardous Waste Sites, 1998: 1 general Superfund site (2 proposed)
Toxic Chemicals Released, 1997: 64,639,656 pounds (EPA Toxic Release Inventory System - TRIS)
  Entergy and Mississippi Power released over 10 million pounds in 1998, well within EPA limits. These two state-regulated utilities provide electric service to about 45% of the state's population.

> Mississippi is 2nd only to Texas in the number of rural water systems with 1,268 systems serving 2.6 million residents.

The Ultimate Reference on the State

Economy of Mississippi

PORTS

Mississippi Manufacturing Exports (millions of dollars): 1998 — $2,348.3   1997 — $2,587.6

Busiest Port: Pascagoula handled 27.5 million tons in 1998 (31,270,055 tons 1997 — the 23th busiest U.S. port). The State Port at Gulfport handled 2,102,656 tons in 1998 and 2,448,429 tons valued at $1.156 billion in 1997. Biloxi handled 2,521,187 tons in 1997.

Cargo Handled by Major River Ports, 1997 (short tons): (49,775,000 at all river ports in Mississippi) Vicksburg — 5,627,234; Greenville — 2,808,368; Natchez — 628,000; Rosedale — 565,000
(MS has 16 river ports — 4 on the Gulf Coast, 6 on the Tenn-Tom, 5 on the Mississippi River & 1 in Yazoo City)

Total Mississippi River Cargo: 322.8 million short tons in 1998 and the same in 1997.

Tennessee-Tombigbee River Tonnage: 1998 — 9,313,514   1997 — 9,154,222   1996 — 8,931,466

Mississippi's Exports, 1996 - 1998			
	FOOD	NON-FOOD	TOTALS
1996	$727,571,944	$2,266,389,402	$2,993,961,346
1997	360,326,988	2,353,358,591	2,713,685,579
1998	71,973,229	2,470,236,270	2,542,209,499

Source: Mississippi Institutions of Higher Learning

Mississippi's Top 10 Export Markets, 1998*			
Canada	$492,760,000	Russia	$41,644,000
Mexico	242,408,000	Italy	41,591,000
Honduras	82,738,000	Belgium	28,823,000
Britain	70,359,000	Germany	26,145,000
Japan	44,266,000	Ireland	23,055,000

*Source: U.S. Census Bureau, Office of Trade and Economic Analysis, International Trade Administration, U.S. Dept. of Commerce.

MISCELLANEOUS

Timber/Lumber Harvested, 1998: 2.8 billion board feet (7.75 million cords of pulpwood in 1997).
Wildfires, FY 1999: 4,360 — 43,082 acres (Five-year average, FY '95-'99: 3,924 — 47,235 acres)
Commercial Fishing, 1998: $48,400,000
No. of Phone Lines, 1/1/2000: BellSouth has about 1.33 million lines (voice & data).
No. Bankruptcies Filed: 1999 — 17,750 (17,549 individuals and 201 businesses)
                              1998 — 18,700 (18,456 individuals and 244 businesses)
No. of U.S. Patents Granted to Mississippi Residents, 1997: 182 (156 inventions and 26 designs)
Percent of Households with Internet Access, Dec. 1998: 13.6%, lowest in the nation.

FORTUNE 500 COMPANIES WITH OPERATIONS IN MISSISSIPPI, 1999

Air Products & Chemicals	E.I. Dupont de Nemours	Owens Corning
Aluminum Company of America	Eaton Corporation	Parker Hannifin
Archer Daniels Midland	Emerson Electric	Pfizer, Inc.
Ashland, Inc.	Engelhard Corporation	Praxair, Inc.
Avery Dennison Corporation	FMC Corporation	Raytheon Company
Baker Hughes, Inc.	Farmland Industries, Inc.	Rohm and Haas
Baxter International, Inc.	Federal-Mogul Corporation	Sara Lee Corporation
Bethlehem Steel Corporation	Fleetwood Enterprises	Sherwin-Williams
Black & Decker Corporation	Fort James Corporation	Smurfit-Stone Container
The Boeing Company	Gannett Company	Temple-Inland, Inc.
Brunswick Corporation	General Electric Company	Tenneco, Inc.
Caterpillar, Inc.	General Motors Corporation	Textron, Inc.
Chevron Corporation	Georgia-Pacific Corporation	Tyson Foods, Inc.
Coca-Cola Enterprises	IMC Global, Inc.	U.S. Industries, Inc.
ConAgra, Inc.	ITT Industries	U.S. Office Products
Cooper Industries	Illinois Tool Works	USG Corporation
Crown Cork & Seal	International Paper	United Technologies
Dana Corporation	Kimberly-Clark	VF Corporation
Dean Foods, Inc.	Knight-Ridder, Inc.	Weyerhaeuser Corporation
R.R. Donnelley & Sons	Leggett & Platt	Whirlpool Corporation
Dover Corporation	Litton Industries, Inc.	WorldCom, Inc.
Dow Chemical	Lockheed Martin	York International

While WorldCom is the only Fortune 500 company headquartered in Mississippi, there were these 65 additional Fortune 500 companies with 183 plants in Mississippi in 1999. SOURCE: *FORTUNE* magazine, April 26, 1999.

Last minute BULLETIN as this book goes to press: Nissan Motor Company announces on Nov. 9, 2000, that it is going to build a $1 billion truck assembly plant in Madison County just south of Canton that will initially employ about 3,000 people and possibly as many as 4,000 workers.

Economy of Mississippi

Largest Publicly Traded Mississippi-Based Companies

Name of Firm	1999 Market* Capitalization	1998	1999	Change	July 14 2000	Oct. 11 2000	Change
WorldCom	$167,632,500,000	$47.83	$53.06	10.9%	$49.13	$25.75	-47.6%
Trustmark Corp.	1,665,262,500	22.19	21.61	-2.6%	19.56	18.06	-7.7%
Delta & Pine Land	1,147,781,250	36.84	17.31	-53.0%	26.69	25.69	-3.7%
BancorpSouth Inc.	1,018,500,000	17.53	16.19	-7.6%	14.94	14.25	-4.6%
Hancock Holding	474,150,000	44.43	38.75	-12.8%	31.75	30.75	-3.1%
ChemFirst Corporation	452,925,000	19.41	21.75	12.1%	23.88	19.31	-19.1%
Parkway Properties	338,017,500	29.35	28.75	-2.0%	32.56	29.19	-10.4%
EastGroup Properties	317,000,000	16.97	18.38	8.3%	22.13	21.56	-2.6%
Friede Goldman	295,425,000	11.38	6.88	-39.6%	8.13	6.63	-18.5%
Mississippi Chemical	267,525,000	13.50	6.00	-55.6%	4.25	3.63	-14.6%
Peoples Holding	197,693,125	31.44	28.88	-8.2%	19.88	20.25	1.9%
Isle of Capri Casinos	197,650,000	3.97	13.19	232.3%	14.56	13.44	-7.7%
Sanderson Farms Inc.	184,175,000	15.06	8.56	-43.1%	7.50	6.50	-13.3%
First M&F Corporation	128,310,000	34.87	30.00	-14.0%	21.00	17.25	-17.9%
Hancock Fabrics Inc.	91,918,750	7.83	3.13	-60.1%	4.25	4.50	5.9%
Callon Petroleum	91,378,125	11.63	14.81	27.4%	14.44	16.63	15.2%
Cal-Maine Foods	64,000,000	4.40	3.56	-19.1%	3.63	3.56	-1.9%

* Market capitalization = outstanding shares times per-share price on July 16, 1999.
** Stock prices adjusted for stock splits and dividends. Figures for 1998 and 1999 cover each entire calendar year.

Market Share for Top-10 Banks in Mississippi

	Market Share 1998	Market Share 1999	Deposits 6/30/99
Trustmark	14.4%	13.8%	$3.9 billion
Deposit Guaranty	13.7%	12.4%	$3.5 billion
BancorpSouth	11.3%	12.0%	$3.4 billion
Union Planters	10.2%	9.3%	$2.6 billion
Hancock Bank	5.6%	5.5%	$1.5 billion
Peoples Bank & Trust	3.2%	3.5%	$980 million
Community Bank	2.0%	2.4%	$682 million
Merchants & Farmers	2.1%	2.3%	$638 million
BankPlus	1.7%	2.1%	$597 million
Nat'l. Bank of Commerce	1.7%	1.9%	$543 million

SOURCE: Federal Deposit Insurance Corp.

As of June 30, 1999, a total of 109 Mississippi banks had $29,410,751,000 in assets and $26,554,679,000 in deposits. Mississippi banks employ about 14,000 Mississippians with an annual payroll of over half a billion dollars. Annually, they loan Mississippians more than $18 billion and they hold about $9 billion worth of public bonds. As of Jan. 1, 2000, a total of 110 Mississippi banks had 1,122 locations statewide (not counting ATMs). SOURCE: The State Dept. of Banking & Consumer Finance and the Miss. Bankers Association.

Between Sept. 1992 and Sept. 1998 (6 years), labor statistics showed that 154,100 new jobs were filled in Mississippi, a 15.9% increase in nonfarm employment, according to the Mississippi Employment Security Commission. The state Department of Economic and Community Development reported that during that time, companies announced plans to bring 170,000 new jobs and $16 billion in capital investment to Mississippi.

Manufactures Summary: 1996

No. of All Employees:	239,000
Total Payroll:	$5,654,000,000
Per Employee Average Wage:	$23,666 year
No. of Production Workers:	190,000
Total Wages:	$3,838,000,000
Average Hourly Earnings:	1996 — $10.18
	1997 — $10.41
	1998 — $10.72
Total Value Added:	$17,295,000,000
Per Production Worker:	$91,024
Value of All Shipments:	$39,564,000,000

Mississippi ranks 10th-best in the nation in terms of small businesses' chances for survival, according to a Washington, D.C. group. The Small Business Survival Committee released their Business Survival Index in May 1999. Here are some selected Miss. components:

Personal Income Tax:	5% (ties for 18th lowest)
Corporate Income Tax:	5% (ranks 9th)
Capital Gains Tax:	0% (ties for best in the nation with 10 other states)
Property Taxes:	$2.66 per $100 of personal income (ranks 13th)
General Sales Taxes:	$4.02 per $100 of personal income (ranks 44th)
Unemployment Taxes:	Ranks 14th
Health Ins. Tax Rate:	3% (ranks 44th)
Electric Utilities Tax:	0% (ranks best in the U.S.)
Workers' Comp.:	Ranks 12th
Crime Rate:	4.63 (ranks 25th)
Bureaucrats:	6.36 p/100 pop.(ranks 47th)
Right to Work State:	Positive (Miss. is one)

The Ultimate Reference on the State

Economy of Mississippi

PER CAPITA PERSONAL INCOME IN MISSISSIPPI COUNTIES BY RANKING, 1998

Rank	County	Income	Rank	County	Income	Rank	County	Income	Rank	County	Income
1.	Madison	$25,096	21.	Leake	$19,259	42.	Attala	$17,289	63.	Copiah	$15,555
2.	Rankin	24,646	22.	Union	19,166	43.	Humphreys	17,204	64.	Walthall	15,504
3.	DeSoto	24,616	23.	Grenada	19,103	44.	Tippah	17,202	65.	Prentiss	15,445
4.	Hinds	24,333	24.	Lafayette	19,034	45.	Wayne	17,032	66.	Panola	15,368
5.	Warren	23,967	25.	Newton	18,944	46.	Carroll	17,029	67.	Jeff. Davis	14,944
6.	Lee	23,486	26.	Tunica	18,857	47.	Yalobusha	17,026	68.	Benton	14,881
7.	Harrison	22,838	27.	Lamar	18,761	48.	Covington	16,885	69.	Wilkinson	14,647
8.	Lauderdale	21,456	28.	Simpson	18,489	49.	Coahoma	16,727	70.	Amite	14,622
9.	Jackson	21,170	29.	Lincoln	18,326	50.	Monroe	16,667	71.	Claiborne	14,501
10.	Tate	20,670	30.	Calhoun	18,159	51.	George	16,572	72.	Franklin	14,300
11.	Jones	20,598	31.	Leflore	17,915	52.	Montgomery	16,566	73.	Choctaw	14,063
12.	Lowndes	20,249	32.	Marshall	17,878	53.	Webster	16,502	74.	Quitman	13,980
13.	Neshoba	20,198	33.	Washington	17,863	54.	Bolivar	16,499	75.	Sunflower	13,884
14.	Smith	19,709	34.	Yazoo	17,847	55.	Kemper	16,460	76.	Perry	13,774
15.	Hancock	19,519	35.	Winston	17,746	56.	Pearl River	16,304	77.	Holmes	13,472
16.	Scott	19,503	36.	Pike	17,737	57.	Tishomingo	16,217	78.	Tallahatchie	13,223
17.	Itawamba	19,484	37.	Clay	17,735	58.	Marion	16,180	79.	Issaquena	12,859
18.	Adams	19,461	38.	Oktibbeha	17,728	59.	Clarke	16,013	80.	Greene	12,833
19.	Alcorn	19,372	39.	Chickasaw	17,435	60.	Stone	15,811	81.	Sharkey	12,734
20.	Forrest	19,313	40.	Lawrence	17,337	61.	Noxubee	15,809	82.	Jefferson	11,390
			41.	Pontotoc	17,333	62.	Jasper	15,687			

SOURCE: U.S. Bureau of Economic Analysis, released June 15, 2000

COST OF LIVING INDEX IN MISSISSIPPI COUNTIES, 1999

County	Index	County	Index	County	Index	County	Index
Adams	0.99	Greene	0.92	Leflore	0.97	Sharkey	0.84
Alcorn	1.00	Grenada	0.97	Lincoln	0.96	Simpson	1.00
Amite	0.91	Hancock	1.03	Lowndes	1.01	Smith	1.01
Attala	0.94	Harrison	1.09	Madison	1.14	Stone	0.98
Benton	0.93	Hinds	1.09	Marion	0.94	Sunflower	0.86
Bolivar	0.93	Holmes	0.90	Marshall	0.96	Tallahatchie	0.90
Calhoun	0.96	Humphreys	0.93	Monroe	0.96	Tate	1.04
Carroll	0.94	Issaquena	0.87	Montgomery	0.95	Tippah	0.98
Chickasaw	0.96	Itawamba	0.98	Neshoba	1.00	Tishomingo	0.96
Choctaw	0.91	Jackson	1.04	Newton	0.97	Tunica	0.95
Claiborne	0.89	Jasper	0.95	Noxubee	0.91	Union	1.02
Clarke	0.95	Jefferson	0.86	Oktibbeha	0.96	Walthall	0.91
Clay	0.95	Jefferson Davis	0.91	Panola	0.94	Warren	1.07
Coahoma	0.96	Jones	1.01	Pearl River	0.99	Washington	0.96
Copiah	0.95	Kemper	0.92	Perry	0.91	Wayne	0.96
Covington	0.98	Lafayette	0.99	Pike	0.96	Webster	0.94
DeSoto	1.22	Lamar	1.03	Pontotoc	0.99	Wilkinson	0.90
Forrest	1.02	Lauderdale	1.03	Prentiss	0.96	Winston	0.94
Franklin	0.92	Lawrence	0.95	Quitman	0.90	Yalobusha	0.98
George	0.97	Leake	0.96	Rankin	1.14	Yazoo	0.97
		Lee	1.08	Scott	0.98		

The average is 1.00. In 1999, it took $1.22 in DeSoto County (the highest) to buy the same goods and services that $0.84 would buy in Sharkey County (the lowest).

SOURCE: The Center for Policy Research and Planning; Jackson, Mississippi

Members of the Mississippi Business Hall of Fame (Through 2000)

NAME	COMPANY	HEADQUARTERS
J. Kelly Allgood (retired president)	BellSouth in Mississippi	Jackson
Hugh Coyt Bailey, Sr.	H. C. Bailey Companies	Madison
Charles D. Bannerman	The Delta Foundation, Inc.	Greenville
Edmund L. Brunini, Sr.	Brunini, Grantham, Grower & Hewes	Jackson
John H. Bryan*[1]	Bryan Foods/Sara Lee Corporation	West Point
Bobby L. Chain	Chain Electric Company	Hattiesburg
Lawrence Owen Cooper, Sr.*	Mississippi Chemical Corporation	Yazoo City
Alf F. Dantzler	Dantzler Boat and Barge Company	Pascagoula
Bernard J. Ebbers*	MCI WorldCom	Clinton
D. G. "Sonny" Fountain	Fountain Construction Company	Jackson
James E. Fowler, Sr.	Fowler Buick-GMC Truck	Jackson
J. Herman Hines	Deposit Guaranty Corporation	Jackson
W. Henry Holman, Jr.	Jitney-Jungle Stores of America, Inc.	Jackson
J. L. Holloway	Friede Goldman International	Jackson
Warren A. Hood	Hood Industries, Inc.	Hattiesburg
Billy & Linda Howard	Howard Industries, Inc.	Laurel
Dudley J. Hughes	Hughes-Rawls Corporation	Jackson
Alvis Hunt	Trustmark National Bank	Jackson
Stuart Chalmers Irby, Jr.	Irby Construction Companies	Jackson
Stuart Chalmers Irby, Sr.	Irby Construction Companies	Jackson
J. Con Maloney	Cowboy Maloney's Electric City	Jackson
Chief Phillip Martin*	Mississippi Band of Choctaw Indians	Philadelphia
H. F. McCarty, Jr.	McCarty Farms, Inc.	Jackson
Richard D. McRae, Sr.*	McRae's Department Stores	Jackson
Norman Crooks Nelson, M.D.	University of Miss. Medical Center	Jackson
John N. Palmer, Sr.*	Skytel, Inc.	Jackson
Aubrey Burns Patterson	Bank of Mississippi/BancorpSouth, Inc.	Tupelo
Hartley D. & Melia M. Peavey*	Peavey Electronics Corporation	Meridian
Jack R. Reed	Reed's (Department Store)	Tupelo
E. B. Robinson, Jr.	Deposit Guaranty Corporation	Jackson
Gerald J. St.Pè	Ingalls Shipbuilding of Litton Industries	Pascagoula
Joe Frank Sanderson, Sr.*	Sanderson Farms, Inc.	Laurel
Leo W. Seal, Jr.	Hancock Bank	Gulfport
Leland R. Speed	EastGroup and Parkway Properties	Jackson
W. A. "Bill" Taylor	Taylor Group, Inc.	Louisville
Sister Josephine Therese	St. Dominic Health Services, Inc.	Jackson
George F. Walker	Delta Wire, Inc.	Clarksdale
LeRoy Walker, Jr.	LTM Enterprises, Inc./McDonald's	Jackson
J. C. Whitehead	Bank of Mississippi/BancorpSouth, Inc.	Tupelo
J. Kelley Williams	ChemFirst, Inc.	Jackson
Lowery Woodall (retired exec. director)	Forrest General Hospital	Hattiesburg

The Mississippi Business Hall of Fame was established in 1989 to honor outstanding business leaders, past and present, for their significant contributions to the growth and development of business in the state. It is also intended to promote a better public understanding of the American business system and how it relates to our national prosperity and freedoms. The Mississippi Business Hall of Fame is a joint venture of Junior Achievement of Mississippi, Inc. and *The Clarion-Ledger* newspaper of Jackson.

Junior Achievement's Mission Statement: To educate and inspire young people to value free enterprise, and understand business and economics to improve the quality of their lives.

The information on this page courtesy of Junior Achievement of Mississippi, Inc.

[1] An asterisk (*) indicates that the person is profiled in the chapter "Profiles of Famous & Notable Mississippians."

The Ultimate Reference on the State

Health in Mississippi

Physicians, 8/1/2000: 8,076 (includes 2,509 from out-of-state licensed to practice in Mississippi)
   5,567 in Mississippi (199.3 per 100,000 people, or 1 doctor for every 502 people)
   White — 4,763; Black — 354; other — 450; Male — 4,683; Female — 884
Registered Nurses, 3/1/2000: 30,082 (1,083 per 100,000 people)
Licensed Practical Nurses, 3/1/2000: 11,884 (428 per 100,000 people)
Optometrists, 4/1/2000: 261 (9.4 per 100,000 people)
Psychologists, 3/1/99: 394 (14.2 per 100,000 people)
Therapists, 4/1/2000: Respiratory — 1,687 (61 per 100,000)
   Physical   — 1,199 (43 per 100,000)
Pharmacists (Registered), 3/1/2000: 2,499 (90 per 100,000 people)
Dentists (General & Specialists), 1/13/2000: 1,454 (52.4 per 100,000 people)
Number of Hospitals, 8/1/2000: 109 (3.9 per 100,000 people)
Hospital Beds, 8/1/2000 (State-licensed): 15,204 (544 per 100,000 people)
Hospital Beds Occupancy Rate, 1997: 62.6%
Patients Admitted: 1997—413,000 (8,100 avg. daily census)   1995—388,000 (7,600 avg. daily census)
Outpatient Visits: 1997 — 3.9 million   1995 — 3.2 million
Average Hospital Costs, 1997: $858.24 per day
Health Care Expenditures by State & Local Governments, 1996: $ 1,593,000,000
Medicare, 1998: $2,201,037,000 in medical cost payments were made on behalf of 408,000 enrollees.
Medicaid & Other Public Assistance Medical Care, 1998: $1,741,379,000 to over 500,000 people.
Medicaid Managed Care Enrollment, FY '97: 81,000 (15% of the total 544,000 Medicaid enrollment)
Total Live Births, 1998: 42,917 (68.2 p/1,000 females ages 15-44) White 22,950 Non-White 19,967
Birth Rate, 1998 (per 1,000 population): 15.59
Live Births to Unmarried Mothers, 1998: 19,500 (45.4% of all live births)
   White 4,680 (24%) 10.9% of all births   Non-White 14,820 (76%) 34.5% of all births
Live Births to Teenage Mothers, 1998: 8,598 (20.6% of all live births)
   White 3,235 (37.6%) 7.5% of all births   Non-White 5,363 (62.4%) 12.5% of all births
Total Live Births, 1997: 41,527 (66.1 p/1,000 females ages 15-44) White 22,021 Non-White 19,506
Birth Rate, 1997 (per 1,000 population): 15.4
Live Births to Unmarried Mothers, 1997: 18,853 (45.4% of all live births)
   White 4,317 (22.9%) 10.4% of all births   Non-White 14,536 (77.1%) 35.0% of all births
Live Births to Teenage Mothers, 1997: 8,575 (20.6% of all live births)
   White 3,098 (36.1%) 7.5% of all births   Non-White 5,477 (63.9%) 13.2% of all births
Total Live Births: **1996** — 40,978   **1995** — 41,332   **1994** — 41,938   **1993** — 42,134
Birth Rate (p/1,000 pop.):   **1996** — 15.2   **1995** — 15.3   **1994** — 16.3   **1993** — 16.4
Births to Teenage Mothers, 1996: 8,745 (21.3% of all live births)
Births to Unmarried Teenage Mothers, 1996: 7,068 (80.8% of births to teenage mothers)
Births to Unmarried Mothers, 1996: 18,458 (45.0% of all live births)
   White 3,995 (21.6% of births to unmarrieds) Non-White 14,463 (78.4% of births to unmarrieds)
Infant Mortality and Rate, 1998: 436 (10.2 per 1,000 live births)   White 146   Non-White 290
   1997: 440 (10.6 per 1,000)   White 156   Non-White 284
Low Birth Weight Babies, 1998: 4,346 (10.1% of all live births)   White 1,657   Non-White 2,689
   1997: 4,193 (10.1% of all live births)   White 1,621   Non-White 2,572
Premature Live Births, 1998:   6,614 (15.4% of all live births)   White 2,762   Non-White 3,852
   1997:   6,338 (15.3% of all live births)   White 2,549   Non-White 3,789
Abortions Performed: 1998 — 3,955   1997 — 4,325   1996 — 4,206   1995 — 3,563
   1994 — 3,979   1993 — 6,002   1992 — 7,555   1991 — 8,184
   1990 — 6,842   1989 — 5,490   1988 — 5,170   1987 — 5,469
Total Abortions Performed in Mississippi, 1987-1998 (12 Years): 64,740 (average of 5,395 per year)
Life Expectancy For Those Born in 1998 (Nationwide Figures in Years):
   White   — Female 79.9   Male 74.6   Both Sexes 77.3
   Black   — Female 75.0   Male 67.8   Both Sexes 71.5
   All Races — Female 79.4   Male 73.9   Both Sexes 76.7

SOURCES for this chapter: State Department of Health and other State & Federal Government Agencies.

Health in Mississippi

Deaths: 1998 — 27,737 (10.1 per 1,000 pop)   White — 18,343   Non-White — 9,394
         (10,333, or 37.25%, were in cities with population of 10,000 or more)
         (17,404, or 62.75%, were in cities, towns & communities with population less than 10,000)
         1997 — 27,380 (10.2 per 1,000 pop.)   White — 18,034   Non-White — 9,346
         1996 — 26,566 (9.9 per 1,000 pop.)   White — 17,488   Non-White — 9,078

Number of Deaths From The Ten Leading Causes, 1998: 22,886 (82.5% of all deaths in the state)

Deaths by The Ten Leading Causes in Mississippi, 1998:
- **Heart Diseases** — 9,501 (345.2 p/100,000)
- **Cancer** — 5,944 (216.0 per 100,000 people)
- **Strokes** — 1,804 (65.6 per 100,000 people)
- **Accidents** — 1,712 (62.2 p/100,000 people)
    - Motor Vehicle Traffic Accidents — 941
    - Water Transport (boats, etc.) — 16
    - Drownings — 81
    - Falls — 181
    - Conflagration & Other Fire & Flames — 105
    - Poisoning — 57
        - by drugs & medication — 45   by alcohol — 1
- **Emphysema/Chronic Lung Diseases** — 1,128 (40.9 p/100,000)
- **Pneumonia & Influenza** — 1,065 (38.6 per 100,000 people)
    - Pneumonia 1,058; Flu 7
- **Diabetes** — 628 (22.8 per 100,000 people)
- **Kidney Diseases** — 416 (15.1 per 100,000)
- **Homicide** — 358 (13.0 per 100,000 people)
- **Suicide** — 330 (12.0 per 100,000 people)

Deaths From Other Selected Causes, 1998:
- **Congenital Anomalies** — 139
- **Diseases of the Digestive System** — 820
- **Endocrine, Nutritional, & Metabolic Diseases** — 881
- **HIV Infection** — 139
- **Mental Disorders** — 322
    - Psychoses — 206
    - Neurotic & Personality Disorders & Other Nonpsychotic Mental Disorders — 107
    - Alcohol Dependence Syndrome — 46   Nondependent Abuse of Drugs (overdose) — 17
- **Chronic Liver Disease & Cirrhosis** — 231
- **Diseases of Blood & Blood-Forming Organs** — 112
- **Viral Hepatitis** — 43   **Tuberculosis** — 15

During the 1999-2000 hunting season, 40 accidents (24 involving firearms or bows & 16 in tree stand falls) left 11 hunters dead — eight in gun/bow accidents (7 deer hunting & one duck hunting) plus three in tree stand mishaps.

State Firearms Deaths (homicide, suicide & accidental)

Year	Number	Rate
1993	662	25.7
1994	626	24.3
1995	589	21.9
1996	549	20.4
1997	593	22.0

Rate is the no. of deaths per 100,000 population.

According to Health Dept. statistics, there was a possible snake bite death in Miss. in 1978. One snake bite death occurred in each of the years of 1982 & 1997, plus a snake bite fatality on June 21, 2000 in Lawrence County.

Ten leading causes of death in the U.S. & mortality rate per 100,000 people, 1998:

Heart disease	268.0
Cancer	199.4
Stroke	58.5
Lung disease	42.3
Pneumonia/flu	35.1
Accidents (incl. auto)	34.5
Diabetes	23.9
Suicide	10.8
Kidney disease	9.7
Liver disease/cirrhosis	9.2
Total All Causes	**865.0**

Source: National Center for Health Statistics, U.S. Dept. of Health and Human Services

During 1999, blacks made up 73.6% of HIV cases and 61.4% of AIDS cases reported in Mississippi.

In FY 1998, there were 653 new HIV infections and 377 AIDS cases reported in Mississippi. There were 969 cases of early syphilis reported.

Percentage of Pop. Who Smoked Cigarettes, 1997: 28.3% of males, 18.6% of females, 23.2% of total
Couples Married, 1998: 20,911   Bride — White 14,222   Non-White 6,689 (12,260 first marriages)
                             Groom — White 14,158   Non-White 6,753 (12,310 first. marriages)
Number of Divorces Granted in Miss., 1998: 13,748 (White 10,310; Non-White 3,004; Unknown 434)
No. of Home Health Care Agencies (State, Hospital & Private), 7/1/2000: 64 (2.3 per 100,000)
Number of State-Licensed Nursing Homes, 7/1/2000: 203 with approx. 18,000 beds
No. of Licensed Child Care Centers, 1998: 1,543 (1,863 family child care providers in 1997)
State Budget for the Dept. of Health, FY 2001: $209 million.
State Budget for the Dept. of Mental Health, FY 2000: $219,402,077 (148% increase)
     The 1999 Legislature approved $17.5 million to build 7 new regional mental facilities across
     Mississippi — in Batesville, Brookhaven, Cleveland, Corinth, Grenada, Laurel, and Newton.
State Budget for Social Programs, FY 2000: $300,798,654
Population Without Health Insurance: 1998 — 554,000 (20%)   1997 — 550,000 (20.1%). According
     to census data, about 144,000 Mississippi children are in families with no health insurance.
Private Establishments Offering One or More Major Health Insurance Plans in 1993:
     24,600 businesses or firms (43.3% of all establishments) with 55% of employees enrolled.

Health in Mississippi

Number of Live Births and Deaths in Cities of 10,000 or More, 1998

	Live Births			Deaths		
	Total	White	Non-White	Total	White	Non-White
Biloxi	824	554	270	460	376	84
Brandon	332	266	66	174	165	9
Brookhaven	176	69	107	228	144	84
Canton	305	35	270	153	45	108
Clarksdale	456	82	374	266	108	158
Cleveland	241	90	151	160	69	91
Clinton	283	188	95	162	125	37
Columbus	439	152	287	318	184	134
Corinth	216	156	60	192	155	37
Gautier	231	140	91	87	78	9
Greenville	865	187	678	500	196	304
Greenwood	400	85	315	231	98	133
Grenada	229	87	142	208	127	81
Gulfport	1,080	605	475	707	515	192
Hattiesburg	718	263	455	491	321	170
Indianola	211	38	173	111	44	67
Jackson	3,188	661	2,527	2,040	972	1,068
Laurel	324	76	248	257	152	105
Long Beach	220	193	27	141	137	4
McComb	231	62	169	210	129	81
Meridian	654	220	434	594	356	238
Moss Point	260	53	207	193	84	109
Natchez	325	107	218	312	147	165
Ocean Springs	269	241	28	202	189	13
Pascagoula	502	331	171	278	225	53
Pearl	293	229	64	145	125	20
Picayune	189	118	71	141	92	49
Ridgeland	281	210	71	91	75	16
Southaven	386	362	24	222	209	13
Starkville	308	137	171	140	75	65
Tupelo	520	299	221	339	270	69
Vicksburg	478	138	340	398	195	203
Yazoo City	281	53	228	182	74	108
TOTALS	15,715*	6,487	9,228	10,333**	6,256	4,077

*36.62% of the total 42,917 live births in MS in 1998   **37.25% percent of the total 27,737 deaths in MS in 1998.

Source: Mississippi Department of Health

Hospitals in Mississippi

ABERDEEN-MONROE COUNTY HOSPITAL; 400 S Chestnut; Aberdeen 39730 (49)[1] .... (662) 369-2455
ALLIANCE HEALTHCARE SYSTEM (formerly Marshall County Memorial Medical Center)
    1430 E Salem Ave; Holly Springs 38635 (40) .... (662) 252-1212
BAPTIST MEMORIAL HOSPITAL BOONEVILLE; 100 Hospital St; Booneville 38829 (114) ... (662) 720-5000
BAPTIST MEMORIAL HOSPITAL DeSOTO CO; 7601 Southcrest Pky; Southaven 38671 (140) . (662) 349-4000
BAPTIST MEM. HOSPITAL/GOLDEN TRIANGLE; 2520 5th St N; Columbus 39701 (328) ..... (662) 243-1500
BAPTIST MEMORIAL HOSP. NORTH MISS.; 2301 S Lamar Blvd; Oxford 38655 (204) .... (662) 232-8100
BAPTIST MEMORIAL HOSPITAL-UNION CO.; 200 Hwy 30W; New Albany 38652 (153) ...... (662) 538-7631
BEACHAM MEMORIAL HOSPITAL; 203 N Cherry St; Magnolia 39652 (37) .... (601) 783-2353
BILOXI REGIONAL MEDICAL CENTER; 150 Reynoir St; Biloxi 39533 (153) .... (228) 436-1104
BOLIVAR MEDICAL CENTER; 901 Hwy 8E; P.O. Box 1380; Cleveland 38732 (165) .... (662) 846-2551
CENTRAL MISSISSIPPI MEDICAL CENTER; 1850 Chadwick Dr; Jackson 39204 (409) .... (601) 376-1000
CHARTER PARKWOOD HOSPITAL; 8135 Goodman Rd; Olive Branch 38654 (66) .... (662) 895-4900
CHOCTAW COUNTY MEDICAL CENTER; 148 W Cherry St; Ackerman 39735 (22) .... (662) 285-6235
CLAIBORNE COUNTY HOSPITAL; 123 McComb Ave; Port Gibson 39150 (32) .... (601) 437-5141
CLAY COUNTY MEDICAL CENTER; 835 Medical Center Dr; West Point 39773 (60) .... (662) 495-2300
COVINGTON COUNTY HOSPITAL; Sixth & Holly; P.O. Box 11149; Collins 39428 (82) .... (601) 765-6711
DELTA REGIONAL MEDICAL CENTER; 1400 E Union St; Greenville 38703 (268) .... (662) 334-2169
DIAMOND GROVE CTR. FOR CHILDREN/ADOLESCENTS; 2311 Hwy 15S; Louisville (20) .. (662) 779-0119
EAST MISSISSIPPI STATE HOSPITAL; 4555 Highland Park Dr; Meridian 39304 (407) .... (601) 482-6186
FIELD MEMORIAL COMMUNITY HOSPITAL; 270 W Main St; Centreville 39631 (66) .... (601) 645-5221
FORREST GENERAL HOSPITAL; 6051 U.S. Hwy 49; Hattiesburg 39401 (537) .... (601) 288-7000
FRANKLIN COUNTY MEM. HOSPITAL; Hwy 84 & Union Church Rd; Meadville 39653 (49) .. (601) 384-5801
G. V. "SONNY" MONTGOMERY VETERANS AFFAIRS MEDICAL CENTER;
    1500 E Woodrow Wilson Dr; Jackson 39216 (163 beds) ----- 1-800-949-1009 or (601) 362-4471
GARDEN PARK COMMUNITY HOSPITAL; 1520 Broad Ave; Gulfport 39501 (130) .... (228) 864-4210
GEORGE COUNTY HOSPITAL; 859 Winter St; P.O. Box 607; Lucedale 39452 (53) .... (601) 947-3161
GILMORE MEMORIAL HOSPITAL; 1105 E Earl Frye Blvd; Amory 38821 (95) .... (662) 256-7111
GREENWOOD LEFLORE HOSPITAL; 1401 River Rd; Greenwood 38930 (260) .... (662) 459-7000
GRENADA LAKE MEDICAL CENTER; 960 Avent Dr; Grenada 38901 (156) .... (662) 227-7000
GULF COAST MEDICAL CENTER; 180 DeBuys Rd; Biloxi 39531 (189) .... (228) 388-6711
H. C. WATKINS MEMORIAL HOSPITAL; 605 S Archusa Ave; Quitman 39355 (32) .... (601) 776-6925
HANCOCK MEDICAL CENTER; 149 Drinkwater Blvd; Bay St. Louis 39520 (104) .... (228) 467-8600
HARDY WILSON MEMORIAL HOSPITAL; 233 Magnolia St; Hazlehurst 39083 (49) .... (601) 894-4541
HILLCREST HOSPITAL; 140 Burke Rd. & Hospital Dr; Calhoun City 38916 (30) .... (662) 628-6611
HUMPHREYS COUNTY MEMORIAL HOSPITAL; 500 CCC Rd; Belzoni 39038 (28) .... (662) 247-3831
IUKA HOSPITAL; 1777 Curtis Dr; P.O. Box 860; Iuka 38852 (48) .... (662) 423-6051
JASPER GENERAL HOSPITAL; 15 South 6th St; Bay Springs 39422 (16) .... (601) 764-2101
JEFF ANDERSON REGIONAL MEDICAL CENTER; 2124 14th St; Meridian 39301 (260) ...... (601) 553-6000
JEFFERSON COUNTY HOSPITAL; 809 S Main St; Fayette 39069 (30) .... (601) 786-3401
KILMICHAEL HOSPITAL; 301 Lamar Ave; P.O. Box 188; Kilmichael 39747 (19) .... (662) 262-4311
KING'S DAUGHTERS HOSPITAL; 300 S Washington Ave; Greenville 38702 (137) .... (662) 378-2020
KING'S DAUGHTERS HOSPITAL; 823 Grand Ave; Yazoo City 39194 (88) .... (662) 746-2261
KING'S DAUGHTERS MEDICAL CENTER; 427 Hwy 51N; Brookhaven 39601 (122) .... (601) 833-6011
L. O. CROSBY MEMORIAL HOSPITAL; 801 Goodyear Blvd; Picayune 39466 (95) .... (601) 798-4711
LAIRD HOSPITAL; 25117 Hwy 15; Union 39365 (50) .... (662) 774-8214
LAUREL WOOD CENTER, INC; 5000 Hwy 39N; Meridian 39301 (109) .... (601) 483-6211
LAWRENCE COUNTY HOSPITAL; 1065 Hwy 84E; P.O. Box 788; Monticello 39654 (53) ...... (601) 587-4051
LEAKE COUNTY MEMORIAL HOSPITAL; 310 Ellis St; Carthage 39051 (32) .... (601) 267-4511
MADISON COUNTY MEDICAL CENTER; Hwy 16E; P. O. Box 1607; Canton 39046 (67) ...... (601) 859-1331
MAGEE GENERAL HOSPITAL; 300 SE 3rd Ave; Magee 39111 (64) .... (601) 849-5070
MAGNOLIA REGIONAL HEALTH CENTER; 611 Alcorn Dr; Corinth 38834 (164) .... (662) 293-1000
MARION GENERAL HOSPITAL; 1560 Sumrall Rd; Columbia 39429 (79) .... (601) 736-6303
MEDICAL/DENTAL FACILITY AT PARCHMAN PRISON; Hwy 49W; Parchman 38738 (56) .. (662) 745-6611
MEMORIAL HOSPITAL AT GULFPORT; 4500 13th St; Gulfport 39501 (425) .... (228) 867-4000

[1] Number in parentheses following the address of each facility indicates the number of licensed beds.

The Ultimate Reference on the State

Hospitals in Mississippi

METHODIST HEALTHCARE MIDDLE MISS.; 239 Bowling Green Rd; Lexington 39095 (84)[1] . (662) 834-1321
MISSISSIPPI BAPTIST MEDICAL CENTER; 1225 N State St; Jackson 39202 (639) .... (601) 968-1000
MISSISSIPPI HOSPITAL FOR RESTORATIVE CARE; 1225 N State St; Jackson 39202 (25) .... (601) 968-1054
MISS. METHODIST HOSP. & REHAB CTR; 1350 E Woodrow Wilson; Jackson 39216 (124) ... (601) 364-3365
MISSISSIPPI STATE HOSPITAL; 3550 Hwy 468W; Whitfield 39193 (1,479) .... (601) 351-8000
MONTFORT JONES MEMORIAL HOSPITAL; 220 Hwy 12W; Kosciusko 39090 (72) .... (662) 289-4311
NATCHEZ COMMUNITY HOSPITAL; 129 Jefferson Davis Blvd; Natchez 39120 (101) .... (601) 445-6205
NATCHEZ REGIONAL MEDICAL CENTER; 54 Sgt. Prentiss Dr; Natchez 39120 (205) .... (601) 443-2100
NESHOBA COUNTY GENERAL HOSPITAL; 1001 Holland Ave; Philadelphia 39350 (82) ...... (601) 663-1200
NEWTON REGIONAL HOSPITAL; 208 S Main St; Newton 39332 (49) .... (601) 683-2031
NORTH MISSISSIPPI MEDICAL CENTER; 830 S Gloster; Tupelo 38801 (650) .... (662) 841-3978
NORTH MISS. MEDICAL CENTER-PONTOTOC; 176 S Main; Pontotoc 38863 (58) .... (662) 489-5510
NORTH MISSISSIPPI STATE HOSPITAL; 1937 Briar Ridge Rd; Tupelo 38801 (50) .... (662) 690-4200
NORTH SUNFLOWER COUNTY HOSPITAL; 840 N Oak Ave; Ruleville 38771 (44) .... (662) 756-2711
NORTHWEST MISS. REGIONAL MEDICAL CTR; 1970 Hospital Dr; Clarksdale 38614 (175) .. (662) 627-3211
NOXUBEE GENERAL HOSPITAL; 606 N Jefferson St; Macon 39341 (49) .... (662) 726-4231
OAK CIRCLE CENTER (Adolescent Psychiatric); 3550 Hwy 468W; Whitfield 39193 (60) .... (601) 351-8000
OCEAN SPRINGS HOSPITAL; 3109 Bienville Blvd; Ocean Springs 39564 (124) .... (228) 818-1195
OKOLONA COMMUNITY HOSPITAL; 512 Rockwell Dr; Okolona 38860 (10) .... (662) 447-3311
OKTIBBEHA COUNTY HOSPITAL; 400 Hospital Rd; Starkville 39759 (96) .... (662) 323-4320
PEARL RIVER COUNTY HOSPITAL; 305 W Moody St; Poplarville 39470 (24) .... (601) 795-4543
PERRY COUNTY GENERAL HOSPITAL; 206 Bay Ave; Richton 39476 (22) .... (601) 788-6316
PRENTISS REGIONAL HOSPITAL; 1102 Rose St; Prentiss 39474 (41) .... (601) 792-4276
QUITMAN COUNTY HOSPITAL; 340 Getwell Dr; Marks 38646 (36) .... (662) 326-8031
RANKIN MEDICAL CENTER; 350 Crossgates Blvd; Brandon 39042 (134) .... (601) 825-1501
RILEY MEMORIAL HOSPITAL; 1102 Constitution Ave; Meridian 39301 (180) .... (601) 693-2511
RIVER OAKS HOSPITAL; 1030 River Oaks Dr; Jackson 39296 (110) .... (601) 932-1030
RIVER REGION HEALTH SYSTEM; 100 McAuley Dr; Vicksburg 39180 (354) .... (601) 636-2131
RUSH FOUNDATION HOSPITAL; 1314 19th Ave; Meridian 39301 (215) .... (601) 483-0011
S. E. LACKEY MEMORIAL HOSPITAL; 330 North Broad St; Forest 39074 (44) .... (601) 469-4151
SAINT DOMINIC HOSPITAL; 969 Lakeland Dr; Jackson 39216 (571) .... (601) 364-6848
SCOTT REGIONAL HOSPITAL; 317 Hwy 13S; Morton 39117 (30) .... (601) 732-6301
SELECT SPECIALTY HOSPITAL OF BILOXI; 648 E Beach Blvd; Biloxi 39530 (42) .... (228) 374-7474
SELECT SPECIALTY HOSPITAL-GULFPORT; 4500 13th St., 5th Floor; Gulfport 39502 (38) .. (228) 867-4820
SENATOBIA COMMUNITY HOSPITAL; 401 Getwell Rd; Senatobia 38668 (76) .... (662) 562-3100
SHARKEY-ISSAQUENA COMMUNITY HOSPITAL; 108 S 4th St; Rolling Fork 39159 (29) .... (662) 873-4395
SIMPSON GENERAL HOSPITAL; 1842 Simpson, Hwy 149; Mendenhall 39114 (49) .... (601) 847-2221
SINGING RIVER HOSPITAL; 2809 Denny Ave; Pascagoula 39581 (427) .... (228) 938-5000
SOUTH CENTRAL REGIONAL MEDICAL CENTER; 1220 Jefferson St; Laurel 39441 (285) ... (601) 426-4507
SOUTH PANOLA COMMUNITY HOSPITAL; 155 Keating Rd; Batesville 38606 (70) .... (662) 563-5611
SOUTH SUNFLOWER COUNTY HOSPITAL; 121 E Baker St; Indianola 38751 (69) .... (662) 887-5235
SOUTHWEST MISS. REGIONAL MEDICAL CENTER; 215 Marion Av; McComb 39648 (160) . (601) 249-5500
SPECIALTY HOSPITAL OF MERIDIAN, THE; 1314 19th Ave; Meridian 39301 (40) .... (601) 486-4211
TALLAHATCHIE GENERAL HOSPITAL; 201 S Market St; Charleston 38921 (16) .... (601) 647-5535
TIPPAH COUNTY HOSPITAL; 1005 City Ave N; Ripley 38663 (70) .... (662) 837-9221
TRACE REGIONAL HOSPITAL; Hwy 8E; P.O. Box 626; Houston 38851 (84) .... (662) 456-3700
TYLER HOLMES MEMORIAL HOSPITAL; 409 Tyler Holmes Dr; Winona 38967 (49) .... (662) 283-4114
U.S. AIR FORCE MEDICAL CENTER; Keesler AFB; Biloxi 39534 (110) .... (228) 377-6550
UNIVERSITY HOSPITAL & CLINICS-DURANT; 713 Northwest Ave; Durant 39063 (29) .... (662) 653-3081
UNIVERSITY OF MISSISSIPPI MEDICAL CENTER; 2500 N State; Jackson 39216 (665) .... (601) 984-1000
VA GULFCOAST VETERANS HEALTH CARE SYSTEM; Pass Road; Biloxi 39531 (117)   .... (228) 523-5000
WALTHALL COUNTY GENERAL HOSPITAL; 100 Hospital Dr; Tylertown 39667 (49) .... (601) 876-2122
WAYNE GENERAL HOSPITAL; 950 Matthew Dr; Waynesboro 39367 (80) .... (601) 735-5151
WEBSTER HEALTH SERVICES; 500 Veterans Memorial Blvd; Eupora 39744 (43) .... (662) 258-6221
WESLEY MEDICAL CENTER; 5001 W Hardy St; Hattiesburg 39402 (211) .... (601) 268-8000

[1] Number in parentheses following the address of each facility indicates the number of licensed beds.

Hospitals in Mississippi

WHITFIELD MEDICAL/SURGICAL HOSPITAL; Bldg 60, Oak Circle; Whitfield 39193 (43) .... (601) 351-8023
WINSTON MEDICAL CENTER; 562 E Main; P.O. Box 967; Louisville 39339 (65) .... (662) 773-6211
WOMEN'S HOSPITAL AT RIVER OAKS; 1026 N Flowood Dr; Flowood 39208 (111) .... (601) 936-2390
YALOBUSHA GENERAL HOSPITAL; Hwy 7S; P.O. Box 728; Water Valley 38965 (26) .... (662) 473-1411

Summary: 109 state-licensed hospitals with a total of 15,204 licensed beds plus 1 military hospitals and 2 Veterans Affairs hospitals.

When University of Mississippi Medical Center opened in 1955, there were 166 students. Today, there are about 1,800 students. About half of Mississippi's practicing physicians are graduates of UMC and more than two-thirds of the School of Medicine's graduates are still in the state. There are 2.5 million square feet under roof on the 164-acre campus. The Center has $211 million in construction and renovation projects authorized that are estimated to create over 5,700 jobs with a $449 million economic impact spread over several years. University Medical Center's $530,349,028 budget for FY 2000 had over a $1 billion economic impact on Jackson and the state! With about 6,500 employees and an annual payroll of close to $200 million, UMC is the greater Jackson area's largest employer and close to the top on the list of largest employers in the state. The teaching hospital admits more than 25,000 patients yearly and treats about 300,000 in its emergency room. Counting staff, students, patients and visitors, the daily peak "population" of UMC ranges from 10,000 to 12,000, which exceeds the population of 87 to 89 percent of Mississippi's incorporated municipalities and 10 Mississippi counties! The annual utility bill alone is $4.5 million. In a year, 4 million pounds (2,000 tons) of linens are laundered and 45 tons of eggs are cooked for breakfast!

According to the Mississippi Hospital Association, the following figures represent the amount of Medicare cuts in each of Mississippi's congressional districts through 2002 caused by the Balanced Budget Act of 1997:

1st. District — $109,858,013	2nd District — $ 55,184,645
3rd District — $ 93,419,324	4th District — $215,103,411
5th District — $173,734,378	Total Cuts — $647,299,771

The Institutions of Higher Learning's University Research Center estimates Medicare and Medicaid cuts authorized by that Balanced Budget Act could cost Mississippi an additional $550 million in personal income and 20,000 jobs. A $20 billion bill passed by Congress in November 1999 would lessen some of these cuts.

AMBULATORY SURGICAL FACILITIES

BETTER LIVING CLINIC ENDOSCOPY CENTER; 3000 Halls Ferry Rd; Vicksburg 39180 ..... (601) 638-9800
BILOXI OUTPATIENT SURGERY & ENDOSCOPY CENTER; 111 Lameuse; Biloxi 39530 ..... (228) 374-2130
CORINTH SURGERY CENTER; 401 Alcorn Dr; Corinth 38834 .... (662) 293-2000
DELTA GASTROENTEROLOGY; 9215 Millbranch Rd; Southaven 38671 .... (662) 280-8222
EAST MISSISSIPPI ENDOSCOPIC CENTER; 1926 23rd Ave; Meridian 39302 .... (601) 485-1131
EAR, NOSE, THROAT & FACIAL PLASTIC SURGERY; 108 Millsaps Dr; Hattiesburg 39402 .. (601) 268-5131
EYE & AESTHETIC SURGERY CENTER; 414-B Marion Dr; McComb 39648 .... (601) 684-9606
FIRST CHOICE SURGICAL CENTER; 114 Jeff Davis Blvd; Natchez 39120 .... (601) 442-5382
GASTROENTEROLOGY CLINIC OF LAUREL; 1020 Adams St; Laurel 39440 .... (601) 649-0633
GULF COAST ENDOSCOPY ASC; 90 Industrial Park Circle; Ocean Springs 39564 .... (228) 872-6290
GULFPORT OUTPATIENT SURGICAL CENTER; 1240 Broad Ave; Gulfport 39501 .... (228) 868-1120
HEALTHSOUTH MISSISSIPPI SURGERY CENTER; 1421 N State St; Jackson 39202 .... (601) 353-8000
HEALTHSOUTH OUTPATIENT CENTER OF GULFPORT; 1206 31st. Ave; Gulfport 39501 ... (228) 864-0008
JACKSON EYE INSTITUTE & ASC; 2500 Lakeland Dr., Suite B; Flowood 39208 .... (601) 933-1197
LOWERY WOODALL OUTPATIENT SURGERY FACILITY; 105 S 28th; Hattiesburg 39401 .. (601) 288-1072
M A E PHYSICIANS SURGERY CENTER; 1190 N State St; Jackson 39202 .... (601) 968-1790
MID SOUTH SURGICAL CENTER; 1693 S Colorado St; Greenville 38703 .... (662) 332-8700
NORTH MISSISSIPPI SURGERY CENTER; 4376 W Eason Blvd; Tupelo 38801 .... (662) 841-4700
PAIN MANAGEMENT CENTER; One Layfair Dr., Suite 400; Flowood 39208 .... (601) 936-8800
PREMIER ENDOSCOPY CENTER OF JACKSON; 501 Marshall St., Suite 501; Jackson 39202 .. (601) 352-2273
RAYNER EYE CLINIC SURGICAL CENTER; 1308 Belk Dr; Oxford 38655 .... (662) 234-6551
SOUTHERN EYE CENTER; 1420 28th Ave; Hattiesburg 39402 .... (601) 264-3937
SOUTHWEST MISS. AMBULATORY SURGERY CENTER; 215 Marion Ave; McComb 39648 . (601) 249-5500
ST. DOMINIC AMBULATORY SURGERY CENTER; 971 Lakeland Dr; Jackson 39216 .... (601) 364-2935
SURGICARE OF JACKSON; 760 Lakeland Dr; Jackson 39216 .... (601) 362-8700

The Ultimate Reference on the State

County Health Departments in Mississippi

Adams; 408 Highway 61 N; Natchez 39120	(601) 445-4601
Alcorn; 3706 Joann Dr; Corinth 38834	(662) 287-6121
Amite; 123 Main; Gloster 39638	(601) 225-4961
Amite; 315 E Main St; Liberty 39645	(601) 657-8351
Attala; 999 N Wells St; Kosciusko 39090	(662) 289-2351
Benton; Ashland 38603	(662) 224-6442
Bolivar; 201 S Court St; Cleveland 38732	(662) 843-2706
Bolivar; Hwy 1 N; Rosedale 38769	(662) 759-3361
Calhoun; Bruce 38915	(662) 983-2301
Calhoun; E Taylor Av; Calhoun City 38916	(662) 628-6631
Carroll; Grenada Rd; Carrollton 38927	(662) 237-9224
Carroll; Vaiden 39176	(662) 464-5277
Chickasaw; 332 N Jefferson; Houston 38851	(662) 456-3737
Chickasaw; Main; Okolona 38860	(662) 447-5492
Choctaw; 123 Chester St; Ackerman 39735	(662) 285-6213
Claiborne; Market St; Port Gibson 39150	(601) 437-5184
Clarke; 124 W Donald St; Quitman 39355	(601) 776-2149
Clay; 218 W Broad St; West Point 39773	(662) 494-4514
Coahoma; 805 Ohio Av; Clarksdale 38614	(662) 624-8316
Copiah; 640 Georgetown St; Hazlehurst	(601) 894-2271
Covington; 502 Beech Av; Collins 39428	(601) 765-4291
Desoto; Hwy 51 S; Hernando 38632	(662) 429-9814
DeSoto; 6569 Cockrum St; Olive Branch	(662) 895-3090
Forrest; 5008 Highway 42; Hattiesburg	(601) 583-0291
Franklin; Meadville 39653	(601) 384-5871
George; 307 S Winter St; Lucedale 39452	(601) 947-4217
Greene; Leakesville 39451	(601) 394-2389
Grenada; 1241 S Mound St; Grenada 38901	(662) 226-3711
Hancock; 3062 Longfellow Rd; Bay Saint Louis 39520	(228) 467-5236
Harrison; 761 Esters Blvd; Biloxi 39530	(228) 435-3641
Harrison; 4521 Old Pass Rd, Gulfport 39501	(228) 863-1036
Harrison; 15th St; Gulfport 39501	(228) 863-1036
Hinds; 408 E Cynthia; Clinton 39056	(601) 924-6012
Hinds; Main Office; 420 E Woodrow Wilson Dr; Jackson 39216	(601) 364-2666
Hinds; Candlestick Park Clinic; 820 Cooper Rd; Jackson 39212	(601) 371-1133
Hinds; South Jackson Clinic; 1221 Ellis Av; Jackson 39209	(601) 355-6377
Hinds; North Clinic 5965 I-55 N; Jackson	(601) 978-1744
Hinds; Clinton Clinic; 408 E Cynthia; Clinton	(601) 924-6012
Hinds; Courthouse Annex; Raymond 39154	(601) 857-5581
Holmes; 100 Westwood Av; Lexington 39095	(662) 834-3142
Holmes; Blake; Tchula 39169	(662) 235-5611
Humphreys; 107 S Hayden St; Belzoni 39038	(662) 247-1861
Issaquena; 416 Race; Rolling Fork 39159	(662) 873-6202
Itawamba; 601 Crane St; Fulton 38843	(662) 862-3710
Jackson; Moss Point 39562	(228) 474-0085
Jackson; 6904 Washington Av; Ocean Springs	(228) 875-1336
Jackson; Hospital Road; Pascagoula 39567	(228) 762-1117
Jackson; 13812 Hwy 57; Vancleave 39565	(228) 826-3908
Jasper; Bay Springs 39422	(601) 764-2419
Jasper; 309 Bay; Heidelberg 39439	(601) 787-3423
Jefferson Co Health Center; Poindexter; Fayette	(601) 786-3061
Jones; Ellisville Blvd; Laurel 39441	(601) 426-3258
Kemper; Hwy 16 W; DeKalb 39328	(601) 743-5865
Lafayette; Hwy 7; Oxford 38655	(662) 234-5231
Lamar; Purvis 39475	(601) 794-1055
Lauderdale; 2119 Hwy 19 N; Meridian 39307	(601) 693-5507
Lawrence; 168 N Washington; Monticello	(601) 587-2561
Leake; 302 Ellis St; Carthage 39051	(601) 267-3072
Lee; 532 S Church St; Tupelo 38801	(662) 841-9096
Leflore; 2600 Browning Rd; Greenwood	(662) 453-0284
Lincoln; 1212 Northpark Ln NE; Brookhaven	(601) 833-3314
Lowndes; 400 Wilkins Wise Rd; Columbus	(662) 328-6158
Lowndes; 1112 Military Rd; Columbus 39703	(601) 328-6091
Madison; 317 N Union St; Canton 39046	(601) 859-3316
Madison; 108 Clark St E; Flora 39071	(601) 879-3602
Marion; 908 Sumrall Rd; Columbia 39429	(601) 736-2676
Marshall; 225 S Market St; Holly Springs	(662) 252-4621
Monroe; 401 Main St S; Amory 38821	(662) 256-5341
Montgomery; Alberta Dr; Winona 38967	(662) 283-3655
Neshoba; Hwy 19 S; Philadelphia 39350	(601) 656-4371
Newton; Newton 39345	(601) 635-2337
Newton; 500 Decatur St; Newton 39350	(601) 683-3331
Noxubee; Macon 39341	(662) 726-4451
Oktibbeha; 203 Yeates St; Starkville 39759	(662) 323-4565
Panola; Batesville 38606	(662) 563-4616
Panola Region Office; Batesville 38606	(662) 563-9334
Panola; Main; Como 38619	(662) 526-5673
Pearl River; Picayune 39466	(601) 798-6212
Pearl River; Poplarville 39470	(601) 795-4937
Perry; New Augusta 39462	(601) 964-3288
Pike; 205 Marion Av; McComb 39648	(601) 684-1030
Pike; Hwy 51 N; Magnolia 39652	(601) 783-5662
Pontotoc; 341 Ridge Dr; Pontotoc 38863	(662) 489-1241
Prentiss; 101 N 1st St; Booneville 38829	(662) 728-4048
Quitman; Chestnut; Marks 38646	(662) 326-2861
Rankin; 100 Tamberlin St; Brandon 39042	(601) 825-2141
Rankin; Florence 39073	(601) 845-6411
Scott; Airport Road; Forest 39074	(601) 469-4941
Sharkey; 416 Race; Rolling Fork 39159	(662) 873-6202
Simpson; Magee 39111	(601) 849-2831
Simpson; 405 N Main St; Mendenhall 39114	(601) 847-2755
Smith; Raleigh 39153	(601) 782-4472
Smith; 102 Dallas St; Taylorsville 39168	(601) 785-4704
Stone; 211 Critz; Wiggins 39577	(601) 928-5293
Sunflower; 119 N Chester; Ruleville 38771	(662) 756-4881
Sunflower; 412 Hwy 49 S; Sunflower 38778	(662) 887-4951
Tallahatchie; 206 E Walnut St; Charleston	(662) 647-5805
Tallahatchie; North Pleasant; Charleston	(662) 647-3404
Tallahatchie; 208 Wilson; Sumner 38957	(662) 375-8345
Tate; 309 Scott St; Senatobia 38668-2830	(662) 562-4428
Tippah; 116 Hospital St; Ripley 38663	(662) 837-3215
Tishomingo; Bettydale Dr; Iuka 38852	(662) 423-6100
Tunica; Hwy 61 S; Tunica 38676	(662) 363-2166
Union; 400 Main St E; New Albany 38652	(662) 534-1926
Walthall; 901 Union Rd; Tylertown 39667	(601) 876-4924
Warren; 807 Monroe St; Vicksburg 39180	(601) 636-4356
Washington; 1633 Hospital St; Greenville	(662) 332-8177
Washington; Hollandale 38748	(662) 827-5626
Washington; 801 N Broad St; Leland 38756	(662) 686-7711
Wayne; Chickasawhay; Waynesboro 39367	(601) 735-2351
Webster; 319 E Gould Av; Eupora 39744	(662) 258-3761
Wilkinson; 991 First St South; Woodville	(601) 888-4202
Winston; Main; Louisville 39339	(662) 773-8087
Yalobusha; 612 Front; Coffeeville 38922	(662) 675-2465
Yalobusha; Simmons St; Water Valley 38965	(662) 473-1424
Yazoo; 230 E Broadway; Yazoo City 39194	(662) 746-3713

Law Enforcement Units in Mississippi

Sheriff's Departments by County

ADAMS; 306 State St; Natchez 39120	(601) 442-2752
ALCORN; 305 S. Fulton Dr; Corinth 38834	(662) 286-5521
AMITE; Courthouse; Liberty 39645	(601) 657-8057
ATTALA; 112 W. Adam St; Kosciusko 39090	(662) 289-5556
BENTON; Ashland 38603	(662) 224-8941
BOLIVAR; Courthouse; Cleveland 38732	(662) 843-5378
BOLIVAR; Rosedale 38769	(662) 759-3536
CALHOUN; Pittsboro 38951	(662) 412-3149
CARROLL; 105 E Washington; Carrollton	(662) 237-9283
CHICKASAW; 210 Harrington St; Houston	(662) 456-2339
CHICKASAW; 110 Oliver St; Okolona	(662) 447-3402
CHOCTAW; Akerman 39725	(662) 285-6129
CLAIBORNE; Port Gibson 39150	(601) 437-5161
CLARKE; 444 W. Donald St; Quitman 39255	(601) 776-5252
CLAY; West Point 39773	(662) 494-5152
COAHOMA; Clarksdale 38614	(662) 624-3081
COPIAH; Hazlehurst 39083	(601) 894-3011
COVINGTON; Covington 39428	(601) 765-8281
DeSOTO; 311 W. South St; Hernando 38632	(662) 429-1470
FORREST; Hattiesburg 39403	(601) 544-7800
FRANKLIN; Meadville 39653	(601) 384-2323
GEORGE; 355 Cox St, Suite B; Lucedale	(601) 947-4811
GREENE; Leaksville 39452	(601) 394-2341
GRENADA; 35 Doak St; Grenada 38901	(662) 226-2721
HANCOCK; Bay Saint Louis 39520	(228) 467-5101
HARRISON; Gulfport 39502	(228) 865-7070
HARRISON; 735 Washington Loop; Biloxi	(228) 435-4220
HINDS; Jackson 39215	(601) 968-6702
HINDS; 1450 County Farm Rd; Raymond	(601) 857-4800
HOLMES; Lexington 39095	(662) 834-1511
HUMPHREYS; 106 Castleman St; Belzoni	(662) 247-2551
ISSAQUENA; Mayersville 39113	(662) 873-2781
ITAWAMBA; 201 S. Cummings St; Fulton	(662) 862-3401
JACKSON; Pascagoula 39568	(228) 769-3095
JASPER; Bay Springs 39422	(601) 764-2588
JEFFERSON; Fayette 39069	(601) 786-3403
JEFFERSON DAVIS; Prentiss 39474	(601) 792-5169
JONES; Laurel 39440	(601) 425-3147
KEMPER; DeKalb 39328	(601) 743-2255
LAFAYETTE; 711 Jackson Ave; Oxford	(662) 234-6421
LAMAR; Purvis 39475	(601) 794-8610
LAUDERDALE; 2001 5th St; Meridian	(601) 482-9800
LAWRENCE; Monticello 39654	(601) 587-2961
LEAKE; Carthage 39051	(601) 267-7361
LEE; 510 N. Commerce; Tupelo 38801	(662) 841-9040
LEFLORE; Courthouse; Greenwood 38931	(662) 453-5141
LINCOLN; 100 S Jackson St; Brookhaven	(601) 833-5231
LOWNDES; 2503 Bell Ave; Columbus 39701	(662) 329-5827
MADISON; Hwy 51S; Canton 39046	(601) 859-2345
MARION; 500 Courthouse Sq. #1; Columbia	(601) 736-5051
MARSHALL; 136 N Alderson; Holly Springs	(662) 252-1311
MONROE; S Chestnut; Aberdeen 39730	(662) 369-2468
MONTGOMERY; 217 Sterling St; Winona	(662) 283-4612
NESHOBA; 401 E Beacon St; Philadelphia	(601) 656-1414
NEWTON; Decatur 39327	(602) 635-2101
NOXUBEE; 505 S Jefferson St; Macon 39341	(662) 726-4166
OKTIBBEHA; 111 N Washington St; Starkville	(662) 323-2421
PANOLA; 151 Public Square; Batesville 38606	(662) 563-6230
PEARL RIVER; 200 S. Main; Poplarville	(601) 795-4716
PERRY; New Augusta 39462	(601) 964-8461
PIKE; 2109 Jesse Hall Rd; Magnolia 39652	(601) 783-2323
PONTOTOC; 116 N Main; Pontotoc 38863	(662) 489-3111
PRENTISS; 1901 E. Chambers Dr; Booneville	(662) 728-6232
QUITMAN; 233 Chestnut; Marks 38646	(662) 326-3131
RANKIN; 221 N Timber; Brandon 39042	(601) 825-1480
SCOTT; 531 Airport Rd; Forest 39074	(601) 469-1511
SHARKEY; 400 Locust St; Rolling Fork 39159	(662) 873-4321
SIMPSON; 111 W. Pine St; Mendenhall 39114	(601) 847-2921
SMITH; Raleigh 39153	(601) 782-4531
STONE; 308 Court St; Wiggins 39577	(601) 928-7251
SUNFLOWER; Indianola 38751	(662) 887-2121
TALLAHATCHIE; Charleston 38921	(662) 647-5511
TALLAHATCHIE; Sumner 38957	(662) 375-8676
TATE; No. One Justice Dr; Senatobia 38668	(662) 562-4434
TIPPAH; 204 W Spring St; Ripley 38663	(662) 837-9336
TISHOMINGO; 1111 Maria Lane; Iuka 38852	(662) 423-7000
TUNICA; Tunica, MS 38676	(662) 363-1411
UNION; 300 Carter Ave; New Albany 38652	(662) 534-1941
WALTHALL; 807 Magnolia Ave; Tylertown	(601) 876-3481
WARREN; 1000 Grove St; Vicksburg 39180	(601) 636-1761
WASHINGTON; Courthouse; Greenville 38701	(662) 334-4523
WAYNE; New Courthouse; Waynesboro 39367	(601) 735-2323
WEBSTER; 321 E. Gould St; Eupora 39744	(662) 258-7701
WILKINSON; 525 Main St; Woodville 39669	(601) 888-3511
WINSTON; 115 S. Court St; Louisville 39339	(662) 773-5881
YALOBUSHA; Coffeeville 38922	(662) 675-2444
YALOBUSHA; Calhoun;Water Valley 38965	(662) 473-2722
YAZOO; 211 E Broadway; Yazoo City	(662) 746-5611

Adams County, Mississippi Sheriff William T. "Tommy" Ferrell was sworn in as second vice president of the National Sheriff's Association in June 2000. He will become Mississippi's first president of the association in 2002, serving for one year. The 60-year old organization, headquartered in Alexandria, Virginia, has over 20,000 members nationwide. Sheriff Ferrell has been been with the group for over ten years, serving on the board of directors and as sergeant-at-arms before being elected seventh vice president in 1996.

Law Enforcement Units in Mississippi

Local Police Departments
(No. of full-time officers as of 10/31/99 in parentheses)

ABERDEEN 39730 (18)	(662) 369-6454
ACKERMAN 39735; 119 W Main St (5)	(662) 285-3600
AMORY 38821 (20)	(662) 256-2676
ANGUILLA 38721	(662) 873-4978
ARCOLA 38722	(662) 827-2063
BALDWYN 38824; S 2nd;	(662) 365-8141
BASSFIELD 39421	(601) 943-6300
BATESVILLE 38606; 103 College St	(662) 563-5653
BAY SPRINGS 39422	(601) 764-3122
BAY ST LOUIS 39521; Old Spanish Trail (34)	(228) 467-9221
BEAUMONT 39423; Hwy 15	(601) 784-3781
BELMONT 38827	(662) 454-3381
BELZONI 39038; 314 N Hayden St (7)	(662) 247-2181
BENOIT 38725	(662) 742-3751
BENTONIA 39040	(662) 755-2281
BILOXI 39530; 1045 Howard Ave (129)	(228) 435-6103
BLUE MOUNTAIN 38610	(662) 685-4721
BOLTON 39041; Municipal Building	(601) 866-7233
BOONEVILLE 38829; 203 N Main St (26)	(662) 728-5611
BRANDON 39042; 203 Town Square (21)	(601) 825-7225
BROOKHAVEN 39601; 300 S Second St (33)	(601) 833-2424
BROOKSVILLE 39739	(662) 738-5531
BRUCE 38915	(662) 983-2450
BRUCE POLICE DEPT; Pittsboro, MS 38951	(662) 983-7391
BUDE POLICE STATION; Meadville 39653	(601) 384-2626
BURNSVILLE 38833	(662) 427-9526
BYHALIA 38611	(662) 838-6000
CALHOUN CITY 38916	(662) 628-6897
CANTON 39046; 347 N Liberty	(601) 859-2121
CARTHAGE 39051; 302 W Main St (10)	(601) 267-8011
CENTREVILLE 39631	(601) 645-5917
CHARLESTON 38921; Courthouse Square	(601) 647-5841
CLARKSDALE 38614; 305 S State St	(662) 627-8455
CLEVELAND 38732; 301 S Sharpe Ave (38)	(662) 843-3611
CLINTON 39056; 205 Monroe St	(601) 924-5252
COFFEEVILLE 38922; Depot St	(662) 675-2411
COLDWATER 38618	(662) 622-7241
COLLINS 39428; Beech St (10)	(601) 765-6541
COLUMBIA 39429; 201 2nd St (23)	(601) 736-8204
COLUMBUS 39701; 523 Main St (76)	(662) 328-7511
COMO 38619	(662) 526-5106
CORINTH 38834 (378)	(662) 286-3377
CRENSHAW 38621	(662) 382-5272
CROSBY 39633	(601) 639-4516
CROWDER 38622	(662) 326-8822
CRYSTAL SPRINGS; 286 W Railroad Ave	(601) 892-2121
DECATUR 39327 (4)	(601) 635-3555
DEKALB 39328	(601) 743-9197
DERMA 38839	(662) 628-6635
DREW 38737; 120 Shaw Ave	(662) 745-2200
DUCK HILL 38925	(662) 565-7200
DURANT 39063; 106 W Mulberry St	(662) 653-6846
ECRU 38841	(662) 489-3881
EDWARDS 39066; 100 Utica St (4)	(601) 852-4213
ELLISVILLE 39437; 102 W Holly St	(601) 477-9352
EUPORA 39744; N Dunn (6)	(662) 258-4121
FAYETTE 39069 (3)	(601) 786-3333
FLORA 39071	(601) 879-8871
FLORENCE 39073; N Church St	(601) 845-8856
FLOWOOD 39208; 3480 Lakeland Dr (28)	(601) 932-5400
FOREST 39074; 850 Park Rd	(601) 469-4141
FRIARS POINT 38631	(662) 383-2233
FULTON 38843 (9)	(662) 862-3441
GALLMAN 39077; Hwy 51	(601) 894-3011
GAUTIER 39553; 718 Hwy 90	(228) 497-2486
GEORGETOWN 39078	(601) 858-2463
GLENDORA; Town Hall; Sumner, MS 38957	(662) 375-9977
GLOSTER 39638; 259 1st St (5)	(601) 225-4771
GOODMAN 39079; 9912 Main St (3)	(662) 472-2263
GREENVILLE 38701; 216 Main St (103)	(662) 378-1515
GREENWOOD 38930; 406 Main St (50)	(662) 453-3311
GRENADA 38901 (39)	(662) 227-3434
GULFPORT 39501; 15th St (175)	(228) 868-5900
HATTIESBURG 39401 (117)	(601) 544-7900
HAZLEHURST 39083; 111 W Frost St	(601) 894-1181
HEIDELBERG 39439; New City Hall (5)	(601) 787-3961
HERNANDO 38632; 190 Commerce (19)	(662) 429-9092
HICKORY 39332	(662) 646-2211
HOLLANDALE; 200 E Ave S; Arcola 38722	(662) 827-2212
HOLLY SPRINGS 38635; 140 E Falconer Ave	(662) 252-2121
HORN LAKE; 2285 Goodman Rd W (32)	(662) 393-6174
HOULKA 38850	(662) 568-2745
HOUSTON 38851; 324 E Madison St (10)	(662) 456-2554
INDIANOLA 38751 (24)	(662) 887-1811
INVERNESS 38753; 802 E Grand Ave (4)	(662) 265-5741
ISOLA 38754; Julia St	(662) 962-6132
ITTA BENA 38941; Humphreys St	(662) 254-6333
IUKA 38852; 118 S Pearl St (9)	(662) 423-6340
JACKSON; 327 E Pascagoula (419 on 9/29/00)	(601) 960-1234
JACKSON; Precinct 1; 2460 Terry Rd	(601) 960-1878
JACKSON; Precinct 2; 805 Westland Plaza	(601) 960-1467
JACKSON; Precinct 3; 350 Woodrow Wilson	(601) 960-1447
JACKSON; Precinct 4; 4940 Old Canton Rd	(601) 960-1453
JONESTOWN 38639	(662) 358-9962
KILMICHAEL 39747	(662) 262-4242
KOSCIUSKO 39090; W Adams St (20)	(662) 289-3131
LAUREL 39440; 317 S Magnolia St (62)	(601) 425-4711
LEAKESVILLE 39451 (4)	(601) 394-2336
LELAND 38756; 320 Broad (20)	(662) 686-7233
LEXINGTON 39095; 207 Tchula St	(662) 834-3508
LIBERTY 39645; 243 W Main St	(601) 657-8021
LONG BEACH 39560; 202 Alexander Rd (31)	(228) 863-7282
LOUIN 39338	(601) 739-3630
LOUISE 39097	(662) 836-5121
LOUISVILLE 39339; 200 S Church Ave (18)	(662) 773-3511
LUCEDALE 39452 (11)	(601) 947-3261

Law Enforcement Units in Mississippi

Local Police Departments

LUMBERTON 39455	(601) 796-8891
MABEN 39750; 2nd Ave W	(662) 263-4212
MACON 39341; 105 W Pulaski St (7)	(662) 726-5255
MADISON 39110; 240 Main St (32)	(601) 856-6111
MAGEE 39111; E Choctaw (13)	(601) 849-2366
MAGNOLIA 39652; E Bay St (2)	(601) 783-2323
MANTACHIE 38855	(662) 282-7936
MARKS 38646; 515 Poplar St	(662) 326-3424
MAYERSVILLE 39113; Courthouse	(662) 873-6439
McCOMB 39648; 110 5th Ave (34)	(601) 684-3213
McCOOL; WEIR 39772	(662) 547-6123
MEADVILLE 39653	(601) 384-5555
MENDENHALL 39114; W Maude Ave (8)	(601) 847-2641
MERIDIAN 39301; 2415 6th (107)	(601) 485-1825
MISS.DEPT OF CORRECTIONS; Prentiss	(601) 792-2700
MIZE 39116	(601) 733-2221
MONTICELLO 39654; City Hall	(601) 587-7732
MORTON 39117; 17 W 1st Ave (13)	(601) 732-8933
MOSS POINT; 4412 Denny Av; Pascagoula (34)	(228) 475-1711
MOUND BAYOU 38762 (5)	(662) 741-2192
MOUNT OLIVE 39119	(662) 797-3232
NATCHEZ 39120; 233 D'Evereux (52)	(601) 445-5565
NETTLETON 38858	(662) 963-2171
NEW ALBANY 38652; 110 Bankhead St E (19)	(662) 534-2222
NEW AUGUSTA 39462	(601) 964-8101
NEW HEBRON 39140	(601) 694-2400
NEWTON 39345 (10)	(601) 683-2041
NORTH CARROLLTON; Town Hall; Carrollton	(662) 237-8281
NOXAPATER 39346	(662) 724-4476
OCEAN SPRINGS 39564; 503 Dewey Av (34)	(228) 875-2211
OKOLONA 38860; 106 E Main St	(662) 447-5427
OLIVE BRANCH 38654 (45)	(662) 895-3166
OSYKA 39657	(601) 542-5041
OXFORD; 715 Molly Barr Rd; University (49)	(662) 232-2400
PACHUTA; Main St; Pachuta 39347	(601) 776-6396
PASCAGOULA 39567; 611 Live Oak Av (53)	(228) 762-2211
PASS CHRISTIAN 39571 (18)	(228) 452-3300
PEARL 39208; 3565 Old Brandon Rd (34)	(601) 939-7000
PELAHATCHIE 39145; Hwy 80E (6)	(601) 854-5223
PETAL 39465; 149 W 8th Ave (16)	(601) 544-5331
PHILADELPHIA 39350	(601) 656-2131
PICAYUNE 39466; 328 S Main St (23)	(601) 798-4682
PICKENS 39146	(662) 468-2171
PLANTERSVILLE 38862; Town Hall; Hwy 6	(662) 844-2012
PONTOTOC 38863; 18 S Liberty St	(662) 489-3631
POPLARVILLE 39470 (9)	(601) 795-8161
PORT GIBSON 39150; 800 Farmer St	(601) 437-5101
POTTS CAMP 38659	(662) 333-7285
PURVIS 39475; 136 Shelby Speights Dr. (7)	(601) 794-6512
QUITMAN 39355; 101 E Church St	(601) 776-6461
RALEIGH 39153	(601) 782-4672
RAYMOND 39154 (6)	(601) 857-8041
RICHLAND 39218; 391 Scarborough Dr	(601) 932-3100
RICHTON 39476; 205 Elm Ave	(601) 788-5551
RIDGELAND 39157 (40 on 7/31/00)	(601) 856-2121
RIPLEY 38663; 500-A South Main St	(662) 837-2215
ROLLING FORK 39159; 400 Walnut St (4)	(662) 873-2212
ROSEDALE 38769	(662) 759-3536
RULEVILLE 38771; 100 Chester Ave	(662) 756-2793
SALTILLO 38866; 115 S 2nd Ave	(662) 869-2100
SANDERSVILLE 39477	(601) 428-0992
SARDIS 38666; 114A W Lee St	(662) 487-1383
SEBASTOPOL; City Hall; Hwy 21; Sebastopol	(601) 625-7200
SENATOBIA 38668; 135 N Front St (19)	(662) 562-5643
SHANNON 38868	(662) 767-3878
SHAW 38773 (6)	(662) 754-5741
SHELBY 38774; 305 Third Ave	(662) 398-5155
SHUBUTA 39360	(601) 687-1536
SHUQUALAK 39361	(662) 793-4521
SILVER CREEK 39663; Town Hall; 242 2nd	(601) 886-7866
SMITHVILLE 38870	(662) 651-4063
SOSO 39480; City Hall	(601) 729-2958
SOUTHAVEN 38671; 8791 Northwest Dr (62)	(662) 393-8652
STARKVILLE 39759; City Hall (35)	(662) 323-4134
STATE LINE 39362	(601) 848-7755
STONEWALL; Hwy 513; Stonewall 39363	(601) 659-4662
SUMMIT 39666; 706 Railroad Ave	(601) 276-9511
SUMRALL 39482; E Center Ave	(601) 758-3531
SUNFLOWER 38778 (2)	(662) 569-3131
TAYLORSVILLE 39168	(601) 785-6531
TCHULA 39169; Front St	(662) 235-4056
TERRY 39170; Hwy 51 (3)	(601) 878-5521
TISHOMINGO 38873	(662) 438-6302
TUNICA 38676	(662) 363-2400
TUPELO 38801; 220 N Front St (114)	(662) 841-6490
TUTWILER 38963; 209 Hancock St	(662) 345-8321
TYLERTOWN 39667; 807 Magnolia Ave	(601) 876-4440
UNION 39365; Bank St	(662) 774-9211
UTICA 39175; 105 Depot (9)	(601) 885-6112
VAIDEN 39176; 202 Mulberry (3)	(662) 464-5628
VARDAMAN 38878	(662) 682-5111
VERONA 38879 (7)	(662) 566-2215
VICKSBURG 39180; 721 Clay St (94)	(601) 636-2511
VICKSBURG CRIMEFIGHTERS; Vicksburg	(601) 636-6393
WALNUT; City Hall; 102 S Main St; Walnut	(662) 223-4405
WALNUT GROVE 39189	(601) 253-2321
WATER VALLEY 38965; 909 N Main St	(662) 473-2933
WAVELAND 39576; Hwy 90 (21)	(228) 467-3669
WAYNESBORO 39367	(601) 735-4612
WEBB 38966	(662) 375-8164
WEIR 39772	(662) 547-6747
WESSON 39191	(601) 643-2211
WEST POINT 39773; 330 W Broad St	(662) 494-1244
WIGGINS 39577 (12)	(601) 928-5444
WINONA 38967; 129 Liberty St (11)	(662) 283-1121
WOODVILLE 39669	(601) 888-4411
YAZOO CITY 39194; 305 Lintonia Ave. (33)	(662) 746-1131

Law Enforcement Units in Mississippi

Department of Public Safety (Highway Patrol)

JACKSON; Main Headquarters; Information number & number for all top officials .... (601) 987-1212
JACKSON; Colonel Tom Blain, Executive Director, Mississippi Bureau of Narcotics .... (601) 359-1570
JACKSON; Major Jimmy Dees; Chief Inspector, Central Region .... (601) 987-1212
HATTIESBURG 39401; 301 S 26th Ave (Major David Wynn; Chief Inspector, Southern Region) .... (601) 264-3529
NEW ALBANY; Major Carlton Hays; Chief Inspector, Northern Region .... (662) 534-4755
DISTRICT 1 OFFICE; Captain Clifton K. Dunlap; PO Box 958; Jackson 30205 .... (601) 987-1212
DISTRICT 2 OFFICE; Captain Jimmy G. Holly; 701 Highway 82 W; Greenwood 38930 .... (662) 453-4515
DISTRICT 3 OFFICE; Captain William C. Ellis; Highway 51 N; Batesville 38606 .... (662) 563-4651
DISTRICT 4 OFFICE; Captain Jihnny E. Kerr; PO Box 866; New Albany 38652 .... (662) 534-4755
DISTRICT 5 OFFICE; Captain James D. Humphries; PO Box 589; Starkville 39759 .... (662) 323-5314
DISTRICT 6 OFFICE; Captain Jon R. Howard; PO Box 4218; Meridian 39301 .... (601) 693-1926
DISTRICT 7 OFFICE; Captain Donald Rawson; 6085 Highway 49; Hattiesburg 39401 .... (601) 264-3529
DISTRICT 8 OFFICE; Captain Albert SantaCruz; 4008 Eighth St; Gulfport 39501 .... (228) 864-1314
DISTRICT 9 OFFICE; Captain James D. Vines; 440 Highway 51 S; Brookhaven 39601 .... (601) 833-7811
JACKSON; Mississippi Crime Laboratory .... (601) 987-1600
BATESVILLE; North Mississippi Crime Laboratory .... (662) 563-5681
GULFPORT; Gulf Coast Crime Laboratory .... (228) 832-9641
MERIDIAN; East Mississippi Crime Laboratory .... (601) 483-5273
PEARL 39208; 3791 Hwy 468 W (Mississippi Law Enforcement Officer's Training Academy) .... (601) 933-2100

Department of Public Safety (Driver's License Examining Stations)

ABERDEEN; City Hall (Monday 8:30-4:30[56]) .... (662) 369-4164
ACKERMAN; National Guard Armory (2nd, 4th & 5th Wednesday 8:30-4:30) .... (662) 285-2035
AMORY; Community Center Building (Tuesday & 1st & 3rd Wed. 8:30-4:30) .... (662) 256-3929
ASHLAND; City Hall (2nd & 4th Friday 8:30-4:30) .... (662) 224-6282
BATESVILLE; Substation (Monday & Tuesday 8:00-5:00) .... (228) 563-8125
BAY SAINT LOUIS; Shoreline Park Community Center (Monday & Tuesday 8:00-5:00) .... (228) 467-0346
BAY SPRINGS; Courthouse Building (Friday 8:00-5:00) .... (601) 764-2248
BELZONI; Old MP&L Bldg.; 314 N Hayden (Monday 8:30-4:30) .... (662) 247-0105
BILOXI; 451 Parker St. (Monday-Friday 8:00-5:00) .... (228) 374-0041
BOONEVILLE; West Side Community Center in Community Park (Wednesday 8:30-4:30) .... (662) 728-1782
BROOKHAVEN; Substation (Monday-Friday 8:00-5:00) .... (601) 833-0808
BRUCE; City Hall (Thursday 8:30-4:30) .... (662) 983-2453
CANTON; Community Center Building (Thursday 8:30-4:30) .... (601) 859-5829
CARTHAGE; Police Dept. (Wednesday 8:00-5:00) .... (601) 267-8011
CHARLESTON; City Hall (1st & 3rd Tuesday 8:30-4:30) .... (662) 647-8421
CLARKSDALE; 144 Ritch (Monday-Friday 8:00-5:00) .... (662) 624-2650
CLEVELAND; Agriculture Center Building (Monday-Friday 8:00-5:00) .... (662) 846-0749
COLLINS; Courthouse (Monday 8:00-5:00) .... (601) 765-4205
COLUMBIA; City Hall (Thursday 8:30-5:00) .... (662) 736-6688
COLUMBUS; Lowndes County Administration Building (Monday-Friday 8:00-4:30) .... (662) 327-1833
CORINTH; Sheriff's Office (Wednesday 8:30-5:00, Thursday 8:00-5:00, Friday 8:00-4:30) .... (662) 286-7704
CRYSTAL SPRINGS; City Hall (1st & 2nd Monday 8:30-4:30) .... (601) 892-1210
DEKALB; Farmer's Market (2nd Tuesday 8:00-5:00) .... (601) 743-2028
EUPORA; County Office Building (Thursday 8:30-4:30) .... (662) 258-2567
FOREST; Police Dept (Thursday & Friday 8:00-5:00) .... (601) 469-3256
FULTON; Courthouse (Tuesday 8:30-4:30) .... (662) 862-7041
GREENVILLE; CDL Office Bldg; 420 Hwy 82W (Monday-Friday 8:00-5:00) .... (662) 332-4734
GREENWOOD; Substation (Monday-Friday 8:00-5:00) .... (662) 453-5743
GRENADA; MHP Building (Wednesday 8:30-5:00, Thursday 8:00-5:00 & Friday 8:00-4:00) .... (662) 226-2341
GULFPORT; Substation (Monday-Friday 8:00-5:00) .... (228) 864-1317
GULFPORT; 10565 E-J Three Rivers Road (Monday-Friday 8:00-5:00) .... (228) 832-1865
HATTIESBURG; CDL Bldg. (Monday-Friday 8:00-5:00) .... (601) 582-3814
HAZLEHURST; City Hall (3rd & 4th. Monday 8:30-4:30) .... (601) 894-3131
HOLLY SPRINGS; DL Office (Monday & Tuesday 8:30-5:00) .... (662) 252-2254
HOUSTON; National Guard Armory (Tuesday 8:30-4:30) .... (662) 456-1402

---

[56] Days and hours officers are present to give examinations and issue licenses.

Law Enforcement Units in Mississippi

INDIANOLA; Justice Court Bldg. (Thursday 8:30-4:30) .... (662) 887-7219
IUKA; Rescue Squad Bldg. (Monday 8:30-5:00, Tuesday 8:00-4:30) .... (662) 423-3781
JACKSON; Headquarters Building (Monday-Friday 8:00-5:00) .... (601) 987-1284
JACKSON; 2460 Terry Road (Monday-Friday 8:00-5:00) .... (601) 987-1288
JACKSON; 442 Highway 49 S; Richland (Monday-Friday 8:00-5:00) .... (601) 939-4217
KOSCIUSKO; Convention Center Building (Monday & Tuesday 8:30-4:30) .... (662) 289-5437
LAUREL; Old Health Dept. Building (Monday-Friday 8:00-5:00) .... (601) 425-3802
LEAKSVILLE; City Hall (2nd Thursday 8:00-5:00) .... (601) 394-2383
LEXINGTON; Old Hospital Building (Wednesday 8:30-4:30) .... (662) 834-4040
LIBERTY; Amite County Building (1st, 2nd & 3rd Thursday 8:00-4:30) .... (601) 657-8602
LOUISVILLE; Courthouse Building (Monday-Friday 8:30-4:30) .... (662) 773-3843
LUCEDALE; Senior Citizens Building (Wednesday 8:00-5:00) .... (601) 947-6587
MACON; E911 Building, 16129 Highway 45 Alternate (2nd & 4th Tuesday 8:30-4:30) .... (662) 726-4812
MAGNOLIA; Community Center (Monday-Friday 8:00-5:00) .... (601) 783-6618
MARKS; Court Room (2nd & 4th Monday 8:30-4:30) .... (662) 326-3131
MEADVILLE; County Extention Office (1st Wednesday 8:00-4:30) .... (601) 384-2048
MENDENHALL; Old MP&L Building (Thursday & Friday 8:00-5:00) .... (601) 847-5733
MERIDIAN; Substation at 841 Hwy 19N (Monday-Friday 8:00-5:00) .... (601) 483-9246
MONTICELLO; City Hall (Tuesday 8:00-4:30) .... (601) 587-7732
NATCHEZ; CDL Building (Monday-Friday 8:00-5:00) .... (601) 442-4879
NESBITT; License Road (Monday-Friday 8:00-5:00) .... (662) 429-5584
NEW ALBANY; Patrol Office (Monday-Friday 8:00-5:00) .... (662) 534-3111
NEWTON; Old Hwy 15N (Monday-Friday 8:00-5:00) .... (601) 683-2576
OKOLONA; National Guard Armory (1st & 3rd Wednesday 8:30-4:30) .... (662) 447-2478
OXFORD; Examining Trailer, Hiway 7S (Monday-Friday, except 2nd & 4th Tuesday 8:00-5:00) ..... (662) 236-2066
PASCAGOULA; Fairgrounds (Monday-Friday 8:00-5:00) .... (228) 769-3266
PHILADELPHIA; Jail (1st, 3rd & 4th Monday & Tuesday 8:00-5:00) .... (228) 656-6120
PICAYUNE; Friendship Park (Wednesday & Thursday 8:00-5:00) .... (601) 799-1428
PONTOTOC; New County Building (1st, 3rd & 5th Friday 8:30-4:30) .... (662) 489-3934
POPLARVILLE; PR Administration Building (1st & 2nd Friday 8:00-5:00) .... (601) 795-3055
PORT GIBSON; Civil Defense Building (1st. & 2nd Wednesday 8:30-4:30) .... (601) 437-8384
PRENTISS; Library Building (Tuesday 8:00-5:00) .... (601) 792-8159
PURVIS; Lamar County Bank (1st Wednesday 8:00-5:00) .... (601) 794-8041
QUITMAN; Central Maintence Building (Wednesday 8:00-4:30) .... (601) 776-6618
RALEIGH; City Hall (Tuesday 8:00-5:00) .... (601) 782-4672
RICHLAND; 442 Hwy 49S (Monday-Friday 8:00-5:00) .... (601) 939-4217
RICHTON; Fire Dept. (1st Thursday 8:00-5:00) .... (601) 788-6172
RIPLEY; DL Building (Thursday 8:30-4:30) .... (662) 837-8409
ROLLING FORK; National Guard Armory (3rd & 4th Wednesday 8:30-4:30) .... (662) 873-4615
SARDIS; I-55 & Hwy 315 (Wednesday, Thursday & Friday 8:00-5:00) .... (662) 487-3001
SENATOBIA; County Extension Office Building (Wed. & Thur., road test only 8:00-5:00) ...... (662) 562-8024
STARKVILLE; Substation (Monday-Friday 8:00-4:30) .... (662) 323-5316
TUNICA; County Community Complex (1st & 3rd Monday 8:30-4:30) .... (662) 363-3914
TUPELO; Tupelo Furniture Market Building (Monday - Friday 8:00-5:00) .... (662) 844-2408
TYLERTOWN; Library (2nd, 3rd, 4th & 5th Wednesday 8:00-4:30) .... (601) 876-4348
VICKSBURG; Juvenile Detention Center (Monday, Tuesday, Thursday & Friday 8:00-5:00) .... (601) 638-5441
WATER VALLEY; Main St (2nd & 4th Tuesday 8:30-4:30) .... (662) 473-2445
WAYNESBORO; Old Hospital Building (Friday 8:00-5:00) .... (662) 735-3242
WEST POINT; Police Dept. (Thursday & Friday 8:30-5:00) .... (662) 494-1244
WIGGINS; City Hall (2rd & 4th Friday 8:00-5:00) .... (601) 928-7221
WINONA; Old Justice Court Building (Tuesday 8:30-4:30) .... (662) 283-4105
WOODVILLE; County Extension Building (2nd & 4th Thursday 8:00-4:30) .... (601) 888-3211
YAZOO CITY; Teen Center Building (Wednesday 8:30-4:30) .... (662) 746-9213

The Miss. Dept. of Public Safety issued 534,882 driver's licenses during the fiscal year ending June 30, 1999.

There were 30 Mississippi law enforcement officers feloniously killed in the line of duty during the 13-year period of 1986 through 1998 with deaths reported every year except 1996, when none were killed.

There are 209 police depts. in Miss. (not counting 82 Sheriff's Depts. and Highway Patrol) & 17,120 in the U.S.

Crime in Mississippi

No. of Full-Time Law Enforcement Employees, as of Oct. 31, 1999: 7,584
   Sworn Officers 4,790 (4,425 male & 365 female); Civilians 2,794 (1,020 male & 1,774 female)
State & Local Government Expenditures on Police Protection, 1996: $287 million.
Number of Sworn Highway Patrol Officers (As of 7/1/2000): 535 (339 traffic enforcement officers)
Number of Sworn Bureau of Narcotics Agents (10/20/2000): 164
Budget for Highway Safety Patrol: FY 2000 — $ 49,045,302   FY 2001 — $ 56,791,711 requested
Budget for Bureau of Narcotics: FY 2000 — $ 16,633,813   FY 2001 — $ 16,079,529 requested
Budget for Dept. of Corrections: FY 2000 — $240,225,462   FY 1999 — $236,461,650
                                      FY 1998 — $202,468,031   FY 1997 — $185,795,368

Category	Year	Count	% Change		Rate[1]	% Change
Crimes, Total	1998	120,647		Rate	4,384.0	
	1999	118,231	-02.0%	Rate:	4,269.8	-02.6% under 1998
[2]Violent Crimes	1998	11,302		Rate	410.7	
	1999	9,671	-14.4%	Rate	349.3	-15.0% under 1998
[3]Property Crimes	1998	109,345		Rate	3,973.3	
	1999	108,560	-00.7%	Rate	3,920.5	-01.3% under 1998
Murder	1998	315		Rate	11.4	
	1999	213	-32.4%	Rate	7.7	-32.5% under 1998
Forcible Rape	1998	1,026		Rate	37.3	
	1999	1,156	+12.7%	Rate	41.7	+11.8% over 1998
Robbery	1998	3,394		Rate	123.3	
	1999	3,091	-08.9%	Rate	111.6	-09.5% under 1998
Aggravated Assault	1998	6,567		Rate	238.6	
	1999	5,211	-20.6%	Rate	188.2	-21.1% under 1998
Burglary	1998	31,498		Rate	1,144.5	
	1999	29,109	-07.6%	Rate	1,051.2	-08.2% under 1998
Larceny-Theft	1998	68,525		Rate	2,490.0	
	1999	65,919	-03.8%	Rate	2,380.6	-04.4% under 1998
Motor Vehicle Theft	1998	9,322		Rate	338.7	
	1999	13,532	+45.2%	Rate	488.7	+44.3% over 1998
Prison Inmates	1996	13,143	+04.5%	Rate	483.9	+03.8% over 1995
	1997	14,548	+10.7%	Rate	532.7	+10.1% over 1996
	Oct. 1, 2000	20,220	(Male 18,590 — Black 13,801; White 4,422; Other 97)			
			(Female 1,630 — Black 1,458; White 158; Other 14)			

Oct. 9, 2000: Parolees — 1,377   **Probationers** — 14,824   **Total Active Offenders** — 36,421
No. Paroled: 1999 — 671   1998 — 1,087   1997 — 1,277   1996 — 1,185

> The state's last execution: Leo Edwards died in the gas chamber on 6/21/1989.

No. in State Penitentiary at Parchman, 3/9/2000: 4,367 (capacity 4,869)
   The average annual cost to keep a prisoner in Parchment is $28,000.
Prisoners on Death Row, Oct. 1, 2000: 61 (0.3%) [method of execution is lethal injection]
Prisoners Executed: Since 1930 — 158   Since 1977 — 4   **Last Execution**: 6/21/89
Lawyers, 1/1/2000: 5,835 (476 persons per lawyer, or 210 lawyers per 100,000 people)

> At the end of 1999, U.S. prisons and jails held 1,890,800 inmates. The figure topped 2 million for the first time ever when counting the additional 135,800 people held in juvenile, military, immigration and other facilities, including those in U.S. territories. In 1998, Mississippi had the fourth highest incarceration *rate* in the nation — 574 prisoners per 100,000 population. Louisiana was first with 736, followed by Texas (724) and Oklahoma (622). Mississippi topped the list of states with the largest percentage increase in prisoners 1997-98 with a 16.7% increase. Mississippi was 6th in increases in prison populations from 1990-1998 with a 8.8% increase. Mississippi followed Texas (12.4%), West Virginia (10.5%), Hawaii (10.0%), Idaho (9.6%) & the Federal system (9.4%).

> On June 30, 1993, Mississippi Department of Corrections had 9,629 prisoners in a system with a capacity for 9,164 prisoners (465 over capacity). By March 9, 2000, the figures were 18,735 prisoners with a capacity for 17,809 (926 over capacity). Mississippi Department of Corrections projections based on 20 construction or renovation projects would give Mississippi 22,733 beds by 2003 with an equal number of inmates, a 148% increase in space in just one decade.

---

[1] Rate per 100,000 population. Resident Population 1998: 2,752,000   1999: 2,769,000
[2] Includes murder & non-negligent manslaughter, forcible rape, robbery and aggravated assault.
[3] Includes burglary, larceny-theft and motor vehicle theft. Does not include arson.

Crime in Mississippi

NUMBER OF MAJOR OFFENSES IN SELECTED CITIES WITH POPULATION 10,000 OR MORE, 1999

City[1]	Pop.	Murder	Forcible Rape	Robbery	Aggravated Assualt	Burglary	Larceny-Theft	Vehicle Theft	Total
Biloxi	47,600	1	31	125	179	652	3,905	341	5,234
Brandon	14,700	--	--	4	6	25	147	3	185
Brookhaven	10,713	2	6	18	23	15	132	--	196
Cleveland	14,923	--	7	29	50	245	1,021	30	1,382
Columbus	22,431	1	12	23	99	243	1,202	83	1,663
Corinth	12,277	1	2	19	54	147	519	35	777
Greenwood	18,327	4	21	57	39	553	1,092	50	1,816
Grenada	11,228	3	8	23	65	175	743	66	1,083
Gulfport	65,151	6	47	115	83	1,017	3,631	488	5,387
Hattiesburg	49,099	3	21	77	75	920	2,283	156	3,535
Horn Lake	13,968	--	1	15	22	80	315	34	467
Indianola	11,583	1	16	26	80	391	838	55	1,407
Jackson	189,930	45	248	1,096	691	4,814	9,703	3,475	20,072
Laurel	18,409	1	18	45	70	319	1,184	84	1,721
Long Beach	16,877	1	4	12	4	91	495	27	634
Madison	12,694	--	1	5	2	17	160	3	188
McComb	11,817	3	3	35	31	162	426	57	717
Meridian	40,497	4	16	80	142	615	1,097	134	2,088
Natchez	18,387	3	8	26	33	256	1,168	39	1,533
Olive Branch	12,135	--	7	7	78	106	487	103	788
Oxford	12,169	--	1	15	15	57	230	24	342
Pascagoula	27,326	2	15	84	96	686	1,970	254	3,107
Pearl	23,427	--	12	12	24	137	707	66	958
Picayune	12,130	--	8	12	29	98	507	28	682
Ridgeland	16,644	1	--	24	13	88	892	70	1,088
Southaven	23,575	2	3	18	9	237	829	97	1,195
Starkville	20,305	--	3	30	33	144	865	97	1,127
Tupelo	35,803	2	17	53	54	447	1,744	129	2,446

NUMBER OF MAJOR OFFENSES BY AREA, 1999

Area	Population	Violent[2]	Property	Totals
MSAs[3]	993,288	4,080	52,593	56,673
Cities outside MSAs	637,473	3,520	40,715	44,235
Rural Areas	1,138,239	2,071	15,252	17,323
State Total	**2,769,000**	**9,671**	**108,560**	**118,231**
Rate per 100,000 population		349	3,921	4,270

NUMBER OF MAJOR OFFENSES FOR THE JACKSON MSA, 1999[4]

Area	Population	Violent	Property	Totals
City of Jackson	189,930	2,080	17,992	20,072
Remainer of MSA	242,643	397	7,172	7,569
Total Jackson MSA	**432,573**	**2,477**	**25,164**	**27,641**
Rate per 100,000 population		573	5,817	6,390

Mississippi Highway Patrol citations issued in FY 1998 amounted to $10.6 million in fines.

[1] Mississippi cities with 10,000 population or more are represented except Canton, Clarksdale, Clinton, Gautier, Greenville, Moss Point, Ocean Springs, Vicksburg and Yazoo City (did not report / no data available).
[2] Violent crimes are murder, forcible rape, robbery & aggravated assault. Property crimes are burglary, larcency-theft & motor vehicle theft.
[3] Metropolitan Statistical Areas — the Biloxi-Gulfport, Pascagoula, Hattiesburg, Jackson and Memphis MSAs.
[4] The Jackson MSA includes Hinds County (and the City of Jackson), Madison County and Rankin County.

Main Sources *Crime In The U.S., Uniform Crime Reports*, 1998 and 1999; U.S. Department of Justice - Federal Bureau of Investigation, and the Mississippi Department of Corrections.

Fire Departments in Mississippi

ABERDEEN; Cedar Creek Vol; Egypt Rd	(662) 369-7557
ABERDEEN; 101 Matubba	(662) 369-9551
ABERDEEN; Fire Chief's Off; 101 Matubba	(662) 369-2011
ABERDEEN; Rural Hill V F D; Whitaker Rd	(662) 369-7719
ACKERMAN	(662) 285-9999
AMORY	(662) 256-2902
AMORY; Becker Athens; Calvary Church Rd	(662) 256-4040
AMORY; Cason Volunteer Dept; Old Hwy 6	(662) 256-9180
AMORY; Hatley Dept	(662) 256-7245
AMORY; Splunge Vol. Dept; Splunge Rd	(662) 256-9800
ARCOLA; Hollandale Dept; E Ave S	(662) 827-2112
ARTESIA	(662) 272-5757
ASHLAND; W Boundary Dr	(662) 224-6282
ASHLAND; Snow Lake Dept; Snow Lake Dr	(662) 224-8919
BALDWYN; Ingram Dept; Ingram Rd	(662) 365-7443
BALDWYN; Dundee Dept	(662) 365-8081
BASSFIELD	(601) 943-5600
BATESVILLE; College St	(662) 563-4703
BATESVILLE; 102 Woodland Rd S	(662) 563-6612
BAY SAINT LOUIS; Old Spanish Trail	(228) 467-4619
BAY SAINT LOUIS; Bayside Park	(228) 466-4619
BAY SAINT LOUIS; Clermont Harbor	(228) 467-3345
BAY SAINT LOUIS; Diamondhead; 4440 Kalani Dr	(228) 255-1314
BAY SAINT LOUIS; East Hancock; Chapman Rd	(228) 466-3932
BEAUMONT; Dolly Ave	(601) 784-3338
BELDEN	(662) 842-2222
BELMONT	(662) 454-9999
BELMONT (To Report Fire)	(662) 454-3311
BELZONI; Chief's Office; 312 N Hayden St	(662) 247-2910
BELZONI; 312 N Hayden St	(662) 247-1313
BILOXI; 710 Beach Blvd	(228) 374-3105
BILOXI; 213 N LeMoyne Blvd	(228) 432-7566
BILOXI; D'Iberville Vol; 10441 LeMoyne Blvd	(228) 392-3473
BILOXI; 310 Main St	(228) 436-3633
BILOXI; Woolmarket Volunteer Dept	(228) 392-5588
BOGUE CHITTO; Ruth Vol. Dept; Hwy 583	(601) 734-6445
BOLTON (To report a fire)	(601) 948-3232
BOONEVILLE	(662) 728-4091
BOONEVILLE; Station No. 2; S Lake St	(662) 728-9616
BRANDON	(601) 825-9999
BRANDON; Lake Harbor Vol; 1551 Hwy 43N	(228) 829-2414
BRANDON; Langford Dept; 1415 Hwy 471	(601) 825-0038
BROOKHAVEN; City Hall	(601) 833-2411
BROOKHAVEN; Industrial Park Rd	(601) 833-7311
BROOKHAVEN; Whitworth Ave	(601) 833-3008
BROOKHAVEN; Willard St	(601) 833-7417
BROOKHAVEN; Lincoln County Dept	(601) 833-5566
BUDE	(601) 384-5100
BYHALIA	(662) 838-6688
CALHOUN CITY	(662) 983-7391
CANTON; W Peace St	(601) 859-8839
CANTON; 745 E Center St	(601) 859-3311
CANTON; Farm Haven Vol. Dept; Hwy 16E	(601) 859-3000
CARTHAGE; 302 W Main St	(601) 267-5711
CARTHAGE; 302 W Main St	(601) 267-8473
CARTHAGE; White St	(601) 267-2711
CAYCE; Volunteer Dept	(662) 851-7698
CENTREVILLE	(601) 645-5432
CHARLESTON	(662) 647-8433
CLARKSDALE; DeSoto Ave	(662) 627-8480
CLARKSDALE; Sasse St	(662) 627-8487
CLEVELAND; S Sharpe Ave	(662) 843-2711
CLEVELAND; 200 S Court St	(662) 843-4252
CLINTON; Stat. No. 1; 301 W Main St	(601) 924-6421
CLINTON; Stat. No. 2; 910 Old Vicksburg Rd	(601) 924-3902
CLINTON; Stat. No. 3; 1659 W Northside Dr	(601) 924-5188
COFFEEVILLE; Depot St	(662) 675-2411
COFFEEVILLE; Depot St. (to report a fire)	(662) 675-2642
COLDWATER	(662) 622-5541
COLLINS; S 1st	(601) 765-4821
COLUMBIA; Pine Burr Vol; Pine Burr Rd	(601) 736-3400
COLUMBUS; 115 6th St. N	(662) 328-7521
COLUMBUS; 205 7th Ave. S	(662) 329-5121
COLUMBUS; Columbus Air Force Base Dept	(662) 434-8881
COMO	(662) 526-5578
CORINTH; E 6th St	(662) 286-8051
CORINTH; S Alcorn Dr	(662) 286-2203
CORINTH; Municipal Bldg	(662) 286-2213
CORINTH; Farmington Vol; Farmington Rd	(662) 287-8161
CRENSHAW	(662) 382-5353
CROSBY	(601) 639-4969
CRYSTAL SPRINGS; 269A S Jackson	(601) 892-1313
DeKALB; Hopper Ave	(601) 743-2422
DECATUR	(601) 635-2000
DREW; 144 N Church St	(662) 745-2323
DUCK HILL	(662) 565-9999
DURANT; 106 W Mulberry St	(662) 653-6846
ECRU; 115 W Main St	(662) 489-4361
EDWARDS (To report a fire)	(601) 948-3232
ELLISVILLE; Main St	(601) 477-8822
ELLISVILLE; 804 Dubose St	(601) 477-2120
ELLISVILLE; 108 Court	(601) 477-9272
ENTERPRISE; Hwy 513W	(601) 659-4454
ESCATAWPA; Volunteer Dept	(228) 475-1621
ETHEL	(662) 674-5222
EUPORA; 102 E Clark Ave. (to report a fire)	(662) 258-6600
FAYETTE; 109 Poindexter	(601) 786-3311
FAYETTE; Union Church Vol; S Main St	(601) 786-8000
FLORA	(601) 879-8871
FLORENCE; Cleary Vol. Dept; Hoover Lake	(601) 845-7181
FLORENCE; Old Pearl Dept	(601) 845-8489
FLORENCE; Volunteer Dept	(601) 845-7399
FLOWOOD; 3601 1st St	(601) 932-4903
FLOWOOD; 3480 Lakeland Dr	(601) 932-6600
FOREST; 337 E 2nd St	(601) 469-2214
FULTON	(662) 862-9716
FULTON; Peppertown Dorsey Dept	(662) 862-9661
FULTON; Itawamba County Dept	(662) 862-7300
GAUTIER; 7510 Martin Bluff Rd	(228) 497-5910
GAUTIER; Vol; 3604 Gautier/Vancleave Rd	(228) 497-1656

Fire Departments in Mississippi

GEORGETOWN; Fire Alert	(601) 858-9999
GLOSTER; Wilkinson County/Amite Co. Vol.	(601) 639-4969
GOLDEN	(662) 454-9645
GRENADA; 76 N Main	(662) 226-1421
GREENVILLE; 532 Central St.	(662) 378-1616
GREENVILLE	(662) 332-1572
GREENWOOD; 404 Main St.	(662) 453-1414
GREENWOOD; Fire Chief; 404 Main St.	(662) 455-7610
GREENWOOD; Fire Marshall	(662) 455-7613
GULFPORT	(228) 865-2333
GULFPORT; 1515 23rd Ave.	(228) 868-5950
GULFPORT; 1506 24th Ave.	(228) 863-1214
GULFPORT; Latimer Vol. Dept; 9525 Scott	(228) 392-7021
GULFPORT; N Gulfport Vol; 4800 Texas Ave.	(228) 864-0332
GULFPORT; Orange Grove VFD; Klein Rd.	(228) 832-1600
GUNTOWN	(662) 348-2319
HAMILTON; Volunteer Dept; Hamilton Rd.	(662) 343-5600
HARRISVILLE; Volunteer Dept; Hwy 469	(601) 847-0712
HATTIESBURG; City Hall	(601) 582-1773
HATTIESBURG; N Main St.	(601) 582-3311
HATTIESBURG; Lamar Co; Oak Grove Rd.	(601) 264-7563
HATTIESBURG; Rawls Springs Dept.	(601) 268-2238
HATTIESBURG; Runnelstown Vol; 420 Forrest	(601) 545-9422
HAZLEHURST; Front St.	(601) 894-4211
HAZLEHURST; W Frost St.	(601) 894-1181
HERMANVILLE; Claiborne County Dept.	(601) 535-9999
HERNANDO; 190 Commerce St.	(662) 429-9092
HERNANDO; 4501 Okeechobee St.	(662) 429-5225
HERNANDO; DeSoto County Dept.	(662) 429-1111
HERNANDO; Eudora; Hwy 304, Harper Rd.	(662) 429-9000
HERNANDO; Love Vol. Dept; 7345 Hwy 51S	(662) 429-9562
HICKORY FLAT	(662) 333-9999
HOLLY BLUFF; Volunteer; Hwy 16	(662) 828-3210
HOLLY BLUFF; Hwy 16 (to report a fire)	(662) 746-2121
HOLLY SPRINGS; 150 E Falconer Ave.	(662) 252-2521
HORN LAKE; 2285 Goodman Rd W	(662) 393-0100
HOUSTON; 324 E Madison St.	(662) 456-4190
HOUSTON; Houlka Dept; 324 E Madison St.	(662) 456-3264
HURLEY; East Central Vol; 21728 Hwy 613	(601) 588-3800
HURLEY; Three Rivers Vol; 16901 Hwy 63	(601) 588-3306
INDIANOLA	(662) 887-1811
INVERNESS; 802 E Grand Ave.	(662) 265-5121
ISOLA	(662) 962-3333
ITTA BENA; 200 Humphreys St.	(662) 254-6333
IUKA; 118 S Pearl St.	(662) 423-5011
IUKA; Tishomingo Volunteer Dept.	(662) 423-1862
JACKSON; Stat. No. 1; 555 S West St.	(601) 960-2101
JACKSON; Stat. No. 2; 836 W Amite St.	(601) 960-2102
JACKSON; Stat. No. 3; 333 E Fortification St.	(601) 960-2103
JACKSON; Stat. No. 5; 1810 N State St.	(601) 960-2105
JACKSON; Stat. No. 6; 101 Livingston Park Dr.	(601) 960-2106
JACKSON; Stat. No. 7; 4625 N State St.	(601) 960-2107
JACKSON; Stat. No. 8; 1706 Terry Rd.	(601) 960-2108
JACKSON; Stat. No. 10; 2410 Livingston Rd.	(601) 960-2110
JACKSON; Stat. No. 11; 3660 Terry Rd.	(601) 960-2111
JACKSON; Stat. No. 12; 2435 McFadden Rd.	(601) 960-2112
JACKSON; Stat. No. 14; 3206 Lynch St.	(601) 960-2114
JACKSON; Stat. No. 15; 4943 Clinton Blvd.	(601) 960-2115
JACKSON; Stat. No. 16; 1400 Lakeland Dr.	(601) 960-2116
JACKSON; Stat. No. 17; 1491 Canton Mart Rd.	(601) 960-2117
JACKSON; Stat. No. 19; 5610 Ridgewood Rd.	(601) 960-2119
JACKSON; Stat. 20; 4445 Medgar Evers Blvd.	(601) 960-2120
JACKSON; Stat. No. 21; 5360 Watkins Dr.	(601) 960-2121
JACKSON; Stat. No. 22; 1560 Lakeshore Rd.	(601) 960-2122
JACKSON; Stat. No. 23; 2460 Raymond Rd.	(601) 960-2123
JACKSON; Stat. No. 24; 1240 Wiggins Rd.	(601) 960-2124
JACKSON; Stat. No. 25; 4064 S Siwell Rd.	(601) 960-2125
JACKSON; Stat. No. 26; 223 Flag Chapel Cir.	(601) 960-2126
JACKSON; Maclean Vol; 1367 Ross Circle	(601) 982-8761
JONESTOWN; 307 Main	(662) 358-9962
KILMICHAEL; 1011 Depot Ave.	(662) 262-7527
KOSCIUSKO; W Jefferson	(662) 289-1171
KOSCIUSKO; Attala Co. Dept; Fairground Rd.	(662) 289-9163
LAMBERT	(662) 326-3951
LAUREL; City Fire Dept.	(601) 426-9999
LAUREL; 101 13th Ave.	(601) 428-6473
LAUREL; 415 Queensburg Ave.	(601) 428-6474
LAUREL; 639 W 26th St.	(601) 428-6475
LAUREL; Hillcrest Dr.	(601) 428-6476
LAUREL; 1247 N Meridian Ave.	(601) 428-6477
LAUREL; 1314 Ellisville Blvd.	(601) 428-6468
LEAKESVILLE; Fire Emergency	(601) 394-9999
LEAKSVILLE; Southeast Greene Co. Dept.	(601) 394-5250
LELAND; W Deer Creek Dr E	(662) 686-2243
LENA	(601) 654-3332
LEXINGTON; Chief's Office; 207 Tchula St.	(662) 834-3965
LEXINGTON; Ebenezer Dept; Hwy 14	(662) 834-1305
LIBERTY; 243 W Main St.	(601) 657-8941
LONG BEACH; Alexander Rd.	(228) 863-7292
LORMAN; Volunteer	(601) 437-3761
LOUISE	(662) 836-5555
LOUISVILLE; N Court	(662) 773-9402
LUCEDALE	(601) 947-3406
LUCEDALE; Greene Co. Beat 4 Vol; Hwy 63N	(601) 947-6034
LULA	(662) 337-2323
LUMBERTON; NE Pearl River Co. Vol.	(601) 796-3473
LYON; Coahoma Central Sta; 130 Roberson Rd.	(662) 624-3033
MABEN; 2nd Ave	(662) 323-8362
MACON; W Pearl	(662) 726-4212
MADISON	(601) 856-4300
MADISON; 620 Old Canton Rd.	(601) 856-8894
MADISON; South Madison Co; Yandell Rd.	(601) 856-1770
MAGEE; 123 N Main Ave.	(601) 849-2202
MAGNOLIA; 135 Laurel St.	(601) 783-2333
MARIETTA; Volunteer Dept.	(662) 728-4460
MARKS; 900 Poplar	(662) 326-2121
McCOMB; 110 5th Ave.	(601) 684-2124
McCOMB; Magnolia Dept; 131 3rd St.	(601) 249-2301
MEADVILLE	(601) 384-5555
MENDENHALL; 167 W Maude Ave.	(601) 847-1511
MENDENHALL; Braxton Dept; Harrisville Rd.	(601) 847-5544
MERIDIAN; 2400 7th St.	(601) 485-1871

The Ultimate Reference on the State

Fire Departments in Mississippi

MERIDIAN; 902 Grand Ave.	(601) 485-1872
MERIDIAN; 529 51st Ave.	(601) 485-1873
MERIDIAN; 2724 40th St.	(601) 485-1874
MERIDIAN; 2302 Hwy 39N	(601) 485-1875
MERIDIAN; 3532 20th St.	(601) 485-1876
MERIDIAN; 910 52nd St.	(601) 485-1877
MERIDIAN; Key Field	(601) 485-1878
MERIDIAN; Naval Air Station; Fuller Rd.	(601) 679-8888
MINTER CITY	(662) 658-1131
MONTICELLO; Broad St.	(601) 587-2721
MONTPELIER; Volunteer Dept.	(662) 494-8421
MOOREVILLE	(662) 844-2363
MORTON; 121 W 1st.	(601) 732-6339
MOORHEAD; 801 Walnut	(662) 246-5611
MOSS POINT; McInnis Ave.	(228) 475-7462
MOSS POINT; 4223 Saracennia Rd.	(228) 474-2402
MOUNT PLEASANT; Cayce; Lee Creek Rd.	(662) 851-3374
NATCHEZ; Martin Luther King Jr Rd.	(601) 442-7621
NATCHEZ; John R Junkin Dr.	(601) 445-4431
NATCHEZ; Liberty Rd.	(601) 445-5081
NESBIT; 901 Pleasant Hill Rd.	(601) 429-6841
NETTLETON	(662) 963-2380
NEW ALBANY; 107 Cleveland St.	(662) 534-4711
NEW AUGUSTA; Volunteer	(601) 964-3333
NEWTON	(601) 683-2095
NICHOLSON; Volunteer Dept.	(601) 798-3412
NOXAPATER	(662) 724-2697
NOXAPATER; Mars Hill Volunteer Dept.	(662) 724-2240
OCEAN SPRINGS; 503 Dewey Ave.	(228) 875-5442
OCEAN SPRINGS; Vol; 6200 Old Spanish Trl	(228) 875-0620
OCEAN SPRINGS; Fort Bayou Vol; 13320 Ruth St.	(228) 875-5131
OCEAN SPRINGS; Gulf Park; Simmons Bayou Dr	(228) 875-1311
OKOLONA; 106 E Main St.	(662) 447-2484
OLIVE BRANCH; Barton Marshall Dept.	(662) 895-6508
OLIVE BRANCH; 8771 Byhalia Rd.	(662) 895-3322
OSYKA; City Hall	(601) 542-5041
OSYKA; Vol; 1005 Magnolia Progress Rd.	(601) 542-5746
OXFORD; Washington Ave; University	(662) 232-2412
OXFORD; 658 N Lamar; University	(662) 232-2411
OXFORD; Lafayette Dept	(662) 234-8789
PASCAGOULA; 1707 Jackson Ave	(228) 762-3066
PASCAGOULA; Franklin Crk; Forts Lake Rd.	(228) 474-2421
PASCAGOULA; Moss Point Chief; 4412 Denny Ave.	(228) 474-1344
PASS CHRISTIAN; E 2nd St.	(228) 452-3323
PASS CHRISTIAN; W North St.	(228) 452-3326
PASS CHRISTIAN; Cuevas Vol; Menge Ave.	(228) 452-3952
PASS CHRISTIAN; Delisle Volunteer Dept.	(228) 255-1234
PEARL; Old Brandon Rd.	(601) 939-7405
PEARL; Old Whitfield Rd.	(601) 939-0791
PEARL; S Pearson Rd.	(601) 939-7240
PEARL; Volunteer Dept.	(601) 939-1031
PELAHATCHIE	(601) 854-8123
PELAHATCHIE; Leesburg Vol; 400 Hwy 481	(601) 854-6900
PETAL; 1 W 8th Ave.	(601) 545-8208
PETAL; 109 W 8th Ave.	(601) 582-9999
PETAL; 102 Fairchild Dr.	(601) 583-0991
PHILADELPHIA; 525 Main St.	(601) 656-1151
PHILADELPHIA; Hwy 19N	(601) 656-5841
PICAYUNE; Carriere Vol. Dept; Hwy 11N	(601) 798-5085
PICAYUNE; 220 S Haugh Ave.	(601) 798-4916
PICAYUNE; Pine Grove Vol; Harvey Burks Rd.	(601) 799-2937
PICAYUNE; SE Pearl River Co; Mt Carmel Rd.	(601) 799-3583
PONTOTOC; 131 N Main St.	(662) 489-3631
POPLARVILLE; 101 Industrial Park Dr.	(601) 795-2200
PORT GIBSON; Main	(601) 437-5001
PORT GIBSON; Pattison Rd.	(601) 437-3021
PORT GIBSON; Claiborne Co. Dept; 412 Main.	(601) 437-8263
PRENTISS	(601) 792-5198
PURVIS; Vol. Dept; 136 Shelby Speights Dr.	(601) 794-6512
QUITMAN; Hwy 45N	(601) 776-6181
RIENZI	(662) 462-5200
RICHLAND; 566 Old Hwy 49S	(601) 932-6056
RICHLAND; Vol; Scarborough & Hwy 49S	(601) 932-2999
RICHTON; 205 Elm Ave.	(601) 788-6767
RIDGELAND	(601) 856-6811
RIPLEY; 205 E Spring St	(662) 837-5421
RIPLEY; 103 Hwy 15S (to report fire)	(662) 837-3004
ROLLING FORK; China St.	(662) 873-4065
ROSEDALE	(662) 759-3342
RULEVILLE; 208 E Floyce St.	(662) 756-2118
SALTILLO	(662) 842-3587
SARDIS; 114A W Lee	(662) 487-1383
SCOOBA	(662) 476-8452
SEMINARY; SE Covington Co; Hwy 598	(601) 722-3748
SENATOBIA; N Front	(662) 562-4221
SENATOBIA; Looxahoma Vol. Dept; Hwy 4E	(662) 562-7272
SHAW	(662) 754-2121
SHELBY	(662) 398-7821
SHUBUTA	(601) 687-1536
SLEDGE	(662) 382-7711
SMITHVILLE	(662) 651-4046
SOUTHAVEN; 8779 Whitworth St.	(662) 393-7466
SOUTHAVEN; Northwest Dr.	(662) 393-7441
SOUTHAVEN; DeSoto Woods; Goodman Rd.	(662) 393-0100
STARKVILLE; Hwy 12	(662) 323-2812
STARKVILLE; Central Oktibbeha; Hwy 12W	(662) 323-2244
STARKVILLE; East Oktibbeha Co; Hwy 182	(662) 323-0044
STARKVILLE; Maben Dept; 2nd Ave.	(662) 323-8362
STARKVILLE; Mathiston Dept.	(662) 323-1212
SUMMIT	(601) 249-2301
TYLERTOWN; Enon Dept.	(601) 876-4609
TYLERTOWN; Lexie Dept.	(601) 876-2933
TAYLORSVILLE	(601) 785-4431
TCHULA	(662) 235-4056
TISHOMINGO; Paden Volunteer Dept.	(662) 438-6560
TISHOMINGO; Volunteer Dept.	(662) 438-6650
TOOMSUBA; Lauderdale Dept; Toomsuba Rd.	(601) 632-5977
TUNICA	(662) 363-1464
TUPELO	(662) 841-6489

Fire Departments in Mississippi

TUPELO; 106 W Jefferson St. .... (662) 841-6439	WATER VALLEY; 909 N Main St .... (662) 473-2111
TUPELO; Station No. 2; W Main St. .... (662) 841-6483	WATERFORD; Volunteer Dept. .... (662) 252-3473
TUPELO; Station No. 3; E Main .... (662) 841-6484	WAVELAND; Station 1 .... (228) 467-6154
TUPELO; Station No. 4; 814 Rial Dr. .... (662) 841-6485	WAYNESBORO: Wayne St. .... (601) 735-4346
TUPELO; Station No. 5; 1804 S Green St. ...... (662) 841-6486	WAYNESBORO; Wayne Co. Dept;
TUPELO; Fire Prevention; 106 W Jackson ...... (662) 841-6481	New Courthouse .... (601) 735-3801
TUTWILER .... (662) 345-8363	WEBB .... (662) 375-8164
TYLERTOWN; Ball Ave. .... (601) 876-3434	WEST; Hwy 51N .... (662) 967-2876
UNION; 404 Bank St. .... (662) 774-9211	WEST POINT; 400 E Brame Ave. .... (662) 494-2311
UTICA .... (601) 885-5901	WEST POINT; 400 E Brame Ave. .... (662) 494-1531
VAIDEN; 201 Mulberry .... (662) 464-5252	WEST POINT; 972 E Broad St. .... (662) 494-4256
VANCLEAVE; Ballpark Rd. .... (228) 826-4206	WEST POINT; Clay Co. Vol; 218 W Broad St. . (662) 494-3989
VERONA; City Hall .... (662) 566-2191	WHEELER; Vol; #663-A CR 5031 .... (662) 365-1111
VICKSBURG; Central Station; 1630 Walnut .... (601) 636-1603	WIGGINS; 150 N Magnolia Dr. .... (601) 928-9999
VICKSBURG; Stat. No. 6; 912 Cherry St. ...... (601) 634-4532	WINONA; Hwy 51N .... (662) 283-4271
VICKSBURG; Stat. 7; 3217 Washington St. .... (601) 634-4533	YAZOO CITY (To report a fire) .... (662) 746-2121
VICKSBURG; Stat. 8; 3506 Hall's Ferry Rd. .... (601) 634-4534	YAZOO CITY; Station No. 1;
VICTORIA/MARSHALL COUNTY; Victoria .. (662) 838-2246	City Hall on Washington St .... (662) 746-2841
WALLS; 5876 Hwy 301 .... (662) 781-2020	YAZOO CITY; Station No. 3; 610 E 15th St. ... (662) 746-5561
WALNUT; 102 S Main .... (662) 223-4045	YAZOO CITY; Benton Vol; 210 S Washington . (662) 746-2121

Most fire departments can be reached by telephone by dialing 911.

Under the Fire Registry Law, insurance companies must report to the Office of the State Fire Marshall any fire "causing $10,000 or more in property damage or in which any person was injured or loses his life."
In FY 1999, there were 799 such claims filed, a decrease of 39, or 5%, from the 838 claims filed in FY 1998.

There were 51 fire related death investigations in FY 1999, a decrease of 39, or 76%, from the 90 in FY 1998.

During FY 1999, the Office of the State Fire Marshall conducted 680 investigations of suspicious fires. Of those, 449 fires were in rural areas, and 231 in urban areas. Of the suspicious fires, 311 were residential, 95 commercial structures, 142 manufactured home fires, 62 vehicular fires and 70 "other" fires. Causes of the investigated fires were 287 incendiary, 260 accidental and 133 undetermined. Of the 680 fires investigated, the estimated property value was $148,203,455 for buildings and $58,484,662 for contents. The amount of insurance coverage on those properties was $864,874,037 for buildings and $25,421,700 for contents. The total property loss of those fires came to $54,265,662, a 10% increase over the $52,178,210 in FY 1998.

Of the 287 incendiary (or arson) fires in FY 1999, a total of 59 arrests were made. For the fiscal years 1995 through 1999, there were a total of 1,682 incendiary fire investigations with a total of 401 arrests made, an overall arrest rate average of 23.84%, well above the national average of less than 17%.

From Jan. 1, 1990 through June 30, 1999, there were 5,573 fires investigated by the State Fire Marshall's Office. Of those, 110 (only 2%) were of places of religious assembly (churches).

Wildfires, FY 2001: 38,736 acres lost in 2,921 wildfires (July 1, 2000 through Oct. 31, 2000)
    FY 2000: 76,562 acres lost in 6,892 wildfires
    FY 1999: 43,082 acres lost in 4,360 wildfires (5-yr. total, FY 95-99 — 236,175 acres in 19,620 fires =
                 5-yr. avg., FY 95-99 — 47,235 acres and 3,924 wildfires)
    FY 1998: 35,451 acres lost in 3,238 wildfires (worst in the 5 year period FY 95-99 was FY 1996 —
                 95,014 acres lost in 6,344 wildfires)

Wildfire statistics furnished by the Mississippi Forestry Commission

FIRE DEPARTMENT SALARIES FOR THE JACKSON METRO AREA, 1996

	Firefighter	Captain	Chief
Clinton	$18,169 - $27,393	$23,493 - $32,520	$36,220 - $50,137
Jackson	$18,490 - $28,791	$28,621 - $40,672	$55,203 - $84,066
Madison	$18,304 - $27,206	$23,462 - $30,784	$34,632 - $45,427
Pearl	$21,120 - $28,872	$28,800 - $35,580	City's Discretion
Richland	$22,120 - $28,861	$29,000 - $37,838	N/A
Ridgeland	$20,587 - $39,137	$26,353 - $47,669	$34,590 - $62,566
Average	$19,788 - $30,043	$26,622 - $37,511	$40,161 - $60,549

Education in Mississippi

GENERAL

Less Than 9th Grade Education, 1990: Black adults 26.6%; White adults 26.4%; Hispanic adults 12.8%; Native American adults 28.0%; Asian American adults 18.0%; all minorities 26.4%; all adults 15.7%

Pop. Ages 25 Years of Age & Older: High School Graduates: March **1999**: 78.0%   **1990**: 64.3%
Bachelor's Degree or more: "   **1999**: 19.2%   **1990**: 14.7%

High School Diploma Only, 1990: Black adults 22.1%; Hispanic adults 23.2%; Native American adults 29.6%; Asian American adults 17.9%; White adults 30.1%

Student/Computer Ratio: **1999** — 7 to 1 (national average, 5.7 to 1)   **1995** — 55 to 1
Of the state's 1,006 schools, 920 were connected to the Internet in 1999.

PUBLIC SCHOOLS, ELEMENTARY & SECONDARY

No. of School Districts, 1998-99: 152 (68 county + 81 separate + 3 agricultural high schools)

No. of Public Schools, 1998-99: 1,021 (518 elementary; 197 secondary; 148 consolidated elementary & secondary; 51 alternative; 88 vocational; 19 special)

Smallest District, Fall 1999 Enrollment: Clay County School District — 248 students

Largest District, Fall 1999 Enrollment: Jackson Public School District — 31,387
Second Largest: DeSoto County School District — 18,917

Largest District, Fall 1998 Enrollment: Jackson Public Schools — 31,772 (1998-99 ADA 30,127)[1]
Second Largest: Desoto County Schools — 18,112 (1998-99 ADA 17,439)

Pre-Kindergarten Enrollment, Fall 1998: 1,067 + 1,548 Special Education Pre-Kindergarten

Kindergarten Enrollment, Fall 1998: 39,509 (ADA — 37,404) + 212 Special Education Kindergarten

Total Enrollment, Fall 1999: 499,362 (the lowest since the fall of 1986 when it was 498,639)
Fall 1998: 502,382 (elementary — 327,435; secondary — 174,947)

Cumulative Enrollment All School Year, 1998-99: 557,209 (elem. — 364,702; secondary 192,507)

Average Daily Attendance (ADA), 1998-99: 470,765 (elementary — 309,906; secondary 160,859)

Pupil/Teacher Ratio, 1998-99: 15.72 pupils per classroom teacher (based on ADA for all grades)

Number of Diploma Graduates: **1998-99** — 24,148 (10,842 male 44.9% and 13,306 female 55.1%)
(12,334 white 51.1% and 11,560 black 47.8%)
1997-98 — 24,477 (11,141 male 45.5% and 13,336 female 54.5%)
1996-97 — 23,388 (10,553 male 45.1% and 12,835 female 54.9%)
1995-96 — 23,032 (10,419 male 46.2% and 12,613 female 54.8%)

> In 1998-99, there were also 1,760 Certificate Recipients and 332 GED Credential Recipients for a total of 26,240 graduates / other completers.

No. of Dropouts: **1998-99** — 9,090 (1.98% of enrollment)   **1997-98** — 10,150 (2.19% of enrollment)

Revenues for Public Schools 1998-99: $2,563,167,327 TOTAL
$1,396,182,101 (State 54.47%)
$ 811,457,775 (Local 31.66%)
$ 355,527,451 (Federal 13.87%)

Expenditures for Public Schools, 1998-99: $2,408,045,907
Instruction: $1,757,862,371
Non-Instructional Services: $ 179,710,694
Support Services: $ 369,069,069
Administration: $ 101,403,773

> 1996 figures for MS, LA & AR showed 89.3% of children attending public schools & 10.7% attending private schools. In Miss., 85% of white children attend public schools & 98% of black children attend public schools.

Average Expenditure per Pupil in ADA, 1998-99: $5,120 (U.S. — $6,734; Southeast — $5,979)
Less Transportation: $4,878   Instructional Cost: $3,032

Number of Classroom Teachers, 1998-99: 29,939 (elementary — 16,331; secondary — 13,608)

Average Experience of All Classroom Teachers, 1998-99: 13.79 years

Number of Superintendents, Principals, Librarians, etc. Requiring Certification, 1998-99: 4,897

No. All Other Public School Staff (Secretarial/Clerical/Support Personnel, etc.), 1998-99: 27,541

Average Teachers' Salaries, 1999-00: $31,897 (30,782 teachers) Southeast $37,072; National $41,575
1998-99: $29,550 (29,939 teachers) Southeast $35,817; National $40,582
1997-98: $28,691 (29,574 teachers)
1989-90: $24,364 (27,506 teachers)
1979-80: $11,851 (25,815 teachers)

> In 1998-99, there were 3,094 Asian students in Mississippi schools, up from 2,118 in 1990 and the number of Hispanic students went from 869 to 2,525, a threefold increase.

[1] ADA stands for Average Daily Attendance.   SOURCE: Miss. Dept. of Education

Education in Mississippi

Public School Transportation, 1998-99:
    5,270 buses traveled 47,943,135 miles (avg. of 9,097.4 miles per bus or 118.24 miles per student).
        405,484 students (ADA) were transported.
            271 accidents involving school buses (avg. of one per 176,912 miles).
    All 271 accidents resulted in property damage.
        165 of the accidents resulted in injuries to pupils.
            (average one injury-causing accident per 290,564 miles).
    There were NO DEATHS from school bus accidents.

HIGHER EDUCATION

THE EIGHT STATE-SUPPORTED UNIVERSITIES

Total For-Credit Enrollment, Fall 1999: 62,726 (49,863 full-time 79.5%; 12,863 part-time 20.5%)
    57,053 on-campus 91.0% (47,277 full-time 82.9%; 8,776 part-time 17.1%)
        From: 44,359 in-state (77.8%); 10,942 other states (19.2%); 1,752 other countries (3.1%)
    50,805 undergraduate (81%) and 11,921 graduate (19%)
    49,577 resident (79.0%) and 13,149 nonresident (21.0%)
    27,462 men (43.8%); 35,264 women (56.2%)
    39,492 white (63.0%); 20,198 black (32.2%) & 3,036 other (4.8%)

A greater percentage of college degrees (associate, bachelor's, master's, doctoral) go to minorities in Miss. than in any other state.

Number of Degrees Awarded, 1998-99: 12,769 (white — 8,767; black — 3,320; other — 682)
        1997-98: 12,210 (8,469 bachlor's; 2,847 master's, 357 doctoral,
            351 professional and 186 other)

Range of Yearly Tuition & Fees for State Residents, 1999-00: $2,556 at MUW to $3,053 at UM
        2000-01: $2,656 at MUW to $3,153 at UM

Faculty Average Salary Range: FY 2000 — $41,514 (MVSU) to $57,006 (MSU); $51,223 average
        FY 1999 — $37,500 (MVSU) to $52,200 (MSU)

Average Pay for All Miss. University Full-Time Faculty, FY 1999: $48,602 ($52,136 in the South)

Total Operating Budgets, FY 2000: $1,780,793,874 ($28,390.04 per student)
    $144,133,186 (8.1%) of the operating budgets went to scholarships and fellowships.

Total State Appropriation (Fiscal Year):
    2001 — $634,366,774   2000 — $639,856,473
    1999 — $552,196,134   1998 — $507 million
    1997 — $507 million   1996 — $461 million

Estimated Replacement Value of All Buildings, 1998: $2,346,800,000

The State of Mississippi university system consists of eight public universities, the University of Mississippi Medical Center, the Mississippi Education and Research Center, the Gulf Coast Research Laboratory, plus six degree-granting off-campus centers and extension classes. Three universities have been designated by the Board of Trustees of the Mississippi Institutions of Higher Learning as **comprehensive universities** — Mississippi State University, the University of Mississippi, and the University of Southern Mississippi offer doctorates in many disciplines, in addition to bachelor's and master's degrees. Jackson State University has the distinction of being designated the **urban university** of the state. Recognized as **regional universities** and primarily offering bachelor's and master's degrees are Alcorn State University, Delta State University, Mississippi University for Women, and Mississippi Valley State University.

Mississippi University for Women was rated the best value among all Southern regional public liberal arts colleges for the 4th year in a row by *U.S. News & World Report* in their 2001 edition of *America's Best Colleges*. The "W" was also ranked in the top 10 for campus diversity. Millsaps College ranked 15th in national liberal arts colleges listed as "Great Schools at Great Prices." Millsaps remained in the top half of national liberal arts colleges for the 4th year in a row. Mississippi College was rated in the top 20 among ragional universities in the South and Jackson State University was listed in tier four in that category. Listing most of Mississippi's historically black colleges — Tougaloo (tier 3), Alcorn State, and Mississippi Valley State (tier 3) — the publication listed Rust College in Holly Springs in tier two among Southern liberal arts colleges. Ole Miss and Mississippi State were listed in tier 3 among national universities. Ole Miss ranked 42nd and Mississippi State ranked 57th on a list of the nation's "100 Best Buys" in public colleges/universities in the Oct. 2000 issue of *Kiplinger's Personal Finance* magazine. Mississippi's schools had favorable reviews in other publications in 2000.

THE FIFTEEN PUBLIC COMMUNITY/JUNIOR COLLEGES

Total Enrollment, Fall 1999: 126,407 (fall 1998 — 122,770)
    Credit — 53,669   Non-Credit — 72,738

No. of Degrees Awarded, 1998-99: 6,218 Associate; 1,549 Certificate

In FY 1999, Mississippi Public Community College libraries had a total of 891,500 books.

Average Salaries at Mississippi's Public Community / Junior Colleges, FY 2000:
    With Master's: $31,036 (starting) to $50,530; With Doctorate: $36,182 (starting) to $54,634

Total Revenue & Expenditures, 1998-99: $305,579,492

    Sources: State Institutions of Higher Learning and the State Board of Community & Junior Colleges

Colleges & Universities in Mississippi

SENIOR (FOUR-YEAR) COLLEGES

ALCORN STATE UNIVERSITY; 1000 ASU Drive; Alcorn State 39096 (est. 1871) 2,871 [1] .... (601) 877-6100
DELTA STATE UNIVERSITY; Cleveland (est. 1925) 4,086 .... (662) 846-3000
JACKSON STATE UNIVERSITY; 1400 Lynch St; Jackson 39217 (est. 1877) 6,354 .... (601) 968-2121
MISSISSIPPI STATE UNIVERSITY; Mississippi State 39762 (est. 1878) 16,076 .... (662) 325-2323
MISSISSIPPI UNIVERSITY FOR WOMEN; Columbus 39701 (est. 1884) 2,953 .... (662) 329-4750
    or Toll Free 877-GO-2-TheW = (877) 462-8439
MISSISSIPPI VALLEY STATE UNIVERSITY; Itta Bena 38941 (est. 1946) 2,509 .... (662) 254-9041
UNIVERSITY OF MISSISSIPPI; University 38677 (est. 1844) 11,746 .... (662) 915-7211
    or Toll Free (800) 653-6477
UNIVERSITY OF MISS. MED'L CTR; 2500 N State St; Jackson 39216 (est. 1955) 1,781 .... (601) 984-1010
UNIVERSITY OF SOUTHERN MISS; 2901 Hardy; Hattiesburg 39406 (est. 1910) 14,350 .... (601) 266-4111

Independent Nonprofit (Private)
BELHAVEN COLLEGE; 1500 Peachtree St; Jackson 39202-1789 (est. 1883) 1,625 (fall 2000) .... (601) 968-5940
BLUE MOUNTAIN COLLEGE; PO Box 160; Blue Mountain 38610-0160 (est. 1873) 455 .... (662) 685-4771
MILLSAPS COLLEGE; 1701 N State; Jackson 39210-0001 (est. 1890) 1,362 .... (601) 354-5201
MISSISSIPPI COLLEGE; 200 W. College St; Clinton 39058 (est. 1826) 3,449 .... (601) 925-3000
RUST COLLEGE; 150 E Rust Ave; Holly Springs 38635 (est. 1866) 852 .... (662) 252-4661
TOUGALOO COLLEGE; 500 West County Line Rd; Tougaloo 39174 (est. 1869) 990 (fall 2000) ..... (601) 956-4941
WILLIAM CAREY COLLEGE; Hattiesburg 39401-5499 (est. 1906) 2,400 (3 campuses) [fall 2000] .. (601) 582-5051

COMMUNITY AND JUNIOR (TWO-YEAR) COLLEGES

COAHOMA COMMUNITY COLLEGE; 3240 Friars Point Rd; Clarksdale 38614 (est. 1949) 1,058 ..... (662) 627-2571
COPIAH-LINCOLN COMMUNITY COLLEGE; Wesson (est. 1928) 2,455 .... (601) 643-5101
EAST CENTRAL COMMUNITY COLLEGE; PO Box 129; Decatur 39327 (est. 1928) 2,076 .... (601) 635-2111
    or Toll Free (877) 462-3222
EAST MISS. COMM. COLLEGE: Golden Triangle; Box 100; Mayhew 39753 (est. 1927) 1,200 .... (662) 243-1900
EAST MISS. COMMUNITY COLLEGE; PO Box 158; Scooba 39358 (est. 1927) 1,079 (2,279) .... (662) 476-8442
HINDS COMMUNITY COLLEGE; Raymond 39154 (est. 1917) 8,990 (6 campuses) .... (601) 857-5261
HOLMES COMMUNITY COLLEGE; 1 Hill St; Goodman 39079 (est. 1928) 892 (2,703) .... (601) 472-2312
HOLMES COMMUNITY COLLEGE; 1060 Avent Dr, Grenada 38901-5063 676 (2,703) .... (601) 226-0830
HOLMES COMMUNITY COLLEGE; 412 W Ridgeland Ave; Ridgeland 39157 1,135 (2,703) .... (601) 856-5400
ITAWAMBA COMMUNITY COLL; 602 W Hill St; Fulton 38843 (est. 1947) 3,596 (2 campuses) ...... (662) 862-8001
JONES COUNTY JUNIOR COLLEGE; 900 S Court St; Ellisville 39437 (est. 1928) 4,428 .... (601) 477-4100
MERIDIAN COMMUNITY COLLEGE; 910 Hwy 19N; Meridian 39301 (est. 1937) 2,927 .... (601) 483-8241
MISSISSIPPI DELTA COMMUNITY COLLEGE; Moorhead 38761 (est. 1926) 2,431 .... (662) 246-6322
MISS. GULF COAST COMMUNITY COLLEGE; Jackson County Campus Gautier (est. 1965) .... (228) 497-9602
MISS. GULF COAST COMMUNITY COLLEGE: Jeff. Davis Campus; Gulfport .... (228) 896-3355
MISS. GULF COAST COMMUNITY COLLEGE; Perkinston (est. 1911) 9,147 (7 campuses) .... (601) 928-6280
NORTHEAST MISSISSIPPI COMMUNITY COLLEGE; Booneville (est. 1948) 2,804 .... (662) 728-7751
NORTHWEST MISSISSIPPI COMMUNITY COLLEGE; Senatobia (est. 1927) 4,451 .... (662) 562-3200
PEARL RIVER COMMUNITY COLLEGE; Poplarville 39470 (est. 1909) 2,777 (2 campuses) .... (601) 795-6801
SOUTHWEST MISSISSIPPI COMMUNITY COLLEGE; Summit 39666 (est. 1918) 1,674 .... (601) 276-2019

Independent Nonprofit (Private)
ANTONELLI COLLEGE; 480 E Woodrow Wilson Dr; Jackson 39216 (est. 1996) 320 (spring 2000) ... (601) 362-9991
MARY HOLMES JUNIOR COLLEGE; PO Box 1257; West Point 39773 (est. 1862) 280 (fall 2000) .. (662) 494-6820
VIRGINIA COLLEGE; 5360 I-55 N; Jackson 39211 (est. 1983) 130 (spring 2000) .... (601) 977-0960
WOOD JUNIOR COLLEGE; Box-C; Mathiston 39752-0289 (est. 1886) 177 ('99) .... (662) 263-8128

SECTARIAN SCHOOLS

JACKSON COLLEGE OF MINISTRIES; 1555 Beasley Rd; Jackson 39206 159 .... (601) 981-1611
MAGNOLIA BIBLE COLLEGE; 822 S Huntington St; Kosciusko 39090 (est. 1976) 61 (fall '99) .... (662) 289-2896
REFORMED THEOLOGICAL SEMINARY; 5422 Clinton Blvd; Jackson 39209 (est. 1963) 250 (spring '00) . (601) 923-1600
SOUTHEASTERN BAPTIST COLLEGE; 4229 Highway 15 N; Laurel 39440 (est. 1950) 64 .... (601) 426-6346
WESLEY BIBLICAL SEMINARY; 5980 Floral Dr; Jackson 39206 (est. 1974) 81 .... (601) 957-1314
WESLEY COLLEGE; 111 Wesley Circle; Florence 39073 (est. 1944) 106 (spring 2000) .... (601) 845-2265

> Enrollment at the 8 state-supported universities for the fall of 1999 was a record 62,726, up 211 over the previous record 62,515 in the fall of 1998. Enrollment at the state's community colleges was 126,407 students in fall 1999 — 53,669 for credit and 72,738 non-credit — compared to 122,770 enrolled in fall 1998.

[1] Enrollment figures represent students enrolled in for-credit classes, both on and off campus and are for fall 1999 for the 8 state-supported universities and for fall 1998 for most of the other schools..

Libraries in Mississippi

PUBLIC LIBRARIES

BENTON COUNTY LIBRARY SYSTEM; PO Box 216; 100 S. Main St; Ashland 38603	(662) 224-6400
Hickory Flat Public Library; PO Box 309; Hickory Flat 38633	(662) 333-7663
Robert M. Bond Memorial Library; PO Box 216; 100 S. Main St; Ashland 38603	(662) 224-6400
BLACKMUR MEMORIAL LIBRARY (independent); 608 Blackmur Dr. & South St; Water Valley 38965	(662) 473-2444
BOLIVAR COUNTY LIBRARY SYSTEM; 104 S Leflore Ave; Cleveland 38732	(662) 843-2774
Benoit Pubic Library; PO Box 307; Main St; Benoit 38725	(662) 742-3402
Cleveland Depot Library; 101 South Bayou Ave; Cleveland 38732	(662) 843-7323
Field Memorial Library; PO Box 387; 132 Peeler Ave; Shaw 38773	(662) 754-6381
Gunnison Public Library; PO Box 91; Town Hall on Main St; Gunnison 38746	(662) 747-2354
Mound Bayou Library Station; at St. Gabriel Education Center; Mound Bayou 38762	(662) 741-2439
Robinson-Carpenter Memorial Library; 104 S Leflore Ave; Cleveland	(662) 843-2774
Rosedale Public Library; PO Box 206; 702 Front St; Rosedale 38769	(662) 759-6332
Shelby Public Library; PO Box 789; Highway 61 South; Shelby 38774	(662) 398-7748
Thelma R. Rayner Memorial Library; 201 S. Front St; Merigold 38759	(662) 748-2105
CARNEGIE PUBLIC LIB. of CLARKSDALE & COAHOMA CO.; Box 280; 114 Delta Av; Clarksdale 38614	(662) 624-4461
CARROLL COUNTY PUBLIC LIBRARY SYSTEM; PO Box 329; Lexington Ave; Carrollton 38917	(662) 237-6268
Carrollton/North Carrollton Public Library; PO Box 329; Lexington Ave; Carrollton 38917	(662) 237-6268
Vaiden Public Library; PO Box 108; Lee St; Vaiden 39176	(662) 464-7736
CENTRAL MISS. REGIONAL LIBRARY SYSTEM; P.O. Box 1749; 104 Office Park Dr.; Brandon 39043	(601) 825-0100
Brandon Public Library; PO Box 1537; 1475 W. Government St; Brandon 39042	(601) 825-2672
D'Lo Public Library; PO Box 147; Poplar St; D'Lo 39062	(601) 847-1721
Evan A. Ford Public Library; PO Box 430; 208 Spring St; Taylorsville 39168	(601) 785-4361
Florence Public Library; PO Box 95; 104 W. Main St; Florence 39073	(601) 845-6032
Floyd J. Robinson Memorial Library; PO Box 266; 150 Main St; Raleigh 39153	(601) 782-4277
Forest Public Library; PO Box 737; 210 S Raleigh St; Forest 39074	(601) 469-1481
Harrisville Public Library; PO Box 307; MS Highway 469; Harrisville 39082	(601) 847-1268
Lake Public Library; PO Box 160; Town Hall on Front St; Lake 39092	(601) 775-3552
Magee Public Library; 120 Northwest 1st St; Magee 39111	(601) 849-3747
Mendenhall Public Library; 1630 Simpson St; Mendenhall 39114	(601) 847-2181
Morton Public Library; 16 East Fourth St; Morton 39117	(601) 732-6288
Northwest Point Reservoir Public Library; 2230 Spillway Rd; Brandon 39042	(601) 992-2539
Pearl Public Library; PO Box 97509; 3470 Highway 80 East; Pearl 39288	(601) 932-3535
Pelahatchie Public Library; P.O. Box 562; 603 Highway 80 East; Pelahatchie 39145	(601) 854-8764
Polkville Public Library; HCR 66, Box 113; Town Hall, Highway 13; Polkville 39117	(601) 537-3115
Puckett Public Library; PO Box 550; 118 Cemetery Rd; Puckett 39151	(601) 824-0180
R. T. Prince Memorial Library; PO Box 247; Highway 28; Mize 39116	(601) 733-9414
Richland Public Library; PO Box 180098; 370 Scarbrough St; Richland 39218	(601) 932-1846
Sandhill Public Library; PO Box 69; 698 Pisgah Rd; Sandhill 39161	(601) 829-1653
Sebastopol Public Library; PO Box 173; Highway 21 North; Sebastopol 39359	(601) 625-7200
COLUMBUS-LOWNDES PUBLIC LIBRARY (SYSTEM); 314 Seventh St N; Columbus 39701	(662) 329-5300
Artesia Public Library; PO Box 186; City Hall on Main St; Artesia 39736	(662) 272-5255
Caledonia Public Library; 754 Main St; Caledonia 39740	(662) 356-6384
Crawford Public Library; PO Box 104; Town Hall at 315 Main St; Crawford 39743	(662) 272-5144
COPIAH-JEFFERSON REGIONAL LIBRARY SYSTEM; 223 S Extension St; Hazlehurst 39083	(601) 894-1672
George W. Covington Memorial Library; 223 S Extension St; Hazlehurst 39083	(601) 894-1681
J. T. Biggs, Jr. Memorial Library; 200 S Jackson St; Crystal Springs 39059	(601) 892-3205
Jefferson County Public Library; PO Box 578; 428 Main St; Fayette 39069	(601) 786-3982
Longie Dale Hamilton Memorial Library; PO Box 299; 1017 Spring St; Wesson 39191	(601) 643-5725
DIXIE REGIONAL LIBRARY SYSTEM; Pontotoc County Library; 111 N Main St; Pontotoc 38863	(662) 489-3960
Calhoun City Public Library; PO Box 646; 113 E. Burkitt; Calhoun City 38916	(662) 628-6331
Dr. J. S. Edmondson Memorial Library; PO Box 174; 109 Stovall St; Vardaman 38878	(662) 682-7333
Houlka Public Library; PO Box 275; City Hall on Walker St; Houlka 38850	(662) 568-2747
Houston Carnegie Library; PO Box 186; 105 W Madison St; Houston 38851	(662) 456-3381
Jesse Yancy Memorial Library; PO Box 96; 314 N. Newberger St; Bruce 38915	(662) 983-2220
Okolona Carnegie Library; PO Box 196; 321 Main St; Okolona 38860	(662) 447-2401
Sherman Public Library; PO Box 181; 20 West Lamar St; Sherman 38851	(662) 840-2513

Libraries in Mississippi

EAST MISSISSIPPI REGIONAL LIBRARY SYSTEM; 116 Water St; Quitman 39355	(601) 776-3881
Bay Springs Municipal Library; PO Drawer N; 81 S Court St; Bay Springs 39422	(601) 764-2291
Enterprise Public Library; Ritchey St; Enterprise 39330	(601) 659-3564
Louin Public Library; PO Box 176; Highway 15 North; Louin 39338	(601) 739-3630
Mary Weems Parker Memorial Library; PO Box 252; 1016 N Pine Ave; Heidelberg 39439	(601) 787-3857
Pachuta Public Library; PO Box 189; Highway 11 North; Pachuta 39347	(601) 776-3131
Quitman Public Library; 116 Water St; Quitman 39355	(601) 776-2492
Shubuta Public Library; PO Box 786; Eucutta Rd; Shubuta 39360	(601) 687-1536
Stonewall Public Library; PO Box 700; 801 Erwin Rd; Stonewall 39363	(601) 659-7033
ELIZABETH JONES LIBRARY; PO Box 130; 1050 Fairfield Ave; Grenada 38901	(662) 226-2072
FIRST REGIONAL LIBRARY SYSTEM; Hernando Public Library; 370 W. Commerce St; Hernando 38632	(662) 429-4439
B. J. Chain Public Library; 6619 S Cockrum St; Olive Branch 38654	(662) 895-5900
Batesville Public Library; 207 Hwy 51N; Batesville 38606	(662) 563-6644
Coldwater Public Library; P O Box 519; Coldwater 38618	(662) 622-5573
Emily Jones Pointer Public Library; P O Box 128; Main Street SE; Como 38619	(662) 526-5283
Lafayette County-Oxford Public Library; 401 Bramlett Blvd; Oxford 38655	(662) 234-5751
M. R. Davis Public Library; 8889 Northwest Dr; Southaven 38671	(662) 342-0102
M. R. Dye Public Library; 2885 Goodman Rd W; Horn Lake 38637	(662) 393-5654
Robert C. Irwin Public Library; PO Box 1057; 1201 Second East Ave; Tunica 38876	(662) 363-2162
Sam Lapidus Memorial Library; PO Box 246; 108 Missouri St; Crenshaw 38621	(662) 382-7479
Sardis Public Library; 101 McLaurin St; Sardis 38666	(662) 487-2126
Senatobia Public Library; 222 S Ward St; Senatobia 38668	(662) 562-6791
Walls Library; 7181 Delta Bluff Parkway; Walls 38680	(662) 781-3664
GREENWOOD-LEFLORE LIBRARY (SYSTEM); 405 W Washington St; Greenwood 38930	(662) 453-3634
Itta Bena Branch Library; 305 Thurman St; Itta Bena 38941	(662) 254-7790
Jodie Wilson Branch Library; 209 E Martin Luther King Dr; Greenwood 38930	(662) 453-1761
HANCOCK COUNTY LIBRARY SYSTEM; 312 Hwy 90; Bay Saint Louis 39520	(228) 467-5282
Bay St. Louis-Hancock County Library; 312 Hwy 90; Bay Saint Louis 39520	(228) 467-5282
Kiln Public Library; PO Box 628; 16603 Hwy 603; Kiln 38556	(228) 255-1724
Waveland Library Literacy Center; 333 Coleman Ave; Waveland 39576	(228) 467-9240
HARRIETTE PERSON MEMORIAL LIBRARY; 606 Main Street; Port Gibson 39150	(601) 437-5202
HARRISON COUNTY LIBRARY SYSTEM; PO Box 4018; 1300 21st Ave; Gulfport 39502	(228) 863-7433
Biloxi Main Library; 139 Lameuse St; Biloxi 39530	(228) 374-0330
D'iberville Public Library; 10391 Auto Mall Parkway; D'Iberville 39532	(228) 392-2279
Division Street Study Center; 595 Division St; Biloxi 39530	(228) 435-2435
Isiah Fredericks Study Center; 3321 Martin Luther King, Jr. Blvd; Gulfport 39501	(228) 868-1268
Gulfport Public Library; 1300 21st Ave; Gulfport 39501	(228) 863-6411
Margaret S. Sherry Memorial Library; 2141 Popps Ferry Rd; Biloxi 39532	(228) 388-1633
Orange Grove Public Library; 12031 Mobile Ave; Gulfport 39503	(228) 832-6924
Pass Christian Public Library; 111 Heirn Ave; Pass Christian 39571	(228) 452-4596
West Biloxi Public Library; 2047 Pass Rd; Biloxi 39531	(228) 388-5696
HOMOCHITTO VALLEY LIBRARY SERVICE; 220 S Commerce; Natchez 39120	(601) 445-8862
Judge George W. Armstrong Library; 220 S Commerce; Natchez 39120	(601) 445-8862
Kevin Poole Vancleave Memorial Library; PO Box 517; 1141 West Park; Centreville 39631	(601) 645-5771
Woodville Public Library; PO Box 397; 489 Main St; Woodville 39669	(601) 888-6712
HUMPHREYS COUNTY LIBRARY (SYSTEM); 105 S Hayden St; Belzoni 39038	(662) 247-3606
Isola Public Library; PO Box 213; Julia Street; Isola 38754	(662) 962-3606
JACKSON-GEORGE REGIONAL LIBRARY SYSTEM; 3214 Pascagoula St; Pascagoula 39567	(228) 769-3060
East Central Library; 21801 Slider Rd; Pascagoula 39581	(228) 588-6263
Gautier Public Library; 2100 Library Lane; Gautier 39553	(228) 497-4531
George County Public Library; 110 Beaver Dam Rd; Lucedale 39452	(601) 947-2123
Moss Point City Library; 4401 McInnis St; Moss Point 39563	(228) 475-7462
Ocean Springs Municipal Library; 1525 Dewey Ave; Ocean Springs 39564	(228) 875-1193
Pascagoula Public Library; 3214 Pascagoula St; Pascagoula 39567	(228) 769-3060
Saint Martin Public Library; 15004 Lemoyne Blvd; Biloxi 39532	(228) 392-3250
Vancleave Public Library; 12604 Highway 57; Vancleave 39565	(228) 826-5857
JACKSON/HINDS LIBRARY SYSTEM; Eudora Welty Library; 300 N State St; Jackson 39201	(601) 968-5811
A. E. Wood Library; 111 Clinton Blvd; Clinton 39056	(601) 924-5684

Libraries in Mississippi

Annie Thompson Jeffers Library; 111 W Madison St; Bolton 39041	(601) 866-4247
Beverly J. Brown Library; PO Box 720013; 5795 South Siwell Rd; (Byram) Jackson 39272	(601) 372-0954
Colonial Mart Library; 5050 Parkway Dr; Jackson 39211	(601) 956-4606
Edwards Library; PO Box 140; Old Edwards Elementary School; Edwards 39066	(601) 852-2230
Ella Bess Austin Library; PO Box 155; 320 W. Cunningham Ave; Terry 39170	(601) 878-5521
Evelyn Taylor Majure Library; PO Box 340; 108 White Oak St; Utica 39175	(601) 885-8381
Fannie Lou Hamer Library; 3540 Albermarle Rd; Jackson 39213	(601) 362-3012
Margaret Walker Alexander Library; 2525 Robinson Rd; Jackson 39209	(601) 354-8911
Medgar Evers Boulevard Branch Library; 4215 Medgar Evers Blvd; Jackson 39213	(601) 982-2867
Northside Library; 807 East Northside Dr; Jackson 39201	(601) 366-0021
Raymond Library; PO Box 14; County Courthouse; Raymond 39154	(601) 857-8721
South Hills Library; 515 West McDowell Rd; Jackson 39204	(601) 371-1621
White Rock Library; 560 Country Club Dr; Jackson 39209	(601) 922-6076
KEMPER-NEWTON REGIONAL LIB. SYSTEM; Union Public Library; 101 Peachtree Street; Union 39365	(601) 774-5096
Chunky Public Library; :PO Box 86; Commerce St; Chunky 39323	(601) 655-8376
Decatur Public Library; PO Box 40; Decatur St; Decatur 39327	(601) 635-2777
DeKalb Public Library; PO Box 710; Bell Street; DeKalb 39328	(601) 743-5981
Hickory Public Library; PO Box 32; Railroad St; Hickory 39332	No Phone
J. Elliot McMullan Library; 300 West Church St; Newton 39345	(601) 683-3367
Scooba Public Library; PO Box 25; 1037 Kemper St; Scooba 39358	(662) 476-8452
LAMAR COUNTY LIBRARY SYSTEM; PO Box 289; 122 Shelby Speights Dr; Purvis 39475	(601) 794-8651
L. R. Boyer Memorial Library; PO Box 327; 103 Poplar St; Sumrall 39482	(601) 758-4711
Lumberton Public Library; 106 E Main Ave; Lumberton 39455	(601) 796-4277
Purvis Public Library; PO Box 289; 122 Shelby Speights Dr; Purvis 39475	(601) 794-8768
LAUREL-JONES COUNTY LIBRARY (SYSTEM); 530 Commerce St; Laurel 39440	(601) 428-4313
Ellisville Public Library; 110 Court St; Ellisville 39437	(601) 477-9271
Sandersville Public Library; PO Box 217; 102 Maple St; Sandersville 39477	(601) 425-3551
LEE-ITAWAMBA LIBRARY SYSTEM; Lee County Library; 219 N Madison St; Tupelo 38801	(662) 841-9027
Itawamba County Pratt Memorial Library; 210 Cedar St; Fulton 38843	(662) 862-4926
LONG BEACH PUBLIC LIBRARY (independent); 209 Jeff Davis Ave; Long Beach 39560	(228) 863-0711
LINCOLN-LAWRENCE-FRANKLIN REGIONAL LIBRARY SYSTEM; Brookhaven 39601	(601) 833-3369
Bude Public Library; PO Box 69; 903-904 Railroad Ave; Bude 39630	(601) 384-2348
Franklin County Public Library; PO Box 336; S. Second St; Meadville 39653	(601) 384-2997
Lawrence County Public Library; PO Box 446; 142 Washington St; Monticello 39654	(601) 587-2471
Lincoln County Public Library; PO Box 541; 100 South Jackson St; Brookhaven 39601	(601) 833-3369
Newhebron Public Library; PO Box 202; West Main at Highway 43; Newhebron 39140	(601) 694-2623
MADISON COUNTY LIBRARY SYSTEM; 102 Priestley St; Canton 39046	(601) 859-3202
Elsie Jurgens Memorial Library; 397 Highway 51; Ridgeland 39157	(601) 856-4536
Flora Public Library; PO Box 356; 168 Carter St; Flora 39071	(601) 879-8835
Madison County-Canton Public Library; 102 Priestley St; Canton 39046	(601) 859-3202
Rebecca Baine Rigby Library; PO Box 1153; 994 Madison Ave; Madison 39110	(601) 856-2749
MARKS-QUITMAN COUNTY PUBLIC LIBRARY (SYSTEM); 315 E Main St; Marks 38646	(662) 326-7141
Sledge Public Library; Sledge City Hall; Sledge 38670	(662) 382-7716
MARSHALL COUNTY LIBRARY (SYSTEM); 109 E Gholson Ave; Holly Springs	(662) 252-3823
Potts Camp Library; PO Box 427; Centre St; Potts Camp 38659	(662) 333-7068
Ruth B. French Library; PO Box 325; 2422 Church St; Byhalia 38611	(662) 838-4024
MERIDIAN-LAUDERDALE COUNTY PUBLIC LIBRARY; 2517 Seventh St; Meridian 39301	(601) 693-6771
Mailibrary; 2517 7th St; Meridian 39301	(601) 486-2263
MID-MISSISSIPPI REGIONAL LIBRARY SYSTEM; 201 Huntington St; Kosciusko 39090	(662) 289-5151
Attala County Library; 201 S Huntington St; Kosciusko 39090	(662) 289-5141
Carthage-Leake County Library; 114 E Franklin St; Carthage 39051	(601) 267-7821
Duck Hill Public Library; PO Box 279; 125 North St; Duck Hill 38925	(662) 565-2391
Durant Public Library; 104 N Jackson St; Durant 39063	(662) 653-3451
Goodman Public Library; PO Box 374; Main St; Goodman 39079	(662) 472-2263
Kilmichael Public Library; PO Box 316; 116 North Depot; Kilmichael 39747	(662) 262-7615
Lexington Public Library; 208 Tchula St; Lexington 39095	(662) 834-4578
Pickens Public Library; PO Box 188; 1301 Highway 51; Pickens 39146	(662) 468-2391
Tchula Public Library; PO Box 248; 201 Mercer St; Tchula 39169	(662) 235-5235

Libraries in Mississippi

MID-MISSISSIPPI REGIONAL LIBRARY SYSTEM (Continued)	
Walnut Grove Public Library; PO Box 206; 140 Main St; Walnut Grove 39189	(601) 253-2483
West Public Library; PO Box 9; 121 Front St; West 39192	(662) 967-2510
Winona-Montgomery County Library; 115 N Quitman St; Winona 38967	(662) 283-3443
Winston County Library; 301 W Park St; Louisville 39339	(662) 773-3212
NESHOBA COUNTY PUBLIC LIBRARY; 230 Beacon St; Philadelphia 39350	(601) 656-4911
NORTHEAST REGIONAL LIBRARY SYSTEM; 1023 Fillmore St; Corinth 38834	(662) 287-7311
Anne Spencer Cox Library; 303 North 3rd St; Baldwyn 38824	(662) 365-3305
Belmont Public Library; PO Box 629; 102 South 3rd St; Belmont 38827	(662) 454-7841
Blue Mountain Public Library; PO Box 37; City Hall, 110 Mill St; Blue Mountain 38610	(662) 685-4721
Burnsville Public Library; PO Box 188; Norman Ave; Burnsville 38833	(662) 427-9258
Chalybeate Public Library; 2501-A Highway 354; Walnut 38683	(662) 223-4620
Corinth Public Library; 1023 Fillmore St; Corinth 38834	(662) 287-2441
George E. Allen Library; 404 W Church St; Booneville 38829	(662) 728-6553
Iuka Public Library; 204 North Main St; Iuka 38852	(662) 423-6300
Margaret McRae Memorial Library; PO Box 128; Main St. (Hwy 25); Tishomingo 38873	(662) 438-7640
Marietta Public Library; PO Box 88; County Road 470, House #7; Marietta 38856	(662) 728-9320
Rienzi Public Library; PO Box 69; 5 School St; Rienzi 38865	(662) 462-5015
Ripley Public Library; 308 North Commerce St; Ripley 38663	(662) 837-7773
Walnut Public Library; 102 South Main St; Walnut 38683	(662) 223-6768
NOXUBEE COUNTY LIBRARY SYSTEM; Ada S. Fant Memorial Library; 103 E King St; Macon 39341	(662) 726-5461
Brooksville Public Library; PO Box 425; 108 West Main St; Brooksville 39739	(662) 738-4559
Vista J. Daniel Memorial Library; PO Box 248; 402 Residence St; Shuqualak 39361	(662) 793-9576
PEARL RIVER COUNTY LIBRARY SYSTEM; 900 Goodyear Rd; Picayune 39466	(601) 798-5081
Margaret Reed Crosby Memorial Library; 900 Goodyear Blvd; Picayune 39466	(601) 798-5081
Poplarville Public Library; 202 West Beers St; Poplarville 39470	(601) 795-8411
PIKE-AMITE-WALTHALL LIBRARY SYSTEM; McComb Public Library; 114 State St; McComb 39648	(601) 684-2661
Alpha Center Library; 414 McComb St; McComb 39648	(601) 684-8312
Crosby Public Library; PO Box 427; Highway 33; Crosby 39633	(601) 639-4633
Gloster Public Library; PO Box 460; Main St; Gloster 39638	(601) 225-4341
Liberty Public Library; PO Box 187; Clinic Dr; Liberty 39645	(601) 657-8781
Magnolia Public Library; 230 S Cherry St; Magnolia 39652	(601) 783-6565
Osyka Public Library; 568 West Railroad Ave N; Osyka 39657	(601) 542-5147
Progress Public Library; 5071 Mt. Herman Rd; McComb 39648	(601) 542-5501
Walthall County Library; 707 Union Rd; Tylertown 39667	(601) 876-4348
PINE FOREST REGIONAL LIBRARY SYSTEM; PO Box 1208; 210 Front St; Richton 39476	(601) 788-6539
Conway Hall Library; 9220 Highway 42; Petal 39465	(601) 584-7469
Jane Blain Brewer Memorial Library; PO Box 279; 203 South St; Mount Olive 39119	(601) 797-4955
Leakesville Public Library; PO Box 1089; 101 Lafayette St; Leaksville 39451	(601) 394-2897
McHenry Public Library; PO Box 14; McHenry Ave; McHenry 39561	No Phone
Mclain Public Library; PO Box 65; 117 Church Ave; McClain 39456	(601) 753-2389
New Augusta Public Library; PO Box 387; 28 Buck Creek Rd; New Augusta 39462	(601) 964-3774
R. E. Blackwell Memorial Library; PO Box 1539; 43 South Fir St; Collins 39428	(601) 765-8582
Richton Public Library; PO Box 1208; 210 Front St; Richton 39476	(601) 788-6539
Seminary Public Library; 101 Willow St; Seminary 39479	(601) 722-9041
State Line Public Library; PO Box 279; 8 Farrier St; State Line 39362	(601) 848-2011
Stone County Library; 242 Second St; Wiggins 39577	(601) 928-4993
William Estes Powell Memorial Library; 1502 Bolton Ave; Beaumont 39423	(601) 784-3471
SOUTH DELTA LIBRARY SERVICES; B. S. Ricks Memorial Library; 310 N Main; Yazoo City 39194	(662) 746-5557
Sharkey-Issaquena County Library; 300 E China St; Rolling Fork 39159	(662) 873-4076
SOUTH MISSISSIPPI REGIONAL LIBRARY SYSTEM; 900 Broad St; Columbia 39429	(601) 736-5516
Bassfield Public Library; PO Box 310; Second and Foote Streets; Bassfield 39421	(601) 943-5420
Columbia-Marion County Library; 900 Broad St; Columbia 39429	(601) 736-5516
Prentiss Public Library; PO Box 1315; 2229 Pearl; Prentiss 39474	(601) 792-5845
STARKVILLE-OKTIBBEHA CO. LIBRARY SYSTEM; PO Box 1406; 326 University Dr; Starkville 39759	(662) 323-2766
Maben Public Library; PO Box 507; 2nd Ave; Maben 39750	(662) 263-5619
Starkville Public Library; PO Box 1406; 326 University Dr; Starkville 39759	(662) 323-2766
Sturgis Public Library; PO Box 8; 529 Main; Sturgis 39769	(662) 465-7493

Libraries in Mississippi

SUNFLOWER COUNTY LIBRARY SYSTEM; 201 Cypress Dr; Indianola 38751	(662) 887-2153
Drew Public Library; 290 W Park Ave; Drew 38737	(662) 745-2237
Henry M. Seymour Library; 200 East Percy St; Indianola 38751	(662) 887-1672
Horace S. Stansel Library; 112 South Ruby St; Ruleville 38771	(662) 756-2226
Inverness Public Library; PO Box 206; 802 East Grand Ave; Inverness 38753	(662) 265-5179
Kathy June Sheriff Library; PO Box 178; 1001 W Delta Ave; Moorhead 38761	(662) 246-8263
Sunflower Public Library; PO Box 280; 111 North railroad St; Sunflower 38778	(662) 569-3423
TALLAHATCHIE COUNTY LIBRARY SYSTEM; PO Box 219; 102 Walnut; Charleston 38921	(662) 647-2638
Charleston Library; PO Box 219; 102 Walnut; Charleston 38921	(662) 647-2638
Sumner Public Library; PO Box 386; 507 North Walnut St; Sumner 38957	(662) 375-8901
Tutwiler Public Library; PO Box 214; 103 Second St; Tutwiler 38963	(662) 345-8475
Webb Public Library; PO Box 618; 199 Laura; Webb 38966	(662) 375-8787
THE LIBRARY OF HATTIESBURG, PETAL & FORREST COUNTY; 329 Hardy Street; Hattiesburg 39401	(601) 582-4461
The Petal Library; 714 Main Street; Petal 39465	(601) 584-7610
TOMBIGBEE REGIONAL LIBRARY SYSTEM; PO Box 675; 338 Commerce St; West Point 39773	(662) 494-4872
Amory Municipal Library; 402 2nd Ave N at 4th St; Amory 38821	(662) 256-5261
Bryan Public Library; PO Box 675; 338 Commerce St; West Point 39773	(662) 494-4872
Choctaw County Public Library; PO Box 755; South Louisville St; Ackerman 39735	(662) 285-6348
Dorothy J. Lowe Memorial Library; PO Box 1310; West Main St; Nettleton 38858	(662) 963-2014
Evans Memorial Library; 105 North Long St; Aberdeen 39731	(662) 369-4601
Hamilton Public Library; PO Box 96; Highway 45 South; Hamilton 39746	(662) 343-8962
Mathiston Public Library; PO Box 82; Scott St; Mathiston 39752	(662) 263-4772
Webster County Public Library; PO Box 205; 202 West Fox Ave; Eupora 39744	(662) 258-7515
Weir Public Library; PO Box 248; 119 Front St; Weir 39772	(662) 547-6747
Wren Public Library; 32655 Highway 45 North; Aberdeen 39730	(662) 256-4957
UNION COUNTY LIBRARY SYSTEM; PO Box 846; 219 King St; New Albany 38652	(662) 534-1991
Jennie Stephens Smith Library; PO Box 846; 219 King St; New Albany 38652	(662) 534-1991
Nance-McNeely Library; PO Box 225; 1177 Springdale Ave; Myrtle 38650	(662) 988-2895
WARREN COUNTY-VICKSBURG PUBLIC LIBRARY; 700 Veto St; Vicksburg 39180	(601) 636-6411
WASHINGTON COUNTY LIBRARY SYSTEM; 341 Main; Greenville 38701	(662) 335-2331
Arcola Library; Po Box 478; 106 Dr. M. L. King Dr; Arcola 38722	(662) 827-5262
Avon Library; PO Box 10; 874 Riverside Rd; Avon 38723	(662) 332-9346
Glen Allan Library; PO Box 39; 970 Eastside Lake Washington R; Glen Allan 38744	(662) 839-4066
Leland Library; 107 N Broad St; Leland 38756	(662) 686-7353
Torrey Wood Memorial Library; 302 East Ave; Hollandale 38748	(662) 827-2335
William Alexander Percy Memorial Library; 341 Main; Greenville 38701	(662) 335-2331
WAYNESBORO-WAYNE COUNTY LIBRARY SYSTEM; 712 Wayne St; Waynesboro 39367	(601) 735-2268
YALOBUSHA COUNTY PUBLIC LIBRARY SYSTEM; PO Box 359; 14432 Main St; Coffeeville 38922	(662) 675-8822
Coffeeville Public Library; PO Box 359; 14432 Main St; Coffeeville 38922	(662) 675-8822
Oakland Public Library; PO Box 359; 714-A Main St; Oakland 38948	(662) 623-8652

MISSISSIPPI PUBLIC LIBRARY STATISTICS, 1998

Books and Other Items Owned: 6,544,729 (2.38 per capita*)

In 1998, Mississippians made 7,028,288 library visits, checked out 9,059,775 items (3.29 per capita) and they asked librarians 1,213,682 reference questions.

Total Local Government Funds:	$ 23,099,133 ($ 8.39 per capita)
State Government Funds:	$ 5,578,289 ($ 2.03 per capita)
Federal Government Funds:	$ 278,327 ($ 0.10 per capita)
Total Government Funding:	$ 28,955,749 ($ 10.52 per capita)
Other Income:	$ 2,713,587 ($ 0.99 per capita)
Total Operating Income:	$ 31,669,336 ($ 11.51 per capita)

Expenditures: Personnel (salaries & benefits) — $ 18,596,605 |66%| ($ 6.76 per capita)
Expenditures: Materials — Printed: $ 3,685,169   Electronic: $ 186,458   Other: $ 283,761
  Total Materials: $ 4,155,388 |15%| ($ 1.51 per capita)
Expenditures: Other (including computer access) — $ 5,599,573 |20%| ($ 2.03 per capita)
Total Operating Expenditures: $ 28,351,566 ($ 10.30 per capita) [$ 20.88 National]
Jan. 1, 2000 — Number of Public Libraries: 243   Number of Library Systems: 47
*Per capita statistics based on Census Bureau figures showing MS with a pop. of 2,751,335 as of 7/1/98.

Libraries in Mississippi

UNIVERSITY AND COLLEGE LIBRARIES

Alcorn State University: J. D. Boyd Library; 1000 ASU Drive #539; Alcorn State 39096-7500 .... (601) 877-6350
Belhaven College: Warren Hood Library; 1500 Peachtree St; Jackson .... (601) 968-5948
Blue Mountain College: Guyton Library; Blue Mountain 38610 .... (662) 685-4771
Delta State University: W. R. Roberts Library; Leflore Circle; Delta State University; Cleveland 38733 .... (662) 846-4430
Jackson State University: H. T. Sampson Library: 1400 Lynch St; Jackson 39217 .... (601) 968-2123
Jackson State-Universities Center Library; Institutions of Higher Learning; 3825 Ridgewood Rd; Jackson ..... (601) 982-6313
Millsaps College: Millsaps-Wilson Library; 1701 North State St; Jackson 39210 .... (601) 974-1073
Mississippi College: Leland Speed Library: 200 West College St; Clinton 39056 .... (601) 925-3232
Mississippi State University: Mitchell Memorial Library; PO Box 5408; Mississippi State 39762 .... (662) 325-7668
Mississippi University for Women: John Clayton Fant Memorial Library: Columbus 39701 .... (662) 329-7332
Mississippi Valley State University: James Herbert White Library: Itta Bena 38941 .... (662) 254-3495
Rust College: Leontyne Price Library; 150 Rust Ave; Holly Springs 38635   (extension 4100) .... (662) 252-8000
Tougaloo College: L. Sonobia Coleman Library; 500 West County Line Rd; Tougaloo 39174 .... (601) 977-7704
The University of Mississippi: John D. Williams Library; University 38677 .... (662) 915-7935
The University of Mississippi Medical Center: Rowland Medical Library; 2500 N. State St; Jackson .... (601) 984-1230
The University of Southern Mississippi: Cook Mem. Library; Southern Stat., Box 5053; Hattiesburg 39406 .... (601) 266-4250
The University of Southern Mississippi: William David McCain Library & Archives; Hattiesburg .... (601) 266-4345
The University of Southern Mississippi, Gulf Coast Campus: Cox Library; .... (228) 865-4510
William Carey College: I. E. Rouse Library; 498 Tuscan Ave; Hattiesburg 39401-5499 .... (601) 582-6169
William Carey College: McMullan Learning Resources Center; 1856 Beach Dr; Gulfpoort 39507 .... (228) 897-7213

COMMUNITY COLLEGE LIBRARIES

Coahoma Community College: Dickerson-Johnson Library; 3240 Friars Point Rd; Clarksdale 38614   [ext. 161] (662) 627-5446
Copiah-Lincoln Community College: Evelyn W. Oswalt Library; PO Boix 649Wesson 39191 .... (601) 643-8364
Copiah-Lincoln Community College: Natchez Campus Library; 30 Campus Dr; Natchez 39120 .... (601) 446-1101
East Central Community College: Burton Library; PO Box 129; Decatur 39327   (toll free 877-462-3222) or (601) 635-2111
East Mississippi Community College: Golden Triangle Campus Library; PO Box 100; Mayhew 39753 .... (662) 243-1900
East Mississippi Community College: Tubb-May Memorial Library; PO Box 158; Scooba 39358 .... (662) 476-5000
Hinds Community College: George M. McClendon Library; 505 East Main St; Raymond 39154 .... (601) 857-3255
Hinds Community College Library; Academy-Technical Center; 3925 Sunset Dr; Jackson .... (601) 987-8123
Hinds Community College Library; Nursing-Allied Health Center; 1750 Chadwick Dr; Jackson .... (601) 371-3523
Hinds Community College Library; Rankin Campus; Highway 80; Pearl .... (601) 936-5538
Hinds Community College Library; Utica Campus; Hwy 18W; Utica 39175 .... (601) 885-7036
Holmes Community College: McMorrough Library; PO Box 369: Goodman 39079 .... (662) 472-2312
Holmes Community College: Grenada Center Library; 1060 Avent Dr; Grenada 38901 .... (662) 226-8885
Holmes Community College: Learning Resources Center; 412 West Ridgeland Ave; Ridgeland 39157 .... (601) 856-5400
Itawamba Community College: Itawamba Learning Resource Center; 602 W. Hill St; Fulton 38843 .... (662) 862-8000
Itawamba Community College: Learning Resources Center; 2176 S. Eason Blvd; Tupelo 38804 .... (662) 620-5310
Jones County Junior College: T. Terrell Tisdale Library; 900 South Court St; Ellisville 39437 .... (601) 477-4055
Mary Holmes College; PO Drawer 1257; Highway 50 West; West Point 39773 .... (662) 494-6820
Meridian Community College: L. O. Todd Library; 910 Highway 19 North; Meridian 39307 .... (601) 483-8241
Mississippi Delta Community College: Stanny Sanders Library; Moorhead 38761 .... (662) 246-6376
Mississippi Gulf Coast Community College: Jackson County Campus Library; PO Box 100; Gautier 39553 ... (228) 497-7642
Mississippi Gulf Coast Comm. College: Jeff. Davis Campus Library; 2226 Switzer Rd; Gulfport 39507 .... (228) 897-3809
Mississippi Gulf Coast Community College: Perkinston Campus Library; PO Box 548; Perkinston 39573 ..... (601) 928-6286
Northeast Mississippi Community College: Eula Dees Mem. Lib; 101 Cunningham Blvd; Booneville 38829 ... (662) 720-7408
Northwest Mississippi Community College: DeSoto Center Library; 5197 W.E. Ross Pkwy; Southaven 38671 . (662) 280-6164
Northwest Mississippi Community College: R. C. Pugh Library; PO Drawer L; Senatobia .... (662) 562-3278
Pearl River Community College Library-Forrest County Center: 5448 Highway 49 S; Hattiesburg 39401 ...... (601) 544-9122
Pearl River Community College Library-Poplarville Campus: 101 Highway 11 North; Poplarville 39470 ...... (601) 795-1332
Southwest Mississippi Community College: Library-Learning Resources Ctr; College Dr; Summit 39666 ...... (601) 276-2004
Wood College: Wood Memorial Library; PO Box 289; Mathiston 39752 .... (662) 263-5352

OTHER LIBRARIES

LIBRARY FOR THE BLIND & PHYSICALLY HANDICAPPED; 5455 Executive Pl; Jackson (800-446-0892) (601) 713-3410
MAGNOLIA BIBLE COLLEGE LIBRARY: 822 South Hunington Street; Kosciusko 39090 .... (601) 289-2896
MISSISSIPPI LIBRARY COMMISSION; PO Box 10700; 1221 Ellis Ave; Jackson 39289   (800-647-7542) or (601) 961-4111
MISSISSIPPI STATE GOVERNMENT-LEGISLATIVE REFERENCE LIBRARY; Jackson .... (601) 359-3135
MISSISSIPPI STATE LAW LIBRARY; Gartin Justice Bldg; Jackson .... (601) 359-3672
REFORMED THEOLOGICAL SEMINARY LIBRARY; 5422 Clinton Blvd; Jackson   (800-543-2703) or (601) 923-4040
WESLEY BIBLICAL SEMINARY LIBRARY; 5980 Floral Dr; Jackson .... (601) 957-1314

Mississippi Agriculture

Principal Crops 1999: order of value — cotton, soybeans, rice, corn, cottonseed, sweet potatoes & wheat)

PRINCIPAL CROPS, 1998

Acres Planted	Acres Harvested	Value of Production
4,780,000	4,658,000	$ 1,133,739,000

CASH RECEIPTS FROM FARM MARKETINGS

	Crops	Livestock & Products	Total
1999	$ 1,031,013,000	$ 2,142,746,000	$ 3,173,759,000
1998	$ 1,289,838,000	$ 2,254,244,000	$ 3,544,082,000
1997	$ 1,372,218,000	$ 2,086,275,000	$ 3,458,493,000
1996	$ 1,488,995,000	$ 2,002,821,000	$ 3,491,816,000

COTTON LINT

	Planted (millions of acres)	Harvested (millions of acres)	Production (millions of bales)	Yield (lbs. lint p/acre)	Value of Production (in current dollars)
2000*	1.360	1.280	1.700	638	$ not available
1999	1.200	1.180	1.731	704	$ 392,544,000
1998	0.950	0.940	1.444	737	$ 418,644,000
1997	0.985	0.970	1.821	901 (record)	$ 567,278,000
1996	1.120	1.100	1.850	807	$ 612,326,000

* Forecast made on Oct. 1, 2000.

OTHER CROPS

	Production		Yield		Value of Production
*Soybeans, 2000	37,260,000	bushels	23.0	bushels p/acre	$ not available
1999	44,650,000	bushels	23.5	bushels p/acre	$ 227,715,000
1998	48,000,000	bushels	24.0	bushels p/acre	$ 270,240,000
Rice, 2000	13,189,000	bushels	6,050.0	lbs. p/acre	$ not available
1999	18,250,000	cwt	5,650.0	lbs. p/acre	$ 95,813,000
1998	15,544,000	cwt	5,800.0	lbs. p/acre	$ 139,741,000
Corn for Grain, 2000	39,520,000	bushels	104.0	bushels p/acre	$ not available
1999	36,270,000	bushels	117.0	bushels p/acre (record)	$ 72,540,000
1998	43,000,000	bushels	86.0	bushels p/acre	$ 87,720,000
Cottonseed, 1999	667,000	tons	- -		$ 48,358,000
1998	561,000	tons	- -		$ 65,076,000
Wheat, 2000	9,750,000	cwt	50.0	bushels p/acre	$ not available
1999	8,250,000	bushels	50.0	bushels p/acre (record)	$ 19,800,000
1998	6,750,000	bushels	45.0	bushels p/acre	$ 16,133,000
Sorghum for Grain, 1999	4,872,000	bushels	87.0	bushels p/acre (record)	$ 9,257,000
1998	2,340,000	bushels	65.0	bushels p/acre	$ 4,469,000
Sweet Potatoes, 1999	1,545,000	cwt	150.0	cwt p/acre	$ 29,849,000
1998	1,358,000	cwt	140.0	cwt p/acre	$ 23,765,000

*Figures for 2000, except for wheat, are from the forecast made on Oct. 1, 2000.

RECORD HIGHS FOR CROPS

	Planted Acres	Harvested Acres	Yield Per Acre	Production
Cotton, All (since 1866)	4,163,000 (1930)	4,142,000 (1930)	901 lbs (1997)	2,692,000 bales (1937)
Corn, for Grain (since 1866)	3,254,000 (1939)	3,237,000 (1921)	117 bu (1999)	60,090,000 bu (1996)
Grain Sorghum (since 1949)	650,000 (1985)	620,000 (1985)	87 bu (1999)	39,680,000 bu (1985)
Wheat (since 1866)	1,100,000 (1982)	950,000 (1982)	50 bu (1999)	36,100,000 bu (1982)
Soybeans (since 1924)	4,200,000 (1979)	4,100,000 (1979)	34 bu (1992)	118,900,000 bu (1979)
Rice (since 1949)	340,000 (1981)	337,000 (1981)	60 cwt (1996)	18,467,000 cwt (1994)
Hay, All (since 1909)	---	1,030,000 (1941)	2.7 tons (1992)	2,025,000 tons (1992)
Sweet Potatoes (since 1869)	103,000 (1934)	103,000 (1934)	170 cwt (1994)	5,212,000 cwt (1934)

RECORD LOWS FOR CROPS

	Planted Acres	Harvested Acres	Yield Per Acre	Production
Cotton, All (since 1866)	687,000 (1983)	675,000 (1983)	86 lbs (1866)	323,000 bales (1866)
Corn, for Grain (since 1866)	100,000 (1983)	55,000 (1983)	9.5 bu (1866)	2,464,000 bu (1980)
Grain Sorghum (since 1949)	7,300 (1914)**	3,000 (1953)	13 bu (1951)	39,000 bu (1951)
Wheat (since 1866)	1,000 (1939)	1,000 (1939)	4 bu (1890)	13,000 bu (1928)
Soybeans (since 1924)	45,000 (1924)	11,000 (1928)	6.5 bu (1930)	78,000 bu (1930)
Rice (since 1949)	5,000 (1949)	5,000 (1949)	23.3 cwt (1952)	135,000 cwt (1949)
Hay, All (since 1909)	---	219,000 (1909)	.9 tons (1924)	262,000 tons (1909)
Sweet Potatoes (since 1869)	3,000 (1989)	3,000 (1989)	29 cwt (1924)	285,000 cwt (1989)

** Only planted acreage prior to 1949.

The Ultimate Reference on the State

Mississippi Agriculture

LIVESTOCK

Broilers Produced, 1997: 720,300,000 birds
1998: 722,400,000 birds
3,467,501,300 pounds
Broilers, Value of Production, 1998: $1,369,663,000
Eggs Produced, 1998: 1,578,000,000 valued at $159,115,000
1997: 1,547,000,000 valued at $145,676,000
Total Value All Poultry & Eggs, 1998: $1,536,021,000
Cattle & Calves: 1/1/00 — 1,070,000 head   1/1/99 — 1,160,000 head
Beef Cows: 1/1/00 — 579,000 head   1/1/99 — 591,000 head
Milk Cows: 1/1/00 — 36,000 head   1/1/99 — 39,000 head
Milk/Cream Marketings, 1999: 548 million pounds valued at $90 million.
Pig Crop For 1998: 523,000 head (29% increase over 1997)
Hogs & Pigs Inventory: 12/1/98 — 275,000 head   **12/1/97** — 240,000 head

> Poultry & eggs first broke the $1 billion mark in 1994 when it was the state's top commodity with $1.078 billion in sales! Figures were $1.536 billion for 1998 and $1.488 billion for 1999.

> Principal 1998 Farm Commodities (Cash Receipts) were broilers/eggs, timber, cotton lint, catfish, and soybeans.

AQUACULTURE (CATFISH)

Water Surface Acres Used for Production, July 1-Dec. 31: 2000 — 111,500   **1999** — 108,000
No. of Fish Operations on July 1: 2000 — 400   **1999** — 390
Inventory Total Foodsize, 7/1/2000: 176,510,000 (193,800,000 lbs.)
7/1/1999: 181,110,000 (198,010,000 lbs.)
Inventory Large Stockers (millions), July 1: 2000 — 288.8 (114.8 lbs.)   **1999** — 268.9 (104.3 lbs.)
Inventory Small Stockers (millions), July 1: 2000 — 270.0 (25.4 lbs.)   **1999** — 284.0 (27.6 lbs.)
Total Catfish Sales: 1999 — $294,103,000   **1998** — $307,229,000   **1997** — $265,934,000
Foodsize Catfish Sales, 1999: 385,000,000 pounds sold for $281,050,000 (.73 per pound)
1998: 390,000,000 pounds sold for $288,600,000 (.74 per pound)
Miss. Share of U.S. Market: 1999 — 61% (with 58% of acreage)   **1998** — 65% (with 60% of acreage)

GENERAL

Number of Farms: 1999 — 43,000   **1998** — 42,000
Land in Farms, 1999: 11,400,000 acres (265 acres per farm)
1998: 11,600,000 acres (276 acres per farm)
Assets (land/buildings), 1/1/1998: $14,140,000,000   **Debt, 1/1/1998:** $2,584,000,000
Estimated Market Value of Machinery & Equipment, 1997: $1,622,303,718 ($51,801 per farm avg.)
Cash Receipts From All Ag Products Sold, 1998: $3,544,082,000
Net Farm Income, 1999: $948,998,000 ($22,070 per farm average)
U.S. Government Payments: 1999 — $431,096,000   **1998** — $281,634,000   **1997** — $169,869,000

> Miss. farmers and ranchers produced $4.8 billion in agricultural and forestry products in 1999, $4.7 billion in 1998 and $4.85 billion in 1997.

> Value of Production of Mississippi Forestry Products was $1,361,746,000 for 1998.

Main Source: *Mississippi Agricultural Statistics, 1997-98*; National Agricultural Statistics Service and Mississippi Dept. of Agriculture.

Mississippi's Top Ag Counties, 1997
(corn, cotton, hay, rice, soybeans & wheat)

County	Value of Production
Bolivar	$ 142,743,622
Coahoma	116,506,414
Washington	114,843,884
Sunflower	111,600,277
Leflore	92,415,893
Tallahatchie	79,100,121
Tunica	67,098,984
Yazoo	62,005,199
Humphreys	56,782,691
Sharkey	49,401,584
Quitman	45,297,351
Holmes	39,535,546

Source: *Mississippi Agriculture 1972-1998* Mississippi Cooperative Extension Service.

Mississippi's Top Timber Counties, 1997

County	Value of Production
Amite	$ 39,296,694
Lauderdale	33,359,895
Wayne	32,998,931
Kemper	31,883,168
Franklin	30,987,131
Copiah	30,123,589

Mississippi Timber: Value of Production

Year	Value
1992	$ 810,000,000
1993	1,021,000,000
1994	1,073,000,000
1995	1,105,000,000
1996	1,188,830,000
1997	1,313,318,000
1998	1,361,746,000

Mississippi's Rank Nationally in 1999

Catfish-foodsize	1
All Cotton	3
Broilers	4
Sweet Potatoes	4
All Rice	4
Sorghum for Grain	11
Sorghum for Silage	12
Soybeans	14
Eggs	15
Watermelons	16
Beef Cows	21
Hogs & Pigs	22
Corn for Grain	22
All Hay	32
Milk Cows	36

Agriculture in Mississippi

Mississippi Farm Income and Expenses, 1996 - 1998			
	1996	1997	1998
Total cash receipts from farm marketings	$ 3,491,816,000	$ 3,458,493,000	$ 3,544,082,000
Cash receipts: livestock & products	2,002,821,000	2,086,275,000	2,254,244,000
Cash receipts: crops	1,488,995,000	1,372,218,000	1,289,838,000
Other income	541,025,000	571,187,000	711,536,000
Government payments	197,666,000	169,869,000	281,899,000
Imputed & misc. income received	343,359,000	401,318,000	429,637,000
Total production expenses	$ 3,297,493,000	$ 3,368,245,000	$ 3,433,158,000
Feed purchased	598,793,000	600,464,000	612,551,000
Livestock purchased	195,339,000	229,688,000	229,231,000
Seed purchased	63,659,000	70,329,000	74,031,000
Fertilizer & lime (incl. ag chemicals)	393,255,000	395,789,000	374,347,000
Petroleum products purchased	100,931,000	106,102,000	93,550,000
Hired hand labor expenses	374,176,000	366,187,000	384,190,000
All other production expenses	1,571,340,000	1,599,686,000	1,665,258,000
Total value inventory change	103,177,000	49,160,000	-135,083,000
Value of inventory change: livestock	-14,412,000	-56,509,000	-12,700,000
Value of inventory change: crops	117,589,000	105,669,000	-122,383,000
Total cash receipts and other income	$ 4,032,841,000	$ 4,029,680,000	$ 4,255,618,000
less: Total production expenses	3,297,493,000	3,368,245,000	3,433,158,000
Realized net income	735,348,000	661,435,000	822,460,000
plus: Value of inventory change	103,177,000	49,160,000	-135,083,000
Total net income incl. corporate farms	838,525,000	710,595,000	678,377,000
less: Net income of corporate farms	70,872,000	50,457,000	30,730,000
Statistical adjustment	-5,000	+6,000	-4,000
Total net farm proprietors' income	$ 767,648,000	$ 660,144,000	$ 656,643,000
plus: Farm wages and perquisites	148,841,000	159,638,000	175,651,000
plus: Farm other labor income	8,095,000	8,515,000	7,484,000
Total farm labor & proprietors' income	$ 924,584,000	$ 828,297,000	$ 839,778,000

SOURCE for the above table: U.S. Bureau of Economic Analysis, released June 15, 2000.

Value Added to the U.S. Economy by the Agriculture Sector in Mississippi, 1997 - 1999			
	1997	1998	1999
Final Crop Output	$ 1,485,428,000	$ 1,161,448,000	$ 1,064,621,000
Final Animal Output	$ 1,954,461,000	$ 2,161,266,000	$ 2,103,295,000
Services and Forestry	$ 454,249,000	$ 490,762,000	$ 569,588,000
Final Agricultural Sector Output	$ 3,894,138,000	$ 3,813,476,000	$ 3,737,504,000
-Total Production Expenses	$ 2,261,589,000	$ 2,256,101,000	$ 2,309,085,000
-Factor Payments (labor, rent, interest)	520,606,000	555,929,000	552,943,000
-Capital Consumption	287,816,000	291,024,000	297,094,000
+Net Government Transactions	110,997,000	221,660,000	370,615,000
Net Farm Income	$ 935,124,000	$ 932,082,000	$ 948,998,000

SOURCE: Economic Research Service.

Mississippi Agriculture (Charts)

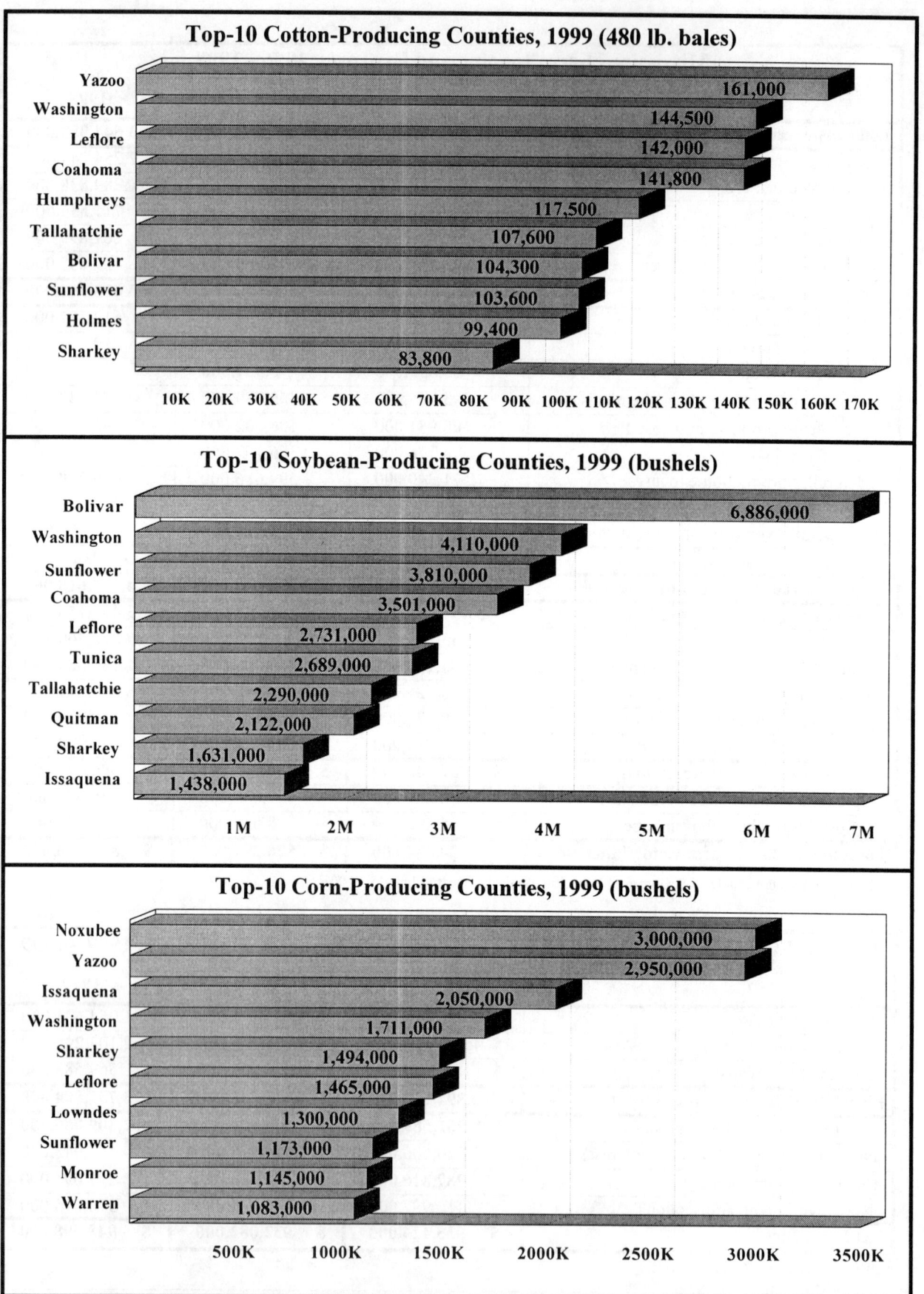

Mississippi Agriculture (Charts)

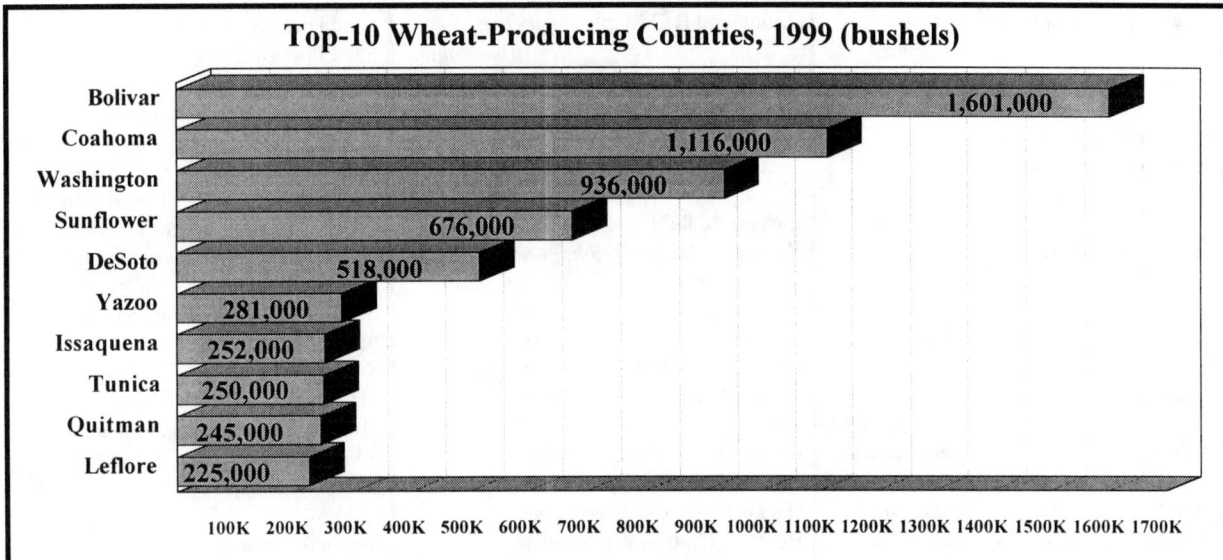

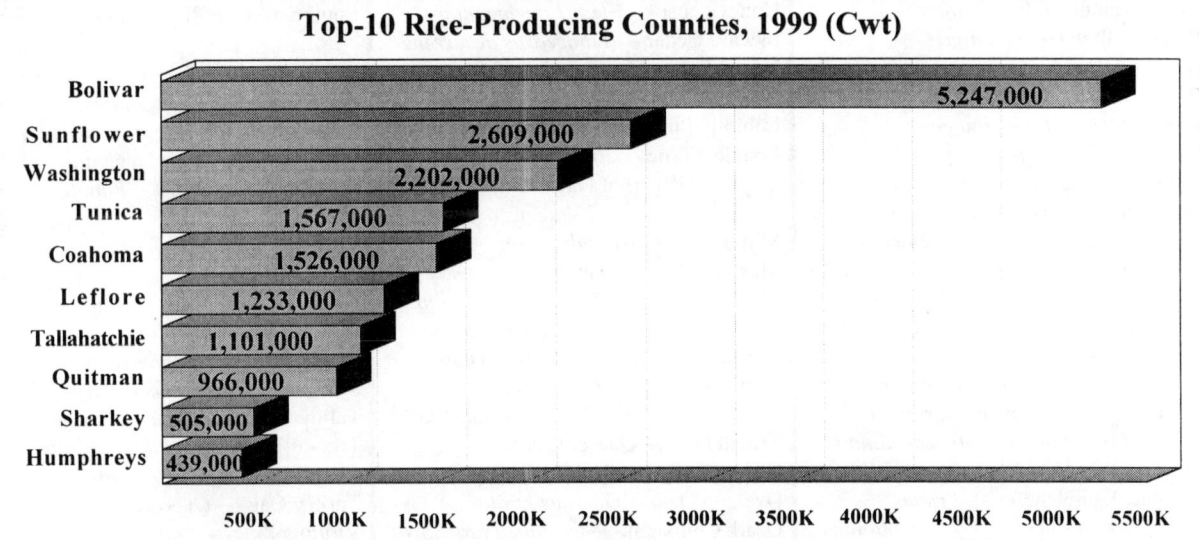

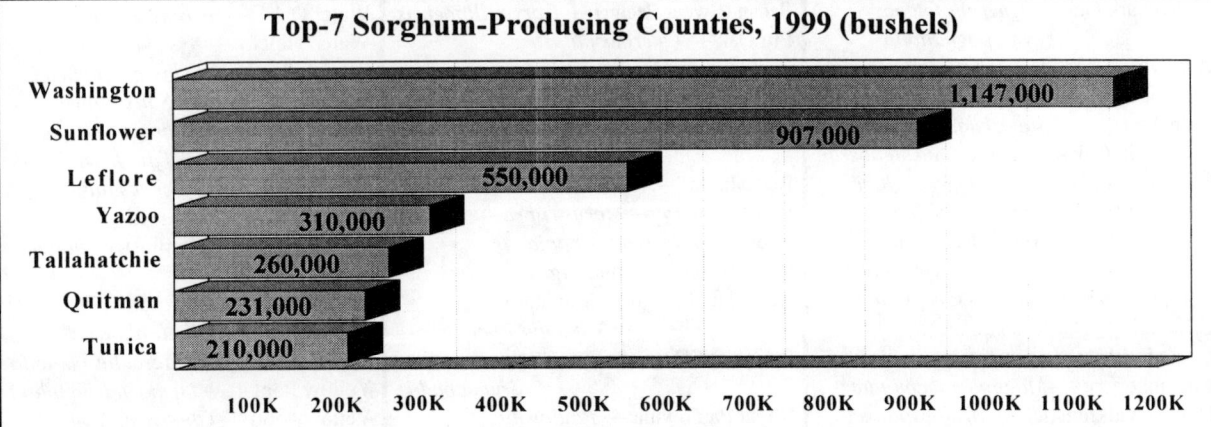

ALL 1999 FIGURES ARE PRELIMINARY ESTIMATES AND SUBJECT TO LATER REVISION

Tree Species of Mississippi

Allegheny Chinkapin —[66]*Castanea pumila*
American Beech — *Fagus grandifolia*
American Chestnut — *Castanea dentata*
American Elm — *Ulmus americana*
American Holly — *Ilex opaca*
American Hornbeam — *Carpinus caroliniana*
American Sycamore — *Platanus occidentalis*
Arizona Cypress — *Cupressus arizonica*
Arkansas Oak — *Quercus arkansana*
Baldcypress — *Taxodium distichum*
Bigleaf Magnolia — *Magnolia macrophylla*
Bitternut Hickory — *Carya cordiformis*
Black Cherry — *Prunus serotina*
Black Locust — *Robinia pseudoacacia*
Black Oak — *Quercus velutina*
Black Tupelo — *Nyssa sylvatica*
Black Walnut — *Juglans nigra*
Black Willow — *Salix nigra*
Blackjack Oak — *Quercus marilandica*
Bluejack Oak — *Quercus incana*
Blue Spruce — *Picea Pungens*
Boxelder — *Acer negundo*
Bur Oak — *Quercus macrocarpa*
Butternut (White Walnut) — *Juglans cinerea*
Buttonbush — *Cephalanthus occidentalis*
Cabbage Palmetto — *Sabal palmetto*
California Privet — *Ligustrum ovalifolium*
Camphor-Tree — *Cinnamomum camphora*
Carolina Ash — *Flaxinus caroliniana*
Carolina Basswood — *Tilia caroliniana*
Carolina Beech — *Fagus grandifolia*
Carolina Laurelcherry — *Prunus caroliniana*
Cedar Elm — *Ulmus crassifolia*
Cherrybark Oak — *Quercus falcata* var. *pagodifolia*
Cherrybark Red Oak — *Quercus pagoda*
Chestnut Oak — *Quercus prinus*
Chinaberry — *Melia azedarach*
Chinkapin Oak — *Quercus muehlenbergii*
Coast Pignut Hickory — *Carya glabra*
Common Pear — *Pyrus communis*
Common Persimmon — *Diospyros virginiana*
Compton Oak — *Quercus comptoniae*
Cow Oak — *Quercus michauxii*
Crapemyrtle — *Lagerstroemia indica*
Cucumbertree — *Magnolia acuminata*
Devils-Walkingstick — *Aralia spinosa*
Drummond Red Maple — *Acer drummondii*
Durand Oak — *Quercus durandii*
Eastern Cottonwood — *Populus deltoides*
Eastern Hemlock — *Tsuga canadensis*
Eastern Hophornbeam — *Ostrya virginiana*
Eastern Redbud — *Cercis canadensis*
Eastern Redcedar — *Juniperus virginiana*
Eastern White Pine — *Pinus strobus*
Florida Maple — *Acer barbatum*
Flowering Dogwood — *Cornus florida*
Fringetree — *Chionanthus virginicus*
Garden Plum — *Prunus domestica*
Georgia Hackberry — *Celtis tenuifolia*
Green Ash — *Fraxinus pennsylvanica*
Gum Bumelia — *Bumelia lanuginosa*
Hackberry — *Celtis occidentalis*
Hercules Club — *Zanthoxylum clava-herculis*
Honeylocust — *Gleditsia triacanthos*
Incense Cedar — *Libocedrus decurrens*
Laurel Oak — *Quercus laurifolia*
Live Oak — *Quercus virginiana*
Loblolly Pine — *Pinus taeda*
Longleaf Pine — *Pinus palustris*
Mayhaw (Riverflat Hawthorn) — *Crataegus opaca*
Mimosa — *Albizia julibrissin*
Mexican Plum — *Prunus Mexicana*
Mockernut Hickory — *Carya tomentosa*
Northern Catalpa — *Catalpa speciosa*
Northern Red Oak — *Quercus rubra*
Northern White Cedar — *Thuja occidentalis*
Nuttall Oak — *Quercus nuttallii*
Osage Orange — *Maclura pomifera*
Overcup Oak — *Quercus lyrata*
Ozark Chinkapin — *Castanea ozarkensis*
Pawpaw — *Asimina triloba*
Pecan (Sweet Pecan) — *Carya illinoensis*
Pin Oak — *Quercus palustris*
Post Oak — *Quercus stellata*
Red Buckeye — *Aesculus pavia*
Red Hickory — *Carya glabra* var. *odorata*
Red Maple — *Acer rubrum*
Red Mulberry — *Morus rubra*
Redbay — *Persea borbonia*
River Birch — *Betula nigra*
Riverflat Hawthorn (Mayhaw) — *Crataegus opaca*
Roughleaf Dogwood — *Cornus drummondii*
Royal Paulownia — *Paulownia tomentosa*
Sand Hickory — *Carya pallida*
Sand Post Oak — *Quercus stellata* var. *margaretta*
Sassafras — *Sassafras albidum*
Scarlet Oak — *Quercus coccinea*
Shagbark Hickory — *Carya ovata*
Shellbark Hickory — *Carya laciniosa*
Shining Sumac — *Rhus copallina*
Shortleaf Pine — *Pinus echinata*
Shumard Red Oak — *Quercus shumardii*
Siberian Elm — *Ulmus pumila*
Silver Maple — *Acer saccharinum*
Silverleaf Poplar — *Populas alba*
Slash Pine — *Pinus elliottii*
Slippery Elm — *Ulmus rubra*
Sourwood — *Oxydendron arboreum*
Southern Catalpa — *Catalpa bignonioides*
Southern Crab Apple — *Malus angustifolia*
Southern Magnolia — *Magnolia grandiflora*
Southern Red Oak — *Quercus falcata*
Spruce Pine — *Pinus glabra*
Sugar Maple — *Acer saccharum*
Sugarberry — *Celtis laevigata*
Swamp Cottonwood — *Populus heterophylla*
Swamp Tupelo — *Nyssa sylvatica* var. *biflora*
Sweet Pecan (Pecan) — *Carya illinoensis*
Sweetbay — *Magnolia virginiana*
Sweetgum — *Liquidambar styraciflua*
Sycamore — *Platanus occidentalis*
Tallowtree — *Sapium sebiferum*
Tree-of-Heaven — *Ailanthus altissima*
Tung-Tree — *Aleurites fordii*
Turkey Oak — *Quercus laevis*
Virginia Pine — *Pinus virginiana*
Water Hickory — *Carya aquatica*
Water Oak — *Quercus nigra*
Water Tupelo — *Nyssa aquatica*
Waterlocust — *Gleditsia aquatica*
Weeping Willow — *Salix babylonica*
White Ash — *Fraxinus americana*
White Basswood — *Tilia heterophylla*
White Mulberry — *Morus alba*
White Oak — *Quercus alba*
White Walnut (Butternut) — *Juglans cinerea*
Willow Oak — *Quercus phellos*
Winged Elm — *Ulmus alata*
Yellow Buckeye — *Aesculus octandra*
Yellow Poplar — *Liriodendron tulipifera*
Yellowwood — *Cladrastis kentukea*

[66] Common name followed by scientific name in *italics*. Although this list does not represent a complete account of woody flora, it does include the most common trees of the state.
Source: Mississippi Forestry Commission

Champion Trees of Mississippi

Tree Species	Circ.	Crown	Height	Points[1]	Nominator(s)	Owner	County
AILANTHUS							
Chinese tree-of-heaven *(Ailanthus altissima)*	6' 8"	41' 0"	126'	216.25	C. Wellborn / B. Brown	Walter Biglane	Adams
APPLE							
Southern crab *(Malus angustifolia)*	2' 11"	30' 0"	25'	67.50	J. Herring / B.E. Brown	MS Dept. of WF & Parks	Madison
ASH							
Carolina *(Fraxinus caroliniana)*	4' 8"	45' 0"	71'	137.80	K. Coursey	U.S. Forest Service	Stone
Green *(Fraxinus pennsylvanica)*	19' 2"	52' 0"	78'	321.00	T. Nipp & M. Alsworth	Grief Brothers	Coahoma
White *(Fraxinus americana)*	10' 11"	64' 7"	93'	240.15	M. Daughdrill / J. Locke	Faye Kaigler	Wilkinson
BALDCYPRESS							
Baldcypress *(Taxodium distichum)* ❀	46' 4"	60' 0"	70'	640.60	Grant & Gary Arinder	Mark Simmons	Humphreys
BASSWOOD							
American *(Tilia americana)*	11' 3"	88' 0"	108'	265.00	P. Hardy	J. Franklin	Warren
White *(Tilia heterophylla)*	7' 2"	52' 0"	63'	162.00	H. P. Bryan	T. Spellman	Carroll
BEECH							
American *(Fagus grandifolia)*	19' 5"	127' 6"	132'	396.88	B. Stevens / D. Hancock / J. H. Smith / J. Bryant	Miss. State Hospital	Rankin
BIRCH							
River *(Betula Nigra)*	10' 2"	80' 0"	100'	242.00	G. Brummett	Georgia Pacific Corp.	Newton
BOXELDER							
Boxelder *(Acer negundo)*	8' 8"	56' 0"	86'	204.00	B. Brown / C. Welborn	Hattie O'Neal	Adams
BUCKEYE							
Red *(Aesculus pavia)*	3' 9"	24' 0"	28'	79.00	B.E. Brown/Green/Herring	Buddy Dixon	Jasper
Ohio *(Aesculus glabra)*	2' 6"	25' 6"	37'	73.40	J. Herring/J. Price/R. Flynt	MS Dept. of WF & Parks	Lowndes
Yellow *(Aesculus octandra)*	10' 5"	46' 3"	60'	196.56	C. Moore	Phil Edge	Issaquena
BUCKTHORN							
Carolina *(Rhamnus caroliniana)*	0' 10"	15' 6"	32'	45.38	J. Herring / B.E. Brown	MS Dept. of WF & Parks	Amite
BUMELIA							
Buckthorn *(Bumelia lycioides)*	1' 6"	26' 0"	31'	55.50	J. Herring / B.E. Brown	MS Dept. W.F. & Parks	Hinds
Gum *(Bumelia lanuginosa)*	4' 3"	16' 0"	59'	114.00	T. Nipp / M. Alsworth	Grief Brothers	Coahoma
BUTTONBUSH							
Common *(Cephalanthus occidentalis)*	4' 9"	22' 8"	18'	80.16	D. Linden / L. Dorris	U.S. Fish & Wildlife Service	Washington
CAMPHOR-TREE							
Camphor-tree *(Cinnamomum camphora)*	5' 3"	34' 6"	59'	130.60	Walter Passmore	Jack E. Logan	Jackson
CATALPA							
Northern *(Catalpa speciosa)*	17' 11"	90' 0"	69'	306.50	D. C. McClurkin	University of Miss.	Lafayette
Southern *(Catalpa bignonioides)*	21' 9"	71' 8"	84'	362.90	J. Ferguson	Dale Camp	Yalobusha
CHERRY							
Black *(Prunus serotina)*	13' 5"	70' 0"	80'	311.00	P. Barbour	James & Dabney Dale	Leflore
CHESTNUT							
American *(Castanea dentata)*	10' 6"	50' 6"	44'	182.63	B. E. Brown / L. Smith / J. Blackwell	Arlene Windham	Smith
CHINABERRY							
Chinaberry *(Melia azedarach)*	13' 10"	55' 9"	54'	233.50	B. Brown / S. Oglesby	Les French	Franklin

[1] Champion trees are selected by points: 1 point for each **inch** in circumference at a point 4½ feet above the ground; 1 point for each **foot** in height (to the nearest foot) & one-fourth point for each **foot** in average crown spread. Those of the same species within 5 points of each other are designated co-champions (🌳). ❀ The Champion tree in the state with the most points. Source: Mississippi Forestry Commission.

The Ultimate Reference on the State

Champion Trees of Mississippi

Tree Species	Circ.	Crown	Height	Points	Nominator(s)	Owner	County
CHINKAPIN							
Allegheny (*Castanea pumila*)	2' 0"	28' 0"	54'	85.40	T. Oakes / J. White	Bernard House	Lauderdale
COFFEETREE							
Kentucky (*Gymnocladus dioicus*)	7' 9"	61' 6"	99'	207.38	K. Cline / R. Cox / G. Byrd / T. Scott	Robert Cox	Tunica
COTTONWOOD							
Eastern (*Populus deltoides*)	23' 8"	141' 0"	120'	439.25	Yazoo-Miss. Delta Levee Board	Yazoo-Miss. Delta Levee Board	Tunica
Swamp (*Populus heterophylla*)	12' 6"	49' 5"	93'	256.58	D. Linden	U.S. Fish & Wildlife	Washington
CRAPEMYRTLE							
Crapemyrtle (*Lagerstroemia indica*)	7' 1"	48' 0"	40'	137.00	S. Kiewit	Curtis & Patricia Shows	Jones
CYPRESS							
Arizona (*Cupressus arizonica*)	3' 6"	31' 0"	19'	68.75	H. P. Bryan	Alice Marshall	Carroll
CYRILLA							
Swamp (*Cyrilla racemiflora*) ♣[1]	3' 9"	38' 0"	55'	109.50	G. Diamond	U.S. Forest Service	Harrison
DEVILS-WALKINGSTICK							
Devils Walkingstick (*Aralia spinosa*)	2' 9"	13' 0"	52'	88.20	J. Hiller	Springfield Plantation	Jefferson
DEVILWOOD							
Devilwood (*Osmanthus americanus*)	0' 4"	15' 0"	34'	41.55	C. Hunt / B. E. Brown	U.S. Forest Service	Stone
DOGWOOD							
Alternate-Leaf (*Cornus alternifolia*)	1' 4"	30' 6"	22'	46.00	J. Herring / E. Brown	MS Dept. WF & Parks	Madison
Flowering (*Cornus florida*)	4' 11"	41' 0"	37'	106.25	C. M. Terry	C. M. Terry	Panola
Roughleaf (*Cornus drummondii*) ♣	2' 7"	13' 0"	30'	64.30	D. Linden / L. Dorris	U.S. Fish & Wildlife	Washington
Swamp (*Cornus stricta*)	1' 0"	16' 0"	21'	37.00	J. Herring / B. E. Brown	MS Dept. WF & Parks	Madison
ELM							
American (*Ulmus americana*)	20' 0"	92' 0"	122'	385.00	C. W. Brasfield	Warren County Hunting & Fishing Club	Claiborne
Cedar (*Ulmus crassifolia*) ♣	10' 9"	49' 0"	102'	243.25	M. Hawkins	Louis Wise	Humphreys
Siberian (*Ulmus pumila*)	4' 9"	35' 0"	46'	111.75	H. P. Bryan	Irene Billups	Carroll
Slippery (*Ulmus rubra*)	11' 9"	92' 0"	81'	245.00	J. Ferguson	U.S. Forest Service	Winston
Winged (*Ulmus alata*)	12' 11"	84' 11"	105'	281.23	B.E. Brown / M. Connerly	William C. Walker	Jasper
FRINGETREE							
Fringetree (*Chionanthus virginicus*)	3' 9"	31' 0"	24'	76.75	H. Smith	Robert Walter	Jones
HACKBERRY							
Common (*Celtis occidentalis*)	14' 10"	87' 0"	92'	291.75	J. Ferguson	Charles Harville	Grenada
Georgia (*Celtis tenuifolia*)	9' 4"	26' 0"	32'	150.50	P. Barbour	Harry Rowland	Carroll
HAWTHORN							
Downy (*Crataegus millis*)	1' 8"	24' 0"	20'	46.00	J. Herring / Watts / Flynt	MS Dept. WF & Parks	Hinds
Green (*Crataegus viridis*)	2' 5"	28' 6"	33'	69.10	P. Barbour	Bob & Cindy Provine	Leflore
Littlehip (*Crataegus spatulata*)	1' 11"	23' 6"	15'	43.88	J. Herring / Price / Flynt	MS Dept. WF & Parks	Lowndes
Parsley (*Crataegus marshallii*) ♣	4' 0"	34' 0"	30'	86.80	B. E. Brown / J. Wallace	City of Collins	Covington
Riverflat (Mayhaw) ♣ (*Crataegus opaca*)	3' 9"	36' 0"	29'	83.00	H. Smith	W. W. Bonner	Jones
Washington (*Crataegus phaenopyrum*)	1' 3"	6' 0"	10'	26.50	B. Yarbrough / K. Stewart	City of Tupelo	Lee
HEMLOCK							
Eastern (*Tsuga canadensis*)	5' 2"	31' 8"	66'	136.00	C. M. Terry / J. Rhodes / A. Taylor	Mrs. R. D. Boult	Panola
HERCULES-CLUB							
Hercules-club (*Zanthoxylum clava-herculis*)	4' 5"	29' 3"	68'	150.40	B. Brown / M. Walters	Spithead, Inc.	Jefferson

[1] ♣ NATIONAL CHAMPION   NOTE: MS Dept. of W.F. & Parks is an abbreviation of Mississippi Department of Wildlife, Fisheries & Parks.

Champion Trees of Mississippi

Tree Species	Circ.	Crown	Height	Points	Nominator(s)	Owner	County
HICKORY							
Bitternut (Carya cordiformis)	8' 6"	77' 6"	116'	237.38	B. Brown / C. Welborn	Robert Y. Wood, Jr.	Adams
Carolina (Southern shagbark) (Carya ovata var. australis)	4' 6"	50' 0"	68'	134.50	G. Green / B. E. Brown	Miss. Dept. of Wildlife, Fisheries and Parks	Jasper
Mockernut (Carya tomentosa)[1] ✿	11' 8"	70' 0"	156'	313.50	D. K. Lee	Mrs. R. C. Bryan	Humphreys
Pignut (Carya glabra)	8' 11"	64' 4"	125'	238.00	C. Terry/Rhodes/Taylor	Dr. Lance Whaley	Panola
Red (Carya glabra var. odorata)	11' 2"	82' 0"	125'	279.30	B. Brown / J. Locke	Henry Davis	Wilkinson
Sand (Carya pallida)	5' 3"	35' 0"	71'	142.75	H. Smith	Herman Smith	Jones
Shagbark (Carya ovata)	8' 3"	56' 0"	104'	216.75	B. E. Brown and Billy Turner	Pearl River Valley Water Supply Dist.	Pearl River
Shellbark (Carya iaciniosa l.)	10' 9"	51' 0"	78'	219.75	J. Herring / P. Windham	USFS / Bienville Forest	Jasper
Water (Carya aquatica)	11' 1"	75' 0"	122'	273.80	Linden/Dorris/B.E. Brown	U.S. Fish & Wildlife	Washington
HOLLY							
American (Ilex opaca)	5' 7"	33' 6"	82'	157.40	J. Herring / C. Hunt	MS Dept. of W.F. & Parks	George
Yaupon (Ilex vomitoria)	1' 5"	10' 0"	27'	42.50	Mac Alford	Amite County Schools	Amite
HONEYLOCUST							
Honey locust (Gleditsia triacanthos)	11' 5"	76' 8"	113'	269.30	A. Duff / R. Walker	Pete Nosser, Jr.	Warren
Water locust (Gleditsia aquatica)	5' 9"	40' 0"	79'	158.00	D. Linden	U.S. Fish & Wildlife	Washington
HOPHORNBEAN							
Eastern (Ostrya virginiana)	4' 2"	51' 6"	64'	126.90	J. Herring / B.E. Brown	MS Dept. WF & Parks	Wilkinson
HORNBEAM							
American (Carpinus caroliniana)	4' 4"	44' 0"	70'	133.00	P. Hardy	Mrs. Leo Mayerhoff	Warren
INCENSE-CEDAR							
Incense-cedar (Libocedrus decurrens)	11' 7"	30' 0"	100'	246.50	S. Lowery / G. Butler	R. Stark	Pontotoc
LAUREL							
Mountain laurel (Kalmia latipolia)	0' 10"	3' 0"	26'	36.75	Mac Alford	John James Audubon Foundation	Amite
LAURELCHERRY							
Carolina (Prunus caroliniana)	6' 0"	29' 4"	60'	139.00	B. Brown	Jefferson Street United Methodist Church	Adams
LOBLOLLY BAY							
Loblolly Bay (Gordonia lasianthus)	4' 11"	37' 11"	104'	172.50	D. Wyrick	U.S. Forest Service Black Creek Dist.	Perry
LOCUST							
Black (Robinia pseudoacacia)	7' 0"	40' 4"	76'	170.10	H. P. Bryan	Bill Lord	Carroll
MAGNOLIA							
Bigleaf (Magnolia macrophylla)	4' 8"	40' 6"	84'	150.13	J. Herring / B.E. Brown	John Palmer	Hinds
Cucumbertree ♣	6' 7"	41' 0"	103'	192.25	J. Harris	Mr. & Mrs. J. Harris	Yazoo
Cucumbertree ♣ (Magnolia acuminata)	6' 7"	44' 0"	110'	201.00	B. E. Brown / J. Herring / J. Stringer	Weyerhaeuser Lumber Co.	Marion
Pyramid (Magnolia pyramidata)	5' 5"	15' 0"	48'	116.25	M. Daughdrill/Dr. S. Russo	Eugene Owen	Wilkinson
Southern ✿ (Magnolia grandiflora)	22' 4"	89' 6"	98'	388.38	J. Yelverton	Jones County Board of Education	Jones
Sweetbay (Magnolia virginiana)	7' 11"	35' 4"	104'	207.83	T. Gamble	Newton County Schools	Newton
Umbrella (Magnolia tripetala) ♣	1' 6"	24' 6"	41'	65.13	J. Herring / B.E. Brown	John Palmer	Hinds
Umbrella (Magnolia tripetala) ♣	1' 9"	24' 0"	36'	63.00	D. Bryant / R. Poore	John Palmer	Hinds
MAPLE							
Florida (Acer barbatum)	11' 1"	66' 4"	92'	241.58	B.E. Brown/G. Brummett	Georgia Pacific Corp.	Wayne
Red (Acer rubrum)	18' 4"	77' 0"	106'	345.25	R. Thornton	Tombigbee River Valley Water District	Prentiss
Silver (Acer saccharinum)	10' 1"	78' 1"	107'	247.52	D. J. Nevels	Jackson Municipal School District	Hinds
Sugar (Acer saccharum)	10' 1"	72' 0"	87'	226.00	J. Ferguson	F. E. Henson, Jr.	Tallahatchie

[1] Mississippi's tallest Champion Tree.   ♣ State Co-Champion   ✿ NATIONAL CHAMPION

Champion Trees of Mississippi

Tree Species	Circ.	Crown	Height	Points	Nominator(s)	Owner	County
MIMOSA							
Mimosa [Silktree] (*Albizia julibrissin*)	9' 5"	77' 0"	51'	183.25	J. Yelverton	Jeff Yelverton	Jasper
MULBERRY							
Paper (*Broussonetia papyrifera*)	14' 2"	41' 6"	37'	217.38	Patti Henson	Kate Eidt	Hinds
Red (*Morus rubra*)	19' 5"	66' 0"	40'	289.50	J. Yelverton and Herman Smith	Martha Davis Welborn & Mary Jane Todd	Jones
White (*Morus alba*)	12' 11"	63' 0"	64'	234.75	T. E. Vowell, Jr.	Chicago Mill/Lumber	Washington
OAK							
Arkansas (*Quercus arkansana*)	12' 2"	106' 0"	95'	267.60	B. E. Brown / J. Wallace	City of Collins	Covington
Bluejack (*Quercus incana*)	4' 8"	40' 6"	40'	106.12	B. E. Brown/J.C. Simmons	Clarko State Park	Clarke
Bluff (*Quercus durandii* var. *austrina*)	2' 5"	31' 0"	22'	58.75	J. Herring / B.E. Brown	MS Dept. of WF & Parks	Madison
Bur (*Quercus macrocarpa*)	11' 10"	119' 6"	102'	273.25	J. Herring/Price/Flynt	MS Dept. WF & Parks	Lowndes
Cherrybark (*Quercus falcata* var. *pagodifolia*)	24' 3"	133' 0"	137'	461.88	H. Davis	G. F. Ferris	Warren
Chestnut (*Quercus prinus*)	10' 6"	62' 0"	60'	201.50	C. O. McGregor	V. E. Miles	Calhoun
Chinkapin (*Quercus muehlenbergii*)	15' 8"	97' 6"	95'	307.38	R. Walker / S. Dixon	Glen R. Triplett	Warren
Compton (*Quercus comptoniae*)	23' 9"	138' 0"	116'	435.50	C. H. Moore	Eddie Garst	Humphreys
Cow (*Quercus michauxii*)	21' 2"	93' 6"	92'	369.38	P. Hardy	Wallace Gay	Warren
Durand (*Quercus durandii*)	12' 3"	99' 0"	100'	271.25	J. Herring/Price/Flynt	MS Dept. WF & Parks	Hinds
Laurel (*Quercus laurifolia*)	19' 9"	108' 0"	131'	395.75	Pepper/Crowell/B. Brown	Ruby Kitchens	Clarke
Live (*Quercus virginiana*)	30' 4"	145' 0"	81'	481.25	B. McGregor	G. F. Watts	Pearl River
Northern Red (*Quercus rubra*)	7' 11"	77' 0"	130'	244.25	D. Hancock / B. Stevens / B. E. Brown	Rankin County Board of Education	Rankin
Nuttall (*Quercus nuttallii*)	21' 8"	96' 0"	110'	394.00	C. Hamberlin	L. B. Stein	Washington
Overcup (*Quercus lyrata*)	19' 9"	89' 3"	124'	383.31	J. Walker / M. Bailey	U.S. Forest Service	Sharkey
Pin (*Quercus palustris*)	14' 5"	98' 6"	110'	307.63	D. K. Lee	Bolivar County Schools	Bolivar
Post (*Quercus stellata*)	15' 2"	109' 0"	94'	303.25	R. Harwell / R. Hyde	Army Corps of Engineers	Lafayette
Sand post (*Quercus stellata* var. *margaretta*)	7' 5"	46' 0"	45'	145.50	B. E. Brown and J. C. Simmons	Clarko State Park	Clarke
Shingle (*Quercus imbricaria*)	2' 6"	27' 8"	34'	71.00	J. Herring / B.E. Brown	MS Dept. of WF & Parks	Madison
Shumard (*Quercus shumardii*) ⚘*[1]	17' 8"	112' 0"	144'	384.00	B. Brown	City of Natchez	Adams
Southern Red (*Quercus falcata*)	22' 9"	117' 0"	94'	396.25	M. Bruce / B. Anderson	Monroe Pointer	Panola
Turkey (*Quercus laevis*)	8' 7"	69' 0"	60'	173.90	R. Nell	Jerry Keel	George
Water (*Quercus nigra*)	22' 1"	108' 0"	114'	406.00	J. Williams / G. Williams / M. McDonald	Jack Williams	Newton
White (*Quercus alba*)	19' 3"	76' 0"	104'	354.00	R. Hanna	McGraw Estate	Yazoo
Willow (*Quercus phellos*)	26' 6"	132' 0"	73'	424.00	B. E. Brown	Louise Stewart	Noxubee
OSAGE-ORANGE							
Osage-Orange (*Maclura pomifera*)	17' 5"	71' 6"	79'	305.87	S. Lowery / S. Patterson	Dr. Forrest Tutor	Pontotoc
PALMETTO							
Cabbage (*Sabal palmetto*)	5' 3"	13' 9"	24'	91.00	S. Lyda	J. C. Mashburn	Wayne
PAULOWNIA							
Royal paulownia (*Paulowinia tomentosa*)	9' 11"	45' 0"	54'	184.25	A. Tapp	U.S. Army Corps of Engineers	Lafayette
PAWPAW							
Pawpaw (*Astrimina triloba*)	7' 7"	59' 8"	60'	159'50	E.L. Hatacher/J. Dunajick	C. A. Montague	Newton
PEAR							
Common (*Pyrus communis*)	7' 3"	17' 3"	42'	133.31	R. Taylor	U.S. Forest Service	Amite
PECAN							
Sweet (*Carya illinoensis*)	21' 2"	115' 0"	132'	415.25	J. Herring and B. Quisenberry	Howard Pritchartt III	Adams

[1] ⚘* NATIONAL CO-CHAMPION   MS Dept. of W.F. & Parks is an abbreviation of Mississippi Department of Wildlife, Fisheries & Parks.

Champion Trees of Mississippi

Tree Species	Circ.	Crown	Height	Points	Nominator(s)	Owner	County
PINE							
Eastern White (*Pinus strobus*)	5' 8"	38' 9"	55'	132.73	J. Rhodes	C. M. Terry	Panola
Loblolly (*Pinus taeda*)	15' 11"	83' 6"	124'	335.87	J. Morgan / R. Watson	Les Lindley and Dr. W. J. Anderson III	Noxubee
Longleaf ꙮ*	7' 7"	38' 0"	134'	234.50	F. Davis	Georgia Pacific Corp.	Wilkinson
Longleaf ꙮ*	9' 7"	50' 0"	110'	237.50	J. Bush & B. E. Brown	Nelda Mitchell	Covington
Longleaf ꙮ* (*Pinus palustris*)	9' 7"	43' 6"	105'	231.00	J. Simmons / R. Scoggin / B. E. Brown	Bay Springs Garden Club	Jasper
Shortleaf (*Pinus echinata*) ꙮ	11' 7"	68' 0"	88'	244.00	G. Coffey	Mary Harris	Union
Slash (*Pinus elliottii*)	9' 7"	52' 0"	103'	231.00	J. Jarrell / B. Rowell	Lillian Powe	Wayne
Spruce[1] (*Pinus glabra*)	11' 11"	60' 6"	154'	302.00	J. Herring / B. E. Brown / A. Bradshaw	U.S. Forest Service	Scott
Virginia (*Pinus virginiana*)	3' 8"	31' 0"	56'	107.75	J. Windham	U.S. Forest Service	Marshall
PLUM							
Mexican (*Prunus mexicana*)	2' 4"	36' 0"	39'	76.00	J. Herring & B. E. Brown	MS Dept. W.F. & Parks	Wilkinson
POPLAR							
Silverleaf [White] (*Populus alba*)	6' 10"	45' 0"	59'	152.25	H. P. Bryan	R. C. Price	Carroll
PRIVET							
California (*Ligustrum ovalifolium*)	4' 2"	30' 0"	28'	85.50	H. P. Bryan	Mrs. G. DeLoach	Carroll
REDBUD							
Eastern (*Cercis canadensis*)	6' 0"	31' 0"	39'	118.75	W. Tally / J. Gardinski	G. Lewis / E. Lewis	Jasper
REDCEDAR							
Eastern (*Juniperus virginiana*)	17' 0"	49' 0"	48'	265.30	W. Passmore	Steve Lott	Jackson
SASSAFRAS							
Sassafras (*Sassafras albidum*)	17' 4"	65' 6"	74'	298.40	J. Cassell	Waterloo Farms	Claiborne
SERVICEBERRY							
Downy serviceberry (shadbush) (*Amelanchier canadensis*)	1' 5"	22' 8"	34'	57.00	J. Herring / B. E. Brown	MS Dept. of WF & Parks	Madison
SILVERBELL							
Two-Wing silverbell (*Halesia diptera*)	4' 3"	16' 0"	39'	94.00	M. Alford	Lawrence Wren	Amite
SNOWBELL							
Bigleaf snowbell (*Styrax grandifolius*)	1' 1"	13' 10"	34'	50.65	J. Herring / B. E. Brown	Miss. Dept. of Wildlife, Fisheries & Parks	Wilkinson
SOURWOOD							
Sourwood (*Oxydendron arboreum*)	6' 10"	45' 0"	123'	216.50	J. Hiller / D. Kelly	Springfield Plantation	Jefferson
SPARKLEBERRY TREE							
Sparkleberry ♣	2' 9"	30' 0"	47'	87.50	G. Lott / W. McCardle	U.S. Forest Service	Harrison
Sparkleberry ♣ (*Vaccinium arboreum*)	3' 2"	29' 0"	40'	85.25	B. Brown / E. Alford	Danny Stringer	Marion
SPRUCE							
Blue Spruce (*Picea pungens*)	3' 4"	17' 0"	20'	64.20	J. Rhodes & R. Olson	Mr./Mrs. Maurice O'Keefe	Panola
SUGARBERRY							
Sugarberry (*Celtis laevigata*)	15' 4"	66' 6"	117'	317.60	A. Yelverton / S. Shaw	Jim Hay	Issaquena
SUMAC							
Shining (*Rhus copallina*)	3' 2"	32' 0"	29'	75.00	R. Harwell / G.W. Poyner	William L. Killough	Pontotoc
Southern (*Rhus glabra*)	1' 3"	13' 6"	29'	47.40	D. Linden / L. Dorris	U.S. Fish & Wildlife	Washington
SWAMP PRIVET							
Swamp privet (*Forestiera acuminata*)	8' 4"	48' 6"	41'	153.12	D. Linden / L. Dorris	U.S. Fish & Wildlife	Washington

[1] Second tallest champion tree in the state.   ꙮ NATIONAL CHAMPION   ꙮ* NATIONAL CO-CHAMPION   ♣ State Co-Champion

The Ultimate Reference on the State

Champion Trees of Mississippi

Tree Species	Circ.	Crown	Height	Points	Nominator(s)	Owner	County
SWEETGUM							
Sweetgum *(Liquidambar styraciflua)*	18' 9"	57' 0"	140'	379.25	C. Moore / W. Henley	U.S. Forest Service	Sharkey
SWEETLEAF							
Sweetleaf *(Symplocos tinctoria)*	2' 10"	27' 6"	61'	101.90	J. Herring / C. Hunt	MS Dept. of W.F. & Parks	George
SYCAMORE							
American *(Platanus occidentalis)*	19' 2"	87' 0"	137'	388.75	B. Hillman	Coahoma Co. Schools	Coahoma
TALLOWTREE							
Chinese *(Sapium sebiferum)*	8' 2"	50' 0"	66'	176.50	P. Connerly / R. Reynolds / M. Draughdrill	Thomas C. Easley	Amite
TUPELO							
Black *(Nyssa sylvatica* var. *silvatica)*	12' 6"	77' 0"	140'	309.25	B. Brown / E. Alford	Emma Lee Brumfield	Amite
Swamp *(Nyssa sylvatica* var. *biflora)*	16' 1"	67' 6"	96'	305.87	J. Jarrell / D. Hinton / J. Gardinski	Lillian Powe	Wayne
Water *(Nyssa aquatica)*	23' 2"	59' 0"	90'	382.75	S. Burgess	T. M. Simmons	Humphreys
VIBURNUM							
Rusty *(Viburnum raffidulum)*	1' 8"	18' 0"	37'	61.00	J. Herring / B.E. Brown	MS Dept. of W.F. & Parks	Hinds
WATER-ELM							
Water-elm *(Planera aquatica)*	7' 9"	49' 0"	45'	149.75	D. Linden / L. Dorris	U.S. Fish & Wildlife	Washington
WATER LOCUST							
Water Locust *(Gleditsia aquatica)*	5' 9"	40' 0"	79'	158.00	D. Linden	U.S. fsih & Wildlife	Washington
WALNUT							
Black *(Juglans nigra)*	17' 2"	88' 0"	136'	364.00	T. Skelton	W. T. Hendricks	DeSoto
White [Butternut] *(Juglans cinerea)*	3' 6"	30' 0"	65'	114.50	P. Barbour	Glenn Miller	Carroll
WAX MYRTLE							
Southern *(Murica cerifera)*	1' 8"	18' 0"	25'	48.50	M. Alford	M. D. Copeland Estate	Amite
WILLOW							
Black *(Salix nigra)*	11' 2"	52' 0"	152'	299.00	B. Brown / M. Walters	Spithead, Inc.	Jefferson
Sandbar *(Salix exigua)*	13' 0"	7' 0"	39'	53.75	D. Linden	U.S. Fish & Wildlife	Washington
Weeping *(Salix babylonica)*	8' 6"	50' 0"	52'	166.50	H. P. Bryan	J. Morgan	Carroll
WINTERBERRY							
Common *(Ilex verticillata)*	0' 10"	13' 0"	15'	28.25	M. Alford	M. D. Copeland Estate	Amite
Mountain *(Ilex montana)*	1' 0"	9' 9"	41'	55.43	J. herring / B. E. Brown	MS Dept. of W.F. & Parks	Amite
WITCH HAZEL							
Witch Hazel *(Hamamelis virginiana)*	0' 11"	17' 3"	36'	50.81	J. Herring / B. E. Brown	MS Dept. of W.F. & Parks	Amite
YELLOW POPLAR							
Yellow poplar *(Liriodendron tulipifera)*	17' 6"	87' 0"	139'	371.95	R. Havard / W. Jenkins	Dorothy Jackson	Amite

Mississippi's **LARGEST** tree is a Baldcypress located 8 miles north of Belzoni in Humphreys County on property owned by Mark Simmons. It's 46 feet, 4 inches in circumference, about 15 feet in diameter, 70 feet in height and is believed to be over 2,000 years old! This state champion is located within 300 feet of the former champion bald cypress which is only slightly smaller. The smaller tree, the 2nd largest tree in the state, would produce enough lumber to build 6 ordinary houses. Mississippi's **TALLEST** champion tree, a Mockernut Hickory (156 feet tall), is also located in Humphreys County.

Mississippi is one of only two states in the nation where the state flower is the blossom of the state tree. The official state tree/flower in Mississippi is the Magnolia/blossom. The official state tree/flower in Virginia is the Dogwood/blossom.

Here's an interesting story about a Mississippi large tree, although it's not a champion tree. The largest tree in the world ever transplanted, a live oak weighing almost 300 tons, was picked up and moved 100 yards during the weekend of April 13-14, 1996, in Biloxi, Mississippi. This giant tree — 593,049 pounds, 50 feet tall, a trunk 52 inches in diameter and branch circumference 95 feet wide — was actually the largest of 3 giant live oaks that Grand Casino contracted to be moved in order to preserve them. This world-record transplant was performed by Environmental Design, a Houston, Texas firm. The cost was $35,000 for the actual uprooting and moving, with the total contract for the project estimated at $60,000.

Champion Trees of Mississippi

THESE SPECIES DO NOT HAVE A MISSISSIPPI CHAMPION LISTED. THOSE WITH AN ASTERISK (*) DO NOT HAVE A NATIONAL CHAMPION.

ALTHEA
Althea (Rose-of-Sharon)*
  (Hibiscus syriacus)

APPLE
Sweet crabapple (Malus coronaria)

ANISE
Florida Anise (Illicium floridanum)

ACACIA
Catclaw Acacia (Acacia greggii)
Sweet Acacia (Acacia farnesiana)

ALDER
Hazel alder (Alnus orientalis)

ARBORVITAE
Oriental (Thuju orientalis)

ASH
Blue ash (Fraxinus guadrangulata)
Carolina ash (F. caroliniana)
Pumpkin ash (F. profunda)

BACCHARIS
Eastern baccharis
  (baccharis halimifolia)

BALDCYPRESS
Pond cypress (Taxodium
  distichum var. nuntans)

BASSWOOD
Carolina (Tilia caroliniana)

BAY
Redbay (Persea borbonia)
Swampbay
  (P. borbonia var. pubescens)

BAYBERRY
Evergreen bayberry*
  (Myrica heterophylla)
Oderless bayberry* (M. inodora)
Southern bayberry (M. cerifera)

BITTER-ORANGE
Tri-foliate orange
  (Poncirus trifoliata)

BUCKEYE
Painted (A. sylvatica)

BUCKWHEAT TREE
Buckwheat tree
  (Cliftonia monophylla)

BURNINGBUSH
Eastern burningbush
  (Euonymus atropurpureus)

CHERRY
Chokecherry (Prunus virginiana)
Sour cherry (P. cerasus)

CHINESE PARASOL TREE
Chinese parasoltree
  (Firmiana simplex)

CHINKAPIN
Floria chinkapin
  (Castanea ahifolia)

CORALBEAN
Southeastern coralbean
  (Erythrina herbacea)

CORKWOOD
Corkwood (Leitneria floridana)

CYRILLA
Littleleaf cyrilla*
  (Cyrilla racemiflora
    var. parvifolia)

DAHOON
Dahoon (Ilex cassine)
Myrtle dahoon* (I. myrtifolia)

DOGWOOD
Smooth dogwood
  (Cornus glabrata)

ELDER
American elder
  (Sambucus canadensis)
Florida
  (S. canadensis var. laciniata)
Silky elder
  (S. canadensis var. laciniata)
Velvet elder* (S. velutina)

ELM
September elm (Ulmus serotina)

FIG
Common fig (Ficus carica)

FORESTIERA
Florida (Forestiera segregata)

HAWTHORN
Barberry hawthorn
  (Crataegus berberifolia)
Blueberry hawthorn
  (C. brachyacantha)
Cockspur hawthorn
  (C. crus-gulli)
Harbison hawthorn*
  (C. harbisonii)
May hawthorn (C. aestivalis)
One flower hawthorn
  (C. uniflora)
Threeflower hawthorn
  (C. trifolia)
Yellow hawthorn (C. flava)

HICKORY
Nutmeg hickory
  (C. myristiciformis)

HOPTREE
Common hoptree
  (Ptelea trifoliata)

HOLLY
Carolina holly (Ilex ambigua)
Common winterberry
  (I. verticillata)
Georgia holly* (I. longipes)
Large gallberry (I. coriacea)
Possumhaw (I. decidua)
Sarvis holly (I. Amelanchier)

INDIAN-FIG
Indian fig*
  (Opuntia ficus-indica)

INDIAN-SPICE
Indian-spice
  (Vitex agnos-castus)

JUJUBE
Common jujube
  (Ziziphus jujuba)

JUNIPER
Common juniper
  (Juniperus communis)

LOCUST
Clammy locust
  (Robinia viscosa)

MANGROVE
Black mangrove
  (Avicennia germinans)

MAPLE
Chalk maple (Acer leucoderme)

MULBERRY
Black mulberry (Morus nigra)
Paper mulberry
  (Broussonetia papyrifera)

OAK
Black (Quercus velutina)
Blackjack (Q. marilandiea)
Chapman (Q. chapmanii)
Delta post oak
  (Q. stellata var. paludosa)
Myrtle oak (Q. myrtifolia)
Sand live oak
  (Q. virginiana var. geminata)
Scarlet (Q. coccinea)
Swamp chestnut oak
  (Q. michauxii)

PALMETTO
Louisiana palmetto (Sabal minor)
Saw palmetto (Serenoa repens)

PAWPAW
Bigflower pawpaw
  (Asimina obvata)
Smallflower (A. parviflora)

PEACH
Common peach (Prunus persica)

PINE
Pond pine (Pinus sorotina)
Sand pine (P. clausa)

PLUM
American plum
  (Prunus americana)
Chickasaw plum (P. angustifolia)
Flatwoods plum (P. umbellata)
Mazzard plum (P. avium)
Wildgoose plum (P. munsoiana)

POPLAR
Black poplar (Populas nigra)
Carolina poplar (P. canadensis)

PRIVET
Chinese privet
  (Ligustrum sinese)
Japanese privet (L. japonica)

RED-CEDAR
Southern red-cedar
  (Juniperus silicicola)

SILVERBELL
Carolina silverbell
  (Halesia caroliniana)
Little silverbell*
  (H. parviflora)

SMOKETREE
American smoketree
  (Cotinus obovatus)

SNOWBELL
American snowbell
  (Styrax americanus)

STEWARTI
Virginia stewarti
  (Stewartia malacodendron)

SUMAC
Poison sumac
  (Toxicodendron vernix)
Smooth sumac
  (Rhus copallina var.
    leucantha)

VIBURNUM
Blackhaw
  (Viburnum prunifolium)
Possumhaw (V. nudum)
Walter (V. obovatum)

WILLOW
Basket willow*
  (Salix viminalis)
Coastal plain willow
  (S. caroliniana)
Silky willow (S. sericea)

YELLOWWOOD
Yellowwood
  (Cladrastis kentukea)

The Ultimate Reference on the State

Wildflowers of Mississippi

Agave — *Agave virginica*
Ageratum — *Conoclinium coelestinum*
Allegheny Spurge — *Pachysandra procumbens*
Alumroot — *Heuchera americana*
American Blue Hearts — *Buchnera americana*
Anglepod — *Cynanchum laeve*
Anise Tree — *Illicium floridanum*
Antelope-Horn — *Asclepias viridis*
Arrow Arum — *Peltandra sagittifolia*
Arrowhead — *Sagittaria latifolia*
Ashy Sunflower — *Helianthus mollis*
Aster — *Aster linariifolius*
Aster — *Aster paludosus*
Aster — *Aster sericocarpoides*
Aster — *Aster shortii*
Atamasco Lily — *Zephyranthes atamasco*
Avens — *Geum canadense*
Bachelor's Button — *Centaurea cyanus*
Balduina — *Balduina uniflora*
Balloon Vine — *Cardiospermum habicababum*
Baneberry — *Actaea pachypoda*
Bastard Toadflax — *Comandra umbellata*
Bay Magnolia (tree) — *Magnolia virginiana*
Beach Morning Glory — *Ipomoea stolonifera*
Beardtongue — *Laxiflorus*
Beardtongue — *Penstemon laevigatus*
Bearsfoot — *Polymnia uvedalia*
Beech-Drops — *Epifagus virginiana*
Beef-Steak Plant — *Perilla frutescens*
Beggar's Ticks — *Desmodium marilandicum*
Beggar's Ticks — *Desmodium nudiflorum*
Beggar's Ticks — *Desmodium paniculatum*
Beggar Ticks — *Bidens aristosa*
Bellwort — *Uvularia grandiflora*
Bent Trillium — *Trillium flexipes*
Bitter Cress (Spring Cress) — *Cardamine bulbosa*
Bitterweed — *Helenium amarum*
Black Eyed Susan — *Rudbeckia hirta*
Black Locust (tree) — *Robinia pseudoacacia*
Black Nightshade — *Solanum americanum*
Black Snakeroot — *Zigadenus densus*
Black Titi — *Cliftonia monophylla*
Blackberry Lily — *Belamanda chinensis*
Bladder Pod — *Sesbania vesicaria*
Bladdernut — *Staphylea trifolia*
Bladderwort — *Utricularia inflata*
Bladderwort — *Utricularia juncea*
Blanket Flower — *Gaillardia pulchella*
Blazing Star — *Liatris aspera*
Blazing Star — *Liatris squarrosa*
Bloodroot — *Sanquinaria canadensis*
Blue-Eyed Grass — *Sisyrinchium augustifolium*
Blue Bells — *Mertensia virginica*
Blue Curis — *Trichostema dichotomum*
Blue Flag — *Iris virginica*
Blue Lobelia — *Lobelia puberula*
Blue Phlox — *Phlox divaricata*
Blue Sage — *Salvia azurea*
Blue Star — *Amsonia tabernaemontana*
Bluestem Goldenrod — *Solidago caesia*
Boltonia — *Boltonia diffusa*
Boneset — *Eupatorium hyssopifolium*
Boneset — *Eupatorium perfoliatum*
Boneset — *Eupatorium rotundifolium*
Boneset — *Eupatorium serotinum*
Bottle Gentian — *Gentiana saponaria*
Bouncing Bet — *Saponaria officinalis*
Brintonia — *Brintonia discoidea*
Bristly Locust — *Robinia hispida*
Buffalo Bur — *Solanum rostratum*
Bull Bay (tree) — *Magnolia grandiflora*
Bull Nettle — *Cnidoscolus stimulosus*
Bunchflower — *Melanthium virginicum*
Burdock — *Arctium minus*
Bush Lespedeza — *Lespedeza capitata*
Butterfly Pea — *Centrosema virginianum*
Butterfly Pea — *Clitoria mariana*
Butterfly Weed — *Asclepias tuberosa*
Butterweed — *Senecio glabellus*
Butterwort — *Pinquicula caerulea*
Butterwort — *Pinquicula lutea*
Button Bush — *Cephalanthus occidentalis*
Calliopsis — *Coreopsis tinctoria*
Camass — *Zigadenus glaberrimus*
Cancer Weed — *Salvia lyrata*
Candy Root — *Polygala cruciata*
Candy Root — *Polygala incarnata*
Candy Root — *Polygala lutea*
Candy Root — *Polygala nana*
Cardinal Flower — *Lobelia cardinalis*
Carolina Cherry — *Prunus caroliniana*
Catalpa — *Catalpa bignonioides*
Celestrial Lily — *Nemastylis geminiflora*
Chaff-Flower — *Alternanthera philoxeroides*
Chickasaw Plum — *Prunus augustifolia*
Cinquefoil — *Potentilla simplex*
Climbing Dogbane — *Trachelospermum difforme*
Climbing Hempweed — *Mikania scandens*
Colic Root — *Aletris farinosa*
Columbine — *Aquilegia canadensis*
Common Chicory — *Cichorium intybus*
Common Morning Glory — *Ipomoea purpurea*
Common Sunflower — *Helianthus annuus*
Compass Plant — *Silphium laciniatum*
Coneflower — *Dracopis amplexicaulis*
Coneflower — *Rudbeckia triloba*
Copper Iris — *Iris fulva*
Coral Bean — *Erythrina herbacea*
Coral Honeysuckle — *Lonicera sempervirens*
Coreopsis — *Coreopsis auriculata*
Coreopsis — *Coreopsis lanceolata* (state wildflower)
Coreopsis — *Coreopsis major*
Coreopsis — *Coreopsis nudata*
Coreopsis — *Coreopsis tripteris*
Corn Speedwell — *Veronica arvensis*
Cottonweed — *Froelichia floridana*
Crane-Fly Orchid — *Tipularia discolor*
Crested Iris — *Iris cristata*
Crimson Clover — *Trifolium incarnatum*
Cross Vine — *Bignonia capreolata*
Crown-Beard — *Verbesina alternifolia*
Crown Vetch — *Coronilla varia*
Cucumber Tree — *Magnolia acuminata*
Culver's Root — *Veronicastrum virginicum*

Wildflowers of Mississippi

Cup Plant — *Silphium perfoliatum*
Cypress Vine — *Ipomoea quamoclit*
Daisy Fleabane — *Erigeron strigosus*
Day Flower — *Commelina communis*
Day Lily — *Hemerocallis fulva*
Deer's Tongue — *Carphephorus odoratissmus*
Devil's Walking Stick — *Aralia spinosa*
Dicliptera — *Dicliptera brachiata*
Dittany — *Cunila origanoides*
Dodder — *Cuscuta gronovii*
Dog Fennel — *Anthemis cotula*
Dog Fennel — *Eupatorium capillifolium*
Dogbane — *Apocynum cannabinum*
Dotted Monarda — *Monarda punctata*
Dutchman's Breeches — *Dicentra cucullaria*
Dutchman's Pipe — *Aristolochia tomentosa*
Dwarf Dandelion — *Krigia dandelion*
Dwarf Iris — *Iris verna*
Ear-Grass — *Yucca flaccida*
Early Buttercup — *Ranunculus fascicularis*
Early Saxifrag — *Saxifraga virginiensis*
Elephant's Foot — *Elephantopus carolinianus*
Elm-Leaf Goldenrod — *Solidago ulmifolia*
Eryngo — *Eryngium integrifolium*
Evening Primrose — *Oenothera speciosa*
Fairy Wand — *Chamaelirium luteum*
False Asphodel — *Tofieldia racemosa*
False Boneset — *Kuhnia eupatorioides*
False Dandelion — *Pyrrhopappus carolinianus*
False Dragonhead — *Physostegia virginiana*
False Indigo — *Amorpha fruticosa*
False Liatris — *Carphephorus pseudoliatris*
False Rue Anemone — *Isopyrum biternatum*
False Solomon's Seal — *Smilacina racemosa*
Featherbells — *Stenanthium gramineum*
Fetter-Bush — *Lyonia lucida*
Fiddler's Trumpet — *Sarracenia leucophylla*
Field Bindweed — *Convolvulus arvensis*
Fire Pink — *Silene virginica*
Flax — *Linum medium*
Flowering Dogwood (tree) — *Cornus florida*
Flowering Spurge — *Euphorbia corollata*
Fly Poison — *Amianthium muscaetoxicum*
Foam Flower — *Tiarella cordifolia*
Foxglove — *Aureolaria pectinata*
Fringed Loosestrife — *Lysimachia lanceolata*
Gay Feather — *Liatris elegans*
Gerardia — *Agalinis purpurea*
Gerardia — *Agalinis tenuifolia*
Giant Chickweed — *Stellaria pubera*
Giant Goldenrod — *Solidago gigantea*
Ginseng — *Panax quinquefolius*
Glasswort — *Salicornia virginica*
Goat's Beard — *Aruncus dioicus*
Goat's Rue — *Tephrosia virginiana*
Gold-Crest — *Lophiola americana*
Golden Aster — *Heterotheca subaxillaris*
Golden Asters — *Chrysopsis camporum*
Golden Asters — *Chrysopsis graminifolia*
Golden Asters — *Chrysopsis mariana*
Golden Club — *Orontium aquaticum*
Goldenrod — *Chrysoma pauciflosculosa*

Goldenrod — *Solidago odora*
Grass-Pink Orchid — *Calopogon pulchellus*
Gray-Head Coneflower — *Ratibida pinnata*
Green-Fly Orchid — *Epidendrum conopseum*
Green Adder's Mouth — *Malaxis unifolia*
Green Dragon — *Arisaema dracontium*
Ground Cherry — *Physalis virginiana*
Ground Ivy — *Glechoma hederacea*
Groundnut — *Apios americana*
Groundsel Tree — *Baccharis halimifolia*
Hairy Phacelia — *Phacelia dubia*
Haplopappus — *Haplopappus divaricatus*
Hardhack — *Spiraea tomentosa*
Harvest-Lice — *Agrimonia pubescens*
Hawkweed — *Hieracium gronovii*
Heal-All — *Prunella vulgaris*
Heart Leaf — *Hexastylis arifolia*
Hedge Bindweed — *Calystegia sepium*
Hedge Parsley — *Torilis arvensis*
Helianthus — *Helinthus Augustifolius*
Henbit — *Lamium amplexicaule*
Henbit — *Lamium purpureum*
Hog-Fennel — *Oxypolis filiformis*
Honey Suckle — *Lonicera japonica*
Honeycomb Head — *Balduina angustifolia*
Horse Balm — *Collinsonia canadensis*
Horse Gentian — *Triosteum angustifolium*
Horse Nettle — *Solanum carolinense*
Hydrolea — *Hydrolea ovata*
Hyptis — *Hyptis alata*
Indian Blanket — *Gaillardia pulchella*
Indian Cucumber Root — *Meleola virginiana*
Indian Hemp — *Apocynum androsaemifolium*
Indian Mallow — *Abutilon theophrasti*
Indian Paint Brush — *Castilleja coccinea*
Indian Pink — *Spigelia marilandica*
Indian Pipe — *Monotropa uniflora*
Indian Plantain — *Cacalia ovata*
Indian Strawberry — *Duchesnea indica*
Ironweed — *Veronia angustifolia*
Ironweed — *Veronia gigantea*
Jack-In-The-Pulpit — *Arisaema triphyllum*
Jacob's Ladder — *Polemonium reptans*
Japanese Honeysuckle — *Lonicera japonica*
Jimpson Weed — *Datura stramonium*
Joe-Pye Weed — *Eupatoriadelphus fistulosus*
June Berry — *Amelanchier arborea*
Kudzu — *Pueraria lobata*
Ladies'-Eardrops — *Brunnichia ovata*
Large-Flowered Vetch — *Vicia grandiflora*
Large Whorled Pogonia — *Isotria verticillata*
Leather Flower — *Clematis crispa*
Leather Flower — *Clematis glaucophylla*
Leatherwood — *Cyrilla racemiflora*
Lemon Mint — *Monarda citriodora*
Little Sweet Betsy — *Trillium cuneatum*
Liverleaf — *Hepatica americana*
Lizard's Tail — *Saururus cernuus*
Loblolly Bay — *Gordonia lasianthus*
Lousewort — *Pedicularis canadensis*
Lupine — *Lupinus villosus*
Man-Root — *Ipomoea pandurata*

Wildflowers of Mississippi

Marsh Fleabane — *Pluchea rosea*
Marsh Pink — *Sabatia stellaris*
Marshallia — *Marshallia tenuifolia*
Mayapple — *Podophyllum peltatum*
Meadow Beauty — *Rhexia alifanus*
Meadow Beauty — *Rhexia mariana*
Meadow Rue — *Thalictrum pubescens*
Melanthera — *Melanthera nivea*
Milkweed — *Asclepias lanceolata*
Milkweed — *Asclepias longifolia*
Mist-Flower — *Conoclinium coelestinum*
Morning Glory — *Ipomoea sagittata*
Morning Glory — *Ipomoea trichocarpa*
Morning Honeysuckle — *Gaura biennis*
Moth Mullein — *Verbascum blattaria*
Mountain Houstonia — *Hedyotis crassifolia*
Mountain Laurel — *Kalmia latifolia*
Mountain Mint — *Pycnanthemum albescens*
Mud Plantain — *Heteranthera reniformis*
Mullein — *Verbascum thapsus*
Multiflora Rose — *Rosa multiflora*
Musk Thistle — *Carduus nutans*
Nestronia — *Nestronia umbellula*
New England Aster — *Aster novae-angliae*
New Jersey Tea — *Ceanothus americanus*
Nodding Ladies' Tresses — *Spiranthes cernua*
Nuttail Indigo — *Baptisia nuttalliana*
Oak-Leaf Hydrangea — *Hydrangea quercifolia*
Obedient Plant — *Physostegia virginiana*
Old Man's Beard — *Chionanthus virginicus*
Orange Puccoon — *Lithospermum caroliniense*
Ox-Eye Daisy — *Chrysanthemum leucanthemum*
Pale Corydalis — *Corydalis flavula*
Parrot-Beaks — *Sarracenia psittacina*
Parsley Haw — *Crataegus marshallii*
Partridge Berry — *Mitchella repens*
Partridge Pea — *Chamaecrista fasciculata*
Passiflora — *Passiflora lutea*
Passion Flower — *Passiflora incarnata*
Pawpaw — *Asimina triloba*
Pencil Flower — *Stylosanthes biflora*
Pennywort — *Obolaria virginica*
Pennyworts — *Hydrocotyle bonariensis*
Phlox — *Phlox maculata*
Pickerelweed — *Pontederia cordata*
Pine Lily — *Lilium catesbaei*
Pineweed — *Hypericum gentianoides*
Pinkweed — *Polygonum pensylvanicum*
Pipewort — *Eriocaulon decangulare*
Pitcher Plant — *Sarracenia alata*
Poison Ivy — *Toxicodendron radicans*
Powdery Thalia — *Thalia dealbata*
Prairie Dock — *Silphium terebinthinaceum*
Prairie Goldenrod — *Solidago rigida*
Prairie Larkspur — *Delphinium carolinianum*
Prairie Mimosa — *Desmanthus illinoensis*
Prairie Phlox — *Phlox pilosa*
Prairie Pink — *Sabatia campestris*
Prickly Mallow — *Sida spinosa*
Prickly Pear (Cactus) — *Opuntia humifusa*
Primrose — *Oenothera speciosa*
Purple Daisy — *Aster patens*

Purple Prairie Clover — *Dalea purpurea*
Purple Trillium — *Trillium recurvatum*
Pussy-Toes — *Antennaria plantaginifolia*
Queen's Delight — *Stillingia sylvatica*
Queen Anne's Lace — *Daucus carota*
Rabbit-Foot Clover — *Trifolium arvense*
Ragged Orchid — *Platanthera lacera*
Ragwort — *Senecia*
Rattle Weed — *Astragalus canadensis*
Rattlebox — *Crotalaria spectabilis*
Rattlebox — *Ludwigia octovalvis*
Rattlesnake Master — *Eryngium yuccifolium*
Rattlesnake Root — *Prenanthes altissima*
Rayless Goldenrod — *Bigelowia nudata*
Red Clover — *Trifolium pratense*
Red Morning Glory — *Ipomoea coccinea*
Red Rattlebox — *Sesbania punicea*
Red Sage — *Salvia coccinea*
Redroot — *Lachnanthes caroliniana*
Richardia — *Richardia scabra*
Rose-Gentian — *Sabatia bartramii*
Rose Mallow — *Hibiscus moscheutos*
Rose Pogonia — *Pogonia ophioglossoides*
Rosin Weed — *Silphium integrifolium*
Rosin Weed — *Silphium trifoliatum*
Rough Buttonweed — *Diodia teres*
Saltwort — *Batis maritima*
Samson's Snakeroot — *Gentiana villosa*
Samson's Snakeroot — *Psoralea psoralioides*
Scarlet Hibiscus — *Hibiscus coccineus*
Sea Lavender — *Limonium carolinianum*
Sea Ox-Eye — *Borrichia frutescens*
Seashore Mallow — *Kosteletzkya virginica*
Seaside Goldenrod — *Solidago sempervirens*
Sebastian Bush — *Sebastiania fruticosa*
Seedbox — *Ludwigia alternifolia*
Sensitive Briar — *Schrankia microphylla*
Sesbania — *Sesbania macrocarpa*
Shooting Star — *Dodecatheon meadia*
Short Milkwort — *Polygala ramosa*
Sicklepod — *Cassia obtusifolia*
Silky Camellia — *Stewartia malachodendron*
Silverbell — *Halesia diptera*
Skullcap — *Scutellaria integrifolia*
Skullcap — *Scutellaria parvula*
Slender Bush Clover — *Lespedeza virginica*
Small Bellwort — *Uvularia perfoliata*
Smooth Foxglove — *Aureolaria flava*
Smooth Vetch — *Vicia villosa*
Sneeze Weed — *Helenium flexuosum*
Sneeze Weed — *Helenium vernale*
Snoutbean — *Rhynchosia tomentosa*
Snowbell — *Styrax grandifolia*
Solomon's Seal — *Polygonatum biflorum*
Sourwood — *Oxydendrum arboreum*
Southern Rein Orchid — *Platanthera flava*
Southern Twayblade — *Listera australis*
Spatter Dock — *Nuphar luteum*
Spearmint — *Mentha spicata*
Spider Flower — *Cleome spinosa*
Spider Lily — *Hymenocallis occidentalis*
Spiderworf — *Tradescantia ohiensis*

Wildflowers of Mississippi

Spiked Lobelia — *Lobelia spicata*
Spotted Touch-Me-Not — *Impatiens capensis*
Sprawling Eryngo — *Eryngium prostratum*
Spreading Pogonia — *Cleistes divaricata*
Spring Beauty — *Claytonia virginica*
Spring Coral Root — *Corallorhiza wisteriana*
Square Flower — *Paronychia erecta*
Squaw Huckleberry — *Vaccinium stamineum*
Squaw Root — *Conopholis americana*
St. John's Wort — *Hypericum brachyphyllum*
St. John's Wort — *Hypericum crux-andreae*
St. John's Wort — *Hypericum denticulatum*
St. John's Wort — *Hypericum galioides*
St. John's Wort — *Hypericum prolificum*
St. John's Wort — *Hypericum punctatum*
St. John's Wort — *Hypericum suffruticosum*
Standing Cypress — *Ipomopsis rubra*
Star Grass — *Aletris lutea*
Starry Champion — *Silene stellata*
Stokesia — *Stokesia laevis*
Stonecrop — *Sedum ternatum*
Strawberry Bush — *Euonymus americanus*
Summer Azalea — *Rhododendron serrulatum*
Sunbonnets — *Chaptalia tomentosa*
Sundew — *Drosera brevifolia*
Sundrops — *Oenothera biennis*
Sundrops — *Oenothera linifolia*
Sundrops — *Oenothera tetragona*
Sunflower — *Helianthus heterophyllus*
Sunflower — *Helianthus hirsutus*
Sunflower — *Helianthus strumosus*
Supple Jack — *Berchemia scandens*
Swamp Lily — *Crinum americanum*
Swamp Milkweed — *Asclepias incarnata*
Sweet Everlasting — *Gnaphalium obtusifolium*
Sweet Shrub — *Calycanthus floridus*
Sweetleaf — *Symplocos tinctoria*
Tall Bluebell — *Campanula americana*
Thistle — *Cirsium carolinianum*
Thread-Leaf Sundew — *Drosera tracyi*
Three Birds Orchid — *Triphora trianthophora*
Tie Vine — *Jacquemontia tamnifolia*
Toadflax — *Linaria canadensis*
Tooth-Cup — *Ammannia coccinea*
Toothwort — *Cardamine concatenata*
Toothwort — *Cardamine diphylla*
Trout Lily — *Erythronium albidum*
Trumpet Vine — *Campsis radicans*
Tulip Tree — *Liriodendron tulipifera*
Turk's Cap Lily — *Lilium superbum*
Turnsole — *Heliotropium indicum*
Turtlehead — *Chelone obliqua*
Twisted Trillium — *Trillium stamineum*
Umbrella Magnolia (tree) — *Magnolia tripetala*
Venus' Looking Glass — *Triodanis perfoliata*
Verbena — *Verbena rigida*
Vetch — *Vicia villosa*
Violet Wood Sorrel — *Oxalis violacea*
Violets — *Viola rostrata*
Violets — *Viola sagittata*
Virgin's Bower — *Clematis virginiana*
Virginia Willow — *Itea virginica*

Water Cress — *Nasturtium officinale*
Water Hemlock — *Cicuta maculata*
Water Horehound — *Lycopus americanus*
Water Hyacinth — *Eichornia crassipes*
Water Lily — *Nelumbo lutea*
Water Lily — *Nymphaea odorata*
Water Loosestrife — *Decodon verticillatus*
Water Shield — *Brasenia schreberi*
Water Spider Orchid — *Habenaria repens*
Water Willow — *Justicia americana*
Waxweed — *Cuphea viscosissima*
White-Flowered Vetch — *Vicia caroliniana*
White-Top Aster — *Aster tortifolius*
White Alder — *Clethra alnifolia*
White Crown-Beard — *Verbesina virginica*
White Heath Aster — *Aster pilosus*
White Sabatia — *Sabatia macrophylla*
White Wild Indigo — *Baptisia lactea*
Wild Azalea — *Rhododendron canescens*
Wild Bergamot — *Monarda fistulosa*
Wild Black Cherry (tree) — *Prunus serotina*
Wild Blueberry — *Vaccinium eliottii*
Wild Comfrey — *Cynoglossum virginianum*
Wild Geranium — *Geranium maculatum*
Wild Ginger — *Asarum canadense*
Wild Hyacinth — *Camassia scilloides*
Wild Hydrangea — *Hydrangea arborescens*
Wild Lettece — *Lactuca floridana*
Wild Onion — *Allium canadense*
Wild Petunia — *Ruellia caroliniensis*
Wild Quinine — *Parthenium integrifolium*
Wild Rose — *Rosa laevigata*
Wild Senna — *Cassia marilandica*
Wild Strawberry — *Fragaria virginiana*
Wild Sweet Cicely — *Osmorhiza longistylis*
Wild Sweet William — *Phlox maculata*
Windflower — *Anemone caroliniana*
Windflower — *Anemonella thalictroides*
Wisteria — *Wisteria frutescens*
Wood Sage — *Teucrium canadense*
Wood Sorrel — *Oxalis stricta*
Wooly Rose Mallow — *Hibiscus lasiocarpus*
Wreath Aster — *Aster ericoides*
Yarrow — *Achillea millefolium*
Yellow-Eyed Grass — *Xyris iridifolia*
Yellow Floating Heart — *Nymphoides peltata*
Yellow Fringed Orchid — *Platanthera ciliaris*
Yellow Jessamine — *Gelsemium sempervirens*
Yellow Lady's Slipper — *Cypripedium calceolus*
Yellow Rhexia — *Rhexia lutea*
Yellow Rocket — *Barbarea vulgaris*
Yellow Root — *Xanthorhiza simplicissima*
Yellow Sensitive Plant — *Neptunia lutea*
Yellow Star Grass — *Hypoxis hirsuta*
Yellow Sweet Clover — *Melilotus officinalis*
Yellow Trumpets — *Sarracenia alata*

Road Mileage Between Mississippi Cities

	Aberdeen	Batesville	Bay St. Louis	Booneville	Brookhaven	Canton	Clarksdale	Cleveland	Columbia	Columbus	Corinth	Crystal Springs	Forest	Greenville	Greenwood	Grenada	Gulfport	Hattiesburg	Holly Springs	Indianola	Jackson	Kosciusko	Laurel
Aberdeen		101	287	66	220	142	135	135	229	27	86	188	140	163	111	77	274	205	95	139	163	91	174
Batesville	101		313	91	199	152	35	71	229	127	110	169	146	105	68	36	305	235	56	83	146	96	212
Bay St. Louis	287	313		349	122	194	323	305	82	261	371	157	167	287	267	278	15	84	359	270	172	217	115
Booneville	66	91	349		260	179	130	166	274	91	18	230	185	198	146	117	328	259	62	179	198	132	228
Brookhaven	220	199	122	260		80	207	193	60	203	277	33	97	171	152	171	146	77	245	156	56	126	86
Canton	142	152	194	179	80		128	119	110	125	201	51	46	102	73	84	182	113	166	87	26	45	107
Clarksdale	135	35	323	130	207	128		36	232	162	148	177	168	72	56	67	308	239	93	59	151	118	234
Cleveland	135	71	305	166	193	119	36		222	152	187	153	159	36	43	55	284	215	129	31	127	110	211
Columbia	229	229	82	274	60	110	232	222		208	309	81	88	197	177	199	91	32	278	188	81	152	61
Columbus	27	127	261	91	203	125	162	152	208		111	178	128	161	108	99	247	178	121	138	147	78	147
Corinth	86	110	371	18	277	201	148	187	309	111		253	207	216	165	137	346	278	60	200	218	150	247
Crystal Springs	188	169	157	230	33	51	177	153	81	178	253		67	132	120	135	165	96	217	125	22	96	91
Forest	140	146	167	185	97	46	168	159	88	128	207	67		151	112	109	158	88	193	137	47	50	64
Greenville	163	105	287	198	171	102	72	36	197	161	216	132	151		52	85	272	203	161	23	115	111	199
Greenwood	111	68	267	146	152	73	56	43	177	108	165	120	112	52		33	253	184	114	29	96	61	177
Grenada	77	36	278	117	171	84	67	55	199	99	137	135	109	85	33		261	192	82	61	113	56	173
Gulfport	274	305	15	328	146	182	308	284	91	247	346	165	158	272	253	261		69	338	259	157	204	100
Hattiesburg	205	235	84	259	77	113	239	215	32	178	278	96	88	203	184	192	69		269	190	88	135	31
Holly Springs	95	56	359	62	245	166	93	129	278	121	60	217	193	161	114	82	338	269		143	196	141	242
Indianola	139	83	270	179	156	87	59	31	188	138	200	125	137	23	29	61	259	190	143		102	91	185
Jackson	163	146	172	198	56	26	151	127	81	147	218	22	47	115	96	113	157	88	196	102		71	84
Kosciusko	91	96	217	132	126	45	118	110	152	78	150	96	50	111	61	56	204	135	141	91	71		116
Laurel	174	212	115	228	86	107	234	211	61	147	247	91	64	199	177	173	100	31	242	185	84	116	
Louisville	67	120	228	118	154	74	148	146	177	53	143	125	72	144	91	91	210	141	138	122	95	36	114
Lucedale	233	285	105	295	137	176	303	286	89	211	316	152	137	270	247	249	71	57	323	254	151	189	71
Magee	190	186	141	234	66	68	198	178	49	180	257	46	49	161	139	152	117	49	233	146	43	101	44
McComb	244	223	100	285	27	110	232	217	39	228	295	57	120	196	177	189	131	72	278	179	81	147	101
Memphis, TN	139	59	375	109	268	186	74	110	294	166	93	234	213	146	130	99	360	291	45	133	212	155	272
Meridian	117	180	172	171	142	94	198	185	118	90	190	114	49	192	142	137	157	88	194	171	93	80	57
Natchez	265	249	201	300	62	127	216	180	110	249	320	87	150	154	172	205	199	139	286	168	102	172	147
New Albany	60	57	339	31	247	167	97	131	262	86	51	219	172	165	118	86	308	239	33	146	181	121	212
Oxford	84	19	339	70	222	138	62	99	250	100	84	188	163	130	83	51	307	239	36	105	165	106	212
Pascagoula	272	326	49	326	176	210	335	312	118	244	344	195	178	300	280	281	34	96	349	286	184	224	108
Philadelphia	94	130	201	147	135	57	157	146	140	79	168	106	52	151	101	97	184	115	167	128	81	36	88
Picayune	264	289	22	326	106	171	299	281	58	238	348	140	147	264	245	257	49	61	336	249	148	200	91
Port Gibson	224	201	194	264	60	85	179	140	122	211	287	47	103	121	135	168	211	141	249	131	60	132	137
Ripley	80	77	360	23	266	187	117	150	282	110	38	239	192	190	137	104	350	278	38	166	214	141	250
Senatobia	123	21	345	97	222	143	57	93	254	150	98	193	170	130	91	59	332	260	36	105	170	119	240
Starkville	37	116	259	98	182	101	142	136	200	22	112	152	102	139	86	77	240	171	123	115	125	55	145
Tunica	150	49	379	126	245	168	36	77	279	180	127	217	200	110	93	89	355	286	66	97	196	148	269
Tupelo	35	72	313	30	226	148	110	139	238	63	49	202	157	169	117	84	298	229	59	145	170	101	198
Vicksburg	201	176	213	239	78	70	146	110	123	186	257	49	88	84	102	135	198	129	216	98	44	108	125
Waynesboro	168	233	140	229	116	137	258	249	90	151	251	119	93	237	201	199	131	60	260	220	117	140	30
West Point	18	109	268	77	201	121	143	142	212	19	98	172	123	150	97	88	252	183	106	127	142	76	152
Winona	90	60	254	126	143	64	82	73	175	82	149	113	87	79	26	22	238	169	105	53	90	35	150
Yazoo City	155	123	212	196	99	28	110	87	139	139	208	67	79	71	55	83	201	132	170	55	44	57	128

(Shortest Route, Center-to-Center)

Louisville	Lucedale	Mcgee	McComb	Memphis, TN	Meridian	Natchez	New Albany	Oxford	Pascagoula	Philadelphia	Picayune	Port Gibson	Ripley	Senatobia	Starkville	Tunica	Tupelo	Vicksburg	Waynesboro	West Point	Winona	Yazoo City	
67	233	190	244	139	117	265	60	84	272	94	264	224	80	123	37	150	35	201	168	18	90	155	Aberdeen
120	285	186	223	59	180	249	57	19	326	130	289	201	77	21	116	49	72	176	233	109	60	123	Batesville
228	105	141	100	375	172	201	339	339	49	201	22	194	360	345	259	379	313	213	140	268	254	212	Bay St. Louis
118	295	234	285	109	171	300	31	70	326	147	326	264	23	97	98	126	30	239	229	77	126	196	Booneville
154	137	66	27	268	142	62	247	222	176	135	106	60	266	222	182	245	226	78	116	201	143	99	Brookhaven
74	176	68	110	186	94	127	167	138	210	57	171	85	187	143	101	168	148	70	137	121	64	28	Canton
148	303	198	232	74	198	216	97	62	335	157	299	179	117	57	142	36	110	146	258	143	82	110	Clarksdale
146	286	178	217	110	185	180	131	99	312	146	281	140	150	93	136	77	139	110	249	142	73	87	Cleveland
177	89	49	39	294	118	110	262	250	118	140	58	122	282	254	200	279	238	123	90	212	175	139	Columbia
53	211	180	228	166	90	249	86	100	244	79	238	211	110	150	22	180	63	186	151	19	82	139	Columbus
143	316	257	295	93	190	320	51	84	344	168	348	287	38	98	112	127	49	257	251	98	149	208	Corinth
125	152	46	57	234	114	87	219	188	195	106	140	47	239	193	152	217	202	49	119	172	113	67	Crystal Springs
72	137	49	120	213	49	150	172	163	178	52	147	103	192	170	102	200	157	88	93	123	87	79	Forest
144	270	161	196	146	192	154	165	130	300	151	264	121	190	130	139	110	169	84	237	150	79	71	Greenville
91	247	139	177	130	142	172	118	83	280	101	245	135	137	91	86	93	117	102	201	97	26	55	Greenwood
91	249	152	189	99	137	205	86	51	281	97	257	168	104	59	77	89	84	135	199	88	22	83	Grenada
210	71	117	131	360	157	199	308	307	34	184	49	211	350	332	240	355	298	198	131	252	238	201	Gulfport
141	57	49	72	291	88	139	239	239	96	115	61	141	278	260	171	286	229	129	60	183	169	132	Hattiesburg
138	323	233	278	45	194	286	33	36	349	167	336	249	38	36	123	66	59	216	260	106	105	170	Holly Springs
122	254	146	179	133	171	168	146	105	286	128	249	131	166	105	115	97	145	98	220	127	53	55	Indianola
95	151	43	81	212	93	102	181	165	184	81	148	60	214	170	125	196	170	44	117	142	90	44	Jackson
36	189	101	147	155	80	172	121	106	224	36	200	132	141	119	55	148	101	108	140	76	35	57	Kosciusko
114	71	44	101	272	57	147	212	212	108	88	91	137	250	240	145	269	198	125	30	152	150	128	Laurel
	187	123	170	173	66	197	108	98	221	26	209	160	128	146	33	176	90	139	121	50	66	94	Louisville
187		106	133	345	117	208	291	303	40	163	84	197	311	310	215	339	267	190	65	216	215	195	Lucedale
123	106		86	249	100	120	223	207	147	101	107	91	244	210	152	237	208	85	73	173	133	89	Magee
170	133	86		293	158	68	275	237	158	163	88	86	293	249	202	270	251	103	134	229	169	127	McComb
173	345	249	293		236	290	80	75	380	195	352	260	82	39	165	40	104	220	295	149	122	184	Memphis, TN
66	117	100	158	236		192	164	164	154	41	148	149	191	206	95	234	141	134	51	95	114	125	Meridian
197	208	120	68	290	192		283	255	226	182	177	47	320	275	226	269	272	70	187	244	182	117	Natchez
108	291	223	275	80	164	283		39	310	136	320	252	18	67	93	97	23	220	227	73	108	174	New Albany
98	303	207	237	75	164	255	39		318	148	309	219	58	39	94	68	48	185	243	91	77	140	Oxford
221	40	147	158	380	154	226	310	318		195	83	240	355	351	249	380	296	226	106	250	258	229	Pascagoula
26	163	101	163	195	41	182	136	148	195		181	140	155	156	56	185	115	125	100	77	72	90	Philadelphia
209	84	107	88	352	148	177	320	309	83	181		170	368	315	240	339	289	192	120	246	235	192	Picayune
160	197	91	86	260	149	47	252	219	240	140	170		271	228	186	218	238	28	165	208	148	78	Port Gibson
128	311	244	293	82	191	320	18	58	355	155	368	271		73	112	103	43	245	246	93	128	194	Ripley
146	310	210	249	39	206	275	67	39	351	156	315	228	73		141	28	93	199	259	131	82	148	Senatobia
33	215	152	202	165	95	226	93	94	249	56	240	186	112	141		169	64	163	151	19	60	113	Starkville
176	339	237	270	40	234	269	97	68	380	185	339	218	103	28	169		121	189	287	161	111	150	Tunica
90	267	208	251	104	141	272	23	48	296	115	289	238	43	93	64	121		209	201	46	95	163	Tupelo
139	190	85	103	220	134	70	220	185	226	125	192	28	245	199	163	189	209		158	181	120	47	Vicksburg
121	65	73	134	295	51	187	227	243	106	100	120	165	246	259	151	287	201	158		152	175	163	Waynesboro
50	216	173	229	149	95	244	73	91	250	77	246	208	93	131	19	161	46	181	152		71	137	West Point
66	215	133	169	122	114	182	108	77	258	72	235	148	128	82	60	111	95	120	175	71		72	Winona
94	195	89	127	184	125	117	174	140	229	90	192	78	194	148	113	150	163	47	163	137	72		Yazoo City

The Ultimate Reference on the State

Travel & Recreation in Mississippi

Interstate Highways: 684 miles (I-10, I-20, I-55 & I-59), rank 32
Primary Highways: U.S. Highways 45, 49, 61, 78, 80, 82 & 98
Number of Major Highway Entrances to the State: 28
Highway Mileage, 1998: 73,295 miles (over 53,000 paved)   **Rural** — 65,371   **Urban** — 7,924
   Interstate 684   **State Highways** 10,651   **County** 53,124   **Cities/Towns** 8,632   **Other** 204
   (As of June 2000, the 1987 Highway Program had 603.17 of four-lane highways open, 957.3 miles under contract, and 824.7 miles left to build for a total of 1,782 miles of new state roadway.)
Workers Driving to Work in Private Vehicles: 91.9% (alone 74.3%; with passengers 25.7%)
In Carpools to Work: 2-person 12.7%; 3-person 2.87%; 4-person 1.16%; 5-person 0.34%
Other Modes of Getting to Work: public transportation 0.8%; taxicabs 0.19%; motorcycle 0.1%;
Travel Time to Work: less than 5 mins. 5.1%; 5-30 mins. 68.2%; 30-60 mins. 21.5%; Mean 20.6 mins.
Domestic Travel Expenditures, 1996 (overnight trips & day trips of 100 miles or more): $3,452,000,000
Average Yearly Cost for Insurance per Insured Vehicle: 1997 — $648   1996 — $604   1995 — $579
Regular Tags, FY Ending 6/30/99: 2,336,190
Special Fee Tags, FY Ending 6/30/99: 114,956 (personalized 63,522; universities & colleges 15,053; wildlife 18,466; antique 13,397; military 1,616; firefighter 1,387; law enforcement 1,070)
Registered Trucks, Trailers & Buses, FY Ending 6/30/99: 70,593
Total Registered Plates & Decals, FY Ending 6/30/99: 2,537,501 (916.5 per 1,000 population)
Number Vehicles per Household: none 12.1%; one 33.7%; two 36.1%; three or more 18.1%
Licensed Drivers, 1998: 1,758,303 (179,175 commercial) 120,000 age 19 & under; 44,500 age 80 & over
Vehicle Miles per Licensed Mississippi Driver, 1997: 18,298 average
Annual Miles Driven per Mississippi Vehicle, 1997: 14,110 average
Est. Miles Driven on Mississippi Roads, 1998: 34,208,624,000 (23.7 billion rural; 10.5 billion urban)
Gallons of Fuel Used per Mississippi Vehicle, 1997: 847 average (16.66 miles per gallon)
Total Gasoline Sold (gallons), 1998: 3,607,135,546 (3,675,270,714 FY 1999)
Total Diesel Fuel Sold (gallons), 1998: 483,641,219 (493,154,965 FY 1999)
Total Motor Fuel (Gasoline & Diesel) Sold, 1998: 4,090,776,765 gallons

> A $58 billion fed'l. transportation bill for FY 2001 would give Miss. $471.8 mil. ($333 mil. for hiways).

Total State Fuel Tax Receipts, FY 1999: $278,816,524 paid on 1,578,368,309 taxable gallons gasoline + $ 58,556,837 on diesel = $337,373,361 total ($121.86 p/capita)
Highway Expenditures: 1998 — $843,443,000   1997 — $809,000,000   1996 — $826,000,000
Federal Payments for Mississippi Highways, 1998: $203,594,000 (plus $506,256,000 capital outlay)
Amount Mississippi Paid into the Federal Highway Trust Fund, FY 1998: $439,570,000
Motor Vehicle Accident Deaths: 1999 — 927   1998 — 948 (27.7 deaths per 100 million miles, highest in the U.S.; about 36% of the deaths in 1999 and 37% of the deaths in 1998 involved alcohol.)
   1997 — 861   1996 — 811   1995 — 868 (123 deaths involved crashes with big trucks)
Railroads: 19 lines as of 4/1/2000 — Burlington Northern & Sante Fe, Canadian National, Columbus & Greenville, CSX Transportation, Gloster Southern, Golden Triangle, Great River, Kansas City Southern, Meridian & Bigbee, Midsouth Rail, Mississippi Central, Mississippi Delta, Mississippi Export, Mississippian, Mississippi & Skunna Valley, Mississippi & Tennessee Railnet, Norfolk Southern, Old Augusta, and Port Bienville.

> 2,800 miles of track with 2,821 hiway rail crossings in the state.

   Six key railroad distribution yards are located in Mississippi, including one in Jackson, one in Gulfport on the Gulf of Mexico, one in Columbus on the Tenn-Tom Waterway, and one in Greenwood on the Yazoo River.
Airports, 5/1/2000 ✈ 202 (7 Public Commercial, 75 Public [6 privately owned], 113 Private, 7 Military).
Largest Airport ✈ Jackson International at Thompson Field in Rankin County, Mississippi.
   (as of June 1, 2000, JIA had nine airlines with 50 daily flights)
Busiest Airports, No. of Operations (Takeoffs & Landings), 1998 ✈ Olive Branch Metro — 115,950; Gulfport/Biloxi Regional — 105,270; Jackson International Airport — 82,585
State Parks (29): Buccaneer, Casey Jones Railroad Museum*, Clarko, Florewood River Plantation*, George Payne Cossar, Golden Memorial, Great River Road, Gulf Marine, Holmes County, Hugh White, J. P. Coleman, John W. Kyle, Lake Lincoln, Lake Lowndes, Lefluer's Bluff, Legion, Leroy Percy, Nanih Waiya Historic Site*, Natchez, Paul B. Johnson, Percy Quin, Roosevelt, Sam Dale Historic Site*, Shepard, Tishomingo, Tombigbee, Trace, Wall Doxey, and Winterville Mounds Historic Site*.

> There are 24 recreational parks and 5 historical parks* in Mississippi.

Travel & Recreation in Mississippi

Area in State Parks: 23,000 acres (35.94 square miles)   **Visitors To State Parks, FY 1997**: 4,745,000
Revenue Generated at State Parks, FY 1997: $5,994,000 (43.5% of operating expenditures)
National Forests (6): Bienville, Delta, DeSoto, Holly Springs, Homochitto, Tombigbee (1.4 million acres)
National Wildlife Refuges (10): Bogue Chitto, Dahomey, Hillside, Horn Island, Mathews Brake,
     Morgan Brake, Noxubee, Panther Swamp, Sandhill Crane and Yazoo.
National Parks in the State (4): Total of 107,600 acres (168.1 square miles) in National Parks;
     Brice's Crossroads (battlefield site) 1 acre
     Gulf Islands National Seashore (approximately 106,000 acres)
     Tupelo Battlefield Monument (1 acre)
     Vicksburg National Military Park (1,620 acres) [designated 1899]

> The Natchez Trace National Parkway, with 10,995 acres in Miss., Ala. & Tenn., had 5,810,094 recreation visits in 1998, the 7th most-visited National Park in the U.S.

Wilderness Areas (3): Black Creek, Gulf Islands National Seashore and Leaf River
Wildlife Management Areas: 36 (Dept. of Wildlife Fisheries & Parks has 21 fishing lakes-5,111 acres)
Federal Indian Reservations & Trust Lands: Over 8,500 members of the Mississippi Band of Choctaws
     live on the 20,486 acres of tribally-owned land near Philadelphia in Neshoba County.
Tourism: Tourism is the state's second largest industry after health care in the service sector of Mississippi,
     producing $5.1 billion in fiscal year 1998, up from $4.8 billion in fiscal year 1997.
     Tourism accounted for 86,000 jobs in FY 1998 compared to 79,000 jobs in FY 1997.
Pro Sports: Baseball — Jackson Diamond Kats (independent Texas-Louisiana League)
Minor League Hockey — Jackson Bandits, Jackson (East Coast Hockey League) associated with the Minnesota
     Wild & Chicago Blackhawks (NHL), Norfolk Admirals (AHL), & Cleveland Lumberjacks (IHL)
     — Memphis River Kings [team plays in Southaven, MS] (Central Hockey League)
     — Mississippi Sea Wolves, Biloxi (East Coast Hockey League)
     — Tupelo T-Rex (Western Professional Hockey League)
NCAA Sports Teams (6):   Alcorn State Braves, Jackson State Tigers, Mississippi State Bulldogs,
     Mississippi Valley State Delta Devils, University of Miss. "Ole Miss" Rebels,
     and University of Southern Mississippi Golden Eagles.

Records of Mississippi's Three Division 1-A Football Teams (Through Nov. 4, 2000):

Team	All-Time	1990 - 1999*	2000
University of Mississippi (Ole Miss) Rebels	550-409-35 (994 games)	66-48-0 (114 games)	6-2
Mississippi State University Bulldogs	444-458-39 (941 games)	63-50-2 (115 games)	6-2
University of Southern Miss. Golden Eagles	462-310-27 (799 games)	66-46-1 (113 games)	6-2

     * The records of all three teams include forfeit wins over Alabama in 1993, games they lost on the field.
     Through the '99 season, Ole Miss has sent 153 players to the NFL or AFL, MSU had sent 98 & Southern Miss 73.
Largest Stadiums: Veterans Memorial, Jackson — 60,000; Vaught-Hemingway, Oxford — 50,000;
     Scott Field, Starkville — 40,656; M.M. Roberts, Hattiesburg — 33,000

> Record crowd at Scott Field in Starkville was 43,917 on Oct. 7, 2000.

The largest crowds for Division I-A football games were 64,112 for the 1981 MSU-USM game, 58,311 for the 1983 MSU-USM game, 54,236 for the 1982 MSU-USM game (all 3 games played at Mississippi Veterans Memorial Stadium) and 52,368 at UM's Vaught-Hemingway Stadium on Sept. 9, 2000.
Ole Miss averaged 46,829 attendance a game in 1999 and just over 46,000 in 1998 at newly expanded Vaught-Hemingway Stadium. Mississippi State University averaged 37,821 in 1999 and 37,400 in 1998. University of Southern Mississippi drew 28,915 per game in 1999 and just over 24,000 per game in 1998.
Athletics Budgets for FY 2001: UM — $21,592,690   MSU — $17,331,164   USM — $9,888,455

Welcome Centers in Mississippi

Welcome Center	Visitors	Phone
Adams County Welcome Center, Hwy 61; 370 Seargent S. Prentiss Dr; Natchez 39120	*86,376	(601) 442-5849
Alcorn County Welcome Center, Harper Rd. off U.S. Hwy 45; Corinth 3883	70,942	(662) 287-9145
DeSoto County Welcome Center, I-55; PO Drawer 249; Hernando 38632	228,609	(662) 429-9969
Hancock County Welcome Center, I-10; PO Box 53; Bay St. Louis 39520	644,845	(228) 533-5554
Itawamba County Welcome Center, Hwy 78; PO Box 121; Tremont 38876	244,684	(662) 652-3330
Jackson County Welcome Center, I-10; PO Box 5181; Kreole Station; Moss Point 39563	672,050	(228) 475-3384
Lauderdale County Welcome Center, I-20; PO Box 50; Toomsuba 39364	372,517	(601) 632-1142
Pearl River County Welcome Center, I-59; PO Box 101; Nicholson 39463	160,845	(601) 798-8184
Pike County Welcome Center, I-55; PO Box 168; Magnolia 39652	212,341	(601) 783-5068
Warren County Welcome Center, I-20; 4210 Washington St; Vicksburg 39180	159,689	(601) 638-4269
Washington County Welcome Center, Hwy 82; PO Box 6022; Greenville 38704	59,266	(662) 332-2378

*Number of actual visitors in FY 2000 — a total of almost 3 million at all 11 Mississippi Welcome Centers.

The Ultimate Reference on the State

Travel & Recreation in Mississippi

Mississippi Welcome Centers - Where Visitors Came From
Fiscal Year 2000 (July 1, 1999 - June 30, 2000)

TOP-10 STATES	NO. OF SIGNED VISITORS	TOP-10 COUNTRIES	NO. OF SIGNED VISITORS
LOUISIANA	585,400	CANADA	17,488
ALABAMA	275,026	GERMANY	11,717
FLORIDA	238,721	ENGLAND	5,860
TEXAS	206,285	FRANCE	4,048
GEORGIA	118,928	MEXICO	2,116
TENNESSEE	83,894	HOLLAND	1,946
ARKANSAS	44,593	AUSTRALIA	1,375
ILLINOIS	42,745	SWITZERLAND	1,232
MISSOURI	41,358	AUSTRIA	767
NORTH CAROLINA	30,573	BELGIUM	723

Figures above reflect only visitors who "signed the books," which usually represents only about 75%-80% of the actual total.

Number of Visitors To Mississippi Welcome Centers, Fiscal Year 2000

WELCOME CENTER	JULY 1999	AUG. 1999	SEPT. 1999	OCT. 1999	NOV. 1999	DEC. 1999	SUB-TOTALS
ADAMS COUNTY	5,580	3,787	7,298	10,703	6,231	3,618	37,217
ALCORN COUNTY	7,243	4,227	4,526	5,483	5,607	4,478	31,564
DESOTO COUNTY	30,254	22,432	20,263	15,886	8,240	6,859	103,934
HANCOCK COUNTY	90,959	60,215	48,643	42,665	37,959	35,649	316,090
ITAWAMBA COUNTY	28,873	23,624	20,731	20,471	19,597	17,367	130,663
JACKSON COUNTY	108,284	77,576	53,990	53,051	50,345	42,508	385,754
LAUDERDALE COUNTY	52,421	37,611	25,973	32,284	28,886	28,504	205,679
PEARL RIVER COUNTY	21,724	14,180	11,636	12,084	13,385	10,193	83,202
PIKE COUNTY	25,391	19,416	12,359	20,590	18,194	13,870	109,820
WARREN COUNTY	26,048	14,671	11,699	12,311	12,984	10,288	88,001
WASHINGTON COUNTY	6,300	4,850	4,814	4,918	3,629	2,839	27,350
SUB-TOTALS	403,077	282,589	221,932	230,446	205,057	176,173	1,519,274

WELCOME CENTER	JAN. 2000	FEB. 2000	MAR. 2000	APR. 2000	MAY 2000	JUNE 2000	SUB-TOTALS	TOTALS
ADAMS COUNTY	3,541	4,538	13,201	12,096	9,923	5,860	49,159	86,376
ALCORN COUNTY	4,399	5,038	5,346	7,446	8,761	8,388	39,378	70,942
DESOTO COUNTY	* 7,553	* 11,045	* 12,911	27,891	31,020	34,255	124,675	228,609
HANCOCK COUNTY	36,746	40,294	53,685	51,375	59,380	87,275	328,755	644,845
ITAWAMBA COUNTY	12,578	14,371	21,083	18,998	21,818	25,173	114,021	244,684
JACKSON COUNTY	49,915	63,554	70,611	55,325	* 34,333	* 12,558	286,296	672,050
LAUDERDALE COUNTY	19,225	19,136	29,386	26,875	29,203	43,013	166,838	372,517
PEARL RIVER COUNTY	8,075	9,359	13,184	13,465	14,131	19,429	77,643	160,845
PIKE COUNTY	11,113	12,752	19,202	20,109	17,784	21,561	102,521	212,341
WARREN COUNTY	5,820	7,668	12,960	10,775	14,351	20,114	71,688	159,689
WASHINGTON COUNTY	2,090	3,660	6,486	5,602	6,542	7,536	31,916	59,266
SUB-TOTALS	161,055	191,415	258,055	249,957	247,246	285,162	1,392,890	
GRAND TOTAL								2,912,164

* These Centers were closed parts of these months for renovation. Source: Mississippi Development Authority - Tourism Division.

Tourist Attractions in Mississippi

ABERDEEN (MONROE COUNTY)　　　　　　　**ABERDEEN VISITORS BUREAU (800-634-3538 OR 662-369-9440)**
Original name was Dundee; Many antebellum mansions and Victorian homes, some open to tours year around by appointment; Evans Memorial Library houses a museum and is nationally known for its historical and genealogical materials, 105 N Long St. FREE (662-369-4601); ANNUAL EVENTS: In April, the North/South Skirmish shooting competition representing specific regiments using Civil War-era weapons; The Tenn-Tom Bassmaster Classic fishing tournament is also held in April; The annual "Blue Bluff River Festival" on the banks of the Tenn-Tom Waterway in mid-Oct. includes a boat & camper show, fireman's rodeo, arts & crafts, plus food. FAMOUS PEOPLE born here: Major league baseball great Guy Bush and bluesman George Robinson.

AMORY (MONROE COUNTY)　　　　　　　**AMORY-MONROE CO. CHAMBER OF COMMERCE (662-256-7194)**
In Frisco Park in the center of town is an old steam locomotive used by President Franklin Roosevelt in his presidential campaign of 1933; The Amory Regional Museum has a collection of railroad artifacts housed in an ex-Frisco passenger coach, placed there by Magnolia State Railway in 1981, plus antique furniture, Indian artifacts, and 1837 log cabin, 715 S. 3rd St. FREE (662-256-2761); ANNUAL EVENTS: Amory Railroad Festival in April features a gigantic arts & crafts exhibit & sale, 10K run, rodeo, antique cars, model airplane show, entertainment & food. FAMOUS PEOPLE born here include football great Bilbo Monaghan, blues singer Lucille Bogan, bluesman Frank Swan and actors John Dye & Gary Grubbs (grew up in Prentiss).

ARKABUTLA (TATE COUNTY)
Arkabutla Lake. The Arkabutla Dam is on the Coldwater River near Arkabutla. Famous actor and "The Voice," announcer James Earl Jones was born here and, his father, actor Robert Earle Jones was born in nearby Coldwater, as was Dumas Malone, famous historian and biographer.

BALDWYN (PRENTISS COUNTY)　　　　　　　**BALDWYN CHAMBER OF COMMERCE (662-365-2383)**
Its first name was Carrollville. The largest bed of huge, ancient (70 million years old) oyster shells and sea fossils in the state; six miles from Baldwyn on hwy. 370 is Brice's Crossroads National Battlefield Site commemorating the heroism of Confederate Gen. Nathan B. Forrest, information on site or at Natchez Trace Visitors Center, FREE (662-680-4025).

BAY SAINT LOUIS (HANCOCK COUNTY)　　　　　　　**HANCOCK CO. TOURISM DEVEOLPMENT BUREAU (800-466-9048)**
Originally known as Shieldsboro. The state's oldest incorporated town; many artist locations: Bay Crafts at 107 Beach Blvd, The Serenity Gallery at 126½ Main St, folk artist Alice Moseley displays her works at her home at 214 Booker St. (228-467-9223); Pirate House; ANNUAL EVENTS: The 4th of July Crab Festival, plenty of food, arts & crafts exhibitors, fireworks, live music, and more (228-467-6509); casino gambling. NEARBY: About 16 miles from Bay St. Louis just off I-10 in Hancock County is NASA's John C. Stennis Space Center. The visitors' center was renovated and enlarged from 8,000 to 14,000 square feet between Sept. 1999 and May 2000. Bus tours include the Space Shuttle Main Engine test complex, the enlarged StenniSphere, a space shuttle simulator, films, lectures, demonstrations by tour guides, the Hall of Achievements for history of NASA & space flight — a massive 154-foot Space Shuttle external fuel tank and other rocket hardware. FREE (228-688-2370 or Toll Free 800-237-1821). FAMOUS PEOPLE born in Bay St. Louis: clarinetist Pete Fountain and political activist and Republican Party leader, the late Evelyn McPhail.

BELZONI (HUMPHREYS COUNTY)　　　　　　　**BELZONI/HUMPHREYS CO. DEVELOP. FOUNDATION (662-247-4838)**
(All phone numbers are Area Code 662). Originally called Fisk's Landing. "The Catfish Capital of the World." Catfish Capital Museum, 110 Magnolia St. (247-4838); Wister Gardens botanical paradise on 14 acres (247-3025); "Mama's Dream World" Art Gallery at 307 Central St. displaying the works of Ethel Wright Mohamed, often called Mississippi's Grandma Moses of stitchery—a permanent collection of her work is at the Smithsonian (247-1433); ANNUAL EVENT: World Catfish Festival held the 1st weekend in April with rock and country bands, catfish-eating contest and crowning of the Catfish Queen. The festival was deemed a Top-100 event by the American Buss Association in 1997 and a Top-20 event by the Southeast Tourism Society in 1998. NEARBY is the largest tree in the state, a Bald Cypress 46½ feet in circumference (15 feet thick) with a height of 70 feet and believed to be over 2,000 years old! The second largest tree in the state, another Blad Cypress, is just a few yards away; FAMOUS PEOPLE born here: Chuck Gordon, film producer (his brother, Larry Gordon, a film producer and former CEO of 20th Century Fox, although born in Yazoo City, grew up in Belzoni); pro basketball player Spencer Haywood (born in nearby Silver City); bluesmen Eddie "Guitar" Burns, Boyd Gilmore, Pinetop Perkins & "Playboy' Vincent; and rockabilly singer Glenn Honeycutt. Although soul/blues singer Denise LaSalle was born in Leflore County, she grew up in Belzoni.

BENTON (YAZOO COUNTY)　　　　　　　**YAZOO CO. CONVENTION AND VISITORS BUREAU (800-381-0662)**
A planned community platted in 1828, its first name was Flagg Springs until it was changed to Benton on Dec. 9, 1829. It served as the first county seat of Yazoo County. It has a pre-Civil War Methodist Church & Masonic Hall. Notable people born here include Jimmy Heidel, former head of the Mississippi Dept. of Economic and Community Development and musician (drummer) Robert Plunkett.

BIGBEE VALLEY (NOXUBEE COUNTY)
The Bigbee Valley General Store on State Highway 388 near the Alabama state line.

Tourist Attractions in Mississippi

BILOXI (HARRISON COUNTY) MISS. GULF COAST CONVENTION/VISITORS BUREAU (888-896-6796)
(All phone numbers are Area Code 228). The Old Biloxi Lighthouse is a 62-foot cast iron structure built in 1848 and the only lighthouse in the nation that stands in the middle of a 4-lane highway (435-6294); Beauvoir Mansion, where Jefferson Davis spent his last years. On the estate is the Jefferson Davis Presidential Library, (800-570-3818); Old French House built in 1737; Old Spanish House built about 1780; Old Brick House built in 1790, at 622 Bayview, donations (432-5498); the Magnolia Hotel built in 1847, only remaining pre-Civil War hotel on the Miss. coast, and Mardi Gras Museum, 119 Rue Magnolia, donations (432-8806); J.L. Scott Marine Education Center & Aquarium at 115 Beach Blvd. (U.S. 90), admission, (374-5550); Moran's Art Studio, 110 Potter Ave. (435-9615); Gulf Coast branch of the Miss. Museum of Art at 136 George Ohr St., FREE (374-5547); Broadwater beach resort; Gulf Marine State Park in E. Biloxi on U.S. 90 at Ocean Springs Bridge (435-4355); Seafood Industry Museum at Point Cadet Plaza, 115 First St., FREE (435-6320); Small Craft Harbor; Keesler Air Force Base, the Air Force Electronics and Computer Training Center (377-2254); Gulf Islands Nat'l. Seashore; Fort Massachusetts, a Civil War fort constructed in 1858 is on Ship Island in the Gulf of Mexico. Point of departure for daily cruises to the island is the Biloxi Point Cadet Marina, Hwy 90 (432-2197); Deep sea fishing; boat cruises; rodeo; ANNUAL EVENTS: Miss. Arts Fair for the Handicapped, mid-June (868-2923); Deep Sea Fishing Rodeo with carnival midway, skydiving exhibitions, fireworks, music, July 4th. weekend (388-2271); Miss Teen USA Pageant is held in Biloxi in Aug. (800-237-9493); Mississippi Gulf Coast Blues Festival, in Sept. (388-8010); Mississippi Coast History Week with historic re-enactments and free public programs, entire 3rd week of Feb; Many seafood festivals throughout the year; casino gambling year 'round; many scheduled events and shows at the Mississippi Coast Coliseum and Convention Center at 2350 Beach Blvd. (388-8010). FAMOUS PEOPLE born here include: country comedian T. Bubba Bechtol; astronaut Fred W. Haise, Jr.; actors Gerald Hopkins and Eric Roberts; country singer/songwriter Chris LeDoux; bluesmen Jimmy Bertrand & Oliver "Dink" Johnson, actress and Miss America (1959) Mary Ann Mobley; historian Grady Howell, Jr.; and potter/artist George Ohr.

BLUE MOUNTAIN (TIPPAH COUNTY)
First known as Prospect Hill; a doll collection that dates back to the first graduating class in the 1800s, in the Administration Building of Blue Mountain College, closed weekends, FREE (662-685-4771). Legal expert, jurist and educator Jerome F. Leavell was born here and grew up in Oxford.

BROOKHAVEN (LINCOLN COUNTY) BROOKHAVEN-LINCOLN CO. CHAMBER OF COMM. (800-613-4667)
Post office was named Bogue Chitto from 1822 until it was changed to Brookhaven on Nov. 14, 1835. The annual Southern Style Christmas Fair with arts & crafts, antiques, food, games, last week in Nov. at the Highland Square Shopping Center (601-833-7430). FAMOUS PEOPLE born here: blueman "Blind Jim" Brewer; record producer Al Perkins; writers Jim Ritchie and Cid Ricketts Sumner; artists Wyatt Waters and Karl Wolfe; and sports writer and Miss. Sports Hall of Famer Jimmie McDowell. Pro football great Lance Alworth, born in Houston, Texas, grew up here.

CANTON (MADISON COUNTY) CANTON CONVENTION & VISITORS BUREAU (800-844-3369)
Courthouse built in 1852, FREE; Old Jail Museum, jail built in 1870, FREE; Tilda Bogue, a restored dogtrot house built c. 1935 (601-859-1307); Multicultural Center and Museum, corner of Center & N. Union Sts; Allison's Wells School of Arts & Crafts teaching center (800-489-2787); ANNUAL EVENTS: Huge Canton Flea Market in spring & fall, the 2nd Thurs. in May & Oct., with over 1,000 arts & crafts exhibitors from 26 states, no Admission (601-859-8055); Mississippi Championship Hot-Air Balloon Fest with at least 50 balloons, balloon glow, fireworks, talent show, barbecue, July 4th weekend (800-844-3369 or 601-895-1307); Canton Historic Square the last weekend in Nov. or 1st weekend in Dec. and Victorian Christmas Festival with over 30,000 lights outlining architecture designs, and Animated Christmas Museum of life-size figures, FREE. Northwest of Canton is Virilla Country Store, built 1869. FAMOUS PEOPLE born here: football great L.C. Greenwood; artist John McCrady; bluesmen William "Do Boy" Diamond, John Lee Henley & Johnnie "Geechie" Temple; and gospel singers Rev. Cleophus Robinson & Harvey "Pop" Watkins, Sr.

CARROLLTON (CARROLL COUNTY)
There are 66 units listed on the National Register of Historic Places including the Old Carroll County Jail Museum (jail built in 1836), Merrill's Store, built in 1834 and the Carroll County Courthouse, built in 1877, which houses the 2nd oldest set of records in the state; the movie *The Reivers*, based on William Faulkner's novel, was filmed here; Jewel Thomas' old farm tools & implements collection — go west from Winona on Hwy 82, turn on the first gravel road past Vaiden-Hwy 35 exit. FREE; FAMOUS PEOPLE born here: bluesman G.L. Crockett; actress Frances E. Neal; Medal of Honor recipient John A. Pittman; novelist Elizabeth Spencer; four-star Admiral John S. McCain, College football player/coach Crawford Mims and Earl L. Brewer, who was Gov. of Miss. 1912-16, were born in Carroll County.

CARTHAGE (LEAKE COUNTY) LEAKE COUNTY CHAMBER OF COMMERCE (662-267-9231)
Its first name was Leaksville. The annual Arts and Crafts Festival in early Oct; Located southeast of Carthage is Bryan's Grocery (country store), take State Hwy 35 south to State Hwy 488 to the Freeny community. Silent screen star Charles Graham and bluesman Little Boyd were born here. Ross Barnett, Gov. of Miss. 1960-64, was born nearby in Leake Co.

CHURCH HILL (JEFFERSON COUNTY)
Its first name was Maryland; Wagner's Country Store, 13 miles north of Natchez on State Hwy 553, built prior to 1870; historic "Maryland Settlement"; Christ Eposcopal Church built in 1857 (601-786-3802).

Tourist Attractions in Mississippi

CLARKSDALE (COAHOMA COUNTY)   COAHOMA COUNTY TOURISM COMMISSION (800-626-3764)
(phone nos. Area Code 662). Its first name was Clarksville. Archaeological Museum, housed in the Carnegie Public Library, 114 Delta Ave., has a collection of Miss. pottery, related artifacts and archaeological research materials, FREE. The Delta Blues Museum in that library draws about 30,000 visitors a year. FREE (627-6820); the Cutrer Mansion, a 1916 Italian Renaissance villa made famous by Tennessee Williams' writings; Stackhouse/Rooster Blues Records at 232 Sunflower Ave. sells blues records, tapes, books & memorabilia and is a key site for fans wanting to know more about the blues (627-2209); the Riverside Hotel (the Blues Hotel) located at 615 Sunflower Ave., which became a blues landmark when Bessie Smith, famous blues singer, died there in 1937 following an auto accident on Hwy 61 (627-6294); Muddy Waters house, 7 miles northwest of Clarksdale; ANNUAL EVENTS: Sunflower River Blues Festival is held the 2nd weekend in Aug. (624-4461); the Tennessee Williams Festival, held in mid-Oct. FAMOUS PEOPLE born here include numerous blues and R&B artists such as Willie Brown, Jackie Brenston, Eddie Calhoun, Sam Cooke, Little Willie Foster, Rev. C.L. Franklin, Lillian "Lil" Green, Lillie Mae Hill, Raymond Hill, Earl Zebedee Hooker, John Lee Hooker, Lurleen Hunter, Johnny "Cool" Johnson, Ernest Lane, Johnny B. Moore, Junior Parker, "Brother" John Sellers, Ike Turner, Robert "Bilbo" Walker and Charles Wright. Other famous people born here include: writer/journalist Lerone Bennett, Jr.; football great Charlie Conerly; and actor/director/impresario Larry Thompson.

CLEVELAND (BOLIVAR COUNTY)   CLEVELAND/BOLIVAR CO. CHAMBER OF COMMERCE (662-843-2712)
It was a village known as Sims until it was named Cleveland on Mar. 25, 1886. On the campus at Delta State University: Fielding Wright Art Center has a permanent collection including Salvador Dali, plus changing exhibits, closed weekends and summer (662-846-4720); Museum of Natural History with Indian artifacts, plus skeleton remains of reptiles, mammals & assorted fossils; the Roy E. Wiley Planetarium (662-846-4250) All FREE.; ANNUAL EVENT: the Crosstie Arts Festival with juried arts & crafts, live entertainment, children's area and food, last weekend in April (800-295-7473). FAMOUS PEOPLE born here: bluemen Little Johnny Christian and "Barkin' " Bill Smith, guitarist "Dr. Mike" James, and Larry Speakes, journalist and press secretary for President Reagan.

CLINTON (HINDS COUNTY)   CLINTON CHAMBER OF COMMERCE (601-924-5912)
First named Mount Salus, it was changed on Sept. 28, 1829. Mississippi College (1826), the first co-ed college in the U.S. to grant degrees to women (601-925-3000); Clinton Cemetery, circa 1800, one of the oldest in central Miss. with graves of pioneer settlers, college presidents & Confederate soldiers; Mississippi's only *Fortune* 500 company, WorldCom, a complete-spectrum communications company and the nation's second-largest long distance carrier, is headquartered here. Poet Sterling D. Plumpp was born here. Former Mississippi Gov. Walter Leake died here in 1825.

COLUMBIA (MARION COUNTY)   MARION COUNTY CHAMBER OF COMMERCE (601-736-6385)
First known as Lott's Bluff. Once the capital of the state. Annual event: Down Home Festival held at the City Park during the Labor Day weekend, features a hog-killing, cracklings frying, jazz dancing, puppet show, carnival rides, live music (601-736-4915); The birthplace of Pro Football great Walter Payton and actress Peggy Dow (Varnadow).

COLUMBUS (LOWNDES COUNTY)   COLUMBUS/LOWNDES COUNTY VISITORS BUREAU (800) 327-2686)
(Phone nos. Area Code 662). First known as Possum Town. Where Hernando DeSoto crossed the Tombigbee River in 1540; Columbus Pilgrimage in early April with tours of more than 100 antebellum homes including Amzi Love, Rosewood Manor, Snowdown, Temple Heights, Waverly & White Arches (329-1191); Franklin Academy, the first free school in the state; sternwheel paddleboat excursions on the Tenn-Tom Waterway (327-2268); Columbus Lock & Dam on the Tenn-Tom (327-2142); Lake Lowndes State Park 6 miles SE of Columbus off Miss. Hwy 69 (328-2110); Miss. University for Women Fine Arts Gallery (329-7341); the Blewett-Harrison-Lee Museum of Civil War memorabilia (327-8888); Friendship Cemetery, site of the country's first Memorial Day observance in 1866, also the burial place of 4 Confederate generals and 2 Miss. governors, Henry Whitfield & James Whitfield, FREE (328-2565); ANNUAL EVENTS: The giant "Trash to Treasures" flea market held the 2nd Sat. in Apr. & Oct. at Columbus Fairgrounds; Golden Triangle Thunder Boat Regatta (May); Folklife Festival at Lake Lowndes State Park in Aug; Possum Town Pig Fest Bar-B-Q cooking contest, 4th weekend in Sept; Calico Fair arts/crafts, 3rd Sat. in Oct; "Christmas on The River"; Columbus Air Force Base Open House with aerial demonstrations, flyovers, aircraft displays, FREE (434-7068). FAMOUS PEOPLE born here: dramatist Tennessee Williams; bluesmen "Blind" Ben Covington, Wylie Dixon & Robbie Montgomery; pro boxer Henry Armstrong, sportscaster Walter "Red" Barber, photographer Birney Imes, research scientist Marietta Eichelberger, college football coach Gene Murphy, floral designer Ralph Null, journalist Frank Trippett, horse trainer/jockey Tom Wilburn, and Glen Graham & Brad Smith (with rock group Blind Melon).

CORINTH (ALCORN COUNTY)   CORINTH AREA TOURISM PROMOTION COUNCIL (800-748-9048)
(Phone nos. Area Code 662). First known as Cross City. Mississippi's "Gateway City." Fort Robinette Memorial Civil War Site; Corinth National Cemetery with over 6,000 markers for Civil War soldiers; Curlee House (287-9501), plus two dozen other restored antebellum homes. The old Duncan House (1857), a National Historic Landmark, which served as headquarters for generals during the Siege of Corinth and the Battles of Corinth and Shiloh, is now renovated and serves as a bed and breakfast known as the Vaughan-Aldridge Guest House; the Corinth jail with gallows in the stairwell; Corinth Train Depot at 213 Fillmore St., FREE (287-5269); the Northeast Mississippi Museum at 4th St. & Washington features Civil War artifacts, Chickasaw Indian artifacts, fossils, exhibits and collections, FREE (287-3120);

Tourist Attractions in Mississippi

CORINTH (Continued)
ANNUAL EVENTS: The Slugburger Festival, a salute to a local culinary favorite (hamburger meat with filler), features a carnival, arts & crafts, and lots of food, around July 10th (287-1550); the Roscoe Turner Balloon Race during the 3rd week in August commemorates the late aviation pioneer, barnstormer and native of Corinth, and features hot-air balloonists from across the country, country music, carnival games & rides, arts & crafts and more (286-9284); the annual Battle of Corinth re-enactment, the state's largest Civil War re-enactment with over 3,000 participants, held the last weekend in Sept; the Hog Wild barbecue festival held the first weekend in Oct. FAMOUS PEOPLE born here: baseball player Don Blasingame; entrepreneur/CEO John N. Palmer, Jr.; novelist/screenwriter Thomas Hal Phillips; and the above-mentioned aviation pioneer Roscoe Turner.

CRYSTAL SPRINGS (COPIAH COUNTY)　　　CRYSTAL SPRINGS CHAMBER OF COMMERCE (601-892-2711)
Once the "Tomato Capital of the World." Annual Labor Day Arts & Crafts on Lake Chautaugua features 5K run, music, more (601-892-2711). FAMOUS PEOPLE born here: bluesmen Dick Bankston & Sam "One-Leg" Norwood; guitarist Major Johnson; research scientist and writer Frances "Fannye" Cook; politician Pat Harrison; and aviator Alton Parker.

D'IBERVILLE (HARRISON COUNTY)　　　D'IBERVILLE/ST. MARTIN CHAMBER OF COMMERCE (601-392-2293)
Warren Fuller's Back Bay Bottles collection of over beer 19,000 bottles, FREE (228-392-2150). College football great Reggie Collier was born here.

DeKALB (KEMPER COUNTY)　　　KEMPER COUNTY CHAMBER OF COMMERCE (601-743-2754)
First known as Holihtasha; Kemper Co. Historical Museum, an old warehouse that belonged to the Stennis family, contains a collection of items from the local office of U.S. Sen. John Stennis (born near DeKalb), plus historical tools and artifacts from around the county, FREE, and Neville-Giles Cemetery, a state historical cemetery dating back to 1825, about 4.5 miles east of Scooba on Hwy 16, (601-743-2754); Jack Webb Country Store, Portersville exit east off Hwy 45, (662-476-5577); Sciple Grist Mill, built in 1790, north of DeKalb off State Hwy 39N and follow signs, FREE.

EDWARDS (HINDS COUNTY)
First known as Liverpool. The World's Only Cactus Plantation with over 3,000 varieties. Just a little east of Vicksburg and just off I-20. Born here were bluesmen Johnny Fuller & "Fiddlin' " Joe Martin and early blues great Charley Patton.

ENTERPRISE (CLARKE COUNTY)　　　CLARKE COUNTY CHAMBER OF COMMERCE (601-776-5701)
Dunn's Falls, a 65-foot waterfall once used to power a gristmill and manufacture Stetson Hats. John B. Stetson learned and practiced his trade here right after the Civil War. The area offers a natural wildlife refuge, picnic areas, gristmill pond, hiking, swimming & more (601-655-9511).

EUDORA (DESOTO COUNTY)　　　DESOTO CO. CONVENTION & VISITORS BUREAU (888-280-9120)
Country Charm Antiques & Museum on Hwy 304, 12 buildings, each containing early American primitive antiques. From I-55, Hernando exit, then 9 miles west on State Hwy 304 (662-429-5359).

FAYETTE (JEFFERSON COUNTY)
Nine miles west of Fayette is Springfield Mansion, built 1786-1791, where Andrew Jackson and Rachel Robards were married in 1791 — the first mansion in the Mississippi Valley to have a full colonnade across the entire facade and one of the first such mansions in America, on the National Register of Historic Places (601-786-3802). Richard H. Truly, who was the first astronaut to head NASA (National Aeronautics and Space Administration) and was born here.

FLORA (MADISON COUNTY)　　　MADISON COUNTY CHAMBER OF COMMERCE (601-605-2554)
Near Flora is the Mississippi Petrified Forest, 36 million years old, declared a Registered National Natural Lankmark in 1966 by the National Park Service, charge (601-879-8189). Three of the (4) Chambers Brothers rock group, George, Lester & Willie Chambers, were born here, as well as politician/women's rights activist Belle Kearney.

FOREST (SCOTT COUNTY)　　　FOREST AREA CHAMBER OF COMMERCE (601-469-4332)
Annual Mississippi Broiler Festival celebrates Scott Co. being the top poultry-producing area in the state and offers a 5K run/walk, 1-mile fun run, antique/classic cars show, arts & crafts booths, fireworks, talent showdown with cash/prizes for performers, a small charge, held last weekend May/1st weekend June. Blues singer/songwriter Arthur "Big Boy" Crudrup, who wrote *That's All Right Mama*, the first hit Elvis Presley had, was born here as was bluesman James "T-Model" Ford. Basketball great Syvia Krebs, born in Jackson, grew up here. Paul B. Johnson, Sr., who was Gov. of Miss. from Jan. 16, 1940 until his death at Hattiesburg on Dec. 26, 1943, was born nearby in Hillsboro.

FRENCH CAMP (CHOCTAW COUNTY)
Colonel James Drane Plantation, a restored 2-story plantation house constructed 1846-1848 with carriage house and French Camp Log Cabin, c. 1846, with period artifacts, operating sorghum mill (seasonally), dogtrot house, workshop, gift shop, Natchez Trace Parkway, Milepost 180.8, FREE (662-547-6657); The Rainwater Observatory, the largest public access observatory in the state features 13 telescopes, including 5 for daytime solar viewing, FREE. E-mail James Hill at jhill@astronomers.org. The compound also has a B&B Inn & lodge rooms (not free), Hwy 413, one mile E of Natchez Trace Parkway at French Camp (662-547-6113 or 662-547-6865); The Harvest Festival is held annually in mid-Oct. James "J.P." Coleman, Gov. of Miss. from 1956-60, was born nearby in Choctaw County at Ackerman.

Tourist Attractions in Mississippi

FRIAR'S POINT (COAHOMA COUNTY) COAHOMA COUNTY TOURISM COMMISSION (800-626-3764)
First known as Union. North Delta Museum with prehistoric Indian artifacts and Civil War exhibits, FREE; FAMOUS PEOPLE born here: bluesman Sam Carr; early movie director B. Reeves Eason; and country/rock star Conway Twitty.

FULTON (ITAWAMBA COUNTY) ITAWAMBA CO. DEVELOPMENT COUNCIL (662-862-4571)
First known as Ironwood Bluff. Fulton Historical Center (662-862-4128). Jazz conductor Jimmie Lunceford born here.

GAUTIER (JACKSON COUNTY) JACKSON COUNTY AREA CHAMBER OF COMMERCE (228-762-3391)
Singing River Boat Cruise; Old Plantation House built in 1856, located 3 miles west of Pascagoula on Hwy 90; Shepard State Park, south of U.S. Hwy 90 (228-497-2244).

GLOSTER (AMITE COUNTY) LIBERTY AREA CHAMBER OF COMMERCE (601-657-8011)
Largest arboretum in Mississippi consisting of 347 acres of plants/flowers of all kinds. Football great and Mississippi Sports Hall of Famer Buster Poole and blues drummer Pearlis Williams were born here.

GREENVILLE (WASHINGTON COUNTY) WASHINGTON CO. CONVENTION/VISITORS BUREAU (800-467-3582)
(All phone nos. Area Code 662). "The Towboat Capital of the World". Port of Greenville ("America's Fifth Seacoast") located on Lake Furguson; the Greenville Flood Museum exhibit focusing on the great 1927 Mississippi River Flood, 915 Washington Ave.; the Greenville Writers' Exhibit showcases works and artifacts of Greenville's large number of prominent writers, at 341 Main St. in the William Alexander Percy Memorial Library, FREE (378-3141); Old Firehouse Museum vintage fire station with antique fire trucks/related exhibits, at 230 Main St. (378-1616); ANNUAL EVENTS: Mississippi International Balloon Classic, the last week in June; the Mississippi Delta Blues and Heritage Festival (the largest blues festival in the nation) is held the 3rd Sat. in Sept. each year (335-3523); Jesse Brent Memorial Labor Day Boat Race; and casino gambling. NEARBY: Winterville Indian Mounds Historic Site State Park & Museum, 3 miles north of Greenville off Hwy 1, one of the largest Indian mound groups in the Mississippi Valley (334-4684); Stoneville, the largest USDA research facility east of the Mississippi; Warfield Point; Paul Love Park; Deerfield Park; Lakes Lee & Washington; Yazoo National Wildlife Refuge; FAMOUS PEOPLE born here: puppeteer Jim Henson (see LELAND); poets Charles Bell, Brooks Haxton & William Alexander Percy; writers William Attaway, David Cohn, Robert Hitt Neill, Bern Keating, Beverly Lowry, John Ramsey Miller & Clifton Taulbert; saxophonist Steve Douglas; sculptors William Beckwith & Leon Koury; soul singers Tyrone Davis & Mary Wilson (the Supremes); bluesmen John "Blackfoot" Colbert, Frank "Left Hand" Craig & David Savage; historian Shelby Foote; TV weatherman and features producer Walt Grayson; Medal of Honor recipient Robert T. Henry; artist Valerie Jaudon; songwriter Ben Peters (grew up in Hollandale); pro football player & College Football Hall of Famer Wilbert Montgomery; major league baseball player George "Boomer" Scott; and actresses Ruth Attaway & Hattie Winston.

GREENWOOD (LEFLORE COUNTY) GREENWOOD CONVENTION & VISITORS CENTER (800-848-9064)
(All phone numbers are Area Code 662). Fist know as Williams Landing. "Cotton Capital of the World." Cottonlandia Museum, U.S. 82W, featuring the history of the Delta — "Indians, lumberjacks, trappers, traders, farmers, heroes, artists, writers, rogues, saints and the women who cared." (453-0925); Cotton Row downtown district, on the National Register of Historic Places (748-9064); Florewood River Plantation State Park, 2 miles west of Greenwood off U.S. 82 (455-3821); Fort Pemberton Confederate Army Civil War site, Hwy 82W, FREE, and Greenwood Cemetery (748-9064), where two Medal of Honor recipients are buried — Mississippian John A. Pittman, who was born in Carrollton, Mississippi and George Wilhelm (not born in Mississippi). Another Medal of Honor recipient, "adopted" Mississippian Hubert H. Lee (b. in Missouri) is buried in Leland-Stoneville Cemetery in nearby Stoneville; Archaeologist Bill Hony's The Prayer Museum at 611 W. Market St., which contains prayer beads, books, church bells & various artifacts about several different religions from around the world (453-7306); Greenwood Civic Center; and Delta Gallery Blues Museum, 933 U.S. Hwy 82W, FREE ((453-2888). ANNUAL EVENTS: C.R.O.P. (Cotton Row On Parade) Day, 1st Saturday in Aug., a downtown festival with music and arts & crafts; the Robert Johnson Blues Memorial is held on hwy. 7 between Itta Bena and Morgan City; Sky Parade (formerly held in Jackson) with airplane displays, flying acrobatics, hundreds of hot air balloons, and much more...one of the largest events of its kind in the U.S., 3rd weekend in Oct.; FAMOUS PEOPLE born in Greenwood: photographer Paul T. Brown (reared in Yazoo City); choreographer John Butler, journalist Clavin Cox; filmmaker/producer Jim Dollarhide; bluesmen Calvin "Fuzz" Jones, Eddie "Guitar Slim" Jones, Walter "Furry" Lewis & Hubert Sumlin; R&B singer Betty Everett, Four-Star Admiral Means Johnston, Jr.; jazz pianist Mulgrew Miller; actresses Carrie Nye and Tonea Stewart; pro football great Kent Hull; and pro baseball manager Clay Hopper (managed Jackie Robinson); pro baseball player Frank White; novelist Donna Tartt (reared in Grenada); and hot air balloon designer Joseph P. Seawright (his brother, electronic sculptor James L. Seawright, Jr., was born in Jackson, but reared in Greenwood).

GRENADA (GRENADA COUNTY) GRENADA TOURISM COUNCIL (800-373-2571)
Known as Pittsburgh from Feb. 28, 1834 until the name was changed to Grenada on Mar. 29, 1836. Grenada Historical Museum has one of the best collections of Indian artifacts in Miss., Poplar St. FREE; Grenada Lake Visitors Center Museum features Indian and Civil War artifacts, Loop 333, Corps of Engineers Bldg., FREE (662-226-5911); 100 sq.-mi. Grenada Lake; ANNUAL EVENT: Thunder on the Water show & festival in June featuring boats races, antique car show, beauty pageant, arts/crafts, fireworks, hot air balloons, 5K walk & big-name entertainment (662-227-1156);...

Tourist Attractions in Mississippi

GRENADA (Continued)
...NEARBY: Hugh White State Park, one mile off Highway 8, just five miles east of Grenada (662-226-4934). FAMOUS PEOPLE born here: saxophonists Ace Cannon & Frank Wright; college football great Jake Gibbs; U.S. Sen. Trent Lott (reared in Pascagoula); William Winter, Gov. of Mississippi 1980-84; bluesmen Walter Davis, Magic Sam, Magic Slim & Billy Stepney; and gospel singer W.C. Taylor. Novelist Donna Tartt (born in Greenwood) grew up here.

GULPORT (HARRISON COUNTY)   MISS. GULF COAST CONVENTION/VISITORS BUREAU **(888-896-6796)**
(All phone nos. Area Code 228). Gillespie Art Gallery with a permanent collection of Mississippi art, William Carey College Campus at 1856 Beach Dr., FREE (865-1500); the Lynn Meadow's Discovery Center (est. May 1998), Mississippi's first children's museum, is not only a "hands-on," but an "ears-and-eyes-open" fun and learning place for children, their families and teachers with activities, playsets & themed areas galore. Designated the Mississippi Travel Attraction of the Year in 1999 by the Governor's Conference on Tourism, 246 Dolan Ave. [Admission](897-6039); Grass Lawn, southern summer home built in 1836, at 720 E Beach Blvd. (864-5019); Marine Life Oceanarium with dolphin and sea lion shows, underwater dive shows, touch pool, bird show in Aqua Stadium, and narrated 25-minute train tour of Gulfport, also Small Craft Harbor, Joseph T. Jones Memorial Park off Hwy 90 (863-0651); Gulf Islands Nat'l. Seashore; Fort Massachusetts, a Civil War fort constructed in 1858 is on Ship Island in the Gulf, daily cruises from the Gulfport Yacht Harbor, hwy. 90 at hwy. 45 (864-1014); the Gulf Coast Winery (muscadine wine), at 1306 29th Ave., FREE wine tasting and tours (800-401-9463); seafood festivals and casino gambling year 'round. FAMOUS PEOPLE born here: pro basketball player Chris Jackson (Mahmoud Abdul-Rauf); Pro Football Hall of Famer Lem Barney; major league baseball player Gerald Walker; actors Don Jeffcoat & Symba Smith; rock guitarist Jaimoe Jai Johanny; bluesmen Jimmy Donley, Albennie Jones & Sollie McElroy and guitarist Lloyd Wells (grew up in Laurel).

HATTIESBURG (FORREST COUNTY)   CONVENTION/VISITORS BUREAU **(601-268-3220 or 800-638-6877)**
(All phone nos. Area Code 601). First named Twin Forks by Indians and traders. Known as the "Hub City." Historic Neighborhoods: four districts listed on the National Register of Historic Places; *The Spirit That Builds Mural* at the Hattiesburg Public Library, 329 Hardy St., FREE (582-4461, www.hptc.lib.ms.us); Arts Council's permanent collection featuring Mississippi artists, at Saenger Center, downtown (583-6005); historic Saenger Theatre, now restored, features the original Mahler pipe organ, Front St., downtown (545-4500); Lucille Parker Art Gallery at William Carey College, 498 Tuscan Ave. (582-6192); The Carey Dinner Theatre and Madrigal Dinner and Theatre Productions at William Carey College (582-6221); The deGrummond Children's Literature Research Center with the world's largest collection of original manuscripts of children's books, housed in the McCain Library at the University of Southern Miss., which also houses the Tennessee Ernie Ford Collection of 2,000 musical arrangements, original manuscripts, recordings and kinescopes, on the campus at USM (266-4349); USM Art Museum featuring the best known Miss. artists FREE (266-4972); All-American Rose Garden on the front lawn at the USM campus, FREE (266-4491); The Studio, a gallery of contemporary art, FREE (545-8534); the George Robert Hall Air Park, dedicated to POW's & MIA's, at Bobby Chain Municipal Airport, FREE (545-4655); ANNUAL EVENTS: USM Coca-Cola Classic Rodeo, PRCA- sanctioned rodeo, last of Apr.; Old Time Festival with 5K run and one-mile fun run/walk, arts, crafts, food, 3 stages of entertainment, a military display and an antique engine/tractor show, weekend before Mother's Day in downtown, FREE (296-7600); TurtleFest arts & crafts, food vendors, KidsFest and a grand finale fireworks display, around July 4th at the Turtle Creek Mall, FREE (794-1011); HubFest with arts & crafts, food vendors and 3 stages of entertainment, in Oct. in downtown, FREE (296-7500); Holiday Fantasy shopping event with 80 booths, weekend before Thanksgiving in Nov. at the Hattiesburg Lake Terrace Convention Ctr., FREE admission (296-7500); Hattiesburg Zoo at Kamper Park hosts the Holiday Lights Zoofari each Dec. (545-4576). NEARBY: Bizzy Bee Farms, muscadines, blueberries, blackberries and honey, 640 Harold Tucker Rd. in the Dixie community, FREE (264-3613); Camp Shelby Armed Forces Museum, 12 miles S of Hattiesburg, South Gate, Bldg. 350, Camp Shelby, FREE (558-2757); Paul B. Johnson State Park with a 225-acre lake, 15 miles S of Hattiesburg on Hwy 49 (582-7721). FAMOUS PEOPLE born here: military heroes Henry A. Comminskey, Jr., Medal of Honor recipient (MOH recipient Jack Lucas now lives here), and Jesse Leroy Brown, the nation's first black naval aviator; jazz trumpetist Bobby Bryant; journalist Robert H. "Ace" Cleveland, Jr.; bluesman Blind John Davis; blueswoman "Mississippi Matilda" Witherspoon; beauty queen/actress Dorothy Dell; basketball coach Tim Floyd; basketball player Danny Manning; Evelyn Gandy, the state's first woman Lt. Gov.; major league baseball player Charlie Hayes; actor Eddie Hodges; the late philanthropist/ humanitarian Oseola McCarty; college/pro basketball great Purvis Short; Miss Mississippi, singer and TV personality Nan Sumrall; and checkers champion Charles C. Walker. Paul B. Johnson, Jr., Gov. of Miss. 1964-68, was born in Hattiesburg and both he and his father (born in Scott Co.), also Gov. of Miss. (1940-43), are buried here in the Oaklawn (City) Cemetery.

HERNANDO (DESOTO COUNTY)   DESOTO COUNTY CONVENTION & VISITORS BUREAU **(888-280-9120)**
First known as Jefferson. Casino gambling galore is nearby in northern Tunica County in the Robinsonville area; FAMOUS PEOPLE born here: guitarist Earl Bell, Bluesmen George "Mojo" Buford, George "Wild Child" Butler, Jim Jackson, and Robert Wilkins. Rock 'n Roll legend Jerry Lee Lewis lives in nearby Nesbit.

HOLLANDALE (Washington County)   WASHINGTON CO. CONVENTION/VISITORS BUREAU **(800-467-3582)**
Five miles west of Hollandale beside Mississippi Hwy 12 is Leroy Percy State Park (662-827-5436). Super songwriter Ben Peters, born in Greenville, grew up in Hollandale. Soul singer Ruby Andrews was born here.

Tourist Attractions in Mississippi

HOLLY SPRINGS (MARSHALL COUNTY)   **HOLLY SPRINGS CHAMBER OF COMMERCE (662-252-2942)**
(All phone numbers are Area Code 662). First called Suavatooky, or "watering place" by the Chickasaw Indians for the spring that bubbled up in a grove of holly. The original post office here was established on Dec. 7, 1835, two years before Marshall County was formed. The state's second oldest pilgrimage city (after Natchez) offers antebellum homes tours during an annual pilgrimage in April; the Kate Freeman Clark Memorial Art Gallery with the largest single collection of paintings by a single artist (Freeman Clark) in the world, located at 292 E College Ave. (252-4211); Marshall County Historical Museum at 220 E. College Ave. (252-3669); state headquarters for the National Audubon Society with a wildlife sanctuary on the 2,400-acre old Strawberry Plains plantation, located just a few blocks off the downtown square, ask for directions; Graceland Too at 200 E Golson Ave. with a huge private collection of Elvis Presley memorabilia (252-7954); ANNUAL EVENTS: the Kudzu Festival & Barbecue with carnival, live music, arts & crafts and more, first weekend in Aug. (252-2943); Northeast Mississippi Blues & Gospel Folk Festival is held the 2nd Saturday in Sept. (252-4661). NEARBY: 8 miles south of Holly Springs on Mississippi Hwy 7 is Wall Doxey State Park (252-4231). FAMOUS PEOPLE born here: artist Kate Freeman Clark (mentioned above); R&B singers & cousins Mel Hardin and Tim McPherson (duo Mel & Tim); bluesman Sylvester "Syl" Johnson; blues guitarists Jimmy Johnson & Mose Vinson; and civil rights activist Ida Bell Wells-Barnett.

INDIANOLA (SUNFLOWER COUNTY)   **INDIANOLA CHAMBER OF COMMERCE (662-887-4454)**
First known as Indian Bayou, then Belingate, then Eureka. The B.B. King Homecoming is the first weekend every June (662-887-4455). B.B. King, although born in nearby Itta Bena, spent a lot of time here in his youth. FAMOUS PEOPLE born here: actress Mary Alice; bluesmen Willie Clayton, Louis "Mr. Bo" Collins, "Jazz" Gillum, Albert King & Beau Shelby; saxophonist Brew Moore; horticulturist/writer Felder Rushing; and writer Steve Yarbrough.

ISSAQUENA COUNTY
Fitler Plantation, the largest cottonwood tree plantation in the world. Issaquena is the least populated county in Miss.

IUKA (TISHOMINGO COUNTY)   **TISHOMINGO COUNTY TOURISM COUNCIL (800-386-4373)**
Old Tishomingo County Courthouse, the original built in 1870, burned in 1886, rebuilt in 1889 and listed on the National Register of Historic Places, it now houses a public museum, FREE, (662-423-1017); also old mansions; mineral springs; Woodall Mountain, the highest point in the state (806 feet) is located 2 miles south of Iuka off Hwy 25; J. P. Coleman State Park 13 miles north of Iuka off Hwy 25 on the Tennessee River at Pickwick Lake (662-423-4516).

JACINTO (ALCORN COUNTY)
Courthouse completed in 1854, on the National Register of Historic Places, FREE (662-286-8662).

JACKSON (HINDS COUNTY)   **JACKSON CONVENTION & VISITORS BUREAU (800-354-7695)**
(All phone numbers for Jackson are Area Code 601). First known as LeFleur's Bluff. The State Capitol (359-3114); Governor's Mansion (359-3175); Old State Capital Historical Museum, where there are 30,000 catalogued items, FREE (359-6920); Mississippi Department of Archives and History, 100 S. State St. FREE (359-6850); War Memorial Building; Jackson City Hall, built in 1847 and one of the few buildings to survive the Civil War, at 219 S President St., FREE (960-1084); The Fire Museum at 355 Woodrow Wilson with educational center and an operational fire station, FREE, but open on request only (call 960-1610 to arrange tours); Mynelle Gardens at 4736 Clinton Blvd. features near 1,000 varieties of botanical plants on 6 acres (960-1894); Mississippi Arts Center including Ballet Mississippi (960-1560). Jackson is one of 4 world cities chosen to host the IBC ballet competition sponsored by the International Theatre Institute Dance Committee. It is rotated among the cities and thus held every 4 years in Jackson—last in 1998 and again in 2002 (355-9853); Ballet Magnificat, 5406 I-55 N (977-1001); Mississippi Museum of Art (960-1515); Smith-Robertson Museum & Cultural Center (960-1457); Black Arts Music Society, 4110 W. Capitol St. (354-1049); the Mississippi Crafts Center at Ridgeland (856-7546); Craftsmen's Guild of Mississippi on Millsaps College Campus. The Guild sponsors the Chimneyville Craft Festival the first weekend in Dec. every year at the Mississippi Trade Mart (981-0019); Arts Alliance of Jackson/Hinds County at 255 E. Pascagoula (960-1557); Mississippi Cultural Arts Coalition (355-2787); Municipal Art Gallery (960-1582); Bryant (art) Galleries at 2845 Lakeland Drive (932-1993); Pearl River Studio/Gallery at 142 Millsaps Ave. FREE (355-0555); Brown's Fine Art (gallery), 630 Fondren Place (982-1900); Gaddis Group Gallery at 4330 N. State St. (981-3150); Twilight Gallery at 101 Upton Dr. FREE (922-6212); Southern Breeze Gallery in Highland Village at 4500 I-55 N., works featured are all by Mississippi artists FREE (982-4222); The F.D. Hall Art Gallery at Jackson State University Music Building, FREE (968-2040); Mississippi Opera Association (960-2300); Jackson Symphony Orchestra (960-1565); New Stage Theatre (948-3531); W. Kessler Ltd., Broadway & off-Broadway productions at Thalia Mara Hall (981-1847); Thalia Mara Hall [Jackson Municipal Auditorium] at 255 E. Pascagoula St. (960-1537); Lefleur's Bluff State Park Golf Course (362-3885); Mississippi Museum of Natural Science at LeFleur's Bluff State Park just off Lakeland Drive, FREE (354-7303); The Oaks, Jackson's oldest house (982-4442); Manship House (961-4724); Russell C. Davis Planetarium & Ronald McNair Space Theater, where you can learn about the Universe with movies, laser-light shows & more (960-1550); The Jackson Zoological Park (the Jackson Zoo), 2918 W. Capitol St. with 430 animals on 110 acres, miniature train ride (352-2580); Mississippi Sports Hall of Fame and Museum at 1170 Lakeland Dr. (982-8264); Mississippi Memorial Stadium (354-6021); lots of boating and recreation at the Ross Barnett Reservoir covering 50 square miles (354-3448);

Tourist Attractions in Mississippi

JACKSON (Continued)
ANNUAL EVENTS: Mississippi Coliseum and Fairgrounds: the Racing Vehicle Extravaganza, the 2nd weekend in Jan; Dixie National Rodeo & Livestock Show, nearly 3 weeks in Feb. & State Fair in Oct. (961-4000) and the annual Mississippi Equine Extravaganza in mid-Nov; the Tour LeFleur pro cyclist race, the second longest of its kind in the country, during the last weekend in May; Jim Buck Ross Agricultural & Forestry Museum (713-3365) which has festivals and celebrations throughout the year, and notably a big Independence Day Celebration July 4th and the barbecue contest, Hog Wild in July during the 3rd weekend in July; Mal's St. Paddy's Parade, third Sat. in March; Jubilee Jam, Mississippi's largest street party with entertainment galore, held the 3rd weekend in May (960-2008); the Mississippi Wildlife Federation's annual "Wildlife Extravaganza," the state's premier hunting, fishing and outdoor show. This 3-day consumer event features seminars, demonstrations, equipment displays and competitions such as the Big Buck contest and fishing contest, held at the Trade Mart the first weekend in Aug; Farish Street Hertiage Festival (blues) is held on Fri. & Sat. in mid-Sept. (960-2384); Jackson State Homecoming Parade, probably the state's biggest parade (968-2272); and Mistletoe Marketplace, the Junior League of Jackson's holiday shopping extravaganza at the Miss. Trade Mart, held the 1st or 2nd week of Nov, Admission (948-2357). FAMOUS PEOPLE born here: major league baseball players Chet Lemon & Dave Parker; pro basketball player Joe Courtney; basketball great Syvia Krebs (reared in Forest); pro football players Edwin "Goat" Hale & Jackie Slater; football coach Bobby Wallace; corporate CEOs James Barksdale, Richard McRae, Sr., Bob Pittman & Joe Frank Sanderson; entrepreneur Will Primos; country singer/songwriter Fred Knobloch; jurist Rueben Anderson; NASA administrator Clifford Charlesworth; journalists Dick Armstrong & Charles Overby; magazine publisher Alyce Alston; inventors Harry Cole & Paul Brammett; jazz guitarist Henry "Skeets" McWilliams; jazz musicians Richard Jess Brown, Teddy Edwards, Dick Griffin (born in nearby Fannin) & Jimmy Henderson; jazz singer Cassandra Wilson (Fowlkes); drummer Freddie Waits; choreographer Hollis Pippin; opera singer Eleni Matos; conductor/composer Lehman Engel; actors Kelly Brown, Robert Harper & Byron Thames; actresses Cynthia Geary, Alice Haining, Ernestine Wade, & Rebecca Walker; dramatists Beth Henley & John Maxwell; movie director Tom Rice; racecar driver Lake Speed; soul singer Dorothy Moore; bluesmen Sam Baker, Columbus Brooks, Andrew Brown, Mel Brown, "Warren" Lee Jackson, Little Johnny Jones, "Papa" Charlie McCoy, McKinley Mitchell, William "Dead Eye" Norris, James "The Black Lone Ranger" Ramsey, Eddie Rasberry, John "Mississippi Johnny Waters" Sandifer, Buddy Scott, King S. Solomon, Otis Spann, Melvin Taylor, Dave Thompson, Leon Washington, Carl Weathersby & "Boogie' Bill Webb; musician Carson Whitsett; blues/ R&B record producers Al Benson & Al Goodman; artists James L. Seawright (reared in Greenwood) & Elizabeth Wolfe; architect/entertainment executive Janet Marie Smith; and writers David Blankenhorn, Anne Carsley, Forrest Lamar Cooper, Richard Ford, Willie Morris (reared in Yazoo City), Mildred D. Taylor & Eudora Welty.

KOSCIUSKO (ATTALA COUNTY)   KOSCIUSKO TOURISM PROMOTION COUNCIL **(662-289-2981)**
Kosciusko was previously known by many names including Red Bud Springs, Peking, Paris and Attala. The Kosciusko Museum and Visitors' Center, at the junction of 35S and Natchez Trace Parkway, FREE; the Natchez Trace Festival and Fiddler's Jamboree the last weekend in Apr. has Arts & Crafts show, flea market, children's play, 10K run, fiddling contest and music; the Annual Fall Gospel Music Jubilee, 2nd Saturday in Sept. FAMOUS PEOPLE born here: Oprah Winfrey, talk-show queen, actress and the world's richest female entertainer, gospel singer Becca Jackson; civil rights activist James Meredith; blues/jazz musician Charlie Musselwhite; bluesman J.D. Suggs, and National Geographic writer/administrator Carolyn Bennett Patterson. Entrepreneur Dumas Milner, who became a wealthy Jackson-based businessman, was born near Kosciusko in Attala County.

LAUREL (JONES COUNTY)   JONES COUNTY CHAMBER OF COMMERCE **(601-428-0574)**
Laurel's Central Historic District has over 360 buildings listed on the National Register of Historic Places; A collection of fine European and Japanese art and one of the finest and largest (about 800) collections of Native American Baskets in the world is in the Lauren-Rogers Memorial Museum of Art, 5th Ave. at 7th St., Mississippi's first art museum and one of only 12 museums in the U.S. founded as memorials to individuals. The museum is also noted for its collection of English Georgian Silver, FREE (601-659-6374, www.lrma.org); Veterans Memorial Museum; Sam Lindsey's model train collection at the Hobby Corner, 1535 N. 1st St. (649-4501); east of Laurel in the Landrum community is Trapper's Gator Farm & Petting Barn with animals such as deer, snakes, birds, bobcats, on Hwy 15S (601-428-4967). FAMOUS PEOPLE born here: pop singer Lance Bass (with group 'N Sync); actor Ray Walston; Olympians Ralph Boston & Lee Calhoun, potter Obie Earl Clark, jazz guitarist/composer James Mundell Lowe, blues harp players Roland "Blue Boy" Hayes & Sam Myers; opera great Leontyne Price (and her brother George Baker Price, the first black U.S. Army general from Miss.); and Medal of Honor recipient James D. Slaton. With two other Medal of Honor recipients born in Jones County — Roy Mitchell Wheat in Moselle and Ira C. Welborn in Mico (now Shady Grove) — the county claims more MOH recipients than any other Mississippi county. Guitarist Lloyd Wells, born in Gulfport, grew up here.

LELAND (WASHINGTON COUNTY)   WASHINGTON CO. CONVENTION/VISITORS BUREAU **(800-467-3582)**
Jim Henson Muppets Museum. Leland was birthplace to Kermit, who was once "just a tadpole in Deer Creek." Henson, born in Greenville, grew up here; Deer Creek Recreational Park; FAMOUS PEOPLE born here: blues guitarist Johnny Winter, blues drummer Junior Blackman, jazz trumpeter Leo "Wadada" Smith; rock singer Joe Frank Carollo, soul singer Thelma Houston, and actor John Daniel "J.D." Evermore (John Moore).

Tourist Attractions in Mississippi

LEXINGTON (HOLMES COUNTY)   HOLMES COUNTY CHAMBER OF COMMERCE (662-834-3372)
Booker-Thomas Museum of life in the early days, on State Hwy 12W, donation (662-834-2672). FAMOUS PEOPLE born here include several bluesmen: Lonnie Pitchford, Rasberry "Raz" Rosby, James Scott, Jr. & Otis "Big Smokey" Smothers; two Medal of Honor recipients — John C. Black, a Medal of Honor recipient during the Civil War was born here & Milton L. Olive, III, a posthumous Medal of Honor recipient during the Vietnam War, was born in Chicago, but grew up about 6 miles from here about halfway between Lexington and Ebenezer and is buried in that area in the West Grove Missionary Baptist Church Cemetery. Edmond F. Noel, Gov. of Miss. 1908-12, was born near Lexington.

LIBERTY (AMITE COUNTY)   LIBERTY AREA CHAMBER OF COMMERCE (601-657-8011)
The Amite Co. Courthouse (1838), listed on the National Register of Historic Places, is the oldest operating courthouse in the state, corner of Hwys 24 & 48, FREE (601-657-8022); Liberty Presbyterian Church, used as a Union hospital during the Civil War. Outside the church stands the first monument to the Confederacy, built in 1871, North Church St., FREE (601-657-8077); Little Red Schoolhouse with museum, on Hwy 569 (Old Jackson Rd.), FREE (601-657-8077); Jerry Clower Museum, 10 miles east of Liberty, full of memorabilia belonging to the late humorist, who was born in Eastfork (601-684-8130). Will D. Campbell, minister, Civil Rights activist and writer was also born in Eastfork. Newspaper columnist and writer Mamie Davis Willoughby (pen name Rose Budd Stevens) was born near Liberty.

LORMAN (JEFFERSON COUNTY)
First known as Lick. Alcorn State Univ., the oldest land-grant college for blacks in the U.S., Hwy 61, (601-877-6130); Canemount Plantation, built in 1855, Hwy 552W (800-423-0684); the Ruins of Windsor — the large columns are the only remains of the largest antebellum home ever built in the state after it burned, Hwy 552W, FREE (601-437-4351).

LOUISVILLE (WINSTON COUNTY)   LOUISVILLE/WINSTON CO. CHAMBER OF COMMERCE (662-773-3921)
American Hertiage "Big Red" Fire Museum at 332 N. Church St., at couple of dozen old fire engines & several hundred pieces of firefighting equipment. FREE (662-773-3421); Legion State Park near Louisville on Old Hwy 25 (662-773-8323). FAMOUS PEOPLE born here: songwriter Carl Jackson and singer/TV personality Lisa Stewart.

LUCEDALE (GEORGE COUNTY)
The Gingham Tree Arts & Crafts show with more than 300 exhibitors, 2nd Sat. in Nov; Palestine Gardens, 12 miles N of Lucedale & 6.5 miles east of Hwy 98, featuring a miniature one-yard-per-mile scale depiction (representing 400 miles on 20 acres) of the Holy Lands such as Jericho, Bethlehem & Jerusalem during the time of Christ (601-947-8422). FAMOUS PEOPLE born here: college basketball player & Harlem Globetrotter, Robert Fairley, college/pro football player Eric Moulds and musician (drummer) Ben Wells.

MACON (NOXUBEE COUNTY)   NOXUBEE COUNTY CHAMBER OF COMMERCE (662-726-4456)
Old Jail Museum (1907), on National Register of Historic Places & Miss. Landmark, FREE (662-726-5461); Noxubee County Historical Society Museum on the Courthouse grounds across from the public library (662-726-5110); Sunshine Farms petting/feeding farm, off hwy. 45, E on Prairie Point Rd. 5 miles (662-726-2264); Touch of Country crafts shop (662-726-4392). FAMOUS PEOPLE born here: bluesmen Carey Bell, Jesse Fortune & Eddy Clearwater; gospel singer "Brother" Joe May; and novelist Ben Ames Williams.

MADISON (MADISON COUNTY)   MADISON CHAMBER OF COMMERCE (601-856-7060)
(Phone nos. Area Code 601). 10 miles N of Jackson; 5 buildings are listed on the National Register of Historic Places: Chapel of the Cross (c. 1850), Strawberry Patch House, Hoy House, Montgomery House and old Madison-Ridgeland High School & Gym; the Madison County Cultural Center and Madison Civic Ballet, 2103 Main St. (853-0291); the Simmons Arboretum, a 10-acre refuge for native trees & other plants, located on St. Augustine Rd., off Hwy 51N (856-1660); Natchez Trace (842-1572); Ross Barnett Reservoir (354-3448); ANNUAL EVENTS: Strawberry Pops Concert, Apr; Mississippi Wing of the Confederate Air Force Open House with vintage aircraft, May (981-0291); Heatwave Classic Triathlon, June (856-8894); Liberty Antique Festival & Classic Car Show, July; Cajun Festival, mid-Sept. at St. Francis of Assisi Catholic Church (856-5556); and Germanfest at nearby Gluckstadt, Sept. (856-4977).

MAGEE (SIMPSON COUNTY)   MAGEE CHAMBER OF COMMERCE (601-849-2517)
First known as Mangum. Annual event: Crazy Day includes square dancing and clogging, antique car show, sky divers, helicopter rides, train rides, puppet show, folk arts, arts/crafts, barbecue, live entertainment, 3rd weekend in Aug. (601-849-2517). College/pro football player/coach Roland Dale and pro football player Kris Mangum were born here.

McCOMB (PIKE COUNTY)   PIKE COUNTY CHAMBER OF COMMERCE (601-684-2291)
First known as Elizabethtown. Nearby: Dixie Springs Lake, on Hwy 51 north of McComb, has one of the few waterfalls in the state; Percy Quin State Park, 6 miles south of McComb (601-684-3938) with Quail Hollow 27-hole golf course, 1-888-GOLFMIS (1-888-465-3647). FAMOUS PEOPLE born in McComb include: jazz guitarist Steve Balilock; R&B great Bo Diddley; bluemen Joe "King Solomon Hill" Holmes & Vasti "Vas-Tie" Jackson; actor Jimmy Boyd; soul singer Brandy (Norwood) and her brother, actor Willie "Ray-J" Norwood, Jr.; newspaperman John O. Emmerich, Jr.; singer/songwriter/conservationist Paul Ott; screenwriter Will Price; country songwriter Dan Tyler; and TV personality Woodie Assaf, weatherman on WLBT-TV in Jackson. Singer/dancer Britney Spears, born in nearby Kentwood, Louisiana, attended school at Parklane Academy in McComb and spent a lot of time in that city.

Tourist Attractions in Mississippi

MERIDIAN (LAUDERDALE COUNTY) **LAUDERDALE COUNTY TOURISM BUREAU (888-868-7720)**
(All phone numbers are Area Code 601). Was known as Sowashee for a short time. Giant Peavey Electronics plant, the Peavey Visitors Center & Museum, 711 A St., FREE (486-1460); the U.S. Naval jet training base for Navy and Marine Corps pilots is open to the public (advance reservations); the Jimmie Rodgers Memorial & Museum (485-1808); the Meridian Museum of Art, on the National Register of Historic Places and Mississippi Landmark, FREE (693-1501); Grand Opera House, on the National Register of Historic Places and state Historic Landmark (693-5239); Walk-About-Meridian Historical Downtown Tour (485-1997); Highland Park Carousel, the only Dentzel carousel in the U.S., National Landmark and on the National Register of Historic Places (485-1850); the Key Brothers Aviation Pictorial Exhibit, at Meridian Regional Airport (Key Field) Hwy 11S, FREE (482-0364); Collectors Car Museum (693-3313); the Rose Hill Cemetery with graves of the Gypsy King and Queen, (483-0083); Okatibbee Water Park (737-2370). ANNUAL EVENTS: The Jimmie Rodgers Memorial Festival, the week that includes May 26, the anniversary of Rodgers death in 1933 (483-5763); Main Street Salutes the Blues Festival in mid-July kicks off the Chunky Rhythm & Blues Festival, complete with European-style beer garden & street dance (485-1996); the Weschler Community Arts Center Expo features a talent show, arts & crafts, live music & food, held end of Aug. (485-8882). NEARBY: Causeyville General Store, on State Hwy 19, eight miles south of Meridian, built in 1895, features musical museum & grist mill, FREE (644-3102); Sam Dale Historic Site, 15 miles north of Meridian off Hwy 39 at Daleville (961-5014). In addition to Jimmie Rodgers, other FAMOUS PEOPLE born here: Miss America Susan Diane Akin; country singer Moe Bandy; historian/writer Howard Bahr; actors Brendon Boone, Alvin Childress, Phil Gordon, Wilbur Higby & James Wheaton; singer/songwriter Paul Davis; folk singer/songwriter Steve Forbert; major league baseball player Dennis "Oil Can" Boyd; creator of the comic strip *Buz Sawyer*, Edwin Phillips Granberry; novelist Barry Hannah, actresses Diane Ladd and Sela Ward, movie costume designer Herschel McCoy, NASA engineer/administrator Richard Mayo; pro basketball player Derrick McKey; Mississippi Sports Hall of Famers Eric McNair (major league baseball), Dr. Walter Reed (coach), and Mike Taylor (amateur golf champ); football great Shorty McWilliams; former Congressman G.V. "Sonny" Montgomery; CEO Hartley Peavey; government administrator Joe Price; director and founder of New Stage Theatre in Jackson, Jane Reid-Petty; pioneering surgeon Leslie Vaughn Rush; soul singers David Ruffin & Al Wilson; blues people Cleo Brown, George Cummings & Louvette Jackson; and writer Brad Watson.

MIZE (SMITH COUNTY)
A big Watermelon Festival held every July with largest melon contest, arts & crafts, live country and gospel music, crowning of the Watermelon Queen, etc. (601-733-5478).

MONTICELLO (LAWRENCE COUNTY) **LAWRENCE COUNTY CHAMBER OF COMMERCE (601-587-3007)**
The Longino House, c. 1884, home of Governor A.H. Longino, who was born in Monticello in 1855 and was governor from Jan. 16, 1900 to Jan. 19, 1904, is fully restored, contains a museum, and is listed on the National Register of Historic Places, 136 Caswell St. (601-587-7732); The Armstrong-Lee House, c. 1856, a 4-room dog-trot house, listed on the National Register of Historic Places and Mississippi Landmark, Hwy 43 one mile north of Arm, FREE (601-886-7128); Fox House, Greek Revival Cottage built in 1848, privately owned, Old Hwy 27 at Wanilla (601-587-7175). FAMOUS PEOPLE born here: bluesmen J.B. Lenoir and Byther Smith; and racecar driver Jim Pace.

MOORHEAD (SUNFLOWER COUNTY) **MOORHEAD CHAMBER OF COMMERCE (662-246-5461)**
First established as a town (pop. 437) on May 24, 1905. Of great interest to blues fans everywhere because it's "Where the Southern crosses the Yellow Dog," immortalized in W.C. Handy's *Yellow Dog Blues*, where the Southern Railroad (Columbus & Greenville) meets with the Yazoo & Mississippi Valley = Yazoo & Delta = Y.D. = Yellow Dog. Bluesman Charlie Booker and country singer/comedian Johnny Russell were born here.

MORGANTOWN (MARION COUNTY) **MARION COUNTY CHAMBER OF COMMERCE (601-736-6385)**
Just west of Columbia, there's colorful Red Bluff, a miniature canyon 300 feet deep, often called "The Grand Canyon of Mississippi." It's on private property, so view it from State Highway 587.

MORTON (SCOTT COUNTY) **MORTON CHAMBER OF COMMERCE (601-732-6135)**
Roosevelt State Park bordering a 150-acre lake is 4 miles S of Morton off hwy 13, take exit 25 off I-20 (601-732-6316).

MOUNT OLIVE (COVINGTON COUNTY) **COVINGTON COUNTY CHAMBER OF COMMERCE (601-765-6012)**
Dry Creek Water Park (601-797-4619); near Mt. Olive on State Hwy 532, are the farms of Bill Diehl, William Diehl & Robert Jamison in the Old Order German Baptist Community. They have a lifestyle and dress similar to the Amish. Homemade goodies & hand-crafted furniture for sale. FAMOUS PEOPLE born here include: bluesman Sterling Magee; football great Steve "Air" McNair; and football player/coach and Mississippi Sports Hall of Famer, Ray Perkins.

NATCHEZ (ADAMS COUNTY) **NATCHEZ CONVENTION & VISITORS BUREAU (800-647-6724)**
(All phone numbers are Area Code 601). The largest number of antebellum structures in the U.S., 600 structures, including 100 houses, on the Nat'l. Register of Historic Places; antebellum homes tours including Ravennaside Historical Party House (442-8015), the Monmouth Plantation at 36 Melrose Ave., (442-5852 or 800-828-4831) along with hundreds more homes. Pilgrimages and tours throughout the year plus the annual Natchez Christmas Pilgrimage with daily tours of homes is held during the last half of December (446-6631 or 800-647-6724); Grand Village of the

Tourist Attractions in Mississippi

Natchez Indians, FREE (446-6502); the state's oldest Masonic Lodge, Harmony Lodge #1, est. Aug. 14, 1818; the Natchez Museum of Afro-American History & Culture, 307A Market St. (445-0728); the Natchez City Cemetery (800-647-6724); the Natchez National Cemetery (445-4981); the oldest known death date cut on a tombstone in Mississippi is that of William Gilbert, who died Nov. 16, 1796, and is located in the Foster Mound Cemetery; Natchez National Historical Park, est. 1988 — 108 acres of mansions, townhouses, and villas related to the history of Natchez (442-7047); Old South (muscadine) Winery, tasting tours available, at 65 S Concord Ave. (445-9924); Natchez Under-the-Hill, historic district famous as 19th century flatboat and steamboat landing, FREE (446-6345); ANNUAL EVENTS: Natchez Bicycle Classic also includes "Best Legs" contest, street dance & more, late June; Steamboat Jubilee & Floozie Contest, a flirt-off between the floozies of the Delta Queen and the Mississippi Queen winds up the annual 12-day race between the two steamboats, late June; the annual Great Mississippi River Balloon Race with hot air balloons, fireworks, music, 3rd weekend in Oct.; and casino gambling year 'round. NEARBY: 6 miles E of Natchez at Washington (once the state capital) is Historic Jefferson College, on the National Register of Historic Places (442-2901); 10 miles NE of Natchez is Emerald Mound on the Natchez Trace, the second largest Indian mound in the U.S., built about 1300 A.D. by ancestors of Creek, Choctaw and Natchez Indians, it covers 8 acres, FREE (445-4211); Natchez State Park, 10 miles north of Natchez off U.S. 61 at Stanton (442-2658); FAMOUS PEOPLE born here: record producer/songwriter Glen Ballard; Civil War Medal of Honor recipient Wilson Brown; historian J.F.H. Claiborne; silent screen actors Frank Cooley & Martha Mattox; novelists Ellen Douglas, Neil McGaughey, and Richard Wright; country singer Mickey Gilley; bluesmen Brint Anderson, Jimmy Anderson, "King Ernest" Baker, Alexander Lightfoot & "Hound Dog" Taylor; modern jazz artist Marion Montgomery; football greats Hugh Green & Billy Shaw, in the Miss. Sports Hall of Fame; and Miss America 1960, Lynda Lee Mead. Three governors were born near Natchez: Gerald C. Brandon, first native-born Mississippian to be governor; John I. Guion (1851); and Bill Allain, governor 1984-88 was born at Washington, just outside Natchez.

NEWTON (NEWTON COUNTY)   **NEWTON CHAMBER OF COMMERCE (601-683-2201)**
Newton Station Depot was burned during the Civil War, but rebuilt in 1905, a Mississippi Landmark and listed on the National Register of Historic Places, FREE (601-683-2201). Bluesman "Prez" Kenneth Kidd was born here. Writer and researcher James F. Brieger (*Hometown Mississippi*) and country/jazz guitarist Bob Saxton were born in Newton Co.

NITTA YUMA (Sharkey County)
A large granite monument with an engraving of the Ten Commandments just off Hwy 61.

NOXAPATER (WINSTON COUNTY)   **LOUISVILLE/WINSTON CO. CHAMBER OF COMMERCE (662-773-3921)**
Nanih Waiya Mound, sacred ground to the Choctaw Indians who consider it the birthplace of their race, listed on the National Register of Historic Places, 12 miles E of Noxapater on Route 39. Nanih Waiya Historic Site (662-773-7988).

OCEAN SPRINGS (JACKSON COUNTY)   **OCEAN SPRINGS CHAMBER OF COMMERCE (228-875-4424)**
(All phone numbers are Area Code 228). Fort Maurepas, a replica of the original built in 1699, corner Washington and Front Beach, FREE (875-4424); Gulf Islands National Seashore Visitors Center, 3500 Park Rd., FREE (875-9057); Walter Anderson Museum of Art at 510 Washington Ave., FREE (872-3164); Art Who? at 623 Washington Ave. (875-3251); Shearwater Pottery, home of the famous Anderson potters, FREE (875-7320); The Doll House, 1201 Hwy 90, hundreds of dolls, doll houses, and stuffed animals, donations (872-3971); the Mississippi Vietnam Veterans Memorial, beside the Ocean Springs Civic Center. Novelist/script writer Al Young were born here.

ONWARD (SHARKEY COUNTY)
The Onward Store on Hwy 61 about 25 miles north of Vicksburg, built in 1913, is located near the site where President Theodore Roosevelt, while on a hunt in 1902, refused to shoot a captured bear. That incident gave birth to the "Teddy Bear." The store displays photographs documenting the hunt.

OXFORD (LAFAYETTE COUNTY)   **OXFORD TOURISM COUNCIL (800-758-9177)**
(phone nos. are Area Code 662). Faulkner's home Rowan Oak (234-4651); Ole Miss (Univ. of Miss.) with much to be seen: the oldest book in the nation, an ancient Biblical manuscript in the library at Ole Miss, the Mississippi Collection with 15,000 catalogued books by Mississippi authors or about the state, and thousands of state documents and other historical & cultural items, the oldest bathtub in the western hemisphere in the archaeology museum, FREE (232-7378), the world's largest collection of Blues music is in the Blues Archive (232-7753), and the Center for the Study of Southern Culture is on campus along with the Barnard antebellum observatory FREE (232-5993); the Mary Buie Museum with an unusual collection of antique dolls and doll furniture, at 510 University Ave; St. Peter's Cemetery with the graves of L.Q.C. Lamar, William and John Faulkner, and Augustus B. Longstreet, former president of the Univ. of Miss.; Nearby on Hiway 7 is the shop of the late Mike McGregor, who worked as Elvis' jeweler (see Water Valley). ANNUAL EVENTS: The Oxford Double Decker Arts Festival with art vendors, a Children's Square Fair, live music and food, last weekend in April; the Faulkner and Yoknapatawpha Conference honoring Faulkner's works, a week-long schedule of activities during the last week of July and/or 1st week of August. FAMOUS PEOPLE born here include bluesman R.L. Burnside, TV and movie set designer Julie Kaye Fanton, and pioneering physician and world-renowned medical writer Dr. Arthur C. Guyton. Lee M. Russell, Gov. of Miss. from 1920-24, was born nearby in Lafayette Co. Educator, attorney and legal expert Dr. Jerome F. Leavell (b. in Blue Mountain, Miss.) grew up here and still lives here.

Tourist Attractions in Mississippi

PASCAGOULA (JACKSON COUNTY)   JACKSON CO. AREA CHAMBER OF COMMERCE (228-762-3391)
First known as Scranton. Ingalls Shipbuilding, the state's largest employer; the La Pointe-Krebs House and Old Spanish Fort, built in 1718, the oldest structure built by white men in the Mississippi Valley, probably the oldest structure of European manufacture between the Appalachians and the Rocky Mountains, now a museum, at 4602 Fort Ave. (228-769-1505); Scranton Floating Museum, a 70-foot commercial shrimp boat and River Park on the Pascagoula River, FREE (228-762-6017); FAMOUS PEOPLE born here: singer-songwriter Jimmy Buffett; R&B singer Margie Joseph; blues singer Libby Rae Watson; artist Eugenia Ann Talbott; college/pro basketball player Antonio Harvey; pro football player Aubrey D. Matthews; college football player and first Conerly Trophy winner Treg Thomas; major league baseball great, the late Harry "The Hat" Walker; and U.S. Senate sergeant-at-arms and doorkeeper Jim Ziglar. U.S. Senator Trent Lott, born in Grenada, grew up in Pascagoula.

PASS CHRISTIAN (HARRISON COUNTY)   MISS. GULF COAST CONVENTION/VITITORS BUREAU (888-896-6796)
Ossian Hall, old mansion; Dixie White House, visited by various presidents; Hillyer House at 207 East Senic Dr., with art, jewelry & pottery (228-452-4810); Seafood Festival held annually in mid-July (228-452-4686). FAMOUS PEOPLE born here: tenor sax player "Capt." John Handy and Pro football great Brett Farve (grew up in nearby Kiln).

PEARL (RANKIN COUNTY)   RANKIN FIRST (601-825-2268) / PEARL C. OF C. (601-939-3338)
Pearl Day Festival with bingo, fireworks, boxing matches, arts & crafts, cloggers, bluegrass, country & gospel music and more, last weekend in June (601-939-3338). Country music singer LeAnn Rimes was born in Pearl.

PETAL (FORREST COUNTY)   HATTIESBURG CONVENTION & VISITORS BUREAU (800-638-6877)
The International Checker Hall of Fame, located on Lynn Rae Road, operated by Charles Walker, Checkers Champion (601-582-7090); Colonel Amos McLemore Homestead, historic site dating to 1830, Hwy 11N (601-583-4994); Isaac Carter Cabin, built in 1846, at 1701 Old Richton Road, FREE (601-584-8279).

PHILADELPHIA (NESHOBA COUNTY)   PHIALDELPHIA/NESHOBA CO. CHAM. OF COMMERCE (601-656-1742)
Choctaw Indian Reservation; Choctaw Museum of Southern Indians, Hwy 16W, FREE (601-656-5251). ANNUAL EVENTS: The Choctaw Indian Fair in mid-July; the Neshoba County Fair, "Mississippi's Giant Houseparty®," held the first week of Aug., 9 miles SW of Philadelphia, the oldest campground fair in the U.S. (started in 1889). There are more than 500 rustic cabins and the week's events include horse harness races, professional rodeo, country bands, carnival rides, beauty pageant, and speeches by politicians from this state and elsewhere. Several Presidents have spoken here (601-656-1742); gambling at Silver Star — the only inland casino in the state (800-557-0711); NEARBY: the Nanih Waiya Historic Site, sacred mound of the Choctaws, dating back to the time of Christ, 20 miles N of Philadelphia off Hwy 21, FREE (601-773-7988). FAMOUS PEOPLE born here: college football player Marcus Dupree; college and pro football player and Miss. Sports Hall of Famer, the late J.T. "Blondy' Back, historian and head of Thomas Jefferson's Monticello home in Charlottesville, Va., Dr. Daniel P. Jordan; writer and photographer Florence Mars; Phillip Martin, Chief of the Miss. Band of Choctaw Indians; gaming industry entrepreneur William Silas "Si" Redd; bluesmen Lester "Mad Dog" Davenport & Otis Rush; journalist Sidney L. "Sid" Salter; and country singer Marty Stuart.

PICAYUNE (PEARL RIVER COUNTY)   GREATER PICAYUNE AREA CHAM. OF COMMERCE (601-798-3122)
First known as Hobolochitto. Was once the "Tung Oil Capital of the World." Crosby Arboretum with native flora of the Pearl River basin, 1801 Goodyear Blvd., (601-798-2311); Annual Fall Classic 10K Run, 5K raceway, one-mile fun run, held the first Sat. in Nov. (601-798-4881). Former world boxing champion Freddie Little was born in Picayune.

PICKENS (HOLMES COUNTY)   HOLMES COUNTY CHAMBER OF COMMERCE (662-834-3372)
Once known as Shiloh. Near Pickens is the Little Red Schoolhouse, the birthplace of the Order of the Eastern Star, an international Masonic order for women, listed on National Historic Register, off I-55 on Hwy 17N, FREE (472-9602).

POCAHANTAS (HINDS COUNTY)
Springdale Hills Arboretum, 104 acres with over 150 species of trees, ponds for fishing, picnic areas, and the ruins of an 1830s mansion, 2116 Springdale Road., nature and historic tours (601-366-4679); ANNUAL EVENTS: Pocahantas Jubilee featuring antique car display & parade, arts & crafts, storytelling, puppet shows, raffle, plenty of food, July 4th, Pine Grove Rd. off Hwy 49N, FREE admission (601-981-9316); the Pocahantas Pow Wow with food, music, hayride tours, mid-Oct., admission FREE, a nominal charge for children's activities. Sax player Gene Porter was born here.

PONTOTOC (PONTOTOC COUNTY)   PONTOTOC COUNTY CHAMBER OF COMMERCE (662-489-5042)
Chickasaw History Exhibit at McDonald's Restaurant on Hwy 145 bypass, FREE (662-489-6100); Trace State Park 10 miles E off Hwy 6 (662-489-2958). FAMOUS PEOPLE born here: U.S. Senator Thad Cochran; novelist Borden Deal, whose book *Dunbar's Cove* (1957) was made into the movie *Wild River* (1960); and songwriter Jim Weatherly. Born nearby in Pontotoc County were Delaney Bramlett and his wife, Bonnie Lynn Bramlett, of "Delaney & Bonnie."

POPLARVILLE (PEARL RIVER COUNTY)   POPLARVILLE AREA CHAMBER OF COMMERCE (601-795-0578)
Located 5 miles from Poplarville is the "Dream House," built by Theodore Bilbo, the colorful governor from 1916-20 & 1928-32 & U.S. Senator from 1935-47; Mississippi Blueberry Jubilee Storytelling Festival annually about the middle of June features a 5K race, lots of arts & crafts plus delicious blueberries (601-795-8378).

Tourist Attractions in Mississippi

PORT GIBSON (CLAIBORNE COUNTY)   PORT GIBSON/CLAIBORNE CO. CHAM. OF COMM. (601-437-4351)
(All phone numbers are Area Code 601). The town Civil War Union General U.S. Grant called "too beautiful to burn." Grand Gulf Military Monument Park includes Grand Gulf Cemetary, a museum containing Civil War artifacts, and historic building restorations, off Hwy 61 on Grand Gulf Rd., 7½ miles NW of Port Gibson (437-5911); Grand Gulf Nuclear Station with the tallest free-standing structure in the state—the cooling tower (520 feet tall)—and the Energy Central exhibit to learn about electricity/nuclear energy (437-6317); a huge 12-foot tall, golden hand tops the spire of the First Presbyterian Church (built in 1859) and points a 5-foot-long forefinger towards the sky. The church has chandeliers from the steamboat Robert E. Lee, Hwy 61S at Church St., FREE (437-4351); Gemiluth Chassed, Mississippi's oldest synagogue, 708 Church St. (729-0240); Planters Hotel, built in 1817; the Irwin Russell Memorial to the prodigy and genius poet who wrote *Christmas Night in the Quarters* published in 1879; many Civil War sites; Resin Bowie, inventor of the bowie knife & brother of Jim Bowie who popularized that knife, is buried in the Catholic Cemetery on Coffee St; the Hermitage, home of Confederate Gen. B.G. Humphreys is nearby. Humphreys, who was Gov. of Miss. from Feb. 3, 1851 to Nov. 4, 1851, is buried in Port Gibson. He was born in Claiborne County when the Mississippi was still a territory, although Claiborne County had been organized. Bluesman J.D. "Jellyjaw" Short was born here. Tall tales storyteller and horse trader Ray Lum was born in nearby Rocky Springs.

PURVIS (LAMAR COUNTY)   LAMAR COUNTY CHAMBER OF COMMERCE (601-794-1011)
Hudson Llama Farm, 44 Chuchwell Rd., 4 miles off Hwy 11, FREE (601-794-5971); Longleaf Plantation on Baker Rd. (800-421-7370 or 601-794-6001): Turkey Trot Farms, hunting & fishing paradise on 1,800 acres, No. 3 Turkey Trot Rd. (601-264-2886); Lamar Co. Historical Museum located in the train depot built in 1883 (601-794-2254). FAMOUS PEOPLE born here: actress Lacey Chabert; Trumpet Records founder and early Rock 'n' Roll and Blues record producer Lillian McMurry; and inventor Joseph Paul Treen, the father of Louisiana Governor David Treen.

QUITMAN (CLARKE COUNTY)   CLARKE COUNTY CHAMBER OF COMMERCE (601-776-5701)
Clarkco State Park (601-776-6651) & Archusa Creek Water Park (601-776-6956), 20 miles south of Meridian. Writer Wyatt Cooper, pro basketball player Antonio McDyess and bluesman "Andy Blake" Blakeney were born in Quitman.

RAYMOND (HINDS COUNTY)   Raymond Chamber of Commerce (601-857-8942)
The Raymond Courthouse, built by slave labor, completed in 1859; home of Hinds Community College — Marie Hull Gallery with permanent exhibits by Miss. artists, changing exhibits of national, regional works, in Denton Art Building at Hinds Community College, FREE (601-857-3275); the Dupree House (circa 1878), available for private luncheon or dinner tours, and adjacent Mamie's Cottage Bed & Breakfast (c. 1840), listed on the National Register of Historic Places. Portions of Eudora Welty's *The Ponder Heart*, a movie for PBS' *Masterpiece Theater*, were filmed in and around the Dupree House in the spring of 2000. Located at 2809 Dupree Rd. (601-857-6051/toll free 877-629-6051); ANNUAL EVENTS: Historic driving tour year 'round, pick up free map and brochure at Hinds County Courthouse or Raymond City Hall; Raymond Country Fair, arts & crafts, food and entertainment, 1st Sat. in May in downtown Raymond, admission FREE; "A Place Called Raymond," fall pilgrimage tour of historic homes and other structures, early Oct. 601-857-8041, Raymond City Hall, or 857-8942. John Bell Williams, Gov. of Miss. 1968-72, was born in Raymond.

RIDGELAND (MADISON COUNTY)   RIDGELAND TOURISM COMMISSION (800-468-6078 EXT. 115)
ANNUAL EVENTS: Pepsi Pops music concert, Old Trace Park on the Ross Barnett Reservoir, 1st weekend in May (601-853-2011); Balloon Glow at Northpark Mall, July 3rd; the Southern Farm Bureau Golf Classic PGA Tour Event at the Annandale Golf Club in October.

RIENZI (ALCORN COUNTY)   CORINTH AREA TOURISM PROMOTION (800-748-9048)
Jacinto Courthouse, once the Tishomingo Co. Courthouse 1854-1870, listed on National Register of Historic Places.

RIPLEY (Tippah County)
The Tippah County Historical Museum; First Monday Trade Day, started in 1893, a 3-day, huge flea-market (the largest in Mississippi) starts Sat. preceding 1st Mon. of each month. Located on Hwy 15 S of Ripley, no admission (662-837-4051). Historical writer Harold Cross and novelist John Faulkner (bro. of William) were born here.

ROBINSONVILLE (TUNICA COUNTY)   TUNICA CO. CONVENTION & VISITORS BUREAU (888-488-6422)
Gambling galore year around 24 hours a day with ten casinos (as of July 1, 2000). Also see the chapter on casinos.

ROCKY SPRINGS (CLAIBORNE COUNTY)   PORT GIBSON/CLAIBORNE CO. CHAM. OF COMM. (601-437-4351)
Virtual ghost town located 17 miles northeast of Natchez, a popular stop on the Natchez Trace. The Methodist Church, built in 1837, is open to the public. The old town graveyard is behind the church. Storyteller was born here.

RODNEY (JEFFERSON COUNTY)
Civil War ghost town once known as Petite Gulf. The Presbyterian Church has a cannonball still lodged in the front wall from the gunboat "Rattler" when Confederate cavalry captured Federal sailors attending services Sept. 13, 1863.

ROSEDALE (BOLIVAR COUNTY)   CLEVELAND/BOLIVAR CO. CHAMBER OF COMMERCE (662-843-2712)
First known as Abel's Point, then Floreyville. Great River Road State Park, off Mississippi Hwy 1 on the Mississippi River (662-759-6762). Soul-jazz drummer Redd Holt and bluesman Dennis "Long Man" Binder were born in Rosedale.

Tourist Attractions in Mississippi

SANDY HOOK (MARION COUNTY)   MARION COUNTY CHAMBER OF COMMERCE (601-736-6385)
John Ford Home built in early 1800's with a stockade for protection against the Indians (601-736-6385).

SARDIS (PANOLA COUNTY)   SARDIS/SARDIS LAKE CHAMBER OF COMMERCE (662-487-3451)
NEARBY: Cobb's Sorghum Molasses Syrup Mill, halfway between Sardis and Batesville off State Highway 51 (662-487-1088); 9 miles east of Sardis off highway 315 is John K. Kyle State Park with Sardis Lake (662-487-1345) and Mallard Point 27-hole golf course, 1-888-TEEMISS (1-888-833-6477). Cliff Finch, Governor of Mississippi from 1976-80 was born nearby in Panola County at Pope.

SEMINARY (COVINGTON COUNTY)   COVINGTON COUNTY CHAMBER OF COMMERCE (601-765-6012)
John Redmon's Arrowhead Collection with 9,000 arrowheads plus other Indian artifacts dating from 8,000 B.C. to 1,200 A.D., off State Highway 535N (601-722-3633).

SHIP ISLAND (GULF OF MEXICO)   MISS. GULF COAST CONVENTION/VISITORS BUREAU (888-896-6796)
Fort Massachusetts, a Civil War fort constructed in 1858. Points of departure for daily cruises to the island are the Biloxi Point Cadet Marina, Hwy 90 (228-432-2197) and Gulfport Yacht Harbor, Hwy 90 at Hwy 45 (228-864-1014).

SOSO (JONES COUNTY)   JONES COUNTY CHAMBER OF COMMERCE (601-428-0574)
The Big Creek Water Park (601-763-8555). Novelist Rebecca Hill lived here.

STARKVILLE (OKTIBBEHA COUNTY)   STARKVILLE VISITORS & CONVENTION COUNCIL (800-649-8687)
(All phone nos. Area Code 662). First known as Boardtown. On the campus at Mississippi State, all FREE: Templeton Ragtime Museum with player pianos & organs, music boxes, sheet music, etc. (325-8301), the MSU Art Gallery (325-6900), the Cobb Institute of Archaeology Museum (325-3826), the Cully Cobb Antique Tool Museum in the Forest Products Utilization Laboratory, the Dunn-Seller Museum with paleontology, mineralogy and geology exhibits (325-3915), the Rose Garden Plant Science Research Center (325-3138), the A.B. McKay Food and Enology Laboratory (325-3200), and the Mississippi Entomological Museum with live exhibits and over 700,000 insect specimens (325-2085) plus much more, all on the campus at MSU; Main Street (art) Gallery & Studio at 111 W. Main St., (320-9550); C.C. Clark Memorial Coca-Cola Museum, FREE (323-4150); Oktibbeha County Hertiage Museum, FREE (323-0211); the Mennonite operated Olde Time Bakery (738-5795). NEARBY: Noxubee National Wildlife Refuge, 8 miles S of Starkville with 3,225 acres [no hunting] (323-5548); Okitibbeha County Lake with fishing, swimming, water-skiing, camping, & picnicking, 8 miles NW of Starkville (323-3350); John W. Starr Memorial Forest with overnight camping, picnicking, hiking, hunting & fishing, 3 miles SW of Starkville (325-2191). FAMOUS PEOPLE born here: the late James "Papa" Bell, the only native Mississippian in the Baseball Hall of Fame; bluesmen Tony Hollins, Little Robert Weaver & John "Boogie Daddy" Wells; journalist and editor-in-chief Eugene Butler; major league baseball player and Miss. Sports Hall of Famer Hughie Critz; first black student at Mississippi State, physician Richard E. Holmes; Olympian Hayes Jones; and geologist Frederic F. Mellen, who discovered the first oil well in the state in Yazoo County. Thomas Bailey, Gov. of Miss. 1944-46, was born nearby in Oktibbeha County near Maben.

SUMRALL (LAMAR COUNTY)   LAMAR COUNTY CHAMBER OF COMMERCE (601-794-1011)
The Country Store with hand-crafted wood products, arts & crafts, and live country music on Saturdays, 4.5 miles south of Sumrall on Highway 589 (601-758-4941). Bluesman Leonard "Baby Doo" Caston was born in Sumrall.

TAYLORSVILLE (SMITH COUNTY)
The Watkins Museum, exhibit of an old newspaper office and printing facilities (601-785-6531).

THAXTON (PONTOTOC COUNTY)   PONTOTOC COUNTY CHAMBER OF COMMERCE (662-489-5042)
First known as Buttermilk Sporings. Annual event: Buttermilk Springs Bluegrass Festival in late June (662-489-5557).

TISHOMINGO (TISHOMINGO COUNTY)   TISHOMINGO CHAMBER OF COMMERCE (662-438-7199)
First known as Good Spring. Tishomingo State Park, off hiway 25 (438-6914); Annual event: The Old Holcut Museum Arts & Crafts Festival the 3rd week in July features hand-crafted goods, fish fry, and gospel music. FREE (462-7065).

TUNICA (TUNCIA COUNTY)   TUNICA COUNTY CONVENTION & VISITORS BUREAU (888-488-6422)
Casino gambling galore with ten world-class casinos in the Robinsonville area (as of July 1, 2000). FAMOUS PEOPLE born in Tunica: bluesmen Isaiah "Doctor" Ross, "Boysaw" Boyson & Arthur "Mississippi" Williams; and blues/R&B record producer Calvin Carter. Portrait-painting artist Marshall Bouldin III and bluesman James Cotton were born in nearby Dundee and Elvis Presley's personal jeweler, Mike McGregor, was born in nearby Tibbs.

TUPELO (LEE COUNTY)   CONVENTION & VISITORS BUREAU 662-841-6521 or 800-533-0611
(All phone nos. are Area Code 662). First known as Gum Pond. Natchez Trace Parkway Visitors Center, FREE (680-4025); Tupelo National Battlefield on W. Main St., FREE (841-6521); Elvis Presley birthplace at 306 Elvis Presley Dr. along with the Elvis Museum & Memorial Chapel (841-1245); just north of Elvis' birthplace is Elvis Presley Lake & Campground with 850 acres (841-1304); Tupelo City Museum with a NASA space exhibit (841-6438); Mississippi Museum of Art, FREE (844-ARTS); Private John Allen National Fish Hatchery, 111 Elizabeth St., FREE (842-1341); ANNUAL EVENTS: gigantic flea markets in the spring; the Gum Tree Festival for 3 days the first part of May features the state's largest 10K run, arts show, crafts, etc.; OLEPUT (Tupelo spelled backwards) Festival in June

Tourist Attractions in Mississippi

features a street dance, Mardi Gras style parade and music; The annual Elvis Presley Festival (first one was in 1999), 1st weekend in Aug., events for adults and children, bike races, classic cars, food vendors, big name entertainment, Front St. downtown Tupelo. NEARBY: Six miles SE of Tupelo off Miss. Hwy 6 is Tombigbee State Park and Tombigbee National Forest which includes Owl Creek Indian Mounds and a Chickasaw village site (842-7669). In addition to Elvis, one of the most famous personalities who ever lived, other FAMOUS PEOPLE born here include: baseball player Dave Clark; jazz tenor sax player Walter Zuber Armstrong; bluesman Richard "Harmonica Slim" Riggins; singers Guy Hovis and "Jumpin'" Gene Simmons; William Lockhart Clayton (government service); children's bookwriter Jim McCafferty; and major league baseball player and Mississippi Sports Hall of Famer Andy Reese.

UTICA (HINDS COUNTY)
First known as Cane Ridge. Museum of the Southern Jewish Experience, at Henry S. Jacobs Camp off Hwy 18 NE of Utica, FREE (601-362-6357). FAMOUS PEOPLE born here: blues great Eugene "Sonny Boy Nelson" Powell and college and pro basketball great Lindsey Hunter.

VALLEY PARK (ISSAQUENA COUNTY)
C. B. "Buddie" Newman Railroad Museum, 21 miles north of Vicksburg on Hwy 61. Former Speaker of the Mississippi House of Representatives who spent 40 years in the state legislature, Buddy will give you a mile-long ride in his miniature, air-powered train. He might even let you blow the whistle. He has a couple of full-size railroad cars plus a caboose on hand plus lots of artifacts, photographs, and memorabilia about railroads. FREE (601-636-0345).

VARDAMAN (CALHOUN COUNTY)
First known as Ticky Ben, then Timberville. "Sweet Potato Capital of the World." The annual National Sweet Potato Fest, the 1st week in Nov. includes crafts, a flea market, tasting booths, sweet potato cooking & pie-eating contests, crowning of Sweet Potato Queen (662-682-7555).

VAUGHAN (YAZOO COUNTY)   **YAZOO COUNTY CONVENTION AND VISITORS BUREAU (800-381-0662)**
Casey Jones Museum State Park, located less than a mile from the actual wreck of the Cannonball number 382 whose engineer, Johnathan 'Casey' Jones, was killed in 1900, interprets history of railroading in the state (662-673-9864); Greg Harkins Chairs ("Chairmaker to the Presidents") woodworking shop is on Possum Bend Road (662-673-8229).

VICKSBURG (WARREN COUNTY)   **CONVENTION & VISITORS BUREAU (800-221-3536 or 601-636-9421)**
(All phone numbers are Area Code 601). First known as Walnut Hills. Convention Center with capacity for 2,400 theater style or 1,000 for a banquet, 1600 Mulberry St. (630-29290); Vicksburg National Military Park with the second largest military cemetery in the U.S. (after Arlington National Cemetery) with 1,620 acres (636-0583, ext. 8023) including the Cairo Museum featuring the restored *U.S.S. Cairo* ironclad ship (636-2199); U.S. Army Corps of Engineers Waterways Experiment Station complex of six major laboratories (one with the most powerful centrifuge in the world!), is one of the world's great research/development centers (FREE group tours 634-2502); Old Court House Museum-Eva W. Davis Memorial, Vicksburg's most historic building constructed by slaves in 1858, where the U.S. flag was raised and the Confederate flag lowered at the surrender of Vicksburg on July 4, 1863. The Museum also has the largest collection of Civil War memorabilia in the South, 1008 Cherry St. (636-0741); Southern Cultural Heritage Complex consists of the former St. Francis Xavier Convent and academy, on the National Register of Historic Places, at 1302 Adams (631-2997); the Biedenharn Museum of Coca-Cola® Memorabilia, where Coke was first bottled anywhere in the world in 1894, at 1107 Washington St. (638-6514); Yesterday's Children Antique Doll & Toy Museum, 1104 Washington St., housed in an 1836 building (638-0650); the Gray and Blue Naval Museum with the world's largest collection of Civil War gunboat models and the only diorama of the Seige of Vicksburg (over 2,500 miniature soldiers), also models of steam boats and modern tow boats, and "The Mississippians Exhibit" displaying naval vessels with names connected to Mississippi, at 1102 Washington St. (638-6500); the Great Animal Adventures Children's Museum dedicated to Dr. Bill Lindley's collection of veterinary artifacts, 721 China St. (629-9920); Joe Gerache's Corner Drug Store, with a display of Civil War and apothecary relics at 1123 Washington Street (636-2756); the Toys and Soldiers Museum at 1100 Cherry St., where over 27,000 toy soldiers are displayed (638-1986); and the Attic Gallery, a salon upstairs over the Sassafras Gift Shop at 1406 Washington St., overflowing with art objects; Antebellum Homes and Mansions include the Martha Vic House (circa 1830), which belonged to the daughter of the founder of Vicksburg, Newitt Vick, 1300 Grove St. (638-7036); the Duff Green Mansion (circa 1856), 1114 East First St. (636-6968 or 800-992-0037); Anchuca (circa 1830), also a B. & B., 1010 East St. (661-0111 or Toll Free 888-686-0111); Balfour House (circa 1835), 1002 Crawford St. (638-7113 or 800-294-7113); Pemberton Headquarters (circa 1835), 1018 Crawford St. (636-9581 or Toll Free 877-636-9581); McRaven Tour Home & Gardens (circa 1797, 1836 & 1849), listed on the National Register of Historic Places, 1445 Harrison St. (636-1663), the Corners (circa 1873), 601 Klein St. (636-7421 or 800-444-7421); Cedar Grove Mansion-Inn (circa 1840-1858), 2200 Oak St. (636-1000 or 800-862-1300); Belle of the Bends (circa 1876), 508 Klein St. (634-0737 or 800-844-2308); Annebelle (circa 1868), 501 Speed St. (638-2000 or 800-791-2000); Shlenker House-Cherry St. Cottages (circa 1890 & 1907), 2212 Cherry St. (601 or 800, then 636-7086); and Stained Glass Manor-Oak Hall (circa 1902-1908), 2430 Drummond St. (638-8893 or toll free 888-VICK-BNB). ANNUAL EVENTS: Vicksburg's Run Through History, March; Spring Pilgrimage Tour of Homes, March & April; Spring Arts & Crafts Show, April; Vicksburg Civil War Living History, May & July; Miss Mississippi

Tourist Attractions in Mississippi

VICKSBURG (Continued)
Beauty Pageant, mid-July at the Vicksburg Auditorium; Over The River Run, Sept.; Fall Arts & Crafts Show, Oct.; Fall Pilgrimage Tour of Homes, Oct.; Balfour Ball, Dec.; and casino gambling year around with 4 casinos. FAMOUS PEOPLE born here: musician and bandleader Walter Barnes, bluesmen Willie Dixon, Iverson "Louisiana Red" Minter; John "Big Bad" Smitty, Percy L. Strother; Joseph "Little Joe Blue" Valery; Artie White & Johnny Young; major league baseball player Ellis Rena Burks; independent film producer Charles Burnett; industrialist Owen Cooper; playwright Mart Crowley, silent screen actor William David; Civil Rights activist and former NAACP head Myrlie Evers-Williams; writer/archivist and government administrator William Ferris, country singer/songwriter Mark Gray; jazz legend and composer Milt Hinton; jazz pianist Hank Jones, college/pro football player, coach and Mississippi Sports Hall of Famer Junie Hovious; fashion designer Patrick Kelly, writers Ellen Douglas and Ellis Nassour; and actress Beah Richards. Storyteller and mule trader Ray Lum, born in Claiborne County, lived here most of his life.

WATER VALLEY (YALOBUSHA COUNTY)   **WATER VALLEY AREA CHAMBER OF COMMERCE (662-473-1122)**
First known as Oke Chukma. Annual Water Valley Watermelon Festival featuring street dance, largest watermelon contest, Watermelon Queen and court pageant, 5K run/walk arts & crafts, and music, first weekend in August (662-473-1122); about 7 miles from Water Valley on the right going toward Oxford on Hwy 7S, is the Mike McGregor Shop. Mike worked for Elvis Presley for 9 years as his jeweler, leather craftsman and horse wrangler. Although Mike died in early 1999, the shop is still open and you can still purchase replicas of Elvis' trademark show belts and Elvis-inspired jewelry and leatherwork along with other great hand-crafted items (662-234-6970). Poet Hubert Creekmore and rockabilly singer Ernie Chaffin were born in Water Valley. NEARBY in Yalobusha County are Yocona Ridge Park and Enid Dam and Reservoir.

WAYNESBORO (WAYNE COUNTY)   **WAYNE COUNTY CHAMBER OF COMMERCE (601-735-2842)**
Maynor Creek Water Park (601-735-4365). FAMOUS PEOPLE born in Waynesboro: major league baseball player Jeff Branson; composer and movie music scorer Tena Clark; and major league baseball player and Mississippi Sports Hall of Famer Claude Passeau.

WESSON (COPIAH COUNTY)   **WESSON CHAMBER OF COMMERCE (601-643-8316)**
The Founders Day Festival Arts & Crafts Flea Market, mid-June (601-643-2636); Mrs. Mississippi/Mrs. America Beauty Pageant is held at Copiah-Lincoln Community College's Rea Auditorium, in late June (601-852-2043). Bluesman Houston Stackhouse was born here.

WEST (HOLMES COUNTY)   **HOLMES COUNTY CHAMBER OF COMMERCE (662-834-3372)**
West Founders Day on July 4th weekend featuring a parade with kids on bikes, go-carts, wagons & skates, wagon rides, storytelling, auction, door prizes, and kissing booth.

WEST POINT (CLAY COUNTY)
First known as Robertson's Cross Roads. Waverly Mansion, built in 1852, off Hwy 50 (662-494-1399); Downhome Blues Festival each July 4th (662-494-8851); Prairie (art) Gallery at 126 W. Main St., FREE (662-494-1900); Prairie Arts Festival, Labor Day weekend, with more than 500 exhibitors, juried fine arts show & flea market, 5K run, street dance & music (662-494-5121); the annual Howlin' Wolf Blues Festival, first weekend in Sept. FAMOUS PEOPLE born here include: businessmen/CEO John H. Bryan, Jr.; entrepreneur/inventor Toxey Haas; bluesmen "Howlin' Wolf" (Chester Arthur Burnett) & Johnny Moore, who worked with Nat King Cole; blues woman Zora Young; president of Mississippi State University, Dr. Malcolm Portera; the first female State Supreme Court Judge Lenore L. Prather; early movie director Larry Semon; rock guitarist Thomas Roger Stevens (with the group Blind Melon); and R&B singer and songwriter Barrett Strong.

WIGGINS (STONE COUNTY)
First known as Niles City. Flint Creek Water Park (601-928-3051); Batson's Log Home with waterwheel & Fish Farm, off Hwy 49 at the Hwy 26 exit, then W (601-928-5271). Anthony Herrera, the actor who played TV soap opera villains, was born here. Major league baseball great Jay Hanna "Dizzy" Dean is buried in nearby Bond, where he grew up.

WOODVILLE (WILKINSON COUNTY)
Many beautiful 19th-century homes including Rosemont Plantation, circa 1810, the boyhood home of Jefferson Davis, 1 mile east of Woodville off State Highway 24E, (601-888-6809); the *Woodville Republican* is the oldest newspaper in the state and also the oldest business in the state; the state's oldest church, the Woodville Baptist, built in 1809; the nation's oldest Episcopal church building west of the Alleghenies, St. Paul's Episcopal Church, erected 1824; the West Feliciana Railroad Building, Mississippi's first railroad chartered in 1831, began operation in 1836 to run the 29 miles between Woodville and St. Francesville, Louisiana, the first standard-gauge line in the nation; NEARBY: 14 miles west of Woodville is the Pond Country Store, built in 1881, at 182 Fort Adams Pond Rd., FREE (601-888-4426); the Clark Creek Natural Area with lush woodlands, waterfalls up to 50 feet high, and winding trails, FREE (601-888-4426); FAMOUS PEOPLE born here: Olympian and Mississippi Sports Hall of Famer Don Scott; musician/composer William Grant Still; jazz musician/composer Lester Young; and bluesman Monroe "Polka Dot Slim" Vincent. Hugh L. White, Gov. of Miss. twice (1936-40 & 1952-56) was born nearby in Wilkinson County at Whitestown (town now extinct).

Tourist Attractions in Mississippi

YAZOO CITY (YAZOO COUNTY) YAZOO COUNTY CONVENTION AND VISITORS BUREAU (800-381-0662)

(All phone numbers are Area Code 662). First known as Hannan's Bluff, then Manchester. "The Gateway to the Delta." B.S. Ricks Memorial Library, the oldest public library building in the state and the first library in the state to computerize its operations (746-5557); Triangle Cultural Center, home of Yazoo Historical Museum including the Jerry Clower Exhibition Center and the Jimmy Carter Room with exhibitions when President Carter stayed at 's home on his visit to Yazoo City in July 1977, North Main St. (746-2273); Historic Downtown area with many churches, public and commercial buildings with 1904-05 architecture, the largest area ever designated when it was placed on the National Register of Historic Places; the Oakes African American Cultural Center on Monroe Street; on the corner of Grand Avenue and Lintonia is the house where much of the movie *Miss Firecracker* was filmed in 1988; the Naval Works Confederate Ship Yards on the Yazoo River where the iron-clad ram *C.S.S. Arkansas* was built. During the *Arkansas's* 24 days of service, it disabled four Union ships and helped hold off the siege of Vicksburg; Kinnison's Kountry Korner store full of antiques, primitives and collectibles, located on the Old Benton Road less than a quarter mile from the Four-Points Intersection, also has a completely furnished replica of an old home place you can tour FREE (746-4164). ANNUAL EVENTS: the Discover Yazoo Festival in May includes a trip to the grave of the Yazoo Witch who, according to legend, burned down the town in 1904. She was made famous by the late Willie Morris in his book *Good Ole Boys* (1972), which was made into a movie released as *The River Pirates*. The Yazoo Witch's grave, in historic Glenwood Cemetery, has chains around it to hold her in! Author Willie Morris, who made her famous in his books, is buried just 13 paces south of her grave; bicycle time trial & road race, held at various times, usually in late spring and early summer; and the Yazoo County Fair, 2nd largest in the state, held the first week in Oct. at Yazoo County Fairgrounds. NEARBY: Fletcher's Chapel Methodist Church, founded in 1849 by John Fletcher, a close friend of John Wesley, founder of Methodism (746-2708); the first oil field in the state, located at Tinsley, where oil was discovered in 1939. FAMOUS PEOPLE born here: actress Stella Stevens; Haley Barbour, former head of the National Republican Party; university presidents John Tyler Caldwell and Priscilla D. Slade (born in Shaw, grew up in Yazoo City); Mike Espy, former congressman and former Secretary of Agriculture; football greats , Houston Hoover, and "Gentle" Ben Williams; pioneering librarian Charlemae Rollins; two pioneering women attorneys — Ruth Campbell, the first women admitted to the Mississippi bar & Helen Carloss, the first women to argue before the U.S. Supreme Court (both are buried in historic Glenwood Cemetery); film producer Larry Gordon (reared in Belzoni); blues/country guitarist and singer Mike Henderson; singer Joshie "Jo" Armstead (with the Ikettes); bluesmen "Uncle" Joe Cooper, Robert Covington, Bo Kirkland, Tommy McClennan & Arthur "Big Boy" Spires; big band leader Herbie Holmes; and inventor/banker Ted Webb, Jr. Like Willie Morris (born in Jackson), motivational expert Zig Ziglar (born in Alabama) grew up in Yazoo City and photographer Paul T. Brown (born in Greenwood) grew up in Yazoo City. The late Jerry Clower, although born at East Fork near Liberty in Amite County, lived in Yazoo City for 34 years (until Oct. 1988) and often mentioned Yazoo City as home in his many hit comedy albums.

CERTIFIED RETIREMENT COMMUNITIES IN MISSISSIPPI

Aberdeen	Columbus	Madison	Natchez	Starkville
Booneville	Corinth	McComb	Oxford	Tupelo
Brookhaven	Hattiesburg	Meridian	Picayune	Vicksburg
Clinton	Holly Springs	Mississippi Gulf Coast	Southaven	West Point

---

Greenville, Hernando and Natchez were named the Most Livable Communities in Mississippi for 1999 by the Mississippi Municipal Association and *The Clarion-Ledger* newspaper of Jackson.

In August 1999, the White House Millennium Council named Laurel and Natchez as Millennium Communities. About 120 communities across the nation were designated through the program.

In August 2000, the American Society of Travel Agents and *Fodor's* travel guide ranked Biloxi, Mississippi third as an "up-and-coming" travel destination, right behind Las Vegas and Orlando. Joe Galloway, ASTA president and CEO, said "As part of the greater Mississippi Gulf Coast, Biloxi has something for everyone."

In millennium polls released Sept. 6, 1999, by *The Clarion-Ledger* of Jackson, readers picked their favorite:
A) Recurring Event — No. 1, Neshoba County Fair and No. 2, Mississippi State Fair.
B) Recreation Destination — No. 1, The Grove at Ole Miss (giant picnic) and No. 2, The Gulf Coast.

According to the state Department of Economic and Community Development, overnight leisure trips to Mississippi increased over 64% (day trips increased over 86%) between 1992 and 1998. The state had 10 million overnight visitors in 1998 with over 35 percent of them coming for casino gaming. Overnight visitors stayed an average of 3.4 days and spent $87 each day. The direct economic impact totaled $2.9 billion!

Jackson's exhibition, *The Majesty of Spain: Royal Collections from the Museo del Prado & Patrimonio Nacional* set for March 1-Sept. 4, 2000, was rated No. 1 on the American Bus Association's 2001 list of Top 100 Events in North America announced in Sept. 2000. It was the second time a Jackson international exhibition nabbed the Number One spot on the ABA list. *The Splendors of Versailles* was named the top U.S. event for 1998.

Convention & Visitors Bureaus of Mississippi

Aberdeen Visitors Bureau; 124 W Commerce St; PO Box 288; Aberdeen 39730 E-mail: aberdeenms@iname.com	662-369-9440 or 800-634-3538 fax 662-369-6489
Bay St. Louis (Hancock County Tourism Development Bureau; PO Box 3002; Bay St. Louis 39521-3002) www.hancockcountyms.org E-mail: tourism@hancockcountyms.org	228-463-9222 or 800-466-9048 fax 228-463-9227
Brandon (Rankin First; PO Box 129; Brandon 39043-0129) www.metroeda.com	601-825-2268 fax 601-825-1877
Canton Convention & Visitors Bureau; PO Box 53; Canton 39046	601-859-1307 or 800-844-3369 fax 601-859-0346
Clarksdale (Coahoma County Tourism Commission; 1540 DeSoto Ave; PO Box 160; Clarksdale 39614-0160) www.clarksdale.com E-mail: ccoc@gmi.com	662-627-7337 or 800-626-3764 fax 662-627-1313
Columbus-Lowndes Convention & Visitors Bureau; PO Drawer 789; Columbus 39703 www.columbus-ms.org E-mail: ccvb@columbus-ms.org	662-329-1191 or 800-327-2686 fax 662-329-8969
Corinth Area Tourism Promotion; PO Box 1089; Corinth 38835-1089 www.corinth.net E-mail: tourism@tsixroads.com	662-287-5269 or 800-748-9048 fax 662-287-5260
DeSoto County Convention & Visitors Bureau; PO Box 804; Southaven 38671-0804	662-280-9120 or 888-280-9120 fax 662-449-1444
Greenville (Washington Co. Convention & Visitors Bureau; 410 Washington Ave; Greenville 38701) www.thedelta.org E-mail: wccvb@tecinfo.com	662-334-2711 or 800-467-3582 fax 662-334-2708
Greenwood Convention & Visitors Bureau; PO Drawer 739; Greenwood 38935 E-mail: gevb@netdoor.com	601-453-9198 or 800-748-9064 fax 662-453-5526
Grenada Tourism Commission; PO Box 1824; Grenada 38902-1824 E-mail: gtourism.aol.com	662-226-2571 or 800-373-2571 fax 662-226-9745
Hattiesburg Convention & Visitors Bureau; PO Box 16122; Hattiesburg 39404 www.hattiesburg.org E-mail: hcvb@netdoor.com	601-268-3220 or 800-638-6877 fax 601-268-3249
Iuka (Tishomingo County Tourism Council; 203 E Quitman; Iuka 38852) www.moad.com/tcdf E-mail: tcdf@tsixroads.com	662-423-0051 or 800-386-4373 fax 662-423-1017
Jackson Convention & Visitors Bureau; 921 N President St; Jackson PO Box 1450; Jackson 39215-1450 www.visitjackson.com	601-960-1891 or 800-354-7695 fax 601-960-1827
Kosciusko Tourist Promotion Council; PO Box 696; Kosciusko 39090-0696 www.kopower.com/coc/coc.htm E-mail: chamber@kopower.com	662-289-2981 fax 662-289-2986
Mississippi Gulf Coast Convention & Visitors Bureau; PO Box 6128; Gulfport 39506 www.gulfcoast.org E-mail: tourism@gulfcoast.org	228-896-6699 or 888-896-6796 fax 228-896-6796

Convention & Visitors Bureaus of Mississippi

Meridian (Lauderdale County Tourism Bureau; PO Box 5313; Meridian 39302) E-mail: abeasley@lauderdalecounty.org	601-482-8001 or 888-868-7720 fax 601-486-4966
Natchez Convention & Visitors Bureau; 640 S Canal St, Box C; Natchez 39120 www.2.bkbank.com/ncvb E-mail: ncvb@bkbank.com	601-446-6345 or 800-647-6724 fax 601-442-0814
New Albany (Union County Development Association; PO Box 125; New Albany 38652	662-534-4354 or 888-534-8232 fax 662-538-4107
Oxford Tourism Council; PO Box 965; Oxford 38655-0965 www.ci.oxford.ms.us E-mail: tourism@oxfordcenter.com	662-234-4680 or 800-758-9177 fax 662-234-0355
Ridgeland Tourism Commission; PO Drawer 2358; Ridgeland 39158 www.visitridgeland.org E-mail: info@visitridgeland.org	601-956-1225 or 800-468-6078 fax 601-956-5224
Senatobia (Tate Economic Development Foundation/Tourism; 105-B Center St; Senatobia 38668 http://www.tatecounty.com E-mail: tatecoef@gmi.net	662-562-8715 fax 662-562-5786
Starkville Visitors & Convention Council; 322 University Dr; Starkville 39759 www.starkville.org E-mail: request@starkville.org	662-323-3322 or 800-649-8687 fax 662-323-5815
Tunica County Convention & Visitors Bureau; PO Box 2739; Tunica 38676-2739 www.tunicamiss.org E-mail: tunicamiss@tunica.net	662-363-3800 or 888-488-6422 fax 662-363-1493
Tupelo Convention & Visitors Bureau; PO Drawer 47; Tupelo 38802 www.tupelo.net E-mail: tour20@tsixroads.com	662-841-6521 or 800-533-0611 fax 662-841-6558
Vicksburg Convention & Visitors Bureau; PO Box 110; Vicksburg 39181-0110 www.vicksburgcvb.org E-mail: mailcvb@vicksburgcvb,org	601-636-9421 or 800-221-3536 fax 601-636-9475
Yazoo County Convention & Visitors Bureau; PO Box 186; Yazoo City 39194-0186 www.yazoo.org E-mail: yazoo@yazoo.org	662-746-1815 or 800-381-0662 fax 662-746-1816
Mississippi Development Authority; Division of Tourism Development; PO Box 849, Jackson 39205 Toll Free 1-800-WARMEST www.visitmississippi.org E-mail: tinquiry@mississippi.org	601-359-3297 or 800-927-6378 fax 601-359-5757

Mississippi State Parks - Parks Operation	601-364-2160
Parks Reservation Information Toll Free 1-800-GO PARKS or	800-467-2757

Mississippi Department of Wildlife, Fisheries & Parks; 2906 N State St; Jackson 39216	601-362-9212
Fax 601-364-3008 Boat Registration & Titling	601-364-2030
Customer Service	601-364-2163

The Ultimate Reference on the State

Chambers of Commerce in Mississippi

Aberdeen/Monroe County Chamber of Commerce; 124 W Commerce; PO Box 727; Aberdeen 39730 (662) 369-6488
    E-mail: asmcoc@tsixroads.com .... Fax (662) 369-6489
Amory/Monroe County Chamber of Commerce; 601 2nd Ave & 6th St; PO Box 128; Amory 38821 .. (662) 256-7194
    Fax (662) 256-5221
Baldwyn Chamber of Commerce; 201 S Second St; PO Box 40; Baldwyn 38824 .... (662) 365-2383
Belzoni/Humphreys County Development Foundation; 111 Magnolia St; PO Box 145; Belzoni 39038 (662) 247-4838
    www.capital2.com/home/catfish.htm   E-mail: catfish@capital2.com .... Fax (662) 247-4805
Biloxi Bay Chamber of Commerce; Po Box 889; Biloxi 39533-0889 .... (228) 435-6149
    www.biloxibaychamber.com   E-mail: bilbaych@olesouth1.com .... Fax (228) 435-6334
Biloxi Chamber of Commerce (member Gulf Coast C of C); 1048 Beach Blvd; PO Box 1928; Biloxi . (228) 374-2717
    E-mail: cxcc@biloxi.org .... Fax (228) 374-2764
Booneville Area Chamber of Commerce; 100 W Church St; PO Box 927; Booneville 38829-0927 .... (662) 728-4130
    www2.tsixroads.com/booneville/chamber   E-mail: bchamber@tsixroads.com ...... Fax (662) 728-4134
Brookhaven/Lincoln County Chamber of Commerce; PO Box 978; Brookhaven 39602-0978 .... (601) 833-1411
    www.brookhavenms.com   E-mail: brookcham@tislink.com   Fax: 601-833-1412 .... (800) 613-4667
Bruce Chamber of Commerce; North Side of Square; PO Box 1013; Bruce 38915-1013 .... (662) 983-2222
    Fax (662) 983-7300
Calhoun City Chmaber of Commerce; 102 S Monroe St, City Hall; PO Box 161; Calhoun City 38916 (662) 628-6990
Canton Chamber of Commerce; 226 E Peace St; PO Box 74; Canton 39045   Fax: 601-855-0149 ..... (601) 859-5816
Chickasaw Development Foundation; PO Box 505; Houston 38851   Fax 662-456-2595 .... (662) 456-2321
Clarke County Chamber of Commerce; PO Box 172; Quitman 39355-0172 .... (601) 776-5701
    www.go-east.org .... Fax (601) 776-5745
Clarksdale/Coahoma County Chamber of Commerce; PO Box 160; Clarksdale 38614-0160 .... (662) 627-7337
    www.clarksdale.com   E-mail: ccoc@clarksdale.com .... Fax (662) 627-1313
Cleveland-Bolivar County Chamber of Commerce/Tourism; PO Box 490; Cleveland 38732-0490 .... (662) 843-2712
    www.ci.cleveland.ms.us   E-mail: gwoods@tecinfo.com   Fax: 662-843-2718 .... (800) 295-7473
Clinton Chamber of Commerce; PO Box 143; Clinton 39060-0143 .... (601) 924-5912
    www.mc.edu/clinton   E-mail: clchamber@aol.com   Fax: 601-925-4009 .... (800) 611-9980
Columbus/Lowndes County Chamber of Commerce; 318 7th St N; PO Box 1016; Columbus 39703 .. (662) 328-4491
    E-mail: chamber@tilc.com.friendship.columbus.ms.us/ .... Fax (662) 327-0976
Covington County Chamber of Commerce; 104 First St; PO Box 1595; Collins 39428-1595 .... (601) 765-6012
Crystal Springs Chamber of Commerce; 210 E Railroad Ave; PO Box 519; Crystal Springs 39059 .... (601) 892-2711
    Fax (601) 892-4870
D'iberville/St. Martin Area Cham. of Comm; 10491 Lemoyne Blvd; POBox 6054; D'Iberville 39532 . (228) 392-2293
    Fax (228) 396-3216
Decatur (Greater Decatur) Chamber of Commerce; PO Box 474; Decatur 39327-0474 .... (601) 635-3863
Drew Chamber of Commerce; 129 Shaw Ave; Drew 38737 .... (662) 745-8975
East Mississippi Business Development Corp; PO Box 790; Meridian 39302-0790 .... (601) 693-1306
    E-mail: embdc1@cybertron.com .... Fax (601) 693-5638
Forest Area Chamber of Commerce; 120 S Davis St; PO Box 266; Forest 39074-0266 .... (601) 469-4332
    www.localink4.com   E-mail: chamberguide@mail.localink4.com .... Fax (601) 469-3224
Greenville Area Chamber Of Commerce; 915 Washington Ave; PO Box 933; Greenville 38702-0933   (662) 378-3141
    www.greenville.ms.us   E-mail: gaccms@tecinfo.com .... Fax (662) 378-3143
Greenwood/Leflore County Chamber of Commerce; 402 Sycamore St; PO Box 848; Greenwood 38935 (662) 453-4152
    Fax (662) 453-8003
Hancock County Chamber Of Commerce; 412 Hwy 90 #6; PO Box 103; Bay St Louis 39520-0103 .. (228) 467-9048
    E-mail: hccoc@goldinc.com .... Fax (228) 467-1573
Hattiesburg Area Development Partnership; One Convention Ctr. Plz; PO Box 751; Hattiesburg 39403 (601) 296-7500
    www.hattiesburg-adp.org   E-mail: adp@hattiesburg-adp.org   Fax 601-296-7505 .... (800) 238-4288
Hazlehurst Chamber of Commerce; PO Box 446; Hazlehurst 39083-0446 .... (601) 894-3752
    www.hazlehurst.net .... Fax (601) 894-3752
Hernando Area Chamber of Commerce; 2475 Memphis St; Hernando 39632   Fax 662-429-0952 ... (662) 429-9055
Holly Springs Chamber of Commerce; 154 S Memphis St; Holly Springs 38635 .... (662) 252-2943
Holmes County Chamber of Commerce; 103 W China St; Lexington 39095   Fax 662-834-4424 ...... (662) 834-3372

Chambers of Commerce in Mississippi

Indianola Chamber of Commerce; PO Box 151; Indianola 38751-0151   Fax 662-887-4454 .... (662) 887-4454
Inverness Chamber of Commerce; PO Box 13; Inverness 38753-0013 .... (662) 265-5511
Itawamba County Development Council; 107 W Wiygul St; Po Box 577; Fulton 38843-0577 .... (662) 862-4571
    www.co.itawamba.ms.us   E-mail: icdc@network.one.com .... Fax (662) 862-5637
Jackson County Chamber of Commerce; PO Drawer 480; Pascagoula 39568-0480 .... (228) 762-3391
    www.jcchamber.com   E-mail: chamber@jcchamber.com .... Fax (228) 769-1726
Jefferson Davis County Chamber of Commerce; PO Box 1797; Prentiss 39474   Fax 601-792-5190 .. (601) 792-5142
Jones County Chamber of Commerce; 153 Base Dr. #3; PO Box 527; Laurel 39441-0527 .... (601) 428-0574
    www.edajones.com   E-mail: edajones@teclink.net   Fax: 601-428-2047 .... (800) 392-9629
Kemper County Chamber of Commerce; 102 Industrial Park Drive; DeKalb 39328 .... (601) 743-2754
    www.kempercounty.com   E-mail: keeda@cybertron.com .... Fax (601) 743-2760
Lamar County Chamber of Commerce; PO Box 598; Purvis 39475-0598 .... (601) 794-1011
    www.lamarcounty.com   E-mail: information@lamarcounty.com   Fax 601-794-1025 ..... (800) 730-5089
Lawrence County Chamber of Commerce; PO Box 996; Monticello 39654-0996 .... (601) 587-3007
    E-mail: lccda@telapex.com .... Fax (601) 587-0750
Leake County Chamber of Commerce; PO Box 209; Carthage 39051-0209 .... (601) 267-9231
    www.leakems.com   E-mail: leakems@netdoor.com .... Fax (601) 267-8123
Leland Chamber of Commerce; S Deer Creek Dr; PO Box 67; Leland 38756-0067 .... (662) 686-2687
Liberty Area Chamber of Commerce; PO Box 18; Liberty 39645-0018 .... (601) 657-8011
Louisville-Winston County Chamber of Commerce; 311 W Park St; PO Box 551; Louisville 39339 ... (662) 773-3921
    E-mail: wceddjo@telapex.com .... Fax (662) 773-8719
Madison Chamber of Commerce; 710 Magnolia St; PO Box 544; Madison 39130-0544 .... (601) 856-7060
    www.ci.madison.ms.us .... Fax (601) 856-4852
Madison Co. Chamber of Commerce; 1062 Highland Colony Pkwy; PO Box 1276; Ridgeland 39158 . (601) 605-2554
    www.co.madison.ms.us   E-mail: info@co.madison.ms.us .... Fax (601) 605-2260
Magee Chamber of Commerce, 117 1st Ave NW; Magee 39111 .... (601) 849-2517
Marion County Chamber of Commerce; 200 Second St; Columbia 39429-2921   Fax: 601-736-6392 (601) 736-6385
Mendenhall Area Chamber of Commerce; 172 W Maude Ave; PO Box 635; Mendenhall 39114-0635 (601) 847-1725
Metro Jackson Chamber of Commerce; 201 S President St; Jackson 39201-4308 .... (601) 948-7575
    www.metrochamber.com   E-mail: donelll@metrochamber.com .... Fax (601) 352-5539
Miss. Gulf Coast Cham. of Comm; 1401 20th Ave; PO Box FF; Gulfport 39502   Fax 228-863-3080 . (228) 863-2933
Mississippi State Chamber of Commerce: 620 North St; Jackson 39202-3140 .... (601) 969-0022
Moorhead Chamber of Commerce; PO Box 396; Moorhead 38761-0396 .... (662) 246-5461
Morton Chamber of Commerce; PO Box 530; Morton 39117-0530   Fax 601-732-7188 .... (601) 732-6135
Natchez/Adams Co. Chamber of Commerce; 108 S Commerce St; PO Box 1403; Natchez 39121 ..... (601) 445-4611
    www.natchezchamber.com   E-mail: astowers@natchezchamber.com .... Fax (601) 445-9361
Newton Chamber of Commerce; 128 S Main St; PO Box 301; Newton 39345-0301 .... (601) 683-2201
Noxubee Co. Cham. of Comm; 503 S Washington; PO Box 308; Macon 39341   Fax 662-726-4080 .. (662) 726-4456
Ocean Springs Chamber of Commerce; PO Box 187; Ocean Springs 39566-0187 .... (228) 875-4424
    www.lillypr.com/oschamber .... Fax (228) 875-0332
Okolona Area Chamber of Commerce; 219 Main St; PO Box 446; Okolona 38860-0446 .... (662) 447-5913
    E-mail: patsyg@tsixroads.com .... Fax (662) 447-3956
Olive Branch Chamber of Commerce; 6820 Cockrum St; PO Box 608; Olive Branch 38654-0608 .... (662) 895-2600
    www.olivebranchms.com   E-mail: olivems@aol.com .... Fax (662) 895-2625
Oxford/Lafayette County Chamber of Commerce; 299 W Jackson Ave; PO Box 147; Oxford 38655 .. (662) 234-4651
    www.oxfordms.com   Fax 622-234-4655 .... (800) 880-6967
Panola Partnership, Inc; 107 Public Square; Batesville 38606 .... (662) 563-3126
    E-mail: panola@panola.com   Fax: 662-563-0704 .... (888) 872-6652
Pearl Chamber of Commerce; 110 George Wallace Dr; PO Box 54125; Pearl 39288-4125 .... (601) 939-3338
    www.pearlms.org   E-mail: pearlcc@earthlink.net .... Fax (601) 936-5717
Philadelphia-Neshoba County Chamber of Commerce; PO Box 51; Philadelphia 39350-0051 .... (601) 656-1742
    www.neshoba.org   E-mail: info@neshoba.org .... Fax (601) 656-1066
Picayune (Greater Picayune Area) Chamber of Commerce; PO Box 448; Picayune 39466-0448 .... (601) 798-3122
    E-mail: chamber@datastar.net .... Fax (601) 798-3122

Chambers of Commerce in Mississippi

Pike County Chamber Of Commerce; PO Box 83; McComb 39649-0083 .... (601) 684-2291
     www.telapex.com/~pcedd/   E-mail: pcedd@telapex.com   Fax: 601-684-4899 .... (800) 399-4404
Pontotoc County Chamber of Commerce; 81 S Main St; PO Box 530; Pontotoc 38863-0530 .... (662) 489-5042
     www.pontotoc.net   E-mail: bill@pontotoc.net .... Fax (662) 489-5263
Poplarville Area Chamber of Commerce; PO Box 367; Poplarville 39470-0367   Fax: 601-795-4941 . (601) 795-0578
Port Gibson/Claiborne County Chamber of Commerce; Hwy 61S; PO Box 491; Port Gibson 39150 ... (601) 437-4351
Rankin First/Rankin County Chamber of Commerce; 101 Service Dr; PO Box 428; Brandon 39043 ... (601) 825-2268
     www.rankinchamber.com   E-mail: info@rankinchamber.com .... Fax (601) 825-1977
Raymond Chamber of Commerce; Raymond .... (601) 857-8942
Ridgeland (City of Ridgeland) Chamber of Commerce; 304 Hwy 51; PO Box 194; Ridgeland 39158 .. (601) 856-0660
     www.ridgelandchamber.com   E-mail: admin@ridgelandchamber.com .... Fax (601) 856-0782
Ruleville Chamber of Commerce; 110 E Floyce St; PO Box 552; Ruleville 38771-0552 .... (662) 756-4836
Sardis-Sardis Lake Cham. of Comm; 114 W Lee; PO Box 377; Sardis 38666 Fax 662-487-3389 ..... (662) 487-3451
Senatobia/Tate Co. Chamber Of Commerce; 105-B Center St; Senatobia 38668 Fax 662-562-5786 .. (662) 562-8715
South Pike Area Chamber of Commerce; 180 Cherry St; Magnolia 39652   Fax 601-783-2386 ..... (601) 783-5267
Southaven Chamber of Commerce; PO Box 211; Southaven 38671-0211 .... (662) 342-6114
     www.southavenchamber.org   Fax: 662-342-6365 .... (800) 272-6551
Starkville Area Chamber of Commerce; 322 University Dr; Starkville 39759-3914 .... (662) 323-5783
     www.starkville.org   E-mail: info@starkville.org .... Fax (662) 323-5815
Tunica County Chamber of Commerce; 1371 Main St; PO Box 2000; Tunica 38676-2000 .... (662) 363-2865
     E-mail: tchamber@tunica.net .... Fax (662) 357-0378
Tupelo Community Development Foundation; Po Box A; Tupelo 38802-1210   Fax 662-841-0693 .. (662) 842-4521
Union Chamber of Commerce; 400 Bank St; Union 39365-2508 .... (601) 774-9586
Verona (City of Verona) Chamber of Commerce; 194 Main St; PO Box 416; Verona 38879-0416 .... (662) 566-2211
Vicksburg/Warren County Chamber of Commerce; 2020 Mission 66; PO Box 709; Vicksburg 39181 . (601) 636-1012
     Fax (601) 636-4422
Walthall County Chamber of Commerce; PO Box 227; Tylertown 39667-0227 .... (601) 876-2680
Water Valley Area Chamber of Commerce; 206Main St; PO Box 726; Water Valley 38965-0726 ..... (662) 473-1122
Wayne County Chamber of Commerce; Azalea Dr; PO Box 864; Waynesboro 39367-0864 .... (601) 735-2842
     www.wayncco.com   E-mail: sbrown@c-gate.net .... Fax (601) 735-6246
Wesson Chamber of Commerce; PO Box 557; Wesson 39191-0557 .... (601) 643-8316
Yazoo County Chamber of Commerce; 212 E Broadway; PO Box 172; Yazoo City 39194-0172 ...... (662) 746-1273
     E-mail: yazoocc@tecinfo.com .... Fax (662) 746-7238

Batesville - see Panola Partnership, Inc.	Lexington - see Holmes County
Bay Saint Louis - see Hancock County	Long Beach - see Miss. Gulf Coast Chamber of Commerce
Bolivar County - see Cleveland	Macon - see Noxubee County
Canton - see Madison County	Magnolia - see South Pike Area Chamber of Commerce
Carthage - see Leake County	McComb - see Pike County
Collins - see Covington County	Meridian - see East Mississippi Business Development
Columbia - see Marion County	Monticello - see Lawrence County
Dekalb - see Kemper County	Pascagoula - see Jackson County
Fulton - see Itawamba Co. Development Council	Prentiss - see Jefferson Davis County
Gulfport - see Miss. Gulf Coast Chamber of Commerce	Purvis - see Lamar County
Horn Lake - see Southaven	Quitman - see Clarke County
Houston - see Chickasaw Development Foundation	Tylertown - see Walthall County
Jackson - see Metro Jackson	Waynesboro - see Wayne County
Laurel - see Jones County	Yazoo City - see Yazoo County

Mississippi Outdoor Sportsmen's Records

BOONE & CROCKET DEER HEADS TAKEN IN MISSISSIPPI[1]

NON-TYPICAL HEADS (MINIMUM SCORE 195)

RANK	SCORE	STATUS	TAKEN BY	SEASON	COUNTY
1	295 6/8**[2]	1	Tony Fulton	1994-95	Winston
2	225 0/8	2	Richard Herring	1988-89	Lowndes
3	221 2/8	1	Milton Parrish	1972-73	Holmes
4	219 2/8	2	Matt Woods	1997-98	Hinds
5	217 5/8	1	Mark Hathcock	1977-78	Carroll
6	212 0/8	2	Wayne Parker	1999-00	Madison
7	209 6/8	1	Ronnie Strickland	1981-82	Franklin
8	205 6/8	1	Joe Shurden	1976-77	Lowndes
9	205 0/8	3	Tommy Yateman[3]	1959	Lowndes
10	204 0/8	2	Denver Eshee	1996-97	Webster
11	202 5/8	2	George Galey	1960s	Carroll
12*	202 1/8	1	Oliver Linding	1983-84	Oktibbeha
12*	202 1/8	3	Bobby Smith	1992-93	Tate
13	201 6/8	2	Jimmy Ashley	1985-86	Wilkinson
14	198 5/8	2	Timothy Watson	1997-98	Oktibbeha
15	196 7/8	2	Eddie Alias, Jr.	1989-90	Yazoo
16	196 5/8	1	Robert Sullivan	1981-82	Wilkinson
17	195 7/8	2	Ken Dye	1986-87	Monroe
18	195 6/8	4	Mark Kinard	1978-79	Oktibbeha
19	195 5/8	1	Kathleen McGehee	1981-82	Adams
20	195 2/8	3	Bill Kimble	1995-96	Copiah

TYPICAL HEADS (MINIMUM SCORE 170)

RANK	SCORE	STATUS	TAKEN BY	SEASON	COUNTY
1	182 7/8**	2	Glen Jourdan	1986-87	Noxubee
2	182 2/8	1	R. L. Bobo	1955-56	Claiborne
3	181 5/8	1	Ronnie Whitaker	1980-81	Wilkinson
4	180 4/8	1	W. F. Smith	1968-69	Leflore
5	180 2/8	3	Steve Greer	1995-96	Madison
6	179 2/8	3	Marlon Stokes	1988-89	Hinds
7	178 5/8	1	Grady Robertson	1951-52	Bolivar
8	176 5/8	1	Sidney Sessions	1952-53	Bolivar
9	176 1/8	3	Mike Steadman	1972-73	Monroe
10	175 2/8	1	Johnnie Leake, Jr.	1977-78	Wilkinson
11*	174 6/8	1	O. P. Gilbert	1960-61	Coahoma
11*	174 6/8	3	Jeremy Boelte	1997-98	Adams
12	174 1/8	3	Bill Makens	1995-96	Coahoma
13	173 5/8	1	Geraline Holliman	1982-83	Lowndes
14	173 3/8	1	Richard Powell	1994-95	Coahoma
15	172 5/8	1	Adrian Stallone	1983-84	Adams
16	172 0/8	1	Nan Foster New	1977-78	Adams
17	170 7/8	1	Warren A. Miller	1920	Issaquena
18	170 6/8	3	Delton Davis	1990-91	Tunica
19	170 4/8	3	Joe Reed Perry	Unknown	Sharkey
20	170 2/8	1	David G. McAdory	1994-95	Madison
21	170 1/8	4	Joe W. Martin	1994-95	Madison

Explanation of Status Numbers
1 — In records of *North American Big Game*
2 — Officially scored and accepted
3 — Officially scored and pending
4 — Officially scored but not entered

[1] This list contains the highest scoring deer ever taken in Mississippi and officially scored. The scoring method is Boone & Crockett, although some heads were never officially submitted for listing in *Boone & Crockett's Record Book of North American Big Game*. * Ties
[2] **Official State Record. Re-scored from 255 6/8 and certified as the **OFFICIAL WORLD RECORD** by Boone & Crockett in April 1998.
[3] Yateman found the deer already dead. SOURCE for this chapter: Mississippi Department of Wildlife, Fisheries and Parks.

Mississippi Outdoor Sportsmen's Records

MISSISSIPPI BEST BUCKS TAKEN WITH BOW & ARROW

Rank	Score	Taken By	Season	County
1	164 7/8	Jimmy House (of Oak Grove, LA)	1999	Issaquena
2	160 1/8	Odis Hill, Jr.	1990	Washington
3	159 6/8	Steve Nichols	1986	Washington
4	159 2/8	Wayne Ray	2000	Holmes
5	158 4/8	John Harvey	1989	Adams
6	155 7/8	Charles B. Neely	1994	Coahoma
7	153 4/8	John M. Johnson	1991	Montgomery
8	151 7/8	Frank Greenlee	1994	Washington
9	150 4/8	Tripp Stennett	1992	Claiborne
10	149 1/8	Chuck Allen	1993	Noxubee
11*	145 2/8	Charles A. Peebles	1988	Issaquena
11*	145 2/8	Robert H. Jarvis	1994	Issaquena
12*	144 6/8	Alan J. Guess	1987	Hancock
12*	144 6/8	Tucker Miller III	1995	Carroll
13	144 5/8	Jim McCrory	1991	Carroll
14	144 4/8	Ronnie G. Richardson	1994	Wilkinson
15	143 7/8	Frank Cascio, Jr.	1978	Oktibbeha
16	142 4/8	Tony Arnold	1995	Montgomery
17	142 0/8	Kirby Deer, Jr.	1992	Sharkey
18	141 5/8	Tommy L. Rose	1993	Pearl River
19	141 2/8	Kim Vickers	1996	Oktibbeha
20	140 7/8	John Robert Moon	1985	Claiborne
21	140 4/8	Bob Bruss	1989	Washington
**	204 0/8	Denver Eshee	1996	Webster
**	165 5/8	James Goss, Jr.	1987	Washington

This list includes the biggest bucks ever officially reported taken by archery equipment in Mississippi and represents a combination of lists compiled by the Mississippi Bowhunters Association and Pope & Young Club's record book *Bowhunting Big Game Records of North America*.
*Ties   **The only non-typical deer on the list — all the rest are typical.

ANIMALS HARVESTED DURING THE 1998-99 SEASON

Deer: During the 1998-99 season, hunters in Mississippi claimed a total of 276,361 deer, 56,211 fewer than 1997-98 (332,572) and 58,639 fewer than the record 335,000 in 1995-96.
There were 142,027 bucks and 133,565 does harvested during the 1998-99 season.

Gun:	223,809	(123,134 bucks & 100,086 does)
Archery:	32,334	(10,347 bucks & 21,978 does)
Primitive weapons:	19,339	(8,243 bucks & 11,089 does)

Other Animals Harvested During The 1998-99 Season (estimates):

Doves:	1,492,879	Raccoons:	127,424	Mallards:	274,742
Squirrels:	901,099	Turkeys (1998):	32,809	Wood Ducks:	104,079
Rabbits:	384,813	Geese:	21,072	Other Ducks:	173,494
Quail:	140,233	Woodcock:	4,736	Coyote:	36,076

ESTIMATED NUMBER OF MISSISSIPPI HUNTERS

	No. of Hunters			Change in No. of
Animal Hunted	1985-86	1990-91	1998-99	Hunters 1986-99
Deer (gun)	183,367	159,983	156,357	-27,010 (-14.7%)
Deer (archery)	38,696	51,717	48,633	+9,937 (+25.7%)
Deer (primitive)	48,863	61,189	43,899	-4,964 (-10.2%)
Dove	110,602	99,708	75,262	-35,340 (-32.0%)
Ducks	34,818	26,040	30,226	-4,592 (-13.2%)
Quail	40,748	25,705	10,987	-29,761 (-73.0%)
Rabbit	97,654	72,000	44,254	-53,400 (-54.7%)
Raccoon	20,945	22,368	11,726	-9,219 (-44.0%)
Squirrel	150,480	114,287	75,392	-75,088 (-49.9%)
Turkey	33,065	55,235	45,626	+12,561 (+38.0%)

Hunting licenses, 1998-99 season: 206,721 small game & 199,825 big game. (see chapter on "Health" for info on hunting accidents)

Mississippi Outdoor Sportsmen's Records

OFFICIAL STATE RECORD FISH

Species	Weight	Angler	Address	Location Caught	Date
Largemouth bass	18.15 lbs.	Anthony Denny	Washington	Natchez State Park Lake	12/31/92
Spotted bass	8 lbs. 2 oz.	S. Ross Grantham	Seminary	Farm Pond, Jones County	09/02/75
Smallmouth bass	7 lbs. 15 oz.	Thomas Wilbanks	Walnut	Yellow Crk. arm Pickwick Lake	01/24/87
Striped bass	37.82 lbs.	Tony C. Graves	Hattiesburg	Bowie River	05/13/93
Striped bass hybrid	17.77 lbs.	Robert F. Fulce	Oxford	Lower Sardis Lake	04/15/91
White bass	5 lbs. 6 oz.	William Mulvihill	Greenwood	Grenada Reservoir Spillway	04/21/79
Yellow bass	15.25 oz.	Milton Smith	Cleveland	Beulah Crevasse, Bolivar Co.	12/13/89
White crappie*	5 lbs. 3 oz.	Fred Bright	Memphis, TN	Enid Reservoir	07/31/57
Black crappie	4 lbs. 4 oz.	Gerald Conlee	Hernando	Arkabutla Reservoir	03/19/91
Bluegill	3.45 lbs.	Gerald E. Thurmond	Blue Mountain	Farm Pond	02/02/95
Redear	3.33 lbs.	James K. Martin	Ripley	Tippah County Lake	11/05/91
Warmouth	1 lb. 8 oz.	Lillian Morris	Ocean Springs	Black Creek	06/17/79
Green sunfish	1.26 lbs.	Craig Jones	Jackson	Waltman's Lake, Canton	05/21/86
Green sunfish hybrid	1.23 lbs.	Troy M. Wright	Horn Lake	Private farm near Olive Branch	04/06/86
Channel catfish	51 lbs. 12 oz.	Tom Edwards	Toomsuba	Lake Tom Bailey	05/31/97
Blue catfish	93.0 lbs.	Carrol Pearson	Gunnison	Miss. River near Rosedale	02/12/97
Flathead catfish	65 lbs. 8 oz.	Wade Arnold	Baldwyn	Pickwick Lake	03/21/87
Black bullhead	5.56 lbs.	Harold B. Alexander	Southaven	Sunrise Lake near Nesbit	06/12/88
Brown bullhead	6.13 lbs.	Bobby L. Gibson, Jr.	Gautier	Farm Pond near Harrisville	01/19/91
Yellow bullhead	2 lbs. 13 oz.	Robert Cason	Greenwood	Mossy Lake	05/26/74
Walleye	9.66 lbs.	Clayton E. Hobbs	Iuka	Tenn. River near Iuka	01/19/85
Sauger	2.52 lbs.	Pete Maucell	Greenville	Miss. River near Greenville	08/05/92
Carp	74.0 lbs.	Curtis Wade	Pelahatchie	Pelahatchie Lake	06/13/63
Grass carp	34.76 lbs.	Dan Robinson	Guntown	Guntown Sportsman Lake	06/03/92
Bigmouth buffalo	42 lbs. 8 oz.	C. B. O'Daniel	Memphis, TN	Sardis Reservoir	11/15/77
Smallmouth buffalo	57 lbs. 12 oz.	Charles M. Cox	Brandon	Ross Barnett Reservoir	11/21/83
Bighead carp	66 lbs. 12 oz	Al Reed	Independence	Sardis Reservoir (lower lake)	03/27/99
Paddlefish	65.0 lbs.	Randy Pues	Jackson	Ross Barnett Reservoir spillway	06/23/74
Drum	25.27 lbs.	George Anderson	Cleveland	MP&L Lake, Cleveland	03/26/89
Chain pickerel	6 lbs. 4 oz.	Ronnie Boren	Marietta	Bay Springs Lake (Tenn-Tom)	10/04/86
Bowfin	18 lbs. 14 oz.	B. H. Toney	Brandon	Ross Barnett Reservoir	11/23/78
Longnose gar	33.0 lbs.	Rod Gilbert	Senatobia	Tunica Cutoff	09/25/73
Shortnose gar**	3 lbs. 1 oz.	Curtis Crosby	Bogue Chitto	Mississippi River	06/02/99
American eel	5 lbs. 1 oz.	Mitch McLendon	Crystal Springs	Mississippi River	07/12/94

*Official world record. **The first shortnose gar ever reported to the MS Dept. of Wildlife, Fisheries and Parks caught on hook & line. All addresses listed are Mississippi locations, except the two noted.

Some Freshwater Fish Found in Mississippi

(There are about 175 species of freshwater fish found in Mississippi)

- Alligator Gar (*Lepisosteus spatula*)
- Black Crappie (*Pomoxis nigromaculatus*)
- Blue Catfish (*Ictalurus furcatus*)
- Bluegill (*Lepomis macrochirus*)
- Bowfin (*Amia calva*)
- Chain Pickerel (*Esox niger*)
- Channel Catfish (*Ictalurus punctatus*)
- Common Carp (*Cyprinus carpio*)
- Flathead Catfish (*Pylodictus olivaris*)
- Freshwater Drum (*Aplodinotus grunniens*)
- Gizzard Shad (*Dorosoma cepedianum*)
- Grass Carp (*Ctenopharyngodon idella*)
- Green Sunfish (*Lepomis cyanellus*)
- Largemouth Bass (*Micropterus salmoides*)
- Longear Sunfish (*Lepomis megalotis*)
- Longnose Gar (*Lepisosteus osseus*)
- Paddlefish (*Polyodon spatula*)
- Redear Sunfish (*Lepomis microlophus*)
- Sauger (*Stizostedion canadense*)
- Shadow Bass (*Ambloplites ariommus*)
- Shovelnose Sturgeon (*Scaphirhynchus platorynchus*)
- Smallmouth Bass (*Micropterus dolomieu*)
- Smallmouth Buffalo (*Itciobus bubalus*)
- Spotted Bass (*Micropterus punctulatus*)
- Spotted Gar (*Lepisosteus oculatus*)
- Striped Bass (*Morone saxatilis*)
- Sunshine Bass (hybrid) (*Morone chrysops x Morone saxatilis*)
- Walleye (*Stizostedion vitreum*)
- Warmouth (*Lepomis gulosus*)
- White Bass (*Morone chrysops*)
- White Crappie (*Pomoxis annularis*)
- Yellow Bass (*Morone mississippiensis*)
- Yellow Bullhead (*Ameiurus natalis*)
- Yellow Perch (*Perca flavescens*)

The Ultimate Reference on the State

State Parks in Mississippi

BUCCANEER STATE PARK — P O Box 180; Waveland 39576 (228) 467-3822
    Location: On the Gulf Coast 2 miles south of Hwy 90 on Beach Blvd in Waveland.
    Offers: Seasonal wave pool and wading pool, game room, tennis & basketball courts, 3 play areas, nature trail, outdoor amphitheater, tent camping with 149 pads.

CASEY JONES RAILROAD MUSEUM STATE PARK — Vaughan 39179 (662) 673-9864
    Location: Just off I-55, Exit 133 (central Mississippi)
    Note: In honor of train engineer Johnathan Luther 'Casey' Jones who died in the historic wreck of the Cannonball in 1900 less than a mile from the museum.
    Offers: 1923 oil-burning steam engine on display. Railroad exhibits. NO CAMPING.
    Hours: 9 am to 5 pm Tues - Sat. Closed Sun & Mon.

CLARKO STATE PARK — Rt 1, Box 186; Quitman 39355 (601) 776-6651
    Location: 20 miles south of Meridian off Hwy 45.
    Offers: Lighted tennis courts, large picnic pavilions, lodge w/meeting rooms, fast food service, camp store, 43 camping pads, 14 cabins w/individual piers on 65-acre Lake Ivy and marked nature trails.

FLOREWOOD RIVER PLANTATION STATE PARK — Greenwood 38930 (662) 455-3821
    Location: 2 miles west of Greenwood off Hwy 82.
    Offers: Recreated 1850s living history plantation and Cotton Museum (no fee).

GEORGE PAYNE COSSAR STATE PARK — Rt 1; Oakland 38948 (662) 623-7356
    Location: On 42-square mile Lake Enid 8 miles east of Oakland off Hwy 32.
    Offers: Famed restaurant with catfish specialty (open year round, Wed - Sun, noon - 9 pm), pool & beach, lodge, nature trail, miniature golf, 8 cabins and 156 camping pads.

GOLDEN MEMORIAL STATE PARK — Rt 1, Box 8; Walnut Grove 39189 (601) 253-2237
    Location: On Hwy 492, 5 miles east of Walnut Grove off Hwy 35 (central Mississippi).
    Note: Memorializes a post-Civil War one-room school once located on the site.
    Offers: Tent camping, picnic tables, grills, 2 picnic pavilions, 7 camping pads.
    Hours: Wed - Sun, 8 am - 5 pm.

GREAT RIVER ROAD STATE PARK — P O Box 292; Rosedale 38769 (662) 759-6762
    Location: In Rosedale off Hwy 1, 35 miles north of Greenville (northwestern MS).
    Note: On the Mississippi River — has a 4-level observation tower to observe the river.
    Offers: fishing, boating, camping pads & lodge w/game room & fast-food service.

GULF MARINE STATE PARK — P O Box 433; Biloxi 39533 (228) 435-4355
    Location: In East Biloxi on U.S. Hwy 90 at Ocean Springs Bridge (coastal Mississippi).
    Note: A recreational/educational complex adjacent to Marine Education Center.

HOLMES COUNTY STATE PARK — Rt 1, Box 153; Durant 39063 (662) 653-3351
    Location: 4 miles south of Durant off I-55, Exit 150 (central Mississippi).
    Note: Most centrally located of the state's parks.
    Offers: 2 fishing lakes, nature trail, group camp w/meeting room & amphitheater, skating rink, archery range, tent camping, 12 cabins & 28 camping pads.

State Parks in Mississippi

HUGH WHITE STATE PARK — P O Box 725; Grenada 38901 (662) 226-4934
    Location: 5 miles east of Grenada off Hwy 8 (north-central Mississippi).
    Note: All popular water sports on 64,600-acre Grenada Lake.
    Offers: Bait shop, beach, pool (for cabin guests), tennis courts, restaurant, 20 cabins, 10-unit motel, group camp for 35 & 173 camping pads.

J. P. COLEMAN STATE PARK — Rt 5, Box 504; Iuka 38852 (662) 423-6515
    Location: 13 miles north of Iuka off Hwy 25 (northeastern Mississippi).
    Note: On the Tennessee River at Pickwick Lake — specializes in all water sports.
    Offers: Rest. w/catering, full-service marina, 20 cabins, 5-unit motel & 45 camping pads.

JOHN KYLE STATE PARK — Rt 1, Box 115; Sardis 38666 (662) 487-1345
    Location: 9 miles east of Sardis of Hwy 315 (northern Mississippi).
    Offers: Sardis Lake, seasonal pool, tennis courts, playing field, indoor sports hall for basketball, volleyball & ping pong, 20 cabins, group camp for 328 camping pads, vacation cabins & the Mallard Pointe 27-hole championship golf course, lighted driving range, putting/chipping greens, pro shop 1-888-TEEMISS (1-888-833-6477).

LAKE LINCOLN STATE PARK — 2573 Sunset Rd, NE; Wesson 39191 (601) 643-9044
    Location: 4.5 miles east off Hwy 51 near Wesson (Southwest Mississippi)
    Offers: 550-acre lake with water sports & excellent fishing, 1.5-acre sand beach, two picnic pavilions, picnic areas, nature trails, 61 improved camping pads (some located lakeside), and a primitive camping area.

LAKE LOWNDES STATE PARK — Rt 4, Box 277-D; Columbus 39702 (662) 328-2110
    Location: 6 miles southeast of Columbus off Hwy 69 (east-central Mississippi).
    Offers: Lodge w/game room & fast-food service, indoor sports hall for basketball, volleyball & badminton, outdoor playing fields, 6 tennis courts, 4 cabins & 50 camping pads.

LeFLEUR'S BLUFF STATE PARK — 2140 Riverside Dr; Jackson (601) 987-3923
    Mayes Lake Campground; Lakeland Dr; Jackson 987-3985
    Mississippi Museum of Natural Science 354-7303
    Golf Course 362-3885

LEGION STATE PARK — Rt 5, Box 32-B; Louisville 39339 (662) 773-8323
    Location: In Louisville on Old Hwy 25 (central Mississippi).
    Offers: 2 lakes, picnicking, tent camping, 2 cabins & nature trail.
    Hours: Wed - Sun, 8 am - 5 pm.

LEROY PERCY STATE PARK — P O Box 176; Hollandale 38748 (662) 827-5436
    Location: 5 miles west of Hollandale off Hwy 12 (northwestern Mississippi).
    Offers: Wildlife hunting, lodge, pool, 5 cabins, group camp for 48 & 16 camping pads.

NANIH WAIYA HISTORIC SITE — Rt 3; Louisville 39339 (662) 773-7988
    Location: 12 miles east of Noxapater off Hwy 490 (central Mississippi).
    Note: Legendary birthplace of Choctaw Indians & site of their sacred mound.
    Offers: Activity building, picnic area & nature trail. NO CAMPING.
    Hours: Wed - Sat, 8 am - 5 pm; Sun 1 - 5 pm.

State Parks in Mississippi

NATCHEZ STATE PARK — Rt 5, Box 465; Natchez 39120   (601) 442-2658
    Location: 10 miles north of Natchez off U.S. Hwy 61 at Stanton (southwestern MS).
    Note: Hamburg Road, an old plantation road, runs through the park.
    Offers: Large lake for fishing & water sports, picnic area, nature trail,
        equestrian trail (no horse rentals), 24 camping pads & tent camping area.

PAUL B. JOHNSON STATE PARK — Rt 3, Box 408; Hattiesburg 39401   (601) 582-7721
    Location: 15 miles south of Hattiesburg of U.S. Hwy 49 (southern Mississippi).
    Note: Situated on spring-fed Geiger Lake.
    Offers: Fishing, water sports, lodge with game room, fast-food service & catering,
        group camp for 150, 16 cabins, 108 camping pads & nature trail.

PERCY QUIN STATE PARK — Rt 3; McComb 39648   (601) 684-3938
    Location: 6 miles south of McComb off I-55, Exit 5 (southwestern Mississippi).
    Offers: Lake Tangipahoa water sports, group camp for 212, 22 cabins, 101
        camping pads, tent camping, lodge with catering, game room, camp store,
        playground, picnic area, railroad museum, plus the Quail Hollow 27-hole
        championship golf course, lighted driving range, putting and chipping greens
        and full-service pro shop (1-888-GOLFMIS = 1888-465-3647).

ROOSEVELT STATE PARK — Morton 39117   (601) 732-6313
    Location: Off I-20, Exit 25 (central Mississippi).
    Offers: Mini-convention center for up to 200 (catering available by reservation),
        game room, group camp for 104, 2 campgrounds, 12 cabins, tent camping,
        lighted tennis courts, softball field, lake & picnicking.

SAM DALE HISTORIC SITE — P O Box 10600; Jackson 39209   (601) 961-5014
    Location: 15 miles north of Meridian off Hwy 39 in Daleville (east-central MS).
    Note: A memorial to General Sam Dale, 19th century frontiersman & patriot.
    Offers: Four picnic shelters. NO RESTROOMS. NO CAMPING.

SHEPARD STATE PARK — 1100 Graveline Rd; Gautier 39553   (228) 497-2244
    Location: 3 miles west of Pascagoula, south of U.S. Hwy 90 in Gautier (southern MS).
    Note: 400 acres replete with trees & wildflowers.
    Offers: Equestrian & bike trails (horses & bikes for rent), hiking trails, tent
        camping & picnicking. Hours: Wed - Sun, 8 am to 5 pm.

TISHOMINGO STATE PARK — Box 880; Tishomingo 38873   (662) 438-6914
    Location: 2 miles south of Tishomingo of Hwy 25 (northeastern Mississippi).
    Offers: An April to October Bear Creek float trip, 13 mile nature trail system,
        swinging bridge, pavilion, lodge, pool, 6 cabins, playing field, group
        camp for 142, tent camping & 20 camping pads.

TOMBIGBEE STATE PARK — Rt 2, Box 336-E; Tupelo 38801   (662) 842-7669
    Location: 6 miles southeast of Tupelo off Hwy 6 (northeastern Mississippi).
    Offers: Catering & fast-food service available in lodge, game room, swim, ski &
        fish in park lake, lakeside group camp with meeting room that houses 200,
        nature trail, archery range, 6 cabins & 20 camping pads.

State Parks in Mississippi

TRACE STATE PARK — Rt 1, Box 254; Belden 38826   (662) 489-2958
     Location: 10 miles east of Pontotoc off Hwy 6 (northeastern Mississippi)
     Offers: 2,500 acres with fishing, water skiing, rental boats, boat launch ramp,
         nature hiking, tent camping and 25 camping pads with electricity & water.

WALL DOXEY STATE PARK — Holly Springs 38635   (662) 252-4231
     Location: 7 miles south of Holly Springs off Hwy 7 (northeastern Mississippi).
     Offers: Spring-fed lake, beach, 3-level diving pier, fishing, multi-purpose
         activity field, playground, archery range, nature trails, lodge with
         catering, group camp for 104, 9 cabins and 64 camping pads.

WINTERVILLE MOUNDS HISTORIC SITE — Greenville 38701   (662) 334-4684
     Location: 3 miles north of Greenville off Hwy 1 (northwestern Mississippi).
     Note: Site of one of the largest Indian mound groups in the Mississippi Valley.
         Believed to be the ceremonial site of the predecessors of the Chickasaw
         and Choctaw Indians.
     Offers: Museum (fee) and picnicking. NO CAMPING.
     Hours: 8 am - 5 pm, Sun, 1 - 5 pm. Closed Mondays & Tuesdays.

A total of 29 state parks — 4 historic parks and 25 recreational parks covering over 23,000 acres (35.94 square miles).

Mississippi State Parks - Parks Operation   **(601) 364-2160**
Parks Reservation Information   **Toll Free 1-800-GO PARKS or (800) 467-2757**

Mississippi State Park facilities are valued at $80 million, not counting land & water values. The State Parks had 4.8 million visitors in fiscal year 1997 and collected $5.4 million in revenues.

PAT HARRISON WATERWAY DISTRICT WATER PARKS (1-800-748-9403)

Archusa Creek Water Park; Route 4, Box 320; Quitman 39355 .... (601) 776-6956
Big Creek Water Park; Route 1; Soso 39480 .... (601) 763-8555
Bluff Creek Water Park; P.O. Box 5044; Vancleave 39565 .... (228) 826-9963
Dry Creek Water Park; Rt. 3, Box 287; Mount Olive 39119 .... (601) 797-4619
Flint Creek Water Park; 1216 Parkway Dr; Wiggins 39577 .... (601) 928-3051
Little Black Creek Water Park; 2159 Little Black Creek Rd, Purvis 39475 ... (601) 794-2957
Maynor Creek Water Park; P.O. Box 591; Waynesboro 39367 .... (601) 735-4365
Okatibbee Water Park; Rt. 12, Box 100A; Meridian 39301 .... (601) 737-2370
Turkey Creek Water Park; Rt. 1, Box 100A; Decatur 39327 .... (601) 635-3314
Dunn's Falls; Rt. 1, Box 115; Enterprise 39330 .... (601) 655-9511

Public & Private Golf Courses in Mississippi

Aberdeen Country Club; Aberdeen .... (662) 369-6251
Ackerman Country Club; Ackerman .... (662) 285-3528
Amory Golf Club; Amory .... (662) 256-9454
Annandale Golf Course; Madison .... (601) 856-3882
Avon Country Club; Greenville .... (662) 332-3861
Back Acres Country Club; Senatobia ...... (662) 562-9838
Bay Breeze Golf Course (Military); Biloxi ... (228) 377-3832
Bay Pointe Country Club; Brandon .... (601) 829-1862
Bay Springs Country Club; Bay Springs .... (601) 764-2621
Bayou Bend Country Club; Sumner .... (662) 375-9381
Bear Creek Golf Club & Pro Shop; Laurel ... (601) 425-5670
Beau Pré Country Club; Natchez .... (601) 442-5493
Beaver Creek Golf Club; Newton .... (601) 683-2986
Bel Air Golf Course; Tupelo .... (662) 841-6446
Belwood Country Club; Natchez .... (601) 442-5493
Benton Country Club; Benton .... (662) 673-9881
Big Oaks Golf Course; Saltillo/Tupelo ...... (662) 840-1218
Blackjack Bay Golf Links; Biloxi .... (228) 392-0400
Booneville Golf & Country Club;
    Booneville .... (662) 728-6812
Briargate Country Club; Southaven .... (662) 393-9914
Briarwood Country Club; Bailey/Meridian ... (601) 681-6183
Bridges at The Casino Magic; Bay St. Louis . (800) 562-4425
Broadwater Beach Resort; Biloxi .... (228) 388-3672
Broadwater Beach Resort; Gulfport .... (228) 896-4482
Brookhaven Country Club; Brookhaven .... (601) 833-9819
Brookwood Country Club; Jackson .... (601) 372-5981
Canebrake Golf Club; Hattiesburg .... (601) 271-2010
Canton Country Club; Canton .... (601) 859-1822
Caroline Golf Club; Madison .... (601) 853-4554
Castlewoods Country Club; Clinton .... (601) 992-1937
Castlewoods Golf Club; Brandon .... (601) 992-1942
Cherokee Valley Golf Club; Olive Branch ... (662) 893-4444
Clarksdale Country Club; Clarksdale ...... (662) 624-4170
Clear Creek Golf Course;
    Vicksburg (Bovina) .... (601) 638-9395
Cleveland Country Club; Cleveland .... (662) 843-3456
Coahoma Country Club; Clarksdale .... (662) 624-9484
Colonial Country Club; Jackson .... (601) 956-4251
Colonial Country Club
    Deerfield Course; Madison .... (601) 856-6966
Columbia Country Club; Columbia .... (601) 736-4413
Columbus Country Club; Columbus .... (662) 328-4837
Confederate Heights Country Club;
    Florence .... (601) 845-6044
Corinth Golf Driving Range; Corinth .... (662) 287-8801
Cottonwoods Golf Course; Robinsonville ... (662) 357-6078
Country Casino and Lady Luck Rythm &
    Blues Casino Golf Course; Lula ... (800) 576-5825
Country Club of Big Oaks; Saltillo .... (662) 844-8002
Country Club of Jackson, The; Jackson .... (601) 956-1411
Dancing Rabbit Golf Course; Philadelphia ... (601) 663-0012
Delta State University Golf; Cleveland ..... (662) 846-4585
Diamondhead Country Club; Diamondhead .. (228) 255-2925
Dixie Golf Club; Laurel .... (601) 649-4254
Dogwood Hills Golf Course; Woolmarket ... (228) 392-9805
Drew Country Club; Drew .... (662) 745-6127
Duncan Park Golf Club; Natchez .... (601) 442-5955
Eagle Ridge Golf Course at Hinds Community
    College; Raymond .... (601) 857-5993

Edgewater Bay Golf Club; Biloxi .... (228) 385-2751
Elm Lake Golf Club; Columbus .... (662) 329-8964
Fernwood Country Club; Fernwood .... (601) 684-6983
Forest Country Club; Forest .... (601) 469-9137
Fulton Country Club; Fulton .... (662) 862-2337
Grand Casino Golf Course;
    Tunica/Robinsonville .... (800) 946-4946
Grand Oaks Golf Course; Oxford .... (662) 236-3008
Great Southern Golf Course; Gulfport ...... (228) 896-3536
Green Hills Country Club; Purvis .... (601) 794-6427
Green Oaks Golf Club; Columbus .... (662) 328-3879
Greenville Municipal Golf Course;
    Greenville .... (662) 332-4079
Greenville Golf & Country Club; Greenville . (662) 332-7210
Greenwood Country Club; Greenwood ..... (662) 453-8792
Grenada Golf Club; Grenada .... (662) 226-3867
Grove Park Municipal Golf Course; Jackson . (601) 960-2074
Gulf Coast Driving Ranges; Gulfport .... (228) 831-0466
Gulf Hills Golf Course; Ocean Springs ..... (228) 872-9663
Gulfport Par 3; Gulfport .... (228) 868-3809
Hamilton Country Club; Hamilton .... (662) 343-8907
Hattiesburg Country Club; Hattiesburg ..... (601) 264-5076
Hernando Hills Country Club; Hernando .... (662) 429-0317
Hickory Hill Country Club; Gautier .... (228) 497-5150
Hillandale Country Club; Corinth .... (662) 287-3507
Hillsdale Country Club; Lumberton .... (601) 796-9005
Holiday Golf Club; Olive Branch .... (662) 895-3500
Holly Springs Country Club; Holly Springs .. (662) 252-7774
Hollywood Casino Golf Course;
    Tunica/Robinsonville .... (800) 871-0711
Holmes County Country Club; Lexington .... (662) 834-9996
Houston Country Club; Houston .... (662) 456-3914
Humphreys County Country Club;
    Silver City .... (662) 247-3141
Indianola Country Club; Indianola .... (662) 887-3832
Isles Golf Club; Pass Christian .... (228) 452-4851
Iuka Country Club; Iuka .... (662) 423-9981
Jerry's Country Club; Mound Bayou .... (662) 741-2727
Kirkwood National Golf Club; Holly Springs (662) 252-4888
Lady Luck Casino Golf Course; Natchez .... (800) 722-5825
Lakeland Golf Center; Jackson .... (601) 936-6840
Lake View Golf Club; Summit .... (601) 276-9311
Lakeview Golf Course; Meridian .... (601) 693-3301
Laurel Country Club; Laurel .... (601) 649-6252
Leake Country Club; Carthage .... (601) 267-9496
Lefleur's Bluff State Park Golf; Jackson ..... (601) 362-3885
Leflore County Country Club; Itta Bena .... (662) 453-2971
Links of Whispering Woods, The;
    Olive Branch .... (662) 895-3500
Live Oaks Golf Club; Jackson .... (601) 982-1231
Louisville Country Club; Louisville .... (662) 773-9964
Lucedale Country Club; Lucedale .... (601) 947-2798
Mallard Pointe Golf Course;
    John Kyle State Park; Sardis ..... (888) 833-6477
Meadows, The; Tupelo .... (662) 840-1985
Meridian Golf Course; Meridian .... (601) 693-3301
Middlefork Country Club; Meadville .... (601) 384-5730
Mid-South Golf Club; Sardis .... (662) 487-9090
Millbrook Country Club; Picayune .... (601) 798-8711
Minglewood Country Club; Morton .... (601) 732-8884

Public & Private Golf Courses in Mississippi

Mississippi National Golf Club/Linkscorp;
    Gautier .... (228) 497-2372
Mississippi State University Golf Course;
    Starkville .... (662) 325-3028
Mosswood Country Club; Port Gibson .... (601) 437-4111
Natchez Trace Golf Club; Saltillo .... (662) 869-2166
New Albany Country Club; New Albany .... (662) 534-4661
Newton Country Club; Newton .... (601) 683-3521
North Creek Golf Course; Southaven .... (662) 280-4653
Northbay Country Club; Madison .... (601) 856-0635
Northwood Country Club; Meridian .... (601) 485-5112
Oak Ridge Driving Range & Golf Course;
    McComb .... (601) 684-7317
Oaks Country Club; New Albany .... (662) 534-7411
Oaks Golf Club, The; Pass Christian .... (228) 452-0909
Okatibbee Creek Golf Course; Meridian ..... (601) 483-4653
Okatoma Golf Club; Collins .... (601) 765-1841
Okolona Country Club; Okolona .... (662) 447-2033
Old Waverly Golf Club; West Point .... (662) 494-6463
Olive Branch Country Club; Olive Branch ... (662) 895-6525
Oxford Country Club; Oxford .... (662) 234-5811
Panola Country Club; Batesville .... (662) 563-9260
Par Three Golf Course; Biloxi .... (228) 388-3631
Pascagoula Country Club; Pascagoula .... (228) 762-1466
Pass Christian Isles Golf Club; Pass Christian (228) 452-4851
Pearl Municipal Golf Course; Pearl .... (601) 932-3534
Pearl River Golf Club; Poplarville .... (601) 795-8887
Pecan Meadows Country Club; Clarksdale ... (662) 624-9484
Philadelphia Country Club; Philadelphia ..... (601) 656-8512
Pine Bayou Golf Course (Military); Gulfport (228) 871-2494
Pine Belt National Golf Club; Moselle .... (601) 584-6531
Pine Burr Country Club; Wiggins .... (601) 928-4911
Pine Burr Golf Club; Gulfport .... (228) 864-0993
Pine Creek Golf Course; Purvis .... (601) 794-6427
Pine Hill Golf & Country Club; Ripley ...... (662) 837-7863
Pine Hills Country Club; Calhoun City ...... (662) 628-5213
Pine Hills Country Club; Gloster .... (601) 225-7741
Pine Island Golf Course; Ocean Springs ..... (228) 875-1674
Pineview Country Club; Macon .... (662) 726-9384
Plantation Golf Club; Olive Branch .... (662) 895-3530
Ponta Creek Golf Course (Military);
    Naval Air Station; Meridian .... (601) 679-2129
Pontotoc Country Club; Pontotoc .... (662) 489-9900
Prentiss Country Club; Prentiss .... (601) 792-5062
Quail Hollow Golf Course;
    Percy Quin State Park; McComb .... (888) 465-3647
Quitman Country Club; Quitman .... (601) 776-2582
Rainbow Bay Golf Club; Biloxi .... (228) 385-2751
Redbud Springs Golf & Country Club;
    Kosciusko .... (662) 289-5446
Refuge, The; Flowood .... (601) 664-1414
River Birch Golf Club; Amory .... (662) 256-3419

Rolling Hills Country Club; Crystal Springs   (601) 892-1621
Royal Gulf Hills Country Club;
    Ocean Springs .... (228) 875-4211
Saint Andrews Golf Club; Ocean Springs .... (228) 875-7730
Sam's Town Hotel & Gambling Hall Golf
    Course; Tunica/Robinsonville ..... (800) 456-0711
Sandy Run Golf Course; Hattiesburg .... (601) 264-5284
Shadow Ridge Golf Club; Hattiesburg ...... (601) 296-0286
Shady Oaks Country Club; Jackson .... (601) 922-2331
Sharkey Country Club; Anguilla .... (662) 873-2222
Shelby Country Club; Shelby .... (662) 398-7777
Shiloh Ridge Golf Estates; Corinth .... (662) 286-8000
Simpson Country Club; Magee .... (601) 849-3567
Sonny Guy Municipal Golf Course; Jackson . (601) 960-1905
Southwind Country Club; Biloxi .... (228) 392-0400
Starkville Country Club; Starkville .... (662) 323-1733
Sunkist Country Club Pro Shop; Biloxi ...... (228) 388-3961
Sunnybrook Driving Range; Ridgeland ...... (601) 856-5573
Tallahatchie Country Club; Charleston ...... (662) 647-9409
Timberton Golf Club; Hattiesburg .... (601) 584-4653
Tramark Golf Club; Gulfport .... (228) 863-7808
Treasure Bay Gulf Hills Golf Course;
    Ocean Springs .... (228) 875-4211
Treasure Oak Country Club; Ocean Springs . (228) 875-9256
Tupelo Country Club; Belden .... (662) 840-2991
Twin Pines Golf Club; Petal .... (601) 544-8318
Tylertown Country Club; Tylertown .... (601) 876-2510
University of Miss. Golf Course; Oxford .... (601) 234-4816
USM's Van Hook Golf Course; Hattiesburg .. (601) 264-1872
Vicksburg Country Club; Vicksburg .... (601) 636-8581
Village Golf Center; Olive Branch .... (662) 895-8223
Walnut Hills Golf Course; Yazoo City .... (662) 716-9667
Walter Sillers Country Club; Rosedale .... (662) 759-3353
Waynesboro Country Club; Waynesboro .... (601) 735-2112
Wedgewood Golf Course; Olive Branch ..... (662) 895-7490
West Hills Family Golf Center; Hattiesburg .. (601) 264-6306
West Point Country Club; West Point .... (662) 494-3535
Whisper Lake Country Club; Madison .... (601) 853-0202
Whispering Pines Golf Club; Columbus
    Air Force Base; Columbus .... (662) 434-7932
Whispering Pines Golf Club; Corinth .... (662) 286-6151
Willow Creek Golf Course; Brandon .... (601) 825-8343
Wilson Lake Country Club; Marks .... (662) 326-2241
Windance Country Club; Gulfport .... (228) 832-5374
Winding Creek Golf Course; Natchez .... (601) 442-6995
Winona Country Club; Winona .... (662) 283-2474
Winstonville Country Club; Winstonville .... (662) 741-2143
Wolf Hollow Golf Course at Copiah-Lincoln
    Community College; Wesson .... (601) 643-8379
Yalobusha Country Club; Water Valley ...... (662) 473-2401
Yazoo Country Club; Yazoo City .... (662) 746-4441
Yoda Creek Golf Club; Bruce .... (662) 983-9632

Total of 201 Courses Listed

The Ultimate Reference on the State

Casinos in Mississippi

Casino Name ♠ ♥ ♦ ♣	Location	Phone Number	Sq. Ft. of Gaming	No. of Slots	No. of Tables	Restaurants, Hotels & Other Amenities
Ameristar Casino	4116 Washington St. Vicksburg	1-800-700-7770	44,388	1,100	50	2 restaurants, 150 hotel rooms, showroom, entertainment
Bally's Saloon & Gambling Hall Hotel	1450 Bally Blvd. Tunica/ Robinsonville	1-800-38-BALLY (1-800-382-2559)	40,000	1,243	54	3 restaurants, 238 hotel rooms, RV park, nightclub, entertainment
Bayou Caddy's Jubilee Casino	211 S. Lakefront Rd. Greenville	1-800-WIN MORE (1-800-946-6673)	28,500	834	23	2 restaurants, 41 hotel rooms, entertainment
Beau Rivage Resort	Intersection I-110 & Beach Blvd. Biloxi	1-888-330-7111 1-888-567-6667 (reservations)	71,669	2,088	95	12 restaurants, 1,780 hotel rooms, golf course w/pkg., marina, entertainment
Boomtown Casino	676 Bayview Ave. Biloxi's Back Bay Biloxi	1-800-627-0777	33,362	1,174	28	2 restaurants, dynamic-motion theater, entertainment
Casino Magic - Bay St. Louis	711 Casino Magic Dr; Bay St. Louis	1-800-5-MAGIC-5 (1-800-562-4425)	39,500	1,111	38	4 restaurants, 201 hotel rms, RV park, golf course, golf pkg., entertainment
Casino Magic - Biloxi	195 Beach Blvd. Biloxi	1-800-562-4425	47,200	1,225	44	4 restaurants, 378 hotel rooms, golf pkg., comedy express, entertainment
Copa Casino	777 Copa Blvd. at Hwys 49 & 90 Gulfport	1-800-WIN-COPA (1-800-946-2672)	27,000	783	23	restaurant, arcade, entertainment
Fitzgerald's Casino	711 Lucky Lane Tunica/ Robinsonville	1-800-766-LUCK (1-800-766-5825)	36,000	1,204	34	4 restaurants, 507 hotel rooms, special events & exhibitions, entertainment
Gold Strike Casino	1010 Casino Ctr. Dr. Tunica/ Robinsonville	1-888-245-7529	47,710	1,374	46	6 restaurants, 1,200 hotel rms (tallest bldg. in MS), theater, entertainment
Grand Casino Biloxi	265 Beach Blvd. (Highway 90) Biloxi	1-800-WIN-2-WIN (1-800-946-2946)	110,000	2,455	100	7 restaurants, 1,000 hotel rooms, golf course, golf pkg., 1,600-seat theater
Grand Casino Gulfport	3215 W. Beach Blvd. Gulfport	1-800-946-7777	85,000	2,392	92	7 restaurants, 1,000 hotel rooms, golf course, golf pkg., theater, arcade
Grand Casino Tunica	13615 Old Hwy 61N Tunica/ Robinsonville	1-800-WIN-4-WIN (800-946-4946)	140,000	3,265	161	7 restaurants, 1,350 hotel rms, RV park, golf course, golf pkg., entertainment
Harrah's Tunica Casino and Hotel	1100 Casino Strip Blvd.; Tunica/ Robinsonville	1-888-789-7900	50,000	1,350	33	3 restaurants, 200 hotel rooms, entertainment
Harrah's Vicksburg	1310 Mulberry St. Vicksburg	1-800-843-2343	18,000	663	30	3 restaurants, 117 hotel rooms, live entertainment
Hollywood Casino	1150 Casino Strip Blvd.; Tunica/ Robinsonville	1-800-871-0711	54,000	1,499	50	3 restaurants, 506 hotel rooms, RV park, golf course, entertainment*
Horseshoe Casino & Hotel	1021 Casino Ctr. Dr. Tunica/ Robinsonville	1-800-303-SHOE (1-800-303-7463)	45,000	1,572	76	4 restaurants, 505 hotel rooms, RV park, film memorabilia, entertainm't.
Imperial Palace	850 Bayview Biloxi	1-800-436-3000	70,000	1,647	53	9 restaurants, 1,100 hotel rooms, golf pkg., auto collection, entertainment

Casinos in Mississippi

Casino Name ♠ ♥ ♦ ♣	Location	Phone Number	Sq. Ft. of Gaming	No. of Slots	No. of Tables	Restaurants, Hotels & Other Amenities
Isle of Capri Casino Crowne Plaza Resort	151 Beach Blvd; Biloxi	1-800-THE-ISLE (1-800-843-4753)	32,500	1,215	37	3 restaurants, 370 hotel rooms, golf pkg., entertainment
Isle of Capri Casino Tunica	1600 Isle of Capri Blvd.; Tunica/Robinsonville	1-800-THE-ISLE (1-800-843-4753)	32,500	870	15	2 restaurants, 225 hotel rooms, Wayne Newton theater, entertainment
Isle of Capri Casino Vicksburg	3990 Washington St. Vicksburg	1-800-WIN-ISLE (1-800-946-4753)	32,500	1,215	37	3 restaurants, 122 hotel rooms, RV park, entertainment
Lady Luck Casino & Hotel	Under-the-Hill at 70 Silver St. Natchez	1-800-722-LUCK (1-800-722-5825)	15,783	664	16	2 restaurants, 143 hotel rooms, golf pkg., entertainment
Lady Luck Rhythm & Blues/Country Casinos	777 Lady Luck Pkwy. at Lula, MS near Clarksdale	1-800-789-5825 1-800-576-5825 (reservations)	63,000	1,514	55	4 restaurants, 593 hotel rooms, golf course, golf pkg., entertainment center
Las Vegas Casino	242 S. Walnut Greenville	1-800-VEGAS-21 (1-800-834-2721)	18,800	800	21	2 restaurants, live entertainment
Lighthouse Point Casino	199 N. Lakefront Rd. Greenville	1-800-878-1777	22,000	782	15	2 restaurants, 148 hotel rooms, entertainment
New Palace Casino	158 Howard Ave. Biloxi	1-800-PALACE-9 (1-800-725-2239)	43,500	773	34	3 restaurants, 239 hotel rooms, theater, entertainment
President Casino	2110 Beach Blvd. Biloxi	1-800-THE-PRES (1-800-843-7737)	38,279	963	38	3 restaurants, 510 hotel rooms, golf course, golf pkg., entertainment
Rainbow Hotel Casino	1380 Warrenton Rd. Vicksburg	1-800-503-3777	31,000	1,000	15	restaurant, 89 hotel rooms, fun park, entertainment
Sam's Town Hotel & Gambling Hall	1477 Casino Strip Blvd.; Tunica/Robinsonville	1-800-456-0711	96,000	1,735	70	5 restaurants, 850 hotel rooms, golf course, golf pkg., entertainment ctr.
Sheraton Casino	1107 Casino Ctr. Dr. Tunica/Robinsonville	1-800-391-3777	32,800	1,354	47	3 restaurants, 140 hotel rooms, comedy zone, live entertainment
Silver Star Resort & Casino	Hwy 16, west of Philadelphia, MS in Neshoba County	1-800-557-0711	90,000+	3,000	108	6 restaurants, 509 hotel rooms, golf course, golf pkg., entertainment
Treasure Bay Casino	1980 Beach Blvd. Biloxi	1-800-PIRATE-9 (1-800-747-2839)	41,000	936	54	4 restaurants, 268 hotel rooms, golf pkg., arcade, show bar, entertainment

STATE GAMING COMMISSION: 1-800-504-PLAY — MISSISSIPPI COUNCIL ON COMPULSIVE GAMBLING: 1-888-777-9696

Gaming is big business in Mississippi — the third largest gambling state in the nation in revenues behind Nevada & New Jersey and the second largest in total area devoted to gaming, behind only Nevada. As of July 1, 2000, there were 32 casinos in the state with over 1.5 million square feet of gaming area, over 43,000 slots and about 1,500 gaming tables. On July 1, 1999, Mississippi casinos directly employed over 36,000 people with an annual payroll over one-half billion dollars. During 1999, over 22 million people visited Mississippi casinos, almost 15 million (67%) of them are from outside the state. Through March 1999, the casino industry had made over $3.5 billion in capital investments in Mississippi. At that time, 27 casinos had 12,819 hotel rooms with an 82% occupancy rate. An additional 1,165 hotel rooms were under construction. The tallest building in Mississippi is the 1,200-room hotel at Gold Strike Casino in Robinsonville (Tunica). The 31-story structure stands 317 feet tall! The largest hotel in the state is the 1,780-room hotel at Beau Rivage Resort in Biloxi, Mississippi.

The Ultimate Reference on the State

Mississippi Casino Gross Gaming Revenues

	1992	1993		1994		
				Gulf Coast Counties	Mississippi River Counties	Totals
Jan.		$ 40,118,995	Jan.	$ 53,322,303	$ 46,644,365	$ 99,966,668
Feb.		42,595,657	Feb.	58,170,877	48,207,481	106,378,358
Mar.		51,243,878	Mar.	60,329,743	59,840,790	120,170,533
Apr.		52,421,280	Apr.	64,221,627	56,862,106	121,083,733
May		58,752,132	May	66,784,833	58,015,782	124,800,615
June		61,396,052	June	62,332,692	57,532,709	119,865,401
July		74,695,230	July	72,102,662	69,809,172	141,911,834
Aug.	$ 10,616,710	78,017,868	Aug.	60,317,077	68,631,095	128,948,172
Sept.	18,455,071	77,061,721	Sept.	61,470,651	66,869,528	128,340,179
Oct.	26,987,124	80,490,318	Oct.	58,208,055	68,520,808	126,728,864
Nov.	32,427,490	82,836,509	Nov.	56,904,455	65,536,548	122,441,002
Dec.	33,321,576	90,206,071	Dec.	53,161,726	68,997,562	122,159,288
Totals	$ 121,807,970	$ 789,835,710	Totals	$ 727,326,701	$ 735,467,945	$1,462,794,646
Running Grand Total		$ 911,643,681		**Running Grand Total**		$2,374,438,327

	1995			1996		
	Gulf Coast Counties	Mississippi River Counties	Totals	Gulf Coast Counties	Mississippi River Counties	Totals
Jan.	$ 57,169,532	$ 76,323,990	$ 133,493,522	$ 57,077,790	$ 84,052,771	$ 141,130,560
Feb.	56,467,579	72,761,744	129,229,322	60,963,023	83,633,806	144,596,830
Mar.	62,368,507	80,836,899	143,205,406	69,349,126	104,634,960	173,984,085
Apr.	61,404,213	84,341,784	145,745,998	62,849,810	89,805,317	152,655,127
May	59,062,693	85,671,861	144,734,554	62,181,216	90,398,796	152,580,012
June	58,613,777	80,215,783	138,829,560	63,232,690	90,176,187	153,408,876
July	70,565,494	98,268,060	168,833,555	70,608,566	101,228,612	171,837,178
Aug.	59,724,280	84,759,463	144,483,743	66,249,144	96,420,867	162,670,011
Sept.	60,160,593	86,232,083	146,392,676	61,132,631	93,899,015	155,031,645
Oct.	55,334,961	87,283,609	142,618,570	57,962,554	93,139,662	151,102,216
Nov.	58,044,361	83,256,656	141,301,016	59,505,895	94,295,404	153,801,299
Dec.	57,100,563	88,374,520	145,475,083	58,226,643	91,021,846	149,248,489
Totals	$ 716,016,554	$1,008,326,452	$1,724,343,006	$ 749,339,088	$1,112,707,243	$1,862,046,331
Running Grand Total			$4,098,781,332	**Running Grand Total**		5,960,827,663

Figures are for state-regulated casinos and do not include revenues from the Silver Star Casino.
Some figures don't add exactly due to rounding. All Totals and Running Grand Totals are correct to the nearest dollar.
SOURCE: State Tax Commission

Mississippi Casino Gross Gaming Revenues

	1997			1998		
	Gulf Coast Counties	Mississippi River Counties	Totals	Gulf Coast Counties	Mississippi River Counties	Totals
Jan.	$ 59,184,097	$ 91,805,085	$ 150,989,182	$ 69,979,277	$ 113,324,734	$ 183,304,011
Feb.	60,505,862	98,907,400	159,413,262	67,563,516	109,184,715	176,748,231
Mar.	65,818,688	110,713,231	176,531,919	74,530,959	119,543,408	194,074,367
Apr.	61,598,936	97,192,944	158,791,880	64,313,823	108,338,990	172,652,813
May	64,419,784	107,785,860	172,205,644	67,695,902	113,527,117	181,223,019
June	64,162,328	104,944,736	169,107,065	68,127,833	110,705,453	178,833,286
July	68,506,249	104,952,519	173,458,768	77,962,370	129,843,216	207,805,586
Aug.	70,580,030	112,360,856	182,940,886	73,636,474	122,271,083	195,907,557
Sept.	61,789,882	97,884,789	159,674,671	57,378,218	108,757,403	166,135,621
Oct.	62,697,914	100,265,065	162,962,978	59,682,650	112,046,007	171,728,657
Nov.	59,929,657	103,822,608	163,752,266	65,715,501	111,568,554	177,284,055
Dec.	58,375,074	96,163,250	154,538,324	67,082,078	101,421,907	168,503,985
Totals	$ 757,568,501	$1,226,798,344	**$1,984,366,845**	$ 813,668,601	$1,360,532,585	**$2,174,201,186**
RUNNING GRAND TOTAL			**$7,945,194,508**	**RUNNING GRAND TOTAL**		**$10,119,395,694**

	1999			2000		
	Gulf Coast Counties	Mississippi River Counties	Totals	Gulf Coast Counties	Mississippi River Counties	Totals
Jan.	$ 76,232,975	$ 116,429,342	$ 192,662,317	$ 89,915,290	$ 126,524,692	$ 216,439,982
Feb.	75,450,129	119,948,022	195,398,151	95,368,657	133,986,047	229,354,704
Mar.	88,450,841	134,690,899	223,141,740	104,209,259	143,772,703	247,981,961
Apr.	92,247,226	125,695,886	217,943,112	89,819,044	128,541,994	218,361,038
May	87,642,275	121,089,606	208,731,881	90,469,218	130,023,532	220,492,751
June	85,839,373	127,998,367	213,837,740	90,254,684	128,881,575	219,136,259
July	102,582,591	144,128,821	246,711,412	107,305,600	142,695,296	250,000,896
Aug.	87,351,834	130,772,218	218,124,052	97,802,072	130,456,125	228,258,197
Sept.	88,374,079	118,724,535	207,098,614	88,748,000	128,076,403	216,824,403
Oct.	86,220,321	119,968,549	206,188,870			
Nov.	81,936,031	118,084,628	200,020,659			
Dec.	77,591,901	108,795,769	186,387,670			
Totals	$1,029,919,576	$1,486,326,643	**$2,516,246,219**	$ 853,891,824	$1,192,958,367	**$2,046,850,191**
RUNNING GRAND TOTAL			**$ 12,635,641,913**	**RUNNING GRAND TOTAL**		**$ 14,682,492,104**

Tax Revenues From Gaming Collected by The Mississippi State Tax Commission

FY 1993	$ 44,411,629.10	FY 1997	$ 233,658,351.91	**TOTAL**	$ 1,656,163,585.89
FY 1994	128,769,795.89	FY 1998	250,345,674.72	General Fund Transfer	$ 914,072,551.88
FY 1995	189,289,451.41	FY 1999	281,509,967.76	To Local Governments	$ 532,192,500.44
FY 1996	213,713,855.43	FY 2000	314,464,859.67	Highway Bond Sinking Fund	$ 209,898,533.57

The Ultimate Reference on the State

Places in Mississippi with Indian Names

Indian tribes that existed in Mississippi before white men: Acolapissa, Bayogoula, Biloxi (Taneks haya), Chakchiuman (Chocchuma), Chickasaw, Choctaw, Choula, Coroa, Grigra, Houma, Ibitoupa, Koroa, Natchez, Ofo (Ofogoula), Pascagoula (Puska Okla), Tapercha, Taposa, Tioux, Tunica, and Yazoo (Yazou).

Most words in this chapter are Choctaw or Chickasaw in origin. The tribe is indicated if it is known. Linguistically, the two dialects are very similar, both being sub-branches of the Western Muskogean dialect. However, there do exist some lexical and phonological differences in the two languages.

STATE

The state got its name from the river that flows along its western boundary, named by the Indians. The name probably came from several different Indian words which translate (depending upon the tribe) as "Ancient Father of Waters," "Beyond Age," "Great River," or "Chief River." A derivation of the Choctaw Indian phrase, "mish sha sippukrie" is "Father of Waters." The name likely derived from Chippewa words mici (great) and zibi (river) or "gathering-in of all the waters." Also Algonquin Indian word "Messipi."

COUNTIES
(20 counties in Mississippi have Indian names or were named after Indian Chiefs)

Amite - Indian word means "friendly river"
Attala - Named for Indian heroine "Attala"
Chickasaw - Named for the Chickasaw Indians (the word Chickasaw means "rebellion")
Choctaw - Named for the Choctaw Indian (the word Choctaw means "separation," although some historians and linguists say the word means "charming voice")
Coahoma - Indian word means "red panther"
Copiah - Indian word means "calling panther"
Issaquena - from the Choctaw "Issiok-hima" meaning "deer river" or "deer branch"
Itawamba - Named for the Chickasaw Indian Chief Itawamba-Mingo, which roughly translates into "Bench-Chief" or "Wooden Seat" (we would call it Chair of State)
Leflore - Named for Greenwood Leflore, Chief of the Choctaw Indians, who was half-French
Neshoba - Indian word means "wolf"
Noxubee - Indian word means "stinking water"
Oktibbeha - Choctaw word means "bloody water" — refers to an actual battle between Indian tribes.
Panola - Indian word means "cotton"
Pontotoc - A compound of the Chickasaw words Ponti and Tokali, which have been translated into three meanings: "land of hanging grapes," "weed prairie" and "battle where the cattails stood."
Tallahatchie - Indian word means "rock river"
Tippah - Indian word means "cut off"
Tishomingo - Indian word means "warrior chief"
Tunica - Indian word means "little people"
Yalobusha - Indian word means "tadpole place" or "tadpoles abounding"
Yazoo - Indian word means "river of death" or, some historians say, "to blow on an instrument" (musical)

> A 1999 survey of the Mississippi Band of Choctaw Indians showed that only 5 percent of tribal members spoke the Choctaw language fluently, 9 percent spoke the language with limited ability, and the remaining 86 percent could speak no Choctaw.

CITIES, TOWNS & COMMUNITIES
(Those that have the same name as a County are not repeated here)

Acona (Holmes County) - Indian word means "whoa"
Alamucha (Lauderdale County) - Indian word means "hiding place"
Biloxi (Harrison County) - named for the Biloxi Indian tribe, the word means "broken pot"
Buckatunna [original spelling Bucatunna] (Wayne County) - Choctaw, means "collected together"
Byhalia (Marshall County) - from the Chickasaw "By halia" meaning "white oak tree"
Chulahoma (Marshall County) - Chickasaw word means "red fox"
Chunky (Newton County) - named for the Choctaw stick-ball game "chunka"
Coila (Carroll County) - named for a Choctaw Princess, the word means "little panther"
Conehatta (Newton County) - from the Choctaw word "Ko-nih-hut-a" meaning "whitish pole cat"
Duck Hill (Montgomery Co.) - named for a Choctaw Indian who called himself "Chief Duck"
Durant (Holmes County) - named for Louis Durant, Choctaw Indian Chief who lived nearby
Escatawpa (Jackson County) - Indian word means "dog"

Places in Mississippi with Indian Names

Greenwood (Leflore County) - Named for Greenwood Leflore, Chief of the Choctaw Indians
Hiwannee (Wayne County) - Indian word means "cut-worm" or "caterpillar"
Huspuckena (Bolivar County) - Choctaw word means "little sunflower"
Itta Bena (Leflore County) - Choctaw words mean "home in the woods"
Iuka (Tishomingo County) - original Chickasaw spelling was "Ai-yu-pi," which means "place of bathing"
Jacinto (Alcorn) - the word is Spanish (meaning "hyacinth"), but was also the name a Chickasaw Chief.
Mashulaville (Noxubee County) - named for Chief Mashulatubbee ("one who perseveres and kills")
Nanachehaw [also known as Allen] (Warren County) - Indian word means "fish hill"
Nanih Waiya (Winston County) - Indian words mean "slanting hill" or "bending hill"
Natchez (Adams County) - named for the Natchez Indian tribe, the word means "to break off from"
Noxapater (Winston County) - possible Indian origin meaning "trigger"
Ofahoma (Leake County) - Choctaw word means "red dog"
Okolona (Chickasaw County) - Choctaw word means "people gathered together"
Osyka (Pike County) - Choctaw word means "the eagle"
Pascagoula (Jackson County) - named for Indian tribe Puska Okla meaning "bread people"
Pachuta (Clarke County) - from the Choctaw "pochi-Ai-etta" meaning "pigeons roost here"
Pelahatchie (Rankin County) - Choctaw word means "crooked as smoke"
Pocahantas (Hinds County) - named for the daughter of Virginia's main Indian Chief Powhatan.
Pushmataha Landing (Coahoma County) - Pushmataha was the name of a famous Indian Chief
Satartia (Yazoo County) - Choctaw word means "pumpkin patch"
Scooba (Kemper County) - from the Choctaw Indian word "oskeba" meaning "reed brake"
Senatobia (Tate County) - from the Indian "Sen-a-to-ho-ba" meaning "rest to the weary"
Shubuta (Clarke County) - Indian word means "smoky"
Shuqualak (Noxubee County) - Choctaw word means either "widely branching" or "hog wallow"
Tchula (Holmes County) - Indian word means "fox"
Teoc (Carroll County) - Choctaw Indian word means "tall pine"
Tilletoba (Yalobusha County) - Choctaw word means "gray rock" (also "blacksmith" & "tall pine")
Toccopola (Pontotoc County) - from Chicksaw "Tok-a-pula" meaning "the crossing of the roads"
Toomsuba (Lauderdale County) - Indian word means "rolling horse"
Tougaloo (Hinds County) - Cherokee Indian word means "where the three creeks (streams) meet"
Tupelo (Lee County) - Chickasaw word "Tuh Pu Lah" means "to scream and make a noise"
Wautubbee (Clarke County) - Indian word means "off-hand killer"
Wenasoga (Alcorn County) - named for an Indian chieftain.
Winona (Montgomery County) - Choctaw word means either "first born daughter" or "the crane"

RIVERS AND CREEKS
(Names that duplicate those of counties, cities, towns or communities are not repeated here)

Bogue Chitto (river) - Choctaw words mean "big river" or "big creek"
Bogue Phalia (river) - Choctaw words mean "long creek"
Buttahatchie (river) - Indian word means "White Sumac River" or just "river"
Chiwapa (creek) - From the Chickasaw word Chiwaipaiya, meaning "a broad expanse of grass"
Loosa-Scoona (river) - from the Choctaw "Lusa-ko-nih" meaning "Black pole cat"
Oaktoma (creek) - Choctaw word means "to be foggy"
Tiak O'Khata (lake in Winston County) - Choctaw word means "Lake of the Pines."
Tibbee (creek) - word means "Water Fight" and refers to an actual battle between Indian
    tribes where the fighting took place primarily in the river.
Tuscalameta (creek) - Indian word means "young warrior"
Yockanookany (river) - from the Choctaw "Yak-ni-nak-ish-wa-na" meaning "catfish land"

> The longest placename in the United States is an Indian word 48-letters long—
> LAKE CHARGOGGAGOGGMACHAUGGAUGGAGOGGCHAUBUNAGUNGAMAUGG.
> The name of the lake, located in Massachusetts, is a Nipmuch Indian word
> meaning "You fish on your side. I fish on my side. Nobody fishes in the middle."

The Ultimate Reference on the State

Broadcasting Stations in Mississippi

PUBLIC / EDUCATIONAL TV STATIONS

BILOXI (McHenry)	— W M A H-TV, Channel 19
BOONEVILLE	— W M A E-TV, Channel 12
BUDE	— W M A U-TV, Channel 17
COLUMBIA	— W45AA, Translator Station
GREENWOOD (Inverness)	— W M A O-TV, Channel 23
HATTIESBURG	— W47BP, Translator Station
JACKSON	— W M P N-TV, Channel 29
MERIDIAN (Rose Hill)	— W M A W-TV, Channel 14
MISS. STATE (Ackerman)	— W M A B-TV, Channel 2
OXFORD	— W M A V-TV, Channel 18

Mississippi Authority For Educational Television
3825 Ridgewood Road
Jackson, MS 39211-6463
(601) 982-6565

COMMERCIAL TV STATIONS

ASHLAND	— W B I I-TV, Channel 20 / IND. — 134 Court Street; 38603	(662) 224-6420
BILOXI	— W L O X-TV, Channel 13 / ABC — 208 Debuys Road; 39531	(228) 896-1313
	W L O X-TV, Channel 13 / ABC (Biloxi); Ocean Springs Phone No.	(228) 875-8080
BOONEVILLE	— W53AF-TV, Channel 53 — 504 North 3rd Street; 38829	(662) 728-6492
BRUCE	— WO7BN-TV, Channel 7/IND. — 100 South Newburger; 38915	(662) 983-2801
BYHALIA	— W B U Y-TV, Channel 40 / TBN — 4240 Highway 309N; 38611	(662) 521-9289
COLUMBUS	— W C B I-TV, Channel 4 / CBS — 201 5th Street South; 39701	(662) 327-4444
	W C B I-TV, Channel 4 / CBS — 1705 South Gloster Street; Tupelo 38801	(662) 841-0044
GREENVILLE	— W A B G-TV, Channel 6 / ABC — 849 Washington Avenue; 38701	(662) 332-0949
	W A B G-TV, Channel 6 / ABC — 2001 Garrard Ave; Greenwood 38930	(662) 453-4001
	W X V T-TV, Channel 15 / CBS — 3015 East Reed Road; 38703	(662) 334-1500
GULFPORT	— W X X V-TV, Channel 25 / FOX — Hiway 49 North; PO Box 2500; 39505	(662) 832-2525
HATTIESBURG	— W D A M-TV, Channel 7 / NBC — Highway 11N; PO Box 16269; 39404	(601) 544-4730
	W D A M-TV, Channel 7 / NBC — Laurel number	(601) 649-3111
	W H L T-TV, Channel 22 / CBS — 990 Hardy Street; 39401	(601) 545-2077
JACKSON	— W23BC-TV, Channel 23 — Jackson State University; Box 17399; 39217	(601) 968-2861
	W27CH-TV, Channel 27 (low power) — WB (Warner Bros.)	(601) 922-1234
	W A P T-TV, Channel 16 / ABC — 7616 Channel 16 Way; 39209	(601) 922-1607
	W D B D-TV, Channel 40 / FOX — Channel 16 Way; 39209	(601) 922-1234
	W J T V-TV, Channel 12 / CBS — 1820 TV Road; 39204	(601) 372-6311
	W L B T-TV, Channel 3 / NBC — 715 South Jefferson Street; 39201	(601) 948-3333
	W M V T-TV, Channel 10, IND — 124 East Amite Street; 39201	(601) 948-7703
MERIDIAN	— W G B C-TV, Channel 30 / NBC — 1151 Crestview Drive; 39302	(601) 485-3030
	W M D M-TV, Channel 24 / CBS — 1151 Crestview Circle; 39302	(601) 693-2424
	W T O K-TV, Channel 11 / ABC — 815 23rd Avenue; 39301	(601) 693-1441
STARKVILLE	— W O B V-TV, Channel 5 — Corner of Meigs & Lampkin; Box 728; 39759	(662) 338-1002
TUPELO	— W L O V -TV, Channel 27 / FOX — 519 South Gloster Street; 38801	(662) 842-7620
	W T V A-TV, Channel 9 / NBC — Beech Spring Road; PO Box 350; 38801	(662) 842-7620
	W T V A-TV, Channel 9 / NBC; 605 2nd Avenue N; Columbus 39701	(662) 327-6464

The first TV station in Mississippi was WJTV in Jackson. It first went on the air Jan. 20, 1953, as a UHF station, channel 25. The station obtained additional power and became channel 12, VHF, on July 1, 1954.

PUBLIC RADIO STATIONS

BILOXI	— WMAH-FM 90.3
BOONEVILLE	— WMAE-FM 89.5
BUDE	— WMAU-FM 88.9
GREENWOOD	— WMAO-FM 90.9
HATTIESBURG	— W207-AU 89.3
JACKSON	— WMPN-FM 91.3
MERIDIAN	— WMAW-FM 88.1
MISS. STATE; Starkville	— WMAB-FM 89.9
OXFORD-UNIVERSITY	— WMAV-FM 90.3

Public Radio In Mississippi
3825 Ridgewood Road
Jackson, MS 39211-6463
(601) 982-0500 or 800-472-2580

Broadcasting Stations in Mississippi

COMMERCIAL RADIO STATIONS

ABERDEEN
WWZQ-AM 1240 & FM 105.3; 1053 South Meridian Street; Aberdeen 39730 .... (662) 369-4561

AMORY
WAFM-FM 95.3 & WAMY-AM 1580; 521 Highway 278W; Amory 38821 .... (662) 256-9726

BATESVILLE
WBLE-FM 100.5 & WJBI-AM 1290; 1040 Highway 6 West; Batesville 38606 .... (662) 563-4664
WHKL-FM 106.9; 1040 Highway 6 West; Batesville 38606 .... (662) 563-1290

BAY SAINT LOUIS
WBSL-AM 1190; 1190 Casino Magic Drive; Bay Street. Louis 39520 .... (228) 467-1190

BAY SPRINGS
WIZK-AM 1570 & FM 94.3; Bay Springs 39422 .... (601) 764-3151

BELZONI
WELZ-AM 1460; Route 3, Brooklyn Road; Belzoni 39038 .... (662) 247-1744

BILOXI
WCPR-FM 97.9; 289 Gulfwater Drive; Biloxi 39531 .... (228) 388-6000
WKNN-FM 99.1 & WMJY-FM 93.7; 286 DeBuys Road; Biloxi 39531 .... (228) 388-2323
WLRK-FM 96.7 & WXRG-FM 105.9 & WXYK-FM 107.1; 212 DeBuys Road; Biloxi 39531 .... (228) 388-6000
WVMI-AM 570; 163 Rue Magnolia; Biloxi 39530 .... (228) 374-1570
WXBD-AM 1490; 212 DeBuys Road; Biloxi 39531 .... (228) 388-1490

BOONEVILLE
WBIP-AM 1400 & FM 99.3; Highway 45 South; 104 S 2nd Street; Booneville 38829-3225 .... (662) 728-5301

BRANDON
WRJH-FM 97.7 & WRKN-AM 970; 1027 Highway 471 North; Brandon 39042 .... (601) 825-5045
WVIV-FM 93.9; 1021-A Highway 471 North; Brandon 39042 .... (601) 825-9432

BROOKHAVEN
WBKN-FM 92.1 & WCHJ-AM 1470; 203 East Monticello Street; Brookhaven 39601-3328 .... (601) 833-9210

BRUCE
WCMR-FM 94.5; 118 South Newberger Street; Bruce 38915 .... (662) 983-6940

CANTON
WMGO-AM 1370; 107 West Peace Street; Canton 39046-4535 .... (601) 859-2373

CARTHAGE
WSSI-AM 1080 & FM 98.3; Radio Road; Carthage 39051 .... (601) 267-8361

CHARLESTON
WTGY-FM 95.7; Marshall Road; Charleston 38921 .... (662) 647-5600

CLARKSDALE
WAID-FM 106.5 & WKDJ-FM 96.5; 112 Leflore Avenue; Clarksdale 38614 -4424 .... (662) 627-2281
WQMA-AM 1520 & WROX-AM 1450; 317 Delta Avenue; Clarksdale 38614 .... (662) 627-1450
WWUN-FM 101.7; 100 Magnolia; Clarksdale 38614 .... (662) 627-1113

CLEVELAND
WCLD-AM 1490 & FM 103.9; 1101 South Davis Avenue; Cleveland 38732 .... (662) 843-4091
WMJW-FM 107.5; PO BOX 780; Cleveland 38732 .... (662) 843-4091
WDSK-AM 1410 & WDTL-FM 92.9 & WOHT-FM 95.3; 309 N Chrisman; Cleveland .... (662) 846-0929

CLINTON
WTWZ-AM 1120; 608C Highway 80 East; Clinton 39056-5123 .... (601) 924-2768

COLUMBIA
WCJU-AM 1450; Highway 98W; 37 South High School Avenue; Columbia 39429-8246 .... (601) 736-2616
WFFF-AM 1360 & FM 96.7; 811 Main Street; Columbia 39429 .... (601) 736-1360

COLUMBUS
WACR-AM 1050 & FM 103.9; 1910 14th Avenue North; Columbus 39701-2406 .... (662) 328-1050
WAJV-FM 98.9; 702 Second Avenue North; Columbus 39703 .... (662) 328-1400
WKOR-FM 94.9 & WSMS-FM 99.9 & WXMU-FM 106.1; 601 2nd Avenue N; Columbus 39701 . (662) 327-1183
WMBC-FM 103.1 & WJWF-AM 1400; 702 Second Avenue North; Columbus 39701-4702 .... (662) 329-1030

CORINTH
WADI-FM 95.3 & WCMA-AM 1230; 1608 S Johns Street; Corinth 38834-6547 .... (662) 287-3101
WXRZ-FM 94.3 & WKCU-AM 1350; 2112 Highway 72 East; Corinth 38834-6735 .... (662) 286-8451

Broadcasting Stations in Mississippi

FOREST
WQST-AM 850; 18844 Highway 80 East; Forest 39074 .... (601) 469-5677
FRENCH CAMP
WFCA-FM 107.9; French Camp Academy Camp; Route 1 Box 12; French Camp 39745 .... (662) 547-6414
GREENVILLE
KDTL-FM 103.5; 1427 South Main, Suite 207; Greenville 38704 .... (662) 378-4103
KUUZ-FM 95.9; 2562 South Main Street Ext; Greenville 38702 .... (662) 332-0025
WBAD-FM 94.3; Seven Oaks Road; Greenville 38704 .... (662) 335-9265
WBAQ-FM 97.9; 136 S Broadway Street; Greenville 38701-4005 .... (662) 335-3383
WDMS-FM 100.7 & WGVM-AM 1260; 1383 Pickett Street; Greenville 38703-2437 .... (662) 334-4559
WESY-AM 1580; Seven Oaks Road; Greenville 38704 .... (662) 378-9405
WGVM-AM 1260 & WDMS-FM 100.7; 1383 Pickett Street; Greenville 38703-2437 .... (662) 334-4559
WIQQ-FM 102.3 & WNIX-AM 1330; Unit 39, Delta Plaza Mall; Highway 1S; Greenville 38702 . (662) 378-2617
GREENWOOD
WABG-AM 960; 2001 Garrard Avenue; Greenwood 38930-5009 .... (662) 453-7822
WGNL-FM 104.3; 503 Ione Street; Greenwood 38930 .... (662) 453-1646
WGRM-AM 1240 & FM (93.9); 1100 Wright Street; Greenwood 38930-2237 .... (662) 453-1240
WYMX-FM 99.1 & WKXG-AM 1540; Browning Road; Greenwood 38930 .... (662) 453-2174
GRENADA
WQXB-FM 100.1 & WYKC-AM 1400; 1348 Sunset Drive (Highway 8W); Grenada 38901 .... (662) 226-1400
GULFPORT
WAOY-FM 91.7; 12280 Ashley Drive; Gulfport 39503 .... (228) 831-3020
WGCM-AM 1240, WGCM-FM 102.3, WZKX-FM 107.9, & WROA-AM 1390;
    11737 Klein Road; Gulfport 39505 .... (228) 832-5111
WJZD-FM 94.5; 1331 Magnolia Street; Gulfport 39507-3514 .... (228) 896-5307
WQFX-AM 1130; 1401 Pass Road; Gulfport 39501-5160 .... (228) 863-6080
WXOR-FM 92.5; 2203 Collins Blvd; Gulfport 39507 .... (228) 896-5280
HATTIESBURG
WBKH-AM 950; 63 Braswell Road; Hattiesburg 39401 .... (601) 582-9595
WFMM-FM 97.3 (simulcasts WFMN-FM to Hattiesburg); 6310 I-55 North; Jackson 39211 ...... (601) 957-1700
WHER-FM 103.7 & WFOR-AM 1400; 2414 West 7th Street; Hattiesburg 39401-3241 .... (601) 544-3232
WJMG-FM 92.1 & WORV-AM 1580; 1204 Graveline Street; Hattiesburg 39401-1372 .... (601) 544-1941
WKNZ-FM 101.7; 7501 Highway 49N; PO Box 15935; Hattiesburg 39402 .... (601) 264-0443
WMXI-FM 98.1; 113 Fairfield Drive; Hattiesburg 39404 .... (601) 261-0898
WXHB-FM 96.5; PO Box 15935; Hattiesburg 39404 .... (601) 268-6965
HAZLEHURST
WDXO-FM 96.5; Hazlehurst .... (601) 894-1441
WMDC-AM 1220 & FM 100.9; 992 Highway 51 North; Hazlehurst 39083 .... (601) 833-0111
HERNANDO
WVIM-FM 95.3; 5555 McCracken Road; Hernando 38632 .... (662) 429-4465
HOLLY SPRINGS
WKRA-AM 1110 & FM 92.7; 1400 Highway 4 East, Suite C; Holly Springs 38635 .... (662) 252-6692
HOUSTON
WCPC-AM 940; 1189 Highway 15 North; Houston 38851 .... (662) 456-3071
INDIANOLA
WNLA-AM 1380 & FM 105.5; Highway 448; Indianola 38751 .... (601) 887-1380
WTCD-FM 96.9; 517 East Baker Street; Indianola 38751-2503 .... (662) 887-1091
IUKA
WFXO-FM 104.9; 311 West Eastport; Iuka 38852-2010 .... (662) 423-6059
JACKSON
WBKJ-FM 105; 900 East County Line Road; Jackson .... (601) 991-1051
WDBT-FM, 95.5, WMSI-FM 102.9, WSTZ-FM 106.7, WQJQ-FM 105.1, & WJDX-AM 620;
    1375 Beasley Road; Jackson 39206 .... (601) 982-1062
WFMN-FM 97.3; 6310 I-55 North; Jackson 39211 .... (601) 957-1700
WIIN-AM 780, WJKK-FM 98.7, & WYOY-FM 101.7; 265 Highpoint Drive; Jackson 39213 ..... (601) 956-0102

The list of commercial radio stations in Jackson continues on the next page.

Broadcasting Stations in Mississippi

WJMI-FM 99.7, WKXI-AM 1300 & FM 107.5 & WOAD-AM 1400;
    731 S Pear Orchard Road, Suite 27; Ridgeland 39157 .... (601) 957-1300
WJNT-AM 1180; 1985 Lakeland Drive; Jackson 39216-5023 .... (601) 366-1150
WJXN-AM 1450 & FM 92.9; 916 Foley Street; Jackson 39202-3406 .... (601) 944-1450
WKXS-FM 96.3; 900 East County Line Road; Jackson 39213 .... (601) 991-9696
WMPR-FM 90.1; 1018 Pecan Park Circle; Jackson 39209 .... (601) 948-5835
WPBQ-AM 1240; 999 Underwood Drive; Flowood 39218 .... (601) 932-1243
WTYX-FM 94.7; 222 Beasley Road; Jackson 39206-2921 .... (601) 957-3000
WWDF-AM 720; 1018 North Flowood Drive; Jackson 39208-9791 .... (601) 932-4848
WYJS-FM 105.9; 102 Business Park Drive, Suite F; Jackson 39213 .... (601) 956-9800
WZRX-AM 1590; 2980 Forest Avenue Extension; Jackson .... (601) 981-9080

KOSCIUSKO
WKOZ-AM 1340 & WLIN-FM 101.1; 105 Golf Course Road; Kosciusko 39090 .... (662) 289-1050

LAUREL
WAML-AM 1340; 1425 Highway 11 South; Laurel Fairgrounds; Laurel 39441 .... (601) 425-0011
WBBN-FM 95.9; 4580 Highway 15 North; Laurel 39440 .... (601) 649-0095
WXRR-FM 104.5; 4580 Highway 15 North; Laurel 39440 .... (601) 544-0095
WEEZ-FM 99.3; 318 West 5th Street; Laurel 39440 .... (601) 425-4390
WKZW-FM 94.3; 4580 Highway 15 North; Laurel 39440 .... (601) 583-9494
WNSL-FM 100.3 & WQIS-AM 890; 51 Victory Road; Laurel 39440 .... (601) 425-1491

LEXINGTON
WAGR-FM 102.5 & WXTN-AM 1000; 100 Radio Road; Lexington 39095 .... (662) 834-1666

LOUISVILLE
WLSM-AM 1270 & FM 107.1; Highway 14 East; Louisville 39339 .... (662) 773-3481

LUCEDALE
WRBE-AM 1440 & FM 106.9; Highway 98 West; Lucedale 39452 .... (601) 947-8151

McCOMB
WAKK-AM 1140, WAKK-FM 104.9, & WAPF-AM 980; 206 North Front St; McComb 39648 ... (601) 684-4116

MERIDIAN
WJDQ-FM 101.3, WMGP-AM 1450, WZKS-FM 104.1 & WZRW-FM 95.1;
    4307 Highway 39 North; Meridian 39301-1008 .... (601) 693-2381
WOKK-FM 97.1 & WALT-AM 910; 3436 Highway 45 North; Meridian 39301 .... (601) 693-2661
WMYQ-FM 97.9; 110 Decatur Street; Newton 39345 / 100 22nd Ave. S, Suite A; Meridian 39301 (601) 963-9898
WMOX-AM 1010; 451 Highway 11/80; Meridian 39301 .... (601) 693-1891
WNBN-AM 1290; 1290 Hawkins Crossing; Meridian 39301 .... (601) 483-3401

MONTICELLO
WMLC-AM 1270; Highway 84 West; Monticello 39654 .... (601) 587-7997
WRQO-FM 102.1; Q-102 Road; Monticello 39654 .... (601) 587-9363

NATCHEZ
WQNZ-FM 95.1 & WNAT-AM 1450; #2 O'Ferrall Street; Natchez 39120 .... (601) 442-4895
WTRC-FM 97.3; #2 O'Ferrall Street; Natchez 39121 .... (601) 446-9730
WTYJ-FM 97.7 & WMIS-AM 1240; 20 East Franklin Street; Natchez 39120 .... (601) 442-2522

NEW ALBANY
WNAU-AM 1470; 204 Moss Hill Drive; New Albany 38652-3400 .... (662) 534-8133

OCEAN SPRINGS
WOSM-FM 103.1; 4720 Radio Road; Ocean Springs 39564-7509 .... (228) 875-9031

OXFORD
WOXD-FM 95.5; 302 Highway 7 South; Oxford 38655 .... (662) 234-9631
WQLJ-FM 93.7; 307 South Lamar Blvd; Oxford 38655-4011 .... (662) 236-0093
WWMS-FM 97.5 & WSUH-AM 1420; 2017 University Avenue East; Oxford 38655-3511 ... (662) 234-6881

PASCAGOULA
WZZJ-AM 1580; 5115 Telephone Road; Pascagoula 39567-1130 .... (228) 762-5683

PETAL
WMFM-FM 106.3; 2571 Old Richton Road; Petal 39465 .... (601) 545-1063

PHILADELPHIA
WWSL-FM 102.3 & WHOC-AM 1490; 1016 West Beacon Street; Philadelphia 39350-3204 ...... (601) 656-1490

Broadcasting Stations in Mississippi

PICAYUNE
WRJW-AM 1320; 2438 Highway 43 East; Picayune 39466 .... (601) 798-4835
WZRH-FM 106.1; 1601 Shortcut Road; Slidell, LA 70458 (licensed to Picayune, MS) .... (504) 641-5672

PONTOTOC
WSEL-AM 1440 & FM 96.7; Highway 6 East; Pontotoc 38863 .... (662) 489-0297

POPLARVILLE
WRPM-AM 1530; 103 Progress Road; Poplarville 39470 .... (601) 795-4900

PORT GIBSON
WVYE-FM 100.5 & WKPG-AM 1320; 911½ Chinquepin Street; Port Gibson 39150 .... (601) 437-5555

PRENTISS
WJDR-FM 98.3; 646 Highway 13S; Prentiss 39474 .... (601) 792-2056

QUITMAN
WYKK-FM 98.9 & WBFN-AM 1500; 311 County Road 140; Quitman 39355 .... (601) 776-2931

RICHTON
WESZ-FM 96.5; 156 Apple Avenue; Richton 39476 .... (601) 788-5801

RIPLEY
WKZU-FM 102.3; 107 East Spring Street; Ripley 38663-2043 .... (662) 837-1023

SENATOBIA
WSAO-AM 1140; Highway 4 East; Senatobia 38668 .... (662) 562-4445

SOUTHAVEN
WAVN-AM 1240; 1336 Brookhaven Drive; Southaven 38671-3749 .... (662) 393-8027

STARKVILLE
WKOR-AM 980, WMSU-FM 92.1 & WSSO-AM 1230; 608 Yellow Jacket Drive; Starkville ..... (662) 323-1230
WLZA-FM 96.1 & WEPA-AM 710; 1105 Stark Road; Starkville 39759 .... (662) 258-7170

TUPELO
WAFR-FM 88.3 & WAJS-FM 99.9; 107 Parkgate Drive; Tupelo 38801 .... (662) 844-8888
WCNA-FM 95.9; 1241 Cliff Gookin Blvd; Tupelo 38801 .... (662) 842-9595
WDFX-FM 98.3; 107 Parkgate Drive; Tupelo 38801 (licensed to Cleveland) .... (662) 844-8888
WESE-FM 92.5, WNRX-AM 1060, WTUP-AM 1490 & WWZD-FM 106.7;
    2812 Cliff Gookin Blvd; PO Box 3300; Tupelo 38803 .... (662) 842-1067
WFTA-FM 101.9 & WFTO-AM 1330; 1241 Cliff Gookin Blvd; Tupelo 38801 .... (662) 842-7625
WSYE FM 93.3; 1705 South Gloster; Tupelo 38801 .... (662) 844-9793
WWKZ-FM 103.5; 3200 West Main Street; Tupelo 38801-9407 .... (662) 844-2134
WZLQ-FM 98.5 & WELO-AM 580; 3216 North Gloster; Tupelo 38802 .... (662) 842-7658

TYLERTOWN
WTYL-AM 1290 & FM 97.7; 930 Union Road; Tylertown 39667 .... (601) 876-2105

VICKSBURG
WBBV-FM 101.1; 899 Highway 61 North; Vicksburg 39180 .... (601) 638-0101
WQBC-AM 1420; 3190 Porters Chapel Road; Vicksburg 39180 .... (601) 636-1108
WRTM-AM 1490; PO Box 820583; Vicksburg 39182 .... (601) 636-7944

WALNUT
WLRC-AM 850; 7760 Highway 72 East; Walnut 38683-9244 .... (662) 223-4071

WATER VALLEY
WLPX-FM 105.5; Highway 7 Bypass; Water Valley 38965 .... (662) 473-5003

WAYNESBORO
WABO-AM 990 & FM 105.5; 6746 Highway 84W; Waynesboro 39367 .... (601) 735-4331

WEST POINT
WKBB-FM 100.9 & WROB-AM 1450; 413 Forest Street; West Point 39773-2327 .... (662) 494-1450

WIGGINS
WLUN-FM 95.3 & WIGG-AM 1420; 959 North Magnolia Drive; Wiggins 39577 .... (601) 928-7281

WINONA
WONA-AM 1570 & FM 95.1; Highway 51 South; Winona 38967 .... (662) 283-1570

YAZOO CITY
WBYP-FM 107.1; PO Box 130; Yazoo City 39194 .... (662) 746-7676
WJNS-FM 92.1; 1405 Enchanted Drive; Yazoo City 39194 .... (662) 746-5921
WMGO-FM 93.1; 1307 East Broadway (Highway 49W); Yazoo City 39194 .... (662) 746-0093

Broadcasting Stations in Mississippi

COMMERCIAL RADIO NETWORKS

LISTEN TO THE EAGLE NETWORK (Radio & TV); PO Box 219; Summit 39666 .... (601) 684-9486
MISSISSIPPI NETWORK; 6310 I-55 North; Jackson 39211 .... (601) 957-1700
NATIONAL WEATHER NETWORK (NWN); 916 Foley Street; Jackson 39202 .... (601) 352-6673
YANCY AGRICULTURE NETWORKS; PO Box 1850; Starkville 39760 .... (662) 324-0949

COLLEGE / UNIVERSITY RADIO STATIONS

Alcorn State University; 1000 ASU Drive; Lorman 39096 (**WPRL-FM 91.7**) .... (601) 877-6290
Copiah-Lincoln Community College; Wesson 39191 (**WCLL-FM**) .... (601) 643-8384
Jackson State University; 1400 J.R. Lynch Street; Jackson 39217 (**WJSU-FM 88.5**) .... (601) 968-2285
Mississippi College; 100 N. Jefferson Street; Clinton 39056 (**WHJT-FM 93.5 & WSLI-AM 930**) (601) 925-3460
    World Wide Web — http://www.mc.edu/alive935
Mississippi State University; Student Media Center; Starkville 39759 (**WMSV-FM 91.1**) .... (662) 325-8034
Mississipi University for Women; Cromwell Communications Center;
    MUW Box 1619; Columbus 39701 (**WMUW-FM 88.5**) .... (662) 329-7255
Mississippi Valley State University; 14000 Highway 82 W; Itta Bena 38941 (**WVSD-FM 91.7**) .. (662) 254-3612
Rust College; 150 Rust Avenue; Holly Springs 39406 (**WURC-FM 88.1**) .... (662) 266-4287
University of Mississippi; UM Student Media Center;
    Farley Hall; University 38677 (**WUMS-FM 92.1**) .... (662) 232-7697
University of Southern Mississippi; PO Box 10045; Hattiesburg 39406 (**WUSM-FM 88.5**) .... (601) 266-4287

MISSISSIPPI ASSOCIATION OF BROADCASTERS

855 S Pear Orchard Road., Suite 403; Ridgeland 39157 .... 1-800-382-0739 or (601) 957-9121

MISCELLANEOUS

Jackson Teleport, Inc. (Satellite Uplink); 916 Foley Street; Jackson 39202 .... (601) 352-6673

NOTE: Keep in mind that radio station call letters are prone to change at any time... and do, indeed, change quite often.

The first commercial radio station in the state was KFNG in Coldwater in Tate County. It went on the air in September 1922 and was owned and operated by broadcasting pioneer Hoyt Wooten. The first *network* radio station in Mississippi was WJDX in Jackson. It went on the air in the Lamar Life Building in Jackson on November 30, 1929.

Newspapers in Mississippi

DAILY NEWSPAPERS

BILOXI	*The Sun Herald*; 205 DeBuys Rd; Biloxi 39535	(228) 896-2100
BROOKHAVEN	*The Daily Leader*; N Railroad Ave; Brookhaven 39601	(601) 833-6961
CLARKSDALE	*Press Register*; 123 2nd St; Clarksdale 38614	(662) 627-2201
CLEVELAND	*Bolivar Commercial*; 821 N Christman; Cleveland 38732	(662) 843-4241
COLUMBUS	*Commercial Dispatch*; 516 Main St; Columbus 39701	(662) 328-2424
CORINTH	*The Daily Corinthian*; 1607 S Harper Rd; Corinth 38834	(662) 287-6111
JACKSON	*The Clarion-Ledger*: 201 S Congress St; Po Box 40; Jackson 39201-0040 http://www.clarionledger.com	1-800-222-8015 or (601) 961-7000
GREENVILLE	*Delta Democrat Times*; 988 N Broadway; Greenville 38701	(662) 335-1155
GREENWOOD	*Commonwealth*; 329 Hwy 82W; Greenwood 38930	(662) 453-5312
GRENADA	*Daily Sentinel-Star*; 158 S Green St; Grenada 38901	(662) 226-4321
HATTIESBURG	*Hattiesburg American*; 825 N Main St; Hattiesburg 39401	(601) 582-4321
LAUREL	*Leader-Call*; 130 Beacon St; Laurel 39440	(601) 428-0551
McCOMB	*Enterprise Journal*; Oliver Emmerich Dr; McComb 39648	(601) 684-2421
MERIDIAN	*Meridian Star, The*; 812 22nd Ave; Meridian 39301	(601) 693-1551
NATCHEZ	*Natchez Democrat*; 503 N Canal St; Natchez 39120	(601) 442-9101
OCEAN SPRINGS	*The Mississippi Press Register*; 1222 Hwy 90; Ocean Springs 39564	(228) 875-8144
OXFORD	*Oxford Eagle*; 916 Jackson Ave; Oxford 38655	(662) 234-4331
PASCAGOULA	*The Mississippi Press Register*; 405 Delmas Ave; Pascagoula 39567	(228) 762-1111
PICAYUNE	*Picayune Item*; 214 Curran Ave; Picayune 39466	(601) 798-4766
STARKVILLE	*Starkville Daily News*; 316 University Dr; Starkville 39759	(662) 323-1642
TUPELO	*Northeast Mississippi Daily Journal*; 1655 S Green St; Tupelo 38801	(662) 842-2611
VICKSBURG	*The Vicksburg Post*; 1601 North Frontage Rd, Suite F; Vicksburg 39180	(601) 636-4545
WEST POINT	*Daily Times Leader*; 227 Court St; West Point 39773	(662) 494-1422

In 1998, Mississippi's 23 daily papers had paid circulation averages of 394,000 daily & 403,000 Sundays (18).

WEEKLY NEWSPAPERS

ABERDEEN	*Aberdeen Examiner*; 209 E Commerce St; Aberdeen 39730	(662) 369-4507
ACKERMAN	*The Choctaw Plain Dealer*; 139 W Main St; Ackerman 39735	(662) 285-6248
AMORY	*Amory Advertiser*; 115 S Main St; Amory 38821	(662) 256-5647
ASHLAND	*Southern Advocate*; Church St; Ashland 38603	(662) 224-6681
BALDWYN	*Baldwyn News*; 111 Front St; Baldwyn 38824	(662) 365-3232
BATESVILLE	*Panolian*; 218 Watt St; Batesville 38606	(662) 563-4591
BAY ST. LOUIS	*Sea Coast Echo*; 124 Court St; Bay Saint Louis 39520	(228) 467-5474
BAY SPRINGS	*Jasper County News*; 5th Ave; Bay Springs 39422	(601) 764-2388
BELMONT	*Belmont-Tishomingo Journal*; 705 N 2nd St; Belmont 38827	(662) 454-7196
BELZONI	*Banner*; 115 Jackson St; Belzoni 39038	(662) 247-3373
BOONEVILLE	*Banner-Independent*; 208 N Main St; Booneville 38829	(662) 728-6214
BILOXI	*Biloxi/D'Iberville Press*; 9450 Central Ave; Biloxi 39533	(228) 392-3307
BRANDON	*Rankin County News*; Brandon	(601) 825-8333
BRUCE	*Calhoun County Journal*; Bruce 38915	(662) 983-2570
CARTHAGE	*The Carthaginian*; 122 Franklin St; Carthage 39051	(601) 267-4501
CALHOUN CITY	*The Monitor Herald*; S Main St; Calhoun City 38916	(662) 628-5241
CANTON	*Madison County Herald*; 159 E Center St; Canton 39046	(601) 859-1221
CARROLLTON	*The Conservative*; 706 Lexington St; Carrollton 38917	(662) 237-4713
CHARLESTON	*The Sun Sentinel*; Court Square #250; Charleston 38921	(662) 647-8462
DREW	*Sunflower County News*; 191 N Main St; Drew 38737	(662) 745-8513
DREW	*Sunflower Progress*; 127 W Shaw Ave; Drew 38737	(662) 745-6269
CLINTON	*Clinton News*; 311 N Jefferson St; Clinton 39056	(601) 924-7142
COFFEEVILLE	*Coffeeville Courier*; Coffeeville 38922	(662) 675-2446
COLLINS	*News Commercial*; Collins 39428	(601) 765-8275
COLUMBIA	*Columbian-Progress*; 318 Second St; Columbia 39429	(601) 736-2611
CRYSTAL SPRINGS	*The Meteor*; 238 E Georgetown St; Crystal Springs 39059	(601) 892-2581
DeKALB	*Kemper County Messenger*; DeKalb 39328	(601) 743-5760

Newspapers in Mississippi

EUPORA	*The Webster Progress Times*; 124 N Dunn St; Eupora 39744	(662) 258-7532
FAYETTE	*Jefferson County Chronicle*; 165 S Main St; Fayette 39069	(601) 786-6397
FOREST	*Scott County Times*; 311 Smith St; Forest 39074	(601) 469-2561
FULTON	*Itawamba County Times*; 106 W Main St; Fulton 38843	(662) 862-3141
GAUTIER	*Gautier Independent*; 3880 Gautier Vancleave Rd; Gautier 39553	(228) 497-4571
GLOSTER	*Wilk-Amite Record*; Main St; Gloster 39638	(601) 225-4531
GRENADA	*Grenada Lake Herald*; 159 S Green St; Grenada 38901	(662) 226-4321
GULFPORT	*Keesler News/Seabee Courier*; 205 Debuys Rd; Gulfport 39507	(228) 896-2492
	The Star Journal; 2507 14th St; Gulfport 39502	(228) 863-4174
HATTIESBURG	*Hub City Community News*; 120 E 8th St; Hattiesburg 39401	(601) 544-6378
HAZLEHURST	*Copiah County Courier*; 103 S Ragsdale Ave; Hazlehurst 39083	(601) 894-3141
HERNANDO	*DeSoto Times*; 28 Losher St; Hernando 38632	(662) 429-6397
HOLLY SPRINGS	*The Marshall Messenger*; 164 Van Dorn Ave; Holly Springs 38635	(662) 252-4193
	The South Reporter; 157 S Center St; Holly Springs 38635	(662) 252-4261
HOUSTON	*Times Post*; 225 E Madison St; Houston 38851	(662) 456-3771
HURLEY	*The Bulletin*; Hwy 613; Hurley 39555	(601) 588-6784
INDIANOLA	*The Enterprise-Tocsin*; 114 Main St; Indianola 38751	(662) 887-2222
IUKA	*Tishomingo County News*; 120 W Front St; Iuka 38852	(662) 423-3666
JACKSON	*Mississippi Link Newspaper*; 206 W Pearl St; Jackson 39201	(601) 355-9103
	Northside Sun; 246 Briarwood Dr; Jackson 39236	(601) 957-1122
	Jackson Advocate; 438 N Mill St; Jackson 39202	(601) 948-4122
	The Rankin Record; 634 Grants Ferry Rd; Jackson 39047	(601) 992-4869
KOSCIUSKO	*The Star Herald*; 317 N Madison St; Kosciusko 39090	(662) 289-2251
LAUREL	*American/Jones County Edition*; 127 N 15th Ave; Laurel 39440	(601) 649-2846
LEAKSVILLE	*Greene County Herald*; Leaksville 39451	(601) 394-5070
LELAND	*Leland Progress*; 128 E 3rd St; Leland 38756	(662) 686-4081
LEXINGTON	*Holmes County Herald*; 308 Court Square; Lexington 39095	(662) 834-1151
LIBERTY	*Southern Herald*; 258 Main St; Liberty 39645	(601) 657-4818
LONG BEACH	*The Progress Newspaper*; 19099-B Pineville Rd; Long Beach 39560	(228) 864-3766
LOUISVILLE	Winston County Journal; N Court St; Louisville 39339	(662) 773-6241
LUCEDALE	*George County Times*; Main St; Lucedale 39452	(601) 947-2967
LUMBERTON	*The Booster*; Box 393; Lumberton 39455	(601) 794-5206
MACON	*Macon Beacon*; 403 S Jefferson St; Macon 39341	(662) 726-4747
MAGEE	*Magee Courier*; 206 N Main; Magee 39111	(601) 849-3434
MAGNOLIA	*Magnolia Gazette*; 267 E Bay St; Magnolia 39652	(601) 783-2441
MARKS	*Quitman County Democrat*; 330 Locust St; Marks 38646	(662) 326-2181
MEADVILLE	*Franklin Advocate*; Main St; Meadville 39653	(601) 384-2484
MENDENHALL	*Simpson County News*; 138 W Maud Ave; Mendenhall 39114	(601) 847-2525
MERIDIAN	*Meridian Memo Digest*; 2511 5th St; Meridian 39301	(601) 693-2372
MONTICELLO	*Lawrence County Press*; 543 Broad St; Monticello 39654	(601) 587-2781
MORTON	*Morton Tribune*; 150 S 4th St; Morton 39117	(601) 732-2210
MOUNT OLIVE	*Mount Olive Tribune*; Mount Olive 39119	(601) 765-8275
NATCHEZ	*Bluff City Post*; 719 Franklin St; Natchez 39120	(601) 446-5218
NEW ALBANY	*New Albany Gazette*; 713 Carter Ave; New Albany 38652	(662) 534-6321
NEWTON	*Newton Record*; 120 S Main St; Newton 39345	(601) 683-2001
OCEAN SPRINGS	*Mississippi Conservative*; 19 Marks Rd; Ocean Springs 39564	(228) 875-5373
	The Ocean Springs Record; 715 Cox Ave; Ocean Springs 39564	(228) 875-2791
OKOLONA	*Okolona Messenger*; 249 Main St; Okolona 38860	(662) 447-5501
OLIVE BRANCH	*DeSoto County Tribune*; 8885 E Goodman; Olive Branch 38654	(662) 895-6220
PETAL	*The Petal Journal*; 119 W Central Ave; Petal 39465	(601) 582-4321
PHILADELPHIA	*Neshoba Democrat*; 439 E Beacon St; Philadelphia 39350	(601) 656-4000
PONTOTOC	*The Pontotoc Progress*; 13 Jefferson St; Pontotoc 38863	(662) 489-3511
POPLARVILLE	*The Poplarville Democrat*; 115 W Pearl St; Poplarville 39470	(601) 795-2247
PORT GIBSON	*Port Gibson Reveille*; 708 Market (Main) St; Port Gibson 39150	(601) 437-5103
PRENTISS	*Prentiss Headlight*; 142 Third St; Prentiss 39474	(601) 792-4221
PURVIS	*Lamar County News*; 106 Shelby Speights Dr; Purvis 39475	(601) 794-2765

Newspapers in Mississippi

WEEKLY NEWSPAPERS (cont'd)

QUITMAN	*Clarke County Tribune*; 101 Main St; Quitman 39355	(601) 776-3726
RALEIGH	*Smith County Reformer*; Main St; Raleigh 39153	(601) 782-4358
RAYMOND	*Hinds County Gazette*; 110 Port Gibson St; Raymond 39154	(601) 857-8071
RICHTON	*The Richton Dispatch*; Richton 39476	(601) 788-6031
RIPLEY	*Southern Sentinel*; 113 Commerce; Ripley 38663	(662) 837-8111
ROLLING FORK	*Deer Creek Pilot*; 203 Locust St; Rolling Fork 39159	(662) 873-4354
SARDIS	*The Southern Reporter*; 105 S Pocahontas; Sardis 38666	(662) 487-1551
SENATOBIA	*Tate County Democrat*; 219 E Main St; Senatobia 38668	(662) 562-4414
TAYLORSVILLE	*Smith County Reformer Hollow*; Taylorsville 39168	(601) 785-6525
	The Taylorsville Post; 124 Main St; Taylorsville 39168	(601) 785-4333
SOUTHAVEN	*DeSoto Times*; 1283 Stateline Rd W; Southaven 38671	(662) 393-6397
	Southaven Press; 1800 Stateline Rd; Southaven 38671	(662) 393-3840
TUNICA	*Tunica Times-Democrat*; Tunica 38676	(662) 363-1511
TYLERTOWN	*Tylertown Times*; 727 Beulah Ave; Tylertown 39667	(601) 876-5111
UNION	*The Union Appeal*; 105 Main St; Union 39365	(662) 774-9433
WATER VALLEY	*North Mississippi Herald*; N Main St; Water Valley 38965	(662) 473-1473
WAYNESBORO	*Wayne County News*; 608 Station St; Waynesboro 39367	(601) 735-4341
WIGGINS	*Stone County Enterprise*; 143 1st SE, Wiggins 39577	(601) 928-4802
WINONA	*Winona Times*; 321 Summit St; Winona 38967	(662) 283-1131
WOODVILLE	*Woodville Republican*; 425 Depot St; Woodville 39669	(601) 888-4293
YAZOO CITY	*The Yazoo Herald*; 1035 Grand Ave; Yazoo City 39194	(662) 746-4911

COLLEGE / UNIVERSITY NEWSPAPERS

Copiah-Lincoln Community College: *Wolf Tales*; Wesson 39191 .... (601) 643-5101
Delta State University: *Delta Statement*; Cleveland 38733 .... (662) 846-4715
East Central Community College: *The Tom-Tom*; Decatur 39327 .... (601) 635-2126
Hinds Community College: *The Hindsonian*; Raymond 39154 .... (601) 857-3323
Holmes Community College: *The Growl*; Goodman 39079 .... (662) 472-2312
Itawamba Community College: *The Chieftain*; Hwy 78W; Fulton 38843 .... (662) 862-3101
Jackson State University: *The Blue & White Flash*; PO Box 18449; Jackson 39217 .... (601) 968-2167
Mary Holmes College: *The Eagle*; West Point 39773 .... (662) 494-6820
Meridian Community College: *MJC News Page*; 5500 Hwy 19 N; Meridian 39305 .... (601) 483-8241
Mississippi State University: *Reflector*; Mississippi State 39762 .... (662) 325-2374
Millsaps College: *Purple & White*; 1701 N State St; Jackson 39210 .... (601) 974-1211
Mississippi College: *Mississippi Collegian*; PO Box 4082; Clinton 39058 .... (601) 925-3244
Mississippi Delta Community College: *Delta Herald*; Moorhead 38761 .... (662) 246-5631
Mississippi State University: *Dawgs' Bite*; S Lafayette; Starkville 39759 .... (662) 323-5108
Mississippi University for Women: *The Spectator*; Cromwell Communications Ctr; Columbus ..... (662) 329-7268
Northwest Mississippi Community College: *The Beacon*; Booneville 38829 .... (662) 728-7751
Rust College: *The Sentinel*; Holly Springs 38635 .... (662) 252-4661
Southwest Mississippi Community College: *The Pine Burr*; Summit 39666 .... (601) 276-2011
Tougaloo College: *Harambee*; 500 West County Line Rd; Tougaloo 39174 .... (601) 977-6159
University of Southern Mississippi: *Student Printz*; Hattiesburg 39406 .... (601) 266-4965
University of Mississippi: *The Daily Mississippian*; **(the state's only *daily* college newspaper)** ... (662) 232-5391
William Carey College: *The Cobbler*; Hattiesburg 39401 .... (601) 582-6148
Wood Community College: *The Breeze*; Mathiston 39752 .... (662) 263-8486

Newspapers in Mississippi

WIRE SERVICES
Associated Press; 125 S Congess; Jackson 39201 .... (601) 948-5897

MEDIA TRADE ASSOCIATIONS
Newsline (Newsletter); Mississippi Association of Broadcasters (MAB);
      855 S Pear Orchard Rd; Suite 403; Ridgeland 39157 .... 1-800-382-0739 or (601) 957-9121

RELIGIOUS PUBLICATIONS
*Baptist Record, Th*e; PO Box 530; 515 E Mississippi St; Jackson 39205-0530 .... (601) 968-3800
Gulf Pine Catholic; Catholic Diocese of Biloxi; PO Box 1189; Biloxi 39533-1189 .... (228) 374-8318
Mississippi Methodist Advocate; 321 Mississippi St; Jackson 39201 .... (601) 354-0515

BUSINESS & PROFESSIONAL JOURNALS
*Catfish Journal, The; 3000 Old Canton Rd; Jackson 39216 .... (601) 714-5327
*Coast Business Journal; 943 33rd Ave; Gulfport 39501 .... (228) 868-1182
*Metro Business Review; 370 Towne Center Blvd; Jackson .... (601) 956-0756
Mississippi Business Journal; 5120 Galaxie Dr; Jackson 39206 .... (601) 364-1000
      World Wide Web — http://www.msbusiness.com
Mississippi Farm Bureau News; 6310 I-55 N; Jackson 39211 .... (601) 977-4153
Mississippi Today; 237 E Amite St; Jackson 39201 .... (601) 969-3581
Today in Mississippi; The Electric Power Associations of MS; 2805 Greenway Dr; Jackson 39204 . (601) 922-2341

EXTRA!!! The Times EXTRA!!!

Mississippi's largest newspaper, *The Clarion-Ledger* of Jackson, is the 98th largest in the nation with an average daily circulation of 107,109 and average circulation on Sunday of 127,962 (audit of Sept. 27, 1998).

The Ultimate Reference on the State

Jackson MSA (Metropolitan Statistical Area)

GEOGRAPHY

Total Area: 2,374 square miles or 1,519,360 acres (approx. 1/20th of the state)
Land: 2,311 square miles or 1,479,040 acres (**Forested, '98**: 1,257 sq mi [804,480 acres] 52.9%)
Water: 63 square miles or 40,320 acres

Area of the City of Jackson is 109 sq. miles (69,760 acres).

PEOPLE, GENERAL[75]

Born in Mississippi: 80.2% of total population   **Foreign Born**: 0.9% of total population
People Speaking Foreign Language at Home (1990 U.S. Census figures age 5 and over): 2.6% total
  Chinese 0.10%; French 0.50%; German 0.30%; Italian 0.05%; Spanish 1.10%; other .5%
Ancestry (per 100,000 people[76]): Arab 219.3; Austrian 29.8; Belgian 11.6; Canadian 31.6; Czech 40.2; Danish 45.0; Dutch 798.7; English 8,612; Finnish 30.6; French 1,654; French Canadian 522.8; German 7,125.5; Greek 154.3; Hungarian 41.2; Irish 9,447.2; Italian 784.5; Lithuanian 15.4; Norwegian 130.8; Polish 254.2; Portuguese 37.7; Romanian 17.7; Russian 65.8; Scotch Irish 3,943.4; Scottish 1,207; Slovak 41.5; Subsaharan African 239.8; Swedish 208.4; Swiss 81.9; Ukrainian 5.1; U.S./American 7,976.3; Welch 281.5; West Indian 24.5; & Yugoslavian 4.1

POPULATION STATISTICS

Pop. City of Jackson: 1990 — 196,637   7/1/98 — 188,419 (the 94th largest city in the U.S.)
Population MSA: 1990 — 395,396 (75.7% urban [299,315] and 24.3% rural [96,081])
Est. Pop. MSA, 7/1/98: 429,741 (white 240,741 - 56.0%; nonwhite 189,000 - 44.0%) Rank 116 of 318
Population Density, 1998: MSA — 180.97 per sq. mile   **City of Jackson** — 1,728.61 per sq. mile
Change in Population of MSA: 1980-1990 — 8.4% increase   1990-1998 — 8.69% increase
Pop. Age Breakdown, 1998 — 0-4 years: 31,544; ages 5-17 years: 82,086; ages 18-24 years: 47,008; 25-44 years: 138,944; ages 45-64 years: 84,559; ages 65 and over: 45,600
Total Age 18 and Older (Voting Age Population), 1998: 316,111 (73.56% of total population)
Incorporated Municipalities Within the Jackson MSA (with 7/1/1998 Estimated Population):
  Hinds County Bolton (783); Clinton (22,067); Edwards (1,195); Jackson (187,433); Learned (99); Terry (619); and Utica (987)
  Madison Co. Canton (12,221); Flora (1,585); Jackson (853); Madison (12,618); Ridgeland (16,545)
  Rankin Co. Brandon (14,612); Florence (2,375); Flowood (4,471); Jackson (133); Pearl (23,287); Pelahatchie (1,597); Puckett (362); and Richland (5,794)

Live Births (Residence Data), 1998: 6,839 (white 3,046 & non-white 3,793)
Deaths, 1998: 3,741 (white 2,120 and nonwhite 1,621)
  Motor Vehicle Deaths: 179   **Total Accidental Deaths**: 300
Number of Households: 7/1/1997 — 151,741 (2.83 persons per household)   1990 — 140,157

HOUSING

Housing Units: 152,493 (Urban: 115,285—75.6%   Suburban: 3,660—2.4%   Rural: 33,548—22.0%)
Homes With...1-3 Rooms: 14.9%; 4-8 Rooms: 80.2%; 9 or More Rooms: 4.9% (average — 5.3 rooms)
Median Value of All Existing Homes: $62,733
Owner-Occupied Units: 92,106 (60.4% of all housing)

Metro Jackson's apartment occupancy fell to 92.6% in the 3rd quarter 2000, down from 94.1% during the 2nd quarter.

  Valued: less than $49,999—37.3%; $50,000-$99,999—47.1%; $100,000-$249,999—14.1%; $250,000-$499,999—1.3%; over $500,000—0.2%
  Owners w/Monthly Cost: below $500—28.4%; $500-$999—56.6%; $1,000-$1,999—13.9%

Median Monthly Homeowner Costs: $680
Average Owner's Income Spent for Housing: 20.9%
Existing Home Sales: 1999 — 4,693 (w/ 438 pending)
                1998 — 4,730 (with 55 pending)

There were 376 homes sold in Metro Jackson in Oct. 1998 at an average price of $98,392. The average selling price a year earlier in Oct. 1997 was $84,130. Source: Miss. Assn. of REALTORS®

Median Price of Homes Sold: 1999 — $95,100   1998 — $93,200
Renter-Occupied Units: 48,035 (31.5% of all homes)
  Median Contract Rent: $320 monthly   **Renters Income Spent for Rent**: 26.0%
  Typical Monthly Rent: $459.50 for 2 bedroom, 2 bath, unfurnished apartment
  Renters with Monthly Rent: under $200—27.7%; $200-$499—65.0%; $500-$749—6.1%

---

[75] 1990 figures only are used in the section "People, General." The Jackson Metropolitan Statistical Area is the largest MSA in the state, encompassing Hinds County (including Jackson, the state capital and largest city in the state), Madison County and Rankin County.
[76] To derive actual number, multiply number given (no. per 100,000 people) by 3.95396.

Jackson MSA (Metropolitan Statistical Area)

Manufactured Housing (mobile homes): 11,894 (7.8% total housing)
Homes That Are Condos: 1.4% of total housing
Average Home Energy Costs: $104.60 per month
Homes Heating with: gas 55.1%; electricity 34.4%

Cost of Living Index, 4th Qtr. 1998 (compared to National Average of 100)	
Grocery Items	86.4
Housing	87.5
Utilities	101.5
Transportation	90.8
Health Care	79.9
Misc. Goods & Services	91.8
TOTAL	89.8

INCOME

Average Salary: 1998 — $27,086 ($23,822 state & $33,381 U.S.)
            1997 — $26,143 ($22,767 state & $31,734 U.S.)
Average Weekly / Hourly Earnings in Manufacturing:
   Apr. 2000 — $526.80 / $13.17   Mar. 2000 — $503.37 / 12.94   Apr. 1999 — $533.66 / $13.08
Avg. Earnings per Job: 1998 — $28,603 (wages/salaries $26,293; nonfarm proprietors' inc. $21,610)
            1997 — $27,663 (wages/salaries $25,331; nonfarm proprietors' inc. $21,086)
Total Personal Income, 1998: $10,546,870,000 (**$24,542 per capita** - Miss. $20,506 - U.S. $28,518)
         $ 7,340,600,000 Net Earnings ($17,081 per capita)
         $ 1,377,976,000 Transfer Payments ($3,207 per capita)
         $ 1,828,294,000 Dividends, Interest, & Rent ($4,254 per capita)
Earnings, 1998: $8,059,431,000
         $6,434,152,000 Wages & Salary Disbursements
         $ 838,928,000 Other Labor Income
         $ 786,351,000 Proprietors Income

Per capita income was $23,273 and median family income was $33,825 in Hinds County in 1998.

Selected Components of Government Transfer Payments, 1998:
   $534,187,000 Retirement & Disability Insurance Payments
   $272,156,000 Medical Payments ($272,156,000 Medicare; $237,571,000 public assist. medical)
   $165,100,000 Income Maintenance Benefit Payments ($58,382,000 SSI; $7,532,000 family
               assistance; $35,591,000 food stamps; $63,595,000 other)

ECONOMY

Total Retail Sales, FY 1999: $6,793,086,667

The City of Jackson total financial budget for FY 2001, which took effect Oct. 1, 2000, was $325 million.

Gross State Sales Tax, FY 1999: $408,869,476 paid by 11,182 retailers.
Real Property Taxes, 1999: $1,413,603,391 assessed
         1998: $1,357,673,110 assessed on 197,033 parcels — true value $9,193,217,603
Personal Prop. Taxes, 1999: $ 964,049,456 assessed
         1998: $ 884,593,453 assessed on 15,470 parcels — true value $4,219,289,187
Personal State Income Taxes, FY 1999: $186,904,874 paid on $3,770,240,369 net taxable income
         by 183,894 taxpayers ($1,016.37 average paid per taxpayer)
Corporate State Income & Franchise Taxes, FY 1999: $56,409,262 paid by 9,102 corporate taxpayers.
Wine/Liquor Sales (w/Taxes), FY 1999: $40,930,415 by 242 permittees (Hinds/Madison Counties - Rankin is dry)
Value of All Construction Contracts, Jan.-Nov.: 1998 — $482.8 million   1997 — $464.1 million
Timber Products Harvested, 1997: 91,284,000 bd. ft. of sawtimber and 348,805 cords of pulpwood
Tourism: Over 40,000 club/organization members visited Jackson Oct. 1998 through Aug. 1999 creating
         an economic impact of $16.6 million, according to the Jackson Convention & Visitors Bureau.
Hotels/Motels, 1999: $54.43 average room price per night with a 57.2% occupancy rate.
Transportation, 1999: 9 airlines; 1 bus line; 2 railroads; 2 freight carrier truck companies.

The Jan. '99 issue of the national P.O.V. magazine ranked Jackson No. 18 among 75 U.S. cities as "Best Cities To Start a Business." A 1999 study by ReliaStar Financial Corp. ranked Metro Jackson 19th among 125 metro areas in the U.S. for people to earn and save money. Among the 24 ranked cities within a 500 mile radius of the city, Jackson was No. 3, behind only Atlanta and Dallas. Jackson ranked No. 85 on the list of "100 Best Places in the U.S. to Do Business" in the May 29, 2000, edition of Forbes magazine.

LABOR

Total Civilian Labor Force:	July 2000 — 239,480	Mar. 2000 — 232,040	July 1999 — 228,390
Total Civilian Employment:	July 2000 — 229,250	Mar. 2000 — 223,460	July 1999 — 220,160
No. Civilian Unemployed:	July 2000 — 10,230	Mar. 2000 — 8,580	July 1999 — 8,230
Unemployment Rate (MSA):	July 2000 — 4.3%	Mar. 2000 — 3.7%	July 1999 — 3.6%
Hinds County:	July 2000 — 5.0%	Mar. 2000 — 4.3%	July 1999 — 4.3%
Madison County:	July 2000 — 4.0%	Mar. 2000 — 3.5%	July 1999 — 3.2%
Rankin County:	July 2000 — 2.8%	Mar. 2000 — 2.5%	July 1999 — 2.3%

Jackson MSA (Metropolitan Statistical Area)

Employed in Government, Apr. 2000: 48,100 (5,400 federal; 25,100 state; 17,600 local)
Largest Industries, 1998 (Percent of Earnings): services 26.5%; state and local government 16.3%; retail trade 9.7%; durable goods manufacturing 6.0%.
State Unemployment Insurance Compensation, 1998: $11,837,000

MAJOR EMPLOYMENT SECTORS OF THE JACKSON MSA			
	Apr. 2000	Mar. 2000	Apr. 1999
TOTAL	227,700	229,000	231,100
Manufacturing	20,500	20,600	19,900
Non-Manufacturing	207,200	208,400	211,200
Construction	11,300	11,400	11,300
Transportation & Public Utilities	17,700	17,800	17,500
Wholesale & Retail Trade	53,800	54,400	56,000
Finance, Insurance & Real Estate	15,200	15,500	16,600
Services	60,500	61,000	60,400
Government (Federal, State, & Local)	48,100	47,600	48,700

SOURCE: Mississippi Employment Security Commission

CRIME

Figures to the right (except for the box) are for Hinds County (incl. the City of Jackson), plus Madison County and Rankin County.

The City of Jackson had 419 police officers as of Sept. 29, 2000.

Major Crimes For the Jackson MSA:	1998	Rate[75]	1997	Rate
Murder & Non-Negligent Manslaughter	68	15.8	79	18.7
Forcible Rape	262	61.0	265	62.8
Robbery	1,373	319.9	1,309	310.4
Aggravated Assault	1,008	234.9	1,059	287.9
All Violent Crimes	**2,711**	**631.7**	**2,712**	**643.2**
Burglary	6,743	1,571.2	7,154	1,696.7
Larceny-Theft	14,836	3,457.0	15,371	3,645.4
Motor Vehicle Theft	4,168	971.2	3,824	906.9
All Property Crime	**25,747**	**5,999.4**	**26,349**	**6,249.0**
Crime Index Total	**28,458**	**6,631.1**	**29,061**	**6,892.2**

CITY OF JACKSON MAJOR CRIME INDEX
1999 — 20,151
1998 — 20,780
1997 — 20,242
1996 — 20,492
1995 — 23,053
1994 — 28,142
1993 — 25,653
1992 — 26,284

Major Crime Figures for the City of Jackson Only, 1999* / 1998:
Homicide: 45 / 60; Forcible Rape: 248 / 221; Robbery: 1,096 / 1,228; Aggravated Assault: 691 / 747;
Burglary: 4,814 / 4,895; Larceny-Theft: 9,703 / 9,897; Auto Theft: 3,475 / 3,626; Arson: 79 / 106
All Violent Crimes: 2,080 / 2,256; All Property Crime: 18,071 / 18,524; **Index Totals: 20,151 / 20,780**

HEALTH

Live Births (Residence Data), 1998: 6,839 (white 3,046 & non-white 3,793)
 Born to Unmarried Teen Mothers: 1,064 (white 182 & non-white 882) 58 under 15 yrs. old
 Born to Unmarried Mothers: 3,113 (white 465 & non-white 2,648)
Deaths, 1998: 3,741 (white 2,120 and nonwhite 1,621) **Motor Vehicle Deaths** — 179
Marriages (by Residence of Bride), 1998: 3,351 (white 1,990; non-white 1,361)
Divorces (by Place of Occurrence), 1998: 2,157 (white 1,396; non-white 747)
Number of Hospitals, Aug. 1, 2000: 13 with 4,437 beds + 1 Veterans Affairs Hospital with 163 beds.[76]
Number of Physicians, Aug. 1, 2000: 1,727   **Average Cost of Hospital Room**: $340.79 per day

Number of motor vehicle deaths in 1999 in the City of Jackson — 54.

University Medical Center has about 1,800 students. Half the physicians practicing in the state graduated from UMC. There are 2.5 million square feet under roof on a campus of 164 acres. With 6,500 employees and an annual budget of over half a billion dollars, including an annual payroll of about $200 million, UMC is the largest single employer in the greater Jackson area! The annual utility bill alone is $4.5 million. In a year at UMC, 4 million pounds of linens are laundered and 45 tons of eggs are cooked for breakfast!

EDUCATION

No. of Public School Districts in Jackson MSA, 1998-99: 7 (3 county + 5 separate) Hinds, Madison, and Rankin Counties; Canton, Clinton, Jackson and Pearl Public; plus Hinds County AHS.
Total Enrollment, Fall 1998: 73,879 (1998-99 Avg. Daily Attendance 70,926 - 96% initial enrollment)
 Pre-Kindergarten: 221
 Kindergarten: 5,545
 Elementary: 36,709 (includes 1,389 in Special Education)
 Secondary: 31,404 (includes 595 in Special Education)

---

[75] Rate is no. per 100,000 pop. *1999 crime figures are preliminary. Source: *Crime In The U.S.*, 1997 & 1998; *Uniform Crime Reports*; FBI.
[76] The City of Jackson has 6 state-licensed hospitals with 2,433 beds plus 1 Veterans Affairs hospital with 163 beds.

Jackson MSA (Metropolitan Statistical Area)

Total Expenditures for Public Schools, 1998-99: $380,511,200 ($5,365 average per pupil in ADA*)

| SOURCE for public school statistics: |
| Mississippi Department of Education |
| *ADA stands for Average Daily Attendance |

$150,643,723 (local sources 40.1%)
$185,343,572 (state sources 48.7%)
$ 42,523,905 (federal sources 11.2%)

Pupil/Teacher Ratio, 1998-99: 16.92 pupils per teacher average (all grades)
Number of Classroom Teachers, 1998-99: 4,192 (2,279 elementary & 1,913 secondary)
Classroom Teacher's Salaries, 1998-99: $30,336 average ($29,550 statewide)
    Elementary — $30,028 average   **Secondary** — $30,703 average
Total of All Classroom Teachers' Salaries, 1998-99: $127.1 million (33.4% of total expenditures)
    Elementary — $68.4 million   **Secondary** — $58.7 million

HIGHER EDUCATION IN THE JACKSON MSA:
No. Enrolled in Colleges & Universities Located within the Jackson MSA: 16,289
    8,135 in 2 state schools in the fall of 1999
        Jackson State University: 6,354 (5,075 full-time 79.9%; 1,279 part-time 20.1%)
            4,971 state resident 78.2%; 1,383 nonresident 21.8%
            2,590 men 40.8%; 3,764 women 59.2%
            162 white 2.5%; 6,050 black 95.2%; 142 other 2.2%
        University of Miss. Medical Center: 1,781 (1,601 full-time 89.9%; 180 part-time 10.1%)
            1,496 state resident 84.0%; 285 nonresident 16.0%
            840 men 47.2%; 941 women 52.8%
            1,435 white 80.6%; 167 black 9.4%; 179 other 10.1%
    8,154 in 10 private schools: 7,348 in 6 schools (fall 1998) plus 806 in 4 schools (spring 2000).

No. Enrolled in Community/Jr. Colleges Located within the MSA, Fall 1998: 10,125
    8,990 on 6 campuses of Hinds Community College and 1,135 on 1 campus of Holmes C.C.
No. of MSA Residents Enrolled in the Eight State-Supported Universities, Fall 1999: 8,432

TRANSPORTATION

Total Number of Registered Vehicles, FY Ending 6/30/1999: 363,357
Workers Driving to Work in Private Vehicles: 93.4%
Workers Driving to Work: Alone — 79.1%   **With Passenger(s)** — 20.9%
Workers Driving in Carpools to Work: 2-person carpool 11.2%; 3-person 1.96%; 4-person 0.62%;
    5-person 0.15%; 6-person 0.10%; and 7-person carpool 0.26% = 14.29% total in carpools
Travel Time to Work: less than 5 minutes 3.0%; 5-30 minutes 71.4%; 30-60 minutes 19.8%;
    60-90 minutes 1.5%; over 90 minutes 4.3%
Mean Travel Time (workers age 16+ who work away from home): 20.0 minutes

ARTS

Number of Institutions: Archives/History 1; Art Museums 6; Aquariums 1; Botanical Gardens 1; Dance Companies 1; General & History Museums & Sites 12; Museums 20; Natural History Museums 1; Opera Companies 1; Performing Arts Companies & Centers 5; Planetariums 1; Science Centers 3; Sports Museums 1; Symphony Orchestras 1; Zoos 1

SPORTS

College NCAA Sports Teams: 2 — Jackson State University Tigers (football & basketball)
Pro Teams: Baseball — The Jackson Diamond Kats (independent Texas-Louisiana League)
    Hockey — The Jackson Bandits (East Coast Hockey League) associated with the
        NHL's Minnesota Wild & Chicago Blackhawks, Norfolk Admirals (AHL),
        and the Cleveland Lumberjacks (IHL).
Stadiums: 1 — Mississippi Veterans Memorial Stadium - seating capacity 60,492
Sports Museums: 1 — Mississippi Sports Hall of Fame & Museum   **Golf Courses**: 6 — all private

VETERANS

World War II Veterans: 1,218 (30.8 per 1,000 people) [the entire state had 58,000 on 7/1/1998]
Korean War Veterans: 668 (16.9 per 1,000 people) [the entire state had 40,000 on 7/1/1998]
Vietnam War Veterans: 1,056 (26.7 per 1,000 people) [the entire state had 67,000 on 7/1/1998]
All Veterans: 2,653 (67.1 per 1,000 people) [the entire state had 223,774 veterans as of July 1, 1998]
Veterans Benefit Payments: **1998** — $43,636,000   **1997** — $42,013,000   **1996** — $41,585,000

How Mississippi Ranks Among All the

Rank ☞	1st	2nd	3rd	4th	5th	6th
Total Area in Square Miles	Florida 59,928	Georgia 58,977	Arkansas 53,182	North Carolina 52,672	Alabama 52,237	Louisiana 49,651
Population, 1990	Florida 12,938,071	North Carolina 6,632,448	Georgia 6,478,149	Virginia 6,189,197	Tennessee 4,877,203	Louisiana 4,372,035
Pop., July 1, 1999	Florida 15,111,244	Georgia 7,788,240	North Carolina 7,650,789	Virginia 6,872,912	Tennessee 5,483,535	Louisiana 4,372,035
Black Population Percentage, 1998	Mississippi 36.5% (1,003,175)	Louisiana 32.2% (1,407,201)	South Carolina 29.9% (1,147,239)	Georgia 28.5% (2,181,455)	Alabama 26.0% (1,132,196)	North Carolina 22.1% (1,665,273)
White Population Percentage, 1998	West Virginia 96.2% (1,741,456)	Kentucky 91.2% (3,618,693)	Arkansas 82.7% (2,098,444)	Florida 82.6% (12,318,852)	Tennessee 82.2% (4,466,360)	Virginia 76.0% (5,162,888)
Unemployment Rate, 1998	Virginia 2.9% (best)	North Carolina 3.5%	South Carolina 3.8%	Alabama* 4.2%	Georgia* 4.2%	Tennessee* 4.2%
Unemployment Benefits Paid, 1998	Florida $638,478,441	North Carolina $378,426,836	Tennessee $300,943,630	Georgia $239,754,196	Kentucky $211,129,913	Alabama $191,465,234
Per Capita Income 1999	Virginia $29,484	Florida $28,023	Georgia $27,198	North Carolina $26,220	Tennessee $25,581	Kentucky $23,161
Disposable Income Per Capita, 1999	Virginia $25,010	Florida $24,201	Georgia $23,225	Tennessee $22,626	North Carolina $22,424	South Carolina $20,491
Gross State Product, 1997	Florida $380.6 billion	Georgia $229.4 billion	North Carolina $218.9 billion	Virginia $211.3	Tennessee $147.0	Louisiana $124.3 billion
Value of Construction, 1997	Florida $25.2 billion	North Carolina $14.0 billion	Georgia $13.6 billion	Virginia $10.1 billion	Tennessee $8.2 billion	South Carolina $6.0 billion
Per Capita State Taxes, F.Y. 1997	Tennessee $1,233 (best)	Alabama $1,270	Louisiana $1,297	Virginia $1,430	South Carolina $1,431	Florida $1,439
State Gen. Fund Revenue, F.Y. '99	Florida $18.185 billion	Georgia $13.649 billion	North Carolina $13.350 billion	Virginia $10.585 billion	Kentucky $6.594 billion	Tennessee $6.573 billion
State Expenditures (Gen. Fund) F.Y. '99	Florida $18.185 billion	Georgia $13.064 billion	North Carolina $13.037 billion	Virginia $10.195 billion	Tennessee $6.421 billion	Kentucky $6.181 billion
State Gen. Fund Exp. Per Capita, F.Y. '99	North Carolina $1,790	Georgia $1,683	Kentucky $1,682	Virginia $1,545	West Virginia $1,512	Louisiana $1,335
State Debt per Capita, F.Y. 1997	Tennessee $618 (best)	North Carolina $765	Georgia $826	Alabama $875	Arkansas $891	Mississippi $899
No. Federal Civilian Employees, March '98	Virginia 117,273	Georgia 62,017	Florida 61,314	Alabama 38,265	Tennessee 32,648	North Carolina 30,895
Teacher's Average Salary, 1999-2000	Georgia $41,257	North Carolina $39,280	Virginia $38,797	Tennessee $36,722	Alabama $36,564	Florida $36,513
Number of Farms 1998	Tennessee 91,000	Kentucky 90,000	North Carolina 58,000	Georgia 50,000	Arkansas 49,500	Alabama* 49,000
Acres per Farm 1998	Arkansas 298	Mississippi 276	Louisiana 273	Florida 236	Georgia 226	South Carolina 196
Cash Receipts Farm Marketings 1998	North Carolina $7,613,296,000	Florida $6,855,313,000	Georgia $5,534,854,000	Arkansas $5,476,417,000	Kentucky $3,963,330,000	Mississippi $3,544,082,000
Per Capita Energy Consumption, 1997	Louisiana 940,000,000 Btu	Kentucky 462,600,000 Btu	Alabama 457,300,000 Btu	West Virginia 445,600,000 Btu	Mississippi 411,200,000 Btu	Arkansas 408,100,000 Btu
Gallons Fuel Used per Vehicle, 1997	Arkansas 1,165	Kentucky 986	South Carolina 892	Georgia 867	Mississippi 847	Alabama 807
No. in Prison at Beginning of 1999	Florida 67,193	Georgia 38,758	Louisiana 32,227	North Carolina 27,193	Virginia 27,191	Alabama 22,655

* States that tied in some categories are listed alphabetically. Rankings are from largest to smallest, but best to worst in some indicated cases.

Southern States in Selected Categories

7th	8th	9th	10th	11th	12th	👉 Rank
Mississippi 48,286	Virginia 42,326	Tennessee 42,146	Kentucky 40,411	South Carolina 31,189	West Virginia 24,231	Total Area in Square Miles
Alabama 4,040,389	Kentucky 3,686,891	South Carolina 3,486,310	Mississippi 2,575,475	Arkansas 2,350,624	West Virginia 1,793,477	Population, 1990
Alabama 4,369,862	Kentucky 3,960,825	South Carolina 3,885,736	Mississippi 2,768,619	Arkansas 2,551,373	West Virginia 1,806,928	Pop., July 1, 1999
Virginia 20.1% (1,362,617)	Tennessee 16.6% (899,546)	Arkansas 16.1% (407,618)	Florida 15.2% (2,267,753)	Kentucky 7.2% (284,860)	West Virginia 3.2% (58,095)	Black Population Percentage, 1998
North Carolina 75.3% (5,684,204)	Alabama 73.0% (3,176,917)	Georgia 69.3% (5,293,151)	South Carolina 69.0% (2,645,077)	Louisiana 66.1% (2,887,280)	Mississippi 62.5% (1,719,480)	White Population Percentage, 1998
Florida 4.3%	Kentucky 4.6%	Mississippi 5.4%	Arkansas 5.5%	Louisiana 5.7%	West Virginia 6.6% (worst)	Unemployment Rate, 1998
Virginia $180,907,809	Arkansas $167,267,262	South Carolina $157,752,812	Louisiana $142,278,850	West Virginia $114,555,007	Mississippi $100,327,276	Unemployment Benefits Paid, 1998
Alabama $22,946	South Carolina $23,496	Louisiana $22,792	Arkansas $22,114	West Virginia $20,888	Mississippi $20,506	Per Capita Income 1999
Alabama $20,068	Louisiana $20,016	Kentucky $19,930	Arkansas $19,412	West Virginia $18,377	Mississippi $18,241	Disposable Income Per Capita, 1999
Alabama $103.1 billion	Kentucky $100.0 billion	South Carolina $93.3 billion	Arkansas $58.4 billion	Mississippi $58.3 billion	West Virginia $38.2 billion	Gross State Product, 1997
Alabama* $4.8 billion	Kentucky* $4.8 billion	Louisiana $4.7 billion	Arkansas $3.0 billion	Mississippi $2.6 billion	West Virginia $1.2 million	Value of Construction, 1997
Georgia $1,456	Mississippi $1,471	Arkansas $1,497	West Virginia $1,600	North Carolina $1,708	Kentucky $1,745 (worst)	Per Capita State Taxes, F.Y. 1997
Louisiana $5.926 billion	South Carolina $5.221 billion	Alabama $4.940 billion	Mississippi $3.319 billion	Arkansas $3.046 billion	West Virginia $2.728 billion	State Gen. Fund Revenue, F.Y. '99
Louisiana $5.819 billion	Alabama $4.906 billion	South Carolina $4.782 billion	Mississippi $3.127 billion	Arkansas $3.009 billion	West Virginia $2.723 billion	State Expenditures (Gen. Fund) F.Y. '99
South Carolina $1,234	Florida $1,207	Arkansas $1,183	Tennessee $1,175	Mississippi $1,133	Alabama $1,126	State Gen. Fund Exp. Per Capita, F.Y. '99
Florida $1,093	South Carolina $1,423	Virginia $1,476	Louisiana $1,615	West Virginia $1,674	Kentucky $1,822 (worst)	State Debt per Capita, F.Y. 1997
Kentucky 20,259	Louisiana 19,923	Mississippi 16,930	South Carolina 15,920	West Virginia 11,211	Arkansas 10,916	No. Federal Civilian Employees, March '98
Kentucky $36,255	South Carolina $36,112	West Virginia $34,994	Arkansas $34,746	Louisiana $32,268	Mississippi $31,913	Teacher's Average Salary, 1999-2000
Virginia* 49,000	Florida 45,000	Mississippi 43,705	Louisiana 30,000	South Carolina 25,000	West Virginia 21,000	Number of Farms 1998
Alabama 194	Virginia 180	West Virginia 176	North Carolina 162	Kentucky 154	Tennessee 131	Acres per Farm 1998
Alabama $3,440,698,000	Virginia $2,435,608,000	Tennessee $2,291,077,000	Louisiana $1,955,077,000	South Carolina $1,545,570,000	West Virginia $434,422,000	Cash Receipts Farm Marketings 1998
South Carolina 389,000,000 Btu	Tennessee 387,800,000 Btu	Georgia 345,400,000 Btu	North Carolina 326,200,000 Btu	Virginia 315,400,000 Btu	Florida 246,200,000 Btu	Per Capita Energy Consumption, 1997
North Carolina 798	West Virginia 794	Tennessee 775	Virginia 740	Florida 719	Louisiana 717	Gallons Fuel Used per Vehicle, 1997
South Carolina 21,236	Tennessee 17,738	Mississippi 15,855	Kentucky 14,987	Arkansas 10,561	West Virginia 3,478	No. in Prison at Beginning of 1999

* States that tied in some categories are listed alphabetically. Rankings are from largest to smallest, but best to worst in some indicated cases.

Mississippi Phone Exchanges

A
Abbeville	(662) 234			
Aberdeen	(662) 319	343		
	369			
Ackerman	(662) 285	387		
Algoma	(662) 489			
Alligator	(662) 624			
Amory	(662) 256	257		
	305			
Anguilla	(662) 873			
Arcola	(662) 827			
Arkabutla	(662) 562			
Artesia	(662) 272			
Ashland	(662) 224			
Avon	(662) 334			

B
Bailey	(601) 681	737		
Baldwyn	(662) 365			
Banner	(662) 414	983		
Barlow	(601) 277			
Bassfield	(601) 943			
Batesville	(662) 561	563		
	578	609*	712	934*	997*
Bay Saint Louis	(228) 216*	342*		
	344*	463	466	467	469
	493*	688	689	797	813
Bay Springs	(601) 670	764		
Beaumont	(601) 588*	784		
Becker	(601) 256			
Belden	(662) 842			
Belen	(662) 326			
Belmont	(662) 454	676		
Belzoni	(662) 247			
Benndale	(601) 945			
Benoit	(662) 742			
Benton	(662) 673			
Bentonia	(662) 755			
Beulah	(662) 759			
Big Creek	(601) 763			
Bigbee Valley	(662) 738			
Biloxi	(228) 209*	212*		
	243*	275*	297*	324*	341*
	348*	349	354	358	374
	377	385	386	388	392
	396	432	435	436	442
	470*	523	546	555	594
	617*	697*	701	702	760*
	806*	860*	861*		
Blue Mountain	(662) 685			
Blue Springs	(662) 534			
Bogue Chitto	(601) 734			
Bolton	(601) 866			
Booneville	(662) 720	728		
	865*			
Boyle	(662) 846			
Brandon	(601) 217	591		
	706	824	825	829
Braxton	(601) 847			

Briarwood	(601) 681			
Brookhaven	(601) 380*	669*		
	695*	734	757*	823	833
	835			
Brooklyn	(601) 598			
Brooksville	(601) 738			
Bruce	(662) 412	413		
	414	983		
Buckatunna	(601) 648			
Bude	(601) 384			
Burnsville	(662) 427			
Byhalia	(662) 838	851		
Byram	(601) 352	353		
	354	355	960	968	969

C
Caledonia	(662) 356			
Calhoun City	(662) 628			
Camden	(662) 468			
Canton	(601) 391	855		
	859			
Carlisle	(601) 535			
Carriere	(601) 798			
Carrollton	(662) 237			
Carson	(601) 943			
Carthage	(601) 253	267		
	298	654		
Cary	(662) 873			
Cascilla	(662) 647			
Causeyville	(601) 644			
Cedar Bluff	(662) 494			
Centreville	(601) 645			
Charleston	(662) 647			
Chatawa	(601) 783			
Chatham	(662) 827			
Chester	(662) 387			
Chulahoma	(662) 564*			
Chunky	(601) 655			
Clara	(601) 735			
Clarksdale	(662) 383	621		
	624	627	902*		
Cleveland	(662) 719*	721		
	843	846		
Clinton	(601) 460	708		
	924	925	926		
Coahoma	(662) 337			
Coffeeville	(662) 675			
Coila	(662) 834			
Coldwater	(662) 233	622		
Collins	(601) 517	641*		
	698	765		
Collinsville	(601) 986			
Columbia	(601) 441*	444		
	731	736	740		
Columbus	(662) 208*	240		
	241	242*	243	244	245
	251*	327	328	329	386*
	435*	574*	889*	904*	

Columbus Air Force Base				
	(662) 434			
Como	(662) 526			
Conehatta	(601) 775			
Corinth	(662) 284	286		
	287	293	396	575*	665
	808*			
Courtland	(662) 563			
Crawford	(662) 272			
Crenshaw	(662) 382			
Crosby	(601) 639			
Crossroads	(601) 772	958		
Crowder	(662) 326			
Cruger	(662) 455			
Crupp	(662) 746			
Crystal Springs	(601) 892			

D
D'Iberville	(228) 392	396		
	435			
D'Lo	(601) 847			
Daleville	(601) 681			
Decatur	(601) 635			
DeKalb	(601) 743			
Delta City	(662) 873			
Dennis	(662) 454			
Derma	(662) 628			
Diamondhead	(228) 435			
Doddsville	(662) 756			
Drew	(662) 745			
Dublin	(662) 624			
Duck Hill	(662) 565			
Duffee	(601) 986			
Dumas	(662) 837			
Duncan	(662) 395			
Dundee	(662) 365			
Durant	(662) 653			

E
Eagle Lake	(601) 279			
Eastabuchie	(601) 582			
Ecru	(662) 489			
Eddiceton	(601) 532			
Eden	(662) 716	746		
Edinburg	(601) 267			
Edwards	(601) 852			
Elizabeth	(662) 686			
Elliott	(662) 226	227		
Ellisville	(601) 433*	477		
	577*			
Enid	(662) 623			
Enterprise	(601) 659	704		
Escatawpa	(228) 475			
Ethel	(662) 674			
Etta	(662) 534			
Eupora	(662) 258	273		
	552*			

F
Fairview	(662) 585
Falcon	(662) 382

* Those with asterisks are used for cellular phones or pagers. All others are regular telephone prefixes. Area codes are in parenrtheses.

Mississippi Phone Exchanges

Falkner	(662) 837			
Farmington	(662) 286	287		
Farrell	(662) 624			
Fayette	(601) 786			
Fernwood	(601) 684			
Fitler	(662) 873			
Flora	(601) 879			
Florence	(601) 845			
Flowood	(601) 932	939		
Forest	(601) 469	507*	625	
Forkville	(601) 732			
Foxworth	(601) 736	752		
French Camp	(662) 547			
Friars Point	(662) 383			
Fulton	(662) 585	862		
G				
Gallman	(601) 888			
Gattman	(662) 256			
Gautier	(228) 374	497	762	
Georgetown	(601) 858			
Glen Allan	(662) 839			
Glendora	(662) 375			
Gloster	(601) 225			
Golden	(662) 585	676		
Goodman	(662) 472			
Gore Springs	(662) 226			
Grace	(662) 873			
Greenville	(662) 332	334	335	347* 378 379 390 496* 522* 806* 820* 931*
Greenwood	(662) 219*	299*	309* 392* 451 453 455 457* 458* 459 466* 475* 514* 515* 555 658 897* 903*	
Greenwood Springs	(662) 256			
Grenada	(662) 226	227	229 230* 294 417* 614* 809* 864*	
Gulfport	(228) 213*	214	263* 313* 314* 323* 336 362* 367 380* 437* 516* 518* 539 547* 563 574 575 604 609* 669* 670* 679 695* 701 770* 808* 822 831 832 850* 863 864 865 867 868 870 871 880* 883* 889* 896 897 918* 931* 993	
Gunnison	(662) 747			
Guntown	(662) 348			
H				
Hamilton	(662) 319			
Harrisville	(601) 792			

Hattiesburg	(601) 261	264	266 268 270* 271 288 296 297* 307* 310* 315* 402* 408* 450* 467* 520* 543* 544 545 549* 550 554 558 570* 579 582 583 584 599 602 705 896 913*	
Hazlehurst	(601) 505*	794	894	
Heidelberg	(601) 787	935*		
Hermanville	(601) 535			
Hernando	(662) 429	449		
Hickory	(601) 646	683		
Hickory Flat	(662) 333			
Hillsboro	(601) 625			
Holcomb	(662) 226			
Hollandale	(662) 827			
Holly Bluff	(662) 828			
Holly Ridge	(662) 887			
Holly Springs	(662) 216*	252	274 333 551 697* 921*	
Homewood	(601) 536			
Horn Lake	(662) 342	349	393	
Houlka	(662) 568			
Houston	(662) 448	456	568	
Hurley	(228) 588			
I				
Independence	(662) 233			
Indianola	(662) 207*	884	887	
Inverness	(662) 265			
Isola	(662) 962			
Itta Bena	(662) 254			
Iuka	(662) 423	424	667 908*	
J				
Jackson (regular telephone prefixes)				
	(601) 206	292	313 321 346 351 352 353 354 355 359 360 362 364 366 368 371 372 373 376 404 420 432 502 503 555 576 592 608 664 709 713 714 718 813 815 863 899 914 919 922 923 944 948 949 952 956 957 960 961 965 968 969 973 974 977 978 979 981 982 984 985 987 991 992 995	

Jackson (cellular phone/pager use)				
	(601) 202*	209*	212* 214* 259* 260* 278* 291* 306* 316* 317* 331* 370* 419* 421* 461* 471* 478* 497* 506* 510* 521* 524* 540* 559* 573* 589* 594* 613* 640* 668* 672* 715* 750* 760* 817* 821* 826* 832* 881* 882* 906* 918* 920* 927* 929* 930* 937* 940* 941* 942* 946* 951* 953* 954* 955* 966*	
Jackson-City of Pearl	932	933	936 939	
Janice	(601) 598			
Jayess	(601) 587	736		
Jonestown	(662) 358			
Jumpertown	(662) 728			
K				
Keesler Air Force Base				
	(228) 432	435		
Kilmichael	(662) 262			
Kiln	(228) 255			
Kokomo	(601) 736			
Kosciusko	(662) 289	290		
Kreole	(228) 474			
L				
Lake	(601) 775			
Lake Cormorant	(662) 781			
Lakeshore	(228) 467			
Lamar	(662) 252	778	840	
Lambert	(662) 326			
Lauderdale	(601) 484	632		
Laurel	(601) 344	399	422 425 426 428 433* 439* 498* 518* 577* 580* 649 804*	
Lawrence	(601) 683			
Leaf	(601) 753			
Leakesville	(601) 394			
Leland	(662) 686			
Lexington	(662) 834			
Liberty	(601) 657			
Little Rock	(601) 774			
Little Yazoo	(662) 755			
Long Beach	(228) 435	868		
Lorman	(601) 877			
Louin	(601) 739			
Louise	(601) 836			
Louisville	(662) 724	773	779 803*	
Lucedale	(601) 394	508*	766 770* 947*	
Lula	(662) 337			
Lumberton	(601) 688*	796		
Lyman	(228) 831	832		
Lynville	(601) 677			
Lyon	(662) 358	627		

The Ultimate Reference on the State

Mississippi Phone Exchanges

M
City	Area Code	Prefixes
Maben	(662)	263
Macon	(662)	361* 726 738
Madden	(601)	267
Madison	(601)	499 605 607 707 853 856 898
Magee	(601)	849 867
Magnolia	(601)	783
Mantachie	(662)	282
Mantee	(662)	456
Marietta	(662)	728
Marion	(601)	482 483
Marks	(662)	326 339
Mathiston	(662)	263
Mattson	(662)	627
Mayersville	(662)	873
Mayhew	(662)	327
McAdams	(662)	289
McCall Creek	(601)	532
McComb	(601)	248* 249 250 276 341* 542 567 684 730* 810*
McCool	(662)	547
McLain	(601)	753
McNeill	(601)	798
Meadville	(601)	384
Mendenhall	(601)	847
Meridian	(601)	409* 479* 480* 481 482 483 484 485 486* 490* 527* 553 581 595* 612* 616* 626 644 655 692 693 696 703 710* 818* 880* 917* 938*
Meridian Naval Air Station	(601)	679
Merigold	(662)	748
Metcalfe	(662)	332 334 378
Michigan City	(662)	768
Midnight	(662)	247
Mineral Wells	(662)	895
Minter City	(662)	658
Mississippi State	(662)	323 325
Mize	(601)	603* 733
Money	(662)	453 455
Monticello	(601)	587
Montpelier	(662)	494
Mooreville	(662)	841 842 844
Moorhead	(662)	246
Morgan City	(662)	254
Morgantown	(601)	736
Morton	(601)	537 732
Moscow	(662)	778
Moselle	(601)	544 582 583 752
Moss	(601)	428 649
Moss Point	(228)	460 474 475
Mound Bayou	(662)	741
Mount Olive	(601)	797
Mount Pleasant	(662)	851
Myrtle	(662)	534 988

N
City	Area Code	Prefixes
Natchez	(601)	210* 304 308* 431* 442 443 445 446 597* 660* 807* 814* 861* 870*
Neely	(601)	525
Nesbit	(662)	429
Neshoba	(601)	656
Nettleton	(662)	963
New Albany	(662)	534 538 539 761*
New Augusta	(601)	964
New Hebron	(601)	694
New Site	(662)	728
Newton	(601)	646 683
Nicholson	(228)	799
Nitta Yuma	(662)	873
North Carrollton	(662)	237
Noxapater	(662)	724

O
City	Area Code	Prefixes
Oak Vale	(601)	736
Oakland	(662)	623
Obadiah	(601)	737
Ocean Springs	(228)	818 872 875
Okolona	(662)	447
Old Taylorsville	(601)	725
Olive Branch	(662)	812* 890 893 895
Osyka	(601)	542
Ovett	(601)	344
Oxford	(662)	232 234 236 238 281 302 513 533* 801* 816* 915 972*

P
City	Area Code	Prefixes
Pace	(662)	723
Pachuta	(601)	776
Panther Burn	(662)	827
Pascagoula	(228)	202 217* 218* 219* 312 366* 381* 407* 497 522 549 596* 602* 623* 627* 691* 696 712 731* 761 762 769 809 931* 934 935 938 990* 994
Pass Christian	(228)	255 452 586
Pattison	(601)	437
Paulding	(601)	727
Pearl	(601)	932 933 936 939
Pearlington	(228)	533
Pelahatchie	(601)	854
Perkinston	(601)	928
Petal	(601)	544 545 582 583 584
Pheba	(662)	494
Philadelphia	(601)	389 416* 650 656 663
Philipp	(662)	658
Picayune	(601)	215* 590* 749 798 799 916*
Pickens	(662)	468
Piney Woods	(601)	845
Pinola	(601)	847
Pittman	(601)	752
Pittsboro	(662)	412 983
Plantersville	(662)	566 842 844
Pocahontas	(601)	362
Polkville	(601)	537
Pontotoc	(662)	488 489 509 860*
Pope	(662)	563
Poplarville	(601)	403 463* 795
Port Gibson	(601)	437 877
Porterville	(662)	476
Potts Camp	(662)	333
Prairie	(662)	369
Prentiss	(601)	792
Preston	(601)	677
Puckett	(601)	269
Pulaski	(601)	536 537
Purvis	(601)	436* 744 794

Q
City	Area Code	Prefixes
Quitman	(601)	776

R
City	Area Code	Prefixes
Raleigh	(601)	374* 782 789
Randolph	(662)	568
Raymond	(601)	857
Red Banks	(662)	252 851
Redwood	(601)	636 638
Reform	(662)	387
Rena Lara	(662)	624
Rich	(662)	337
Richland	(601)	932 939 960
Richton	(601)	689* 788 989
Rienzi	(662)	462
Ripley	(662)	512 837 993*
Robinsonville	(662)	363
Rolling Fork	(662)	873 907*
Rome	(662)	345
Rose Hill	(601)	727

* Those with asterisks are used for cellular phones or pagers. All others are regular telephone prefixes. Area codes are in parenrtheses.

Mississippi Phone Exchanges

Location	Area Code	Prefixes
Rosedale	(662)	723 759
Roxie	(601)	322
Ruleville	(662)	756
Ruth	(601)	734
S		
Saltillo	(662)	842 844 869
Sand Hill	(601)	989
Sandersville	(601)	425 426 428 649
Sandy Hook	(601)	736
Sanatorium	(601)	849
Sarah	(662)	562
Sardis	(662)	487
Satartia	(662)	746
Saucier	(228)	831 832
Schlater	(662)	658
Scobey	(662)	226
Scooba	(662)	476
Scott	(601)	742
Seminary	(601)	722
Senatobia	(662)	301 388* 560 562
Shannon	(662)	767
Sharon	(601)	859
Shaw	(662)	754
Shelby	(662)	398
Sherman	(662)	840 844
Shubuta	(601)	687
Shuqualak	(662)	793
Sibley	(601)	442
Sidon	(662)	453
Silver City	(662)	247
Silver Creek	(601)	886
Skene	(662)	843
Slate Spring	(662)	637
Sledge	(662)	382
Smithdale	(601)	567
Smithville	(662)	651
Snow Lake Shores	(662)	224
Soso	(601)	729 763
Southaven	(662)	280 342 349 393 470* 996*
Star	(601)	845
Starkville	(662)	312* 320* 323 324 325 338 418* 465 615 617* 717 769*
State Line	(601)	848
Steens	(662)	327 328
Stennis Space Center	(228)	688
Stewart	(662)	262
Stoneville	(662)	686
Stonewall	(601)	659
Stringer	(601)	425 725
Sturgis	(662)	465
Summit	(601)	276
Sumner	(662)	375
Sumrall	(601)	516* 758
Sunflower	(662)	569
Sunnyside	(662)	658
Swan Lake	(662)	375
Swiftown	(662)	254
Sylvarena	(601)	789
T		
Taylor	(662)	234
Taylorsville	(601)	452* 785
Tchula	(662)	235
Terry	(601)	878
Thaxton	(662)	489
Thomastown	(662)	289
Thornton	(662)	235
Tillatoba	(662)	623
Tinsley	(662)	746
Tiplersville	(662)	223
Tippo	(662)	647
Tishomingo	(662)	438
Toccopola	(662)	258
Toomsuba	(601)	632
Tougaloo	(601)	956 957
Trebloc	(662)	456
Tremont	(662)	652
Tribbett	(662)	686
Tunica	(662)	357 363 367* 519* 702* 910* 980*
Tupelo	(662)	213* 231* 255* 377 397* 401* 491* 523* 610* 620 678 680 690 691* 790 791 805* 819* 840 841 842 844 869 871* 891 909* 910* 990*
Tutwiler	(662)	345
Tylertown	(601)	222 303* 876
U		
Union	(662)	774
Union Church	(601)	277
University	(662)	915
Utica	(601)	885
V		
Vaiden	(662)	464
Valley Park	(662)	873
Vancleave	(228)	826
Van Vleet	(662)	447
Vance	(662)	345
Vardaman	(662)	682
Vaughan	(662)	673
Verona	(662)	566
Vicksburg	(601)	218* 415* 529* 618* 619 629 630 631 634 636 638 642* 661 802 831* 868* 883 994*
Victoria	(662)	838
Vossburg	(601)	787
W		
Wade	(228)	762
Walls	(662)	781
Walnut	(662)	223
Walnut Grove	(601)	253
Walters	(601)	546
Walthall	(662)	258
Washington	(601)	442
Water Valley	(662)	413 473
Waveland	(228)	466 467
Waynesboro	(601)	381* 410* 671 735
Wayside	(662)	334
Webb	(662)	375
Weir	(662)	547
Wesson	(601)	643
West	(662)	967
West Point	(662)	295* 492 494 495
Wheeler	(662)	465
White Oak	(601)	269
Whitfield	(601)	351
Wiggins	(601)	528 762 928
Winona	(662)	283
Winstonville	(662)	741
Winterville	(662)	332
Woodland	(662)	456
Woodville	(601)	888
Y		
Yazoo City	(662)	314 571* 716 746 751 875*
Yellow Creek	(662)	667

These numbers are "prefixes" or "phone exchange numbers." Phone companies call them "Central Office Codes." They are the first 3 digits of 7-digit phone numbers. At the time this list was compiled (6-1-2000), there were 856 assigned prefixes in use in Mississippi.

Mississippi Phone Exchanges

Area Code **228** covers the three Gulf Coast counties of Hancock, Harrison and Jackson and includes these 132 prefixes:*

202	209*	212*	213*	214	216*
217*	218*	219*	243*	255	263*
275*	297*	312	313*	314*	323*
324*	336	341*	342*	344*	348*
349	354	358	362*	366*	367*
374	377	380*	381*	385	386
388	392	396	407*	432	435
436	437*	442	452	460	463
466	467	469	470*	474	475
493*	497	516*	518*	522	523
533	539	546	547*	549	555
563	574	575	586	588	594
596*	602*	604	609*	617*	623*
627*	669*	670*	679	688	689
691*	695*	696	697*	701	702
712	731*	760*	761	762	769
770*	797	806*	808*	809	813
818	822	826	831	832	850*
860*	861*	863	864	865	867
868	870	871	872	875	880*
883*	889*	896	897	918*	931*
934	935	938	990*	993	994

Area Code **601** covers most of central Mississippi southward to the northern boundaries of the three Gulf Coast counties and includes these 417 prefixes:

202*	206	209*	210*	212*	214*
215*	217*	218*	222	225	248*
249	250	253	259*	260*	261
264	266	267	268	269	270*
271	276	277	278*	279	288
291*	292	296	297*	298	303*
304	306*	307*	308*	310*	313
315*	316*	317*	321	322	331*
341*	344	346	351	352	353
354	355	359	360	362	364
366	368	370*	371	372	373
374*	376	380*	381*	384	389
391	394	399	402*	403	404
408*	409*	410*	415*	416*	419*
420	421*	422	425	426	428
431*	432	433*	436*	437	439*
441*	442	443	444	445	446
450*	452*	460	461*	463*	467*
469	471*	477	478*	479*	480*
481	482	483	484	485	486*
490*	497	498*	499	502	503
505*	506*	507*	508*	510*	516*
517*	518*	520*	521*	524*	525
527*	528	529*	532	535	536
537	540*	542	543*	544	545
546	549*	550*	553	554	555
558	559*	567	570*	573*	576
577*	579	580*	581	582	583
584	587	588*	589*	590*	591
592	594*	595*	597*	598	599
602	603*	605	607	608	612*
613*	616*	618*	619*	625	626
629	630	631	632	634	635
636	638	639	640*	641*	642*
643	644	645	646	648	649
650	654	655	656	657	659
660*	661	663	664	668*	669*
670	671	672*	677	679	681
683	684	687	688*	689*	692
693	694	695*	696	698	703
704	705	706	707	708	709
710*	713	714	715*	718	722
725	727	729	730*	731	732
733	734	735	736	737	739
740	743	744	749	750*	752
753	757*	758	760*	762	763
764	765	766	770*	772	774
775	776	782	783	784	785
786	787	788	789	792	794
795	796	797	798	799	802
804*	807*	810*	813	814*	815
817*	818*	821*	823	824	825
826*	829	831*	832*	833	835
845	847	848	849	852	853
854	855	856	857	858	859
861*	863	866	867	868*	870*
876	877	878	879	880*	881*
882*	883	885	886	888	892
894	896	898	899	906*	913*
914	916*	917*	918*	919	920*
922	923	924	925	926	927*
928	929*	930*	932	933	935*
936	937*	938*	939	940*	941*
942*	943	944	945	946*	947*
948	949	951*	952	953*	954*
955*	956	957	958	960	961
964	965	966*	968	969	973
974	977	978	979	981	982
984	985	986	987	989	991
992	994*	995			

Area Code **662** is the state's newest area code (first used in April 1999). It covers about the northern half of Mississippi and includes these 307 prefixes:

207*	208*	213*	216*	219*	223
224	226	227	229	230*	231*
232	233	234	235	236	237
238	240	241	242*	243	244
245	246	247	251*	252	254
255	256	257	258	262	263
265	272	273	274	280	281
282	283	284	285	286	287
289	290	293	294	295*	299*
301	302	305	309*	312*	314
319	320*	323	324	325	326
327	328	329	332	333	334
335	337	338	339	342	343
345	347*	348	349	356	357
358	361*	363	365	367	369
375	377	378	379	382	383
386	387	388*	390	392*	393
395	396	397*	398	401*	412
413	414	417*	418*	423	424
427	429	434	435*	438	447
448	449	451	453	454	455
456	457*	458*	459	462	464
465	466*	468	470*	472	473
475*	476	487	488	489	491*
492	494	495	496*	509	512
513	514*	515*	519	522*	523*
526	533*	534	538	539	547
551	552*	555	560	561	562
563	564*	565	566	568	569
571	574*	575*	578	585	609*
610*	614*	615	617*	620	621
622	623	624	627	628	637
647	651	652	653	658	665
667	673	674	675	676	678
680	682	685	686	690	691*
697*	702*	712	716	717	719*
720	721	723	724	726	728
738	741	742	745	746	747
748	751	754	755	756	759
761*	767	768	769*	773	778
779	781	790	791	793	801*
803*	805*	806*	808*	809*	812*
816*	819*	820*	827	828	834
836	837	838	839	840	841
842	843	844	846	851	860*
862	864	865*	869	871*	873
875*	884	887	889*	890	891
893	895	897*	902*	903*	904*
907*	908*	909*	910*	915	921*
931*	934*	962	963	967	972*
980*	983	988	990*	993*	996*
997*					

* Those with asterisks indicate prefixes used for cellular phones or pagers. All others are telephone prefixes.

Mississippi Phone Exchanges — Numerical Cross Reference

Area Code 228
202	Pascagoula
209	Biloxi (cellular)
212	Biloxi (cellular)
213	Gulfport (cellular)
214	Gulfport
216	Bay Saint Louis (cellular)
217	Pascagoula (cellular)
218	Pascagoula (cellular)
219	Pascagoula (cellular)
243	Biloxi (cellular)
255	Kiln, Pass Christian
263	Gulfport (cellular)
275	Biloxi (cell/pager)
297	Biloxi (cell/pager)
312	Pascagoula
313	Gulfport (cellular)
314	Gulfport (cellular)
323	Gulfport (cellular)
324	Biloxi (cellular)
336	Gulfport
341	Biloxi (cellular)
342	Bay St. Louis
344	Bay St. Louis
348	Biloxi (cellular)
349	Biloxi
354	Biloxi
358	Biloxi
362	Gulfport
366	Pascagoula (cellular)
367	Gulfport (cellular)
374	Biloxi, Gautier
377	Biloxi
380	Gulfport (cellular)
381	Pascagoula (cellular)
385	Biloxi
386	Biloxi
388	Biloxi
392	Biloxi, D'Iberville
396	Biloxi, D'Iberville
407	Pascagoula (cellular)
432	Biloxi, Keesler Air Force Base
435	Biloxi, D'Iberville, Diamondhead, Keesler Air Force Base, Long Beach
436	Biloxi
437	Gulfport (cellular)
442	Biloxi
452	Pass Christian
460	Moss Point
463	Bay Saint Louis
466	Bay Saint Louis, Waveland
467	Bay Saint Louis, Lakeshore, Waveland
469	Bay St. Louis
470	Biloxi (cellular)
474	Kreole, Moss Point
475	Escatawpa, Moss Point
493	Bay Saint Louis (cellular)
497	Gautier, Pascagoula
516	Gulfport (pager)
518	Gulfport (cellular)
522	Pascagoula
523	Biloxi
533	Pearlington
539	Gulfport
546	Biloxi
547	Gulfport (cellular)
549	Pascagoula
555	Biloxi
563	Gulfport
574	Gulfport
575	Gulfport
586	Pass Christian
588	Hurley
594	Biloxi
596	Pascagoula (cellular)
602	Pascagoula (pager)
604	Gulfport
609	Gulfport (cellular)
617	Biloxi (cell/pager)
623	Pascagoula (cellular)
627	Pascagoula (cellular)
669	Gulfport (cellular)
670	Gulfport (pager)
679	Gulfport
688	Bay Saint Louis, Nicholson, Stennis Space Center
689	Bay Saint Louis, Nicholson
691	Pascagoula (cellular)
695	Gulfport (cellular)
696	Pascagoula
697	Biloxi (cellular)
701	Gulfport
702	Biloxi
712	Pascagoula
731	Pascagoula (cellular)
760	Biloxi (cellular)
761	Pascagoula
762	Gautier, Pascagoula, Wade
769	Pascagoula
770	Gulfport (pager)
797	Bay St. Louis
806	Biloxi (cellular)
808	Gulfport (cell/pager)
809	Pascagoula
813	Bay Saint Louis
818	Ocean Springs
822	Gulfport
826	Vancleave
831	Gulfport, Lyman, Saucier
832	Gulfport, Lyman, Saucier
850	Gulfport (cellular)
860	Biloxi (cellular)
861	Biloxi (cellular)
863	Gulfport
864	Gulfport
865	Gulfport
867	Gulfport
868	Gulfport, Long Beach
870	Gulfport
871	Gulfport
872	Ocean Springs
875	Ocean Springs
880	Gulfport (cellular)
883	Guflport (cellular)
889	Gulfport (cellular)
896	Gulfport
897	Gulfport
918	Gulfport (cell/pager)
931	Pascagoula (pager)
934	Gautier, Pascagoula
935	Pascagoula
938	Pascagoula
990	Pascagoula (cell/pager)
993	Gulfport
994	Pascagoula

Area Code 601
202	Jackson (pager)
206	Jackson
209	Jackson (cellular)
210	Natchez (pager)
212	Jackson (cellular)
214	Jackson (cellular)
215	Picayune (cellular)
217	Brandon (cellular)
218	Vickaburg (cellular)
222	Tylertown
225	Gloster
248	McComb (cellular)
249	McComb
250	McComb
253	Carthage, Walnut Grove
259	Jackson (cellular)
260	Jackson (cellular)
261	Hattiesburg
264	Hattiesburg
266	Hattieburg
267	Carthage, Edinburg, Madden
268	Hattiesburg
269	Puckett, White Oak
270	Hattiesburg (cellular)
271	Hattiesburg
276	McComb, Summit
277	Barlow, Union Church
278	Jackson (cellular)
279	Eagle Lake
288	Hattiesburg
291	Jackson (cell/pager)
292	Jackson
296	Hattiesburg
297	Hattiesburg (cellular)
298	Carthage
303	Tylertown (cellular)
304	Natchez
306	Jackson (pager)
307	Hattiesburg (cell/pager)
308	Natchez (cellular)
310	Hattiesburg (cellular)

The Ultimate Reference on the State

Mississippi Phone Exchanges — Numerical Cross Reference

Area Code 601 (continued)		445	Natchez	573	Jackson (cellular)
313	Jackson	446	Natchez	576	Jackson
315	Hattiesburg (cellular)	450	Hattiesburg (cellular)	577	Ellisville, Laurel (cellular)
316	Jackson (cell/pager)	452	Taylorsville (cellular)	579	Hattiesburg
317	Jackson (cellular)	460	Clinton	580	Laurel (cellular)
321	Jackson	461	Jackson (pager)	581	Meridian
322	Roxie	463	Poplarville (cellular)	582	Eastabuchie, Hattiesburg, Moselle, Petal
331	Jackson (cellular)	467	Hattiesburg (cellular)		
341	McComb (cellular)	469	Forest	583	Hattiesburg, Moselle, Petal
344	Laurel, Ovett	471	Jackson (cellular)	584	Hattiesburg, Petal
346	Jackson	477	Ellisville	587	Jayess, Monticello
351	Jackson, Whitfield	478	Jackson cellular)	588	Beaumont (cellular)
352	Byram, Jackson	479	Meridian (cellular)	589	Jackson (pager)
353	Byram, Jackson	480	Meridian (cellular)	590	Picayune (cellular)
354	Byram, Jackson	481	Meridian	591	Brandon
355	Byram, Jackson	482	Marion, Meridian	592	Jackson
359	Jackson	483	Marion, Meridian	594	Jackson (cellular)
360	Jackson	484	Lauderdale, Meridian	595	Meridian (cellular)
362	Jackson, Pocahontas	485	Meridian	597	Natchez (cellular)
364	Jackson	486	Meridian (cellular)	598	Brooklyn, Janice
366	Jackson	490	Meridian (cellular)	599	Hattiesburg
368	Jackson	497	Jackson (cellular)	602	Hattiesburg
370	Jackson (pager)	498	Laurel (cellular)	603	Mize (cellular)
371	Jackson	499	Madison	605	Madison
372	Jackson	502	Jackson	607	Madison
373	Jackson	503	Jackson	608	Jackson
374	Raleigh (cellular)	505	Hazlehurst (cellular)	612	Meridian (pager)
376	Jackson	506	Jackson (cellular)	613	Jackson (cellular)
380	Brookhaven (cellular)	507	Forest (cellular)	616	Meridian (cellular)
381	Waynesboro (cellular)	508	Lucedale (cellular)	618	Vicksburg (cellular)
384	Bude, Meadville	510	Jackson (cell/pager)	619	Vicksburg
389	Philadelphia	516	Sumrall (cellular)	625	Forest, Hillsboro
391	Canton	517	Collins (cellular)	626	Meridian
394	Leakesville, Lucedale	518	Laurel (cellular)	629	Vicksburg
399	Laurel	520	Hattiesburg (cellular)	630	Vicksburg
402	Hattiesburg (cellular)	521	Jackson (pager)	631	Vicksburg
403	Poplarville	524	Jackson (pager)	632	Lauderdale, Toomsuba
404	Jackson	525	Neely	634	Vicksburg
408	Hattiesburg (cellular)	527	Meridian (cellular)	635	Decatur
409	Meridian (cellular)	528	Wiggins	636	Redwood, Vicksburg
410	Waynesboro (cellular)	529	Vicksburg (cellular)	638	Redwood, Vicksburg
415	Vicksburg (cellular)	532	Eddiceton, McCall Creek	639	Crosby
416	Philadelphia (cellular)	535	Carlisle, Hermanville	640	Jackson (pager)
419	Jackson (pager)	536	Homewood, Pulaski	641	Collins (cellular)
420	Jackson	537	Morton, Polkville, Pulaski	642	Vicksburg (cellular)
421	Jackson (cellular)	540	Jackson (cellular)	643	Wesson
422	Laurel	542	McComb, Osyka	644	Causeyville, Meridian
425	Laurel, Sandersville, Stringer	543	Hattiesburg (cellular)	645	Centreville
426	Laurel, Sandersville	544	Hattiesburg, Moselle, Petal	646	Hickory, Newton
428	Laurel, Moss, Sandersville	545	Hattiesburg, Petal	648	Buckatunna
431	Natchez (cellular)	546	Walters	649	Laurel, Moss, Sandersville
432	Jackson	549	Hattiesburg (cellular)	650	Philadelphia
433	Ellisville, Laurel (cellular)	550	Hattiesburg (cellular)	654	Carthage
436	Purvis (cellular)	553	Meridian	655	Chunky, Meridian
437	Pattison, Port Gibson	554	Hattiesburg	656	Neshoba, Philadelphia
439	Laurel (cellular)	555	Jackson	657	Liberty
441	Columbia (cellular)	558	Hattiesburg	659	Enterprise, Stonewall
442	Natchez, Sibley, Washington	559	Jackson (cellular)	660	Natchez (cellular)
443	Natchez	567	McComb, Smithdale	661	Vicksburg
444	Columbia	570	Hattiesburg (pager)	663	Philadelphia

Mississippi Phone Exchanges — Numerical Cross Reference

664	Jackson	764	Bay Springs	876	Tylertown
668	Jackson (cellular)	765	Collins	877	Lorman, Port Gibson
669	Brookhaven (cellular)	766	Lucedale	878	Terry
670	Bay Springs	772	Crossroads	879	Flora
671	Waynesboro	774	Little Rock, Union	880	Meridian (cell/pager)
672	Jackson (cellular)	775	Conehatta, Lake	881	Jackson (cellular)
677	Lynville, Preston	776	Pachuta, Quitman	882	Jackson (cellular)
679	Meridian Naval Air Station	782	Raleigh	883	Vicksburg
681	Bailey, Briarwood, Daleville	783	Chatawa, Magnolia	885	Utica
683	Hickory, Lawrence, Newton	784	Beaumont	886	Silver Creek
684	Fernwood, McComb	785	Taylorsville	888	Gallman, Woodville
687	Shubuta	786	Fayette	892	Crystal Springs
688	Lumberton (cellular)	787	Heidelberg, Vossberg	894	Hazlehurst
689	Richton (cellular)	788	Richton	896	Hattiesburg
692	Meridian	789	Raleigh, Sylvarena	898	Madison
693	Meridian	792	Harrisville, Prentiss	899	Jackson
694	New Hebron	794	Hazlehurst, Purvis	906	Jackson (cellular)
695	Brookhaven (cellular)	795	Poplarville	913	Hattiesburg (cell/pager)
696	Meridian	796	Lumberton	914	Jackson
698	Collins	797	Mount Olive	916	Picayune (cellular)
703	Meridian	798	Carriere, McNeill, Picayune	917	Meridian (cellular)
704	Enterprise	799	Nicholson, Picayune	918	Jackson (cell/pager)
705	Hattiesburg	802	Vicksburg	919	Jackson
706	Brandon	804	Laurel (cellular)	920	Jackson (pager)
707	Madison	807	Natchez (cellular)	922	Jackson
708	Clinton	810	McComb (cellular)	923	Jackson
709	Jackson	813	Jackson	924	Clinton
710	Meridian (cellular)	814	Natchez (cellular)	925	Clinton
713	Jackson	815	Jackson	926	Clinton
714	Jackson	817	Jackson (pager)	927	Jackson (cellular)
715	Jackson (pager)	818	Meridian (cellular)	928	Perkinston, Wiggins
718	Jackson	821	Jackson (cellular)	929	Jackson (pager)
722	Seminary	823	Brookhaven	930	Jackson (pager)
725	Old Taylorsville, Stringer	824	Brandon	932	Flowood, Pearl, Richland
727	Paulding, Rose Hill	825	Brandon	933	Pearl
729	Soso	826	Jackson (cellular)	935	Heidelberg (cellular)
730	McComb (cellular)	829	Brandon	936	Pearl
731	Columbia	831	Vicksburg (cellular)	937	Jackson (cellular)
732	Forkville, Morton	832	Jackson (cellular)	938	Meridian (cellular)
733	Mize	833	Brookhaven	939	Flowood, Pearl, Richland
734	Bogue Chitto, Brookhaven, Ruth	835	Brookhaven	940	Jackson (cellular)
735	Clara, Waynesboro	845	Florence, Piney Woods, Star	941	Jackson (cellular)
736	Columbia, Foworth, Jayess, Kokomo, Morgantown, Oak Vale, Sandy Hook	847	Braton, D'Lo, Mendenhall, Pinola	942	Jackson (cellular)
		848	State Line	943	Bassfield, Carson
		849	Magee, Sanatorium	944	Jackson
737	Bailey, Obadiah	852	Edwards	945	Benndale
739	Louin	853	Madison	946	Jackson (cellular)
740	Columbia	854	Pelahatchie	947	Lucedale (cellular)
743	DeKalb	855	Canton	948	Jackson
744	Purvis	856	Madison	949	Jackson
749	Picayune	857	Raymond	951	Jackson (cellular)
750	Jackson (cellular)	858	Georgetown	952	Jackson
752	Foxworth, Moselle, Pittman	859	Canton, Sharon	953	Jackson (cellular)
753	Leaf, McLain	861	Natchez (cellular)	954	Jackson (cellular)
757	Brookhaven (cellular)	863	Jackson	955	Jackson (cellular)
758	Sumrall	866	Bolton	956	Jackson, Tougaloo
760	Jackson (cellular)	867	Magee	957	Jackson, Tougaloo
762	Wiggins	868	Vicksburg (cellular)	958	Crossroads
763	Big Creek, Soso	870	Natchez (cellular)	960	Byram, Jackson, Richland
				961	Jackson

The Ultimate Reference on the State

Mississippi Phone Exchanges — Numerical Cross Reference

	Area Code 601 (Continued)				
964	New Augusta	258	Eupora, Toccopola, Walthall	369	Aberdeen, Prairie
965	Jackson	262	Kilmichael, Stewart	375	Glendora, Sumner, Swan Lake, Webb
966	Jackson (cellular)	263	Maben, Mathiston		
968	Byram, Jackson	265	Inverness	377	Tupelo
969	Byram, Jackson	272	Artesia, Crawford	378	Greenville, Metcalfe
973	Jackson	273	Eupora	379	Greenville
974	Jackson	274	Holly Springs	382	Crenshaw, Falcon, Sledge
977	Jackson	280	Southaven	383	Clarksdale, Friars Point
978	Jackson	281	Oxford	386	Columbus (cellular)
979	Jackson	282	Mantachie	387	Ackerman, Chester, Reform
981	Jackson	283	Winona	388	Senatobia (cellular)
982	Jackson	284	Corinth	390	Greenville
984	Jackson	285	Ackerman	392	Greenwood (cellular)
985	Jackson	286	Corinth, Farmington	393	Horn Lake, Southaven
986	Collinsville, Duffee	287	Corinth, Farmington	395	Duncan
987	Jackson	289	Kosciusko, McAdams	396	Corinth
989	Richton, Sand Hill	290	Kosciusko	397	Tupelo (cellular)
991	Jackson	293	Corinth	398	Shelby
992	Jackson	294	Grenada	401	Tupelo (cellular)
994	Vicksburg (cellular)	295	West Point (cellular)	412	Bruce, Pittsboro
995	Jackson	299	Greenwood (cellular)	413	Bruce, Water Valley
		301	Senatobia	414	Banner, Bruce
	Area Code 662	302	Oxford	417	Grenada (cellular)
207	Indianola (cellular)	305	Amory	418	Starkville (cellular)
208	Columbus (pager)	309	Greenwood (pager)	423	Iuka
213	Tupelo (cellular)	312	Starkville (cellular)	424	Iuka
216	Holly Springs (cellular)	314	Yazoo City	427	Burnsville
219	Greenwood (cellular)	319	Aberdeen, Hamilton	429	Hernando, Nesbit
223	Tiplersville, Walnut	320	Starkville (cellular)	434	Columbus Air Force Base
224	Ashland, Snow Lake Shores	323	Mississippi State, Starkville	435	Columbus (cellular)
226	Elliot, Gore Springs, Grenada, Holcomb, Scobey	324	Starkville	438	Tishomingo
		325	Mississippi State, Starkville	447	Okolona, Van Vleet
227	Elliott, Grenada	326	Belen, Crowder, Lambert, Marks	448	Houston
229	Grenada			449	Hernando
230	Grenada (cellular)	327	Columbus, Mayhew, Steens	451	Greenwood
231	Tupelo (cellular)	328	Columbus, Steens	453	Greenwood, Money, Sidon
232	Oxford	329	Columbus	454	Belmont, Dennis
233	Coldwater, Independence	332	Greenville, Metcalfe, Winterville	455	Cruger, Greenwood, Money
234	Abbeville, Oxford, Taylor			456	Houston, Mantee, Trebloc, Woodland
235	Tchula, Thornton	333	Hickory Flat, Holly Springs, Potts Camp		
236	Oxford			457	Greenwood (cellular)
237	Carrollton, North Carrollton	334	Avon, Greenville, Metcalfe, Wayside	458	Greenwood (cellular)
238	Oxford			459	Greenwood
240	Columbus	335	Greenville	462	Rienzi
241	Columbus	337	Coahoma, Lula, Rich	464	Vaiden
242	Columbus (cellular)	338	Starkville	465	Starkville, Sturgis, Wheeler
243	Columbus	339	Marks	466	Grenwood (cellular)
244	Columbus	342	Horn Lake, Southaven	468	Camden, Pickens
245	Columbus	343	Aberdeen	470	Southaven (cellular)
246	Moorhead	345	Rome, Tutwiler, Vance	472	Goodman
247	Belzoni, Midnight, Silver City	347	Greenvillle (cellular)	473	Water Valley
251	Columbus (cellular)	348	Guntown	475	Greenwood (cellular)
252	Holly Springs, Red Banks	349	Horn Lake, Southaven	476	Porterville, Scooba
254	Itta Bena, Morgan City, Swiftown	356	Caledonia	487	Sardis
		357	Tunica	488	Pontotoc
255	Tupelo (cellular)	358	Jonestown, Lyon	489	Algoma, Ecru, Pontotoc, Thaxton
256	Amory, Becker, Gattman, Greenwood Springs	361	Macon (cellular)		
		363	Robinsonville, Tunica	491	Tupelo (cellular)
		365	Baldwyn, Dundee	492	West Point
257	Amory	367	Tunica		

Mississippi Phone Exchanges — Numerical Cross Reference

494	Cedar Bluff, Montpelier, Pheba, West Point
495	West Point
496	Greenville (pager)
509	Pontotoc
512	Ripley
513	Oxford
514	Greenwood (cellular)
415	Greenwood (cellular)
519	Tunica (cell/pager)
522	Grenville (cellular)
523	Tupelo (cellular)
526	Como
533	Oxford (cellular)
534	Blue Springs, Etta, Myrtle, New Albany
538	New Albany
539	New Albany
547	French Camp, McCool, Weir
551	Holly Springs
552	Eupora (cellular)
555	Greenwood
560	Senatobia
561	Batesville
562	Arkabutla, Sarah, Senatobia
563	Batesville, Courtland, Pope
564	Chulahoma (cellular)
565	Duck Hill
566	Planterville, Verona
568	Houlka, Houston, Randolph
569	Sunflower
571	Yazoo City (cellular)
574	Columbus (cellular)
575	Corinth (cellular)
578	Batesville
585	Fairview, Fulton, Golden
609	Batesville (cellular)
610	Tupelo (cellular)
614	Grenada (cellular)
615	Starkville
617	Starkville (cellular)
620	Tupelo
621	Clarksdale
622	Coldwater
623	Enid, Oakland, Tillatoba
624	Alligator, Clarksdale, Dublin, Farrell, Rena Lara
627	Clarksdale, Lyon, Mattson
628	Calhoun City, Derma
637	Slate Spring
647	Cascilla, Charleston, Tippo
651	Smithville
652	Tremont
653	Durant
658	Greenwood, Minter City, Philipp, Schlater, Sunnyside
665	Corinth
667	Iuka, Yellow Creek
673	Benton, Vaughan
674	Ethel
675	Coffeeville
676	Belmont, Golden
678	Tupelo
680	Tupelo
682	Vardaman
685	Blue Mountain
686	Elizabeth, Leland, Stoneville, Tribbett
690	Tupelo
691	Tupelo (cellular)
697	Holly Springs (cellular)
702	Tunica (cellular)
712	Batesville
716	Eden, Yazoo City
717	Starkville
719	Cleveland (cellular)
720	Booneville
721	Cleveland
723	Pace, Rosedale
724	Louisville, Noxapater
726	Macon
728	Booneville, Jumpertown, Marietta, New Site
738	Bigbee Valley, Brooksville, Macon
741	Mound Bayou, Winstonville
742	Benoit, Scott
745	Drew
746	Crupp, Eden, Satartia, Tinsley, Yazoo City
747	Gunnison
748	Merigold
751	Yazoo City
754	Shaw
755	Bentonia, Little Yazoo
756	Doddsville, Ruleville
759	Beulah, Rosedale
761	New Albany (cellular)
767	Shannon
768	Michigan City
769	Starkville (cellular)
773	Louisville
778	Lamar, Moscow
779	Louisville
781	Lake Cormorant, Walls
790	Tupelo
791	Tupelo
793	Shuqualak
801	Oxford (cellular)
803	Louisville (cellular)
805	Tupelo (pager)
806	Greenville (pager)
808	Corinth (cellular)
809	Grenada (cellular)
812	Olive Branch (cell/pager)
816	Oxford (cellular)
819	Tupelo (pager)
820	Greenville (cellular)
827	Arcola, Chatham, Hollandale, Panther Burn
828	Holly Bluff
834	Coila, Lexington
836	Louise
837	Dumas, Falkner, Ripley
838	Byhalia, Victoria
839	Glen Allan
840	Lamar, Sherman, Tupelo
841	Mooreville, Tupelo
842	Belden, Mooreville, Planterville, Saltillo, Tupelo
843	Cleveland, Skene
844	Sherman, Mooreville, Planterville, Saltillo, Tupelo
846	Boyle, Cleveland
851	Byhalia, Mount Pleasant, Red Banks
860	Pontotoc (cellular)
862	Fulton
864	Grenada (cellular)
865	Booneville (cellular)
869	Saltillo, Tupelo
871	Tupelo (cellular)
873	Anguilla, Cary, Delta City, Fitler, Grace, Mayersville, Nitta Yuma, Rolling Fork, Valley Park
875	Yazoo City (cellular)
884	Indianola
887	Holly Ridge, Indianola
889	Columbus (cellular)
890	Olive Branch
891	Tupelo
893	Olive Branch
895	Mineral Wells, Olive Branch
897	Greenwood (cellular)
902	Clarksdale (cellular)
903	Greenwood (cellular)
904	Columbus (cellular)
907	Rolling Fork (cellular)
908	Iuka (cellular)
909	Tupelo (cellular)
910	Tunica (cellular)
915	University (of Mississippi)
921	Holly Springs (pager)
931	Greenville (cellular)
934	Batesville (cellular)
962	Isola
963	Nettleton
967	West
972	Oxford (pager)
980	Tunica (pager)
983	Banner, Bruce, Pittsboro
988	Myrtle
990	Tupelo (cellular)
993	Ripley (cellular)
996	Southaven (cellular)
997	Batesville (cellular)

The Ultimate Reference on the State

Mississippi ZIP Codes

PLACE (COUNTY)	ZIP	PLACE (COUNTY)	ZIP	PLACE (COUNTY)	ZIP
Abbeville (Lafayette)	38601	Bay Saint Louis [boxes](Hancock)	39529	Bolivar (Bolivar)	38725
Abbott (Clay)	39773	Bay Springs (Jasper)	39422	Bolton (Hinds)	39041
Aberdeen (Monroe)	39730	Bayside Park (Hancock)	39520	Bond (Neshoba)	39350
Ackerman (Choctaw)	39735	Bear Garden (Washington)	38748	Bonita (Lauderdale)	39301
Adaton (Oktibbeha)	39759	Bear Town (Pike)	39648	Booneville (Prentiss)	38829
Agricola (George)	39452	Beasley (Clay)	39755	Bowdre (Tunica)	38664
Airey (Harrison)	39574	Beaumont (Perry)	39423	Bowman (Tate)	38618
Albin (Tallahatchie)	38966	Becker ((Monroe)	38825	Boyer (Sunflower)	38751
Alcorn State Univ. (Jefferson)	39096	Beechwood (Amite)	39645	Boyle (Bolivar)	38730
Algoma (Pontotoc)	38820	Bee Lake (Holmes)	39169	Bradley (Oktibbeha)	39759
Alligator (Bolivar)	38720	Belden (Lee)	38826	Brandon (Rankin)	39042
Alma (Lee)	38849	Belen (Quitman)	38609	Brandon (Rankin)	39043
Alpine (Union)	38828	Belhaven College (Hinds)	39202	Brandon (Rankin)	39047
Altitude (Prentiss)	38829	Belle Isle (Hancock)	39572	Branyan (Union)	38828
Alva (Montgomery)	38925	Bellefontaine (Webster)	39737	Braxton (Simpson)	39044
Amistead (Coahoma)	38631	Belleville (Perry)	39462	Brazil (Tallahatchie)	38963
Amory (Monroe)	38821	Bellewood (Humphreys)	38754	Brewer (Lee)	38868
Anchor (Chickasaw)	39776	Bells School (Oktibbeha)	39759	Bristers Store (Lawrence)	39641
Anding (Yazoo)	39040	Belmont (Tishomingo)	38827	Brookhaven (Lincoln)	39601
Anguilla (Sharkey)	38721	Belzoni (Humphreys)	39038	Brookhaven (Lincoln)	39602
Ansley (Hancock)	39558	Benndale (Greene)	39456	Brookhaven (Lincoln)	39603
Antioch (Jones)	39440	Benoit (Bolivar)	38725	Brooklyn (Forrest)	39425
Anvil (Tippah)	38674	Bentley (Calhoun)	39751	Brooks (Tallahatchie)	38737
Arcola (Washington)	38722	Benton (Yazoo)	39039	Brooksville (Noxubee)	39739
Ariel (Amite)	39638	Bentonia (Yazoo)	39040	Brownfield (Tippah)	38683
Arkabutla (Tate)	38602	Benwood (Yalobusha)	38922	Bruce (Calhoun)	38915
Arlington (Lincoln)`	39629	Berclair (Leflore)	38941	Bryant (Yalobusha)	38922
Arm (Lawrence)	39663	Berwick (Amite)	39645	Buckatunna (Wayne)	39322
Arnold Line (Lamar)	39402	Bethany (Lee)	38824	Buckhorn (Pontotoc)	38864
Artesia (Lowndes)	39701	Bethlehem (Marshall)	38659	Bude (Franklin)	39630
Ashland (Benton)	38603	Beulah (Bolivar)	38726	Buena Vista (Tippah)	38663
Ashwood (Wilkinson)	39669	Bewelcome (Amite)	39638	Buena Vista (Chickasaw)	38851
Askew (Panola)	38621	Bexley (George)	39452	Bunkley (Franklin)	39653
Atlanta (Chickasaw)	39776	Big Creek (Calhoun)	38914	Burns (Smith)	39153
Auburn (Amite)	39664	Big Level (Stone)	39573	Burnsville (Tishomingo)	38833
Austin (Tunica)	38676	Bigbee (Monroe)	38821	Burrow (Tippah)	38674
Avalon (Carroll)	38912	Bigbee Valley (Noxubee)	39738	Burtons (Prentiss)	38829
Avent (Greene)	39456	Biggersville (Alcorn)	38834	Busy Corner (Amite)	39645
Avon (Washington)	38723	Bigpoint (Jackson)	39567	Buxton (Panola)	38665
Bacots (Pike)	39648	Biloxi (Harrison)	39530	By (Alcorn)	38834
Bailey (Lauderdale)	39320	Biloxi (Harrison)	39531	Byhalia (Marshall)	38611
Baird (Sunflower)	38751	Biloxi (Harrison)	39532	Byram (Hinds)	39272
Baldwyn (Lee)	38824	Biloxi [PO Boxes](Harrison)	39533	Cademy (Itawamba)	38876
Ballardsville (Lee)	38801	Biloxi [PO Boxes](Harrison)	39534	Cadaretta (Webster)	38829
Ballentine (Panola)	38621	Biloxi [PO Boxes](Harrison)	39535	Caesar (Pearl River)	39466
Baltzer (Coahoma)	38614	Binford (Monroe)	39730	Caile (Humphreys)	38754
Banks (Tunica)	38664	Birdie (Coahoma)	38617	Caledonia (Monroe)	39740
Bankston (Choctaw)	39772	Bissell (Lee)	38801	Calhoun (Jones)	39440
Banner (Calhoun)	38913	Black Hawk (Carroll)	38923	Calhoun City (Calhoun)	38916
Barr (Tate)	38668	Blackjack (Oktibbeha)	39759	Camden (Madison)	39045
Barrontown (Forrest)	39465	Blackland (Prentiss)	38829	Camp Shelby (Forrest)	39407
Bartahatchie (Monroe)	39740	Blackwater (Lafayette)	38685	Campbell (Tippah)	38663
Barth (Pearl River)	39470	Blaine (Sunflower)	38736	Camphill (Tippah)	38683
Barto (Pike)	39648	Blair (Lee)	38849	Cannon (Benton)	38603
Basin (George)	39452	Blodgett (Jones)	39464	Canaan (Benton)	38647
Bassfield (Jefferson Davis)	39421	Bloody Springs (Tishomingo)	38827	Canton (Madison)	39046
Batesville (Panola)	38606	Blue Lake (Tallahatchie)	38737	Cardsville (Itawamba)	38858
Batson (Forrest)	39465	Blue Mountain (Tippah)	38610	Carlisle (Claiborne)	39049
Baugh (Coahoma)	38669	Blue Springs (Union)	38828	Carmichael (Perry)	39423
Baxterville (Lamar)	39455	Bluff (Tippah)	38610	Carnes (Lamar)	39455
Bay Saint Louis (Hancock)	39520	Bobo (Coahoma)	38614	Carolina (Itawamba)	38858
Bay Saint Louis [boxes](Hancock)	39521	Boggan Bend (Lee)	38849	Carpenter (Copiah)	39059
Bay Saint Louis (Hancock)	39522	Bogue Chitto (Lincoln)	39629	Carriere (Pearl River)	39426

Mississippi ZIP Codes

PLACE (COUNTY)	ZIP	PLACE (COUNTY)	ZIP	PLACE (COUNTY)	ZIP
Carrollton (Carroll)	38917	Corinth (Alcorn)	38834	Dubbs (Tunica)	38626
Carson (Jefferson Davis)	39427	Cornersville (Marshall)	38659	Dublin (Coahoma)	38739
Carterville (Forrest)	39465	Corrona (Lee)	38849	Duck Hill (Montgomery)	38925
Carthage (Leake)	39051	Cotton Plant (Tippah)	38610	Dumas (Tippah)	38625
Cary (Sharkey)	39054	Cottonville (Tate)	38618	Duncan (Bolivar)	38740
Cascilla (Tallahatchie)	38920	Courtland (Panola)	38620	Dundee (Tunica)	38626
Cassels (Amite)	39638	Cowart (Tallahatchie)	38921	Dunleith (Washington)	38756
Cedar Hill (Montgomery)	38925	Craig Springs (Oktibbeha)	39769	Durant (Holmes)	39063
Cedarbluff (Clay)	39741	Crane Creek (Stone)	39573	Dwiggins (Tallahatchie)	38737
Center (Union)	38828	Cranfield (Franklin)	39661	Dwyer (Sunflower)	38761
Central Grove (Monroe)	39730	Crawford (Lowndes)	39743	Early Grove (Marshall)	38642
Centreville (Wilkinson)	39631	Crenshaw (Panola)	38621	East Central Community College	
Chaltbeate (Tippah)	38683	Crockett (Tate)	38668	(Newton)	39327
Charleston (Tallahatchie)	38921	Crosby (Amite)	39633	East Fork (Amite)	39664
Chatawa (Pike)	39632	Crossroads (Pearl River)	39470	East Mississippi Comm. College	
Chatham (Washington)	38731	Crossroads (Washington)	38701	(Kemper)	39358
Cheraw (Marion)	39483	Crotts (Jones)	39437	East Moss Point (Jackson)	39563
Cherry Creek (Union)	38828	Crowder (Panola & Quitman)	38622	East Side (Perry)	39476
Chester (Choctaw)	39735	Cruger (Holmes)	38924	Eastbuchie (Jones)	39436
Chesterville (Lee)	38801	Crupp (Yazoo)	39194	Eastlawn (Jackson)	39567
Chiwapa (Pontotoc)	38863	Crystal Springs (Copiah)	39059	Eastport (Tishomingo)	38852
Choctaw (Bolivar)	38773	Cuevas (Harrison)	39571	Eastside (Jackson)	39563
Chunky (Newton)	39323	Cumberland (Webster)	39750	Eatonville (Forrest)	39401
Church Hill (Jefferson)	39055	Curtis Station (Panola)	38606	Ebenezer (Holmes)	39064
Clack (Tunica)	38664	Cybur (Pearl River)	39466	Ecru (Pontotoc)	38841
Clara (Wayne)	39324	D'Iberville (Harrison)	39532	Eddiceton (Franklin)	39647
Clarksdale (Coahoma)	38614	D'Lo (Simpson)	39062	Eden (Yazoo)	39194
Clarkson (Webster)	39752	Dahomey (Bolivar)	38725	Edinburg (Leake)	39051
Clayton (Tunica)	38626	Daisy Vestry (Stone)	39573	Edwards (Hinds)	39066
Clayton Village (Oktibbeha)	39759	Daleville (Lauderdale)	39326	Effie (Tallahatchie)	38921
Cleo (Jones)	39440	Dancy (Webster)	39751	Eggville (Lee)	38866
Cleveland (Bolivar)	38732	Darbun (Walthall)	39667	Egypt (Chickasaw)	38860
Cleveland (Bolivar)	38733	Darling (Quitman)	38623	Electric Mills (Kemper)	39358
Cliftonville (Noxubee)	39739	Darlove (Washington)	38748	Elizabeth (Washington)	38756
Clinton (Hinds)	39056	Darracott (Monroe)	39730	Ellard (Calhoun)	38915
Clinton [Miss. College](Hinds)	39058	Darrington (Wilkinson)	39669	Elliott (Grenada)	38926
Clinton [PO Boxes](Hinds)	39060	Days (DeSoto)	38641	Ellistown (Tishomingo)	38838
Clove Hill (Coahoma)	38645	Decatur (Newton)	39327	Ellisville (Jones)	39437
Coahoma (Coahoma)	38617	Deerbrook (Noxubee)	39739	Elsie (Calhoun)	38878
Coahoma Community College		Deeson (Bolivar)	38740	Eminence (Covington)	39479
(Coahoma)	38614	DeKalb (Kemper)	39328	Endville (Union)	38828
Cobbs (Lincoln)	39602	Delta (Panola)	38621	Enid (Tallahatchie)	38927
Coffeeville (Yalobusha)	38922	Delta City (Sharkey)	39061	Enon (Lawrence)	39641
Coila (Carroll)	38923	Delta State Univ. (Bolivar)	38732	Enterprise (Amite)	39638
Coldwater (Tate)	38618	Dennis (Tishomingo)	38838	Enterprise (Clarke)	39330
Coles (Amite)	39633	Dennis Landing (Bolivar)	38746	Enterprise (Lincoln)	39629
Coles Creek (Calhoun)	38914	Dentontown (Calhoun)	38955	Enterprise (Union)	38627
Collins (Covington)	39428	Derby (Pearl River)	39470	Errata (Jones)	39440
Collinsville (Lauderdale)	39325	Derma (Calhoun)	38839	Erwin (Washington)	38731
Colony Town (Leflore)	38941	Dexter (Walthall)	39667	Escatawpa (Jackson)	39552
Colsub (Monroe)	38821	Diamondhead (Hancock)	39525	Eskridge (Montgomery)	38967
Columbia (Marion)	39429	Dixie (Forrest)	39425	Estill (Washington)	38748
Columbus (Lowndes)	39701	Dixie Pine (Forrest)	39401	Ethel (Attala)	39067
Columbus (Lowndes)	39702	Doddsville (Sunflower)	38736	Etta (Union)	38627
Columbus [PO Boxes](Lowndes)	39703	Dolorosa (Wilkinson)	39669	Eunice (Amite)	39638
Columbus [PO Boxes](Lowndes)	39704	Donegal (Wilkinson)	39669	Eupora (Webster)	39744
Columbus [PO Boxes](Lowndes)	39705	Dorsey (Itawamba)	38843	Eutaw (Bolivar)	38725
Columbus AF Base (Lowndes)	39710	Doskie (Tishomingo)	38833	Evansville (Tate)	38618
Commerce (Tunica)	38664	Dover (Neshoba)	39350	Evansville (Tunica)	38676
Como (Panola)	38619	Dover (Yazoo)	39040	Fair Oaks Springs (Lincoln)	39601
Conehatta (Newton)	39057	Drew (Tallahatchie)	38737	Fair River (Lincoln)	39601
Copiah-Lincoln Comm. College		Dry Creek (Covington)	39428	Fairfield (Union)	38828
(Copiah)	39191	Dubard (Grenada)	38901	Fairlane (Lowndes)	39701

The Ultimate Reference on the State

Mississippi ZIP Codes

PLACE (COUNTY)	ZIP	PLACE (COUNTY)	ZIP	PLACE (COUNTY)	ZIP
Fairview (Itawamba)	38847	Gravestown (Tippah)	38663	Hinds Comm. College, Raymond (Hinds)	39154
Fairview (Sunflower)	38751	Greenville (Washington)	38701	Hinds Comm. College, Utica (Hinds)	39175
Falcon (Quitman)	38628	Greenville [boxes](Washington)	38702		
Falkner (Tippah)	38629	Greenville [boxes](Washington)	38703	Hinkle (Alcorn)	38865
Fame (Webster)	39744	Greenville (Washington)	38704	Hintonville (Perry)	39462
Fannin (Rankin)	39042	Greenwood (Itawamba)	38843	Hobo Station (Prentiss)	38829
Fannin (Rankin)	39047	Greenwood (Leflore)	38930	Hohenlinden (Calhoun)	39751
Farmhaven (Madison)	39046	Greenwood (Leflore)	38935	Holcomb (Grenada)	38940
Farmington (Alcorn)	38834	Greenwood Springs (Monroe)	38848	Holcut (Tishomingo)	38852
Farrell (Coahoma)	38630	Grenada (Grenada)	38901	Hollandale (Washington)	38748
Fayette (Jefferson)	39069	Grenada (Grenada)	38902	Hollis (Calhoun)	38878
Fentress (Choctaw)	39735	Griffith (Clay)	39741	Holly Bluff (Yazoo)	39088
Fernwood (Pike)	39635	Gulf Hills (Jackson)	39564	Holly Grove (Carroll)	38954
Fitler (Issaquena)	39070	Gulf Park Estates (Jackson)	39564	Holly Ridge (Sunflower)	38749
Fitzhugh (Tallahatchie)	38737	Gulfport (Harrison)	39500	Holly Springs [boxes](Marshall)	38634
Flora (Madison)	39071	Gulfport (Harrison)	39501	Holly Springs (Marshall)	38635
Florence (Rankin)	39073	Gulfport [PO Boxes](Harrison)	39502	Hollywood (Tunica)	38676
Flowood (Rankin)	39208	Gulfport (Harrison)	39503	Holmes Community College (Holmes)	39079
Flowood (Rankin)[eff. Feb. 2000]	39232	Gulfport [PO Boxes](Harrison)	39505		
Fontainbleau (Jackson)	39564	Gulfport [PO Boxes](Harrison)	39506	Holmesville (Pike)	39648
Foote (Washington)	38748	Gulfport (Harrison)	39507	Holts (Tishomingo)	38833
Fords Creek (Pearl River)	39470	Gums (Yalobusha)	38922	Homochitto (Amite)	39638
Forest (Scott)	39074	Gunnison (Bolivar)	38746	Horn Lake (DeSoto)	38637
Forkville (Scott)	39076	Guntown (Lee)	38849	Hot Coffee (Covington)	39428
Fort Adams (Wilkinson)	39669	Hamburg (Franklin)	39661	Houlka (Chickasaw)	38850
Foxworth (Marion)	39483	Hamilton (Monroe)	39746	Houston (Chickasaw)	38851
Francis (Bolivar)	38740	Hampton (Washington)	38744	Howison (Harrison)	39574
French Camp (Choctaw)	39745	Hardy (Grenada)	38901	Hoy (Jones)	39440
Friars Point (Coahoma)	38631	Harleston (George)	39452	Hurley (Jackson)	39555
Friendship (Pontotoc)	38841	Harmontown (Panola)	38619	Hurricane (Pontotoc)	38871
Fruitland Park (Stone)	39577	Harperville (Scott)	39080	Hushpuckena (Bolivar)	38774
Fulton (Itawamba)	38843	Harriston (Jefferson)	39081	Ida Wells Station (Marshall)	38634
Furrs (Pontotoc)	38863	Harrisville (Simpson)	39082	Inda (Stone)	39573
Futheyville (Grenada)	38901	Harvey (Forrest)	39465	Independence (Tate)	38638
Gallman (Copiah)	39077	Hatley (Monroe)	38821	Indian Springs (Alcorn)	38846
Gandsi (Covington)	39479	Hattiesburg (Forrest)	39400	Indianola (Sunflower)	38751
Garden City (Franklin)	39661	Hattiesburg (Forrest)	39401	Industrial (Pearl River)	39466
Gatewood (Yalobusha)	38922	Hattiesburg (Forrest)	39402	Ingomar (Union)	38652
Gattman (Monroe)	38844	Hattiesburg [PO Boxes](Forrest)	39403	Inverness (Sunflower)	38753
Gautier (Jackson)	39553	Hattiesburg (Forrest)	39404	Iowana (Jackson)	39553
Geeslin Corner (Grenada)	38901	Hattiesburg [PO Boxes](Forrest)	39406	Ireland (Wilkinson)	39669
Geeville (Lee)	38824	Hazlehurst (Copiah)	39083	Irene (Pike)	39666
Georgetown (Copiah)	39078	Heads (Washington)	38756	Isola (Humphreys)	38754
Gibson (Monroe)	39730	Heathman (Sunflower)	38751	Itawamba Community College (Itawamba)	38843
Gillsburg (Pike)	39657	Heidelberg (Jasper)	39439		
Glade (Jones)	39440	Helena (Jackson)	39567	Itta Bena (Leflore)	38941
Glen (Alcorn)	38846	Helm (Washington)	38756	Iuka (Tishomingo)	38852
Glen Allan (Washington)	38744	Hendrix (Montgomery)	39747	Jacinto (Alcorn)	38865
Glendale (Forrest)	39401	Henleyfield (Pearl River)	39426	Jackson (Hinds)	39200
Glendora (Tallahatchie)	38928	Hermanville (Claiborne)	39086	Jackson (Hinds)	39201
Gloster (Amite)	39638	Hernando (DeSoto)	38632	Jackson (Hinds)	39202
Glover (DeSoto)	38680	Heucks (Lincoln)	39601	Jackson (Hinds)	39203
Gluckstadt (Madison)	39110	Hickory (Newton)	39332	Jackson (Hinds)	39204
Golden (Itawamba)	38847	Hickory Flat (Benton)	38633	Jackson (Hinds)	39206
Goldfield (Tallahatchie)	38737	Hickory Grove (Oktibbeha)	39759	Jackson (Hinds)	39209
Goodhope (Perry)	39476	Higgins (Lamar)	39482	Jackson (Hinds)	39210
Goodfood (Pontotoc)	38863	Highlandale (Leflore)	38944	Jackson (Hinds)	39211
Goodman (Holmes)	39079	Highway Village (Wilkinson)	39669	Jackson (Hinds)	39212
Gore Springs (Webster)	38929	Hillhouse (Coahoma)	38720	Jackson (Hinds)	39213
Grace (Issaquena)	38745	Hillman (Greene)	39451	Jackson (Hinds)	39216
Grady (Webster)	39744	Hillsboro (Scott)	39087	Jackson (Hinds)	39217
Graham (Lee)	38824	Hillsdale (Pearl River)	39470		
Grapeland (Bolivar)	38725	Hinchcliff (Quitman)	38646	Jackson [Fed'l. Bldg.](Hinds)	39269

Mississippi ZIP Codes

PLACE (COUNTY)	ZIP	PLACE (COUNTY)	ZIP	PLACE (COUNTY)	ZIP
Jackson [PO Boxes](Hinds)	39205	Laneheart (Wilkinson)	39669	Madison [PO Boxes](Madison)	39130
Jackson [PO Boxes](Hinds)	39207	Lantrip (Calhoun)	38915	Magee (Simpson)	39111
Jackson [PO Boxes](Hinds)	39215	Larue (Jackson)	39564	Magenta (Washington)	38756
Jackson [PO Boxes](Hinds)	39225	Latimer (Jackson)	39564	Magnolia (Pike)	39652
Jackson [PO Boxes](Hinds)	39236	Latonia (George)	39452	Mahned (Perry)	39462
Jackson [PO Boxes](Hinds)	39250	Lauderdale (Lauderdale)	39335	Malvina (Bolivar)	38769
Jackson [PO Boxes](Hinds)	39271	Laurel (Jones)	39440	Mantachie (Itawamba)	38855
Jackson [PO Boxes](Hinds)	39272	Laurel [PO Boxes](Jones)	39441	Mantee (Calhoun)	39751
Jackson [PO Boxes](Hinds)	39282	Laurel [PO Boxes](Jones)	39442	Marie (Sunflower)	38751
Jackson [PO Boxes](Hinds)	39283	Laurel (Jones)	39443	Marietta (Prentiss)	38856
Jackson [PO Boxes](Hinds)	39284	Lawrence (Newton)	39336	Marion (Lauderdale)	39342
Jackson [PO Boxes](Hinds)	39286	Laws Hill (Lafayette)	38685	Marks (Quitman)	38646
Jackson [PO Boxes](Hinds)	39289	Leaf (Greene)	39456	Mars Hill (Pike)	39666
Jackson [PO Boxes](Hinds)	39296	Leaksville (Greene)	39451	Mary Holmes College (Clay)	39773
Jackson [boxes-airport](Hinds)	39298	Learned (Hinds)	39154	Matherville (Clarke)	39360
Jackson [boxes-Pearl](Rankin)	39288	Lebanon (Marshall)	38659	Mathiston (Webster)	39752
Jackson [Pearl](Rankin)	39208	Leedy (Tishomingo)	38833	Mattson (Coahoma)	38758
Jackson [Richland](Rankin)	39218	Leesdale (Franklin)	39661	Maxie (Forrest)	39425
Jackson Internat'l. Airport (Rankin)	39208	Leeville (Forrest)	39465	Maybank (Forrest)	39401
Jackson State Univ. (Hinds)	39217	Leland (Washington)	38756	Maybell (Jones)	39437
Jago (DeSoto)	38637	Lena (Leake)	39094	Mayersville (Issaquena)	39113
James (Washington)	38748	Lessley (Wilkinson)	39669	Mayhew (Lowndes)	39753
Jamestown (Marion)	39483	Leverett (Tallahatchie)	38920	McAdams (Attala)	39107
Jayess (Lawrence)	39641	Lexie (Walthall)	39667	McCall Creek (Franklin)	39647
Jefferson (Carroll)	38917	Lexington (Holmes)	39095	McCallum (Forrest)	39401
Jeffries (Tunica)	38626	Liberty (Amite)	39645	McCarley (Carroll)	38943
Jennings (Pike)	39652	Lightsey (Wayne)	39367	McComb (Pike)	39648
Johns (Rankin)	39042	Linn (Sunflower)	38736	McComb (Pike)	39649
Johnson (Jones)	39437	Little Creek (Perry)	39423	McCondy (Chickasaw)	38854
Johnston (Pike)	39666	Little Rock (Newton)	39337	McCool (Attala)	39108
Jonathan (Greene)	39451	Little Texas (Tunica)	38676	McCrary (Lowndes)	39701
Jones County College (Jones)	39437	Litton (Bolivar)	38773	McCutcheon (Washington)	38722
Jonestown (Coahoma)	38639	Lobdell (Bolivar)	38726	McElveen (Pike)	39666
Jug Fork (Union)	38828	Locke Station (Panola)	38606	McHenry (Stone)	39561
Jumpertown (Prentiss)	38829	Locum (Tippah)	38625	McLain (Greene)	39456
Keesler Air Force Base (Harrison)	39534	Lodi (Montgomery)	39767	McLaurin (Forrest)	39401
Kendrick (Alcorn)	38834	Lombardy (Bolivar)	38774	McNeill (Pearl River)	39457
Keownville (Union)	38652	Long (Washington)	38756	McRaney (Covington)	39428
Kerin (Holmes)	38924	Long Beach (Harrison)	39560	McSwain (Perry)	39476
Kilmichael (Montgomery)	39747	Longshot (Bolivar)	38732	Meadville (Franklin)	39653
Kiln (Hancock)	39556	Longtown (Panola)	38665	Meeham (Lauderdale)	39301
King And Anderson (Coahoma)	38614	Longview (Oktibbeha)	39759	Melba (Lamar)	39482
Kinlock (Sunflower)	38751	Looxahoma (Tate)	38668	Mendenhall (Simpson)	39114
Kirby (Franklin)	39661	Lorman (Jefferson)	39096	Meridian (Lauderdale)	39301
Kirkville (Lee)	38824	Louin (Jasper)	39338	Meridian [PO Boxes](Lauderdale)	39302
Knoxo (Walthall)	39667	Louise (Humphreys)	39097	Meridian [PO Boxes](Lauderdale)	39303
Knoxville (Franklin)	39661	Louisville (Winston)	39339	Meridian [PO Boxes](Lauderdale)	39304
Kokomo (Marion)	39643	Loyd (Calhoun)	38878	Meridian (Lauderdale)	39305
Kola (Covington)	39428	Lucas (Jefferson Davis)	39474	Meridian (Lauderdale)	39307
Kolola Springs (Monroe)	39740	Lucedale (George)	39452	Meridian Community College (Lauderdale)	39301
Kosciusko (Attala)	39090	Lucien (Lincoln)	39601		
Kossuth (Alcorn)	38834	Ludlow (Scott)	39098	Meridian Naval Air Station (Lauderdale)	39309
Kreole (Jackson)	39563	Lula (Coahoma)	38644		
Lackey (Monroe)	39730	Lumberton (Lamar)	39455	Merigold (Bolivar)	38759
Lafayette (Lafayette)	38655	Lux (Covingtont)	39479	Merrill (George)	39452
Lake (Scott)	39092	Lynn Creek (Noxubee)	39739	Mesa (Walthall)	39667
Lake Cormorant (DeSoto)	38641	Lyon (Coahoma)	38645	Metcalfe (Washington)	38760
Lake View (DeSoto)	38680	Maben (Webster)	39750	Michigan City (Benton)	38647
Lakeshore (Hancock)	39558	Macedonia (Forrest)	39465	Midnight (Humphreys)	39115
Lamar (Marshall)	38642	Macel (Tallahatchie)	38950	Midway (Tishomingo)	38852
Lamar Park (Lamar)	39402	Macon (Noxubee)	39341	Mile Branch (Franklin)	39653
Lambert (Quitman)	38643	Madden (Leake)	39109	Mileston (Holmes)	39169
Lamont (Bolivar)	38755	Madison (Madison)	39110	Mill Creek (Pearl River)	39426

Mississippi ZIP Codes

PLACE (COUNTY)	ZIP
Mill Creek (Jones)	39440
Millsaps College (Hinds)	39210
Mineral Wells (DeSoto)	38648
Mingo (Tishomingo)	38873
Minter City (Leflore)	38944
Mississippi College (Hinds)	39058
Mississippi Delta Comm. College (Sunflower)	38761
Miss. Gulf Coast Comm. College (Stone)	39573
Mississippi State University (Oktibbeha)	39762
Mississippi Univ. for Women (Lowndes)	39701
Mississippi Valley State Univ. (Leflore)	38941
Mitchell (Tippah)	38663
Mize (Smith)	39116
Mocarter (Tunica)	38664
Money (Leflore)	38945
Monroe (Franklin)	39653
Monte Vista (Webster)	39771
Monticello (Lawrence)	39654
Montpelier (Clay)	39754
Montrose (Jasper)	39338
Moores Mill (Tishomingo)	38838
Mooreville (Lee)	38857
Moorhead (Sunflower)	38761
Morgan City (Leflore)	38946
Morgantown (Marion)	39484
Morgantown (Oktibbeha)	39759
Morriston (Forrest)	39465
Morton (Scott)	39117
Moselle (Jones)	39459
Moss (Jasper)	39460
Moss Point (Jackson)	39562
Moss Point (Jackson)	39563
Mound Bayou (Bolivar)	38762
Mound City (Bolivar)	38726
Mound City (Union)	38828
Mount Carmel (Jefferson Davis)	39474
Mount Olive (Amite)	39664
Mount Olive (Covington)	39119
Mount Olive (Franklin)	39653
Mount Pleasant (Itawamba)	38876
Mount Pleasant (Marshall)	38649
Mount Vernon (Lee)	38801
Movella (George)	39452
Muldon (Monroe)	39730
Muldrow (Oktibbeha)	39759
Murdock Crossing (Leflore)	38941
Murphreesboro (Tallahatchie)	38961
Murphy (Washington)	38748
Murry (Tippah)	38663
Myrick (Jones)	39440
Myrtle (Union)	38650
Nason (Grenada)	38940
Natchez (Adams)	39120
Natchez [PO Boxes](Adams)	39121
Natchez (Adams)	39122
National Space Technology Lab. (Hancock)	39529
Naval Air Station (Lauderdale)	39309
Necaise (Stone)	39573
Neely (Greene)	39461
Nesbit (DeSoto)	38651
Nettleton (Lee & Monroe)	38858
New Albany (Union)	38652
New Augusta (Perry)	39462
New Harmony (Union)	38828
New Hope (Lowndes)	39701
New Sight (Lincoln)	39601
New Site (Prentiss)	38859
New Town (Tate)	38668
New Wren (Monroe)	39730
Newhebron (Lawrence)	39140
Newport (DeSoto)	38641
Newton (Newton)	39345
Nicholson (Pearl River)	39463
Niles (Bolivar)	38769
Nitta Yuma (Sharkey)	38763
Nixon (Pontotoc)	38863
Nola (Lawrence)	39665
Norfield (Lincoln)	39629
North Carrollton (Carroll)	38947
Northeast Miss. Comm. College (Prentiss)	38829
Northwest Mississippi Community College (Tate)	38668
Noxapater (Winston)	39346
Oak Bowery (Jones)	39437
Oak Grove (Jones)	39459
Oak Vale (Lawrence)	39656
Oakland (Yalobusha)	38948
Oakland (Pike)	39666
Ocean Springs (Jackson)	39564
Ocean Springs (Jackson)	39566
Oil City (Yazoo)	39040
Okolona (Chickasaw)	38860
Oktibbeha (Webster)	39750
Oktoc (Oktibbeha)	39759
Old Cairo (Prentiss)	38829
Old Hamilton (Monroe)	39746
Old Houlka (Chickasaw)	38850
Old Union (Lee)	38868
Oldenburg (Franklin)	39661
Oldham (Tishomingo)	38852
Olive Branch (DeSoto)	38654
Oloh (Lamar)	39482
Oma (Lawrence)	39654
Ora (Covington)	39428
Orange Grove (Harrison)	39503
Orange Grove (Jackson)	39567
Osborn (Oktibbeha)	39759
Osborne Creek (Prentiss)	38829
Osyka (Pike)	39657
Ovett (Jones)	39464
Oxberry (Grenada)	38940
Oxford (Amite)	39638
Oxford (Lafayette)	38655
Ozona (Pearl River)	39426
Pace (Bolivar)	38764
Pachuta (Clarke)	39347
Paden (Tishomingo)	38873
Palmers Crossing (Forrest)	39401
Panther Burn (Sharkey)	38765
Parchman (Sunflower)	38738
Parham (Monroe)	38848
Paris (Lafayette)	38949
Pascagoula (Jackson)	39567
Pascagoula (Jackson)	39569
Pascagoula (Jackson)	39581
Pascagoula (Jackson)	39595
Pascagoula [PO boxes](Jackson)	39568
Pass Christian (Harrison)	39571
Patrick (Oktibbeha)	39759
Pattison (Claiborne)	39144
Paul (Tallahatchie)	38920
Paulding (Jasper)	39348
Paynes (Tallahatchie)	38920
Pearl (Rankin)	39208
Pearl [PO Boxes](Rankin)	39288
Pearl River Community College (Pearl River)	39470
Pearlhaven (Lincoln)	39601
Pearlington (Hancock)	39572
Pecan (Jackson)	39567
Pecan Grove (Jones)	39437
Pelahatchie (Rankin)	39145
Pendorff (Jones)	39440
Penns (Lowndes)	39743
Penton (Tunica)	38664
Peoples (Tippah)	38663
Peoria (Amite)	39645
Percy (Washington)	38748
Perkinston (Stone)	39573
Perrytown (Amite)	39633
Perthshire (Bolivar)	38746
Petal (Forrest)	39465
Pheba (Clay)	39755
Philadelphia (Neshoba)	39350
Phillipp (Tallahatchie)	38950
Phillipstown (Carroll)	38954
Piave (Perry)	39476
Picayune (Pearl River)	39466
Pickens (Holmes)	39146
Pickwick (Marion)	39483
Pinckneyville (Wilkinson)	39669
Pine Belt Regional Airport (Jones)	39440
Pine Flat (Yalobusha)	38965
Pine Grove (Forrest)	39465
Pine Grove (Lee)	38868
Pine Grove (Prentiss)	38829
Pine Ridge (Lamar)	39475
Pine Valley (Yalobusha)	38965
Pinebluff (Calhoun)	39751
Pinedale (Union)	38627
Pinegrove (Benton)	38633
Piney Woods (Rankin)	39148
Pinola (Simpson)	39149
Pisgah (Alcorn)	38865
Pistol Ridge (Lamar)	39455
Pittman (Marion)	39483
Pittsboro (Calhoun)	38951
Plantersville (Lee)	38862
Pleasant Grove (Panola)	38657
Pleasant Hill (DeSoto)	38651
Pleasant Hill (Jefferson)	39668
Pleasant Hill (Union)	38652

Mississippi ZIP Codes

PLACE (COUNTY)	ZIP	PLACE (COUNTY)	ZIP	PLACE (COUNTY)	ZIP
Pleasant Ridge (Tippah)	38625	Robinwood (Lawrence)	39654	Shellmound (Leflore)	38930
Plymouth (Pontotoc)	38863	Rochdale (Bolivar)	38740	Shepherd (Calhoun)	38915
Poagville (Tate)	38618	Rock Hill (Lamar)	39475	Sherard (Coahoma)	38669
Pocahantas (Hinds)	39072	Rocky Hill (Oktibbeha)	39759	Sherman (Pontotoc)	38869
Polfry (Jackson)	39564	Roebuck (Carroll)	38954	Sherwood (Webster)	39752
Pollock (Sunflower)	38751	Rogerslacy (Jones)	39477	Shipman (George)	39452
Pontotoc (Pontotoc)	38863	Rolling Fork (Sharkey)	39159	Shivers (Simpson)	39149
Pope (Panola)	38658	Rome (Sunflower)	38768	Shocco (Madison)	39163
Poplar Corners (DeSoto)	38680	Rose Hill (Jasper)	39356	Shubuta (Clarke)	39360
Poplar Creek (Montgomery)	39747	Rosebloom (Tallahatchie)	38920	Shuqualak (Noxubee)	39361
Poplar Springs (Montgomery)	39747	Rosedale (Bolivar)	38769	Sibleton (Montgomery)	39747
Poplarville (Pearl River)	39470	Rosella (Lawrence)	39654	Sibley (Adams)	39165
Port Gibson (Claiborne)	39150	Rosetta (Amite)	39633	Sidon (Carroll)	38954
Porterville (Kemper)	39352	Rough Edge (Pontotoc)	38863	Silver City (Humphreys)	39166
Possum Trot (Pontotoc)	38863	Roundaway (Coahoma)	38614	Silver Creek (Lawrence)	39663
Possumneck (Holmes)	39192	Roundlake (Bolivar)	38740	Silver Run (Stone)	39573
Potts Camp (Marshall)	38659	Roxie (Franklin)	39661	Skene (Bolivar)	38775
Powell (Tunica)	38626	Rudyard (Coahoma)	38617	Skuna (Calhoun)	38915
Powers (Jones)	39440	Ruleville (Sunflower)	38771	Slate Spring (Calhoun)	38955
Prairie (Monroe)	39756	Runnelstown (Forrest)	39401	Slayden (Marshall)	38642
Prairie Point (Noxubee)	39353	Rust College (Marshall)	38635	Sledge (Tunica)	38670
Prentiss (Jefferson Davis)	39474	Ruth (Lincoln)	39662	Smith (Covington)	39428
Preston (Kemper)	39354	Sabino (Quitman)	38646	Smithdale (Amite)	39664
Pricedale (Pike)	39666	Sabougla (Calhoun)	38955	Smithville (Monroe)	38870
Prichard (Tunica)	38676	Saints Rest (Sunflower)	38751	Snow Lake Shores (Benton)	38603
Progress (Pike)	39648	Salem (Walthall)	39667	Society Hill (Lawrence)	39656
Puckett (Rankin)	39151	Sallis (Attala)	39160	Somerville (Leflore)	38944
Pulaski (Scott)	39152	Saltillo (Lee)	38866	Sonora (Chickasaw)	38851
Pumkin Corner (Union)	38652	Sand Hill (Jones)	39437	Sontag (Lawrence)	39665
Purvis (Lamar)	39475	Sand Hill (Perry)	39476	Soso (Jones)	39480
Pyland (Chickasaw)	38851	Sandersville (Jones)	39477	Southaven (DeSoto)	38671
Quentin (Franklin)	39647	Sandhill (Rankin)	39161	Southwest Miss. Comm. College (Pike)	39666
Quincy (Monroe)	38848	Sandy Hook (Marion)	39478	Splunge (Monroe)	38848
Quitman (Clarke)	39355	Sanford (Covington)	39479	Spring Hill (Benton)	38647
Quito (Leflore)	38941	Sanitorium (Simpson)	39112	Spring Hill (Lafayette)	38874
Rainey (Jones)	39459	Sapa (Webster)	39744	Springdale (Yalobusha)	38965
Raleigh (Smith)	39153	Sarah (Panola)	38665	Springville (Pontotoc)	38863
Randolph (Pontotoc)	38864	Sardis (Panola)	38666	Stafford Springs (Jasper)	39439
Ratliff (Lee)	38849	Sarepta (Pontotoc)	38864	Star (Rankin)	39167
Rawls Springs (Forrest)	39402	Sartinsville (Lawrence)	39641	Starkville (Oktibbeha)	39759
Raymond (Hinds)	39154	Satartia (Yazoo)	39162	Starkville (Oktibbeha)	39760
Red Banks (Marshall)	38661	Saucier (Harrison)	39574	State Line (Greene)	39362
Redstar (Lincoln)	39601	Saukum (Amite)	39633	Steens (Lowndes)	39766
Redwood (Warren)	39156	Sauls (Lincoln)	39662	Steiner (Bolivar)	38773
Reform (Choctaw)	39757	Savage (Panola)	38665	Stennis Space Center (Hancock)	39529
Refuge (Washington)	38701	Savannah (Pearl River)	39470	Stewart (Montgomery)	39767
Reid (Calhoun)	38878	Schlater (Leflore)	38952	Stoneville (Washington)	38776
Rena Lara (Coahoma)	38767	Scobey (Yalabusha)	38953	Stonewall (Clarke)	39363
Rexburg (Washington)	38756	Scooba (Kemper)	39358	Stovall (Coahoma)	38614
Rhodes (Perry)	39476	Scott (Bolivar)	38772	Strayhorn (Panola)	38665
Riceville (Stone)	39573	Sebastopol (Scott)	39359	Strengthford (Wayne)	39367
Rich (Coahoma)	38662	Sellers (Stone)	39573	Stringer (Jasper)	39481
Richardson (Pearl River)	39466	Seminary (Covington)	39479	Stringtown (Bolivar)	38773
Richland (Rankin)	39218	Senatobia (Tate)	38668	Strongs (Monroe)	39730
Richmond (Lee)	38862	Seneca (Lamar)	39455	Sturgis (Oktibbeha)	39769
Richton (Perry)	39476	Sessums (Oktibbeha)	39759	Success (Harrison)	39574
Ridgeland (Madison)	39157	Shady Grove (Jones)	39440	Summit (Pike)	39666
Ridgeland [PO Boxes](Madison)	39158	Shannon (Lee)	38868	Sumner (Tallahatchie)	38957
Rienzi (Alcorn)	38865	Sharkey (Tallahatchie)	38921	Sumrall (Lamar)	39482
Ripley (Tippah)	38663	Sharon (Jones)	39440	Sunflower (Sunflower)	38778
Rising Sun (Carroll)	38954	Sharon (Madison)	39163	Sunnycrest (Grenada)	38901
Riverton (Coahoma)	38614	Shaw (Bolivar)	38773	Sunnyside (Leflore)	38944
Robinsonville (Tunica)	38664	Shelby (Bolivar)	38774		

The Ultimate Reference on the State

Mississippi ZIP Codes

PLACE (COUNTY)	ZIP	PLACE (COUNTY)	ZIP	PLACE (COUNTY)	ZIP
Sunrise (Forrest)	39401	Tupelo (Lee)	38804	Water Valley (Yalobusha)	38965
Swan Lake (Tallahatchie)	38958	Turnbull (Wilkinson)	39669	Waterford (Lafayette)	38685
Sweatman (Montgomery)	38925	Turon (Monroe)	38870	Waveland (Hancock)	39576
Swiftown (Leflore)	38959	Tutwiler (Tallahatchie)	38963	Waxhaw (Bolivar)	38746
Swiftwater (Washington)	38701	Tylertown (Walthall)	39667	Way (Madison)	39046
Sylvarena (Smith)	39153	Tyro (Tate)	38668	Waynesboro (Wayne)	39367
Symonds (Bolivar)	38769	Tyson (Yalobusha)	38922	Wayside (Washington)	38780
Talowah (Lamar)	39455	Union (Lee)	38862	Webb (Tallahatchie)	38966
Taska (Marshall)	38661	Union (Newton)	39365	Weir (Choctaw)	39772
Tatum (Amite)	39638	Union Church (Jefferson)	39668	Wells Town (Lamar)	39455
Taylor (Lafayette)	38673	Union Hall (Lincoln)	39601	Wenasoga (Alcorn)	38834
Taylorsville (Smith)	39168	University (Lafayette)	38677	Wesson (Copiah)	39191
Tchula (Holmes)	39169	University of Miss. (Lafayette)	38677	West (Holmes)	39192
Teasdale (Tallahatchie)	38927	University of Southern Mississippi		West Biloxi (Harrison)	39531
Ten Mile (Stone)	39573	(Forrest)	39406	West Days (DeSoto)	38641
Terrell (Jefferson Davis)	39474	Utica (Hinds)	39175	West Lincoln (Lincoln)	39601
Terry (Hinds)	39170	Vaiden (Carroll)	39176	West Point (Clay)	39773
Terza (Panola)	38606	Valewood (Washington)	38744	West Poplarville (Pearl River)	39470
Thaxton (Pontotoc)	38871	Valley Hill (Carroll)	38917	Wheeler (Prentiss)	38880
Thomastown (Leake)	39171	Valley Park (Issaquena)	39177	White Apple (Franklin)	39661
Thompson (Amite)	39664	Value (Rankin)	39042	White Cap (Amite)	39638
Thorn (Chickasaw)	38851	Van Buren (Itawamba)	38858	White Sand (Monroe)	39740
Thornton (Holmes)	39172	Van Vleet (Chickasaw)	38877	Whitebluff (Marion)	39483
Thrashers (Prentiss)	38829	Vance (Quitman)	38964	Whitehead (Tallahatchie)	38928
Three Rivers (Jackson)	39567	Vancleave (Jackson)	39565	Whites (Clay)	39773
Thyatira (Tate)	38668	Vardaman (Calhoun)	38878	Whites Crossing (Stone)	39577
Tibbee (Clay)	39773	Vaughan (Yazoo)	39179	Whitfield (Rankin)	39193
Tibbs (Tunica)	38670	Velma (Yalobusha)	38965	Whitney (Tallahatchie)	38737
Tie Plant (Grenada)	38960	Vernal (George)	39452	Wiggins (Stone)	39577
Tillatobia (Tallahatchie)	38961	Verona (Lee)	38879	Wilkinson (Wilkinson)	39669
Tilton (Lawrence)	39654	Vicksburg (Warren)	39180	Willet (Washington)	38748
Tinsley (Yazoo)	39173	Vicksburg [PO Boxes](Warren)	39181	William Carey College (Forrest)	39401
Tiplersville (Tippah)	38674	Vicksburg [PO Boxes](Warren)	39182	Williamsburg (Covington)	39428
Tippo (Tallahatchie)	38962	Vicksburg (Warren)	39183	Winborn (Marshall)	38659
Tishomingo (Tishomingo)	38873	Victoria (Marshall)	38679	Windsor Park (Jackson)	39564
Toccopola (Lafayette)	38874	Villa Ridge (Lamar)	39455	Wingate (Perry)	39462
Tomnolen (Webster)	39744	Vossburg (Jasper)	39366	Winona (Montgomery)	38967
Toomsuba (Lauderdale)	39364	Waco (Sunflower)	38753	Winstonville (Bolivar)	38781
Topeka (Lawrence)	39641	Waddell (Clay)	39741	Winterville (Washington)	38782
Topisaw (Pike)	39666	Wade (Tallahatchie)	38737	Wood Junior College (Webster)	39752
Tougaloo College (Hinds)	39174	Wade (Jackson)	39567	Woodburn (Sunflower)	38751
Trebloc (Chickasaw)	38875	Wakefield (Tate)	38618	Woodland (Chickasaw)	39776
Tremont (Itawamba)	38876	Wallerville (Union)	38652	Woodland (Pontotoc)	38863
Triangle (Harrison)	39534	Wallhill (Tate)	38618	Woodville (Wilkinson)	39669
Tribbett (Washington)	38779	Walls (DeSoto)	38680	Wortham (Harrison)	39574
Trinity (Lowndes)	39743	Walnut (Tippah)	38683	Wren (Monroe)	39730
Troy (Pontotoc)	38863	Walnut (Quitman)	38964	Wright (Bolivar)	38769
Tuckers Crossing (Jones)	39440	Walnut Grove (Leake)	39189	Wyatte (Tate)	38668
Tula (Lafayette)	38675	Walters (Jones)	39437	Yazoo City (Yazoo)	39194
Tunica (Tunica)	38676	Walthall (Webster)	39771	Youngs (Yalobusha)	38922
Tupelo (Lee)	38801	Wanilla (Lawrence)	39654	Zetus (Lincoln)	39601
Tupelo [PO Boxes](Lee)	38802	Wardwell (Calhoun)	38878	Zion (Pontotoc)	38863
Tupelo [PO Boxes](Lee)	38803	Washington (Adams)	39190	Zumbro (Bolivar)	38732

Rural mail delivery points outnumber urban sites by a 55% to 45% (603,500 to 496,500) margin statewide. There are just over 409,000 mail delivery points in the Jackson metro area (MSA), with about 88,800 in the city of

Mississippi ZIP Codes — Numerical Cross Reference

ZIP	PLACE[S] (COUNTY)
38601	Abbeville (Lafayette)
38602	Arkabutla (Tate)
38603	Ashland, Cannon, Snow Lake Shores (Benton)
38606	Batesville, Curtis Station, Locke Station, Terza (Panola)
38609	Belen (Quitman)
38610	Blue Mountain, Bluff, Cotton Plant (Tippah)
38611	Byhalia (Marshall)
38614	Baltzer, Bobo, Clarksdale, Coahoma Community College, King And Anderson, Riverton, Roundaway, Stovall (Coahoma)
38617	Birdie, Coahoma, Rudyard (Coahoma)
38618	Bowman, Coldwater, Cottonville, Evansville, Poagville, Wakefield, Wallhill (Tate)
38619	Como, Harmontown (Panola)
38620	Courtland (Panola)
38621	Askew, Ballentine, Crenshaw, Delta (Panola)
38622	Crowder (Panola & Quitman)
38623	Darling (Quitman)
38625	Dumas, Locum, Pleasant Ridge (Tippah)
38626	Clayton, Dubbs, Dundee, Jeffries, Powell (Tunica)
38627	Enterprise, Etta, Pinedale (Union)
38628	Falcon (Quitman)
38629	Falkner (Tippah)
38630	Farrell (Coahoma)
38631	Amistead, Friars Point (Coahoma)
38632	Hernando (DeSoto)
38633	Hickory Flat, Pinegrove (Benton)
38634	Holly Springs [boxes], Ida Wells Station (Marshall)
38635	Holly Springs, Rust College (Marshall)
38637	Horn Lake, Jago (DeSoto)
38638	Independence (Tate)
38639	Jonestown (Coahoma)
38641	Days, Lake Cormorant, Newport, West Days (DeSoto)
38642	Early Grove, Lamar, Slayden (Marshall)
38643	Lambert (Quitman)
38644	Lula (Coahoma)
38645	Clove Hill, Lyon (Coahoma)
38646	Hinchcliff, Marks, Sabino (Quitman)
38647	Canaan, Michigan City, Spring Hill (Benton)
38648	Mineral Wells (DeSoto)
38649	Mount Pleasant (Marshall)
38650	Myrtle (Union)
38651	Nesbit, Pleasant Hill (DeSoto)
38652	Ingomar, Keownville, New Albany, Pleasant Hill, Pumkin Corner, Wallerville (Union)
38654	Olive Branch (DeSoto)
38655	Lafayette, Oxford (Lafayette)
38657	Pleasant Grove (Panola)
38658	Pope (Panola)
38659	Bethlehem, Cornersville, Lebanon, Potts Camp, Winborn (Marshall)
38661	Red Banks, Taska (Marshall)
38662	Rich (Coahoma)
38663	Buena Vista, Campbell, Gravestown, Mitchell, Murry, Peoples, Ripley (Tippah)
38664	Banks, Bowdre, Clack, Commerce, Mocarter, Penton, Robinsonville (Tunica)
38665	Buxton, Longtown, Sarah, Savage, Strayhorn (Panola)
38666	Sardis (Panola)
38668	Barr, Crockett, Looxahoma, New Town, Northwest Miss. Community College, Senatobia, Thyatira, Tyro, Wyatte (Tate)
38669	Baugh, Sherard (Coahoma)
38670	Sledge, Tibbs (Tunica)
38671	Southaven (DeSoto)
38673	Taylor (Lafayette)
38674	Anvil, Burrow, Tiplersville (Tippah)
38675	Tula (Lafayette)
38676	Austin, Evansville, Hollywood, Little Texas, Prichard, Tunica (Tunica)
38677	University of Mississippi, University (Lafayette)
38679	Victoria (Marshall)
38680	Glover, Lake View, Poplar Corners, Walls (DeSoto)
38683	Brownfield, Camphill, Chaltbeate, Walnut (Tippah)
38685	Blackwater, Laws Hill, Waterford (Lafayette)
38701	Crossroads, Greenville, Refuge, Swiftwater (Washington)
38702	Greenville [boxes] (Washington)
38703	Greenville [boxes] (Washington)
38704	Greenville (Washington)
38720	Alligator (Bolivar); Hillhouse (Coahoma)
38721	Anguilla (Sharkey)
38722	Arcola, McCutcheon (Washington)
38723	Avon (Washington)
38725	Benoit, Bolivar, Dahomey, Eutaw, Grapeland (Bolivar)
38726	Beulah, Lobdell, Mound City (Bolivar)
38730	Boyle (Bolivar)
38731	Chatham, Erwin (Washington)
38732	Cleveland, Delta State Univ., Longshot, Zumbro (Bolivar)
38733	Cleveland (Bolivar)
38736	Blaine, Doddsville, Linn (Sunflower)
38737	Blue Lake, Brooks, Drew, Dwiggins, Fitzhugh, Goldfield, Wade, Whitney (Tallahatchie)
38738	Parchman (Sunflower)
38739	Dublin (Coahoma)
38740	Duncan, Francis, Rochdale, Roundlake (Bolivar)
38744	Glen Allan, Hampton, Valewood (Washington)
38745	Grace (Issaquena)
38746	Dennis Landing, Gunnison, Perthshire, Waxhaw (Bolivar)
38748	Bear Garden, Darlove, Estill, Foote, Hollandale, James, Murphy, Percy, Willet (Washington)
38749	Holly Ridge (Sunflower)
38751	Baird, Boyer, Fairview, Heathman, Indianola, Kinlock, Marie, Pollock, Saints Rest, Woodburn (Sunflower)
38753	Inverness, Waco (Sunflower)
38754	Bellewood, Caile, Isola (Humphreys)
38755	Lamont (Bolivar)
38756	Dunleith, Elizabeth, Heads, Helm, Leland, Long, Magenta, Rexburg (Washington)
38758	Mattson (Coahoma)
38759	Merigold (Bolivar)
38760	Metcalfe (Washington)
38761	Dwyer, Mississippi Delta Comm. College, Moorhead, Sunflower (Sunflower)
38762	Mound Bayou (Bolivar)
38763	Nitta Yuma (Sharkey)
38764	Pace (Bolivar)
38765	Panther Burn (Sharkey)
38767	Rena Lara (Coahoma)
38768	Rome (Sunflower)
38769	Malvina, Niles, Rosedale, Symonds, Wright (Bolivar)
38771	Ruleville (Sunflower)
38772	Scott (Bolivar)
38773	Choctaw, Litton, Shaw, Steiner, Stringtown (Bolivar)
38774	Hushpuckena, Lombardy, Shelby (Bolivar)

The Ultimate Reference on the State

Mississippi ZIP Codes — Numerical Cross Reference

ZIP	PLACE[S] (COUNTY)
38775	Skene (Bolivar)
38776	Stoneville (Washington)
38778	Sunflower (Sunflower)
38779	Tribbett (Washington)
38780	Wayside (Washington)
38781	Winstonville (Bolivar)
38782	Winterville (Washington)
38801	Ballardsville, Bissell, Chesterville, Mount Vernon, Tupelo (Lee)
38802	Tupelo [PO Boxes](Lee)
38803	Tupelo [PO Boxes](Lee)
38804	Tupelo (Lee)
38820	Algoma (Pontotoc)
38821	Amory, Bigbee, Colsub, Hatley (Monroe)
38824	Baldwyn, Bethany, Geeville, Graham, Kirkville (Lee)
38825	Becker ((Monroe)
38826	Belden (Lee)
38827	Belmont, Bloody Springs (Tishomingo)
38828	Alpine, Blue Springs, Branyan, Center, Cherry Creek, Endville, Fairfield, Jug Fork, Mound City, New Harmony (Union)
38829	Altitude, Blackland, Booneville, Burtons, Hobo Station, Jumpertown, Northeast Mississippi Community College, Old Cairo, Osborne Creek, Pine Grove, Thrashers (Prentiss)
38833 Leedy,	Burnsville, Doskie, Holts, (Tishomingo)
38834	Biggersville, By, Corinth, Farmington, Kendrick, Kossuth, Wenasoga (Alcorn)
38838	Dennis, Ellistown, Moores Mill (Tishomingo)
38839	Derma (Calhoun)
38841	Ecru, Friendship (Pontotoc)
38843	Dorsey, Fulton, Greenwood, Itawamba Community College (Itawamba)
38844	Gattman (Monroe)
38846	Glen, Indian Springs (Alcorn)
38847	Fairview, Golden (Itawamba)
38848	Greenwood Springs, Parham, Quincy, Splunge (Monroe)
38849	Alma, Blair, Boggan Bend, Corrona, Guntown, Ratliff (Lee)
38850	Houlka, Old Houlka (Chickasaw)
38851	Buena Vista, Houston, Pyland, Sonora, Thorn (Chickasaw)
38852	Eastport, Holcut, Iuka, Midway, Oldham (Tishomingo)
38854	McCondy (Chickasaw)
38855	Mantachie (Itawamba)
38856	Marietta (Prentiss)
38857	Mooreville (Lee)
38858	Cardsville, Carolina, Van Buren (Itawamba); Nettleton (Lee & Monroe)
38859	New Site (Prentiss)
38860	Egypt, Okolona (Chickasaw)
38862	Plantersville, Richmond, Union (Lee)
38863	Chiwapa, Furrs, Goodfood, Nixon, Plymouth, Pontotoc, Possum Trot, Rough Edge, Springville, Troy, Woodland, Zion (Pontotoc)
38864	Buckhorn, Randolph, Sarepta (Pontotoc)
38865	Hinkle, Jacinto, Pisgah, Rienzi (Alcorn)
38866	Eggville, Saltillo (Lee)
38868	Brewer, Old Union, Pine Grove, Shannon (Lee)
38869	Sherman (Pontotoc)
38870	Smithville, Turon (Monroe)
38871	Hurricane, Thaxton (Pontotoc)
38873	Mingo, Paden, Tishomingo (Tishomingo)
38874	Spring Hill, Toccopola (Lafayette)
38875	Trebloc (Chickasaw)
38876	Cademy, Mount Pleasant, Tremont (Itawamba)
38877	Van Vleet (Chickasaw)
38878	Elsie, Hollis, Loyd, Reid, Vardaman, Wardwell (Calhoun)
38879	Verona (Lee)
38880	Wheeler (Prentiss)
38901	Dubard, Futheyville, Geeslin Corner, Grenada, Hardy, Sunnycrest (Grenada)
38902	Grenada (Grenada)
38912	Avalon (Carroll)
38913	Banner (Calhoun)
38914	Big Creek, Coles Creek (Calhoun)
38915	Bruce, Ellard, Lantrip, Shepherd, Skuna (Calhoun)
38916	Calhoun City (Calhoun)
38917	Carrollton, Jefferson, Valley Hill (Carroll)
38920	Cascilla, Leverett, Paul, Paynes, Rosebloom (Tallahatchie)
38921	Charleston, Cowart, Effie, Sharkey (Tallahatchie)
38922	Benwood, Bryant, Coffeeville, Gatewood, Gums, Tyson, Youngs (Yalobusha)
38923	Black Hawk, Coila (Carroll)
38924	Cruger, Kerin (Holmes)
38925	Alva, Cedar Hill, Duck Hill Sweatman (Montgomery)
38926	Elliott (Grenada)
38927	Enid, Teasdale (Tallahatchie)
38928	Glendora, Whitehead (Tallahatchie)
38929	Cadaretta, Gore Springs (Webster)
38930	Greenwood, Shellmound (Leflore)
38935	Greenwood (Leflore)
38940	Holcomb, Nason, Oxberry (Grenada)
38941	Berclair, Colony Town, Itta Bena, Mississippi Valley State Univ., Murdock Crossing, Quito (Leflore)
38943	McCarley (Carroll)
38944	Highlandale, Minnter City, Somerville, Sunnyside (Leflore)
38945	Money (Leflore)
38946	Morgan City (Leflore)
38947	North Carrollton (Carroll)
38948	Oakland (Yalobusha)
38949	Paris (Lafayette)
38950	Macel, Phillipp (Tallahatchie)
38951	Pittsboro (Calhoun)
38952	Schlater (Leflore)
38953	Scobey (Yalabusha)
38954	Holly Grove, Phillipstown, Rising Sun, Roebuck, Sidon (Carroll)
38955	Dentontown, Sabougla, Slate Spring (Calhoun)
38957	Sumner (Tallahatchie)
38958	Swan Lake (Tallahatchie)
38959	Swiftown (Leflore)
38960	Tie Plant (Grenada)
38961	Murphreesboro, Tillatobia (Tallahatchie)
38962	Tippo (Tallahatchie)
38963	Brazil, Tutwiler (Tallahatchie)
38964	Vance, Walnut (Quitman)
38965	Pine Valley, Pine Flat, Springdale, Velma, Water Valley (Yalobusha)
38966	Albin, Webb (Tallahatchie)
38967	Eskridge, Winona (Montgomery)
39038	Belzoni (Humphreys)
39039	Benton (Yazoo)
39040	Anding, Bentonia, Dover, Oil City (Yazoo)
39041	Bolton (Hinds)
39042	Brandon, Fannin, Johns, Value (Rankin)
39043	Brandon (Rankin)
39044	Braxton (Simpson)
39045	Camden (Madison)

Mississippi ZIP Codes — Numerical Cross Reference

ZIP	PLACE[S] (COUNTY)	ZIP	PLACE[S] (COUNTY)	ZIP	PLACE[S] (COUNTY)
39046	Canton, Farmhaven, Way (Madison)	39121	Natchez [PO Boxes](Adams)	39206	Jackson (Hinds)
		39122	Natchez (Adams)	39207	Jackson [PO Boxes](Hinds)
39047	Brandon, Fannin (Rankin)	39130	Madison [PO Boxes](Madison)	39208	Flowood, Jackson International Airport, Pearl (Rankin)
39049	Carlisle (Claiborne)	39140	Newhebron (Lawrence)		
39051	Carthage, Edinburg (Leake)	39144	Pattison (Claiborne)	39209	Jackson (Hinds)
39054	Cary (Sharkey)	39145	Pelahatchie (Rankin)	39210	Jackson, Millsaps College (Hinds)
39055	Church Hill (Jefferson)	39146	Pickens (Holmes)		
39056	Clinton (Hinds)	39148	Piney Woods (Rankin)	39211	Jackson (Hinds)
39057	Conehatta (Newton)	39149	Pinola, Shivers (Simpson)	39212	Jackson (Hinds)
39058	Clinton, Mississippi College (Hinds)	39150	Port Gibson (Claiborne)	39213	Jackson (Hinds)
		39151	Puckett (Rankin)	39215	Jackson [PO Boxes](Hinds)
39059	Carpenter, Crystal Springs (Copiah)	39152	Pulaski (Scott)	39216	Jackson (Hinds)
		39153	Burns, Raleigh, Sylvarena (Smith)	39217	Jackson, Jackson State University (Hinds)
39060	Clinton [PO Boxes](Hinds)				
39061	Delta City (Sharkey)	39154	Hinds Community College, Learned, Raymond (Hinds)	39218	Richland (Rankin)
39062	D'Lo (Simpson)			39225	Jackson [PO Boxes](Hinds)
39063	Durant (Holmes)	39156	Redwood (Warren)	39232	Flowood [eff. Feb. 2000](Hinds)
39064	Ebenezer (Holmes)	39157	Ridgeland (Madison)	39236	Jackson [PO Boxes](Hinds)
39066	Edwards (Hinds)	39158	Ridgeland [PO Boxes](Madison)	39250	Jackson [PO Boxes](Hinds)
39067	Ethel (Attala)	39159	Rolling Fork (Sharkey)	39269	Jackson [Fed'l. Bldg.](Hinds)
39069	Fayette (Jefferson)	39160	Sallis (Attala)	39271	Jackson [PO Boxes](Hinds)
39070	Fitler (Issaquena)	39161	Sandhill (Rankin)	39272	Byram, Jackson [PO Boxes] (Hinds)
39071	Flora (Madison)	39162	Satartia (Yazoo)		
39072	Pocahantas (Hinds)	39163	Sharon, Shocco (Madison)	39282	Jackson [PO Boxes](Hinds)
39073	Florence (Rankin)	39165	Sibley (Adams)	39283	Jackson [PO Boxes](Hinds)
39074	Forest (Scott)	39166	Silver City (Humphreys)	39284	Jackson [PO Boxes](Hinds)
39076	Forkville (Scott)	39167	Star (Rankin)	39286	Jackson [PO Boxes](Hinds)
39077	Gallman (Copiah)	39168	Taylorsville (Smith)	39288	Pearl [PO Boxes](Rankin)
39078	Georgetown (Copiah)	39169	Bee Lake, Mileston, Tchula (Holmes)	39289	Jackson [PO Boxes](Hinds)
39079	Goodman, Holmes Community College (Holmes)			39296	Jackson [PO Boxes](Hinds)
		39170	Terry (Hinds)	39298	Jackson [boxes-airport](Hinds)
39080	Harperville (Scott)	39171	Thomastown (Leake)	39301	Bonita, Meeham, Meridian, Meridian Community College (Lauderdale)
39081	Harriston (Jefferson)	39172	Thornton (Holmes)		
39082	Harrisville (Simpson)	39173	Tinsley (Yazoo)		
39083	Hazlehurst (Copiah)	39174	Tougaloo College (Hinds)	39302	Meridian [PO Boxes] (Lauderdale)
39086	Hermanville (Claiborne)	39175	Hinds Community College, Utica (Hinds)		
39087	Hillsboro (Scott)			39303	Meridian [PO Boxes] (Lauderdale)
39088	Holly Bluff (Yazoo)	39176	Vaiden (Carroll)		
39090	Kosciusko (Attala)	39177	Valley Park (Issaquena)	39304	Meridian [PO Boxes] (Lauderdale)
39092	Lake (Scott)	39179	Vaughan (Yazoo)		
39094	Lena (Leake)	39180	Vicksburg (Warren)	39305	Meridian (Lauderdale)
39095	Lexington (Holmes)	39181	Vicksburg [PO Boxes](Warren)	39307	Meridian (Lauderdale)
39096	Alcorn State University, Lorman (Jefferson)	39182	Vicksburg [PO Boxes](Warren)	39309	Meridian Naval Air Station (Lauderdale)
		39183	Vicksburg (Warren)		
39097	Louise (Humphreys)	39189	Walnut Grove (Leake)	39320	Bailey (Lauderdale)
39098	Ludlow (Scott)	39190	Washington (Adams)	39322	Buckatunna (Wayne)
39107	McAdams (Attala)	39191	Copiah-Lincoln Community College, Wesson (Copiah)	39323	Chunky (Newton)
39108	McCool (Attala)			39324	Clara (Wayne)
39109	Madden (Leake)	39192	Possumneck, West (Holmes)	39325	Collinsville (Lauderdale)
39110	Gluckstadt, Madison (Madison)	39193	Whitfield (Rankin)	39326	Daleville (Lauderdale)
39111	Magee (Simpson)	39194	Crupp, Eden, Yazoo City (Yazoo)	39327	Decatur, East Central Community College (Newton)
39112	Sanitorium (Simpson)				
39113	Mayersville (Issaquena)	39200	Jackson (Hinds)	39328	DeKalb (Kemper)
39114	Mendenhall (Simpson)	39201	Jackson (Hinds)	39330	Enterprise (Clarke)
39115	Midnight (Humphreys)	39202	Belhaven College, Jackson (Hinds)	39332	Hickory (Newton)
39116	Mize (Smith)			39335	Lauderdale (Lauderdale)
39117	Morton (Scott)	39203	Jackson (Hinds)	39336	Lawrence (Newton)
39119	Mount Olive (Covington)	39204	Jackson (Hinds)	39337	Little Rock (Newton)
39120	Natchez (Adams)	39205	Jackson [PO Boxes](Hinds)	39338	Louin, Montrose (Jasper)

Mississippi ZIP Codes — Numerical Cross Reference

ZIP	PLACE[S] (COUNTY)
39339	Louisville (Winston)
39341	Macon (Noxubee)
39342	Marion (Lauderdale)
39345	Newton (Newton)
39346	Noxapater (Winston)
39347	Pachuta (Clarke)
39348	Paulding (Jasper)
39350	Bond, Dover, Philadelphia (Neshoba)
39352	Porterville (Kemper)
39353	Prairie Point (Noxubee)
39354	Preston (Kemper)
39355	Quitman (Clarke)
39356	Rose Hill (Jasper)
39358	East Mississippi Community College Electric Mills, Scooba (Kemper)
39359	Sebastopol (Scott)
39360	Matherville, Shubuta (Clarke)
39361	Shuqualak (Noxubee)
39362	State Line (Greene)
39363	Stonewall (Clarke)
39364	Toomsuba (Lauderdale)
39365	Union (Newton)
39366	Vossburg (Jasper)
39367	Lightsey, Strengthford, Waynesboro (Wayne)
39400	Hattiesburg (Forrest)
39401	Dixie Pine, Eatonville, Glendale, Hattiesburg, Maybank, McCallum, McLaurin, Palmers Crossing, Sunrise, William Carey College (Forrest)
39402	Hattiesburg, Arnold Line, Lamar Park (Lamar); Rawls Springs (Forrest)
39403	Hattiesburg [PO Boxes](Forrest)
39404	Hattiesburg (Forrest)
39406	Hattiesburg [PO Boxes], Univ. of So. Miss. (Forrest)
39407	Camp Shelby (Forrest)
39421	Bassfield (Jefferson Davis)
39422	Bay Springs (Jasper)
39423	Beaumont, Carmichael, Little Creek (Perry)
39425	Brooklyn, Dixie, Maxie (Forrest)
39426	Carriere. Henleyfield, Mill Creek, Ozona (Pearl River)
39427	Carson (Jefferson Davis)
39428	Collins, Dry Creek, Hot Coffee, Kola, McRaney, Ora, Smith, Williamsburg (Covington)
39429	Columbia (Marion)
39436	Eastbuchie (Jones)
39437	Crotts, Ellisville, Johnson, Jones County Jr. College, Maybell, Oak Bowery, Pecan Grove, Sand Hill, Walters (Jones)
39439	Heidelberg, Stafford Springs (Jasper)
39440	Antioch, Calhoun, Cleo, Errata, Glade, Hoy, Laurel, Mill Creek, Myrick, Pendorff, Pine Belt Regional Airport, Powers, Shady Grove, Sharon, Tuckers Crossing (Jones)
39441	Laurel [PO Boxes](Jones)
39442	Laurel [PO Boxes](Jones)
39443	Laurel (Jones)
39451	Hillman, Jonathan, Leaksville (Greene)
39452	Agricola, Basin, Bexley, Harleston, Latonia, Lucedale, Merrill, Movella, Shipman, Vernal (George)
39455	Baxterville, Carnes, Lumberton, Pistol Ridge, Seneca, Talowah, Villa Ridge, Wells Town (Lamar)
39456	Avent, Benndale, Leaf, McLain (Greene)
39457	McNeill (Pearl River)
39459	Moselle, Oak Grove, Rainey (Jones)
39460	Moss (Jasper)
39461	Neely (Greene)
39462	Belleville, Hintonvillel, Mahned, New Augusta, Wingate (Perry)
39463	Nicholson (Pearl River)
39464	Blodgett, Ovett (Jones)
39465	Barrontown, Batson, Carterville, Harvey, Leeville, Macedonia, Morriston, Petal, Pine Grove (Forrest)
39466	Caesar, Cybur, Industrial, Picayune, Richardson (Pearl River)
39470	Barth, Crossroads, Derby, Fords Creek, Hillsdale, Pearl River Community College, Poplarville, Savannah, West Poplarville (Pearl River)
39474	Lucas, Mount Carmel, Prentiss, Terrell (Jefferson Davis)
39475	Pine Ridge, Purvis, Rock Hill (Lamar)
39476	East Side, Goodhope, McSwain, Piave, Rhodes, Richton, Sand Hill (Perry)
39477	Rogerslacy, Sandersville (Jones)
39478	Sandy Hook (Marion)
39479	Eminence, Gandsi, Lux, Sanford, Seminary (Covington)
39480	Soso (Jones)
39481	Stringer (Jasper)
39482	Higgins, Melba, Oloh, Sumrall (Lamar)
39483	Cheraw, Foxworth, Jamestown, Pickwick, Pittman, Whitebluff (Marion)
39484	Morgantown (Marion)
39500	Gulfport (Harrison)
39501	Gulfport (Harrison)
39502	Gulfport [PO Boxes](Harrison)
39503	Gulfport, Orange Grove (Harrison)
39505	Gulfport [PO Boxes](Harrison)
39506	Gulfport [PO Boxes](Harrison)
39507	Gulfport (Harrison)
39520	Bay Saint Louis, Bayside Park, (Hancock)
39521	Bay Saint Louis [PO Boxes] (Hancock)
39522	Bay Saint Louis (Hancock)
39525	Diamondhead (Hancock)
39529	Bay Saint Louis [PO Boxes], National Space Technology Laboratories, Stennis Space Center (Hancock)
39530	Biloxi (Harrison)
39531	Biloxi, West Biloxi (Harrison)
39532	Biloxi, D'Iberville (Harrison)
39533	Biloxi [PO Boxes](Harrison)
39534	Biloxi [PO Boxes], Keesler Air Force Base, Triangle (Harrison)
39535	Biloxi [PO Boxes](Harrison)
39552	Escatawpa (Jackson)
39553	Gautier, Iowana (Jackson)
39555	Hurley (Jackson)
39556	Kiln (Hancock)
39558	Ansley, Lakeshore (Hancock)
39560	Long Beach (Harrison)
39561	McHenry (Stone)
39562	Moss Point (Jackson)
39563	East Moss Point, Eastside. Kreole. Moss Point (Jackson)
39564	Fontainbleau, Gulf Park Estates, Gulf Hills, Larue, Latimer, Ocean Springs, Polfry, Windsor Park (Jackson)
39565	Vancleave (Jackson)
39566	Ocean Springs (Jackson)
39567	Bigpoint, Eastlawn, Helena, Orange Grove, Pascagoula, Pecan, Three Rivers, Wade (Jackson)
39568	Pascagoula [PO boxes](Jackson)
39569	Pascagoula (Jackson)
39571	Cuevas, Pass Christian (Harrison)

Mississippi ZIP Codes — Numerical Cross Reference

ZIP	PLACE[S] (COUNTY)
39572	Belle Isle, Pearlington (Hancock)
39573	Big Level, Crane Creek, Daisy Vestry, Miss. Gulf Coast Comm. College, Inda, Necaise, Perkinston, Riceville, Sellers, Silver Run, Ten Mile (Stone)
39574	Airey, Howison, Saucier, Success, Wortham (Harrison)
39576	Waveland (Hancock)
39577	Fruitland Park, Whites Crossing, Wiggins (Stone)
39581	Pascagoula (Jackson)
39595	Pascagoula (Jackson)
39601	Brookhaven, Fair River, Fair Oaks Springs, Heucks, Lucien, New Sight, Pearlhaven, Redstar, Union Hall, West Lincoln, Zetus (Lincoln)
39602	Brookhaven, Cobbs (Lincoln)
39603	Brookhaven (Lincoln)
39629	Arlington, Bogue Chitto, Enterprise, Norfield (Lincoln)
39630	Bude (Franklin)
39631	Centreville (Wilkinson)
39632	Chatawa (Pike)
39633	Coles, Crosby, Perrytown, Rosetta, Saukum (Amite)
39635	Fernwood (Pike)
39638	Ariel, Bewelcome, Cassels, Enterprise, Eunice, Gloster, Homochitto, Oxford, Tatum, White Cap (Amite)
39641	Bristers Store, Enon, Jayess, Sartinsville, Topeka (Lawrence)
39643	Kokomo (Marion)
39645	Beechwood, Berwick, Busy Corner, Liberty, Peoria (Amite)
39647	Eddiceton, McCall Creek, Quentin (Franklin)
39648	Bacots, Barto, Bear Town, Holmesville, McComb, Progress (Pike)
39649	McComb (Pike)
39652	Jennings, Magnolia (Pike)
39653	Bunkley, Meadville, Mile Branch, Monroe, Mount Olive (Franklin)
39654	Monticello, Oma, Robinwood, Rosella, Tilton, Wanilla (Lawrence)
39656	Oak Vale, Society Hill (Lawrence)
39657	Gillsburg, Osyka (Pike)
39661	Cranfield, Garden City, Hamburg, Kirby, Knoxville, Leesdale, Oldenburg, Roxie, White Apple (Franklin)
39662	Ruth, Sauls (Lincoln)
39663	Arm, Silver Creek (Lawrence)
39664	Auburn, East Fork, Mount Olive, Smithdale, Thompson (Amite)
39665	Nola, Sontag (Lawrence)
39666	Irene, Johnston, Mars Hill, McElveen, Oakland, Pricedale, Southwest Miss. Community College, Summit, Topisaw (Pike)
39667	Darbun, Dexter, Knoxo, Lexie, Mesa, Salem, Tylertown (Walthall)
39668	Pleasant Hill, Union Church (Jefferson)
39669	Ashwood, Darrington, Dolorosa, Donegal, Fort Adams, Highway Village, Ireland, Laneheart, Lessley, Pinckneyville, Turnbull, Wilkinson, Woodville (Wilkinson)
39701	Columbus, Fairlane, McCrary, Mississippi Univ. for Women, New Hope (Lowndes)
39702	Columbus (Lowndes)
39703	Columbus [PO Boxes] (Lowndes)
39704	Columbus [PO Boxes] (Lowndes)
39705	Columbus [PO Boxes] (Lowndes)
39710	Columbus AF Base (Lowndes)
39730	Aberdeen, Binford, Central Grove, Darracott, Gibson, Lackey, Muldon, New Wren, Strongs, Wren (Monroe)
39735	Ackerman, Chester, Fentress (Choctaw)
39736	Artesia (Lowndes)
39737	Bellefontaine (Webster)
39738	Bigbee Valley (Noxubee)
39739	Brooksville, Deerbrook, Cliftonville, Lynn Creek, (Noxubee)
39740 Deeson	Bartahatchie, Caledonia, Kolola Springs, White Sand (Monroe)
39741	Cedarbluff, Griffith, Waddell (Clay)
39743	Crawford, Penns, Trinity (Lowndes)
39744	Eupora, Fame, Grady, Sapa, Tomnolen (Webster)
39745	French Camp (Choctaw)
39746	Hamilton, Old Hamilton (Monroe)
39747	Hendrix, Kilmichael, Poplar Springs, Poplar Creek, Sibleton (Montgomery)
39750	Cumberland, Maben, Oktibbeha (Webster)
39751	Bentley, Dancy, Hohenlinden, Mantee, Pinebluff (Calhoun)
39752	Clarkson, Mathiston, Sherwood, Wood Junior College (Webster)
39753	Mayhew (Lowndes)
39754	Montpelier (Clay)
39755	Beasley, Pheba (Clay)
39756	Prairie (Monroe)
39757	Reform (Choctaw)
39759	Adaton, Bells School, Blackjack, Bradley, Clayton Village, Hickory Grove, Longview, Morgantown, Muldrow, Oktoc, Osborn, Patrick, Rocky Hill, Sessums, Starkville (Oktibbeha)
39760	Starkville (Oktibbeha)
39762	Mississippi State University (Oktibbeha)
39766	Steens (Lowndes)
39767	Lodi, Stewart (Montgomery)
39769	Craig Springs, Sturgis (Oktibbeha)
39771	Monte Vista, Walthall (Webster)
39772	Bankston, Weir (Choctaw)
39773	Abbott, Mary Holmes College, Tibbee, West Point, Whites (Clay)
39776	Anchor, Atlanta, Woodland (Chickasaw)

ZIP is an acronym that stands for Zoning Improvement Program.

The Ultimate Reference on the State

Pop. of Mississippi Cities/Towns (Numerically — Census Estimates 7/1/1998)

City	Population	City	Population	City	Population
Jackson	188,419	Aberdeen	6,915	Magnolia	2,259
Gulfport	64,762	Kosciusko	6,774	Rolling Fork	2,228
Hattiesburg	48,806	Pass Christian	6,190	Drew	2,136
Biloxi	47,316	Leland	5,970	Sardis	2,136
Greenville	42,042	Crystal Springs	5,832	Mound Bayou	2,102
Meridian	40,255	Richland	5,794	Bruce	2,041
Tupelo	35,589	Winona	5,647	Lexington	2,027
Vicksburg	27,221	Ripley	5,623	Raymond	2,016
Pascagoula	27,163	Senatobia	5,428	Tylertown	1,992
Southaven	23,434	Waynesboro	5,400	Saltillo	1,915
Pearl	23,287	Forest	5,324	Union	1,873
Columbus	22,297	Pontotoc	5,219	Bay Springs	1,855
Clinton	22,067	Flowood	4,471	Fayette	1,822
Clarksdale	20,461	Hazlehurst	4,228	Port Gibson	1,750
Starkville	20,184	Hernando	4,088	Calhoun City	1,736
Laurel	18,299	Carthage	4,084	Monticello	1,732
Natchez	18,277	Wiggins	3,977	Ackerman	1,705
Greenwood	18,218	Magee	3,930	Marks	1,635
Moss Point	18,095	Houston	3,902	Belmont	1,627
Long Beach	16,776	Ellisville	3,770	Pelahatchie	1,597
Ridgeland	16,545	Newton	3,749	Shannon	1,589
Ocean Springs	16,519	Fulton	3,668	Flora	1,585
Cleveland	14,834	Water Valley	3,661	Marion	1,565
Brandon	14,612	Hollandale	3,524	Summit	1,562
Horn Lake	13,885	Baldwyn	3,416	Centreville	1,543
Madison	12,618	Verona	3,347	Wesson	1,520
Canton	12,221	Morton	3,261	Coldwater	1,482
Corinth	12,204	Iuka	3,122	Jonestown	1,462
Oxford	12,096	Okolona	3,059	Como	1,441
Olive Branch	12,063	Ruleville	3,049	Plantersville	1,394
Picayune	12,058	Lucedale	3,041	Taylorsville	1,388
Yazoo City	11,941	Quitman	2,839	Pickens	1,381
McComb	11,746	Poplarville	2,834	Decatur	1,352
Indianola	11,514	Durant	2,686	Goodman	1,348
Grenada	11,161	Shelby	2,686	Tutwiler	1,348
Gautier	11,139	Collins	2,657	Friars Point	1,337
Brookhaven	10,649	Nettleton	2,612	Duck Hill	1,331
Bay Saint Louis	9,841	Lumberton	2,563	Gloster	1,304
Petal	8,888	Purvis	2,532	Woodville	1,297
West Point	8,848	Mendenhall	2,528	Beaumont	1,278
Booneville	8,387	Rosedale	2,507	Prentiss	1,275
D'Iberville	8,211	Florence	2,375	Raleigh	1,266
Philadelphia	7,725	Belzoni	2,367	Metcalfe	1,240
Batesville	7,416	Tchula	2,367	Edwards	1,195
New Albany	7,238	Charleston	2,331	Stonewall	1,161
Holly Springs	7,195	Moorhead	2,315	Sumrall	1,141
Amory	7,144	Eupora	2,312	Leaksville	1,111
Louisville	7,085	Macon	2,298	Inverness	1,103
Waveland	6,986	Shaw	2,290	Richton	1,092
Columbia	6,935	Itta Bena	2,264	DeKalb	1,075

Pop. of Mississippi Cities/Towns (Numerically — Census Estimates 7/1/1998)

City	Pop.	City	Pop.	City	Pop.
Lambert	1,075	Weir	545	Louin	282
Mantachie	1,068	Hickory Flat	544	Pachuta	276
Brooksville	1,044	New Houlka	540	Sebastopol	276
Burnsville	1,017	Arcola	537	Pittsboro	272
Tunica	1,015	Hickory	531	Winstonville	262
Crenshaw	1,007	Artesia	528	Coahoma	250
Utica	987	Scooba	519	Kossuth	244
Mount Olive	963	Ashland	508	Falkner	239
Ecru	958	Osyka	489	Bassfield	238
Byhalia	951	Enterprise	483	Seminary	236
Bude	950	Potts Camp	483	Glen	229
Derma	948	Thaxton	483	Beauregard	226
Heidelberg	937	Beulah	474	Carrollton	220
Vardaman	919	Algoma	458	Lula	218
Smithville	898	Sledge	452	Alligator	213
Sandersville	894	Dumas	450	Golden	209
Caledonia	877	Jumpertown	450	Silver Creek	192
Mathiston	832	Crosby	443	Woodland	183
Vaiden	831	Ethel	440	Sturgis	181
Anguilla	820	Noxapater	438	Pope	178
Coffeeville	795	Lyon	427	Lena	171
Crowder	794	State Line	425	McCool	168
Kilmichael	784	Abbeville	422	Walthall	168
Bolton	783	Schlater	419	West	166
Sunflower	781	D'Lo	412	Toccopola	163
Maben	742	Meadville	411	Glendora	161
Crawford	739	Duncan	394	Blue Springs	154
Guntown	739	Walnut Grove	394	Braxton	142
New Augusta	723	Bentonia	391	Doddsville	138
Blue Mountain	704	Cary	386	Mantee	135
Boyle	696	Myrtle	383	Polkville	135
Liberty	680	New Hebron	382	Falcon	133
Isola	666	Soso	377	Gattman	131
Sherman	620	Lake	364	Sallis	130
Terry	619	Courtland	362	Morgan City	128
Benoit	609	Puckett	362	Paden	126
Sidon	609	Rienzi	358	Slate Spring	119
Gunnison	608	Georgetown	350	Big Creek	117
North Carrollton	607	Pace	348	Sylvarena	111
McLain	606	Sumner	348	Montrose	108
Shubuta	596	Tremont	345	Learned	99
Renova	593	Silver City	322	Eden	90
Webb	587	Mize	321	Memphis	90
Shuqualak	578	Chunky	315	Satartia	61
Walnut	561	French Camp	315		
Merigold	560	Louise	314		
Oakland	559	Taylor	303		
Hatley	558	Tishomingo	302		
Roxie	556	Marietta	295		
Cruger	554	Mayersville	288		

Total: 294 incorporated municipalities with a total population of 1,394,843 (about 50.7% of Mississippi's estimated 1998 population of 2,751,335).

The Ultimate Reference on the State

Pop. of Mississippi Cities/Towns (Alpha. Cross Reference — 1998 Estimates)

City	Pop.	City	Pop.	City	Pop.
Abbeville	422	Coffeeville	795	Greenville	42,042
Aberdeen	6,915	Coldwater	1,482	Greenwood	18,218
Ackerman	1,705	Collins	2,657	Grenada	11,161
Algoma	458	Columbia	6,935	Gulfport	64,762
Alligator	213	Columbus	22,297	Gunnison	608
Amory	7,144	Como	1,441	Guntown	739
Anguilla	820	Corinth	12,204	Hatley	558
Arcola	537	Courtland	362	Hattiesburg	48,806
Artesia	528	Crawford	739	Hazlehurst	4,228
Ashland	508	Crenshaw	1,007	Heidelberg	937
Baldwyn	3,416	Crosby	443	Hernando	4,088
Bassfield	238	Crowder	794	Hickory	531
Batesville	7,416	Cruger	554	Hickory Flat	544
Bay Saint Louis	9,841	Crystal Springs	5,832	Hollandale	3,524
Bay Springs	1,855	D'Iberville	8,211	Holly Springs	7,195
Beaumont	1,278	D'Lo	412	Horn Lake	13,885
Beauregard	226	Decatur	1,352	Houston	3,902
Belmont	1,627	DeKalb	1,075	Indianola	11,514
Belzoni	2,367	Derma	948	Inverness	1,103
Benoit	609	Doddsville	138	Isola	666
Bentonia	391	Drew	2,136	Itta Bena	2,264
Beulah	474	Duck Hill	1,331	Iuka	3,122
Big Creek	117	Dumas	450	Jackson	188,419
Biloxi	47,316	Duncan	394	Jonestown	1,462
Blue Mountain	704	Durant	2,686	Jumpertown	450
Blue Springs	154	Ecru	958	Kilmichael	784
Bolton	783	Eden	90	Kosciusko	6,774
Booneville	8,387	Edwards	1,195	Kossuth	244
Boyle	696	Ellisville	3,770	Lake	364
Brandon	14,612	Enterprise	483	Lambert	1,075
Braxton	142	Ethel	440	Laurel	18,299
Brookhaven	10,649	Eupora	2,312	Leaksville	1,111
Brooksville	1,044	Falcon	133	Learned	99
Bruce	2,041	Falkner	239	Leland	5,970
Bude	950	Fayette	1,822	Lena	171
Burnsville	1,017	Flora	1,585	Lexington	2,027
Byhalia	951	Florence	2,375	Liberty	680
Caledonia	877	Flowood	4,471	Long Beach	16,776
Calhoun City	1,736	Forest	5,324	Louin	282
Canton	12,221	French Camp	315	Louise	314
Carrollton	220	Friars Point	1,337	Louisville	7,085
Carthage	4,084	Fulton	3,668	Lucedale	3,041
Cary	386	Gattman	131	Lula	218
Centreville	1,543	Gautier	11,139	Lumberton	2,563
Charleston	2,331	Georgetown	350	Lyon	427
Chunky	315	Glen	229	Maben	742
Clarksdale	20,461	Glendora	161	Macon	2,298
Cleveland	14,834	Gloster	1,304	Madison	12,618
Clinton	22,067	Golden	209	Magee	3,930
Coahoma	250	Goodman	1,348	Magnolia	2,259

Pop. of Mississippi Cities/Towns (Alpha. Cross Reference — 1998 Estimates)

City	Pop.	City	Pop.	City	Pop.
Mantachie	1,068	Picayune	12,058	Starkville	20,184
Mantee	135	Pickens	1,381	State Line	425
Marietta	295	Pittsboro	272	Stonewall	1,161
Marion	1,565	Plantersville	1,394	Sturgis	181
Marks	1,635	Polkville	135	Summit	1,562
Mathiston	832	Pontotoc	5,219	Sumner	348
Mayersville	288	Pope	178	Sumrall	1,141
McComb	11,746	Poplarville	2,834	Sunflower	781
McCool	168	Port Gibson	1,750	Sylvarena	111
McLain	606	Potts Camp	483	Taylor	303
Meadville	411	Prentiss	1,275	Taylorsville	1,388
Memphis	90	Puckett	362	Tchula	2,367
Mendenhall	2,528	Purvis	2,532	Terry	619
Meridian	40,255	Quitman	2,839	Thaxton	483
Merigold	560	Raleigh	1,266	Tishomingo	302
Metcalfe	1,240	Raymond	2,016	Toccopola	163
Mize	321	Renova	593	Tremont	345
Monticello	1,732	Richland	5,794	Tunica	1,015
Montrose	108	Richton	1,092	Tupelo	35,589
Moorhead	2,315	Ridgeland	16,545	Tutwiler	1,348
Morgan City	128	Rienzi	358	Tylertown	1,992
Morton	3,261	Ripley	5,623	Union	1,873
Moss Point	18,095	Rolling Fork	2,228	Utica	987
Mound Bayou	2,102	Rosedale	2,507	Vaiden	831
Mount Olive	963	Roxie	556	Vardaman	919
Myrtle	383	Ruleville	3,049	Verona	3,347
Natchez	18,277	Sallis	130	Vicksburg	27,221
Nettleton	2,612	Saltillo	1,915	Walnut	561
New Albany	7,238	Sandersville	894	Walnut Grove	394
New Augusta	723	Sardis	2,136	Walthall	168
New Hebron	382	Satartia	61	Water Valley	3,661
New Houlka	540	Schlater	419	Waveland	6,986
Newton	3,749	Scooba	519	Waynesboro	5,400
North Carrollton	607	Sebastopol	276	Webb	587
Noxapater	438	Seminary	236	Weir	545
Oakland	559	Senatobia	5,428	Wesson	1,520
Ocean Springs	16,519	Shannon	1,589	West	166
Okolona	3,059	Shaw	2,290	West Point	8,848
Olive Branch	12,063	Shelby	2,686	Wiggins	3,977
Osyka	489	Sherman	620	Winona	5,647
Oxford	12,096	Shubuta	596	Winstonville	262
Pace	348	Shuqualak	578	Woodland	183
Pachuta	276	Sidon	609	Woodville	1,297
Paden	126	Silver City	322	Yazoo City	11,941
Pascagoula	27,163	Silver Creek	192		
Pass Christian	6,190	Slate Spring	119		
Pearl	23,287	Sledge	452		
Pelahatchie	1,597	Smithville	898		
Petal	8,888	Soso	377		
Philadelphia	7,725	Southaven	23,434		

Total: 294 incorporated municipalities with a total population of 1,394,843 (about 50.7% of Mississippi's estimated 1998 population of 2,751,335)

The Ultimate Reference on the State

Counties of Mississippi by Pop. (Ranking by Census Estimates of 7/1/1999)

	7/1/1999	1990		7/1/1999	1990		7/1/1999	1990
Hinds	245,737	254,441	Lincoln	32,105	30,278	Smith	15,431	14,798
Harrison	178,567	165,365	Coahoma	31,094	31,665	Calhoun	14,891	14,908
Jackson	133,120	115,243	Copiah	28,892	27,592	Tallahatchie	14,587	15,210
Rankin	112,348	87,161	Neshoba	27,639	24,800	Walthall	14,211	14,352
DeSoto	102,131	67,910	Marion	26,538	25,544	Amite	13,906	13,328
Lauderdale	75,978	75,555	Pontotoc	25,685	22,237	Jefferson Davis	13,770	14,051
Lee	75,211	65,579	Simpson	25,375	23,953	Stone	13,488	10,750
Forrest	74,927	68,314	Yazoo	25,208	25,506	Lawrence	13,066	12,458
Madison	74,562	53,794	Scott	24,911	24,137	Greene	12,630	10,220
Washington	64,265	67,935	Prentiss	24,497	23,278	Yalobusha	12,627	12,033
Jones	63,054	62,031	Tate	24,417	21,432	Noxubee	12,497	12,604
Lowndes	60,527	59,308	Union	24,121	22,085	Montgomery	12,394	12,387
Warren	49,148	47,880	Grenada	22,450	21,555	Perry	12,039	10,865
Pearl River	47,969	38,714	Clay	21,657	21,120	Claiborne	11,596	11,370
Hancock	41,518	31,760	Newton	21,741	20,291	Humphreys	11,214	12,134
Bolivar	39,826	41,875	Holmes	21,562	21,604	Webster	10,633	10,222
Oktibbeha	39,765	38,375	Itawamba	21,085	20,017	Kemper	10,487	10,356
Monroe	38,230	36,582	Tippah	21,069	19,523	Carroll	9,967	9,237
Lamar	38,127	30,424	Wayne	20,637	19,517	Quitman	9,780	10,490
Pike	37,910	36,882	George	20,185	16,673	Choctaw	9,366	9,071
Leflore	36,816	37,341	Leake	19,602	18,436	Wilkinson	9,042	9,678
Lafayette	34,912	31,826	Winston	19,253	19,433	Jefferson	8,385	8,653
Panola	33,913	29,996	Tishomingo	18,742	17,683	Franklin	8,160	8,377
Adams	33,657	35,356	Clarke	18,445	17,313	Benton	8,091	8,046
Sunflower	33,257	35,129	Attala	18,338	18,481	Tunica	7,935	8,164
Alcorn	33,080	31,722	Chickasaw	18,121	18,085	Sharkey	6,543	7,066
Marshall	32,323	30,361	Jasper	18,110	17,114	Issaquena	1,635	1,909
			Covington	17,889	16,527			

The County 1999 Population Pie

1999 State Population Estimate 2,768,619

- HINDS COUNTY / THE OTHER 81 COUNTIES 2,522,882
- TOP-3 COUNTIES 557,424 / THE OTHER 79 COUNTIES 2,211,195
- TOP-10 COUNTIES 1,136,846 / THE OTHER 72 COUNTIES 1,631,773
- TOP-15 COUNTIES 1,399,062 / THE OTHER 67 COUNTIES 1,369,557

1990 State Population 2,575,475

From 1990 to 1999, a gain of 193,144 — a 7.5% increase.

Mississippi Counties Population Charts (1998 Census Estimates)

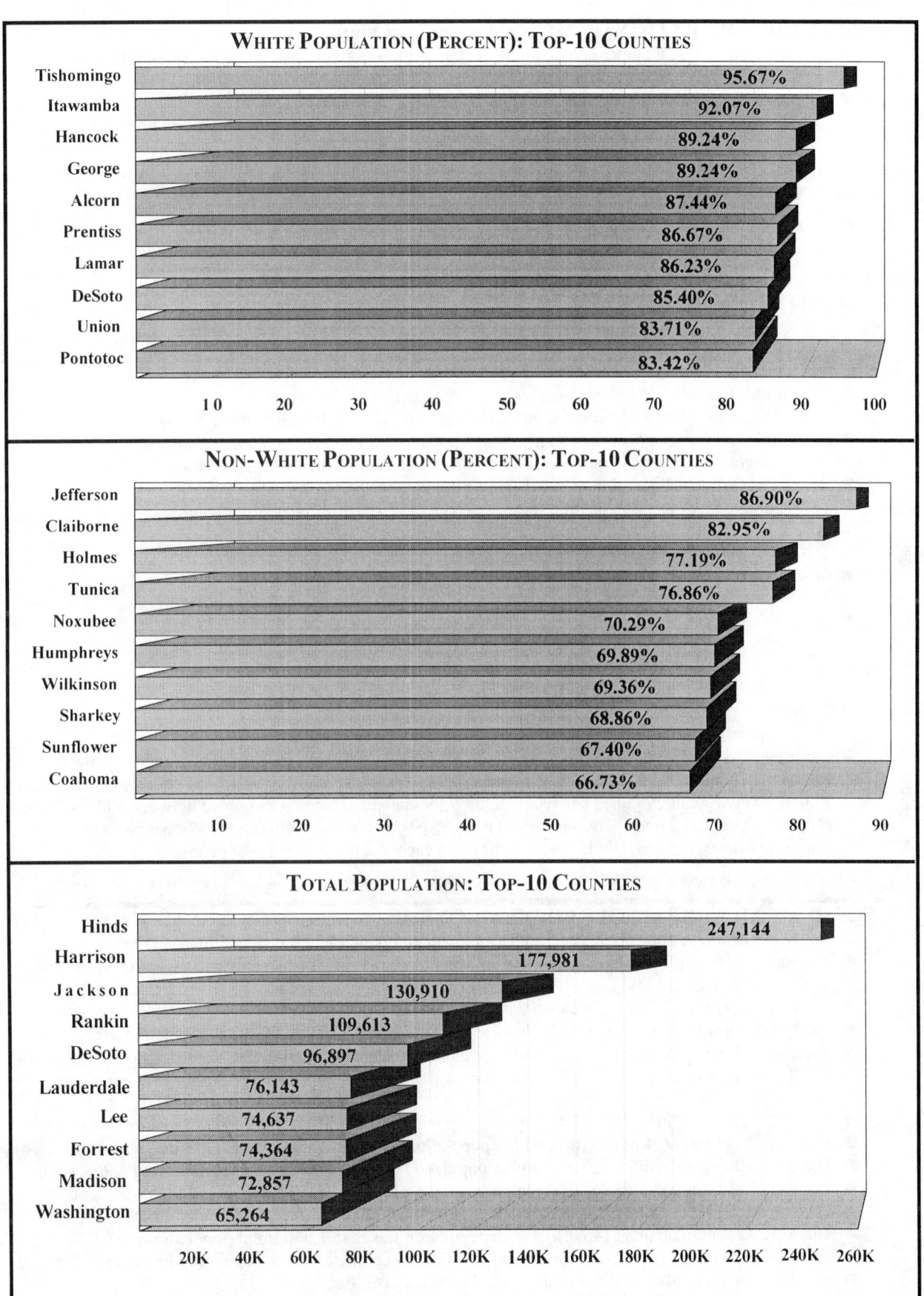

The Ultimate Reference on the State

Analysis of Mississippi Population Figures (1998 Census Estimates)

ANALYSIS OF POPULATION OF MSAs (Metropolitan Statistical Areas)

- Jackson: This MSA includes Hinds, Madison and Rankin Counties and is the largest totally within Miss. 429,614 (rank 93 in the nation) about 15.6% of Mississippi's population.
- Biloxi-Gulfport-Pascagoula: This MSA includes Hancock, Harrison and Jackson Counties. 349,218 (rank 113 in the nation) about 12.7% of Mississippi's population.
- Hattiesburg: This MSA includes Forrest and Lamar Counties. 111,252 (rank 244 in the nation) about 4% of Mississippi's estimated 1998 population.
- Memphis (TN, AR & MS): DeSoto Co., MS, is part of this MSA with 96,897 (3.5% of the state's pop.)

> Almost a million people (986,981), or 35.9% of the state's 1998 estimated population of 2,751,335 (revised), live in the 9 MSA counties: DeSoto, Forrest, Hancock, Harrison, Hinds, Jackson, Lamar, Madison and Rankin.

ANALYSIS OF COUNTIES POPULATION

> Hinds County has over 151 times the population of Issaquena County!

- Most Populated County: Hinds — 247,144 (282.45 persons per square mile) Almost 9% of the state's population lives in Hinds County.
- Least Populated County: Issaquena — 1,629 (4.01 persons per square mile) Less than 6/100th of 1% of Mississippians live in Issaquena County.
- 12 counties (about 14.6% of the counties) have populations 50,000 or more. Population of these 12 counties total 1,250,479 (45.4% of the state's population)
- 70 counties (about 85.4% of the counties) have populations less than 50,000. Population of these 70 counties total 1,501,613 (54.6% of the state's population)
- 34 counties (about 41.5% of the counties) have populations between 20,000 & 50,000. Population of these 34 counties total 1,036,701 (37.7% of the state's population)
- 46 counties (about 56.1% of the counties) have populations 20,000 or more. Population of these 46 counties total 2,287,180 (83.1% of the state's population)
- 36 counties (about 43.9% of the counties) have populations less than 20,000. Population of these 36 counties total 464,912 (16.9% of the state's population)
- 26 counties (about 31.7% of the counties) have populations between 10,000 & 20,000. Population of these 26 counties total 385,240 (14% of the state's population)
- 72 counties (about 87.8% of the counties) have populations 10,000 or more. Population of these 72 counties total 2,672,420 (97.1% of the state's population)
- 10 counties (about 12.2% of the counties) have populations less than 10,000. Population of these 10 counties total 79,672 (only 2.9% of the state's population).
- From 1990 to 1998 — DeSoto County gained 28,987 people, the largest gain of any county in the state. Rankin Co. gained 22,452; Madison Co. gained 19,063; Jackson Co. gained 15,667; Harrison Co. gained 12,616; twelve counties gained between 2,000 - 9,999 people; 16 counties gained between 1,000 - 1,999 people; 26 counties gained between 0 - 999 people; 19 counties lost between 0 - 999 people; and 4 counties (Adams, Bolivar, Hinds, and Washington) each lost more than 1,000 people.

> About 12.7% of the state's population live in the coastal counties of Hancock, Harrison and Jackson.

ANALYSIS OF MUNICIPALITIES POPULATION
(State Code defines a municipality with a population 2,000 or greater as a city, population 300-1,999 as a town, and population less than 300 as a village)

- The state has 108 cities, 140 towns, and 46 villages for a total of 294 municipalities with total population of 1,394,843 (50.7%) — a little over half of Mississippi's people live in incorporated places.
- There are 15 cities (13.9% of all cities) with a population 20,000 or more (total population of 653,303).
- Of all 294 municipalities, 279 (94.9%) have a population less than 20,000 (total population of 741,540).
- There are 22 cities (20% of all cities) with a population between 10,000 & 20,000 (total pop. of 307,470).
- Of all 294 municipalities, 37 (12.6%) cities have a population 10,000 or more with a total population of 960,773, or 68.9% of the population of all incorporated places, or 34.9% of the state's population.
- Of all 294 municipalities, 257 (87.4%) have a population less than 10,000 (total population of 434,070).
- There are 71 cities (66% of all cities) with a population between 2,000 and 10,000 (total pop. of 305,670).
- There are 108 municipalities (36.7%) with a population 2,000 or more (total population of 1,266,443).
- There are 186 municipalities (63.3%) with a population less than 2,000 (total population of 128,400).
- There are 156 municipalities (53.1%) with a population 1,000 or more (total population of 1,334,074).
- There are 138 municipalities (46.9%) with a population less than 1,000 (total population of 60,769).
- Of 92 county seats (10 counties have 2 seats), 67 (72.8%) of them have a population less than 10,000.
- The population of only two cities in the state, Jackson and Gulfport, exceed 50,000.

Population Growth in Mississippi 1830 - 1999

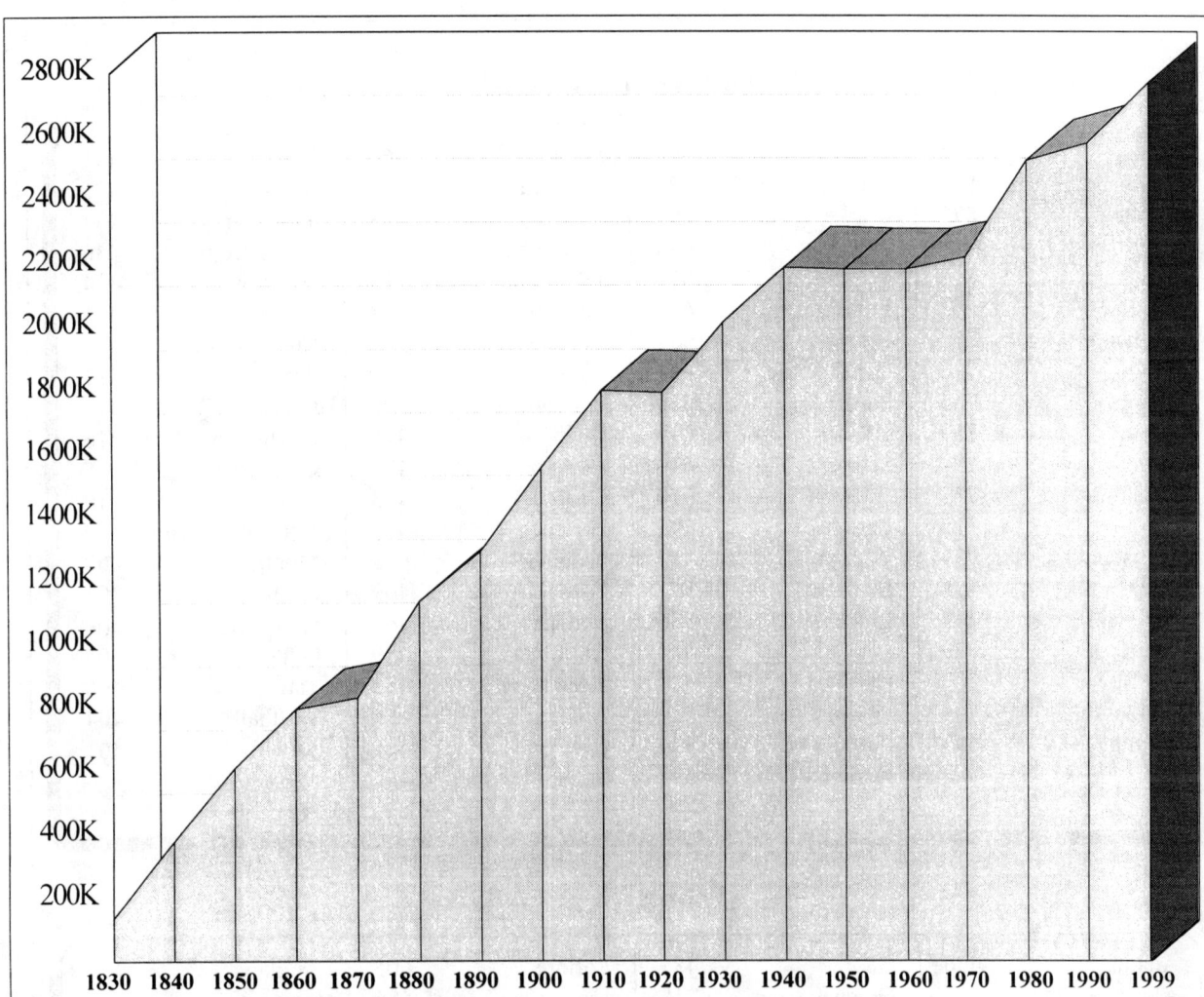

The Changing Population of Mississippi

Census	Population	Census	Population
1800	8,850	1900	1,551,270
1810	40,352	1910	1,797,114
1820	75,448	1920	1,790,618
1830	136,621	1930	2,009,821
1840	375,651	1940	2,183,796
1850	606,555	1950	2,178,914
1860	791,305	1960	2,178,141
1870	827,922	1970	2,216,994
1880	1,131,597	1980	2,520,770
1890	1,289,600	1990	2,575,475
		1998 estimate	2,751,335
		1999 estimate	2,768,619

Increase rates in hundred-year periods (figures rounded): 1800-1900, 175.3x; 1810-1910, 44.5x; 1820-1920, 23.7x; 1830-1930, 14.7x; 1840-1940, 5.8x; 1850-1950, 3.6x; 1860-1960, 2.75x; 1870-1970, 2.7x; 1880-1980, 2.2x; 1890-1990, 2x. The increase rate from 1800-1999 is 312.8x

The Counties of Mississippi by Area (Total Square Miles)

In Order By Size

County	Sq Mi	County	Sq Mi	County	Sq Mi	County	Sq Mi
Yazoo	933	Jones	695	Franklin	566	Lawrence	435
Bolivar	892	Panola	695	Coahoma	559	Sharkey	435
Hinds	875	Clarke	692	Marion	548	Tishomingo	434
Pearl River	819	Jasper	678	Itawamba	541	Humphreys	430
Wayne	813	Wilkinson	678	Jefferson	523	Webster	424
Rankin	782	Lafayette	669	Lowndes	517	Grenada	421
Copiah	779	Perry	651	Chickasaw	503	Choctaw	420
Monroe	772	Tallahatchie	651	Lamar	499	Prentiss	417
Kemper	766	Smith	635	Pontotoc	499	Union	417
Holmes	759	Carroll	634	Claiborne	494	Covington	416
Attala	737	Scott	610	DeSoto	483	Clay	415
Washington	733	Winston	610	George	483	Pike	410
Amite	732	Leflore	605	Hancock	478	Jefferson Davis	409
Jackson	731	Warren	597	Yalobusha	478	Montgomery	408
Greene	718	Simpson	591	Forrest	469	Benton	407
Madison	717	Lincoln	586	Tunica	460	Issaquena	406
Marshall	709	Leake	584	Oktibbeha	459	Quitman	406
Sunflower	707	Harrison	581	Tippah	458	Tate	406
Lauderdale	705	Newton	580	Adams	456	Walthall	404
Noxubee	698	Calhoun	573	Lee	451	Alcorn	401
		Neshoba	571	Stone	446		

In Alphabetical Order

County	Sq Mi	County	Sq Mi	County	Sq Mi	County	Sq Mi
Adams	456	George	483	Leflore	605	Sharkey	435
Alcorn	401	Greene	718	Lincoln	586	Simpson	591
Amite	732	Grenada	421	Lowndes	517	Smith	635
Attala	737	Hancock	478	Madison	717	Stone	446
Benton	407	Harrison	581	Marion	548	Sunflower	707
Bolivar	892	Holmes	759	Marshall	709	Tallahatchie	651
Hinds	875	Humphreys	430	Monroe	772	Tate	406
Calhoun	573	Issaquena	406	Montgomery	408	Tippah	458
Carroll	634	Itawamba	541	Neshoba	571	Tishomingo	434
Chickasaw	503	Jackson	731	Newton	580	Tunica	460
Choctaw	420	Jasper	678	Noxubee	698	Union	417
Claiborne	494	Jefferson Davis	409	Oktibbeha	459	Walthall	404
Clarke	692	Jefferson	523	Panola	695	Warren	597
Clay	415	Jones	695	Pearl River	819	Washington	733
Coahoma	559	Kemper	766	Perry	651	Wayne	813
Copiah	779	Lafayette	669	Pike	410	Webster	424
Covington	416	Lamar	499	Pontotoc	499	Wilkinson	678
DeSoto	483	Lauderdale	705	Prentiss	417	Winston	610
Forrest	469	Lawrence	435	Quitman	406	Yalobusha	478
Franklin	566	Leake	584	Rankin	782	Yazoo	933
		Lee	451	Scott	610		

The Counties of Mississippi

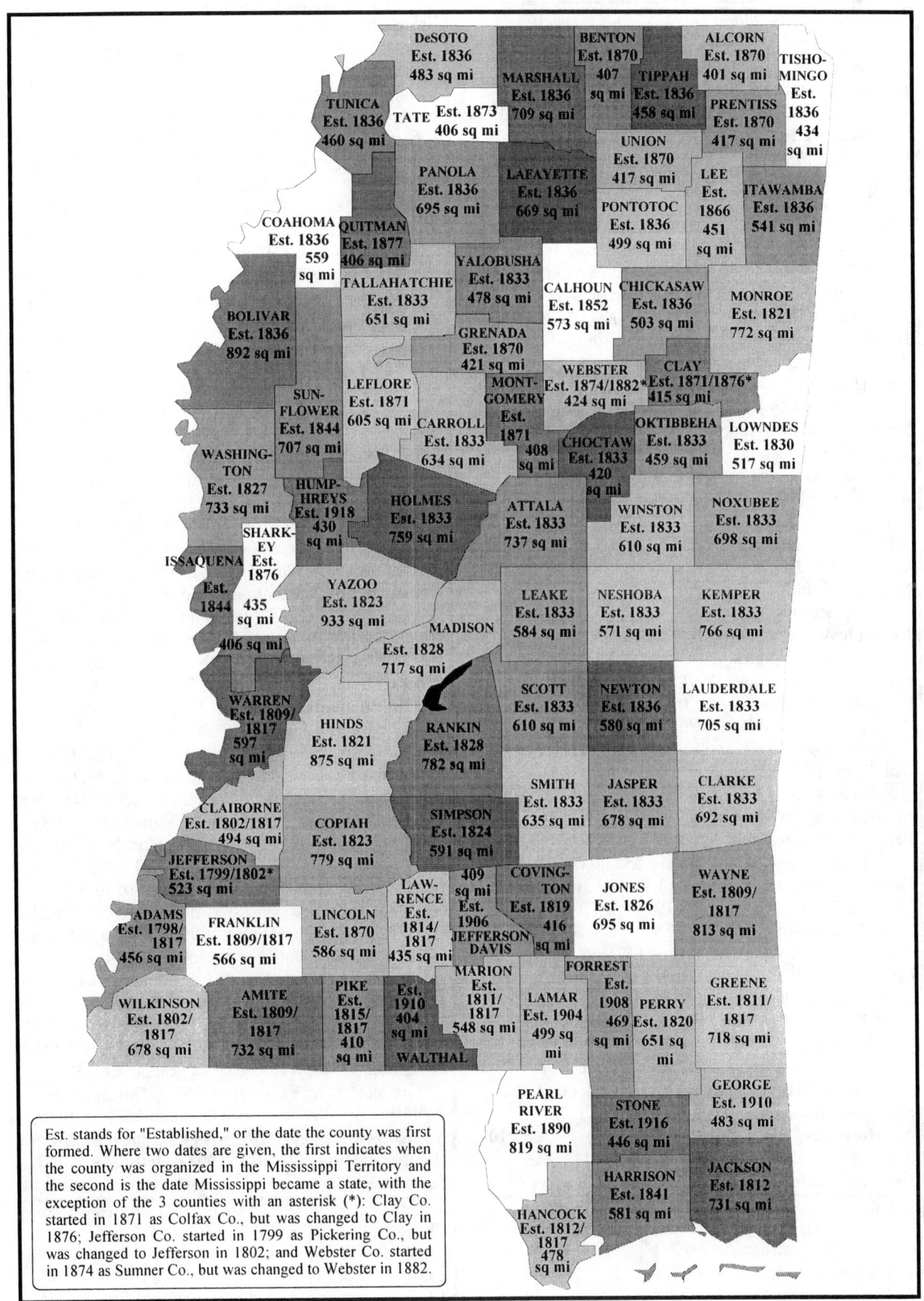

The Ultimate Reference on the State

Adams County

Established: 1798 (oldest county)   Seat: Natchez
Area in Square Miles: 456
Named for President John Adams
Located in southwest Mississippi bordering Louisiana
Incorporated Places with Estimated Population, 7/1/1998:
   Natchez 18,277
County Pop., 7/1/99: 33,657 (73.81 persons p/sq. mi.)
County Pop., 7/1/98: 34,225 (Voting Age: 25,093)
   White: 16,713 (48.83%)   Nonwhite: 17,512 (51.17%)
   Males: 15,672 (45.79%)   Females: 18,553 (54.21%)
   Ages — 0-4: 2,415; 5-17: 6,717; 18-24: 2,785;
   25-44: 9,447; 45-64: 7,552; 65 & older: 5,309
County Pop., 1990: 35,356 (55.0% urban—45.0% rural)
   White: 18,027 (50.99%)   Nonwhite: 17,329 (49.01%)
Households / Persons Per Household, 1998: **12,838** / 2.7
Average Household Income, 1998: $51,755 (rank 32)
1995 Households with Income: Under $15,000—36.45%
   $25,000-49,999—24.52% $75,000 or more—8.52%
Per Capita Personal Income, 1998: $19,461 (rank 18)
Total Personal Income, 1998: $664,412,000
Total Wages & Salaries, 1998: $350,296,000
Avg. Wages, 1998: Week $426 (rank 27); Year $22,157
   FY 1997: Manufacturing —$714 week $18.10 hour
             Services   —$372 week $ 9.30 hour
Labor Force / **Employed** (July 2000): 14,860 / **13,730**
Non-Agri. Employment *in* the County, July 2000: 13,980
   Manufacturing: 1,840 / Nonmanufacturing: 12,140
Unemployed / Rate (July 2000): **1,130** / 7.6%
No. Medicaid Eligibles, FY 1997: 8,614 (24.4% of pop.)
Federal Funds & Grants, 1998: $161,635,000
Cost of Living Index, 1999: 0.99 (average is 1.00)
Average County Millage, 1999: 97.42
Real Property, 1999 Assessed Value: $90,586,427
Real Property, 1998 Assessed Value: $88,498,019
   True Value / No. of Parcels: **$721,664,745** / 16,888
Personal Property, 1999 Assessed Value: $98,414,968
Personal Property, 1998 Assessed Value: $95,417,600
   True Value / No. of Parcels: **$532,047,168** /1,340
Number of Personal Taxpayers, FY 1999: 12,619
Net State Taxable Income, FY 1999: $ 179,150,080
Gross State Income Tax, FY 1999: $ 8,491,267
No. of State Corporate Taxpayers, FY 1999: 644
Corp. Income & Franchise Taxes, FY 1999: $723,939
Retail Sales: 1999—$510,025,546   1998—$431.9 m
Sales Tax / **No. Retailers** (1999): $28,299,836 / **1,350**
No. Vehicles Registered, FY Ending 6/30/99: 30,220
Education, 1990 - Average: 11.6 years (rank 18)
   Graduates: High School 67.3%   College 14.8%
Residents Enrolled in 8 State Universities, Fall 1999: 795
No. Hospitals / Beds / **Doctors** (8/1/2000): **2** / 306 / **103**
Number of Births / **Deaths** (1998): 534 / **446**
Land in Farms / No. Farms (1997): **64,561 acres** / 132

Sheriff; 306 State St; Natchez	(601) 442-2752
Chancery Clerk; Courthouse; Natchez	446-6684
Circuit Clerk; Natchez	446-6326
Tax Assessor; Natchez	446-6732
Tax Collector; Natchez	442-8601

Alcorn County

Established: 1870   Seat: Corinth
Area in Square Miles: 401 (smallest county)
Named for Governor James L. Alcorn
Located in northeast Mississippi bordering Tennessee
Incorporated Places with Estimated Population, 7/1/1998:
   Corinth 12,204   Glen 229   Kossuth 244   Rienzi 358
County Pop., 7/1/99: 33,080 (82.49 persons p/sq. mi.)
County Pop., 7/1/98: 32,716 (Voting Age: 24,763)
   White: 28,607 (87.44%)   Nonwhite: 4,109 (12.56%)
   Males: 15,695 (47.97%)   Females: 17,021 (52.03%)
   Ages — 0-4: 1,971; 5-17: 5,982; 18-24: 2,835;
   25-44: 9,275; 45-64: 7,702; 65 & older: 4,951
County Pop., 1990: 31,722 (37.3% urban—62.7% rural)
   White: 27,993 (88.24%)   Nonwhite: 3,729 (11.76%)
Households / Persons Per Household, 1998: **12,840** / 2.6
Average Household Income, 1998: $49,419 (rank 39)
1995 Households with Income: Under $15,000—32.44%
   $25,000-49,999—28.72% $75,000 or more—5.94%
Per Capita Personal Income, 1998: $19,372 (rank 19)
Total Personal Income, 1998: $634,544,000
Total Wages & Salaries, 1998: $341,481,000
Avg. Wages, 1998: Week $459 (rank 12); Year $23,842
   FY 1997: Manufacturing —$553 week $13.83 hour
             Services   —$409 week $10.23 hour
Labor Force / **Employed** (July 2000): 15,760 / **15,000**
Non-Agri. Employment *in* the County, July 2000: 14,300
   Manufacturing: 5,370 / Nonmanufacturing: 8,930
Unemployed / Rate (July 2000): **760** / 4.8%
No. Medicaid Eligibles, FY 1997: 6,002 (18.9% of pop.)
Federal Funds & Grants, 1998: $142,777,000
Cost of Living Index, 1999: 1.00 (average is 1.00)
Average County Millage, 1999: 81.68
Real Property, 1999 Assessed Value: $79,183,076
Real Property, 1998 Assessed Value: $77,285,719
   True Value / No. of Parcels: **$644,760,445** / 18,146
Personal Property, 1999 Assessed Value: $85,855,590
Personal Property, 1998 Assessed Value: $78,370,452
   True Value / No. of Parcels: **$421,038,046** /1,088
Number of Personal Taxpayers, FY 1999: 12,281
Net State Taxable Income, FY 1999: $ 205,802,628
Gross State Income Tax, FY 1999: $ 9,628,804
No. of State Corporate Taxpayers, FY 1999: 452
Corp. Income & Franchise Taxes, FY 1999: $475,195
Retail Sales: 1999—$398,846,446   1998—$369.6 m
Sales Tax / **No. Retailers** (1999): $25,228,380 / **1,127**
No. Vehicles Registered, FY Ending 6/30/99: 32,148
Education, 1990 - Average: 10.8 years (rank 55)
   Graduates: High School 56.3%   College 9.6%
Residents Enrolled in 8 State Universities, Fall 1999: 313
No. Hospitals / Beds / **Doctors** (8/1/2000): **1** / 164 / **62**
Number of Births / **Deaths** (1998): 460 / **385**
Land in Farms / No. Farms (1997): **80,607 acres** / 449

Sheriff; 305 Fulton St; Corinth	(662) 286-5521
Chancery Clerk; Corinth	286-7702
Circuit Clerk; Courthouse; Corinth	286-7740
Tax Assessor; Corinth	286-7733
Tax Collector; 600 E Waldron; Corinth	286-5713

Amite County

Established: 1809 Seat: Liberty
Area in Square Miles: 732
Named for the Indian word meaning "friendly river"
Located in southwest Mississippi bordering Louisiana
Incorporated Places with Estimated Population, 7/1/1998:
  Centreville 288   Crosby (part) 162
  Gloster 1,304   Liberty 680
County Pop., 7/1/99: 13,906 (19.00 persons p/sq. mi.)
County Pop., 7/1/98: 13,752 (Voting Age: 9,920)
  White: 7,200 (52.36%)   Nonwhite: 6,552 (47.64%)
  Males: 6,623 (48.16%)   Females: 7,129 (51.84%)
  Ages — 0-4: 965; 5-17: 2,867; 18-24: 1,259;
  25-44: 3,612; 45-64: 3,044; 65 & older: 2,005
County Pop., 1990: 13,328 (0.0% urban—100.0% rural)
  White: 7,263 (54.49%)   Nonwhite: 6,065 (45.51%)
Households / Persons Per Household, 1998: **5,042** / 2.7
Average Household Income, 1998: $40,170 (rank 75)
1995 Households with Income: Under $15,000—38.91%
  $25,000-49,999—27.01% $75,000 or more—4.50%
Per Capita Personal Income, 1998: $14,622 (rank 70)
Total Personal Income, 1998: $202,550,000
Total Wages & Salaries, 1998: $54,149,000
Avg. Wages, 1998: Week $403 (rank 41); Year $20,953
  FY 1997: Manufacturing —$484 week $12.10 hour
            Services   —$340 week $ 8.50 hour
Labor Force / **Employed** (July 2000): 6,120 / **5,820**
Non-Agri. Employment *in* the County, July 2000: 2,440
  Manufacturing: 1,020 / Nonmanufacturing: 1,420
Unemployed / Rate (July 2000): **300** / 4.9%
No. Medicaid Eligibles, FY 1997: 3,885 (29.2% of pop.)
Federal Funds & Grants, 1998: $53,694,000
Cost of Living Index, 1999: 0.91 (average is 1.00)
Average County Millage, 1999: 68.31
Real Property, 1999 Assessed Value: $38,448,604
Real Property, 1998 Assessed Value: $36,270,617
  True Value / No. of Parcels: **$287,178,250** / 12,608
Personal Property, 1999 Assessed Value: $22,374,341
Personal Property, 1998 Assessed Value: $21,676,991
  True Value / No. of Parcels: **$95,430,788** / 404
Number of Personal Taxpayers, FY 1999: 3,504
Net State Taxable Income, FY 1999: $ 42,794,672
Gross State Income Tax, FY 1999: $ 1,984,862
No. of State Corporate Taxpayers, FY 1999: 95
Corp. Income & Franchise Taxes, FY 1999: $47,753
Retail Sales: 1999—$47,469,727   1998—$37.6 m
Sales Tax / **No. Retailers** (1999): $2,790,259 / **210**
No. Vehicles Registered, FY Ending 6/30/99: 13,423
Education, 1990 - Average: 10.8 years (rank 59)
  Graduates: High School 57.1%   College 8.7%
Residents Enrolled in 8 State Universities, Fall 1999: 156
No. Hospitals / Beds / **Doctors** (8/1/2000): 0 / 0 / 3
Number of Births / **Deaths** (1998): 165 / **123**
Land in Farms / No. Farms (1997): **118,137 acres** / 471

Sheriff; Liberty	(601) 657-8057
Chancery Clerk; Liberty	657-8022
Circuit Clerk; 243 W Main St; Liberty	657-8932
Tax Assessor & Collector; Liberty	657-8973

Attala County

Established: 1833 Seat: Kosciusko
Area in Square Miles: 737
Named for the Indian Heroine "Attala"
Located in central Mississippi
Incorporated Places with Estimated Population, 7/1/1998:
  Ethel 440   Kosciusko 6,774
  McCool 168   Sallis 130
County Pop., 7/1/99: 18,338 (24.88 persons p/sq. mi.)
County Pop., 7/1/98: 18,404 (Voting Age: 13,619)
  White: 10,642 (57.82%)   Nonwhite: 7,762 (42.18%)
  Males: 8,650 (47.00%)   Females: 9,754 (53.00%)
  Ages — 0-4: 1,217; 5-17: 3,568; 18-24: 1,696;
  25-44: 4,628; 45-64: 4,104; 65 & older: 3,191
County Pop., 1990: 18,481 (37.8% urban—62.2% rural)
  White: 11,081 (59.96%)   Nonwhite: 7,400 (40.04%)
Households / Persons Per Household, 1998: **6,894** / 2.7
Average Household Income, 1998: $45,957 (rank 57)
1995 Households with Income: Under $15,000—39.86%
  $25,000-49,999—27.45% $75,000 or more—4.37%
Per Capita Personal Income, 1998: $17,289 (rank 42)
Total Personal Income, 1998: $316,816,000
Total Wages & Salaries, 1998: $123,234,000
Avg. Wages, 1998: Week $378 (rank 54); Year $19,644
  FY 1997: Manufacturing —$355 week $8.88 hour
            Services   —$383 week $9.58 hour
Labor Force / **Employed** (July 2000): 8,110 / **7,470**
Non-Agri. Employment *in* the County, July 2000: 6,120
  Manufacturing: 1,650 / Nonmanufacturing: 4,470
Unemployed / Rate (July 2000): **640** / 7.9%
No. Medicaid Eligibles, FY 1997: 4,398 (23.8% of pop.)
Federal Funds & Grants, 1998: $99,912,000
Cost of Living Index, 1999: 0.94 (average is 1.00)
Average County Millage, 1999: 95.44
Real Property, 1999 Assessed Value: $45,255,593
Real Property, 1998 Assessed Value: $43,113,597
  True Value / No. of Parcels: **$347,800,000** / 14,931
Personal Property, 1999 Assessed Value: $30,602,354
Personal Property, 1998 Assessed Value: $28,880,860
  True Value / No. of Parcels: **$128,537,815** / 708
Number of Personal Taxpayers, FY 1999: 6,537
Net State Taxable Income, FY 1999: $ 82,803,697
Gross State Income Tax, FY 1999: $ 3,855,490
No. of State Corporate Taxpayers, FY 1999: 187
Corp. Income & Franchise Taxes, FY 1999: $813,439
Retail Sales: 1999—$175,620,121   1998—$155.4 m
Sales Tax / **No. Retailers** (1999): $10,838,539 / **500**
No. Vehicles Registered, FY Ending 6/30/99: 17,277
Education, 1990 - Average: 10.8 years (rank 62)
  Graduates: High School 51.4%   College 10.0%
Residents Enrolled in 8 State Universities, Fall 1999: 387
No. Hospitals / Beds / **Doctors** (8/1/2000): 1 / 72 / 17
Number of Births / **Deaths** (1998): 259 / **306**
Land in Farms / No. Farms (1997): **128,723 acres** / 385

Sheriff; Kosciusko	(662) 289-5556
Chancery Clerk; Kosciusko	289-2921
Circuit Clerk; Kosciusko	289-1471
Tax Assessor & Collector; West	289-4711

The Ultimate Reference on the State

Benton County

Established: 1870   Seat: Ashland
Area in Square Miles: 407
Named for Confederate Army General Samual Benton
Located in northern Mississippi bordering Tennessee
Incorporated Places with Estimated Population, 7/1/1998:
    Ashland 508   Hickory Flat 544
County Pop., 7/1/99: 8,091 (19.88 persons p/sq. mi.)
County Pop., 7/1/98: 8,140 (Voting Age: 5,846)
   White: 4,779 (58.71%)   Nonwhite: 3,361 (41.29%)
   Males: 3,949 (48.51%)   Females: 4,191 (51.49%)
     Ages — 0-4: 564; 5-17: 1,730; 18-24: 786;
     25-44: 2,082; 45-64: 1,721; 65 & older: 1,257
County Pop., 1990: 8,046 (0.0% urban—100.0% rural)
    White: 4,869 (60.51%)   Nonwhite: 3,177 (39.49%)
Households / Persons Per Household, 1998: **2,863** / 2.8
Average Household Income, 1998: $42,025 (rank 70)
1995 Households with Income: Under $15,000—37.42%
   $25,000-49,999—30.38% $75,000 or more—2.45%
Per Capita Personal Income, 1998: $14,881 (rank 68)
Total Personal Income, 1998: $120,328,000
Total Wages & Salaries, 1998: $34,992,000
Avg. Wages, 1998: Week $406 (rank 39); Year $21,101
Labor Force / **Employed** (July 2000): 3,560 / **3,330**
Non-Agri. Employment *in* the County, July 2000: 1,600
    Manufacturing: 470 / Nonmanufacturing: 1,130
Unemployed / Rate (July 2000): **230** / **6.5%**
No. Medicaid Eligibles, FY 1997: 1,814 (22.6% of pop.)
Federal Funds & Grants, 1998: $48,723,000
Cost of Living Index, 1999: 0.93 (average is 1.00)
Average County Millage, 1999: 116.48
Real Property, 1999 Assessed Value: $15,929,403
Real Property, 1998 Assessed Value: $15,366,537
   True Value / No. of Parcels: **$123,594,890** / 7,375
Personal Property, 1999 Assessed Value: $9,340,169
Personal Property, 1998 Assessed Value: $8,354,960
   True Value / No. of Parcels: **$38,454,346** / 198
Number of Personal Taxpayers, FY 1999: 2,928
Net State Taxable Income, FY 1999: $ 33,881,539
Gross State Income Tax, FY 1998: $ 1,534,018
No. of State Corporate Taxpayers, FY 1999: 41
Corp. Income & Franchise Taxes, FY 1999: $12,918
Retail Sales: 1999—$29,899,221   1998—$24.9 m
Sales Tax / **No. Retailers** (1999): $1,584,810 / **151**
No. Vehicles Registered, FY Ending 6/30/99: 6,850
Education, 1990 - Average: 10.2 years (rank 79)
   Graduates: High School 46.4% (rank 79)
                 College 7.8% (rank 75)
Residents Enrolled in 8 State Universities, Fall 1999: 47
No. Hospitals / Beds / **Doctors** (8/1/2000): **0** / 0 / **3**
Number of Births / **Deaths** (1998): 108/ **118**
Land in Farms / No. Farms (1997): **81,444 acres** / 213

Sheriff; Ashland	(662) 224-8941
Chancery Clerk; Ashland	224-6300
Circuit Clerk; Ashland	224-6310
Tax Assessor & Collector; Ashland	224-6315

Bolivar County

Est.: 1836   Seats: Cleveland & Rosedale   892 sq. mi.
Named for South American hero Simon Bolivar
Located in the Delta bordering on Miss. River & Arkansas
Incorporated Places with Estimated Population, 7/1/1998:
Alligator 213   Benoit 609   Beulah 474
Boyle 696   Cleveland 14,834   Duncan 394
Gunnison 608   Merigold 560   Mound Bayou 2,102
Pace 348   Renova 593   Rosedale 2,507
Shaw (pt) 2,283   Shelby 2,686   Winstonville 262
County Pop., 7/1/99: 39,826 (44.65 persons p/sq. mi.)
County Pop., 7/1/98: 40,318 (Voting Age: 27,462)
   White: 14,045 (34.84%)   Nonwhite: 26,273 (65.16%)
   Males: 18,553 (46.02%)   Females: 21,765 (53.98%)
     Ages — 0-4: 3,428; 5-17: 9,428; 18-24: 5,929;
     25-44: 10,333; 45-64: 6,730; 65 & older: 4,470
County Pop., 1990: 41,875 (49.6% urban—50.4% rural)
   White: 15,166 (36.22%)   Nonwhite: 26,709 (63.78%)
Households / Persons Per Household, 1998: **12,765** / 3.1
Average Household Income, 1998: $51,941 (rank 31)
1995 Households with Income: Under $15,000—41.34%
   $25,000-49,999—23.28% $75,000 or more—7.60%
Per Capita Personal Income, 1998: $16,499 (rank 54)
Total Personal Income, 1998: $663,011,000
Total Wages & Salaries, 1998: $319,247,000
Avg. Wages, 1998: Week $430 (rank 25); Year $22,375
   FY 1997:   Manufacturing —$480 week $12.00 hour
                 Services   —$389 week $ 9.73 hour
Labor Force / **Employed** (July 2000): 17,220 / **15,910**
Non-Agri. Employment *in* the County, July 2000: 12,910
    Manufacturing: 2,660 / Nonmanufacturing: 10,250
Unemployed / Rate (July 2000): **1,310** / **7.6%**
No. Medicaid Eligibles, FY 1997: 14,784 (35.3% of pop.)
Federal Funds & Grants, 1998: $202,207,000
Cost of Living Index, 1999: 0.93 (average is 1.00)
Average County Millage, 1999: 110.67
Real Property, 1999 Assessed Value: $100,358,374
Real Property, 1998 Assessed Value: $ 97,099,677
   True Value / No. of Parcels: **$750,114,490** / 21,633
Personal Property, 1999 Assessed Value: $54,367,669
Personal Property, 1998 Assessed Value: $52,343,287
   True Value / No. of Parcels: **$245,715,207** / 1,515
Number of Personal Taxpayers, FY 1999: 12,666
Net State Taxable Income, FY 1999: $ 169,373,527
Gross State Income Tax, FY 1999: $ 7,974,149
Corp. Inc./Franchise Taxes, FY '99: $930,262 (772 payers)
Retail Sales: 1999—$313,949,303   1998—$296.2 m
Sales Tax / **No. Retailers** (1999): $18,947,972 / **1,013**
No. Vehicles Registered, FY Ending 6/30/99: 25,948
Edu., '90 - Avg. 11 yrs; Hi School 54.6%; College 15.2%
Residents Enrolled in 8 State Universities, Fall '99: 1,722
No. Hospitals / Beds / **Doctors** (8/1/2000): **1** / 165 / **41**
Number of Births / **Deaths** (1998): 689 / **411**
Land in Farms / No. Farms (1997): **454,870 acres** / 394

Sheriff: Cleveland/Rosedale	(662) 843-5378/759-3536
Chancery Clerk; Cleveland/Rosedale	843-2071/759-3762
Circuit Clerk; Cleveland/Rosedale	843-2061/759-6521
Tax Assessor & Collector; Cleveland	843-2285/759-6244

CALHOUN COUNTY

Established: 1852   Seat: Pittsboro   Area: 573 sq. mi.
Named for U.S. Vice-President John C. Calhoun
Located in northeast Mississippi
Incorporated Places with Estimated Population, 7/1/1998:
   Big Creek 117   Bruce 2,041   Calhoun City 1,736
   Derma 948   Pittsboro 272   Slate Spring 119
   Vardaman 919
County Pop., 7/1/99: 14,891 (25.99 persons p/sq. mi.)
County Pop., 7/1/98: 14,822 (Voting Age: 11,106)
   White: 10,541 (71.12%)   Nonwhite: 4,281 (28.88%)
   Males: 7,078 (47.75%)   Females: 7,744 (52.25%)
   Ages — 0-4: 965; 5-17: 2,751; 18-24: 1,447;
   25-44: 3,867; 45-64: 3,289; 65 & older: 2,503
County Pop., 1990: 14,908 (0.0% urban—100.0% rural)
   White: 10,840 (72.71%)   Nonwhite: 4,068 (27.29%)
Households / Persons Per Household, 1998: **5,650** / 2.6
Average Household Income, 1998: $47,861 (rank 49)
1995 Households with Income: Under $15,000—33.35%
   $25,000-49,999—32.42% $75,000 or more—3.73%
Per Capita Personal Income, 1998: $18,159 (rank 30)
Total Personal Income, 1998: $270,401,000
Total Wages & Salaries, 1998: $87,670,000
Avg. Wages, 1998: Week $368 (rank 58); Year $19,159
   FY 1997:   Manufacturing —$377 week $9.43 hour
         Services   —$349 week $8.73 hour
Labor Force / **Employed** (July 2000): 6,450 / **6,040**
Non-Agri. Employment *in* the County, July 2000: 4,150
   Manufacturing: 1,740 / Nonmanufacturing: 2,410
Unemployed / Rate (July 2000): **410** / 6.4%
No. Medicaid Eligibles, FY 1997: 3,151 (21.1% of pop.)
Federal Funds & Grants, 1998: $65,557,000
Cost of Living Index, 1999: 0.96 (average is 1.00)
Average County Millage, 1999: 108.05
Real Property, 1999 Assessed Value: $29,358,120
Real Property, 1998 Assessed Value: $28,474,319
   True Value / No. of Parcels: **$232,460,620** / 12,254
Personal Property, 1999 Assessed Value: $22,582,178
Personal Property, 1998 Assessed Value: $22,682,820
   True Value / No. of Parcels: **$107,936,038** / 552
Number of Personal Taxpayers, FY 1999: 5,527
Net State Taxable Income, FY 1999: $ 66,446,375
Gross State Income Tax, FY 1999: $ 2,979,340
No. of State Corporate Taxpayers, FY 1999: 160
Corp. Income & Franchise Taxes, FY 1999: $176,697
Retail Sales: 1999—$86,042,678   1998—$81.7 m
Sales Tax / **No. Retailers** (1999): $5,170,659 / **416**
No. Vehicles Registered, FY Ending 6/30/99: 13,193
Education, 1990 - Average: 10.7 years (rank 67)
   Graduates: High School 52.8%   College 8.2%
Residents Enrolled in 8 State Universities, Fall 1999: 222
No. Hospitals / Beds / **Doctors** (8/1/2000): **1** / 30 / **5**
Number of Births / **Deaths** (1998): 202 / **186**
Land in Farms / No. Farms (1997): **141,817 acres** / 427

Sheriff; Pittsboro	(662) 412-3149
Chancery Clerk; Pittsboro	412-3149
Circuit Clerk; Pittsboro	412-3101
Tax Assessor & Collector; Pittsboro	412-3140

CARROLL COUNTY

Established: 1833   Seats: Carrollton and Vaiden
Area in Square Miles: 634
Named for Charles Carroll, the last surviving signer of the
   Declaration of Independence (d. 1832 at age 95)
Located in central Mississippi
Incorporated Places with Estimated Population, 7/1/1998:
   Carrollton 220   North Carrollton 607   Vaiden 831
County Pop., 7/1/99: 9,967 (15.72 persons p/sq. mi.)
County Pop., 7/1/98: 9,995 (Voting Age: 7,308)
   White: 5,775 (57.78%)   Nonwhite: 4,220 (42.22%)
   Males: 4,804 (48.06%)   Females: 5,191 (51.94%)
   Ages — 0-4: 692; 5-17: 1,995; 18-24: 875;
   25-44: 2,648; 45-64: 2,340; 65 & older: 1,445
County Pop., 1990: 9,237 (0.0% urban—100.0% rural)
   White: 5,571 (60.31%)   Nonwhite: 3,666 (39.69%)
Households / Persons Per Household, 1998: **3,624** / 2.8
Average Household Income, 1998: $46,936 (rank 51)
1995 Households with Income: Under $15,000—36.34%
   $25,000-49,999—28.39% $75,000 or more—5.76%
Per Capita Personal Income, 1998: $17,029 (rank 46)
Total Personal Income, 1998: $170,107,000
Total Wages & Salaries, 1998: $25,959,000
Avg. Wages, 1998: Week $346 (rank 73); Year $17,988
   FY 1997:   Manufacturing —$353 week $8.83 hour
         Services   —$369 week $9.23 hour
Labor Force / **Employed** (July 2000): 4,610 / **4,290**
Non-Agri. Employment *in* the County, July 2000: 1,340
   Manufacturing: 310 / Nonmanufacturing: 1,030
Unemployed / Rate (July 2000): **320** / 6.9%
No. Medicaid Eligibles, FY 1997: 1,807 (19.6% of pop.)
Federal Funds & Grants, 1998: $37,079,000
Cost of Living Index, 1999: 0.94 (average is 1.00)
Average County Millage, 1999: 89.95
Real Property, 1999 Assessed Value: $30,023,275
Real Property, 1998 Assessed Value: $28,403,029
   True Value / No. of Parcels: **$228,402,056** / 8,934
Personal Property, 1999 Assessed Value: $18,052,081
Personal Property, 1998 Assessed Value: $15,943,144
   True Value / No. of Parcels: **$60,980,867** / 254
Number of Personal Taxpayers, FY 1999: 3,105
Net State Taxable Income, FY 1999: $ 39,442,352
Gross State Income Tax, FY 1999: $ 1,801,763
No. of State Corporate Taxpayers, FY 1999: 39
Corp. Income & Franchise Taxes, FY 1999: $5,783
Retail Sales: 1999—$27,305,131   1998—$26.0 m
Sales Tax / **No. Retailers** (1999): $1,499,894 / **238**
No. Vehicles Registered, FY Ending 6/30/99: 10,765
Education, 1990 - Average: 10.7 years (rank 66)
   Graduates: High School 54.0%   College 10.3%
Residents Enrolled in 8 State Universities, Fall 1999: 248
No. Hospitals / Beds / **Doctors** (8/1/2000): **0** / 0 / **3**
Number of Births / **Deaths** (1998): 107 / **102**
Land in Farms / No. Farms (1997): **142,892 acres** / 423

Sheriff; Carrollton	(662) 237-9283
Chancery Clerk; Carrollton/Vaiden	237-9274/464-5476
Circuit Clerk; Carrollton/Vaiden	237-9274/464-5476
Tax Assess./Coll.; Carrollton/Vaiden	237-9217/464-5476

The Ultimate Reference on the State

CHICKASAW COUNTY

Established: 1836   Seats: Houston and Okolona
Area in Square Miles: 503
Named for Chickasaw Indian tribe (means "rebellion")
Located in northeastern Mississippi
Incorporated Places with Estimated Population, 7/1/1998:
    Houston 3,902   New Houlka 540
    Okolona 3,059   Woodland 183
County Pop., 7/1/99: 18,121 (36.03 persons p/sq. mi.)
County Pop., 7/1/98: 18,013 (Voting Age: 14,900)
    White: 10,588 (58.78%)   Nonwhite: 7,425 (41.22%)
    Males: 8,585 (47.66%)   Females: 9,428 (52.34%)
    Ages — 0-4: 1,425; 5-17: 1,688; 18-24: 1,797;
    25-44: 4,966; 45-64: 3,676; 65 & older: 2,461
County Pop., 1990: 18,085 (39.6% urban—60.4% rural)
    White: 11,026 (60.97%)   Nonwhite: 7,059 (39.03%)
Households / Persons Per Household, 1998: **6,451** / 2.8
Average Household Income, 1998: $49,643 (rank 41)
1995 Households with Income: Under $15,000—30.84%
    $25,000-49,999—31.21% $75,000 or more—3.46%
Per Capita Personal Income, 1998: $17,643 (rank 39)
Total Personal Income, 1998: $318,263,000
Total Wages & Salaries, 1998: $152,674,000
Avg. Wages, 1998: Week $373 (rank 56); Year $19,401
    FY 1997: Manufacturing —$373 week $9.33 hour
              Services   —$368 week $9.20 hour
Labor Force / **Employed** (July 2000): 8,350 / **7,690**
Non-Agri. Employment *in* the County, July 2000: 7,990
    Manufacturing: 4,840 / Nonmanufacturing: 3,150
Unemployed / Rate (July 2000): **660** / **7.9%**
No. Medicaid Eligibles, FY 1997: 3,664 (20.3% of pop.)
Federal Funds & Grants, 1998: $81,228,000
Cost of Living Index, 1999: 0.96 (average is 1.00)
Average County Millage, 1999: 122.30
Real Property, 1999 Assessed Value: $37,736,440
Real Property, 1998 Assessed Value: $36,696,170
    True Value / No. of Parcels: **$295,551,820** / 10,497
Personal Property, 1999 Assessed Value: $27,883,524
Personal Property, 1998 Assessed Value: $27,606,365
    True Value / No. of Parcels: **$133,448,068** / 945
Number of Personal Taxpayers, FY 1999: 7,804
Net State Taxable Income, FY 1999: $ 99,071,413
Gross State Income Tax, FY 1999: $ 4,505,370
No. of State Corporate Taxpayers, FY 1999: 323
Corp. Income & Franchise Taxes, FY 1999: $371,569
Retail Sales: 1999—$132,101,630   1998—$126.1 m
Sales Tax / **No. Retailers** (1999): $7,811,762 / **502**
No. Vehicles Registered, FY Ending 6/30/99: 15,634
Education, 1990 - Average: 10.8 years (rank 57)
    Graduates: High School 52.9%   College 9.5%
Residents Enrolled in 8 State Universities, Fall 1999: 290
No. Hospitals / Beds / **Doctors** (8/1/2000): **2** / 94 / **14**
Number of Births / **Deaths** (1998): 310 / **182**
Land in Farms / No. Farms (1997): **138,040 acres** / 447

Sheriff; Houston/Okolona   (662) 456-2339/447-5781
Chancery Clerk; Houston/Okolona   456-2513/447-2092
Circuit Clerk; Houston/Okolona   456-2331/447-2838
Tax Assess./Coll.; Houston/Okolona 456-3327/447-2242

CHOCTAW COUNTY

Established: 1833   Seat: Ackerman
Area in Square Miles: 420
Named for Choctaw Indian tribe (means "separation")
Located in east-central Mississippi
Incorporated Places with Estimated Population, 7/1/1998:
    Ackerman 1,705   French Camp 315
    Mathiston (part) 98 Weir 545
County Pop., 7/1/99: 9,366 (22.30 persons p/sq. mi.)
County Pop., 7/1/98: 9,385 (Voting Age: 6,666)
    White: 6,355 (67.71%)   Nonwhite: 3,030 (32.29%)
    Males: 4,446 (47.37%)   Females: 4,939 (52.63%)
    Ages — 0-4: 636; 5-17: 2,083; 18-24: 790;
    25-44: 2,502; 45-64: 2,080; 65 & older: 1,294
County Pop., 1990: 9,071 (0.0% urban—100.0% rural)
    White: 6,289 (69.33%)   Nonwhite: 2,782 (30.67%)
Households / Persons Per Household, 1998: **3,328** / 2.8
Average Household Income, 1998: $39,728 (rank 77)
1995 Households with Income: Under $15,000—40.89%
    $25,000-49,999—29.29% $75,000 or more—2.61%
Per Capita Personal Income, 1998: $14,063 (rank 73)
Total Personal Income, 1998: $132,205,000
Total Wages & Salaries, 1998: $40,691,000
Avg. Wages, 1998: Week $388 (rank 50); Year $20,188
    FY 1997: Manufacturing —$452 week $11.30 hour
              Services   —$323 week $ 8.08 hour
Labor Force / **Employed** (July 2000): 3,050 / **2,690**
Non-Agri. Employment *in* the County, July 2000: 1,870
    Manufacturing: 420 / Nonmanufacturing: 1,450
Unemployed / Rate (July 2000): **360** / **11.8%**
No. Medicaid Eligibles, FY 1997: 1,952 (21.5% of pop.)
Federal Funds & Grants, 1998: $33,121,000
Cost of Living Index, 1999: 0.91 (average is 1.00)
Average County Millage, 1999: 97.15
Real Property, 1999 Assessed Value: $19,338,630
Real Property, 1998 Assessed Value: $17,897,962
    True Value / No. of Parcels: **$146,009,455** / 8,061
Personal Property, 1999 Assessed Value: $16,973,041
Personal Property, 1998 Assessed Value: $13,228,380
    True Value / No. of Parcels: **$60,575,201** / 273
Number of Personal Taxpayers, FY 1999: 2,722
Net State Taxable Income, FY 1999: $ 34,730,577
Gross State Income Tax, FY 1999: $ 1,582,759
No. of State Corporate Taxpayers, FY 1999: 77
Corp. Income & Franchise Taxes, FY 1999: $97,184
Retail Sales: 1999—$49,304,170   1998—$34.3 m
Sales Tax / **No. Retailers** (1999): $2,549,590 / **195**
No. Vehicles Registered, FY Ending 6/30/99: 8,287
Education, 1990 - Average: 11.0 years (rank 34)
    Graduates: High School 57.6%   College 10.8%
Residents Enrolled in 8 State Universities, Fall 1999: 196
No. Hospitals / Beds / **Doctors** (8/1/2000): **1** / 22 / **4**
Number of Births / **Deaths** (1998): 129 / **85**
Land in Farms / No. Farms (1997): **57,859 acres** / 217

Sheriff; Ackerman   (662) 285-6129
Chancery Clerk; Ackerman   285-6329
Circuit Clerk; Ackerman   285-6245
Tax Assessor & Collector; Ackerman   285-3444

Claiborne County

Established: 1802   Seat: Port Gibson
Area in Square Miles: 494
Named for William C.C. Claiborne, territorial governor
Located in southwest bordering Miss. River & Louisiana
Incorporated Places with Estimated Population, 7/1/1998:
    Port Gibson 1,750
County Pop., 7/1/99: 11,596 (23.47 persons p/sq. mi.)
County Pop., 7/1/98: 11,662 (Voting Age: 8,509)
    White: 1,988 (17.05%)   Nonwhite: 9,674 (82.95%)
    Males: 5,412 (46.41%)   Females: 6,250 (53.59%)
    Ages — 0-4: 788; 5-17: 2,365; 18-24: 2,691;
    25-44: 2,727; 45-64: 1,837; 65 & older: 1,254
County Pop., 1990: 11,370 (0.0% urban—100.0% rural)
    White: 1,994 (17.54%)   Nonwhite: 9,376 (82.46%)
Households / Persons Per Household, 1998: **3,383** / 3.4
Average Household Income, 1998: $49,352 (rank 40)
1995 Households with Income: Under $15,000—47.80%
    $25,000-49,999—18.78% $75,000 or more—4.25%
Per Capita Personal Income, 1998: $14,501 (rank 71)
Total Personal Income, 1998: $166,945,000
Total Wages & Salaries, 1998: $157,918,000
Avg. Wages, 1998: Week $677 (rank 1); Year $35,100
    FY 1997: Manufacturing —$443 week $11.08 hour
                Services   —$475 week $11.88 hour
Labor Force / **Employed** (July 2000): 3,000 / **2,660**
Non-Agri. Employment *in* the County, July 2000: 3,780
    Manufacturing: 600 / Nonmanufacturing: 3,180
Unemployed / Rate (July 2000): **340** / **11.3%**
No. Medicaid Eligibles, FY 1997: 3,373 (29.8% of pop.)
Federal Funds & Grants, 1998: $47,573,000
Cost of Living Index, 1999: 0.89 (average is 1.00)
Average County Millage, 1999: 64.25
Real Property, 1999 Assessed Value: $21,588,908
Real Property, 1998 Assessed Value: $20,210,961
    True Value / No. of Parcels: **$158,136,466** / 7,283
Personal Property, 1999 Assessed Value: $20,264,548
Personal Property, 1998 Assessed Value: $19,451,589
    True Value / No. of Parcels: **$88,503,590** / 271
Number of Personal Taxpayers, FY 1999: 3,489
Net State Taxable Income, FY 1999: $ 40,623,324
Gross State Income Tax, FY 1999: $ 1,886,450
No. of State Corporate Taxpayers, FY 1999: 92
Corp. Income & Franchise Taxes, FY 1999: $137,011
Retail Sales: 1999—$53,082,495   1998—$52.0 m
Sales Tax / **No. Retailers** (1999): $2,684,108 / **195**
No. Vehicles Registered, FY Ending 6/30/99: 9,101
Education, 1990 - Average: 11.3 years (rank 21)
    Graduates: High School 58.7%   College 16.1%
Residents Enrolled in 8 State Universities, Fall 1999: 369
No. Hospitals / Beds / **Doctors** (8/1/2000): **1** / 32 / **5**
Number of Births / **Deaths** (1998): 163 / **109**
Land in Farms / No. Farms (1997): **81,229 acres** / 170

Sheriff; Port Gibson	(601) 437-5161
Chancery Clerk; 503 Main St; Port Gibson	437-4992
Circuit Clerk; Port Gibson	437-5841
Tax Assessor & Collector; Port Gibson	437-5591

Clarke County

Established: 1833   Seat: Quitman
Area in Square Miles: 692
Named for Judge Joshua Clarke, 1st Chancellor of Miss.
Located in southeast Mississippi
Incorporated Places with Estimated Population, 7/1/1998:
    Enterprise 483   Pachuta 276   Quitman 2,839
    Shubuta 596   Stonewall 1,161
County Pop., 7/1/99: 18,445 (26.65 persons p/sq. mi.)
County Pop., 7/1/98: 18,231 (Voting Age: 13,267)
    White: 11,535 (63.27%)   Nonwhite: 6,696 (36.73%)
    Males: 8,650 (47.45%)   Females: 9,581 (52.55%)
    Ages — 0-4: 1,244; 5-17: 3,720; 18-24: 1,707;
    25-44: 4,946; 45-64: 3,853; 65 & older: 2,761
County Pop., 1990: 17,313 (15.6% urban—84.4% rural)
    White: 11,306 (65.30%)   Nonwhite: 6,007 (34.70%)
Households / Persons Per Household, 1998: **6,677** / 2.7
Average Household Income, 1998: $43,744 (rank 66)
1995 Households with Income: Under $15,000—31.95%
    $25,000-49,999—28.89% $75,000 or more—4.12%
Per Capita Personal Income, 1998: $16,013 (rank 59)
Total Personal Income, 1998: $292,066,000
Total Wages & Salaries, 1998: $97,549,000
Avg. Wages, 1998: Week $390 (rank 49); Year $20,304
    FY 1997: Manufacturing —$419 week $10.48 hour
                Services   —$331 week $ 8.28 hour
Labor Force / **Employed** (July 2000): 9,130 / **8,340**
Non-Agri. Employment *in* the County, July 2000: 4,810
    Manufacturing: 2,370 / Nonmanufacturing: 2,440
Unemployed / Rate (July 2000): **790** / 8.7%
No. Medicaid Eligibles, FY 1997: 2,805 (16.2% of pop.)
Federal Funds & Grants, 1998: $76,282,000
Cost of Living Index, 1999: 0.95 (average is 1.00)
Average County Millage, 1999: 90.39
Real Property, 1999 Assessed Value: $40,372,195
Real Property, 1998 Assessed Value: $37,809,083
    True Value / No. of Parcels: **$306,122,500** / 14,700
Personal Property, 1999 Assessed Value: $34,487,258
Personal Property, 1998 Assessed Value: $32,437,470
    True Value / No. of Parcels: **$159,673,234** / 802
Number of Personal Taxpayers, FY 1999: 6,362
Net State Taxable Income, FY 1999: $ 82,050,304
Gross State Income Tax, FY 1999: $ 3,741,852
No. of State Corporate Taxpayers, FY 1999: 117
Corp. Income & Franchise Taxes, FY 1999: $99,441
Retail Sales: 1999—$88,083,518   1998—$92.7 m
Sales Tax / **No. Retailers** (1999): $4,663,624 / **422**
No. Vehicles Registered, FY Ending 6/30/99: 15,804
Education, 1990 - Average: 11.1 years (rank 33)
    Graduates: High School 61.6%   College 8.2%
Residents Enrolled in 8 State Universities, Fall 1999: 203
No. Hospitals / Beds / **Doctors** (8/1/2000): **1** / 32 / **9**
Number of Births / **Deaths** (1998): 223 / **161**
Land in Farms / No. Farms (1997): **52,018 acres** / 269

Sheriff; 444 W, Donald St; Quitman	(601) 776-5252
Chancery Clerk; Courthouse; Quitman	776-2126
Circuit Clerk; Courthouse; Quitman	776-3111
Tax Assessor & Collector; Quitman	776-6931

The Ultimate Reference on the State

CLAY COUNTY

Established: 1871*/1876 *First est. as "Colfax"
Seat: West Point Area in Square Miles: 415
Named for Henry Clay, Kentucky statesman
Located in the northeast part of the state
Incorporated Places with Estimated Population, 7/1/1998:
  West Point 8,848
County Pop., 7/1/99: 21,657 (52.19 persons p/sq. mi.)
County Pop., 7/1/98: 21,637 (Voting Age: 15,307)
  White: 9,581 (44.28%) Nonwhite: 12,056 (55.72%)
  Males: 10,210 (47.19%) Females: 11,427 (52.81%)
  Ages — 0-4: 1,628; 5-17: 4,702; 18-24: 2,355;
  25-44: 5,989; 45-64: 4,119; 65 & older: 2,844
County Pop., 1990: 21,120 (40.2% urban—59.8% rural)
  White: 9,693 (45.89%) Nonwhite: 11,427 (54.11%)
Households / Persons Per Household, 1998: **7,415** / 2.9
Average Household Income, 1998: $51,713 (rank 33)
1995 Households with Income: Under $15,000—34.62%
  $25,000-49,999—28.94% $75,000 or more—6.00%
Per Capita Personal Income, 1998: $17,735 (rank 37)
Total Personal Income, 1998: $383,476,000
Total Wages & Salaries, 1998: $222,045,000
Avg. Wages, 1998: Week $486 (rank 8); Year $25,247
  FY 1997: Manufacturing —$603 week $15.08 hour
            Services   —$383 week $ 9.58 hour
Labor Force / **Employed** (July 2000): 9,430 / **8,640**
Non-Agri. Employment *in* the County, July 2000: 8,900
  Manufacturing: 4,040 / Nonmanufacturing: 4,860
Unemployed / Rate (July 2000): **790** / 8.4%
No. Medicaid Eligibles, FY 1997: 5,327 (25.2% of pop.)
Federal Funds & Grants, 1998: $95,285,000
Cost of Living Index, 1999: 0.95 (average is 1.00)
Average County Millage, 1999: 90.40
Real Property, 1999 Assessed Value: $54,997,788
Real Property, 1998 Assessed Value: $52,970,893
  True Value / No. of Parcels: **$427,394,979** / 11,839
Personal Property, 1999 Assessed Value: $42,587,754
Personal Property, 1998 Assessed Value: $44,582,152
  True Value / No. of Parcels: **$229,282,489** / 809
Number of Personal Taxpayers, FY 1999: 7,679
Net State Taxable Income, FY 1999: $ 122,600,176
Gross State Income Tax, FY 1999: $ 5,808,918
No. of State Corporate Taxpayers, FY 1999: 181
Corp. Income & Franchise Taxes, FY 1999: $312,766
Retail Sales: 1999—$173,473,998 1998—$144.9 m
Sales Tax / **No. Retailers** (1999): $10,247,115 / **566**
No. Vehicles Registered, FY Ending 6/30/99: 16,769
Education, 1990 - Average: 11.3 years (rank 24)
  Graduates: High School 60.44% College 12.9%
Residents Enrolled in 8 State Universities, Fall 1999: 510
No. Hospitals / Beds / **Doctors** (8/1/2000): **1** / 60 / **23**
Number of Births / **Deaths** (1998): 355 / **242**
Land in Farms / No. Farms (1997): **131,666 acres** / 367

Sheriff; West Point (662) 494-5152
Chancery Clerk; 205 Court St; West Point 494-3124
Circuit Clerk; 205 Court St; West Point 494-3384
Tax Assessor & Collector; West Point 494-3432

COAHOMA COUNTY

Established: 1836 Seat: Clarksdale
Area in Square Miles: 559
Named for the Indian word meaning "red panther"
Located in northwest bordering Miss. River & Arkansas
Incorporated Places with Estimated Population, 7/1/1998:
  Clarksdale 20,461 Coahoma 250 Friars Point 1,337
  Jonestown 1,462 Lula 218 Lyon 427
County Pop., 7/1/99: 31,094 (55.62 persons p/sq. mi.)
County Pop., 7/1/98: 31,089 (Voting Age: 20,896)
  White: 10,344 (33.27%) Nonwhite: 20,745 (66.73%)
  Males: 14,146 (45.50%) Females: 16,943 (54.50%)
  Ages — 0-4: 2,698; 5-17: 7,495; 18-24: 3,222;
  25-44: 7,950; 45-64: 5,887; 65 & older: 3,837
County Pop., 1990: 31,665 (62.3% urban—37.7% rural)
  White: 10,984 (34.69%) Nonwhite: 20,681 (65.31%)
Households / Persons Per Household, 1998: **10,432** / 3.0
Average Household Income, 1998: $50,152 (rank 37)
1995 Households with Income: Under $15,000—43.79%
  $25,000-49,999—22.64% $75,000 or more—5.27%
Per Capita Personal Income, 1998: $16,727 (rank 49)
Total Personal Income, 1998: $523,159,000
Total Wages & Salaries, 1998: $257,451,000
Avg. Wages, 1998: Week $413 (rank 36); Year $21,488
  FY 1997: Manufacturing —$512 week $12.80 hour
            Services   —$392 week $ 9.80 hour
Labor Force / **Employed** (July 2000): 11,910 / **10,810**
Non-Agri. Employment *in* the County, July 2000: 10,440
  Manufacturing: 1,180 / Nonmanufacturing: 9,260
Unemployed / Rate (July 2000): **1,100** / 9.2%
No. Medicaid Eligibles, FY 1997: 12,039 (38% of pop.)
Federal Funds & Grants, 1998: $180,433,000
Cost of Living Index, 1999: 0.96 (average is 1.00)
Average County Millage, 1999: 84.76
Real Property, 1999 Assessed Value: $83,117,542
Real Property, 1998 Assessed Value: $81,059,008
  True Value / No. of Parcels: **$616,367,947** / 15,413
Personal Property, 1999 Assessed Value: $49,800,864
Personal Property, 1998 Assessed Value: $47,615,391
  True Value / No. of Parcels: **$237,620,704** / 1,196
Number of Personal Taxpayers, FY 1999: 9,796
Net State Taxable Income, FY 1999: $ 133,488,845
Gross State Income Tax, FY 1999: $ 6,376,446
No. of State Corporate Taxpayers, FY 1999: 693
Corp. Income & Franchise Taxes, FY 1999: $738,919
Retail Sales: 1999—$283,976,098 1998—$267.2 m
Sales Tax / **No. Retailers** (1999): $17,392,568 / **840**
No. Vehicles Registered, FY Ending 6/30/99: 19,372
Education, 1990 - Average: 11.0 years (rank 44)
  Graduates: High School 54.0% College 14.7%
Residents Enrolled in 8 State Universities, Fall 1999: 731
No. Hospitals / Beds / **Doctors** (8/1/2000): **1** / 175 / **56**
Number of Births / **Deaths** (1998): 629 / **355**
Land in Farms / No. Farms (1997): **272,809 acres** / 181

Sheriff; Clarksdale (662) 624-3081
Chancery Clerk; Clarksdale 624-3000
Circuit Clerk; Clarksdale 624-3014
Tax Assessor & Collector; Clarksdale 624-3020

COPIAH COUNTY

Established: 1823 Seat: Hazlehurst
Area in Square Miles: 779
Named for the Indian word meaning "calling panther"
Located in southwest Mississippi
Incorporated Places with Estimated Population, 7/1/1998:
  Beauregard 226   Crystal Springs 5,832
  Georgetown 350   Hazlehurst 4,228   Wesson 1,520
County Pop., 7/1/99: 28,892 (37.09 persons p/sq. mi.)
County Pop., 7/1/98: 28,944 (Voting Age: 20,794)
    White: 13,658 (47.19%)   Nonwhite: 15,286 (52.81%)
    Males: 13,793 (47.65%)   Females: 15,151 (52.35%)
    Ages — 0-4: 2,122; 5-17: 6,028; 18-24: 3,490;
    25-44: 7,725; 45-64: 5,672; 65 & older: 3,907
County Pop., 1990: 27,592 (35.7% urban—64.3% rural)
    White: 13,608 (49.32%)   Nonwhite: 13,984 (50.68%)
Households / Persons Per Household, 1998: **9,705** / 3.0
Average Household Income, 1998: $46,202 (rank 54)
1995 Households with Income: Under $15,000—38.27%
    $25,000-49,999—26.40% $75,000 or more—4.4%
Per Capita Personal Income, 1998: $15,555 (rank 63)
Total Personal Income, 1998: $448,404,000
Total Wages & Salaries, 1998: $150,462,000
Avg. Wages, 1998: Week $371 (rank 57); Year $19,306
    FY 1997: Manufacturing —$405 week $10.13 hour
              Services   —$356 week $ 8.90 hour
Labor Force / **Employed** (July 2000): 11,440 / **10,490**
Non-Agri. Employment in the County, July 2000: 7,500
    Manufacturing: 2,490 / Nonmanufacturing: 5,010
Unemployed / Rate (July 2000): **950** / 8.3%
No. Medicaid Eligibles, FY 1997: 6,851 (24.8% of pop.)
Federal Funds & Grants, 1998: $140,436,000
Cost of Living Index, 1999: 0.95 (average is 1.00)
Average County Millage, 1999: 95.88
Real Property, 1999 Assessed Value: $53,503,236
Real Property, 1998 Assessed Value: $50,942,969
    True Value / No. of Parcels: **$414,680,060** / 18,424
Personal Property, 1999 Assessed Value: $48,619,259
Personal Property, 1998 Assessed Value: $44,256,312
    True Value / No. of Parcels: **$200,248,827** / 846
Number of Personal Taxpayers, FY 1999: 10,142
Net State Taxable Income, FY 1999: $ 128,097,187
Gross State Income Tax, FY 1999: $ 5,903,542
No. of State Corporate Taxpayers, FY 1999: 291
Corp. Income & Franchise Taxes, FY 1999: $192,224
Retail Sales: 1999—$160,035,940   1998—$147.2 m
Sales Tax / **No. Retailers** (1999): $9,817,065 / **561**
No. Vehicles Registered, FY Ending 6/30/99: 23,751
Education, 1990 - Average: 11.2 years (rank 26)
    Graduates: High School 61.1%   College 9.4%
Residents Enrolled in 8 State Universities, Fall 1999: 353
No. Hospitals / Beds / **Doctors** (8/1/2000): **1** / 49 / **14**
Number of Births / **Deaths** (1998): 435 / **287**
Land in Farms / No. Farms (1997): **120,681 acres** / 510

Sheriff; Hazlehurst	(601) 894-3011
Chancery Clerk; Courthouse; Hazlehurst	894-3021
Circuit Clerk; Courthouse; Hazlehurst	894-1241
Tax Assessor & Collector; Hazlehurst	894-2731

COVINGTON COUNTY

Established: 1819 Seat: Collins
Area in Square Miles: 416
Named for Gen. Leonard Covington, killed in 1812 War
Located in southeast Mississippi
Incorporated Places with Estimated Population, 7/1/1998:
    Collins 2,657   Mount Olive 963   Seminary 236
County Pop., 7/1/99: 17,889 (43.00 persons p/sq. mi.)
County Pop., 7/1/98: 17,802 (Voting Age: 12,549)
    White: 11,116 (62.44%)   Nonwhite: 6,686 (37.56%)
    Males: 8,577 (48.18%)   Females: 9,225 (51.82%)
    Ages — 0-4: 1,381; 5-17: 3,872; 18-24: 1,806;
    25-44: 4,788; 45-64: 3,820; 65 & older: 2,135
County Pop., 1990: 16,527 (15.4% urban—84.6% rural)
    White: 10,697 (64.72%)   Nonwhite: 5,830 (35.28%)
Households / Persons Per Household, 1998: **6,199** / 2.9
Average Household Income, 1998: $48,274 (rank 45)
1995 Households with Income: Under $15,000—36.81%
    $25,000-49,999—30.18% $75,000 or more—4.34%
Per Capita Personal Income, 1998: $16,885 (rank 48)
Total Personal Income, 1998: $299,250,000
Total Wages & Salaries, 1998: $92,501,000
Avg. Wages, 1998: Week $353 (rank 66); Year $18,347
    FY 1997: Manufacturing —$331 week $8.28 hour
              Services   —$358 week $8.95 hour
Labor Force / **Employed** (July 2000): 8,340 / **7,910**
Non-Agri. Employment in the County, July 2000: 4,510
    Manufacturing: 1,720 / Nonmanufacturing: 2,890
Unemployed / Rate (July 2000): **430** / 5.2%
No. Medicaid Eligibles, FY 1997: 3,904 (23.6% of pop.)
Federal Funds & Grants, 1998: $78,039,000
Cost of Living Index, 1999: 0.98 (average is 1.00)
Average County Millage, 1999: 75.05
Real Property, 1999 Assessed Value: $333,216,888
Real Property, 1998 Assessed Value: $32,022,836
    True Value / No. of Parcels: **$262,134,070** / 13,494
Personal Property, 1999 Assessed Value: $32,123,375
Personal Property, 1998 Assessed Value: $30,456,270
    True Value / No. of Parcels: **$142,273,797** / 515
Number of Personal Taxpayers, FY 1999: 6,106
Net State Taxable Income, FY 1999: $ 73,771,946
Gross State Income Tax, FY 1999: $ 3,374,191
No. of State Corporate Taxpayers, FY 1999: 143
Corp. Income & Franchise Taxes, FY 1999: $159,905
Retail Sales: 1999—$122,542,424   1998—$104.8 m
Sales Tax / **No. Retailers** (1999): $6,696,113 / **436**
No. Vehicles Registered, FY Ending 6/30/99: 17,638
Education, 1990 - Average: 11.0 years (rank 43)
    Graduates: High School 55.5%   College 8.6%
Residents Enrolled in 8 State Universities, Fall 1999: 248
No. Hospitals / Beds / **Doctors** (8/1/2000): **1** / 82 / **10**
Number of Births / **Deaths** (1998): 320 / **230**
Land in Farms / No. Farms (1997): **85,666 acres** / 475

Sheriff; Collins	(601) 765-8281
Chancery Clerk; Collins	765-4242
Circuit Clerk; Collins	765-6506
Tax Assessor & Collector; Collins	765-6402

The Ultimate Reference on the State

DeSoto County

Established: 1836   Seat: Hernando   Area: 483 sq. mi.
Named for Hernando DeSoto, discoverer of Miss. River
In extreme northwest bordering Miss. River & Tenn.
Incorporated Places with Estimated Population, 7/1/1998:
   Hernando 4,088   Horn Lake 13,885   Memphis 90
   Olive Branch 12,063   Southaven 23,434
County Pop., 7/1/99: 102,131 (211.45 persons p/sq. mi.)
County Pop., 7/1/98: 96,897 (Voting Age: 70,406)
   White: 82,754 (85.40%)   Nonwhite: 14,143 (14.60%)
   Males: 47,569 (49.09%)   Females: 49,328 (50.91%)
   Ages — 0-4: 7,308; 5-17: 19,183; 18-24: 8,976;
   25-44: 30,561; 45-64: 22,114; 65 & older: 8,755
County Pop., 1990: 67,910 (53.0% urban—% rural)
   White: 58,901 (86.73%)   Nonwhite: 9,009 (13.27%)
Households / Persons Per Household, 1998: **32,947** / 2.9
Average Household Income, 1998: $72,554 (rank 1)
1995 Households with Income: Under $15,000—18.12%
   $25,000-49,999—35.82% $75,000 or more—10.01%
Per Capita Personal Income, 1998: $24,616 (rank 3)
Total Personal Income, 1998: $2,390,466,000
Total Wages & Salaries, 1998: $761,713,000
Avg. Wages, 1998: Week $452 (rank 18); Year $23,492
   FY 1997: Manufacturing —$575 week $14.38 hour
             Services   —$360 week $ 9.00 hour
Labor Force / **Employed** (July 2000): 56,120 / **54,600**
Non-Agri. Employment *in* the County, July 2000: 32,070
   Manufacturing: 7,960 / Nonmanufacturing: 24,110
Unemployed / Rate (July 2000): **1,520** / 2.9%
No. Medicaid Eligibles, FY 1997: 6,514 (9.6% of pop.)
Federal Funds & Grants, 1998: $236,225,000
Cost of Living Index, '99: 1.22 (avg. 1.00) [state's highest]
Average County Millage, 1999: 86.39
Real Property, 1999 Assessed Value: $392,362,600
Real Property, 1998 Assessed Value: $356,612,340
   True Value / No. Parcels: **$3,080,036,670** / 42,952
Personal Property, 1999 Assessed Value: $231,082,101
Personal Property, 1998 Assessed Value: $207,251,293
   True Value / No. of Parcels: **$962,078,155** / 2,676
Number of Personal Taxpayers, FY 1999: 36,549
Net State Taxable Income, FY 1999: $ 749,157,892
Gross State Income Tax, FY 1999: $ 35,738,482
No. of State Corporate Taxpayers, FY 1999: 842
Corp. Income & Franchise Taxes, FY 1999: $1,935,688
Retail Sales: 1999—$1,098,139,877   1998—$896.5 m
Sales Tax / **No. Retailers** (1999): $66,264,975 / **2,021**
No. Vehicles Registered, FY Ending 6/30/99: 95,319
Education, 1990 - Average: 11.7 years (rank 16)
   Graduates: High School 71.2%   College 9.5%
Residents Enrolled in 8 State Universities, Fall 1999: 967
No. Hospitals / Beds / **Doctors** (8/1/2000): 2 / 206 / 320
Number of Births / **Deaths** (1998): 1,570 / **674**
Land in Farms / No. Farms (1997): **149,312 acres** / 467

Sheriff; 311 W. South St; Hernando	(662) 429-1470
Chancery Clerk; 2535 Hwy 51S; Hernando	429-1318
Circuit Clerk; 2535 Hwy 51S; Hernando	429-1325
Tax Assessor; 2535 Hwy 51S; Hernando	429-1335
Tax Collector; 2535 Hwy 51S; Hernando	429-1340

Forrest County

Established: 1908   Seat: Hattiesburg
Area in Square Miles: 469
Named for Confederate General Nathan Bedford Forrest
Located in southwest Mississippi
Incorporated Places with Estimated Population, 7/1/1998:
   Hattiesburg (part) 45,996   Petal 8,888
County Pop., 7/1/99: 74,927 (159.76 persons p/sq. mi.)
County Pop., 7/1/98: 74,364 (Voting Age: 55,769)
   White: 49,062 (65.98%)   Nonwhite: 25,302 (34.02%)
   Males: 34,703 (46.67%)   Females: 39,661 (53.33%)
   Ages — 0-4: 5,310 5-17: 13,285; 18-24: 12,666;
   25-44: 20,924; 45-64: 13,639; 65 & older: 8,540
County Pop., 1990: 68,314 (75.9% urban—24.1% rural)
   White: 46,626 (68.25%)   Nonwhite: 21,688 (31.75%)
Households / Persons Per Household, 1998: **27,417** / 2.7
Average Household Income, 1998: $52,468 (rank 26)
1995 Households with Income: Under $15,000—37.82%
   $25,000-49,999—26.10% $75,000 or more—6.18%
Per Capita Personal Income, 1998: $19,313 (rank 20)
Total Personal Income, 1998: $1,438,540,000
Total Wages & Salaries, 1998: $905,060,000
Avg. Wages, 1998: Week $465 (rank 11); Year $24,167
   FY 1997: Manufacturing —$505 week $12.63 hour
             Services   —$510 week $12.75 hour
Labor Force / **Employed** (July 2000): 34,630 / **32,940**
Non-Agri. Employment *in* the County, July 2000: 36,860
   Manufacturing: 4,150 / Nonmanufacturing: 32,710
Unemployed / Rate (July 2000): **1,690** / 4.9%
No. Medicaid Eligibles, FY 1997: 13,494 (19.7% of pop.)
Federal Funds & Grants, 1998: $361,012,000
Cost of Living Index, 1999: 1.02 (average is 1.00)
Average County Millage, 1999: 98.26
Real Property, 1999 Assessed Value: $190,361,304
Real Property, 1998 Assessed Value: $184,591,358
   True Value / No. Parcels: **$1,501,860,890** / 35,194
Personal Property, 1999 Assessed Value: $126,500,065
Personal Property, 1998 Assessed Value: $110,896,415
   True Value / No. of Parcels: **$561,644,074** / 2,472
Number of Personal Taxpayers, FY 1999: 27,162
Net State Taxable Income, FY 1999: $ 471,304,567
Gross State Income Tax, FY 1999: $ 22,803,208
No. of State Corporate Taxpayers, FY 1999: 1,378
Corp. Income & Franchise Taxes, FY 1999: $3,981,183
Retail Sales: 1999—$954,108,853   1998—$902.8 m
Sales Tax / **No. Retailers** (1999): $55,946,797 / **2,172**
No. Vehicles Registered, FY Ending 6/30/99: 51,285
Education, 1990 - Average: 12.1 years (rank 8)
   Graduates: High School 72.1%   College 19.8%
Residents Enrolled in 8 State Universities, Fall '99: 2,328
No. Hospitals / Beds / **Doctors** (8/1/2000): 1 / 537 / 345
Number of Births / **Deaths** (1998): 1,076 / **707**
Land in Farms / No. Farms (1997): **46,036 acres** / 291

Sheriff; Hattiesburg	(601) 544-7800
Chancery Clerk; Hattiesburg	545-6014
Circuit Clerk; Hattiesburg	544-6014
Tax Assessor; Hattiesburg	545-6130
Tax Collector; Hattiesburg	582-8228

FRANKLIN COUNTY

Established: 1809   Seat: Meadville
Area in Square Miles: 566
Named for Ben Franklin, colonial statesman & scientist
Located in southwest Mississippi
Incorporated Places with Estimated Population, 7/1/1998:
    Bude 950   Meadville 411   Roxie 556
County Pop., 7/1/99: 8,160 (14.42 persons p/sq. mi.)
County Pop., 7/1/98: 8,319 (Voting Age: 5,972)
    White: 5,095 (61.25)   Nonwhite: 3,224 (38.75%)
    Males: 3,969 (47.71%)   Females: 4,350 (52.29%)
    Ages — 0-4: 609; 5-17: 1,738; 18-24: 682;
    25-44: 2,237; 45-64: 1,774; 65 & older: 1,279
County Pop., 1990: 8,377 (0.0% urban—100.0% rural)
    White: 5,292 (63.17%)   Nonwhite: 3,085 (36.83%)
Households / Persons Per Household, 1998: **3,066** / 2.7
Average Household Income, 1998: $38,651 (rank 81)
1995 Households with Income: Under $15,000—39.04%
    $25,000-49,999—24.15% $75,000 or more—4.33%
Per Capita Personal Income, 1998: $14,300 (rank 72)
Total Personal Income, 1998: $118,507,000
Total Wages & Salaries, 1998: $45,128,000
Avg. Wages, 1998: Week $403 (rank 40); Year $20,961
    FY 1997: Manufacturing —$400 week $10.00 hour
        Services   —$366 week $ 9.15 hour
Labor Force / **Employed** (July 2000): 3,430 / **3,160**
Non-Agri. Employment *in* the County, July 2000: 2,110
    Manufacturing: 510 / Nonmanufacturing: 1,600
Unemployed / Rate (July 2000): **270** / 7.9%
No. Medicaid Eligibles, FY 1997: 1,875 (22.4% of pop.)
Federal Funds & Grants, 1998: $36,408,000
Cost of Living Index, 1999: 0.92 (average is 1.00)
Average County Millage, 1999: 89.35
Real Property, 1999 Assessed Value: $19,903,352
Real Property, 1998 Assessed Value: $19,063,361
    True Value / No. of Parcels: **$151,481,610** / 8,667
Personal Property, 1999 Assessed Value: $12,367,565
Personal Property, 1998 Assessed Value: $11,684,811
    True Value / No. of Parcels: **$50,527,737** / 320
Number of Personal Taxpayers, FY 1999: 2,428
Net State Taxable Income, FY 1999: $ 31,874,092
Gross State Income Tax, FY 1999: $ 1,458,779
No. of State Corporate Taxpayers, FY 1999: 68
Corp. Income & Franchise Taxes, FY 1999: $116,259
Retail Sales: 1999—$27,485,107   1998—$30.5 m
Sales Tax / **No. Retailers** (1999): $1,569,765 / **165**
No. Vehicles Registered, FY Ending 6/30/99: 8,159
Education, 1990 - Average: 10.9 years (rank 53)
    Graduates: High School 58.1%   College 7.4%
Residents Enrolled in 8 State Universities, Fall 1999: 132
No. Hospitals / Beds / **Doctors** (8/1/2000): **1** / 49 / **4**
Number of Births / **Deaths** (1998): 132 / **126**
Land in Farms / No. Farms (1997): **42,495 acres** / 158

Sheriff; Meadville	(601) 384-2323
Chancery Clerk; Meadville	384-2330
Circuit Clerk; Meadville	384-2320
Tax Assessor & Collector; Meadville	384-2359

GEORGE COUNTY

Established: 1910   Seat: Lucedale
Area in Square Miles: 483
Named for U.S. Senator J.Z. George, jurist & statesman
Located in southeast Mississippi bordering Alabama
Incorporated Places with Estimated Population, 7/1/1998:
    Lucedale 3,041
County Pop., 7/1/99: 20,185 (41.79 persons p/sq. mi.)
County Pop., 7/1/98: 19,645 (Voting Age: 13,917)
    White: 17,531 (89.24%)   Nonwhite: 2,114 (10.76%)
    Males: 9,665 (49.20%)   Females: 9,980 (50.80%)
    Ages — 0-4: 1,431; 5-17: 4,297; 18-24: 1,909;
    25-44: 5,498; 45-64: 4,276; 65 & older: 2,234
County Pop., 1990: 16,673 (15.7% urban—84.3% rural)
    White: 15,007 (90.00%)   Nonwhite: 1,666 (10.00%)
Households / Persons Per Household, 1998: **6,773** / 2.9
Average Household Income, 1998: $47,955 (rank 48)
1995 Households with Income: Under $15,000—31.12%
    $25,000-49,999—28.81% $75,000 or more—5.69%
Per Capita Personal Income, 1998: $16,572 (rank 51)
Total Personal Income, 1998: $324,818,000
Total Wages & Salaries, 1998: $78,162,000
Avg. Wages, 1998: Week $360 (rank 60); Year $18,698
    FY 1997: Manufacturing —$392 week $9.80 hour
        Services   —$375 week $9.38 hour
Labor Force / **Employed** (July 2000): 9,250 / **8,420**
Non-Agri. Employment *in* the County, July 2000: 4,080
    Manufacturing: 490 / Nonmanufacturing: 3,590
Unemployed / Rate (July 2000): **830** / 9.0%
No. Medicaid Eligibles, FY 1997: 2,965 (17.8% of pop.)
Federal Funds & Grants, 1998: $71,784,000
Cost of Living Index, 1999: 0.97 (average is 1.00)
Average County Millage, 1999: 120.72
Real Property, 1999 Assessed Value: $37,443,535
Real Property, 1998 Assessed Value: $36,202,886
    True Value / No. of Parcels: **$307,052,306** / 13,476
Personal Property, 1999 Assessed Value: $25,177,569
Personal Property, 1998 Assessed Value: $22,631,320
    True Value / No. of Parcels: **$89,431,309** / 650
Number of Personal Taxpayers, FY 1999: 7,006
Net State Taxable Income, FY 1999: $ 100,864,815
Gross State Income Tax, FY 1999: $ 4,634,594
No. of State Corporate Taxpayers, FY 1999: 183
Corp. Income & Franchise Taxes, FY 1999: $228,988
Retail Sales: 1999—$133,423,547   1998—$137.2 m
Sales Tax / **No. Retailers** (1999): $8,113,888 / **458**
No. Vehicles Registered, FY Ending 6/30/99: 17,330
Education, 1990 - Average: 11.0 years (rank 35)
    Graduates: High School 58.8%   College 8.3%
Residents Enrolled in 8 State Universities, Fall 1999: 183
No. Hospitals / Beds / **Doctors** (8/1/2000): **1** / 53 / **40**
Number of Births / **Deaths** (1998): 365 / **171**
Land in Farms / No. Farms (1997): **41,744 acres** / 419

Sheriff; 355 Cox St, Suite B; Lucedale	(601) 947-4811
Chancery Clerk; 355 Cox St, Ste A; Lucedale	947-4801
Circuit Clerk; 355 Cox St, Ste C; Lucedale	947-4881
Tax Assessor & Collector; Lucedale	947-7541

GREENE COUNTY

Established: 1811 Seat: Leaksville
Area in Square Miles: 718
Named for Nathaniel Greene, Revolutionary War hero
Located in southeast Mississippi bordering Alabama
Incorporated Places with Estimated Population, 7/1/1998:
  Leaksville 1,111   McLain 606
  State Line (part) 269
County Pop., 7/1/99: 12,630 (17.59 persons p/sq. mi.)
County Pop., 7/1/98: 11,766 (Voting Age: 8,487)
  White: 8,869 (75.38%)   Nonwhite: 2,897 (24.62%)
  Males: 6,264 (53.24%)   Females: 5,502 (46.76%)
  Ages — 0-4: 784; 5-17: 2,495; 18-24: 1,155;
  25-44: 3,706; 45-64: 2,381; 65 & older: 1,245
County Pop., 1990: 10,220 (0.0% urban—100.0% rural)
  White: 7,987 (78.15%)   Nonwhite: 2,233 (21.85%)
Households / Persons Per Household, 1998: **4,136** / 3.1
Average Household Income, 1998: $39,833 (rank 78)
1995 Households with Income: Under $15,000—36.26%
  $25,000-49,999—31.10% $75,000 or more—3.45%
Per Capita Personal Income, 1998: $12,833 (rank 80)
Total Personal Income, 1998: $163,559,000
Total Wages & Salaries, 1998: $41,702,000
Avg. Wages, 1998: Week $348 (rank 70); Year $18,074
  FY 1997: Manufacturing —$349 week $8.73 hour
           Services: —$318 week $7.95 hour
Labor Force / **Employed** (July 2000): 5,790 / **5,250**
Non-Agri. Employment *in* the County, July 2000: 2,140
  Manufacturing: 360 / Nonmanufacturing: 1,780
Unemployed / Rate (July 2000): **540** / 9.3%
No. Medicaid Eligibles, FY 1997: 2,257 (22.1% of pop.)
Federal Funds & Grants, 1998: $37,010,000
Cost of Living Index, 1999: 0.92 (average is 1.00)
Average County Millage, 1999: 102.99
Real Property, 1999 Assessed Value: $25,815,520
Real Property, 1998 Assessed Value: $24,456,924
  True Value / No. of Parcels: **$191,518,772** / 9,709
Personal Property, 1999 Assessed Value: $14,379,103
Personal Property, 1998 Assessed Value: $13,802,497
  True Value / No. of Parcels: **$58,714,087** / 267
Number of Personal Taxpayers, FY 1999: 3,193
Net State Taxable Income, FY 1999: $ 37,109,255
Gross State Income Tax, FY 1999: $ 1,676,781
No. of State Corporate Taxpayers, FY 1999: 67
Corp. Income & Franchise Taxes, FY 1999: $36,793
Retail Sales: 1999—$32,714,460   1998—$31.7 m
Sales Tax / **No. Retailers** (1999): $1,969,305 / **193**
No. Vehicles Registered, FY Ending 6/30/99: 9,602
Education, 1990 - Average: 11.0 years (rank 40)
  Graduates: High School 62.4%   College 6.0%
Residents Enrolled in 8 State Universities, Fall 1999: 76
No. Hospitals / Beds / **Doctors** (8/1/2000): **0** / 0 / **4**
Number of Births / **Deaths** (1998): 159 / **89**
Land in Farms / No. Farms (1997): **58,916 acres** / 334

Sheriff; Leaksville	(601) 394-2341
Chancery Clerk; Leaksville	394-2377
Circuit Clerk; Leaksville	394-2379
Tax Assessor & Collector; Leaksville	394-2378

GRENADA COUNTY

Established: 1870 Seat: Grenada
Area in Square Miles: 421
Named for the city of Grenada, Spain
Located in north-central Mississippi
Incorporated Places with Estimated Population, 7/1/1998:
  Grenada 11,161
County Pop., 7/1/99: 22,450 (53.33 persons p/sq. mi.)
County Pop., 7/1/98: 22,427 (Voting Age: 16,236)
  White: 12,524 (55.84%)   Nonwhite: 9,903 (44.16%)
  Males: 10,450 (46.60%)   Females: 11,977 (53.40%)
  Ages — 0-4: 1,658; 5-17: 4,533 18-24: 2,153;
  25-44: 6,415; 45-64: 4,637; 65 & older: 3,031
County Pop., 1990: 21,555 (50.4% urban—49.6% rural)
  White: 12,589 (58.40%)   Nonwhite: 8,966 (41.60%)
Households / Persons Per Household, 1998: **7,995** / 2.8
Average Household Income, 1998: $53,543 (rank 20)
1995 Households with Income: Under $15,000—35.67%
  $25,000-49,999—29.15% $75,000 or more—4.22%
Per Capita Personal Income, 1998: $19,103 (rank 23)
Total Personal Income, 1998: $428,071,000
Total Wages & Salaries, 1998: $277,534,000
Avg. Wages, 1998: Week $459 (rank 12); Year $23,866
  FY 1997: Manufacturing —$546 week $13.65 hour
           Services   —$376 week $ 9.40 hour
Labor Force / **Employed** (July 2000): 10,610 / **9,930**
Non-Agri. Employment *in* the County, July 2000: 11,590
  Manufacturing: 4,170 / Nonmanufacturing: 7,420
Unemployed / Rate (July 2000): **680** / 6.4%
No. Medicaid Eligibles, FY 1997: 5,012 (23.3% of pop.)
Federal Funds & Grants, 1998: $124,218,000
Cost of Living Index, 1999: 0.97 (average is 1.00)
Average County Millage, 1999: 88.46
Real Property, 1999 Assessed Value: $67,685,284
Real Property, 1998 Assessed Value: $66,791,501
  True Value / No. of Parcels: **$533,156,583** / 14,477
Personal Property, 1999 Assessed Value: $64,705,014
Personal Property, 1998 Assessed Value: $68,158,772
  True Value / No. of Parcels: **$372,008,254** / 997
Number of Personal Taxpayers, FY 1999: 8,752
Net State Taxable Income, FY 1999: $ 134,307,927
Gross State Income Tax, FY 1999: $ 6,293,361
No. of State Corporate Taxpayers, FY 1999: 278
Corp. Income & Franchise Taxes, FY 1999: $484,347
Retail Sales: 1999—$315,665,755   1998—$298.3 m
Sales Tax / **No. Retailers** (1999): $19,436,694 / **770**
No. Vehicles Registered, FY Ending 6/30/99: 19,440
Education, 1990 - Average: 10.9 years (rank 48)
  Graduates: High School 56.5%   College 10.8%
Residents Enrolled in 8 State Universities, Fall 1999: 470
No. Hospitals / Beds / **Doctors** (8/1/2000): **1** / 156 / **44**
Number of Births / **Deaths** (1998): 343 / **278**
Land in Farms / No. Farms (1997): **91,002 acres** / 211

Sheriff; 35 Doak St; Grenada	(662) 226-2721
Chancery Clerk; Courthouse; Grenada	226-1821
Circuit Clerk; Courthouse; Grenada	226-1941
Tax Assessor & Collector; Grenada	226-1741

Hancock County

Established: 1812 Seat: Bay Saint Louis
Area in Square Miles: 478
Named for John Hancock, 1st signer of the Decl. of Indep.
Located on coast bordering Gulf of Mexico & Louisiana
Incorporated Places with Estimated Population, 7/1/1998:
  Bay St. Louis 9,841   Waveland 6,986
County Pop., 7/1/99: 41,518 (86.86 persons p/sq. mi.)
County Pop., 7/1/98: 40,327 (Voting Age: 29,832)
  White: 35,988 (89.24%) Nonwhite: 4,339 (10.76%)
  Males: 20,007 (49.61%) Females: 20,320 (50.39%)
  Ages — 0-4: 2,839; 5-17: 7,656; 18-24: 3,239;
  25-44: 11,014; 45-64: 9,611; 65 & older: 5,968
County Pop., 1990: 31,760 (60.1% urban—39.9% rural)
  White: 28,532 (89.84%) Nonwhite: 3,228 (10.16%)
Households / Persons Per Household, 1998: **14,923** / 2.7
Average Household Income, 1998: $52,673 (rank 24)
1995 Households with Income: Under $15,000—31.84%
  $25,000-49,999—28.89% $75,000 or more—7.46%
Per Capita Personal Income, 1998: $19,519 (rank 15)
Total Personal Income, 1998: $786,067,000
Total Wages & Salaries, 1998: $420,350,000
Avg. Wages, 1998: Week $498 (rank 5); Year $25,907
  FY 1997: Manufacturing —$780 week $19.50 hour
       Services: —$466 week $11.65 hour
Labor Force / **Employed** (July 2000): 18,800 / **18,060**
Non-Agri. Employment *in* the County, July 2000: 14,260
  Manufacturing: 1,430 / Nonmanufacturing: 12,830
Unemployed / Rate (July 2000): **740** / 3.9%
No. Medicaid Eligibles, FY 1997: 5,508 (17.3% of pop.)
Federal Funds & Grants, 1998: $455,117,000
Cost of Living Index, 1999: 1.03 (average is 1.00)
Average County Millage, 1999: 100.50
Real Property, 1999 Assessed Value: $169,476,622
Real Property, 1998 Assessed Value: $157,229,684
  True Value / No. Parcels: **$1,279,758,560** / 47,630
Personal Property, 1999 Assessed Value: $112,709,252
Personal Property, 1998 Assessed Value: $78,745,552
  True Value / No. of Parcels: **$381,331,747** / 847
Number of Personal Taxpayers, FY 1999: 12,047
Net State Taxable Income, FY 1999: $ 204,760,711
Gross State Income Tax, FY 1999: $ 9,825,583
No. of State Corporate Taxpayers, FY 1999: 435
Corp. Income & Franchise Taxes, FY 1999: $416,048
Retail Sales: 1999—$409,711,472   1998—$362.0 m
Sales Tax / **No. Retailers** (1999): $23,007,735 / **1,096**
No. Vehicles Registered, FY Ending 6/30/99: 41,139
Education, 1990 - Average: 11.8 years (rank 15)
  Graduates: High School 68.0%   College 14.3%
Residents Enrolled in 8 State Universities, Fall 1999: 537
No. Hospitals / Beds / **Doctors** (8/1/2000): **1** / 104 / **63**
Number of Births / **Deaths** (1998): 458 / **409**
Land in Farms / No. Farms (1997): **36,327 acres** / 239

Sheriff; Bay St. Louis	(228) 467-5101
Chancery Clerk; 150 Main St; Bay St. Louis	467-5404
Circuit Clerk; Courthouse; Bay St. Louis	467-5265
Tax Assessor & Collector; Bay St. Louis	467-4425

Harrison County

Established: 1841 Seats: Gulfport and Biloxi
Area in Square Miles: 581
Named for William H. Harrison, 9th president of the U.S.
Located on the coast bordering the Gulf of Mexico
Incorporated Places with Estimated Population, 7/1/1998:
  Biloxi 47,316   D'Iberville 8,211   Gulfport 64,762
  Long Beach 16,776   Pass Christian 6,190
County Pop., 7/1/99: 178,567 (307.34 persons p/sq. mi.)
County Pop., 7/1/98: 177,981 (Voting Age: 130,501)
  White: 133,624 (75.08%) Nonwhite: 44,357 (24.92%)
  Males: 87,289 (49.04%) Females: 90,692 (50.96%)
  Ages — 0-4: 14,218; 5-17: 33,262; 18-24: 18,779;
  25-44: 54,396; 45-64: 35,824; 65 & older: 21,502
County Pop., 1990: 165,365 (84.3% urban—15.7% rural)
  White: 127,750 (77.25%) Nonwhite: 37,615 (22.75%)
Households / Persons Per Household, 1998: **63,868** / 2.8
Average Household Income, 1998: $63,361 (rank 6)
1995 Households with Income: Under $15,000—25.94%
  $25,000-49,999—33.20% $75,000 or more—7.78%
Per Capita Personal Income, 1998: $22,838 (rank 7)
Total Personal Income, 1998: $4,046,780,000
Total Wages & Salaries, 1998: $2,498,765,000
Avg. Wages, 1998: Week $432 (rank 24); Year $22,465
  FY 1997: Manufacturing —$552 week $13.80 hour
       Services   —$405 week $10.13 hour
Labor Force / **Employed** (July 2000): 90,420 / **86,730**
Non-Agri. Employment *in* the County, July 2000: 93,830
  Manufacturing: 5,550 / Nonmanufacturing: 88,280
Unemployed / Rate (July 2000): **3,690** / 4.1%
No. Medicaid Eligibles, FY 1997: 27,055 (16.4% of pop.)
Federal Funds & Grants, 1998: $1,321,593,000
Cost of Living Index, 1999: 1.09 (average is 1.00)
Average County Millage, 1999: 99.89
Real Property, 1999 Assessed Value: $583,819,998
Real Property, 1998 Assessed Value: $558,358,823
  True Value / No. Parcels: **$4,471,478,340** / 81,895
Personal Property, 1999 Assessed Value: $349,109,254
Personal Property, 1998 Assessed Value: $325,069,093
  True Value / No. of Parcels: **$1,644,149,278** / 6,671
Number of Personal Taxpayers, FY 1999: 67,796
Net State Taxable Income, FY 1999: $ 1,111,300,667
Gross State Income Tax, FY 1999: $ 55,444,215
No. of State Corporate Taxpayers, FY 1999: 2,855
Corp. Income & Franchise Taxes, FY 1999: $11,178,197
Retail Sales: 1999—$3,154,592,532   1998—$2,601.2 m
Sales Tax / **No. Retailers** (1999): $187,575,766 / **4,964**
No. Vehicles Registered, FY Ending 6/30/99: 156,692
Edu., '90 - Avg 12.2 yrs; Hi School 74.7%; College 16.3%
Residents Enrolled in 8 State Universities, Fall '99: 2,415
No. Hospitals / Beds/**Doctors** (8/1/2000): **6** / 977 / **521**
Number of Births / **Deaths** (1998): 2,866 / **1,753**
Land in Farms / No. Farms (1997): **17,871 acres** / 275

Sheriff; Gulfport/Biloxi	(228) 865-7071/435-4220
Chancery Clerk; Gulfport/Biloxi	865-4036/435-8220
Circuit Clerk; Gulfport/Biloxi	865-4167/435-8233
Tax Assessor; Gulfport/Biloxi	865-4077/435-8266
Tax Collector; Gulfport/Biloxi	865-4040/435-8241

The Ultimate Reference on the State

Hinds County

Est: 1821   Seats: Jackson & Raymond   Area: 875 sq. mi.
Named for Gen. Thomas Hinds, Battle of New Orleans
Located in west-central Mississippi
Incorporated Places with Estimated Population, 7/1/1998:
   Bolton 783   Clinton 22,067   Edwards 1,195
   Jackson (part) 187,433   Learned 99
   Terry 619   Utica 987
County Pop., 7/1/99: 245,737 (280.84 persons p/sq. mi.)
County Pop., 7/1/98: 247,144 (Voting Age: 182,423)
   White: 113,778 (46.04%) Nonwhite: 133,366 (53.96%)
   Males: 115,732 (46.83%) Females: 131,412 (53.17%)
   Ages — 0-4: 18,193; 5-17: 46,528; 18-24: 29,383;
   25-44: 77,865; 45-64: 47,653; 65 & older: 27,522
County Pop., 1990: 254,441 (86.7% urban—13.3% rural)
   White: 123,179 (48.41%) Nonwhite 131,262 (51.59%)
Households / Persons Per Household, 1998: **88,477** / 2.8
Average Household Income, 1998: $68,002 (rank 4)
1995 Households with Income: Under $15,000—25.83%
   $25,000-49,999—30.22% $75,000 or more—11.98%
Per Capita Personal Income, 1998: $24,333 (rank 4)
Total Personal Income, 1998: $6,016,667,000
Total Wages & Salaries, 1998: $4,523,099,000
Avg. Wages, 1998: Week $528 (rank 3); Year $27,467
   FY 1997: Manufacturing —570 week $14.25 hour
               Services —489 week $12.23 hour
Labor Force / **Employed** (July 2000): 136,700 / **129,830**
Non-Agri. Employment *in* the County, July 2000: 156,170
   Manufacturing: 10,440 / Nonmanufacturing: 145,730
Unemployed / Rate (July 2000): **6,870** / 5.0%
No. Medicaid Eligibles, FY 1997: 48,920 (19.2% of pop.)
Federal Funds & Grants, 1998: $1,755,117,000
Cost of Living Index, 1999: 1.09 (average is 1.00)
Average County Millage, 1999: 89.55
Real Property, 1999 Assessed Value: $756,719,549
Real Property, 1998 Assessed Value: $745,696,768
   True Value / No. Parcels: **$5,985,588,470** / 105,941
Personal Property, 1999 Assessed Value: $502,515,163
Personal Property, 1998 Assessed Value: $472,019,256
   True Value / No. Parcels: **$2,370,185,673** / 9,841
Number of Personal Taxpayers, FY 1999: 115,918
Net State Taxable Income, FY 1999: $ 2,095,148,525
Gross State Income Tax, FY 1999: $ 102,572,046
No. of State Corporate Taxpayers, FY 1999: 6,103
Corp. Income & Franchise Taxes, FY 1999: $54,120,510
Retail Sales: 1999—$4,106,614,746   1998—$3,878.0 m
Sales Tax / **No. Retailers** (1999): $248,735,422 / **6,566**
No. Vehicles Registered, FY Ending 6/30/99: 184,228
Edu., '90 - Avg 12.6 yrs; Hi School 75.2%; College 26.4%
Residents Enrolled in 8 State Universities, Fall '99: 5,552
No. Hospitals/Beds/Doctors (8/1/2000): **6** / 2,433 / **1,474**
Number of Births / **Deaths** (1998): 4,027 / **2,467**
Land in Farms / No. Farms (1997): **196,393 acres** / 723

Sheriff; Jackson/Raymond   (601) 968-6702/857-4800
Chancery Clerk; Jackson/Raymond   968-6537/857-8055
Circuit Clerk; Jackson/Raymond   968-6628/857-8038
Tax Assessor; Jackson/Raymond   968-6626/857-8787
Tax Collector; Jackson/Raymond   968-6585/857-5574

Holmes County

Est: 1833   Seat: Lexington   Area: 759 sq. mi.
Named for David Holmes, the first governor of the state
Located in north-central Mississippi
Incorporated Places with Estimated Population, 7/1/1998:
   Cruger 554   Durant 2,686   Goodman 1,348
   Lexington 2,027 Pickens 1,381   Tchula 2,367
   West 166
County Pop., 7/1/99: 21,562 (28.41 persons p/sq. mi.)
County Pop., 7/1/98: 21,522 (Voting Age: 14,421)
   White: 4,909 (22.81%)   Nonwhite: 16,613 (77.19%)
   Males: 9,974 (46.34%)   Females: 11,548 (53.66%)
   Ages — 0-4: 1,830; 5-17: 5,271; 18-24: 2,634;
   25-44: 5,278; 45-64: 3,744; 65 & older: 2,765
County Pop., 1990: 21,604 (13.2% urban—86.8% rural)
   White: 5,176 (23.96%)   Nonwhite: 16,428 (76.04%)
Households / Persons Per Household, 1998: **7,122** / 3.0
Average Household Income, 1998: $40,693 (rank 74)
1995 Households with Income: Under $15,000—59.94%
   $25,000-49,999—16.15% $75,000 or more—3.32%
Per Capita Personal Income, 1998: $13,472 (rank 77)
Total Personal Income, 1998: $289,820,000
Total Wages & Salaries, 1998: $104,203,000
Avg. Wages, 1998: Week $364 (rank 59); Year $18,946
   FY 1997: Manufacturing —$360 week $9.00 hour
               Services —$397 week $9.93 hour
Labor Force / **Employed** (July 2000): 7,330 / **5,910**
Non-Agri. Employment *in* the County, July 2000: 4,580
   Manufacturing: 930 / Nonmanufacturing: 3,650
Unemployed / Rate (July 2000): **1,420** / 19.4%
No. Medicaid Eligibles, FY 1997: 9,253 (42.8% of pop.)
Federal Funds & Grants, 1998: $129,064,000
Cost of Living Index, 1999: 0.90 (average is 1.00)
Average County Millage, 1999: 90.08
Real Property, 1999 Assessed Value: $43,860,767
Real Property, 1998 Assessed Value: $41,824,416
   True Value / No. of Parcels: **$317,786,176** / 14,337
Personal Property, 1999 Assessed Value: $25,426,292
Personal Property, 1998 Assessed Value: $24,044,477
   True Value / No. of Parcels: **$109,588,993** / 561
Number of Personal Taxpayers, FY 1999: 6,310
Net State Taxable Income, FY 1999: $ 58,974,080
Gross State Income Tax, FY 1999: $ 2,698,625
No. of State Corporate Taxpayers, FY 1999: 173
Corp. Income & Franchise Taxes, FY 1999: $249,421
Retail Sales: 1999—$96,009,499   1998—$96.1 m
Sales Tax / **No. Retailers** (1999): $5,696,163 / **440**
No. Vehicles Registered, FY Ending 6/30/99: 14,614
Education, 1990 - Average: 10.5 years (rank 73)
   Graduates: High School 48.0%   College 9.7%
Residents Enrolled in 8 State Universities, Fall 1999: 446
No. Hospitals / Beds / **Doctors** (8/1/2000): **2** / 113 / **20**
Number of Births / **Deaths** (1998): 409 / **272**
Land in Farms / No. Farms (1997): **189,866 acres** / 352

Sheriff; Lexington   (662) 834-1511
Chancery Clerk; Courthouse; Lexington   834-2508
Circuit Clerk; Courthouse; Lexington   834-2476
Tax Assessor & Collector; Lexington   834-2865

The Mississippi Almanac

Humphreys County

Est: 1918 (youngest co.)   Seat: Belzoni   Area: 430 sq. mi.
Named for Benjamin Humphreys, 26th governor of Miss.
Located in the Delta area of west-central Mississippi
Incorporated Places with Estimated Population, 7/1/1998:
   Belzoni 2,367   Isola 666
   Louise 314   Silver City 322
County Pop., 7/1/99: 11,214 (26.08 persons p/sq. mi.)
County Pop., 7/1/98: 11,344 (Voting Age: 7,502)
    White: 3,416 (30.11%)   Nonwhite: 7,928 (69.89%)
    Males: 5,260 (46.37%)   Females: 6,084 (53.63%)
      Ages — 0-4: 1,006; 5-17: 2,836; 18-24: 1,216;
      25-44: 2,906; 45-64: 2,029; 65 & older: 1,351
County Pop., 1990: 12,134 (20.9% urban—79.1% rural)
     White: 3,856 (31.78%)   Nonwhite: 8,278 (68.22%)
Households / Persons Per Household, 1998: **3,676** / 3.1
Average Household Income, 1998: $52,970 (rank 22)
1995 Households with Income: Under $15,000—46.19%
   $25,000-49,999—21.60% $75,000 or more—6.39%
Per Capita Personal Income, 1998: $17,204 (rank 43)
Total Personal Income, 1998: $194,715,000
Total Wages & Salaries, 1998: $76,736,000
Avg. Wages, 1998: Week $331 (rank 79); Year $17,217
    FY 1997: Manufacturing —$389 week $9.73 hour
               Services   —$376 week $9.40 hour
Labor Force / **Employed** (July 2000): 5,150 / **4,460**
Non-Agri. Employment *in* the County, July 2000: 3,170
   Manufacturing: 1,130 / Nonmanufacturing: 2,040
Unemployed / Rate (July 2000): **690** / 13.4%
No. Medicaid Eligibles, FY 1997: 4,341 (35.8% of pop.)
Federal Funds & Grants, 1998: $65,983,000
Cost of Living Index, 1999: 0.93 (average is 1.00)
Average County Millage, 1999: 104.85
Real Property, 1999 Assessed Value: $26,625,792
Real Property, 1998 Assessed Value: $25,830,897
   True Value / No. of Parcels: **$194,294,936** / 8,300
Personal Property, 1999 Assessed Value: $15,173,811
Personal Property, 1998 Assessed Value: $14,534,000
   True Value / No. of Parcels: **$63,493,626** / 482
Number of Personal Taxpayers, FY 1999: 2,848
Net State Taxable Income, FY 1999: $ 39,465,292
Gross State Income Tax, FY 1999: $ 1,910,085
No. of State Corporate Taxpayers, FY 1999: 185
Corp. Income & Franchise Taxes, FY 1999: $1,093,996
Retail Sales: 1999—$72,521,948   1998—$74.8 m
Sales Tax / **No. Retailers** (1999): $4,129,641 / **280**
No. Vehicles Registered, FY Ending 6/30/99: 7,528
Education, 1990 - Average: 10.4 years (rank 76)
    Graduates: High School 46.4%   College 10.4%
Residents Enrolled in 8 State Universities, Fall 1999: 297
No. Hospitals / Beds / **Doctors** (8/1/2000): **1** / 28 / **3**
Number of Births / **Deaths** (1998): 210 / **103**
Land in Farms / No. Farms (1997): **198,236 acres** / 240

Sheriff; 102 Castleman St; Belzoni	(662) 247-2551
Chancery Clerk; 102 Castleman St; Belzoni	247-1740
Circuit Clerk; 102 Castleman St; Belzoni	247-3065
Tax Assessor; 102 Castleman St; Belzoni	247-3174
Tax Collector; 102 Castleman St; Belzoni	247-2552

Issaquena County

Established: 1844   Seat: Mayersville
Area in Square Miles: 406
Named for the Indian word meaning "deer river"
Located in the western part bordering Miss. River & LA
Incorporated Places with Estimated Population, 7/1/1998:
    Mayersville 288
County Pop., 7/1/99: 1,635 (4.03 persons p/sq. mi.)
County Pop., 7/1/98: 1,629 (Voting Age: 1,111)
    White: 665 (40.82%)   Nonwhite: 964 (59.18%)
    Males: 789 (48.43%)   Females: 840 (51.57%)
      Ages — 0-4: 146; 5-17: 372; 18-24: 166;
      25-44: 413; 45-64: 368; 65 & older: 164
County Pop., 1990: 1,909 (0.0% urban—100.0% rural)
     White: 833 (43.63%)   Nonwhite: 1,076 (56.36%)
Households / Persons Per Household, 1998: **543** / 3.0
Average Household Income, 1998: $38,719 (rank 80)
1995 Households with Income: Under $15,000—41.67%
   $25,000-49,999—23.23% $75,000 or more—5.14%
Per Capita Personal Income, 1998: $12,859 (rank 79)
Total Personal Income, 1998: $21,038,000
Total Wages & Salaries, 1998: $7,258,000
Avg. Wages, 1998: Week $310 (rank 82); Year $16,115
Labor Force / **Employed** (July 2000):   660 / **580**
Non-Agri. Employment *in* the County, July 2000: 240
   Manufacturing: 10 / Nonmanufacturing: 230
Unemployed / Rate (July 2000): **80** / 12.1%
No. Medicaid Eligibles, FY 1997: 533 (27.9% of pop.)
Federal Funds & Grants, 1998: $10,491,000
Cost of Living Index, 1999: 0.87 (average is 1.00)
Average County Millage, 1999: 91.97
Real Property, 1999 Assessed Value: $13,082,328
Real Property, 1998 Assessed Value: $12,353,991
   True Value / No. of Parcels: **$85,126,252** / 2,501
Personal Property, 1999 Assessed Value: $2,458,514
Personal Property, 1998 Assessed Value: $2,393,711
   True Value / No. of Parcels: **$9,447,828** / 88
Number of Personal Taxpayers, FY 1999: 367
Net State Taxable Income, FY 1999: $ 6,489,422
Gross State Income Tax, FY 1999: $ 316,876
No. of State Corporate Taxpayers, FY 1999: 41
Corp. Income & Franchise Taxes, FY 1999: $21,100
Retail Sales: 1999—$5,109,394   1998—$5.5 m
Sales Tax / **No. Retailers** (1999): $211,689 / **27**
No. Vehicles Registered, FY Ending 6/30/99: 1,661
Education, 1990 - Average: 10.0 years (rank 82)
    Graduates: High School 43.7% (rank 82)
             College 5.6% (rank 82)
Residents Enrolled in 8 State Universities, Fall 1999: 26
No. Hospitals / Beds / **Doctors** (8/1/2000): **0** / 0 / **1**
Number of Births / **Deaths** (1998): 24 / **11**
Land in Farms / No. Farms (1997): **112,746 acres** / 82

Sheriff; Mayersville	(662) 873-2781
Chancery Clerk; Mayersville	873-2761
Circuit Clerk; Mayersville	873-2761
Tax Assessor & Collector; Mayersville	873-4665

ITAWAMBA COUNTY

Established: 1836 Seat: Fulton
Area in Square Miles: 541
Named for the Indian Chief Itawamba
Located in northeastern Mississippi bordering Alabama
Incorporated Places with Estimated Population, 7/1/1998:
  Fulton 3,668 Mantachie 1,068 Tremont 345
County Pop., 7/1/99: 21,085 (38.97 persons p/sq. mi.)
County Pop., 7/1/98: 21,072 (Voting Age: 16,108)
  White: 19,400 (92.07%) Nonwhite: 1,672 (7.93%)
  Males: 10,340 (49.07%) Females: 10,732 (50.93%)
  Ages — 0-4: 1,263; 5-17: 3,701; 18-24: 2,339;
  25-44: 5,664; 45-64: 5,085; 65 & older: 3,020
County Pop., 1990: 20,017 (16.9% urban—83.1% rural)
  White: 18,604 (92.94%) Nonwhite: 1,413 (7.06%)
Households / Persons Per Household, 1998: **7,885** / 2.7
Average Household Income, 1998: $52,118 (rank 30)
1995 Households with Income: Under $15,000—27.96%
  $25,000-49,999—34.14% $75,000 or more—4.83%
Per Capita Personal Income, 1998: $19,484 (rank 17)
Total Personal Income, 1998: $410,970,000
Total Wages & Salaries, 1998: $127,476,000
Avg. Wages, 1998: Week $417 (rank 33); Year $21,673
  FY 1997: Manufacturing —$441 week $11.03 hour
        Services   —$409 week $10.23 hour
Labor Force / **Employed** (July 2000): 11,900 / **11,180**
Non-Agri. Employment *in* the County, July 2000: 6,140
  Manufacturing: 1,960 / Nonmanufacturing: 4,180
Unemployed / Rate (July 2000): **720** / 6.1%
No. Medicaid Eligibles, FY 1997: 2,563 (12.8% of pop.)
Federal Funds & Grants, 1998: $71,012,000
Cost of Living Index, 1999: 0.98 (average is 1.00)
Average County Millage, 1999: 94.00
Real Property, 1999 Assessed Value: $44,846,205
Real Property, 1998 Assessed Value: $42,615,308
  True Value / No. of Parcels: **$356,018,115** / 14,425
Personal Property, 1999 Assessed Value: $39,379,920
Personal Property, 1998 Assessed Value: $38,667,931
  True Value / No. of Parcels: **$184,196,212** / 497
Number of Personal Taxpayers, FY 1999: 7,684
Net State Taxable Income, FY 1999: $ 126,058,614
Gross State Income Tax, FY 1999: $ 5,790,113
No. of State Corporate Taxpayers, FY 1999: 190
Corp. Income & Franchise Taxes, FY 1999: $235,217
Retail Sales: 1999—$126,894,652 1998—$122.9 m
Sales Tax / **No. Retailers** (1999): $7,429,606 / **515**
No. Vehicles Registered, FY Ending 6/30/99: 20,275
Education, 1990 - Average: 10.5 years (rank 74)
  Graduates: High School 49.0% College 6.7%
Residents Enrolled in 8 State Universities, Fall 1999: 234
No. Hospitals / Beds / **Doctors** (8/1/2000): **0** / 0 / **9**
Number of Births / **Deaths** (1998): 242 / **264**
Land in Farms / No. Farms (1997): **81,566 acres** / 387

Sheriff; 201 S Cummings St; Fulton	(662) 862-3401
Chancery Clerk; 201 W Main St; Fulton	862-3421
Circuit Clerk; 201 W Main St; Fulton	862-3511
Tax Assessor/Collector; 201 W Main; Fulton	862-4304

JACKSON COUNTY

Est: 1812 Seat: Pascagoula Area: 731 sq. mi.
Named for General Andrew Jackson
Located on coast bordering Gulf of Mexico & Alabama
Incorporated Places with Estimated Population, 7/1/1998:
  Gautier 11,139   Moss Point 18,095
  Ocean Springs 16,519 Pascagoula 27,163
County Pop., 7/1/99: 133,120 (182.11 persons p/sq. mi.)
County Pop., 7/1/98: 130,910 (Voting Age: 94,493)
  White: 99,974 (76.37%) Nonwhite: 30,936 (23.63%)
  Males: 64,742 (49.46%) Females: 66,168 (50.54%)
  Ages — 0-4: 9,476; 5-17: 26,941; 18-24: 12,479;
  25-44: 39,423; 45-64: 29,343; 65 & older: 13,248
County Pop., 1990: 115,243 (80.4% urban—19.6% rural)
  White: 90,275 (78.33%) Nonwhite: 24,968 (21.67%)
Households / Persons Per Household, 1998: **45,954** / 2.8
Average Household Income, 1998: $60,256 (rank 10)
1995 Households with Income: Under $15,000—21.60%
  $25,000-49,999—31.09% $75,000 or more—12.35%
Per Capita Personal Income, 1998: $21,170 (rank 9)
Total Personal Income, 1998: $2,768,954,000
Total Wages & Salaries, 1998: $1,768,586,000
Avg. Wages, 1998: Week $579 (rank 2); Year $30,130
  FY 1997: Manufacturing —$696 week $17.40 hour
        Services   —$482 week $12.05 hour
Labor Force / **Employed** (July 2000): 73,410 / **69,720**
Non-Agri. Employment *in* the County, July 2000: 55,160
  Manufacturing: 19,660 / Nonmanufacturing: 35,500
Unemployed / Rate (July 2000): **3,690** / 5.0%
No. Medicaid Eligibles, FY 1997: 16,450 (14.3% of pop.)
Federal Funds & Grants, 1998: $1,276,477,000
Cost of Living Index, 1999: 1.04 (average is 1.00)
Average County Millage, 1999: 126.97
Real Property, 1999 Assessed Value: $355,524,203
Real Property, 1998 Assessed Value: $354,199,511
  True Value / No. Parcels: **$2,960,062,089** / 73,966
Personal Property, 1999 Assessed Value: $370,433,844
Personal Property, 1998 Assessed Value: $328,398,795
  True Value / No. of Parcels: **$1,775,919,969** / 2,718
Number of Personal Taxpayers, FY 1999: 45,292
Net State Taxable Income, FY 1999: $ 858,155,294
Gross State Income Tax, FY 1999: $ 42,908,459
No. of State Corporate Taxpayers, FY 1999: 1,237
Corp. Income & Franchise Taxes, FY 1999: $8,883,739
Retail Sales: 1999—$1,348,220,655 1998—$1,170.4 m
Sales Tax / **No. Retailers** (1999): $79,916,018 / **2,724**
No. Vehicles Registered, FY Ending 6/30/99: 113,514
Education, 1990 - Average: 12.1 years (rank 9)
  Graduates: High School 74.4% College 14.4%
Residents Enrolled in 8 State Universities, Fall '99: 1,788
No. Hospitals / Beds / **Doctors** (8/1/2000): **2** / 551 / **246**
Number of Births / **Deaths** (1998): 1,862 / **1,112**
Land in Farms / No. Farms (1997): **32,610 acres** / 321

Sheriff; Pascagoula	(228) 769-3095
Chancery Clerk; Pascagoula	769-3131
Circuit Clerk; Pascagoula	769-3040
Tax Assessor; Pascagoula	769-3070
Tax Collector; Pascagoula	769-3200

JASPER COUNTY

Established: 1833   Seats: Bay Springs & Paulding
Area in Square Miles: 678
Named for Sergeant Jasper, Revolutionary War hero
Located in south-central Mississippi
Incorporated Places with Estimated Population, 7/1/1998:
  Bay Springs 1,855   Heidelberg 937
  Louin 282   Montrose 108
County Pop., 7/1/99: 18,110 (26.71 persons p/sq. mi.)
County Pop., 7/1/98: 17,672 (Voting Age: 12,568)
  White: 8,269 (46.79%)   Nonwhite: 9,403 (53.21%)
  Males: 8,482 (48.00%)   Females: 9,190 (52.00%)
  Ages — 0-4: 1,193; 5-17: 3,911; 18-24: 1,721;
    25-44: 4,758; 45-64: 3,598; 65 & older: 2,491
County Pop., 1990: 17,114 (0.0% urban—100.0% rural)
  White: 8,402 (49.09%)   Nonwhite: 8,712 (50.91%)
Households / Persons Per Household, 1998: **6,151** / 2.9
Average Household Income, 1998: $45,051 (rank 63)
1995 Households with Income: Under $15,000—37.64%
  $25,000-49,999—27.84% $75,000 or more—6.11%
Per Capita Personal Income, 1998: $15,687 (rank 62)
Total Personal Income, 1998: $277,120,000
Total Wages & Salaries, 1998: $103,468,000
Avg. Wages, 1998: Week $384 (rank 52); Year $19,963
  FY 1997: Manufacturing —$373 week $9.33 hour
           Services   —$362 week $9.05 hour
Labor Force / **Employed** (July 2000): 8,550 / **8,090**
Non-Agri. Employment *in* the County, July 2000: 4,780
  Manufacturing: 1,860 / Nonmanufacturing: 2,920
Unemployed / Rate (July 2000): **460** / 5.4%
No. Medicaid Eligibles, FY 1997: 3,862 (22.6% of pop.)
Federal Funds & Grants, 1998: $76,061,000
Cost of Living Index, 1999: 0.95 (average is 1.00)
Average County Millage, 1999: 106.27
Real Property, 1999 Assessed Value: $41,590,957
Real Property, 1998 Assessed Value: $39,769,169
  True Value / No. of Parcels: **$321,569,680** / 16,169
Personal Property, 1999 Assessed Value: $29,202,534
Personal Property, 1998 Assessed Value: $25,817,422
  True Value / No. of Parcels: **$113,515,621** / 536
Number of Personal Taxpayers, FY 1999: 6,065
Net State Taxable Income, FY 1999: $ 89,244,011
Gross State Income Tax, FY 1999: $ 4,227,629
No. of State Corporate Taxpayers, FY 1999: 196
Corp. Income & Franchise Taxes, FY 1999: $357,086
Retail Sales: 1999—$100,728,170   1998—$93.9 m
Sales Tax / **No. Retailers** (1999): $5,893,832 / **363**
No. Vehicles Registered, FY Ending 6/30/99: 16,034
Education, 1990 - Average: 11.1 years (rank 30)
  Graduates: High School 60.0%   College 9.8%
Residents Enrolled in 8 State Universities, Fall 1999: 224
No. Hospitals / Beds / **Doctors** (8/1/2000): **1** / 16 / **4**
Number of Births / **Deaths** (1998): 309 / **193**
Land in Farms / No. Farms (1997): **74,714 acres** / 367

Sheriff; Bay Springs	(601) 764-2588
Chancery Clk; Bay Springs/Paulding	764-3368/727-4941
Circuit Clerk; Bay Springs/Paulding	764-2245/727-4941
Tx Asses./Coll.; Bay Sprgs/Paulding	764-2813/727-4971

JEFFERSON COUNTY

Established: 1799*/ 1802   *1st established as "Pickering"
Seat: Fayette   Area in Square Miles: 523
Named for President Thomas Jefferson
Located in the southwest bordering the Mississippi River
Incorporated Places with Estimated Population, 7/1/1998:
  Fayette 1,822
County Pop., 7/1/99: 8,385 (16.03 persons p/sq. mi.)
County Pop., 7/1/98: 8,427 (Voting Age: 5,681)
  White: 1,104 (13.10%)   Nonwhite: 7,323 (86.90%)
  Males: 3,966 (47.06%)   Females: 4,461 (52.94%)
  Ages — 0-4: 677; 5-17: 2,069; 18-24: 874;
    25-44: 2,225; 45-64: 1,586; 65 & older: 996
County Pop., 1990: 8,653 (0.0% urban—100.0% rural)
  White: 1,194 (13.80%)   Nonwhite: 7,459 (86.20%)
Households / Persons Per Household, 1998: **2,764** / 3.1
Average Household Income, 1998: $34,826 (rank 82)
1995 Households with Income: Under $15,000—53.17%
  $25,000-49,999—18.07% $75,000 or more—3.17%
Per Capita Personal Income, 1998: $11,390 (rank 82)
Total Personal Income, 1998: $96,260,000
Total Wages & Salaries, 1998: $26,494,000
Avg. Wages, 1998: Week $347 (rank 72); Year $18,043
  FY 1997: Manufacturing —$398 week $9.95 hour
           Services   —$317 week $7.93 hour
Labor Force / **Employed** (July 2000): 2,820 / **2,260**
Non-Agri. Employment *in* the County, July 2000: 1,320
  Manufacturing: 100 / Nonmanufacturing: 1,220
Unemployed / Rate (July 2000): **560** / 19.9 %
No. Medicaid Eligibles, FY 1997: 2,992 (34.6% of pop.)
Federal Funds & Grants, 1998: $54,445,000
Cost of Living Index, 1999: 0.86 (average is 1.00)
Average County Millage, 1999: 126.52
Real Property, 1999 Assessed Value: $19,999,085
Real Property, 1998 Assessed Value: $18,893,107
  True Value / No. of Parcels: **$142,165,550** / 7,234
Personal Property, 1999 Assessed Value: $8,351,712
Personal Property, 1998 Assessed Value: $7,222,839
  True Value / No. of Parcels: **$29,656,862** / 228
Number of Personal Taxpayers, FY 1999: 2,616
Net State Taxable Income, FY 1999: $ 22,244,948
Gross State Income Tax, FY 1999: $ 995,729
No. of State Corporate Taxpayers, FY 1999: 30
Corp. Income & Franchise Taxes, FY 1999: $11,834
Retail Sales: 1999—$26,897,384   1998—$24.1 m
Sales Tax / **No. Retailers** (1999): $1,381,529 / **139**
No. Vehicles Registered, FY Ending 6/30/99: 5,796
Education, 1990 - Average: 10.7 years (rank 42)
  Graduates: High School 53.0%   College 10.3%
Residents Enrolled in 8 State Universities, Fall 1999: 310
No. Hospitals / Beds / **Doctors** (8/1/2000): **1** / 30 / **4**
Number of Births / **Deaths** (1998): 114 / **100**
Land in Farms / No. Farms (1997): **63,517 acres** / 158

Sheriff; Fayette	(601) 786-3403
Chancery Clerk; Fayette	786-3021
Circuit Clerk; 225 Community Dr; Fayette	786-3422
Tax Assessor & Collector; Fayette	786-3781

The Ultimate Reference on the State

JEFFERSON DAVIS COUNTY

Established: 1906 Seat: Prentiss
Area in Square Miles: 409
Named for Confederate President Jefferson Davis
Located in south-central Mississippi
Incorporated Places with Estimated Population, 7/1/1998:
    Bassfield 238   Prentiss 1,275
County Pop., 7/1/99: 13,770 (33.67 persons p/sq. mi.)
County Pop., 7/1/98: 13,860 (Voting Age: 9,799)
    White: 5,944 (42.89%)   Nonwhite: 7,916 (57.11%)
    Males: 6,551 (47.27%)   Females: 7,309 (52.73%)
    Ages — 0-4: 990; 5-17: 3,071; 18-24: 1,432;
    25-44: 3,627; 45-64: 2,825; 65 & older: 1,915
County Pop., 1990: 14,051 (0.0% urban—100.0% rural)
    White: 6,325 (45.01%)   Nonwhite: 7,726 (54.99%)
Households / Persons Per Household, 1998: **4,721** / 2.9
Average Household Income, 1998: $43,730 (rank 67)
1995 Households with Income: Under $15,000—42.96%
    $25,000-49,999—24.69% $75,000 or more—3.06%
Per Capita Personal Income, 1998: $14,944 (rank 67)
Total Personal Income, 1998: $206,446,000
Total Wages & Salaries, 1998: $54,321,000
Avg. Wages, 1998: Week $336 (rank 77); Year $17,473
    FY 1997: Manufacturing —$254 week $6.35 hour
             Services   —$376 week $9.40 hour
Labor Force / **Employed** (July 2000): 4,940 / **4,240**
Non-Agri. Employment *in* the County, July 2000: 2,570
    Manufacturing: 480 / Nonmanufacturing: 2,090
Unemployed / Rate (July 2000): **700** / 14.2%
No. Medicaid Eligibles, FY 1997: 3,747 (26.7% of pop.)
Federal Funds & Grants, 1998: $56,393,000
Cost of Living Index, 1999: 0.91 (average is 1.00)
Average County Millage, 1999: 90.00
Real Property, 1999 Assessed Value: $31,340,339
Real Property, 1998 Assessed Value: $29,219,538
    True Value / No. of Parcels: **$239,394,350** / 12,618
Personal Property, 1999 Assessed Value: $19,146,564
Personal Property, 1998 Assessed Value: $16,501,652
    True Value / No. of Parcels: **$65,820,575** / 387
Number of Personal Taxpayers, FY 1999: 4,558
Net State Taxable Income, FY 1999: $ 43,241,840
Gross State Income Tax, FY 1999: $ 1,973,049
No. of State Corporate Taxpayers, FY 1999: 66
Corp. Income & Franchise Taxes, FY 1999: $65,517
Retail Sales: 1999—$63,096,470   1998—$61.2 m
Sales Tax / **No. Retailers** (1999): $3,824,424 / **248**
No. Vehicles Registered, FY Ending 6/30/99: 12,852
Education, 1990 - Average: 11.0 years (rank 68)
    Graduates: High School 57.4%   College 8.9%
Residents Enrolled in 8 State Universities, Fall 1999: 193
No. Hospitals / Beds / **Doctors** (8/1/2000): **1** / 41 / **9**
Number of Births / **Deaths** (1998): 223 / **142**
Land in Farms / No. Farms (1997): **78,668 acres** / 389

Sheriff; Prentiss	(601) 792-5169
Chancery Clerk; Prentiss	792-4204
Circuit Clerk; Prentiss	792-4231
Tax Assessor & Collector; Prentiss	792-4291

JONES COUNTY

Established: 1826 Seats: Ellisville and Laurel
Area in Square Miles: 695
Named for John Paul Jones, Revoluntionary War hero
Located in southeastern Mississippi
Incorporated Places with Estimated Population, 7/1/1998:
    Ellisville 3,770   Laurel 18,299
    Sandersville 894   Soso 377
County Pop., 7/1/99: 63,054 (90.73 persons p/sq. mi.)
County Pop., 7/1/98: 63,461 (Voting Age: 46,941)
    White: 46,151 (72.72%)   Nonwhite: 17,310 (27.28%)
    Males: 30,222 (47.62%)   Females: 33,239 (52.38%)
    Ages — 0-4: 4,188; 5-17: 12,332; 18-24: 5,980;
    25-44: 17,864; 45-64: 14,105; 65 & older: 8,992
County Pop., 1990: 62,031 (36.2% urban—63.8% rural)
    White: 46,151 (74.40%)   Nonwhite: 15,880 (25.60%)
Households / Persons Per Household, 1998: **23,118** / 2.8
Average Household Income, 1998: $56,682 (rank 12)
1995 Households with Income: Under $15,000—30.65%
    $25,000-49,999—29.33% $75,000 or more—7.17%
Per Capita Personal Income, 1998: $20,598 (rank 11)
Total Personal Income, 1998: $1,310,332,000
Total Wages & Salaries, 1998: $676,407,000
Avg. Wages, 1998: Week $442 (rank 21); Year $23,002
    FY 1997: Manufacturing —$484 week $12.10 hour
             Services   —$422 week $10.55 hour
Labor Force / **Employed** (July 2000): 33,330 / **32,220**
Non-Agri. Employment *in* the County, July 2000: 29,300
    Manufacturing: 8,550 / Nonmanufacturing: 20,750
Unemployed / Rate (July 2000): **1,110** / 3.3%
No. Medicaid Eligibles, FY 1997: 12,090 (19.5% of pop.)
Federal Funds & Grants, 1998: $300,255,000
Cost of Living Index, 1999: 1.01 (average is 1.00)
Average County Millage, 1999: 99.95
Real Property, 1999 Assessed Value: $130,914,194
Real Property, 1998 Assessed Value: $127,067,493
    True Value / No. Parcels: **$1,049,160,440** / 32,330
Personal Property, 1999 Assessed Value: $122,040,524
Personal Property, 1998 Assessed Value: $114,349,867
    True Value / No. of Parcels: **$540,993,756** / 2,009
Number of Personal Taxpayers, FY 1999: 21,171
Net State Taxable Income, FY 1999: $ 334,764,176
Gross State Income Tax, FY 1999: $ 15,733,734
No. of State Corporate Taxpayers, FY 1999: 788
Corp. Income & Franchise Taxes, FY 1999: $3,709,968
Retail Sales: 1999—$749,057,107   1998—$777.7 m
Sales Tax / **No. Retailers** (1999): $46,055,948 / **1,899**
No. Vehicles Registered, FY Ending 6/30/99: 52,766
Education, 1990 - Average: 11.5 years (rank 19)
    Graduates: High School 64.3%   College 12.2%
Residents Enrolled in 8 State Universities, Fall 1999: 858
No. Hospitals / Beds/**Doctors** (8/1/2000): **1** / 285 / **104**
Number of Births / **Deaths** (1998): 904 / **625**
Land in Farms / No. Farms (1997): **91,116 acres** / 773

Sheriff; Laurel	(601) 425-3147
Chancery Clerk; Ellisville/Laurel	477-3307/428-0527
Circuit Clerk; Ellisville/Laurel	477-8538/428-3602
Tax Assess./Coll; Ellisville/Laurel	477-3261/649-1636

Kemper County

Established: 1833　　　　　Seat: DeKalb
Area in Square Miles: 766
Named for Reuben Kemper, who led a company of men from the Miss. Territory against Spanish Mobile in 1811
Located in east-central Mississippi bordering Alabama
Incorporated Places with Estimated Population, 7/1/1998:
　DeKalb 1,075　　　　　Scooba 519
County Pop., 7/1/99: 10,487 (13.69 persons p/sq. mi.)
County Pop., 7/1/98: 10,575 (Voting Age: 7,637)
　White: 4,271 (40.39%)　　Nonwhite: 6,304 (59.61%)
　Males: 5,109 (48.31%)　　Females: 5,466 (51.69%)
　Ages — 0-4: 719; 5-17: 2,219; 18-24: 1,273;
　25-44: 2,675; 45-64: 2,104; 65 & older: 1,585
County Pop., 1990: 10,356 (0.0% urban—100.0% rural)
　White: 4,405 (42.54%)　　Nonwhite: 5,951 (57.46%)
Households / Persons Per Household, 1998: **3,711** / 2.8
Average Household Income, 1998: $46,901 (rank 52)
1995 Households with Income: Under $15,000—38.55%
　$25,000-49,999—26.65%　$75,000 or more—5.03%
Per Capita Personal Income, 1998: $16,460 (rank 55)
Total Personal Income, 1998: $174,034,000
Total Wages & Salaries, 1998: $42,027,000
Avg. Wages, 1998: Week $342 (rank 75); Year $17,784
　FY 1997: Manufacturing —$248 week　$6.20 hour
　　　　　Services　　　—$372 week　$9.30 hour
Labor Force / **Employed** (July 2000): 4,540 / **4,090**
Non-Agri. Employment *in* the County, July 2000: 2,040
　Manufacturing: 710 / Nonmanufacturing: 1,330
Unemployed / Rate (July 2000): **450** / 9.9%
No. Medicaid Eligibles, FY 1997: 2,093 (20.2% of pop.)
Federal Funds & Grants, 1998: $43,080,000
Cost of Living Index, 1999: 0.92 (average is 1.00)
Average County Millage, 1999: 111.97
Real Property, 1999 Assessed Value: $24,589,995
Real Property, 1998 Assessed Value: $23,372,340
　True Value / No. of Parcels: **$185,392,739** / 11,008
Personal Property, 1999 Assessed Value: $9,297,692
Personal Property, 1998 Assessed Value: $8,148,515
　True Value / No. of Parcels: **$30,388,982** / 216
Number of Personal Taxpayers, FY 1999: 3,231
Net State Taxable Income, FY 1999: $ 34,324,449
Gross State Income Tax, FY 1999: $ 1,566,402
No. of State Corporate Taxpayers, FY 1999: 49
Corp. Income & Franchise Taxes, FY 1999: $95,557
Retail Sales: 1999—$30,286,071　　　1998—$29.3 m
Sales Tax / **No. Retailers** (1999): $1,815,103 / **192**
No. Vehicles Registered, FY Ending 6/30/99: 7,777
Education, 1990 - Average: 10.8 years (rank 60)
　Graduates: High School 56.3%　　College 7.9%
Residents Enrolled in 8 State Universities, Fall 1999: 104
No. Hospitals / Beds / **Doctors** (8/1/2000): **0** / 0 / **5**
Number of Births / **Deaths** (1998): 149 / **101**
Land in Farms / No. Farms (1997): **96,760 acres** / 382

Sheriff; DeKalb	(601) 743-2255
Chancery Clerk; DeKalb	743-2460
Circuit Clerk; DeKalb	743-2224
Tax Assessor & Collector; DeKalb	743-2693

Lafayette County

Established: 1836　　　　　Seat: Oxford
Area in Square Miles: 669
Named for General Marquis de La Fayette
Located in north-central Mississippi
Incorporated Places with Estimated Population, 7/1/1998:
　Abbeville 422　　Oxford 12,096　　Taylor 303
County Pop., 7/1/99: 34,914 (52.19 persons p/sq. mi.)
County Pop., 7/1/98: 34,555 (Voting Age: 27,426)
　White: 24,097 (69.74%)　Nonwhite: 10,458 (30.26%)
　Males: 16,860 (48.79%)　Females: 17,695 (51.21%)
　Ages — 0-4: 1,926; 5-17: 5,203; 18-24: 8,660;
　25-44: 9,353; 45-64: 6,033; 65 & older: 3,380
County Pop., 1990: 31,826 (31.4% urban—68.6% rural)
　White: 23,190 (72.86%)　　Nonwhite: 8,636 (27.14%)
Households / Persons Per Household, 1998: **12,085** / 2.9
Average Household Income, 1998: $54,742 (rank 17)
1995 Households with Income: Under $15,000—32.80%
　$25,000-49,999—27.93%　$75,000 or more—8.83%
Per Capita Personal Income, 1998: $19,034 (rank 24)
Total Personal Income, 1998: $661,550,000
Total Wages & Salaries, 1998: $361,750,000
Avg. Wages, 1998: Week $417 (rank 32); Year $21,706
　FY 1997: Manufacturing —$459 week　$11.48 hour
　　　　　Services　　　—$460 week　$11.50 hour
Labor Force / **Employed** (July 2000): 18,590 / **18,050**
Non-Agri. Employment *in* the County, July 2000: 17,830
　Manufacturing: 2,070 / Nonmanufacturing: 15,760
Unemployed / Rate (July 2000): **540** / 2.9%
No. Medicaid Eligibles, FY 1997: 3,703 (11.6% of pop.)
Federal Funds & Grants, 1998: $122,530,000
Cost of Living Index, 1999: 0.99 (average is 1.00)
Average County Millage, 1999: 123.50
Real Property, 1999 Assessed Value: $97,641,844
Real Property, 1998 Assessed Value: $88,783,306
　True Value / No. of Parcels: **$729,587,525** / 15,991
Personal Property, 1999 Assessed Value: $59,697,361
Personal Property, 1998 Assessed Value: $51,228,437
　True Value / No. of Parcels: **$237,544,576** / 989
Number of Personal Taxpayers, FY 1999: 10,974
Net State Taxable Income, FY 1999: $ 200,204,770
Gross State Income Tax, FY 1999: $ 9,623,692
No. of State Corporate Taxpayers, FY 1999: 441
Corp. Income & Franchise Taxes, FY 1999: $477,194
Retail Sales: 1999—$371,038,163　　　1998—$359.7 m
Sales Tax / **No. Retailers** (1999): $23,396,709 / **942**
No. Vehicles Registered, FY Ending 6/30/99: 25,754
Education, 1990 - Average: 12.4 years (rank 4)
　Graduates: High School 70.2%　　College 29.2%
Residents Enrolled in 8 State Universities, Fall '99: 1,326
No. Hospitals / Beds / **Doctors** (8/1/2000): **1** / 204 / **96**
Number of Births / **Deaths** (1998): 419 / **319**
Land in Farms / No. Farms (1997): **102,123 acres** / 372

Sheriff; 711 Jackson Ave; Oxford	(662) 234-6421
Chancery Clerk; Courthouse; Oxford	234-7563
Circuit Clerk; Courthouse; Oxford	234-4951
Tax Assessor & Collector; Courthse; Oxford	234-5562

LAMAR COUNTY

Established: 1904　　　　　　Seat: Purvis
Area in Square Miles: 499
Named for L.Q.C. Lamar, U.S. Senator from Mississippi
Located in the south part of Mississippi
Incorporated Places with Estimated Population, 7/1/1998:
　　Hattiesburg (part) 2,810　　　Lumberton (part) 2,553
　　Purvis 2,532　　　　　　　　Sumrall 1,141
County Pop., 7/1/99: 38,127 (76.41 persons p/sq. mi.)
County Pop., 7/1/98: 36,888 (Voting Age: 26,227)
　　White: 31,809 (86.23%)　Nonwhite: 5,079 (13.77%)
　　Males: 17,937 (48.63%)　Females: 18,951 (51.37%)
　　Ages — 0-4: 2,882; 5-17: 7,779; 18-24: 3,733;
　　25-44: 11,801; 45-64: 7,347; 65 & older: 3,346
County Pop., 1990: 30,424 (26.6% urban—73.4% rural)
　　White: 26,663 (87.64%)　Nonwhite: 3,761 (12.36%)
Households / Persons Per Household, 1998: **13,226** / 2.8
Average Household Income, 1998: $52,544 (rank 25)
1995 Households with Income: Under $15,000—27.13%
　　$25,000-49,999—29.26%　$75,000 or more—11.45%
Per Capita Personal Income, 1998: $18,761 (rank 27)
Total Personal Income, 1998: $694,934,000
Total Wages & Salaries, 1998: $265,205,000
Avg. Wages, 1998: Week $359 (rank 61); Year $18,644
　　FY 1997:　Manufacturing —$424 week　　$10.60 hour
　　　　　　　Services　　　　—$454 week　　$11.35 hour
Labor Force / **Employed** (July 2000): 17,750 / **17,110**
Non-Agri. Employment *in* the County, July 2000: 12,900
　　Manufacturing: 1,170 / Nonmanufacturing: 11,730
Unemployed / Rate (July 2000): **640** / 3.6%
No. Medicaid Eligibles, FY 1997: 4,451 (14.6% of pop.)
Federal Funds & Grants, 1998: $86,246,000
Cost of Living Index, 1999: 1.03 (average is 1.00)
Average County Millage, 1999: 96.45
Real Property, 1999 Assessed Value: $129,981,329
Real Property, 1998 Assessed Value: $120,010,189
　　True Value / No. of Parcels: **$995,993,700** / 22,446
Personal Property, 1999 Assessed Value: $82,993,176
Personal Property, 1998 Assessed Value: $75,753,989
　　True Value / No. of Parcels: **$342,790,991** / 1,194
Number of Personal Taxpayers, FY 1999: 10,273
Net State Taxable Income, FY 1999: $ 194,184,851
Gross State Income Tax, FY 1999:　　$　9,302,475
No. of State Corporate Taxpayers, FY 1999: 191
Corp. Income & Franchise Taxes, FY 1999: $272,864
Retail Sales: 1999—$729,145,217　　　1998—$655.5 m
Sales Tax / **No. Retailers** (1999): $48,392,298 / **1,095**
No. Vehicles Registered, FY Ending 6/30/99: 37,145
Education, 1990 - Average: 12.27 years (rank 5)
　　Graduates: High School 73.3%　　College 20.9%
Residents Enrolled in 8 State Universities, Fall 1999: 770
No. Hospitals / Beds / **Doctors** (8/1/2000): **1** / 211 / **7**
Number of Births / **Deaths** (1998): 635 / **274**
Land in Farms / No. Farms (1997): **74,162 acres** / 401

Sheriff; Purvis	(601) 794-8610
Chancery Clerk; Purvis	794-8504
Circuit Clerk; Purvis	794-8504
Tax Assessor & Collector; Purvis	794-1020

LAUDERDALE COUNTY

Established: 1833　　　　　　Seat: Meridian
Area in Square Miles: 705
Named for James Lauderdale, killed in Battle of New Orl.
Located in east-central Mississippi bordering Alabama
Incorporated Places with Estimated Population, 7/1/1998:
　　Marion 1,565　　　　　　Meridian 40,255
County Pop., 7/1/99: 75,978 (107.77 persons p/sq. mi.)
County Pop., 7/1/98: 76,143 (Voting Age: 55,977)
　　White: 47,452 (62.32%)　Nonwhite: 28,691 (37.68%)
　　Males: 35,868 (47.11%)　Females: 40,275 (52.89%)
　　Ages — 0-4: 5,551; 5-17: 14,615; 18-24: 7,976;
　　25-44: 21,991; 45-64: 15,563; 65 & older: 10,447
County Pop., 1990: 75,555 (57.6% urban—42.4% rural)
　　White: 48,667 (64.41%)　Nonwhite: 26,888 (35.59%)
Households / Persons Per Household, 1998: **28,455** / 2.7
Average Household Income, 1998: $57,388 (rank 11)
1995 Households with Income: Under $15,000—32.37%
　　$25,000-49,999—28.77%　$75,000 or more—7.79%
Per Capita Personal Income, 1998: $21,456 (rank 8)
Total Personal Income, 1998: $1,632,922,000
Total Wages & Salaries, 1998: $991,425,000
Avg. Wages, 1998: Week $454 (rank 17); Year $23,588
　　FY 1997:　Manufacturing —$551 week　　$13.78 hour
　　　　　　　Services　　　　—$469 week　　$11.73 hour
Labor Force / **Employed** (July 2000): 35,840 / **33,680**
Non-Agri. Employment *in* the County, July 2000: 36,580
　　Manufacturing: 4,770 / Nonmanufacturing: 31,810
Unemployed / Rate (July 2000): **2,160** / 6.0%
No. Medicaid Eligibles, FY 1997: 14,505 (19.2% of pop.)
Federal Funds & Grants, 1998: $431,933,000
Cost of Living Index, 1999: 1.03 (average is 1.00)
Average County Millage, 1999: 98.64
Real Property, 1999 Assessed Value: $211,072,589
Real Property, 1998 Assessed Value: $203,740,688
　　True Value / No. Parcels: **$1,668,902,215** / 40,328
Personal Property, 1999 Assessed Value: $127,061,358
Personal Property, 1998 Assessed Value: $125,862,278
　　True Value / No. of Parcels: **$590,125,051** / 2,174
Number of Personal Taxpayers, FY 1999: 28,209
Net State Taxable Income, FY 1999: $ 497,247,459
Gross State Income Tax, FY 1999:　　$ 24,514,286
No. of State Corporate Taxpayers, FY 1999: 1,204
Corp. Income & Franchise Taxes, FY 1999: $2,659,581
Retail Sales: 1999—$1,123,204,608　　1998—$1,094.3 m
Sales Tax / **No. Retailers** (1999): $69,616,963 / **2,485**
No. Vehicles Registered, FY Ending 6/30/99: 61,771
Education, 1990 - Average: 11.86 years (rank 12)
　　Graduates: High School 69.7%　　College 13.3%
Residents Enrolled in 8 State Universities, Fall '99: 1,136
No. Hospitals / Beds / **Doctors** (8/1/2000): **6** / 1,211 / **259**
Number of Births / **Deaths** (1998): 1,187 / **890**
Land in Farms / No. Farms (1997): **74,752 acres** / 357

Sheriff; 500 21st Ave; Meridian	(601) 482-9800
Chancery Clerk; Courthouse; Meridian	482-9701
Circuit Clerk; Meridian	482-9731
Tax Assessor; Meridian	482-9779
Tax Collector; Meridian	482-9786

LAWRENCE COUNTY

Established: 1814   Seat: Monticello
Area in Square Miles: 435
Named for Capt. James Lawrence, hero of War of 1812
Located in south-central Mississippi
Incorporated Places with Estimated Population, 7/1/1998:
     Monticello 1,732   New Hebron 382
     Silver Creek 192
County Pop., 7/1/99: 13,066 (30.04 persons p/sq. mi.)
County Pop., 7/1/98: 13,053 (Voting Age: 9,363)
    White: 8,412 (64.44%)   Nonwhite: 4,641 (35.56%)
    Males: 6,220 (47.65%)   Females: 6,833 (52.35%)
    Ages — 0-4: 890; 5-17: 2,800; 18-24: 1,161;
    25-44: 3,495; 45-64: 2,845; 65 & older: 1,862
County Pop., 1990: 12,458 (0.0% urban—100.0% rural)
    White: 8,290 (66.54%)   Nonwhite: 4,168 (33.46%)
Households / Persons Per Household, 1998: **4,699** / 2.8
Average Household Income, 1998: $47,960 (rank 47)
1995 Households with Income: Under $15,000—34.56%
    $25,000-49,999—30.11% $75,000 or more—5.79%
Per Capita Personal Income, 1998: $17,337 (rank 40)
Total Personal Income, 1998: $225,362,000
Total Wages & Salaries, 1998: $92,165,000
Avg. Wages, 1998: Week $497 (rank 6); Year $25,842
    FY 1997: Manufacturing —$677 week $16.93 hour
                 Services   —$370 week $ 9.25 hour
Labor Force / **Employed** (July 2000): 5,610 / **4,970**
Non-Agri. Employment *in* the County, July 2000: 3,340
    Manufacturing: 1,040 / Nonmanufacturing: 2,300
Unemployed / Rate (July 2000): **640** / 11.4%
No. Medicaid Eligibles, FY 1997: 2,646 (21.2% of pop.)
Federal Funds & Grants, 1998: $66,831,000
Cost of Living Index, 1999: 0.95 (average is 1.00)
Average County Millage, 1999: 97.45
Real Property, 1999 Assessed Value: $33,180,267
Real Property, 1998 Assessed Value: $32,017,599
    True Value / No. of Parcels: **$257,775,933** / 11,538
Personal Property, 1999 Assessed Value: $43,726,618
Personal Property, 1998 Assessed Value: $39,211,119
    True Value / No. of Parcels: **$226,234,705** / 487
Number of Personal Taxpayers, FY 1999: 4,729
Net State Taxable Income, FY 1999: $ 68,190,705
Gross State Income Tax, FY 1999: $ 3,193,186
No. of State Corporate Taxpayers, FY 1999: 112
Corp. Income & Franchise Taxes, FY 1999: $91,535
Retail Sales: 1999—$58,095,584   1998—$57.3 m
Sales Tax / **No. Retailers** (1999): $3,327,712 / **281**
No. Vehicles Registered, FY Ending 6/30/99: 12,307
Education, 1990 - Average: 11.13 years (rank 31)
    Graduates: High School 61.9%   College 9.2%
Residents Enrolled in 8 State Universities, Fall 1999: 205
No. Hospitals / Beds / **Doctors** (8/1/2000): **1** / 53 / **7**
Number of Births / **Deaths** (1998): 185 / **151**
Land in Farms / No. Farms (1997): **55,146 acres** / 308

Sheriff; Monticello	(601) 587-2961
Chancery Clerk; Monticello	587-7162
Circuit Clerk; Monticello	587-4791
Tax Assessor & Collector; Monticello	587-4543

LEAKE COUNTY

Established: 1833   Seat: Carthage
Area in Square Miles: 584
Named for Walther Leake, 3rd governor of Mississippi
Located in central Mississippi
Incorporated Places with Estimated Population, 7/1/1998:
     Carthage 4,084   Lena 171   Walnut Grove 394
County Pop., 7/1/99: 19,602 (33.57 persons p/sq. mi.)
County Pop., 7/1/98: 19,372 (Voting Age: 14,109)
    White: 11,185 (57.74%)   Nonwhite: 8,187 (42.26%)
    Males: 9,266 (47.83%)   Females: 10,106 (52.17%)
    Ages — 0-4: 1,317; 5-17: 3,946; 18-24: 1,798;
    25-44: 5,074; 45-64: 4,247; 65 & older: 2,990
County Pop., 1990: 18,436 (20.7% urban—79.3% rural)
    White: 11,081 (60.11%)   Nonwhite: 7,355 (39.89%)
Households / Persons Per Household, 1998: **7,142** / 2.7
Average Household Income, 1998: $52,412 (rank 27)
1995 Households with Income: Under $15,000—37.19%
    $25,000-49,999—29.90% $75,000 or more—4.04%
Per Capita Personal Income, 1998: $19,259 (rank 21)
Total Personal Income, 1998: $374,335,000
Total Wages & Salaries, 1998: $132,129,000
Avg. Wages, 1998: Week $337 (rank 76); Year $17,511
    FY 1997: Manufacturing —$290 week $7.25 hour
                 Services   —$364 week $9.10 hour
Labor Force / **Employed** (July 2000): 10,820 / **10,100**
Non-Agri. Employment *in* the County, July 2000: 7,010
    Manufacturing: 3,190 / Nonmanufacturing: 3,820
Unemployed / Rate (July 2000): **720** / 6.7%
No. Medicaid Eligibles, FY 1997: 4,165 (22.6% of pop.)
Federal Funds & Grants, 1998: $94,221,000
Cost of Living Index, 1999: 0.96 (average is 1.00)
Average County Millage, 1999: 95.66
Real Property, 1999 Assessed Value: $44,018,877
Real Property, 1998 Assessed Value: $42,740,939
    True Value / No. of Parcels: **$342,631,819** / 14,016
Personal Property, 1999 Assessed Value: $30,176,985
Personal Property, 1998 Assessed Value: $27,667,495
    True Value / No. of Parcels: **$126,365,882** / 658
Number of Personal Taxpayers, FY 1999: 6,835
Net State Taxable Income, FY 1999: $ 83,393,042
Gross State Income Tax, FY 1999: $ 3,802,383
No. of State Corporate Taxpayers, FY 1999: 148
Corp. Income & Franchise Taxes, FY 1999: $251,091
Retail Sales: 1999—$165,906,231   1998—$148.3 m
Sales Tax / **No. Retailers** (1999): $9,079,457 / **428**
No. Vehicles Registered, FY Ending 6/30/99: 17,495
Education, 1990 - Average: 10.83 years (rank 56)
    Graduates: High School 54.3%   College 9.2%
Residents Enrolled in 8 State Universities, Fall 1999: 280
No. Hospitals / Beds / **Doctors** (8/1/2000): **1** / 32 / **11**
Number of Births / **Deaths** (1998): 344 / **252**
Land in Farms / No. Farms (1997): **104,050 acres** / 583

Sheriff; Carthage	(601) 267-7361
Chancery Clerk; Courthouse; Carthage	267-7371
Circuit Clerk; Courthouse; Carthage	267-8357
Tax Assessor & Collector; Carthage	267-3021

Lee County

Established: 1866 Seat: Tupelo Area: 451 sq. mi.
Named for Robert E. Lee, General of the Confederacy
Located in the northeastern part of Mississippi
Incorporated Places with Estimated Population, 7/1/1998:
  Baldwyn (pt.) 1,582 Guntown 739 Nettleton (pt.) 1,208
  Plantersville 1,394 Saltillo 1,915 Shannon 1,589
  Tupelo 35,589 Verona 3,347
County Pop., 7/1/99: 75,211 (166.76 persons p/sq. mi.)
County Pop., 7/1/98: 74,637 (Voting Age: 54,470)
  White: 57,008 (76.66%) Nonwhite: 17,359 (23.34%)
  Males: 35,654 (47.77%) Females: 38,983 (52.23%)
  Ages — 0-4: 5,787; 5-17: 14,380; 18-24: 6,969;
  25-44: 23,275; 45-64: 15,858; 65 & older: 8,368
County Pop., 1990: 65,581 (53.1% urban—46.9% rural)
  White: 51,256 (78.16%) Nonwhite: 14,325 (21.84%)
Households / Persons Per Household, 1998: **27,713** / 2.7
Average Household Income, 1998: $63,240 (rank 7)
1995 Households with Income: Under $15,000—24.32%
  $25,000-49,999—32.83% $75,000 or more—10.32%
Per Capita Personal Income, 1998: $23,486 (rank 6)
Total Personal Income, 1998: $1,752,559,000
Total Wages & Salaries, 1998: $1,422,128,000
Avg. Wages, 1998: Week $485 (rank 9); Year $25,203
  FY 1997: Manufacturing —$524 week $13.10 hour
            Services   —$452 week $11.30 hour
Labor Force / **Employed** (July 2000): 41,980 / **40,040**
Non-Agri. Employment *in* the County, July 2000: 54,460
  Manufacturing: 17,420 / Nonmanufacturing: 37,040
Unemployed / Rate (July 2000): **1,940** / 4.6%
No. Medicaid Eligibles, FY 1997: 9,984 (15.2% of pop.)
Federal Funds & Grants, 1998: $291,249,000
Cost of Living Index, 1999: 1.08 (average is 1.00)
Average County Millage, 1999: 85.18
Real Property, 1999 Assessed Value: $259,838,745
Real Property, 1998 Assessed Value: $250,188,742
  True Value / No. Parcels: **$2,008,233,050** / 34,309
Personal Property, 1999 Assessed Value: $256,502,215
Personal Property, 1998 Assessed Value: $247,438,735
  True Value / No. of Parcels: **$1,377,686,600** / 3,801
Number of Personal Taxpayers, FY 1999: 32,616
Net State Taxable Income, FY 1999: $ 612,707,564
Gross State Income Tax, FY 1999: $ 29,781,373
No. of State Corporate Taxpayers, FY 1999: 1,394
Corp. Income & Franchise Taxes, FY 1999: $6,376,233
Retail Sales: 1999—$1,402,868,210 1998—$1,332.6 m
Sales Tax / **No. Retailers** (1999): $85,708,944 / **3,212**
No. Vehicles Registered, FY Ending 6/30/99: 67,886
Edu., '90 - Avg 11.8 yrs; Hi School 67.8%; College 15.0%
Residents Enrolled in 8 State Universities, Fall '99: 1,119
No. Hospitals/Beds / **Doctors** (8/1/2000): **2** / 700 / **260**
Number of Births / **Deaths** (1998): 1,199 / **671**
Land in Farms / No. Farms (1997): **135,004 acres** / 488

Sheriff; 301 Front St; Tupelo   (662) 841-9040
Chancery Clerk; 300 W Main St; Tupelo   841-9100
Circuit Clerk; Tupelo   841-9024
Tax Assessor; 201 Jefferson; Tupelo   841-9030
Tax Collector; Tupelo   841-9034

Leflore County

Established: 1871 Seat: Greenwood
Area in Square Miles: 605
Named for Greenwood Leflore, Chief of the Choctaws
Located in the northwestern part of Mississippi
Incorporated Places with Estimated Population, 7/1/1998:
  Greenwood 18,218 Itta Bena 2,264
  Morgan City 128 Schlater 419 Sidon 609
County Pop., 7/1/99: 36,816 (60.85 persons p/sq. mi.)
County Pop., 7/1/98: 36,951 (Voting Age: 25,810)
  White: 13,530 (36.62%) Nonwhite: 23,421 (63.38%)
  Males: 17,385 (46.05%) Females: 19,566 (52.95%)
  Ages — 0-4: 2,942; 5-17: 8,199; 18-24: 4,573;
  25-44: 9,851; 45-64: 6,728; 65 & older: 4,658
County Pop., 1990: 37,341 (50.6% urban—49.4% rural)
  White: 14,431 (38.65%) Nonwhite: 22,910 (61.35%)
Households / Persons Per Household, 1998: **12,735** / 2.9
Average Household Income, 1998: $52,388 (rank 28)
1995 Households with Income: Under $15,000—39.27%
  $25,000-49,999—25.73% $75,000 or more—7.82%
Per Capita Personal Income, 1998: $17,915 (rank 31)
Total Personal Income, 1998: $667,171,000
Total Wages & Salaries, 1998: $368,754,000
Avg. Wages, 1998: Week $399 (rank 43); Year $20,723
  FY 1997: Manufacturing —$384 week $9.60 hour
            Services   —$397 week $9.93 hour
Labor Force / **Employed** (July 2000): 16,050 / **14,490**
Non-Agri. Employment *in* the County, July 2000: 16,100
  Manufacturing: 3,820 / Nonmanufacturing: 12,280
Unemployed / Rate (July 2000): **1,560** / 9.7%
No. Medicaid Eligibles, FY 1997: 13,341 (35.4% of pop.)
Federal Funds & Grants, 1998: $199,414,000
Cost of Living Index, 1999: 0.97 (average is 1.00)
Average County Millage, 1999: 114.34
Real Property, 1999 Assessed Value: $86,524,520
Real Property, 1998 Assessed Value: $84,558,799
  True Value / No. of Parcels: **$662,323,914** / 16,328
Personal Property, 1999 Assessed Value: $54,646,756
Personal Property, 1998 Assessed Value: $51,422,203
  True Value / No. of Parcels: **$254,722,431** / 1,209
Number of Personal Taxpayers, FY 1999: 11,583
Net State Taxable Income, FY 1999: $ 160,858,162
Gross State Income Tax, FY 1999: $ 7,646,561
No. of State Corporate Taxpayers, FY 1999: 746
Corp. Income & Franchise Taxes, FY 1999: $954,890
Retail Sales: 1999—$383,399,999 1998—$374.3 m
Sales Tax / **No. Retailers** (1999): $23,827,298 / **1,005**
No. Vehicles Registered, FY Ending 6/30/99: 22,517
Edu., '90 - Avg 11.0 yrs; Hi School 55.3%; College 15.7%
Residents Enrolled in 8 State Universities, Fall '99: 1,219
No. Hospitals / Beds / **Doctors** (8/1/2000): **1** / 260 / **71**
Number of Births / **Deaths** (1998): 645 / **385**
Land in Farms / No. Farms (1997): **267,357 acres** / 246

Sheriff; Greenwood   (662) 453-5141
Chancery Clerk; Greenwood   453-6203
Circuit Clerk; Greenwood   453-1435
Tax Assessor; Greenwood   455-7900
Tax Collector; Greenwood   453-6205

Lincoln County

Established: 1870　　　　Seat: Brookhaven
Area in Square Miles: 586
Named for Abraham Lincoln, 16th. President of the U.S.
Located in southwest Mississippi
Incorporated Places with Estimated Population, 7/1/1998:
　　Brookhaven 10,649
County Pop., 7/1/99: 32,105 (54.79 persons p/sq. mi.)
County Pop., 7/1/98: 31,771 (Voting Age: 23,225)
　　White: 21,467 (67.57%)　　Nonwhite: 10,304 (32.43%)
　　Males: 15,122 (47.60%)　　Females: 16,649 (52.40%)
　　Ages — 0-4: 1,983; 5-17: 6,563; 18-24: 2,886;
　　25-44: 8,892; 45-64: 6,872; 65 & older: 4,575
County Pop., 1990: 30,278 (33.8% urban—66.2% rural)
　　White: 21,128 (69.78%)　　Nonwhite: 9,150 (30.22%)
Households / Persons Per Household, 1998: **11,662** / 2.7
Average Household Income, 1998: $50,063 (rank 38)
1995 Households with Income: Under $15,000—35.85%
　$25,000-49,999—27.02%　$75,000 or more—6.12%
Per Capita Personal Income, 1998: $18,326 (rank 29)
Total Personal Income, 1998: $583,860,000
Total Wages & Salaries, 1998: $275,292,000
Avg. Wages, 1998: Week $415 (rank 34); Year $21,579
　FY 1997:　Manufacturing —$516 week　　$12.90 hour
　　　　　　Services　　—$373 week　$ 9.33 hour
Labor Force / **Employed** (July 2000): 14,650 / **13,870**
Non-Agri. Employment *in* the County, July 2000: 12,400
　Manufacturing: 1,750 / Nonmanufacturing: 10,650
Unemployed / Rate (July 2000): **780** / 5.3%
No. Medicaid Eligibles, FY 1997: 6,010 (19.8% of pop.)
Federal Funds & Grants, 1998: $130,470,000
Cost of Living Index, 1999: 0.96 (average is 1.00)
Average County Millage, 1999: 87.79
Real Property, 1999 Assessed Value: $81,051,329
Real Property, 1998 Assessed Value: $78,956,498
　True Value / No. of Parcels: **$641,590,830** / 20,050
Personal Property, 1999 Assessed Value: $63,936,806
Personal Property, 1998 Assessed Value: $59,978,780
　True Value / No. of Parcels: **$273,316,029** / 1,390
Number of Personal Taxpayers, FY 1999: 10,937
Net State Taxable Income, FY 1999: $ 172,016,953
Gross State Income Tax, FY 1999: 　$ 8,139,357
No. of State Corporate Taxpayers, FY 1999: 381
Corp. Income & Franchise Taxes, FY 1999: $5115,804
Retail Sales: 1999—$400,447,870　　1998—$377.4 m
Sales Tax / **No. Retailers** (1999): $23,895,187 / **945**
No. Vehicles Registered, FY Ending 6/30/99: 30,220
Education, 1990 - Average: 11.44 years (rank 20)
　Graduates: High School 63.0%　　College 11.6%
Residents Enrolled in 8 State Universities, Fall 1999: 384
No. Hospitals / Beds / **Doctors** (8/1/2000): **1** / 122 / **37**
Number of Births / **Deaths** (1998): 510 / **401**
Land in Farms / No. Farms (1997): **98,854 acres** / 499

Sheriff; Brookhaven	(601) 833-5231
Chancery Clerk; Courthouse; Brookhaven	835-3411
Circuit Clerk; Courthouse; Brookhaven	835-3435
Tax Assessor; 301 S First; Brookhaven	835-3425
Tax Collector; 301 S First; Brookhaven	835-3427

Lowndes County

Established: 1830　　　　Seat: Columbus
Area in Square Miles: 517
Named for William Lowndes-noted Carolina congressman
Located in east-central Mississippi bordering Alabama
Incorporated Places with Estimated Population, 7/1/1998:
　　Artesia 528　　　　　Caledonia 877
　　Columbus 22,297　　　Crawford 739
County Pop., 7/1/99: 60,527 (117.07 persons p/sq. mi.)
County Pop., 7/1/98: 61,208 (Voting Age: 44,034)
　　White: 36,591 (59.78%)　　Nonwhite: 24,617 (40.22%)
　　Males: 28,984 (47.35%)　　Females: 32,224 (52.65%)
　　Ages — 0-4: 5,017; 5-17: 12,157; 18-24: 7,242;
　　25-44: 18,854; 45-64: 11,514; 65 & older: 6,424
County Pop., 1990: 59,308 (45.0% urban—55.0% rural)
　　White: 36,769 (62.00%)　　Nonwhite: 22,539 (38.00%)
Households / Persons Per Household, 1998: **21,948** / 2.8
Average Household Income, 1998: $56,319 (rank 14)
1995 Households with Income: Under $15,000—30.40%
　$25,000-49,999—31.11%　$75,000 or more—7.01%
Per Capita Personal Income, 1998: $20,249 (rank 12)
Total Personal Income, 1998: $1,236,108,000
Total Wages & Salaries, 1998: $780,371,000
Avg. Wages, 1998: Week $475 (rank 10); Year $24,716
　FY 1997:　Manufacturing —$588 week　　$14.70 hour
　　　　　　Services　　—$413 week　$10.33 hour
Labor Force / **Employed** (July 2000): 26,800 / **25,190**
Non-Agri. Employment *in* the County, July 2000: 26,680
　Manufacturing: 6,410 / Nonmanufacturing: 20,270
Unemployed / Rate (July 2000): **1,610** / 6.0%
No. Medicaid Eligibles, FY 1997: 11,828 (19.9% of pop.)
Federal Funds & Grants, 1998: $384,161,000
Cost of Living Index, 1999: 1.01 (average is 1.00)
Average County Millage, 1999: 97.40
Real Property, 1999 Assessed Value: $171,764,170
Real Property, 1998 Assessed Value: $167,765,779
　True Value / No. of Parcels: **$1,364,840,959** / 27,551
Personal Property, 1999 Assessed Value: $174,779,544
Personal Property, 1998 Assessed Value: $173,998,856
　True Value / No. of Parcels: **$976,411,600** / 2,260
Number of Personal Taxpayers, FY 1999: 22,757
Net State Taxable Income, FY 1999: $ 372,451,687
Gross State Income Tax, FY 1999:　$ 17,779,481
No. of State Corporate Taxpayers, FY 1999: 908
Corp. Income & Franchise Taxes, FY 1999: $2,322,887
Retail Sales: 1999—$836,821,925　　1998—$761.2 m
Sales Tax / **No. Retailers** (1999): $50,231,357 / **1,868**
No. Vehicles Registered, FY Ending 6/30/99: 49,405
Edu., '90 - Avg 11.9 yrs; Hi School 69.0%; College 18.6%
Residents Enrolled in 8 State Universities, Fall '99: 2,190
No. Hospitals / Beds / **Doctors** (8/1/2000): **1** / 328 / **96**
Number of Births / **Deaths** (1998): 983 / **526**
Land in Farms / No. Farms (1997): **145,098 acres** / 378

Sheriff; Columbus	(662) 329-5827
County Administrator; Columbus	329-5896
Chancery Clerk; 2nd Ave N; Columbus	329-5800
Circuit Clerk; Columbus	329-5900
Tax Assessor & Collector; Columbus	329-5707

Madison County

Established: 1828   Seat: Canton   Area: 717 sq. mi.
Named for James Madison, 4th President of the U.S.
Located in the central part of Mississippi
Incorporated Places with Estimated Population, 7/1/1998:
  Canton 12,221   Flora 1,585
  Jackson (part) 853   Madison 12,618   Ridgeland 16,545
County Pop., 7/1/99: 74,562 (103.99 persons p/sq. mi.)
County Pop., 7/1/98: 72,857 (Voting Age: 52,253)
  White: 38,452 (52.78%)   Nonwhite: 34,405 (47.22%)
  Males: 34,485 (47.33%)   Females: 38,372 (52.67%)
  Ages — 0-4: 6,180; 5-17: 14,424; 18-24: 7,759;
  25-44: 24,717; 45-64: 12,940; 65 & older: 6,837
County Pop., 1990: 53,794 (58.0% urban—42.0% rural)
  White: 29,773 (55.35%)   Nonwhite: 24,021 (44.65%)
Households / Persons Per Household, 1998: **25,878** / 2.8
Average Household Income, 1998: $70,678 (rank 3)
1995 Households with Income: Under $15,000—26.24%
  $25,000-49,999—29.01% $75,000 or more—11.69%
Per Capita Personal Income, 1998: $25,096 (rank 1)
Total Personal Income, 1998: $1,828,987,000
Total Wages & Salaries, 1998: $652,203,000
Avg. Wages, 1998: Week $454 (rank 16); Year $23,589
  FY 1997: Manufacturing —$473 week $11.83 hour
           Services   —$438 week $10.95 hour
Labor Force / **Employed** (July 2000): 39,190 / **37,630**
Non-Agri. Employment *in* the County, July 2000: 25,440
  Manufacturing: 3,190 / Nonmanufacturing: 22,250
Unemployed / Rate (July 2000): **1,560** / 4.0%
No. Medicaid Eligibles, FY 1997: 10,750 (20% of pop.)
Federal Funds & Grants, 1998: $312,960,000
Cost of Living Index, 1999: 1.14 (average is 1.00)
Average County Millage, 1999: 83.36
Real Property, 1999 Assessed Value: $294,060,910
Real Property, 1998 Assessed Value: $274,230,750
  True Value / No. Parcels: **$2,322,599,380** / 35,782
Personal Property, 1999 Assessed Value: $183,704,085
Personal Property, 1998 Assessed Value: $169,916,650
  True Value / No. of Parcels: **$732,050,667** / 2,480
Number of Personal Taxpayers, FY 1999: 27,168
Net State Taxable Income, FY 1999: $ 781,331,018
Gross State Income Tax, FY 1999: $ 41,509,844
No. of State Corporate Taxpayers, FY 1999: 1,404
Corp. Income & Franchise Taxes, FY 1999: $1,398,186
Retail Sales: 1999—$1,094,094,279   1998—$961.1 m
Sales Tax / **No. Retailers** (1999): $68,366,594 / **1,963**
No. Vehicles Registered, FY Ending 6/30/99: 67,013
Education, 1990 - Average: 12.44 years (rank 3)
  Graduates: High School 71.5%   College 29.3%
Residents Enrolled in 8 State Universities, Fall '99: 1,234
No. Hospitals / Beds / **Doctors** (8/1/2000): **1** / 67 / **105**
Number of Births / **Deaths** (1998): 1,243 / **518**
Land in Farms / No. Farms (1997): **182,095 acres** / 465

Sheriff; Canton	(601) 859-2345
Chancery Clerk; 135 W Center; Canton	859-1177
Circuit Clerk; Canton	859-4365
Tax Assessor; Canton/Ridgeland	859-1921/856-1796
Tax Collector; Canton/Ridgeland	859-5226/856-4472

Marion County

Established: 1811   Seat: Columbia
Area in Square Miles: 548
Named for Frances Marion, Revoluntionary War General
Located in south-central Mississippi bordering Louisiana
Incorporated Places with Estimated Population, 7/1/1998:
  Columbia 6,935
County Pop., 7/1/99: 26,538 (48.43 persons p/sq. mi.)
County Pop., 7/1/98: 26,386 (Voting Age: 18,723)
  White: 17,734 (67.21%)   Nonwhite: 8,,652 (32.79%)
  Males: 12,735 (48.26%)   Females: 13,651 (51.74%)
  Ages — 0-4: 1,811; 5-17: 5,852; 18-24: 2,363;
  25-44: 7,182; 45-64: 5,438; 65 & older: 3,740
County Pop., 1990: 25,544 (26.7% urban—73.3% rural)
  White: 17,692 (69.26%)   Nonwhite: 7,852 (30.74%)
Households / Persons Per Household, 1998: **9,428** / 2.8
Average Household Income, 1998: $45,313 (rank 61)
1995 Households with Income: Under $15,000—37.40%
  $25,000-49,999—27.65% $75,000 or more—4.59%
Per Capita Personal Income, 1998: $16,180 (rank 58)
Total Personal Income, 1998: $427,219,000
Total Wages & Salaries, 1998: $165,914,000
Avg. Wages, 1998: Week $356 (rank 65); Year $18,493
  FY 1997: Manufacturing —$291 week $7.28 hour
           Services   —$370 week $9.25 hour
Labor Force / **Employed** (July 2000): 11,110 / **10,160**
Non-Agri. Employment *in* the County, July 2000: 8,140
  Manufacturing: 1,410 / Nonmanufacturing: 6,730
Unemployed / Rate (July 2000): **950** / 8.6%
No. Medicaid Eligibles, FY 1997: 6,443 (25.2% of pop.)
Federal Funds & Grants, 1998: $131,370,000
Cost of Living Index, 1999: 0.94 (average is 1.00)
Average County Millage, 1999: 95.28
Real Property, 1999 Assessed Value: $55,455,876
Real Property, 1998 Assessed Value: $53,587,412
  True Value / No. of Parcels: **$438,827,130** / 15,560
Personal Property, 1999 Assessed Value: $40,841,256
Personal Property, 1998 Assessed Value: $37,709,495
  True Value / No. of Parcels: **$167,288,742** / 986
Number of Personal Taxpayers, FY 1999: 8,705
Net State Taxable Income, FY 1999: $ 98,003,381
Gross State Income Tax, FY 1999: $ 4,516,692
No. of State Corporate Taxpayers, FY 1999: 350
Corp. Income & Franchise Taxes, FY 1999: $602,214
Retail Sales: 1999—$235,810,569   1998—$217.3 m
Sales Tax / **No. Retailers** (1999): $14,551,187 / **719**
No. Vehicles Registered, FY Ending 6/30/99: 24,209
Education, 1990 - Average: 11.00 years (rank 38)
  Graduates: High School 58.8%   College 8.4%
Residents Enrolled in 8 State Universities, Fall 1999: 416
No. Hospitals / Beds / **Doctors** (8/1/2000): **1** / 79 / **19**
Number of Births / **Deaths** (1998): 374 / **316**
Land in Farms / No. Farms (1997): **97,378 acres** / 485

Sheriff; 500 Courthouse Sq. #1 Columbia	(601) 736-5051
Chancery Clerk; 250 Broad St; Columbia	736-2691
Circuit Clerk; 250 Broad St; Columbia	736-8246
Tax Assessor; 250 Broad St; Columbia	736-3157
Tax Collector; 250 Broad St; Columbia	736-8256

Marshall County

Established: 1836   Seat: Holly Springs
Area in Square Miles: 709
Named for John Marshall, Chief Justice of Supreme Court
Located in northern Mississippi bordering Tennessee
Incorporated Places with Estimated Population, 7/1/1998:
    Byhalia 951   Holly Springs 7,195   Potts Camp 483
County Pop., 7/1/99: 32,323 (45.59 persons p/sq. mi.)
County Pop., 7/1/98: 32,296 (Voting Age: 23,167)
    White: 15,124 (46.83%)   Nonwhite: 17,172 (53.17%)
    Males: 15,397 (47.67%)   Females: 16,899 (52.33%)
    Ages — 0-4: 2,483; 5-17: 6,646; 18-24: 3,801;
    25-44: 9,102; 45-64: 6,606; 65 & older: 3,658
County Pop., 1990: 30,361 (23.9% urban—76.1% rural)
    White: 14,869 (48.97%)   Nonwhite: 15,492 (51.03%)
Households / Persons Per Household, 1998: **10,650** / 3.0
Average Household Income, 1998: $54,003 (rank 18)
1995 Households with Income: Under $15,000—36.35%
    $25,000-49,999—29.56% $75,000 or more—4.02%
Per Capita Personal Income, 1998: $17,878 (rank 32)
Total Personal Income, 1998: $575,122,000
Total Wages & Salaries, 1998: $160,794,000
Avg. Wages, 1998: Week $377 (rank 55); Year $19,581
    FY 1997:   Manufacturing —$457 week $11.43 hour
                    Services   —$339 week $ 8.48 hour
Labor Force / **Employed** (July 2000): 15,000 / **14,220**
Non-Agri. Employment *in* the County, July 2000: 8,380
    Manufacturing: 2,130 / Nonmanufacturing: 6,250
Unemployed / Rate (July 2000): **870** / 5.8%
No. Medicaid Eligibles, FY 1997: 7,534 (24.8% of pop.)
Federal Funds & Grants, 1998: $133,929,000
Cost of Living Index, 1999: 0.96 (average is 1.00)
Average County Millage, 1999: 114.79
Real Property, 1999 Assessed Value: $72,252,029
Real Property, 1998 Assessed Value: $68,116,241
    True Value / No. of Parcels: **$558,620,670** / 20,033
Personal Property, 1999 Assessed Value: $47,902,250
Personal Property, 1998 Assessed Value: $44,300,066
    True Value / No. of Parcels: **$212,619,972** / 1,088
Number of Personal Taxpayers, FY 1999: 12,848
Net State Taxable Income, FY 1999: $ 152,556,578
Gross State Income Tax, FY 1999: $ 6,988,293
No. of State Corporate Taxpayers, FY 1999: 163
Corp. Income & Franchise Taxes, FY 1999: $403,346
Retail Sales: 1999—$168,382,695   1998—$149.3 m
Sales Tax / **No. Retailers** (1999): $10,136,336 / **669**
No. Vehicles Registered, FY Ending 6/30/99: 28,258
Education, 1990 - Average: 10.65 years (rank 69)
    Graduates: High School 51.7%   College 9.4%
Residents Enrolled in 8 State Universities, Fall 1999: 287
No. Hospitals / Beds / **Doctors** (8/1/2000): **1** / **40** / **16**
Number of Births / **Deaths** (1998): 500 / **305**
Land in Farms / No. Farms (1997): **181,342 acres** / 469

Sheriff; 136 N Anderson; Holly Springs   (662) 252-1311
Chancery Clerk; Holly Springs   252-4431
Circuit Clerk; Courthouse; Holly Springs   252-3434
Tax Assessor; Holly Springs   252-6209
Tax Collector; Holly Springs   252-3661

Monroe County

Established: 1821   Seat: Aberdeen
Area in Square Miles: 772
Named for U.S. President James Monroe
Located in northeast Mississippi bordering Alabama
Incorporated Places with Estimated Population, 7/1/1998:
    Aberdeen 6,915   Amory 7,144   Gattman 131
    Hatley 558   Nettleton (pt) 1,404   Smithville 898
County Pop., 7/1/99: 38,230 (49.52 persons p/sq. mi.)
County Pop., 7/1/98: 38,263 (Voting Age: 27,743)
    White: 25,754 (67.31%)   Nonwhite: 12,509 (32.69%)
    Males: 18,050 (47.17%)   Females: 20,213 (52.83%)
    Ages — 0-4: 2,767; 5-17: 7,753; 18-24: 3,695;
    25-44: 10,629; 45-64: 8,276; 65 & older: 5,143
County Pop., 1990: 36,582 (38.1% urban—61.9% rural)
    White: 25,325 (69.23%)   Nonwhite: 11,257 (30.77%)
Households / Persons Per Household, 1998: **13,891** / 2.7
Average Household Income, 1998: $45,719 (rank 58)
1995 Households with Income: Under $15,000—33.19%
    $25,000-49,999—30.58% $75,000 or more—4.39%
Per Capita Personal Income, 1998: $16,667 (rank 50)
Total Personal Income, 1998: $635,085,000
Total Wages & Salaries, 1998: $282,280,000
Avg. Wages, 1998: Week $456 (rank 14); Year $23,733
    FY 1997:   Manufacturing —$528 week $13.20 hour
                    Services   —$381 week $ 9.53 hour
Labor Force / **Employed** (July 2000): 15,980 / **13,910**
Non-Agri. Employment *in* the County, July 2000: 11,160
    Manufacturing: 4,010 / Nonmanufacturing: 7,150
Unemployed / Rate (July 2000): **2,070** / 13.0%
No. Medicaid Eligibles, FY 1997: 6,307 (17.2% of pop.)
Federal Funds & Grants, 1998: $145,299,000
Cost of Living Index, 1999: 0.96 (average is 1.00)
Average County Millage, 1999: 87.92
Real Property, 1999 Assessed Value: $73,178,504
Real Property, 1998 Assessed Value: $71,714,081
    True Value / No. of Parcels: **$600,839,751** / 25,312
Personal Property, 1999 Assessed Value: $98,146,007
Personal Property, 1998 Assessed Value: $94,100,164
    True Value / No. of Parcels: **$510,873,267** / 1,380
Number of Personal Taxpayers, FY 1999: 13,966
Net State Taxable Income, FY 1999: $ 194,353,814
Gross State Income Tax, FY 1999: $ 8,882,710
No. of State Corporate Taxpayers, FY 1999: 364
Corp. Income & Franchise Taxes, FY 1999: $666,419
Retail Sales: 1999—$290,054,455   1998—$293.2 m
Sales Tax / **No. Retailers** (1999): $16,870,753 / **955**
No. Vehicles Registered, FY Ending 6/30/99: 32,944
Edu., '90 - Avg. 10.83 yrs; Hi School 55.6%; College 8.4%
Residents Enrolled in 8 State Universities, Fall 1999: 600
No. Hospitals / Beds / **Doctors** (8/1/2000): **2** / **144** / **46**
Number of Births / **Deaths** (1998): 545 / **404**
Land in Farms / No. Farms (1997): **162,346 acres** / 504

Sheriff; Aberdeen   (662) 369-2468
Chancery Clerk; 201 W Commerce; Aberdeen   369-8143
Circuit Clerk; Courthouse; Aberdeen   369-8695
Tax Assessor & Collector; Aberdeen   369-2033
Tax Collector; Aberdeen   369-6484

The Ultimate Reference on the State

MONTGOMERY COUNTY

Established: 1871   Seat: Winona
Area in Square Miles: 408
Named for Richard Montgomery, Revol. War General
Located in the central part of Mississippi
Incorporated Places with Estimated Population, 7/1/1998:
    Duck Hill 1,331   Kilmichael 784   Winona 5,647
County Pop., 7/1/99: 12,394 (30.38 persons p/sq. mi.)
County Pop., 7/1/98: 12,425 (Voting Age: 9,078)
    White: 6,670 (53.68%)   Nonwhite: 5,755 (46.32%)
    Males: 5,783 (46.54%)   Females: 6,642 (53.46%)
        Ages — 0-4: 821; 5-17: 2,526; 18-24: 1,190;
        25-44: 3,120; 45-64: 2,756; 65 & older: 2,012
County Pop., 1990: 12,388 (46.1% urban—53.9% rural)
    White: 6,929 (55.93%)   Nonwhite: 5,459 (44.07%)
Households / Persons Per Household, 1998: **4,531** / 2.7
Average Household Income, 1998: $45,348 (rank 60)
1995 Households with Income: Under $15,000—37.81%
    $25,000-49,999—25.65% $75,000 or more—4.92%
Per Capita Personal Income, 1998: $16,566 (rank 52)
Total Personal Income, 1998: $205,451,000
Total Wages & Salaries, 1998: $61,633,000
Avg. Wages, 1998: Week $324 (rank 80); Year $16,873
    FY 1997: Manufacturing —$322 week $8.05 hour
              Services   —$346 week $8.65 hour
Labor Force / **Employed** (July 2000): 5,720 / **5,350**
Non-Agri. Employment *in* the County, July 2000: 3,420
    Manufacturing: 660 / Nonmanufacturing: 2,760
Unemployed / Rate (July 2000): **370** / 6.5%
No. Medicaid Eligibles, FY 1997: 3,080 (24.9% of pop.)
Federal Funds & Grants, 1998: $72,563,000
Cost of Living Index, 1999: 0.95 (average is 1.00)
Average County Millage, 1999: 101.47
Real Property, 1999 Assessed Value: $25,444,281
Real Property, 1998 Assessed Value: $24,714,333
    True Value / No. of Parcels: **$202,542,484** / 9,532
Personal Property, 1999 Assessed Value: $15,483,930
Personal Property, 1998 Assessed Value: $15,213,838
    True Value / No. of Parcels: **$66,568,242** / 471
Number of Personal Taxpayers, FY 1999: 4,569
Net State Taxable Income, FY 1999: $ 47,856,637
Gross State Income Tax, FY 1999: $ 2,155,874
No. of State Corporate Taxpayers, FY 1999: 79
Corp. Income & Franchise Taxes, FY 1999: $232,069
Retail Sales: 1999—$86,539,592   1998—$84.1 m
Sales Tax / **No. Retailers** (1999): $5,290,775 / **341**
No. Vehicles Registered, FY Ending 6/30/99: 9,676
Education, 1990 - Average: 10.95 years (rank 46)
    Graduates: High School 56.6%   College 9.5%
Residents Enrolled in 8 State Universities, Fall 1999: 281
No. Hospitals / Beds / **Doctors** (8/1/2000): **2** / 68 / **11**
Number of Births / **Deaths** (1998): 191 / **155**
Land in Farms / No. Farms (1997): **92,299 acres** / 286

Sheriff; Winona   (662) 283-4612
Chancery Clerk; N Summit; Winona   283-2333
Circuit Clerk; N Summit; Winona   283-4161
Tax Assessor & Collector; N Summit; Winona   283-2112

NESHOBA COUNTY

Established: 1833   Seat: Philadelphia
Area in Square Miles: 571
Named for the Indian word meaning "wolf"
Located in east-central Mississippi
Incorporated Places with Estimated Population, 7/1/1998:
    Philadelphia 7,725   Union (part) 466
County Pop., 7/1/99: 27,639 (48.40 persons p/sq. mi.)
County Pop., 7/1/98: 27,653 (Voting Age: 19,630)
    White: 18,278 (66.10%)   Nonwhite: 9,375 (33.90%)
    Males: 13,271(48.00%)   Females: 14,382 (52.00%)
        Ages — 0-4: 1,963; 5-17: 6,060; 18-24: 2,603;
        25-44: 7,452; 45-64: 5,788; 65 & older: 3,787
County Pop., 1990: 24,800 (27.3% urban—72.7% rural)
    White: 16,990 (68.51%)   Nonwhite: 7,810 (31.49%)
Households / Persons Per Household, 1998: **9,806** / 2.8
Average Household Income, 1998: $56,647 (rank 13)
1995 Households with Income: Under $15,000—32.08%
    $25,000-49,999—31.14% $75,000 or more—5.05%
Per Capita Personal Income, 1998: $20,198 (rank 13)
Total Personal Income, 1998: $555,491,000
Total Wages & Salaries, 1998: $320,196,000
Avg. Wages, 1998: Week $420 (rank 31); Year $21,818
    FY 1997: Manufacturing —$387 week $9.68 hour
              Services   —$386 week $9.65 hour
Labor Force / **Employed** (July 2000): 16,300 / **15,430**
Non-Agri. Employment *in* the County, July 2000: 13,340
    Manufacturing: 2,670 / Nonmanufacturing: 10,670
Unemployed / Rate (July 2000): **870** / 5.3%
No. Medicaid Eligibles, FY 1997: 5,341 (21.5% of pop.)
Federal Funds & Grants, 1998: $125,184,000
Cost of Living Index, 1999: 1.00 (average is 1.00)
Average County Millage, 1999: 96.21
Real Property, 1999 Assessed Value: $53,615,967
Real Property, 1998 Assessed Value: $51,943,668
    True Value / No. of Parcels: **$427,406,485** / 16,499
Personal Property, 1999 Assessed Value: $40,958,960
Personal Property, 1998 Assessed Value: $43,205,596
    True Value / No. of Parcels: **$213,236,790** / 866
Number of Personal Taxpayers, FY 1999: 8,280
Net State Taxable Income, FY 1999: $ 118,146,714
Gross State Income Tax, FY 1999: $ 5,454,818
No. of State Corporate Taxpayers, FY 1999: 200
Corp. Income & Franchise Taxes, FY 1999: $1,190,038
Retail Sales: 1999—$306,541,788   1998—$326.3 m
Sales Tax / **No. Retailers** (1999): $17,638,785 / **657**
No. Vehicles Registered, FY Ending 6/30/99: 24,778
Education, 1990 - Average: 11.20 years (rank 28)
    Graduates: High School 60.9%   College 10.1%
Residents Enrolled in 8 State Universities, Fall 1999: 334
No. Hospitals / Beds / **Doctors** (8/1/2000): **1** / 82 / **21**
Number of Births / **Deaths** (1998): 447 / **331**
Land in Farms / No. Farms (1997): **140,511 acres** / 608

Sheriff; 401 E Beacon St; Philadelphia   (601) 656-1414
Chancery Clerk; 401 E Beacon; Philadelphia   656-3581
Circuit Clerk; 401 E Beacon St; Philadelphia 656-4781
Tax Assessor & Collector; Philadelphia   656-4541

Newton County

Established: 1836　　　　　　Seat: Decatur
Area in Square Miles: 580
Named for scientist and mathematician Sir Isaac Newton
Located in east-central Mississippi
Incorporated Places with Estimated Population, 7/1/1998:
　　Chunky 315　　　Decatur 1,352　　　Hickory 531
　　Lake (part) 21　　Newton 3,749　　Union (pt) 1,407
County Pop., 7/1/99: 21,741 (37.48 persons p/sq. mi.)
County Pop., 7/1/98: 21,516 (Voting Age: 15,822)
　　White: 14,026 (65.19%)　　Nonwhite: 7,490 (34.81%)
　　Males: 10,305 (47.89%)　　Females: 11,211 (52.11%)
　　Ages — 0-4: 1,427; 5-17: 4,267; 18-24: 2,431;
　　25-44: 5,666; 45-64: 4,581; 65 & older: 3,144
County Pop., 1990: 20,291 (18.2% urban—81.8% rural)
　　White: 13,704 (67.54%)　　Nonwhite: 6,587 (32.46%)
Households / Persons Per Household, 1998: **7,813** / 2.8
Average Household Income, 1998: $52,362 (rank 29)
1995 Households with Income: Under $15,000—34.50%
　　$25,000-49,999—31.25%　$75,000 or more—4.73%
Per Capita Personal Income, 1998: $18,944 (rank 25)
Total Personal Income, 1998: $409,128,000
Total Wages & Salaries, 1998: $155,258,000
Avg. Wages, 1998: Week $392 (rank 47); Year $20,358
　　FY 1997: Manufacturing —$421 week　　$10.53 hour
　　　　　　　Services 　　—$377 week　　$ 9.43 hour
Labor Force / **Employed** (July 2000): 8,810 / **8,300**
Non-Agri. Employment in the County, July 2000: 7,000
　　Manufacturing: 2,350 / Nonmanufacturing: 4,650
Unemployed / Rate (July 2000): **510** / 5.8%
No. Medicaid Eligibles, FY 1997: 4,033 (19.9% of pop.)
Federal Funds & Grants, 1998: $106,752,000
Cost of Living Index, 1999: 0.97 (average is 1.00)
Average County Millage, 1999: 104.98
Real Property, 1999 Assessed Value: $43,293,180
Real Property, 1998 Assessed Value: $43,015,399
　　True Value / No. of Parcels: **$350,081,173** / 14,209
Personal Property, 1999 Assessed Value: $30,896,867
Personal Property, 1998 Assessed Value: $31,444,771
　　True Value / No. of Parcels: **$147,478,994** / 713
Number of Personal Taxpayers, FY 1999: 7,984
Net State Taxable Income, FY 1999:　$ 99,296,162
Gross State Income Tax, FY 1999:　　$ 4,499,388
No. of State Corporate Taxpayers, FY 1999: 149
Corp. Income & Franchise Taxes, FY 1999: $119,813
Retail Sales: 1999—$126,311,514　　　1998—$122.7 m
Sales Tax / **No. Retailers** (1999): $7,537,356 / **458**
No. Vehicles Registered, FY Ending 6/30/99: 18,437
Education, 1990 - Average: 11.25 years (rank 25)
　　Graduates: High School 60.1%　　College 9.7%
Residents Enrolled in 8 State Universities, Fall 1999: 271
No. Hospitals / Beds / **Doctors** (8/1/2000): **2** / 99 / **17**
Number of Births / **Deaths** (1998): 346 / **243**
Land in Farms / No. Farms (1997): **100,328 acres** / 543

Sheriff; Decatur	(601) 635-2101
Chancery Clerk; Decatur	635-2367
Circuit Clerk; Decatur	635-2368
Tax Assessor & Collector; Decatur	635-2517

Noxubee County

Established: 1833　　　　　　Seat: Macon
Area in Square Miles: 698
Named for the Indian word meaning "stinking water"
Located in eastern Mississippi bordering Alabama
Incorporated Places with Estimated Population, 7/1/1998:
　　Brooksville 1,044　　Macon 2,298　　Shuqualak 578
County Pop., 7/1/99: 12,497 (17.90 persons p/sq. mi.)
County Pop., 7/1/98: 12,366 (Voting Age: 8,402)
　　White: 3,674 (29.71%)　　Nonwhite: 8,692 (70.29%)
　　Males: 5,839 (47.22%)　　Females: 6,527 (52.78%)
　　Ages — 0-4: 1,091; 5-17: 2,873; 18-24: 1,297;
　　25-44: 3,260; 45-64: 2,294; 65 & older: 1,551
County Pop., 1990: 12,604 (0.0% urban—100.0% rural)
　　White: 3,960 (31.42%)　　Nonwhite: 8,644 (68.58%)
Households / Persons Per Household, 1998: **4,074** / 3.0
Average Household Income, 1998: $48,172 (rank 46)
1995 Households with Income: Under $15,000—38.07%
　　$25,000-49,999—27.44%　$75,000 or more—5.56%
Per Capita Personal Income, 1998: $15,809 (rank 61)
Total Personal Income, 1998: $196,237,000
Total Wages & Salaries, 1998: $72,942,000
Avg. Wages, 1998: Week $352 (rank 68); Year $18,304
　　FY 1997: Manufacturing —$367 week　　$9.18 hour
　　　　　　　Services 　　—$347 week　　$8.68 hour
Labor Force / **Employed** (July 2000): 4,340 / **3,950**
Non-Agri. Employment in the County, July 2000: 3,760
　　Manufacturing: 1,730 / Nonmanufacturing: 2,030
Unemployed / Rate (July 2000): **390** / 9.0%
No. Medicaid Eligibles, FY 1997: 4,293 (34.1% of pop.)
Federal Funds & Grants, 1998: $52,525,000
Cost of Living Index, 1999: 0.91 (average is 1.00)
Average County Millage, 1999: 103.30
Real Property, 1999 Assessed Value: $28,219,043
Real Property, 1998 Assessed Value: $27,227,858
　　True Value / No. of Parcels: **$211,546,477** / 9,140
Personal Property, 1999 Assessed Value: $18,354,434
Personal Property, 1998 Assessed Value: $17,529,055
　　True Value / No. of Parcels: **$89,289,456** / 475
Number of Personal Taxpayers, FY 1999: 4,347
Net State Taxable Income, FY 1999:　$ 46,871,275
Gross State Income Tax, FY 1999:　　$ 2,208,081
No. of State Corporate Taxpayers, FY 1999: 107
Corp. Income & Franchise Taxes, FY 1999: $308,846
Retail Sales: 1999—$60,938,218　　　1998—$63.9 m
Sales Tax / **No. Retailers** (1999): $3,592,596 / **286**
No. Vehicles Registered, FY Ending 6/30/99: 8,643
Education, 1990 - Average: 10.38 years (rank 75)
　　Graduates: High School 49.6%　　College 7.9%
Residents Enrolled in 8 State Universities, Fall 1999: 212
No. Hospitals / Beds / **Doctors** (8/1/2000): **1** / 49 / **12**
Number of Births / **Deaths** (1998): 207 / **121**
Land in Farms / No. Farms (1997): **193,558 acres** / 454

Sheriff; 505 S Jefferson St; Macon	(662) 726-4166
Chancery Clerk; 505 S Jefferson St; Macon	726-4243
Circuit Clerk; 505 S Jefferson St; Macon	726-5737
Tax Assessor & Collector; Macon	726-2679

Oktibbeha County

Established: 1833   Seat: Starkville
Area in Square Miles: 459
Named for the Indian word meaning "bloody water"
Located in northeast Mississippi
Incorporated Places with Estimated Population, 7/1/1998:
    Maben (part) 491   Starkville 20,184   Sturgis 181
County Pop., 7/1/99: 39,765 (86.63 persons p/sq. mi.)
County Pop., 7/1/98: 39,291 (Voting Age: 30,633)
    White: 23,439 (59.65%)   Nonwhite: 15,852 (40.35%)
    Males: 19,527 (49.70%)   Females: 19,764 (50.30%)
    Ages — 0-4: 2,502; 5-17: 6,156; 18-24: 10,276;
    25-44: 10,401; 45-64: 6,283; 65 & older: 3,673
County Pop., 1990: 38,375 (48.1% urban—51.9% rural)
    White: 24,178 (63.00%)   Nonwhite: 14,197 (37.00%)
Households / Persons Per Household, 1998: **13,331** / 3.0
Average Household Income, 1998: $52,708 (rank 23)
1995 Households with Income: Under $15,000—37.93%
   $25,000-49,999—24.04% $75,000 or more—8.71%
Per Capita Personal Income, 1998: $17,728 (rank 38)
Total Personal Income, 1998: $703,660,000
Total Wages & Salaries, 1998: $383,065,000
Avg. Wages, 1998: Week $433 (rank 23); Year $22,501
    FY 1997:   Manufacturing —$481 week $12.03 hour
                 Services   —$471 week $11.78 hour
Labor Force / **Employed** (July 2000): 19,660 / **18,870**
Non-Agri. Employment *in* the County, July 2000: 18,040
    Manufacturing: 2,430 / Nonmanufacturing: 15,610
Unemployed / Rate (July 2000): **730** / 3.7%
No. Medicaid Eligibles, FY 1997: 6,452 (16.8% of pop.)
Federal Funds & Grants, 1998: $185,606,000
Cost of Living Index, 1999: 0.96 (average is 1.00)
Average County Millage, 1999: 98.39
Real Property, 1999 Assessed Value: $107,870,427
Real Property, 1998 Assessed Value: $104,538,467
    True Value / No. of Parcels: **$848,075,271** / 18,120
Personal Property, 1999 Assessed Value: $59,039,914
Personal Property, 1998 Assessed Value: $55,321,535
    True Value / No. of Parcels: **$253,953,764** / 1,295
Number of Personal Taxpayers, FY 1999: 12,475
Net State Taxable Income, FY 1999: $ 195,622,597
Gross State Income Tax, FY 1999: $ 9,253,645
No. of State Corporate Taxpayers, FY 1999: 351
Corp. Income & Franchise Taxes, FY 1999: $1,321,398
Retail Sales: 1999—$375,175,023   1998—$363.5 m
Sales Tax / **No. Retailers** (1999): $23,379,524 / **854**
No. Vehicles Registered, FY Ending 6/30/99: 25,646
Education, 1990 - Average: 12.71 years (rank 1)
    Graduates: High School 73.0%   College 31.7%
Residents Enrolled in 8 State Universities, Fall '99: 1,669
No. Hospitals / Beds / **Doctors** (8/1/2000): **1** / 96 / **48**
Number of Births / **Deaths** (1998): 502 / **283**
Land in Farms / No. Farms (1997): **85,286 acres** / 329

Sheriff; 111 N Washington; Starkville   (662) 323-2421
Chancery Clerk; Courthouse; Starkville   323-5834
Circuit Clerk; Courthouse; Starkville   323-1356
Tax Assessor & Collector; Starkville   323-1273

Panola County

Est: 1836   Seats: Batesville & Sardis   Area: 695 sq. mi.
Named for the Indian word meaning "cotton"
Located in northwest Mississippi
Incorporated Places with Estimated Population, 7/1/1998:
    Batesville 7,416   Como 1,441   Courtland 362
    Crenshaw (part) 784   Crowder (part) 335
    Pope 178   Sardis 2,136
County Pop., 7/1/99: 33,913 (48.80 persons p/sq. mi.)
County Pop., 7/1/98: 33,400 (Voting Age: 23,172)
    White: 16,394 (49.08%)   Nonwhite: 17,006 (50.92%)
    Males: 15,838 (47.42%)   Females: 17,562 (52.58%)
    Ages — 0-4: 2,672; 5-17: 7,556; 18-24: 3,510;
    25-44: 9,095; 45-64: 6,594; 65 & older: 3,973
County Pop., 1990: 29,996 (21.3% urban—78.7% rural)
    White: 15,366 (51.23%)   Nonwhite: 14,630 (48.77%)
Households / Persons Per Household, 1998: **11,211** / 3.0
Average Household Income, 1998: $45,682 (rank 59)
1995 Households with Income: Under $15,000—36.63%
   $25,000-49,999—30.51% $75,000 or more—4.07%
Per Capita Personal Income, 1998: $15,368 (rank 66)
Total Personal Income, 1998: $512,154,000
Total Wages & Salaries, 1998: $243,333,000
Avg. Wages, 1998: Week $396 (rank 44); Year $20,613
    FY 1997:   Manufacturing —$424 week $10.60 hour
                 Services   —$347 week $ 8.68 hour
Labor Force / **Employed** (July 2000): 13,210 / **11,860**
Non-Agri. Employment *in* the County, July 2000: 10,790
    Manufacturing: 3,090 / Nonmanufacturing: 7,700
Unemployed / Rate (July 2000): **1,350** / 10.2%
No. Medicaid Eligibles, FY 1997: 8,364 (27.9% of pop.)
Federal Funds & Grants, 1998: $148,101,000
Cost of Living Index, 1999: 0.94 (average is 1.00)
Average County Millage, 1999: 110.25
Real Property, 1999 Assessed Value: $79,556,981
Real Property, 1998 Assessed Value: $73,857,548
    True Value / No. of Parcels: **$596,001,886** / 20,585
Personal Property, 1999 Assessed Value: $59,922,412
Personal Property, 1998 Assessed Value: $55,631,542
    True Value / No. of Parcels: **$288,028,535** / 1,273
Number of Personal Taxpayers, FY 1999: 12,204
Net State Taxable Income, FY 1999: $ 150,323,295
Gross State Income Tax, FY 1999: $ 6,955,095
No. of State Corporate Taxpayers, FY 1999: 369
Corp. Income & Franchise Taxes, FY 1999: $443,559
Retail Sales: 1999—$360,644,458   1998—$298.8 m
Sales Tax / **No. Retailers** (1999): $19,690,660 / **868**
No. Vehicles Registered, FY Ending 6/30/99: 25,423
Edu., '90 - Avg 10.8 yrs; Hi School 54.3%; College 8.7%
Residents Enrolled in 8 State Universities, Fall 1999: 490
No. Hospitals / Beds / **Doctors** (8/1/2000): **1** / 70 / **33**
Number of Births / **Deaths** (1998): 553 / **382**
Land in Farms / No. Farms (1997): **238,468 acres** / 573

Sheriff; 151 Public Square; Batesville   (662) 563-6230
County Administrator; Batesville   563-6200
Chancery Clerk; Batesville/Sardis   563-6205/487-2070
Circuit Clerk; Batesville/Sardis   563-6210/487-2073
Tax Assess./Coll; Batesville/Sardis   563-6270/487-2092

Pearl River County

Established: 1890 Seat: Poplarville
Area in Square Miles: 819
Named for the Pearl River
Located in southern Mississippi bordering Louisiana
Incorporated Places with Estimated Population, 7/1/1998:
　　Lumberton (part) 10　　Picayune 12,058
　　Poplarville 2,834
County Pop., 7/1/99: 47,969 (58.57 persons p/sq. mi.)
County Pop., 7/1/98: 46,862 (Voting Age: 33,980)
　　White: 39,236 (83.73%)　Nonwhite: 7,626 (16.27%)
　　Males: 22,651 (48.34%)　Females: 24,211 (51.66%)
　　　Ages — 0-4: 3,339; 5-17: 9,543; 18-24: 4,459;
　　　25-44: 12,974; 45-64: 10,953; 65 & older: 5,594
County Pop., 1990: 38,714 (34.4% urban—65.6% rural)
　　White: 32,819 (84.77%)　Nonwhite: 5,895 (15.23%)
Households / Persons Per Household, 1998: **16,597** / 2.8
Average Household Income, 1998: $46,005 (rank 56)
1995 Households with Income: Under $15,000—33.46%
　　$25,000-49,999—28.55%　$75,000 or more—5.61%
Per Capita Personal Income, 1998: $16,304 (rank 56)
Total Personal Income, 1998: $763,553,000
Total Wages & Salaries, 1998: $187,723,000
Avg. Wages, 1998: Week $353 (rank 67); Year $18,340
　　FY 1997: Manufacturing —$455 week　$11.38 hour
　　　　　　　Services　　　—$369 week　$ 9.23 hour
Labor Force / **Employed** (July 2000): 20,460 / **19,540**
Non-Agri. Employment *in* the County, July 2000: 9,580
　　Manufacturing: 940 / Nonmanufacturing: 8,640
Unemployed / Rate (July 2000): **920** / 4.5%
No. Medicaid Eligibles, FY 1997: 8,072 (20.8% of pop.)
Federal Funds & Grants, 1998: $195,660,000
Cost of Living Index, 1999: 0.99 (average is 1.00)
Average County Millage, 1999: 98.07
Real Property, 1999 Assessed Value: $112,638,617
Real Property, 1998 Assessed Value: $107,498,520
　　True Value / No. of Parcels: **$905,984,780** / 35,563
Personal Property, 1999 Assessed Value: $65,739,901
Personal Property, 1998 Assessed Value: $60,533,038
　　True Value / No. of Parcels: **$248,770,119** / 1,794
Number of Personal Taxpayers, FY 1999: 13,592
Net State Taxable Income, FY 1999: $ 180,489,155
Gross State Income Tax, FY 1999: $ 8,453,708
No. of State Corporate Taxpayers, FY 1999: 497
Corp. Income & Franchise Taxes, FY 1999: $1,450,712
Retail Sales: 1999—$350,508,185　　1998—$311.9 m
Sales Tax / **No. Retailers** (1999): $22,139,628 / **1,202**
No. Vehicles Registered, FY Ending 6/30/99: 44,252
Education, 1990 - Average: 11.67 years (rank 17)
　　Graduates: High School 68.4%　　College 11.4%
Residents Enrolled in 8 State Universities, Fall 1999: 568
No. Hospitals / Beds / **Doctors** (8/1/2000): **2** / 119 / **50**
Number of Births / **Deaths** (1998): 635 / **461**
Land in Farms / No. Farms (1997): **103,128 acres** / 609

Sheriff; 200 S Main; Poplarville	(601) 795-4716
Chancery Clerk; Poplarville	795-3001
Circuit Clerk; Courthouse; Poplarville	795-4911
Tax Assessor & Collector; Poplarville	795-4081

Perry County

Established: 1820　　Seat: New Augusta
Area in Square Miles: 651
Named for Commodore Oliver Perry, Battle of Lake Erie
Located in southeast Mississippi
Incorporated Places with Estimated Population, 7/1/1998:
　　Beaumont 1,278　New Augusta 723　Richton 1,092
County Pop., 7/1/99: 12,039 (18.49 persons p/sq. mi.)
County Pop., 7/1/98: 11,798 (Voting Age: 8,270)
　　White: 8,822 (74.78%)　Nonwhite: 2,976 (25.22%)
　　Males: 5,707 (48.37%)　Females: 6,091 (51.63%)
　　　Ages — 0-4: 881; 5-17: 2,647; 18-24: 1,153;
　　　25-44: 3,304; 45-64: 2,442; 65 & older: 1,371
County Pop., 1990: 10,865 (0.0% urban—100.0% rural)
　　White: 8,306 (76.45%)　Nonwhite: 2,559 (23.55%)
Households / Persons Per Household, 1998: **4,156** / 2.9
Average Household Income, 1998: $39,297 (rank 79)
1995 Households with Income: Under $15,000—40.13%
　　$25,000-49,999—28.21%　$75,000 or more—3.28%
Per Capita Personal Income, 1998: $13,774 (rank 76)
Total Personal Income, 1998: $163,336,000
Total Wages & Salaries, 1998: $71,200,000
Avg. Wages, 1998: Week $496 (rank 7); Year $25,798
　　FY 1997: Manufacturing —$736 week　$18.40 hour
　　　　　　　Services　　　—$310 week　$ 7.75 hour
Labor Force / **Employed** (July 2000): 4,790 / **4,380**
Non-Agri. Employment *in* the County, July 2000: 2,900
　　Manufacturing: 1,010 / Nonmanufacturing: 1,890
Unemployed / Rate (July 2000): **410** / 8.6%
No. Medicaid Eligibles, FY 1997: 2,603 (24% of pop.)
Federal Funds & Grants, 1998: $42,017,000
Cost of Living Index, 1999: 0.91 (average is 1.00)
Average County Millage, 1999: 94.54
Real Property, 1999 Assessed Value: $20,560,754
Real Property, 1998 Assessed Value: $19,635,516
　　True Value / No. of Parcels: **$158,950,731** / 8,973
Personal Property, 1999 Assessed Value: $26,880,866
Personal Property, 1998 Assessed Value: $26,523,946
　　True Value / No. of Parcels: **$140,824,822** / 368
Number of Personal Taxpayers, FY 1999: 3,562
Net State Taxable Income, FY 1999: $ 42,904,995
Gross State Income Tax, FY 1999: $ 1,939,007
No. of State Corporate Taxpayers, FY 1999: 58
Corp. Income & Franchise Taxes, FY 1999: $51,399
Retail Sales: 1999—$45,152,495　　1998—$43.2 m
Sales Tax / **No. Retailers** (1999): $2,606,641 / **245**
No. Vehicles Registered, FY Ending 6/30/99: 11,162
Education, 1990 - Average: 11.09 years (rank 32)
　　Graduates: High School 61.8%　　College 7.1%
Residents Enrolled in 8 State Universities, Fall 1999: 105
No. Hospitals / Beds / **Doctors** (8/1/2000): **1** / 22 / **6**
Number of Births / **Deaths** (1998): 197 / **89**
Land in Farms / No. Farms (1997): **31,903 acres** / 246

Sheriff; New Augusta	(601) 964-8461
Chancery Clerk; New Augusta	964-8398
Circuit Clerk; New Augusta	964-8663
Tax Assessor & Collector; New Augusta	964-3398

The Ultimate Reference on the State

PIKE COUNTY

Established: 1815 Seat: Magnolia
Area in Square Miles: 410
Named for Gen. Zebulon Pike, army commander/explorer
Located in southwest Mississippi bordering Louisiana
Incorporated Places with Estimated Population, 7/1/1998:
   McComb 11,746   Magnolia 2,259
   Osyka 489   Summit 1,562
County Pop., 7/1/99: 37,910 (92.46 persons p/sq. mi.)
County Pop., 7/1/98: 37,920 (Voting Age: 27,103)
   White: 19,430 (51.24%)   Nonwhite: 18,490 (48.76%)
   Males: 17,702 (46.68%)   Females: 20,218 (53.32%)
     Ages — 0-4: 2,587; 5-17: 8,230; 18-24: 3,712;
   25-44: 10,339; 45-64: 7,783; 65 & older: 5,269
County Pop., 1990: 36,882 (31.4% urban—68.6% rural)
   White: 19,946 (54.08%)   Nonwhite: 16,936 (45.92%)
Households / Persons Per Household, 1998: **13,782** / 2.7
Average Household Income, 1998: $48,691 (rank 43)
1995 Households with Income: Under $15,000—40.96%
   $25,000-49,999—23.87% $75,000 or more—5.47%
Per Capita Personal Income, 1998: $17,737 (rank 36)
Total Personal Income, 1998: $671,096,000
Total Wages & Salaries, 1998: $345,985,000
Avg. Wages, 1998: Week $383 (rank 53); Year $19,917
   FY 1997: Manufacturing —$373 week $ 9.33 hour
              Services   —$421 week $10.53 hour
Labor Force / **Employed** (July 2000): 18,250 / **17,050**
Non-Agri. Employment *in* the County, July 2000: 17,140
   Manufacturing: 4,850 / Nonmanufacturing: 12,290
Unemployed / Rate (July 2000): **1,200** / **6.6%**
No. Medicaid Eligibles, FY 1997: 9,807 (26.6% of pop.)
Federal Funds & Grants, 1998: $179,881,000
Cost of Living Index, 1999: 0.96 (average is 1.00)
Average County Millage, 1999: 99.33
Real Property, 1999 Assessed Value: $90,477,574
Real Property, 1998 Assessed Value: $81,162,352
   True Value / No. of Parcels: **$661,540,091** / 22,623
Personal Property, 1999 Assessed Value: $66,046,822
Personal Property, 1998 Assessed Value: $62,505,451
   True Value / No. of Parcels: **$299,244,712**/ 1,409
Number of Personal Taxpayers, FY 1999: 12,610
Net State Taxable Income, FY 1999: $ 168,190,981
Gross State Income Tax, FY 1999: $ 7,934,832
No. of State Corporate Taxpayers, FY 1999: 501
Corp. Income & Franchise Taxes, FY 1999: $774,825
Retail Sales: 1999—$459,005,806   1998—$420.7 m
Sales Tax / **No. Retailers** (1999): $28,079,649 / **1,117**
No. Vehicles Registered, FY Ending 6/30/99: 32,993
Education, 1990 - Average: 11.30 years (rank 22)
   Graduates: High School 60.6%   College 12.8%
Residents Enrolled in 8 State Universities, Fall 1999: 619
No. Hospitals / Beds / **Doctors** (8/1/2000): **2** / 197 / **81**
Number of Births / **Deaths** (1998): 631 / **436**
Land in Farms / No. Farms (1997): **70,507 acres** / 437

Sheriff; Magnolia   (601) 783-2323
Chancery Clerk; Courthouse; Magnolia   783-3362
Circuit Clerk; Courthouse; Magnolia   783-2581
Tax Assessor & Collector; Magnolia   783-5511

PONTOTOC COUNTY

Established: 1836   Seat: Pontotoc
Area in Square Miles: 499
Named for the Indian word meaning "weed prairie"
Located in northeast Mississippi
Incorporated Places with Estimated Population, 7/1/1998:
   Algoma 458   Ecru 958   Pontotoc 5,219
   Sherman 449   Thaxton 483   Toccopola 163
County Pop., 7/1/99: 25,685 (51.47 persons p/sq. mi.)
County Pop., 7/1/98: 25,397 (Voting Age: 18,678)
   White: 21,185 (83.42%)   Nonwhite: 4,212 (16.58%)
   Males: 12,335 (48.57%)   Females: 13,062 (51.43%)
     Ages — 0-4: 1,777; 5-17: 4,942; 18-24: 2,462;
   25-44: 7,407; 45-64: 5,582; 65 & older: 3,227
County Pop., 1990: 22,237 (20.6% urban—79.4% rural)
   White: 18,860 (84.81%)   Nonwhite: 3,377 (15.19%)
Households / Persons Per Household, 1998: **9,459** / 2.7
Average Household Income, 1998: $46,373 (rank 53)
1995 Households with Income: Under $15,000—29.69%
   $25,000-49,999—31.54% $75,000 or more—4.54%
Per Capita Personal Income, 1998: $17,333 (rank 41)
Total Personal Income, 1998: $438,650,000
Total Wages & Salaries, 1998: $214,344,000
Avg. Wages, 1998: Week $412 (rank 37); Year $21,437
   FY 1997: Manufacturing —$433 week $10.83 hour
              Services   —$353 week $ 8.83 hour
Labor Force / **Employed** (July 2000): 14,040 / **13,460**
Non-Agri. Employment *in* the County, July 2000: 10,460
   Manufacturing: 6,390 / Nonmanufacturing: 4,070
Unemployed / Rate (July 2000): **580** / **4.1%**
No. Medicaid Eligibles, FY 1997: 3,184 (14.3% of pop.)
Federal Funds & Grants, 1998: $85,850,000
Cost of Living Index, 1999: 0.99 (average is 1.00)
Average County Millage, 1999: 89.70
Real Property, 1999 Assessed Value: $58,553,001
Real Property, 1998 Assessed Value: $54,880,709
   True Value / No. of Parcels: **$457,710,735** / 15,807
Personal Property, 1999 Assessed Value: $45,590,027
Personal Property, 1998 Assessed Value: $43,272,773
   True Value / No. of Parcels: **$210,090,846** / 822
Number of Personal Taxpayers, FY 1999: 9,403
Net State Taxable Income, FY 1999: $ 144,235,209
Gross State Income Tax, FY 1999: $ 6,541,295
No. of State Corporate Taxpayers, FY 1999: 237
Corp. Income & Franchise Taxes, FY 1999: $344,883
Retail Sales: 1999—$146,807,421   1998—$136.9 m
Sales Tax / **No. Retailers** (1999): $8,822,142 / **650**
No. Vehicles Registered, FY Ending 6/30/99: 23,886
Education, 1990 - Average: 10.95 years (rank 45)
   Graduates: High School 57.4%   College 8.1%
Residents Enrolled in 8 State Universities, Fall 1999: 297
No. Hospitals / Beds / **Doctors** (8/1/2000): **1** / 58 / **15**
Number of Births / **Deaths** (1998): 372 / **244**
Land in Farms / No. Farms (1997): **114,658 acres** / 552

Sheriff; 116 N Main; Pontotoc   (662) 489-3111
Chancery Clerk; Courthouse; Pontotoc   489-3900
Circuit Clerk; Courthouse; Pontotoc   489-3908
Tax Assessor & Collector; Crthouse; Pontotoc 489-3904

Prentiss County

Established: 1870　　　　　　Seat: Booneville
Area in Square Miles: 417
Named for Sargent S. Prentiss, Mississippi orator
Located in the northeastern hills of the state
Incorporated Places with Estimated Population, 7/1/1998:
　　Baldwyn (part) 1,834　　　Booneville 8,387
　　Jumpertown 450　　　　　Marietta 295
County Pop., 7/1/99: 24,497 (58.75 persons p/sq. mi.)
County Pop., 7/1/98: 24,295 (Voting Age: 18,424)
　　White: 21,056 (86.67%)　　Nonwhite: 3,239 (13.33%)
　　Males: 11,652 (47.96%)　　Females: 12,643 (52.04%)
　　Ages — 0-4: 1,586; 5-17: 4,285; 18-24: 2,902;
　　25-44: 6,399; 45-64: 5,411; 65 & older: 3,712
County Pop., 1990: 23,278 (41.5% urban—58.5% rural)
　　White: 20,482 (87.99%)　　Nonwhite: 2,796 (12.01%)
Households / Persons Per Household, 1998: **9,049** / 2.7
Average Household Income, 1998: $41,573 (rank 71)
1995 Households with Income: Under $15,000—31.41%
　　$25,000-49,999—31.61%　$75,000 or more—5.62%
Per Capita Personal Income, 1998: $15,445 (rank 65)
Total Personal Income, 1998: $376,172,000
Total Wages & Salaries, 1998: $186,560,000
Avg. Wages, 1998: Week $395 (rank 45); Year $20,534
　　FY 1997: Manufacturing —$395 week　$ 9.88 hour
　　　　　　　Services　　—$403 week　$10.08 hour
Labor Force / **Employed** (July 2000): 12,740 / **12,000**
Non-Agri. Employment *in* the County, July 2000: 8,610
　　Manufacturing: 3,570 / Nonmanufacturing: 5,040
Unemployed / Rate (July 2000): **740** / **5.8%**
No. Medicaid Eligibles, FY 1997: 3,887 (16.7% of pop.)
Federal Funds & Grants, 1998: $92,703,000
Cost of Living Index, 1999: 0.96 (average is 1.00)
Average County Millage, 1999: 108.34
Real Property, 1999 Assessed Value: $43,975,307
Real Property, 1998 Assessed Value: $42,597,068
　　True Value / No. of Parcels: **$353,791,597** / 13,980
Personal Property, 1999 Assessed Value: $40,793,698
Personal Property, 1998 Assessed Value: $39,632,271
　　True Value / No. of Parcels: **$202,471,002** / 997
Number of Personal Taxpayers, FY 1999: 10,182
Net State Taxable Income, FY 1999: $ 139,754,360
Gross State Income Tax, FY 1999:　$　6,338,186
No. of State Corporate Taxpayers, FY 1999: 310
Corp. Income & Franchise Taxes, FY 1999: $552,453
Retail Sales: 1999—$177,246,557　　1998—$162.8 m
Sales Tax / **No. Retailers** (1999): $10,461,559 / **695**
No. Vehicles Registered, FY Ending 6/30/99: 21,939
Education, 1990 - Average: 10.80 years (rank 61)
　　Graduates: High School 52.9%　　College 8.4%
Residents Enrolled in 8 State Universities, Fall 1999: 218
No. Hospitals / Beds / **Doctors** (8/1/2000): **1** / 114 / **30**
Number of Births / **Deaths** (1998): 352 / **202**
Land in Farms / No. Farms (1997): **88,081 acres** / 412

Sheriff; 1901 E Chambers Dr; Booneville (662) 728-6232
Chancery Clerk; Courthouse; Booneville　　　　728-8151
Circuit Clerk; 101-A N Main St; Booneville　　　728-4611
Tax Assessor & Collector; Booneville　　　　　　728-5044

Quitman County

Established: 1877　　　　　　Seat: Marks
Area in Square Miles: 406
Named for John A. Quitman, 10th governor of Mississippi
Located in the northwest Delta area of Mississippi
Incorporated Places with Estimated Pop. 7/1/1998:
　　Crenshaw (part) 223　Crowder (part) 459　Falcon 133
　　Lambert 1,075　　　Marks 1.635　　　　Sledge 452
County Pop., 7/1/99: 9,780 (24.09 persons p/sq. mi.)
County Pop., 7/1/98: 9,914 (Voting Age: 6,751)
　　White: 3,813 (38.46%)　　Nonwhite: 6,101 (61.54%)
　　Males: 4,643 (46.83%)　　Females: 5,271 (53.17%)
　　Ages — 0-4: 833; 5-17: 2,330; 18-24: 1,051;
　　25-44: 2,508; 45-64: 1,813; 65 & older: 1,379
County Pop., 1990: 10,490 (0.0% urban—100.0% rural)
　　White: 4,249 (40.51%)　　Nonwhite: 6,241 (59.49%)
Households / Persons Per Household, 1998: **3,329** / 3.0
Average Household Income, 1998: $41,400 (rank 72)
1995 Households with Income: Under $15,000—42.27%
　　$25,000-49,999—25.07%　$75,000 or more—4.93%
Per Capita Personal Income, 1998: $13,980 (rank 74)
Total Personal Income, 1998: $137,813,000
Total Wages & Salaries, 1998: $39,824,000
Avg. Wages, 1998: Week $358 (rank 62); Year $18,622
　　FY 1997: Manufacturing —$428 week　$10.70 hour
　　　　　　　Services　　—$338 week　$ 8.45 hour
Labor Force / **Employed** (July 2000): 3,540 / **3,180**
Non-Agri. Employment *in* the County, July 2000: 1,880
　　Manufacturing: 330 / Nonmanufacturing: 1,550
Unemployed / Rate (July 2000): **360** / **10.2%**
No. Medicaid Eligibles, FY 1997: 3,938 (37.5% of pop.)
Federal Funds & Grants, 1998: $56,426,000
Cost of Living Index, 1999: 0.90 (average is 1.00)
Average County Millage, 1999: 107.53
Real Property, 1999 Assessed Value: $24,361,101
Real Property, 1998 Assessed Value: $23,367,614
　　True Value / No. of Parcels: **$174,938,850** / 7,924
Personal Property, 1999 Assessed Value: $ 9,778,594
Personal Property, 1998 Assessed Value: $12,090,118
　　True Value / No. of Parcels: **$57,322,406** / 392
Number of Personal Taxpayers, FY 1999: 3,037
Net State Taxable Income, FY 1999: $ 28,915,606
Gross State Income Tax, FY 1999:　$　1,320,480
No. of State Corporate Taxpayers, FY 1999: 139
Corp. Income & Franchise Taxes, FY 1999: $141,181
Retail Sales: 1999—$38,802,057　　　1998—$33.8 m
Sales Tax / **No. Retailers** (1999): $2,306,936 / **212**
No. Vehicles Registered, FY Ending 6/30/99: 6,678
Education, 1990 - Average: 10.27 years (rank 77)
　　Graduates: High School 45.5%　　College 9.0%
Residents Enrolled in 8 State Universities, Fall 1999: 162
No. Hospitals / Beds / **Doctors** (8/1/2000): **1** / 36 / **4**
Number of Births / **Deaths** (1998): 176 / **132**
Land in Farms / No. Farms (1997): **169,557 acres** / 179

Sheriff; Marks　　　　　　　　　　　　　(662) 326-3131
Chancery Clerk; Courthouse; Marks　　　　　　326-2661
Circuit Clerk; Courthouse; Marks　　　　　　　326-8003
Tax Assessor & Collector; Crthouse; Marks　　　326-8928

The Ultimate Reference on the State

Rankin County

Established: 1828   Seat: Brandon   Area: 782 sq. mi.
Named for Christopher Rankin, congressman
Located in central Mississippi
Incorporated Places with Estimated Population, 7/1/1998:
  Brandon 14,612   Florence 2,375   Flowood 4,471
  Jackson (part) 133   Pearl 23,287   Pelahatchie 1,597
  Puckett 362   Richland 5,794
County Pop., 7/1/99: 112,348 (143.67 persons p/sq. mi.)
County Pop., 7/1/98: 109,613 (Voting Age: 81,341)
   White: 88,440 (80.68%)   Nonwhite: 21,173 (19.32%)
   Males: 53,926 (49.20%)   Females: 55,687 (50.80%)
   Ages — 0-4: 7,162; 5-17: 21,110; 18-24: 9,852;
   25-44: 36,321; 45-64: 23,941; 65 & older: 11,227
County Pop., 1990: 87,161 (54.5% urban—45.5% rural)
   White: 71,942 (82.54%)   Nonwhite: 15,219 (17.46%)
Households / Persons Per Household, 1998: **37,333** / 2.9
Average Household Income, 1998: $72,354 (rank 2)
1995 Households with Income: Under $15,000—17.96%
   $25,000-49,999—32.80% $75,000 or more—12.76%
Per Capita Personal Income, 1998: $24,646 (rank 2)
Total Personal Income, 1998: $2,701,216,000
Total Wages & Salaries, 1998: $1,258,750,000
Avg. Wages, 1998: Week $499 (rank 4); Year $25,934
   FY 1997: Manufacturing —$570 week $14.25 hour
             Services   —$420 week $10.50 hour
Labor Force / **Employed** (July 2000): 63,590 / **61,790**
Non-Agri. Employment *in* the County, July 2000: 48,690
   Manufacturing: 6,850 / Nonmanufacturing: 41,840
Unemployed / Rate (July 2000): **1,800** / 2.8%
No. Medicaid Eligibles, FY 1997: 10,531 (12.1% of pop.)
Federal Funds & Grants, 1998: $316,238,000
Cost of Living Index, 1999: 1.14 (average is 1.00)
Average County Millage, 1999: 81.91
Real Property, 1999 Assessed Value: $362,822,932
Real Property, 1998 Assessed Value: $337,745,592
   True Value / No. Parcels: **$2,885,029,753** / 55,310
Personal Property, 1999 Assessed Value: $277,830,208
Personal Property, 1998 Assessed Value: $242,657,547
   True Value / No. of Parcels: **$1,117,052,847** / 3,149
Number of Personal Taxpayers, FY 1999: 40,808
Net State Taxable Income, FY 1999: $ 893,760,826
Gross State Income Tax, FY 1999: $ 42,822,984
No. of State Corporate Taxpayers, FY 1999: 1,595
Corp. Income & Franchise Taxes, FY 1999: $890,566
Retail Sales: 1999—$1,592,377,642   1998—$1,408.2 m
Sales Tax / **No. Retailers** (1999): $91,767,460 / **2,653**
No. Vehicles Registered, FY Ending 6/30/99: 112,116
Edu., '90 - Avg 12.2 yrs; Hi School 73.8%; College 19.0%
Residents Enrolled in 8 State Universities, Fall '99: 1,646
No. Hospitals/Beds/**Doctors** (8/1/2000): **6** / 1,937 / **148**
Number of Births / **Deaths** (1998): 1,569 / **756**
Land in Farms / No. Farms (1997): **117,296 acres** / 558

Sheriff; 221 N Timber; Brandon   (601) 825-1480
Chancery Clerk; Brandon   825-1469
Circuit Clerk; Brandon   825-1466
Tax Assessor; 211 E Government St; Brandon   825-1470
Tax Collector; 211 E Government St; Brandon 825-1467

Scott County

Established: 1833   Seat: Forest
Area in Square Miles: 610
Named for Abram Scott, 7th governor of Mississippi
Located in central Mississippi
Incorporated Places with Estimated Population, 7/1/1998:
   Forest 5,324   Lake (part) 343
   Morton 3,261   Sebastopol 276
County Pop., 7/1/99: 24,911 (40.84 persons p/sq. mi.)
County Pop., 7/1/98: 25,001 (Voting Age: 17,889)
   White: 14,865 (59.46%)   Nonwhite: 10,136 (40.54%)
   Males: 11,950 (47.80%)   Females: 13,051 (52.20%)
   Ages — 0-4: 1,976; 5-17: 5,136; 18-24: 2,449;
   25-44: 6,809; 45-64: 5,160; 65 & older: 3,471
County Pop., 1990: 24,137 (34.3% urban—65.7% rural)
   White: 14,830 (61.44%)   Nonwhite: 9,307 (38.56%)
Households / Persons Per Household, 1998: **8,800** / 2.8
Average Household Income, 1998: $55,441 (rank 15)
1995 Households with Income: Under $15,000—33.45%
   $25,000-49,999—28.71% $75,000 or more—7.45%
Per Capita Personal Income, 1998: $19,503 (rank 16)
Total Personal Income, 1998: $487,879,000
Total Wages & Salaries, 1998: $228,883,000
Avg. Wages, 1998: Week $349 (rank 69); Year $18,157
   FY 1997: Manufacturing —$328 week $8.50 hour
             Services   —$352 week $8.80 hour
Labor Force / **Employed** (July 2000): 13,710 / **13,000**
Non-Agri. Employment *in* the County, July 2000: 12,700
   Manufacturing: 6,430 / Nonmanufacturing: 6,270
Unemployed / Rate (July 2000): **710** / 5.2%
No. Medicaid Eligibles, FY 1997: 5,627 (23.3% of pop.)
Federal Funds & Grants, 1998: $117,732,000
Cost of Living Index, 1999: 0.98 (average is 1.00)
Average County Millage, 1999: 92.50
Real Property, 1999 Assessed Value: $52,394,693
Real Property, 1998 Assessed Value: $49,546,329
   True Value / No. of Parcels: **$398,010,209** / 16,063
Personal Property, 1999 Assessed Value: $46,091,796
Personal Property, 1998 Assessed Value: $41,573,912
   True Value / No. of Parcels: **$201,276,975** / 976
Number of Personal Taxpayers, FY 1999: 10,840
Net State Taxable Income, FY 1999: $ 119,585,647
Gross State Income Tax, FY 1999: $ 5,430,938
No. of State Corporate Taxpayers, FY 1999: 301
Corp. Income & Franchise Taxes, FY 1999: $379,123
Retail Sales: 1999—$211,508,221   1998—$206.1 m
Sales Tax / **No. Retailers** (1999): $12,640,184 / **659**
No. Vehicles Registered, FY Ending 6/30/99: 22,952
Education, 1990 - Average: 10.85 years (rank 54)
   Graduates: High School 53.1%   College 9.4%
Residents Enrolled in 8 State Universities, Fall 1999: 272
No. Hospitals / Beds / **Doctors** (8/1/2000): **2** / 74 / **15**
Number of Births / **Deaths** (1998): 439 / **321**
Land in Farms / No. Farms (1997): **107,468 acres** / 674

Sheriff; 531 Airport Rd; Forest   (601) 469-1511
Chancery Clerk; Courthouse; Forest   469-1922
Circuit Clerk; Courthouse; Forest   469-3601
Tax Assessor & Collector; 100 E 1st; Forest   469-4051

SHARKEY COUNTY

Established: 1876   Seat: Rolling Fork
Area in Square Miles: 435
Named for W.L. Sharkey, provincial governor of Mississippi following the Civil War
Located in the Delta bordering Miss. River & Arkansas
Incorporated Places with Estimated Population, 7/1/1998:
     Anguilla 820   Cary 386   Rolling Fork 2,228
County Pop., 7/1/99: 6,543 (15.04 persons p/sq. mi.)
County Pop., 7/1/98: 6,650 (Voting Age: 4,339)
     White: 2,071 (31.14%)   Nonwhite: 4,579 (68.86%)
     Males: 3,070 (46.17%)   Females: 3,580 (53.83%)
     Ages — 0-4: 585; 5-17: 1,726; 18-24: 760;
     25-44: 1,741; 45-64: 1,106; 65 & older: 732
County Pop., 1990: 7,066 (0.0% urban—100.0% rural)
     White: 2,352 (33.29%)   Nonwhite: 4,714 (66.71%)
Households / Persons Per Household, 1998: **1,957** / 3.4
Average Household Income, 1998: $42,950 (rank 68)
1995 Households with Income: Under $15,000—42.93%
     $25,000-49,999—22.64% $75,000 or more—6.06%
Per Capita Personal Income, 1998: $12,734 (rank 81)
Total Personal Income, 1998: $84,071,000
Total Wages & Salaries, 1998: $36,539,000
Avg. Wages, 1998: Week $332 (rank 78); Year $17,260
     FY 1997:   Manufacturing —$ NA
               Services   —$ 351 week $8.78 hour
Labor Force / **Employed** (July 2000): 2,480 / **2,230**
Non-Agri. Employment *in* the County, July 2000: 1,340
     Manufacturing: 0 / Nonmanufacturing: 1,340
Unemployed / Rate (July 2000): **250** / 10.1%
No. Medicaid Eligibles, FY 1997: 2,683 (38% of pop.)
Federal Funds & Grants, 1998: $39,891,000
Cost of Living Index, '99: 0.84 (avg. 1.00) [state's lowest]
Average County Millage, 1999: 85.77
Real Property, 1999 Assessed Value: $21,679,369
Real Property, 1998 Assessed Value: $18,059,280
     True Value / No. of Parcels: **$132,864,489** / 4,533
Personal Property, 1999 Assessed Value: $8,056,947
Personal Property, 1998 Assessed Value: $8,266,116
     True Value / No. of Parcels: **$36,095,096** / 287
Number of Personal Taxpayers, FY 1999: 1,514
Net State Taxable Income, FY 1999: $ 20,335,676
Gross State Income Tax, FY 1999: $ 970,006
No. of State Corporate Taxpayers, FY 1999: 268
Corp. Income & Franchise Taxes, FY 1999: $388,563
Retail Sales: 1999—$38,549,443   1998—$34.1 m
Sales Tax / **No. Retailers** (1999): $2,281,216 / **140**
No. Vehicles Registered, FY Ending 6/30/99: 4,431
Education, 1990 - Average: 10.53 years (rank 72)
     Graduates: High School 51.3%   College 12.4%
Residents Enrolled in 8 State Universities, Fall 1999: 163
No. Hospitals / Beds / **Doctors** (8/1/2000): **1** / 29 / **3**
Number of Births / **Deaths** (1998): 126 / **82**
Land in Farms / No. Farms (1997): **165,581 acres** / 110

Sheriff; Courthouse; Rolling Fork   (662) 873-4321
Chancery Clerk; 400 Locust St; Rolling Fork   873-2755
Circuit Clerk; 400 Locust St; Rolling Fork   873-2755
Tax Assessor & Collector; Rolling Fork   873-4317

SIMPSON COUNTY

Established: 1824   Seat: Mendenhall
Area in Square Miles: 591
Named for Josiah Simpson, Mississippi Territory judge
Located in south-central Mississippi
Incorporated Places with Estimated Population, 7/1/1998:
     Braxton 142   D'Lo 412
     Magee 3,930   Mendenhall 2,528
County Pop., 7/1/99: 25,375 (42.94 persons p/sq. mi.)
County Pop., 7/1/98: 25,338 (Voting Age: 18,221)
     White: 16,533 (65.25%)   Nonwhite: 8,806 (34.75%)
     Males: 12,365 (48.80%)   Females: 12,973 (51.20%)
     Ages — 0-4: 1,819; 5-17: 5,298; 18-24: 2,280;
     25-44: 7,231; 45-64: 5,374; 65 & older: 3,336
County Pop., 1990: 23,953 (15.1% urban—84.9% rural)
     White: 16,163 (67.48%)   Nonwhite: 7,790 (32.52%)
Households / Persons Per Household, 1998: **8,816** / 2.9
Average Household Income, 1998: $53,047 (rank 21)
1995 Households with Income: Under $15,000—31.32%
     $25,000-49,999—31.48% $75,000 or more—5.70%
Per Capita Personal Income, 1998: $18,489 (rank 28)
Total Personal Income, 1998: $467,680,000
Total Wages & Salaries, 1998: $135,274,000
Avg. Wages, 1998: Week $356 (rank 64); Year $18,508
     FY 1997:   Manufacturing —$412 week $10.30 hour
               Services   —$326 week $ 8.15 hour
Labor Force / **Employed** (July 2000): 10,440 / **9,960**
Non-Agri. Employment *in* the County, July 2000: 6,800
     Manufacturing: 540 / Nonmanufacturing: 6,260
Unemployed / Rate (July 2000): **480** / 4.6%
No. Medicaid Eligibles, FY 1997: 5,294 (22.1% of pop.)
Federal Funds & Grants, 1998: $113,353,000
Cost of Living Index, 1999: 1.00 (average is 1.00)
Average County Millage, 1999: 97.46
Real Property, 1999 Assessed Value: $50,436,240
Real Property, 1998 Assessed Value: $49,317,643
     True Value / No. of Parcels: **$399,410,850** / 18,295
Personal Property, 1999 Assessed Value: $35,270,374
Personal Property, 1998 Assessed Value: $35,717,541
     True Value / No. of Parcels: **$158,122,321** / 812
Number of Personal Taxpayers, FY 1999: 8,854
Net State Taxable Income, FY 1999: $ 116,302,677
Gross State Income Tax, FY 1999: $ 5,359,132
No. of State Corporate Taxpayers, FY 1999: 210
Corp. Income & Franchise Taxes, FY 1999: $181,232
Retail Sales: 1999—$205,743,201   1998—$176.3 m
Sales Tax / **No. Retailers** (1999): $12,103,112 / **568**
No. Vehicles Registered, FY Ending 6/30/99: 23,201
Education, 1990 - Average: 11.01 years (rank 37)
     Graduates: High School 58.0%   College 8.7%
Residents Enrolled in 8 State Universities, Fall 1999: 314
No. Hospitals / Beds / **Doctors** (8/1/2000): **2** / 113 / **20**
Number of Births / **Deaths** (1998): 424 / **318**
Land in Farms / No. Farms (1997): **93,715 acres** / 550

Sheriff; Mendenhall   (601) 847-2921
Chancery Clerk; 1015 Bob St; Mendenhall   847-2626
Circuit Clerk; Mendenhall   847-2474
Tax Assessor & Collector; Crthse; Mendenhall   847-1744

The Ultimate Reference on the State

Smith County

Established: 1833　　　　Seat: Raleigh
Area in Square Miles: 635
Named for Major David Smith of Hinds County
Located in southeast Mississippi
Incorporated Places with Estimated Population, 7/1/1998:
　　Mize 321　　　Polkville 135　　　Raleigh 1,266
　　Sylvarena 111　　　Taylorsville 1,388
County Pop., 7/1/99: 15,431 (24.30 persons p/sq. mi.)
County Pop., 7/1/98: 15,296 (Voting Age: 11,125)
　　White: 11,622 (75.98%)　　Nonwhite: 3,674 (24.02%)
　　Males: 7,514 (49.12%)　　Females: 7,782 (50.88%)
　　Ages — 0-4: 1,078; 5-17: 3,093; 18-24: 1,432;
　　25-44: 4,177; 45-64: 3,468; 65 & older: 2,048
County Pop., 1990: 14,798 (0.0% urban—100.0% rural)
　　White: 11,528 (77.90%)　　Nonwhite: 3,270 (22.10%)
Households / Persons Per Household, 1998: **5,457** / 2.8
Average Household Income, 1998: $55,141 (rank 16)
1995 Households with Income: Under $15,000—33.49%
　　$25,000-49,999—31.00%　$75,000 or more—5.84%
Per Capita Personal Income, 1998: $19,709 (rank 14)
Total Personal Income, 1998: $300,918,000
Total Wages & Salaries, 1998: $96,112,000
Avg. Wages, 1998: Week $422 (rank 30); Year $21,947
　　FY 1997:　Manufacturing —$445 week　　$11.13 hour
　　　　　　　Services　　　—$331 week　$ 8.28 hour
Labor Force / **Employed** (July 2000): 5,940 / **5,690**
Non-Agri. Employment *in* the County, July 2000: 3,890
　　Manufacturing: 1,920 / Nonmanufacturing: 1,970
Unemployed / Rate (July 2000): **250** / 4.2%
No. Medicaid Eligibles, FY 1997: 2,946 (19.9% of pop.)
Federal Funds & Grants, 1998: $57,167,000
Cost of Living Index, 1999: 1.01 (average is 1.00)
Average County Millage, 1999: 91.35
Real Property, 1999 Assessed Value: $32,926,798
Real Property, 1998 Assessed Value: $31,310,844
　　True Value / No. of Parcels: **$253,221,351** / 13,423
Personal Property, 1999 Assessed Value: $33,640,961
Personal Property, 1998 Assessed Value: $34,523,434
　　True Value / No. of Parcels: **$173,447,573** / 490
Number of Personal Taxpayers, FY 1999: 4,655
Net State Taxable Income, FY 1999: $ 63,954,409
Gross State Income Tax, FY 1999:　$ 2,941,699
No. of State Corporate Taxpayers, FY 1999: 76
Corp. Income & Franchise Taxes, FY 1999: $60,303
Retail Sales: 1999—$68,582,146　　　1998—$51.0 m
Sales Tax / **No. Retailers** (1999): $3,534,801 / **290**
No. Vehicles Registered, FY Ending 6/30/99: 15,072
Education, 1990 - Average: 10.89 years (rank 51)
　　Graduates: High School 57.0%　　College 7.6%
Residents Enrolled in 8 State Universities, Fall 1999: 160
No. Hospitals / Beds / **Doctors** (8/1/2000): **0** / 0 / **5**
Number of Births / **Deaths** (1998): 241 / **163**
Land in Farms / No. Farms (1997): **94,798 acres** / 635

Sheriff; Raleigh	(601) 782-4531
Chancery Clerk; Raleigh	782-9811
Circuit Clerk; Raleigh	782-4751
Tax Assessor & Collector; Raleigh	782-9803

Stone County

Established: 1916　　　　Seat: Wiggins
Area in Square Miles: 446
Named for John Marshall Stone, 31st governor of Miss.
Located in southeast Mississippi
Incorporated Places with Estimated Population, 7/1/1998:
　　Wiggins 3,977
County Pop., 7/1/99: 13,488 (30.24 persons p/sq. mi.)
County Pop., 7/1/98: 13,166 (Voting Age: 9,510)
　　White: 9,980 (75.80%)　　Nonwhite: 3,186 (24.20%)
　　Males: 6,457 (49.04%)　　Females: 6,709 (50.96%)
　　Ages — 0-4: 1,000; 5-17: 2,656; 18-24: 1,603;
　　25-44: 3,692; 45-64: 2,743; 65 & older: 1,472
County Pop., 1990: 10,750 (29.6% urban—70.4% rural)
　　White: 8,352 (77.69%)　　Nonwhite: 2,398 (22.31%)
Households / Persons Per Household, 1998: **4,530** / 2.9
Average Household Income, 1998: $46,154 (rank 55)
1995 Households with Income: Under $15,000—31.75%
　　$25,000-49,999—29.07%　$75,000 or more—6.24%
Per Capita Personal Income, 1998: $15,811 (rank 60)
Total Personal Income, 1998: $209,104,000
Total Wages & Salaries, 1998: $82,220,000
Avg. Wages, 1998: Week $414 (rank 35); Year $21,528
　　FY 1997:　Manufacturing —$488 week　　$12.20 hour
　　　　　　　Services　　　—$422 week　$10.55 hour
Labor Force / **Employed** (July 2000): 5,430 / **5,040**
Non-Agri. Employment *in* the County, July 2000: 3,650
　　Manufacturing: 810 / Nonmanufacturing: 2,840
Unemployed / Rate (July 2000): **390** / 7.2%
No. Medicaid Eligibles, FY 1997: 2,792 (26% of pop.)
Federal Funds & Grants, 1998: $63,412,000
Cost of Living Index, 1999: 0.98 (average is 1.00)
Average County Millage, 1999: 129.00
Real Property, 1999 Assessed Value: $27,235,019
Real Property, 1998 Assessed Value: $25,784,942
　　True Value / No. of Parcels: **$210,829,154** / 8,756
Personal Property, 1999 Assessed Value: $20,694,296
Personal Property, 1998 Assessed Value: $19,550,841
　　True Value / No. of Parcels: **$89,084,108** / 495
Number of Personal Taxpayers, FY 1999: 4,561
Net State Taxable Income, FY 1998: $ 62,894,897
Gross State Income Tax, FY 1999:　$ 2,891,465
No. of State Corporate Taxpayers, FY 1999: 173
Corp. Income & Franchise Taxes, FY 1999: $147,824
Retail Sales: 1999—$95,658,342　　　1998—$87.7 m
Sales Tax / **No. Retailers** (1999): $5,635,252 / **354**
No. Vehicles Registered, FY Ending 6/30/99: 11,886
Education, 1990 - Average: 11.79 years (rank 13)
　　Graduates: High School 68.1%　　College 12.4%
Residents Enrolled in 8 State Universities, Fall 1999: 184
No. Hospitals / Beds / **Doctors** (8/1/2000): **0** / 0 / **18**
Number of Births / **Deaths** (1998): 185 / **131**
Land in Farms / No. Farms (1997): **41,544 acres** / 212

Sheriff; 308 Court St; Wiggins	(601) 928-7251
Chancery Clerk; Courthouse; Wiggins	928-5266
Circuit Clerk; 323 Cavers Ave; Wiggins	928-5246
Tax Assessor & Collector; Wiggins	928-3121

Sunflower County

Est: 1844   Seat: Indianola   Area: 707 sq. mi.
Named for the Sunflower River
Located in the Delta area of northwest Mississippi
Incorporated Places with Estimated Population, 7/1/1998:
    Doddsville 138   Drew 2,136   Indianola 11,514
    Inverness 1,103   Moorhead 2,315   Ruleville 3,049
    Shaw (part) 7   Sunflower 781
County Pop., 7/1/99: 33,257 (47.04 persons p/sq. mi.)
County Pop., 7/1/98: 34,577 (Voting Age: 25,123)
    White: 11,273 (32.60%)   Nonwhite: 23,304 (67.40%)
    Males: 18,986 (54.91%)   Females: 15,591 (45.09%)
    Ages — 0-4: 2,381; 5-17: 7,073; 18-24: 4,203;
    25-44: 11,416; 45-64: 5,890; 65 & older: 3,614
County Pop., 1990: 35,129 (45.7% urban—54.3% rural)
    White: 11,614 (33.06%)   Nonwhite: 23,515 (66.94%)
Households / Persons Per Household, 1998: **9,231** / 3.6
Average Household Income, 1998: $50,441 (rank 36)
1995 Households with Income: Under $15,000—44.23%
    $25,000-49,999—23.09% $75,000 or more—5.45%
Per Capita Personal Income, 1998: $13,884 (rank 75)
Total Personal Income, 1998: $465,623,000
Total Wages & Salaries, 1998: $266,038,000
Avg. Wages, 1998: Week $395 (rank 46); Year $20,516
    FY 1997: Manufacturing —$390 week $9.75 hour
    Services   —$376 week $9.40 hour
Labor Force / **Employed** (July 2000): 11,510 / **10,290**
Non-Agri. Employment *in* the County, July 2000: 11,740
    Manufacturing: 2,670 / Nonmanufacturing: 9,070
Unemployed / Rate (July 2000): **1,220** / 10.6%
No. Medicaid Eligibles, FY 1997: 10,841 (33% of pop.)
Federal Funds & Grants, 1998: $144,833,000
Cost of Living Index, 1999: 0.86 (average is 1.00)
Average County Millage, 1999: 94.64
Real Property, 1999 Assessed Value: $76,239,626
Real Property, 1998 Assessed Value: $69,964,832
    True Value / No. of Parcels: **$542,139,413** / 15,480
Personal Property, 1999 Assessed Value: $46,670,293
Personal Property, 1998 Assessed Value: $42,808,912
    True Value / No. of Parcels: **$198,479,237** / 894
Number of Personal Taxpayers, FY 1999: 8,514
Net State Taxable Income, FY 1999: $ 103,679,872
Gross State Income Tax, FY 1999: $ 4,850,460
No. of State Corporate Taxpayers, FY 1999: 526
Corp. Income & Franchise Taxes, FY 1999: $485,286
Retail Sales: 1999—$209,726,891   1998—$183.3 m
Sales Tax / **No. Retailers** (1999): $12,286,829 / **646**
No. Vehicles Registered, FY Ending 6/30/99: 19,229
Education, 1990 - Average: 10.62 years (rank 71)
    Graduates: High School 49.2%   College 12.3%
Residents Enrolled in 8 State Universities, Fall 1999: 755
No. Hospitals / Beds / **Doctors** (8/1/2000): **3** / 169 / **20**
Number of Births / **Deaths** (1998): 528 / **341**
Land in Farms / No. Farms (1997): **348,290 acres** / 350

Sheriff; 1300 Allen Rd; Indianola   (662) 887-2121
Chancery Clerk; Courthouse; Indianola   887-4703
Circuit Clerk; Courthouse; Indianola   887-1252
Tax Assessor & Collector; Indianola   887-1454

Tallahatchie County

Established: 1833   Seats: Charleston and Sumner
Area in Square Miles: 651
Named for the Indian word meaning "rock river"
Located in the Delta area of northwest Mississippi
Incorporated Places with Estimated Population, 7/1/1998:
    Charleston 2,331   Glendora 161   Sumner 348
    Tutwiler 1,348   Webb 587
County Pop., 7/1/99: 14,587 (22.41 persons p/sq. mi.)
County Pop., 7/1/98: 14,893 (Voting Age: 10,193)
    White: 5,802 (38.96%)   Nonwhite: 9,091 (61.04%)
    Males: 7,005 (47.04%)   Females: 7,888 (52.96%)
    Ages — 0-4: 1,249; 5-17: 3,451; 18-24: 1,618;
    25-44: 3,777; 45-64: 2,866; 65 & older: 1,932
County Pop., 1990: 15,210 (0.0% urban—100.0% rural)
    White: 6,269 (41.22%)   Nonwhite: 8,941 (58.78%)
Households / Persons Per Household, 1998: **4,899** / 3.0
Average Household Income, 1998: $39,911 (rank 76)
1995 Households with Income: Under $15,000—43.07%
    $25,000-49,999—25.93% $75,000 or more—2.93%
Per Capita Personal Income, 1998: $13,223 (rank 78)
Total Personal Income, 1998: $195,524,000
Total Wages & Salaries, 1998: $53,063,000
Avg. Wages, 1998: Week $319 (rank 81); Year $16,576
    FY 1997: Manufacturing —$311 week $7.78 hour
    Services   —$351 week $8.78 hour
Labor Force / **Employed** (July 2000): 5,430 / **4,910**
Non-Agri. Employment *in* the County, July 2000: 2,470
    Manufacturing: 380 / Nonmanufacturing: 2,090
Unemployed / Rate (July 2000): **520** / 9.6%
No. Medicaid Eligibles, FY 1997: 4,863 (32% of pop.)
Federal Funds & Grants, 1998: $78,274,000
Cost of Living Index, 1999: 0.90 (average is 1.00)
Average County Millage, 1999: 99.20
Real Property, 1999 Assessed Value: $36,421,694
Real Property, 1998 Assessed Value: $34,216,463
    True Value / No. of Parcels: **$257,486,337** / 9,830
Personal Property, 1999 Assessed Value: $15,549,795
Personal Property, 1998 Assessed Value: $14,902,397
    True Value / No. of Parcels: **$61,106,170** / 502
Number of Personal Taxpayers, FY 1999: 3,962
Net State Taxable Income, FY 1999: $ 45,776,789
Gross State Income Tax, FY 1999: $ 2,136,013
No. of State Corporate Taxpayers, FY 1999: 189
Corp. Income & Franchise Taxes, FY 1999: $225,111
Retail Sales: 1999—$51,940,161   1998—$51.9 m
Sales Tax / **No. Retailers** (1999): $3,151,385 / **331**
No. Vehicles Registered, FY Ending 6/30/99: 10,544
Education, 1990 - Average: 10.25 years (rank 78)
    Graduates: High School 48.2%   College 7.9%
Residents Enrolled in 8 State Universities, Fall 1999: 255
No. Hospitals / Beds / **Doctors** (8/1/2000): **1** / 16 / **7**
Number of Births / **Deaths** (1998): 219 / **152**
Land in Farms / No. Farms (1997): **296,881 acres** / 355

Sheriff; Charleston/Sumner   (662) 647-5511/375-8676
Chancery Clerk; Charleston   647-5551
Circuit Clerk; Charleston/Sumner   647-8758/375-8515
Tax Assessor & Collector; Sumner   375-8386

The Ultimate Reference on the State

TATE COUNTY

Established: 1873   Seat: Senatobia
Area in Square Miles: 406
Named for T.S. Tate, pioneer settler
Located in northwest Mississippi
Incorporated Places with Estimated Population, 7/1/1998:
     Coldwater 1,482   Senatobia 5,428
County Pop., 7/1/99: 24,417 (60.14 persons p/sq. mi.)
County Pop., 7/1/98: 23,923 (Voting Age: 17,236)
    White: 15,051 (62.91%)   Nonwhite: 8,872 (37.09%)
    Males: 11,529 (48.19%)   Females: 12,394 (51.81%)
      Ages — 0-4: 1,759; 5-17: 4,928; 18-24: 2,911;
      25-44: 6,724; 45-64: 4,871; 65 & older: 2,730
County Pop., 1990: 21,432 (22.3% urban—77.7% rural)
    White: 13,975 (65.21%)   Nonwhite: 7,457 (33.79%)
Households / Persons Per Household, 1998: **7,854** / 3.1
Average Household Income, 1998: $63,090 (rank 8)
1995 Households with Income: Under $15,000—29.53%
   $25,000-49,999—31.99% $75,000 or more—7.06%
Per Capita Personal Income, 1998: $20,670 (rank 10)
Total Personal Income, 1998: $495,511,000
Total Wages & Salaries, 1998: $149,182,000
Avg. Wages, 1998: Week $391 (rank 48); Year $20,335
    FY 1997:   Manufacturing —$426 week $10.65 hour
                   Services   —$386 week $ 9.65 hour
Labor Force / **Employed** (July 2000): 10,450 / **9,810**
Non-Agri. Employment *in* the County, July 2000: 6,500
    Manufacturing: 1,900 / Nonmanufacturing: 4,600
Unemployed / Rate (July 2000): **640** / 6.1%
No. Medicaid Eligibles, FY 1997: 3,895 (18.2% of pop.)
Federal Funds & Grants, 1998: $81,394,000
Cost of Living Index, 1999: 1.04 (average is 1.00)
Average County Millage, 1999: 94.79
Real Property, 1999 Assessed Value: $59,143,329
Real Property, 1998 Assessed Value: $56,210,355
    True Value / No. of Parcels: **$483,885,284** / 12,840
Personal Property, 1999 Assessed Value: $40,062,614
Personal Property, 1998 Assessed Value: $33,979,632
    True Value / No. of Parcels: **$145,285,857** / 689
Number of Personal Taxpayers, FY 1999: 9,424
Net State Taxable Income, FY 1999: $ 139,026,262
Gross State Income Tax, FY 1999: $ 6,451,874
No. of State Corporate Taxpayers, FY 1999: 149
Corp. Income & Franchise Taxes, FY 1999: $297,028
Retail Sales: 1999—$205,220,532   1998—$193.6 m
Sales Tax / **No. Retailers** (1999): $12,671,182 / **545**
No. Vehicles Registered, FY Ending 6/30/99: 20,309
Education, 1990 - Average: 11.26 years (rank 23)
     Graduates: High School 61.0%   College 11.7%
Residents Enrolled in 8 State Universities, Fall 1999: 276
No. Hospitals / Beds / **Doctors** (8/1/2000): **1** / 76 / **23**
Number of Births / **Deaths** (1998): 385 / **216**
Land in Farms / No. Farms (1997): **134,657 acres** / 508

Sheriff; No. One Justice Dr; Senatobia   (662) 562-4434
Chancery Clerk; 201 Ward St; Senatobia   562-5661
Circuit Clerk; 201 Ward St; Senatobia   562-5211
Tax Assessor; Senatobia   562-6011
Tax Collector; Senatobia   562-4404

TIPPAH COUNTY

Established: 1836   Seat: Ripley
Area in Square Miles: 458
Named for the Indian word meaning "cut off"
Located in northeast Mississippi bordering Tennessee
Incorporated Places with Estimated Population, 7/1/1998:
     Blue Mountain 704   Dumas 450   Falkner 239
     Ripley 5,623   Walnut 561
County Pop., 7/1/99: 21,069 (46.00 persons p/sq. mi.)
County Pop., 7/1/98: 21,031 (Voting Age: 15,583)
    White: 17,207 (81.82%)   Nonwhite: 3,824 (18.18%)
    Males: 10,112 (48.08%)   Females: 10,919 (51.92%)
      Ages — 0-4: 1,420; 5-17: 4,028; 18-24: 2,097;
      25-44: 5,704; 45-64: 4,605; 65 & older: 3,177
County Pop., 1990: 19,523 (27.5% urban—72.5% rural)
    White: 16,267 (83.32%)   Nonwhite: 2,256 (16.68%)
Households / Persons Per Household, 1998: **7,692** / 2.7
Average Household Income, 1998: $47,001 (rank 50)
1995 Households with Income: Under $15,000—33.39%
   $25,000-49,999—31.45% $75,000 or more—4.08%
Per Capita Personal Income, 1998: $17,202 (rank 44)
Total Personal Income, 1998: $361,517,000
Total Wages & Salaries, 1998: $176,656,000
Avg. Wages, 1998: Week $429 (rank 26); Year $22,290
    FY 1997:   Manufacturing —$454 week $11.35 hour
                   Services   —$367 week $ 9.18 hour
Labor Force / **Employed** (July 2000): 11,030 / **10,430**
Non-Agri. Employment *in* the County, July 2000: 8,000
    Manufacturing: 4,000 / Nonmanufacturing: 4,000
Unemployed / Rate (July 2000): **600** / 5.4%
No. Medicaid Eligibles, FY 1997: 4,104 (21% of pop.)
Federal Funds & Grants, 1998: $96,458,000
Cost of Living Index, 1999: 0.98 (average is 1.00)
Average County Millage, 1999: 99.80
Real Property, 1999 Assessed Value: $40,594,495
Real Property, 1998 Assessed Value: $39,022,055
    True Value / No. of Parcels: **$321,715,492** / 14,146
Personal Property, 1999 Assessed Value: $35,222,417
Personal Property, 1998 Assessed Value: $30,456,814
    True Value / No. of Parcels: **$151,232,222** / 1,148
Number of Personal Taxpayers, FY 1999: 8,263
Net State Taxable Income, FY 1999: $ 109,285,261
Gross State Income Tax, FY 1999: $ 4,861,254
No. of State Corporate Taxpayers, FY 1999: 223
Corp. Income & Franchise Taxes, FY 1999: $614,540
Retail Sales: 1999—$143,923,845   1998—$134.4 m
Sales Tax / **No. Retailers** (1999): $8,497,585 / **535**
No. Vehicles Registered, FY Ending 6/30/99: 19,628
Education, 1990 - Average: 10.77 years (rank 63)
     Graduates: High School 54.4%   College 9.0%
Residents Enrolled in 8 State Universities, Fall 1999: 214
No. Hospitals / Beds / **Doctors** (8/1/2000): **1** / 70 / **15**
Number of Births / **Deaths** (1998): 316 / **256**
Land in Farms / No. Farms (1997): **113,847 acres** / 501

Sheriff; 204 W Spring St; Ripley   (662) 837-9336
Chancery Clerk; Courthouse; Ripley   837-7374
Circuit Clerk; Courthouse; Ripley   837-7370
Tax Assessor & Collector; Courthouse; Ripley   837-9410

TISHOMINGO COUNTY

Established: 1836   Seat: Iuka
Area in Square Miles: 434
Named for the Indian word meaning "Warrior Chief"
Located in the extreme northeast bordering Al & TN
Incorporated Places with Estimated Population, 7/1/1998:
    Belmont 1,627   Burnsville 1,017   Golden 209
    Iuka 3,122   Paden 126   Tishomingo 302
County Pop., 7/1/99: 18,742 (43.18 persons p/sq. mi.)
County Pop., 7/1/98: 18,654 (Voting Age: 14,464)
    White: 17,846 (95.67%)   Nonwhite: 808 (4.33%)
    Males: 8,893 (47.67%)   Females: 9,761 (52.33%)
    Ages — 0-4: 1,131; 5-17: 3,059; 18-24: 1,630;
       25-44: 5,006; 45-64: 4,596; 65 & older: 3,232
County Pop., 1990: 17,683 (17.7% urban—82.3% rural)
    White: 16,970 (95.97%)   Nonwhite: 713 (4.03%)
Households / Persons Per Household, 1998: **7,434** / 2.5
Average Household Income, 1998: $40,707 (rank 73)
1995 Households with Income: Under $15,000—32.54%
    $25,000-49,999—31.84% $75,000 or more—4.21%
Per Capita Personal Income, 1998: $16,217 (rank 57)
Total Personal Income, 1998: $302,613,000
Total Wages & Salaries, 1998: $136,533,000
Avg. Wages, 1998: Week $401 (rank 42); Year $20,832
    FY 1997: Manufacturing —$379 week $9.48 hour
         Services   —$380 week $9.50 hour
Labor Force / **Employed** (July 2000): 9,310 / **8,560**
Non-Agri. Employment *in* the County, July 2000: 6,270
    Manufacturing: 2,770 / Nonmanufacturing: 3,500
Unemployed / Rate (July 2000): **750** / 8.1%
No. Medicaid Eligibles, FY 1997: 2,879 (16.3% of pop.)
Federal Funds & Grants, 1998: $112,365,000
Cost of Living Index, 1999: 0.96 (average is 1.00)
Average County Millage, 1999: 71.00
Real Property, 1999 Assessed Value: $49,969,622
Real Property, 1998 Assessed Value: $49,271,377
    True Value / No. of Parcels: **$400,525,826** / 13,690
Personal Property, 1999 Assessed Value: $31,623,949
Personal Property, 1998 Assessed Value: $28,157,300
    True Value / No. of Parcels: **$125,336,075** / 735
Number of Personal Taxpayers, FY 1999: 6,870
Net State Taxable Income, FY 1999: $ 97,967,098
Gross State Income Tax, FY 1999: $ 4,448,898
No. of State Corporate Taxpayers, FY 1999: 201
Corp. Income & Franchise Taxes, FY 1999: $322,015
Retail Sales: 1999—$131,904,464   1998—$123.6 m
Sales Tax / **No. Retailers** (1999): $8,101,201 / **591**
No. Vehicles Registered, FY Ending 6/30/99: 20,049
Edu., '90 - Avg 10.64 yrs; Hi School 55.0%; College 6.6%
Residents Enrolled in 8 State Universities, Fall 1999: 138
No. Hospitals / Beds / **Doctors** (8/1/2000): **1** / 48 / **21**
Number of Births / **Deaths** (1998): 246 / **281**
Land in Farms / No. Farms (1997): **44,866 acres** / 258

Sheriff; 1111 Maria Lane; Iuka	(662) 423-7000
Chancery Clerk; 1008 Hwy 25S; Iuka	423-7010
Circuit Clerk; 1008 Hwy 24S; Iuka	423-7026
Tax Assessor & Collector; Iuka	423-7059
Tax Collector; Iuka	423-7048

TUNICA COUNTY

Established: 1836   Seat: Tunica
Area in Square Miles: 460
Named for the Indian word meaning "little people"
Located in northwest Delta bordering the Miss. River
Incorporated Places with Estimated Population, 7/1/1998:
    Tunica 1,015
County Pop., 7/1/99: 7,935 (17.25 persons p/sq. mi.)
County Pop., 7/1/98: 8,039 (Voting Age: 5,146)
    White: 1,860 (23.14%)   Nonwhite: 6,179 (76.86%)
    Males: 3,736 (46.47%)   Females: 4,303 (53.53%)
    Ages — 0-4: 776; 5-17: 2,117; 18-24: 927;
       25-44: 2,015; 45-64: 1,351; 65 & older: 853
County Pop., 1990: 8,164 (0.0% urban—100.0% rural)
    White: 1,991 (24.39%)   Nonwhite: 6,173 (75.61%)
Households / Persons Per Household, 1998: **2,496** / 3.2
Average Household Income, 1998: $60,751 (rank 9)
1995 Households with Income: Under $15,000—49.92%
    $25,000-49,999—18.49% $75,000 or more—5.71%
Per Capita Personal Income, 1998: $18,857 (rank 26)
Total Personal Income, 1998: $151,627,000
Total Wages & Salaries, 1998: $419,526,000
Avg. Wages, 1998: Week $423 (rank 29); Year $22,021
    FY 1997: Manufacturing —$349 week $ 8.73 hour
         Services   —$430 week $10.75 hour
Labor Force / **Employed** (July 2000): 5,250 / **4,980**
Non-Agri. Employment *in* the County, July 2000: 16,390
    Manufacturing: 520 / Nonmanufacturing: 15,870
Unemployed / Rate (July 2000): **270** / 5.1%
No. Medicaid Eligibles, FY 1997: 2,722 (33.3% of pop.)
Federal Funds & Grants, 1998: $44,487,000
Cost of Living Index, 1999: 0.95 (average is 1.00)
Average County Millage, 1999: 39.30
Real Property, 1999 Assessed Value: $107,687,633
Real Property, 1998 Assessed Value: $101,043,910
    True Value / No. of Parcels: **$691,825,560** / 5,242
Personal Property, 1999 Assessed Value: $99,764,414
Personal Property, 1998 Assessed Value: $94,855,585
    True Value / No. of Parcels: **$598,108,455** / 375
Number of Personal Taxpayers, FY 1999: 3,306
Net State Taxable Income, FY 1999: $ 38,432,386
Gross State Income Tax, FY 1999: $ 1,829,228
No. of State Corporate Taxpayers, FY 1999: 271
Corp. Income & Franchise Taxes, FY 1999: $397,935
Retail Sales: 1999—$325,821,691   1998—$337.6 m
Sales Tax / **No. Retailers** (1999): $18,670,902 / **290**
No. Vehicles Registered, FY Ending 6/30/99: 7,672
Education, 1990 - Average: 10.17 years (rank 81)
    Graduates: High School 45.9%   College 8.5%
Residents Enrolled in 8 State Universities, Fall 1999: 100
No. Hospitals / Beds / **Doctors** (8/1/2000): **0** / 0 / **4**
Number of Births / **Deaths** (1998): 173 / **90**
Land in Farms / No. Farms (1997): **202,353 acres** / 95

Sheriff; Tunica	(662) 363-2593
Chancery Clerk; Tunica	363-2451
Circuit Clerk; Tunica	363-2842
Tax Assessor & Collector; Tunica	363-1266

The Ultimate Reference on the State

UNION COUNTY

Established: 1870 Seat: New Albany
Area in Square Miles: 417
Named for the nickname of the U.S., "the Union"
Located in northeast Mississippi
Incorporated Places with Estimated Population, 7/1/1998:
    Blue Springs 154   Myrtle 383
    New Albany 7,238   Sherman (part) 171
County Pop., 7/1/99: 24,121 (57.84 persons p/sq. mi.)
County Pop., 7/1/98: 23,828 (Voting Age: 17,749)
    White: 19,946 (83.71%)   Nonwhite: 3,882 (16.29%)
    Males: 11,507 (48.29%)   Females: 12,321 (51.71%)
    Ages — 0-4: 1,544; 5-17: 4,535; 18-24: 2,247;
    25-44: 6,722; 45-64: 5,389; 65 & older: 3,391
County Pop., 1990: 22,085 (30.7% urban—69.3% rural)
    White: 18,754 (84.92%)   Nonwhite: 3,331 (15.08%)
Households / Persons Per Household, 1998: **9,043** / 2.6
Average Household Income, 1998: $50,573 (rank 35)
1995 Households with Income: Under $15,000—27.33%
    $25,000-49,999—34.80% $75,000 or more—5.90%
Per Capita Personal Income, 1998: $19,166 (rank 22)
Total Personal Income, 1998: $457,309,000
Total Wages & Salaries, 1998: $202,148,000
Avg. Wages, 1998: Week $424 (rank 28); Year $22,022
    FY 1997: Manufacturing —$494 week $12.35 hour
              Services   —$386 week $ 9.65 hour
Labor Force / **Employed** (July 2000): 12,880 / **12,380**
Non-Agri. Employment *in* the County, July 2000: 9,280
    Manufacturing: 3,530 / Nonmanufacturing: 5,750
Unemployed / Rate (July 2000): **500** / 3.9%
No. Medicaid Eligibles, FY 1997: 3,643 (16.5% of pop.)
Federal Funds & Grants, 1998: $84,423,000
Cost of Living Index, 1999: 1.02 (average is 1.00)
Average County Millage, 1999: 97.60
Real Property, 1999 Assessed Value: $57,133,098
Real Property, 1998 Assessed Value: $55,294,561
    True Value / No. of Parcels: **$446,087,577** / 15,923
Personal Property, 1999 Assessed Value: $52,769,558
Personal Property, 1998 Assessed Value: $47,635,691
    True Value / No. of Parcels: **$244,790,343** / 777
Number of Personal Taxpayers, FY 1999: 9,522
Net State Taxable Income, FY 1999: $ 142,396,264
Gross State Income Tax, FY 1999: $ 6,445,409
No. of State Corporate Taxpayers, FY 1999: 246
Corp. Income & Franchise Taxes, FY 1999: $126,247
Retail Sales: 1999—$212,148,204   1998—$180.1 m
Sales Tax / **No. Retailers** (1999): $12,773,796 / **613**
No. Vehicles Registered, FY Ending 6/30/99: 22,727
Education, 1990 - Average: 10.94 years (rank 47)
    Graduates: High School 57.3%   College 10.1%
Residents Enrolled in 8 State Universities, Fall 1999: 273
No. Hospitals / Beds / **Doctors** (8/1/2000): **1** / 153 / **32**
Number of Births / **Deaths** (1998): 358 / **263**
Land in Farms / No. Farms (1997): **102,243 acres** / 549

Sheriff; 300 Carter Ave; New Albany	(662) 534-1941
Chancery Clerk; New Albany	534-1900
Circuit Clerk; New Albany	534-1910
Tax Assessor & Collector; New Albany	534-1972

WALTHALL COUNTY

Established: 1910   Seat: Tylertown
Area in Square Miles: 404
Named for Edward Walthall, Confed. Gen. & U.S. senator
Located in southern Mississippi bordering Louisiana
Incorporated Places with Estimated Population, 7/1/1998:
    Tylertown 1,992
County Pop., 7/1/99: 14,211 (35.18 persons p/sq. mi.)
County Pop., 7/1/98: 14,369 (Voting Age: 10,062)
    White: 7,924 (55.15%)   Nonwhite: 6,445 (44.85%)
    Males: 6,948 (48.35%)   Females: 7,421 (51.65%)
    Ages — 0-4: 1,041; 5-17: 3,266; 18-24: 1,373;
    25-44: 1,695; 45-64: 3,019; 65 & older: 1,975
County Pop., 1990: 14,352 (0.0% urban—100.0% rural)
    White: 8,252 (57.50%)   Nonwhite: 6,100 (42.50%)
Households / Persons Per Household, 1998: **4,932** / 2.9
Average Household Income, 1998: $45,241 (rank 62)
1995 Households with Income: Under $15,000—42.41%
    $25,000-49,999—22.79% $75,000 or more—4.51%
Per Capita Personal Income, 1998: $15,504 (rank 64)
Total Personal Income, 1998: $223,119,000
Total Wages & Salaries, 1998: $67,013,000
Avg. Wages, 1998: Week $347 (rank 71); Year $18,058
    FY 1997: Manufacturing —$325 week $8.13 hour
              Services   —$386 week $9.65 hour
Labor Force / **Employed** (July 2000): 6,510 / **5,830**
Non-Agri. Employment *in* the County, July 2000: 3,500
    Manufacturing: 1,090 / Nonmanufacturing: 2,410
Unemployed / Rate (July 2000): **680** / 10.4%
No. Medicaid Eligibles, FY 1997: 3,976 (27.7% of pop.)
Federal Funds & Grants, 1998: $59,063,000
Cost of Living Index, 1999: 0.91 (average is 1.00)
Average County Millage, 1999: 86.20
Real Property, 1999 Assessed Value: $31,862,648
Real Property, 1998 Assessed Value: $30,958,496
    True Value / No. of Parcels: **$253,553,893** / 11,928
Personal Property, 1999 Assessed Value: $20,604,601
Personal Property, 1998 Assessed Value: $19,593,516
    True Value / No. of Parcels: **$81,382,644** / 433
Number of Personal Taxpayers, FY 1999: 3,788
Net State Taxable Income, FY 1999: $ 40,967,332
Gross State Income Tax, FY 1999: $ 1,877,819
No. of State Corporate Taxpayers, FY 1999: 115
Corp. Income & Franchise Taxes, FY 1999: $118,700
Retail Sales: 1999—$69,801,856   1998—$65.1 m
Sales Tax / **No. Retailers** (1999): $4,216,314 / **307**
No. Vehicles Registered, FY Ending 6/30/99: 13,928
Education, 1990 - Average: 10.90 years (rank 50)
    Graduates: High School 55.0%   College 10.1%
Residents Enrolled in 8 State Universities, Fall 1999: 190
No. Hospitals / Beds / **Doctors** (8/1/2000): **1** / 49 / **10**
Number of Births / **Deaths** (1998): 227 / **171**
Land in Farms / No. Farms (1997): **110,322 acres** / 538

Sheriff; 807 Magnolia Ave; Tylertown	(601) 876-3481
Chancery Clerk; Tylertown	876-3553
Circuit Clerk; 200 Ball Ave; Tylertown	876-5677
Tax Assessor & Collector; Tylertown	876-4932

WARREN COUNTY

Established: 1809　　　　Seat: Vicksburg
Area in Square Miles: 597
Named for Joseph Warren, Revolutionary War hero
Located in west-central Mississippi
Incorporated Places with Estimated Population, 7/1/1998:
　　Vicksburg 27,221
County Pop., 7/1/99: 49,148 (82.32 persons p/sq. mi.)
County Pop., 7/1/98: 49,404 (Voting Age: 35,313)
　　White: 28,668 (58.03%)　　Nonwhite: 20,736 (41.97%)
　　Males: 23,347 (47.26%)　　Females: 26,057 (52.74%)
　　Ages — 0-4: 3,505;　5-17: 10,586;　18-24: 4,389;
　　25-44: 14,800;　45-64: 10,272;　65 & older: 5,852
County Pop., 1990: 47,880 (43.7% urban—56.3% rural)
　　White: 28,827 (60.21%)　　Nonwhite: 19,053 (39.79%)
Households / Persons Per Household, 1998: **17,982** / 2.7
Average Household Income, 1998: $65,784 (rank 5)
1995 Households with Income: Under $15,000—29.45%
　　$25,000-49,999—27.64%　$75,000 or more—10.81%
Per Capita Personal Income, 1998: $23,967 (rank 5)
Total Personal Income, 1998: $1,182,957,000
Total Wages & Salaries, 1998: $704,303,000
Avg. Wages, 1998: Week $447 (rank 20); Year $23,225
　　FY 1997:　Manufacturing —$572 week　　$14.30 hour
　　　　　　　Services　　　　—$410 week　　$10.25 hour
Labor Force / **Employed** (July 2000): 27,110 / **25,730**
Non-Agri. Employment *in* the County, July 2000: 26,040
　　Manufacturing: 4,750 / Nonmanufacturing: 21,290
Unemployed / Rate (July 2000): **1,380** / 5.1%
No. Medicaid Eligibles, FY 1997: 9,832 (20.5% of pop.)
Federal Funds & Grants, 1998: $378,851,000
Cost of Living Index, 1999: 1.07 (average is 1.00)
Average County Millage, 1999: 77.71
Real Property, 1999 Assessed Value: $197,528,288
Real Property, 1998 Assessed Value: $190,199,933
　　True Value / No. Parcels: **$1,503,189,840** / 23,833
Personal Property, 1999 Assessed Value: $145,281,590
Personal Property, 1998 Assessed Value: $139,662,888
　　True Value / No. of Parcels: **$742,738,711** / 1,628
Number of Personal Taxpayers, FY 1999: 19,834
Net State Taxable Income, FY 1999:　$ 351,717,851
Gross State Income Tax, FY 1999:　　$ 16,872,922
No. of State Corporate Taxpayers, FY 1999: 778
Corp. Income & Franchise Taxes, FY 1999: $965,852
Retail Sales: 1999—$656,518,332　　　1998—$594.5 m
Sales Tax / **No. Retailers** (1999): $40,425,937 / **1,416**
No. Vehicles Registered, FY Ending 6/30/99: 42,495
Education, 1990 - Average: 11.94 years (rank 10)
　　Graduates: High School 67.7%　　College 19.1%
Residents Enrolled in 8 State Universities, Fall '99: 1,039
No. Hospitals / Beds / **Doctors** (8/1/2000): **1** / 354 / **91**
Number of Births / **Deaths** (1998): 781 / **513**
Land in Farms / No. Farms (1997): **97,829 acres** / 159

Sheriff; 1000 Grove St; Vicksburg	(601) 636-1761
Chancery Clerk; Courthouse; Vicksburg	636-4415
Circuit Clerk; Courthouse; Vicksburg	636-3961
Tax Assessor; Courthouse; Vicksburg	638-6161
Tax Collector; Courthouse; Vicksburg	638-6181

WASHINGTON COUNTY

Established: 1827　　Seat: Greenville　　　733 sq. mi.
Named for President George Washington
Located in the Delta northwest bordering Miss. River/AR
Incorporated Places with Estimated Population, 7/1/1998:
　　Arcola 537　　　　　Greenville 42,042
　　Hollandale 3,524　Leland 5,870　　　Matcalfe 1,240
County Pop., 7/1/99: 64,265 (87.67 persons p/sq. mi.)
County Pop., 7/1/98: 65,264 (Voting Age: 44,269)
　　White: 25,782 (39.50%)　　Nonwhite: 39,482 (60.50%)
　　Males: 30,511 (46.75%)　　Females: 34,753 (53.25%)
　　Ages — 0-4: 5,510;　5-17: 15,485;　18-24: 6,750;
　　25-44: 18,202;　45-64: 12,121;　65 & older: 7,196
County Pop., 1990: 67,935 (81.2% urban—18.8% rural)
　　White: 28,194 (41.50%)　　Nonwhite: 39,741 (58.50%)
Households / Persons Per Household, 1998: **21,704** / 3.0
Average Household Income, 1998: $53,640 (rank 19)
1995 Households with Income: Under $15,000—37.94%
　　$25,000-49,999—25.75%　$75,000 or more—7.49%
Per Capita Personal Income, 1998: $17,863 (rank 33)
Total Personal Income, 1998: $1,164,165,000
Total Wages & Salaries, 1998: $632,766,000
Avg. Wages, 1998: Week $433 (rank 22); Year $22,511
　　FY 1997:　Manufacturing —$499 week　　$12.48 hour
　　　　　　　Services　　　　—$391 week　　$ 9.78 hour
Labor Force / **Employed** (July 2000): 27,440 / **24,590**
Non-Agri. Employment *in* the County, July 2000: 23,570
　　Manufacturing: 5,110 / Nonmanufacturing: 18,460
Unemployed / Rate (July 2000): **2,850** / 10.4%
No. Medicaid Eligibles, FY 1997: 21,718 (32% of pop.)
Federal Funds & Grants, 1998: $299,612,000
Cost of Living Index, 1999: 0.96 (average is 1.00)
Average County Millage, 1999: 90.52
Real Property, 1999 Assessed Value: $158,816,105
Real Property, 1998 Assessed Value: $145,513,420
　　True Value / No. Parcels: **$1,149,422,573** / 27,567
Personal Property, 1999 Assessed Value: $113,238,421
Personal Property, 1998 Assessed Value: $113,577,253
　　True Value / No. of Parcels: **$584,810,081** / 2,417
Number of Personal Taxpayers, FY 1999: 20,777
Net State Taxable Income, FY 1999:　$ 301,294,424
Gross State Income Tax, FY 1999:　　$ 14,913,403
No. of State Corporate Taxpayers, FY 1999: 1,190
Corp. Income & Franchise Taxes, FY 1999: $1,706,831
Retail Sales: 1999—$652,100,142　　　1998—$641.8 m
Sales Tax / **No. Retailers** (1999): $41,006,606 / **1,691**
No. Vehicles Registered, FY Ending 6/30/99: 43,056
Education, 1990 - Average: 11.19 years (rank 29)
　　Graduates: High School 58.8%　　College 14.3%
Residents Enrolled in 8 State Universities, Fall '99: 1,683
No. Hospitals/Beds / **Doctors** (8/1/2000): **2** / 405 / **112**
Number of Births / **Deaths** (1998): 1,222 / **696**
Land in Farms / No. Farms (1997): **342,781 acres** / 283

Sheriff; Greenville	(662) 334-4523
Chancery Clerk; Courthouse; Greenville	332-1595
Circuit Clerk; Courthouse; Greenville	378-2747
Tax Assessor; Courthouse; Greenville	334-2651
Tax Collector; Courthouse; Greenville	378-2922

The Ultimate Reference on the State

WAYNE COUNTY

Established: 1809   Seat: Waynesboro
Area in Square Miles: 813
Named for General Anthony Wayne,
    A Revolutionary War hero
Located in southeast Mississippi bordering Alabama
Incorporated Places with Estimated Population, 7/1/1998:
    State Line (part) 156   Waynesboro 5,400
County Pop., 7/1/99: 20,637 (25.38 persons p/sq. mi.)
County Pop., 7/1/98: 20,368 (Voting Age: 14,274)
    White: 12,543 (61.58%)   Nonwhite: 7,825 (38.42%)
    Males: 9,733 (47.79%)   Females: 10,635 (52.21%)
    Ages — 0-4: 1,540; 5-17: 4,554; 18-24: 1,993;
    25-44: 5,864; 45-64: 4,207; 65 & older: 2,210
County Pop., 1990: 19,517 (26.7% urban—73.6% rural)
    White: 12,478 (63.93%)   Nonwhite: 7,039 (36.07%)
Households / Persons Per Household, 1998: **7,128** / 2.8
Average Household Income, 1998: $48,496 (rank 44)
1995 Households with Income: Under $15,000—34.86%
    $25,000-49,999—28.41% $75,000 or more—5.32%
Per Capita Personal Income, 1998: $17,032 (rank 45)
Total Personal Income, 1998: $345,700,000
Total Wages & Salaries, 1998: $142,628,000
Avg. Wages, 1998: Week $408 (rank 38); Year $21,194
    FY 1997: Manufacturing —$435 week $10.88 hour
                 Services   —$362 week $ 9.05 hour
Labor Force / **Employed** (July 2000): 9,020 / **8,410**
Non-Agri. Employment *in* the County, July 2000: 5,950
    Manufacturing: 1,490 / Nonmanufacturing: 4,460
Unemployed / Rate (July 2000): **610** / 6.8%
No. Medicaid Eligibles, FY 1997: 4,905 (25.1% of pop.)
Federal Funds & Grants, 1998: $66,645,000
Cost of Living Index, 1999: 0.96 (average is 1.00)
Average County Millage, 1999: 82.60
Real Property, 1999 Assessed Value: $46,927,187
Real Property, 1998 Assessed Value: $44,529,333
    True Value / No. of Parcels: **$359,893,318** / 14,121
Personal Property, 1999 Assessed Value: $40,096,487
Personal Property, 1998 Assessed Value: $35,537,346
    True Value / No. of Parcels: **$170,666,945** / 837
Number of Personal Taxpayers, FY 1999: 6,539
Net State Taxable Income, FY 1999: $ 81,436,583
Gross State Income Tax, FY 1999: $ 3,750,314
No. of State Corporate Taxpayers, FY 1999: 189
Corp. Income & Franchise Taxes, FY 1999: $380,033
Retail Sales: 1999—$204,587,833   1998—$219.1 m
Sales Tax / **No. Retailers** (1999): $112,072,731 / **539**
No. Vehicles Registered, FY Ending 6/30/99: 18,513
Education, 1990 - Average: 10.93 years (rank 49)
    Graduates: High School 56.1%   College 8.9%
Residents Enrolled in 8 State Universities, Fall 1999: 202
No. Hospitals / Beds / **Doctors** (8/1/2000): **1** / 80 / **15**
Number of Births / **Deaths** (1998): 368 / **212**
Land in Farms / No. Farms (1997): **75,766 acres** / 458

Sheriff; Waynesboro	(601) 735-2323
Chancery Clerk; Waynesboro	735-2873
Circuit Clerk; Courthouse; Waynesboro	735-1171
Tax Assessor & Collector; Waynesboro	735-3381

WEBSTER COUNTY

Established: 1874*/1882   *1st established as "Sumner"
Seat: Walthall   Area in Square Miles: 424
Named for Daniel Webster, early statesman
Located in northeast Mississippi
Incorporated Places with Estimated Population, 7/1/1998:
    Eupora 2,312   Maben (part) 251   Mantee 135
    Mathiston (part) 734   Walthall 168
County Pop., 7/1/99: 10,633 (25.08 persons p/sq. mi.)
County Pop., 7/1/98: 10,547 (Voting Age: 7,805)
    White: 8,044 (76.27%)   Nonwhite: 2,503 (23.73%)
    Males: 5,065 (48.02%)   Females: 5,482 (51.98%)
    Ages — 0-4: 671; 5-17: 2,071; 18-24: 998;
    25-44: 2,734; 45-64: 2,332; 65 & older: 1,741
County Pop., 1990: 10,222 (0.0% urban—100.0% rural)
    White: 7,950 (77.77%)   Nonwhite: 2,272 (22.23%)
Households / Persons Per Household, 1998: **3,967** / 2.7
Average Household Income, 1998: $44,033 (rank 65)
1995 Households with Income: Under $15,000—37.09%
    $25,000-49,999—30.41% $75,000 or more—4.97%
Per Capita Personal Income, 1998: $16,502 (rank 53)
Total Personal Income, 1998: $174,677.000
Total Wages & Salaries, 1998: $67,015,000
Avg. Wages, 1998: Week $344 (rank 74); Year $17,877
    FY 1997: Manufacturing —$336 week $8.40 hour
                 Services   —$352 week $8.80 hour
Labor Force / **Employed** (July 2000): 4,510 / **4,320**
Non-Agri. Employment *in* the County, July 2000: 3,530
    Manufacturing: 1,640 / Nonmanufacturing: 1,890
Unemployed / Rate (July 2000): **190** / 4.2%
No. Medicaid Eligibles, FY 1997: 2,186 (21.4% of pop.)
Federal Funds & Grants, 1998: $48,946,000
Cost of Living Index, 1999: 0.94 (average is 1.00)
Average County Millage, 1999: 81.66
Real Property, 1999 Assessed Value: $29,212,427
Real Property, 1998 Assessed Value: $27,810,939
    True Value / No. of Parcels: **$228,206,529** / 8,787
Personal Property, 1999 Assessed Value: $21,035,275
Personal Property, 1998 Assessed Value: $18,440,215
    True Value / No. of Parcels: **$85,722,408** / 434
Number of Personal Taxpayers, FY 1999: 3,520
Net State Taxable Income, FY 1999: $ 46,517,365
Gross State Income Tax, FY 1999: $ 2,113,281
No. of State Corporate Taxpayers, FY 1999: 94
Corp. Income & Franchise Taxes, FY 1999: $132,727
Retail Sales: 1999—$60,089,889   1998—$52.1 m
Sales Tax / **No. Retailers** (1999): $3,510,985 / **258**
No. Vehicles Registered, FY Ending 6/30/99: 10,000
Education, 1990 - Average: 11.00 years (rank 39)
    Graduates: High School 58.6%   College 10.8%
Residents Enrolled in 8 State Universities, Fall 1999: 262
No. Hospitals / Beds / **Doctors** (8/1/2000): **1** / 43 / **4**
Number of Births / **Deaths** (1998): 132 / **133**
Land in Farms / No. Farms (1997): **78,623 acres** / 289

Sheriff; 321 E Gould St; Eupora	(662) 258-7701
Chancery Clerk; Walthall	258-4131
Circuit Clerk; Walthall	258-6287
Tax Assessor & Collector; Walthall	258-6446

WILKINSON COUNTY

Established: 1802 Seat: Woodville
Area in Square Miles: 678
Named for General James Wilkinson
Located in southwest Mississippi bordering Louisiana
Incorporated Places with Estimated Population, 7/1/1998:
 Centreville (part) 1,255 Crosby (part) 281
 Woodville 1,297
County Pop., 7/1/99: 9,042 (13.34 persons p/sq. mi.)
County Pop., 7/1/98: 9,174 (Voting Age: 6,562)
 White: 2,811 (30.64%) Nonwhite: 6,363 (69.36%)
 Males: 4,289 (46.75%) Females: 4,885 (53.25%)
 Ages — 0-4: 703; 5-17: 1,909; 18-24: 884;
 25-44: 2,526; 45-64: 1,826; 65 & older: 1,326
County Pop., 1990: 9,678 (0.0% urban—100.0% rural)
 White: 3,123 (32.27%) Nonwhite: 6,555 (67.73%)
Households / Persons Per Household, 1998: **3,160** / 2.9
Average Household Income, 1998: $42,449 (rank 69)
1995 Households with Income: Under $15,000—44.95%
 $25,000-49,999—24.83% $75,000 or more—3.66%
Per Capita Personal Income, 1998: $14,647 (rank 69)
Total Personal Income, 1998: $134,135,000
Total Wages & Salaries, 1998: $43,093,000
Avg. Wages, 1998: Week $357 (rank 63); Year $18,560
Labor Force / **Employed** (July 2000): 2,980 / **2,590**
Non-Agri. Employment *in* the County, July 2000: 1,810
 Manufacturing: 260 / Nonmanufacturing: 1,550
Unemployed / Rate (July 2000): **390** / 13.1%
No. Medicaid Eligibles, FY 1997: 2,994 (31% of pop.)
Federal Funds & Grants, 1998: $42,841,000
Cost of Living Index, 1999: 0.90 (average is 1.00)
Average County Millage, 1999: 93.08
Real Property, 1999 Assessed Value: $26,820,390
Real Property, 1998 Assessed Value: $26,639,955
 True Value / No. of Parcels: **$203,362,170** / 9,118
Personal Property, 1999 Assessed Value: $12,203,166
Personal Property, 1998 Assessed Value: $11,418,422
 True Value / No. of Parcels: **$46,916,097** / 405
Number of Personal Taxpayers, FY 1999: 2,680
Net State Taxable Income, FY 1999: $ 30,269,765
Gross State Income Tax, FY 1999: $ 1,402,081
No. of State Corporate Taxpayers, FY 1999: 99
Corp. Income & Franchise Taxes, FY 1999: $142,224
Retail Sales: 1999—$49,121,762   1998—$62.7 m
Sales Tax / **No. Retailers** (1999): $2,921,426 / **215**
No. Vehicles Registered, FY Ending 6/30/99: 7,859
Education, 1990 - Average: 10.21 years (rank 80)
 Graduates: High School 48.3% College 8.9%
Residents Enrolled in 8 State Universities, Fall 1999: 145
No. Hospitals / Beds / **Doctors** (8/1/2000): **1** / 66 / **18**
Number of Births / **Deaths** (1998): 144 / **121**
Land in Farms / No. Farms (1997): **109,267 acres** / 196

Sheriff; Woodville	(601) 888-3511
Chancery Clerk; Woodville	888-4381
Circuit Clerk; Woodville	888-6697
Tax Assessor & Collector; Woodville	888-4562

WINSTON COUNTY

Established: 1833 Seat: Louisville
Area in Square Miles: 610
Named for Louis Winston, distinguished citizen of Miss.
Located in east-central Mississippi
Incorporated Places with Estimated Population, 7/1/1998:
 Louisville 7,085   Noxapater 438
County Pop., 7/1/99: 19,253 (31.56 persons p/sq. mi.)
County Pop., 7/1/98: 19,387 (Voting Age: 14,017)
 White: 10,740 (55.40%) Nonwhite: 8,647 (44.60%)
 Males: 9,138 (47.13%) Females: 10,249 (52.87%)
 Ages — 0-4: 1,312; 5-17: 4,058; 18-24: 1,725;
 25-44: 5,122; 45-64: 4,168; 65 & older: 3,002
County Pop., 1990: 19,433 (36.9% urban—63.1% rural)
 White: 11,164 (57.45%) Nonwhite: 8,269 (42.55%)
Households / Persons Per Household, 1998: **7,010** / 2.8
Average Household Income, 1998: $48,825 (rank 42)
1995 Households with Income: Under $15,000—37.56%
 $25,000-49,999—29.36% $75,000 or more—3.77%
Per Capita Personal Income, 1998: $17,746 (rank 35)
Total Personal Income, 1998: $342,248,000
Total Wages & Salaries, 1998: $151,462,000
Avg. Wages, 1998: Week $452 (rank 19); Year $23,479
 FY 1997: Manufacturing —$586 week $14.65 hour
   Services —$382 week $ 9.55 hour
Labor Force / **Employed** (July 2000): 8,010 / **7,240**
Non-Agri. Employment *in* the County, July 2000: 6,060
 Manufacturing: 2,040 / Nonmanufacturing: 4,020
Unemployed / Rate (July 2000): **770** / 9.6%
No. Medicaid Eligibles, FY 1997: 4,226 (21.7% of pop.)
Federal Funds & Grants, 1998: $78,950,000
Cost of Living Index, 1999: 0.94 (average is 1.00)
Average County Millage, 1999: 83.58
Real Property, 1999 Assessed Value: $44,983,821
Real Property, 1998 Assessed Value: $43,021,397
 True Value / No. of Parcels: **$361,475,018** / 14,156
Personal Property, 1999 Assessed Value: $41,096,618
Personal Property, 1998 Assessed Value: $32,532,086
 True Value / No. of Parcels: **$154,092,141** / 563
Number of Personal Taxpayers, FY 1999: 7,327
Net State Taxable Income, FY 1999: $ 96,789,723
Gross State Income Tax, FY 1999: $ 4,489,502
No. of State Corporate Taxpayers, FY 1999: 160
Corp. Income & Franchise Taxes, FY 1999: $395,752
Retail Sales: 1999—$160,337,140   1998—$148.5 m
Sales Tax / **No. Retailers** (1999): $9,234,326 / **429**
No. Vehicles Registered, FY Ending 6/30/99: 17,379
Education, 1990 - Average: 11.21 years (rank 27)
 Graduates: High School 59.1% College 10.8%
Residents Enrolled in 8 State Universities, Fall 1999: 345
No. Hospitals / Beds / **Doctors** (8/1/2000): **2** / 85 / **13**
Number of Births / **Deaths** (1998): 245 / **218**
Land in Farms / No. Farms (1997): **88,045 acres** / 458

Sheriff; 115 S Court St; Louisville	(662) 773-5881
Chancery Clerk; Main St; Louisville	773-3631
Circuit Clerk; Main St; Louisville	773-3581
Tax Assessor & Collector; Main St; Louisville	773-3694

The Ultimate Reference on the State

YALOBUSHA COUNTY

Established: 1833   Seats: Coffeeville & Water Valley
Area in Square Miles: 478
Named for the Indian word meaning "tadpole place"
Located in northern Mississippi
Incorporated Places with Estimated Population, 7/1/1998:
  Coffeeville 795   Oakland 559   Water Valley 3,661
County Pop., 7/1/99: 12,627 (26.42 persons p/sq. mi.)
County Pop., 7/1/98: 12,366 (Voting Age: 9,076)
  White: 7,409 (59.91%)   Nonwhite: 4,957 (40.09%)
  Males: 5,784 (46.77%)   Females: 6,582 (53.23%)
  Ages — 0-4: 857; 5-17: 2,433; 18-24: 1,098;
    25-44: 3,291; 45-64: 2,686; 65 & older: 2,001
County Pop., 1990: 12,033 (30.0% urban—70.0% rural)
  White: 7,492 (62.26%)   Nonwhite: 4,541 (37.74%)
Households / Persons Per Household, 1998: **4,746** / 2.6
Average Household Income, 1998: $44,543 (rank 64)
1995 Households with Income: Under $15,000—40.84%
  $25,000-49,999—29.63% $75,000 or more—3.44%
Per Capita Personal Income, 1998: $17,026 (rank 47)
Total Personal Income, 1998: $211,392,000
Total Wages & Salaries, 1998: $74,285,000
Avg. Wages, 1998: Week $388 (rank 51); Year $20,160
  FY 1997: Manufacturing —$423 week $10.58 hour
           Services   —$322 week $ 8.05 hour
Labor Force / **Employed** (July 2000): 4,830 / **4,450**
Non-Agri. Employment *in* the County, July 2000: 3,350
  Manufacturing: 1,300 / Nonmanufacturing: 2,050
Unemployed / Rate (July 2000): **380** / 7.9%
No. Medicaid Eligibles, FY 1997: 3,039 (25.3% of pop.)
Federal Funds & Grants, 1998: $68,473,000
Cost of Living Index, 1999: 0.98 (average is 1.00)
Average County Millage, 1999: 120.38
Real Property, 1999 Assessed Value: $22,221,783
Real Property, 1998 Assessed Value: $21,406,711
  True Value / No. of Parcels: **$178,213,803** / 11,421
Personal Property, 1999 Assessed Value: $14,385,123
Personal Property, 1998 Assessed Value: $14,614,098
  True Value / No. of Parcels: **$60,223,833** / 375
Number of Personal Taxpayers, FY 1999: 5,074
Net State Taxable Income, FY 1999: $ 68,763,985
Gross State Income Tax, FY 1999: $ 3,164,421
No. of State Corporate Taxpayers, FY 1999: 83
Corp. Income & Franchise Taxes, FY 1999: $210,464
Retail Sales: 1999—$62,875,599   1998—$52.3 m
Sales Tax / **No. Retailers** (1999): $3,699,833 / **335**
No. Vehicles Registered, FY Ending 6/30/99: 11,078
Education, 1990 - Average: 10.77 years (rank 64)
  Graduates: High School 55.7%   College 9.9%
Residents Enrolled in 8 State Universities, Fall 1999: 235
No. Hospitals / Beds / **Doctors** (8/1/2000): **1** / 26 / **5**
Number of Births / **Deaths** (1998): 192 / **184**
Land in Farms / No. Farms (1997): **85,547 acres** / 278

All numbers for all offices are Coffeeville / Water Valley
Sheriff   (662) 675-2444/473-2722
Chancery Clerk   675-2716/473-2091
Circuit Clerk   675-8187/473-1341
Tax Assessor & Collector   675-8707/473-1235

YAZOO COUNTY

Established: 1823   Seat: Yazoo City
Area in Square Miles: 933 (largest county in the state)
Named for the Indian word meaning "river of death"
Located in west-central Mississippi
Incorporated Places with Estimated Population, 7/1/1998:
  Bentonia 391   Eden 90   Satartia 61
  Yazoo City 11,941
County Pop., 7/1/99: 25,208 (27.02 persons p/sq. mi.)
County Pop., 7/1/98: 25,510 (Voting Age: 17,641)
  White: 11,447 (44.87%)   Nonwhite: 14,063 (55.13%)
  Males: 11,932 (46.77%)   Females: 13,578 (53.23%)
  Ages — 0-4: 2,061; 5-17: 5,808; 18-24: 2,372;
    25-44: 6,656; 45-64: 5,172; 65 & older: 3,441
County Pop., 1990: 25,506 (48.7% urban—51.3% rural)
  White: 11,983 (46.98%)   Nonwhite: 13,523 (53.02%)
Households / Persons Per Household, 1998: **8,817** / 2.9
Average Household Income, 1998: $51,613 (rank 34)
1995 Households with Income: Under $15,000—44.60%
  $25,000-49,999—22.95% $75,000 or more—5.45%
Per Capita Personal Income, 1998: $17,847 (rank 34)
Total Personal Income, 1998: $455,097,000
Total Wages & Salaries, 1998: $187,714,000
Avg. Wages, 1998: Week $455 (rank 15); Year $23,680
  FY 1997: Manufacturing —$426 week $10.65 hour
           Services   —$368 week $ 9.20 hour
Labor Force / **Employed** (July 2000): 10,330 / **8,990**
Non-Agri. Employment *in* the County, July 2000: 6,860
  Manufacturing: 1,630 / Nonmanufacturing: 5,230
Unemployed / Rate (July 2000): **1,340** / 13.0%
No. Medicaid Eligibles, FY 1997: 7,896 (31% of pop.)
Federal Funds & Grants, 1998: $150,719,000
Cost of Living Index, 1999: 0.97 (average is 1.00)
Average County Millage, 1999: 102.54
Real Property, 1999 Assessed Value: $60,402,374
Real Property, 1998 Assessed Value: $58,239,860
  True Value / No. of Parcels: **$450,904,560** / 18,014
Personal Property, 1999 Assessed Value: $47,967,341
Personal Property, 1998 Assessed Value: $46,124,766
  True Value / No. of Parcels: **$231,257,408** / 809
Number of Personal Taxpayers, FY 1999: 8,026
Net State Taxable Income, FY 1999: $ 116,898,594
Gross State Income Tax, FY 1999: $ 5,556,050
No. of State Corporate Taxpayers, FY 1999: 352
Corp. Income & Franchise Taxes, FY 1999: $1,246,418
Retail Sales: 1999—$210,446,456   1998—$182.7 m
Sales Tax / **No. Retailers** (1999): $12,441,782 / **605**
No. Vehicles Registered, FY Ending 6/30/99: 18,827
Edu., '90 - Avg 10.9 yrs; Hi School 53.4%; College 12.0%
Residents Enrolled in 8 State Universities, Fall 1999: 404
No. Hospitals / Beds / **Doctors** (8/1/2000): **1** / 88 / **18**
Number of Births / **Deaths** (1998): 489 / **303**
Land in Farms / No. Farms (1997): **312,298 acres** / 392

Sheriff; Yazoo City   (662) 746-5611
County Administrator; Yazoo City   746-8668
Chancery Clerk; Yazoo City   746-2661
Circuit Clerk; Courthouse; Yazoo City   746-1872
Tax Assessor & Collector; Yazoo City   746-1583

Former Names of Some Mississippi Communities

Community	Former Name(s)	County	Community	Former Name(s)	County
Aberdeen	Dundee	Monroe	Blair	Cedar Hill	Lee
Adelle	Little Texas	Madison	Blakeney	Beaverdam	Smith
Adelle	Smith School	Madison	Blanch	Ball Hill	Scott
Air Mount *	Honey Cut	Yalobusha	Blanton	Watsonia	Sharkey
Alamucha	Old Town	Lauderdale	Bloomfield	West Calico	Kemper
Alcorn	Oakland Station	Claiborne	Blue Mountain	Prospect Hill	Tippah
Aldridge	Ditchley	Washington	Bobo	Annis Ridge	Coahoma
Alene *	Fox's Mill	Jones	Bogue	Ingram's	Washington
Allen	Nanachehaw	Warren	Bogue Chitto	Lick Skillet	Lincoln
Alva	Stateland	Montgomery	Bowen	McDaniel's Mill	Itawamba
Anguilla	McKinneyville	Sharkey	Bowerton	Pine Ridge	Copiah
Arbo	Leake's Switch	Covington	Boyette	Bodone	Attala
Ardon *	Armstrong	Prentiss	Boykin	Bethel	Smith
Ariel	Mutrie	Amite	Brackett	Pineville	Lawrence
Arklet *	McInnis Crossing	Lauderdale	Bradley Chapel	Bell Hill	Warren
Ashland	Clover Hill	Issaquena	Branch	Groveton	Scott
Athens	Senath	Monroe	Branchville	Seneasha	Attala
Auburn	Adams Camp Ground	Lincoln	Brand	Bishassa	Newton
Auris *	Kelly's Store	Attala	Brandywine	Wells	Claiborne
Auter	Robinson	Sharkey	Brazil	Lay	Tallahatchie
Avon	Pettit	Washington	Brazil	Bessie	Tallahatchie
Avon	Riverside	Washington	Brazil	Murphree's Spur	Tallahatchie
Baldwyn	Carrollville	Lee/Prentiss	Broach *	Lowrey Mill	Scott
Baptist	White Oak	Panola	Broach *	Fairchild Mill	Scott
Barton	Oak Grove	Marshall	Broach *	Donohue	Scott
Basin	Helveston	George	Brookfield	Brooks	Warren
Baugh	Woodmere	Coahoma	Brooklyn	Bullis	Forrest
Bay St. Louis	Shieldsboro	Hancock	Brownfield	Gatlin	Tippah
Bean's Ferry	Boatright's Ferry	Itawamba	Brunswick	Altorf	Warren
Bear Creek	Fancher	Attala	Bryant	Perryville	Yalobusha
Beatrice	Cooper's Spur	Clarke	Brayantville	Gayden	Carroll
Beauregard	Bahala	Copiah	Brayantville	Geren or Gerenton	Carroll
Becker	Howell's Crossing	Monroe	Buckleytown	Shermon Hill	Scott
Belden	Leighton	Lee	Buckner	Buckland	Washington
Belden	Bells	Lee	Buena Vista	Monterey	Chickasaw
Belmont	Gum Springs	Tishomingo	Burgess	Welcometon	Lafayette
Belzoni	Fisk's Landing	Humphreys	Burgess	Morganville	Lafayette
Benoit	Ingomar	Bolivar	Burnside	Pearl Valley	Neshoba
Bent Oak	Cobb's Switch	Lowndes	Burnside	Lake Burnside	Neshoba
Benton	Flagg Spring	Yazoo	Buttercup	Jackson Springs	Lauderdale
Bentonia	Pritchett's Cross Roads	Yazoo	Cahn's Switch	Moseley's Switch	Clay
Berclair	Blue Lake	Leflore	Caile	Ark	Sunflower
Bertram	Ray's Sand Flat	Attala	Cairo	Odum Hill	Prentiss
Bethany	Brice's Crossroads	Lee	Cairo	Clausell Hill	Prentiss
Beulah	Dicken's Town	Attala	Calhoun City	Burkett	Calhoun
Beulah	Rocky Point	Leake	Calvary	Coulter	Winston
Bigbee Valley	White Hall	Noxubee	Cameron	Eureka School	Madison
Bigbee	Johnson's Mill	Monroe	Cameron's Ferry	Ford's Ferry	Pearl River
Bigby Fork	Pannel's Store	Itawamba	Cameta	Weeping Willow	Sharkey
Biggersville	New Hope	Alcorn	Canaan	Hood's Mill	Benton
Binford	Reynolds	Monroe	Capell	Rose Hill	Amite
Bissel	Colbert's Tavern	Lee	Carmack	Providence	Attala
Bissel	Walker's Cross Roads	Lee	Carmichael	Maxville	Clarke
Blackwater	Jacksonville	Kemper	Carnes	Helena	Forrest
Blackwater	Zada	Kemper	Carriere	Highlands	Pearl River
Blair	Parker Neighborhood	Lee	Carriere	Lacey	Pearl River

* The name the place was last known by has now become extinct along with its former name or names. For places that have had more than one former name, the previous placenames are listed chronologically with the first name listed first, second name listed second, etc.

Former Names of Some Mississippi Communities

Community	Former Name(s)	County	Community	Former Name(s)	County
Carson Ridge	Turkey Creek	Attala	Davenport *	Beverly	Coahoma
Carthage	Leakesville	Leake	DeKalb	Holihtasha	Kemper
Cary	Leighton	Sharkey	DeLisle	La Rivieres Des Loups	Harrison
Cascilla	Ashland	Tallahatchie	DeLisle	Wolftown	Harrison
Cascilla	Calista	Tallahatchie	Delta	Gerald	Coahoma
Caswell	Graham's Mill	Lafayette	Delta City	Catchings	Sharkey
Causeyville	Edbony	Lauderdale	Dennis	Old Hillside	Tishomingo
Causeyville	Increase	Lauderdale	Dentville	Pine Bluff	Copiah
Cayce	Bainsville	Marshall	Dodds	Dean's Crossing	Attala
Cedars	South Vicksburg	Warren	Dolorosa	Cold Springs	Wilkinson
Centerville	Mallory	Carroll	Dry Creek	Vex	Covington
Centreville	Elysian Fields	Wilkinson	Dry Run	Crossroads	Prentiss
Chalybeate	Jonesboro	Tippah	Dubbs	Slabtown	Tunica
Chambers	Winstonville	Bolivar	Dublin	Hopson Bayou Settlement	Coahoma
Chambers	Wyandotte	Bolivar	Dundee	Carnesville	Tunica
Chatawa	Carter's Hill	Pike	Dwiggins	Sandy Bayou	Sunflower
Chita	New Salem	Attala	Eastman *	Maxey's Mill	Itawamba
Chotard	Woodland	Issaquena	Eastman *	Bounds Crossroads	Itawamba
Church Hill	Maryland	Jefferson	Eastman *	Mount Gilliard	Itawamba
Claiborne	Grand Plains	Hancock	Ebenezer	Bucksnort	Holmes
Clara	Big Creek	Wayne	Ebenezer	Manchester	Holmes
Clarksdale	Clarksville	Coahoma	Edwards	Liverpool	Hinds
Clarkson	Pine Chapel	Webster	Egypt	Pineville	Chickasaw
Cleveland	Simms	Bolivar	Elfin	Spencer's Store	Itawamba
Cliff	Cromean's Store	Itawamba	Eliphaz	Hunters Chapel	Tate
Clinton	Mount Dexter	Hinds	Ellisville	Leesburg	Jones
Clinton	Mount Salus	Hinds	Elzy	Cherry Hill	Calhoun
Clisby	Dupree	Clay	Endville	Reagh	Pontotoc
Coar's Springs	Coarsville	Copiah	Endville	Brazille	Pontotoc
Coke	Coke Spur	Alcorn	Endville	Oakdale	Pontotoc
Coldwater	Elm Grove	Tate	Enid	Harrison	Tallahatchie
Collins	Williamsburg Depot	Covington	Essex	McPherson	Quitman
Colony Town	Cude	Leflore	Essex	Stalls	Quitman
Columbia	Lott's Bluff	Marion	Ethel	Stonewall	Attala
Columbus	Possum Town	Lowndes	Eton	Toby Tubby's Ferry	Lafayette
Concordia	Maysonia	Bolivar	Etta	Rocky Ford	Union
Cooksville	Pleasant Ridge	Noxubee	Eudora	Ellaville	DeSoto
Corinth	Cross City	Alcorn	Eudora	Dixie	DeSoto
Corona	Camp Creek	Lee	Eupora	Early Grove	Webster
Cotton Gin Port	Tollamstoxa	Monroe	Faisonia	Lee's Landing	Sunflower
Cottonwood	Carnarvon	Issaquena	Farce	Fairmont	Smith
Counts Spur	Traynham	Coahoma	Farmer *	Wayside	Alcorn
Courtland	Randolph's Crossing	Panola	Farmhaven	Williamstown	Madison
Crosby	Dayton	Amite	Farrell	McLemore Flat	Coahoma
Crosby	Stephenson	Amite	Fellowship	Buckley's Store	Jasper
Crossroads	Strahan's Ferry	Pearl River	Fellowship	Masengale	Jasper
Cruger	Elmwood	Holmes	Ferrell	McLemone	Hinds
Cumberland	Choctaw Ridge	Webster	Ferrell	Farror	Hinds
Daleville	Spring Hill	Lauderdale	Finkmount	Tip Top	Bolivar
Dancy	Sheba	Webster	Flautt	Duggers	Tallahatchie
Danforth	Dowd's Landing	Coahoma	Florence	Steen's Creek	Rankin
Dantzler	Ramsey	Jackson	Foote	Dudley	Washington
Danville *	Troy	Alcorn	Foote	Colmere	Washington
Darlove	Yerger	Washington	Ford	Smith's Mill	Simpson
Darnall	Big Oak	Kemper	Ford	Simonfield	Winston
Darrington	Crooked Creek	Wilkinson	Forkville	New Beach	Scott

* The name the place was last known by has now become extinct along with its former name or names. For places that have had more than one former name, the previous placenames are listed chronologically with the first name listed first, second name listed second, etc.

Former Names of Some Mississippi Communities

Community	Former Name(s)	County	Community	Former Name(s)	County
Fort Adams	Roche a Davion	Wilkinson	Hiwanee	Red Bluff	Wayne
Fort Adams	Loftus Heights	Wilkinson	Hoffman	Megee Switch	Holmes
Fort Stephens	Snowden	Lauderdale	Hollywood	Holly Grove	Tunica
Fostoria	Speed's	Warren	Holston	Annie	Hinds
Four Mile	Lotus	Humphreys	Homewood	Hell's Half-acre	Scott
Foxworth	West Columbia	Marion	Homewood	Buck Snort	Scott
Friar's Point	Union	Coahoma	Hooker	Crooked Creek	Lawrence
Friendship	Little Texas	Attala	Hopewell	Laird	Benton
Fulcher	Mount Airey	Choctaw	Hopewell	Ruby	Copiah
Fulton	Ironwood Bluff	Itawamba	Hosea	Betts	Pontotoc
Furr's	Brame	Pontotoc	House	Emuckalushia	Neshoba
Gail	Salmon	Scott	House	Herbert	Neshoba
Gandercleugh	Gander Slough	Yazoo	House	Java	Neshoba
Gatewood	Walthall	Yalobusha	Hudson	Gregory Crossing	Attala
Gattman	Gothman	Monroe	Hudsonville	Scale's Station	Marshall
Gault	Pine Flat	Lafayette	Hugo	Stump Valley	Tallahatchie
Gautier	West Pascagoula	Jackson	Hurricane	Pleasant	Attala
George	Cardill	Yazoo	Ihrie	Lake Place	Jefferson
Gershorm	Williams	Pontotoc	Ina	Fork	Simpson
Gholson	Summerville	Noxubee	Indianola	Indian Bayou	Sunflower
Gift	Jones	Alcorn	Indianola	Belingate	Sunflower
Gilton	Forest	Marshall	Indianola	Eureka	Sunflower
Gilvo	Allen's Chapel	Lee	Ingram	Passena	Coahoma
Glancy	Centerpoint	Copiah	Insmore	McCaleb	Claiborne
Glen	Glendale	Alcorn	Inverness	Burnfield	Sunflower
Glendale	Hickory Grove	Forrest	Isola	Dawson Lake	Humphreys
Gluckstadt	Calhoun Station	Madison	Issaquena	Valley	Sharkey
Goss	Prince	Marion	Jackson	Le Fleur's Bluff	Hinds
Grange	West Fork	Lawrence	Jackson Landing	Bing's Ferry	Pearl River
Green Pond	Beauchamp	Attala	Janet	Pleasant Hill	Greene
Greenwood	Williams Landing	Leflore	Jefferiesville	Greenwood	Claiborne
Grenada	Pittsburgh	Grenada	Jobes	Alcorn Switch	Alcorn
Grenada	Tulahoma	Grenada	Jobes	Meadows	Alcorn
Gum Branch	Gum Springs	Winston	Johns	Gates	Rankin
Hamage	Old Buford	Marion	Johnsonville*	Mound Bayou	Sunflower
Hampton	Linden	Washington	Johnsonville*	Johnson's Landing	Sunflower
Handsboro	Buena Vista	Harrison	Jonestown	Swan Lake	Coahoma
Hankinson	St. Albans	Claiborne	Kalem	Concord	Scott
Hannah	Nugent	Bolivar	Kilmichael	Rutherford	Montgomery
Hardin Town	Hopewell	Calhoun	Kingston	Jersey Town	Adams
Harrisville	Buck Snort	Simpson	Klein	Mount Carmel	Smith
Hattiesburg	Twin Forks	Forrest	Knox	Pickletown	Attala
Hattiesburg	Gordonville	Forrest	Kolola	Shinn's Springs	Lowndes
Hatton	Hughes' Store	Yalobusha	Kosciusko	Red Bud Springs	Attala
Hatley	Tubb's Cross Roads	Monroe	Kosciusko	Peking	Attala
Heard's Landing	Vick's Landing	Sunflower	Kosciusko	Peakedend	Attala
Heartease	Mir-a-mar	Harrison	Kosciusko	Paris	Attala
Hebron	Bethel	Jones	Kosciusko	Parrish	Attala
Hebron	Reddoch	Jones	Kosciusko	Parish	Attala
Hebron	Fuller	Jones	Kosciusko	Attala	Attala
Hemingway	Bright's Corner	Carroll	Kossuth	New Hope	Alcorn
Hernando	Jefferson	DeSoto	Kushakbolukta	Concha	Kemper
Hervey	East Place	Claiborne	Lackey	Gum Springs	Monroe
Hesterville	Palmer's Springs	Attala	Lackey	Noah	Monroe
Hesterville	Cedar Grove	Attala	Lake Cormorant	Blytheville	DeSoto
High Point	Hathorn	Winston	Lake	Maryville	Scott

* The name the place was last known by has now become extinct along with its former name or names. For places that have had more than one former name, the previous placenames are listed chronologically with the first name listed first, second name listed second, etc.

The Ultimate Reference on the State

Former Names of Some Mississippi Communities

Community	Former Name(s)	County	Community	Former Name(s)	County
Lakeshore	Fig Orchard	Hancock	Melba	Lottstown	Jeff. Davis
Lambert	O'Neal's Switch	Quitman	Melwyn	Pigford	Lauderdale
Lamkin	Gibbon	Humphreys	Mendenhall	Edna	Simpson
Landon	Pecan Grove	Harrison	Meridian	Sowashee (for a short time)	Lauderdale
Laneheart	Bunker Hill	Wilkinson	Meridian	Baldwin (for only 17 days)	Lauderdale
Langford	Oakdale	Rankin	Metcalf	Wilczinski	Washington
Larkin*	Stallona	Sharkey	Metcalf	Elena	Washington
Larkin*	Patmos	Sharkey	Michigan City	Davis Mills	Benton
Lathamtown	Vera	Scott	Midway	Evans	Yazoo
Lauderdale	Spring's Depot	Lauderdale	Mineral Wells	Kelly	DeSoto
Leaf	Salem	Greene	Mingo	Mann's	Tishomingo
Leesdale	Franklin	Adams	Mollie	Lone Pine	Madison
Leesdale	Turnerville	Adams	Money	Woodstock	Leflore
Lena	Friendship	Leake	Monroe	Holly	Franklin
Lespedeza	Hays	Panola	Monterey	Brier Hill	Rankin
Lewisburg	Kileton	DeSoto	Montpelier	Joe Cross	Clay
Limerick	Stuart's Landing	Yazoo	Montpelier	Crosstown	Clay
Litton	Ivy	Bolivar	Montpelier	LaCross	Clay
Locopolis	Denman	Tallahatchie	Moon	Walton	Coahoma
Lodge	Sand Flat	Lauderdale	Morrow	Andrews Chapel	Lauderdale
Lodi	Store	Montgomery	Moselle	Tusconola	Jones
Long Beach	Scott's Station	Harrison	Mound Springs	Bog	Lee
Longview	Cedar Grove	Pontotoc	Mound Springs	Bucy	Lee
Longview	Cox	Pontotoc	Mount Herman	Mayo Town	Attala
Lorman	Lick	Jefferson	Mountain	Strengthville	George
Lorman	Hayes	Jefferson	Muldon	Louhatten	Monroe
Lorraine	Stonewall	Harrison	Munson	Higgins	Attala
Louise	Upshaw	Humphreys	Murphreesboro	New Hope	Tallahatchie
Loyd Star	East's Mill	Lincoln	Myrtle	Candy Hill	Union
Loyd Star	Red Star	Lincoln	Neely	Washington	Greene
Luckney	Lucknow	Rankin	Neil	Pines	Tishomingo
Lurline	Greenleaf	Tate	Neshoba	Crenshaw	Neshoba
Lux	Bryant	Covington	New Salem	Prudeville	Pontotoc
Lynn Creek	Buck Snort	Noxubee	New Wren	Wren	Monroe
Lyon	Shufordsville	Coahoma	Newman	Baldwin's Ferry	Hinds
Maben	Good Water	Oktibbeha	Newman's	Newbell	Warren
Macedonia	Rochester	Attala	North Carrollton	Rathbone	Carroll
Magee	Mangum	Simpson	Nugent	Maysville	Harrison
Malvina	Phalia	Bolivar	Oak Hill	Nixon	Pontotoc
Mantee	Center Grove	Webster	Oldham	Archer	Tishomingo
Marks	Riverside	Quitman	Olive Branch	Cow Pens	DeSoto
Marksville	Ashton Plantation	Holmes	Olive Branch	Watson's Crossroads	DeSoto
Marvin's Chapel	East Union	Attala	Ophelia	Ratliff's Ferry	Rankin
Mathiston	Spring Valley	Webster	Ora	Duckworth	Covington
Maud	Busby	Tunica	Orange Grove	Murray Station	Jackson
Maxie	Hog Pen Branch	Forrest	Orangeville	Orange Hill	Hinds
Maybank	Monroe	Forrest	Osborn	Camp Oaks	Oktibbeha
Mayersville	Gibson's Landing	Issaquena	Osborn	Muldrow	Oktibbeha
Mayersville	Wadelawn	Issaquena	Otis	Harmond	Scott
Mayersville	Mount Level	Issaquena	Owen's Wells	Gray's Mill	Holmes
McComb	Elizabethtown	Pike	Pace	Arnold	Bolivar
McCool	Barksdale	Attala	Paden	Castle Garden	Tishomingo
McDonald	Sol	Neshoba	Paden	Burnt Hill	Tishomingo
McVille	Yockanookany	Attala	Palmyra	Davis Island	Warren
Meadville	Franklin	Franklin	Pascagoula	Scranton	Jackson
Meehan	Siding	Lauderdale	Pattison	Martin	Claiborne

* The name the place was last known by has now become extinct along with its former name or names. For places that have had more than one former name, the previous placenames are listed chronologically with the first name listed first, second name listed second, etc.

Former Names of Some Mississippi Communities

Community	Former Name(s)	County	Community	Former Name(s)	County
Paulette	Tarbore	Noxubee	Roseacres	Priddy	Coahoma
Paynes	Pages on Sculmore	Tallahatchie	Rosedale	Abel's Point	Bolivar
Paynes	Dogwood Flats	Tallahatchie	Rosedale	Floreyville	Bolivar
Pearlington	Little Jerusalem	Hancock	Rosetta	Harvard Ferry	Wilkinson
Peck	Ryan	Union	Ruleville	Key's Deadening	Sunflower
Peoria	Robinson	Amite	Sabougla	Davis Town	Calhoun
Philadelphia	Neshoba Courthouse	Neshoba	Saint Paul*	Sweetwater	Marion
Phoenix	Claiborneville	Yazoo	Saint Paul*	Hickman	Marion
Picayune	Hobolochitto	Pearl River	Salem	Varnell	Walthall
Pickens	Bole's Ferry	Holmes	Salem	Melis	Walthall
Pickens	Montgomery	Holmes	Sand Hill	Sand Rock	Greene
Pickens	Shiloh	Holmes	Sandy Bayou	Dwiggins	Sunflower
Pickens	Pickens Station	Holmes	Sandy Ridge	Dabney	Leflore
Pine Hills	Shell Beach	Harrison	Sandy Ridge	Geren	Leflore
Pineview	Pines	Jones	Sandy Ridge	Gwin	Leflore
Pineville	Pine Village	Smith	Sandy Ridge	Ruby	Leflore
Piney Woods	Taylor Hill	Rankin	Saukum	Ashley	Wilkinson
Pittsboro	Orrsville	Calhoun	Sauls	Mullin's Town	Lawrence
Pleasant Hill	Robertson's Cross Roads	DeSoto	Savannah Grove	A & V Junction	Lauderdale
Pleasant Grove	Chiwapa	Pontotoc	Savoy	Corrine	Lauderdale
Pontetok*	Allen's Agency	Pontotoc	Savoy	Corry	Lauderdale
Pontetok*	Bonner Community	Pontotoc	Scobey	Garner Station	Yalobusha
Pontetok*	Camp Ground	Pontotoc	Second Creek	White Apple Village	Adams
Prentiss *	Indian Point	Bolivar	Seven Springs	Mississippi Springs	Hinds
Pretoria	Pugh's Store	Noxubee	Shady Grove	Mico	Jones
Prismatic	Smith's Shops	Kemper	Shankstown	Louisville	Jefferson
Puckett	Clear Creek	Rankin	Sharon	Choctaw Purchase	Madison
Queensburg	Wausau	Jones	Sharon	Purchase	Madison
Quito	Alexandria	Leflore	Shelby	Bellevue	Bolivar
Ragland	Usher	Newton	Shepard	Southern	Jeff. Davis
Raleigh	Idian Springs	Smith	Sherwood	Livingston	Choctaw
Rankin	Spears Cut	Rankin	Shiloh	Petersburg	Lee
Ransom	Ransomville	Lauderdale	Shiloh	Allenburg	Lee
Ratliff	Oak Grove	Itawamba	Shiloh	Rands	Lee
Redland	McIntoshville	Pontotoc	Shinault	Holder	Lafayette
Reese	Jackson's Point	Coahoma	Shipman	Brushy	George
Regan	Morey	Madison	Shore Crest	Moccasin Point	Harrison
Regan	Forlorn	Madison	Shucktown	Snowden	Lauderdale
Renshaw	Redding Switch	Yazoo	Sidon	Marion Landing	Leflore
Rex	Moore Station	Bolivar	Silver City	Palmetto Home	Humphreys
Rich	Yazoo Pass	Coahoma	Silver Creek	The Hall	Lawrence
Richardson	Mitchel Station	Pearl River	Sisloff Junction	Mills Bayou Junction	Leflore
Richton	Rich's Mill	Perry	Slayden	Gourd Neck	Marshall
Ridgeland	Highland Colony	Madison	Smith	Yawn	Covington
Rio	Pinder	Kemper	Smith's Spur	Tonic	Lauderdale
River Hill	Lake City	Madison	Smith's Spur	Blank's Station	Lauderdale
Riverton*	The Wood Yard	Bolivar	Snave	Cammack	Issaquena
Riverton*	Pride's Point	Bolivar	Soso	Woodbury	Jones
Roberts	Colon	Newton	Spring Hill	Blands	Lafayette
Robinwood*	Riverside	Lawrence	Springport	Big Sandy	Panola
Robinwood*	Wilson's Station	Lawrence	Springville	Spring Hill	Pontotoc
Robinwood*	Folwell	Lawrence	Stafford	Brownsville	Bolivar
Rodney	Petite Gulf	Jefferson	Stage	Track	Scott
Rome	Shafter	Sunflower	Stallo	Maurine	Neshoba
Roscoe	Skinamadink	Newton	Starkville	Boardtown	Oktibbeha
Roseacres	Mound Place	Coahoma	Steens	Jamison's Mill	Lowndes

* The name the place was last known by has now become extinct along with its former name or names. For places that have had more than one former name, the previous placenames are listed chronologically with the first name listed first, second name listed second, etc.

Former Names of Some Mississippi Communities

Community	Former Name(s)	County	Community	Former Name(s)	County
Sterling	Okitibbee	Lauderdale	Waldo	Woodland	Neshoba
Sterling	Sageville	Lauderdale	Wallfield	Elvira	Pontotoc
Stinson	Jones' Store	Lauderdale	Walls	Alpika	DeSoto
Stratton	Pinkney	Newton	Walnut	Hopkins	Tippah
Stratton	Stamper	Newton	Wanilla	Smith's Ferry	Lawrence
Strengthford	Progression	Wayne	Wanilla	Berkson	Lawrence
Stringer	P. K.	Jasper	Warsaw	Crossroads	Marshall
Sturgis	Whitefield	Oktibbeha	Warsaw	Oak Hill	Marshall
Sturgis	Palestine (part of town)	Oktibbeha	Water Valley	Oke Chukma	Yalobusha
Sulphur Springs	Springfield	Madison	Wautubbee	Hell's Valley	Clarke
Summerland	Chestnut Springs	Smith	Way	Way's Bluff	Madison
Sunnyside	Emmaville	Leflore	Weathersby	Carraway	Simpson
Sunrise	Roan	Leake	Webb	Hood	Tallahatchie
Teckville	Bedenbaugh	Lafayette	Webster	Crossroads	Winston
Terry	New Town	Hinds	Wells	Marx	Lowndes
Thaxton	Buttermilk Springs	Pontotoc	West Point	Robertson's Cross Roads	Clay
Thayer	Sutton's Switch	Lincoln	Westside	Bethel	Claiborne
Thomasville	Dry Creek	Rankin	Whaley	Dodd's Ferry	Carroll
Thompson	Harmoney	Attala	Whites	Clear Branch	Rankin
Thompsonville	Hollingsworth	Hinds	Whitestown *	Newtonia	Wilkinson
Thrasher	Rugg	Prentiss	Wiggins	Niles City	Stone
Tileville	Niles	Bolivar	Wilkinson	Buffalo	Wilkinson
Tillatoba	Dame Station	Yalobusha	Williamson	Reynolds	Panola
Tilton	Sauls	Lawrence	Willis	Robinsonville	Coahoma
Tinsley	Taylor's Switch	Yazoo	Willis Heights	West Tupelo	Lee
Tishomingo	Good Spring	Tishomingo	Wiltshire	Mount Ida	Carroll
Tralake	Trail Lake	Washington	Winborn	Reed's Switch	Benton
Trapp	Darden Ridge	Neshoba	Winstonville	Chambers	Bolivar
Trapp	Coldwater	Neshoba	Wolf	Ringgold	Scott
Trenton	Dutch Colony	Smith	Woodland	Dewey	Chickasaw
Trotter's Landing	Glendale Landing	Tunica	Woodlawn	Kidd's Tavern	Lowndes
Tupelo	Gum Pond	Lee	Wortham	Redmon's Crossing	Harrison
Turnbull	Johnson's Station	Wilkinson	Wright's	Webb	Lauderdale
Turon	Prospect	Itawamba	Wyatt	Mitchell's Bluff	Lafayette
Tuscan	Blanton's Gap	Choctaw	Yazoo City	Hannan's Bluff	Yazoo
Tuscola	Pensacola	Leake	Yazoo City	Manchester	Yazoo
Tylertown	Magee's Settlement	Walthall	Yocony	Grissom's Mill	Itawamba
Tylertown	Conerly's Post Office	Walthall	Zama	Ayres	Attala
Union	Rusk	Lee	Zeiglerville	New Prospect	Yazoo
Union	Chauki	Newton	Zelleria	Sim's Switch	Yazoo
Union	Ina	Simpson	Zemuly	Bolatusha	Attala
Union Church	Buie	Jefferson	Zero	Pleasant Hill	Lauderdale
Unity	North West	Attala	Zion Hill	Scotland	Amite
Updike	Lanhark	Sharkey			
Urbo	Skinner's Switch	Newton			
Urbo	Yarbo	Newton			
Utica	Cane Ridge	Hinds			
Vaiden	Shongola	Carroll			
Vancleave	Bluff Creek	Jackson			
Vardaman	Ticky Bin	Calhoun			
Vardaman	Timberville	Calhoun			
Velma	Dixon Switch	Yalobusha			
Vicksburg	Walnut Hills	Warren			
Vimville	Coker's Chapel	Lauderdale			
Voy	Beam's Store	Itawamba			
Walden	Johnson's Crossing	Monroe			

* The name the place was last known by has now become extinct along with its former name or names. For places that have had more than one former name, the previous placenames are listed chronologically with the first name listed first, second name listed second, etc.

Counties of Mississippi With Placenames

ADAMS
Alloway Landing
Anna
Arnot
Briar Landing
Butler Lake
Callon Lake
Carthage
Carthage Landing
Cerro Gordo Landing
Cloverdale
Cowpen Point Landing
Cranfield
Dies Slough
Ellis Cliffs
Eureka Landing
Fenwick
Fields Lake
Foster
Giles Landing
Hawthorne
Homochitto National
    Forest (part)
Hutchins Landing
Jackson Point Landing
Jeannette Johnsville
Kaiser-Carlton Lake
Kienstra
Kingston
Leesdale
Linwood
Long Lake
Mississippi River
McMillan
Monmouth
Morgantown
Natchez[1] 18,277
Natchez Nat'l. Cemetery
Natchez State Park
Natchez Trace Parkway
    (part)
Pandella Landing
Parker Landing
Pine Ridge
Rawles
Risher Lake
Saint Catherine
Scotia
Selma
Sibley
Stanton
Stokes
Washington
Waverly Place Landing

ALCORN
Alcorn
Allentown
Bennett Ridge
Biggersville
Browder Ridge
By
Coke
Collins Crossing
Collinstown
Corinth 12,204
Corinth Nat'l. Cemetery
Crow
Crumtown
Cuba
Gift
Glen 229
Glens Glen
Hightown
Hinkle
Indian Springs
Jacinto
Jobes
Jones Hollow
Jonestown
Kendrick
Kossuth 244
Lewis Hollow
Liddon Lake
Lone Pine
Oakland
Rienzi 358
Ross Crossing
Ruslor Junction
Searcy Town
Smith Bridge
Sorghum Hollow
Springer Glade
Strickland
Synagogue
Theo
Waukomis Lake
Wenasoga
Winbush Ridge

AMITE
Ariel
Beechwood
Berwick
Bewelcome
Brookside
Busy Corner
Capell
Carruth Lake
Cassels
Centreville 288
    (1,543 total)
    [part in Wilkinson Co.]
Coles
Compromise
Crosby 162 (443 total)
    [part in Wilkinson Co.]
East Fork
Enterprise
Eunice
Gillsburg
Glading
Gloster 1,304
Hebron
Hiram
Homochitto
Homochitto National
    Forest (part)
Huron
Hustler
Liberty 680
Line Creek
Mars Hill
McElveen
Mixon
Mount Olive
O'Neil
Olio
Oxford
Peoria
Sansing Lake
Smithdale
Street
Tangipahoa
Tatum
Terrys Creek
Thompson
Ustane
White Cap
Zion Hill

ATTALA
Antioch
Aponaug
Bear Creek
Beulah
Bluff Springs
Bowies Chapel
Boyette
Branchville
Burkettsville
Carmack
Carson Ridge
Center
Center Point
Chapel Hill
Chita
Cowpen
Dodds
Dossville (part)
Doty Springs
Earlyville
East Macedonia
Edgefield
Ethel 440
Forrest
Friendship
Glendale
Gregory
Hesterville
Hurricane
Joplin
Joseph
Kosciusko 6,774
Knox
Langley
Liberty Chapel
Liberty Hill
Macedonia
Marvins Chapel
McAdams
McCool 168
McVille
Mercer
Mount Herman
Multona Springs
Munson
Natchez Trace Parkway
    (part)
New Hope
Newport
Newtonville
Nile
North Center
North Union
Oak Ridge
Patterson
Pierces Chapel
Pilgrims Rest
Plantation
Pleasant Ridge
Possumneck
Rockport
Rutherford
Sallis 130
Sand Hill
Sandridge Lake
Shady Grove
Shrock
Smyrna
Springdale
Steele
Tabernacle
Thompson
Thweatt
Unity
Valena
Wamba
Williamsville
Youth Center Lake
Zama
Zemuly

BENTON
Ashland 508
Bethel
Black Jack
Brody
Canaan
Cannon
Dardun
Hamilton
Hickory Flat 544
Holly Springs National
    Forest (part)
Hopewell
Jobe Hollow
Lamar
Michigan City
New Canaan
Pine Grove
Richmond Hollow
Robinson Bottom
Snow Lake Shores
Spring Hill
Winborn

BOLIVAR
Alligator 213
Alligator Lake
Appeal
Australia Landing
Benoit 609
Beulah 474
Beulah Island Landing
Beulah Lake
Bolivar
Bolivar Lake
    (Lake Charlie Capps)
Bolivar Landing
Boyle 696
Buffalo Bayou
Busey
Catfish Point
Catfish Point Landing
Catfish Towhead
Caulk Neck
Caulk Point
Cessions Landing
Chambers (Winstonville)
Choctaw
Christmas
Cleveland 14,834
Cleveland Crossing
Clifford
Concordia
Conservation League
    Lake
Cypress Bend
Dahomey National
    Wildlife Refuge
Deeson
Dennis Landing
Dixie
Duncan 394
Eldridge
Eutaw
Eutaw Landing
Francis
Gill
Grapeland
Great River Road State
    Park
Gunnison 608
Hannah
Harlow
Home Landing
Hurricane Point
Hushpuckena
Hog Pen Slough
Huntington Point
Kimball Lake
Lake Charlie Capps
    (formerly Bolivar Lake)
Lake Vista

[1] COUNTY SEATS ARE IN *ITALICS*. A NUMBER AFTER A PLACENAME DENOTES THE 1998 POPULATION ESTIMATE.

The Ultimate Reference on the State

Counties of Mississippi With Placenames

BOLIVAR (continued)
Lamont
Laughlin
Litton
Lobdell
Longshot
Malvina
Mason Landing
Meltonia
Merigold 560
Mississippi River
Mound Bayou 2,102
Mound City
Mound Landing
Niblett Landing
Niles
O'Reilly
Old River Lake
Old Tar Paper Shack Lake
Pace 348
Perthshire
Prentiss Bar
Renova 593
Riverton Landing
Rochdale
Rosedale[1] 2,507
Round Lake
Saw Grass Lake
Scott
Shaw 283 (2,290 total)
    [part in Sunflower Co.]
Shelby 2,686
Skene
Smith Point
Stringtown
Symonds
Terrene Landing
Tileville
Turners Flat
Victor
Vista Lake
Waxhaw
Whiskey Chute
Whittington Lake
Willow Slough
Winstonville (Chambers) 262
Wright
Yellow Bend
Zumbro

CALHOUN
Banner
Benela
Bently
Big Creek 117
Bounds
Bruce 2,041
Calhoun City 1,736
Coles Creek
Dentontown
Derma 948

Ellard
Elsie
Hollis
Lantrip
Loyd
New Liberty
Partee
Pittman
Pittsboro 272
Reid
Retreat
Sabougla
Sarepta
Shepherd
Skuna
Slate Spring 119
Vance
Vardaman 919
Varden
Wardwell

CARROLL
Adair
Avalon
Bailey Lake
Beatty
Black Hawk
Booths Lake
Carrollton 220
Centerville
Coila
Donley
Gravel Hill
Holly Grove
Jefferson
Little Texas
Malmaison
McCarley
Miles
North Carrollton 607
Oklahoma
Pine Bluff
Seven Pines
Shady Grove
Teoc
Vaiden 831
Valley Hill
Whaley
Wiltshire

CHICKASAW
Anchor
Atlanta
Bacon
Bethel
Bowles
Buena Vista
Camp Bellewood
Chalk Bluff
Coleville
Congress
Egypt
Elize

Enon
Hall
Hickory Flat
Holladay
Houlka 540
Houston 3,902
Jolly
Leotis
Macedonia
McCondy
Natchez Trace Parkway
    (part)
Neals
New York
Newport
Oak Grove
Okolona 3,059
Old Houlka
Parkersburg
Pikeville
Poplar Springs
Prairie Mount
Prospect
Pyland
Ridge
Salem
Scarbrough Lake
Shake Rag
Simpson Lake
Sonora
Sparta
Tabbville
Thelma
Thorn
Tombigbee National Forest (part)
Trebloc
Van Vleet
Woodland 183

CHOCTAW
Ackerman 1,705
Ashfordville
Bankston
Bywy
Bywy Overlook
Chester
Choctaw Lake
Fentress
French Camp 315
Fulcher
Kerr
Mathiston 98 (832 total)
    [part in Webster Co.]
Natchez Trace Parkway
    (part)
Reform
Sherwood
Tollison
Tombigbee National Forest (part)
Tuscan
Weir 545

Williams
Wood Springs

CLAIBORNE
Alcorn
Allen
Barland
Brooks Light
Bruinsburg
Burnell
Carlisle
Claiborne Lake
Galloway
Gin Lake
Gordon
Grand Gulf
Grand Gulf Military Park
Grand Gulf Nuclear Station
Green Meadow
Hamilton Lake
Hankinson
Hermanville
Hervey
Humphreys
Ingleside
Insmore
Lake Bruin State park
Mississippi River
Natchez Trace Parkway
    (part)
Oaklawn
Pattison
Pattona
Peyton
Pierre Bayou
Port Gibson 1,750
Reganton
Rocky Springs
Russum
Saint Elmo
Sarepta
Shelby
Spring Plains
Tillman
Westside
Willows
Windsor Ruins

CLARKE
Barnett
Basic
Beatrice
Beaver Dam
Brewer
Camp Pine Crest
Carmichael
Chancellor
Clarkco State Park
Choctaw
Crandall
Creek
Davis

Davidson
Dedwylder
DeSoto
East Enterprise
Elwood
Energy
Enterprise 483
Goodwater
Hale
Harmony
Horn
Hurricane Creek
Indian Mound
Junction City
Langsdale
Linton
Mannassa
Martinere Bend
Matherville
Mayhoff Springs
Middleton
Nancy
Pachuta 276
Pierces Springs
Pine Ridge
Quitman 2,839
Roy
Sable
Sels Prairie
Shiloh
Shubuta 596
Snell
Stonewall 1,161
Sykes
Threadville
Wautubbee
West Enterprise
West Pachuta
White House

CLAY
Abbot
Beasley
Cairo
Cedar Bluff
Griffith
Hopewell
Mary Holmes
Mhoons Valley
Montpelier
Natchez Trace Parkway
    (part)
Northgate
Palestine
Palo Alto
Pheba
Pine Acres
Pinebluff
Point Harbor
Siloam
Stephen
Tibbee
Una

[1] COUNTY SEATS ARE IN *ITALICS*. A NUMBER AFTER A PLACENAME DENOTES THE 1998 POPULATION ESTIMATE.

Counties of Mississippi With Placenames

Vinton
Waddell
Walkers Gin
Waverly
Waverly Ferry
West Point 8,848
Whites

COAHOMA
Africa
Anderson Landing
Armistead
Barbee
Baugh
Beverly
   (Davenport Station)
Black Bayou
Bobo
Boone
Burke Landing
Carter
Claremont
Clarksdale[1] 20,461
Cleary
Clover Hill
Coahoma 250
Corndike Brake
Counts
Danforth
Delta
DeSoto Lake
Dickerson
Dublin
Durham
Eagles Nest
Eleanor
Farrell
Fitch
Friar's Point 1,337
Glen Aubin
Glendale
Green Grove
Harrs Place
Hillhouse Landing
Hopson
Horseshoe Lake
Humber
Ingram
Iris
Jeffries
Jonestown 1,462
Kay Bayou
King And Anderson
Lake Charles Landing
Long Lake
Lula 218
Lurand
Lyon 427
Malone Landing
Mascot
Matagorda
Mattson
Miller Point

Mississippi River
Montezuma Bar
Moon
Moon Lake
Old Town Bend
Popsons
Powell
Pullen
Pushmataha Landing
Reese Landing
Rena Lara
Rescue Landing
Rich
Riverton
Robertsville
Roseacres
Roundaway
Rowen Bayou
Rudyard
Rucks
Rush Bayou
Sandy Bayou
Sessions
Sherard
Shutersville
State Levee
Stillons
Stokely
Stokes
Stovall
Sunday
Sunflower Landing
Swan Lake
Walnut Grove
Wildwood
Willis

COPIAH
Allen
Ashley
Barlow
Beauregard 226
Beechgrove
Bowerton
Browns Wells
Burtonton
Camp Wesley Pines
Carpenter
Coaler
Coars Springs
Conn
Cowanville
Crystal Springs 5,832
Dentville
Egypt Hill
Gallatin
Gallman
Gatesville
Georgetown 350
Glancy
Harperville
Hazlehurst 4,228
Hermanville

Homochitto National
   Forest (part)
Hoodtown
Hopewell
It
Jack
Linden
Martinsville
Meadows Store
Midway
Myles
Old Georgetown
Pierre Bayou
Pleasant Hill
Rockport
Sand Hill
Sardis
Shady Grove
Smyrna
Stronghope
Tillman
Wesson 1,520
Willing

COVINGTON
Arbo
Bethel
Cold Springs
Collins 2,657
Cooley Springs
Dont
Dry Creek (Lone Star)
Eminence
Friendship
Gandsi
Gilmore
Hopewell
Hot Coffee
Kelly
Kola
Liberty
Lone Star (Dry Creek)
Lux
McDonald
McNair
McRaney
Mike Conner Lake
Moscos
Mount Olive 963
Mount Pleasant
Ora
Pickering
Providence
Reddochs
Rock Hill
Salem
Sanford
Seminary 236
Shady Oak
Smith
Speedtown
Sunset
Union

Vennie Park
Williamsburg
Willowtown

DE SOTO
Alden
Alphaba
Arkabutla Dam
Arkabutla Lake/Reservoir
   (part in Tate Co.)
Barnesville
Bright
Camp Currier
Cedarview Cockrum
Cow Island Bend
Cublake
Days
Dead Negro Slough
Deans Corner
Eudora
Fairhaven
Frees Corners
Glover
Handy Corner
Hernando 4,088
Hernando Point
Holly Hills
Horn Lake 13,885
Horn Lake (body of water)
Howards Store
Ingrams Mill
Jago
Lake Cormorant
Lake View
Lewisburg
Love
Lynchburg
Marienette
Maywood
Memphis 90
Miller
Mineral Wells
Mississippi River
Nesbit
Newport
Norfolk
Norfolk Bayou
Olive Branch 12,063
Overpark
Penton
Pleasant Hill
Plum Point
Poplar Corners
Robinson Gin
Southaven 23,434
Stonewall
Trinity
Twin Lakes
Walls
West Days
Wilson Store
Wrights Store

FORREST
Barron
Barrontown
Batson
Bedford Woods
Bonhomie
Bowie
Brooklyn
Buena Vista Lakes
Camp Dantzler
Camp Shelby (military)
Carnes
Carterville
Corinth
Currie
DeSoto National Forest
   (part)
Dixie
Dixie Pine
Dragon
Dreyfus
Eastside
Eatonville
Elks Lake
Epps
Forrest Park
Four Points
Fruitland Park
Glendale
Goodluck
Harvey
Hattiesburg 45,996
   (48,806 total)
   [part in Lamar Co.]
Innswood South
Kirkwood
Leeville
Macedonia
Mars Hill
Maxie
Maybank
McCallum
McLaurin
Meyers
Morriston
Palmer
Palmers Crossing
Paul B. Johnson State
   Park
Petal 8,888
Pine Grove
Pistol Ridge
Providence
Ragland
Ralston
Rawles Springs
Riverside
Rock Hill
Sharon Acres
Shelby Lake
Southern
Sunrise
Tiak

[1] COUNTY SEATS ARE IN *ITALICS*. A NUMBER AFTER A PLACENAME DENOTES THE 1998 POPULATION ESTIMATE.

Counties of Mississippi With Placenames

FORREST (continued)
Wallis
Westwood
Woodhaven
Woodlawn Court

FRANKLIN
Bude 950
Bunckley
Dick
Eddiceton
Flat Rock
Freewoods
Garden City
Hamburg
Homochitto National Forest (part)
Kennolia
Kirby
Knoxville
Little Springs
Lucien
McCall Creek
Meadville[1] 411
Mile Branch
Monroe
Mount Olive
New Hope
Okhissa Lake
Oldenburg
Orange
Quentin
Roxie 556
Shucktown
Suffolk
Veto
White Apple

GEORGE
Agricola
Avent
Barton
Basin
Benndale
Bexley
Bull Bay Bend
Central
Central Lookout
Crossroads
Dale
Dean Landing
Donovan
Eubanks
Evanston
Gibson Landing
Howell
Isabell
Latonia
Lucedale 3,041
Marsha
McCrea Dead River
Mengel
Merrill
Mountain
Movella
Parker Lookout
Reed Flat
Rock Creek
Ruble
Sandy Wash Bend
Shipman
Slavonia
Vaughan
Ward
Waters Landing
Wilkinson Ferry

GREENE
Adamsville
Avent Station
Avera
Benjoe
Bothwell
Bradley
Brown Town
Bud Bluff
Byrd
Carson City
Chat High Bluff
Churchwell High Bluff
Clark
Coaker Bend
Coaker Bluff
DeSoto National Forest (part)
Dueitt
Ferry Bend
Gants Bluff
Hillman
Indian Hill
James
Jonathan
Kitrell Creek Reservoir
Kittrell
Knobtown
Leaf
Leakesville 1,111
McLain 606
Meeting House Bluff
Mohoba
Neely
Old Avera
Piave
Pisgah
Rancho Ande
Red Bluff
Rounsaville
Royce
Sand Hill
Shell Bluff
Stalworth Camp
State Line 269 (425 tot.) [part in Wayne Co.]
Turner Store
Vernal
Wilson

GRENADA
Bew Springs
Camp McCain (military)
Cape Retreat
Carver Bluff
Carver Point
Cedar Point
Choctaw
Crescent Ridge
Dubard
Elliott
Futheyville
Geeslin Corner
Glenwild
Gore Springs
Graysport Crossing
Grenada 11,161
Grenada dam
Grenada Lake/Reservoir
Grenada Landing
Hardy
Hardy Station
Haserway
Holcomb
Hugh White State Park
Hurricane Branch
Kincaid
Kirkman Landing
Leflore
Maxey Bayou
Memphis Junction
Misterton
Nason
Oxberry
Oxberry Bayou
Parsons
Piney Woods
Redding
Riverdale
Sorghum Lake
Sunnycrest
Tie Plant
Vaney Bayou
Youngs

HANCOCK
Ansley
Bay Saint Louis 9,841
Bayou Bolan
Bayside Park
Belle Isle
Bennett
Beppo
Breath Bayou
Buccaneer State Park
Campbell Bayous
Catahoula
Catfish Bayou
Cedar Point
Center
Clermont Harbor
Cowand Point
Crane Creek
Cross Bayou
Cutoff Bayou
Diamondhead
East Double Bayou
Fenton
Flat Top
Foster Bayou
Four Dollar Bayou
Gainesville
Grand Plains Bayou
Gulfside
Henderson Point
Heron Bay Bayou
Holy Cross Boys Camp
Jackson Landing
Jackson Ridge
Kiln
King Bee Bayou
Leetown
Lakeshore
Lighthouse Point
Logtown
Long Point
Napoleon
NASA's John C. Stennis Space Center Test Site
Necaise
Necaise Crossing
North Side
Pearlington
Point Clear
Redfish Bayou
Saint Joseph Point
Sand Bayou
Santa Rosa
Sawmill Bayou
Sellers
Sellers Lookout
Shoreline Park
Silver Creek Acres
Standard
Trout Bayou
Waveland 6,986
Westonia Lookout
Wiehe
Woody Bayou

HARRISON
Airey
Beauvoir
Big Lake
Biloxi 47,316
Bulah
Camp Wilkes
Cedar Lake
Cedar Point
Coalville
Cuevas
D'Iberville 8,211
De Buys
De Lisle
Dedeaux
DeSoto National Forest (part)
Devils Elbow
Ditch Bayou
Edgewater Park
Gaston Point
Goose Point
Grassy Point
Gulf Islands National Seashore
Gulfport 64,762
Handsboro
Heartease
Henderson Point
Hovey
Howison
Jones Mill
Keesler Air Force Base
Landon
Lizana
Long Beach 16,776
Loraine
Lyman
Mallini Point
Mississippi City (extinct)
New Hope
North Bay
North Biloxi
North Gulfport
Nugent
Orange Grove
Pass Christian 6,190
Pine Hills
Pitcher Point
Rawhide
Riceville
Sandard
Saucier
Seymour
Shallow Point
Success
Timber Ridge
Ton Lake
Vidalia
West Biloxi
West Gulfport
White Harbor
White Plains
Wool Market
Wortham

HINDS
Adams
Bear Creek
Bernard
Bethesda
Bolton 783
Bottom Acres
Bradie
Breckenridge
Briarcliff
Brookhollow Place
Brookleigh

[1] COUNTY SEATS ARE IN *ITALICS*. A NUMBER AFTER A PLACENAME DENOTES THE 1998 POPULATION ESTIMATE.

Counties of Mississippi With Placenames

Brookwood	Newman	Choctaw	**HUMPHREYS**	Tallula
Brookwood Pines	Nogan	Coxburg	Anchorage	Valewood
Brownsville	North Colony	Cruger 554	Bellewood	Valley Park
Byram	Northpointe	Dulweber	*Belzoni* 2,367	Woodside
Carmichael	Norwood	Durant 2,686	Brooklyn	
Carriage Hills	Oak Creek	Ebenezer	Castleman	**ITAWAMBA**
Catherine Lake	Oakley	Edsville	Craig	Abney
Cayuga	Orangeville	Egypt	Deovolente	Authority
Cedar Hills	Palestine	Emory	Eagle Lake	Ballardsville
Champion Hill	Pine Grove	Eulogy	Famosla	Beans Ferry
Chapel Hill	Pine Lea	Franklin	Fisk Bayou	Beaver Lake
Cherry Park	Pocahontas	Garden Chapel	Four Mile	Beene's Ferry
Choctaw Village	Queens Hill	Good Hope	French Bayou	Cadamy
Clinton 22,067	Queens Lane	Goodman 1,348	Gooden Lake	Cardsville
Coopers Wells	Raintree Place	Gum Grove	Grass Lake	Carolina
Coxs Ferry	*Raymond* 2,016	Gwin	Gum Bayou	Centerville
Cynthia	Red Hill	Hillside National	Hard Cash	Clay
Dabney Crossroads	Reedtown	Wildlife Refuge	Hidi	Credille Dam
Dixie Acres	Rolling Meadows	Hoffman	Honey Island	Dorsey
Dixon	Rosemary	Holmes County	Isola 666	Evergreen
Dry Grove	St. Thomas	State Park	Jaketown	Fairview
Duke	Salem	Horseshoe	Lamkin	*Fulton* 3,668
Easthaven	Seven Springs	Horseshoe Lake	Lodi	Greenwood
Eastover	Sherwood Forest	Howard	Louise 314	Kirkville
Edgewood Acres	Siwell	Ituma	Midnight	Lunch
Edwards[1] 1,195	Smiths	Jones Crossing	Refuge	Mantachie 1,068
Elton	Spring Ridge	Keirn	Richland	Mount Pleasant
Elton Place	Sunkist	Lebanon	Romeo	Natchez Trace Parkway
Fairchilds Crossing	Taylorsville	*Lexington* 2,027	Silent Shade	(part)
Forest Green	Terry 619	Marcella	Silver City 322	New Salem
Forest Hill	The Briars	Marksville	Sleepy Hollow	Oakland
Garden Park	The Cascades	Matthew's Brake Nat'l.	Wilzone	Ozark
Green Acres	The Islands	Wildlife Refuge	Wolf Lake	Peppertown
Green Crossing	Thompson	McMillan		Rara Avis
Highland Meadows	Thompsonville	Meeks	**ISSAQUENA**	Ratliff
Hope Springs	Tinnin	Mileston	Adams Landing	Sandy Springs
Hubbard	Tougaloo	Montgomery	Addie	Shiloh
Jackson 187,433	Trailwood	Morgan Bayou	Albemarle Lake	Tennessee-Tombigbee
(188,419 total)[part in	Turnage Trails Camp	Morgan Brake National	Alexander	Waterway (part)
Madison & Rankin]	Utica 987	Wildlife Refuge	Arcadia	Tilden
Kickapoo Camp	Van Winkle	Oak Grove	Ashland	Tremont 345
Kentwood	Warren Place	Omega	Black Bayou	Turon
Lake Hico	Wateroaks	Oregon	Booth	Van Buren
Lakeover	West View	Oswego	Chotard	West Fulton
Lakeridge	Willowood	Owens Wells	Cypress Lake	Yale
Lakeside	Windsor Forest	Pickens 1,381	Delta National Forest	
Learned 99	Wingfield Place	Pinchback	(part in Sharkey)	**JACKSON**
Lebanon	Woodhaven	Pine Grove	Elleslie	Back Bayou
LeFleur's Bluff State Park	Woodland Hills	Pluto	Fitler	Bangs Bayou
Leavell Woods	Woodmoor	Poplar Springs	Goose Lake Flats	Bangs Lake
Lost Lake		Quofaloma	Grace	Bayou Chemise
Lynchburg	**HOLMES**	Richland	Gross Bayou	Belle Fontaine Point
Magnolia Terrace	Aberdeen Junction	Roseneath	Hardee	Big Bear Bayou
Mayfair	Acona	Shackleford	Homochitto	Big Lake
McRaven	Bee Lake (community)	Stonewall	Hopedale	Big Point
Meadow Oaks	Bee Lake	Tchula 2,367	Ingomar	Black Creek Slough
Midway	Black	Thornton	Magna Vista	Camp Ground Slough
Moncure	Blissdale	Tolarville	*Mayersville* 288	Camp Lamotte
Morgans Store	Bowling Green	West 166	Millers Landing	Coleson Bayou
Morning Star	Brozville	West Hill	Mills Bayou	Coll Town
Natchez Trace Parkway	Butler	Westfield	Mississippi River	Crooked Bayou
(part)	Camp Castolians Springs	Wyatt	New Fitler	Dantzler
Nevada	Castalians Springs		Parks Place	Dees Landing

[1] COUNTY SEATS ARE IN *ITALICS*. A NUMBER AFTER A PLACENAME DENOTES THE 1998 POPULATION ESTIMATE.

Counties of Mississippi With Placenames

JACKSON (continued)
Delmas Bayou
DeSoto National Forest (part)
East Moss Point
East Pascagoula
Eastlawn
East Side
Escatawpa
Evergreen
Fontainebleau
Ford (part of Moss Point)
Forts Lake
Gautier 11,139
Graham Ferry
Graveline Bayou
Griffin Point
Gulf Hills
Gulf Marine State Park
Gurlie Bayou
Harleston
Helena
Hilda
Hollingsworth Point
Holly Landing
Hurley
Hurley Lookout
Iowana
Jose Bayou
Kreole
Lang Bayou
Larue
Latimer
Laughter Flat Landing
Longview Bayou
Macon Bend
Marsh Lake
Martin Bluff
McCall Landing
McInnis Bayou
Miles Bluff
Missala
Moss Point[1] 18,095
Nut Bank
Ocean Springs 16,519
Old Americus
Orange Grove
Orange Lake
Parish Lake Bayou
Pascagoula 27,163
Pascagoula Naval Home Port
Pasgoula
Pecan
Point Tuasaine
Polfry
Popetown
Poticaw Landing
Red Bluff
Rogers Bend
Saint Martin
Sandhill Crane Complex Nat'l. Wildlife Refuge

Sawmill Point
Shepard State Park
Sikes Bluff
Slaughter Flat Landing
South Pascagoula
Spanish Point
Ss Bayou
St. Martin
Swift Bayou
The Horseshoe
The Prairie
Third Bayou
Three Rivers
Vancleave
Vaughn Bayou
Vestry
Wade
White Bluff
Windsor Park
Yellow Bluff

JASPER
Acme
Baxter
Bay Springs 1,855
Bienville National Forest (part)
Blacks Dam
Blue Ridge
Burns
Claiborne
Claude Bennett Lake
Davisville
Etchehoma
Fellowship
Fouke
Garlandville
Goshen
Gridley
Hamlet
Heidelberg 937
Hero
Holt
Jewells Hill
Kelona
Lake Como
Louin 282
Markwald
McNeal
Missionary
Montrose 108
Moss
Mulberry
New Fellowship
Oak Bowery
Orange
Paulding
Ras
Roberts
Rose Hill
Stafford Springs
Stevens
Stringer

Tallahoma
Turkey Ridge
Turnerville
Verba
Vernon
Vossburg
Vrue
Waldrup
Weems

JEFFERSON
Ashland
Baptizing Slough
Blue Hill
Buena Vista
Cadillac
Cannonsburg
Church Hill
Clifton
Coon Box
Deane
Dennis Crossroads
Elmo
Fayette 1,822
Four Forks
Gilliam Chute
Gum Ridge
Harriston
Holmes Lake
Homochitto National Forest (part)
Huntley
Ihrie
Jefferson
Kings Point
Leedo
Long Bayou
Lorman
Malcolm
McBride
McNair
Melton
Mississippi River
Natchez Trace Parkway (part)
North Fork
Perth
Phoenix
Pumping Station Slough
Red Lick
Rodney
Shankstown
Spithead Towhead
Springfield
Stampley
Stonington
Union Church
Uniontown
Violet

JEFFERSON DAVIS
Bassfield 238
Cantwell Mill

Carson
Clem
Deen
Double Churches
Gwinville
Hathorn
Haw Pond
Hebron
Jeff Davis Lake
Lucas
Melba
Morris
Mount Carmel
Old Bassfield
Prentiss 1,275
Progress
Society Hill
Story
Terrell
Watts Hollow
Whitesand

JONES
Albeison
Antioch
Benson
Blodgett
Bogue Homa
Bogue Homa Lake
Bonner
Calhoun
Cleo
Crotts
Currie
Eastabutchie
Eastview
Ellisville 3,770
Ellisville Junction
Errata
Flynt
Gitano
Glade
Haney
Hawkes Hebron
Hoy
Jenkins
Johnson
Landrum
Lanham
Laurel 18,299
Limbert
Matthews
Maybell
Mill Creek
Monarch
Moselle
Mount Olive
Mount Zion
Myrick
Oak Bowery
Oak Grove
Ouetti
Ovett

Pecan Grove
Pendorff
Pine Belt Regional Airport
Pleasant Ridge
Powers
Queensburg
Rainey
Rogerslacy
Sand Hill
Sandersville 894
Service
Shady Grove
Sharon
Shelton
Soso 377
Springhill
Summerland
Tawanta
Tuckers Crossing
Union
Walters
Whitfield

KEMPER
Akron
Antioch
Ayanabi
Beckville
Binnsville
Blackwater
Bloomfield
Bluff Springs
Bogue Toocolo Chitto
Carters
Center Ridge
Chomontakali
Cleveland
Cow Creek
Coy
Cullum
Cuthi
Damascus
DeKalb 1,075
East Coongetto
East Yazo Skatane
Electric Mills
Enondale
Giles
Haanka Ullah
Hatchette
Herbert
Kellis Store
Kemper County Lake
Kemper Springs
Kipling
Klondike
Liberty
Lynville
Millington
Moscow
Moses
Mount Nebo

[1] COUNTY SEATS ARE IN *ITALICS*. A NUMBER AFTER A PLACENAME DENOTES THE 1998 POPULATION ESTIMATE.

Counties of Mississippi With Placenames

Narkeeta
Oak Grove
Oktibbeha
Old Narkeetah
Old Scooba
Old Wahalak
Peden
Porterville
Preston
Prince Chapel
Prismatic
Red Bud
Rio
Rocky Mount
Sciples Mill
Scooba 519
Spinks
Sucarnoochee
Tamola
Texas
Townsend
Wahalak

LAFAYETTE
Abbeville[1] 422
Altus
Bagley
Brittany Woods
Burgess
Burt
College Hill
College Hill Station
Coon Creek Lake
Cornish
Dallas Jones Crossing
De Lay
Denmark
Dogtown
East Goose Valley
Free Springs
Harmontown
Holly Springs National
    Forest (part)
Keel
Lafayette Springs
Markette
Molly Barr Cove
Oxford 12,096
Paris
Piera
Piney Point
Porterton
Potlockney
Puskus Lake
Ridgeland
Riverside
Rolling Woods
Russell Lake
Sardis Lake/Reservoir
    (part in Panola Co.)
Splinter
Spring Hill
Springdale

Tatum Point
Taylor 303
Teckville
The Dell
Tula
University
Waterford
West Goose Valley
Woodlawn
Yocona

LAMAR
Arnold Line
Baxterville
Bedford Woods West
Bellevue
Bennett York
Boggy Hollow
Breland
Bynum
Clyde
Coral
East Lakewood
Epley
Fanning
Forrest Hills
Hanford
Harmon
Hattiesburg 2,810
    (48,806 total)
    [part in Forrest Co.]
Hickory Grove
Hickory Hollow
Higgins
Lake Serene North
Lake Serene South
Lakewood
Lamar Park
Lumberton 2,553
    (2,563 total) [part in
    Pearl River County]
Oak Grove
Okahola
Oloh
Pat Harrison Watrway
Lake
Pine Grove
Pine Ridge
Purvis 2,532
Richburg
Rocky Branch
Rouse
Seneca
Serene Lake
Shadow Wood
Sumrall 1,141
Tall Pines
Talowah
Varnado
Villa Del Ray
Villa Ridge
Wardwell
Wells Town

West Hattiesburg
West Hills
West Lake Manor
Westgate
Westover

LAUDERDALE
Alamucha
Arundel
Bailey
Bonita
Bonita Reservoirs
Camp Binachi
Causeyville (Increase)
Center Hill
Cliff Williams
Collinsville
Complete
Cresant Lake
Dalesville
Dalewood Shores Lake
Enzor
Fort Stephens
    (Shucktown)
Graham
Hookston
Houston
Increase (Causeyville)
Kewanee
Key Field
Lake Helen Dam
Lauderdale
Lizelia
Lockhart
Lost Gap
Marion 1,565
Martin
Meehan
Meridale Camp
Meridian 40,255
Meridian Naval Air
    Station
Meridian Station
Moseley
Nellieburg
Obadiah
Okatibbee Dam
Okatibbee Lake/
    Reservoir
Pine Springs
Pleasant Hill
Point
Poplar Springs
Post
Russell
Sam Dale State Hist. Site
Sampson
Savannah Grove
Savoy
Schamberville
Shucktown (Fort
    Stephens)
Smith

Sterling
Stinson
Suqualena
Tom Bailey Lake
Toomsuba
Topton
Vimville
Whynot
Wolf Springs
Zero

LAWRENCE
Arm
Bristers Store
Divide
Ferguson
Grange
Hardscrabble
Hooker
Hooker Hollow
Jayess
Lamberts Store
Mary Crawford Lake
Monticello 1,732
New Hebron 382
Nola
Oak Vale
Oma
Robinwood
Rosella
Silver Creek 192
Soegaard
Sontag
Tilton
Topeka
Tryus
Verna
Wanilla

LEAKE
Abdan
Barnes
Battle Bluff
Bertrice
Carthage 4,084
Conway
Coosa
Crossroad
Dossville (part)
Dowell
Drysdale
Duck Pond Slough
Ebenezer
Edinburg
Estesmill
Forest Grove
Free Trade
Freeny
Gill
Good Hope
Goshen
Gray
Harmony

High Hill
Hopoca
Lena 171
Madden
Marydell
McAfee
Midway
Natchez Trace Parkway
    (part)
Ofahoma
Palmetto Flats
Pearl Hill
Piggtown
Pilgrim Rest
Redwater
Remus
Renfroe
Rosebud
Saint Ann
Salem
Singleton
Standing Pine
Sunrise
Thomastown
Tuckers Crossing
Tuscola
Walnut Grove 394
Wiggins
Williston
Yellow Bluff

LEE
Ackia Gardens
Alma
Applewood
Auburn
Baldwyn 1,582
    (3,416 total)
    [part in Prentiss Co.]
Beech Springs
Belden
Belledeer Hills
Bethany
Birmingham
Birmingham Ridge
Bissel
Blair
Boggan Bend
Boggan Grove
Brewer
Briarwood
Brices Crossroads site
Bristow Acres
Campbellton
Chapelville
Chateau Le Blanc
Chickasaw Village
Confederate Park
Corrana
East Tupelo
Eastwood Place
Edgemont
Eggville

[1] COUNTY SEATS ARE IN *ITALICS*. A NUMBER AFTER A PLACENAME DENOTES THE 1998 POPULATION ESTIMATE.

Counties of Mississippi With Placenames

LEE (continued)
Flowerdale
Foxmoor
Frog Island
Graves
Green Acres
Guntown 739
Highland Circle
Indian Hills
Jug Fork
Knights Acres
Lake Piomingo
Lakeview
Lakewood Park
Lamar Bruce Lake
Lar-eli-do
Macedonia
Meadowhill
Meadowview
Mooreville
Morganwood Camp
Mount Vernon
Natchez Trace Parkway (part)
Nettleton[1] 1,208 (2,612 total) [part in Monroe Co.]
North Park
Oakridge
Old Town Overlook
Old Union
Palmetto
Park Monceau
Parkway
Pea Ridge
Piamingo Lake
Pine Grove
Pine Hill
Pinecrest
Pinehurst
Plantersville 1,394
Pratts
Priceville
Richmond
Saltillo 1,915
Shannon 1,589
Sharon Hills
Shiloh
Skyline
Smithey
Terrace Park
Tombigbee State Park
Traceland
Tracewood
Tupelo 35,589
Tupelo National Battlefield Union
Unity
Verona 3,347
Wildwood

LEFLORE
Alligator Bayou
Beckham Branch
Berclair
Black Bayou Junction
Black Democrat Bayou
Bright Corner
Browning
Catfish Bayou
Colony Town
Craigside
Crenfree
Eagleston Spur
Florewood River Plantation State Park
Fort Loring Landing
Geren
Greenwood 18,218
Grenada Junction
Hatten
Hells Halfacre
Highlandale
Itta Bena 2,264
Leflore Co. Legion State Park
Little Tippo
Marsh Bayou
Mathews Crossing
Mayday
McLean Spur
McNutt
Minter City
Money
Morgan City 128
Murdock Crossing
Nichols
Old Dominion
Peteet
Pelucia Bayou
Phillipstown
Purnell
Quito
Rising Sun
Rixwood
Robinson Bayou
Roebuck
Ruby
Runnymede
Sandy Ridge
Schlater 419
Shellmound
Sheppardtown
Sidon 609
Sisloff Junction
Somerville
Sunnyside
Swiftown
Tackett Lake
Tippo Bayou
Wakeland
Wildwood
Williamson Bayou

LINCOLN
Arlington
Auburn
Blueberry Hill
Bogue Chitto
Bristerville
Brookhaven 10,649
Cam
Carlos
Caseyville
Center Point
Cobbs (Vaughn)
Enterprise
East Lincoln
Fair Oak Springs
Fair River
Friendship
Harmony
Hartman
Heucks Retreat
Hog Chain
Hurricane Lake
Loyd Star (Red Star)
Montgomery
New Sight
Norfield
Old Malcum
Old Red Star
Pearlhaven
Rafn
Rain
Red Star (Loyd Star)
Ruth
Sauls
Thayer
Union Hall
Vaughn (Cobbs)
Wellman
West Lincoln
Wilkinson
Williams
Williams Lake
Woolworth
Zetus

LOWNDES
Allendale
Artesia 528
Bartahatchie
Bent Oak
Billups
Border Springs
Briarwood
Bunker Hill
Cady Hills
Caledonia 877
Camp Pratt
Cedar Creek
Chins Springs
Christopher Hills
College
Columbus 22,297
Columbus Air Force Base
Columbus Lake
Crawford 739
Dean Acres
Eastwood Hills
Eskridge
Fairlane
Flint Hill
Flynn
Forreston
Fox Run
Fox Run Colony
Golden Triangle Regional Airport
Grattam
Greenacres
Hairston Bend
Hedgemoor
Holly Hills
Kolola Springs
Lake Lowndes State Park
Mayhew
McCrary
McIntyre
Mount Zion
Nashville
New Hope
New Hope Park
Northaven Woods
Oakdale Park
Penns
Pinecrest
Plum Grove
Plymouth
Prairie Hill
Propst Highlands
Sherwood Forest
Shula Grove
Sleepy Hollow
Steens
Tennessee-Tombigbee Waterway (part)
Trinity
Wells
West Port
White Sand
Whitebury
Wolfe Creek
Woodlawn

MADISON
Adelle
Allison's Wells
Anderson
Annandale
Ballard
Beatties Bluff
Beaver Creek
Beech Ridge
Bourne McGehee
Camden
Cameron
Canton 12,221
Castle Lake
Cavalier Lake
Cedar Hill
Charlton
Cobbville
Costas Lake
Davis
Farmhaven
Flora 1,585
Gateway North
Gluckstadt
Greenbrook
Havendale
Hunters Creek
Jackson 853 (188,419 total)[part in Hinds & Rankin]
Kearney Park
Lake Castle
Lake Cavalier
Lake Lorman
Livingston
Loring
Lorman Lake
Madison 12,618
Madison Station
Madisonville
Mannsdale
Maris Town
Meltonville
Milltown
Millville
Mississippi Petrified Forest
Natchez Trace Parkway (part)
Natchez Trace Village
New Hope Grove
Oaks
Pecan Creek
Ratliff Ferry
Raytown
Revive
Richton
Ridgeland 16,545
Robinson Springs
Rose Hill Center
Roses Bluff
Ross Barnett Reservoir
Sandalwood
Sandhill
Sharon
Sharpsburg
Shocco
Sloan
Squirrel Hill
Stokes
Stonegate
Stribling Lake
Summertree
Tavern Hill
The Breakers
Tidewater
Tithelo Lake
Traceland North
Treasure Cove

[1] COUNTY SEATS ARE IN *ITALICS*. A NUMBER AFTER A PLACENAME DENOTES THE 1998 POPULATION ESTIMATE.

Counties of Mississippi With Placenames

Truitt
Turnetta
Twelve Oaks
Twin Harbor
Vernon
Village Glen
Village Square
Virillia
Way

MARION
Bethel
Bill Waller Lake
Bunker Hill
Carmich
Cheraw
Columbia 6,935
Columbia Lake
Ebenezer
Edna
Enon
Expose
Fordsville
Fortenberry
Foxworth
Good Hope
Goss
Hamage
Harmony
Holly Springs
Hopewell
Hub
Hurricane Creek
Improve
Jamestown
Keno
Kokomo
Lampton
Lovelace
Mildred
Morgantown
Natcole
New Hope
New Union
Newsom
Pickwick
Pinebur
Pittman
Red Bluff
Revive
Saint Paul
Sandy Hook
Sauer
Saxon
Spring Cottage
Sumbax
Twin
Veneer
White Bluff

MARSHALL
Atway
Barton

Bethlehem
Blackwater
Byhalia[1] 951
Cayce
Chewalla Lake
Chulahoma
Coal Oil Corner
Colbert
Cornersville
Early Grove
Galena
Gilton
Higdon
Holly Springs 7,195
Holly Springs National
    Forest (part)
Hudsonville
Lake Center
Laws Hill
Mack
Mahon
Malone
Marianna
Mount Pleasant
Orion
Potts Camp 483
Red Banks
Sand Flats
Slayden
Spraggins
Taska
Victoria
Waites
Wall Doxey State Park
Wallhill
Warsaw
Waterford
Watson
Watson Center
Wyatt Crossing

MONROE
Aberdeen 6,915
Aberdeen Lake
Acker
Ales
Amory 7,144
Ashland
Athens
Becker
Bigbee
Binford
Bolivar
Bristol
Bristow
Buttahatchie
Caledonia
Camargo
Camp Wrenwoods
Cauhorn
Central Grove
Central Park
Colsub

Coon Tail
Corrine
Cotton Gin Port
Darracott
East Aberdeen
Easthaven
Evergreen
Flinn
Gardenspot
Gattman 131
Gibson
Gladneyville
Glenwood
Goose Pond
Green Acres
Greenbrier
Greenwood Springs
Grubb Springs
Hamilton
Hatley 558
Highland Park
Hillcrest
Lackey
Lake Martha Dam
Lake Monroe
Lakewood
Lawrence
Longview
Malone Lake
McCluney
Monroe Lake
Muldon
Nettleton 1,404
    (2,612 total)
    [part in Lee Co.]
New Hamilton
New Wren
Parham
Parkview
Pinehurst
Piney Grove
Prairie
Quincy
Riggins
Rodgers
Rye
Sipsey Fork
Smithville 898
South Amory
Splunge
Stanford
Strong
Sykes
Tanglewood
Temperence Hill
Tennessee-Tombigbee
    Waterway (part)
Terrells
Tranquil
Tucker Place
Vassar
Walden
Wesley

Westville
Wise Gap
White Springs
Wildwood
Willcox
Woodcrest

MONTGOMERY
Alva
Cedar Hill
Duck Hill 1,331
Eskridge
Foltz
Fox
Hendrix
Huntsville
Kilmichael 784
Lilac
Lodi
Minerva
Poplar Creek
Poplar Springs
Sawyer
Sibleyton
Sugar Hill
Sweatman
Windham Dam
Winona 5,647

NESHOBA
Alice
Arlington
Barfoot
Beatline
Bethsaida
Bloomfield
Bogue Chitto
Bond
Burnside
Center
Choctaw Indian
    Reservation
Crossroads
Deemer
Deweese
Dixon
Dover
Dowdville
Fairgrounds
Fairview
Forestdale
Foxtrap
Golden Grove
Good Hope
Herbert Springs
Hope
House
King Bee
Kitchener
Laurel Hill
Linwood
Longino
McDonald

Neshoba
Neshoba County Legion
    Lake
Neville
North Bend
Ocobla
Pearl River
Philadelphia 7,725
Sandtown
Spring Creek
Spring Hill
Stallo
Trapp
Tucker
Union 466 (1,873 total)
    [part in Newton Co.]
Waldo
Williamsville
Zaphyr Hill

NEWTON
Bartlett
Battlefield
Bethel
Beulah
Bienville National Forest
    (part)
Bissaasha
Blounts Store
Calhoun
Cedar Grove
Center Ridge
Chunky 315
Coatraw
Conehatta
Decatur 1,352
Doolittle
Duffee
Ebenezer
Evergreen
Goodhope
Greenfield
Greenland
Hazel
Hickory 531
Hubbard
Jeff
Lake 21 (364 total)
    [part in Scott County]
Lawrence
Lebanon
Liberty
Little Rock
Lucern
Mount Vernon
New Ireland
New Providence
Newton
Oka Kapassa
Okahta Talaia
Patrons Union
Perdue
Perota

[1] COUNTY SEATS ARE IN *ITALICS*. A NUMBER AFTER A PLACENAME DENOTES THE 1998 POPULATION ESTIMATE.

Counties of Mississippi With Placenames

NEWTON (continued)
Pine Bluff
Poplar Springs
Prospect
Roberts
Rock Branch
Rock Creek
Roscoe
Scalon
Six Towns
Stratton
Tanglewood
Toomer
Union 1,407
    (1,873 total)
    [part in Neshoba Co.]
Urbo
Volcan
Wickward
Willoughby

NOXUBEE
Aliceville Lake
Allgoods Mill
Aubrey
Avery
Bells
Big Lake
Bigbee Valley
Bluff Lake
Brazelia
Brooklyn
Brooksville[1] 1,044
Calyx
Camp Rockbrook
Center Point
Clearman
Cliftonville
Cooksville
Cross Roads
Crow
Deerbrook
Dinsmore
Dixie
Eli
Fairhill
Fairport
Fairview
Farewells
Gholson
Griffin Slough
Harlan
Hashuqua
Heard Lake Dam
Jeff Davis
Lake Forest Ranch Camp
Land-O-Lakes
Loakfoma Lake
Lynn Creek Macedonia
Macon 2,298
Marsh Hollow
Mashulaville
May Spring

McLeod
Noxubee National
    Wildlife Refuge
Parkeville
Paulette
Prairie Point
Ravine
Shavers
Shuqualak 578
Taylors
Togo
X-Prairie

OKTIBBEHA
Academy Park
Adaton
Avondale
Bells
Bells School
Black Jack
Bradley
Bugh
Cedar Point
Center Grove
Clayton Village
College View
College Vista
Craig Springs
Deerfield
Didlake
Double Springs
Fairfield Commons
Glendale
Green Acres
Green Oaks
Green Timber Reservoir 3
Greenbriar
Hancock Circle
Hillbrook
Hillcrest
Landers
Longview
Lyle
Maben 491 (742 total)
    [part in Webster Co.]
Mississippi State
Morgantown
Montgomery Park
Nashdale
Northgate
Northwood
Northwood Hills
Noxubee National
    Wildlife Refuge
Ocktok
Oktibbeha County Lake
Oktibbeha Gardens
Osborn
Parkdale
Parker Slough
Patrick
Pecan Acres
Plairs

Plantation Homes
Pleasant Acres
Pleasant Ridge
Pressly Place
Quail Valley
Rocky Hill
Rolling Hills
Rosedale
Self Creek
Sessums
Sheely Hills
Sherwood Forest
Southdale
Starkville 20,184
State College
Stonegate
Strickland
Sturgis 181
Sunset
Tanglewood
Templeton Meadows
Terza
Timbercove
Valley View
West End
Westwood
Whispering Pines
Wood Dale
Wood Manor

PANOLA
Asa
Askew
Ballentine
Baptist
Batesville 7,416
Black Jack Point
Bluff Springs
Buxton
Cemetery Ridge
Central Academy
Chapeltown
Como 1,441
Courtland 362
Crenshaw 784
    (1,007 total)
    [part in Quitman Co.]
Crowder 335 (794 total)
    [part in Quitman Co.]
Curtis Station
Cypress Point
Delta
Eureka Springs
Glenville
Goode
Hayes Crossing
Hideaway Hills
Horatio
John W. Kyle State Park
Kings Corner
Kjirksey
Lake Carrier
Lespideza Point
Locke Station

Longtown
Lower Lake Beach
McGhee
McIvor
Mims
Moccasin Point
Mount Olivet
Oak Ridge
Orwood
Parksplace
Pleasant Grove
Pope 178
Rayburn Bayou
Sand Bayou
Sardis 2,136
Sardis dam
Sardis Lake/Reservoir
    (part in Lafayette Co.)
Shuford
Tallahatchie
Terza
Tocawa
Viney Rough
Wallace
Yellow Lake

PEARL RIVER
Anchor Lake
Barth
Bird Line School
Bogue Chitto National
    Wildlife Refuge
Caesar
Carriere
Centre
Crossroads
Cybur
Cypress Bayou
Derby
Farr Slough
Ferris Slough
Fords Creek
Goodyear (part of
    Picayune)
Greenbriar Park
Hawthorne
Henleyfield
Hickory Grove
Hide-A-Way Lake
Hillsdale
Hunt Bluff
Industrial
Juniper Grove
Leslie Slough
Lumberton 10
    (2,563 total)
    [part in Lamar Co.]
Mars Slough
McCall River
McNeill
Middle Creek
Mill Creek
Millard

Nicholson
Nortac
Orvisburg
Ozona
Palestine
Parker Bayou
Paul H. Barrett Lake
Picayune 12,058
Poplarville 2,834
Red Top
Riceville
Richardson
Rowlands
Savannah
Silver Run
Stewarts Bluff
Thomas School
Tyler
Walkiah
West Poplarville
White Sand
Willis Slough
Yamacraw
Young

PERRY
Agnes
Barbara
Batt Place
Beaumont 1,278
Belleville
Benmore
Bland Bluff
Breakover Sandbar
Brewer
Buzzard Bay
Carmichael
Corinth
Deep Creek
DeSoto National Forest
    (part)
East Side
Fairhope Bluff
Ferguston
Good Hope
Hercules Station
Hintonville
Indian Springs
Janice
Kittrell
Little Creek
Mahned
McSwain
New Augusta 723
Oak Grove
Old Augusta
Perry Lake
Progress
Racetrack Bend
Redhill
Rhodes
Richton 1,092
Runnelstown

[1] COUNTY SEATS ARE IN *ITALICS*. A NUMBER AFTER A PLACENAME DENOTES THE 1998 POPULATION ESTIMATE.

Counties of Mississippi With Placenames

Scott Bend
Steep Hollow
Tallahala
Wingate

PIKE
Bacots
Barto
Bear Town
Beardens
Chatawa
Conerly
Dixie Springs
Dykes Crossing
Emerald
Felders Campground
Fernwood
Gladhurst
Holmesville
Irene
Jennings
Johnston
Johnstons Station
Kirkville
Lake Tangipahoa
Leggett
Magnolia 2,259
Martin
McComb 11,746
Oakland
Osyka[1] 489
Percy Quin State Park
Pitts
Pricedale
Progress
Quinlivan
Quins Station
Simmonsville
Smithburg
Stella
Stephens
Summit 1,562
Tangipahoa Lake
Terry's Creek
Topisaw
Vaughts
Yale Community

PONTOTOC
Algoma 458
Buchannan
Buckhorn
Cairo
Camp Yocona
Cherry Creek
Chesterville
Connewah Bottom
Ecru 958
Endville
Esperanza (Hurricane)
Fawn Meadows
Friendship
Furrs

Gershorn
Good Food
Hebron
Hortontown
Hurricane (Esperanza)
Longview
Matthews
Natchez Trace Lake
Natchez Trace Parkway
 (part)
North Junction
Oak Hill
Pannell
Pleasant Grove
Plymouth
Pontotoc 5,219
Pontotoc Ridge
 Experiment Lake
Poplar Springs
Possum Trot
Randolph
Robbs
Rough Edge
Shady Grove
Sherman 449 (620 total)
 [part in Union Co.]
Springville
Thaxton 483
Toccopola 163
Trace State park
Troy
Turnpike
Wallfield
Wilson Bottom
Woodland
Zion

PRENTISS
Altitude
Baldwyn 1,834
 (3,416 total)
 [part in Lee Co.]
Big Rock Hollow
Blackland
Blythe's Chapel
 (Claudville)
Booneville 8,387
Burtons
Bynum
Cairo
Claudville (Blythe's
 Chapel)
East prentiss
Frankstown
Gaston
Geeville
Heading Mill Hollow
Hills Chapel
Hobo Station
Hodges Chapel
Hopewell
Horseshoe Bend
Jumpertown 450

King Hollow
Lake City
Lebanon
Marietta 295

Natchez Trace Parkway
 (part)
New Hope
New Site
Old Cairo
Osborne Creek
Piney Grove Hollow
Pisgah
Riddle Wind Ridge
Sunflower
Thrasher
Wheeler

QUITMAN
Allen
Ash Log Bayou
Barksdale
Bear Lake
Belen
Birdie
Buck Bayou
Chancy
Crenshaw 223
 (1,007 total)
 [part in Panola Co.]
Crowder 459 (794 total)
 [part in Panola Co.]
Darling
Denton
Essex
Falcon 133
Hinchcliff
Lambert 1,075
Little Whiting Lake
Longstreet
Marks 1,635
Oliverfried
Posey Mound
Riverview
Sabino
Sledge 452
Vance
Walnut
West Marks
Whiting Lake
Wilson Bayou
Wilson Brake
Yarbrough

RANKIN
Abernathy
Allen C. Thompson Field
 (Jackson Internat'l
 Airport)
Alonzo
Anse
Arrowhead Point
Audubon Point

Bafrick
Barnes Prairie
Bates Park
Beldine
Bellegrove
Bilbros Corner
Brandon 14,612
Brandon Depot
Bridlewood
Burnham
Camp Pioneer
Castlewoods
Cato
Cedar Point
Cleary
Comeby
Cross Roads
Crossgates
Dobson
Dogwood Place
Easthaven
Eureka
Fannin
Fannin Station
Fink Bine
Florence 2,375
Flowood 4,471
Forest Point
Forty
Frenchs Store
Galilee
George
Goshen Springs
Goshen Springs Station
Green (Greenfield)
Grove Park
Gulde
Harbourview
Hickory Glen
Howell
Hunters Woods
Jackson 133
 (188,419 total)[part
 in Hinds & Madison]
Joe
Johns
King
Koch
Lakeland
Lakeshore
Langford
Leesburg
Linden
Luckney
Mayton
Mill Creek
Mill Creek Corners
Mill Creek Place
Mill Run
Millro
Monterey
Moseley
Mountain Creek

New Fannin
Northwoods
Ophelia
Paradise Point
Pat
Patton Place
Pearl 23,287
Pearson
Pelahatchie 1,597
Pine Park
Piney Woods
Pisgah
Plain
Plainview
Puckett 362
Randall Place
Rankin
Ratliff
Reservoir
Richland 5,794
Richmond
Robinhood lakes
Rock Hill
Rollison Prairie
Ross Barnett Reservoir
Round Prairie
Rufus
Sand Hill
Shady Dell
Sherwood Forest
Shiloh
Sinai
Star
Sunrise Point
Terrapin Landing
The Commons
Thomasville
Timber Lakes
Tupelo Gum Slough
Turtle Creek
Value
Wansley Bend
Waterwood
Wells
West Leesburg
Whites
Whitfield
Woodlake

SCOTT
Bald Prairie
Beach
Bienville National Forest
 (part)
Branch
Buckleytown
Cash
Clarksburg
Clifton
Cooperville
Damascus
Dennis Settlement
Donohoe

[1] COUNTY SEATS ARE IN *ITALICS*. A NUMBER AFTER A PLACENAME DENOTES THE 1998 POPULATION ESTIMATE.

Counties of Mississippi With Placenames

SCOTT (continued)
East Hillsboro
Fikestown
Forest 5,324
Forkville
Frogtown
Golden Memorial State Park
Gum Spring
Harperville
Hays
Hillsboro
Homewood
Horseshoe
Hunter Town
Independence
Kalem
Kracker Station
Lake 343 (364 total)
 [part in Newton Co.]
Lillian
Line Prairie
Little Italy
Ludlow
Midway
Morton 3,261
Muskegon
Norris
Otho
Peagler Store
Piketown
Pulaski
Raworth
Roosevelt State Park
Roosevelt State Park Lake
Sebastopol 276
Singleton Settlement
Stage
Steele
Sun
Usrytown
Wolf

SHARKEY
Anguilla 820
Auter
Big Basin
Big Eddy Landing
Blanton
Bommers Ferry
Buck Point
Cameta
Cary[1] 386
Chapel Landing
Choctaw Landing
Crippen Point
Cypress Bend
Delta City
Delta National Forest
 (part in Issaquena Co.)
Devils Elbow Bayou
Dogwood Landing
Dowling Bayou
Egremont

Harworth
Hickman Landing
Holland Landing
Hollands
Issaquena
Kelso
Larkin (Poor Joe Larkin)
Little Atchafalaya Landing
Little Basin
Little Sunflower
Lorenzen
Lucre
McCann Bayou
Mont Helena
Mud Lake Bayou
Nitta Yuma
Onward
Panther Burn
Plaquemine Bayou
Poor Joe Larkin (Larkin)
Ratliff Landing
Red Rock
Richey
Riverside Junction
Rolling Fork 2,228
Sago
Shraderville
Smedes
Spanish Fort
Straight Bayou
Tisdale Landing
Turnertown
Updike
Vickland
White House Landing

SIMPSON
Braxton 142
Bridgeport
Bush
Camp Mondamin
Coats
Cyclone
D'Lo 412
Everett
Fayettehill
Gama
Geren
Gum Springs
Harrisville
Jaynesville
Maddox
Magee 3,930
Martinville
Mendenhall 2,528
Merit
Merry Hell
Pearl
Pine Lake
Pinola
Rexford
Sanatorium

Saratoga
Schley
Shivers
Simpson Co. Legion Lake
Touchstone
Union
Upton
Weathersby
Westville
Zion Hill

SMITH
Bezer
Bienville National Forest
 (part)
Bunker Hill
Burns
Center Ridge
Clear Springs
Cohay
Daniel
Flat Rock Hill
Gambrell
Gunn
Heater
Klein
Lemon
Lingle
Lorena
Milton
Mineral Springs
Mize 321
Mount Pleasant
New Haven
Old Taylorsville
Pineville
Polkville 135
Raleigh 1,266
Ross Barnett Lake
Sand Point
Shady Grove
Shongelo
Simpson
Sullivan's Hollow
Sylvarena 111
Taylorsville 1,388
Ted
Trazler
Trenton
Union
White Oak
Wicker
Wisner
Zion Hill

STONE
Beatrice
Big Island
Big Level
Bond
Camp Towanda
City Bridge
Daisy Vestry

De Soto National. Forest
 (part)
Flint Creek Reservoir
Fruitland Park
Inda
Lake-A-Way
Little Island
McHenry
Open Gap
Perkinston
Perry
Ramsey Springs
Smith Town
Stillmore
Sweet Bay Bog
Ten Mile
Texas
Whites Crossing
Wiggins 3,977

SUNFLOWER
Baird
Ballaston
Baltzer
Blaine
Bowles
Boyer
Brooks
Caile
Cordy Brake
Cottondale
Crahen
Dabney Brake
Dockery
Doddsville 138
Drew 2,136
Dwyer
Eastland
Fairview
Faisonia
Fitzhugh
Frazier
Furry
Galen
Goldfield
Halstead
Heathman
Holly Ridge
Indianola 11,514
Inverness 1,103
Inwood
Jaquith
Johnsonville
Kinick
Kinlock
Linn
Lombardy
Marie
Markham
Mattoon
McDaniels
Milroy
Minot

Moorhead 2,315
New Town
Parchman
Pentecost
Pine Land
Pollock
Powell Bayou
Promised Land
Rome
Roundaway
Ruleville 3,049
Saints Rest
Sandy Bayou
Shaw 7 (2,290 total)
 [most in Bolivar Co.]
Southside
Steiner
Sunflower 781
Waco
Wade
Waltonia
White City
Whitney
Woodburn

TALLAHATCHIE
Albin
Black Bayou
Blue Lake Community
Brazil
Cascilla
Center Point
Charleston 2,331
Cowart
Crevi
Distall
East Tippo Bayou
Effie
Enid
Fewell
Flautt
Glendora 161
Grassy Lake
Hardtime Bayou
Hiram
Hugo
Leverett
Locopolis Bayou
Macel
Mehr
Midway
Mikona
Mitchner
Murphreesboro
Needmore
Paul
Paynes
Pecan Bayou
Philipp
Possum Bayou
Rosebloom
Sharkey
Starck Hollow

[1] COUNTY SEATS ARE IN *ITALICS*. A NUMBER AFTER A PLACENAME DENOTES THE 1998 POPULATION ESTIMATE.

Counties of Mississippi With Placenames

Stover	Dry Creek	Holcut	Commerce Landing	Center
Sumner 348	Dumas 450	Holt Hollow	Dooley	Concord
Swan Lake	Falkner 239	Holts Spur	Dry Bayou	Darden
Tandy	Gravestown	Horseshoe Bend	Dubbs	Darden Lake
Teasdale	Green Bottom	*Iuka* 3,122	Dundee	Ellistown
Tippo	Gus Bottom	J. P. Coleman State Park	Eagle Landing	Enterprise
Turner	Holly Springs National	Leedy	Evansville	Etta (Rocky Ford)
Tutwiler 1,348	Forest (part)	Meat Hollow	Fish Lake Bayou	Fairfield
Webb 587	Howell Siding	Midway	Flat Bayou	Fairview
Whitehead	Lowrey	Mingo	Fletcher Bayou	Flatwood
	Mitchell	Moores Mill	Flower Lake	Gallway
TATE	Mohawk Lake		Flower Lake Bar	Glenfield
Aiken	Mount Moriah	Natchez Trace Parkway	Floyd Bayou	Graham
Antioch	Mount Zion	(part)	Fox Island Bend	Halltown
Arkabutla	Mowell Siding	Neil	Gerlach Mill	Holly Springs National
Arkabutla Lake/Reservoir	Murry	New Bethel	Green River	Forest (part)
(part in DeSoto Co.)	New Hope	North Crossroads	Hally	Ingomar
Barr	Peoples	Null Hollow	Hamlin	Jericho
Bayou Point	Pine Grove	Oldham	Harbert Landing	Keownville
Bett	*Ripley* 5,623	Oldham Hollow	Harbert Point	Locum
Bowman	Shady Grove	Owens Hollow	Hardin Point	Locust Grove
Coldwater 1,482	Silver Springs	Paden 126	Herron Bayou	Macedonia
Cottonville	Tiplersville	Petertown	Hollywood	Martintown
Crockett	Tippah County Lake	Pickwick Lake (part)	Jack Lake Bayou	Mitchell
Crossroad	Walnut 561	Pine Flat	Kyles Brake	Molino
Cypress Corner	Walnut Creek	Pinedale	Little Texas	Mound City
Eliphaz	Whitten Town	Sanders Hollow	Lost Lake	Myrtle 383
Evansville		Sandy Creek	Mathis Bayou	*New Albany* 7,238
Goode	**TISHOMINGO**	Shaw Landing	Maud	New Harmony
Independence	Ada Hollow	Shop Hollow	McKinney Bayou	North Haven
Kelley's Crossing	Bacon Springs	Short	Mhoon Landing	Old Myrtle
Linwood	Barnes Hollow	Snowdown (extinct)	Minton Bayou	Parks
Looxahoma	Bay Springs Lake	Steam Mill Hollow	Mississippi River	Pea Ridge
Lurline	Belmont 1,627	Stinett Hollow	Mocarter	Pinedale
New Garden	Big Spring Hollow	Ten Island	Nails Bayou	Pleasant Hill
New Town	Blackard Hollow	Tennessee-Tombigbee	North Tunica	Pleasant Ridge
Poagville	Bloody Springs	Waterway (part)	OK Bend	Poolville
Rockhill	Blythe Crossing	Tishomingo 302	Pink	Pumpkin Center
Savage	Boo Hollow	Tishomingo State Park	Prichard	Reese
Senatobia[1] 5,428	Brogdan Hollow	Walker Siding	River Bend	Rocky Ford (Etta)
Senatobia Lakes	Burnsville 1,017	Windbush Hollow	Robinsonville	Shari
Springfield	Camp Hollow	Woodall mountain	Sarah	Sherman 171 (620 total)
Strayhorn	Carter Branch	Yankee Charles Ridge	Shoo Fly Bar	[part in Prentiss Co.]
Thyatira	Castleberry Hollow	Yellow Creek	Stringer Bayou	Smalco
Tyro	Chalk Hollow		St. Frances Island	Union Hill
Wakefield	Chalk Mine Hollow	**TUNICA**	Landing	Wallerville
Wyatte	Chestnut Ridge	Anderson Bayou	Sunrise Bayou	
	Coke	Austin	Tee Bayou	**WALTHALL**
TIPPAH	Cooks Landing	Austin Bar	Tibbs	Babington
Adkins Bottom	Cooper Hollow	Banks	Trotter Landing	Barrett Dam
Anvil	Cross Roads	Beaverdam	*Tunica* 1,015	Bridges
Blue Mountain 704	Dennis	Beaverdam Bayou	Tunica Lake	Carto
Bluff	Dixon Hollow	Beaverdam Lake	Tunica North	China Grove
Brownfield	Doskie	Boggy Bayou	Walnut Bend	Conerby
Buena Vista	Eastport	Bordeaux Point	White Oak	Darburn
Burrow	Ellistown	Bowdre		Davo
Camp Hill Campbell	Fred Hollow	Brushy Bayou	**UNION**	Dexter
Campbell Siding	Golden 209	Buck Island Bar	Alpine	Dillion
Chalybeate	Gravel Siding	Buck Island Bayou	Baker	Dinan
Clarysville	Happy Hollow	Clack	Bald Hill	Enon
Cliff Siding	Hazard Switch	Clark Towhead	Beacon Hill	Flowers
Cotton Plant	Hicks Hollow	Clayton	Blue Springs 154	Kioto
Cuba	High Point	Commerce	Branyan	Kirklin

[1] COUNTY SEATS ARE IN *ITALICS*. A NUMBER AFTER A PLACENAME DENOTES THE 1998 POPULATION ESTIMATE.

The Ultimate Reference on the State

Counties of Mississippi With Placenames

WALTHALL (cont'd)
Knoxo
Lehr
Lexie
Mesa
Rushing
Salem
Sartinville
Simonds
Tylertown 1,992
Walthall Lake

WARREN
Allen
Antioch
Ballground
Beechwood
Ben Slough
Bellemeade
Bernard Acres
Big Black
Blakely
Boat Slough
Bovina
Brunswick
Cedars
Centennial Lake
Chickasaw Bayou
Chotard
Culkin
Eagle Bend
Eagle Lake
Eagle Lake Community
Eagle Lake Pass
Eldorado
Floweree
Flowers
Forest Home Chute
Forest Home Towhead
Fort Saint Peter (site)
Grange Hall
Greenbriar
Halpino Lake
Haynes Bluff
Hurricane
Jeff Davis
Jetts
Jonestown
Katzenmeyer
Kimberly
Kings
Kings Ferry
Lake Forest
Lake Park
Lakewood
Le Tourneau
Long Lake
Long Lake Community
Mississippi River
Muddy Bayou
Newmans
Newmans Grove
Oak Ridge

Openwood Plantation
Peelers
Porters Chapel
Possum Hollow
Rawhide
Redbone
Redwood
Rose Hill
Russellville
Sherwood Forest
Signal
Simrall
Southhaven
Speeds Addition
Stout
Timberlane
Twin Lake
Valley Mills
Vicksburg[1] 27,221
Vicksburg National Military Park
Villanova
Walsh
Waltersville
Warrenton
Woodlawn
Yokena
Youngton

WASHINGTON
Alder Grove
Aldridge
Alhambra
Almy
Arcola 537
Ashley Crossing
Ashwood
Avon
Bear Garden
Bourbon
Brighton
Buddy Bridges Camp
Burdette
Byrne City
Carolina Chute
Catchings
Chatham
Cletonia
Crossroads
Darlove
Deer Lake Slough
Dredge
Dunkirk
Dunleith
Elizabeth
Empire
Erwin
Estill
Ferguson Lake
Floyd
Foote
Forkland
Forrest City

Gin Slough
Granny Baker Bayou
Geneill
Glen Allan
Greenville 42,042
Hampton
Hays
Heads
Helm
Hollandale 3,524
Hollyknowe
Hunt
Isenberg
James
Johnston
Jones Chapel
Lake Washington
Lamont
Lee Lake
Leland 5,970
Leota
Leroy Percy State Park
Linsey
Long
Longwood
Magenta
Manhattan
Marathon
McCutcheon
McGrath
Metcalfe 1,240
Mississippi River
Murphy
Muskedine
Napanee
Osseola
Overby
Paducah
Percy
Port Anderson
Princeton
Priscilla
Randolph
Refuge
Rexburg
Silver Lake
Spencer
Stoneville
Swiftwater
Tamburo
Tarpley Neck
Tralake
Tribbett
Warsaw
Wayside
Willet
Wilmot
Winterville
Winterville Mounds Historical site
Woodside
Yazoo National Wildlife Refuge

WAYNE
Battles
Belmont
Boyce
Buckatunna
Chicora
Clara
Denham
De Soto National Forest (part)
Eret
Eucutta
Frost Bridge Camp
Gretna
Henderson
Hiwannee
Hollis Creek
Lightsey
Matherville
Mulberry
Pat Harrison Waterway Lake
Pineview
Pleasant Grove
Robinsons Junction
Smithtown
State Line 156 (425 total) [part in Greene Co.]
Strengthford
Tokio
Water Oil
Waynesboro 5,400
West King
Whistler
Winchester
Woodwards

WEBSTER
Bellefontaine
Bentley
Cadaretta
Center
Clarkson
Cumberland
Dancy
Embry
Eupora 2,312
Fame
Gibson
Grady
Hohenlinden
Maben 251 (742 total) [part in Oktibbeha Co.]
Mantee 135
Mathiston 734 (832 total) [part in Choctaw Co.]
Montevista
Pellez
Sapa
Shady Grove
Southland Park

Spring Hill
Stewart
Tomnolen
Walthall 168
Westwood
Whites Creek East
Whites Creek West

WILKINSON
Artonish
Artonish Lake
Ashwood
Centreville 1,255 (1,543 total) [part in Amite Co.]
Crosby 281 (443 total) [part in Amite Co.]
Darrington
Doloroso
Donegal
Fort Adams
Highway Village
Homochitto National Forest (part)
Ireland
Laneheart
Lessley
Loch Leven
Mississippi River
Mount Pleasant
Old River Lake
Palmetto Point
Perrytown
Pinckneyville
Pond
Possum Corner
Rosetta
Saukum
Turnbull
Whitaker
Whitestown
Wilkinson
Woodville 1,297

WINSTON
Betheden
Boone
Calvary
Center Ridge
Claytown
Coonwood
Deposit
Deweese Lake Dam
Ellison Ridge
Estes
Evergreen
Fearns Springs
Finis Hook
Ford
Four Corners
Gum Branch
Handle
Highpoint

[1] COUNTY SEATS ARE IN *ITALICS*. A NUMBER AFTER A PLACENAME DENOTES THE 1998 POPULATION ESTIMATE.

Counties of Mississippi With Placenames

Hinze	**YALOBUSHA**	Tyson	Eagle Bend	Miller Landing
Lake Tiak O'Khata	Benwood	Velma	Eden 90	Mills Crossing
Legion State Park	Blanche	Wallace Creek	Ellwood Landing	Monkeytown
Liberty	Bruce Junction	*Water Valley* 3,661	Enola	Myrleville
Loakfoma	Bryant	Water Valley Landing	Enola Landing	Nod
Lobutcha	Camp Ground	Yocona Ridge	Evans	Norway
Louisville 7,085	*Coffeeville* 795		Fairview Landing	Oil City
McMillan	Enid Dam	**YAZOO**	Fifteen Mile Bayou	Panther Swamp National
Millcreek	Enid Lake/Reservoir	Anding	Fordyke	Wildlife Refuge
Nanih Waiya	Gatewood	Bayland	Four Points	Patosi
Nanih Waiya State	George P. Cossar State	Belle Prairie	Free Run	Phoenix
Historical Site	Park Gums	Benton	Fugate	Pierce Crossroad
Noxapater 438	Gums Crossing	Bentonia 391	George	Pleasant Home Landing
Noxubee National	Hawkins Crossing	Berryville	George Lake	Plumville
Wildlife Refuge	Holly Springs National	Bethesda	Germania	Possum Bend
Perkinsville	Forest (part)	Black Bayou	Hilton	Potato Hill Bayou
Plattsburg	Hubbard Creek	Broad Lake	Holly Bluff	Renshaw
Randalls Bluff	Hyde	Campbellsville	Home Park	Roadside
Rome	Lakeside	Carter	Horn Place Landing	Ryans L'argent Landing
Ross Branch Reservoir	Long Branch	Casey Jones Railroad	Jonestown	Satartia 61
Rural Hill	New Hope	Museum State Park	(part of Yazoo City)	Scotland
Singleton	Oakland 559	Cedar Hill	Kansas Landing	Scotland Fork
Tampa	Palestine	Center Ridge	Kearney	The Basin
Tombigbee National	Pine Flat	Chethams	Lake City	Tinsley
Forest (part)	Pine Valley	Claibornesville	Lake Dick	Tinsley Oil Field
Triplets Corner	Plum Point	Colby	Limerick	Valley
Vernon	Point Pleasant	Crump	Linwood	Vaughan
Vowell	Scobey	Crupp	Little Yazoo	Woodlawn
Webster	Spearman	Deasonville	Liverpool	*Yazoo City* 11,941
White Lake	Tillatoba	Deep Bayou	Loch Lomond	Yazoo Junction
Winston	Torrence	Deep Slough	Mechanicsburg	Zeiglerville
	Turkey Creek	Dover Dump Lake	Midway	Zelleria

Mississippi has 82 of the 3,142 counties in the United States. That's about 1/38th, or 2.6%, of the number of counties in the U.S.

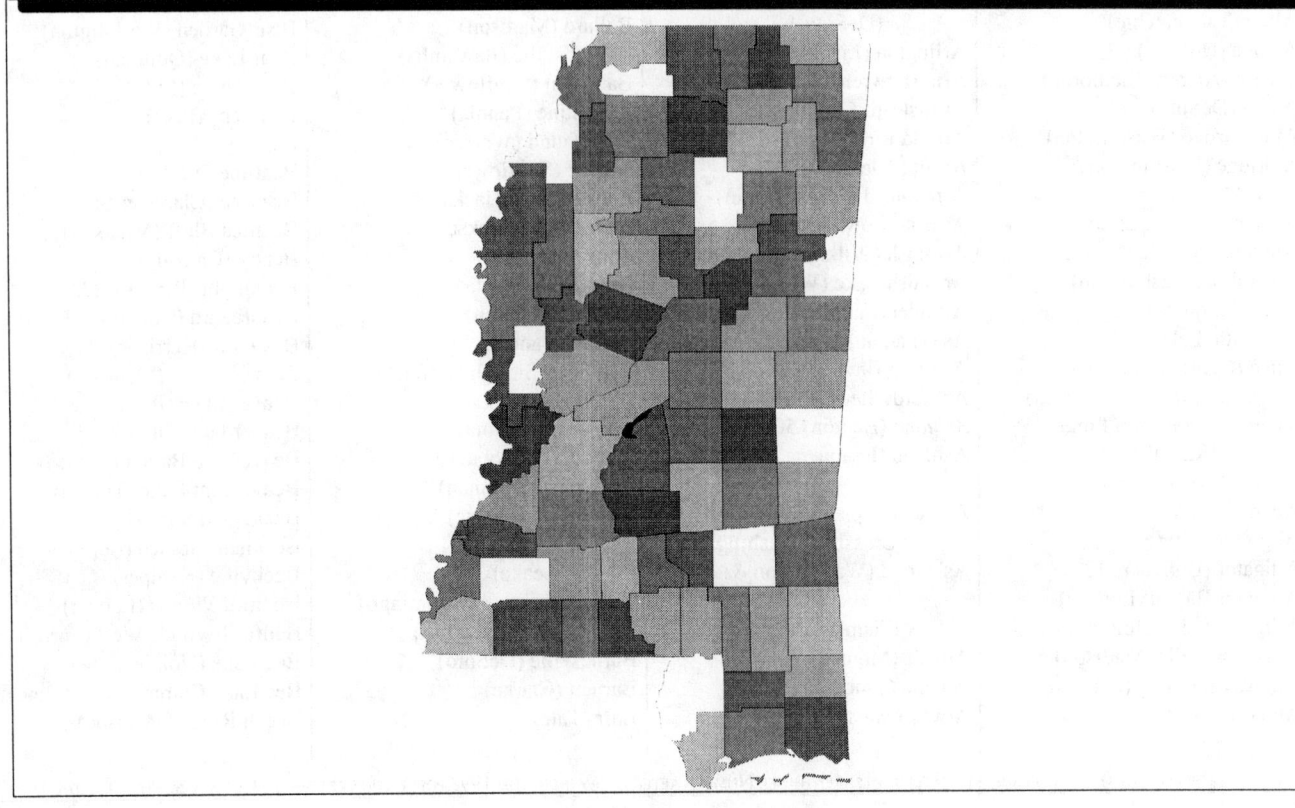

The Ultimate Reference on the State

Master List of Mississippi Placenames

A
Abbeville (Lafayette) 422[1]
Abbot (Clay)
Abdan (Leake)
Aberdeen (Monroe) 6,915
Aberdeen Junction (Holmes)
Aberdeen Lake (Monroe)
Abernathy (Rankin)
Abney (Itawamba)
Academy Park (Oktibbeha)
Acker (Montgomery)
Ackerman (Choctaw) 1,705
Ackia Gardens (Lee)
Acme (Jasper)
Acona (Holmes)
Ada Hollow (Tishomingo)
Adair (Carroll)
Adams (Hinds)
Adams Landing (Issaquena)
Adamsville (Greene)
Adaton (Oktibbeha)
Addie (Issaquena)
Adelle (Madison)
Adkins Bottom (Tippah)
Africa (Coahoma)
Agnes (Perry)
Agricola (George)
Aiken (Tate)
Airey (Harrison)
Akron (Kemper)
Alamucha (Lauderdale)
Albeison (Jones)
Albemarle Lake (Issaquena)
Albin (Tallahatchie)
Alcona (Holmes)
Alcorn (Alcorn Claiborne)
Alden (DeSoto)
Alder Grove (Washington)
Aldridge (Washington)
Ales (Monroe)
Alexander (Issaquena)
Algoma (Pontotoc) 458
Alhambra (Washington)
Alice (Neshoba)
Aliceville Lake
Allen (Clairborne, Copiah, Quitman & Warren)
Allen C. Thompson Field (Rankin)
Allendale (Lowndes)
Allentown (Alcorn)
Allgoods Mill (Noxubee)
Alligator (Bolivar) 213
Alligator Bayou (Leflore)
Alligator Lake (Bolivar)
Allison's Wells (Madison)
Alloway Landing (Adams)
Alma (Lee)

Almy (Washington)
Alonzo (Rankin)
Alphaba (DeSoto)
Alpine (Union)
Altitude (Prentiss)
Altus (Lafayette)
Alva (Montgomery)
Amory (Monroe) 7,144
Anchor (Chickasaw)
Anchor Lake (Pearl River)
Anchorage (Humphreys)
Anderson (Madison)
Anderson Bayou (Tunica)
Anderson Landing (Coahoma)
Anding (Yazoo)
Anguilla (Sharkey) 820
Anna (Adams)
Annandale (Madison)
Anse (Rankin)
Ansley (Hancock)
Antioch (Attala, Jones, Kemper, Tate & Warren)
Anvil (Tippah)
Aponaug (Attala)
Appeal (Bolivar)
Applewood (Lee)
Arbo (Covington)
Arcadia (Issaquena)
Arcola (Washington) 537
Ariel (Amite)
Arkabutla (Tate)
Arkabutla Dam (DeSoto)
Arkabutla Lake/Reservoir (DeSoto & Tate)
Arlington (Lincoln & Neshoba)
Arm (Lawrence)
Armistead (Coahoma)
Arnold Line (Lamar)
Arnot (Adams)
Arrowhead Point (Rankin)
Artesia (Lowndes) 528
Artonish (Wilkinson)
Artonish Lake (Wilkinson)
Arundel (Lauderdale)
Asa (Panola)
Ash Log Bayou (Quitman)
Ashfordville (Choctaw)
Ashland (Benton) 508
Ashland (Issaquena, Jefferson & Monroe)
Ashley (Copiah)
Ashley Crossing (Washington)
Ashwood (Washington & Wilkinson)
Askew (Panola)
Athens (Monroe)
Atlanta (Chickasaw)
Atway (Marshall)

Aubrey (Noxubee)
Auburn (Lee & Lincoln)
Audubon Point (Rankin)
Auris (Attala)[extinct]
Austin (Tunica)
Austin Bar (Tunica)
Australia Landing (Bolivar)
Auter (Sharkey)
Authority (Itawamba)
Avalon (Carroll)
Avent (George)
Avent Station (Greene)
Avera (Greene)
Avery (Noxubee)
Avon (Washington)
Avondale (Oktibbeha)
Ayanabi (Kemper)

B
Babington (Walthall)
Back Bayou (Jackson)
Bacon (Chickasaw)
Bacon Springs (Tishomingo)
Bacots (Pike)
Bafrick (Rankin)
Bagley (Lafayette)
Bailey (Lauderdale)
Bailey Lake (Carroll)
Baird (Sunflower)
Baker (Union)
Bald Hill (Union)
Bald Prairie (Scott)
Baldwyn (Prentiss/Lee) 1,834 + 1,582 = 3,416
Ballard (Madison)
Ballardsville (Itawamba)
Ballaston (Sunflower)
Ballentine (Panola)
Ballground (Warren)
Baltzer (Sunflower)
Bangs Bayou (Jackson)
Bangs Lake (Jackson)
Banks (Tunica)
Bankston (Choctaw)
Banner (Calhoun)
Baptist (Panola)
Baptizing Slough (Jefferson)
Barbara (Perry)
Barbee (Coahoma)
Barfoot (Neshoba)
Barksdale (Quitman)
Barland (Claiborne)
Barlow (Copiah)
Barnes (Leake)
Barnes Hollow (Tishomingo)
Barnes Prairie (Rankin)
Barnesville (DeSoto)
Barnett (Clarke)
Barr (Tate)

Barrett Dam (Walthall)
Barron (Forrest)
Barrontown (Forrest)
Bartahatchie (Lowndes)
Barth (Pearl River)
Bartlett (Newton)
Barto (Pike)
Barton (George & Marshall)
Basic (Clarke)
Basin (George)
Bassfield (Jeff. Davis) 238
Bates Park (Rankin)
Batesville (Panola) 7,416
Batson (Forrest)
Batt Place (Perry)
Battle Bluff (Leake)
Battlefield (Newton)
Battles (Wayne)
Baugh (Coahoma)
Baxter (Jasper)
Baxterville (Lamar)
Bay Saint Louis (Hancock) 9,841
Bay Springs Lake (Tishomingo)
Bay Springs (Jasper) 1,855
Bayland (Yazoo)
Bayou Bolan (Hancock)
Bayou Chemise (Jackson)
Bayou Point (Tate)
Bayside Park (Hancock)
Beach (Scott)
Beacon Hill (Union)
Bean's Ferry (Itawamba)
Bear Creek (Attala & Hinds)
Bear Garden (Washington)
Bear Lake (Quitman)
Bear Town (Pike)
Beardens (Pike)
Beasley (Clay)
Beatline (Neshoba)
Beatrice (Clarke & Stone)
Beatties Bluff (Madison)
Beatty (Carroll)
Beaumont (Perry) 1,278
Beauregard (Copiah) 226
Beauvoir (Harrison)
Beaver Creek (Madison)
Beaver Lake (Itawamba)
Beaverdam (Tunica)
Beaverdam Bayou (Tunica)
Beaverdam Lake (Tunica)
Becker (Monroe)
Beckham Branch (Leflore)
Beckville (Kemper)
Bedford Woods (Forrest)
Bedford Woods West (Forrest)
Bee Lake (Holmes)
Bee Lake Community (Holmes)
Beech Ridge (Madison)

[1] COUNTY (OR COUNTIES) WHERE PLACE IS LOCATED IS IN PARENTHESIS. NUMBER AFTER ENTRY INDICATES 1998 POPULATION ESTIMATE. COUNTY SEATS ARE IN *ITALICS*.

Master List of Mississippi Placenames

Beech Springs (Lee)
Beechgrove (Copiah)
Beechwood (Amite & Warren)
Beene's Ferry (Itawamba)
Belden (Lee)
Beldine (Rankin)
Belen (Quitman)
Belle Fontaine Point (Jackson)
Belle Isle (Hancock)
Belle Prairie (Yazoo)
Belledeer Hills (Lee)
Bellefontaine (Webster)
Bellegrove (Rankin)
Bellemeade (Warren)
Belleville (Perry)
Bellevue (Lamar)
Bellewood (Humphreys)
Bells (Noxubee & Oktibbeha)
Bells School (Oktibbeha)
Belmont (Wayne)
Belmont (Tishomingo) 1,627
Belzoni (Humphreys) 2,367
Ben Slough (Warren)
Benela (Calhoun)
Benjoe (Greene)
Benmore (Perry)
Benndale (George)
Bennett (Hancock)
Bennett Ridge (Alcorn)
Bennett York (Lamar)
Benoit (Bolivar) 609
Benson (Jones)
Bent Oak (Lowndes)
Bentley (Webster)
Bently (Calhoun)
Benton (Yazoo)
Bentonia (Yazoo) 391
Benwood (Yalobusha)
Beppo (Hancock)
Berclair (Leflore)
Bernard (Hinds)
Bernard Acres (Warren)
Berryville (Yazoo)
Bertrice (Leake)
Berwick (Amite)
Bethany (Lee)
Betheden (Winston)
Bethel (Benton, Chickasaw, Covington, Marion & Newton)
Bethesda (Hinds & Yazoo)
Bethlehem (Marshall)
Bethsaida (Neshoba)
Bett (Tate)
Beulah (Attala & Newton)
Beulah (Bolivar) 474
Beulah Island Landing (Bolivar)
Beulah Lake (Bolivar)
Beverly [Davenport Station] (Coahoma)
Bew Springs (Grenada)

Bewelcome (Amite)
Bexley (George)
Bezer (Smith)
Bienville National Forest (Jasper, Newton, Scott & Smith)
Big Basin (Sharkey)
Big Bear Bayou (Jackson)
Big Black (Warren)
Big Creek (Calhoun) 117
Big Eddy Landing (Sharkey)
Big Island (Stone)
Big Lake (Harrison, Jackson & Noxubee)
Big Level (Stone)
Big Point (Jackson)
Big Rock Hollow (Prentiss)
Big Spring Hollow (Tishomingo)
Bigbee (Monroe)
Bigbee Valley (Noxubee)
Biggersville (Alcorn)
Bilbros Corner (Rankin)
Bill Waller Lake (Marion)
Billups (Lowndes)
Biloxi (Harrison) 47,316
Binford (Monroe)
Binnsville (Kemper)
Bird Line School (Pearl River)
Birdie (Quitman)
Birmingham (Lee)
Birmingham Ridge (Lee)
Bissaasha (Newton)
Bissel (Lee)
Black (Holmes)
Black Bayou (Coahoma, Issaquena, Tallahatchie & Yazoo)
Black Bayou Junction (Leflore)
Black Creek Slough (Jackson)
Black Democrat Bayou (Leflore)
Black Hawk (Carroll)
Black Jack (Benton, Oktibbeha)
Black Jack Point (Panola)
Blackard Hollow (Tishomingo)
Blackland (Prentiss)
Blacks Dam (Jasper)
Blackwater (Marshall)
Blackwater [Zada] (Kemper)
Blaine (Sunflower)
Blair (Lee)
Blakely (Warren)
Blanche (Yalobusha)
Bland Bluff (Perry)
Blanton (Sharkey)
Blissdale (Holmes)
Blodgett (Jones)
Bloody Springs (Tishomingo)
Bloomfield (Kemper, Neshoba)
Blounts Store (Newton)

Blue Hill (Jefferson)
Blue Lake Community (Tallahatchie)
Blue Mountain (Tippah) 704
Blue Ridge (Jasper)
Blue Springs (Union) 154
Blueberry Hill (Lincoln)
Bluff (Tippah)
Bluff Lake (Noxubee)
Bluff Springs (Attala, Kemper & Panola)
Blythe Crossing (Tishomingo)
Blythe's Chapel [Claudville] (Prentiss)
Boat Slough (Warren)
Bobo (Coahoma)
Boggan Bend (Lee)
Boggan Grove (Lee)
Boggy Bayou (Tunica)
Boggy Hollow (Lamar)
Bogue Chitto (Lincoln & Neshoba)
Bogue Chitto National Wildlife Refuge (Pearl River)
Bogue Homa (Jones)
Bogue Homa Lake (Jones)
Bogue Toocolo Chitto (Kemper)
Boice (Wayne)
Bolivar (Bolivar & Monroe)
Bolivar Lake [Lake Charlie Capps] (Bolivar)
Bolivar Landing (Bolivar)
Bolton (Hinds) 783
Bommers Ferry (Sharkey)
Bond (Neshoba & Stone)
Bonhomie (Forrest)
Bonita (Lauderdale)
Bonita Reservoirs (Lauderdale)
Bonner (Jones)
Boo Hollow (Tishomingo)
Boon (Winston)
Boone (Coahoma)
Booneville (Prentiss) 8,387
Booth (Issaquena)
Booths Lake (Carroll)
Bordeaux Point (Tunica)
Border Springs (Lowndes)
Bothwell (Greene)
Bottom Acres (Hinds)
Bounds (Calhoun)
Bourbon (Washington)
Bourne McGehee (Madison)
Bovina (Warren)
Bowdre (Tunica)
Bowerton (Copiah)
Bowie (Forrest)
Bowies Chapel (Attala)
Bowles (Chickasaw, Sunflower)
Bowling Green (Holmes)
Bowman (Tate)

Boyer (Sunflower)
Boyette (Attala)
Boyle (Bolivar) 696
Bradie (Hinds)
Bradley (Greene & Oktibbeha)
Branch (Scott)
Branchville (Attala)
Brandon (Rankin) 14,612
Brandon Depot (Rankin)
Branyan (Union)
Braxton (Simpson) 142
Brazelia (Noxubee)
Brazil (Tallahatchie)
Breakover Sandbar (Perry)
Breath Bayou (Hancock)
Breckenridge (Hinds)
Breland (Lamar)
Brewer (Clarke, Lee & Perry)
Briar Landing (Adams)
Briarcliff (Hinds)
Briarwood (Lee & Lowndes)
Brices Crossroads National Battlefield Site (Lee)
Bridgeport (Simpson)
Bridges (Walthall)
Bridlewood (Rankin)
Bright (DeSoto)
Bright Corner (Leflore)
Brighton (Washington)
Bristers Store (Lawrence)
Bristerville (Lincoln)
Bristol (Monroe)
Bristow (Monroe)
Bristow Acres (Lee)
Brittany Woods (Lafayette)
Broad Lake (Yazoo)
Brody (Benton)
Brogdan Hollow (Tishomingo)
Brookhaven (Lincoln) 10,649
Brookhollow Place (Hinds)
Brookleigh (Hinds)
Brooklyn (Forrest, Humphreys & Noxubee)
Brooks (Sunflower)
Brooks Light (Claiborne)
Brookside (Amite)
Brooksville (Noxubee) 1,044
Brookwood (Hinds)
Brookwood Pines (Hinds)
Browder ridge (Alcorn)
Brown Town (Greene)
Brownfield (Tippah)
Browning (Leflore)
Browns Wells (Copiah)
Brownsville (Hinds)
Brozville (Holmes)
Bruce (Calhoun) 2,041
Bruce Junction (Yalobusha)
Bruinsburg (Claiborne)
Brunswick (Warren)

The Ultimate Reference on the State

Master List of Mississippi Placenames

Brushy Bayou (Tunica)
Bryant (Yalobusha)
Buccaneer State Park (Hancock)
Buchannan (Pontotoc)
Buck Bayou (Quitman)
Buck Island Bar (Tunica)
Buck Island Bayou (Tunica)
Buck Point (Sharkey)
Buckatunna (Wayne)
Buckhorn (Pontotoc)
Buckleytown (Scott)
Bud Bluff (Greene)
Buddy Bridges Camp (Washington)
Bude (Franklin) 950
Buena Vista (Chickasaw, Jefferson & Tippah)
Buffalo Bayou (Bolivar)
Bugh (Oktibbeha)
Bulah (Harrison)
Bull Bay Bend (George)
Bunker Hill (Lowndes, Marion & Smith)
Bunkley (Franklin)
Burdette (Washington)
Burgess (Lafayette)
Burke Landing (Coahoma)
Burkettsville (Attala)
Burnell (Claiborne)
Burnham (Rankin)
Burns (Jasper & Smith)
Burnside (Neshoba)
Burnsville (Tishomingo) 1,017
Burrow (Tippah)
Burt (Lafayette)
Burton (Prentiss)
Burtonton (Copiah)
Busey (Bolivar)
Bush (Simpson)
Busy Corner (Amite)
Butler (Holmes)
Butler Lake (Adams)
Buttahatchie (Monroe)
Buxton (Panola)
Buzzard Bay (Perry)
By (Alcorn)
Byhalia (Marshall) 951
Bynum (Lamar & Prentiss)
Byram (Hinds)
Byrd (Greene)
Byrne City (Washington)
Bywy (Choctaw)
Bywy Overlook (Choctaw)
C
Cadamy (Itawamba)
Cadaretta (Webster)
Cadillac (Jefferson)
Cady Hills (Lowndes)
Caesar (Pearl River)
Caile (Sunflower)
Cairo (Clay, Pontotoc, Prentiss)
Caledonia (Lowndes) 877
Caledonia (Monroe)
Calhoun (Jones & Newton)
Calhoun City (Calhoun) 1,736
Callon Lake (Adams)
Calvary (Winston)
Calyx (Noxubee)
Cam (Lincoln)
Camargo (Monroe)
Camden (Madison)
Cameron (Madison)
Cameta (Sharkey)
Camp Bellewood (Chickasaw)
Camp Binachi (Lauderdale)
Camp Castalian Springs (Holmes)
Camp Currier (DeSoto)
Camp Dantzler (Forrest)
Camp Ground (Yalobusha)
Camp Ground Slough (Jackson)
Camp Hill (Tippah)
Camp Hollow (Tishomingo)
Camp Lamotte (Jackson)
Camp McCain [Military] (Grenada)
Camp Mondamin (Simpson)
Camp Pine Crest (Clarke)
Camp Pioneer (Rankin)
Camp Pratt (Lowndes)
Camp Rockbrook (Noxubee)
Camp Shelby [Military] (Forrest)
Camp Towanda (Stone)
Camp Wesley Pines (Copiah)
Camp Wilkes (Harrison)
Camp Wrenwoods (Monroe)
Camp Yocona (Pontotoc)
Campbell (Tippah)
Campbell Bayous (Hancock)
Campbell Siding (Tippah)
Campbellton (Lee)
Campbellville (Yazoo)
Canaan (Benton)
Cannon (Benton)
Cannonsburg (Jefferson)
Canton (Madison) 12,221
Cantwell Mill (Jeff. Davis)
Cape Retreat (Grenada)
Capell (Amite)
Cardsville (Itawamba)
Carlisle (Claiborne)
Carlos (Lincoln)
Carmack (Attala)
Carmich (Marion)
Carmichael (Clarke, Hinds & Perry)
Carnes (Forrest)
Carolina (Itawamba)
Carolina Chute (Washington)
Carpenter (Copiah)
Carriage Hills (Hinds)
Carriere (Pearl River)
Carrollton (Carroll) 220
Carruth Lake (Amite)
Carson (Jefferson Davis)
Carson City (Greene)
Carson Ridge (Attala)
Carter (Coahoma & Yazoo)
Carter Branch (Tishomingo)
Carters (Kemper)
Carterville (Forrest)
Carthage (Adams)
Carthage (Leake) 4,084
Carthage Landing (Adams)
Carto (Walthall)
Carver Bluff (Grenada)
Carver Point (Grenada)
Cary (Sharkey) 386
Cascilla (Tallahatchie)
Casey Jones Railroad Museum State Park (Yazoo)
Caseyville (Lincoln)
Cash (Scott)
Cassels (Amite)
Castalian Springs (Holmes)
Castle Lake (Madison)
Castleberry Hollow (Tishomingo)
Castleman (Humphreys)
Castlewoods (Rankin)
Catahoula (Hancock)
Catfish Bayou (Hancock, Leflore)
Catfish Point (Bolivar)
Catfish Point Landing (Bolivar)
Catfish Towhead (Bolivar)
Catherine Lake (Hinds)
Cato (Rankin)
Cauhorn (Monroe)
Caulk Neck (Bolivar)
Caulk Point (Bolivar)
Causeyville (Lauderdale)
Cavalier Lake (Madison)
Cayce (Marshall)
Cayuga (Hinds)
Cedar Bluff (Clay)
Cedar Creek (Lowndes)
Cedar Grove (Newton)
Cedar Hill (Madison, Montgomery & Yazoo)
Cedar Hills (Hinds)
Cedar Lake (Harrison)
Cedar Point (Grenada, Hancock, Harrison, Oktibbeha & Rankin)
Cedars (Warren)
Cedarview (DeSoto)
Cemetery Ridge (Panola)
Centennial Lake (Warren)
Center (Attala, Hancock, Neshoba, Union & Webster)
Center Grove (Oktibbeha)
Center Hill (Lauderdale)
Center Point (Attala, Lincoln, Noxubee & Tallahatchie)
Center Ridge (Kemper, Newton, Smith, Winston & Yazoo)
Centerville (Carroll & Itawamba)
Central (George)
Central Academy (Panola)
Central Grove (Monroe)
Central Lookout (George)
Central Park (Monroe)
Centre (Pearl River)
Centreville (Wilkinson/Amite) 1,255 + 288 = 1,543
Cessions Landing (Bolivar)
Chalk Bluff (Chickasaw)
Chalk Hollow (Tishomingo)
Chalk Mine Hollow (Tishomingo)
Chalybeate (Tippah)
Chambers [Winstonville] (Bolivar)
Champion Hill (Hinds)
Chancellor (Clarke)
Chancy (Quitman)
Chapel Hill (Attala & Hinds)
Chapel Landing (Sharkey)
Chapeltown (Panola)
Chapelville (Lee)
Charleston (Tallahatchie) 2,331
Charlton (Madison)
Chat High Bluff (Greene)
Chatawa (Pike)
Chateau Le Blanc (Lee)
Chatham (Washington)
Cheraw (Marion)
Cherry Creek (Pontotoc)
Cherry Park (Hinds)
Chester (Choctaw)
Chesterville (Pontotoc)
Chestnut Ridge (Tishomingo)
Chethams (Yazoo)
Chewalla Lake (Marshall)
Chickasaw Bayou (Warren)
Chickasaw Village (Lee)
Chicora (Wayne)
China Grove (Walthall)
Chins Springs (Lowndes)
Chita (Attala)
Choctaw (Bolivar, Clarke, Grenada & Holmes)
Choctaw Indian Reservation (Neshoba)
Choctaw Lake (Choctaw)
Choctaw Landing (Sharkey)
Choctaw Village (Hinds)
Chomontakali (Kemper)

Master List of Mississippi Placenames

Chotard (Issaquena)
Christmas (Bolivar)
Christopher Hills (Lowndes)
Chulahoma (Marshall)
Chunky (Newton) 315
Church Hill (Jefferson)
Churchwell High Bluff (Greene)
City Bridge (Stone)
Clack (Tunica)
Claiborne (Jasper)
Claiborne Lake (Claiborne)
Claibornesville (Yazoo)
Clara (Wayne)
Claremont (Coahoma)
Clark (Greene)
Clark Towhead (Tunica)
Clarkco State Park (Clarke)
Clarksburg (Scott)
Clarksdale (Coahoma) 20,461
Clarkson (Webster)
Clarysville (Tippah)
Claude Bennett Lake (Jasper)
Claudville [Blythe's Chapel] (Prentiss)
Clay (Itawamba)
Clayton (Tunica)
Clayton Village (Oktibbeha)
Claytown (Winston)
Clear Springs (Smith)
Clearman (Noxubee)
Cleary (Coahoma & Rankin)
Clem (Jefferson Davis)
Cleo (Jones)
Clermont Harbor (Hancock)
Cletonia (Washington)
Cleveland (Bolivar) 14,834
Cleveland (Kemper)
Cleveland Crossing (Bolivar)
Cliff Siding (Tippah)
Cliff Williams (Lauderdale)
Clifford (Bolivar)
Clifton (Jefferson & Scott)
Cliftonville (Noxubee)
Clinton (Hinds) 22,067
Clover Hill (Coahoma)
Cloverdale (Adams)
Clyde (Lamar)
Coahoma (Coahoma) 250
Coaker Bend (Greene)
Coaker Bluff (Greene)
Coal Oil Corner (Marshall)
Coaler (Copiah)
Coalville (Harrison)
Coars Springs (Copiah)
Coatraw (Newton)
Coats (Simpson)
Cobbs [Vaughn] (Lincoln)
Cobbville (Madison)
Cockrum (DeSoto)
Coffeeville (Yalobusha) 795

Cohay (Smith)
Coila (Carroll)
Coke (Alcorn & Tishomingo)
Colbert (Marshall)
Colby (Yazoo)
Cold Springs (Covington)
Coldwater (Tate) 1,482
Coles (Amite)
Coles Creek (Calhoun)
Coleson Bayou (Jackson)
Coleville (Chickasaw)
Coll Town (Jackson)
College (Lowndes)
College Hill (Lafayette)
College Hill Station (Lafayette)
College View (Oktibbeha)
College Vista (Oktibbeha)
Collins (Covington) 2,657
Collins Crossing (Alcorn)
Collinstown (Alcorn)
Collinsville (Lauderdale)
Colonytown (Leflore)
Colsub (Monroe)
Columbia (Marion) 6,935
Columbia Lake (Marion)
Columbus (Lowndes) 22,297
Columbus Air Force Base (Lowndes)
Columbus Lake (Lowndes)
Comeby (Rankin)
Commerce (Tunica)
Commerce Landing (Tunica)
Como (Panola) 1,441
Complete (Lauderdale)
Compromise (Amite)
Concord (Union)
Concordia (Bolivar)
Conehatta (Newton)
Conerby (Walthall)
Conerly (Pike)
Confederate Park (Lee)
Congress (Chickasaw)
Conn (Copiah)
Connewah Bottom (Pontotoc)
Conservation League Lake (Bolivar)
Conway (Leake)
Cooks Landing (Tishomingo)
Cooksville (Noxubee)
Cooley Springs (Covington)
Coon Box (Jefferson)
Coon Creek Lake (Lafayette)
Coon Tail (Monroe)
Coonwood (Winston)
Cooper Hollow (Tishomingo)
Cooperville (Scott)
Coosa (Leake)
Coral (Lamar)
Cordy Brake (Sunflower)
Corinth (Alcorn) 12,204

Corinth (Forrest & Perry)
Corinth Nat'l. Cemetery (Alcorn)
Corndike Brake (Coahoma)
Cornersville (Marshall)
Cornish (Lafayette)
Corrine (Monroe)
Corrona (Lee)
Costas Lake (Madison)
Cotton Gin Port (Monroe)
Cotton Plant (Tippah)
Cottondale (Sunflower)
Cottonville (Tate)
Counts (Coahoma)
Courtland (Panola) 362
Cow Creek (Kemper)
Cow Island Bend (DeSoto)
Cowand Point (Hancock)
Cowanville (Copiah)
Cowart (Tallahatchie)
Cowpen (Attala)
Cowpen Point Landing (Adams)
Coxburg (Holmes)
Coxs Ferry (Hinds)
Coy (Kemper)
Crahen (Sunflower)
Craig (Humphreys)
Craig Springs (Oktibbeha)
Craigside (Leflore)
Crandall (Clarke)
Crane Creek (Hancock)
Cranfield (Adams)
Crawford (Lowndes) 739
Credille Dam (Itawamba)
Creek (Clarke)
Crenfree (Leflore)
Crenshaw (Panola/Quitman) 784 + 223 = 1,007
Cresant Lake (Lauderdale)
Crescent Ridge (Grenada)
Crevi (Tallahatchie)
Crippen Point (Sharkey)
Crockett (Tate)
Crooked Bayou (Jackson)
Crosby (Wilkinson/Amite) 281 + 162 = 443
Cross Bayou (Hancock)
Cross Roads (Noxubee, Rankin & Tishomingo)
Crossgates (Rankin)
Crossroad (Leake & Tate)
Crossroads (George, Neshoba, Pearl River & Washington)
Crotts (Jones)
Crow (Alcorn & Noxubee)
Crowder (Quitman/Panola) 459 + 335 = 794
Cruger (Holmes) 554
Crump (Yazoo)
Crumtown (Alcorn)
Crupp (Yazoo)

Crystal Springs (Copiah) 5,832
Cub Lake (DeSoto)
Cuba (Alcorn)
Cuevas (Harrison)
Culkin (Warren)
Cullum (Kemper)
Cumberland (Webster)
Currie (Forrest & Jones)
Curtis Station (Panola)
Cuthi Uckehaca (Kemper)
Cutoff Bayou (Hancock)
Cybur (Pearl River)
Cyclone (Simpson)
Cynthia (Hinds)
Cypress Bayou (Pearl River)
Cypress Bend (Bolivar, Sharkey)
Cypress Corner (Tate)
Cypress Lake (Issaquena)
Cypress Point (Panola)

D

D'Iberville (Harrison) 8,211
D'Lo (Simpson) 412
Dabney Brake (Sunflower)
Dabney Crossroads (Hinds)
Dahomey (Bolivar)
Daisy Vestry (Stone)
Dale (George)
Daleville (Lauderdale)
Dalewood Shores Lake (Lauderdale)
Dallas Jones Crossing (Lafayette)
Damascus (Kemper & Scott)
Dancy (Webster)
Danforth (Coahoma)
Daniel (Smith)
Dantzler (Jackson)
Darbun (Walthall)
Darden (Union)
Darden Lake (Union)
Dardun (Benton)
Darling (Quitman)
Darlove (Washington)
Darracott (Monroe)
Darrington (Wilkinson)
Davenport Station [Beverly] (Coahoma)
Davidson (Clarke)
Davis (Clarke & Madison)
Davisville (Jasper)
Davo (Walthall)
Days (DeSoto)
De Buys (Harrison)
De Lisle (Harrison)
Dead Negro Slough (DeSoto)
Dean Acres (Lowndes)
Dean Landing (George)
Deane (Jefferson)
Deans Corner (DeSoto)
Deasonville (Yazoo)
Decatur (Newton) 1,352

The Ultimate Reference on the State

Master List of Mississippi Placenames

Dedeaux (Harrison)[1]
Dedwylder (Clarke)
Deemer (Neshoba)
Deen (Jefferson Davis)
Deep Bayou (Yazoo)
Deep Creek (Perry)
Deep Slough (Yazoo)
Deer Lake Slough (Washington)
Deerbrook (Noxubee)
Deerfield (Oktibbeha)
Dees Landing (Jackson)
Deeson (Bolivar)
DeKalb (Kemper) 1,075
Delay (Lafayette)
Delmas Bayou (Jackson)
Delta (Coahoma & Panola)
Delta City (Sharkey)
Delta National Forest (Issaquena & Sharkey)
Denham (Wayne)
Denmark (Lafayette)
Dennis (Tishomingo)
Dennis Crossroads (Jefferson)
Dennis Landing (Bolivar)
Dennis Settlement (Scott)
Denton (Quitman)
Dentontown (Calhoun)
Dentville (Copiah)
Deovolente (Humphreys)
Deposit (Winston)
Derby (Pearl River)
Derma (Calhoun) 948
DeSoto (Clarke)
DeSoto Lake (Coahoma)
DeSoto National Forest (Forrest, Greene, Harrison, Jackson, Perry, Stone & Wayne)
Devils Elbow (Harrison)
Devils Elbow Bayou (Sharkey)
Deweese (Neshoba)
Deweese Lake Dam (Winston)
Dexter (Walthall)
Diamondhead (Hancock)
Dick (Franklin)
Dickerson (Coahoma)
Didlake (Oktibbeha)
Dies Slough (Adams)
Dillon (Walthall)
Dinan (Walthall)
Dinsmore (Noxubee)
Distall (Tallahatchie)
Ditch Bayou (Harrison)
Divide (Lawrence)
Dixie (Bolivar, Forrest, Noxubee)
Dixie Pine (Forrest)
Dixie Springs (Pike)
Dixon (Hinds & Neshoba)
Dixon Acres (Hinds)
Dixon Hollow (Tishomingo)
Dobson (Rankin)
Dockery (Sunflower)
Dodds (Attala)
Doddsville (Sunflower) 138
Dogtown (Lafayette)
Dogwood Landing (Sharkey)
Dogwood Place (Rankin)
Doloroso (Wilkinson)
Donegal (Wilkinson)
Donley (Carroll)
Donohoe (Scott)
Donovan (George)
Dont (Covington)
Dooley (Tunica)
Doolittle (Newton)
Dorsey (Itawamba)
Doskie (Tishomingo)
Dossville (Amite/Leake)
Doty Springs (Attala)
Double Churches (Jeff. Davis)
Double Springs (Oktibbeha)
Dover (Neshoba & Yazoo)
Dowdville (Neshoba)
Dowell (Leake)
Dowling Bayou (Sharkey)
Dragon (Forrest)
Dredge (Washington)
Drew (Sunflower) 2,136
Dreyfus (Forrest)
Dry Bayou (Tunica)
Dry Creek (Tippah)
Dry Creek [Lone Star] (Covington)
Dry Grove (Hinds)
Drysdale (Leake)
Dubard (Grenada)
Dubbs (Tunica)
Dublin (Coahoma)
Duck Hill (Montgomery) 1,331
Duck Pond Slough (Leake)
Dueitt (Greene)
Duffee (Newton)
Duke (Hinds)
Dulweber (Holmes)
Dumas (Tippah) 450
Dump Lake (Yazoo)
Duncan (Bolivar) 394
Dundee (Tunica)
Dunkirk (Washington)
Dunleith (Washington)
Durant (Holmes) 2,686
Durham (Coahoma)
Dwyer (Sunflower)
Dykes Crossing (Pike)
E
Eagle Bend (Warren, Yazoo)
Eagle Lake (Humphreys, Warren)
Eagle Lake community (Warren)
Eagle Lake Pass (Warren)
Eagle Landing (Tunica)
Eagles Nest (Coahoma)
Eagleston Spur (Leflore)
Early Grove (Marshall)
Earlyville (Attala)
East Aberdeen (Monroe)
East Coongetto (Kemper)
East Double Bayou (Hancock)
East Enterprise (Clarke)
East Fork (Amite)
East Goose Valley (Lafayette)
East Hillsboro (Scott)
East Lakewood (Lamar)
East Lincoln (Lincoln)
East Macedonia (Attala)
East Moss Point (Jackson)
East Pascogoula (Jackson)
East Prentiss (Prentiss)
East Side (Jackson & Perry)
East Tippo Bayou (Tallahatchie)
East Yazo Skatane (Kemper)
Eastabutchie (Jones)
Easthaven (Hinds, Monroe & Rankin)
Eastland (Sunflower)
Eastlawn (Jackson)
Eastover (Hinds)
Eastport (Tishomingo)
Eastside (Forrest)
Eastview (Jones)
Eastwood Hills (Lowndes)
Eastwood Place (Lee)
Eatonville (Forrest)
Ebenezer (Holmes, Leake, Marion & Newton)
Ecru (Pontotoc) 958
Eddiceton (Franklin)
Eden (Yazoo) 90
Edgefield (Attala)
Edgemont (Lee)
Edgewater Park (Harrison)
Edgewood Acres (Hinds)
Edinburg (Leake)
Edna (Marion)
Edsville (Holmes)
Edwards (Hinds) 1,195
Effie (Tallahatchie)
Eggville (Lee)
Egremont (Sharkey)
Egypt (Chickasaw & Holmes)
Egypt Hill (Copiah)
Eldorado (Warren)
Eldridge (Bolivar)
Eleanor (Coahoma)
Electric Mills (Kemper)
Eli (Noxubee)
Eliphaz (Tate)
Elizabeth (Washington)
Elize (Chickasaw)
Elks Lake (Forrest)
Ellard (Calhoun)
Elleslie (Issaquena)
Elliott (Grenada)
Ellis Cliffs (Adams)
Ellison Ridge (Winston)
Ellistown (Tishomingo & Union)
Ellisville (Jones) 3,770
Ellisville Junction (Jones)
Ellwood Landing (Yazoo)
Elmo (Jefferson)
Elsie (Calhoun)
Elton (Hinds)
Elton Place (Hinds)
Elwood (Clarke)
Embry (Webster)
Emerald (Pike)
Eminence (Covington)
Emory (Holmes)
Empire (Washington)
Endville (Pontotoc)
Energy (Clarke)
Enid (Tallahatchie)
Enid Dam (Yalobusha)
Enid Lake/Reservoir (Yalobusha)
Enola (Yazoo)
Enola Landing (Yazoo)
Enon (Chickasaw, Marion & Walthall)
Enondale (Kemper)
Enterprise (Clarke) 483
Enterprise (Amite, Lincoln, & Union)
Enzor (Lauderdale)
Epley (Lamar)
Epps (Forrest)
Eret (Wayne)
Errata (Jones)
Erwin (Washington)
Escatawpa (Jackson)
Eskridge (Lowndes & Montgomery)
Esperanza [Hurricane](Pontotoc)
Essex (Quitman)
Estes (Winston)
Estesmill (Leake)
Estill (Washington)
Etchehoma (Jasper)
Ethel (Attala) 440
Etta [Rocky Ford] (Union)
Eubanks (George)
Eucutta (Wayne)
Eudora (DeSoto)
Eulogy (Holmes)

[1] County (or counties) where place is located is in parenthesis. Number after entry indicates 1998 population estimate. County seats are in *italics*.

Master List of Mississippi Placenames

Eunice (Amite)
Eupora (Webster) 2,312
Eureka (Rankin)
Eureka Landing (Adams)
Eureka Springs (Panola)
Eutaw (Bolivar)
Eutaw Landing (Bolivar)
Evans (Yazoo)
Evanston (George)
Evansville (Tate & Tunica)
Everett (Simpson)
Evergreen (Itawamba, Jackson, Monroe, Newton & Winston)
Expose (Marion)

F

Fair Oak Springs (Lincoln)
Fair River (Lincoln)
Fairchilds Crossing (Hinds)
Fairfield (Union)
Fairfield Commons (Oktibbeha)
Fairground (Neshoba)
Fairhaven (DeSoto)
Fairhill (Noxubee)
Fairhope Bluff (Perry)
Fairlane (Lowndes)
Fairport (Noxubee)
Fairview (Itawamba, Neshoba, Noxubee, Sunflower & Union)
Fairview Landing (Yazoo)
Faisonia (Sunflower)
Falcon (Quitman) 133
Falkner (Tippah) 239
Fame (Webster)
Famosla (Humphreys)
Fannin (Rankin)
Fannin Station (Rankin)
Fanning (Lamar)
Farewells (Noxubee)
Farmhaven (Madison)
Farr Slough (Pearl River)
Farrell (Coahoma)
Fawn Meadows (Pontotoc)
Fayette (Jefferson) 1,822
Fayettehill (Simpson)
Fearns Springs (Winston)
Felders Campground (Pike)
Fellowship (Jasper)
Fenton (Hancock)
Fentress (Choctaw)
Fenwick (Adams)
Ferguson (Lawrence & Perry)
Ferguson Lake (Washington)
Fernwood (Pike)
Ferris Slough (Pearl River)
Ferry Bend (Greene)
Fewell (Tallahatchie)
Fields Lake (Adams)
Fifteen Mile Bayou (Yazoo)

Fikestown (Scott)
Finis Hook (Winston)
Fink Bine (Rankin)
Fish Lake Bayou (Tunica)
Fisk Bayou (Humphreys)
Fitch (Coahoma)
Fitler (Issaquena)
Fitzhugh (Sunflower)
Flat Bayou (Tunica)
Flat Rock (Franklin)
Flat Rock Hill (Smith)
Flat Top (Hancock)
Flatwood (Union)
Flautt (Tallahatchie)
Fletcher Bayou (Tunica)
Flinn (Monroe)
Flint Creek Reservoir (Stone)
Flint Hill (Lowndes)
Flora (Madison) 1,585
Florence (Rankin) 2,375
Florewood River Plantation (Leflore)
Flower Lake (Tunica)
Flower Lake Bar (Tunica)
Flowerdale (Lee)
Floweree (Warren)
Flowers (Walthall & Warren)
Flowood (Rankin) 4,471
Floyd (Washington)
Floyd Bayou (Tunica)
Flynt (Jones)
Foltz (Montgomery)
Fontainebleau (Jackson)
Foote (Washington)
Ford (Jackson & Winston)
Fords Creek (Pearl River)
Fordsville (Marion)
Fordyke (Yazoo)
Forest (Scott) 5,324
Forest Green (Hinds)
Forest Grove (Leake)
Forest Hill (Hinds)
Forest Home Chute (Warren)
Forest Home Towhead (Warren)
Forest Point (Rankin)
Forestdale (Neshoba)
Forkland (Washington)
Forkville (Scott)
Forrest (Attala)
Forrest City (Washington)
Forrest Hills (Lamar)
Forrest Park (Forrest)
Forreston (Lowndes)
Fort Adams (Wilkinson)
Fort Loring Landing (Leflore)
Fort Saint Peter [site] (Warren)
Fort Stephens [Shucktown] (Lauderdale)
Fortenberry (Marion)
Forts Lake (Jackson)

Forty (Rankin)
Foster (Adams)
Foster Bayou (Hancock)
Fouke (Jasper)
Four Corners (Winston)
Four Dollar Bayou (Hancock)
Four Forks (Jefferson)
Four Mile (Humphreys)
Four Points (Forrest & Yazoo)
Fox (Montgomery)
Fox Island Bend (Tunica)
Fox Run (Lowndes)
Fox Run Colony (Lowndes)
Foxmoor (Lee)
Foxtrap (Noxubee)
Foxworth (Marion)
Francis (Bolivar)
Franklin (Holmes)
Frankstown (Prentiss)
Frazier (Sunflower)
Fred Hollow (Tishomingo)
Free Run (Yazoo)
Free Springs (Lafayette)
Free Trade (Leake)
Freeny (Leake)
Frees Corners (DeSoto)
Freewoods (Franklin)
French Bayou (Humphreys)
French Camp (Choctaw) 315
Frenchs Store (Rankin)
Friar's Point (Coahoma) 1,337
Friendship (Attala, Covington, Lincoln & Pontotoc)
Frog Island (Lee)
Frogtown (Scott)
Frost Bridge Camp (Wayne)
Fruitland Park (Forrest & Stone)
Fugate (Yazoo)
Fulcher (Choctaw)
Fulton (Itawamba) 3,668
Furrs (Pontotoc)
Furry (Sunflower)
Futheyville (Grenada)

G

Gainesville (Hancock)
Galen (Sunflower)
Galena (Marshall)
Galilee (Rankin)
Gallatin (Copiah)
Gallman (Copiah)
Galloway (Claiborne)
Gallway (Union)
Gama (Simpson)
Gambrell (Smith)
Gandsi (Covington)
Gants Bluff (Greene)
Garden Chapel (Holmes)
Garden City (Franklin)
Garden Park (Hinds)
Garlandville (Jasper)

Gaston (Prentiss)
Gaston Point (Harrison)
Gatesville (Copiah)
Gateway North (Madison)
Gatewood (Yalobusha)
Gattman (Monroe) 131
Gautier (Jackson) 11,139
Geeslin Corner (Grenada)
Geeville (Prentiss)
Geneill (Washington)
George (Rankin & Yazoo)
George Lake (Yazoo)
George P. Cossar State Park (Yalobusha)
Georgetown (Copiah) 350
Gerlach Mill (Tunica)
Germania (Yazoo)
Gershorn (Pontotoc)
Gholson (Noxubee)
Gibson (Monroe & Webster)
Gibson Landing (George)
Gift (Alcorn)
Giles (Kemper)
Giles Landing (Adams)
Gill (Bolivar & Leake)
Gilliam Chute (Jefferson)
Gillsburg (Amite)
Gilmore (Covington)
Gilton (Marshall)
Gin Lake (Claiborne)
Gin Slough (Washington)
Gitano (Jones)
Glade (Jones)
Gladhurst (Pike)
Glading (Amite)
Gladneyville (Monroe)
Glancy (Copiah)
Glen (Alcorn) 229
Glen Allan (Washington)
Glen Aubin (Coahoma)
Glendale (Attala, Coahoma, Forrest & Oktibbeha)
Glendora (Tallahatchie) 161
Glenfield (Union)
Glens Glen (Alcorn)
Glenville (Panola)
Glenwild (Grenada)
Glenwood (Monroe)
Gloster (Amite) 1,304
Glover (DeSoto)
Gluckstadt (Madison)
Golden (Tishomingo) 209
Golden Grove (Neshoba)
Golden Memorial State Park (Scott)
Golden Triangle Regional Airport (Lowndes)
Goldfield (Sunflower)
Good Food (Pontotoc)

The Ultimate Reference on the State

Master List of Mississippi Placenames

Good Hope (Holmes, Leake, Marion, Neshoba & Perry)
Goode (Tate)
Gooden Lake (Humphreys)
Goodhope (Newton)
Goodluck (Forrest)
Goodman (Holmes) 1,348
Goodwater (Clarke)
Goodyear (Pearl River)
Goose Lake Flats (Issaquena)
Goose Point (Harrison)
Goose Pond (Monroe)
Gordon (Claiborne)
Gore Springs (Grenada)
Goshen (Jasper & Leake)
Goshen Springs (Rankin)
Goshen Springs Station (Rankin)
Goss (Marion)
Grace (Issaquena)
Grady (Webster)
Graham (Lauderdale & Union)
Graham Ferry (Jackson)
Grand Gulf (Claiborne)
Grand Gulf Military Park (Claiborne)
Grand Gulf Nuclear Power Station (Claiborne)
Grand Plains Bayou (Hancock)
Grange (Lawrence)
Grange Hall (Warren)
Granny Baker Bayou (Washington)
Grapeland (Bolivar)
Grass Lake (Humphreys)
Grassy Lake (Tallahatchie)
Grassy Point (Harrison)
Grattam (Lowndes)
Gravel Hill (Carroll)
Gravel Siding (Tishomingo)
Graveline Bayou (Jackson)
Graves (Lee)
Gravestown (Tippah)
Gray (Leake)
Graysport Crossing (Grenada)
Great River Road State Park (Bolivar)
Green [Greenfield] (Rankin)
Green Acres (Hinds, Lee, Monroe & Oktibbeha)
Green Bottom (Tippah)
Green Crossing (Hinds)
Green Grove (Coahoma)
Green Meadow (Claiborne)
Green Oaks (Oktibbeha)
Green River (Tunica)
Green Timber Reservoir 3 (Oktibbeha)
Greenacres (Lowndes)
Greenbriar (Oktibbeha, Warren)
Greenbriar Park (Pearl River)

Greenbrier (Monroe)
Greenbrook (Madison)
Greenfield (Newton)
Greenfield [Green] (Rankin)
Greenland (Newton)
Greenville (Washington) 42,042
Greenwood (Leflore) 18,218
Greenwood (Itawamba)
Greenwood Springs (Monroe)
Gregory (Attala)
Grenada (Grenada) 11,161
Grenada Dam (Grenada)
Grenada Junction (Leflore)
Grenada Lake/Reservoir (Grenada)
Grenada Landing (Grenada)
Gretna (Wayne)
Gridley (Jasper)
Griffin Point (Jackson)
Griffin Slough (Noxubee)
Griffith (Clay)
Gross Bayou (Issaquena)
Grove Park (Rankin)
Grubb Springs (Monroe)
Gulde (Rankin)
Gulf Hills (Jackson)
Gulf Islands National Seashore (Harrison)
Gulf Marine State Park (Jackson)
Gulfport (Harrison) 64,762
Gulfside (Hancock)
Gum Bayou (Humphreys)
Gum Branch (Winston)
Gum Grove (Holmes)
Gum Ridge (Jefferson)
Gum Spring (Scott)
Gum Springs (Simpson)
Gums (Yalobusha)
Gums Crossing (Yalobusha)
Gunn (Smith)
Gunnison (Bolivar) 608
Guntown (Lee) 739
Gurlie Bayou (Jackson)
Gus Bottom (Tippah)
Gwin (Holmes)
Gwinville (Jefferson Davis)

H

Haanka Ullah (Kemper)
Hairston Bend (Lowndes)
Hale (Clarke)
Hall (Chickasaw)
Halltown (Union)
Hally (Tunica)
Halpino Lake (Warren)
Halstead (Sunflower)
Hamage (Marion)
Hamburg (Franklin)
Hamilton (Benton & Monroe)
Hamilton Lake (Claiborne)
Hamlet (Jasper)

Hamlin (Tunica)
Hampton (Washington)
Hancock Circle (Oktibbeha)
Handle (Winston)
Handsboro (Harrison)
Handy Corner (DeSoto)
Haney (Jones)
Hanford (Lamar)
Hankinson (Claiborne)
Hannah (Bolivar)
Happy Hollow (Tishomingo)
Harbert Landing (Tunica)
Harbert Point (Tunica)
Harbourview (Rankin)
Hard Cash (Humphreys)
Hardee (Issaquena)
Hardin Point (Tunica)
Hardscrabble (Lawrence)
Hardtime Bayou (Tallahatchie)
Hardy (Grenada)
Harlan (Noxubee)
Harleston (Jackson)
Harmon (Lamar)
Harmontown (Lafayette)
Harmony (Clarke, Leake, Lincoln & Marion)
Harperville (Covington & Scott)
Harriston (Jefferson)
Harrisville (Simpson)
Harrs Place (Coahoma)
Hartman (Lincoln)
Harvey (Forrest)
Harworth (Sharkey)
Hashuqua (Noxubee)
Hatchette (Kemper)
Hathorn (Jefferson Davis)
Hatley (Monroe) 558
Hatten (Leflore)
Hattiesburg (Forrest/Lamar) 45,996 + 2,810 = 48,806
Havendale (Madison)
Haw Pond (Jefferson Davis)
Hawkes (Jones)
Hawkins Crossing (Yalobusha)
Hawthorne (Adams, Pearl River)
Hayes Crossing (Panola)
Haynes Bluff (Warren)
Hays (Scott & Washington)
Hazard Switch (Tishomingo)
Hazel (Newton)
Hazlehurst (Copiah) 4,228
Heading Mill Hollow (Prentiss)
Heads (Washington)
Heard Lake Dam (Noxubee)
Heartease (Harrison)
Heater (Smith)
Heathman (Sunflower)
Hebron (Amite, Jeff. Davis, Jones & Pontotoc)
Hedgemoor (Monroe)

Heidelberg (Jasper) 937
Helena (Jackson)
Hell's Halfacre (Leflore)
Helm (Washington)
Henderson (Wayne)
Henderson Point (Hancock & Harrison)
Hendrix (Montgomery)
Henleyfield (Pearl River)
Herbert (Kemper)
Herbert Springs (Neshoba)
Hercules Station (Perry)
Hermanville (Claiborne, Copiah)
Hernando (DeSoto) 4,088
Hernando Point (DeSoto)
Hero (Jasper)
Heron Bay Bayou (Hancock)
Herron Bayou (Tunica)
Hervey (Claiborne)
Hesterville (Attala)
Heucks Retreat (Lincoln)
Hickman Landing (Sharkey)
Hickory (Newton) 531
Hickory Flat (Chickasaw)
Hickory Flat (Benton) 544
Hickory Glen (Rankin)
Hickory Grove (Lamar & Pearl River)
Hickory Hollow (Lamar)
Hicks Hollow (Tishomingo)
Hide-A-Way Lake (Pearl River)
Hideaway Hills (Panola)
Hidi (Humphreys)
Higdon (Marshall)
Higgins (Lamar)
High Hill (Leake)
High Point (Tishomingo & Winston)
Highland Circle (Lee)
Highland Meadows (Hinds)
Highland Park (Monroe)
Highlandale (Leflore)
Hightown (Alcorn)
Highway Village (Wilkinson)
Hilda (Jackson)
Hillbrook (Oktibbeha)
Hillcrest (Monroe, Oktibbeha)
Hillhouse Landing (Coahoma)
Hillman (Greene)
Hills Chapel (Prentiss)
Hillsboro (Scott)
Hillsdale (Pearl River)
Hillside National Wildlife Refuge (Holmes)
Hilton (Yazoo)
Hinchcliff (Quitman)
Hinkle (Alcorn)
Hintonville (Perry)
Hinze (Winston)

Master List of Mississippi Placenames

Hiram (Tallahatchie, Wilkinson)
Hiwannee (Wayne)
Hobo Station (Prentiss)
Hodges Chapel (Prentiss)
Hoffman (Holmes)
Hog Chain (Lincoln)
Hog Pen Slough (Bolivar)
Hohenlinden (Webster)
Holcomb (Grenada)
Holcut (Tishomingo)
Holladay (Chickasaw)
Holland Landing (Sharkey)
Hollandale (Washington) 3,524
Hollands (Sharkey)
Hollingsworth Point (Jackson)
Hollis (Calhoun)
Hollis Creek (Wayne)
Holly Bluff (Yazoo)
Holly Grove (Carroll)
Holly Hills (DeSoto & Lowndes)
Holly Landing (Jackson)
Holly Ridge (Sunflower)
Holly Springs (Marshall) 7,195
Holly Springs (Marion)
Holly Springs National Forest
   (Benton, Lafayette,
   Marshall, Tippah,
   Union & Yalobusha)
Hollyknowe (Washington)
Hollywood (Tunica)
Holmes Co. State Park (Holmes)
Holmes Lake (Jefferson)
Holmesville (Pike)
Holt (Jasper)
Holt Hollow (Tishomingo)
Holts Spur (Tishomingo)
Holy Cross Boys Camp
   (Hancock)
Home Landing (Bolivar)
Home Park (Yazoo)
Homewood (Scott)
Homochitto (Amite, Issaquena)
Homochitto National Forest
   (Adams, Amite, Copiah,
   Franklin, Jefferson
   & Wilkinson)
Honey Island (Humphreys)
Hoodtown (Copiah)
Hooker (Lawrence)
Hooker Hollow (Lawrence)
Hookston (Lauderdale)
Hope (Neshoba)
Hope Springs (Hinds)
Hopedale (Issaquena)
Hopewell (Benton, Clay,
   Copiah, Covington,
   Marion & Prentiss)
Hopoca (Leake)
Hopson (Coahoma)
Horatio (Panola)

Horn (Clarke)
Horn Lake (DeSoto)
Horn Lake (DeSoto) 13,885
Horn Place Landing (Yazoo)
Horseshoe (Holmes & Scott)
Horseshoe Bend (Prentiss &
   Tishomingo)
Horseshoe Lake (Coahoma &
   Holmes)
Hortontown (Pontotoc)
Hot Coffee (Covington)
Houlka (Chickasaw) 540
House (Neshoba)
Houston (Chickasaw) 3,902
Houston (Lauderdale)
Hovey (Harrison)
Howard (Holmes)
Howards Store (DeSoto)
Howell (George & Rankin)
Howell Siding (Tippah)
Howison (Harrison)
Hoy (Jones)
Hub (Marion)
Hubbard (Hinds & Newton)
Hubbard Creek (Yalobusha)
Hudsonville (Marshall)
Hugh White State Park (Grenada)
Hugo (Tallahatchie)
Humber (Coahoma)
Humphreys (Claiborne)
Hunt (Washington)
Hunt Bluff (Pearl River)
Hunter Town (Scott)
Hunters Creek (Madison)
Hunters Woods (Rankin)
Huntington Point (Bolivar)
Huntley (Jefferson)
Huntsville (Montgomery)
Hurley (Jackson)
Hurley Lookout (Jackson)
Huron (Amite)
Hurricane (Attala & Warren)
Hurricane [Esperanza](Pontotoc)
Hurricane Branch (Grenada)
Hurricane Creek (Clarke,
   & Marion)
Hurricane Lake (Lincoln)
Hurricane Point (Bolivar)
Hushpuckena (Bolivar)
Hustler (Amite)
Hutchins Landing (Adams)
Hyde (Yalobusha)
I
Ihrie (Jefferson)
Improve (Marion)
Increase [Causeyville]
   Lauderdale)
Inda (Stone)
Independence (Scott & Tate)
Indian Hill (Greene)

Indian Hills (Lee)
Indian Mound (Clarke)
Indian Springs (Alcorn)
Indianola (Sunflower) 11,514
Industrial (Pearl River)
Ingleside (Claiborne)
Ingomar (Issaquena & Union)
Ingram (Coahoma)
Ingrams Mill (DeSoto)
Innswood South (Forrest)
Insmore (Claiborne)
Inverness (Sunflower) 1,103
Inwood (Sunflower)
Iowana (Jackson)
Ireland (Wilkinson)
Irene (Pike)
Iris (Coahoma)
Isabell (George)
Isenberg (Washington)
Isola (Humphreys) 666
Issaquena (Sharkey)
It (Copiah)
Itta Bena (Leflore) 2,264
Ituma (Holmes)
Iuka (Tishomingo) 3,122
J
J. P. Coleman State Park
   (Tishomingo)
Jacinto (Alcorn)
Jack (Copiah)
Jack Lake Bayou (Tunica)
Jackson (Hinds/Madison/
   Rankin)
   187,433 + 853 + 133 =
   188,419
Jackson International Airport
   (Rankin)
Jackson Landing (Hancock)
Jackson Point Landing (Adams)
Jackson Ridge (Hancock)
Jago (DeSoto)
Jaketown (Humphreys)
James (Greene & Washington)
Jamestown (Marion)
Janice (Perry)
Jaquith (Sunflower)
Jayess (Lawrence)
Jaynesville (Simpson)
Jeannette (Adams)
Jeff (Newton)
Jeff Davis (Noxubee & Warren)
Jeff Davis Lake (Jeff. Davis)
Jefferson (Carroll & Jefferson)
Jeffries (Coahoma)
Jenkins (Jones)
Jennings (Pike)
Jericho (Union)
Jetts (Warren)
Jewells Hills (Jasper)
Jobe Hollow (Benton)

Jobes (Alcorn)
Joe (Rankin)
John C. Stennis Space Center
   (Hancock)
John W. Kyle State Park (Panola)
Johns (Rankin)
Johnson (Jones)
Johnsonville (Sunflower)
Johnston (Pike &
   Washington)
Johnstons Station (Pike)
Johnsville (Adams)
Jolly (Chickasaw)
Jonathan (Greene)
Jones Chapel (Washington)
Jones Crossing (Holmes)
Jones Hollow (Alcorn)
Jones Mill (Harrison)
Jonestown (Alcorn & Yazoo)
Jonestown (Coahoma) 1,462
Joplin (Attala)
Jose Bayou (Jackson)
Joseph (Attala)
Jug Fork (Lee)
Jumpertown (Prentiss) 450
Junction City (Clarke)
Juniper Grove (Pearl River)
K
Kaiser-Carlton Lake (Adams)
Kalem (Scott)
Kansas Landing (Yazoo)
Katzenmeyer (Warren)
Kay Bayou (Coahoma)
Kearney (Yazoo)
Kearney Park (Madison)
Keel (Lafayette)
Keesler Air Force Base
   [military] (Harrison)
Keirn (Holmes)
Kelley's Crossing (Tate)
Kellis Store (Kemper)
Kelly (Covington)
Kelona (Jasper)
Kelso (Sharkey)
Kemper County Lake (Kemper)
Kemper Springs (Kemper)
Kendrick (Alcorn)
Kennolia (Franklin)
Keno (Marion)
Kentwood (Hinds)
Keownville (Union)
Kerr (Choctaw)
Kewanee (Lauderdale)
Key Field [airport] (Lauderdale)
Kickapoo Camp (Hinds)
Kienstra (Adams)
Kilmichael (Montgomery) 784
Kiln (Hancock)
Kimball Lake (Bolivar)
Kimberly (Warren)

The Ultimate Reference on the State

Master List of Mississippi Placenames

Kincaid (Grenada)
King (Rankin)
King And Anderson (Coahoma)
King Bee (Neshoba)
King Bee Bayou (Hancock)
King Hollow (Prentiss)
Kings (Warren)
Kings Corner (Panola)
Kings Ferry (Warren)
Kings Point (Jefferson)
Kingston (Adams)
Kinlock (Sunflower)
Kioto (Walthall)
Kipling (Kemper)
Kirby (Franklin)
Kirklin (Walthall)
Kirkman Landing (Grenada)
Kirkville (Itawamba & Pike)
Kirkwood Park (Forrest)
Kitchener (Neshoba)
Kitrell Creek Reservoir (Greene)
Kittrell (Greene & Perry)
Kjirsey (Panola)
Klein (Smith)
Klondike (Kemper)
Knights Acres (Lee)
Knobtown (Greene)
Knox (Attala)
Knoxo (Walthall)
Knoxville (Franklin)
Koch (Rankin)
Kokomo (Marion)
Kola (Covington)
Kolola Springs (Lowndes)
Kosciusko (Attala) 6,774
Kossuth (Alcorn) 244
Kracker Station (Scott)
Kreole (Jackson)
Kyles Brake (Tunica)
L
Lackey (Monroe)
Lafayette Springs (Lafayette)
Lake-A-Way (Stone)
Lake (Scott/Newton)
    343 + 21 = 364
Lake Bruin State Park
    (Claiborne)
Lake Carrier (Panola)
Lake Castle (Madison)
Lake Cavalier (Madison)
Lake Center (Marshall)
Lake Charles Landing (Coahoma)
Lake Charlie Capps [formerly
    Bolivar Lake](Bolivar)
Lake City (Prentiss & Yazoo)
Lake Como (Jasper)
Lake Cormorant (DeSoto)
Lake Dick (Yazoo)
Lake Forest (Warren)

Lake Forest Ranch Camp
    (Noxubee)
Lake Helen Dam (Lauderdale)
Lake Hico (Hinds)
Lake Lorman (Madison)
Lake Lowndes State Park
    (Lowndes)
Lake Martha Dam (Monroe)
Lake Monroe (Monroe)
Lake Park (Warren)
Lake Piomingo (Lee)
Lake Serene North (Lamar)
Lake Serene South (Lamar)
Lake Tangipahoa (Pike)
Lake Tiak O'Khata (Winston)
Lake View (DeSoto)
Lake Vista (Bolivar)
Lake Washington
    (Washington)
Lakeland (Rankin)
Lakeover (Hinds)
Lakeridge (Hinds)
Lakeshore (Hancock & Rankin)
Lakeside (Hinds & Yalobusha)
Lakeview (Lee)
Lakewood (Lamar, Monroe
    & Warren)
Lakewood Park (Lee)
Lamar (Benton)
Lamar Bruce Lake (Lee)
Lamar Park (Lamar)
Lambert (Quitman) 1,075
Lamberts Store (Lawrence)
Lamkin (Humphreys)
Lamont (Bolivar & Washington)
Lampton (Marion)
Land-O-Lakes (Noxubee)
Landers (Oktibbeha)
Landon (Harrison)
Landrum (Jones)
Laneheart (Wilkinson)
Lang Bayou (Jackson)
Langford (Rankin)
Langley (Attala)
Langsdale (Clarke)
Lanham (Jones)
Lantrip (Calhoun)
Lar-eli-do (Lee)
Larkin (Sharkey)
Larue (Jackson)
Latimer (Jackson)
Latonia (George)
Lauderdale (Lauderdale)
Laughlin (Bolivar)
Laughter Flat Landing (Jackson)
Laurel (Jones) 18,299
Laurel Hill (Neshoba)
Lawrence (Monroe & Newton)
Laws Hill (Marshall)
Le Tourneau (Warren)

Leaf (Greene)
Leakesville (Greene) 1,111
Learned (Hinds) 99
Leavell Woods (Hinds)
Lebanon (Hinds, Holmes,
    Newton & Prentiss)
Lee Lake (Washington)
Leedo (Jefferson)
Leedy (Tishomingo)
Leesburg (Rankin)
Leesdale (Adams)
Leetown (Hancock)
Leeville (Forrest)
LeFleur's Bluff State Park
    (Hinds)
Leflore (Grenada)
Leflore County Legion State
    Park (Leflore)
Leggett (Pike)
Legion State Park (Winston)
Lehr (Walthall)
Leland (Washington) 5,970
Lemon (Smith)
Lena (Leake) 171
Leota (Washington)
Leotis (Chickasaw)
Leroy Percy State Park
    (Washington)
Leslie Slough (Pearl River)
Lespideza Point (Panola)
Lessley (Wilkinson)
Leverett (Tallahatchie)
Lewis Hollow (Alcorn)
Lewisburg (DeSoto)
Lexie (Walthall)
Lexington (Holmes) 2,027
Liberty (Amite) 680
Liberty (Covington, Kemper,
    Newton & Winston)
Liberty Chapel (Attala)
Liberty Hill (Attala)
Liddon Lake (Alcorn)
Lighthouse Point (Hancock)
Lightsey (Wayne)
Lilac (Montgomery)
Lillian (Scott)
Limbert (Jones)
Limerick (Yazoo)
Linden (Copiah & Rankin)
Line Creek (Amite)
Line Prairie (Scott)
Lingle (Smith)
Linn (Sunflower)
Linsey (Washington)
Linton (Clarke)
Linwood (Adams)
Linwood (Neshoba, Tate, Yazoo)
Little Atchafalaya Landing
    (Sharkey)
Little Basin (Sharkey)

Little Creek (Perry)
Little Island (Stone)
Little Italy (Scott)
Little Rock (Newton)
Little Springs (Franklin)
Little Sunflower (Sharkey)
Little Texas (Carroll & Tunica)
Little Tippo (Leflore)
Little Whiting Lake (Quitman)
Little Yazoo (Yazoo)
Litton (Bolivar)
Liverpool (Yazoo)
Livingston (Madison)
Lizana (Harrison)
Lizelia (Lauderdale)
Loakfoma (Winston)
Loakfoma Lake (Noxubee)
Lobdell (Bolivar)
Lobutcha (Winston)
Loch Leven (Wilkinson)
Loch Lomond (Yazoo)
Locke Station (Panola)
Lockhart (Lauderdale)
Locopolis Bayou
    (Tallahatchie)
Locum (Union)
Locust Grove (Union)
Lodi (Humphreys, Montgomery)
Logtown (Hancock)
Lombardy (Sunflower)
Lone Pine (Alcorn)
Lone Star [Dry Creek]
    (Covington)
Long (Washington)
Long Bayou (Jefferson)
Long Beach (Harrison) 16,776
Long Branch (Yalobusha)
Long Lake (Adams, Coahoma
    & Warren)
Long Lake Comm. (Warren)
Long Point (Hancock)
Longino (Neshoba)
Longshot (Bolivar)
Longstreet (Quitman)
Longtown (Panola)
Longview (Monroe, Oktibbeha
    & Pontotoc)
Longview Bayou (Jackson)
Longwood (Washington)
Looxahoma (Tate)
Loraine (Harrison)
Lorena (Smith)
Lorenzen (Sharkey)
Loring (Madison)
Lorman (Jefferson)
Lorman Lake (Madison)
Lost Gap (Lauderdale)
Lost Lake (Hinds & Tunica)
Louin (Jasper) 282
Louise (Humphreys) 314

Master List of Mississippi Placenames

Louisville (Winston) 7,085
Love (DeSoto)
Lovelace (Marion)
Lower Lake Beach (Panola)
Lowrey (Tippah)
Loyd (Calhoun)
Loyd Star [Red Star] (Lincoln)
Lucas (Jefferson Davis)
Lucedale (George) 3,041
Lucern (Newton)
Lucien (Franklin)
Luckney (Rankin)
Lucre (Sharkey)
Ludlow (Scott)
Lula (Coahoma) 218
Lumberton (Lamar/Pearl
    River) 2,553 + 10 = 2,563
Lunch (Itawamba)
Lurand (Coahoma)
Lurline (Tate)
Lux (Covington)
Lyle (Oktibbeha)
Lyman (Harrison)
Lynchburg (DeSoto & Hinds)
Lynn Creek (Noxubee)
Lynville (Kemper)
Lyon (Coahoma) 427
M
Maben (Oktibbeha/Webster)
    491 + 251 = 742
Macedonia (Attala,
    Chickasaw, Forrest, Lee,
    Noxubee & Union)
Macel (Tallahatchie)
Mack (Marshall)
Macon (Noxubee) 2,298
Macon Bend (Jackson)
Madden (Leake)
Maddox (Simpson)
Madison (Madison) 12,618
Madison Station (Madison)
Madisonville (Madison)
Magee (Simpson) 3,930
Magenta (Washington)
Magna Vista (Issaquena)
Magnolia (Pike) 2,259
Magnolia Terrace (Hinds)
Mahned (Perry)
Mahon (Marshall)
Malcolm (Jefferson)
Mallini Point (Harrison)
Malmaison (Carroll)
Malone (Marshall)
Malone Lake (Monroe)
Malone Landing (Coahoma)
Malvina (Bolivar)
Manhattan (Washington)
Mannassa (Clarke)
Mannsdale (Madison)
Mantachie (Itawamba) 1,068

Mantee (Webster) 135
Marathon (Washington)
Marcella (Holmes)
Marianna (Marshall)
Marie (Sunflower)
Marienette (DeSoto)
Marietta (Prentiss) 295
Marion (Lauderdale) 1,565
Maris Town (Madison)
Markette (Lafayette)
Markham (Sunflower)
Marks (Quitman) 1,635
Marksville (Holmes)
Markwald (Jasper)
Mars Hill (Amite & Forrest)
Mars Slough (Pearl River)
Marsh Bayou (Leflore)
Marsh Hollow (Noxubee)
Marsh Lake (Jackson)
Marsha (George)
Martin (Lauderdale & Pike)
Martin Bluff (Jackson)
Martinere Bend (Clarke)
Martinville (Simpson)
Martinsville (Copiah)
Martintown (Union)
Marvins Chapel (Attala)
Mary Crawford Lake (Lawrence)
Mary Holmes (Clay)
Marydell (Leake)
Mascot (Coahoma)
Mashulaville (Noxubee)
Mason Landing (Bolivar)
Matagorda (Coahoma)
Matherville (Clarke & Wayne)
Mathews Crossing (Leflore)
Mathis Bayou (Tunica)
Mathiston (Webster/Choctaw)
    734 + 98 = 832
Matthew's Brake National
    Wildlife Refuge (Holmes)
Matthews (Jones & Pontotoc)
Mattoon (Sunflower)
Mattson (Coahoma)
Maud (Tunica)
Maxey Bayou (Grenada)
Maxie (Forrest)
May Spring (Noxubee)
Maybank (Forrest)
Maybell (Jones)
Mayday (Leflore)
Mayersville (Issaquena) 288
Mayfair (Hinds)
Mayhew (Lowndes)
Mayhoff Springs (Clarke)
Mayton (Rankin)
Maywood (DeSoto)
McAdams (Attala)
McAfee (Leake)
McBride (Jefferson)

McCall Creek (Franklin)
McCall Landing (Jackson)
McCall River (Pearl River)
McCallum (Forrest)
McCann Bayou (Sharkey)
McCarley (Carroll)
McCluney (Monroe)
McComb (Pike) 11,746
McCondy (Chickasaw)
McCool (Attala) 168
McCrary (Lowndes)
McCutcheon (Washington)
McDaniels (Sunflower)
McDonald (Covington, Neshoba)
McElveen (Amite)
McGhee (Panola)
McGrath (Washington)
McHenry (Stone)
McInnis Bayou (Jackson)
McIntyre (Lowndes)
McIvor (Panola)
McKinney Bayou (Tunica)
McLain (Greene) 606
McLaurin (Forrest)
McLean Spur (Leflore)
McLeod (Noxubee)
McMillan (Adams, Holmes &
    Winston)
McNair (Jefferson)
McNeal (Jasper)
McNeill (Pearl River)
McNutt (Leflore)
McRaney (Covington)
McRaven (Hinds)
McSwain (Perry)
McVille (Attala)
Meadow Oaks (Hinds)
Meadowhill (Hinds)
Meadows Store (Copiah)
Meadowview (Lee)
Meadville (Franklin) 411
Meat Hollow (Tishomingo)
Mechanicsburg (Yazoo)
Meehan (Lauderdale)
Meeks (Holmes)
Meeting House Bluff (Greene)
Mehr (Tallahatchie)
Melba (Jefferson Davis)
Melton (Jefferson)
Meltonia (Bolivar)
Meltonville (Madison)
Memphis (DeSoto) 90
Memphis Junction (Grenada)
Mendenhall (Simpson) 2,528
Mengel (George)
Meridale Camp (Lauderdale)
Meridian (Lauderdale) 40,255
Meridian Naval Air Station
    (Lauderdale)
Merigold (Bolivar) 560

Merit (Simpson)
Merrill (George)
Mesa (Walthall)
Metcalfe (Washington) 1,240
Meyers (Forrest)
Mhoon Landing (Tunica)
Mhoons Valley (Clay)
Michigan City (Benton)
Middle Creek (Pearl River)
Middleton (Clarke)
Midnight (Humphreys)
Midway (Copiah, Hinds, Leake,
    Scott, Tallahatchie,
    Tishomingo & Yazoo)
Mike Conner Lake (Covington)
Mikoma (Tallahatchie)
Mildred (Marion)
Mile Branch (Franklin)
Miles (Carroll)
Miles Bluff (Jackson)
Mileston (Holmes)
Mill Creek (Jones, Pearl River
    & Rankin)
Millard (Pearl River)
Millcreek (Winston)
Miller (DeSoto)
Miller Landing (Yazoo)
Miller Point (Coahoma)
Millers Landing (Issaquena)
Millington (Kemper)
Mills Bayou (Issaquena)
Mills Crossing (Yazoo)
Milltown (Madison)
Millville (Madison)
Milroy (Sunflower)
Mims (Panola)
Mineral Wells (DeSoto)
Minerva (Montgomery)
Mingo (Tishomingo)
Minot (Sunflower)
Minter City (Leflore)
Minton Bayou (Tunica)
Missala (Jackson)
Missionary (Jasper)
Mississippi City (Harrison)
Miss. Petrified Forest (Madison)
Mississippi River (bordering)
    Adams, Bolivar, Claiborne,
    Coahoma, DeSoto, Issaquena,
    Jefferson, Tunica, Warren,
    Washington, & Wilkinson)
Mississippi State (Oktibbeha)
Misterton (Grenada)
Mitchell (Tippah & Union)
Mixon (Amite)
Mize (Smith) 321
Mocarter (Tunica)
Moccasin Point (Panola)
Mohawk Lake (Tippah)
Molino (Union)

The Ultimate Reference on the State

Master List of Mississippi Placenames

Monarch (Jones)[1]
Moncure (Hinds)
Money (Leflore)
Monkeytown (Yazoo)
Monroe (Franklin)
Monroe Lake (Monroe)
Mont Helena (Sharkey)
Monterey (Rankin)
Montevista (Webster)
Montezuma Bar (Coahoma)
Montgomery (Holmes, Lincoln)
Monticello (Lawrence) 1,732
Montpelier (Clay)
Montrose (Jasper) 108
Moon (Coahoma)
Moon Lake (Coahoma)
Moores Mill (Tishomingo)
Mooreville (Lee)
Moorhead (Sunflower) 2,315
Morgan Bayou (Holmes)
Morgan Brake National.
   Wildlife Refuge (Holmes)
Morgan City (Leflore) 128
Morgans Store (Hinds)
Morgantown (Adams, Marion
   & Otibbeha)
Morganwood Camp (Lee)
Morning Star (Hinds)
Morris (Jefferson Davis)
Morriston (Forrest)
Morton (Scott) 3,261
Moscos (Covington)
Moscow (Kemper)
Moseley (Lauderdale, Rankin)
Moselle (Jones)
Moses (Kemper)
Moss (Jasper)
Moss Point (Jackson) 18,095
Mound Bayou (Bolivar) 2,102
Mound City (Bolivar, Union)
Mound Landing (Bolivar)
Mount Carmel (Jeff. Davis)
Mount Herman (Attala)
Mount Moriah (Tippah)
Mount Nebo (Kemper)
Mount Olive (Amite, Franklin
   & Jones)
Mount Olive (Covington) 963
Mount Olivet (Panola)
Mount Pleasant (Covington,
   Itawamba, Marshall,
   Smith & Wayne)
Mount Vernon (Lee & Newton)
Mount Zion (Jones, Lowndes
   & Tippah)
Mountain (George)
Mountain Creek (Rankin)
Movella (George)

Mowell Siding (Tippah)
Mud Lake Bayou (Sharkey)
Muddy Bayou (Warren)
Mulberry (Jasper & Wayne)
Muldon (Monroe)
Multona Springs (Attala)
Munson (Attala)
Murdock Crossing (Leflore)
Murphreesboro (Tallahatchie)
Murphy (Washington)
Murry (Tippah)
Muskedine (Washington)
Muskegon (Scott)
Myles (Copiah)
Myrick (Jones)
Myrleville (Yazoo)
Myrtle (Union) 383

N
Nails Bayou (Tunica)
Nancy (Clarke)
Nanih Waiya (Winston)
Nanih Waiya State Historical
   Site (Winston)
Napanee (Washington)
Napoleon (Hancock)
Narkeeta (Kemper)
NASA's John C. Stennis
   Space Center (Hancock)
Nashdale (Oktibbeha)
Nashville (Lowndes)
Nason (Grenada)
Natchez (Adams) 18,277
Natchez Nat'l. Cemetery (Adams)
Natchez State Park (Adams)
Natchez Trace Lake (Pontotoc)
Natchez Trace Parkway
   (Adams, Attala, Chickasaw,
   Choctaw, Claiborne, Clay,
   Hinds, Itawamba, Jefferson,
   Leake, Lee, Madison, Pontotoc,
   Prentiss & Tishomingo)
Natchez Trace Village (Madison)
Natcole (Marion)
Neals (Chickasaw)
Necaise (Hancock)
Necaise Crossing (Hancock)
Needmore (Tallahatchie)
Neely (Greene)
Neil (Tishomingo)
Nellieburg (Lauderdale)
Nesbit (DeSoto)
Neshoba (Neshoba)
Neshoba County Legion Lake
   (Neshoba)

Nettleton (Monroe 1,404 /
   Lee 1,208) = 2,612
Nevada (Hinds)

Neville (Neshoba)
New Albany (Union) 7,238
New Augusta (Perry) 723
New Bethel (Tishomingo)
New Canaan (Benton)
New Fannin (Rankin)
New Fellowship (Jasper)
New Fitler (Issaquena)
New Garden (Tate)
New Hamilton (Monroe)
New Harmony (Union)
New Haven (Smith)
New Hebron (Lawrence) 382
New Hope (Attala, Franklin,
   Harrison, Lowndes,
   Marion, Prentiss,
   Tippah & Yalobusha)
New Hope Grove (Madison)
New Hope Park (Lowndes)
New Ireland (Newton)
New Liberty (Calhoun)
New Providence (Newton)
New Salem (Itawamba)
New Sight (Lincoln)
New Site (Prentiss)
New Town (Sunflower & Tate)
New Union (Marion)
New Wren (Monroe)
New York (Chickasaw)
Newman (Hinds)
Newmans (Warren)
Newmans Grove (Warren)
Newport (DeSoto)
Newport (Attala & Chickasaw)
Newsom (Marion)
Newton (Newton) 3,749
Newtonville (Attala)
Niblett Landing (Bolivar)
Nichols (Leflore)
Nicholson (Pearl River)
Nile (Attala)
Niles (Bolivar)
Nitta Yuma (Sharkey)
Nod (Yazoo)
Nogan (Hinds)
Nola (Lawrence)
Norfield (Lincoln)
Norfolk (DeSoto)
Norfolk Bayou (DeSoto)
Norris (Scott)
Nortac (Pearl River)
North Bay (Harrison)
North Bend (Neshoba)
North Biloxi (Harrison)
North Carrollton (Carroll) 607
North Center (Attala)
North Colony (Hinds)
North Crossroads (Tishomingo)

North Fork (Jefferson)
North Gulfport (Harrison)
North Haven (Union)
North Junction (Pontotoc)
North Park (Lee)
North Side (Hancock)
North Tunica (Tunica)
North Union (Attala)
Northaven Woods (Lowndes)
Northgate (Clay & Oktibbeha)
Northpointe (Hinds)
Northwood (Oktibbeha)
Northwood Hills (Oktibbeha)
Northwoods (Rankin)
Norway (Yazoo)
Norwood (Hinds)
Noxapater (Winston) 438
Noxubee National Wildlife
   Refuge (Noxubee, Oktibbeha
   & Winston)
Nugent (Harrison)
Null Hollow (Tishomingo)
Nut Bank (Jackson)

O
O'Neil (Amite)
O'Reilly (Bolivar)
Oak Bowery (Jasper & Jones)
Oak Creek (Hinds)
Oak Grove (Chickasaw, Holmes,
   Jones, Kemper, Lamar
   & Perry)
Oak Hill (Pontotoc)
Oak Ridge (Attala, Panola &
   Warren)
Oak Vale (Lawrence)
Oakdale Park (Lowndes)
Oakland (Yalobusha) 559
Oakland (Alcorn, Itawamba,
   & Pike)
Oaklawn (Claiborne)
Oakley (Hinds)
Oakridge (Lee)
Oaks (Madison)
Obadiah (Lauderdale)
Ocean Springs (Jackson) 16,519
Ocobla (Neshoba)
Ocktok (Oktibbeha)
Ofahoma (Leake)
Oil City (Yazoo)
OK Bend (Tunica)
Oka Kapassa (Newton)
Okahola (Lamar)
Okahta Talaia (Newton)
Okatibbee Dam (Lauderdale)
Okatibbee Lake/Reservoir
   (Lauderdale)
Okhissa Lake (Franklin)
Oklahoma (Carroll)

[1] County (or counties) where place is located is in parenthesis. Number after entry indicates 1998 population estimate. County Seats in *italics*.

Master List of Mississippi Placenames

Okolona (Chickasaw) 3,059
Oktibbeha (Kemper)
Oktibbeha County Lake
    (Oktibbeha)
Oktibbeha Gardens
    (Oktibbeha)
Old Americus (Jackson)
Old Augusta (Perry)
Old Avera (Greene)
Old Bassfield (Jeff. Davis)
Old Cairo (Prentiss)
Old Dominion (Leflore)
Old Georgetown (Copiah)
Old Houlka (Chickasaw)
Old Malcum (Lincoln)
Old Myrtle (Union)
Old Narkeetah (Kemper)
Old Red Star (Lincoln)
Old River Lake (Bolivar & Wilkinson)
Old Scooba (Kemper)
Old Tar Paper Shack Lake
    (Bolivar)
Old Taylorsville (Smith)
Old Town Bend (Coahoma)
Old Town Overlook (Lee)
Old Union (Lee)
Old Wahalak (Kemper)
Oldenburg (Franklin)
Oldham (Tishomingo)
Oldham Hollow (Tishomingo)
Olio (Amite)
Olive Branch (DeSoto) 12,063
Oliverfried (Quitman)
Oloh (Lamar)
Oma (Lawrence)
Omega (Holmes)
Onward (Sharkey)
Open Gap (Stone)
Openwood Plantation (Warren)
Ophelia (Rankin)
Ora (Covington)
Orange (Franklin & Jasper)
Orange Grove (Harrison & Jackson)
Orange Lake (Jackson)
Orangeville (Hinds)
Oregon (Holmes)
Orion (Marshall)
Orvisburg (Pearl River)
Orwood (Panola)
Osborn (Oktibbeha)
Osborne Creek (Prentiss)
Osseola (Washington)
Oswego (Holmes)
Osyka (Pike) 489
Otho (Scott)
Ouetti (Jones)
Overby (Washington)
Overpark (DeSoto)

Ovett (Jones)
Owens Hollow (Tishomingo)
Owens Wells (Holmes)
Oxberry (Grenada)
Oxberry Bayou (Grenada)
Oxford (Amite)
Oxford (Lafayette) 12,096
Ozark (Itawamba)
Ozona (Pearl River)

P

Pace (Bolivar) 348
Pachuta (Clarke) 276
Paden (Tishomingo) 126
Paducah (Washington)
Palestine (Clay, Hinds,
    Pearl River & Yalobusha)
Palmer (Forrest)
Palmers Crossing (Forrest)
Palmetto (Lee)
Palmetto Flats (Leake)
Palmetto Point (Wilkinson)
Palo Alto (Clay)
Pandella Landing (Adams)
Pannell (Pontotoc)
Panther Burn (Sharkey)

Panther Swamp National
    Wildlife Refuge (Yazoo)
Paradise Point (Rankin)
Parchman (Sunflower)
Parham (Monroe)
Paris (Lafayette)
Parish Lake Bayou (Jackson)
Park Monceau (Lee)
Parkdale (Oktibbeha)
Parker Bayou (Pearl River)
Parker Landing (Adams)
Parker Lookout (George)
Parker Slough (Oktibbeha)
Parkersburg (Chickasaw)
Parkeville (Noxubee)
Parks (Union)
Parks Place (Issaquena)
Parksplace (Panola)
Parkview (Monroe)
Parkway (Lee)
Parsons (Grenada)
Partee (Calhoun)
Pascagoula (Jackson) 27,163
Pascagoula Naval Home Port
    (Jackson)
Pasgoula (Jackson)
Pass Christian (Harrison) 6,190
Pat (Rankin)
Pat Harrison Waterway Lake
    (Lamar/Wayne)
Patosi (Yazoo)
Patrick (Oktibbeha)
Patrons Union (Newton)
Patterson (Attala)

Pattison (Claiborne)
Patton Place (Rankin)
Pattona (Claiborne)
Paul (Tallahatchie)
Paul B. Johnson State Park
    (Forrest)
Paul H. Barrett Lake
    (Pearl River)
Paulding (Jasper)
Paulette (Noxubee)
Paynes (Tallahatchie)
Pea Ridge (Lee & Union)
Peagler Store (Scott)
Pearl (Simpson)
Pearl (Rankin) 23,287
Pearl Hill (Leake)
Pearl River (Neshoba)
Pearlhaven (Lincoln)
Pearlington (Hancock)
Pearson (Rankin)
Pecan (Jackson)
Pecan Acres (Oktibbeha)
Pecan Bayou (Tallahatchie)
Pecan Creek (Madison)
Pecan Grove (Jones)
Peden (Kemper)
Peelers (Warren)
Pelahatchie (Rankin) 1,597
Pellez (Webster)
Pelucia Bayou (Leflore)
Pendorff (Jones)
Penns (Lowndes)
Pentecost (Sunflower)
Penton (DeSoto)
Peoples (Tippah)
Peoria (Amite)
Peppertown (Itawamba)
Percy (Washington)
Percy Quin State Park (Pike)
Perdue (Newton)
Perkinston (Stone)
Perkinsville (Winston)
Perota (Newton)
Perry (Stone)
Perry Lake (Perry)
Perrytown (Wilkinson)
Perth (Jefferson)
Perthshire (Bolivar)
Petal (Forrest) 8,888
Peteet (Leflore)
Petertown (Tishomingo)
Peyton (Claiborne)
Pheba (Clay)
Philadelphia (Neshoba) 7,725
Philipp (Tallahatchie)
Phillipstown (Leflore)
Phoenix (Jefferson & Yazoo)
Piamingo Lake (Lee)
Piave (Greene)
Picayune (Pearl River) 12,058

Pickens (Holmes) 1,381
Pickering (Covington)
Pickwick (Marion)
Pickwick Lake (Tishomingo)
Piera (Lafayette)
Pierce Crossroad (Yazoo)
Pierces Chapel (Attala)
Pierces Springs (Clarke)
Pierre Bayou (Claiborne, Copiah)
Piggtown (Leake)
Piketown (Scott)
Pikeville (Chickasaw)
Pilgrim Rest (Leake)
Pilgrims Rest (Attala)
Pinchback (Holmes)
Pinckneyville (Wilkinson)
Pine Acres (Clay)
Pine Belt Reg'l. Airport (Jones)
Pine Bluff (Carroll & Newton)
Pine Flat (Tishomingo &
    Yalobusha)
Pine Grove (Benton, Forrest,
    Hinds, Holmes, Lamar,
    Lee & Tippah)
Pine Hill (Lee)
Pine Hills (Harrison)
Pine Lake (Simpson)
Pine Land (Sunflower)
Pine Lea (Hinds)
Pine Park (Rankin)
Pine Ridge (Adams, Clarke
    & Lamar)
Pine Springs (Lauderdale)
Pine Valley (Yalobusha)
Pinebluff (Clay)
Pinebur (Marion)
Pinecrest (Lee & Lowndes)
Pinedale (Tishomingo & Union)
Pinehurst (Lee & Monroe)
Pineview (Wayne)
Pineville (Smith)
Piney Grove (Monroe)
Piney Grove Hollow (Prentiss)
Piney Point (Lafayette)
Piney Woods (Grenada, Rankin)
Pink (Tunica)
Pinola (Simpson)
Pisgah (Greene, Prentiss &
    Rankin)
Pistol Ridge (Forrest)
Pitcher Point (Harrison)
Pittman (Calhoun & Marion)
Pitts (Pike)
Pittsboro (Calhoun) 272
Plain (Rankin)
Plainview (Rankin)
Plairs (Oktibbeha)
Plantation (Attala)
Plantation Homes (Oktibbeha)
Plantersville (Lee) 1,394

The Ultimate Reference on the State

Master List of Mississippi Placenames

Plaquemine Bayou (Sharkey)
Plattsburg (Winston)
Pleasant Acres (Oktibbeha)
Pleasant Grove (Panola, Pontotoc & Wayne)
Pleasant Hill (Copiah, Desoto, Lauderdale & Union)
Pleasant Home Landing (Yazoo)
Pleasant Ridge (Attala, Jones, Oktibbeha & Union)
Plum Grove (Lowndes)
Plum Point (DeSoto, Yalobusha)
Plumville (Yazoo)
Pluto (Holmes)
Plymouth (Lowndes, Pontotoc)
Poagville (Tate)
Pocahontas (Hinds)
Point (Lauderdale)
Point Clear (Hancock)
Point Harbor (Clay)
Point Pleasant (Yalobusha)
Point Tuasaine (Jackson)
Polfry (Jackson)
Polkville (Smith) 135
Pollock (Sunflower)
Pond (Wilkinson)
Pontotoc (Pontotoc) 5,219
Pontotoc Ridge Experiment Lake (Pontotoc)
Poolville (Union)
Poor Joe Larkin (Sharkey)
Pope (Panola) 178
Popetown (Jackson)
Poplar Corners (DeSoto)
Poplar Creek (Montgomery)
Poplar Springs (Chickasaw, Holmes, Lauderdale, Montgomery, Newton & Pontotoc)
Poplarville (Pearl River) 2,834
Popsons (Coahoma)
Port Anderson (Washington)
Port Gibson (Claiborne) 1,750
Porters Chapel (Warren)
Porterton (Lafayette)
Porterville (Kemper)
Posey Mound (Quitman)
Possum Bayou (Tallahatchie)
Possum Bend (Yazoo)
Possum Corner (Wilkinson)
Possum Hollow (Warren)
Possum Trot (Pontotoc)
Possumneck (Attala)
Post (Lauderdale)
Potato Hill Bayou (Yazoo)
Poticaw Landing (Jackson)
Potlockney (Lafayette)
Potts Camp (Marshall) 483
Powell (Coahoma)
Powell Bayou (Sunflower)

Powers (Jones)
Prairie (Monroe)
Prairie Hill (Lowndes)
Prairie Mount (Chickasaw)
Prairie Point (Noxubee)
Praise Acres (Lee)
Pratts (Lee)
Prentiss (Jeff. Davis) 1,275
Prentiss Bar (Bolivar)
Pressly Place (Oktibbeha)
Preston (Kemper)
Pricedale (Pike)
Priceville (Lee)
Prichard (Tunica)
Prince Chapel (Lee)
Princeton (Washington)
Priscilla (Washington)
Prismatic (Kemper)
Progress (Jefferson Davis, Perry & Pike)
Promised Land (Sunflower)
Propst Highlands (Lowndes)
Prospect (Chickasaw, Newton)
Providence (Covington, Forrest)
Puckett (Rankin) 362
Pulaski (Scott)
Pullen (Coahoma)
Pumping Station Slough (Jefferson)
Pumpkin Center (Union)
Purnell (Leflore)
Purvis (Lamar) 2,532
Pushmataha Landing (Coahoma)
Puskus Lake (Lafayette)
Pyland (Chickasaw)

Q
Quail Valley (Oktibbeha)
Queens Hill (Hinds)
Queens Lane (Hinds)
Queensburg (Jones)
Quentin (Franklin)
Quincy (Monroe)
Quinlivan (Pike)
Quins Station (Pike)
Quitman (Clarke) 2,839
Quito (Leflore)
Quofaloma (Holmes)

R
Racetrack Bend (Perry)
Rafn (Lincoln)
Ragland (Forrest)
Rain (Lincoln)
Rainey (Jones)
Raintree Place (Hinds)
Raleigh (Smith) 1,266
Ralston (Forrest)
Ramsey Springs (Stone)
Rancho Ande (Greene)
Randall Place (Rankin)
Randalls Bluff (Winston)

Randolph (Pontotoc, Washington)
Rankin (Rankin)
Rara Avis (Itawamba)
Ras (Jasper)
Ratliff (Itawamba & Rankin)
Ratliff Ferry (Madison)
Ratliff Landing (Sharkey)
Ravine (Noxubee)
Rawhide (Harrison & Warren)
Rawles (Adams)
Rawles Springs (Forrest)
Raworth (Scott)
Rayburn Bayou (Panola)
Raymond (Hinds) 2,016
Raytown (Madison)
Red Banks (Marshall)
Red Bluff (Greene, Jackson & Marion)
Red Bud (Kemper)
Red Hill (Hinds)
Red Lick (Jefferson)
Red Rock (Sharkey)
Red Star [Loyd Star] (Lincoln)
Red Top (Pearl River)
Redbone (Warren)
Redding (Grenada)
Reddochs (Covington)
Redfish Bayou (Hancock)
Redhill (Perry)
Redwater (Leake)
Redwood (Warren)
Reed Flat (George)
Reedtown (Hinds)
Reese (Union)
Reese Landing (Coahoma)
Reform (Choctaw)
Refuge (Hunphreys, Washington)
Reganton (Claiborne)
Reid (Calhoun)
Remus (Leake)
Rena Lara (Coahoma)
Renfroe (Leake)
Renova (Bolivar) 593
Renshaw (Yazoo)
Rescue Landing (Coahoma)
Reservoir (Rankin)
Retreat (Calhoun)
Revive (Madison & Marion)
Rexburg (Washington)
Rexford (Simpson)
Rhodes (Perry)
Riceville (Harrison, Pearl River)
Rich (Coahoma)
Richardson (Pearl River)
Richburg (Lamar)
Richey (Sharkey)
Richland (Rankin) 5,794
Richland (Holmes, Humphreys)
Richmond (Lee & Rankin)
Richmond Hollow (Benton)

Richton (Madison)
Richton (Perry) 1,092
Riddle Wind Ridge (Prentiss)
Ridge (Chickasaw)
Ridgeland (Lafayette)
Ridgeland (Madison) 16,545
Rienzi (Alcorn) 358
Riggins (Monroe)
Rio (Kemper)
Ripley (Tippah) 5,623
Risher Lake (Adams)
Rising Sun (Leflore)
River Bend (Tunica)
Riverdale (Grenada)
Riverside (Forrest & Lafayette)
Riverside Junction (Sharkey)
Riverton (Coahoma)
Riverton Landing (Bolivar)
Riverview (Quitman)
Rixwood (Leflore)
Roadside (Yazoo)
Robbs (Pontotoc)
Roberts (Jasper & Newton)
Robertsville (Coahoma)
Robinhood Lakes (Rankin)
Robinson Bayou (Leflore)
Robinson Bottom (Benton)
Robinson Gin (DeSoto)
Robinson Springs (Madison)
Robinsons Junction (Wayne)
Robinsonville (Tunica)
Robinwood (Lawrence)
Rochdale (Bolivar)
Rock Branch (Newton)
Rock Creek (George, Newton)
Rock Hill (Covington, Forrest & Rankin)
Rockhill (Tate)
Rockport (Attala & Copiah)
Rocky Branch (Lamar)
Rocky Ford [Etta] (Union)
Rocky Hill (Oktibbeha)
Rocky Mount (Kemper)
Rocky Springs (Claiborne)
Rodgers (Monroe)
Rodney (Jefferson)
Roebuck (Leflore)
Rogers Bend (Jackson)
Rogerslacy (Jones)
Rolling Fork (Sharkey) 2,228
Rolling Hills (Oktibbeha)
Rolling Meadows (Hinds)
Rolling Woods (Lafayette)
Rollinson Prairie (Rankin)
Rome (Sunflower & Winston)
Romeo (Humphreys)
Roosevelt State Park (Scott)
Roosevelt State Park Lake (Scott)
Roscoe (Newton)

Master List of Mississippi Placenames

Rose Hill (Jasper & Warren)
Rose Hill Center (Madison)
Roseacres (Coahoma)
Rosebloom (Tallahatchie)
Rosebud (Leake)
Rosedale (Bolivar) 2,507
Rosedale (Oktibbeha)
Rosella (Lawrence)
Rosemary (Hinds)
Roseneath (Holmes)
Roses Bluff (Madison)
Rosetta (Wilkinson)
Ross Barnett Lake (Smith)
Ross Barnett Reservoir
    (Madison & Rankin)
Ross Branch Reservoir (Winston)
Ross Crossing (Alcorn)
Rough Edge (Pontotoc)
Round Lake (Bolivar)
Round Prairie (Rankin)
Roundaway (Coahoma &
    Sunflower)
Rounsaville (Greene)
Rouse (Lamar)
Rowen Bayou (Coahoma)
Rowlands (Pearl River)
Roxie (Franklin) 556
Roy (Clarke)
Royce (Greene)
Ruble (George)
Ruby (Leflore)
Rucks (Coahoma)
Rudyard (Coahoma)
Rufus (Rankin)
Ruleville (Sunflower) 3,049
Runnelstown (Perry)
Runnymede (Leflore)
Rural Hill (Winston)
Rush Bayou (Coahoma)
Rushing (Walthall)
Ruslor Junction (Alcorn)
Russell (Lauderdale)
Russell Lake (Lafayette)
Russellville (Warren)
Russum (Claiborne)
Ruth (Lincoln)
Rutherford (Attala)
Ryans L'argent Landing (Yazoo)
Rye (Monroe)
S
Sabino (Quitman)
Sable (Clarke)
Sabougla (Calhoun)
Sago (Sharkey)
Saint Ann (Leake)
Saint Catherine (Adams)
Saint Elmo (Claiborne)
Saint Frances Island
    Landing (Tunica)
Saint Joseph Point (Hancock)

St. Martin (Jackson)
Saint Paul (Marion)
St. Thomas (Hinds)
Saints Rest (Sunflower)
Salem (Chickasaw, Covington,
    Hinds, Leake &
    Walthall)
Sallis (Attala) 130
Saltillo (Lee) 1,915
Sam Dale State Historical
    Site (Lauderdale)
Sampson (Lauderdale)
Sanatorium (Simpson)
Sand Bayou (Hancock, Panola)
Sand Flats (Marshall)
Sand Hill (Attala, Copiah,
    Greene, Jones & Rankin)
Sand Point (Smith)
Sandalwood (Madison)
Sandard (Harrison)
Sanders Hollow (Tishomingo)
Sandersville (Jones) 894
Sandhill (Madison)
Sandhill Crane Complex Nat'l.
    Wildlife Refuge (Jackson)
Sandridge Lake (Attala)
Sandtown (Neshoba)
Sandy Bayou (Coahoma &
    Sunflower)
Sandy Creek (Tishomingo)
Sandy Hook (Marion)
Sandy Ridge (Leflore)
Sandy Springs (Itawamba)
Sandy Wash Bend (George)
Sanford (Covington)
Sansing Lake (Amite)
Santa Rosa (Hancock)
Sapa (Webster)
Sarah (Tunica)
Saratoga (Simpson)
Sardis (Copiah)
Sardis (Panola) 2,136
Sardis Dam (Panola)
Sardis Lake/Reservoir
    (Lafayette & Panola)
Sarepta (Calhoun & Claiborne)
Sartinville (Walthall)
Satartia (Yazoo) 61
Saucier (Harrison)
Sauer (Marion)
Saukum (Wilkinson)
Sauls (Lincoln)
Savage (Tate)
Savannah (Pearl River)
Savannah Grove (Lauderdale)
Savoy (Lauderdale)
Saw Grass Lake (Bolivar)
Sawmill Bayou (Hancock)
Sawmill Pointe (Jackson)
Sawyer (Montgomery)

Saxon (Marion)
Scanlon (Newton)
Scarbrough Lake (Chickasaw)
Schamberville (Lauderdale)
Schlater (Leflore) 419
Schley (Simpson)
Sciples Mill (Kemper)
Scobey (Yalobusha)
Scooba (Kemper) 519
Scotia (Adams)
Scotland (Yazoo)
Scotland Fork (Yazoo)
Scott (Bolivar)
Scott Bend (Perry)
Searcy Town (Alcorn)
Sebastopol (Scott) 276
Self Creek (Oktibbeha)
Sellers (Hancock)
Selma (Adams)
Sels Prairie (Clarke)
Seminary (Covington) 236
Senatobia (Tate) 5,428
Senatobia Lakes (Tate)
Seneca (Lamar)
Serene Lake (Lamar)
Service (Jones)
Sessions (Coahoma)
Sessums (Oktibbeha)
Seven Pines (Carroll)
Seven Springs (Hinds)
Seymour (Harrison)
Shackleford (Holmes)
Shadow Wood (Lamar)
Shady Dell (Rankin)
Shady Grove (Attala, Carroll
    Copiah, Jones, Pontotoc,
    Smith, Tippah & Webster)
Shady Oak (Covington)
Shake Rag (Chickasaw)
Shallow Point (Harrison)
Shankstown (Jefferson)
Shannon (Lee) 1,589
Shari (Union)
Sharkey (Tallahatchie)
Sharon (Jones & Madison)
Sharon Acres (Forrest)
Sharpsburg (Madison)
Shavers (Noxubee)
Shaw (Bolivar/Sunflower)
    2,283 + 7 = 2,290
Shaw Landing (Tishomingo)
Sheely Hills (Oktibbeha)
Shelby (Bolivar) 2,686
Shelby (Claiborne)
Shelby Lake (Forrest)
Shell Bluff (Greene)
Shellmound (Leflore)
Shelton (Jones)
Shepard State Park (Jackson)
Shepherd (Calhoun)

Sheppardtown (Leflore)
Sherard (Coahoma)
Sherman (Pontotoc/Union)
    449 + 171 = 620
Sherwood (Choctaw)
Sherwood Forest (Hinds,
    Lowndes, Oktibbeha,
    Rankin & Warren)
Shiloh (Clarke, Itawamba,
    Lee & Rankin)
Shipman (George)
Shivers (Simpson)
Shocco (Madison)
Shongelo (Smith)
Shoo Fly Bar (Tunica)
Shop Hollow (Tishomingo)
Shoreline Park (Hancock)
Short (Tishomingo)
Shraderville (Sharkey)
Shrock (Attala)
Shubuta (Clarke) 596
Shucktown (Franklin)
Shucktown [Fort Stephens]
    (Lauderdale)
Shuford (Panola)
Shula Grove (Lowndes)
Shuqualak (Noxubee) 578
Shutersville (Coahoma)
Sibley (Adams)
Sibleyton (Montgomery)
Sidon (Leflore) 609
Signal (Warren)
Sikes Bluff (Jackson)
Silent Shade (Humphreys)
Siloam (Clay)
Silver City (Humphreys) 322
Silver Creek (Lawrence) 192
Silver Creek Acres (Hancock)
Silver Lake (Washington)
Silver Run (Pearl River)
Silver Springs (Tippah)
Simmonsville (Pike)
Simonds (Walthall)
Simpson (Smith)
Simpson County Legion Lake
    (Simpson)
Simpson Lake (Chickasaw)
Simrall (Warren)
Sinai (Rankin)
Singleton (Leake & Winston)
Singleton Settlement (Scott)
Sipsey Fork (Monroe)
Sisloff Junction (Leflore)
Siwell (Hinds)
Six Towns (Newton)
Skene (Bolivar)
Skuna (Calhoun)
Skyline (Lee)
Slate Spring (Calhoun) 119
Slaughter Flat Landing (Jackson)

Master List of Mississippi Placenames

Slavonia (George)[1]
Slayden (Marshall)
Sledge (Quitman) 452
Sleepy Hollow (Humphreys & Lowndes)
Sloan (Madison)
Smalco (Union)
Smedes (Sharkey)
Smith (Covington, Lauderdale)
Smith Bridge (Alcorn)
Smith Point (Bolivar)
Smith Town (Stone)
Smithburg (Pike)
Smithdale (Amite)
Smithey (Lee)
Smiths (Hinds)
Smithtown (Wayne)
Smithville (Monroe) 898
Smyrna (Attala & Copiah)
Snell (Clarke)
Snow Lake Shores (Benton)
Snowdown (Tishomingo)[ext.]
Society Hill (Jefferson Davis)
Soegaard (Lawrence)
Somerville (Leflore)
Sonora (Chickasaw)
Sontag (Lawrence)
Sorghum Hollow (Alcorn)
Sorghum Lake (Grenada)
Soso (Jones) 377
South Amory (Monroe)
South Pascagoula (Jackson)
Southaven (DeSoto) 23,434
Southdale (Oktibbeha)
Southern (Forrest)
Southhaven (Warren)
Southland Park (Webster)
Southside (Sunflower)
Spanish Fort (Sharkey)
Spanish Point (Jackson)
Sparta (Chickasaw)
Spearman (Yalobusha)
Speeds Addition (Warren)
Speedtown (Covington)
Spencer (Washington)
Spinks (Kemper)
Spithead Towhead (Jefferson)
Splinter (Lafayette)
Splunge (Monroe)
Spraggins (Marshall)
Spring Cottage (Marion)
Spring Creek (Neshoba)
Spring Hill (Benton, Lafayette, Neshoba & Webster)
Spring Plains (Claiborne)
Spring Ridge (Hinds)
Springdale (Attala & Lafayette)
Springer Glade (Alcorn)

Springfield (Jefferson & Tate)
Springhill (Jones)
Springville (Pontotoc)
Squirrel Hill (Madison)
Ss Bayou (Jackson)
Stafford Springs (Jasper)
Stage (Scott)
Stallo (Neshoba)
Stalworth Camp (Greene)
Stampley (Jefferson)
Standard (Hancock)
Standing Pine (Leake)
Stanford (Monroe)
Stanton (Adams)
Star (Rankin)
Starck Hollow (Tallahatchie)
Starkville (Oktibbeha) 20,184
State College (Oktibbeha)
State Levee (Coahoma)
State Line (Greene/Wayne) 269 + 156 = 425
Steam Mill Hollow (Tishomingo)
Steele (Attala & Scott)
Steens (Lowndes)
Steep Hollow (Perry)
Steiner (Sunflower)
Stella (Pike)
Stennis NASA Space Center (Hancock)
Stephen (Clay)
Stephens (Pike)
Stephenville (Sunflower)
Sterling (Lauderdale)
Stevens (Jasper)
Stewart (Webster)
Stewarts Bluff (Pearl River)
Stillmore (Stone)
Stillons (Coahoma)
Stinett Hollow (Tishomingo)
Stinson (Lauderdale)
Stokely (Coahoma)
Stokes (Adams, Coahoma & Madison)
Stonegate (Madison, Oktibbeha)
Stoneville (Washington)
Stonewall (Clarke) 1,161
Stonewall (DeSoto & Holmes)
Stonington (Jefferson)
Story (Jefferson Davis)
Stout (Warren)
Stovall (Coahoma)
Stover (Tallahatchie)
Straight Bayou (Sharkey)
Stratton (Newton)
Strayhorn (Tate)
Street (Amite)
Strengthford (Wayne)

Stribling Lake (Madison)
Strickland (Alcorn, Oktibbeha)
Stringer (Jasper)
Stringer Bayou (Tunica)
Stringtown (Bolivar)
Strong (Monroe)
Stronghope (Copiah)
Sturgis (Oktibbeha) 181
Sucarnoochee (Kemper)
Success (Harrison)
Suffolk (Franklin)
Sugar Hill (Montgomery)
Sullivan's Hollow (Smith)
Sumbax (Marion)
Summerland (Jones)
Summertree (Madison)
Summit (Pike) 1,562
Sumner (Tallahatchie) 348
Sumrall (Lamar) 1,141
Sun (Scott)
Sunday (Coahoma)
Sunflower (Sunflower) 781
Sunflower (Prentiss)
Sunflower Landing (Coahoma)
Sunkist (Hinds)
Sunnycrest (Grenada)
Sunnyside (Leflore)
Sunrise (Forrest & Leake)
Sunrise Bayou (Tunica)
Sunrise Point (Rankin)
Sunset (Covington & Oktibbeha)
Suqualena (Lauderdale)
Swan Lake (Coahoma & Tallahatchie)
Sweatman (Montgomery)
Sweet Bay Bog (Stone)
Swift Bayou (Jackson)
Swiftown (Leflore)
Swiftwater (Washington)
Sykes (Clarke & Monroe)
Sylvarena (Smith) 111
Symonds (Bolivar)
Synagogue (Alcorn)
T
Tabbville (Chickasaw)
Tabernacle (Attala)
Tackett Lake (Leflore)
Tall Pines (Lamar)
Tallahala (Perry)
Tallahatchie (Panola)
Tallahoma (Jasper)
Tallula (Issaquena)
Talowah (Lamar)
Tamburo (Washington)
Tamola (Kemper)
Tampa (Winston)
Tandy (Tallahatchie)
Tangipahoa (Amite)

Tangipahoa Lake (Pike)
Tanglewood (Monroe, Newton & Oktibbeha)
Tarpley Neck (Washington)
Taska (Marshall)
Tatum (Amite)
Tatum Point (Lafayette)
Tavern Hill (Madison)
Tawanta (Jones)
Taylor (Lafayette) 303
Taylors (Noxubee)
Taylorsville (Hinds)
Taylorsville (Smith) 1,388
Tchula (Holmes) 2,367
Teasdale (Tallahatchie)
Teckville (Lafayette)
Ted (Smith)
Tee Bayou (Tunica)
Temperence Hill (Monroe)
Templeton Meadows (Oktibbeha)
Ten Island (Tishomingo)
Ten Mile (Stone)
Tennessee-Tombigbee Waterway (Itawamba, Lowndes, Monroe & Tishomingo)
Teoc (Carroll)
Terrace Park (Lee)
Terrapin Landing (Rankin)
Terrell (Jefferson Davis)
Terrells (Monroe)
Terrene Landing (Bolivar)
Terry (Hinds) 619
Terrys Creek (Amite)
Terry's Creek (Pike)
Terza (Panola)
Texas (Kemper & Stone)
Thaxton (Pontotoc) 483
Thayer (Lincoln)
The Basin (Yazoo)
The Breakers (Madison)
The Briars (Hinds)
The Cascades (Hinds)
The Commons (Rankin)
The Dell (Lafayette)
The Horseshoe (Jackson)
The Islands (Hinds)
The Prairie (Jackson)
Thelma (Chickasaw)
Theo (Alcorn)
Third Bayou (Jackson)
Thomas School (Pearl River)
Thomastown (Leake)
Thomasville (Rankin)
Thompson (Amite, Attala, Hinds)
Thompsonville (Hinds)
Thorn (Chickasaw)
Thornton (Holmes)
Thrasher (Prentiss)

[1] County (or counties) where place is located is in parenthesis. Number after entry indicates 1998 population estimate. County seats are in *italics*.

Master List of Mississippi Placenames

Threadville (Clarke)
Three Rivers (Jackson)
Thweatt (Attala)
Thyatira (Tate)
Tiak (Forrest)
Tibbee (Clay)
Tibbs (Tunica)
Tidewater (Madison)
Tie Plant (Grenada)
Tilden (Itawamba)
Tileville (Bolivar)
Tillatoba (Yalobusha) 124
Tillman (Claiborne & Copiah)
Tilton (Lawrence)
Timber Lakes (Rankin)
Timber Ridge (Harrison)
Timbercove (Oktibbeha)
Timberlane (Warren)
Tinnin (Hinds)
Tinsley (Yazoo)
Tinsley Oil Field (Yazoo)
Tiplersville (Tippah)
Tippah County Lake (Tippah)
Tippo (Tallahatchie)
Tippo Bayou (Leflore)
Tisdell Landing (Sharkey)
Tishomingo (Tishomingo)302
Tishomingo State Park
   (Tishomingo)
Tithelo Lake (Madison)
Tocawa (Panola)
Toccopola (Pontotoc) 163
Togo (Noxubee)
Tokio (Wayne)
Tolarville (Holmes)
Tollison (Choctaw)
Tom Bailey Lake (Lauderdale)
Tombigbee National Forest
   (Chickasaw, Choctaw
      & Winston)
Tombigbee State Park (Lee)
Tomnolen (Webster)
Ton Lake (Harrison)
Toomer (Newton)
Toomsuba (Lauderdale)
Topeka (Lawrence)
Topisaw (Pike)
Topton (Lauderdale)
Torrence (Yalobusha)
Touchstone (Simpson)
Tougaloo (Hinds)
Townsend (Kemper)
Trace State Park (Pontotoc)
Traceland (Lee)
Traceland North (Madison)
Tracewood (Lee)
Trailwood (Hinds)
Tralake (Washington)
Tranquil (Monroe)
Trapp (Neshoba)

Trasher (Prentiss)
Traxler (Smith)
Treasure Cove (Madison)
Trebloc (Chickasaw)
Tremont (Itawamba) 345
Trenton (Smith)
Tribbett (Washington)
Trinity (DeSoto & Lowndes)
Triplets Corners (Winston)
Trotter Landing (Tunica)
Trout Bayou (Hancock)
Troy (Pontotoc)
Truitt (Madison)
Tryus (Lawrence)
Tucker (Neshoba)
Tucker Place (Monroe)
Tuckers Crossing (Jones, Leake)
Tula (Lafayette)
Tully Seale Lake (Adams)
Tunica (Tunica) 1,015
Tunica Lake (Tunica)
Tunica North (Tunica)
Tupelo (Lee) 35,589
Tupelo Gum Slough (Rankin)
Tupelo Nat'l. Battlefield (Lee)
Turkey Creek (Yalobusha)
Turkey Ridge (Jasper)
Turnage Trails Camp (Hinds)
Turnbull (Wilkinson)
Turner (Tallahatchie)
Turners Flat (Bolivar)
Turners Store (Greene)
Turnerville (Jasper)
Turnetta (Madison)
Turnpike (Pontotoc)
Turon (Itawamba)
Turtle Creek (Rankin)
Tuscan (Choctaw)
Tuscola (Leake)
Tutwiler (Tallahatchie) 1,348
Twelve Oaks (Madison)
Twin (Marion)
Twin Harbor (Madison)
Twin Lake (Warren)
Twin Lakes (DeSoto)
Tyler (Pearl River)
Tylertown (Walthall) 1,992
Tyro (Tate)
Tyson (Yalobusha)

U
Una (Clay)
Union (Covington, Jones, Lee,
   Simpson & Smith)
Union (Newton/Neshoba)
   1,407 + 466 = 1,873
Union Church (Jefferson)
Union Hall (Lincoln)
Union Hill (Union)
Uniontown (Jefferson)
Unity (Attala & Lee)

University (Lafayette)
Updike (Sharkey)
Upton (Simpson)
Urbo (Newton)
Usrytown (Scott)
Ustane (Amite)
Utica (Hinds) 987

V
Vaiden (Carroll) 831
Valena (Attala)
Valewood (Issaquena)
Valley (Yazoo)
Valley Hill (Carroll)
Valley Mills (Warren)
Valley Park (Issaquena)
Valley View (Oktibbeha)
Value (Rankin)
Van Buren (Itawamba)
Van Vleet (Chickasaw)
Van Winkle (Hinds)
Vance (Calhoun & Quitman)
Vancleave (Jackson)
Vaney Bayou (Grenada)
Vardaman (Calhoun) 919
Varden (Calhoun)
Varnado (Lamar)
Vassar (Monroe)
Vaughan (George & Yazoo)
Vaughn [Cobbs] (Lincoln)
Vaughn Bayou (Jackson)
Vaughts (Pike)
Velma (Yalobusha)
Veneer (Marion)
Vennie Park (Covington)
Verba (Jasper)
Verna (Lawrence)
Vernal (Greene)
Vernon (Jasper, Madison &
      Winston)
Verona (Lee) 3,347
Vestry (Jackson)
Veto (Franklin)
Vickland (Sharkey)
Vicksburg (Warren) 27,221
Vicksburg National Military
   Park (Warren)
Victor (Bolivar)
Victoria (Marshall)
Vidalia (Harrison)
Villa Del Ray (Lamar)
Villa Ridge (Lamar)
Village Glen (Madison)
Village Square (Madison)
Villanova (Warren)
Vimville (Lauderdale)
Viney Rough (Panola)
Vinton (Clay)
Violet (Jefferson)
Virilia (Madison)
Vista Lake (Bolivar)

Volcan (Newton)
Vossburg (Jasper)
Vowell (Winston)
Vrue (Jasper)

W
Waco (Sunflower)
Waddell (Clay)
Wade (Jackson & Sunflower)
Wahalak (Kemper)
Waites (Marshall)
Wakefield (Tate)
Wakeland (Leflore)
Walden (Monroe)
Waldo (Neshoba)
Waldrup (Jasper)
Walker Siding (Tishomingo)
Walkers Gin (Clay)
Walkiah (Pearl River)
Wall Doxey State Park Marshall)
Wallerville (Union)
Wallace (Panola)
Wallace Creek (Yalobusha)
Wallfield (Pontotoc)
Wallhill (Marshall)
Wallis (Forrest)
Walls (DeSoto)
Walnut (Tippah) 561
Walnut (Quitman)
Walnut Bend (Tunica)
Walnut Creek (Tippah)
Walnut Grove (Leake) 394
Walnut Grove (Coahoma)
Walsh (Warren)
Walters (Jones)
Waltersville (Warren)
Walthall (Webster) 168
Walthall Lake (Walthall)
Waltonia (Sunflower)
Wamba (Attala)
Wanilla (Lawrence)
Wansley Bend (Rankin)
Ward (George)
Wardwell (Calhoun & Lamar)
Warren Place (Hinds)
Warrenton (Warren)
Warsaw (Marshall, Washington)
Washington (Adams)
Water Oil (Wayne)
Water Valley (Yalobusha) 3,661
Water Valley Landing
      (Yalobusha)
Waterford (Lafayette, Marshall)
Wateroaks (Hinds)
Waters Landing (George)
Waterwood (Rankin)
Watson (Marshall)
Watson Center (Marshall)
Watts Hollow (Jeff. Davis)
Waukomis Lake (Alcorn)
Wautubbee (Clarke)

Master List of Mississippi Placenames

Waveland (Hancock) 6,986
Waverly (Clay)
Waverly Ferry (Clay)
Waverly Place Landing (Adams)
Waxhaw (Bolivar)
Way (Madison)
Waynesboro (Wayne) 5,400
Wayside (Washington)
Weathersby (Simpson)
Webb (Tallahatchie) 587
Webster (Winston)
Weems (Jasper)
Weir (Choctaw) 545
Wellman (Lincoln)
Wells (Lowndes & Rankin)
Wells Town (Lamar)
Wenasoga (Alcorn)
Wesley (Monroe)
Wesson (Copiah) 1,520
West (Holmes) 166
West Biloxi (Harrison)
West Days (DeSoto)
West End (Oktibbeha)
West Enterprise (Clarke)
West Fulton (Itawamba)
West Goose Valley (Lafayette)
West Gulfport (Harrison)
West Hattiesburg (Lamar)
West Hill (Holmes)
West Hills (Lamar)
West King (Wayne)
West Lake Manor (Lamar)
West Leesburg (Rankin)
West Lincoln (Lincoln)
West Marks (Quitman)
West Pachuta (Clarke)
West Point (Clay) 8,848
West Poplarville (Pearl River)
West Port (Lowndes)
West View (Hinds)
Westfield (Holmes)
Westgate (Lamar)
Westonia Lookout (Hancock)
Westover (Lamar)
Westside (Claiborne)
Westville (Monroe & Simpson)
Westwood (Forrest, Oktibbeha & Webster)
Whaley (Carroll)
Wheeler (Prentiss)
Whiskey Chute (Bolivar)
Whispering Pines (Oktibbeha)
Whistler (Wayne)
Whitaker (Wilkinson)
White Apple (Franklin)
White Bluff (Jackson & Marion)
White Cap (Amite)
White City (Sunflower)
White Harbor (Harrison)
White House (Clarke)
White House Landing (Sharkey)
White Lake (Winston)
White Oak (Smith & Tunica)
White Plains (Harrison)
White Sand (Lowndes & Pearl River)
White Springs (Monroe)
Whitebury (Lowndes)
Whitehead (Tallahatchie)
Whites (Clay & Rankin)
Whites Creek East (Webster)
Whites Creek West (Webster)
Whites Crossing (Stone)
Whitesand (Jefferson Davis)
Whitestown (Wilkinson)
Whitfield (Jones & Rankin)
Whiting Lake (Quitman)
Whitney (Sunflower)
Whitten Town (Tippah)
Whittington Lake (Bolivar)
Whynot (Lauderdale)
Wicker (Smith)
Wickward (Newton)
Wiehe (Hancock)
Wiggins (Stone) 3,977
Wiggins (Leake)
Wildwood (Coahoma, Lee, Leflore & Monroe)
Wilkinson (Lincoln, Wilkinson)
Wilkinson Ferry (George)
Willcox (Monroe)
Willet (Washington)
Williams (Choctaw, Lincoln)
Williams Lake (Lincoln)
Williamsburg (Covington)
Williamson Bayou (Leflore)
Williamsville (Attala, Neshoba)
Willing (Copiah)
Willis (Coahoma)
Willis Slough (Pearl River)
Williston (Leake)
Willoughby (Newton)
Willow Slough (Bolivar)
Willowood (Hinds)
Willows (Claiborne)
Willowtown (Covington)
Wilmot (Washington)
Wilson (Greene)
Wilson Bayou (Quitman)
Wilson Bottom (Pontotoc)
Wilson Brake (Quitman)
Wilson Store (DeSoto)
Wiltshire (Carroll)
Wilzone (Humphreys)
Winborn (Benton)
Winbush Ridge (Alcorn)
Winchester (Wayne)
Windbush Hollow (Tishomingo)
Windham Dam (Montgomery)
Windsor Forest (Hinds)
Windsor Park (Jackson)
Windsor Ruins (Claiborne)
Wingate (Perry)
Wingfield Place (Hinds)
Winona (Montgomery) 5,647
Winston (Winston)
Winstonville [Chambers] (Bolivar) 262
Winterville (Washington)
Winterville Mounds Historical Site (Washington)
Wise Gap (Monroe)
Wisner (Smith)
Wolf (Scott)
Wolf Lake (Humphreys)
Wolf Springs (Lauderdale)
Wolfe Creek (Lowndes)
Wood Dale (Oktibbeha)
Wood Manor (Oktibbeha)
Wood Springs (Choctaw)
Woodall Mountain (Tishomingo)
Woodburn (Sunflower)
Woodcrest (Monroe)
Woodhaven (Forrest & Hinds)
Woodlake (Rankin)
Woodland (Chickasaw) 183
Woodland (Pontotoc)
Woodland Hills (Hinds)
Woodlawn (Lafayette, Lowndes, Warren & Yazoo)
Woodlawn Court (Forrest)
Woodmoor (Hinds)
Woodside (Issaquena & Washington)
Woodville (Wilkinson) 1,297
Woodwards (Wayne)
Woody Bayou (Hancock)
Wool Market (Harrison)
Woolworth (Lincoln)
Wortham (Harrison)
Wright (Bolivar)
Wrights Store (DeSoto)
Wyatt (Holmes)
Wyatt Crossing (Marshall)
Wyatte (Tate)

X

X-Prairie (Noxubee)

Y

Yale (Itawamba)
Yale Community (Pike)
Yamacraw (Pearl River)
Yankee Charlie Ridge (Tishomingo)
Yarbrough (Quitman)
Yazoo City (Yazoo) 11,941
Yazoo Junction (Yazoo)
Yazoo National Wildlife Refuge (Washington)
Yellow Bend (Bolivar)
Yellow Bluff (Jackson, Leake)
Yellow Creek (Tishomingo)
Yellow Lake (Panola)
Yocona (Lafayette)
Yocona Ridge (Yalobusha)
Yokena (Warren)
Young (Pearl River)
Youngs (Grenada)
Youngton (Warren)
Youth Center Lake (Attala)

Z

Zada [Blackwater] (Kemper)
Zama (Attala)
Zaphyr Hill (Neshoba)
Zeiglerville (Yazoo)
Zelleria (Yazoo)
Zemuly (Attala)
Zero (Lauderdale)
Zetus (Lincoln)
Zion (Pontotoc)
Zion Hill (Amite, Simpson & Smith)
Zumbro (Bolivar)

Mississippi has no places with really long names. The longest single-word placename we could find in the state was Claibornesville in Yazoo County, which has 15 letters. The longest placename in the U.S. is in the state of Massachusetts — Lake CHARGOGGAGOGGMACHAUGGAUGGAGOGGCHAUBUNAGUNGAMAUGG (48 letters). The name is a Nipmuch Indian word transated as: "You fish on your side. I fish on my side. Nobody fishes in the middle."

Selected Bibliography

HERE ARE SOME OF THE MANY PUBLICATIONS AND SOURCES THAT HAVE HELPED IN OUR RESEARCH:

American Weather Book, The, by David M. Ludlum; Houghton Mifflin Company, 1982.

Billboard Book of Top 40 Hits, The, 4th edition; by Joel Whitburn. Billboard Books, an imprint of Watson-Guptill Publications, 1989. Indexed. Later editions are available. Excellent!

Encyclopedia of Southern Culture; Many contributors; Charles Reagan Wilson & William Ferris, Coeditors; Center for the Study of Southern Culture at the University of Mississippi; The University of North Carolina Press, 1989. This huge, 1,600-page volume covers hundreds of topics about many subjects and has hundreds of biographies. Indexed.

History of Mississippi, A; Many contributors; Richard Aubrey McLemore, Chief Editor; Mississippi Department of Archives and History, 1973; University and College Press, Hattiesburg, MS. This exhaustive 1,350 page, two-volume set is the definitive reference work on the subject and offers a large bibliography and index, plus complete footnotes.

Hometown Mississippi, 2nd edition; compiled and published by James F. Brieger, Jackson, Mississippi; 1980. This excellent, detailed reference work is an exhaustive compilation of Mississippi placenames, both present and past (many towns and places are now extinct), and gives in-depth information on how these places came to be, how they got their names, and much of their early history. Research for this large volume took 15 years! Indexed.

Mississippi Matters of Fact Calenders, 1998, 1999 & 2000; Compiled by Forrest Lamar Cooper; Florence, Mississippi.

Mississippi Official and Statistical Register, 1996-2000; State of Mississippi, Eric Clark; Secretary of State, 1997. The "Blue Book," is a statistical compilation facts and information about state & local government and public officials. Indexed.

Mississippi Trivia, Vol. I, 1984, Vol. II, 1985, Vol. III, 1986, Vol. IV, 1990; Written and published by Forrest Lamar Cooper; Florence, Mississippi.

Mississippi Writers: Reflections of Childhood and Youth, Vol. I: Fiction; edited by Dorothy Abbott; the University Press of Mississippi, 1986. Indexed.

Mississippi Writers: Reflections of Childhood and Youth, Vol. II: Nonfiction; edited by Dorothy Abbott; the University Press of Mississippi, 1986. Indexed.

Wildflowers of Mississippi; S. Lee Timme; University Press of Mississippi, 1989. An authoritative guide to identifying more than 500 Mississippi wildflowers with beautiful, full-color photographs. Indexed.

World Almanac and Book of Facts 2000; World Almanac Books, an imprint of PRIMEDIA Reference Inc.; One International Blvd., Suite 630; Mahwah, NJ 07495-0017, 1999. Indexed.

JUST A FEW OF THE MANY MISSISSIPPI STATE GOVERNMENT PUBLICATIONS REFERENCED:

Annual Report, 1997-1998; Mississippi Forestry Commission; Jackson, Mississippi.

Annual Report of the State Superintendent of Education 2000 (School Year 1998-1999; **2000**; State Department of Education.

Champion Trees of Mississippi, MFC Publication No. 35, Oct. 1995 & Revision 1999; Mississippi Forestry Commission.

Facts at a Glance, July 1997-June 1998; Mississippi Forestry Commission; Jackson, Mississippi.

IHL System Profile: A Report From the Board of Trustees of State Institutions of Higher Learning; January 2000

Mississippi Agricultural Statistics, (Supplements 32 & 33), 1999; National Agricultural Statistics Service and Mississippi Department of Agriculture and Commerce; Jackson, Mississippi.

Mississippi Agriculture, 1972-1998, Dec. 1998; Agricultural Economics Department; Cooperative Extension Service; Mississippi State University

Mississippi Department of Corrections Annual Report, Fiscal Year 1999; State Dept. of Corrections

Mississippi Economic Review and Outlook, June 1999; Center for Policy Research and Planning, Mississippi Institutions of Higher Learning; Jackson, Mississippi.

Mississippi Handbook of Selected Data, 1999; Center of Policy Research and Planning, Mississippi Institutions of Higher Learning; Jackson, Mississippi.

Mississippi State Tax Commission Annual Reports, FYs Ending June 30, 1998 & June 30, 1999

Mississippi Statistical Abstract, 1997; Mississippi State University, College of Business & Industry, Division of Research; Mississippi State, Mississippi

Mississippi Trees, 1992; Clair A. Brown; Mississippi Forestry Commission; Jackson, Mississippi.

Mississippi Trivia, 1993; Compiled by Lawanda Turnage, Mississippi Division of Tourism; Jackson.

Mississippi Universities: Fall 1999 Enrollment Fact Book; The Board of Trustees of State Institutions of Higher Learning; Jackson, Mississippi.

Mississippi's Public Community and Junior Colleges, 1998-1999 Statistical Data; 2000; State Board for Community and Junior Colleges; Jackson, Mississippi.

Vital Statistics, Mississippi, 1997 & 1998; Mississippi State Department of Health; Jackson, Mississippi.

In addition, we utilized scores of publications (and Websites) from U.S. Government agencies, especially the Census Bureau. We searched hundreds of databases, newspapers and thousands of sites on the World Wide Web. We talked to many of the famous/notable Mississippians or their relatives, plus hundreds of other people in gathering information for this book.

Index of People

3 Doors Down, 335
'N Sync, 335, 440
Abbott, Dorothy, 597
Abdul-Rauf, Mahmoud, 29, 145, 239, 256, 259, 438
Abernethy, Thomas Gerstle, 366
Adams, Billy Ray, 274
Adams, Frank M., 304
Adams, Jon, 43
Adams, Robert, 365
Adams, Stan, 41
Adams, Stanley, 36
Adams, Stephen, 365
Adams, Wirt, 8
Adams, Woodrow Wilson, 263
Agnes M. Fitzhugh, 274
Akers, Garfield, 263
Akin, Susan Diane, 28, 224, 243, 254, 260, 268, 442
Alcorn, Gov. James L., 9, 11, 324, 353-54, 359, 365
Alexander, James, 263
Alexander, Karen 269
Alexander, Margaret Walker, 42, 123, 224, 243, 253, 256
Alice, Mary, 248, 254, 259, 281-83, 439
Allain, Gov. Bill, 27, 78, 124, 306, 353-54, 362, 443
Allen, Betsy, 4, 301
Allen, John Mills, 366
Allen, Mary Imogene, 268
Allen, Pete, 263
Allen, "Private" John, 13, 224, 242, 249, 255, 262
Allgood, J. Kelly, 383
Allison, Mose, 77, 244, 247, 255, 261
Alston, Alyce, 77-8, 220, 224, 241, 255, 259, 440
Alworth, Lance, 78, 130, 179, 189, 224, 243, 256, 270, 273-74, 310, 434
Ambrose, Stephen, 289, 293
Ames, Gov. Adelbert, 9, 15, 275, 303, 305, 352, 353-54, 358-59, 365
Anderson, Andy, 78, 224, 241, 255
Anderson, Brint, 263, 443
Anderson, Carolyn, 269
Anderson, Chapman Levy, 366
Anderson, Jimmy, 263, 443
Anderson, Lt. George, 314
Anderson, Rashard, 49, 273
Anderson, Rueben, 27, 78, 224, 245, 254, 259, 306, 440
Anderson, Seneca, 48
Anderson, Walter, 21, 78-9, 204, 224, 245, 250, 254
Andrews, Dana, 31, 224, 236, 252, 254, 258, 281-92, 327, 328
Andrews, Ruby, 263, 438
Applegate, Sharon, 269
Arians, Bruce, 35
Armistead, John, 224, 241, 256
Armstead, Joshie "Jo", 263, 449
Armstrong, Artie, 42-44
Armstrong, Charles, 274
Armstrong, Dick, 440
Armstrong, Henry, 29, 224, 248, 252, 256, 258, 311, 435
Armstrong, Louis, 42-44, 47, 263
Armstrong, Richard, 31, 224, 244, 252, 255, 259
Armstrong, Walter Zuber, 263, 447
Arnold, Bonner, 274
Arnold, Brad, 335
Ashmore, James, 274
Assaf, Woodie, 45, 79-80, 224, 239, 254, 260, 321, 346, 441
Ates, Roscoe, 20, 80, 224, 237, 250, 254, 259, 281-82, 284-86, 293, 328
Attaway, Ruth, 29, 80, 224, 242, 251, 254, 259, 276, 281, 283, 288-89, 291, 437
Attaway, William, 9, 28, 80, 247, 224, 251, 256, 306, 437
Austin, Kent, 158, 167
Autry, James A., 80, 224, 239, 257, 258
Avery, John, 273
Baer, Max Sr., 296
Baggett, Blaine, 80-1, 224, 243, 256, 259
Bahr, Howard, 81, 224, 243, 257, 260, 442
Bailey, Gov. Thomas L., 17, 354, 446
Bailey, Hugh Coyt Sr., 383
Bailey, Kitty Bevens, 268
Bailey, Thomas L., 16, 353, 361
Baker, Buddy, 30
Baker, Johnny, 274
Baker, "King" Ernest, 262, 441
Baker, Sam, 263, 440
Ball, Coolidge, 81, 224, 247, 256, 259
Ballard, Glen, 81, 224, 240, 255, 261, 335, 443
Ballay, Matthieu, 39
Baloni, Louis, 81, 224, 244, 254, 261
Bandy, Moe, 81, 224, 238, 255, 260, 442
Bankhead, Tommy, 263, 267
Banks, Fred, 27
Banks, Willie, 263
Bankston, Dick, 146, 263, 436
Bannerman, Charles D., 383
Barber, Frank D., 40
Barber, Walter Lanier "Red", 31, 81-2, 238, 252, 254, 258, 433
Barbour, Calvin, 274
Barbour, Haley, 26, 37, 42, 82, 224, 246, 254, 262, 318, 347, 449
Barbour, William H. Jr., 28, 33, 36
Barfoot, Van T., 82, 156, 219, 224, 241, 255, 259, 275, 305
Barginear, Myra, 268
Barksdale, Ethelbert, 366
Barksdale, Gen. William, 303, 366
Barksdale, James, 82, 182, 224, 237, 254, 259, 440
Barkum, Jerome, 273
Barnes, Prentiss, 82-3, 224, 240, 255, 260, 332
Barnes, Rod, 43
Barnes, Roosevelt "Booba", 38, 83, 200, 224, 245, 252, 254, 260
Barnes, Walter, 263, 448
Barnett, Fred, 83, 224, 241, 256, 261
Barnett, Gov. Ross R., 19-20, 27, 29, 353-54, 359, 361, 434
Barnett, William, 33
Barney, Lem, 83, 224, 241, 244, 259, 274, 310, 438
Barr, Nevada, 83, 224, 238, 257
Barranco, Johnny, 83, 224, 242, 254
Barrett, Bucky, 83-84, 87-88, 156, 165, 194, 214, 224, 245, 255, 341, 342
Barrett, Paul, 34, 35
Barrier, B. J. Jr., 18, 84, 224, 242, 249, 254, 262
Barry, Frederick George, 366
Barry, Henry W., 366
Barry, Marion Jr., 84, 224, 238, 255, 259
Barry, William Taylor Sullivan, 366
Bartling, Doby, 274
Barton, Dee, 84, 224, 245, 255, 259, 283-85, 287-88, 291, 293, 329
Basch, Harry, 84, 224, 239, 254, 259
Bass, Jack, 84, 224, 242, 257
Bass, Lance, 84, 224, 240, 255, 260, 335, 440
Bates, Leroy, 263
Batts, Will, 263, 266
Baxter, James, 274
Bayless, Luster, 84, 224, 246, 255, 261, 282, 289, 290, 291, 292, 329
Beard, Joe, 263
Beatty, Ed, 273
Beauregard, Nathan, 263
Bechtol, T. Bubba, 85, 224, 240, 254, 258, 434
Beck, Crafton, 47
Beckett, Frederic Lee, 263
Beckwith, Byron De La, 20, 31, 117, 279
Beckwith, William, 85, 118, 150, 224, 239, 254, 259, 437
Beeman, Joseph Henry, 366
Bell, Carey, 85, 224, 247, 254, 260, 263, 441
Bell, Charles, 85, 224, 247, 257, 259, 437
Bell, Earl, 263, 438
Bell, James "Cool Papa", 30, 33, 85-6, 121, 224, 241, 252, 256, 261, 274, 309, 446
Bellande, Mickey, 274
Bellard, Emory, 28
Bender, Jonathan, 273, 312
Bennett, Charles, 224, 255
Bennett, Hendley Stone, 366
Bennett, Lerone Jr., 86, 224, 246, 255, 258, 307, 435
Bennett, Marshall, 319, 348
Bennett, Tony, 273
Benson, Al, 91, 263, 440
Berry, Pamela, 36
Bertrand, Jimmy, 263, 434
Bessey, Charles C., 275, 344
Best, Willie, 20, 86, 224, 241, 250, 254, 261, 328
Bevel, Charles, 263
Bianco, Mike, 49
Biedenharn, Joseph A., 313
Biggers, Judge Neal, 33, 36

Index of People

Biggs, Thomas, 45, 86, 224, 237, 253, 254
Biggs, Verlon, 270, 271
Bilbo, Gov. Theodore G., 13, 15, 17, 353-54, 360, 444
Billingsley, William Devotie, 315
Billington, Johnnie, 263
Billiot, James, 26
Binder, Dennis, 263, 445
Black, Becky, 269
Black, J.T., 48, 86, 224, 244, 253, 256, 261, 274
Black, John C., 86-7, 224, 237, 249, 255, 260, 275, 305, 441
Blacklidge, Therman, 274
Blackman, Junior, 263, 440
Blackmore, Richard, 270
Blackwell, Bernard, 274
Blackwood, Cecil 224, 247, 255, 258
Blackwood, Doyle, 23, 224, 244, 250, 255, 258, 342
Blackwood, James, 224, 243, 255, 258, 342
Blackwood, R.W., 18, 224, 246, 249, 255, 258
Blackwood, Roy, 23, 224, 248, 250, 255, 259, 342
Blades, Courtney, 46, 49, 309
Blailock, Steve, 84, 87-88, 156, 165, 194, 224, 242, 255, 260, 341, 342, 441
Blain, Tom, 46
Blair, Jennifer Jo, 268
Blakeney, Andrew, 263, 445
Blakes, Clennon Lee "Sonny", 263
Blalock, Chester, 25
Blanchard, Felix "Doc", 88, 165, 224, 248, 256, 274
Blankenhorn, David, 88, 224, 241, 257, 259, 440
Blasingame, Don, 88, 224, 239, 256, 258, 274, 436
Blind Melon, 88, 228, 234, 334, 435, 448
Blouin, Becky, 268
Blount, David, 35
Blues Brothers, the 139, 158, 173, 189, 332-33
Bodron, Ellis, 40
Bogan, Lucille, 17, 88, 239, 225, 249, 254, 258, 433
Boines, Huston, 263
Bolton, Ruthie, 38
Bolton-Holifield, Ruthie, 88, 225, 241, 256, 260, 311
Bonnin, Ashley, 43
Bonnin, June, 43
Booker, Charlie, 263, 442
Boone, Brendon, 88-90, 225, 238, 254, 260, 442
Boone, Pete, 38
Booth, Jerry, 89, 225, 239, 252, 255, 260
Borden, Gail, 5, 6, 14, 297
Boston, Ralph, 19, 89, 225, 241, 256, 260, 274, 440
Bouldin, Marshall III, 89, 225, 244, 254, 258, 446
Bounds, Carol Diane, 268

Bowen, David Reece, 366
Bowens, Tim, 89, 199, 225, 238, 256, 261, 273
Bower, Jeff, 89-90, 225, 241, 256
Bowers, Eaton Jackson, 366
Bowers, Sam, 20, 21, 42
Bowie, Jim, 343, 445
Bowie, Resin, 343, 445
Boyd, Dennis "Oil Can", 90, 225, 246, 256, 260, 284, 440
Boyd, Eddie, 32, 90-91, 225, 247, 252, 254, 261
Boyd, Jimmy, 91, 225, 236, 254, 260, 285-86, 288-89, 291-92, 441
Boyd, Little, 263, 434
Boyette, Grant, 42, 47
Boyette, LaFrance, 268
Boyll, Jamie, 47
Boyson, Cornelius 'Boysaw", 263, 446
Bracey, Ishmon, 22, 91, 146, 225, 236, 250, 254, 258, 330
Brackeen, Denver, 274
Braddy, Bob, 48
Braddy, Pauline, 263
Bradford, Bobby Lee, 263
Bradley, Addie, 263
Brady, Bruce H., 48, 91, 225, 244, 253, 254, 258
Bramlett, Bonnie Lynn, 91, 225, 247, 255, 261, 444
Bramlett, Delaney, 91, 225, 242, 255, 261, 444
Bramlett, Leon, 274
Brandon, Gov. Gerald C., 3, 5, 352, 354, 356, 443
Brandy (Norwood), 92, 175, 225, 238, 255, 260, 286, 334, 441
Brannon, William T., 92, 225, 238, 257, 261
Branson, Jeff, 92, 225, 237, 256, 262, 446
Brantley, Jeff, 92, 101, 177, 183, 225, 244, 256
Brasfield, Rod, 19, 92, 225, 244, 250, 254, 261, 284
Brazile, Robert, 273
Brenston, Jackie, 25, 92, 106, 207, 225, 243, 251, 255, 258, 265, 334, 435
Brewer, Billy, 27, 28, 33, 44
Brewer, Gov. Earl LeRoy, 13, 16, 353-54, 360, 434
Brewer, James "Blind Jim", 263, 434
Brewer, Jim, 92-3, 225, 244, 257, 259
Brice, Alundis, 270
Brickell, Henry Herschel, 18, 93, 225, 245, 249, 255, 261
Brieger, James F., 93, 225, 240, 255, 261, 443, 597
Brien, Bobby, 274
Briggs, Eddie, 34, 44
Brooks, Columbus, 263, 440
Brooks, Danny, 41
Brooks, Leon, 263
Brooks, Melissa, 38
Brooks, Tommy, 27
Brooke, Walker, 365

Broom, Susan, 269
Broonzy, Big Bill, 19, 93, 96, 99, 126, 128, 215, 225, 242, 249, 254, 261, 266
Brown, Alice Regina, 311
Brown, Andrew, 263, 440
Brown, Arelean, 263
Brown, Bud, 270
Brown, Cheri Lynn, 268
Brown, Cleo, 263, 442
Brown, Dusty, 263
Brown, Gov. Albert G., 5, 10, 352, 344, 354, 357, 365, 366
Brown, James Thomas, 263
Brown, Jesse Leroy, 17-18, 93, 225, 246, 249, 255, 259, 306, 438
Brown, John Henry, 263
Brown, Kelly, 25, 93, 225, 245, 251, 254, 260, 283, 284, 290, 440
Brown, Ladora, 316
Brown, Larry, 93, 225, 242, 257, 262
Brown, Mel, 263, 440
Brown, Paul T., 93, 225, 241, 255, 259, 437, 449
Brown, Richard Jess Jr., 93, 225, 245, 255, 260, 440
Brown, Rickey, 273
Brown, Robert, 263
Brown, Tashaila, 316
Brown, Willie (football player), 33, 94, 146, 225, 248, 256, 262, 270-71, 274, 310, 447
Brown, Willie Lee, 263, 435
Brown, Wilson, 94, 122, 225, 249, 255, 261, 275, 305, 344, 443
Brownell, Wesley, 40, 41
Brownlee, Archie, 19, 94, 120, 225, 250, 254, 262
Bruce, Blanche K., 9, 11, 94, 225, 238, 249, 255, 365
Brumfield, Jackson, 274
Brummett, Paul, 94, 225, 243, 255, 260, 440
Brunini, Edmund L., Sr., 383
Bryan, John H. Jr., 94-5, 225, 246, 254, 262, 383, 448
Bryan, George, 46
Bryant, Bobby, 42, 95, 135, 225, 241, 253, 255, 259, 438
Bryant, Dr. Charles, 299
Bryant, Phil, 37, 348
Buchanan, Bill, 95, 225, 237, 257
Buckley, Terrell, 273
Buffett, Jimmy, 95, 160, 225, 248, 255, 261, 335, 337, 444
Buford, George, 263, 438
Bullen, Rev. Joseph, 2
Burghard, Julius, 274
Burgin, Bill, 24
Burks, Eddie, 263
Burks, Ellis, 95, 225, 245, 256, 262, 448
Burleson, Roseanne, 269
Burnett, Charles, 86, 95-6, 225, 239-40, 255, 262, 285, 288, 290, 328-29, 448

Index of People

Burnett, Chester A. (see "Howlin' Wolf")
Burns, J.C., 46
Burns, Eddie 'Guitar", 96, 225, 238, 254, 258, 433
Burns, Jimmy, 263
Burnside, R.L., 96, 225, 247, 254, 261, 443
Burrell, Ode, 96, 225, 245, 256, 259, 274
Burton, Aron, 263
Burton, Larry, 263
Busby, Cherry, 268
Busby, Jeff, 15
Busby, Thomas Jefferson, 366
Bush, Anne, 269
Bush, Guy T., 28, 96, 225, 244, 251, 256, 258, 274, 309, 433
Butler, Eugene, 35, 96, 225, 241, 252, 255, 261, 446
Butler, George, 246, 263
Butler, Jack 96, 225, 240, 257, 258
Butler, Jerry, 96, 116, 225, 248, 255, 261, 263, 332
Butler, John, 437
Butler, Ray, 41
Byrd, Adam Monroe, 366
Byrd, James D., 307, 313
Cadillac, Antoine de la Mothe, 1
Cage, Harry, 366
Cage, James, 263
Cain, Glenn, 18
Cain, Mary, 18
Cain, P.C., 346
Caldwell, Charles, 9
Caldwell, John Tyler, 35, 96-7, 225, 248, 252, 255, 262, 449
Caldwell, Isaac, 4
Calhoun, Eddie, 263, 435
Calhoun, Lee, 29, 97, 238, 225, 252, 256, 260, 311, 440
Calicott, "Mississippi Joe", 263
Cameron, "Buck", 274
Cameron, Mark, 274
Campbell, Eddie C., 263
Campbell, Lucie E., 263
Campbell, Milton (see Milton, Little)
Campbell, V. Ruth, 97, 225, 237, 250, 254, 262, 301, 344, 449
Campbell, Walter, 264
Campbell, Will D., 97, 172, 225, 243, 257, 259, 307, 347, 441
Canby, Gen. Edward, 8
Candler, Ezekiel Samuel Jr., 366
Cannon, Ace 97, 225, 240, 255, 259, 438
Cannon, Gus, 25, 97, 225, 245, 251, 254, 261
Canton Spirituals, the, 211, 342
Canzoneri, Robert, 97-8, 225, 247, 257
Capers, Charlotte, 38, 98, 225, 241, 252, 257
Carlisle, Gene, 300
Carlisle, Helen, 98, 247, 257, 262
Carlisle, Jennifer, 98, 124, 225, 247, 256, 259, 308
Carloss, Helen, 17, 98, 225, 240, 249, 254, 262, 301, 344, 449

Carmichael, Gil, 24, 25
Carmody, Jim, 26, 29, 30
Carollo, Joe Frank, 98, 225, 244, 255, 260, 334, 440
Carpenter, James Ray, 154
Carr, Harriet Jane, 268
Carr, James, 264
Carr, Sam, 98, 145, 225, 240, 254, 259, 437
Carroll, Charlotte Ann, 268
Carroll, Jeanne, 264
Carsley, Anne, 98, 225, 240, 257, 260, 440
Carson, James, 35, 45
Carter, Bo, 21, 98-9, 209, 225, 239, 250, 254, 258
Carter, Calvin, 264, 446
Carter, Hodding, Jr., 17, 23, 37, 99, 150, 225, 237, 250, 255, 321, 343
Carter, Hodding III, 99, 226, 239, 255
Carter, Joe, 270
Carter, Mary Rose, 167
Carthan, Eddie, 26
Cartlidge, Jacob, 34
Carver, Johnny, 99, 226, 247, 255, 260
Casem, Marino, 274
Cassibry, Nap, 25
Caster, Richard, 270
Caston, Charles E., 45
Caston, James "Doc", 45
Caston, Leonard, 264, 446
Catchings, Thomas Clendinen, 366
Cates, Edward L., 27
Catledge, Turner, 27, 99, 174, 226, 239, 251, 255, 258, 307
Cavalier, Robert Rene, 1
Cazalas, James K., 34
Centobia, Mario, 41
Chabert, Lacey, 99, 226, 246, 254, 261, 287, 445
Chadwick, Gene, 274
Chaffin, Ernie, 40, 99, 226, 236, 253, 255, 262, 448
Chain, Bobby L., 383
Chalmers, James Ronald, 366
Chalmers, Joseph Williams, 365
Chambers Brothers, the, 99, 436
Chambers, George, 99, 226, 245, 255, 259, 436
Chambers, Joe, 99, 226, 244, 255, 261
Chambers, Lester, 99, 226, 240, 255, 259, 436
Chambers, Willie, 99, 226, 238, 255, 259, 436
Chamblee, LaMar, 30
Chancellor, Van, 40
Chaney, James, 20, 45
Chapman, Judge Clyde, 44
Charlesworth, Clifford E., 99, 226, 248, 254, 260, 307, 440
Chatmon, Sam, 27, 99, 169, 212, 226, 236, 251, 254, 258
Cheesman, Bob, 313
Childress, Alvin, 28, 99-100, 209, 217, 226, 244, 251, 254, 260, 291, 442
Christian, Little Johnny, 264, 435

Chrowder, Rett, 49, 107, 241, 256, 310
Claiborne, Craig, 48, 100, 226, 244, 253, 255, 261
Claiborne, J.F.H., 10, 100, 226, 240, 249, 255, 261, 366, 443
Claiborne, L.M. Jr., 46
Claiborne, W.C.C., 354
Claiborne, William C.C., 3, 324, 352, 354-55
Clark, Charles, 8, 10, 352, 354, 358
Clark, Dave, 100, 226, 244, 256, 262, 447
Clark, Eric, 348, 597
Clark, Kate Freeman, 19, 100, 226, 249, 254, 259, 437, 439
Clark, Obie Earl, 440
Clark, Robert, 21, 24
Clark, Sam, 264
Clark, Tena, 100-1, 226, 248, 255, 262, 287, 292-93, 448
Clark, Will, 28, 30, 101, 177, 226, 239, 256
Clay, Bill, 35
Clayton, William Lockhart, 21, 101, 226, 237, 250, 255, 262, 307, 447
Clayton, Willie, 264, 439
Clearwater, Eddy, 101, 133, 226, 236, 254, 260, 441
Cleveland, Robert H. 'Ace" Sr., 34, 101, 226, 243, 252, 255, 259, 274, 438
Cloud, Rev. Adam, 3
Clower, Jerry, 42, 97, 101-2, 226, 245, 253, 254, 259, 307, 441, 449
Cobbs, Willie, 102, 226, 242, 254
Cockran, Carolyn, 268
Cochran, Commodore S., 22, 102, 103, 226, 237, 250, 256, 261, 311
Cochran, Hank, 102-3, 226, 243, 256, 259, 285, 339
Cochran, Roy, 26, 102-3, 226, 237, 251, 256, 261, 274, 311
Cochran, Thad, 24, 32, 36-37, 43, 102-03, 114, 155, 226, 248, 255, 261, 318, 348, 365-66, 369, 444
Coday, Bill, 264
Coe, Frederick H., 25, 103, 226, 248, 251, 256, 258, 287
Coggins, Doris, 268, 302
Cohn, David L., 19, 103, 226, 246, 250, 257, 259, 437
Colbert, Chief Levi, 4
Colbert, John, 264, 437
Cole, Harry A. Sr., 103, 168, 226, 236, 250, 255, 260, 314, 440
Cole, Suzanne, 43
Cole, W.Q., 12
Cole, West, 27
Coleman, Bracy, 40, 41, 44
Coleman, Gov. James P., "J.P.", 18, 30, 194, 202, 353-54, 361, 436
Collier, Holt, 12
Collier, James William, 366
Collier, Reggie, 25, 89, 103, 104, 220, 226, 241, 256, 258, 436
Collins, Bobby, 26, 90, 104, 108, 219, 226, 246, 256, 260, 274

The Ultimate Reference on the State 601

Index of People

Collins, Glen, 273
Collins, Louis Bo, 264, 439
Collins, Ross Alexander, 314, 366
Colmer, Bill, 155
Colmer, William Meyers, 366
Comfort, Joe, 264
Comminskey, Henry A., 104-5, 226, 236, 250, 255, 259, 275, 305, 438
Conerly, Charlie, 38, 105, 118, 209, 226, 245, 252, 256, 258, 274, 435
Conner, Gov. Martin 'Mike' S., 15, 18, 344, 353-54, 361
Cook, Frances A., 20, 105, 226, 243, 250, 255, 258, 436
Cook, Hamp, 274
Cook, James "Bus", 39
Cooke, Sam, 21, 105, 226, 237, 250, 255, 258, 334, 336, 435
Cooks, Johnie, 270, 273
Coole, Kathleen (Kathy) Ann, 268
Cooley, Archie, 29
Cooley, Frank L., 16, 105, 226, 249, 254, 261, 327, 443
Cooper, Dorree, 105-6, 226, 238, 255, 279, 281, 283-85, 287-89, 293, 329
Cooper, Forrest Lamar, 106, 226, 246, 257, 260, 440, 597
Cooper, Hank, 313
Cooper, James, 312
Cooper, Owen, 24, 28, 106, 226, 240, 251, 254, 262, 383, 448
Cooper, "Uncle" Joe, 264, 449
Cooper, Wyatt, 25, 106, 226, 244, 251, 255, 261, 445
Corhern, Hunter, 274
Cotton Blossom Singers, 106, 120, 226
Cotton, James, 92, 106, 201, 207, 226, 242, 254, 258, 334, 446
Couch, Tommy, 106-7, 226, 247, 254
Courtney, Joe, 107, 226, 246, 256, 260, 440
Covington, "Blind" Ben, 264, 435
Covington, Robert, 264, 449
Cox, Calvin, 107, 226, 248, 255, 259, 435
Cox, Diane, 269
Craft, Dwight, 36
Craft, Harry, 35, 226, 240, 252, 256, 259, 274
Craft, Willie Dwight, 41
Craig, Frank, 264, 437
Crawford, A.G., 274
Crawford, Dorothy Painter, 18
Creekmore, Hubert, 21, 107, 226, 237, 250, 257, 262, 448
Creson, Ann, 44
Crespino, Bobby, 273, 274
Crews, David, 308
Crimm, Hal, 45
Cristil, Jack, 107, 226, 248, 254, 274
Critz, Hughie, 107, 226, 245, 251, 256, 261, 274, 446
Crockett, George "G.L.", 264, 434
Crook, General, 264
Crosby, Bryant, 316
Cross, Harold, 226, 245, 257, 261, 445

Crowder, Rett, 49, 107-8, 226, 241, 256, 310
Crowley, Mart, 108, 226, 244, 255, 262, 282, 284, 286, 290, 448
Crudup, Arthur "Big Boy", 23, 108, 153, 185, 226, 244, 250, 254, 259, 436
Cruz, Antonio, 311
Cummings, George, 264, 442
Curry, Pinell, 264
Curtis, James, 264
Cutcliffe, David, 43
Cutrer, T. Tommy, 42, 108, 226, 242, 253, 254, 261
Dahmer, Ellie, 42
Dahmer, Vernon Sr., 21, 42
Dale, George, 36, 348
Dale, Roland, 33, 108-9, 226, 247, 256, 260, 274, 441
Dampier, Erick, 46, 109, 226, 242, 256, 261, 273, 346
Daniels, Quicy, 311
Danks, Dale, 27
Dantzler, Alf F., 383
Darby, Ike, 264
Davenport, Jim, 274
Davenport, Lester, 264, 444
David, William, 21, 109, 226, 246, 250, 254, 262, 327, 448
Davidson, J.W., 274
Davion, Father, 1
Davis, Alexander K., 9
Davis, Arthur "Art", 273, 274
Davis, Blind John, 28, 93, 109, 226, 237, 251, 254, 259, 438
Davis, Charles, 264
Davis, Clifton III, 30, 167, 312
Davis, Harper, 274
Davis, Janet, 312
Davis, Jefferson, 5-6, 10, 15, 85, 109, 124, 153, 179, 193, 226, 241, 249, 257, 280, 303, 319, 348, 365-66, 434, 446
Davis, "Little" Sammy, 264
Davis, Mamie, 264
Davis, Paul, 109, 226, 240, 255, 260, 338, 442
Davis, Reuben, 366
Davis, Tyrone, 107, 109, 226, 240, 255, 259, 334, 437
Davis, Walter, 20, 109-10, 226, 238, 250, 254, 259, 438
Dawkins, James Henry, 264
Day, Eagle, 274
De Chiaro, John, 110, 226, 237, 255
de La Pointe, Joseph Simon, 294
de Pineda, Alonso, 1
De Soto, Hernando, 1, 435
de Tonti, Lt. Henri, 1, 348
Deal, Borden, 28, 110, 227, 246, 251, 257, 261, 292, 444
Dean, James D., 307
Dean, Jay Hanna "Dizzy", 18, 23, 110, 227, 237, 250, 256, 274, 448
DeCell, Herman Brister, 28
DeChaunac, Sebastien, 39

Dee, Henry Hezekiah, 20
Dell, Dorothy, 15, 86, 110, 227, 237, 249, 254, 259, 328, 438
Delta Rhythm Boys, the, 264
Denley, S. Gale, 110, 227, 238, 255, 258
Dennis, Mike, 273
Denny, Walter McKennon, 366
Denton, Betty, 269
Dern, Laura, 328
DeShay, James, 264
Devenney, Matt, 30
Diamond, James H., 110-11, 176, 227, 240, 249, 255, 275, 305, 344
Diamond, William, 264, 434
Dickson, David, 3, 366
Dickson, William Alexander, 366
Diddley, Bo, 111, 227, 248, 255, 260, 267, 292, 330, 332, 336, 441
Dilworth, Marcus R., 27, 307
Ditto, Mayor Kane, 31, 32
Dixie Humingbirds, the, 267
Dixon, Hanford, 273
Dixon, Louisa, 111, 227, 239, 257
Dixon, Willie, 31, 85, 111, 153, 173, 227, 242, 252, 254, 262-64, 330, 332, 336, 448
Dixon, Wylie, 264, 435
Dobbs, C. D., 264
Dodds, Johnny, 263
Dollarhide, Jim, 111, 227, 241, 254, 259, 280, 437
Donald, David Herbert, 111-12, 227, 246, 255, 259, 308, 343
Donley, Jimmy, 264, 438
Donnelly, Mary, 268
Donovan, Joe, 36
Dorley, August, 87, 112, 157, 227, 248, 249, 255, 275, 305, 343, 344
Dorman, Harold, 29, 112, 227, 248, 251, 255, 261, 341
Dottley, John "Kayo", 274
Dougherty, Ed, 35
Douglas, Ben H., 112, 227, 238, 255, 261
Douglas, Ellen, 112, 135, 227, 242, 257, 261, 443, 448
Douglas, K.C., 24, 112, 146, 227, 247, 250, 254, 261
Douglas, Steve, 112, 227, 238, 255, 259, 437
Douglass, Mary Angie, 112, 227, 239, 251, 257, 262, 300
Dow, Peggy, 112-13, 209, 227, 239, 254, 258, 285, 435
Dowdy, Charles Wayne, 366
Dowe, Sheena Johnson, 43
Doxey, Wall, 365, 366
Drain, Charles, 264
Dugger, Suzanne, 268
Dunaway, Jim, 273, 274
Dunbar, Scott, 264
Duncan, Dr. Stephen, 5
Duncan, Michael, 281, 285, 292-93, 329
Dunlap, Bill, 113, 227, 237, 254, 260
Dunn, Aubert Culberson, 366
Dupré, Thomas, 39

Index of People

Dupree, Marcus, 26, 27, 33, 113, 163, 172, 227, 241, 257, 261, 444
Durr, Buddy, 113, 227, 245, 256, 259
Dye, John, 113, 227, 237, 254, 258, 433
Dyer, Howard, 28
Dyer, Johnnie, 264
Eagles, Charles W., 113, 227, 245, 255
Earles, Kristen, 269
Eason, B. Reeves, 19, 113, 227, 246, 249, 255, 259, 281, 285, 293, 327-28, 437
Eastland, James, 24, 28, 40, 103, 113-14, 201, 227, 247, 251, 255, 258, 318, 365
Eatem, Robert, 264
Eatmon, Narvel, 264
Ebbers, Bernard "Bernie" J., 37, 48, 114, 227, 244, 254, 347, 383
Edwards, Brad, 114, 227, 241, 256, 260
Edwards, Charles Marcus, 20
Edwards, David 'Honeyboy", 114, 227, 242, 254, 261, 265
Edwards, Jim, 21, 114, 227, 248, 250, 256, 258, 274
Edwards, Leo, 29
Edwards, Theodore "Teddy", 114-15, 227, 240, 255, 260, 440
Eichelberger, Marietta, 115, 227, 244, 251, 255, 260, 300, 435
El, Eddie, 264
Eleni, Matos, 160, 231, 238, 256, 260
Ellett, Henry Thomas, 366
Ellis, Powhatan, 365
Ellis, Tellis "T.B.", 48, 115, 227, 241, 253, 256, 262
Ellis, Tim, 115, 227, 241, 256, 260
Ellzey, Lawrence Russell, 366
Elmore, Doug, 274
Elrod, E.B. "Buddy", 42, 115, 227, 247, 253, 256, 274
Embry, Joey, 42
Emling, Ward, 115, 227, 237, 255
Emmerich, John O. Jr., 34, 115, 227, 240, 252, 255, 260, 321, 441
Engel, Lehman, 26, 116, 227, 245, 251, 254, 260, 440
Espy, Mike, 28, 31, 32, 42, 116, 227, 248, 255, 262, 306, 348, 366, 449
Etheridge, Kevin, 116, 227, 245, 256, 259, 308
Evans, Dianne, 268
Evans, Donald Leroy, 30, 43
Evans, Jo, 264
Evans, Larry, 270
Evans, Leo, 264
Everett, Betty, 96, 116, 227, 247, 255, 259, 332, 437
Evermore, John Daniel "J.D.", 116, 171, 227, 247, 254, 260, 292, 440
Evers, Charles, 22-24, 116, 227, 244, 254, 258
Evers, Medgar, 27, 31, 116-17, 194, 227, 242, 254, 258-59, 279, 301
Evers-Williams, Myrlie, 117, 227, 239, 254, 262, 301, 448
Ewert, Terry, 117, 227, 241, 256
Ezell, Ralph, 264
Fairley, Christy, 312
Fairley, Robert, 117, 227, 243, 256, 260, 441
Fanaka, Jamaa, 117, 227, 244, 255, 260, 288
Fanning, Sharon, 48
Fanton, Julie Kaye, 117, 227, 241, 255, 261, 283, 287, 443
Farragut, Admiral David G., 7
Farrior, Marvin M., 44
Fatherbee, Jane, 269
Fatheree, Jess, 274
Faulkner, John, 20, 117, 227, 245, 250, 257, 261, 443, 445
Faulkner, William, 11, 15, 18, 20, 45, 81, 85, 91, 117-18, 121, 150, 160, 214, 222, 227, 245, 250, 257, 261, 276, 281, 285, 286, 287, 289, 290, 291, 328, 337, 343, 346, 434, 443
Favors, Greg, 270
Favre, Brett, 35, 39, 40, 42, 89, 90, 104, 118-19, 220, 227, 246, 256, 261, 270, 271, 309, 444
Feathers, Charlie, 42, 119, 149, 227, 241, 253, 255, 261, 274
Featherston, Winfield Scott, 366
Felder, Ebony, 48
Felker, Rockey, 29
Felts, Nollie, 274
Ferguson, Robert B., 119, 227, 248, 255
Ferrell, Sheriff William T. 391
Ferris, William R., 113, 119-20, 157, 227, 237, 257, 262, 448, 597
Ferriss, Dave "Boo", 120, 227, 248, 256, 261, 274
Finch, Gov. Cliff, 24, 28, 353-54, 446
Finch, Francis Miles, 303
Finkelberg, Arty, 120, 227, 236, 257
Finneran, James, 29
Fisher, Doxey, 24
Fisher, Mary Beth, 269
Five Blind Boys of Mississippi, the, 19, 94, 106, 120, 227
Flamingos, the, 266
Fleming, Fisher, 269
Fleming, Horace W. Jr., 37
Fleming, Phillip Dean, 32
Fletcher, Bettye Ward, 46
Fletcher, John, 447
Florence, Mars, 231
Floyd, Frank, 264
Floyd, John, M. 120, 227, 247, 257, 260
Floyd, Lee, 274
Floyd, Tim, 43, 120, 227, 238, 256, 259, 438
Foley, Larry, 41
Fontaine, Major Lamar, 303
Foote, Gov. Henry, 10, 352, 354, 357, 365
Foote, Harry, 5
Foote, Shelby, 112, 120, 123, 227, 247, 355, 259, 343, 437
Forbert, Steve, 121, 227, 248, 255, 260, 442
Ford, Aaron Lane, 366
Ford, Ebenezer James, 12, 299
Ford, Helen, 24, 302
Ford, James "T-Model", 264, 436
Ford, Richard, 112, 121, 227, 238, 257, 260, 343, 440
Ford, Ruth, 121, 227, 242, 254, 259, 286, 290, 291, 329
Fordice, Gov. Kirk, 30-32, 34, 37-39, 41, 44, 327, 353-54
Fordice, Pat, 44
Forrest, Lt. Gen. Nathan Bedford, 303, 324, 433
Fortenberry, John, 286
Fortner, Neil, 311
Fortunato, Joe, 274
Fortune, Jesse, 264, 441
Fortune, Porter, 27
Foshee, Jane Carol, 268
Foster, Bobby, 264
Foster, Leroy, 264
Foster, Little Willie, 264, 435
Foster, Willie (baseball player), 24, 121, 227, 241, 251, 256, 309
Fountain, D. G., 383
Fountain, Pete, 87, 121, 228, 242, 255, 258, 433
Fowler, Carol, 301
Fowler, James E. Sr., 383
Fowlkes, Herman B., 217
Fox, Andrew Fuller, 366
Fox, Dorothy Elizabeth, 268
Foxworth, Jo, 121, 228, 242, 254, 262
Fraiser, Jim, 121-22, 228, 246, 257, 277-78, 280
Francis, Olin, 18, 122, 228, 245, 249, 254, 260, 285, 289
Franklin, Aretha, 122
Franklin, Rev. C.L., 122, 228, 237, 251, 257-58, 435
Franklin, William Webster, 366
Frazier, Leslie, 270
Freedman, Nicole, 311
Freeman, Cliff, 122, 228, 238, 254, 262, 308
Freeman, John D., 366
Freeman, Martin, 94, 122, 157, 228, 241, 249, 255, 275, 305, 344
Freeman, Michael, 43
Freeman, Morgan, 45, 122-23, 205, 228, 241, 254, 281-93, 327, 328, 346
Frezzell, Betty, 35
Fritts, Edward O., 123, 228, 238, 257
Frye, Theodore, 264
Fulgear, Willie, 347
Fuller, Johnny, 264, 436
Fulton, Doss Golden, 274
Fulton, Tony, 345
Funchess, John Wesley, 264
Funk, Fred, 43
Futurion, Morris, 17, 296
Gaddy, Tranny Lee, 274
Gainwell, Jackie, 48
Gaither, Frances Jones, 18, 123, 241, 228, 249, 257

Index of People

Gallagher, Cissye, 49
Gallagher, Jim Jr., 123, 228, 239, 256
Gandy, Evelyn, 123-24, 228, 244, 255, 259, 438
Gant, Joe, 40
Gatchell, K.P., 274
Gayoso, Manuel 2, 12
Geary, Cynthia Lynn, 124, 228, 239, 254, 260, 280, 283, 440
Gebhart, Smylie, 274
Geddie, Wanda Gayle, 268
Gentry, Bobbie, 124, 194, 203, 228, 243, 255, 259, 277, 337, 341
George, James Z., 11, 15, 94, 124, 170, 228, 246, 249, 255, 319, 365
Gex, Judge Walter, 37
Gholson, Samuel Jameson, 366
Ghosh, Shayon, 98, 124, 228, 246, 256, 308
Gibbon, J.C., 274
Gibbs, Jake, 35, 125, 164, 228, 247, 256, 259, 274, 438
Gibbs, Phillip L., 22
Gibson, Tobias, 2
Gilbert, Kline, 274
Gilbert, Lafayette, 264
Gilbert, William, 343, 443
Gilchrist, Ellen, 125, 228, 238, 257, 262
Gill, Mary Elizabeth, 269
Gilley, Mickey, 125, 154, 228, 239, 255, 261, 292, 337, 443
Gillom, Jennifer, 29, 46, 125, 228, 241, 256, 258, 346
Gillom, Peggy, 43, 125-26, 228, 240, 256, 258, 274, 311
Gillum, William M. "Jazz", 21, 126, 228, 244, 250, 254, 259, 439
Gilmore, Boyd, 264, 433
Glass, Gerald, 273
Goggin, Michael, 126, 199, 228, 241, 256, 259, 308
Gooch, Randy, 36
Goode, Tom "T.G.", 270, 274
Gooden, Rhonda, 301
Goodman, Al, 264, 440
Goodman, Andrew, 20, 45
Gorden, W.C., 126, 228, 242, 256, 274
Gordon, Charles "Chuck", 126-27, 228, 241, 255, 258, 292, 328, 433
Gordon, Edward Lansing Jr., 311
Gordon, Gavin, 27, 127, 228, 239, 251, 254, 258, 281-82, 289, 291-92
Gordon, James, 365
Gordon, Larry, 126-27, 228, 239, 255, 262, 281-89, 291-93, 328, 433, 449
Gordon, Phil, 127, 228, 240, 254, 260, 442
Gore, Samuel Marshall, 127, 228, 247, 254
Graham, Bonnie, 274
Graham, Charles, 16, 127, 228, 238, 249, 254, 258, 327, 434
Graham, Glen, 88, 338, 248, 255, 258, 334, 435
Granberry, Edwin Phillips, 29, 127, 228, 240, 252, 254, 260, 442
Granberry, Jeremy, 41

Grant, Gen. Ulysses S., 7, 8, 445
Grantham, Larry, 270, 274
Graves, Roosevelt, 264
Graves, Latrisha, 48
Graves, Sgt. First Class Todd, 311
Gray, Jimmy Lee, 27
Gray, Mark, 127, 228, 246, 256, 262, 448
Gray, Paul, 127, 228, 255, 260
Grayson, Walt, 80, 127-28, 228, 239, 254, 259, 437
Green, Allen, 343
Green, Cleveland, 270-71
Green, Garland, 264
Green, Henry, 264
Green, Hugh, 128, 196, 228, 243, 256, 261, 273, 443
Green, James, 38
Green, James Earl 22
Green, L. C., 264
Green, Lillian, 18, 128, 228, 248, 249, 254, 258, 435
Green, Reed, 274
Green, Willie, 43, 270-71
Greenfield, Elizabeth Taylor, 9
Greenwood, L.C., 128, 228, 244, 256, 258, 270-71, 274, 434
Gregory, General Frank, 314
Gregory, Jack, 128, 129, 228, 246, 256, 262, 274
Gregory, Paul, 23, 24, 45, 129, 228, 241, 253, 256, 262, 274
Griffin, A.C., 17
Griffin, Charles Hudson, 366
Griffin, Dick, 129, 237, 255, 259, 440
Griffin, James Richard, 228
Griffith, Shirley, 264
Grisham, John, 35, 129, 149, 169, 203, 228, 238, 257, 278-79, 284, 288-89, 293, 347
Griswold, David, 308
Grubbs, Gary, 129-30, 228, 247, 254, 258, 281, 286, 292, 433
Guice, William Wade, 38
Guion, Gov. John I., 5, 6, 343-44, 352, 354, 357, 443
Guy, Ray, 78, 104, 130, 179, 220, 228, 248, 256, 270-71, 273-74, 310
Guyton, Dr. Arthur C., 130, 228, 244, 255, 261, 315, 441
Gwin, Samuel, 4
Gwin, William McKendree, 366
Haag, Carla, 268
Haas, Toxey, 130-31, 228, 237, 255, 262, 313, 448
Haddix, Michael, 273
Haddix, Travis, 131, 228, 247, 254, 262
Hagan, James, 5
Haile, William, 366
Haining, Alice, 131, 228, 246, 254, 260, 440
Haise, Fred W. Jr., 131, 181, 207, 228, 247, 256, 258, 314-15, 434
Hale, Edwin, 13, 27, 131, 228, 237, 251, 256, 260, 274, 440
Haley, Alex, 299

Hall, Robert Samuel, 366
Hall, Emily, 269
Hall, John E., 131, 228, 243, 255
Hall, L.P., 274
Hall, Parker, 273
Hall, Rick, 264
Hallman, Curley, 29
Hamblett, Theora, 131, 228, 237, 251, 254, 261
Hamel, William L., 345
Hamer, Fannie Lou, 132, 228, 246, 251, 254, 260
Hammett, Evelyn Allen, 28, 132, 228, 241, 251, 255, 260
Hammett, William Henry, 367
Hammons, Earle W., 132, 228, 248, 250, 255, 262, 327
Handy, John, 265, 444
Handy, W.C., 10, 19, 97, 132, 139, 228, 247, 249, 254, 267, 313
Hannah, Barry, 132, 228, 240, 257, 260, 442
Hanson, Jack G., 132-33, 228, 245, 249, 255, 259, 275, 305, 344
Hapes, Merle, 273
Hardin, Glen, 274
Hardin, Mel (see Mel & Tim)
Hardwick, Phil, 133, 228, 242, 257, 260
Hardy, Dr. James D., 20, 45, 133, 228, 241, 255, 315
Hardy, Hattie Lott, 10
Harkey, Ira B. Jr., 20, 133, 228, 237, 255, 321, 343
Harkins, Greg, 133, 228, 239, 257, 260, 447
Harlem Globetrotters, the, 117, 145, 187
Harlem Hamfats, the, 267
Harmon, Clarence, 270
Harmon, George, 47
Harney, Richard, 265
Harper, Joe, 265
Harper, Robert, 133, 228, 254, 260, 277, 280, 283-84, 287-89, 292, 440
Harrell, Todd, 335
Harrington, Eddy (see Eddy Clearwater)
Harrington, Othello, 133, 229, 237, 256, 260
Harrington, Perry, 270
Harris, George E., 318, 367
Harris, Homer, 265
Harris, Lusia (see Stewart, Lusia Harris)
Harris, Thomas, 134, 195, 229, 245, 257, 281, 285, 287, 290, 293, 328
Harris, Walt, 273
Harris, Wiley Pope, 367
Harrison, Amy, 269
Harrison, David E., 134, 229, 246, 252, 255, 313
Harrison, Dr. Robert, 26
Harrison, Pat, 16, 49, 113, 134, 229, 244, 249, 255, 258, 318, 365, 367, 436
Harrison, Pat (coach), 49
Hartley, Bob, 274
Harvey, Antonio, 134, 229, 242, 256, 261, 444

Index of People

Harvey, Jim, 270
Harvey, Richard, 270
Harvey, Thomas, 313
Haskell, Sam, 134, 229, 242, 254
Hatch, Provine Jr., 265
Hawkins, Ted, 134-35, 229, 247, 252, 254, 260
Haxton, Brooks, 135, 229, 248, 257, 259, 437
Hayes, Charlie, 135, 229, 241, 256, 259, 438
Hayes, P. T., 265
Hayes, Roland, 265, 440
Haymond, Saul, 135, 229, 236, 254, 259
Haynes, George, 24
Haywood, Spencer, 135, 229, 240, 256, 261, 433
Heard, John W., 135, 213, 229, 239, 249, 255, 262, 275, 305
Hearin, Robert and Annie Laurie, 29, 30
Hebron, John, 6
Heidel, Jimmy, 135, 229, 248, 255, 258, 433
Hemingway, Judge William, 209
Hemphill, Jessie Mae, 265
Hemphill, Sidney, 265
Henderson, Chris, 335
Henderson, Jimmy, 136, 229, 241, 255, 260, 440
Henderson, Joe, 265
Henderson, John, 365
Henderson, Mike, 136, 229, 242, 255, 262, 449
Henderson, Renee, 269
Henley, Beth, 25, 136, 190, 229, 240, 255, 260, 278, 283, 288, 291-92, 327, 343, 440
Henley, John Lee, 265, 434
Henley, Marion, 274
Henninger, Brian, 46
Henry, Aaron, 24, 40, 78, 136, 229, 242, 253-54, 258
Henry, Patrick, 367
Henry, R.H., 9, 10
Henry, Robert T., 136, 229, 247, 249, 255, 259, 275, 305, 344, 437
Henson, Jim, 30, 136, 229, 245, 252, 257, 259, 283, 286-87, 291, 293, 437, 440
Herdahl, Lisa, 36
Herndon, Ty, 136-37, 137, 229, 240, 255, 260
Herrera, Anthony, 137, 229, 237, 254, 262, 448
Hester, John Jr., 30
Hester, W.E., 274
Hickerson, Gene, 274
Hickson, Charles, 23
Higby, Wilbur, 15, 137, 229, 244, 249, 254, 260, 442
Higby, William, 327
Hilburn, Judge L. Breland, 31
Hill, Faith, 45, 137, 229, 245, 255, 261, 338, 346
Hill, Lillie Mae, 265, 435

Hill, Paul, 32
Hill, Raymond, 265, 435
Hill, Rebecca, 137-38, 229, 237, 257, 446
Hill, Rosa Lee, 265
Hill, Wilson Shedric, 367
Hillery, Arthur "Art", 138, 229, 247, 255
Hilliard, Elbert R., 325
Hilton, Roy 270, 271
Hindman, Stan 273, 274
Hinds, Major Gen. Thomas, 3, 367
Hines, J. Herman, 383
Hinson, Jon C., 25, 367
Hinton, Milt, 138, 229, 242, 255, 262, 448
Hitt, Joel, 274
Hitt, Thomas S., 28, 274
Hodges, Earl, 21
Hodges, Eddie, 138, 229, 238, 254, 259, 281, 285, 438
Holden, T.D., 274
Holder, Lenena, 268
Holiday, Jimmy, 265
Holland, Steve, 345
Holliman, W.G. Jr., 138, 229, 245, 254, 261
Hollingsworth, Gerald M., 138, 229, 255, 258
Hollingsworth, Virginia Joyce, 268
Hollingsworth, William, 17, 138, 229, 238, 249, 254
Hollins, Tony, 265, 446
Holloway, J.L., 48, 296, 383
Holman, W. Henry Jr., 383
Holmes, Dr. Richard E., 139, 229, 238, 257, 261, 446
Holmes, Gov. David, 2-4, 324, 352, 354-56, 365
Holmes, Herbie, 26, 138, 229, 245, 251, 257, 262, 449
Holmes, Joe, 265, 441
Holmes, Lester, 273
Holt, Isaac, 265, 270
Holt, Morris "Magic Slim", 265, 438
Holt, Redd, 445
Holts, Roosevelt, 265
Holyfield, D.Q., 36
Honeycutt, Glenn, 139, 229, 240, 255, 258, 433
Hood, Warren A., 383
Hooker, Charles Edward, 367
Hooker, Earl Z., 22, 139, 173, 180, 229, 236, 250, 254, 258, 267, 435
Hooker, John Lee, 96, 111, 139, 142, 178, 210, 229, 244, 254, 258, 282, 330-31, 336, 435
Hooks, Maurice, 41
Hoover, Houston, 139, 229, 237, 256, 262, 449
Hopkins, Gerald, 139, 229, 248, 254, 258, 434
Hopper, Clay, 139, 229, 246, 251, 256, 259, 437
Hopson, Karen, 268
Horhn, John, 41
Horton, Big Walter, 26, 114, 139-40, 223, 229, 239, 251, 254, 259, 267

Horwitz, Harry Moses, 346
Hosemann, Delbert, 42
House, Eddie James "Son", 29, 140, 215, 229, 239, 252, 254, 261
Houston, Thelma, 140, 220, 229, 240, 255, 260, 329, 334, 440
Hovious, Junie, 42, 140, 229, 246, 253, 256, 262, 274, 448
Hovis, Guy, 140, 229, 245, 255, 262, 369, 447
Howard, Billy & Linda, 383
Howard, Moe (see Horwitz, Harry Moses)
Howe, Albert Richards, 367
Howell, Bailey, 46, 140-41, 229, 237, 256, 273-74, 346
Howell, Beth, 268
Howell, Grady Jr., 141, 229, 239, 255, 258, 434
Howlin' Wolf, Little, 154-55, 194, 243, 259
Howlin' Wolf, 83, 96, 141, 144, 146, 154, 173, 178, 200, 263, 265, 266, 330-31, 336, 448
Hubbard, Robert, 141, 229, 240, 255
Hubbard, Sylvia, 260
Hudson, Anne, 301
Huff, Luther Henry, 265
Huff, Percy, 265
Huggins, David, 46, 47
Hughes, Col. Henry, 6, 307
Hughes, Dudley J., 383
Hull, Kent, 141, 229, 237, 256, 259, 270-71, 437
Hull, Marie Atkinson, 141, 229, 245, 251, 254, 261
Humphreys, Gov. Benjamin G., 8, 10, 324, 352, 354, 358, 367, 445
Humphreys, Michael, 141, 229, 254, 259, 284, 293, 328
Humphreys, William Yerger, 367
Hunt, Alvis, 383
Hunt, Lee, 27, 29
Hunter, Lindsey, 46, 141-42, 229, 248, 256, 262, 273, 346, 447
Hunter, Lurleen, 265, 435
Hurdle, Missy, 268
Hurt, Mississippi John, 21, 142, 215, 229, 239, 250, 254, 261, 332, 336
Hutton, Doug, 33, 142, 229, 239, 256, 258, 274

Ikettes, the, 263, 266, 449
Iles, Greg, 142, 229, 239, 257
Imbragulio, John Vincent, 48, 142-43, 209, 229, 246, 253, 255, 259
Imes, Birney, 143, 229, 244, 255, 258, 435
Ingraham, Joseph Holt, 299
Ingraham, Prentiss, 12, 343
Ingram, Noah, 312
Inkster, Juli, 45
Irby, Stuart Chalmers (Jr. & Sr.), 383
Irons, Olivia, 269

Jabaley, Michael, 143, 229, 242, 255
Jackson, Andrew, J3
Jackson, Becca, 143, 229, 255, 260, 440
Jackson, Bessie, 88

Index of People

Jackson, Carl, 143, 229, 245, 256, 260, 340, 441
Jackson, Fruteland, 265
Jackson, George, 143, 229, 239, 256, 259, 265
Jackson, Harold, 274
Jackson, Jim, 265, 438
Jackson, Kate, 301
Jackson, Kirby, 270, 271
Jackson, Lee, 265, 440
Jackson, Louvette, 265, 442
Jackson Southeraires, the, 31
Jackson, Thomas, 303
Jackson, Vasti, 265, 441
Jackson, Wharlest, 21
James, D. Clayton, 143-44, 229, 238, 255
James, Elmore, 20, 114, 144, 163, 200, 229, 237, 250, 254, 261, 265-67, 330, 336
James, Michael, 265
James, Skip, 22, 144, 177, 205, 215, 229, 241, 250, 254, 258, 267, 331
Jaudon, Valerie, 144, 229, 243, 254, 259, 437
Jeanes, William, 295
Jeffcoat, Don, 144, 230, 238, 254, 259, 438
Jefferson, Wesley, 265
Jeffords, Elza, 367
Jenkins, Bert, 144-45, 230, 248, 256, 261, 274
Jenkins, Daron, 145, 230, 238, 256, 260
Jenkins, Harold (see Twitty, Conway)
Jenkins, Lucy, 269
Jernigan, Annice Ray, 268
Jesse, Austin, 263
Johanny, Jaimoe Jai, 145, 230, 242, 255, 259, 438
Johnson, Carl Ray, 34
Johnson, George Ellis, 145, 230, 241, 254, 261, 306
Johnson, Gov. Paul B. Jr., 20, 28, 353-54, 361-62, 438
Johnson, Gov. Paul B. Sr., 16, 353-54, 361, 367, 436
Johnson, J.J., 43, 105
Johnson, Jack, 145, 230, 243, 254, 260
Johnson, James, 265
Johnson, Jimmy (bluesman), 230, 439
Johnson, Jimmy (cartoonist), 145, 230, 238, 247, 254, 259, 347
Johnson, Johnny, 265, 435
Johnson, Lonnie, 173, 265
Johnson, Luther, 145, 230, 240, 254, 259
Johnson, M.C., 274
Johnson, Major Gen. Walter, 22
Johnson, Major, 265, 436
Johnson, Mayor Harvey, 41
Johnson, Oliver, 265, 434
Johnson, Pete, 29
Johnson, Robert, 16, 40, 93, 114, 140-41, 144-46, 173, 178, 182, 205, 230, 240, 249, 254, 259, 277, 280, 331
Johnson, Robert (policeman), 32, 47
Johnson, Samuel, 26
Johnson, "Signifyin' " Mary, 265
Johnson, Sylvester, 265, 439
Johnson, Tammy, 269
Johnson, Tommy, 19, 91, 146, 230, 249, 254, 261, 330
Johnson, Willie Lee, 265
Johnston, Admiral Means Jr., 29, 146, 230, 248, 252, 255, 259, 304, 437
Johnston, Gen. Albert Sidney, 7
Johnston, John, 146, 230, 238, 257, 260
Johnston, Joseph E., 303
Joiner, Robert E., 25, 319
Jolliet, Louis, 1
Jones, Albennie, 265, 438
Jones, Alfred, 311
Jones, Arthneice, 265
Jones, Calvin, 265, 437
Jones, Casey, 9, 47
Jones, David "Deacon", 146-47, 230, 248, 256, 310
Jones, Eddie "Guitar Slim", 19, 146-47, 230, 248, 250, 254, 259, 437
Jones, Hayes, 147, 230, 243, 256, 261, 311, 446
Jones, Henry, 147, 230, 243, 255, 262, 448
Jones, James Earl, 28, 96, 147, 190, 230, 237, 254, 258, 281-91, 293, 327-28, 433
Jones, Jennie, 269
Jones, John Luther (Casey), 11, 265, 447
Jones, John Allen, 34
Jones, Kevin, 163, 312
Jones, Laurence C., 13, 24, 147, 230, 247, 250, 255
Jones, Little Johnny, 265, 440
Jones, Lloyd, 34
Jones, Otha, 34
Jones, Robert Earl, 147, 230, 237, 254, 258, 283, 285, 290, 292-3, 433
Jones, Teneeshia, 49
Jordan, Daniel P., 147-48, 230, 243, 255, 261, 307, 444
Jordan, Mack A., 132, 148, 230, 248-49, 255, 258, 275, 305, 344
Jordan, Orsmond Jr., 274
Jordan, Winthrop D., 148, 230, 247, 255
Joseph, Margie, 148, 230, 256, 261, 444
Junkin, John R., 23, 24
Karls, Deborah, 269
Kearney, Belle, 14, 16, 148, 230, 238, 249, 257, 259, 301, 436
Keating, Bern, 437
Keith, Don Lee, 148, 230, 246, 255, 262
Keith, Thomas, 280
Keller, Dr. Candace, 301
Kellum, Murry 30, 148, 230, 248, 252, 256
Kelly, John T., 26
Kelly, Patrick, 30, 148, 230, 245, 252, 257, 262, 307, 448
Kemp, Charlie, 307
Kenn, E.D., 17
Kenna, Doug Jr., 274
Kent, Willie, 265
Kessinger, Donnie, 38, 274
Key, Al and Fred, 15, 314
Keyes, Tyrone, 270
Keys, Randolph, 149, 230, 240, 256, 258, 273
Khayat, Edna, 269
Khayat, Robert C., 33, 149, 230, 240, 255, 261, 274
Kidd, Kenneth, 265, 443
Kilrain, Jake, 311
Kimball, Jeanette S., 265
Kimbrough, Junior, 42, 96, 149, 230, 243, 253-54, 259
Kinard, Frank "Bruiser" 28, 149, 183, 230, 246, 251, 256, 261, 274, 310
King, Albert, 31, 149, 154, 155, 189, 230, 240, 252, 254, 259, 263, 331, 333, 336, 439
King, B. B., 14, 27, 45, 91, 131, 135, 141, 144, 149-50, 154-55, 158, 178, 187, 191, 201, 215, 221, 230, 245, 254, 259, 263, 265-66, 331, 336, 346, 439
King, Dr. Martin Luther, 21
King, John Wayne, 35
King Louis XIV, 1
King, Melinda, 268
King, Riley B. (see King, B. B.)
Kinsey, Lester, 265
Kirby, Pat, 150, 230, 246, 255, 262
Kirkland, Bo, 265, 449
Kitchens, Ann, 269
Kitchens, John, 41
Kizart, Lee, 265
Kizart, Willie, 265
Knobloch, Fred, 150, 230, 240, 256, 260, 338, 440
Knox, Ike, 274
Koury, Leon Z., 31, 150, 230, 247, 252, 254, 259, 437
Krebs, Sylvia Howell, 150, 230, 244, 256, 260, 274, 436, 440
Kyle, John Curtis, 367
La Salle, 1
Lacy, Reubin, 265
Ladd, Diane 150, 230, 248, 254, 260, 278-79, 281-83, 286-87, 289-90, 292, 328, 442
Ladner, Wendell, 274
Lake, William Augustus, 367
Lamar, L.Q.C., 10, 11, 150-51, 155, 230, 245, 249, 254, 319, 324, 348, 365, 367, 443
Lambert, A.C. "Buttch", 151, 230, 256, 259, 274
Lambert, Flavous, 24
Lance, Major, 32, 151, 230, 239, 252, 256, 262, 334
Landsberg, Johan, 39
Lane, Ernest, 265, 435
Lang, Gene, 270, 271
Langham, Billy Morris, 26
LaSalle, Denise, 107, 143, 145, 151, 230, 243, 256, 260, 433
Lattimore, William, 3
Laurie E. Parker, 178, 243, 257, 258

Index of People

Law, John, 1
Le Moyne de Bienville, 1
Leach, Wardell, 41
Leake, Gov. Walter 3, 324, 352, 354-55, 356, 365, 435
Leake, Lafayette, 265
Lear, Jimmy, 274
Leathers, T. P., 343
Leavell, Jerome F., 152, 230, 238, 255, 258, 434, 443
LeDoux, Chris, 152, 230, 246, 256, 258, 434
Lee, George W. Sr., 265
Lee, Hal, 29, 152, 230, 238, 252, 256, 260, 274
Lee, Hubert L., 152-53, 230, 237, 251, 255, 275, 305, 344, 437
Lee, Robert E., 8
Lee, Stephen Dill, 12, 153, 230, 245, 249, 255
Lee, Warren, 265
Leflore, Chief Greenwood, 2, 3, 8, 37
Lemon, Chet, 153, 230, 238, 256, 260, 440
Lenoir, J.B., 21, 153, 230, 240, 250, 254, 260, 266, 442
Leslie, Sam, 153, 230, 243, 251, 256, 261, 274
Lester, Tom, 153, 230, 245, 254, 260, 281
Lett, Leon, 270, 271
Levitz, Jacqueline, 34
Lewis, Clarke, 367
Lewis, D.D., 270-71, 274
Lewis, Jerry Lee, 78, 91, 125, 153-54, 181, 230, 246, 256, 285, 336-37, 339, 438
Lewis, R. V., 34
Lewis, Walter "Furry", 230, 238, 251, 254, 259, 437, 153
Lightfoot, Alexander, 265, 443
Liles, Jack, 48
Liles, Richard, 335
Lindsay, Ken, 154, 230, 242, 256, 274
Lindsey, Jake W., 154, 230, 240, 251, 255, 275, 305, 344
Lipps, Louis, 273
Lipscomb, Dr. Eddie, 345
Lipscomb, Lacey, 43
Lipscomb, Raney, 43
Lipsey, Elaine, 269
Little, Freddie, 33, 154, 230, 240, 256, 261, 274, 444
Littlejohn, Johnny, 200, 266
Litton, Kari, 268
Livingston, Dick, 48
Livingston, Dora Lee, 268
Lloyd, Edgar, 25
Loesch, Margaret, 300
Lofton, James Harol, 274
Logan, Andrew, 265
Lomax, Alan, 114, 120, 140, 162, 173
Lomax, John A., 17, 155, 230, 245, 249, 257, 259
London, Mel, 265
Longino, Gov. Andrew H., 11, 16, 353-54, 359-60, 442

Longstreet, Augustus B., 9, 151, 155, 230, 245, 249, 255, 443
Longstreet, James, 18
Lott, Senator Trent, 32, 36-37, 43, 46, 155, 223, 230, 246, 255, 259, 318, 348, 365, 367, 369, 438, 444
Louwerens, Monica, 268
Love, Clayton, 265, 266
Love, William Franklin, 367
Love, Willie, 265
Lowe, Mundell, 84, 88, 155-56, 165, 194, 214, 230, 240, 255, 260, 281, 284, 291, 342, 440
Lowe, Peggy, 25, 26, 44
Lowrey, Bill Green, 367
Lowry, Beverly, 156, 230, 243, 257, 437
Lowry, Gov. Robert, 10, 13, 353-54, 359
Luandrew, Albert (see Sunnyland Slim)
Lucas, Aubrey, 37
Lucas, Jack H., 82, 156-57, 219, 231, 238, 255, 275, 305, 438
Lucas, Leigh, 269
Lucas-Tauchar, Frances, 46
Luckett, Celeste Hill, 268
Lum, Ray, 24, 157, 231, 242, 251, 257, 261, 445, 448
Lunceford, Jimmie, 17, 157, 218, 231, 241, 249, 257, 259, 437
Lynch, Charles, 4-5, 344, 352, 354, 356
Lynch, John R., 9, 16, 157, 231, 244, 249, 255, 306, 367
Mabus, Gov. Ray Jr., 29, 31, 353-4, 363
Mack, Brandy, 49
Macon, John Wesley, 265
Maddox, Carl, 274
Madison, Earlean, 44
Madison, James J., 157, 231, 241, 249, 255, 275, 305
Magee, Mollie, 268
Magee, Sterling, 265, 442
Magee, Sylvester Mack, 23, 303
Maghett, Samuel (see Magic Sam)
Magic Sam, 22, 101, 154, 157-58, 231, 238, 250, 254, 259, 438
Mahmoud, Abdul-Rauf, 29, 224, 273, 438
Majure, Jim, 158, 231, 244, 252, 257-58
Maley, Helaine, 308
Malone, Dumas, 28, 158, 213, 236, 251, 255, 258, 343, 433
Malone, Jeff, 27, 46, 141, 158, 231, 242, 256, 273, 346
Malone, Tom, 158, 231, 241, 255, 259
Maloney, J. Con, 383
Mangum, Kris, 158, 231, 243, 256, 260, 441
Mannery, Jerry, 169
Manning, Archie, 26-27, 30, 46, 158, 164, 167, 231, 239, 256, 258, 273-74, 346
Manning, Danny, 159, 231, 241, 256, 259, 438
Manning, Kathy, 268
Manning, Vannoy Hartrog, 367
Mara, Thalia, 159, 214, 231, 242, 254
Marlette, Doug, 347

Marquette, Father Jacques, 1
Mars, Florence, 159, 236, 255, 261, 444
Marsallis, Jim, 270
Marschalk, Andrew, 2-3
Marsh, Mike, 41
Martin, Chief Phillip, 23, 47, 159, 239, 261, 383, 444
Martin, General W. T., 343
Martin, Joe, 265, 436
Martin, Michael, 43
Martin, Phillip, 231, 257
Martin, Roy, 159, 231, 237, 251, 257
Martino, Angel, 38
Mary, Alice, 224
Massey, Patra, 269
Masterson, Bat, 311
Mathews, Burnita Shelton, 301
Matos, Eleni, 160, 238, 260, 440
Matthews, Aubrey D., 160, 231, 245, 256, 261, 444
Matthews, Joseph W., 5, 7, 352, 354, 357
Mattox, Martha, 15, 160, 231, 241, 249, 254, 261, 281, 327, 443
Matulich, Robin, 269
Mauney, Gary W., 34
Maxwell, John, 160, 231, 242, 255, 260, 440
May, Christy, 268
May, Joe, 265, 441
May, Shondra, 28
Mayo, Richard, 231
Mayo, Richard E., 160, 243, 254, 260, 442
McAfee, Fred, 270
McAllister, "Deuce", 46, 49, 105, 158, 310
McAnally, Mac, 160, 231, 242, 256, 258, 337
McCafferty, Jim, 160, 231, 239, 257, 262, 447
McCain, Admiral John Sidney, 17, 160-61, 231, 243, 249, 255, 261, 304, 434
McCarthy, "Babe", 274
McCarty, H. F. Jr., 383
McCarty, Oseola, 38, 45, 97, 130, 161, 194, 231, 239, 253, 255, 259, 346, 438
McClamroch, Christine Joyce, 268
McClellan, Eric, 161, 231, 247, 254
McClennan, Tommy, 96, 114, 266, 449
McCleon, Dexter, 270
McClinton, O.B., 29, 161, 231, 240, 251, 256, 261
McCoy, Herschel, 161-62, 231, 255, 260, 286, 289, 292, 329, 442
McCoy, Charlie, 91, 146, 209, 266, 330, 440
McCoy, Dr. A. H., 306
McCoy, Joe, 266
McCrady, John, 21, 161-62, 231, 244, 250, 254, 258, 434
McDaniel, Luke, 31, 162, 231, 237, 252, 256, 259
McDaniel, Otha Ellas Bates (see Diddley, Bo)
McDowell, Jimmie, 2311, 239, 255, 258, 274, 434

Index of People

McDowell, "Mississippi" Fred, 23, 96, 106, 142, 162, 200, 231, 237, 250, 254
McDyess, Antonio, 162-63, 231, 244, 256, 261, 273, 311, 445
McElroy, Bucky, 274
McElroy, Sollie Jr., 266, 332, 438
McGaughey, Neil, 45, 163, 231, 246, 253, 257, 261, 443
McGee, Keffer, 40
McGehee, Daniel Rayford, 367
McGill, Gary, 33, 113, 163, 231, 240, 256, 261, 312
McGill, Lawrence B., 327
McGraw, Tim, 137
McGregor, Mike, 163, 231, 240, 253, 257, 261, 443, 448
McGuffee, Kimberly, 268
McHugh, Robert P., 42, 163, 231, 238, 253, 255
McIntosh, David, 274
McKee, George Colin, 367
McKeen, Allyn, 274
McKey, Derrick, 163, 231, 246, 256, 260, 442
McLain, Frank Alexander, 367
McLaurin, Gov. Anselm Joseph, 11, 13, 353-54, 359, 365
McLean, George, 37
McLellan, Bill, 45
McLemore, Richard Aubrey, 597
McMillan, Terry, 49
McMurry, Lillian, 45, 163, 217, 231, 248, 253, 255, 261, 445
McNair, Caleb, 43
McNair, Eric, 17, 163, 231, 240, 249, 256, 260, 274, 442
McNair, Steve, 33, 35, 41, 48, 163-64, 231, 238, 256, 261, 270-71, 273, 309, 442
McNutt, Alexander Gallatin, 4, 5, 344, 352, 354, 356
McPhail, Evelyn, 37, 39, 42, 164, 231, 241, 253, 257-58, 318, 433
McPherson, Tim (see Mel & Tim)
McRae, Chuck, 33, 35, 44
McRae, John Jones, 5, 9, 352, 354, 358, 365, 367
McRae, Richard D. Sr., 164, 231, 238, 254, 260, 383, 440
McRaney, Gerald, 164-65, 231, 244, 254, 258, 288
McRaney, Patricia Ann, 268
McWilliams, Elsie, 28, 165, 231, 241, 251, 256, 259, 339
McWilliams, Henry, 231, 255
McWilliams, Skeets, 88, 156, 165, 194, 214, 243, 260, 341-2
McWilliams, Thomas "Shorty", 40, 165, 231, 241, 252, 256, 260, 274, 442
McWillie, Gov. William, 6, 9, 352, 354, 358, 367
Mead, Cowles, 3
Mead, Lynda Lee, 19, 165, 231, 240, 254, 268, 443

Meadows, Glenda, 130, 268
Means, Jimmy, 25
Meiners, Don, 44
Mel & Tim, 133, 164-65, 228, 231, 255-56, 259, 439
Mellen, Frederic F., 165, 231, 244, 252, 257, 261, 446
Meredith, James, 20, 21, 29, 165, 194, 231, 242, 254, 260, 440
Meriwether, David, 3
Merrell, H. T. "Dick", 165-66, 231, 237, 251, 254, 259, 314
Merrins, Eddie, 166, 231, 243, 256, 260, 274
Mickal, Abe, 274
Middlecoff, Cary, 42, 166, 231, 236, 253, 256, 274
Miley, Major Gen. William "Bud", 40, 166, 231, 248, 253, 255, 314
Miller, Dicenzo, 163, 166-67, 231, 242, 256, 259, 312
Miller, Edmund Sr. & Hannah, 44
Miller, Howard, 45
Miller, Jim, 270
Miller, John Ramsey, 167, 231, 246, 257, 259, 437
Miller, Mary Carol, 167, 231, 239, 257, 259
Miller, Mulgrew, 167, 231, 243, 255, 259, 437
Miller, Romaro, 158, 167, 231, 245, 256, 261, 312
Mills, Mary Bentley, 274
Mills, Mary Linda, 268
Millsaps, Reuben W., 13, 167-68, 231, 241, 249, 255, 259
Milner, Dumas, 31, 103, 168, 231, 237, 252, 254, 258, 440
Milton, Little, 83, 97, 102, 155, 221, 230, 244, 259, 331
Mims, Crawford 33, 168, 231, 239, 256, 258, 274, 434
Ming, Hoyt Lester 28, 168-69, 232, 246, 251, 255, 258
Minter, Iverson, 266, 438
Mississippi Mass Choir, the, 107, 169, 232, 342
Mississippi Sheiks, the, 99, 169, 209, 232
Mitchell, Emil and Kelly, 344
Mitchell, James, 266
Mitchell, Judith Paige, 169, 232, 247, 255
Mitchell, McKinley, 266, 440
Mitchell, Willie (baseball player), 23, 169, 232, 248, 250, 256, 261, 274, 309
Mitchell, Willie, 169, 232, 238, 255, 258
Mobley, Mary Ann, 19, 45, 169-70, 232, 238, 254, 258, 268, 284-85, 302, 346, 434
Moffett, Tim, 163
Mohamed, Ethel Wright, 31, 169-70, 232, 246, 252, 254, 259, 433
Monaghan, Bilbo, 32, 170, 232, 242, 252, 256, 258, 274, 310, 433
Money, Hernando De Soto, 13, 170, 232, 244, 249, 255, 259, 365, 367

Montgomery, G.V. "Sonny", 32, 34, 36-7, 170-71, 232, 243, 255, 260, 318, 367, 442
Montgomery, Isaiah T., 10, 11
Montgomery, Johnny, 274
Montgomery, Keith, 33
Montgomery, Marion, 266, 443
Montgomery, Mary Lacy, 269
Montgomery, Robbie, 266
Montgomery, Wilbert, N. 38, 171, 232, 245, 256, 259, 437
Moody, Anne, 171, 232, 245, 254, 258, 300
Moody, George, 30
Moore, Allen, 30
Moore, Archie, 42, 171, 232, 248, 253, 256, 258, 281, 282, 284, 288, 311
Moore, Brew, 439
Moore, "Bucky", 274
Moore, Charles Eddie, 20
Moore, Dorothy, 171, 232, 246, 256, 260, 333, 440
Moore, Johnny (actor)
   (see Evermore, John Daniel "J.D.")
Moore, Johnny (bluesman), 266
Moore, Johnny B. (Belle), 266, 435
Moore, Mike, 29, 32, 35, 39, 43, 348
Moore, Milton A. Jr., 266
Moore, Royce and Barbara, 37
Moree, Don, 36, 41
Morgan, James Bright, 367
Morgan, Jessie Wynn, 268
Morganfield, McKinley
   (see Muddy Waters)
Morphis, Joseph L., 318, 367
Morphis, Mary Kathrine, 269
Morris, George, 274
Morris, Sylvester, 49, 273
Morris, Willie, 45, 171-72, 232, 248, 253, 257, 260, 266, 278, 280, 343-44, 346, 440, 449
Morrison, Jordan, 308
Morrissey, Thomas M., 345
Mortensen, Davis K., 172, 232, 240, 254
Moseley, Alice, 172, 232, 248, 254, 258, 433
Moulds, Eric, 172-73, 232, 243, 256, 260, 273, 441
Mounger Billy II, 297
Muddy Waters, 22, 27, 85, 90-91, 96, 101-02, 106, 111, 139-41, 145-46, 155, 171, 173, 180, 200-01, 204, 220-21, 223, 261, 265-66, 331, 336, 435
Muldrow, Henry Lowndes, 367
Mullens, Maianne, 269
Mullins, Chucky, 30
Murphree, Gov. Dennis H., 16, 17, 353-54, 360-61
Murphy, Dot, 173, 232, 245, 256, 260, 274
Murphy, Ed, 29
Murphy, Gene, 173, 232, 246, 256, 258, 435
Murphy, Matt, 173, 232, 248, 254, 261, 332

Index of People

Musgrove, Gov. Ronnie, 34-35, 37, 46, 44-8, 319, 348, 353-54, 363
Musselwhite, Charlie, 173, 232, 237, 254, 260, 330, 440
Myer, Buddy, 23, 173, 232, 239, 250, 256, 259
Myer, C.S., 274
Myers, David, 266
Myers, Louis, 32, 173, 232, 245, 252, 254, 258
Myers, Robert L., 266
Myers, Sam, 143, 200, 263, 266, 440
Myricks, Larry 29, 274
Nabers, Benjamin Duke, 367
Nail, Pamela 173, 232, 243, 254, 302
Nassour, Ellis, 174, 232, 246, 257, 262, 448
Nave, Barbara Jan, 268
Neal, Frances E., 174, 232, 242, 254, 258, 282, 328, 434
Needham, Theresa, 266
Neill, Robert Hitt, 437
Nelson, Ben, 174, 232, 243, 256, 258
Nelson, Jack, 174, 232, 246, 255, 343
Nelson, Norman Crooks, 383
Neville, Thomas Jr., 274
Newman, C. B. "Buddie", 23, 29, 447
Newman, Joseph W. "Joe", 28, 174, 232, 242, 255
Newman, Lester C., 41
Newton, Dennis Howell, 44-45
Neyland, Leedell W., 174, 232, 243, 257, 259
Nichols, Alvin, 266
Nighthawk, Robert, 267
Niles, Jason, 367
Nix, Jack C., 274
Nixon, Walter L., 28, 29
Noble, Billy, 28
Noble, C.R., 274
Nobles, Lennie Josephine, 268
Nobles, Lewis, 32-34, 36
Noel, Gov. Edmond F., 12, 14, 353-54, 360, 441
Nordan, Lewis, 174-75, 232, 244, 257, 259
Norris, William J. "Dead Eye", 266, 438
Norwood, Sam, 266, 436
Norwood, Willie "Ray-J" Jr., 175, 232, 254, 260, 441
Null, Ralph, 175, 232, 239, 257, 258, 435
Nunn, Freddie Joe, 273
Nutt, Dr. Haller Rush, 3, 4, 325
Nutter, Patrick, 48
Nye, Carrie, 175, 232, 254, 259, 283, 285, 290, 291, 437
O'Keefe, Jerry, 34
O'Neal, Frederick, 31, 175, 232, 244, 252, 254, 258, 288, 290-91
Oakman, Jack H., 175, 232, 241, 257, 261
Ogunkoya, Falilatu 38, 175, 232, 248, 256
Ohr, George, 13, 175, 232, 242, 249, 254, 258, 434
Olive, Milton L. (III), 111, 175-76, 215, 232, 247, 250, 255, 275, 305, 344, 441
Oliver, Tami, 269
Ormond, Loren, 269
Orr, Simeon, 346
Oswalt, Roy, 311
Otis, Clay, 264
Ott, Paul, 176, 232, 245, 257, 260, 441
Overby, Charles L., 176, 232, 245, 254, 260, 440
Overstreet, Paul, 176, 232, 239, 256, 261, 338
Overton, David, 24
Owen, Garry, 176-77, 232, 238, 249, 254, 258
Owens, Ginny, 342
Owens, Jack, 40, 176-77, 232, 247, 252, 254, 258, 267
Pace, Jim, 177, 232, 237, 256, 260, 442
Palmeiro, Rafael, 28, 101, 177, 183, 232, 245, 256
Palmer, John N. Sr., 177, 232, 242, 254, 258, 383, 436
Parish, Laura, 269
Parker, Alton N., 254, 314, 436
Parker, Calvin Jr., 23
Parker, Dave, 177, 232, 241, 258, 256, 440
Parker, Herman, 178
Parker, J.D., 274
Parker, Laurie E., 178, 232, 243, 257, 258
Parker, Little Junior, 23, 154, 177, 232, 239, 250, 254, 258, 435
Parker, Mike, 32, 34, 37, 42, 44-46, 319, 348, 367
Passeau, Claude, 178, 233, 239, 256, 262, 274, 448
Pates, Robert Eugene, 26
Patridge, Stewart, 40, 46, 105
Patterson, Aubrey Burns, 383
Patterson, Carolyn Bennett, 178, 232, 240, 255, 440
Patterson, Steve, 37
Patton, Charley, 15, 114, 139-40, 146, 178, 215, 232, 240, 249, 254, 259, 266, 331, 436
Patton, Jimmy, 274
Patton, Ricky, 270
Paul, Suzanne, 269
Payton, Walter, 27, 28, 29, 38, 45, 78, 118, 130, 152, 171, 178-79, 188-89, 232, 243, 253, 256, 258, 270, 273-74, 310, 435
Pease, Henry Roberts, 365
Peavey, Hartley D., 42, 179, 232, 248, 254, 260, 383, 442
Peavey, Hartley D. & Melia M., 383
Peavey, Melia M., 42, 179, 383
Peck, Wiley, 273
Pemberton, Gen. John C., 7, 179, 232, 243, 249, 255
Pennbaker, John, 106
Peoples, John A. Jr., 27
Pepper, Hugh, 274
Perce, Legrand Winfield, 367
Percy, Le Roy, 365
Percy, Walker, 30, 112, 122, 179, 232, 241, 252, 257, 343
Percy, William Alexander, 16, 180, 232, 241, 249, 257, 259, 437
Perkins, Al, 266, 434
Perkins, "Pinetop", 180, 201, 221, 232, 242, 254, 258, 332, 336, 433
Perkins, Ray, 180, 232, 247, 256, 261, 270-71, 274, 442
Perkins, Thomas (see Wayne, Thomas)
Perlozzo, Sam, 33
Perry, Vernon, 180, 232, 245, 256, 260
Peters, Ben, 180-81, 233, 242, 256, 259, 339, 437, 438
Peterson, Col. Teresa M., 315
Peterson, Donald H., 131, 181, 207, 233, 246, 254, 262, 314
Pettus, Gov. John J., 5, 6, 9, 352, 354, 357
Peyton, Annie C., 11, 181, 233, 245, 249, 255, 260
Pharr, Cynthia Ivy, 300
Phenix, Perry, 270
Phillips, Brewer, 266
Phillips, J.M., 274
Phillips, Sam, 92, 97, 106, 139, 153, 162, 180, 185, 221
Phillips, Thomas Hal, 181, 233, 246, 255, 258, 277, 282, 287, 289, 292, 328, 436
Phillips, William, 308
Philpot, Cory, 181, 233, 241, 256
Pickering, Charles W. (Chip), Jr., 37, 348, 353, 362, 367, 369
Pillers, Lawrence, 270, 271
Pillow, George D., 274
Pippin, Hollis, 32, 181, 233, 240, 252, 254, 260, 278, 440
Pitchford, Lonnie, 42, 181-82, 233, 246, 253, 254, 260, 441
Pittman, Bob, 25, 46, 182, 233, 248, 254, 260, 307, 440
Pittman, Gail, 308
Pittman, John A., 182, 233, 246, 252, 255, 258, 275, 305, 344, 434, 437
Pittman, Shane, 269
Pittman, William II, 182, 233, 239, 256
Pitts, Kimber Lynn, 269
Plummer, Bruce, 270
Plummer, Franklin E., 367
Plumpp, Sterling D., 182-83, 233, 237, 257-58, 435
Plunkett, Robert, 266, 433
Poindexter, Gov. George, 3, 5, 352, 354-56, 365, 368
Polanski, Frank, 182-83, 233, 246, 255
Polanski, Sandra, 183, 233, 241, 255, 259
Polk, Ron, 24, 45, 101, 177, 183, 233, 237, 256, 274
Pollard, Rev. Frank, 23
Pollock, Oliver, 345
Pool, Rainey, 44-5
Poole, Barney, 274
Poole, J. E. "Buster", 32, 183, 233, 244, 252, 256, 259, 274, 437
Poole, Ray Smith, 274
Pope John Paul II, 110, 127, 133, 169
Pope, Donna Marie, 268

Index of People

Pope, Maj. Gen. John, 7
Porter, Betty Jane, 268
Porter, David, 266
Porter, Gene, 266
Portera, Malcolm, 41, 183,-84 233, 237, 255, 262, 448
Posey, James, 26
Posey, Pam, 49
Posey, Parker, 184, 233, 247, 254, 283, 289, 292-93, 329
Pott, Johnny, 274
Powell, Eugene, 266, 447
Power, John Logan, 10
Powers, Gov. Ridgely C., 9, 13, 353-4, 359
Prather, Judge Lenore L., 26, 27, 46, 184, 233, 245, 254, 262, 448
Prentiss, Seargent Smith, 368
Presley, Elvis, 15, 18, 23-24, 45, 78, 80, 87, 91, 102, 108, 112, 119, 138-39, 162-63, 169, 171, 178, 184-85, 202, 221, 233, 236, 251, 256, 262, 277-79, 282-83, 285-92, 302, 327, 335-36, 339-40, 346, 436, 439, 443, 446-8
Presley, Lisa Marie, 81, 185
Prewitt, Cheryl, 185, 233, 238, 254, 258, 268
Price, Brig. Gen. George B., 185, 233, 244, 255, 260, 306, 440
Price, Joe, 307, 442
Price, Leontyne, 27, 45, 123, 131, 185-86, 233, 238, 256, 260, 306, 346, 440
Price, Major Gen. Sterling, 7
Price, Toni, 269
Price, Will A., 20, 186, 233, 250, 255, 260, 285, 293, 328-29, 441
Pride, Charley, 29, 112, 119, 181, 186, 221, 233, 239, 256, 261, 339-41
Primer, John, 266
Primos, Will, 186, 233, 238, 254, 260, 296, 440
Pritchett, Kelvin, 273
Pruett, Marion Albert, 25-26, 44
Pryor, James "Snooky", 186, 233, 245, 254, 260
Puckett, Patricia (Patsy) Alice, 268
Pugh, Virginia Wynette (see Wynette, Tammy)
Pulliam, Trent, 186-87, 233, 243, 256, 259
Pushamataha, Chief, 2, 3, 471
Pyron, W. H., 25, 319
Quin, Percy Edwards, 368
Quitman, Gov. John A., 4-6, 324, 343, 352, 354, 356, 368
Radvanyi, Janos, 187, 233, 244, 257
Ramsey, Claude, 28
Ramsey, James, 266, 440
Rankin, Christopher, 368
Rankin, John Elliott, 368
Rankin, William Edward, 347
Rasberry, Eddie, 266, 440
Raspberry, William, 187, 233, 246, 255, 261
Rayborn, Tena, 269
Read, Charles W. "Savez", 344

Redd, William Silas, 187, 233, 247, 254, 261, 444
Reed, Jack R., 29, 383
Reed, Jimmy, 24, 91, 139, 154-55, 187, 233, 244, 251, 254, 258, 263, 267, 330, 336
Reed, Samuel Leroy, 30
Reed, Thomas Buck, 365
Reed, Walter, 187-88, 233, 245, 260, 274, 442
Reese, Andy, 21, 188, 233, 237, 250, 256, 262, 274, 447
Reese, Donald, 273
Reeves, Anna, 188, 233, 239, 256, 262
Reid-Petty, Jane, 42, 188, 233, 241, 253, 255, 260, 442
Renfroe, Joe, 274
Rent, Clyda S., 29, 47
Revels, Hiram, 9, 12, 37, 188, 233, 245, 249, 255, 306, 365
Revon, Nick, 274
Rice, Darius, 49
Rice, Floyd, 270
Rice, Jerry, 27, 30, 33, 35, 38, 40, 78, 89, 118, 130, 178-79, 188-89, 199, 212, 233, 246, 256, 258, 270-71, 273, 310
Rice, "Sir" Mack, 189, 233, 247, 256, 258, 333, 336
Rice, Tom, 146, 189, 233, 247, 255, 260, 280, 440
Richard, Willie, 266
Richards, Beah, 189-90, 220, 233, 242, 253-54, 262, 281, 283, 285-87, 328-29, 448
Richardson, Gloster, 270, 271
Richardson, Willie, 270, 274
Riggins, Richard, 266, 447
Riley, Virginia Helen, 268
Rimes, LeAnn, 190, 233, 256, 261, 244, 338, 444
Ritchie, Jim, 190, 233, 240, 257, 258, 434
Rivers, Boyd, 266
Robbins, John Richard "Rick", 36, 41
Roberts, Alton Wayne, 45
Roberts, Annie Laurie, 268
Roberts, Eric, 136, 190, 233, 240, 254, 258, 281-82, 284-90, 292, 327, 434
Roberts, Matt, 335
Roberts, Robert Whyte, 368
Robinson, E. B. Jr., 383
Robinson, Fenton, 266
Robinson, George, 266, 433
Robinson, Jackie, 130, 139
Robinson, James, 190-91, 233, 244, 256, 260
Robinson, Rev. Cleophus, 266, 434
Robertson, Robbie Lee, 268, 435
Robertson, Ronnie, 308
Robinson, Stanley L., 274
Rocha, Alex, 49
Rodgers, Jimmie 11, 15, 28, 40, 191, 233, 244, 249, 256, 261, 336, 339, 442
Rogers, Jimmy, 40, 140, 173, 191, 233, 241, 253, 254, 261

Rollins, Charlemae, 25, 191, 233, 242, 251, 257, 262, 449
Rommerdale, Eric H., 191
Rommerdale, Rick, 233, 247, 255
Roosa, Stuart A., 191-92, 233
Roosevelt, President Theodore, 12-13
Rosby, Rasberry, 266, 441
Rosecrans, Maj. Gen. William, 7
Ross, Captain Isaac, 346
Ross, Craig, 192, 233, 247, 256, 262, 308
Ross, Isaiah "Doctor", 192, 233, 246, 254, 262, 446
Ross, Jim Buck, 36, 45, 127, 133, 192, 233, 243, 253, 255, 261
Rosser, Dr. James C. Jr., 192-93, 233, 245, 255, 261
Routh, Beatrice Louise, 30, 43
Rowland, Dunbar, 12, 16, 141, 192-93, 233, 244, 249, 255, 261
Rudd, Dwayne, 273
Ruffin, David, 30, 193, 233, 237, 252, 256, 262, 332, 336, 442
Ruffin, Jimmy 193, 233, 240, 256, 258, 332
Runnels, Gov. Hiram G., 2, 4, 37, 352, 354, 356
Runnels, Jeanna, 269
Rush, Bobby, 107, 155, 193, 221, 233, 247, 256
Rush, Dr. Leslie V., 16, 29, 193, 233, 238, 251, 255, 260, 316, 442
Rush, Otis, 101, 145, 149, 158, 173, 193, 233, 240, 254, 261, 266, 330, 331, 444
Rushen, Tom, 266
Rushing, Felder, 2333, 242, 257, 259, 439
Russell, Donna Hild, 28, 193, 233, 242, 254, 258, 302
Russell, Gov. Lee M., 14, 16, 344, 353-54, 360, 443
Russell, Irwin, 10, 346, 445
Russell, John Richard, 20, 315
Russell, Johnny, 193, 194, 233, 237, 256, 261, 442
Ryan, Paddy, 311
Sack, Lester M., 274
Saggus, James S., 34, 193-94, 233, 243, 252, 255
Sain, Oliver, 155, 266
Salter, Sidney L., 194, 233, 237, 255, 261, 444
Sanders, Jill, 269
Sanderson, Joe Frank Sr., 42, 194, 234, 243, 253, 254, 260, 383, 440
Sandifer, John, 266, 438
Sane, Dan, 266
Sargent, Winthrop, 2-3, 352, 354-55
Satterfield, Louis, 266
Saunders, Wallace, 308
Savage, David, 266, 437
Savage, Father William, 1
Savarese, Ralph, 346
Sawyer, R. Tom, 274
Saxton, Bob, 84, 88, 156, 165, 194, 214, 234, 243, 255, 341, 342, 443

Index of People

Scarborough, Chuck, 194, 234, 247, 254
Scarborough, Sandra, 269
Schwerner, Michael, 20, 45
Scott, Arminta, 268
Scott, Buddy, 440
Scott, Don, 194, 247, 251, 234, 256, 262, 274, 311, 448
Scott, Esther Mae, 266
Scott, George "Boomer", 195, 234, 239, 256, 259, 437
Scott, Gov. Abram M., 4, 11, 27-28, 34, 40, 48, 89, 97, 324, 344, 352, 354, 356
Scott, James Jr., 266, 441
Scott, Kenneth, 266
Scott, W.A., 307
Scruggs, Irene, 266
Sea, Johnny, 195, 234, 242, 256, 259
Seal, Leo W. Jr., 383
Seale, James Ford, 20
Seals, Leon, 270, 271
Seawright, James L. Jr., 195, 234, 241, 254, 260, 435, 437, 440
Seawright, Joseph P., 195, 234, 244, 257, 259, 437
Seawright, Toni, 29, 268
Seay, Virgil, 270, 271
Sellers, John, 266, 435
Semon, Larry, 15, 195, 234, 242, 249, 254, 262, 292, 327, 448
Sesay, Ansu, 43
Sewell, Dr. Patrick, 315-16
Shackleford, Steven Jr., 98, 124, 308
Shafter, John, 43, 49
Shaman, Floyd D., 195, 234, 248, 254
Shanks, Carolyn C., 44, 300
Sharkey, Gov. William L., 8, 9, 324, 344, 352, 354, 358
Shaw, Billy, 195, 234, 248, 256, 261, 274, 443
Shaw, Charles, 266
Shaw, Delbert Allen, 42
Shaw, Eddie, 264, 266
Shaw, Sherard, 35
Shelby, Beau, 266, 439
Sherman, Gen. William T., 7, 8, 346
Sherrill, Jackie, 195-96, 234, 248, 256, 310
Sherry, Margaret & Vincent, 29
Shoemake, Larry Wayne, 36
Short, Eugene, 273
Short, J. D., 266
Short, Purvis, 196-97, 234, 244, 256, 259, 273-74, 312, 438
Shower, Hudson, 266
Shows, Ronnie, 42, 368-9
Simino, Judith Marion, 268
Simmons, Alberta Jean, 264
Simmons, Jean F., 197, 234, 241, 255
Simmons, "Jumpin' Gene, 197, 234, 242, 256, 262, 447
Simmons, Sherye, 268
Simon, Carolyn, 268
Sims, Henry, 266
Singleton, Otho Robards, 368
Sisson, Thomas Upton, 368

Skelton, Amy Jo, 269
Skutnik, Lennie, 26
Slade, Prescilla D., 197, 234, 245, 255, 261, 449
Slater, Elizabeth, 47
Slater, Jackie, 197, 234, 241, 256, 260, 270, 440
Slaton, James D., 197, 234, 239, 250, 255, 260, 275, 305, 344, 440
Sledge, Justin, 40, 42
Sloan, Steve, 26
Small, Torrance, 198, 234, 242, 256
Smith, Larkin I., 368
Smith, Patrick D., 234
Smith, Tony, 273
Smith, Ben Barrett, 47
Smith, Bessie, 435
Smith, Bill, 266, 435
Smith, Brad, 88, 234, 246, 255, 258, 334, 435
Smith, Byther, 266, 442
Smith, Calvin, 26-27, 198, 234, 236, 256, 258, 311
Smith, Connie, 119, 204, 337
Smith, Don, 270
Smith, Frank E., 40, 198, 234, 238, 253, 255, 261, 368
Smith, Frederick W. 198, 234, 243, 254, 260
Smith, Gen. A. J., 8
Smith, Hamilton, 16, 198, 234, 246, 249, 255, 261, 327
Smith, Hazel Brannon, 20, 32, 198, 234, 237, 252, 255, 321, 343
Smith, Janet Marie, 198-99, 234, 248, 254, 260, 440
Smith, Jimmy, 89, 199, 234, 238, 256, 270
Smith, John D., 30
Smith, Kimberly R., 126, 199, 234, 245, 256, 308
Smith, L.T. 199-200, 234, 244, 256, 260, 274
Smith, Larkin, 29
Smith. Leo, 266, 440
Smith, Lucius, 266
Smith, Madeline Theresa, 268
Smith, Moses, 266
Smith, Patrick D., 200, 246, 257, 260
Smith, Rachel Ann, 268, 302
Smith, Riley H., 274
Smith, Seth, 312
Smith, Symba, 200, 234, 242, 254, 259, 281, 286, 438
Smith, Tad, 274
Smith, Warren, 200, 234, 237, 251, 256, 260
Smith, Willie Mae Ford, 32, 200, 234, 242, 252, 254, 261
Smitty, John "Big Bad", 200, 234, 238, 254, 262, 267, 448
Smothers, Albert, 266
Smothers, Otis "Big Smokey", 266, 441
Snedden, James, 275, 344
Solomon, King S., 267, 440
Soriano, Heather, 268

Southern, Willie B. Jr., 44
Spann, Lucille, 267
Spann, Otis, 22, 146, 180, 200-01, 223, 234, 239, 250, 254, 260, 267, 440
Sparks, Aaron, 267
Sparks, Milton "Lindberg", 267
Speakes, Larry, 130, 201, 234, 245, 255, 258, 435
Spears, Britney, 201, 234, 248, 256, 337, 441
Speed, Lake, 201, 234, 237, 256, 260, 440
Speed, Leland R., 383
Speight, Jesse, 365
Spell, Lester, 36, 348
Spencer, Elizabeth, 201-02, 234, 243, 257-58, 434
Spencer, James Grafton, 368
Spencer, William O., 274
Sperber, Julie Ann Cook, 42
Spight, Thomas, 368
Spinks, Johnny R. "Jack", 32, 202, 234, 237, 252, 256, 262, 274
Spinks, W.L., 6
Spires, Arthur "Big Boy", 173, 267, 449
Spires, Benjamin "Bud", 177, 267
Spry, Ralph, 27
Spurlock, Michael, 312
Spurrier, Topp, Mildred, 235
St. Pè, Gerald J., 383
Stacey, Billy, 202, 234, 243, 256, 262, 273-74
Stackhouse, Houston, 267, 448
Stamps, Terrance D., 44
Staples, Cleotha, 202, 267, 333
Staples, Pervis, 202, 267, 333
Staples, Roebuck "Pop", 202, 234, 248, 256, 262, 292, 333
Staple Singers, the, 91, 333, 336
Starks, Duane, 273
Starnes, Mike, 202, 234, 238, 254
Stennis, Senator John C., 23, 26, 29, 34, 45, 171, 172, 176, 194, 202, 234, 243, 252, 255, 260, 318, 346, 365, 436
Stephen, Adams, 365, 366
Stephens, Hubert Durrett, 365, 368
Stepney, Billy, 267, 438
Stetson, John B., 345, 436
Stevens, Rose Budd
  (see Willoughby, Mamie Davis)
Stevens, Stella, 202, 234, 246, 254, 262, 281, 283-84, 287-91, 329, 449
Stevens, Thomas Roger, 88, 234, 247, 255, 262, 334, 448
Stevenson, Arthur Lee, 267
Stewart, Lisa, 202, 234, 243, 256, 260, 441
Stewart, Lusia Harris, 133, 203, 210, 234, 238, 256, 260, 274
Stewart, Tonea, 203, 234, 254, 259, 437
Stewart, Zach, 33
Still, William Grant, 25, 203, 234, 241, 251, 254, 262, 306, 448
Stinson, Katherine, 165
Stockdale, Thomas Ringland, 368
Stokes, Benjamin M., 2

Index of People

Stone, Gov. John, 9-11, 324, 353-4, 359
Stone, H.L., 274
Stovall, Jewell, 267
Strange, Don, 47
Strawberry, Darryl, 26
Street, James Howell, 18, 203, 234, 246, 249, 257, 260
Streeter, Sarah, 267
Stribling, Roger, 24
Stringer, Jessie, 47
Stringfellow, Savante, 46, 48-49
Strong, Barrett, 203, 234, 237, 256, 262, 332, 336, 448
Strother, Percy L., 267, 448
Stroud, W.D., 274
Stuart A. Roosa, 191, 243, 252, 254
Stuart, Clyde, 274
Stuart, Marty, 203-04, 234, 246, 256, 261, 337, 444
Stuckey, Henry, 267
Suber, Billie Scott, 274
Suggs, James Douglas "J.D.", 267, 440
Sullivan, Charles, 25
Sullivan, John L., 10, 311
Sullivan, Judge Michael, 48
Sullivan, R.B., 274
Sullivan, W.R., 274
Sullivan, William Van Amberg, 365, 368
Sumlin, Hubert, 204, 234, 247, 254, 259, 437
Summers, Jimmy, 267
Sumner, Cid Ricketts, 234, 257
Sumner, Cid Ricketts, 22, 204, 234, 245, 250, 257-58, 291, 329, 434
Sumrall, Nan, 204, 234, 247, 256, 259, 268, 438
Sunnyland Slim, 34, 114, 156, 204, 234, 244, 252, 254, 262, 264
Swain, Vivian Brown, 301
Swalm, Dave C., 204, 234, 247, 255
Swan, Frank, 267, 433
Swayze, T.K., 274
Sweet, Judge Denise, 47
Sykes, Frances Carlisle, 268
Talbott, Eugenia Ann, 204, 24, 243, 254, 261, 444
Tartt, Donna, 204-05, 234, 248, 257, 259, 437-38
Tate, Arthur, 25
Taulbert, Clifton L., 204-05, 234, 238, 257, 259, 288, 437
Taylor, Eddie, 263, 267
Taylor, Gary Eugene, 368
Taylor, Gene, 32, 348, 369, 444
Taylor, "Hound Dog", 136, 154, 205, 234, 240, 250, 254, 261, 266, 443
Taylor, Jim, 270
Taylor, Melvin, 267, 440
Taylor, Mike, 205, 234, 243, 256, 274, 442
Taylor, Mildred D., 205, 234, 245, 257, 260, 289, 440
Taylor, Pete, 274
Taylor, W. A., 383
Taylor, W. C. Jr., 205, 235, 247, 256, 259, 342, 438

Teasdale, Martha Annette, 268
Temple, Johnnie "Geechie", 146, 205, 235, 246, 250, 254, 258, 434
Terrell, Marvin, 274
Terry, Doc, 267
Thames, Byron, 205, 235, 240, 254, 260, 281, 285-86, 440
Therese, Sister Josephine, 383
Theriot, Herbert, 205, 235, 245, 256
Thibodeaux, Kathy, 205, 235, 247, 254
Thibodeaux, Keith R., 205-06, 235, 248, 254
Thierry, John, 273
Thomae, Dr. Keith, 37
Thomas, Charles S. Sr., 35, 205-06, 235, 246, 252, 256, 262, 274
Thomas James "Son", 31, 144, 206, 235, 246, 252, 254, 259
Thomas, Mamie, 301
Thomas, Neville Jr., 274
Thomas, Rufus, 206, 221, 235, 239, 256, 258
Thomas, Treg, 38, 105, 206, 235, 239, 256, 261, 444
Thomas, Willie B., 267
Thompson, A. Sonny, 267
Thompson, Bennie, 32, 42, 348, 368-9
Thompson, Charles W., 267
Thompson, Dave, 267, 440
Thompson, Jacob, 348, 368
Thompson, Larry A., 206, 235, 243, 255, 258, 435
Thompson, Mac, 267
Thompson, Mayor Allen C., 21
Thompson, Richard, 41
Thorn, Paul, 206, 235, 242, 256, 340
Till, Emmett, 18
Tillman, Lewis, 29, 270
Todd, Howell, 35
Topp, Mildred Spurrier, 20, 206, 236, 250, 257
Topp, Sarah Ann, 268
Tornes, Kenneth, 36, 41, 48
Townsend, Andre, 270-71
Townsend, Henry J., 267
Treen, David, 28, 314, 445
Treen, Joseph Paul, 28, 206, 240, 251, 255, 261, 314, 445
Treen, Joseph Paul, 235
Tribbett, First Lt. Karen Fuller, 315
Trippett, Frank, 42, 206-07, 235, 242, 253, 255, 258, 435
Trotter, James Fisher, 365
Truly, Richard, 28-30, 131, 181, 195, 206, 235, 247, 254, 259, 314-15, 436
Tuberville, Tommy, 33, 35, 43
Tuck, Amy, 46-47, 348
Tucker, Gov. Tilghman M., 5-6, 352, 354, 357, 368
Tudury, Henry Jetton, 13, 304
Turk, M.K., 38, 108
Turner, Gerald, 33
Turner, Ike , 91-92, 106, 155, 207, 217, 235, 247, 256, 258, 265, 267, 333, 334, 435

Turner, Ike & Tina, 189, 207, 221, 333, 336
Turner, Jo Ann, 269
Turner, Othar, 267
Turner, Roscoe, 15, 22, 207-08, 235, 245, 250, 254, 258, 314, 436
Twitty, Conway, 31, 181, 208, 235, 244, 252, 256, 259, 282, 288, 290, 339, 437
Tyler, Adele Brown, 340
Tyler, Dan, 208, 235, 247, 256, 260, 340, 441
Underwood, 'Bear", 274
Underwood, Dr. Felix J., 14-16, 19, 37, 235, 208, 247, 250, 255, 261
Unser, Del, 208-09, 235, 248, 267, 274
Valery, Joseph Jr., 267, 448
Van Dorn, Maj. Gen. Earl, 7
Van Eaton, Henry Smith, 368
Van Hook, B.O., 274
Van Zant, Ronnie, 24
Vann, Thad, 274
Vardaman, Gov. James K., 12, 15, 344, 353-54, 360, 365
Varnado, Christine M., 126, 199, 209, 235, 237, 256, 308
Vaughan, Marvin, 312
Vaught, Johnny, 108, 168, 183, 209, 235, 240, 256, 274
Veal, C. V., 267
Venable, William Webb, 368
Venson, "Playboy", 267
Vest, Dorothy, 274
Vick, Newet, 3
Vick, S.B., 209, 235, 240, 251, 256, 258, 274, 309
Vidal, Jose, 343
Vincent, Johnny, 142, 200, 209
Vincent, Monroe, 267, 448
Vinson, Mose, 267, 439
Vinson, Walter, 99, 146, 169, 209, 235, 237, 250, 254
Voss, Henry, 4
Wade, Ernestine, 27, 100, 209, 217, 235, 243, 251, 254, 260, 440
Wade, Margaret, 34, 203, 209, 235, 248, 252, 256, 260, 274
Waits, Freddie 29, 210, 235, 240, 252, 255, 260, 440
Walker, Brig. General George, 48
Walker, Charles C. 210, 235, 248, 256, 259, 309, 438, 444
Walker, Clifford, 20
Walker, Dontae, 210, 235, 237, 256, 260
Walker, George F., 383
Walker, Gerald, 25, 210, 235, 239, 251, 256, 259, 274, 309, 438
Walker, Harry "The Hat", 45, 210, 235, 246, 253, 256, 261, 444
Walker, James, 267
Walker, Johnny, 267
Walker, LeRoy Jr., 383
Walker, Prentiss Lafayette, 368
Walker, Rebecca, 210, 235, 257, 260, 289, 440

Index of People

Walker, Robert John, 365
Walker, Robert J., 5, 267, 348, 435
Walker, Shirley, 48
Wallace, Bobby, 210-11, 235, 245, 256, 440
Waller, Bill L. 23, 353-4, 362
Waller, Bill L. Jr., 41
Walls, Wesley, 29, 41, 211, 235, 239, 256, 258, 270
Walls, Paul Sr., 37
Walston, Ray, 211, 235, 248, 254, 260, 281, 283-84, 286-93, 327, 328, 440
Walter, Little, 173
Walters, Carl Sr., 274
Walters, J. E. "Fred", 274
Walthall, Edward Cary, 365
Walton, Wade, 267
Ward, Charlie, 274
Ward, Sela, 211, 235, 242, 254, 260, 284-85, 287-89, 293, 442
Ware, Hayes, 267
Washington, Leon, 267, 440
Waters, Wyatt, 211, 235, 239, 254, 434
Watkins, Harvey "Pop" Sr., 33, 211, 248, 252, 256, 258, 342, 434
Watson, Brad, 212, 235, 243, 257, 260, 442
Watson, Libby Rae, 212, 235-36, 254, 261, 444
Watts, Joann, 269
Watts, Louis Thomas, 267
Wayne (Perkins), Thomas, 23, 212, 235, 243, 250, 256, 258
Weatherly, Jim, 212, 235, 239, 256, 261, 444
Weathersby, Carl, 267, 440
Weatherspoon, Clarence, 46, 104, 212-13, 220, 235, 244, 256, 258, 273, 346
Weaver, Little Robert, 267, 446
Webb, "Boogie" Bill, 146, 235, 267
Webb, J.L. "Skeeter", 28, 213, 247, 251, 256, 260, 274
Webb, Jimmy, 273
Webb, Peggy, 213, 235, 238, 257, 261, 302
Webb, Ted. J. Jr., 213, 235, 247, 255, 262, 449
Weddington, H.G., 274
Weese, Norris, 34, 213, 235, 243, 252, 256, 270
Welborn, Ira C., 235, 238, 249, 255, 260, 275, 305, 344, 440
Wells, Ben, 267, 441
Wells, Guilford Wiley, 368
Wells, John "Boogie Daddy" 267, 448
Wells, Mary Ann, 214, 235, 242, 257, 258
Wells, Paul L., 274
Wells, Lloyd, 84, 87-88, 156, 165, 194, 213-14, 235, 240, 255, 259, 341-42, 438, 440
Wells-Barnett, Ida Bell, 15, 214, 235, 242, 249, 254, 259, 439
Welty, Eudora, 23, 45, 112, 118, 120, 121, 123, 157, 159, 188, 214, 222, 235, 240, 257, 260, 343, 346, 440, 445

Wesley, John, 449
Westerfield, Louis, 38, 214, 235, 243, 252, 255, 260, 306
Westerfield, Scott, 46
Wheat, Roy M., 21, 176, 214-15, 236, 243, 250, 255, 261, 275, 305, 344, 440
Wheaton, James, 442
Whitaker, Jessica, 43
White, Artie, 107, 215, 235, 240, 254, 262-63, 448
White, Bukka, 24, 215, 235, 247, 251, 254, 259
White, Frank, 215, 235, 244, 256, 259, 437
White, Gov. Hugh L., 15, 18, 21, 353-4, 361, 448
White, Willye B., 20, 215, 235-6, 256, 260, 274, 311
Whitehead, J. C., 383
Whitfield, Gov. James, 5, 9, 344, 352, 357, 435
Whitfield, Gov. Henry L. 14, 344, 353-4, 360, 435
Whitney, Davey Jr., 48, 274
Whitsett, Carson, 267, 440
Whitten, Jamie L., 30-32, 35, 215-16, 235, 240, 252, 255, 258, 318, 368
Whittington, William Madison, 368
Whitworth, Rev. M. J., 6
Wicker, Roger, 32, 37, 215, 318, 348, 368-9
Wilbanks, Hilliard A., 275, 344
Wilborn, Nelson, 267
Wilburn, Barry, 270
Wilburn, Tom, 215-16, 235, 248, 256, 258, 435
Wilcox, John A., 368
Wilhelm, George, 275, 344, 437
Wilke, Mike, 35
Wilkerson, Suzanne, 269
Wilkins, Joe Willie, 267
Wilkins, Robert, 29, 216, 237, 251, 254, 259, 438
Wilkins, Robert, 235
Williams, Arthur "Mississippi", 267, 446
Williams, Ben Ames, 18, 216, 236, 239, 249, 257, 260, 441
Williams, Big Joe, 26, 114, 173, 216, 236, 251, 254, 258, 330, 336
Williams, Blanche C., 301
Williams Brothers, the, 267
Williams, Bunny, 267
Williams, Douglas, 267
Williams, Frank, 236
Williams, Frank, 31, 169, 216, 242, 252, 256, 261
Williams, "Gentle" Ben, 216, 235, 244, 256, 262, 274, 449
Williams, Gov. John Bell, 21-22, 27, 353-4, 362, 368, 445
Williams, Greg, 270
Williams, Hank, 337
Williams, J. Kelley, 383
Williams, Joe, 236
Williams, John Sharp, 14-15, 148, 216, 236, 243, 249, 255, 318, 365. 368

Williams, John 270
Williams, Kandace, 268
Williams, Lee, 267
Williams, Milan B., 216, 236, 239, 255, 261, 333
Williams, Pearlis, 267, 437
Williams, Richard, 30, 38-39, 43
Williams, Robert, 2, 4, 44, 352, 354-5
Williams, Spencer Jr., 100, 209, 216-17, 236, 242, 250, 254
Williams, Tennessee, 13, 17-18, 27, 116, 150, 200, 217, 236, 239, 251, 255, 258, 276, 279, 282, 284, 286, 288-89, 291, 328, 343, 435
Williams, Thomas Hickman, 365
Williams, Thomas Hill, 365
Williams, Thomas Lanier, 217
Williamson, Allen, 19
Williamson, Harriet G., 316
Williamson, Sonny Boy II, 21, 85, 163, 211, 217, 221, 236, 239, 250, 2544, 259, 267, 330
Willing, John, 267
Willoughby, Mamie Davis, 38, 202, 217, 236, 247, 252, 257, 260, 441
Wilson, Al, 217, 236, 242, 256, 260, 334, 442
Wilson, B.F., 274
Wilson, Cassandra, 217-18, 236, 248, 256, 260, 341, 440
Wilson, Charles, 218, 236, 243, 257
Wilson, Elder Roma, 218, 236, 248, 254, 259
Wilson, Gen. Lewis H. Jr., 82, 156, 218-19, 236, 238, 255, 258, 275, 304-05
Wilson, Gerald Stanley, 218, 236, 244, 255, 261
Wilson, Jerrell, 270
Wilson, Margie Lou, 268
Wilson, Mary, 219, 238, 256, 259, 333, 336, 437
Wilson, Pat, 274
Wilson, Robert Lee, 267
Wilson, Thomas Webber, 368
Wiman, Richard, 219, 236, 243, 257, 258
Winder, Sammy, 90, 104, 219-20, 236, 242, 256, 260, 270, 271, 274
Winfrey, Oprah, 18, 133, 140, 190, 220, 236-37, 256, 260, 281-82, 288, 301, 329, 347, 440
Wingate, Judge Henry T., 44
Winn, Newton Alfred, 29
Winstead, William Arthur, 368
Winston, Hattie, 220, 238, 254, 259, 281, 437
Winston, Hattie, 236
Winter, Ken, 47
Winter, Johnny, 236, 254
Winter, Gov. William, 23-7, 48, 78, 106, 124, 172, 198, 306, 353-54, 362, 438
Winter, Johnny, 173, 220, 238, 260, 330, 331, 440
Wiss, Rosa, 11

Indices

Index of People (continued)

Witherspoon, Frances, 307
Witherspoon, Matilda, 267, 438
Witherspoon, Samuel Andrew, 368
Wiygul, Brenda, 269
Wolfe, Elizabeth, 220, 236, 241, 254, 260, 440
Wolfe, Karl, 27, 220-21, 236-37, 251, 254, 258, 434
Wolfe, Karl and Mildred, 17
Wolfe, Mildred, 221, 236, 244, 254
Wonsley, Otis, 270
Wood, Bobbye, 268
Wood, June, 269
Wood, Willy, 38
Woodall, Lowery, 383
Woodard, Robert, 312
Woodham, Luke, 39, 41, 42, 44, 47
Woods, Johnny, 267
Wooten, Hoyt B., 22, 221, 236, 245, 250, 254, 258, 321, 477
Word, Thomas Jefferson, 368
Worsham, Charlie, 221, 236, 244, 255
Wrencher, John Thomas, 267
Wright, Amos, 23
Wright, Charles, 221, 236, 256, 258, 435
Wright, Daniel Boone, 368
Wright, Early, 45, 221, 236, 238, 253-54, 260
Wright, Fielding Lewis, 354
Wright, Frank, 30, 221, 236, 242, 252, 255, 259, 438
Wright, Gov. Fielding L., 17, 19, 353, 361
Wright, Katherine, 268, 269
Wright, Richard, 16, 19, 118, 214, 221-22, 236, 244, 250, 257, 261, 288, 343, 443
Wyatt, Elizabeth Pharr, 269
Wynette, Tammy, 42, 181, 222, 236, 240, 253, 256, 262, 339-40
Yarbrough, Steve, 222, 236, 244, 257, 259, 439
Young, Al, 152, 222, 236, 241, 257, 261, 443
Young, Billie Jean, 222, 236, 243, 254
Young, Donnie, 296
Young, Ed, 267
Young, G. D., 267
Young, Johnny, 23, 222-23, 236, 250, 254, 262, 448
Young, Lester W., 19, 156, 223, 236, 244, 250, 255, 262, 328, 342, 448
Young, Mark, 158, 167
Young, Ronnie, 345
Young, Roynell, 273
Young, Stark, 20, 223, 236, 246, 250, 255, 258
Young, Willie, 270
Young, Zora, 267, 448
Zacharias, Donald, 41, 183
Zaninelli, Luigi, 223, 236, 239, 254
Zhu, Ruopeng, 308
Ziglar, Jim, 223, 236, 248, 255, 261, 444
Ziglar, Zig, 223, 236, 247, 257, 449

General Index

NOTE: placenames are not indexed here.
A.B. McKay Food and Enology Lab, 446
ABC permit holders, 351
ABCA's Hall of Fame, 183
abortions performed, 76, 384
Aberdeen Examiner, The, 194
Academy Award(s), 150, 162, 217, 220, 276-77, 279, 281-92, 327-29
Academy of Country Music Awards, 125, 137, 190, 203, 208, 222, 337, 339, 340
accidents, deaths from, 385
Ace Records, 48, 142, 143, 189, 200
ad agency of the year, 122
Admiral Byrd's personal pilot, 314
date Miss. admitted to the union, 348
AFDC, 350
African-American men who served during the Civil War, 303
African American Literary Hall of Fame,
African Comet, 294
age of buying alcohol, 351
age of leaving school, 351
age of majority-full civil rights, 351
age of marriage, 351
Agricultural & Mechanical College est., 10
agricultural sector output, 413
agriculture, 411
Agriculture Commissioner, 348, 369
aid to families with dependent children, 350
aids cases reported, number of, 385
airports, 430
album set a record for first-week sales, 81
alcohol taxes, 351
Alcorn A&M named Alcorn State Univ., 23
Alcorn A&M College est., 9
Aldelbert Ames resigns, 9
All-American Bowl, 90, 272
All-American Football Foundation, 80
All-American Rose Garden, 438
all-time favorite country music singer, 137
all-time favorite entertainer, 185, 346
all-time favorite in blues/jazz/R&B, 150
all-time favorite movie filmed in and/or about Mississippi, 279
all-time favorite pop/rock singer, 185
all-time leading NFL rusher, 310
all-time leading touchdown scorers, 178
all-time NFL team, 78, 130, 146, 179, 189
Aloha Bowl, 90, 104, 180
Alligator Records, 173
Allison's Wells School of Arts, 434
Allure women's magazine, 78
ambulatory surgical facilities, list of, 389
American Bar Journal, The, 122
America's Fifth Seacoast, 437
America's best colleges, 403
America's first black naval aviator, 17
America Online, 82, 161, 182
American Academy of Arts and Letters, 81, 202, 212
American Advertising Federation's Hall of Fame, 121
American Bar Association, 184
American Bar Assn. Silver Gavel, 206
American Baseball Coaches Association, 129, 183
American Black Achievement Award, 145, 306
American Book Award, 222
American Civil Liberties Union, 28, 38, 307
American Football Coaches Assn., 104
American Library Association Best Book of the Year Award, 171
American Music Award(s), 137, 190, 222, 338, 340
American Queen (ship), 33
American Woodworker magazine, 133
Amite County Courthouse, 441
Amoco-Silver Circle Awards, 182
among the first Mississippi politicians to denounce segregation, 198
Amory Advertiser, The, 194
amount of diesel fuel sold, 430
amount of gasoline sold, 430
AmSouth Bancorp buys First American Corp., 44
analysis of counties population, 514
analysis of municipalities population, 514
analysis of population of MSAs, 514
ancestry, 73, 482
Andrew Jackson visits Jackson, 4
animals harvested by hunters, 456
annual employment averages by sector in Mississippi, 378
annual mean temperature in Jackson, 63
annual rain, 52
antebellum homes, 325, 435, 439, 442, 447
antique car tags, 430
Apollo 11 and Apollo 13, 131
aquaculture, 412
Archaeological Museum, 435
architect of the Miss. Constitution of 1890, 124, 319
area in state parks, 431
Arkabutla Lake & Dam, 433
Army's greatest fullback, 88
arson fires, number of, 401
Artist's Achievement Award of the Governor's Awards, 89, 112, 337
Arts Education Award of the Governor's Awards, 197
assessed value of all property, 377
assests of all Mississippi banks, 376, 381
first top $1 billion, 18
first pass $2 billion, 21
Associated Press, 115, 125, 167, 193, 194
Associated Press All-American, 211
Association of Film Commissioners International, 115
astronaut(s), 28-30, 131, 181, 191, 195, 207, 294, 297, 314-15, 434, 436
athletic director at Jackson State from 1977-1988, 187

General Index

Atlanta Constitution, The, 107, 174
Atlanta Daily World, 86, 307
Atlanta Journal Constitution, 221
Atlanta Press Club, 107
Atlantic Monthly magazine, 85, 93-94, 103, 217, 303
Attic Gallery, 447
Attorney General, 348, 369
Auditor, 348
auto speed limits
    in 1906, 12   in 1920, 14
    changed in 1996, 36
Auto World Weekly magazine, 295
average annual precipitation statewide, 59
average cost of electricity, 379
average elevation of Mississippi, 50
average experience of all classroom teachers, 402
average home energy costs, 483
average hospital costs, 384
average owner's income spent for housing, 75, 482
average pay for university faculty, 403
average pay statewide, 76
average precipitation & temperatures, 59
average salary, 483
avg. wind direction/speed in Jackson, 64
average earnings per job, 377, 483
aviation pioneer, 22, 84, 165, 207
Ayers Desegregation Case, 32-33
B.B. King Homecoming, 439
B.G. Humphreys Bridge opens, 16
Ballet Magnificat, 205, 439
Baltimore Sun, 115
Bancroft Prize, 148
Baptists organize first state convention, 3
barges, 380
Barksdale Reading Institute, 300
Barnard antebellum observatory, 443
Barq's Root Beer, 295
Baseball Hall of Fame, 23, 30-31, 82, 86, 110, 121, 309
Basketball Hall of Fame, 141, 203, 210
bass singer for the Moonglows, 332
Battle of Champion Hill, 141, 303
Battle of Corinth, 7
Battle of Farmington, 7
Battle of Harrisburg, 8
Battle of New Orleans, 3
Battle of Shiloh, 7
Beauvoir Mansion, 434
beef cows, 412
Belhaven College founded, 13
Belle of the Bends, 447
BellSouth sells MobileComm paging, 34
below poverty level, 75, 376
Belzoni Banner, The, 219
Bendix Trophy, 207
Bessie Smith dies in Miss., 16
BEST
    basketball player in state, 140
    Book of the Year Award, 300
    buck deer taken with bow/arrow, 456
    highway system in the South, 321
    Jazz Vocal, 341

    New Male Vocalist, 203
    professor at a master's degree-granting university, 301
    small corporation in the nation, 296
    snow sled made, 297
    start in football in Mississippi State's history, 310
    Studio Guitarist, 341
    Traditional Blues Album, 333
best-attended sports event, 45
best-known modern bluesman, 331
best-selling album ever by a woman, 335
Better Homes and Gardens, 80, 301
Biedenharn Candy Co. & Coca-Cola Museum, 447
Big Black River Bridge Battle, 7
BIGGEST
    country gospel chart in world, 342
    deer heads taken in Mississippi, 455
    Rock & Roll hits of all time, 184, 335
    Rock & Roll singles of all time, 19
Billboard magazine, 78, 81, 95, 97, 102, 109, 137-38, 143, 150, 169, 171, 181, 185-86, 189-90, 201, 203, 208, 331, 333, 335, 337-38, 340, 342
Billboard's Gospel Music Chart, 211
Billboard's No. One Gospel album, 342
Billboard's Top Female Country Artist, 338
Biloxi Daily Herald, 131
Biloxi first incorporated, 4
Biloxi Indians, 294, 468
Biloxi Lighthouse, 326
Biloxi Point Cadet Marina, 434, 446
Birmingham News, 180
birth of the Civil Rights movement in Mississippi, 18
birth rate, 384
birthplace of corn clubs, 313
birthplace of the Blues, 313
birthplace of the National Association of Junior Auxiliaries, 313
birthplace of the Order of the Eastern Star, 313, 444
birthplace of the PTA, 313
births, number of, 76, 482, 484
births to unmarried teens, 384
Black and Tan constitution, 9
Black Code, 8-9
black elected officials, 348
black population, 73-74
blacks who fought for the South, 303
Blewett-Harrison-Lee Museum, 435
blimps that fly by remote control, 313
Blue and Gray magazine, 303
blue laws of the state rescinded, 24
Bluebonnet Bowl, 21, 272
Bluegrass Hall of Fame, 191
Blues Archive, 443
Blues Foundation, 143, 173, 330
Blues Foundation's Hall of Fame, 93, 140, 143-44, 149, 146, 192, 216, 331
Blues Foundation's Lifetime Achievement Award, 330

BMI (Broadcast Music, Inc.) Awards, 339
Board of Optometry created, 14
Board of Pardons abolished, 14
Board of Pardons established, 13
Board of Pharmacy created, 14
Board of State Park Supervisors est., 15
Bolivar Commercial, The, 194
boll weevil first detected in Mississippi, 12
Boone & Crocket deer heads, 455
Boone & Crockett Club record, 345
Bowhunter of the Year, 188
branches & departments of state government, 370-72
Brice's Crossroads, 8, 52
Brice's Crossroads Civil War Museum opens, 20
Brice's Crossroads National Battlefield Site, 431, 433
broadcasting pioneer, 22, 221
broilers, 412
broke Michael Jordan's record, 312
Brookhaven Ledger, 10
Brotherhood of Locomotive Engineers, 9
Brown vs. Board of Education case, 18
budget for the state for FY 2001, 377
budgets for Bureau of Narcotics, Dept. of Corrections & Highway Patrol, 396
Bureau of Vital Statistics created, 13
busiest airports, 430
busiest port, 380
business & trade associations, 374
business journals, 479
business survival index, 381
Business Week magazine, 114, 295, 296
C. B. Newman Railroad Museum, 447
C.R.O.P. (Cotton Row On Parade) Day, 437
C.S.S. Arkansas, 7, 447
Cable Ace Award, 211
Cairo Museum, 447
Camp McCain, 16
Camp Shelby, 13, 16, 22
Camp Shelby Armed Forces Museum, 438
Canadian Football League, 35, 181
cancer, deaths from, 385
Canemount Plantation, 441
Canton Flea Market, 434
capital, name of, 348
Capital Press Club, 187
Car and Driver magazine, 295
Carey Dinner Theatre, 438
Carl Sandburg Literary Prize, 182
carpools, 430
Carroll County Courthouse, 434
Carrollton Massacre, 10
Casey Jones Museum, 52, 430, 447, 458
cash receipts from all ag products sold, 412
cash receipts from farm marketings, 411, 413
Cashbox (magazine), 78, 97, 102, 186, 205, 340
casino gambling, 433-34, 437-38, 443-46,
casino revenue, 466-67
casinos, 312, 464-67
catfish, 412

The Ultimate Reference on the State   615

General Index

Catfish Capital Museum, 433
Catfish Capital of the World, 320, 433
Catfish Farmers of America chartered, 21
catfish sales, 412
cattle & calves, 412
census figures (historical), 6, 11, 15, 18, 21-22, 30
Centennial Olympic Games, 343
Center for Study of Southern Culture, 443
Central Female Academy founded, 5
Chairmaker to the Presidents, 133, 447
Champion Hill, 7
changing population of Mississippi, 515
Chapel of the Cross, 441
Charles Frankel Award, 120
Charter psychiatric hospital to close, 46
Cherokee Indian, 469
Chevron refinery is built in Pascagoula, 20
Chicago Sun-Times, 222
Chicago World's Fair, 221
Chickasaw Cession, 4
Chickasaw History Exhibit, 444
Chickasaw Indians, 1-2, 4, 301, 435, 439, 461, 468-69
Chimneyville, 8
Choctaw Indian Fair, 326, 444
Choctaw Indian Reservation, 119, 326, 444
Choctaw Indians, 1-3, 23, 47, 312, 326, 348, 444, 457, 461, 468-69
Choctaw Museum of Southern Indians, 444
Choir of the Year Award, 169
Chris Schenkel Award for broadcasting excellence, 107
Christopher Award, 112
Chronicle newspaper, 12
Citizens Council, 20
Civil Rights, 8, 15, 19-21, 23-24, 28-29, 40-41, 45, 78, 97, 99, 102, 106, 112-13, 115-17, 132-33, 136, 159, 165, 171, 300-01
Civil War, 7-8, 12, 15, 18, 23, 36, 81, 86-87, 93-94, 100, 112, 120, 122, 124, 141, 147-48, 151, 153, 155, 157, 167, 170, 179, 188, 303-04, 320, 325-26, 343-46, 433-39, 441, 443, 445-47
Civilian Conservation Corps, 15
civilian labor force, 76, 377, 483
Clarion-Ledger, The, 4, 9-10, 16, 19, 26-27, 32, 35-36, 38-39, 41, 44-46, 48, 101, 110, 115, 118, 122, 133, 145, 163-64, 167, 172, 176, 185, 193-94, 209, 217, 302, 318, 343, 346-47, 383, 447, 476, 479, 481
Clarion-Ledger Division I Men's Basketball Team of the Century, 109, 141-42, 158, 213
Clarion-Ledger occupies new building, 35
Clark Creek Natural Area, 446
classroom teachers, number of, 402
climate, 52
closest gubernatorial election of the 20th Century, 44, 46, 319, 353, 363

CMA Awards, 137, 338, 340
co-founder Alcorn A&M College, 306
co-founder of Legal Advice Bureau, 307
co-lead singer of the Temptations, 30, 193
Coach of the Year, 27, 33, 35, 104, 108, 115, 126, 129, 145, 166, 180, 183, 196, 211
Cobb Institute Archaeology Museum, 446
Coca-Cola first bottled, 313
coined the word "sociology", 307
coldest weather in Jackson, 63
Collage Football Hall of Fame, 171
Collectors Car Museum, 442
college/university newspapers, 478
college/university radio stations, 475
college/university operating budgets, 403
college enrollment, 403-04
College Football Hall of Fame, 28, 30, 35, 38, 78, 88, 105, 125, 128, 131, 149, 158, 162, 179, 209, 310
College Football magazine, 158
College World Series, 23, 26, 28, 40, 43, 45-46, 49, 101, 129, 177, 183
college yearly tuition & fees, 403
Collier's magazine, 217
Columbus Air Force Base, 378, 435
Columbus Lock & Dam, 435
commander of *CSS Arkansas* ironclad, 344
commercial fishing, 380
commercial radio networks, 475
commercial radio stations, 471-74
commercial tv stations, 470
Commonwealth Magazine, 148
Communications Hall of Fame, 198
community and junior colleges, list of, 404
community college libraries, list of, 410
composed original ballad Casey Jones, 308
comprehensive universities, 403
Concorde supersonic jet lands in Miss., 29
conductor and arranger for Tennessee Ernie Ford's orchestra, 214
Conerly Trophy, 38, 40, 43, 46, 105, 206, 444
Confederate deaths, 8, 303
Confederate Monument, 303
Confederate States of America, 303, 324
Conference USA, 90
Congressional Medal of Honor, 82, 87, 104, 110-11, 132, 136, 148, 152, 154, 156, 175-76, 182, 197-98, 215, 218-19, 304-05
Consolidated School Law passed, 13
Constitution of 1865 framed, 8
construction, nonresidential, 377
construction begins on Sillers State Office Building, 22
construction begins on the Natchez Trace Parkway, 16
construction in Mississippi, 377
Consumer Reports magazine, 297
Corcoran Gallery, 100, 113
CORE (Congress of Racial Equality), 171
Corinth National Cemetery, 435
corporate state income taxes, 377, 483
cost of electricity, 379

cost of living index in Miss. counties, 382
cost of the state capitol building, 326
Cotton Bowl, 19-20, 43, 45, 90, 104, 196, 272
Cotton Capital of the World, 320, 437
cotton gin first introduced in Natchez, 2
cotton & major crops - planted, harvested, production, yield & value, 411
Cotton Row, 437
Cottonlandia Museum, 437
Council on Compulsive Gambling, 465
counties named for Indians, 324
counties of Miss. by population, 512
counties with duel county seats, 324
Country Comic of the Year, 102
Country Living Gardens mag., 193
Country Music Association, 81, 83, 186, 190, 203, 208, 222, 339, 340-41
Country Music DJ Hall of Fame, 108
Country Music Hall of Fame, 92, 185, 186, 191, 208, 222, 284, 339
county health departments created, 14
county population charts, 513
county population pie, 512
Craftsmen's Guild of Mississippi, 439
creeks, list of, 50-51
crimes, 396-97, 482
Crosby Arboretum, 444
Daily Herald, 131, 163
Daily Mississippian, The, 110, 122
Daily News, 98, 101, 145, 162, 168, 174
daily newspapers, 476
daily water use, 379
Davis Planetarium, 86, 439
deaths in Miss., number of, 385, 482
Decoration Day, 344
dedication of the new capitol, 12
defense facilities, 350
deGrummond Children's Literature Research Center, 438
Delta's first great blues star, 331
Delta Air Lines first service in Jackson, 15
Delta Blues Festival, 437
Delta Blues Museum, 435
Delta Bowl, 17, 272
Delta Comm. College Hall of Fame, 206
Delta Democrat-Times, 23, 34, 99, 321
Delta Gallery Blues Museum, 437
Delta Queen (boat), 443
Delta State Teachers College renamed Delta State University, 23
Democratic National Convention, 37
dentists, number of, 384
Dentzel Carousel, 326
Department of Archives & History, 12, 37
Department of Game and Fish est., 13
Dept. of Public Safety, 394
Deposit Guaranty Plaza opens, 23
deposits in Mississippi banks, 376, 381
Derringer Award, 120
designed ceramic dinnerware for *Today* co-host Katie Couric, 308
DeSoto Times Today newspaper, 182
developed new procedure to treat lung cancer, 316

General Index

diabetes, deaths from, 385
discovered the lost Biblical town of Trogylium, 299
discovered the Tinsley oil dome in Yazoo County, 165
disposable personal income, 376
distance around state boundary, 50
Dixie National Rodeo & Livestock Show (Dixie Nationals), 182, 192, 440
Doctors Hospital in Jackson opens, 21
domestic travel expenditures, 430
double Royal Slam, 345
Dove Awards, 87, 169
Downbeat mag., 94, 165, 218, 223, 342
Dr. Tichener's antiseptic, 297
Dred Scott decision, 6
driest years/seasons/months in Jackson, 64
driest year statewide, 59
driver's license examining stations, 394
dropouts, number of public school, 402
dry counties, 350
Dunn's Falls, 436, 461
Dunn-Seller Museum, 446
Earliest first freeze date in Jackson, 63
earnings in Mississippi, 376
east-to-west transcontinental flight record, 314
East-West Shrine Bowl, 219
Easter flood, 25, 80
Eastern Clarion newspaper, 4
easternmost point of Mississippi, 50
Ebony magazine, 86, 145, 218, 306, 307
economic indicators, 378
Edgewater Mall opens at Biloxi, 20
education, 76, 402-04, 482-83
education associations, 374
Education Commission est., 13
educational TV stations, list of, 472
Egg Bowl, 35, 38, 43, 46, 196
eggs produced, 412
eight state-supported universities, 403
electoral votes, 348
electric energy production 7 sales, 379
electric energy use by residences, 75
electric power associations of Miss., 379
Eli Whitney invents the cotton gin, 2
Elizabeth Female Academy chartered, 3
Elvis Presley
    birthplace, 446
    Commemorative Postage Stamp, 185
    Festival, 447
    makes his public debut, 18
Elvis Presley's first movie released, 19
Emancipation Proclamation, 7
Emerald Mound, 325, 443
Emmy (Emmy Award), 86, 124, 136, 147, 150, 173, 181, 211, 220, 321, 329
emphysema, deaths from, 385
employment distribution, 76, 377
employment in government, 484
employment figures, 76, 377, 483-84
Encyclopedia of Southern Culture, 113, 120, 597
end of the Korean War, 18
energy consumption / expenditures, 379

energy machine, Newman's, 174
energy use by residences, 75
Enid Dam and Reservoir, 448
enrollment in community colleges, 403
enrollment in public schools, 402
    in the Jackson MSA, 484
enrollment in the eight state-supported universities, 485
Enterprise Journal, 115
Entertainment Weekly magazine, 185
Espy appointed Secretary of Agri., 31, 116
Espy is acquitted, 42, 116
Resigns as Secretary of USDA, 32, 116
Esquire magazine, 132, 133, 218
Essence magazine, 149, 210, 218, 341
estimated state population July 1, 1998 — breakdown by age group, 74
ethnic origins of Mississippians, 73
Eudora Welty Library opens, 28
evergreen magnolia, 349
execution of Jimmy Lee Gray, 27
executive term, 348
existing single family home sales, 75, 482
expenditures for public schools, 402, 485
export products, 380
extreme breadth/length of Mississippi, 50
F.D. Hall Art Gallery, 439
farm commodities, 412
farm cash receipts, income, expenses, 413
farm marketings, 411
farm proprietors' income, 413
fastest-rising single record with the longest stay on the charts for a new act, 84
FASTEST
    baseball player ever, 30, 86, 309
    female quarter-miler in state history, 312
    growth in Southeast in no. of single-family building permits, 75, 377
    man in world over 200 pounds, 86
    selling album in history, 84, 335
    time in the world for 100 meters, 26
Father of Country Music, 191
Father of Jackson State athletics, the, 115
Father of Mississippi History, 100
Faulkner Award, 132
Faulkner/Yoknapatawpha Conference, 443
FAVORITE
    actor from Mississippi, 123, 346
    athlete, male & female, 346
    blues/jazz/R&B singer/musician, 346
    country music singer/musician, 346
    fiction writer, 346
    Miss Mississippi, 268, 302, 346
    Mississippi TV personality, 80
    new soul-R&B artist, 334
    non-fiction writer, 343, 346
    pop/rock singer, 346
    recurring events, 45
FEDERAL
    Correctional Institution, 378
    employees, 350
    facilities, 378
    funds received, 350
    government phone numbers, 373

government toll-free phone nos, 373
Indian Reservation, 52, 431
marijuana farm, 21
payments for Miss. highways, 430
spending in Mississippi, 350, 377
transfer payments to Mississippi, 350
transportation bill for FY 2001, 430
federally-owned land, 52
Female Vocalist of Year, 218, 222, 340
Field & Stream magazine, 93
Fielding Wright Art Center, 435
Fiesta Bowl, 196
Financial World magazine, 114
Fine Gardening magazine, 193
fire at Ross Barnett Reservoir, 47
fire department salaries, 401
Fire Museum, 439
fire nearly destroys Yazoo City, 12
Fire Registry Law, 401
fire related deaths, 401
Firearms Deaths, 385
first-ever basket in Olympic women's basketball competition, 203
FIRST
    adrenal glands transplant in humans, 20, 133, 315
    agricultural commodity to break the billion dollar mark, 31
    American company to reach billion-dollar mark in one decade, 198
    American designer ever inducted into Chamble Syndicale, 148, 307
    American sociologist, 6
    American to fly over Antartica, 314
    American to set foot on Antartica, 314
    American to win a medal at the 1996 Olympics, 38
    and only federal marijuana farm in the nation, 298
    and only first-class battleship to visit an inland city, 13
    animal-to-human transplant, 20, 45, 133, 315
    anti-pollution law in America, 302
    astronaut to become administrator, 207
    blockbuster movie of the 21st Century, 329
    blues artist to record on Alligator Records, 205
    boxer inducted into the Mississippi Sports Hall of Fame, 154
    can of evaporated condensed milk, 6, 297
    casino in the state, 30, 312
    Catholic seminary for black priests in the U.S., 299
    Citizens Council is formed, 18
    city in the U.S. to receive electric power from TVA, 15
    city in the U.S. to use electricity from the TVA, 302
    city in the world where Digital Satellite Systems were sold, 302

The Ultimate Reference on the State

General Index

FIRST

- co-ed college in the U.S. to grant degrees to women, 435
- co-op in the U.S. financed by REA to electrify, 302
- coast-to-coast, non-stop passenger flight, 207
- coast-to-coast, non-stop passenger flight ever made, 15
- coast-to-coast, non-stop passenger flight in the U.S, 314
- Coca-Cola bottling plant, 30
- college football squad in America to fly on an airplane, 314
- college squad in the U.S. to fly on an airplane, 16
- concrete highway in the state, 13
- concrete road south in the South, 13
- Conerly Trophy winner, 444
- Confederate monument, 9
- cotton crop commercially produced entirely by machinery, 17, 298
- country humorist to earn a gold record, 42, 102
- country star to have a stamp dedicated to him, 191
- court decision in the U.S. to grant property rights to women, 4, 301
- deaf parents in America to legally adopt hearing children, 170, 310
- deaf player in the country to play a full year of pro football, 32
- deaf player in history to play a full year of pro football, 170, 310
- deaf principal of the Mississippi School for the Deaf, 29
- dial telephone system in Miss., 16
- director in the New York Players Guild, 80
- director of the Mississippi Dept. of Archives and History, 16, 193
- electrically powered cotton gin in the state, 14
- endowed chair of nursing in the world, 316
- Episcopal church in the state, 3
- european permanent settlement, 348
- ever 7,000-yard rusher, 312
- federal prison in the state, 32
- football player pictured on Wheaties cereal box, 178, 310
- free public library established, 11, 13
- free public high school, 3
- free school in the state, 435
- full-time female assistant football coach on the collegiate level in the U.S., 173
- furniture assembly line, 17, 296
- gospel group to record a long play album, 87
- governor's race ever decided in the House, 319
- governor in the 20th Century to win back-to-back terms, 353, 363
- Governor of State of Mississippi, 355

FIRST

- governor to live in the Governor's Mansion, 352, 357
- gubernatorial election ever decided in the House, 46, 353, 363
- hard surface road in South, 13, 321
- heart transplant in the world, 20, 133, 315
- hit recorded on Sun Records, 206
- hospital in the U.S. to use Cryoablation, 315
- improved road in the state, 2
- in tornado-related deaths, 60
- Jewish congregation in U.S. to call a woman to exercise a rabbi's function, 299
- Jitney Jungle store opens, 13
- junior colleges in the nation, 14
- library in the state to computerize operations, 447
- lung transplant in the world, 20, 133, 315
- Lutheran church in the state, 5
- major college game played at Miss. Veterans Memorial Stadium, 18
- major rock star to change to country, 208, 339
- manager of Mississippi Memorial Stadium, 28
- mansion in Miss. Valley with full colonnade across facade, 436
- member of Congress to lead the House of Representatives in the Pledge of Allegiance, 170
- milk condensing plant in South, 14
- Mississippi collegian to make a serious run for the Heisman, 105
- Mississippi planter to use steam power to drive ginstand, 3
- Miss. state income tax law passed, 13
- monument to the Confederacy, 441
- national bank branch, 294
- national Emmy for any broadcaster in the area, 321
- national guard unit to receive giant Starlifter transport jet, 304
- nationally-known country star, 191, 339
- native-born Mississippi governor, 3, 352, 356, 443
- natural gas field discovered, 14
- naval aviator killed in a plane crash, 315
- Negro to conduct a major American orchestra, 203
- network radio station in Mississippi, 321, 477
- newspaper in Mississippi, 2
- NFL player with 1,000 career receptions, 38
- non-athlete ever inducted into the Miss. Sports Hall of Fame, 107
- nuclear detonation east of the Mississippi, 20, 317
- nuclear submarine built in South, 294

FIRST

- oil field in the state, 447
- Olympic qualifying event ever held in Mississippi, 49, 311
- permanent colony in Mississippi, 1
- person elected into the Country Music Hall of Fame, 339
- person in the state to be sentenced to die by lethal injection, 27
- pitcher to face Babe Ruth in an American League game, 23, 309
- place in the nation to sell shoes in boxes in pairs, 346
- player ever with five 30-touchdown seasons, 119, 309
- player in the NFL to stay with same team for two decades, 197
- predominately black land-grant college in the nation, 3
- preparatory school established in the Miss. Territory, 299
- Presbyterian Church in the state, 2
- president of Miss. A&M College, 12
- president of Mississippi Agricultural & Mechanical College, 153
- radio station in Miss., 22, 321, 477
- railroad chartered in Mississippi, 4
- REA-financed co-op to electrify, 16
- real-life mother / daughter nominated for one film in the same year, 150
- first real-life mother and daughter to receive Academy Award, 328
- Rebel player inducted into College Football Hall of Fame, 149, 310
- recipient of the Miss. Institute of Arts and Letters Literature Award, 112
- regional shopping center on the Miss. Gulf Coast, 20
- Republican governor, 353, 359
- Republican governor since reconstruction, 30, 35, 363
- Republican Senator from Mississippi since reconstruction, 103
- Republican to win the 1st District in the 20th Century, 318
- Rhodes Scholar from Miss., 12, 299
- Rock 'n' Roll hit, 106, 207
- Rock 'n' Roll record, 25, 92, 334
- rock and country superstar, 339
- Rock and Roll record distributed on a worldwide basis, 78
- round trip transoceanic flight, 314
- rural electric coop in U.S., 15, 302
- school in the U.S. authorized to grant degrees to women, 3, 299
- single record in history to sell a million advance copies, 335
- song broadcast in space, 208, 339
- Southerner to ever serve as Secretary of Agriculture, 116
- Southerner to use Negro dialect in poetry, 346
- spacewalk of Shuttle program, 181
- Special Horatio Alger Award, 168
- standard-gauge railroad, 295, 446

General Index

FIRST
- statewide elected official in modern times to resign, 37
- student ever at Mississippi State to have a perfect ACT score, 116
- successful Biblical novel, 299
- successful intramedullary bone-pinning operation, 16, 193, 316
- sudden-death game in NFL championship history, 105
- tenured African-American law professor at Ole Miss, 214, 306
- territorial governor, 2
- time 2 senators from the same state ran for Majority Leader, 318
- time Coke was sold in bottles, 313
- TV station in Mississippi, 321, 472
- two-way paging network, 177, 295
- U.S. Senator in the nation elected by popular ballot, 216, 318
- war vessel ever sunk by a water-floated mine or torpedo, 303
- white person to win the W.C. Handy Blues Award, 191

FIRST BLACK
- admitted to Univ. of Miss., 20
- and first Southerner and youngest person to serve as Secretary of Agriculture, 31, 306
- appointed to an administrative position on a state board, 23
- athlete at the University of Miss., 81
- bank in the nation, 157
- Catholic bishop consecrated in the U.S., 299
- chairman of State College Board, 26
- concert singer, 9
- congressman from Mississippi since Reconstruction, 28, 31, 116, 306
- dean of the University of Miss. School of Law, 214, 306
- elected to full term in U.S. Senate, 9
- enrolled in Ole Miss, 165
- football players to sign with Ole Miss, 216
- fraternity house at Ole Miss, 29
- graduate of University of Miss. School of Law, 306
- in the U.S. Senate, 306
- inducted into the Miss. Sports Hall of Fame, 89
- law dean at North Carolina Central University, 214
- mayor in the state, 22
- Mississippian drafted by the NFL, 32
- Mississippian with the rank of Gen. in the Army, 185, 306, 440
- naval aviator to lose his life in combat, 18
- naval aviator in the nation, 306, 438
- naval officer to have a ship named in his honor, 93
- novelist to achive fame, 221
- owned bank in Miss. since 1928, 31
- owned bank in the U.S., 306

FIRST BLACK
- owned company listed on American Stock Exchange, 145, 306
- Senator, 188
- senator to preside over a Senate session, 94
- state Supreme Court Justice, 27, 306
- statewide candidate, 23
- student at Mississippi State, 139, 446
- student at the University of Miss., 29
- symphonic work performed in the U.S., 306
- to deliver keynote address before a national political convention, 306
- to have a U.S. Federal Building named after him, 306
- to head the Miss. Bar Assn., 78, 306
- to serve a full term in the U.S. Senate, 11, 94
- to win Miss Mississippi, 29
- U.S. Senator, 9, 12, 188
- writer to write scripts for TV and films, 80, 306

FIRST FEMALE
- admitted to the Miss. state bar, 97, 301, 344, 447
- candidate for governor, 18
- Chief Justice of the State Supreme Court, 184
- combat jet pilot in the U.S. Marine Corps, 315
- elected to chair the national NAACP board, 117
- federal judge in the U.S., 301
- in Miss. elected to a constitutional statewide office, 124
- in Miss. to get a medical degree, 11
- in the nation to argue cases before the U.S. Supreme Court, 98, 301
- in the South to become a state senator, 14, 16, 148, 301
- inducted into the Miss. Sports Hall of Fame, 34, 209
- inducted into the National Basketball Hall of Fame, 34, 210
- lieutenant governor, 124
- permanent president of MUW, 29
- president of the Mississippi State Medical Association, 301
- rural route mail carrier in U.S., 301
- State Supreme Court Judge, 26, 446
- to address a joint session of the Miss. legislature, 148
- to argue cases before the U.S. Supreme Court, 344, 447
- to rank No. 1 on *Forbes*' 40 highest paid entertainers, 220, 301
- to fly in Japan, 166
- to fly at night, 166
- to hold Chancellorship in Miss., 184
- to lead Millsaps College, 47
- to receive a doctorate in mathematics from Tulane, 301
- wing commander in the U.S. Air Force, 315

first of 14 Poole family members to play at Ole Miss, 183
first of four Yale graduates to serve as president of Ole Miss, 155

FIRST MISSISSIPPIAN
- and first woman to chair the board of the NAACP, 301
- chosen president of American Legion Boys Nation, 307
- elected National Commander of the American Legion, 307
- elected Senate Majority Leader, 318
- selected for the Pro Football Hall of Fame, 149, 310
- to be a candidate for vice-president of the U.S., 17
- to be president pro temp of the U.S. Senate, 318
- to become a cabinet member, 5
- to go directly to the NBA from high school, 312
- to play in baseball's major leagues, 23, 169, 309

FIRST STATE
- aid highway law passed, 13
- attorney general to sue tobacco industry, 35, 319
- in the nation to have a planned system of junior colleges, 299
- in the U.S. to abolish imprisonment for debtors, 3, 302
- mental hospital built, 6
- operated university exclusively for women in the U.S., 299
- to adopt a homestead exemption, 302
- to erect Confederate monument, 303
- to establish a state-endowed college for women, 181
- to ratify 18th amendment, 13
- to organize a State Bar, 302

First Lady of Country Music, 42
Five Hundred Songs That Shaped Rock And Roll, 105, 111, 139, 141-42, 144, 146, 149-50, 154, 173, 185, 187, 191, 193, 202-03, 207, 216, 330, 331-36, 339
Florida Citrus Bowl, 272
Florida Times newspaper, 206
Folk Arts Hall of Fame, 177, 218
food stamp recipients, number of, 350
Football Digest, 158
Football Hall of Fame, 130
Football News, 158
Football Writer's Assn. of America, 130
Forbes magazine, 82, 95, 114, 347
Forbes list of 400 Richest Americans, 347
foreign-born population, 73
foreign-owned businesses, 376
foreign born in Jackson MSA, 482
forest fires, 52, 401
forested area, 52
forestry products, 412
Fort Massachusetts, 434, 438, 446
Fort Maurepas, 1, 294, 443
Fort Nogales, 2

General Index

Fort Panmure, 1
Fort Pemberton Confederate Army Civil War site, 437
Fort Robinette Memorial Civil War Site, 435
Fort Rosalie, 1, 2
Fort Sumter, 6
Fortune 500 companies with operations in Mississippi, 380
Fortune magazine, 31, 114, 168
Foster General Army Hospital becomes the VA Hospital, 17
Foster General Hospital, 16
founded Federal Express, 198
founded MTV, 307
founded *Eastern Clarion* newspaper, 358
founded the Mississippi Mass Choir, 216
founder O. Henry Short Story Awards, 301
founder of Mississippi Chemical Corp., 28
founder of Miss. Sports Hall of Fame, 162
founder of Trumpet Records, 45
four Mississippians die in Amtrack wreck, 43
fourth largest church organ in U.S., 299
Franklin Academy, 435
Franklin Academy established, 2-3
Freedom Bowl, 188
freeze data, 58
French and Indian War, 1
freshwater fish common to Miss., 457
Friede Goldman International merges with Halter Marine, 44
Friendship Cemetery, 344, 435
Fulbright Fellowship, 222
Fulton Historical Center, 437
Gallons of fuel used per vehicle, 430
gaming tables, number of, 465
Garden Design, 193
Garden Writers Assn. of America, 193
gas utility industry, 379
gasoline used, 430
Gateway City, 435
Gator Bowl, 19, 23, 30, 196, 272
general business, 376
geographic center of Mississippi, 50
George Robert Hall Air Park, 438
Gideon Lincecum, 3
Glamour magazine's Ten Outstanding Working Women, 300
Golden Globe Award, 99, 123, 159, 190, 211
Golden Hugo Award, the, 111
golf courses in Mississippi, 462-63
Golf magazine, 166
Good Housekeeping magazine, 308
Gospel Music Assn. Hall of Fame, 87, 212
Gospel Record of the Year, 342
government expenditures on police, 396
government payments to farmers, 412
government transfer payments, 376, 483
governmental units, number of, 351
Governor's Awards for Excellence in the Arts, 86, 93, 103, 106, 120, 123, 138, 171-73, 177, 186, 188, 214, 218, 222, 327, 333

Governor's Mansion, 439
governor who served longest term, 359
Grambling State Univ. Hall of Fame, 94
Grammy Awards (or Grammy), 31, 48, 81, 83, 87-88, 92, 106, 111, 124, 137, 139-40, 143, 149, 152, 162, 169, 171, 173, 176, 181, 185-86, 190, 201-04, 208, 211-12, 217-18, 222, 330-31, 333-35, 337-42
Grand Gulf, 379
Grand Gulf Advertiser newspaper, 4
Grand Gulf Cemetary, 445
Grand Gulf Military Monument Park, 445
Grand Gulf Nuclear Power Plant, 320, 445
Grand Gulf nuclear station starts up, 27
Grand Gulf Historical Park Museum, 20
Grand Ole Opry, 19, 42, 85, 92, 102, 108, 143, 185-86, 193-95, 203-04, 221, 284, 337, 340-41
Grand Opera House, 442
Grand Village of the Natchez Indian, 443
Grandparents Magazine, 301
grants to state & local governments, 350
Gray and Blue Naval Museum, 447
Great Animal Adventures Children's Museum, 447
Great Depression, 4, 15
Great Seal of Mississippi adopted, 3
Great Seal of the State of Mississippi, 349
greater Jackson area's largest employer, 316, 389
greatest snows in Jackson, 65-66
greatest temperature falls in Jackson, 63
greatest tenor saxophonist ever, 19
greatest winds in Jackson, 59, 64
Greenville Delta Democrat-Times, 17
Greenville Flood Museum, 437
Greenville Writers' Exhibit, 437
Greenwood Commonwealth, The, 107, 321
Grenada Historical Museum, 437
Grenada Lake Visitors Ctr. Museum, 437
Grisham wins court case, 35
gross state product, 376
groundbreaking for a federal prison, 32
groundbreaking for Miss. Sports Hall of Fame, 33
Guggenheim Fellowship, 110, 112, 156, 181, 202, 222
Guinness Book of World Records, 107, 129, 210, 297, 309, 316, 319, 346
Guitar Player Awards, 341
Gulf Coast Winery, 438
Gulf Islands National Seashore, 52, 431, 434, 438, 443
Gulf of Mexico, area & depth, 50
Gulfport Yacht Harbor, 438, 446
Gypsy King and Queen, 442
Hall of Fame Bowl, 26, 272
Hampstead Academy established, 3
Hancock County's largest employer, 317
Harmon Trophy, 207, 314
Harper's magazine, 45, 210, 222, 343
Harper's Bazaar, 85
Hattieburg American paper, 30, 34, 101
Hattiesburg Zoo at Kamper Park, 438

hazardous waste sites, 379
heads Thomas Jefferson Foundation, 147
health care expenditures by state & local governments, 384
Health Departments, listing of, 390
heart diseases, deaths from, 385
Heatwave 2000, 62
Heatwave Classic Triathlon, 441
Hederman family sells *Clarion-Ledger*, 26
Heisman Trophy, 33, 49, 88, 96, 103, 105, 125, 128, 158, 164-65, 196, 309
Henry Clay visits Vicksburg & Jackson, 5
high school football career TD passes, 312
high school graduates, number of, 76, 402
high school rodeo champion, 182
higher education, 403
higher education, Jackson MSA, 485
HIGHEST
    ranking military officer from Mississippi, 218-19, 275, 304
    national office ever held by a Mississippian, 114, 318
    natural point in Miss., 50, 320, 439
    paid female entertainer, 329
    temperature / wind in Miss., 59
Highland Park Carousel, 442
Highway Commission established, 13
highway statistics including mileage, 430
Historic Jefferson College, 443
historic sites (parks) 52, 430, 437, 442-44
HIV Infection, deaths from, 385
hogs & pigs Inventory, 412
Hollywood Rock & Roll Walk of Fame, 179
Hollywood Walk of Fame, 150, 154, 186, 331, 340
home ownership, 75
homestead exemption program begins, 16
homicide, 385
hospital beds, number of, 384
hospital outpatient visits, number of, 384
Hospitality State, 348
hospitals, listing of, 387-89
hospitals, number of, 384, 482
hourly wages, 377
households, number of 75
households with Internet access, 380
households with telephone, 75
houses first numbered in Vicksburg, 11
housing units, number of, 75
Houston Cronicle newspaper, 115
how some Mississippi places got their names, 323
Howlin' Wolf Blues Festival, 446
Hula Bowl, 213
Humanitarian Bowl, 43, 272
hunting accidents & deaths, 385
hurricane (s), 11-12, 17, 19-22, 25, 27, 34, 38, 60
Hurricane Camille, 22, 80, 163
Hurricane Georges, 42
IBC ballet competition, 439
ice storm(s), 18, 24, 26, 31, 35, 42
Illinois Harness Racing Hall of Fame, 216
Illustrated Newspaper, 8

General Index

Imperial Wizard, 20, 21, 42
income, 381
income from construction, 377
income per capita, 376
income spent for housing, 75
incorporated municipalities, 513
Independence Bowl, 25, 27, 29, 43, 46, 90, 104, 167, 219, 272
Independence Bowl-record three TD passes, 167
independent (private) colleges, list of, 404
Indian(s), 325, 348, 433, 435, 437, 443, 446-47, 457, 461, 468-69
Indian tribes of Mississippi history, 468
Industrial Institute & College est., 10
infant mortality rate, 384
Ingalls Shipbuilding/Shiyard, 16-17, 294, 350, 377, 444
Ingalls Shipyard begins operation, 16
Institute for Arts and Letters Performing Arts Award, 188
Insurance Commissioner, 348, 369
insurance companies, business by, 376
International Ballet Competition, 25, 30
Internat'l. Boxing Hall of Fame, 171, 311
International Checker Hall of Fame, 210, 309, 444
International Country Gospel Music Assn, 205, 342
International Women's Sports Hall of Fame, 215
interstate highways, 430
invented Pine-Sol household cleaner, 103
inventor of the bowie knife, 445
Iron Mountain vanishes, 347
Jacinto Courthouse, 445
Jackson Business Journal, 122
Jackson Daily News, 14, 17, 24, 26, 34, 41, 98, 101, 145, 347
Jackson Diamond Kats baseball team makes debut, 49
Jackson International Airport, 29, 33, 35-37, 45, 430
Jackson Military Road, 3
Jackson Mississippian newspaper, 6
Jackson MSA statistics, 480-83
Jackson Municipal Airport, 20, 28, 29 dedicated, 20 renamed, 29
Jackson State's all-time leading rusher, 29
Jackson State Hall of Fame, 115, 188
Jackson State Homecoming Parade, 440
Jackson Symphony Orchestra, 439
Jackson Touchdown Club, 274
Jackson Zoological Park, 439
Jackson's extinct volcano, 326
Jazz Times magazine, 218
Jefferson College chartered, 2
Jefferson Davis dies, 10
Jefferson Davis elected President of the Confederacy, 6
Jefferson Davis Presidential Library, 434
Jefferson Davis released from prison, 9
Jerry Clower's Museum, 441
Jerry Clower Exhibition Center, 447
Jesse M. Unruh Award, 319

Jet magazine, 86
Jim Buck Ross Agricultural & Forestry Museum, 440
Jim Crow laws, 10
Jim Henson Muppets Museum, 136, 440
Jim Thorpe Trophy, 105, 178
Jimmie Rodgers Memorial & Museum, 442
Jimmie Rodgers Memorial Festival, 442
Jitney Jungle Stores of America files Chapter 11 bankruptcy, 44
Jitney Jungle Stores of America sold, 34
Joe Gerache's Corner Drug Store, 447
John C. Stennis Space Center, 294, 317, 328, 378, 433
John Wayne's personal costume designer, 329
Jones County claims more MOH recipients than any other Miss. county, 440
JSU basketball scoring record, 312
Jubilee Jam, 440
judiciary, 348
Junior Achievement of Mississippi, 383
Junior College Commission est., 15
Kate Freeman Clark Art Gallery, 20, 439
Kayden Nat'l. University Press Award, 148
Keesler Air Force Base, 16, 378, 434
Keesler Air Force Base established, 16
Kemper County Historical Museum, 436
Kennedy Center Honor, 150, 186, 217
Key brothers aviation pictorial exhibit, 442
kickstand for bicycles & motorcycles, 314
kidney diseases, deaths from, 385
kindergarten enrollment, 402
Korean War veterans, 76, 485
Kosciusko Museum & Visitors Center, 440
Ku Klux Klan, 9, 42
Kudzu is brought to Miss. from Japan, 15
Labor in Mississippi, 76, 377, 481-82
Ladies' Home Journal, 80, 85, 301
lakes / reservoirs, list of, 51
Lamar County Historical Museum, 445
land area of state, 50
land in farms, 412
land in national parks, 52
land use, 52
LARGEST
    airport in Mississippi, 430
    amphibious operation in history, 7
    antebellum home ever built in the state, 326, 441
    arboretum in the state, 437
    area ever designated when first placed on National Register of Historic Places, 447
    arena floor in the state, 345
    baby ever born at Forrest General Hospital, 316
    baby ever born in the state, 316
    bed of sea fossils in the state, 433
    Bible rebinding company in the U.S., 299
    blues festival in the nation, 437
    casino between Las Vegas and Atlantic City, 312

    collection of Civil War memorabilia in the South, 447
    college dormitory under one roof, 19
    consolidated school in U.S., 15, 326
    cottonwood tree plantation in the world, 439
    county in Mississippi, 52, 351
    cruise ships built in America, 294
    express delivery company in the world, 198
    fed'l. criminal fine in state history, 37
    floating casino in the world, 312
    frozenated beverage company, 295
    gin laboratory in the world, 298
    home in the state, 347
    honky-tonk in the world, 337
    hotel in the state, 465
    independent R&B and gospel label in the U.S., 107
    individual financial contributor to the War of Independence, 345
    jury award in the state's history, 33
    manufacturer of musical instruments in the U.S., 297
    merger in U.S. history, 182, 295
    national cemetery, 344
    National Guard and reserve training camp in the nation, 304
    non-government employer, 377
    number of antebellum structures in the U.S., 442
    pager refurbisher in the U.S., 317
    percentage of casualties of any state in the Confederacy, 8
    private gift to Ole Miss, 82
    public access observatory in the state, 436
    publicly traded Mississippi-based companies, 381
    remaining octagonal house in the U.S., 325
    rural mail carrier in the U.S., 347
    school district in the state, 402
    sculpture in the U.S., 294
    sculpture of a shark head in the world, 294
    collection of paintings by a single artist in world, 19-20, 100, 439
    single donation to advance literacy in the nation's history, 82, 300
    single earth excavation project in history, 27, 345
    single gift ever made to the Ole Miss athletic dept., 138
    snowfalls in Jackson, 66
    stadiums, 431
    sternwheeler ever built, 23, 326
    syndicator of outdoors media programming, 296
    teacher pay plan in state history, 47
    tree in the state, 433
    tree in the world ever transplanted, 295, 423
    USDA research facility east of the Mississippi, 437

General Index

LAST
- bare pro knuckles sanctioned fight in the U.S., 10, 311
- battle between U.S. Navy and foreign foe in American waters, 304
- county in the state organized, 13
- documented duel, 9, 295
- execution in Mississippi, 396
- state to allow legally sold alcoholic beverages, 320
- survivor of all Generals of the Civil War, 15, 352, 359
- survivor of the Civil War, 23, 303
- territorial governor, 2

Lauren-Rogers Memorial Museum of Art, 440
law enforcement officers feloniously killed, number of, 395
lawyers, number of, 396
leading international authority on cybersurgery, 192
leading lifetime touchdown scorers, 78
leading New York critic, 223
leading scorer in the AFC in 1987, 220
least populated county in Miss., 351, 514
LeFleur's Bluff, 3
Lefty Gomez Award, 183
Legends Society, 104, 119, 130, 213, 220
Legion of Honor, 214
legislators ratify 13th Amendment, 33
legislature refuses to ratify 13th Amendment abolishing slavery, 8
length of Mississippi coastline, 50
Leo Edwards is executed, 29
Lexington Advertiser, 20, 32, 198, 321
Liberty Bowl, 20-21, 30-31, 40, 46, 90, 96, 196, 272
library visits, number of, 409
libraries, list of public, 405-09
licensed child care centers, 350
licensed practical nurses, number of, 384
Lieutenant Governor, 348, 369
life expectancy, 76, 384
Life magazine, 162, 168, 206, 220
Lifetime Achievement Award from Miss. Institute of Arts and Letters, 186
Lifetime Achievement Award by the Miss. Women Lawyers Assn., 124
Lincoln's assassination, 8
Lincoln Award, 112
Little Red Schoolhouse, 444
Little Yazoo destroyed by tornado, 22
Litton Industries buys Ingalls Shipyard, 20
live births to teenage mothers, 384
live births to unmarried mothers, 384
liver disease, deaths from, 385
livestock, 411-12
Living Blues Award, 193
Living Blues magazine, 98, 145
local police departments, 392-93
London Times, 174
longest-selling paperback on the Publishers Weekly best-seller list, 129
longest-serving elected insurance commissioner in the U.S., 318

longest-serving sheriff in state history, 44
LONGEST
- board in the world, 297
- placename in the U.S., 469, 596
- placename in Mississippi, 596
- running album on Billboard's Gospel Chart, 342
- service in the U.S. House, 30
- serving TV weatherman in U.S., 321
- stint ever for a female country music singer's debut song, 338
- stretch of flat highway in U.S., 321
- sudden-death playoff in golf, 166
- tenure ever in the senate, 202

Los Angeles Times, 101, 174, 221
Lott elected Senate Majority Leader, 36
Louisiana Territory, 2
low birth weight babies, 384
lower 18-hole golf score than anybody has ever shot on the PGA Tour, 107, 310
lowest and flattest coast in the U.S., 294
lowest point of Mississippi, 50
lowest temperature ever in Miss., 59
lowest temperature in Jackson, 63
lowest winning score in the 83-year history of the State Am, 310
lung diseases, deaths from, 385
Lynn Meadow's Discovery Center, 438
Mademoiselle magazine, 149
Madison County Cultural Center, 441
magnolia becomes the state tree, 16
Magnolia State, 348
mail delivery points, number of, 502
major crimes for the Jackson MSA, 484
major flood in Jackson, 25-26, 80
major lakes/reservoirs, 51
major national credit bureaus, 375
major watersheds, 50
Mal's St. Paddy's Parade, 440
Malaco Records, 106-07, 109, 151, 155, 162, 169, 171, 193, 335, 342
Malaco Records formed in 1968, 106
Man of the Year honors, 134
man who created MTV (Music Television Video), 182
man who invented the dollar sign ($), 345
Manship House, 439
manufactured housing, 75, 483
manufacturing earnings, 377
map coordinates of Miss. cities, 53
Mardi Gras Museum, 434
Marie Hull Gallery, 445
Marine Life Oceanarium, 438
Marion Albert Pruett convicted, 26
market share for top banks in Miss., 381
market value of farm machinery & equipment, 412
married actor Zachary Scott, 329
married actress Maureen O'Hara, 329
married singer Connie Smith, 337
married singer George Jones, 222, 340
married singer Tim McGraw, 338
Marshall County Historical Museum, 439
Mary Buie Museum, 443
Matty Hersee Hospital founded, 12

maximum monthly snowfall in Jackson, 66
Maxwell Cup, 88
McCarty Farms sold, 33
McComb Enterprise Journal, 321
McNair signs rookie-record contract, 35
McRae Foundation, 164
McRaven Tour Home & Gardens, 447
mechanical cotton pickers demonstrated, 17
Medal of Honor, Congressional, 94, 104, 112, 122, 135, 157, 213, 215, 275, 303-05, 331, 343-44, 434, 437-38, 440-41, 443
Medger Evers murdered, 20
media trade associations, 479
median age of population, 75
median contract rent, 75, 482
median household income, 76, 376
median monthly homeowner costs, 75, 482
median price for homes in Jackson, 75
median price of homes sold, 482
Medicaid, 75, 350, 384
Medicaid eligibles, 75, 350
Medicaid managed care enrollment, 384
medical pioneer, 193
Medicare, 350, 384, 389
Medicare cuts, 389
Medicare expenditures, 384
Memorial Day started in Mississippi, 303
Memphis Free Speech, 214
mental hospitals, 484
Meridian Museum of Art, 442
Meridian Naval Air Station, 378
Meridian Star newspaper, 162, 206
Meridian, The, 6
Metro Jackson's apartment occupancy rate, 480
Metrocenter Mall opens, 24
Metropolitan Opera, 186
Metropolitan Statistical Areas, 514
military bases, 378
military contracts in mississippi, 350, 378
military family called "Fightin' McCains" started in Mississippi, 161
military installations, 350
milk/cream marketings, 412
milk cows, 412
Millennium polls, 45-46, 318, 343, 346, 447
"Million-Aires" Award, 119
Millsaps College opens, 11
Minneapolis Tribune, 115
minor watersheds, 50
minority whip, 155
Mirage Bowl, 104
miscellaneous associations, 375
Miss America, 19, 25, 28, 29, 110, 165, 169, 185, 285, 302, 434, 442-43
Miss Black America, 24, 302
Miss Mississippi, 130, 134, 169, 193, 204, 268, 302, 346, 446
Miss Mississippi Beauty Pageant, 446
Miss Teen All American, 200
Miss Teen USA Pageant, 434
Miss Universe, 110

General Index

MISSISSIPPI
    A&M College first football win, 12
    admitted as a state, 3
    Agriculture Service Dept. est., 15
    Arts Association, 197
    Arts Center, 439
    Arts Commission, 120, 133, 135
    Association of Broadcasters, 475
    Association of Coaches Hall of Fame, 145, 200
    Athletic Commisssion est., 15
    Author of the Year in 1988, 193
    Ballet, 197
    Band Directors Hall of Fame, 160
    Band of Choctaw Indians, 23, 159, 468
    Bankers Association formed, 10
    Baptist Association formed, 2
    Bar, 78, 103, 155, 157, 184
    Bar Foundation, 184
    blue laws abolished, 28
    Bowhunter's Association, 188
    Business Hall of Fame, 95, 106, 114, 159, 164, 177, 179, 194, 296, 383
    Chemical Corp., 17, 106, 298, 307
    Chemical Corp., startup bond issue approved, 17
    Coast Coliseum & Convention Center, 434
    Coliseum & Fairgrounds, 440
    Comm. on Hospital Care est., 17
    company's product on the moon, 297
    company's products have been to Jupiter, 297
    Congressional Delegation, 369
    Crafts Center, 439
    Cultural Arts Coalition, 439
    Dental Association formed, 9
    Dept. of Archives and History, 98, 99, 193, 325, 439
    Economic Development Council, 133
    Education Association organized, 10
    elected officials, 369
    Entomological Museum, 446
    exports, 380
    Firefighters Memorial Burn Center opens, 26
    Flood of 1927, 25, 64
    Folklore Society formed, 14
    Game and Fish Commission, 105
    Gaming Commission, 37
    Hall of Fame, 99
    Highway Patrol citations, 397
    Historical Society founded, 6
    House of Representatives, 369
    Illiteracy Commission est., 13
    Institute of Arts and Letters Award for Music, 223
    Institute of Arts and Letters Literature Award, 97, 112-13, 138, 143-44, 156, 163, 179, 222
    Library Association, 178
    Library Association Award, 222
    Library Association founded, 13

MISSISSIPPI
    Medical Center, first graduates, 19
    Medical Center groundbreaking, 18
    Museum of Natural History, 21, 105, 439
    Museum of Art, 106, 141, 144, 221, 439, 446
    Museum of Natural Science, 15, 346
    Museum of Natural Science est., 15
    Musicians Hall of Fame, 84, 87-88, 93, 95, 105, 107, 111, 116, 138, 146, 150, 156, 165, 169, 181, 185-86, 191, 194, 203, 214, 216, 222-23, 342
    Negro Training School founded, 16
    Normal College renamed Miss. State Teachers College, 14
    Normal College est. / opens, 13
    Opera Association, 439
    Petrified Forest, 436
    phone exchanges (prefixes), 486-95
    placed under Federal military rule, 9
    Poetry Society organized, 14
    Power and Light first organized, 14
    Press Asociation, 110, 115, 163, 187
    Press Association's Hall of Fame, 110, 116, 187
    Professional Athlete of the Year, 199
    readmitted to the Union, 9
    River at Vicksburg, level of, 64
    River flood, 14, 25
    River flood of 1927, 25, 64
    Scheme, 1
    Senate, 369
    Sports Hall of Fame, 28, 30, 32-35, 38, 42, 48, 78, 83, 86, 88-89, 91, 94, 96, 101, 103-05, 107-10, 114-15, 120, 125-26, 128-31, 140-42, 145, 149-54, 158, 162-63, 165-66, 168-70, 173, 178-80, 183, 188, 192, 195, 197, 199, 200, 202, 205-06, 209-10, 213, 215-16, 220, 309-12, 439, 443
    Sports Hall of Fame and Museum, 274, 311, 439, 485
    Sports Hall of Fame and Museum opens, 38, 311
    Sports Writers Association, 164
    Sportscasters Association, 80
    Sportwriters Hall of Fame, 194
    State awarded its first honorary degrees, 95
    State baseball team goes to its first College World Series, 23
    State basketball team makes Sweet 16, 35
    State Charity Hospital opens, 13
    State College for Women becomes Miss. University for Women, 23
    State College renamed, 19
    State Parks, 52, 430-31, 434-35, 437-39, 441-47, 451
    State School for Mentally Handicapped established, 14

MISSISSIPPI
    State University Sports Hall of Fame, 107, 115, 120, 139, 141-42, 165, 169, 173-74, 183, 202, 209
    Symphony Chamber Orchestra, 183
    Symphony Orchestra, 183, 197
    Territory, 2-3, 12
    Trade Mart, 439
    Veterans Memorial Stadium, 485
    Vietnam Veterans Memorial, 443
    Welcome Centers, 431
    Women Lawyers Association, 184
Miss. Statesman & Natchez Gazette, 3
Mississippi Statesman newspaper, 3
Mississippi Business Journal, 133
Mississippi Herald, 2
Mississippi Magazine, 141, 167, 193
Mississippi Queen (boat), 443
Mississsippi Review, 156
Mississippi State's all-time scoring leader in basketball, 158
Mississippi State's women's basketball team makes first trip to NCAA Tournament, 46

MISSISSIPPI'S
    first and only professional theater, 42
    first & only publisher of newspaper chain located in Miss., 115
    first art museum, 440
    first baseball legend, 309
    first black member of the U.S. House of Representatives, 16, 157, 306
    first capitol building, 3
    first children's museum, 438
    first governor, 3
    first museum for 21st Century, 311
    first railroad, 446
    greatest college football game, 115
    high school basketball career scoring leader, 312
    last execution in the 20th Century, 29
    Man of the Century, 185, 346
    most decorated soldier of WWI, 13
    oldest synagogue, 445
    only black circuit judge, 27
    only state-based Fortune 500 company, 114, 435
    proportionate share of nat'l. debt, 377
    tallest building, 23
    Top 10 export markets, 380
    Woman of the Century, 214, 346
mockingbird, one of state's symbols, 349
mockingbird chosen official state bird, 16
Montgomery GI Bill, 170
Montgomery VA Medical Center, 171
monthly rent, 482
more college career football yards than anyone in history, 309
more No. 1 records than any other artist, 208, 339

MOST
    accomplished golf instructor in the world, 166
    accurate mine-hunting devise the U.S. Army has, 318

The Ultimate Reference on the State

General Index

MOST
- charted singles (records), 184, 335
- churches per capita, 299
- common surnames in Miss., 347
- destructive ice storms, 59
- famous of early bluesmen, 331
- hit albums, 185, 335
- influential slide guitarist of the postwar period, 144
- livable communities in Mississippi for 1999, 447
- lynchings, 14
- one-sided football win in Ole Miss history, 12
- populated county, 351, 514
- powerful centrifuge in the world, 447
- prolific offensive player in NCAA's 125-year history, 164
- rainfall, snowfall, 59
- successful event of its kind in the state's history, 37, 345
- successful talk show host, 329
- times of running 1,000 yards or more in a season, 310
- Top-10 & Top 40 records, 185, 335
- unusual weather occurrence, 59
- watched hunting video series in the U.S., 296

Motor City Bowl, 272
Motor Sports Hall of Fame, 208
motor vehicle accident deaths, 430
Motor Voter Law upheld, 42
Mound Bayou founded, 10
Mount Hermon Female Seminary opens, 9
movies filmed in Mississippi, 29, 80, 115, 117-18, 124, 129, 150, 168, 222, 276-80, 328, 337
Mrs. America, 28, 174, 193, 302, 446
Mrs. Mississippi, 174, 446
Mrs. World, 174, 193, 302
Ms magazine, 210
MSU's 16th president, 183
MTV on air for the first time, 25
Museum of Classical Archaeology, 17
Museum of the Southern Jewish Experience, 447
Music City News awards, 205, 208, 339
Music City News Male Artist of the Year, 186, 340
music director of Opryland USA, 214, 341
Music Operators of America, 186, 340
Music Operators of America Record of the Year, 181
Musical America Magazine, 110
musical arranger at NBC, 342
Mynelle Gardens, 439

NAACP, 20-21, 24, 40, 78, 116-17, 136, 171, 214
narrowest recorded percentage win in any election, 25, 319
NASA, 20, 28-31, 89, 95, 99, 110, 130-31, 160, 191-92, 195, 207, 294, 297, 307, 313, 315, 320, 433, 436, 440, 446
NASA's Space Technology Labs open, 21

NASCAR, 201
Nashville Songwriters Hall of Fame, 103, 181, 208, 339
NATCHEZ
- City Cemetery, 443
- dance hall fire, 16
- Hospital (Charity), 2, 4
- Indians, 325, 443, 468-69
- Museum of Afro-American History & Culture, 443
- National Cemetery, 343-44, 443
- National Historical Park, 443
- tornado of 1840, 5
- Trace, 2, 15, 430, 441, 443, 445
- Trace Parkway, 325-26, 431, 436, 440, 446
- Trace Parkway Museum opens, 20
- Under-The-Hill, 325

Natchez Gazette, 3
Natchez Statesman and Gazette, 100
Natchez Times, The, 17
National Rifleman, The, 141
NATION'S
- best fiscal leader, 319
- first black aviator killed in combat, 93, 306
- first color educational TV station, 22
- largest catfish processor, 30
- largest independent R&B and Gospel record label, 342
- largest producer and distributor of fresh shell chicken eggs, 298
- leading catfish research center, 298
- oldest and largest all-black city, 29
- oldest land grant college for African-Americans, 299
- second largest manufacturer of off-premises ATMs, 296
- second largest national cemetery, 344
- second oldest yacht club, 294
- top Abraham Lincoln scholar, 308

National Assn. of Attorneys General, 319
National Assn. of State Treasurers, 319
Nat'l. Aviation Hall of Fame, 22, 208, 314
Nat'l. Basketball Hall of Fame, 203, 210
National Black College Hall of Fame, 89, 203, 220
National Book Award, 179
National Book Circle Award, 121
National Coach of the Year, 104, 145, 183, 196
national credit bureaus, 375
National Endowment of the Arts, 121, 135, 150, 175, 177
National Film Registry, 80, 86, 95, 110, 118, 223, 328
National Finals Rodeo, 205
National Football Foundation, 102, 107, 129, 162
national forests and parks, 52, 431
National Geographic magazine, 178
National Heritage Fellowship, 150, 218
national high school record for victories by an undefeated team, 312
National Medal of the Arts, 147

National Military Park, 303, 447
national publication with its editorial offices in Mississippi, 295
National Republican Committee, 42
National Republican Pary, 447
National Sweet Potato Fest, 447
National Track & Field Hall of Fame, 89, 97, 147, 215, 311
national wildlife refuges, 52, 431
National Women's Hall of Fame, 132, 214, 220
native American population, 73
natural gas production, 379
natural resources, 52
Naval Works Confederate Ship Yards, 447
NBA All-Star, 141
NCAA Division II Football Hall of Fame, 179
NCAA sports teams, 431
needle regiments, 8
Negro regiments, 8
Neshoba County Fair, 10, 326, 444
- first held, 10
Neshoba Democrat, The, 99, 194
net domestic migration, 73
net farm income, 412-13
net international migration, 73
new businesses, 376
new graduated income tax law, 14
new housing starts, 377
New Orleans Magazine, 88, 148
New Orleans Review, 96
New Orleans States, 178
New Orleans Times, 8
New Republic, 223
new single family housing permits, 75
new speed records for Atlantic crossing and a westerly crossing of the Atlantic, 166
New Stage Theatre, 439
New York Critics' Circle award, 136, 217
New York Film Critics Award, 96
New York Times, the, 27-28, 48, 81, 88-89, 98-101, 112-13, 123, 142, 156, 159, 171, 174, 193, 201, 205, 212, 217, 221-22, 300, 307, 346
New York Times best-seller list, 129, 214
New York World's Fair, 141, 150, 178, 221
New Yorker, 96, 202, 214
Newbery Medal, 205
Newsday, 212
Newseum, 176
newspapers in the state, list of, 476-79
Newsweek magazine, 42, 88, 94, 206, 347
Newton Station Depot, 443
NFL All-Time Team, 130
NFL MVP award for an unprecedented 3rd straight year, 118, 309
NFL Offensive Player of the Year, 118, 189
nine 9 MSA counties, 514
Nissan Motor Company, 49, 380
NOAA weather radio, 58
Nobel Prize for Literature, 117, 200

General Index

noncontiguous areas (islands), 50
nonfuel minerals, 379
nonwhite population, 73-74
nonwhite population chart, 513
nonwhite pop. of Jackson MSA, 480
normal (average) lows for each month in Jackson, 63
Normal Monthly Precip. in Jackson, 64
Normal Yearly Precipitation in Jackson, 64
International Hall of Fame, 205
North Delta Museum, 437
North Mississippi Business Journal, 122
Northeast Mississippi Daily Journal, 37
Northeast Mississippi Museum, 435
northernmost point of Mississippi, 50
Northpark Mall opens, 27
Noxubee County Historical Society Museum, 441
Noxubee National Wildlife Refuge, 446
nuclear device exploded inside salt dome in Lamar County, 20
Nuclear power plants, 379
NUMBER OF
   ABC Permit Holders, 351
   annual miles driven per vehicle, 430
   bankruptcies Filed, 380
   banks, 376
   blacks in legislature, 348
   businesses, 376
   classroom teachers, 402, 485
   couples married, 73, 385
   crimes, 396
   deaths, 76
   degrees awarded, 403
   degrees awarded at community colleges, 403
   Democrats in the legislature, 348
   diploma graduates, 402
   divorces granted, 73, 76, 385
   driver's licenses issued, 395
   dropouts, 402
   employed / unemployed, 76, 377-78, 481-82
   enrolled in colleges & universities in the Jackson MSA, 485
   farms, 412
   federal government employees, 378
   foster care homes, 350
   full-time law enforcement employees, 396
   highway rail crossings in Miss., 430
   home health care agencies, 385
   hospitals, 384
   households, 75, 482
   landfills, 379
   lawyers, 396
   licensed drivers, 430
   licensed child care centers, 385
   live births, 76, 384
   live births and deaths in cities, 386
   major crime for Jackson MSA, 397
   major crime offenses in cities, 397
   marriages, 76
   miles driven by all Mississippi drivers, 321, 420

NUMBER OF
   miles driven on Miss. Roads, 430
   minority members in legislature, 348
   Mississippi hunters, 456
   Mississippi Landmarks, 325
   Mississippians killed in wars, 304
   motor vehicle deaths in 1999 in the City of Jackson, 484
   paroled, 396
   phone Lines, 380
   physicians, 384
   police officers in Jackson, 484
   police depts. in Miss., 395
   prisoners in State Penitentiary at Parchman, 396
   public schools, number of, 402
   public school districts, 402, 484
   registered voters, 348
   registered vehicles, 430, 485
   Republicans in the legislature, 348
   rural water systems, 379
   seasonal heating degree days in Jackson, 63
   state government employees, 349
   state entries on the National Register of Historic Places, 325
   state-licensed nursing homes, 385
   sworn highway patrol officers, 396
   sworn Bureau of Narcotics Agents, 396
   union members, 377
   vehicles per household, 430
   veterans, 76, 350
   visitors to Mississippi casinos, 465
   vistors to Mississippi Welcome Centers, 432
   war veterans, 76
   winter heating degree days in Jackson, 63
   women in legislature, 348
   workers in State Government, 378
NUMBER ONE
   banana port in the U.S., 14, 294
   movie of all time, 328
   tree farming state in the nation, 21
   deer ever killed by a hunter with a firearm, 345
   record on the Adult Contemporary Christian charts, 342
   record on *Time* magazine's Best Music of 1996, 341
   farm state in the nation, 298
O, The Oprah Magazine, 78, 220
Oakes African American Cultural Center, 447
Oakland College (later Alcorn State) est., 3
officer who ordered the first shot in the Civil War, 12
official state record fish, 457
official world record deer, 455
Old Biloxi Lighthouse, 434
Old Courthouse Museum, 303, 447
Old Main at Mississippi State burns, 19
Old Spanish Fort Museum, 294, 444
Old State Capital Historical Museum, 439

OLDEST
   American swimmer to ever win an Olympic medal, 38
   bathtub in western the hemisphere, 299, 443
   book in the nation, 299, 443
   business in the state, 3, 446
   campground fair in U.S., 326, 444
   county in Mississippi, 351
   death date on a tombstone, 343, 443
   edifice in the U.S. west of the Atlantic coast, 294
   Episcopal church building west of the Alleghenies, 299, 448
   existing industrial building in the state, 326
   family-owned phone company, 295
   field game in America, 326
   governor to ever serve, 353, 360
   house in Jackson, 439
   land-grant college for blacks in the U.S., 441
   law firm in the nation, 152
   newspaper in the state, 446
   operating courthouse in the state, 441
   public library building in Miss., 447
   structure built by white men in the Mississippi Valley, 444
   synagogue in the state, 445
   university building and second oldest school building in Miss., 326
Ole Miss Alumni Hall of Fame, 80, 138, 140, 148
Ole Miss Athletic Hall of Fame, 213
Ole Miss football team first named Rebels, 16
Ole Miss football team plays its first night game, 15
Ole Miss Jazz Alumni Hall of Fame, 139
Ole Miss Law Alumna of the Year, 184
Ole Miss Rebels first football win, 11
Ole Miss record for QB sacks, 216
Ole Miss record for touchdown passes, 167
Ole Miss Sports Hall of Fame, 81
Ole Miss Team of the Century, 216
Olympic(s), 19-20, 22, 25-27, 29, 36, 38, 49, 80, 86-89, 97, 101-03, 114, 117-18, 125, 135, 137, 147, 150, 158, 161, 163, 172, 175, 179, 183, 199, 203, 214, 222, 311, 341, 343
Olympic Gold Medal(s), 19-20, 22, 26-27, 29, 38, 88, 103, 198
Olympic Hall of Fame, 89, 97
on Billboard's chart for 45 consecutive weeks, setting a new record, 169
once the "Tomato Capital of the World", 320, 436
ONE OF
   America's "15 Most Beautiful Black Women", 218
   only four black boarding schools in the nation, 147
   only four Mississippians to hold the Juridical Science Doctoris (J.S.D) degree, 152

General Index

ONE OF
   People magazine's "50 Most Beautiful People", 337, 338
   Teen People magazine's "21 Hottest Stars Under 21", 337

ONE OF THE
   10 all-time Favorite Wheaties® Champions, 310
   25 most influential people in America, 220
   100 hottest new U.S. businesses, 296
   all-time great jazz guitarists, 341
   fastest growing small businesses in the country, 296
   first American women to fly, 165
   first elected to the Songwriters Hall of Fame, 339
   first houses in America built with full colonnade across full facade, 326
   first librarians to stress pride in black heritage, 191
   greatest and most prolific songwriters, 180
   longest continuous-running radio shows in the nation, 221
   nation's longest serving agriculture commissioners, 192
   state's greatest football coaching legends, 209
   ten attorneys who established the law dept./ at Merrill Lynch, 152
   Top-15 best-selling recording artists of all time, 340
   two PGA tournament directors, 174
   world's top blues pianists, 180

ONLY
   5th cabinet member ever from the state, 306
   American to have ever won Mrs. World, 174, 302
   artist in the music history to have had 21 top-5 hits in a row, 208, 339
   black-owned bank closes, 3
   boxer to ever hold 3 world champion titles simultaneously, 29, 79, 311
   boxer to fight both Muhammad Ali and Rocky Marciano, 311
   brothers ever to win Olympic Gold, 102, 103, 311
   cabinet member from Mississippi in the 20th Century, 116, 306, 319
   Confederate soldier to lie in state in the Old Capitol, 303
   county in the nation named for Simon Bolivar, 324
   county in the nation named for the city of Grenada, Spain, 324
   Dentzel carousel in U.S., 442
   federal prison in Mississippi, 346
   Fortune 500 company headquartered in Mississippi, 295, 380
   Governor of Mississippi to receive the Medal of Honor, 359
   Governor of the state to entertain a member of a royal family, 16

ONLY
   governor to be lieutenant governor 3 times, 353
   governor to resign from office, 352, 355
   house in America on United Nations' World Heritage List, 147
   inland casino in the state, 444
   Lady Rebel to ever score over 2,000 points and pull down over 1,000 rebounds, 125
   lighthouse in U.S. in the middle of a four-lane highway, 326, 434
   man to ever pinch hit for Babe Ruth, 209, 309
   minister to ever become a comic strip character, 97
   Miss. governor buried outside the continental U.S., 9, 352, 358
   Mississippi governor 20th Century to serve back-to-back terms, 35
   Mississippian in the Nat'l. Aviation Hall of Fame, 208, 314
   Mississippian to serve on the nation's highest court, 151, 155, 319
   Mississippian to receive the Medal of Honor during Vietnam, 21
   Mississippian to receive the MOH for World War I, 157
   native Mississippian in Baseball Hall of Fame, 30, 86, 446
   opening day cycle in major league baseball history, 210, 309
   petrified forest in eastern U.S., 326
   pilot to have won the Thompson air race three times, 208
   player in NCAA history to gain over 16,000 yards, 164
   record label, inducted into the Miss. Musicians Hall of Fame, 107
   state to ever have a Miss Hospitality Pageant, 302
   the second Mississippian to be president of the PGA, 311
   truly original America music, 313
   two American aviators who ever 'double-crossed' the ocean, 166

Onward Store, 443
Oprah Winfrey Show, the, 161, 220
Opryland USA, 341
optometrists, number of, 384
Orange Bowl, 16, 180, 272
Order of the Eastern Star organized, 5, 313
origin of name Mississippi, 348
original lead singer of the Flamingos, 332
original Marlboro Man, 105
originator of the historic Marshall Plan following World War II, 101
Oscar® (Academy Award), 106, 121, 123, 136, 147, 281-88, 290-92
Outdoor Life Magazine, 91
Outer Critics Circle award, 147
Outstanding Mississippi Woman Lawyer Award, 184
Outstanding Women of America, 173

Owen Cooper Memorial Award, 106
Oxford American magazine, 129, 132
Oxford Falcon, 9
Palaces of St. Petersburg, 35, 37, 345
Palestine Gardens, 441
Parade magazine, 167
parolees, number of, 396
Pascagoula Chronicle, 133, 321
Pascagoula Indians, 294
Pascagoula Naval Home Port, 378
passed or ran for 127 TDs, a state record, 167
pasture land, 52
Pat Harrison Waterway District Water Parks, 442, 445-46, 448, 461
patents granted to Miss. residents, 380
patients admitted to hospitals, 384
Peach Bowl, 23, 31, 35, 46, 196, 213, 272
Pearl Harbor, Mississippi deaths at, 304
Peavey Visitors Center & Museum, 442
pellagra experiment at Parchman Penitentiary, 13
Pemberton Headquarters, 447
PEN/Faulkner Award, 121
People magazine, 165, 167, 218, 220
People magazine's list "50 Most Beautiful People", 137, 201, 211, 220
per capita personal income in Mississippi Counties, 382
percentage in the state with bachelor's degree or higher, 76
percentage of population of Mississippi who smoke cigarettes, 385
percentage of possible sunshine in Jackson, 63
percentage of tribal members who speak the Choctaw language, 468
Perry County Courthouse burns again in 1990, 30
Persian Gulf War veterans, 76
personal income, 376, 483
personal property, 377
personalized car tags, 430
Petrified Forest, 436
petroleum production, 379
PGA Hall of Fame, 166
PGA Tour, 174
PGA Tour record book, 166
Pharmacists, number of, 384
Phi Beta Kappa, 85, 137, 143, 149, 172, 308
physical therapists, number of, 384
physicians, number of, 384
physiographic region of Mississippi, 50
pig crop, 412
pilgrimage(s), 435, 439, 442, 445, 447
Pine-Sol®, 168, 314
Piney Woods Country Life School, 13, 147
place where Memorial Day started, 344
placenames, 322-24, 559-96
pneumonia, deaths from, 385
police departments, 392-93
political-geographic division of Miss., 50
political parties, 374
popular dinner silverware patterns, 325

General Index

population statistics, 74-76, 384-85, 480, 482, 508-15
population born in Mississippi, 73
population density, 73
population of Miss. cities/towns, 508-511
population without health insurance, 385
ports, 50, 294, 380
poultry, 298
pre-kindergarten enrollment, 402
prehistoric whale, 349
premature live births, 384
present constitution adopted, 348
President Davis captured, 8
president of 20th Century-Fox, 328
President of the Confederacy, 109
president of the PGA of America, 154
President pro temp of the Senate, 113, 134
Presidential Citation, 315
Presidential Medal of Freedom, 131, 186, 214, 217
Presidential Medal of Honor, 150
Press Club of New Orleans, 148
primary highways, 430
principal crops, 411
principal manufactured goods, 377
prison inmates, number of, 396
prisoners, executed & on death row, 396
Private John Allen National Fish Hatchery, 446
private schools, number of, 402
Pro Bowl, 83, 89, 94, 96, 118, 128, 130, 141, 149, 158, 173, 178, 189, 195, 199, 211, 220, 310
Pro Football Hall of Fame, 28, 78, 83, 94, 105, 146, 149, 179, 195, 310
pro sports teams in Mississippi, 431
probationers, number of, 396
professional associations, 375
professional journals, 479
Professional Rodeo Cowboys Assn., 205
Progressive Farmer magazine, 35, 96, 217
projected population, 75
property crimes, 396-97
psychologists, number of, 384
Public/Educational TV & Radio, 470
public community/junior colleges, 403
public libraries statistics, 409
public schools, number of, 402
Publishers Weekly, 129, 204, 212
Pulitzer Gold Medal, 343
Pulitzer Prize (or Pulitzer), 17-18, 20, 23, 25, 27, 32, 99, 112, 117, 120-21, 133, 136, 148, 158, 174, 176, 187, 198, 205, 214, 217, 282-83, 291, 307-08, 321, 343, 347
pupil/teacher ratio, 402, 485
Pushcart Prize, 120, 222
Queen and King of all gypsies in North America, 344
Quizquiz, 1
R&B Foundation's Pioneer Award, 109
radio stations, list of, 473, 475-77
radiofrequency lung tumor ablation, 316
railroad(s), 430, 433, 442, 446-47, 456, 460

Rainwater Observatory, 436
Rankin General Hospital opens, 21
rarest of North American cranes, 347
RCA's best-selling artist since Elvis, 340
Reader's Digest, 206
readmission of Mississippi, 348
real property, 377
real property taxes, 483
Rebels win first Nat'l. Championship, 209
Reconstruction, 9, 21-22, 24, 28, 31, 34-35, 306, 318
record for the longest service in the U.S. House of Representatives, 215, 318
record highs for crops, 411
record lows for crops, 411
record low temperatures in Jackson, 63
Record World magazine, 102, 181
Records of Mississippi's Three Division 1-A Football Teams, 431
Red Bluff miniature canyon, 442
regional universities, 403
registered nurses, number of, 384
registered regular tags, 430
religions, 73
religious publications, 479
Republic of Jones, 7
Republican Conference Chairman, 103
Republican National Committee, 82, 164, 318
Republican National Convention, 37
Republican whip, 155
reservoirs, 51
resigned under threat of impeachment, 359
respiratory therapists, no. of, 384
restoration of Old Capitol completed, 19
retail sales, 376, 381, 483
retirement communities, 447
revenue & expenditures at community colleges, 403
revenue generated at state parks, 431
revenues for public schools, 402
Revolutionary War, 1
Rhythm & Blues Foundation, 111, 139, 155
Richmond Times-Dispatch, 148
Ripley's Believe It-or-Not largest and 2nd largest checkerboards, 210
river cargo, 380
river ports, 380
rivers, list of major, 50
Riverside Hotel (the Blues Hotel), 435
Robert F. Kennedy Journalism Awards, 145
Robert Johnson Blues Memorial, 437
Rock & Roll Hall of Fame, 78, 83, 99, 105, 108, 111, 119, 139, 141, 144, 146, 149, 154, 162, 173, 185, 187, 191, 197, 200, 207, 212, 330-34, 339
Rolling Stone magazine, 88, 134, 220, 222, 334
Ronald McNair Space Theater, 439
Rose Garden Plant Science Research Center, 446
Rose Hill Cemetery, 344, 442
Rosemont Plantation, 446

Ross Barnett Reservoir, 64, 439, 441, 445
Ross Barnett Reservoir hits record low, 64
Rowan Oak, 443
Roy E. Wiley Planetarium, 435
Royal Slam, 345
Ruins of Windsor, 276, 326, 441
Rural Electrification Administration (REA) started, 15
Russell C. Davis Planetarium, 86, 439
Saenger Center and Theatre, 438
salaries at Mississippi's public community colleges, 403
sales tax collected, 377
sales tax goes from 6% to 7%, 30
San Francisco Examiner, 86
Saturday Evening Post magazine, 31
Saturday Night Live band, 158
Saturday Review, 206
school bus accidents, 403
school districts, number of, 402
School for the Blind established, 5
School for the Deaf, 29, 32
School for the Deaf established, 5
school lunch program, 350
School of Pharmacy started at University of Mississippi, 12
school transportation, 403
scored a perfect 36 on the ACT, 98, 116, 124, 126, 192, 199, 209
Scott County Times, 194
Scott Marine Education Center & Aquarium, 434
Scranton Floating Museum, 444
Screen Actors Guild, 122-23, 211
Seafood Industry Museum, 434
SEC Team of the Decade for 1950-59, 209
seceded from the union, 348
SECOND
    longest punt in college football history, 130
    most attended art / cultural event in the Southeast in 1998, 42
    biggest gaming state in the nation in gaming space, 312
    chancellor of the Univ. of Miss., 155
    county in the U.S. to establish a Board of Health, 295
    highest attended exhibit in the U.S. in 1996, 37, 345
    largest gambling state in total gaming area, 465
    largest Indian mound in U.S., 443
    largest military cemetery in U.S., 447
    largest reinforced concrete building in the world, 320
    municipal streetcar system in U.S., 12
    oldest executive residence in the U.S. continuously occupied, 325
    oldest pilgrimage city, 439
    state in the nation to establish a State Archives Dept., 347
    tallest free-standing structure in the state, 320
Secretary of Agriculture, 306

General Index

Secretary of State, 348, 369
sectarian colleges, list of, 404
Seminary For Freedmen established, 10
Senate Majority Leader, 155, 223, 318
Senior Bowl, 96, 168, 180, 219
sent more men to war in WWII than any town its size in the U.S., 304
service industry job growth, 379
set 2 Ole Miss records, 310
set an Orange Bowl record, 180
senior (four-year) colleges, list of, 404
settlement with the tobacco industry, 319
Shaw University (later Rust College), 9
Shaw University renamed Rust College, 11
Shearwater Pottery, , 443
Sheriff's Departments, list of, 391
Sheriff Paul Barrett sentenced, 35
Sherman necktie, 346
Ship Island, 434, 438, 446
shopping centers/malls, 376
shortest gubernatorial term, 352, 357
shortest of any single-term governor of Mississippi, 357
shortest placenames, 323
Siege of Vicksburg, 8
Silver Medal (Olympic), 311
Silver Medalist in the 1982 International Ballet Competition, 205
single largest donation in Mississippi State's 116-year history, 204
site of the country's first Memorial Day observance, 435
SkyTel 2-way paging launched, 34
slave(s)[slavery], 1, 2, 5-9, 16, 33, 96-97, 100, 118, 132, 147-48, 157, 160, 214, 445, 447
slavery in Mississippi abolished, 8
slogans of cities/towns, 322
slot machines, number of, 465
smallest county in Mississippi, 52, 351
smallest public school district, 402
Smith-Robertson Museum & Cultural Center, 439
Smith-Wills Stadium, 86, 309
Smithsonian Institute, 175, 297, 208, 433
Smithsonian Museum, 22, 208
snake bite deaths, 385
SNCC (Student Non-Violent Coordinating Committee), 171
snow in Jackson, 65
social security, 350
soft toilet seat, 313
soil erosion, 52
sold more country-comedy albums than any other artist, 102, 307
solid waste, 379
solo artist that received the most RIAA awards, 335
some preliminary results of the 2000 Census, 75
Songwriters Hall of Fame, 150, 165, 191, 339
Soul Train Awards, 92, 169, 217, 334, 341
South's first diesel-powered streamliner locomotive, 15

South's largest collection of Civil War memorabilia, 303
South's largest retail furniture store, 296
South Miss. Charity Hospital opens, 13
South Mississippi Magazine, 141
South Mississippi Sun, 163
Southern Baptist Convention, 5
Southern Christian Leadership Conference, 97
Southern Farm Bureau Golf Classic PGA Tour Event, 46, 445
Southern Living magazine, 35, 96
Southern Miss Sports Hall of Fame, 90
Southern Outdoors magazine, 93
Southern states, data for each, 484-85
southernmost point of Miss., 50
Sovereignty Commission, 18, 24, 36, 41
    created, 18   disbanded, 24
Soybeans, 412
Space Shuttle, 131, 160, 192, 297, 433
Splendors of Versailles exhibition ends, 42
Sporting News, 130, 158
Sporting News NFL Player of the Year, 189
Sports Afield magazine, 132
Sports Illustrated, 49, 118, 125, 158, 164, 167, 171, 173, 189
Sportsman of the Year, 91, 213
Sprague, The (boat), 23, 326
Springarn Medal, 117
Springdale Hills Arboretum, 444
SS Argentina, SS Brasil, & SS Exchequer, 294
St. Dominic-Jackson Memorial Hospital dedicated, 18
St. Dominic's Hospital, 17, 36
St. Peter's Cemetery, 443
Stackhouse/Rooster Blues Records, 435
Starkville Daily News, 194
Stars Over Mississippi fundraiser, 134
STATE
    appropriation for higher education, 403
    Auditor, 369
    Baptist Convention, 5
    Bar Association, 302
    Bar Association formed, 10
    Beverage, Bird, butterfly, fish, tree and other official symbols, 349
    Board of Accountancy created, 14
    Board of Architecture est., 15
    Board of Law Examiners est., 13
    boundary, 50
    budget for the Departments of Health & Mental Health, 385
    budget for FY 2001, 377
    champion tree, 298
    Coat of Arms, 348
    Commission for the Blind est., 15
    Constitution of 1890, 11
    Dept. of Public Welfare est., 15
    employee averages, 349
    expenditures, 377
    Fair held for first time, 9
    firearms deaths, 385

STATE
    Flag & Coat of Arms adopted, 11
    Flag, 348
    Flower, 298, 349, 423
    fuel tax receipts, 430
    General Fund, 350
    government debt, expenditures & revenues, 350
    government toll-free phone nos., 372
    high school football records, 312
    Historical Museum, 346
    income taxes, 377
    income tax rate for individuals, 377
    Insurance Commission est., 14
    legislators, 348
    motto, 348
    nicknames, 348
    of Miss. Hall of Fame, 37, 208, 306
    paid holidays, 349
    Parks, 52, 430-31, 434-35, 437-39, 441-47, 451, 458-61
    ratifies Prohibition Amendment, 320
    revenue, 377
    sales tax, 483
    sales tax increases, 18
    statute making state flag official emblem repealed in 1906, 48
    Supreme Court Justice Chuck McRae, 33
    Symbols, 349
    Tax Commission established, 13
    Tree, 298, 349, 423
STATE'S, the
    all-time favorite politician, 202, 318
    biggest parade, 440
    first $1 billion ag. commodity, 298
    first and only billionaire, 114
    first black Circuit Court judge since Reconstruction, 306
    first ever 3-game bowl sweep, 46
    first ever popularly elected Republican senator, 318
    first garbage-powered energy plant begins operation, 27
    first Mardi-Gras parade, 12
    first prison, 4
    first Republican governor, 9
    first woman Lt. Gov., 438
    greatest scientific accomplishment of the Millennium, 133
    largest single private employer, 294
    largest tree, 298, 423
    largest construction company, 296
    largest employer, 444
    largest hotel, 465
    largest public library, 28
    oldest church, 446
    oldest incorporated town, 433
    oldest Masonic Lodge, 443
    only daily college newspaper, 480
    second favorite politician, 171
    tallest building, 320, 465
    tallest champion tree, 298
    top scientific contribution, 45
    two charity hospitals close, 29

General Index

steamboats: *Natchez*, 343
    New Orleans, 2   *Robert E. Lee*, 343
Stellar Awards, 169
Stephen Dill Lee started the Civil War, 153
sternwheel paddleboat, 435
strokes, deaths from, 385
Sullivan Trophy, 88
student/computer Ratio, 402
Sue Kaufman Prize for first fiction, 212
Sugar Bowl, 18-22, 180, 196, 272
suicide, rate of, 385
Sun Bowl, 18, 21, 23, 25, 90, 104, 180, 272
Sun Herald, The, 163
Sun Records (& studio), 78, 92, 97, 99, 112, 119, 139, 141, 153, 155, 162, 185, 192, 197, 206, 211, 221, 336
Sunderland Society, 143
Super-Bowl-record 81 yard TD pass, 309
Super Bowl, 28, 30, 41, 48, 78, 94, 118, 128, 137, 141, 164, 171, 189, 195, 211, 213, 220, 309, 310
Super Bowl record for a quarterback, 164
Super Bowl records by Jerry Rice, 189
supercomputer center of the South, 317
Superconducting Super Collider, 29
Supplemental Security Income (SSI), 350
Supreme Court, 348
surface area of state, 50
surprise snowstorm, 66
SWAC Athletic Director of the Year, 188
SWAC Hall of Fame, 94, 197
Sweet Potato Capital of World, 320, 447
TALLEST
    building in Mississippi, 320, 465
    champion tree, 420, 423
    free-standing structure in Miss., 320, 445
    structure east of the Mississippi, 320
Tangerine Bowl, 19, 26, 90, 104, 108, 219, 272
Tatum salt dome, 317
Tax Commission receipts, 377
tax revenues from gaming, 465
taxes in Mississippi, 377
teachers salaries, 402, 485
Teddy Bear gets its start in Miss., 12, 160, 313, 443
Teen People magazine's "21 Hottest Stars Under 21", 201
teenage mothers, 384
Temperature/precipitation data for:
    Biloxi & Brookhaven, 54
    Clarksdale & Columbus, 55
    Greenwood & Hattiesburg, 56
    Jackson, 62-72
    Meridian & Tupelo, 57
ten leading causes of death in Miss. & the U.S., 385
Ten Most Fascinating People of '95, 161
Tenn-Tom Waterway opens, 27
Tennessee-Tombigbee Waterway, 23, 215, 345, 380, 435
    construction begins, 23
Tennessee Ernie Ford Collection, 438

Tennessee Valley Authority (TVA), 15, 23, 26, 198
terrain of Mississippi, 51
Thalia Mara Hall, 159, 439
Theater Hall of Fame, 147
third biggest gaming state in the nation, 312, 465
third highest home-ownership rate in the U.S., 75
third most prolific writer in literary history, 343
third movie ever to win the top five Academy Awards, 134
Thompson Field, 22
Thompson Trophy Race, 207, 314
Three-Chopped Way Road, 2
timber / lumber production, 380
timber products harvested, 483
Time magazine, 31, 42, 127, 130, 149, 159, 206-07, 210, 217-18, 220
Tippah County Historical Museum, 445
TNN/*Music City News* Country Awards, 137, 204, 338
Tombigbee National Forest, 447
Tony Award, 26, 28, 103, 116, 147, 211, 283, 285
Top-10 counties for cotton, soybeans, rice, corn, wheat & sorghum (charts), 414
Top-20 Largest Companies, 381
Top 100 Greatest American Movies of All Time, 123, 141, 147, 150, 174, 186, 190, 211, 217, 281-85, 290-92, 328
Top Female Vocalist of the Year, 338
Top Humanitarian, 346
top Lincoln scholar in the nation, 112
top manufacturing employers, 376
top movie of all time, 174
top poultry-producing area in the state, 436
topography of Mississipp, 51
tornado(s), 5, 10, 12, 14, 16-19, 21-27, 29-30, 32-33, 44, 60-61
Tornes found guilty, sentenced to die, 41
Tour LeFleur pro cyclist race, 440
tourism, 376, 431, 483
Towboat Capital of the World, 320, 437
toxic chemicals released, 379
Toys and Soldiers Museum, 447
Trade Mart, 440
Trail of Tears, 4
transportation in Jackson MSA, 483
travel time to work, 430, 485
Traveling Leisure Magazine, 172
Treaty of Chickasaw Council House, 3
Treaty of Dancing Rabbit Creek, 3
Treaty of Doak's Stand, 3
Treaty of Paris, 1
Treaty of Pontotoc, 4
Treaty of San Lorenzo, 2
tree, largest in Mississippi, 298
tree species, 416-23
Triangle Cultural Center, 447
true value of all real and personal property in Mississippi, 347, 377
Trumpet Records, 45, 144, 162-63, 217, 445

Truth® video series, the, 186, 296
tung oil tree introduced to Mississippi, 14
Tupelo Battlefield Monument, 52, 431
Tupelo City Museum, 446
Tupelo National Battlefield, 446
TV Guide, 78, 185, 220
TV towers among the tallest in nation, 320
twister(s) [tornado], 16, 22, 23, 60-61
typical monthly rent, 482
U.S. House of Representatives, 369
U.S. Army Corps of Engineers Waterway Experiment Station, 317, 378, 447
U.S. Cabinet Members from Miss., 348
U.S. News and World Report, 88, 403
U.S. Senators from Miss., listing of, 348
U.S. Women's Open golf championship held in West Point, Miss., 45
UFO abductees, 23
unemployment figures, 377, 483
unemployment insurance benefits, 350, 377, 484
Union Co. Courthouse burns, 10
university and college libraries, 410
university enrollment, 403
University Medical Center, 18, 20, 35, 37, 45, 315-16, 389, 484
University Medical Center established, 18
Univ. of Miss. Alumni Hall of Fame, 184
Univ. of Miss. Athletic Hall of Fame, 109
University of Mississippi established, 4
University of Miss. Law School est., 5
University of Southern Mississippi, 37
university system, 403
unusual placenames, 323
upholstery capital of the world, 296
UPI's SEC Player of the Year, 158
urban university, 403
USA Today, 26, 42, 43, 90, 95, 108, 167, 176, 196, 209-10, 213, 218
USA Today best-seller list, 218
USM's Alumni Hall of Fame, 214
USM Athletic Hall of Fame, 104
USM wins their 3rd Conference USA championship, 46
USM's all-time leading rebounder, 212
USS Arizona, 304
USS Cairo, 7, 303, 447
USS Constitution, 7
USS Jesse L. Brown, 306
USS John C. Stennis commissioned, 34
USS Massachusetts, 6
USS Mississippi, 13
USS Nautilus, 304
USS Sculpin, 294
USS Vicksburg christened at Ingalls, 30
VA Medical Center renamed the G.V. "Sonny" Montgomery VA Medical Center, 37, 171
valedictorian of high school class at Miss. School for the Blind, 342
value added to the u.s. economy by the agriculture sector, 413
value of all construction contracts, 483
value of all existing homes, 482
value of all university buildings, 403

General Index

value of construction, 377
value of poultry & eggs, 412
value of residential remodeling, 75
Vanity Fair magazine, 156
Vaught-Hemingway Stadium, 167, 209
veterans, 76, 485
veterans benefit payments, 350
veterans medical services, 350
Veterans Memorial Museum, 440
Veterans Memorial Stadium, 485
  largest crowd, 26
Vicksburg Civil War Living History, 447
Vicksburg Military Park, 34
Vicksburg National Cemetery, 344
Vicksburg National Military Park, 44, 52, 303, 431
Vicksburg Sentinel, 5
Vicksburg Sunday Post-Herald, 18, 343
Vicksburg surrenders, 8
Vietnam War veterans, 76, 485
Viking range rated best, 297
violent crimes, 396-7
violent weather, 60
Vision Award, 212
vital statistics, 76
Vocal Event of the Year, 337, 338, 340
Vogue magazine, 149
voted NFL Player of the Century, 179
voted one of the 10 all-time Favorite Wheaties Champions, 178

W.C. Handy Blues Award(s), 139, 143, 155, 173, 177, 191, 193, 330-31
wages & salaries, 376
Wall Street Journal, 133, 213
Walter Anderson Museum of Art, 443
Walter Payton Award, 164
Walter Sillers State Office Building officially dedicated, 23
War Memorial Building, 439
War of 1812, 2-3, 304
war veterans, 76
Washington Post, The, 88, 187, 221
Washington Republican, 2
water area of the state, 50
water uses, 379
water parks, 442, 445-46, 448, 461
water withdrawn, 52
Waterways Experiment Station, 317, 447
Waterways Experiment Station opens in Vicksburg, 22
Watkins Museum, 446
weather phone numbers, 59
Weekly Clarion-Ledger, 12
weekly newspapers, 476-78
Welcome Centers in Mississippi, 431
westernmost point of Mississippi, 50
wet counties, 350
wettest days/months/seasons in Jackson, 64
white-tailed deer, 349
White Knights, 20
white population, 73-74, 513
white population of Jackson MSA, 480
Whitworth College founded, 6
Wilderness Areas, 52, 431
wildfires, number of, 52, 401

Wildlife Management Areas, 52, 431
Windsor, 10
wine and liquor sales, 351, 483
winningest coach in Mississippi State and SEC history, 183
winningest coach in Mississippi State University basketball history, 43
wire services, list of, 479
Wister Gardens, 433
Witch of Yazoo, 172, 278, 449
Woman's World, 120
Women's Basketball Hall of Fame, 203, 210
Women's College World Series, 309
won the MIAL in music an unprecedented 5th time, 223
Woodall Mountain, 320, 439
Woodville Republican, 3, 446
Woolmarket Consolidated School, 13
work begins on new capitol, 12
workers' compensation, 350, 377
World Catfish Festival, 433
WORLD'S
  largest and heaviest mobile off-shore self-elevating oil rigs, 296
  longest/largest man-made beach, 294
  most powerful centrifuge, 317
  most widely used medical textbook, 130, 315
  richest female entertainer, 440
  strongest archaeologist, 324
WORLD'S FIRST
  all-welded iron ship, 294
  all-welded passenger ship, 16, 294
  bone-pinning operation, 16
  Eskimo Catholic priest, 299
  farmer-owned nitrogen plant, 298
  heart transplant, 45, 295
  kidney transplant, 20, 133, 315
  interactive musical biography, 150
WORLD'S LARGEST
  collection of blues music, 299, 443
  collection of Civil War gunboat models, 447
  collection of original manuscripts and illustrations of children's books, 299, 438
  commercial breeder, producer, seller of cotton planting seed, 298
  cotton merchant, 81
cottonwood tree plantation, 298
  farmer-owned fertilizer plant, 298
  forest products company, 172
  General Motors dealer, 168, 298
  hardboard manufacturing plant, 297
  hydrology laboratory, 317
  industrial forklift, 297
  manufacturer of aerospace hydraulic pumps, 297
  shrimp, 294
WORLD'S ONLY
  documented case of pregnancy by bullet, 304
  cactus plantation, 298, 436
  stationary Dentzel menagerie, 326

WORLD RECORD
  closest election ever by percentage, 25, 319
  deer, 345, 455
  for sustained endurance in the air, 15, 314
  playing game of checkers, 210, 309
  largest hog and ox, 346
  Olympic jump, 89
  one hundred meter run, 198
  westerly crossing of the Atlantic, 166
  yield for corn on one acre, 18, 313
  yield for oats on one acre, 16
World Series, 88, 90, 92, 96, 101, 107, 110, 120-21, 129, 135, 153, 163, 173, 177-78, 183, 195, 208, 210, 215
WORLDCOM, 26, 37-38, 42, 44, 48, 114, 380-81
  buys SkyTel paging, 44, 114
  first formed as LDDS, 26, 114
  market capitalization, 381
  merger with Sprint aborted, 48, 114
  merges with MFS, 38, 114
  MCI merger finalized, 42, 114
  moves to Clinton, 37, 114
  sales & earnings, 114
  stock performance, 381
worst Amtrak accident ever, 31
worst hurricanes & tornadoes, 60
Writer's Digest, 120
wrote or cowrote 38 of the 110 songs recorded by her brother-in-law, 165

Yalobusha Baptist Female Institute est., 5
Yazoo Historical Museum, 447
Yazoo Indians, 468-69
Yazoo Witch, the, 172, 278, 344, 447
yearly cost for car insurance, 430
Yesterday's Children Antique Doll & Toy Museum, 447
Yocona Ridge Park, 446
YOUNGEST
  artist ever to sell so many copies of an album, 201, 337
  county in Mississippi, 351
  editor ever of the nation's oldest magazine, 45, 172, 343
  governor to ever serve, 352
  general in the Confederacy, 12, 153
  man ever elected to the House of Representatives, 306
  man to ever serve as governor of Mississippi, 357
  Marine and the youngest man in the 20th century to be given the CMOH, 156, 275, 305
  ordained Baptist minister in the U.S., 18
  person ever nominated for a CMA award, 190
  person ever nominated for a Country Music Association award, 338

ZIP Codes of Mississippi, 496-507

About the Author

James (Jim) L. Cox was born in the southwestern part of Virginia in the small town of Richlands. He spent his childhood years alternately between the beautiful mountain hollows of Appalachia and the busy city streets of Baltimore, Maryland.

A teenage prodigy in math and science, especially astronomy, he lectured to college students and others on subjects such as Einstein's Theory of Relativity and space exploration while he was still in high school. At the advent of the space age, he spoke to civic groups such as Lions Clubs and Kiwanis Clubs about space travel and other scientific subjects. In 1957, at age 16, he accurately predicted that man would land on the moon in 1969, twelve years before the fact! During that same time period, young Cox devised a system for naming very large numbers, which he claims he has used to name the largest numbers ever conceived. Today, after years of studying the subject, he considers himself one of the world's few experts on very large numbers.

He attended Southwest Virginia Community College and the University of Virginia. His plans to become an astrophysicist, however, were shelved by a stint in the U.S. Army. During a tour of duty in Korea, he became actively involved in radio broadcasting and pursued a career in this field upon his honorable discharge from active duty.

His radio career spanned over three decades during which time he worked at several stations in four different states as a disc jockey, news reporter, news writer, copywriter, commercial production manager, program director, and vice-president and general manager of a two-station operation in Virginia for over eleven years. It was during this period when he also became part-owner of a 16-track professional recording studio. He later sold his share of that operation and eventually found his way to Yazoo City, Mississippi in 1979. There, he continued his career in broadcasting and worked for over 12 years at both radio stations in that city while also doing some audio/video consulting work as a sideline. He retired from radio in 1992 and began writing.

This book is the third in a series from Cox's publishing company, Computer Search & Research, which is located in Yazoo City.